Part of the **UWorld** Family

THE REVIEW PROGRAMS TRUSTED
BY TOP STUDENTS, SCHOOLS AND EMPLOYERS

pharmacy.uworld.c

The RxPrep® Difference

NAPLEX,® MPJE® & CPJE Reviews

Not sure how to learn it all? Prepare for the NAPLEX the smart way with our comprehensive RxPrep online course. The RxPrep video lectures and QBanks match to each chapter in this course book. The questions in the QBank cover the must-know basic competency drug information. Track your progress, then test your readiness prior to exam day.

READ: Includes the simplest and most complete calculations and biostatistics reviews. It's all here, in easy steps, for complete exam know-how.
The RxPrep course book is the student-preferred resource for the NAPLEX. It includes all topics tested with must-know key drugs and study tips.

WATCH: Pair the course book with video lectures that emphasize the required drug information.
Focus on topics that need a fresh review, or use a video lecture to bring up a topic score.

PRACTICE: Over 3,700 QBank questions to apply what you've learned and assess your performance.
The RxPrep QBank contain case-rich, exam-style questions that cover all the required material, plus a cumulative practice exam.

ATTEND: Live or streaming video review sessions.

UPDATED: Annually. Current, complete and ready for exam preparation.

PURCHASE THE VIDEO LECTURES AND QBANK ONLINE AT PHARMACY.UWORLD.COM

CONTACT RXPREP FOR LIVE REVIEWS AND GROUP RATES

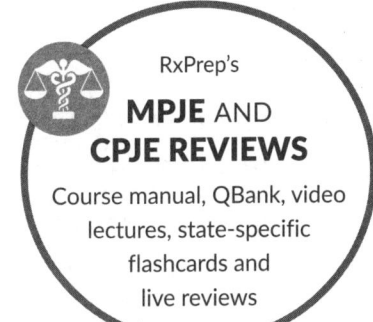

RxPrep's
MPJE AND **CPJE REVIEWS**
Course manual, QBank, video lectures, state-specific flashcards and live reviews

Part of the UWorld Family

2023 NAPLEX®

COURSE BOOK

Study Guide for the NAPLEX®
for those testing in 2023

EDITORS

CHELSEA BOMBATCH, PharmD, BCPS

STEPHANIE BRIAN, PharmD, BCPS

PETER COLLEY, PharmD, BCPS AQ-ID, AAHIVP

CAITLIN DAVIS, PharmD, BCPS

LAUREN DEVINE, PharmD, BCPS, BCCP

AMY DREW, PharmD, BCPS

STEPHANIE D. GARRETT, PharmD, BCPS

ANGIE VEVERKA, PharmD, BCPS

2023 Associate Editors

DEEATRA CRADDOCK, PharmD, BCACP
YASAR TASNIF, PharmD, BCPS, FAST
BOBBIE VARGHESE, PharmD

Book Design and Production

JONI HUTTON

CHAPTER TABLE OF CONTENTS
INCLUDING REQUIRED FORMULAS

CHAPTER TABLE OF CONTENTS
INCLUDING REQUIRED FORMULAS

CONTENT LEGEND

⣿ = Required Formula

KEY DRUG GUY AND STUDY TIP GAL
PAGE NUMBERS

CONTENT LEGEND

= Study Tip Gal      = Key Drug Guy

KEY DRUG GUY AND STUDY TIP GAL
PAGE NUMBERS CONT.

CONTENT LEGEND

= Study Tip Gal   = Key Drug Guy

PREPARING FOR THE NAPLEX

CONTENTS

CHAPTER CONTENT

iStock.com/ipopba

CHAPTER 1

PREPARING FOR THE NAPLEX®
WITH RxPREP

RxPREP STUDY MATERIALS

There is no such thing as luck when taking licensure exams; there is only drug knowledge and the skill required to apply the knowledge to case-based questions. All topics must be mastered, and all calculations must be completed with adequate speed and accuracy. Thorough preparation is necessary to pass the NAPLEX®; apply the tips provided in this chapter to have the greatest chance of passing.

The RxPrep online course includes a question bank (or QBank for short) and video lectures that are used in conjunction with the RxPrep course book. These materials are available online at pharmacy.uworld. com. The online course includes everything you need to be successful on the NAPLEX.

COURSE BOOK UPDATES AND ERRATA

The course book is updated annually to be current for the pharmacist licensure exam. It is best to study from the most current edition available for your period of testing.

The RxPrep pharmacists review new drug approvals and new guidelines that are released after the current course book is published. When new information could be relevant for testing, a summary of the changes will be posted online. Any course book corrections are posted in the same location.

Refer to pharmacy.uworld.com to find relevant updates for the NAPLEX.

HOW TO USE THE RxPREP COURSE BOOK

The RxPrep course book includes several tools to simplify the information. Drugs are bolded if they are top sellers or have major safety issues. These are important drugs for the NAPLEX and should be known well (including the brand name, if bolded). If information is underlined, it is essential to know for the exam.

Study Tip Gals and Key Drug Guys are used to highlight important information. Study Tip Gals contain an explanation, simplification or summary of points, and Key Drug Guys are there to help you learn drugs with similar traits. Do not skip these; they contain highly testable information! These are marked with a light bulb (for a Study Tip Gal) or a key (for a Key Drug Guy) on the table of contents for the chapter. You can also find them using the table of contents for the course book.

Example Drug Table

BOLDED DRUG = TOP SELLER "MUST KNOW" →

DRUG	DOSING	SAFETY/SIDE EFFECTS/MONITORING
Levetiracetam (Keppra, Keppra XR, Roweepra, Spritam) Tablet, ODT, oral solution, injection	**Initial:** 500 mg BID or 1,000 mg daily (XR) **Maximum:** 3,000 mg/day **CrCl ≤ 80 mL/min:** ↓ dose IV:PO ratio 1:1	**WARNINGS** <u>Psychiatric reactions, including psychotic symptoms, somnolence, fatigue, suicidal behavior, anaphylaxis, angioedema, coordination difficulties, severe skin reactions (SJS/TEN), hematologic abnormalities (mainly anemias), ↑ BP, loss of seizure control during pregnancy</u> **SIDE EFFECTS** Irritability, dizziness, weakness, asthenia, vomiting (children and adolescents) **NOTES** <u>No significant drug interactions</u>

UNDERLINED INFORMATION = ESSENTIAL "MUST KNOW"

Study Tip Gal Box

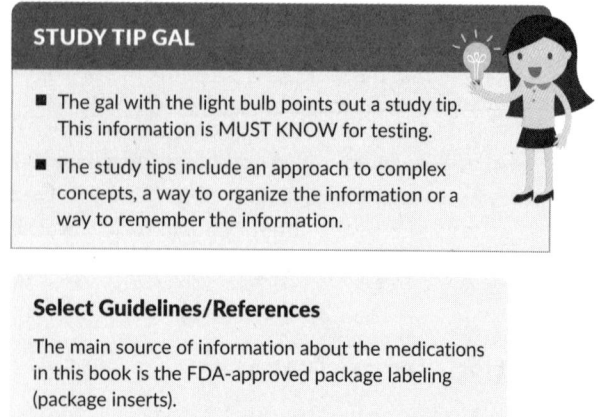

STUDY TIP GAL

- The gal with the light bulb points out a study tip. This information is MUST KNOW for testing.

- The study tips include an approach to complex concepts, a way to organize the information or a way to remember the information.

Select Guidelines/References

The main source of information about the medications in this book is the FDA-approved package labeling (package inserts).

Key Drug Guy Box

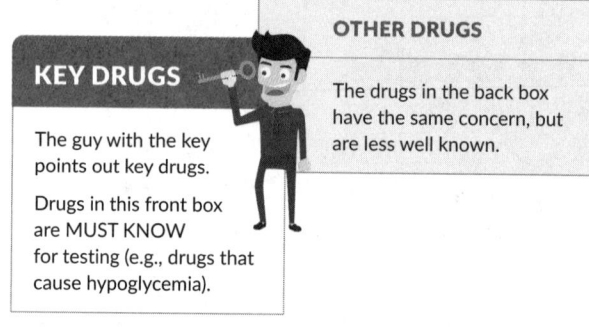

KEY DRUGS

The guy with the key points out key drugs.

Drugs in this front box are MUST KNOW for testing (e.g., drugs that cause hypoglycemia).

OTHER DRUGS

The drugs in the back box have the same concern, but are less well known.

FOUNDATION CHAPTERS

There are foundation chapters at the beginning and end of the course book (in the sections titled Pharmacy Foundations Part 1 and Part 2). Information in these chapters will apply to other topics. Complete these early; learning this material will help you throughout your studies. Then, revisit them at the end of your studies to make sure the information was retained. Foundation material may be required to answer questions in any QBank.

PRACTICE CASES, QUESTIONS AND CASE SCENARIOS

You will need to obtain information from a case to answer questions on the NAPLEX. For example, how many grams of protein per day are being provided by the parenteral nutrition? Or, which drug is the best option to treat the patient's infection? Practice cases and sample questions that are designed to be similar to cases you might see on the exam can be found at the end of the course book and in several chapters. They allow you to test your knowledge. Look for case scenarios in grey shaded boxes. These are a complement to the QBank, which is the best place to apply what you have learned.

GETTING STARTED WITH A STUDY PLAN

Begin by creating a study plan. To help you get started, the RxPrep pharmacists have organized the course book topics based on the time it usually takes to complete them (see table below). Sample study schedules and templates can be found online at pharmacy.uworld.com.

HELPFUL POINTERS FOR CREATING YOUR STUDY SCHEDULE

- Fill in the schedule by allocating adequate time for each of the topics. Use the time estimates below, with your best guess if you will need more or less time to complete a topic.

- Include math early in your study schedule and allow time to practice frequently. Repetition is required for mastery.

- Alternate between math, foundation and clinical topics to stay engaged.

- Always leave weekly catch-up time. It is normal to fall behind; catch-up time will keep you on track. If you fall behind on your study schedule and are unable to catch up, it may be best to postpone your exam. Do not skip chapters and QBanks as any topic can appear on the exam.

- Leave the two weeks before your estimated test date open. The last two weeks are used to take the RxPrep Practice Exam, remediate any missed areas, and review the math and other topics that may have been forgotten.

Alternate your study time between math and clinical topics.

Estimated Topic Completion Time		
1-2 hours per Topic (~1 weekday night)	**2-4 hours per Topic** (~1-2 weekday nights)	**> 4 hours per Topic** (~2-5 weeknights or 1-2 weekend days)
Allergic Rhinitis, Cough & Cold	Acute & Critical Care Medicine	Anticoagulation
Alzheimer's Disease	Acute Coronary Syndromes	Biostatistics
Anemia	ADHD	Calculations II
Answering Case-Based Exam Questions	Arrhythmias	Calculations III
Anxiety Disorders	Asthma	Calculations IV
Basic Science Concepts	Calculations I	Common Skin Conditions
Benign Prostatic Hyperplasia (BPH)	Calculations V	Diabetes
Bipolar Disorder	Chronic Heart Failure	Dyslipidemia
Cases, Exam-Style Practice	Compounding I	HIV
Common Conditions of the Eyes and Ears	Compounding II	Infectious Diseases I
Constipation & Diarrhea	Compounding III	Infectious Diseases II
COPD	Contraception & Infertility	Oncology I
Cystic Fibrosis	Depression	Oncology II
Drug Allergies & Adverse Drug Reactions	Dietary Supplements, Natural & Complementary Medicine	Osteoporosis, Menopause & Testosterone Use
Drug Formulations & Patient Counseling	Drug Interactions	Pain
Drug References	GERD & PUD	Seizures/Epilepsy
Drug Use in Pregnancy & Lactation	Hepatitis & Liver Disease	Systemic Steroids & Autoimmune Conditions
Gout	Hypertension	
Infectious Diseases IV	Immunizations	
Intravenous Medication Principles	Infectious Diseases III	
Migraine	Inflammatory Bowel Disease	
Motion Sickness	Lab Values & Drug Monitoring	
Parkinson Disease	Medication Safety & Quality Improvement	
Pediatric Conditions	Pharmacokinetics	
Pharmacogenomics	Renal Disease	
Pulmonary Arterial Hypertension	Schizophrenia/Psychosis	
Sexual Dysfunction	Transplant	
Sickle Cell Disease		
Sleep Disorders		
Stable Ischemic Heart Disease		
Stroke		
Thyroid Disorders		
Tobacco Cessation		
Toxicology & Antidotes		
Travelers		
Urinary Incontinence		
Weight Loss		

TIPS FOR STUDYING

STUDYING CLINICAL CHAPTERS

- If you know a topic well, review the course book chapter quickly with a focus on bolded drugs, underlined information, Study Tip Gals and Key Drug Guys. Then proceed to the QBank to test your knowledge.

- If you are not confident with a topic, you will need to review it before proceeding to the QBank. Read the chapter, or watch the video lecture while following along with the chapter. Highlight the information you will need to review and review it before taking the matching QBank.

- After completing the topic QBank, review any questions you answered incorrectly. Use the available QBank tools to make flashcards or notes for content you want to revisit later.

STUDYING CALCULATIONS

Math is an important part of the exam, and calculations are best mastered through repetition. Start by completing the Calculations chapters in the course book, then move on to the QBanks. There are five Calculations chapters:

- Calculations I, II, III and IV can be completed in any order.

- The last Calculations chapter (Calculations V) contains exam-style math practice; review this chapter after the other four have been completed.

Other essential calculations are found in these chapters:

- Biostatistics
- Pharmacokinetics
- Select clinical chapters (e.g., corrected phenytoin in Seizures/Epilepsy, insulin math in Diabetes).

Use the Required Formulas Sheet (found in the quick guides and the end of the course book) while you are learning. Repeat each of the calculations QBanks until you can do all of the problems with decent speed and accuracy. You will be ready for math on the NAPLEX when you are completing math problems on "auto pilot"; you see a problem, and the calculation automatically flows out from your pen. This happens because you have seen this type of problem many times.

As your scores improve, shift to completing the QBanks without using the Required Formulas Sheet. Turn off "Tutor" mode so answer explanations are hidden, allowing you to assess your timing. The goal is to complete each question in ~1 minute and 36 seconds to mimic timing on the NAPLEX (see The Format of the NAPLEX section later in this chapter).

> Repeat the math QBanks until all formulas on the Required Formulas Sheet are known and easy to use.
>
> Math starts out difficult. With practice, math becomes automatic. Like learning to drive!

Test your Knowledge

The formulas on the Required Formulas Sheet must be memorized. To assess what you know, take the Required Formulas Practice Test and check off items on the Required Formulas Checklist as you go (see next page) if you have memorized the formula.

ASSESSING READINESS FOR THE NAPLEX

You will know you are ready for the NAPLEX when the following conditions are met:

- Each calculation is marked off on the Required Formulas Checklist, which indicates that the formula is known by heart, and the math can be completed flawlessly.

- All topics in the course book have been reviewed. Any topic can appear on the NAPLEX; skipping topics and taking a chance on the NAPLEX is not advised.

- All questions in the QBank show as "used" (indicating they have been completed), and questions answered incorrectly have been reviewed.

THE RxPREP PRACTICE EXAM

Once you have completed your studies and feel prepared to take the NAPLEX, take the RxPrep Practice Exam. The questions on this exam have been selected to align with the NAPLEX Competency Statements (discussed later).

- The Practice Exam has 150 questions. To have the same time per question as the NAPLEX, it should be taken as a timed, 4-hour exam.

- Use a calculator only. Do not use your course book, notes or the Required Formula Sheet.

Evaluate your performance on the Practice Exam to determine your readiness to take the NAPLEX. If you did not score well, you may need to postpone your exam to allow for additional time to study. If you feel ready to take the NAPLEX, use the remaining time left to review missed information from the Practice Exam and items that are easily forgotten, such as math (including clinical math, Biostatistics and Pharmacokinetics) and compounding. If you did not score well in a few areas, review those topics more thoroughly using the course book, video lectures and QBank.

REQUIRED FORMULAS CHECKLIST

Calculations
- ❑ Liquid (Volume) Conversions p. 117
- ❑ Solid (Weight) Conversions p. 117
- ❑ mEq to mmol Conversion p. 117
- ❑ Height Conversions p. 117
- ❑ Percentage Strength p. 128
- ❑ Ratio Strength p. 132
- ❑ Parts Per Million (PPM) p. 134
- ❑ Specific Gravity (SG) p. 135
- ❑ Dilution & Concentration (Q1C1, Changing Strength or Quantity) p. 136
- ❑ Alligation p. 137
- ❑ Osmolarity p. 140
- ❑ Isotonicity (E Value) p. 143
- ❑ Moles and Millimoles p. 144
- ❑ Milliequivalents p. 146
- ❑ Determining Fluid Needs p. 150
- ❑ Total Energy Expenditure p. 151
- ❑ Parenteral Nutrition Calories p. 152
- ❑ Enteral Nutrition Calories p. 152
- ❑ Grams of Nitrogen From Protein p. 153
- ❑ Corrected Calcium for Albumin < 3.5 p. 160
- ❑ Body Mass Index (BMI) p. 169
- ❑ Ideal Body Weight (IBW) p. 170
- ❑ Adjusted Body Weight (AdjBW$_{0.4}$) p. 170
- ❑ Which Weight to Use for Drug Dosing (mg/kg) p. 171
- ❑ Flow Rates/Drop Factor p. 172 & p. 175
- ❑ Dehydration p. 177
- ❑ Cockcroft-Gault Equation p. 178
- ❑ Arterial Blood Gas (ABG) p. 180
- ❑ Anion Gap p. 181
- ❑ pH Calculations p. 182
- ❑ Percent Ionization p. 185
- ❑ Absolute Neutrophil Count (ANC) p. 187

Answering Case-Based Exam Questions
- ❑ Temperature Conversions p. 108

Biostatistics
- ❑ Mean, Median and Mode p. 204
- ❑ Risk, Relative Risk (RR) p. 209
- ❑ Relative Risk Reduction (RRR) p. 210
- ❑ Absolute Risk Reduction (ARR) p. 210
- ❑ Number Needed to Treat (NNT) p. 211
- ❑ Number Needed to Harm (NNH) p. 212
- ❑ Odds Ratio (OR) p. 212
- ❑ Hazard Ratio (HR) p. 213
- ❑ Incremental Cost-Effectiveness Ratio p. 223

Compounding II
- ❑ Minimum Weighable Quantity (MWQ) p. 251

Dyslipidemia
- ❑ Friedewald Equation p. 423

Common Skin Conditions
- ❑ Time to Burn (TTB) p. 562

Tobacco Cessation
- ❑ Pack-Year Smoking History p. 598

Diabetes
- ❑ Initiating Basal-Bolus Insulin in Type 1 Diabetes p. 617
- ❑ Insulin-to-Carbohydrate Ratio: Rule of 500 for Rapid-Acting Insulin p. 619
- ❑ Insulin-to-Carbohydrate Ratio: Rule of 450 for Regular Insulin p. 619
- ❑ Correction Factor: 1,800 Rule for Rapid-Acting Insulin p. 619
- ❑ Correction Factor: 1,500 Rule for Regular Insulin p. 619
- ❑ Correction Dose p. 619

Acute & Critical Care Medicine
- ❑ Mean Arterial Pressure (MAP) p. 713

Oncology II
- ❑ BSA Calculations, using Mosteller p. 817

Seizures/Epilepsy
- ❑ Phenytoin Correction for Albumin < 3.5 p. 898

Pharmacokinetics
- ❑ Bioavailability (F) p. 958
- ❑ Volume of Distribution (Vd) p. 959
- ❑ Clearance p. 961 & p. 963
- ❑ Elimination Rate Constant (ke) p. 963
- ❑ Predicting Drug Concentrations p. 963
- ❑ Half-Life ($t_{1/2}$) p. 964
- ❑ Loading Dose (LD) p. 966

Drug-Dose Conversions
- ❑ KCl Solution (Oral) to Tablets p. 147
- ❑ Calcium Salts p. 186
- ❑ Aminophylline ↔ Theophylline p. 186
- ❑ Statins p. 426
- ❑ Metoprolol p. 445
- ❑ Loop Diuretics p. 470
- ❑ Iron, Elemental p. 518
- ❑ Insulin p. 620
- ❑ Levothyroxine p. 629
- ❑ Steroids p. 636
- ❑ Opioids (methodology) p. 762
- ❑ Lithium p. 855

NOTE: The required formulas can be found in the quick guides section at the end of this chapter, plus in an easy "tear out" page at the end of the course book.

THE NAPLEX COMPETENCY STATEMENTS

The NAPLEX Competency Statements are available on the National Association of Boards of Pharmacy (NABP) website at https://nabp.pharmacy. The Competency Statements provide a blueprint (outline) of tested items, split into six "areas" or sections.

AREA	TITLE
1	Obtain, interpret, or assess data, medical, or patient information
2	Identify drug characteristics
3	Develop or manage treatment plans
4	Perform calculations
5	Compound, dispense, or administer drugs or manage delivery systems
6	Develop or manage practice or medication-use systems to ensure safety and quality

The key points for each competency area are summarized below, but you are encouraged to read the complete Competency Statements on the NABP website.

AREA #1 (~18% OF THE EXAM)

- Questions are largely asked in a case-based format. It will be important to quickly identify pertinent information from a case (e.g., abnormal labs, past medical history, medication use history, diagnostic tests) or an abstract (e.g., results from a study). It is critical to master the Lab Values & Drug Monitoring chapter; lab reference ranges will be provided.

AREA #2 (~14% OF THE EXAM)

- This section includes pharmacology, mechanism of action, therapeutic class, boxed warnings, safety in pregnancy or lactation and prescription vs. OTC status.

- Brand/generics are tested, along with common dosage forms.

AREA #3 (~35% OF THE EXAM)

- This area focuses on defining therapeutic goals, outcomes and clinical endpoints. You should be able to identify medications without an indication, untreated conditions, and duplications of therapy. Drug dosing, dosing adjustments and duration of therapy may be tested.

- Strong knowledge of drug contraindications, precautions, adverse effects and drug interactions is essential.

- The ability to apply guidelines to patient care (e.g., evidence-based practice) is covered in Area #3.

AREA #4 (~14% OF THE EXAM)

- Calculations involving patient parameters (e.g., BSA, body weight) and laboratory measures (e.g., CrCl, corrected phenytoin, ANC) are essential to making drug therapy decisions.

- The ability to calculate quantities of drugs to be dispensed or ingredients to be compounded is tested in this section.

- Nutritional calculations, rates of administration (e.g., flow rates), dose conversions and drug concentrations are covered.

- Biostatistics and pharmacokinetic calculations are included in Area #4.

AREA #5 (~11% OF THE EXAM)

- Techniques, procedures and equipment used for sterile and non-sterile compounding, including hazardous drugs, are a requirement.

- Properties of drug products that affect compatibility/ stability, onset/duration or pharmacokinetics are covered.

- Familiarity with proper storage, packaging, handling and medication disposal is expected.

- Instructions and techniques for medication administration are tested in this section.

AREA #6 (~7% OF THE EXAM)

- Medication safety concepts, including the role of pharmacy informatics in the medication-use system, are included in Area #6.

- Disease prevention, screening programs and stewardship are covered. Knowledge of vaccinations will be important.

THE FORMAT OF THE NAPLEX

The NAPLEX is a 6-hour exam with 225 questions. Of these, 200 questions are used to determine the exam result (e.g., pass or fail). The other 25 questions are pretest questions that are being evaluated for inclusion on future exams. Pretest questions are interspersed throughout the exam; it is not possible to identify them.

- The majority of the questions (including calculations) are asked in a case-based format (such as patient profiles with an accompanying question). There are also stand-alone questions without a case.

- All questions must be answered in the order they are presented. You cannot skip questions or go back to a question at a later time.

The computer screen will display a prompt for two optional 10-minute breaks; these do not count towards the 6-hour time limit. Any other non-scheduled breaks that you request will be subtracted from the total test time.

QUESTION TYPES

There are five question types on the NAPLEX. Each of the five types are in the RxPrep QBank:

- Multiple-Choice: select the one correct answer.

- Multiple-Response: select all of the correct responses and no incorrect response for credit.

- Constructed-Response: enter the answer using the computer keyboard (usually for math problems).

- Ordered-Response: put the items in a specified order.

- Hot Spot: select the correct area on a diagram or picture by clicking on it.

CALCULATORS

- Personal calculators are not permitted during the exam. The Pearson VUE testing center dashboard uses an on-screen calculator that is similar to the Texas Instruments TI-30XS Multiview and other comparable hand-held, non-graphing calculators. The on-screen calculator can be opened in a pop-up window during the exam at any time.

- A candidate requesting a handheld calculator will be given a basic, non-scientific calculator. Some of the calculations may require advanced functions that require the use of the on-screen calculator (e.g., order of operands, exponents and multi-step problems). Refer to the Calculations chapters for detailed information.

- Pearson VUE offers a demo test on their website, available at: home.pearsonvue.com/nabp.

ARRIVAL DETAILS, TUTORIAL

On the day of the exam, arrive at least 30 minutes prior to your appointment for check-in procedures (ID verification, palm vein scan, digital signature and photograph). Review the Candidate Application Bulletin on the NABP website for details on acceptable forms of ID, prohibited items and exam misconduct.

- If you arrive more than 30 minutes after your scheduled appointment and are refused admission to sit for the exam, you will be required to forfeit your appointment.

- Take the online exam tutorial before starting the exam. The tutorial will explain how to navigate the cases, enter answers, etc. The tutorial is important and does not take away from your test time.

PHARMACY LAW EXAMS

MPJE®

Many people study for the MPJE after the NAPLEX has been completed. There is little overlap between the NAPLEX and MPJE.

Depending on a person's prior knowledge and work experience, MPJE preparation will take about 2 – 5 weeks. The RxPrep MPJE Course and state-specific flashcard decks will provide the content needed to do well.

CPJE

Unlike the MPJE, the law exam in California (the CPJE), contains clinical content that overlaps with the NAPLEX. The RxPrep course book includes the topics that overlap with the CPJE (Medication Safety, Infectious Diseases, Immunizations, HIV, others). The clinical topics not covered on the NAPLEX that are tested on the CPJE are included in the separate CPJE course (e.g., therapeutic interchange). California law is covered completely in the CPJE course.

Best wishes for your exam preparation,

The RxPrep Pharmacy Team

QUICK GUIDES

CONTENTS

TOP PRESCRIPTION DRUGS

Top selling/must know prescription drugs are included in this list and bolded throughout the course book. Refer to the clinical chapters for essential underlined information about them. These are oral formulations unless otherwise noted. Top prescription drugs that are injectable only and top OTC medications are listed separately. Note that some prescription medications are also available OTC (see Top OTC Drugs list).

QUICK GUIDES

DRUG	BRAND NAME
Abacavir	
Abacavir/Lamivudine	Epzicom
Acetaminophen	Tylenol (oral/suppository), Ofirmev (injection)
Acetaminophen/Codeine	Tylenol with Codeine #2, #3, #4
Acyclovir	Zovirax (oral, injection, topical)
Adapalene	Differin (topical)
Albuterol	ProAir HFA, ProAir RespiClick, Proventil HFA, Ventolin HFA (inhalation)
Albuterol/Ipratropium	Combivent Respimat (inhalation)
Alendronate	Fosamax
Allopurinol	Zyloprim (oral), Aloprim (injection)
Alprazolam	Xanax
Alvimopan	Entereg
Amiodarone	Pacerone (oral), Nexterone (injection)
Amitriptyline	Elavil
Amlodipine	Norvasc
Amlodipine/Benazepril	Lotrel
Amoxicillin	
Amoxicillin/Clarithromycin/Lansoprazole	Prevpac
Amoxicillin/Clavulanate	Augmentin
Amphetamine/Dextroamphetamine	Adderall
Ampicillin	Generics (oral, injection)
Anastrozole	Arimidex
Apixaban	Eliquis

DRUG	BRAND NAME
Aprepitant	Emend
Aripiprazole	Abilify
Atazanavir	Reyataz
Atenolol	Tenormin
Atenolol/Chlorthalidone	Tenoretic
Atomoxetine	Strattera
Atorvastatin	Lipitor
Azelastine	Astepro (nasal), generics (ophthalmic)
Azithromycin	Zithromax (oral, injection), Z-Pak (oral)
Bacitracin/Neomycin/Polymyxin B/Hydrocortisone	Cortisporin (topical)
Baclofen	Lioresal (intrathecal), generics (oral)
Beclomethasone	QVAR RediHaler (inhalation)
Benazepril	Lotensin
Benzonatate	Tessalon Perles
Benztropine	Cogentin
Betamethasone dipropionate	Diprolene Cream AF (topical)
Betamethasone/Clotrimazole	Lotrisone (topical)
Bictegravir/Emtricitabine/Tenofovir alafenamide	Biktarvy
Bimatoprost	Lumigan, Latisse (ophthalmic)
Bismuth/Metronidazole/Tetracycline	Pylera
Bisoprolol/Hydrochlorothiazide	Ziac
Brompheniramine/Pseudoephedrine/Dextromethorphan	Bromfed DM

DRUG	BRAND NAME
Budesonide	Pulmicort, Pulmicort Flexhaler (inhalation), Entocort EC, Uceris (oral)
Budesonide/Formoterol	Symbicort (inhalation)
Bumetanide	Bumex (oral), generics (injection)
Buprenorphine	Belbuca (buccal film), Butrans (patch)
Buprenorphine/Naloxone	Suboxone (SL film), Zubsolv (SL tablet)
Bupropion	Wellbutrin SR, Wellbutrin XL, Zyban
Buspirone	
Butoconazole	Gynazole-1 (topical)
Calcitonin	Miacalcin (injection), generics (nasal)
Canagliflozin	Invokana
Canagliflozin/Metformin	Invokamet
Capecitabine	Xeloda
Carbamazepine	Tegretol
Carbidopa/Levodopa	Sinemet
Carisoprodol	Soma
Carvedilol	Coreg
Cefdinir	
Cefuroxime	Generics (oral, injection)
Celecoxib	Celebrex
Cephalexin	Keflex
Chlorpheniramine/Hydrocodone	TussiCaps
Chlorthalidone	
Cholecalciferol, vitamin D3	

Top Prescription Drugs Continued

DRUG	BRAND NAME
Cinacalcet	*Sensipar*
Ciprofloxacin	*Cipro* (oral), generics (injection)
Ciprofloxacin/ Dexamethasone	*Ciprodex* (otic)
Citalopram	*Celexa*
Clarithromycin	
Clindamycin	*Cleocin* (injection, oral), *Cleocin-T, Clindagel* (topical)
Clobetasol	*Clobex, Temovate, Olux* (topical)
Clonazepam	*Klonopin*
Clonidine	*Catapres, Kapvay* (oral), *Catapres-TTS* (patch)
Clopidogrel	*Plavix*
Clozapine	*Clozaril*
Cobicistat	*Tybost*
Codeine	
Codeine/Promethazine	
Colchicine	*Colcrys*
Colesevelam	*Welchol*
Cyanocobalamin, vitamin B12	Generics (injection, nasal)
Cyclobenzaprine	*Amrix, Fexmid, Flexeril*
Cyclophosphamide	Generics (oral, injection)
Cyclosporine	*Neoral, Gengraf* (modified; oral) *Sandimmune* (non-modified; oral, injection), *Restasis* (ophthalmic)
Dabigatran	*Pradaxa*
Dapagliflozin	*Farxiga*
Darunavir	*Prezista*
Desvenlafaxine	*Pristiq*
Dexamethasone	*DexPak* (oral), *Decadron* (oral, injection)
Dexlansoprazole	*Dexilant*

DRUG	BRAND NAME
Dextromethorphan/ Promethazine	
Diazepam	*Valium* (oral), *Diastat AcuDial* (rectal gel), generics (injection)
Diclofenac	*Voltaren* (topical), generics (oral, patch)
Dicyclomine	*Bentyl*
Digoxin	*Digitek, Digox* (oral), *Lanoxin* (oral, injection)
Dihydroergotamine	*D.H.E. 45* (injection), *Migranal* (nasal)
Diltiazem	*Tiazac* (oral), *Cardizem* (oral), generics (injection)
Diphenhydramine	*Benadryl* (oral, topical, injection)
Diphenoxylate/Atropine	*Lomotil*
Dipyridamole/Aspirin	*Aggrenox*
Dolutegravir	*Tivicay*
Dolutegravir/Abacavir/ Lamivudine	*Triumeq*
Dolutegravir/ Lamivudine	*Dovato*
Donepezil	*Aricept*
Dornase alfa	*Pulmozyme* (inhalation)
Doxazosin	*Cardura*
Doxepin	
Doxycycline	*Vibramycin* (oral), generics (injection)
Dronabinol	*Marinol*
Duloxetine	*Cymbalta*
Efavirenz	
Efavirenz/ Emtricitabine/Tenofovir disoproxil fumarate	*Atripla*
Elvitegravir/Cobicistat/ Emtricitabine/Tenofovir alafenamide	*Genvoya*
Elvitegravir/Cobicistat/ Emtricitabine/Tenofovir disoproxil fumarate	*Stribild*

DRUG	BRAND NAME
Empagliflozin	*Jardiance*
Emtricitabine	
Emtricitabine/Tenofovir alafenamide	*Descovy*
Emtricitabine/Tenofovir disoproxil fumarate	*Truvada*
Enalapril	*Vasotec*
Entecavir	*Baraclude*
Ergocalciferol, vitamin D2	*Calciferol*
Erythromycin	*E.E.S., Ery-Tab* (oral), *Erythrocin* (oral, injection)
Escitalopram	*Lexapro*
Esomeprazole	*Nexium, Nexium 24HR* (oral), *Nexium IV* (injection)
Estradiol	*Estrace* (vaginal cream), *Estring* (vaginal ring), *Vagifem* (vaginal tablet), *Vivelle-Dot, Alora, Climara* (patch)
Estrogens, conjugated (equine)	*Premarin* (vaginal cream, oral, injection)
Estrogens, conjugated (equine)/ Medroxyprogesterone	
Eszopiclone	*Lunesta*
Ethinyl estradiol/ Drospirenone	*Yasmin, Yaz*
Ethinyl estradiol/ Etonogestrel	*NuvaRing* (vaginal ring)
Ethinyl estradiol/ Levonorgestrel	*Seasonique*
Ethinyl estradiol/ Norethindrone	*Junel, Loestrin, Lo Loestrin Microgestin*
Ethinyl estradiol/ Norgestimate	*Ortho Tri-Cyclen Lo, Tri-Sprintec, Sprintec 28*
Ethosuximide	*Zarontin*
Ezetimibe	*Zetia*
Famotidine	*Pepcid* (oral, injection), *Zantac 360*
Fenofibrate	*Antara, Tricor, Trilipix*

QUICK GUIDES

Top Prescription Drugs Continued

DRUG	BRAND NAME
Fentanyl	*Duragesic* (patch), *Sublimaze* (injection)
Fidaxomicin	*Dificid*
Finasteride	*Proscar, Propecia*
Fluconazole	*Diflucan* (oral, injection)
Fluocinonide	*Vanos* (topical)
Fluoxetine	*Prozac*
Fluticasone	*Flovent Diskus, Flovent HFA, Arnuity Ellipta* (inhalation)
Fluticasone/Salmeterol	*Advair Diskus, Advair HFA* (inhalation)
Fluticasone/Vilanterol	*Breo Ellipta* (inhalation)
Formoterol	Inhalation
Furosemide	*Lasix* (oral), generics (injection)
Gabapentin	*Neurontin*
Gemfibrozil	*Lopid*
Glecaprevir/Pibrentasvir	*Mavyret*
Glimepiride	*Amaryl*
Glipizide	*Glucotrol*
Glyburide	
Glyburide, micronized	*Glynase*
Granisetron	*Sancuso* (patch), generics (injection, oral)
Guanfacine ER	*Intuniv*
Haloperidol	*Haldol* (oral, injection)
Hydralazine	Generics (oral, injection)
Hydralazine/Isosorbide dinitrate	*BiDil*
Hydrochlorothiazide	
Hydrocodone/ Acetaminophen	*Lortab, Lorcet, Norco, Vicodin*
Hydrocortisone	*Solu-Cortef* (injection), generics (oral)

DRUG	BRAND NAME
Hydromorphone	*Dilaudid* (oral, injection)
Hydroxychloroquine	*Plaquenil*
Hydroxyurea	
Hydroxyzine	*Vistaril*
Ibandronate	*Boniva* (oral, injection)
Ibuprofen	*Advil, Motrin IB* (oral), *Caldolor* (injection)
Icosapent ethyl	*Vascepa*
Imatinib	*Gleevec*
Indomethacin	*Indocin* (oral, injection, suppository)
Influenza vaccine, live attenuated (LAIV4)	*FluMist Quadrivalent* (nasal)
Ipratropium bromide	*Atrovent HFA* (inhalation)
Irbesartan	*Avapro*
Isocarboxazid	*Marplan*
Isoniazid (INH)	
Isosorbide mononitrate	
Isotretinoin	*Absorica, Amnesteem*
Ketoconazole	Generics (topical, oral)
Ketorolac	*Toradol* (oral, injection), *Acular* (ophthalmic), *Sprix* (nasal)
Labetalol	Generics (oral, injection)
Lacosamide	*Vimpat* (oral, injection)
Lactulose	
Lamivudine	*Epivir, Epivir HBV*
Lamotrigine	*Lamictal, Lamictal ODT, Lamictal Starter Kit*
Lansoprazole	*Prevacid, Prevacid 24HR, Prevacid SoluTab*
Latanoprost	*Xalatan* (ophthalmic)
Levetiracetam	*Keppra* (oral, injection)

DRUG	BRAND NAME
Levofloxacin	*Levaquin* (oral, injection)
Levothyroxine	*Levoxyl, Synthroid, Unithroid* (oral), generics (injection)
Lidocaine	*Lidoderm* (patch), generics (topical, oral solution)
Linaclotide	*Linzess*
Linagliptin	*Tradjenta*
Linezolid	*Zyvox* (oral, injection)
Liothyronine	*Cytomel*
Lisdexamfetamine	*Vyvanse*
Lisinopril	*Prinivil, Zestril*
Lisinopril/ Hydrochlorothiazide	*Zestoretic*
Lithium	*Lithobid*
Lorazepam	*Ativan* (oral, injection)
Losartan	*Cozaar*
Losartan/ Hydrochlorothiazide	*Hyzaar*
Lovastatin	*Altoprev*
Lubiprostone	*Amitiza*
Lurasidone	*Latuda*
Medroxyprogesterone	*Provera* (oral), *Depo-Provera* (injection)
Meloxicam	*Mobic*
Memantine	*Namenda*
Meperidine	*Demerol* (oral, injection)
Mesalamine	*Asacol HD, Pentasa, Canasa* (suppository), *Rowasa* (enema)
Metformin	*Glucophage, Glucophage XR, Fortamet, Glumetza*
Metformin/Pioglitazone	*Actoplus Met*
Metformin/Sitagliptin	*Janumet*

Top Prescription Drugs Continued

DRUG	BRAND NAME
Methadone	*Dolophine*
Methimazole	
Methocarbamol	*Robaxin*
Methotrexate	*Trexall* (oral), *Otrexup, Rasuvo* (injection)
Methylnaltrexone	*Relistor* (oral, injection)
Methylphenidate	*Concerta, Ritalin, Ritalin LA* (oral), *Daytrana* (patch)
Methylprednisolone	*Medrol* (oral), *Solu-Medrol* (injection)
Metoclopramide	*Reglan* (oral), generics (injection)
Metoprolol succinate ER	*Toprol XL*
Metoprolol tartrate IR	*Lopressor* (oral), generics (injection)
Metronidazole	*Flagyl* (oral, injection)
Minocycline	*Solodyn* (oral), *Minocin* (oral, injection)
Mirtazapine	*Remeron, Remeron SolTab*
Mometasone	Generics (topical)
Mometasone/ Formoterol	*Dulera* (inhalation)
Montelukast	*Singulair*
Morphine	*MS Contin, Kadian* (oral), *Duramorph, Infumorph* (injection)
Moxifloxacin	*Avelox* (oral), *Vigamox, Moxeza* (ophthalmic), generics (injection)
Mupirocin	*Bactroban* (topical)
Mycophenolate mofetil	*CellCept* (oral, injection)
Mycophenolic acid	*Myfortic*
N-acetylcysteine	*Acetadote* (injection), generics (oral)

DRUG	BRAND NAME
Nabilone	*Cesamet*
Nabumetone	
Nadolol	*Corgard*
Naloxegol	*Movantik*
Naloxone	*Narcan* (nasal), generics (injection)
Naproxen	*Aleve*
Naproxen/ Esomeprazole	*Vimovo*
Nebivolol	*Bystolic*
Neomycin/Polymyxin B/Dexamethasone	*Maxitrol* (ophthalmic)
Niacin	*Niaspan*
Nifedipine ER	*Adalat CC, Procardia XL*
Nitrofurantoin	*Macrobid, Macrodantin*
Nitroglycerin	*Nitro-BID* (ointment), *Nitrostat* (SL tablet), *Nitrolingual, NitroMist* (SL spray), generics (injection)
Norethindrone	*Errin, Camila, Nora-BE*
Nortriptyline	*Pamelor*
Nystatin	
Ofloxacin	*Ocuflox* (ophthalmic)
Olanzapine	*Zyprexa*
Olmesartan	*Benicar*
Olmesartan/ Hydrochlorothiazide	*Benicar HCT*
Olopatadine	*Pataday* (ophthalmic)
Omega-3 fatty acids	*Lovaza*
Omeprazole	*Prilosec, Prilosec OTC*
Ondansetron	*Zofran* (oral), *Zuplenz* (oral film), generics (injection)

DRUG	BRAND NAME
Orlistat	*Xenical, Alli*
Oseltamivir	*Tamiflu*
Oxcarbazepine	*Trileptal*
Oxybutynin	*Ditropan XL* (oral), *Oxytrol, Oxytrol for Women* (patch)
Oxycodone	*Oxycontin* (oral, ER), *Roxicodone* (oral, IR)
Oxycodone/ Acetaminophen	*Percocet, Endocet*
Paliperidone	*Invega*
Pancrelipase	*Creon, Viokace, Zenpep*
Pantoprazole	*Protonix* (oral, injection)
Paroxetine	*Paxil*
Penicillin VK	
Phenazopyridine	*Pyridium*
Phenelzine	*Nardil*
Phenobarbital	Generics (oral, injection)
Phentermine	*Adipex-P*
Phenytoin	*Dilantin, Dilantin Infatabs* (oral), generics (oral, injection)
Pioglitazone	*Actos*
Polyethylene glycol 3350	*MiraLax*
Polyethylene glycol-electrolyte solution	*Colyte, GoLytely, NuLytely*
Polymyxin/ Trimethoprim	*Polytrim* (ophthalmic)
Posaconazole	*Noxafil* (oral, injection)
Potassium chloride	*Klor-Con, K-Tab, Micro-K* (oral), generics (oral, injection)
Pramipexole	*Mirapex, Mirapex ER*
Prasugrel	*Effient*

Top Prescription Drugs Continued

DRUG	BRAND NAME
Pravastatin	Pravachol
Prednisolone	Millipred, Orapred ODT (oral), Pred Forte, Pred Mild (ophthalmic)
Prednisone	Deltasone
Pregabalin	Lyrica
Progesterone, micronized	Prometrium
Prochlorperazine	Compazine (oral, injection)
Promethazine	Phenergan (oral, injection, suppository)
Propranolol	Inderal LA, Inderal XL (oral), generics (injection)
Propylthiouracil (PTU)	
Quetiapine	Seroquel
Quinapril	Accupril
Raltegravir	Isentress, Isentress HD
Ramipril	Altace
Rifampin	
Rifaximin	Xifaxan
Rilpivirine	
Rilpivirine/ Emtricitabine/Tenofovir alafenamide	Odefsey
Rilpivirine/ Emtricitabine/Tenofovir disoproxil fumarate	Complera
Risperidone	Risperdal
Ritonavir	Norvir
Rivaroxaban	Xarelto
Rivastigmine	Exelon (patch), generics (oral)
Ropinirole ER	Requip XL
Rosiglitazone	Avandia

DRUG	BRAND NAME
Rosuvastatin	Crestor
Rotavirus 1 vaccine	Rotarix
Rotavirus 5 vaccine	RotaTeq
Sacubitril/Valsartan	Entresto
Salmeterol	Serevent Diskus (inhalation)
Scopolamine	Transderm Scop (patch)
Selenium sulfide	Selsun (topical)
Sertraline	Zoloft
Sevelamer carbonate	Renvela
Sevelamer hydrochloride	Renagel
Sildenafil	Viagra (oral), Revatio (oral, injection)
Simvastatin	Zocor
Sitagliptin	Januvia
Sodium phosphates	OsmoPrep (oral), generics (injection)
Sodium polystyrene sulfonate	SPS, Kayexalate (oral, enema)
Sodium/Potassium/ Magnesium sulfate	Suprep Bowel Prep Kit
Sofosbuvir/Velpatasvir	Epclusa
Solifenacin	Vesicare
Spironolactone	Aldactone
Sucralfate	Carafate
Sulfamethoxazole/ Trimethoprim	Bactrim DS (oral), Bactrim (oral, injection)
Sumatriptan	Imitrex (oral, injection, nasal), Imitrex STATdose (injection), Onzetra Xsail (nasal)
Sumatriptan/Naproxen	Treximet
Tacrolimus	Prograf (oral, injection)

DRUG	BRAND NAME
Tadalafil	Cialis, Adcirca
Tamoxifen	
Tamsulosin	Flomax
Temazepam	Restoril
Tenofovir alafenamide	Vemlidy
Tenofovir disoproxil fumarate	Viread
Terazosin	
Terbinafine	Generics (oral)
Terconazole	Generics (topical, vaginal)
Testosterone	AndroGel, AndroGel Pump (topical)
Theophylline	
Thyroid, desiccated	Armour Thyroid
Ticagrelor	Brilinta
Timolol	Timoptic, Istalol, Timoptic-XE (ophthalmic)
Timolol/Dorzolamide	Cosopt, Cosopt PF (ophthalmic)
Tiotropium	Spiriva HandiHaler, Spiriva Respimat (inhalation)
Tizanidine	Zanaflex
Tobramycin	Generics (inhalation, injection)
Tolterodine	Detrol
Tolvaptan	Samsca
Topiramate	Topamax
Torsemide	
Tramadol	Ultram
Tranexamic acid	Cyklokapron (injection), Lysteda (oral)

Top Prescription Drugs Continued

DRUG	BRAND NAME
Tranylcypromine	*Parnate*
Travoprost	*Travatan Z* (ophthalmic)
Trazodone	
Tretinoin	*Atralin, Renova, Retin-A, Retin-A Micro* (topical)
Triamcinolone	*Kenalog* (topical, injection)
Triamterene/ Hydrochlorothiazide	*Dyazide, Maxzide*
Valacyclovir	*Valtrex*
Valganciclovir	*Valcyte*
Valproic acid/ Divalproex	*Depakote, Depakote ER, Depakote Sprinkle, Depakene* (oral), generics (injection)
Valsartan	*Diovan*
Valsartan/Amlodipine	*Exforge*
Valsartan/ Hydrochlorothiazide	*Diovan HCT*
Vancomycin	*Vancocin* (oral, injection)
Varenicline	*Chantix*
Venlafaxine	*Effexor XR*
Verapamil	*Calan SR*
Vitamin K, phytonadione	*Mephyton* (oral), generics (injection)
Voriconazole	*Vfend* (oral), *Vfend IV* (injection)
Warfarin	*Coumadin, Jantoven*
Zidovudine	*Retrovir* (oral, injection)
Ziprasidone	*Geodon* (oral, injection)
Zolpidem	*Ambien* (oral), *Edluar, Intermezzo* (SL tablet)

TOP PRESCRIPTION DRUGS: INJECTABLE ONLY

Top selling/must know prescription drugs that are injectable only are included in this list and are bolded throughout the course book. Refer to the clinical chapters for essential underlined information about them.

DRUG	BRAND NAME
Adalimumab	Humira
Albumin	Albutein, AlbuRx
Alteplase	Activase
Amikacin	
Amphotericin B, conventional	
Amphotericin B, liposomal	Ambisome
Ampicillin/Sulbactam	Unasyn
Andexanet alfa	Andexxa
Antithymocyte globulin (equine)	Atgam
Antithymocyte globulin (rabbit)	Thymoglobulin
Argatroban	
Aztreonam	Azactam
Belimumab	Benlysta
Bevacizumab	Avastin
Bivalirudin	Angiomax
Bleomycin	
Busulfan	
Carboplatin	
Carmustine	
Caspofungin	Cancidas
Cefazolin	
Cefepime	
Cefotaxime	
Cefotetan	Cefotan
Ceftaroline	Teflaro
Ceftazidime	Fortaz
Ceftriaxone	
Certolizumab pegol	Cimzia

DRUG	BRAND NAME
Cetuximab	
Cisatracurium	Nimbex
Cisplatin	
Crotalidae polyvalent immune Fab	CroFab
D5W	
Daptomycin	Cubicin
Darbepoetin alfa	Aranesp
Denosumab	Prolia, Xgeva
Dexmedetomidine	Precedex
Digoxin immune Fab	DigiFab
Diphtheria and Tetanus Toxoids, Acellular Pertussis (Tdap) vaccine	Adacel, Boostrix
Docetaxel	
Dopamine	
Doxorubicin	
DTaP-HepB-IPV vaccine	Pediarix
Dulaglutide	Trulicity
Enalaprilat	
Enoxaparin	Lovenox
Epinephrine	Adrenalin, EpiPen
Epoetin alfa	Epogen, Procrit
Epoprostenol	Flolan
Eptifibatide	Integrilin
Ertapenem	Invanz
Esmolol	Brevibloc
Etanercept	Enbrel
Factor VIIa recombinant	NovoSeven RT
Ferumoxytol	Feraheme

DRUG	BRAND NAME
Filgrastim	Neupogen
Flumazenil	
Fluorouracil, 5-FU	
Fosaprepitant	Emend
Fosphenytoin	Cerebyx
Four factor prothrombin complex concentrate	Kcentra
Fulvestrant	
Ganciclovir	
Gentamicin	
Glatiramer acetate	Copaxone
Golimumab	Simponi
Goserelin	Zoladex
Hepatitis A vaccine	Havrix, VAQTA
Hepatitis B vaccine	Engerix-B, Heplisav-B, Recombivax HB
Human Papillomavirus (HPV) vaccine (9-valent)	Gardasil 9
Idarucizumab	Praxbind
Ifosfamide	
Immunoglobulin	Gammagard, Octagam, Privigen, Carimune NF, Flebogamma DIF, Gamunex-C
Inactivated Quadrivalent Influenza vaccine (IIV4)	Afluria Quadrivalent, Fluarix Quadrivalent, FluLaval Quadrivalent, Flucelvax Quadrivalent, Fluzone Quadrivalent, Fluzone High-Dose Quadrivalent
Infliximab	Remicade

Top Prescription Drugs: Injectable Only Continued

DRUG	BRAND NAME
Insulin aspart	Novolog
Insulin detemir	Levemir
Insulin glargine	Lantus, Toujeo
Insulin lispro	Humalog
Insulin NPH	Humulin N, Novolin N
Insulin regular	Humulin R, Novolin R
Insulin, premixed (70% NPH/30% regular)	Humulin 70/30, Novolin 70/30
Irinotecan	
Iron sucrose	Venofer
Lactated Ringer's	
Leuprolide	Lupron Depot
Liraglutide	Victoza, Saxenda
Measles-Mumps-Rubella vaccine (MMR)	M-M-R II
Measles-Mumps-Rubella-Varicella vaccine (MMRV)	ProQuad
Meningococcal vaccine (MCV4)	Menactra, MenQuadfi, Menveo
Meropenem	
Micafungin	Mycamine
Midazolam	Versed
Mitoxantrone	
Natalizumab	Tysabri
Nicardipine	Cardene IV
Nitroprusside	Nipride
Norepinephrine	Levophed
NS (½NS, ¼NS)	
Octreotide	Sandostatin
Omalizumab	Xolair
Paclitaxel	
Palivizumab	Synagis

DRUG	BRAND NAME
Palonosetron	Aloxi
Pegfilgrastim	Neulasta
Penicillin G benzathine	Bicillin L-A
Piperacillin/Tazobactam	Zosyn
Plasma-Lyte A	
Pneumococcal Conjugate vaccine (PCV13)	Prevnar 13
Pneumococcal Conjugate vaccine (PCV15)	Vaxneuvance
Pneumococcal Conjugate vaccine (PCV20)	Prevnar 20
Pneumococcal Polysaccharide vaccine (PPSV23)	Pneumovax 23
Propofol	Diprivan
Protamine sulfate	
Rabies vaccine	RabAvert
Rasburicase	Elitek
Rituximab	Rituxan
Succinylcholine	
Tenecteplase	TNKase
Testosterone cypionate	
Trastuzumab	Herceptin
Unfractionated heparin	
Varicella (Chickenpox) Virus vaccine	Varivax
Vasopressin	
Vedolizumab	Entyvio
Vinblastine	
Vincristine	
Zoledronic acid	Reclast, Zometa
Zoster (Shingles) Virus vaccine	Shingrix

TOP OTC DRUGS

For drugs that are available in both OTC and Rx (prescription) versions, the Rx doses are generally higher than the OTC doses. The brand names can be different [e.g., orlistat OTC (*Alli*) is 60 mg/dose, orlistat Rx (*Xenical*) is 120 mg/dose] and are provided as a study aid (generic may be the top-seller).

DRUG

ALLERGIC RHINITIS, COUGH AND COLD

Antihistamines, Non-Sedating

Fexofenadine (*Allegra Allergy 24-HR, Children's Allegra Allergy*)

Loratadine (*Claritin, Children's Claritin*)

Cetirizine (*Zyrtec, Children's Zyrtec*)

Levocetirizine (*Xyzal Allergy 24HR, Children's Xyzal Allergy 24HR*)

Antihistamines, Sedating

Diphenhydramine (*Benadryl*), **OTC and Rx**

Chlorpheniramine

Cough Suppressant

Dextromethorphan (*Delsym, Robitussin*)

Mucolytic-Expectorant

Guaifenesin (*Mucinex, Robafen*)

Cough Suppressant/Mucolytic-Expectorant

Dextromethorphan/Guaifenesin (*Robafen DM, Robitussin DM*)

Decongestants

Oxymetazoline (*Afrin*) – nasal

Phenylephrine (*Sudafed PE*) – systemic

Pseudoephedrine (*Sudafed, Nexafed, Zephrex-D*) – systemic, behind the counter

Decongestants/Antihistamines, Non-Sedating

Cetirizine/Pseudoephedrine (*Zyrtec-D*)

Fexofenadine/Pseudoephedrine (*Allegra-D*)

Loratadine/Pseudoephedrine ER (*Claritin-D*)

Nasal Steroid Inhalers

Budesonide (*Rhinocort Allergy*)

Fluticasone (*Flonase Allergy Relief, Flonase Sensimist, Children's Flonase Sensimist*)

Triamcinolone (*Nasacort Allergy 24HR, Nasacort Allergy 24HR Children*)

Nasal Mast Cell Stabilizer

Cromolyn (*NasalCrom*)

DRUG

COMMON SKIN CONDITIONS

Acne

Adapalene (*Differin*), **OTC and Rx**

Azelaic acid

Benzoyl peroxide

Salicylic acid

Alopecia

Minoxidil (*Rogaine*) – topical

Cold Sores, for Herpes Simplex

Docosanol (*Abreva*)

Dandruff Shampoos

Ketoconazole 1% (*Nizoral A-D*)

Pyrithione zinc (*Head & Shoulders*)

Selenium sulfide (*Selsun*)

Coal tar (*T/Gel*)

Diaper Rash

Petrolatum/Zinc Oxide (*Desitin*)

Topical Antifungals, for Tinea Infections

Butenafine (*Lotrimin Ultra*) – cream

Clotrimazole (*Lotrimin AF*) – cream

Miconazole (*Lotrimin AF*) – powder and spray

Terbinafine (*Lamisil AT*) – cream

Tolnaftate (*Tinactin*) – cream and spray

Undecylenic acid (*Fungi-Nail*)

Vaginal Antifungals, for Candida Infections

Clotrimazole (*Gyne-Lotrimin*)

Miconazole (*Monistat*)

Hemorrhoids

Phenylephrine (*Preparation H*)

Lice

Permethrin 1% (*Nix*)

Piperonyl butoxide/Pyrethrin (*RID*)

DRUG

Minor wounds

Polymyxin B/Bacitracin/Neomycin (*Neosporin*) – topical antibiotic

Pinworm

Pyrantel pamoate

Inflammation and Rash

Hydrocortisone cream 0.5% and 1% (*Cortaid, Cortisone, Cortizone-10*) – topical, **OTC and Rx**

CONSTIPATION AND DIARRHEA

Antidiarrheals

Bismuth subsalicylate (*Pepto-Bismol*)

Loperamide (*Imodium A-D*)

Constipation

Bisacodyl (*Dulcolax*) – oral, enema, suppository

Calcium polycarbophil (*FiberCon*)

Docusate sodium (*Colace*) – oral, enema

Glycerin suppository

Magnesium hydroxide (*Milk of Magnesia*)

Methylcellulose (*Citrucel*)

Mineral oil – oral, enema

Polyethylene glycol 3350 (*MiraLax*), **OTC and Rx**

Psyllium (*Metamucil*)

Sodium phosphates (*Fleet Enema*) – enema

Senna (*Ex-Lax, Senokot*)

Senna/Docusate (*Senokot S, Senna S*)

Wheat dextrin (*Benefiber*)

CONTRACEPTION

Condoms

Diaphragm

Nonoxynol-9 spermicide

Emergency Contraception

Levonorgestrel (*Plan B One-Step*), **OTC and Rx**

Top OTC Drugs Continued

DRUG

DIABETES: INSULIN, OTC and Rx

NPH Insulin

Humulin N, Novolin N

Premixed Insulins

Humulin 70/30, Novolin 70/30

Regular Insulin

Humulin R, Novolin R

DIETARY SUPPLEMENTS, NATURAL & COMPLEMENTARY MEDICINE

Calcium carbonate (*Tums, Oscal*)

Calcium citrate (*Citracal, Cal-Citrate*)

Coenzyme Q10

Ferrous sulfate (*Slow Fe, Fer-In-Sol*)

Omega-3 fatty acids (fish oils)

Magnesium citrate

Magnesium oxide

Probiotics

Lactobacillus (Culturelle)

Bifidobacterium longum (Align)

Saccharomyces boulardii (Florastor)

Vitamins

Niacin Controlled Release (*Slo-Niacin*)

Multivitamin (*One-A-Day*, others)

Prenatal multivitamin, **OTC and Rx**

Vitamin B complex

Vitamin B12, cyanocobalamin, **OTC and Rx**

Vitamin B9, folic acid, folate, **OTC and Rx**

Vitamin C, ascorbic acid

Vitamin D2, ergocalciferol, **OTC and Rx**

Vitamin D3, cholecalciferol, **OTC and Rx**

GASTROESOPHAGEAL REFLUX DISEASE & PEPTIC ULCER DISEASE

Proton Pump Inhibitors, OTC and Rx

Esomeprazole 20 mg (*Nexium 24HR*)

Omeprazole 20 mg (*Prilosec OTC*)

Lansoprazole 15 mg (*Prevacid 24HR*), Lansoprazole 15 mg ODT

DRUG

H2-Receptor Antagonists, OTC and Rx

Cimetidine 200 mg (*Tagamet*)

Famotidine 10/20 mg (*Pepcid AC, Zantac 360*)

Antacids & Antigas

Aluminum/Magnesium/Simethicone (*Mylanta Classic*)

Calcium carbonate (*Tums*)

Calcium carbonate/Magnesium (*Mylanta Supreme*)

Calcium carbonate/Simethicone (*Maalox Advanced Maximum Strength*)

Anhydrous citric acid/Aspirin/Sodium bicarbonate (*Alka-Seltzer*)

Simethicone (*Gas-X*)

Alpha-Galactosidase enzyme (*Beano*)

Lactase enzyme (*Lactaid*)

MOTION SICKNESS

Dimenhydrinate (*Dramamine*)

Meclizine (*Dramamine All Day Less Drowsy*)

OPHTHALMICS AND OTICS

Artificial tears (*Systane, Refresh*) – dry eye

Carbamide peroxide (*Debrox*) – ear wax removal

Ketotifen (*Alaway, Zaditor*) – red eyes/allergies

Naphazoline (*Clear Eyes Redness Relief*) – red eye

Naphazoline/Pheniramine (*Naphcon-A, Visine-A*) – red eyes/allergies

Olopatadine (*Pataday*) – red eyes/allergies, **OTC and Rx**

Tetrahydrozoline (*Visine*) – red eye

PAIN

Acetaminophen 325/500/650 mg (*Tylenol, FeverAll* rectal suppository)

Acetaminophen/Caffeine (*Excedrin Tension Headache*)

Acetaminophen/Aspirin/Caffeine (*Excedrin Extra Strength, Excedrin Migraine*)

Acetaminophen/Caffeine/Pyrilamine (*Midol Complete*)

Aspirin (*Bayer, Ecotrin, Bufferin, Ascriptin*)

Capsaicin 0.025% and 0.075% cream (*Zostrix, Zostrix HP*)

DRUG

Diclofenac gel (*Voltaren*), **OTC and Rx**

Ibuprofen 200 mg (*Motrin, Advil*), **OTC and Rx**

Lidocaine patches (*LidoPatch*), **OTC and Rx**

Magnesium salicylate (*Doan's Extra Strength*)

Methyl salicylate and menthol topical (*BenGay, Salonpas, IcyHot*)

Naproxen sodium 220 mg (*Aleve*), **OTC and Rx**

Trolamine salicylate (*Aspercreme*)

SLEEP DISORDERS

Diphenhydramine (*Benadryl*), **OTC and Rx**

Doxylamine (*Unisom SleepTabs*)

Melatonin

TOBACCO CESSATION

Nicotine gum (*Nicorette*)

Nicotine lozenge (*Nicorette, Nicorette Mini*)

Nicotine transdermal patch (*Nicoderm CQ*)

URINARY INCONTINENCE

Oxybutynin (*Oxytrol for Women*), **OTC and Rx**

WEIGHT LOSS

Orlistat (*Alli*), **OTC and Rx**

REQUIRED FORMULAS

Calculations

Liquid (Volume) Conversions p. 117

1 tsp (t) = 5 mL, tbsp (T) = 15 mL

1 fl oz = 30 mL (approx.); 29.57 mL (actual)

1 cup = 8 oz, 240 mL (approx.); 236.56 mL (actual)

1 pint = 16 oz, 480 mL (approx.); 473 mL (actual)

1 quart = 2 pints, 960 mL (approx.); 946 mL (actual)

1 gallon = 4 quarts, 3,840 mL (approx.); 3,785 mL (actual)

Solid (Weight) Conversions p. 117

1 kg = 2.2 pounds (lbs)

1 oz = 28.4 grams (g)

1 lb = 454 g

1 grain = 65 mg (approx.); 64.8 mg (actual)

mEq to mmol is 1:1 for monovalent ions, 1:0.5 for divalent ions

Height Conversions p. 117

1 inch (in) = 2.54 centimeters (cm)

1 meter (m) = 100 cm

Percentage Strength p. 128

$$\% \text{ w/v} = \frac{X \text{ g}}{100 \text{ mL}} \qquad \% \text{ v/v} = \frac{X \text{ mL}}{100 \text{ mL}} \qquad \% \text{ w/w} = \frac{X \text{ g}}{100 \text{ g}}$$

Ratio Strength p. 132

Percentage strength = 100 / Ratio strength

Ratio strength = 100 / Percentage strength

Parts Per Million (PPM) p. 134

PPM → Percentage strength   Move the decimal left 4 places

Percentage strength → PPM   Move the decimal right 4 places

Specific Gravity (SG) p. 135

$$SG = \frac{\text{weight of substance (g)}}{\text{weight of equal volume of water (g)}} \quad \text{or} \quad SG = \frac{g}{mL}$$

Dilution & Concentration (Changing Strength or Quantity) p. 136

Q1 x C1 = Q2 x C2   Q1 = old quantity   Q2 = new quantity

                           C1 = old concentration   C2 = new concentration

Alligation p. 137

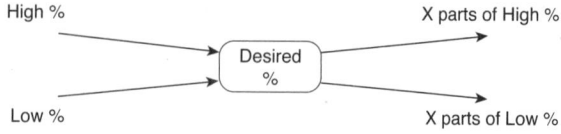

High %

Desired %

Low %

X parts of High %

X parts of Low %

Use proportions to calculate amount of high % and/or low % required

Osmolarity p. 140

$$\text{mOsmol/L} = \frac{\text{Wt of substance (g/L)}}{\text{MW (g/mole)}} \times (\text{\# of particles}) \times 1{,}000$$

Isotonicity (E Value) p. 143

$$E = \frac{(58.5)(i)}{(\text{MW of drug})(1.8)}$$

Moles and Millimoles p. 144

$$\text{mols} = \frac{g}{MW} \quad \text{or} \quad \text{mmols} = \frac{mg}{MW}$$

Milliequivalents p. 146

$$\text{mEq} = \frac{mg \times valence}{MW} \quad \text{or} \quad \text{mEq} = \text{mmols} \times valence$$

Enteral Nutrition Calories p. 152

Carbs, Protein = 4 kcal/gram   Fat = 9 kcal/gram

Parenteral Nutrition Calories p. 152

Dextrose monohydrate = 3.4 kcal/gram   ILE 10% = 1.1 kcal/mL

Amino acid solutions = 4 kcal/gram   ILE 20% = 2 kcal/mL

                                     ILE 30% = 3 kcal/mL

Determining Fluid Needs p. 150

When weight > 20 kg: 1,500 mL + (20 mL)(weight in kg − 20)

can estimate using 30-40 mL/kg/day

Total Energy Expenditure p. 151

TEE = BEE x activity factor x stress factor

Grams of Nitrogen From Protein p. 153

$$\text{Nitrogen (g)} = \frac{\text{protein intake (g)}}{6.25}$$

Corrected Calcium for Albumin < 3.5 (not needed with ionized Ca) p. 160

$Ca_{corrected}$ (mg/dL) = $calcium_{reported(serum)}$ + [(4.0 − albumin) x (0.8)]

Body Mass Index (BMI) p. 169

$$\text{BMI (kg/m}^2\text{)} = \frac{\text{weight (kg)}}{[\text{height (m)}]^2} \quad \text{or} \quad \frac{\text{weight (lbs)}}{[\text{height (inches)}]^2} \times 703$$

Ideal Body Weight (IBW) p. 170

IBW (males) = 50 kg + (2.3 kg)(number of inches over 5 feet)

IBW (females) = 45.5 kg + (2.3 kg)(number of inches over 5 feet)

Adjusted Body Weight (AdjBW$_{0.4}$) p. 170

$AdjBW_{0.4}$ = IBW + 0.4(TBW − IBW)

Which Weight to Use for Drug Dosing (mg/kg) p. 171

All drugs (if underweight)   Total Body Weight (TBW)

Most drugs (if normal weight or obese)   TBW

Exceptions

Acyclovir, Aminophylline, Levothyroxine,   IBW

Theophylline (normal weight, obese)

Aminoglycosides (obese) $AdjBW_{0.4}$

Flow Rates/Drop Factor (drops/min) p. 172 & p. 175

$$\frac{\text{\# drops}}{mL} \times \frac{mL}{hr} \times \frac{hr}{60 \text{ min}} = \frac{\text{\# drops}}{min}$$

Dehydration p. 177

BUN:SCr > 20:1

Cockcroft-Gault Equation p. 178

$$\text{CrCl (mL/min)} = \frac{140 - (\text{age of patient})}{72 \times SCr} \times \text{weight (kg) (x 0.85 if female)}$$

Arterial Blood Gas (ABG) p. 180

ABG: pH/pCO$_2$/pO$_2$/HCO$_3$/O$_2$ Sat

1. pH < 7.35 → acidosis, pH > 7.45 → alkalosis
2. Respiratory: pCO$_2$ < 35 → alkalosis, pCO$_2$ > 45 → acidosis
   Metabolic: HCO$_3$ > 26 → alkalosis, HCO$_3$ < 22 → acidosis
3. Which abnormal value (pCO$_2$ or HCO$_3$) matches the pH from Step #1?
   Ex: ↓ pH + ↑ pCO$_2$ → <u>respiratory</u> acidosis
   Ex: ↓ pH + ↓ HCO$_3$ → <u>metabolic</u> acidosis

Anion Gap p. 181

Anion gap (AG) = Na − Cl − HCO$_3$

pH Calculations p. 182

Weak acid   Weak base

$$\text{pH} = pK_a + \log\left[\frac{salt}{acid}\right] \qquad \text{pH} = pK_a + \log\left[\frac{base}{salt}\right]$$

Percent Ionization p. 185

Weak acid   Weak base

$$\% \text{ ionization} = \frac{100}{1+10^{(pKa-pH)}} \qquad \% \text{ ionization} = \frac{100}{1+10^{(pH-pKa)}}$$

Absolute Neutrophil Count (ANC) p. 187

ANC (cells/mm^3) = WBC x [(% segs + % bands)/100]

Answering Case-Based Exam Questions

Temperature Conversions (Fahrenheit ↔ Celsius) p. 108

°C = (°F − 32)/1.8   °F = (°C x 1.8) + 32

Common Skin Conditions

Time to Burn (TTB) p. 562

TTB (with sunscreen in min) = SPF X TTB (without sunscreen)

Biostatistics

Mean, Median and Mode p. 204

Mean - average value

Median - value in the middle of an ordered list

Mode - value that occurs most frequently

Risk, Relative Risk (RR) p. 209, Relative Risk Reduction (RRR) & Absolute Risk Reduction (ARR) p. 210

$$\text{Risk} = \frac{\text{Number of subjects in group with an unfavorable event}}{\text{Total number of subjects in group}}$$

$$\text{RR} = \frac{\text{Risk in treatment group}}{\text{Risk in control group}}$$

$$\text{RRR} = \frac{(\% \text{ risk in control group} - \% \text{ risk in treatment group})}{\% \text{ risk in the control group}}$$

$$\text{ARR} = (\% \text{ risk in control group}) - (\% \text{ risk in treatment group})$$

Number Needed to Treat or Harm (NNT, NNH) p. 211-212

$$\text{NNT or NNH} = \frac{1}{\text{ARR}^*}$$
*expressed as decimal

Odds Ratio (OR) p. 212

Exposure	Outcome Present	Outcome Absent
Present	A	B
Absent	C	D

$$\text{OR} = \frac{AD}{BC}$$

Hazard Ratio (HR) p. 213

$$\text{HR} = \frac{\text{Hazard rate in the treatment group}}{\text{Hazard rate in the control group}}$$

Incremental Cost-Effectiveness Ratio p. 223

$$\text{Incremental cost ratio} = \frac{(C_2 - C_1)}{(E_2 - E_1)}$$
*C = costs, E = effects

Tobacco Cessation

Pack-Year Smoking History p. 598

$$\text{Pack-year smoking history} = \text{Cigarette packs / day} \times \text{years smoked}$$

Diabetes

Initiating Basal-Bolus Insulin in Type 1 Diabetes p. 617

1. Calculate total daily dose (TDD) of 0.5 units/kg/day using TBW.
2. Divide into 1/2 basal & 1/2 rapid-acting. If using NPH/R, use 2/3 & 1/3.
3. Split rapid-acting among meals.

Insulin-to-Carbohydrate Ratio: Rule of 450 for Regular Insulin p. 619

$$\frac{450}{\text{total daily dose of insulin (TDD)}} = \text{grams of carbohydrate covered by 1 unit of regular insulin}$$

Insulin-to-Carbohydrate Ratio: Rule of 500 for Rapid-Acting Insulin p. 619

$$\frac{500}{\text{total daily dose of insulin (TDD)}} = \text{grams of carbohydrate covered by 1 unit of rapid-acting insulin}$$

Correction Factor: 1,500 Rule for Regular Insulin p. 619

$$\frac{1{,}500}{\text{total daily dose of insulin (TDD)}} = \text{correction factor for 1 unit of regular insulin}$$

Correction Factor: 1,800 Rule for Rapid-Acting Insulin p. 619

$$\frac{1{,}800}{\text{total daily dose of insulin (TDD)}} = \text{correction factor for 1 unit of rapid-acting insulin}$$

Correction Dose p. 619

$$\frac{(\text{blood glucose now}) - (\text{target blood glucose})}{\text{correction factor}} = \text{correction dose}$$

Dyslipidemia

Friedewald Equation p. 423

$$\text{LDL} = \text{TC} - \text{HDL} - \frac{\text{TG}^*}{5}$$
*do not use if TG > 400

Compounding II

Minimum Weighable Quantity (MWQ) p. 251

$$\text{MWQ} = \frac{\text{Sensitivity requirement}}{\text{Acceptable error rate (usually 0.05)}}$$

Oncology II

BSA Calculations, Mosteller p. 817
(review how to use Dubois-Dubois)

$$\text{BSA (m}^2) = \sqrt{\frac{\text{Ht (cm)} \times \text{Wt (kg)}}{3{,}600}}$$

Pharmacokinetics

Bioavailability (F) p. 958

$$F (\%) = 100 \times \frac{\text{AUC}_{extravascular}}{\text{AUC}_{intravascular}} \times \frac{\text{Dose}_{intravenous}}{\text{Dose}_{extravascular}}$$

Volume of Distribution (Vd) p. 959

$$\text{Vd} = \frac{\text{Amount of drug in body}}{\text{Concentration of drug in plasma}}$$

Clearance p. 961 & p. 963

$$\text{Cl} = \frac{\text{F} \times \text{dose}}{\text{AUC}} \quad \text{or} \quad \text{Cl} = \text{ke} \times \text{Vd}$$

Elimination Rate Constant (ke) p. 963

$$\text{ke} = \frac{\text{Cl}}{\text{Vd}}$$

Predicting Drug Concentrations p. 963

$$C_2 = C_1 \times e^{-kt} \qquad \text{ke} = \frac{\ln(C_1/C_2)}{t}$$

Half-Life (t½) p. 964

$$t_{½} = \frac{0.693}{\text{ke}}$$

Loading Dose (LD) p. 966

$$\text{LD} = \frac{\text{Desired concentration} \times \text{Vd}}{\text{F}}$$

Acute & Critical Care Medicine

Mean Arterial Pressure (MAP) p. 713

$$\text{MAP} = [(2 \times \text{diastolic pressure}) + \text{systolic pressure}] / 3$$

Seizures/Epilepsy

Phenytoin (Total) Correction for Albumin < 3.5 p. 898

$$\text{Phenytoin}_{corrected} \text{ (mcg/mL)} = \frac{\text{Total phenytoin measured}}{(0.2 \times \text{albumin}) + 0.1}$$

DRUG-DOSE CONVERSIONS

KCl Solution (Oral) to Tablets p. 147 (see problem #61)
KCl 10% = 20 mEq/15 mL

Calcium Salts p. 186
Calcium carbonate = 40% elemental calcium
Calcium citrate = 21% elemental calcium

Aminophylline ↔ Theophylline p. 186
Aminophylline to Theophylline: Multiply by 0.8 (remember: **ATM**)
Theophylline to Aminophylline: Divide by 0.8

Statins p. 426

Pitavastatin	2 mg	Lovastatin	40 mg
Rosuvastatin	5 mg	Pravastatin	40 mg
Atorvastatin	10 mg	Fluvastatin	80 mg
Simvastatin	20 mg		

Metoprolol p. 445
IV:PO = 1:2.5

Loop Diuretics p. 470

Ethacrynic acid	50 mg	Bumetanide	1 mg
Furosemide	40 mg	Furosemide	IV:PO = 1:2
Torsemide	20 mg	Other Loops	IV:PO = 1:1

Iron, Elemental p. 518
Ferrous Sulfate = 20% elemental iron (e.g., 325 mg x 0.2 = 65 mg)

Insulin p. 620
Usually, 1:1 conversion
Exceptions:
NPH dosed BID → glargine dosed daily, use 80% of NPH dose
Toujeo → other forms of glargine or detemir, use 80% of *Toujeo* dose

Levothyroxine p. 629
IV:PO = 0.75:1

Steroids p. 636

Cortisone	25 mg	Methylprednisolone	4 mg
Hydrocortisone	20 mg	Triamcinolone	4 mg
Prednisone	5 mg	Dexamethasone	0.75 mg
Prednisolone	5 mg	Betamethasone	0.6 mg

Opioids (methodology) p. 762

Lithium p. 855
5 mL lithium citrate syrup = 300 mg lithium carbonate = 8 mEq Li$^+$ ion

DIAGNOSTIC TESTS

DISORDER/CONDITION	DIAGNOSTIC TESTS (REFER TO SPECIFIC CHAPTER FOR MORE INFORMATION)
AUTOIMMUNE CONDITIONS	
Autoimmune, Various	↑ erythrocyte sedimentation rate **(ESR)**, ↑ C-reactive protein **(CRP)**, positive rheumatoid factor **(RF)** antibodies, positive anti-nuclear antibody **(ANA)**
Rheumatoid Arthritis (RA)	Above autoimmune tests plus positive anti-citrullinated peptide antibody (ACPA)
Systemic Lupus Erythematosus (SLE)	Above autoimmune tests plus positive anti-dsDNA antibodies
Multiple Sclerosis	Magnetic resonance imaging **(MRI)**
ANTICOAGULATION AND BLOOD DISORDERS	
Anemia	All: **↓ Hgb/Hct/RBCs** **Microcytic (or Fe-deficiency): ↓ MCV** (cell size is smaller, MCV < 80 fL) **Macrocytic (or B12 or folate deficiency): ↑ MCV** (cell size is larger, MCV > 100 fL), Schilling test
Venous Thromboembolism (VTE)	**D-dimer** test (marker of fibrinolysis) Deep vein thrombosis (DVT): **ultrasound (US),** venography, MRI Pulmonary embolism (PE): pulmonary computed tomographic angiography (CTA)
Stroke Prevention	**CHA$_2$DS$_2$-VASc** scoring system (score directs need for anticoagulation in patients with atrial fibrillation)
Heparin-Induced Thrombocytopenia (HIT)	Unexplained **↓ platelets (> 50% drop from baseline)** 5-14 days after starting heparin, positive antibodies based on a heparin-platelet factor 4 (PF4) ELISA and/or serotonin release assay (SRA)
CARDIOVASCULAR CONDITIONS	
Acute Coronary Syndromes (ACS)	Electrocardiogram **(ECG, or EKG),** cardiac enzymes [creatine kinase muscle/brain (CK-MB), **troponin** I, T]
Arrhythmias	**ECG** (or EKG), **Holter monitor** (a portable ECG device), heart rate (HR)
Cerebrovascular Accident (CVA, or Stroke)	Computed tomography **(CT), MRI**
Chronic Heart Failure	Echocardiogram **(echo),** ↑ B-type natriuretic peptide (BNP), ↑ N-terminal proBNP (NT-proBNP)
Stable Ischemic Heart Disease (SIHD)/Chronic Stable Angina	**Cardiac stress test,** angiography
Dyslipidemia	**↑ TC, Non-HDL, LDL, TGs,** coronary artery calcium (CAC, a non-invasive CT scan of the heart that measures calcium-containing plaque)
Hypertension	↑ systolic blood pressure (SBP)/diastolic blood pressure (DBP)
Hypertensive Emergency or Urgency	Emergency: **↑ BP (≥ 180/120 mmHg) with acute target organ damage** Urgency: **↑ BP (≥ 180/120 mmHg) without acute target organ damage**
10-Year Risk for Atherosclerotic Cardiovascular Disease (ASCVD)	10-year **ASCVD risk tool** [use if no history of ASCVD (ACS/IHD, stroke, PAD)]
ENDOCRINE CONDITIONS	
Diabetes, Prediabetes	Fasting plasma glucose **(FPG),** oral glucose tolerance test **(OGTT),** hemoglobin A1C **(A1C)**
Hyperthyroidism	↓ thyroid stimulating hormone **(TSH)**, ↑ free T4 **(FT4)**
Hypothyroidism	**↑ TSH, ↓ FT4**
FEMALE HEALTH	
Ovulation	Luteinizing hormone **(LH),** peak value provides optimal timing for intercourse to become pregnant
Pregnancy	Positive human chorionic gonadotropin **(hCG)** in urine (outpatient test kit) or in blood
Bacterial Vaginitis	Clear, white or gray vaginal discharge, with a **fishy odor** and **pH > 4.5,** little or no pain
Candida Vaginitis	**White, thicker** vaginal discharge, **pruritus**
Trichomoniasis	**Yellow, green frothy,** foul-smelling vaginal discharge, **pH > 4.5,** soreness and pain with intercourse

Diagnostic Tests Continued

DISORDER/CONDITION	DIAGNOSTIC TESTS (REFER TO SPECIFIC CHAPTER FOR MORE INFORMATION)
GASTROINTESTINAL DISORDERS	
Peptic Ulcer Disease	Upper gastrointestinal endoscopy (mouth to small intestine) **Duodenal ulcer:** pain 2-3 hrs after eating **(without food in stomach), pain relief** with food/antacids **Gastric ulcer:** pain right after eating **(with food in stomach),** little/**no pain relief** with food/antacids
GERD	**Esophageal pH monitoring,** endoscopy
H. pylori	**Urea breath test (UBT),** fecal antigen test
Inflammatory Bowel Disease (Ulcerative Colitis, Crohn's Disease)	Endoscopy (for Crohn's disease, which affects more of the GI tract) Sigmoidoscopy (for ulcerative colitis, which affects the colon and rectum) For both: colonoscopy, biopsy, CT, MRI
PULMONARY DISORDERS	
Bronchospastic Diseases	**Spirometry,** measures three main variables: **FEV1:** how much air can be forcefully exhaled in one second **FVC:** the maximum amount of air that can be forcefully exhaled **FEV1/FVC:** the percentage of total air capacity ("vital capacity") that can be forcefully exhaled in one second
Asthma	**FVC, FEV1** and peak expiratory flow rate (PEFR) Allergic asthma: **skin test** (to detect an allergen)
Chronic Obstructive Pulmonary Disease (COPD)	**Post-bronchodilator FEV1/FVC < 0.7** Eosinophils ≥ 300 cells/μL indicates inflammation and better response to inhaled corticosteroids
ACID/BASE DISORDERS	
Metabolic Acidosis	**Arterial blood gas, measures pH, pCO2, HCO3** ↓ pH, ↓ HCO3; compensation: respiratory alkalosis
Respiratory Acidosis	↓ pH, ↑ pCO2; compensation: metabolic alkalosis
Metabolic Alkalosis	↑ pH, ↑ HCO3; compensation: respiratory acidosis
Respiratory Alkalosis	↑ pH, ↓ pCO2; compensation: metabolic acidosis
Anion Gap Metabolic Acidosis	Anion gap > 12 mEq/L
INFECTIONS	
General Infection	**Fever** (temperature ≥ 100.4°F or 38°C), **↑ WBC** count, left shift (↑ bands, or immature neutrophils)
C. difficile	**Positive *C. difficile* stool toxin** [enzyme immunoassay plus glutamate dehydrogenase (GDH) test] or **PCR**
HIV	**HIV antigen/antibody immunoassay, HIV-1/HIV-2 antibody** differentiation immunoassay, **HIV RNA viral load,** nucleic acid test
Infective Endocarditis	Echo (to check for vegetation), blood culture (to identify causative organism)
Lyme Disease	Round, red bullseye rash, enzyme-linked immunosorbent assay **(ELISA)** test
Meningitis	**Lumbar puncture (LP),** plus symptoms of severe headache, stiff neck and altered mental status
Onychomycosis (Fungal Infection of Toenail or Fingernail)	**20% KOH smear**
Lice (*Pediculosis*)	**Pruritus,** visible lice on the scalp and **nits (eggs)** on hair shafts
Pinworm (*Vermicularis*)	**Tape test** (on skin adjacent to anus to check presence of eggs), **helminths** (worms) in blood, feces or urine
Pneumonia	**Chest X-ray** showing infiltrates, consolidations or opacities
Syphilis	Positive nontreponemal assay [rapid plasma reagin **(RPR)** or Venereal Diseases Research Laboratory **(VDRL)** blood test] and treponemal assay
***Toxoplasma gondii* Encephalitis**	Toxoplasma IgG test
Tuberculosis (TB)	Latent TB: positive tuberculin skin test **(TST)** [also known as a purified protein derivative **(PPD)],** or interferon-gamma release assay **(IGRA)** blood test Active TB: positive sputum **acid-fast bacilli (AFB) stain** and culture, chest X-ray with cavitation
Urinary Tract Infection (UTI)	**Urinalysis** (positive leukocyte esterase or WBC > 10 cells/mm³, nitrites, bacteria), urine culture

Diagnostic Tests Continued

DISORDER/CONDITION	DIAGNOSTIC TESTS (REFER TO SPECIFIC CHAPTER FOR MORE INFORMATION)
CANCER	
Initial screenings; all followed by biopsy (tissue sample sent to pathology)	
Breast	**Mammogram, ultrasound, MRI**
Cervical	**Pap smear, HPV test**
Colon	**Colonoscopy, sigmoidoscopy**, double-contrast barium enema, CT colonography, stool DNA, fecal occult blood test (FOBT), fecal immunochemical test
Lung	**CT chest**
Skin	Skin biopsy
Prostate	**Digital rectal exam (DRE), prostate-specific antigen (PSA)**
General	Carcinoembryonic antigen (CEA) test (a marker to identify cancer), positron emission tomography (PET)
ADDITIONAL COMMON CONDITIONS	
Allergic Reactions	**Skin prick** (scratch) test (immediate), immunoglobulin E **(IgE) antibodies** (blood)
Bleeding	↓ Hgb/Hct, visible blood or bruising, coffee ground emesis or dark/tarry stools (upper GI bleeding), red blood in stool (lower GI bleeding or hemorrhoid)
Cholestasis (Bile Duct Blockage)	↑ alkaline phosphatase (Alk Phos), ↑ total bilirubin (Tbili), ↑ gamma-glutamyltransferase (GGT)
Cognitive Impairment (e.g., Alzheimer's)	Mini-mental state exam **(MMSE),** score < 24 indicates impairment
Cystic Fibrosis	**Sweat test**
Glaucoma	↑ intraocular pressure **(IOP),** visual field test (to identify optic nerve damage)
Gout	↑ uric acid **(UA)** level
Liver Disease	Liver function tests **(LFTs):** ↑ **AST/ALT,** ↑ **Alk Phos,** ↑ **Tbili,** ↑ lactate dehydrogenase (LDH)
	Cirrhosis (chronic liver disease): ↑ **PT/INR,** ↓ **Albumin**
	Alcoholic liver disease: ↑ AST > ↑ ALT, ↑ GGT
	Hepatic encephalopathy: ↑ **ammonia** level (blood)
Movement Disorders (e.g. Parkinson Disease)	**Abnormal involuntary movement scale (AIMS),** rating scale used to measure involuntary movements, or tardive dyskinesias, as monitoring for patient improvement
Myopathy	↑ creatine kinase or **creatine phosphokinase (CPK)**
Neuropathy, Peripheral	Assess sensation with **10-g monofilament,** pinprick, temperature and/or vibration tests
Osteoarthritis	X-ray, MRI
Osteoporosis	Bone mineral density **(BMD)** using dual energy X-ray absorptiometry **(DEXA** or **DXA), T-score ≤ -2.5**
	Osteopenia: T-score -1 to -2.4
Pain	**Pain scales,** non-verbal signs (e.g., moaning, grimacing, agitation)
Pancreatitis	↑ **amylase/lipase**
Psychiatric Disease (e.g., Depression, Schizophrenia)	**DSM-5** diagnostic criteria
	Depression-specific: **Ham-D or HDRS assessment scale**
Renal Disease	↑ **BUN/SCr,** creatinine clearance **(CrCl),** glomerular filtration rate **(eGFR), urine albumin**
	Dehydration: BUN/SCr ratio > 20:1, plus symptoms (e.g., ↓ urine output, dry mucus membranes, tachycardia)
Seizures/epilepsy	Electroencephalogram **(EEG)**
Weight: Underweight, Normal Weight, Overweight, Obesity	**BMI** (plus **waist circumference** for risks associated with overweight/obesity), ideal body weight **(IBW),** total body weight **(TBW)**

MEDICAL TERMS

This is not a complete list. Some medical definitions are described in the chapters that follow (e.g., blood cell terminology in the Lab Values & Drug Monitoring and Anemia chapters, compounding terminology in the Compounding chapters, oncology terminology in the Oncology I chapter).

COMMON PREFIXES AND SUFFIXES

A-	Not, no, or lack of
-algia	Pain or soreness
Audio-	Hearing
Brady-	Slow
Dys-	Difficult, abnormal or painful
-ectomy	Surgical removal
Hem-	Blood
Hepato-	Liver
Hyper-	High, above normal or excessive
Hypo-	Low or below normal
-itis	Inflammation
Myo-	Muscle
Nephro-	Kidney
Oligo-	Too few or too little
Patho- or -pathy	Disease or suffering
-pnea	Breathing
Tachy-	Fast

MEDICAL TERMS

Abscess	A local collection of pus anywhere in the body.
Agranulocytosis	A lack of granulocytes (white blood cells) produced by the bone marrow.
Akathisia	An inability to stay still with constant movement (restlessness).
Akinesia	A lack of body movement.
Alogia	A lack of speech (also called aphasia).
Alopecia	Hair loss.
Amenorrhea	The absence or cessation of menstruation.
Amnesia, anterograde	A loss of memory related to events that occur after a traumatic event.
Amnesia, retrograde	A loss of memory related to events occurring before a traumatic event.
Anaphylaxis	A severe, life-threatening allergic reaction occurring within 30-60 minutes of an exposure. Symptoms can include hypotension, swelling of the mouth and throat, difficulty breathing (bronchospasm, wheezing), hives, abdominal pain.
Angioedema	Subcutaneous or submucosal swelling, typically in the tissues of the face, lips, mouth and throat. Can occur in isolation or as a component of anaphylaxis.
Anion	A negatively charged ion (e.g. chloride).
Anorexia	A significant loss of appetite or aversion to food.
Anorgasmia	An inability to achieve orgasm.
Anuria	No urine output.

Medical Terms Continued

Aortic Dissection	A tear in the wall of the aorta, which allows blood to flow between the wall layers, separating (dissecting) them.
Aphasia	A lack of speech (also called alogia).
Apoptosis	Cell death.
Arrhythmia	An abnormal heart rhythm.
Arthralgia	Joint pain.
Arthritis	Joint inflammation.
Ascites	Fluid accumulation within the peritoneal space of the abdomen.
Asplenia	Decreased spleen function or the absence of a spleen.
Asthenia	Lack of energy and strength; weakness.
Ataxia	A lack of muscle control and uncoordinated body movements.
Atherosclerosis	The buildup of fats, cholesterol and other substances within arterial walls, which leads to plaques and a narrowing of the arterial space.
Attenuated	Weakened.
Atypical	Unusual.
Auscultation	Listening to internal organs (e.g., heart and lungs) with a stethoscope.
Axillary	Armpit.
Avolition	A total lack of motivation.
Azotemia	A buildup of urea (a nitrogen waste product normally eliminated by the kidneys) in the blood (also called uremia).
Beyond Use Date (BUD)	An expiration date applied to a compounded product, beyond which the drug should not be used.
Bilateral	On both sides of the body.
Bioavailability	The proportion (expressed as a percentage) of a drug that enters into the systemic circulation and is available to exert its biological action.
Blepharitis	Eyelid inflammation.
Bolus	A single intravenous dose of a medication administered all at once over a short period of time.
Bradycardia	Slow heart rate (< 60 bpm).
Bradykinesia	Slow body movement.
Bronchitis	Inflammation of the bronchial tubes in the lungs.
Bulimia	An eating disorder characterized by binging (over-eating) followed by self-induced vomiting.
Cachexia	Extreme weight loss and muscle wasting due to a chronic illness.
Carbuncle	A red, inflamed cluster of furuncles (boils) that contain pus and can form an abscess.
Cardiomegaly	Enlarged heart.
Cataplexy	A sudden, temporary loss of muscle control and an inability to move while the person is awake, often triggered by strong emotions such as laughing, crying or fear.
Cataract	A cloudiness covering the lens in the eye, caused by a breakdown of proteins and resulting in blurred vision.
Cation	A positively charged ion (e.g., sodium).
Cellulitis	A spreading bacterial infection in the skin or subcutaneous tissue, characterized by redness, swelling, warmth and pain.
Central line	A long catheter inserted into a neck, upper chest or groin vein and guided into a large central vein (superior vena cava) to administer intravenous medications and fluids.
Cerebrovascular Accident	When blood flow to a part of the brain is blocked (e.g., by a clot or a ruptured vessel) and brain cells die. Also called a stroke.
Cerumen	Ear wax.

Medical Terms Continued

Chancre	A painless ulcer (usually located on the genitals) associated with primary syphilis.
Chelation	The process by which ions and molecules (e.g., drugs) bind to metal ions, forming a non-absorbable complex.
Cholecystectomy	Surgical removal of the gallbladder.
Cholelithiasis	The formation of stones (calculi) in the gallbladder.
Cholestasis	A reduction or blockage of bile flow.
Cirrhosis	Advanced, irreversible fibrosis (scarring) of the liver.
Coagulopathy	A condition associated with excessive bleeding and impaired clot formation.
Conjunctivitis	Inflammation of the thin clear membrane that covers the eyeball and lines the inside of the eyelid.
Continuous Positive Airway Pressure (CPAP)	A treatment for obstructive sleep apnea that uses a machine to pump air through the airways, keeping the windpipe open during sleep.
Crystalluria	The presence of crystals in the urine caused by metabolic disorders or drugs.
Cystitis	Bladder inflammation, usually due to a bacterial infection.
Delirium	An acute change in mental status characterized by incoherent thoughts and speech, disorientation, agitation, hallucinations, delusions and/or paranoia.
Delusion	A false or irrational belief based on an incorrect interpretation of reality.
Dementia	Memory loss and difficulty with thinking, problem-solving and language that interferes with daily life.
Desiccant	A substance that preserves something by removing moisture and keeping it dry.
Diabetic Ketoacidosis (DKA)	A life-threatening hyperglycemic crisis characterized by high blood glucose, anion gap metabolic acidosis and ketones in the blood or urine.
Dialysis	The process of removing waste products and excess electrolytes and fluid from the blood.
Diaphoresis	Excessive or abnormal sweating not explained by the environmental temperature or a person's activity level.
Diplopia	Double vision.
Dissection	A tear within the wall of a blood vessel (e.g., the aorta), which allows blood to flow between the wall layers, separating (dissecting) them.
Dyscrasia	Any disease or abnormal condition of the body.
Dysentery	An infection of the intestines characterized by severe, bloody diarrhea and abdominal pain.
Dysgeusia	An altered sense of taste.
Dyskinesia	Abnormal, involuntary movements.
Dysmenorrhea	Discomfort and pain during the menstrual period.
Dyspepsia	Indigestion.
Dysphagia	Difficulty swallowing.
Dysphonia	An impairment of the voice (e.g., hoarseness) and difficulty speaking.
Dyspnea	Difficult or labored breathing; shortness of breath.
Dystonia	Involuntary movements and prolonged contractions of muscles that result in twisting body motions and abnormal posture.
Ectopic	In an abnormal place or position.
Embolism	A foreign substance or blood clot that travels through the bloodstream and lodges in a blood vessel causing an obstruction.
Empyema	A collection of pus and fluid in a body cavity, usually the pleural space (the space between the lung and the inner surface of the chest wall).
Encephalitis	Inflammation of the brain.
Encephalopathy	Brain disease, damage, or malfunction that results in an altered mental state.

QUICK GUIDES

Medical Terms Continued

Endocarditis	Inflammation of the heart valves or lining of the heart chambers.
Endometriosis	A painful condition in which tissue that normally lines the uterus (endometrium) has grown outside the uterus.
Enteral	Involving the intestine.
Enuresis	Involuntary urination.
Epistaxis	Nosebleed.
Eructation	Burping or belching.
Erythema	Skin redness.
Etiology	The cause (e.g., of a disease).
Euphoria	A feeling of happiness; elevated mood.
Euthyroid	Normal thyroid gland function.
Exacerbation	An increase or worsening (e.g., in the severity of a disease).
Excoriation	The scraping or wearing off of skin resulting in a skin abrasion.
Exophthalmos	Bulging (protruding) eyeballs.
Extravasation	When fluid (e.g., drug, blood) leaks outside of a vessel into the surrounding tissue.
Fibromyalgia	A condition of widespread pain accompanied by stiffness, fatigue, sleep disturbances, headaches and emotional or mental distress (e.g., anxiety).
Fibrosis	Scarring (with stiffness) in connective tissue.
Flatulence	Excess gas in the gastrointestinal tract.
Folliculitis	Hair follicle inflammation, usually caused by infection; can look like acne.
Galactorrhea	The production of breast milk in men or women who are not breastfeeding.
Gastritis	Inflammation, irritation or erosion of the lining of the stomach.
Gastroparesis	Decreased function of the nerves controlling the stomach muscles, resulting in inadequate digestion and delayed gastric emptying.
Genotype	The set of unique genes that determine a specific trait in an individual.
Gingival Bleeding	Bleeding of the gums (gingiva).
Gingival Hyperplasia	Gum (gingiva) overgrowth.
Glossitis	Tongue inflammation.
Gynecomastia	Breast enlargement in men.
Hallucination	A distortion of reality whereby a person hears, sees or feels something that is not there.
Heimlich Maneuver	The procedure for removing or dislodging an obstruction (e.g., food) from a person's airway by applying forceful abdominal thrusts in an inward and upward direction.
Hematemesis	Vomiting blood.
Hematologic	Having to do with blood or blood disorders.
Hematoma	A collection of blood within an organ or localized body tissue.
Hematuria	Blood in the urine.
Hemolysis	The destruction of red blood cells (RBCs).
Hemoptysis	Coughing or spitting up blood from the respiratory tract.
Hemorrhoid	An enlarged or swollen blood vessel near the anus or within the rectum.
Hemostasis	The stopping of blood flow.
Hepatotoxicity	Liver damage.

Medical Terms Continued

Hirsutism	Male-pattern hair growth in women.
Hot Flashes	Episodes of flushing with a sensation of warmth or heat in the upper body and face.
Hyperbilirubinemia	Increased bilirubin in the blood; can cause jaundice.
Hyperhidrosis	Excessive sweating.
Hyperosmolar Hyperglycemic State (HHS)	A hyperglycemic crisis characterized by very high blood glucose, severe dehydration, and confusion.
Hyperplasia	An increase in the number of cells in an organ or body tissue.
Hyperthermia	A body temperature well above normal.
Hypertrichosis	Excessive hair growth; can be all over the body or in patches.
Hypertrophy	The enlargement of an organ or tissue resulting from an increase in cell size.
Hypohidrosis	Reduced sweat production (also called oligohydrosis).
Intraarticular	Into the joint.
Intracranial Hemorrhage (ICH)	Bleeding in the brain.
Intrathecal	Introduced into or occurring in the space between the layers of tissue that cover the brain and spinal cord.
Ischemia	An inadequate blood supply to an organ or part of the body.
Jaundice	A yellowing of the skin and sclerae (the whites of the eyes).
Leukocytosis	Increased (higher than normal) white blood cell count.
Libido	Sexual desire.
Lymphadenopathy	Swollen lymph node (also called glands).
Lyophilized	Freeze-dried.
Malaise	A general feeling of discomfort or illness.
Malignant	Severe and progressively worsening. In cancer, the ability to spread to other parts of the body and invade and destroy tissue.
Medication Guide (MedGuide)	A handout that provides drug-specific information to help the patient avoid serious adverse events.
Melasma	Skin pigmentation, usually appearing as dark spots on the cheeks of the face.
Menorrhagia	Heavy menstrual bleeding.
Metatarsophalangeal Joint	The big toe joint.
Morbidity	Illness or disease.
Mortality	Death.
Mucositis	Inflammation or ulceration of the mucous membranes in the digestive tract (often in the mouth).
Myalgia	Muscle pain.
Mydriasis	Pupil dilation.
Myelosuppression	Decreased bone marrow activity resulting in low white blood cells (WBCs), red blood cells (RBCs) and platelets.
Myocardial Infarction	A heart attack.
Myocarditis	Inflammation of the myocardium (heart muscle).
Myoclonus	Involuntary and abnormal muscle contractions.
Myopathy	Muscle weakness or any muscle disease.

Medical Terms Continued

Necrosis	Cell or tissue death.
Nephrolithiasis	The formation of kidney stones.
Nephrotoxicity	Kidney (renal) toxicity or damage.
Neuropathy	Nerve damage.
Nosocomial	Originating in a hospital.
Nystagmus	Repetitive, uncontrolled movements of the eye.
Oligohidrosis	Reduced sweat production (also called hypohidrosis).
Orthopnea	Shortness of breath when lying flat.
Orthostasis	A drop in blood pressure that happens soon after standing.
Osteomalacia	Softening of the bones.
Osteomyelitis	An infection inside the bone.
Osteoporosis	Low bone mass (density) resulting in porous and brittle bones.
Otalgia	Ear pain.
Otorrhea	Drainage of liquid from the ear.
Ototoxicity	Ear damage.
Palliative care	Medical (or comfort) care to improve the quality of life and provide symptom relief in patients with a serious, life-threatening or terminal illness, but does not cure the disease.
Pallor	Pale skin color.
Parasomnia	Unusual, odd, or dangerous behavior occurring during sleep.
Paresthesia	A burning, prickling or "pins and needles" sensation.
Peak Level	The highest concentration of a drug in the bloodstream.
Pediculosis	Lice infestation.
Pegylation	The addition of polyethylene glycol (PEG) to a molecule.
Perinatal	The time immediately before and after birth.
Peripheral Line	A short catheter inserted into a peripheral vein, usually in the hand or the lower part of the arm or foot, to administer intravenous medications and fluids.
Peripherally Inserted Central Line (PICC)	A central line inserted peripherally (in a vein in the arm) and advanced through the vein until the tip reaches a large vessel (often the superior vena cava).
Peripheral Neuropathy	Peripheral weakness, numbness, and pain from nerve damage.
Peristalsis	Wave-like muscle movements of the gastrointestinal tract that help digest food and push the contents forward.
Pharmacodynamics	The effect that a drug has on the body.
Pharmacokinetics	The effect that the body has on a drug as it goes through the processes of absorption, distribution, metabolism and excretion.
Pharyngitis	Inflammation of the pharynx resulting in a sore throat.
Phenotype	An observable trait (e.g., hair color) that is the outward expression of a person's genotype.
Phlebitis	Inflammation of a vein.
Photosensitivity	An oversensitivity of the skin to light.
Pleural Effusion	Fluid between the layers of the pleura, the thin membranes that line the outside of the lungs.
Pneumonia	An infection that inflames one or both lungs.
Polydipsia	Extreme thirst.

Medical Terms Continued

Polyp	An abnormal growth of tissue projecting from a mucous membrane.
Polyphagia	Excessive hunger or increased appetite.
Polyuria	Excessive urination.
Porphyria	A group of disorders (commonly affecting the skin and nervous system) resulting from abnormalities in heme (an oxygen transporter) production and a subsequent increase in the formation of intermediate chemicals (porphyrins).
Postprandial	After a meal.
Preeclampsia	A serious, potentially fatal complication of pregnancy characterized by high blood pressure, protein in the urine and peripheral edema.
Preprandial	Before a meal.
Priapism	Prolonged, often painful, erection of the penis.
Prophylaxis	Prevention (e.g., of a disease).
Pruritus	Itchy skin.
Pulse Oximetry	A noninvasive test that measures the level of oxygen in the blood (also called oxygen saturation).
Purulent	Consisting of, containing, or discharging pus.
Pyelonephritis	A type of urinary tract infection where one or both kidneys become infected.
Pyrexia	Fever.
Rales	An abnormal rattling or crackling sound heard when examining the lungs with a stethoscope.
Rhonchi	Continuous, deep rattling sounds (that resemble snoring) heard when examining the lungs with a stethoscope.
Risk Evaluation and Mitigation Strategy (REMS)	A drug safety program required by the FDA for some medications with serious safety concerns to ensure the benefits of the medication outweigh the risks.
Retrograde Ejaculation	Semen enters the bladder instead of exiting through the penis during orgasm.
Rhabdomyolysis	A condition where skeletal muscle breaks down, releasing creatine phosphokinase (CPK), myoglobin and other muscle components into the blood; can lead to kidney failure.
Rhinitis	Inflammation and swelling in the nose.
Rhinorrhea	Runny nose, with a thin mucus nasal discharge.
Rigidity	Stiffness or an inability to bend.
Rigor	A sudden feeling of cold with shivering accompanied by a rise in temperature.
Scabies	An infestation of the skin by an itchy, contagious mite (*Sarcoptes scabiei*).
Sepsis	A life-threatening immune response to infection that can lead to tissue damage, organ dysfunction and death.
Septicemia	A severe bloodstream infection (also called bacteremia or blood poisoning).
Shock	A medical emergency (with high mortality), most often characterized by severe hypotension and hypoperfusion of vital organs.
Sialorrhea	Excessive salivation or drooling.
Sinusitis	Inflammation of the sinuses (the hollow areas of the skull around the nose).
Somnambulism	Sleepwalking.
Somnolence	Sleepiness or drowsiness.
Spirometry	A pulmonary function test that measures the volume of air someone can inhale, the volume they can exhale and how fast they can exhale.
Steatorrhea	Excess fat in the feces due to decreased intestinal fat absorption.
Steatosis	Abnormal fat accumulation.
Stenosis	The narrowing of a body space.

Medical Terms Continued

Stevens-Johnson Syndrome/Toxic Epidermal Necrolysis (SJS/TEN)	A severe systemic reaction that causes rash, blisters and peeling of the skin and the mucus membranes of the mouth, airways, eyes and genitalia.
Stomatitis	Inflammation and/or ulceration of the mouth.
Striae	Stretch marks on the skin.
Stricture	An abnormal narrowing of a body passage.
Subtherapeutic	Lower than what is considered to be safe and effective (e.g., drug level, dose, laboratory value).
Supratherapeutic	Above what is considered to be safe and effective (e.g., drug level, dose, laboratory value).
Syncope	A temporary loss of consciousness caused by a drop in blood pressure and blood flow to the brain (also called fainting).
Synergy	When the combined effect is greater than the sum of the parts.
Systemic Lupus Erythematosus (SLE)	An autoimmune condition that causes inflammation and tissue damage in many parts of the body including the joints, skin, brain, lungs, kidney and heart (also called lupus).
Tachycardia	Fast heart rate (> 100 bpm).
Tachyphylaxis	A diminished response to successive doses of a drug.
Tardive Dyskinesia	Uncontrollable, involuntary, repetitive movements of the face (most common) and other body parts.
Teratogenic	A drug that will cause birth defects if taken during pregnancy.
Thrombocytopenia	Low platelet count.
Thrombotic Thrombocytopenic Purpura (TTP)	A serious blood disorder that causes blood clots (thrombosis from platelet clumping) to form in small blood vessels throughout the body. This leads to a low platelet count and subsequent bleeding under the skin which appears as purple bruises (purpura).
Thrush	A yeast infection characterized by white patches in the mouth and/or throat caused by Candida albicans.
Tinnitus	A ringing or buzzing in the ears.
Torsades de Pointes (TdP)	A life-threatening type of ventricular tachycardia characterized by changes in the QRS complexes and a prolonged QT interval.
Transient Ischemic Attack (TIA)	A temporary blockage of blood flow to the brain that causes symptoms of a stroke that resolve within a short period of time (also called a "mini-stroke").
Trough Level	The lowest concentration of a drug in the bloodstream or the concentration measured immediately before the next dose.
Unilateral	On one side of the body.
Uremia	A buildup of urea (a nitrogen waste product normally eliminated by the kidneys) in the blood (also called azotemia).
Urethra	The tube that carries urine from the bladder out of the body. It runs through the penis in males and the vaginal opening in females.
Ureter	The tubes that run from each kidney into the bladder, delivering the "renal filtrate" that will be excreted as urine.
Urolithiasis	The formation of stones in the kidney, urethra, bladder or ureters.
Urticaria	Raised, itchy areas of skin (also called hives).
Vesicant	A drug that can cause severe tissue damage or blistering.
Xerophthalmia	Extreme dryness of the eyes (conjunctiva and cornea).
Xerostomia	Severe dry mouth caused by decreased saliva.

COMMON MEDICAL ABBREVIATIONS

ABBREVIATION	MEANING
5-HT	Serotonin
A & O	Alert & Oriented
ABG	Arterial Blood Gas
AC	Before Meals
ACE	Angiotensin Converting Enzyme
ACh	Acetylcholine
ACIP	Advisory Committee on Immunization Practices
ACOG	American College of Obstetricians and Gynecologists
ACS	Acute Coronary Syndrome
ACTH	Adrenocorticotropic Hormone
AD	Right Ear
ADH	Antidiuretic Hormone
ADHD	Attention Deficit Hyperactivity Disorder
ADHF	Acute Decompensated Heart Failure
ADL	Activity of Daily Living
ADR	Adverse Drug Reaction
ADT	Alternate Day Therapy, Androgen Deprivation Therapy
AED	Antiepileptic Drug, Automated External Defibrillator
AF, AFib	Atrial Fibrillation
AGEP	Acute Generalized Exanthematous Pustulosis
AIDS	Acquired Immunodeficiency Syndrome
AIN	Acute Interstitial Nephritis
AKI	Acute Kidney Injury
ALT	Alanine Aminotransferase
ANA	Antinuclear Antibody
ANC	Absolute Neutrophil Count
ANS	Autonomic Nervous System
AOM	Acute Otitis Media
aPTT, PTT	Activated Partial Thromboplastin Time
ARA	Aldosterone Receptor Antagonist
ARB	Angiotensin Receptor Blocker
ARDS	Acute Respiratory Distress Syndrome
ARF	Acute Renal Failure
ARNI	Angiotensin Receptor and Neprilysin Inhibitor
ART	Antiretroviral Therapy

ABBREVIATION	MEANING
AS	Left Ear
ASCVD	Atherosclerotic Cardiovascular Disease
AST	Aspartate Aminotransferase
ATC	Around The Clock
ATN	Acute Tubular Necrosis
AU	Each Ear
AVP	Arginine Vasopressin
BEE	Basal Energy Expenditure
BG	Blood Glucose
BGM	Blood Glucose Monitoring
BID	Twice a Day
BIW	Two Times Per Week
BM	Bowel Movement
BMD	Bone Mineral Density
BMI	Body Mass Index
BMP	Basic Metabolic Panel
BP	Blood Pressure
BPH	Benign Prostatic Hyperplasia (or Hypertrophy)
BPM	Beats Per Minute, Breaths Per Minute
BSA	Body Surface Area
BUN	Blood Urea Nitrogen
$\bar{c}$ or w/	With
C-I, C-II, C-III, C-IV, C-V	Refers to Controlled Substance Schedule
C & S	Culture and Susceptibility
c/o	Complaining of
CA	Cancer, Cardiac Arrest
CABG	Coronary Artery Bypass Graft
CAD	Coronary Artery Disease
cAMP	Cyclic Adenosine Monophosphate
CA-MRSA	Community-Acquired Methicillin-Resistant *Staphylococcus aureus*
CAP	Community-Acquired Pneumonia
CAPES	*Citrobacter, Acinetobacter, Providencia, Enterobacter, Serratia*
CBC	Complete Blood Count
CBT	Cognitive Behavioral Therapy
CC	Chief Complaint
CCB	Calcium Channel Blocker

Common Medical Abbreviations Continued

ABBREVIATION	MEANING
CD	Crohn's Disease
CDI	*C. difficile* Infection
CF	Cystic Fibrosis
CHF	Chronic (or Congestive) Heart Failure
CI	Cardiac Index, Contraindicated
CK	Creatine Kinase (same as CPK)
CKD	Chronic Kidney Disease
CMV	Cytomegalovirus
CNS	Central Nervous System
CO	Cardiac Output
COC	Combination Oral Contraceptive
COPD	Chronic Obstructive Pulmonary Disease
CP	Chest Pain, Cerebral Palsy
CPAP	Continuous Positive Airway Pressure
CPK	Creatine Phosphokinase (same as CK)
CPR	Cardiopulmonary Resuscitation
CrCl	Creatinine Clearance
CRE	Carbapenem-Resistant *Enterobacteriaceae*
CRF	Chronic Renal Failure
CRP	C-reactive Protein
CSF	Cerebrospinal Fluid, Colony Stimulating Factor
CT, CAT	Computerized (or Computed) Tomography
CV	Cardiovascular
CVA	Cerebrovascular Accident
CVP	Central Venous Pressure
CXR	Chest X-Ray
D/C	Discontinue, Discharge
D5W	5% Dextrose in Water
DA	Dopamine
DDI	Drug-Drug Interaction
DHP CCB	Dihydropyridine Calcium Channel Blocker
DILE	Drug-Induced Lupus Erythematous
DJD	Degenerative Joint Disease (Osteoarthritis)
DKA	Diabetic Ketoacidosis
DM	Diabetes Mellitus
DMARD	Disease-Modifying Antirheumatic Drug
DOAC	Direct-Acting Oral Anticoagulant (same as NOAC)
DOC	Drug of Choice

ABBREVIATION	MEANING
DOE	Dyspnea on Exertion
DPI	Dry Powder Inhaler
DRESS	Drug Reaction with Eosinophilia and Systemic Symptoms
dtd	Of Such Doses
DVT	Deep Vein Thrombosis
Dx	Diagnosis
EC	Enteric Coated
ECG, EKG	Electrocardiogram
ED	Emergency Department, Erectile Dysfunction
EF	Ejection Fraction
Epi	Epinephrine
EPS	Extrapyramidal Symptoms
ERA	Endothelin Receptor Antagonist
ESBL	Extended-Spectrum Beta-Lactamase
ESR	Erythrocyte Sedimentation Rate
ESRD	End Stage Renal Disease
ETOH	Ethanol
f/u	Follow-Up
FBG	Fasting Blood Glucose
FDA	Food and Drug Administration
FEV1	Forced Expiratory Volume in 1 Second
FPG	Fasting Plasma Glucose
FSH	Follicle Stimulating Hormone
FT4	Free Thyroxine (T4)
G6PD	Glucose-6-Phosphate Dehydrogenase
GERD	Gastroesophageal Reflux Disease
GFR	Glomerular Filtration Rate
GI	Gastrointestinal
GNR	Gram-Negative Rod
GnRH	Gonadotropin-Releasing Hormone
gtt, gtts	Drop, Drops
h/o	History of
HA	Headache
HACEK	*Haemophilus, Actinobacillus, Cardiobacterium, Eikenella, Kingella*
HAP	Hospital-Acquired Pneumonia
HBV	Hepatitis B Virus
hCG	Human Chorionic Gonadotropin

QUICK GUIDES

Common Medical Abbreviations Continued

ABBREVIATION	MEANING
Hct	Hematocrit
HCTZ, HCT	Hydrochlorothiazide
HCV	Hepatitis C Virus
HDL, HDL-C	High Density Lipoprotein
HEENT	Head, Eyes, Ears, Nose and Throat
HF	Heart Failure
HFrEF	Heart Failure with Reduced Ejection Fraction
HFpEF	Heart Failure with Preserved Ejection Fraction
Hgb	Hemoglobin
HIPAA	Health Insurance Portability and Accountability Act
HIT	Heparin-Induced Thrombocytopenia
HIV	Human Immunodeficiency Virus
HJR	Hepatojugular Reflux
HNPEK	*Haemophilus influenzae, Neisseria* spp., *Proteus mirabilis, Escherichia coli, Klebsiella pneumonia*
HPA	Hypothalamic-Pituitary-Adrenal
HPI	History of Present Illness
HR	Heart Rate
HS	At Bedtime
HSV	Herpes Simplex Virus
HTN	Hypertension
HUS	Hemolytic Uremic Syndrome
Hx	History
I & O	Intake and Output, Input and Output
IBD	Inflammatory Bowel Disease
IBS	Irritable Bowel Syndrome
IBW	Ideal Body Weight
ICD	International Classification of Diseases
ICH	Intracranial Hemorrhage
ICS	Inhaled Corticosteroid
ICU	Intensive Care Unit
ID	Intradermal, Infectious Disease
IE	Infective Endocarditis
IFIS	Intraoperative Floppy Iris Syndrome
IHD	Ischemic Heart Disease
IM	Intramuscular
Inj	Injection
INR	International Normalized Ratio
IOP	Intraocular Pressure

ABBREVIATION	MEANING
IUD	Intrauterine Device
IV	Intravenous
IVP	Intravenous Push
IVPB	Intravenous Piggyback
LABA	Long-Acting Beta-2 Agonist
LAMA	Long-Acting Muscarinic Antagonist
LD	Loading Dose
LDH	Lactate Dehydrogenase
LDL, LDL-C	Low-Density Lipoprotein
LFT	Liver Function Test
LH	Luteinizing Hormone
LMWH	Low Molecular Weight Heparin
LP	Lumbar Puncture
LR	Lactated Ringer's
LVEF	Left Ventricular Ejection Fraction
LVH	Left Ventricular Hypertrophy
M. ft.	Mix and Make
MAO	Monoamine Oxidase
MAP	Mean Arterial Pressure
MCH	Mean Corpuscular Hemoglobin
MCHC	Mean Corpuscular Hemoglobin Concentration
MCV	Mean Corpuscular Volume
MD	Maintenance Dose
MDI	Metered-Dose Inhaler
MDR	Multidrug-Resistant
MI	Myocardial Infarction
MIC	Minimum Inhibitory Concentration
mL	Milliliter
mPAP	Mean Pulmonary Artery Pressure
MRI	Magnetic Resonance Imaging
MRSA	Methicillin-Resistant *Staphylococcus aureus*
MS	Multiple Sclerosis (Do not use this abbreviation for Morphine Sulfate – potential med error)
MSSA	Methicillin-Sensitive *Staphylococcus aureus*
MVA	Motor Vehicle Accident
MVC	Motor Vehicle Crash (or Collision)
MVI	Multivitamin Injection
MW	Molecular Weight

Common Medical Abbreviations Continued

ABBREVIATION	MEANING
N/V, N & V	Nausea and Vomiting
N/V/D	Nausea, Vomiting, Diarrhea
NE	Norepinephrine
NG	Nasogastric
NJ	Nasojejunal
NKA	No Known Allergies
NKDA	No Known Drug Allergies
NMS	Neuroleptic Malignant Syndrome
NOAC	Non-Vitamin K Oral Anticoagulant (same as DOAC)
Non-DHP CCB	Non-Dihydropyridine Calcium Channel Blocker
nPEP	Nonoccupational Post-Exposure Prophylaxis
NPO	Nothing By Mouth
NR	No Refills
NRT	Nicotine Replacement Therapy
NS	Normal Saline
NSAID	Non-Steroidal Anti-Inflammatory Drug
NSR	Normal Sinus Rhythm
NSTEMI	Non-ST Segment Elevation Myocardial Infarction
NTE	Not To Exceed
NTG	Nitroglycerin
OB-GYN	Obstetrics and Gynecology
OCP	Oral Contraceptive Pill
OD	Right Eye
ODT	Orally-Disintegrating Tablet
OGTT	Oral Glucose Tolerance Test
oPEP	Occupational Post-Exposure Prophylaxis
OROS	Osmotic Release Delivery System
OS	Left Eye
OSA	Obstructive Sleep Apnea
OTC	Over-The-Counter
OU	Each Eye
P-gp	P-glycoprotein
PAD	Peripheral Arterial Disease
PAP	Pulmonary Artery Pressure
PCA	Patient-Controlled Analgesia
PC	After Meals
PCC	Prothrombin Complex Concentrate

ABBREVIATION	MEANING
PCI	Percutaneous Coronary Intervention
PCN	Penicillin
PCOS	Polycystic Ovary Syndrome
PCP	Primary Care Physician (or Provider)
PCV13	Pneumococcal Conjugate Vaccine (13-valent)
PCV15	Pneumococcal Conjugate Vaccine (15-valent)
PCV20	Pneumococcal Conjugate Vaccine (20-valent)
PCWP	Pulmonary Capillary Wedge Pressure
PD	Parkinson Disease
PDA	Patent Ductus Arteriosus
PE	Pulmonary Embolus, Physical Exam
PEK	*Proteus mirabilis, Escherichia coli, Klebsiella pneumonia*
PEP	Post-Exposure Prophylaxis
PET	Positron Emission Tomography
PFT	Pulmonary Function Test
PHN	Postherpetic Neuralgia
PICC	Peripherally Inserted Central Catheter
PKU	Phenylketonuria
PMH	Past Medical History
PO	By Mouth, Oral
POP	Progestin-Only Pill
PPD	Purified Protein Derivative
PPG	Postprandial Glucose
PPI	Proton Pump Inhibitor, Patient Package Insert
PPSV23	Pneumococcal Polysaccharide Vaccine (23-valent)
PRBCs	Packed Red Blood Cells
PR	Per Rectum
PrEP	Pre-Exposure Prophylaxis
PRN	As Needed
PSA	Prostate Specific Antigen
PT	Prothrombin Time, Physical Therapy
Pt	Patient
PTH	Parathyroid Hormone
PUD	Peptic Ulcer Disease
PV	Per Vagina
PVC	Polyvinyl Chloride
Q	Every
QD	Every Day

Common Medical Abbreviations Continued

ABBREVIATION	MEANING	ABBREVIATION	MEANING
QID	Four Times a Day	Supp, sup	Suppository
QOD	Every Other Day	SVR	Systemic Vascular Resistance
QS	Sufficient Quantity	TB	Tuberculosis
QS AD	Sufficient Quantity to Make	TC	Total Cholesterol
r/o	Rule Out	TCA	Tricyclic Antidepressant
RA	Rheumatoid Arthritis	TD	Tardive Dyskinesia
RASS	Richmond Agitation and Sedation Scale	TdP	Torsade de Pointes
RBC	Red Blood Cell	TEN	Toxic Epidermal Necrolysis
RML	Right Middle Lobe	TG	Triglycerides
ROS	Review of Systems	TIA	Transient Ischemic Attack
RSV	Respiratory Syncytial Virus	TIBC	Total Iron Binding Capacity
Rx	Prescription	TID	Three Times a Day
Rxn	Reaction	TIW	Three Times Per Week
s̄ or w/o	Without	TNF	Tumor Necrosis Factor
s/p	Status Post	TOP	Topically
SABA	Short-Acting Beta-2 Agonist	TPN	Total Parenteral Nutrition
SAMA	Short-Acting Muscarinic Antagonist	TSH	Thyroid Stimulating Hormone
SC, SQ, subc, subq	Subcutaneous	TTP	Thrombotic Thrombocytopenic Purpura
SCr	Serum Creatinine	TBW	Total Body Weight
SERM	Selective Estrogen Receptor Modulator	Tx	Treatment
SIADH	Syndrome of Inappropriate Antidiuretic Hormone	UA	Urinalysis, Unstable Angina
Sig	Write on Label	UC	Ulcerative Colitis
SJS	Stevens-Johnson Syndrome	UFH	Unfractionated Heparin
SL	Sublingual	ULN	Upper Limit of Normal
SLE	Systemic Lupus Erythematous	Ung	Ointment
SNRI	Serotonin and Norepinephrine Reuptake Inhibitor	URTI	Upper Respiratory Tract Infection
SOAP	Subjective, Objective, Assessment, Plan	UTI	Urinary Tract Infection
SOB	Shortness of Breath	VAP	Ventilator-Associated Pneumonia
Spp.	Species	VF, VFib	Ventricular Fibrillation
ss	One-half	VRE	Vancomycin-Resistant *Enterococcus*
S/Sx	Signs and Symptoms	VT, VTach	Ventricular Tachycardia
SSRI	Selective Serotonin Reuptake Inhibitor	VTE	Venous Thromboembolism
SSTI	Skin and Soft-Tissue Infection, Skin and Skin-Structure Infection	WA	While Awake
STAT	Immediately	WBC	White Blood Cell
STD	Sexually Transmitted Disease	WNL	Within Normal Limits
STEMI	ST Segment Elevation Myocardial Infarction	y/o	Year Old
STI	Sexually Transmitted Infection	yr	Year

Meanings of abbreviations may vary. Not all of these abbreviations are considered safe but may be used in practice. Unapproved abbreviations should be avoided (see Medication Safety & Quality Improvement chapter).

PHARMACY FOUNDATIONS
PART 1

CONTENTS

CHAPTER CONTENT

Acetylsalicylic Acid

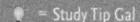

📷 ©RxPrep

CHAPTER 2

BASIC SCIENCE CONCEPTS

BACKGROUND

An understanding of basic science concepts is essential to a pharmacist's role as the drug information expert. This chapter describes common terminology and foundational concepts that should be known for the NAPLEX. They may be tested directly, or application of knowledge may be required when answering case-based drug therapy questions.

Important drug mechanisms are reviewed in more detail in the specific disease state chapters.

DEFINITIONS

Substrate (or Ligand)
A substance that creates a signal or produces an effect by binding to a receptor, enzyme or transporter.

Endogenous
A substance that is produced by the body (such as a naturally-produced substrate).

Exogenous
A substance that is produced outside of the body (such as a drug or other chemical).

Agonist
A substance that combines with a receptor to initiate a reaction.
Can be endogenous or exogenous (mimicking an endogenous substrate).

Antagonist
A substance that reduces or blocks a reaction. Can be endogenous or exogenous.

Induction
When a substance increases the activity of an enzyme.

Inhibition
When a substance decreases or blocks the activity of an enzyme.

CONTENT LEGEND

OVERVIEW OF THE NERVOUS SYSTEM

The <u>central nervous system</u> (CNS) includes the brain and the spinal cord. The CNS controls the functions of the rest of the body by sending signals to the <u>peripheral nervous system</u> (PNS). The PNS has two main systems (somatic and autonomic). The <u>somatic nervous system</u> (voluntary) controls <u>muscle movement</u> while the <u>autonomic nervous system</u> (involuntary) controls other bodily functions, such as digestion, cardiac output and blood pressure (BP).

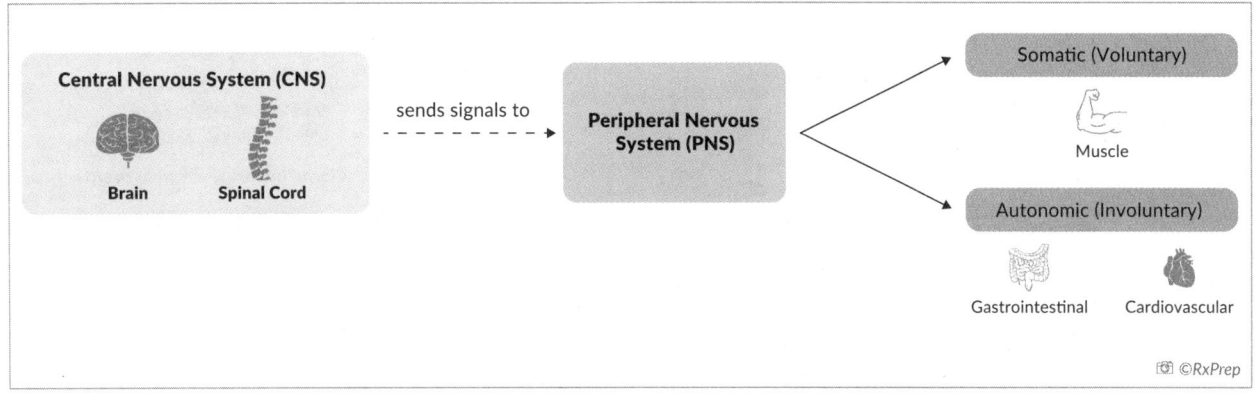

iStock.com/Alex_Doubovitsky, ambassador806, Mack15, sabelskaya

NEUROTRANSMITTERS

Signal transmission in the CNS and PNS is accomplished by <u>neurotransmitters</u> (NTs), which are the body's chemical messengers (i.e., substrates/ligands). NTs are released from presynaptic neurons into the synaptic cleft, then they travel to postsynaptic neurons or other parts of the body to exert their effect (see image).

Common NTs discussed in this chapter include <u>acetylcholine</u> (ACh), <u>epinephrine</u> (Epi), <u>norepinephrine</u> (NE), <u>dopamine</u> (DA) and <u>serotonin</u> (5-HT).

<u>ACh</u> is the primary NT involved in the <u>somatic nervous system</u>. It is released in response to neuron signals and binds to <u>nicotinic receptors</u> (Nn) in <u>skeletal muscles</u> to affect muscle movement. Neurotransmitters involved in the autonomic nervous system are discussed below.

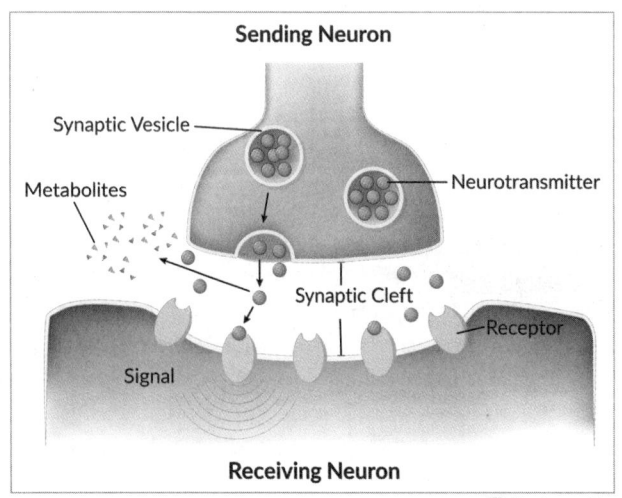

iStock.com/ttsz

AUTONOMIC NERVOUS SYSTEM

There are two main divisions of the autonomic nervous system, parasympathetic and sympathetic (see the diagram on the following page). The <u>parasympathetic nervous system</u> (PSNS) is known as the "<u>rest and digest</u>" system. The PSNS works by releasing <u>ACh</u>, which binds to <u>muscarinic receptors</u> located throughout the body, including the GI tract, the bladder and the eyes. This results in a physiologic response known as <u>SLUDD (salivation, lacrimation, urination, defecation and digestion)</u>.

The <u>sympathetic nervous system</u> (SNS) is known as the "<u>fight or flight</u>" system. The SNS works by releasing <u>Epi</u> and <u>NE</u>, which act on <u>adrenergic receptors (alpha-1, beta-1 and beta-2)</u> in the cardiovascular and respiratory systems. Activation of this system results in increased <u>BP, HR and bronchodilation</u>. Stimulation of beta-2 receptors in the GI tract increases glucose production to provide muscles with oxygen and energy. When the SNS is activated, functions like digestion and urination are minimized to focus on the more important bodily functions for "fight or flight."

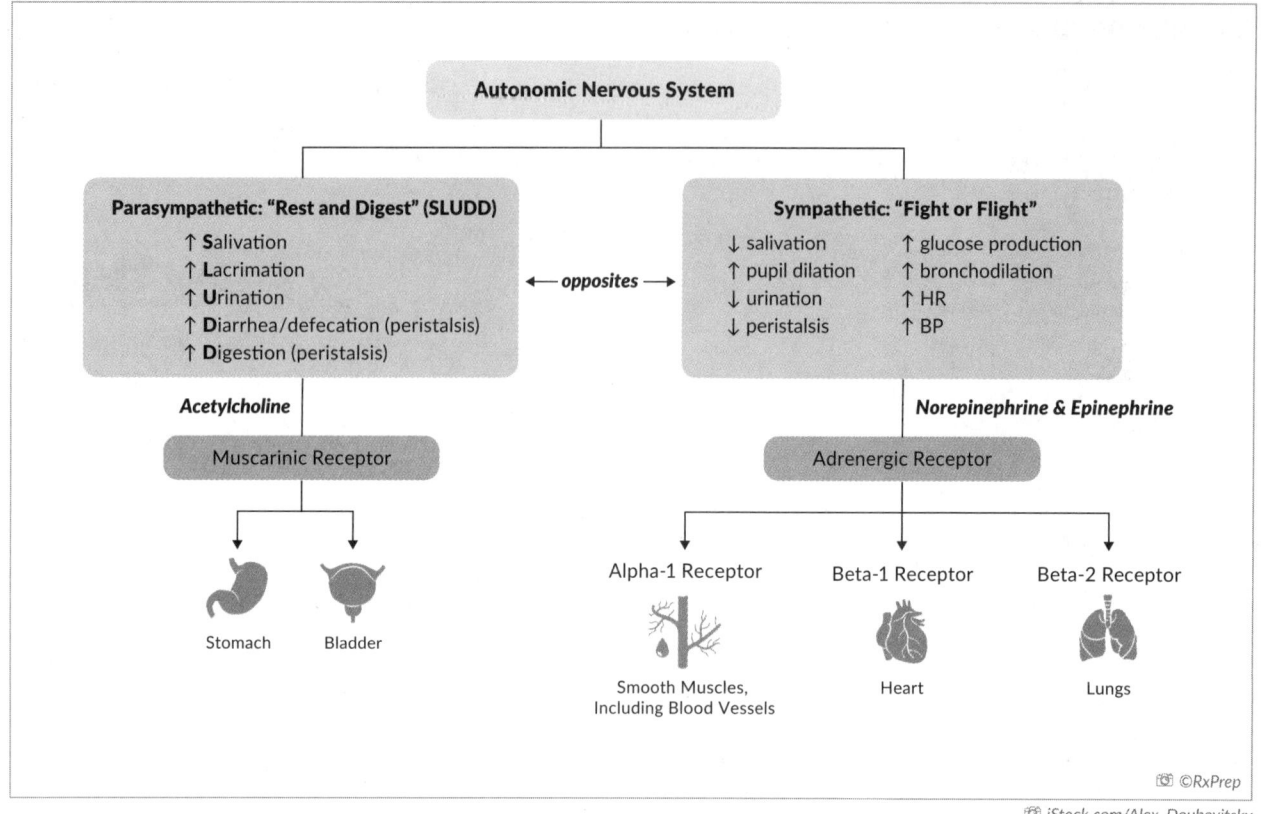

©RxPrep

iStock.com/Alex_Doubovitsky

RECEPTORS AND SUBSTRATES

Chemical substances (e.g., neurotransmitters) released by cells in the body act as substrates (or ligands) by interacting with other cells to communicate and send signals. The substrate binds to receptors on the receiving cell to cause a signal or change. Substrates can be endogenous or exogenous. Once bound, the receptor-substrate complex causes some change that results in a biological effect (e.g., secretion of a hormone, contraction of a muscle, activation of an enzyme).

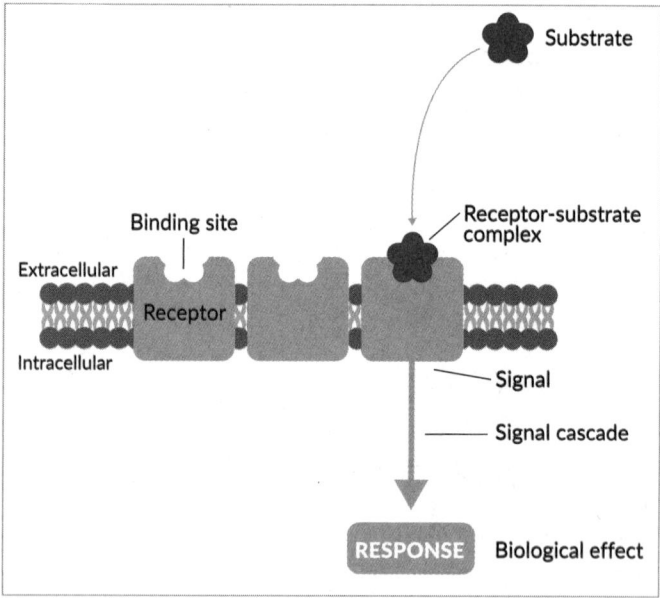

RxPrep

Substrates that bind to receptors can be agonists or antagonists. An agonist is a substance that binds to and activates a receptor, producing some type of response. An antagonist (sometimes called a blocker or inhibitor) binds to a receptor but does not produce a subsequent reaction; the antagonist blocks the agonist from binding and inhibits the subsequent reaction.

The interaction of an antagonist with a receptor can be competitive or non-competitive. Competitive inhibition occurs when an antagonist binds to the same active site of a receptor as the endogenous substrate, preventing it from binding and causing a reaction. With non-competitive inhibition, the antagonist binds to the receptor at a site other than the active site (called the allosteric site), which changes the shape of the active site and prevents the endogenous substrate from binding.

DRUG-RECEPTOR INTERACTIONS

Drugs are exogenous substances that can act as agonists or antagonists. Examples of drugs agonists and antagonists include:

- Albuterol, a beta-2 agonist that behaves similarly to epinephrine. It binds to beta-2 receptors in the lungs, which activates several steps [e.g., increased cyclic adenosine monophosphate (cAMP) production and decreased intracellular calcium] and results in bronchial smooth muscle relaxation.

- Beta-1 blockers, which prevent adrenergic neurotransmitters (e.g., epinephrine) from binding to beta-1 receptors in the heart. Epinephrine normally increases heart rate and contractility when it binds to beta-1 receptors. By blocking the receptor, beta-1 blockers decrease heart rate and contractility.

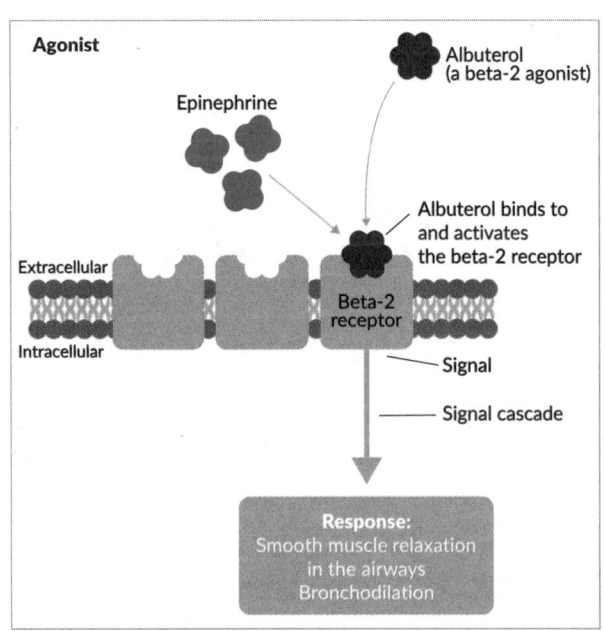

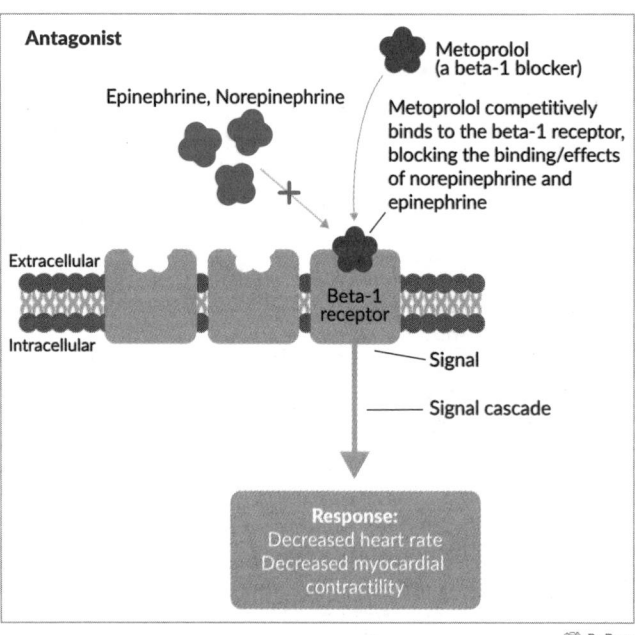

COMMON DRUG RECEPTOR TARGETS

The Study Tip Gal on the following page lists receptors that are common drug targets along with their endogenous substrates. Example drugs that have an agonist or antagonist effect at the receptor, along with the resulting biological effect, are included. How drugs work at these receptors is closely related to the conditions they treat. For example, muscarinic and alpha-1 receptors are targets for medications used to reduce bladder contractions (e.g., oxybutynin) and to relax the bladder (e.g., doxazosin) (see the Urinary Incontinence and Benign Prostatic Hyperplasia chapters). Terbutaline is a beta-2 agonist used in acute, severe asthma exacerbations.

Some medications affect multiple receptors. Isoproterenol is a mixed beta-1 and beta-2 agonist; it is used for bradycardia and causes bronchodilation. Carvedilol inhibits alpha-1, beta-1 and beta-2 receptors. It is used to decrease BP (by causing peripheral vasodilation and a decrease in HR), but it can cause bronchoconstriction. Vasopressors, such as epinephrine and norepinephrine, stimulate multiple receptors, including alpha-1 and beta-1, leading to increased vasoconstriction, HR and BP.

Other medications work in the CNS to affect the amount of neurotransmitter released and availabile to act on PNS receptors. Clonidine is a centrally acting alpha-2 adrenergic agonist. When presynaptic alpha-2 receptors located in the brain are stimulated, there is a decrease in overall sympathetic output (i.e., neurotransmitter release). Decreased release and availability of NE and Epi to bind to adrenergic receptors results in vasodilation (decreased BP) and a decrease in HR. Refer to the Overview of the Nervous System section for more on this process.

COMMON RECEPTORS, SUBSTRATES AND DRUG EXAMPLES

RECEPTOR	ENDOGENOUS SUBSTRATE	AGONIST ACTION	DRUG AGONISTS	ANTAGONIST ACTION	DRUG ANTAGONISTS
Muscarinic	Acetylcholine	↑ SLUDD*	Pilocarpine, bethanechol	↓ SLUDD*	Atropine, oxybutynin
Nicotinic	Acetylcholine	↑ HR, BP	Nicotine	Neuromuscular blockade	Neuromuscular blockers (e.g., rocuronium)
Alpha-1 (mainly peripheral)	Epinephrine, norepinephrine	Smooth muscle vasoconstriction, ↑ BP	Phenylephrine, dopamine (dose-dependent)	Smooth muscle vasodilation, ↓ BP	Alpha-1 blockers (e.g., doxazosin, carvedilol, phentolamine)
Alpha-2 (mainly brain; central)	Epinephrine, norepinephrine	↓ release of epinephrine and norepinephrine, ↓ BP, HR	Clonidine, brimonidine (ophthalmic, for glaucoma)	↑ BP, HR	Ergot alkaloids, yohimbine
Beta-1 (mainly heart)	Epinephrine, norepinephrine	↑ myocardial contractility, CO, HR	Dobutamine, isoproterenol, dopamine (dose-dependent)	↓ CO, HR	Beta-1 selective blockers (e.g., metoprolol) and non-selective beta-blockers (e.g., propranolol, carvedilol)
Beta-2 (mainly lungs)	Epinephrine	Bronchodilation	Albuterol, terbutaline, isoproterenol	Bronchoconstriction	Non-selective beta-blockers (e.g., propranolol, carvedilol)
Dopamine	Dopamine	Many, including renal, cardiac and CNS effects	Levodopa, pramipexole	Many, including renal, cardiac and CNS effects	First-generation antipsychotics (e.g., haloperidol), metoclopramide
Serotonin	Serotonin	Many, including platelet, GI and psychiatric effects	Triptans (e.g., sumatriptan)	Many, including platelet, GI and psychiatric effects	Ondansetron, second-generation antipsychotics (e.g., quetiapine)

*SLUDD = salivation, lacrimation, urination, diarrhea/defecation and digestion (see Autonomic Nervous System section).

ENZYMES

Enzymes are compounds that speed up (catalyze) a reaction (e.g., creating a new compound or breaking down a compound into smaller parts). The interaction of a substrate with an enzyme can be agonistic or antagonistic, competitive or non-competitive (similar to receptors).

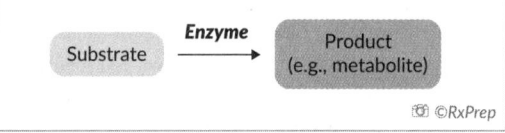

©RxPrep

An example enzyme is monoamine oxidase (MAO), which is responsible for breaking down catecholamines (e.g., dopamine, norepinephrine, epinephrine and serotonin) as shown in the pathway below. The Study Tip Gal on the following page describes common enzyme systems and drug targets that alter enzyme effects.

Catecholamine Metabolism: Endogenous Pathways

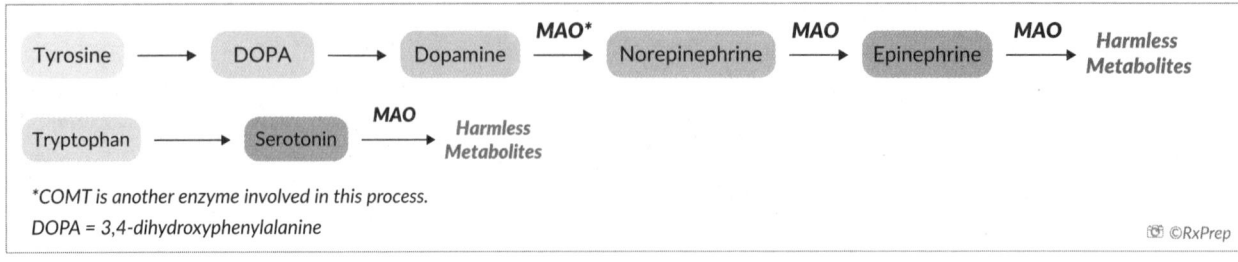

*COMT is another enzyme involved in this process.
DOPA = 3,4-dihydroxyphenylalanine

©RxPrep

COMMON ENZYME TARGETS FOR MEDICATIONS

ENZYME	ENDOGENOUS EFFECTS	DRUG EXAMPLES	DRUG ACTION
Acetylcholinesterase	Breaks down acetylcholine	Acetylcholinesterase inhibitors: donepezil, rivastigmine, galantamine	Block acetylcholinesterase, resulting in ↑ ACh levels; used to treat Alzheimer's disease.
Angiotensin-converting enzyme (ACE)	Converts angiotensin I to angiotensin II (a potent vasoconstrictor)	ACE inhibitors (e.g., lisinopril, ramipril)	Inhibit production of angiotensin II, resulting in ↓ vasoconstriction and ↓ aldosterone secretion; used to treat hypertension, heart failure and kidney disease.
Catechol-O-methyltransferase (COMT)	Breaks down levodopa	COMT inhibitor: entacapone	Blocks COMT enzyme to prevent peripheral breakdown of levodopa, resulting in ↑ duration of action of levodopa; used to treat Parkinson disease.
Cyclooxygenase (COX)	Converts arachidonic acid to prostaglandins (cause inflammation) and thromboxane A2 (causes platelet aggregation)	NSAIDs (e.g., aspirin, ibuprofen)	Block COX enzymes to ↓ prostaglandins and thromboxane A2; used to treat pain/inflammation and ↓ platelet activation/aggregation (aspirin).
Monoamine oxidase (MAO)	Breaks down catecholamines (e.g., DA, NE, Epi, 5-HT)	MAO inhibitors: phenelzine, tranylcypromine, isocarboxazid, selegiline, rasagiline, methylene blue, linezolid	Block MAO which ↑ catecholamine levels; used to treat depression. If catecholamines ↑ too much (due to additive effects with other drugs or foods), toxic effects can occur, such as hypertensive crisis or serotonin syndrome (see MAO Inhibitors, Hypertensive Crisis and Serotonin Syndrome section below).
Phosphodiesterase (PDE)	Breaks down cyclic guanosine monophosphate (cGMP), a smooth muscle relaxant	PDE-5 inhibitors (e.g., sildenafil, tadalafil)	Competitively bind to the same active site as cGMP on the PDE-5 enzyme, preventing the breakdown of cGMP and prolonging smooth muscle relaxation (e.g., in the arteries of the penis); used to treat erectile dysfunction.
Vitamin K epoxide reductase	Converts vitamin K to the active form required for production of select clotting factors	Warfarin	Blocks vitamin K epoxide reductase enzyme which ↓ production of clotting factors II, VII, IX and X; used to treat or prevent blood clots.
Xanthine oxidase	Breaks down hypoxanthine and xanthine into uric acid	Xanthine oxidase inhibitor: allopurinol	Blocks xanthine oxidase enzyme which decreases uric acid production; used to prevent gout attacks.

MAO INHIBITORS, HYPERTENSIVE CRISIS AND SEROTONIN SYNDROME

When multiple drugs work similarly at the same receptor or enzyme, additive effects can occur, which can be detrimental. For example, when MAO is blocked by an MAO inhibitor, there is a buildup of catecholamines. This is beneficial for treating depression, but if too many catecholamines accumulate (e.g., due to multiple drugs being used together that increase catecholamines), hypertensive crisis or serotonin syndrome can develop. The diagrams on the following page list the drugs and foods that contribute to either hypertensive crisis or serotonin syndrome, along with the symptoms indicative of each condition. These types of additive drug interactions are discussed further in the Drug Interactions and Depression chapters.

Catecholamine Metabolism: Additive Effects with MAO Inhibitors

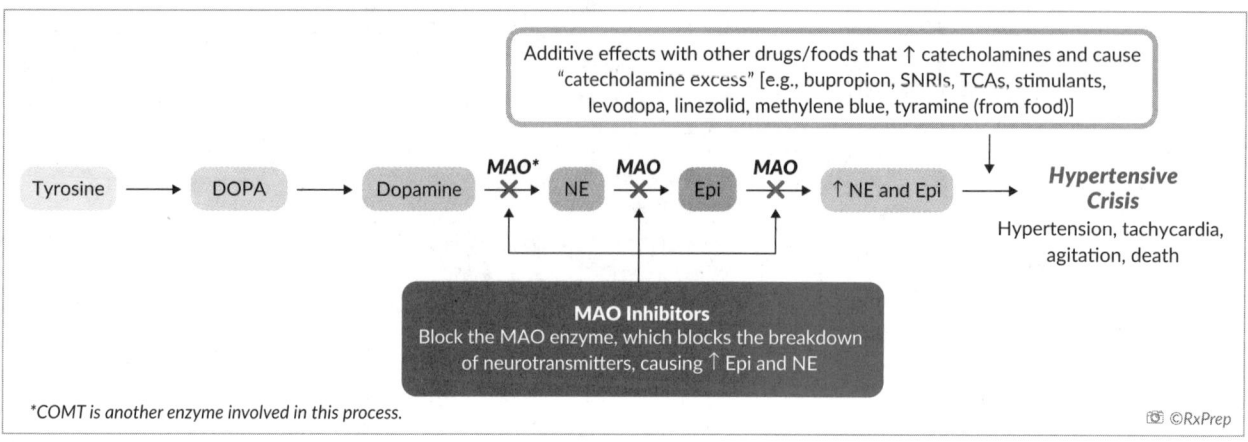

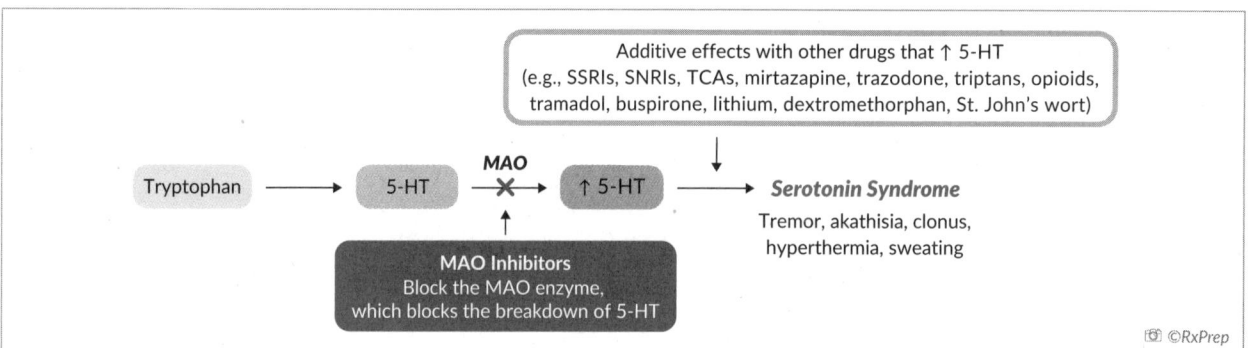

CHEMICAL STRUCTURES

The expected <u>effect</u> of a drug can be <u>predicted</u> from its mechanism of action and chemical structure. The relationship between the structure of a compound and its activity is referred to as the <u>structure-activity relationship</u>.

The common functional groups and <u>drug structures that should be recognized</u> for the exam are shown in the tables starting on the following page. Knowledge of these functional groups allows a pharmacist to predict certain effects or adverse effects of drugs. For example, identification of the <u>sulfonamide</u> functional group on the <u>celecoxib</u> compound (enclosed in the dotted lines of the structure below) explains why celecoxib is contraindicated in patients with a history of hypersensitivity (e.g., allergic) reactions to sulfonamides.

Differences in functional groups within a drug class can be important. If a patient has a hypersensitivity reaction to one type of drug in the class (e.g., an ester-type anesthetic such as procaine), other drugs in the class with the same functional group (e.g., benzocaine) should be avoided due to the potential for cross-reactivity. Selection of an anesthetic with a different functional group (e.g., an amide-type anesthetic such as lidocaine) would be reasonable. Amide-type anesthetics can be recognized by the "i" in their name before the "-caine" ending (e.g., l<u>i</u>docaine, bup<u>i</u>vacaine, rop<u>i</u>vacaine).

COMMON FUNCTIONAL GROUPS

Neutral Functional Groups

HYDROXYL OR ALCOHOL (PRIMARY)	KETONE	ALDEHYDE	AMIDE

NITRATE	NITRO	AROMATIC (BENZENE) RING	UREA

CARBONATE	CARBAMATE	ETHER	THIOETHER

Acidic Functional Groups

CARBOXYL	PHENOL	IMIDE	SULFONAMIDE

Basic Functional Groups

AMINE (PRIMARY)	AMINE (TERTIARY)	IMINE	AMIDINE

©RxPrep

ESSENTIAL DRUG STRUCTURES

Beta-Lactam Antibiotics

AMOXICILLIN

Beta-lactam, penicillin antibiotic

Contains a beta-lactam ring fused to a 5-sided ring

Hypersensitivity: cross-reactive to other drugs with a beta-lactam ring (see ceftriaxone and ertapenem)

CEFTRIAXONE

Beta-lactam, cephalosporin antibiotic

Contains a beta-lactam ring fused to a 6-sided ring

Hypersensitivity: cross-reactive to other drugs with a beta-lactam ring (see amoxicillin and ertapenem)

ERTAPENEM

Beta-lactam, carbapenem antibiotic

Contains a beta-lactam ring fused to a 5-sided ring

Hypersensitivity: cross-reactive to other drugs with a beta-lactam ring (see amoxicillin and ceftriaxone)

Other Antibiotics

AZTREONAM

Monobactam antibiotic

Contains a lactam ring not fused to another ring (note "mono" in monobactam means one)

Hypersensitivity: not cross-reactive with beta-lactam antibiotics

GENTAMICIN

Aminoglycoside antibiotic

Contains an amine (amino) group* and a sugar (glycoside) group**

©RxPrep

SULFAMETHOXAZOLE

Sulfonamide antibiotic

Contains a sulfonamide group

Hypersensitivity: cross-reactive to other drugs containing a sulfonamide group (e.g., celecoxib)

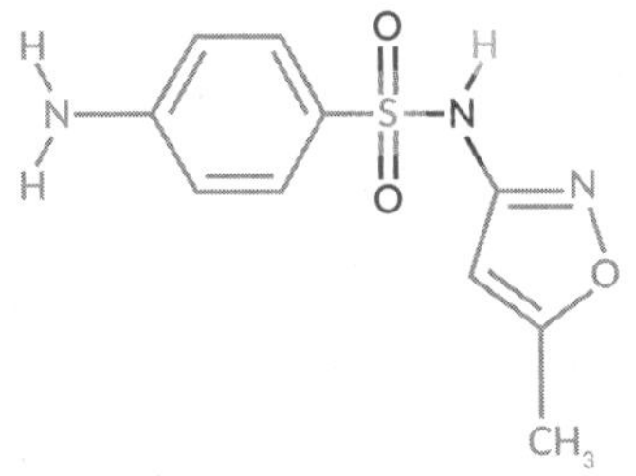

Non-Steroidal Anti-Inflammatory Drugs (NSAIDs)

ASPIRIN

Salicylate non-steroidal anti-inflammatory analgesic

Contains an acidic, carboxyl group

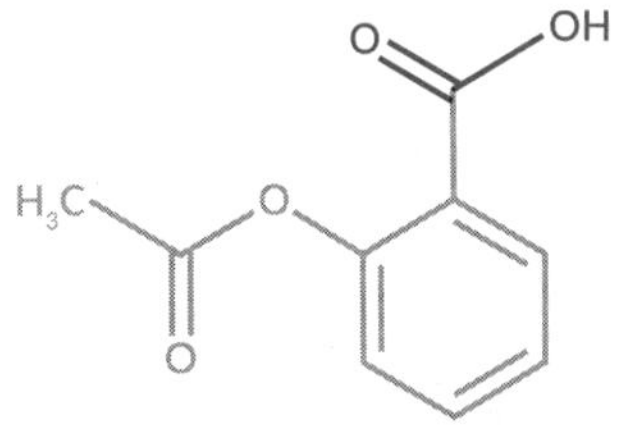

IBUPROFEN

Non-steroidal anti-inflammatory analgesic

Contains a carboxyl group

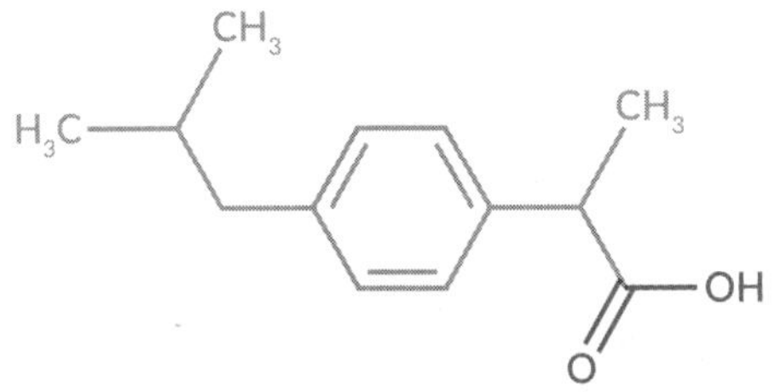

Other Well-Known Structures

AMPHETAMINE

Stimulant

Contains a primary amine functional group (note "amine" in the name)

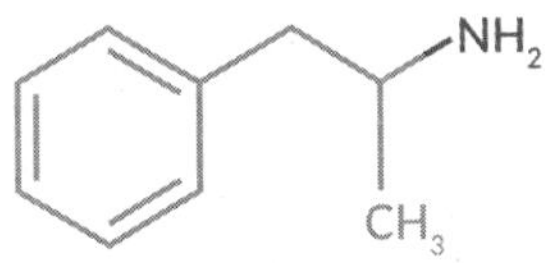

LEVOTHYROXINE

Thyroid hormone (T4)

Contains four iodine molecules in the structure (note the "4" in T4); converted to T3 (triiodothyronine) in the body (note "tri" meaning 3 and "iod" for iodine)

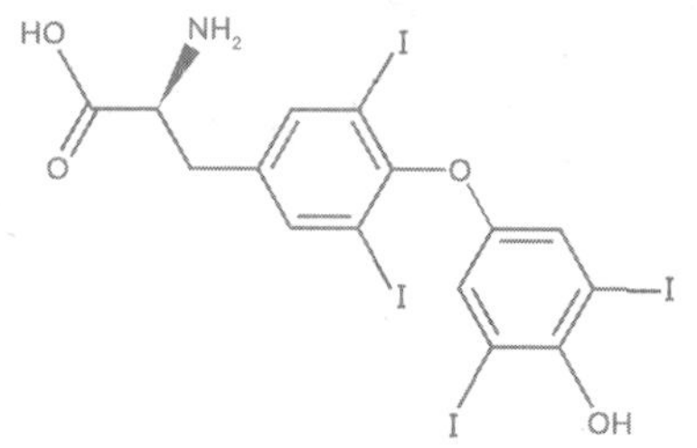

AMIODARONE

Class III antiarrhythmic

Contains two iodine molecules in the structure (note "iod" in the name)

Explains the hyper- and hypothyroid effects and contraindication in patients with an iodine allergy

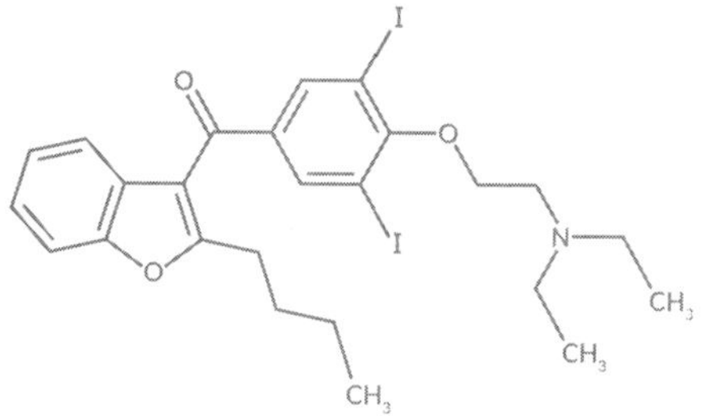

FENOFIBRATE

Fibrate, for high cholesterol

Contains ketone groups

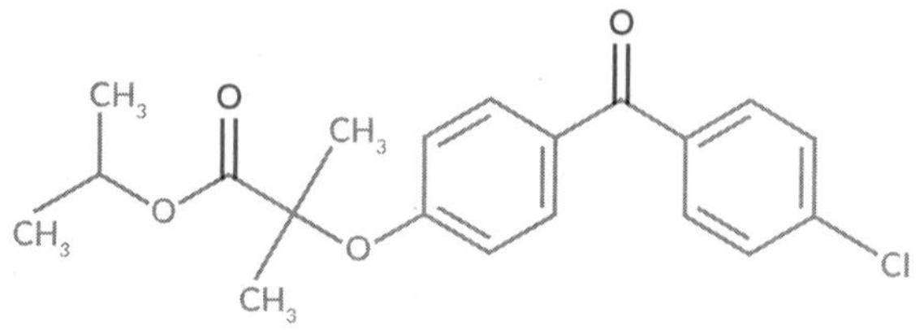

AMITRIPTYLINE

Tricyclic antidepressant

Contains three rings in the structure (note the "tri" in the name)

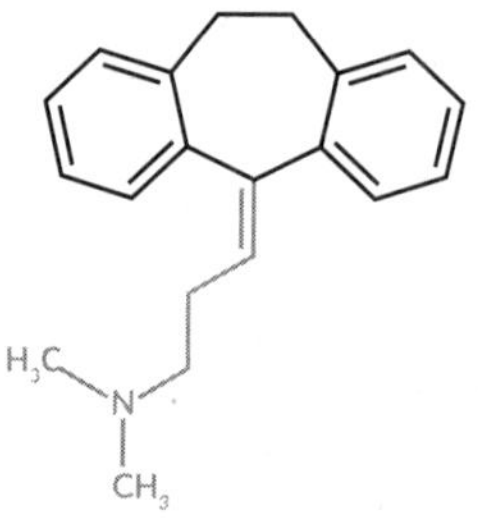

CHLORPROMAZINE

Phenothiazine antipsychotic

Contains a thioether group

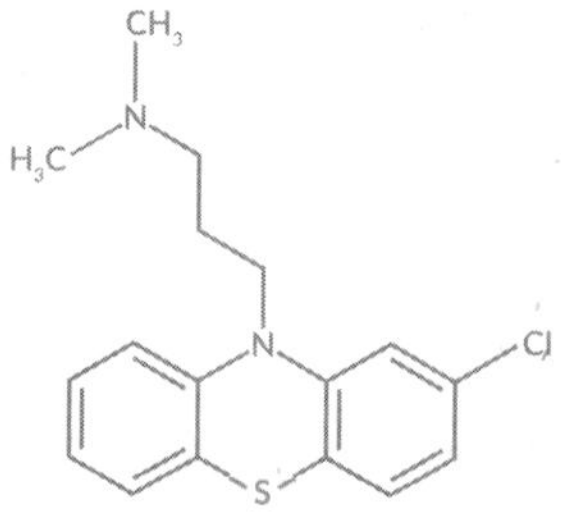

©RxPrep

CHAPTER CONTENT

CONTENT LEGEND

● = Study Tip Gal

Is that a protein, carbohydrate, fat, vitamin, mineral or other type of nutrient?

No. It could be a toxin. I will eliminate it. Hmm...renal or hepatic clearance?

CHAPTER 3

DRUG INTERACTIONS

TYPES OF DRUG INTERACTIONS

PHARMACODYNAMIC DRUG INTERACTIONS

Pharmacodynamics refers to the effect or change that a drug has on the body or some other type of organism (see Study Tip Gal below). A pharmacodynamic (PD) drug interaction occurs when two or more drugs are given together, and their end effects impact each other.

PHARMACODYNAMICS: PHARMACO + DYNAMICS

"Pharmaco" refers to a drug. "Dynamic" refers to an activity, such as a type of process or change.

Pharmacodynamics = the effect that a drug has on the body. The effect can be therapeutic (e.g., morphine provides pain relief when it binds to the mu receptor) or toxic (excessive morphine can be fatal).

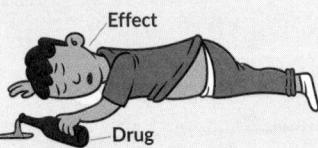

Effect

Drug

PD drug interactions can occur when two or more drugs are given together. The effects can be additive (such as more sedation), antagonistic (one drug blocks the effect of another drug) or synergistic, with an amplified (more than additive) effect.

Additive Effects: Agonists Binding to the Same Receptor

Multiple drugs that are agonists at the same receptor can cause additive effects.

Example: opioids are mu-receptor agonists, providing analgesia, but with a risk of fatal toxicity when overdosed. If two opioids (e.g., morphine and oxycodone) are taken together, the effects would be additive, with increased side effects (e.g., excessive sedation, respiratory depression and death).

Additive Effects: Agonists Binding to Different Receptors

Drugs that have similar end effects through different mechanisms/receptors can cause additive effects.

Example: benzodiazepines are sedating and can suppress respiration. The effects are similar to opioids but caused by a different mechanism. Benzodiazepines bind to and enhance the effect of the endogenous inhibitory neurotransmitter gamma-aminobutyric acid (GABA), causing anxiolytic, hypnotic, anticonvulsant and muscle relaxant effects (including relaxing the diaphragm, which is how respiration becomes suppressed). When taken concurrently with opioids, the additive effects increase the risk of a fatal overdose. Drugs in both classes have a boxed warning about this risk (see Study Tip Gal below).

RISK WITH CONCURRENT USE OF BENZODIAZEPINES AND OPIOIDS

Due to the heightened fatality risk when opioids and benzodiazepines are taken together, the FDA added a boxed warning to all drugs in both classes.

WARNING: RISKS FROM CONCOMITANT USE WITH OPIOIDS
Concomitant use of benzodiazepines and opioids may result in profound sedation, respiratory depression, coma and death.

- Limit concomitant prescribing of these drugs to patients for whom alternative treatment options are inadequate.
- Restrict dosages and durations to the minimum required.
- Monitor patients for signs and symptoms of respiratory depression and sedation.

Another example: warfarin causes anticoagulation through inhibition of vitamin K-dependent clotting factors. Aspirin blocks the effects of platelets. Although they work through different mechanisms, both can cause increased bleeding, and when used together, the risk is greater.

Antagonists Block the Action of Agonists

An antagonist blocks the agonist from binding to its receptor. The agonist is unable to initiate a change that would have resulted in some effect (e.g., analgesia from an opioid, or respiratory depression when the opioid dose is excessive).

Example: naloxone is a mu-receptor antagonist; it saturates mu-receptors and blocks the opioid from binding. Naloxone is used to reverse respiratory depression, but will also reverse the analgesic effect.

Synergistic Effects

Synergism is present when two drugs taken in combination have a greater effect than that obtained by simply adding the two individual effects together.

Example: oxycodone provides analgesia as a mu-receptor agonist. Acetaminophen provides analgesia by a different mechanism, which is not fully understood (some of the analgesic effect is thought to occur via inhibition of prostaglandin synthesis in the central nervous system). The mechanisms that produce analgesia with opioids and acetaminophen do not overlap. Acetaminophen taken with oxycodone produces more analgesia than the effect that would be expected from adding together the analgesic effects provided by each drug.

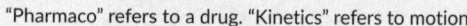

PHARMACOKINETIC DRUG INTERACTIONS

Pharmacokinetics (PK) refers to the effect or change that the body has on a drug (see Study Tip Gal below).

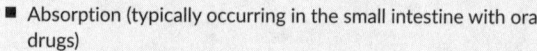

PHARMACOKINETICS: PHARMACO + KINETICS

"Pharmaco" refers to a drug. "Kinetics" refers to motion.

Pharmacokinetics = the effect the body has on the drug as it goes through the absorption, distribution, metabolism and excretion (ADME) processes.

- Absorption (typically occurring in the small intestine with oral drugs)
- Distribution (through the blood and dispersed throughout the tissues)
- Metabolism (including enzymatic reactions)
- Excretion [removal of the drug or end products (metabolites) from the body]

PK drug interactions occur when one drug alters the absorption, distribution, metabolism or excretion of another drug. PK drug interactions can be beneficial or harmful.

Reduced Absorption

Chelation occurs when a drug binds to polyvalent cations (e.g., Mg^{++}, Ca^{++}, Fe^{++}) in another compound (e.g., antacids or iron supplements). The chelated complex cannot dissolve in the gut fluid and will pass out in the stool.

Example: quinolone antibiotics bind to calcium-containing drugs and dairy products. When taken together, the antibiotic will not dissolve, will not be absorbed, and the infection may not be adequately treated.

Drugs with polyvalent cations or other binding properties (e.g., antacids, multivitamins, sucralfate, bile acid resins, aluminum, calcium, iron, magnesium, zinc, phosphate binders) should be separated from quinolones, tetracyclines, levothyroxine and oral bisphosphonates.

Some drugs require an acidic gut for adequate absorption. If gastrointestinal pH is increased, absorption will be decreased.

Example: acid-suppressing drugs (e.g., H2RAs, proton pump inhibitors) decrease the absorption of some antifungals (e.g., itraconazole) if taken together. This can result in untreated or resistant infections.

The Gastroesophageal Reflux Disease & Peptic Ulcer Disease chapter contains a more comprehensive list of the most common drugs that have binding interactions or require an acidic gut for absorption.

Induction or Inhibition of Metabolism

The majority of PK drug interactions occur during metabolism (e.g., Phase I or Phase II reactions) in the liver. Drug-drug interactions can be harmful or beneficial.

Example of a beneficial interaction: ritonavir and darunavir are used together. Ritonavir inhibits the metabolism of darunavir, which "boosts" darunavir levels and increases its efficacy in treating HIV.

Examples of harmful interactions: clarithromycin inhibits warfarin metabolism (which increases the INR and risk of bleeding), and rifampin induces warfarin metabolism (which decreases the INR and increases the risk for blood clots). Both reactions are potentially harmful, but treatment with these drug combinations may be necessary. The dose of warfarin can be decreased (with clarithromycin) or increased (with rifampin) to keep the INR in the desired range.

Decreased or Increased Excretion

Renal excretion is the primary route of drug excretion. Drug interactions can block or enhance renal excretion.

Example of decreased renal excretion: probenecid blocks the renal excretion of penicillin. Giving probenecid with penicillin can be beneficial when high penicillin levels are needed to cross the blood-brain barrier (BBB) and provide effective treatment of neurosyphilis.

Example of increased renal excretion: salicylate (e.g., aspirin) overdose results in toxicity. Intravenous sodium bicarbonate alkalinizes the urine, which causes the salicylate to become ionized. Ionized compounds are more hydrophilic (water-loving) and will stay in the urine. Less will be reabsorbed through the renal tubules (i.e., across a lipid membrane) back into the blood. Compounds that stay in the urine will be renally excreted.

ENZYME SYSTEMS, DRUG METABOLISM AND DRUG INTERACTIONS

CYTOCHROME P450 ENZYMES

The purpose of cytochrome P450 (CYP450) enzymes is to catalyze Phase I reactions that either produce essential compounds (e.g., cholesterol and cortisol) or uncover or insert a polar (i.e., water-loving) group on a compound to facilitate renal excretion. CYP450 enzymes are primarily expressed in the liver.

How CYP450 Enzymes Metabolize Drugs

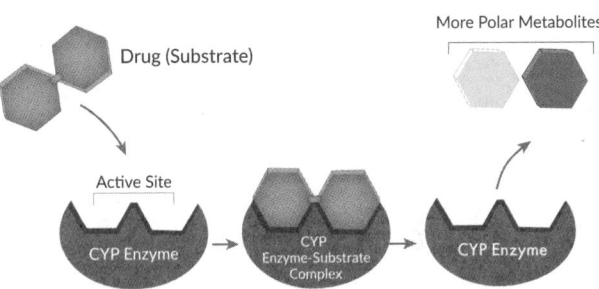

More than 50 CYP enzymes have been identified, with six of them metabolizing most drugs. CYP3A4 metabolizes ~34% of all CYP450 drug substrates. The function of CYP450 enzymes can be affected by genetics (see Pharmacogenomics chapter) and other drugs that act as enzyme inhibitors or inducers.

A table of common CYP450 enzyme substrates, inducers and inhibitors is provided at the end of the chapter.

PRODRUGS: INACTIVE DRUGS CONVERTED BY CYP ENZYMES TO ACTIVE DRUGS

Prodrugs are taken by the patient in an inactive form and are converted by CYP450 enzymes into the active form.

How CYP450 Enzymes Metabolize Prodrugs

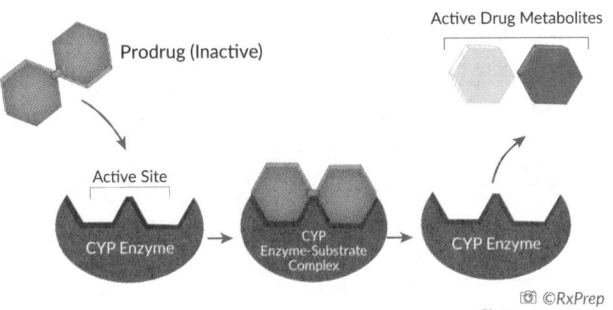

Prodrugs are used by drug manufacturers to:

- Extend the dosing interval. An example of this is valacyclovir, which is metabolized to the active drug acyclovir. Valacyclovir has higher bioavailability than acyclovir and is dosed less frequently.

- Prevent drug abuse. An example of this is lisdexamfetamine *(Vyvanse)*, which is formulated with an amino acid (lysine) attached to the amphetamine. This renders the amphetamine inactive, until the lysine is detached by enzymatic cleavage, which prevents the crushing and snorting of the drug.

The Study Tip Gal below lists some common prodrugs and their active metabolites along with some example safety concerns that can arise when a prodrug is used in patients with altered drug metabolism (e.g., due to genetics or a drug interaction).

COMMON PRODRUGS AND EXAMPLE SAFETY CONSIDERATIONS

PRODRUG AND ACTIVE METABOLITE	EXAMPLE SAFETY CONSIDERATIONS
Capecitabine → Fluorouracil	Codeine, by itself, and in combination products such as *Tylenol #3*:
Clopidogrel → Active metabolite	■ Risk of toxicity with ultra-rapid metabolizers (UMs) of CYP2D6 due to a more rapid conversion to morphine.
Codeine → Morphine	❑ Do not use codeine in UMs of 2D6.
Colistimethate → Colistin	■ Risk of poor analgesia with poor metabolizers (PMs) of CYP2D6.
Cortisone → Cortisol	❑ Use an alternative analgesic in patients identified as PMs of 2D6.
Famciclovir → Penciclovir	
Fosphenytoin → Phenytoin	
Isavuconazonium sulfate → Isavuconazole	Clopidogrel *(Plavix)*:
Levodopa → Dopamine	■ Risk with CYP2C19 inhibitors, which can block conversion to the active form.
Lisdexamfetamine → Dextroamphetamine	❑ Do not use with CYP2C19 inhibitors, including omeprazole and esomeprazole (can decrease antiplatelet effects).
Prednisone → Prednisolone	■ Risk with PMs of CYP2C19 (low conversion to the active form, with reduced antiplatelet activity).
Primidone → Phenobarbital	
Tramadol → Active metabolite	❑ Use an alternative P2Y12 inhibitor in patients identified as PMs of 2C19.
Valacyclovir → Acyclovir	
Valganciclovir → Ganciclovir	

NON-CYP450 ENZYMES

CYP450 enzymes are involved in Phase I reactions. Other enzymes, including those active in Phase II reactions, can also alter drug levels. For example, bictegravir, an antiretroviral drug for HIV, is a substrate of CYP3A4 and the Phase II enzyme uridine diphosphate glucuronosyltransferase (UGT) 1A1. Inducers or inhibitors of CYP3A4 or UGT1A1 will change the metabolism of bictegravir.

Another type of Phase II enzyme, N-acetyltransferase (NAT), is well known due to its identification early in the history of pharmacogenomic studies. NATs are highly polymorphic; differences in the degree of isoniazid toxicity were found to be due to differences in the rate of acetylation by NAT.

CYP ENZYME INHIBITORS INCREASE THE CONCENTRATION OF SUBSTRATE DRUGS

Drugs that are CYP enzyme inhibitors decrease enzyme function and the ability to metabolize compounds. Drugs that are substrates for the same CYP enzyme will have a decreased rate of drug metabolism and an increased serum drug level. In some cases, less drug will be lost to first-pass metabolism. Enzyme inhibition is fast; effects are seen within a few days and will end quickly when the inhibitor is discontinued.

With prodrugs, inhibitors and inducers have an opposite effect on drug levels. With an inhibitor, there are less functional enzymes to convert the prodrug and the concentration of the active drug decreases (see clopidogrel example in the Common Prodrugs Study Tip Gal on the previous page).

The FDA labels enzyme inhibitors as strong, moderate or weak, based on the effect on metabolism of substrate drugs. The Study Tip Gal below describes CYP inhibitors that are commonly involved in drug interactions. For most, the interaction occurs because the drug listed is a moderate or strong CYP3A4 inhibitor. For others (e.g., amiodarone), interactions occur due to the drug's ability to inhibit multiple CYP enzymes (e.g., 3A4, 2C9, 1A2).

COMMON CYP INHIBITORS INVOLVED IN DRUG INTERACTIONS

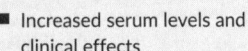

G ♥ PACMAN

Grapefruit

♥

Protease inhibitors (PIs), especially ritonavir, but many PIs are potent inhibitors

Azole antifungals (fluconazole, itraconazole, ketoconazole, posaconazole, voriconazole and isavuconazonium)

Cyclosporine, cobicistat

Macrolides (clarithromycin and erythromycin, not azithromycin)

Amiodarone (and dronedarone)

Non-DHP CCBs (diltiazem and verapamil)

Effect on Substrates
- Decreased metabolism
- Increased serum levels and clinical effects
- **IN**hibitors = **IN**creased effects/levels/ADRs/toxicities

Effect on Prodrugs
- Decreased conversion to the active drug (↓ serum levels and clinical effects)

Recognizing the Problem
- Perform therapeutic drug monitoring
- Monitor for therapeutic effect, ADRs, toxicity

Possible Actions: decrease dose of substrate (unless a prodrug), use alternate drug to avoid combination

CASE SCENARIO: TOXICITY WITH AN INHIBITOR

A 76-year-old male presents to the pharmacy with a voriconazole prescription to treat aspergillosis.

His medication profile includes betaxolol 1 drop OU BID, simvastatin 40 mg PO QHS and hydrochlorothiazide 25 mg PO QAM.

Recognizing the Problem
Voriconazole is a strong CYP3A4 inhibitor and simvastatin is a major CYP3A4 substrate. Voriconazole will increase the simvastatin level, increasing the risk of muscle toxicity and rhabdomyolysis.

Pharmacist Actions
The combination of voriconazole and simvastatin is contraindicated.

Ensure that the drugs are not used concurrently. Recommend an alternative statin, such as rosuvastatin.

CYP ENZYME INDUCERS DECREASE THE CONCENTRATION OF SUBSTRATE DRUGS

Drugs that are CYP enzyme inducers increase enzyme production or activity. Drugs that are substrates for the same CYP enzyme will have an increased rate of drug metabolism and a decreased serum drug level. In some cases, more drug will be lost to first-pass metabolism. Inducers can cause therapeutic failure.

With an inducer, there are more enzymes to catalyze the conversion of a prodrug and the concentration of the active drug increases.

Similar to inhibitors, the FDA labels enzyme inducers as strong, moderate or weak, based on the effect on metabolism of substrate drugs. The Study Tip Gal below describes CYP inducers that are commonly involved in drug interactions. For most, the interaction occurs because the drug listed is a moderate or strong CYP3A4 inducer and/or it induces multiple CYP enzymes (e.g., rifampin).

COMMON CYP INDUCERS INVOLVED IN DRUG INTERACTIONS

PS PORCS

Phenytoin

Smoking

Phenobarbital

Oxcarbazepine

Rifampin (and rifabutin, rifapentine)

Carbamazepine (also an auto-inducer)

St. John's wort

Effect on Substrates
- Increased metabolism
- Decreased serum levels and clinical effects
- In**D**ucers = **D**ecreased effects/levels

Effect on Prodrugs
- Increased conversion to the active drug (↑ serum levels and clinical effects)

Recognizing the Problem
- Perform therapeutic drug monitoring
- Monitor for therapeutic effect

Possible Actions: increase dose of substrate (unless a prodrug), use alternate drug to avoid combination

CASE SCENARIO: SUBTHERAPEUTIC LEVEL WITH AN INDUCER

A 34-year-old female with a mechanical mitral valve has been taking warfarin chronically to prevent thrombosis.

Warfarin dose: 5 mg PO daily

INR range for the past 6 months: 2.6-3.1 (INR goal 2.5-3.5)

She was admitted for infective endocarditis and started on gentamicin, ceftriaxone, rifampin and vancomycin.

Recognizing the Problem
Rifampin is an inducer of P-gp, CYP2C9, 3A4, 1A2 and 2C19.

Warfarin is metabolized by CYP2C9 (major), 1A2, 2C19 and 3A4.

Pharmacist Actions
Monitor INR more frequently; increase warfarin dose as needed.

"Lag" Time for Enzyme Induction

Induction most often requires additional enzyme production, which takes time. The full effect on drug levels may not be seen for up to four weeks. When the inducer is stopped, it could take 2 – 4 weeks for the induction effects to disappear completely; the excess enzymes will degrade based on their half-lives.

GUT EXCRETION BY DRUG TRANSPORTERS

P-GLYCOPROTEIN EFFLUX PUMPS

Permeability glycoprotein (P-gp) efflux pumps (or transporters) are located in many tissue membranes where they protect against foreign substances by moving them out of critical areas. The term efflux means to flow out, and P-gp pumps in the cell membranes of the GI tract transport drugs and their metabolites out of the body by pumping them into the gut, where they can be excreted in the stool.

When a drug blocks (or inhibits) P-gp, a drug that is a P-gp substrate will have increased absorption (less drug is pumped into the gut) and the substrate drug level will increase. There are other transporters in other parts of the body that are not described here, including efflux pumps that cause resistance by pumping chemotherapeutics out of cancer cells, and the organic ion transporter OATP1B1/3, which pumps drugs and other compounds from the blood into the liver.

There is overlap among the enzymes and transporters that protect the body from perceived toxins, including drugs. Many drugs which are substrates, inhibitors or inducers of P-gp have the same effect on CYP450 enzymes. The table below lists common P-gp substrates, inducers and inhibitors. A chart of common CYP450 substrates, inducers and inhibitors can be found at the end of the chapter.

P-gp Common Substrates, Inducers and Inhibitors

SUBSTRATES	INDUCERS	INHIBITORS
Anticoagulants (apixaban, edoxaban, dabigatran, rivaroxaban) **Cardiovascular drugs** (digoxin, diltiazem, carvedilol, ranolazine, verapamil) **Immunosuppressants** (cyclosporine, sirolimus, tacrolimus) **HCV drugs** (dasabuvir, ombitasvir, paritaprevir, sofosbuvir) **Others** (atazanavir, colchicine, dolutegravir, posaconazole, raltegravir, saxagliptin)	Carbamazepine, dexamethasone, phenobarbital, phenytoin, rifampin, St. John's wort, tipranavir	**Anti-infectives** (clarithromycin, itraconazole, posaconazole) **Cardiovascular drugs** (amiodarone, carvedilol, conivaptan, diltiazem, dronedarone, quinidine, verapamil) **HIV drugs** (cobicistat, ritonavir) **HCV drugs** (ledipasvir, paritaprevir) **Others** (cyclosporine, flibanserin, ticagrelor)

ENTEROHEPATIC RECYCLING

After a drug has been metabolized in the liver, it can be transported through the bile back to the gut. From the gut, the drug can be reabsorbed (primarily in the small intestine, where most drugs are absorbed), enter into the portal vein and travel back to the liver. The recycling of an already-metabolized drug is called enterohepatic recycling, which increases the duration of action of many drugs, including some antibiotics, some NSAIDs and the cholesterol-lowering drug ezetimibe.

COMMON DRUG INTERACTIONS

Drug interactions are an important part of pharmacy practice. This chapter covers common drug interactions that involve major drug classes (e.g., CNS depressants) or drugs with specific properties (e.g., QT-prolonging drugs). Other important drug interactions involving specific drugs (e.g., warfarin, lithium, theophylline and more) are discussed in depth in their respective chapters (e.g., Anticoagulation, Bipolar Disorder, Asthma).

The major categories of drug interactions discussed in the tables that follow include:

- Common Cardiovascular Drug Interactions
- Inhibitors Increase Substrate Drugs
- Inducers Decrease Substrate Drugs
- Drugs with Additive Risks

COMMON CARDIOVASCULAR DRUG INTERACTIONS

INTERACTION	RISK	ACTIONS BY PHARMACIST/NOTES
AMIODARONE **+ Warfarin** Can be used together for atrial fibrillation treatment: amiodarone (for rhythm control), warfarin (to reduce clot risk). Dronedarone has similar drug interaction issues.	Amiodarone inhibits multiple enzymes, including CYP2C9, which metabolizes the more potent warfarin isomer. ↓ warfarin metabolism causes ↑ INR and bleeding risk.	**If using amiodarone 1st and adding warfarin** ■ Start warfarin at a lower dose of ≤ 5 mg. **If using warfarin 1st and adding amiodarone** ■ ↓ warfarin dose 30-50%, depending on the INR. **Taking both** ■ Monitor INR; adjust as needed.
AMIODARONE **+ Digoxin** Can be given together for atrial fibrillation treatment: amiodarone (for rhythm control), digoxin [for rate control (↓ HR), or for symptom improvement in a patient with HF].	Amiodarone inhibits P-gp; digoxin is a P-gp substrate. ↓ digoxin excretion, ↑ ADRs/toxicity. Amiodarone and digoxin both ↓ HR, ↑ risk of bradycardia, arrhythmia, fatality.	**If using amiodarone 1st and adding digoxin** ■ Start oral digoxin at a low dose, such as 0.125 mg daily. **If using digoxin 1st and adding amiodarone** ■ ↓ oral digoxin dose 50% (e.g., change 0.25 mg daily to 0.125 mg daily, or change 0.125 mg daily to 0.125 mg every other day). **Taking both amiodarone and digoxin** ■ Instruct patient to monitor for symptoms of digoxin toxicity: nausea, vomiting, vision changes; if present, contact prescriber.
DIGOXIN **+ Loop diuretic** Can be given together for heart failure treatment: digoxin (for symptom improvement), loop diuretics (to alleviate symptoms due to fluid overload).	Loop diuretics ↓ K, Mg, Ca and Na. Low K, Mg or Ca will worsen arrhythmias. Digoxin toxicity risk is increased with ↓ K and Mg levels and ↑ Ca levels. Caution: HF and renal impairment often occur together. Digoxin is cleared by P-gp and excreted by the kidneys; renal impairment (which can be exacerbated by loop diuretics) ↑ digoxin levels and toxicity risk.	■ Monitor HR; normal is 60-100 BPM (can be lower, based on patient's history and physical state). Check for other drugs that ↓ HR: beta-blockers, clonidine, diltiazem, verapamil, dexmedetomidine (Precedex). ■ If digoxin is being used for rate control, inform prescribers to consider beta-blockers or non-DHP CCBs instead. **Taking digoxin and a loop diuretic** ■ Monitor electrolytes and correct if abnormal. ■ Renal impairment: ↓ digoxin dose or frequency, or discontinue.
DRUGS THAT DECREASE HEART RATE Diltiazem/verapamil or beta-blockers for rate control; clonidine and beta-blockers to lower blood pressure.	Additive effects when drugs that ↓ HR are used together, including amiodarone, digoxin, beta-blockers, clonidine, diltiazem, verapamil and dexmedetomidine (Precedex).	Monitor HR; normal is 60-100 BPM (can be lower, based on patient's history and physical state).
STATINS **+ Strong CYP3A4 inhibitors** Inhibitors: protease inhibitors (including ritonavir), cobicistat, clarithromycin, erythromycin, azole antifungals, cyclosporine, grapefruit/grapefruit juice	↑ levels of CYP3A4 substrates: lovastatin, simvastatin, atorvastatin. ↑ myopathy risk; if severe (with high CPK), can cause rhabdomyolysis with acute renal failure (ARF).	Simvastatin and lovastatin are contraindicated with strong CYP3A4 inhibitors. Recommend a statin not metabolized by CYP450 enzymes (e.g., pitavastatin, pravastatin, rosuvastatin).
WARFARIN **+ CYP2C9 inhibitors and inducers** Inhibitors: azole antifungals, sulfamethoxazole/trimethoprim, amiodarone, metronidazole Inducers: rifampin, St. John's wort	↑ levels of warfarin (↑ INR and bleeding risk) with CYP2C9 inhibitors. ↓ levels of warfarin (↓ INR and ↑ clotting risk) with CYP2C9 inducers.	Monitor INR; therapeutic range is 2-3 for most conditions (2.5-3.5 for some high-risk indications, such as mechanical mitral valve). Some drugs (e.g., amiodarone) require prophylactic warfarin dose adjustment when started (see above).

INHIBITORS INCREASE SUBSTRATE DRUGS

INTERACTION	RISK	ACTIONS BY PHARMACIST/NOTES
CYP3A4 INHIBITORS **+ CYP3A4 substrates (many)** Includes the opioids fentanyl, hydrocodone, oxycodone, methadone.	↓ CYP3A4 substrate (i.e., drug) metabolism will cause ↑ drug levels and ↑ ADRs/toxicity. If an opioid is the substrate, sedation will increase, followed by respiratory depression, which can quickly cause fatality.	Do not use a CYP3A4 inhibitor with an opioid metabolized by CYP3A4; the combination will cause increased ADRs, including sedation, and can be fatal. Grapefruit/grapefruit juice: do not take with CYP3A4 substrates. Drugs that specifically include instructions not to take with grapefruit include amiodarone, simvastatin, lovastatin, nifedipine and tacrolimus; many other drugs have similar risk.
VALPROATE **+ Lamotrigine** Valproate is an inhibitor of lamotrigine metabolism.	Valproate ↓ lamotrigine metabolism and ↑ lamotrigine levels causing ↑ risk of serious skin reactions, including SJS/TEN (can be fatal).	Initiate lamotrigine using the starter kit that begins with lower lamotrigine doses. Titrate carefully every 2 weeks. Counsel patients to get emergency help if rash develops.
MONOAMINE OXIDASE (MAO) INHIBITORS Isocarboxazid, phenelzine, tranylcypromine, rasagiline, selegiline, linezolid, methylene blue **+** **Drugs/foods that ↑ epinephrine (Epi), norepinephrine (NE), dopamine (DA)** SNRIs, TCAs, bupropion, levodopa, stimulants, including amphetamines used for ADHD (e.g., methylphenidate, lisdexamfetamine, dextroamphetamine), tyramine (from foods) **+** **Drugs that ↑ serotonin (5-HT)** Antidepressants: SSRIs, SNRIs, TCAs, mirtazapine, trazodone Opioids and analgesics: fentanyl, methadone, tramadol Others: buspirone, dextromethorphan (when high doses taken as drug of abuse), lithium, St. John's wort	The MAO enzyme metabolizes Epi, NE, DA, tyramine and 5-HT. Blocking MAO with an MAO-inhibitor will ↑ Epi, NE, DA and 5-HT. High Epi, NE and DA can cause hypertensive crisis. High 5-HT can cause serotonin syndrome; see Serotonergic Toxicity in the Drugs with Additive Risks section.	Do not use together. Use a 2-week washout period when switching between drugs with MAO inhibition or serotonergic properties (except with fluoxetine, wait 5 weeks). Tyramine-rich foods have been aged, pickled, fermented or smoked, including aged cheeses, air-dried meats, sauerkraut, some wines and beers.
CYP2D6 INHIBITORS Amiodarone, fluoxetine, paroxetine, fluvoxamine **+ CYP2D6 substrates** Many, including codeine, meperidine, tramadol, tamoxifen	↓ drug substrate metabolism, ↑ ADRs/toxicity (or decreased clinical efficacy if a prodrug).	Avoid using together if possible.
CYP3A4, P-GP INHIBITORS **+** **Calcineurin inhibitors (CNIs)** Tacrolimus, cyclosporine **or** **mTOR kinase inhibitors** Sirolimus, everolimus	↓ drug substrate metabolism, ↑ ADRs/toxicity, including ↑ blood pressure, nephrotoxicity, metabolic syndrome and other adverse effects (see Transplant chapter).	Avoid using together or ↓ dose of CNI or mTOR kinase inhibitor cautiously and based on drug levels. Monitor transplant drug levels.

INDUCERS DECREASE SUBSTRATE DRUGS

INTERACTION	RISK	ACTIONS BY PHARMACIST/NOTES
ANTIEPILEPTIC DRUG (AED) CYP INDUCERS Phenytoin, phenobarbital, primidone, carbamazepine, oxcarbazepine **+** **Other drugs metabolized by CYP enzymes** Oral contraceptives, other AEDs, carbamazepine (auto-inducer, induces its own metabolism), others	↑ substrate (drug) metabolism will cause ↓ drug levels. ↓ drug effects; with AEDs, loss of seizure control.	Monitor drug levels; induction takes up to 4 weeks for the full effect. Consider increasing the dose of the substrate drug. If substrate is lamotrigine, use the starter kit that begins with higher lamotrigine doses.
RIFAMPIN **+ CYP and P-gp substrates**	The concentration of substrate drugs will greatly decrease.	Monitor drug levels or other appropriate monitoring parameters, such as an INR with warfarin. Increase the dose of the substrate drug as necessary.
CYP3A4 INDUCERS **+** **Opioids that are CYP3A4 substrates** Fentanyl, hydrocodone, oxycodone, methadone	↑ metabolism results in ↓ opioid concentration; analgesia (pain relief) will decrease.	Assess the patient's use of breakthrough pain medication to determine if an increased maintenance dose is necessary. Use caution; opioids cause respiratory depression when overdosed, and induction has a lag time.
CYP2D6 UMs **+** **Prodrugs that are CYP2D6 substrates** Codeine, tramadol	There are no CYP2D6 inducers (it is not an inducible enzyme). With 2D6 UMs (who produce about twice as many enzymes), the effect is similar to the effect from an inducer and the prodrug will be converted more rapidly to the active drug. ↑ active drug concentration, which can cause toxicity/risk and possible fatality.	Do not use codeine or tramadol in children ≤ 12 years or < 18 years following tonsillectomy and/or adenoidectomy (contraindication). Do not use an opioid prodrug that is metabolized by CYP2D6 (codeine, tramadol) in a breast-feeding mother unless it is known that she is not a 2D6 UM.
CYP3A4, P-GP INDUCERS **+** **Calcineurin inhibitors (CNIs)** Tacrolimus, cyclosporine **or** **mTOR kinase inhibitors** Sirolimus, everolimus	↑ drug metabolism results in ↓ transplant drug level and ↑ risk of transplant (organ) rejection.	Avoid using together or ↑ dose of CNI or mTOR kinase inhibitor carefully. Monitor transplant drug levels for efficacy.
SMOKING Primarily induces CYP1A2; includes smoking tobacco and marijuana **+** **Some antipsychotics, antidepressants, hypnotics, anxiolytics, caffeine, theophylline, warfarin (R-isomer)**	**Smokers who quit** When the inducer (cigarettes) is stopped, drug concentrations of CYP1A2 substrates will ↑, causing toxicity.	Counsel/advocate for smoking cessation. When a smoker quits, monitor the INR if taking warfarin; the R-isomer of warfarin (less potent isomer) is metabolized by CYP1A2, but the therapeutic range is narrow and could be affected. Nicotine replacement products (NRT, such as the patch and gum) do not induce CYP enzymes.
	Current smoker CYP1A2 substrates (i.e., drugs) will have ↓ levels.	When a current smoker starts a drug that is a CYP1A2 substrate, a higher dose can be required.

DRUGS WITH ADDITIVE RISK

ADDITIVE SIDE EFFECT	RISK	ACTIONS BY PHARMACIST/NOTES
SEROTONERGIC TOXICITY		
Antidepressants SSRIs, SNRIs, TCAs, mirtazapine, trazodone **MAO inhibitors** Antidepressants: isocarboxazid, phenelzine, tranylcypromine Selective MAO-B inhibitors: selegiline, rasagiline Others: linezolid, methylene blue **Opioids** Fentanyl, meperidine, methadone, tramadol, tapentadol (though there is risk when any opioid is used in combination with serotonergic drugs) **Triptans** Occasional (PRN) triptan use may be safe; more frequent use can increase risk **Natural products** St. John's wort, L-tryptophan **Others** Buspirone, lithium, dextromethorphan (when taken in excess as a drug of abuse)	Serotonin syndrome risk increases when <u>two or more drugs</u> that affect serotonin are used <u>together</u>. Higher doses ↑ risk. Symptoms range from mild to severe and fatal: ■ Autonomic dysfunction (diaphoresis, nausea, vomiting, hyperthermia) ■ Altered mental status (akathisia, anxiety, <u>agitation</u>, delirium) ■ Neuromuscular excitation (hyperreflexia, tremor, <u>rigidity</u>, tonic-clonic seizures)	<u>Avoid using serotonergic drugs together</u>; if used, doses should be within recommended ranges. Check for inhibitors of serotonergic drugs. Counsel patients to report symptoms, even if mild. If severe symptoms, counsel to go to the emergency department. Recommend eliminating an initial serotonergic drug prior to starting a new serotonergic drug by using a <u>washout period</u>: use <u>2 weeks</u> between the drugs, or use <u>5 weeks</u> for drugs with a longer duration of action, such as <u>fluoxetine</u>.
BLEEDING		
Anticoagulants Warfarin, dabigatran, apixaban, edoxaban, rivaroxaban, heparin, enoxaparin, dalteparin, fondaparinux, argatroban, bivalirudin **Antiplatelets** Salicylates (including aspirin), dipyridamole, clopidogrel, prasugrel, ticagrelor **NSAIDs** Ibuprofen, naproxen, diclofenac, indomethacin, others **SSRIs, SNRIs** Citalopram, escitalopram, fluoxetine, paroxetine, sertraline, duloxetine, venlafaxine, others **Natural products** 5G's: garlic, ginger, ginkgo biloba, ginseng, glucosamine Vitamin E, willow bark, fish oils (high doses)	↑ <u>bleeding risk</u>; can occur with or without changing an anticoagulation monitoring parameter, such as the INR (with warfarin).	<u>Avoid using in combination</u>, with a few exceptions: ■ Aspirin (for cardioprotection) and occasional NSAID use for pain, fever or inflammation. ■ SSRI/SNRI use and occasional NSAID use for pain, fever or inflammation. ■ Dual antiplatelet therapy may be recommended for select patients (e.g., to prevent cardiac stent thrombosis). ■ Bridging/overlap treatment, such as enoxaparin + warfarin, until INR therapeutic ≥ 24 hrs.
HYPERKALEMIA		
Renin-angiotensin-aldosterone system drugs ACE inhibitors, ARBs, aliskiren, sacubitril/valsartan, spironolactone, eplerenone (highest risk with aldosterone receptor antagonists) **Potassium-sparing diuretics** Amiloride, triamterene **Others** Salt substitutes (KCl), calcineurin inhibitors (tacrolimus and cyclosporine), SMX/TMP, canagliflozin, drospirenone-containing oral contraceptives	<u>Hyperkalemia</u>; symptoms include weakness, heart palpitations, arrhythmia. Higher risk with renal impairment.	<u>Do not use ACE inhibitors with ARBs.</u> <u>Do not use sacubitril/valsartan with ACE inhibitors or ARBs.</u> If risk of hyperkalemia, suggest alternatives to canagliflozin (for diabetes), SMX/TMP (for infection) or drospirenone-containing oral contraceptives. Counsel patient to <u>avoid salt substitutes</u> that contain KCl. Monitor potassium.

ADDITIVE SIDE EFFECT	RISK	ACTIONS BY PHARMACIST/NOTES
QT PROLONGATION		
Antiarrhythmics Class 1a, 1c and III (see Arrhythmias chapter) **Anti-infectives** Antimalarials (e.g., hydroxychloroquine) Azole antifungals, except isavuconazonium Lefamulin Macrolides Quinolones **Antidepressants** SSRIs: highest risk with citalopram, escitalopram TCAs Others: mirtazapine, trazodone, venlafaxine **Antipsychotics** First-generation (e.g., haloperidol, thioridazine) Second-generation: highest risk with ziprasidone **Antiemetics** 5-HT3 receptor antagonists (e.g., ondansetron) Others: droperidol, metoclopramide, promethazine **Oncology medications** Androgen deprivation therapy (e.g., leuprolide) Tyrosine kinase inhibitors (e.g., nilotinib) Other: oxaliplatin **Others** Cilostazol, donepezil, fingolimod, hydroxyzine, loperamide, ranolazine, solifenacin, methadone, tacrolimus	QT prolongation ↑ the risk of torsades de pointes (TdP), an often fatal arrhythmia. The risk increases with: ■ Higher doses. ■ Higher drug levels due to concurrent enzyme inhibitors. ■ Higher drug levels due to reduced drug clearance, such as with renal or liver disease. ■ Multiple QT-prolonging drugs used together. ■ Elderly (> 60 years) and patients with CVD, including arrhythmias, HF, MI.	With all QT-prolonging drugs, avoid/reduce risk of TdP: ■ Limit use of QT-prolonging drugs or select drugs with lower QT risk, especially with arrhythmias, CVD or CVD risk (exception: amiodarone is the drug of choice to treat an arrhythmia in patients with HF). ■ Carefully dose QT-prolonging drugs; use lower doses/caution use in elderly patients. ❑ Do not exceed citalopram 40 mg daily or 20 mg daily in elderly (> 60 years), liver disease or with enzyme inhibitors that decrease clearance. ❑ Do not exceed escitalopram 20 mg daily or 10 mg daily in elderly. ❑ Among SSRIs, sertraline is considered safest in patients with CVD. ■ Avoid concurrent QT-prolonging drugs, if possible. ■ Avoid use of inhibitors that block a QT-prolonging drug's metabolism. ■ Do not use droperidol for inpatient N/V (droperidol is injection only and has restricted use due to QT prolongation risk).
CNS DEPRESSION		
Many Drugs/Drug Classes Opioids Skeletal muscle relaxants Antiepileptic drugs Benzodiazepines Barbiturates Hypnotics Antidepressants: mirtazapine, trazodone Antihypertensives: propranolol, clonidine Cannabis-related drugs: dronabinol, nabilone Sedating antihistamines Cough syrups with an antihistamine or opioid Some NSAIDs **Highest risk for fatality when used in combination:** Opioids + Benzodiazepines or other CNS depressants	CNS depressant-effects: somnolence, dizziness, confusion/cognitive impairment, altered consciousness/delirium, gait instability/imbalance/risk of falls/accidents, including motor vehicle accidents. Benzodiazepines are a drug of abuse, and are often prescribed inappropriately (for anxiety or insomnia), adding unnecessary risk of CNS depression. Benzodiazepines are appropriate for status epilepticus, alcohol withdrawal, as an antidote for stimulant overdose, prior to medical procedures, in acute high-anxiety situations and for anticipatory emesis with chemotherapy. Opioids: due to the risks of abuse, dependence and addiction, reserve for severe pain that is not responsive to other measures.	Provide patient counseling: ■ Do not use alcohol. ■ Do not operate a car or other vehicles/machines. ■ Can increase risk of falls, confusion. Monitor for sedation, slow and shallow breathing, and shortness of breath. Avoid combining CNS depressants when possible. Suggest alternatives for anxiety (e.g., SSRI, SNRI), insomnia (lifestyle treatments preferred) or pain (e.g., acetaminophen, NSAIDs, antidepressants). **For opioids specifically:** ■ Do not use in combination with benzodiazepines; use of other CNS depressants, including alcohol, have a high risk of fatality with opioids. ■ Extended-release formulations have additional risk: several become shorter-acting when taken with alcohol, which increases the risk of fatality. ■ Recommend naloxone for at-risk patients, including use of high doses, rapid dose increases or reduced clearance (e.g., renal impairment with morphine). ■ Avoid codeine if pharmacogenomic profile is unknown (highest risk with CYP2D6 UMs). ■ See other CYP3A4 and 2D6 interaction information discussed previously.

ADDITIVE SIDE EFFECT	RISK	ACTIONS BY PHARMACIST/NOTES
OTOTOXICITY		
Aminoglycosides Gentamicin, tobramycin, amikacin, others **Cisplatin** **Loop diuretics (especially rapid IV administration)** Furosemide, bumetanide, ethacrynic acid **Salicylates** Aspirin, salsalate, magnesium salicylate, others **Vancomycin**	Hearing loss, tinnitus, vertigo.	■ Consider an audiology consult at start of treatment for baseline hearing assessment, continue to monitor. ■ Avoid using multiple ototoxic drugs at the same time, when possible.
NEPHROTOXICITY		
Anti-infectives Aminoglycosides, amphotericin B, polymyxins, vancomycin **Cisplatin** **Calcineurin inhibitors** Cyclosporine, tacrolimus **Loop diuretics** Furosemide, torsemide, bumetanide, ethacrynic acid **NSAIDs** **Radiographic-contrast dye**	Worsening renal function/ acute renal failure (ARF), can be evidenced by ↓ in urine output and ↑ SCr/BUN.	■ Cisplatin: use amifostine (Ethyol) to protect kidneys. ■ Maintain adequate hydration (dehydration can worsen kidney function). ■ Monitor drug levels (e.g., aminoglycosides, vancomycin, tacrolimus), as appropriate. ■ Discontinue offending drugs if acute renal failure occurs. ■ Monitor urine output, SCr/BUN.
ANTICHOLINERGIC TOXICITY		
Antidepressants/antipsychotics Paroxetine, TCAs, first-generation antipsychotics **Sedating antihistamines** Diphenhydramine, brompheniramine, chlorpheniramine, doxylamine, hydroxyzine, cyproheptadine, meclizine **Centrally-acting anticholinergics** Benztropine, trihexyphenidyl **Muscle relaxants** Baclofen, carisoprodol, cyclobenzaprine **Antimuscarinics (for urinary incontinence)** Oxybutynin, darifenacin, tolterodine **Others** Atropine, belladonna, dicyclomine	Anticholinergic symptoms: CNS depression, including sedation, and peripheral anticholinergic side effects of dry mouth, dry eyes, blurry vision, constipation, urinary retention. Highest risk in elderly.	■ Recommend alternatives to sedating antihistamines, such as loratadine, fexofenadine, cetirizine, or suggest saline nasal spray/drops that clear allergens out of the nasal passages. ■ If using diphenhydramine or other sedating antihistamines for sleep, suggest lifestyle changes (sleep hygiene). ■ Recommend treatments for dry mouth, dry eyes (see Sjogren's Syndrome in the Systemic Steroids & Autoimmune Conditions chapter); recommend laxatives for constipation (see Constipation & Diarrhea chapter).
HYPOTENSION/ORTHOSTASIS		
PDE-5 inhibitors Sildenafil, tadalafil, avanafil, vardenafil + **CYP3A4 inhibitors** or **Nitrates** or **Alpha-1 blockers** Non-selective (e.g., doxazosin, terazosin) or selective (e.g., tamsulosin)	With CYP3A4 inhibitors: ↓ PDE-5 inhibitor metabolism causes ↑ side effects, including headache, dizziness, flushing (causing ↑ risk of falls/injury). PDE-5 inhibitors, nitrates and alpha-1 blockers all cause vasodilation. Additive effects can lead to hypotension/orthostasis, dizziness and falls. With nitrates, severe hypotension can cause chest pain and CV events, which can be fatal.	**If taking a CYP3A4 inhibitor** ■ Start with half the usual starting dose of the PDE-5 inhibitor (see Sexual Dysfunction chapter). **PDE-5 inhibitors and nitrates** ■ Do not use together (contraindicated); check for use of sublingual nitroglycerin PRN for chest pain; can consider use of nitroglycerin in emergent situations (UA/NSTEMI/STEMI) with close monitoring. **PDE-5 inhibitors and alpha-1 blockers** ■ Start with a low dose when adding a drug from either class (e.g., if taking an alpha-1 blocker, start at half the usual PDE-5 inhibitor starting dose). Do not start a PDE-5 inhibitor unless stable (e.g., no symptoms of hypotension) on an alpha-1 blocker.

CYP450 ENZYMES: COMMON SUBSTRATES, INDUCERS AND INHIBITORS

CYP	SUBSTRATES	INDUCERS	INHIBITORS
3A4	**Analgesics** (buprenorphine, diclofenac, fentanyl, hydrocodone, meloxicam, methadone, oxycodone, tramadol) **Anticoagulants** (apixaban, rivaroxaban, R-warfarin) **Cardiovascular drugs** (amiodarone, amlodipine, bosentan, diltiazem, eplerenone, ivabradine, nifedipine, quinidine, ranolazine, tolvaptan, verapamil) **Immunosuppressants** (cyclosporine, tacrolimus, sirolimus) **Statins** (atorvastatin, lovastatin, simvastatin) **Key HIV drugs** (atazanavir, efavirenz and other NNRTIs, ritonavir, tipranavir) **PDE-5 inhibitors** (avanafil, sildenafil, tadalafil, vardenafil) **Others** (alfuzosin, aprepitant, aripiprazole, benzodiazepines, brexpiprazole, buspirone, carbamazepine, citalopram, clarithromycin, colchicine, dapsone, dutasteride, erythromycin, escitalopram, ethinyl estradiol, felbamate, haloperidol, ketoconazole, levonorgestrel, mirtazapine, modafinil, ondansetron, paritaprevir, progesterone, quetiapine, tamoxifen, trazodone, venlafaxine, zolpidem)	Carbamazepine, efavirenz, etravirine, oxcarbazepine, phenobarbital, phenytoin, primidone, rifabutin, rifampin, rifapentine, smoking, St. John's wort	**Anti-infectives** (clarithromycin, erythromycin, azole antifungals, isoniazid) **Cardiovascular drugs** (amiodarone, diltiazem, dronedarone, quinidine, ranolazine, verapamil) **Key HIV drugs** (cobicistat, efavirenz, ritonavir and other protease inhibitors) **Others** (aprepitant, cimetidine, cyclosporine, fluvoxamine, grapefruit juice, haloperidol, nefazodone, sertraline)
1A2	Alosetron, aprepitant, clozapine, cyclobenzaprine, duloxetine, ethinyl estradiol, fluvoxamine, methadone, mirtazapine, olanzapine, ondansetron, pimozide, propranolol, rasagiline, ropinirole, theophylline, tizanidine, R-warfarin, zolpidem	Carbamazepine, phenobarbital, phenytoin, primidone, rifampin, ritonavir, smoking, St. John's wort	Atazanavir, cimetidine, ciprofloxacin, fluvoxamine, zileuton
2C8	Amiodarone, dasabuvir, pioglitazone, repaglinide, rosiglitazone	Phenytoin, rifampin	Amiodarone, atazanavir, clopidogrel, gemfibrozil, ketoconazole, trimethoprim/sulfamethoxazole, ritonavir
2C9	Alosetron, carvedilol, celecoxib, diazepam, diclofenac, fluvastatin, glyburide, glipizide, glimepiride, meloxicam, nateglinide, phenytoin, ramelteon, S-warfarin, tamoxifen, zolpidem	Aprepitant, carbamazepine, phenobarbital, phenytoin, primidone, rifampin, rifapentine, ritonavir, smoking, St. John's wort	Amiodarone, atazanavir, capecitabine, cimetidine, efavirenz, etravirine, gemfibrozil, fluconazole, fluvoxamine, fluorouracil, isoniazid, ketoconazole, metronidazole, oritavancin, tamoxifen, trimethoprim/sulfamethoxazole, valproic acid, voriconazole, zafirlukast
2C19	Clopidogrel, phenytoin, thioridazine, voriconazole	Carbamazepine, phenobarbital, phenytoin, rifampin	Cimetidine, esomeprazole, efavirenz, etravirine, fluoxetine, fluvoxamine, isoniazid, ketoconazole, modafinil, omeprazole, topiramate, voriconazole
2D6	**Analgesics** (codeine, hydrocodone, meperidine, methadone, oxycodone, tramadol) **Antipsychotics/Antidepressants** (aripiprazole, brexpiprazole, doxepin, fluoxetine, haloperidol, mirtazapine, risperidone, thioridazine, trazodone, tricyclic antidepressants, venlafaxine) **Others** (atomoxetine, carvedilol, dextromethorphan, flecainide, methamphetamine, metoprolol, propafenone, propranolol, tamoxifen)		Amiodarone, bupropion, cimetidine, cobicistat, darifenacin, dronedarone, duloxetine, fluoxetine, mirabegron, paroxetine, propafenone, quinidine, ritonavir, sertraline

CONTENT LEGEND

 = Key Drug Guy

![Clinical laboratory requisition form with syringe and blood collection tubes]

© iStock.com/Michael Burrell

CHAPTER 4

LAB VALUES & DRUG MONITORING

BACKGROUND

Laboratory values assist healthcare providers in diagnosing and monitoring diseases and drug therapies. Blood or other samples can be sent to a hospital or an outside laboratory, or alternate methods can be used. Point-of-care (POC) testing provides rapid results at the site of patient care. There are many POC tests, including tests for cardiac enzymes, A1C, INR, and various infections. Home testing kits, many of which are available OTC, provide convenience and privacy and are available to test for pregnancy, ovulation, HIV infection, herpes, fecal occult blood or the presence of illicit substances or opioids.

Therapeutic drug monitoring (TDM) involves obtaining a drug level or other relevant labs to monitor efficacy and safety. TDM is reviewed in detail at the end of this chapter.

Pharmacists in many states can order and interpret lab tests for a variety of purposes, including screening for and diagnosing disease, monitoring drug levels and other related lab values, checking for medication adherence or screening for drugs of abuse.

DEFINITIONS

COMPLETE BLOOD COUNT

The complete blood count (CBC) is a commonly ordered lab panel that analyzes white blood cells (WBCs), or neutrophils, red blood cells (RBCs) and platelets (PLTs). The CBC includes hemoglobin (oxygen-carrying protein in RBCs) and hematocrit (the level of RBCs in the fluid component of the blood, or plasma). When a CBC with differential is ordered, the types of neutrophils are analyzed.

BASIC METABOLIC PANEL/COMPREHENSIVE METABOLIC PANEL

The basic metabolic panel (BMP) includes seven to eight tests that analyze electrolytes, glucose, renal function and acid/base (with HCO3, or bicarbonate) status. Some labs calculate and report an anion gap along with the BMP (see Calculations IV chapter).

A comprehensive metabolic panel (CMP) includes the tests in a BMP plus albumin, alanine aminotransferase (ALT), aspartate aminotransferase (AST), total bilirubin and total protein. The additional tests are used primarily to assess liver function. The BMP and CMP are groups of labs that are ordered together for convenience.

The stick diagrams below are used in practice when writing a paper chart note to denote the primary components of the CBC or BMP. Pharmacists should know which values are contained in the stick diagrams below.

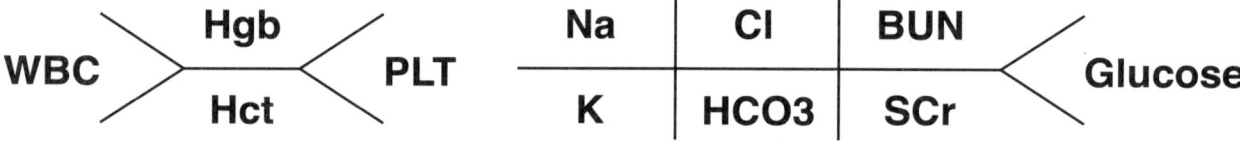

BLOOD CELL LINES

Stem cells in the bone marrow produce red blood cells, white blood cells and platelets (see figure). White blood cells can be called leukocytes, and red blood cells can be called erythrocytes. An immature red blood cell is called a reticulocyte (discussed in the Anemia section of the Common Laboratory Reference Ranges table).

Changes in Blood Cell Lines

Increase in Individual Cell Lines	
↑ WBC	Leukocytosis
↑ RBC	Polycythemia
↑ Platelets	Thrombocytosis
Decrease in Individual Cell Lines	
↓ WBC	Leukopenia
↓ RBC (or ↓ Hgb)	Anemia
↓ Platelets	Thrombocytopenia
Decrease in Multiple Cell Lines	
Myelosuppression	↓ WBCs, RBCs and platelets
Agranulocytosis Drug causes: clozapine, propylthiouracil, methimazole, procainamide, carbamazepine, sulfamethoxazole/trimethoprim, isoniazid	↓ granulocytes (WBCs that have secretory granules in the cytoplasm); includes ↓ neutrophils, basophils and eosinophils

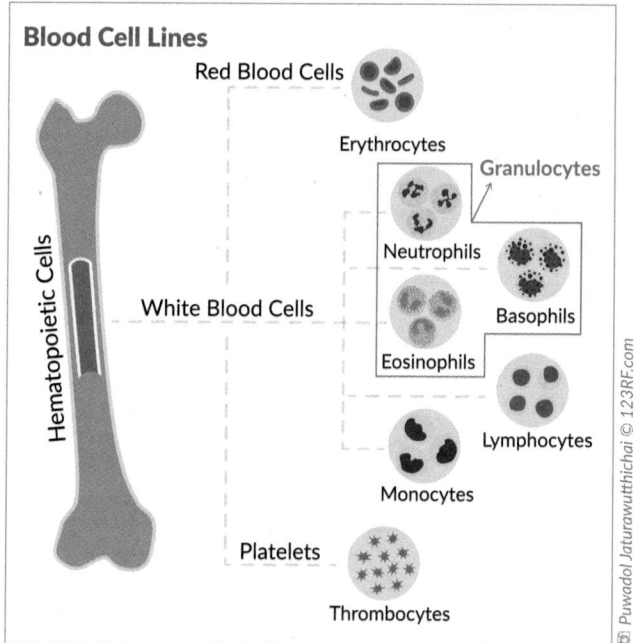

Blood Cell Lines

© Puwadol Jaturawutthichai © 123RF.com

LAB RESULTS

Lab results are usually reported as a numerical value (e.g., sodium = 139 mEq/L). Some are reported as "positive" or "negative" or indicate a specific finding, such as "Gram-positive cocci." Reference ranges can vary slightly from one facility to another (due to slight variances in products and techniques) and between pediatric and adult populations. A patient's lab results may be within the reference ranges (normal) or outside of the reference ranges (can indicate a condition that needs to be addressed). A value that is termed critical can be life-threatening unless corrective action is taken quickly. The Joint Commission requires that all accredited facilities create and follow a protocol to identify and report critical values to the responsible healthcare provider, who has an established time frame to manage the result. This applies to critical lab values and diagnostic procedure results.

COMMON LABORATORY REFERENCE RANGES – ADULT

Reference ranges for labs are generally <u>provided</u> on the NAPLEX, but may not be provided on the California Practice Standards and Jurisprudence Exam (CPJE). Familiarity with lab tests and their interpretation will greatly reduce the time required to evaluate cases on the exam. "Must know" labs for pharmacists are bolded in the following table, though others are likely to be included in patient cases. The reference range for a healthy adult is provided unless otherwise noted. Drugs specifically indicated to treat a lab abnormality (e.g., urate-lowering therapies) are included in the respective chapters (e.g., the Gout chapter). Studying this table will be much easier after mastering all of the associated disease state chapters in this book.

ITEM	COMMON REFERENCE RANGE	NOTES
BMP and Electrolytes		
Calcium, total Calcium, ionized **(Ca)**	8.5–10.5 mg/dL 4.5–5.1 mg/dL	<u>Calculate corrected calcium if albumin is low</u> (see Calculations III chapter for formula). Correction is not needed for ionized calcium. ↑ due to calcium supplementation, <u>vitamin D, thiazide diuretics</u>. ↓ due to <u>long-term heparin, loop diuretics, bisphosphonates, cinacalcet</u>, systemic steroids, calcitonin, foscarnet, topiramate. Supplement calcium in pregnancy, osteoporosis/osteopenia and with certain drugs (see Dietary Supplements, Natural & Complementary Medicine chapter).
Chloride (Cl)	95–106 mEq/L	Used with other labs to assess acid-base status and fluid balance.
Magnesium (Mg)	1.3–2.1 mEq/L	↑ due to magnesium-containing antacids and laxatives (higher risk with renal impairment). ↓ due to <u>PPIs, diuretics, amphotericin B</u>, foscarnet, echinocandins, diarrhea, chronic alcohol intake.
Phosphate (PO4)	2.3–4.7 mg/dL	↑ in <u>chronic kidney disease</u>. ↓ due to phosphate binders, foscarnet, oral calcium intake.
Potassium (K)	3.5–5 mEq/L	↑ due to <u>ACE inhibitors, ARBs, aldosterone receptor antagonists (ARAs), aliskiren, canagliflozin, cyclosporine, tacrolimus</u>, mycophenolate, <u>potassium supplements, sulfamethoxazole/trimethoprim, drospirenone-containing oral contraceptives, chronic heparin use, NSAIDs</u>, pentamidine. ↓ due to <u>beta-2 agonists, diuretics, insulin</u>, steroids, conivaptan, mycophenolate (both ↑ and ↓ reported).
Sodium (Na)	135–145 mEq/L	↑ due to <u>hypertonic saline, tolvaptan</u>, conivaptan. ↓ due to <u>carbamazepine, oxcarbazepine, SSRIs, diuretics</u>, desmopressin.
Bicarbonate **(HCO3 or "bicarb")**	Venous: 24–30 mEq/L Arterial: 22–26 mEq/L (varies by method)	Used to assess acid-base status. ↑ due to loop diuretics, systemic steroids. ↓ due to <u>topiramate</u>, zonisamide, salicylate overdose.
Blood Urea Nitrogen **(BUN)**	7–20 mg/dL	↑ in <u>renal impairment and dehydration</u>. Used with SCr (e.g., BUN:SCr ratio) to assess fluid status and renal function.
Serum Creatinine **(SCr)**	0.6–1.3 mg/dL	↑ due to many drugs that impair renal function (e.g., <u>aminoglycosides</u>, <u>amphotericin B, cisplatin, colistimethate, cyclosporine, loop diuretics, polymyxin, NSAIDs, radiocontrast dye, tacrolimus, vancomycin</u>). False ↑ due to sulfamethoxazole/trimethoprim, H2RAs, cobicistat. ↓ with low muscle mass, amputation, hemodilution.
Anion Gap (AG)	5–12 mEq/L	A calculated value, but often reported on the BMP (see Calculations IV chapter). An ↑ <u>anion gap</u> suggests <u>metabolic acidosis</u>.

ITEM	COMMON REFERENCE RANGE	NOTES
WBC Count and Differential		
Many drugs (including chemotherapy, immunosuppressants and antivirals) have the potential to affect WBCs, Hgb and PLTs.		
White Blood Cells (WBCs)	4,000–11,000 cells/mm³	Used to diagnose and monitor infection/inflammation. Can ↑ as an acute phase reactant, indicating a systemic reaction to inflammation or stress (e.g., surgery). ↑ due to systemic steroids, colony stimulating factors, epinephrine. ↓ due to clozapine, chemotherapy that targets the bone marrow, carbamazepine, cephalosporins, immunosuppressants (e.g., DMARDs, biologics), procainamide, vancomycin.
Neutrophils	45–73%	Neutrophils and bands are used with clinical s/sx to assess the likelihood of acute infection. WBCs are used in the absolute neutrophil count (ANC) calculation (see Calculations IV chapter). Neutrophils are also called polymorphonuclear cells (PMNs or polys) or segmented neutrophils (segs).
Bands	3–5%	Bands are immature neutrophils released from the bone marrow to fight infection (called a "left shift" when elevated).
Eosinophils	0–5%	↑ in drug allergy, asthma, inflammation, parasitic infection.
Basophils	0–1%	↑ in inflammation, hypersensitivity reactions, leukemia.
Lymphocytes	20–40%	↑ in viral infections, lymphoma. ↓ in bone marrow suppression, HIV or due to systemic steroids.
Monocytes	2–8%	↑ in chronic infections, inflammation, stress.
Anemia		
Red Blood Cells (RBCs)	Males: 4.5–5.5 x 10⁶ cells/µL Females: 4.1–4.9 x 10⁶ cells/µL	RBCs have an average life span of 120 days. ↑ due to erythropoiesis-stimulating agents (ESAs), smoking and polycythemia (a condition that causes high RBCs). ↓ due to chemotherapy that targets the bone marrow, low production, blood loss, deficiency anemias (e.g., B12, folate), hemolytic anemia, sickle cell anemia.
Hemoglobin (Hgb, Hb)	Males: 13.5–18 g/dL Females: 12–16 g/dL	Hgb is the iron-containing protein that carries oxygen in RBCs. The Hct mirrors the Hgb result (providing the same clinical information). ↑ due to ESAs (see Anemia chapter).
Hematocrit (Hct)	Males: 38–50% Females: 36–46%	↓ in anemias and bleeding (risk with anticoagulants, antiplatelets, fibrinolytics). See Coombs Test and G6PD for drug-induced anemias.
Mean Corpuscular Volume (MCV)	80–100 fL	Reflects the size and average volume of RBCs. ↑ (macrocytic anemia) due to B12 or folate deficiency. ↓ (microcytic anemia) due to iron deficiency.
Mean Corpuscular Hemoglobin (MCH)	26–34 pg/cell	Additional tests used in an anemia workup. Together MCV, MCHC and RDW are called "RBC indices."
Mean Corpuscular Hgb Concentration (MCHC)	31–37 g/dL	
RBC Distribution Width (RDW)	11.5–14.5%	RDW measures the variability in RBC size.
Iron	65–150 mcg/dL	↑ due to iron supplementation. ↓ due to blood loss or poor nutrition.
Total Iron Binding Capacity (TIBC)	250–400 mcg/dL	Monitored as part of the workup and treatment for iron deficiency anemia or anemia of chronic disease (e.g., CKD).
Transferrin	> 200 mg/dL	
Transferrin Saturation (TSAT)	Males: 15–50% Females: 12–45%	
Ferritin	11–300 ng/mL	
Erythropoietin	2–25 mIU/mL	

ITEM	COMMON REFERENCE RANGE	NOTES
Folic Acid (folate)	5–25 mcg/L	B12 and folate are ordered for further workup of macrocytic anemia. ↓ due to phenytoin/fosphenytoin, phenobarbital, primidone, methotrexate, sulfamethoxazole/trimethoprim, sulfasalazine. Supplement folate in women of childbearing age and alcoholism (see Dietary Supplements, Natural & Complementary Medicine chapter).
Vitamin B12	> 200 pg/mL	↓ due to PPIs, metformin, colchicine, chloramphenicol.
Methylmalonate (MMA)	Varies	Used for further workup of macrocytic anemia when B12 deficiency is suspected. Schilling test has also been used.
Reticulocyte Count	0.5–2.5%	Measures the amount of reticulocytes (immature red blood cells) being made by the bone marrow; reticulocyte count is ↑ in blood loss, ↓ in untreated anemia, due to iron, folate or B12 deficiency, and with bone marrow suppression.
Coombs Test, Direct Also known as: Direct Antiglobulin Test (DAT)	Negative	Used in the diagnosis of hemolytic anemia when the cause is unclear (i.e., an immune mechanism vs. another cause). See Anemia chapter. Drugs that can cause hemolytic anemia include penicillins and cephalosporins (prolonged use/high concentrations), dapsone, isoniazid, levodopa, methyldopa, methylene blue, nitrofurantoin, pegloticase, primaquine, quinidine, quinine, rasburicase, rifampin and sulfonamides. If the Coombs test is positive and a drug-induced cause is suspected, discontinue the offending drug.
Glucose-6-Phosphate Dehydrogenase (G6PD)	5–14 units/gram	Used to determine if hemolytic anemia is due to G6PD deficiency. RBC destruction with G6PD deficiency is triggered by stress, foods (fava beans) or these drugs: dapsone, methylene blue, nitrofurantoin, pegloticase, primaquine, rasburicase, sulfonamides (see Anemia chapter).

Anticoagulation
These tests evaluate different aspects of clotting and are used to monitor specific drugs.

ITEM	COMMON REFERENCE RANGE	NOTES
Antifactor Xa Activity (Anti-Xa)	Therapeutic doses of LMWH (obtain a peak anti-Xa level 4 hours after a SC LMWH dose): 1.0-2.0 IU/mL Unfractionated heparin (obtain 6 hours after IV infusion starts and every 6 hours until therapeutic): 0.3-0.7 IU/mL	Used to monitor low molecular weight heparins (LMWHs) and unfractionated heparin (UFH). Monitoring for LMWH is recommended in pregnancy and may be used in obesity, low body weight, pediatrics, elderly, renal insufficiency (see Anticoagulation chapter).
Prothrombin Time / International Normalized Ratio (PT / INR)	PT: 10–13 seconds (varies) INR: < 1.2 (for those not on warfarin)	Used to monitor warfarin. INR ↑ (without warfarin) is typically due to liver disease. False ↑ can occur with daptomycin, oritavancin, telavancin. Many interactions can cause an ↑ or ↓ INR (see Anticoagulation chapter).
Activated Partial Thromboplastin Time (aPTT or PTT)	22–38 seconds (varies, this is called the "control") UFH: obtain 6 hours after IV infusion starts and every 6 hours until therapeutic Goal (on UFH): 1.5-2.5x control	Used to monitor (UFH) and direct thrombin inhibitors (e.g., argatroban). False ↑ can occur with oritavancin, telavancin.
Activated Clotting Time (ACT)	70–180 seconds (varies)	Used to monitor anticoagulation in the cardiac catheterization lab during percutaneous coronary intervention (PCI) and surgery.
Platelets (PLTs)	150,000–450,000 cells/mm³	Platelets have an average life span of 7-10 days. Platelets are required for clot formation. Spontaneous bleeding can occur when platelets are < 20,000 cells/mm³. ↓ due to heparin, LMWHs, fondaparinux, glycoprotein IIb/IIIa receptor antagonists, linezolid, valproic acid, chemotherapy that targets the bone marrow.
Heparin-Induced Platelet Antibodies: ELISA test 1st, then an SRA (serotonin release assay)	Negative	Heparin-induced thrombocytopenia (HIT) is suspected when platelets drop > 50% from baseline as a result of treatment with UFH or LMWH. Antibody testing is used to confirm a diagnosis of HIT. If the ELISA test is positive, a positive SRA is confirmatory.

ITEM	COMMON REFERENCE RANGE	NOTES
Liver and Gastroenterology		
Albumin	3.5–5 g/dL	↓ due to cirrhosis and malnutrition.
		Serum levels of highly protein-bound drugs (e.g., warfarin, calcium, phenytoin) are impacted by low albumin. Phenytoin, valproic acid and calcium serum concentrations require correction for low albumin (see Seizures/Epilepsy, Pharmacokinetics and Calculations III chapters). A "free" phenytoin level or ionized calcium do not require adjustment.
Alkaline Phosphatase (Alk Phos or ALP)	33–131 IU/L	Used with other labs to assess liver, biliary tract (cholestatic) and bone disease.
Aspartate Aminotransferase (AST)	10–40 units/L	AST and ALT are enzymes released from injured hepatocytes (liver cells). Numerous medications and herbals can ↑ AST and ALT (see Hepatitis & Liver Disease chapter).
Alanine Aminotransferase (ALT)	10–40 units/L	
Gamma-Glutamyl Transpeptidase (GGT)	9–58 units/L	Used with other labs to assess liver, biliary tract (cholestasis) and pancreas.
Bilirubin, total (T Bili)	0.1–1.2 mg/dL	Used along with other liver tests to determine causes of liver damage and detect bile duct blockage.
Ammonia	19–60 mcg/dL	Though not diagnostic, often measured in suspected hepatic encephalopathy (HE). ↑ due to valproic acid, topiramate. ↓ due to lactulose.
Hepatic (liver) panel AST, ALT, Tbili, Albumin and Alk Phos	See above	A group of liver function tests (LFTs) ordered together to assess acute and chronic liver inflammation/disease and baseline and routine monitoring of hepatotoxic drugs. The panel can include other tests to evaluate liver function (e.g., PT/INR, total protein).
Pancreatic Enzymes		
Amylase	60–180 units/L	↑ in pancreatitis, which can be caused by didanosine, stavudine, GLP-1 agonists, DPP-4 inhibitors, valproic acid, hypertriglyceridemia.
Lipase	5–160 units/L	
Cardiovascular		
Creatine Kinase or **Creatine Phosphokinase (CK or CPK)**	Males: 55–170 IU/L Females: 30–135 IU/L	Use to assess muscle inflammation (myositis), or more serious muscle damage, and to diagnose cardiac conditions. ↑ due to daptomycin, quinupristin/dalfopristin, statins, fibrates (especially if given with a statin), emtricitabine, tenofovir, tipranavir, raltegravir, dolutegravir.
CK-MB Isoenzymes, total	≤ 6.0 ng/mL	As a group, these are called "cardiac enzymes."
Troponin T (TnT)	0–0.1 ng/mL (assay dependent)	CK-MB, TnT and TnI are used in the diagnosis of MI. Troponins can be elevated with a few other conditions (e.g., sepsis, PE, CKD).
Troponin I (TnI)	0–0.5 ng/mL (assay dependent)	BNP and NT-proBNP are both markers of cardiac stress. They are not heart failure (HF) nor heart disease-specific, but higher values indicate a higher likelihood of HF when consistent with HF symptoms. Renal failure is the second most common cause of ↑ BNP and NT-proBNP.
B-Type Natriuretic Peptide (BNP)	< 100 pg/mL or ng/L	Myoglobin and CK-MB are not interchangeable; they are two separate markers. Myoglobin is a sensitive marker for muscle injury but has relatively low specificity for acute MI and therefore is not routinely used for diagnosis (see Acute Coronary Syndromes chapter).
N-Terminal-ProBNP (NT-proBNP)	Males: < 61 pg/mL Females: 12–151 pg/mL	
Respiratory		
Eosinophil Count	< 100 cells/mcL	Used, along with a history of COPD exacerbations, to determine if inhaled corticosteroids (ICS) will be beneficial in COPD treatment (See Chronic Obstructive Pulmonary Disease chapter).

ITEM	COMMON REFERENCE RANGE	NOTES
Lipids and Cardiovascular Risk		
Total Cholesterol (TC)	< 200 mg/dL	For complete discussion, see Dyslipidemia chapter. Fasting begins 9-12 hours prior to lipid blood draw.
Low Density Lipoprotein (LDL)	< 100 mg/dL, desirable	Non-HDL = TC – HDL. Guidelines do not support specific TC, HDL or TG goals; they support a statin intensity level for LDL-C reductions based on those most likely to benefit. This means that the target values are not being used as goals for treatment, but elevations should be recognized. In some individuals, additional treatment is considered if LDL ≥ 70 mg/dL.
High Density Lipoprotein (HDL)	< 40 mg/dL, low (male) ≥ 60 mg/dL, desirable	
Non-HDL	< 130 mg/dL, desirable	
Triglycerides (TG)	< 150 mg/dL	
Lipid panel TC, HDL, LDL, TG	See above	A group of labs ordered together to assess the major cholesterol types and determine cardiovascular risk. A fasting lipid panel is preferred.
Lipoprotein-a, Lp(a) Apoliprotein-B, Apo B	< 10 mg/dL < 130 mg/dL	↑ Lp(a) and ↑ ApoB are being used more commonly; these are associated with ↑ coagulation and ↑ risk of CVD.
C-reactive Protein (CRP)	0–0.5 mg/dL	↑ CRP indicates inflammation, which could be due to many conditions (infection, trauma, malignancy). Higher levels indicate ↑ risk. High-sensitivity CRP (hs-CRP) is more sensitive for CVD.
Coronary Artery Calcium score	< 300 Agatston units or < 75th percentile for age, sex and ethnicity; higher score indicates a higher risk	The coronary artery calcium score measures calcium build-up in the coronary arteries.
Ankle Brachial Index (ABI)	1–1.4	The ankle brachial index measures the ratio of the BP in the lower legs to the BP in the arms. It is used to assess severity of peripheral artery disease (PAD). An ABI < 1 indicates some degree of PAD.
Diabetes		
Fasting Plasma Glucose (FPG)	≥ 126 mg/dL is positive for diabetes 100–125 mg/dL is positive for pre-diabetes	Fasting begins ≥ 8 hours prior to the blood draw. See Diabetes chapter for complete discussion and medications that can cause hyper- and hypoglycemia.
Hemoglobin A1C (A1C)	< 7% (ADA), ≤ 6.5% (AACE)	Average blood glucose over the past 3 months; based on attachment of glucose to hemoglobin; ↑ glucose = ↑ BG attached to Hgb = ↑ A1C.
Estimated Average Glucose (eAG)	< 154 mg/dL (ADA)	Used to correlate a finger stick glucose with an A1C; an eAG of 126 mg/dL corresponds to an A1C of 6%.
Preprandial Blood Glucose	80–130 mg/dL (ADA) < 110 mg/dL (AACE)	Blood glucose measurement taken before a meal.
Postprandial Blood Glucose	< 180 mg/dL (ADA) < 140 mg/dL (AACE)	Blood glucose measurement taken after a meal (1-2 hours after the start of eating).
C-Peptide (fasting)	0.78–1.89 ng/mL	Insulin breakdown product used to evaluate beta-cell function (distinguishes type 1 from type 2 diabetes). ↓ or absent in type 1 diabetes.
Urine Albumin to Creatinine Ratio or Albumin to Creatinine Ratio (UACR or ACR) or **Urinary Albumin Excretion (UAE)**	Males: < 17 mg/gram Females: < 25 mg/gram < 30 mg/24 hours	See Diabetes and Renal Disease chapters.

ITEM	COMMON REFERENCE RANGE	NOTES
Thyroid Function		
Thyroid Stimulating Hormone **(TSH)**	0.3–3 mIU/L	TSH is used with FT4 to diagnose hypothyroidism and hyperthyroidism, and is used alone (sometimes with FT4) to monitor patients being treated. ↑ TSH = hypothyroidism, ↓ TSH = hyperthyroidism. ↑ or ↓ due to amiodarone, interferons. ↑ (hypothyroidism) due to tyrosine kinase inhibitors, lithium, carbamazepine.
Total Thyroxine (T4)	4.5–10.9 mcg/dL	T4 and FT4 are two of several tests used for a detailed assessment of thyroid function (see Thyroid Disorders chapter).
Free Thyroxine (FT4)	0.9–2.3 ng/dL	
Uric Acid/Gout		
Uric Acid	Males: 3.5–7.2 mg/dL Females: 2–6.5 mg/dL	Used in the diagnosis and treatment of gout. ↑ due to diuretics, niacin, low doses of aspirin, pyrazinamide, cyclosporine, tacrolimus, select pancreatic enzyme products, select chemotherapy (due to tumor lysis syndrome).
Inflammation/Autoimmune Disease		
C-Reactive Protein **(CRP)**	Normal: 0–0.5 mg/dL High risk: > 3 mg/dL	Nonspecific tests used in autoimmune disorders, inflammation, infections. If ANA is positive, an anti-dsDNA test will help establish a diagnosis of systemic lupus erythematosus, which can be drug-induced (see below).
Rheumatoid Factor **(RF)**	Negative, or ≤ upper limit of normal (ULN) for the lab (usually < 20 IU/mL)	Drug-induced lupus erythematosus (DILE) can be caused by many drugs. More likely with anti-TNF agents, hydralazine, isoniazid, methimazole, methyldopa, minocycline, procainamide, propylthiouracil, quinidine, terbinafine. The causative drug must be discontinued (see Systemic Steroids & Autoimmune Conditions chapter).
Erythrocyte Sedimentation Rate **(ESR)**	Males: ≤ 20 mm/hr Females: ≤ 30 mm/hr	
Antinuclear Antibodies **(ANA)**	Negative (titers may be provided)	
Antihistone Antibodies (Detected by ELISA)	Negative	
HIV		
CD4 T Lymphocyte Count	Immunocompromised state: < 200 cells/mm³	Used to assess HIV and monitor treatment (see HIV chapter). CD4 count is an indicator of immune function and helps establish the need for opportunistic infection prophylaxis.
HIV RNA Concentration **(Viral Load)**	Undetectable Measured in copies/mL	
HIV Antibody (Ab)	Negative (non-reactive)	Detects infection with the virus; may not become positive until several weeks after exposure.
HIV DNA PCR	Negative	Useful for early detection.
HIV p24 Antigen	Undetectable	
Acid-Base (Arterial Sample)		
pH	7.35–7.45	Together these values make up an arterial blood gas (ABG). This blood must be drawn from an artery (not a vein, as with other labs).
pCO2	35–45 mmHg	Often written in chart notes with a stick diagram: pH/pCO2/pO2/HCO3/O2 Sat (see Calculations IV chapter for ABG interpretation). Bicarbonate on the ABG is a calculated value, and the reference range may differ from venous samples (reported with a BMP).
pO2	80–100 mmHg	
HCO3	22–26 mEq/L	
O2 Sat	> 95%	

ITEM	COMMON REFERENCE RANGE	NOTES
Hormonal		
Testosterone total, free	Males: 300–950 ng/dL	↑ with testosterone supplementation.
Prostate-Specific Antigen (PSA)	< 4 ng/mL	Can ↑ with testosterone supplementation. Used in detecting prostate cancer and BPH.
Human Chorionic Gonadotropin (hCG)	Varies by test	A positive result from a blood or urine test indicates pregnancy.
Luteinizing Hormone (LH)	Varies during cycle	Rises mid-cycle, causing egg release from the ovaries (ovulation). Tested in urine with ovulation predictor kits for women attempting pregnancy.
Parathyroid Hormone (PTH)	Varies	Used in evaluation of parathyroid disorders, hypercalcemia and chronic kidney disease (CKD) (see Renal Disease chapter).
Other		
Cosyntropin Stimulation Test	Baseline and timed increase are measured	Used to test for adrenal suppression; medications that affect baseline cortisol or suppress adrenal response will impact test and may need to be held prior (e.g., steroids).
Lactic Acid (lactate)	0.5–2.2 mEq/L	Lactic acidosis indicates anaerobic metabolism, which occurs in long-distance running and in certain medical conditions (e.g., sepsis). ↑ due to NRTIs (see HIV chapter), metformin (low risk/mostly with renal disease and heart failure), alcohol, cyanide.
Procalcitonin	≤ 0.15 ng/mL	↑ due to systemic bacterial infections or severe localized infections.
Prolactin	1–25 ng/mL	Secretion is regulated by dopamine; can ↑ with haloperidol, risperidone, paliperidone, methyldopa. Can ↓ with bromocriptine.
Purified Protein Derivative (PPD) or Tuberculin Skin Test (TST)	No induration (raised area); induration is measured to assess TB exposure	TB skin test (TST) administered by intradermal injection. Not used alone for diagnosis of active TB. Response is measured by diameter (mm) of induration at 48-72 hours (see ID II: Bacterial Infections chapter).
Rapid Plasma Reagin (RPR) or Venereal Diseases Reseach Laboratory (VDRL)	Negative	Non-treponemal antibody tests used to screen for syphilis. If the RPR or VDRL is positive, confirmatory testing with a treponemal assay is performed. Titers may be reported and are used to monitor response to therapy.
Serum Osmolality	275–290 mOsm/kg H2O	Used with Na, BUN/SCr, and clinical volume status to evaluate hypo/hypernatremia. ↑ due to mannitol, toxicities (e.g., ethylene glycol, methanol, propylene glycol).
Thiopurine Methyltransferase (TPMT)	≥ 15 units/mL	Those with a genetic deficiency of TPMT are at ↑ risk for myelosuppression (bone marrow suppression) and may require lower doses of azathioprine and mercaptopurine.
Vitamin D, serum 25(OH)	> 30 ng/mL	↓ levels increase risk of osteoporosis, osteomalacia (rickets), CVD, diabetes, hypertension, infectious diseases and other conditions. Supplement vitamin D with various conditions and drugs (see Dietary Supplements, Natural & Complementary Medicine chapter).

ASSESSING PATIENT CASES QUICKLY

Cases can be evaluated more quickly by recognizing lab patterns and signs and symptoms that provide a clue to the patient's diagnosis. Watch for drug-induced signs/symptoms and lab changes. Look for lab contraindications to drugs (e.g., +hCG, hyperkalemia). Additional information can be found in the chapters on these disease states.

Lab patterns and likely diagnoses can be located in the first chapter of this course book. Lab patterns due to an infectious disease can be found in the Infectious Diseases chapters.

THERAPEUTIC DRUG MONITORING

Drug levels or other values (such as anti-Xa levels for LMWHs) are used to reach dosing goals and avoid toxicity. Therapeutic drug monitoring (TDM) is increasingly common due to the need to target highly resistant infectious organisms and dose medications properly in overweight and obese patients. The <u>peak</u> level is the highest concentration in the blood a drug will reach; it requires time for the drug to distribute to body's tissues. The <u>trough</u> level is the lowest concentration a drug will reach in the blood and is <u>drawn right before the next dose</u> or some short period of time before the next dose (30 minutes is common). This allows time to assess the level before another dose is given, so the next dose can be withheld if the level is high. The time that drug levels are drawn is critical for accurate interpretation. For example, a tobramycin level of 6 mcg/mL would be interpreted differently if the level was a trough versus a peak. Obtaining drug levels at <u>steady state</u> is often (but not always) preferred. See the Pharmacokinetics chapter for further discussion.

<u>Narrow therapeutic index (NTI)</u> drugs have a <u>narrow separation</u> between the subtherapeutic (low), therapeutic (desired) and supratherapeutic (high) drug levels. Supratherapeutic drug levels can be toxic.

TDM is commonly <u>performed by pharmacists</u>. The following <u>Key Drugs Guy</u> lists drugs that are routinely monitored. These drugs and usual therapeutic ranges are felt to be <u>essential for the NAPLEX</u>.

THERAPEUTIC DRUG LEVELS

DRUG	USUAL THERAPEUTIC RANGE
Carbamazepine	4–12 mcg/mL
Digoxin	0.8–2 ng/mL (AF)
	0.5–0.9 ng/mL (HF)
Gentamicin (traditional dosing)	Peak: 5–10 mcg/mL
	Trough: < 2 mcg/mL
Lithium	0.6–1.2 mEq/L (up to 1.5 mEq/L for acute symptoms), drawn as a trough
Phenytoin/Fosphenytoin	10–20 mcg/mL; if albumin is low, calculate a corrected level; see Seizures/Epilepsy chapter
Free Phenytoin	1–2.5 mcg/mL
Procainamide	4–10 mcg/mL
NAPA (procainamide active metabolite)	15–25 mcg/mL
Combined	10–30 mcg/mL
Theophylline	5–15 mcg/mL
Tobramycin (traditional dosing)	Peak: 5–10 mcg/mL
	Trough: < 2 mcg/mL
Valproic acid	50–100 mcg/mL (up to 150 mcg/mL in some patients); see Seizures/Epilepsy chapter
Vancomycin*	Trough: 15–20 mcg/mL for most serious infections (pneumonia, endocarditis, osteomyelitis, meningitis, and bacteremia)
	Trough: 10–15 mcg/mL for others
Warfarin	Goal INR is 2–3 for most indications, use higher range (2.5–3.5) for high-risk conditions, such as mechanical mitral valves

*AUC can be used to monitor vancomycin.
Refer to the Pharmacokinetics chapter for detailed information.

Select Guidelines/References

Lab Tests Online. https://labtestsonline.org (accessed 2022 Jan 11).
Lee M. Basic Skills in Interpreting Laboratory Data. 6th ed. Betheseda, MD: ASHP; 2017.
Schmidt J, Wieczorkiewicz J. Interpreting Laboratory Data: A Point-of-Care Guide. Betheseda, MD: ASHP; 2012.

©Michael J. Freudiger

CHAPTER 5
DRUG REFERENCES

BACKGROUND

Providing drug information to patients and other healthcare professionals is a critical function of pharmacists, the drug therapy experts. Pharmacists need to select appropriate resources and provide accurate responses that reflect the most current drug information.

This chapter covers the essential content contained in a package insert (PI) and other general drug information resources used in pharmacy practice. It includes the most common resources for locating specialty healthcare content (such as drug shortages or travel vaccines), consumer information and databases to retrieve clinical studies.

> Pharmacists respond to drug questions around the clock. Knowing where to locate drug information is a must in all practice settings.

CASE SCENARIO
MJ presents with a prescription for *Keppra* 500 mg tablets by mouth BID for her 5-year-old, 40 lb daughter. She asks the pharmacist a few questions:

- Is the medication dosed properly for her daughter's age and weight?
- Is it possible to crush the tablets or switch to a liquid?
- Is it safe to take melatonin for sleep with *Keppra*?

RESOURCES
- Drug dosing in a child may (or may not) be in the drug's PI, which includes only FDA-approved indications. It may be included in the off-label section of a general drug information resource, such as *Lexicomp*. A <u>pediatric</u> resource such as *The Harriet Lane Handbook* includes pediatric dosing that might otherwise be unavailable. The clinical guidelines for the condition might have recommended dosing for children, especially for common conditions in children, such as epilepsy and various infectious diseases.
- Administration recommendations (e.g., if the tablets can be crushed) and the product formulations (e.g., if a solution is available) will be reflected in the PI and general drug information resources. If a formulation is not available, a compounding pharmacist might be able to prepare an oral formulation following the preparation recommendations in USP 795, and according to a master formula (recipe) for oral *Keppra* liquid.
- A drug-natural product interaction tool should be used to evaluate the safety of taking melatonin and *Keppra*, which can be found in most general drug information resources. A specific natural medicine resource might provide more detail.

CONTENT LEGEND

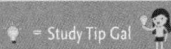 = Study Tip Gal

PHARMACY FOUNDATIONS PART 1

PACKAGE INSERTS

The PI is the FDA-approved drug information that is part of the drug's official labeling. The example PI below shows the common categories included in a PI (and in the drug monographs from general drug information resources, discussed later in the chapter). The table at the bottom of the page describes methods for locating a PI.

The FDA approves drugs and their labeling. The PI is part of the labeling. PIs contain only the information approved by the FDA. They do not include, for example, off-label uses or drug costs.

COMMON CONTENT CATEGORIES IN A DRUG PACKAGE INSERT

PRESCRIBING INFORMATION
EVISTA (raloxifene hydrochloride) Tablet for Oral Use

BOXED WARNING
Increased Risk of Venous Thromboembolism and Death from Stroke.

-----------------------Recent Major Changes-----------------------
None.

-----------------------Indications and Usage-----------------------
EVISTA is an estrogen agonist/antagonist indicated for:
- Treatment and prevention of osteoporosis in postmenopausal women.
- Reduction in risk of invasive breast cancer in postmenopausal women.

-----------------------Dosage and Administration-----------------------
60 mg tablet orally once daily.
Calcium and vitamin D should be added if insufficient.

-----------------------Dosage Forms and Strengths-----------------------
Tablets (not scored) 60 mg.

-----------------------Contraindications-----------------------
- Active or past venous thromboembolism.
- Pregnancy, women who might become pregnant.

-----------------------Warnings and Precautions-----------------------
- Venous thromboembolism.
- Death due to stroke in patients with cardiovascular disease.
- Do not use to prevent cardiovascular disease.
- Hypertriglyceridemia.

-----------------------Adverse Reactions-----------------------
Adverse reactions (> 2% and more common than with placebo) include: hot flashes, leg cramps, peripheral edema, arthralgia...

-----------------------Drug Interactions-----------------------
- Cholestyramine: use with EVISTA is not recommended. Reduces raloxifene absorption.
- Warfarin: monitor prothrombin time.

-----------------------Use in Specific Populations-----------------------
Renal impairment: EVISTA should be used with caution in patients with moderate or severe renal impairment.

-----------------------Drug Abuse and Dependence-----------------------
Not applicable.

-----------------------Overdosage/Toxicology-----------------------
In an 8-week study of 63 postmenopausal women, a dose of raloxifene 600 mg/day was safely tolerated.
In clinical trials, no raloxifene overdose has been reported.

-----------------------Pharmacology/Mechanism of Action-----------------------
Raloxifene is an estrogen agonist/antagonist, commonly referred to as a selective estrogen receptor modulator (SERM). The biological actions of raloxifene are largely mediated through binding to estrogen receptors.

-----------------------Additional Categories-----------------------
Description (active and inactive ingredients)

Pharmacokinetics and Pharmacodynamics

Clinical Studies

How Supplied/Storage and Handling

Patient Counseling Information

Revised; not actual Evista Package Insert.

PACKAGE INSERT LOCATIONS	FORMATS	WEBSITE
DailyMed (NLM)	Online	https://dailymed.nlm.nih.gov
Drugs@FDA	Online and Mobile App	www.accessdata.fda.gov/scripts/cder/daf
The Drug Manufacturer's Website	Individual URL Addresses	The manufacturer's website (e.g., www.pfizer.com) or the drug-specific website (common with new drugs; the website URL will be the drug's brand name, such as www.eliquis.com)
Attached to the physical product (e.g., the bottle or box)	Printed	N/A

THE PI INCLUDES THE DRUG'S SAFETY INFORMATION

All drugs, OTC and prescription, have some degree of risk. When a decision is made to prescribe a drug (and the patient agrees to take the drug), the benefit must outweigh the risk. Important drug safety information in the PI is split into the categories below. Dispensing of the drug may require separate patient handouts alerting of the drug's toxicity (Medication Guides) and/or a strategy to manage the risk (REMS). These are discussed in the Drug Allergies & Adverse Drug Reactions chapter.

When drug safety information changes (e.g., new warnings or withdrawal from the market), the FDA publishes a safety communication or alert on their website, and an updated PI will reflect the drug's safety-related labeling changes.

- **Boxed Warnings**: the strictest warnings. The black box around the warning (see example on previous page) alerts prescribers to the risk of death or permanent disability (e.g., increased risk of venous thromboembolism and death from stroke with raloxifene).

- **Contraindications**: when a patient has a contraindication to a drug, the drug cannot be used in that patient. The risk will outweigh any possible benefit (e.g., a history of venous thromboembolism is a contraindication to the use of raloxifene). If there are no known contraindications for a drug, the section will state "None."

- **Warnings** and **Precautions**: includes serious reactions that can result in death, hospitalization, medical intervention, disability or teratogenicity (e.g., raloxifene has a warning for venous thromboembolism). Warnings and precautions may or may not change a prescribing decision.

- **Adverse Reactions**: refers to undesirable, uncomfortable or dangerous effects from a drug (e.g., arthralgia from raloxifene). The risk-benefit assessment is patient-specific (e.g., arthralgia from raloxifene will be a concern for a patient with chronic joint pain versus a patient with no joint pain).

GENERAL DRUG INFORMATION RESOURCES

General drug information resources rely on the PI for much of their drug monograph content. The table on the following page describes the general drug information resources commonly used by pharmacists. These resources are managed by different companies, and the additional information they contain beyond standard package labeling content varies (see the Unique Features table).

Most general drug information resources require a paid subscription, but a few (e.g., *Drugs.com, RxList*) can be accessed by anyone at no cost to the user. Many resources are available online (as websites, electronic books or

General drug information resources contain monographs on each drug. The monographs include the FDA-approved information from the drug's PI, plus some other items, depending on the resource.

comprehensive, searchable databases). Some can be used as a mobile application to help direct real-time patient care decisions.

Trissel's → Lexicomp
→ Micromedex
→ Clinical Pharmacology

Drug monograph sites pull in information from the PI and other sources. *Clinical Pharmacology, Facts and Comparisons, Lexicomp* and *Micromedex* are commonly used. Each contains information that pharmacists find useful, including Trissel's IV drug compatibility and stability data, drug class comparisons, natural products, drug (tablet/capsule) identification and international drug names. Most sites provide drug pricing, with either the drug's average wholesale price (AWP), which is usually reported by the manufacturer, or the average price charged at pharmacies, which tends to be lower (~17% less than the AWP). The pricing provides a rough ballpark estimate.

The *American Hospital Formulary Service (AHFS) Clinical Drug Information* provides comprehensive monographs that link to supporting evidence and references, which makes it a very useful resource for researching a topic in detail. The off-label drug use section is well-researched, with linked references.

Caution: pharmacists rely on the data in the drug information resource at their practice site, but when drug information is updated, there can be a lag time until the PI and the drug's monograph include the update (especially printed versions). Pharmacists may need to check multiple sources to confirm they are retrieving the most current content.

SUMMARY OF GENERAL DRUG INFORMATION RESOURCES

REFERENCE	FORMATS	DESCRIPTION
American Hospital Formulary Service (AHFS)* www.ahfsdruginformation.com An ASHP product	AHFS Drug Information: Book	Collection of drug monographs for medications available in the U.S.
	AHFS DI Essentials: Part of AHFS CDI (below)	Select drug monographs from AHFS Drug Information re-formatted for point-of-care decision making; expands on therapeutic evidence and includes additional information (e.g., patient counseling).
	AHFS Clinical Drug Information (AHFS CDI): Online and Mobile App	AHFS Drug Information and AHFS DI Essentials databases, plus real-time updates (e.g., drug shortages, FDA safety alerts).
	Included with Lexicomp Online	
Clinical Pharmacology www.clinicalpharmacology.com	Online and Mobile App	Monographs for Rx and OTC drugs, natural products and investigational drugs.
Drug Information Portal (NLM) https://druginfo.nlm.nih.gov/drugportal/	Online	Free from the National Library of Medicine (NLM). Drug searches link directly to other NLM databases for related information (e.g., DailyMed for the PI, LactMed for breastfeeding considerations).
Epocrates/Epocrates + www.epocrates.com	Online and Mobile App	Free with registration; drug information plus guideline summaries.
		Epocrates + (fee required) expands into evidence-based disease management and includes sections on natural products, lab and diagnostic information and ICD-10 coding (for billing purposes).
Facts & Comparisons eAnswers www.wolterskluwercdi.com/facts-comparisons-online/	Online	Collection of databases; includes drug monographs, comparative drug charts and other unique resources (e.g., search drugs based on a specific adverse reaction).
Lexicomp www.wolterskluwercdi.com/lexicomp-online/	Drug Information Handbook: Book	Drug monographs organized alphabetically; includes useful appendices (e.g., drug class comparisons, equivalent dosing charts).
	Lexi-Drugs: Online and Mobile App	Multiple clinical databases (beyond Lexi-Drugs) depending on subscription level purchased (see the Locating Specific Types of Information table).
Micromedex truvenhealth.com/Products/Micromedex	DRUGDEX: Online and Mobile App	Multiple clinical databases beyond DRUGDEX (see the Locating Specific Types of Information table).
Prescriber's Digital Reference (*mobilePDR*) www.pdr.net/resources/mobilePDR/	Online and Mobile App	Free with registration; previously the Physician's Desk Reference (no longer in print); includes information for drugs, vaccines and biologics. Detail is more than the drug's PI, and includes practical information, such as where injections can be given, and time to reach clinical effect.
Drugs.com www.drugs.com	Online and Mobile App	Free for professionals and consumers; drug information is primarily sourced from other products, including AHFS Drug Information, Micromedex and Cerner Multum.
RxList www.rxlist.com	Online	Free for professionals and consumers; drug information is primarily sourced from other products, including the FDA, Cerner Multum and First Databank, Inc.

Only resource designated by the U.S. Congress as acceptable for determining reimbursement for off-label uses under Medicare Part D and Medicaid.

UNIQUE FEATURES OF COMMON DRUG INFORMATION RESOURCES

The table below describes some of the popular features of general drug information resources that are useful in daily practice and commonly accessed by pharmacists. Many online databases link to external sites that have public access (e.g., *Lexicomp* includes vaccine monographs and immunization schedules and provides links to the CDC website).

REFERENCE	Off-Label Uses	IV Drug Compatibility	Drug/Pill Identification	Natural Products	Drug Class Comparisons	Pricing	International Drug Names
AHFS/AHFS CDI	✓	✓					✓ (via USP Dictionary of USAN and International Drug Names)
Clinical Pharmacology	✓	✓ (via Trissel's*)	✓	✓	✓	✓	✓ (via Index Nominum)
Drugs.com	✓		✓	✓	✓	✓	✓
Epocrates/ Epocrates +	✓		✓	✓ (Epocrates +)	✓	✓	
Facts & Comparisons eAnswers	✓	✓ (via Trissel's*)	✓	✓	✓		✓ (via Martindale)
Lexicomp	✓	✓ (via Trissel's*)	✓ (Lexi-Drug ID)	✓ (Lexi-Natural Products)	✓ (via Facts & Comparisons)	✓	✓ (via Martindale)
Micromedex	✓	✓ (via Trissel's*)	✓ (IDENTIDEX)	✓ (AltMedDex)	✓	✓ (Red Book)	✓ (via Martindale, Index Nominum and others)
***mobile*PDR**			✓		✓		

Data from Trissel's 2 Clinical Pharmaceutics Database

Pharmacist's Letter

Pharmacist's Letter does not contain traditional drug monographs, but is a valuable resource that provides evidence-based drug information. The same company provides similar products called *Prescriber's Letter* and *Pharmacy Technician's Letter*. Subscribers receive a monthly newsletter with short summaries on new or updated drug information, and have online access to helpful practice tools, including:

- New drug approvals, drug withdrawals, new dosage forms and first-time generics
- Charts (e.g., drug class comparisons, disease-state treatment summaries)
- Patient education summaries and patient flyers
- Continuing education (CE)
- Training materials for technicians and intern pharmacists

OTC DRUG INFORMATION

OTC, or nonprescription drugs, are considered safe and effective for self-diagnosed conditions by the general public, have adequate written directions for self-use, and do not require physician supervision. A prescription is not needed to purchase OTC products.

LABELING REQUIREMENTS FOR OTC DRUGS

The labeling on prescription drugs is written for healthcare providers. The labeling on OTC drugs is written for patients who may not have medical training. The language needs to be written in a manner that a layperson can understand, in order to be able to use the drug safely and for its intended purpose. The package labeling information for OTC drugs is in the Drug Facts Panel (see figure to the right) and must include:

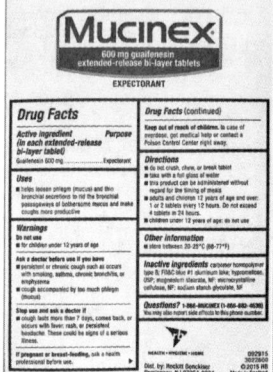

- The active ingredients, including the amount in each dosage unit and the purpose
- The uses (simpler word than indications) for the product
- Specific warnings, including when the drug should not be used (e.g., kidney disease), and when it is appropriate to consult with a doctor or pharmacist
- Side effects, and substances or activities to avoid
- Dosage instructions
- The inactive ingredients

OTC Drug Approval

There are two methods that a manufacturer can use to market an OTC product: the New Drug Application (NDA) process and the OTC Monograph process. The NDA approval process for prescription drugs is managed through the FDA's Center for Drug Evaluation and Research (CDER). OTC drugs can go through the same drug approval process, or the manufacturer can opt to stick to the standards in the OTC monograph for that therapeutic drug class. The monograph for the class will cover the acceptable ingredients, doses, formulations, and labeling, plus study data on the drug's safety and effectiveness.

OTC drugs that have gone through the NDA approval process become FDA-approved drugs. The OTC drug labeling can be found on the FDA website through Drugs@FDA, and will be listed in common general drug information resources (e.g., Lexicomp, Micromedex). The labeling for OTC drugs does not need to be a separate document, but can be the container itself, as long as the items specified above are included.

PRACTICE GUIDELINES

Major medical groups and organizations publish practice guidelines to promote evidence-based treatment of conditions. Commonly used guidelines (and the organizations that publish them) should be known for the NAPLEX (see Study Tip Gal).

LOCATING GUIDELINES FOR COMMON CONDITIONS

ANTICOAGULATION
Guidelines from the American College of Chest Physicians (known as CHEST guidelines):

    Stroke Prevention in Atrial Fibrillation
    Venous Thromboembolism

CARDIOVASCULAR DISEASES
Guidelines from the American College of Cardiology/American Heart Association (ACC/AHA):

    Acute Coronary Syndromes
    Atrial Fibrillation
    Heart Failure
    High Cholesterol
    Hypertension

DIABETES
American Association of Clinical Endocrinologists (AACE)
American Diabetes Association (ADA)

INFECTIOUS DISEASES
Infectious Diseases Society of America (IDSA)
HIV/AIDS: US Dept. of Health and Human Services (ClinicalInfo.HIV.gov)
Sexually transmitted infections: Centers for Disease Control (CDC)

ONCOLOGY
American Society of Clinical Oncology (ASCO)
National Comprehensive Cancer Network (NCCN)

PEDIATRICS
The American Academy of Pediatrics (AAP)

PREGNANCY/WOMEN'S HEALTH
The American College of Obstetricians and Gynecologists (ACOG)

PSYCHIATRIC CONDITIONS
American Psychiatric Association (APA) Diagnostic and Statistical Manual of Mental disorders, 5th Edition (DSM-5)

PULMONARY CONDITIONS
Asthma: Global Initiative for Asthma (GINA) and National Heart, Lung and Blood Institute (NHLBI)
COPD: Global Initiative for Chronic Obstructive Lung Disease (GOLD)

RENAL DISEASE
Kidney Disease Improving Global Outcomes (KDIGO)

VACCINES
Advisory Committee on Immunization Practices (ACIP)
Centers for Disease Control (CDC)

LOCATING SPECIFIC TYPES OF INFORMATION

The table below highlights select specialty references that may be encountered on the licensure exam. General drug information resources described previously (e.g., *Lexicomp* and *Micromedex*) provide some of the same information.

SPECIALTY REFERENCES BY TOPIC

ADVERSE REACTIONS

ASHP's Drug-Induced Diseases: Prevention, Detection, and Management

FDAble: FDA searchable database of adverse reactions caused by medicines, vaccines, devices, tobacco products, dietary supplements

- MedWatch: FDA's Adverse Event Reporting System (FAERS)
- Vaccine Adverse Event Reporting System (VAERS)
- Manufacturer and User Facility Device Experience (MAUDE)
- Safety Reporting Portal

Meyler's Side Effects of Drugs

COMPOUNDING AND PHARMACEUTICS

Allen's The Art, Science, and Technology of Pharmaceutical Compounding

ASHP Guidelines on Compounding Sterile Preparations

Handbook of Pharmaceutical Excipients

Safety Data Sheets (SDS), previously called Material Safety Data Sheets (MSDS)

Merck Index: An Encyclopedia of Chemicals, Drugs, and Biologicals

Remington: The Science and Practice of Pharmacy

Trissel's Stability of Compounded Formulations

USP Compounding Compendium:

- USP 795: Non-Sterile Preparations
- USP 797: Sterile Preparations
- USP 800: Hazardous Drugs - Handling in Healthcare Settings
- USP-NF: monographs for drug substances, dosage forms, compounded preparations and excipients

ASHP's Extemporaneous Formulations for Pediatric, Geriatric, and Special Needs Patients

Pediatric Drug Formulations

International Journal of Pharmaceutical Compounding

DRUG INTERACTIONS

Hansten and Horn's Drug Interactions Analysis and Management

Drug Interaction Facts: Facts & Comparisons

DRUG PRICING

Red Book (Micromedex)

Medi-Span Price Rx

DRUG SHORTAGES

ASHP Current Drug Shortages

FDA Drug Shortages

CDC Current Vaccine Shortages & Delays

American Hospital Formulary Service Clinical Drug Information (AHFS CDI)

DRUG SUBSTITUTION

FDA's Orange Book: Approved Drug Products with Therapeutic Equivalence Evaluations

FDA's Purple Book: Lists of Licensed Biological Products with Reference Product Exclusivity and Biosimilarity or Interchangeability Evaluations

GERIATRICS

American Geriatrics Society (AGS) Beers Criteria for Potentially Inappropriate Medication Use in Older Adults

ASHP's Fundamentals of Geriatric Pharmacotherapy

Geriatric Dosage Handbook (Lexicomp)

IMMUNIZATIONS (ADULT AND PEDIATRIC)

CDC Advisory Committee on Immunization Practices (ACIP)

- Updates published in the Morbidity and Mortality Weekly Report (MMWR)

CDC Pink Book: Epidemiology and Prevention of Vaccine-Preventable Diseases

Immunization Action Coalition

American Pharmacists Association (APhA) Immunization Center

Vaccines, Blood & Biologics (FDA)

INFECTIOUS DISEASES

Infectious Diseases Society of America (IDSA) Practice Guidelines

Sanford Guide to Antimicrobial Therapy

Human Immunodeficiency Virus (HIV)

HIVInfo.NIH.gov from the US Dept. of Health and Human Services

Sanford Guide to HIV/AIDS Therapy

Johns Hopkins ABX and HIV Guides

Travel Medicine

World Health Organization (WHO)

CDC

- Yellow Book: Health Information for International Travel
- Travelers' Health: resources for travelers and healthcare professionals

International Society of Travel Medicine (ISTM)

International Association For Medical Assistance To Travelers (IAMAT)

INTERNATIONAL DRUG INFORMATION

Index Nominum: International Drug Directory

Martindale: The Complete Drug Reference

USP Dictionary of United States Adopted Names (USAN) and International Drug Names

Drug Information Handbook with International Trade Names Index (Lexicomp)

European Drug Index

SPECIALTY REFERENCES BY TOPIC (CONTINUED)

INVESTIGATIONAL DRUGS
Clinicaltrials.gov (NIH)

IV DRUG COMPATIBILITY AND STABILITY
ASHP's Handbook on Injectable Drugs

King Guide to Parenteral Admixtures

Trissel's 2 Clinical Pharmaceutics Database

MEDICATION SAFETY
FDA MedWatch (report adverse events and medication errors)

Institute for Safe Medication Practices (ISMP)

- Report medication errors to the ISMP Medication Errors Reporting Program (ISMP MERP)

NIOSH List of Antineoplastic (Chemotherapy) and Other Hazardous Drugs in Healthcare Settings

Crediblemeds.org (QT Drugs Lists)

FDA:

- Drug and Biologic Recalls
- Drug Safety Label Changes database
- Medication Guides
- Drug Communications and Safety Alerts

NATURAL PRODUCTS/ALTERNATIVE MEDICINE
Natural Medicines Database (Therapeutic Research Center)

Dietary Supplements Label Database (NIH)

USP Dietary Supplements Compendium

OVERDOSES, POISONING AND TOXICOLOGY
Lexi-Tox (Lexicomp)

Micromedex Toxicology Management (previously POISINDEX)

TOXLINE in PubMed

Goldfrank's Toxicologic Emergencies

State Poison Control Center

The American Association of Poison Control Centers

PEDIATRICS
NeoFax and Pediatrics (Micromedex)

Pediatric & Neonatal Dosage Handbook (Lexicomp)

Red Book: Report of the Committee on Infectious Diseases (AAP)

The Harriet Lane Handbook

American Academy of Pediatrics (AAP)

ASHP's Pediatric Injectable Drugs (The Teddy Bear Book)

Nelson Textbook of Pediatrics

Pediatric Pharmacy Association (PPA) Key Potentially Inappropriate Drugs in Pediatrics: The KIDs List

PHARMACOLOGY
Goodman and Gilman's The Pharmacological Basis of Therapeutics

Katzung's Basic and Clinical Pharmacology

PREGNANCY AND LACTATION
Briggs' Drugs in Pregnancy and Lactation

CDC: Medications during Pregnancy/Breastfeeding

Hale's Medications and Mothers' Milk

LactMed (NLM)

Reprotox and Reprorisk (Micromedex)

MotherToBaby

REGULATORY AND BUSINESS DEVELOPMENT
FDA Center for Drug Evaluation and Research (CDER)

Pink Sheet

THERAPEUTICS AND DISEASE MANAGEMENT
DiPiro's Pharmacotherapy: A Pathophysiologic Approach

Handbook of Nonprescription Drugs: An Interactive Approach to Self-Care (OTC)

Koda-Kimble's Applied Therapeutics: The Clinical Use of Drugs

The Merck Manual

UpToDate

CDC: Diseases & Conditions

Harrison's Principles of Internal Medicine

Medscape

VETERINARY
Plumb's Veterinary Drug Handbook

SELECTING THE CORRECT "COLOR" DRUG REFERENCE

A number of important references are referred to by a color (see Study Tip Gal on next page). One of the more frequently accessed resources is the FDA's *Orange Book,* available online at www.accessdata.fda.gov/scripts/cder/ob/. This resource is used to determine if a generic substitution of a branded product is acceptable based on an AB rating, which indicates therapeutic equivalence to the brand.

Below is an example of the methylphenidate extended-release tablet entry from the online *Orange Book* indicating therapeutic equivalence to *Concerta.*

Mkt. Status	Active Ingredient	Proprietary Name	Appl No	Dosage Form	Route	Strength	TE Code	RLD	RS	Applicant Holder
RX	METHYLPHENIDATE HYDROCHLORIDE	CONCERTA	N021121	TABLET, EXTENDED RELEASE	ORAL	18MG	AB	RLD		JANSSEN PHARMACEUTICALS INC
RX	METHYLPHENIDATE HYDROCHLORIDE	CONCERTA	N021121	TABLET, EXTENDED RELEASE	ORAL	27MG	AB	RLD		JANSSEN PHARMACEUTICALS INC
RX	METHYLPHENIDATE HYDROCHLORIDE	CONCERTA	N021121	TABLET, EXTENDED RELEASE	ORAL	36MG	AB	RLD		JANSSEN PHARMACEUTICALS INC
RX	METHYLPHENIDATE HYDROCHLORIDE	CONCERTA	N021121	TABLET, EXTENDED RELEASE	ORAL	54MG	AB	RLD	RS	JANSSEN PHARMACEUTICALS INC

"COLOR" DRUG REFERENCES

Orange Book (FDA)
List of approved drugs that can be interchanged with generics based on therapeutic equivalence.

Pink Book (CDC)
Information on epidemiology and vaccine-preventable diseases.

Pink Sheet (Pharma Intelligence)
News reports on regulatory, legislative, legal and business developments.

Purple Book (FDA)
List of biological drug products, including biosimilars.

Red Book, Pharmacy
Drug pricing information.

Red Book, Pediatrics (AAP)
Summaries of pediatric infectious diseases, antimicrobial treatment and vaccinations.

Yellow Book (CDC)
Information on the health risks of international travel, required vaccines and prophylaxis medications.

Green Book (FDA)
Information on approved animal drug products.

LOCATING CLINICAL STUDY DATA AND RESEARCH SUMMARIES

Pharmacists use several databases to search for published studies, systematic reviews, meta-analyses and review articles. Searches can be done using Medical Subject Headings (MeSH) terms, which are used to group articles with the same content. Two of the more common databases are:

- *PubMed:* accesses MEDLINE (journal articles in medicine, nursing, dentistry, veterinary medicine, life sciences and more) and is a free service available from the NLM (www.ncbi.nlm.nih.gov/pubmed/).

- *Cochrane Library:* provides evidence-based information to guide clinical decision making. The database of Cochrane Systematic Reviews contains > 7,500 reviews [e.g., *Diagnostic Tests for Autism Spectrum Disorder (ASD) in Preschool Children*]. This important work is supported by government funds and donations, with no cost for users. It can be accessed at www.cochranelibrary.com.

CONSUMER RESOURCES

Pharmacists should be able to recommend reputable websites for patient-friendly information on medical conditions and drug treatment.

- The CDC (www.CDC.gov) has a symptom checker and provides information on infectious diseases, immunizations and travelers' health.

- *Drugs.com* (www.drugs.com) and *RxList* (www.rxlist.com) provide drug monographs and other information (see earlier descriptions in the General Drug Information Resources section).

- *Mayo Clinic* (www.mayoclinic.org) provides comprehensive patient information for diseases, symptoms, tests and procedures, and drugs and supplements.

- *MedlinePlus* (medlineplus.gov/, from the NLM) has sections on health topics, drugs and supplements, health-related videos, lab tests and a medical encyclopedia with images.

- *WebMD* (www.webmd.com) covers diseases, healthy living, pregnancy, prescription and OTC drug information, plus it has a pill identifier and interaction checker.

- FDA For Consumers website (www.fda.gov/ForConsumers/default.htm) provides comprehensive information on drugs (including recalls), food products, medical devices, vaccines, tobacco products and other topics that fall under the FDA's jurisdiction. Content can be selected by audience type (e.g., women, children or minority health).

- *MyHealthfinder* (https://health.gov/myhealthfinder, from the U.S. Department of Health and Human Services) has a mission to encourage healthy living through various topics (e.g., how to eat in a healthy manner, types of physical activity).

- *SafeMedication* (www.safemedication.com, from ASHP) includes medication tips and tools and a searchable database for patient-focused drug monographs, pulled from AHFS.

© iStock.com/luchschen

CHAPTER CONTENT

CONTENT LEGEND

= Study Tip Gal

CHAPTER 6

DRUG FORMULATIONS & PATIENT COUNSELING

DRUG FORMULATION CONSIDERATIONS

Compressed tablets are the most common formulation type and the least expensive to manufacture. Capsules are also relatively inexpensive to make. If a pharmaceutical company develops a drug in another formulation, the cost will be higher, and there must be a patient group that would benefit from the new formulation. For example, methylphenidate 10 mg immediate-release tablets cost ~$1.00 per tablet. The branded patch, *Daytrana*, is ~$16 per patch. The higher-priced formulation is beneficial in a child who can't swallow tablets or doesn't want to take doses during the day while at school.

It is helpful to recall drug formulation types by asking two questions:

1. Who uses this drug (e.g., which condition/patient population)?

2. Is there a reason to have this type of formulation for this patient population?

These questions can be useful on the exam when unsure if a particular formulation exists.

EXAMPLE: OLANZAPINE

Olanzapine is an antipsychotic that has various formulation options: immediate-release (IR) tablet, orally disintegrating tablet (ODT), short-acting injection and long-acting injection.

Who uses this drug?
People with schizophrenia, bipolar disorder or some type of psychosis.

Why are different formulations beneficial?
Patients with schizophrenia often discontinue their antipsychotics. A long-acting injection can improve adherence. ODTs dissolve quickly in the mouth; they are useful to prevent the patient from hiding the

medication in the mouth ("cheeking") and then spitting it out when no one is watching. The likelihood of "cheeking" is further reduced by giving a drink of water after the ODT. The short-acting injection works quickly and is useful for acute agitation.

EXAMPLE: ONDANSETRON

Ondansetron is a 5HT-3 receptor antagonist (5HT3-RA) used to prevent or treat nausea. It is available in various formulations: IR tablet, oral solution, ODT, oral film and short-acting injection.

Who uses this drug?

Patients receiving emetogenic drugs (e.g., chemotherapy), post-surgical patients or patients with any condition that causes nausea/vomiting.

Why are different formulations beneficial?

Oral medications will not be very effective when a patient is vomiting; an injection would be useful in this case if the patient is in a medical setting. An ODT or oral film can be useful for nausea without vomiting. Dysphagia (difficulty swallowing) is common in patients receiving chemotherapy and with other conditions (e.g., post-stroke, elderly). It would be difficult to swallow tablets with painful esophageal ulcers, strictures or tumors. An oral solution would be preferred in many of these cases. Though tablets can sometimes be crushed and put down a nasogastric (NG) tube, oral solutions are typically preferred when giving medications via NG tube.

Another 5HT3-RA, granisetron, comes in a long-acting patch (Sancuso) that prevents chemotherapy-induced nausea for up to seven days. The patch is applied before the chemotherapy to allow time for the drug to be absorbed through the skin.

ORAL FORMULATIONS

The majority of solid tablets and capsules and are designed to be swallowed whole. These can be short-acting or long-acting formulations. Other oral medications include liquids (mainly solutions and suspensions), ODTs, chewable tablets, sublingual tablets/films and granules/powders. See the table below for a summary of oral formulations and their common uses.

COMMON ORAL FORMULATIONS

FORMULATION	EXAMPLES	REASONS FOR USE
Long-acting oral tablets/capsules	*Concerta* – methylphenidate *Detrol LA* – tolterodine The following suffixes indicate a long-acting formulation: XL, XR, ER, LA, SR, CR, CRT, SA, TR, "cont" (for controlled release); other products may have 24, timecaps or sprinkles in the name. **Osmotic Release Oral System (OROS)** *Concerta, Cardura XL, Procardia XL, Asacol HD, Delzicol* and several other long-acting medications use an OROS to provide fast drug delivery, followed by an extended-release. Water from the gut is absorbed into the delivery system by osmosis, which increases the pressure inside and forces the drug out through a small opening. The tablet/capsule shell may be visible in the patient's stool (called a ghost tablet/capsule), but the drug has been released (important counseling point).	Drugs may be designed to release slowly to avoid nausea or to provide a long duration of action. Providing a smooth level of drug release over time reduces high "peaks," which reduces side effects (e.g., less drug hitting the "wrong" receptor) and provides a safe level of drug over the dosing interval. Patients must be counseled to not crush or chew any drug that is a long-acting formulation (including ER opioids). It could release all the medication at once, and a fatal dose could be released. Some long-acting opioid capsules (e.g., *Kadian*, Xtampza ER)* can be opened and the contents sprinkled on certain foods. The capsule contents should not be crushed or chewed. Always consult package labeling, as not all formulations have been studied in this way. ISMP's "Do Not Crush List" is a useful resource for drugs that should not be crushed. There are a few long-acting formulations that should not be crushed but can be cut on the score line (e.g., *Toprol XL, Sinemet CR*).*
Liquid oral suspensions	*Augmentin* – amoxicillin/clavulanate *Tylenol Children's* – acetaminophen, for children	Useful in patients with swallowing difficulty or who are unable to follow directions (e.g., infants and young children, adults with altered mental status, animals). Liquid medications can be administered in the side of the mouth using a dropper, and most can be administered via a feeding tube.
Liquid oral solutions	*Constulose* – lactulose, for hepatic encephalopathy *Neurontin* – gabapentin, for neuropathic pain *Rapamune* – sirolimus, for prevention of rejection after organ transplant	Suspensions must be shaken to redisperse the medication prior to administration. Shaking is not required for solutions, as the drug is evenly distributed in the solvent.

Brand discontinued but name still used in practice.

FORMULATION	EXAMPLES	REASONS FOR USE
Chewable tablets	*Suprax* – cefixime *Singulair* – montelukast *Lamictal* – lamotrigine	Primarily used for children who are unable to swallow tablets. A few chewable products are used by adults. Chewable calcium products are popular because calcium tablets are large and hard for many people to swallow. Lanthanum carbonate (*Fosrenol*) is a phosphate binder that must be chewed for the drug to bind phosphate in the gut.
Lozenges/troches for oral mucosa drug administration	*Mycelex* – clotrimazole, for oral thrush *Cepacol* – benzocaine/menthol, for sore throat	Used to treat a condition in the oral mucosa; the drug is held in the mouth while the troche slowly dissolves.
Orally disintegrating tablets (ODTs) Placed on the tongue and disintegrates rapidly in saliva Films that dissolve in the mouth are similar to ODTs (e.g., *Zuplenz* – ondansetron film)	*Lamictal ODT* – lamotrigine, for seizures *Remeron SolTab* – mirtazapine, for depression *Zyprexa Zydis* – olanzapine, for schizophrenia Ondansetron – for nausea, dysphagia	An ODT may be helpful when a patient cannot swallow tablets/capsules due to dysphagia (difficulty swallowing). Paralysis of the throat muscles from stroke is the most common cause. Other causes of dysphagia include: esophagitis, esophageal tumors, ↓ LES pressure/reflux, facial swelling from an allergic reaction and conditions that worsen motor function, including Parkinson disease. Children are often unable to swallow tablets or capsules. Nausea can make it difficult to tolerate anything orally. If vomiting is present or expected, a non-oral route should be used (e.g., a suppository). Non-adherence: ODTs dissolve quickly. This can help with compliance since it is harder for uncooperative patients to spit the drug out.
Sublingual (SL) or buccal delivery with a tablet, film, powder or spray	*Edluar* – zolpidem SL tablet *Nitrostat* – nitroglycerin SL tablet *Subsys, Actiq, Fentora* – various fentanyl formulations	SL and buccal formulations have the same benefits as ODTs. With SL/buccal absorption, the onset of action is faster than with a tablet or capsule that is swallowed; the drug is readily absorbed into the venous circulation at the administration site (e.g., under the tongue). Less drug is lost to gut degradation and first-pass metabolism.
Granules, powders or capsules that can be opened and sprinkled into soft food or water*	**Sprinkled on Applesauce** *Adderall XR* – dextroamphetamine/amphetamine ER *Coreg CR* – carvedilol *Dexilant* – dexlansoprazole *Focalin XR* – dexmethylphenidate *Namenda XR* – memantine *Nexium* – esomeprazole *Ritalin LA* – methylphenidate **Other Specific Instructions** *Cambia* – diclofenac powder, in water *Creon* and other pancreatic enzyme products – pancrelipase, on soft food with a low pH (applesauce, pureed pears or banana) *Depakote Sprinkles* – valproic acid, on soft food *Kadian** – morphine, on applesauce or soft food Potassium chloride ER capsules – on applesauce or pudding *Questran, Questran Light* – cholestyramine, in 2-6 oz water or non-carbonated liquid *Singulair* – montelukast granules, in 5 mL of baby formula or breast milk or in a spoonful of applesauce, carrots, rice or ice cream *Vyvanse* – lisdexamfetamine, in water, yogurt or orange juice	These formulations are primarily for pediatric or geriatric patients who have difficulty swallowing. Hospital implications: it is usually cheaper to give an oral medication via NG tube rather than converting to IV administration. Some medications are not available in an IV formulation. Instruct the patient on the following: ■ Do not chew any long-acting pellets or beads that are emptied out from a capsule. ■ If capsule contents are mixed in food or liquid, do not let the mixture sit too long (take within the time directed). ■ Do not add to anything warm or hot (the contents will dissolve too quickly). *Always refer to the product labeling for instructions; not all capsule medications should be opened and administered (refer to long-acting capsules section earlier in this table). Medications should only be mixed in the specific foods/liquids that were studied, because the pH of the food/liquid could be critical. Many medications have specific instructions for oral vs. NG tube administration.

Brand discontinued but name still used in practice.

WARNING: SWEETENERS ARE NOT SWEET FOR ALL

Formulations that are exposed to taste buds (e.g., ODTs) often contain sweeteners (e.g., aspartame, saccharin), which are generally well-tolerated but can be problematic for some people. Sorbitol metabolism produces gas, cramping and bloating in sensitive patients, including those with irritable bowel syndrome (IBS). Phenylalanine is used in many ODT, chewable and granule medication formulations. It is a dangerous sweetener for those with phenylketonuria (PKU), a genetic defect in which the enzyme that degrades phenylalanine is absent. Lactose is the most commonly used excipient in drug formulations. It may be an issue in patients with lactose intolerance, though sensitivity to lactose is variable and changes with age. Additional sweeteners and excipients are reviewed in the Compounding chapters.

ODT AND ORAL FILM COUNSELING

- Orally disintegrating tablets: do not attempt to push the tablets through foil backing. With dry hands, peel back the foil of one blister and remove the tablet.
- Place tablet (or film) on the tongue; it will dissolve in seconds. Once dissolved, you may swallow with saliva. Administration with liquid is not necessary. Wash hands after administration.

SELECT MEDICATIONS IN UNIQUE FORMULATIONS

Medications are increasingly offered in new, unique formulations (e.g., *Onzetra Xsail*, a nasal powder for migraine, or *Cotempla XR-ODT*, a long-acting ODT for ADHD). These formulations are reviewed in the disease state chapters of this book. The following sections summarize commonly encountered unique formulations, including example products and general counseling information. More specific counseling points for drugs that are available in these formulations can be found in the individual disease state chapters.

INJECTIONS

Injections can be given by various routes, including intradermal, subcutaneous, intramuscular (for short- or long-acting effects) and intravenous (see examples in the table below). Injections that patients give themselves are almost always given by SC injection. IM injections use a longer needle and generally hurt more (e.g., result in subsequent muscle soreness). *EpiPen* is an IM injection that is given in the thigh for acute need (e.g., bronchoconstriction, wheezing); see the Drug Allergies & Adverse Drug Reactions chapter.

Monoclonal antibodies ("-mabs") are injectable proteins used to treat many diseases (e.g., cancer, autoimmune conditions). Most monoclonal antibodies can cause injection reactions, and can require premedication (e.g., acetaminophen and diphenhydramine) to prevent severe symptoms. Select drugs must be administered in a healthcare setting under medical supervision to monitor for reactions (e.g., omalizumab).

FORMULATION	EXAMPLES	REASONS FOR USE
Subcutaneous (SC) injections that patients can mostly self-administer	See self-administered injections on the following page Naloxone – for opioid overdose reversal *Imitrex* – sumatriptan, avoids worsening nausea (from migraine), fast onset Insulins, GLP-1 agonists – see Diabetes chapter	SC administration is used for rapid effect (e.g., for pain or opioid overdose) or for drugs that would degrade or not be absorbed if given by oral administration (e.g., enoxaparin, etanercept).
Long-acting intramuscular (IM) injections	*Abilify Maintena* – aripiprazole *Haldol* – haloperidol decanoate *Invega Sustenna, Invega Trinza* – paliperidone *Lupron Depot* – leuprolide *Risperdal Consta* – risperidone *Vivitrol* – naltrexone *Zyprexa Relprevv* – olanzapine	Various drugs come as long-acting injections to improve adherence (such as antipsychotics) or to ↓ the need for more frequent (painful) injections.
Intravenous (IV) injections	Many acute care drugs	Bypasses the oral route for patients who are intubated or sedated; fast response (can quickly achieve desired concentrations), avoids loss of drug due to N/V.

Self-Administered Injections

	ROOM TEMP STABILITY	INJECTION LOCATION	FREQUENCY
Refrigerated*			
Glatiramer (Copaxone)	Up to 30 days	Abdomen, arms, hips, thighs	Daily or 3 times per week
Etanercept (Enbrel)	Up to 14 days	Thigh (preferred), abdomen, upper arm	Weekly or twice weekly
Adalimumab (Humira)	Up to 14 days	Abdomen, thigh	Every other week
Certolizumab pegol (Cimzia)	Prefilled syringes: up to 7 days	Abdomen, thigh	Every 2-4 weeks
Golimumab (Simponi)	Up to 30 days	Thigh, lower abdomen (below navel), upper arm	Monthly
Teriparatide (Forteo)	Minimize, should be stored in the refrigerator at all times	Thigh, abdomen	Daily
Abaloparatide (Tymlos)	Up to 30 days	Abdomen	Daily
Not Refrigerated			
Enoxaparin (Lovenox)		Abdomen, > 1 inch from navel	Once or twice daily
Fondaparinux (Arixtra)		Abdomen, > 1 inch from navel	Daily
Methotrexate (Otrexup, others)		Abdomen, thigh	Weekly
Sumatriptan (Imitrex, Zembrace, SymTouch)		Upper arm, thigh	PRN, at first sign of migraine

*Let sit at room temperature for 15-30 minutes prior to injecting.

Injectable Medication Counseling

STEP 1	STEP 2	STEP 3	STEP 4	STEP 5
Wash hands	Prepare injection	Select and clean injection site	Inject	Discard syringes, pen needles or entire assembly in sharps container

iStock.com/ZernLiew
Luciano Cosmo © 123RF.com

- Inject at least 1 inch away from the previous injection site.
- Never use the same needle more than once.
- Some injections "click" when the needle enters the skin and/or "click" when the injection is complete.
- With single-use devices, discard the needle or entire assembly (with attached needle) in a sharps container.
- Do not rub the skin near anticoagulant injections (e.g., enoxaparin, fondaparinux); rubbing can cause severe bruising.
- Do not use any device to heat up cold injections; let the injection sit at room temperature for ~20 minutes.
- Liquids can degrade; if a solution is discolored or contains particles, do not use. Do not use beyond the expiration date.

Safe Handling of Monoclonal Antibodies

Regardless of the condition being treated, monoclonal antibodies have similar counseling points for storage and handling. Proteins can easily denature (break apart) if handled incorrectly. Patients should be instructed not to shake the medication, and to avoid exposing the drug to extreme temperatures (hot or cold). These drugs should be stored in the refrigerator prior to use, and be slowly brought to room temperature prior to injecting (injecting cold drug is painful).

PATCHES

Patch Administration Sites

Most patches (e.g., *Catapres-TTS, Duragesic*) can be applied to one or more of these <u>common application sites</u>, on either side of the body:

- <u>Chest</u> (upper)
- <u>Back</u> (upper and lower)
- <u>Upper arm</u> (on the part facing out)
- <u>Flanks</u> (sides of the body, abdomen level)

<u>Exelon</u> is applied to the same sites, but <u>not the flanks</u>. *Butrans* is applied to the same sites, except rather than the sides of the body near the abdomen, it is applied to the sides of the body, level to the chest. Some pain patches (such as *Flector, Lidoderm* and *Salonpas*) treat local pain, and are applied over the painful area/s.

The patches in the <u>figures below</u> have unusual application sites. <u>*Daytrana*</u> is applied on the <u>hip</u>, alternating right and left hips daily. <u>*Transderm Scop*</u> is applied <u>behind the ear</u>, at least four hours before needed, alternating ears every 72 hours. Never apply patches with estrogen on the breasts, or testosterone on the scrotum (testicles and surrounding area). Patches can <u>irritate the skin</u>; <u>sites</u> where the patch is placed, with the exception of the topical pain patches, should be <u>alternated</u>.

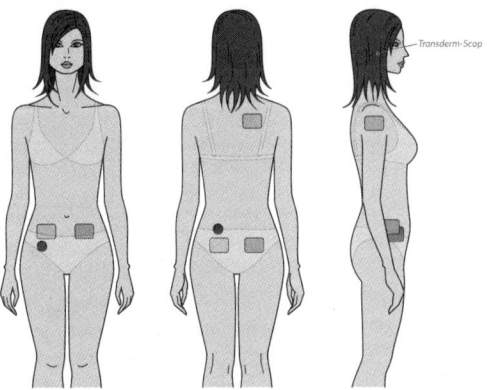
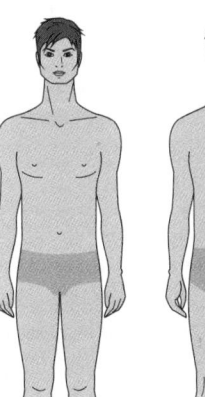
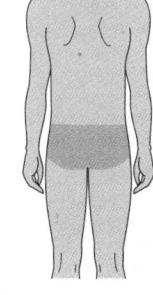
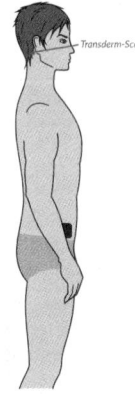

Transderm-Scop

© pushinka © 123RF.com

Xulane (back, abdomen, arm or buttock)
Daytrana (hip)
Oxytrol (abdomen, hip or buttock)

Vivelle-Dot (lower abdomen or buttock)
Transderm-Scop (behind the ear)

Daytrana (hip)
Transderm-Scop (behind the ear)

PATCH FREQUENCY

Daily
Methylphenidate (*Daytrana*): QAM, 2 hours prior to school

Nicotine (*NicoDerm CQ*)

Rivastigmine (*Exelon*)

Rotigotine (*Neupro*)

Selegiline (*Emsam*)

Testosterone (*Androderm*): nightly, not on scrotum

Daily (With Special Instructions)
Lidocaine (*Lidoderm*): 1-3 patches (as needed), on for 12 hours, off for 12 hours

Nitroglycerin: on for 12-14 hours, then off for 10-12 hours

Twice Daily
Diclofenac

Twice Weekly
Estradiol* (*Alora, Vivelle-Dot*)

Oxybutynin (*Oxytrol*)

Weekly
Buprenorphine (*Butrans*)

Clonidine (*Catapres-TTS*)

Estradiol* (*Climara*)

Estradiol/Levonorgestrel

Ethinyl estradiol/Norelgestromin (*Xulane*): weekly for 3 weeks, off for 1 week

Every 72 Hours
Fentanyl (*Duragesic*): Q72H, if it wears off after 48 hours, change to Q48H

Scopolamine (*Transderm Scop*): Q72H, if needed

Estradiol patches may be used on continuous or cyclic (3 weeks on, 1 week off) schedules at the frequency listed above.

Patch Counseling

QUESTION	RESPONSE
Can I cut the patch into pieces?	■ Usually no, <u>except</u> *Lidoderm*, which is designed to be cut and applied over the painful regions.
Can the patch be exposed to heat from an electric blanket, heating pad or body temperature > 38°C (> 100.4°F)?	■ Avoid heat exposure with most patches. <u>Heat causes rapid absorption</u> of the medication from the patch, resulting in toxicity. With fentanyl and buprenorphine, this can be quickly toxic (fatal).
The patch is bothering my skin. What can I do?	■ <u>Never</u> apply to <u>skin that is irritated</u>. ■ <u>Alternate</u> the application site. ■ The skin should <u>not be shaved</u> shortly before applying; shaving is irritating to the skin. If needed, cut the hair short with scissors. A <u>topical steroid</u>, such as hydrocortisone, can be applied after the patch is removed.

Which patches need to be removed prior to an MRI?	■ Patches <u>containing metal</u> (e.g., aluminum) need to be <u>removed prior to an MRI</u> or the metal will burn the skin:
	
	    ❑ Clonidine *(Catapres-TTS)*
	    ❑ Rotigotine *(Neupro)*
	    ❑ Scopolamine *(Transderm Scop)*
	    ❑ Testosterone *(Androderm)*
	
	■ Patches containing the same medication (e.g., generics) may vary in metal content between different manufacturers. It is widely recommended that estradiol patches (e.g., *Alora*, generic estradiol) be removed prior to an MRI. Other patches with variable recommendations include nitroglycerin, oxybutynin, diclofenac, nicotine and fentanyl. Always verify the labeling for a specific product.

Can the patch be covered with tape if it will not stick or falls off?	■ <u>Most</u> patches <u>cannot be covered</u> with tape. A few patches can be taped around the edges. ■ Fentanyl *(Duragesic)* and buprenorphine *(Butrans)* can be covered only with the <u>permitted</u> adhesive film dressings, <u>Bioclusive</u> or <u>Tegaderm</u>. ■ *Catapres-TTS* comes with <u>its own adhesive cover</u>, which goes over the patch to hold it in place. ■ Never apply patches to skin that is oily. ■ When applied, patches have to be smoothed out on the skin, and then pressed down for a number of seconds, usually 10-30 seconds.
Where is the patch applied?	■ Common application sites include the upper chest or upper/sides of the back (below the neck), upper thigh or upper outer arm; select patches have unique application sites (see previous page). Always verify with product labeling.
How do I dispose of used patches?	■ In most cases, remove and fold the patch to <u>press adhesive surfaces together</u> for disposal. Used drugs should be disposed of according to the manufacturer's instructions, which can include throwing it away in a lidded container or flushing it down the toilet. ■ Some highly potent narcotic patches (e.g., *Duragesic, Butrans)* and *Daytrana* can be fatal, especially if ingested by a child or pet. For these drugs, the FDA and/or manufacturer may recommend <u>flushing</u> the used patch down the toilet to remove it from the home immediately.
Where is the drug located?	■ The drug can be in a raised pouch, a <u>reservoir</u> (containing a gel or a semi-solid form) or directly incorporated into the <u>adhesive</u> of the patch (the side that adheres to the patient's skin).

TOPICALS

Medications applied to the skin can be used for both <u>local effects</u> on the skin or <u>systemic effects</u> throughout the body.

<u>Topical medications</u> used for their <u>local effects</u> have <u>decreased systemic side effects</u> and generally provide faster relief. This includes creams, ointments, gels and solutions. Common conditions treated topically include <u>muscle/joint pain or inflammation, cold sores, acne, eczema or other skin rashes, mild skin infections</u> and <u>hair loss</u>.

Examples of topical medications used for their localized effect include:

■ *Voltaren* – diclofenac gel, treats pain near the skin surface

■ Mupirocin ointment, treats some skin infections

Topical medications used for systemic effects can be used as an alternative to injections. Patches are a unique type of topical medication (discussed earlier) that are usually used for systemic effects. Another example includes testosterone *(AndroGel)*, which is used for hypogonadism/testosterone deficiency.

NASAL SPRAYS

The nasal route has a <u>faster onset</u> than the oral route and is <u>useful for acute conditions</u> that should be treated quickly, including pain. Nasal sprays bypass gut absorption; some <u>proteins</u> that would get <u>destroyed in the gut</u> (e.g., calcitonin) can be given nasally. Patients with certain conditions may absorb a drug better nasally vs. orally (e.g., patients lacking intrinsic factor needed for oral absorption of vitamin B12). Examples of nasal sprays include:

- *Imitrex* – sumatriptan, fast onset, alternative to injection
- *Afrin* – oxymetazoline
- *Flonase Allergy Relief* – fluticasone

Afrin and *Flonase* are used primarily to treat <u>localized</u> nasal symptoms.

Nasal Spray Counseling

Before use
- <u>Shake</u> the bottle <u>gently</u> and remove the cap.
- <u>Prime</u> the pump before first use or when you have not used it recently (7 – 14 days on average).
- <u>Blow</u> your <u>nose</u> to clear your nostrils.

Using the spray
- <u>Close one nostril</u> and insert the nasal applicator into the other nostril.
- Start to <u>breathe in</u> through your <u>nose</u>, and <u>press</u> firmly and quickly <u>down</u> once on the applicator to release the spray.

- <u>Breathe out</u> through your <u>mouth</u>.
- If a second spray is needed (in the same nostril or in the other nostril), repeat the above steps.
- Wipe the nasal applicator with a clean tissue and replace the cap.
- Use the bottle for the <u>labeled number of sprays</u> then discard, even if it is not completely empty.
- <u>Do not blow your nose</u> right after using the nasal spray.

EYE AND EAR DROPS

Eye drops and ear drops are used for <u>local effects</u>. <u>Eye drops</u> must be <u>sterile</u> (to prevent infection) and close to the <u>pH of the body</u> (to avoid pain upon administration). The ear is less sensitive, so ear drops have less stringent requirements. Because of this, <u>eye drops</u> can be <u>administered in the ear</u>, but <u>ear drops</u> can <u>never</u> be administered <u>in the eye</u>.

Eye Drop Counseling
- Wash your hands before and after using eye drops.
- Before you open the bottle, <u>shake it a few times</u>. <u>Gels</u> should be inverted and <u>shaken once</u> prior to use (to help the medication reach the tip).
- Bend your neck back so that you are <u>looking up</u>. Use one finger to <u>pull down your lower eyelid</u>. It is helpful, at least initially, to use a mirror.
- <u>Without</u> letting the tip of the bottle <u>touch your eye</u> or eyelid, release one drop of the medication by either squeezing the bottle or tapping on the bottom of the bottle. The drop should go into the space <u>between</u> your <u>eye</u> and your <u>lower eyelid</u>. If you squeeze in more than one drop, you are wasting medication.
- After you squeeze the drop of medication into your eye, <u>close your eye</u>. <u>Press a finger between your eye and the top of your nose</u> for at least <u>one minute</u> so more of the medication stays in your eye and you are less likely to have side effects. Blot extra solution from the eyelid with a tissue.
- If you need to use more than one eye drop:
  - ❏ If there are two drops of the same medication being given at the same time, wait five minutes between drops (do not administer two drops at once).
  - ❏ <u>Wait</u> at least <u>5 – 10 minutes</u> to put a <u>second medication</u> in the same eye. If administering a <u>gel</u>, wait <u>10 minutes</u>.
- If the eye drop contains a <u>preservative</u> called <u>benzalkonium chloride (BAK)</u> and you wear soft contact lenses, <u>remove lenses prior to administration and wait 15 minutes</u> to reinsert them.

Ear Drop Counseling
- If cold, gently shake the bottle or roll it in your hands for 1 – 2 minutes to warm the solution. Do not drop cold medication into the ear, as discomfort and dizziness can occur.
- Lie down or tilt the head so that the <u>affected ear faces up</u>.
- Gently pull the earlobe <u>up</u> and <u>back</u> for <u>adults</u> to straighten the ear canal. Pull <u>down</u> and <u>back</u> for <u>children < 3 years</u>.

- Administer the prescribed number of drops into the ear canal. Keep the ear facing up for about five minutes to allow the medication to coat the ear canal.
- Do not touch the dropper tip to any surface. To clean, wipe with a clean tissue.

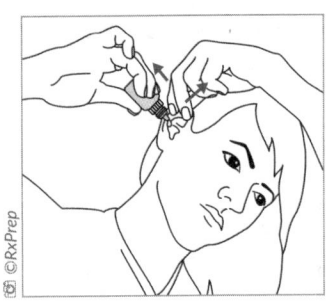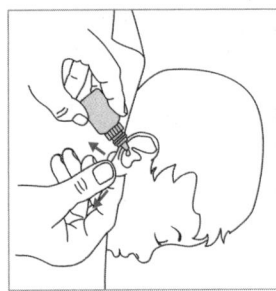

©RxPrep

RECTAL MEDICATIONS

Medications given rectally, such as suppositories and enemas, are used either for localized treatment (e.g., constipation, hemorrhoids) or for systemic treatment (e.g., diazepam rectal gel for acute seizures). Suppositories can also be used when the patient is NPO and systemic treatment is needed (e.g., acetaminophen for pain or fever in an infant). Examples of common rectal medications include:

- *Rowasa* – mesalamine enema, treats local disease (distal ulcerative colitis)
- *Pedia-Lax* – glycerin suppository, treats constipation (stool is in rectum)
- *FeverAll* – acetaminophen suppository, treats pain/fever

Rectal Medication Counseling

All rectal products
- For best results, empty the bowel immediately before use.

Enemas
- Remove the bottle from the pouch and shake well. Remove the protective sheath from the applicator tip. Hold the bottle at the neck to prevent any of the medication from being discharged.
- Best results are obtained by lying on the left side with the left leg extended and the right leg flexed forward for balance. Gently insert the medication or applicator tip into the rectum, pointed slightly toward the navel to prevent damage to the rectal wall.
- Grasp the bottle firmly, and then tilt slightly so that the nozzle is aimed towards the back; squeeze slowly to instill the medication. Steady hand pressure will discharge most of the medication. After administering, withdraw and discard the bottle.
- Remain in position for at least 30 minutes, or preferably all night for maximum benefit.

Suppositories
- Detach one suppository from the strip. Remove the foil wrapper carefully while holding the suppository upright. Do not handle the suppository too much; heat from your hands and body can cause it to melt.
- Insert the suppository, with the pointed end first, completely into your rectum, using gentle pressure. You can put a little bit of lubricating gel on the suppository if you have trouble.
- For best results, keep the suppository in your rectum for at least 1 – 3 hours.

INHALATIONS

Inhaled medications provide immediate (rescue) and long-lasting (maintenance) benefits in lung disorders (e.g., asthma or COPD). The drug is delivered directly to the lungs and this minimizes systemic toxicities. Instructions for use are dependent on the type of device and the medication (see the Asthma and Chronic Obstructive Pulmonary Disease chapters for details). Inhaled antibiotics are discussed in the Cystic Fibrosis chapter.

OTHER PATIENT COUNSELING

Counseling patients on safe and effective medication use is an essential role of pharmacists. This section reviews common counseling points for most drugs, as well as recommended language to use when counseling.

MISSED DOSES
- Most medications follow this general rule for when a dose is missed:
  - If you miss a dose, take it as soon as you remember. If it is almost time for your next dose, skip the missed dose and take the next dose at your regularly scheduled time. Do not take two doses at the same time unless instructed by your healthcare provider.
- Exceptions that do not follow these instructions are discussed in the individual chapters. This includes:
  - High-risk drugs (e.g., anticoagulants, transplant medications)
  - Oral contraceptives
  - Drugs that must be taken at specific times (e.g., phosphate binders, pancreatic enzymes and prandial insulin that must be taken before a meal)

MEDICATION STORAGE

Most medications can be stored in any cool, dry place (e.g., a medicine cabinet, not in a bathroom to avoid steam/humidity). Medications that require unique storage (e.g., in a refrigerator or in the original container) are highlighted throughout the individual disease state chapters.

ADHERENCE COUNSELING AND MONITORING

Adherence counseling and assessment is a key role of a pharmacist, especially in the community/outpatient setting. Pharmacists often review refill histories of medications to understand how a patient is actually using their medication at home. If the medication is used to prevent/control a disease, nonadherence can imply that the patient does not understand how to use their medication, the importance of their medication (common with conditions that have limited symptoms, such as hypertension), is experiencing side effects or requires assistance in remembering to take the drug (e.g., pill boxes or refill reminders).

If the medication is used as needed for acute symptoms (e.g., a rescue inhaler), a refill history can reveal how well the patient's condition is controlled. Infrequent use of a rescue/as needed medication means that the patient is not having symptoms frequently, whereas frequent use can imply that the patient is suffering from symptoms or not using the medication correctly.

When assessing adherence, remember to evaluate the reason for the drug first. Then use a refill history (and patient reports) to better understand what issues may be impacting medication use (see the Case Scenario below).

Counseling on adherence can be challenging; use of motivational interviewing techniques can help the pharmacist to better understand the patient and their individual needs. Motivational interviewing is a counseling approach that focuses on the patient's priorities to help facilitate change. Asking open-ended questions, employing empathy and reserving judgments will help to build patient relationships.

CASE SCENARIO
PK is a 43-year-old male with anxiety. He presents to the pharmacy today (11/14) for a refill of his medications. Upon reviewing his chart, the pharmacist sees the following refill history:

Last Fill	Rx	Medication	Sig	Quantity	Refills
10/24	64255	Sertraline 50 mg	Take one tablet by mouth daily for anxiety	30	1
10/24	64301	Lorazepam 1 mg	Take one tablet by mouth daily as needed for anxiety	30	1
10/1	64255	Sertraline 50 mg	Take one tablet by mouth daily for anxiety	30	2
10/1	64301	Lorazepam 1 mg	Take one tablet by mouth daily as needed for anxiety	30	2
9/12	64255	Sertraline 50 mg	Take one tablet by mouth daily for anxiety	30	3
9/12	64301	Lorazepam 1 mg	Take one tablet by mouth daily as needed for anxiety	30	3

Based on the instructions and your understanding of these medications, what is the purpose of each medication?
Sertraline is being used for maintenance/control of anxiety and lorazepam is being used as needed for acute symptoms of anxiety.

How long should each fill last, if used as instructed?
Each fill of sertraline (30 tablets) should last 30 days.
Each fill of lorazepam (30 tablets) should last at least 30 days, but longer if PK's anxiety is well controlled.

What does the refill history tell you?
PK is likely using both medications in the same way, as he is getting refills of both medications consistently at the same time. He may not be aware that his lorazepam should be used only when needed for symptoms, and that his sertraline should be taken daily (regardless of symptoms).

Furthermore, his refills do not appear to be lasting a full month; he may be taking both medications more frequently than prescribed. A discussion with PK is warranted to determine why these trends have occurred and if he understands how these medications should be taken. Open-ended, non-judgmental questions should be used to best evaluate his understanding.

COUNSELING LANGUAGE

Key counseling points for medications are presented in individual chapters throughout this course book, in simplified lists for easier learning. When counseling a patient, layman's language should be used for a better understanding. In the following table you will find example language that can be used when counseling a patient on common drug-related issues.

PATIENT COUNSELING	LANGUAGE TO USE
Allergy/anaphylaxis	Seek immediate medical help if you develop symptoms of a severe allergic reaction: severe rash with itching, redness or swelling, swelling in your face, lips, tongue or throat, wheezing or trouble breathing, or severe dizziness.
Anticholinergic effects	This medication can cause dry mouth, constipation, difficulty urinating, dry eyes and blurred vision. For select anticholinergic medications, include: this medication can make you feel drowsy.
Avoid grapefruit	Avoid eating grapefruit or drinking grapefruit juice while using this medication. Grapefruit can lead to higher levels of the medication in your blood, which will increase side effects.
Avoid in pregnancy (teratogenic)	This medication can cause birth defects if taken during pregnancy. Women who are pregnant or planning to become pregnant must not use this medication. Effective contraception is required.
Bleeding/bruising	This medication can cause bleeding, such as nosebleeds, bleeding gums and bruising. If you develop serious symptoms, such as coughing up blood or vomit that looks like coffee grounds, dark, tarry-looking stool, or bleeding in unusual places, such as blood in the urine or very large bruises, contact your prescriber immediately. Over-the-counter pain medications and natural products can increase bleeding risk. Talk to your pharmacist before taking any new medications.
Blood clot	This medication can increase the risk of a blood clot, which can be serious. Seek immediate medical help if you have symptoms of a clot. This can occur in your limbs, with symptoms such as swelling, redness or warmth in the lower leg (around the calf muscle) or arm. A blood clot in a lung or the heart can cause chest pain and trouble breathing. A clot in the brain (a stroke) can cause sudden confusion, numbness/weakness on one side of the body, trouble speaking or loss of consciousness.
Body fluid discoloration	This medication can change the color of your urine, saliva and sweat, and may stain clothing. This is not harmful. Some drugs can stain contact lenses.
Cancer	You are more likely to develop certain types of cancers while taking this medication, including skin cancer. Protect your skin from the sun. Use a broad-spectrum sunscreen that covers UVA and UVB rays, with an SPF of 30 or higher. Follow the recommendations you are given for cancer screenings.
Constipation	This medication can cause constipation. A laxative or stool softener can be helpful. Drink plenty of water, exercise regularly and eat food with fiber such as fruits, vegetables and grains.
Contains phenylalanine – do not use if you have phenylketonuria (PKU)	This medication contains an artificial sweetener called phenylalanine. People with phenylketonuria (PKU) should not use products that contain phenylalanine.
Decreased heart rate	This medication can decrease heart rate, which can cause dizziness. When you rise from a sitting or lying position, move slowly and carefully to prevent a fall. You may be instructed to monitor your heart rate.
Delirium	This medication can cause confused thinking and unusual behaviors. Contact your healthcare provider if this develops.
Dehydration	This medication can cause dehydration. Symptoms include dry mouth, increased thirst, less frequent urination, dizziness, headache and dry skin. If you develop severe symptoms, such as a rapid breathing and dark-colored urine, contact your healthcare provider immediately. Dehydration in an infant is dangerous. Symptoms can include a sunken soft spot of the head (called a fontanelle), no tears (i.e., when crying), lethargy and listlessness. Products like *Pedialyte* and *Enfalyte* can be used to replace fluids and minerals, such as sodium and potassium. Severe dehydration can require emergency medical treatment.
Depression/psychosis (also see suicidal ideation)	This medication can worsen or cause changes to your mood, including suicidal thoughts and behaviors. In some cases, your thoughts can become strange or psychotic. Notify your healthcare provider right away if your mood or behavior worsens.
Diarrhea	This medication can cause diarrhea. Drink fluids with electrolytes to prevent dehydration. Contact a healthcare provider if symptoms do not improve after a few days or if any of the following are present: age < 6 months, pregnancy, high fever (> 101°F), severe abdominal pain or blood in the stool.
Dizziness	This medication can cause dizziness, which is more likely to occur when you rise from a sitting or lying position. Rise slowly and carefully to prevent a fall.
Drowsiness	This medication can make you feel tired. Use caution when driving, operating machinery or performing other hazardous activities. Alcohol, sleeping pills, pain medications, antihistamines, antidepressants and other medications that cause drowsiness can make this side effect worse, which could be dangerous.

PATIENT COUNSELING	LANGUAGE TO USE
Drug interactions due to binding	This medication can bind to other medications and food, which can change the drug's absorption. Separate antacids, multivitamins/minerals, iron, magnesium, calcium, dairy products and calcium-rich foods from medications that can bind.
Drug interactions due to high gastric pH	This medication uses the acid in your stomach to be absorbed. If you are taking other medications to lower the acid in your stomach, such as heartburn medication, this medication will not work well. Talk to your pharmacist before taking medications to lower stomach acid.
Dry mouth	This medication can cause or worsen dry mouth. Sucking on sugarless hard candy or ice chips, sipping water or chewing sugarless gum can help. With dry mouth, it is especially important to keep your teeth clean to prevent cavities. Over-the-counter saliva substitutes can be helpful.
Dyspepsia	This medication can cause indigestion. Symptoms can include bloating, upset stomach, nausea, burping or heartburn. Taking the medication with food can be helpful. If the symptoms do not improve or worsen, contact your healthcare provider.
Edema	This medication can cause fluid and water to accumulate and cause swelling, especially in the ankles and legs. If you have heart disease, discuss the use of this medication with your healthcare provider, and monitor your weight.
Eye damage	Tell your healthcare provider immediately if you develop any eye pain or vision changes, such as seeing halos or having blurry vision.
Ghost tablet in stool	The tablet that contains this medication can pass into the stool. If there is a tablet in your stool, it is nothing to worry about; it is an empty tablet.
Gingival hyperplasia	This medication can cause swelling and growth of the gums around your teeth. Brush and floss often, and see your dentist for regular cleanings.
Heart failure	This medication can cause or worsen heart failure. Contact your healthcare provider if you develop symptoms, including trouble breathing, shortness of breath, rapid weight gain or swelling in the legs, ankles and feet.
Hyperglycemia	This medication can cause high blood sugar. Symptoms include more frequent urination and increased thirst and hunger. Check your blood sugar if you have a glucose meter. Tell your healthcare provider if you develop symptoms of high blood sugar.
Hyperthyroidism	This medication can change how your thyroid gland works. Tell your healthcare provider if you develop symptoms of an overactive thyroid, including increased sensitivity to heat, unexplained weight loss, thinning hair, unusual sweating, nervousness, irritability or restlessness. Tests can be ordered to check your thyroid function.
Hypoglycemia	This medication can cause low blood sugar. Symptoms can include dizziness, irritability, shakiness, sweating, hunger, confusion, fast heart rate and blurred vision. Check your blood sugar, if able, and eat or drink something with sugar, such as a ½ cup of orange juice or regular soda, 1 cup of milk, 1 tablespoon of honey or 3-4 glucose tablets or gel.
Hypothyroidism	This medication can lower the amount of thyroid hormone you produce. Tell your healthcare provider if you develop symptoms of low thyroid, including feeling tired or cold, weight gain, constipation or hair loss. Tests can be ordered to check your thyroid function.
Increased blood pressure	This medication can increase blood pressure. Monitor blood pressure as directed by your healthcare provider, especially if you have hypertension.
Increased heart rate	This medication can increase heart rate, which can cause dizziness. When you rise from a sitting or lying position, move slowly and carefully to prevent a fall. You may be instructed to monitor your heart rate.
Infection	This medication can lower your body's ability to fight infections. Avoid contact with people who are sick. Regular handwashing is one of the best ways to remove germs and avoid getting sick.
Injection site reaction	The spot where you inject this medication can become red, swollen, painful and itchy. If the area looks especially worrisome or is very painful, let your healthcare provider know.
Insomnia	This medication can cause difficulty sleeping. To improve your sleep, keep a regular sleep schedule and keep the bedroom dark, comfortable and quiet.
Lactic acidosis	This medication can cause a buildup of acid in the blood. Get immediate medical help if you feel very weak or tired, have unusual muscle pain, trouble breathing and/or stomach pain with nausea and vomiting.
Liver damage	This medication can damage the liver. Get medical help if you develop any of the following: yellowing of the white part of your eyes, yellowing of your skin, dark-colored urine, light-colored stool or bad stomach pain and nausea.
Lung damage	This medication can damage the lungs. Get medical help if you develop any of the following: severe/persistent cough, shortness of breath, chest pain or breathing that is difficult or painful.
Many drug interactions	There are many medications that can interact with this drug. Check with your healthcare provider or pharmacist before starting any new medications, including over-the-counter medications, vitamins and/or herbal products.

PHARMACY FOUNDATIONS PART 1

PATIENT COUNSELING	LANGUAGE TO USE
MedGuide required	This MedGuide contains important information about your medication. Take the MedGuide home and read it carefully so you understand the medication, and how to use it as safely as possible.
Muscle damage	This medication can cause muscle damage. If you develop unusual muscle pain, tenderness or weakness, or if you are urinating less than usual, get medical help.
Nausea	This medication can make you feel nauseous. Taking the medication with food and a glass of water can be helpful.
Nephrotoxicity	This medication can cause problems with the kidneys. Contact your prescriber right away if you have little or no urination, blood in the urine, swelling in your feet or ankles or rapid weight gain.
Orthostasis	This medication can cause the blood pressure to drop when you stand up, which can cause dizziness and light-headedness. This can cause falls and injuries. It is important to get up slowly when lying down or sitting, and to hold onto the bed rail or a strong tabletop until you feel steady.
Pancreatitis	This medication can damage the pancreas. If you are nauseous and have sharp pain in the upper abdomen that feels like it's radiating to your back, get medical help.
Paresthesia	This medication can cause a feeling of "pins and needles" in the legs, hands and feet. It is usually harmless.
Peripheral neuropathy	This medication can cause the nerves in your legs, feet, arms and/or fingers to become damaged. If you develop tingling, stabbing pain or numbness, such as in your feet, contact your prescriber.
Photosensitivity	This medication can cause your skin to be more sensitive to the sun. Stay out of the sun during midday hours, use sun-protective clothing and broad-spectrum sunscreen with an SPF of at least 30.
Priapism	If you develop a prolonged and painful erection that lasts more than four hours, stop using this medication and get medical help right away to avoid permanent damage to the penis.
QT prolongation	This medication can cause a condition called "QT prolongation," which makes the heartbeat too fast and not regular. This can cause dizziness and sudden fainting. If this happens, get immediate medical help. Check with your pharmacist before taking any new medications; other medications can make this more likely.
Rash	Mild rash: this drug can cause a mild rash. If it is itchy, taking 25 or 50 mg of diphenhydramine (Benadryl) should help. Severe rash: this medication can cause a severe rash that begins with a fever and flu-like symptoms, followed by a bright red rash. This is an allergic reaction that requires immediate medical help. Some medications can cause both a mild and severe rash.
Reduces ADEK absorption	This medication can block the amount of fat-soluble vitamins (A, D, E, K) that your body absorbs. Take a multivitamin at a different time of day than this medication.
Remove patch before an MRI	Some brands of this patch contain metal, which will burn your skin during an MRI. Remove the patch before an MRI.
Serotonin syndrome	This medication increases the level of serotonin in your blood. If it is taken with other over-the-counter or prescription medications that also increase serotonin, toxicity can occur. Seek urgent medical help if you feel dizzy, shaky, agitated, feverish and have a racing heartbeat.
Sexual dysfunction	This medication can cause sexual problems, including (select counseling point based on medication-specific side effects): ■ Decreased libido: low sexual drive/interest. ■ Ejaculation difficulties: anorgasmia (no ejaculation) or retrograde ejaculation (a "dry orgasm" or very little ejaculate during orgasm). ■ Erectile dysfunction (impotence): difficulty getting or maintaining an erection.
Stomach bleeding (especially for NSAIDs)	This medication can cause stomach bleeding. If your stools are black or tarry-looking, or if you are coughing or vomiting up blood that looks like coffee grounds, contact your healthcare provider immediately.
Subcutaneous injection	This medication is injected under the skin with a very short needle. Before injecting, wash your hands. Rotate where you inject, and do not inject into skin that is injured, tender or bruised.
Suicidal ideation (also see depression/psychosis)	This medication can increase the risk of having suicidal thoughts. Contact your prescriber right away if you notice symptoms of depression, unusual behavior, changes in mood or thoughts of hurting yourself.
Urinary tract infection	This medication increases the risk of a urinary tract infection. Contact your prescriber if you experience burning when you urinate, or if you need to go to the bathroom more often, and suddenly. The urine can also be darker than usual.
Vision changes	This medication can cause vision changes. Tell your healthcare provider if you notice that colors seem different, if there are halos around lights or if your vision becomes blurry.

CONTENT LEGEND

= Key Drug Guy

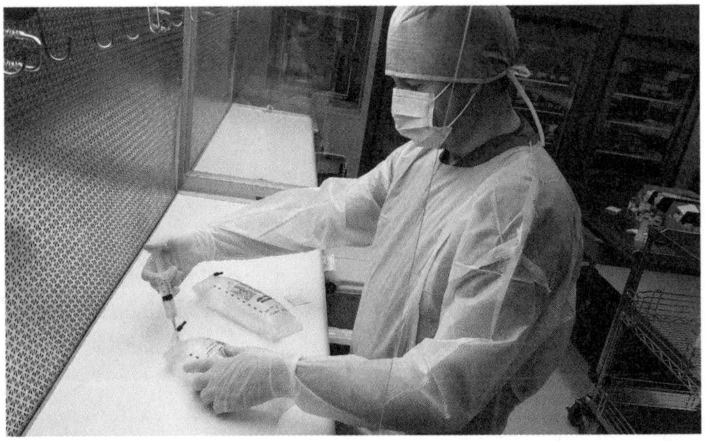

©Michael J. Freudiger

CHAPTER 7

INTRAVENOUS MEDICATION PRINCIPLES

BACKGROUND

Enteral administration [through the gastrointestinal (GI) tract] is the preferred route for drug delivery. When the enteral route is not feasible, a parenteral route (outside of the GI tract) is used. Common routes for parenteral drug administration include intravenous (IV), intramuscular, subcutaneous or transdermal administration. Other parenteral routes are used for specific purposes, including intra-articular (into the joint) and intrathecal (into the space under the arachnoid membrane of the brain/spinal cord). The intrathecal route is often used by anesthesiologists and for some chemotherapy, but when contraindicated (e.g., with vincristine), intrathecal administration can be fatal.

IV DRUG DELIVERY

The IV route is required in hospitalized patients who are NPO (unable to take anything by mouth) and with gastrointestinal conditions when the gut needs to be bypassed (e.g., surgery, malabsorption). Drugs with poor oral bioavailability are often given IV (e.g., vancomycin for conditions other than *C. difficile* treatment). In a critical situation where fast (stat) onset is required (e.g., using a vasopressor to quickly raise cardiac output), IV administration is a must. Oral medications require gut dissolution and absorption, which takes time.

This chapter focuses on the aspects of intravenous administration that are important to the pharmacist, including venous access (IV lines), compatibility and stability issues and administration requirements.

VENOUS CATHETERS

A catheter is a piece of plastic tubing that goes into a part of the body to put fluids in or take them out (e.g., with a urinary catheter). A catheter inserted into a vein is called a <u>venous catheter</u> and is used for fluid and drug delivery. A venous catheter is called a <u>line</u>, and the patient is said to have IV access. Lines come in two primary types: peripheral and central.

PERIPHERAL LINES

Percutaneous means through the skin and peripheral refers to locations away from the body's central compartment, including the arms and legs. Most IV drugs can be delivered through percutaneous, <u>peripheral venous catheters</u> that are inserted into <u>smaller veins</u>. Common veins used for peripheral venous catheters are the <u>cephalic vein</u> in the arm and the saphenous vein near the ankle.

Peripheral lines are simpler and less expensive to insert than central lines, but they have limitations. Administering drugs into smaller veins can cause <u>phlebitis</u> (vein irritation), venous <u>thrombosis</u> (clots) and interstitial <u>fluid extravasation</u>; this is when the catheter becomes dislodged from the vein and the infusion contents enter surrounding tissue.

CENTRAL LINES

A <u>central line</u> empties into a <u>larger vein</u> and the contents are quickly diluted. Central lines provide secure, long-term vascular (i.e., blood vessel) access and are required for administration of:

- <u>Highly concentrated drugs</u> (e.g., potassium chloride > 20 mEq/100 mL)

- <u>Long-term antibiotics</u> (e.g., to treat osteomyelitis)

- Toxic drugs that would cause severe phlebitis [e.g., chemotherapy, especially with <u>vesicants</u> (see next column)]

- Drugs with a <u>pH</u> or <u>osmolality</u> that is not close to blood pH or osmolality (e.g., <u>parenteral nutrition</u>)

Central lines are sometimes used for patients with poor peripheral venous access (e.g., a person with IV drug abuse with collapsed veins). Additional benefits with a central line include the ability to administer higher volumes and use faster infusion rates.

Central Line Placement

To be considered a central venous catheter, also called a central line, the catheter tip must be located in a <u>large vessel</u> (i.e., <u>superior vena cava</u>, right atrium or inferior vena cava). The catheter can reach one of these locations by being inserted into a proximal central vein or a peripheral vein. A line inserted in a proximal central vein can be placed in the internal jugular vein (near the top of the chest), subclavian vein (under the collarbone) or femoral vein (in the groin). These are in close proximity to the large vessels and do not require long catheters. Dialysis catheters are placed in this manner.

Peripherally inserted central catheters (PICC) are inserted by placing the line into a <u>peripheral vein</u> and advancing (pushing) the catheter through the vein until the tip <u>ends</u> in the <u>superior vena cava</u> (where the infusion contents will be released). It is simpler to insert a PICC line than a direct central line; a PICC line can be inserted at the bedside, and a quick x-ray will confirm that the tip has reached the right location.

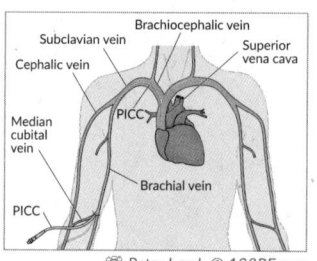

A PICC empties into the superior vena cava from a line placed into a peripheral vein (see figure on left).

Peter Lamb © 123RF.com

Vesicants are Safer with a Central Line

A vesicant is a drug that will cause <u>severe tissue damage</u> if the catheter tip comes out of the vein, allowing the drug to seep into the surrounding tissues (i.e., <u>extravasate</u>). Vesicants are preferentially administered through a central line because the line is less likely to become dislodged from the vein. <u>Vesicants</u> include <u>vasopressors</u> (e.g., dopamine, <u>norepinephrine</u>), <u>anthracyclines</u> (e.g., doxorubicin), <u>vinca alkaloids</u> (e.g., vincristine, vinblastine), digoxin, foscarnet, nafcillin, mannitol, mitomycin and promethazine.

PROMETHAZINE CAN CAUSE SEVERE TISSUE INJURY
Some hospitals removed it from formulary due to this risk.
Not to be given intra-arterial or SC; IM is preferred but this has tissue injury risk, too.
Minimally: do <u>not</u> give to <u>children < 2 years</u>, dilute the drug, limit the dose and concentration and be careful.

INCOMPATIBILITIES

Incompatible means that substances are <u>unsuitable for use together</u>. The end result could be a physical (e.g., color changes, precipitation) or chemical (e.g., drug degradation) interaction. When substances deemed incompatible are used together, it can lead to a safety concern for the patient.

The pharmacist is the primary resource for compatibility questions; reputable resources are required. The primary resources include the *Handbook on Injectable Drugs* (commonly called *Trissel's*), the <u>*King Guide to Parenteral Admixtures*</u> (commonly called *King's*) and the drug's <u>package insert</u>. Some drug information databases use the IV compatibility information from *Trissel's* (see Drug References chapter). Recent concerns regarding compatibility issues can also be found in *Pharmacy Practice News* and in *Hospital Pharmacy*.

CHEMICAL AND PHYSICAL INCOMPATIBILITY

<u>Chemical</u> incompatibility causes drug degradation or toxicity due to a <u>hydrolysis, oxidation or decomposition</u> reaction.

<u>Physical</u> incompatibilities occur <u>between a drug</u> and one of the <u>following</u>:

- The <u>container</u> (e.g., polyvinyl chloride containers)
- The <u>diluent</u> (solution) (e.g., dextrose or saline)
- Another <u>drug</u>

CONTAINER INCOMPATIBILITY

DEHP from the Container

The majority of polyvinyl chloride (PVC) containers use diethylhexyl phthalate (<u>DEHP</u>) as a "plasticizer" to make the plastic bag more flexible. DEHP can <u>leach</u> from the container and into the solution. DEHP is toxic and can harm the liver and testes.

Container Absorption/Adsorption

Absorption occurs when drug moves into the PVC container and adsorption occurs when drug adheres (or "sticks") to the container; either will reduce the drug's concentration.

Alternative (Non-PVC) Containers

Drugs that have leaching or absorption/adsorption issues with PVC containers can be placed in <u>polyolefin, polypropylene</u> or <u>glass</u> containers (although glass is heavy and can break).

Insulin and PVC Containers

Insulin adsorbs to PVC. Clinicians adjust the rate of insulin infusions to obtain blood glucose control, <u>regardless</u> of the type of <u>IV container and tubing</u> used. It might be useful to know that insulin does adsorb to PVC for testing purposes.

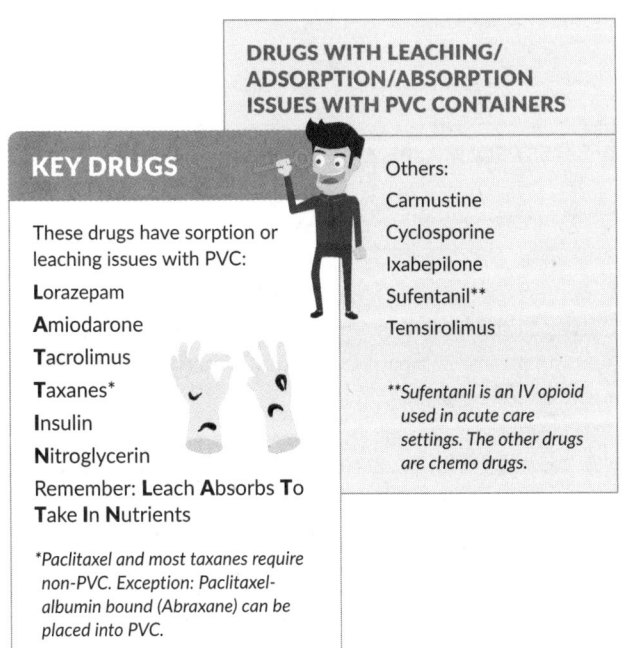

DRUGS WITH LEACHING/ADSORPTION/ABSORPTION ISSUES WITH PVC CONTAINERS

KEY DRUGS

These drugs have sorption or leaching issues with PVC:

Lorazepam
Amiodarone
Tacrolimus
Taxanes*
Insulin
Nitroglycerin

Remember: **L**each **A**bsorbs **T**o **T**ake **I**n **N**utrients

Paclitaxel and most taxanes require non-PVC. Exception: Paclitaxel-albumin bound (Abraxane) can be placed into PVC.

Others:
Carmustine
Cyclosporine
Ixabepilone
Sufentanil**
Temsirolimus

**Sufentanil is an IV opioid used in acute care settings. The other drugs are chemo drugs.*

iStock.com/grivina, VikiVector

COMMON DRUGS WITH DILUENT SOLUTION REQUIREMENTS

KEY DRUGS

SALINE (No Dextrose)

Remember:
A DIAbetic **C**an't **E**at **P**ie

Ampicillin
Daptomycin (*Cubicin*)
Infliximab (*Remicade*)
Ampicillin/Sulbactam (*Unasyn*)
Caspofungin (*Cancidas*)
Ertapenem (*Invanz*)
Phenytoin (Dilantin)

DEXTROSE (No Saline)

Remember: **O**utrageous **B**akers **A**void **S**alt

Oxaliplatin
Bactrim — SMX/TMP
Amphotericin B (all)
Synercid — Quinupristin/Dalfopristin

Others:

Saline (No Dextrose)
Abatacept (*Orencia*)
Azacitidine (*Vidaza*)
Belimumab (*Benlysta*)
Bevacizumab (*Avastin*)
Idarucizumab (*Praxbind*)
Iron Sucrose (*Venofer*)
Sodium Ferric Gluconate Complex (*Ferrlecit*)
Natalizumab (*Tysabri*)
Trastuzumab (*Herceptin*)

Dextrose (No Saline)
Carfilzomib (*Kyprolis*)
Mycophenolate (*CellCept IV*)
Pentamidine

DILUENT INCOMPATIBILITY

When drugs are diluted in solution for IV administration, they are commonly placed into 50 mL or larger IV <u>piggybacks</u> that contain <u>5% dextrose</u> (D5W) or <u>0.9% sodium chloride</u> (normal saline, NS). For most drugs, either solution is acceptable, but some drugs cannot be put into dextrose, and others cannot be put into saline (see <u>Key Drugs Guy</u> above). These drugs may also be compatible with sterile water, but that would be for reconstitution (e.g., for a drug that comes as a powder) and not for diluting in large volumes for infusion into a patient.

DRUG-DRUG INCOMPATIBILITY

Hospitalized patients are usually receiving IV fluids with multiple IV medications. To minimize the number of inserted peripheral and central lines, infusion bags are often joined together in a Y-site and run together in the same line during administration.

Y-Site Administration: Mixing Drugs in the Line

A Y-site describes the shape that forms when the lines (from different IV containers) are joined prior to entering the patient. Often, the large (1 liter) container is the patient's fluids and the smaller IV piggybacks contain the

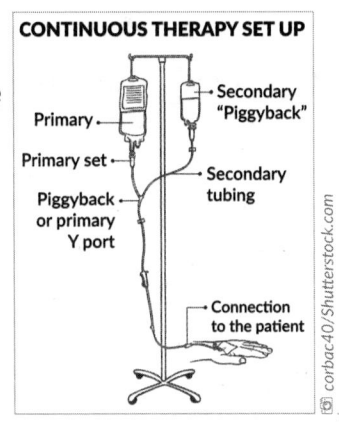

CONTINUOUS THERAPY SET UP

Primary
Primary set
Piggyback or primary Y port

Secondary "Piggyback"
Secondary tubing

Connection to the patient

corbac-40/Shutterstock.com

drugs. Since the drugs mix together briefly in the common portion of the IV tubing, it is important that the drugs and solutions are compatible with Y-site administration.

Additive Compatibility: Mixing Drugs in the Same Container

Additive compatibility needs to be confirmed when putting multiple drugs together in the same container or syringe. Additive compatibility and Y-site compatibility are listed separately in *Trissel's* and other drug reference sources.

There are more compatibility issues with mixing drugs in the same container (compared to Y-site administration) because the drugs are together for a longer period of time. Y-site incompatibilities are important because this type of administration is common, and many drugs that cannot be mixed in the same container are compatible when the drugs are mixed together for a short period in the line.

HIGH-RISK INCOMPATIBILITIES

A dangerous example of incompatibility involves ceftriaxone and calcium. Ceftriaxone cannot be mixed with any calcium-containing solutions due to the risk of precipitates. Lactated Ringers, a common IV fluid, contains calcium and cannot be mixed with ceftriaxone, including Y-site administration. This combination must be avoided in all age groups; neonates have the highest risk for lethal effects.

Calcium and phosphate can form a deadly precipitate in intravenous fluids. Methods to prevent calcium-phosphate precipitation when preparing parenteral nutrition are discussed in the Calculations III chapter.

Amphotericin B and sodium bicarbonate are incompatible with the majority of IV drugs with any type of IV administration. The common hospital drug piperacillin/tazobactam forms a precipitate when it mixes with acyclovir, amphotericin B and many other IV drugs.

Heparin is incompatible when administered with many drugs, including those often given concurrently in a patient requiring heparin (e.g., nitroglycerin, alteplase and hydromorphone). Caspofungin, another common hospital drug for treating *Candida* infections, has many Y-site incompatibilities. All of the IV quinolones are incompatible with Y-site infusion of many drugs. Information is extensive for incompatibilities; there are many others.

> **BEWARE!**
> **Mixing Together Can Be Fatal**
>
> Risk of precipitates→ emboli→ fatality
>
> Calcium & Ceftriaxone*
>
> Calcium & Phosphate**
>
> *Lactated Ringers contains calcium.
> **When calcium and phosphate are both put into PN, methods must be used to reduced the risk of a precipitate.

REFERENCE TABLE INTERPRETATION

The tables shown in this section are similar to tables that a pharmacist would need to interpret to check drug compatibility. The reference drug is listed in the table (cefepime, in the example below). The drug tested with it for compatibility issues is listed in the row below (gentamicin). A pharmacist can check to see if cefepime can be mixed with gentamicin in the same container. The table below reports that cefepime and gentamicin are incompatible (I in the last column) when mixed together in either D5W or NS, at the concentrations listed. In addition to the C/I rating, the remarks include that a precipitate had formed.

Cefepime

DRUG	MFR	CONC/L	MFR	CONC/L	TEST SOLN	REMARKS	REF	C/I
Gentamicin	ES	1.2 g	BR	40 g	D5W, NS	Cloudiness forms in 18 hr at room temp	588	I

C = compatible; I = incompatible
Y-Site Injection Compatibility (1:1 Mixture)

In this next example, a pharmacist can check if cefepime can be given in the same line when gentamicin is infusing (Y-site administration). The pharmacist will find that cefepime and gentamicin are compatible for Y-site administration at the concentrations listed, indicated by the "C" in the far right column and by the remarks.

Cefepime

DRUG	MFR	CONC	MFR	CONC	REMARKS	REF	C/I
Gentamicin	ES	6 mg/mL	BMS	120 mg/mL	Physically compatible with less than 10% cefepime loss. Gentamicin was not tested.	2212	C

C = compatible; I = incompatible

FILTERS

Filters can be required during compounding, administration or both. In-line filters (attached to the IV tubing) are used with drugs that have a risk of particulates, precipitates, crystals, contaminants or entrapped air in the final solution. The size of the filter required is determined by the size of the particles to be removed. The majority of drugs in which filters are necessary use a 0.22 micron filter (1 micron = 1/1,000 mm); another common filter size is 1.2 microns, which is used for lipids. Parenteral nutrition is filtered with a 0.22 micron filter, which will catch a calcium-phosphate particulate. If lipids are included, the filter size will need to be larger. Some drugs come packaged with the required filter. Large molecule drugs, including many liposomal formulations of chemotherapy drugs, must not be filtered due to the size of the drug particle.

If compounding IV medications packaged in glass ampules, filter needles or filter straws are used to prevent particulates from entering the IV bag and a filter may be required in the line.

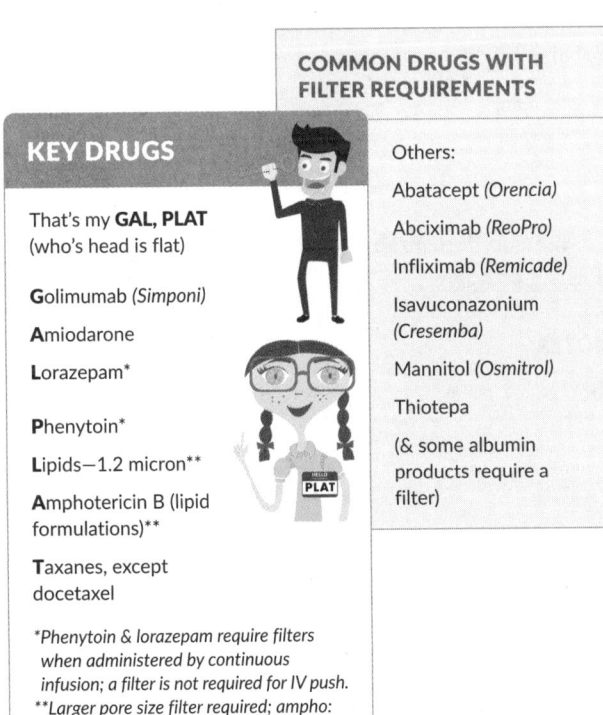

COMMON DRUGS WITH FILTER REQUIREMENTS

KEY DRUGS

That's my **GAL, PLAT** (who's head is flat)

Golimumab (Simponi)

Amiodarone

Lorazepam*

Phenytoin*

Lipids—1.2 micron**

Amphotericin B (lipid formulations)**

Taxanes, except docetaxel

*Phenytoin & lorazepam require filters when administered by continuous infusion; a filter is not required for IV push.
**Larger pore size filter required; ampho: prepare using a 5 micron filter

Others:

Abatacept (Orencia)

Abciximab (ReoPro)

Infliximab (Remicade)

Isavuconazonium (Cresemba)

Mannitol (Osmitrol)

Thiotepa

(& some albumin products require a filter)

iStock.com/littlemissk

TEMPERATURE & STABILITY

A drug that is "stable" will be stable only at a given concentration, for a certain time, at a certain temperature and with a certain degree of light exposure.

Time in Solution

Solutions decompose faster than solid (e.g., powder) formulations. The likelihood of a chemical reaction that would degrade the drug increases with time. Compatibility concerns due to longer infusion times have become an important issue in recent years with piperacillin/tazobactam (Zosyn) extended infusions. The same drug is commonly used with shorter infusions, without stability issues. The longer infusion period is used to increase time above the minimum inhibitory concentration (T > MIC) in order to counter drug resistance with nosocomial pathogens, including Pseudomonas, Enterobacter and Acinetobacter. The higher T > MIC is beneficial, but the longer infusion times result in more compatibility issues. Interactions with various antibiotics (e.g., piperacillin/tazobactam, azithromycin, ciprofloxacin, tobramycin, vancomycin), insulin and some of the vasopressors occur more commonly when given as a longer infusion.

Temperature

Higher temperatures speed up chemical reactions and break down proteins. The majority of IV drugs are refrigerated in order to permit longer stability (i.e., a longer period until the beyond-use-date). There are exceptions; for example, furosemide and phenytoin crystallize if kept cold and are stored at room temperature. See the Key Drugs Guy below for IV drugs that are kept at room temperature.

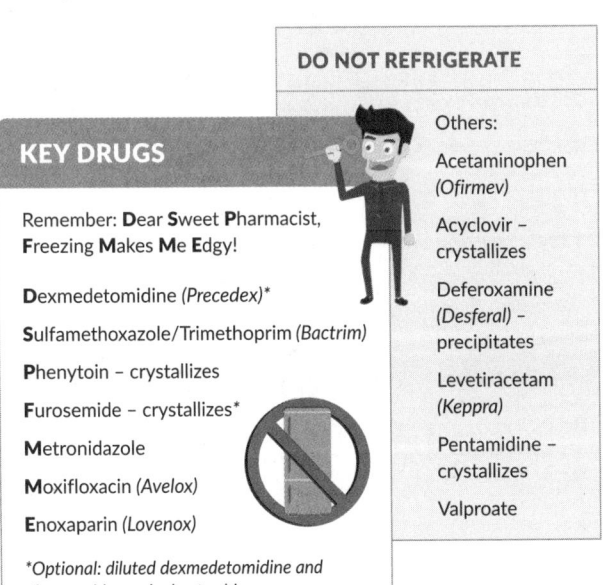

DO NOT REFRIGERATE

KEY DRUGS

Remember: **D**ear **S**weet **P**harmacist, **F**reezing **M**akes **M**e **E**dgy!

Dexmedetomidine (Precedex)*

Sulfamethoxazole/Trimethoprim (Bactrim)

Phenytoin – crystallizes

Furosemide – crystallizes*

Metronidazole

Moxifloxacin (Avelox)

Enoxaparin (Lovenox)

*Optional: diluted dexmedetomidine and furosemide can be kept cold.

Others:

Acetaminophen (Ofirmev)

Acyclovir – crystallizes

Deferoxamine (Desferal) – precipitates

Levetiracetam (Keppra)

Pentamidine – crystallizes

Valproate

iStock.com/hendart, igorshi

Light Exposure

Light exposure causes photo-degradation, which destroys some drugs, and in some cases, increases a drug's toxicity (e.g., nitroprusside). Many medications should be protected from light during storage to avoid degradation. Some medications are supplied in amber (light-protected) vials, and others are stored in the original packaging (foil overwrap or box) until needed. A small number of drugs are so light-sensitive that they require protection from light during administration. Pharmacy staff dispense these medications with a light-protective cover. In some cases, light-protective tubing (generally amber-colored) is needed. See the Key Drugs Guy on the right for a list of photosensitive drugs that require light-protection during administration.

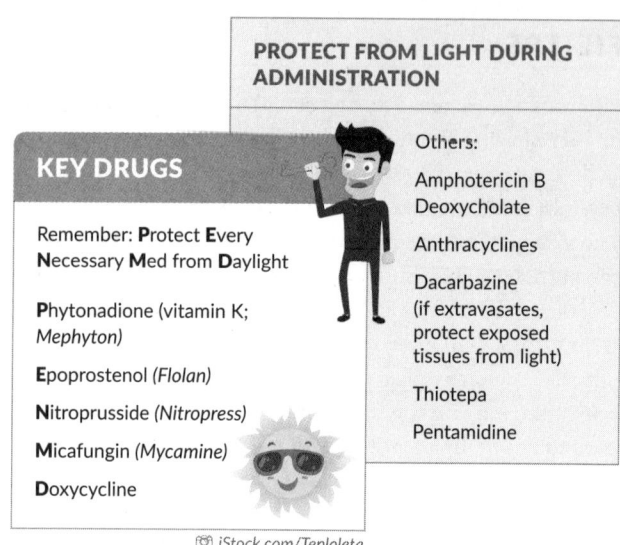

PROTECT FROM LIGHT DURING ADMINISTRATION

KEY DRUGS

Remember: **P**rotect **E**very **N**ecessary **M**ed from **D**aylight

Phytonadione (vitamin K; *Mephyton*)

Epoprostenol (*Flolan*)

Nitroprusside (*Nitropress*)

Micafungin (*Mycamine*)

Doxycycline

Others:

Amphotericin B Deoxycholate

Anthracyclines

Dacarbazine (if extravasates, protect exposed tissues from light)

Thiotepa

Pentamidine

iStock.com/Teploleta

Do Not Shake/Agitate

Agitation destroys some drugs, including hormones and other proteins. Drugs that are easily destroyed/damaged should not be shaken during compounding or transport, and can not be transported via pneumatic tube systems. Examples include:

- Protein/blood products, such as albumin, immune globulins, monoclonal antibodies and insulins (note: some manufacturers allow insulin to be transported via pneumatic tube one time)
- Products that foam, such as alteplase, etanercept (*Enbrel*), rasburicase, quinupristin/dalfopristin (*Synercid*) or caspofungin; these drugs should only be swirled when reconstituting, do not shake; wait for the foam to dissolve
- Vaccines that have been reconstituted, such as varicella zoster virus vaccine
- Emulsions, such as propofol and injectable lipid emulsions

Check Solutions for Color Changes

Most intravenous medications are clear and colorless. In some cases, discoloration can be of little or no consequence. However, in most cases, discoloration indicates oxidation or another type of decomposition.

DRUG	DO NOT USE WITH COLOR CHANGE	NOTES
Chlorpromazine	Darker than slight yellow	Slight yellow: potency retained, okay to use
Dacarbazine	Pink	
Dobutamine		Oxidation turns the solution slightly pink, but potency is not lost
Dopamine	Darker than slight yellow	Slight yellow: potency retained, okay to use
Epinephrine	Pink, then brown	
Isoproterenol	Pink or darker	Damaged by air, light, heat
Morphine	Dark	
Nitroprusside	Orange → brown → blue	Blue indicates nearly complete dissociation to cyanide
Norepinephrine	Brown or any discoloration	Normal color: yellow/orange
Tigecycline	Green/black	

IV Drugs that Come as Colored Solutions (i.e., not clear)

DRUG	COLOR OF IV FLUID		SKIN AND SECRETIONS DISCOLORATION
Anthracyclines (e.g., doxorubicin)	Red		Sweat and urine
Rifampin	Red		Body fluids and teeth
Mitoxantrone	Blue		Skin, eyes, urine
Methotrexate	Yellow		None
Multivitamins for Infusion (MVI)	Yellow		None
Tigecycline	Yellow/Orange		Teeth (if used during teeth development)
IV Iron, various	Brown		Urine

iStock.com/LisLud

Check Solutions for Particulates

The clinician (or the patient if using a self-injectable) should always check parenteral solutions for particulate matter. If particulates are present, the drug should be discarded.

Select Guidelines/References

Handbook on Injectable Drugs, 19th Ed. American Society of Health-System Pharmacists. 2016.

King Guide to Parenteral Admixtures. https://www.kingguide.com/online.html (accessed 2022 Jan 13).

CHAPTER CONTENT

CONTENT LEGEND

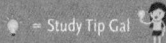 = Study Tip Gal   = Required Formula

CHAPTER 8

ANSWERING CASE-BASED EXAM QUESTIONS

iStock.com/ipopba

BACKGROUND

Increased use of electronic health records (EHRs) provides pharmacists with greater access to patient-specific information, including labs, test results and progress notes from other healthcare providers. Pharmacists must be prepared to effectively use all of this information to make decisions about drug therapy.

Questions on the NAPLEX are presented mainly in a case-based format. Some of the information provided in the case will be needed to correctly answer the questions. The goal is to assess whether the pharmacist can make the best choices for a specific patient vs. simply recalling facts. This better reflects the role of pharmacists in healthcare today.

This chapter reviews the patient medical record and discusses how to use the information to correctly answer case-based questions on the exam. Practice the techniques discussed in the RxPrep QBank.

THE PATIENT MEDICAL RECORD

ELECTRONIC HEALTH RECORDS

The patient medical record (PMR) provides complete documentation of a patient's medical history at a particular institution. The PMR can be referred to as the "medical record" or the "patient chart." These terms are from the era of paper records when all of the patient's medical information was gathered into ring binders. Paper charts have been phased out in most healthcare settings and replaced by EHRs, which improve accuracy and efficiency.

The EHR is quicker and easier to review. For example, if a patient is admitted to the hospital with an elevated SCr, the EHR provides current and previous lab results (by selecting a date range that can go back years in time) which are used to determine if this is a new or an old finding, and what recent workup has been completed. Procedures with results recorded on paper or faxed records from another facility can be quickly scanned into the EHR. EHRs allow providers to have immediate access to information when they are off-site. Some community pharmacies have access to EHRs of affiliated clinics.

When the EHR is linked to Computerized Prescriber Order Entry (CPOE) and electronic prescribing (e-prescribing), the problem of illegible handwriting is eliminated. The CPOE system can be designed to present only formulary drugs with proper dosing as options. As a result, pharmacists spend less time clarifying orders or changing to a formulary drug. Clinical decision support (CDS) tools can be built into the order entry process. Examples include order sets, pathways, limited drop-down menus that reflect the preferred drug/s, drug interaction and dose checking alerts. Refer to the Medication Safety & Quality Improvement chapter for additional information.

The Health Insurance Portability and Accountability Act of 1996 (HIPAA) requires security protections for all individually identifiable health information, called protected health information (PHI). These protections apply to both paper records and electronic records. For electronic records, access is limited with PINs and passwords. The information is encrypted, and there is an "audit trail" to track access. Security can still be breached; individuals can access medical records for patients they are not involved with, an employee can forget to log out or the system can be hacked. All personnel using the EHR are responsible for security. Education on security must be continual, and the software must be continuously evaluated for breaches. As part of the HIPAA requirements, patients have a right to access their own medical records kept in either paper or electronic formats.

SECTIONS OF THE PATIENT MEDICAL RECORD

The first additions to the patient medical record (PMR) (paper or EHR) are the patient's demographic data (including insurance information), admission sheet, a service agreement form ("this is what I am having done at this facility"), a page describing the patient's rights (a Joint Commission requirement) and an advance directive. An advance directive documents the patient's wishes concerning medical treatment if they are unable to make decisions on their own behalf. Allergies may be here or listed in a separate area of the chart.

Certain religious groups will refuse blood transfusions and blood products, which will need to be documented in the PMR. Blood products primarily involve albumin and immune globulins, but some patients will refuse drugs buffered in blood (*Epogen/Procrit, Kogenate* – used for hemophilia), natural clotting factors/tissue adhesives/interferons and a few other uncommon products. A few vaccines contain

porcine-derived gelatin as a stabilizer. The major religious groups consider this use acceptable, but a specific patient may not.

Other forms or sections in the PMR include progress notes, the vital signs record, laboratory tests, monitoring records used for some medications (e.g., warfarin to track the INR history), medication administration records and procedure records, including the diagnostic and operating room (OR) records. At the end of the hospital stay, the planning and discharge forms are added to the EHR.

When documenting information in the PMR, it is important to avoid abbreviations that could be interpreted to mean something else. The list of "Do Not Use" abbreviations should be easily available (refer to the Medication Safety & Quality Improvement chapter).

REQUIREMENTS FOR REIMBURSEMENT: DOCUMENTATION AND QUALITY OF CARE

Pharmacists are involved with many patient care activities and frequently make verbal patient care recommendations. While verbal recommendations may be effective, they are not part of the PMR and do not allow the information to be shared with other healthcare providers involved in the patient's care who are not present at that time. Interventions require documentation for reimbursement since the quality of the care is (increasingly) tied to the payment. Departments of pharmacy should have policies in place that describe the authority of pharmacists to document in the PMR, what activities will be documented and the proper format for documentation. Some activities that pharmacists document in the PMR include patient counseling, medication histories, consultations (e.g., pharmacokinetics, anticoagulation) and dosage adjustments. Documenting in the PMR is critical to establishing pharmacists as central members of the healthcare team.

The Centers for Medicare and Medicaid Services (CMS) provides health insurance to many Americans. CMS is directly involved with quality measurements and cost control. CMS has penalties for poor care and incentives for quality care. Two areas in which the penalties are steep are the rate of hospital-acquired infections and the hospital's readmission rate. These measures are chosen because they are expensive and are often, but not always, avoidable.

The Joint Commission, the Pharmacy Quality Alliance (PQA) and the Agency for Healthcare Research and Quality (AHRQ) are involved in setting the criteria to measure the quality of care. The PQA quality measurements focus on medications. Specific goals include increasing adherence, avoiding unnecessary or unsafe medications (such as high-risk medications in the elderly) and increasing the use of medications indicated for certain conditions.

MEDICARE & MEDICAID

Medicare is the federal health insurance program for people ≥ 65 years old, < 65 with disability and all ages with end stage renal disease (ESRD).

The prescription drug benefit under Medicare is called Part D.

Part A covers the hospital visit and Part B covers medical costs, such as doctor visits and some vaccines.

Medicaid provides health insurance for all ages with very low income (< 133% of the federal poverty level). Medicaid is a federal and state program. A senior who qualifies for both Medicare and Medicaid has "dual coverage."

THE SOAP NOTE FORMAT

A progress note records a patient encounter. One common method of organizing a progress note is the SOAP format, which organizes the information into four parts: Subjective, Objective, Assessment and Plan (SOAP). Prior to the use of SOAP notes, it was difficult to understand patient chart entries because the format was not standardized. Pharmacists may write SOAP notes to document their activities and read the SOAP notes of others while providing patient care. An example SOAP note from an EHR is included at the end of this chapter.

SUBJECTIVE

The 1st section in a SOAP note is the subjective information recorded from the patient. It is the patient's narrative of their symptoms. Only the relevant information is recorded. The person conducting the interview should use open-ended and direct questions while avoiding closed-ended and leading questions. For example, the leading question: "You always take your blood pressure pills, right?" is not likely to get a useful response. Phrasing the question in a direct manner that is worded to avoid a "yes or no" response will be more useful: "In a typical week, about how many mornings do you forget to take your blood pressure pills?"

The subjective section contains:

- A one-line Chief Complaint (CC). This is the specific reason the patient is being seen today, such as "I've had a stabbing pain in my right hip for three days."

- A detailed history of present illness (HPI). The HPI contains the onset and duration of the complaint, the quality and severity (e.g., a numerical pain rating), any modifying factors that reduce or aggravate the condition, treatments that have been tried and the effect of the treatment.

- A detailed past medical history (PMH) with social history (alcohol, tobacco and illicit drug use), family history (first-degree relatives only – parents and siblings), allergies and

patient-reported medication use. Medications include prescriptions, over-the-counter (OTC) drugs, vitamins and natural products. Information on start date and last refill is important when recording medication information.

OBJECTIVE

The 2nd section in a SOAP note is the objective information obtained by the clinician, either through observation or analysis. This includes:

- Vital signs (respiration rate, heart rate, blood pressure and temperature). Note that on the top of the sample EHR at the end of this chapter, the vitals are recorded at the top of the page, but vital signs are objective data.

- Other measurements (e.g., height and weight), physical findings, diagnostic tests performed (e.g., ECG, chest X-ray, urinalysis) and laboratory results go into this section.

- The medication list if it is obtained from a source other than the patient (e.g., recording information from prescription bottles or calling another pharmacy) because it was objectively verified.

Critical results are lab values significantly outside the reference range. Since these can indicate a life-threatening situation, they must be reported to a healthcare provider and addressed quickly. This is a Joint Commission National Patient Safety Goal.

Units of Measure

It is important to document measurements according to the policies of the institution. Documentation is generally done in metric system units (e.g., kg, cm). Recording weights and heights with incorrect units (150 pounds vs. 150 kg) can have fatal consequences in terms of dosing medications. Refer to the Calculations chapters to practice common height and weight conversions.

In the U.S., temperatures are still frequently recorded in degrees Fahrenheit and may need to be converted to degrees Celsius. The route that the temperature was taken should be recorded (i.e., rectal, oral, axillary, tympanic). Temperatures taken rectally or orally are more accurate than if taken by axillary (under the arm) or tympanic (in the ear) methods.

Temperature Conversions

$°C = (°F - 32)/1.8$	$°F = (°C \times 1.8) + 32$

CASE SCENARIO
A patient presented with a temperature of 101.6°F. What is this temperature in degrees Celsius? Round to the nearest TENTH.

$$°C = \frac{(101.6°F - 32)}{1.8} = 38.7°C$$

Select Drugs and Conditions that Alter Vital Signs

Make note of drugs that cause "↓ HR" or "↑ BP" while studying. On the exam, you might be asked about the possible cause of an abnormal vital sign. The table below is not all-inclusive; some conditions have variable effects on vital signs depending on severity (e.g., infection, withdrawal, poisoning). This information will be covered in more detail in the individual disease state chapters.

VITAL SIGN	INCREASED	DECREASED
Blood Pressure (BP)	"Hypertension" **Drugs** See Key Drugs Guy in Hypertension chapter **Conditions** ■ Renal insufficiency/failure ■ Pregnancy ■ Excess salt intake ■ Obesity ■ Adrenal tumors	"Hypotension" **Drugs** ■ Antihypertensives ■ Vasodilators ■ Opioids ■ Benzodiazepines ■ Anesthetics ■ Phosphodiesterase inhibitors **Conditions** ■ Anaphylaxis ■ Blood loss ■ Infection (esp. sepsis) ■ Dehydration (orthostatic hypotension)
Heart Rate (HR)	"Tachycardia" **Drugs** ■ Stimulants (ADHD, weight loss drugs) ■ Decongestants ■ Beta-agonists (esp. overuse) ■ Theophylline (esp. in toxicity) ■ Anticholinergics (tricyclics, antihistamines) ■ Bupropion ■ Antipsychotics ■ Excess caffeine/nicotine, illicit drug use ■ Vasodilators (e.g., nitrates, hydralazine, dihydropyridine CCBs) cause reflex tachycardia **Conditions** ■ Some arrhythmias (e.g., atrial fibrillation, ventricular tachycardia) ■ Hyperthyroidism ■ Anemia ■ Dehydration ■ Anxiety, stress, pain ■ Hypoglycemia ■ Infection ■ Drug withdrawal ■ Serotonin syndrome	"Bradycardia" **Drugs** ■ Beta-blockers ■ Non-dihydropyridine CCBs ■ Digoxin ■ Clonidine, guanfacine ■ Antiarrhythmics (esp. Class III) ■ Opioids ■ Sedatives ■ Anesthetics ■ Neuromuscular blockers ■ Acetylcholinesterase inhibitors **Conditions** ■ Some arrhythmias (sinus bradycardia) ■ Hypothyroidism
Respiratory Rate (RR)	"Tachypnea" **Drugs** ■ Stimulants **Conditions** ■ Asthma and COPD (esp. when poorly controlled) ■ Anxiety, stress ■ Ketoacidosis ■ Pneumonia	"Respiratory depression" **Drugs** ■ Opioids ■ Sedatives **Conditions** ■ Hypothyroidism
Temperature (Temp)	"Hyperthermia" **Drugs** ■ Inhaled anesthetics (malignant hyperthermia) ■ Antipsychotics (neuroleptic malignant syndrome) ■ Topiramate **Conditions** ■ Fever ■ Hyperthyroidism (esp. thyroid storm) ■ Trauma ■ Cancer ■ Serotonin syndrome	"Hypothermia" **Conditions** ■ Exposure to cold ■ Hypothyroidism (esp. myxedema coma) ■ Hypoglycemia

ASSESSMENT

The 3rd section is the assessment. This is the provider's thought process of possible causes of the current situation. Many conditions present with similar signs and symptoms; the assessment will often include a differential diagnosis, which is a list of possible diagnoses that could explain the patient's current signs and symptoms. Each diagnosis on the list will be investigated.

PLAN

The 4th section is the plan. This is how the problem/s will be addressed. The plan should be as specific as possible. Labs might be ordered, the patient might require diagnostic exams, referrals may be requested or the patient may require education (e.g., suspected nonadherence, poor device technique, nutritional education or smoking cessation support). If there is a differential diagnosis, there will be multiple steps in the plan to eliminate ("rule out") some of the possible conditions. Patients often have many medical problems that must be addressed, and they may be vastly different from the complaint that prompted the patient to seek medical attention.

MILITARY TIME

In all medical records, including the SOAP note, time is recorded with a 24-hour clock, rather than splitting the day into two 12-hour segments (AM/PM). The 24-hour clock is called "military time." The day begins at midnight, which is called 24:00 (pronounced "twenty-four hundred"). This is the start of the day and is sometimes referred to as 00:00. After 12:00 noon the time continues on the same number scale for the rest of the day: 1:00 PM is 13:00, 2:00 PM is 14:00, and so on. The last minute of the day is 23:59, then 24:00 (midnight), and then the next day begins. Some clocks are labeled for military time (see image).

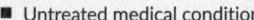

To convert military time back to 12-hour segments (AM/PM), simply subtract 12 from any number ≥ 13 (e.g., 16:00 = 4 pm, because 16 – 12 = 4).

ANSWERING CASE-BASED QUESTIONS ON THE EXAM

Pharmacists caring for patients (or taking the NAPLEX) are often faced with complex medication regimens. In order to provide the best care possible, a systematic approach to the assessment of the treatment plan and medication regimen is warranted.

IDENTIFYING MEDICATION THERAPY PROBLEMS

Pharmacists should assess for medication therapy problems, intervene when appropriate and document the intervention/s in the PMR as policy permits. Cases on the exam will require the same type of systematic assessment to identify risks to the patient and potential solutions to problems.

Pharmacists develop a process for thoroughly identifying medication problems. One method is shown below (see Study Tip Gal). Ask yourself each question listed: Are there any therapeutic duplications? Are there any drug interactions? You may not be able to answer every question with the information provided. Strong mastery of the material (e.g., brand or generic name identification, drug interactions, guideline recommendations) is essential. The Case Scenario below illustrates how you could be asked several different types of questions about a case.

HOW TO LOOK FOR MEDICATION PROBLEMS IN A PATIENT CASE

Review the case for the following medication problems:

- Untreated medical condition
- Medications used without an indication
- Improper drug selection
- Dose that is too low or high
- Therapeutic duplication
- Lack of patient understanding about medication
- Drug allergy
- Drug interaction
- Improper use of medication
- Failure to receive medication
- Adverse drug reaction
- Nonadherence

Practice reviewing cases until it becomes routine to check for each of these problems, every time. This is essential for a pharmacist.

CASE SCENARIO

A new patient transfers the following prescriptions to a community pharmacy on December 15th: *Benicar* 20 mg daily, *Zocor* 20 mg daily, *Stribild* 1 daily (last refilled November 1st) and *Avapro* 150 mg TID. All are written for a 30-day supply.

Identify the potential problems (see Study Tip Gal above):

- Therapeutic duplication: two ARBs
- Drug interaction: cobicistat is contraindicated with simvastatin
- Dose too high: *Avapro* should be dosed once daily
- Potential nonadherence: *Stribild* should be refilled every 30 days

MATCHING DRUGS TO MEDICAL PROBLEMS

How will you determine whether there are untreated medical conditions, drugs without an indication or duplications of therapy? Pharmacists are skilled at matching up medical problems and drugs as a quick way to assess this.

CASE SCENARIO

Match the medications to the condition being treated. Some conditions may require more than one medication.

Past Medical History	Medications	Past Medical History	Medications
Hypertension	Keflex	Hypertension ⟶	Hydrochlorothiazide
Arthritis	Synthroid	Arthritis ⟶	Meloxicam
Depression	Hydrochlorothiazide	Depression ⟶	Cymbalta
Cellulitis	Renova cream	Cellulitis ⟶	Keflex
Diabetes	Ambien	Diabetes	?
	Meloxicam	? Insomnia	Ambien
	Cymbalta	? Hypothyroidism	Synthroid
		? Acne	Renova cream

- There are several medications without a documented indication in the patient's past medical history. The pharmacist should interview the patient and/or review labs/vitals (PRN) to determine if these medications are still required or were possibly prescribed in error. It is very common for the medical record to be incomplete or incorrect, but pharmacists must ensure that medications are used properly.

- There is one condition (diabetes) that is not being treated with a medication. Many patients are able to control type 2 diabetes with diet alone, which might be the case. A review of the labs (blood glucose, A1C) would help answer this question. Again, notice that mastery of brand/generic names is critical.

QUESTIONS ABOUT THE MEDICATION PROFILE

Use the Case Scenario below to answer questions about the medication profile.

CASE SCENARIO

The pharmacist is filling new prescriptions for a patient with the following home medication list:

Advair
Clozapine
Roflumilast
Depakote ER
Dutasteride
Fenofibrate
Hyzaar
ProAir
Spiriva
Tamsulosin

Based on the medication profile, which group of medical problems does this patient have?

A. Asthma, glaucoma and gout
B. Atrial fibrillation, depression and schizophrenia
C. Hypertriglyceridemia, migraine and Parkinson disease
D. BPH, COPD and hypertension
E. Seizures, diabetes and anemia

One of the new prescriptions is for *Flomax*. This is a duplication of therapy with which of the patient's current medications?

A. Advair
B. Roflumilast
C. Dutasteride
D. Hyzaar
E. Tamsulosin

The patient's labs reveal an increased ammonia level. Which of the home medications is most likely responsible?

A. Advair
B. Clozapine
C. Depakote ER
D. Spiriva
E. Tamsulosin

Answers:

D, E, C

RECOMMENDING DRUG THERAPY

Some exam questions will ask you to make a drug therapy recommendation. This requires strong knowledge of guidelines and indications/contraindications for drugs. Read the question and answer choices first, before extensively evaluating the case. After you read the question, you should be able to quickly determine what information you need from the case.

CASE SCENARIO

A patient has a past medical history of type 2 diabetes and is not taking any medications. Which of the following medications should be recommended to treat the patient's diabetes?

A. *Glucophage XR*

B. *Actos*

C. *Januvia*

D. *Glucotrol*

E. Regular insulin given by IV infusion

How will you decide which answer to pick? Here is the correct approach to the question:

- Metformin is a recommended first-line medication, along with lifestyle modifications, for type 2 diabetes. It is very likely the correct answer, but the question may be testing something more advanced than a simple recall of the recommended first-line medication. Before selecting metformin, make sure it is a safe choice in this specific patient and that nothing was missed in the case that would make another choice better:

  ❑ Insulin is one of the answer choices. Could this patient have hyperglycemia hyperosmolar state (HHS) or diabetic ketoacidosis (DKA), which would require an insulin infusion? Read the HPI. Look for signs, symptoms and labs that help (e.g., very high blood glucose, altered mental status, extreme dehydration; refer to the Diabetes chapter).

  ❑ Metformin should not be started if eGFR is < 45 mL/min/1.73 m². If eGFR is not provided, calculate the patient's CrCl and use this as an eGFR estimate. Metformin may not be safe for this patient.

  ❑ Check the progress notes and other information provided. Metformin should not be used within 48 hours of receiving IV iodinated contrast media.

If the patient does not require an insulin infusion to treat DKA or HHS, and there are no contraindications or safety concerns with metformin, select it as the correct answer choice. If metformin is not a safe choice, use a similar process to determine which of the other choices is best for this patient.

PATIENT COMMUNICATION

HEALTH LITERACY

Good communication skills are essential for pharmacists and are linked to patient satisfaction and trust. Pharmacists provide valuable information to patients, but the effort is wasted if the information is not understood. Only about 12% of adults have proficient health literacy. Health literacy is the degree to which individuals are able to obtain, process and understand basic health and medication information to make appropriate health decisions (e.g., being able to correctly interpret a prescription label). Health literacy is different than simply being able to read or being well educated. Low health literacy is common in the elderly, minority populations, those with lower income, poor health, and limited English proficiency, but it can be an issue for any patient. A person's health literacy is dependent on age, communication skills, knowledge, experience and culture. Low health literacy is linked to poor health outcomes.

EFFECTIVE COMMUNICATION AND EDUCATION STRATEGIES

- Approach all patients as if they may not understand the health information presented. Do not assume that it is easy to tell who has low health literacy.

- Use non-medical language ("layman's" language) that patients can understand (see the Drug Formulations and Patient Counseling chapter for more details). Example: say "tired" instead of "fatigued" or "high blood pressure" instead of "hypertension."

- Ask open-ended questions that require more than a "yes" or "no" answer. Example: "what questions can I answer about your medication today?" instead of "do you have questions?"

- Avoid leading questions. Example: "what about your high blood pressure concerns you?" instead of "are you concerned about the side effects from the high blood pressure medication?"

- Confirm understanding. Ask the patient to repeat the information or ask what they would tell their spouse or friend about the new medication.

- Use different communication strategies (verbal, written, visual aids) to enhance understanding. Ask the patient how he/she prefers to receive the information.

- Use active listening. Clarifying or summarizing what the patient has said is helpful and gives the patient an opportunity to offer correction.

- Speak clearly, make eye contact, introduce yourself and refer to patients by their name. Avoid "sweetie," "dear" and other similar terms.

EXAMPLE ELECTRONIC HEALTH RECORD SOAP NOTE

JB (MRN: JB747114): SOAP Note for 9/25
Age: 40 years
Allergies: NKDA

VS

Height:	Weight:	BMI	Blood Pressure	Pulse	Resp Rate	Oral Temp:
67 in	88.6 kg	30.5 kg/m²	154/92 mmHg	80 bpm	12 rpm	36.6 °C

CC | "I feel limp."

S | JB is a 40 y/o female who presents with a 3-month history of increasing fatigue. She first noticed that she felt tired when working long hours at work but has been working her usual 8 hours a day for the past 2 months and has not regained her energy. She described her fatigue as "feeling limp." It is present throughout the day and is worse with significant exertion (e.g., walking > 3-4 blocks or going up stairs). She has tried sleeping up to 10 hours/night (increased from 8 hours/night), and it has not helped. She is concerned that there is something seriously wrong, as she is usually full of energy and her family and friends are starting to ask if she is sick. She has not been able to exercise, which she usually enjoys. She has gained about 2.7-3.2 kgs in the last few months, which she attributes to inactivity due to fatigue. Her husband states that she has "always" snored quite loudly. Her menses are regular on timing, heavy flow for 1-2 days, then lighter for another 2-3 days. The pattern is unchanged from before the onset of her fatigue. Her last menstrual period was one week ago.

Denies: chest pain, shortness of breath, abdominal pain, N/V/D, changes in her stool, fever, chills, night sweats and changes in mood.

She reports a history of GERD, HTN, heart murmur and depression. She states that she takes her medications regularly "except the one for her blood pressure because she doesn't feel like her pressure is high."

Her reported medications include *Pepcid AC* 10 mg PO BID, chlorthalidone 25 mg PO Daily, *Zoloft* 100 mg Daily and *Caltrate + D* 600 mg BID.

O | Well-appearing Black female in no acute distress.

SKIN: not pale, no rashes

NECK: no thyromegaly or thyroid nodules

NODES: no cervical, axillary or inguinal lymphadenopathy

CHEST: clear to auscultation and percussion bilaterally

CV: RRR, 2/6 systolic ejection murmur heard best at the LLSB that radiates to the apex, no S3 or S4

ABD: normal active bowel sounds, no hepatosplenomegaly by palpation or percussion, no abdominal tenderness

EXT: no edema, pulses normal

A | Recent onset of fatigue with no obvious inciting event. Hypothyroidism is possible given her weight gain, though this may have occurred from her inactivity. Anemia is possible, though her menstrual periods have not lengthened or increased, and there are no other apparent sources of blood loss. A recent menses makes pregnancy unlikely. Given her history of snoring, sleep apnea is possible, but her history of snoring over many years is not entirely consistent with her more recent onset of fatigue. She does not seem to have a recurrence of her depression since she has no new symptoms. She does not have symptoms of infection, nor has her murmur changed, so subacute bacterial endocarditis is unlikely. BP is elevated, and she has been noncompliant with prescribed therapy for HTN.

P | #1. Check TSH to rule out hypothyroidism

#2. Check CBC to rule out anemia

#3. If the above are unremarkable, consider a sleep study to rule out sleep apnea

#4. Pharmacy consult for medication adherence

#5. Follow-up visit in 1 week to discuss test results and further workup

---

Select Guidelines/References

American Society of Health-System Pharmacists. ASHP Guidelines on Pharmacist-Conducted Patient Education and Counseling. *Am J Health-Syst Pharm.* 1997;54:431-4.

Office of Disease Prevention and Health Promotion. Health Literacy and Communication at http://health.gov/communication/ (accessed 2022 January 4).

Image credit, middle of page 110: 📷 *iStock.com/AndrewScherbackov*

CALCULATIONS

CONTENTS

This chapter covers basic math concepts that must be mastered for NAPLEX. These topics may be a review for some, but they are the foundation for solving more complex problems.

CONTENT LEGEND

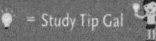

 = Study Tip Gal   = Key Drug Guy

CHAPTER 9

CALCULATIONS I: MATH BASICS

EQUIVALENT MEASUREMENTS

Drugs can be measured in different ways:

- Weights [grams (g), milligrams (mg), micrograms (mcg), nanograms (ng)].

- Liquid volumes [liters (L), milliliters (mL)].

- Percentage strengths (g in 100 mL, g in 100 g, or mL in 100 mL).

- Concentrations of a given amount of a drug in a given volume of liquid (mcg/mL or mg/L). Very small amounts are measured in ng/mL. BUN and serum creatinine concentrations are measured in mg/dL (one liter is 10 dL).

- Concentrations using milliequivalents (mEq) per liter (mEq/L) (e.g., lithium and common electrolytes).

Common conversions must be known for the exam (see Study Tip Gal on the next page); they may or may not be provided. Actual or approximate conversions can be used if a specific conversion is not provided in the question. The rounding instructions provided on the exam questions will account for any differences in using actual vs. approximate conversions. If a specific conversion is provided in the question, always use it (see problem #2).

1. **A prescription reads: "take 2 tsp PO Q6H x 7 days." How many milliliters must be dispensed to complete 7 days of therapy?**

$$2 \text{ tsp } \times \frac{5 \text{ mL}}{1 \text{ tsp}} = 10 \text{ mL per dose}$$

$$\frac{10 \text{ mL}}{\text{dose}} \times \frac{4 \text{ doses}}{\text{day}} \times 7 \text{ days } = 280 \text{ mL}$$

2. **If 1 ounce = 30 mL, how many milliliters of sterile water will remain after 50 mL are used from a 16 ounce bottle?**

$$16 \text{ oz} \times \frac{30 \text{ mL}}{1 \text{ oz}} = 480 \text{ mL bottle of sterile water}$$

480 mL – 50 mL = 430 mL of sterile water will remain

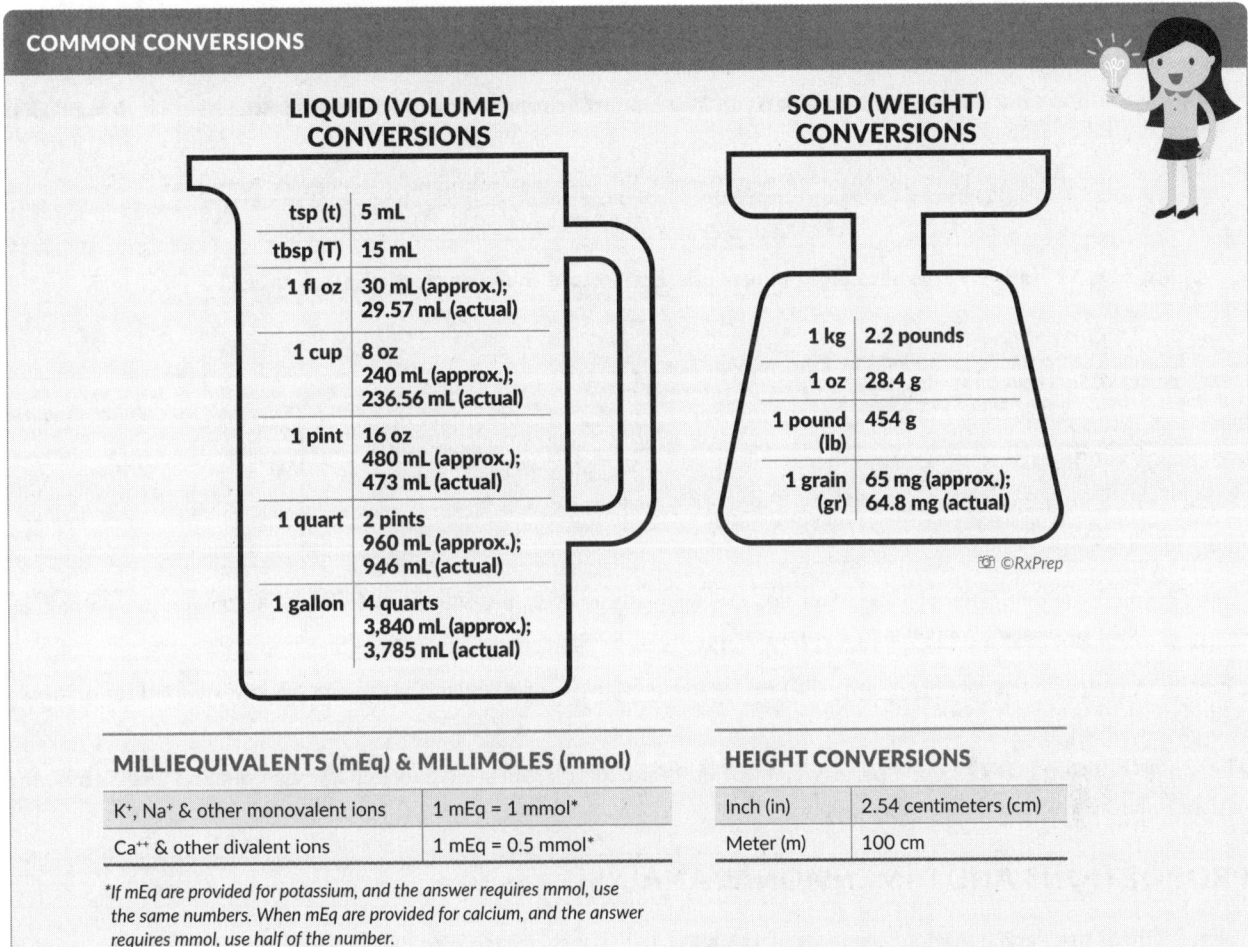

COMMON CONVERSIONS

LIQUID (VOLUME) CONVERSIONS

tsp (t)	5 mL
tbsp (T)	15 mL
1 fl oz	30 mL (approx.); 29.57 mL (actual)
1 cup	8 oz 240 mL (approx.); 236.56 mL (actual)
1 pint	16 oz 480 mL (approx.); 473 mL (actual)
1 quart	2 pints 960 mL (approx.); 946 mL (actual)
1 gallon	4 quarts 3,840 mL (approx.); 3,785 mL (actual)

SOLID (WEIGHT) CONVERSIONS

1 kg	2.2 pounds
1 oz	28.4 g
1 pound (lb)	454 g
1 grain (gr)	65 mg (approx.); 64.8 mg (actual)

©RxPrep

MILLIEQUIVALENTS (mEq) & MILLIMOLES (mmol)

K⁺, Na⁺ & other monovalent ions	1 mEq = 1 mmol*
Ca⁺⁺ & other divalent ions	1 mEq = 0.5 mmol*

HEIGHT CONVERSIONS

Inch (in)	2.54 centimeters (cm)
Meter (m)	100 cm

If mEq are provided for potassium, and the answer requires mmol, use the same numbers. When mEq are provided for calcium, and the answer requires mmol, use half of the number.

ROUNDING

Rounding correctly is very important on NAPLEX (see Study Tip Gal to the right). The majority of problems that require rounding will specify to round to the nearest whole number.

3. **A pediatric patient is receiving 5.25 mL of drug every 4 hours. How many milliliters will be required for the entire day? Round to the nearest whole number.**

5.25 mL (per dose) x 6 times/day = 31.5 mL
Round to the nearest whole number = 32 mL

HOW TO ROUND ON THE EXAM

- Underline the number to the right of what is being rounded. If rounding to the nearest whole number, underline the 4 in this example: 347.4̲8
- Look at the number that is underlined and apply one of these rules:
  - If the underlined number is 5, 6, 7, 8, or 9, round up.
  - If the underlined number is 0, 1, 2, 3, or 4, round down.
- 347.48 rounded to the nearest whole number is 347.

Never round until the last step in the calculation.*

Round only once on the last step; use the calculator's memory or parentheses function on the exam for the intermediate steps. In the RxPrep course book, some intermediate steps (that do not affect the final answer) have been rounded for simplicity and space.

4. A patient requires 410.9 mg of a drug daily. The daily dose will be divided for BID administration. How many milligrams will the patient receive BID? Round to the nearest whole number.

> 410.9 mg daily/2 times per day = 205.45 mg BID
> Round to the nearest whole number = 205 mg BID

What if the problem said "round to the nearest tenth?" The correct answer would then be 205.5 mg. Rounding to the nearest tenth is the same as rounding to one decimal place.

5. Enoxaparin 56.5 mg was ordered for a patient. The hospital rounds enoxaparin doses to the nearest 10 mg. What dose should be dispensed?

Correct answer: 60 mg. Rounding to the nearest 10 mg is different than rounding to the nearest tenth.

6. A patient is 5'2" tall. What is her height in centimeters? Round to the nearest whole number.

> 5 feet x 12 inches / 1 foot = 60 inches + 2 inches = 62 inches

> 62 inches x 2.54 cm / 1 inch = 157.48 cm
> Round to the nearest whole number = 157 cm

Watch for products that cannot be split. You cannot dispense part of an insulin vial or part of a *Byetta* pen to a patient, so rounding to the nearest vial or pen would be required.

Example: A patient takes *Novolog* 16 units TID before meals. How many vials of *Novolog* should be dispensed for a 30-day supply?

Answer: The patient takes 48 units per day or 1,440 units per month. Since each vial of *Novolog* contains 1,000 units, the patient requires two vials for a 30-day supply.

PROPORTIONS AND DIMENSIONAL ANALYSIS

These methods are very important for most of the math that pharmacists do routinely. Pharmacists tend to either love dimensional analysis, or they prefer to do individual proportion calculations (or a combination of the two). When performed correctly, both methods provide the same answer. Pick the method that works best for you.

PROPORTIONS

Proportions are two fractions (ratios) that are set equal to each other. One variable is unknown and labeled "X." When setting up proportions, make sure that the units for the numerators match to each other and the units for the denominators match to each other or make sure the items in the left fraction match and the items in the right fraction match (see Study Tip Gal and problem #7 for an example).

DIMENSIONAL ANALYSIS

Dimensional analysis allows multiple proportion calculations to be completed quickly. Diagonal units that are the same can be crossed out ("canceled out"), leaving the desired units. The numbers can be plugged into the calculator exactly as written.

SETTING UP PROPORTIONS

Two methods of matching:

Match both numerators and both denominators: Every item in the left numerator (drug, route, units) must match to every item in the right numerator (except the values of the numbers).

Every item in the left denominator must match to every item in the right denominator (except the values of the numbers).

Match numerator and denominator of each fraction: Items in the left fraction (numerator and denominator) must match, and items in the right fraction (numerator and denominator) must match (except the value of the numbers).

Carefully review problem #7 to see how both methods provide the same answer.

7. **A patient weighs 176 pounds. What is the patient's weight in kilograms?**

Method 1: Proportion. Solve for X by multiplying diagonally and then dividing. Set up in either of the two ways shown.

Method 2: Dimensional analysis. Cancel out the same units diagonally, leaving the desired units.

$$\frac{176 \text{ lbs}}{X \text{ kg}} = \frac{2.2 \text{ lbs}}{1 \text{ kg}} \quad X = 80 \text{ kg}$$

$$176 \text{ lbs} \times \frac{1 \text{ kg}}{2.2 \text{ lbs}} = 80 \text{ kg}$$

or

$$\frac{176 \text{ lbs}}{2.2 \text{ lbs}} = \frac{X \text{ kg}}{1 \text{ kg}} \quad X = 80 \text{ kg}$$

Notice that there is an equal sign (=) between the fractions in a proportion and a multiplication symbol (x) between the fractions in dimensional analysis.

CONVERTING COMMON UNITS

LARGER → SMALLER VOLUME

Liters (L) → milliliters (mL)

8. **How many milliliters are in 5 liters?**

Method 1: Proportion

$$\frac{5 \text{ L}}{X \text{ mL}} = \frac{1 \text{ L}}{1,000 \text{ mL}} \quad X = 5,000 \text{ mL}$$

or

Method 2: Dimensional analysis

$$5 \text{ L} \times \frac{1,000 \text{ mL}}{1 \text{ L}} = 5,000 \text{ mL}$$

SMALLER → LARGER VOLUME

Milliliters (mL) → liters (L)

9. **Convert 5,000 mL to liters.**

$$5,000 \text{ mL} \times \frac{1 \text{ L}}{1,000 \text{ mL}} = 5 \text{ L}$$

LARGER → SMALLER WEIGHT

Kilograms (kg) → grams (g) → milligrams (mg) → micrograms (mcg) → nanograms (ng)

10. **How many nanograms are equal to 5 kg?**

This example requires 4 separate proportions or dimensional analysis (shown).

$$5 \text{ kg} \times \frac{1,000 \text{ g}}{1 \text{ kg}} \times \frac{1,000 \text{ mg}}{1 \text{ g}} \times \frac{1,000 \text{ mcg}}{1 \text{ mg}} \times \frac{1,000 \text{ ng}}{1 \text{ mcg}} = 5 \text{ trillion ng (or } 5 \times 10^{12} \text{ ng)}$$

SMALLER → LARGER WEIGHT

Nanograms (ng) → micrograms (mcg) → milligrams (mg) → grams (g) → kilograms (kg)

11. **How many grams are equal to 50,000,000 nanograms?**

$$50,000,000 \text{ ng} \times \frac{1 \text{ mcg}}{1,000 \text{ ng}} \times \frac{1 \text{ mg}}{1,000 \text{ mcg}} \times \frac{1 \text{ g}}{1,000 \text{ mg}} = 0.05 \text{ g}$$

When dimensional analysis is presented from this point forward, the strike through lines will be omitted for readability.

CALCULATIONS INVOLVING PRESCRIPTIONS

Interpretation of prescriptions, orders and compounding instructions will be necessary on the exam. Refer to Chapter 1 for common abbreviations used in prescriptions and medical charts.

12. **A pharmacist receives this prescription for hydrocodone/ acetaminophen. How many tablets should be dispensed?**

    A. 6 tablets

    B. 8 tablets

    C. 12 tablets

    D. 16 tablets

    E. 24 tablets

    The correct answer is (C). The dispense quantity is indicated and consistent with the "not to exceed" instructions.

John Smith, MD
123 Anywhere Street
Anytown, USA 00000
Phone: (555) 555-5555
DEA # AS1234563

Name Mary Smith   DOB May 15, XXXX
Address 177 Green Street   Date August 23, XXXX
Touch Rx symbol, color will disappear then reappear.

Rx Hydrocodone/Acetaminophen 5/325 mg #12
Sig: i-ii tabs PO q 4-6 hrs prn pain X 2 days. NTE 6/d.

SUBSTITUTION PERMISSABLE_____ DO NOT SUBSTITUTE _____

✔ DO NOT REFILL ___ REFILL ___ TIMES | SIGNATURE OF PRESCRIBER
John Smith

Prescription is void if more than one controlled substance is written per blank.
Security Features. Details on Back.

©RxPrep

13. **A pharmacist receives a prescription for "Vigamox 0.5%. Dispense 3 mL. 1 gtt tid ou x 7d." How many drops will the patient use per day?**

    A. 1 drop

    B. 2 drops

    C. 3 drops

    D. 6 drops

    E. 21 drops

    The correct answer is (D). Abbreviations commonly used on prescriptions must be known. Refer to the table of Common Medical Abbreviations in the quick guides at the front of the book.

14. **A 7-year-old male child (48 pounds) presents to the urgent care clinic with a fever of 102°F, and nausea/vomiting that started the previous day. He will receive an acetaminophen 5 grain suppository for the fever. A pharmacist receives a prescription for the suppository with the instructions: Use 1 PR Q4-6H PRN temperature > 102°F. How many milligrams per kilogram (mg/kg) will the child receive per dose? Round to the nearest whole number.**

$$5 \text{ grains} \times \frac{65 \text{ mg}}{1 \text{ grain}} = 325 \text{ mg per suppository}$$

$$48 \text{ lbs} \times \frac{1 \text{ kg}}{2.2 \text{ lbs}} = {\sim}21.8182 \text{ kg}$$

Note: if a proportion is used to solve the step above, the repeating decimals must be addressed. It is best to use the calculator's memory or parentheses function on the exam so that all decimals can be carried forward to the next step. Round only once on the last step.

$$325 \text{ mg}/21.8182 \text{ kg} = {\sim}14.896 \text{ mg/kg, round to } 15 \text{ mg/kg}$$

Try the problem again with the actual conversion (64.8 mg/grain). Notice that the answer will be the same.

15. **How many milliliters of *Mylanta* suspension are contained in each dose of the prescription below? Round to the nearest whole number.**

PRESCRIPTION	QUANTITY
Belladonna Tincture	10 mL
Phenobarbital	60 mL
Mylanta susp. qs. ad	120 mL
Sig. 5 mL BID	

The total prescription is 120 mL; 10 mL belladonna, 60 mL of phenobarbital, and that leaves 50 mL for the *Mylanta*.

$$\frac{50 \text{ mL } Mylanta}{120 \text{ mL total Rx}} = \frac{X \text{ mL } Mylanta}{5 \text{ mL total Rx dose}} \quad X = 2.08, \text{ or } 2 \text{ mL } Mylanta \text{ per dose}$$

16. **A pharmacist received this sulfamethoxazole/trimethoprim prescription and dispensed 3 oz to the patient. How many days of therapy will they be short? Use 30 mL for 1 fluid ounce.**

    A. 1
    B. 3
    C. 9
    D. 10
    E. 90

The correct answer is (A).

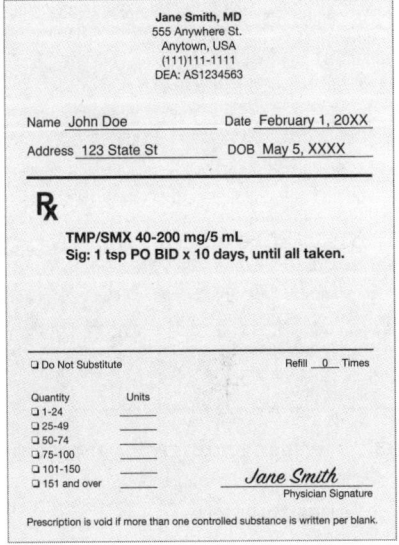

5 mL (per dose) x 2 times/day x 10 days = 100 mL

Quantity dispensed: 3 oz x 30 mL/oz = 90 mL dispensed

Difference: 100 mL – 90 mL = 10 mL, which is 1 day of therapy

A common mistake is selecting answer (D). Yes, the patient will be 10 mL short, but the question asked for "days of therapy." Each tsp (t) is 5 mL. The patient must take 2 tsp (t) daily (or 10 mL), so she is one day short for her prescribed course of therapy.

Jane Smith, MD
555 Anywhere St.
Anytown, USA
(111)111-1111
DEA: AS1234563

Name John Doe   Date February 1, 20XX
Address 123 State St   DOB May 5, XXXX

℞

TMP/SMX 40-200 mg/5 mL
Sig: 1 tsp PO BID x 10 days, until all taken.

❑ Do Not Substitute   Refill   0   Times

Quantity	Units
❑ 1-24	____
❑ 25-49	____
❑ 50-74	____
❑ 75-100	____
❑ 101-150	____
❑ 151 and over	____

Jane Smith
Physician Signature

Prescription is void if more than one controlled substance is written per blank.

©RxPrep

17. **A pharmacist has tablets that contain 0.25 mg of levothyroxine per tablet. The tablets will be crushed and mixed with glycerol and water to prepare a prescription for a child weighing 36 pounds. How many levothyroxine tablets will be needed to compound the following prescription?**

PRESCRIPTION	QUANTITY
Levothyroxine Liq.	0.1 mg/mL
Disp.	60 mL
Sig. 0.01 mg per kg PO BID	

$$60 \text{ mL total Rx} \times \frac{0.1 \text{ mg levo}}{\text{mL}} = 6 \text{ mg of levothyroxine needed}$$

$$6 \text{ mg levo} \times \frac{1 \text{ tab}}{0.25 \text{ mg levo}} = 24 \text{ tabs of levothyroxine needed}$$

The first step can also be performed as a proportion. <u>If the proportion is set up correctly, the answers will be the same.</u>

$$\frac{0.1 \text{ mg levo}}{1 \text{ mL}} = \frac{X \text{ mg levo}}{60 \text{ mL}} \quad X = 6 \text{ mg of levothyroxine needed}$$

$$6 \text{ mg levo} \times \frac{1 \text{ tab}}{0.25 \text{ mg levo}} = 24 \text{ tabs of levothyroxine needed}$$

Or, it can be solved by <u>dimensional analysis</u>:

$$\frac{1 \text{ tab levo}}{0.25 \text{ mg levo}} \times \frac{0.1 \text{ mg levo}}{\text{mL}} \times 60 \text{ mL total Rx} = 24 \text{ tabs of levothyroxine needed}$$

18. **How many milligrams of codeine will be contained in each capsule?**

PRESCRIPTION	QUANTITY
Codeine Sulfate	0.6 g
Guaifenesin	1.2 g
Caffeine	0.15 g
M. ft. caps. no. 24	
Sig. One capsule TID PRN cough	

Begin by converting to the units requested in the answer (mg).

$$0.6 \text{ g codeine} \times \frac{1,000 \text{ mg}}{1 \text{ g}} = 600 \text{ mg of codeine for the total prescription}$$

The prescription order is for 24 capsules.

$$\frac{600 \text{ mg codeine total}}{24 \text{ caps}} = 25 \text{ mg of codeine/capsule}$$

After solving the problem, read the question again to be certain the question was answered with the correct units (mg of codeine per capsule).

19. **How many grains of aspirin will be contained in each capsule? Round to the nearest tenth.**

PRESCRIPTION	QUANTITY
Aspirin	6 g
Phenacetin	3.2 g
Caffeine	0.48 g
M. ft. no. 20 caps	
Sig. One capsule Q6H PRN pain	

$$6 \text{ g aspirin} \times \frac{1{,}000 \text{ mg}}{1 \text{ g}} \times \frac{1 \text{ grain}}{65 \text{ mg}} = 92.3 \text{ grains}$$

We have 92.3 grains of aspirin that will be divided into 20 capsules.

$$\frac{92.3 \text{ grains}}{20 \text{ capsules}} = 4.6 \text{ grains/capsule}$$

After solving the problem, read the question again to be certain the question was answered with the correct units (grains per capsule).

---

20. **A 45 milliliter nasal spray delivers 20 sprays per milliliter of solution. Each spray contains 1.5 mg of active drug. How many milligrams of drug are contained in the 45 mL package?**

First calculate the amount of drug per mL.

$$\frac{1.5 \text{ mg drug}}{\text{spray}} \times \frac{20 \text{ sprays}}{\text{mL}} = 30 \text{ mg/mL}$$

Then solve for milligrams of drug in 45 mL.

$$\frac{30 \text{ mg}}{\text{mL}} = \frac{X \text{ mg}}{45 \text{ mL}} \quad X = 1{,}350 \text{ mg}$$

---

21. **A metered-dose inhaler provides 90 micrograms of albuterol sulfate with each inhalation. The canister provides 200 inhalations. If the patient uses the entire canister, how many total milligrams will the patient have received?**

$$200 \text{ inhalations} \times \frac{90 \text{ mcg}}{\text{inhalation}} \times \frac{1 \text{ mg}}{1{,}000 \text{ mcg}} = 18 \text{ mg}$$

22. Digoxin injection is supplied in ampules of 500 mcg per 2 mL. How many milliliters must a nurse administer to provide a dose of 0.2 mg?

Method 1: Two steps using a proportion.

First, convert micrograms to milligrams.

$$500 \text{ mcg} \times \frac{1 \text{ mg}}{1{,}000 \text{ mcg}} = 0.5 \text{ mg}$$

Then use a proportion to calculate the number of milliliters for a 0.2 mg dose.

$$\frac{0.5 \text{ mg digoxin}}{2 \text{ mL}} = \frac{0.2 \text{ mg digoxin}}{X \text{ mL}} \qquad X = 0.8 \text{ mL}$$

Method 2: Dimensional analysis.

$$0.2 \text{ mg} \times \frac{1{,}000 \text{ mcg}}{1 \text{ mg}} \times \frac{2 \text{ mL}}{500 \text{ mcg}} = 0.8 \text{ mL}$$

---

23. If one 10 mL vial contains 0.05 g of diltiazem, how many milliliters should be administered to provide a 25 mg dose of diltiazem?

Method 1: Two steps using a proportion.

First, convert grams to milligrams. It is usually best practice to convert to the units required for the answer when beginning the problem.

$$0.05 \text{ g diltiazem} \times \frac{1{,}000 \text{ mg}}{1 \text{ g}} = 50 \text{ mg}$$

Next, calculate the number of milliliters for a 25 mg dose.

$$\frac{50 \text{ mg}}{10 \text{ mL}} = \frac{25 \text{ mg}}{X \text{ mL}} \qquad X = 5 \text{ mL}$$

Method 2: Dimensional analysis.

$$25 \text{ mg dose} \times \frac{1 \text{ g}}{1{,}000 \text{ mg}} \times \frac{10 \text{ mL}}{0.05 \text{ g}} = 5 \text{ mL}$$

CONVERTING FROM ONE DRUG TO ANOTHER

Another common application for proportions is converting from one drug and dose to another drug and dose. Common conversions that pharmacists perform are shown (see Key Drugs Guy). These common drug-dose conversions can also be found on the RxPrep Required Formulas Sheet.

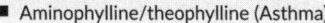

24. **The pharmacist is consulted to convert a patient from prednisone 10 mg PO BID to an equivalent dose of oral dexamethasone given once daily. What is the equivalent daily dose? Prednisone 5 mg = dexamethasone 0.75 mg.**

$$\frac{20 \text{ mg prednisone}}{X \text{ mg dexamethasone}} = \frac{5 \text{ mg prednisone}}{0.75 \text{ mg dexamethasone}} \qquad X = 3 \text{ mg of dexamethasone daily}$$

Notice that the numerators match each other (drug name and units) and the denominators match each other. For the exam, the equivalencies (e.g., prednisone 5 mg = dexamethasone 0.75 mg) must be memorized (see the Systemic Steroids & Autoimmune Conditions chapter for steroid equivalencies).

DRUG-DOSE CONVERSIONS

These drug-dose conversions must be known for the exam. The conversions are discussed in the disease state chapters noted.

- Aminophylline/theophylline (Asthma)
- Calcium salts (Osteoporosis, Menopause & Testosterone Use, Calculations IV)
- Insulin (Diabetes)
- Iron salts (Anemia)
- Lithium salts (Bipolar Disorder, Calculations II)
- Loop diuretics (Chronic Heart Failure)
- Opioids (Pain)
- Potassium chloride (Chronic Heart Failure, Calculations II)
- Statins (Dyslipidemia)
- Steroids (Systemic Steroids & Autoimmune Conditions)
- IV:PO conversions
  - ❑ Furosemide (Chronic Heart Failure)
  - ❑ Levothyroxine (Thyroid Disorders)
  - ❑ Metoprolol (Chronic Heart Failure)

RATIOS

A ratio is a comparison between two numbers. Ratios can be used to describe how ingredients should be mixed. If compounding instructions state "mix petrolatum and lanolin in a 3:1 ratio," it means 3 parts of petrolatum should be mixed with 1 part of lanolin. The pharmacist needs to know the weight of one part in order to calculate the weight of the other or the weight of the final mixture. The ratio is usually converted to a fraction (e.g., 3:1 = 3/1) for use in math.

25. **How many grams of bacitracin and nystatin are required to prepare 150 g of a 2:3 topical bacitracin:nystatin ointment?**

Since the total weight is provided (150 g) and the total number of parts can be calculated (2 parts + 3 parts = 5 total parts), the value of 1 part can be determined using a proportion.

$$\frac{5 \text{ total parts}}{150 \text{ g}} = \frac{1 \text{ part}}{X \text{ g}} \qquad X = 30 \text{ g per 1 part}$$

$$2 \text{ parts bacitracin} \times \frac{30 \text{ grams}}{1 \text{ part}} = 60 \text{ g bacitracin}$$

$$3 \text{ parts nystatin} \times \frac{30 \text{ grams}}{1 \text{ part}} = 90 \text{ g nystatin}$$

Add the weights to confirm that they match the total weight:

60 g bacitracin + 90 g nystatin = 150 g of 2:3 bacitracin:nystatin ointment

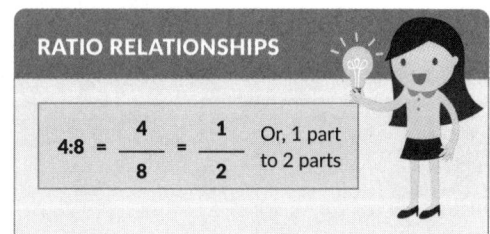

RATIO RELATIONSHIPS

$$4:8 = \frac{4}{8} = \frac{1}{2} \qquad \text{Or, 1 part to 2 parts}$$

CALCULATIONS

DECIMALS AND PERCENTAGE CONVERSION

To convert a <u>decimal to a percentage</u>, <u>multiply</u> the decimal by 100.

To convert a <u>percentage to a decimal</u>, <u>divide</u> the percentage by 100.

26. **HT is a 16-year-old female who complains of weakness, fatigue and heavy menstrual periods. She is diagnosed with anemia. HT takes ferrous sulfate 220 mg once daily. How many milligrams of elemental iron does HT receive from the supplement? Ferrous sulfate is 20% elemental iron.**

> Divide the percentage by 100: 20%/100 = 0.2

Multiply the total amount of ferrous sulfate by 0.2 to determine the amount of elemental iron in mg:

> 220 mg x 0.2 = 44 mg elemental iron

SQUARING A NUMBER

27. **Calculate 3.5^2.**

Either method will provide the answer:

Method 1: Multiply the number by itself:

> 3.5 x 3.5 = 12.25

Method 2: Use the x^2 key on the calculator:

1. Enter the number to square on the calculator: 3.5

2. Hit the x^2 key

3. This will provide the same answer: 12.25

EXPONENTS

28. **Calculate 2^4.**

1. Enter the first number (in this example, enter 2)

2. Hit the x^y key

3. Enter the exponent (in this example, enter 4)

4. This will provide the answer; in this example, the answer is 16

ORDER OF OPERATIONS

Math calculations that involve more than one function need to be completed in a specified order (see Study Tip Gal). The order is brackets (first), then parentheses, then exponents, then multiplication and division (left to right), then addition and subtraction (left to right). In fractions, the fraction bar is a grouping symbol; the entire numerator and the entire denominator are calculated before dividing the denominator into the numerator.

Phenytoin requires a specific formula to calculate the corrected drug level when the albumin is low (< 3.5 g/dL). Refer to the Seizures/Epilepsy chapter for additional discussion. The order of operations must be followed in order to get the correct result.

FOLLOW THE RULES OF MATH

Brackets → Parentheses (and other grouping symbols) → Exponents → Multiplication and Division → Addition and Subtraction

Remember: **B-PEMDAS**

Billy, **P**lease **E**at **M**om's **D**elicious **A**pple **S**trudel

---

29. **SJ is a female patient in the internal medicine unit receiving treatment following a motor vehicle accident. Her medications include lorazepam, morphine and phenytoin. Her serum albumin is 1.8 g/dL and her phenytoin level is 9.6 mcg/mL. Calculate SJ's corrected phenytoin level using the formula provided. Round to the nearest one decimal place.**

$$\text{Phenytoin corrected (mcg/mL)} = \frac{\text{Total phenytoin measured}}{(0.2 \times \text{albumin}) + 0.1} \quad \dagger$$

† *Use serum phenytoin in mcg/mL (same as mg/L) and albumin in g/dL (standard units in the U.S.) in the corrected phenytoin formula. The units are not intended to cancel out.*

$$\text{Phenytoin corrected} = \frac{9.6}{(0.2 \times 1.8) + 0.1} = \begin{array}{l}\sim 20.8696 \text{ mcg/mL} \\ \text{Round to the nearest one decimal place} = 20.9 \text{ mcg/mL}\end{array}$$

1. Do the math inside parentheses first: 0.2 x 1.8 = 0.36

2. Add 0.1 to the answer: 0.36 + 0.1 = 0.46

3. Divide 9.6 by the answer: 9.6 divided by 0.46 = 20.9 (per rounding instructions provided)

READY TO SUBMIT YOUR ANSWER?

Not so fast. Do a double check first!

Ask yourself these questions to avoid common mistakes:

- Does the answer match the question?
  - ❏ Re-read the question. Did you solve for the right thing? Remember, many problems on the exam require more than one step.
- Is the answer in the correct units? This is a common mistake. The problem may have been done correctly, but one more step is required to convert the answer to the specified units.
- Is the answer rounded correctly? The rounding instructions must be followed to get the problems right on the exam.
- Does the answer make sense?
  - ❏ If the problem asks how many liters of fluid a patient will receive in one day, 20,000 liters is unlikely to be the right answer. It does not make sense.

iStock.com/Gligatron

CHAPTER 10

CALCULATIONS II: COMPOUNDING

PERCENTAGE STRENGTH

Drug concentrations can be expressed in many ways, but they are a ratio of the amount of an ingredient to the total amount of the product. A percent is the number of parts in 100. Percents are often written as decimals or fractions (e.g., 25% = 0.25 = 25/100). The types of percentage concentrations are defined as follows:

- Percent weight-in-volume (% w/v) is expressed as g/100 mL (a solid mixed into a liquid). This applies to common IV fluids (see Study Tip Gal on the next page).

- Percent volume-in-volume (% v/v) is expressed as mL/100 mL (a liquid mixed into a liquid).

- Percent weight-in-weight (% w/w) is expressed as g/100 g (a solid mixed into a solid).

---

1. **How many grams of NaCl are in 1 liter of normal saline (NS)?**

    Normal saline contains 0.9 g NaCl per 100 mL of solution (see Study Tip Gal on the next page). Percentage strength problems are solved with simple proportions (reviewed in detail in Calculations I).

    $$\frac{0.9 \text{ g}}{100 \text{ mL}} = \frac{X \text{ g}}{1{,}000 \text{ mL}} \qquad X = 9 \text{ g}$$

 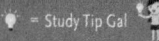

2. **How many grams of NaCl are in 500 mL of 1/2NS? Round to the nearest hundredth.**

   Since NS is 0.9% NaCl, 1/2NS is 0.45%.

   $$\frac{0.45 \text{ g}}{100 \text{ mL}} = \frac{X \text{ g}}{500 \text{ mL}} \qquad X = 2.25 \text{ g}$$

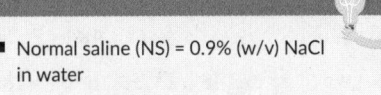

3. **How many grams of dextrose are in 250 mL of D5W? Round to the nearest tenth.**

   $$\frac{5 \text{ g}}{100 \text{ mL}} = \frac{X \text{ g}}{250 \text{ mL}} \qquad X = 12.5 \text{ g}$$

4. **How many milligrams of triamcinolone should be used in preparing the following prescription? Round to the nearest whole number.**

PRESCRIPTION	QUANTITY
Triamcinolone (w/v)	5%
Glycerin qs	60 mL
Sig. Two drops in right ear once daily	

   $$\frac{5 \text{ g}}{100 \text{ mL}} = \frac{X \text{ g}}{60 \text{ mL}} \qquad X = 3 \text{ g, or 3,000 mg}$$

5. **A prescription reads as follows: "Prepare a 3% w/w coal tar preparation; qs with petrolatum to 150 grams." How many grams of petrolatum are required to compound the prescription? Round to the nearest tenth.**

   $$\frac{3 \text{ g coal tar}}{100 \text{ g preparation}} = \frac{X \text{ g coal tar}}{150 \text{ g preparation}} \qquad X = 4.5 \text{ g coal tar}$$

   150 g (total weight of preparation) − 4.5 g (coal tar) = 145.5 g petrolatum

6. **A pharmacist is compounding a vancomycin oral suspension. The master formulation record says to reconstitute a 5 g vial of vancomycin powder for injection with 50 mL of sterile water, then dilute with sterile water to 200 mL. What is the final percentage strength of the compounded product (w/v)?**

   $$\frac{5 \text{ g}}{200 \text{ mL}} = \frac{X \text{ g}}{100 \text{ mL}} \qquad X = 2.5 \text{ g, which is 2.5\%}$$

7. **If 1,250 grams of a mixture contains 80 grams of a drug, what is the percentage strength (w/w) of the mixture? Round to the nearest tenth.**

   $$\frac{80 \text{ g}}{1,250 \text{ g}} = \frac{X \text{ g}}{100 \text{ g}} \qquad X = 6.4 \text{ g, which is 6.4\%}$$

8. **A mouth rinse contains 1/12% (w/v) of chlorhexidine gluconate. How many grams of chlorhexidine gluconate should be used to prepare 18 liters of mouth rinse? Round to the nearest whole number.**

First, convert 1/12% to a decimal. 1/12% = 0.083 g per 100 mL (w/v).

Next, convert L to mL. 18 L x 1,000 mL/L = 18,000 mL.

Then, solve for grams of chlorhexidine gluconate needed.

$$\frac{0.083 \text{ g}}{100 \text{ mL}} = \frac{X \text{ g}}{18{,}000 \text{ mL}} \qquad X = 14.94 \text{ g, rounded to 15 g}$$

9. **SS is a 79-year-old female with dry mouth and dry eyes from Sjögren's syndrome. She is picking up the prescription below. What is the maximum milligrams of pilocarpine she will receive per day?**

PRESCRIPTION	QUANTITY
Pilocarpine	1% (w/v)
Sodium chloride qs ad	15 mL
Sig: 2 gtts (0.05 mL/gtt) po TID prn up to 5 days for dry mouth	

First, calculate the amount of pilocarpine in the prescription.

$$\frac{1 \text{ g}}{100 \text{ mL}} = \frac{X \text{ g}}{15 \text{ mL}} \qquad X = 0.15 \text{ g}$$

Then, convert to mg since the problem asks for mg of pilocarpine.

$$0.15 \text{ g} \times \frac{1{,}000 \text{ mg}}{1 \text{ g}} = 150 \text{ mg of pilocarpine}$$

The patient will receive up to 3 doses per day (0.1 mL x 3 = 0.3 mL). Calculate the amount of pilocarpine in 0.3 mL.

$$\frac{150 \text{ mg pilocarpine}}{15 \text{ mL}} = \frac{X \text{ mg}}{0.3 \text{ mL}} \qquad X = 3 \text{ mg pilocarpine}$$

10. **A pharmacist dissolves 6 tablets. Each tablet contains 250 mg of metronidazole. The pharmacist will put the drug into a liquid base to prepare 60 mL of a topical solution. What is the percentage strength (w/v) of metronidazole in the prescription? Round to the nearest tenth.**

$$6 \text{ tablets} \times \frac{250 \text{ mg}}{1 \text{ tab}} = 1{,}500 \text{ mg, or 1.5 g metronidazole}$$

$$\frac{1.5 \text{ g}}{60 \text{ mL}} = \frac{X \text{ g}}{100 \text{ mL}} \qquad X = 2.5 \text{ g, which is 2.5\% w/v}$$

11. **If 12 grams of lanolin are combined with 2 grams of white wax and 36 grams of petrolatum to make an ointment, what is the percentage strength (w/w) of lanolin in the ointment?**

$$\frac{12 \text{ g lanolin}}{50 \text{ g ointment}} = \frac{X \text{ g}}{100 \text{ g}} \qquad X = 24\% \text{ w/w}$$

12. **A pharmacist adds 5.3 grams of hydrocortisone to 150 grams of a 2.5% hydrocortisone ointment. What is the percentage (w/w) of hydrocortisone in the finished product? Round to the nearest whole number.**

    First, determine the amount of hydrocortisone (HC) in the current product.

    $$\frac{2.5 \text{ g HC}}{100 \text{ g ointment}} = \frac{X \text{ g HC}}{150 \text{ g ointment}} \qquad X = 3.75 \text{ g HC}$$

    5.3 grams of HC is being added to the existing product, which contains 3.75 g of HC: 5.3 g + 3.75 g = 9.05 g.

    Next, find the percent concentration of the final product (5.3 g + 150 g = 155.3 g).

    $$\frac{9.05 \text{ g HC}}{155.3 \text{ g ointment}} = \frac{X \text{ g HC}}{100 \text{ g ointment}} \qquad X = 5.8274 \text{ g, rounded to 6\% w/w}$$

13. **How many milliliters of hydrocortisone liquid (40 mg/mL) will be needed to prepare 30 grams of a 0.25% cream (w/w)? Round to the nearest hundredth.**

    First, calculate the amount of hydrocortisone needed in the final product.

    $$\frac{0.25 \text{ g}}{100 \text{ g}} = \frac{X \text{ g}}{30 \text{ g}} \qquad X = 0.075 \text{ g or 75 mg}$$

    Then, solve for mL of hydrocortisone liquid needed.

    $$\frac{40 \text{ mg}}{\text{mL}} = \frac{75 \text{ mg}}{X \text{ mL}} \qquad X = 1.875 \text{ mL, rounded to 1.88 mL}$$

    After solving the problem, read the question again to be certain the question was answered with the correct units (mL).

14. **What is the percentage strength of imiquimod in the following prescription? Round to the nearest hundredth.**

PRESCRIPTION	QUANTITY
Imiquimod 5% cream	15 g
Xylocaine	20 g
Hydrophilic ointment	25 g

    First, calculate the amount of imiquimod (5%) in the prescription.

    $$\frac{5 \text{ g}}{100 \text{ g}} \times 15 \text{ g} = 0.75 \text{ grams of imiquimod}$$

    The total weight of the prescription is 60 g (15 g + 20 g + 25 g).

    $$\frac{0.75 \text{ g}}{60 \text{ g}} = \frac{X \text{ g}}{100 \text{ g}} \qquad X = 1.25 \text{ g, which is 1.25\% w/w}$$

RATIO STRENGTH

The concentration of a weak solution can be expressed as a ratio strength. It is denoted as <u>one unit of solute</u> contained <u>in the total amount</u> of the solution or mixture (e.g., 1:500). Ratio strength is another way of presenting a percentage strength. This makes sense because percentages are ratios of parts per hundred.

In clinical practice, ratio strengths have been associated with medication errors. The FDA now requires removal of ratio strengths from the labeling of injectable drug products with only one active ingredient (e.g., epinephrine, isoproterenol). Ratio strength is still commonly used in compounding.

15. **Express 0.04% as a ratio strength.**

$$\frac{0.04}{100} = \frac{1 \text{ part}}{X \text{ parts}} \quad X = 2{,}500. \text{ Ratio strength is } 1{:}2{,}500$$

Convert back to 0.04% by taking 1/2,500 x 100 or simply 100/2,500. Try it.

On the exam there will be instructions for how to enter your answer. Usually you will enter the numbers after the colon in the ratio strength (e.g., for this problem, you would enter 2500). The instructions could read "Calculate the ratio strength. Enter only the numbers after the colon, as shown here with Xs: 1:XXX."

16. **Express 1:4,000 as a percentage strength.**

$$\frac{1 \text{ part}}{4{,}000 \text{ parts}} = \frac{X}{100} \quad X = 0.025, \text{ which is } 0.025\%$$

Problem #16 can be done using the shortcut in the box above for converting between ratio and percentage strength:

Percentage strength = 100 / 4,000 = 0.025%

17. **There are 50 mg of drug in 50 mL of solution. Express the concentration as a ratio strength.**

First, convert 50 mg to grams. 50 mg x 1 g/1,000 mg = 0.05 g

Then, calculate grams per 100 mL.

$$\frac{0.05 \text{ g}}{50 \text{ mL}} = \frac{X \text{ g}}{100 \text{ mL}} \quad X = 0.1 \text{ g}$$

Now solve for ratio strength.

$$\frac{0.1 \text{ g}}{100 \text{ mL}} = \frac{1 \text{ part}}{X \text{ parts}} \quad X = 1{,}000, \text{ or } 1{:}1{,}000$$

18. How many milligrams of iodine should be used in compounding the following prescription?

ITEM	QUANTITY
Iodine	1:400
Hydrophilic ointment qs ad	10 g
Sig. Apply as directed.	

First, convert the ratio strength to a percentage strength.

$$\frac{1 \text{ part}}{400 \text{ parts}} = \frac{X \text{ g}}{100 \text{ g}} \quad X = 0.25\% \text{ w/w}$$

Then, determine how much iodine will be needed for the prescription.

$$\frac{0.25 \text{ g}}{100 \text{ g}} = \frac{X \text{ g}}{10 \text{ g}} \quad X = 0.025 \text{ g, or 25 mg}$$

Or, solve another way:

1:400 means 1 g in 400 g of ointment.

$$\frac{1 \text{ g}}{400 \text{ g}} = \frac{X \text{ g}}{10 \text{ g}} \quad X = 0.025 \text{ g, or 25 mg}$$

19. A 10 mL mixture contains 0.25 mL of active drug. Express the concentration as a percentage strength (v/v) and a ratio strength.

First, find out how much drug is in 100 mL.

$$\frac{0.25 \text{ mL drug}}{10 \text{ mL}} = \frac{X \text{ mL drug}}{100 \text{ mL}} \quad X = 2.5 \text{ mL, or 2.5\% (v/v)}$$

Now solve for ratio strength.

$$\frac{2.5 \text{ mL drug}}{100 \text{ mL}} = \frac{1 \text{ part}}{X \text{ parts}} \quad X = 40; \text{ or 1:40}$$

20. What is the concentration, in ratio strength, of a trituration made by combining 150 mg of albuterol sulfate and 4.05 grams of lactose?

First, add up the total weight of the prescription.

$$0.150 \text{ g} + 4.05 \text{ g} = 4.2 \text{ g}$$

Now solve for ratio strength.

$$\frac{0.150 \text{ g}}{4.2 \text{ g}} = \frac{1 \text{ part}}{X \text{ parts}} \quad X = 28, \text{ or 1:28}$$

Refer to the Compounding chapters for discussion of trituration and other compounding terminology.

PARTS PER MILLION

Parts per million (PPM) and parts per billion (PPB) are used to express the strength of very dilute solutions. They are defined as the number of parts of the drug per 1 million (or 1 billion) parts of the whole. The same designations are used as for percentage strength (% w/w, % w/v and % v/v).

SHORTCUT FOR PARTS PER MILLION

- PPM → Percentage strength
  - ☐ Move the decimal left 4 places
- Percentage strength → PPM
  - ☐ Move the decimal right 4 places

21. Express 0.00022% (w/v) as PPM. Round to the nearest tenth.

$$\frac{0.00022\ g}{100\ mL} = \frac{X\ parts}{1,000,000} \quad X = 2.2\ PPM$$

22. Express 30 PPM of copper in solution as a percentage.

$$\frac{30\ parts}{1,000,000} = \frac{X\ g}{100\ mL} \quad X = 0.003\%$$

23. Express 5 PPM of iron in water as a percentage.

$$\frac{5\ parts}{1,000,000} = \frac{X\ g}{100\ mL} \quad X = 0.0005\%$$

24. A patient's blood contains 0.085 PPM of selenium. How many micrograms of selenium does the patient's blood contain if the blood volume is 6 liters?

$$\frac{0.085\ parts}{1,000,000} = \frac{X\ g}{6,000\ mL} \quad X = 0.00051\ g,\ or\ 510\ mcg$$

25. A sample of an intravenous solution is found to contain 0.4 PPM of DEHP. How much of the solution, in milliliters, will contain 50 micrograms of DEHP?

$$\frac{0.4\ parts}{1,000,000} = \frac{0.00005\ g}{X\ mL} \quad X = 125\ mL$$

If asked to express something in PPB (parts per billion), divide by 1,000,000,000 (9 zeros).

SPECIFIC GRAVITY

Specific gravity (SG) is the ratio of the density of a substance to the density of water. SG can be important for calculating doses of IV medications, in compounding and in interpreting a urinalysis. Water has a specific gravity of 1; 1 g water = 1 mL water. Substances with a SG < 1 are lighter than water and those with SG > 1 are heavier than water.

$$SG = \frac{\text{weight of substance (g)}}{\text{weight of equal volume of water (g)}} \quad \text{or more simply:} \quad SG = \frac{g}{mL}$$

26. **What is the specific gravity of 150 mL of glycerin weighing 165 grams? Round to the nearest tenth.**

$$SG = \frac{165\ g}{150\ mL} \qquad SG = 1.1$$

Check the answer: 150 mL x 1.1 = 165 g

27. **What is the weight of 750 mL of concentrated acetic acid (SG = 1.2)?**

$$1.2 = \frac{X\ g}{750\ mL} \qquad X = 900\ g$$

Check the answer: 900 g/750 mL = 1.2

28. **How many milliliters of polysorbate 80 (SG = 1.08) are needed to prepare a prescription that includes 48 grams of the surfactant/emulsifier (polysorbate)? Round to the nearest hundredth.**

$$1.08 = \frac{48\ g}{X\ mL} \qquad X = 44.44\ mL$$

29. **What is the specific gravity of 30 mL of a liquid weighing 23,400 milligrams? Round to the nearest hundredth.**

$$SG = \frac{23.4\ g}{30\ mL} \qquad SG = 0.78$$

30. **What is the weight of 0.5 L of polyethylene glycol 400 (SG = 1.13)?**

$$1.13 = \frac{X\ g}{500\ mL} \qquad X = 565\ grams$$

31. **Nitroglycerin has a specific gravity of 1.59. How much would 1 quart weigh in grams? Use 1 quart = 946 mL. Round to the nearest whole number.**

$$1.59 = \frac{X\ g}{946\ mL} \qquad X = 1,504\ g$$

Check the answer: 1,504 g/946 mL = 1.59

Note that the SG is equivalent to the density in g/mL (with units). If asked for the density in the above problem, the answer would be 1.59 g/mL.

DILUTION AND CONCENTRATION

Q1C1

This formula can be used to change the strength or quantity. Q1C1 is used when the problem deals with two concentrations. Be careful: the units on each side must match and one or more may need to be changed, such as mg to gram, or vice-versa.

> Q1 x C1 = Q2 x C2
>
> Q1 = old quantity   Q2 = new quantity
>
> C1 = old concentration   C2 = new concentration

0% AND 100%

If the prescription calls for an ingredient that is pure, the concentration is 100%.

A diluent (e.g., petrolatum, lanolin, alcohol, ointment base, inert base, lactose, *Aquaphor*) does not contain any drug – the concentration of the diluent is 0%.

32. **A pharmacist has an order for parenteral nutrition that includes 550 mL of D70%. The pharmacist checks the supplies and finds the closest strength he has available is D50%. How many milliliters of D50% will provide an equivalent energy requirement?**

> 550 mL x 70% = Q2 x 50%

> Q2 = 770 mL of D50%

33. **How many grams of petrolatum (diluent) should be added to 250 grams of a 20% ichthammol ointment to make a 7% ichthammol ointment? Round to the nearest tenth.**

Note the difference from the previous problem. In this example, the problem asks how much diluent should be added to make the final weight.

> 250 g x 20% = Q2 x 7%

> Q2 = 714.3 g of 7% ichthammol ointment

Read the question again to be certain about what is being asked. Since the question did not ask how much of the 7% ointment can be prepared, but rather how much diluent is required, an additional step is needed:

> 714.3 g total weight – 250 g (already present) = 464.3 g petrolatum required

34. **A patient has been receiving 200 mL of an enteral mixture that contains 432 mOsm/L. The pharmacist will reduce the contents to 278 mOsm/L. How many milliliters of bacteriostatic water should be added to the bag? Round to the nearest mL.**

> 200 mL x 432 mOsm/L = Q2 x 278 mOsm/L   X = 311 mL

> Q2 = 311 mL of the 278 mOsm/L enteral mixture can be prepared

There are 200 mL in the original bag. The final volume will be 311 mL.

> 311 mL – 200 mL = 111 mL of bacteriostatic water

35. If 1 gallon of a 20% (w/v) solution is evaporated to a solution with a 50% (w/v) strength, what will be the new volume (in milliliters)? Round to the nearest 100 mL.

3,785 mL x 20% = Q2 x 50%

Q2 = 1,514 mL, rounded to the nearest 100 mL = 1,500 mL

This answer will be the same regardless of which conversion is used for gallon to mL.

36. Using 20 grams of a 9% boric acid ointment base, the pharmacist will manufacture a 5% ointment. How much diluent is required?

20 g x 9% = Q2 x 5%

Q2 = 36 g of the 5% ointment can be prepared

36 g total weight − 20 g (already present) = 16 g diluent required

ALLIGATION

Alligation is used to obtain a new strength (percentage) that is between two strengths the pharmacist has in stock. It is used when the problem deals with <u>three concentrations</u>.

37. A pharmacist is asked to prepare 80 grams of a 12.5% ichthammol ointment with 16% and 12% ichthammol ointments that she has in stock. How many grams of the 16% and 12% ointment are required?

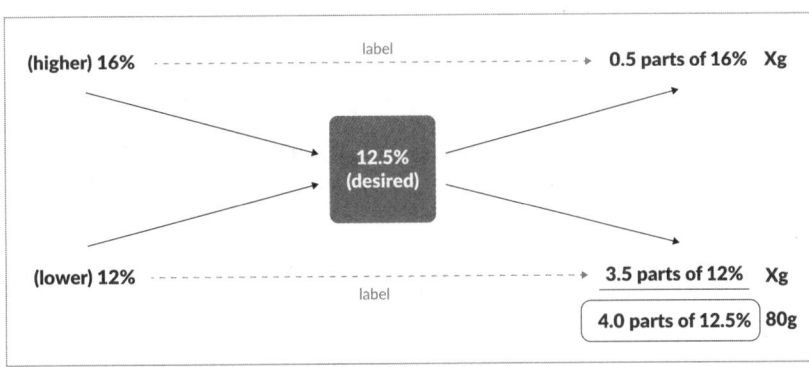

Setting Up An Alligation

- High goes high: write the higher concentration at the top left.
- Low goes low: write the lower concentration on the lower left.
- Write the desired concentration in the middle.
- Subtract diagonally along the X lines to obtain the number of parts. Write the absolute number (no negative sign) on the right side of the X.
  - ❑ 16% − 12.5% = 3.5 parts
  - ❑ 12% − 12.5% = 0.5 parts
- Label horizontally along the dashed lines; the starting concentrations are carried across.
- For some problems, it will be necessary to add up the total number of parts (as shown).

Divide the total weight (80 g) by the number of parts to get the weight per part.

$$\frac{80\ g}{4\ parts} = 20\ grams\ per\ part$$

Take the amount per part (20 g) and multiply it by the parts from each of the concentrations (from the high, and from the low).

$$0.5\ parts\ of\ 16\%\ \ x\ \ \frac{20\ g}{part} = 10\ g\ of\ the\ 16\%\ ichthammol\ ointment$$

$$3.5\ parts\ of\ 12\%\ \ x\ \ \frac{20\ g}{part} = 70\ g\ of\ the\ 12\%\ ichthammol\ ointment$$

When the two quantities are mixed together, the pharmacist will have 80 g of a 12.5% ichthammol ointment.

38. A pharmacist is asked to prepare 1 gallon of tincture containing 5.5% iodine. The pharmacy has 3% iodine tincture and 8.5% iodine tincture in stock. How many milliliters of the 3% and 8.5% iodine tincture should be used? (Use 1 gallon = 3,785 mL)

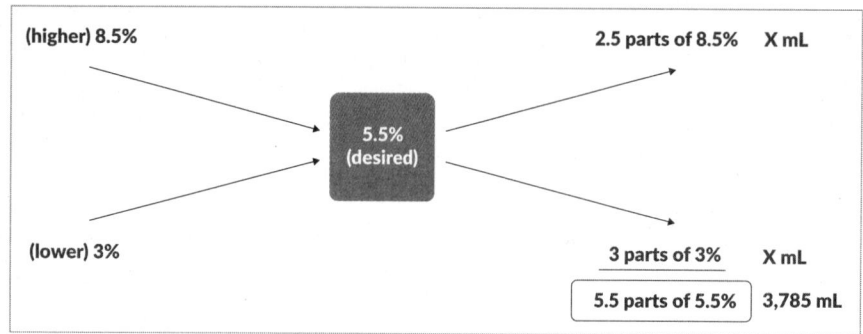

Divide the total volume (3,785 mL) by the number of parts to obtain the volume per part.

$$\frac{3{,}785 \text{ mL}}{5.5 \text{ parts}} = 688.2 \text{ mL per part}$$

$$2.5 \text{ parts} \times \frac{688.2 \text{ mL}}{\text{part}} = 1{,}720 \text{ mL of the 8.5\% iodine tincture}$$

$$3 \text{ parts} \times \frac{688.2 \text{ mL}}{\text{part}} = 2{,}065 \text{ mL of the 3\% iodine tincture}$$

The end product provides 3,785 mL of a 5.5% iodine tincture. Alligation can also be used when the final volume is not known, as shown in the next problem.

---

39. A hospice pharmacist receives a prescription for 1% morphine sulfate oral solution. She has a 120 mL bottle of morphine sulfate labeled 20 mg/5 mL and a 240 mL bottle of morphine sulfate labeled 100 mg/5 mL. How much of the 100 mg/5 mL product must be mixed with the contents of the 20 mg/5 mL morphine sulfate bottle to prepare the desired percentage strength for the patient?

First determine the percentage strengths of the two available products.

$$20 \text{ mg/5 mL} \quad \frac{0.02 \text{ g}}{5 \text{ mL}} = \frac{X \text{ g}}{100 \text{ mL}} \quad X = 0.4\% \qquad 100 \text{ mg/5 mL} \quad \frac{0.1 \text{ g}}{5 \text{ mL}} = \frac{X \text{ g}}{100 \text{ mL}} \quad X = 2\%$$

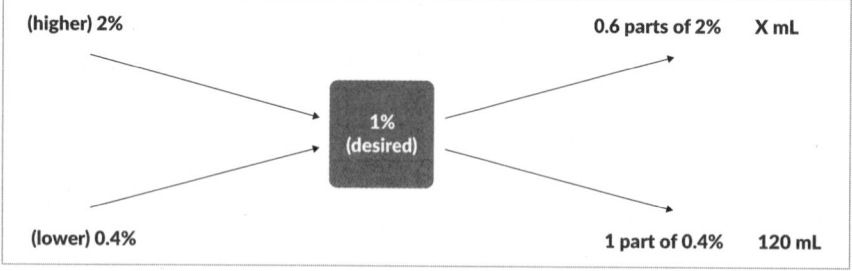

In this case, we do not know the final volume of the product, but we know the proper ratio of the parts (0.6:1).

$$\frac{1 \text{ part of 0.4\% morphine}}{0.6 \text{ parts of 2\% morphine}} = \frac{120 \text{ mL of 0.4\% morphine}}{X \text{ mL of 2\% morphine}} \quad X = 72 \text{ mL of 2\% morphine sulfate}$$

72 mL of 2% (100 mg/5 mL) morphine sulfate must be added to the 120 mL of 0.4% (20 mg/5 mL) morphine sulfate to get a 1% solution. Ultimately, 192 mL of 1% product can be prepared, but the alligation must be solved to determine that.

40. A pharmacist must prepare 100 grams of a 50% hydrocortisone powder using the 25% and 75% powders that she has in stock. How much of each is required?

Since the desired strength is exactly in the middle of the strengths available, divide the desired quantity in half:

100 g / 2 = 50 grams. Use 50 g of the 75% and 50 g of the 25% to prepare 100 g of a 50% powder.

DILUTION AND CONCENTRATION EXTRA CREDIT

How many milliliters of sargramostim 500 mcg/mL must be diluted with 250 mL of normal saline to prepare a concentration of 20 mcg/mL?

The final volume is not 250 mL. When the final volume is unknown, you cannot use simple Q1C1. Two methods to solve this problem are shown: the algebraic method (below) and alligation (below, right; which is set up like #39 with unknown final volume). Notice in the alligation, the normal saline is labeled "0 mcg/mL." It is serving as a diluent here. Normal saline contains 0 mcg/mL of sargramostim.

Q1C1 + Q2C2 = (Q1+Q2)(C3)

250 mL (0 mcg/mL) + X mL (500 mcg/mL) = (250 mL + X mL)(20 mcg/mL)

0 + 500X = 5,000 + 20X

480X = 5,000

X = 10.417 mL

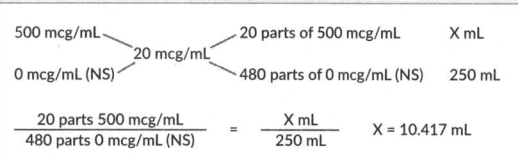

Solve in reverse to check yourself:

500 mcg/mL = X mcg/10.417 mL

X = 5,208.5 mcg

Total volume = 10.417 mL + 250 mL = 260.417 mL

5,208.5 mcg/260.417 mL = 20 mcg/mL final concentration

OSMOLARITY

The total number of particles in a given solution is directly proportional to its osmotic pressure. The particles are usually measured in milliosmoles. Osmolarity is the measure of total number of particles (or solutes) per liter of solution, defined as osmoles/liter (Osmol/L) or, more commonly as milliosmoles/liter (mOsmol/L). Solutes can be either <u>ionic</u> (such as NaCl, which <u>dissociates</u> into two solutes in solution, Na^+ and Cl^-) or <u>non-ionic</u> (which <u>do not dissociate</u>, such as glucose and urea).

Since the volume of water changes according to temperature, the term osmolality (mOsmol/kg) is used in clinical practice; it is independent of temperature. When solute concentrations are very low, osmolarity and osmolality are similar.

Milliosmole calculation problems differ from osmolarity calculation problems in that <u>osmolarity will always need to be normalized to a volume of 1 liter</u>. <u>Math problems</u> usually use <u>osmolarity</u>. The compounds and dissociation particles shown in the table should be known for the exam.

COMPOUND	# OF DISSOCIATION PARTICLES
Dextrose	1
Mannitol	
Potassium chloride (KCl)	2
Sodium chloride (NaCl)	
Sodium acetate ($NaC_2H_3O_2$)	
Magnesium sulfate ($MgSO_4$)	
Calcium chloride ($CaCl_2$)	3
Sodium citrate ($Na_3C_6H_5O_7$)	4

CALCULATIONS

$$mOsmol/L \ = \ \frac{Wt \ of \ substance \ (g/L)}{MW \ (g/mole)} \ \times \ (\# \ of \ particles) \ \times \ 1{,}000$$

Step 1. Add up the number of particles into which the compound dissociates.

Step 2. Calculate the number of grams of the compound present in 1 L.

Step 3. Use the molecular weight (MW) to solve the problem.

Milliosmole calculations do not normalize to 1 liter.

41. **What is the osmolarity, in mOsmol/L, of normal saline (0.9% NaCl)? MW = 58.5 g/mol. Round to the nearest whole number.**

NaCl dissociates into 2 particles; Na^+ and Cl^-.

Calculate the number of grams of the compound (NaCl) present in 1 L.

$$\frac{0.9 \ g}{100 \ mL} \ = \ \frac{X \ g}{1{,}000 \ mL} \qquad X = 9 \ g$$

Use the molecular weight to solve for mOsmol/L.

$$mOsmol/L \ = \ \frac{9 \ g/L}{58.5 \ g/mol} \ \times \ 2 \ \times \ 1{,}000 \ = \ 308 \ mOsmol/L$$

42. **What is the osmolarity, in mOsmol/L, of D5W? MW = 198 g/mol. Round to the nearest tenth.**

Dextrose does not dissociate and is counted as 1 particle.

$$\frac{5 \ g}{100 \ mL} \ = \ \frac{X \ g}{1{,}000 \ mL} \qquad X = 50 \ g$$

Use the molecular weight to solve for mOsmol/L.

$$mOsmol/L \ = \ \frac{50 \ g/L}{198 \ g/mol} \ \times \ 1 \ \times \ 1{,}000 \ = \ 252.5 \ mOsmol/L$$

43. **How many milliosmoles of $CaCl_2$ (MW = 111 g/mol) are represented in 150 mL of a 10% (w/v) calcium chloride solution? Round to the nearest whole number.**

$$\frac{10 \ g}{100 \ mL} \ = \ \frac{X \ g}{150 \ mL} \qquad X = 15 \ g$$

$$mOsmol \ = \ \frac{15 \ g}{111 \ g/mol} \ \times \ 3 \ \times \ 1{,}000 \ = \ 405 \ mOsmol$$

Note that the problem is asking for milliosmoles and not osmolarity. The answer is in milliosmoles and not mOsmol/L. It is not normalized to 1 liter.

44. **A solution contains 373 mg Na ions per liter. How many milliosmoles are represented in the solution? MW = 23 g/mol. Round to the nearest tenth.**

First, convert the units to match the formula.

$$\frac{373 \text{ mg Na}}{L} \times \frac{1 \text{ g}}{1,000 \text{ mg}} = 0.373 \text{ g/L}$$

$$mOsmol = \frac{0.373 \text{ g/L}}{23 \text{ g/mol}} \times 1 \times 1,000 = 16.2 \text{ mOsmol}$$

The problem asks for milliosmoles and not osmolarity. Since the problem provides the amount of Na ions in 1 liter, the numerical answer is the same (mOsmol or mOsmol/L).

45. **How many grams of potassium chloride are needed to make 200 mL of a solution containing 250 mOsmol/L? Round to the nearest hundredth. K (MW = 39 g/mol), Cl (MW = 35.5 g/mol)**

First calculate the MW of KCl.

MW of KCl = MW of K + MW of Cl = 39 + 35.5 = 74.5

$$250 \text{ mOsmol/L} = \frac{X}{74.5} \times 2 \times 1,000 \qquad X = 9.31 \text{ g/L}$$

$$\frac{9.31 \text{ g}}{1,000 \text{ mL}} = \frac{X \text{ g}}{200 \text{ mL}} \qquad X = 1.86 \text{ g}$$

You may be provided with the molecular weight on the exam or asked to calculate it.

46. **A solution contains 200 mg of Ca ions per liter. How many milliosmoles are represented in the solution? MW = 40 g/mol.**

$$mOsmol = \frac{0.2 \text{ g/L}}{40 \text{ g/mol}} \times 1 \times 1,000 = 5 \text{ mOsmol}$$

The problem is asking for milliosmoles and not osmolarity. The answer is in milliosmoles and not mOsmol/L. It is not normalized to 1 liter.

47. **Calculate the osmolar concentration, in milliosmoles, represented by 1 liter of a 10% (w/v) solution of anhydrous dextrose (MW = 180 g/mol) in water. Round to the nearest one decimal place.**

$$\frac{10 \text{ g}}{100 \text{ mL}} = \frac{X \text{ g}}{1,000 \text{ mL}} \qquad X = 100 \text{ g}$$

$$mOsmol = \frac{100 \text{ g/L}}{180 \text{ g/mol}} \times 1 \times 1,000 = 555.6 \text{ mOsmol}$$

The problem asks for milliosmoles and not osmolarity. Since the problem asks for mOsmol of dextrose in 1 liter, the numerical answer is the same (mOsmol or mOsmol/L).

CALCULATIONS

48. **A patient was ordered 1 liter of D5NS with 20 mEq of KCl for dehydration. How many milliosmoles are in 1 liter of this fluid (MW dextrose = 198 g/mol, Na = 23 g/mol, K = 39 g/mol, Cl = 35.5 g/mol)? Round to the nearest whole number.**

First, solve for the osmolarity of the dextrose component.

$$\frac{5 \text{ g Dextrose}}{100 \text{ mL}} \times \frac{X \text{ g}}{1{,}000 \text{ mL}} = 50 \text{ g/L}$$

$$mOsmol = \frac{50 \text{ g/L}}{198 \text{ g/mol}} \times 1 \times 1{,}000 = 252.5252 \text{ mOsmol/L}$$

Next, solve for the osmolarity of the NS component.

$$\frac{0.9 \text{ g NaCl}}{100 \text{ mL}} \times \frac{X \text{ g}}{1{,}000 \text{ mL}} = 9 \text{ g/L}$$

$$mOsmol = \frac{9 \text{ g/L}}{58.5 \text{ g/mol}} \times 2 \times 1{,}000 = 307.6922 \text{ mOsmol/L}$$

Then, solve for the osmolarity of the KCl component, using the milliequivalent formula (reviewed later in this chapter).

$$20 \text{ mEq} = \frac{X \text{ mg} \times 1}{74.5} = 1{,}490 \text{ mg} = 1.49 \text{ g}$$

$$mOsmol = \frac{1.49 \text{ g/L}}{74.5 \text{ g/mol}} \times 2 \times 1{,}000 = 40 \text{ mOsmol/L}$$

The final step is to add the three components together to find the total osmolarity.

$$252.5252 \text{ mOsmol/L dextrose} + 307.6922 \text{ mOsmol/L NaCl} + 40 \text{ mOsmol/L KCl} = 600.217 \text{ mOsmol/L, or } 600 \text{ mOsmol/L}$$

ISOTONICITY

When discussing osmotic pressure gradients between fluids, the term tonicity is used; solutions can be isotonic (osmolality is the same as blood, which is ~300 mOsmol/kg), hypotonic or hypertonic. When solutions are prepared, they need to match the tonicity of the body fluid as closely as possible. If the osmolality is higher in one cellular compartment, it will cause water to move from the lower to the higher concentration of solutes. If a parenteral nutrition (PN) solution is injected with a higher osmolality than blood, fluid will flow into the vein, resulting in edema, inflammation, phlebitis and possible thrombosis. Isotonicity is desired when preparing eye drops and nasal solutions.

Since isotonicity is related to the number of particles in solution, the dissociation factor (or ionization), symbolized by the letter i, is determined for the compound (drug). Non-ionic compounds do not dissociate and will have a dissociation factor, i, of one. The table shows the dissociation factors (i) based on the percentage that dissociates into ions; for example, a dissociation factor of 1.8 means that 80% of the compound will dissociate in a weak solution.

NUMBER OF DISSOCIATED IONS	DISSOCIATION FACTOR (OR IONIZATION) i
1	1
2	1.8
3	2.6
4	3.4
5	4.2

(+ 0.8 between each consecutive value)

As mentioned previously, <u>body fluids are isotonic</u>, having an <u>osmotic pressure equivalent to 0.9% sodium chloride</u>. When making a medication to place into a body fluid, the <u>drug provides solutes</u> to the solvent and needs to be accounted for in the prescription in order to avoid making the prescription hypertonic. The relationship between the amount of drug that produces a particular osmolarity and the amount of sodium chloride that produces the same osmolarity is called the <u>sodium chloride equivalent</u>, or "E value" for short. This is the formula for calculating the E value of a compound:

$$E = \frac{(58.5)(i)}{(MW\ of\ drug)(1.8)}$$

The "E value" formula takes into account the molecular weight of NaCl (58.5) and the <u>dissociation factor of 1.8 since normal saline is around 80% ionized, adding 0.8 for each additional ion beyond 1</u> into which the drug dissociates. The compound being prepared is compared to NaCl because NaCl is the major determinant of the isotonicity of body fluid.

Once the "E value" is determined, the following steps outline the process of doing isotonicity problems:

Step 1. Calculate the total amount of NaCl needed to make the final product/prescription isotonic by multiplying 0.9% NS by the desired volume of the prescription.

Step 2. Calculate the amount of NaCl represented by the drug. To do this, multiply the total drug amount (in milligrams or grams) by the "E value."

Step 3. Subtract step 2 from step 1 to determine the total amount of NaCl needed to prepare an isotonic prescription.

---

49. Calculate the E value for mannitol (MW = 182 g/mol). Round to the nearest hundredth.

$$\frac{(58.5)(i)}{(MW\ of\ drug)(1.8)} = \frac{58.5\ (1)}{182\ (1.8)} = 0.18$$

---

50. The E value for ephedrine sulfate is 0.23. How many grams of sodium chloride are needed to compound the following prescription? Round to 3 decimal places.

PRESCRIPTION	QUANTITY
Ephedrine sulfate	0.4 g
Sodium chloride	qs
Purified water qs	30 mL
Make isotonic soln.	
Sig. Use 2 drops in each nostril as directed.	

Step 1. Determine how much NaCl would make the product isotonic.

$$\frac{0.9\ g}{100\ mL} = \frac{X}{30\ mL} \quad X = 0.27\ g$$

Step 2. Determine amount of sodium chloride represented from ephedrine sulfate.

0.4 g x 0.23 ("E value") = 0.092 g of sodium chloride

Step 3. Subtract step 2 from step 1.

0.27 g – 0.092 g = 0.178 g of NaCl are needed to make an isotonic solution

51. Calculate the E value for potassium iodide, which dissociates into 2 particles (MW = 166 g/mol). Round to two decimal places.

$$\frac{(58.5)(i)}{(MW\ of\ drug)(1.8)} = \frac{58.5\ (1.8)}{166\ (1.8)} = 0.35$$

52. Physostigmine salicylate (MW = 413 g/mol) is a 2-ion electrolyte, dissociating 80% in a given concentration (i.e., use a dissociation factor of 1.8). Calculate its sodium chloride equivalent. Round to two decimal places.

$$\frac{(58.5)(i)}{(MW\ of\ drug)(1.8)} = \frac{58.5\ (1.8)}{413\ (1.8)} = 0.14$$

53. The pharmacist receives an order for 10 mL of tobramycin 1% ophthalmic solution. He has tobramycin 40 mg/mL solution. Tobramycin does not dissociate and has a MW of 468 g/mol. Find the E value for tobramycin and determine how many milligrams of NaCl are needed to make the solution isotonic.

$$\frac{(58.5)(i)}{(MW\ of\ drug)(1.8)} = \frac{58.5\ (1)}{468\ (1.8)} = 0.07, \text{ which is the "E value" for tobramycin}$$

The "E value" for tobramycin is 0.07. The prescription asks for 10 mL of 1% solution.

Step 1. Determine how much NaCl would make the product isotonic (if that is all you were using).

$$\frac{0.9\ g}{100\ mL} = \frac{X}{10\ mL} \quad X = 0.09\ g, \text{ or } 90\ mg$$

Step 2. Determine amount of sodium chloride represented from tobramycin.

$$\frac{1\ g}{100\ mL} = \frac{X}{10\ mL} \quad X = 0.1\ g, \text{ or } 100\ mg$$

100 mg x 0.07 ("E value") = 7 mg of sodium chloride

Step 3. Subtract step 2 from step 1. You are using tobramycin, so you do not need all the NaCl. Subtract out the equivalent amount of tonicity provided by the tobramycin, which is 7 mg.

90 mg – 7 mg = 83 mg (83 mg additional sodium chloride is needed to make an isotonic solution)

MOLES AND MILLIMOLES

A mole (mol) is the molecular weight of a substance in grams, or g/mole. A millimole (mmol) is 1/1,000 of the molecular weight in grams, or 1/1,000 of a mole. For monovalent species, the numeric value of the milliequivalent and millimole are identical.

$$mols = \frac{g}{MW} \quad or \quad mmols = \frac{mg}{MW}$$

54. How many moles of anhydrous magnesium sulfate (MW = 120.4 g/mol) are present in 250 grams of the substance? Round to the nearest hundredth.

$$mols = \frac{250\ g}{120.4} = 2.076, \text{ or } 2.08\ mols$$

55. **How many moles are equivalent to 875 milligrams of aluminum acetate (MW = 204 g/mol)? Round to 3 decimal places.**

First, convert 875 mg to grams.

$$875 \text{ mg} \times \frac{1 \text{ g}}{1,000 \text{ mg}} = 0.875 \text{ g}$$

Next, solve for mols.

$$\text{mols} = \frac{0.875 \text{ g}}{204} = 0.004 \text{ mols}$$

---

56. **How many millimoles of sodium phosphate (MW = 138 g/mol) are present in 90 g of the substance? Round to the nearest whole number.**

$$\text{mmols} = \frac{90,000 \text{ mg}}{138} = 652 \text{ mmols}$$

Or, solve another way:

$$\frac{90 \text{ g}}{138} = 0.652 \text{ mols, which is } 652 \text{ mmols}$$

---

57. **How many moles are equivalent to 45 grams of potassium carbonate (MW = 138 g/mol)? Round to the nearest thousandth.**

$$\text{mols} = \frac{45 \text{ g}}{138} = 0.326 \text{ mols}$$

---

58. **How many millimoles of calcium chloride (MW = 147 g/mol) are represented in 147 mL of a 10% (w/v) calcium chloride solution?**

Step 1: Calculate the amount (g) of $CaCl_2$ in 147 mL of 10% $CaCl_2$ solution.

$$\frac{10 \text{ g}}{100 \text{ mL}} = \frac{X \text{ g}}{147 \text{ mL}} \qquad X = 14.7 \text{ g}$$

Step 2: Calculate the mols of $CaCl_2$ in 147 mL of 10% $CaCl_2$ solution.

$$\text{mols} = \frac{14.7 \text{ g}}{147} = 0.1 \text{ mol}$$

Step 3: Solve the problem by converting moles to millimoles:

$$0.1 \text{ mol} \times 1,000 = 100 \text{ mmols}$$

---

59. **How many milligrams of sodium chloride (MW = 58.5 g/mol) represent 0.25 mmol? Do not round the answer.**

$$0.25 \text{ mmols} = \frac{X \text{ mg}}{58.5} \qquad X = 14.625 \text{ mg}$$

60. How many grams of sodium chloride (MW = 58.5 g/mol) should be used to prepare this solution? Do not round the answer.

PRESCRIPTION	QUANTITY
Methylprednisolone	0.5 g
NaCl solution	60 mL
Each 5 mL should contain 0.6 mmols of NaCl	

First determine how many mmols of NaCl will be in 60 mL of the compounded preparation.

$$\frac{0.6 \text{ mmols}}{5 \text{ mL}} = \frac{X \text{ mmols}}{60 \text{ mL}} \qquad X = 7.2 \text{ mmols NaCl}$$

Next, use the total mmols of NaCl to calculate grams of NaCl.

$$7.2 \text{ mmols} = \frac{X \text{ mg}}{58.5} \qquad X = 421.2 \text{ mg or } 0.4212 \text{ g NaCl}$$

MILLIEQUIVALENTS

Drugs can be expressed in solution in different ways:

- Milliosmoles refers to the number of particles in solution.

- Millimoles refers to the molecular weight (MW).

- Milliequivalents (mEq) represent the amount, in milligrams (mg), of a solute equal to 1/1,000 of its gram equivalent weight, taking into account the valence of the ions. Like osmolarity, the quantity of particles is important – but so is the electrical charge. Milliequivalents refers to the chemical activity of an electrolyte and is related to the total number of ionic charges in solution and considers the valence (charge) of each ion.

To count the valence, divide the compound into its positive and negative components, and then count the number of either the positive or the negative charges. For a given compound, the milliequivalents of cations equals that of anions. Some common compounds and their valences are listed in the table to the right. A comparison of valence and dissociation particles is presented in the Study Tip Gal on the next page. Remember, there are a lot of chelation drug interactions with "divalent" cations (calcium, magnesium and iron). Use that interaction to remember which compounds have a valence of 2.

COMPOUND	VALENCE
Ammonium chloride (NH_4Cl)	
Potassium chloride (KCl)	
Potassium gluconate ($KC_6H_{11}O_7$)	
Sodium acetate ($NaC_2H_3O_2$)	1
Sodium bicarbonate ($NaHCO_3$)	
Sodium chloride (NaCl)	
Calcium carbonate ($CaCO_3$)	
Calcium chloride ($CaCl_2$)	
Ferrous sulfate ($FeSO_4$)	2
Lithium carbonate (Li_2CO_3)	
Magnesium sulfate ($MgSO_4$)	

$$mEq = \frac{mg \times valence}{MW} \qquad or \qquad mEq = mmols \times valence$$

DISSOCIATION PARTICLES VS. VALENCE

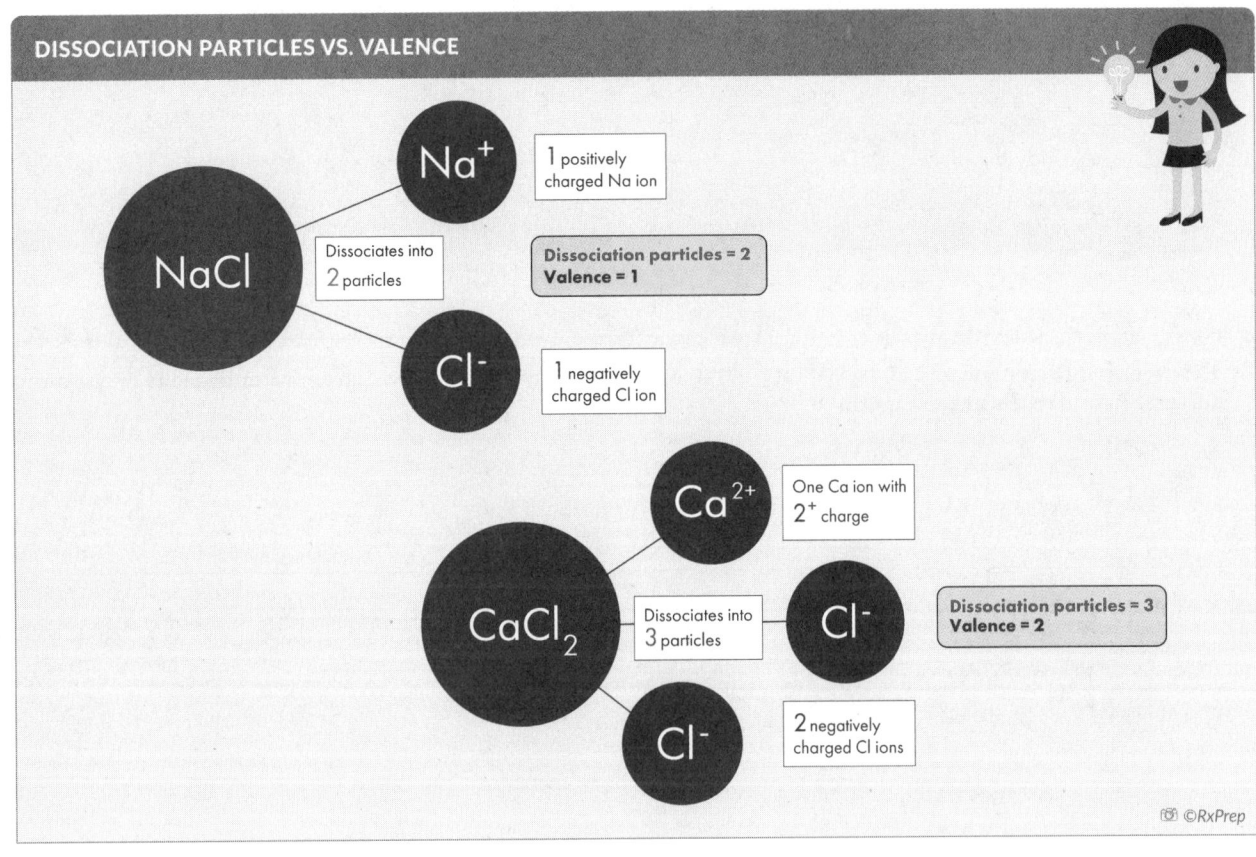

---

61. **A 20 mL vial is labeled potassium chloride (2 mEq/mL). How many grams of potassium chloride (MW = 74.5 g/mol) are present? Round to the nearest hundredth.**

$$20 \text{ mL} \times \frac{2 \text{ mEq}}{\text{mL}} = 40 \text{ mEq KCl total}$$

$$40 \text{ mEq} = \frac{\text{mg} \times 1}{74.5} = 2{,}980 \text{ mg, which is } 2.98 \text{ g}$$

If asked to convert <u>KCl liquid to tablets</u> or vice versa, use a simple proportion since <u>KCl 10% = 20 mEq/15 mL (see Required Formulas Sheet)</u>. For example, if someone is using *Klor-Con* 20 mEq BID, the total daily dose is 40 mEq. Convert to KCl 10%, as follows:

$$\frac{40 \text{ mEq}}{X \text{ mL}} = \frac{20 \text{ mEq}}{15 \text{ mL}} \quad X = 30 \text{ mL of KCl 10% liquid (15 mL PO BID) is equal to Klor-Con 40 mEq (20 mEq PO BID)}$$

---

62. **How many milliequivalents of potassium chloride are present in a 12 mL dose of a 10% (w/v) potassium chloride (MW = 74.5 g/mol) elixir? Round to 1 decimal place.**

$$\frac{10 \text{ g}}{100 \text{ mL}} = \frac{X \text{ g}}{12 \text{ mL}} \quad X = 1.2 \text{ g, or } 1{,}200 \text{ mg}$$

$$\text{mEq} = \frac{1{,}200 \text{ mg} \times 1}{74.5} = 16.1 \text{ mEq}$$

63. Calculate the milliequivalents of a standard ammonium chloride (MW = 53.5 g/mol) 21.4 mg/mL sterile solution in a 500 mL container.

$$\frac{21.4 \text{ mg}}{\text{mL}} \times 500 \text{ mL} = 10{,}700 \text{ mg}$$

$$\text{mEq} = \frac{10{,}700 \text{ mg} \times 1}{53.5} = 200 \text{ mEq}$$

64. How many milliequivalents of $MgSO_4$ (MW = 120.4 g/mol) are represented in 1 gram of anhydrous magnesium sulfate? Round to the nearest tenth.

$$\text{mEq} = \frac{1{,}000 \text{ mg} \times 2}{120.4} = 16.6 \text{ mEq}$$

65. How many milliequivalents of sodium are in a 50 mL vial of 8.4% sodium bicarbonate (MW = 84 g/mol)?

$$\frac{8.4 \text{ g}}{100 \text{ mL}} = \frac{X \text{ g}}{50 \text{ mL}} \qquad X = 4.2 \text{ g, or } 4{,}200 \text{ mg}$$

$$\text{mEq} = \frac{4{,}200 \text{ mg} \times 1}{84} = 50 \text{ mEq}$$

66. A 74-year-old male takes *Lithobid* (lithium carbonate, Li_2CO_3) 450 mg PO BID, but reports difficulty swallowing the capsules. How many milliliters of lithium citrate syrup provide an equivalent daily dose of lithium? Round to the nearest whole number. (MW of lithium carbonate = 74 g/mol)

The problem can be solved with the milliequivalent formula if the MW is provided. The valence of lithium carbonate is 2 (2 positively charged lithium ions and carbonate, which carries a negative 2 charge).

$$\text{mEq} = \frac{900 \text{ mg} \times 2}{74} = 24.324 \text{ mEq of Li ion per day}$$

Refer to the <u>Required Formulas Sheet</u> for the conversion between lithium salts:

$$\frac{24.324 \text{ mEq Li ion}}{X \text{ mL}} = \frac{8 \text{ mEq Li ion}}{5 \text{ mL lithium citrate syrup}} \qquad X = 15 \text{ mL of lithium citrate per day}$$

Alternative method:

$$\frac{900 \text{ mg } Li_2CO_3}{X \text{ mEq}} = \frac{300 \text{ mg } Li_2CO_3}{8 \text{ mEq}} \qquad X = 24 \text{ mEq Li ion per day}$$

$$\frac{24 \text{ mEq Li ion}}{X \text{ mL}} = \frac{8 \text{ mEq Li ion}}{5 \text{ mL lithium citrate syrup}} \qquad X = 15 \text{ mL of lithium citrate per day}$$

© iStock.com/i_frontier

CHAPTER 11

CALCULATIONS III: PARENTERAL & ENTERAL NUTRITION

CONTENT LEGEND

☀ = Study Tip Gal 🧑

BACKGROUND

When a patient cannot eat enough to stay healthy, nutrition support may be required. Examples include patients with stroke, cancer, GI disorders (e.g., bowel obstruction, Crohn's disease, ulcerative colitis) or patients in a coma. Enteral nutrition (EN) uses the GI tract to deliver all or part of a patient's caloric needs (e.g., eating food orally or delivering a formula via a feeding tube into the stomach or intestine). Parenteral nutrition (PN), also referred to as total parenteral nutrition (TPN), delivers calories into a vein through a peripheral or central line. When the GI tract is working, enteral nutrition is preferred; it is most physiologic, has fewer complications and is generally less expensive. Parenteral nutrition can be used when the GI tract is not functioning, or in patients who cannot maintain nutritional status enterally.

CALORIE SOURCES

A calorie is a measurement of the energy, or heat, it takes to raise the temperature of 1 gram of water by 1°C. Calories are associated with nutrition because humans obtain energy from the food they consume orally or from EN/PN. Calories are provided by these 3 components: carbohydrates, fat and protein (called macronutrients).

A calorie is a very small unit, and these are therefore measured in kilocalories, or kcals, where 1,000 calories = 1 kcal. It is common to find the term "calories" used interchangeably for kcals. For example, the "Nutrition Facts" box on the side of a container of Honey Nut Cheerios® states that a ¾ cup serving of the cereal provides 110 Calories. Precisely, this is 110 kcals. Looking at the box, the word "Calories" is written with a capital "C" which is sometimes used to indicate kcals, versus a lower case "c." For pharmacy calculations, "calories" or "Calories" are meant to refer to kilocalories, or kcals.

CALCULATIONS

PARENTERAL NUTRITION

Compared to EN, PN is more <u>invasive, less physiologic</u> and has a higher risk of complications (e.g., infection and thrombosis). PN may be indicated when the patient is not able to absorb adequate nutrition via the GI tract for <u>> 5 days</u>. Conditions that often require PN include bowel obstruction, ileus, severe diarrhea, radiation enteritis and untreatable malabsorption.

There are 2 types of PN admixtures. Both types contain sterile water for injection, electrolytes, vitamins and minerals.

- <u>2-in-1 formulations</u> contain <u>two macronutrients (dextrose and amino acids)</u> in one container. Lipids are infused separately, if needed.

- <u>3-in-1 formulations</u> contain <u>three macronutrients (dextrose, amino acids and lipids)</u> in one container. 3-in-1 formulations are also called total nutrient admixture (TNA) or "all-in-one" formulations.

PN admixtures are <u>compounded sterile products (CSPs)</u> and their preparation must comply with <u>USP Chapter 797</u> requirements. They are also classified as <u>high-alert</u> medications by the Institute for Safe Medication Practices (ISMP). Many large hospitals use automated compounding devices to combine the ingredients into a single container, but <u>multi-chamber bags</u> can be purchased for convenience. Two-chamber premixed PN products have an amino acid solution in one chamber and a dextrose solution in another chamber. The seal between the chambers is broken before administration to mix the solutions together. Three-chamber options (with lipid emulsion in the third chamber) are also available. *Clinimix* is one of the commonly used multi-chamber products. *Clinimix-E* products contain electrolytes.

If the PN is expected to be used short-term (< 1 week), peripheral administration may be possible, but has a high risk of phlebitis (inflammation of the vein) and vein damage. <u>Central line</u> placement allows for a higher osmolarity and wider variation in pH. Common types of central lines include <u>peripherally inserted central catheters ("PICC" lines)</u>, Hickman, Broviac, Groshong and others. Administration of <u>PN requires a filter due to the risk of a precipitate</u>.

Each patient's fluid, kcal, protein and lipid requirements, plus the initial electrolyte, vitamin and trace element requirements will be determined. PN requires careful monitoring, including assessing the degree of glucose intolerance and the risk of refeeding syndrome, which is an intracellular loss of electrolytes, particularly phosphate, that causes serious complications.

DETERMINING FLUID NEEDS

Fluid requirements are determined first when designing a PN regimen. Enough fluid needs to be given to maintain adequate hydration, but not too much to cause accumulation. Daily fluid needs can be calculated using this formula:

When weight > 20 kg: 1,500 mL + (20 mL)(weight in kg* − 20)

Total body weight (the patient's weight on the scale) is used for most PN calculations, unless the question specifies otherwise.

Some institutions estimate adult fluid requirements using a general guideline of 30 – 40 mL/kg/day. The PN and fluid volume should be tailored to the patient. If the patient has problems with fluid accumulation (e.g., heart failure or renal dysfunction), the amount of fluid provided should be reduced. Fluid volume from medications, including intravenous piggybacks (IVPBs), should be included in the calculation of the overall volume the patient is receiving.

1. **GG is a 57-year-old female admitted to the hospital with bowel obstruction. She will be NPO for the next 5 – 7 days. The decision was made to start PN therapy. She weighs 65 kg. Her SCr is 1.3 mg/dL. Calculate GG's daily fluid requirements.**

    1,500 mL + (20 mL) (65 − 20) = 2,400 mL/day

2. **A 76-year-old, 154-pound patient is NPO and needs hydration. She is afebrile and does not have heart failure, renal disease or ascites. What volume of fluid should the patient receive per day?**

    1,500 mL + (20 mL) (70 − 20) = 2,500 mL/day

DETERMINING CALORIC NEEDS

Basal Energy Expenditure

The basal energy expenditure (BEE), otherwise referred to as the basal metabolic rate (BMR), is the energy expenditure in the resting state, exclusive of eating and activity. It is <u>estimated differently in male and female adults using the Harris-Benedict equations</u> below. Most pharmacists do not memorize these equations; they will likely be provided on the exam.

> BEE (males): 66.47 + 13.75 (weight in kg*) + 5 (height in cm) – 6.76 (age in years)
>
> BEE (females): 655.1 + 9.6 (weight in kg*) + 1.85 (height in cm) – 4.68 (age in years)

Total body weight (the patient's weight on the scale) is used for most PN calculations, unless the question specifies otherwise.

Total Energy Expenditure

<u>Total energy expenditure</u> (TEE; or total daily expenditure, TDE) is a measure of <u>BEE plus excess metabolic demands</u> as a result of stress, the thermal effects of feeding and energy expenditure from activity. Once the BEE is calculated, calculate the TEE by taking the BEE calories and multiplying by the appropriate activity factor and stress factor. This will increase the calories required. Energy requirements are increased 12% with each degree of fever over 37°C.

> TEE = BEE x activity factor x stress factor

The activity factor is either 1.2 if confined to bed (non-ambulatory), or 1.3 if out of bed (ambulatory). Commonly used stress factors are listed in the table. The formula for BEE and patient-specific stress factors are likely to be provided if needed on the exam.

STATE OF STRESS	STRESS FACTOR
Minor surgery	1.2
Infection	1.4
Major trauma, sepsis, burns up to 30% BSA	1.5
Burns over 30% BSA	1.5–2

3. **Using the Harris-Benedict equation, calculate the basal energy expenditure for a 66-year-old male with major trauma (stress factor 1.5). He weighs 174 pounds and is 5'10". Activity factor is 1.2. Round to the nearest whole number.**

   Height = 70 inches x 2.54 cm/inch = 177.8 cm. Weight = 174 pounds x 1 kg/2.2 pounds = 79.0909 kg.

   BEE (males): 66.47 + 13.75 (weight in kg) + 5 (height in cm) – 6.76 (age in years)

   > BEE = 66.47 + (13.75 x 79.0909) + (5 x 177.8) – (6.76 x 66)

   > BEE = 66.47 + 1,087.5 + 889 – 446.16 = 1,596.81, or 1,597 kcal/day

   The stress factor is not needed in this calculation, because you were asked to calculate BEE only. The <u>BEE can be estimated using 15 – 25 kcal/kg/day (adults)</u>. It may be helpful to check the calculation with this estimate and see if the numbers are close. In this case, an estimation using 20 kcal/kg/day would provide 1,582 kcal/day (very close to 1,597 kcal/day as above).

4. **Calculate the total energy expenditure for a major trauma patient (stress factor is 1.5, activity factor is 1.2) who is a 66-year-old male, weighing 174 pounds and measuring 5'10" in height. (Use the BEE calculated from the patient in the previous problem.) Round to the nearest whole number.**

   TEE = BEE x activity factor x stress factor. BEE was calculated above.

   > TEE = 1,597 kcal/day x 1.2 x 1.5 = 2,875 kcal/day

5. **A 25-year-old female major trauma patient survives surgery and is recovering in the surgical intensive care unit. The medical team wants to start PN therapy. She is 122 pounds, 5'7" with some mild renal impairment. Calculate her BEE using the Harris-Benedict equation and her TEE (stress factor = 1.7 and activity factor = 1.2). Round each to the nearest whole number.**

Height = 67 inches x 2.54 cm/inch = 170.18 cm. Weight = 122 pounds x 1 kg/2.2 pounds = 55.4545 kg.

BEE (females): 655.1 + 9.6 (weight in kg) + 1.85 (height in cm) – 4.68 (age in years)

BEE = 655.1 + (9.6 x 55.4545) + (1.85 x 170.18) – (4.68 x 25)

BEE = 655.1 + 532.3632 + 314.833 – 117 = 1,385.2962, or 1,385 kcal/day

TEE = BEE x activity factor x stress factor

TEE = 1,385 kcal/day x 1.2 x 1.7 = 2,825 kcal/day

Once the total caloric needs are determined, the calories provided from each macronutrient can be calculated using the conversions shown in the Study Tip Gal below.

Calories Provided from Macronutrients

USUAL DIET*			EN FORMULAS*		PN FORMULAS	
Carbs	Bread, Rice....	4 kcal/gram	Corn syrup solids, cornstarch, sucrose....	Premixed solutions that contain carbohydrates, fat and protein. See Enteral Nutrition at the end of this chapter.	Dextrose Monohydrate	3.4 kcal/gram
					Glycerol/Glycerin**	4.3 kcal/gram
Fat	Butter, Oil....	9 kcal/gram	Borage oil, canola oil, corn oil....		Injectable Lipid Emulsion (ILE) 10%	1.1 kcal/mL
				Examples of EN formulas: *Ensure, Osmolite, Jevity, Glucerna* and others	Injectable Lipid Emulsion (ILE) 20% (*Intralipid, Smoflipid*)	2 kcal/mL
					Injectable Lipid Emulsion (ILE) 30%	3 kcal/mL
Protein	Fish, Meat....	4 kcal/gram	Casein, soy, whey....		Amino Acid Solutions (*Aminosyn, FreAmine*, others)	4 kcal/gram

*The diet and enteral formula components shown are common examples; there are others.
**Glycerol may be used to decrease hyperglycemia; more commonly, the dextrose load is decreased or the insulin dose is increased.

PROTEIN

Protein is used either to repair or build muscle cells or as a source of energy. Protein in enteral intake is present in various forms, and in PN as the constituent amino acids. Because critically ill patients are catabolic (protein breakdown occurs faster than synthesis), many clinicians prefer to use "protein sparing" techniques in this population. This means that most or all of the TEE calories are provided by dextrose and fat. If adequate energy is provided by carbohydrates and fat, the protein may be "spared" and can be used by muscle (although the protein calories may not end up in the intended location). If "protein sparing" is used, the energy required by the patient will come from only the dextrose and lipids, which are the "non-protein calories" (NPC). Overall, whether to include the calories from protein in the total calories provided by a PN regimen is controversial.

Protein from food, enteral nutrition formulas or parenteral amino acid solutions provides 4 kcal/gram. The typical protein requirement for a non-stressed, ambulatory patient is 0.8 – 1 g/kg/day. The weight to use to calculate the protein requirement will likely be specified (if needed) in an exam scenario. Some prescribers order protein based on the patient's ideal body weight (IBW). Protein requirements increase if the patient is placed under stress, which is defined as illness severity. The more severely ill, the greater the protein requirements will be. In patients with a high degree of metabolic stress the protein requirements can be as high as 2 g/kg/day.

CONDITION	PROTEIN REQUIREMENTS
Ambulatory, non-hospitalized (non-stressed)	0.8–1 g/kg/day
Hospitalized or malnourished	1.2–2 g/kg/day

6. MK is a 62-year-old female who has been admitted with enteritis and pneumonia. She has a history of Crohn's disease and COPD. Her IBW is 54.7 kg. The staff gastroenterologist has ordered PN therapy with 1.5 g/kg IBW/day of protein. How many grams of protein will MK receive per day? Round to the nearest whole number.

> 54.7 kg x 1.5 g/kg IBW/day = 82 g protein/day

7. PP is a 46-year-old male who weighs 207 pounds. He is admitted for bowel resection surgery. Post surgery, he is to be started on PN therapy. The physician wants the patient to receive 1.3 g/kg/day of protein. Calculate his protein requirement. Round to the nearest whole number.

First, convert pounds to kg: 207 pounds x 1 kg/2.2 pounds = 94.1 kg.

Then, calculate the protein requirement.

> 94.1 kg x 1.3 g/kg/day = 122 g protein/day

NITROGEN BALANCE

Grams of Nitrogen from Protein

Nitrogen is released during protein catabolism and is mainly excreted as urea in the urine. Nitrogen balance is the difference between the body's nitrogen gains and losses. While grams of protein are calculated in a nutritional plan, grams of nitrogen are used as an expression of the amount of protein received by the patient. There is 1 g of nitrogen (N) for each 6.25 g of protein. To calculate the grams of nitrogen in a certain weight of protein, divide the protein grams by 6.25.

$$\text{Nitrogen intake} = \frac{\text{grams of protein intake}}{6.25}$$

8. A patient is receiving PN containing 540 mL of 12.5% amino acids per day. How many grams of nitrogen is the patient receiving? Round to the nearest tenth.

$$\frac{12.5 \text{ g}}{100 \text{ mL}} = \frac{X \text{ g}}{540 \text{ mL}} \qquad X = 67.5 \text{ g of protein}$$

$$\frac{67.5 \text{ g of protein}}{6.25} = 10.8 \text{ g of nitrogen}$$

Non-Protein Calories to Nitrogen Ratio

The non-protein calorie to nitrogen ratio (NPC:N) is calculated as follows:

■ First, calculate the grams of nitrogen supplied per day (1 g N = 6.25 g of protein).

■ Then, divide the total non-protein calories (dextrose + lipids) by the grams of nitrogen.

Desirable NPC:N ratios are:

■ 80:1 in the most severely stressed patients

■ 100:1 in severely stressed patients

■ 150:1 in an unstressed patient

CALCULATIONS

9. **A patient is receiving PN containing 480 mL of dextrose 50% and 50 grams of amino acids plus electrolytes. Calculate the non-protein calories to nitrogen ratio for this patient.**

First, calculate the nitrogen intake.

$$\text{Nitrogen} \ = \ \frac{50 \text{ g of protein}}{6.25} \ = \ 8 \text{ g}$$

Next, calculate the non-protein calories.

$$\frac{50 \text{ g dextrose}}{100 \text{ mL}} \ = \ \frac{X \text{ g}}{480 \text{ mL}} \qquad X = 240 \text{ g dextrose}$$

$$240 \text{ g dextrose} \ \times \ \frac{3.4 \text{ kcal dextrose}}{1 \text{ g}} \ = \ 816 \text{ kcal of dextrose}$$

Then, set up the NPC:N ratio.

NPC:N ratio is 816:8, or 102:1

AMINO ACID CALCULATIONS

Amino acids are the protein source in PN. Amino acids come in stock preparations of 5%, 8.5%, 10%, 15% and others. They all provide 4 kcal/gram. Branded amino acid solutions commonly used for PN include *Aminosyn, FreAmine, Travasol, TrophAmine* and *Clinisol*.

10. **If the pharmacy stocks *Aminosyn* 8.5%, how many milliliters will be needed to provide 108 grams of protein? Round to the nearest whole number.**

$$\frac{8.5 \text{ g}}{100 \text{ mL}} \ = \ \frac{108 \text{ g}}{X \text{ mL}} \qquad X = 1{,}270.58, \text{ or } 1{,}271 \text{ mL}$$

11. **How many calories are provided by 108 grams of protein?**

$$\frac{4 \text{ kcal}}{g} \ \times \ 108 \text{ g} \ = \ 432 \text{ kcal of protein}$$

12. **The pharmacy stocks *FreAmine* 10%. A patient requires 122 grams of protein per day. How many milliliters of *FreAmine* will the patient need?**

$$\frac{10 \text{ g}}{100 \text{ mL}} \ = \ \frac{122 \text{ g}}{X \text{ mL}} \qquad X = 1{,}220 \text{ mL}$$

13. **JR is a 55-year-old male (weight 189 pounds) who is confined to bed (activity factor 1.2) due to his current infection (stress factor 1.5). JR requires 1.4 g/kg/day of protein and the pharmacy stocks *Aminosyn* 8.5%. Calculate the amount of *Aminosyn*, in milliliters, JR should receive. Round to the nearest whole number.**

First, convert weight to kg: 189 pounds x 1 kg/2.2 pounds = 85.90 kg

Next, calculate the protein requirement: 1.4 g/kg/day x 85.9090 kg = 120.27 g/day

Then, calculate the amount of *Aminosyn* (mL) needed. Note that the activity factor and stress factor are not required to calculate the protein requirement.

$$\frac{8.5 \text{ g}}{100 \text{ mL}} = \frac{120.27 \text{ g}}{X \text{ mL}} \qquad X = 1,414.97, \text{ or } 1,415 \text{ mL}$$

14. **JR is receiving 97 grams of protein in an *Aminosyn* 8.5% solution on day 8 of his hospitalization. How many calories are provided by this amount of protein?**

$$\frac{4 \text{ kcal}}{\text{g}} \times 97 \text{ g} = 388 \text{ kcal of protein}$$

15. **A PN order is written to include 800 mL of 10% amino acid solution. The pharmacy only has 15% amino acid solution in stock. Using the 15% amino acid solution instead, how many milliliters should be added to the PN bag? Round to the nearest whole number.**

First, calculate the grams of protein that would be provided with the 10% solution.

$$\frac{10 \text{ g}}{100 \text{ mL}} = \frac{X \text{ g}}{800 \text{ mL}} \qquad X = 80 \text{ g}$$

Next, calculate how much of the 15% amino acid solution will supply 80 grams of protein.

$$\frac{15 \text{ g}}{100 \text{ mL}} = \frac{80 \text{ g}}{X \text{ mL}} \qquad X = 533 \text{ mL}$$

CARBOHYDRATES

Glucose is the <u>primary energy source</u>. Unless a patient purchases glucose tablets or gel, carbohydrates are consumed as simple sugars, such as fruit juice, or complex "starchy" sugars, such as legumes and grains. These are hydrolyzed by the gut into the monosaccharides fructose, galactose and glucose, which are absorbed. The liver converts the first two into glucose, and excess glucose is stored as glycogen.

<u>Carbohydrates from food or in enteral nutrition formulas provide 4 kcal/gram</u>. In PN, <u>dextrose monohydrate</u> provides the <u>carbohydrate source</u>. This is the isomer of glucose (D-glucose) which can be metabolized for energy. The <u>dextrose in PN provides 3.4 kcal/gram</u>. Occasionally, glycerol is used as an alternative to dextrose in patients with impaired insulin secretion. Glycerol provides 4.3 kcal/gram and comes premixed with amino acids.

The usual distribution of non-protein calories is 70 – 85% as carbohydrate (dextrose) and 15 – 30% as fat (lipids). Dextrose comes in concentrations of 5%, 10%, 20%, 30%, 50%, 70% and others. The higher concentrations are used for PN. When calculating the dextrose, do not exceed 4 mg/kg/min (some use 7 g/kg/day). These are conservative estimates of the maximum amount of dextrose that the liver can handle.

16. **Using 50% dextrose in water, how many milliliters are required to fulfill a PN order for 405 grams of dextrose?**

$$\frac{50 \text{ g}}{100 \text{ mL}} = \frac{405 \text{ g}}{X \text{ mL}} = 810 \text{ mL}$$

17. **DF, a 44-year-old male, is receiving 1,235 mL of D30W, 1,010 mL of *FreAmine* 8.5%, 200 mL of *Intralipid* 20% and 50 mL of electrolytes/minerals in his PN. How many calories from dextrose is DF receiving from the PN? Round to the nearest whole number.**

$$\frac{30 \text{ g}}{100 \text{ mL}} \times \frac{1,235 \text{ mL}}{\text{day}} \times \frac{3.4 \text{ kcal}}{\text{g}} = 1,260 \text{ kcal/day}$$

---

18. **A pharmacist mixed 200 mL D20% with 100 mL D5%. What is the percentage strength of dextrose in the final bag?**

The 200 mL bag has 40 g of dextrose (20 g/100 mL x 200 mL).

The 100 mL bag has 5 g of dextrose. There are a total of 45 g of dextrose in the bag.

$$\frac{45 \text{ g}}{300 \text{ mL}} = \frac{X \text{ g}}{100 \text{ mL}} \qquad X = 15 \text{ g; the percentage strength is } 15\%$$

---

19. **If a 50% dextrose injection provides 170 kcal in each 100 mL, how many milliliters of a 70% dextrose injection would provide the same caloric value? Round to the nearest tenth.**

There are several ways to solve this problem. Option 1:

$$\frac{70 \text{ g}}{100 \text{ mL}} = \frac{50 \text{ g}}{X \text{ mL}} = 71.4 \text{ mL}$$

Option 2:

$$\frac{100 \text{ mL}}{70 \text{ g}} \times \frac{1 \text{ g}}{3.4 \text{ kcal}} \times 170 \text{ kcal} = 71.4 \text{ mL}$$

Option 3: since the calories are from 50% dextrose and the pharmacist is using 70% dextrose, the Q1C1 (dilution and concentration) method can be used (see the Calculations II chapter):

$$100 \text{ mL} \times 50\% = Q2 \times 70\%$$

$$Q2 = 71.4 \text{ mL}$$

---

20. **AH is receiving 640 mL of D50W in her PN. How many calories does this provide?**

$$\frac{50 \text{ g}}{100 \text{ mL}} \times \frac{640 \text{ mL}}{\text{day}} \times \frac{3.4 \text{ kcal}}{\text{g}} = 1,088 \text{ kcal}$$

---

21. **A PN order is written for 500 mL of 50% dextrose. The pharmacy only has D70W in stock. How many milliliters of D70W should be added to the PN bag? Round to the nearest whole number.**

First, calculate the grams of dextrose needed for the PN as written.

$$\frac{50 \text{ g}}{100 \text{ mL}} = \frac{X \text{ g}}{500 \text{ mL}} \qquad X = 250 \text{ g}$$

Next, calculate how much of the 70% dextrose solution provides 250 grams of dextrose.

$$\frac{70 \text{ g}}{100 \text{ mL}} = \frac{250 \text{ g}}{X \text{ mL}} \qquad X = 357 \text{ mL of D70W}$$

FAT

Fats, or lipids, are used by the body for energy and various critical functions (e.g., they are an essential component of cell membranes, a solvent for fat-soluble vitamins, and play a role in hormone production and activity, as well as in cell signaling). In food and EN formulas, fat is provided as four types: saturated, *trans*, monounsaturated and polyunsaturated. Each of these provides 9 kcal/gram. In PN, injectable lipid emulsion (ILE) is the fat source. Fat calories in PN are not measured in kcal/gram; they are measured in kcal/mL due to the caloric contribution provided by the egg phospholipid and glycerol components in the ILE. A 10% ILE provides 1.1 kcal/mL, 20% provides 2 kcal/mL and 30% provides 3 kcal/mL.

Non-protein calories are comprised of 70 – 85% carbohydrate (dextrose) and 15 – 30% fat (lipids). Lipids are available as 10%, 20% or 30% emulsions, with brand names *Intralipid* (all concentrations) and *Smoflipid* (20% only); *Smoflipid* contains 4 oils, while traditional ILE contains only soybean oil, so they are not interchangeable. ISMP has received numerous reports of mix-ups between them.

Lipids do not need to be given daily; if a patient has high triglycerides, lipid administration may be reduced to three times per week or once weekly. If lipids are given once weekly, divide the total calories by 7 to determine the daily amount of fat the patient receives. Due to the risk of infection, the recommended hang time limit for ILE is 12 hours when infused alone. However, an admixture containing fat emulsion, such as a TNA, may be administered over 24 hours. Lipid emulsions cannot be filtered through 0.22 micron filters; 1.2 micron filters are commonly used for lipids.

Some medications are formulated in a lipid emulsion (propofol and clevidipine) that provides fat calories. If a patient is receiving PN along with one or both of these medications, the calorie contribution from the medication must be considered. Refer to the Acute & Critical Care Medicine and Hypertension chapters for further discussion.

---

22. **A patient is receiving 500 mL of 10% lipids. How many calories is the patient receiving from the lipids? Round to the nearest whole number.**

$$\frac{1.1 \text{ kcal}}{\text{mL}} = \frac{X \text{ kcal}}{500 \text{ mL}} \quad X = 550 \text{ kcal}$$

---

23. **The total energy expenditure (TEE) for a critically ill patient is 2,435 kcal/day. The patient is receiving 1,446 kcal from dextrose and 810 kcal from protein. In this critical care unit, clinicians do not include protein calories in the TEE estimation. How many kcal should be provided by the lipids?**

As stated in the problem, at this institution TEE refers to the non-protein calories.

2,435 kcal (total non-protein) – 1,446 kcal (dextrose) = 989 kcal remaining from lipids

---

24. **Using 20% *Smoflipid*, how many milliliters are required to meet 989 calories? Round to the nearest whole number.**

$$\frac{2 \text{ kcal}}{\text{mL}} = \frac{989 \text{ kcal}}{X \text{ mL}} \quad X = 495 \text{ mL}$$

---

25. **A patient is receiving 660 mL of 10% *Intralipid* on Saturdays along with his normal daily PN therapy of 1,420 mL of D20W, 450 mL *Aminosyn* 15%, and 30 mL of electrolytes. What is the daily amount of calories provided by the lipids? Round to the nearest whole number.**

$$\frac{1.1 \text{ kcal}}{\text{mL}} = \frac{X \text{ kcal}}{660 \text{ mL}} \quad X = 726 \text{ kcal/week. Divide by 7 to get kcal/day} = 104 \text{ kcal/day}$$

---

26. **A patient is receiving 180 mL of 30% lipids. How many calories is the patient receiving from the lipids?**

$$\frac{3 \text{ kcal}}{\text{mL}} = \frac{X \text{ kcal}}{180 \text{ mL}} \quad X = 540 \text{ kcal}$$

27. **A PN order calls for 475 calories to be provided by lipids. The pharmacy has 10% lipid emulsion in stock. How many milliliters should be administered to the patient? Round to the nearest whole number.**

$$\frac{1.1 \text{ kcal}}{\text{mL}} = \frac{475 \text{ kcal}}{X \text{ mL}} \qquad X = 432 \text{ mL}$$

ELECTROLYTES

Electrolytes in the PN must be individualized to the patient's needs. Electrolytes include sodium, potassium, phosphate, chloride and calcium. More or less of an electrolyte may be needed based on the patient's conditions (e.g., renal disease).

SODIUM

Sodium is the principal <u>extracellular</u> cation. Sodium may need to be reduced in renal dysfunction or cardiovascular disease, including hypertension. Sodium chloride (NaCl) comes in many concentrations, such as 0.9% (normal saline, or NS), 0.45% (½NS) and others. Sodium chloride 23.4% is used for PN preparation and contains 4 mEq/mL of sodium. Hypertonic saline (greater than 0.9%) is dangerous if used incorrectly and is discussed in the Medication Safety & Quality Improvement chapter.

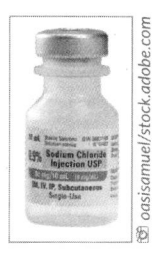 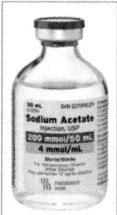

Sodium can be added to PN as either sodium <u>chloride</u>, sodium <u>acetate</u>, sodium <u>phosphate</u> or a combination of these. If <u>acidosis</u> is present, <u>sodium acetate</u> should be used; sodium acetate is converted to sodium bicarbonate and may help correct the acidosis.

28. **The pharmacist is going to add 80 mEq of sodium to the PN; half will be given as sodium acetate (2 mEq/mL) and half as sodium chloride (4 mEq/mL). How many milliliters of sodium chloride will be needed?**

40 mEq will be provided by the NaCl.

$$\frac{4 \text{ mEq}}{\text{mL}} = \frac{40 \text{ mEq}}{X \text{ mL}} \qquad X = 10 \text{ mL}$$

29. **The pharmacist is making PN that needs to contain 80 mEq of sodium and 45 mEq of acetate. The available pharmacy stock solutions include sodium chloride (4 mEq/mL of sodium) and sodium acetate (2 mEq/mL of sodium). The final volume of the PN will be 2.5 liters to be infused at 100 mL/hr. What quantity, in milliliters, of each stock solution should be added to the PN to meet the requirements? Round to the nearest hundredth.**

First, calculate the volume of sodium acetate needed (since acetate can only be provided by sodium acetate and sodium will also be provided by this solution).

$$\frac{2 \text{ mEq}}{\text{mL}} = \frac{45 \text{ mEq}}{X \text{ mL}} \qquad X = 22.5 \text{ mL of sodium acetate}$$

Next, determine how many mEq of sodium are supplied by 22.5 mL sodium acetate.

$$\frac{2 \text{ mEq}}{\text{mL}} \times 22.5 \text{ mL sodium acetate} = 45 \text{ mEq of sodium}$$

So, 45 mEq (22.5 mL) of sodium acetate supplies 45 mEq of acetate and 45 mEq of sodium. How many mEq of sodium are left to be provided by the sodium chloride?

$$80 \text{ mEq Na total} - 45 \text{ mEq Na from Na Acetate} = 35 \text{ mEq of sodium still needed from NaCl}$$

Calculate the volume of sodium chloride that will supply the remaining sodium (35 mEq).

$$\frac{4 \text{ mEq}}{\text{mL}} = \frac{35 \text{ mEq}}{X \text{ mL}} \qquad X = 8.75 \text{ mL of sodium chloride}$$

30. **A 2 liter PN solution is to contain 60 mEq of sodium and 30 mEq of acetate. The pharmacy has in stock sodium chloride (4 mEq/mL) and sodium acetate (2 mEq/mL). What quantity, in milliliters, of each solution should be added to the PN? Round to the nearest tenth.**

First, calculate the amount of sodium acetate needed.

$$\frac{2 \text{ mEq}}{\text{mL}} = \frac{30 \text{ mEq}}{X \text{ mL}} \qquad X = 15 \text{ mL of sodium acetate}$$

This amount (15 mL of sodium acetate) supplies 30 mEq of sodium (15 mL x 2 mEq/mL = 30 mEq). The additional amount of sodium required is 30 mEq from NaCl (60 mEq – 30 mEq).

Now, calculate the amount of sodium chloride needed.

$$\frac{4 \text{ mEq}}{\text{mL}} = \frac{30 \text{ mEq}}{X \text{ mL}} \qquad X = 7.5 \text{ mL of NaCl}$$

POTASSIUM

Potassium is the principal intracellular cation. Potassium may need to be reduced in renal or cardiovascular disease. Potassium can be provided by potassium chloride (KCl), potassium phosphate (KPhos, KPO4), potassium acetate or a combination of these. The normal range for serum potassium is 3.5 – 5 mEq/L.

PHOSPHATE

Phosphorus (or phosphate, PO4) is present in DNA, cell membranes and ATP. It acts as an acid-base buffer and is vital in bone metabolism. Phosphate can be provided by sodium phosphate (NaPO4) or potassium phosphate (KPhos, KPO4). The two forms do not provide equivalent amounts of phosphate. The PN order should be written in mmol of phosphate, followed by the type of salt form (potassium or sodium). Phosphate will often need to be reduced in renal disease.

31. **The pharmacist has calculated that a patient requires 30 mmol of phosphate and 80 mEq of potassium. The pharmacy has stock solutions of potassium phosphate (3 mmol of phosphate with 4.4 mEq of potassium/mL) and potassium chloride (2 mEq K/mL). How many milliliters each of potassium phosphate and potassium chloride will be required to meet the patient's needs?**

First, calculate the volume of potassium phosphate required (since phosphate can only be provided by KPO4 and potassium will also be provided by this solution).

$$\frac{3 \text{ mmol phosphate}}{\text{mL}} = \frac{30 \text{ mmol phosphate}}{X \text{ mL}} \qquad X = 10 \text{ mL KPO4}$$

Each mL of the potassium phosphate (KPO4) supplies 4.4 mEq of potassium. Calculate the amount of potassium the patient will receive from the 10 mL of KPO4.

10 mL x 4.4 mEq/mL = 44 mEq potassium from KPO4

The remaining potassium will be provided by KCl.

80 mEq K required – 44 mEq K (from KPO4) = 36 mEq to be obtained from KCl

$$\frac{2 \text{ mEq K}}{\text{mL}} = \frac{36 \text{ mEq K}}{X \text{ mL}} \qquad X = 18 \text{ mL KCl}$$

The patient requires 10 mL of potassium phosphate and 18 mL of potassium chloride.

CALCIUM

Calcium is important for many functions, including cardiac conduction, muscle contraction and bone homeostasis. The normal serum calcium level is 8.5 – 10.5 mg/dL. Almost half of serum calcium is bound to albumin. Low albumin will lead to a measured serum calcium concentration that is falsely low. If albumin is low (< 3.5 g/dL), the calcium level must be corrected with the equation below prior to determining the calcium needs in the PN or providing calcium replacement in any manner:

$$Ca_{corrected}\ (mg/dL) = calcium_{reported(serum)} + [(4.0 - albumin) \times (0.8)]\ †$$

†Use serum calcium in mg/dL and albumin in g/dL (standard units in the U.S.) in the corrected calcium formula

32. Calculate the corrected calcium value for a patient with the following reported lab values:

LAB	REFERENCE RANGE	RESULT
Calcium (mg/dL)	8.5–10.5	7.6
Albumin (g/dL)	3.5–5	1.5

$$Ca_{corrected} = 7.6 + [(4.0 - 1.5) \times (0.8)] = 9.6\ mg/dL$$

The corrected calcium provides a more accurate estimate of the patient's true serum calcium level (i.e., what it would be if the albumin was normal). In this example, the patient's corrected calcium is within the reference range for the lab.

33. A patient is to receive 8 mEq of calcium. The pharmacy has calcium gluconate 10% in stock which provides 0.465 mEq/mL. How many milliliters of calcium gluconate should be added to the PN? Round to the nearest whole number.

$$8\ mEq\ Ca \times \frac{1\ mL}{0.465\ mEq\ Ca} = 17.2,\ or\ 17\ mL\ calcium\ gluconate$$

Calcium and Phosphate Solubility

Phosphate and calcium can bind together and precipitate, which can cause a pulmonary embolus. This can be fatal. The following steps can help reduce the risk of a calcium-phosphate precipitate:

- Choose calcium gluconate over calcium chloride ($CaCl_2$) because it has a lower risk of precipitation with phosphates. Calcium gluconate has a lower dissociation constant than calcium chloride, leaving less free calcium available in solution to bind phosphates.

- Add phosphate first (after the dextrose and amino acids), followed by other PN components, agitate the solution, then add calcium near the end to take advantage of the maximum volume of the PN formulation.

- The calcium and phosphate added together (units must be the same to do this) should not exceed 45 mEq/L.

  - Automated PN compounding software may use a calcium phosphate solubility curve to assess risk. Generally, when calcium and phosphate concentrations are plotted on the X- and Y-axis of the solubility graph, the lines should meet below the curve. Values that plot above the curve indicate a risk for precipitation.

- Maintain a proper pH (lower pH = less risk of precipitation) and refrigerate the bag once prepared. When temperature increases, more calcium and phosphate dissociate in solution and precipitation risk increases.

34. A patient is receiving 30 mmol of phosphate and 8 mEq of calcium. The volume of the PN is 2,000 mL. There are 2 mEq PO4/mmol. Confirm that the sum of the calcium and phosphorus does not exceed 45 mEq/L.

First, calculate the mEq of phosphate.

$$\frac{2 \text{ mEq PO4}}{\text{mmol}} \times 30 \text{ mmol PO4} = 60 \text{ mEq phosphate}$$

Then, add the phosphate and calcium mEq together. 60 mEq phosphate + 8 mEq calcium = 68 mEq.

Read the question again. Has it been answered? The volume of the PN is 2,000 mL, or 2 L. Calculate the <u>mEq per liter</u>.

68 mEq/2 L = 34 mEq/L, which is less than 45 mEq/L.

OTHER ADDITIVES

Multivitamins and trace elements are usually added to the PN formula. Insulin and histamine-2 receptor antagonists (H2RAs) are occasionally added. Adding any other IV medications to the PN is generally discouraged, because the entire PN would be wasted if a medication was discontinued or changed during the day.

MULTIVITAMINS

There are 4 fat-soluble vitamins (A, D, E, K) and 9 water-soluble vitamins (thiamine, riboflavin, niacin, pantothenic acid, pyridoxine, ascorbic acid, folic acid, cyanocobalamin, biotin) in the standard MVI-13 mixture. The MVI-12 mixture does not contain vitamin K since certain patients may need less or more of this vitamin. If a patient on PN therapy is taking warfarin, the INR must be monitored.

TRACE ELEMENTS

The standard mix includes zinc, copper, chromium and manganese (and possibly selenium). Manganese and copper should be withheld in severe liver disease. Chromium, molybdenum and selenium should be withheld in severe renal disease. <u>Iron is not routinely given in PN</u>.

INSULIN

Because of the large carbohydrate component of PN, insulin may be required (even in patients without diabetes). Half the sliding scale requirement from the previous day (or less) can be added to the PN as <u>regular insulin</u> to safely control blood glucose. This can be supplemented by SC insulin as needed. PN formulas are often titrated on and off (e.g., started at less than the goal rate and not abruptly stopped) to facilitate physiologic glucose regulation.

ENTERAL NUTRITION

EN, which provides nutrients via the GI tract, is the preferred method of feeding for patients who cannot meet their nutritional needs through voluntary oral intake. Several <u>advantages</u> of EN over PN include <u>lower cost</u>, it <u>uses the gut (which prevents atrophy</u> and other problems) and it has a <u>lower risk of complications</u> (less infections, less hyperglycemia, reduced risk of cholelithiasis and cholestasis). EN is sometimes administered through a feeding tube (see section on following page).

Example EN formulas include *Ensure, Osmolite, Jevity, Glucerna, Novasource* and many others. Some are specialized for certain types of patients (e.g., *Nepro* is a renal formula, *Glucerna* is for patients with diabetes), and some can be purchased OTC for meal replacement or those needing additional calories.

CALCULATIONS

FEEDING TUBES

- A tube in the nose to the stomach is called a <u>nasogastric (NG)</u>, or nasoenteral, tube.

- A tube that goes through the skin into the stomach is called a <u>gastrostomy, or percutaneous endoscopic gastrostomy (PEG or G) tube</u>.

- A tube into the small intestine is called a <u>jejunostomy, or percutaneous endoscopic jejunostomy (PEJ or J) tube</u>.

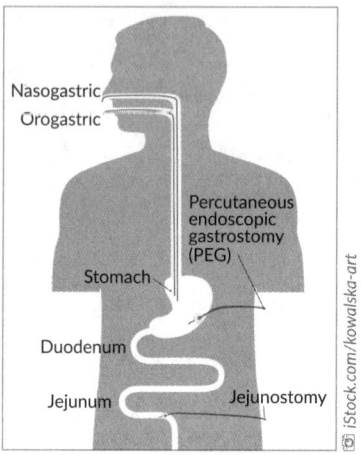

NG tubes are often used, primarily for short-term enteral nutrition administration. For longer-term, or if the stomach cannot be used, tubes are placed further down the GI tract. Tube feedings can range from providing adjunctive support to providing complete nutrition support.

The most common risk associated with tube feeding is aspiration, which can lead to pneumonia. Tube feeds do not, by themselves, provide enough water. Water is given in addition to the tube feeds. If fluid intake is inadequate, it will be uncomfortable for the patient and put them at risk for complications, including hypernatremia.

DRUG ADMINISTRATION VIA FEEDING TUBES

Drug administration through a feeding tube is an important part of patient care but can be prone to errors. Medications should never be added directly to the EN formula, and oral dosage forms (solid and liquid) are not always compatible with tube administration. Drug physical and chemical changes (e.g., from crushing and diluting an oral tablet), alterations in absorption, or interactions with nutrients (see below) can reduce the effect or increase the toxicity of a drug. Additionally, improper administration can cause blockage of the feeding tube. It is prudent to always consult package labeling for product-specific information, but in general, the following types of drugs <u>should not</u> be crushed and administered via a feeding tube:

- Enteric-coated products

- Delayed- or extended-release products

- Sublingual or buccal formulations

- Hazardous drugs (e.g., chemotherapeutics, hormones, teratogens)

Drug-Nutrient Interactions

The general rule for preventing drug/enteral feeding interactions is to <u>hold the feedings 1 hour before and 1 – 2 hours after</u> drug administration.

- <u>Warfarin</u>: many enteral products bind warfarin, resulting in low INRs and the need for dose adjustments. <u>Hold tube feeds one hour before and one hour after warfarin</u> administration. EN formulas contain varying amounts of vitamin K, which can complicate warfarin dosing in some patients.

- <u>Tetracyclines, quinolones and levothyroxine</u>: will <u>chelate</u> with polyvalent cations, including calcium, magnesium and iron, which reduces drug bioavailability; <u>separate</u> from tube feeds.

- <u>Ciprofloxacin</u>: the oral suspension is not compatible with tube feeds because the oil-based suspension adheres to the tube. <u>Immediate-release tablets</u> are used instead; <u>crush and mix</u> with water, and flush the line with water before and after administration.

- <u>Phenytoin</u> (*Dilantin* suspension): <u>levels are reduced</u> when the drug binds to the feeding solution, leading to less free drug availability and subtherapeutic levels; <u>separate</u> tube feeds by 2 hours.

Patient Case (For Questions 35 – 37)

WT is a patient starting enteral nutrition therapy. She has a past medical history significant for type 2 diabetes. She will be started on *Glucerna* ready-to-drink vanilla shakes. See the Nutrition Facts label provided.

Nutrition Facts	
Serving Size	8 fl oz (237 mL)
Amount Per Serving	
Calories	**356 kcal**
Total Fat 17.8 g	
Protein 19.6 g	
Total Carbohydrate 31.5 g	
Dietary Fiber	3.8 g
L-Carnitine	51 mg
Taurine	40 mg
m-Inositol	205 mg
Vitamin A	
Viamin C	
Iron	

35. **What percent of calories will WT receive from the protein component? Round to the nearest whole number.**

First, calculate the amount of calories provided by the protein component.

$$19.6 \text{ g protein} \times \frac{4 \text{ kcal}}{\text{g}} = 78.4 \text{ kcal}$$

Next, find the percentage of protein calories.

$$\frac{78.4 \text{ kcal}}{356 \text{ kcal}} \times 100 = 22\%$$

36. **How many calories will WT receive from the fat component of one (8 fl oz) shake? Round to the nearest whole number.**

$$17.8 \text{ g} \times \frac{9 \text{ kcal}}{\text{g}} = 160.2, \text{ or } 160 \text{ kcal}$$

37. **What percent of calories are derived from the fat component? Round to the nearest whole number.**

$$\frac{160.2 \text{ kcal}}{356 \text{ kcal}} \times 100 = 45\%$$

Patient Case (For Questions 38 – 40)

JB is a patient receiving *Osmolite* (a high-protein, low-residue enteral nutrition formula) through a PEG tube. See the Nutrition Facts label provided.

Nutrition Facts	
Serving Size	8 fl oz (237 mL)
Amount Per Serving	
Calories	**285 kcal**
Total Fat 9.2 g	
Protein 13.2 g	
Total Carbohydrate 37.4 g	
L-Carnitine	36 mg
Taurine	36 mg
Vitamin A	
Viamin C	
Iron	

38. **How many calories will JB receive from the carbohydrate component if he receives 4 fl oz? Round to the nearest whole number.**

First, calculate the total calories from carbohydrates in one carton (8 fl oz).

$$37.4 \text{ g carbohydrate} \times \frac{4 \text{ kcal}}{\text{g}} = 149.6 \text{ kcal from 8 fl oz}$$

The question asks about calories in 4 fl oz (½ carton).

$$\frac{149.6 \text{ kcal}}{2} = 74.8, \text{ or } 75 \text{ kcal from 4 fl oz}$$

CALCULATIONS

39. What percent of calories will JB receive from the carbohydrate component? Round to the nearest whole number.

First, calculate the amount of calories from the carbohydrate component.

$$37.4 \text{ g carbohydrate} \quad \times \quad \frac{4 \text{ kcal}}{g} \quad = \quad 149.6 \text{ kcal}$$

Next, find the percentage of carbohydrate calories.

$$\frac{149.6 \text{ kcal}}{285 \text{ kcal}} \quad \times \quad 100 \quad = \quad 52.49, \text{ or } 52\%$$

40. The nurse was administering one carton (8 fl oz) of *Osmolite* to JB when she accidentally spilled 2 fl oz on the floor. The remaining amount in the carton was accurately delivered to the patient. How many calories did he actually receive? Do not round the answer.

$$\frac{8 \text{ fl oz}}{285 \text{ kcal}} \quad = \quad \frac{6 \text{ fl oz}}{X \text{ kcal}} \qquad X = 213.75 \text{ kcal}$$

ADDITIONAL PN PRACTICE

Use the following PN order to answer questions 41 – 42:

Parenteral Nutrition Order Form

Macronutrients 2-in-1

Premixed:
☐ **Clinimix (5/15)**   Amino acids 5% / Dextrose 15%
☐ **Clinimix (5/15) with electrolytes**   Amino acids 5% / Dextrose 15%
☐ **Clinimix (4.25/10)**   Amino acids 4.25% / Dextrose 10%
☒ **Clinimix (4.25/10) with electrolytes**   Amino acids 4.25% / Dextrose 10%

Directions (2-in-1 PN)

Infuse: ☒ Daily   ☐ _____ times weekly

Select rate or volume:

Rate:
☒ Continuous infusion __75__ mL/hr

☐ 12-hour infusion _____ mL/hr

Volume (liters/day):
☐ 1   ☐ 2   ☐ Other _____

©RxPrep

41. How many calories will the PN provide from protein each day? Round to the nearest whole number.

Using the rate specified on the PN order form, calculate how many milliliters of PN the patient will receive each day:

75 mL/hr x 24 hrs = 1,800 mL/day

Then use the percentage strength of protein from the product ordered to calculate kcals/day from protein:

$$\frac{4.25 \text{ g protein}}{100 \text{ mL}} \quad \times \quad \frac{4 \text{ kcal}}{g \text{ protein}} \quad \times \quad \frac{1,800 \text{ mL}}{day} \quad = \quad 306 \text{ kcal/day from protein}$$

42. How many calories will the PN provide from carbohydrates each day? Round to the nearest whole number.

$$\frac{10 \text{ g}}{100 \text{ mL}} \quad \times \quad \frac{3.4 \text{ kcal}}{g} \quad \times \quad \frac{1,800 \text{ mL}}{day} \quad = \quad 612 \text{ kcal from carbohydrates}$$

CALCULATIONS

43. How many liters of this PN should be ordered to provide 1,420 kcals per day? Round to the nearest whole number.

Parenteral Nutrition Order Form

Macronutrients 2-in-1

Premixed:
☐ **Clinimix (5/15)**   Amino acids 5% / Dextrose 15%
☒ **Clinimix (5/15) with electrolytes**   Amino acids 5% / Dextrose 15%
☐ **Clinimix (4.25/10)**   Amino acids 4.25% / Dextrose 10%
☐ **Clinimix (4.25/10) with electrolytes**   Amino acids 4.25% / Dextrose 10%

Directions (2-in-1 PN)

Infuse: ☒ Daily   ☐ _____ times weekly

Select rate or volume:

Rate:

☐ Continuous infusion _____ mL/hr

☐ 12-hour infusion _____ mL/hr

Volume (liters/day):

☐ 1   ☐ 2   ☐ Other _____

☐ ©RxPrep

First, calculate how many kcals/L the PN provides:

Protein

$$\frac{5 \text{ g protein}}{100 \text{ mL}} = \frac{X \text{ g}}{1{,}000 \text{ mL}} \qquad X = 50 \text{ g protein/L}$$

$$\frac{50 \text{ g protein}}{L} \times \frac{4 \text{ kcal}}{g} = 200 \text{ kcal protein/L}$$

Dextrose

$$\frac{15 \text{ g dextrose}}{100 \text{ mL}} = \frac{X \text{ g}}{1{,}000 \text{ mL}} \qquad X = 150 \text{ g dextrose/L}$$

$$\frac{150 \text{ g dextrose}}{L} \times \frac{3.4 \text{ kcal}}{g} = 510 \text{ kcal dextrose/L}$$

Total

200 kcal/L protein + 510 kcal/L dextrose = 710 kcal/L for PN

Now determine how many liters will provide 1,420 kcals:

$$\frac{710 \text{ kcals}}{L} = \frac{1{,}420 \text{ kcals}}{X \text{ L}} \qquad X = 2 \text{ L}$$

44. How many calories will this PN provide per day? Round to the nearest whole number.

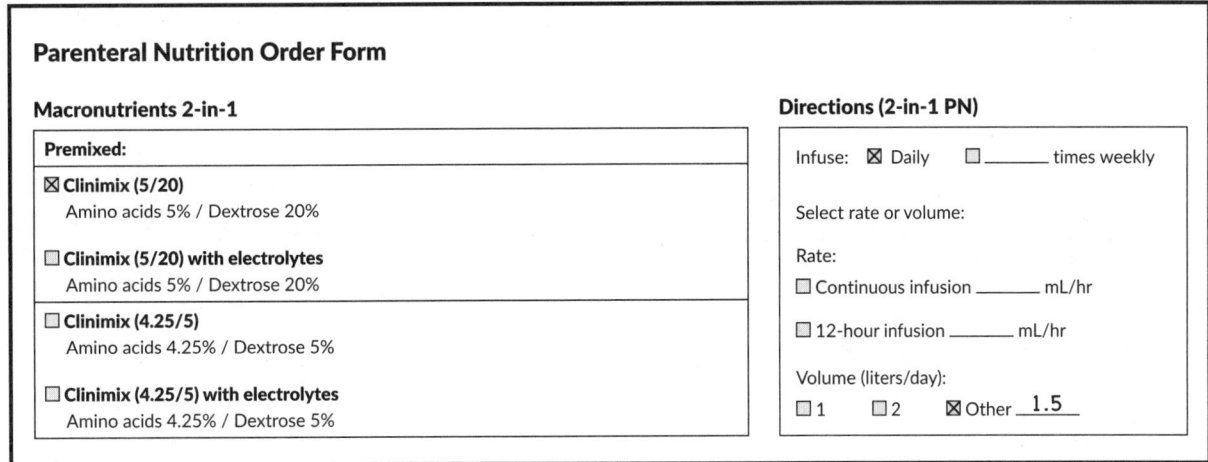

Parenteral Nutrition Order Form

Macronutrients 2-in-1

Premixed:
☒ **Clinimix (5/20)**   Amino acids 5% / Dextrose 20%
☐ **Clinimix (5/20) with electrolytes**   Amino acids 5% / Dextrose 20%
☐ **Clinimix (4.25/5)**   Amino acids 4.25% / Dextrose 5%
☐ **Clinimix (4.25/5) with electrolytes**   Amino acids 4.25% / Dextrose 5%

Directions (2-in-1 PN)

Infuse: ☒ Daily   ☐ _____ times weekly

Select rate or volume:

Rate:
☐ Continuous infusion _____ mL/hr

☐ 12-hour infusion _____ mL/hr

Volume (liters/day):
☐ 1   ☐ 2   ☒ Other _1.5_

☐ ©RxPrep

Question 44 continued on next page.

CALCULATIONS

$$\frac{5\ g}{100\ mL} \times \frac{4\ kcal}{g} \times \frac{1{,}500\ mL}{day} = 300\ kcal/day\ from\ protein$$

$$\frac{20\ g}{100\ mL} \times \frac{3.4\ kcal}{g} \times \frac{1{,}500\ mL}{day} = 1{,}020\ kcal/day\ from\ dextrose$$

300 kcal/day protein + 1,020 kcal/day dextrose = 1,320 kcal per day

45. **TE is a 35-year-old female who is receiving PN therapy with 325 grams of dextrose, 85 grams of amino acids and 300 mL of 10% lipids. What percentage of total calories is provided by the protein content? Round to the nearest whole number.**

First, calculate the calories from all sources; dextrose, amino acids and lipids.

Dextrose

$$\frac{3.4\ kcal}{g} \times 325\ g = 1{,}105\ kcal\ of\ dextrose$$

Protein

$$\frac{4\ kcal}{g} \times 85\ g = 340\ kcal\ of\ protein$$

Lipids

$$\frac{1.1\ kcal}{mL} \times 300\ mL = 330\ kcal\ of\ fat$$

Then, add up the total calories from all the sources. 1,105 + 340 + 330 = 1,775 kcal

Finally, calculate the percent of calories from protein.

$$\frac{340\ kcal}{1{,}775\ kcal} \times 100 = 19\%$$

Use the following PN order to answer questions 46 – 54:

ITEM	QUANTITY		ITEM	QUANTITY
Dextrose 70%	250 g		Calcium	12 mEq
Amino acids	50 g		MVI-12	5 mL
Sodium chloride (M.W. 58.5)	44 mEq		Trace elements-5	1 mL
Sodium acetate (M.W. 82)	20 mEq		Vitamin K-1	0.5 mg
Potassium	40 mEq		Famotidine	10 mg
Magnesium sulfate	12 mEq		Regular insulin	20 units
Phosphate	18 mmol		Sterile water qs ad	960 mL

46. **How many milliliters of dextrose 70% should be added to the PN? Round to the nearest whole number.**

$$\frac{70\ g}{100\ mL} = \frac{250\ g}{X\ mL} \qquad X = 357\ mL\ of\ dextrose\ 70\%$$

47. Using potassium phosphate (3 mmol of phosphate and 4.4 mEq of potassium/mL) vials in stock, calculate the amount of potassium phosphate that should be added to the PN to meet the phosphate requirement.

$$\frac{3 \text{ mmol phosphate}}{\text{mL}} = \frac{18 \text{ mmol phosphate}}{X \text{ mL}} \qquad X = 6 \text{ mL potassium phosphate}$$

48. If the pharmacist adds 6 mL of potassium phosphate (3 mmol/mL of phosphate and 4.4 mEq/mL of potassium) to the 2-in-1 product, how much potassium chloride (2 mEq/mL), in milliliters, should be added to fulfill the order? Round to the nearest tenth.

First, calculate the amount of K already added to the PN in the form of potassium phosphate.

$$\frac{4.4 \text{ mEq K}}{\text{mL}} \times 6 \text{ mL} = 26.4 \text{ mEq K}$$

Total K needed is 40 mEq. 40 mEq – 26.4 mEq = 13.6 mEq still needed from KCl

$$\frac{2 \text{ mEq K}}{\text{mL}} = \frac{13.6 \text{ mEq K}}{X \text{ mL}} \qquad X = 6.8 \text{ mL KCl}$$

49. The pharmacy has calcium gluconate 10% (0.465 mEq/mL) in stock. How many milliliters of calcium gluconate 10% should be added to the PN? Round to the nearest whole number.

$$\frac{0.465 \text{ mEq Ca}}{\text{mL}} = \frac{12 \text{ mEq Ca}}{X \text{ mL}} \qquad X = 25.8, \text{ or } 26 \text{ mL calcium gluconate 10\%}$$

50. The PN calls for 18 mmol of phosphate and 12 mEq of calcium (provided by 26 mL of calcium gluconate 10%, as calculated in the previous problem) in a volume of 960 mL. There are 2 mEq PO4/mmol. Confirm that the sum of the calcium and phosphorus do not exceed 45 mEq/L.

First, calculate the mEq of phosphate.

$$\frac{2 \text{ mEq PO4}}{\text{mmol}} \times 18 \text{ mmol PO4} = 36 \text{ mEq phosphate}$$

Then, add up the milliequivalents of phosphate and calcium. 36 mEq phosphate + 12 mEq calcium = 48 mEq.

The volume of the PN is 960 mL, or 0.96 L. Calculate the mEq per liter.

48 mEq/0.96 L = 50 mEq/L, which is greater than 45 mEq/L

When the sum of calcium and phosphate milliequivalents exceeds 45 mEq/L, there is a risk of precipitation (see previous discussion of Calcium and Phosphate Solubility in this chapter). The pharmacist should contact the prescriber to amend the order.

51. Calculate the amount of magnesium sulfate (4 mEq/mL) that should be added to the PN.

$$\frac{4 \text{ mEq}}{\text{mL}} = \frac{12 \text{ mEq}}{X \text{ mL}} \qquad X = 3 \text{ mL magnesium sulfate}$$

52. What percentage of the total calories from the PN are represented by the protein component? Round to the nearest whole number.

First, calculate the total calories.

Dextrose

$$\frac{3.4 \text{ kcal dextrose}}{g} \times 250 \text{ g dextrose} = 850 \text{ kcal of dextrose}$$

Protein

$$\frac{4 \text{ kcal protein}}{g} \times 50 \text{ g protein} = 200 \text{ kcal of protein}$$

Total calories = 850 + 200 = 1,050 kcal. Now, calculate the percent of calories from protein.

$$\frac{200 \text{ kcal}}{1,050 \text{ kcal}} \times 100 = 19\%$$

Questions 53 – 54 require knowledge of milliequivalents from the Calculations II chapter.

53. How many milliliters of 23.4% sodium chloride should be added to the PN?

$$44 \text{ mEq} = \frac{X \text{ mg} \times 1}{58.5} \qquad X = 2,574 \text{ mg, or } 2.574 \text{ g}$$

$$\frac{23.4 \text{ g}}{100 \text{ mL}} = \frac{2.574 \text{ g}}{X \text{ mL}} \qquad X = 11 \text{ mL of } 23.4\% \text{ NaCl}$$

This concentration of NaCl is hypertonic and is a high-alert drug due to heightened risk of patient harm when dosed incorrectly. Refer to the Medication Safety & Quality Improvement chapter.

---

54. Calculate the amount of 16.4% sodium acetate that should be added to the PN.

$$20 \text{ mEq} = \frac{X \text{ mg} \times 1}{82} \qquad X = 1,640 \text{ mg, or } 1.64 \text{ g}$$

$$\frac{16.4 \text{ g}}{100 \text{ mL}} = \frac{1.64 \text{ g}}{X \text{ mL}} \qquad X = 10 \text{ mL of } 16.4\% \text{ sodium acetate}$$

CONTENT LEGEND

 = Study Tip Gal

iStock.com/Jacoblund

CHAPTER 12

CALCULATIONS IV: CLINICAL

BODY MASS INDEX

Overweight and obesity are health problems associated with increased morbidity from hypertension, dyslipidemia, diabetes, coronary heart disease, stroke, gallbladder disease, osteoarthritis and other conditions. Higher body weights are also associated with increases in all-cause mortality. Body mass index (BMI) is a measure of body fat based on height and weight that applies to adult men and women. BMI is a useful measure of body fat, but the BMI can over-estimate body fat in persons who are muscular, and can under-estimate body fat in frail elderly persons and others who have lost muscle mass. Waist circumference is used concurrently with BMI. If most of the fat is around the waist, there is higher disease risk. High risk is defined as a waist size > 35 inches for women or > 40 inches for men. Underweight can be a problem if a person is fighting a disease such as a frail, hospitalized patient with an infection.

BMI should be calculated as follows:

$$\text{BMI (kg/m}^2) = \frac{\text{weight (kg)}}{[\text{height (m)}]^2}$$

Alternatively, BMI can be calculated with weight in pounds and height in inches using a conversion factor to convert to units of kg/m²:

$$\text{BMI (kg/m}^2) = \frac{\text{weight (pounds)}}{[\text{height (in)}]^2} \times 703 \text{ (to convert to kg/m}^2)$$

BMI CLASSIFICATIONS

BMI (kg/m²)	CLASSIFICATION
< 18.5	Underweight
18.5 – 24.9	Normal weight
25 – 29.9	Overweight
≥ 30	Obese

1. A male patient comes to the pharmacy and tells the pharmacist he is 6'7" tall and 250 pounds. His waist circumference is 43 inches. Calculate his BMI. Round to the nearest whole number. Is the patient underweight, normal weight, overweight or obese?

   - Convert weight to kg: 250 pounds x 1 kg/2.2 lbs = 113.6363 kg

   - Convert height to cm: 6'7" = 79 inches x 2.54 cm/inch = 200.66 cm

$$200.66 \text{ cm} \times \frac{1 \text{ m}}{100 \text{ cm}} = 2.0066 \text{ m}$$

$$\text{BMI (kg/m}^2) = \frac{113.6363 \text{ kg}}{(2.0066 \text{ m})^2} = 28.2 \text{ kg/m}^2, \text{ rounded to 28, overweight}$$

Because of the rounding specifications in the question, the answer is the same regardless of the formula used. Expect the same on the exam.

2. Calculate the BMI for a male who is 6' tall and weighs 198 lbs. Round to the nearest tenth. Is the patient underweight, normal weight, overweight or obese?

$$\text{BMI (kg/m}^2) = \frac{198 \text{ pounds}}{(72 \text{ in})^2} \times 703 = 26.9 \text{ kg/m}^2, \text{ overweight}$$

Because of the rounding specifications in the question, the answer is the same regardless of the formula used. Expect the same on the exam.

BODY WEIGHT

There are three potential measures of body weight for a patient: actual (or total) body weight, ideal body weight and adjusted body weight. In pharmacy, weights are used to calculate drug doses, flow rates, creatinine clearance and more. The weight that should be used for each type of calculation (in an individual patient) is not always the same.

ACTUAL BODY WEIGHT OR TOTAL BODY WEIGHT

Actual body weight or total body weight (TBW) is the weight of the patient when weighed on a scale.

IDEAL BODY WEIGHT

Ideal body weight (IBW) is the healthy (ideal) weight for a person.

IBW (males) = 50 kg + (2.3 kg)(number of inches over 5 feet)

IBW (females) = 45.5 kg + (2.3 kg)(number of inches over 5 feet)

There are alternate methods of calculating IBW in children and adults < 5 feet.

ADJUSTED BODY WEIGHT

Adjusted body weight is calculated when patients are obese or overweight.

$\text{AdjBW}_{0.4} = \text{IBW} + 0.4(\text{TBW} - \text{IBW})$

Adult doses are generally the same for all patients (e.g., lisinopril 10 mg daily). Weight-based (mg/kg) dosing is common in pediatrics and is recommended for some medications in adult patients. Total body weight is used for weight-based dosing of most drugs in adults, but there are exceptions. Some drugs with a narrow therapeutic index (e.g., aminophylline, theophylline) are dosed based on IBW to avoid toxicity. Some drugs (e.g., enoxaparin, vancomycin) are dosed based on total body weight (even if a patient is obese) because of the results of clinical trials. Dosing drugs in obesity is challenging because there is a risk of underdosing (when standard doses are used) and overdosing (when dosing based on total body weight). In clinical practice, consult primary literature for the best dosing strategy in obese patients. Refer to the algorithm on the next page for guidance on selecting the correct weight for drug dosing (mg/kg).

WHICH WEIGHT TO USE FOR DRUG DOSING (mg/kg)?

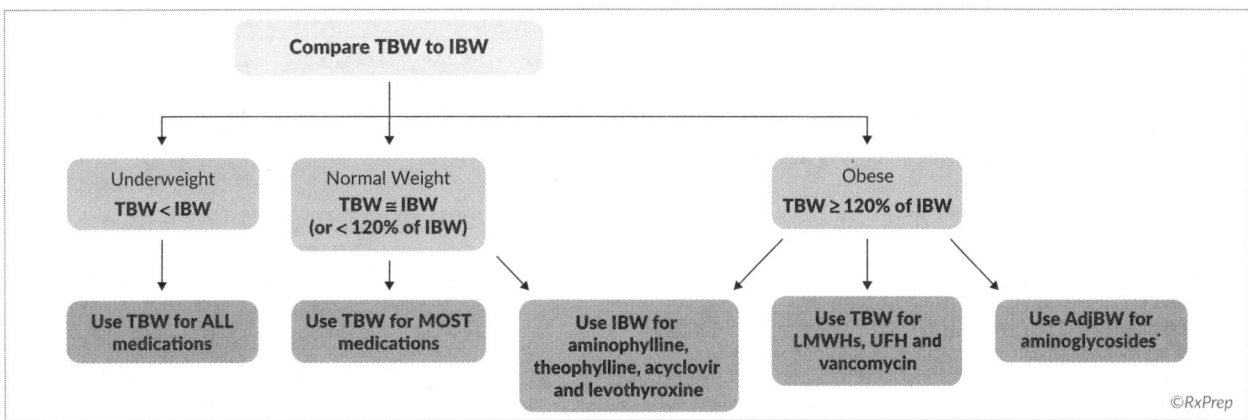

If a question specifies what weight to use (even if different from above), use it. Follow all instructions on the exam.
*Aminoglycosides are dosed based on TBW or IBW, unless the patient is obese, then AdjBW is used.

---

3. **A female patient is to receive 5 mg/kg/day of theophylline. The patient is 5'7" and weighs 243 pounds. Calculate the daily theophylline dose the patient should receive.**

$$\text{Total Body Weight} = 243 \text{ lb} \times \frac{1 \text{ kg}}{2.2 \text{ lbs}} = 110.4545 \text{ kg}$$

$$\text{IBW (female)} = 45.5 \text{ kg} + (2.3 \times 7 \text{ in}) = 61.6 \text{ kg}$$

$$\text{\% above IBW} = \frac{110.4545 \text{ kg}}{61.6 \text{ kg}} = \sim 1.8 \text{, she is 180\% of her IBW or 80\% above her IBW}$$

Use the algorithm to determine which weight to use to dose the theophylline. This patient is obese. <u>Theophylline, aminophylline, acyclovir and levothyroxine</u> are narrow therapeutic index drugs. They are <u>dosed on IBW</u> in normal weight and obese patients for safety.

$$\text{Theophylline 5 mg/kg} \times 61.6 \text{ kg} = 308 \text{ mg}$$

---

4. **A 34-year-old male (height 6'7", weight 287 pounds) is hospitalized after a motor vehicle accident. He develops a *Pseudomonas aeruginosa* infection. The physician orders tobramycin 2 mg/kg IV Q8H. Calculate the tobramycin dose. Round to the nearest 10 milligrams.**

$$\text{Total Body Weight} = 287 \text{ lb} \times \frac{1 \text{ kg}}{2.2 \text{ lbs}} = 130.4545 \text{ kg}$$

$$\text{IBW (male)} = 50 \text{ kg} + (2.3 \times 19 \text{ in}) = 93.7 \text{ kg}$$

$$\text{\% above IBW} = \frac{130.4545 \text{ kg}}{93.7 \text{ kg}} = 1.39 \text{, he is 139\% of his IBW or 39\% above his IBW}$$

Use the algorithm to determine which weight to use to dose the aminoglycoside. This patient is obese. Aminoglycosides are dosed using adjusted body weight in obese patients.

$$\text{AdjBW}_{0.4} = 93.7 + 0.4 (130.4545 - 93.7) = 108.4 \text{ kg}$$

$$\text{Tobramycin 2 mg/kg} \times 108.4 \text{ kg} = 216.8 \text{ mg, round to 220 mg IV Q8H}$$

HEIGHT IN INCHES

In the U.S., heights are generally presented in feet and inches vs using the metric system.

- Example 1: A patient is 5 feet 6 inches tall (often written 5'6"). How many inches tall is the patient?
  - ❑ 1 ft = 12 inches, so 5 ft = 60 inches
  - ❑ Next, add the additional 6 inches
  - ❑ 5'6" = 66 inches
  - ❑ For IBW calculation: patient is 6 inches over 5 feet
- Example 2: A patient is 6'3". How many inches tall is this patient?
  - ❑ 6 ft x 12 inches/ft = 72 inches
  - ❑ Next, add the additional 3 inches
  - ❑ 6'3" = 75 inches
  - ❑ For IBW calculation: patient is 15 inches over 5 feet

FLOW RATES

Intravenous (IV) infusions or continuous infusions are commonly used to deliver medications in different settings, including hospitals. Flow rates are used to specify the volume or amount of drug a patient will receive over a given period of time. An order can specify the flow rate in many ways. Some examples include: milliliters per hour, milligrams per hour, mcg/kg/min or as the total time to administer the entire volume of the infusion (e.g., give over 8 hours). Sometimes flow rates are expressed in drops/min, which is discussed later in this chapter.

Flow rate problems can be performed with proportions or dimensional analysis. Principles of each are reviewed in Calculations I. Some of the following problems will be illustrated using both methods, but not all. Feel free to use whichever method is most comfortable.

5. **A patient will receive 400 mg of a drug that has been put in a 250 mL IV bag. The rate of drug administration is 375 mcg per minute. Calculate the flow rate in milliliters per hour. Round to the nearest whole number.**

   The order specifies the rate of administration as 375 mcg/min. Many infusion pumps are set to deliver a certain volume of fluid per unit of time (e.g., mL/hr). This requires a conversion.

   Dimensional analysis works well for flow rate problems. Here is a breakdown of the steps:

   1. The 1st fraction is the drug concentration. Since you are solving for mL/hr, milliliters needs to be in the numerator.

   2. The 2nd fraction converts the drug weight from milligrams to micrograms.

   3. The 3rd fraction is the rate of drug administration.

   4. The 4th fraction converts minutes to hours.

   5. This combines the individual steps into one calculation. If using dimensional analysis, make sure that all <u>units cancel out</u> to leave the correct units:

$$\frac{250\,\text{mL}}{400\,\text{mg}} \times \frac{1\,\text{mg}}{1{,}000\,\text{mcg}} \times \frac{375\,\text{mcg}}{\text{min}} \times \frac{60\,\text{min}}{1\,\text{hr}} = 14\,\text{mL/hr}$$

   Flow rates depend on the <u>dose</u> of the medication and the <u>concentration</u> available. If the concentration of the medication is 400 mg/250 mL (in the example above), then the IV needs to run at 14 mL/hr to deliver 375 mcg/min.

   If the pharmacy prepared a more concentrated product (e.g., 800 mg/250 mL, or twice as concentrated), then the IV will only need to run at 7 mL/hr to deliver the same dose. See math below:

$$\frac{250\,\text{mL}}{800\,\text{mg}} \times \frac{1\,\text{mg}}{1{,}000\,\text{mcg}} \times \frac{375\,\text{mcg}}{\text{min}} \times \frac{60\,\text{min}}{1\,\text{hr}} = 7\,\text{mL/hr}$$

6. **The pharmacist has an order for heparin 25,000 units in 250 mL D5W to infuse at 1,000 units/hour. The pharmacy has the following premixed heparin bags in stock: 25,000 units in 500 mL ½ NS, 10,000 units in 250 mL D5W, and 25,000 units in 250 mL D5W. What should the infusion rate be set at in mL/hour?**

   The pharmacy has the heparin product that was ordered. First, calculate the concentration (units per mL).

$$\frac{25{,}000\,\text{units}}{250\,\text{mL}} = 100\,\text{units/mL}$$

   Next calculate the infusion rate.

$$\frac{1{,}000\,\text{units}}{1\,\text{hr}} \times \frac{1\,\text{mL}}{100\,\text{units}} = 10\,\text{mL/hr}$$

   Since 1,000 units/hour must be delivered to the patient and there are 100 units in each mL, the pump should be programmed for an infusion rate of 10 mL/hr.

Question 6 continued on next page

A second way to solve flow rate problems is using dimensional analysis:

$$\frac{250 \text{ mL}}{25,000 \text{ units}} \times \frac{1,000 \text{ units}}{1 \text{ hr}} = 10 \text{ mL/hr}$$

Another way to solve these problems is to use a proportion:

$$\frac{25,000 \text{ units}}{250 \text{ mL}} = \frac{1,000 \text{ units}}{X \text{ mL}} \quad X = 10 \text{ mL (10 mL/hr since we need to administer 1,000 units in 1 hour)}$$

Try solving the problems in this section both ways and decide which you prefer.

---

7. **If 200 mg of drug are added to a 500 mL bag, what rate of flow, in milliliters per hour, will deliver 500 mcg of drug per hour? Round to the nearest hundredth.**

$$200 \text{ mg} \times \frac{1,000 \text{ mcg}}{1 \text{ mg}} = 200,000 \text{ mcg}$$

$$\frac{200,000 \text{ mcg}}{500 \text{ mL}} = \frac{500 \text{ mcg}}{X} \quad X = 1.25 \text{ mL/hour}$$

---

8. **A nurse is hanging a 4% lidocaine drip for a patient. If the dose ordered is 6 mg/min, how many hours will a 250 mL bag last? Round to the nearest tenth.**

$$\frac{4 \text{ g}}{100 \text{ mL}} = \frac{X \text{ g}}{250 \text{ mL}} \quad X = 10 \text{ g or 10,000 mg}$$

$$\frac{6 \text{ mg}}{\text{min}} = \frac{10,000 \text{ mg}}{X \text{ min}} \quad X = 1,666.67 \text{ minutes}$$

Convert to hours = 27.777 hrs, or 27.8 hrs

Or, solve another way:

$$\frac{1 \text{ hr}}{60 \text{ min}} \times \frac{1 \text{ min}}{6 \text{ mg}} \times \frac{1,000 \text{ mg}}{1 \text{ g}} \times \frac{4 \text{ g}}{100 \text{ mL}} \times 250 \text{ mL} = 27.8 \text{ hours}$$

---

9. **A 68 kg patient is receiving a drug in a standard concentration of 400 mg/250 mL of ½ NS running at 15 mL/hr. Calculate the dose in mcg/kg/min. Round to the nearest hundredth.**

$$\frac{15 \text{ mL}}{\text{hr}} \times \frac{400 \text{ mg}}{250 \text{ mL}} = 24 \text{ mg/hr}$$

$$\frac{24 \text{ mg}}{\text{hr}} \times \frac{1,000 \text{ mcg}}{1 \text{ mg}} = 24,000 \text{ mcg/hr}$$

$$\frac{24,000 \text{ mcg}}{\text{hr}} \times \frac{1 \text{ hr}}{60 \text{ min}} = 400 \text{ mcg/min}$$

$$\frac{400 \text{ mcg/min}}{68 \text{ kg}} = 5.88 \text{ mcg/kg/min}$$

Or, solve another way:

$$\frac{15 \text{ mL}}{1 \text{ hr}} \times \frac{400 \text{ mg}}{250 \text{ mL}} \times \frac{1,000 \text{ mcg}}{1 \text{ mg}} \times \frac{1 \text{ hr}}{60 \text{ min}} \div 68 \text{ kg} = 5.88 \text{ mcg/kg/min}$$

10. The pharmacist has an order for heparin 25,000 units in 250 mL D5W to infuse at 1,000 units/hour. How many hours will it take to infuse the entire bag?

$$25,000 \text{ units} \times \frac{1 \text{ hr}}{1,000 \text{ units}} = 25 \text{ hrs}$$

11. If 50 mg of drug are added to a 500 mL bag, what rate of flow, in milliliters per hour, will deliver 5 mg of drug per hour?

$$\frac{500 \text{ mL}}{50 \text{ mg}} \times \frac{5 \text{ mg}}{\text{hr}} = 50 \text{ mL/hour}$$

12. A patient is to receive *Keppra* at a rate of 5 mg/min. The pharmacy has a 5 mL *Keppra* vial (100 mg/mL) which will be diluted in 100 mL of NS. What is the *Keppra* infusion rate, in mL/min? Do not include the volume of the 5 mL additive.

First, calculate the amount of *Keppra* in the vial.

$$\frac{100 \text{ mg}}{\text{mL}} = \frac{X \text{ mg}}{5 \text{ mL}} \qquad X = 500 \text{ mg}$$

Then, solve for the answer in mL/min.

$$\frac{100 \text{ mL}}{500 \text{ mg}} \times \frac{5 \text{ mg}}{\text{min}} = 1 \text{ mL/min}$$

FINAL VOLUME OF COMPOUNDED IV SOLUTIONS

Why does problem #12 say "do not include the volume of the 5 mL additive"? Because the answer might be different (depending on the rounding instructions) if you used 100 mL vs 105 mL for the final volume.

■ Exam scenarios:

❏ Explicit instructions (e.g., #12).

❏ Language stating that a specific volume is "added to" some volume of a fluid (e.g., #22).

❏ Rounding instructions are such that either method will yield the correct answer or volumes of additives are not provided.

❏ Language stating that a specific volume is added "to make 1 liter" or "for a final volume of 1 L."

This can be handled in many ways in clinical practice, but institutions should have clear policies to avoid medication errors.

13. A patient is to receive 600,000 units of penicillin G potassium in 100 mL D5W. A vial of penicillin G potassium 1,000,000 units is available. The manufacturer states that when 4.6 mL of diluent is added, a 200,000 units/mL solution will result. How many milliliters of reconstituted solution should be withdrawn and added to the bag of D5W?

$$\frac{200,000 \text{ units}}{\text{mL}} = \frac{600,000 \text{ units}}{X \text{ mL}} \qquad X = 3 \text{ mL}$$

14. A patient is to receive *Flagyl* at a rate of 12.5 mg/min. The pharmacy has a 5 mL (100 mg/mL) *Flagyl* injection vial to be diluted in 100 mL of NS. How much drug in milligrams will the patient receive over 20 minutes?

$$\frac{12.5 \text{ mg}}{\text{min}} \times 20 \text{ minutes} = 250 \text{ mg}$$

15. A physician has ordered 2 grams of cefotetan to be added to 100 mL NS for a 56-year-old female with an anaerobic infection. Using a reconstituted injection containing 154 mg/mL, how many milliliters should be added to prepare the order? Round to the nearest whole number.

$$2,000 \text{ mg} \times \frac{1 \text{ mL}}{154 \text{ mg}} = 13 \text{ mL}$$

16. **JY is a 58-year-old male hospitalized for a total knee replacement. He was given unfractionated heparin and developed heparin-induced thrombocytopenia (HIT). Argatroban was ordered at a dose of 2 mcg/kg/min. The pharmacy mixes a concentration of 100 mg argatroban in 250 mL of D5W. JY weighs 187 lbs. At what rate (mL/hour) should the nurse infuse argatroban to provide the desired dose? Round to the nearest whole number.**

First, determine the amount of drug needed based on the body weight provided.

$$2 \text{ mcg/kg/min} \times 85 \text{ kg} = 170 \text{ mcg/min}$$

Then, calculate mL/hr.

$$\frac{250 \text{ mL}}{100 \text{ mg}} \times \frac{1 \text{ mg}}{1{,}000 \text{ mcg}} \times \frac{170 \text{ mcg}}{\text{min}} \times \frac{60 \text{ min}}{\text{hr}} = 25.5 \text{ mL/hr, rounded to } 26 \text{ mL/hr}$$

17. **A 165-pound patient is to receive 250 mL of a dopamine drip at a rate of 17 mcg/kg/min. The pharmacy has dopamine premixed in a concentration of 3.2 mg/mL in D5W. Calculate the infusion rate in mL/minute. Round to the nearest tenth.**

Step 1: Calculate amount of drug in the 250 mL bag.

$$\frac{3.2 \text{ mg}}{\text{mL}} \times 250 \text{ mL} = 800 \text{ mg}$$

Step 2: Calculate amount of drug the patient needs per minute.

$$\frac{17 \text{ mcg}}{\text{kg/min}} \times \frac{1 \text{ kg}}{2.2 \text{ lbs}} \times 165 \text{ lbs} = 1{,}275 \text{ mcg/min or } 1.275 \text{ mg/min}$$

Step 3: Solve for milliliters per minute.

$$\frac{250 \text{ mL}}{800 \text{ mg}} \times \frac{1.275 \text{ mg}}{\text{min}} = 0.4 \text{ mL/min}$$

18. **An order is written for phenytoin IV. A loading dose of 15 mg/kg is to be infused at 0.5 mg/kg/min for a 33-pound child. The pharmacy has phenytoin injection solution 50 mg/mL in a 5 mL vial in stock. The pharmacist will put the dose into 50 mL NS. Over how many minutes should the dose be administered? Round to the nearest whole number.**

First, calculate the child's body weight in kg.

$$33 \text{ lbs} \times \frac{1 \text{ kg}}{2.2 \text{ lbs}} = 15 \text{ kg}$$

Next, find the dose the child will receive.

$$\frac{15 \text{ mg}}{\text{kg}} \times 15 \text{ kg} = 225 \text{ mg}$$

Then, calculate the time it will take to infuse this amount of drug at the given rate.

$$0.5 \text{ mg/kg/min} \times 15 \text{ kg} = 7.5 \text{ mg/min}$$

$$\frac{1 \text{ min}}{7.5 \text{ mg}} \times 225 \text{ mg} = 30 \text{ minutes}$$

DROP FACTOR

IV tubing is set to deliver a certain number of drops per minute (gtts/min). There are various types of IV tubing and each has a hollow plastic chamber called a drip chamber. The number of drops per minute can be counted by looking at the drip chamber. It is important to know how big the drops are to calibrate the tubing in terms of drops/mL. This is called the drop factor. Calculating flow rates from a drop factor is not as common with the prevalence of programmable "smart" pumps. It is a good skill to know for situations when a programmable pump is not available (or fails) and as a "double check."

CALCULATIONS

19. A physician orders an IV infusion of D5W 1 liter to be delivered over 8 hours. The IV infusion set delivers 15 drops/mL. How many drops/min will the patient receive? Round to the nearest whole number.

$$\frac{15 \text{ drops}}{1 \text{ mL}} \times \frac{1,000 \text{ mL}}{8 \text{ hr}} \times \frac{1 \text{ hr}}{60 \text{ min}} = 31.25 \text{ drops/min, rounded to 31 drops/min}$$

20. A physician orders 15 units of regular insulin in 1 liter of D5W to be given over 10 hours. What is the infusion rate, in drops/minute, if the IV set delivers 15 drops/mL? Do not include the insulin volume in the calculation.

$$\frac{15 \text{ drops}}{\text{mL}} \times \frac{1,000 \text{ mL}}{10 \text{ hrs}} \times \frac{1 \text{ hr}}{60 \text{ min}} = 25 \text{ drops/min}$$

21. The pharmacy has insulin vials containing 100 units of insulin/mL. A physician orders 15 units of regular insulin in 1 liter of D5W to be given over 10 hours. How many units of insulin will the patient receive each hour if the IV set delivers 15 drops/mL? Do not round the answer.

$$\frac{15 \text{ units}}{10 \text{ hrs}} = \frac{X \text{ units}}{1 \text{ hr}} \quad X = 1.5 \text{ units/hr}$$

22. An order is written for 10 mL of a 10% calcium chloride injection and 10 mL of multivitamin injection (MVI) to be added to 500 mL of D5W. The infusion is to be administered over 6 hours. The IV set delivers 15 drops/mL. What should be the rate of flow in drops/minute to deliver this infusion? Round to the nearest whole number.

Total volume of the infusion = 500 mL (D5W) + 10 mL (CaCl$_2$) + 10 mL (MVI) = 520 mL

$$\frac{15 \text{ drops}}{\text{mL}} \times \frac{520 \text{ mL}}{6 \text{ hr}} \times \frac{1 \text{ hr}}{60 \text{ min}} = 21.6666, \text{ rounded to 22 drops/min}$$

23. RS is a 45-year-old male, 5'5", 168 pounds, hospitalized with a diabetic foot infection. The pharmacist prepared a 500 mL bag of D5W containing 1 gram of vancomycin to be infused over 4 hours using a 20 gtts/mL IV tubing set. How many milligrams of vancomycin will the patient receive each minute? Round to the nearest tenth.

$$\frac{1,000 \text{ mg vanco}}{4 \text{ hrs}} \times \frac{1 \text{ hr}}{60 \text{ min}} = 4.16 \text{ mg/min, rounded to 4.2 mg/min}$$

Notice that the patient's height and weight are not needed to solve this problem.

24. A patient is to receive 1.5 liters of NS running at 45 gtts/min using a 15 gtts/mL IV tubing set. Calculate the total infusion time in hours. Round to the nearest tenth.

$$\frac{15 \text{ gtts}}{1 \text{ mL}} = \frac{45 \text{ gtts}}{X \text{ mL}} \quad X = 3 \text{ mL}$$

$$\frac{3 \text{ mL}}{\text{min}} = \frac{1,500 \text{ mL}}{X \text{ min}} \quad X = 500 \text{ min}$$

$$500 \text{ min} \times \frac{1 \text{ hr}}{60 \text{ min}} = 8.3 \text{ hrs}$$

25. The 8 AM medications scheduled for a patient include *Tygacil* dosed at 6 mg/kg. The patient weighs 142 pounds. The nurse has *Tygacil* labeled 500 mg/50 mL NS. The dose will be administered over thirty minutes. The IV tubing in the unit delivers 15 drops per milliliter. What is the correct rate of flow in drops per minute? Round to the nearest drop.

$$\frac{142 \text{ pounds}}{2.2 \text{ pounds/kg}} \times \frac{6 \text{ mg}}{\text{kg}} = 387.27 \text{ mg required dose}$$

$$387.27 \text{ mg} \times \frac{50 \text{ mL}}{500 \text{ mg}} = 38.727 \text{ mL}$$

$$\frac{38.727 \text{ mL}}{30 \text{ min}} \times \frac{15 \text{ drops}}{\text{mL}} = 19.36 \text{ drops/min, rounded to 19 drops/min for 30 minutes}$$

RENAL FUNCTION AND CREATININE CLEARANCE ESTIMATION

Creatinine is a break-down product produced when muscle tissue makes energy. The normal range for serum creatinine is approximately 0.6 – 1.3 mg/dL. If kidney function declines and creatinine cannot be cleared (excreted), the creatinine level will increase in the blood and the creatinine clearance (CrCl) will decrease. This tells us that the concentration of drugs that are renally cleared will also increase and a dose reduction may be required. Sometimes the serum creatinine can appear normal even when renal function is compromised (e.g., in the elderly). Refer to the Lab Values & Drug Monitoring and Renal Disease chapters.

Patients should be assessed for dehydration when the serum creatinine is elevated. Dehydration can cause both the serum creatinine (SCr) and the blood urea nitrogen (BUN) to increase. A BUN:SCr ratio > 20:1 indicates dehydration. Correcting the dehydration will reduce both BUN and SCr, and can prevent or treat acute renal failure. Signs of dehydration should also be assessed and these can include decreased urine output, tachycardia, tachypnea, dry skin/mouth/mucous membranes, skin tenting (skin does not bounce back when pinched into a fold) and possibly fever. Dehydration is usually caused by diarrhea, vomiting and/or a lack of adequate fluid intake.

26. Looking at the laboratory values below, make an assessment of the patient's hydration status.

	PATIENT'S VALUE	REFERENCE RANGE
BUN	54 mg/dL	7–20 mg/dL
Creatinine	1.8 mg/dL	0.6–1.3 mg/dL

   A. The patient appears to be well hydrated.
   B. The patient appears to be too hydrated.
   C. The patient is not experiencing dehydration.
   D. The patient is experiencing dehydration.
   E. The patient is experiencing fluid accumulation.

The correct answer is (D). The patient's BUN:SCr ratio is 54/1.8 = 30:1. Since 30:1 > 20:1, the BUN is disproportionately elevated relative to the creatinine, indicating that the patient is dehydrated.

27. NK is receiving a furosemide infusion at 5 mg/hr. The nurse notices her urine output has decreased in the last hour. Laboratory values are drawn and the patient has a SCr of 1.5 mg/dL and a BUN of 26 mg/dL. The nurse wants to know if she should stop the furosemide infusion due to the patient becoming dehydrated. What is the correct assessment of the patient's hydration status?

   A. The patient appears to be too hydrated given the laboratory results.
   B. The patient is not experiencing dehydration given the laboratory results.
   C. The patient is experiencing dehydration and may need to be started on fluids.
   D. The patient has objective information indicating dehydration but the patient needs to be assessed subjectively as well.
   E. None of the above are correct.

The correct answer is (B). The BUN:SCr ratio is 26/1.5 = 17.3:1, which is < 20:1. Continue to monitor the patient.

THE COCKCROFT-GAULT EQUATION

This formula is used by pharmacists to estimate renal function. It is <u>not reliable</u> in very <u>young children, ESRD</u> patients or when <u>renal function is fluctuating</u> rapidly. There are different methods used to estimate renal function in these circumstances. <u>The Cockcroft-Gault equation should be known, as it is commonly used in practice</u>.

$$CrCl \text{ (mL/min)} = \frac{140 - (\text{age of patient})}{72 \times SCr} \times \text{weight in kg (}\times 0.85 \text{ if female)}$$

Use age in years, weight in kg and SCr in mg/dL (same as mmol/L) in the Cockcroft-Gault equation

WHICH WEIGHT TO USE FOR CALCULATING CrCl?

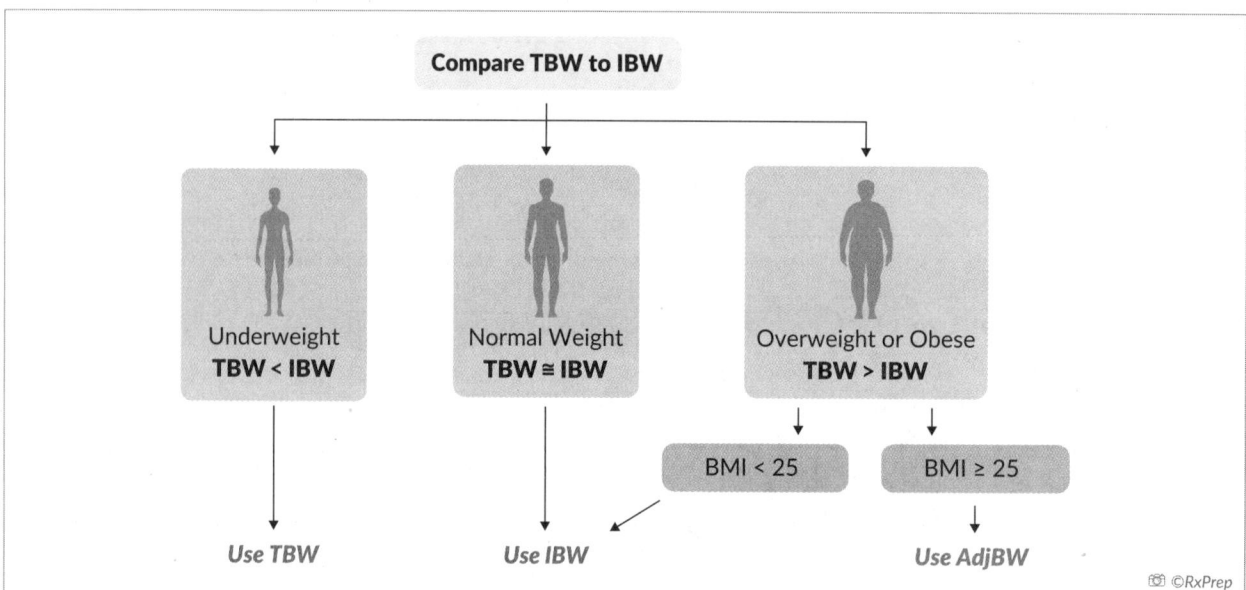

The CrCl is used to renally adjust most necessary medications [some medications are adjusted based on eGFR (e.g., metformin, SGLT2 inhibitors)]. The proper weight to use in the Cockcroft-Gault equation <u>will not always be the same</u> weight used to calculate a weight-based (mg/kg) dose (see previous algorithm). The following examples illustrate this point.

28. **A 64-year-old female patient (height 5'5", weight 205 pounds) is hospitalized with a nosocomial pneumonia which is responding to treatment. Her current antibiotic medications include ciprofloxacin, *Primaxin* and vancomycin. Her morning laboratory values include: K 4 mEq/L, BUN 60 mg/dL, SCr 2.7 mg/dL and glucose 222 mg/dL. Based on the renal dosage recommendations from the package labeling below, what is the correct dose of *Primaxin* for this patient?**

CrCl	≥ 90 mL/min	60–89 mL/min	30–59 mL/min	15–29 mL/min
Primaxin Dose	1,000 mg IV Q8H	500 mg IV Q6H	500 mg IV Q8H	500 mg IV Q12H

Use the algorithm to determine which weight to use to calculate CrCl.

Total Body Weight = 93.1818 kg

IBW = 45.5 kg + (2.3 x 5 in) = 57 kg

$$BMI = \frac{205\ lbs}{(65\ inches)^2} \times 703 = 34.1\ kg/m^2,\ obese$$

Now calculate her adjusted body weight:

$AdjBW_{0.4}$ = 57 + 0.4 (93.1818 – 57) = 71.47 kg

Then, solve using the Cockcroft-Gault equation:

$$CrCl = \frac{140 - 64}{72 \times 2.7} \times 71.47\ (0.85) = 23.75\ mL/min$$

The correct dose of *Primaxin* is 500 mg IV Q12H.

---

29. **Levofloxacin, dosing per pharmacy, is ordered for an 87-year-old female patient (height 5'4", weight 103 pounds). Her labs include BUN 22 mg/dL and SCr 1 mg/dL. Choose the correct dosing regimen based on the renal dosage adjustments from the package labeling below.**

CrCl	≥ 50 mL/min	20–49 mL/min	< 20 mL/min
Levofloxacin Dose	500 mg Q24 hours	250 mg Q24 hours	250 mg Q48 hours

First, determine which weight to use in calculating the CrCl.

Total Body Weight = 46.8181 kg

IBW = 45.5 kg + (2.3 x 4 in) = 54.7 kg

Use total body weight for calculating CrCl since the patient's total body weight is less than her IBW.

$$CrCl = \frac{140 - 87}{72 \times 1} \times 46.8181\ kg\ (x\ 0.85) = 29\ mL/min$$

The correct dose of levofloxacin is 250 mg Q24H.

30. A 50-year-old male (height 6'1", weight 177 pounds) has HIV and is being started on tenofovir disoproxil fumarate, emtricitabine and efavirenz therapy. His laboratory values include K 4.4 mEq/L, BUN 40 mg/dL, SCr 1.8 mg/dL, and CD4 count of 455 cells/mm³. Using the renal dosage recommendations from the package labeling below, what is the correct dose of tenofovir for this patient?

CrCl	≥ 50 mL/min	30–49 mL/min	10–29 mL/min	< 10 mL/min
Tenofovir Dose	300 mg daily	300 mg Q48 hours	300 mg Q72-96 hours	300 mg weekly

First, determine which weight to use in calculating the CrCl.

Total Body Weight = 80.4545 kg

IBW = 50 kg + (2.3 x 13 in) = 79.9, or 80 kg

The IBW is almost the same as the actual weight. Either weight will yield a similar CrCl.

Next, calculate the CrCl.

$$CrCl = \frac{140 - 50}{72 \times 1.8} \times 80 \text{ kg} = 55 \text{ mL/min}$$

The dose of tenofovir should be 300 mg daily.

ACID-BASE AND ARTERIAL BLOOD GASES

pH

The pH refers to the acidity or basicity of a solution. As a solution becomes more acidic (the concentration of protons increases), the pH decreases. Conversely, when the concentration of protons decrease, the pH increases and the solution is more basic, or alkaline. Pure water is neutral at a pH of 7, and blood, with a pH of 7.4, is slightly alkaline. Stomach acid has a pH of ~2, and is therefore acidic, with many protons in solution.

ARTERIAL BLOOD GASES

The acid-base status of a patient can be determined with an arterial blood gas (ABG). The primary buffering system of the body is the bicarbonate/carbonic acid system. The kidneys help to maintain a neutral pH by controlling bicarbonate (HCO3) reabsorption and elimination. Bicarbonate acts as a buffer and a base. The lungs help maintain a neutral pH by controlling carbonic acid (which is directly proportional to the partial pressure of carbon dioxide or pCO2) retained or released from the body. Carbon dioxide acts as a buffer and an acid. Alterations from the normal values lead to acid-base disorders. Diet and cellular metabolism lead to a large production of hydrogen ions (protons) that need to be excreted to maintain acid-base balance. ABGs are presented as follows in a written chart note:

ABG: pH/pCO2/pO2/HCO3/O2 Sat

INTERPRETING ABGs

- Step #1: Is it an acidosis or alkalosis?
  - ☐ ↓ pH = acidosis
  - ☐ ↑ pH = alkalosis
- Step #2: What other values are abnormal?
  - ☐ Respiratory: ↓ CO2 = alkalosis   ↑ CO2 = acidosis
  - ☐ Metabolic: ↑ HCO3 = alkalosis   ↓ HCO3 = acidosis
- Step #3: Which of the abnormal values in Step #2 matches with the pH in Step #1?
  - ☐ Example: ↓ pH, ↑ CO2 and normal HCO3
  - ☐ pH = acidosis and ↑ CO2 = acidosis; this is a respiratory acidosis
- Step #4: What if both CO2 and HCO3 are abnormal?
  - ☐ Usually only one of the values will match the pH, the other will go in the opposite direction as expected from the pH. This is called compensation.
  - ☐ Example: ↓ pH, ↓ CO2 and ↓ HCO3
  - ☐ ↓ pH = acidosis, ↓ HCO3 = acidosis and ↓ CO2 = alkalosis; this is a metabolic acidosis with some degree of respiratory compensation

An acid-base disorder that leads to a <u>pH < 7.35</u> is called an acidosis. If the disorder leads to a <u>pH > 7.45</u>, it is called an alkalosis. These disorders are further classified as either <u>metabolic</u> or <u>respiratory</u> in origin. The <u>primary</u> disturbance in a metabolic acid-base disorder is the plasma HCO_3 concentration. A <u>metabolic acidosis</u> is characterized primarily by a <u>decrease</u> in plasma HCO_3 concentration. In a <u>metabolic alkalosis</u>, the plasma HCO_3 concentration is <u>increased</u>. Metabolic acidosis may be associated with an increase in the anion gap. The primary disturbance in a respiratory acid-base disorder is pCO_2. In <u>respiratory acidosis</u>, the pCO_2 is <u>elevated</u> and in <u>respiratory alkalosis</u>, the pCO_2 is <u>decreased</u>. Each disturbance has a <u>compensatory</u> (secondary) response that attempts to correct the imbalance toward normal and keep the pH neutral (see <u>Study Tip Gal</u> on previous page for the steps to interpret ABGs).

ABG PARAMETER	REFERENCE RANGE
pH	7.35 – 7.45
pCO2	35 – 45 mmHg
pO2	80 – 100 mmHg
HCO3	22 – 26 mEq/L
O2 Sat	> 95%

Reference ranges for an arterial sample. Bicarbonate reported on ABG is a calculated value and the reference range will differ from a venous sample.

31. **A baby sitter brings a 7-year-old boy to the Emergency Department. He is unarousable. Labs are ordered and an ABG is drawn. The ABG results are as follows: 6.72/40/89/12/94%. What acid-base disorder does the child have?**

    Based on the pH, this is an acidosis. The pCO2 is normal and the HCO3 is decreased (low bicarbonate indicates acidosis). This is a metabolic acidosis.

32. **An elderly female is admitted to the hospital after a motor vehicle accident. She suffered a head injury and is in the ICU. An ABG is obtained and the results are as follows: 8.25/29/97/26/98%. What acid-base disorder does the patient have?**

    Based on the pH, this is an alkalosis. The pCO2 is decreased (low pCO2 indicates alkalosis) and the HCO3 is normal. This is a respiratory alkalosis.

ANION GAP

When a patient is experiencing <u>metabolic acidosis</u>, it is common to calculate an anion gap. The anion gap is the difference in the measured cations and the measured anions in the blood. An anion gap assists in determining the cause of the acidosis. A mnemonic to remember the <u>causes of a gap acidosis</u> is <u>CUTE DIMPLES</u> [cyanide, uremia, toluene, ethanol (alcoholic ketoacidosis), diabetic ketoacidosis, isoniazid, methanol, propylene glycol, lactic acidosis, ethylene glycol, salicylates]. The anion gap is considered high if it is > 12 mEq/L (meaning the patient has a gap acidosis). The anion gap can be low, which is less common. A non-gap acidosis is caused by other factors, mainly hyperchloremic acidosis. Anion gap is calculated with this formula, using the values from the basic metabolic panel (venous sample).

> Anion gap (AG) = Na – Cl – HCO3

33. **A patient in the ICU has recently developed an acidosis. Using the laboratory parameters below, calculate the patient's anion gap.**

Na	139
Cl	101
K	4.6
HCO3	19
SCr	1.6
BUN	38

    > Anion Gap = 139 – 101 – 19 = 19; therefore, the patient has a positive anion gap acidosis

CALCULATIONS

34. SJ was recently admitted to the ICU with a pH of 7.27. Below is her laboratory data. Calculate SJ's anion gap.

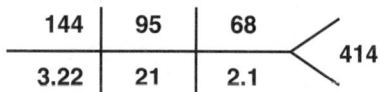

The stick diagram method of presenting a basic metabolic panel (BMP) and complete blood count (CBC) is presented in the Lab Values & Drug Monitoring chapter

Anion Gap = 144 − 95 − 21 = 28; therefore, SJ has a positive anion gap acidosis

BUFFER SYSTEMS AND IONIZATION

Buffer systems help to reduce the impact of too few or too many hydrogen ions in body fluids. These hydrogen ions could cause harm, including degrading some drugs, destabilizing proteins, inhibiting cellular functions and, with too much of a change outside of the narrow range, cells die and death can occur. Therefore, buffers minimize fluctuations in pH so that harm is avoided. Buffer systems are common in the body and are composed of either a weak acid and salt of the acid (e.g., acetic acid and sodium acetate), or a weak base and salt of the base (e.g., ammonium hydroxide and ammonium chloride). An <u>acid</u> is a compound that dissociates, <u>releasing (donating) protons into solution</u>. Once the proton is released, the compound is now a conjugate base, or its salt form. For example, HCl in solution is an acid and dissociates (giving up the proton) into H^+ and Cl^-. A <u>base picks up, or binds, the proton</u>. For example, NH_3 is a base that can pick up a proton and become NH_4^+.

Acid-base reactions are equilibrium reactions; there is drug moving back and forth between the acid and base state. The pH and the pKa are used to determine if the drug is acting as an acid or a base. When the pH = pKa, the molar concentration of the salt form and the molar concentration of the acid form of the buffer acid-base pair will be equal: 50% of the buffer will be in salt form and 50% in acid form. Notice that the percentage of buffer in the acid form when added to the percentage of buffer in the salt form will equal 100%. <u>When the pH = pKa, this is the point at which half the compound is not protonated (ionized), and half is protonated (un-ionized).</u>

A 'strong' acid or base means 100% dissociation and a 'weak' acid or base means very limited dissociation. Any time a pKa is provided, it refers to the acid form losing protons to give to the base, or salt, form.

If the 'pKb' is provided, think 'base' simply because of the definitions of the two terms.

<u>If the pH > pKa, more of the acid is ionized</u>, and more of the conjugate base is un-ionized.

<u>If the pH = pKa, the ionized and un-ionized forms are equal</u>.

<u>If the pH < pKa, more of the acid is un-ionized</u>, and more of the conjugate base is ionized.

The percentage of drug in the ionized versus un-ionized state is important because <u>an ionized drug is soluble but cannot easily cross lipid membranes. An un-ionized drug is not soluble but can cross the membranes and reach the proper receptor site. Most drugs are weak acids.</u> They are soluble, and can pick up a proton to cross the lipid layer.

Most drug molecules are weak acids (or weak bases). These molecules can exist in either the un-ionized or the ionized state, and the degree of ionization depends on the dissociation constant (Ka) of the drug and the pH of the environment. This leads to the <u>Henderson-Hasselbalch</u> equation, also known as the buffer equation, <u>which is used to solve for the pH.</u>

THE pH OF A SOLUTION

Weak Acid Formula

$$pH = pK_a + \log\left[\frac{salt}{acid}\right]$$

Weak Base Formulas

$$pH = (pK_{w^*} - pK_b) + \log\left[\frac{base}{salt}\right] \quad or \quad pH = pK_a + \log\left[\frac{base}{salt}\right]$$

*where pKw = 14

CALCULATING THE LOG OF A NUMBER

35. Calculate log (1/0.5). Round to the nearest tenth.

$$\log\left[\frac{1}{0.5}\right]$$

1. If there is a division, solve the division first: 1/0.5 = 2.

2. The number 2 will be on the calculator screen. Solve for log[2] by hitting the log₁₀ or log key.

   Some hand-held and on-screen calculators may require you to press the log key first, followed by "2" to solve this problem.

3. This will provide the answer, in this example, the answer is 0.3 (rounded to the nearest tenth).

Some calculators have parenthesis that allow you to enter the calculation as written in the problem, rather than performing each step separately. Practice these steps until you are familiar with them.

36. What is the pH of a solution prepared to be 0.5 M sodium citrate and 0.05 M citric acid (pKa for citric acid = 3.13)? Round to the nearest hundredth.

$$pH = pK_a + \log\left[\frac{salt}{acid}\right]$$

$$pH = 3.13 + \log\left[\frac{0.5M}{0.05M}\right]$$

$$pH = 3.13 + \log[10]$$

$$pH = 3.13 + 1$$

$$pH = 4.13$$

37. What is the pH of a solution prepared to be 0.4 M ammonia and 0.04 M ammonium chloride (pKb for ammonia = 4.76)? Round to the nearest hundredth.

$$pH = (pK_w - pK_b) + \log\left[\frac{base}{salt}\right]$$

$$pH = (14 - 4.76) + \log\left[\frac{0.4}{0.04}\right]$$

$$pH = 9.24 + \log[10]$$

$$pH = 9.24 + 1$$

$$pH = 10.24$$

38. **What is the pH of a buffer solution containing 0.5 M acetic acid and 1 M sodium acetate in 1 liter of solution (pKa for acetic acid = 4.76)? Round to the nearest hundredth.**

$$pH = pK_a + \log\left[\frac{salt}{acid}\right]$$

$$pH = 4.76 + \log\left[\frac{1}{0.5}\right]$$

$$pH = 4.76 + \log[2]$$

$$pH = 4.76 + 0.301$$

$$pH = 5.06$$

39. **A buffer solution is prepared using 0.3 mole of a weakly basic drug and an unknown quantity of its salt (pKa of the drug = 10.1). The final solution has a pH of 8.99. How much of the salt was used? Round to the nearest hundredth.**

$$pH = pK_a + \log\left[\frac{base}{salt}\right]$$

$$8.99 = 10.1 + \log\left[\frac{0.3}{X}\right]$$

$$8.99 - 10.1 = \log\left[\frac{0.3}{X}\right]$$

$$10^{-1.11} = \frac{0.3}{X}$$

$$X = 3.86 \text{ mole of the salt}$$

PERCENTAGE OF DRUG IONIZATION IN A SOLUTION

The Henderson-Hasselbalch equation can be modified to calculate the percent of ionization of a drug. Since the pH is a measurement of the hydrogen ions (protons) in the solution, the percent ionization is the percentage of the drug in the solution that has deprotonated.

To calculate the % ionization of a weak acid:

$$\% \text{ ionization} = \frac{100}{1+10^{(pKa-pH)}}$$

To calculate the % ionization of a weak base:

$$\% \text{ ionization} = \frac{100}{1+10^{(pH-pKa)}}$$

40. **What is the percent ionization of amitriptyline, a weak base with a pKa = 9.4, at a physiologic pH of 7.4?**

    Use the weak base formula:

    $$\% \text{ ionization} = \frac{100}{1+10^{(pH-pKa)}}$$

    $$\% \text{ ionization} = \frac{100}{1+10^{(7.4-9.4)}}$$

    $$\% \text{ ionization} = \frac{100}{1+10^{(-2)}}$$

    $$\% \text{ ionization} = \frac{100}{1.01}$$

    $$\% \text{ ionization} = 99\%$$

41. **What is the percent ionization of naproxen, a weak acid with a pKa of 4.2, in the stomach at a pH of 3? Round to the nearest whole number.**

    Use the weak acid formula:

    $$\% \text{ ionization} = \frac{100}{1+10^{(pKa-pH)}}$$

    $$\% \text{ ionization} = \frac{100}{16.85}$$

    $$\% \text{ ionization} = 6\%$$

DRUG CONVERSIONS

CALCIUM SALT CONVERSIONS

Calcium carbonate (*Oscal, Tums*) has acid-dependent absorption and should be taken with meals. Calcium carbonate is a dense form of calcium and contains 40% elemental calcium. A tablet that advertises 500 mg of elemental calcium weighs 1,250 mg. If 1,250 mg is multiplied by 0.40 (which is 40%), it will yield 500 mg elemental calcium.

Calcium citrate (*Citracal*) has acid-independent absorption and can be taken with or without food. Calcium citrate is less dense and contains 21% elemental calcium. A tablet that advertises 315 mg calcium weighs 1,500 mg. If 1,500 mg is multiplied by 0.21 (or 21%), it will yield 315 mg elemental calcium. This is why the larger calcium citrate tablets provide less elemental calcium per tablet. They may be preferred if the gut fluid is basic, rather than acidic.

Calcium acetate is used as a phosphate binder and not for calcium replacement. Though the capsules contain 25% elemental calcium, absorption from this formulation is poor. Calcium carbonate and citrate are most commonly used for calcium replacement.

42. **A patient is taking 3 calcium citrate tablets daily (one tablet, TID). Each weighs 1,500 mg total (non-elemental) weight. She wishes to trade her calcium tablets for the carbonate form. If she is going to use 1,250 mg carbonate tablets (by weight), how many tablets will she need to take to provide the same total daily dose of elemental calcium?**

> 1,500 mg/tablet x 3 tablets/day x 0.21 = 945 mg elemental calcium daily

Each of the carbonate tablets (1,250 mg x 0.4) has 500 mg elemental calcium per tablet.

$$\frac{945 \text{ mg elemental calcium}}{X \text{ tablets}} = \frac{500 \text{ mg elemental calcium}}{1 \text{ tablet}} \qquad X = 1.89 \text{ tablets}$$

She would need to take 2 tablets daily to provide a similar dose. Calcium absorption increases with lower doses, so this patient should be instructed to take one tablet with the morning meal and one with the evening meal.

AMINOPHYLLINE TO THEOPHYLLINE

Aminophylline and theophylline are narrow therapeutic index drugs. They are dosed using IBW in normal weight and obese patients for safety (see Body Weight section at the beginning of this chapter). Conversions between aminophylline and theophylline must be known for the exam. To convert aminophylline to theophylline, remember "ATM":

- **A**minophylline to **T**heophylline: **M**ultiply by 0.8
- Theophylline to Aminophylline: Divide by 0.8

43. **A physician writes an order for aminophylline 500 mg IV, dosed at 0.5 mg per kg per hour for a female patient (185 pounds, 5'1"). There is only theophylline in stock. How many milligrams of theophylline will the patient receive per hour? Round to the nearest whole number.**

> IBW (female) = 45.5 kg + (2.3 x 1 in) = 47.8 kg

$$\frac{0.5 \text{ mg aminophylline}}{\text{kg/hr}} \times 47.8 \text{ kg} = 23.9 \text{ mg/hr aminophylline}$$

The aminophylline dose must now be converted to theophylline.

> 23.9 mg/hr aminophylline x 0.8 = 19.12 mg/hr, rounded to the nearest whole number = 19 mg/hr of theophylline

After solving the problem, read the question again to be certain the question was answered with the correct units (mg per hour of theophylline).

ABSOLUTE NEUTROPHIL COUNT

Neutrophils are our body's main defense against infection. The lower a patient's neutrophil count, the more susceptible that patient is to infection (see table below). The Clozapine REMS Program is designed to reduce the risk of severe clozapine-induced neutropenia; clozapine cannot be refilled if the ANC is < 1,000 cells/mm³. A neutropenic patient should be monitored for signs of infection, including fever, shaking, general weakness or flu-like symptoms. Precautions to reduce infection risk, such as proper hand-washing and avoiding others with infection, should be followed. Further information is available in the Lab Values & Drug Monitoring chapter.

ANC (CELLS/MM³)	DEFINITION
2,200 – 8,000	Normal
< 1,000	Neutropenia (at risk for infection)
< 500	Severe neutropenia
< 100	Profound neutropenia

CALCULATING THE ANC

Multiply the WBC (in total cells/mm³) by the percentage of neutrophils (the segs plus the bands) and divide by 100. Neutrophils can be labeled polymorphonuclear cells (PMNs or polys) or segmented neutrophils (segs) on a lab report.

ANC (cells/mm³) = WBC x [(% segs + % bands)/100]

44. **A patient is being seen at the oncology clinic today after her first round of chemotherapy one week ago. A CBC with differential is ordered and reported back as WBC = 14.8 x 10³ cells/mm³, segs 10% and bands 11%. Calculate this patient's ANC.**

WBC = 14,800 cells/mm³, Segs = 10% Bands = 11%

ANC = 14,800 x [(10% + 11%)/100] = 14,800 x 0.21 = 3,108 cells/mm³

45. **A patient is taking clozapine and is at the clinic for a routine visit. Today's labs include WBC = 4,300 cells/mm³ with 48% segs and 2% bands. Calculate this patient's ANC.**

WBC = 4,300 cells/mm³, Segs = 48% Bands = 2%

ANC = 4,300 x [(48% + 2%)/100] = 4,300 x 0.5 = 2,150 cells/mm³

CHAPTER 13

CALCULATIONS V:
EXAM-STYLE MATH PRACTICE

PRACTICE WHAT YOU'VE LEARNED

After all of the math concepts in Calculations I – IV have been mastered, test yourself with this exam-style math practice. Put all of your notes and formula sheets away. Grab a calculator and some scrap paper. <u>Time yourself</u> to finish the following 30 questions in ≤ 50 minutes. An answer key with detailed explanations follows.

TOOLS YOU WILL NEED

- Pen or Pencil

- Scrap paper

- Calculator
  (use yours or an online scientific calculator)

CONTENT LEGEND

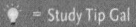 = Study Tip Gal

Images credits, above: 📷 *iStock.com/Dmitry Volkov, nidwlw, rzarek, kondak*

EXAM-STYLE MATH PRACTICE

1. A pharmacist receives a prescription for a 1.5% (w/w) hydrocortisone cream using cold cream as the base. She will use hydrocortisone injection (100 mg/mL, SG 1.5) to prepare the prescription because she has no hydrocortisone powder in stock. How many grams of cold cream are required to compound 60 grams of the preparation? Round to the nearest one decimal place.

2. How many milliliters of a 1:2,500 (w/v) solution of aluminum acetate can be made from 100 mL of a 0.2% solution?

3. A pharmacist will prepare an amoxicillin suspension to provide a 1600 mg daily dose for a child with an otitis media infection. The dose will be divided BID. To prepare amoxicillin 200 mg/5 mL, the pharmacist should add 76 mL of water to the powder for a final volume of 100 mL. The pharmacist mistakenly adds too much water and finds that the final volume is 110 mL. The pharmacy has no other bottles of amoxicillin, so the pharmacist will dispense the bottle with the extra water added. How many milliliters should the patient take twice daily to receive the correct dose? Round to the nearest whole number.

4. What is the ratio strength (w/v) of 50 mL containing a 1:20 (w/v) ammonia solution diluted to 1 liter?

5. A pharmacist receives an order for sodium chloride 4 mEq/kg/day for a patient who weighs 165 pounds. Using ½NS, how many liters will the patient require per day? Round to the nearest tenth. (M.W. of Na = 23, M.W. of Cl = 35.5)

6. How many milligrams of aminophylline will Mr. Kelly receive per day based on the order in the profile? Round to the nearest whole number.

PATIENT PROFILE

Patient Name:	Mike Kelly			
Address:	65 Laney Road			
Age:	22	Sex:	M	
Allergies:	NKDA			

DIAGNOSES

Asthma

Allergies

MEDICATIONS

Date	Prescriber	Drug/Strength/Sig
8/23	Sanchez	*Singulair* 10 mg 1 tablet in the evening daily
8/23	Sanchez	*Qvar* 1 puff (40 mcg) BID
9/29	Williams	Methylprednisolone 40 mg IV Q12H
9/29	Williams	Aminophylline 0.5 mg/kg/hr
9/29	Williams	D5½NS at 80 mL/hr
9/29	Williams	Albuterol nebulization 2.5 mg Q6H

LAB/DIAGNOSTIC TESTS

Test	Normal Value	Results		
		Date: 1/7	Date: 3/23	Date: 9/29
Weight		125 pounds	141 pounds	160 pounds
Height		5'9"		5'9"
WBC	4,000-11,000 cells/mm³	12,000		11,225
K	3.5-5 mEq/L	3.7	4.1	3.6
Glu	65-99 mg/dL	101		142

7. A patient is receiving D5½NS with potassium chloride at 20 drops/min. After 10 hours, the patient has received a total of 40 mEq of potassium chloride using tubing that delivers 15 drops/mL. What is the percentage concentration of potassium chloride in the patient's IV fluid? Round to 2 decimal places. (M.W. of K = 39, M.W. of Cl = 36)

8. An order is written for a dopamine drip in the ICU. The order reads: "Start dopamine drip at 3 mcg/kg/min, titrate by 5 mcg/kg/min Q5 minutes to achieve SBP > 100 mmHg. Page the critical care resident for additional orders if maximum dose of 20 mcg/kg/min is reached." The patient weighs 165 pounds and the ICU stocks premixed dopamine drips (400 mg/250 mL) in the automated dispensing cabinet (ADC). What rate (mL/hr) should the dopamine drip be started at? Round to the nearest whole number.

9. A 46-year-old female with radiation enteritis is receiving 1,800 kcal from her parenteral nutrition. The solution contains amino acids, dextrose and electrolytes. There are 84.5 grams of protein in the PN and it is running at 85 mL/hour over 24 hours. What is the final concentration of dextrose in the PN solution? Express the answer as a percentage. Round to the nearest whole number.

10. ML is a 165-pound male receiving a premixed dopamine drip (400 mg/250 mL) in the ICU. The order states that the drip can be titrated to a maximum dose of 20 mcg/kg/min. What is the maximum rate (mL/hr) at which the drip can be run? Round to the nearest whole number.

11. A pharmacist in an oncology clinic receives the following prescription for a patient with Hodgkin's lymphoma: "Prednisone 40 mg/m²/day PO on days 1-14." The patient is 5'1" and weighs 116 pounds. The hospital uses the following formula for BSA (m²) = 0.007184 x height(cm)$^{0.725}$ x weight(kg)$^{0.425}$. How many 20 mg prednisone tablets should be dispensed to the patient?

12. A nephrologist is treating a patient with hyponatremia. She estimates the patient's sodium deficit to be 210 mEq. How many milliliters of normal saline (M.W. Na = 23, M.W. Cl = 35.5) will be required to replace the deficit?

13. A pharmacy technician is asked to compound three 500 mL doses of 5% albumin. How many 50 mL vials of 25% albumin will be required?

14. A patient is to receive a potassium acetate infusion prepared by adding 9 mL of 39.2% potassium acetate ($KC_2H_3O_2$) to 0.45% NS to make 1 liter. The patient is to receive the potassium acetate at 5 mEq/hr. What rate (mL/hr) will provide this dose? Round to the nearest whole number. (M.W. of K = 39, M.W of $C_2H_3O_2$ = 59)

15. An intravenous infusion contains 2 mL of a 1:1,000 (w/v) solution of epinephrine and 250 mL of D5W. At what flow rate (mL/min) should the infusion be administered to provide 0.3 mcg/kg/min of epinephrine to an 80 kg patient? Round to the nearest whole number.

16. A cough syrup contains 4 grams of brompheniramine maleate per liter. How many milligrams are contained in one teaspoonful of the elixir?

17. A patient is to receive acyclovir 5 mg/kg every 8 hours for an acute outbreak of herpes zoster. What daily dose, in milligrams, should a 110-pound female receive?

Use the following case to answer questions 18-20:

PATIENT PROFILE

Patient Name:	Helene Gudot						
Address:	1365 Stephens Avenue						
Age:	64	Sex:	F	Height:	5'5"	Weight:	135 pounds
Allergies:	Bactrim						

DIAGNOSES

Type 2 Diabetes	Dyslipidemia
Hypertension	Heart Failure

MEDICATIONS

Date	Prescriber	Drug/Strength/Sig
12/10	Marks	Metformin 1 gram BID
12/10	Marks	Regular insulin sliding scale per protocol
12/11	Marks	Lantus 10 units SC QHS
12/12	Ventrakhan	D51/4NS + 20 mEq KCl at 75 mL/hr
12/12	King	Coreg 6.25 mg BID
12/13	Marks	D51/2NS + 10 mEq KCl at 60 mL/hr
12/13	Marks	Lasix 40 mg IV Q12H
12/13	Ventrakhan	Altace 5 mg BID

LAB/DIAGNOSTIC TESTS

Test	Normal Value	Results		
		Date: 12/13	Date: 12/12	Date: 12/11
WBC	4,000-11,000 cells/mm^3	10.7	10.1	12.2
Na	135-146 mEq/L	139	142	145
K	3.5-5.3 mEq/L	4.3	4.1	3.3
Cl	98-110 mEq/L	104	105	101
HCO3	22-28 mEq/L	26	26	25
BUN	7-25 mg/dL	23	26	28
Creatinine	0.6-1.2 mg/dL	1.1	1.3	1.4
Glu	65-99 mg/dL	180 @ 0700	140 @ 0700	260 @ 0700
Glu	65-99 mg/dL	280 @ 1100	280 @ 1100	320 @ 1100
Glu	65-99 mg/dL	220 @ 1700	300 @ 1700	280 @ 1700
Glu	65-99 mg/dL	100 @ 2100	220 @ 2100	220 @ 2100

18. Mrs. Gudot uses the following regular insulin sliding scale: "take 1 unit of insulin SC for every 20 mg/dL of blood sugar > 160 mg/dL." How many units of sliding scale insulin should have been administered on December 12th?

19. The pharmacist is asked to convert several of Mrs. Gudot's labs to different units so her case can be compared to a published case report. Convert her serum potassium (M.W. of potassium = 39) on December 13th to mg/dL. Round to the nearest tenth.

20. Convert Mrs. Gudot's serum sodium level on December 11th to mmol/L. Round to the nearest whole number. (M.W. of Na = 23)

21. A patient received 4 mg of IV morphine. What is an equivalent dose of oral hydromorphone? Round to the nearest whole number. (10 mg of IV morphine is equivalent to 7.5 mg of oral hydromorphone)

22. If 200 capsules contain 500 mg of an active ingredient, how many milligrams of the active ingredient will 76 capsules contain?

23. If phenobarbital elixir contains 18.2 mg of phenobarbital per 5 mL, how many grams of phenobarbital would be used in preparing a pint of the elixir? Round to the nearest tenth.

24. **How many calories will the patient receive each day from the following PN order? Round to the nearest whole number.**

Parenteral Nutrition Order Form

Macronutrients 2-in-1

Premixed:
☐ **Clinimix (5/15)** Amino acids 5% / Dextrose 15%
☒ **Clinimix (5/15) with electrolytes** Amino acids 5% / Dextrose 15%
☐ **Clinimix (4.25/10)** Amino acids 4.25% / Dextrose 10%
☐ **Clinimix (4.25/10) with electrolytes** Amino acids 4.25% / Dextrose 10%

Directions (2-in-1 PN)

Infuse: ☒ Daily   ☐ _____ times weekly

Select rate or volume:

Rate:
☒ Continuous infusion ___60___ mL/hr

☐ 12-hour infusion _____ mL/hr

Volume (liters/day):
☐ 1   ☐ 2   ☐ Other _____

©RxPrep

25. **A penicillin V 250 mg tablet equals 400,000 units of penicillin activity. A patient is taking penicillin V 500 mg tablets QID for 7 days. How much penicillin activity, in units, will this patient receive in the total prescription?**

26. **Oral potassium chloride 20% solution contains 40 mEq of potassium per 15 milliliters of solution. A patient needs 25 mEq of potassium daily. How many milliliters of 20% potassium chloride should the patient take? Round to the nearest tenth.**

27. **The pharmacist reviews Ms. Hoydt's *Lovenox* order and labs in the profile. At this hospital, pharmacists have the authority to make renal dosage adjustments per package labeling when necessary. What is the correct *Lovenox* dose for Ms. Hoydt?**

PATIENT PROFILE

Patient Name:	Carolyn Hoydt					
Address:	13 Windgate Road					
Age:	37	Sex:	F	Height:	5'6"	Weight: 175 pounds
Allergies:	NKDA					

DIAGNOSES

DVT confirmed by ultrasound

MEDICATIONS

Date	Prescriber	Drug/Strength/Sig
7/5	Langston	*Ortho Tri-Cyclen* 1 PO daily
7/5	Langston	*Centrum* 1 PO daily
11/15	Mason	*Lovenox* 1 mg/kg SC Q12H
11/15	Mason	D5½NS @ 70 mL/hr

LAB/DIAGNOSTIC TESTS

Test	Normal Value	Results Date: 7/5	Date: 11/15	Date:
Na	135-146 mEq/L	136	142	
K	3.5-5.3 mEq/L	3.5	5.2	
Cl	98-110 mEq/L	109	105	
HCO3	22-28 mEq/L	25	26	
BUN	7-25 mg/dL	10	22	
Creatinine	0.6-1.2 mg/dL	0.7	1.4	
Glu	65-99 mg/dL	100	120	
Hgb	12-16 g/dL	12	13.6	
Hct	36-46%	37	41	

A. 175 mg SC Q12H

B. 175 mg SC once daily

C. 80 mg SC once daily

D. 80 mg SC Q12H

E. 60 mg SC Q12H

28. **The pharmacist reviews the order for IV *Bactrim* and the labs for Mr. Ross in the profile. What dose should Mr. Ross receive given the renal dosage recommendations below?**

CrCl	> 30 mL/min	15–30 mL/min	< 15 mL/min
Sulfamethoxazole/ Trimethoprim (SMX/TMP)	No dosage adjustment required	Administer 50% of the recommended dose	Use is not recommended

PATIENT PROFILE

Patient Name:	Jeremy Ross						
Address:	22 Harris Lane						
Age:	41	**Sex:**	M	**Height:**	6'1"	**Weight:**	70 kg
Allergies:	NKDA						

DIAGNOSES

Depression	Dyslipidemia
HIV	

MEDICATIONS

Date	Prescriber	Drug/Strength/Sig
5/5	Sangler	Nicotine patch 21 mg/day – apply 1 patch daily
5/5	Sangler	*Stribild* 1 tablet daily
6/15	Sangler	*Celexa* 20 mg 1 tablet daily
11/15	Mason	*Lipitor* 10 mg 1 tablet daily
12/1	Hern	*Bactrim* 20 mg TMP/kg/day IV divided Q6H

LAB/DIAGNOSTIC TESTS

Test	Normal Value	Results Date: 12/1	Date: 5/5	
WBC	4,000-11,000 cells/mm³	10.7	9.5	
CD4	800–1,100 cells/mm³	187	226	
Na	135-146 mEq/L	139	142	
K	3.5-5.3 mEq/L	3.7	4.1	
Cl	98-110 mEq/L	109	105	
HCO3	22-28 mEq/L	24	26	
BUN	7-25 mg/dL	7	9	
Creatinine	0.6-1.2 mg/dL	0.6	0.8	
Glu	65-99 mg/dL	120	136	

A. 1400 mg TMP IV Q6H

B. 700 mg TMP IV Q6H

C. 400 mg TMP IV Q12H

D. 350 mg TMP IV Q6H

E. Mr. Ross should not receive *Bactrim*

29. **MH is a 72-year-old male patient hospitalized with decompensated heart failure and fever. Cultures are positive for aspergillosis. MH weighs 110 kg and will receive 0.25 mg/kg per day of amphotericin B (reconstituted and diluted to 0.1 mg/mL) by IV infusion. How many milliliters of amphotericin solution are required to deliver the daily dose?**

30. **What is the pH of a solution containing 0.2 mole of a weakly basic drug and 0.02 mole of its salt per liter of solution (pKa of the drug = 9.36)? Round to the nearest hundredth.**

13 CALCULATIONS V: EXAM-STYLE MATH PRACTICE

ANSWER KEY AND EXPLANATIONS

1. **First, calculate the grams of hydrocortisone required for the prescription.**

$$\frac{1.5 \text{ g}}{100 \text{ g}} = \frac{X \text{ g}}{60 \text{ g}} \qquad X = 0.9 \text{ grams of hydrocortisone required}$$

Calculate the volume of hydrocortisone injection required.

$$\frac{100 \text{ mg}}{1 \text{ mL}} = \frac{900 \text{ mg}}{X \text{ mL}} \qquad X = 9 \text{ mL}$$

Calculate the weight of 9 mL of hydrocortisone injection using the SG provided.

$$1.5 = \frac{X \text{ g}}{9 \text{ mL}} \qquad X = 13.5 \text{ grams (weight of hydrocortisone injection)}$$

Calculate the grams of cold cream required.

$$60 \text{ g final product} \quad - \quad 13.5 \text{ g (weight of hydrocortisone)} \quad = \quad 46.5 \text{ g of cold cream}$$

2. **Both concentrations must be in the same units to use the Q1C1 = Q2C2 formula. So, 1:2,500 must be converted to a percentage strength first.**

$$\frac{1 \text{ part}}{2,500 \text{ parts}} = \frac{X \text{ g}}{100 \text{ mL}} \qquad X = 0.04 \text{ g, or } 0.04\%$$

Now use the formula.

$$100 \text{ mL} \quad \times \quad 0.2\% \quad = \quad Q2 \quad \times \quad 0.04\%$$

$$Q2 = 500 \text{ mL}$$

3. **Two methods to solve this calculation are shown:**

$$\frac{200 \text{ mg}}{5 \text{ mL}} = \frac{X \text{ mg}}{100 \text{ mL}} \qquad X = 4,000 \text{ mg}$$

$$\frac{4,000 \text{ mg}}{110 \text{ mL}} = \frac{X \text{ mg}}{\text{mL}} \qquad X = 36.36 \text{ mg/mL}$$

$$\frac{4,000 \text{ mg}}{110 \text{ mL}} = \frac{800 \text{ mg}}{X \text{ mL}} \qquad X = 22 \text{ mL}$$

$$\frac{36.36 \text{ mg}}{1 \text{ mL}} = \frac{800 \text{ mg}}{X \text{ mL}} \qquad X = 22 \text{ mL}$$

4. **First, convert 1:20 to a percentage strength.**

$$\frac{1 \text{ part}}{20 \text{ parts}} = \frac{X \text{ g}}{100 \text{ mL}} \qquad X = 5 \text{ g, or } 5\%$$

$$50 \text{ mL} \quad \times \quad 5\% \quad = \quad 1,000 \text{ mL} \quad \times \quad C2$$

$$C2 = 0.25\%$$

$$\text{Convert } 0.25\% \text{ to ratio strength} \quad = \quad 1:400$$

5.

$$\frac{4 \text{ mEq}}{\text{kg}} \times 75 \text{ kg} = 300 \text{ mEq/day}$$

$$300 \text{ mEq} = \frac{X \text{ mg} \times 1}{58.5} = 17{,}550 \text{ mg, or } 17.55 \text{ g}$$

$$\frac{0.45 \text{ g}}{100 \text{ mL}} = \frac{17.55 \text{ g}}{X \text{ mL}} \qquad X = 3{,}900 \text{ mL or } 3.9 \text{ L}$$

6. Aminophylline is dosed based on IBW.

$$IBW \text{ (male)} = 50 \text{ kg} + (2.3 \times 9 \text{ in}) = 70.7 \text{ kg}$$

$$Aminophylline \ 0.5 \text{ mg/kg/hr} \times 70.7 \text{ kg} \times 24 \text{ hrs} = 848.4 \text{ mg/day, round to } 848 \text{ mg/day}$$

7.

$$40 \text{ mEq} = \frac{X \text{ mg} \times 1}{75} = 3{,}000 \text{ mg, or } 3 \text{ g of KCl have been given in 10 hours}$$

$$\frac{20 \text{ drops}}{\text{min}} \times \frac{60 \text{ min}}{1 \text{ hr}} \times 10 \text{ hrs} = 12{,}000 \text{ drops infused in 10 hours}$$

$$\frac{15 \text{ drops}}{\text{mL}} = \frac{12{,}000 \text{ drops}}{X \text{ mL}} \qquad X = 800 \text{ mL have infused in 10 hours}$$

$$\frac{3 \text{ g KCl}}{800 \text{ mL}} = \frac{X \text{ g}}{100 \text{ mL}} \qquad X = 0.375 \text{ g, or } 0.38\%$$

8.

$$3 \text{ mcg/kg/min} \times 75 \text{ kg} = 225 \text{ mcg/min}$$

$$\frac{250 \text{ mL}}{400 \text{ mg}} \times \frac{1 \text{ mg}}{1000 \text{ mcg}} \times \frac{225 \text{ mcg}}{\text{min}} \times \frac{60 \text{ min}}{1 \text{ hr}} = 8.4 \text{ mL/hr, or } 8 \text{ mL/hr}$$

9. First, calculate the calories from dextrose by subtracting out the protein component.

$$84.5 \text{ g} \times \frac{4 \text{ kcal}}{\text{g}} = 338 \text{ kcal}$$

$$1{,}800 \text{ kcal} - 338 \text{ kcal of protein} = 1{,}462 \text{ kcal from dextrose}$$

Next, calculate the grams of dextrose in this PN.

$$1{,}462 \text{ kcal} \times \frac{1 \text{ g}}{3.4 \text{ kcal}} = 430 \text{ grams of dextrose}$$

Then, calculate the final concentration. This requires calculating the total volume the patient is receiving.

$$\frac{85 \text{ mL}}{\text{hr}} \times 24 \text{ hours} = 2{,}040 \text{ mL}$$

$$\frac{430 \text{ g dextrose}}{2{,}040 \text{ mL}} = \frac{X \text{ g}}{100 \text{ mL}} \qquad X = 21\%$$

10.

$$20 \text{ mcg/kg/min} \times 75 \text{ kg} = 1500 \text{ mcg/min}$$

$$\frac{250 \text{ mL}}{400 \text{ mg}} \times \frac{1 \text{ mg}}{1000 \text{ mcg}} \times \frac{1500 \text{ mcg}}{\text{min}} \times \frac{60 \text{ min}}{1 \text{ hr}} = \begin{array}{l} 56.25 \text{ mL/hr – max rate per order} \\ \text{Round to the nearest whole number} = 56 \text{ mL/hr} \end{array}$$

11.

$$\text{BSA (m}^2) = 0.007184 \times (154.94)^{0.725} \times (52.7272)^{0.425} = 1.5 \text{ m}^2$$

$$40 \text{ mg/m}^2\text{/day} \times 1.5 \text{ m}^2 = 60 \text{ mg/day}$$

Refer to Oncology II chapter for discussion of BSA.

The patient will take 60 mg of prednisone (three 20 mg tablets) per day for 14 days. The pharmacist should dispense 42 of the 20 mg prednisone tablets.

12.

$$210 \text{ mEq} = \frac{\text{mg} \times 1}{58.5} \qquad 12{,}285 \text{ mg or } 12.285 \text{ g}$$

$$\frac{0.9 \text{ g}}{100 \text{ mL}} = \frac{12.285 \text{ g}}{X \text{ mL}} \qquad X = 1{,}365 \text{ mL of NS are required}$$

13.

$$\frac{5 \text{ g}}{100 \text{ mL}} = \frac{X \text{ g}}{500 \text{ mL}} \qquad X = 25 \text{ g, or 75 g for the three required doses}$$

$$\frac{25 \text{ g}}{100 \text{ mL}} = \frac{X \text{ g}}{50 \text{ mL}} \qquad X = 12.5 \text{ g per 50 mL vial}$$

$$75 \text{ g required} \times \frac{1 \text{ vial}}{12.5 \text{ g}} \qquad X = 6 \text{ vials of 25\% albumin required}$$

14.

$$\frac{39.2 \text{ g}}{100 \text{ mL}} = \frac{X \text{ g}}{9 \text{ mL}} \qquad X = 3.528 \text{ g or 3,528 mg}$$

$$X \text{ mEq} = \frac{3{,}528 \text{ mg} \times 1}{98} = 36 \text{ mEq}$$

$$\frac{1{,}000 \text{ mL}}{36 \text{ mEq}} \times \frac{5 \text{ mEq}}{\text{hr}} = 138.88 \text{ mL/hr, or 139 mL/hr}$$

CALCULATIONS

15.

1:1,000 ratio strength = 0.1% (w/v)

$$\frac{0.1 \text{ g}}{100 \text{ mL}} = \frac{X \text{ g}}{2 \text{ mL}} \qquad X = 0.002 \text{ g, or 2 mg}$$

The patient is 80 kg x 0.3 mcg/kg/min = 24 mcg/min

$$\frac{252 \text{ mL}}{2 \text{ mg}} \times \frac{1 \text{ mg}}{1{,}000 \text{ mcg}} \times \frac{24 \text{ mcg}}{\text{min}} = 3 \text{ mL/min}$$

16. First, convert grams to milligrams.

$$4 \text{ g} \times \frac{1000 \text{ mg}}{1 \text{ g}} = 4{,}000 \text{ mg per 1 liter}$$

1 L = 1,000 mL

1 teaspoonful = 5 mL

Next, solve using a proportion.

$$\frac{4{,}000 \text{ mg}}{1{,}000 \text{ mL}} = \frac{X \text{ mg}}{5 \text{ mL}} \qquad X = 20 \text{ mg}$$

17. Begin by converting the patient's weight in pounds (lbs) to kilograms (kg).

$$110 \text{ pounds} \times \frac{1 \text{ kg}}{2.2 \text{ pounds}} = 50 \text{ kg}$$

Acyclovir should be dosed based on IBW in normal weight or obese patients [refer to Which Weight to Use for Drug Dosing (mg/kg) in Calculations IV].
Since no height is provided in the question, the only option is to use the weight provided. An adult female weighing 110 pounds is likely very close to IBW.

$$\frac{5 \text{ mg}}{1 \text{ kg}} = \frac{X \text{ mg}}{50 \text{ kg}} \qquad X = 250 \text{ mg/dose} \times 3 \text{ doses/day} = 750 \text{ mg/day}$$

18.

140 mg/dL = no insulin

280 mg/dL – 160 mg/dL = 120 mg/dL; 120 mg/dL / 20 mg/dL = 6 units

300 mg/dL – 160 mg/dL = 140 mg/dL / 20 mg/dL = 7 units

220 mg/dL – 160 mg/dL = 60 mg/dL / 20 mg/dL = 3 units

Total sliding scale units for December 12th = 6 + 7 + 3 = 16 units

19.

$$4.3 \text{ mEq} = \frac{X \text{ mg} \times 1}{39} \qquad X = 167.7 \text{ mg}$$

4.3 mEq = 167.7 mg. The patient's serum potassium is reported as 4.3 mEq/L, which equals 167.7 mg/L.

$$\frac{167.7 \text{ mg}}{1 \text{ L}} \times \frac{1 \text{ L}}{10 \text{ dL}} = 16.8 \text{ mg/dL}$$

20.

$$145 \text{ mEq} = \frac{X \text{ mg} \times 1}{23} \qquad X = 3{,}335 \text{ mg}$$

$$X \text{ mmols} = \frac{3{,}335 \text{ mg}}{23} \qquad X = 145 \text{ mmols, therefore } 145 \text{ mEq/L} = 145 \text{ mmol/L for sodium}$$

Note that mmols = mEq in this problem. For Na and K, the mmol and mEq are the same; 1 mmol = 1 mEq.

21.

$$\frac{4 \text{ mg IV morphine}}{X \text{ mg oral hydromorphone}} = \frac{10 \text{ mg IV morphine}}{7.5 \text{ mg oral hydromorphone}} \qquad X = 3 \text{ mg oral hydromorphone}$$

22.

$$\frac{200 \text{ caps}}{500 \text{ mg}} = \frac{76 \text{ caps}}{X \text{ mg}} \qquad X = 190 \text{ mg}$$

23. First, convert milligrams to grams.

$$18.2 \text{ mg} \times \frac{1 \text{ g}}{1{,}000 \text{ mg}} = 0.0182 \text{ g}$$

Use a proportion to calculate the grams needed for 1 pint.

$$\frac{0.0182 \text{ g}}{5 \text{ mL}} = \frac{X \text{ g}}{473 \text{ mL}} \qquad X = 1.7 \text{ g}$$

Because of the rounding specifications in the question, the answer is the same regardless of the pint conversion used. Expect the same on the exam.

24. First, calculate how many milliliters of PN the patient will receive in 24 hours based on the rate ordered:

$$60 \text{ mL/hr} \times 24 \text{ hours} = 1{,}440 \text{ mL/day}$$

Use the percentage strength of dextrose from the product ordered to calculate the calories from dextrose:

$$\frac{3.4 \text{ kcal}}{g} \times \frac{15 \text{ g}}{100 \text{ mL}} \times 1{,}440 \text{ mL} = 734.4 \text{ kcal from dextrose}$$

Use the percentage strength of amino acids from the product ordered to calculate the calories from protein:

$$\frac{4 \text{ kcal}}{g} \times \frac{5 \text{ g}}{100 \text{ mL}} \times 1{,}440 \text{ mL} = 288 \text{ kcal from protein}$$

Since no lipids were ordered, add the dextrose and protein calories to get the total calories:

$$734.4 \text{ kcals} + 288 \text{ kcals} = 1{,}022.4, \text{ or } 1{,}022 \text{ kcals/day}$$

25. If 250 mg contains 400,000 units, then 500 mg contains 800,000 units. The patient is taking 4 tablets daily, for 7 days (or 28 total tablets), at 800,000 units each.

$$\frac{800{,}000 \text{ units}}{1 \text{ tab}} = \frac{X \text{ units}}{28 \text{ tabs}} \qquad X = 22{,}400{,}000 \text{ units}$$

26.

$$\frac{40 \text{ mEq K}}{15 \text{ mL}} = \frac{25 \text{ mEq K}}{X \text{ mL}} \qquad X = 9.375, \text{ or } 9.4 \text{ mL}$$

27. The correct answer is (D). Total body weight is used to determine the weight-based dose of LMWHs. Since the patient's BMI is 28.3 kg/m² (overweight), her adjusted body weight is used in the Cockcroft-Gault equation to calculate CrCl. Her CrCl is 58.5 mL/min (well above the threshold of 30 mL/min, for changing the dosing interval of *Lovenox* to once daily).

28. The correct answer is (D). Mr. Ross is of normal weight per BMI (BMI = 20.4 kg/m²). His *Bactrim* dose will be calculated with his total body weight (20 mg TMP/kg/day x 70 kg = 1400 mg TMP/day or 350 mg TMP Q6H for normal renal function). His TBW is less than his IBW, so his CrCl should be calculated with his TBW and is ~160 ml/min. Renal dose adjustments will not be needed for any medications at this level of CrCl.

29. Begin by calculating the total daily dose (mg) for this patient.

$$\frac{0.25 \text{ mg}}{1 \text{ kg}} = \frac{X \text{ mg}}{110 \text{ kg}} \qquad X = 27.5 \text{ mg daily}$$

Calculate the volume of reconstituted amphotericin B solution needed per day.

$$\frac{27.5 \text{ mg}}{X \text{ mL}} = \frac{0.1 \text{ mg}}{1 \text{ mL}} \qquad X = 275 \text{ mL}$$

30.

$$pH = pK_a + \log\left[\frac{base}{salt}\right]$$

$$pH = 9.36 + \log\left[\frac{0.2}{0.02}\right]$$

$$pH = 9.36 + 1$$

$$pH = 10.36$$

CALCULATIONS

ARE YOU READY FOR THE MATH ON THE NAPLEX?

Remember, math is very important on the NAPLEX. How will you know that you have sufficiently studied math for the exam? This small sample of questions is not enough to make that determination. The RxPrep QBank contains exam-style questions that cover many additional calculation problems. See the Preparing for the NAPLEX with RxPrep chapter and the Study Tip Gal to the right for tips on how to study the calculations content and recognize when you are ready for math on the exam.

ASSESSING READINESS FOR MATH

You are ready to tackle calculations on the NAPLEX when:

- Each calculations QBank (including biostatistics and pharmacokinetics) has been reviewed multiple times and math mistakes have become a thing of the past.

- The formulas can be quickly recalled in response to a problem ("automatic recall").

- Math problems are able to be completed efficiently (meaning, in the same time as you will have available on the exam). The goal is to complete each question in ~1.6 minutes (1 minute and 36 seconds).

Track Your Scores	
Calculations #1	48, 78, 96, 100 Yeah!
Calculations #2	55, 82, 92, 100 Yeah!
Calculations #3	60, 77 keep going…
Calculations #4	66, 74 keep going…
Calculations #5	48, 65 keep going…
Biostats math	48, 59 don't give up…

Keep track of your scores as you practice (either in the QBank or in a separate place, like this). Keep going until the math is flawless. Math mistakes can greatly impact the exam result. A math mistake in pharmacy means the patient received the wrong dose.

BIOSTATISTICS

CONTENTS

CONTENT LEGEND

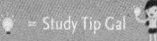 = Study Tip Gal    = Required Formula

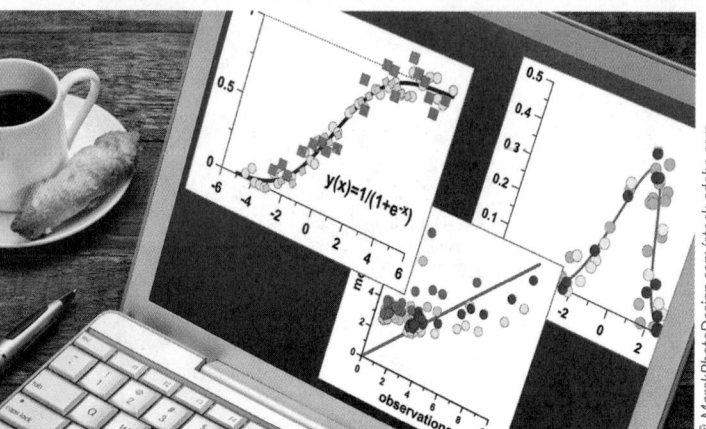

CHAPTER 14

BIOSTATISTICS

PURPOSE OF BIOSTATISTICS

Statistics involves the collection and analysis of all types of data, from the average number of cars on a freeway to the blood pressure reduction expected from a calcium channel blocker. When statistics are used to understand the effects of a drug or medical procedure on people and animals, the statistical analysis is called biostatistical analysis, or simply, biostatistics.

A basic understanding of biostatistics is required to interpret studies in medical and pharmacy journals, such as the *New England Journal of Medicine* or *Pharmacotherapy*. Simple formulas and definitions, described here, prepare the reader to interpret most journal articles and feel confident tackling common practice-based situations, such as:

A physician asks if a patient should be switched from standard of care treatment to a new drug based on the relative risk reduction reported in a clinical trial.

A patient taking warfarin wants to know if he should switch to Xarelto because he saw a commercial claiming that "it prevents DVT or PE in 98% of patients."

STEPS TO JOURNAL PUBLICATION

The path to publication for the classic type of research study is shown in the figure on the next page. A study manuscript (description of the research, with results) can be submitted for publication in a professional, peer-reviewed journal. The editor of the journal selects potential publications and sends them to experts in the topic area for peer review. Peer review is intended to assess the research design and methods, the value of the results and conclusions to the field of study, how well the manuscript is written, and whether it is appropriate for the readership of the journal. The reviewers make a recommendation to the editor to either accept the article (usually with revisions) or reject it. Data that contradicts a previous recommendation, or presents new information, can change treatment guidelines.

BEGIN with a **RESEARCH QUESTION**	**DESIGN** the **STUDY**	**ENROLL** the **SUBJECTS**	**COLLECT** the **DATA**	**ANALYZE** the **DATA**	**PUBLISH**
Write a null hypothesis to answer the research question, such as: New drug is not as effective as current drug.	Is it randomized, placebo-controlled, a case-control or other type of study?	Assign to a treatment group or control group, or identify subjects belonging to a cohort or other group.	Prospectively (going into the future for a set period of time) or retrospectively (looking back in time using medical records).	Enter the data into statistical software; assess the results (e.g., risk reductions, confidence intervals).	

©RxPrep   iStock.com/dilyanah

BIOSTATISTICS

ORGANIZATION OF A PUBLISHED CLINICAL TRIAL

A published clinical trial begins with an abstract that provides a brief summary of the article. The introduction to the study comes next, which includes background information, such as disease history and prevalence, and the research hypothesis. This is followed by the study methods, which describe the variables and outcomes, and the statistical methods used to analyze the data.

The results section includes figures, tables and graphs. A reader needs to interpret basic statistics and common graphs in order to understand the study results. The researchers conclude the article with an interpretation of the results and the implications for current practice.

TYPES OF STUDY DATA

When data points, or values, are collected during a study, they can be analyzed to determine the degree of difference between groups, or some other type of association. The statistical tests used to perform the analysis depend on the type of data.

CONTINUOUS DATA

Continuous data has a logical order with values that continuously increase (or decrease) by the same amount (e.g., a HR of 120 BPM is twice as fast as a HR of 60 BPM). The two types of continuous data are interval data and ratio data. The difference between them is that interval data has no meaningful zero (zero does not equal none) and ratio data has a meaningful zero (zero equals none). The Celsius temperature scale is an example of interval data because it has no meaningful zero (0°C does not mean no temperature; it is the freezing point of water). Heart rate is an example of ratio data; a HR of 0 BPM is cardiac arrest (zero equals none; the heart is not beating).

DISCRETE (CATEGORICAL) DATA

The two types of discrete data, nominal and ordinal, have categories, and are sometimes called categorical data. Nominal and name are derived from the same word; with nominal data, subjects are sorted into arbitrary categories (names), such as male or female (0 = male, 1 = female or 0 = female, 1 = male). It is sometimes described as "yes/no" data. Ordinal comes from the word order; ordinal data is ranked and has a logical order, such as a pain scale. In contrast to continuous data, ordinal scale categories do not increase by the same amount; a pain scale rating of 4 is worse than a pain scale rating of 2, but it does not mean that there is twice as much pain.

CONTINUOUS DATA		DISCRETE (CATEGORICAL) DATA	
Data is provided by some type of measurement which has unlimited options (theoretically) of continuous values		Data fits into a limited number of categories	
RATIO DATA	**INTERVAL DATA**	**NOMINAL DATA**	**ORDINAL DATA**
Equal difference between values, with a true, meaningful zero	Equal difference between values, but without a meaningful zero	Categories are in an arbitrary order	Categories are ranked in a logical order, but the difference between categories is not equal
(0 = NONE)	(0 ≠ NONE)	*Order of categories does not matter*	
Examples: age, height, weight, time, blood pressure	**Examples:** Celsius and Fahrenheit temperature scales	**Examples:** gender, ethnicity, marital status, mortality	*Order of categories matters*
			Examples: NYHA Functional Class I-IV; 0-10 pain scale
Ordered, Equal	Ordered, Equal	No Set Order	Ordered, Ranked

SUMMARIZING THE DATA

MEASURES OF CENTRAL TENDENCY

Descriptive statistics provide simple summaries of the data. The typical descriptive values are called the <u>measures of central tendency</u>, and include the mean, the median and the mode (see <u>Study Tip Gal</u> below for mean, median and mode calculation examples).

- <u>Mean</u>: the <u>average</u> value; it is calculated by <u>adding up</u> the values and <u>dividing the sum</u> by the <u>number of values</u>. The mean is preferred for <u>continuous data</u> that is <u>normally distributed</u> (described below).

- <u>Median</u>: the value <u>in the middle</u> when the values are arranged from <u>lowest to highest</u>. When there are <u>two</u> center values (as with an even number of values), <u>take the average</u> of the two center values. The median is preferred for <u>ordinal data</u> or <u>continuous data</u> that is <u>skewed</u> (not normally distributed).

- <u>Mode</u>: the value that occurs <u>most frequently</u>. The mode is preferred for <u>nominal data</u>.

SPREAD (VARIABILITY) OF DATA

Two common methods of describing the variability, or spread, in data are the range and the standard deviation (SD).

- <u>Range</u>: the difference between the highest and lowest values.

- <u>Standard deviation (SD)</u>: indicates <u>how spread out</u> the data is, and to what degree the data is dispersed <u>away from the mean</u> (i.e., spread out over a smaller or larger range). A large number of data values close to the mean has a smaller SD. Data that is <u>highly dispersed</u> has a <u>larger SD</u>.

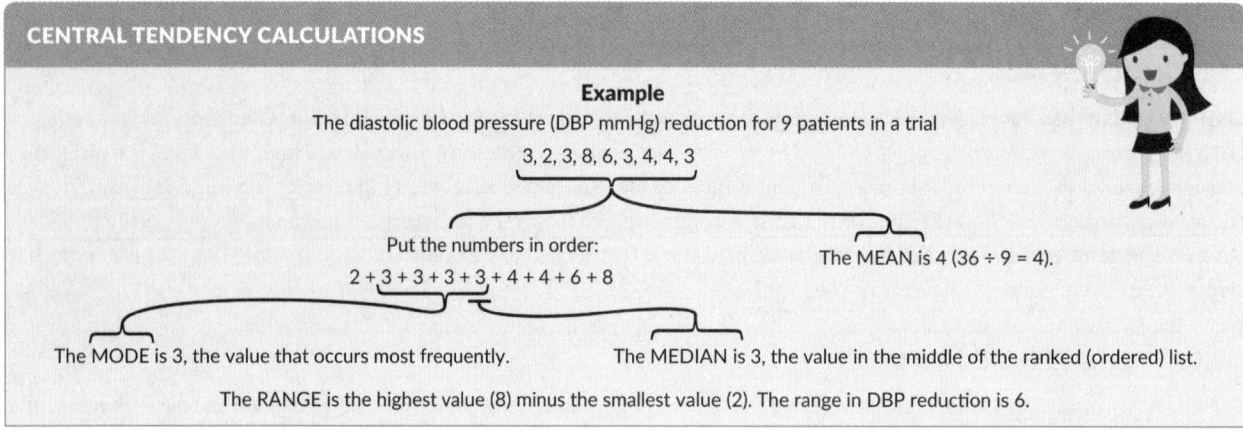

CENTRAL TENDENCY CALCULATIONS

Example

The diastolic blood pressure (DBP mmHg) reduction for 9 patients in a trial

3, 2, 3, 8, 6, 3, 4, 4, 3

Put the numbers in order:

2 + 3 + 3 + 3 + 3 + 4 + 4 + 6 + 8

The MEAN is 4 (36 ÷ 9 = 4).

The MODE is 3, the value that occurs most frequently.

The MEDIAN is 3, the value in the middle of the ranked (ordered) list.

The RANGE is the highest value (8) minus the smallest value (2). The range in DBP reduction is 6.

GAUSSIAN (NORMAL) DISTRIBUTIONS

<u>Large sample sets</u> of <u>continuous data</u> tend to form a <u>Gaussian</u>, or "<u>normal</u>" (bell-shaped), distribution (see the figure at the top of the next page). For example, if a researcher collects 5,000 blood pressure measurements (continuous data) from Idaho residents and plots the values, the graph would form a normal distribution.

Characteristics of a Gaussian Distribution

When the distribution of data is <u>normal</u>, the curve is <u>symmetrical</u> (even on both sides), with most of the values closer to the middle. <u>Half of the values</u> are on the <u>left side</u> of the curve, and <u>half of the values</u> are on the <u>right side</u>. A small number of values are in the <u>tails</u>. When data is normally distributed:

- The <u>mean, median</u> and <u>mode</u> are the <u>same</u> value, and are at the center point of the curve.

- <u>68% of the values</u> fall within <u>1 SD</u> of the mean and <u>95% of the values</u> fall within <u>2 SDs</u> of the mean.

Normal Distribution Shapes

The examples to the right show how the curve of normally distributed data changes based on the spread (or range) of the data. The curve gets taller and skinnier as the range of data narrows. The curve gets shorter and wider as the range of data widens (or is more spread out).

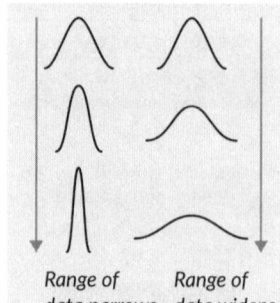

Range of data narrows   Range of data widens

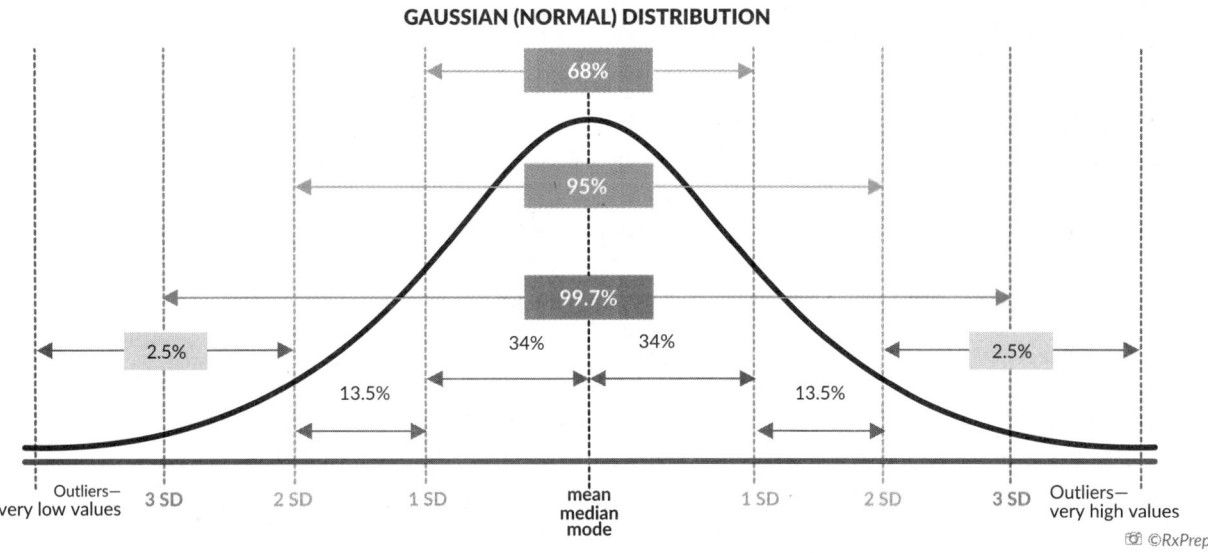

GAUSSIAN (NORMAL) DISTRIBUTION

SKEWED DISTRIBUTIONS

Data that are skewed do not have the characteristics of a normal distribution; the curve is not symmetrical, 68% of the values do not fall within 1 SD from the mean, and the mean, median and mode are not the same value. This usually occurs when the number of values (sample size) is small and/or there are outliers in the data.

Outliers (Extreme Values)

An outlier is an extreme value, either very low or very high, compared to the norm. For example, if a study reports the mean weight of included adult patients as 90 kg, then a patient in the same study with a weight of 40 kg or 186 kg is an outlier. When there are a small number of values, an outlier has a large impact on the mean and the data becomes skewed. In this case, the median is a better measure of central tendency. In the examples to the right, the median is right in the middle of the data and is not affected by outliers.

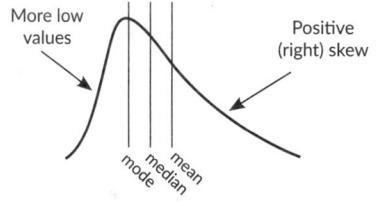

The distortion of the central tendency caused by outliers is decreased by collecting more values; as the number of values increases, the effect of outliers on the mean decreases.

Skew Refers to the Direction of the Tail

Data is skewed towards outliers. When there are more low values in a data set and the outliers are the high values, data is skewed to the right (positive skew). When there are more high values in the data set and the outliers are the low values, the data is skewed to the left (negative skew).

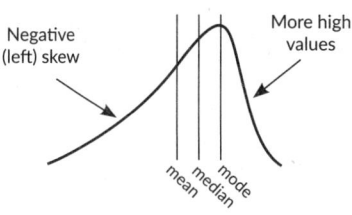

DEPENDENT AND INDEPENDENT VARIABLES

A variable in a study is any data point or characteristic that can be measured or counted. Examples include age, gender, blood pressure or pain. Variables can be clinical endpoints such as death, stroke, hospitalization or an adverse event, or they can be intermediate (or surrogate) endpoints used to assess an outcome, such as measuring serum creatinine to assess the degree of renal impairment.

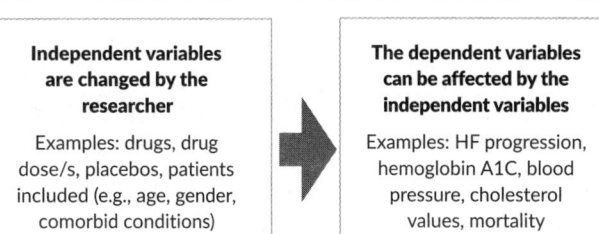

Independent variables are changed by the researcher	The dependent variables can be affected by the independent variables
Examples: drugs, drug dose/s, placebos, patients included (e.g., age, gender, comorbid conditions)	Examples: HF progression, hemoglobin A1C, blood pressure, cholesterol values, mortality

An independent variable is changed (manipulated) by the researcher in order to determine whether it has an effect on the dependent variable (the outcome). Independent variables are the characteristics of the subject groups (treatment and control) selected for inclusion (e.g., age, gender, presence or absence of hypertension, diabetes or other comorbid conditions), or any other characteristic that could have an effect on the dependent variable.

BIOSTATISTICS

TESTING THE HYPOTHESIS FOR SIGNIFICANCE

If a drug or device manufacturer wants to sell their product and make money, they will want research data that demonstrates that their product is significantly better than (or superior to) the current treatment or a placebo (no treatment). To show significance, the trial needs to demonstrate that the null hypothesis is not true and should be rejected, and the alternative hypothesis can be accepted. The null hypothesis and alternative hypothesis are always complementary; when one is accepted, the other is rejected.

THE NULL HYPOTHESIS AND ALTERNATIVE HYPOTHESIS

Null means none or no; a null hypothesis (H_0) states that there is no statistically significant difference between groups. A researcher who is studying a drug versus a placebo would write a null hypothesis that states that there is no difference in efficacy between the drug and the placebo (drug efficacy = placebo efficacy). The null hypothesis is what the researcher tries to disprove or reject.

The alternative hypothesis (H_A) states that there is a statistically significant difference between the groups (drug efficacy ≠ placebo efficacy). The alternative hypothesis is what the researcher hopes to prove or accept.

ALPHA LEVEL: THE STANDARD FOR SIGNIFICANCE

When investigators design a study, they select a maximum permissible error margin, called alpha (α). Alpha is the threshold for rejecting the null hypothesis. In medical research, alpha is commonly set at 5% (or 0.05). A smaller alpha value can be chosen (e.g., 1%, or 0.01), but this requires more data, more subjects (which means more expense) and/or a larger treatment effect.

ALPHA CORRELATES WITH THE VALUES IN THE TAILS WHEN DATA HAS A NORMAL DISTRIBUTION

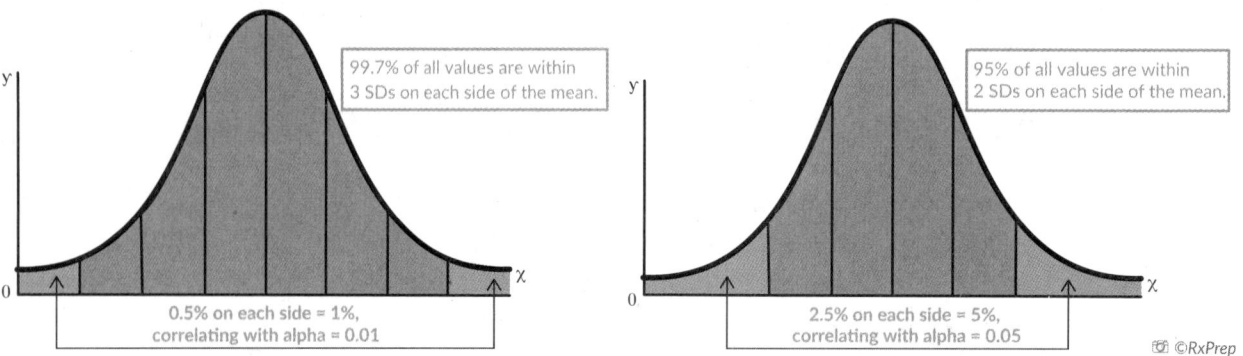

99.7% of all values are within 3 SDs on each side of the mean.

0.5% on each side = 1%, correlating with alpha = 0.01

95% of all values are within 2 SDs on each side of the mean.

2.5% on each side = 5%, correlating with alpha = 0.05

©RxPrep

Comparing the P-Value to Alpha

Once the alpha value is determined, statistical tests are performed to compare the data, and a p-value is calculated. The p-value is compared to alpha. If alpha is set at 0.05 and the p-value is less than 0.05, the null hypothesis is rejected, and the result is termed statistically significant. If the p-value is greater than or equal to alpha (p ≥ 0.05), the study has failed to reject the null hypothesis, and the result is not statistically significant.

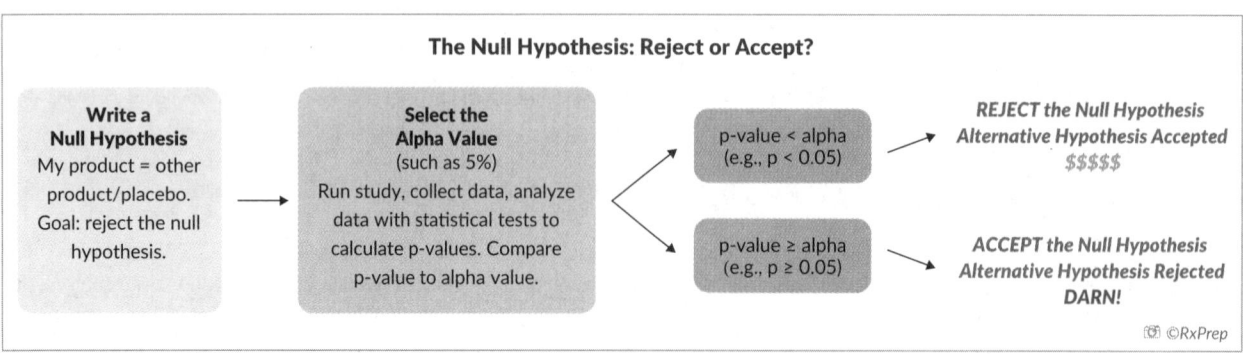

The Null Hypothesis: Reject or Accept?

Write a Null Hypothesis
My product = other product/placebo. Goal: reject the null hypothesis.

Select the Alpha Value (such as 5%)
Run study, collect data, analyze data with statistical tests to calculate p-values. Compare p-value to alpha value.

p-value < alpha (e.g., p < 0.05)

p-value ≥ alpha (e.g., p ≥ 0.05)

REJECT the Null Hypothesis Alternative Hypothesis Accepted $$$$$

ACCEPT the Null Hypothesis Alternative Hypothesis Rejected DARN!

©RxPrep

CONFIDENCE INTERVALS

A confidence interval (CI) provides the same information about significance as the p-value, plus the precision of the result. Alpha and the CI in a study will correlate with each other.

$$CI = 1 - \alpha$$

If alpha is 0.05, the study reports 95% CIs; an alpha of 0.01 corresponds to a CI of 99%. The relationship between alpha, the p-value and the CI is described in the table here and in the figure on the previous page.

ALPHA	P-VALUE	MEANING	
0.05	≥ 0.05	Not statistically significant	
0.05	< 0.05	95% probability (confidence) that the conclusion is correct; less than 5% chance it's not.	
0.01	< 0.01	99% probability (confidence) that the conclusion is correct; less than 1% chance it's not.	*Statistically Significant*
0.001	< 0.001	99.9% probability (confidence) that the conclusion is correct; less than 0.1% chance it's not.	

INTERPRETING CONFIDENCE INTERVALS

- **The values in the CI range are used to determine whether significance has been reached**
- **Determining statistical significance using the CI alone (without a p-value) is required for the exam**

COMPARING DIFFERENCE DATA (MEANS)
- Difference data is based on subtraction [e.g., the difference in Δ FEV1 between roflumilast and placebo (below) was 38 (46 – 8 = 38)]
- The result is statistically significant if the CI range does not include zero (e.g., zero is not present in the range of values); for example:
  - ❏ The 95% CI for the difference in Δ FEV1 (18-58 mL) does not include zero → the result is statistically significant
  - ❏ The 95% CI for the difference in Δ FEV1/FVC (-0.26-0.89%) includes zero → the result is not statistically significant

LUNG FUNCTION	DRUG* (N = 745)	PLACEBO (N = 745)	DIFFERENCE (95% CI)
Δ FEV1 (mL)	46	8	38 (18-58)
Δ FEV1/FVC (%)	0.314	0.001	0.313 (-0.26-0.89)

*Roflumilast

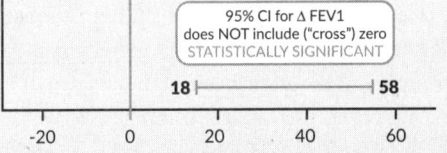
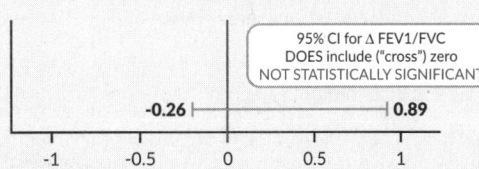

COMPARING RATIO DATA (RELATIVE RISK, ODDS RATIO, HAZARD RATIO)
- Ratio data is based on division [e.g., the ratio of severe exacerbations between roflumilast and placebo (below) was 0.92 (0.11/0.12 = 0.92)]
- The result is statistically significant if the CI range does not include one (e.g., one is not present in the range of values); for example:
  - ❏ The 95% CI for the relative risk of severe exacerbations (0.61-1.29) includes one → the result is not statistically significant
  - ❏ The 95% CI for the relative risk of moderate exacerbations (0.72-0.99) does not include one → the result is statistically significant

EXACERBATIONS*	DRUG** (N = 745)	PLACEBO (N = 745)	RELATIVE RISK (95% CI)
Severe	0.11	0.12	0.92 (0.61-1.29)
Moderate	0.94	1.11	0.85 (0.72-0.99)

*Mean rate, per patient per year
**Roflumilast

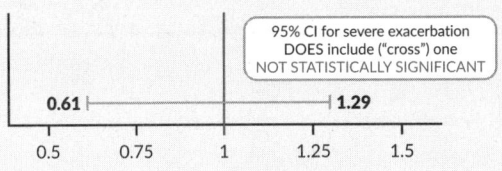
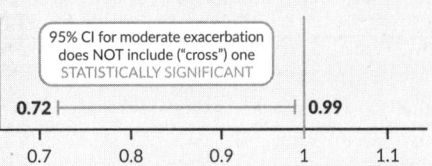

©RxPrep

Confidence Intervals and Estimation (Extent and Variability in the Data)

The goal of the majority of medical research is to use the study results to promote the procedure or drug for use in the general population of patients with the same medical condition. Clinicians need to understand how their patients would benefit. The CI includes the treatment effect and the range; both are helpful in estimating the effect on others.

A CI can be written in slightly different formats. For example, a study comparing metoprolol to placebo finds a 12% absolute risk reduction (ARR) in heart failure progression, with a 95% CI range of 6 – 35%. This can be written as ARR 12% (95% CI 6% – 35%) or as decimals, with commas in the range, such as ARR 0.12 (0.95 CI 0.06, 0.35). The CI indicates that you are 95% confident that the true value of the ARR for the general (or true) population lies somewhere within the range of 6% – 35%, with some values as low as 6% and others as high as 35%.

A narrow CI range implies high precision, and a wide CI range implies poor precision. If the reported CI range was 4% – 68%, the true value would still be within the range, but where? The range is wider, and therefore less precise. Cardiologists who interpret the results for their patients would not know whether to expect a result closer to 4% or 68%. A large range correlates to a large dispersion in the data. A narrower range is preferable.

In some studies, specific patient types will cause a wider distribution in data. For example, fibrates are used to lower triglyceride levels; they cause a greater reduction in patients with higher triglycerides. The consideration of where the patient is likely to fall within the range will become part of the assessment of the individual's baseline risk.

TYPE I AND TYPE II ERRORS

Consider what would happen if a drug manufacturer developed and marketed a new drug as better for heart failure than the standard of care, when in fact the new, expensive drug has similar benefits to the old drug (it is not better at all). The null hypothesis stated that the new drug and the old drug are equal. The statistical tests found a significant benefit with the new drug, and the null hypothesis was rejected when it should have been accepted.

Type I Errors: False-Positives

In the scenario described above, the conclusion was wrong and a type I error was made. The alternative hypothesis was accepted and the null hypothesis was rejected in error. The probability, or risk, of making a type I error is determined by alpha and it relates to the confidence interval.

$$CI = 1 - \alpha \text{ (type I error)}$$

When alpha is 0.05 and a study result is reported with $p < 0.05$, it is statistically significant and the probability of a type I error (making the wrong conclusion) is $\leq 5\%$. You are 95% confident (0.95 = 1 – 0.05) that your result is correct and not due to chance.

Type II Errors: False-Negatives

The probability of a type II error, denoted as beta (β), occurs when the null hypothesis is accepted when it should have been rejected. Beta is set by the investigators during the design of a study. It is typically set at 0.1 or 0.2, meaning the risk of a type II error is 10% or 20%. The risk of a type II error increases if the sample size is too small. To decrease this risk, a power analysis is performed to determine the sample size needed to detect a true difference between groups.

Study Power

Power is the probability that a test will reject the null hypothesis correctly (i.e., the power to avoid a type II error). Power = 1 – β. As the power increases, the chance of a type II error decreases. Power is determined by the number of outcome values collected, the difference in outcome rates between the groups, and the significance (alpha) level. If beta is set at 0.2, the study has 80% power (there is a 20% chance of missing a true difference and making a type II error). If beta is set at 0.1, the study has 90% power. A larger sample size is needed to increase study power and decrease the risk of a type II error.

	H_0 ACCEPTED	H_0 REJECTED
H_0 is TRUE (NO difference between groups)	Correct Conclusion	Type I Error Committed FALSE POSITIVE
H_0 is FALSE (There IS a difference between groups)	Type II Error Committed FALSE NEGATIVE	Correct Conclusion

H_0 = the null hypothesis

RISK

In healthcare, risk refers to the probability of an event (how likely it is to occur) when an intervention, such as a drug, is given. The lack of intervention is measured as the effect in the placebo (or control) group.

RELATIVE RISK (OR RISK RATIO)

The <u>relative risk</u> (RR) is the ratio of <u>risk in the exposed group</u> (treatment) <u>divided by risk in the control group</u>.

RR Formula

$$\text{Risk} = \frac{\text{Number of subjects in group with an unfavorable event}}{\text{Total number of subjects in group}}$$

$$\text{RR} = \frac{\text{Risk in treatment group}}{\text{Risk in control group}}$$

RR Calculation

A placebo-controlled study was performed to evaluate whether metoprolol reduces disease progression in patients with heart failure (HF). A total of 10,111 patients were enrolled and followed for 12 months. What is the relative risk of HF progression in the metoprolol-treated group versus the placebo group?

Calculate the risk of HF progression in each group. Then calculate RR.

	METOPROLOL N = 5,123	CONTROL N = 4,988
HF progression	823	1,397

Metoprolol Risk	Control Risk
$\frac{823}{5,123} = 0.16$	$\frac{1,397}{4,988} = 0.28$

$$\text{RR} = \frac{0.16}{0.28} = 0.57 \times 100 = 57\%$$

Answer can be expressed as a decimal or a percentage; the exam question will specify with instructions

RR Interpretation

RR = 1 (or 100%) implies <u>no difference</u> in risk of the outcome between the groups.
RR > 1 (or 100%) implies <u>greater risk</u> of the outcome in the treatment group.
RR < 1 (or 100%) implies <u>lower risk</u> (reduced risk) of the outcome in the treatment group.

In the metoprolol study, the RR of HF progression was 57%. Patients treated with metoprolol were 57% <u>as likely</u> to have progression of disease as placebo-treated patients.

INTERPRETING THE RELATIVE RISK (RR)

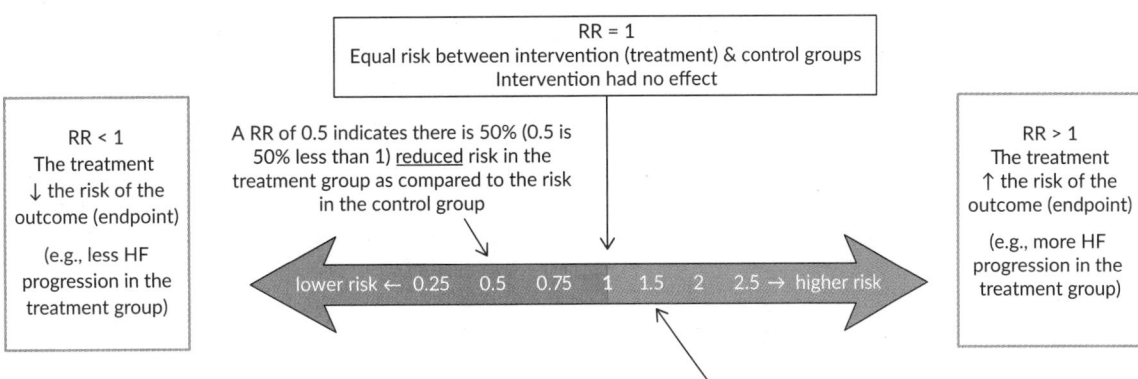

RR = 1
Equal risk between intervention (treatment) & control groups
Intervention had no effect

RR < 1
The treatment ↓ the risk of the outcome (endpoint)
(e.g., less HF progression in the treatment group)

A RR of 0.5 indicates there is 50% (0.5 is 50% less than 1) <u>reduced</u> risk in the treatment group as compared to the risk in the control group

RR > 1
The treatment ↑ the risk of the outcome (endpoint)
(e.g., more HF progression in the treatment group)

lower risk ← 0.25   0.5   0.75   1   1.5   2   2.5 → higher risk

A RR of 1.5 indicates there is 50% (1.5 is 50% greater than 1) <u>increased</u> risk in the treatment group as compared to the risk in the control group

©RxPrep

RELATIVE RISK REDUCTION

The RR calculation determines whether there is less risk (RR < 1) or more risk (RR > 1). The <u>relative risk reduction</u> (RRR) is calculated after the RR and indicates <u>how much the risk is reduced</u> in the treatment group compared to the control group.

RRR Formula

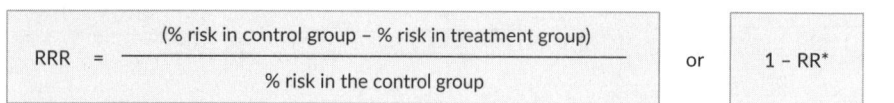

$$RRR = \frac{(\% \text{ risk in control group} - \% \text{ risk in treatment group})}{\% \text{ risk in the control group}} \quad \text{or} \quad 1 - RR^*$$

Decimals or percentages may be used for risks   **Must use decimal form of RR*

RRR Calculation

Using the risks previously calculated for HF progression in the treatment and control groups (metoprolol: 16% and placebo: 28%), calculate the RRR of HF progression.

$$RRR = \frac{(28\% - 16\%)}{28\%} = 0.43 \quad \text{or} \quad RRR = 1 - 0.57 = 0.43$$

Answer can be expressed as a decimal or percentage; the exam question will specify with instructions

RRR Interpretation

The RRR is 43%. Metoprolol-treated patients were 43% <u>less likely</u> to have HF progression than placebo-treated patients.

INTERPRETING THE RELATIVE RISK REDUCTION (RRR)

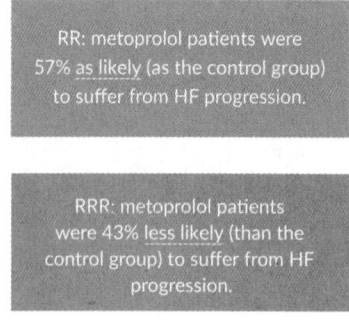

RR: metoprolol patients were 57% <u>as likely</u> (as the control group) to suffer from HF progression.

RRR: metoprolol patients were 43% <u>less likely</u> (than the control group) to suffer from HF progression.

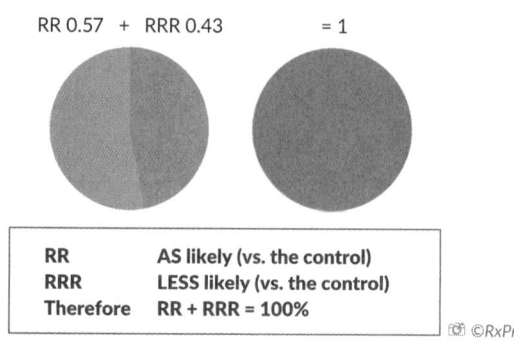

RR 0.57 + RRR 0.43   = 1

RR	AS likely (vs. the control)
RRR	LESS likely (vs. the control)
Therefore	RR + RRR = 100%

©RxPrep

ABSOLUTE RISK REDUCTION

A clinician is listening to a presentation on a drug. The drug manufacturer representative reports that the drug causes 48% less nausea than the standard treatment. The result sounds great; the clinician asks the pharmaceutical representative: what is the absolute risk reduction (ARR)?

The RR and RRR provide relative (proportional) differences in risk between the treatment group and the control group; they have no meaning in terms of absolute risk.

<u>Absolute risk reduction</u> is more useful because it includes the <u>reduction</u> in risk <u>and</u> the <u>incidence rate</u> of the outcome. If the risk of nausea is reduced, but the risk was small to begin with (perhaps the drug caused very little nausea), the large risk reduction has little practical benefit.

It is best if a study reports both ARR and RRR, and for clinicians to understand how to interpret the risk for their patients. If the ARR is not reported, it is possible that the risk reduction, in terms of a decrease in absolute risk, is minimal.

ARR Formula

$$ARR = (\% \text{ risk in control group}) - (\% \text{ risk in treatment group})$$

ARR Calculation

Using the risks previously calculated for HF progression in the metoprolol study, calculate the ARR of HF progression.

Metoprolol Risk		Control Risk	
$\dfrac{823}{5,123}$	$= 0.16$	$\dfrac{1,397}{4,988}$	$= 0.28$

ARR = 0.28 − 0.16 = 0.12 × 100 = 12%

Answer can be expressed as a decimal or a percentage; the exam question will specify with instructions

ARR Interpretation

The ARR is 12%, meaning 12 out of every 100 patients benefit from the treatment. Said another way, for every 100 patients treated with metoprolol, 12 fewer patients will have HF progression.

An additional benefit of calculating the ARR is to be able to use the inverse of the ARR to determine the number needed to treat (NNT) and number needed to harm (NNH). These concepts are discussed next.

INTERPRETING THE ABSOLUTE RISK REDUCTION (ARR)

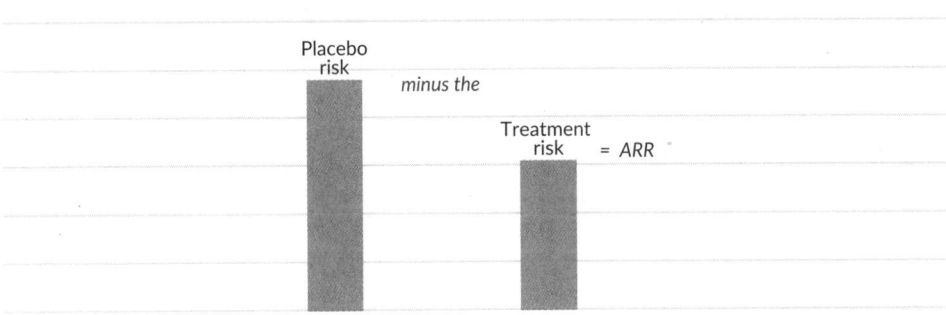

The absolute risk reduction is the true difference in risk between the treatment and the placebo groups.
Said another way, the ARR is the net effect (benefit) beyond the effect obtained from a placebo.

©RxPrep

NUMBER NEEDED TO TREAT OR HARM

NNT and NNH help clinicians answer the question: how many patients need to receive the drug for one patient to get benefit (NNT) or harm (NNH)? This information, taken into consideration with the patient's individual risk, helps guide decisions.

NUMBER NEEDED TO TREAT

NNT is the number of patients who need to be treated for a certain period of time (e.g., one year) in order for one patient to benefit (e.g., avoid HF progression).

NNT Formula

$$NNT = \frac{1}{\text{(risk in control group)} - \text{(risk in treatment group)}^*} \quad \text{or} \quad \frac{1}{ARR^*}$$

Risk and ARR are expressed as decimals

NNT Calculation

The ARR in the metoprolol study was 12%. The duration of the study period was one year. Calculate the number of patients that need to be treated with metoprolol for one year in order to prevent one case of HF progression.

$$NNT = \frac{1}{0.12} = 8.3, \text{ rounded up to } 9^*$$

Numbers greater than a whole number are rounded up

NNT Interpretation

For every 9 patients who receive metoprolol for one year, HF progression is prevented in one patient.

NUMBER NEEDED TO HARM

NNH is the number of patients who need to be treated for a certain period of time in order for one patient to experience harm.

NNT and NNH are calculated with the same formula (see the NNT formula on the previous page). There are two differences:

1. NNT is rounded up, and NNH is rounded down (see Study Tip Gal).

2. The absolute value of the ARR is used with NNH, as shown in the following example.

NNH Calculation

A study evaluated the efficacy of clopidogrel versus placebo, both given in addition to aspirin, in reducing the risk of cardiovascular death, MI and stroke. The study reported a 3.9% risk of major bleeding in the treatment group and a 2.8% risk of major bleeding in the control group.

ARR = 2.8% – 3.9% = –1.1%; the absolute value is the difference between the two groups. There is a 1.1% higher risk of major bleeding in the treatment group.

$$NNH = \frac{1}{0.011} = 90.9, \text{ rounded down to } 90^*$$

*Numbers greater than a whole number are rounded down

NNH Interpretation

One additional case of major bleeding is expected to occur for every 90 patients taking clopidogrel instead of placebo.

ROUNDING RULES FOR NNT AND NNH

Normal rounding rules do not apply:

- For NNT:
  - Anything greater than a whole number, round up to the next whole number. This avoids overstating the potential benefit of an intervention.
  - Example: NNT of 52.1 → round up to 53

- For NNH:
  - Anything greater than a whole number, round down to the nearest whole number. This avoids understating the potential harm of an intervention.
  - Example: NNH of 41.9 → round down to 41

ODDS RATIO AND HAZARD RATIO

ODDS RATIO

Odds are the probability that an event will occur versus the probability that it will not occur. Case-control studies, described in the Types of Medical Studies section, are not suitable for relative risk calculations. In case-control studies, the odds ratio is used to estimate the risk of unfavorable events associated with a treatment or intervention.

Case-control studies enroll patients who have a clinical outcome or disease that has already occurred (e.g., lung cancer). The patient medical charts are reviewed retrospectively (in the past) to search for possible exposures (e.g., smoking) that increased the risk of the clinical outcome or disease. In this case, the odds ratio (OR) is used to calculate the odds of an outcome occurring with an exposure, compared to the odds of the outcome occurring without the exposure. ORs are used most commonly with case-control studies but can be used in cohort and cross-sectional studies.

OR Formula

EXPOSURE/TREATMENT	OUTCOME PRESENT	OUTCOME ABSENT
Present	A	B
Absent	C	D

$$OR = \frac{AD}{BC}$$

A = # that have the outcome, with exposure

B = # without the outcome, with exposure

C = # that have the outcome, without exposure

D = # without the outcome, without exposure

OR Calculation

A case-control study was conducted to assess the risk of falls with fracture (outcome) associated with serotonergic antidepressant (AD) use (exposure) among a cohort of Chinese females ≥ 65 years old. Cases were matched with 33,000 controls (1:4, by age, sex and cohort entry date).

EXPOSURE/ TREATMENT	FALLS W/ FRACTURE (CASES)	FALLS W/O FRACTURE (CONTROLS)
Serotonergic AD-YES	4,991	18,270
Serotonergic AD-NO	3,259	14,730

$$AD = 4{,}991 \times 14{,}730 = 73{,}517{,}430$$

$$BC = 18{,}270 \times 3{,}259 = 59{,}541{,}930$$

$$OR = \frac{73{,}517{,}430}{59{,}541{,}930} = 1.23$$

Conclusion: serotonergic ADs are associated with a 23% increased risk of falls with fracture (see OR and HR Interpretation below).

HAZARD RATIO

In a survival analysis (e.g. analysis of death or disease progression), instead of using "risk," a hazard rate is used. A hazard rate is the rate at which an unfavorable event occurs within a short period of time. Similar to RR, the hazard ratio (HR) is the ratio between the hazard rate in the treatment group and the hazard rate in the control group.

HR Formula

$$HR = \frac{\text{Hazard rate in the treatment group}}{\text{Hazard rate in the control group}}$$

HR Calculation

A placebo-controlled study was performed to evaluate whether niacin, when added to intensive statin therapy, reduces cardiovascular risk in patients with established cardiovascular disease. The primary endpoint was the first event of the composite endpoint (death from coronary heart disease, nonfatal myocardial infarction, ischemic stroke, hospitalization for an acute coronary syndrome or coronary or cerebral revascularization). A total of 3,414 patients were enrolled and followed for three years.

Calculate the hazard ratio.

	NIACIN	PLACEBO
Primary endpoint	N = 1,718	N = 1,696
	282	274

Niacin Hazard Rate	Control Hazard Rate
$\dfrac{282}{1{,}718} = 0.16$	$\dfrac{274}{1{,}696} = 0.16$

$$HR = \frac{0.16}{0.16} = 1 \times 100 = 100\%$$

Answer can be expressed as a decimal or a percentage; the exam question will specify with instructions

Conclusion: there is no benefit to cardiovascular risk when adding niacin to intensive statin therapy (see OR and HR Interpretation below).

OR AND HR INTERPRETATION

OR and HR are interpreted in a similar way to RR:

OR or HR = 1: the event rate is the same in the treatment and control arms. There is no advantage to the treatment.

OR or HR > 1: the event rate in the treatment group is higher than the event rate in the control group; for example, a HR of 2 for an outcome of death indicates that there are twice as many deaths in the treatment group.

OR or HR < 1: the event rate in the treatment group is lower than the event rate in the control group; for example, a HR of 0.5 for an outcome of death indicates that there are half as many deaths in the treatment group.

PRIMARY AND COMPOSITE ENDPOINTS

The <u>primary endpoint</u> is the main (primary) result that is measured to see if the treatment had a significant benefit. In the metoprolol trial, the primary endpoint was HF progression.

A <u>composite endpoint</u> combines <u>multiple</u> individual endpoints into <u>one measurement</u>. This is attractive to researchers, as combining several endpoints increases the likelihood of reaching a statistically significant benefit with a smaller, less costly trial.

When a composite endpoint is used, each individual endpoint gets counted toward the same (composite) outcome.

Primary Endpoints (distinct and separate)	Composite Endpoint (combined into one)
Death from cardiovascular causes	Death from cardiovascular causes
or	and
Nonfatal stroke	Nonfatal stroke
or	and
Nonfatal MI	Nonfatal MI

COMPOSITE ENDPOINTS: CAUTION

All endpoints in a composite must be <u>similar</u> in magnitude and have similar, meaningful importance to the patient. For example, the composite endpoint of blood pressure reduction should not be included with heart attack and stroke reduction. The FDA requires each individual endpoint to be measured and reported when a composite endpoint is used. When assessing a <u>composite</u> measurement, it is important to <u>use the composite</u> endpoint <u>value</u>, rather than adding together the values for the individual endpoints. The value of the sum of the individual endpoints may <u>not equal</u> the value of the composite endpoint, since a patient can have more than one non-fatal endpoint during a trial.

TYPES OF STATISTICAL TESTS

The next step following data collection (and calculation of risks, RR, ARR, HR, etc.) is to analyze the data to check if differences between the treatment and control groups are <u>statistically significant</u> or if there is an association or relationship in the data. Selecting the correct test to analyze the data depends on the type of data and the outcomes measured.

CONTINUOUS DATA

With continuous data, the type of test used to determine statistical significance depends on the distribution of data (discussed previously). If it is <u>normally distributed, parametric</u> methods are appropriate. If the data is <u>not normally distributed</u>, <u>nonparametric</u> methods are appropriate.

T-Tests

This is a parametric method used when the endpoint has <u>continuous data</u> and the data is <u>normally distributed</u>. When data from a single sample group is compared with known data from the general population, a <u>one-sample t-test</u> is performed. If a single sample group is used for a pre-/post-measurement (i.e., the patient serves as their own control), a <u>paired t-test</u> is appropriate.

A <u>student t-test</u> is used when the study has <u>two</u> independent samples: the <u>treatment</u> and the <u>control</u> groups. For example, a study comparing the reduction in hemoglobin A1C values between metformin and placebo would use an independent or unpaired student t-test.

Analysis of Variance

Analysis of variance (<u>ANOVA</u>), or the F-test, is used to test for statistical significance when using <u>continuous data</u> with <u>3 or more</u> samples, or groups.

DISCRETE (CATEGORICAL) DATA

Chi-Square Test

For <u>nominal or ordinal data</u>, a <u>chi-square</u> test is used to determine statistical significance between treatment groups. For example, if a study assesses the difference in mortality (nominal data) between two groups, or pain scores based on a pain scale (ordinal data), a chi-square test could be used.

SELECTING A TEST TO ANALYZE THE DATA

NUMBER OF GROUPS	TYPE OF DATA		
	Continuous		Discrete/Categorical
	PARAMETRIC TESTS (data has normal distribution)	**NON-PARAMETRIC TESTS** (data has skewed distribution)	
1	One-sample t-test	Sign test	Chi-square test
1 (with before & after measures)	Dependent/paired t-test	Wilcoxon Signed-Rank test	Wilcoxon Signed-Rank test
2 (treatment & control)	Independent/unpaired student t-test	Mann-Whitney (Wilcoxon Rank-Sum) test	Chi-square test or Fisher's exact test / Mann-Whitney (Wilcoxon Rank-Sum) test (may be preferred for ordinal data)
≥ 3	ANOVA (or F-test)	Kruskal-Wallis test	Kruskal-Wallis test

EXAMPLES OF TEST TYPE SELECTION

Example 1

A study is performed to assess the safety and efficacy of ketamine-dexmedetomidine (KD) versus ketamine-propofol (KP) for sedation in patients after coronary artery bypass graft surgery.

ENDPOINT (MEAN VALUES)	KD	KP
Fentanyl dose, mcg	41.94 ± 20.43	152.8 ± 51.2
Weaning/extubation time, min	374.05 ± 20.25	445.23 ± 21.7

Measurements of dose and time are both continuous data. The trial has two independent samples, or groups (KD and KP). An appropriate test is an independent/unpaired student t-test. If the trial included a third group, ANOVA would be used.

Example 2

An emergency medical team wants to see if there is a statistically significant difference in death due to multiple drug overdose (OD) with at least one opioid taken, versus no opioid taken. Which test can determine a statistically significant difference in death?

ENDPOINT	YES OPIOID N = 250	NO OPIOID N = 150
Death (n, %)	52 (20.8%)	35 (23.3%)

The variable (dead or alive) is nominal. The chi-square test is used to test for significance when there are two groups.

CORRELATION AND REGRESSION

CORRELATION

Correlation is a statistical technique that is used to determine if one variable (such as number of days hospitalized) changes, or is related to, another variable (such as incidence of hospital-acquired infection). When the independent variable (number of hospital days) causes the dependent variable (infections) to increase, the direction of the correlation is positive (increases to the right). When the independent variable causes the dependent variable to decrease, the direction of the correlation is negative (decreases to the right).

Different types of data require different tests for correlation. Spearman's rank-order correlation, referred to as Rho, is used to test correlation with ordinal, ranked data. The primary test used for continuous data is the Pearson's correlation coefficient, denoted as r, which is a calculated score that indicates the strength and direction of the relationship between two variables. The values range from –1 to +1, and are described in the figure on the next page.

It is not possible to conclude from a correlation analysis that the change in a variable causes the change in another variable. A correlation, whether positive or negative, does not prove a causal relationship.

TESTING FOR CORRELATION WITH THE PEARSON CORRELATION COEFFICIENT

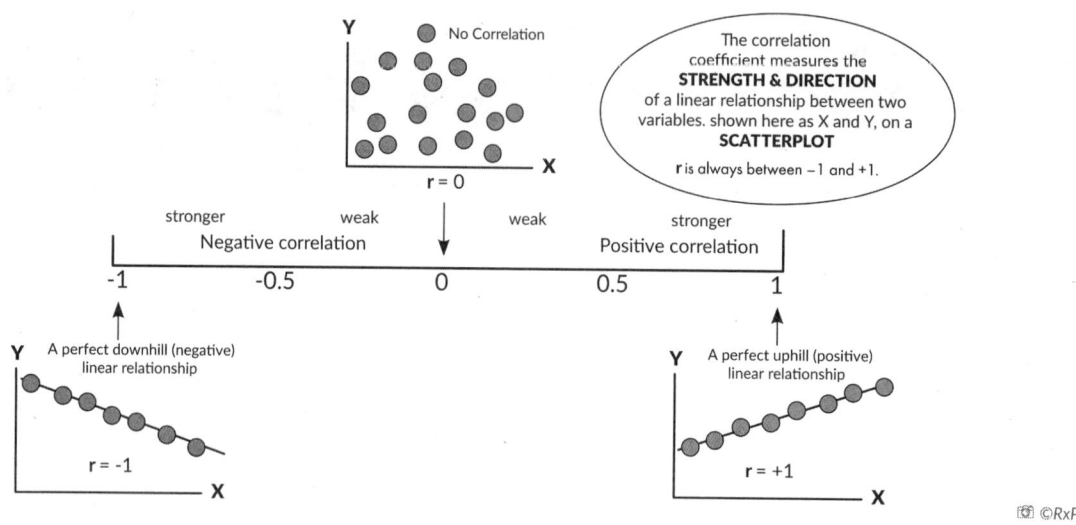

REGRESSION

Regression is used to describe the relationship between a dependent variable and one or more independent (or explanatory) variables, or how much the value of the dependent variable changes when the independent variables changes. Regression is common in observational studies where researchers need to assess multiple independent variables or need to control for many confounding factors. There are three typical types of regressions: 1) linear, for continuous data, 2) logistic, for categorical data, and 3) Cox regression, for categorical data in a survival analysis.

SENSITIVITY AND SPECIFICITY

Lab and diagnostic tests are used to screen for and diagnose medical conditions. Interpreting sensitivity and specificity correctly is required to answer these two questions concerning the validity of lab or diagnostic test results:

- If the result is positive, what is the likelihood of having the disease?

- If the result is negative, what is the likelihood of not having the disease?

SENSITIVITY, THE TRUE POSITIVE

Sensitivity describes how effectively a test identifies patients with the condition. The higher the sensitivity, the better; a test with 100% sensitivity will be positive in all patients with the condition. Sensitivity is calculated from the number of patients who test positive, out of those who actually have the condition (sensitivity is the percentage of "true-positive" results).

SPECIFICITY, THE TRUE NEGATIVE

Specificity describes how effectively a test identifies patients without the condition. The higher the specificity the better; a test with 100% specificity will be negative in all patients without the condition. Specificity is calculated from the number who test negative, out of those who actually do not have the condition (specificity is the percentage of "true-negative" results).

Sensitivity and Specificity Formula

TEST RESULT	HAVE CONDITION	NO CONDITION
Positive	A	B
Negative	C	D
Total	A + C	B + D

$$\text{Sensitivity} = \frac{A}{A + C} \times 100$$

$$\text{Specificity} = \frac{D}{B + D} \times 100$$

A = # that have the condition, with a positive test result
B = # without the condition, with a positive test result
C = # that have the condition, with a negative test result
D = # without the condition, with a negative test result

Sensitivity and Specificity Calculation and Interpretation

The tables below show how sensitivity and specificity is calculated for two lab tests used in the diagnosis of rheumatoid arthritis (RA), cyclic citrulline peptide (CCP) and rheumatoid factor (RF). Based on study data, CCP has a sensitivity of 98% and a specificity of 98% for RA, while RF has a sensitivity of 28% and a specificity of 87%.

Using the RF lab test as an example, a sensitivity of 28% means that only 28% of patients with the condition will have a positive RF result; the test is negative in 72% of patients with the disease (and the diagnosis can be missed). A specificity of 87% means that the test is negative in 87% of patients without the disease; but 13% of patients without the disease can test positive (potentially causing an incorrect diagnosis).

CCP RESULTS	HAVE CONDITION	NO CONDITION
Positive	A = 147	B = 9
Negative	C = 3	D = 441
Total	A + C = 150	B + D = 450
Sensitivity	147/150 x 100 = 98%	
Specificity		441/450 x 100 = 98%

RF RESULTS	HAVE CONDITION	NO CONDITION
Positive	A = 21	B = 26
Negative	C = 54	D = 174
Total	A + C = 75	B + D = 200
Sensitivity	21/75 x 100 = 28%	
Specificity		174/200 x 100 = 87%

Sensitivity and Specificity Application

If an elderly female patient with swollen finger joints is referred to a rheumatologist and lab tests reveal a positive CCP and a positive RF, the positive CCP indicates a very strong likelihood that the patient has RA because it has high sensitivity and specificity (98%). If the RF is positive and the CCP is negative, the rheumatologist would consider the possibility of other autoimmune/inflammatory conditions that could be contributing to swollen joints because of the low sensitivity of RF (28%).

INTENTION-TO-TREAT AND PER PROTOCOL ANALYSIS

Data from clinical trials can be analyzed in two different ways; intention-to-treat or per protocol. Intention-to-treat analysis includes data for all patients originally allocated to each treatment group (active and control) even if the patient did not complete the trial according to the study protocol (e.g., due to non-compliance, protocol violations or study withdrawal). This method provides a conservative (real-world) estimate of the treatment effect. A per protocol analysis is conducted for the subset of the trial population who completed the study according to the protocol (or at least without any major protocol violations). This method can provide an optimistic estimate of treatment effect since it is limited to the subset of patients who were adherent to the protocol.

NONINFERIORITY AND EQUIVALENCE TRIAL DESIGNS

The standard design of most trials is to establish that a treatment is superior to another treatment; the researcher wishes to show that the new drug is better than the old drug or a placebo. Perhaps a new treatment is developed that is less expensive or less toxic than the standard of care. Researchers would hope to demonstrate that the new drug is roughly equivalent, or at least not inferior, to the standard of care. Two types of trials are used for this purpose: equivalence and non-inferiority trials.

Equivalence trials attempt to demonstrate that the new treatment has roughly the same effect as the old (or reference) treatment. These trials test for effect in two directions, for higher or lower effectiveness, which is called a two-way margin. Non-inferiority trials attempt to demonstrate that the new treatment is no worse than the current standard based on the predefined non-inferiority (delta) margin. The delta margin is the minimal difference in effect between the two groups that is considered clinically acceptable based on previous research.

FOREST PLOTS AND CONFIDENCE INTERVALS

Forest plots are graphs that have a "forest" of lines. Forest plots can be used for a single study in which individual endpoints are pooled (gathered together) into a composite endpoint (see figure labeled Pogue, et al. below). More commonly, forest plots are used when the results from multiple studies are pooled into a single study, such as with a meta-analysis (see figure labeled Miller, et al. below).

Forest plots provide CIs for difference data or ratio data. Interpreting forest plots correctly can help identify whether a statistically significant benefit has been reached. When interpreting statistical significance using a forest plot:

- The boxes show the effect estimate. In a meta-analysis, the size of the box correlates with the size of the effect from the single study shown. Diamonds (at the bottom of the forest plot) represent pooled results from multiple studies.

- The horizontal lines through the boxes illustrate the length of the confidence interval for that particular endpoint (in a single study) or for the particular study (in a meta-analysis). The longer the line, the wider the interval, and the less reliable the study results. The width of the diamond in a meta-analysis serves the same purpose.

- The vertical solid line is the line of no effect; a significant benefit has been reached when data falls to the left of the line; data to the right of the line indicates significant harm. The vertical line is set at zero for difference data and at one for ratio data.

COMPARING DIFFERENCE DATA

The study shown to the right (a meta-analysis by Miller, et al.) uses a forest plot to test for significance with difference data. Recall for difference data, a result is not statistically significant if the confidence interval crosses zero, so the vertical line (line of no difference) is set at zero. Examples (for high-dosage vitamin E):

- 3rd study (PPS): shows a statistically significant benefit; the data point, plus the entire confidence interval, is to the left of the vertical line and does not cross zero.

- 5th study (CHAOS): the result is not statistically significant; the confidence interval crosses zero.

- 9th study (WAVE): shows a statistically significant harmful outcome; the data point, plus the entire confidence interval, is all to the right of the vertical line and does not cross zero.

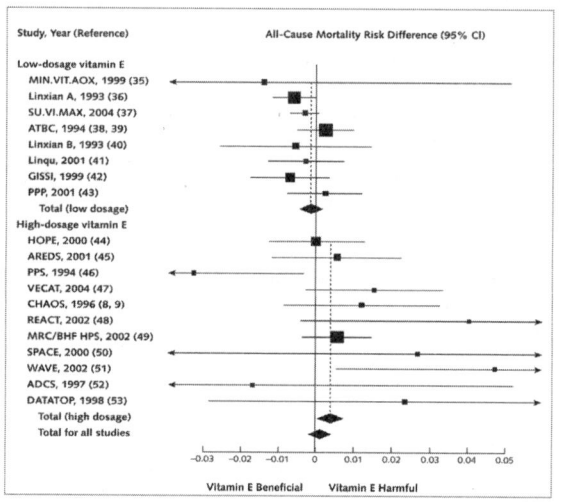

Miller, et al. Ann Intern Med. 2005 Jan 4;142(1):37-46.

COMPARING RATIO DATA

The study shown to the right (by Pogue, et al.) uses a forest plot to test for significance of a composite endpoint reported as ratio data, in this case hazard ratio. Recall for ratio data, the result is not statistically significant if the confidence interval crosses one, so the vertical line (line of no difference) is set at one. Examples:

- Primary composite endpoint: a statistically significant benefit was shown with treatment; the CI (0.7 – 0.99) does not cross one (and the horizontal line representing the CI does not touch or cross the vertical line at one).

- CV death: shows no statistically significant benefit (or harm); the CI (0.92 – 1.83) crosses one (and the horizontal line representing the CI crosses the vertical line at one).

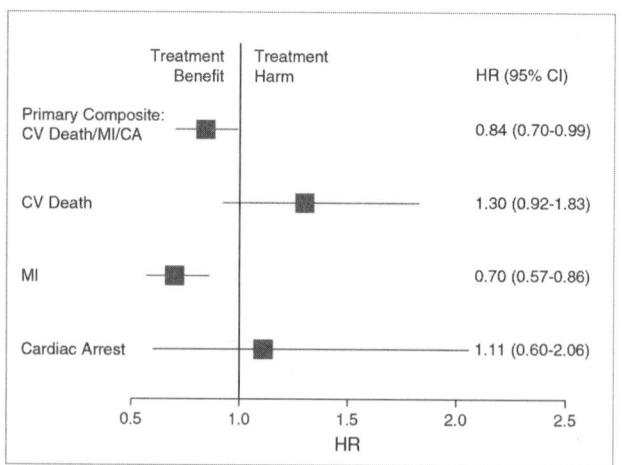

Pogue, et al. PLoS One 2012; 7(4): e34785.

TYPES OF MEDICAL STUDIES

Evidence-based medicine (EBM), which is largely guideline and protocol-driven, is the foundation of practice and most patient care recommendations are based on valid study data. The type of study that a researcher chooses is a major factor in determining the quality of the study data and the clinical value or impact. The pyramid figure to the right depicts the reliability of each of the major study types.

Common types of studies include:

- Case-control studies: retrospective comparisons of cases (patients with a disease) and controls (patients without a disease).

- Cohort studies: retrospective or prospective comparisons of patients with an exposure to those without an exposure.

- Randomized controlled trials: prospective comparison of patients who were randomly assigned to groups.

- Meta-analyses: analyzes the results of multiple studies.

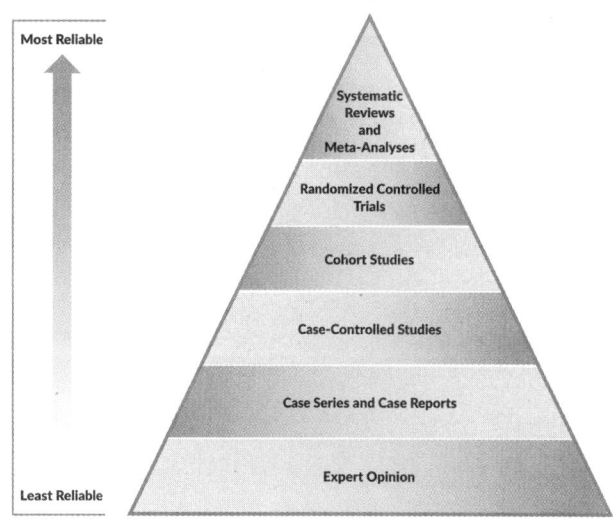

Each type of study has benefits and limitations. The table below describes the various study types and provides an example of each study.

STUDY TYPE, BENEFITS AND LIMITATIONS	STUDY TYPE EXAMPLE
CASE-CONTROL STUDY Compares patients with a disease (cases) to those without the disease (controls). The outcome of the cases and controls is already known, but the researcher looks back in time (retrospectively) to see if a relationship exists between the disease (outcome) and various risk factors. **Benefits** Data is easy to get from medical records. Good for looking at outcomes when the intervention is unethical (e.g., exposing patients to a pesticide to test an association with cancer; cases that occurred are used instead). Less expensive than a RCT. **Limitations** Cause and effect cannot reliably be determined (associations may be proven to be non-existent).	***Predictors of surgical site infection after open lower extremity bypass (LEB) revascularization.*** **Methods** Data was pulled from 35 hospitals for all patients who had LEB during a 3-year period. Cases of surgical site infection (SSI) were identified and compared to those who did not develop an SSI (controls). An odds ratio (OR) was calculated for various risk factors that might increase SSI risk. **Statistical Data** Renal failure OR: 4.35 (95% CI 3.45-5.47; p < 0.001). Hypertension OR: 4.29 (95% CI 2.74-6.72; p < 0.001). BMI ≥ 25 kg/m² OR: 1.78 (95% CI 1.23-2.57; p = 0.002). **Conclusion** Renal failure, hypertension and BMI ≥ 25 kg/m² were all associated with an increased risk of SSI.
COHORT STUDY Compares outcomes of a group of patients exposed and not exposed to a treatment; the researcher follows both groups prospectively (in the future) or retrospectively (less common) to see if they develop the outcome. **Benefits** Good for looking at outcomes when the intervention would be unethical. **Limitations** More time-consuming and expensive than a retrospective study. Can be influenced by confounders, which are other factors that affect the outcome (e.g., smoking, lipid levels).	***Statin use and cognitive function in adults with type 1 diabetes.*** **Methods** Patients with type 1 diabetes who were taking statins (exposed) were compared to those not taking statins (not exposed) and followed for 7-12 years to see if statin use was associated with cognitive impairment (outcome). **Statistical Data** Statin use and odds of cognitive impairment OR: 4.84 (95% CI 1.63-14.44; p = 0.005). **Conclusion** In type 1 diabetes, patients taking statins were more likely to develop cognitive impairment compared to those who did not take statins.

STUDY TYPE, BENEFITS AND LIMITATIONS	STUDY TYPE EXAMPLE
CROSS-SECTIONAL SURVEY Estimates the relationship between variables and outcomes (prevalence) at one particular time (cross-section) in a defined population. **Benefits** Can identify associations that need further study (hypothesis-generating). **Limitations** Does not determine causality (further studies needed if association found).	*Association of selective serotonin reuptake inhibitors and bone mineral density (BMD) in elderly women.* **Methods** A cross-sectional analysis of 250 elderly women (defined population) from August 2010 to April 2015 (time period) was performed. Data was collected retrospectively for two groups: SSRI users (variable) and SSRI nonusers (variable) to compare the prevalence of low BMD. **Statistical Data** No difference in the prevalence of low BMD at the femoral neck ($p = 0.887$) or the spine ($p = 0.275$). **Conclusion** There was no difference in the prevalence of low BMD between elderly women on SSRIs and not on SSRIs.
CASE REPORT AND CASE SERIES Describes an adverse reaction or a unique condition that appears in a single patient (case report) or a few patients (case series). The outcome of the case in each of these is already known. A case series is more reliable than a case report. **Benefits** Can identify new diseases, drug side effects or potential uses. Generates hypotheses that can be tested with other study designs. **Limitations** Conclusions cannot be drawn from a single or few cases.	*Tardive oculogyric crisis during treatment with clozapine: report of three cases.* **Methods** A psychiatrist identified three cases of patients at his center who experienced the adverse effect, wrote it up, and it was printed in a medical journal. **Statistical Data** No statistical validity; risk cannot be compared to the general population as there is no control. **Conclusion** The findings of oculogyric crisis in patients treated with clozapine are interesting but do not provide important information on prevalence.
RANDOMIZED CONTROLLED TRIAL (RCT) Compares an experimental treatment to a control (placebo or existing treatment) to determine which is better. Subjects with the desired characteristics (inclusion criteria) are carefully selected, and patients with characteristics that may influence the outcome are excluded (exclusion criteria). Patients are randomized (have an equal chance of being assigned to the treatment or control group) and sometimes blinded (unaware if they are receiving treatment or control). Common types of blinding designs include: ■ Double-blind: both the patient and the investigator are unaware of the treatment assignment. ■ Single-blind: the patient is unaware of the treatment assignment, but the investigator knows. ■ Open label (or unblinded): all parties know which treatment is being given to the patient. **Benefits** Preferred study type to determine cause and effect or superiority. Less potential for bias. **Limitations** Time-consuming and expensive. May not reflect real-life scenarios (when rigorous exclusion criteria are used).	*Angiotensin-neprilysin inhibition versus enalapril in heart failure (PARADIGM-HF study).* **Methods** Patients with heart failure were randomized in a double-blind manner to receive a new drug (angiotensin-neprilysin inhibitor) or the current standard of care (enalapril). The effectiveness of the treatments was measured as a primary composite outcome of death from cardiovascular causes or hospitalization for heart failure. **Statistical Data** Primary outcome HR: 0.8 (95% CI 0.73-0.87, $p < 0.001$). **Conclusion** The new drug demonstrated a statistically significant benefit in reducing death from cardiovascular causes or hospitalizations due to heart failure. The null hypothesis (that there was no difference between the two arms) was rejected.
PARALLEL RCT Subjects are randomized to the treatment or control arm for the entire study.	The PARADIGM-HF study (discussed above) is an example of a parallel study design and is the most common type of RCT.

STUDY TYPE, BENEFITS AND LIMITATIONS	STUDY TYPE EXAMPLE
CROSSOVER RCT Patients are randomized to one of two sequential treatments: Group 1 – receive treatment A first, then crossover (change) to treatment B. Group 2 – receive treatment B first, then crossover (change) to treatment A. **Benefits** Patients serve as their own control; this minimizes the effects from confounders. **Limitations** A washout period is needed to minimize the influence of the first drug during the second treatment.	***Crossover comparison of timolol and latanoprost in chronic primary angle-closure glaucoma.*** **Methods** Patients with chronic primary angle-closure glaucoma were randomized after surgery to latanoprost or timolol. Three months after treatment with the first drug, the second drug was substituted. Intraocular pressure (IOP) was recorded before starting and at 3 and 7 months in both groups. **Statistical Data** Decrease in IOP from baseline was 8.2 ± 2 mmHg with latanoprost ($p < 0.001$) and 6.1 ± 1.7 mmHg with timolol ($p = 0.01$). **Conclusion** Latanoprost was associated with a greater decrease in IOP from baseline than timolol.
FACTORIAL DESIGN Randomizes to more than the usual two groups to test a number of experimental conditions. **Benefits** Evaluates multiple interventions (multiple drugs or dosing regimens) in a single experiment. **Limitations** With each arm added, more subjects are needed to have adequate power.	***Prednisolone or pentoxifylline for alcoholic hepatitis.*** **Methods** A 2-by-2 factorial design was used to evaluate the effect of prednisolone or pentoxifylline on 28-day mortality in patients with alcoholic hepatitis. Patients were randomized to 1 of 4 groups: prednisolone (PR)-pentoxifylline (PE), PR-placebo, PE-placebo, or placebo-placebo. **Statistical Data** Pentoxifylline (PE-PR and PE-placebo groups) OR: 1.04 (95% CI 0.77-1.49; $p = 0.69$). Prednisolone (PR-placebo) OR: 0.72 (95% CI 0.52-1.01; $p = 0.06$). **Conclusion** Pentoxifylline (alone or in combination with prednisolone) and prednisolone alone did not reduce mortality in patients with alcoholic hepatitis.
META-ANALYSIS Combines results from multiple studies in order to develop a conclusion that has greater statistical power than is possible from the individual smaller studies. **Benefits** Smaller studies can be pooled instead of performing a large, expensive study. See previous forest plot explanation for how data can be presented. **Limitations** Studies may not be uniform (size, inclusion and exclusion criteria, etc). Validity can be compromised if lower quality studies are weighted equally to higher quality studies.	***Antioxidants for chronic kidney disease (CKD).*** **Methods** The authors searched the PubMed database to locate studies investigating the use of antioxidants in people with CKD. Ten studies were identified, and the results were pooled to determine whether antioxidants had an effect on cardiovascular disease and mortality in patients with CKD. **Statistical Data** Antioxidant use and cardiovascular disease RR: 0.78 (95% CI 0.52-1.18; $p = 0.24$). All-cause mortality RR: 0.93 (95% CI 0.76-1.14; $p = 0.48$). **Conclusion** Antioxidant use did not reduce cardiovascular disease or mortality in CKD patients.
SYSTEMATIC REVIEW ARTICLE Summary of the clinical literature that focuses on a specific topic or question (e.g., treatment options for a condition). Begins with a question followed by a literature search, then the information is summarized, and sometimes includes a meta-analysis to synthesize results. **Benefits** Inexpensive (studies already exist).	***The evolving treatment landscape of advanced renal cell carcinoma (RCC) in patients progressing after VEGF inhibition.*** **Methods** It is still unclear which patients benefit most from VEGF and mTOR inhibitors and the ideal sequence, timing and duration of therapy. The review wanted to define the appropriate treatment sequence after first-line treatment failure. **Statistical Data** No statistical tests reported. **Conclusion** There are no predictive biomarkers that determine the best therapy for the right patient or the best sequence of treatment. More studies are needed.

PHARMACOECONOMICS

BACKGROUND

Healthcare costs in the United States rank among the highest of all industrialized countries. In 2017, total healthcare expenditures reached $3.5 trillion, which translates to an average of $10,739 per person, or about 17.9% of the national gross domestic product. The increasing costs have highlighted the need to understand how limited resources can be used most effectively and efficiently in the care of individual patients and society as a whole. It is necessary to scientifically evaluate the value (i.e., costs vs. outcomes) of interventions such as medical procedures or drugs.

DEFINITIONS

Pharmacoeconomics is a collection of descriptive and analytic techniques for evaluating pharmaceutical interventions (e.g., drugs, devices, procedures) in the healthcare system. Pharmacoeconomic research identifies, measures and compares the costs (direct, indirect and intangible) and the consequences (clinical, economic and humanistic) of pharmaceutical products and services.

Various research methods can be used to determine the impact of the pharmaceutical product or service. These methods include cost-effectiveness analysis, cost-minimization analysis, cost-utility analysis and cost-benefit analysis. The term "pharmacoeconomics" is sometimes referred to as "outcomes research," but they are not the same thing. Pharmacoeconomic methods are specific to assessing the costs and consequences of pharmaceutical products and services. Outcomes research represents a broader research discipline that attempts to identify, measure and evaluate the end result of healthcare services.

Healthcare providers, payers and other decision makers use these methods to evaluate and compare the total costs and consequences of pharmaceutical products and services. The results of pharmacoeconomic analyses can vary significantly based on the point of view of the analyst; the study perspective is critical for interpretation. What may be viewed as good value for society or for the patient may not be deemed as such from an institutional or provider perspective (e.g., the costs of lost productivity due to illness are critically important to a patient or employer, but perhaps less so to a health plan).

Pharmacoeconomic analyses provide useful supplemental evidence to traditional efficacy and safety endpoints. They help translate important clinical benefits into economic and patient-centered terms, and can assist providers and payers in determining where, or if, a drug fits into the treatment paradigm for a specific condition. Pharmacoeconomic studies serve to guide optimal healthcare resource allocation in a standardized and evidence-based manner.

The ECHO model (Economic, Clinical and Humanistic Outcomes) provides a broad evaluative framework to assess the outcomes associated with diseases and treatments.

- Economic outcomes: include direct, indirect and intangible costs of the drug compared to a medical intervention.
- Clinical outcomes: include medical events that occur as a result of the treatment or intervention.
- Humanistic Outcomes: include consequences of the disease or treatment as reported by the patient or caregiver (e.g., patient satisfaction, quality of life).

MEDICAL COST CATEGORIES: DIRECT, INDIRECT AND INTANGIBLE

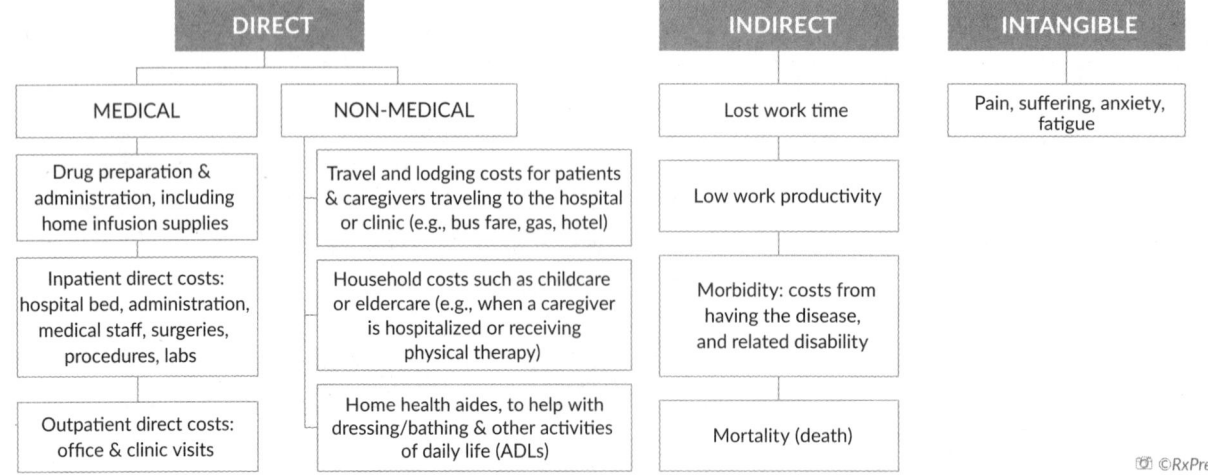

AVERAGE AND INCREMENTAL COST-EFFECTIVENESS RATIOS

The results of a pharmacoeconomic analysis are commonly expressed in terms of a cost ratio, representing the costs incurred to achieve a particular outcome [e.g., cost per case cured, cost per treatment success, cost per quality-adjusted life year (QALY) gained]. Two fundamental cost ratios are commonly used to communicate results of a pharmacoeconomic analysis.

Average Cost-Effectiveness Ratios

Average cost-effectiveness ratios reflect the cost per outcome of one treatment independent of other treatment alternatives. For example, if a treatment costs $50 to generate successful outcomes in two patients, the average cost-effectiveness ratio is $25/treatment success ($50/2 successfully treated patients).

Incremental Cost-Effectiveness Ratios

Incremental cost-effectiveness ratios represent the change in costs and outcomes when two treatment alternatives are compared. An incremental cost-effectiveness ratio is calculated when evaluating costs and outcomes between competing alternatives, and represents the additional costs required to produce an additional unit of effect. It is calculated as shown to the right, where C is for costs and E is for effects.

$$\text{Incremental Cost Ratio} = \frac{(C_2 - C_1)}{(E_2 - E_1)}$$

- Example: if spending $200 on Drug A results in 5 treatment successes while spending $300 on Drug B results in 7 treatment successes, what is the incremental cost ratio?

$$\text{Incremental Cost Ratio} = \frac{(\$300 - \$200)}{(7 - 5)} = \frac{\$100}{2} = \$50$$

Conclusion: Drug B costs $50 more relative to Drug A for each additional treatment success.

PHARMACOECONOMIC METHODOLOGIES

Cost-Minimization Analysis

Cost-minimization analysis (CMA) is used when two or more interventions have demonstrated equivalence in outcomes, and the costs of each intervention are being compared. CMA measures and compares the input costs of treatment alternatives that have equivalent outcomes. This determination of equivalence is a key consideration in adopting this methodology. Ideally, evidence exists to support the clinical equivalence of the alternatives. In some instances, assumptions are made in the absence of relevant evidence.

For example, two ACE inhibitors, captopril and lisinopril, are considered therapeutically equivalent in the literature, but the acquisition cost (the price paid for the drug) and administrative costs may be different (captopril is administered TID and lisinopril is administered once daily). A CMA looks at "minimizing costs" when multiple drugs have equal efficacy and tolerability. Another example of CMA is looking at the same drug regimen given in two different settings (e.g., hospital versus home health care). CMA is considered the easiest analysis to perform, but use of this method is limited given its ability to compare only alternatives with demonstrated equivalent outcomes.

Cost-Benefit Analysis

Cost-benefit analysis (CBA) is a systematic process for calculating and comparing benefits and costs of an intervention in terms of monetary units (dollars). CBA consists of identifying all the benefits from an intervention and converting them into dollars in the year that they will occur. The costs associated with the intervention are identified, allocated to the year when they occur, and then discounted back to their present day value. Given that all other factors remain constant, the program with the largest present day value of benefits minus costs is the best economic value. In CBA, it can be difficult to assign a dollar amount to a benefit (e.g., measuring the benefit of patient quality of life, which is difficult to quantify, and assigning a dollar value to it). One advantage to using CBA is the ability to determine if the benefits of the intervention exceed the costs of implementation. CBA can also be used to compare multiple programs for similar or unrelated outcomes, as long as the outcome measures can be converted to dollars.

Cost-Effectiveness Analysis

Cost-effectiveness analysis (CEA) is used to compare the clinical effects of two or more interventions to the respective costs. The resources associated with the intervention are usually measured in dollars, and clinical outcomes are usually measured in natural health units (e.g., LDL values in mg/dL, % clinical cures, length of stay). The main advantage of this method is that the outcomes are easier to quantify when compared to other analyses, and clinicians are familiar with these types of outcomes since they are similar to outcomes seen in clinical trials and practice. CEA is the most common pharmacoeconomic methodology seen in biomedical literature.

A disadvantage of CEA is the inability to directly compare different types of outcomes. For example, one cannot compare the cost-effectiveness of implementing a diabetes program with implementing an asthma program where the outcome units are different (e.g., blood glucose values versus asthma exacerbations). It is also difficult to combine two or more outcomes into one value of measurement (e.g., comparing one chemotherapeutic agent that prolongs survival, but has significant side effects, to another chemotherapeutic agent that has less effect on prolonging survival but fewer side effects).

Cost-Utility Analysis

Cost-utility analysis (CUA) is a specialized form of CEA that includes a quality-of-life component of morbidity assessments, using common health indices such as quality-adjusted life years (QALYs) and disability-adjusted life years (DALYs). CEA can measure the quantity of life (years gained) but not the "quality" or "utility" of those years. In CUA, the intervention outcome is measured in terms of QALYs gained. QALY takes into account both the quality (morbidity) and the quantity (mortality) of life gained.

CUA measures outcomes based on years of life that are adjusted by utility weights, which range from 1 for "perfect health" to 0 for "dead." These weights can take into account patient and society preferences for specific health states. There is no consensus on the measurement, since both patient and society preferences can vary based on culture. An advantage of CUA is that different types of outcomes, and diseases with multiple outcomes of interest, can be compared (unlike CEA which can only compare one common unit).

Four Basic Pharmacoeconomic Methodologies

METHODOLOGY	COST MEASUREMENT UNIT	OUTCOME UNIT
Cost-minimization analysis	Dollars	Demonstrated or assumed to be equivalent in comparative groups
Cost-benefit analysis	Dollars	Dollars
Cost-effectiveness analysis	Dollars	Natural units (e.g., life-years gained, mmHg blood pressure, % at treatment goal)
Cost-utility analysis	Dollars	Quality-adjusted-life year (QALY) or other utilities

HEALTH-RELATED QUALITY OF LIFE

Health-related quality of life (HRQOL) refers to the effects of a disease and its treatment on an individual's function and well-being, as perceived by that individual. It is commonly included under a broad umbrella of assessments known as patient-reported outcomes (PROs). HRQOL is comprised of several important domains, including physical and mental functioning, role functioning, vitality, social functioning and general health perceptions.

HRQOL assessments can provide important patient-centered information related to the effects of a disease or treatment on patient functioning and well-being. These assessments are typically developed as either general (or generic) health status instruments that can be used across a number of disease areas (e.g., the SF-36 Health Survey can be used for asthma, diabetes and other conditions) or disease-specific measures applicable to a limited disease population (e.g., the Asthma Quality of Life Questionnaire). Prior to their use in practice, it is critical that the reliability and validity of HRQOL assessments in specific patient populations has been documented.

COMPOUNDING & HAZARDOUS DRUGS

CONTENTS

CONTENT LEGEND

💡 = Study Tip Gal   🔑 = Key Drug Guy

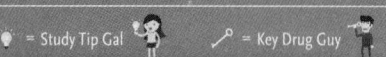

CHAPTER 15
COMPOUNDING I: BASICS

WHAT ARE COMPOUNDED DRUGS?

Compounding is the process of combining or altering ingredients to create a medication. A traditional compounded drug is prepared by a pharmacist for an individual patient based on a prescription. Compounded drugs meet unique needs and are not FDA-approved. The dose or formulation cannot be commercially available as a manufactured product.

THE DIFFERENT TYPES OF COMPOUNDING

Compounded drugs are either non-sterile or sterile. Both non-sterile and sterile compounded drugs can be further subdivided into two categories: non-hazardous and hazardous (see Study Tip Gal on next page). The formulation of the drug determines if it is non-sterile or sterile; the drug being used determines if the compound is deemed hazardous (e.g., causes cancer or adverse reproductive effects).

COMPOUNDING STANDARDS AND RESOURCES

U.S. Pharmacopeia

The U.S. Pharmacopeia (USP) sets the standards for compounding preparations. The USP Chapters related to compounding include USP 795 (Non-Sterile Compounding), USP 797 (Sterile Compounding) and USP 800 (Handling Hazardous Drugs). USP does not determine which drugs are hazardous; it simply sets the requirements for safe handling of hazardous drugs (HDs).

USP 795, 797 and 800 are considered to be minimum acceptable standards for compounding by the Food and Drug Administration (FDA), the state boards of pharmacy and the Joint Commission. USP standards apply to all who engage in compounding (pharmacy staff, nurses and physicians), and all practice settings (hospitals, other healthcare institutions, clinics and pharmacies).

USP COMPOUNDING CHAPTERS

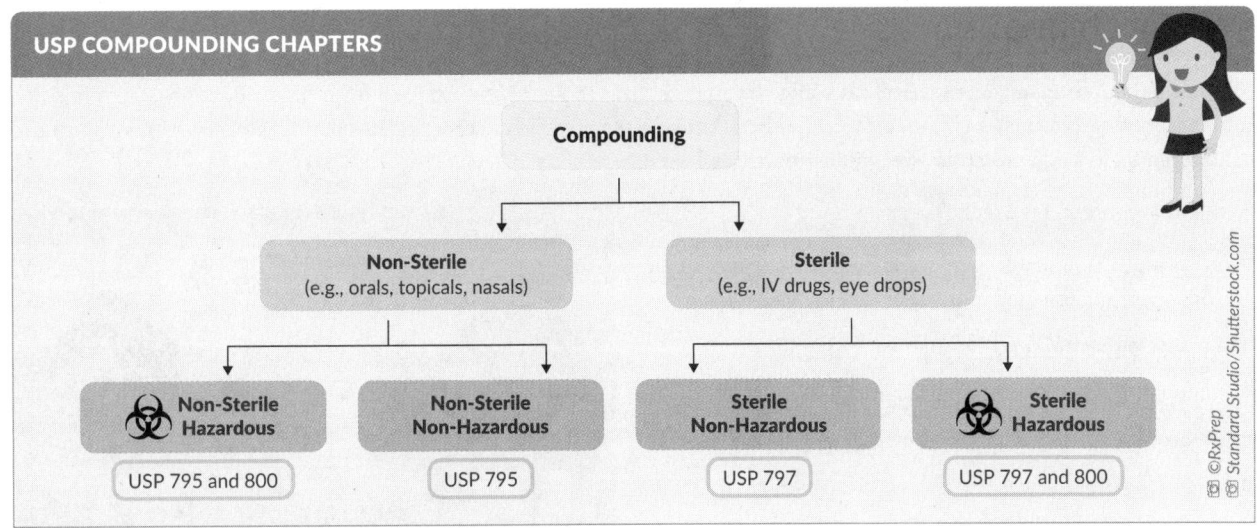

U.S. PHARMACOPEIA

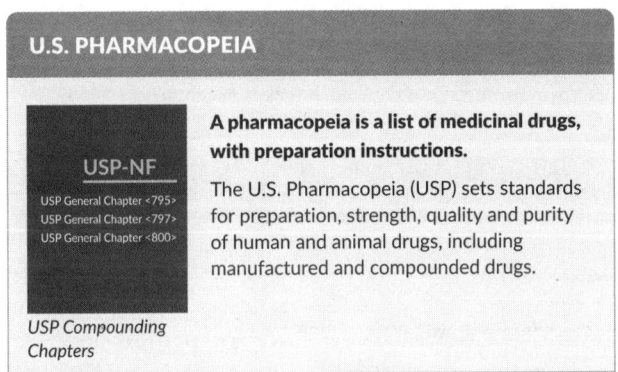

USP Compounding Chapters

A pharmacopeia is a list of medicinal drugs, with preparation instructions.

The U.S. Pharmacopeia (USP) sets standards for preparation, strength, quality and purity of human and animal drugs, including manufactured and compounded drugs.

In June 2019, USP published revisions to chapters 795 and 797. They are currently under appeal and have not yet been finalized. The current versions of USP 795 (2014) and USP 797 (2008) remain official until further notice from USP.

American Society of Health-System Pharmacists

Hospital pharmacists rely on the American Society of Health-System Pharmacists (ASHP) for detailed guidance on implementing USP standards.

NON-STERILE COMPOUNDING

Non-sterile compounding is primarily used to:

- Prepare a dose or formulation that is not commercially available, such as:

   ❏ Changing a solid tablet to a liquid for a patient who cannot swallow the tablet

   ❏ Compounding a 10% ointment when only 5% and 15% are available

- Avoid an excipient (e.g., gluten or red dye)

- Add a flavor to a medication to make it more palatable (e.g., a cherry-flavored antiviral suspension for a child)

Non-sterile preparations include those administered by mouth, via tube, rectally, vaginally, topically, nasally or in the ear.

USP 795 divides non-sterile compounding into three categories based on complexity:

- Simple: requires (simply) following instructions (e.g., preparing a product using a compounding kit that has clear step-by-step instructions, or following a USP monograph)

- Moderate: involves specialized calculations or procedures, or making a preparation that has no established stability data (e.g., mixing two topical creams when stability data for the mixture is not available)

- Complex: requires specialized training, equipment, facilities or procedures (e.g., transdermal dosage forms)

PHYSICAL SPACE BASICS

The compounding space should be specifically designated for non-sterile compounding. Sterile compounds should be prepared in a distinctly separate location. Non-sterile compounding can be performed in ambient air (room air), but must be separated from the dispensing part of the pharmacy.

Adequate space is needed to avoid mix-ups of ingredients, containers and other components. The space should include shelving and storage. All components, equipment and containers should be stored off the floor. The space should be clean and well-lit. Heating, ventilation and air conditioning systems must be controlled to avoid drug deterioration.

There needs to be adequate plumbing and two types of water:

1. Potable (drinkable, such as from the tap), for hand and equipment washing

2. Purified (e.g., distilled), for use in water-containing formulations, and for rinsing equipment and utensils

The sink must be easily accessible to the compounding area, be clean and be emptied of items unrelated to compounding. Soap, detergent and a sanitary method of drying hands (e.g., single-use towels) should be available.

STERILE COMPOUNDING

Sterile compounding must be carried out using strict procedures to keep products free from contamination. Drugs injected into the blood or administered into certain other body sites must be free of microorganisms (e.g., bacteria, viruses, fungi) and contaminants (e.g., glass shards, precipitates, particles).

Sterile compounding is used to prepare:

- <u>Intravenous (IV)</u> drugs (e.g., 1 gram of vancomycin taken from a vial and injected into a 250 mL D5W IV bag)

- <u>Intramuscular (IM) and subcutaneous (SC, SQ)</u> drugs

- Radiopharmaceuticals (nuclear medicine drugs)

- <u>Eye drops</u> (e.g., moxifloxacin and prednisolone eye drops)

- <u>Irrigations</u> (liquid "washes" that go into a body cavity, such as a gentamicin bladder irrigation)

- Pulmonary <u>inhalations</u> (does not include nasal inhalations)

Before getting into the details, review the terminology used by USP, which is provided in the <u>Study Tip Gal</u> below.

INTERPRETING USP TERMINOLOGY

ACRONYM	MEANING	COMMON TERMS
CSPs	Compounded Sterile Products	IVs or other drugs that require sterile manipulation
SVP	Small Volume Parenteral	IV bag or container containing ≤ 100 mL
LVP	Large Volume Parenteral	IV bag or container containing > 100 mL
PPE	Personal Protective Equipment	Garb (e.g., gown, gloves, mask); "don" means to put on, "doff" is to take off
PEC	Primary Engineering Control	Sterile hood that provides ISO 5 air for compounding
LAFW	Laminar Airflow Workbench	Type of sterile hood (PEC); parallel air streams flow in one direction
C-PEC	Containment Primary Engineering Control	Ventilated (negative pressure) chemo hood used for HDs
BSC	Biological Safety Cabinet	Chemo hood (Class II or III for sterile HD), a type of C-PEC
SEC	Secondary Engineering Control	ISO 7 "buffer room" where the sterile hood (PEC) is located
C-SEC	Containment Secondary Engineering Control	Ventilated (negative pressure) buffer room for HDs (room where the C-PEC is located)
SCA	Segregated Compounding Area	Designated space that contains an ISO 5 hood but is not part of a cleanroom suite (air is not ISO-rated)
C-SCA	Containment Segregated Compounding Area	Ventilated (negative pressure) room used for HDs; not in a cleanroom suite (air is not ISO-rated)
CAI	Compounding Aseptic Isolator	"Glovebox" for non-HDs, a closed-front sterile hood (PEC)
CACI	Compounding Aseptic Containment Isolator	"Glovebox" for HDs, a type of closed-front C-PEC
RABS	Restricted Access Barrier System	"Glovebox"/closed-front sterile hood (includes CAIs and CACIs)
CSTD	Closed System Transfer Device	Device preventing escape of HD/vapors when transferring (e.g., from a vial to a syringe)
CVE	Containment Ventilated Enclosure	Ventilated "powder hood" for non-sterile products (can be used for HDs if USP 800 standards are met)

USP 797 SPACE REQUIREMENTS FOR STERILE COMPOUNDING

There are greater (and stricter) compounding space requirements for sterile compounding than non-sterile compounding.

AIR QUALITY AND HEPA FILTERS

Clean air in the compounding area reduces the risk of contamination. The International Standards Organization (ISO) sets the standards for air quality, which is determined by the number and size of particles per volume of air. The lower the particle count, the cleaner the air.

In critical areas that are closest to exposed sterile drugs and containers [i.e., inside the sterile hood(PEC)], the air quality must be at least ISO 5. This means that there are no more than 3,520 particles per cubic meter. Particles are included in this count if they are 0.5 microns (micrometers) or larger.

The farther away from the PEC, the dirtier the air. The buffer area (the SEC, which contains PECs) must be at least ISO 7. The anteroom (the room adjacent to the SEC, where hand washing and garbing occurs) must be at least ISO 8 if it opens into a positive-pressure buffer area (non-HD sterile compounding), or at least ISO 7 if it opens into a negative-pressure buffer area (HD sterile compounding).

COMPOUNDING AREA	ISO RATING	PARTICLES/m³
Primary engineering control (PEC, called the sterile hood, or isolator, if using a glove box)	5	3,520
Not applicable (ISO 6 is not used for pharmacy spaces)	6	35,200
Secondary engineering control (SEC, called the buffer room or buffer area) Anteroom, if it opens into a negative pressure SEC (same ISO # as the SEC)	7	352,000
Anteroom, if it opens into a positive pressure SEC	8	3,520,000

High-Efficiency Particulate Air Filters

High-efficiency particulate air (HEPA) filters pick up particles when the air runs through the filter. HEPA filters are > 99.97% efficient in removing particles as small as 0.3 microns wide or larger, including bacteria, viruses, fungi and dust.

In a vertical airflow biological safety cabinet (BSC) or C-PEC, the HEPA filter is at the top of the sterile hood. In a laminar airflow workbench (LAFW) or PEC, the HEPA filter is at the back of the sterile hood (horizontal airflow). The filter is covered by a protective stainless-steel grill. A blower pushes the air through the HEPA filter. The filter catches contaminants before the air enters the inside of the PEC. Compounding should be done in the cleanest air, which is the air coming directly out of the HEPA filter. This is called the direct compounding area (DCA), and the air from the HEPA filter is called the first air (see the Study Tip Gal on the following page).

The HEPA filter must be recertified by a specialist every 6 months and anytime a PEC has been moved.

The dots in the image below show the relevant amount of particles in the air. Ambient (room) air is not rated; if it were, most room air would be about ISO 9.

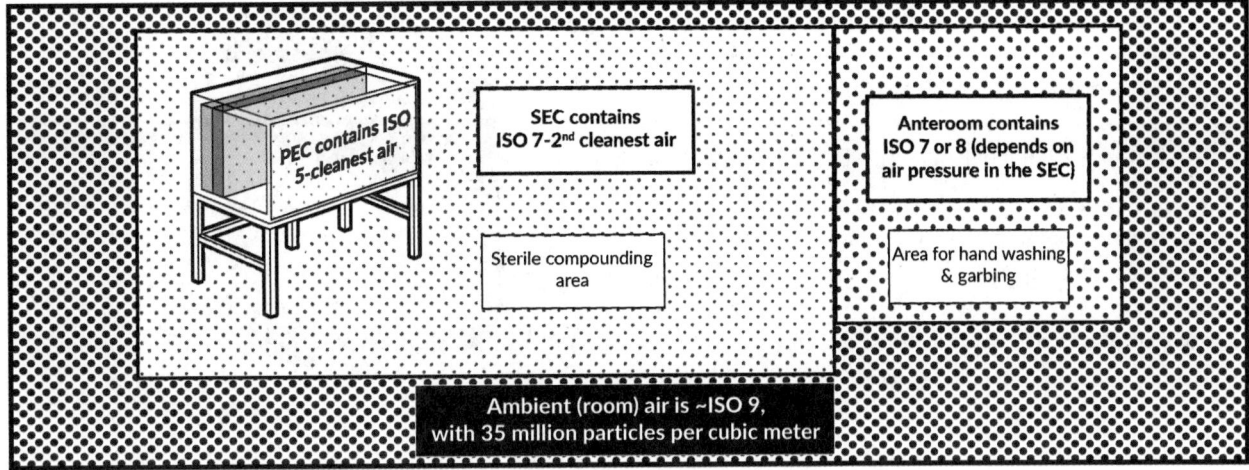

ISO AIR QUALITY INSIDE THE PEC

The Direct Compounding Area and First Air

The PEC provides ISO 5 air quality for sterile compounding. The air coming directly out of the HEPA filter is called the first air, which is cleaner than the rest of the air in the sterile hood. To prevent contamination of CSPs during compounding, the injection port of the vial and the syringe needle must be kept in the first air (see image).

- Do not obstruct first air, especially the area where the needle enters the vial or ampule.
- Do not block airflow from the HEPA filter with hands or supplies.
- Place items correctly inside the PEC (see the Compounding III chapter) to avoid creating turbulence, which can lead to contamination of the CSPs.

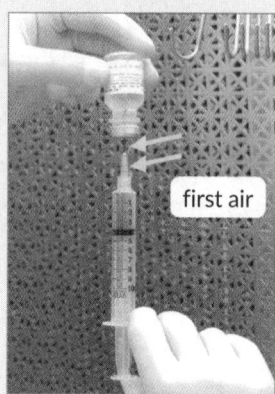

first air

Prevent Contamination by Keeping the Air in the PEC Clean

- Wipe off the outside of all materials (e.g., vials, syringes) with 70% isopropyl alcohol (IPA) before bringing them into the PEC.
- Open packages along the designated tear line, if present; do not rip open packages or punch needles or syringes through the wrappers which contaminates the air with particles.
- Compound at least 6 inches inside the sterile hood to prevent exposing CSPs to dirtier ISO 7 air from the SEC.
- Move waste out of the PEC shortly after it is created; do not let it accumulate inside the sterile hood.

Most contamination to CSPs comes from the compounding staff, largely from inadequate hand hygiene and garbing; correct technique is essential, and is described later in this chapter.

AIR PRESSURE

In addition to the ISO air quality in a space, the air pressure in the space relative to the adjacent space is important.

There must be a differential (i.e., a difference) in air pressure between spaces to keep the air inside a space enclosed, or conversely, to permit the air to enter adjacent areas.

For non-hazardous compounding, the air pressure inside the PEC and SEC are both positive since the air will not cause toxicity if it moves into adjacent spaces. Positive air pressure helps protect the compounded sterile products (CSPs) from contamination.

With hazardous compounding, the containment PEC (C-PEC) and the containment SEC (C-SEC) must have negative pressure to contain and exhaust the toxic air in the space. Negative air pressure protects the compounding staff.

PHYSICAL SPACE BASICS

Surfaces of ceilings, walls, floors, fixtures, shelving, counters and cabinets must be smooth, impervious, and free from cracks and crevices to make them easy to clean and disinfect. Stainless steel equipment is often used. Objects that shed particles (e.g., cardboard boxes) should not be brought into the cleanroom.

TYPES OF STERILE COMPOUNDING AREAS

- Cleanroom suite: one or more sterile hoods (ISO 5 PECs) inside an ISO 7 buffer room (SEC) that is entered through an adjacent anteroom.
- Segregated compounding area (SCA) with an ISO 5 PEC: a sterile hood, often an isolator (glovebox) with a closed front, located in a segregated space with unclassified air.

PRIMARY ENGINEERING CONTROL

The PEC is a device or room that provides an ISO 5 environment for sterile compounding. In a pharmacy, the most common way to achieve ISO 5 air is by using a sterile hood. In other industries and larger hospital pharmacies, whole rooms may have ISO 5 air.

PECs for Non-Hazardous Sterile Preparations

PECs used for non-hazardous sterile compounding have HEPA-filtered air and positive air pressure, to protect the CSPs from contamination, and are not externally ventilated.

- A laminar airflow workbench (LAFW) is an open-front PEC where air flows out in parallel lines from the HEPA filter, typically from the back of the hood, i.e., horizontal laminar airflow (see image). Laminar airflow keeps the cleaner air in the PEC from mixing with the dirtier air in the buffer room and keeps particles from colliding with each other and landing on the DCA surface or CSPs.

© Courtesy of Germfree

→ Room Air
→ Filtered Air

Horizontal laminar airflow

- A <u>compounding aseptic isolator (CAI)</u> is a closed-front PEC that can be located in a buffer room (SEC), but is often located in a <u>segregated compounding area (SCA)</u>. The closed front keeps the unclassified room air around it from mixing with the clean air inside the PEC. It is commonly referred to as a glovebox because the pharmacist or technician inserts their hands through the ports on the front into gloves that reside within the PEC. Garb required when compounding in a CAI depends on the manufacturer's instructions, but minimally <u>hand hygiene</u> must be performed and <u>sterile, powder-free gloves</u> should be used inside the CAI (placed over the long gloves attached to the isolator).

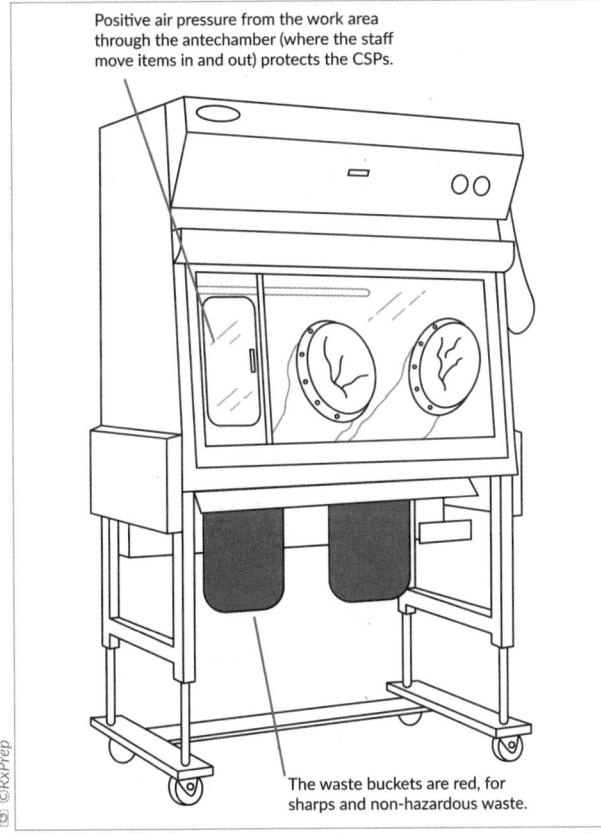

Positive air pressure from the work area through the antechamber (where the staff move items in and out) protects the CSPs.

The waste buckets are red, for sharps and non-hazardous waste.

©RxPrep

Compounding Aseptic Isolator

SECONDARY ENGINEERING CONTROL

The SEC is the room that contains the PEC or multiple PECs. The SEC is commonly called the <u>buffer area</u> or buffer room because it provides a "buffer" of relatively clean air (<u>ISO 7</u>) around the PEC (ISO 5).

ANTEROOM

The anteroom (sometimes called the ante-area) connects the rest of the pharmacy to the buffer room (SEC). It contains a sink, cabinets and benches to facilitate <u>garbing</u> and preparation for compounding. Running down the center of the anteroom is a large visible line called the <u>line of demarcation</u>, which separates the room into <u>clean</u> and <u>dirty</u> <u>sections</u>. The side closest to the other areas of the pharmacy is

considered to be the dirty side of the anteroom. This is where hair and face covers are donned. The side of the anteroom closest to the buffer room is considered to be the clean side. <u>Shoe covers must be applied one at a time while stepping over the demarcation line</u>, placing the covered shoe on the clean side. Handwashing and donning of the gown occur on the clean side of the anteroom.

STERILE COMPOUNDING FOR EMERGENCIES

The requirements described in this chapter for compounding sterile products, including putting on protective garb and cleaning the PEC (described later), take time.

In certain circumstances, IV drugs are needed stat (i.e., immediately), with no time for aseptic preparation, such as in an ambulance or during a code blue when quick action is needed to save a life. This is emergency use, and because the drug has been prepared for that patient under suboptimal conditions for sterility, the CSP will have a very short beyond-use date (BUD) of 1 hour, after which the drug can no longer be used and must be discarded. BUDs are described in the Compounding III chapter.

SEGREGATED COMPOUNDING AREA

An SCA is an option when a cleanroom is not able to be installed. It is a designated area with <u>unclassified air</u>, such as a corner of the pharmacy. It does not have a buffer area or anteroom, and can only be used for certain (low-risk) CSPs. The maximum <u>beyond use date (BUD)</u> for a CSP made in an SCA is <u>12 hours</u>. CSP risk categories are discussed further in the Compounding III chapter.

SCAs are useful for satellite pharmacies that are a distance away from the main pharmacy in a large hospital, for infusion centers, clinics and small hospitals.

Segregated means kept apart from other areas of the pharmacy to minimize contamination, interruptions and noise. SCAs cannot be located adjacent to food preparation, warehouses, construction sites, or unsealed windows/doors near busy areas (e.g., not near the pharmacy pick-up area).

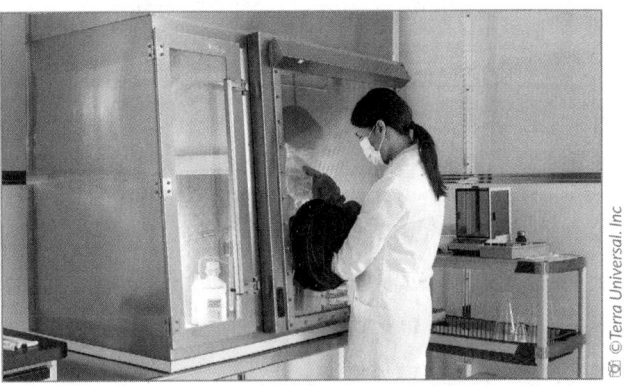

©Terra Universal, Inc

CAI in a Segregated Compounding Area

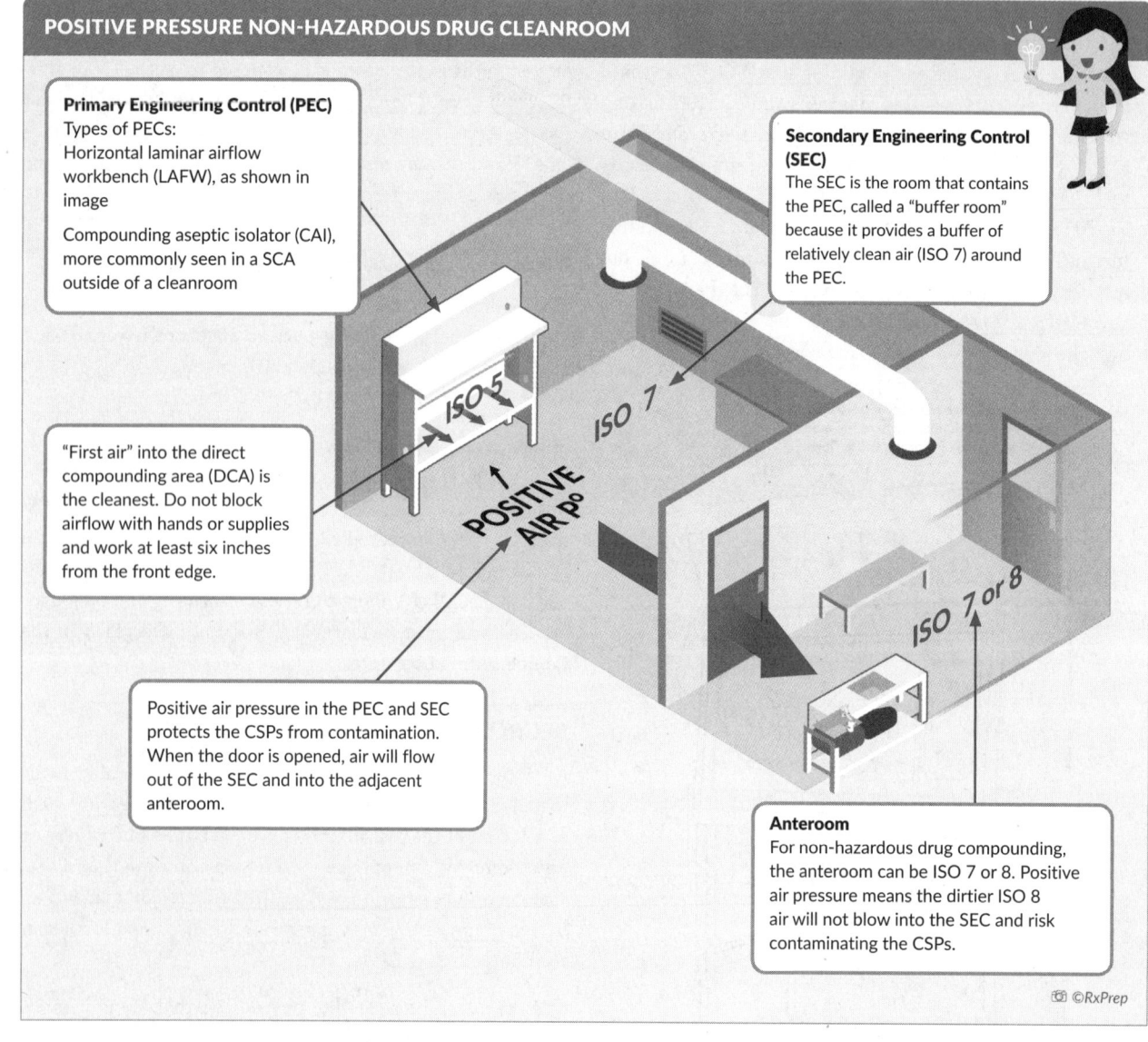

POSITIVE PRESSURE NON-HAZARDOUS DRUG CLEANROOM

Primary Engineering Control (PEC)
Types of PECs:
Horizontal laminar airflow workbench (LAFW), as shown in image

Compounding aseptic isolator (CAI), more commonly seen in a SCA outside of a cleanroom

Secondary Engineering Control (SEC)
The SEC is the room that contains the PEC, called a "buffer room" because it provides a buffer of relatively clean air (ISO 7) around the PEC.

"First air" into the direct compounding area (DCA) is the cleanest. Do not block airflow with hands or supplies and work at least six inches from the front edge.

Positive air pressure in the PEC and SEC protects the CSPs from contamination. When the door is opened, air will flow out of the SEC and into the adjacent anteroom.

Anteroom
For non-hazardous drug compounding, the anteroom can be ISO 7 or 8. Positive air pressure means the dirtier ISO 8 air will not blow into the SEC and risk contaminating the CSPs.

©RxPrep

HAZARDOUS DRUGS

Hazardous drugs (HDs) can cause toxicity to the healthcare workers who handle them in any manner, including unloading the drugs in the receiving dock, stocking the shelves, preparing the drugs in the pharmacy, administering the drugs to a patient and obtaining and cleaning up body fluids that contain hazardous drug residues.

HDs require workspaces, equipment and devices that are designed to reduce exposure of the drug to the staff. The standards for handling HDs are set by USP in chapter 800.

THE NATIONAL INSTITUTE FOR OCCUPATIONAL SAFETY AND HEALTH

The National Institute for Occupational Safety and Health (NIOSH) determines which drugs are hazardous. NIOSH keeps a list of all HDs called the *NIOSH List of Antineoplastic and Other Hazardous Drugs in Healthcare Settings* (see Key Drugs Guy on the following page). A drugs is considered hazardous if it is:

- Carcinogenic (cancer-causing)
- Teratogenic (causes congenital disabilities) or reproductive toxicity (e.g., infertility)
- Genotoxic (damages DNA, which can cause cancer)
- Toxic to organs at low doses
- Labeled by the manufacturer with special handling instructions

HAZARDOUS KEY DRUGS ON THE NIOSH LIST

Antineoplastic Drugs (Chemotherapeutics)

Non-Antineoplastic Hazardous Drugs on the NIOSH List:

Abortifacient
Mifepristone, Misoprostol

Antibiotics
Chloramphenicol

Anticoagulants
Warfarin

Antifungals
Fluconazole, Voriconazole

Antiretrovirals
Abacavir, Entecavir, Zidovudine

Antivirals
Cidofovir, Ganciclovir, Valganciclovir

Acne
Isotretinoin

Arrhythmias
Dronedarone

Autoimmune Conditions
Acitretin, Azathioprine, Leflunomide

Fingolimod, Teriflunomide

Benign Prostatic Hyperplasia (BPH)
Dutasteride, Finasteride

Bisphosphonates
Pamidronate, Zoledronic Acid

Chemoprotectant (Cardiac)
Dexrazoxane

Depression
Paroxetine

Diabetes
Exenatide, Liraglutide

Dyslipidemia
Lomitapide

Seizures/Epilepsy
Clobazam, Clonazepam

Carbamazepine, Oxcarbazepine, Eslicarbazepine, Divalproex, Fosphenytoin, Phenytoin, Topiramate, Vigabatrin, Zonisamide

Gout
Colchicine

Heart Failure
Ivabradine, Spironolactone

Hepatitis
Ribavirin

Hormonal Agents
Androgens (e.g., testosterone)

Estrogens (e.g., estradiol)

Oxytocin, Dinoprostone

Progesterones (e.g., medroxyprogesterone)

SERD/SERMs (e.g., fulvestrant, tamoxifen)

Ulipristal

Hyperthyroidism
Methimazole, Propylthiouracil

Insomnia
Temazepam, Triazolam

Iron Overload
Deferiprone

Migraine
Dihydroergotamine

Parkinson Disease
Apomorphine, Rasagiline

Pulmonary Arterial Hypertension (PAH)
Ambrisentan, Bosentan, Macitentan, Riociguat

Schizophrenia
Ziprasidone

Transplant
Cyclosporine, Mycophenolate, Tacrolimus, Sirolimus

SAFETY DATA SHEETS (SDS)

SDS (previously called MSDS) are a series of safety documents required by the Occupational Safety and Health Administration (OSHA) to be accessible to all employees who are working with hazardous materials, including drugs. Each hazardous drug has its own document, which provides guidance on drug-specific safety information including:

- Personal protective equipment (PPE)
- First aid procedures
- Spill clean-up procedures

HAZARD COMMUNICATION PROGRAM

Each facility must have a designated individual who is responsible for creating Standard Operating Procedures (SOPs) focused on worker safety during all aspects of hazardous drug handling. This hazard communication program includes a written plan that details implementation of HD safety procedures, proper training of personnel, competency assessment and maintaining all required HD documentation. Pharmacies must maintain a list of all hazardous drugs stocked. The list must be reviewed every 12 months or whenever a new drug or dosage form is stocked or used. Prior to handling any HDs, both men and women with reproductive capability (the ability to have children) must confirm in writing that they understand the risks associated with handling HDs.

ASSESSING RISK FOR HAZARDOUS DRUGS

Risk is defined differently in USP 797 and 800. USP 797 risk categories are based on risk of contamination of the sterile product. With hazardous drug compounding (USP 800), higher risk means a higher chance of causing harm to the workers exposed to the drug.

The USP 800 requirements for safe handling of HDs are extensive, but some activities are not as risky as others. Some examples of lower-risk activities include counting and packaging tablets. A pharmacy can conduct an Assessment of Risk (AoR) for drugs with lower risk to avoid having to follow all USP 800 requirements for drugs that will be dispensed without manipulation.

As part of the AoR, SOPs must be developed, which include actions to limit staff exposure, such as:

- Putting HDs in distinctive shelf bins to alert staff

- Wearing ASTM D6978-rated gloves when counting or packaging drugs

- Dedicating a counting tray and spatula for counting HDs and decontaminating both after use

- Placing prepared HD containers into a sealable plastic bag

If any manipulation of the low-risk hazardous drug is required (e.g., using powder to prepare a solution, cutting tablets in half, adding a vial of HD to a large volume fluid), USP 800 requirements must be followed. If no AoR is conducted, the pharmacy must follow the full USP 800 requirements. AoR documents must be reviewed at least every 12 months and the review must be documented.

USP 800 SPACE REQUIREMENTS

PHYSICAL SPACE BASICS

Hoods and buffer rooms used for compounding HDs include the word containment:

- Containment-primary engineering control (C-PEC)

- Containment-secondary engineering control (C-SEC)

- Containment-segregated compounding area (C-SCA)

- Compounding aseptic containment isolator (CACI)

Containment is required to keep hazardous drugs, particles and vapors contained within the space due to toxicity risk.

C-PECs for Hazardous Drug Compounding

Both sterile and non-sterile hazardous compounds must be prepared in a C-PEC that is located in a C-SEC or C-SCA. Types of C-PECs are listed below.

- Biological safety cabinets (BSCs) have vertical laminar airflow (air flows down from the HEPA filter at the top of the hood) and negative air pressure, which protects the worker from being exposed to the hazardous drug they are working with. For sterile hazardous drug compounding, the BSC must be Class II (most common) or Class III.

- Containment ventilated enclosures (CVEs) are powder containment hoods with HEPA-filtered air and negative air pressure used for non-sterile compounding only.

- Compounding aseptic containment isolators (CACIs) are closed-front C-PECs (gloveboxes) that can be located in a buffer room (SEC), but are often located in a C-SCA.

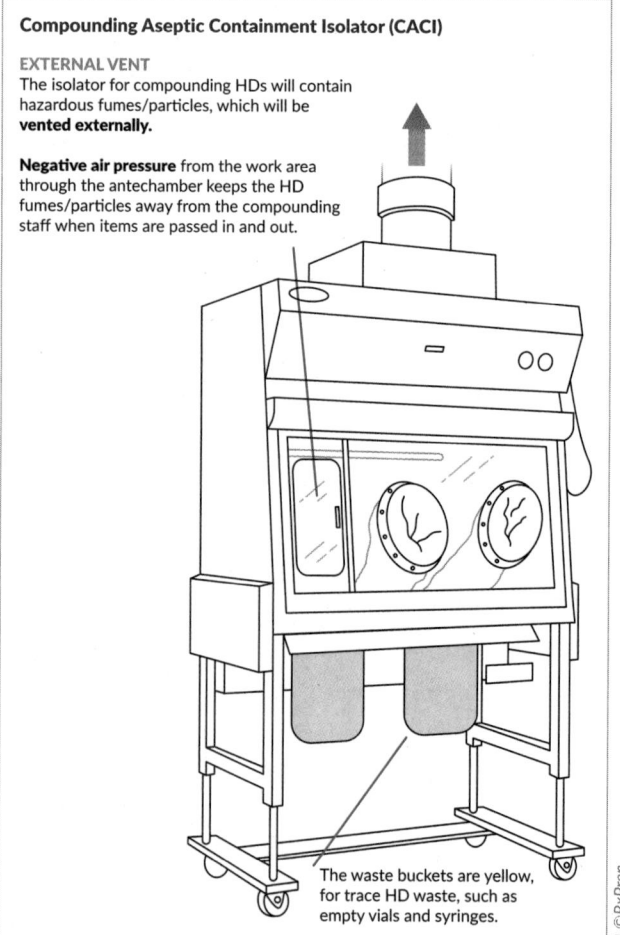

Compounding Aseptic Containment Isolator (CACI)

EXTERNAL VENT
The isolator for compounding HDs will contain hazardous fumes/particles, which will be **vented externally.**

Negative air pressure from the work area through the antechamber keeps the HD fumes/particles away from the compounding staff when items are passed in and out.

The waste buckets are yellow, for trace HD waste, such as empty vials and syringes.

©RxPrep

Compounding Aseptic Containment Isolator

Non-Sterile and Sterile HD Compounding in the Same Space

While it is preferable to keep <u>non-sterile</u> and <u>sterile</u> compounding space separate, an exception can be made to prepare non-sterile hazardous drugs in a C-PEC inside a C-SEC, if these requirements are met:

- The C-SEC must <u>maintain ISO 7</u> air even when it is being used for non-sterile HD compounding.

- If there are <u>separate sterile and non-sterile C-PECs</u> in the same C-SEC, they must be kept at least <u>1 meter apart</u>.

- Particle-generating activity, such as working with powders, cannot be performed when any sterile compounding is being performed in the same C-SEC.

- Occasional non-sterile HD compounding can be completed in a sterile C-PEC, but it must be properly decontaminated, cleaned and disinfected before using again to compound sterile HDs.

AIR HANDLING FOR HAZARDOUS DRUGS

Negative Air Pressure

<u>C-PECs</u>, <u>C-SECs</u> and <u>C-SCAs</u> must have <u>negative air pressure</u>.

- Negative air pressure in the C-PEC causes the air to flow into the C-PEC (away from the person who is standing at the front of the hood), and then to flow out of the C-PEC through the external exhaust at the top of the hood.

- Negative air pressure in the C-SEC keeps air from flowing into the anteroom. It is removed through the room exhaust.

Air Changes

Air in spaces used for HD compounding can get contaminated and needs to be regularly replaced. The <u>air changes per hour</u> (<u>ACPH</u>) is the <u>number of times</u> (per hour) that the <u>air is replaced</u> in the room.

- In space where <u>non-sterile HDs</u> are compounded there must be at least <u>12 ACPH</u>.

- In a <u>sterile C-SEC</u> there must be at least <u>30 ACPH</u>. This requirement also applies to a sterile SEC for non-HDs.

- In a <u>C-SCA</u> there must be at least <u>12 ACPH</u>.

External Exhaust

Air that has been contaminated with HDs must be <u>externally exhausted</u>. This means that the air is moved out of the space (from the C-PEC, from the C-SEC or from the non-sterile HD compounding space) and <u>cannot be recirculated</u> and returned to the room. It is sent outside and takes any contamination out with it.

Redundant HEPA Filters Instead of External Exhaust

Community pharmacies can be located in areas that would not welcome contaminated air exhaust, such as a compounding pharmacy that prepares HDs that is located adjacent to a busy park.

An <u>alternative</u> option to an external exhaust (for <u>non-sterile HD</u> compounding only) is to use <u>redundant HEPA filters</u>. Air is passed through two or more HEPA filters in a series (see the illustration below).

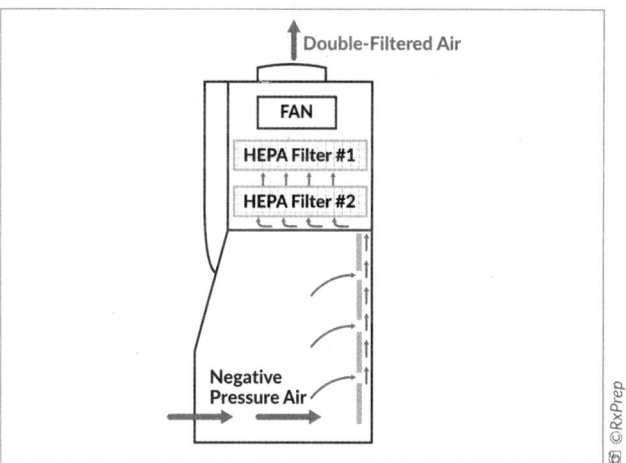

Redundant HEPA Filters

HAZARDOUS DRUG STORAGE

Hazardous drugs must be <u>stored separately</u> from non-hazardous drugs in an externally ventilated, <u>negative-pressure</u> room with at least <u>12 ACPH</u>.

COMPOUNDING & HAZARDOUS DRUGS

NEGATIVE PRESSURE HAZARDOUS DRUG CLEANROOM

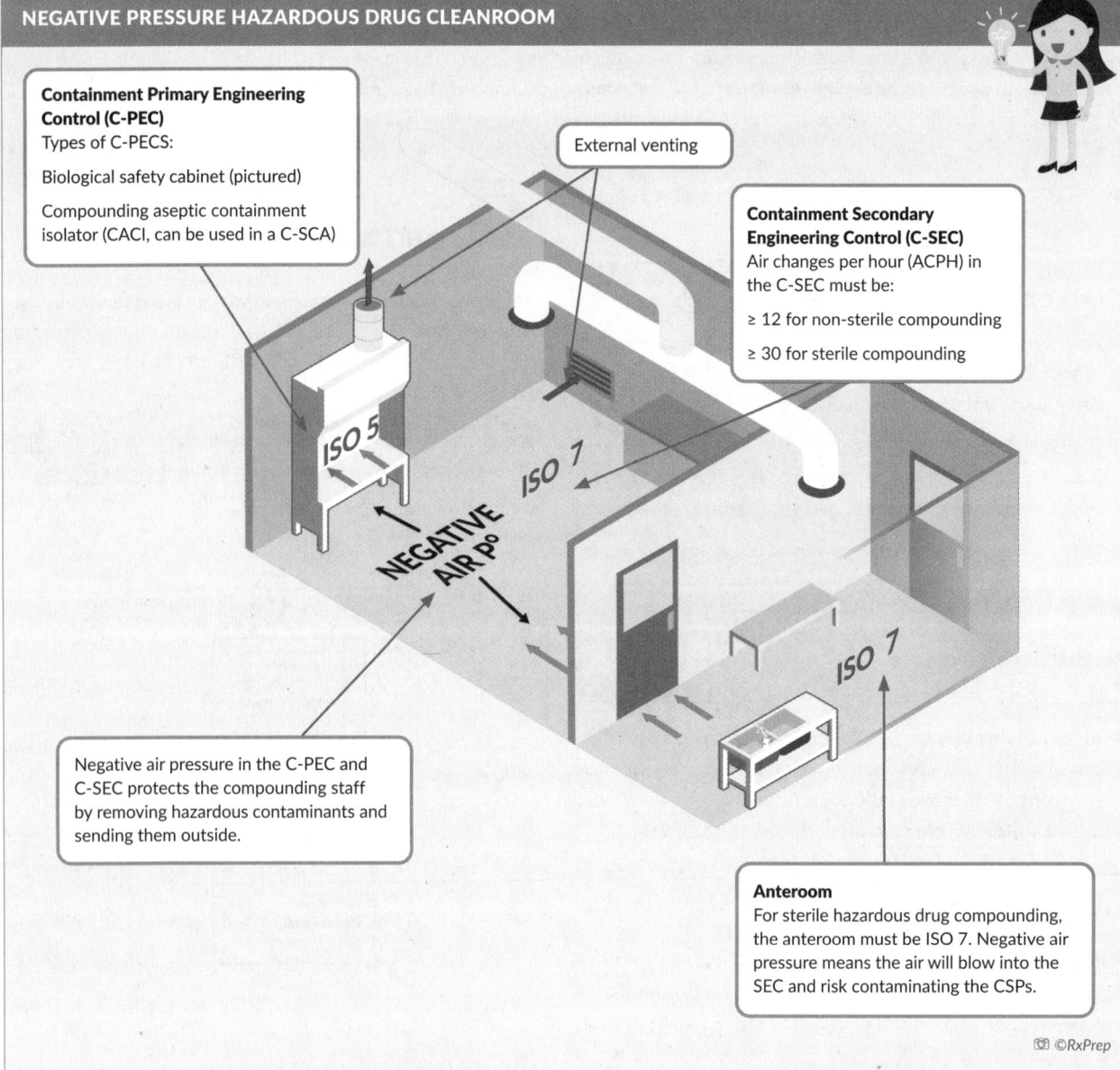

Containment Primary Engineering Control (C-PEC)
Types of C-PECS:

Biological safety cabinet (pictured)

Compounding aseptic containment isolator (CACI, can be used in a C-SCA)

External venting

Containment Secondary Engineering Control (C-SEC)
Air changes per hour (ACPH) in the C-SEC must be:

≥ 12 for non-sterile compounding

≥ 30 for sterile compounding

ISO 5

ISO 7

NEGATIVE AIR P°

ISO 7

Negative air pressure in the C-PEC and C-SEC protects the compounding staff by removing hazardous contaminants and sending them outside.

Anteroom
For sterile hazardous drug compounding, the anteroom must be ISO 7. Negative air pressure means the air will blow into the SEC and risk contaminating the CSPs.

©RxPrep

COMPOUNDING STAFF TRAINING

Personnel (i.e., staff) must have proper training for each type of compounding they perform. All training must be documented.

- Initial training includes didactic training (teaching, with lectures or videos) and hands-on training (compounding), which must be observed by the designated person in charge of compounding (i.e., compounding supervisor) or a staff expert.

- Continuous (ongoing) training must also be completed. When work is new or different for any reason, the compounding staff must receive additional training. This can include new drugs, revised drug information, changes in equipment and new or revised procedures.

REQUIRED TRAINING AND TESTING FOR STERILE COMPOUNDING

Staff must demonstrate that they can follow adequate aseptic procedures for each of these items prior to independently compounding sterile products:

- Hand hygiene
- Garbing and gloving technique
- Cleaning and disinfecting procedures for the sterile space and equipment
- Sterile drug preparation

Adequate aseptic technique in hand hygiene, garbing and gloving is demonstrated by passing the gloved fingertip test.

Adequate aseptic technique in sterile drug preparation is demonstrated by passing the media-fill test.

GLOVED FINGERTIP TEST

A passing score on the gloved fingertip test is required initially, then annually (if compounding only low- and medium-risk CSPs) or semi-annually (if compounding high-risk CSPs). The evaluator collects a gloved sample from each hand of the compounder by rolling the pads of the fingers and thumb over a surface which contains tryptic soy agar (TSA).

If microorganisms are present, they will use the TSA as a food source and replicate. The plates are incubated (heated, to facilitate growth) for 2 - 3 days and then inspected for microbial growth, which will be visible as spots on the plates. Spots that form are called colony-forming units (CFUs) and indicate contamination was present on the gloves.

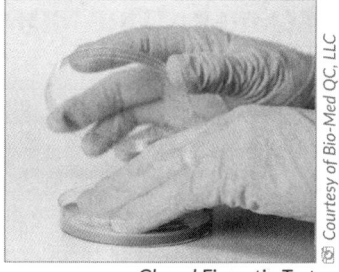

Gloved Fingertip Test

Passing a Gloved Fingertip Test

- Initial test: passing requires three consecutive gloved fingertip samples, taken after garbing, with zero CFUs for both hands.

- Ongoing competency: at least one sample taken from each hand immediately after completion of the media-fill test, with a goal of ≤ 3 CFUs total for both hands.

MEDIA-FILL TEST

The media-fill test is used to determine if a compounder is preparing CSPs in an aseptic manner. The test must be performed initially during training and at least annually for low- and medium-risk level compounding and semiannually for high-risk compounding.

Tryptic soy broth (TSB) takes the place of the drug in the preparation. TSB is a growth medium used by the organisms to replicate. A small IV bag or vial can be used for the test. Multiple aseptic manipulations (transfers using the same syringe) are done and then the product is incubated and checked for bacterial growth. Turbidity (cloudiness) means contamination is present.

Passing a Media-Fill Test

If the liquid stays clear after 14 days of incubation, the compounder passed the test.

Media Fill Test

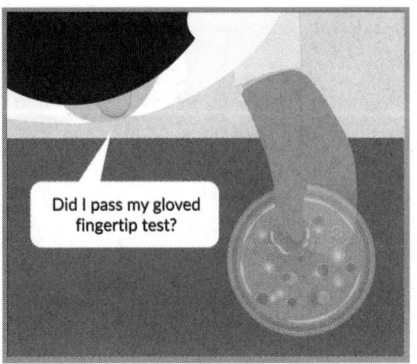

COMPOUNDING & HAZARDOUS DRUGS

TEMPERATURE MONITORING

Temperatures must be kept in the appropriate range and documented on the temperature log sheet (see clipboard). The SEC (buffer room) should be checked once daily and be maintained at 20°C (68°F), or cooler. The refrigerator and freezer should be monitored daily unless they contain vaccines, which require twice daily monitoring. The refrigerator temperature should be between 2 – 8°C. If a freezer contains only CSPs (no vaccines), then the freezer temperature should be between -25 and -10°C, according to USP 797. If the freezer also contains vaccines, the required freezer temperature is -50 to -15°C, per CDC guidance. If the temperature is out of range, action must be taken and documented.

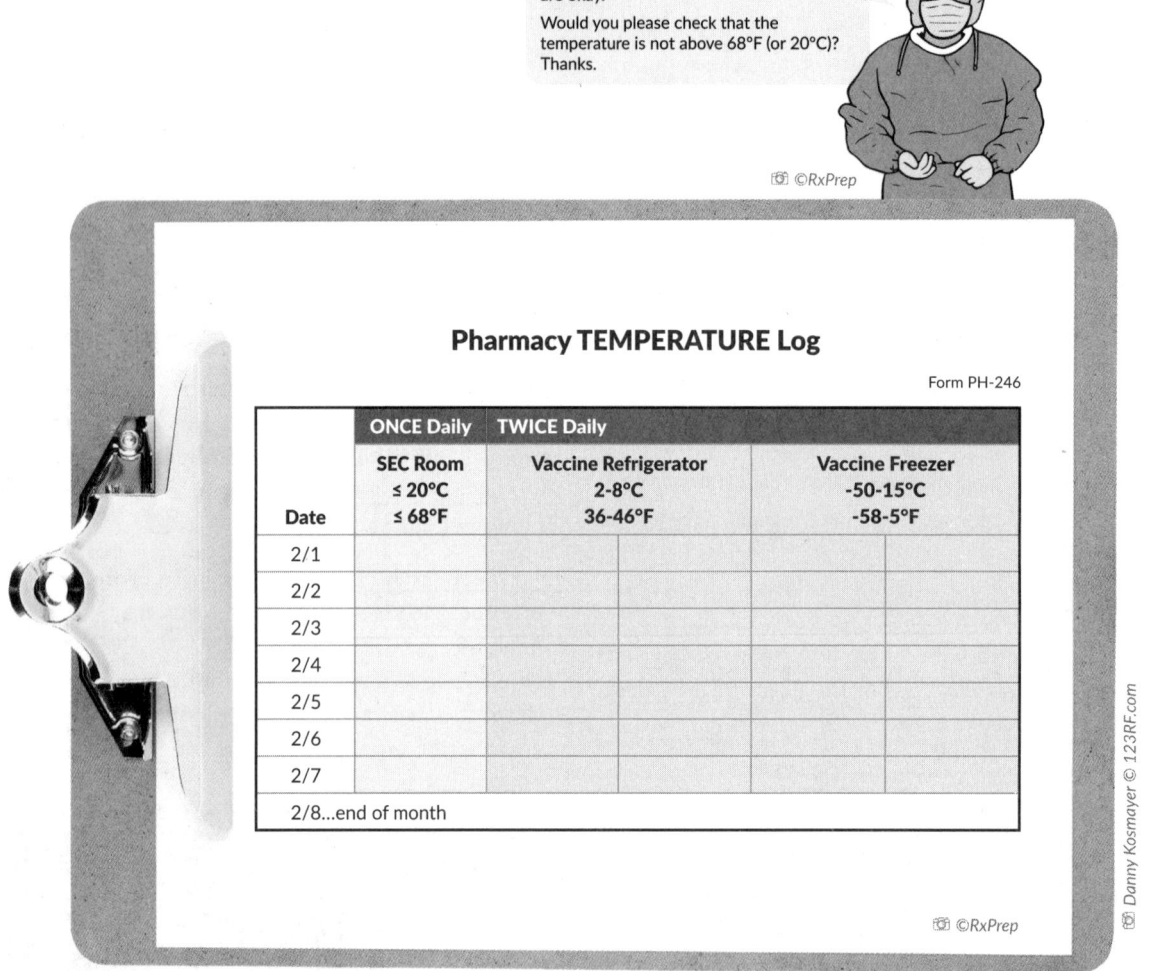

It feels hot in the SEC. I hope the CSPs are okay.

Would you please check that the temperature is not above 68°F (or 20°C)? Thanks.

©RxPrep

Pharmacy TEMPERATURE Log

Form PH-246

Date	ONCE Daily	TWICE Daily	
	SEC Room ≤ 20°C ≤ 68°F	Vaccine Refrigerator 2-8°C 36-46°F	Vaccine Freezer -50-15°C -58-5°F
2/1			
2/2			
2/3			
2/4			
2/5			
2/6			
2/7			
2/8...end of month			

©RxPrep

Danny Kosmayer © 123RF.com

AIR AND SURFACE TESTING

In addition to personnel testing with the gloved fingertip test and the media-fill test, there are other tests that are used to ensure that the environment for compounding sterile products is acceptably free of contaminants.

AIR SAMPLING

Air sampling identifies contaminants in the air. It should be performed at least every 6 months by a person certified in air sampling, or by a qualified compounding staff member.

SURFACE SAMPLING

© RxPrep

USP requires that surfaces be tested <u>periodically</u>. <u>Tryptic soy agar (TSA)</u> provides a good growth medium. <u>Polysorbate 80 and lecithin</u> are added, to the TSA to <u>neutralize</u> the effect of any <u>disinfecting agents</u> on the surfaces.

The testing should occur at the <u>end of the day</u> when the surfaces are in the poorest state. All surfaces that are regularly exposed to staff (e.g., <u>inside the PECs</u> and <u>other work surfaces</u>, door handles, equipment) should be tested. At least one surface sample must be taken from each ISO 5, 7 and 8 area. After the plates have been incubated for 2 – 3 days, the results should <u>indicate zero CFUs</u> (preferred).

Action must be taken if <u>> 3 CFUs</u> are identified in the ISO 5 area, <u>> 5 CFUs</u> in the ISO 7 area and <u>> 100 CFUs</u> in the ISO 8 area. If action is needed, polymerase chain reaction (PCR) can be used to identify the microorganisms present, which can help determine the source (e.g., *Staphylococci* are likely from the compounding staff; *Pseudomonas* can be due to water condensation from poor air conditioning or personnel contamination).

AIR PRESSURE TESTING

Air pressure testing confirms there is the correct <u>differential</u> (difference in pressures) <u>between two spaces</u> and ensures that the <u>airflow</u> is <u>unidirectional</u> (i.e., in one direction out from or into a space). Pressure gauges are installed in the cleanroom space, and <u>checked (minimally) once daily</u> or <u>with every work shift</u>.

HUMIDITY CONTROL

Humidity must be carefully controlled to prevent the presence of excess moisture in the sterile compounding area, which can lead to bacterial growth. The humidity should be below 60% and should be checked at least once daily.

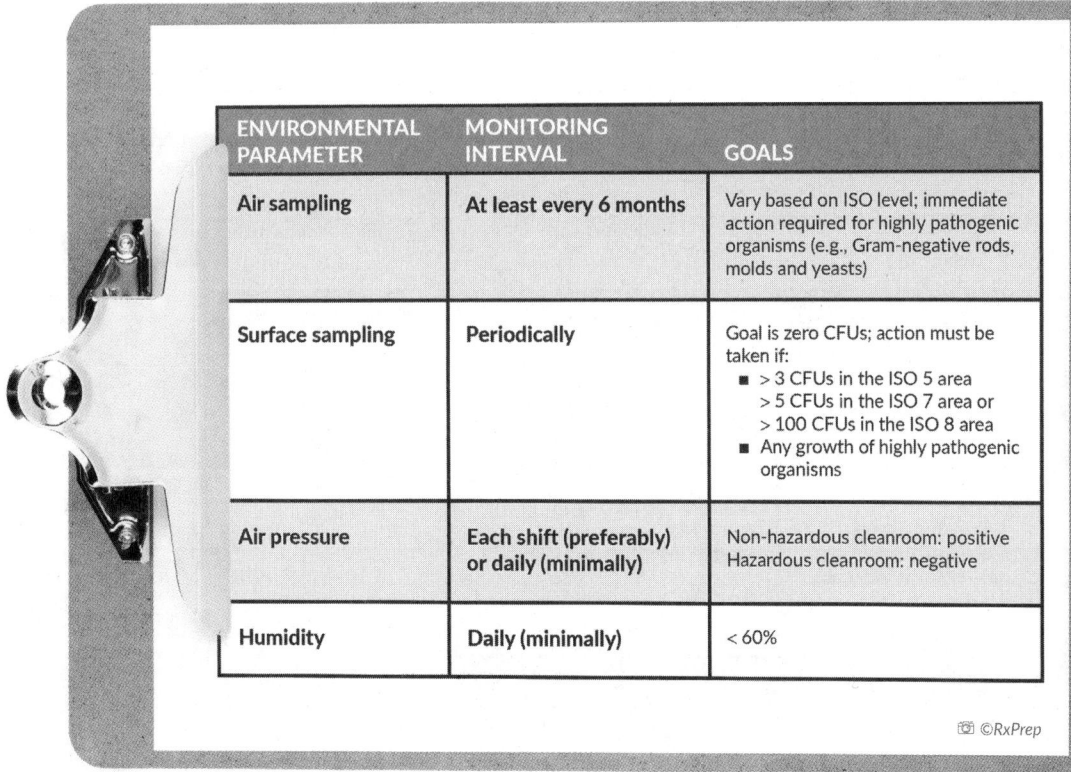

ENVIRONMENTAL PARAMETER	MONITORING INTERVAL	GOALS
Air sampling	At least every 6 months	Vary based on ISO level; immediate action required for highly pathogenic organisms (e.g., Gram-negative rods, molds and yeasts)
Surface sampling	Periodically	Goal is zero CFUs; action must be taken if: ■ > 3 CFUs in the ISO 5 area > 5 CFUs in the ISO 7 area or > 100 CFUs in the ISO 8 area ■ Any growth of highly pathogenic organisms
Air pressure	Each shift (preferably) or daily (minimally)	Non-hazardous cleanroom: positive Hazardous cleanroom: negative
Humidity	Daily (minimally)	< 60%

© RxPrep

Danny Kosmayer © 123RF.com

KEEPING THE STERILE COMPOUNDING AREA CLEAN

KEEP THE PEC RUNNING

All PECs and C-PECs are preferably kept <u>running at all times</u> to help keep the surfaces clean. If there is a power outage, all compounding must stop, and the PECs will need to be <u>cleaned</u> with a <u>germicidal detergent</u> and then <u>disinfected</u> with <u>sterile 70% isopropyl alcohol (IPA)</u> prior to re-initiation of compounding activity.

If the PEC is a <u>C-PEC, sanitization</u> will be needed if the power has been turned off. The sanitization process is more complex, and is described on the following page.

If the power has been off, in addition to cleaning and disinfecting (or sanitization for C-PECs), the PEC or C-PEC must be on for at least <u>30 minutes</u> before compounding can begin.

CLEAN THE PEC CONTINUOUSLY

The PEC is cleaned throughout the day (see below), and at the end of the day it is cleaned again (first) before cleaning the SEC and the anteroom. <u>Lint-free sterile</u> wipes are used to clean the PEC. First, the PEC is cleaned with a <u>germicidal detergent</u>, then <u>disinfected</u> with <u>70% IPA</u>. There are wipes that come pre-soaked with the appropriate agent. Alternatively, a spray bottle can be used to wet a dry wipe. Never spray inside the PEC. Use <u>slightly overlapping, unidirectional</u> strokes rather than circular motions. Use a new side of the wipe for the next area cleaned, and <u>replace used wipes</u> often.

PECs are cleaned from <u>top to bottom, back to front</u>. This means that the <u>cleanest</u> areas will be <u>cleaned first</u>, and the <u>dirtiest</u> areas will be <u>cleaned last</u>.

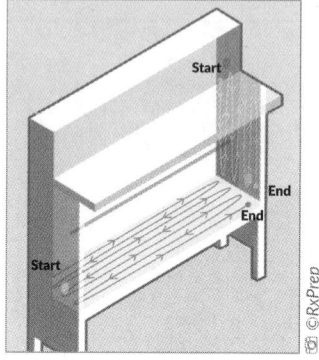

Clean side walls and work surface from back to front in long sweeps.

Cleaning a Horizontal Laminar Airflow PEC

This is an example of the order of cleaning for a PEC.

1. Clean the ceiling of the hood, from back to front.

2. Clean the grill over the HEPA filter, from top to bottom.

3. Clean the side walls starting from back to front, wiping up and down in a long sweeping motion. Clean the IV bar and hooks. Either the side walls or the bar can be cleaned first.

4. Clean anything kept in the hood [e.g., automated compounding device (used for parenteral nutrition), or other equipment].

5. Clean the bottom surface (the work area) starting from back to front, with a side to side motion.

Do not start compounding until the surfaces have dried.

DAILY		MONTHLY
All Sterile Work	**For Hazardous Drugs**	**Ceiling**
Before entering the cleanroom, wipe the outside container of all supplies	<u>Always</u> sanitize the work area at the end of a shift: Deactivate, Decontaminate, Clean, Disinfect	**Walls**
		Shelving
Clean with germicidal cleaner and disinfect with sterile 70% IPA, every day: <u>counters & floors</u>	Leaving HD residue for the next shift is NOT acceptable and is likely a justification for termination	**Chairs**
		Bins
		Carts

ISO 5 PECs, all types, are cleaned often:

✓ Before each shift

✓ Every 30 minutes while working

✓ Before and after each batch of CSPs

✓ Whenever needed, including after spills

©RxPrep

HAZARDOUS DRUG COMPOUNDING CLEANING SPECIFICS

SANITIZATION

All areas and equipment used for handling HDs must be sanitized, which includes deactivating, decontaminating and cleaning at least once daily. Sterile compounding areas and equipment must be disinfected as a final step. It is important to perform the sanitizing steps in the correct order; if the disinfecting step is done before deactivating, it will spread the HD residue.

DEACTIVATION and **DECONTAMINATION**
2% Bleach (Sodium Hypochlorite) or Peroxide
Reduce HD toxicity, then remove HD residues

CLEANING
Germicidal Detergent, such as Quat, Ammonium, Phenolics
Removes dirt and microbial contamination

DISINFECTION
Sterile 70% Isopropyl Alcohol (IPA)
Inhibits or destroys microorganisms; required step in sterile compounding

When using the sanitizing agents, wetted wipes should be used instead of using a spray bottle to directly spray onto the surfaces and equipment. This is because the spray can cause any HD residue to aerosolize and spread to other areas. All workers performing these activities must wear appropriate PPE. A NIOSH approved fit-tested respirator should be used if the sash of the BSC or the front cover of the CACI is opened.

There are several commercially available kits which simplify the sanitization process, and multi-purpose agents that combine deactivation and decontamination, such as *Peridox RTU*. Bleach or peroxide can be used for both steps. Bleach can cause corrosion on stainless steel surfaces, which includes the surfaces of C-PECs. To prevent corrosion, neutralize the bleach by wiping surfaces afterwards with sodium thiosulfate, sterile alcohol, sterile water or a germicidal detergent.

All areas where HDs are handled (receiving, transporting, compounding, administering, disposal), reusable equipment and devices must be routinely deactivated/decontaminated and cleaned. The cleaning and disinfecting schedule from USP 800 applies to both sterile and non-sterile HD compounding areas. Decontamination is required anytime a spill occurs.

SURFACE SAMPLING FOR HAZARDOUS DRUGS

Pharmacies involved in hazardous compounding should perform wipe sampling of all compounding surfaces initially and at least every 6 months to ensure that hazardous residue is adequately contained. Areas in the C-PEC, C-SEC and anteroom should be tested for contamination. If contamination is present, the designated individual must identify the source and implement a plan to contain it.

DRUG EXPOSURE

The most urgent action to take when a staff member has an exposure (whether to a non-HD, a chemical in the workplace or a HD) is to get the drug or chemical off the person as soon as possible. The first 10 to 15 seconds after exposure are critical. Delaying treatment, even for a few seconds, may cause serious injury.

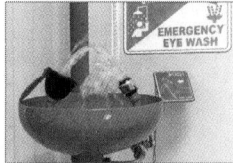
settapong/stock.adobe.com

Protocols for emergency procedures should be kept in the pharmacy. Minimal actions to take:

1. For an exposure to gloves or gown, immediately remove the garb that has the drug on it.

2. Immediately cleanse any affected skin with soap and water.

3. For an eye exposure, flood the affected eye at an eyewash fountain (see image above), or with water or an isotonic eyewash for at least 15 minutes. Depending on the chemical, the time required for flushing can be longer.

4. Obtain medical attention, when warranted.

5. Document the exposure in the employee's record.

HAZARDOUS DRUG EXPOSURE & SPILL MANAGEMENT

Remove any HD exposed to the skin as soon as possible (see details above). Emergency medical treatment must be sought with significant skin exposure (see following section on managing a spill) and with mucus membrane and inhalation exposure. Chemotherapeutics and some other HDs can irritate the eyes and mucus membranes in the nose and mouth and cause lung damage.

Eye and face protection must be worn when there is a risk for HD spills or splashes, including when working in a PEC and when working outside of a PEC (e.g., when administering the drug to a patient or cleaning up a spill).

Goggles are used for eye protection. Eye glasses alone or safety glasses with side shields do not protect the eyes adequately from splashes; face shields in combination with goggles is preferable and provides complete protection against splashes to the face and eyes.

RESPIRATORY PROTECTION

When HDs are unpacked and they are not contained in plastic, the staff member should wear an elastomeric half-mask, with a multi-gas cartridge and P100-filter, until assessment of the packaging integrity ensures that no breakage or spillage occurred during transport.

An N95 respirator is sufficient for most HD compounding, but does not provide adequate protection against gases, vapors or direct liquid splashes. Additional respiratory protection is needed in situations with direct HD exposure including:

- Cleaning up spills that need more supplies to clean up than provided by a spill kit.

- Deactivating, decontaminating and cleaning underneath the work surface of a C-PEC.

- When there is a known or suspected airborne exposure to HD powders or vapors.

- Disposal of PPE used when handling HDs, which will be contaminated with (minimally) trace amounts.

When there is a risk of respiratory exposure, one of the following should be worn:

- A fit-tested respirator mask with attached gas canisters (a "gas mask"); see picture below on the left.

© CDC.gov

Respirator mask with gas canisters

Powered Air-Purifying Respirator (PAPR)

- A powered air-purifying respirator (PAPR) that blows air through the filter to the user (see picture above on the right). PAPRs are easier to breathe through than the gas mask type but require a fully charged battery to work properly. They use the same filters as gas masks.

HAZARDOUS DRUG SPILLS

HD spills must be cleaned up immediately. Depending on the facility, all of the compounding staff can be trained to handle HD spills, or the facility can have a trained spill response team. The Safety Data Sheet (SDS) should be consulted for guidance on spill clean-up procedures.

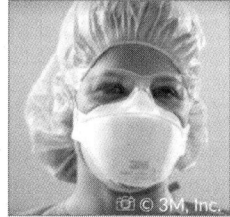
© 3M, Inc.
N95 Respirator Mask plus Goggles with Side Shields

Establish the Who, What and When

- Who refers to the staff who will respond to assist with people exposed to the spill and who will respond to clean up the spill. If HD exposure has occurred, emergency medical help will be needed.

- What refers to the rapid assessment of the situation to determine if additional help will be needed.

- When refers to the urgent need to clean up hazardous spills immediately.

Managing the Spill

- Spill kits for HDs must be kept in areas where HDs are prepared, stored and administered. The spill kits must be available immediately wherever HDs travel, which is where they can spill.

- Quickly limit access to the area, and post warning signs around the perimeter of the spill. Multiple signs can be needed if more than one entry opens into the area with the spill. Pregnant women should not be involved with any clean-up activities and should immediately leave the area.

- The warning sign should state **Caution: Hazardous Spill, Proceed with Care!** or something similar.

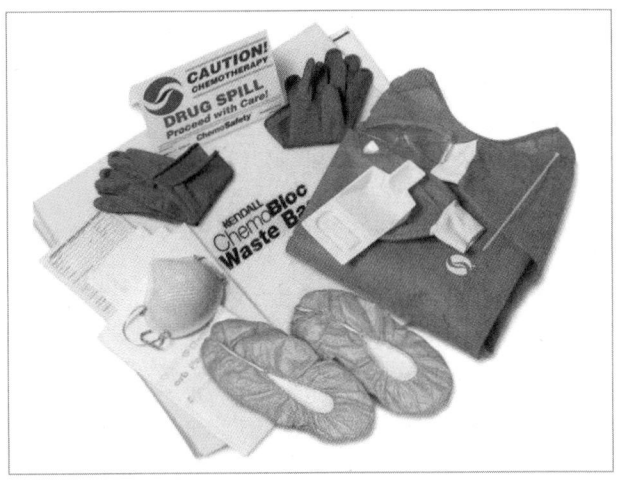

Spill Kit Contents

- Protective <u>gown</u>, latex <u>gloves</u> (minimally), <u>N95 respirator</u> mask plus <u>goggles</u> with side shields

- <u>HD waste bag</u>, scoop and scraper to get spill waste into the waste bag, <u>chemo pads</u> to absorb hazardous liquid

- <u>HD spill report exposure form</u> to document HD exposure

Procedure for Cleaning up a Spill

Open the spill kit. The PPE should be donned immediately to protect the staff cleaning up the spill.

- Put the heavy-duty gloves over the <u>ASTM D6978 (chemotherapy)-rated gloves</u>, which are the type used for HD compounding. The heavy-duty gloves protect the hands from broken glass.

- Clean up macro amounts (big amounts) of spilled drug and broken glass.

  - Never use a brush to clean up broken glass and powder that is contaminated with HDs. Brushes can cause particles to become airborne.

- If liquid is present, cover the liquid with an absorbent spill pad.

- Next, decontaminate the surfaces on which the HD has spilled from the area of lesser contamination to areas of greater contamination to avoid spreading the hazard.

- If moistened pads are not available, pour the solution on the pads. Do not spray.

- Put trash into a hazardous waste bag, and seal. This is <u>bulk hazardous waste</u>, which is discarded in the <u>black</u> bulk hazardous <u>waste bin</u>.

After the Spill is Cleaned

- Doff (remove) garb and perform hand hygiene.

- Decontaminate the respirator and replace the cartridges.

- Replace the spill kit.

ADMINISTRATION OF HAZARDOUS DRUGS

Appropriate PPE must be worn when <u>administering</u> HDs. <u>Two pairs of chemotherapy gloves</u> are required when administering all <u>HDs</u>. A chemotherapy <u>gown</u> is required when administering <u>IV HDs</u> and recommended when administering other HDs (e.g., oral).

<u>Closed-system drug transfer devices</u> (CSTDs) <u>must</u> be used by <u>nurses</u> for drug <u>administration</u>, if available for the formulation being used. Chemotherapy <u>pins</u> are used to prevent HDs from <u>aerosolizing</u> by reducing air pressure with venting. They can be used during reconstitution and during administration. The pins attach with a luer lock connection, described in the Compounding II chapter.

<u>CSTDs</u> should be used to transfer drugs whenever possible to keep the HDs <u>contained</u> within the device. CSTDs reduce leaks and spills when withdrawing solutions from vials, injecting solutions into IV bags, <u>reconstituting</u> dried powders into solutions and for syringe to syringe transfers. CSTDs are <u>recommended</u> when <u>compounding HDs</u> and <u>required</u> for <u>administering</u> antineoplastics, if available. CSTDs have a <u>built-in valve</u> that <u>equalizes</u> the <u>air pressure</u> when fluid is added or withdrawn from the vial.

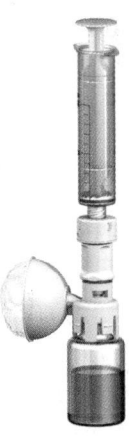

Example of a Closed System Transfer Device

Pharmacy and nursing should try to avoid manipulating oral HDs, such as crushing tablets and opening capsules. If a liquid formulation of the drug is available, it should be used. If manipulation is required (e.g., crushing tablets) it should be done in a <u>plastic bag</u> to contain any dust or particles.

COMPOUNDING & HAZARDOUS DRUGS

DISPOSAL

All PPE worn when handling HDs is considered contaminated with trace amounts. The <u>outer chemotherapy gloves</u> worn during compounding are discarded in a <u>yellow trace chemotherapy waste bin</u> located <u>inside</u> the C-PEC or put in a <u>sealable bag</u> if discarding outside the C-PEC. Remove the outer glove before handling and labeling the compounded preparation. The <u>chemotherapy gown</u> and <u>outer shoe covers</u> must be taken off before exiting the <u>negative-pressure area</u> and thrown away in the <u>yellow trace chemotherapy waste bin</u>. The rest of the garb is removed when leaving the ante-room or C-SCA once the compounding session is complete.

Trace Chemo Waste Bin: Yellow *Bulk Chemo Waste Bin: Black*

📷 *New Africa/stock.adobe.com*

<u>All trace antineoplastic waste</u> (i.e., empty vials, empty syringes, empty IV bags, IV tubes, used gloves, used gowns, used pads) is thrown away in a <u>yellow container</u>, which will be destroyed by incineration (burning) at a waste facility.

<u>Bulk antineoplastic waste</u>, which includes unused or partially empty IV bags, syringes and vials, are thrown away in a <u>black container</u>, which will be incinerated at a waste facility.

TRANSPORTING HAZARDOUS DRUGS

When HDs need to be transported, they must be properly labeled and packaged to minimize the risk of spillage or breakage. <u>Pneumatic tube</u> systems <u>cannot</u> be used to transport any <u>liquid</u> HDs or any <u>antineoplastics</u> because of the potential for breakage and contamination.

GARBING FOR ALL TYPES OF COMPOUNDING

Garb attire includes hair covers (bonnets), beard covers, special shoes or shoe covers, gowns, gloves, face masks, eye shields and aprons. The <u>garb attire</u> required <u>depends on the type of compounding</u> performed. The staff have to be protected from chemical exposure (some drugs are more toxic than others), and the drug needs to be protected from contamination. Hand hygiene and garbing is more detailed for sterile compounding.

GARB FOR HAZARDOUS DRUGS

Appropriate PPE must be worn with each step involving HDs: receiving, storage, transporting, compounding (sterile and non-sterile), administration, sanitation and during spill control. <u>Double ASTM D6978 (chemotherapy)-rated gloves</u> are required when <u>compounding or cleaning up spills</u>. <u>Single gloves</u> can be used for HD <u>receiving and storage</u>.

Non-Sterile Hazardous Drugs

Placing intact tablets or capsules into unit-dose or multidose containers on an occasional basis poses relatively low risk to the healthcare worker. A single pair of gloves may be adequate. When USP 800 is not being followed completely (which requires 2 pairs of gloves), it must be based on an AoR that has identified the drugs which can have less stringent requirements, and the procedures put in place to reduce risk.

Repeatedly counting, cutting or crushing tablets poses a higher risk for worker exposure and contamination to the workplace if exposure controls are not in place. If a BSC or CACI is not available, then PPE should be used that includes:

- <u>Double gloves, a gown, a mask</u> and
- A <u>disposable pad</u> to protect the <u>work surface</u>

Sterile Hazardous Drugs

PPE for sterile hazardous drug compounding includes:

- <u>Head</u> covers, a <u>face mask</u> and (if applicable) <u>beard</u> covers
- <u>Two pairs</u> of <u>shoe covers</u>
- A gown <u>impermeable</u> to liquids
- <u>Two pairs</u> of <u>ASTM D6978 (chemotherapy)-rated gloves</u>
- A <u>full-facepiece respirator</u> or a <u>face shield with goggles</u> when there is a risk for spills or splashes

The following pages illustrate how to don garb for <u>sterile compounding</u>, followed by <u>requirements</u> for sterile <u>hazardous</u> garb. <u>Removing coats, sweaters, makeup</u> and visible <u>jewelry</u> is required <u>before entering the ante-area</u>. Some pharmacies have compounders change into scrubs at work; these may be cleaner than street clothes, and are light and comfortable. The scrubs are laundered and kept on site to decrease the flow of microbes from the outside.

GARBING FOR STERILE COMPOUNDING

Garb is donned in the <u>ante-area</u>. The order in which the garb should be donned is from <u>dirtiest to cleanest</u>.

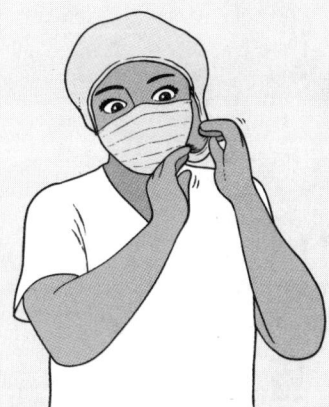

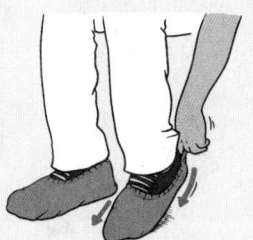

- Remove coats, <u>rings, watches,</u> bracelets and <u>makeup</u> before entering the ante-area. <u>Artificial or long nails are not</u> permitted.

- No make-up is permitted because it sheds.

- Don <u>head and facial hair covers</u> and <u>face masks</u>, then <u>shoe covers</u> while stepping over the <u>line of demarcation</u> that separates the dirty side of the anteroom from the clean side. A <u>second pair</u> of shoe covers are needed for compounding <u>HDs</u>. The ante-area should have a mirror that is used to check that the hair is completely covered. An eye shield is optional, except if preparing a hazardous drug.

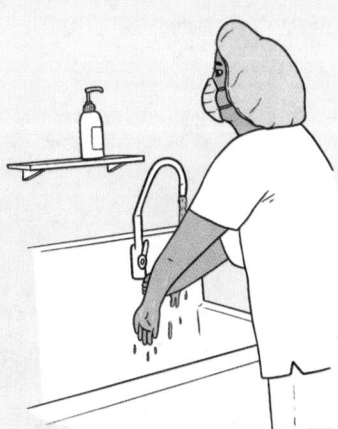

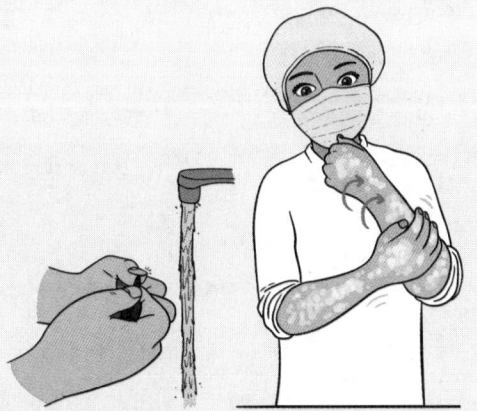

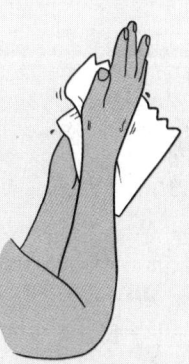

- Perform <u>hand hygiene</u> with <u>soap and warm water</u>. Most contamination of CSPs comes from the hands.

- Under warm water, <u>clean under fingernails</u> to remove debris.

- Working from the <u>fingertips to the elbows</u>, wash vigorously in <u>circular motions for 30 seconds</u>.

- Dry hands and forearms with lint-free disposable towels.

©RxPrep

COMPOUNDING & HAZARDOUS DRUGS

GARBING FOR STERILE COMPOUNDING continued

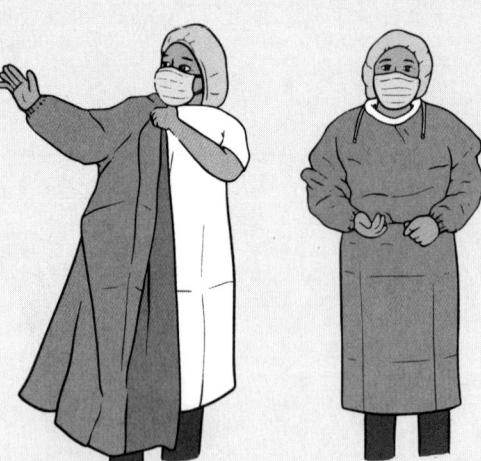
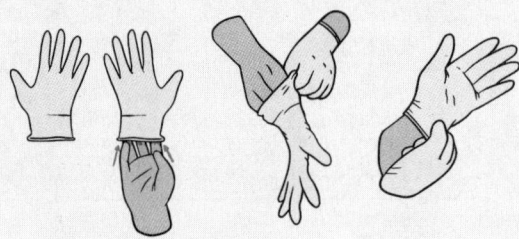

- Don a <u>non-shedding gown</u> that fits snugly around the wrists and has an enclosure at the neck. <u>Disposable</u> gowns are required for HD compounding and preferred for non-HD compounding. If gowns are reusable, they must be laundered prior to reuse.

- Enter the <u>buffer area (SEC)</u>.

- Apply an <u>alcohol-based surgical hand scrub</u> with persistent antimicrobial activity for the recommended amount of time (per manufacturer) and allow to dry. The FDA has issued a warning for serious allergic reactions to <u>chlorhexidine</u>, which <u>many compounders use</u>. Another option is <u>povidone-iodine</u> (*Betadine*), which can be used if there has been an allergic reaction to chlorhexidine.

- Don <u>sterile, powder-free gloves</u>. For compounding HDs, <u>two pairs of ASTM D6978 (chemotherapy)-rated gloves</u> are required.

- Sanitize the gloves with <u>70% IPA routinely</u> during compounding and whenever the gloves touch non-sterile surfaces. Do not resume compounding until the alcohol has dried. Continually inspect gloves for tears.

- All garb must be used when compounding with an isolator (glove box) <u>unless</u> the isolator's manufacturer provides written documentation that garb is not required.

- When the compounding is completed and the compounding personnel leaves the cleanroom/compounding area, all garb except for the gown goes into the disposal container. If the <u>gown</u> is not visibly soiled, it can be taken off and <u>kept</u> on the clean side of the <u>anteroom</u> in order to be <u>re-worn for the current work shift</u>. The gown cannot leave the ante-area if it is going to be re-worn. Hand hygiene is repeated, and all other garb is replaced when re-entering the compounding area.

©RxPrep

WHEN TO RE-GARB

- Garb should not be worn outside of the anteroom; if the anteroom has been exited, complete regarbing is required, including hand hygiene.

- If working in an SCA and it is left for any reason, regarbing is required.

GARBING FOR HAZARDOUS DRUGS

Garb is donned in the <u>ante-area</u>. The order in which the garb should be donned is from <u>dirtiest to cleanest</u>.

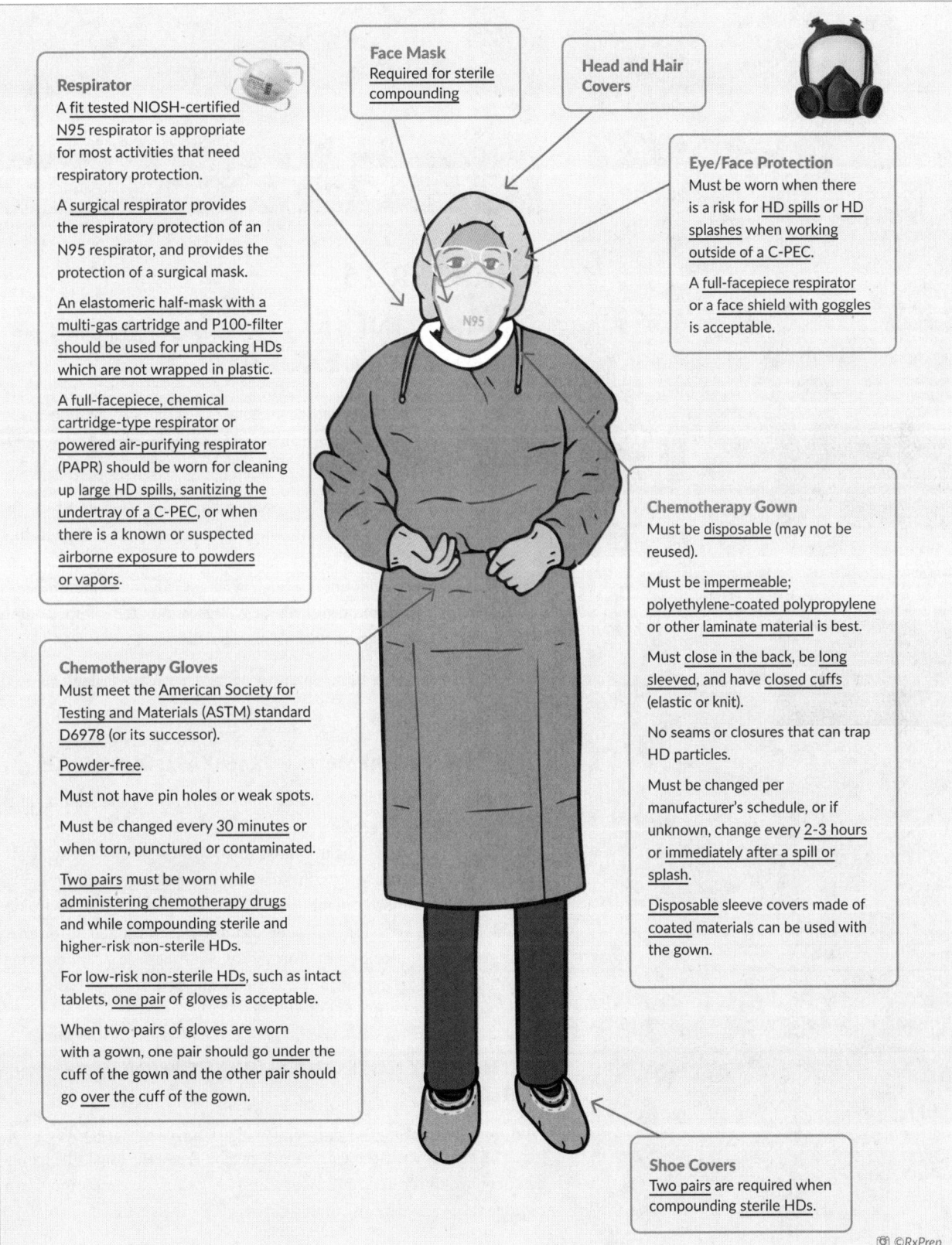

Respirator

A <u>fit tested NIOSH-certified N95</u> respirator is appropriate for most activities that need respiratory protection.

A <u>surgical respirator</u> provides the respiratory protection of an N95 respirator, and provides the protection of a surgical mask.

An <u>elastomeric half-mask with a multi-gas cartridge</u> and <u>P100-filter</u> should be used for unpacking HDs which are not wrapped in plastic.

A <u>full-facepiece, chemical cartridge-type respirator</u> or <u>powered air-purifying respirator (PAPR)</u> should be worn for cleaning up <u>large HD spills</u>, sanitizing the <u>undertray of a C-PEC</u>, or when there is a known or suspected <u>airborne exposure to powders or vapors</u>.

Face Mask
<u>Required for sterile compounding</u>

Head and Hair Covers

Eye/Face Protection

Must be worn when there is a risk for <u>HD spills</u> or <u>HD splashes</u> when <u>working outside of a C-PEC</u>.

A <u>full-facepiece respirator</u> or a <u>face shield with goggles</u> is acceptable.

Chemotherapy Gloves

Must meet the <u>American Society for Testing and Materials (ASTM) standard D6978</u> (or its successor).

<u>Powder-free</u>.

Must not have pin holes or weak spots.

Must be changed every <u>30 minutes</u> or when torn, punctured or contaminated.

<u>Two pairs</u> must be worn while <u>administering chemotherapy drugs</u> and while <u>compounding</u> sterile and higher-risk non-sterile HDs.

For <u>low-risk non-sterile HDs</u>, such as intact tablets, <u>one pair</u> of gloves is acceptable.

When two pairs of gloves are worn with a gown, one pair should go <u>under</u> the cuff of the gown and the other pair should go <u>over</u> the cuff of the gown.

Chemotherapy Gown

Must be <u>disposable</u> (may not be reused).

Must be <u>impermeable</u>; <u>polyethylene-coated polypropylene</u> or other <u>laminate material</u> is best.

Must <u>close in the back</u>, be <u>long sleeved</u>, and have <u>closed cuffs</u> (elastic or knit).

No seams or closures that can trap HD particles.

Must be changed per manufacturer's schedule, or if unknown, change every <u>2-3 hours</u> or <u>immediately after a spill or splash</u>.

<u>Disposable</u> sleeve covers made of <u>coated</u> materials can be used with the gown.

Shoe Covers
<u>Two pairs</u> are required when compounding <u>sterile HDs</u>.

©RxPrep

CONTENT LEGEND

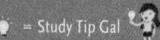 = Study Tip Gal    = Required Formula

---

CHAPTER 16

COMPOUNDING II: EQUIPMENT, STABILITY & EXCIPIENTS

EQUIPMENT

The first section of this chapter covers equipment used for compounding. Most equipment is used for non-sterile compounding (e.g., ointment mills and tablet molds), some is used for both non-sterile and sterile compounding (e.g., syringes) and a small number is used for sterile compounding only (e.g., the automated compounding equipment used to prepare parenteral nutrition).

Equipment should be kept clean, in proper working order and free from contamination.

DEDICATED EQUIPMENT FOR HAZARDOUS DRUGS

The Compounding I chapter describes the space (and equipment) requirements for hazardous drug (HD) preparation and how non-hazardous drugs should be prepared in separate spaces with separate equipment. HDs cause contamination. Equipment used for HDs, including routine equipment such as counting trays and spatulas, should be dedicated for HD preparation and sanitized after use. Equipment that cannot be thoroughly sanitized (e.g., automated counting or packaging machines) should not be used for HDs as any residue could contaminate other drugs.

CAUTIONARY NOTE ON CALIBRATION AND MATERIALS

Equipment must be calibrated regularly to confirm accuracy. For some types of equipment, the calibration can be frequent (e.g., electronic balances are calibrated routinely before use). Complex equipment can require calibration by an outside expert.

Equipment should be made of material that does not react with the compounding ingredients (e.g., metal spatulas should not be used with compounds containing metal ions).

MEASURING VOLUME

Pharmacists use various equipment to measure the <u>volume</u> of ingredients, and nurses and patients use some of the same equipment (such as oral syringes and pipettes) to administer medication.

When measuring, select a device that has a measuring capacity <u>equal to</u> or <u>slightly larger</u> than the amount being measured to get the most <u>accurate</u> measurement (e.g., if an 8 mL dose is needed, and the syringe sizes available are 1 mL, 3 mL, 5 mL, 7.5 mL and 10 mL, the 10 mL syringe should be used). <u>Measurements</u> should be made in the <u>metric system</u>.

Cylindrical and Conical Graduates

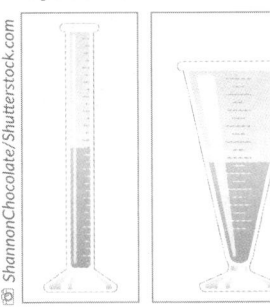

Graduated cylinder   Conical graduate

Graduates are measuring equipment with <u>lines</u> on the glass that are used to <u>measure</u> the <u>volume</u>, and include graduated cylinders (left image), conical (cone-shaped) graduates (right image), graduated beakers and graduated medication containers.

A <u>graduated cylinder</u> has the <u>same diameter</u> from the <u>top to the bottom</u> of the container and provides <u>more accurate</u> measurements than conical graduates or beakers, which have wide mouths (makes it easier to stir mixtures with a <u>glass stirring rod</u>). The <u>wider</u> the <u>mouth</u>, the <u>lower</u> the <u>accuracy</u>.

Some important points about measuring volume using graduates include:

- A graduate should not be used to measure volumes <u>less</u> than <u>20%</u> of the graduate's <u>capacity</u>.

    ❑ The smaller the percentage of the graduate's measuring capacity that is used, the higher the measuring error (e.g., measuring 5 mL in a 100 mL graduate will have a higher measuring error than measuring 87 mL in a 100 mL graduate. A 5 mL measurement needs a smaller graduate.)

- To <u>read the volume</u> in a graduate, place it on a flat surface and view the height of the liquid in the cylinder at <u>eye level</u>.

- The liquid can curve downward from both sides, especially with viscous liquids. This curve is called the <u>meniscus</u>.

- The <u>bottom of the meniscus</u>, at the <u>center</u> is where the measurement is read (see image).

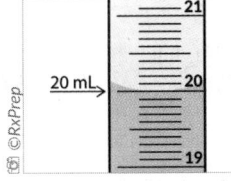

Measure the level at the bottom of the meniscus (i.e., the curve), at eye level. This graduated cylinder contains 20 mL.

Syringes

Syringes used for Non-Sterile Compounding

Oral syringes and <u>hypodermic</u> (injection) syringes (also called <u>parenteral</u> syringes) can be used for measuring volume. See images on the next page.

- <u>Syringes</u> are <u>most accurate</u> for measuring <u>small volumes</u>.

- They are especially <u>useful</u> for measuring <u>viscous</u> (thick) liquids, such as glycerin and mineral oil.

- Patients receiving a liquid who require a <u>very accurate dose</u> should use an <u>oral syringe</u> for measurement rather than a small dosing cup, which has lower accuracy.

- Oral syringes are useful for squirting the medication into the side of the mouth (as are small pipettes or droppers), which can be useful for children and animals. Oral syringes can be used to deliver small amounts of topical preparations.

Caution with Oral Syringes in an Acute Care Setting

There have been multiple deaths due to patients receiving oral medications as an injection. Safety measures must be in place to prevent oral medications from being given by the wrong route (see next page).

Syringes used for Sterile Compounding

<u>Hypodermic</u> (parenteral) syringes are commonly used for sterile compounding to <u>transfer</u> drugs and additives <u>into</u> IV bags.

- All syringe packages should be <u>wiped off with isopropyl alcohol (IPA) 70%</u> to remove contaminants and dust, <u>prior</u> to being brought <u>into</u> the secondary engineering control (SEC) or into the primary engineering control (PEC) if working in a segregated compounding area.

- Sterile syringes are individually wrapped, and must be <u>opened along the seal</u> (not torn open) to avoid <u>shedding</u> (i.e., <u>release of particles</u> into the sterile space).

Caution with Hypodermic Syringe Needle-Sticks

<u>Recapping</u> needles leads to <u>needle-stick injuries</u>. In sterile compounding, a needle-stick can <u>injure</u> the staff and cause <u>contamination</u> to the compounded sterile products (CSPs). In patient care settings, <u>needle-stick injuries</u> carry <u>infection risk</u>.

- In general, <u>do not recap</u> syringes.

- It is preferable to <u>use syringes with safety features</u>, such as safety shields that cover the needle immediately after use.

- If the needle must be recapped, it is safer to place the cap on the work surface (rather than holding it) and slip the tip of the needle into the cap, without letting the needle tip touch the work surface.

Luer Locks Improve Patient Safety

Luer locks make <u>secure, leak-free connections</u> between syringes, catheters and IV lines. They have male and female ends that screw together, forming a tight seal (see image).

Using a Syringe

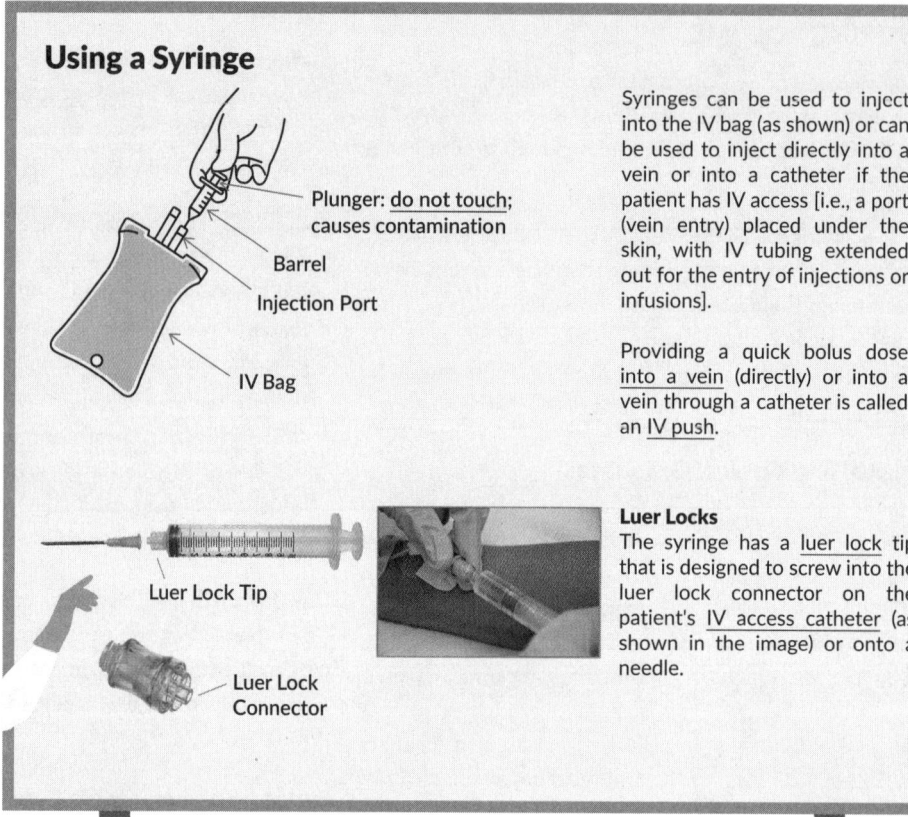

Plunger: <u>do not touch</u>; causes contamination

Barrel

Injection Port

IV Bag

Syringes can be used to inject into the IV bag (as shown) or can be used to inject directly into a vein or into a catheter if the patient has IV access [i.e., a port (vein entry) placed under the skin, with IV tubing extended out for the entry of injections or infusions].

Providing a quick bolus dose <u>into a vein</u> (directly) or into a vein through a catheter is called an <u>IV push</u>.

Luer Lock Tip

Luer Lock Connector

Luer Locks

The syringe has a <u>luer lock</u> tip that is designed to screw into the luer lock connector on the patient's <u>IV access catheter</u> (as shown in the image) or onto a needle.

©RxPrep

Syringe Types

Hypodermic (Injection) Syringes

These come with <u>cannulas</u> (needles) attached, or the cannula is separate and can be screwed onto the tip of the syringe. Hypodermic (or parenteral injection) syringes are available in many sizes, (e.g., 1 mL, 3 mL, 5 mL, 10 mL and others).

Choose the Correct Size Syringe

For drawing up medication, <u>do not</u> use the <u>exact size</u> syringe needed because the plunger can easily become dislodged. Select the <u>closest syringe size</u> above the size needed. Do <u>not add two</u> different syringe sizes for a dose.

Oral Syringes

These are used to administer drugs <u>orally</u> or through a feeding tube [e.g., <u>nasogastric</u> (NG)]. To avoid fatal medication errors, safety measures include:

- Placing a "<u>For Oral Use Only</u>" sticker over the syringe cap
- Using a syringe design that prevents connection to an IV port
- Using oral syringes with brightly colored plungers/caps that differentiate them from IV syringes
- Clearly communicating the correct route of administration to the nurse

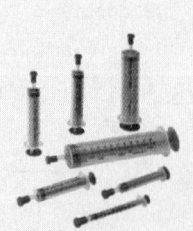

©RxPrep

Pipettes and Droppers

Pipettes

<u>Pipettes</u> are <u>thin plastic</u> or <u>glass tubes</u> used to measure small volumes. Pipettes can be used by patients to take medication because they are easy to draw up a dose (insert tip into liquid medication, squeeze and release the bulb, remove). If the pipette is being inserted into an opening such as a mouth or nose, it is important to keep the bulb squeezed after the dose is delivered and when withdrawing it, to avoid contaminating the inside of the pipette.

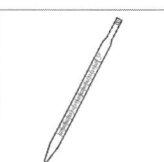

Mohr pipette (graduated)

Disposable pipette

Pipettes can be referred to as droppers, because they release drops. Medicine droppers are also called droppers.

- A <u>volumetric pipette</u> draws up a set volume only, which is the volume the pipette can hold.

- A <u>Mohr pipette</u> is <u>graduated</u> and is used to measure different volumes. Mohr pipettes are commonly used in compounding.

Medicine Droppers

Medicine droppers come in graduated and non-graduated versions. Graduated droppers that meet USP criteria (such as the dropper in the image) release drops of water that weigh 45 – 55 mg, when held vertically.

Graduated dropper

- The weight is given for water drops; other compounds will have different weights for the same size drops, depending on the liquid's specific gravity.

- Non-graduated medicine droppers that meet the USP criteria release a similarly-sized drop.

WEIGHING EQUIPMENT

Balances

There are two types of balances used to weigh ingredients. The older balance is the <u>Class III torsion balance</u> (sometimes called a <u>Class A balance</u>). This type of balance is still used, though less commonly than the electronic balance [see "Ye Old Torsion Balance" for a description and the calculation for the <u>minimum weighable quantity (MWQ)</u>].

YE OLD TORSION BALANCE

<u>Class III (Class A) torsion balances</u> have internal weights, which are used to weigh quantities ≤ 1 gram. When weighing > 1 gram, external weights (see picture) are placed on one pan and the substance to be weighed is placed on the other. The external weights must be handled with a forceps (pincers) to avoid getting oil from the skin on the weights.

Torsion balances have a <u>sensitivity requirement</u> (SR) that is most often 6 mg, meaning 6 mg can be added or removed before the dial moves 1 division.

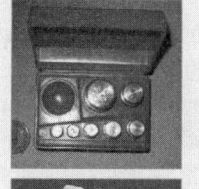

Torsion balance

The <u>minimum weighable quantity</u> (the minimum amount that can be weighed) is calculated based on the SR and <u>acceptable error rate</u> (typically <u>0.05 or 5%</u>):

MWQ	=	SR / acceptable error rate (0.05 or 5%)

MWQ = 6 mg / 0.05 = 120 mg

The top-loading <u>electronic balance</u> (called an <u>analytical balance</u> or a <u>scale</u>) is used most commonly.

- This type of balance is <u>simple</u> to use and has <u>higher sensitivity</u> (i.e., can weigh with more precision, including very small amounts). It is not necessary to calculate the MWQ with a modern electronic balance.

- When using an electronic balance, the compounder must "<u>tare</u>" or "<u>zero out</u>" the balance after placing the weigh boat or glassine paper on the scale. This ensures that <u>only the ingredients</u> are weighed and the container or paper used to hold the ingredients are not included in the weight.

With either balance, <u>never place material</u> to be <u>weighed</u> (e.g., powder) <u>directly on the balance</u>. The material will be placed on a <u>weigh boat</u> (a shallow dish) or on <u>glassine weighing paper</u>, which is coated to reduce moisture penetration. The weigh boats are made of plastic or other material.

Electronic balance

Fagron©

Weigh boats

GRINDING, MIXING AND TRANSFERRING EQUIPMENT

Mortars and Pestles

Mortars and pestles are used to grind substances into a finer consistency, and can be used to stir and mix small amounts of ingredients. The mortar is the bowl, and the pestle is the blunt, heavy stick. A compounding pharmacy needs at least one glass and one Wedgwood or porcelain mortar and pestle.

- Glass mortars are used for liquids, such as suspensions and solutions, and for mixing compounds that are oily or can stain.

- Wedgwood mortars have a rough surface, and are preferred for grinding dry crystals and hard powders.

- Porcelain mortars have a smooth surface, and are preferred for blending powders and pulverizing gummy consistencies.

Fagron©

Glass mortar & pestle   Wedgwood mortar & pestle   Porcelain mortar & pestle

Spatulas

Spatulas are used to mix and transfer (move) ingredients from one place (such as an ointment slab) to another place (such as a container). The flat part of the blade can be used to flatten and grind down ingredients, and to pack preparations such as ointments into containers. Spatulas are made of stainless steel, plastic or hard rubber. Stainless steel and disposable plastic spatulas are used commonly. The type of spatula used depends on what ingredients are being transferred or mixed.

- A steel (metal) spatula would not be used if making a mixture that contains metallic ions.

- A rubber spatula is used to handle corrosive material.

Ointment Slabs

Ingredients are mixed into ointments on a compounding (or ointment) slab, which is a flat board made of porcelain or glass.

Fagron©

Slab and spatula

- Ointment slabs are used as a work surface for other purposes besides making ointments since the material is hard and non-reactive. For example, an ointment slab can be used to form pills (in which case it can be referred to as a pill tile) and for rolling out suppositories.

- Disposable parchment ointment pads can be used as a work surface if the water content of the mixture will not cause the paper to tear.

- Mixtures that have a higher water content than an ointment, such as a cream, can be mixed on an ointment slab if the mixture will hold its shape (and not flow off the slab). Otherwise, different equipment can be used to hold the preparation, such as a mortar bowl or a beaker.

Powder Sieves

Sieves are sifters similar to those used in baking.

Sieve

- After a powder has been ground fine, it is sifted in order to ensure a uniform particle size.

ELECTRIC MIXING EQUIPMENT

Mixing can be performed manually or with electric mixing equipment. Electric mixing speeds up the process.

- Ointment mills, homogenizers and grinders are used to mix ingredients.

- Ointment mills and grinders reduce the particle size, which increases the surface area and the rate of drug absorption.

Ointment Mills

An ointment mill draws the ointment (or another semi-solid preparation) between rollers that grind and homogenize (i.e., make non-gritty, smooth and uniform) the ingredients in the preparation (see image).

Fagron©

Ointment mill

Homogenizers

A homogenizer (also called an electric mortar and pestle) can be used to mix ointments, creams or other semi-solid preparations.

GAKO®

Homogenizer (also called an electric mortar & pestle)

- The homogenizer is similar to a smoothie blender, although with more power, and at a higher cost (see image). Homogenizers can be small and hand-held.

- A popular brand of homogenizer is called the *Unguator*.

- There are other homogenizer manufacturers that make various models (e.g., *PharmaRAM* or *Mazerustar Mixer*).

Grinders

Electric grinders are similar to coffee bean grinders. In fact, coffee bean grinders are used in some pharmacies. When used for compounding, they must be dedicated for compounding use only (i.e., not for coffee bean grinding). A grinder is useful for grinding hard tablets down. The powder will need further preparation to produce a fine powder.

Hot Plate with Magnetic Stirrer

A hot plate (see next section) with a magnetic stirrer can save time by continuously stirring the mixture to dissolve and mix the ingredients.

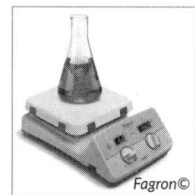

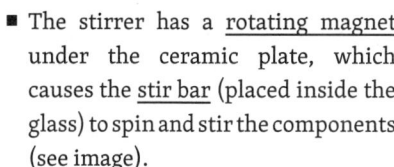

Hot plate with a stir bar in the glass. A magnet inside the hot plate moves the stir bar.

- The stirrer has a rotating magnet under the ceramic plate, which causes the stir bar (placed inside the glass) to spin and stir the components (see image).

- Hot plates are used without the stir bar to heat only (a glass stirring rod can be used to mix contents manually).

HEATING DEVICES

Heating with Hot Plates

Hot plates provide direct heat to soften and melt ingredients, and to hasten chemical reactions. Heat must be carefully controlled to avoid burning.

- A water bath is helpful when the temperature needs to be carefully controlled. The water bath protects the ingredients from overheating and burning.

- The ingredients to be melted will be in a container (e.g., a beaker) that is placed into a larger container filled with water.

- The water in the outer container separates the inner container from the direct heat source, to prevent burning.

Heating with Microwave Ovens

Microwave ovens heat quickly; be careful that the heat is applied uniformly as some microwaves provide uneven heat.

MOLDS, TABLET PRESSES AND CAPSULE MACHINES

Reusable or disposable molds are used to prepare tablets, lozenges/troches (orally-dissolving tablets) and suppositories.

- With soft delivery vehicles, such as suppositories and lozenges, the medication is often dispensed in a disposable plastic mold. This helps keep the product in the correct shape. Refrigeration helps soft products retain shape.

Tablets

A tablet press (or tablet mold) is two plastic or metal plates used to compress damp powder into tablets.

- Similar to forcing *Play-Doh* into a mold to form a shape, the compounder takes the pasty mass and uses the tablet press to form tablet shapes.

- After the mold shapes the tablets, the tablets are removed, and given time to dry.

Capsules

Capsules can be soft gels or hard shells, which are more commonly used for compounding. The shells are made of gelatin, which is pork-derived and will not be suitable for some patients, or from hypromellose or a similar plant-derived product. Hypromellose is a cellulose product, as the name implies.

- Capsule sizes for human use range from 000 (the largest size) to 5 (the smallest size). Veterinary pharmacists can order larger capsule sizes for use in large animals.

- Capsule bodies are filled with the drugs and excipients, and the capsule caps are placed over the bodies by hand or with a capsule machine.

Tube Sealers

Tube-sealers heat and squeeze the ends of tubes shut; the end will look similar to the crimped end of a toothpaste tube.

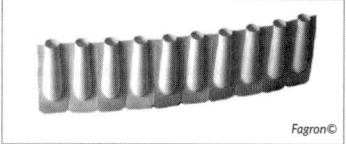

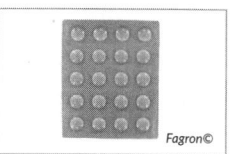

Suppository mold   *Lozenge mold*

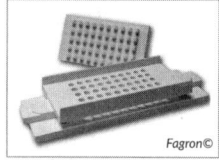

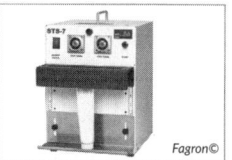

Tablet press   *Tube sealer (sealed at bottom)*

COMPOUNDING INGREDIENTS

All medications, whether compounded or not, include the drug/s (called the active pharmaceutical ingredients, or APIs) and the excipients. Excipients do not produce therapeutic effect, but are needed to make the dosage form stable, functional and, with some oral dosage forms, palatable.

HIGH QUALITY INGREDIENTS REQUIRED

High-quality ingredients ensure the purity and safety of the formulation. Ingredients that are recommended for use will be listed in either:

- The USP National Formulary (USP-NF)

- The Food Chemicals Codex (FCC) substances list

Preferably, ingredients should be manufactured at an FDA-registered facility. If any substance comes from a non-FDA registered facility, a Certificate of Analysis (CoA) should be obtained that confirms the specifications and quality.

If any component is moved to a different container, the new container should be labeled with the component name, original supplier, lot or control number, transfer date and expiration date.

MISSING EXPIRATION DATE

Ingredients <u>degrade</u>, and <u>expiration dates</u> are important to ensure that the product <u>retains potency</u> and is <u>non-toxic</u>. If there is an ingredient <u>without</u> an <u>expiration date</u>, the pharmacist will <u>assign</u> a conservative (cautious) date that is <u>no more than 3 years</u> from the date of receipt (the day the pharmacy received the item). The label on the container should include:

- The <u>date of receipt</u>
- The <u>assigned expiration date</u>

SURFACTANTS

SALAD DRESSING CHEMISTRY

Preparations can have multiple phases, similar to an oil and vinegar salad dressing, which has an oil phase that will become dispersed in the watery phase (the vinegar) when shaken. The dressing will quickly settle back into the two distinct phases because the "<u>tension</u>" between the two <u>surfaces</u> is <u>high</u>; the oil and water will repel each other. A surfactant added to the salad dressing will lower the tension between the two surfaces, and <u>keep</u> the <u>phases from</u> quickly <u>separating</u>.

Lowering the Surface Tension

<u>Surfactant</u> is a contraction of the words <u>surface active agent</u>. Surfactants <u>lower</u> the <u>surface tension</u> (i.e., the <u>interfacial tension</u>) between <u>two ingredients (or phases)</u> in a preparation to make them more <u>miscible</u> (i.e., easier to <u>mix together</u>). The side of the phase that is close to the other phase is the "face" of the phase, and the interfacial tension is the tension at the interface. The surfactant lowers the interfacial tension, to help the phases move closer together.

SURFACTANT MECHANISM OF ACTION

The common mechanism of action of a surfactant involves forming a micelle structure (see micelle figure, in first box to the right), which can reverse (turn inside-out). If oil and water are mixed, the oil will interact with the <u>lipophilic (lipid-loving) end</u> of the surfactant, and the water will interact with the <u>hydrophilic (water-loving) end</u> of the surfactant. <u>Surfactants</u> are <u>amphiphilic</u>; they are both hydrophilic (on one side) and hydrophobic (on the other side).

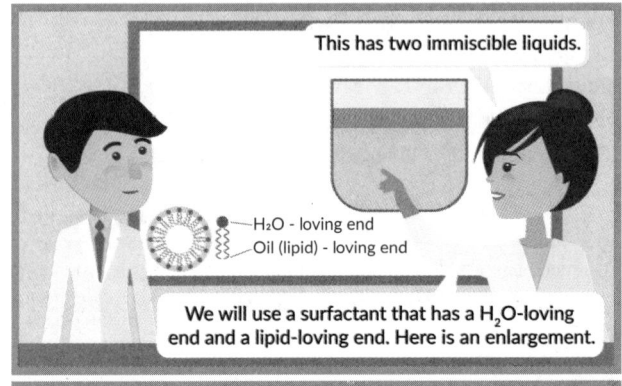

This has two immiscible liquids.

H₂O - loving end
Oil (lipid) - loving end

We will use a surfactant that has a H$_2$O-loving end and a lipid-loving end. Here is an enlargement.

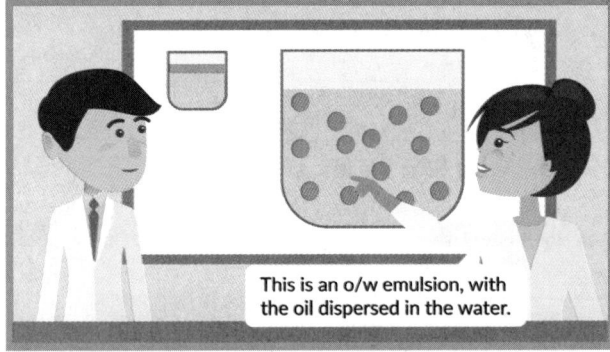

This is an o/w emulsion, with the oil dispersed in the water.

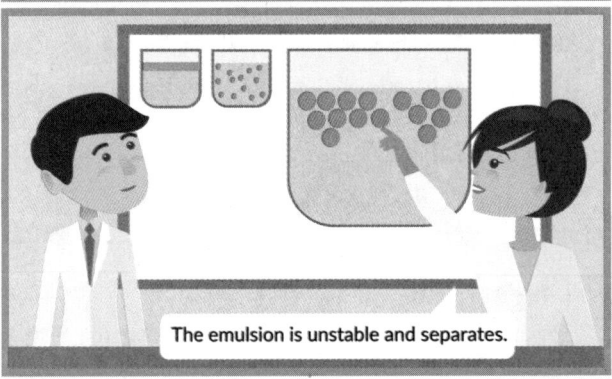

The emulsion is unstable and separates.

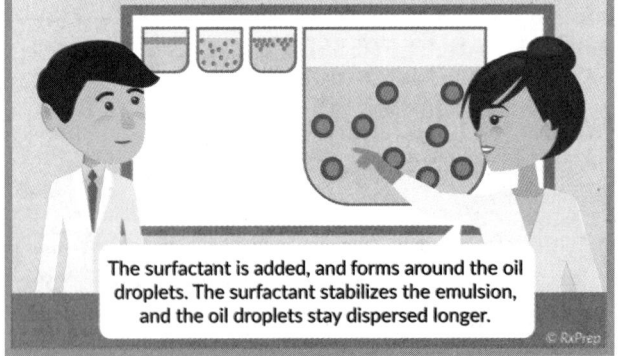

The surfactant is added, and forms around the oil droplets. The surfactant stabilizes the emulsion, and the oil droplets stay dispersed longer.

Non-Micelle Mechanisms

Surfactants do not always form micelles; some form a film between the surfaces, or form an electrically-charged layer to keep the phases separate. With all mechanisms, the surface tension is lowered, which helps with drug preparation and stabilization.

SURFACTANTS HAVE MANY USES

Surfactants have practical uses in addition to aiding in the formation of homogenous preparations. By keeping the drug dispersed, a consistent dose is delivered. In manufacturing, the micelles formed by surfactants are used to facilitate gut absorption of lipophilic drugs, similar to the way bile acids facilitate absorption of cholesterol, and are used to control the rate of drug release.

When the surface tension is lowered, it is easier to grind particles down, and to mix ingredients. Surfactants are called by a variety of names, depending on the use or the type of preparation, as described below.

TYPES OF SURFACTANTS

Wetting Agents

Wetting agents are substances that reduce the surface tension between a liquid and a solid to permit the substance to more easily spread. A fine powder that will be incorporated into a suspension is wetted with a wetting agent and stirred into a thick paste prior to being put into the delivery vehicle. Levigating agents (see next column) can be referred to as wetting agents.

Emulsifiers

An emulsion is two or more liquids which are not able to be blended together (immiscible), such as water droplets dispersed in oil, or oil droplets dispersed in water. Emulsifiers are added to an emulsion to help keep the liquid droplets dispersed throughout the liquid vehicle. This helps prevent the two liquids from separating into distinct (separate) phases. Emulsifiers can be called emulgents.

Suspending Agents

A suspension is a solid dispersed in a liquid (e.g., sulfamethoxazole powder does not dissolve in water, and is delivered as a suspension). Suspending agents are added to suspensions to help keep the solid particles from settling. Suspending agents do not keep suspensions separated for long, and suspensions must be shaken to redisperse the solid prior to use. Suspending agents can be called dispersants (or dispersing agents). A suspending agent can be a plasticizer, where plasticizer means that it will make the preparation easier to shape or mold. Sorbitol can be used as a plasticizer for gelatin capsules.

COMMERCIALLY AVAILABLE SUSPENDING AGENTS

Ora-Plus:
- Composed of a gel-like structure that keeps drug particles suspended and prevents settling
- Slightly acidic to prevent drug degradation through oxidation
- Bland taste; must be combined with *Ora-Sweet* for flavor

Ora-Sweet:
- Similar to simple syrup
- Provides flavor to *Ora-Plus*

Ora-Blend is a commercially available combination of *Ora-Plus* and *Ora-Sweet*

Ora-Sweet and *Ora-Blend* are available in sugar-free formulations sweetened with saccharin (*Ora-Sweet SF, Ora-Blend SF*)

Levigating Agents

Levigation and trituration are both used to grind down particles (i.e., make particles smaller); the difference is that levigation uses a levigating agent (also called a levigant) such as glycerin or mineral oil to aid in the grinding. Trituration is the grinding of particles without the addition of a liquid (the powder stays dry). Mineral oil is a commonly used levigating agent for lipophilic (oil-soluble) compounds, and glycerin or propylene glycol are used for aqueous (water-soluble) compounds.

Foaming Agent

Foaming agents help foam to form (e.g., in soap) by lowering the surface tension of water. A major use of surfactants in manufacturing is in detergents, where they foam and remove dirt. In non-sterile compounding, anti-foaming agents are more commonly used (e.g., simethicone).

Glycols & Gels are Used as Surfactants and Delivery Vehicles

The commonly used products polyethylene glycol (PEG) and poloxamer, by itself or as the P in PLO gel (described later), are both delivery vehicles and surfactants.

PEG and poloxamer have both hydrophilic and hydrophobic parts, which makes them useful for a variety of preparations. For example, poloxamer gel can be used to distribute ingredients in a preparation into the "like" phase [i.e., the hydrophobic compound distributes into the organic (lipophilic) phase, and the hydrophilic compound distributes into the water-based phase]. Poloxamer is useful for topical drug delivery.

THE HYDROPHILIC-LIPOPHILIC BALANCE

When a pharmacist wishes to disperse a liquid into a liquid to form an emulsion, selecting the right surfactant is important to keep the liquid droplets adequately dispersed.

A primary consideration in selecting the surfactant to use in an emulsion will be whether the emulsion is a water-in-oil (w/o) emulsion or an oil-in-water (o/w) emulsion.

- The taste of w/o formulations is not palatable; they are primarily used topically.

- Oral formulations are typically o/w formulations.

The hydrophilic-lipophilic balance (HLB) number determines the type of surfactant required to make an emulsion (see Study Tip Gal to the right).

The following table has examples of surfactants and their HLB values. There are many available surfactants; these are just a handful.

In the table, PEG 400 and *Tween 85* have HLB values greater than 10, and would be possible options for forming an o/w emulsion. The HLB values that are less than 10 (e.g., *Span 65*) would be possible options for forming a w/o emulsion.

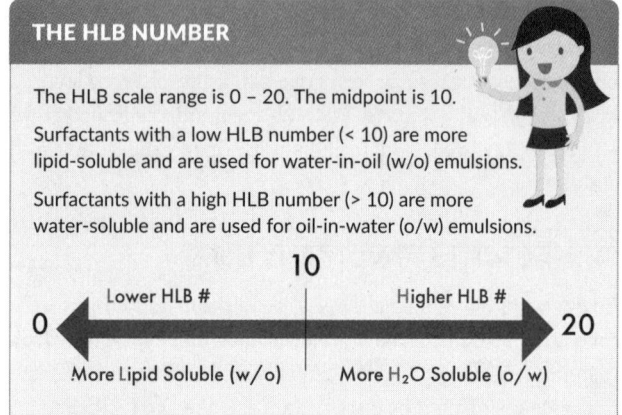

THE HLB NUMBER

The HLB scale range is 0 – 20. The midpoint is 10.

Surfactants with a low HLB number (< 10) are more lipid-soluble and are used for water-in-oil (w/o) emulsions.

Surfactants with a high HLB number (> 10) are more water-soluble and are used for oil-in-water (o/w) emulsions.

10

Lower HLB #   Higher HLB #

0   20

More Lipid Soluble (w/o)   More H_2O Soluble (o/w)

We are Miscible.
We mix well together.

No, we are Immiscible.
We do not mix well at all.

© RxPrep

Examples of Surfactants and their HLB Values

COMMERCIAL NAME	CHEMICAL NAME	HLB VALUE
Glyceryl monostearate	Glyceryl monostearate	3.8
PEG 400 monooleate	Polyoxyethylene monooleate	11.4
Span 65	Sorbitan tristearate	2.1
Tween 81	Polyoxyethylene sorbitan monooleate	10
Tween 85	Polyoxyethylene sorbitan trioleate	11

STABILITY AND DEGRADATION

STABILITY OF COMPOUNDED PREPARATIONS

USP defines stability as the extent to which a product retains, within specified limits, and throughout its period of storage and use (i.e., the shelf-life), the same properties and characteristics it possessed at the time it was made. The stability of compounded products can be easily compromised if they are not prepared or stored properly. This can be recognized by changes in texture, color, smell or development of precipitates.

Functional Groups Are Susceptible to Degradation

The differences between drugs with similar chemical structures lies in the functional groups that are attached to the compound's core structure and the bonds that hold the compound together. Reactions involving the functional groups are common causes of drug degradation and can make the drug ineffective, unpalatable and toxic.

Reactions that Cause Drug Degradation

USP emphasizes three types of chemical reactions that cause most drug products to become unstable and degrade:

- Oxidation-Reduction
- Hydrolysis
- Photolysis

The following section describes each of these reactions and methods that reduce the likelihood of these reactions (e.g., light and moisture protection) to extend the stability of the preparation. Drug degradation in the body (i.e., metabolism) is reviewed in the Drug Interactions and Pharmacokinetics chapters.

OXIDATION

A compound is <u>oxidized</u> when it <u>loses electrons</u> and is <u>reduced</u> when it <u>gains electrons</u>. Oxidation and reduction reactions occur together; when one compound is oxidized, another must be reduced at the same time. This is called the <u>re-dox</u> reaction. With some drugs, <u>oxidation</u> is visible with a <u>color change</u>, such as epinephrine becoming <u>amber-colored (yellow/orangish)</u>. Other compounds turn <u>pink/reddish</u> when <u>oxidized</u>.

Which Compounds are Likely to Become Oxidized?

The molecular structures most likely to oxidize are those with a <u>hydroxyl (–OH) group</u> directly bonded to an aromatic ring, such as catecholamines (e.g., epinephrine), phenolics (e.g., phenylephrine) and aldehydes (e.g., various structures used as flavorings).

An example <u>epinephrine oxidation</u> is shown below. Another example of oxidation that can be seen (and enjoyed) is cooking onions to cause <u>caramelization</u>. The sugar is caramelized in a series of reactions, which begins when the <u>alcohol functional group</u> in the sugar is <u>oxidized</u>. An <u>alcohol</u> is a <u>hydroxyl</u> functional group (<u>–OH) bound</u> to a <u>carbon</u>. The <u>water</u> is removed when the steam <u>evaporates</u>. The end product has a visible color change and a change in taste (i.e., brown, caramel-flavored onions).

Example: Oxidation of Epinephrine. The presence of the hydroxyl groups on the ring make oxidation more likely.

How can Oxidation be Prevented?

Oxidation is catalyzed by heat, light and metal ions. Changes in temperature and pH must be carefully controlled; either can exponentially increase <u>oxidation</u> (and will do the same for <u>hydrolysis</u> reactions, described next).

Light protection	With <u>amber</u> glass, UV light-blocking containers (e.g., plastic) and light-protective sleeves (bags) for IV bags, IV lines and syringes.
Adequate storage	Temperature control with <u>refrigeration</u>, control of room temperatures and (occasionally) freezer storage.
Chelating agents	Use chelators to <u>chelate metal ions</u> that have an <u>unshared electron</u> in the outer shell. These are <u>free radicals</u>, which can catalyze <u>oxidation chain reactions</u>. The <u>chelating agent</u> ties up the catalyst, <u>preventing the reaction</u>. Common chelators have the letters **ED**: EDetate disodium (<u>EDTA</u>), EDetate calcium disodium and EDetic Acid.
Antioxidants Also called: <u>free radical scavengers</u>	<u>Oxidation</u> produces <u>free radicals</u>, which are highly reactive with other compounds, and cause a chain reaction that damages the compound (see chelating agents above). Autoxidation is when oxidation reactions occur routinely during preparation and storage. <u>Antioxidants</u> inhibit free radicals. Common antioxidants include <u>ascorbic acid (vitamin C), tocopherols (vitamin E)</u>, ascorbyl palmitate, Na ascorbate, Na bisulfate, Na sulfoxylate and Na thiosulfate.
Control pH	<u>Maintain pH</u> with a <u>buffer</u>; see pH discussion that follows.

HYDROLYSIS

<u>Hydrolysis</u> occurs when <u>water</u> causes the cleavage of a bond in a molecule. Compounds likely to undergo hydrolysis should not be exposed to moisture. Counseling should include to avoid storing products susceptible to hydrolysis in the bathroom and to close containers tightly. <u>Desiccants</u> are sometimes used to soak up any moisture that enters the container.

Which Compounds are Likely to Become Hydrolyzed?

The most common functional groups susceptible to hydrolysis are esters, amides and lactams. The carbonyl group is subject to hydrolysis.

Ester Carbonyl group bonded to an OR group	
Amide Carbonyl group bonded to a Nitrogen	
Lactam, a cyclic amide This is a beta-lactam ring, present in penicillins, carbapenems, cephalosporins and monobactams.	

Example: Hydrolysis of the ester group on acetylsalicylic acid (aspirin) to form acetic acid and salicylic acid. In this case, hydrolysis is beneficial. The analgesic is salicylic acid, which is formed by hydrolysis of the prodrug acetylsalicylic acid.

Aspirin - acetylsalicylic acid → Salicylic acid + Acetic acid

How Can Hydrolysis be Prevented?

To reduce hydrolysis, the compound should be protected from moisture (water) exposure and other factors that favor degradation, including light exposure, metal ions and changes in temperature and pH.

Light protection	See Oxidation table.
Adsorbents (desiccants)	To adsorb any moisture that enters the container.
Lyophilized powders	Drugs can be stored as a lyophilized (freeze-dried) powder instead of in solution.
Chelating agents	See Oxidation table.
Hygroscopic salt	Hygroscopic means water-absorbing. In some cases, a salt form of the drug can be chosen that is less hygroscopic, will absorb less water and will be less likely to degrade from hydrolysis.
Prodrug formulation	Prodrugs that release the active drug by a hydrolysis reaction can be formulated [e.g., acetylsalicylic acid (aspirin) is hydrolyzed to salicylic acid (the analgesic) and acetic acid].
Control temperature	Control the temperature in which the product is stored; hydrolysis occurs more rapidly at higher temperatures.
Control pH	Maintain pH with a buffer; see pH discussion that follows.

PHOTOLYSIS

Many drugs are sensitive to UV light exposure, which causes photolysis (breakage) of covalent bonds and drug degradation. Photolysis can be prevented with light protection.

Which Compounds are Likely to Become Degraded by Light Exposure?

Compounds that are sensitive to light include ascorbic acid, folic acid, nitroprusside and phytonadione injection. Intravenous drugs that require light protection are discussed in the Intravenous Medication Principles chapter.

ADDITIONAL PROCESSES THAT DEGRADE DRUGS

Other reactions that degrade drugs include:

- Isomerization, when a compound changes into a form with the same atoms but an inactive structure.

- Epimerization, when a compound changes into an isomer that differs only in the configuration of the atoms. The two compounds are stereoisomers. Epimerization creates a chiral counterpart. The epimer can be inactive, or active (e.g., doxorubicin is active, and epirubicin, the epimer, is also active).

- Decarboxylation can happen to compounds with dissolved carboxylic acids. When heated, the carbon dioxide is lost from the carboxyl group. Drugs at risk of decarboxylation can be kept refrigerated.

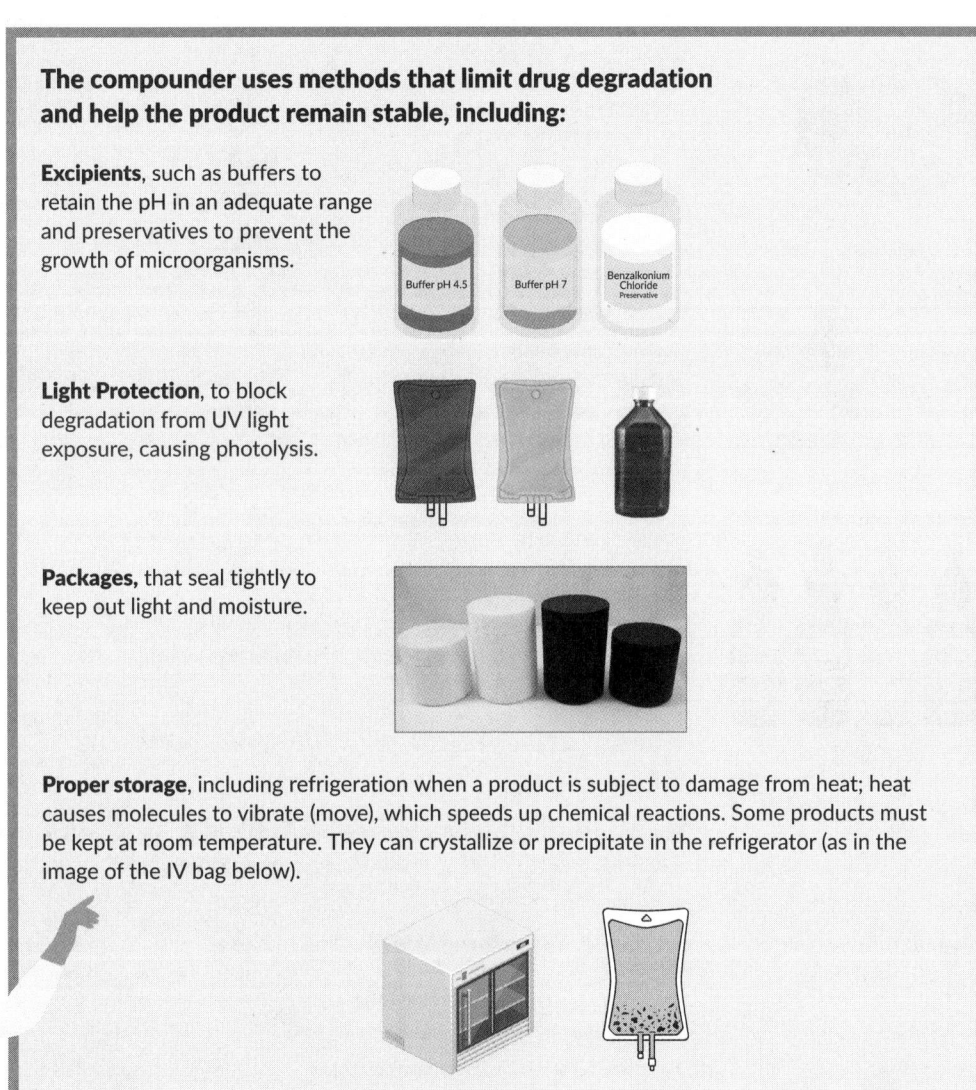

The compounder uses methods that limit drug degradation and help the product remain stable, including:

Excipients, such as buffers to retain the pH in an adequate range and preservatives to prevent the growth of microorganisms.

Buffer pH 4.5   Buffer pH 7   Benzalkonium Chloride Preservative

Light Protection, to block degradation from UV light exposure, causing photolysis.

Packages, that seal tightly to keep out light and moisture.

Proper storage, including refrigeration when a product is subject to damage from heat; heat causes molecules to vibrate (move), which speeds up chemical reactions. Some products must be kept at room temperature. They can crystallize or precipitate in the refrigerator (as in the image of the IV bag below).

©RxPrep

EXCIPIENTS

MAJOR EXCIPIENTS

MAJOR EXCIPIENTS	PURPOSE AND NOTES	EXAMPLES
Binders *ahasoft2000 © 123RF.com*	Binders allow the contents of a tablet to stick together while permitting the contents to be released once ingested. They can provide stability and strength.	Acacia Starch paste Sucrose syrup Compressible sugar (e.g., *Nu-Tab*)

Diluents and fillers
 	
 iStock.com/Anna_zabella
	Diluents (to make something more dilute) and fillers (to bulk up a small amount) add size to very small dosages.
	
	 In liquids, the diluent helps suspend the drug and facilitates disintegration, which is required for absorption (see disintegrants below).
		Tablets/capsules:
		 Sugars:
		   Lactose
		   Mannitol
		   Sorbitol
		 Starches
		 Calcium salts
		 Cellulose powder (many uses)
		
		 Liquids:
		 Water
		 Glycerin
		 Alcohol
		
		 Topicals:
		 Petrolatum
		 Mineral oil
		 Lanolin
		 Waxes

Disintegrants *ahasoft2000 © 123RF.com*	Facilitates the breakup of a tablet after oral administration. Oral products have to be dissolved in order to be absorbed in the small intestine, where most drugs are absorbed. Alginates and cellulose absorb water, causing the tablet to swell and release its contents.	Alginic acid Cellulose products Polacrilin potassium (e.g., *Amberlite*) Starches

Flavorings and coloring agents
 	
 Olzas/Shutterstock.com
	Flavorings and coloring agents make the product look and taste better.
	
	 Salty or sweet tastes mask a bitter flavor. Mint and spices mask poor flavor. Acids (such as citric acid) enhance fruit flavors.
		Coloring agents:
		 D&C Red No. 3
		 Yellow No. 6
		 Caramel
		 Ferric oxide (red)
		
		 Sweeteners:
		 Non-caloric, artificial:
		   Aspartame
		   Saccharin
		   Sucralose
		 Glycerin
		 Dextrose
		 Sugar alcohols (e.g., mannitol, sorbitol, xylitol)
		 Stevia, monk fruit extract

Lubricants	Can be called glidants or anti-adherents. Lubricants and anti-adherents prevent ingredients from sticking to each other and to equipment. This can be useful for tablet molds and punches, suppository molds and for capsule filling. Glidants improve powder flowability by reducing interparticle friction.	Magnesium stearate, calcium stearate, stearic acid Colloidal silica PEG Glycerin Mineral oil Talc
Preservatives	Preservatives slow or prevent microorganism growth. They are required in most preparations except if sterile and used immediately or if sealed in single-use preparations. Ophthalmic (eye) preparations in multi-dose containers need a preservative. Do not use preservatives in neonates. Alcohols and acids are often used as preservatives. Preservatives commonly have "benz," "cetyl," "phenyl/ol" and "parabens" in the name.	Chlorhexidine [also used as an antiseptic in surgical scrubs to eliminate or reduce microorganisms (*Hibiclens*) and as a dental rinse (*Peridex*)] Povidone iodine (used as a topical antiseptic and as a preservative in some ophthalmics) Sodium benzoate/benzoic acid, benzalkonium chloride, benzyl alcohol Sorbic acid/potassium sorbate Methyl/ethyl/propyl parabens EDTA Thimerosal (contains mercury, used in some vaccines) Cetylpyridinium chloride

MAJOR EXCIPIENTS	PURPOSE AND NOTES	EXAMPLES
Buffers Buffer pH 4.5 Buffer pH 7 📷 iStock.com/Cathal Stadler	Buffers keep the pH within a certain range, which can improve stability and solubility and decrease irritation to sensitive tissues in the body. Ionized compounds are more polar, which makes them more water-soluble. The pKa determines how much of a compound is ionized when placed into a solution with a set pH. The pH of a buffer system can be calculated with the Henderson-Hasselbalch equation (see the Calculations IV and Compounding III chapters).	**Buffers used to maintain acidic pH:** Hydrochloric acid Acetic acid/sodium acetate Citric acid/sodium citrate **Buffers used to maintain alkaline pH:** Sodium hydroxide Boric acid/sodium borate Sodium bicarbonate/sodium carbonate **Buffers used to maintain neutral pH:** Sodium biphosphate/sodium phosphate Potassium phosphate/metaphosphate

SOLVENTS

Hydrophilic Solvents

SOLVENTS	PURPOSE AND NOTES	EXAMPLES
Water 	Water is commonly used as a solvent, as a delivery vehicle and for cleaning equipment and tools. As a delivery vehicle, water is used for oral liquid formulations (e.g., solutions, suspensions, emulsions), topicals (e.g., creams, lotions) and in all types of injectable medications.	USP specifies that purified water must be used in compounding, unless otherwise specified. Purified water has been treated to remove chemicals and contaminants. Types of purification include distillation, deionization, reverse osmosis and carbon filtration. Distilled water is used for reconstitution [i.e., adding water to lyophilized (freeze-dried) powder] to prepare oral suspensions and in non-sterile compounding preparations. Potable water (drinking/tap water) is safe to drink and used for hand washing and initial equipment cleaning.
Sterile Water 📷 Burlingham/Shutterstock.com	For preparation and reconstitution of sterile drugs. Sterile water must be free of microorganisms.	Sterile water for injection (SWFI) must be free of bacterial endotoxins (pyrogens) produced by microorganisms that inhabit water. Bacteriostatic water for injection: SWFI with antimicrobial preservatives. Sterile water for irrigation: sterile water packaged in large containers for washing, rinsing and dilution of products used for irrigating body cavities, wounds, urinary catheters or surgical drainage tubes.
Alcohols 📷 Mohd Syis Zulkipli/Shutterstock.com	Alcohols have high miscibility (mixes easily) with water and can be used to dissolve solutes that would be insoluble in water alone. Isopropyl alcohols (IPAs) are used as disinfectants on equipment or on skin (e.g., on an alcohol swab for skin disinfection prior to a needle stick). They can be used as solvents when compounding topicals.	Benzyl alcohol: used as a solvent, preservative and for the aroma (fragrance). Alcohol USP: ethanol (grain alcohol, ethyl alcohol or drinking alcohol), can be used as an alternative to fomepizole for methanol or ethylene glycol toxicity. Methanol (toxic): fuel, used to make many chemicals. IPA 70%: preferred disinfectant in sterile compounding.
Glycols Polyethylene glycol (PEG) is a long, synthetic polymer. PEGs are numbered based on the molecular weight (e.g., PEG 400 and PEG 3350). The size/molecular weight depends on the number of times the structure inside the parentheses repeats: H–(O–CH2–CH2)n–OH	Glycols have a low freezing point (which makes antifreeze possible), a high boiling point and are water-soluble. PEG has low toxicity and low systemic absorption, making it a useful excipient. It is used as a surfactant, solvent, plasticizer, suppository base, ointment base, lubricant and troche base. It is water-soluble and water-miscible (mixes well with water into a homogenous mixture).	PEG 400 is used commonly in compounding and PEG 3350 is used as a laxative. When PEG is linked to a protein drug (pegylated), such as PEG-filgrastim, it increases the half-life. Polybase is a PEG mixture used as a suppository base. It is a good delivery vehicle and slides out of molds without the need for a lubricant. It is also a good emulsifier. Methoxy-polyethylene glycol (MPEG) Glycerin Propylene glycol: used in small quantities as a solvent (large quantities are toxic) Ethylene glycol (toxic): antifreeze

Hydrophobic Solvents

SOLVENTS	PURPOSE AND NOTES	EXAMPLES
Oils and Fats Oils are hydrocarbon liquids derived from plants, animals or petroleum [i.e., petrolatum (*Vaseline petroleum jelly*)]. Oils are immiscible in water; they are hydrophobic, lipophilic compounds.	Oils are used as delivery vehicles, for therapeutic or nutritional use, and some are used as scents and flavorings.	Mineral oil: derived from petroleum, and is the ingredient in *Baby Oil* Almond, borage, canola, castor, coconut Omega-3 (alpha-linolenic fatty acids, DHA/EPA) Omega-6 (gamma-linoleic fatty acids)

EMOLLIENTS (MOISTURIZERS)

Prior to reviewing the emollients below, it is helpful to note the differences between emollients. An emollient refers to a product that softens and soothes the skin. Occlusive ointments, including petroleum jelly (i.e., white petrolatum), theobroma oil (i.e., cocoa butter), beeswax, paraffin and other waxes form a protective barrier to prevent the loss of water molecules from the top layer of the skin (epidermis). Humectants are put into many emollient formulations to pull in water from the atmosphere to moisturize the skin. They can be sticky-feeling, and are combined with other more soothing ingredients. Humectants include glycerin or glycerol, propylene glycol, PEG, urea and hyaluronic acid.

Ointments have 80 – 100% oil, 0 – 20% water, and are best for extremely dry skin and thick skin, such as on elbows and feet. Creams are usually about half oil, half water (minimally greater than 20% water and up to 50% oil) and are best for normal and dry skin. Lotions have the most water, and are best for oily skin.

EMOLLIENT	PURPOSE AND NOTES	EXAMPLES
Ointments USP separates ointments into 4 groups. Some contain water and some do not, which is important in determining the BUD; see the Compounding III chapter. The four ointment groups are listed below.	Ointments are defined as semisolids, with 0 – 20% water hydrocarbons, waxes and/or polyols (compounds with multiple OH groups). Provide a barrier to water loss from the skin and are used as vehicles for topical drug delivery. In some products the emollient components are mixed with humectants, which draw water into the skin, and make the product less greasy.	Common emollients: Petrolatum, lanolin, mineral oil, dimethicone Common combination products: *Polybase*: PEG 400, PEG 8000, polysorbate 80; water-soluble, water-miscible *Aquaphor* (OTC): 41% petrolatum, with mineral oil, lanolin, glycerin + other ingredients. Semi-occlusive barrier, less greasy than petrolatum. *Aquabase* (OTC): similar to *Aquaphor*
1. Hydrocarbon Bases	Called "oleaginous" ointments (oil-containing, no water); good for drug delivery and forming a protective barrier, hard to wash off/greasy.	White ointment, white petrolatum (e.g., *Vaseline petroleum jelly*)
2. Absorption Bases	Can be used to form water-in-oil emulsions, useful as emollients.	Hydrophilic petrolatum, lanolin
3. Water-Removable Bases	Hydrophilic, oil-in-water emulsions. Per USP, more correctly called creams; more easily diluted, and easier to wash off the skin.	Hydrophilic ointment
4. Water-Soluble Bases	Do not contain petrolatum; per USP, are more correctly called gels.	Polyethylene glycol ointment
Creams More water than ointments.	Creams are semi-solid preparations that have a soft, spreadable consistency. Most creams are water-in-oil or oil-in-water emulsions. Water-in-oil creams feel more greasy.	*Lipoderm* cream *Eucerin*: water, petrolatum, mineral oil, ceresin, lanolin + other ingredients *Cetaphil*: water, glycerin, petrolatum, dimethicone, benzyl alcohol, PEG + other ingredients
Lotions More water than creams, which makes them more fluid. Lotions are sometimes poured from a container, which is not feasible with creams.	Lotions can be aqueous or hydroalcoholic, with a small amount of alcohol added to solubilize ingredients, or to hasten evaporation of the solvent from the skin.	*Versabase* lotion

Gels Gels are semisolid preparations of small inorganic particles or large organic molecules interpenetrated by a liquid. If the gel has small discrete particles in it, it is classified as a two-phase system. If the particles are distributed uniformly so that the gel does not appear to have any discrete particles, it is a single-phase system.	Gels can be used to administer medications by various routes, including topical, oral, intranasal, vaginal and rectal. Aqueous solutions of poloxamers are <u>liquid when refrigerated</u> and form a <u>gel at room temperature</u>, in a reversible process. PLO gel is used often because of this property; compounds are easily mixed into the liquid (when taken from the refrigerator), which then forms a gel when stored at room temperature (see comic below).	Polyethylene + mineral oil (*Plastibase, Jelene*) Poloxamer 407NF <u>Poloxamer (Pluronic) Lecithin Organogel (PLO) gel</u> <u>Poloxamers</u> contain a <u>hydrophobic</u> chain of polyoxypropylene with two <u>hydrophilic</u> chains of polyoxyethylene. This means poloxamer gel can be used for hydrophobic or hydrophilic drug delivery.
Pastes	Pastes contain powder in an ointment base.	Zinc oxide paste, used for diaper rash; zinc oxide is a desiccant (draws water from the baby's bottom).
Suppository bases, made of various fats and glycols	Suppository bases have to stay intact for insertion, and melt once inserted. Theobroma oil (cocoa butter) used to be a common base for suppositories, but it melts easily. Newer bases are now more popular.	*Polybase*, cocoa butter (theobroma oil), <u>hydrogenated vegetable oils</u> (palm, palm kernel, and coconut oils), PEG polymers, glycerinated <u>gelatin</u>

COMPOUNDING & HAZARDOUS DRUGS

OTHER EXCIPIENTS

EXCIPIENTS	PURPOSE AND NOTES	EXAMPLES
Adsorbents	To keep powders dry, to prevent hydrolysis reactions.	Magnesium oxide/carbonate, kaolin
Anti-foaming agent	Breaks up and inhibits the formation of foams.	Simethicone, dimethicone
Coatings (regular)	Prevent degradation due to oxygen, light, moisture, mask unpalatable taste.	Shellac, gelatin, gluten (food grade)
Emulsifiers	Reduce the surface tension between two liquids (e.g., oil and water), allowing the two phases to come closer together. Emulsifiers are a type of surfactant.	Acacia, agar, carbomers, glyceryl monostearate, pectin, PEG, sodium lauryl sulfate, sorbitan lipophilic esters (Arlacel, Span), sorbitan hydrophilic esters (Myrj, Tween)
Enteric-coating	Most drugs dissolve in the stomach and are absorbed in the small intestine. Some drugs would be destroyed by stomach acid and require an acid-resistant (enteric-coated) protective layer to prevent dissolution in the stomach. The coating can also be used to mask poor taste.	Cellulose acetate phthalate Shellac (a natural polymer resin, from insects)
Gelling (thickening) agent, stabilizer	Increases the viscosity of a substance; can stabilize the mixture. Gelatin, cellulose and bentonite are used commonly; they swell well when mixed with water.	Agar, alginates, various gums [guar, xanthan, acacia (a natural gum)], gelatins, bentonite (a type of clay), carbomer, cellulose, starches, tragacanth, acrylates, cetyl alcohol, magnesium aluminum silicate (Veegum), poloxamer (pluronic) gels, polyvinyl alcohol (eye lubricant), sorbitol
Humectant	Prevents preparations from becoming dry and brittle; when put into emollients, draws water into the skin to moisturize.	Glycerin or glycerol, propylene glycol, PEG, lecithin, urea, hyaluronic acid
Levigating (wetting) agent	Liquid used in the process of reducing the particle size to reduce the surface tension.	Mineral oil, glycerin, glycols, PEG, propylene glycol

EXCIPIENTS TO BE AVOIDED IN SOME PATIENTS

EXCIPIENT	AVOID IN	ALTERNATIVE
Alcohol, used as a solvent.	Children	Select alternative solvent; see excipient table.
Aspartame (contains phenylalanine), used as a sweetener.	Phenylketonuria (PKU), not able to metabolize phenylalanine	Select alternative sweeteners; see excipient table.
Gelatin, used to form capsule shells.	Vegetarians and vegans, anyone who wishes to avoid pork	Hypromellose capsule shells are made from cellulose and are vegan (no meat or dairy) and vegetarian (no meat).
Gluten, used as a starch (filler). Gluten is in wheat, barley and rye. Gluten as a starch in drugs is primarily from wheat.	Celiac disease, anyone who wishes to avoid gluten	Starch can come from non-gluten sources (e.g., corn, potato, tapioca).
Lactose, used as a sweetener, to compress tablets and as a filler/diluent.	Lactose intolerance or lactose allergy	Lactose content may/may not cause symptoms (with intolerance) as the amount in compounded products can be small. Select an alternative (with lactose allergy, and possibly with lactose intolerance), depending on the purpose.
Preservatives (e.g., benzyl alcohol).	Neonates	Use preservative-free formulations.
Sorbitol, used as a sweetener.	Irritable bowel syndrome (IBS); sorbitol can cause GI distress in IBS	Select alternative sweeteners; see excipient table.
Sucrose (table sugar), used as a sweetener and coating.	Diabetes	The amount used may/may not cause the blood glucose to increase. Select alternative sweeteners; see excipient table.
Xylitol, used as a sweetener.	Do not use in dogs; it can cause xylitol toxicosis (hypoglycemia and liver damage). Xylitol can cause GI upset in humans.	Select alternative sweeteners; see excipient table.

CONTENT LEGEND

💡 = Study Tip Gal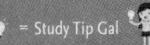

CHAPTER 17

COMPOUNDING III: DOCUMENTATION & PREPARATION

NON-STERILE PREPARATIONS

DOCUMENTATION

Two very important records that each compounded product must have are the master formula record and the compounding record. The master formula record is the recipe that is followed to compound a preparation. The compounding log (or record) is the log book of all products made at the pharmacy (see images on the following pages).

The documentation in the compounding log must be detailed enough that another trained person can replicate the steps involved in the preparation, evaluate if the procedure was correct and trace the origin of all components.

The pharmacy must keep records of steps and processes that relate to the compounded product, such as equipment cleaning, calibration and maintenance, temperature logs for the refrigerator, freezer and room (ambient) air, and records of chemicals, bulk drugs and drug products.

PREPARATION STEPS

Prior to preparing to compound, the pharmacist will need to evaluate the prescription and determine if it is appropriate for the patient, and whether the proposed formulation is reasonable (e.g., is the formulation likely to have acceptable stability and palatability?).

When ready to compound, the initial steps will be similar for most formulations, such as calibrating equipment and weighing ingredients. The final steps will be similar, and include packaging and performing quality control (QC). What changes most are the steps in between, which depend on the type of formulation to be prepared.

Always review the Safety Data Sheets (SDS) for each bulk ingredient to determine safety procedures for the staff who will compound the preparation, including the recommended personal protective equipment (PPE).

MASTER FORMULA #3755
IBUPROFEN 200 mg SUPPOSITORIES

Formula:

Ibuprofen 200mg Suppositories

Strength:	200mg		**Quantity:**	1

Ingredients:	**Quantity:**
Ibuprofen	0.2 gm
SilicaGel	0.02 gm
Base MBK (Fatty Acid Base)	Calculate

Procedure:

Note: calculations should be made to make an excess amount of 10% of the amount needed.

1. Calculate and weigh ingredients to prepare 10 Ibuprofen 200mg suppositories in the blue mold which is calibrated to 1.28 gm of *Base MBK* per suppository. Use the Suppository, General Formula worksheet.

2. Melt *Base MBK* at 50 degrees C using a hot water bath.

3. Using a mortar and pestle, triturate ibuprofen and *SilicaGel* together to a fine powder.

4. Sift the powder from Step 3 into the melted *Base MBK* while stirring. The use of a strainer helps to ensure small particle size.

5. Turn off heat and stir until mixture looks consistently suspended.

6. Pour into molds (may use a large bore syringe if available) and allow to cool to room temperature.

7. Package in universal sleeve and label.

Recommended Expiration:	180 days
Recommended Storage/ Auxiliary Labels:	Refrigerate
Notes:	

MASTER FORMULA
Compound's Official or Assigned Name
Strength, Dosage Form

Calculations

Ingredients, with quantities

Stability & Compatibility data, with references

Equipment

Preparation/Mixing instructions

Labeling information

Packaging/Storage requirements

Quality Control (QC) procedures, with expected results

BUD, recommended

Description of final product

What you SHOULD do

Formula # 3755

Raindrop Compounding Pharmacy
COMPOUNDING RECORD

PRODUCT

Drug Name and Strength	Use/Dosage Form	Quantity	Control/Rx #	Date
Ibuprofen 200 mg	Suppositories	#10	37-865	6-7-21

INGREDIENTS

Ingredient	NDC or Manufacturer #	QTY	LOT	EXP
Ibuprofen powder USP	IB100-25, Spectrum	2 g	A3472-19	3/24
Silica gel	S1935, Spectrum	0.2 g	S1008-19	12/23
MBK base	30-156, PCCA	12.8 g	1234-18	2/23
Disposable supp molds	Apothecary			

COMPOUNDING DIRECTIONS & PROCEDURES

1.	Calcs: Ibuprofen 0.2 g x 10 = 2 g, Silica 0.02 g x 10 = 0.2 g, MBK base 1.28 g x 10 = 12.8 g
2.	Weighed 12.8 g MBK base
3.	Placed base in beaker, heated in hot-water bath at warm temp of 50 °C
4.	Weighed 2 g ibuprofen, triturated in mortar & pestle with silica gel
5.	Added to melted base through 125 um powder sieve
6.	Stirred 8 minutes with heat off
7.	Poured into molds, slightly overfilled
8.	Solidified at room temp for 20 minutes, placed in refrigerator to harden for 1 hour
9.	Trimmed excess off top.
10.	QC Weight 1.5 g, smooth uniform surface, even color
11.	Description 1.5 g white suppositori

Weighed by: Dacy L

Prepared by: Dacy L

COMPOUNDING RECORD OR LOG

Compound's Official Name or Assigned Name
Reference # for the Master Formula
Strength, Dosage Form

Specific to this preparation

Ingredients (including manufacturers/sources, lot numbers & expiration dates)

Steps followed

QC results

BUD, actual (assigned)

Description of final product

The product's assigned lot or prescription number— a duplicate prescription label can be attached to the log

Staff involved with the preparation

(1) Compounder, (2) Person who did QC, (3) RPh who approved final product, with dates

What you DID

©RxPrep, Inc.

Preparation of Non-Sterile HDs

Non-sterile hazardous drugs (HDs) should preferably be compounded in a containment primary engineering control (C-PEC), discussed in the Compounding I chapter. This option is not always available, and efforts must be made to protect the staff with techniques to reduce exposure (e.g., splitting tablets while enclosed in a sealed plastic bag). All equipment used for HDs, including counting trays and spatulas, must be dedicated for HDs only, and sanitized after use.

The final formulations, when possible, should be placed into unit-dose sealed packaging, and placed into a plastic bag with a hazardous label (see the image on the right).

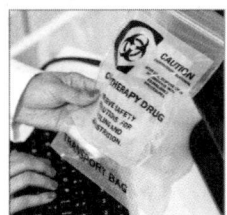
©Teva Canada Limited

The Formulation Determines the Type of Garb

Minimally, PPE (i.e., garb) should include a clean lab coat and gloves when preparing non-sterile, non-hazardous preparations. The SDS will provide information if other PPE is needed. For example, the SDS for benzalkonium chloride recommends using gloves, a gown and eye/face protection. Benzalkonium chloride should not be exposed to skin or mucus membranes, and the SDS provides instructions to manage exposure, such as steps to take if the compound is inhaled.

PPE is reviewed in the Compounding I chapter.

Initial Steps

1. Calculate the quantities needed for each component.

2. Gather all the components and the equipment needed.

3. Wash equipment, if needed, and calibrate.

4. Perform hand hygiene and garb.

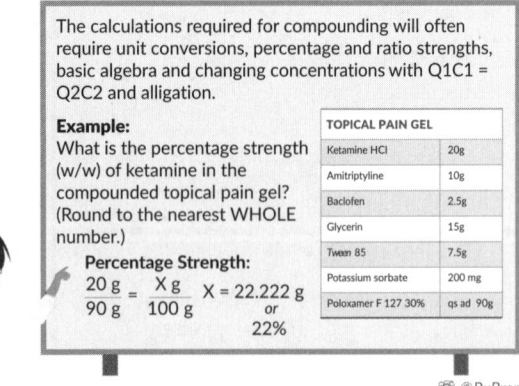

The calculations required for compounding will often require unit conversions, percentage and ratio strengths, basic algebra and changing concentrations with Q1C1 = Q2C2 and alligation.

Example:
What is the percentage strength (w/w) of ketamine in the compounded topical pain gel? (Round to the nearest WHOLE number.)

Percentage Strength:
$$\frac{20\,g}{90\,g} = \frac{X\,g}{100\,g} \quad X = 22.222\,g$$
$$\text{or}\quad 22\%$$

TOPICAL PAIN GEL	
Ketamine HCl	20g
Amitriptyline	10g
Baclofen	2.5g
Glycerin	15g
Tween 85	7.5g
Potassium sorbate	200 mg
Poloxamer F 127 30%	qs ad 90g

©RxPrep

Compounding Steps

Make the product according to the master formula.

- Most formulations will require common techniques, such as trituration, levigation and geometric dilution.

- Other steps are unique to the formulation type, such as calculating the density factor to make suppositories.

Completion Steps

1. Package the product and apply the container label and any needed auxiliary labels. A duplicate container label can be placed on the compounding record.

2. Perform QC: validate the weight, check the product for mixing adequacy, color, clarity, odor, consistency and pH. Enter the measurements and observations in the compounding record.

3. Counsel the patient, and if any subsequent adverse drug reactions (ADRs) are reported, add them to the compounding record.

PREPARING POWDERS

REDUCING PARTICLE SIZE

When making a compound with dry ingredients, the goal is to make an evenly-distributed mixture with fine powder. Comminution means to reduce particle size by grinding, crushing, milling, vibrating or other processes (manual or mechanical).

The compounder likely starts off with coarse granules or broken tablet pieces. Powders will be finely ground into particles that range in size from 0.1 – 10 microns. After the powder has been ground, it is placed into a sieve.

Using a powder sieve ensures uniform particle size
Magicleaf/Shutterstock.com

Sieves, which are sifters, are used to ensure that the particle size is uniform. The powder is put into the sieve and sifted through the mesh. Once placed into the sieve, the powder is stirred with a sieve brush or a plastic spatula to force the particles through the mesh. A high mesh size has many wires that make many holes, and only a fine powder will get through the mesh. The sieve number is based on the number of holes per inch (e.g., #100 sieve has 100 openings/inch).

Three Main Methods of Comminution

■ Trituration: a general term used to mean "mix thoroughly" (or make the product homogenous). Pharmacists most commonly associate trituration with grinding tablets with a mortar and pestle until a fine powder is achieved, but the term can describe liquids (e.g., triturating an emulsion by shaking it).

■ Levigation and spatulation:

❏ Levigation involves triturating the powder with a mortar and pestle and incorporating a small amount of liquid (called a levigating agent or wetting agent). This helps with the grinding process and creates a uniform paste.

❏ Spatulation is similar to levigation, but performed on an ointment slab with a spatula (not with a mortar and pestle).

■ Pulverization by intervention is used for crystalline powders that will not crush easily. The crystals are dissolved with an intervening solvent and mixed until the solvent evaporates. When the powder recrystallizes, the particles are finer.

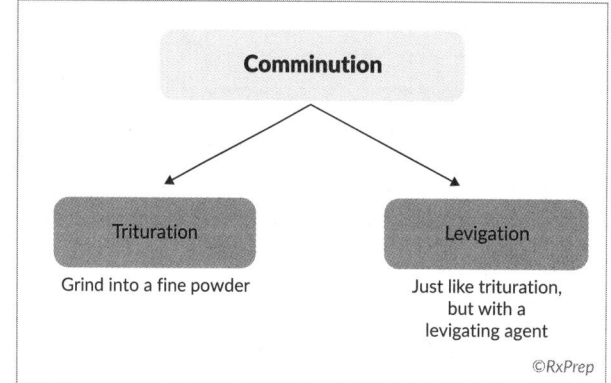

MIXING INGREDIENTS

Geometric dilution is a method of mixing ingredients to ensure that ingredients are evenly distributed in a diluent or delivery vehicle. A small amount of the drug is mixed into an equal amount of the diluent. After the initial small amount is thoroughly mixed, another equal amount of the ingredients is mixed in. This is repeated until all the ingredients are mixed together. Geometric dilution can be used with dry powder ingredients alone, or when making a paste. When using multiple ingredients, begin with the ingredient that has the smallest quantity, followed by the ingredient with the next smallest quantity, and up until each has been added. With each addition, the amount should be roughly doubled.

Geometric Dilution is used to Prepare Homogenous Products

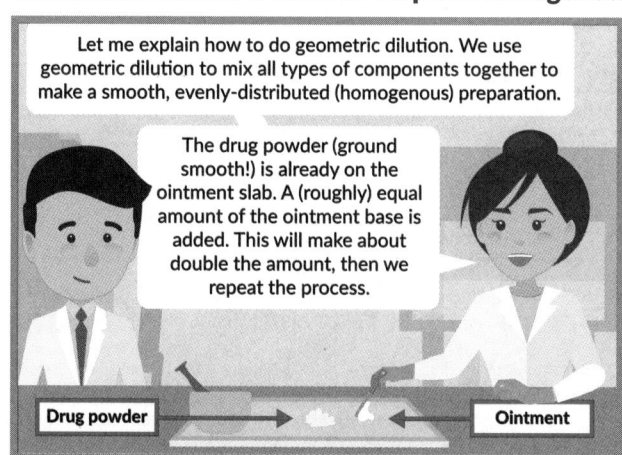

DOSAGE FORMS

SOLUTIONS, SUSPENSIONS AND EMULSIONS

A **SOLUTION** is a solute dissolved in a solvent (such as NaCl, dissolved in water).

Solutions are homogenous (i.e., consistent, uniform throughout). If the solute concentration is too high, it can lead to unwanted precipitation (see below).

Solutions are usually for oral use. Lotions are topical solutions.

TYPES OF SOLUTIONS:

- Syrups are oral solutions with sucrose, other sugars or artificial sugars.

- Elixirs are sweet hydroalcoholic solutions used for drugs that would be insoluble in a purely aqueous formulation. Hydroalcohol is a mixture of alcohol and water.

- Tinctures are plant or animal extracts dissolved in alcohol or hydroalcohol.

- Spirits are alcohols or hydroalcohols of volatile, aromatic compounds such as camphor. Volatile means the compound vaporizes (evaporates) easily.

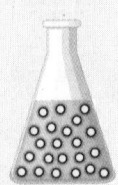

A **SUSPENSION** is a solid dispersed in a liquid. It is a two-phase heterogeneous (i.e., not uniform) mixture.

A wetting agent/levigating agent is a type of surfactant used to incorporate an insoluble drug into a liquid, which makes a suspension.

A desirable suspension does not have rapid precipitation of the solids; particles can be redispersed easily by shaking.

An **EMULSION** is a liquid dispersed in a liquid. It is a two-phase heterogeneous mixture. Emulsions are oil-in-water (oil droplets in an aqueous vehicle) or water-in-oil.*

An emulsifier is a type of surfactant that is used to reduce the surface tension between two liquids (e.g., oil and water). The emulsifier allows the two phases to come closer together.

To make the emulsion, the emulsifier will need to be carefully chosen, according to the hydrophilic-lipophilic balance (HLB) number (see the Compounding II chapter).

The phase that is present as droplets is the dispersed, internal phase or discontinuous phase, and the phase in which the droplets are suspended is the continuous or external phase.

PRECIPITATION/SEDIMENTATION is when the dispersed phase settles (clumps) together. The process of a solid settling on the bottom of a container is sedimentation.

This can happen with suspensions and emulsions, and less commonly with solutions. Shake or gently roll to re-disperse.

© GraphicsRF.com/Shutterstock.com

How to Prepare Solutions

Prepare the ingredients, and reduce the particle size of the drug/s to form a fine powder. The initial step in preparing any solution will be to determine if the solute will dissolve in the solution. The drug should remain soluble at different temperatures that may be encountered, including during refrigeration, if required for stability. If the drug is not soluble (e.g., will not dissolve in water), a suspension or a different solvent may be preferable. The dissolution rate can be used to determine the time it will take for the solute to dissolve. The dissolution rate is calculated using Fick's First Law of Diffusion. A larger surface area (i.e., smaller particles), stirring the preparation and using heat will increase the dissolution rate.

Determine if the solution will be stable at the desired temperature. A buffer system may be needed to resist changes in pH (see the end of this chapter). A preservative may be needed to protect against microbial growth, including bacteria, fungi and yeast. Flavorings, sweeteners and coloring agents can be added. Package the solution and apply a BUD and appropriate auxiliary labels.

How to Prepare Suspensions

Prepare the ingredients, and reduce the particle size of the drug/s to form a fine powder. Wet the powder, and levigate to form a paste. Continue to add liquid in portions. Add a surfactant to help keep the suspension dispersed. Transfer the mixture into a conical graduate or the container in which it will be dispensed, and QS to the final volume. A homogenizer will help make a uniform suspension. A preservative may be needed to protect against microbial growth, including bacteria, fungi and yeast. Flavorings, sweeteners and coloring agents can be added. Package the suspension and apply a BUD.

Even with surfactants used as suspending agents, suspensions are inherently unstable, and will need to be redispersed (i.e., shaken) prior to use.

How to Prepare Emulsions

| 4 parts oil | + | 2 parts water | + | 1 part gum (e.g., acacia) |

Emulsions can be made by either the Continental or English gum method; mixing oil, water, and an emulsifier (gum) in a 4:2:1 ratio.

Continental (dry gum) method:
1. Levigate the gum with oil.
2. Add the water all at once.
3. Triturate by shaking in a bottle or mixing in a mortar until a cracking sound is heard and mixture is creamy white.
4. Add other ingredients by dissolving them first in solution and adding a quantity of water sufficient to make (QS) up to the final volume.
5. Homogenize (with a homogenizer machine).

English (wet gum) method:
1. Triturate the gum with water to form a mucilage (thick and sticky like mucus).
2. Add oil slowly while shaking or mixing.
3. Add other ingredients as in the dry gum method.

Hint: It rains a lot in England (wet), and the oil is added slowly because you cannot drive too fast in the rain. The continent is dry, and you can add the water quickly (all at once).

iStock.com/Anna_zabella

POWDERS

Powders are fine particles of a solid. A dose of medication can be given as the dry powder (put into liquid or a small amount of soft food) for someone who is not able to swallow capsules or tablets, such as a small child or an elderly person with dysphagia. Powders are used to prepare tablets, capsules, inhalations, suspensions, ointments, creams and other topical treatments. Powders often include excipients, such as:

- Glidant/lubricant to improve the flowability of a powder: magnesium stearate.
- Surfactant to neutralize the static charge and keep the powder from floating away: sodium lauryl sulfate.

How to Prepare Powders

Reduce the size of the powder. This may require breaking down tablets with a grinder, followed by trituration or levigation. Sift the powder through a sieve (pictured previously) onto glassine paper.

If the amount of powder per dose is very small, it will be necessary to add an inert filler (diluent). A filler could also be needed to provide a minimum weighable quantity if using a torsion balance (see the Compounding II chapter). A common diluent is lactose. Add the filler and other excipients using geometric dilution.

Melting Point Order

Heat is sometimes used when compounding with powders to help with mixing. If melting ingredients (for any formulation), melt the ingredient with the highest melting point prior to adding the ingredient/s with lower melting points. Line up the ingredients by the melting temperature, and melt in that order, starting with the highest melting point.

Eutectic Mixtures

A eutectic mixture means that the combination of the ingredients (when mixed together) will melt at a lower temperature than either of the individual component's melting temperatures (see comic). The lower melting point of the eutectic mixture allows it to penetrate the skin more easily than the individual components.

Eutectic mixtures can create difficulty during compounding:

- If a pharmacist is not aware that the components form a eutectic mixture, the temperature on the hot plate can be set too high and the mixture can burn.
- If the components are solid powders at room temperature, the mixture of the powders can melt and turn the mixture into a sticky mess, ruining the dry preparation. An adsorbent powder (magnesium oxide, magnesium carbonate or kaolin) can be used to keep the powder dry.

©RxPrep

CAPSULES

Capsules are soluble shells of gelatin (an animal product) or hypromellose (a vegetable product), which are filled with the active drug, diluents (fillers) and any other excipients. Hard-shell capsules are used most commonly in compounding, and are filled with powders. Soft-shell capsules are used mostly for oils. Glycerol and sorbitol are used as plasticizers to make the capsules less brittle and more flexible.

Capsule-filling machine
📷 *felipe caparros/Shutterstock.com*

How to Prepare Capsules

Capsules are made by first triturating the dry ingredients and geometrically mixing with the fillers/other excipients. The powder is put into the capsules by either hand filling (also known as the "punch method") or by using a capsule-filling machine (see the Compounding II chapter for information on equipment).

Hand filling: to begin, the powder is placed on powder paper or on an ointment slab. The pile of powder is smoothed with a spatula to a height about a third of the length of the capsule. The open end of the capsule is repeatedly "punched" into the pile of powder until the capsule is filled. When the base is filled, it is fitted with the cap.

Manual capsule-filling machine: these are small devices that help the pharmacist quickly load 50, 100 or 300 capsules. Plates help sort the capsule bodies and hold them upright and in place. The powder is put above the capsules on to a plastic sheet where a plastic spreader is used to move the powder into the capsules. A comb or tamper and a spreader are used repeatedly until the powder is packed into the capsules. Then, the caps are put over the capsule bodies.

Common capsule sizes range from largest (size 000, ~1 inch long) to smallest (size 5, ~0.4 inches long).

- Capsule bodies can be filled by hand (for a small number) or with a capsule-filling machine (for larger amounts).
- In addition to using a capsule-filling machine to add a powder formulation, liquids can be added to upright capsule bodies with a pipette or dropper.

TABLETS

There are many types of tablets, including molded tablets, sublingual tablets, buccal tablets, orally disintegrating tablets, chewable tablets, effervescent tablets and compressed tablets. The molded tablet is the most common tablet type made in compounding, and the compressed tablet is the most common type made in manufacturing.

How to Prepare Molded Tablets

The first step to compound a molded tablet is to triturate the dry ingredients and mix by geometric dilution. Alcohol and/or water is added to moisten the powder. The powder mixture should have a pasty consistency, which can be molded into tablets (using tablet molds), and allowed to dry. Coloring and a coating may be added.

LOZENGES/TROCHES

Lozenges (or troches) can be hard or soft tablets that slowly dissolve in the mouth, or chewable tablets that are easily chewed and swallowed. Lozenges/troches are generally used to deliver a medication that acts locally in the mouth. A commercially available example is a clotrimazole troche for treatment of oral thrush.

A lozenge contains the active drug in a base of sucrose or syrup for hard lozenges, polyethylene glycol (PEG) for soft lozenges and glycerin or gelatin for chewable lozenges. Flavoring agents and coloring agents may be added. The base is melted, mixed with the API and excipients, placed into a mold and allowed to cool back into a solid.

CREAMS

Creams, lotions, ointments, pastes and gels are delivery vehicles, and are described in more detail in the Compounding II chapter. Creams are semi-solid formulations intended for topical use. They contain more than 20% water and up to 50% oil. They spread easily and are reasonably hydrating. Creams are packaged in tubes and tubs.

LOTIONS

Lotions contain the most water (compared to other topicals), are more fluid than creams, and can be poured. They are easy to spread on the skin and they absorb quickly. Since lotions contain a lot of water, they can be delivered in pumps.

OINTMENTS

Ointments contain the least water, 0 – 20%, with the remainder composed of oil-based product/s. Ointments are a good delivery vehicle to provide a barrier to exposure (e.g., organisms, sun) and they prevent moisture loss which helps burn and scar healing. They are packaged in tubes or tubs.

How to Prepare Ointments

Powders should be triturated well, using a levigating agent. The levigating agent must be miscible with the base, which means they can mix together well (mixing "like with like" is a common compounding principle). The powder will be mixed into the ointment base, using geometric dilution.

Certain ointments will require heat in order to mix the components together well. This is called the fusion method. Always use the lowest temperature possible. First, melt the ingredients with the highest melting point, then add the others, according to their decreasing melting points. Otherwise, undesired chemical reactions could occur. A water bath used to heat the ointment components will help prevent over-heating.

PASTES

The ingredients in pastes are similar to ointments, but they are made thicker by adding more solid ingredients. They provide a protective barrier because they do not melt significantly at body temperature.

GELS

Gels are semisolids interpenetrated by a liquid. Gels serve as a versatile drug delivery system for various routes of administration; they can be used orally, topically (for local or transdermal drug delivery), vaginally and rectally. Gelling agents are added to increase the viscosity and thicken the product. Alcohol is added to some gels to decrease the viscosity. Pluronic lecithin organogel ("PLO gel") can be used for transdermal drug administration. Pre-mixed PLO gels are available. See the Compounding II chapter for details.

SUPPOSITORIES

A suppository base is either oil-soluble (oleaginous) or water-soluble. Oil-soluble bases include cocoa butter (known as theobroma oil) and hydrogenated vegetable oils (palm, palm kernel and coconut oils). Water-soluble bases include PEG polymers and glycerinated gelatin. If a drug powder is added to a base, the powder should be triturated to a fine consistency.

- If the preparation softens or melts easily, such as with theobroma oil (cocoa butter), the molds will need to be stored in the refrigerator. The melting point of theobroma oil is slightly below human body temperature. When theobroma oil is used as a suppository base, the suppository will start to melt when held in the hand. It is not possible to insert a melting suppository. Storing it in the refrigerator will make the suppository hard, and easier to insert. Storing it in the mold in which it was formed would be preferable.

The drug will displace part of the base. If the drug has the same density as the base, it will displace an equal amount of volume. If the density is greater, it will displace less, and if it is lower, it will displace more. To calculate the amount of base displaced, the density factor of the drug is needed. The density factor can be found in compounding references, or calculated with the Paddock Method:

$$\text{Density Factor} = \frac{B}{A - C + B}$$

A = weight of the suppository blank, B = weight of medication per suppository, C = weight of medicated suppository.

How to Prepare Suppositories

There are three methods to prepare a suppository:

Hand molding can be used when only a few suppositories are to be prepared, using a cocoa butter base. The cocoa butter is not melted. It is grated and then mixed with the drug/s in a mortar and pestle or on a pill tile with a spatula. The mass is rolled into a cylinder, which is cut into suppository-size pieces. A tip is formed on one end to make insertion easier.

In the commonly-used fusion molding method, the base is gently heated, the ingredients are added, the mixture is poured into room temperature molds, and left to harden. If the base is poured into a cold mold, it can cause the suppository to crack and split. If the suppository does not harden, the molds can be refrigerated. Disposable plastic molds can be used for molding. Often, the suppositories are dispensed in the mold; suppositories are soft, and easily damaged. They are stored in the mold until needed.

In the compression molding method, the pharmacist will need to know the weight of each mold, and the drug's density factor (see last section). The amount of base required to fill each mold is calculated, the base is grated, mixed with the drug and put into a cold compression mold.

Lubricants can be applied to the mold so the suppositories can be removed more easily. If a lubricant is used it must be opposite of the suppository base in terms of solubility. The goal is to reduce friction. For example: glycerin or propylene glycol (both water-soluble) are good lubricants for suppositories made with oil-soluble suppository bases, while mineral oil or vegetable oil spray (oil-soluble) are good lubricants for water-soluble bases.

USE OF SUPPOSITORIES

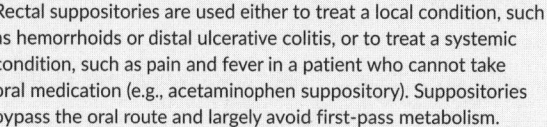

Vaginal suppositories are used to treat conditions inside the vagina, such as a *Candida* infection, or conditions related to the female reproductive system, such as hormone replacement in a patient with menopausal symptoms.

Rectal suppositories are used either to treat a local condition, such as hemorrhoids or distal ulcerative colitis, or to treat a systemic condition, such as pain and fever in a patient who cannot take oral medication (e.g., acetaminophen suppository). Suppositories bypass the oral route and largely avoid first-pass metabolism.

Suppository bases must be hard enough to be briefly handled, but soft enough to melt easily once inserted. Storing the suppository in the refrigerator can make insertion easier.

COMPOUNDING KITS

There are some companies that package pre-measured ingredients for a compounded product into "compounding kits." If the pharmacy does not routinely receive prescriptions for a certain product, it can be cost-effective (and easier) to purchase compounding kits as needed instead of purchasing the bulk ingredients.

SELECTING THE BEYOND-USE DATE FOR NON-STERILE PREPARATIONS

The beyond-use date (BUD) is the date or time after which the compounded product should not be used. The Study Tip Gal provides the default BUDs for non-sterile compounded preparations that are packaged in tight, light-resistant containers, per USP 795 standards.

USP specifies refrigeration for water-containing oral formulations only. Individual products may have shorter stability and/or different storage requirements which will override USP-provided defaults. Other exceptions include:

- If any ingredient expires before the BUD, use the earlier expiration date.

- BUDs can be extended if stability data is obtained that determines the drug is stable for a longer period.

BEYOND-USE DATES FOR NON-STERILE COMPOUNDED PRODUCTS

FORMULATION	BEYOND-USE DATE
Nonaqueous Formulations (e.g., a drug in petrolatum)	Not later than 6 months (180 days). Store at room temperature.
Water-Containing Oral Formulations (such as an oral suspension)	Not later than 14 days when stored at controlled cold temperatures. Store in refrigerator.
Water-Containing Topical/Dermal and Mucosal Liquid and Semisolid Formulations (such as a cream or lotion)	Not later than 30 days. Store at room temperature.

Beyond-Use Date Examples

PREPARATION	FORMULATION	MAXIMUM BUD
Metronidazole topical solution prepared with propylene glycol and distilled water	Topical, aqueous	30 days
Acetaminophen, diphenhydramine and hydroxyzine oral suspension prepared in lemon syrup (citric acid, purified water, lemon flavoring)	Oral, aqueous	14 days, refrigerated
Topical preparation of zinc oxide in white petrolatum	Non-aqueous	180 days
Nystatin in a strawberry-flavored popsicle with an 80% sorbitol and purified water solution	Oral, aqueous	14 days, refrigerated
Polymyxin and hydrocortisone prepared in a commercial emulsion cream for skin rash	Topical, aqueous	30 days
Ciprofloxacin and dexamethasone in *Versabase* lotion	Topical, aqueous	30 days
Estradiol powder, black cohosh powder and soybean oil preparation in hypromellose capsules	Non-aqueous	180 days
Morphine powder with stevia sweetener in a PEG lozenge	Non-aqueous	180 days
Progesterone suppository in an oleaginous base	Non-aqueous	180 days
Calamine powder prepared with glycerin in 70% isopropyl alcohol for poison ivy	Topical, aqueous	30 days
Lidocaine and diphenhydramine in poloxamer gel with lecithin/isopropyl palmitate	Topical, aqueous	30 days
Diclofenac powder in propylene glycol	Non-aqueous	180 days
Lidocaine, alcohol USP and distilled water buccal dental gel	Topical, aqueous	30 days

Unit-Dose Repackaging

A unit-dose refers to a small package that contains one dose of a medication. Unit-dose preparations can come from the manufacturer or a repackaging company, or a pharmacy can repackage multi-dose containers into unit-dose packages.

- Example: repackaging clopidogrel 75 mg from a multi-dose container of 100 tablets, with each unit-dose package containing one 75 mg tablet, which is the usual dose.

Unit-dose repackaging is not compounding, but shares some commonalities, including the assignment of a BUD, and safety requirements if repackaging HDs. BUDs for repackaged drugs should be the manufacturer's expiration date from the original container or 6 months from the repackaging date, whichever is earlier.

NON-STERILE QUALITY ASSURANCE

A quality assurance (QA) plan outlines the steps and actions that ensure proper standards are maintained. It includes the Standard Operating Procedures (SOPs), which are itemized steps on how to perform routine and expected tasks. The QA plan must be reviewed and updated regularly.

The QA program should include periodic testing of the finished compounded preparations. A pharmacy may do some QA testing in-house (e.g., confirming weight and consistency) and outsource others (e.g., sending products out to another company for sterility or stability testing).

QA records need to include the names of the compounding staff, including their job orientation and training records.

APPLYING PRODUCT AND AUXILIARY LABELS

The labeling of all compounded products must include the <u>BUD</u> and <u>storage and handling</u> information. There should be a label indicating that it is a compounded product. All HDs should be labeled appropriately.

Certain formulations may need additional auxiliary labels (see below).

Topical products:

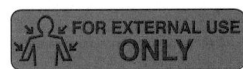

Emulsions, suspensions:

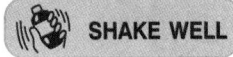

Suppositories, some troches, some suspensions:

*

PATIENT COUNSELING

The pharmacist must counsel the patient or caregiver about the proper use of a compounded product, with similar information as required for prescription drugs. <u>ADRs</u> resulting from a compounded product should be <u>reported</u> to the pharmacy, and the pharmacist will need to <u>record the ADR in the compounding record</u>. The patient's profile should include the ADR. Depending on the reaction, further action may be necessary.

STERILE PREPARATIONS

PHYSIOCHEMICAL CONSIDERATIONS

Human blood and body tissues have an osmotic pressure (number of particles in solution) equivalent to 0.9% sodium chloride (which is considered isotonic). Most sterile preparations, including intravenous (IV) solutions and ophthalmic products, should be <u>isotonic</u> to human blood and contain a similar number of particles in solution (i.e., osmolarity) of <u>~285 mOsm/L</u>. This prevents fluid transfer across biological semipermeable membranes. Osmolarity and isotonicity are discussed later in this chapter and in the Calculations II chapter.

The pH of sterile preparations should be close to <u>neutral</u> (pH of 7); blood is slightly alkaline at a pH of 7.35 – 7.45. <u>Non-PVC bags</u> should be used for IV medications that have <u>leaching or sorption</u> issues (see the Intravenous Medication Principles chapter). The IV tubing must be sterile and nonpyrogenic.

COMMON PRODUCTS USED IN STERILE COMPOUNDING

AMPULES AND VIALS

Ampules: ampules are small, sealed glass containers with a long neck that contain liquid medication. The ampule is broken by snapping the neck at the narrowest part. The glass is weaker in that area and will snap off. This can introduce glass particles into the drug solution. A <u>filter needle</u> or <u>filter straw</u> will be required to remove the glass.

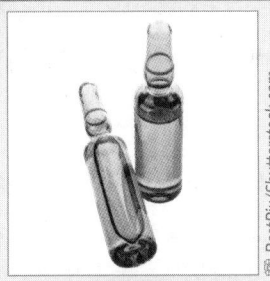
BestPix/Shutterstock.com

Vials that contain liquids: a volume of drug from the vial is drawn up in a syringe, which can then be added to an IV bag.

The compounder will inject a volume of air equal to the volume of drug that is withdrawn to equalize the pressure. A different process is used for hazardous drugs due to risk of exposure of the personnel (discussed later in the chapter).

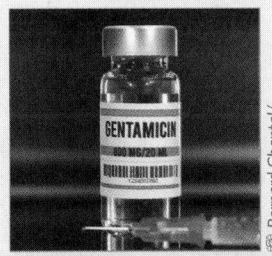
Bernard Chantal/Shutterstock.com

Vials that contain lyophilized or freeze-dried powder: the powder needs to be <u>reconstituted</u> by adding <u>sterile water</u> for injection, bacteriostatic water for injection or a diluent supplied by the manufacturer. Drugs may be commercially available as powders because they are unstable as a solution. The image to the right shows a vial of lyophilized powder before and after reconstitution.

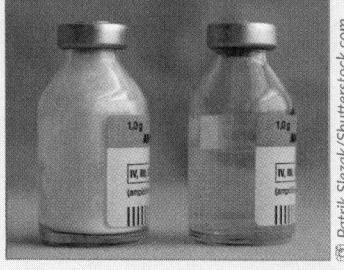
Patrik Slezak/Shutterstock.com

📷 *Labels courtesy of* 🍀 shamrocklabels
📷 *©RxPrep, Inc.*

COMPOUNDING & HAZARDOUS DRUGS

IV BAGS

Small volume parenteral (SVP): SVPs are IV bags or syringes that contain a small volume (100 mL or less) of fluid. SVPs can contain plain fluid, such as NS or D5W, that can be sent to the patient care area for floor stock or labeled for a specific patient. SVPs can also contain a drug with or without a diluent. These can be compounded in the pharmacy or come in ready-to-use containers from the manufacturer (see section below).

The SVPs are often "piggybacked" onto a large volume parenteral (LVP). These are called IV piggybacks (IVPBs); see figure. This reduces the need to have multiple lines running into the patient. The drugs will mix together in the tubing so they must be compatible in the IV line.

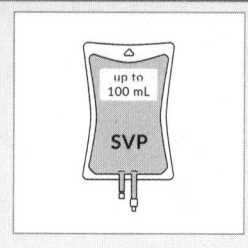

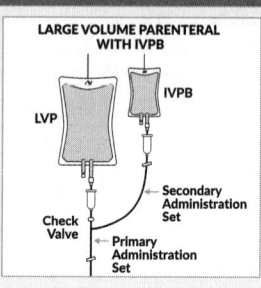

Large volume parenteral (LVP): LVPs are IV containers that contain more than 100 mL. 1 liter bags are commonly used to provide fluids, and are available in a variety of formulations: NS, ½NS, D5W, D5½NS, D5NS, lactated ringers (LR) and others used less commonly, including D10NS, D2.5½NS, D5⅓NS, D5¼NS. Parenteral nutrition (PN) for adults is prepared as a LVP.

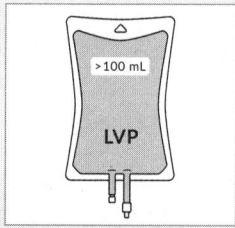

READY-TO-USE STERILE MEDICATIONS

Ready-to-use medications (RTUs): are available as prepared IV bags or prefilled syringes. The pharmacy staff opens the outer container and applies the patient label. These do not have a CSP risk level, as they are not compounded. The expiration date is provided by the manufacturer, and is on the packaging.

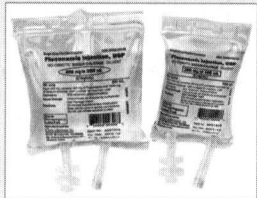

Ready-to-use vial/bag systems (ADD-Vantage, Minibag Plus, others): vials and bags are supplied together. The vial can be attached to the bags at the bedside by the nurse for immediate use. If the vial is attached in the pharmacy cleanroom (in an ISO 5 hood inside an ISO 7 buffer room; see the Compounding I chapter), it can be saved for an extended period of time as indicated by the manufacturer on the packaging. Each of the proprietary bag and vial systems are different in design, but all involve an activation step of releasing IV fluid into the drug vial and then returning the reconstituted drug back into the bag.

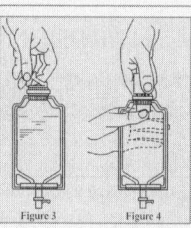

WORKFLOW FOR CSP PREPARATION

- Pharmacist reviews the order.

- Gather and inspect all materials.

- Clean hood. Place only needed items in the hood.

- Prepare CSPs with aseptic technique.

- Properly dispose of syringes and needles into the sharps container (see the Medication Safety & Quality Improvement chapter).

- Visually inspect all finished CSPs.

- If the CSP is high-risk, complete terminal sterilization (discussed later in this chapter).

HOW TO SET UP ITEMS IN THE STERILE HOOD

Space requirements for sterile compounding are discussed in detail in the Compounding I chapter; refer there for information on ISO air ratings, laminar airflow hood requirements and more.

- Only required items can be placed in the hood. No paper, pens, labels, calculators or trays.

- All work must be done within the sterile hood at least six inches from the front to prevent the hood air (ISO 5) and buffer room air (ISO 7) from mingling.

- Place all items in the sterile hood side-by-side. Items should not be closer than six inches from the back of the hood.

- Nothing should be between the sterile object and the HEPA filter in a horizontal airflow hood or above a sterile object in a vertical airflow hood.

- Do not tear open components. Open along the seal within the hood. Do not touch the syringe tip or plunger, even with gloved hands.

HOW TO TRANSFER SOLUTIONS AND INJECT INTO IV BAGS

- For greatest accuracy, use the <u>smallest syringe</u> that can hold the <u>desired amount</u> of solution. The syringe should not be larger than twice the volume to be measured.

- Powders are <u>reconstituted</u> by introducing a diluent such as <u>sterile water for injection</u>, bacteriostatic water for injection (which is sterile) or a diluent provided by the manufacturer. In some cases, dilution is done with saline or dextrose solution.

- <u>Swab</u> the rubber top of the vial (or ampule neck) with <u>70% IPA</u>, and wait for it to air-dry; do not blow on or wave over it to dry faster.

- Prior to withdrawing any liquid from a vial, <u>inject a volume of air equal to the volume of fluid to be removed</u>. Exception: <u>do not inject air</u> prior to removing <u>hazardous</u> drugs from vials. The negative-pressure technique (described in the next section) or a closed-system transfer device (CSTD) should be used. As part of their mechanism, CSTDs equalize the pressure in the vial which eliminates the need to inject air.

- Puncture the rubber top of the vial with the needle, <u>bevel up</u> and at a 45-degree angle. Then bring the syringe and needle <u>straight up</u> to a 90-degree angle while penetrating the stopper. Depress the plunger of the syringe, emptying the air into the vial. <u>Invert</u> the vial with the attached syringe. Draw up the amount of liquid required. Withdraw the needle from the vial. In the case of a multi-dose vial, the rubber cap will close, sealing the contents of the vial.

- The volume of solution drawn into a syringe is measured at the point of contact between the <u>rubber piston</u> and the <u>side of the syringe barrel</u>.

- <u>Coring</u> occurs when a small piece of rubber from the stopper is aspirated into the needle, and is put into the solution in the vial. The rubber piece can get injected into a patient. <u>Look for small cored pieces</u> floating near the top of the solution during the <u>visual inspection</u> of the CSP.

- If the medication is in a glass ampule, <u>open the ampule</u> by <u>snapping the neck away</u> from you. Tilt the ampule, then withdraw the fluid using a filter straw or filter needle to remove any glass particles that may have fallen into the ampule. The <u>needle must be changed</u> before injecting the syringe contents into an IV bag to avoid introducing glass or particles into the bag. A standard needle could be used to withdraw the drug from the ampule, as long as it is then replaced with a filter device before the drug is pushed out of the syringe.

Negative-Pressure Technique

<u>Air should not be injected into a vial containing a HD</u>. Positive pressure can cause the HD to spray out around the needle, contaminating the workspace and endangering personnel. Instead, the <u>negative-pressure technique</u> should be used. First, pull the plunger back to fill the syringe with a volume of air equal to the volume of drug to be removed. Insert the needle into the vial, invert the vial and pull on the plunger. This will create a vacuum that pulls the drug out of the vial and into the syringe. This should be done in small increments, pausing to allow the air to move out of the syringe and into the vial, until the desired volume of drug has been drawn up.

VISUAL INSPECTION

- The supervising pharmacist should <u>verify that the correct volume of product</u> is in the syringe <u>before</u> compounding continues. This is the safest method because the pharmacist can <u>see the actual volume in the syringe</u>. The "<u>syringe pull-back method</u>" is when the pharmacist verifies the volume in an empty syringe <u>after</u> the compounding is done; the technician "pulls-back" the plunger of the syringe to the volume of product that was added into the IV admixture and places the empty syringe next to the vial. This method relies on memory and is not recommended.

- Finished CSPs are <u>visually inspected</u> immediately after preparation, against a dark background, for <u>particulates</u>, <u>cored pieces, precipitates and cloudiness</u>. The container should be <u>lightly squeezed</u> to check for leakage.

TERMINAL STERILIZATION

Terminal <u>sterilization</u> is required for high-risk CSPs (discussed on the next page). Terminal sterilization methods include <u>steam</u> sterilization (with an <u>autoclave</u>), dry-heat sterilization (depyrogenation), gas sterilization, ionizing radiation and unidirectional aseptic processing. <u>Do not use heat</u> on <u>heat-sensitive</u> drugs (e.g., proteins, including hormones and insulin).

Bubble-Point Test and Filter Integrity

CSPs that are <u>heat-labile</u> (e.g., hormones, insulin, other proteins) can be sterilized with <u>filtration</u> using a <u>0.22-micron filter</u>. The filter will remove microorganisms larger than 0.22 microns, including bacteria, viruses, yeast and fungi.

If <u>filtering</u> is used, the <u>bubble-point test</u> must be performed. This test uses pressure to force liquid to "bubble" out of the filter to test the <u>filter integrity</u>.

LABEL REQUIREMENTS

The labels of CSPs must have the names and amounts or concentrations of ingredients, the total volume, the BUD, the route of administration, the storage requirements and other information for safe use.

All hazardous preparations must have a label that reads "Chemotherapy - dispose of properly" or something similar.

Auxiliary labels should be placed on CSPs that require special handling (e.g., if a filter or light protection is required, or if the CSP should not be refrigerated).

High-alert medications (defined by ISMP) are drugs that have a high risk of causing significant patient harm when used incorrectly. Appropriate auxiliary labels such as "Contains Potassium" or "Warning: Paralyzing Agent" should be used.

PYROGEN (BACTERIAL ENDOTOXIN) TESTING

Endotoxins are produced by both Gram-positive and Gram-negative bacteria and fungi. Endotoxins from Gram-negative bacteria are more potent and represent a serious threat to patient safety. Pyrogens can come from using equipment (such as glassware and utensils) washed with tap water. To avoid this issue, glassware and utensils should be rinsed with sterile water and depyrogenated using dry-heat (steam) sterilization with an autoclave.

Certain CSPs must be tested for endotoxins. The reagent for the bacterial endotoxins test (BET) is called the Limulus Amebocyte Lysate (LAL).

STERILE PREPARATION AND RISK

USP categorizes CSPs by the risk of contamination, which is based on the compounding area, ingredients and equipment used, and the complexity of the preparation. A sterile product that is contaminated with microorganisms or any other type of contaminant can cause severe illness and death.

The risk levels are low, medium and high. Categorization into these three levels assumes that compounding is done in a cleanroom (i.e., an ISO 5 PEC contained within an ISO 7 SEC). Low-risk and medium-risk CSPs are commonly prepared by pharmacy staff. There are two other special categories: low with less than 12-hour BUD and immediate-use. These risk levels are used to determine an appropriate BUD.

LOW-RISK STERILE COMPOUNDING

The majority of sterile compounds prepared by pharmacists are low-risk. Low-risk sterile compounding uses 1 to 3 components (including the diluent) that are supplied as sterile from the manufacturer.

Typically, the sterile additives (i.e., drugs) come in solution and are ready to be withdrawn from the vial and used. The additives are injected into a sterile diluent contained in an IV bag, or drawn up into a sterile syringe.

Low-risk sterile drugs have the lowest contamination risk, and the longest BUD.

MEDIUM-RISK STERILE COMPOUNDING

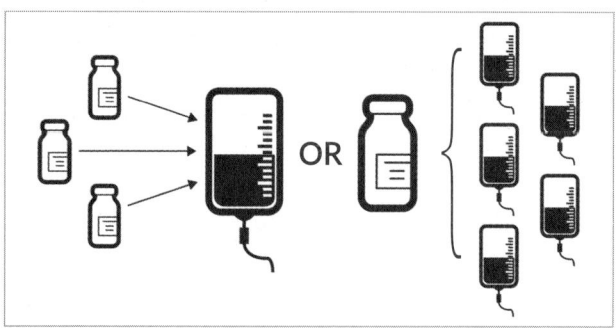

Kirill Mlayshev, winnievinzence/Shutterstock.com

The contamination risk increases each time the bag is entered (i.e., with a syringe, to place in an additive). If more than 3 sterile components are needed (including the diluent), the CSP is medium-risk. Parenteral nutrition preparations require many additives (see image below) including dextrose, lipids, amino acids, multivitamins, minerals, electrolytes and other sterile ingredients. A compounded parenteral nutrition would be medium-risk. Another type of medium-risk compounding is making a batch of drugs; for example, preparing ten IV bags of cefazolin in 50 mL D5W for the ten total knee arthroplasty surgeries scheduled that day.

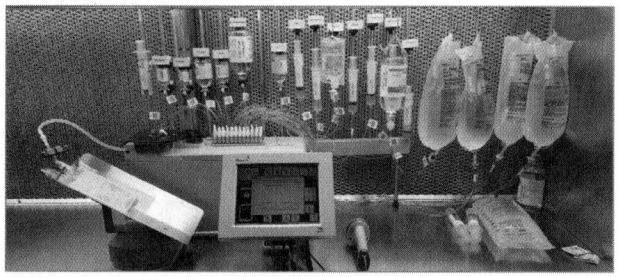

HIGH-RISK STERILE COMPOUNDING

High-risk sterile compounding is not common in most practice settings. High-risk sterile compounding uses non-sterile ingredients and equipment, including some of the equipment that is normally used for non-sterile compounding. Consequently, the end product will need to be sterilized prior to use. High-risk sterile drugs have the highest contamination risk, and the shortest BUD, with the exception of immediate-use CSPs. These are CSPs prepared in emergency situations in which there is inadequate time to prepare the CSP aseptically, such as during a code blue. Immediate-use CSPs have the shortest BUD.

Certain high-risk CSPs and CSPs intended for use beyond the recommended BUD must have sterility testing. The sterility testing should use either tryptic soy broth (TSB) or fluid thioglycollate medium (FTM), and include bacterial endotoxin (pyrogen) testing prior to use.

DETERMINING THE CSP RISK LEVEL

AREA REQUIREMENTS*	RISK LEVEL	CHARACTERISTICS	EXAMPLES
INSIDE A CLEANROOM			
ISO 5 PEC ISO 7 buffer area ISO 7 ante area (HD) ISO 8 ante area (non-HD)	Low	■ ≤ 3 sterile ingredients (including diluent) ■ No more than 2 entries into any 1 sterile container or device ■ Limited to transferring, measuring and mixing manipulations	Reconstituting a single-dose vial of antibiotic with sterile water and transferring it to a normal saline IV bag.
	Medium	■ > 3 sterile ingredients OR ■ Multiple doses of a sterile product withdrawn from the same vial to make several CSPs of the same product (a batch) ■ Complex aseptic manipulations	Preparing parenteral nutrition. Using a multi-dose vial of antibiotic and transferring single-doses to several normal saline IV bags for multiple patients. This process is called batch preparation.
	High	■ Non-sterile ingredients ■ Non-sterile equipment	Using a non-sterile bulk drug powder or non-sterile equipment to a make a preparation that will be terminally sterilized. Sterile components were held outside of ISO 5 air for more than 1 hour.
OUTSIDE OF A CLEANROOM			
ISO 5 PEC in an SCA ISO 5 C-PEC in a C-SCA	Low-risk CSPs with 12-hr or less BUD	■ See characteristics for low-risk	Reconstituting a single-dose vial of antibiotic and transferring to a small IV bag in a CAI in an SCA in a satellite pharmacy (not in a cleanroom).
Clean, uncluttered, functionally separate area	Immediate-use	■ Only intended for emergency administration ■ Must be for administration within 1 hour	Providing stat IV drug administration in a medical setting or ambulance.

Requirements are discussed in detail in the Compounding I chapter.

DETERMINING THE BEYOND-USE DATE BASED ON CSP RISK LEVEL

The BUD is the date or time after which the CSP should not be used. The BUD is determined by USP 797 standards and the stability/expiration date of the individual ingredients, whichever is shorter. The higher the CSP risk level, the shorter the BUD, and the colder the storage temperature, the longer the BUD. Sterility testing can be done to see if a longer BUD is possible.

BEYOND-USE DATES FOR COMPOUNDED STERILE PRODUCTS

CSP RISK LEVEL	ROOM TEMP BUD	REFRIGERATED BUD	FROZEN BUD
Low	48 hours	14 days	45 days
Medium	30 hours	9 days	
High	24 hours	3 days	
Low-risk CSP prepared in an ISO 5 PEC or C-PEC in an SCA or C-SCA (not in a cleanroom)	12 hours	12 hours	N/A
Immediate-use	1 hour	N/A	N/A

BUDs for Single-Dose Containers (SDC) and Multi-Dose Containers (MDC)

The BUDs in this table are for the vials, bags, bottles, syringes and ampules that contain the drugs, electrolytes and other items that are being put into the CSPs. For example, a single-dose 1 g vial of vancomycin, once opened, can be used for up to 6 hours if the vial was opened in and remains in the PEC, which has ISO 5 air.

DOSE	BUD
SDC – vial, bag, bottle, syringe Outside an ISO 5 environment	1 hour from the time of puncture or opening
SDC – vial, bag, bottle, syringe Inside an ISO 5 environment	Up to 6 hours from the time of puncture or opening
SDC – ampule Inside or outside an ISO 5 environment	Any unused contents left in the ampule cannot be stored and must be discarded
MDC Inside or outside an ISO 5 environment	Up to 28 days from the time of puncture or opening, unless otherwise specified by the manufacturer

CSP QUALITY ASSURANCE

Every facility that prepares CSPs must have a quality assurance (QA) plan that evaluates, corrects and improves the quality processes. The plan should minimally include:

- Personnel training and assessment
- Environmental monitoring
- Equipment calibration and maintenance

Each part of the QA plan must be documented and the follow-up actions identified must have assigned personnel responsible for each item, with expected dates of completion. If a problem has been identified or a medication error or safety issue has occurred, a root cause analysis should be started as soon as possible, discussed in the Medication Safety & Quality Improvement chapter. A failure mode and effects analysis of new techniques can help to identify problems with new procedures in advance. Standard Operating Procedures (SOPs), described earlier, should be developed, followed and periodically reviewed to determine if revisions are needed.

RECALLS

When high-risk level CSPs are dispensed before receiving the results of their sterility tests, there must be a written procedure requiring daily observation of the incubating test specimens and immediate recall of the dispensed CSPs if there is evidence of microbial growth. All patients and physicians who received the recalled CSPs are notified of the potential risk.

If sterility test results come back positive, there should be an investigation of aseptic technique, environmental control and other sterility assurance measures to determine the source of contamination and improve the methods or processes.

Recalls apply to both sterile and non-sterile preparations and are discussed further in RxPrep's MPJE Course.

CLASS	DESCRIPTION
Class I Recall	A situation in which there is a reasonable probability that the use or exposure will cause serious adverse health consequences or death. For example, microbial growth is observed in an intrathecal injection.
Class II Recall	A situation in which use or exposure can cause temporary or reversible adverse health consequences or where the probability of harm is remote. For example, ketorolac injections have been recalled in 2010 and 2015 due to the possibility of particles in the vials.
Class III Recall	A situation in which use or exposure is not likely to cause adverse health consequences. For example, the coloring on tablets may have been applied inconsistently.

OSMOLARITY AND INTRAVENOUS DRUGS

OSMOLARITY AND TONICITY

Osmolarity and tonicity are related terms; both are used to express the solute concentration in solution. Osmolarity includes all solutes and tonicity includes only the solutes that do not cross the vasculature (i.e., the biological membrane).

Osmolarity in Intravenous Formulations

Saline concentrations greater than 0.9% are referred to as hypertonic. Hypertonic saline injections, given erroneously, can be fatal.

Hypertonic saline (commonly 3% or 23.4%) is used for various indications in the acute care setting, such as treating hyponatremia (3%) and for use in preparing parenteral nutrition (23.4%). When hypertonic saline is administered into a peripheral vein, the high concentration of solutes relative to the concentration in the blood will cause water to move out of the red blood cells (RBCs) in an attempt to dilute the solute concentration. This will cause the RBCs to become shriveled and dysfunctional.

To avoid adverse outcomes, hypertonic saline is often restricted to the pharmacy and only dispensed for administration in areas of the hospital where safety can be monitored (e.g., a critical care unit).

The osmolarity of an IV formulation can impact its administration. The highest osmolarity acceptable for peripheral IV administration is ~900 mOsmol/L. Solutions with higher osmolarity should be administered via a central line (i.e., not by peripheral administration) to avoid damaging the vein (i.e., phlebitis). The central line delivers intravenous medications and fluids into a larger blood volume, which quickly dilutes the solution.

When a preparation has lower osmolarity than blood (i.e., it is hypotonic), the RBCs will absorb fluid. This can cause hemolysis (i.e., the RBCs will burst), which can be fatal.

In general, ½NS (0.45%), which has an osmolarity of 154 mOsm/L, is the lowest osmolarity of saline that should be administered intravenously alone. Lower concentrations of saline, such as ¼NS (0.225%) can be administered if combined with other fluids, such as 5% dextrose, which will increase the total osmolarity of the fluid.

RESISTING CHANGES IN pH WITH BUFFER SYSTEMS

As stated earlier, the blood has a slightly alkaline pH of 7.35 – 7.45. Tissues and cells (e.g. the nose, eyes, skin) are very sensitive to changes in pH (defined as the number of protons in solution). The body uses the carbonic acid-bicarbonate buffer system to resist changes in pH in both directions:

- When the pH rises, the blood becomes more basic. Hydrogen ions (protons) will be released from carbonic acid, which causes the pH of the blood to lower. The blood becomes more acidic.

- When the pH falls, the blood becomes more acidic. Hydrogen ions get picked up (more bicarbonate binds with protons), which causes the pH of the blood to rise. The blood becomes more basic.

The above scenario is referring to the carbonic acid-bicarbonate buffer system. There are two other buffer systems that resist changes in pH; the phosphate buffer system and the protein buffer system.

Preparations that are administered in sensitive tissue (e.g., eye drops, injections) must be formulated to keep the pH within a narrow range to avoid damaging the tissue and causing pain.

In addition to providing acceptable formulations for patient care, the pH will be an important consideration to provide stability for the drug in the solution.

Similar to human blood, compounding preparations that require a narrow pH range will need a buffer system that can resist changes in pH. Buffer systems, similar to the buffer systems in the body, consist of an acid and its salt. For example, acetic acid is used with sodium acetate, its salt, in a common buffer system:

- Acetic acid serves as the proton donor to decrease the pH.

- Sodium acetate serves as the proton acceptor, to increase the pH.

In the Calculations IV chapter, the Henderson-Hasselbalch equation is used to calculate the pH of a solution when the molar (M) concentrations of the buffer components are provided. A variation of the Henderson-Hasselbalch can be used to determine the amount of buffer required.

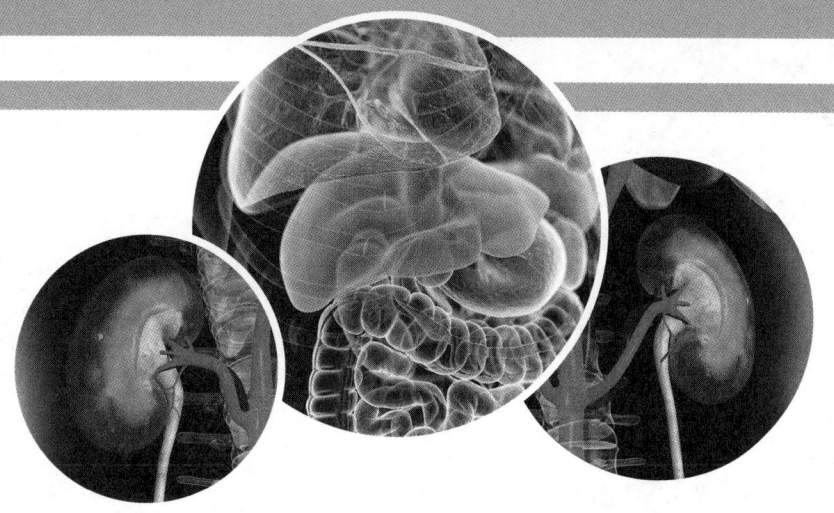

RENAL & LIVER DISEASE

CONTENTS

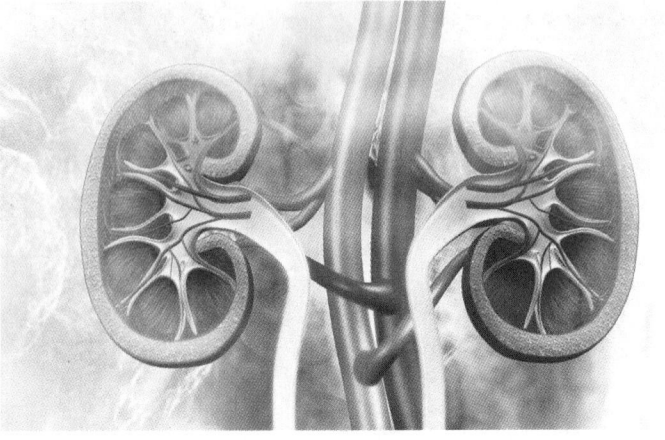

© crystal light/Shutterstock.com

CHAPTER 18
RENAL DISEASE

BACKGROUND

Approximately 30 million U.S. adults (more than one in seven) have chronic kidney disease (CKD). The risk is highest in African Americans, Hispanic Americans, American Indians and Asians. The most common causes are diabetes and hypertension; controlling blood glucose and blood pressure can prevent renal damage and delay progression to kidney failure [i.e., end-stage renal disease (ESRD)].

Less common causes of CKD include polycystic kidney disease, some types of infections, renal artery stenosis (a blocked artery that prevents blood flow to the kidney) and drug-induced kidney disease (caused by nephrotoxic medications).

Pharmacists can assess the degree of kidney impairment in CKD patients to ensure safe and effective medication dosing. They can recognize and recommend treatment for related disorders, such as anemia, hypertension, acid-base and electrolyte disturbances and disorders of bone and mineral metabolism (e.g., management of parathyroid hormone, phosphate, calcium and vitamin D levels).

RENAL PHYSIOLOGY

The nephron is the functional unit of the kidney. Its primary function is to control the concentration of sodium and water. The nephrons reabsorb what is needed back into the blood, and the remainder is excreted in the urine. This regulates blood volume, and in turn, blood pressure. The major parts of the nephron include Bowman's capsule, the glomerulus, the proximal tubule, the loop of Henle, the distal convoluted tubule and the collecting duct (see the figure on the following page). There are roughly one million nephrons in each kidney.

CHAPTER CONTENT

DEFINITIONS

Acute Kidney Injury (AKI)
A sudden loss of kidney function due to a non-renal condition (e.g., drugs). Often reversible (temporary), but can be permanent if the precipitating condition is not corrected. A common cause is dehydration (can present with BUN:SCr ratio > 20:1 plus decreased urine output, dry mucus membranes, tachycardia).

Chronic Kidney Disease (CKD)
A progressive loss of kidney function over months or years. The degree of kidney function is measured by the glomerular filtration rate (GFR) or creatinine clearance (CrCl), and by how much albumin is in the urine.

Kidney Failure [End-Stage Renal Disease (ESRD)]
Total and permanent kidney failure. Fluid and waste accumulates. Dialysis (or transplant) is needed to perform the functions of the kidneys.

CONTENT LEGEND

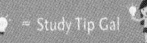 = Study Tip Gal  = Key Drug Guy

GLOMERULUS

The afferent arteriole delivers blood into the glomerulus, a large filtering unit that is located within Bowman's capsule. Substances with a molecular weight < 40,000 daltons, including most drugs, pass through the glomerular capillaries into the filtrate (inside the lumen, or tube, of the nephron) and are excreted in the urine. If the glomerulus is healthy, larger substances (e.g., proteins and protein-bound drugs) are not filtered and stay in the blood (exiting the nephron via the efferent arteriole). If the glomerulus is damaged, some albumin passes into the urine. The amount of albumin in the urine is used, along with the glomerular filtration rate (GFR), to assess the severity of kidney disease (also called nephropathy). See the GFR and Albuminuria for Staging Kidney Disease section for further discussion.

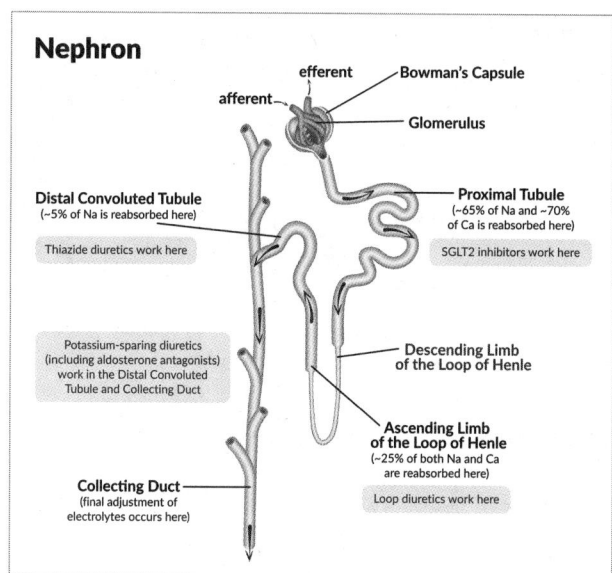

iStock.com/TefiM

PROXIMAL TUBULE

Proximal means "close to." The proximal tubule is closest to Bowman's capsule (the entry point of the nephron). Much of the sodium (Na), chloride (Cl), calcium (Ca) and water that are initially filtered out of the blood are reabsorbed back into the bloodstream here. Blood pH is regulated by the exchange of hydrogen and bicarbonate ions. Medications that work here include the sodium-glucose cotransporter 2 (SGLT2) inhibitors (see the Diabetes chapter for details).

LOOP OF HENLE

As filtrate moves down the loop of Henle (the descending limb), water is reabsorbed into the blood, but Na and Cl ions are not, which increases the concentration of Na and Cl in the filtrate. As the filtrate moves up the loop of Henle (the ascending limb), Na and Cl ions are reabsorbed back into the blood, but water is not. If antidiuretic hormone (ADH) is present, water passes through the walls of the ascending limb and is reabsorbed into the blood; less water is then excreted in the urine (anti-diuresis). ADH is also called vasopressin.

The ascending limb of the loop of Henle is the site of reabsorption for about 25% of the filtered Na. When loop diuretics inhibit the Na-K pump in the thick ascending limb of the loop of Henle, less Na is reabsorbed back into the blood. There is a significant increase in the concentration of Na in the filtrate, causing less water to be reabsorbed (more stays in the filtrate and is excreted in the urine along with Na). By blocking the pump, loop diuretics cause less Ca reabsorption back into the blood, leading to Ca depletion. Long-term use of loop diuretics can decrease bone density because of this.

DISTAL CONVOLUTED TUBULE

Distal means "farther away." The distal convoluted tubule is the farthest point away from entry into the nephron.

It is involved in regulating potassium (K), Na, Ca and pH. Thiazide diuretics inhibit the Na-Cl pump in the distal convoluted tubule. Only about 5% of Na is reabsorbed at this point, making thiazides weaker diuretics than loops. Thiazides increase Ca reabsorption at the Ca pump in the distal convoluted tubule. Unlike loop diuretics, the long-term use of thiazide diuretics has a protective effect on bones.

COLLECTING DUCT

The collecting duct is a network of tubules and ducts that connect the nephrons in each kidney to a ureter. The urine filtrate passes from the ureters into the bladder and then out of the body via the urethra (see figure at right). The collecting duct is involved with water and electrolyte balance, which is affected by levels of ADH and aldosterone. Potassium-sparing diuretics, including aldosterone antagonists (e.g., spironolactone, eplerenone), work in the distal convoluted tubule and collecting duct to ultimately decrease Na and water reabsorption and increase K retention.

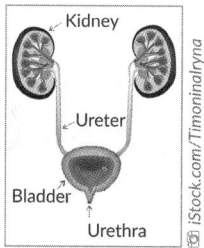

iStock.com/Timoninalryna

DRUG-INDUCED KIDNEY DISEASE

Drug-induced kidney disease (DIKD) is linked to numerous medications; it can be acute and reversible if the medication is stopped, but it can be irreversible and progress to CKD. DIKD is especially common in the hospital setting and contributes to morbidity and mortality. Risk factors include reduced renal blood flow (e.g., preexisting kidney disease, chronic or acute heart failure, dehydration, hypotension), increased age, use of multiple nephrotoxic medications at the same time and frequent use or large doses of nephrotoxic medications.

RENAL & LIVER DISEASE

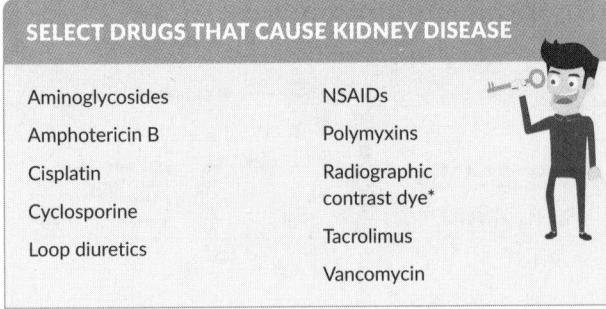

SELECT DRUGS THAT CAUSE KIDNEY DISEASE

Aminoglycosides	NSAIDs
Amphotericin B	Polymyxins
Cisplatin	Radiographic contrast dye*
Cyclosporine	Tacrolimus
Loop diuretics	Vancomycin

Sometimes called contrast media or contrast agent; used during imaging tests (e.g., angiography, MRI, CT).

ESTIMATING KIDNEY FUNCTION

Two common laboratory markers used to estimate kidney function are blood urea nitrogen (BUN) and serum creatinine (SCr). BUN measures the amount of nitrogen in the blood that comes from urea, a waste product of protein metabolism. As kidney function declines, BUN increases. BUN is not used alone to estimate kidney function because other factors besides renal impairment can increase the BUN (primarily dehydration).

Creatinine, a waste product of muscle metabolism, is mostly filtered by the glomerulus and is easily measured. As kidney function declines, creatinine increases (similar to BUN). The normal range of SCr is ~0.6 – 1.3 mg/dL. Any creatinine that is not filtered is secreted into the nephron tubules. The amount secreted increases as renal function declines and less creatinine is filtered (a compensatory mechanism).

CREATININE CLEARANCE

The Cockcroft-Gault equation for CrCl is most commonly used to estimate kidney function when dosing medications. The accuracy of creatinine-based estimation equations is decreased when a patient has very low muscle mass, which is often the case in frail elderly patients (low muscle mass = low SCr). This can lead to an overestimation of CrCl and inappropriate drug dosing for the patient's true kidney function.

Obesity, liver disease, pregnancy, high muscle mass and other conditions associated with abnormal muscle turnover can affect the estimation of kidney function using measured SCr. The Cockcroft-Gault equation is not preferable in very young children, in kidney failure or in unstable renal function (e.g., SCr is fluctuating or changing over a short period of time).

Drug dosing recommendations are generally based on CrCl (using the Cockcroft-Gault equation). A few specific drugs use GFR for dosing adjustment purposes, including the SGLT2 inhibitors and metformin.

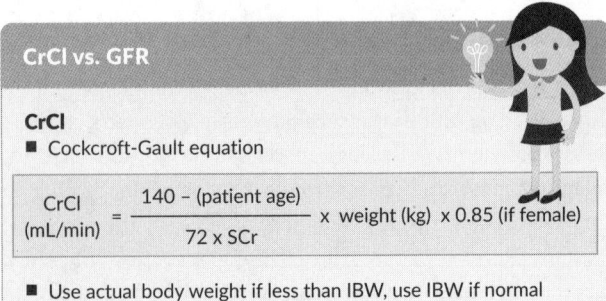

CrCl vs. GFR

CrCl
- Cockcroft-Gault equation

$$CrCl\ (mL/min) = \frac{140 - (patient\ age)}{72 \times SCr} \times weight\ (kg) \times 0.85\ (if\ female)$$

- Use actual body weight if less than IBW, use IBW if normal weight (by BMI), use adjusted body weight if overweight (by BMI)*
- Medication contraindications and dosing adjustments are typically based on CrCl calculated using the Cockcroft-Gault equation

GFR
- Not commonly calculated by pharmacists, but may be reported with a basic metabolic panel (BMP)
- CKD-EPI and MDRD equations are used
- Used for staging kidney disease and for dosing select drugs (e.g., metformin, SGLT2 inhibitors)
- For the exam, if GFR is not provided, CrCl provides a close estimate to determine contraindications and dosing adjustments

See the Calculations IV chapter for more information on weights and CrCl.

GFR AND ALBUMINURIA FOR STAGING KIDNEY DISEASE

GFR [or estimated GFR (eGFR)] is calculated using the Modification of Diet in Renal Disease (MDRD) and Chronic Kidney Disease Epidemiology Collaboration (CKD-EPI) equations. Albumin is the primary protein that is measured in the urine to assess kidney disease; albuminuria is sometimes referred to as proteinuria.

The Kidney Disease Improving Global Outcomes (KDIGO) and Kidney Disease Outcomes Quality Initiative (KDOQI) guidelines recommend using the GFR and degree of albuminuria (level of albumin present in the urine), along with the cause of CKD, to determine the degree/stage of renal impairment. The two tables on the following page show how the GFR and degree of albuminuria are used to assess the severity of kidney disease. In the first table, the GFR value is used to determine the severity of renal impairment. The degree of albuminuria is classified according to the second table, where the 1st and 2nd columns are measurements of albumin (in different units) and the 3rd column contains an interpretation of these measurements.

The values in these tables, on the following page, do not need to be memorized, but it is important to recognize that a GFR < 60 mL/min/1.73 m^2 and/or albuminuria (ACR or AER ≥ 30) indicates that the patient has CKD and specific treatments are warranted to prevent progression of disease (see Hypertension section).

GFR Categories

GFR (mL/min/1.73 m²)	TERMS	GFR CATEGORY (KDIGO 2012)	CKD STAGE (KDOQI 2002)
≥ 90 + kidney damage*	Normal or high	G1	Stage 1
60-89 + kidney damage*	Mild decrease	G2	Stage 2
45-59	Mild to moderate decrease	G3a	Stage 3
30-44	Moderate to severe decrease	G3b	
15-29	Severe decrease	G4	Stage 4
< 15 or dialysis dependent	Kidney failure	G5	Stage 5

*Markers of kidney damage include a history of kidney transplant, structural abnormalities on imaging, presence of albuminuria and other factors.

Degree of Albuminuria

ACR (mg/g) or AER (mg/24 hr)	ACR (mg/mmol)	TERMS	ALBUMINURIA CATEGORY (KDIGO 2012)
< 30	< 3	Normal to mild increase (previously called normoalbuminuria)	A1
30-300	3-30	Moderate increase (previously called microalbuminuria)	A2
> 300	> 30	Severe increase (previously called macroalbuminuria)	A3

ACR: albumin to creatinine ratio; AER: albumin excretion rate

HYPERTENSION AND DIABETES IN CHRONIC KIDNEY DISEASE

HYPERTENSION

Hypertension causes and worsens CKD. The 2021 KDIGO Guideline on Blood Pressure in CKD recommends a target SBP < 120 mmHg (with strict, standardized office BP monitoring) for those with hypertension and CKD. This is lower than the target BP recommended in the ACC/AHA guidelines for the general population with hypertension, but unlikely to be tested.

An ACE inhibitor or ARB is first-line for patients with CKD, hypertension and albuminuria (with or without diabetes). Renin-angiotensin-aldosterone system (RAAS) inhibition with an ACE inhibitor or ARB reduces CKD progression (see Study Tip Gal below).

ACE INHIBITORS AND ARBs FOR ALBUMINURIA

Who?
Recommended in all patients with albuminuria

Why?
To prevent kidney disease progression

How?
Inhibit renin-angiotensin-aldosterone system (RAAS), causing efferent arteriolar dilation

What?
Reduce pressure in the glomerulus, decrease albuminuria and provide cardiovascular protection

When starting treatment with an ACE inhibitor or ARB, the baseline SCr can increase by up to 30%. This is expected, and treatment should not be stopped. If SCr increases by > 30%, the treatment should be discontinued and the patient will generally be referred to a nephrologist.

ACE inhibitors and ARBs should never be used together. They increase potassium, which can result in hyperkalemia. The serum creatinine and potassium should be monitored 1 – 2 weeks after initiating an ACE inhibitor or ARB. Patients should be counseled to avoid potassium supplements and salt substitutes (with KCl). It is important to maximize the dose of the ACE inhibitor or ARB for renal protection. Refer to the Hypertension chapter for additional detail.

DIABETES

The 2020 KDIGO Guideline on Diabetes Management in CKD recommends first-line treatment with metformin and a sodium-glucose cotransporter 2 (SGLT2) inhibitor for patients with CKD, type 2 diabetes and eGFR ≥ 30 mL/min/1.73 m². SGLT2 inhibitors (specifically canagliflozin, dapagliflozin and empagliflozin) have demonstrated a reduction in cardiovascular events and CKD progression. If the patient is unable to use these medications or cannot meet glycemic targets on them, a glucagon-like peptide 1 (GLP-1) receptor agonist is recommended. Finerenone, a nonsteroidal mineralocorticoid receptor antagonist, was recently FDA-approved for patients with CKD associated with type 2 diabetes to reduce CKD progression and cardiovascular risks. Refer to the Diabetes chapter for additional detail.

RENAL & LIVER DISEASE

MODIFYING DRUG THERAPY

Common scenarios related to medications and kidney disease include:

- The drug is eliminated through the kidneys. The <u>dose</u> is <u>reduced</u> and/or the dosing <u>interval</u> is <u>extended</u> to <u>avoid accumulation</u> and side effects/toxicity.

- The drug can <u>cause or worsen kidney disease</u> (it is nephrotoxic).

- The drug becomes <u>less effective</u> as kidney function declines (e.g., thiazide diuretics, nitrofurantoin).

- The drug is <u>contraindicated</u> at a specific level of kidney impairment because <u>drug accumulation</u> is <u>unsafe</u> (e.g., increased bleeding risk with some anticoagulants), the drug can cause further <u>kidney damage</u> (e.g., NSAIDs) or the drug may cause more <u>harmful effects</u> than usual when kidney function is reduced (e.g., hyperkalemia with aldosterone receptor antagonists).

Remember the basic principles of medication dosing in patients with impaired renal function. <u>Dose adjustments</u> may be necessary when CrCl is <u>< 60 mL/min</u>; when CrCl is <u>≤ 30 mL/min</u>, additional adjustments may be needed or the drug may be <u>contraindicated</u> (see <u>Key Drugs Guys</u> below).

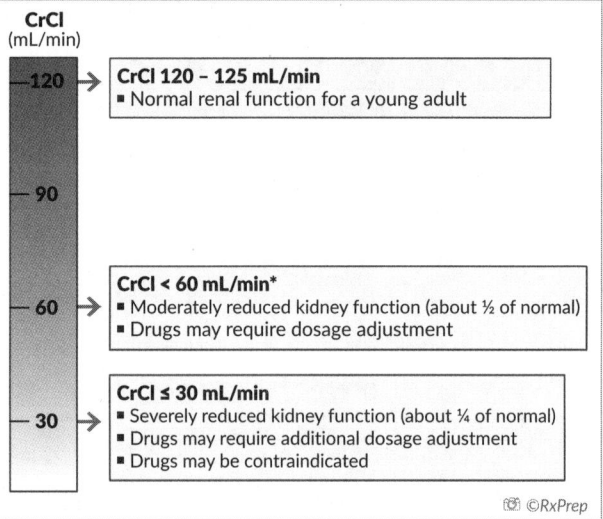

Check package labeling for individual drug requirements.

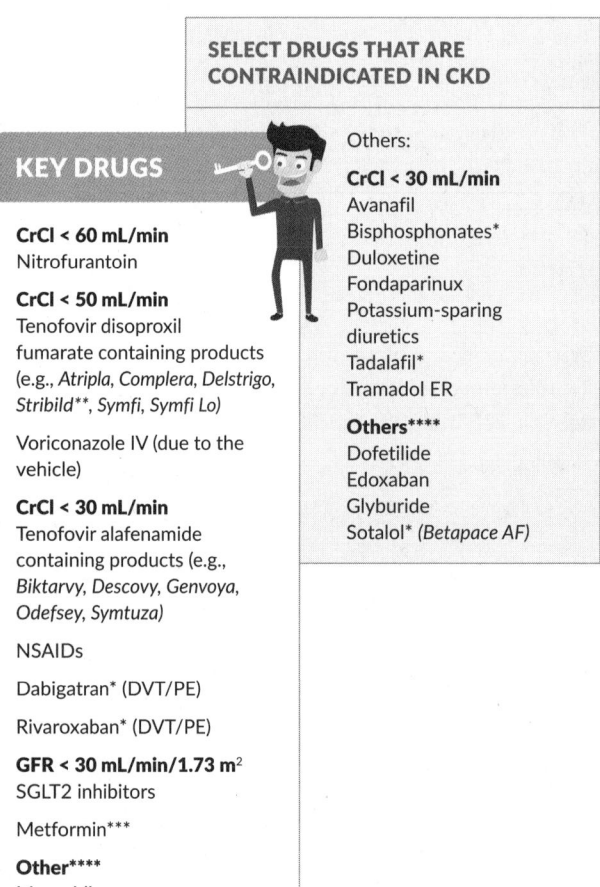

SELECT DRUGS THAT REQUIRE ↓ DOSE OR ↑ INTERVAL IN CKD

KEY DRUGS

Anti-Infectives
Aminoglycosides (↑ dosing interval primarily)

Beta-lactam antibiotics (except antistaphylococcal penicillins and ceftriaxone)

Fluconazole

Quinolones (except moxifloxacin)

Vancomycin

Cardiovascular Drugs
LMWHs (enoxaparin)

Rivaroxaban* (for AF)

Apixaban* (for AF)

Dabigatran* (for AF)

Gastrointestinal Drugs
H2RAs (famotidine, ranitidine)

Metoclopramide

Other
Bisphosphonates*

Lithium

Others:

Anti-Infectives
Amphotericin B
Anti-tuberculosis medications (ethambutol, pyrazinamide)
Antivirals (acyclovir, valacyclovir, ganciclovir, valganciclovir, oseltamivir)
Aztreonam
NRTIs, including tenofovir
Polymyxins
Sulfamethoxazole/Trimethoprim

Cardiovascular Drugs
Antiarrhythmics (digoxin, disopyramide, dofetilide, procainamide, sotalol*)
Statins (most)

Pain/Gout Drugs
Allopurinol
Colchicine
Gabapentin, pregabalin
Morphine and codeine
Tramadol ER

Others
Cyclosporine
Tacrolimus
Topiramate

Medication has indication-specific recommendations.

SELECT DRUGS THAT ARE CONTRAINDICATED IN CKD

KEY DRUGS

CrCl < 60 mL/min
Nitrofurantoin

CrCl < 50 mL/min
Tenofovir disoproxil fumarate containing products (e.g., *Atripla, Complera, Delstrigo, Stribild**, Symfi, Symfi Lo*)

Voriconazole IV (due to the vehicle)

CrCl < 30 mL/min
Tenofovir alafenamide containing products (e.g., *Biktarvy, Descovy, Genvoya, Odefsey, Symtuza*)

NSAIDs

Dabigatran* (DVT/PE)

Rivaroxaban* (DVT/PE)

GFR < 30 mL/min/1.73 m²
SGLT2 inhibitors

Metformin***

Other**
Meperidine

Others:

CrCl < 30 mL/min
Avanafil
Bisphosphonates*
Duloxetine
Fondaparinux
Potassium-sparing diuretics
Tadalafil*
Tramadol ER

Others**
Dofetilide
Edoxaban
Glyburide
Sotalol* (*Betapace AF*)

* Medication has indication-specific recommendations.
** For treated patients; do not start treatment if CrCl < 70 mL/min.
*** For treated patients; do not start treatment if GFR ≤ 45 mL/min/1.73 m².
**** Not specified or another CrCl cut-off is used.

COMPLICATIONS OF CHRONIC KIDNEY DISEASE

See the figure illustrating the common complications of chronic kidney disease (exam studies should focus on the treatments).

CKD MINERAL AND BONE DISORDER

CKD mineral and bone disorder (CKD-MBD) is common in patients with renal impairment and affects almost all patients receiving dialysis. CKD-MBD is associated with fractures, cardiovascular disease and increased mortality. Patients with advanced kidney disease require monitoring of parathyroid hormone (PTH), phosphorus (phosphate, PO4), Ca and vitamin D levels.

Hyperphosphatemia

Hyperphosphatemia contributes to chronically elevated PTH levels (secondary hyperparathyroidism) and must be treated to prevent bone disease and fractures. Treatment is initially focused on restricting dietary phosphate (e.g., avoid dairy products, cola, chocolate and nuts). As CKD progresses, phosphate binders are often required. Phosphate binders block the absorption of dietary PO4 by binding to it in the intestine. They are taken just prior to (or at the start of) each meal. If a dose is missed (and the food is absorbed), the phosphate binder should be skipped, and the patient should resume normal dosing at the next meal or snack. There are three types of phosphate binders: 1) aluminum-based, 2) calcium-based and 3) aluminum-free, calcium-free drugs.

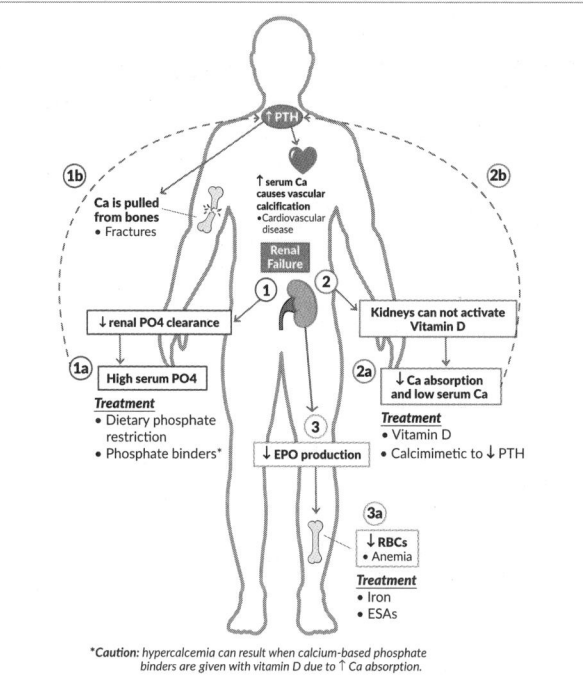

Caution: hypercalcemia can result when calcium-based phosphate binders are given with vitamin D due to ↑ Ca absorption.

The interactions of Ca, PO4 and vitamin D in CKD are complex. **1)** PO4 levels increase (because the kidneys cannot eliminate excess PO4 absorbed from the diet). **2)** Vitamin D can not be activated by the kidney, causing dietary calcium absorption to decrease. Both high PO4 **(1a)** and low Ca **(2a)** cause increased release of PTH. In a patient with healthy kidneys, PTH would cause the kidneys to increase Ca reabsorption, but in CKD this is not possible and Ca is pulled from the bones, leading to bone demineralization and increased fractures. Normally, when Ca levels return to normal, PTH release is shut down, but the chronically high PO4 levels continue to stimulate PTH release and hypercalcemia can persist, causing calcification and cardiovascular disease. **3)** In CKD, the kidneys produce less erythropoietin (EPO), resulting in decreased RBC production in the bone marrow which causes anemia.

©RxPrep
MaskaRad/Shutterstock.com

Phosphate Binders

DRUG	DOSE	SAFETY/SIDE EFFECTS/MONITORING
Aluminum-based: potent phosphate binders, but rarely used due to the risk of aluminum accumulation (which can cause nervous system and bone toxicity). Treatment duration is limited to 4 weeks.		
Aluminum hydroxide Suspension	300-600 mg PO TID with meals	**SIDE EFFECTS** Aluminum intoxication, "dialysis dementia," osteomalacia, constipation, nausea **MONITORING** Ca, PO4, PTH, s/sx of aluminum toxicity
Calcium-based: first-line.		
Calcium acetate (Phoslyra, PhosLo*, others) Tablet, capsule, solution	1,334 mg PO TID with meals, titrate based on PO4 levels	**SIDE EFFECTS** Hypercalcemia, constipation, nausea **MONITORING** Ca, PO4, PTH
Calcium carbonate (Tums, others) Tablet, chewable tablet	500 mg PO TID with meals (can vary with formulation used), titrate based on PO4 levels Total daily dose of elemental calcium should be < 2,000 mg (from diet and supplements)	**NOTES** Calcium acetate binds more dietary phosphorus on an elemental calcium basis compared to calcium carbonate Hypercalcemia is especially problematic with concomitant use of vitamin D (due to increased calcium absorption)

RENAL & LIVER DISEASE

DRUG	DOSE	SAFETY/SIDE EFFECTS/MONITORING
Aluminum-free, calcium-free: no aluminum accumulation, less hypercalcemia, but more expensive.		
Sucroferric oxyhydroxide (*Velphoro*) Chewable tablet	500 mg PO TID with meals, titrate based on PO4 levels	**WARNINGS** Iron absorption occurs with ferric citrate; dosage reduction of IV iron may be necessary; store out of reach of children to prevent accidental overdose
Ferric citrate (*Auryxia*) Tablet	2 tablets (420 mg) PO TID with meals, titrate based on PO4 levels	**SIDE EFFECTS** Diarrhea, constipation, discolored (black) feces **MONITORING** Iron, ferritin, TSAT (only with ferric citrate), PO4, PTH **NOTES** Absorption is minimal with sucroferric oxyhydroxide
Lanthanum carbonate (*Fosrenol*) Chewable tablet, powder	500 mg PO TID with meals, titrate based on PO4 levels Must chew tablet thoroughly to reduce risk of severe GI adverse effects Use powder if unable to chew tablets	**CONTRAINDICATIONS** GI obstruction, fecal impaction, ileus **WARNINGS** GI perforation **SIDE EFFECTS** Nausea/vomiting, diarrhea, constipation, abdominal pain **MONITORING** Ca, PO4, PTH
Sevelamer: a non-calcium, non-aluminum based phosphate binder that is not systemically absorbed.		
Sevelamer carbonate (*Renvela*) Tablet, powder **Sevelamer hydrochloride (*Renagel*)** Tablet	800-1,600 mg PO TID with meals, titrate based on PO4 levels	**CONTRAINDICATIONS** Bowel obstruction **WARNINGS** Can reduce dietary absorption of vitamins D, E, K and folic acid; consider vitamin supplementation Tablets can cause dysphagia and get stuck in the esophagus; consider using powder if swallowing difficulty is present **SIDE EFFECTS** Nausea/vomiting/diarrhea (all > 20%), dyspepsia, constipation, abdominal pain, flatulence **MONITORING** Ca, PO4, HCO3, Cl, PTH **NOTES** Can lower total cholesterol and LDL by 15-30%. Sevelamer carbonate can maintain bicarbonate concentrations

Brand discontinued but name still used in practice.

Phosphate Binder Drug Interactions

- Phosphate binders are designed to "bind" and because of this have many drug interactions. Separate administration from levothyroxine and antibiotics that chelate (e.g., quinolones, tetracyclines).

- Calcium-based phosphate binders interact with many drugs, including quinolones, tetracyclines, oral bisphosphonates and thyroid products.

- Sucroferric oxyhydroxide and ferric citrate are iron-based phosphate binders. Doxycycline should be taken one hour before both products. Ciprofloxacin should be separated by two hours from ferric citrate. Levothyroxine should not be used with sucroferric oxyhydroxide.

- Lanthanum carbonate can bind to aluminum-, calcium- or magnesium-containing antacids; administration of these products should be separated from the lanthanum dose by two hours. Quinolone antibiotics should be given one hour before or four hours after lanthanum. Separate levothyroxine by at least two hours.

- Sevelamer can decrease absorption of some medications. Quinolone antibiotics should be given two hours before or six hours after the sevelamer dose. Mycophenolate, tacrolimus and levothyroxine serum concentrations can be decreased and doses of these medications should be given several hours before sevelamer.

Vitamin D Deficiency & Secondary Hyperparathyroidism

After controlling hyperphosphatemia, elevations in PTH are treated primarily with vitamin D. Vitamin D deficiency occurs when the kidney is unable to hydroxylate vitamin D to its final active form, 1,25-dihydroxy vitamin D. Vitamin D deficiency worsens bone disease, impairs immunity and increases the risk of cardiovascular disease.

Vitamin D occurs in two primary forms: vitamin D3 (or cholecalciferol), which is synthesized in the skin after exposure to ultraviolet light (e.g., the sun), and vitamin D2 (or ergocalciferol), which is produced from plant sterols and is the primary dietary source of vitamin D. Supplementation with oral ergocalciferol or cholecalciferol may be necessary, especially in patients with early CKD (e.g., stage 3 and 4).

The vitamin D analogs are used in patients with later stages of CKD, or kidney failure, to increase calcium absorption from the gut, raise serum calcium concentrations and inhibit PTH secretion. Calcitriol (Rocaltrol) is the active form of vitamin D3. Newer vitamin D analogs, such as paricalcitol and doxercalciferol, are alternatives that cause less hypercalcemia than calcitriol.

Another method of inhibiting PTH release is by increasing the sensitivity of the calcium receptor on the parathyroid gland. Cinacalcet (Sensipar) is a "calcimimetic" which mimics the actions of calcium on the parathyroid gland and causes a further reduction in PTH. It is only used in dialysis patients.

Drugs for the Treatment of Secondary Hyperparathyroidism

DRUG	DOSING	SAFETY/SIDE EFFECTS/MONITORING
Vitamin D analogs: ↑ intestinal absorption of Ca, which provides negative feedback to the parathyroid gland.		
Calcitriol (Rocaltrol) Capsule, solution, injection	CKD: 0.25-0.5 mcg PO daily Dialysis: 0.25-1 mcg PO daily or 0.5-4 mcg IV 3x weekly	**CONTRAINDICATIONS** Hypercalcemia, vitamin D toxicity **WARNINGS** Digitalis toxicity potentiated by hypercalcemia **SIDE EFFECTS** Hypercalcemia, hyperphosphatemia, N/V/D (> 10%) **MONITORING** Ca, PO4, PTH, 25-hydroxy vitamin D (calcifediol) **NOTES** Take with food or shortly after a meal to ↓ GI upset (calcitriol) Calcifediol is a prodrug of calcitriol
Calcifediol (Rayaldee) ER capsule	CKD Stage 3 or 4: 30 mcg PO QHS	
Doxercalciferol (Hectorol) Capsule, injection	CKD: 1-3.5 mcg PO daily Dialysis: 10-20 mcg PO 3x weekly or 4-18 mcg IV 3x weekly	
Paricalcitol (Zemplar) Capsule, injection	CKD: 1-2 mcg PO daily or 2-4 mcg PO 3x weekly Dialysis: 2.8-7 mcg IV 3x weekly	
Calcimimetic: ↑ sensitivity of the calcium-sensing receptor on the parathyroid gland, which causes ↓ PTH, ↓ Ca, ↓ PO4.		
Cinacalcet (Sensipar)	Dialysis: 30-180 mg PO daily with food Take tablet whole, do not crush or chew	**CONTRAINDICATIONS** Hypocalcemia **WARNING** Caution in patients with a history of seizures **SIDE EFFECTS** Hypocalcemia, N/V/D, paresthesia, HA, fatigue, depression, anorexia, constipation, bone fracture, weakness, arthralgia, myalgia, limb pain, URTIs **MONITORING** Ca, PO4, PTH
Etelcalcetide (Parsabiv)	Dialysis: 2.5-15 mg IV 3x weekly	**WARNINGS** Hypocalcemia, worsening HF, GI bleeding, decreased bone turnover **SIDE EFFECTS** Muscle spasms, paresthesia, N/V/D **MONITORING** Ca, PO4, PTH

RENAL & LIVER DISEASE

ANEMIA OF CKD

Anemia is defined as a hemoglobin level < 13 g/dL. It is common in CKD and is due to a combination of factors. The primary problem is a lack of erythropoietin (EPO), which is normally produced by the kidneys and travels to the bone marrow to stimulate the production of red blood cells (RBCs). RBCs (which contain hemoglobin) are released into the blood where they transport oxygen.

As kidney function declines, EPO production decreases. This leads to reduced hemoglobin levels and symptoms of anemia (e.g., fatigue, pale skin). These processes are exacerbated by CKD, causing an inflammatory state, which contributes to decreased EPO production. Anemia of CKD is sometimes referred to as anemia of chronic disease.

Erythropoiesis-stimulating agents (ESAs) work like EPO to produce more RBCs and can prevent the need for blood transfusions. ESAs include epoetin alfa (*Procrit, Epogen, Retacrit*) and the longer-lasting formulation darbepoetin alfa (*Aranesp*). ESAs have risks, including elevated blood pressure and thrombosis. They should only be used when the hemoglobin is < 10 g/dL. The dose should be held or discontinued if the hemoglobin exceeds 11 g/dL, as the risk for thromboembolic disease (DVT, PE, MI, stroke) is increased with higher hemoglobin levels.

ESAs are only effective if adequate iron is available to make hemoglobin. It is important to assess an iron panel (iron, ferritin and TSAT) and provide supplementation to prevent iron deficiency. In kidney failure, iron levels can be low due to reduced GI absorption and blood loss from dialysis treatments. Intravenous (IV) iron is given at the dialysis center. See the Anemia chapter for more information on identifying different types of anemia and use of ESAs and IV iron.

HYPERKALEMIA

A normal potassium level is 3.5 – 5 mEq/L. Hyperkalemia can be defined as a potassium level > 5.3 or > 5.5 mEq/L (ranges vary), though clinicians will be concerned with any level > 5 mEq/L.

Potassium is the most abundant intracellular cation and is essential for life. Humans obtain potassium through the diet from many foods, including meats, beans and fruits. Normal daily intake through the GI tract is about 1 mEq/kg/day. Excess intake is excreted, primarily via the kidneys and partially via the gut. Renal potassium excretion is increased by the hormone aldosterone, diuretics (loops > thiazides),

by a high urine flow (via osmotic diuresis) and by negatively charged ions in the distal tubule (e.g., bicarbonate).

High dietary potassium intake does not typically cause hyperkalemia unless there is significant renal damage. With normal kidney function, the acute rise in potassium from a meal would be offset by the release of insulin, which causes potassium to shift into the cells.

The most common cause of hyperkalemia is decreased renal excretion due to kidney failure. The risk can be increased with a high dietary potassium intake or use of drugs that interfere with potassium excretion.

Patients with diabetes are at a higher risk for hyperkalemia, as insulin deficiency reduces the ability to shift potassium into the cells, and many patients with diabetes take ACE inhibitors or ARBs. Hospitalized patients are at higher risk of hyperkalemia than outpatients, primarily due to the concurrent use of drugs and IV solutions. Rarely, acute hyperkalemia can be due to tumor lysis, rhabdomyolysis or succinylcholine administration.

A patient with an elevated potassium level may be asymptomatic. When symptoms are present, they can include muscle weakness, bradycardia and fatal arrhythmias. If the potassium is high or the heart rate/rhythm is abnormal, the patient is usually monitored with an ECG. The risk for severe, negative outcomes increases as the potassium level increases.

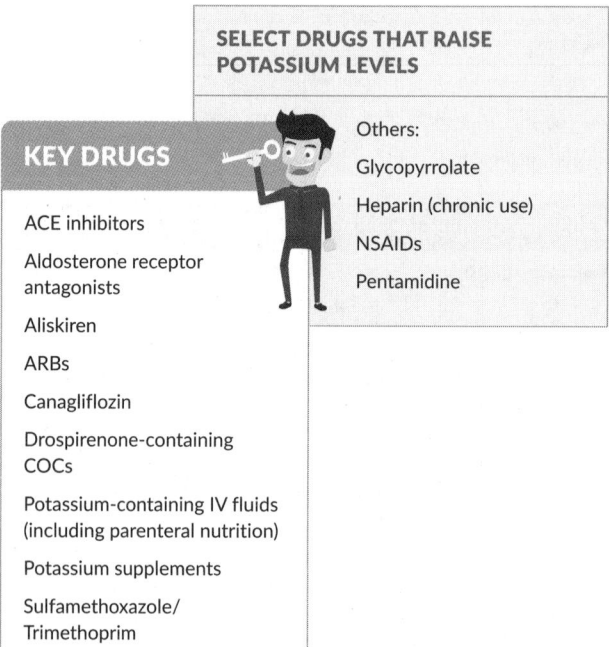

SELECT DRUGS THAT RAISE POTASSIUM LEVELS

KEY DRUGS

ACE inhibitors

Aldosterone receptor antagonists

Aliskiren

ARBs

Canagliflozin

Drospirenone-containing COCs

Potassium-containing IV fluids (including parenteral nutrition)

Potassium supplements

Sulfamethoxazole/Trimethoprim

Transplant drugs (cyclosporine, everolimus, tacrolimus)

Others:

Glycopyrrolate

Heparin (chronic use)

NSAIDs

Pentamidine

Treatment of Hyperkalemia

All potassium sources must be discontinued. If hyperkalemia is severe, there is an urgent clinical need to stabilize the myocardial cells (to prevent arrhythmias, this is done first) and to rapidly shift potassium intracellularly or induce elimination from the body.

The Study Tip Gal below lists the medication options for management of hyperkalemia. Several medications move potassium from the extracellular to the intracellular compartment. One or more of these methods are used in severe hyperkalemia. These drugs work quickly, but they do not lower total body potassium. Interventions to enhance potassium elimination can be used. These methods take longer to reduce potassium and are only used alone in less severe situations; they are mostly used in combination with a drug that shifts potassium intracellularly.

STEPS FOR TREATING SEVERE HYPERKALEMIA

MECHANISM	INTERVENTION	ROUTE OF ADMINISTRATION	ONSET	NOTES
Stabilize the heart Prevent arrhythmias	Calcium gluconate	IV	1-2 minutes	Does not decrease potassium. Stabilizes myocardial cells to prevent arrhythmias.
Move it Shift K intracellularly	Regular insulin	IV	30 minutes	Co-administered with glucose or dextrose to prevent hypoglycemia.
	Dextrose	IV		Stimulates insulin secretion, but does not shift K intracellularly on its own.
	Sodium bicarbonate	IV		Used when metabolic acidosis is present.
	Albuterol	Nebulized		Monitor for tachycardia and chest pain.
Remove it Eliminate K from the body	Furosemide	IV	5 minutes	Eliminates K in the urine. Monitor volume status.
	Sodium polystyrene sulfonate	Oral or rectal	2-24 hours	Binds K in the GI tract. Due to adverse effects (GI necrosis), used for emergency situations only. Oral may take hours to days to work. Rectal route has a faster onset and can be used in acute (emergency) treatment.
	Patiromer	Oral	~7 hours	Binds K in the GI tract. Delayed onset limits use in life-threatening emergencies.
	Sodium zirconium cyclosilicate	Oral	1 hour	Binds K in the GI tract. Potassium binder with fastest onset of action; may be preferred for emergency situations.
	Hemodialysis		Immediate, once started	Removes K from the blood. It takes several hours to set up/complete dialysis. Other methods are generally used in conjunction.

Drugs for Treatment of Hyperkalemia

DRUG	DOSE	SAFETY/SIDE EFFECTS/MONITORING
Sodium polystyrene sulfonate (*SPS, Kayexalate**, *Kionex*) Powder, oral suspension, rectal suspension Non-absorbed cation exchange resin	Oral: 15 grams 1-4 times/day Rectal: 30-50 grams Q6H	**WARNINGS** Electrolyte disturbances (hypernatremia, hypokalemia, hypomagnesemia, hypocalcemia), fecal impaction, GI necrosis (↑ risk when administered with sorbitol; do not use together) Can bind other oral medications (check for drug interactions and separate administration) **SIDE EFFECTS** N/V, constipation or diarrhea **MONITORING** K, Mg, Na, Ca **NOTES** Do not mix oral products with fruit juices containing K Variable onset of action; rectal formulation is faster Due to the risk of GI necrosis, limit use to specific situations (e.g., life-threatening hyperkalemia and other therapies to remove potassium are not available or possible)
Patiromer (*Veltassa*) Powder for oral suspension Non-absorbed cation exchange polymer	8.4 grams PO once daily; max dose is 25.2 grams once daily Instructions: measure 1/3 cup of water and pour half into an empty cup; empty the *Veltassa* packet contents into the water and stir well; add the remaining water to the mixture and stir well (the mixture will be cloudy); drink the mixture right away (if powder remains in the cup, add additional water and drink; repeat as needed)	**WARNINGS** Can worsen GI motility, hypomagnesemia Binds to many oral drugs; separate by at least 3 hours before or 3 hours after **SIDE EFFECTS** Constipation, nausea, diarrhea **MONITORING** K, Mg **NOTES** Delayed onset of action limits the use in life-threatening hyperkalemia Store powder in the refrigerator (must be used within 3 months if stored at room temperature)
Sodium zirconium cyclosilicate (*Lokelma*) Powder for oral suspension Non-absorbed cation exchange polymer	10 g PO TID for up to 48 hours Instructions: empty packet contents into a cup with at least 3 tablespoons of water; stir well and drink immediately (if powder remains in the cup, add additional water and drink; repeat as needed)	**WARNINGS** Can worsen GI motility, edema, contains sodium (may need to adjust dietary sodium intake) Can bind other drugs; separate by at least 2 hours before or 2 hours after **SIDE EFFECTS** Peripheral edema **NOTES** Generally the preferred potassium binder due to fastest onset of action Store at room temperature

*Brand discontinued but name still used in practice.

METABOLIC ACIDOSIS

The ability of the kidney to reabsorb bicarbonate decreases as CKD progresses. This can result in the development of metabolic acidosis. In the ambulatory care setting, treatment of metabolic acidosis is initiated when the serum bicarbonate concentration is < 22 mEq/L. Drugs to replace bicarbonate include:

- Sodium bicarbonate (*Neut*)
    - Sodium load can cause fluid retention.
    - Monitor sodium level and use caution in patients with hypertension or cardiovascular disease.
- Sodium citrate/citric acid solution (*Cytra-2, Oracit, Shohl's solution*)
    - Monitor sodium level.
    - Metabolized to bicarbonate by the liver; may not be effective in patients with liver failure.

DIALYSIS

If CKD progresses to failure (stage 5 disease), dialysis is required in all patients who do not receive a kidney transplant. The two primary types of dialysis are hemodialysis (HD) and peritoneal dialysis (PD). In HD, the patient's blood is pumped to the dialyzer (dialysis machine) and runs through a semipermeable dialysis filter, which, using a concentration gradient, removes waste products, electrolytes and excess fluid. HD is a 3 – 4 hour process, several times per week (usually three times). Patients who do HD at home can do it more frequently (e.g., 5 – 6 times per week).

In PD, a dialysis solution (usually containing glucose) is pumped into the peritoneal cavity (the abdominal cavity surrounding the internal organs). The peritoneal membrane acts as the semipermeable membrane (i.e., as the dialyzer). The solution is left in the abdomen to "dwell" for a period of time, then is drained. This cycle is repeated throughout the day, every day. PD is performed by the patient at home.

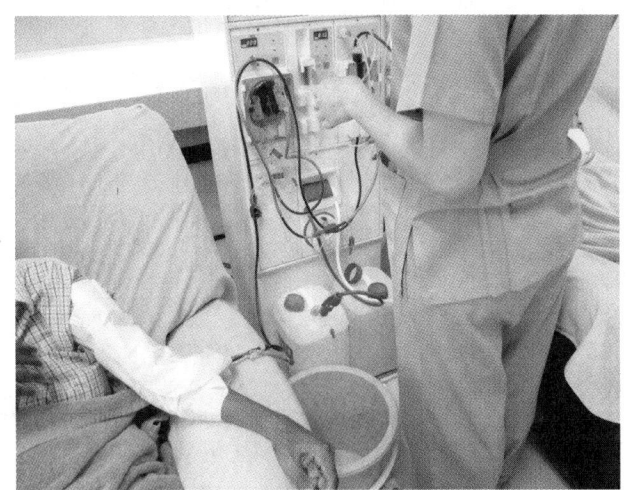

khawfangenvi16/Shutterstock.com

FACTORS AFFECTING DRUG REMOVAL DURING DIALYSIS

When a patient receives dialysis, the pharmacist must consider the amount of medication cleared during dialysis in order to recommend the correct dose and interval. Medications that are removed during dialysis (including many antibiotics) must be given after dialysis or may require a supplemental dose following dialysis. Drug removal during dialysis depends primarily on the factors below.

FACTOR	EFFECT
Drug Characteristic	
Molecular weight/size	Smaller molecules are more readily removed by dialysis
Volume of distribution	Drugs with a large Vd are less likely to be removed by dialysis
Protein-binding	Highly protein-bound drugs are less likely to be removed by dialysis
Dialysis Factors	
Membrane	High-flux (large pore size) and high-efficiency (large surface area) HD filters remove more substances than conventional/low-flux filters
Blood flow rate	Higher dialysis blood flow rates increase drug removal over a given time interval

Select Guidelines/References

Kidney Disease: Improving Global Outcomes (KDIGO) CKD Work Group. KDIGO 2012 Clinical Practice Guideline for the Evaluation and Management of Chronic Kidney Disease. *Kidney Int.*, Suppl. 2013;3:1-150.

Kidney Disease: Improving Global Outcomes (KDIGO) Blood Pressure Work Group. KDIGO 2021 Clinical Practice Guideline for the Management of Blood Pressure in Chronic Kidney Disease. *Kidney Int.* 2021;99(3S):S1-S87.

Kidney Disease: Improving Global Outcomes (KDIGO) Diabetes Work Group. KDIGO 2020 Clinical Practice Guideline for Diabetes Management in Chronic Kidney Disease. *Kidney Int.* 2020;98(4S):S1-S115.

CONTENT LEGEND

 = Study Tip Gal   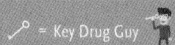 = Key Drug Guy

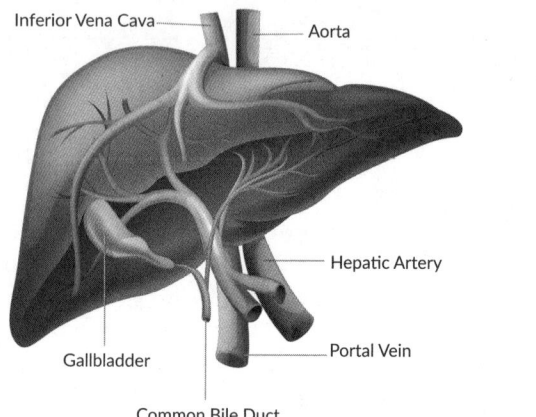

Inferior Vena Cava —   Aorta

Hepatic Artery

Gallbladder   Portal Vein

Common Bile Duct

📷 iStock.com/blueringmedia

CHAPTER 19

HEPATITIS & LIVER DISEASE

HEPATITIS

BACKGROUND

Hepatitis means <u>inflammation of the liver</u>. Hepatitis viruses are the most common cause, but alcohol, certain drugs, autoimmune diseases and other viruses/infections can cause hepatitis. Viruses that damage the liver include hepatitis A through E (most cases of viral hepatitis are caused by hepatitis A, B or C), herpes viruses, cytomegalovirus, Epstein-Barr virus and adenoviruses. Symptoms and treatment differ depending on the cause of hepatitis and extent of liver damage. Many patients with hepatitis B and C do not know they are infected.

HEPATITIS A, B AND C

The <u>Study Tip Gal</u> on the following page provides a comparison of the hepatitis viruses. Hepatitis A virus (HAV) usually causes an <u>acute, self-limiting illness</u>. Transmission occurs primarily via the <u>fecal-oral</u> route, due to either <u>improper handwashing</u> after exposure to an infected person or ingestion of <u>contaminated food/water</u>. Symptoms are generally mild and non-specific.

Hepatitis B virus (HBV) and hepatitis C virus (HCV) can cause <u>acute illness</u> and can lead to <u>chronic infection, cirrhosis of the liver, liver cancer, liver failure and death</u>. Transmission occurs from contact with infectious <u>blood</u> or other <u>body fluids</u> (e.g., having sex with an infected person), sharing contaminated needles to inject drugs or from an infected mother to her newborn (perinatal transmission).

Routine screening for HBV in otherwise healthy individuals is not required; screening (and subsequent vaccination) is based on risk. Due to the increasing prevalence of HCV, a one-time screening is recommended in all individuals ≥ 18 years. Periodic, repeat screening is recommended in those with enhanced risk. Pregnant women should be screened for HBV and HCV with each pregnancy.

Comparison of Hepatitis Viruses

	HEPATITIS A	HEPATITIS B	HEPATITIS C
Acute vs. Chronic	Acute	Both	Both
Transmission	Fecal-oral	Blood, body fluid	Blood, body fluid
Vaccine	Yes*	Yes*	No
First-Line Treatment	Supportive	PEG-INF or NRTI (tenofovir or entecavir)	Treatment naïve: DAA combination
Other Treatments for Select Patients			DAA combination + RBV or DAA combination + RBV + PEG-INF**

DAA = direct-acting antivirals, PEG-INF = pegylated interferon, RBV = ribavirin
*See Immunizations chapter
**HCV guidelines no longer routinely recommend interferon alfa (see text for discussion)

DRUG TREATMENT FOR HEPATITIS C

There are six different HCV genotypes (1 – 6) and various subtypes (e.g., 1a or 1b). Treatment options and duration of therapy depend on the genotype, the presence of cirrhosis and whether the patient has been treated before. Preferred HCV regimens consist of 2 – 3 direct-acting antivirals (DAAs) with different mechanisms, usually for 8 – 12 weeks. Some combinations include ritonavir, which is not active for HCV, but is used to boost (increase) levels of HCV protease inhibitors.

Ribavirin can be added to DAA therapy as an alternative treatment option. Interferon is no longer recommended in combination regimens, but could play a role when DAAs are contraindicated or too expensive. Because treatment of HCV is rapidly changing, drug selection is typically handled by specialists. Healthcare providers should consult the American Association for the Study of Liver Diseases (AASLD) website for the most up-to-date recommendations (www.hcvguidelines.org).

DIRECT-ACTING ANTIVIRALS (DAAs)

DAAs have revolutionized the treatment of HCV, almost entirely eliminating older, poorly tolerated treatments (e.g., interferon and ribavirin) and offering a cure for most patients. Treatment of HCV is approached much like HIV, with regimens consisting of combinations of drugs that target different phases of the HCV life cycle. DAAs include NS3/4A protease inhibitors, NS5A replication complex inhibitors and NS5B polymerase inhibitors (see Study Tip Gal). Many DAAs are available only in combination products. For treatment-naive patients without cirrhosis, recommended regimens are:

- Glecaprevir/pibrentasvir
- Sofosbuvir/velpatasvir

DAA MECHANISMS AND REGIMENS

Preferred HCV regimens include 2-3 DAAs with different mechanisms of action (often in one tablet)

MECHANISM	NAME CLUE	EXAMPLES
NS3/4A Protease Inhibitors	–previr P for PI	Glecaprevir Grazoprevir Paritaprevir Voxilaprevir
NS5A Replication Complex Inhibitors	–asvir A for NS5A	Elbasvir Ledipasvir Ombitasvir Pibrentasvir Velpatasvir
NS5B Polymerase Inhibitors	–buvir B for NS5B	Dasabuvir Sofosbuvir

Be able to recognize appropriate and inappropriate combinations.

Example:

Velpatasvir + sofosbuvir: preferred regimen combining 2 different MOAs.

Dasabuvir + sofosbuvir: two DAAs with the same MOA; should not be used together in a combination regimen.

What do the protease inhibitors used for HIV and HCV have in common? They are taken with food.

Remember: **P**rotease **I**nhibitors & **G**rub (**PIG**) **Take With Food***

*Exceptions: elbasvir/grazoprevir (Zepatier) for HCV (without regard to food) and fosamprenavir oral susp for HIV (without food in adults)

iStock.com/Tigatelu

DRUG	DOSING	SAFETY/SIDE EFFECTS/MONITORING
All DAAs		**BOXED WARNING (FOR ENTIRE CLASS)** Risk of reactivating HBV; test all patients for HBV before starting a DAA **WARNINGS** For sofosbuvir-containing regimens: do not use amiodarone with sofosbuvir as serious symptomatic bradycardia has been reported Hypoglycemia can occur when DAAs are used with insulin or other hypoglycemic drugs, unless the dose of the diabetes medication is reduced; DAAs improve glucose metabolism **SIDE EFFECTS** Well-tolerated; HA, fatigue, diarrhea, nausea **MONITORING** LFTs (including bilirubin), HCV-RNA
Glecaprevir/ pibrentasvir (Mavyret) Tablet	3 tablets once daily with food	**CONTRAINDICATIONS** Mavyret: moderate-severe hepatic impairment (Child-Pugh B or C) or history of hepatic decompensation
Sofosbuvir/velpatasvir (Epclusa) Tablet	1 tablet daily with or without food	**WARNINGS** Potentially serious drug interactions (see DAA Drug Interactions on the following page) **NOTES** Sofosbuvir monotherapy is not effective and not recommended
Sofosbuvir/ledipasvir (Harvoni) Tablet	1 tablet daily with or without food	*Sovaldi, Epclusa, Harvoni, Vosevi*: protect from moisture; dispense in original container *Epclusa, Harvoni* and *Vosevi*: avoid or minimize acid-suppressive therapy during treatment (see DAA Drug Interactions) *Mavyret, Vosevi*: rare cases of liver failure or worsening liver function
Sofosbuvir/velpatasvir/ voxilaprevir (Vosevi) Tablet	1 tablet daily with food	**Pan-Genotypic (approved for all 6 HCV genotypes) for Treatment-Naïve Patients** *Epclusa* and *Mavyret* **Approved for 8-Week Course of Therapy (select patients)** *Mavyret*
Sofosbuvir (Sovaldi) Tablet	400 mg daily with or without food	**Approved for Salvage Therapy (failed previous therapy)** *Vosevi* and *Mavyret* (select patients)
Paritaprevir/ ritonavir/ombitasvir + dasabuvir (Viekira Pak*) Tablets Paritaprevir/ritonavir/ ombitasvir combination tablets copackaged with dasabuvir tablets	*Viekira Pak:* 2 tablets of paritaprevir/ritonavir/ ombitasvir once daily in the morning and 1 dasabuvir tablet twice daily with meals	**CONTRAINDICATIONS** Moderate-severe hepatic impairment (Child-Pugh B or C), history of hepatic decompensation, use with CYP3A4 substrates or inducers (↑ levels can cause serious events), use with ethinyl estradiol products (avoid use during treatment and for 2 weeks after stopping) *Viekira Pak*: do not use with strong inducers or inhibitors of CYP2C8 **WARNINGS** Hepatic decompensation/failure in patients with cirrhosis, ↑ LFTs (> 5 x ULN) within 4 wks of treatment, significant drug interaction potential, risk of HIV protease inhibitor resistance **SIDE EFFECTS** Insomnia, pruritus
Elbasvir/grazoprevir (Zepatier) Tablet	1 tablet daily with or without food	**CONTRAINDICATIONS** Moderate-severe hepatic impairment (Child-Pugh B or C); use with strong inducers of CYP3A4, OATP1B1/3 inhibitors and efavirenz; all contraindications to ribavirin apply when used in combination regimens **WARNINGS** ↑ LFTs (> 5 x ULN) within 4 wks of treatment, significant drug interaction potential **NOTES** Screening for NS5A polymorphism is recommended when treating HCV genotype 1a *Zepatier*: rare cases of liver failure or worsening liver function

Viekira Pak is available but mainly used outside the U.S.

DAA DRUG INTERACTIONS

All DAAs have <u>significant drug interaction potential</u>. This summary is not all-inclusive. Consult the package labeling of each drug for additional detail.

All DAAs

- <u>Contraindicated with strong inducers of CYP3A4</u> (e.g., <u>carbamazepine, oxcarbazepine, phenobarbital, phenytoin, rifampin, rifabutin and St. John's wort</u>).

- Most DAAs ↑ statin concentrations and myopathy risk.

- ↓ BG can occur with insulin and other diabetes medications. Monitor BG and ↓ diabetes medication dose as needed.

Harvoni, Epclusa and Vosevi

- Contains sofosbuvir: do not use with amiodarone due to the risk of bradycardia.

- <u>Antacids, H2RAs and PPIs</u> can ↓ concentrations of <u>ledipasvir and velpatasvir</u>.

  ❏ Separate from antacids by four hours.

  ❏ Take H2RAs at the same time or separated (~12 hours) and use famotidine ≤ 40 mg BID or equivalent.

  ❏ <u>PPIs are not recommended with Epclusa</u>.

Mavyret

- Do not use with efavirenz, HIV protease inhibitors (specifically atazanavir, darunavir, lopinavir, ritonavir), ethinyl estradiol-containing products or cyclosporine.

Viekira Pak

- Contraindicated with: <u>strong inducers of CYP3A4, ethinyl estradiol-containing products, lovastatin, simvastatin</u>, alfuzosin, cisapride, colchicine, ranolazine, dronedarone, lurasidone, pimozide, ergotamine derivatives, efavirenz, sildenafil (dosed for PAH), triazolam and oral midazolam.

- Dasabuvir (component of *Viekira Pak)* is a substrate (major) of CYP2C8; do not use with strong inducers or inhibitors of CYP2C8 (e.g., gemfibrozil).

- See HIV chapter for additional ritonavir drug interactions.

Zepatier

- Do not use with efavirenz, HIV protease inhibitors (specifically atazanavir, darunavir, lopinavir, saquinavir, tipranavir) or cyclosporine.

- Not recommended with nafcillin, ketoconazole, bosentan, tacrolimus, etravirine, *Stribild, Genvoya* and modafinil.

RIBAVIRIN

Ribavirin (RBV) is an oral antiviral drug that inhibits replication of RNA and DNA viruses. It can be used for <u>HCV in combination</u> with other drugs (DAAs and/or interferon alfa), but <u>never as monotherapy</u>. <u>Aerosolized ribavirin</u> has been used for <u>respiratory syncytial virus (RSV)</u> (see the Pediatric Conditions chapter).

DRUG	DOSING	SAFETY/SIDE EFFECTS/MONITORING
Ribavirin Capsule, tablet *Virazole* – for RSV	400-600 mg BID, varies based on indication, patient weight and genotype ↑ tolerability if given with food Hgb < 10 g/dL: ↓ dose (avoid if Hgb < 8.5 g/dL) Capsule should not be crushed, chewed, opened or broken	**BOXED WARNINGS** <u>Significant teratogenic</u> effects; <u>not effective for monotherapy of HCV</u>; <u>hemolytic anemia</u> (primary toxicity of oral therapy, mostly occurring within 1-2 wks of initiation) **CONTRAINDICATIONS** <u>Pregnancy</u>, women of childbearing age who will not use contraception reliably, male partners of pregnant women, hemoglobinopathies, CrCl < 50 mL/min (capsule), autoimmune hepatitis **SIDE EFFECTS** <u>Hemolytic anemia</u> (can worsen cardiac disease and lead to MI; do not use in unstable cardiac disease), fatigue, HA, insomnia, N/V/D, anorexia, myalgias, hypothyroidism **MONITORING** CBC with differential, platelets, electrolytes, LFTs/bili, HCV-RNA, TSH, monthly pregnancy tests **NOTES** <u>Avoid pregnancy in females (including in female partners of male patients) during therapy</u> and <u>6 months after</u> completion; at least <u>2 reliable forms of effective contraception</u> are required <u>during treatment and in the 6-month post-treatment</u> follow-up period

Ribavirin Drug Interactions

- Ribavirin can ↑ hepatotoxic effects of NRTIs; lactic acidosis can occur.

- Zidovudine can ↑ risk and severity of anemia from ribavirin.

- Do not use with didanosine due to cases of fatal hepatic failure, peripheral neuropathy and pancreatitis.

RENAL & LIVER DISEASE

INTERFERON ALFA

Interferons are naturally-produced cytokines that have antiviral, antiproliferative and immunomodulatory effects. Interferon alfa (INF-alfa) is approved for <u>treatment of HBV and HCV</u>. The <u>pegylated forms</u> (PEG-INF-alfa) have polyethylene glycol added, which <u>prolongs the half-life</u>, reducing the dosing to once weekly. INF-alfa monotherapy and combination therapy have been used to treat HCV. Combination therapy for HCV consists of INF + RBV or INF + RBV + DAAs. HCV guidelines do not recommend interferon products, but they will continue to be used when other treatments are contraindicated or too costly. <u>Interferons have toxicities and lab abnormalities</u> that limit their use.

DRUG	DOSING	SAFETY/SIDE EFFECTS/MONITORING
Interferon-alfa-2b (*Intron A*) – for HBV, HCV, many cancers	<u>SC</u> dosing varies by indication and product:	**BOXED WARNINGS** Can cause or exacerbate <u>neuropsychiatric, autoimmune, ischemic or infectious</u> disorders; if used with <u>ribavirin, teratogenic/anemia risk</u>
Pegylated interferon-alfa-2a (*Pegasys*) – for HBV and HCV	*Intron A*: 3 times weekly *Pegasys* and *PegIntron*: weekly	**CONTRAINDICATIONS** Autoimmune hepatitis, decompensated liver disease in cirrhotic patients, infants/neonates (*Pegasys*)
Pegylated interferon-alfa-2b (*PegIntron, Sylatron*) – for HCV		**WARNINGS** Neuropsychiatric events, cardiovascular events, endocrine disorders (hypo/hyperthyroidism, hypo/hyperglycemia), visual disorders (retinopathy, decrease in vision), pancreatitis, myelosuppression, skin reactions

INTERFERONS

- Alfa: HBV, HCV and some cancers

- Beta: Multiple sclerosis (MS)

Interferons do not provide a cure and are hard to take. A flu-like syndrome after the injection is common. The list of boxed warnings and warnings is long.

SIDE EFFECTS
<u>CNS effects (fatigue, depression</u>, anxiety, weakness), <u>GI upset, ↑ LFTs (5-10 x ULN during treatment), myelosuppression</u>, mild alopecia

<u>Flu-like syndrome (fever, chills, HA, malaise); pre-treat with acetaminophen and an antihistamine</u>

MONITORING
CBC with differential, platelets, LFTs, uric acid, SCr, electrolytes, TGs, thyroid function tests, serum HBV-DNA or HCV-RNA levels

DRUG TREATMENT FOR HEPATITIS B

INTERFERON ALFA

Interferon alfa (see previous page) is approved as monotherapy and is a preferred treatment for HBV.

NUCLEOSIDE/TIDE REVERSE TRANSCRIPTASE INHIBITORS (NRTIs)

These drugs inhibit HBV replication by inhibiting HBV polymerase resulting in DNA chain termination. The NRTIs listed below are approved as monotherapy options for HBV. Prior to starting HBV therapy, all patients should be tested for HIV. Antivirals used for HBV can have activity against HIV, and if a patient is co-infected with both HIV and HBV, it is important that the chosen therapy is appropriate for both viruses to minimize risk of HIV antiviral resistance.

DRUG	DOSING	SAFETY/SIDE EFFECTS/MONITORING
All HBV NRTIs	CrCl < 50 mL/min: ↓ dose or frequency Exception: *Vemlidy* (see below)	**BOXED WARNINGS (FOR ALL HBV NRTIs)** Lactic acidosis and severe hepatomegaly with steatosis, which can be fatal (downgraded from boxed warning to warning for both tenofovir formulations and lamivudine) Exacerbations of HBV can occur upon discontinuation, monitor closely Can cause HIV resistance in HBV patients with unrecognized or untreated HIV infection (downgraded from boxed warning to warning for both tenofovir formulations) See HIV chapter for further information
Tenofovir disoproxil fumarate, TDF *(Viread)* Tablet, powder (oral) Preferred therapy	300 mg daily	**WARNINGS** Renal toxicity including acute renal failure and/or Fanconi syndrome, osteomalacia and ↓ bone mineral density **SIDE EFFECTS** TDF: renal impairment, ↓ bone mineral density, N/V/D, ↑ LFTs, ↑ CPK, headache, depression
Tenofovir alafenamide, TAF *(Vemlidy)* Tablet Preferred therapy	25 mg daily with food CrCl < 15 mL/min: not recommended	TAF: nausea, headache, abdominal pain, fatigue, cough, ↓ bone mineral density, ↑ LFTs **NOTES** *Viread* tablets and *Vemlidy*: protect from moisture; dispense only in original container TAF is associated with ↓ renal and bone toxicity compared to TDF *Vemlidy* is approved only for treating HBV; see HIV chapter for tenofovir alafenamide combination products used for HIV
Entecavir *(Baraclude)* Tablet, oral solution Preferred therapy	Nucleoside-treatment naïve: 0.5 mg daily Lamivudine-resistant: 1 mg daily Take on empty stomach	**SIDE EFFECTS** Peripheral edema, pyrexia, ascites, ↑ LFTs, hematuria, nephrotoxicity, ↑ SCr **NOTES** Food reduces AUC by 18-20%; take on an empty stomach (2 hours before or after a meal)
Lamivudine *(Epivir HBV)* Tablet, oral solution	100 mg daily 150 mg BID or 300 mg daily if co-infected with HIV	**BOXED WARNING** Do not use *Epivir HBV* for treatment of HIV (contains lower dose of lamivudine); can result in HIV resistance **SIDE EFFECTS** Headache, N/V/D, fatigue, insomnia, myalgias, ↑ LFTs, pancreatitis (rare)
Adefovir *(Hepsera)* Tablet	10 mg daily	**BOXED WARNING** Caution in patients with renal impairment or those at risk of renal toxicity (including concurrent nephrotoxic drugs or NSAIDs) **SIDE EFFECTS** HA, weakness, abdominal pain, hematuria, rash, nephrotoxicity

NRTI Drug Interactions

- Ribavirin can ↑ hepatotoxic effects of all NRTIs; lactic acidosis can occur.

- Tenofovir formulations: do not use with adefovir due to ↑ risk of virologic failure and potential for ↑ side effects.

- Tenofovir alafenamide is a P-gp substrate; do not use with oxcarbazepine, phenytoin, phenobarbital, rifampin and St. John's wort.

- SMX/TMP can ↑ lamivudine levels due to ↓ excretion.

LIVER DISEASE AND CIRRHOSIS

BACKGROUND

Cirrhosis is advanced fibrosis (scarring) of the liver that is usually irreversible. There are many causes, but the most common in the U.S. are hepatitis C and alcohol consumption. As scar tissue replaces the healthy liver tissue, blood flow through the liver is impaired, leading to numerous complications including portal hypertension, gastroesophageal varices, ascites and hepatic encephalopathy.

CLINICAL PRESENTATION

Symptoms can include nausea, loss of appetite, vomiting, diarrhea, malaise, pain in the upper right quadrant of the abdomen, yellowed skin and yellowed whites of the eyes (jaundice) and darkened urine. Stool can become lighter in color (white or clay-colored) due to decreased bile (from decreased production or a blocked bile duct).

OBJECTIVE CRITERIA

Cirrhosis is definitively diagnosed with a liver biopsy, but certain lab results can suggest cirrhosis or other types of liver damage (see Study Tip Gal). Aspartate aminotransferase (AST) and alanine aminotransferase (ALT) are liver enzymes. The normal range for both is 10 – 40 units/L. In general, the higher the values, the more active (acute) the liver disease or inflammation. Clinical signs of liver disease, in addition to ↑ ALT and ↑ AST, include ↓ albumin (protein produced by the liver; normal range 3.5 – 5.5 g/dL), ↑ alkaline phosphatase (Alk Phos or ALP), ↑ total bilirubin (Tbili), ↑ lactate dehydrogenase (LDH), and ↑ prothrombin time (PT) and INR.

A hepatic panel (AST, ALT, Tbili and Alk Phos), also called liver function tests (LFTs), is used to assess acute and chronic liver inflammation/disease, and for baseline and routine monitoring of hepatotoxic drugs. Albumin and PT/INR are markers of synthetic liver function (production ability) and are likely to be altered in chronic liver disease (particularly cirrhosis). Liver disease can be classified as hepatocellular (↑ ALT and ↑ AST), cholestatic (↑ Alk Phos and ↑ Tbili) or mixed (↑ AST, ALT, Alk Phos and Tbili). See the Lab Values & Drug Monitoring chapter for additional information.

ASSESSING SEVERITY OF LIVER DISEASE

The severity of liver disease serves as a predictor of patient survival, surgical outcomes and the risk of complications, such as variceal bleeding. The Child-Turcotte-Pugh (CTP) or Child-Pugh classification system is widely used and online calculators are available. The score ranges from 0 – 15. Class A (mild disease) is defined as a score < 7; Class B (moderate disease) is a score of 7 – 9, and Class C (severe disease) is

---

LAB TESTS FOR LIVER DISEASE

Specific liver function test (LFT) abnormalities can help distinguish between types of liver disease.

Acute liver toxicity, including from drugs
- ↑ AST/ALT

Chronic liver disease (e.g., cirrhosis)
- ↑ AST/ALT, Alk Phos, Tbili, LDH, PT/INR
- ↓ Albumin

Alcoholic liver disease
- ↑ AST > ↑ ALT (AST will be about double the ALT), ↑ gamma-glutamyl transpeptidase (GGT)

Hepatic encephalopathy
- ↑ Ammonia

Jaundice
- ↑ Tbili

---

a score of 10 – 15. The model for end-stage liver disease (MELD) is another scoring system that ranges from 0 – 40. Higher numbers indicate a greater risk of death within three months. Noninvasive tests are increasingly used to predict fibrosis and cirrhosis.

Unlike drug dosing in renal failure, information to guide drug dosing of hepatically cleared drugs in liver failure is not as widely available. It is becoming more common to see package labeling for medications make specific recommendations based on Child-Pugh class. In general, caution is advised when using hepatically cleared drugs in severe liver disease (Class C) and, in select cases, dose adjustment could be necessary. For drugs that are extensively hepatically metabolized, it is best to start at lower doses and titrate to clinical effect.

NATURAL PRODUCTS

Milk thistle, an extract derived from a member of the daisy family, is sometimes used by patients with liver disease. Milk thistle does not appear to be harmful, but there is limited data to demonstrate efficacy. A possible side effect is mild diarrhea and there are concerns for possible drug interactions between milk thistle and antiviral hepatitis C medications. Kava, comfrey and flavocoxid (Limbrel, a medical food) are known hepatotoxins.

DRUG-INDUCED LIVER INJURY

Many drugs can cause liver damage (see Key Drugs Guy on next page). The primary treatment (in most cases) is to stop the drug. Hepatotoxic drugs are typically discontinued when the LFTs are > 3 times the upper limit of normal (> 150 units/L of ALT or AST), but clinical judgment is warranted. Rechallenging with the drug can be considered if clinically necessary. An excellent reference for drug-induced liver injury (DILI) is http://livertox.nih.gov.

Acetaminophen is a known hepatotoxic drug and can cause severe injury. Acetaminophen can be used by patients with cirrhosis, for limited periods of time and at lower dosages. Patients with alcoholic cirrhosis who are actively drinking and/or malnourished are more susceptible to further liver damage. NSAIDs should be avoided in patients with cirrhosis because these drugs can lead to decompensation, including bleeding.

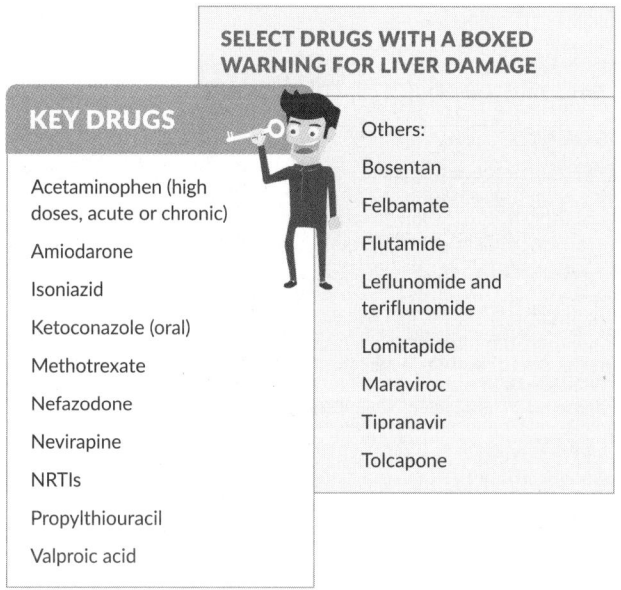

SELECT DRUGS WITH A BOXED WARNING FOR LIVER DAMAGE

KEY DRUGS

Acetaminophen (high doses, acute or chronic)

Amiodarone

Isoniazid

Ketoconazole (oral)

Methotrexate

Nefazodone

Nevirapine

NRTIs

Propylthiouracil

Valproic acid

Others:

Bosentan

Felbamate

Flutamide

Leflunomide and teriflunomide

Lomitapide

Maraviroc

Tipranavir

Tolcapone

ALCOHOL-ASSOCIATED LIVER DISEASE

Alcohol-associated liver disease (ALD), sometimes called alcoholic liver disease, is the most common type of drug-induced liver disease. Risk increases with the duration and amount of alcohol consumed, and women have a higher risk than men. ALD can include fatty liver, alcoholic hepatitis and chronic hepatitis with hepatic fibrosis or cirrhosis. Chronic alcohol ingestion over a long period of time causes "steatosis" or fatty liver, due to fat deposition in the hepatocytes. This can be reversible and self-limited (if drinking is stopped) or can lead to fibrosis and cirrhosis. Some patients develop alcoholic hepatitis, an acute process with poor short-term survival. Of all chronic heavy drinkers, only 15 – 20% develop hepatitis or cirrhosis.

Chronic consumption of alcohol results in the secretion of pro-inflammatory cytokines (TNF-alpha, IL-6 and IL-8), oxidative stress, lipid peroxidation and acetaldehyde toxicity. These factors cause inflammation, apoptosis (cell death) and eventually fibrosis of liver cells. If the patient stops drinking, the liver can possibly regenerate to some extent.

TREATMENT

The most important part of treatment is alcohol cessation. Maintenance of abstinence is essential to improving outcomes and should include the use of drug treatment to control cravings. Treatment programs primarily use

benzodiazepines for alcohol withdrawal in inpatients, whereas anticonvulsants are commonly used for outpatients. Naltrexone (Vivitrol), acamprosate and disulfiram (formerly Antabuse) are used to prevent relapses. A few off-label treatments include gabapentin, baclofen and topiramate. An alcohol rehabilitation program and a support group whose members share common experiences and problems are extremely helpful in breaking the addiction to alcohol.

Proper nutrition is essential to help the liver recover. Vitamins and trace minerals, including vitamin A, vitamin D, thiamine (vitamin B1), folate, pyridoxine (vitamin B6) and zinc can help reverse malnutrition. Thiamine is used to prevent and treat Wernicke-Korsakoff syndrome. Wernicke's encephalopathy and Korsakoff syndrome are different conditions that are both due to brain damage caused by a lack of vitamin B1. Hepatotoxic drugs should be avoided if possible or doses should be adjusted as appropriate.

COMPLICATIONS OF LIVER DISEASE AND CIRRHOSIS

PORTAL HYPERTENSION AND VARICEAL BLEEDING

Portal hypertension (increased blood pressure in the portal vein) can cause complications, including the development of esophageal varices (enlarged veins in the lower part of the esophagus). When blood flow through the liver is blocked by scar tissue, it backs up and flows into smaller blood vessels. These vessels can balloon out and bleed if they break open.

Esophageal Varices

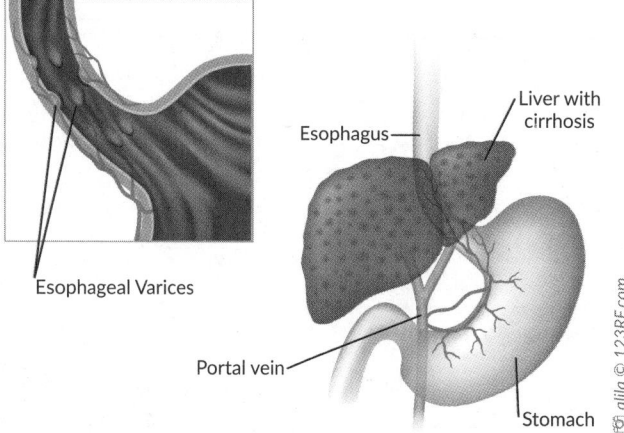

Esophageal Varices

Esophagus

Liver with cirrhosis

Portal vein

Stomach

alila © 123RF.com

Acute variceal bleeding can be fatal. Patients are stabilized with supportive therapies, such as blood volume resuscitation (blood products), mechanical ventilation, correction of coagulopathy, and attempts to stop the bleeding and prevent rebleeding. Band ligation (putting a band around the vessel) or sclerotherapy (injecting a solution into the vessel to make it collapse and close) are recommended first-line treatments for bleeding varices. These procedures are performed by a physician using endoscopy. Medications that vasoconstrict the splanchnic (GI) circulation can stop or minimize the bleeding. Octreotide is selective for the splanchnic vessels whereas vasopressin is non-selective. Surgical interventions can be considered if the patient is not responding to treatment or to prevent future rebleeding episodes. Common surgical procedures include balloon tamponade (can help control current bleeding) or transjugular intrahepatic portosystemic shunt (TIPS), in which a stent is placed in the liver to allow blood to flow directly from the portal vein to the hepatic vein (bypassing the scarred liver tissue). Short-term antibiotic prophylaxis (ceftriaxone or quinolone for up to 7 days) should be given to cirrhotic patients with a variceal bleed to reduce bacterial infections and mortality. Non-selective beta-blockers can be used for primary and secondary prevention of variceal bleeding (see below).

Vasoconstricting Medications for Bleeding Varices

DRUG	DOSING	SAFETY/SIDE EFFECTS/MONITORING
Octreotide (Sandostatin, *Sandostatin LAR Depot,* others) Analog of somatostatin with greater potency and longer duration of action	Bolus: 25-100 mcg IV (usual 50 mcg), can repeat in 1 hr if hemorrhage not controlled Continuous infusion: 25-50 mcg/hr x 2-5 days	**SIDE EFFECTS** Bradycardia, cholelithiasis, biliary sludge, chest pain, fatigue, HA, pruritus, hyperglycemia, hypoglycemia (highest risk in type 1 diabetes), N/V/D, hypothyroidism, abdominal pain, malaise, fever, dizziness, flatulence, constipation, injection site pain, arthropathy, myalgias, URTIs **MONITORING** Blood glucose, HR, ECG
Vasopressin *(Vasostrict)* Antidiuretic hormone analog Not first line (usually used with nitroglycerin IV to prevent myocardial ischemia)	Infusion: 0.2-0.4 units/min IV (max 0.8 units/min), max duration 24 hours	**SIDE EFFECTS** Arrhythmias, chest pain, MI, ↓ cardiac output, ↑ BP, N/V **MONITORING** BP, HR, ECG, fluid balance

Non-Selective Beta-Blockers for Portal Hypertension

Non-selective beta-blockers (e.g., nadolol, propranolol) are used for primary and secondary prevention of variceal bleeding. Beta-blockers reduce portal pressure, by reducing portal venous inflow, through two mechanisms: 1) decreased cardiac output (via beta-1 blockade) and 2) decreased splanchnic blood flow due to vasoconstriction (via beta-2 blockade and unopposed alpha activity). The beta-blocker is titrated to the maximal tolerated dose (target HR 55 – 60 BPM) and continued indefinitely.

DRUG	DOSING	SAFETY/SIDE EFFECTS/MONITORING
Nadolol (Corgard)	Initial: 40 mg PO daily	Refer to the Hypertension chapter for a complete review of beta-blockers. **BOXED WARNING** Do not withdraw beta-blockers abruptly (particularly in patients with CAD), gradually taper over 1-2 wks to avoid acute tachycardia, HTN and/or ischemia **CONTRAINDICATIONS** Sinus bradycardia, 2nd or 3rd degree heart block, sick sinus syndrome (unless patient has a functioning artificial pacemaker) or cardiogenic shock; do not initiate in patients with an active asthma exacerbation
Propranolol (Inderal LA, Inderal XL, *InnoPran XL, Hemangeol)*	Initial: 20 mg PO BID	**WARNING** Non-selective drugs are used for portal hypertension; use extreme caution with asthma, severe COPD, peripheral vascular disease or Raynaud's disease (a condition with vasospasms in the extremities) Can mask signs of hyperthyroidism and aggravate psychiatric conditions; use caution in patients with diabetes (particularly with recurrent hypoglycemia) **MONITORING** HR, BP

HEPATIC ENCEPHALOPATHY

Hepatic encephalopathy (HE) is caused by acute or chronic hepatic insufficiency. Symptoms include musty odor of the breath and/or urine, changes in thinking, confusion, forgetfulness, drowsiness, disorientation, mood changes, poor concentration, worsening handwriting, hand tremor (asterixis), sluggish movements and risk of coma. The symptoms of HE result from an accumulation of gut-derived nitrogenous substances in the blood (such as ammonia, glutamate). These substances would normally be cleared by the liver, but when the liver is not functioning properly, blood is shunted through collateral vessels that empty directly into the circulation instead.

Treatment includes identifying and treating precipitating factors and reducing blood ammonia levels through diet (by limiting the amount of animal protein) and drug therapy. Patients should have a daily protein intake of 1 – 1.5 g/kg. Vegetable and dairy sources of protein are preferred to animal sources due to the lower calorie to nitrogen ratio. Branched-chain amino acids (BCAAs) (e.g., leucine, isoleucine, valine) are favored over aromatic amino acids (AAAs); they interfere with AAAs ability to cross the blood-brain barrier and increase hepatocyte growth factor synthesis.

Drug therapy consists of nonabsorbable disaccharides (such as lactulose) and antibiotics (rifaximin, neomycin, others) for acute and chronic therapy. Lactulose is first line for both acute and chronic (prevention) therapy. It works by converting ammonia produced by intestinal bacteria to ammonium, which is polar and therefore cannot readily diffuse into the blood. Lactulose also enhances diffusion of ammonia into the colon for excretion. Rifaximin is the preferred second-line treatment. Antibiotics work by inhibiting the activity of urease-producing bacteria, which decreases ammonia production. Zinc (220 mg PO BID) may also be used; it can serve as a cofactor for enzymes of the urea cycle, further decreasing ammonia concentrations, and can correct a zinc deficiency.

RENAL & LIVER DISEASE

DRUG	DOSING	SAFETY/SIDE EFFECTS/MONITORING
Lactulose (*Enulose, Constulose, Generlac, Kristalose*) Oral solution and packet	Treatment: 30-45 mL (or 20-30 grams) PO every hour until stool evacuation; then 30-45 mL (20-30 grams) PO 3-4 times/day, titrated to produce 2-3 soft bowel movements daily Enema: Q4-6H PRN Prevention: 30-45 mL (or 20-30 grams) PO 3-4 times/day, titrated to produce 2-3 soft bowel movements daily	**CONTRAINDICATIONS** Low galactose diet **SIDE EFFECTS** Flatulence, diarrhea, dyspepsia, abdominal discomfort, dehydration, hypernatremia, hypokalemia **MONITORING** Mental status, bowel movements, ammonia, fluid status, electrolytes
Rifaximin (*Xifaxan*) Tablet	Treatment (off-label): 400 mg PO Q8H x 5-10 days Prevention: 550 mg PO BID	**SIDE EFFECTS** Peripheral edema, dizziness, fatigue, nausea, ascites, flatulence, headache **MONITORING** Mental status, ammonia
Neomycin	4-12 grams daily divided Q4-6H x 5-6 days	**BOXED WARNINGS** Neurotoxicity (hearing loss, vertigo, ataxia); nephrotoxicity (particularly in renal impairment or with concurrent use of other nephrotoxic drugs); can cause neuromuscular blockade and respiratory paralysis especially when given soon after anesthesia or with muscle relaxants **SIDE EFFECTS** GI upset, ototoxicity, nephrotoxicity, irritation/soreness of mouth/rectal area **MONITORING** Mental status, renal function, hearing, ammonia
Metronidazole (*Flagyl*)	250 mg PO Q6-12H	**NOTES** Do not use long term due to peripheral neuropathies See Infectious Diseases I chapter for additional information

ASCITES

Ascites is fluid accumulation within the peritoneal space that can lead to the development of spontaneous bacterial peritonitis (SBP) and hepatorenal syndrome (HRS). There are many treatment approaches to managing ascites, which are chosen based on the severity; all patients with cirrhosis and ascites should be considered for liver transplantation.

Patients with ascites due to portal hypertension should restrict dietary sodium intake to < 2 grams/day, avoid sodium-retaining medications (including NSAIDs) and use diuretics to increase fluid loss. Restriction of fluid is recommended only in patients with symptomatic severe hyponatremia (serum Na < 120 mEq/L).

Diuretic therapy for ascites can be initiated with either spironolactone monotherapy or with a combination of furosemide and spironolactone. Furosemide by itself is ineffective. Spironolactone is initiated at a single daily dose of 50 – 100 mg and increased to a maximum of 400 mg per day. When used in combination, the drugs should be titrated to a maximal weight loss of 0.5 kg/day; if possible, a ratio of 40 mg furosemide to 100 mg spironolactone should be used to maintain potassium balance.

The spironolactone oral suspension (CaroSpir) is not therapeutically equivalent to oral tablets (Aldactone). The approved CaroSpir dose for treating edema associated with

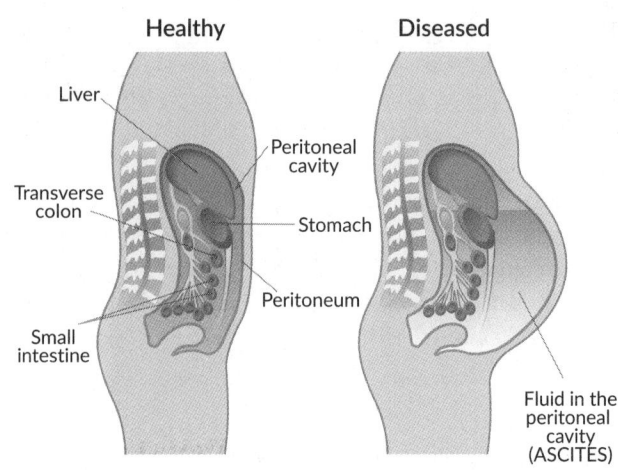

Healthy   Diseased

Liver

Peritoneal cavity

Transverse colon

Stomach

Peritoneum

Small intestine

Fluid in the peritoneal cavity (ASCITES)

cirrhosis is 20 – 75 mg (4 – 15 mL) in single or divided doses (see Chronic Heart Failure and Hypertension chapters for additional information).

In severe cases, abdominal paracentesis is needed to directly remove ascitic fluid. Large volume paracentesis (removal of > 5 L) is associated with significant fluid shifts and the addition of albumin (6 – 8 grams per liter of fluid removed) is recommended to prevent paracentesis-induced circulatory dysfunction and progression to hepatorenal syndrome.

SPONTANEOUS BACTERIAL PERITONITIS

Spontaneous bacterial peritonitis (SBP) is an acute infection of the ascitic fluid. Diagnosis is guided by cell and microbiologic analysis. Targeting *Streptococci* and enteric Gram-negative pathogens with ceftriaxone (or an equivalent) for 5 – 7 days is recommended. The addition of albumin (1.5 grams/kg of body weight on day 1 and 1 gram/kg on day 3) can improve survival in some patients. Patients who have survived an episode of SBP should receive secondary prophylaxis with oral ciprofloxacin or sulfamethoxazole/trimethoprim.

HEPATORENAL SYNDROME

Hepatorenal syndrome (HRS) is the development of renal failure in patients with advanced cirrhosis. It occurs as a result of renal vasoconstriction, mediated by activation of the renin-angiotensin-aldosterone system (RAAS) and the sympathetic nervous system (SNS) through a feedback mechanism known as hepatorenal reflex. Appropriately treating the various stages and complications of cirrhosis, and avoiding nephrotoxins and renal hypoperfusion, helps prevent progression to HRS. HRS can be directly treated with albumin, octreotide and midodrine, but prevention is critical given the difficulty in managing HRS in this patient population.

KEY COUNSELING POINTS

See the Drug Formulations and Patient Counseling chapter for counseling language/layman's terminology.

ALL DIRECT-ACTING ANTIVIRALS

- Many drug interactions.

Mavyret
- Take with food.

Viekira Pak
- Can cause liver damage.
- *Viekira Pak* contains two different types of tablets. You must take both types of tablets exactly as prescribed to treat your chronic hepatitis C virus (HCV) infection.
  - ❏ One tablet contains the medicines ombitasvir, paritaprevir and ritonavir (take two tablets once daily).
  - ❏ The other tablet contains the medicine dasabuvir (take one tablet twice daily).

RIBAVIRIN
- Avoid in pregnancy (teratogenic), including in male partners of pregnant women.
- Can cause hemolytic anemia.

NRTIs
- Can cause lactic acidosis.
- *Epivir HBV* tablets and oral solution are not interchangeable with the *Epivir* tablets and solution used in HIV (which have higher doses).
- Take entecavir on an empty stomach.

BETA-BLOCKERS
- Do not abruptly discontinue without consulting your healthcare provider.

Select Guidelines/References

American Association of Liver Diseases-Infectious Diseases Society of America (AASLD-IDSA) HCV Guidance: Recommendations for Testing, Managing, and Treating Hepatitis C. www.hcvguidelines.org (accessed 2022 Jan 18).

Diagnosis and Treatment of Alcohol-Associated Liver Diseases: 2019 Practice Guidance From the American Association for the Study of Liver Diseases. *Hepatology.* 2020;71(1):306-333.

Update on Prevention, Diagnosis, and Treatment of Chronic Hepatitis B: AASLD 2018 Hepatitis B Guidance. *Hepatology.* 2018;67(4):1560-1599.

IMMUNIZATIONS
& TRAVELERS

CONTENTS

CONTENT LEGEND

= Study Tip Gal   = Key Drug Guy

© iStock.com/tronand

CHAPTER 20
IMMUNIZATIONS

BACKGROUND

Vaccines prevent patients from acquiring serious or potentially fatal diseases. Childhood diseases that used to be common (e.g., diphtheria, meningitis, polio, tetanus) are now rare because children are vaccinated to prevent the illness, or are protected by herd immunity (when vaccinated people protect the unvaccinated, making them less likely to become infected). If vaccination rates drop below 85% – 95%, vaccine-preventable diseases can become a threat, as demonstrated by U.S. pertussis and measles outbreaks in recent years.

VACCINE RESOURCES

- The FDA approves the indication for a vaccine based on the demonstrated safety and efficacy.

- The Advisory Committee on Immunization Practices (ACIP) provides the recommendations for vaccine administration in children and adults (i.e., who gets what vaccine and when).

- The Centers for Disease Control and Prevention (CDC) approves the ACIP recommendations and publishes them in the CDC's Morbidity and Mortality Weekly Report (MMWR) and The Pink Book (Epidemiology and Prevention of Vaccine-Preventable Diseases).

- Other helpful resources for pharmacists related to immunizations are available on the following websites:

  ❏ American Pharmacists Association (www.pharmacist.com/immunization-center).

  ❏ Immunization Action Coalition (www.immunize.org).

Reliable Vaccine Information for Patients

Vaccine Information Statements (VISs) are prepared by the CDC for each vaccine to explain their benefits and risks. Federal law requires that a VIS be handed to the patient (or parent) before a vaccination is administered. VISs can be found on the CDC and Immunization Action Coalition websites.

VACCINES AND AUTISM

Some people believe that vaccines cause autism. The causes of autism are not fully understood, but there is <u>no evidence</u> that autism is caused by vaccines. Parents often first notice the behaviors of autism at an age when most childhood vaccine series are near completion (e.g., 18 – 24 months). Abnormal brain structure that is present in children with autism can be identified in the prefrontal and temporal cortical tissue before a child is born, prior to receiving vaccines. Genetic studies have confirmed that genes play an important role. For example, if one twin has autism, the other twin is also highly likely to have autism.

Thimerosal

Thimerosal is a mercury-containing preservative used in some vaccines; it was alleged to be contributing to the increase in autism since mercury has been linked to some brain disorders. There is <u>no evidence</u> that thimerosal poses a risk for autism. Thimerosal was removed from childhood vaccines in 2001, and the rates of autism have continued to increase. Thimerosal is contained in some multidose flu vaccines; parents may request a single-dose flu vaccine that does not contain a preservative, or a multidose vaccine without thimerosal.

GELATIN-CONTAINING PRODUCTS

Gelatin is porcine-derived (from pigs) and is used in some vaccines as a stabilizer. Most religious leaders for faiths with dietary rules that prohibit pork products permit the use of gelatin-containing vaccines.

IMMUNITY

The purpose of the immune system is to identify self substances (normal body parts/components) and non-self (foreign) substances, which are called antigens. When an <u>antigen</u> is detected, <u>antibodies</u> are produced naturally to <u>provide immunity</u> and <u>destroy</u> the antigen. <u>Immunoglobulin</u> is the medical term for antibody.

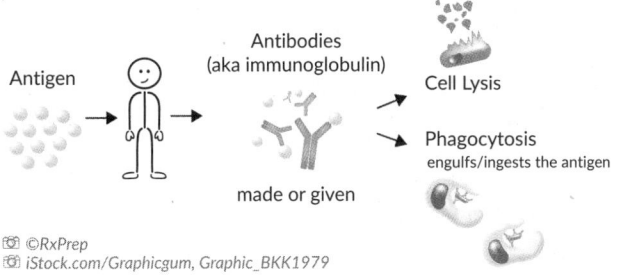

Antigen → Antibodies (aka immunoglobulin) → Cell Lysis / Phagocytosis (engulfs/ingests the antigen)

made or given

Immunity is acquired actively or passively. <u>Active immunity</u> develops when the person's <u>own immune system produces antibodies</u> to fight an infection or in response to vaccine administration. <u>Passive immunity</u> is acquired when <u>antibodies</u> are <u>provided from someone else</u> (see below).

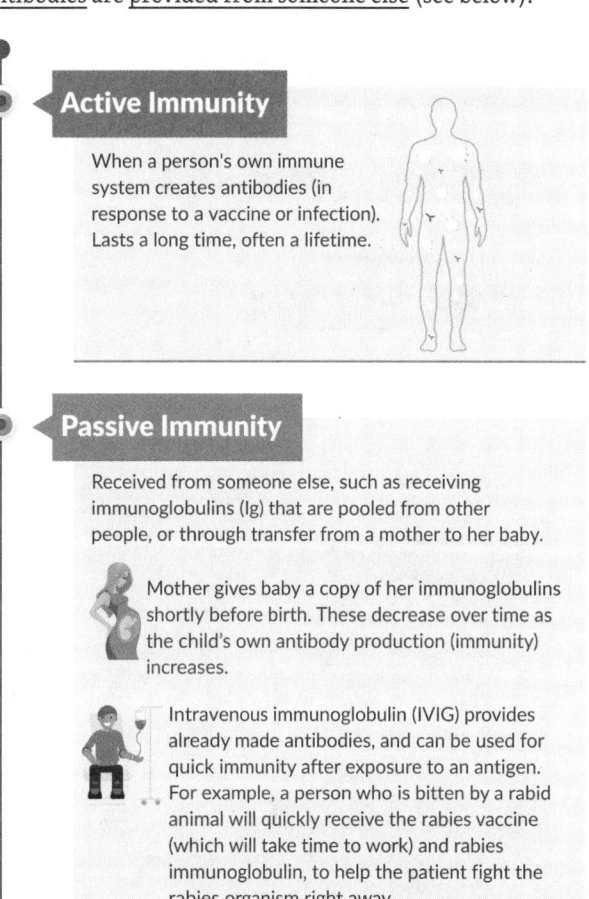

Active Immunity

When a person's own immune system creates antibodies (in response to a vaccine or infection). Lasts a long time, often a lifetime.

Passive Immunity

Received from someone else, such as receiving immunoglobulins (Ig) that are pooled from other people, or through transfer from a mother to her baby.

Mother gives baby a copy of her immunoglobulins shortly before birth. These decrease over time as the child's own antibody production (immunity) increases.

Intravenous immunoglobulin (IVIG) provides already made antibodies, and can be used for quick immunity after exposure to an antigen. For example, a person who is bitten by a rabid animal will quickly receive the rabies vaccine (which will take time to work) and rabies immunoglobulin, to help the patient fight the rabies organism right away.

TYPES OF VACCINES

<u>Live attenuated</u> (weakened) vaccines are produced by modifying a disease-producing ("wild") virus or bacterium in a laboratory; they have the ability to <u>replicate</u> (grow) and produce immunity but usually do not cause illness. Live attenuated vaccines are most similar to the actual disease and produce a <u>strong immune response</u> to the vaccine; they are <u>contraindicated</u> in <u>immunocompromised and pregnant</u> patients since uncontrolled replication of the pathogen can occur.

Most <u>inactivated</u> vaccines are composed of either a whole virus or bacterium, or fractions of either. Immunity resulting from an inactivated vaccine can diminish with time and <u>supplemental doses</u> may be required to increase, or "boost," immunity.

IMMUNIZATIONS & TRAVELERS

INACTIVATED VACCINES

Inactivated vaccines use the killed version of a wild virus or bacteria that causes the disease. Inactivated vaccines cannot replicate (and cause disease). They are less affected by circulating antibodies than live vaccines.*

Limitation: immunity is not as strong as with live vaccines; boosters may be required for ongoing immunity.

Polysaccharide, Conjugate and Recombinant Vaccines

Target a section of the organism, such as a protein, sugar, or capsid (outer casing).

Polysaccharide Vaccines

Polysaccharide (sugar) molecules are taken from the outside layer of encapsulated bacteria (such as pneumococcal serotypes; each serotype matches to a circulating strain of the organism). Polysaccharide vaccines do not produce a good immune response in children < 2 years of age.

Ex: Pneumococcal Polysaccharide Vaccine (Pneumovax 23)

Conjugate Vaccines

Conjugate vaccines use polysaccharide (sugar) molecules from the outside layer of encapsulated bacteria and join the molecules to carrier proteins. Conjugation increases the immune response in infants, and the antibody booster response to multiple doses of vaccine.

Ex: Pneumococcal Conjugate Vaccine (Prevnar 13), Meningococcal Conjugate Vaccine (e.g., Menactra)

Recombinant Vaccines

A gene segment of a protein from the organism is inserted into the gene of another cell, such as a yeast cell, where it replicates.

Ex: Human Papillomavirus Vaccine (Gardasil 9), Recombinant Influenza Vaccine (FluBlok Quadrivalent)

Toxoid Vaccines

The vaccine targets a toxin produced by the disease.

Ex: Diptheria Toxoid vaccine, Tetanus Toxoid vaccine

mRNA Vaccines

The vaccine gives instructions to the body's cells (in the form of mRNA) to produce a protein specific to the pathogen, which then triggers an immune response.

Ex: select COVID-19 vaccines

LIVE VACCINES

Live vaccines are most similar to the actual disease and provide a strong, long-lasting immune response.

Limitations: 1) Patients who are immunocompromised may not be able to halt replication; vaccination could cause the disease. 2) Circulating antibodies can interfere with vaccine replication.*

See the Key Drugs Guy for a list of common live vaccines.

*See the Live Vaccines and Antibody section

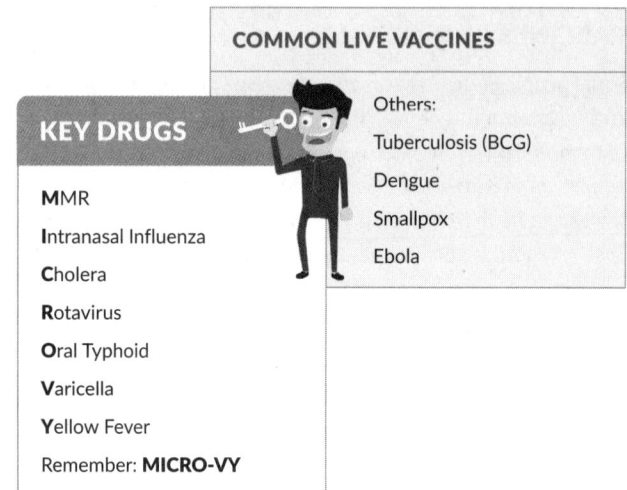

COMMON LIVE VACCINES

KEY DRUGS

MMR
Intranasal Influenza
Cholera
Rotavirus
Oral Typhoid
Varicella
Yellow Fever
Remember: **MICRO-VY**

Others:
Tuberculosis (BCG)
Dengue
Smallpox
Ebola

TIMING AND SPACING OF VACCINES

SIMULTANEOUS ADMINISTRATION

Most live or inactivated vaccines can be administered simultaneously (on the same day or at the same visit) without decreasing the antibody response or increasing the risk of adverse reactions (see the Study Tip Gal on the following page). Simultaneous administration of all vaccines for which a child is eligible is very important in childhood vaccination. Every effort should be made to provide all necessary vaccinations at one visit to improve compliance and increase the probability that a child will be fully immunized at the appropriate age. Combination vaccines help accomplish this with less injections.

VACCINES GIVEN IN A SERIES

Increasing the interval between the doses of a vaccine given in a series does not diminish the effectiveness of the vaccine after completion of the series. It may delay complete protection. Decreasing the interval between doses of vaccine can interfere with antibody response and is generally avoided. In a few cases, the interval can be shortened for high-risk patients (e.g., between doses of two different pneumococcal vaccines in an immunocompromised patient).

LIVE VACCINES AND ANTIBODY

Antibodies, in some blood and IVIG products, can interfere with live vaccine replication and a separation period may be required (see the Study Tip Gal on the following page). This is a concern with live vaccines because replication is required to produce an immune response.

The interval between an antibody-containing product and a measles, mumps and rubella-containing vaccine (MMR) or a varicella-containing vaccine (Varivax or MMRV) is a minimum of 3 months and can be up to 11 months. The specific product and dose determines the separation time.

Maternal antibodies are passed from the mother to the baby before birth, and will reduce the baby's response to live vaccines. Most live vaccines are withheld until the child is 12 months of age; at this time, the mother's antibodies will be depleted. An exception is live rotavirus vaccine, which is given to infants. It has been shown to be effective at preventing rotavirus-induced gastroenteritis despite the presence of maternal antibodies.

Inactivated vaccines can be given at any time. Inactivated vaccines are started when a baby is two months old, except for the hepatitis B vaccine series, which is started at birth.

LIVE VACCINES AND THE TB SKIN TEST

The tuberculin skin test (TST), also called a purified protein derivative (PPD) test, can be used to diagnose latent tuberculosis (TB). Live vaccines can cause a false-negative TST result. Options to reduce this risk include:

1. Give the live vaccine on the same day as the TST.

2. Wait 4 weeks after a live vaccine to perform the TST.

3. Administer the TST first, wait 48 – 72 hours to get the result, then give the live vaccine.

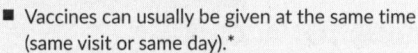

VACCINE TIMING & SPACING

General Rules for All Vaccines
- Vaccines can usually be given at the same time (same visit or same day).*

- Multiple live vaccines can be given on the same day or (if not given on the same day) spaced 4 weeks apart.**

- If a vaccine series requires > 1 dose, the intervals between doses can be extended without restarting the series, but they should not be shortened in most cases.

Live Vaccines and Antibody
- MMR and varicella-containing vaccines require separation from antibody-containing products (e.g., blood transfusions, IVIG). The recommended spacing is:

  ❏ Vaccine → 2 weeks → antibody-containing product

  ❏ Antibody-containing product → 3 months or longer → vaccine

- Simultaneous administration of vaccine and antibody (in the form of immunoglobulin) is recommended for post-exposure prophylaxis of certain diseases (e.g., hepatitis A and B, rabies, tetanus).

Exception: in patients with asplenia, Prevnar and Menactra should be separated by 4 weeks.

**Exception: no separation is required for oral rotavirus vaccines.*

VACCINE ADVERSE REACTIONS

All vaccines have the potential to cause an adverse reaction. Reactions can range from local (e.g., soreness, redness, itching) to severe and life-threatening (e.g., anaphylaxis).

Patients are screened for precautions and contraindications before vaccine administration to reduce the risk of severe reactions (see the Screening Prior to Vaccine Administration section on the following page). The patient should be monitored for at least 15 minutes after vaccination (to watch for an allergic reaction, syncope, dizziness or falls).

Pharmacists who administer vaccines need a plan (protocol) that covers emergency management of severe reactions until emergency medical help arrives (see the Management of Severe Allergic Reactions section on the following page). Adverse reactions that require some type of assistance should be reported to patient's healthcare provider and the FDA's Vaccine Adverse Event Reporting System (VAERS).

LOCAL REACTIONS

Local reactions occur at or near the injection site. These are common, more so with inactivated vaccines, and include pain, swelling and redness. Rarely, local reactions may be very exaggerated or severe.

SYSTEMIC REACTIONS

Systemic reactions are less common than local reactions. They include fever, malaise, myalgias (muscle pain), headache, loss of appetite or a mild illness that has similarities to the disease being prevented, such as a few chickenpox vesicles after receiving the varicella vaccine. Patients who have experienced systemic symptoms after a flu shot might think (incorrectly) that the vaccine caused the flu. The flu shot is an inactivated (killed) vaccine and cannot cause disease.

With live vaccines, mild systemic reactions can occur 3 – 21 days after the vaccine is given (i.e., after an incubation period). Intranasal flu vaccine can replicate in the upper airways (nose and throat) and can cause mild cold-like symptoms, such as a runny nose.

True Allergic Reactions

These are uncommon, and can be caused by the vaccine itself or a component of the vaccine product, such as a stabilizer, preservative or antibiotic (used to inhibit bacterial growth). Minor allergic reactions will resolve quickly and can be treated with diphenhydramine (OTC) or hydroxyzine (prescription). A minor reaction is not a contraindication to future vaccinations.

Severe allergic reactions are very rare (< 1 in 500,000 doses). A severe reaction with anaphylaxis can be life-threatening if not managed correctly. Anaphylactic reactions are IgE-mediated and occur within 30 – 60 minutes of receiving the vaccine. Symptoms can include urticaria (hives), swelling of the mouth and throat, difficulty breathing, wheezing, abdominal cramping and hypotension or shock.

The protocol for emergency management (see below) will include the use of epinephrine, which must be available to quickly reverse breathing difficulty.

MANAGEMENT OF SEVERE ALLERGIC REACTIONS

All providers who administer vaccines must have emergency protocols and supplies to treat anaphylaxis. If symptoms are severe, a second person should activate the emergency medical system (EMS) by calling 911. The primary healthcare provider should remain with the patient, assessing the airway, breathing, circulation and level of consciousness.

Care should be provided until EMS arrives:

- For adults, administer aqueous epinephrine 1 mg/mL (1:1,000 dilution) intramuscularly, 0.01 mg/kg (maximum dose is 0.5 mg). Most pharmacies use prefilled epinephrine auto-injectors. At least three adult (0.3 mg) auto-injectors should be available. Most adults will require 1 – 3 doses administered every 5 – 15 minutes.

- Diphenhydramine can be given to reduce swelling and pruritus. Drugs cannot be given orally if airway swelling is present due to a risk of choking.

- The patient should be placed in a supine position (flat on the back), unless there is breathing difficulty. Elevating the head will help breathing, but caution must be taken to keep the blood pressure adequate. If the blood pressure is low, elevate the legs only. Monitor the blood pressure and pulse every 5 minutes.

- Provide cardiopulmonary resuscitation (CPR), if necessary. Immunizing pharmacists need current basic life support (BLS or CPR) certification.

- Record all vital signs and administered medications

VACCINE CONTRAINDICATIONS AND PRECAUTIONS

There are specific circumstances when vaccines should not be given. Most precautions are temporary, and the vaccine can be given at a later time. For example, if the patient has a moderate or severe acute illness, vaccine administration should be delayed until it resolves. Mild acute illness is not a precaution, and the vaccine can be administered.

A contraindication is a condition that significantly increases the potential of a serious adverse reaction. Pregnancy and immunosuppression are two important contraindications to the use of live vaccines. Live vaccine administration must be timed carefully in patients who have recently received an antibody-containing blood product, as previously described. A severe or anaphylactic reaction following a vaccine dose is a contraindication to any subsequent doses of the same vaccine.

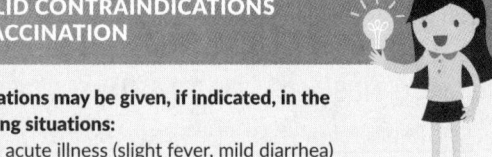

INVALID CONTRAINDICATIONS TO VACCINATION

Vaccinations may be given, if indicated, in the following situations:

- Mild acute illness (slight fever, mild diarrhea)
- Current antimicrobial treatment (some exceptions: see varicella, live influenza and oral typhoid vaccines)
- Previous local skin reaction (mild/moderate) from a vaccine
- Allergies: bird feathers, penicillin, allergies to products not in the vaccine
- Pregnancy (except live vaccines), breastfeeding, preterm birth
- Recent tuberculin skin test (see text for timing and spacing with live vaccines only)
- Immunosuppressed person in the household, recent exposure to the disease or convalescence
- Family history of adverse events to the vaccine

SCREENING PRIOR TO VACCINE ADMINISTRATION

Use a screening form to rule out specific contraindications and precautions to the vaccine in adults. Note that a "yes" response to some of these questions will indicate a type of vaccine to use, rather than a contraindication to all formulations (e.g., if a person has an allergy to thimerosal, then a single-dose vial or prefilled syringe may be required to avoid the preservative).

1. Are you sick today?

2. Do you have allergies to medications, food, a vaccine component or latex?

3. Have you ever had a serious reaction after receiving a vaccine?

4. Do you have a long-term health problem caused by heart disease, lung disease, asthma, kidney disease, metabolic disease (e.g., diabetes), anemia or other blood disorder?

5. Do you have cancer, leukemia, AIDS or any other immune system problem?

6. Do you take cortisone, prednisone, other steroids, anticancer drugs or have you had radiation treatments?

7. Have you ever had a seizure or nervous system problem?

8. During the past year, have you received a transfusion of blood or blood products, or been given immune (gamma) globulin or an antiviral drug?

9. For patients of child-bearing potential: are you pregnant or do you plan to become pregnant during the next month?

10. Have you received any vaccinations in the past 4 weeks?

Vaccine Contraindications and Precautions

VACCINE	CONTRAINDICATIONS	PRECAUTIONS
All vaccines	Severe allergic reaction (e.g., anaphylaxis) to a vaccine or vaccine component after a previous dose.	Illness: If a child or adult has only a mild illness (such as a cold), vaccines should be given (see the Study Tip Gal on the previous page). Treatment with antibiotics is not a valid reason to delay vaccines. If the person has a moderate or severe acute illness (regardless of antibiotic use) it is reasonable to delay vaccines until the condition has improved.
Live vaccines	Pregnancy (do not attempt pregnancy until 4 weeks after receiving a live vaccine). Immunosuppression (see the Vaccinations for Specific Conditions/Populations chart on the following page).	Recent administration of an antibody-containing blood product (see the section on Live Vaccines and Antibody).
Diphtheria, tetanus and pertussis vaccines	For pertussis-containing vaccines: encephalopathy (e.g., coma, decreased level of consciousness, prolonged seizures) that is not attributable to another cause within 7 days after receiving the vaccine.	Guillain-Barré syndrome (GBS) within 6 weeks of a previous diphtheria, tetanus and/or pertussis vaccine. For DTaP and Tdap only: infantile spasms, uncontrolled seizures.
Hepatitis B vaccines Human papillomavirus vaccine (HPV)	Hypersensitivity to yeast.	
Influenza vaccines	Live, attenuated influenza vaccine (LAIV4): severe egg allergy (e.g., anaphylaxis), use of aspirin-containing products (children and adolescents), recent use of influenza antiviral medications (oseltamivir or zanamivir in the past 48 hours, peramivir in the last 5 days or baloxavir in the last 17 days), children age 2-4 years with asthma or a wheezing episode in the last 12 months, close contact with an immunosuppressed person.	All influenza vaccines: history of GBS within 6 weeks of a previous influenza vaccination. LAIV4: asthma in any patient age ≥ 5 years, underlying conditions that predispose to influenza complications (e.g., chronic lung, heart, renal, hepatic, neurologic, hematologic and metabolic disorders, including diabetes). Inactivated influenza vaccines (IIV): egg allergy other than hives (e.g., angioedema, respiratory distress, recurrent emesis or required emergency medical intervention) – if a vaccine other than ccIIV4 (Flucelvax) or RIV4 (Flublok) is used, it should be administered in a medical setting under the supervision of a healthcare provider who can manage severe allergic reactions.
Recombinant zoster vaccine (RZV)		Pregnancy, breastfeeding: consider delaying vaccination.
Varicella vaccines	History of severe allergic reaction (e.g., anaphylaxis) to gelatin or neomycin.	Use of acyclovir, famciclovir or valacyclovir in the 24 hours before vaccination; avoid these antivirals for 14 days after vaccination.
Rotavirus vaccines	History of intussusception (when part of the intestine slides into an adjacent intestine part, blocking food/fluids).	Chronic gastrointestinal disease.
Yellow fever vaccine	Severe allergic reaction (e.g., anaphylaxis) to eggs.	
Latex present on vial stoppers and in prefilled syringes	Most latex sensitivities are a contact-type allergy, which does not prohibit vaccine administration; if the reaction to latex is severe (e.g., anaphylactic), avoid vaccines with latex.	

IMMUNIZATIONS & TRAVELERS

VACCINATIONS FOR SPECIFIC CONDITIONS/POPULATIONS

VACCINATIONS FOR SPECIAL GROUPS*

*An annual influenza vaccine is recommended for all special groups (age ≥ 6 months).

Infants and Children

- 3-dose hepatitis B vaccine started at birth
- Other vaccine series start at age 2 months, including: PCV13, DTaP, Hib, polio, rotavirus
- Live vaccine series generally start at age ≥ 12 months, including: MMR, varicella
- No polysaccharide vaccines before age 2 years

Adolescents and Young Adults

- Meningococcal vaccine (MCV4; *Menactra, Menveo* or *MenQuadfi*)
  - ❑ 2 doses: 1 dose at age 11-12 years and 1 dose at age 16 years
  - ❑ First-year college students in residential housing (if not previously vaccinated): 1 dose
- Human papillomavirus vaccine
  - ❑ Recommended at age 11-12 years
  - ❑ 2 or 3 doses (depending on age at start)
- Tdap: first dose at age > 11 years

Pregnancy

- Live vaccines are contraindicated
- Influenza vaccine, inactivated (not live), can be given in any trimester
- Tdap x 1 with each pregnancy (weeks 27-36, optimally)*

*It's not just Mom who needs Tdap x 1 to protect the infant from pertussis; vaccinate others in close contact with the infant (e.g., father, grandparents, child-care providers), if not up-to-date.

Older Adults

- Herpes zoster vaccine (*Shingrix*): age ≥ 50 years, 2 doses, 2-6 months apart
- Pneumococcal vaccine (age ≥ 65 years), give one of the following regimens:
  - ❑ PCV20 x 1
  - ❑ PCV15 x 1, then PPSV23 x 1 ≥ 12 months later (or ≥ 8 weeks later if immunocompromised)

Diabetes

- Pneumococcal vaccine (age 19-64 years), give one of the following regimens:
  - ❑ PCV20 x 1
  - ❑ PCV15 x 1, then PPSV23 x 1 ≥ 12 months later (or ≥ 8 weeks later if immunocompromised)
- Hepatitis B: age 19-59 years (or age ≥ 60 years if at risk for hepatitis B infection)

Healthcare Professionals
—including pharmacists, nurses, physicians

- Annual influenza vaccine is usually required (with proof/documentation of vaccination)
- Hepatitis B: if there is no evidence of vaccine series completion or a blood test showing immunity
- Tdap: 1 dose, if not up-to-date, then Td or Tdap every 10 years
- Varicella: if there is no history of vaccination or chickenpox infection
- MMR: if there is no history of vaccination or a blood test showing immunity

Sickle Cell Disease & Other Causes of Asplenia (Damaged/Missing Spleen)
—the spleen contains T-cells and B-cells; a damaged or missing spleen (e.g., splenectomy) causes a type of immunodeficiency

- *H. influenzae* type b (Hib) vaccine
- Pneumococcal vaccine (age 19-64 years), give one of the following regimens:
  - ❑ PCV20 x 1
  - ❑ PCV15 x 1, then PPSV23 x 1 ≥ 8 weeks later
- Meningococcal vaccines
  - ❑ Meningococcal conjugate vaccine (*Menactra, Menveo* or *MenQuadfi*)
  - ❑ Serogroup B meningococcal vaccine (*Bexsero* or *Trumenba*)

Immunodeficiency
—called altered immunocompetence, immunosuppresion or immunocompromise; caused by drugs or conditions**

- Live vaccines are contraindicated
- Pneumococcal vaccine (age 19-64 years), give one of the following regimens:
  - ❑ PCV20 x 1
  - ❑ PCV15 x 1, then PPSV23 x 1 ≥ 8 weeks later
- HIV infection
  - ❑ Meningococcal conjugate vaccine (*Menactra, Menveo* or *MenQuadfi*)
  - ❑ Hepatitis A vaccine
  - ❑ Hepatitis B vaccine

**Immunocompromising conditions:
- Chronic renal failure or nephrotic syndrome
- Malignancy
- HIV infection
- Solid organ transplant
- Treatment with immunosuppressive drugs [e.g., chemotherapy, TNF-alpha inhibitors, transplant medications, systemic steroids ≥ 14 days at doses equivalent to ≥ 20 mg (or 2 mg/kg) prednisone daily]

VACCINATIONS FOR ADULTS*

Does not include routine childhood vaccines.

Influenza

Annually for all patients ≥ 6 months old

Tdap, Td

Tdap x 1 if not received previously
Td or Tdap every 10 years

Shingles

Shingrix:

Vaccinate all adults ≥ 50 years or ≥ 19 years if immunosuppressed (or expected to become immunosuppressed)

2-dose series, with second dose given 2-6 months after the first dose (can shorten to 1-2 months if immunosuppressed)

Vaccinate even if patient previously had chickenpox or shingles or received *Zostavax*

Human Papillomavirus (HPV)

Adults ≤ 26 years who did not complete the HPV series*

Indicated up to age 45 years

Pneumococcal

Age 19-64 years with a specific medical condition* or age ≥ 65 years (if never received before): PCV20 x 1 or PCV15 x 1 followed by PPSV23 ≥ 12 months later (or ≥ 8 weeks later if immunocompromised)

Alcohol use disorder, cigarette smoking, diabetes, chronic heart, lung or liver disease, sickle cell disease/asplenia, HIV infection, malignancy, solid organ transplant, chronic renal failure, taking immunosuppressive drugs (e.g., chemotherapy, long-term systemic steroids)

Meningococcal
2 VACCINES, ADULTS NEED 1 OR BOTH

Serogroup B vaccines (*Bexsero, Trumenba*): give if complement component deficiency, taking eculizumab or ravulizumab, asplenia, microbiologist with exposure to *Neisseria meningitidis*, serogroup B meningococcal disease outbreak exposure

Conjugate vaccines (*Menactra, Menveo, MenQuadfi*):
same groups as above, plus: HIV, travelers/residents to countries in which the disease is common, military recruits, first year college students living in dorms, if not up-to-date

Hepatitis B

All adults age 19-59 years and patients ≥ 60 years with risk factors, including chronic liver disease, HIV infection, exposure via sexual activity (e.g., men who have sex with men, multiple sex partners), IV drug use, incarcerated, travel to an endemic area, blood exposure (e.g., healthcare personnel, diabetes, dialysis)

Give alone (*Engerix-B, Recombivax HB, Heplisav-B*) or with hepatitis A vaccine (*Twinrix*)

Hepatitis A

Adults traveling to undeveloped countries outside of the U.S., household members and other close contacts of adopted children newly arriving from countries with moderate-high infection risk, liver disease, hemophilia, men who have sex with men, IV drug users, homeless individuals, HIV

Give alone (*Havrix, VAQTA*) or with hepatitis B vaccine (*Twinrix*)

ROUTINE VACCINES

VACCINE	ADMINISTRATION RECOMMENDATIONS	STORAGE/ADMINISTRATION
Diphtheria Toxoid-, Tetanus Toxoid- and acellular Pertussis-Containing Vaccines The pediatric formulations (with the upper-case D, as in DTaP) have 3-5 times as much diphtheria component than the adult formulations. The adult formulations have a lower case d (Tdap or Td).		
DTaP: *Daptacel, Infanrix* DTaP-IPV: *Kinrix, Quadracel* **DTaP-HepB-IPV: *Pediarix*** DTaP-IPV / Hib: *Pentacel* DTaP-IPV / Hib / HepB: *Vaxelis* DT Td: *Tenivac, TDVax* **Tdap: *Adacel, Boostrix***	**DTaP** A routine childhood vaccine series; 5 doses given at ages 2, 4, 6, 12-18 months and 4-6 years. For children younger than 7 years of age. **DT** Used for routine vaccine series in infants and children < 7 years old who have a contraindication to the acellular pertussis antigen in DTaP. **Td or Tdap** Tdap booster typically given at age ≥ 11 years (if not previously received). Routine booster given every 10 years in patients age ≥ 7 years. Wound prophylaxis: for deep or dirty wounds, revaccinate with Td or Tdap if it has been more than 5 years since the last dose. Tetanus immunoglobulin (TIG) may be required if no previous tetanus vaccines have been given. Recommended in: 1. Pregnant or postpartum women, with each pregnancy (see Vaccinations for Specific Conditions/Populations). 2. Close contacts of infants younger than age 12 months (e.g., father, grandparents, child-care providers), if not up-to-date. 3. Healthcare personnel with direct patient contact, if not up-to-date. 4. Children age 7-10 years who did not get fully vaccinated with the DTaP series; give a single dose of Tdap instead of DTaP.	Store in the refrigerator. Do not freeze. Shake the prefilled syringe or vial before use. Give IM.
Haemophilus influenzae Type B (Hib)-Containing Vaccines		
Hib: *ActHIB, Hiberix, PedvaxHIB* DTaP-IPV / Hib: *Pentacel* DTaP-IPV / Hib / HepB: *Vaxelis*	Hib: a routine childhood vaccine series given between ages 2-15 months. *ActHIB* and *Hiberix* are 4-dose series, *PedvaxHIB* is a 3-dose series. Given to adults with asplenia.	Store in the refrigerator. Do not freeze. Shake the prefilled syringe or vial before use. Give IM.
Hepatitis-Containing Vaccines		
Hepatitis A: *Havrix, VAQTA* **Hepatitis B: *Engerix-B, Heplisav-B, Recombivax HB*, *PreHevbrio*** High-dose *Recombivax HB* (40 mcg/mL) is indicated for dialysis patients Hepatitis A and B: *Twinrix* **DTaP-HepB-IPV: *Pediarix*** DTaP-IPV / Hib / HepB: *Vaxelis*	**Hepatitis A** Children: a routine childhood vaccine series; 2 doses given at age 12 months and then 6-18 months later. Adults: men who have sex with men, illicit drug users, chronic liver disease, homeless individuals, HIV, travelers to countries with high hepatitis A incidence, or anyone else who wants it. **Hepatitis B** Children: routine childhood vaccine series started within 24 hours after birth; 3 doses given at age 0, 1-2 and 6-18 months. Adults: all aged 19-59 years or those ≥ 60 years with risk factors, including chronic liver disease, HIV infection, blood exposure (e.g., healthcare workers, on dialysis, diabetes), IV drug use, exposure via sexual activity (e.g., men who have sex with men, anyone with multiple sex partners), incarcerated people, travel to an endemic area. *Engerix-B, Recombivax HB* and *PreHevbrio* (age ≥ 18 years): 3-dose series given at month 0, 1 and 6 (can be completed in 4 months if necessary, but requires a booster at 1 year if the series is accelerated). *Heplisav-B* (age ≥ 18 years): 2-dose series given at month 0 and 1. Do not use in pregnant women. **Hepatitis A and B** 3-dose series given at months 0, 1 and 6; can be completed faster if needed for use prior to travel to high-risk areas.	Store in the refrigerator. Do not freeze. Shake the vial or prefilled syringe before use. Give IM.

VACCINE	ADMINISTRATION RECOMMENDATIONS	STORAGE/ADMINISTRATION
Human Papillomavirus Vaccines **Prevents** ~90% of <u>cervical cancers</u>, as well as vulvar, vaginal, oropharyngeal, penile and anal cancers, and <u>genital warts</u>.		
HPV9 (9-Valent): *Gardasil 9*	**Ages 9-26 Years*** Recommended age: 11-12 years (may be started at age 9**). Use is contraindicated with a severe yeast allergy. **Regimens** If started <u>before age 15</u> → <u>2 doses</u> (at month 0 and 6-12 months later) If started at <u>age 15 or older</u>, or if immunocompromised → <u>3 doses</u> (at months 0, 1-2 and 6)	Store in refrigerator. Do not freeze. Shake the prefilled syringe or vial before use. Give IM. Caution for fainting (incidence is similar to other vaccines); administer to seated patient and monitor after vaccination.

*FDA-approved up to age 45 years. ACIP recommends use for anyone ≤ 26 years, and for some adults age 27-45 years with patient/physician discussion of benefits.

**Start at age 9 years in anyone with a history of sexual abuse.

INFLUENZA VACCINES

<u>Influenza (the flu)</u> is one of the <u>most common vaccine preventable illnesses in the U.S</u>. Influenza A and B are the two types of influenza viruses that cause epidemic human disease. Influenza A virus has subtypes based on the two surface antigens, <u>hemagglutinin and neuraminidase</u>. Immunity to the surface antigens reduces the likelihood of infection, and severity of disease if infection occurs.

The influenza vaccine is given <u>annually</u>. The vaccine changes every year to account for antigenic drift, which causes variations in the virus. More dramatic antigenic changes, or shifts, occur approximately every 30 years and can result in the emergence of a novel influenza virus, with the potential to cause a pandemic.

<u>The virus spreads</u> from person to person, primarily through <u>respiratory droplet transmission</u>. This can happen when an infected person coughs or sneezes in close proximity to an uninfected person. Influenza illness has an <u>abrupt onset of symptoms</u> (fever, myalgia, headache, malaise, nonproductive cough, sore throat and rhinitis). In children, otitis media, nausea and vomiting are commonly reported.

Uncomplicated influenza illness typically resolves after 3 – 7 days, though cough and malaise can persist for more than 2 weeks. In some people, influenza can exacerbate underlying medical conditions (e.g., pulmonary or cardiac disease) and lead to secondary bacterial pneumonia or primary influenza viral pneumonia (as with elderly or immunocompromised patients). Hospitalization and death are more common in people age < 5 years, ≥ 65 years or those with comorbid conditions. See the Infectious Diseases III chapter for treatment of influenza with antiviral medications. See the <u>Study Tip Gal</u> to the right for important details about influenza vaccines.

INFLUENZA VACCINE TIPS

RECOMMENDED ANNUALLY*
All patients age ≥ 6 months, unless contraindicated.

Any vaccine can be used within the FDA indications (ACIP does not give preference to any one type of influenza vaccine).

All brand names have **FLU** in the name (e.g., A**flu**ria, **Flu**zone, **Flu**Mist).

SPECIFIC PATIENT CONSIDERATIONS
- **Age 6 months to 8 years (not previously vaccinated)**
  - ❑ Give 2 doses (4 weeks apart).

- **Patients with an egg allergy**
  - ❑ Can receive any age-appropriate inactivated influenza vaccine (see the drug table for details), even if severe allergy symptoms (e.g., wheezing, requiring epinephrine, hypotension or cardiovascular changes). No additional observation period is recommended (beyond the required 15 minutes).
  - ❑ *Flublok* (an egg-free product) is approved for age ≥ 18 years only. *Flucelvax* (egg-free; grown in a cell culture) is approved for age ≥ 4 years. Other influenza vaccines might contain trace amounts of egg proteins.
  - ❑ If using an influenza vaccine other than *Flublok* or *Flucelvax* in a patient with a severe egg allergy (i.e., more than hives), the vaccine should be administered in a medical setting under the supervision of a healthcare provider who is able to recognize and treat severe allergic reactions.
  - ❑ Do not administer the live influenza vaccine (*FluMist*).

- **Pregnant patients**
  - ❑ Can receive any age-appropriate inactivated influenza vaccine (see the drug table for details). Do not administer the live influenza vaccine (*FluMist*).

- **Indicated only for patients age ≥ 65 years**
  - ❑ *Fluzone High-Dose Quadrivalent* and *Fluad Quadrivalent*.

*If there is a vaccine shortage, the highest risk patients will be vaccinated first. The CDC website will provide information on who is at highest risk.

IMMUNIZATIONS & TRAVELERS

VACCINE	ADMINISTRATION RECOMMENDATIONS	STORAGE/ADMINISTRATION
Influenza Vaccines There are many formulations of quadrivalent influenza vaccine. Key differences between them include whether the virus is inactivated (IIV) or live attenuated (LAIV4), the route (IM, intranasal), the antigen dose or the presence of adjuvant. Inactivated influenza vaccines (IIV) are produced using eggs unless otherwise noted.		
Quadrivalent Inactivated Influenza Vaccines (IIV4) ■ **Afluria** *Quadrivalent*, **Fluarix** *Quadrivalent*, **FluLaval** *Quadrivalent*, **Fluzone** *Quadrivalent*: approved for age ≥ 6 months ■ **Flucelvax** *Quadrivalent* (grown in cell culture, ccIIV4, egg-free): approved for age ≥ 6 months ■ *Flublok Quadrivalent* (recombinant inactivated vaccine, RIV4, egg-free): approved for age ≥ 18 years ■ **Fluzone High-Dose** *Quadrivalent*, **Fluad** *Quadrivalent*: approved for ages ≥ 65 years **Quadrivalent Live Attenuated Influenza Vaccine (LAIV4)** ■ **FluMist** *Quadrivalent*: approved for healthy people age 2-49 years	Seasonal influenza vaccine recommendations are updated annually and can be found at www.cdc.gov. **Quadrivalent** Quadrivalent flu vaccines protect against two influenza A's and two influenza B's. **Vaccine Timing** Give vaccine as soon as it is available, even if it arrives in late summer. It is preferable to administer the vaccine before October, but individuals should still be vaccinated later in the season. Outbreaks usually peak by February. **Live Attenuated Vaccine** LAIV4 is indicated for healthy patients age 2-49 years. See the previous table with vaccine contraindications and precautions for details. Do not use in pregnancy or if immunocompromised, or if influenza medications were recently used (oseltamivir or zanamivir within past 48 hours, peramivir in the past 5 days or baloxavir in the past 17 days). **Egg Allergy** See Study Tip Gal on the previous page.	Store in the refrigerator. Do not freeze. **Administer IM Except:** *FluMist Quadrivalent* is given as 0.2 mL, divided between the two nostrils. **Product Notes:** *Fluzone High-Dose Quadrivalent* contains 4x the antigen dose of standard dose IM vaccines, to increase antibody production. *Fluad Quadrivalent* contains an oil-in-water emulsion of MF59 (an adjuvant), to increase antibody production. *Afluria Quadrivalent*: can be given with a needle-free jet injector.
Measles, Mumps and Rubella-Containing Vaccines (Live Attenuated)		
MMR: *M-M-R II* **MMRV** (MMR + Varicella): **ProQuad**	Children: a routine vaccination series; 2 doses given at age 12-15 months and age 4-6 years. *ProQuad*: indicated for patients age 12 months-12 years. Adults: 1-2 doses if no evidence of immunity. Give 2 doses (4 weeks apart) to: healthcare workers, HIV patients with a CD4 count ≥ 200 cells/mm³ for at least 6 months, nonpregnant patients of childbearing age (with no evidence of immunity to rubella), international travelers, household contacts of immunocompromised people and students in postsecondary educational institutions. Do not use in pregnancy or if immunocompromised. Adults born before 1957 are generally considered immune to measles and mumps.	MMR: store in the refrigerator or freezer. MMRV: store vaccine in the freezer only due to the varicella component. Store diluents at room temperature or in the refrigerator. Give SC.

VACCINE	ADMINISTRATION RECOMMENDATIONS	STORAGE/ADMINISTRATION
Meningococcal Vaccines Quadrivalent meningococcal conjugate vaccines (MCV4) include serogroups A, C, W and Y. Serogroup B (MenB) is available in a separate vaccine.		
MCV4 (Conjugate Vaccines) *Menactra:* for age 9 months-55 years *MenQuadfi:* for age ≥ 2 years *Menveo:* for age 2 months-55 years *Menactra* and *Menveo* can be used in adults ≥ 56 years, if needed	**Routine Vaccination:** Adolescents: 2-dose series given at age 11-12 years and at age 16 years (booster dose). **Special Populations at High Risk:** Travelers to certain countries, such as the meningitis belt in Sub-Saharan Africa. Age 2 months and older with: HIV, asplenia/sickle cell disease, complement component deficiencies or use of eculizumab or ravulizumab. Lab workers with *N. meningitidis* exposure. First-year college students (age ≤ 21 years) living in resident housing, if not up-to-date. Military recruits. The number of doses and timing (intervals) will depend on age and specific risk. People with ongoing risk of meningococcal disease should be revaccinated every 5 years.	Store in the refrigerator. Do not freeze. Give IM. *Menveo:* both vials (the powder and the liquid) contain vaccine; use only the supplied liquid for reconstitution. MCV4 vaccine is required by Saudi Arabia for travel to the Hajj and Umrah pilgrimages; proof of vaccination is required.
MenB: *Bexsero, Trumenba* For age 10-25 years	**Age ≥ 10 Years with High Risk:** Asplenia/sickle cell disease, complement component deficiencies or use of eculizumab or ravulizumab. Lab workers with *N. meningitidis* exposure. During an outbreak. *Bexsero:* 2 doses (given 1 month apart). *Trumenba:* 2 doses (given 6 months apart). If high risk of meningococcal disease or during an outbreak: give 3 doses (at months 0, 1-2 and 6). Optional for patients age 16-23 years who are not at high risk but want the vaccine (if given, the preferred age is 16-18 years).	Store in the refrigerator. Do not freeze. Give IM. *Bexsero* and *Trumenba* cover the serogroup B strain and are used in addition to the quadrivalent meningococcal conjugate vaccines.

IMMUNIZATIONS & TRAVELERS (side)

PNEUMOCOCCAL VACCINES

The bacteria *S. pneumoniae*, referred to as pneumococcus, is the most common cause of otitis media, pneumonia, meningitis and bloodstream infections in children. Adults age 65 years and older and those with certain chronic conditions or altered immunocompetence are at increased risk of pneumococcal disease. As you learn the pneumococcal vaccine recommendations, keep these key concepts in mind:

- There are three pneumococcal conjugate vaccines [PCV13 (*Prevnar 13*), PCV15 (*Vaxneuvance*), PCV20 (*Prevnar 20*)] and one polysaccharide vaccine, PPSV23 (*Pneumovax 23*).

- Children age ≤ 5 years receive PCV13 (*Prevnar 13*) as part of routine childhood vaccinations.
  - Young children (< 2 years) should not receive *Pneumovax 23* as they do not produce an adequate antibody response to polysaccharide vaccines.

- Adults should receive either PCV20 (*Prevnar 20*) alone, or PCV15 (*Vaxneuvance*) followed by PPSV23 (*Pneumovax 23*). The recommended age of administration in adults is based on the presence or absence of underlying medical conditions (see table below).

VACCINE	ADMINISTRATION RECOMMENDATIONS	STORAGE/ADMINISTRATION
Pneumococcal Vaccines		
Conjugate Vaccines *Prevnar 13* **(PCV13)** *Vaxneuvance* **(PCV15)** *Prevnar 20* **(PCV20)**	Children < 5 years: 4-dose series of PCV13 given at age 2, 4, 6 and 12-15 months. **Adults age 19-64 years with specific medical conditions (see below) or age ≥ 65 years (if never received before):** PCV20 x 1 or PCV15 x 1 followed by PPSV23 x 1 ≥ 12 months later (PPSV23 may be given ≥ 8 weeks later if immunocompromised) Specific medical conditions (*indicates an immunocompromised state): alcohol use disorder, cigarette smoking, diabetes, chronic heart, lung or liver disease, sickle cell disease/asplenia*, HIV infection*, malignancy*, solid organ transplant*, chronic renal failure*, taking immunosuppressive drugs* (e.g., chemotherapy, long-term systemic steroids) **Other Scenarios** Patients who previously received PPSV23: administer 1 dose of PCV15 or PCV20 ≥ 12 months after the last PPSV23 dose; additional doses of PPSV23 are not needed. Patients who previously received PCV13: consult the CDC recommendations for guidance on additional PPSV23 doses that may be recommended.	Store in the refrigerator. Do not freeze. Shake the vial or prefilled syringe prior to use. **PCV13, PCV15, PCV20** Give IM. **PPSV23** Give IM or SC.
Polysaccharide Vaccine *Pneumovax 23* **(PPSV23)**	Children age 2-18 years: indicated after completion of the PCV13 series in patients with select medical conditions. Adults: indicated after PCV15 (see above).	
Poliovirus-Containing Vaccines Only inactivated poliovirus vaccine (IPV) is available in the U.S. Oral polio vaccine (live attenuated) may be administered in other countries.		
IPV: *IPOL* DTaP-IPV: *Kinrix, Quadracel* **DTaP-HepB-IPV:** *Pediarix* DTaP-IPV / Hib: *Pentacel* DTaP-IPV / Hib / HepB: *Vaxelis*	A routine childhood vaccine series; 4 doses given at age 2, 4, 6-18 months and 4-6 years.	Store in the refrigerator. Do not freeze. Shake the prefilled syringe or vial before use. IPV (*IPOL*): give IM or SC.
Rotavirus Vaccines (Live Attenuated)		
RV1: *Rotarix* RV5: *RotaTeq*	Given to all infants. Do not initiate the series after age 15 weeks. *Rotarix*: 2 doses at age 2 and 4 months. *RotaTeq*: 3 doses at age 2, 4 and 6 months.	Store in the refrigerator. Do not freeze. Give orally.

VACCINE	ADMINISTRATION RECOMMENDATIONS	STORAGE/ADMINISTRATION
Varicella-Containing Vaccines Varicella virus-containing vaccines are <u>live</u> attenuated vaccines. *<u>Shingrix</u>* is a <u>recombinant (non-live)</u> vaccine.		
Varicella Virus Vaccine (for chickenpox): *Varivax* **MMRV:** *ProQuad* **Zoster Virus Vaccine (for herpes zoster / shingles):** *Shingrix*	***Varivax*** A routine childhood vaccine series; 2 doses, given at age 12-15 months and 4-6 years. Any adolescent or adult without evidence of immunity to varicella: give <u>2 doses</u>. Do <u>not</u> use in <u>pregnancy</u> or if <u>immunocompromised</u>. <u>Some antivirals</u> (e.g., acyclovir, valacyclovir, famciclovir) can <u>interfere with</u> *Varivax* (<u>live</u> vaccine). <u>Stop 24 hours before</u> vaccine administration and do not take for 14 days after vaccination. ***Shingrix*** All adults ≥ 50 years or adults ≥ 19 years who are or will be immunosuppressed: <u>2 doses</u> given at month 0 and month 2-6 (2nd dose may be given at month 1-2 if immunocompromised). <u>Vaccinate even if</u> the patient has previously received *Varivax* or *Zostavax* (live zoster vaccine no longer available) or has a <u>history of zoster infection</u>, since recurrence is possible. The zoster vaccine is indicated for the prevention of shingles (not for treatment of an active case). It can reduce complications, such as the severity of postherpetic neuralgia following infections.	***Varivax*** Store vaccine <u>in the freezer</u>. Store the diluent in the refrigerator or at room temperature. <u>Reconstitute immediately</u> upon removal from the freezer <u>and inject</u>; short stability (30 minutes). Do <u>not</u> give if there is a hypersensitivity to <u>gelatin or neomycin</u>. <u>Give SC</u>. ***Shingrix*** Store vaccine and adjuvant liquid in the refrigerator. <u>Do not freeze</u>. <u>Give IM</u>.

NON-ROUTINE VACCINES

The vaccines in the table below are administered only when there is exposure or risk of exposure to a particular infectious pathogen. For the majority, the risk is incurred when traveling to a high-risk area. COVID-19 vaccines are included here as long-term recommendations are still under development; however, it is anticipated that COVID-19 vaccination will become routine for select populations.

DRUG	ADMINISTRATION RECOMMENDATIONS	STORAGE/ADMINISTRATION
Rabies Vaccine: *RabAvert, Imovax Rabies*	Prevention when there is a high risk exposure (e.g., animal handlers, traveling to a high risk area): 3 doses. Post-exposure (with previous vaccination): 2 doses. Post-exposure (without previous vaccination): 4 doses; <u>1 dose of rabies immune globulin</u> (RIG) should be given <u>with the first vaccine dose</u>.	Store in the refrigerator. Reconstitute with the provided diluent. Give IM.
Typhoid Vaccine: *Vivotif* (<u>live vaccine</u>) <u>Oral</u> *Typhim Vi* (inactivated polysaccharide vaccine) <u>Injection</u>	To prevent typhoid fever caused by *Salmonella typhi* (see the Travelers chapter for disease information). Oral: take 1 capsule PO on alternate days (day 0, 2, 4 and 6). <u>Complete at least 1 week prior</u> to possible exposure. Give every 5 years if continued risk or exposure. Injection: give 1 dose <u>at least 2 weeks prior</u> to possible exposure. Give every 2 years if continued risk or exposure.	<u>Oral</u> capsules: <u>store in the refrigerator</u>. Take on an <u>empty stomach</u> (1 hour before a meal) <u>with cold or lukewarm water</u>. Injection: store in the refrigerator. Do not freeze. Injection: give IM.
Japanese Encephalitis Virus Vaccine: *Ixiaro*	Give if spending ≥ 1 month in endemic areas during transmission season, especially if travel will include rural areas. Give 2 doses, 28 days apart. Complete at least 1 week prior to potential exposure (see the Travelers chapter for disease information).	Store in the refrigerator. Do not freeze. Give IM.
Tuberculosis Bacille Calmette-Guerin (BCG) Vaccine Live vaccine	Not used in the U.S. Given to infants and small children in countries with higher TB incidence. Provides weak protection for pulmonary TB.	Can cause a <u>positive reaction</u> to the <u>TB skin test</u> (see the Infectious Diseases II chapter).

IMMUNIZATIONS & TRAVELERS

DRUG	ADMINISTRATION RECOMMENDATIONS	STORAGE/ADMINISTRATION
Yellow Fever Vaccine: *YF-VAX* Live vaccine	Give to those who travel to, or live in, areas of risk and to travelers to countries that require vaccination (see the Travelers chapter). Contraindicated with a severe (life-threatening) allergy to eggs or gelatin, immunosuppression, age < 6 month or breastfeeding. Avoid donating blood for 2 weeks after receiving the vaccine. The International Certificate of Vaccination (yellow card) is provided and is valid for 10 years, starting 10 days after vaccination. It may be required to enter endemic areas.	Store in the refrigerator. Reconstitute with the provided diluent; swirl, do not shake. Give SC.
Cholera vaccine: *Vaxchora* Live vaccine	Give to people age 18-64 years who are traveling to an area of active toxigenic *Vibrio cholerae* transmission. Give 1 oral dose ≥ 10 days prior to exposure.	Store the packet for reconstitution in the freezer. Remove no more than 15 minutes prior to reconstitution. Dissolve the buffer packet in 100 mL of cold or room temperature water, then add the active component packet; stir for 30 seconds and drink within 15 minutes.
Dengue vaccine: *Dengvaxia* Live vaccine	Give to people age 9-16 years who have previously tested positive for dengue infection and live in endemic areas. Not indicated for primary prevention. Give 3 doses at months 0, 6 and 12.	Store in the refrigerator. Reconstitute with the provided diluent; swirl, do not shake. Give SC.
Smallpox and monkeypox vaccine: *Jynneos* Live vaccine	Give to adults ≥ 18 years who are at high risk for infection. Give 2 doses, four weeks apart.	Keep frozen. Allow vaccine to thaw and reach room temperature before use. Swirl for at least 30 seconds. Give SC.
Ebola vaccine: *Ervebo* Live vaccine	Give to adults ≥ 18 years for the prevention of disease caused by the *Zaire ebolavirus*. Not protective against other species of *Ebolavirus* or *Marburgvirus*. Give 1 dose.	Keep frozen. Allow vaccine to thaw at room temperature (do not thaw in the refrigerator) until no visible ice is present before use. Give IM.
COVID-19 vaccines mRNA vaccines: *Comirnaty* (Pfizer-BioNTech) *Spikevax* (Moderna) Viral vector vaccine: Janssen COVID-19 vaccine	mRNA vaccines are preferred for the primary series and booster doses. Pfizer vaccine (FDA-approved for persons age ≥ 16 years): Primary series (age ≥ 5 years): 2 doses*, 21 days apart Booster (age ≥ 12 years): ≥ 5 months after the last primary series dose Moderna vaccine (FDA-approved for adults age ≥ 18 years): Primary series: 2 doses*, 28 days apart Booster: ≥ 5 months after the last primary series dose Janssen vaccine (FDA emergency-use authorization for adults ≥ 18 years) Primary series: 1 dose Booster: 2 months after the primary series dose	Storage varies by product. Give IM.

A 3rd primary series dose ≥ 28 days after the second dose is recommended for immunocompromised individuals.

STORAGE

Vaccines should be properly stored and <u>kept in the original packaging</u> (box) until use. Some vaccines require protection from light. Vaccines should be stored in the refrigerator or freezer units designed for storing biologics (including vaccines) or in separate, free-standing freezer and refrigerator units. Household freezer units or dormitory-style refrigerators should not be used for vaccine storage. Vaccines should be stored on the shelves away from the walls; <u>never</u> place vaccines <u>in the doors</u> of the freezer or the refrigerator as the temperature there is unstable. <u>Rotate stock</u>, so vaccines and diluents <u>with the earliest expiration date are used first</u>.

The CDC recommends a calibrated thermometer or a digital data logger be connected to a <u>buffered temperature probe</u> in the refrigerator and freezer. An example of a buffered probe is one immersed in a vial of liquid (e.g., glycol). This prevents false readings due to the rapid changes in air temperature that occur when refrigerator doors are opened. Read and <u>document</u> refrigerator and freezer <u>temperatures</u> at least <u>twice each workday</u> (in the morning and before the end of the workday). Maintain a consistent power source. <u>Keep temperature logs for 3 years</u> (<u>or longer</u>, as required by individual states).

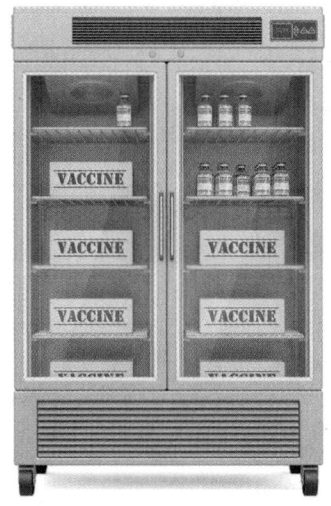

Staff can easily confuse the vaccines within the storage unit. Use labels and separate containers.

VACCINE STORAGE REQUIREMENTS

- <u>Most</u> vaccines are stored in the <u>refrigerator</u> (between 36°F and 46°F, or 2°C and 8°C).

- Vaccines that should be stored in the freezer (between –58°F and +5°F, or –50°C and –15°C) include: <u>varicella vaccine, MMRV</u>, oral <u>cholera</u> vaccine, ebola vaccine, and smallpox and monkeypox vaccine.

- <u>MMR</u> is stored either in the <u>refrigerator or freezer</u>.

Diluents

- Some vaccines require reconstitution with a diluent before use. The diluents that come with varicella, MMR and MMRV vaccines can be stored in the <u>refrigerator</u> or at <u>room temperature</u>.

- Vaccines that are reconstituted should be used shortly after preparation.

ADMINISTRATION

ROUTES OF ADMINISTRATION

IM ONLY	SC ONLY	IM OR SC	INTRANASAL	PO
<u>Most</u> vaccines are given IM. The vaccines listed in the following sections of the table are exceptions.	<u>MMR, MMRV, Varicella, Yellow Fever</u>, Dengue, Smallpox and Monkeypox	PPSV23, IPV *(IPOL)*	*FluMist* Quadrivalent (Live Attenuated Vaccine)	<u>Typhoid</u> *(Vivotif)* capsules Oral solutions: Cholera *(Vaxchora)* and <u>Rotavirus</u> *(RotaTeq, Rotarix)*

ADMINISTRATION TECHNIQUE

- <u>SC</u>: use a 23 – 25 gauge, <u>5/8" needle</u> at a <u>45-degree</u> angle. Adults: inject into the <u>fatty tissue over the triceps</u>. Infants: inject into the anterolateral mid-thigh muscle.

- <u>IM</u>: use a 22 – 25 gauge needle. Inject at a <u>90-degree</u> angle. Adults: inject into the <u>deltoid</u> muscle above the level of the armpit and below the shoulder joint. Infants: inject into the anterolateral mid-thigh muscle. <u>IM needle length</u>: 1" in adults.

    - <u>Exceptions</u>: weight < 130 pounds, use a 5/8 – 1" needle and males > 260 pounds or females > 200 pounds, use a 1½" needle.

- Never mix vaccines in the same syringe.

- Use of acetaminophen before vaccine administration, to prevent adverse effects, is not recommended. It can be given if symptoms occur.

IMMUNIZATION REGISTRIES

Immunization registries are computerized information systems that collect vaccination histories and help ensure correct and timely immunizations, especially for children. They are useful for healthcare providers, who can use the registries to obtain the patient's history, produce vaccine records and manage vaccine inventories, among other benefits. It helps the community at-large to identify groups who are not receiving vaccines in order to target outreach efforts. Some systems are able to notify patients if vaccines are needed. Where allowed, pharmacists should strive to report all vaccines administrated to their state or local registry.

Select Guidelines/References

CDC Vaccine and Immunization websites: https://www.cdc.gov/vaccines, https://www.cdc.gov/vaccines/hcp/acip-recs/index.html and https://www.cdc.gov/travel (accessed 2022 Feb 9). The pediatric and adult schedules are updated annually and published in January.

The CDC's Pink Book, Epidemiology and Prevention of Vaccine Preventable Diseases (published every 2 years). https://www.cdc.gov/vaccines/pubs/pinkbook/index.html (accessed 2022 Feb 9).

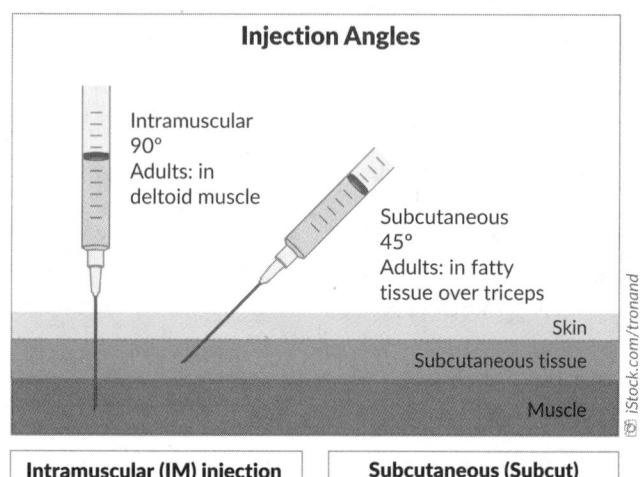

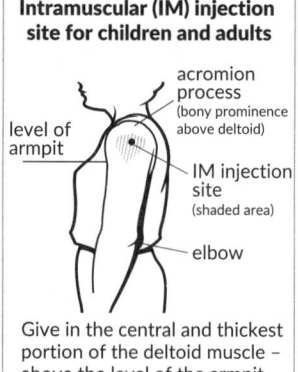

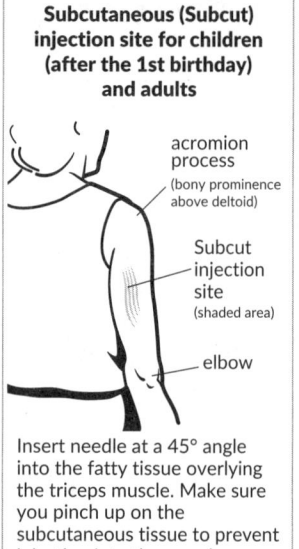

© http://www.immunize.org/catg.d/p2020.pdf

CONTENT LEGEND

 = Study Tip Gal   = Key Drug Guy

© iStock.com/seb_ra

CHAPTER 21

TRAVELERS

BACKGROUND

In 2019, U.S. residents made more than 79 million trips with at least one night outside the United States. Pharmacists assist travelers by providing formal advice, travel vaccines, malaria prophylaxis and other medications prior to travel. Consultative services provided by pharmacists can include educational awareness of country-specific risks, and ways to prevent and address them.

Travelers should have a list of their medical conditions and medications (prescription and OTC). Travel vaccinations should be documented on the International Certificate of Vaccination or Prophylaxis (ICVP) card, sometimes called the "yellow card." Prescription medications should be stored in the original prescription containers. Medications and medical supplies should be packed in carry-on luggage.

When preparing a patient for travel, healthcare professionals should consider: 1) diseases spread through food and water, 2) diseases spread through blood and bodily fluids, and 3) diseases transmitted by insects. A traveler's risk for contracting disease is assessed based upon travel duration, destination-specific risks, itinerary and patient-specific health concerns. CDC's Health Information for International Travel (the "Yellow Book") is available on the CDC website and contains travel health information, including travel health insurance recommendations. Travel advisories and visa requirements can be checked on the U.S. State Department website.

DISEASES TRANSMITTED THROUGH CONTAMINATED FOOD AND WATER

Contaminated food and water cause many travel-related illnesses. Many international travel destinations (especially developing countries) vary in the availability of clean water, plumbing and refrigeration. These factors can lead to unsafe food handling practices and food and water contamination with fecal matter, leading to an increased risk of illness.

IMMUNIZATIONS & TRAVELERS

TRAVELERS' DIARRHEA

Travelers' diarrhea (TD) is the most common travel-related illness, occurring in 30 – 70% of travelers, depending on the destination and season. Areas of highest risk include most of Asia, the Middle East, Africa, Mexico, and Central and South America. TD is the sudden onset of abnormally loose or liquid, frequent stools. If blood is mixed in with the stool, it is classified as dysentery, which is often accompanied by more severe systemic symptoms such as fever. Severity is assessed by the patient as mild, moderate or severe, and this determines initial treatment (see Study Tip Gal on the following page). Dysentery is classified as severe.

Symptoms usually begin within 6 – 72 hours if caused by a bacterial or viral pathogen. More than 80% of TD cases are bacterial. The primary pathogen is E. coli, followed by Campylobacter jejuni, Shigella species and Salmonella species. Untreated bacterial diarrhea can last 3 – 7 days, and some pathogens can cause invasive infections outside of the GI tract. Persistent TD, defined as diarrhea lasting ≥ 14 days, is more likely to occur with certain bacterial and protozoal pathogens and requires additional testing.

TD Prevention

Safe food and water habits can reduce, but do not eliminate, the risk of TD. The rule "boil it, cook it, peel it or forget it" is helpful when discussing food safety. These food and water precautions can be recommended:

- Eat only food that is cooked and served hot. Avoid food that has been sitting on a buffet.

- Eat raw fruits and vegetables only if washed in clean water or peeled (e.g., oranges).

- Use bottled water or boil for approximately one minute before drinking or using to brush teeth. Avoid ice.

- Eating at well-known restaurants can help reduce risk. Poor hygiene practices can increase the risk of contracting TD.

- Keep hands clean and out of the mouth. Wash hands often with soap and water, especially after using the bathroom and before eating. If soap and water are not available, use an alcohol-based hand sanitizer.

Prophylaxis with bismuth subsalicylate (BSS), the active ingredient of Pepto-Bismol, reduces the incidence of TD by ~50%. Do not use BSS in patients with an aspirin allergy, pregnancy, renal insufficiency, gout, ulcer, or anyone taking anticoagulants, probenecid or methotrexate. Taking BSS with aspirin or other salicylates can cause salicylate toxicity.

BSS is FDA-approved for OTC use in children ≥ 12 years old, but has been used off-label in younger children (≥ 3 years old) as long as they have had no recent or current viral infections (due to the risk of Reye's syndrome). BSS tablets or liquid can be recommended as prophylaxis in any appropriate traveler.

Antibiotic prophylaxis should not be used by most travelers. It can be used by people who are at high risk of developing complications of TD (e.g., immunosuppressed patients or significant comorbidities) or those with travel for performance reasons (e.g., a professional athlete). If antibiotic prophylaxis is indicated, rifaximin is preferred. Alternatives include azithromycin and rifamycin.

TD Treatment

Hydration (with increased fluid and salt intake) is essential for all TD cases. In an elderly patient with severe diarrhea or any traveler with prolonged watery diarrhea or vomiting, oral rehydration solution is preferred for fluid replacement. The packets are available in pharmacies throughout the world. They are easy to prepare: mix one packet with one liter of boiled, purified water.

Medications are not required for non-severe, non-cholera-like diarrhea. OTC anti-diarrheal drugs will reduce the number of bowel movements, allowing travelers to continue their planned itinerary. The primary antimotility drug used for acute diarrhea is loperamide (Imodium A-D). Loperamide decreases the frequency and urgency of bowel movements, making it easier for a person with diarrhea to continue travel activities (e.g., ride on a bus or airplane). The dose is 4 mg after the first loose stool and 2 mg after each subsequent loose stool, up to a maximum dose of 16 mg/day by prescription or 8 mg/day OTC. Loperamide can be used for self-treatment for up to two days. If symptoms remain after 48 hours, a healthcare provider should be seen. It should not be used in children < 2 years old (< 6 years old if OTC) or in patients with bloody diarrhea. See the Constipation & Diarrhea chapter for more information on loperamide.

BSS is another treatment option. The salicylate portion of BSS has antisecretory, anti-diarrheal properties and can reduce stools passed by ~40%. See the Constipation & Diarrhea chapter for specific information on contraindications and side effects, such as black tongue/stools, risk of Reye's syndrome in children and salicylate toxicity.

Compared with BSS, loperamide showed a greater reduction in the number of diarrheal stools passed and has been shown to shorten the duration of acute diarrhea in both children and adults.

DRUGS FOR TRAVELERS' DIARRHEA

Prophylaxis
- Bismuth subsalicylate 524-1050 mg PO 4 times daily (with meals and at bedtime)
- Antibiotics (rifaximin preferred)
  - ❏ Only used if there is a high risk of complications from TD

Treatment
- Mild TD: loperamide or bismuth subsalicylate
- Moderate TD: loperamide ± antibiotics
  - ❏ Azithromycin or a quinolone (if low resistance)
  - ❏ Rifaximin is an alternative
- Severe TD (including dysentery): antibiotics ± loperamide
  - ❏ Azithromycin preferred
  - ❏ Quinolones or rifaximin as alternatives

Antibiotics shorten the duration of moderate-to-severe TD to a little over 24 hours. Azithromycin, quinolones or rifaximin can be used (typically a single-dose regimen), depending on the TD severity and antibiotic resistance patterns. Azithromycin is preferred for severe TD and dysentery. Quinolones, rifaximin or rifamycin can be used for severe TD if no dysentery is present. Rifaximin and rifamycin cannot be used to treat infections in which invasive pathogens (e.g., *Campylobacter jejuni, Salmonella* species) are suspected. Rifamycin *(Aemcolo)* is FDA-approved for treatment of TD caused by noninvasive strains of *E. coli* in adults.

TYPHOID FEVER

Typhoid fever is caused by the bacterium *Salmonella typhi*. The disease can be life-threatening. The highest risk areas for contracting typhoid fever include East and Southeast Asia, Africa, the Caribbean, and Central and South America.

Humans are the only source for this bacteria. Disease is spread through food or water contaminated by the feces of someone with either an acute infection or from a chronic, asymptomatic carrier. The incubation period of typhoid fever and paratyphoid fever (a similar illness) is 6 – 30 days. Patients present with fatigue and increasing fever over 3 – 4 days. Additional symptoms may include headache, malaise, anorexia, rash and enlargement of the liver and spleen. Intestinal hemorrhage or perforation can occur 2 – 3 weeks later and can be fatal.

Typhoid vaccines are recommended but are only 50 – 80% effective; even vaccinated travelers should follow safe food and water precautions and wash their hands frequently. These precautions are the only prevention method for paratyphoid fever because there is not a vaccine available.

Typhoid vaccines include *Vivotif*, an oral, live-attenuated vaccine, and *Typhim Vi*, an inactivated, intramuscular injection. The oral vaccine regimen should be completed ≥ 1 week prior to travel. It should not be used in children < 6 years old, patients taking antibiotics or in those with an extremely sensitive stomach. The intramuscular vaccine must be given ≥ 2 weeks before the expected exposure and is not recommended for children < 2 years old. Revaccination is recommended every five years for *Vivotif* and every two years for *Typhim Vi* in patients who remain at risk.

CHOLERA

Cholera is a bacterial infection caused by *Vibrio cholerae*. The disease is very rare in the U.S., but still occurs in many places, including Africa, Southeast Asia and Haiti. The infection is often mild or asymptomatic, but in severe cases, it can present with profuse diarrhea and vomiting, and eventual dehydration that can be life-threatening. The most common symptom includes watery diarrhea, which is referred to as "rice-water stools."

In addition to food and water precautions, a live-attenuated vaccine (Vaxchora) is recommended for those traveling to a region with active cholera transmission. *Vaxchora* is administered as a single, oral liquid dose at least 10 days before travel and is approved for use in ages 2 through 64 years. In December 2020, the maker of *Vaxchora* temporarily stopped manufacturing, which may lead to drug shortages.

POLIO

Most people in the U.S. received the polio vaccine in childhood, but the virus is not eradicated worldwide. Many countries remain endemic and have had an active spread of poliovirus in the recent past. These include Afghanistan, Myanmar (Burma), Guinea, Laos, Nigeria, Madagascar, Pakistan and Ukraine. The CDC recommends a single lifetime booster dose of inactivated poliovirus vaccine at least four weeks prior to travel for adults who have previously completed a poliovirus vaccine series and who are traveling to regions where poliovirus is circulating. Travelers might be required to show proof of polio vaccination when leaving a polio-infected country.

IMMUNIZATIONS & TRAVELERS

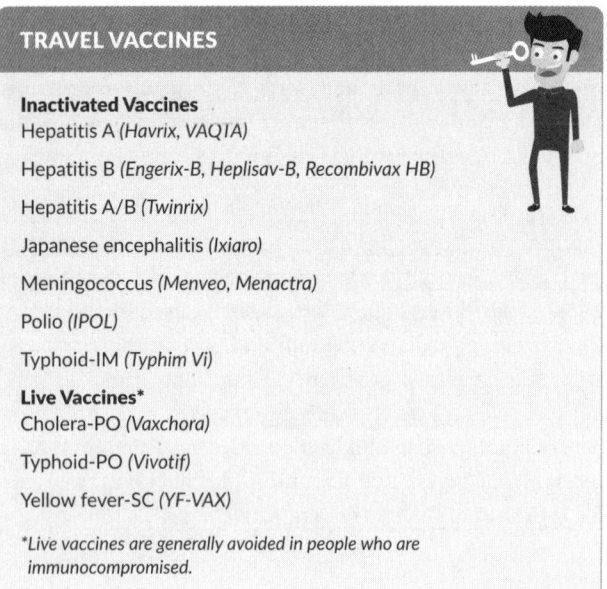

TRAVEL VACCINES

Inactivated Vaccines
Hepatitis A (Havrix, VAQTA)

Hepatitis B (Engerix-B, Heplisav-B, Recombivax HB)

Hepatitis A/B (Twinrix)

Japanese encephalitis (Ixiaro)

Meningococcus (Menveo, Menactra)

Polio (IPOL)

Typhoid-IM (Typhim Vi)

Live Vaccines*
Cholera-PO (Vaxchora)

Typhoid-PO (Vivotif)

Yellow fever-SC (YF-VAX)

*Live vaccines are generally avoided in people who are immunocompromised.

HEPATITIS A

Hepatitis A is a common vaccine-preventable infection among international travelers. People from developed countries who travel to developing countries are at the highest risk. The infected patient can be asymptomatic or might have symptoms that include fever, malaise, jaundice, nausea and abdominal discomfort that can last up to six months. Vaccination should be considered for travelers to most parts of the world, except Canada, Western Europe, Scandinavia, Japan, New Zealand and Australia.

DISEASES TRANSMITTED THROUGH BLOOD AND BODILY FLUIDS

HEPATITIS B

Hepatitis B is transmitted through contact with contaminated blood or other body fluids. The risk for travelers who do not participate in high-risk behaviors is low. Hepatitis B has an incubation period of about 90 days. Infection can present as malaise, jaundice, nausea and abdominal discomfort. Chronic infection with Hepatitis B can result in chronic liver disease and liver cancer.

Hepatitis B vaccination is extremely important for travelers who plan to receive medical care, volunteer to provide medical work or have unprotected sexual encounters with new partners. Piercings and tattoos can also transmit the virus and should be avoided. The 3-dose vaccine series takes six months to complete. If a traveler is unable to receive all three doses before departure, administer as many doses as possible before departure and complete the series upon return. In instances of high risk, an accelerated series can be administered; when the accelerated series is used, a booster dose is required at one year for long-term immunity.

MENINGOCOCCAL MENINGITIS

Bacterial meningitis involving *N. meningitidis* has a high mortality rate and is a medical emergency. Patients with symptoms of fever, severe and unrelenting headache, nausea, stiff neck (nuchal rigidity) and mental status changes require urgent treatment to avoid the risk of permanent neurological damage and death. Diagnosis is made by a lumbar puncture (LP). See the Infectious Diseases II chapter.

Meningitis is spread by respiratory secretions and is widespread in many parts of the world. Vaccination is recommended for people who travel to or reside in countries where *N. meningitidis* is hyperendemic or epidemic, particularly if spending a long time in contact with the local population. High-risk regions include the meningitis belt of Africa during the dry season (December – June). The government of Saudi Arabia requires the meningococcal vaccine for travel during the annual Hajj and Umrah pilgrimages. Current recommendations include only the quadrivalent vaccines (*Menactra, Menveo* and *MenQuadfi*) which contain four bacterial types: ACWY. There are no recommendations to use the serogroup B meningococcal vaccines for travelers.

DISEASES TRANSMITTED BY INSECT BITES

Insects that transmit disease are vectors; a vector carries an organism to an individual, causing infection. A reservoir is any place (such as an animal, insect, soil or plant) in which the disease lives and can multiply. The primary insects that transmit infections to travelers are mosquitoes, which transmit Japanese encephalitis, yellow fever, dengue, malaria and Zika virus. The following strategies should be employed to avoid insect bites as much as possible:

- Stay and sleep in screened or air-conditioned rooms and use a bed net, which can be pre-treated with mosquito repellent, such as those listed below.

- Cover exposed skin by wearing long-sleeved shirts, long pants and hats.

- Use proper application of mosquito repellents containing 20% – 50% DEET as the active ingredient on exposed skin. DEET also protects against ticks. Other insect repellents that can be used topically for mosquitoes (but not for ticks) are picaridin, oil of lemon, eucalyptus or IR3535.

- Use permethrin to treat clothing, gear and bed nets but do not apply directly to the skin.

DENGUE

Dengue is transmitted by *Aedes aegypti* and *Aedes albopictus* mosquitoes. In many parts of the tropics and subtropics, dengue is endemic; it occurs every year, usually during a season when mosquito populations are high and rainfall is optimal for breeding. An estimated 75% of infections are asymptomatic, but up to 5% of patients develop severe, life-threatening disease. Severe dengue can include shock, severe bleeding or organ failure. Treatment is supportive, as there are no specific medications to treat dengue infection. *Dengvaxia* is a live-attenuated recombinant vaccine recommended only to those with a past dengue infection. Protection from mosquito bites is essential.

JAPANESE ENCEPHALITIS

The Japanese Encephalitis (JE) virus is transmitted by mosquitoes. Infection is usually asymptomatic, but can develop into encephalitis (swelling around the brain) with rigors, risk of seizures, coma and death. Infection risk is highest in rural agricultural areas. The best prevention is to reduce exposure to mosquitoes. The JE vaccine is sometimes recommended with travel to Asia and parts of the western Pacific. The vaccine (*Ixiaro*) is recommended for travelers older than two months of age who are planning extended exposure to the outdoors (e.g., campers) or who plan to spend at least one month in endemic areas during the JE virus transmission season. There is an accelerated schedule available for those traveling with little notice.

MALARIA

Malaria is transmitted by the Anopheles mosquito. Once in a human host, it multiplies first in the liver and then moves into the red blood cells, multiplying and destroying them. Classic symptoms of malaria include shaking, chills, high fever and flu-like illness; these should not be ignored in a patient with recent travel. Malaria is endemic in Asia, Latin America, North Africa, Eastern Europe and the South Pacific. *Plasmodium vivax* is the most common of four human malaria species (*P. falciparum, P. malariae, P. ovale* and *P. vivax*). *P. vivax* causes 50% of malaria cases in India and is becoming increasingly resistant to malaria drugs. *P. falciparum* is the most deadly species. About 1,700 cases of malaria are diagnosed in the U.S. annually, mostly in returned travelers. Even with treatment, malaria can be fatal, so prophylactic medications are recommended for travelers to certain regions. The CDC website features maps of malaria presence by country, the species of malaria, and resistance patterns. All of this information is incorporated into the CDC's region-specific prophylaxis medication recommendations. Recommendations can change year-to-year.

Malaria Prophylaxis Regimens

Malaria prophylaxis must be started prior to travel and continue after returning (see following tables for specific requirements). Malaria drugs cause nausea; taking with sufficient water, food or milk decreases nausea.

Quick Starts

DRUG	DOSING	SAFETY/SIDE EFFECTS/NOTES
These medications are initiated just 1-2 days prior to travel, which makes them ideal when traveling with little advance notice		
Doxycycline (Doryx, Vibramycin)	Stop: 4 weeks after travel	Causes photosensitivity*
		Not used in:
Also prevents rickettsial infections and leptospirosis, so preferred in hiking/ camping	Taken daily	Pregnancy
		Children < 8 years old (due to tooth development/ discoloration)
Atovaquone/Proguanil (*Malarone*)	Stop: 1 week after travel	**Not used in:**
		Pregnancy
Good coverage	Taken daily	Breastfeeding
		Severe renal impairment
Primaquine	Stop: 1 week after travel	**Not used in:**
		G6PD deficiency (CDC requires screening prior to use due to risk of hemolytic anemia)
Most effective drug against *P. vivax*	Taken daily	Pregnancy
		Breastfeeding (unless infant is tested for G6PD deficiency)

Daily regimens

Avoid these in pregnancy

Cause nausea; to decrease, take with food, milk or water

Use broad-spectrum sunscreen (protects against UVA and UVB rays) with Sun Protection Factor (SPF) 30 or higher, plus water resistant. Other strategies: seek shade, wear protective clothing, avoid mid-day sun.

Advance Starts

Weekly regimens

Safe in children, pregnancy

Choice depends on resistance in the region

DRUG	DOSING	SAFETY/SIDE EFFECTS/NOTES
These medications must be started 1-2 weeks prior to travel		
Chloroquine Resistance issues with *P. falciparum* and *P. vivax*	Start: 1-2 weeks before travel Stop: 4 weeks after travel Taken weekly Patients taking chronic hydroxychloroquine are covered (depending on resistance)	**SIDE EFFECTS** Retinal toxicity/visual changes, exacerbation of psoriasis, serious skin rash (rare), blue-gray skin pigmentation (rare with short-term use) Contraindicated for prophylaxis if underlying retinal or visual changes **Not used in:** Areas of chloroquine or mefloquine resistance
Mefloquine	Start: ≥ 2 weeks before travel Stop: 4 weeks after travel Taken weekly	**Not used in:** Underlying psychiatric conditions Seizures Arrhythmias Areas of mefloquine resistance
Tafenoquine *(Arakoda)* May be used for up to 6 months of continuous dosing	Loading dose: 3 days before travel, taken daily Maintenance dose: 7 days after last dose of loading regimen Taken weekly Terminal dose: single dose after the last dose of the maintenance regimen	**Not used in:** G6PD deficiency (CDC requires screening prior to use due to risk of hemolytic anemia) Pregnancy Breastfeeding (unless infant is tested for G6PD deficiency) Underlying psychiatric conditions

YELLOW FEVER

Yellow fever is caused by a virus and transmitted by mosquitoes found in tropical and subtropical areas in Africa and Central and South America. Reducing mosquito exposure is essential. Most infections are asymptomatic. If symptoms develop, the initial illness presents with influenza-like symptoms. Most patients will improve, but ~15% progress to a more toxic form of the disease with risk of shock, bleeding and organ failure. There is no specific treatment for acute infection except symptomatic relief with fluids, analgesics and antipyretics. Aspirin and other NSAIDs cannot be used due to an increased risk of bleeding.

A live-attenuated vaccine (YF-VAX) is available to prevent yellow fever and stop transmission. After vaccination, patients are provided an ICVP ("yellow card"), which is required as a condition of entry for some countries. The card is valid beginning 10 days after date of vaccination. In 2015, the CDC Advisory Committee on Immunization Practices (ACIP) approved a new recommendation that a single dose of yellow fever vaccine provides life-long protection and is adequate for most travelers. Healthcare providers should review the entry requirements for destination countries, as some countries continue to require a booster vaccine dose every 10 years (as previous guidelines recommended).

The vaccine is contraindicated with hypersensitivity to eggs and in people who are severely immunocompromised. Due to the risks of serious adverse effects, vaccination is recommended only in travelers at a high risk of exposure or who require proof of vaccination to enter a country. Mild adverse effects are common (occurring in 10 – 30% of patients) and include low-grade fever and headache lasting for 5 – 10 days. In rare cases, severe adverse effects occur, such as yellow fever vaccine-associated neurologic disease.

ZIKA VIRUS

The Zika virus is transmitted primarily by the *Aedes* species mosquito. Sexual and possible blood transfusion-associated transmission have been reported. Most Zika virus infections are asymptomatic. Symptomatic infections are generally mild with symptoms consisting of fever, maculopapular rash, arthralgia (joint pain) and conjunctivitis (red eyes).

The most pressing concern with Zika virus arose in 2015 when Brazil observed a marked increase in the number of infants born with microcephaly, a birth defect that can cause significant disability and can be life-threatening in severe cases. Zika virus RNA was subsequently identified in tissues from infants with microcephaly and from fetal losses in women infected during pregnancy. Zika infection during pregnancy can cause birth defects of the brain and eyes, hearing deficits and impaired growth. Reports of Guillain-Barré syndrome, an uncommon sickness of the nervous system, have also increased in areas affected by Zika.

No vaccine is available yet for the Zika virus. Avoiding mosquito bites and using condoms during sexual contact with people with possible Zika virus infection reduces transmission risk.

The CDC recommends against pregnant women traveling to any area with ongoing transmission of Zika virus. Women who are trying to become pregnant should consult with their healthcare provider prior to travel. Men who have a pregnant partner and have traveled to an area with Zika should use condoms or avoid sex during the pregnancy. These recommendations might change as more data about the Zika virus become available.

ADDITIONAL CONCERNS FOR TRAVELING INDIVIDUALS

VENOUS THROMBOEMBOLISM PREVENTION

Travelers are at increased risk for deep vein thrombosis (DVT) and pulmonary embolism (PE) due to limited movement with long air travel. Wearing compression stockings during long trips reduces risk; these are sold in pharmacies. Travelers should be instructed to stand up, walk and perform lower leg exercises when sitting. Patients should know the symptoms of a DVT and PE and be instructed to seek immediate medical care if suspected. DVT risk factors, symptoms and treatment are discussed in the Anticoagulation chapter.

ALTITUDE SICKNESS AND MOTION SICKNESS

Acute mountain sickness (AMS) occurs when people climb rapidly to a high altitude. It occurs commonly above 8,000 feet and is more likely in individuals who live close to sea level and those who have had the condition previously. Symptoms include dizziness, headache, tachycardia and shortness of breath. The primary prophylactic medication is acetazolamide (Diamox) 125 mg twice daily, started the day before (preferred) or on the day of ascent. Higher doses are used for treatment. This can improve breathing, but is not without side effects (polyuria, photosensitivity, taste alteration, risk of dehydration, urticaria and a possibility of severe skin rashes). Acetazolamide is contraindicated with a sulfa allergy. Sun protection and hydration are recommended. In acute cases of altitude sickness, oxygen, inhaled beta-agonists and dexamethasone are given to reduce cerebral edema.

Motion sickness is common among travelers and is discussed in the Motion Sickness chapter.

THE RETURNED TRAVELER

It is imperative that travelers who are ill upon returning home see a healthcare provider. It is important for patients to communicate travel specifics to the healthcare provider, including the travel itinerary, the trip duration, accommodations (where they stayed), travel activities and any precautions that were taken to reduce infection risk, including vaccination history prior to leaving the U.S.

Some diseases have longer incubation periods and symptoms might not appear for weeks or months. Travelers often return home before their symptoms begin. This can lead to epidemics and the spread of disease from country to country. An example of this is the 2014 outbreak of the Ebola virus in West Africa, the largest Ebola outbreak in history. Ebola is transmitted by direct contact with blood or bodily fluids of a symptomatic person. Symptoms (fever, headache, diarrhea and hemorrhaging) can appear from 2 – 21 days after exposure. Due to the potentially long incubation, an infected person could be asymptomatic when returning to the U.S. and spread the disease before a diagnosis is made. Isolation upon return can reduce transmission.

Another example of this is illustrated by the Zika outbreak discussed previously in this chapter. In 2015, the Zika virus was identified for the first time in the Western hemisphere, with large outbreaks reported in Brazil. Since then, the virus has spread throughout much of the Americas and is still a concern for travelers, especially for those who are pregnant or are planning a pregnancy in the near future.

Select Guidelines/References

Centers for Disease Control (CDC) Center on Travelers Health. Available at http://wwwnc.cdc.gov/travel (accessed 2022 Jan 20).

International Society of Travel Medicine (ISTM), Pharmacist Professional Group of the ISTM. Available at www.istm.org (accessed 2022 Jan 20).

Riddle MS, Connor BA, Beeching, NJ, et al. Guidelines for the prevention and treatment of travelers' diarrhea: a graded expert panel report. J Travel Med 2017; 24(Suppl 1):S63-S80.

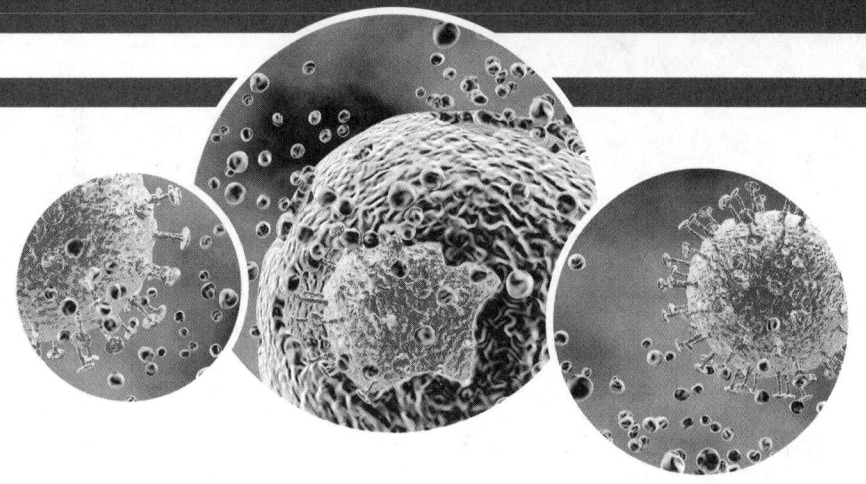

INFECTIOUS DISEASES

CONTENTS

CONTENT LEGEND

= Study Tip Gal   = Key Drug Guy

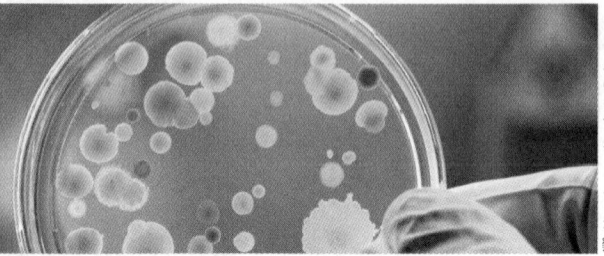

© iStock.com/AndreasReh

CHAPTER 22

INFECTIOUS DISEASES I: BACKGROUND & ANTIBIOTICS BY DRUG CLASS

BACKGROUND

An infectious disease (ID) is caused by one or more pathogens [viruses, bacteria, fungi, protozoa, parasites and/or infectious proteins (prions)]. Infectious diseases are transmitted through various mechanisms, including physical contact with an infected individual or their body fluids, consuming contaminated food or water or by touching contaminated objects. Some conditions are transmitted by airborne inhalation and others are spread by a vector (carrier). Transmissible diseases that are spread from <u>person to person</u> are referred to as <u>communicable</u> or <u>contagious</u>.

HOW TO APPROACH INFECTIOUS DISEASES

Infectious diseases is organized into four chapters:

- ID I covers the principles of infectious diseases and provides summaries of antibacterial drugs by class.

- ID II reviews treatment of specific bacterial infections.

- ID III discusses antifungals, antivirals and select diseases.

- ID IV reviews prophylaxis and treatment of opportunistic infections in immunocompromised patients.

Three primary factors impact treatment decisions in infectious diseases: the <u>bug</u> (pathogen), the <u>drug</u> (antibiotic) and the <u>patient</u> (host). Do not be tempted to think of bugs, drugs and infectious diseases as separate sections to memorize; they must be considered together.

HOW DO I START?

- Recognize common organisms and groups of organisms.
- Focus on resistant organisms and the drugs that treat them.
- Learn the basic spectrum of activity for antimicrobial classes.
- Use bolded drugs, underlined information and Study Tip Gals to identify important points (and think about how to assess the patient profile on the exam).

ANTIBIOTIC SELECTION

- Infection characteristics include the <u>infection site</u>, infection <u>severity</u> and whether it is <u>community-</u> or <u>hospital-acquired</u>. Infections that are hospital-acquired often involve multidrug-resistant (MDR) organisms.

- The <u>presence of an infection</u> is determined by <u>signs and symptoms</u>. For example, the presence of bacteria in a urine culture does not mean there is an infection. The diagnosis is based on symptoms (e.g., dysuria, urgency, leukocytosis, fever) plus a positive urinalysis and/or urine culture.

- <u>Antibiotic</u> characteristics include the <u>spectrum of activity</u> and ability to <u>penetrate</u> the <u>site of infection</u>. Lipophilic antimicrobials have better tissue penetration. Antibiotics that are not cleared renally may not achieve adequate drug concentrations in the urine.

- Patient characteristics impact treatment choices. These include <u>age, body weight, renal and hepatic function</u>, <u>allergies</u>, recent antibiotic use, colonization with resistant bacteria, recent environmental exposure, vaccination status, pregnancy status, immune function and <u>comorbid</u> conditions.

EMPIRIC TREATMENT

- Antibiotics are often started <u>before the pathogen is identified</u>. This <u>empiric</u> treatment is usually <u>broad-spectrum</u> (covers several different types of bacteria) and is based on a best guess of the <u>likely organisms</u> causing the infection (see image below). Local resistance patterns (e.g., the antibiogram) and antibiotic use guidelines should be considered when selecting empiric treatment.

Common Bacterial Pathogens for Select Sites of Infection

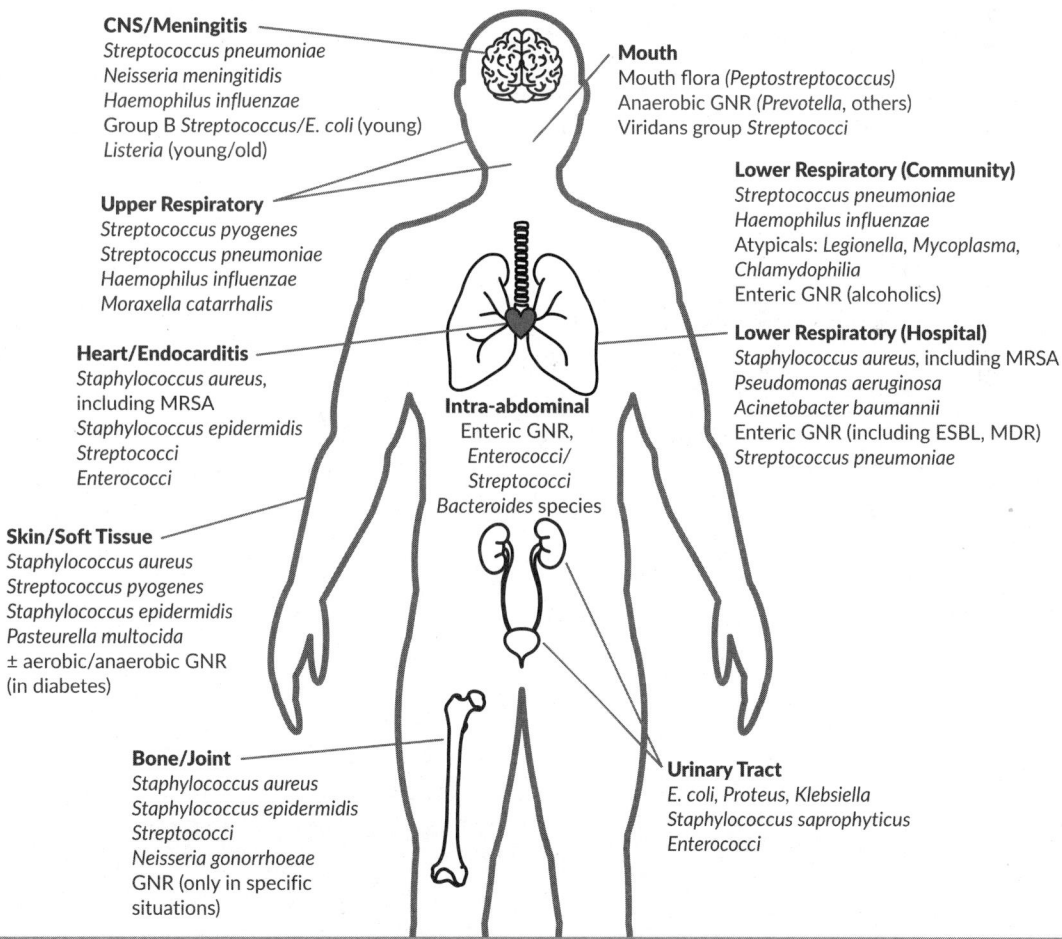

CNS = central nervous system; GNR = Gram-negative rods; Enteric GNR = *Proteus, E. coli, Klebsiella, Enterobacter, Serratia*; ESBL = extended-spectrum beta-lactamase; MDR = multidrug-resistant; MRSA = methicillin-resistant *Staphylococcus aureus*

©RxPrep
MaskaRad, Rvector, D things/Shutterstock.com

GRAM STAIN

Cultures are taken from the infection site (e.g., urine, blood, lung secretions, wound tissue or abscess fluid) and sent to the microbiology lab. The Gram stain categorizes the organism by <u>shape</u> (or <u>morphology</u>), see <u>Study Tip Gal</u> below, and provides <u>quick, preliminary results</u> (e.g., Gram-negative rods). While it <u>does not identify the exact organism</u> (e.g., *Klebsiella pneumoniae*), it provides a clue about what organism may be causing the infection and an opportunity to adjust the empiric antibiotic regimen before the species is formally identified.

- **Gram-positive** organisms: have a <u>thick cell wall</u> and stain dark <u>purple or bluish</u> from the <u>crystal violet stain</u>.

- **Gram-negative** organisms: have a <u>thin cell wall</u> and take up the <u>safranin</u> counterstain, resulting in a <u>pink or reddish</u> color.

- **Atypical** organisms: do not have a cell wall and <u>do not stain</u> well.

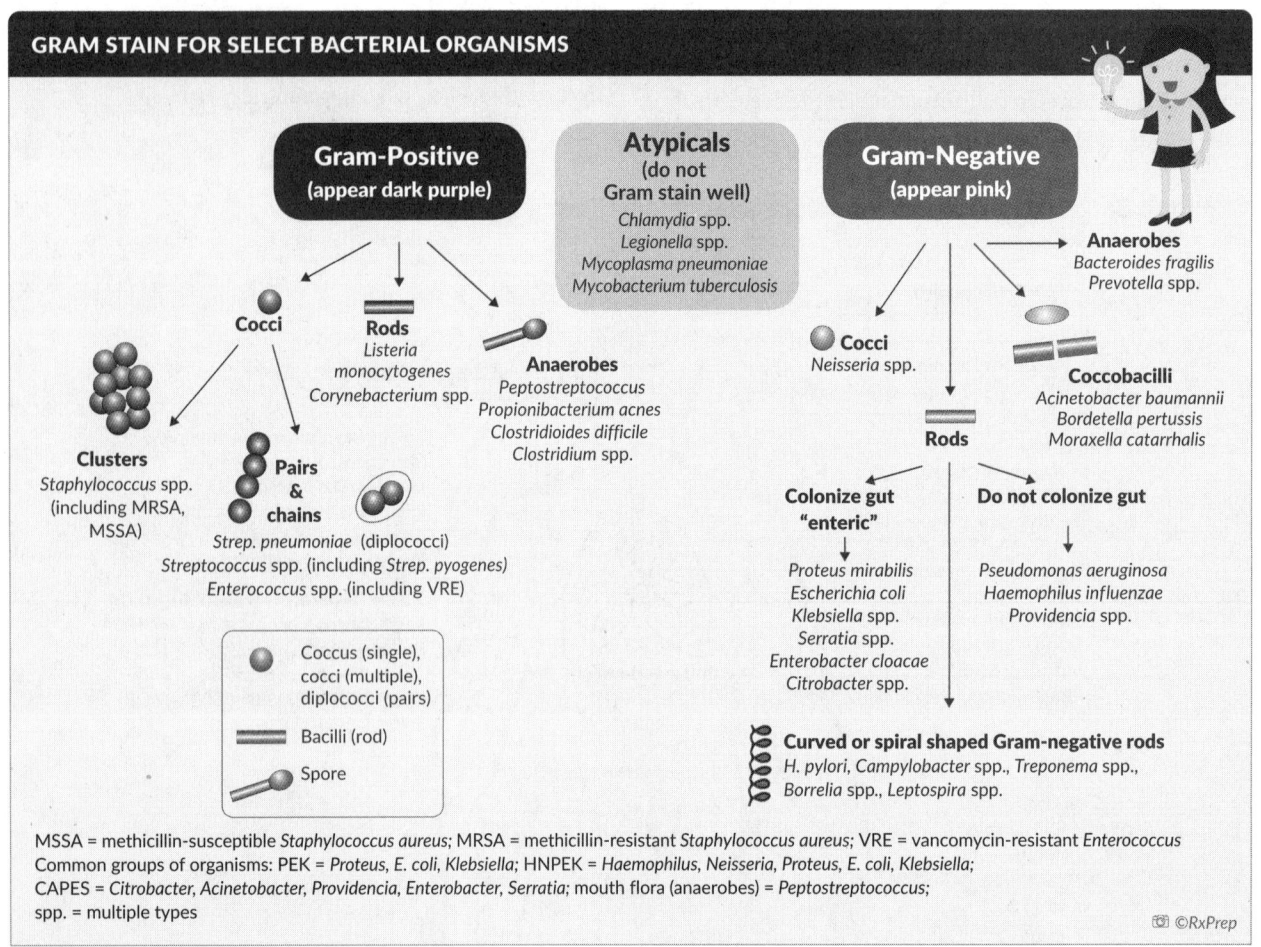

GRAM STAIN FOR SELECT BACTERIAL ORGANISMS

Gram-Positive (appear dark purple)

Cocci

Clusters
Staphylococcus spp. (including MRSA, MSSA)

Pairs & chains
Strep. pneumoniae (diplococci)
Streptococcus spp. (including *Strep. pyogenes*)
Enterococcus spp. (including VRE)

Rods
Listeria monocytogenes
Corynebacterium spp.

Anaerobes
Peptostreptococcus
Propionibacterium acnes
Clostridioides difficile
Clostridium spp.

Atypicals (do not Gram stain well)
Chlamydia spp.
Legionella spp.
Mycoplasma pneumoniae
Mycobacterium tuberculosis

Gram-Negative (appear pink)

Anaerobes
Bacteroides fragilis
Prevotella spp.

Cocci
Neisseria spp.

Coccobacilli
Acinetobacter baumannii
Bordetella pertussis
Moraxella catarrhalis

Rods

Colonize gut "enteric"
Proteus mirabilis
Escherichia coli
Klebsiella spp.
Serratia spp.
Enterobacter cloacae
Citrobacter spp.

Do not colonize gut
Pseudomonas aeruginosa
Haemophilus influenzae
Providencia spp.

Curved or spiral shaped Gram-negative rods
H. pylori, Campylobacter spp., *Treponema* spp., *Borrelia* spp., *Leptospira* spp.

Legend:
- Coccus (single), cocci (multiple), diplococci (pairs)
- Bacilli (rod)
- Spore

MSSA = methicillin-susceptible *Staphylococcus aureus*; MRSA = methicillin-resistant *Staphylococcus aureus*; VRE = vancomycin-resistant *Enterococcus*
Common groups of organisms: PEK = *Proteus, E. coli, Klebsiella*; HNPEK = *Haemophilus, Neisseria, Proteus, E. coli, Klebsiella*;
CAPES = *Citrobacter, Acinetobacter, Providencia, Enterobacter, Serratia*; mouth flora (anaerobes) = *Peptostreptococcus*;
spp. = multiple types

©RxPrep

ANTIBIOGRAM

An antibiogram combines culture data from patients at a single institution into one chart (such as all Gram-positive organisms cultured at a hospital) to show <u>susceptibility patterns</u> over a specific time period (generally 1 year). Refer to the <u>example antibiogram</u> on the next page. Bacteria are listed vertically, and drugs are listed horizontally. The numbers inside the table are the <u>percent susceptibility</u> of each organism to the listed drug.

Antibiograms aid in selecting <u>empiric</u> treatment (see Case Scenario) and are used to monitor <u>resistance trends</u> over time.

CASE SCENARIO

A 77-year-old female is admitted to the ICU from home with confusion, cough, temperature = 101.9°F, respiratory rate = 32 breaths per minute and oxygen saturation = 88% on room air. Her chest X-ray is consistent with pneumonia and a sputum Gram stain shows Gram-positive cocci in pairs. The pharmacist is asked to choose a beta-lactam (in addition to azithromycin) for empiric treatment.

After reviewing the institutional antibiogram (see example on next page), the pharmacist recommends ceftriaxone. Local susceptibility patterns are consistent with national guidelines, showing that third-generation cephalosporins are highly active against the likely pathogen (*S. pneumoniae*).

Hospital Antibiogram Example (Abridged)

JANUARY-DECEMBER	# OF ISOLATES	PENICILLIN	OXACILLIN	AMPICILLIN	CEFTRIAXONE	CLINDAMYCIN	ERYTHROMYCIN	GENTAMICIN	LEVOFLOXACIN	LINEZOLID	TETRACYCLINE	SMX/TMP	VANCOMYCIN
Gram-Positive Organisms (All Isolates)					REPORTED AS % SUSCEPTIBLE								
Staphylococcus aureus	1360												
MSSA	830	–	100	–	–	88	78	98§	87	100	93	98	100
MRSA	530	–	–	–	–	78	10	92§	15	100	93	92	100
Streptococcus pneumoniae	42	91	–	–	100	–	79	–	97	–	85	80	100
Enterococcus spp.	663	–	–	93	–	–	–	69§	–	99	–	–	100
Enterococcus faecalis	99	–	–	98	–	–	–	62§	–	99	–	–	87
Enterococcus faecium	164	–	–	10	–	–	–	90§	100	99	–	–	15
Urine Isolates													
Enterococcus spp.	153	–	–	79	–	–	–	–	61	100	–	–	81

§Synergy only

ANTIBIOTIC STREAMLINING

CULTURE AND SUSCEPTIBILITY

The culture and susceptibility (C & S) report is usually available within 24 – 72 hours. The C & S report identifies the organism and the results of the susceptibility testing (see Study Tip Gal below). The empiric antibiotics can then be streamlined, which can include discontinuing one or more antibiotics and/or changing to a more narrow-spectrum treatment.

EXAMPLE CULTURE AND SUSCEPTIBILITY REPORT

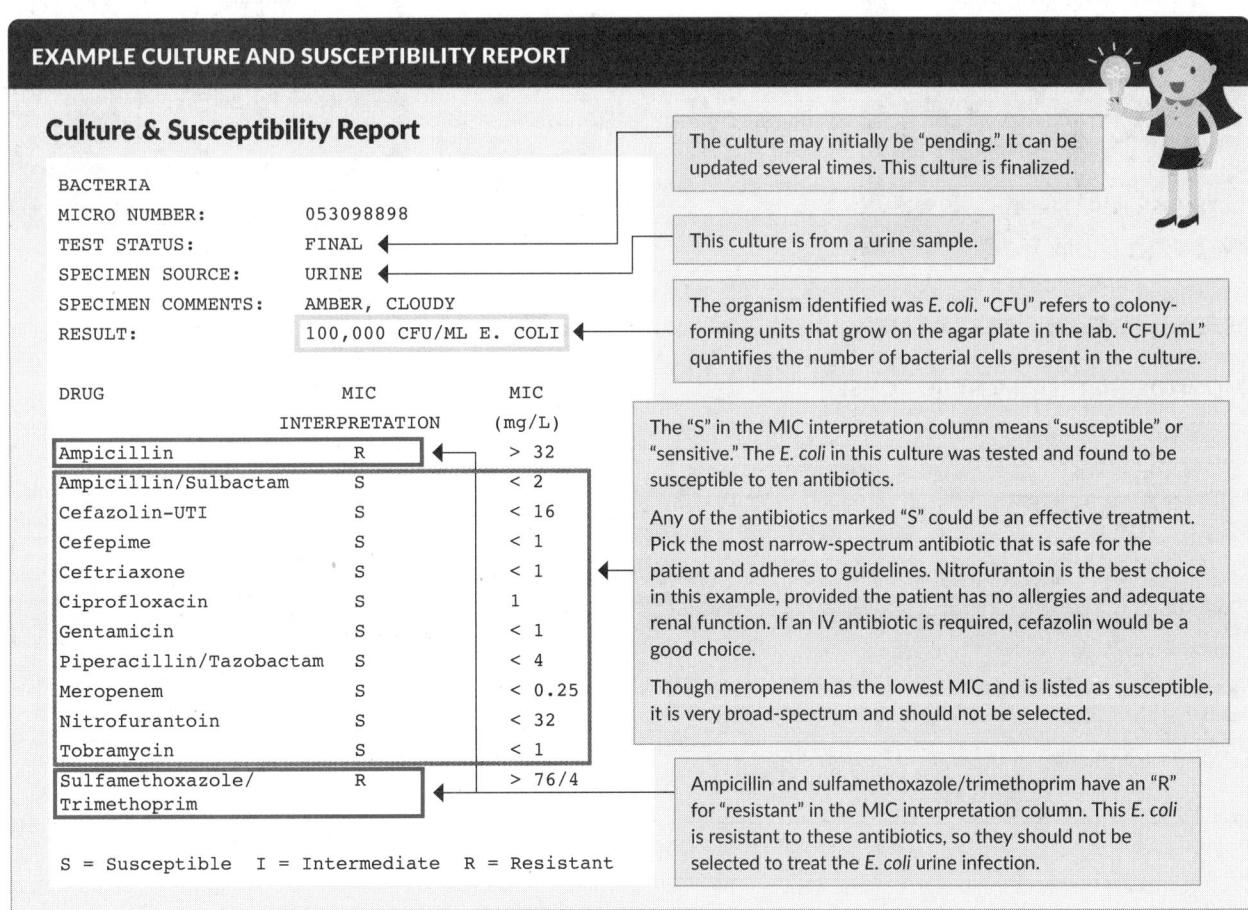

Culture & Susceptibility Report

```
BACTERIA
MICRO NUMBER:        053098898
TEST STATUS:         FINAL
SPECIMEN SOURCE:     URINE
SPECIMEN COMMENTS:   AMBER, CLOUDY
RESULT:              100,000 CFU/ML E. COLI

DRUG                      MIC              MIC
                          INTERPRETATION   (mg/L)
Ampicillin                R                > 32
Ampicillin/Sulbactam      S                < 2
Cefazolin-UTI             S                < 16
Cefepime                  S                < 1
Ceftriaxone               S                < 1
Ciprofloxacin             S                1
Gentamicin                S                < 1
Piperacillin/Tazobactam   S                < 4
Meropenem                 S                < 0.25
Nitrofurantoin            S                < 32
Tobramycin                S                < 1
Sulfamethoxazole/         R                > 76/4
Trimethoprim

S = Susceptible   I = Intermediate   R = Resistant
```

The culture may initially be "pending." It can be updated several times. This culture is finalized.

This culture is from a urine sample.

The organism identified was *E. coli*. "CFU" refers to colony-forming units that grow on the agar plate in the lab. "CFU/mL" quantifies the number of bacterial cells present in the culture.

The "S" in the MIC interpretation column means "susceptible" or "sensitive." The *E. coli* in this culture was tested and found to be susceptible to ten antibiotics.

Any of the antibiotics marked "S" could be an effective treatment. Pick the most narrow-spectrum antibiotic that is safe for the patient and adheres to guidelines. Nitrofurantoin is the best choice in this example, provided the patient has no allergies and adequate renal function. If an IV antibiotic is required, cefazolin would be a good choice.

Though meropenem has the lowest MIC and is listed as susceptible, it is very broad-spectrum and should not be selected.

Ampicillin and sulfamethoxazole/trimethoprim have an "R" for "resistant" in the MIC interpretation column. This *E. coli* is resistant to these antibiotics, so they should not be selected to treat the *E. coli* urine infection.

INFECTIOUS DISEASES

The microbiology lab uses various methods to determine which organism is present in the sample; for example, some Gram-negative bacteria (e.g., *E. coli*) break down lactose (a sugar) in a unique way and some do not (e.g., *Pseudomonas*). Lactose can be used to help determine the types of bacteria that may be present.

Once the organism has been identified, susceptibility testing is performed to determine which antibiotics are useful for treatment. The bacteria is cultured (grown on an agar plate) and exposed to varying concentrations of select antibiotics. The lab identifies the minimum concentration of each antibiotic that inhibits bacterial growth, which is called the minimum inhibitory concentration (MIC). MICs are specific to each antibiotic and organism and should not be compared among different antibiotics. The lab compares the MIC to the susceptibility breakpoint, which is the usual drug concentration that inhibits bacterial growth [as determined by the Clinical & Laboratory Standards Institute (CLSI)]. An interpretation is made as to which drugs inhibit growth (and at what concentration) and which drugs do not.

An antibiotic marked susceptible (S) should be selected. Drugs listed as intermediate (I) may be effective under specific circumstances (e.g., higher doses, extended infusions), but usually would not be selected over a drug that is reported as susceptible. Drugs listed as resistant (R) should not be selected.

Synergy

An infection could require more than one antibiotic for successful treatment. The effect of two antibiotics can be additive (an effect equal to the sum of the individual drugs) or synergistic (an effect greater than the sum of the individual drugs). In certain infections, synergy is useful. For example, aminoglycosides and beta-lactams can be used together synergistically to treat certain invasive Gram-positive infections (e.g., infective endocarditis); the beta-lactam allows the aminoglycoside to reach its intracellular target (the ribosome), where it causes lethal damage to the bacteria. Without the beta-lactam, aminoglycosides cannot penetrate the cell wall at safe doses. This synergy permits a lower dose of aminoglycoside and clears the bloodstream infection more quickly.

Empiric Treatment
Select empiric treatment based on the likely organisms at the infection site (e.g., lower respiratory tract, CNS, skin/soft tissue).

Is the patient at risk for MRSA? MDR bacteria? If yes, provide coverage.

Use the antibiogram and Gram stain (if available) to guide the treatment selection.

Streamline
When the C & S results are available, streamline to more narrow-spectrum antibiotics as soon as possible; if > 1 organism is present, try to find one antibiotic that will treat both.

Consider IV:PO conversion if the patient is clinically stable, eating and there is an appropriate oral drug (e.g., that can penetrate the infection site).

Assess the Patient
Throughout treatment, monitor for improvement. The patient's condition can override the culture information (e.g., if no improvement, perhaps an unidentified organism is the cause of the illness).

With all antibiotics, set the duration of treatment; do not let antibiotics continue unnecessarily.

ASSESSMENT OF TREATMENT

MONITORING TREATMENT RESPONSE	REASONS FOR LACK OF RESPONSE
Clinical status of the patient: 1. Fever trend and other vital signs depending on the infection (e.g., O2 saturation in pneumonia) 2. WBC trend 3. Reduction in signs and symptoms of infection (e.g., improved mentation in meningitis, decreased pain/inflammation in cellulitus) Improved radiographic findings (such as chest X-ray results) Repeat cultures are negative (particularly blood and CNS cultures; sputum and urine cultures do not need to be repeated) Markers of inflammation are decreased: procalcitonin levels (more specific to bacterial infections), C-reactive protein (CRP) and erythrocyte sedimentation rate (ESR)	**Antibiotic factors** Inadequate spectrum of activity and/or dose, poor tissue penetration, drug-drug interactions, non-adherence, inadequate duration of treatment, inability to tolerate/toxicity **Microbiologic factors** Resistance, superinfection (*C. difficile*), alternative etiology [viral, fungal, noninfectious cause (e.g., CHF exacerbation vs. pneumonia)] **Host factors** Uncontrolled source of infection (e.g., abscess or fluid collection, implanted devices with biofilm), immunocompromised

ANTIBIOTIC RESISTANCE

Antibiotic resistance is the ability of an organism to multiply in the presence of a drug that normally limits its growth or kills it. The CDC estimates that there are ~2,000,000 infections a year where the causative organism is resistant to the usual treatment. These infections are difficult to treat and often require drugs that are costly and/or toxic.

Common mechanisms of resistance include:

- Intrinsic resistance: the resistance is natural to the organism. For example, *E. coli* is resistant to vancomycin because this antibiotic is too large to penetrate the bacterial cell wall of *E. coli*.

- Selection pressure: resistance occurs when antibiotics kill off susceptible bacteria, leaving behind more resistant strains to multiply. For example, normal GI flora includes *Enterococcus*. When antibiotics (e.g., vancomycin) eliminate susceptible *Enterococci*, vancomycin-resistant *enterococcus* (VRE) can become predominant.

- Acquired resistance: bacterial DNA containing resistant genes can be transferred between different species and/or picked up from dead bacterial fragments in the environment.

- Enzyme inactivation: enzymes produced by bacteria break down the antibiotic.

  - Bacteria that produce beta-lactamases break down beta-lactams (e.g., penicillins) before they can bind to their site of activity. Beta-lactamase inhibitors (clavulanate, sulbactam, tazobactam, avibactam) are combined with some beta-lactams to preserve or increase their spectrum of activity.

  - Extended-spectrum beta-lactamases (ESBLs) are beta-lactamases that can break down all penicillins and most cephalosporins. Organisms that produce ESBLs can be difficult to kill, and serious infections involving these organisms are treated with carbapenems or newer cephalosporin/beta-lactamase inhibitors.

  - Carbapenem-resistant *Enterobacteriaceae* (CRE) are MDR Gram-negative organisms (e.g., *Klebsiella* spp., *E. coli)* that produce enzymes (e.g., carbapenemase) capable of breaking down penicillins, most cephalosporins and carbapenems. CRE infections typically require treatment with a combination of antibiotics that include drugs such as the polymyxins, which have a high risk for toxicity (see the Polymyxins drug table). Newer, costly drugs, such as ceftazidime/avibactam (*Avycaz)* are also used.

COMMON RESISTANT PATHOGENS

Klebsiella pneumoniae (E**SBL, CRE)**

Escherichia coli (ESBL, CRE)

Acinetobacter baumannii

Enterococcus faecalis, Enterococcus faecium (VRE)

Staphylococcus aureus (MRSA)

Pseudomonas aeruginosa

Remember: **K**ill **E**ach **A**nd **E**very **S**trong **P**athogen

ESBL = extended-spectrum beta-lactamase
CRE = carbapenem-resistant Enterobacteriaceae
VRE = vancomycin-resistant Enterococcus

CLOSTRIDIOIDES DIFFICILE INFECTION

Inactive *C. difficile* spores are present in normal GI flora. When an antibiotic kills normal, healthy GI flora along with the targeted pathogens, *C. difficile* spores can become activated, producing toxins that inflame the GI mucosa. An overgrowth of drug-resistant organisms can occur, leading to superinfections, such as *Clostridioides difficile* infection (CDI).

Symptoms can be mild (loose stools and abdominal cramping) to severe (pseudomembranous colitis that can require colectomy or be fatal). In recent years, *C. difficile* infections have become more common, more severe and more difficult to treat. All antibiotics have a warning for the risk of CDI, but the risk is highest with broad-spectrum penicillins and cephalosporins, quinolones, carbapenems, and clindamycin, which has a boxed warning. When appropriate, antibiotics are streamlined or discontinued to reduce CDI risk.

ANTIMICROBIAL STEWARDSHIP PROGRAMS

Antimicrobial stewardship programs (ASPs) are designed to improve patient safety and outcomes, curb resistance, reduce adverse effects and promote cost-effectiveness.

ASPs consist of collaborative teams (e.g., ID physicians, ID pharmacists, microbiology lab and infection prevention personnel) that establish antibiotic guidance for their facility. ASPs conduct audits of prescribing habits and provide education to change suboptimal practices and improve care.

Examples ASP interventions: 1) pharmacokinetic monitoring of aminoglycosides and vancomycin, 2) use of clinical decision support software to rapidly identify pathogens and shorten the time to starting effective treatment, 3) preauthorization of select antimicrobials, 4) prospective audit and feedback to prescribers of selected antibiotics and 5) timely transitions from IV to PO antibiotics.

ANTIBIOTIC MECHANISMS OF ACTION

Knowledge of drug mechanisms of action can help distinguish what types of organisms can be treated with a given antibiotic. The target sites of common antibacterials are outlined in the following diagram. Generally, cell wall and cell membrane inhibitors, DNA/RNA inhibitors and aminoglycosides are bactericidal (kill bacteria), while most protein and folic acid synthesis inhibitors are bacteriostatic (inhibit bacterial growth). A detailed description of the mechanism of action for each antibiotic or antibiotic class is included on the following pages.

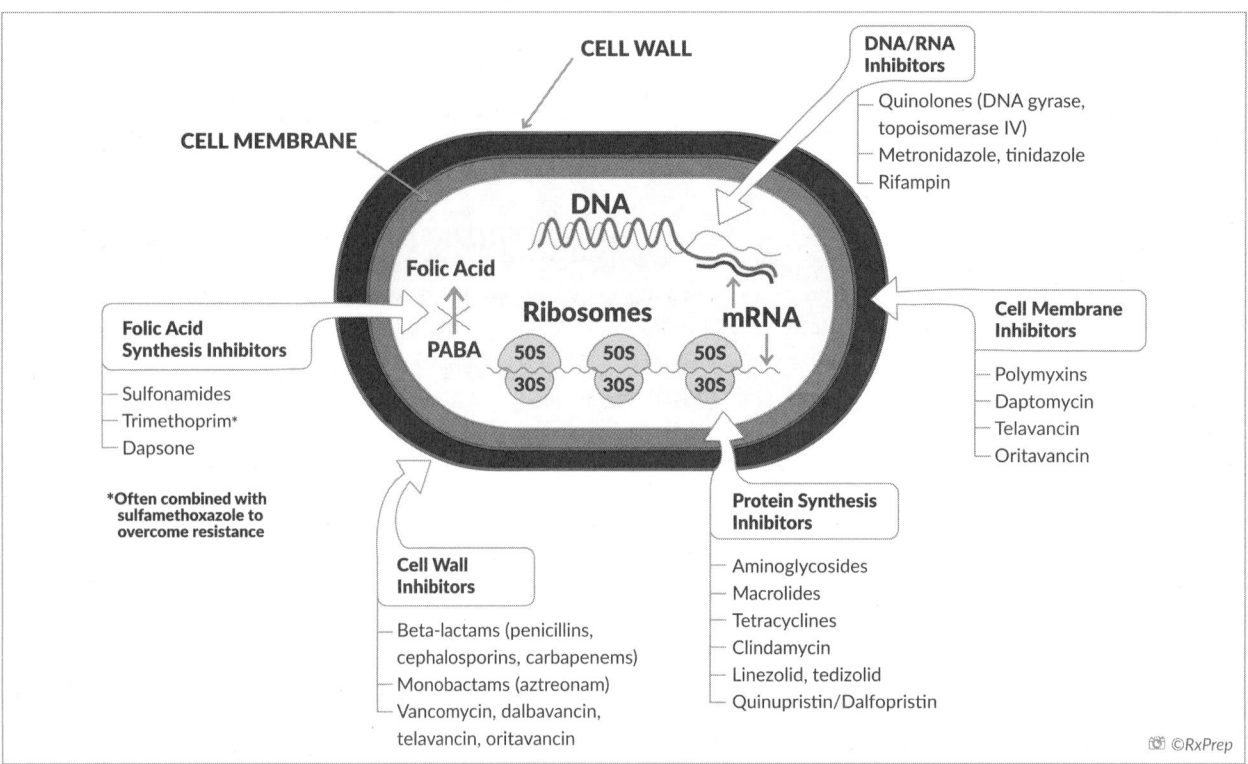

ANTIBIOTIC PHARMACOKINETICS AND PHARMACODYNAMICS

Appropriate selection of an antibiotic regimen requires an understanding of antibiotic pharmacokinetic (PK) principles (absorption, distribution, metabolism and excretion – refer to the Pharmacokinetics chapter) and pharmacodynamic principles (concentration-dependent or time-dependent killing).

HYDROPHILIC AND LIPOPHILIC DRUGS

Hydrophilicity or lipophilicity of an antibiotic can be used to predict a number of PK parameters (see figure below).

HYDROPHILIC AGENTS	
Beta-lactams	1) Small volume of distribution → Poor tissue penetration
Aminoglycosides	2) Renal elimination → Drug accumulation and side effects (e.g., nephrotoxicity, seizures) can occur if not dose adjusted
Vancomycin	3) Low intracellular concentrations → Not active against atypical (intracellular) pathogens
Daptomycin	4) Increased clearance and/or distribution in sepsis → Consider loading doses and aggressive dosing in sepsis
Polymyxins	5) Poor-moderate bioavailability → Not used PO or IV:PO ratio is not 1:1

LIPOPHILIC AGENTS	
Quinolones	1) Large volume of distribution → Excellent tissue penetration— including bone, lung and brain tissues
Macrolides	2) Hepatic metabolism → Potential for hepatotoxicity and drug-drug interactions
Rifampin	3) Achieve intracellular concentrations → Active against atypical (intracellular) pathogens
Linezolid	4) Clearance/distribution is changed minimally in sepsis → Dose adjustments generally not needed in sepsis
Tetracyclines	5) Excellent bioavailability → IV:PO ratio is often 1:1

PO = oral, IV = intravenous

DOSE OPTIMIZATION

The pharmacodynamics of select antibiotics are displayed in the figure below. Drugs with concentration-dependent killing (such as aminoglycosides) can be dosed less frequently and in higher doses to maximize the concentration above the MIC. Drugs with time-dependent killing (such as beta-lactams) can be dosed more frequently or each dose can be administered for a longer duration to maximize the time above the MIC. Examples include extending the infusion time of beta-lactam antibiotics (e.g., from 30 minutes to 4 hours) or administering the drug as a continuous infusion. Studies have documented that extended/continuous infusions of beta-lactams reduce hospital length of stay, mortality and costs, particularly when treating pneumonia caused by MDR Gram-negative pathogens (e.g., *Pseudomonas*).

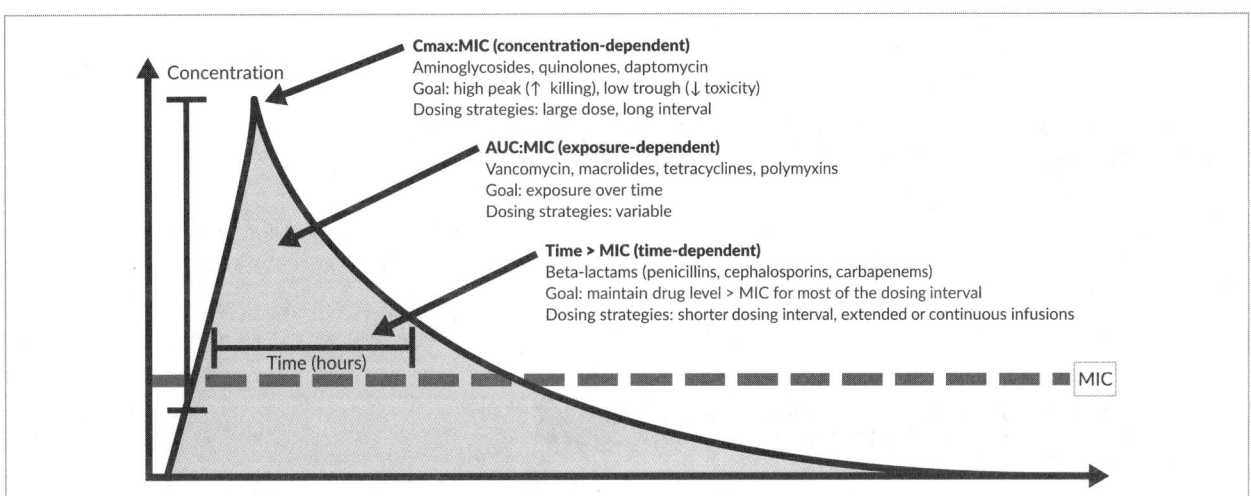

AUC = area under the concentration-time curve, Cmax = maximum plasma concentration, MIC = minimum inhibitory concentration

BETA-LACTAM ANTIBIOTICS

Beta-lactam antibiotics (penicillins, cephalosporins and carbapenems) have a chemical structure that is characterized by a beta-lactam ring (see the Basic Science Concepts chapter). They inhibit bacterial cell wall synthesis by binding to penicillin-binding proteins (PBPs). This prevents the final step of peptidoglycan synthesis in bacterial cell walls.

PENICILLINS

Coverage varies by subgroup, or type, of penicillin. As a class, they are not active against MRSA or atypical organisms.

- Natural penicillins are active against Gram-positive cocci (*Streptococci* and *Enterococci*, but not *Staphylococci*) and Gram-positive anaerobes (mouth flora). They have no appreciable Gram-negative activity.

- Antistaphylococcal penicillins cover *Streptococci* and have enhanced activity against methicillin-susceptible *Staphylococcus aureus* (MSSA), but they lack activity against *Enterococcus*, Gram-negative pathogens and anaerobes.

- Aminopenicillins cover *Streptococci*, *Enterococci* and Gram-positive anaerobes (mouth flora) plus (with the addition of the amino group) the Gram-negative bacteria *Haemophilus*, *Neisseria*, *Proteus* and *E. coli*.

  - Aminopenicillins combined with beta-lactamase inhibitors (e.g., clavulanate, sulbactam) have added activity against MSSA, more resistant strains of Gram-negative bacteria [e.g., *Haemophilus*, *Neisseria*, *Proteus*, *E. coli* and *Klebsiella* (HNPEK)] and Gram-negative anaerobes (*B. fragilis*).

- Extended-spectrum penicillins, combined with a beta-lactamase inhibitor (e.g., piperacillin/tazobactam), have broad-spectrum activity. They cover the same organisms as aminopenicillin/beta-lactamase inhibitor combinations (see above) plus have expanded coverage of other Gram-negative bacteria, including *Citrobacter*, *Acinetobacter*, *Providencia*, *Enterobacter*, *Serratia* (CAPES) and *Pseudomonas*.

Select Penicillins

DRUG	DOSING	SAFETY/SIDE EFFECTS/MONITORING
Natural Penicillins		**BOXED WARNING**
Penicillin V Potassium Tablet, suspension	PO: 125-500 mg Q6-12H on an empty stomach	Penicillin G benzathine: not for IV use; can cause cardio-respiratory arrest and death
Penicillin G Aqueous (*Pfizerpen*) Injection	IV: 2-4 million units Q4-6H	**CONTRAINDICATIONS** *Augmentin and Unasyn*: history of cholestatic jaundice or hepatic dysfunction associated with previous use
Penicillin G Benzathine **(*Bicillin L-A*)** Penicillin G Benzathine and Penicillin G Procaine (*Bicillin C-R*)	IM: 1.2-2.4 million units x 1 (frequency varies)	Severe renal impairment (CrCl < 30 mL/min): do not use extended-release oral forms of amoxicillin and amoxicillin/clavulanate (*Augmentin XR*), or the 875 mg strength of amoxicillin/clavulanate
Antistaphylococcal Penicillins		**SIDE EFFECTS**
Dicloxacillin Capsule	PO: 125-500 mg Q6H	Seizures (with accumulation when not correctly dose adjusted in renal dysfunction), GI upset, diarrhea, rash (including SJS/TEN)/allergic reactions/anaphylaxis, hemolytic anemia (identified with a positive Coombs test), renal failure, myelosuppression with prolonged use, ↑ LFTs
Nafcillin Injection	IV/IM: 1-2 grams Q4-6H	
Oxacillin Injection	IV: 250-2,000 mg Q4-6H	**MONITORING** Renal function, symptoms of anaphylaxis with 1st dose, CBC and LFTs with prolonged courses
Aminopenicillins		**NOTES**
Amoxicillin Tablet, capsule, chewable, suspension	PO: dosing varies with formulation; 24-hr ER tablet is taken once daily	**Antistaphylococcal Penicillins** Preferred for MSSA soft tissue, bone and joint, endocarditis and bloodstream infections No renal dose adjustments
Amoxicillin/Clavulanate (*Augmentin*, *Augmentin ES-600*) Tablet, chewable, suspension	PO: dosing varies with formulation; XR tablet is taken Q12H with food	Nafcillin is a vesicant – administration through a central line is preferred; if extravasation occurs, use cold packs and hyaluronidase injections
Ampicillin Injection, capsule, suspension	PO: 250-500 mg Q6H on an empty stomach 1 hr before or 2 hrs after meals IV/IM: 1-2 grams Q4-6H	**Aminopenicillins** Ampicillin PO is rarely used due to poor bioavailability; amoxicillin is preferred if switching from IV ampicillin
Ampicillin/Sulbactam (*Unasyn*) Injection	IV: 1.5-3 grams Q6H	Amoxicillin/clavulanate: use a 14:1 ratio to ↓ diarrhea caused by the clavulanate component IV ampicillin and ampicillin/sulbactam must be diluted in NS only
Extended-Spectrum Penicillins		
Piperacillin/Tazobactam (*Zosyn*) Injection	IV: 3.375 grams Q6H or 4.5 grams Q6-8H Prolonged or extended infusions: 3.375-4.5 grams IV Q8H (each dose infused over 4 hours)	**Extended-Spectrum Penicillins** Piperacillin/tazobactam contains 65 mg Na per 1 gram of piperacillin

See lab interactions, storage requirements and renal dosage information near the end of this chapter.

Penicillin Drug Interactions

- Probenecid can ↑ the levels of beta-lactams by interfering with renal excretion. This combination is sometimes used intentionally in severe infections to ↑ antibiotic levels.

- Beta-lactams (except nafcillin and dicloxacillin) can enhance the anticoagulant effect of warfarin by inhibiting the production of vitamin K-dependent clotting factors. Nafcillin and dicloxacillin can inhibit the anticoagulant effect of warfarin.

- Penicillins can ↑ the serum concentration of methotrexate; they can ↓ the serum concentration of mycophenolate active metabolites due to impaired enterohepatic recirculation.

KEY FEATURES OF PENICILLINS

CLASS EFFECTS

- All penicillins should be avoided in patients with a beta-lactam allergy

  - Exceptions: treatment of syphilis during pregnancy (all patients) or in patients with poor compliance/follow-up – desensitize and treat with penicillin G benzathine

- All penicillins increase the risk of seizures if accumulation occurs (e.g., failure to dose adjust in renal dysfunction)

OUTPATIENT (ORAL)

Penicillin VK

- A first-line treatment for strep throat and mild nonpurulent skin infections (no abscess)

Amoxicillin

- First-line treatment for acute otitis media (pediatric dose: 80-90 mg/kg/day)

- Drug of choice for infective endocarditis prophylaxis before dental procedures (2 grams PO x 1, 30-60 minutes before procedure)

- Used in *H. pylori* treatment*

Amoxicillin/Clavulanate (*Augmentin*)

- First-line treatment for acute otitis media (pediatric dose: 90 mg/kg/day) and bacterial sinusitis (if antibiotics indicated)

- Use the lowest dose of clavulanate to ↓ diarrhea

Dicloxacillin

- Covers MSSA only (no MRSA)

- No renal dose adjustment needed

INPATIENT (PARENTERAL)

Penicillin G Benzathine (*Bicillin L-A*)

- Drug of choice for syphilis (2.4 million units IM x 1)

- Not for IV use; can cause death

Nafcillin and Oxacillin

- See dicloxacillin above

Piperacillin/Tazobactam (*Zosyn*)

- Only penicillin active against *Pseudomonas*

- Extended infusions (4 hours) can be used to maximize T > MIC

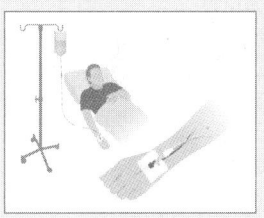

See the Gastroesophageal Reflux Disease & Peptic Ulcer Disease chapter

CEPHALOSPORINS

The spectrum of activity varies by cephalosporin "generation." Generally, the Gram-negative spectrum increases with each generation. As a class, they are not active against *Enterococcus* spp. or atypical organisms.

- First generation: excellent activity against Gram-positive cocci (e.g., *Streptococci* and *Staphylococci*) and preferred when a cephalosporin is used for MSSA infections. They have some activity against the Gram-negative rods *Proteus*, *E. coli* and *Klebsiella* (PEK), but in general, Gram-negative activity is decreased compared to 2nd, 3rd and 4th generation cephalosporins.

- Second generation: there are two types. Drugs such as cefuroxime cover *Staphylococci*, more resistant strains of *S. pneumoniae* plus *Haemophilus, Neisseria, Proteus, E. coli* and *Klebsiella* (HNPEK). The second type includes cefotetan and cefoxitin, which have added activity against Gram-negative anaerobes (*B. fragilis*).

- Third generation: there are two groups.

  - Group 1: includes ceftriaxone, cefotaxime and oral drugs (e.g., cefdinir); they cover resistant *Streptococci* (*S. pneumoniae* and viridans group *Streptococci*), *Staphylococci* (MSSA), Gram-positive anaerobes and resistant strains of HNPEK.

  - Group 2: includes ceftazidime, which lacks Gram-positive activity but covers *Pseudomonas*.

- Fourth generation: only includes cefepime, which has broad Gram-negative activity (HNPEK, CAPES and *Pseudomonas*), and Gram-positive activity similar to ceftriaxone.

- Fifth generation: only includes ceftaroline, which has Gram-negative activity similar to ceftriaxone, but broad Gram-positive activity; it is the only beta-lactam that covers MRSA.

- Other cephalosporins:

  - Beta-lactamase inhibitor combinations: ceftazidime/avibactam and ceftolozane/tazobactam have a similar spectrum as ceftazidime but with added activity against MDR *Pseudomonas* and other MDR Gram-negative rods.

  - Siderophore cephalosporin: cefiderocol uses the iron transport system to enter the Gram-negative cell wall. It is approved for complicated UTI/pyelonephritis and active against *E. coli, Enterobacter, Klebsiella, Proteus* and *Pseudomonas*.

INFECTIOUS DISEASES

DRUG	DOSING	SAFETY/SIDE EFFECTS/MONITORING
1st Generation		**CONTRAINDICATIONS (CEFTRIAXONE)** Hyperbilirubinemic neonates (causes biliary sludging, kernicterus)
Cefazolin	IV/IM: 1-2 grams Q8H	
Cephalexin (Keflex*)	PO: 250-500 mg Q6-12H	Concurrent use with calcium-containing IV products in neonates ≤ 28 days old
Cefadroxil	PO: 1-2 grams Q12-24H	**WARNINGS**
2nd Generation		Cross-sensitivity with PCN allergy (< 10%, higher risk with 1st generation cephalosporins): do not use in patients with a type 1 hypersensitivity to PCN (swelling, angioedema, anaphylaxis)
Cefuroxime	PO/IV/IM: 250-1,500 mg Q8-12H	
Cefotetan (Cefotan)	IV/IM: 1-2 grams Q12H	Cefotetan contains a side chain [N-methylthiotetrazole (NMTT or 1-MTT)] which can ↑ the risk of bleeding and cause a disulfiram-like reaction with alcohol ingestion
Cefaclor	PO: 250-500 mg Q8H	
Cefoxitin	IV/IM: 1-2 grams Q6-8H	Anaphylaxis/hypersensitivity reactions
Cefprozil	PO: 250-500 mg Q12-24H	Some drugs can ↑ INR in patients taking warfarin
3rd Generation Group 1		**SIDE EFFECTS** Seizures (with accumulation when not correctly dose adjusted in renal dysfunction), GI upset, diarrhea, rash/allergic reactions/anaphylaxis, acute interstitial nephritis, hemolytic anemia (identified with a positive Coombs test), myelosuppression with prolonged use, ↑ LFTs, drug fever, serious skin reactions (SJS/TEN)
Cefdinir	PO: 300 mg Q12H or 600 mg daily	
Ceftriaxone	IV/IM: 1-2 grams Q12-24H	
Cefotaxime	IV/IM: 1-2 grams Q4-12H	
Cefditoren	PO: 200-400 mg Q12H with food	
Cefixime (Suprax)	PO: 400 mg divided Q12-24H	**MONITORING** Renal function, signs of anaphylaxis with 1st dose, CBC, LFTs
Cefpodoxime	PO: 100-400 mg Q12H	
Ceftibuten	PO: 400 mg daily on an empty stomach	**NOTES** Ceftriaxone: no renal adjustment, CNS penetration at high doses (e.g., 2 grams Q12H) when meninges inflamed
3rd Generation Group 2		
Ceftazidime (Fortaz, Tazicef)	IV/IM: 1-2 grams Q8-12H	Cefixime available in a chewable tablet
4th Generation		Ceftazidime/avibactam: activity against some carbapenem-resistant Enterobacteriaceae (CRE)
Cefepime	IV/IM: 1-2 grams Q8-12H	
5th Generation		Cefiderocol: increase to 2 grams Q6H if CrCl ≥ 120 mL/min
Ceftaroline fosamil (Teflaro)	IV: 600 mg Q12H	
Cephalosporin Combinations		
Ceftazidime/Avibactam (Avycaz)	IV: 2.5 grams Q8H	
Ceftolozane/Tazobactam (Zerbaxa)	IV: 1.5-3 grams Q8H	
Siderophore Cephalosporin		
Cefiderocol (Fetroja)	IV: 2 grams IV Q8H (each dose infused over 3 hours)	

*Brand discontinued but name still used in practice.
See lab interactions, storage requirements and renal dosage information near the end of this chapter.

Cephalosporin Drug Interactions

- Drugs that decrease stomach acid can decrease the bioavailability of some oral cephalosporins. Cefuroxime, cefpodoxime, cefdinir and cefditoren should be separated by two hours from short-acting antacids. H2RAs and PPIs should be avoided.

- Insoluble precipitates may form when ceftriaxone is administered with calcium-containing IV fluids (do not use together in neonates; see Contraindications section in table above). In adults, the IV line should be flushed with a compatible fluid between administration of each product.

KEY FEATURES OF CEPHALOSPORINS

CLASS EFFECTS

- Due to a small risk of cross-reactivity, do not choose a cephalosporin on the exam if the patient has a penicillin allergy (exception: pediatric patients with acute otitis media and a mild penicillin allergy*)
- Risk of seizures if accumulation occurs (e.g., failure to dose adjust in renal dysfunction)

OUTPATIENT (ORAL)

1st Generation: Cephalexin

- Common uses: skin infections (MSSA), strep throat

2nd Generation: Cefuroxime

- Common uses: acute otitis media, community-acquired pneumonia (CAP)

3rd Generation: Cefdinir

- Common uses: acute otitis media

INPATIENT (PARENTERAL)

1st Generation: Cefazolin

- Common use: surgical prophylaxis

2nd Generation: Cefotetan and Cefoxitin

- Anaerobic coverage (*B. fragilis*)
- Common use: surgical prophylaxis (gastrointestinal procedures)
- Cefotetan can cause a disulfiram-like reaction with alcohol ingestion

3rd Generation: Ceftriaxone and Cefotaxime

- Common uses: CAP, meningitis, spontaneous bacterial peritonitis, pyelonephritis
- Ceftriaxone
  - ❏ No renal dose adjustment
  - ❏ Do not use ceftriaxone in neonates (age 0-28 days)

Ceftazidime (3rd Generation) and Cefepime (4th Generation)

- Active against *Pseudomonas*

Ceftolozane/Tazobactam and Ceftazidime/Avibactam

- Used for MDR Gram-negative organisms (including *Pseudomonas*)

Ceftaroline

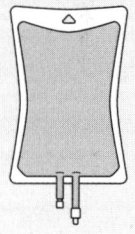

- Only beta-lactam active against MRSA
- Common uses: CAP, skin and soft tissue infections

Delayed-onset reaction (> 48 hours after the first antibiotic dose) appearing as a nonpruritic or mildly pruritic, maculopapular rash, but lacking systemic symptoms (e.g., hives, bronchospasm, anaphylaxis) or other serious reactions (e.g., Stevens-Johnson syndrome).

CASE SCENARIO

When studying the carbapenems (on the next page), think of how you would approach a case on the exam in which one of the answer choices is *Invanz* 1 gram IV Q24H. How can you decide if this is the best answer choice? Assess the following, using the underlined information in the carbapenem drug table:

- Allergies: if the patient has a penicillin allergy, there is likely a better answer choice because of the possibility of cross-reactivity.
- Culture and susceptibility: if the culture is growing ESBL-positive *E. coli*, ertapenem may be a good choice. If *Pseudomonas* is growing, ertapenem can be immediately ruled out based on a lack of activity against this pathogen.
- Past medical history and medication profile: if the patient has a history of seizures or takes an antiepileptic drug, such as phenytoin, there is likely a better choice than a carbapenem, which can increase the risk for seizures.

INFECTIOUS DISEASES

CARBAPENEMS

Carbapenems are very broad-spectrum antibiotics that are generally <u>reserved for MDR Gram-negative</u> infections. They are active against most Gram-positive, Gram-negative (including <u>ESBL-producing bacteria</u>) and anaerobic pathogens. They provide <u>no coverage</u> of <u>atypical pathogens, MRSA, VRE</u>, *C. difficile* or *Stenotrophomonas*.

<u>Ertapenem is different</u> from other carbapenems as it has <u>no activity against *Pseudomonas, Acinetobacter*</u> or *Enterococcus*. Carbapenem/beta-lactamase inhibitor combinations are typically reserved for highly resistant infections (e.g., CRE) that are not able to be treated with a single entity carbapenem.

DRUG	DOSING	SAFETY/SIDE EFFECTS/MONITORING
Doripenem Injection	IV: 500 mg Q8H	**CONTRAINDICATIONS** Anaphylactic reactions to beta-lactam antibiotics **WARNINGS** <u>Do not use in patients with PCN allergy</u> (small risk of cross-reactivity)
Imipenem/Cilastatin *(Primaxin I.V.)* Imipenem/Cilastatin/ Relebactam *(Recarbrio)* Injection	IV: 250-1,000 mg Q6-8H IV: 1.25 grams Q6H	CNS adverse effects, including states of confusion and <u>seizures</u> Doripenem: do not use for the treatment of pneumonia, including hospital-acquired pneumonia (HAP) and ventilator-associated pneumonia (VAP) **SIDE EFFECTS** Diarrhea, rash/severe skin reaction (DRESS), seizures with higher doses and in patients with impaired renal function (mainly imipenem), bone marrow suppression with prolonged use, ↑ LFTs
Meropenem Meropenem/Vaborbactam *(Vabomere)* Injection	IV: 500-1,000 mg Q8H IV: 4 grams Q8H (each dose infused over 3 hrs)	**MONITORING** <u>Renal function</u>, symptoms of anaphylaxis with 1st dose, CBC, LFTs **NOTES** Imipenem is combined with cilastatin to prevent drug degradation by renal tubular dehydropeptidase
Ertapenem *(Invanz)* Injection <u>Stable in NS only</u>	IV/IM: 1 gram daily	As above plus: **NOTES** No coverage of *Pseudomonas, Acinetobacter* or *Enterococcus* Commonly used for diabetic foot infections

See lab interactions, storage requirements and renal dosage information near the end of this chapter.

Carbapenem Drug Interactions

- Carbapenems can ↓ serum concentrations of valproic acid, leading to a loss of seizure control.

- Use with caution in patients with a history of seizure disorder, or in combination with other drugs known to lower the seizure threshold (e.g., ganciclovir, quinolones, bupropion, tramadol). See the Seizures/Epilepsy chapter for a complete list.

KEY FEATURES OF CARBAPENEMS

Class effects
- All active against ESBL-producing organisms and (except ertapenem) *Pseudomonas*

- Do not use with penicillin allergy

- Seizure risk (with higher doses, failure to dose adjust in renal dysfunction, or use of imipenem/cilastatin)

Remember what they do not cover
- Atypicals, VRE, MRSA, *C. difficile, Stenotrophomonas*

- **ErtAPenem** does not cover **PEA:** *Pseudomonas, Enterococcus, Acinetobacter*

Common uses
- Polymicrobial infections (e.g., severe diabetic foot infection)

- Empiric therapy when resistant organisms are suspected

- ESBL-positive infections

- Resistant *Pseudomonas* or *Acinetobacter* infections (except ertapenem)

All are IV only. Ertapenem must be diluted in normal saline.

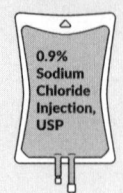

0.9% Sodium Chloride Injection, USP

MONOBACTAM

AZTREONAM

Aztreonam has a mechanism of action similar to beta-lactams; it inhibits bacterial cell wall synthesis by binding to penicillin-binding proteins (PBPs), which prevents the final step of peptidoglycan synthesis in bacterial cell walls. The monobactam structure makes cross-reactivity with a beta-lactam unlikely. Aztreonam is primarily used when a beta-lactam allergy is present.

Aztreonam covers many Gram-negative organisms, including *Pseudomonas*. It has no Gram-positive or anaerobic activity.

DRUG	DOSING	SAFETY/SIDE EFFECTS/MONITORING
Aztreonam (*Azactam*) Injection *Cayston* – inhaled, for cystic fibrosis	IV: 500-2,000 mg Q6-12H CrCl < 30 mL/min: dose adjustment required	**SIDE EFFECTS** Similar to penicillins, including rash, N/V/D, ↑ LFTs **NOTES** Can be used with a penicillin allergy

See lab interactions, storage requirements and renal dosage information near the end of this chapter.

SPECTRUM OF ACTIVITY SUMMARY

The chart below provides a visual representation of the general spectrum of activity for select beta-lactams and aztreonam. It can be used to identify antibiotics with activity against common pathogens, drugs with unique coverage (e.g., drugs active against *Pseudomonas* or MRSA) or where coverage is lacking (e.g., drugs that do not cover *Enterococcus*).

Column headers: MRSA | S. aureus (MSSA) | S. pneumoniae | Viridans group Streptococcus | Enterococcus (not VRE) | PEK | HNPEK | CAPES | Pseudomonas | Gram-positive anaerobes (mouth flora) | Bacteroides fragilis | Atypical organisms

Drug coverage bars:
- Penicillin — covers S. pneumoniae through Enterococcus (not VRE); and Gram-positive anaerobes (mouth flora)
- Amoxicillin[a] — covers S. pneumoniae through HNPEK; and Gram-positive anaerobes (mouth flora)
- Oxacillin — covers S. aureus (MSSA), S. pneumoniae, Viridans group Streptococcus
- Nafcillin — covers S. aureus (MSSA), S. pneumoniae, Viridans group Streptococcus
- Amoxicillin/Clavulanate, Ampicillin/Sulbactam — covers S. aureus (MSSA) through HNPEK; and Gram-positive anaerobes (mouth flora) and Bacteroides fragilis
- Piperacillin/Tazobactam — covers S. aureus (MSSA) through Pseudomonas; and Gram-positive anaerobes (mouth flora) and Bacteroides fragilis
- Cefazolin, Cephalexin — covers S. aureus (MSSA) through Viridans group Streptococcus; PEK; and Gram-positive anaerobes (mouth flora)
- Cefuroxime, Cefotetan, Cefoxitin — covers S. aureus (MSSA) through Viridans group Streptococcus; PEK, HNPEK; and Bacteroides fragilis (Cefotetan, Cefoxitin)
- Cefotaxime, Ceftriaxone — covers S. aureus (MSSA) through Viridans group Streptococcus; PEK, HNPEK, CAPES; and Gram-positive anaerobes (mouth flora)
- Ceftazidime, Aztreonam — covers PEK through Pseudomonas
- Cefepime — covers S. aureus (MSSA) through Viridans group Streptococcus; PEK through Pseudomonas
- Ceftaroline — covers MRSA through Viridans group Streptococcus; PEK through CAPES[b]; Gram-positive anaerobes (mouth flora)
- Ceftazidime/Avibactam, Ceftolozane/Tazobactam — covers S. aureus (MSSA) through Viridans group Streptococcus; PEK through Pseudomonas[c]
- Imipenem/Cilastatin[d], Meropenem[d], Doripenem[d] — covers S. aureus (MSSA) through Pseudomonas; Gram-positive anaerobes (mouth flora) and Bacteroides fragilis
- Ertapenem — covers S. aureus (MSSA) through Enterococcus (not VRE); PEK through CAPES[e]; Gram-positive anaerobes (mouth flora) and Bacteroides fragilis

[a] No Klebsiella coverage
[b] No Acinetobacter or Providencia coverage
[c] Must be given with metronidazole for adequate anaerobic coverage
[d] E. faecalis only
[e] No Acinetobacter coverage

INFECTIOUS DISEASES

AMINOGLYCOSIDES

Aminoglycosides bind to the ribosome, which interferes with bacterial protein synthesis and results in a defective bacterial cell membrane. They are active against Gram-negative bacteria (including *Pseudomonas)* and are primarily used as part of an empiric regimen with other antibiotics (generally not used as monotherapy). Gentamicin and streptomycin are used for synergy, in combination with a beta-lactam or vancomycin, when treating Gram-positive infections (e.g., enterococcal endocarditis). Streptomycin and amikacin are used as second-line treatments for *Mycobacterial* infections.

There are two dosing strategies for aminoglycosides; traditional dosing uses lower doses more frequently (e.g., Q8H if renal function is normal). Extended interval dosing uses higher doses (to attain higher peaks) less frequently (e.g., once daily if renal function is normal). With extended interval dosing, there is less accumulation of drug, lower risk of nephrotoxicity and decreased cost. While there is a better chance of achieving the target Cmax:MIC, this dosing strategy has not been shown to be clinically superior to traditional dosing. See Study Tip Gal for more on aminoglycosides.

AMINOGLYCOSIDES: GOOD NEWS, BAD NEWS

GOOD NEWS
Aminoglycosides kill Gram-negative pathogens, are synergistic with beta-lactams for some Gram-positive organisms, and have low resistance and drug cost.

Aminoglycosides demonstrate concentration-dependent activity and have a post-antibiotic effect (the bacterial killing continues after the serum level drops below the MIC).

BAD NEWS
They have notable toxicities that require monitoring: renal damage and ototoxicity, which may be irreversible (hearing loss/tinnitus/balance problems).

SMART IDEA
Take advantage of the concentration-dependent kinetics → give larger doses less frequently → this gives the kidneys time to recover between doses.

DRUG	DOSING	SAFETY/SIDE EFFECTS/MONITORING
Gentamicin IV, IM, ophthalmic, topical **Tobramycin** IV, IM, ophthalmic, inhaled Tobramycin inhalation for CF *(Tobi, Tobi Podhaler, Bethkis, Kitabis Pak)* **Amikacin** IV, IM	If underweight (< ideal body weight): use total body weight for dosing If normal weight (not obese or underweight): ideal body weight or total body weight can be used for dosing (follow the institutional protocol) If obese, use adjusted body weight for dosing (see Notes) **Traditional IV Dosing** Gentamicin and tobramycin: 1-2.5 mg/kg/dose; lower doses are used for Gram-positive infections; higher doses are used for Gram-negative infections Amikacin: 5-7.5 mg/kg/dose Q8H **Renal Dose Adjustments (Traditional Dosing)** CrCl ≥ 60 mL/min: Q8H CrCl 40-60 mL/min: Q12H CrCl 20-40 mL/min: Q24H CrCl < 20 mL/min: 1x dose, then dose per levels	**BOXED WARNINGS** Nephrotoxicity, ototoxicity (hearing loss, vertigo, ataxia), neuromuscular blockade and respiratory paralysis, avoid with other neurotoxic/nephrotoxic drugs, fetal harm if given in pregnancy **WARNINGS** Use caution in patients with impaired renal function, in the elderly, and those taking other nephrotoxic drugs (amphotericin B, cisplatin, polymyxins, cyclosporine, loop diuretics, NSAIDs, radiocontrast dye, tacrolimus and vancomycin) **SIDE EFFECTS** Nephrotoxicity (acute tubular necrosis), hearing loss (early toxicity associated with high-pitched sounds), vestibular toxicity (resulting in balance deficits) **MONITORING** Drug levels, renal function, urine output, hearing tests Traditional dosing: draw a trough level right before (or 30 minutes before) the 4th dose; draw a peak level 30 minutes after the end of the 30-minute infusion for the 4th dose (see table on the following page for target peaks and troughs)
Streptomycin IM	**Extended Interval IV Dosing (Gentamicin/Tobramycin)** 4-7 mg/kg/dose (commonly 7 mg/kg) Frequency (dosing interval) is determined by a nomogram (see example on following page) but the shortest interval is Q24H if renal function is normal	Extended interval dosing: draw a random level per the timing on the nomogram (see example on following page) **NOTES** Amikacin is the most active against *Pseudomonas*
Plazomicin *(Zemdri)* IV For complicated UTI only (see Notes)	Avoid when clearance and/or volume of distribution are altered [e.g., pregnancy, ascites, burns, cystic fibrosis, CrCl < 30 mL/min (including end-stage renal disease on dialysis)] **Other Dosing** Plazomicin 15 mg/kg IV Q24H (dose adjustments required if CrCl < 60 mL/min)	The clinical definition of obesity varies (but TBW > 120% IBW is commonly used for drug dosing); on the exam, obesity will be obvious, and may be stated in the question, indicating that adjusted body weight should be used for weight-based dosing (see the Calculations IV chapter for more information) Plazomicin is reserved for MDR Gram-negative UTIs and should only be used when there are no alternative treatment options

See lab interactions, storage requirements and renal dosage information near the end of this chapter.

TRADITIONAL DOSING: TARGET DRUG CONCENTRATIONS

When peak and trough levels are drawn with the 4th aminoglycoside dose (see the Monitoring section of the drug table on the previous page), the levels are compared to the goal peaks and troughs to determine if dose adjustments are needed. Hospitals have protocols that guide dose adjustments. See the Pharmacokinetics chapter for details.

DRUG	PEAK	TROUGH
Gentamicin, Gram-positive infection (synergy)	3-4 mcg/mL	< 1 mcg/mL
Gentamicin, Gram-negative infection	5-10 mcg/mL	< 2 mcg/mL
Tobramycin		
Amikacin	20-30 mcg/mL	< 5 mcg/mL

Organism-specific peak goals are typically ≥ 10 times the MIC of the bacteria causing the infection.

EXTENDED INTERVAL DOSING NOMOGRAM

With extended interval dosing nomograms, a <u>random level</u> is drawn after the <u>first dose</u> (the timing depends on the nomogram; the <u>Hartford nomogram</u> shown below uses a window of 6 – 14 hours after the start of the infusion). The nomogram is used to plot the patient's level and determine the appropriate dosing interval. If the level plots <u>on a line, round up</u> to the next dosing <u>interval</u> to avoid potential toxicity.

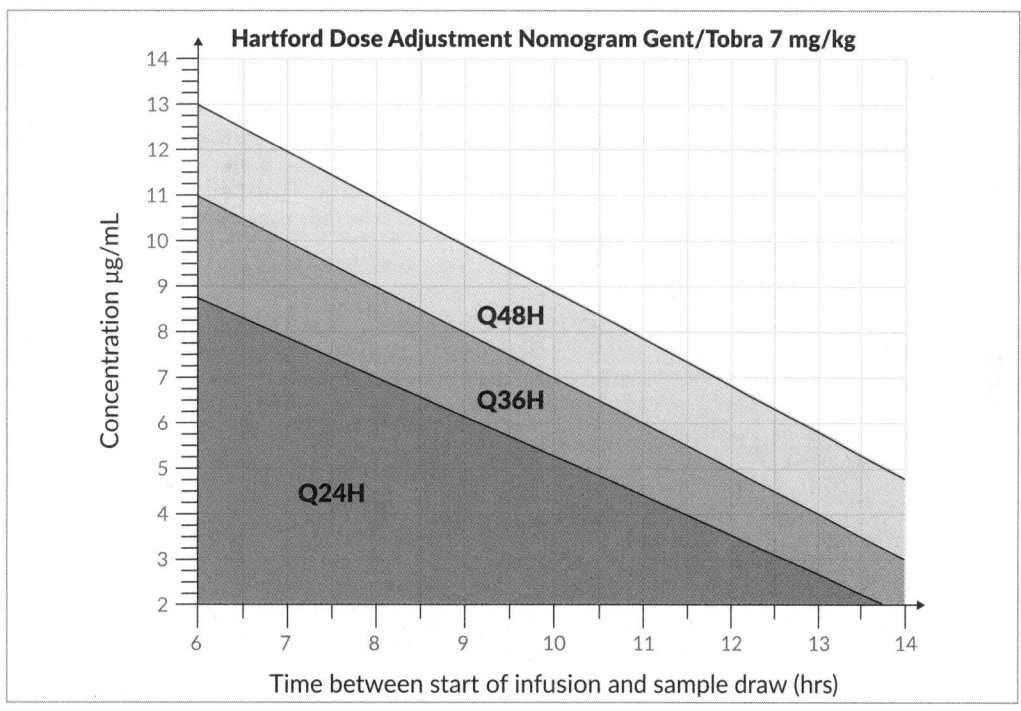

CASE SCENARIO

PR, a 56-year-old hospitalized female (height: 5'4", weight: 79 kg), is prescribed an antibiotic regimen that includes extended-interval tobramycin "pharmacy to dose." The pharmacy aminoglycoside dosing protocol includes the Hartford nomogram method for dosing.

First, calculate the initial tobramycin dose.

■ Determine which weight to use: since PR's TBW of 79 kg is > 120% greater than her IBW of 54.7 kg, adjusted body weight should be used. PR's adusted body weight is 64.4 kg.

■ Calculate the inital dose: 7 mg/kg x 64.4 kg = ~450 mg.

Next, determine the frequency of dosing.

■ A random tobramycin level drawn 10 hours after the start of the 450 mg infusion is 6 mcg/mL.

■ When plotted on the nomogram above (by drawing a line up from 10 hours on the X-axis and a line over from 6 mcg/mL on the Y-axis), the lines meet in the Q36H dosing section.

PR can receive 450 mg tobramycin IV Q36H.

INFECTIOUS DISEASES

QUINOLONES

Quinolones inhibit bacterial DNA topoisomerase IV and DNA gyrase (topoisomerase II) inside the bacteria. This prevents supercoiling of DNA and promotes breakage of double-stranded DNA. Quinolones have concentration-dependent antibacterial activity and a broad-spectrum of activity against a variety of Gram-negative, Gram-positive and atypical pathogens. Some notable distinctions in the class include:

- Levofloxacin, moxifloxacin and gemifloxacin are referred to as respiratory quinolones due to enhanced coverage of S. pneumoniae and atypical pathogens.

- Ciprofloxacin and levofloxacin have enhanced Gram-negative activity, including activity against Pseudomonas.

They may be used empirically in combination with another agent (e.g., a beta-lactam) when Pseudomonas infections are suspected, or as monotherapy if the final C & S report indicates susceptibility.

- Moxifloxacin has enhanced Gram-positive and anaerobic activity and can be used alone for polymicrobial infections (e.g., intra-abdominal infections). It is the only quinolone that cannot be used to treat urinary tract infections.

- Delafloxacin is active against MRSA and is the preferred quinolone if treating skin infections suspected to be caused by MRSA. Other quinolones should generally be avoided due to high rates of MRSA resistance.

DRUG	DOSING	SAFETY/SIDE EFFECTS/MONITORING
Ciprofloxacin (Cipro, Ciloxan eye drops, Cetraxal and Otiprio ear drops) Tablet, suspension, injection, ointment, ophthalmic, otic Combination ear drops: + dexamethasone **(Ciprodex)** + fluocinolone (Otovel) + hydrocortisone (Cipro HC)	PO: 250-750 mg Q12H IV: 200-400 mg Q8-12H CrCl 30-50 mL/min: Q12H CrCl < 30 mL/min: Q18-24H	**BOXED WARNINGS** Tendon inflammation and/or rupture (often in the Achilles tendon) within hours/days of starting, or up to several months after completion of treatment; ↑ risk with concurrent use of systemic steroids, in organ transplant patients and age > 60 years. Discontinue immediately if symptoms occur. Peripheral neuropathy; can last months to years after discontinuation of the drug and may become permanent. Discontinue immediately if symptoms occur. CNS effects [seizures, tremor, restlessness, confusion, hallucinations, depression (and suicidal thoughts), paranoia, nightmares, insomnia, ↑ intracranial pressure (including pseudotumor cerebri)]. Use caution in patients with CNS disorders or with drugs that cause seizures or lower the seizure threshold (see the Seizures/Epilepsy chapter).
Levofloxacin (Levaquin*) Tablet, solution, injection, ophthalmic	PO/IV: 250-750 mg daily CrCl < 50 mL/min: Q48H and/or ↓ dose; adjustment varies by indication and renal function	Avoid in patients with myasthenia gravis (may exacerbate muscle weakness). Use last-line (only if no other possible treatments) for: acute bacterial sinusitis, acute exacerbation of chronic bronchitis and uncomplicated UTI (do not use moxifloxacin).
Moxifloxacin (Avelox*, Moxeza and Vigamox eye drops) Tablet, injection, ophthalmic	IV/PO: 400 mg Q24H No renal dose adjustments required	**CONTRAINDICATIONS** Ciprofloxacin: concurrent administration of tizanidine. **WARNINGS** QT prolongation (highest risk with moxifloxacin > levofloxacin > ciprofloxacin); avoid in patients with known QT prolongation, or those with additive risks (hypokalemia, use of other drugs that prolong the QT interval, including Class Ia and Class III antiarrhythmics – see the Arrhythmias chapter).
Delafloxacin (Baxdela) Tablet, injection	PO: 450 mg Q12H IV: 300 mg Q12H CrCl < 15-29 mL/min: dose adjustment required (IV only) CrCl < 15 mL/min: not recommended (IV or PO)	Hypoglycemia and hyperglycemia; hypoglycemia can lead to coma. Psychiatric disturbances (agitation, disorientation, lack of attention, nervousness, memory impairment and delirium). Avoid systemic quinolones in children and in pregnancy/breastfeeding due to the risk of musculoskeletal toxicity (exception: for anthrax exposure, the benefit outweighs the risk).
Gatifloxacin (Zymaxid eye drops)	No oral formulation	Aortic aneurysm and dissection (↑ risk with longer durations of therapy or history of peripheral vascular disease, atherosclerosis or prior aneurysms). Other: photosensitivity, hepatotoxicity, crystalluria (must stay hydrated).
Gemifloxacin Tablet	PO: 320 mg daily CrCl ≤ 40 mL/min: dose adjustment required	**SIDE EFFECTS** Nausea/diarrhea, headache, dizziness, serious skin reactions (SJS/TEN). **NOTES** Cipro oral suspension: shake vigorously for 15 seconds before each dose. Do not put through an NG or other feeding tube (the oil-based suspension adheres to tubing).
Ofloxacin (Ocuflox eye drops) Tablet, ophthalmic, otic	PO: 200-400 mg Q12H CrCl < 30 mL/min: dose adjustment required	Cipro: can crush immediate-release tablets, mix with water and give via a feeding tube. Hold tube feedings at least 1 hour before and 2 hours after the dose. Moxifloxacin should not be used for UTIs (does not concentrate in the urine).

Brand discontinued but name still used in practice.
See lab interactions, storage requirements and renal dosage information near the end of this chapter.

Quinolone Drug Interactions

- <u>Antacids</u> and other <u>polyvalent cations</u> (e.g., magnesium, aluminum, phosphate, calcium, iron, zinc), multivitamins, sucralfate, and bile acid resins <u>can chelate and inhibit quinolone absorption</u> and should not be taken at the same time (separate administration).

- The phosphate binders <u>lanthanum</u> carbonate *(Fosrenol)* and <u>sevelamer *(Renvela, Renagel)*</u> can ↓ the serum concentration of oral quinolones; <u>separate administration</u> by at least 2 hours before, and at least 2 hours after (with lanthanum) or 6 hours after (with sevelamer).

- Quinolones can ↑ the effects of warfarin.

- Quinolones can ↑ the effects of sulfonylureas, insulin and other hypoglycemic drugs.

- Caution with CVD, ↓ potassium and magnesium and with other <u>QT-prolonging drugs</u> (e.g., azole antifungals, antipsychotics, methadone, macrolides).

- Probenecid and NSAIDs can ↑ quinolone levels.

- Ciprofloxacin is a strong <u>CYP1A2 inhibitor</u>, a weak CYP3A4 inhibitor, and a P-glycoprotein (P-gp) substrate; ciprofloxacin can ↑ <u>levels</u> of caffeine, <u>theophylline</u> and tizanidine by reducing metabolism.

KEY FEATURES OF QUINOLONES

Common Uses
- Can vary by agent: pneumonias, UTIs, intra-abdominal infections, travelers' diarrhea

Respiratory Quinolones
- Levofloxacin, moxifloxacin, gemifloxacin
- Reliable *S. pneumoniae* activity (in pneumonia)

Antipseudomonal Quinolones
- Ciprofloxacin, levofloxacin
- Used for *Pseudomonas* infections (including pneumonia)

Moxifloxacin
- Only quinolone that is not renally adjusted (do not use for UTIs)

IV to PO Ratio 1:1
- Levofloxacin and moxifloxacin

Profile Review Tips
- Caution with CVD, ↓ K/Mg and with other QT-prolonging drugs (e.g., azole antifungals, antipsychotics, methadone, macrolides)
- Avoid in patients with a seizure history or if using seizure drugs
- Avoid in children

Counseling
- Avoid sun exposure, separate from polyvalent cations, monitor blood glucose (in diabetes)
- Watch for tendon rupture, neuropathy, CNS or psychiatric side effects

MACROLIDES

Macrolides bind to the <u>50S ribosomal subunit</u>, resulting in inhibition of RNA-dependent protein synthesis. They have excellent coverage of <u>atypicals</u> (*Legionella, Chlamydia, Mycoplasma* and *Mycobacterium avium* complex) and *Haemophilus*. Macrolides are treatment options for <u>community-acquired</u> upper and lower <u>respiratory tract infections</u> and certain sexually transmitted infections (e.g., <u>chlamydia</u>), but utility against *S. pneumoniae, Haemophilus, Chlamydia* and *Moraxella* can be limited due to increasing resistance.

DRUG	DOSING	SAFETY/SIDE EFFECTS/MONITORING
Azithromycin (*Zithromax, Z-Pak*, Zithromax Tri-Pak, *AzaSite* eye drops) Tablet, suspension, injection, ophthalmic Better Gram-negative activity than erythromycin	Z-Pak: <u>500 mg on day 1, then 250 mg on days 2-5</u> *Tri-Pak*: <u>500 mg daily for 3 days</u> Dosing regimens vary depending on indication IV: 250-500 mg daily No renal dose adjustments required	**CONTRAINDICATIONS** History of cholestatic jaundice/hepatic dysfunction with prior use <u>Clarithromycin and erythromycin: do not use with lovastatin or simvastatin,</u> pimozide, ergotamine or dihydroergotamine Clarithromycin: concurrent use with colchicine in patients with renal or hepatic impairment
Clarithromycin Tablet, ER tablet, suspension Better Gram-positive activity	PO: 250-500 mg Q12H or 1 gram (ER tablet) daily CrCl < 30 mL/min: dose adjustment required	**WARNINGS** <u>QT prolongation</u> (highest risk with erythromycin > azithromycin > clarithromycin); avoid in patients with known QT prolongation, or those with additive risks (hypokalemia, use of other drugs that prolong the QT interval, including Class Ia and Class III antiarrhythmics – see the Arrhythmias chapter)
Erythromycin (*E.E.S., Ery-Tab, Erythrocin*, EryPed, Ery and *Erygel* topical) Capsule, tablet, suspension, injection, ophthalmic, topical E.E.S = erythromycin ethylsuccinate	Dosing varies by product E.E.S 400 mg = 250 mg erythromycin base or stearate Erythromycin lactobionate is the IV form No renal dose adjustments required	<u>Hepatotoxicity</u>; use caution in patients with liver disease Exacerbation of myasthenia gravis Clarithromycin: caution in patients with <u>CAD</u> (↑ mortality has been documented ≥ 1 year after the end of a 2-week course of treatment) **SIDE EFFECTS** <u>GI upset</u> (diarrhea, abdominal pain, cramping), taste perversion, ototoxicity (rare, reversible), severe (but rare) skin reactions (SJS/TEN/DRESS)

Brand discontinued but name still used in practice.
See lab interactions, storage requirements and renal dosage information near the end of this chapter.

INFECTIOUS DISEASES

Macrolide Drug Interactions

- Erythromycin and clarithromycin are major substrates of CYP3A4 and are CYP3A4 inhibitors (moderate for erythromycin, strong for clarithromycin). Some medications metabolized by CYP3A4 should be avoided (e.g., simvastatin and lovastatin are contraindicated) and others may require close monitoring, or should be used with caution in combination with erythromycin and clarithromycin. Some examples include apixaban, colchicine, dabigatran, rivaroxaban, theophylline and warfarin. Refer to the Drug Interactions chapter for more information.

- Azithromycin is a minor substrate of CYP3A4 and a weak inhibitor of CYP1A2 and P-gp; it has fewer clinically significant drug interactions than other macrolides.

- All macrolides: use caution with CVD, ↓ potassium and magnesium and with other QT-prolonging drugs (e.g., azole antifungals, antipsychotics, methadone, quinolones).

KEY FEATURES OF MACROLIDES

Common Uses
- All macrolides: CAP, and as an alternative to a beta-lactam for strep throat

- Azithromycin: COPD exacerbations, pertussis, chlamydia (in pregnant patients), prophylaxis for *Mycobacterium avium* complex, severe travelers' diarrhea (including dysentery, diarrhea with bloody stools)

- Clarithromycin: used in *H. pylori* treatment regimens (see the Gastroesophageal Reflux Disease & Peptic Ulcer Disease chapter)

- Erythromycin ↑ gastric motility and is used for gastroparesis

Common Azithromycin Dosing (Z-Pak)
- Two 250 mg tablets PO x 1, then 250 mg PO daily x 4 days

QT Prolongation
- Caution with CVD, ↓ K/Mg and other QT-prolonging drugs (e.g., azole antifungals, antipsychotics, methadone, quinolones)

Drug Interactions
- Clarithromycin and erythromycin are strong CYP3A4 inhibitors; lovastatin and simvastatin are contraindicated (↑ risk of muscle toxicity)

TETRACYCLINES

Tetracyclines inhibit bacterial protein synthesis by reversibly binding to the 30S ribosomal subunit. They cover many Gram-positive bacteria (*Staphylococci, Streptococci, Enterococci, Propionibacterium* spp.), Gram-negative bacteria, including respiratory flora (*Haemophilus, Moraxella*, atypicals) and other unique pathogens (e.g., *Rickettsiae, Bacillus anthracis, Treponema pallidum* and other spirochetes).

Doxycycline has broader indications than the other tetracyclines, including respiratory tract infections (e.g., CAP), tick-borne/rickettsial diseases, spirochetes and sexually transmitted infections (e.g., chlamydia). Doxycycline is an option for the treatment of mild CA-MRSA skin infections and VRE urinary tract infections. Minocycline is often preferred for acne.

DRUG	DOSING	SAFETY/SIDE EFFECTS/MONITORING
Doxycycline (Vibramycin, *Doryx, Oracea, Acticlate,* others) Capsule, tablet, suspension, syrup, injection	PO/IV: 100-200 mg daily in 1-2 divided doses Take with food to ↓ GI irritation (except take *Oracea* on an empty stomach, 1 hr before or 2 hrs after meals) No renal dose adjustments required	**WARNINGS** Children < 8 years of age, pregnancy and breastfeeding (suppresses bone growth and skeletal development, and permanently discolors teeth) Photosensitivity, tissue hyperpigmentation, severe skin reactions (DRESS/SJS/TEN), exfoliative dermatitis Gastrointestinal inflammation/ulceration (see Notes section)
Minocycline (Minocin, **Solodyn,** *CoreMino, Minolira, Ximino)* Capsule, tablet, injection	PO/IV: 200 mg x 1, then 50-100 mg Q12H CrCl < 80 mL/min: max 200 mg/day	Minocycline: drug-induced lupus erythematosus (DILE) **SIDE EFFECTS** N/V/D, rash
Eravacycline (*Xerava*) Injection	1 mg/kg IV Q12H Only approved for complicated intra-abdominal infections	**MONITORING** LFTs, renal function, CBC
Omadacycline (*Nuzyra*) Tablet, injection	Dose varies by indication (approved for CAP and skin infections)	**NOTES** IV:PO ratio is 1:1 (doxycycline, minocycline)
Sarecycline (*Seysara*) Tablet	Dose varies based on body weight Only approved for moderate-severe acne vulgaris	Tablets and capsules should be taken with 8 oz of water; with doxycycline, sit upright for at least 30 minutes after dose to avoid esophageal irritation
Tetracycline Capsule	PO: 250-500 mg Q6H on an empty stomach CrCl ≤ 50 mL/min: dose adjustment required	

See lab interactions, storage requirements and renal dosage information near the end of this chapter.

Tetracycline Drug Interactions

- <u>Antacids</u> and other <u>polyvalent cations</u> (e.g., magnesium, aluminum, phosphate, calcium, iron, zinc), multivitamins, <u>sucralfate, bismuth subsalicylate and bile acid resins</u> can <u>chelate</u> and <u>inhibit tetracycline absorption</u>. Separate doses of tetracyclines (1 – 2 hours before or 4 hours after the chelating drug). Dairy products should be avoided 1 hour before or 2 hours after tetracycline.

- Lanthanum carbonate *(Fosrenol)* can ↓ the concentration of tetracycline derivatives; take tetracycline at least 2 hours before or after lanthanum.

- Tetracycline is a major substrate of CYP3A4 and a moderate CYP3A4 inhibitor. Use caution with CYP3A4 inhibitors, which ↑ levels, and CYP3A4 inducers, which ↓ levels.

- Tetracyclines can enhance the effects of warfarin and neuromuscular blocking drugs.

KEY FEATURES OF TETRACYCLINES

Common Uses

- Doxycycline and minocycline: CA-MRSA skin infections, acne

- Doxycycline: first-line treatment for Lyme disease and Rocky Mountain Spotted Fever (tick-borne illnesses), CAP, COPD exacerbations, bacterial sinusitis (if antibiotic indicated), VRE UTI, chlamydia

- Tetracycline: used in *H. pylori* treatment regimens (see the Gastroesophageal Reflux Disease & Peptic Ulcer Disease chapter)

Do not use in pregnancy, breastfeeding or children < 8 years old

---

SULFONAMIDES

Sulfamethoxazole (SMX) inhibits dihydrofolic acid formation from para-aminobenzoic acid, which interferes with bacterial folic acid synthesis. Trimethoprim (TMP) inhibits dihydrofolic acid reduction to tetrahydrofolate, resulting in <u>inhibition of the folic acid pathway</u>.

Sulfamethoxazole/trimethoprim has activity against *Staphylococci* (including MRSA and <u>CA-MRSA</u>); *S. pneumoniae* and Group A *Streptococcus* activity is unreliable. Activity against Gram-negative bacteria is broad and includes *Haemophilus, Proteus, E. coli, Klebsiella, Enterobacter, Shigella, Salmonella* and *Stenotrophomonas*. SMX/TMP is active against some <u>opportunistic pathogens</u> (*Nocardia, Pneumocystis, Toxoplasmosis*), but <u>does not</u> have activity against *Pseudomonas, Enterococci*, atypicals or anaerobes.

DRUG	DOSING	SAFETY/SIDE EFFECTS/MONITORING
Sulfamethoxazole/ Trimethoprim *(Bactrim, Bactrim DS*, *Sulfatrim Pediatric)* Tablet, suspension, injection **Single Strength (SS) 400 mg SMX/80 mg TMP **Double Strength (DS)** 800 mg SMX/160 mg TMP All products are formulated with a SMX:TMP ratio = 5:1	Dose based on the TMP component **Severe Infections** PO/IV: 10-20 mg TMP/kg/day, divided Q6-8H (e.g., 2 DS tablets BID-TID) **Uncomplicated UTI** 1 DS tablet PO BID x 3 days ***Pneumocystis* Pneumonia (PCP) Prophylaxis** 1 DS or SS tablet daily **PCP Treatment** IV/PO: 15-20 mg TMP/kg/day divided Q6H CrCl 15-30 mL/min: dose adjustment required CrCl < 15 mL/min: not recommended	**CONTRAINDICATIONS** Sulfa allergy, anemia due to folate deficiency, renal or hepatic disease, infants < 2 months **WARNINGS** Blood dyscrasias, including agranulocytosis and aplastic anemia Skin reactions: SJS/TEN, thrombotic thrombocytopenic purpura (TTP) G6PD deficiency (hemolysis risk): do not use with known deficiency and discontinue drug if hemolysis occurs Hypoglycemia, thrombocytopenia Pregnancy: use only if benefit outweighs risk (blocks folic acid metabolism, leading to congenital defects) **SIDE EFFECTS** Photosensitivity, ↑ K, hemolytic anemia (identified with a positive Coombs test), crystalluria (take with 8 oz of water), N/V/D, anorexia, skin rash, ↓ folate, false elevations in SCr (due to inhibition of creatinine tubular secretion), renal failure **MONITORING** Renal function, electrolytes, CBC, folate **NOTES** See ID II chapter for a discussion on use for UTIs during pregnancy

See lab interactions, storage requirements and renal dosage information near the end of this chapter.

Sulfonamide Drug Interactions

- SMX/TMP is a moderate-strong CYP2C8 and CYP2C9 inhibitor and can cause significantly ↑ INR if used in combination with warfarin (see the Drug Interactions chapter for more information).

- Levels of SMX/TMP can be ↓ by CYP2C8 and CYP2C9 inducers.

- SMX/TMP can enhance the toxic effects of methotrexate. The therapeutic effects of SMX/TMP can be diminished by the use of leucovorin or levoleucovorin.

- The risk for hyperkalemia will ↑ in patients with renal dysfunction or if used in combination with ACE inhibitors, ARBs, aliskiren, aldosterone receptor antagonists (ARAs), potassium-sparing diuretics, cyclosporine, tacrolimus, NSAIDs, drospirenone-containing oral contraceptives or canagliflozin.

KEY FEATURES OF SULFAMETHOXAZOLE/TRIMETHOPRIM

Common Uses
- CA-MRSA skin infections, UTI, *Pneumocystis* pneumonia (PCP)

5:1 Ratio of SMX/TMP (Dose Based on TMP)
- Single strength (SS) tablet contains 80 mg TMP
- Double strength (DS) tablet contains 160 mg TMP – usual dose is one tablet BID

Sulfa Allergy
- Most sulfa allergies occur with SMX/TMP (rash/hives common)
- Rarely, severe skin reactions (e.g., SJS or TEN) can occur; if rash is accompanied by a fever or systemic symptoms, seek emergency care

INR ↑ when used with warfarin. Use alternative antibiotic when possible.

ANTIBIOTICS FOR GRAM-POSITIVE INFECTIONS

VANCOMYCIN

Vancomycin is a glycopeptide that inhibits bacterial cell wall synthesis by binding to the D-alanyl-D-alanine cell wall precursor and blocking peptidoglycan polymerization. Vancomycin only covers Gram-positive bacteria, including *Staphylococci* (MRSA), *Streptococci, Enterococci* (not VRE) and *C. difficile* (using the PO route only).

DRUG	DOSING	SAFETY/SIDE EFFECTS/MONITORING
Vancomycin (*Vancocin*, *Firvanq* oral solution) Capsule, oral solution, injection First-line treatment for moderate-severe systemic MRSA infections Consider an alternative drug when MRSA MIC ≥ 2 mcg/mL	**Systemic infections (IV only)** IV: 15-20 mg/kg Q8-12H Dose based on total body weight CrCl 20-49 mL/min: Q24H CrCl < 20 mL/min: give one dose, then dose per levels Peripheral IV infusions should not exceed 5 mg/mL **C. difficile infections (PO only)** PO: 125 QID x 10 days 500 mg QID used for severe, complicated disease (in combination with IV metronidazole) No renal dose adjustments required	**WARNINGS** Ototoxicity and nephrotoxicity; caution with use of other nephrotoxic or ototoxic drugs or with prolonged high serum concentrations (dose adjustment required in renal impairment) PO formulation is used only for *C. difficile* colitis and enterocolitis, not for systemic infections; IV formulation is not effective for *C. difficile* (does not cross into the GI tract) Vancomycin infusion reaction (maculopapular rash, hypotension, flushing and chills) from too rapid of an infusion rate; do not infuse faster than 1 gram per hour **SIDE EFFECTS** Abdominal pain, nausea (oral route), phlebitis (irritation to vein), myelosuppression (neutropenia/thrombocytopenia), drug fever, severe skin reactions (SJS/TEN) **MONITORING** Renal function, drug levels (see below), WBC AUC/MIC ratio (improved outcomes and less toxicity) or steady state trough (drawn 30 minutes before the 4th or 5th dose) Serious MRSA infections (e.g., bacteremia, sepsis, endocarditis, pneumonia, osteomyelitis, meningitis): AUC/MIC ratio of 400-600 recommended or goal trough 15-20 mcg/mL Other infections (e.g., UTI, skin infections): goal trough 10-15 mcg/mL

See lab interactions, storage requirements and renal dosage information near the end of this chapter.

Vancomycin Drug Interactions

- The risk of nephrotoxicity is ↑ when used with other nephrotoxic drugs (e.g., aminoglycosides, amphotericin B, cisplatin, polymyxins, cyclosporine, tacrolimus, loop diuretics, NSAIDs and radiographic contrast dye).

- Vancomycin can ↑ the risk of ototoxicity when used with other ototoxic drugs (e.g., aminoglycosides, cisplatin, loop diuretics).

LIPOGLYCOPEPTIDES

Lipoglycopeptides (with the generic name suffix "-vancin") inhibit bacterial cell wall synthesis by 1) binding to the D-alanyl-D-alanine portion of the cell wall, blocking polymerization and cross-linking of peptidoglycan, and 2) disrupting bacterial membrane potential and changing cell permeability (due to the presence of a lipophilic side chain). They have concentration-dependent activity against similar pathogens as vancomycin (with the exception that they only come in IV form and cannot be used to treat *C. difficile* infections).

DRUG	DOSING	SAFETY/SIDE EFFECTS/MONITORING
Telavancin (*Vibativ*) Injection Approved for complicated skin and soft-tissue infections (SSTI) and hospital-acquired and ventilator-associated pneumonia	IV: 10 mg/kg daily CrCl ≤ 50 mL/min: dose adjustment required Infuse over 60 minutes to prevent infusion reaction	**BOXED WARNINGS** Fetal risk – obtain pregnancy test prior to starting therapy; nephrotoxicity; ↑ mortality with pre-existing moderate-to-severe renal impairment (CrCl ≤ 50 mL/min) when compared to vancomycin in pneumonia trials **CONTRAINDICATIONS** Concurrent use of IV unfractionated heparin (UFH) **WARNINGS** Can falsely ↑ coagulation tests (e.g., aPTT/PT/INR), but does not ↑ bleeding risk; infusion reaction (similar to vancomycin) with rapid IV administration (give over ≥ 60 minutes); QT prolongation **SIDE EFFECTS** Metallic taste, N/V, ↑ SCr, foamy urine **MONITORING** Renal function, pregnancy status
Oritavancin (*Orbactiv*) Injection Approved for SSTI	Single-dose IV regimen: 1,200 mg Infuse over 3 hours CrCl < 30 mL/min: has not been studied, use with caution	**CONTRAINDICATIONS** Oritavancin: do not use IV UFH for 120 hours (5 days) after oritavancin administration due to interference (false elevations) with aPTT laboratory results **WARNINGS** Can cause falsely ↑ PT/INR for up to 12 hours and aPTT for up to 120 hours after a dose Oritavancin: use a different antibiotic if osteomyelitis is confirmed or suspected Dalbavancin: ↑ ALT > 3x the upper limit of normal **SIDE EFFECTS** Infusion reaction (similar to vancomycin), N/V/D, headache, rash **MONITORING** Signs of osteomyelitis (oritavancin), LFTs, renal function **NOTES** Extremely long half-life allows a single-dose regimen for both
Dalbavancin (*Dalvance*) Injection Approved for SSTI	Single-dose IV regimen: 1,500 mg Two-dose IV regimen: 1,000 mg x 1, then 500 mg one week later Infuse over 30 minutes CrCl < 30 mL/min (not on dialysis): dose adjustment required	

See lab interactions, storage requirements and renal dosage information near the end of this chapter.

Telavancin/Oritavancin Drug Interactions

- Avoid telavancin in patients with congenital long QT syndrome, known QT prolongation or uncompensated heart failure. Use caution with other medications known to prolong the QT interval (see the Arrhythmias chapter).

- Oritavancin is a weak inhibitor of CYP2C9 and CYP2C19, and a weak inducer of CYP3A4 and CYP2D6. Use caution when coadministered with drugs metabolized by these enzymes (including warfarin).

DAPTOMYCIN

Daptomycin is a cyclic lipopeptide. It binds to cell membrane components, causing rapid depolarization; this inhibits all intracellular replication processes, including protein synthesis, and causes cell death. Daptomycin has concentration-dependent activity against most Gram-positive bacteria, including *Staphylococci* (MRSA) and *Enterococci* (both species of VRE, *E. faecium* and *E. faecalis)*. It has no activity against Gram-negative pathogens.

DRUG	DOSING	SAFETY/SIDE EFFECTS/MONITORING
Daptomycin (Cubicin, Cubicin RF) Injection Approved for complicated skin and soft-tissue infections (SSTI) and *S. aureus* (including MRSA) bloodstream infections and right-sided endocarditis Do not use to treat pneumonia; drug is inactivated in the lungs by surfactant	SSTI: 4 mg/kg IV daily Bacteremia/right-sided endocarditis: 6 mg/kg IV daily (per package labeling; doses up to 10 mg/kg IV daily may be used in practice) CrCl < 30 mL/min: dose adjustment required	**WARNINGS** Myopathy and rhabdomyolysis: discontinue in patients with s/sx and CPK > 1,000 units/L (5x ULN), or in asymptomatic patients with a CPK ≥ 2,000 units/L (10x ULN); consider temporarily withholding other drugs that can cause muscle damage (e.g., statins) during treatment Can falsely ↑ PT/INR, but does not ↑ bleeding risk Peripheral neuropathy Eosinophilic pneumonia – generally develops 2-4 weeks after treatment initiation **SIDE EFFECTS** ↑ CPK, abdominal pain, pruritus, chest pain, edema, hypertension, acute kidney injury **MONITORING** CPK level weekly (more frequently if on a statin or with renal impairment); muscle pain/weakness, s/sx of neuropathy, dyspnea **NOTES** *Cubicin:* compatible with NS and LR (no dextrose) *Cubicin RF:* compatible with NS (no dextrose) but must use only sterile or bacteriostatic water for injection to reconstitute the lyophilized powder (before diluting further with NS)

See lab interactions, storage requirements and renal dosage information near the end of this chapter.

Daptomycin Drug Interactions

- Daptomycin can have additive risk of muscle toxicity when used in conjunction with statins.

OXAZOLIDINONES

Linezolid and tedizolid bind to the 50S subunit of the bacterial ribosome, inhibiting translation and protein synthesis. They have activity against similar pathogens as vancomycin (e.g., MRSA), but also cover VRE (*E. faecium* and *E. faecalis)*.

DRUG	DOSING	SAFETY/SIDE EFFECTS/MONITORING
Linezolid (Zyvox) Tablet, suspension, injection	PO/IV: 600 mg Q12H No renal dose adjustments required IV:PO ratio is 1:1	**CONTRAINDICATIONS** Do not use with or within 2 weeks of MAO inhibitors **WARNINGS** Duration-related myelosuppression (thrombocytopenia, anemia, leukopenia) when used > 14 days, peripheral and optic neuropathy when used > 28 days, serotonin syndrome, hypoglycemia (caution with insulin or other hypoglycemic drugs), seizures, lactic acidosis, ↑ BP (caution and monitor BP in patients with uncontrolled hypertension and untreated hyperthyroidism) **SIDE EFFECTS** ↓ platelets, ↓ Hgb, ↓ WBC, HA, nausea, diarrhea,↑ LFTs **MONITORING** HR, BP, BG (in diabetes), weekly CBC, visual function **NOTES** Do not shake linezolid suspension
Tedizolid (Sivextro) Tablet, injection Approved for SSTI	PO/IV: 200 mg daily for 6 days No renal dose adjustments required IV:PO ratio is 1:1	**WARNINGS** Consider alternative treatment in patients with neutropenia **SIDE EFFECTS** Nausea, diarrhea, paresthesias, hypertension, visual impairment, blurred vision (less GI side effects and myelosuppression compared to linezolid)

See lab interactions, storage requirements and renal dosage information near the end of this chapter.

Linezolid/Tedizolid Drug Interactions

- Linezolid and tedizolid are <u>reversible monoamine oxidase inhibitors</u>. Avoid <u>tyramine-containing foods</u> and <u>serotonergic drugs</u> (see the Drug Interactions chapter).

- Linezolid can exacerbate hypoglycemic episodes; use caution in patients receiving insulin or oral hypoglycemic drugs (e.g., sulfonylureas).

QUINUPRISTIN/DALFOPRISTIN

This drug is a streptogramin; it binds to the <u>50S ribosomal subunit</u> inhibiting protein synthesis. Quinupristin/dalfopristin is active against most <u>Gram-positive bacteria</u>, including *Staphylococci* (MRSA) and *Enterococcus faecium* (VRE, but <u>not *E. faecalis*</u>). It is approved for complicated skin and soft-tissue infections, but is <u>not well-tolerated</u>; use is typically limited to vancomycin-resistant *E. faecium* infections.

DRUG	DOSING	SAFETY/SIDE EFFECTS/MONITORING
Quinupristin/ Dalfopristin (*Synercid*) Injection	IV: 7.5 mg/kg Q8-12H Infuse over 60 minutes No renal dose adjustments required	**SIDE EFFECTS** <u>Arthralgias/myalgias</u> (up to 47% of patients), <u>infusion reactions</u>, including edema and pain at infusion site (up to 44% of patients), phlebitis (up to 40% of patients), <u>hyperbilirubinemia</u> (up to 35% of patients), CPK elevations, GI upset, ↑ LFTs **NOTES** Dilute in <u>D5W only</u> Administer via <u>central line</u>, such as a peripherally inserted central catheter (<u>PICC</u>), to avoid phlebitis

See lab interactions, storage requirements and renal dosage information near the end of this chapter.

Quinupristin/Dalfopristin Drug Interactions

- Quinupristin/dalfopristin is a weak CYP3A4 inhibitor; it can ↑ levels of CCBs, cyclosporine, dofetilide and others.

ADDITIONAL BROAD-SPECTRUM DRUGS

TIGECYCLINE

Tigecycline is a glycylcycline. It binds to the 30S ribosomal subunit inhibiting protein synthesis; structurally, it is <u>related to the tetracyclines</u>. Tigecycline has <u>broad-spectrum</u> activity against Gram-positive bacteria, including *Staphylococci* (MRSA) and *Enterococci* (VRE), Gram-negative bacteria, anaerobes and atypical organisms. Among the Gram-negatives, it has <u>no activity against the "3 P's"</u>: *Pseudomonas, Proteus, Providencia* species. Tigecycline is approved for complicated skin and soft-tissue infections, intra-abdominal infections and community-acquired pneumonia; use is limited (see Boxed Warning).

DRUG	DOSING	SAFETY/SIDE EFFECTS/MONITORING
Tigecycline (*Tygacil*) Injection Derivative of minocycline	IV: 100 mg x 1 dose, then 50 mg Q12H Severe hepatic impairment: dose adjustment required No renal dose adjustments required	**BOXED WARNING** ↑ risk of death, use only when alternative treatments are not suitable **WARNINGS** Hepatotoxicity, pancreatitis, photosensitivity, teeth discoloration in children < 8 years old (avoid use) Lower cure rates in ventilator-associated pneumonia **SIDE EFFECTS** N/V (can be intractable), diarrhea, headache, dizziness, ↑ LFTs, rash/severe skin reactions (SJS) **NOTES** <u>Do not use for bloodstream infections</u>; it does not achieve adequate concentrations in the blood since it is lipophilic (drug distributes quickly out of the blood into tissues) Reconstituted <u>solution</u> should be <u>yellow-orange</u>; discard if not this color

See lab interactions, storage requirements and renal dosage information near the end of this chapter.

Tigecycline Drug Interactions

- Tigecycline can ↑ the INR in patients taking warfarin.

INFECTIOUS DISEASES

POLYMYXINS

The polymyxin class consists of two drugs, colistimethate (sometimes referred to as colistin) and polymyxin B. Colistimethate is an inactive prodrug that is hydrolyzed to colistin. Colistin acts as a cationic detergent and damages the bacterial cytoplasmic membrane, causing leakage of intracellular substances and cell death. Polymyxins have activity against Gram-negative bacteria, such as *Enterobacter* spp., *E. coli*, *Klebsiella pneumoniae* and *Pseudomonas aeruginosa* (but not *Proteus* spp.). Due to the risk of toxicities, they are used primarily for MDR Gram-negative pathogens in combination with other antibiotics.

DRUG	DOSING	SAFETY/SIDE EFFECTS/MONITORING
Colistimethate (*Coly-Mycin M*) Injection (can be used for inhalation administration)	IV/IM: 2.5-5 mg/kg/day in 2-4 divided doses Dose is expressed in terms of colistin base activity CrCl < 80 mL/min: dose adjustment required Solutions for inhalation must be mixed immediately prior to administration	**WARNING** Dose-dependent nephrotoxicity (monitor renal function and electrolytes), neurotoxicity (dizziness, headache, tingling, oral paresthesia, vertigo) **NOTES** Colistimethate is a prodrug that is converted to colistin (the active form); assess dose carefully, as it can be represented in units of colistimethate, mg of colistimethate, or mg of colistin base activity Avoid use with other nephrotoxic medications Neurotoxicity can result in respiratory paralysis from neuromuscular blockade
Polymyxin B Injection	IV: 15,000-25,000 units/kg/day divided every 12 hours CrCl < 80 mL/min: dose adjustment required	**BOXED WARNINGS** Nephrotoxicity (dose-dependent) Neurotoxicity (dizziness, tingling, numbness, paresthesia, vertigo) Should only be administered to hospitalized patients Avoid concurrent or sequential use of other neurotoxic or nephrotoxic drugs Neurotoxicity can result in respiratory paralysis from neuromuscular blockade **MONITORING** Renal function **NOTES** 1 mg = 10,000 units polymyxin B

See lab interactions, storage requirements and renal dosage information near the end of this chapter.

Polymyxin Drug Interactions

- Other nephrotoxic drugs can enhance the nephrotoxic effects (refer to the Aminoglycosides section).

CHLORAMPHENICOL

Chloramphenicol reversibly binds to the 50S subunit of the bacterial ribosome, inhibiting protein synthesis. It has activity against Gram-positive, Gram-negative, anaerobic and atypical organisms.

DRUG	DOSING	SAFETY/SIDE EFFECTS/MONITORING
Chloramphenicol Injection Rarely used due to adverse effects	IV: 50-100 mg/kg/day in divided doses Q6H (max 4 grams/day) No dose adjustments in renal impairment, but use with caution	**BOXED WARNING** Serious and fatal blood dyscrasias (aplastic anemia, pancytopenia – may be irreversible) **WARNINGS** Gray syndrome with high serum levels – circulatory collapse, cyanosis, acidosis, abdominal distention, myocardial depression, coma and death **MONITORING** CBC at baseline and every 2 days during therapy, LFTs, renal function, serum drug concentrations

See lab interactions, storage requirements and renal dosage information near the end of this chapter.

MISCELLANEOUS ANTIBIOTICS

CLINDAMYCIN

Clindamycin is a lincosamide that reversibly binds to the 50S subunit of the bacterial ribosome, inhibiting protein synthesis. It has activity against most Gram-positive bacteria, including some CA-MRSA and anaerobes. It does not cover *Enterococcus* or Gram-negative pathogens and has limited to no Gram-negative anaerobic activity.

DRUG	DOSING	SAFETY/SIDE EFFECTS/MONITORING
Clindamycin (Cleocin) Injection, capsule, suspension Topical formulations: **Cleocin-T, Clindagel,** Clindacin ETZ, Clindacin Pac, Clindacin-P, Evoclin Foam, gel, lotion, kit, solution, swab *Clindesse*, Cleocin Vaginal cream, suppository	PO: 150-450 mg Q6H IV: 600-900 mg Q8H No renal dose adjustments required	**BOXED WARNING** Colitis (*C. difficile*) **WARNING** Severe or fatal skin reactions (SJS/TEN/DRESS) **SIDE EFFECTS** N/V/D, rash, urticaria, ↑ LFTs (rare) **NOTES** An induction test (D-test) should be performed on *S. aureus* that is susceptible to clindamycin but resistant to erythromycin; a flattened zone between the disks (positive D-test) indicates inducible clindamycin resistance and clindamycin should not be used Common uses: purulent and non-purulent skin infections, beta-lactam alternative for dental abscesses, surgery prophylaxis and infective endocarditis prophylaxis

See lab interactions, storage requirements and renal dosage information near the end of this chapter.

METRONIDAZOLE AND RELATED DRUGS

These antibiotics cause a loss of helical DNA structure and strand breakage resulting in inhibition of protein synthesis. Metronidazole has activity against anaerobes and protozoal organisms. It is effective for bacterial vaginosis, trichomoniasis, giardiasis, amebiasis, *C. difficile* (though not preferred) and is used in combination regimens for intra-abdominal infections.

Tinidazole is structurally related to metronidazole, but activity is limited to protozoa (giardiasis, amebiasis), trichomoniasis and bacterial vaginosis organisms. Secnidazole is only indicated for bacterial vaginosis.

DRUG	DOSING	SAFETY/SIDE EFFECTS/MONITORING
Metronidazole (Flagyl) Tablet, capsule, injection Topical: *MetroCream, Metrogel, MetroLotion, Noritate, Rosadan* Vaginal: *Nuvessa, Vandazole*	PO/IV: 500-750 mg Q8-12H or 250-500 mg Q6-8H No renal dose adjustments required Take immediate-release tablets with food to ↓ GI upset IV:PO ratio is 1:1	**BOXED WARNING** Possibly carcinogenic based on animal data **CONTRAINDICATIONS** Pregnancy (1st trimester), use of alcohol or propylene glycol-containing products during treatment or within 3 days of treatment discontinuation (disulfiram reaction) Metronidazole: use of disulfiram within the past 2 weeks Tinidazole: breastfeeding **WARNINGS** CNS effects: seizures, peripheral neuropathy Metronidazole: aseptic meningitis, encephalopathy, optic neuropathy
Tinidazole Tablet	2 grams PO daily Take with food to minimize GI effects No renal dose adjustments required	**SIDE EFFECTS** Metallic taste, HA, nausea, furry tongue, darkened urine, dizziness, rash/severe skin reactions (SJS/TEN) **NOTES** See the ID II chapter for a discussion of use for STIs in pregnancy
Secnidazole (*Solosec*) Granule packet Approved only for bacterial vaginosis	PO: 2 gram single dose Sprinkle contents of 1 packet onto applesauce, yogurt, or pudding and consume within 30 minutes; do not chew the granules	**WARNINGS** Possibly carcinogenic (based on animal data with structurally similar drugs) **SIDE EFFECTS** Vulvovaginal candidiasis, HA, N/D

See lab interactions, storage requirements and renal dosage information near the end of this chapter.

Metronidazole and Tinidazole Drug Interactions

- Metronidazole and tinidazole should not be used with alcohol (during and for 3 days after discontinuation of treatment) due to a potential disulfiram-like reaction (abdominal cramping, nausea/vomiting, headaches, and flushing).

- Metronidazole is a weak inhibitor of CYP2C9 and can cause an ↑ INR in patients taking warfarin.

LEFAMULIN

Lefamulin is a first-in-class pleuromutilin. It inhibits bacterial protein synthesis by binding to the peptidyl transferase center of the 50S ribosomal subunit.

DRUG	DOSING	SAFETY/SIDE EFFECTS/MONITORING
Lefamulin (Xenleta) Tablet, injection	PO: 600 mg Q12H IV: 150 mg Q12H	**CONTRAINDICATIONS** Use with CYP3A4 substrates that prolong the QT interval **WARNINGS** Avoid in pregnancy (teratogenic), QT prolongation, C. difficile-associated diarrhea **SIDE EFFECTS** Diarrhea, nausea, injection site reactions **NOTES** Approved for CAP

See lab interactions, storage requirements and renal dosage information near the end of this chapter.

FIDAXOMICIN

Fidaxomicin inhibits RNA polymerase, resulting in inhibition of protein synthesis and cell death. It is used for *C. difficile* infections.

DRUG	DOSING	SAFETY/SIDE EFFECTS/MONITORING
Fidaxomicin (Dificid) Tablet, suspension	PO: 200 mg BID x 10 days No renal dose adjustments required	**WARNINGS** Not effective for systemic infections – absorption is minimal **SIDE EFFECTS** N/V, abdominal pain, GI bleeding, anemia

See lab interactions, storage requirements and renal dosage information near the end of this chapter.

RIFAXIMIN

Rifaximin inhibits bacterial RNA synthesis by binding to bacterial DNA-dependent RNA polymerase. It is structurally related to rifampin.

DRUG	DOSING	SAFETY/SIDE EFFECTS/MONITORING
Rifaximin (Xifaxan) Tablet	**Travelers' diarrhea** PO: 200 mg TID x 3 days **↓ recurrence of hepatic encephalopathy** PO: 550 mg BID **Irritable bowel syndrome w/diarrhea (IBS-D)** PO: 550 mg TID x 14 days No renal dose adjustments required	**SIDE EFFECTS** Peripheral edema, dizziness, headache, flatulence, nausea, abdominal pain, rash/pruritus **NOTES** Not effective for systemic infections (< 1% absorption) Used off-label for *C. difficile* infection (second or subsequent recurrence) and treatment of hepatic encephalopathy

See lab interactions, storage requirements and renal dosage information near the end of this chapter.

URINARY AGENTS

FOSFOMYCIN

Inhibits bacterial cell wall synthesis by inactivating the enzyme pyruval transferase, which is critical in the synthesis of cell walls. It has activity against _E. coli_ (including ESBLs) and _E. faecalis_ (including VRE). A single-dose regimen is used for uncomplicated UTI (cystitis only).

DRUG	DOSING	SAFETY/SIDE EFFECTS/MONITORING
Fosfomycin _(Monurol)_ Packet granules = 3 gram per packet	**Female, uncomplicated UTI** 3 grams PO x 1, mixed in 3-4 oz of cold water	**SIDE EFFECTS** Headache, diarrhea, nausea **NOTES** Concentrates in the urine

See lab interactions, storage requirements and renal dosage information near the end of this chapter.

NITROFURANTOIN

Nitrofurantoin is a bacterial cell wall inhibitor. It is used for uncomplicated UTI (cystitis only). It covers _E. coli, Klebsiella, Enterobacter, S. aureus_ and _Enterococcus_ (VRE).

DRUG	DOSING	SAFETY/SIDE EFFECTS/MONITORING
Nitrofurantoin _(Macrobid, Macrodantin)_ Capsule, suspension	_Macrodantin_ PO: 50-100 mg QID x 3-7 days; 50-100 mg QHS for prophylaxis _Macrobid_ PO: 100 mg BID x 5 days The macrocrystal formulation _(Macrobid)_ dissolves more slowly and is given BID	**CONTRAINDICATIONS** Renal impairment (CrCl < 60 mL/min*): inadequate urine concentrations and risk for accumulation of neurotoxins; previous history of cholestatic jaundice/hepatic dysfunction; pregnancy (at term) **WARNINGS** Optic neuritis, hepatotoxicity, peripheral neuropathy, pulmonary toxicity, hemolytic anemia (identified with a positive Coombs test; use caution in patients with G6PD deficiency) **SIDE EFFECTS** GI upset (take with food), headache, rash, brown urine discoloration (harmless) **NOTES** Concentrates in the urine

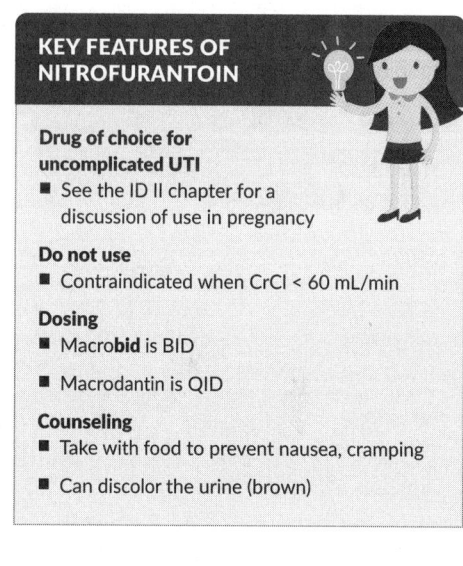

KEY FEATURES OF NITROFURANTOIN

Drug of choice for uncomplicated UTI
- See the ID II chapter for a discussion of use in pregnancy

Do not use
- Contraindicated when CrCl < 60 mL/min

Dosing
- Macro**bid** is BID
- Macrodantin is QID

Counseling
- Take with food to prevent nausea, cramping
- Can discolor the urine (brown)

*Per package labeling. Some sources (e.g., Beers Criteria) recommend use if CrCl > 30 mL/min.
See lab interactions, storage requirements and renal dosage information near the end of this chapter.

TOPICAL DECOLONIZATION

MUPIROCIN NASAL OINTMENT

Mupirocin is a topical antimicrobial ointment used to eliminate _Staphylococci_ (MRSA) colonization of the nares. See the Common Skin Conditions chapter for a discussion of topical mupirocin use for infected skin lesions.

DRUG	DOSING	SAFETY/SIDE EFFECTS/MONITORING
Mupirocin _(Bactroban*)_ 1 gram tubes	**Decolonization** ½ tube in each nostril BID x 5 days	**SIDE EFFECTS** Headache, burning, localized irritation, rhinitis, pharyngitis

*Brand discontinued but name still used in practice.
See lab interactions, storage requirements and renal dosage information near the end of this chapter.

SUMMARY TABLES

COMMONLY USED/ACTIVE DRUGS FOR SPECIFIC PATHOGENS

Methicillin-sensitive _Staphylococcus aureus_ (MSSA)

Dicloxacillin, nafcillin, oxacillin

Cefazolin, cephalexin (and other 1st and 2nd generation cephalosporins)

Amoxicillin/clavulanate, ampicillin/sulbactam

Doxycycline, minocycline

SMX/TMP

Community-associated methicillin-resistant _Staphylococcus aureus_ (CA-MRSA) skin & soft tissue infections (SSTIs)

SMX/TMP

Doxycycline, minocycline

Clindamycin*

Linezolid

Severe SSTIs requiring IV treatment or hospitalization (cover MRSA and _Streptococci_)

Vancomycin (consider using alternative if MIC ≥ 2)

Linezolid, tedizolid

Daptomycin

Ceftaroline

Telavancin

Oritavancin

Dalbavancin

Quinupristin/Dalfopristin

Tigecycline

Nosocomial MRSA

Vancomycin (consider using alternative if MIC ≥ 2)

Linezolid

Daptomycin (not in pneumonia)

Telavancin

VRE (_E. faecalis_)

Pen G or ampicillin

Linezolid

Daptomycin

Tigecycline

Cystitis only: nitrofurantoin, fosfomycin, doxycycline

VRE (_E. faecium_)

Daptomycin

Linezolid

Quinupristin/Dalfopristin

Tigecycline

Cystitis only: nitrofurantoin, fosfomycin, doxycycline

HNPEK

Beta-lactam/beta-lactamase inhibitor

Amoxicillin (if beta-lactamase negative)

Cephalosporins (except 1st generation)

Carbapenems

SMX/TMP

Aminoglycosides

Quinolones

Atypical Organisms

Azithromycin, clarithromycin

Doxycycline, minocycline

Quinolones

Pseudomonas aeruginosa

Piperacillin/tazobactam

Cefepime

Ceftazidime

Ceftazidime/avibactam

Ceftolozane/tazobactam

Carbapenems (except ertapenem)

Ciprofloxacin, levofloxacin

Aztreonam

Aminoglycosides

Colistimethate, polymyxin B

Acinetobacter baumannii

Carbapenems (except ertapenem)

Ampicillin/sulbactam

Minocycline

Tigecycline

Quinolones

SMX/TMP

Amikacin

Colistimethate, polymyxin B

Extended-spectrum beta-lactamase producing Gram-negative rods (ESBL GNR) – _E. coli_, _K. pneumoniae_, _P. mirabilis_

Carbapenems

Ceftazidime/avibactam

Ceftolozane/tazobactam

Aminoglycosides

Cystitis only: fosfomycin

Carbapenem-resistant Gram-negative rods (CRE)

Ceftazidime/avibactam

Colistimethate, polymyxin B

Meropenem/vaborbactam

Imipenem/cilastatin/relebactam

Bacteroides fragilis

Metronidazole

Beta-lactam/beta-lactamase inhibitor

Cefotetan, cefoxitin

Carbapenems

Tigecycline

Others (reduced activity): moxifloxacin

C. difficile

Vancomycin (oral)

Fidaxomicin

Metronidazole

*A D-test must be performed before using clindamycin.

STORAGE REQUIREMENTS: LIQUID ORAL ANTIBIOTICS*

REFRIGERATION REQUIRED AFTER RECONSTITUTION

Penicillin VK	Cefadroxil	Cefaclor
Ampicillin	Cefpodoxime	Ceftibuten
Amoxicillin/Clavulanate	Cefprozil	Vancomycin oral
Cephalexin	Cefuroxime	Valganciclovir**

REFRIGERATION RECOMMENDED

Amoxicillin – improves taste

DO NOT REFRIGERATE

Cefdinir	Ciprofloxacin	Acyclovir**
Azithromycin	Levofloxacin	Fluconazole**
Clarithromycin – bitter taste, thickens/gels	Clindamycin – thickens, may crystallize	Posaconazole**
	Linezolid	Voriconazole**
Doxycycline	Sulfamethoxazole/Trimethoprim	Nystatin**

Most oral suspensions should be discarded 10-14 days after reconstitution.
***Discussed in the ID III chapter.*

STORAGE REQUIREMENTS: IV ANTIBIOTICS

Most IV medications are refrigerated; the list below represents a few that are not.

DO NOT REFRIGERATE

Metronidazole	Sulfamethoxazole/Trimethoprim
Moxifloxacin	Acyclovir** – refrigeration causes crystallization

***Brand discontinued but name still used in practice.*
***Discussed in the ID III chapter.*

DRUG-LABORATORY INTERACTIONS

Some antimicrobials can cause abnormalities in laboratory values, necessitating a change in treatment (e.g., a positive Coombs test in combination with bleeding indicates that a patient could be experiencing drug-related hemolysis and the antibiotic should be discontinued). Some medications can interfere with the result of the test, even if there are no clinical effects (e.g., daptomycin can cause a falsely elevated INR, but does not cause bleeding). In other cases, a drug should not be started in patients with certain laboratory test results (e.g., primaquine in patients with G6PD deficiency).

See the Lab Values & Drug Monitoring chapter for a complete list of drugs (antibiotics and other drugs) that interfere with lab tests. Refer to the Anemia chapter for a complete discussion on hemolytic anemia and drugs that can cause hemolysis and/or should be avoided with G6PD deficiency.

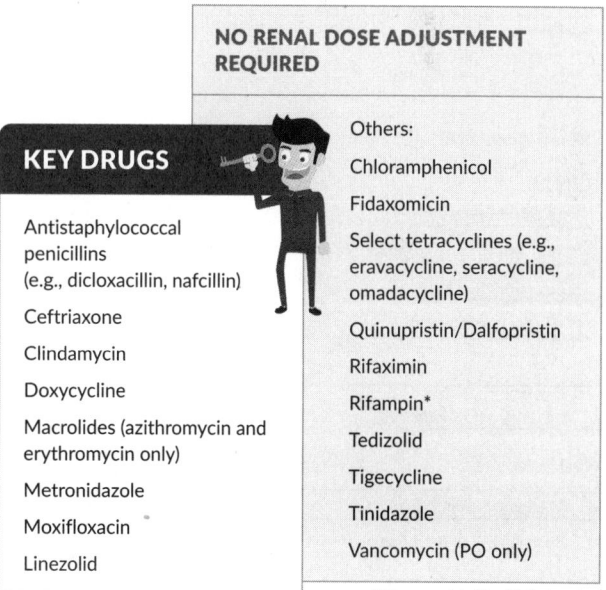

KEY DRUGS

NO RENAL DOSE ADJUSTMENT REQUIRED

Antistaphylococcal penicillins (e.g., dicloxacillin, nafcillin)

Ceftriaxone

Clindamycin

Doxycycline

Macrolides (azithromycin and erythromycin only)

Metronidazole

Moxifloxacin

Linezolid

Others:

Chloramphenicol

Fidaxomicin

Select tetracyclines (e.g., eravacycline, seracycline, omadacycline)

Quinupristin/Dalfopristin

Rifaximin

Rifampin*

Tedizolid

Tigecycline

Tinidazole

Vancomycin (PO only)

Discussed in the ID II chapter.

RENAL DOSE ADJUSTMENTS

Many antibiotics are cleared through the kidneys and require dose adjustments based on renal function. This includes most beta-lactams and quinolones. See Key Drugs Guy for antibiotics that do not require renal adjustment.

SPECIAL REQUIREMENTS

TAKE WITH/WITHOUT FOOD

Most antibiotics can be taken with food to decrease GI upset

Exceptions:

Take on an empty stomach: ampicillin oral capsules and suspension, ceftibuten suspension, levofloxacin oral solution, penicillin VK, rifampin*, isoniazid*, itraconazole solution*, voriconazole*

Take within one hour of finishing a meal: amoxicillin ER

1:1 IV TO ORAL DOSING
For these drugs, the oral and IV doses are the same.

Levofloxacin, moxifloxacin

Doxycycline, minocycline

Linezolid, tedizolid

Metronidazole

Sulfamethoxazole/Trimethoprim

Fluconazole*, isavuconazonium*, posaconazole* (oral tablets and IV), voriconazole*

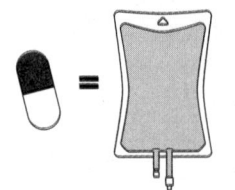

LIGHT PROTECTION DURING ADMINISTRATION
See the Intravenous Medication Principles chapter for a complete list of drugs (including antibiotics) that require specific light protection.

Doxycycline

Micafungin*

Pentamidine*

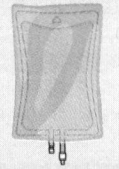

DILUENT COMPATIBILITY REQUIREMENTS
See the Intravenous Medication Principles chapter for a complete list of drugs (including antibiotics and other drugs) that require specific diluents.

Compatible with dextrose only

Quinupristin/Dalfopristin

Sulfamethoxazole/Trimethoprim

Amphotericin B* (conventional, *Abelcet*, *Ambisome*)

Dalbavancin, oritavancin

Pentamidine*

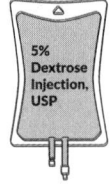

5% Dextrose Injection, USP

Compatible with saline only

Ampicillin

Ampicillin/Sulbactam

Ertapenem

Daptomycin (*Cubicin RF* – see the daptomycin drug table for reconstitution requirements prior to dilution)

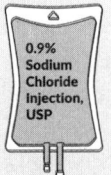

0.9% Sodium Chloride Injection, USP

Compatible with NS/LR only

Caspofungin*

Daptomycin (*Cubicin*)

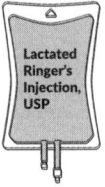

Lactated Ringer's Injection, USP

Discussed in the ID II-IV chapters.

KEY COUNSELING POINTS

See the Drug Formulations and Patient Counseling chapter for counseling language/layman's terminology.

ALL ANTIBIOTICS

- Proper storage (refrigeration or room temperature) and administration (with or without food) is essential. See the previous pages.
- Shake suspensions well.
- Antibiotics treat bacterial infections. They do not treat viral infections, such as the common cold.
- Complete the full course of therapy even if symptoms improve.
- Measure liquid doses carefully using the measuring device/syringe that comes with the medication. Do not use household spoons.
- Some oral liquid and chewable dosage forms contain phenylalanine. Do not use if you have phenylketonuria (PKU).
- Can cause:
  - ❑ Rash.
  - ❑ Nausea.
  - ❑ Diarrhea, including _C. difficile_-associated diarrhea (abdominal pain, cramps, watery or bloody stool).

QUINOLONES

- Can cause:
  - ❑ CNS effects, including seizures.
  - ❑ Hypo/hyperglycemia.
  - ❑ Peripheral neuropathy.
  - ❑ Photosensitivity.
  - ❑ QT prolongation.
  - ❑ Tendon inflammation (tendinitis) or tendon rupture. Can present with a "pop" or pain/swelling in the back of the ankle (Achilles), shoulder or hand.
- Avoid in pregnancy, breastfeeding and children.
- Drug interactions due to binding.

MACROLIDES

- Can cause:
  - ❑ GI upset.
  - ❑ QT prolongation.

Azithromycin

- _Z-Pak:_ take two tablets on day 1, followed by one tablet daily on days 2 – 5.

TETRACYCLINES

- Avoid in pregnancy, breastfeeding and children < 8 years old.
- Drug interactions due to binding.
- Can cause photosensitivity.

Doxycycline (oral)

- Take with a full glass of water and remain upright for 30 minutes after the dose to avoid GI irritation.

SULFAMETHOXAZOLE/TRIMETHOPRIM

- Avoid in:
  - ❑ Pregnancy or breastfeeding.
  - ❑ Sulfa allergy.
- Can cause:
  - ❑ Photosensitivity.
  - ❑ Crystals in the urine. Take with a full glass of water.

METRONIDAZOLE

- Do not use any alcohol products while using this medication, and for at least three days afterward.
- Can cause:
  - ❑ Nausea.
  - ❑ Metallic taste in the mouth.

NITROFURANTOIN

- Take with food to ↓ nausea.
- Can cause:
  - ❑ Nausea
  - ❑ Brown discoloration of urine (temporary and harmless).

MUPIROCIN NASAL OINTMENT

- Place ½ the ointment from the tube into one nostril and the other ½ into the other nostril. Press the nostrils at the same time and let go; do this many times (for about 1 minute) to spread the ointment into the nose.
- Wash hands after use.
- Can cause burning and itching in the nose.

Select Guidelines/References

Guidelines available at the Infectious Diseases Society of America website (www.idsociety.org)

CHAPTER CONTENT

CONTENT LEGEND

✦ = Study Tip Gal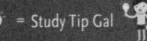

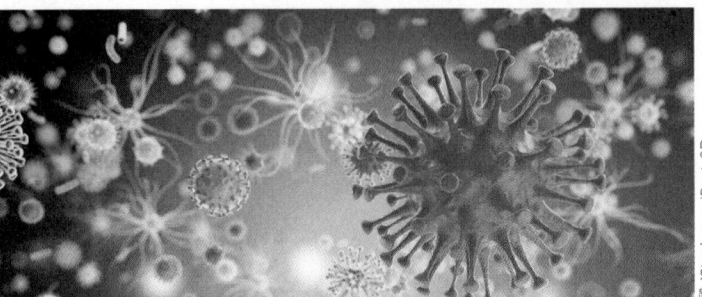

Ⓘ iStock.com/Rost-9D

CHAPTER 23

INFECTIOUS DISEASES II: BACTERIAL INFECTIONS

BACKGROUND

Review the Infectious Diseases I chapter before this chapter to gain a working knowledge of bacterial pathogens, microbiology reports, bacterial resistance and antimicrobial (antibiotic) drugs, including their spectrum of activity and pharmacokinetic/pharmacodynamic properties that play an important role in selecting the optimal treatment for infections.

PERIOPERATIVE ANTIBIOTIC PROPHYLAXIS

When a surgeon cuts into the skin during an operative (surgical) procedure, local bacterial flora at the incision site can cause contamination and subsequent infection. Skin flora (e.g., staphylococci and streptococci) are common causes of infection, with Gram-negative and anaerobic organisms playing a role in select surgeries (e.g., intra-abdominal procedures). Intravenous (IV) antibiotics are given prior to surgery to reduce this risk. The preferred regimens and alternatives are shown in the Perioperative Antibiotic Selection table on the following page.

The recommended start time for antibiotics is based on drug half-life and infusion time to ensure adequate tissue concentrations are achieved by the time surgery begins. The Study Tip Gal flow diagram below provides details on the timing of antibiotics.

Timing of Perioperative Antibiotics

PRE-OPERATIVE (PRIOR TO SURGERY)

Prevent Infection
Hang before surgery

1g Cefazolin 50mL

Infuse antibiotic (e.g., cefazolin or cefuroxime)* within 60 min before first incision

If a quinolone or vancomycin are used,* start the infusion 120 min before first incision

INTRA-OPERATIVE (DURING SURGERY)

Additional doses may be administered for longer surgeries (e.g., > 4 hours) or if there is major blood loss

POST-OPERATIVE (AFTER SURGERY)

Antibiotics are not usually needed; if used, discontinue within 24 hours

See Perioperative Antibiotic Selection table on the next page.

PERIOPERATIVE ANTIBIOTIC SELECTION

- Cefazolin, a first-generation cephalosporin (or cefuroxime, a second-generation cephalosporin), is preferred for most surgeries to prevent methicillin-susceptible *S. aureus* (MSSA) and streptococcal infections.

- Clindamycin is an alternative if the patient has a beta-lactam allergy.

- In gastrointestinal surgeries, the prophylactic antibiotic regimen needs to cover skin flora plus broad Gram-negative and anaerobic organisms.

- Vancomycin should be included in the regimen if MRSA colonization or risk is present. Vancomycin is also an alternative (instead of clindamycin) if the patient has a beta-lactam allergy.

SURGICAL PROCEDURE	RECOMMENDED ANTIBIOTICS*	BETA-LACTAM ALLERGY
Cardiac or vascular	Cefazolin or cefuroxime	Clindamycin or vancomycin
Orthopedic (e.g., joint replacement, hip fracture repair)	Cefazolin	
Gastrointestinal (e.g., appendectomy, colorectal surgery)	Cefazolin + metronidazole, cefotetan, cefoxitin, or ampicillin/sulbactam	Clindamycin or metronidazole + aminoglycoside or quinolone

* For patients colonized with MRSA or procedures in hospitals with a high prevalence of post-operative MRSA infections, include vancomycin in the regimen.

MENINGITIS

Meningitis is an inflammation of the meninges (membranes) that cover the brain and spinal cord. The meninges swell, causing classic symptoms of fever, headache, nuchal rigidity (stiff neck) and altered mental status. Other symptoms include chills, vomiting, seizures, rash and photophobia. Meningitis symptoms must be quickly recognized and treated to avoid severe complications, including death.

Diagnosis is made via a lumbar puncture (LP), whereby a sample of cerebrospinal fluid (CSF) is collected and analyzed to help guide empiric antibiotic treatment until culture and susceptibility results are available. A high CSF pressure (sometimes referred to as the "opening pressure") detected during the LP procedure is another sign of possible infection. It is preferable to perform the LP prior to starting antibiotics; however, treatment should be initiated if the LP is delayed.

Meningitis is mostly caused by viral infections but can be due to bacteria or fungi. The most common bacterial causes are *Neisseria meningitidis, Streptococcus pneumoniae* and *Haemophilus influenzae*; the risk of infection with these pathogens has decreased with routine vaccinations (see the Immunizations chapter). The risk of meningitis due to *Listeria monocytogenes* is higher in neonates, patients age > 50 years and immunocompromised patients.

ACUTE BACTERIAL MENINGITIS TREATMENT (COMMUNITY-ACQUIRED)

- The recommended empiric antibiotic regimens are based on the likely causative pathogens according to patient age and immune status (see Study Tip Gal on the following page). Aggressive (high) doses are used to adequately penetrate the CNS.

- Antibiotic durations are pathogen-dependent:

  - 7 days for *N. meningitidis* and *H. influenzae*

  - 10 – 14 days for *S. pneumoniae*

  - At least 21 days for *Listeria monocytogenes*

- Dexamethasone, administered 15 – 20 minutes prior to or with the first antibiotic dose, can prevent neurological complications (e.g., hearing loss) and death from pneumococcal meningitis. Since the causative pathogen is not known at the time empiric treatment is initiated, it is appropriate to administer dexamethasone in all cases. The adult dose is 0.15 mg/kg (rounded to the nearest 10 mg) IV Q6H. Steroid treatment should be continued for 4 days. If *S. pneumoniae* is not identified as the cause of meningitis, dexamethasone can be discontinued.

MENINGITIS: EMPIRIC TREATMENT*

COVER THE MOST COMMON BACTERIA

- *Streptococcus pneumoniae* and *Neisseria meningitidis* for most adult patients.

- Add coverage for *Listeria monocytogenes* in neonates, age > 50 years and immunocompromised patients.

- Add vancomycin in patients ≥ 1-month-old for double coverage of *Streptococcus pneumoniae*.

AGE < 1 MONTH (NEONATES)	AGE 1 MONTH TO 50 YEARS	AGE > 50 YEARS OR IMMUNOCOMPROMISED
Ampicillin (for *Listeria* coverage) + Cefotaxime (no ceftriaxone) or Gentamicin	Ceftriaxone or cefotaxime + Vancomycin	Ampicillin (for *Listeria* coverage) + Cetriaxone or cefotaxime + Vancomycin

Annasunny24/Shutterstock.com

DO NOT USE CEFTRIAXONE IN NEONATES

- Ceftriaxone can cause biliary sludging (solids that precipitate from bile) and kernicterus (brain damage from high bilirubin) in neonates.

If severe penicillin allergy (adults): treat with a quinolone (e.g., moxifloxacin) + vancomycin ± SMX/TMP (for Listeria coverage); obtain Infectious Diseases consult

UPPER RESPIRATORY TRACT INFECTIONS

ACUTE OTITIS MEDIA (AOM)

Acute otitis media (AOM) is the most common childhood infection in the United States requiring antibiotic treatment. Signs and symptoms often have a rapid onset and can include bulging tympanic (eardrum) membranes, otorrhea (middle ear effusion/fluid), otalgia (ear pain), fever, crying and tugging or rubbing the ears.

- Most AOM is viral and antibiotics will be ineffective.

- Bacterial infection is typically caused by *S. pneumoniae, H. influenzae* or *Moraxella catarrhalis*.

- Observation for 48 – 72 hours is an option for select patients age ≥ 6 months with non-severe AOM (see Study Tip Gal). Severe AOM is defined as having an ill appearance, otorrhea, otalgia > 48 hours or a temperature ≥ 102.2°F (39°C). Observation is not an option for children < 6 months old and antibiotics should be prescribed.

AOM TREATMENT IN KIDS: WHEN TO CONSIDER OBSERVATION

Try observation for 2-3 days if symptoms are non-severe [(otalgia < 48 hrs, no otorrhea, temperature < 102.2°F (39°C)] and:

- Age 6-23 months: symptoms in one ear only.

- Age ≥ 2 years: symptoms in one or both ears.

If symptoms do not improve, or worsen, use antibiotics.

Example
A physician gives a prescription for amoxicillin to a parent whose son has non-severe AOM on the right-side only, and advises the parent:

"Don't fill it right away; hold on to it for a couple of days and see if he improves without medication. If he does not get any better, go ahead and get the medication filled for him."

blueringmedia © 123RF.com

Antibiotic Treatment

- High-dose amoxicillin or amoxicillin/clavulanate are first-line (see table on the following page). A high dose of amoxicillin is needed to cover most strains of *S. pneumoniae*.

- With amoxicillin/clavulanate, the formulation with the least amount of clavulanate should be used to decrease the risk of diarrhea. The target amoxicillin to clavulanate ratio is 14:1, making *Augmentin ES-600* (amoxicillin 600 mg and clavulanate 42.9 mg per 5 mL) a preferred formulation.

- In children with a non-severe penicillin allergy, the American Academy of Pediatrics (AAP) recommends a second- or third-generation cephalosporin as there is a low risk of cross-reactivity. Non-beta-lactam antibiotics that are suitable for use in children (e.g., azithromycin) have limited efficacy against the typical AOM pathogens due to resistance.

- The treatment duration with oral medications is:

  ❏ 10 days for children < 2 years

  ❏ 7 days for ages 2 – 5 years

  ❏ 5 – 7 days for ages ≥ 6 years

Acute Otitis Media: Antibiotic Treatment

FIRST-LINE TREATMENT	ALTERNATIVE TREATMENT (MILD PENICILLIN ALLERGY**)	TREATMENT FAILURE (NOT IMPROVED AFTER 2-3 DAYS)
Amoxicillin: 90 mg/kg/day in 2 divided doses or Amoxicillin/clavulanate*: 90 mg/kg/day of amoxicillin with 6.4 mg/kg/day of clavulanate, in 2 divided doses	Cefdinir 14 mg/kg/day in 1 or 2 doses	Amoxicillin/clavulanate (if amoxicillin was the initial therapy): 90 mg/kg/day of amoxicillin with 6.4 mg/kg/day of clavulanate, in 2 divided doses or Ceftriaxone 50 mg/kg IM daily for 3 days
	Cefuroxime 30 mg/kg/day in 2 divided doses	
	Cefpodoxime 10 mg/kg/day in 2 divided doses	
	Ceftriaxone 50 mg/kg IM daily for 1 or 3 days	

*Preferred in patients who have received amoxicillin in the past 30 days.
**Delayed-onset reaction (> 48 hours after the first antibiotic dose) appearing as a nonpruritic or mildly pruritic, maculopapular rash, but lacking systemic symptoms (e.g., hives, bronchospasm, anaphylaxis) or other serious reactions (e.g., Stevens-Johnson syndrome).

OVERVIEW OF NON-AOM UPPER RESPIRATORY TRACT INFECTIONS

The majority of upper respiratory tract infections are viral and antibiotics are not beneficial. With pharyngitis and sinusitis, antibiotics can be used if symptoms are severe or chronic and/or if there is diagnostic evidence of a bacterial infection.

	COMMON COLD	INFLUENZA	PHARYNGITIS	ACUTE SINUSITIS
Typical Etiology	Respiratory viruses (rhinovirus, seasonal coronavirus)	Influenza virus	Respiratory viruses, Group A Streptococcus (S. pyogenes); commonly referred to as "Strep throat"	Respiratory viruses, S. pneumoniae, H. influenzae, M. catarrhalis
Clinical Presentation	Sneezing, runny nose, mild sore throat and/or cough, congestion	Sudden onset fever, chills, fatigue, myalgia, dry cough, sore throat, headache Symptoms are more severe than the common cold	Sore throat, fever, swollen lymph nodes, white patches (exudates) on the tonsils There is an absence of cough, runny nose or congestion	Nasal congestion, purulent nasal discharge, facial/ear/dental pain or pressure, headache, fever
Criteria for Anti-Infective Treatment	None; generally resolves in a few days	Suspected or confirmed infection (e.g., positive rapid influenza antigen test) and: Symptoms < 48 hours, or Severe illness (e.g., hospitalized), or Symptoms plus risk factors for influenza complications	Rapid antigen test (tonsil swab) or throat culture positive for S. pyogenes	≥ 10 days of persistent symptoms or ≥ 3 days of severe symptoms (face pain, purulent nasal discharge, temperature > 102°F) or Worsening symptoms after initial improvement
Treatment Options	Symptomatic care: OTC analgesics, decongestants, cough suppressants, expectorants and/or antihistamines; see the Allergic Rhinitis, Cough & Cold chapter	Symptomatic care with or without antiviral therapy (see the Infectious Diseases III chapter)	Penicillin or amoxicillin Mild penicillin allergy: 1st or 2nd generation cephalosporin Severe reaction (e.g., anaphylaxis) to penicillin: macrolide (clarithromycin, azithromycin) or clindamycin	Amoxicillin/clavulanate or Symptomatic care for up to 7 days with OTC decongestants, antihistamines, expectorants and/or analgesics; antibiotics can be used if symptoms worsen or do not improve

iStock.com/blueringmedia
Igor Zakowski © 123RF.com

INFECTIOUS DISEASES

LOWER RESPIRATORY TRACT INFECTIONS

ACUTE BRONCHITIS

Bronchitis is an inflammation of the mucous membranes of the bronchi. The key defining features include:

- Non-productive or productive <u>cough</u> lasting <u>1 – 3 weeks</u>, chest wall tenderness, wheezing and/or rhonchi. Systemic symptoms (e.g., fever, chills, malaise) are rare.

- Usually preceded by an upper respiratory tract <u>virus</u>, such as rhinovirus, coronavirus or influenza virus.

- Bacterial causes are rare but can include *S. pneumoniae*, *H. influenzae* or atypical pathogens (e.g., *Mycoplasma pneumoniae*).

- Diagnosis is made by ruling out other causes of acute cough (e.g., pneumonia, COPD exacerbation). <u>Chest X-ray</u> findings are typically <u>normal</u> and cultures are not routinely performed.

- <u>Antibiotics are not recommended</u>. The symptoms are generally self-limiting and can be managed with <u>supportive care</u> (e.g., cough suppressants, expectorants, analgesics).

Pertussis

Acute bronchitis caused by <u>*Bordetella pertussis*</u> (and commonly known as <u>whooping cough</u>) can be distinguished from other causes of bronchitis by the characteristic series of forceful coughs followed by an inspiratory "whoop" sound. Diagnosis can be confirmed with a nasopharyngeal swab culture or PCR test for *B. pertussis*.

Pertussis is <u>highly contagious</u> and should be treated with <u>macrolides</u> (azithromycin, clarithromycin), which are highly effective at eradicating *B. pertussis* and preventing transmission to vulnerable populations (e.g., infants).

ACUTE BACTERIAL EXACERBATION OF COPD

- COPD is often diagnosed in older patients who smoke (or have a long history of smoking). The Global Initiative for Chronic Obstructive Lung Disease (<u>GOLD</u>) <u>guideline</u> defines a <u>COPD exacerbation</u> as an <u>acute increase in symptoms</u>, beyond normal day-to-day variation, that necessitates a change in COPD medications.

- The <u>three cardinal symptoms</u> of a COPD exacerbation are: <u>increased dyspnea, increased sputum volume</u> and <u>increased sputum purulence</u>.

- Exacerbations can be triggered by viral infections, bacterial infections (e.g., <u>*H. influenzae, M. catarrhalis, S. pneumoniae*</u>), environmental pollution or an unknown cause.

- Supportive treatment (e.g., oxygen, systemic steroids, inhaled bronchodilators) is often adequate, but <u>antibiotics</u> should be administered to patients who meet select criteria (see diagram that follows).

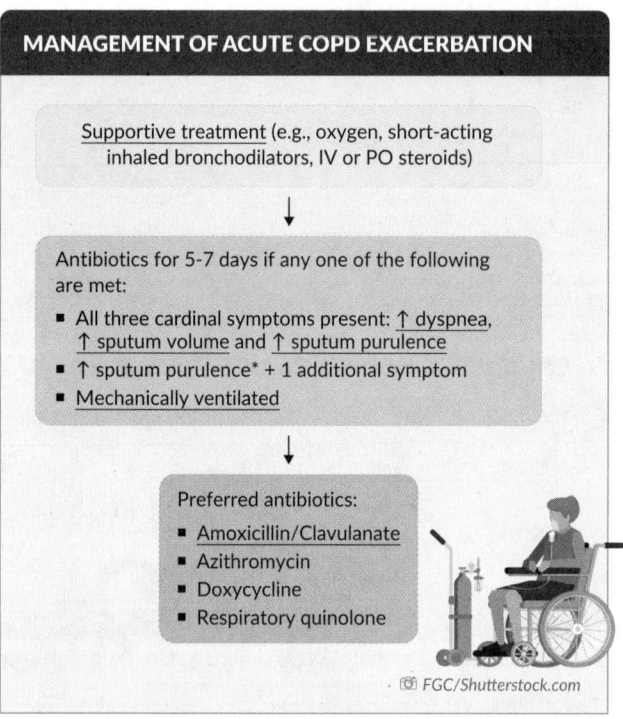

MANAGEMENT OF ACUTE COPD EXACERBATION

Supportive treatment (e.g., oxygen, short-acting inhaled bronchodilators, IV or PO steroids)

↓

Antibiotics for 5-7 days if any one of the following are met:
- All three cardinal symptoms present: ↑ dyspnea, ↑ sputum volume and ↑ sputum purulence
- ↑ sputum purulence* + 1 additional symptom
- Mechanically ventilated

↓

Preferred antibiotics:
- <u>Amoxicillin/Clavulanate</u>
- Azithromycin
- Doxycycline
- Respiratory quinolone

FGC/Shutterstock.com

Purulent sputum is thick and often yellow or green. If sputum purulence is increased, only 1 additional cardinal symptom (↑ dyspnea or ↑ sputum volume) is needed to justify antibiotic treatment.

COMMUNITY-ACQUIRED PNEUMONIA

Common pneumonia symptoms include <u>shortness of breath</u>, <u>fever, cough</u> with <u>purulent sputum</u>, pleuritic chest pain, <u>rales</u> (crackling noises in the lungs), <u>tachypnea (increased respiratory rate)</u> and decreased breath sounds. A <u>chest X-ray</u> is the <u>gold standard</u> diagnostic test and will have "<u>infiltrates</u>," "<u>opacities</u>" or "<u>consolidations</u>" to indicate pneumonia.

Community-acquired pneumonia (<u>CAP</u>) is a lung infection contracted outside of healthcare facilities and can be bacterial, viral or fungal (rare). When symptoms are <u>mild</u> (e.g., the patient is not hospitalized and is able to complete daily activities), it can be termed "<u>walking pneumonia</u>." Most bacterial cases are caused by *S. pneumoniae, H. influenzae, M. pneumoniae* and possibly *C. pneumoniae*.

Antibiotic regimens for CAP are designed to provide reliable activity against the likely causative pathogens, including resistant strains. The spectrum of activity of the specific antibiotic must be considered rather than using class trends (e.g., <u>ciprofloxacin</u> is not used for CAP; it is not a respiratory quinolone because it <u>does not</u> reliably <u>cover *S. pneumoniae*</u>). The usual <u>duration of treatment</u> for CAP is <u>5 – 7 days</u>.

INFECTIOUS DISEASES

Outpatient CAP Treatment

Outpatient treatment of CAP requires an assessment of patient comorbidities, which increase the risk of antibiotic resistance (e.g., drug-resistant *S. pneumoniae*) and requires broader coverage.

The Study Tip Gal and Case Scenario below describe a stepwise approach to selecting an empiric CAP regimen based on patient-specific criteria and known safety issues with select drugs/drug classes (as detailed in the Infectious Diseases I chapter). Lefamulin *(Xenleta)* is FDA-approved for CAP treatment but has not yet been incorporated into guidelines and is not included in the recommendations below.

OUTPATIENT CAP ASSESSMENT AND TREATMENT

Step 1: look for comorbidities (chronic heart, lung, liver or renal disease; diabetes mellitus; alcohol use disorder; malignancy; or asplenia)

Step 2: decide if the patient falls into the category of "Healthy" or "High-Risk" (see below)

Step 3: choose one option within the assigned category; be sure to look for allergies, drug-disease interactions (e.g., quinolones and seizures), drug-drug interactions (e.g., QT prolongation) and culture results (if available)

PATIENT CHARACTERISTICS	RECOMMENDED EMPIRIC REGIMEN
Healthy **No comorbidities (see Step 1 above)**	■ Amoxicillin high-dose (1 gram TID), or ■ Doxycycline, or ■ Macrolide (azithromycin or clarithromycin) if local pneumococcal resistance is < 25%
High-Risk **With comorbidities (see Step 1 above)**	■ Beta-lactam + macrolide or doxycycline ❑ Amoxicillin/clavulanate or cephalosporin (e.g., cefpodoxime, cefuroxime) plus ❑ Macrolide or doxycycline ■ Respiratory quinolone monotherapy ❑ Moxifloxacin, levofloxacin or gemifloxacin

CASE SCENARIO

RP is a 46-year-old female who presents to the urgent care clinic with shortness of breath, productive cough and a temperature of 100.8°F. A chest X-ray reveals a left lower lobe infiltrate. Her past medical history includes back pain, schizophrenia and a penicillin allergy (hives). Her scheduled medications include *Geodon* 40 mg PO BID and trazodone 50 mg PO QHS. Which empiric antibiotic regimen should RP receive for pneumonia?

Stepwise approach: RP's past medical history does not include any of the chronic comorbidities listed in Step 1. She is not at risk for drug-resistant *S. pneumoniae* and can be treated per the "Healthy" patient category. The choice is between high-dose amoxicillin, doxycycline or a macrolide. Amoxicillin should be avoided given her penicillin allergy. Macrolides can prolong the QT interval. Since *Geodon* and trazodone can also prolong the QT interval, causing additive risk, doxycycline would be the best choice in this patient with outpatient CAP.

Inpatient CAP Treatment

Selection of an empiric regimen is based on the severity of illness and often includes IV antibiotics initially.

Nonsevere (admission to a general medicine unit):

■ Beta-lactam + macrolide or doxycycline
❑ Preferred beta-lactams: ceftriaxone, cefotaxime, ceftaroline or ampicillin/sulbactam
■ Respiratory quinolone monotherapy

Severe (admission to the ICU):

■ Beta-lactam + macrolide
■ Beta-lactam + respiratory quinolone (do not use quinolone monotherapy)

Risk factors for *Pseudomonas* and/or MRSA:

■ MRSA (prior respiratory isolation or positive nasal swab): add coverage with vancomycin or linezolid
■ *Pseudomonas* (prior respiratory isolation): use a beta-lactam antibiotic with activity against *Pseudomonas*, such as piperacillin/tazobactam, cefepime, ceftazidime, imipenem/cilastatin or meropenem.
■ Hospitalization, and use of parenteral antibiotics, in the past 90 days: use a regimen with antibiotics active against both MRSA and *Pseudomonas*

INFECTIOUS DISEASES

HOSPITAL-ACQUIRED AND VENTILATOR-ASSOCIATED PNEUMONIA

Hospital-acquired pneumonia (HAP) has an onset > 48 hours after hospital admission. HAP is the leading infectious cause of death in ICU patients.

Ventilator-associated pneumonia (VAP) occurs > 48 hours after the start of mechanical ventilation and can lead to a prolonged duration of ventilation and hospitalization. The rate of VAP can be reduced by proper hand-washing, elevating the head of the bed ≥ 30 degrees, weaning off the ventilator as soon as possible, removing nasogastric (NG) tubes when possible and discontinuing unnecessary stress ulcer prophylaxis (e.g., with proton pump inhibitors).

Common pathogens in HAP and VAP

Nosocomial pathogens are common in HAP and VAP. The risk for MRSA and MDR Gram-negative rods, including _P. aeruginosa_, _Acinetobacter_ spp., _Enterobacter_ spp., _E. coli_ and _Klebsiella_ spp., is increased in select cases.

Treatment of HAP and VAP

The degree of risk helps guide empiric treatment. The Study Tip Gal below lists the recommended antibiotics for coverage of MRSA and _Pseudomonas_ in HAP and VAP and tips for selecting the correct regimen on the exam. Treat for 7 days; shorter or longer treatment durations may be indicated based on clinical, radiologic and laboratory parameters.

HAP/VAP: SELECTING AN EMPIRIC REGIMEN

All patients need an antibiotic for _Pseudomonas_ and MSSA
- Example agents:
  - ❏ Cefepime
  - ❏ Piperacillin/tazobactam
  - ❏ Levofloxacin

Add vancomycin or linezolid if risk for MRSA
- Risk factors: IV antibiotic use in the past 90 days, MRSA prevalence in hospital unit is > 20% or uknown, prior MRSA infection or positive MRSA nasal swab
- Example regimens:
  - ❏ Cefepime + vancomycin
  - ❏ Meropenem + linezolid
  - ❏ Aztreonam + vancomycin

Use two antibiotics for _Pseudomonas_ if risk for MDR Gram-negative pathogens
- Risk factors: IV antibiotic use in the past 90 days, prevalence of Gram-negative resistance in hospital unit is > 10%, hospitalized ≥ 5 days prior to the onset of VAP
- Example regimens (typically MRSA risk is also present):
  - ❏ Piperacillin/tazobactam + ciprofloxacin + vancomycin
  - ❏ Cefepime + gentamicin + linezolid

Antibiotics for _Pseudomonas_ (do not use two beta-lactams together)
Beta-lactams: piperacillin/tazobactam, cefepime, ceftazidime, imipenem/cilastatin, meropenem

Levofloxacin or ciprofloxacin

Aztreonam

Tobramycin, gentamicin or amikacin*

*These agents are always used in combination with another antipseudomonal drug.

TUBERCULOSIS

Tuberculosis (TB) is caused by _Mycobacterium tuberculosis_ (an aerobic, non-spore forming bacillus). It primarily infects the lungs but can disseminate (spread) to other organs. The disease has two phases: latent and active.

With latent disease, the immune system is able to contain the infection and the patient lacks symptoms. Active pulmonary TB is transmitted by aerosolized droplets (e.g., sneezing, coughing, talking) and is highly contagious. It most often presents with cough/hemoptysis (coughing up blood), purulent sputum, fever, night sweats and unintentional weight loss. Hospitalized patients require isolation in a single negative-pressure room and healthcare workers caring for them must wear a respirator mask (e.g., an N95 face mask).

Latent Tuberculosis Diagnosis

Latent disease can be diagnosed using the tuberculin skin test (TST), also called a purified protein derivative (PPD) test, or an interferon-gamma release assay (IGRA) blood test. With a TST, a solution is injected intradermally and the skin area is inspected for induration (a raised area) 48 – 72 hours later (see criteria for a positive result in the box on the following page). Since a false-positive TST can occur in those who have received the bacille Calmette-Guerin (BCG) vaccine (used in countries with high TB rates), an IGRA blood test is preferred in these patients (does not require a follow-up visit). Any patient with a positive TST or IGRA test should be screened for the presence of active TB (e.g., clinical symptoms, chest X-ray) before latent TB treatment is initiated.

DIAGNOSIS OF LATENT TB: CRITERIA FOR POSITIVE TB SKIN TEST (TST) RESULTS

≥ 5 mm induration
Close contacts of recent active TB cases
HIV infection
Immunosuppression (e.g., organ transplantation, chemotherapy)

≥ 10 mm induration
Immigrants from high burden countries
Clinical risk (e.g., IV drug users, diabetes)
Residents/employees of "high-risk" congregate settings (e.g., prisons, healthcare facilities, homeless shelters)

≥ 15 mm induration
Patients with no risk factors

© Gritsalak Karalak © 123RF.com

Induration = raised area

Latent Tuberculosis Treatment

Treatment of latent TB with one of the following regimens greatly reduces the risk of developing active disease. There are advantages and disadvantages of each, but in general, shorter regimens (e.g., 3 or 4 months) are preferred in most adults due to higher completion rates and less risk of hepatotoxicity compared to longer courses of isoniazid (INH). Drug interactions are the biggest barrier to rifampin- and rifapentine-based regimens (see the drug table on the following page).

Regimen options:

- INH and rifapentine once weekly for 12 weeks via directly observed therapy (DOT) or self-administered. Do not use this regimen in pregnant patients.

- INH with rifampin daily for 3 months.

- Rifampin 600 mg daily for 4 months.

- INH 300 mg daily for 6 or 9 months.

  - May be preferred in HIV-positive patients taking antiretroviral therapy (due to the risk for drug interactions). If used, a 9-month course of treatment is recommended.

Active Tuberculosis Diagnosis

A positive TST or IGRA is likely with active TB, but the diagnosis must be confirmed. *M. tuberculosis* (MTB) is an acid-fast bacilli (AFB). It can be detected with an AFB smear of sputum samples, however the AFB stain is not specific to MTB and a definitive diagnosis must be made with polymerase chain reaction (PCR) or sputum culture results. MTB is a slow-growing organism; the final culture and susceptibility results can take up to 6 weeks.

Active Tuberculosis Treatment

Active TB treatment is divided into two phases (intensive and continuation). To avoid resistance, the preferred intensive phase regimen consists of four drugs: rifampin, isoniazid, pyrazinamide and ethambutol for two months (this regimen is known as "RIPE" therapy).

In the continuation phase (typically four months) treatment can be scaled back to two drugs (commonly rifampin and isoniazid) depending on the drug susceptibility of the isolate. The continuation phase is extended to seven months in select cases (e.g., the sputum culture remains positive after two months of treatment, or if intensive phase treatment did not include pyrazinamide).

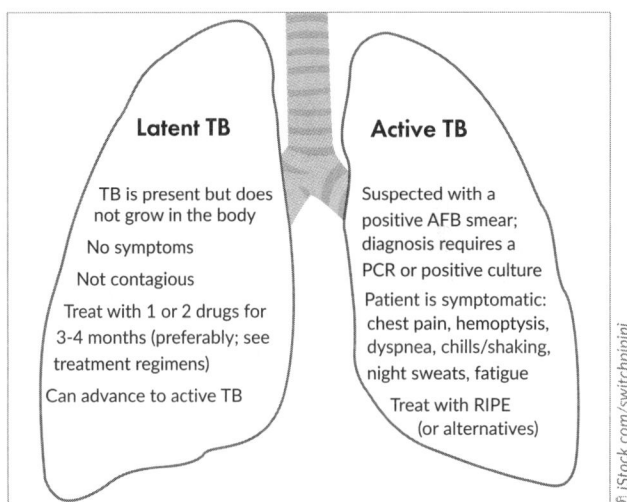

Latent TB

TB is present but does not grow in the body

No symptoms

Not contagious

Treat with 1 or 2 drugs for 3-4 months (preferably; see treatment regimens)

Can advance to active TB

Active TB

Suspected with a positive AFB smear; diagnosis requires a PCR or positive culture

Patient is symptomatic: chest pain, hemoptysis, dyspnea, chills/shaking, night sweats, fatigue

Treat with RIPE (or alternatives)

© iStock.com/switchpipipi

DOT is used to increase medication adherence and is preferred in select populations (homeless, drug-resistant disease, adherence issues, positive sputum smears and delayed culture positivity). Alternative dosing regimens (e.g., drugs administered 2 – 3 times per week) can be used in this setting. Daily dosing regimens are strongly encouraged if DOT is not possible.

TB can be resistant to INH or rifampin; if TB is resistant to both, it is called multidrug-resistant TB (MDR-TB). Resistant TB requires use of second-line agents and longer durations of treatment (up to 24 months). While many agents can be used, preferred drugs include quinolones (moxifloxacin or levofloxacin) or injectables (streptomycin, amikacin or kanamycin).

In extremely drug-resistant TB (XDR-TB), bedaquiline (*Sirturo*) can be used, but it has boxed warnings for QT prolongation and an increased risk of death compared to placebo. Pretomanid is approved for MDR-TB or XDR-TB of the lung, in combination with bedaquiline and linezolid. It has many side effects, including hepatotoxicity, peripheral neuropathy (can be severe), optic neuropathy, myelosuppression and QT prolongation.

PREFERRED ACTIVE TB REGIMEN (TOTAL TREATMENT DURATION: 6 MONTHS)

Intensive Phase	
4 drugs for 2 months (until cultures and susceptibilities are available)	RIPE: Rifampin (RIF) + Isoniazid (INH) + Pyrazinamide (PZA) + Ethambutol; daily or 5x per week Duration: 8 weeks
Continuation Phase	
2 drugs for 4 months (based on culture and susceptibility results)	INH and RIF; daily, 5x per week or 3x per week Duration: 18 weeks

RIPE Therapy for Active TB

DRUG	DOSING	SAFETY/SIDE EFFECTS/MONITORING
Rifampin *(Rifadin)*	10 mg/kg (max 600 mg) PO daily or 2-3x/week Doses differ for other indications Take on an empty stomach	**CONTRAINDICATIONS** Do not use with protease inhibitors **SIDE EFFECTS** ↑ LFTs, hemolytic anemia (detected with a positive Coombs test), flu-like syndrome, GI upset, rash/pruritus Orange-red discoloration of body secretions (sputum, urine, sweat, tears, teeth); can stain contact lenses, clothing and bedsheets **NOTES** Rifampin has many drug-drug interactions (see Rifampin Drug Interactions on the following page); rifabutin has fewer drug interactions and can replace rifampin in some cases (e.g., HIV patients taking protease inhibitors), though a drug-drug interaction screen is still needed
Isoniazid	5 mg/kg (max 300 mg) PO daily or 15 mg/kg (max 900 mg) 1-3x/week Take on an empty stomach Use pyridoxine (vitamin B6) 25-50 mg PO daily to ↓ the risk of INH-associated peripheral neuropathy	**BOXED WARNING** Severe (and fatal) hepatitis **CONTRAINDICATIONS** Active liver disease, previous severe adverse reaction to isoniazid **WARNINGS** Peripheral neuropathy, higher risk in patients predisposed to neuropathy (e.g., diabetes, HIV, renal failure, alcohol use disorder, elderly, malnourished); pyridoxine (vitamin B6) supplementation is recommended for these patients and patients who are pregnant or breastfeeding **SIDE EFFECTS** ↑ LFTs (usually asymptomatic), drug-induced lupus erythematosus (DILE), hemolytic anemia (detected with a positive Coombs test), agranulocytosis, aplastic anemia, hyperglycemia, headache, GI upset, pancreatitis, severe skin reactions (SJS/DRESS), optic neuritis
Pyrazinamide	20-25 mg/kg PO daily (max daily doses vary based on weight) CrCl < 30 mL/min: extend interval	**CONTRAINDICATIONS** Acute gout, severe hepatic damage **SIDE EFFECTS** ↑ LFTs, hyperuricemia/gout, GI upset, malaise, arthralgia, myalgia, rash
Ethambutol *(Myambutol)*	15-20 mg/kg (max 1.6 grams) PO daily or 25-30 mg/kg (max 2.4 grams) 3x/week or 50 mg/kg (max 4 grams) 2x/week CrCl < 50 mL/min: extend interval	**CONTRAINDICATIONS** Optic neuritis (risk vs. benefit decision); do not use in young children, unconscious patients or any patient who cannot discern and report visual changes **SIDE EFFECTS** ↑ LFTs, optic neuritis (dose-related), ↓ visual acuity, partial loss of vision/blind spot and/or color blindness (usually reversible), rash, headache, confusion, hallucinations, N/V

Rifampin Drug Interactions

- <u>Rifampin</u> is a <u>potent inducer</u> of CYP450 1A2, 2C8, 2C9, 2C19, <u>3A4</u> and <u>P-glycoprotein</u>. It can significantly ↓ the concentration and therapeutic <u>effect of many other drugs</u>.

- Some notable interactions include ↓ serum concentrations of:

  - <u>Protease inhibitors</u> (substitute rifabutin).

  - <u>Warfarin</u> (a <u>very large ↓ in INR</u> is common; requires increased doses of warfarin).

  - <u>Oral contraceptives</u> (↓ efficacy; requires additional backup contraceptive methods).

- <u>Do not use</u> rifampin with <u>apixaban, rivaroxaban</u>, edoxaban, or dabigatran.

- It is important to <u>screen the medication profile for drug interactions</u> with rifampin. See the Drug Interactions chapter for more information.

RIPE THERAPY FOR TB

MONITOR INFECTION
Sputum sample (for culture), symptoms and chest X-ray (are lungs clear or clearing up?)

DRUG-SPECIFIC KEY POINTS
All RIPE Drugs
↑ LFTs, including total bilirubin – monitor

Rifampin
Orange bodily secretions

Strong CYP450 inducer (can use rifabutin if unacceptable DDIs)

Flu-like symptoms

Isoniazid
Peripheral neuropathy: give with pyridoxine (vitamin B6) 25-50 mg PO daily

Monitor for symptoms of DILE

Rifampin and Isoniazid
Risk for hemolytic anemia (identified by a positive Coombs test)

Pyrazinamide
↑ uric acid – do not use with acute gout

Ethambutol
Visual damage (requires baseline and monthly vision exams)

Confusion/hallucinations

INFECTIVE ENDOCARDITIS

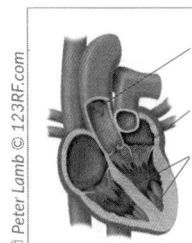

Free bacterial "vegetation" causing systemic embolus

Bacterial infection on valve

Bacterial infection on endocardial surface

© Peter Lamb © 123RF.com

An infection of the inner tissue of the heart, typically the <u>heart valves</u>, is called infective endocarditis (IE). Patients who have prosthetic heart valves, chronic IV access, IV drug abuse or frequent and chronic healthcare exposure are some of those who are most at risk. The majority of patients present with fever, with or without a heart murmur. IE is diagnosed using the Modified Duke Criteria, which includes an <u>echocardiogram</u> to visualize the vegetation and <u>positive blood cultures</u>. The three most common species of organisms that cause IE are <u>staphylococci, streptococci</u> and <u>enterococci</u>.

IE is generally fatal if left untreated. Empiric treatment often includes vancomycin and ceftriaxone. Definitive treatment, and antibiotic duration for IE, are dependent on the pathogen, the type of infected valve (native or prosthetic) and the susceptibility results. <u>Gentamicin</u> is added to the antimicrobial regimen for <u>synergy</u> when the infection is more difficult to eradicate, such as with prosthetic valve infections or when treating more resistant organisms. In some cases, the risk of additive nephrotoxicity outweighs the benefit and it is left off of the regimen (e.g., when vancomycin is used for streptococcal endocarditis in patients with a beta-lactam allergy).

In general, 4 – 6 weeks of <u>IV antibiotic treatment is required</u>; when prosthetic valves and/or more resistant organisms are involved, treatment durations are at the upper end of this range or longer. The duration of gentamicin synergy varies from 2 – 6 weeks, depending on the organism being treated and the presence or absence of a prosthetic valve. When <u>gentamicin</u> is used for <u>synergy</u>, traditional dosing is typically used to target <u>peak levels of 3 – 4 mcg/mL</u> and <u>trough levels < 1 mcg/mL</u>. Extended interval dosing of aminoglycosides is less common when treating IE.

Some bacteria can form a biofilm (slime layer), especially on prosthetic valves. This is difficult for some antibiotics to penetrate. Rifampin may be used in cases of staphylococcal prosthetic valve endocarditis due to its ability to treat organisms in a biofilm.

INFECTIVE ENDOCARDITIS TREATMENT

ORGANISM	PREFERRED ANTIBIOTIC REGIMEN
Viridans group streptococci	Penicillin or ceftriaxone (± gentamicin)
	If beta-lactam allergy, use vancomycin monotherapy
Staphylococci (MSSA)	Nafcillin or cefazolin (+ gentamicin and rifampin if prosthetic valve)
	If beta-lactam allergy, use vancomycin* (+ gentamicin and rifampin if prosthetic valve)
Staphylococci (MRSA)	Vancomycin* (+ gentamicin and rifampin if prosthetic valve)
Enterococci	For both native and prosthetic valve IE: penicillin or ampicillin + gentamicin or ampicillin + high-dose ceftriaxone
	If beta-lactam allergy, use vancomycin + gentamicin
	If VRE, use daptomycin or linezolid

*Daptomycin monotherapy is an alternative for MSSA and MRSA IE when the patient has a beta-lactam allergy and no prosthetic valve.

INFECTIVE ENDOCARDITIS DENTAL PROPHYLAXIS

The mouth contains bacteria that can enter the blood during dental procedures. The bacteria can travel to the heart, where they can settle on the myocardial lining, a heart valve or a blood vessel. IE after dental procedures is rare, but the risk is increased with certain cardiac conditions. In patients at high risk, antibiotics should be used before all dental procedures that involve manipulation of gingival tissue (gums), the periapical region (near the root of the tooth) or perforation of the oral mucosa. See the following table for the risk criteria and recommended prophylaxis regimens.

PATIENTS AT HIGH RISK FOR IE	ADULT PROPHYLAXIS REGIMENS*
Dental work needed, such as a root canal **+** **Select cardiac conditions, including:** 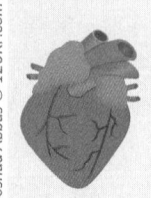 ■ Artificial (prosthetic) heart valve or heart valve repaired with artificial material ■ History of endocarditis ■ Heart transplant with abnormal heart valve function ■ Certain congenital heart defects including heart/heart valve disease	All given as a single dose 30-60 minutes before the dental procedure **First line:** Amoxicillin 2 grams PO **If unable to take oral medication:** Ampicillin 2 grams IM/IV, or Cefazolin or ceftriaxone 1 gram IM/IV **If able to take oral medication but allergic to penicillin**: Azithromycin or clarithromycin 500 mg, or Doxycyline 100 mg

*In pediatric patients, use weight-based doses of the same antibiotics.
**In practice, cephalosporins may be considered if penicillin reaction is mild (no history of anaphylaxis, angioedema or urticaria); on the exam, look for a safer option.

INTRA-ABDOMINAL INFECTIONS

Intra-abdominal infections are a common cause of hospital admission and the second most common cause of infectious mortality in ICU patients. They are usually polymicrobial and can occur in any intra-abdominal organ or space. Types of infections include: primary, secondary and tertiary peritonitis, and biliary tract infections (cholecystitis and cholangitis).

Primary peritonitis, referred to as spontaneous bacterial peritonitis (SBP), is an infection of the peritoneal space that often occurs in patients with liver disease (e.g., cirrhosis). The most likely pathogens are streptococci, enteric Gram-negative organisms (Proteus, E. Coli and Klebsiella, or PEK) and, rarely, anaerobes.

The drug of choice is ceftriaxone for 5 – 7 days. Alternative treatments include ampicillin, gentamicin or a quinolone. SMX/TMP, ofloxacin or ciprofloxacin can be used for primary or secondary prophylaxis of SBP.

Secondary peritonitis is caused by a traumatic event (e.g., ulceration, ischemia, obstruction or surgery). Abscesses are common and should be drained, and damaged tissue may require surgery. The most likely pathogens are streptococci, enteric Gram-negatives and anaerobes (Bacteroides fragilis). In more severe cases (critically ill patients in the ICU), coverage of Pseudomonas and CAPES organisms may be necessary.

Cholecystitis is an acute inflammation of the gallbladder due to an obstructive stone. It is usually managed surgically with a cholecystectomy. Infection may not be the precipitating factor but is present in ~50% of cases. If an infection is present, likely pathogens and antimicrobial selection are similar to primary peritonitis.

Cholangitis is an infection of the common bile duct and is generally managed with bile decompression and antimicrobial therapy. Likely pathogens and antimicrobial selection are similar to secondary peritonitis.

Treatment of intra-abdominal infections (except primary peritonitis) involves selecting one or more antibiotics that will cover the likely pathogens, including anaerobes. This is accomplished with a single drug in some cases. If the antibiotic selected does not have anaerobic coverage, an additional antibiotic (usually metronidazole) must be added (see the Infectious Diseases I chapter for a discussion of antibiotic spectrum of activity).

The duration of treatment is 4 – 7 days for mild-moderate cases and 7 – 14 days for severe cases. If an intra-abdominal abscess is present, ≥ 14 days of treatment may be required.

MANAGEMENT OF SECONDARY PERITONITIS AND CHOLANGITIS

MILD-TO-MODERATE INFECTIONS	HIGH-SEVERITY INFECTIONS (ICU PATIENT)
Cover PEK, anaerobes, streptococci ± enterococci	Cover PEK, CAPES, *Pseudomonas*, anaerobes, streptococci ± enterococci
Possible regimens include:	Possible regimens include:
Cefoxitin	Carbapenem (except ertapenem)
Ertapenem	Piperacillin/tazobactam
Moxifloxacin	(Cefepime or ceftazidime) + metronidazole
(Cefazolin, cefuroxime or ceftriaxone) + metronidazole	(Ciprofloxacin or levofloxacin) + metronidazole
(Ciprofloxacin or levofloxacin) + metronidazole	Cefazolin + (aztreonam or aminoglycoside) + metronidazole

PEK (enteric GNRs) = Proteus, E. coli, Klebsiella; CAPES (nosocomial GNRs) = Citrobacter, Acinetobacter, Providencia, Enterobacter, Serratia

SKIN AND SOFT-TISSUE INFECTIONS (SSTIs)

Skin and soft-tissue infections (SSTIs) can involve any or all layers of the skin (epidermis, dermis and subcutaneous fat), fascia and muscle. SSTIs usually result from the introduction of bacteria through breaks in the skin barrier, and less frequently from an infection that spreads from the bloodstream to the skin. Minor local trauma (small cuts, insect bites) can be the provoking event and can progress to a deeper infection.

SSTIs can be broadly divided into infections that are superficial (impetigo, furuncles and carbuncles), nonpurulent infections that penetrate the subcutaneous tissues (cellulitis) and purulent (contains pus) infections (abscesses). Each is further categorized as mild, moderate or severe, which impacts the choice of antibiotics and the route (topical, PO or IV). Common antibiotics used for outpatient treatment of mild-moderate infections are listed in the table on the following page. The list is not all-inclusive but represents commonly used oral antibiotics.

SSTI CLASSIFICATIONS

Mild infection
Systemic signs absent

Moderate infection
Systemic signs present

Systemic signs:
Temperature > 100.4°F

Heart rate > 90 BPM

WBC > 12,000 or < 4000 cells/mm³

Severe infection
Systemic signs present, signs of a deeper infection (e.g., fluid-filled blisters, skin sloughing, hypotension or evidence of organ dysfunction), patient is immunocompromised or failed oral antibiotics + incision and drainage (for purulent infections).

INFECTIOUS DISEASES

OUTPATIENT TREATMENT OF COMMON SKIN AND SOFT-TISSUE INFECTIONS

INFECTION	PRESENTATION	TREATMENT/COMMENTS
Superficial Infections		
Impetigo *Strep.* spp., *S. aureus* (most often MSSA) 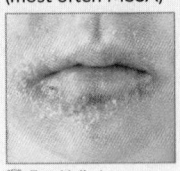 FotoHelin/ Shutterstock.com	Common in children. A blister-like rash found anywhere on the skin, usually around the nose, mouth, hands and arms. Blisters produce a thick, yellowish clear fluid that dries and forms honey-colored crusts over the area.	Use warm, wet compresses to help remove dried crusts. Apply a topical antibiotic, typically mupirocin. Retapamulin (*Altabax*) and ozenoxacin (*Xepi*) are alternative treatments approved for impetigo. **If numerous lesions, use systemic antibiotics that cover MSSA:** ■ Cephalexin 250 mg PO QID
Folliculitis/furuncles/ carbuncles *S. aureus*, including community-acquired MRSA (CA-MRSA) 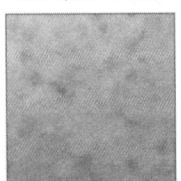 ocskaymark © 123RF.com	Folliculitis: a hair follicle infection that looks like a red pimple. Furuncle (boil): an infection in the hair follicle and surrounding tissue. Carbuncle: a group of infected furuncles.	Folliculitis and furuncles may require only warm compresses to ↓ inflammation and help with drainage. Carbuncles require incision & drainage (I&D) to drain pus. **If systemic signs, use antibiotics that cover MSSA:** ■ Cephalexin 500 mg PO QID **If non-responsive to initial treatment, change to a drug with CA-MRSA coverage:** ■ SMX/TMP DS 1-2 tablets PO BID ■ Doxycycline 100 mg PO BID Occasionally, folliculitis is due to a fungal infection and can be treated with ketoconazole cream.
Cellulitis (Non-Purulent Infections)		
Mild infection Streptococci, including *S. pyogenes* (Group A strep, GAS), *S. aureus* 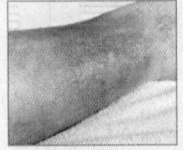 Blueee77/ Shutterstock.com	Mild symptoms: localized pain, swelling, redness, warmth. Often occurs on the legs, generally unilateral, and spreads to other areas.	**Oral antibiotics must be active against streptococci (± MSSA):** ■ Cephalexin 500 mg PO QID ■ Clindamycin 300 mg PO QID (if beta-lactam allergy) Other antibiotics that cover *Streptococcus* can be used (e.g., penicillin VK, dicloxacillin). Duration of treatment: 5 days (longer if no improvement within 5 days). Moderate-severe infections require IV treatment; refer to chapter text for severity classification.
Abscess (Purulent Infections)		
Mild-moderate purulent infection Commonly caused by *S. aureus*, including CA-MRSA 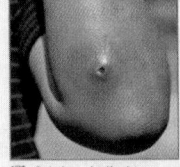 Criniger kolio/ Shutterstock.com	Initially appears as a localized fluid collection (abscess). Recurrent MRSA infections: consider nasal decolonization with nasal mupirocin, and skin decolonization with chlorhexidine or dilute bleach. Contagious; to avoid spreading, keep the lesion covered, do not share personal towels and wash sheets/towels/clothing in hot water.	Single abscess, no systemic signs (mild infection): primary treatment is I&D. **If systemic signs or multiple sites (moderate infection), perform I&D, culture fluid and use oral antibiotics that cover CA-MRSA:** ■ SMX/TMP DS 1-2 tablets PO BID ■ Doxycycline 100 mg PO BID ■ Minocycline 200 mg PO x 1, then 100 mg PO BID ■ Clindamycin 300 mg PO QID Linezolid covers CA-MRSA, but is more expensive. If cultures show MSSA, use cephalexin.

SEVERE SKIN AND SOFT TISSUE INFECTIONS

Severe purulent infections or those in more complicated patients (e.g., failed initial treatment, immunocompromised) can cause more critical conditions (e.g., sepsis) and require IV antibiotics initially. Drugs that are active against MRSA should be selected. Once the patient is stable and the pathogen/s have been identified, it is often possible to transition to oral antibiotics to complete treatment.

INFECTION	NOTES	TREATMENT
Severe purulent SSTI	Duration of therapy: 7-14 days	Use antibiotics with MRSA activity: Vancomycin (goal trough 10-15 mcg/mL) Daptomycin Linezolid Others: ceftaroline, tedizolid, telavancin Once clinically stable, transition to PO antibiotics
Necrotizing fasciitis *S. pyogenes* (Group A Strep, GAS) is common, as well as some other bacteria, such as *Clostridium* spp.	A life-threatening, fast-moving type of skin infection that rapidly destroys tissue and can quickly penetrate down to the muscle. Presentation: intense pain/tenderness over affected skin and underlying muscle, with skin discoloration, edema and systemic signs. Requires emergency treatment in a hospital.	Empiric therapy is broad: Vancomycin + beta-lactam (piperacillin/tazobactam, imipenem/cilastatin or meropenem)

DIABETIC FOOT INFECTIONS

Patients with diabetes are at high risk for foot infections because of neuropathic damage and compromised blood flow to the lower extremities. Foot infections are the most common cause of amputation. Ulcers are evaluated for the presence of inflammation and purulence and then classified by severity, which guides management (e.g., surgery and/or antibiotics). *Staphylococcus* spp. and *Streptococcus* spp. are the predominant pathogens in diabetic foot infections. Since infections can be polymicrobial, broad-spectrum empiric treatment is usually necessary. Cultures should be performed in order to narrow therapy whenever possible. Knowledge of antibiotics that cover common MDR pathogens (e.g., MRSA, *Pseudomonas*) and anaerobic organisms is important for identifying appropriate treatment on the exam.

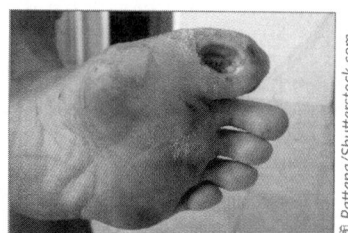

Most common cause of amputations. Starts in soft tissue, can spread into bone (osteomyelitis). Proper foot care is crucial to avoid infections.

It is imperative that patients follow proper foot care and evaluation, as discussed in the Diabetes chapter. If a deeper infection is present, such as osteomyelitis, longer courses of antibiotics (often IV) are required.

ETIOLOGY	GRAM-POSITIVE	GRAM-NEGATIVE
Aerobic	*S. aureus* (including MRSA) Group A *Streptococcus* Viridans group streptococci *S. epidermidis*	*E. coli* *Klebsiella pneumoniae* *Proteus mirabilis* *Enterobacter cloacae* *Pseudomonas aeruginosa*
Anaerobic	*Peptostreptococcus* *Clostridium perfringens*	*Bacteroides fragilis* and others

TREATMENT OF MODERATE-SEVERE DIABETIC FOOT INFECTIONS

TYPE OF REGIMEN	TREATMENT	DURATION OF TREATMENT
Monotherapy (when no MRSA coverage needed; cover MSSA)	Ampicillin/sulbactam, piperacillin/tazobactam,* a carbapenem (imipenem/cilastatin,* meropenem,* ertapenem) or moxifloxacin	7-14 days More severe, deep tissue infection: 2-4 weeks Severe, limb-threatening or bone/joint infection: 4-6 weeks Osteomyelitis: requires longer courses of therapy and may require chronic suppressive therapy
Combination therapy (when MRSA and *Pseudomonas* coverage needed)	Vancomycin plus one of the following: Ceftazidime,* cefepime,* piperacillin/tazobactam,* aztreonam* or a carbapenem* (except ertapenem) Note: consider adding anaerobic coverage (metronidazole) if ceftazidime, cefepime or aztreonam are selected Vancomycin alternatives: daptomycin or linezolid	

*Has Pseudomonas coverage.

URINARY TRACT INFECTIONS (UTIs)

Most urinary tract infections (UTIs) occur in the lower urinary tract, which includes the bladder (cystitis) and the urethra. More severe infections can occur in the kidneys (pyelonephritis), or the upper urinary tract. UTIs are more common in females than males, as the female urethra provides a shorter route for organisms to travel up into the bladder. Sexual intercourse can facilitate this movement; women who commonly develop UTIs after intercourse may be prescribed prophylactic antibiotics.

UTIs are classified as uncomplicated or complicated. Uncomplicated UTIs are those that occur in non-pregnant, premenopausal women who have no urologic abnormalities or comorbidities. An infection in males is considered to be complicated because it is likely due to some type of abnormality or obstruction, such as an enlarged prostate. Complicated infections can also result from a neurogenic bladder (e.g., spinal cord injury, stroke, multiple sclerosis), an obstruction (e.g., a stone) or the presence of an indwelling catheter (see the Medication Safety & Quality Improvement chapter for a discussion of ways to reduce catheter-associated infections).

Cystitis can be diagnosed based on the typical symptoms (see box to the right). For more complicated or severe infections, a urinalysis can indicate if an infection is present, and is considered positive when there is evidence of pyuria (positive leukocyte esterase or > 10 WBCs/mm^3) and bacteriuria (positive nitrite test or ≥ 10^5 bacteria/mL in asymptomatic patients, ≥ 10^3 bacteria/mL in symptomatic males and ≥ 10^2 bacteria/mL in symptomatic females and catheterized patients). The presence of bacteria alone is not indicative of a UTI and does not require treatment (exception: asymptomatic bacteriuria in pregnancy). A positive urinalysis can be followed by a urine culture to identify a causative organism.

UTI SYMPTOMS

Cystitis (Lower UTI)
- Urgency and frequency (the feeling of needing to go often and quickly), including overnight (nocturia)
- Dysuria (painful urination, burning)
- Suprapubic heaviness
- Hematuria (blood in the urine)

Pyelonephritis (Upper UTI)
- Flank/costovertebral angle pain
- Abdominal pain, nausea and vomiting
- Fever and malaise

Pyelonephritis

E. coli/other organisms

Cysitis (UTI)

designua © 123RF.com

UTI TREATMENT

DIAGNOSIS	DRUGS OF CHOICE		COMMENTS
Acute uncomplicated cystitis Occurs in females of child-bearing age (~15-45 years) Common pathogens: *Proteus*, <u>*E. coli*</u> (vast majority), *Klebsiella*, *S. saprophyticus*, enterococci	<u>Nitrofurantoin *(Macrobid)* 100 mg PO BID with food x 5 days</u> <u>(contraindicated if CrCl < 60 mL/min)</u> or <u>SMX/TMP DS 1 tablet PO BID x 3 days</u> (do not use if sulfa allergy or ≥ 20% *E. coli* resistance rate) or <u>Fosfomycin 3 grams x 1 dose</u> (inferior efficacy)		Usually treated empirically as an outpatient. If no response with first-line treatment, check a urine culture and treat accordingly. <u>Do not use moxifloxacin for UTIs</u> (does not reach high levels in the urine). Prophylaxis: if ≥ 3 episodes in 1 year, can use SMX/TMP SS 1 tablet daily, nitrofurantoin 50 mg PO daily, or SMX/TMP DS 1 tablet after sexual intercourse.
	Alternative Options		
	Beta-lactam (amoxicillin/clavulanate or cephalosporin) x 3-7 days or Ciprofloxacin 250 mg PO BID x 3 days* or Levofloxacin 250 mg PO daily x 3 days* *Quinolones: do not use in children, pregnant patients, those with seizures, neuropathy or QT prolongation risk; watch for tendinitis/rupture and BG changes (especially in patients with diabetes)	<u>Pregnancy:</u> <u>Amoxicillin</u> <u>Cephalexin</u> Fosfomycin (if beta-lactam allergy) Pregnant women with acute cystitis (symptomatic) should be treated for 7 days See the following page for a discussion on asymptomatic bacteriuria during pregnancy	
Acute pyelonephritis Common pathogens: *E. coli*, enterococci, *Proteus*, *Klebsiella*, *Pseudomonas*	**Moderately ill outpatient (PO)** <u>If local quinolone resistance ≤ 10%:</u> Ciprofloxacin 500 mg PO BID x 7 days Levofloxacin 750 mg PO daily x 5 days <u>If local quinolone resistance > 10%:</u> Ceftriaxone 1 gram IV/IM x 1, ertapenem 1 gram IV/IM x 1 or aminoglycoside extended-interval dose IV/IM x 1, then continue with a quinolone (as above) x 5-7 days SMX/TMP x 14 days Beta-lactam (amoxicillin/clavulanate, cefdinir, cefadroxil or cefpodoxime) x 10-14 days **Severely ill hospitalized patient (IV)** Initial: ceftriaxone, piperacillin/tazobactam, a quinolone (ciprofloxacin or levofloxacin) or a carbapenem (if ESBL-producing organism suspected) Step down to oral treatment options based on culture & susceptibility results Treatment duration: 5-14 days depending on regimen and clinical response		If risk for or documented *Pseudomonas* infection, consider piperacillin/tazobactam or an antipseudomonal carbapenem (meropenem, doripenem, imipenem/ cilastatin). Last-line options (in adults with pyelonephritis and complicated UTIs and no other treatment options): Cefiderocol *(Fetroja)* Imipenem/cilastatin/relebactam *(Recarbrio)* Meropenem/vaborbactam *(Vabomere)* Plazomicin *(Zemdri)*
Complicated UTI Common pathogens: *E. coli*, *Klebsiella*, *Enterobacter*, *Serratia*, *Pseudomonas*, enterococci, staphylococci	Similar options as noted above for pyelonephritis Use a <u>carbapenem</u> if <u>ESBL-producing</u> bacteria are present Treat for 7 days if there is prompt symptom relief Treat for 10-14 days if there is a delayed response		Urinalysis, urine and blood cultures are required. May be due to an obstruction or catheterization; remove or change catheter if appropriate.

INFECTIOUS DISEASES

Urinary Analgesic

Phenazopyridine can help with dysuria (pain/burning with urination). Appropriate antibiotics will resolve symptoms promptly.

DRUG	DOSING	SAFETY/SIDE EFFECTS/MONITORING	
Phenazopyridine **(Pyridium, Azo** **Urinary Pain Relief)** OTC and Rx	200 mg PO TID x 2 days (max) Take with 8 oz of water, with or immediately following food, to minimize stomach upset	**CONTRAINDICATIONS** Do not use in patients with renal impairment or liver disease **SIDE EFFECTS** Headache, dizziness, stomach cramps, body secretion discoloration **NOTES** Can cause red-orange coloring of the urine and other body fluids; contact lenses/clothes can be stained Hemolytic anemia with G6PD deficiency (discontinue if hemolysis occurs)	orange urine color

© iStock.com/sanlas

BACTERIURIA AND PREGNANCY

Bacteriuria ($\geq 10^5$ bacteria/mL on a urinalysis) in pregnant women must be treated even if asymptomatic. If not treated, bacteriuria can lead to pyelonephritis, premature birth and neonatal meningitis.

- Beta-lactams are preferred (amoxicillin ± clavulanate or an oral cephalosporin).

- Nitrofurantoin and SMX/TMP can be used in patients with a beta-lactam allergy. The American College of Obstetricians and Gynecologists (ACOG) states that they should be avoided in the 1st trimester, if possible, and there

are safety risks when used later in pregnancy (SMX/TMP can cause hyperbilirubinemia and kernicterus in the newborn if used close to delivery, and nitrofurantoin should be avoided in the 3rd trimester due to the possibility of hemolytic anemia in the infant).

- Fosfomycin can be considered in pregnant patients who have drug allergies.

- Quinolones should be avoided due to cartilage toxicity and arthropathies (see the Infectious Diseases I chapter for more information).

© iStock.com/Volhah

TRAVELERS' DIARRHEA

Travelers' diarrhea (TD) is a common travel-related illness and is primarily caused by ingestion of contaminated food or water. *Escherichia coli* causes 80 – 90% of TD cases. *Campylobacter jejuni, Shigella* spp. and *Salmonella* spp. are other possible bacterial causes. Viral diarrhea can involve a number of pathogens, most commonly norovirus and rotavirus.

Patients present with a sudden onset of symptoms, including loose stools, abdominal cramps/pain, fever, vomiting or dysentery (bloody diarrhea). These symptoms limit traveler activity.

Azithromycin is the preferred treatment if dysentery is present. Quinolones (for 1 – 3 days) or rifaximin (for 3 days) can be used when bloody diarrhea is not present. Travel destination can also impact the preferred treatment; in practice, always consult specific recommendations. Antimotility agents (e.g., loperamide), provide symptomatic relief but should not be used if bloody diarrhea is present (see the Travelers and Constipation & Diarrhea chapters for information on prevention and symptomatic treatment).

TRAVELERS' DIARRHEA TREATMENT

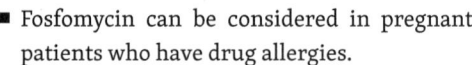

Preferred treatment if fever, blood in stools, pregnant or pediatric:
Azithromycin 1,000 mg PO x 1 or 500 mg PO daily x 1-3 days

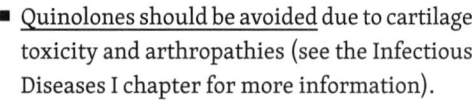

Otherwise, choose one of the following:
Ciprofloxacin 750 mg PO x 1 or 500 mg PO BID x 3 days

Levofloxacin 500 mg PO x 1 or daily x 1-3 days

Ofloxacin 400 mg PO x 1 or BID x 3 days

Rifaximin 200 mg PO TID x 3 days

© iStock.com/Bibigon

CLOSTRIDIOIDES DIFFICILE INFECTION

The GI tract contains > 1,000 species of organisms as part of the normal flora. Antibiotics can eliminate much of the "healthy" bacteria, allowing an overgrowth of *Clostridioides difficile*, a Gram-positive, obligate anaerobic, spore-forming rod. Some types of *C. difficile* release toxins (toxin A and B) that attack the intestinal lining, causing inflammation of the colon (colitis). Symptoms of *C. difficile* infection (CDI) include at least three, watery stools per day, abdominal cramps, fever and an elevated white blood cell count. Inflammation of the colon can lead to pseudomembranous colitis, which can progress to toxic megacolon and result in the need for colectomy or death. Other risk factors include recent healthcare exposure, use of proton pump inhibitors, advanced age, immunocompromised state, obesity and previous CDI.

CDI TREATMENT

Treatment recommendations vary based on whether it is the first infection or a recurrence (see Study Tip Gal below). Review the patient profile to determine the recommended treatment. Probiotics are not beneficial for treatment but may be useful for prophylaxis. When the monoclonal antibody bezlotoxumab *(Zinplava)* is administered, it binds to toxin B and neutralizes its adverse effects. Bezlotoxumab decreases the risk of CDI recurrence but does not treat the active infection and must be administered in conjunction with antibacterial therapy. It should be used with caution in patients with underlying heart failure.

C. DIFFICILE GUIDELINE RECOMMENDATIONS

- When infection is suspected, discontinue unnecessary antibiotics and other possible causative agents (e.g., PPIs) if possible
- Isolate patients (in a single room with a dedicated bathroom; use contact precautions – gown and gloves)
- After patient care/visits: wash hands with soap and water (more effective than alcohol-containing hand sanitizers)
- Diagnosis: positive *C. difficile* stool toxin (enzyme immunoassay combined with a glutamate dehydrogenase test) or PCR
- Adjunct bezlotoxumab (i.e., in addition to antibacterial treatment) can be considered for high-risk patients: ≥ age 65 years, immunocompromised status, severe presentation and/or experiencing a 2nd episode of CDI within the past 6 months

1ST EPISODE
FDX 200 mg PO BID x 10 days, or
VAN 125 mg PO QID x 10 days (standard regimen)
MET 500 mg PO TID x 10 days (option only if non-severe* and treatments above are unavailable)

2nd EPISODE (1st Recurrence)
FDX 200 mg PO BID x 10 days, or
VAN standard regimen followed by a prolonged pulse/tapered course** (the standard regimen without a prolonged taper is acceptable if MET was used for the initial episode)

3rd OR SUBSEQUENT EPISODES
FDX 200 mg PO BID x 10 days, or
VAN standard regimen followed by a prolonged pulse/tapered course**, or
VAN standard regimen followed by rifaximin 400 mg TID x 20 days, or
Fecal microbiota transplantation

Fulminant/Complicated Disease
Diagnosed when significant systemic toxic effects are present, such as hypotension, shock, ileus or toxic megacolon; can occur with any episode/recurrence
VAN 500 mg PO/NG/PR QID + metronidazole 500 mg IV Q8H

FDX = fidaxomicin (Dificid); VAN = vancomycin; MET = metronidazole
*Non-severe = WBC < 15,000 cells/mm³ and SCr < 1.5 mg/dL
**Example vancomycin tapered and pulsed regimen = 125 mg PO QID x 10 days, BID x 1 week, daily x 1 week, then 125 mg every 2-3 days for 2-8 weeks.

SEXUALLY TRANSMITTED INFECTIONS

Safe sex practices and education are important to prevent sexually transmitted infections (STIs). Condoms (male and female) can help decrease transmission. Oral sex has a much lower risk of HIV transmission than vaginal or anal sex, but still carries risk for herpes, syphilis, hepatitis B, gonorrhea and human papillomavirus (HPV).

Screening should be performed for timely diagnosis of STIs and prevention of complications, including cervical cancer, infertility or transmission to partners. Sexual partners should be treated concurrently to prevent re-infection, except in bacterial vaginosis. See Study Tip Gal for usual symptoms of common STIs and the table below for treatment recommendations (refer to the Infectious Diseases III chapter for a discussion of herpes simplex virus).

SYMPTOMS OF COMMON STIs

Chlamydia:	genital discharge or no symptoms
Gonorrhea:	genital discharge or no symptoms
Genital warts:	single or multiple pink/skin-toned lesions
Latent syphilis:	asymptomatic
Primary syphilis:	painless, smooth genital sores (chancre)

Females only

Bacterial vaginosis: vaginal discharge (clear, white or gray) that has a "fishy" odor and pH > 4.5; little or no pain

Trichomoniasis: yellow/green, frothy vaginal discharge with pH > 4.5; soreness, pain with intercourse

TREATMENT OF SEXUALLY TRANSMITTED INFECTIONS

INFECTION	DRUG OF CHOICE	DOSING/DURATION	ALTERNATIVES/NOTES
Syphilis (primary, secondary or early latent) *Treponema pallidum*, a spirochete Early latent: acquired within the past year, asymptomatic	Penicillin G benzathine (*Bicillin L-A*, do not substitute with *Bicillin C-R*)	2.4 million units IM x 1	Beta-lactam allergy ■ Doxycycline 100 mg PO BID x 14 days ■ If pregnant, nonadherent with treatment or unlikely to follow up, desensitize and treat with *Bicillin L-A* (see Study Tip Gal on next page) Diagnosis: positive non-treponemal test, such as a rapid plasma reagin (RPR) or Venereal Diseases Research Lab (VDRL) blood test, and treponemal assay
Syphilis (late latent or tertiary) Late latent: acquired > 1 year ago or unknown duration, asymptomatic	As above	2.4 million units IM weekly x 3 weeks (7.2 million units total)	Beta-lactam allergy ■ Doxycycline 100 mg PO BID x 28 days (see notes above for pregnant or nonadherent patients)
Neurosyphilis Can occur at any stage of disease	Penicillin G aqueous crystalline	3-4 million units IV Q4H x 10-14 days	Penicillin G procaine Beta-lactam allergy: desensitization followed by administration of penicillin G aqueous IV
Gonorrhea *Neisseria gonorrhoeae*, a Gram-negative diplococcus Commonly diagnosed via urethral, vaginal, cervical, rectal and/or pharyngeal swabs	Ceftriaxone If chlamydia has not been excluded: add doxycycline (see below)	< 150 kg: 500 mg IM x 1 ≥ 150 kg: 1 gram IM x 1	Treatment is the same for pregnant patients If ceftriaxone is not available: cefixime 800 mg PO x 1 If cephalosporin allergy: gentamicin 240 mg IM x 1 + azithromycin 2 grams PO x 1 Ceftriaxone is most effective for pharyngeal infections (if severe cephalosporin allergy, consult an ID specialist)
Chlamydia *Chlamydia trachomatis*, an intracellular obligate Gram-negative organism Testing as per gonorrhea	Non-pregnant: doxycycline Pregnant: azithromycin	100 mg PO BID x 7 days 1 gram PO x 1	Erythromycin base 500 mg PO QID x 7 days, or Levofloxacin 500 mg PO daily x 7 days Pregnancy: amoxicillin 500 mg PO TID x 7 days

INFECTION	DRUG OF CHOICE	DOSING/DURATION	ALTERNATIVES/NOTES
Bacterial Vaginosis Many different organisms, including *Gardnerella vaginalis*	Metronidazole or Metronidazole 0.75% gel or Clindamycin 2% cream	500 mg PO BID x 7 days 1 applicator intravaginally daily x 5 days 1 applicator intravaginally at bedtime x 7 days	Clindamycin 300 mg PO BID x 7 days (or clindamycin ovules* 100 mg intravaginally at bedtime x 3 days), or Tinidazole 2 g PO daily x 2 days (or 1 g PO daily x 5 days), or Secnidazole 2 g PO x 1 dose Females with bacterial vaginosis should not douche
Trichomoniasis *Trichomonas vaginalis*, a flagellated protozoan	Metronidazole	Females: 500 mg PO BID x 7 days Males: 2 grams PO x 1	Pregnancy: metronidazole (per package labeling) is contraindicated in the 1st trimester, but based on additional safety data (and the adverse outcomes associated with infection), the CDC recommends metronidazole for trichomoniasis in all trimesters
Genital Warts Human papillomavirus (HPV) strains 6 & 11 *Gardasil* vaccine reduces the risk of genital warts as well as cervical and other cancers (see the Immunizations chapter)	Imiquimod cream (*Aldara, Zyclara*)	Apply topically to clean, dry, warty tissue and wash off in 6-10 hours Apply 3x/week until cleared (or 16 weeks)	Treatment not required if asymptomatic (warts generally resolve spontaneously within one year) Local side effects of erythema, burning, scaling, ulcers and vesicles can occur with imiquimod treatment Imiquimod cream can weaken condoms and diaphrams and irritate anogenital mucosa; patients should abstain from sexual activity while the cream is on the skin

Clindamycin ovules use a base that can weaken latex or rubber products (e.g., condoms); alternative contraception methods should be used within 72 hours of clindamycin ovules.

SYPHILIS: PENICILLIN DESENSITIZATION REQUIRED?

Syphilis must be treated with penicillin in select patients with a penicillin allergy because the alternative, doxycycline, is not suitable and poorly studied.

- A pregnant patient cannot take doxycycline due to the adverse effects on the fetus (suppressed bone growth and skeletal development).
- A patient with poor compliance/follow-up is at risk for treatment failure with a twice-daily regimen that must be taken for 14-28 days.

Per the CDC, follow these steps:

1. Confirm the allergic reaction with a skin test.
2. Temporarily desensitize the patient with an approved desensitization protocol.
3. Treat with IM penicillin G benzathine (*Bicillin L-A*).

INFECTIOUS DISEASES

RICKETTSIAL DISEASES AND RELATED INFECTIONS

Rickettsial infections are caused by a variety of bacteria that are carried by many ticks, fleas and lice. The rickettsial diseases caused in humans are listed in the table below, along with the recommended treatments. Rocky Mountain spotted fever is the most common and most fatal rickettsial illness in the U.S. Initial signs and symptoms include fever, headache and muscle pain, followed by the development of a rash.

DISEASE	ORGANISM	TREATMENT
Rocky Mountain Spotted Fever	*Rickettsia rickettsii* Gram-negative obligate intracellular bacteria	Doxycycline 100 mg PO/IV BID x 5-7 days (the drug of choice in pediatric patients)
Typhus	*Rickettsia typhi* Gram-negative obligate intracellular bacteria	Doxycycline 100 mg PO/IV BID x 7 days
Lyme Disease	*Borrelia burgdorferi, Borrelia mayonii* Spirochetes	Doxycycline 100 mg PO BID x 10 days, or Amoxicillin 500 mg PO TID x 14 days, or Cefuroxime 500 mg PO BID x 14 days
Ehrlichiosis	*Ehrlichia chaffeensis* Obligate intracellular bacteria	Doxycycline 100 mg PO/IV BID x 7-14 days
Tularemia	*Francisella tularensis* Aerobic Gram-negative coccobacilli	Gentamicin or tobramycin 5 mg/kg/day IV divided Q8H x 7-14 days

Select Guidelines/References

Bratzler DW, Dellinger EP, Olsen KM, et al. Clinical practice guidelines for antimicrobial prophylaxis for surgery. *Am J Health-Syst Pharm.* 2013;70:195-283.

Lieberthal AS, Carroll AE, Chonmaitree T, et al. The diagnosis and management acute otitis media. *Pediatrics.* 2013;31:e964-e999.

Metlay JP, Waterer GW, Long AC, et al. Diagnosis and treatment of adults with community-acquired pneumonia. An official clinical practice guideline of the American Thoracic Society and Infectious Diseases Society of America. *Am J Respir Crit Care Med.* 2019;200:e45-e67.

Sterling TR, Njie G, Zenner D, et al. Guidelines for the treatment of latent tuberculosis infection: Recommendations from the National Tuberculosis Controllers Association and CDC, 2020. *MMWR Recomm Rep* 2020;69(No.RR-1):1-11.

Johnson S, Lavergne V, Skinner AM, et al. Clinical practice guideline by the Infectious Diseases Society of America (IDSA) and Society for Healthcare Epidemiology of America (SHEA): 2021 focused update guidelines on management of for *Clostridioides difficile* infection in adults. *Clinical Infectious Diseases.* 2021;73:e1029-e1044.

Workowski KA, Golan GA. Sexually transmitted infections treatment guidelines, 2021. *MMWR Recomm Rep* 2021;70(No. RR-4):1-187.

Guidelines available at the Infectious Diseases Society of America website (www.idsociety.org).

LYME DISEASE OR RINGWORM?

Lyme Disease

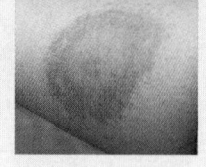

Bacterial (spirochete) infection *Borrelia burgdorferi* and *Borrelia mayonii*, spread by ticks

Bullseye rash (round, red), achy joints, fever

Diagnosis: enzyme immunoassay (EIA) identifies antibodies
Treatment: doxycycline 100 mg BID PO/IV

Ringworm

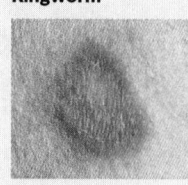

Fungal infection
Tinea corporis

1+ reddish, raised rings, can be itchy
Treatments: clotrimazole or another topical antifungal

FUNGAL CLASSIFICATIONS

Yeasts
Candida species
C. albicans
C. tropicalis
C. parapsilosis
C. glabrata
C. krusei

Cryptococcus neoformans

Molds
Aspergillus species

Zygomycetes (Mucor and Rhizopus species)

Dimorphic fungi
Histoplasma capsulatum

Blastomyces dermatitidis

Coccidioides immitis

CONTENT LEGEND

● = Study Tip Gal

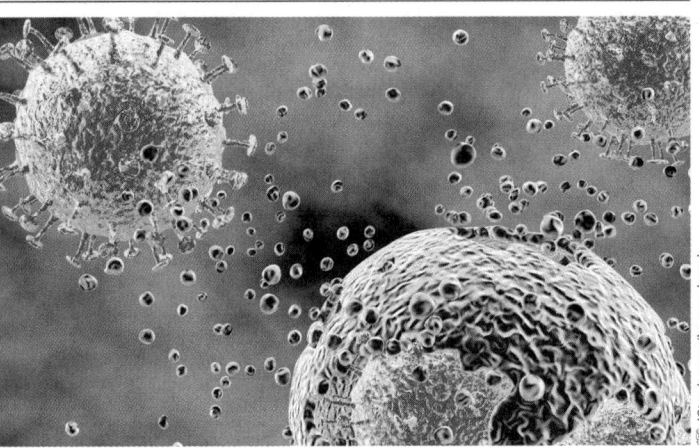

© iStock.com/image_jungle

CHAPTER 24

INFECTIOUS DISEASES III: ANTIFUNGALS & ANTIVIRALS

SYSTEMIC FUNGAL INFECTIONS

Fungal infections cause a wide spectrum of diseases, from mild infections of the nail bed to severe infections such as meningitis or pneumonia. Invasive fungal infections are associated with high morbidity and mortality. Diagnosis of fungal infections can be made by culture, serologic studies or histologic features of a tissue specimen.

Fungi are classified as either yeasts, molds or dimorphic species (see box). Dimorphic fungi exist as mold forms at lower temperatures and yeast forms at higher temperatures ("mold in the cold, yeast in the heat"). *Zygomycetes* refers to a class of fungi which includes *Mucor* species and *Rhizopus* species; invasive disease caused by these species is commonly referred to as "mucormycosis."

Certain types of fungi (including yeasts such as *Candida*) can colonize body surfaces and are considered to be normal flora in the intestine. They do not normally cause serious infections unless they contaminate a sterile space (e.g., the blood) or the immune system is weakened by drugs or diseases (e.g., chemotherapy, HIV), increasing the risk of opportunistic infections. See the Infectious Diseases IV: Opportunistic Infections chapter for more information.

Some fungi reproduce by spreading microscopic spores. These spores are often present in the air, where they can be inhaled or come into contact with the skin, causing lung, skin and (in some cases) central nervous system infections. Long-term, systemic antifungals are necessary for certain invasive fungal infections (e.g., *Cryptococcus*, *Coccidioides*) in someone who is chronically immunosuppressed.

C. albicans is the most susceptible of the *Candida* species to drug treatment. *C. glabrata* and *C. krusei* tend to be more difficult to treat due to resistance to certain azole antifungals. Of the molds, *Aspergillus* and *Zygomycetes* require the use of specific agents with an adequate spectrum of activity.

INFECTIOUS DISEASES

AMPHOTERICIN B

Amphotericin B binds to ergosterol, altering cell membrane permeability and causing cell death. It is a broad-spectrum drug that can be used as initial treatment for many invasive infections, including cryptococcal meningitis (in combination with flucytosine), histoplasmosis and mucormycosis. It is active against:

- Yeasts: most *Candida* species and *Cryptococcus neoformans*
- Molds: *Aspergillus* species and *Zygomycetes*
- Dimorphic fungi: *Histoplasma capsulatum*, *Blastomyces dermatitidis* and *Coccidioides immitis*

Amphotericin B deoxycholate (the conventional formulation) has many toxicities. The amphotericin B lipid formulations are a complex of the active medication and a lipid component; they are associated with fewer toxicities (e.g., decreased infusion reactions, decreased nephrotoxicity) compared to the conventional (deoxycholate) formulation.

FORMULATIONS	DOSING	SAFETY/SIDE EFFECTS/MONITORING
Conventional Formulation		**BOXED WARNINGS**
Amphotericin B Deoxycholate Injection	0.1-1.5 mg/kg/day	Medication errors confusing the lipid-based forms of amphotericin (*AmBisome* and *Abelcet*) and conventional amphotericin B have resulted in cardiopulmonary arrest and death; conventional amphotericin B doses should not exceed 1.5 mg/kg/day (verify product name and dosage if dose exceeds 1.5 mg/kg/day)
		SIDE EFFECTS
		Infusion-related: fever, chills, headache, malaise, rigors, ↓ or ↑ BP, thrombophlebitis, N/V
		Other: ↓ K, ↓ Mg, nephrotoxicity, anemia
		Ambisome: severe back/chest pain with the first dose
Lipid Formulations		**MONITORING**
Amphotericin B Lipid Complex (*Abelcet*) Injection	5 mg/kg/day	Renal function, LFTs, electrolytes (especially K and Mg), CBC
		NOTES
		Preparation: compatible with D5W only, lipid formulations must be filtered during preparation
		Amphotericin B deoxycholate (conventional formulation) requires premedication to reduce infusion-related reactions; give the following 30-60 minutes prior to the infusion:
Liposomal Amphotericin B (*AmBisome*) Injection	3-6 mg/kg/day	■ Acetaminophen or NSAID ■ Diphenhydramine and/or hydrocortisone ■ NS boluses to ↓ the risk of nephrotoxicity ■ ± meperidine to ↓ the duration of severe rigors
		Both conventional and lipid formulations are yellow-orange in color

Amphotericin B Drug Interactions

- Additive risk of nephrotoxicity when used with other nephrotoxic agents such as aminoglycosides, cisplatin, polymyxins, cyclosporine, loop diuretics, NSAIDs, radiocontrast dye, tacrolimus and vancomycin.

- Can ↑ the risk of digoxin toxicity due to hypokalemia. Use caution with any agent that ↓ potassium or magnesium since amphotericin decreases both. Scheduled replacement of potassium and/or magnesium should be considered.

FLUCYTOSINE

Flucytosine penetrates fungal cells and is converted to fluorouracil, which competes with uracil, interfering with fungal RNA and protein synthesis. Due to the development of resistance, flucytosine should not be used alone. It is recommended in combination with amphotericin B for the treatment of invasive cryptococcal (e.g., meningitis) or *Candida* infections.

DRUG	DOSING	SAFETY/SIDE EFFECTS/MONITORING
Flucytosine, 5-FC (*Ancobon*)	50-150 mg/kg/day PO divided Q6H CrCl ≤ 40 mL/min: adjustment required	**BOXED WARNING** Use with extreme caution in patients with renal dysfunction; monitor hematologic, renal and hepatic status **SIDE EFFECTS** Dose-related myelosuppression (anemia, neutropenia, thrombocytopenia), ↑ SCr, ↑ BUN, liver injury, ↑ bilirubin, many CNS effects, hypoglycemia, ↓ K, aplastic anemia

AZOLE ANTIFUNGALS

Azole antifungals decrease ergosterol synthesis and cell membrane formation. The coverage and indications of azoles vary widely, and their use is sometimes limited due to significant drug interactions caused by their CYP450 (mainly CYP3A4) inhibition. Ketoconazole was the first azole antifungal, but due to toxicities and many drug interactions, it is now most often used topically.

Fluconazole has activity against *C. albicans, C. parapsilosis* and *C. tropicalis*. It has limited efficacy against *C. glabrata* due to resistance, and *C. krusei* is considered fluconazole-resistant. Fluconazole can be used for many infections, including yeast infections (e.g., oral, esophageal, vaginal) and nail bed infections (onychomycosis). A yeast infection in the mouth, called oral thrush or oral candidiasis, presents with white-colored, sore patches on the tongue and oral mucosa.

Itraconazole use is often limited by drug interactions, lack of available data and expense. The primary uses for itraconazole are for the dimorphic fungi *Blastomycosis* and *Histoplasmosis* and nail bed infections. Voriconazole is the treatment of choice for *Aspergillus*.

See the Common Skin Conditions chapter for treatment of non-invasive fungal infections, including onychomycosis.

KEY ISSUES WITH AZOLE ANTIFUNGALS

Class Effects
- ↑ LFTs
- QT prolongation (except isavuconazonium)
- Many drug interactions

Drug-Specific Concerns
- Fluconazole: the only azole that requires renal dose adjustment
- Ketoconazole: hepatotoxicity has led to liver transplantation
- Itraconazole: can cause heart failure
- Voriconazole: can cause visual changes and phototoxicity
- Posaconazole:
  - Tablet dose ≠ suspension dose (due to different bioavailability)
  - Take with food

IV Administration
- IV to PO ratio is 1:1 for all azoles
- Drugs with sulfobutyl ether beta-cyclodextrin (SBECD) vehicle: voriconazole, posaconazole

---

DRUG	DOSING	SAFETY/SIDE EFFECTS/MONITORING
Fluconazole (*Diflucan*) Tablet, suspension, injection	50-800 mg PO/IV daily Vaginal candidiasis: 150 mg PO x 1 CrCl ≤ 50 mL/min: ↓ dose by 50% IV:PO ratio is 1:1	**BOXED WARNINGS** **Itraconazole** Can worsen or cause heart failure; do not use to treat onychomycosis in patients with ventricular dysfunction or a history of heart failure Can cause ↑ plasma concentrations of certain drugs and can lead to QT prolongation and ventricular tachyarrhythmias, including Torsades de Pointes (TdP)
Itraconazole (*Sporanox, Tolsura*) Capsule, solution	200 mg PO daily or BID *Tolsura:* 130 mg PO daily or BID Formulations have different bioavailability and are not interchangeable; the oral solution is better absorbed Solution is taken on an empty stomach; capsules are taken with food Limited data on use in renal impairment (use with caution)	**Ketoconazole** Hepatotoxicity which has led to liver transplantation and/or death QT prolongation Use oral tablets only when other effective antifungal therapy is unavailable or not tolerated and the benefits outweigh the risks (hepatotoxicity, drug interactions) **WARNINGS** Hepatotoxicity Fluconazole: not recommended in pregnancy, exfoliative skin disorders can occur
Ketoconazole topical (**Nizoral A-D**, *Extina, Ketozole, Xolegel*) Tablet, cream, foam, gel, shampoo *Nizoral A-D* is OTC	200-400 mg PO daily No adjustment in renal impairment	**SIDE EFFECTS** ↑ LFTs, QT prolongation, headache, N/V, abdominal pain, rash/pruritus, dizziness, hair loss (or possible hair growth) and altered hair texture with ketoconazole shampoo **NOTES** All azoles are cleared hepatically except fluconazole, which requires renal dose adjustment Fluconazole and voriconazole penetrate the CNS adequately to treat fungal meningitis (see voriconazole on the following page)

DRUG	DOSING	SAFETY/SIDE EFFECTS/MONITORING
Voriconazole (Vfend, Vfend IV) Tablet, suspension, injection	Loading dose: 6 mg/kg IV Q12H x 2 doses Maintenance dose: 4 mg/kg IV Q12H or 200 mg PO Q12H Mild-moderate hepatic impairment: reduce maintenance dose by 50% Severe hepatic impairment: only use if benefit outweighs risk, monitor closely CrCl < 50 mL/min: the intravenous vehicle SBECD accumulates; oral voriconazole is preferred Monitor SCr if IV voriconazole is used; change to oral when possible Therapeutic range (trough): 1-5 mcg/mL IV:PO ratio is 1:1	**CONTRAINDICATIONS** Coadministration with barbiturates (long-acting), carbamazepine, efavirenz (≥ 400 mg/day), ergot alkaloids, pimozide, quinidine, rifabutin, rifampin, ritonavir (≥ 800 mg/day), sirolimus or St. John's wort **WARNINGS** Hepatotoxicity, visual disturbances (optic neuritis and papilledema), phototoxicity, QT prolongation (correct K, Ca and Mg prior to initiating treatment), nephrotoxicity, avoid in pregnancy, infusion-related reactions, serious skin reactions (SJS/TEN), skeletal adverse effects (fluorosis, periostitis), pancreatitis **SIDE EFFECTS** Visual changes (~20% - blurred vision, photophobia, altered color perception, altered visual acuity), ↑ LFTs, ↑ SCr, CNS toxicity (hallucinations, headache, dizziness), photosensitivity, ↑ or ↓ K **MONITORING** LFTs, renal function, electrolytes, visual function (when used > 28 days), trough concentrations (toxicity more likely with troughs > 5 mcg/mL) **NOTES** *Vfend:* take on an empty stomach, at least 1 hour before or after a meal; hold tube feedings for 1 hour before and after doses Use caution when driving at night due to vision changes Avoid direct sunlight Suspension: shake for 10 seconds before each use; do not refrigerate
Posaconazole (Noxafil) Delayed-release tablet, suspension, injection	Suspension: 200 mg TID or 400 mg BID Give with a full meal (during or within 20 minutes following a meal) Tablets: 300 mg PO BID on day 1, then 300 mg PO daily with food (can range from 100-400 mg/day, divided in 1-3 doses) IV: 300 mg BID on day 1, then 300 mg daily eGFR < 50 mL/min/1.73m²: the intravenous vehicle SBECD can accumulate and worsen renal function; oral treatment is preferred IV:PO ratio is 1:1	**CONTRAINDICATIONS** Coadministration with sirolimus, ergot alkaloids, pimozide, quinidine, atorvastatin, lovastatin and simvastatin **WARNINGS** QT prolongation (correct K, Ca and Mg prior to initiating treatment) Prescribing and dispensing errors: suspension and tablet are not interchangeable as dosing regimens differ (tablet is better absorbed) Neurotoxicity when used with vincristine, due to increased vincristine levels (seizures, peripheral neuropathy, SIADH, paralytic ileus) **SIDE EFFECTS** N/V/D, fever, headache, ↑ LFTs, rash, ↓ K, ↓ Mg, cough **MONITORING** LFTs, renal function, electrolytes, CBC
Isavuconazonium sulfate (*Cresemba*) Capsules, injection Prodrug of isavuconazole	IV/PO: 372 mg Q8H for 6 doses, then 372 mg daily No adjustment for renal dysfunction, use with caution in severe hepatic impairment Swallow capsules whole, do not crush or open IV:PO ratio is 1:1	**CONTRAINDICATIONS** Use with strong CYP3A4 inhibitors or inducers, familial short QT syndrome (causes QT shortening, not prolongation) **WARNINGS** Hepatotoxicity, infusion-related reactions (hypotension, dyspnea, chills, dizziness, tingling and numbness), hypersensitivity reactions (anaphylaxis, SJS/TEN), teratogenic, drug interactions, particulates (undissolved intravenous drug) **SIDE EFFECTS** N/V/D, headache, injection site reactions, peripheral edema, ↓ K, ↑ LFTs **MONITORING** LFTs, electrolytes **NOTES** Requires a filter (0.2-1.2 micron) during administration due to possible particulates Capsules must be protected from moisture; original container has a desiccant

Azole Antifungal Drug Interactions

- <u>All</u> azoles are moderate-strong <u>CYP3A4 inhibitors</u>; monitor for drug interactions.

- Itraconazole and ketoconazole inhibit P-glycoprotein.

- <u>Fluconazole</u> and voriconazole <u>inhibit CYP2C9</u>, which can ↑ the effects of <u>warfarin</u>. <u>Monitor INR</u> and signs/symptoms of bleeding.

- Azoles can ↑ the concentrations of apixaban and rivaroxaban. Monitor for signs/symptoms of bleeding.

- Caution use in combination with other <u>QT-prolonging</u> drugs [e.g., antiarrhythmics, quinolones, macrolides, antidepressants (tricyclics, SSRIs, mirtazapine, trazodone, venlafaxine), antipsychotics, 5HT-3 receptor antagonists, others (see the Arrhythmias chapter)].

- PPIs and cimetidine can decrease the absorption of posaconazole suspension and should be stopped during therapy to avoid treatment failure.

- The absorption of <u>itraconazole (Sporanox brand capsules)</u> and <u>ketoconazole</u> requires an <u>acidic gut</u>; ↑ pH will ↓ absorption. Separate antacids two hours before and after doses.

  - If PPIs or H2RAs must be used while on ketoconazole, take an acidic beverage (such as <u>non-diet cola</u>) to provide an <u>acidic environment for absorption</u>.

- Voriconazole:

  - Concentrations can ↑ dangerously when given with drugs that inhibit CYP2C19, 2C9 or 3A4, or with small dose increases. Exhibits first-order, followed by zero-order (non-linear), kinetics.

  - Do not use with barbiturates (long-acting), carbamazepine, efavirenz (≥ 400 mg/day), ergot alkaloids, pimozide, quinidine, rifabutin, rifampin, ritonavir (≥ 800 mg/day), sirolimus or St. John's wort.

ECHINOCANDINS

Echinocandins <u>inhibit</u> the <u>synthesis of beta (1,3)-D-glucan</u>, an essential component of the <u>fungal cell wall</u>. They are <u>effective against most Candida species</u>, including strains typically resistant to azole antifungals (e.g., *C. glabrata* and *C. krusei*). Though they have activity against *Aspergillus* species, they should only be used as part of a combination regimen, and other medications are generally preferred. Echinocandins are available <u>only as injections</u>. They are typically well-tolerated and are not associated with significant renal or hepatic toxicity.

DRUG	DOSING	SAFETY/SIDE EFFECTS/MONITORING
Caspofungin (*Cancidas*) Injection	70 mg IV on day 1, then 50 mg IV daily Moderate hepatic impairment: 70 mg IV on day 1, then 35 mg IV daily ↑ dose to 70 mg IV daily when used in combination with rifampin or other strong enzyme inducers	**WARNINGS** <u>Histamine-mediated symptoms</u> (rash, pruritus, facial swelling, flushing, hypotension) have occurred; anaphylaxis **SIDE EFFECTS** ↑ LFTs, headache, hypotension, ↑ or ↓ K, ↓ Mg, fever, N/V/D, hyperglycemia, anemia, ↑ SCr, rash Severe skin reactions, including SJS/TEN (caspofungin)
Micafungin (*Mycamine**) Injection	**Candidemia** 100 mg IV daily **Esophageal Candidiasis** 150 mg IV daily	**MONITORING** LFTs **NOTES** All are given <u>once daily</u> and <u>do not require dose adjustment in renal impairment</u> Very few drug interactions
Anidulafungin (*Eraxis*) Injection	**Candidemia** 200 mg IV on day 1, then 100 mg IV daily **Esophageal Candidiasis** 100 mg IV on day 1, then 50 mg daily	

Brand discontinued but name still used in practice.

OTHER ANTIFUNGAL AGENTS

Superficial fungal infections are easier to treat than invasive fungal infections, and topical antifungal products are preferred in most cases (see the Common Skin Conditions chapter); systemic medications (e.g., griseofulvin) are considered second-line. Griseofulvin has a narrow antifungal spectrum, is less effective than other systemic drugs (e.g., itraconazole or terbinafine) and requires prolonged courses. Nystatin suspension, clotrimazole troches/lozenges and buccal miconazole are useful for treating mild, localized *Candida* infections (e.g., thrush).

DRUG	DOSING	SAFETY/SIDE EFFECTS/MONITORING
Nystatin Suspension, tablet Topical forms (*Nyamyc, Nystop*)	**Oral Candidiasis** Suspension: 400,000-600,000 units 4 times/day x 7-14 days **Intestinal Infections** Oral tablets: 500,000-1,000,000 units Q8H	**SIDE EFFECTS** N/V/D, stomach pain Minimal GI absorption, low systemic risk **NOTES** Suspension: swish in the mouth and retain for as long as possible (several minutes) before swallowing
Griseofulvin Tablet (microsize, ultramicrosize), suspension (microsize) Indicated for fungal infections of the skin, hair and nails	Microsize: 500-1,000 mg/day in 1-2 divided doses Ultramicrosize: 375-750 mg/day in 1-2 divided doses Duration of therapy depends on the site of infection: Tinea corporis: 2-4 weeks Tinea pedis: 4-8 weeks	**CONTRAINDICATIONS** Pregnancy, severe liver disease, porphyria **SIDE EFFECTS** Photosensitivity, ↑ LFTs, HA, rash, urticaria, dizziness, leukopenia, severe skin reactions **MONITORING** LFTs, renal function, CBC **NOTES** Cross reaction possible with PCN allergy Take with a fatty meal to ↑ absorption or with food/milk to avoid GI upset
Terbinafine (*Lamisil AT*) Tablet, topical Topical forms (Rx, OTC)	250 mg/day in 1-2 divided doses without regard to meals	**CONTRAINDICATIONS** Chronic or active liver disease **WARNINGS** Hepatotoxicity, taste/smell disturbance (including permanent loss of taste or smell), depression, neutropenia, thrombotic thrombocytopenic purpura (TTP), hemolytic uremic syndrome (HUS), serious skin reactions (SJS/TEN/DRESS/erythema multiforme), can cause/worsen systemic lupus erythematosus Confirm fungal infection prior to use due to toxicities **SIDE EFFECTS** Headache, ↑ LFTs, skin rash, abdominal pain, pruritus, diarrhea, dyspepsia **MONITORING** CBC, LFTs
Clotrimazole 10 mg troche/lozenge Topical and vaginal forms (multiple brand names)	**Oropharyngeal Candidiasis** Prophylaxis: 10 mg 3 times/day Treatment: 10 mg 5 times/day x 7-14 days Allow troche to dissolve slowly over 15-30 minutes	**SIDE EFFECTS** ↑ LFTs, nausea, dysgeusia **MONITORING** LFTs
Miconazole Buccal tablet (*Oravig*) Topical and vaginal forms	**Oropharyngeal Candidiasis** 50 mg (1 tablet) applied to the upper gum region daily for 7-14 days	**CONTRAINDICATIONS** Hypersensitivity to milk protein concentrate **SIDE EFFECTS** Local application site reactions (pain, burning, pruritus, edema, toothache)

Drug Interactions

- Griseofulvin: can ↑ the metabolism of hormonal contraceptives (estrogen and progestin) which can lead to contraceptive failure. Use a nonhormonal form of contraception.

- Terbinafine is a strong CYP2D6 inhibitor and a weak/moderate CYP3A4 inducer.

EMPIRIC TREATMENT FOR SELECT FUNGAL PATHOGENS/INFECTIONS*

PATHOGEN	PREFERRED REGIMEN	ALTERNATIVE REGIMEN
Candida albicans Oropharyngeal infection (thrush)	Mild disease: topical antifungals (clotrimazole, miconazole) Moderate-severe disease or HIV+: fluconazole	Nystatin
Candida albicans Esophageal infection	Fluconazole	Echinocandin
Candida krusei and *glabrata*** All *Candida* species bloodstream infections	Echinocandin	Amphotericin B, high-dose fluconazole (susceptible isolates only)
Aspergillus Invasive	Voriconazole	Amphotericin B, isavuconazonium
Cryptococcus neoformans Meningitis	Amphotericin B + flucytosine (5-FC)	High-dose fluconazole + flucytosine (5-FC)
Dermatophytes Nail bed infection	Terbinafine or itraconazole (confirm fungal infection prior to treatment); see the Common Skin Conditions chapter	Fluconazole

De-escalate and tailor therapy based on a culture and susceptibility report.
See the Infectious Disease IV chapter for opportunistic fungal infections that affect immunocompromised patients.
**Candida krusei and glabrata are more resistant to azole antifungals.*

ANTIFUNGAL KEY COUNSELING POINTS

See the Drug Formulations and Patient Counseling chapter for counseling language/layman's terminology.

AZOLE ANTIFUNGALS
- Can cause:
  - Liver damage.
  - QT prolongation (except isavuconazonium).
- Many drug interactions.

Ketoconazole and Itraconazole
- Itraconazole
  - Tablets and capsules: take with food.
  - Solution: take on an empty stomach.
  - Can cause heart failure.
- Possible drug interactions due to high gastric pH.

Posaconazole (*Noxafil*)
- Posaconazole tablets: take with food.
- Posaconazole suspension: take with a full meal or oral liquid nutritional supplement.

Voriconazole (*Vfend*)
- Take on an empty stomach, at least one hour before or one hour after meals.
- Can cause:
  - Photosensitivity.
  - Vision changes.
- Store reconstituted oral suspension at room temperature.

NYSTATIN
- Oral suspension: shake well before using.

TERBINAFINE
- Oral terbinafine can cause liver damage.
- Can take several months after finishing treatment to see the full benefit of this drug. It takes time for new healthy nails to grow and replace the infected ones.

INFECTIOUS DISEASES

VIRAL INFECTIONS

Viruses depend on host cell metabolic processes for survival; for that reason, they are sometimes referred to as obligate intracellular parasites. Many viral infections have no effective drug treatment. Medications are available to treat influenza virus, COVID-19, herpes simplex virus [genital herpes, herpes labialis (cold sores) and systemic herpes virus infections], varicella zoster virus (VZV) and cytomegalovirus (CMV).

Treatments for viral infections work by directly inhibiting viruses (antiviral agents) or augmenting or modifying host defenses to the viral infection (immunomodulating agents). Antivirals target critical steps in the viral life cycle, such as entry into the cell or replication; since viruses depend on the host cell machinery for metabolism/replication, antivirals can also injure or destroy the host cell.

INFLUENZA

Influenza is a respiratory virus that affects 3 – 11% of the U.S. population annually, with peak activity typically occurring between late November and March. Influenza A and B are the strains that commonly infect humans. Many diagnostic tests are available to test for influenza (e.g., molecular assays, antigen detection tests). The rapid influenza diagnostic test is often done as a nasopharyngeal swab.

Both influenza A and B can cause severe illness leading to hospitalization and death, particularly in at-risk patients, including pregnant patients, immunocompromised patients, children < 5 years, adults ≥ 65 years, and those with comorbid conditions (e.g., diabetes, asthma, cardiovascular disease). Influenza spreads via respiratory droplets generated by coughing and sneezing. A person with influenza can be contagious one day prior to developing symptoms and for up to 5 – 7 days after becoming ill.

Influenza commonly presents with fever, chills, fatigue, myalgia, non-productive cough, sore throat and headache. The seasonal influenza vaccine is the most effective prevention for influenza infection and is recommended for all patients age ≥ 6 months who have no contraindications. See the Immunizations chapter for details.

Antivirals for Influenza

The Centers for Disease Control and Prevention (CDC) provides annual updates to the antiviral treatment recommendations based on the type of circulating virus each influenza season. Neuraminidase inhibitors (oseltamivir, zanamivir and peramivir) reduce the amount of virus in the body by inhibiting the enzyme which enables release of new viral particles from infected cells. They are active against influenza A and B, decreasing the duration of symptoms by about one day and reducing complications. To be most effective, neuraminidase inhibitors should be started within 48 hours of illness onset. In hospitalized, severely ill patients and those at high risk of complications, neuraminidase inhibitors should still be started > 48 hours after symptom onset, though there is less benefit if started later, after the virus has already damaged respiratory epithelial cells.

Baloxavir marboxil (Xofluza) is an endonuclease inhibitor approved for the treatment and post-exposure prevention of influenza. It has the advantage of being a single-dose regimen. Similar to neuraminidase inhibitors, it should be started within 48 hours of symptom onset.

The adamantanes (rimantadine and amantadine) were previously used to treat and prevent influenza A, but they are no longer recommended due to widespread resistance. Amantadine is used for Parkinson disease (see the Parkinson Disease chapter).

Neuraminidase Inhibitors

DRUG	DOSING	SAFETY/SIDE EFFECTS/MONITORING
Oseltamivir (Tamiflu) 30, 45, 75 mg capsules 6 mg/mL (60 mL) suspension 📷 Stuart Monk/Shutterstock.com	**Treatment, age > 12 years:** 75 mg BID x 5 days **Prophylaxis, age > 12 years:** 75 mg daily x 10 days CrCl ≤ 60 mL/min: adjustment required **Pediatric patients:** dose based on body weight	**WARNINGS** Neuropsychiatric events (sudden confusion, delirium, hallucinations, unusual behavior or self-injury), serious skin reactions (SJS/TEN), anaphylaxis **SIDE EFFECTS** Headache, nausea, vomiting, diarrhea, abdominal pain **NOTES** Preferred in pregnancy over other neuraminidase inhibitors Store reconstituted suspension at room temperature for 10 days or in the refrigerator for 17 days
Zanamivir (Relenza Diskhaler)	**Treatment, age ≥ 7 years:** 10 mg (two 5 mg inhalations) BID x 5 days **Prophylaxis, age ≥ 5 years:** 10 mg (two 5 mg inhalations) once daily x 10 days (household setting) or 28 days (community outbreak)	**WARNINGS** Neuropsychiatric events, bronchospasm (do not use in asthma/COPD or with any breathing problems); stop the drug if wheezing or breathing problems develop **SIDE EFFECTS** Headache, throat pain, cough
Peramivir (Rapivab) Injection	**Treatment (adult):** 600 mg IV as a single dose CrCl < 50 mL/min: adjustment required	**WARNINGS** Neuropsychiatric events, serious skin reactions (SJS/TEN), anaphylaxis, renal impairment **SIDE EFFECTS** Hypertension, insomnia, ↑ blood glucose, diarrhea, constipation, neutropenia, ↑ AST/ALT

Endonuclease Inhibitors

DRUG	DOSING	SAFETY/SIDE EFFECTS/MONITORING
Baloxavir marboxil (Xofluza) 20, 40 mg capsules 2 mg/mL (20 mL) suspension	**Treatment and prophylaxis, age ≥ 12 years:** 40 to < 80 kg: 40 mg PO x 1 dose ≥ 80 kg: 80 mg PO x 1 dose Use with caution in renal or hepatic impairment (limited data)	**WARNINGS** Hypersensitivity including skin reactions (erythema multiforme, urticaria) Prescribers should look for secondary bacterial infections and treat accordingly **SIDE EFFECTS** Diarrhea **NOTES** Avoid administration with dairy products, antacids or other supplements containing polyvalent cations (e.g., calcium, magnesium, selenium, zinc) Store in original blister packaging Once reconstituted, the oral suspension must be administered within 10 hours (store at room temp); dose may require more than 1 bottle

COVID-19

There are many different types of coronaviruses. Seasonal coronaviruses are a frequent cause of respiratory infections, including the common cold. Severe acute respiratory syndrome coronavirus 2 (SARS-CoV-2), a novel coronavirus that emerged in late 2019, causes coronavirus disease 2019 (COVID-19). It has a wide range of clinical presentations, from asymptomatic to severe illness requiring ICU admission and mechanical ventilation. Advanced age and comorbidities (e.g., cardiovascular or respiratory disease, diabetes, cancer) increase the risk of severe illness and death.

Like influenza, COVID-19 is spread through respiratory droplets released when coughing or sneezing. Spread can be reduced by maintaining a distance of at least 6 feet from others, wearing masks and frequent handwashing. Infected individuals may be contagious for up to 48 hours before symptom onset. Symptoms most often present within 4 – 5 days of exposure (up to 14 days) and can include fever, chills, cough, shortness of breath, fatigue, myalgia, loss of taste or smell, sore throat, runny nose and GI symptoms. Available vaccines to prevent COVID-19 are discussed in the Immunizations chapter.

COVID-19 Testing and Treatment

The recommendations on testing, treatment, isolation of infected individuals and quarantine of those potentially exposed continue to evolve; consult the CDC, National Institutes of Health (NIH) and Infectious Diseases Society of America (IDSA) websites for the most current recommendations. Generally, all symptomatic patients and select asymptomatic individuals (e.g., travelers, those with close contact with an infected person, people with repeated exposures, including healthcare workers) should be tested for COVID-19. Diagnosis usually involves a polymerase chain reaction (PCR) test using a nasopharyngeal swab specimen and/or a rapid antigen test, which is generally less sensitive than PCR.

Symptomatic care (e.g., hydration, analgesics/antipyretics, antitussives) is appropriate in all patients. It is essential to counsel patients to seek medical care if symptoms worsen (e.g., new-onset dyspnea) or interfere with daily activities. There are some medications [e.g., remdesivir *(Veklury)*, nirmatrelvir/ritonavir *(Paxlovid)*, tocilizumab] that are available to treat COVID-19 in nonhospitalized or hospitalized patients, if deemed appropriate by a healthcare provider. Most are available under an FDA emergency-use authorization; remdesivir is the only agent with an FDA-approved indication. Systemic steroids (e.g., dexamethasone) can be added to antiviral and/or immunomodulator treatment in hospitalized patients who require supplemental oxygen. Virus-neutralizing monoclonal antibodies are still under investigation.

HERPES VIRUSES

There are hundreds of herpes viruses in existence, but not all are responsible for causing human disease. Clinically significant herpes viruses include herpes simplex viruses 1 and 2 (HSV-1, HSV-2), varicella zoster virus (VZV), cytomegalovirus (CMV), Epstein-Barr virus (EBV), human herpesviruses (HHV-6, HHV-7) and Kaposi sarcoma associated herpes virus (HHV-8).

Both HSV-1 and HSV-2 can cause various infections, including orofacial, esophageal, genital, ophthalmic, pulmonary and CNS (e.g., encephalitis) infections. HSV-1 is most commonly associated with oropharyngeal disease. HSV-2 is more closely associated with genital disease. Each virus is capable of causing infections clinically indistinguishable at both anatomic sites.

Antivirals for Herpes Simplex Virus and Varicella Zoster Virus

INFECTIOUS DISEASES

DRUG	SAFETY/SIDE EFFECTS/MONITORING
Acyclovir (*Zovirax*, Sitavig) Capsule, tablet, buccal tablet, suspension, injection, topical	**WARNINGS** Caution in patients with renal impairment, the elderly and/or those receiving nephrotoxic drugs; infuse acyclovir over at least 1 hour and maintain adequate hydration to reduce the risk of renal tubular damage Thrombotic thrombocytopenic purpura/hemolytic uremic syndrome (TTP/HUS) has been reported in immunocompromised patients
Valacyclovir (*Valtrex*) Tablet Prodrug of acyclovir	**SIDE EFFECTS** Malaise, headache, N/V/D, rash, pruritus, ↑ LFTs, neutropenia, ↑ seizures (especially with IV acyclovir and famciclovir), transient burning or stinging with topical formulations (acyclovir) Anaphylaxis (famciclovir) ↑ SCr/BUN with crystal nephropathy (IV acyclovir)
Famciclovir Tablet Prodrug of penciclovir	**MONITORING** Renal function, LFTs, CBC **NOTES** Acyclovir dose is based on IBW, including in obese patients (see the Calculations IV chapter) ↓ dose and/or extend interval in renal impairment In general, 5 mg/kg IV acyclovir = 1,000 mg PO valacyclovir

Herpes Simplex Labialis (Cold Sores)

Cold sores are common and highly contagious. Children often contract the infection from family members; infection is usually due to HSV-1 in children but can be caused by HSV-2 due to adult oral/genital sex. The virus can shed when the patient is asymptomatic, but is more commonly spread when there are active lesions. Patients should avoid kissing and sharing drinks when the lesions are oozing.

Cold sores usually appear in the same location repeatedly. The most common site is the junction between the upper and lower lip. Triggers that cause sore outbreaks include stress/fatigue, stress to the skin (e.g., sun exposure, acid peels) and dental work. Patients should identify their triggers and attempt to avoid them.

Cold sore eruption is preceded by a prodrome (symptoms that occur before the lesions appear) of tingling, itching or soreness, which is the optimal time to take topical or oral medication to reduce blister duration. If recurrences are frequent (> 4 times/year), chronic suppression treatment can be taken daily. OTC and prescription topicals shorten the duration of cold sores by up to one day; oral (systemic) antivirals shorten the duration by up to two days.

Topical Treatment for Herpes Labialis

DRUGS	DOSING	NOTES
Docosanol (*Abreva*) – OTC Cream	Apply 5x daily at first sign of outbreak, continue until healed.	Systemic antivirals are more effective. _Marten_House/Shutterstock.com_
Acyclovir (*Zovirax*) – Rx Cream	Apply 5x daily for 4 days (can be used on genital sores).	
Acyclovir (*Sitavig*) – Rx Buccal tablet	Apply 50 mg tablet as a single dose to the upper gum region.	
Penciclovir (*Denavir*) – Rx Cream	Apply every 2 hours during waking hours for 4 days.	

Systemic (Oral) Treatment of Herpes Labialis

EPISODE	ACYCLOVIR	VALACYCLOVIR	FAMCICLOVIR
Initial (treat for 7-10 days)	200 mg 5x daily or 400 mg TID	1 gram BID	250 mg 3x daily or 500 mg BID
Recurrence	400 mg TID x 5-10 days	2 grams BID x 1 day	1.5 grams x 1 dose
Chronic suppression	400 mg BID	500 mg or 1 gram daily	

Genital Herpes

Genital herpes, caused by HSV-2, is a chronic, life-long viral infection that affects 1 in 6 people in the U.S. The first episode of genital herpes usually begins within 2 – 14 days after exposure. Up to 50% of patients are asymptomatic, but others experience a prodrome of flu-like symptoms, fever, headache, malaise and myalgia before the development of pustular or ulcerative lesions on external genitalia. Lesions usually begin as papules or vesicles that rapidly spread. Clusters of lesions form, crust and then re-epithelialize. Lesions are painful and associated with itching, dysuria and vaginal or urethral discharge.

Treatment must be initiated during the prodrome period or within one day of lesion onset. Acyclovir (Zovirax) is the least expensive regimen, but it must be dosed up to five times per day. Valacyclovir (Valtrex) is a prodrug of acyclovir; it can reach higher concentrations than oral acyclovir and the less frequent dosing can enhance adherence. If the virus is found to be resistant to acyclovir, it will be resistant to valacyclovir and (usually) famciclovir. Infections caused by acyclovir-resistant HSV are treated with foscarnet until the lesions heal.

Recurrent infections are not associated with systemic manifestations. Symptoms are localized to the genital area, are milder and of shorter duration. Patients typically experience a prodrome of mild tingling or shooting pain in the legs, hips, thighs or buttocks. Suppressive therapy (antivirals taken chronically) reduces the frequency of genital herpes recurrences by 70 – 80% and is recommended for patients who have frequent recurrences (e.g., > 6 recurrences/year). With suppressive therapy, many report no symptomatic outbreaks and viral transmission is also reduced.

Oral Treatment of Genital Herpes in Non-HIV Patients

EPISODE	ACYCLOVIR	VALACYCLOVIR	FAMCICLOVIR
Initial (treat for 7-10 days)*	400 mg TID or 200 mg 5x daily	1 gram BID	250 mg TID
Recurrence	400 mg TID x 5 days or 800 mg BID x 5 days or 800 mg TID x 2 days	500 mg BID x 3 days or 1 gram daily x 5 days	125 mg BID x 5 days or 500 mg x 1, then 250 mg BID x 2 days or 1 gram BID x 1 day
Chronic suppression	400 mg BID	500 mg or 1 gram daily	250 mg BID

Treatment can be extended if healing is incomplete after 10 days of therapy

Invasive HSV Infections

HSV is the most commonly identified cause of viral encephalitis in the U.S. (10 – 20% of all cases). HSV encephalitis occurs more frequently in young patients (ages 5 - 30 years) and older adults (age > 50 years). Hallmark symptoms include acute onset of fever, focal neurologic symptoms and altered mental status. HSV encephalitis is treated with IV acyclovir 10 mg/kg/dose Q8H x 14 – 21 days. Other invasive infections (e.g., esophagitis and pneumonitis) occur infrequently, typically in the immunosuppressed population, and are treated with IV acyclovir 5 mg/kg/dose Q8H.

Varicella Zoster Virus and Herpes Zoster

Most adults in the U.S. had varicella zoster virus (chickenpox) infection during childhood. The virus can lie dormant in the nerve for decades without causing any symptoms. The recurrence of viral symptoms is called herpes zoster or shingles. An outbreak can occur as the patient ages and is often due to acute stress. Although herpes zoster can occur at any age, adults > 60 years old are most often affected. The shingles rash is distinctive; it can be itchy or tingly, is very painful and often manifests unilaterally (on only one side of the body). Pharmacists should recognize the classic presentation of a shingles rash and inform patients to see a healthcare provider.

Antiviral therapy should be initiated at the earliest sign or symptom of shingles and is most effective when started within 72 hours of the onset of zoster rash. Pain can be treated with topical medications (Lidoderm patch, lidocaine gel), neuropathic pain medications (e.g., pregabalin, gabapentin, duloxetine, tricyclic antidepressants), NSAIDs or opioids. Most patients recover without long-term effects, but 5 – 10% have chronic pain [called postherpetic neuralgia (PHN)], which can be debilitating. Older patients are more likely to experience PHN, non-pain complications, hospitalizations and interference with activities of daily living. The treatment of PHN is similar to the treatment of acute shingles pain.

The Advisory Committee on Immunization Practices (ACIP) recommends the shingles vaccines (Shingrix) in immunocompetent adults ≥ 50 years and adults ≥ 19 years who are or will be immunosppressed. Patients previously vaccinated with Zostavax (no longer marketed) should be re-vaccinated with Shingrix. Patients who have had a previous shingles outbreak should be vaccinated to decrease the likelihood of recurrence and severity of postherpetic neuralgia. See the Immunizations chapter.

Herpes Zoster (Shingles) Treatment

DRUG	DOSING	DESCRIPTION
Acyclovir (Zovirax)	800 mg PO 5x daily for <u>7 days</u> (or 10 days)	
Valacyclovir (Valtrex)	1 gram PO TID for <u>7 days</u>	
Famciclovir	500 mg PO TID for <u>7 days</u>	

📷 Toey Toey/Shutterstock.com

<u>A cluster of fluid-filled blisters, often in a band</u> around one side of the waist, on one side of the forehead, around an eye or on the neck (less common on other areas of the body)

Cytomegalovirus

Cytomegalovirus (CMV) is a double-stranded DNA virus within the herpes virus family (HHV-5). It occurs in severely <u>immunocompromised</u> states (e.g., AIDS, transplant recipients) and most commonly causes <u>retinitis, colitis or esophagitis</u>. <u>Ganciclovir and valganciclovir</u> are the <u>treatments of choice for CMV</u> infection. <u>Foscarnet and cidofovir</u> should be <u>reserved</u> for <u>refractory cases</u>, as an alternative when treatment-limiting toxicities occur with ganciclovir and/or when the CMV strain is resistant to (val)ganciclovir. Maribavir *(Livtencity)* is an option for post-transplant CMV disease refractory to all other treatments. Secondary prophylaxis (also called maintenance therapy) is necessary for some patients. Letermovir *(Prevymis)* is FDA-approved for the prophylaxis of CMV in patients receiving a hematopoietic stem cell transplant who screen positive for CMV. Ganciclovir and valganciclovir are used for prophylaxis of CMV infection in solid organ transplant recipients at high risk (donor is positive for CMV/recipient is negative for CMV).

DRUG	DOSING	SAFETY/SIDE EFFECTS/MONITORING
Ganciclovir Injection *Zirgan* (ophthalmic gel)	Treatment: 5 mg/kg IV BID x 14-21 days Maintenance/prophylaxis: 5 mg/kg IV daily ↓ dose and extend interval when CrCl < 70 mL/min Injection: reconstitute with sterile water, <u>not</u> bacteriostatic water Hazardous agent: special handling required	**BOXED WARNINGS** <u>Myelosuppression</u>; carcinogenic and teratogenic effects and inhibition of spermatogenesis in animals **SIDE EFFECTS** Fever, N/V/D, anorexia, thrombocytopenia, neutropenia, leukopenia, anemia, ↑ SCr, seizures (rare), retinal detachment (in patients with CMV retinitis) **MONITORING** CBC with differential, PLT, SCr, retinal exam
Valganciclovir **(Valcyte)** Tablet, solution <u>Prodrug of ganciclovir</u> (with better bioavailability)	Treatment: 900 mg PO BID x 21 days Maintenance/prophylaxis: 900 mg PO daily ↓ dose and extend interval when CrCl < 60 mL/min Hazardous agent: special handling required	**NOTES** Females should use contraception during treatment and for 30 days after, males should use a barrier contraceptive for 90 days after IV ganciclovir 5 mg/kg = PO valganciclovir 900 mg Ganciclovir and valganciclovir are the drugs of choice for CMV disease Both compete with tenofovir for elimination via tubular secretion, concentrations of either tenofovir or ganciclovir may be increased <u>Solution: refrigerate</u>; discard after 49 days

INFECTIOUS DISEASES

DRUG	DOSING	SAFETY/SIDE EFFECTS/MONITORING
Cidofovir Injection CMV retinitis in HIV patients only	5 mg/kg/wk IV x 2 weeks, then 5 mg/kg once every 2 weeks Hazardous agent: special handling required Renal impairment: ↓ dose or discontinue based on level of SCr increase (also see Contraindications)	**BOXED WARNINGS** Dose-dependent nephrotoxicity, neutropenia, carcinogenic/teratogenic **CONTRAINDICATIONS** SCr > 1.5 mg/dL, CrCl ≤ 55 mL/min, urine protein ≥ 100 mg/dL (≥ 2+ proteinuria), sulfa allergy, use with or within 7 days of other nephrotoxic drugs, direct intraocular injection **SIDE EFFECTS** Nephrotoxicity, myelosuppression (less than ganciclovir), metabolic acidosis **NOTES** Patient should receive hydration before each dose and probenecid before and after each dose to decrease nephrotoxicity Competes with tenofovir for tubular secretion, concentrations of either drug can be increased
Foscarnet *(Foscavir)* Injection CMV retinitis, resistant HSV	Induction: 90 mg/kg IV Q12H or 60 mg/kg Q8H x 2-3 weeks Maintenance: 90-120 mg/kg IV daily Renal impairment: ↓ dose and extend interval	**BOXED WARNINGS** Renal impairment occurs to some degree in the majority of patients (prehydration recommended); seizures due to electrolyte imbalances (can lead to status epilepticus or death) **SIDE EFFECTS** Electrolyte abnormalities (↓ K, ↓ Ca, ↓ Mg, ↓ Phos), ↑ SCr, ↑ BUN, QT prolongation **NOTES** Do not exceed maximum infusion rate (increases toxicity)

Epstein-Barr Virus

Epstein-Barr virus (EBV) is a member of the herpes virus family. Infectious EBV is called mononucleosis or "mono," and most people get infected with EBV at some point in their lives. It is transmitted through bodily fluids, primarily saliva, and can spread by kissing, sharing drinks or food, or by contact with an object that has been in the mouth of an infected person (e.g., child's toys). Common symptoms include fatigue, fever, sore throat and swollen lymph nodes. They usually resolve in 2 – 4 weeks. No drug treatment or vaccine exists for mononucleosis.

Amoxicillin or ampicillin treatment in a child with EBV can cause a non-pruritic (i.e., non-itchy) rash that appears similar to an allergic reaction; it is not and should not be included as an "allergy" in the medical record.

ANTIVIRAL KEY COUNSELING POINTS

See the Drug Formulations and Patient Counseling chapter for counseling language/layman's terminology.

Oseltamivir *(Tamiflu)*
- Treatment should begin within two days of onset of influenza symptoms.
- Can cause delirium.

Acyclovir *(Zovirax)* and Valacyclovir *(Valtrex)*
- This medication does not cure herpes infections (cold sores, chickenpox, shingles or genital herpes). Use safe sex practices to lower transmission risk.
- Start treatment within 24 hours of the onset of symptoms.
- Acyclovir:
  - Drink plenty of fluids.
  - The topical cream can cause temporary burning or stinging.

Select Guidelines/References

Patterson TF, Thompson GR 3rd, Denning DW, et al. Practice Guidelines for the Diagnosis and Management of Aspergillosis: 2016 Update by IDSA. *Clin Infect Dis*. 2016;63:e1-e60.

Pappas PG, Kauffman CA, Andes DR, et al. Clinical Practice Guideline for Management of Candidiasis: 2016 Update by IDSA. *Clin Infect Dis*. 2016;62:409-17.

Uyeki TM, Bernstein HH, Bradley JS, et al. Clinical Practice Guidelines by the Infectious Diseases Society of America: 2018 Update on Diagnosis, Treatment, Chemoprophylaxis, and Institutional Outbreak Management of Seasonal Influenza. *Clin Infect Dis*. 2018;48:1003-1032.

COVID-19 Treatment Guidelines Panel. Coronavirus Disease 2019 (COVID-19) Treatment Guidelines. National Institutes of Health. Available at https://www.covid19treatmentguidelines.nih.gov/ (accessed 2022 Jan 27).

Protozoa
Rheumatoid
Methotrexate
Virus
Immunosuppressed
AIDS
Bacteria
Dexamethasone
Leukemia
Fungus
Prednisone

CHAPTER 25

INFECTIOUS DISEASES IV: OPPORTUNISTIC INFECTIONS

BACKGROUND

Immunocompromised patients are predisposed to opportunistic infections (OIs), which occur when the immune system is weak and unable to respond normally to invading bacteria, fungi, viruses and protozoa. The risk can be related to a disease or drug treatment that suppresses the immune system. Immunocompromised states include:

- Diseases that destroy key components of the immune response, primarily HIV with a CD4 T lymphocyte count < 200 cells/mm³ (which is a defining criteria for AIDS).

- Use of systemic steroids for 14 days or longer at a prednisone dose (or prednisone equivalent dose) ≥ 20 mg/day or ≥ 2 mg/kg/day.

- Asplenia (lack of a functioning spleen), due to sickle cell disease or splenectomy.

- Use of immunosuppressants for autoimmune conditions or post-transplant (e.g., TNF-alpha inhibitors).

- Use of cancer chemotherapy agents that destroy white blood cells, particularly with severe neutropenia (ANC < 500 cells/mm³).

INFECTIOUS DISEASES

PRIMARY PROPHYLAXIS

Common opportunistic infections requiring primary prophylaxis include:

- *Pneumocystis jirovecii* pneumonia (PJP or PCP)
- *Toxoplasmosis gondii* encephalitis
- *Mycobacterium avium* complex (MAC)

Candida infections in the mouth/esophagus (e.g., thrush) are more likely in immunocompromised states, but prophylaxis is not usually recommended.

OIs can be prevented with antibiotics, antifungals and/or antivirals; this is referred to as chemoprophylaxis, or simply prophylaxis. The criteria for starting and stopping primary prophylaxis in HIV patients are discussed below. Criteria for other disease states will differ; for example, in the setting of malignancy, primary prophylaxis is warranted when a patient is expected to develop profound neutropenia (ANC < 100 cells/mm³ for ≥ 7 days), and is continued for the duration of neutropenia.

PRIMARY PROPHYLAXIS REGIMENS IN HIV

The table below outlines select OIs, the CD4 count at which a patient with HIV becomes at risk for the infection and the primary prophylaxis regimen used to prevent the infection.

Selection of alternative regimens (for prophylaxis or treatment) depends on patient-specific factors (e.g., allergies or G6PD deficiency). For example, atovaquone, dapsone and pentamidine are options for PCP in the setting of a sulfa allergy, and atovaquone and pentamidine are options in the setting of a G6PD deficiency. Leucovorin is added to all pyrimethamine-containing regimens as rescue therapy to reduce the risk of pyrimethamine-induced myelosuppression.

OPPORTUNISTIC INFECTION	CRITERIA FOR STARTING	PRIMARY PROPHYLAXIS REGIMEN	CRITERIA FOR DISCONTINUING
Pneumocystis jirovecii pneumonia (PJP or PCP)	CD4 count < 200 cells/mm³ or AIDS-defining illness (see Human Immunodeficiency Virus chapter)	**PREFERRED** SMX/TMP* DS or SS daily **ALTERNATIVES** SMX/TMP DS 3x/week or Dapsone or Dapsone + pyrimethamine + leucovorin or Atovaquone or Atovaquone + pyrimethamine + leucovorin Inhaled pentamidine	CD4 count > 200 cells/mm³ for > 3 months on ART Can consider when CD4 count is 100-200 cells/mm³ and viral load has been undetectable for ≥ 3-6 months
Toxoplasma gondii encephalitis	Toxoplasma IgG positive and CD4 count < 100 cells/mm³	**PREFERRED** SMX/TMP DS daily **ALTERNATIVES** SMX/TMP DS 3x/week or SS daily or Dapsone + pyrimethamine + leucovorin or Atovaquone or Atovaquone + pyrimethamine + leucovorin	CD4 count > 200 cells/mm³ for > 3 months on ART Can consider when CD4 count is 100-200 cells/mm³ and viral load has been undetectable for ≥ 3-6 months
Mycobacterium avium complex (MAC)	Not recommended if ART is started immediately Initiate if not taking ART and CD4 count < 50 cells/mm³ Must rule out active disseminated MAC disease	**PREFERRED** Azithromycin 1,200 mg weekly **ALTERNATIVES** Azithromycin 600 mg twice weekly or Clarithromycin 500 mg BID	Taking fully suppressive ART

SMX/TMP = sulfamethoxazole/trimethoprim

TREATMENT OF OPPORTUNISTIC INFECTIONS

The following table lists select OIs and the recommended medications for treatment, which is the same regardless of the cause of immunosuppression. After completing initial treatment, secondary prophylaxis is given to prevent recurrence of the infection in patients who continue to be at risk.

When treating thrush in patients with HIV, even with mild disease, systemic treatment is preferred (rather than localized treatment with agents such as clotrimazole, miconazole or nystatin).

OPPORTUNISTIC INFECTION	PREFERRED REGIMEN	ALTERNATIVE REGIMEN	SECONDARY PROPHYLAXIS
Candidiasis (thrush) (oropharyngeal/esophageal) Appears as a white film in the mouth/throat	Fluconazole	Oropharyngeal: itraconazole, posaconazole, topicals (e.g., clotrimazole troche, nystatin) Esophageal: voriconazole, isavuconazonium or an echinocandin (e.g., caspofungin)	Not usually recommended
Cryptococcal meningitis	Amphotericin B (deoxycholate or liposomal) + flucytosine	Fluconazole + flucytosine or Amphotericin B + fluconazole	Fluconazole (low dose)
Cytomegalovirus (CMV)	Valganciclovir or Ganciclovir	If toxicities to ganciclovir or resistant strains: foscarnet or cidofovir	None; maintain CD4 count > 100 cells/mm^3
Mycobacterium avium complex (MAC)	(Clarithromycin or azithromycin) + ethambutol	Add a 3rd or 4th agent using rifabutin, amikacin, streptomycin, moxifloxacin or levofloxacin	Same as treatment regimen
Pneumocystis jirovecii pneumonia (PJP, or PCP)	SMX/TMP (high-dose, see Infectious Diseases I chapter) ± prednisone or methylprednisolone Duration: 21 days	Atovaquone or Pentamidine IV or Clindamycin + primaquine or Dapsone + trimethoprim	Same as primary prophylaxis
Toxoplasmosis gondii encephalitis Risks: exposure to the parasite via ingestion of undercooked/raw meat or raw shellfish, or contact with cat feces/litter	Pyrimethamine + leucovorin + sulfadiazine	SMX/TMP or Clindamycin + pyrimethamine + leucovorin or Atovaquone or Atovaquone + sulfadiazine or Atovaquone + pyrimethamine + leucovorin	Same as treatment (but with reduced doses)

Select Guidelines/References

Panel on Opportunistic Infections in HIV-Infected Adults and Adolescents. Guidelines for the Prevention and Treatment of Opportunistic Infections in HIV-Infected Adults and Adolescents: Recommendations from the Centers for Disease Control and Prevention, the National Institutes of Health, and the HIV Medicine Association of the Infectious Diseases Society of America. Available at https://clinicalinfo.hiv.gov/sites/default/files/guidelines/documents/Adult_OI.pdf (accessed 2022 Jan 30).

National Comprehensive Cancer Network (NCCN) Clinical Practice Guidelines in Oncology. Prevention and Treatment of Cancer-Related Infections. Version 2.2020. http://www.nccn.org/professionals/physician_gls/pdf/infections.pdf (accessed 2022 Jan 30).

Antimicrobial Prophylaxis for Adult Patients With Cancer-Related Immunosuppression: ASCO and IDSA Clinical Practice Guideline Update. Available at https://www.idsociety.org/globalassets/idsa/practice-guidelines/jco.18.00374.pdf (accessed 2022 Jan 30).

CHAPTER CONTENT

CONTENT LEGEND

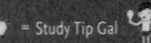 ● = Study Tip Gal

Adapted from ©https://aidsinfo.nih.gov/

CHAPTER 26

HUMAN IMMUNODEFICIENCY VIRUS

BACKGROUND

There are ~1.2 million people infected with human immunodeficiency virus (HIV) in the U.S., and ~13% of those are unaware that they are infected. Annually, ~38,000 people are newly diagnosed with HIV. If left untreated, HIV can progress to an advanced and severe stage of infection called acquired immunodeficiency syndrome (AIDS).

HIV CAUSES T-CELL DEATH

HIV is a single-stranded RNA retrovirus that uses the machinery in host CD4 T-helper cells (T cells) to replicate. Once replicated, the viral copies burst through the CD4 cell membrane, destroying the cell in the process. Billions of T cells are destroyed every day if HIV is not treated adequately with antiretroviral therapy (ART).

- When HIV continues to replicate, the viral load increases and the CD4 count decreases.

- AIDS is diagnosed when the CD4 count falls below 200 cells/mm³ or the patient develops an AIDS-defining condition (discussed later in the chapter).
  - At this point, the immune system is very weak and can no longer ward off opportunistic infections (OIs) (e.g., infections caused by normal environmental exposures that would not otherwise occur in a host with an intact immune system) and specific malignancies that are indicative of AIDS (e.g., Kaposi's sarcoma, an AIDS-defining condition).

The ART regimens currently available allow people with HIV to live long and healthy lives if adherent to treatment. When HIV/AIDS was first recognized in 1981, there was no effective treatment.

TRANSMISSION

Infection is spread by direct contact with <u>blood, semen, vaginal secretions</u> or <u>rectal secretions</u>, or ingestion of <u>breast milk</u>. Most infections are caused by <u>unprotected vaginal or rectal sex</u>, and <u>sharing injection</u> drug equipment, including needles. Infection can spread from a <u>woman</u> with HIV <u>to her child</u> during <u>pregnancy, childbirth</u> or <u>breastfeeding</u>. This is called <u>mother-to-child</u> or <u>vertical</u> transmission.

SCREENING AND DIAGNOSIS

The CDC recommends routine HIV screening at least <u>once for all patients</u> who are 13 – 64 years old. If a person is <u>high-risk</u> for infection, testing should be done at least <u>annually</u>. The <u>high-risk</u> indicators for becoming infected with HIV are:

- <u>Sharing drug-injection equipment</u>: needles, syringes and cookers (used to mix up or "cook" drugs).

- <u>High-risk sexual behaviors</u>: men who have sex with men, sex with multiple partners, sex with a person known to be infected with HIV, sexual activity resulting in a history of <u>sexually transmitted infections</u> (e.g., syphilis, chlamydia, gonorrhea).

- A history of <u>hepatitis</u> or <u>tuberculosis</u> (TB) infection.

STAGES OF INFECTION AND DIAGNOSTIC TESTING

<u>Acute HIV infection</u> presents with non-specific <u>flu-like symptoms</u> that can last a few days to several weeks, including fever, myalgias, headache, lymphadenopathy (i.e., swollen lymph glands), pharyngitis and rash. An antibody response can take weeks or months to develop and, in most cases, is not fully able to fend off the virus. Patients become asymptomatic after this initial phase, but the virus is still replicating and capable of being transmitted. Over time, the CD4 count decreases, but it can take several years for an untreated patient to develop AIDS.

- ~2 weeks post-infection, the viral load is high enough for <u>HIV RNA and HIV p24 antigens</u> to be <u>detected</u> with an initial <u>HIV-1/HIV-2 antigen/antibody</u> screening test (see algorithm below).

  - <u>Positive</u> results should be <u>confirmed</u> with an <u>antibody differentiation immunoassay</u> which <u>differentiates HIV-1</u> (the most common subtype in the U.S.) from <u>HIV-2 antibodies</u>. Antibodies can be <u>detected</u> in most people about <u>4 – 12 weeks</u> after contracting the disease, but it can take up to 6 months for some and repeat testing may be needed.

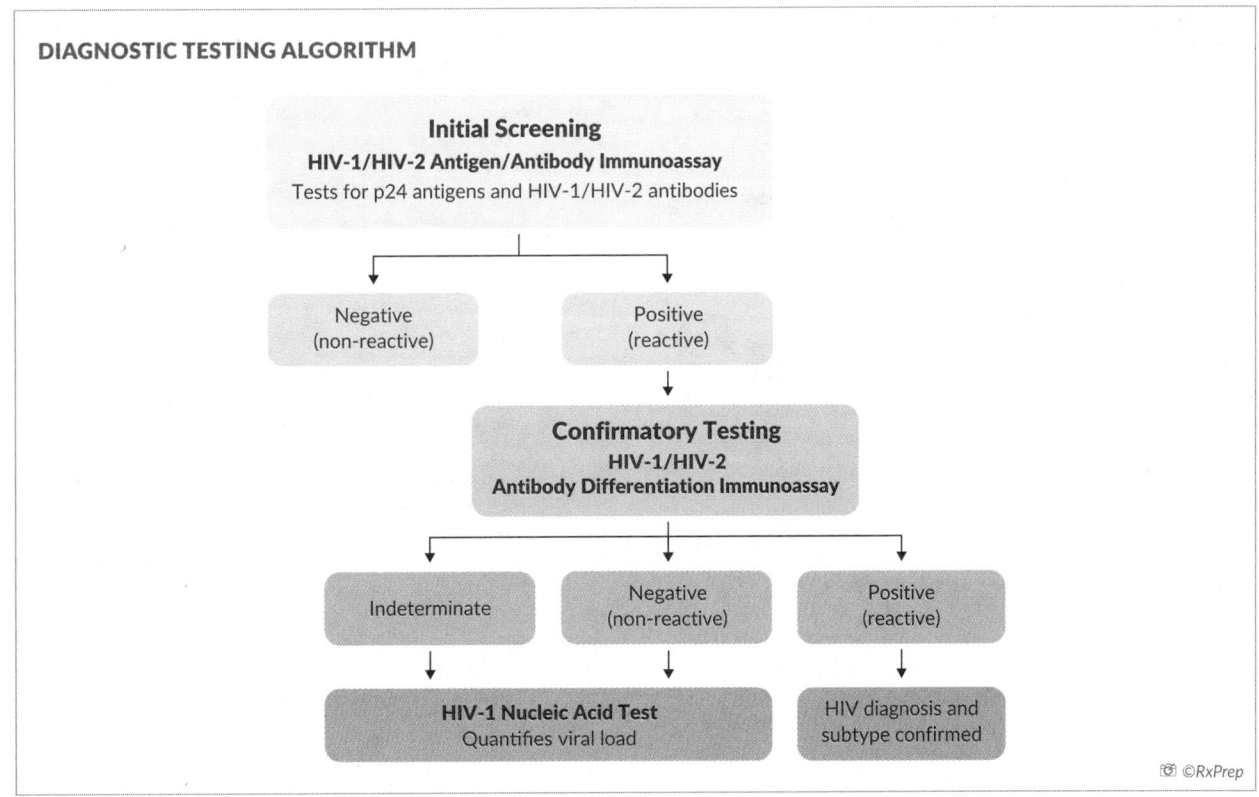

DIAGNOSTIC TESTING ALGORITHM

©RxPrep

OVER-THE-COUNTER HIV TESTING

The _OraQuick In-Home HIV Test_ detects the presence of <u>HIV antibodies</u> and provides immediate results (other OTC test kits require that a sample be sent to a lab). Individuals with a <u>positive</u> _OraQuick_ result must <u>follow up</u> with a <u>confirmatory</u> laboratory test (see previous Diagnostic Testing Algorithm).

To use the _OraQuick_ test, the upper and lower gums are swabbed with a test stick, which is then inserted into a test tube containing liquid. After 20 minutes, the test stick can be read (see picture for interpretation). The tests should be used ≥ 3 months from exposure due to the <u>lag in antibody production</u>; testing <u>sooner</u> can cause a <u>false negative</u> result.

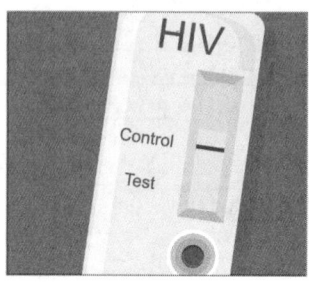 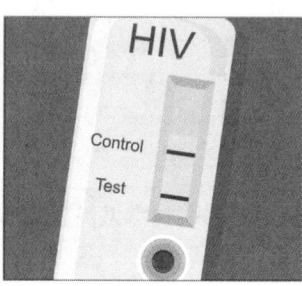

1 line = negative result. The 1st line is the control line, which should always be present.

2 lines = positive result. Many test kits are like _OraQuick_: 2 lines is a positive for whatever is being tested (e.g., pregnancy).

HIV REPLICATION STAGES AND ANTIRETROVIRAL SITES OF ACTION

It is <u>important to understand the steps (or stages)</u> involved in <u>HIV viral replication</u> and know where <u>each drug class works</u>.

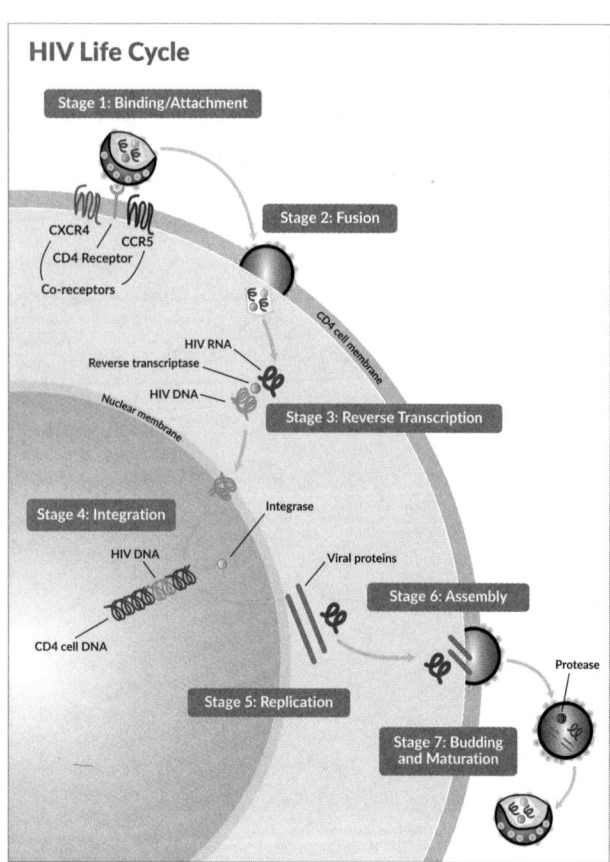

HIV Life Cycle

STAGE AND DESCRIPTION	DRUGS/DRUG CLASSES*
Stage 1: Binding/Attachment HIV attaches to a CD4 receptor and the CCR5 and/or CXCR4 co-receptors on the surface of the CD4 host cell.	CCR5 antagonist: maraviroc Attachment inhibitor: fostemsavir Post-attachment inhibitor: ibalizumab-uiyk
Stage 2: Fusion The HIV viral envelope fuses with the CD4 cell membrane. HIV enters the host cell and releases HIV RNA, viral proteins and enzymes needed for replication.	Fusion inhibitor: enfuvirtide
Stage 3: Reverse Transcription HIV RNA is converted to HIV DNA by reverse transcriptase (an HIV enzyme). HIV DNA can then enter the CD4 cell nucleus.	Nucleoside reverse transcriptase inhibitors (NRTIs) (e.g., emtricitabine, tenofovir) Non-nucleoside reverse transcriptase inhibitors (NNRTIs) (e.g., efavirenz, rilpivirine)
Stage 4: Integration Once inside the CD4 cell nucleus, integrase (an HIV enzyme) is released and used to insert HIV DNA into the host cell DNA.	Integrase strand transfer inhibitors (INSTIs) (e.g., bictegravir, dolutegravir, raltegravir)
Stage 5: Replication Host cell machinery is used to transcribe and translate HIV DNA into HIV RNA and long-chain proteins (the HIV building blocks).	None
Stage 6: Assembly New HIV RNA, proteins and enzymes (including protease) move to the cell surface and assemble into immature HIV.	None
Stage 7: Budding and Maturation Immature HIV pushes out of the CD4 cell and protease (an HIV enzyme) breaks up the long viral protein chains, creating mature virus that can infect other cells.	Protease inhibitors (PIs) (e.g., atazanavir, darunavir)

*See Drug Tables later in the chapter for more detail on mechanisms of action for each drug/drug class.

INITIAL EVALUATION AND MONITORING

The initial evaluation and follow-up monitoring of patients with HIV is extensive. Vaccinations can be indicated (or contraindicated) based on the CD4 count (see the Immunizations chapter). Routine lab tests are listed below.

- CD4 count: the major indicator of immune function used to determine the need for OI prophylaxis (see the Infectious Diseases IV chapter).

- HIV viral load: indicates how much HIV RNA is in the blood. It is the most important indicator of response to ART. A high viral load can be due to medication nonadherence or drug resistance. The treatment goal is an undetectable HIV viral load.

- Drug resistance genotypic testing.

- Comprehensive metabolic panel (includes LFTs), CBC with differential, random or fasting lipid panel, random or fasting blood glucose level and a urinalysis.

- Hepatitis B and C screening.

- Pregnancy test (patients of child-bearing potential).

- HLA-B*5701 allele (if considering using abacavir) or a tropism assay (if considering using maraviroc).

ANTIRETROVIRAL THERAPY

ART should be started as soon as possible in all HIV-infected individuals. The goal is to reduce disease progression by suppressing the HIV viral load, preserving the immune system and reducing HIV-associated morbidity and mortality. Treatment adherence is essential to prevent drug resistance.

The Study Tip Gal below shows the guideline-recommended initial regimens for most patients with newly diagnosed HIV and the table on the following page lists other complete ART regimens that are effective and tolerable if a preferred initial regimen is not suitable for a patient.

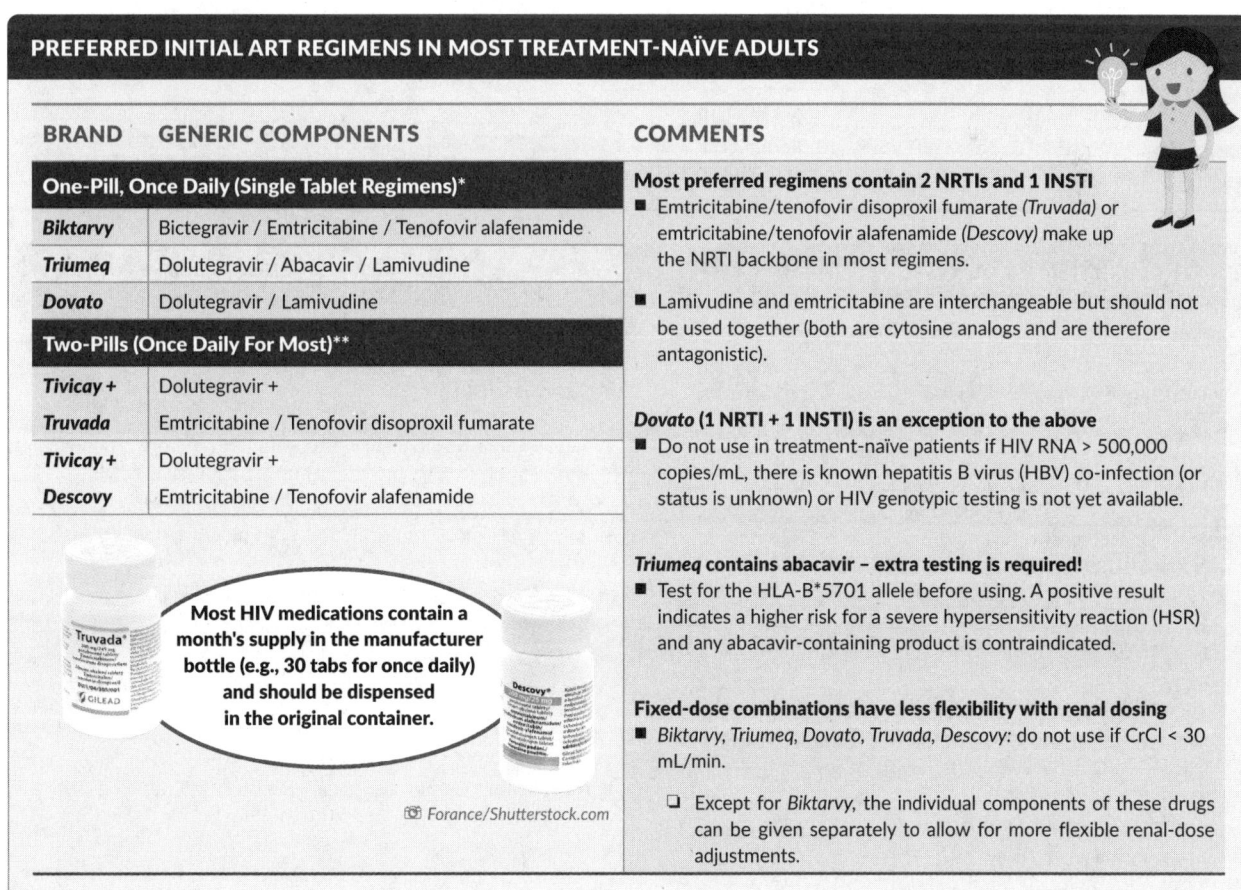

*A "/" indicates that the generic components are available in the same pill

There are multiple ways to "make" alternative ART regimens using single entity and/or combination products (see the Combination Antiretroviral Products tables later in the chapter to learn which branded products to combine).

ALTERNATIVE ART REGIMENS

A complete HIV ART regimen has <u>one "base"</u> plus <u>two NRTIs</u> to serve as the "backbone." The "base" can be a PI, an NNRTI, or an INSTI.

PI-based (boosted with cobicistat or ritonavir)
- Darunavir or atazanavir

NNRTI-based
- Efavirenz or rilpivirine

INSTI-based
- Elvitegravir (only available in combination products)
- Raltegravir

NRTI backbone (2 drugs, 1 from each row)
- TDF or TAF or abacavir PLUS
- Emtricitabine or lamivudine

Complete regimen examples
- Rilpivirine + TDF + emtricitabine
- Raltegravir + TAF + emtricitabine

TDF = tenofovir disoproxil fumarate; TAF = tenofovir alafenamide

DRUGS USED IN ART REGIMENS

DRUGS IN CLASS	MECHANISM OF ACTION	ADMINISTRATION
Nucleoside/Nucleotide Reverse Transcriptase Inhibitors (NRTIs)		
Abacavir *(Ziagen)* **Emtricitabine** *(Emtriva)* **Lamivudine** *(Epivir)* **Tenofovir disoproxil fumarate**, TDF *(Viread)* **Tenofovir alafenamide**, TAF Only in combination products for HIV; *Vemlidy* is a single-entity product for HBV **Zidovudine** *(Retrovir)* No longer recommended: Didanosine Stavudine	Competitively <u>inhibit</u> the <u>reverse transcriptase</u> enzyme, preventing the conversion of HIV RNA to HIV DNA in <u>stage 3</u> (reverse transcription) of the HIV life cycle NRTIs have a low barrier to resistance (i.e., resistance develops easily) **NAME TIP...** Remember the NRTIs with **ZDS** ♥ **LATTE**	Tenofovir (both formulations): <u>once daily</u> Abacavir and lamivudine: <u>once daily</u> and twice daily regimens Zidovudine: twice daily All NRTIs, except abacavir: ↓ dose with <u>renal</u> impairment TDF oral powder: mix with 2-4 oz of soft food (applesauce, yogurt) to avoid a bitter taste; contains lactose Zidovudine: administered <u>IV</u> during <u>labor and delivery</u> in patients with HIV RNA > 1,000 copies/mL (to <u>protect</u> the <u>baby</u>)

NRTI KEY FEATURES AND SAFETY ISSUES

All NRTIs
- Warning: lactic acidosis and hepatomegaly with steatosis (fatty liver); boxed warning for didanosine, stavudine and zidovudine
- Common side effects: nausea, diarrhea, headache, ↑ LFTs

HBV and HIV Coinfection Boxed Warnings
- Severe acute HBV exacerbation can occur if emtricitabine, lamivudine or tenofovir-containing products are discontinued (some NRTIs treat HBV)
- Do not use *Epivir-HBV* for the treatment of HIV (contains a lower dose of lamivudine)

Abacavir
- Boxed warning: risk for hypersensitivity reaction (HSR)
  - ❏ Screen for HLA-B*5701 allele before starting; abacavir is contraindicated if positive (higher risk of HSR)
  - ❏ Patients must carry a medication card indicating that HSR (e.g., fever, rash, N/V/D, abdominal pain, fatigue, dyspnea, cough) is an emergency
  - ❏ Never re-challenge patients with a history of HSR
- Consider avoiding with CVD due to a potential ↑ risk of MI

Emtricitabine
- Hyperpigmentation of the palms of the hands or soles of the feet

Tenofovir Formulations (Higher Risk with TDF)
- Renal impairment, including acute renal failure and Fanconi syndrome (renal tubular injury with hyperphosphatemia)
- ↓ dose with renal impairment and avoid other nephrotoxic drugs (e.g., NSAIDs)
- ↓ bone mineral density: consider calcium/vitamin D supplementation and DEXA scan if at risk
- Note: monitor lipids if switching from TDF to TAF for an improved side effect profile (TAF is associated with a higher risk of lipid abnormalities)

Zidovudine
- Hematologic toxicity: neutropenia and anemia (↑ MCV is a sign of adherence)
- Myopathy

Didanosine and Stavudine
- Pancreatitis, peripheral neuropathy (can be irreversible)

DRUGS IN CLASS	MECHANISM OF ACTION	ADMINISTRATION

Integrase Strand Transfer Inhibitors (INSTIs)

Bictegravir
Only in the combination drug *Biktarvy*

Cabotegravir *(Vocabria, Apretude)*

Dolutegravir *(Tivicay)*

Elvitegravir
Only in the combination drugs *Genvoya* and *Stribild*

Raltegravir *(Isentress, Isentress HD)*

Block the <u>integrase</u> enzyme, preventing HIV DNA from <u>inserting</u> into the host cell DNA in <u>stage 4</u> (integration) of the HIV life cycle

INSTIs have a higher barrier to resistance than NRTIs and NNRTIs

NAME TIPS...
Generic names end in "-tegravir"

Remember the common INSTIs with **BRED**

Biktarvy, Stribild, Genvoya, Isentress HD, Tivicay: <u>once daily</u>

Isentress, Tivicay (treatment-experienced patients, those with INSTI resistance or those taking UGT1A1 or CYP3A4 inducers): <u>twice daily</u>

<u>CrCl < 70 mL/min: do not start *Stribild*</u>

<u>CrCl < 50 mL/min: discontinue *Stribild*</u>

<u>CrCl < 30 mL/min: do not start *Biktarvy* or *Genvoya*</u>

Cabotegravir PO *(Vocabria):* indicated only for lead-in treatment to assess tolerability prior to initiation of cabotegravir/rilpivirine *(Cabenuva)* injection, or as bridge therapy in patients who will miss a scheduled cabotegravir/rilpivirine injection for > 7 days

Cabotegravir extended-release intramuscular injection *(Apretude):* indicated only for pre-exposure prophylaxis (PrEP); see HIV Prevention Strategies section later in the chapter

INFECTIOUS DISEASES

INSTI KEY FEATURES AND SAFETY ISSUES

Side Effects and Warnings
- **B**ictegravir, dolutegravir: ↑ SCr (by inhibiting tubular secretion) with no effect on GFR
- **R**altegravir: ↑ CPK, myopathy and rhabdomyolysis
- **E**lvitegravir: proteinuria
- **D**olutegravir:
  - ❑ Hypersensitivity reaction (HSR) with severe rash and organ dysfunction, including hepatotoxicity
  - ❑ Small risk of neural tube defects in a dveloping fetus (though still a preferred drug for treatment of HIV during pregnancy)
  - ❑ ↑ CPK, myalgia
- All INSTIs: headache, insomnia, diarrhea, weight gain, rare risk of depression and suicidal ideation in patients with pre-existing psychiatric conditions (except bictegravir)

Drug Interactions with Polyvalent Cations
- Separate from polyvalent cations (see image to the right); exceptions:
  - ❑ Dolutegravir and bictegravir can be taken with oral calcium or iron if also taken with food
  - ❑ Dose separations with raltegravir may not be effective; avoid polyvalent cations if possible

Cations and INSTIs don't go together

Take INSTIs **2 hours before** or **6 hours after:** aluminum, calcium, magnesium and iron-containing products.

INFECTIOUS DISEASES

DRUGS IN CLASS	MECHANISM OF ACTION	ADMINISTRATION

Non-Nucleoside Reverse Transcriptase Inhibitors (NNRTIs)

Efavirenz *(Sustiva)*

Rilpivirine *(Edurant)*

Doravirine *(Pifeltro)*

Etravirine *(Intelence)*

Nevirapine *(Viramune XR)*

No longer recommended:

Delavirdine

Non-competitively <u>inhibit</u> the <u>reverse transcriptase</u> enzyme, preventing the conversion of HIV RNA to HIV DNA in <u>stage 3</u> (reverse transcription) of the HIV life cycle

NNRTIs have a lower barrier to resistance than INSTIs or PIs

> **NAME TIPS...**
> Generic names contain "-vir-"
>
> Remember the NNRTIs with **REDDEN**

Rilpivirine

- Take with a <u>meal</u> and water (do <u>not</u> substitute with a <u>protein</u> drink)

- Requires an <u>acidic</u> environment for <u>absorption</u>; do <u>not use with</u> PPIs and <u>separate from H2RAs</u> and <u>antacids</u> (see <u>Study Tip Gal</u> below)

Efavirenz

- Food increases the bioavailability and risk for CNS effects; take on an <u>empty stomach QHS</u> to ↓ (and sleep through) CNS effects

NNRTI KEY FEATURES AND SAFETY ISSUES

Used in alternative ART regimens (not first line in most patients): 1 NNRTI plus 2 NRTIs

All NNRTIs
- Hepatotoxicity and rash/severe rash, including SJS/TEN: highest risk with nevirapine

Efavirenz
- Psychiatric symptoms (depression, suicidal thoughts)
- CNS effects (impaired concentration, abnormal dreams, confusion), generally resolve in 2-4 weeks
- ↑ total cholesterol and triglycerides

Drug Interactions
- All NNRTIs are major CYP3A4 substrates (and some are substrates of other CYP enzymes)
  - ❏ Rilpivirine and doravirine: do not use with strong CYP3A4 inducers (carbamazepine, oxcarbazepine, phenobarbital, phenytoin, rifampin, rifapentine, St. John's wort)
- Efavirenz and etravirine are moderate CYP3A4 inducers (many drug interactions)
- Rilpivirine and acid-suppressants (see image to the right)

Rilpivirine
- Depression
- ↑ SCr with no effect on GFR
- Do not use if viral load > 100,000 copies/mL and/or CD4 count < 200 cells/mm³ (higher failure rate)

Rilpivirine needs an acidic gut for absorption.

DO NOT USE WITH PPIs

Separate H2RAs
Take H2RAs at least 12 hours before or 4 hours after rilpivirine

Separate Antacids
Take antacids at least 2 hours before or 4 hours after rilpivirine*

Approximate; separation times vary between antacid brands.

DRUGS IN CLASS	MECHANISM OF ACTION	ADMINISTRATION

Protease Inhibitors (PIs)

Atazanavir (Reyataz)

Darunavir (Prezista)

Fosamprenavir (Lexiva)

Lopinavir / ritonavir, LPV/r (Kaletra)*

Saquinavir (Invirase)

Tipranavir (Aptivus)

* Small r indicates ritonavir is used as a booster for lopinavir; ritonavir is in the Boosters table on the following page.

No longer recommended:

Indinavir

Nelfinavir

Inhibit the HIV protease enzyme, preventing long viral protein chains from being broken down into the smaller chains needed to produce mature (infectious) virus in stage 7 (budding and maturation) of the HIV life cycle; HIV continues to replicate, but produces immature virions that are not infectious

PIs (especially darunavir) have a high barrier to resistance

> **NAME TIP...**
> Generic names end in "-navir"

All PIs
- Recommended to take with a booster (ritonavir or cobicistat)
- No renal dose adjustments
- Take with food to ↓ GI upset except:
  - ❏ Fosamprenavir oral solution (in adults) is without food
  - ❏ Lopinavir/ritonavir (Kaletra) tablets are with or without food

Atazanavir
- Needs an acidic gut for absorption (see Study Tip Gal below)

Ritonavir
- Only used for pharmacokinetic boosting (see the table on the following page)

PI KEY FEATURES AND SAFETY ISSUES

Used in alternative ART regimens (not first line in most patients): 1 PI (boosted with ritonavir or cobicistat) plus 2 NRTIs

All PIs
- Metabolic abnormalities: hyperglycemia/insulin resistance, dyslipidemia (↑ LDL, ↑ TGs), ↑ body fat and lipodystrophy
  - ❏ PIs ↑ CVD risk (lower risk with atazanavir and darunavir, higher risk with lopinavir/ritonavir)
- Hepatic dysfunction: ↑ LFTs, hepatitis (highest risk with tipranavir), and/or exacerbation of preexisting hepatic disease
- Hypersensitivity reactions: rash (including SJS/TEN), bronchospasm, angioedema, anaphylaxis
- Common side effects: diarrhea, nausea

Atazanavir
- Hyperbilirubinemia (jaundice or scleral icterus, remember with "bananavir"): reversible, does not require discontinuation
- Requires acidic gut for absorption:
  - ❏ Antacids: take atazanavir 2 hours before or 1 hour after
  - ❏ H2RAs: avoid or take atazanavir 2 hours before or 10 hours after
  - ❏ PPIs: avoid with unboosted atazanavir; take boosted atazanavir at least 12 hours after the PPI (dose should not exceed omeprazole 20 mg or equivalent)

Darunavir, Fosamprenavir, Tipranavir
- Caution with sulfa allergy

Lopinavir/Ritonavir (Kaletra)
- Oral solution contains 42% alcohol: can cause a disulfiram reaction if taken with metronidazole

Tipranavir
- Intracranial hemorrhage

CYP3A4 Drug Interactions (Many)
- All PIs are major CYP3A4 substrates and most are strong CYP3A4 inhibitors
- Do not use the following drugs with PIs*:
  - ❏ Alfuzosin
  - ❏ Colchicine
  - ❏ Dronedarone
  - ❏ Lovastatin and simvastatin (rosuvastatin or atorvastatin are preferred with PIs)
  - ❏ CYP3A4 inducers (e.g., carbamazepine, phenytoin, phenobarbital, rifampin, St. John's wort)
  - ❏ Anticoagulants/antiplatelets: apixaban, edoxaban, rivaroxaban, ticagrelor (warfarin is not contraindicated but INR should be monitored closely)
  - ❏ Direct-acting antivirals (DAAs) for hepatitis C
  - ❏ Some hormonal contraceptives (counsel on use of additional/ alternative contraceptive methods)
  - ❏ Steroids (systemic, intranasal and inhaled, with the exception of beclomethasone; increased risk of Cushing's syndrome)

*List not all inclusive, includes common drugs that could be tested

PROTEASE INHIBITORS

↓ HDL
↑ LDL and TG
↑ Blood Glucose → **Metabolic Syndrome**
Insulin Resistance
Abdominal Adiposity

Better call the pharmacist for help.

+ DRUG INTERACTIONS

INFECTIOUS DISEASES

DRUGS	ADMINISTRATION	KEY FEATURES
Pharmacokinetic Boosters (Enhancers)		
Ritonavir (Norvir) Difficult to co-formulate (often used as a single entity product) **Cobicistat (Tybost)** Can be co-formulated (found in many combination products) *For combinations with boosters, identify the booster with r and c. Example: LPV/r in Kaletra indicates ritonavir is boosting lopinavir.*	**Ritonavir** 100 to 400 mg PO daily (in 1-2 divided doses) with food Oral solution contains 43% alcohol: can cause a disulfiram reaction if taken with metronidazole Powder: mix with soft food or liquid and take within 2 hrs **Cobicistat** 150 mg PO daily with the boosted drug (e.g., darunavir, atazanavir) and with food	▪ Ritonavir and cobicistat are inhibitors of CYP3A4. They inhibit ART metabolism, which increases (boosts) the ART level and therapeutic effect. ▪ Ritonavir is a PI (has antiretroviral activity), but is used as a booster because it is a strong inhibitor and is not well tolerated at the higher doses needed for antiretroviral activity. Booster dosing is lower than treatment dosing, making metabolic side effects much less of a concern. ▪ Ritonavir and cobicistat are not interchangeable. Do not use both together. ▪ Both have many drug interactions (see Study Tip Gal below).

BOOSTER DRUG INTERACTIONS

Ritonavir and cobicistat are strong inhibitors of CYP3A4 and they also inhibit CYP2D6, P-gp transporters and some of the OAT family of transporters.

They increase the levels of many other drugs; knowing which ART combinations contain these boosters is important to identify possible interactions with other CYP substrates, inhibitors and inducers.

Drugs that are contraindicated with ritonavir and cobicistat include*:

- Alfuzosin, tamsulosin
- Colchicine (with hepatic or renal impairment)
- Lovastatin and simvastatin
- Azole antifungals (especially isavuconazonium, itraconazole and voriconazole)
- Cardiovascular drugs: amiodarone (ritonavir only), dronedarone, eplerenone, ivabradine, ranolazine
- PDE-5 inhibitors used for pulmonary hypertension (tadalafil, sildenafil) (dose-reductions required if taking for erectile dysfunction or BPH)
- Many tyrosine kinase inhibitors ("nibs")
- CYP3A4 inducers: carbamazepine, phenytoin, phenobarbital, rifampin, St. John's wort
- Any narrow therapeutic index drug that is highly dependent on CYP3A4 for clearance

List not all inclusive, includes common drugs that could be tested

DRUGS	MECHANISM OF ACTION	SAFETY ISSUES AND NOTES
Entry and Attachment Inhibitors		
CCR5 Antagonist Maraviroc (Selzentry) Tablet, solution	Blocks HIV from binding (and subsequently entering) the CD4 cell in virus strains that use the CCR5 co-receptor in stage 1 of the HIV life cycle (binding/attachment)	**SAFETY ISSUES** Hepatotoxicity (boxed warning), hypersensitivity reactions (including SJS/TEN), CV events (including MI), orthostatic hypotension in patients with renal impairment Do not use if severe renal impairment (CrCl < 30 mL/min) and taking potent CYP3A4 inhibitors/inducers **BASELINE TEST REQUIRED** Must have tropism assay results before starting (tropism test determines if the HIV strain infecting the patient can only bind to the CCR5 co-receptor) If the HIV strain can bind to CXCR4 or mixed (CXCR4/CCR5) co-receptors, maraviroc will not work and HIV will still be able to enter the CD4 cell
Attachment Inhibitor Fostemsavir (Rukobia) Tablet	Converted to temsavir (active form), which binds to the gp120 subunit of HIV envelope proteins, inhibiting the interaction between the virus and the CD4 host cell in stage 1 of the HIV life cycle (binding/attachment)	**SAFETY ISSUES** Do not use with strong CYP3A4 inducers Must maintain effective HBV treatment in patients coinfected with HBV Can ↑ SCr (higher risk if underlying renal disease) **NOTES** Indicated in combination with other ARTs in heavily treatment-experienced patients who are failing current therapy

DRUGS	MECHANISM OF ACTION	SAFETY ISSUES AND NOTES
Entry and Attachment Inhibitors (Cont.)		
Post-Attachment Inhibitor Ibalizumab-uiyk *(Trogarzo)* Injection (administered IV)	Monoclonal antibody that binds to a select domain of CD4 cell receptors in stage 1 (binding/attachment) of the HIV life cycle, blocking entry of the virus into the cell	**SAFETY ISSUES** Infusion-related reactions (observe for 1 hour after the first infusion), diarrhea, dizziness, nausea, rash **NOTES** Refrigerate unused vials and administer immediately after dilution Indicated in combination with other ARTs in heavily treatment-experienced patients who are failing current therapy
Fusion Inhibitor Enfuvirtide *(Fuzeon)* Powder for injection (administered by SC self-injection into the abdomen, the front of the thigh or the back of the arm)	Prevents HIV from fusing to the CD4 cell membrane in stage 2 (fusion) of the HIV life cycle, which prevents virus entry into the cell	**SAFETY ISSUES** Risk of bacterial pneumonia, hypersensitivity reactions Local injection site reactions (occur in nearly all patients): pain, erythema, nodules and cysts, ecchymosis, nausea, diarrhea and fatigue **NOTES** Store unused drug/supplies at room temperature; once reconstituted, refrigerate and use within 24 hours

COMBINATION ANTIRETROVIRAL PRODUCTS

Combination products lower the pill burden and improve adherence. The table below lists commonly used combination drugs and relevant notes. Additional notes on "first-line" (i.e., preferred initial) ART regimens are presented earlier in the chapter.

SINGLE TABLET REGIMENS

GENERIC NAME	BRAND	NOTES
Complete regimens (1 tablet once daily unless noted).		
INSTI-based		
Bictegravir / emtricitabine / tenofovir alafenamide	***Biktarvy***	*Biktarvy, Triumeq, Dovato*: first line.
Cabotegravir / rilpivirine	*Cabenuva*	*Cabenuva*: administered IM once monthly by a healthcare professional (must be preceded by one month of lead-in treatment with oral cabotegravir to assess tolerability).
Dolutegravir / abacavir / lamivudine	***Triumeq***	*Cabenuva, Dovato, Juluca*: can be used to replace a current stable ART regimen in patients with virologic suppression and no history of treatment failure or known resistance.
Dolutegravir / lamivudine	***Dovato***	
Dolutegravir / rilpivirine	*Juluca*	CrCl < 50 mL/min: do not start tenofovir disoproxil fumarate-containing products (< 70 mL/min for *Stribild*).
Elvitegravir / cobicistat / emtricitabine / tenofovir disoproxil fumarate	***Stribild***	CrCl < 30 mL/min: do not start tenofovir alafenamide-containing products.
Elvitegravir / cobicistat / emtricitabine / tenofovir alafenamide	***Genvoya***	*Stribild, Genvoya*: take with food.
NNRTI-based		
Doravirine / lamivudine / tenofovir disoproxil fumarate	*Delstrigo*	Same renal dosing criteria as above for tenofovir-containing products.
Efavirenz / emtricitabine / tenofovir disoproxil fumarate	***Atripla***	*Atripla, Symfi, Symfi Lo*: take on an empty stomach (contains efavirenz).
Efavirenz / lamivudine / tenofovir disoproxil fumarate	*Symfi, Symfi Lo*	*Complera, Odefsey*: take with food (contains rilpivirine).
Rilpivirine / emtricitabine / tenofovir disoproxil fumarate	***Complera***	
Rilpivirine / emtricitabine / tenofovir alafenamide	***Odefsey***	
PI-based		
Darunavir / cobicistat / emtricitabine / tenofovir alafenamide	*Symtuza*	Take with food. Do not start if CrCl < 30 mL/min (contains tenofovir alafenamide).

OTHER COMBINATION PRODUCTS

GENERIC NAME	BRAND	NOTES
Must be used with additional ARTs to make a complete regimen.		
NRTI Combination Products (1 tablet daily unless noted)		
Abacavir / lamivudine	*Epzicom*	*Epzicom, Trizivir*: require baseline testing for HLA-B*5701 (contain abacavir).
Abacavir / lamivudine / zidovudine	*Trizivir*	*Descovy, Truvada*: part of first-line regimens. Do not use if CrCl < 30 mL/min [< 60 mL/min for *Truvada* if using for PrEP (see HIV Prevention Strategies section)].
Emtricitabine / tenofovir alafenamide	*Descovy*	
Emtricitabine / tenofovir disoproxil fumarate	*Truvada*	*Trizivir, Combivir*: twice daily.
Lamivudine / zidovudine	*Combivir*	*Cimduo*: do not use if < 50 mL/min.
Lamivudine / tenofovir disoproxil fumarate	*Cimduo*	
Common PI Combination Products (1 tablet daily)		
Atazanavir / cobicistat	*Evotaz*	Take cobicistat-containing products with food.
Darunavir / cobicistat	*Prezcobix*	

AIDS-DEFINING CONDITIONS

Despite the effectiveness of current ART regimens in reducing the viral load to undetectable levels, nearly 17,000 people in the U.S. will progress to AIDS annually. AIDS is diagnosed when the CD4 count is < 200 cells/mm³ or by the presence of an AIDS-defining condition, which includes:

- Opportunistic infections (OIs) [e.g., *Mycobacterium avium* complex (MAC), *Pneumocystis jirovecii* pneumonia (PJP or PCP), *Cryptococcus neoformans*, *Histoplasmosis*, severe *Candida albicans* infections, including esophageal and bronchial thrush, tuberculosis]. The prophylaxis and treatment of OIs is discussed in the Infectious Diseases IV: Opportunistic Infections chapter.

- Several cancers, including Kaposi's sarcoma.

- HIV wasting syndrome, a debilitating condition with loss of fat tissue (lipoatrophy), muscle mass and appetite (anorexia), and diarrhea. Options to increase appetite are slim and include the cannabis-related drugs dronabinol *(Syndros)* and nabilone, and megestrol, a progestin that stimulates appetite.

IMMUNE RECONSTITUTION INFLAMMATORY SYNDROME

Immune reconstitution inflammatory syndrome (IRIS) is a paradoxical (unexpected) worsening of a known underlying condition, or a previously unidentified condition, after ART is started or treatment is changed to a more effective regimen. As the immune system begins to recover, it becomes capable of mounting an inflammatory response, and symptoms of the underlying condition can become unmasked.

Key points about IRIS:

- It is more likely to occur as the viral load decreases and the CD4 count recovers.

- Underlying conditions that can appear or worsen include common OIs, hepatitis B and C, herpes simplex virus (HSV), varicella zoster virus (VZV, shingles), autoimmune conditions and some cancers (e.g., Kaposi's sarcoma). In some cases, a known underlying condition will be treated for a short time prior to starting ART to help prevent IRIS.

- IRIS symptoms can range from mild to severe (most commonly mild) and are typically self-limiting. ART should be continued, and the unmasked condition should be treated.

HIV TREATMENT DURING PREGNANCY

All pregnant patients with HIV should take ART during pregnancy for their own health and to prevent mother-to-child transmission. Most HIV medications are considered safe to use during pregnancy, without an increased risk of birth defects.

In most cases, patients who are already taking an effective ART regimen should continue using the same regimen throughout their pregnancy. If not already taking ART, a regimen should be started as soon as possible using one of the options below (note: though there is a very small risk of neural tube defects with dolutegravir, the benefits outweigh the risks, making it a preferred drug). Breastfeeding should be avoided.

RECOMMENDATIONS FOR TREATMENT-NAÏVE PREGNANT PATIENTS

Treatment should consist of three drugs: two NRTIs plus either an INSTI or a boosted PI. Choose one of the NRTI combination options in column 1 below and either an INSTI (from column 2) or a boosted PI (from column 3).

NRTI COMBINATIONS	INSTI	BOOSTED PI
Abacavir / lamivudine	Raltegravir	Atazanavir + ritonavir
Tenofovir disoproxil fumarate / emtricitabine	Dolutegravir	Darunavir + ritonavir
Tenofovir disoproxil fumarate / lamivudine		

HIV PREVENTION STRATEGIES

TREATMENT AS PREVENTION

Treatment of HIV with current ART regimens is so effective that adherent patients can achieve a viral load low enough to prevent infecting other people. When appropriate, PrEP and PEP are two other ways to reduce HIV infection risk before or after exposure (see the Study Tip Gal on the following page).

PRE-EXPOSURE PROPHYLAXIS (PrEP)

Pre-exposure prophylaxis (PrEP) is a prevention method whereby people with high risk behaviors who do not have HIV take medication to prevent infection.

PrEP Treatment Options

- An oral regimen of either *Truvada* or *Descovy*, taken daily, with no more than a 90-day supply provided at a time.

- A long-acting intramuscular injection of cabotegravir (*Apretude*); administered by a healthcare provider monthly for 2 doses, then every 2 months.

Before Starting PrEP

- Confirm that the person is HIV-negative with an HIV Ab test (use of a PrEP regimen in an HIV-positive person could cause resistance to commonly used treatments).

- Ask about recent symptoms that could indicate HIV infection, due to the lag time for detectable antibody.

- Confirm CrCl ≥ 60 mL/min (if using *Truvada)* or ≥ 30 mL/min (if using *Descovy*). [Note: the CrCl cutoff for *Truvada* is higher for PrEP than when used for HIV treatment.]

- Screen for hepatitis B (if using oral PrEP) and sexually transmitted infections (STIs).

PrEP Follow-Up Visits

At each visit, test for HIV and confirm a negative result before refilling or administering PrEP treatment:

- *Truvada* and *Descovy:* every 3 months.

- Cabotegravir: 1 month after the first injection, then every 2 months.

Screening for STIs and monitoring of renal function and other drug adverse effects (e.g., lipid abnormalities with *Descovy)* is recommended during follow-up visits, but the suggested frequency varies between treatment strategies.

POST-EXPOSURE PROPHYLAXIS (PEP)

Post-exposure prophylaxis (PEP) is for emergency situations whereby a non-infected person is exposed to body fluids that are known to be or could be infected with HIV. The two types of PEP are: nonoccupational (nPEP) and occupational (oPEP).

- nPEP can be used after sex without a condom (e.g., condom broke, unplanned sex, sexual assault), injection drug use or some other type of nonoccupational exposure.

- oPEP is typically used for healthcare personnel who are exposed to body fluids that could be infectious, such as from a needlestick (prick from a needle).

- For both types, treatment should be started as soon as possible within 72 hours (3 days) of the exposure and continued for 28 days.

- The exposed individual should receive a baseline HIV Ab test and a follow-up test at 4 – 6 weeks, 3 months and 6 months after the exposure.

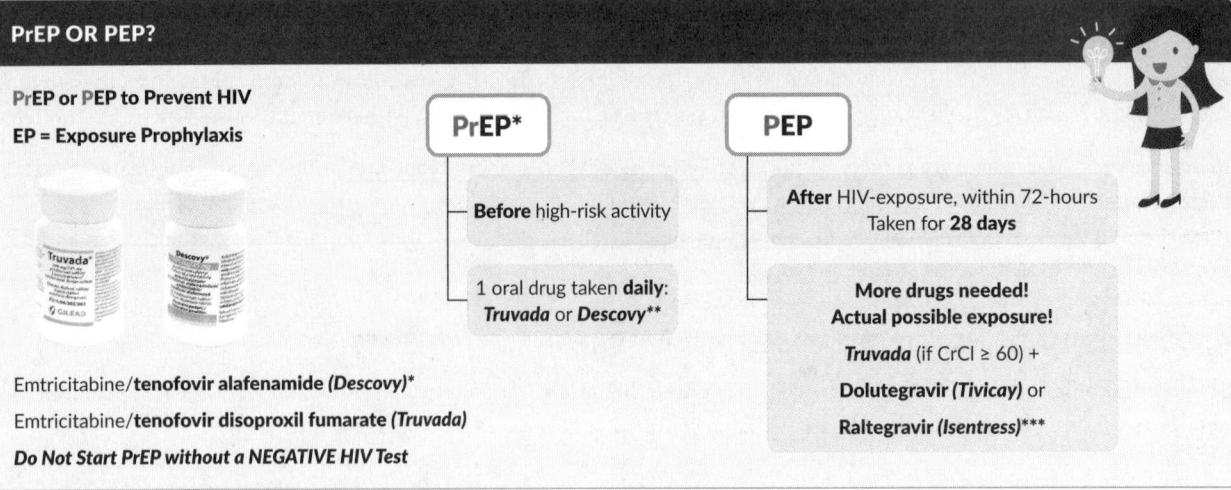

PrEP OR PEP?

PrEP or PEP to Prevent HIV

EP = Exposure Prophylaxis

PrEP*

— **Before** high-risk activity

— 1 oral drug taken **daily**: *Truvada* or *Descovy***

PEP

— **After** HIV-exposure, within 72-hours Taken for **28 days**

More drugs needed! Actual possible exposure!

Truvada (if CrCl ≥ 60) +

Dolutegravir *(Tivicay)* or

Raltegravir *(Isentress)***

Emtricitabine/**tenofovir alafenamide *(Descovy)****

Emtricitabine/**tenofovir disoproxil fumarate *(Truvada)***

Do Not Start PrEP without a NEGATIVE HIV Test

*An alternative to oral treatment is intramuscular cabotegravir (Apretude), administered (by a healthcare professional) monthly x 2 doses, then every 2 months.
**Descovy: not approved for PrEP in patients assigned female at birth (i.e., at risk of getting HIV from vaginal sex), and not approved for PEP.
***May be preferred in patients of child-bearing potential (due to a small risk of neural tube defects with dolutegravir).

STUDY GUIDE FOR ANTIRETROVIRAL TREATMENTS

Test yourself on the names and ingredients of select ART products. Write in the missing brand or generic names then include any pertinent notes about the drug or it's components based on what you learned in the chapter [e.g., mechanism, administration (with/without food), baseline tests required, major safety issues]. Refer back to the chapter as needed.

BRAND NAME	INGREDIENTS	NOTES
Atripla		
	Bictegravir / Emtricitabine / Tenofovir AF	
	Rilpivirine / Emtricitabine / Tenofovir DF	
Descovy		
Dovato		
	Lamivudine	
	Abacavir / Lamivudine	
Genvoya		
	Raltegravir	
Odefsey		
	Ritonavir	
Prezista		
	Atazanavir	
Retrovir		
	Elvitegravir / Cobicistat / Emtricitabine / Tenofovir DF	
Tivicay		
	Abacavir / Lamivudine / Dolutegravir	
	Emtricitabine / Tenofovir DF	
Tybost		
	Tenofovir DF	

KEY COUNSELING POINTS

See the Drug Formulations and Patient Counseling chapter for counseling language/layman's terminology.

All HIV Medications

- Do not skip doses or stop taking HIV medications unless instructed to do so by your healthcare provider (see strategies to improve adherence to the right); get refills before running out.
- This medication is not a cure for HIV. Do not share needles or other drug mixing equipment. Use safe sex practices.
- IRIS: do not stop taking ART; notify your healthcare provider of a new or worsening condition.

All NRTIs

- If you have hepatitis B, do not stop taking this medication without discussing with your healthcare provider, as a severe worsening of the hepatitis can occur.
- Can cause lactic acidosis.

Abacavir

- Before using this medication, your blood should be tested to see if you are at high risk for a severe reaction.

Emtricitabine

- This medication can cause darkened spots on the palms of the hands and on the soles of the feet.

Tenofovir Disoproxil Fumarate and Tenofovir Alafenamide

- Can cause (less with alafenamide):
  - Kidney impairment.
  - Low bone density/fracture risk.

All INSTIs

- This medication can interact with antacids. Take 2 hours before or 6 hours after this medication.

All NNRTIs

- Can cause:
  - Rash/severe rash.
  - Hepatotoxicity.

Efavirenz

- Take at bedtime on an empty stomach to reduce side effects.
- Can cause (at the start, improves in 2 – 4 weeks):
  - Depression/psychosis.
  - Confusion and abnormal dreams.

STRATEGIES TO IMPROVE ADHERENCE TO ANTIRETROVIRAL THERAPY

Multidisciplinary team approach (e.g., nurses, social workers, pharmacists, psychologists, physicians).

Accessible, non-judgmental healthcare team; establish a trusting relationship with the patient.

Evaluate the patient's knowledge of HIV disease, prevention and treatment, and provide information as needed; establish patient readiness to start ART and involve them in ART regimen selection.

Identify potential barriers to adherence (e.g., psychosocial or cognitive issues, substance abuse, low literacy, busy daily schedule, lack of prescription coverage and/or social support).

Assess adherence at every clinic visit, and simplify ART regimen when possible; provide positive reinforcement to foster adherence success.

Identify non-adherence and reasons for non-adherence (e.g., adverse effects from medications, complex regimen, difficulty swallowing large pills, forgetfulness, pill fatigue, food requirements, stigma, change or lapse of insurance coverage).

Provide resources (e.g., referrals for mental health and/or substance abuse treatment, prescription drug assistance programs, pillboxes, reminder tools, medication lists or calendars).

Rilpivirine

- Take with a full meal (not a protein drink) and water.
- Do not use proton pump inhibitors; take H2RAs 12 hours before or 4 hours after, and antacids 2 hours before or 4 hours after rilpivirine.
- Can cause depression.

All PIs

- Take with food (except fosamprenavir oral solution in adults).
- Can cause high blood glucose, high triglycerides or body fat redistribution.

Atazanavir or Darunavir

- If taking ritonavir, make sure to take both at the same time.

Atazanavir

- Do not take acid-suppressing medications with atazanavir.
- Can cause hyperbilirubinemia.

Darunavir, Fosamprenavir, Tipranavir

- Caution with sulfa allergy.

Select Guidelines/References

Panel on Antiretroviral Guidelines for Adults and Adolescents. Guidelines for the Use of Antiretroviral Agents in Adults and Adolescents with HIV. Department of Health and Human Services. Available at: https://clinicalinfo.hiv.gov/sites/default/files/inline-files/AdultandAdolescentGL.pdf. (accessed 2022 Jan 18).

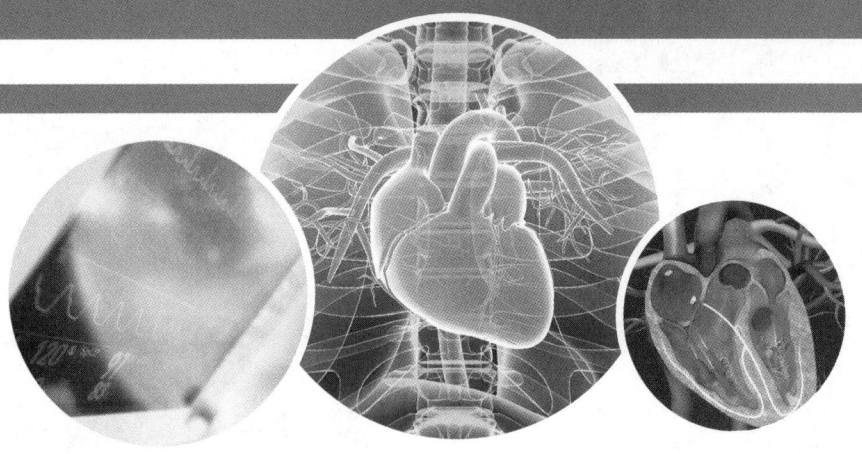

CARDIOVASCULAR CONDITIONS

CONTENTS

CHAPTER CONTENT

CONTENT LEGEND

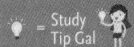 = Study Tip Gal   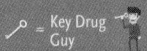 = Key Drug Guy    = Required Formula

---

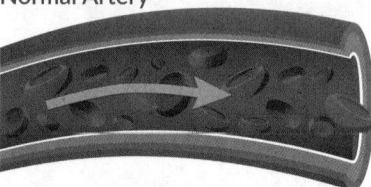

Normal Artery

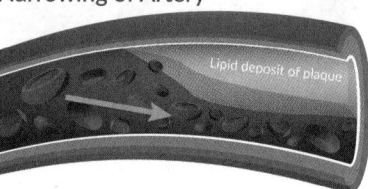

Narrowing of Artery

Lipid deposit of plaque

iStock.com/newannyart

CHAPTER 27

DYSLIPIDEMIA

BACKGROUND

Cholesterol is an important component of healthy cells and tissues, including the brain. It is a structural component of cell walls, a precursor in hormone synthesis and is used in the production of bile acids.

- Bile acids are needed to absorb lipids, including fat-soluble vitamins. They are produced in the liver, then travel through the bile ducts (with free cholesterol and waste products) into the small intestine. They are converted from bile acids into bile salts in the intestine, then bile salts are recycled from the intestine and returned to the liver.

- This process, referred to as enterohepatic recycling, involves the gut (enteric system) and the liver (hepatic). Drugs can be involved in this recycling process as well; see Drug Interactions and Pharmacokinetics chapters for details.

Cholesterol exits the body either as free cholesterol or as bile acid.

ATHEROSCLEROSIS AND ASCVD

While cholesterol is an essential substance in the body, elevated cholesterol increases the risk of heart disease. Atherosclerosis is the formation of plaque from a buildup of fats, cholesterol and other substances on the inner walls of arteries. Atherosclerosis is asymptomatic, but leads to atherosclerotic cardiovascular disease (ASCVD), which includes myocardial infarction, stroke/transient ischemic attacks, angina and peripheral arterial disease. Different types of cholesterol protect from or contribute to ASCVD risk.

Cholesterol in the body can be decreased by reducing the formation (as seen with statins), blocking absorption (such as with ezetimibe) or blocking the enterohepatic recirculation of bile salts (such as with bile acid sequestrants like colesevelam).

TYPES OF CHOLESTEROL

Total cholesterol (TC) includes the three major types of lipoproteins: low-density lipoprotein (LDL), high-density lipoprotein (HDL) and very-low density lipoprotein (VLDL).

- HDL (i.e., "good" cholesterol) takes cholesterol from the blood and delivers it to the liver for removal from the body. High HDL lowers ASCVD risk.

- Non-HDL includes the lipoproteins that contribute to atherosclerosis: LDL, intermediate-density lipoproteins (IDL), VLDL, chylomicron remnants and lipoprotein(a).

  ❑ Non-HDL is a strong predictor of ASCVD.

  ❑ Non-HDL calculation: non-HDL = TC – HDL

- Lipoprotein(a) is a genetic variant of LDL. High lipoprotein(a) indicates high risk of ASCVD.

- High triglycerides (TGs), or hypertriglyceridemia, are associated with high ASCVD risk. TGs > 500 mg/dL can cause acute pancreatitis.

CLASSIFICATION OF DYSLIPIDEMIA

Abnormal lipoprotein levels are called dyslipidemias, which are either primary (genetic cause) or secondary (due to some lifestyle and/or medical condition/s).

PRIMARY (OR FAMILIAL)

Primary (familial) hypercholesterolemias (FH) are genetic defects that cause severe cholesterol elevations. FHs include heterozygous familial hypercholesterolemia (HeFH) and homozygous familial hypercholesterolemia (HoFH). Familial dyslipidemias are categorized by the Fredrickson classification.

SECONDARY (OR ACQUIRED)

Most dyslipidemias are due to poor diet and lack of physical activity that result in central adiposity. Medical conditions that cause dyslipidemia include hypothyroidism and diabetes. See the Key Drugs Guy on the right. Severe elevations (including LDL ≥ 190 and TG ≥ 500 mg/dL) are very high risk and must be treated.

CHOLESTEROL (LIPOPROTEIN) TYPES AND NORMAL VALUES

Lipid panels (i.e., TC, HDL, TG) are taken after a 9 – 12 hour fast. If the LDL is not reported, it can be calculated using the Friedewald equation:

$$LDL = TC - HDL - \frac{TG}{5}$$

This formula is not used when the TGs are > 400 mg/dL.

SELECT DRUGS/CONDITIONS THAT CAN RAISE LDL AND/OR TRIGLYCERIDES

KEY DRUGS

↑ LDL and TG:
Diuretics

Efavirenz

Steroids

Immunosuppressants (e.g., cyclosporine, tacrolimus)

Atypical antipsychotics

Protease inhibitors

↑ LDL Only:

Fish oils (except *Vascepa*)

↑ TG Only:
IV lipid emulsions

Propofol

Bile acid sequestrants (~5%)

Conditions:
Obesity, poor diet, hypothyroidism, alcoholism, smoking, diabetes, renal/liver disease, nephrotic syndrome

Others:

↑ LDL and TG:
Retinoids

↑ LDL Only:
Anabolic steroids

Fibrates

Progestins

SGLT2 inhibitors

↑ TG Only:
Estrogen

Tamoxifen

Clevidipine

Beta-blockers

Conditions:
Pregnancy, polycystic ovarian syndrome, anorexia

CLASSIFICATION OF CHOLESTEROL AND TG LEVELS (MG/DL)

NON-HDL*	
< 130	Desirable

LDL	
< 100	Desirable
≥ 190	Very high

HDL	
≥ 40 (men)	Desirable
≥ 50 (women)	Desirable

Triglycerides	
< 150	Desirable
≥ 500	Very high**

HDL = high-density lipoprotein cholesterol, LDL = low-density lipoprotein cholesterol, non-HDL = non-high-density lipoprotein cholesterol
*Non-HDL = total cholesterol minus HDL
**Severe hypertriglyceridemia is another term used for very high triglycerides in pharmaceutical product labeling

Non-HDL and apoB do not require fasting for accurate assessment. If not fasting, the TG level can be falsely elevated, which can cause an incorrect LDL calculation. See Case Scenario on the next page.

CASE SCENARIO

JS is a 47-year-old male with dyslipidemia and type 2 diabetes. He stopped taking his simvastatin about 5 months ago due to muscle aches. His cholesterol panel has the following values: TC 202 mg/dL, HDL 36 mg/dL and TG 280 mg/dL.

Calculate the patient's LDL cholesterol:

LDL is calculated using the Friedewald equation* LDL = TC – HDL – (TG/5)

$$202 - 36 - \frac{280}{5} = 110$$

*This formula is not used when the TGs are > 400 mg/dL

TREATMENT PRINCIPLES

Treatment of dyslipidemia is important, as lowering LDL by 1% reduces heart disease and stroke by 1%. The 2018 American College of Cardiology and the American Heart Association guidelines (ACC/AHA) on cholesterol management provide consensus recommendations from a large number of organizations, including the National Lipid Association (NLA). The recommendations in this chapter primarily reflect these guidelines. Recommendations for managing cholesterol in certain populations are addressed in disease-specific guidelines (e.g., diabetes and the ADA guidelines).

CALCULATING ASCVD RISK

The ASCVD risk calculation is used to provide an estimate of an individual's risk of having a first cardiovascular event (e.g., MI, stroke or death) during the next 10 years. Healthcare providers use the estimated risk to determine whether they should prescribe risk-reducing treatments, including statins and antihypertensives. An elevated risk level can also motivate the patient to address modifiable risk factors. The online calculator is used to determine risk (http://tools.acc.org/ASCVD-Risk-Estimator-Plus/). The clinician inputs:

- The patient's gender, age (20 – 79 years) and race
- TC and HDL
- Systolic blood pressure, and whether antihypertensive treatment is used
- The presence of diabetes and smoking status

This risk assessment should be repeated every 4 – 6 years in those found to be at a low 10-year risk (< 7.5%). Note that the risk score is not needed for patients with clinical ASCVD, diabetes or LDL ≥ 190 mg/dL, as all patients in these groups should be started on a statin.

If a risk-based treatment decision is still uncertain after a quantitative risk assessment, additional risk-enhancing factors should be considered to assist with decision making.

These factors include very high LDL, family history of premature ASCVD, metabolic syndrome, chronic kidney disease, history of preeclampsia or premature menopause, chronic inflammatory disorders, high CRP, high coronary artery calcium score (CAC) and abnormal ankle brachial index. The CAC measurement is helpful in deciding if statins should be initiated in those with 10-year ASCVD risk of 7.5 – 19.9%. A CAC score ≥ 100 Agatston units indicates statins should be initiated.

Atherosclerosis

Atherosclerosis can occur anywhere in the body (see image below), and if it is present in one location, it is present everywhere. People are often unaware they have atherosclerosis until an ASCVD event occurs (e.g., CVA, TIA, ACS, MI).

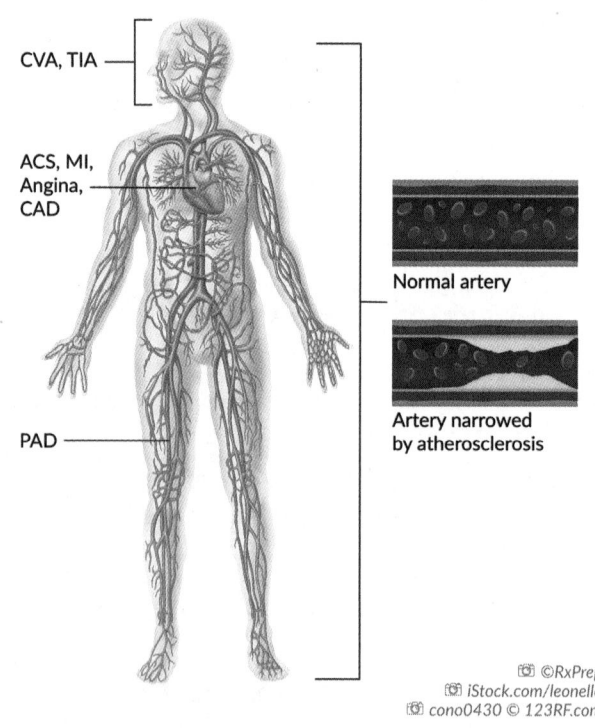

CVA, TIA

ACS, MI, Angina, CAD

PAD

Normal artery

Artery narrowed by atherosclerosis

©RxPrep
iStock.com/leonello
cono0430 © 123RF.com

NON-DRUG TREATMENT

Lifestyle modifications are an important part of management and include:

- Consuming a diet to maintain a healthy weight (BMI 18.5 – 24.9 kg/m^2).
  - Diet should be rich in vegetables, fruits, whole grains and high-fiber foods, such as in plant-based and Mediterranean diets.
  - Consume fish, especially fish with high-fat content (rich in omega-3 fatty acids).
  - Limit intake of saturated fat, *trans* fat (partially hydrogenated) and cholesterol by choosing lean meats, non-meat alternatives and low-fat dairy products. Aim for 5 – 6% of calories from saturated fat.
  - Limit intake of added sugars and salt.
- Engaging in aerobic physical activity 3 – 4 times per week, lasting 40 minutes/session (decreases LDL 3 – 6 mg/dL).
- Avoiding tobacco products and limiting alcohol.

NATURAL PRODUCTS

Red yeast rice is yeast grown on rice that contains naturally occurring HMG-CoA reductase inhibitors in low amounts.

Plant stanols, sterols, fibrous foods (found in psyllium, barley, oat bran) and a specific type of artichoke extract are each effective in lowering LDL. OTC fish oils can be used to lower TG, but some products can increase LDL. Garlic used to be recommended for dyslipidemia, but the effect is not significant. Fish oils and niacin are discussed later in this chapter. See Dietary Supplements, Natural & Complementary Medicine chapter.

DRUG TREATMENT

Statins are the primary drugs of choice in treating high non-HDL and LDL; they are used in patients with ASCVD and those at risk for ASCVD. Patients are classified into statin-benefit groups to determine the appropriate intensity of statin treatment (see Study Tip Gal below). If a patient is statin intolerant or needs additional LDL lowering, other cholesterol-lowering drugs may be used. Guidelines focus on using ezetimibe and PCSK9 inhibitors over other non-statin drugs because of the clinical benefits shown.

LIVER DAMAGE

Many cholesterol-lowering drugs cause liver damage (niacin, fibrates, potentially statins and ezetimibe). These drugs should not be used if the AST or ALT is > 3 times the upper limit of normal. Statins do not increase liver enzymes greater than the increases seen in the general population; however, LFTs should still be monitored.

STATINS

Statins inhibit the enzyme 3-hydroxy-3-methylglutaryl coenzyme A (HMG-CoA) reductase, which prevents the conversion of HMG-CoA to mevalonate. This is the rate-limiting step in cholesterol synthesis. Statin treatment decreases ASCVD risk when given at the right intensity to the right people (i.e., statin-benefit groups).

DETERMINING STATIN TREATMENT INTENSITY BASED ON PATIENT RISK

STATIN BENEFIT GROUPS	PATIENT CRITERIA	STATIN TREATMENT
Secondary Prevention		
Clinical ASCVD	Includes CHD*, stroke, TIA or peripheral arterial disease thought to be of atherosclerotic origin	High-intensity**
Primary Prevention		
Primary elevation of LDL ≥ 190 mg/dL	Primary elevation of LDL ≥ 190 mg/dL	High-intensity**
Diabetes and age 40-75 years with LDL between 70-189 mg/dL***	Multiple ASCVD risk factors	High-intensity**
	Regardless of 10-year ASCVD risk	Moderate-intensity
Age 40-75 years with LDL between 70-189 mg/dL	10-year ASCVD risk ≥ 20%	High-intensity**
	10-year ASCVD risk 7.5-19.9% + risk-enhancing factors	Moderate-intensity

*CHD = coronary heart disease, which includes: ACS, s/p MI, stable or unstable angina, coronary or other arterial revascularization
**Consider moderate-intensity statin if not a candidate for high-intensity or patient > 75 years with LDL 70-189 mg/dL
*** 2019 ACC/AHA Guideline on the Primary Prevention of Cardiovascular Disease eliminates LDL 70-189 mg/dL from this statin benefit group

Statin Treatment Intensity Definitions and Selection Options

Doses in mg	ATORVASTATIN	ROSUVASTATIN	SIMVASTATIN	PRAVASTATIN	LOVASTATIN	FLUVASTATIN	PITAVASTATIN
HIGH	40-80	20-40					
MODERATE	10-20	5-10	20-40	40-80	40	40 BID/80 XL	2-4
LOW			10	10-20	20	20-40	1

High-intensity: ↓ LDL ≥ 50%; Moderate-intensity: ↓ LDL 30-49%; Low-intensity: ↓ LDL < 30%

Statin Equivalent Doses

Equivalent doses are used to change one statin to another (see Study Tip Gal below). This might be done in the case of drug interactions, intolerance or cost.

STATIN EQUIVALENT DOSES

Pitavastatin 2 mg

Rosuvastatin 5 mg

Atorvastatin 10 mg

Simvastatin 20 mg

Lovastatin 40 mg

Pravastatin 40 mg

Fluvastatin 80 mg

Remember: **P**harmacists **R**ock **At S**aving Lives and **Pr**eventing **F**atty deposits

CASE SCENARIO

TM is a 57-year-old male with dyslipidemia and is currently taking simvastatin 40 mg. His physician would like to switch to an equivalent atorvastatin dose.

Calculate the equivalent dose of atorvastatin:

$$\frac{\text{Atorvastatin 10 mg}}{\text{Simvastatin 20 mg}} = \frac{\text{Atorvastatin X mg}}{\text{Simvastatin 40 mg}} \quad X = 20 \text{ mg}$$

A cholesterol panel is drawn before TM leaves the physician's office. The LDL is found to be 195 mg/dL. The physician calls the pharmacy to change to a high-intensity dose of atorvastatin.

To change from moderate-intensity to high-intensity:

Increase lower dose by multiplying by 4 and increase higher dose the same way.

10-20 mg becomes 40-80 mg.

High-intensity atorvastatin is 40-80 mg; the physician can select a dose in this range.

Muscle Damage from Statins

Muscle damage is the most important adverse effect of statins. This generally presents as muscle soreness, tiredness or weakness that is symmetrical (on both sides of the body) in large adjacent muscle groups in the legs, back or arms. Symptoms usually occur within six weeks of starting treatment, but can develop at any time. The severity of these muscle effects can present in a variety of ways, including:

- Myalgias: muscle soreness and tenderness
- Myopathy: muscle weakness ± CPK elevations
- Myositis: muscle inflammation
- Rhabdomyolysis: muscle symptoms with very high CPK (> 10,000 IU/L) plus muscle protein in the urine (myoglobinuria), which can lead to acute renal failure

Coenzyme Q10 may provide benefit for mild symptoms. The primary management includes holding the statin and rechallenging once symptoms resolve; see Study Tip Gal.

MANAGING MYALGIAS

REDUCE THE RISK

Avoid drug interactions, including OTC products.

Do not use simvastatin 80 mg/day.

Do not use gemfibrozil + statin.

MANAGING MYALGIAS

Hold statin, check CPK, investigate other possible causes.

After 2-4 weeks: re-challenge with same statin at same or ↓ dose. Most patients who did not tolerate a statin will tolerate it when re-challenged, or will tolerate a different statin.

If myalgias return, discontinue statin. Once muscle symptoms resolve, use a low dose of a different statin; gradually ↑ dose.

Statins

DRUG	DOSING	SAFETY/SIDE EFFECTS/MONITORING
Atorvastatin (*Lipitor*) + amlodipine (*Caduet*)	10-80 mg daily	**CONTRAINDICATIONS** Do not use in pregnancy, breastfeeding for most patients; can consider continuing a statin in individuals at very high risk for cardiovascular events (e.g., stroke, myocardial infarction) Do not use with liver disease, including any unexplained ↑ LFTs Do not use strong CYP3A4 inhibitors with simvastatin and lovastatin; do not use cyclosporine with pitavastatin
Fluvastatin (*Lescol**, *Lescol XL*)	20-80 mg *Lescol* once daily is taken in the evening *Lescol XL* is taken daily	**WARNINGS** Muscle damage: myopathy/rhabdomyolysis with ↑ CPK ± acute renal failure, higher risk with higher dose (e.g., simvastatin 80 mg), advanced age (≥ 65 years), niacin, fibrates (e.g., gemfibrozil), CYP3A4 inhibitors, hypothyroidism (uncontrolled), renal impairment
Lovastatin (*Altoprev*, *Mevacor**)	20-80 mg Lovastatin (immediate release) is taken with evening meal *Altoprev* (extended release) is taken at bedtime	Diabetes: ↑ A1C/FBG; benefit of statin outweighs risk Hepatotoxicity, with ↑ LFTs (rare), immune-mediated necrotizing myopathy (IMNM) (rare) Rosuvastatin: proteinuria, hematuria – usually transient Atorvastatin: hemorrhagic stroke (if recent stroke or TIAs); benefit of statin outweighs risk
Pitavastatin (*Livalo*, *Zypitamag*)	1-4 mg daily	**SIDE EFFECTS** Generally well-tolerated, can cause myalgia/myopathy
Pravastatin (*Pravachol*)	10-80 mg daily	**MONITORING** **Baseline/Routine** Lipid panel (TC, LDL, HDL, TGs) 4-12 weeks after starting treatment, then every 3-12 months (usually annually), LFTs **Symptomatic** Myalgia/myopathy: check CPK Little/no urine: check SCr/BUN for acute renal failure due to rhabdomyolysis
Rosuvastatin (*Crestor*, *Ezallor Sprinkle*)	5-40 mg daily Consider 5 mg starting dose in Asian patients – exposures are 2 times higher	Abdominal pain or jaundice: check LFTs for possible hepatotoxicity **NOTES** Can take *Crestor*, *Lipitor*, *Livalo*, *Lescol XL* and *Pravachol* at any time of day *FloLipid* is taken on an empty stomach
Simvastatin (*Zocor*, *FloLipid*) Tablet, suspension + ezetimibe (*Vytorin*)	10-40 mg daily in the evening Do not initiate 80 mg dose	For CrCl < 30 mL/min, use lower starting doses of lovastatin, simvastatin and rosuvastatin For eGFR < 60 mL/min, use lower starting dose of pitavastatin **Lipid Effects** ↓ LDL ~20-55%, ↑ HDL ~5-15%, ↓ TG ~10-30%

*Lescol and Mevacor brands discontinued but names still used in practice.

Statin Drug Interactions

Drug interactions with statins increase the risk of adverse effects (e.g., muscle damage). Significant interactions are listed in the box to the right. Most interactions are CYP enzyme mediated, with CYP3A4 being most common. Atorvastatin, lovastatin and simvastatin are CYP3A4 substrates. In general, rosuvastatin and pravastatin have less drug interactions.

Fibrates (especially gemfibrozil) and niacin can ↑ the risk of myopathies and rhabdomyolysis. Do not use statins with gemfibrozil.

Amlodipine can ↑ the concentration of atorvastatin, lovastatin and simvastatin (max daily dose 20 mg/day).

SIGNIFICANT DRUG INTERACTIONS

Do not use with simvastatin or lovastatin	Remember **G ♥ PACMAN***	**MAX DAILY DOSE**
	Grapefruit	
	♥	
	Protease Inhibitors	
	Azole Antifungals	
	C – Cyclosporine, Cobicistat	Rosuvastatin 5 mg/day max with cyclosporine only Atorvastatin 20 mg/day max with cobicistat only
	Macrolides (except Azithromycin)	
	Amiodarone	Simvastatin 20 mg/day max Lovastatin 40 mg/day max
	Non-DHP CCBs	Simvastatin 10 mg/day max Lovastatin 20 mg/day max

*See the Drug Interactions chapter for major CYP3A4 inhibitors

©RxPrep

NON-STATIN ADD-ON TREATMENT

When the LDL remains above goal despite statin treatment, additional medications may be needed. The statin dose should be maximized (i.e., up to the maximum dose tolerated) before other drugs are added.

Ezetimibe and PCSK9 inhibitors are discussed most in clinical guidelines due to their demonstrated cardiovascular benefits. In most cases, ezetimibe is preferred because PCSK9 inhibitors are injectable and much more expensive.

Other medications would be added in select populations. Fish oils and fibrates are used to target high triglycerides. Icosapent ethyl (a fish oil) is also recommended for ASCVD reduction in certain high-risk patients. Bile acid sequestrants are rarely used, except when statins cannot be tolerated.

Determining Add-On Treatment

PATIENT CRITERIA	NON-STATIN TREATMENT
Very high-risk*, statin at max dose & LDL remains ≥ 70 mg/dL	Ezetimibe (preferred) or PCSK9 inhibitors
Primary hypercholesterolemia (LDL ≥ 190 mg/dL), statin at max dose & LDL remains ≥ 100 mg/dL	Ezetimibe (preferred) or PCSK9 inhibitors

*History of multiple ASCVD events or one ASCVD event in a high-risk patient (e.g., diabetes).

EZETIMIBE

Ezetimibe inhibits absorption of cholesterol in the small intestine.

DRUG	DOSING	SAFETY/SIDE EFFECTS/MONITORING
Ezetimibe (Zetia) + simvastatin (Vytorin)	10 mg daily If eGFR < 60 mL/min, do not exceed simvastatin 20 mg/day when using combination product (Vytorin)	**CONTRAINDICATIONS** Vytorin: statin contraindications apply; active liver disease (including any unexplained ↑ in LFTs), pregnancy/breastfeeding **WARNINGS** Avoid use in moderate or severe hepatic impairment Skeletal muscle effects (e.g., myopathy, rhabdomyolysis), risk ↑ when combined with a statin **SIDE EFFECTS** Myalgias, diarrhea, URTIs, arthralgias, pain in extremities, sinusitis **MONITORING** When used with a statin and/or fibrate: LFTs at baseline and as clinically indicated thereafter **NOTES** **Lipid effects with ezetimibe monotherapy** ↓ LDL 18-23%, ↑ HDL 1-3%, ↓ TG 5-10%

Ezetimibe Drug Interactions

- When ezetimibe and cyclosporine are given together, the concentration of both can ↑; monitor levels of cyclosporine.

- Concurrent bile acid sequestrants ↓ ezetimibe; give ezetimibe two hours before or four hours after bile acid sequestrants.

- Can ↑ risk of cholelithiasis when used with fenofibrate and gemfibrozil. Do not use with gemfibrozil.

PROPROTEIN CONVERTASE SUBTILISIN KEXIN TYPE 9 INHIBITORS

The LDL receptor clears circulating LDL. Proprotein convertase subtilisin kexin type 9 (PCSK9) is an enzyme that increases LDL receptor degradation. The PCSK9 inhibitors, alirocumab and evolocumab, are monoclonal antibodies (MAb) that block the ability of PCSK9 to bind to the LDL receptor. They dramatically ↓ LDL cholesterol and reduce the risk of cardiac events. They are costly and given by SC injection.

DRUG	DOSING	SAFETY/SIDE EFFECTS/MONITORING
Alirocumab (*Praluent*) 75 mg/mL, 150 mg/mL prefilled syringes or prefilled pen	**HeFH or ASCVD** 75-150 mg SC once every 2 weeks or 300 mg (150 mg x 2 sites) SC monthly	**WARNINGS** Allergic reactions **SIDE EFFECTS** Injection site reactions, nasopharyngitis, influenza, URTIs, UTI, back pain (evolocumab), ↑ LFTs (alirocumab)
Evolocumab (*Repatha, Repatha SureClick, Pushtronex*) 140 mg/mL prefilled syringe or autoinjector 420 mg/3.5mL prefilled cartridge	**HeFH or ASCVD** 140 mg SC once every 2 weeks or 420 mg monthly **HoFH** 420 mg SC once monthly The 420 mg dose is given as three consecutive 140 mg injections within 30 minutes or as a 420 mg single injection	**MONITORING** LDL at baseline and at 4-8 weeks to assess response **NOTES** Store in the refrigerator in the original carton to protect from light; can be kept at room temperature for up to 30 days; discard after 30 days if stored at room temperature Prior to administration, allow prefilled pen to warm to room temperature (~30 minutes, 45 minutes for *Pushtronex*) and inspect for particulate matter and discoloration **Lipid Effects** ↓ LDL ~60%, ↓ non-HDL ~35%, ↓ apoB ~50%, ↓ TC ~36%

BILE ACID SEQUESTRANTS/BILE ACID BINDING RESINS

These drugs bind bile acids in the intestine, forming a complex that is excreted in the feces. This non-systemic action results in a partial removal of the bile acids from the enterohepatic circulation, preventing their reabsorption.

DRUG	DOSING	SAFETY/SIDE EFFECTS/MONITORING
Cholestyramine (*Prevalite, Questran*, Questran Light**) Also approved for pruritus due to increased levels of bile acids, and regression of atherosclerosis 4 gram powder packet	Initial: 4 grams daily or BID Maintenance: 8-16 grams/day divided BID with meals (max 24 grams/day)	**CONTRAINDICATIONS** Cholestyramine: complete biliary obstruction Colesevelam: bowel obstruction, TG > 500 mg/dL, history of hypertriglyceridemia-induced pancreatitis **WARNINGS** Cholestyramine "light" formulations and colesevelam granules contain phenylalanine and should not be used in patients with PKU ↑ bleeding tendency due to vitamin K deficiency
Colesevelam (*Welchol*) 625 mg tablet, 3.75 gram granule packet Also approved for glycemic control in type 2 DM (↓ A1C ~0.5%)	Tablets/granules: 3.75 grams daily or in divided doses with a meal and liquid	**SIDE EFFECTS** Constipation (may need dose reduction or laxative), abdominal pain, cramping, bloating, gas, ↑ TG, dyspepsia, nausea, esophageal obstruction **NOTES** Not recommended when TG are ≥ 300 mg/dL Cholestyramine packet: mix powder with 2-6 oz. water or non-carbonated liquid; sipping or holding the resin suspension in the mouth for prolonged periods may lead to changes in the surface of the teeth resulting in discoloration, erosion of enamel or decay; use good oral hygiene
Colestipol (*Colestid*) 1 gram tablet, 5 gram packet and granules	Tablets: 2 grams daily or BID (max 16 grams/day) Packet and granules: 5 grams daily or BID (max 30 grams/day)	Colesevelam is an option in a pregnant patient Colesevelam packet: empty 1 packet into a glass; add 8 oz. of water, fruit juice or a diet soft drink and mix well Colestipol packet: empty 1 packet into at least 3 oz. of liquid and stir until mixed **Lipid Effects** ↓ LDL ~10-30%, ↑ HDL ~3-5%, no change or ↑ TG ~5%

*Brands discontinued but names still used in practice.

Bile Acid Sequestrants Drug Interactions

- Colesevelam has fewer drug interactions than the other two bile acid sequestrants and is more commonly used. For cholestyramine or colestipol, take all other drugs at least 1 – 4 hours before or 4 – 6 hours after the bile acid sequestrants.

- With warfarin, monitor INR frequently during initiation and after a dose change.

- The following medications should be taken four hours prior to colesevelam: cyclosporine, glimepiride, glipizide, glyburide, levothyroxine, olmesartan, phenytoin, and oral contraceptives containing ethinyl estradiol and norethindrone. Colesevelam ↑ levels of metformin ER.

- Bile acid sequestrants can ↓ absorption of fat-soluble vitamins (A, D, E, K), folate and iron. A multivitamin may be needed, but separate administration time from the bile acid sequestrant.

FIBRATES

Fibrates are peroxisome proliferator receptor alpha (PPARα) activators, which upregulate the expression of apolipoprotein C2 (apoC-II) and apolipoprotein A1 (apoA-I). ApoC-II increases lipoprotein lipase activity leading to increased catabolism of VLDL particles. This will decrease TG significantly, but in the setting of high TG (increased VLDL particles), fibrate therapy can lead to an increase of LDL particles and subsequently increase LDL cholesterol. The decreased TG can lead to an increase in HDL cholesterol.

DRUG	DOSING	SAFETY/SIDE EFFECTS/MONITORING
Fenofibrate, Fenofibric Acid **(Antara, Tricor, Trilipix,** Fenoglide, Fibricor, Lipofen, Triglide, generics)	Fenofibrate (micronized): 43-130 mg daily Antara (micronized capsule): 30-90 mg daily Antara, micronized (brand) and fenofibrate, micronized (generic) have slightly different dosing regimens for treatment of hypertriglyceridemia Fenoglide: 40-120 mg daily with meals Fibricor: 35-105 mg daily Lipofen: 50-150 mg daily with meals Tricor: 48-145 mg daily Triglide: 160 mg daily Trilipix: 45-135 mg daily	**CONTRAINDICATIONS** Severe liver disease, including primary biliary cirrhosis Severe renal disease (CrCl ≤ 30 mL/min) Gallbladder disease Breastfeeding (fenofibrate derivatives only) Concurrent use with repaglinide or simvastatin (gemfibrozil only) **WARNINGS** Myopathy, ↑ risk when coadministered with a statin, particularly in the elderly, diabetes, renal failure or hypothyroidism Cholelithiasis Reversible ↑ SCr (> 2 mg/dL); clinical significance unknown **SIDE EFFECTS** Dyspepsia (gemfibrozil), ↑ LFTs (dose-related), abdominal pain, ↑ CPK, URTIs
Gemfibrozil (Lopid)	600 mg BID, 30 minutes before breakfast and dinner	**MONITORING** LFTs, renal function **NOTES** Reduce dose if CrCl 31-80 mL/min (fenofibrates) **Lipid Effects** ↓ TG ~20-50%, ↑ HDL ~15%, ↓ LDL ~5-20% (can ↑ LDL when TG are high)

Fibrate Drug Interactions

- Fibrates (especially gemfibrozil) can ↑ the risk of myopathies and rhabdomyolysis. Gemfibrozil should not be given with ezetimibe or statins.

- Colchicine can ↑ the risk of myopathy when coadministered with fenofibrate.

- Gemfibrozil is contraindicated with repaglinide as it can ↑ hypoglycemic effects.

- Fibrates can ↑ the effects of sulfonylureas and warfarin.

NIACIN

Niacin decreases the rate of hepatic synthesis of VLDL (decreases TG) and LDL and can also increase the rate of chylomicron TG removal from plasma. It alters the binding of HDL particles to scavenger receptor B-1 in the liver, which removes the cholesterol inside, but does not take up the HDL particle, which leaves it free to return to the circulation for reverse cholesterol transport. Niacin is also known as nicotinic acid or vitamin B3, although doses for cholesterol reduction are much higher than doses found in multivitamin products.

DRUG	DOSING	SAFETY/SIDE EFFECTS/MONITORING
Niacin Immediate-release (IR) (crystalline): *Niacor* Generic OTC Extended-release (ER): *Niaspan* Controlled-release (CR)/sustained-release (SR): *Slo-Niacin*, OTC	Titrate slowly IR: 250-3,000 mg in 3 divided doses with food ER: 500-2,000 mg at bedtime after a low-fat snack CR/SR: 250-750 mg daily with food	**CONTRAINDICATIONS** Do not use with active liver disease, active PUD or arterial bleeding **WARNINGS** Rhabdomyolysis with niacin doses ≥ 1 gram/day combined with statins Hepatotoxicity Lab abnormalities: ↑ BG, ↑ uric acid, ↓ phosphate Use with caution in patients with unstable angina or the acute phase of an MI **SIDE EFFECTS** Flushing, pruritus (itching), vomiting, diarrhea, ↑ BG, hyperuricemia (or gout), nausea, cough, orthostatic hypotension, hypophosphatemia, ↓ platelets **MONITORING** Check LFTs at the start (baseline); every 6-12 weeks for the first year and then about every 6 months, blood glucose (if diabetic), uric acid (if gout history), INR (if on warfarin), lipid profile **NOTES** IR niacin has poor tolerability due to flushing/itching CR/SR have less (but still significant) flushing but more hepatotoxicity The best clinical choice is ER *Niaspan*, with less flushing and less hepatotoxicity (compared to CR/SR formulations), but it is the most expensive To reduce flushing: take aspirin 325 mg (or ibuprofen 200 mg) 30-60 minutes before the dose; take with food, but avoid spicy food, alcohol and hot beverages (which can worsen flushing) Formulations of niacin (IR vs. ER) are not interchangeable Flush-free niacins (inositol hexaniacinate or hexanicotinate), niacinamide or nicotinamide are not effective **Lipid Effects** ↓ LDL 5-25%, ↑ HDL 15-35%, ↓ TG 20-50%

Niacin Drug Interactions

- Monitor for other concurrent drugs that are potentially hepatotoxic.

- Take niacin 4 – 6 hours after bile acid sequestrants.

FISH OILS

The mechanism is not completely understood; it may reduce hepatic synthesis of TG. These are indicated as an adjunct to diet when TG ≥ 500 mg/dL. Fish oil is also known as omega-3 fatty acids. Icosapent ethyl (Vascepa) is recommended for ASCVD risk reduction in select patients (clinical ASCVD or type 2 diabetes and additional risk factors) with triglycerides that are 135 – 499 mg/dL despite maximally tolerated statin.

DRUG	DOSING	SAFETY/SIDE EFFECTS/MONITORING
Omega-3 Acid Ethyl Esters *(Lovaza)* 1 gram capsule contains 465 mg eicosapentaenoic (EPA) acid and 375 mg docosahexaenoic acid (DHA)	4 capsules daily or 2 capsules BID	**WARNINGS** Use with caution in patients with known hypersensitivity to fish and/or shellfish Monitor LFTs (in patients with hepatic impairment) and LDL periodically during therapy *Lovaza:* can ↑ levels of LDL; possible association with more frequent recurrences of symptomatic atrial fibrillation (AF) or flutter in patients with AF, particularly within the first months of initiation **SIDE EFFECTS** Eructation (burping), dyspepsia, taste perversions *(Lovaza)*, arthralgias *(Vascepa)*
Icosapent ethyl *(Vascepa)* Contains 0.5 or 1 gram of icosapent ethyl, an ethyl ester of omega-3 fatty acid EPA	0.5 gram capsules- 4 BID with food or 1 gram capsules- 2 BID with food	**NOTES** Many OTC omega-3 fatty acid products are marketed as dietary supplements; only prescription medications *Lovaza* and *Vascepa* are FDA-approved for TG lowering, in addition to diet, when TG ≥ 500 mg/dL Stop prior to elective surgeries due to increased risk of bleeding **Lipid Effects** ↓ TG up to 45%, ↑ HDL ~9%, can ↑ LDL (up to 44% with *Lovaza*, no ↑ seen with *Vascepa)*

Fish Oil Drug Interactions

- Omega-3-fatty acids can prolong bleeding time; use with caution with other medications that can ↑ bleeding risk (e.g., antiplatelets, anticoagulants). Monitor INR if patients are taking warfarin at dose initiation or dose change.

OTHER DRUGS

Lomitapide is a specialty drug that decreases apoB, the main component of LDL and VLDL (the precursor to LDL). Lomitapide binds to and inhibits microsomal triglyceride transfer protein (MTP), which prevents the assembly of apoB containing lipoproteins. It is approved for use in homozygous familial hypercholesterolemia (HoFH).

Novel treatments include evinacumab-dgnb *(Evkeeza)*, which is approved for HoFH. It blocks the function of angiopoietin-like 3 (ANGPTL3), a protein involved in lipid metabolism. Bempedoic acid *(Nexletol)* inhibits cholesterol synthesis in the liver by inhibiting adenosine triphosphate-citrate lyase (ACL). It is approved for use in HeFH and ASCVD requiring additional LDL lowering. Inclisiran *(Leqvio)* is an injectable approved for HeFH and secondary prevention of cardiovascular events that works by increasing LDL receptor recycling and expression through ribonucleic acid (RNA) interference.

DRUG	DOSING	SAFETY/SIDE EFFECTS/MONITORING
Lomitapide *(Juxtapid)* Capsule Due to the risk of hepatotoxicity, this agent is only available through the *Juxtapid* Risk Evaluation and Mitigation Strategy (REMS) program	5-60 mg daily Hepatic impairment or ESRD: dosage adjustment required Take whole, with water, but without food, at least two hours after the evening meal	**BOXED WARNINGS** Hepatotoxicity (↑ LFTs, steatosis) **CONTRAINDICATIONS** Active liver disease (including unexplained ↑ LFTs), moderate or severe hepatic impairment Pregnancy Do not use with moderate or strong CYP3A4 inhibitors **SIDE EFFECTS** N/V/D, dyspepsia, abdominal pain, constipation, flatulence, ↑ LFTs, chest pain, back pain, fatigue, weight loss, influenza, nasopharyngitis **MONITORING** LFTs (including total bilirubin), alkaline phosphatase, lipids, pregnancy test in females of reproductive potential at baseline **NOTES** Drug interactions involving CYP3A4 and P-glycoprotein (see Drug Interactions chapter)

KEY COUNSELING POINTS

See the Drug Formulations and Patient Counseling chapter for counseling language/layman's terminology.

See Drug Interactions section for each drug class.

ALL CHOLESTEROL MEDICATIONS

- Follow lifestyle recommendations, including heart-healthy eating habits and exercise.

Statins

- Take simvastatin and fluvastatin IR in the evening (if taken once daily), lovastatin IR with the evening meal and lovastatin ER at bedtime. Other statins can be taken at any time of the day.
- Can cause:
  - ❏ Muscle damage.
  - ❏ Liver damage.
- Avoid grapefruit.
- Avoid in pregnancy (teratogenic) in most cases.

Ezetimibe

- Can cause:
  - ❏ Muscle damage.
  - ❏ Liver damage.

PCSK9 Inhibitors

- Subcutaneous injection. Inject into the thigh, abdomen or upper arm.
- Can cause:
  - ❏ Allergy/anaphylaxis.
  - ❏ Injection site reaction.
- Store in the refrigerator. Allow to warm to room temperature before injecting. Can be kept at room temperature for 30 days.

Bile Acid Sequestrants

- Take at mealtimes with plenty of water or other liquid.
- Can cause constipation.
- Reduces ADEK absorption.

Fibrates

- *Fenoglide* and *Lipofen:* take with food.
- *Lopid:* take twice daily, 30 minutes before breakfast and dinner.
- Can cause:
  - ❏ Muscle damage.
  - ❏ Liver damage.
  - ❏ Cholelithiasis (i.e., gallstones); contact prescriber for severe abdominal pain, nausea or vomiting.
  - ❏ Pancreatitis.

Niacin

- *Niaspan:* take at bedtime after a low-fat snack.
- Other niacins: take with food.
- Can cause:
  - ❏ Hyperglycemia.
  - ❏ Liver damage.
  - ❏ Flushing (warmth, redness, itching and/or tingling of the skin). May subside after several weeks of consistent use. With *Niaspan*, flushing will occur mostly at night; use caution if awakened due to dizziness.
- To reduce flushing, take aspirin 325 mg (or 200 mg of ibuprofen) 30 – 60 minutes before the dose. Taking with food and avoiding drinking alcohol or hot beverages or eating spicy foods around niacin administration can help reduce flushing.

Fish Oil

- *Vascepa:* take with food.
- Can cause dyspepsia (all fish oils), burping or abnormal sense of taste (*Lovaza*) or joint pain (*Vascepa*).

Select Guidelines/References

Grundy SM, Stone NJ, Bailey AL, et al. 2018 AHA/ACC/AACVPR/AAPA/ABC/ACPM/ADA/AGS/APhA/ASPC/NLA/PCNA guideline on the management of blood cholesterol: a report of the American College of Cardiology/American Heart Association Task Force on Clinical Practice Guidelines. *Circulation.* 2018;000:e000–e000. DOI: 10.1161/CIR.0000000000000625.

2019 ACC/AHA Guideline on the Primary Prevention of Cardiovascular Disease: A Report of the American College of Cardiology/American Heart Association Task Force on Clinical Practice Guidelines. *Circulation.* 2019;140(11):e596-e646.

CONTENT LEGEND

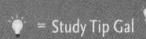 = Study Tip Gal   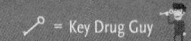 = Key Drug Guy

---

CHAPTER 28
HYPERTENSION

BACKGROUND

Hypertension, or high blood pressure (BP), affects one in three American adults and is a common disease managed in primary care. Hypertension is mostly asymptomatic, which can delay diagnosis and can contribute to medication non-adherence. Medication side effects, cost and pill burden can also lead to discontinuation of treatment. Uncontrolled hypertension places the patient at greater risk for heart disease, stroke and kidney disease. Pharmacists play a vital role by screening and monitoring patients and providing counseling about the importance of lifestyle management (e.g., healthy diet, sodium restriction, physical activity, smoking cessation) and medication adherence. Patient self-monitoring of blood pressure at home can improve motivation and treatment success.

ETIOLOGY AND PATHOPHYSIOLOGY

Most patients (~95%) have primary, or essential, hypertension. The cause is unknown, but a combination of risk factors (e.g., obesity, sedentary lifestyle, excessive salt intake, smoking, family history, diabetes, dyslipidemia) is usually present. Secondary hypertension can be caused by renal disease (e.g., chronic kidney disease), adrenal disease (e.g., excess aldosterone secretion), obstructive sleep apnea or drugs (see Key Drugs Guy later in the chapter). There is increased activity of the sympathetic nervous system (SNS) and the renin-angiotensin-aldosterone system (RAAS), leading to increased levels of neurohormones (e.g., norepinephrine, angiotensin II, aldosterone) that can increase blood pressure. Most medications used to treat hypertension target these neurohormonal pathways (see the Compensatory Mechanisms in Hypertension flow diagram on the next page).

COMPENSATORY MECHANISMS IN HYPERTENSION

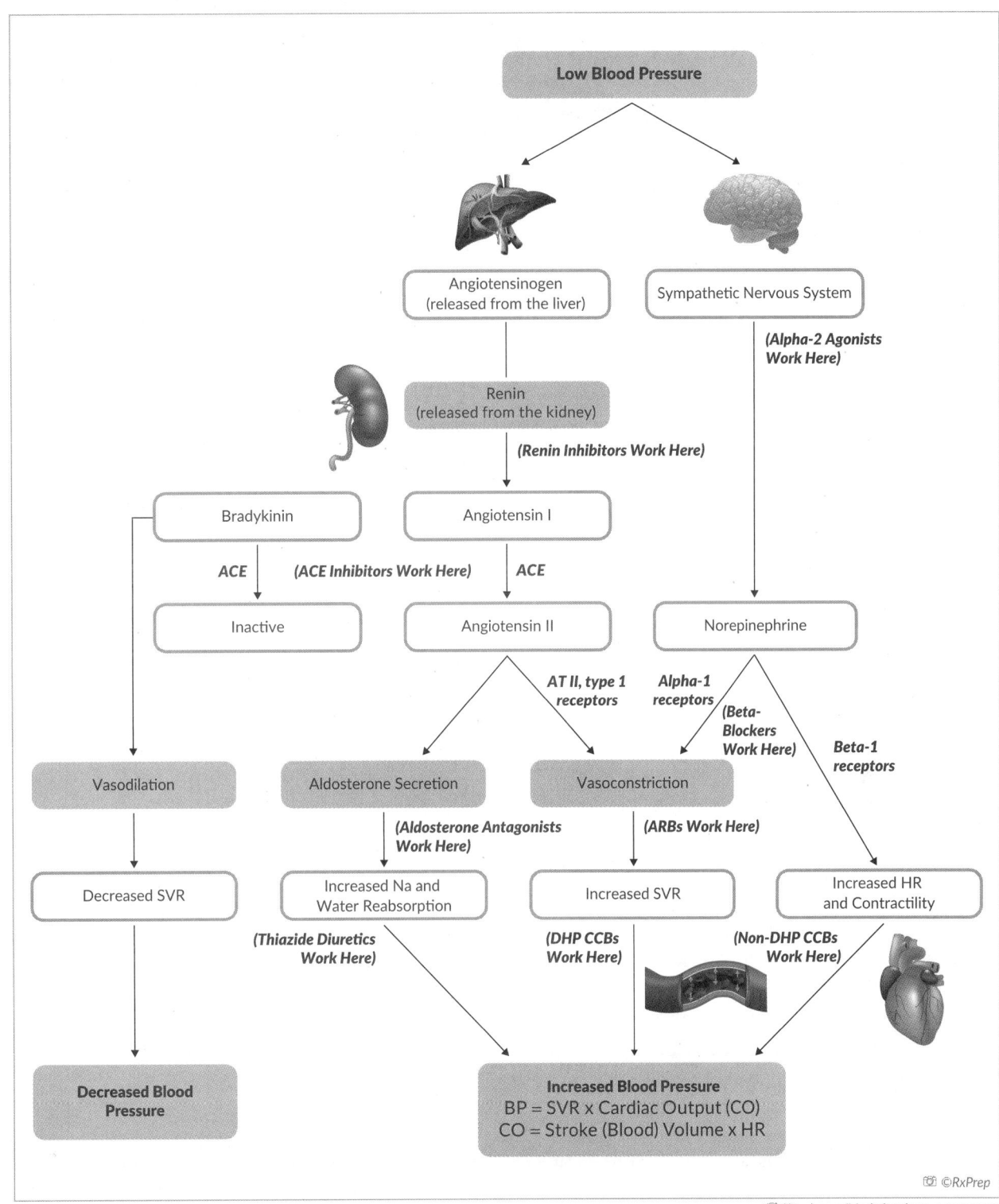

iStock.com/MariaAverburg, newannyart

CARDIOVASCULAR CONDITIONS

SCREENING AND DIAGNOSIS

Accurate measurement of BP (see Study Tip Gal) is essential for diagnosing hypertension and assessing if titration of medication is needed. BP readings in the same individual can vary during the day due to stress, exercise, medications, eating and other activities of daily living. BP usually decreases during the night and increases again in the early morning. BP assessments should be based on an average of at least two readings on two separate occasions, preferably standardized to the timing of medication administration.

Self-monitoring of BP, using an automated home or an ambulatory monitoring device is preferred. BP readings in a clinical office setting tend to be higher, leading to inaccurate clinical decisions related to patient risk and treatment. The American College of Cardiology/American Heart Association (ACC/AHA) has defined four categories of BP in adults, based on systolic BP (SBP) and/or diastolic BP (DBP) readings:

- Normal: SBP < 120 mmHg and DBP < 80 mmHg
- Elevated: SBP 120 – 129 mmHg and DBP < 80 mmHg
- Hypertension:
  - Stage 1: SBP 130 – 139 mmHg or DBP 80 – 89 mmHg
  - Stage 2: SBP ≥ 140 mmHg or DBP ≥ 90 mmHg

LIFESTYLE MANAGEMENT

Lifestyle interventions are essential to prevent hypertension (in patients with normal or elevated blood pressure) and during the treatment of hypertension, in conjunction with medications. Proven interventions include:

- Weight loss (1 kg of weight loss decreases BP by ~1 mmHg)
- A heart-healthy diet [e.g., the DASH eating plan (Dietary Approaches to Stop Hypertension)] that is high in fruits, vegetables, fiber and low-fat dairy products, and low in saturated fats and sugar
- Adequate dietary potassium intake or supplementation, unless contraindicated (e.g., chronic kidney disease)
- Reducing sodium intake to < 1,500 mg daily
- Routine physical activity
- Limiting alcohol consumption to one drink daily for women and two drinks daily for men
- Tobacco cessation
- Controlling blood glucose and cholesterol to reduce cardiovascular disease risk

BLOOD PRESSURE MONITORING

Correct use of your blood pressure monitoring device

DO	DON'T
Go to the restroom and empty the bladder	Talk
Sit in a chair (both feet on the floor) and relax for at least 5 minutes	Sit or lie down on an examination table
Use the correct cuff size	Drink caffeine, exercise or smoke for 30 minutes prior
Support the arm at heart level (e.g., resting on a desk)	Use a finger or wrist monitor (less accurate)
Wait 1-2 minutes in between measurements	

Self-monitoring: bring device and BP reading log to clinic visits
Ambulatory BP monitoring devices: wear during daily activities; obtains readings every 15-60 minutes, day and night

Home BP monitoring devices: record the average of 2-3 readings in the morning and/or evening before eating or taking any medications

DRUGS THAT CAN INCREASE BLOOD PRESSURE

KEY DRUGS

Amphetamines and ADHD drugs

Cocaine

Decongestants (e.g., pseudoephedrine, phenylephrine)

Erythropoiesis-stimulating agents

Immunosuppressants (e.g., cyclosporine)

NSAIDs

Systemic steroids

Others:

Alcohol (excessive)

Appetite suppressants (e.g., phentermine)

Caffeine

Herbals (e.g., ma huang, licorice, yohimbine)

Oral contraceptives

Select oncology drugs (e.g., bevacizumab, tyrosine kinase inhibitors)

Antidepressants (e.g., TCAs, SNRIs, MAO inhibitors)

NATURAL PRODUCTS

In addition to fiber and potassium consumed in a heart-healthy diet, some patients may supplement drug treatment with natural medicines. Although not recommended by guidelines, fish oil, coenzyme Q10, L-arginine and garlic have some evidence for reducing blood pressure and overall cardiovascular risk. Patients should be advised that fish oil and garlic can increase bleeding risk.

TREATMENT PRINCIPLES (ACC/AHA)

- Emphasize lifestyle modifications throughout treatment.

- Once-daily regimens are preferred for medication adherence.

- Four preferred drug classes are recommended for initial and/or titration of treatment before selecting medications from alternate drug classes:

  - ACE inhibitors, ARBs, dihydropyridine calcium channel blockers (DHP CCBs) or thiazide diuretics (see Study Tip Gal for initial drug selection based on patient-specific criteria).

  - Do not use ACE inhibitors and ARBs in combination.

- Most patients will require two or more drugs (see Combination Blood Pressure Drugs table on next page). Additional drugs needed for blood pressure control, after initial drug selection, should be selected from the four preferred drug classes before moving to alternative classes.

- When titrating medications, adding a second drug before reaching maximum doses of the first medication can be more effective and cause fewer side effects.

- Patients with hypertension and comorbid conditions (e.g., heart failure, stable ischemic heart disease) should be treated according to the specific disease-state guideline recommendations. Refer to individual course book chapters as appropriate.

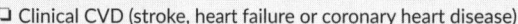

HYPERTENSION GUIDELINE RECOMMENDATIONS

WHEN TO START TREATMENT
- Stage 2 HTN (SBP ≥ 140 mmHg or DBP ≥ 90 mmHg)
- Stage 1 HTN (SBP 130-139 mmHg or DBP 80-89 mmHg) and:
  - Clinical CVD (stroke, heart failure or coronary heart disease)
  - 10-year ASCVD risk ≥ 10%*
  - Does not meet BP goal after 6 months of lifestyle modifications

BP GOAL
- All patients: < 130/80 mmHg**

INITIAL DRUG SELECTION
- Non-black: thiazide, DHP CCB, ACE inhibitor or ARB
- Black: thiazide or DHP CCB
- CKD*** (all races): ACE inhibitor or ARB (to slow progression to ESRD)
- Diabetes with albuminuria (all races): ACE inhibitor or ARB
- Diabetes with CAD**** (all races): ACE inhibitor or ARB
- Start 2 first-line drugs (from preferred drug classes) in Stage 2 HTN when average SBP and DBP > 20/10 mmHg above goal (e.g., 150/90 mmHg)

MONITORING
- Check BP every month and titrate medication if not at goal

*ASCVD = atherosclerotic cardiovascular disease; risk can be assessed using an online tool (http://tools.acc.org/ASCVD-Risk-Estimator/)
**The ADA recommends a goal BP < 130/80 mmHg for patients with diabetes and high ASCVD risk and < 140/90 mmHg for patients at lower risk (see Diabetes chapter). The 2021 KDIGO guideline recommends goal SBP < 120 mmHg for patients with hypertension and CKD (see Renal Disease chapter); exam questions should specify which guideline to follow
***CKD: stage 3 (eGFR < 60 mL/min/1.73 m²) and/or albuminuria (urine albumin ≥ 300 mg/day or albumin:creatinine ratio ≥ 300 mg/g)
****The ADA recommends use of an ACE inhibitor or ARB to reduce the risk of cardiovascular events

PREGNANCY AND HYPERTENSION

Teratogenic drugs can cause fetal harm and should be discontinued if planning a pregnancy. ACE inhibitors, ARBs and the direct renin inhibitor aliskiren have a boxed warning for fetal toxicity in pregnancy and should be stopped immediately.

Antihypertensive drugs can be used during pregnancy to treat preeclampsia, gestational hypertension (hypertension that develops during pregnancy) or chronic hypertension (hypertension before pregnancy). Preeclampsia occurs after week 20 of the pregnancy and is evident by elevated blood pressure and proteinuria in the majority of cases. It is more common in women who are overweight, have pre-existing hypertension, renal disease or diabetes. In patients at high risk of preeclampsia, daily low-dose aspirin is recommended after the first trimester.

Pregnant patients with chronic hypertension should receive drug treatment if SBP is ≥ 160 mmHg or DBP is ≥ 105 mmHg. The American College of Obstetricians and Gynecologists (ACOG) recommend labetalol and nifedipine extended-release as first-line treatments. Methyldopa is recommended but may be less effective at BP lowering. The BP should be maintained between 120 – 160 mmHg systolic and 80 – 110 mmHg diastolic.

COMBINATION BLOOD PRESSURE DRUGS

Tip: the brand names of many diuretic combinations end in HCT, -ide or -etic

ACE INHIBITOR OR ARB + DIURETIC
Lisinopril/Hydrochlorothiazide (Zestoretic)

Losartan/Hydrochlorothiazide (Hyzaar)

Olmesartan/Hydrochlorothiazide (Benicar HCT)

Valsartan/Hydrochlorothiazide (Diovan HCT)

Azilsartan/Chlorthalidone (Edarbyclor)

Benazepril/Hydrochlorothiazide (Lotensin HCT)

Candesartan/Hydrochlorothiazide

Captopril/Hydrochlorothiazide

Enalapril/Hydrochlorothiazide (Vaseretic)

Fosinopril/Hydrochlorothiazide

Irbesartan/Hydrochlorothiazide (Avalide)

Moexipril/Hydrochlorothiazide

Quinapril/Hydrochlorothiazide (Accuretic)

Telmisartan/Hydrochlorothiazide (Micardis HCT)

ACE INHIBITOR OR ARB + CCB
Benazepril/Amlodipine (Lotrel)

Valsartan/Amlodipine (Exforge)

Olmesartan/Amlodipine (Azor)

Perindopril/Amlodipine (Prestalia)

Telmisartan/Amlodipine (Twynsta)

Trandolapril/Verapamil (Tarka)

DIRECT RENIN INHIBITOR + DIURETIC
Aliskiren/Hydrochlorothiazide (Tekturna HCT)

ALPHA-2 AGONIST + DIURETIC
Methyldopa/Hydrochlorothiazide

BETA BLOCKER + DIURETIC
Atenolol/Chlorthalidone (Tenoretic)

Bisoprolol/Hydrochlorothiazide (Ziac)

Metoprolol Tartrate/Hydrochlorothiazide (Lopressor HCT)

Metoprolol Succinate/Hydrochlorothiazide (Dutoprol)

Nadolol/Bendroflumethiazide

Propranolol/Hydrochlorothiazide

K-SPARING + THIAZIDE-TYPE DIURETIC
Triamterene/Hydrochlorothiazide (Maxzide, Maxzide-25, Dyazide)

Amiloride/Hydrochlorothiazide

Spironolactone/Hydrochlorothiazide (Aldactazide)

TRIPLE COMBINATIONS
Olmesartan/Amlodipine/Hydrochlorothiazide (Tribenzor)

Valsartan/Amlodipine/Hydrochlorothiazide (Exforge HCT)

THIAZIDE-TYPE DIURETICS

Thiazide-type diuretics are inexpensive, effective and have mild side effects in most patients. They are one of four drug classes that can be considered for initial treatment. Loop diuretics are used primarily in heart failure (see Chronic Heart Failure chapter).

Thiazides and thiazide-type diuretics <u>inhibit sodium reabsorption</u> in the <u>distal convoluted tubules</u> (see <u>Nephron diagram</u>), causing <u>increased excretion</u> of <u>sodium, chloride, water and potassium</u>.

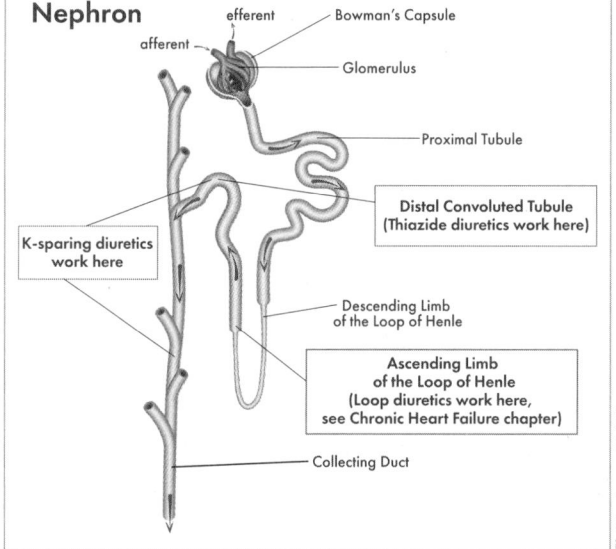

Nephron

efferent

afferent

Bowman's Capsule

Glomerulus

Proximal Tubule

Distal Convoluted Tubule (Thiazide diuretics work here)

K-sparing diuretics work here

Descending Limb of the Loop of Henle

Ascending Limb of the Loop of Henle (Loop diuretics work here, see Chronic Heart Failure chapter)

Collecting Duct

iStock.com/TefiM

DRUG	DOSING	SAFETY/SIDE EFFECTS/MONITORING
Chlorthalidone Tablet	12.5-25 mg daily (max dose is 100 mg daily but doses > 25 mg/day have limited clinical benefit)	**CONTRAINDICATIONS** Hypersensitivity to sulfonamide-derived drugs (not likely to cross-react – see Drug Allergies & Adverse Drug Reactions chapter); anuria **WARNINGS** Severe renal disease (can precipitate azotemia), progressive liver disease (fluid and electrolyte changes can precipitate hepatic coma), can precipitate or exacerbate conditions such as systemic lupus erythematosus (SLE), gout and diabetes, transient myopia or acute angle-closure glaucoma (hydrochlorothiazide)
Hydrochlorothiazide (*Microzide**) Tablet, capsule	12.5-50 mg daily (max dose is 100 mg daily but doses > 50 mg/day have limited clinical benefit and ↑ risk of adverse effects)	**SIDE EFFECTS** ↓ electrolytes: K, Mg, Na ↑ electrolytes/labs: Ca, UA, LDL, TG, BG Photosensitivity (including a small ↑ risk of non-melanoma skin cancer), impotence, dizziness, rash
Chlorothiazide (*Diuril, Sodium Diuril*) Tablet, oral suspension, injection	500-2,000 mg daily in 1-2 divided doses	**MONITORING** Electrolytes, renal function, BP, fluid status (input and output, weight), BG (in diabetes) **NOTES** Thiazides are not effective when CrCl < 30 mL/min (except metolazone, which may work with reduced renal function or diuretic resistance)
Indapamide Tablet	1.25-5 mg daily	Take early in the day to avoid nocturia Chlorothiazide is the only medication in this class available IV
Metolazone Tablet	2.5-5 mg daily	Chlorthalidone may be preferred over hydrochlorothiazide due to longer duration (if a patient is doing well on hydrochlorothiazide, no need to switch) Hypokalemia can be avoided with regular intake of potassium-rich foods or potassium supplements

Brand discontinued but name still used in practice

Thiazide-Type Diuretic Drug Interactions

- All antihypertensives can enhance the blood pressure lowering effects of other drugs; carefully monitor blood pressure when adding medications.

- Drugs that can cause sodium and water retention (e.g., NSAIDs) can decrease the effectiveness of antihypertensive medications. Do not use in combination.

- Thiazide diuretics can ↓ lithium renal clearance and ↑ the risk of lithium toxicity. Do not use in combination if possible.

- Thiazide diuretics can ↑ dofetilide serum concentrations leading to an ↑ risk of QT prolongation; do not use in combination.

CALCIUM CHANNEL BLOCKERS

There are two types of calcium channel blockers (CCBs), dihydropyridines (DHP) and non-dihydropyridines (non-DHP). Nifedipine (a DHP CCB) and diltiazem (a non-DHP CCB) have many long-acting formulations. Not all generic products are therapeutically equivalent to the brand-name products. If the pharmacist is substituting a generic product for a brand-name product, they should check the *Orange Book* and choose a generic product that is AB-rated to the brand product.

DIHYDROPYRIDINE CCBs

DHP CCBs have generic names that end in "-pine"; they are used for hypertension, chronic stable angina and Prinzmetal's angina (see Stable Ischemic Heart Disease chapter). They inhibit Ca ions from entering vascular smooth muscle and myocardial cells; this causes peripheral arterial vasodilation (which ↓ SVR and BP) and coronary artery vasodilation. Peripheral vasodilation leads to common side effects of reflex tachycardia/palpitations, headache, flushing and peripheral edema.

DRUG	DOSING	SAFETY/SIDE EFFECTS/MONITORING
Amlodipine (Norvasc, Katerzia) Tablet, suspension	2.5-10 mg daily	**CONTRAINDICATIONS** Nicardipine should not be used in advanced aortic stenosis **WARNINGS** Hypotension (especially with severe aortic stenosis), worsening angina and/or MI, severe hepatic impairment, use caution in heart failure (see Notes) Nifedipine IR: do not use for chronic hypertension or acute BP reduction in non-pregnant adults (profound hypotension, MI and/or death has occurred)
Nicardipine IV (Cardene IV) Nicardipine IR Capsule, injection	IV: 5 mg/hr, ↑ by 2.5 mg/hr every 5-15 mins to max dose of 15 mg/hr IR: 20-40 mg TID	**SIDE EFFECTS** Generally well-tolerated, can cause peripheral edema/headache/flushing/palpitations/reflex tachycardia/fatigue (worse with nifedipine IR), nausea, gingival hyperplasia (more gingival hyperplasia with non-DHPs)
Nifedipine ER (Adalat CC, Procardia XL) Nifedipine IR (Procardia)	30-90 mg daily	**MONITORING** Peripheral edema, BP, HR **NOTES** Amlodipine is considered the safest if a CCB must be used to lower BP in heart failure with reduced ejection fraction
Felodipine ER	2.5-10 mg daily	Nifedipine ER is a drug of choice in pregnancy
Isradipine	2.5-10 mg BID	DHP CCBs (e.g., nifedipine ER) are used to prevent peripheral vasoconstriction in Raynaud's (i.e., cold/blue fingers)
Nisoldipine ER (Sular)	8.5-34 mg daily	*Adalat CC* and *Procardia XL*: OROS/gel matrix formulations (see Drug Formulations and
Nisoldipine ER (original formulation)	10-60 mg daily	Patient Counseling chapter) can leave a ghost tablet (empty shell) in the stool
Clevidipine (Cleviprex) Injection	1-21 mg/hr	**CONTRAINDICATIONS** Allergy to soybeans, soy products or eggs; defective lipid metabolism (e.g., lipoid nephrosis, hyperlipidemia with acute pancreatitis); severe aortic stenosis **WARNINGS** Hypotension, reflex tachycardia, infections (see Notes) **SIDE EFFECTS** Hypertriglyceridemia, headache, atrial fibrillation, nausea **MONITORING** BP, HR **NOTES** A lipid emulsion (provides 2 kcal/mL); it is milky-white in color Use strict aseptic technique due to infection risk; maximum time of use after vial puncture is 12 hrs

CASE SCENARIO

TW is a 54-year-old female admitted to the medical ICU with a hypertensive emergency. She is receiving clevidipine 50 mg/100 mL at a rate of 3 mg/hr. The bottle has 52 mL remaining at 1400.

- **How many calories per day is TW receiving from clevidipine?**

Calculate using the flow rate, product concentration and known kcal/mL provided.

$$\frac{3 \text{ mg}}{\text{hr}} \times \frac{24 \text{ hrs}}{\text{day}} \times \frac{100 \text{ mL}}{50 \text{ mg}} \times \frac{2 \text{ kcal}}{\text{mL}} = 288 \text{ kcal/day}$$

- **At what time should the bottle of clevidipine be removed and replaced?**

48 mL of clevidipine have been used. First, calculate how long the bottle has been hanging.

$$48 \text{ mL} \times \frac{50 \text{ mg}}{100 \text{ mL}} \times \frac{1 \text{ hr}}{3 \text{ mg}} = 8 \text{ hrs}$$

The bottle needs to be replaced every 12 hours (or in 4 more hours). It is currently 1400. A new bottle should be hung at 1800.

- **What other drugs may require similar calculations?**

Propofol (*Diprivan*) is another lipid emulsion that provides calories (1.1 kcal/mL) and requires tubing/vial changes every 12 hours (refer to the Acute & Critical Care Medicine chapter for more information).

NON-DIHYDROPYRIDINE CCBs

The non-DHP CCBs, verapamil and diltiazem, are primarily used to control HR in certain arrhythmias (e.g., atrial fibrillation) and are sometimes used for hypertension and angina. They inhibit Ca ions from entering vascular smooth muscle and myocardial cells, but they are more selective for the myocardium than the DHP CCBs. The decrease in BP produced by non-DHP CCBs is due to negative inotropic (↓ force of ventricular contraction) and negative chronotropic (↓ HR) effects.

DRUG	DOSING	SAFETY/SIDE EFFECTS/MONITORING
Diltiazem (Cardizem, Tiazac, Cardizem CD, Cardizem LA, Cartia XT, others) IR tablet, ER tablet (24-HR), ER capsule (12-HR), ER capsule (24-HR), injection	120-360 mg daily; max dose varies with product IR tablet: daily dose given in 4 divided doses ER capsule (12-HR): daily dose given in 2 divided doses	**CONTRAINDICATIONS** Hypotension (SBP < 90 mmHg) or cardiogenic shock; 2nd or 3rd degree AV block or sick sinus syndrome (unless has a functioning artificial ventricular pacemaker), acute MI and pulmonary congestion (diltiazem), severe left ventricular dysfunction (verapamil), atrial flutter or atrial fibrillation and an accessory bypass tract (verapamil) **WARNINGS** Heart failure (may worsen symptoms), bradycardia, hypotension, acute liver injury/↑ LFTs, cardiac conduction abnormalities (diltiazem), hypertrophic cardiomyopathy (verapamil)
Verapamil (Calan SR, Verelan, Verelan PM) IR tablet, ER tablet, ER capsule (24-HR), injection	240-480 mg daily IR tablet: daily dose given in 3 divided doses Calan SR: daily dose can be given in 2 divided doses (QAM and QPM) Verelan PM: daily dose given QHS	**SIDE EFFECTS** Edema, constipation (more with verapamil), gingival hyperplasia, headache, dizziness **MONITORING** BP, HR, ECG, LFTs **NOTES** IV:PO dose conversions are not 1:1 Non-DHP CCBs are used to reduce rapid heart rate in atrial fibrillation

Calcium Channel Blocker Drug Interactions

- Use caution with other drugs that ↓ HR, including beta-blockers, digoxin, clonidine, amiodarone and dexmedetomidine (*Precedex*).

- All CCBs (except clevidipine) are major substrates of CYP450 3A4. Use caution with strong CYP3A4 inducers and inhibitors, and in some cases, do not use in combination. Check for drug interactions. Do not use with grapefruit juice.

- Diltiazem and verapamil are substrates and inhibitors of P-gp and moderate inhibitors of CYP3A4, increasing the concentration of many other drugs. Patients who take statins should use lower doses of simvastatin or lovastatin (see Dyslipidemia chapter) or use a statin that is not metabolized by CYP3A4 (e.g., pitavastatin, pravastatin, rosuvastatin).

RENIN-ANGIOTENSIN ALDOSTERONE SYSTEM INHIBITORS

Angiotensin II (Ang II) causes vasoconstriction and increased release of aldosterone; this results in sodium and water retention. RAAS inhibitors decrease BP by inhibiting the effects of Ang II. Some drugs (ACE inhibitors and ARBs) have been shown to slow the progression of kidney disease in patients with albuminuria (e.g., due to diabetes, hypertension). Ang II constricts the efferent arterioles of the nephron (see Nephron diagram earlier in chapter), causing increased workload in the glomeruli; over time, this results in kidney damage. Blocking Ang II causes efferent arteriole vasodilation and decreases glomerular filtration pressure. In heart failure, ACE inhibitors and ARBs protect the myocardium from the remodeling effects of Ang II.

RAAS inhibitors should not be used in combination (e.g., ACE inhibitor ± ARB ± aliskiren ± ARNI) due to an increased risk for adverse effects (see RAAS Inhibitor Drug Interactions). Angioedema is a potentially fatal adverse effect that can occur with the use of any drug. It is more common with ACE inhibitors than ARBs or aliskiren, and black patients have a higher risk. For testing purposes, if a patient develops angioedema with any RAAS inhibitor, other RAAS inhibitors should be avoided.

ANGIOTENSIN-CONVERTING ENZYME INHIBITORS

ACE inhibitors end in "-pril." They block the conversion of angiotensin I (Ang I) to Ang II, resulting in ↓ vasoconstriction and ↓ aldosterone secretion. They block the degradation of bradykinin, which is thought to contribute to the vasodilatory effects (and side effects of a dry and hacking cough and angioedema).

DRUG	DOSING	SAFETY/SIDE EFFECTS/MONITORING
Benazepril (Lotensin)	5-40 mg daily	**BOXED WARNINGS** Can cause injury and death to the developing fetus when used in the 2nd and 3rd trimesters; discontinue as soon as pregnancy is detected
Enalapril (Vasotec, Epaned powder for oral solution) **Enalaprilat (Vasotec IV)**	PO: 5-20 mg daily or BID IV (enalaprilat): 0.625-5 mg Q6H	**CONTRAINDICATIONS** Do not use with history of angioedema Do not use within 36 hrs of sacubitril/valsartan (Entresto)
Lisinopril (Prinivil, Zestril, Qbrelis oral solution)	5-40 mg daily	Do not use with aliskiren in diabetes
Quinapril (Accupril)	5-40 mg daily	**WARNINGS** Angioedema, hyperkalemia, hypotension, renal impairment, bilateral renal artery stenosis (avoid use)
Ramipril (Altace)	2.5-20 mg daily	
Captopril	12.5 mg BID-50 mg TID	**SIDE EFFECTS** Generally well-tolerated, can cause cough, hyperkalemia, ↑ SCr, hypotension/dizziness [↑ risk if volume-depleted (e.g., with concurrent diuretic)], headache
Fosinopril	10-40 mg daily	
Moexipril	3.75-30 mg daily	**MONITORING** BP, K, renal function, s/sx of angioedema
Perindopril	4-16 mg daily	**NOTES** Once-daily drugs can be used BID if needed
Trandolapril	1-8 mg daily	

ANGIOTENSIN RECEPTOR BLOCKERS

ARBs <u>end in "-sartan."</u> They <u>block Ang II</u> from binding to the angiotensin II type-1 (AT1) receptor on vascular smooth muscle, <u>preventing vasoconstriction.</u>

DRUG	DOSING	SAFETY/SIDE EFFECTS/MONITORING
Irbesartan (*Avapro*)	75-300 mg daily	Same as ACE inhibitors except:
Losartan (*Cozaar*)	25-100 mg daily in 1-2 divided doses	<u>Less</u> cough <u>Less</u> angioedema <u>No washout period required</u> with sacubitril/valsartan (*Entresto*)
Olmesartan (*Benicar*)	10-40 mg daily	
Valsartan (*Diovan*)	80-320 mg daily	Additional safety issues unique to ARBs include:
Azilsartan (*Edarbi*)	40-80 mg daily	**WARNINGS** <u>Olmesartan: sprue-like enteropathy</u> – severe, chronic diarrhea with substantial
Candesartan (*Atacand*)	8-32 mg daily in 1-2 divided doses	weight loss; can occur months to years after drug initiation
Eprosartan	400-800 mg daily in 1-2 divided doses	**NOTES** Azilsartan: keep in original container to protect from light and moisture
Telmisartan (*Micardis*)	20-80 mg daily	

DIRECT RENIN INHIBITOR

Aliskiren directly inhibits renin, which is responsible for the conversion of angiotensinogen to Ang I. A decrease in the formation of Ang I results in a decrease in the formation of Ang II.

DRUG	DOSING	SAFETY/SIDE EFFECTS/MONITORING
Aliskiren (*Tekturna*)	150-300 mg daily Take with or without food but be consistent in administration with regard to meals Avoid high fat foods (reduces absorption)	Same as ACE inhibitors and ARBs except: **CONTRAINDICATIONS** <u>Do not use with ACE inhibitors or ARBs in patients with diabetes</u> **NOTES** *Tekturna:* tablets must be protected from moisture *Tekturna HCT* (see the Combination Blood Pressure Drugs table earlier in chapter): the original container contains a desiccant

RAAS INHIBITOR DRUG INTERACTIONS

- <u>All RAAS inhibitors</u> ↑ the risk of <u>hyperkalemia</u>. Other medications that increase potassium (e.g., potassium-sparing diuretics) should be used cautiously. Patients should avoid salt substitutes that contain potassium chloride (instead of sodium chloride).

- <u>Do not use more than one RAAS inhibitor together</u> (ACE inhibitor ± ARB ± aliskiren ± ARNI) due to an ↑ risk of renal impairment, hypotension and hyperkalemia. <u>Aliskiren</u> in combination <u>with an ACE inhibitor or ARB</u> is specifically <u>contraindicated in patients with diabetes.</u>

- ACE inhibitors and ARBs should not be used in combination with sacubitril/valsartan (*Entresto*). If switching from an <u>ACE inhibitor to *Entresto*</u>, or vice versa, a <u>36-hour washout period</u> is required. See the Chronic Heart Failure chapter for additional information.

- ACE inhibitors and ARBs can ↓ <u>lithium renal clearance</u> and ↑ the <u>risk of lithium toxicity.</u>

CARDIOVASCULAR CONDITIONS

ADDITIONAL DRUGS FOR TREATING HYPERTENSION

POTASSIUM-SPARING DIURETICS

The potassium-sparing diuretics triamterene and amiloride have minimal BP-lowering effects. They are often used in combination with hydrochlorothiazide (e.g., *Maxzide)* to counteract the mild potassium losses seen with thiazide diuretics. The aldosterone receptor antagonists, spironolactone and eplerenone, are the preferred add-on drugs in resistant hypertension (uncontrolled BP despite maximum tolerated doses of a CCB + thiazide diuretic + ACE inhibitor or ARB), and they are commonly used in heart failure.

Spironolactone is a non-selective aldosterone receptor antagonist (also blocks androgen), while eplerenone is a selective aldosterone receptor antagonist that does not exhibit endocrine side effects. These medications compete with aldosterone at receptor sites in the distal convoluted tubule and collecting ducts of the nephron (see Nephron diagram earlier in the chapter), increasing sodium and water excretion and conserving potassium.

DRUG	DOSING	SAFETY/SIDE EFFECTS/MONITORING
Spironolactone (*Aldactone,* *CaroSpir* oral suspension)	25-100 mg daily in 1-2 divided doses	**BOXED WARNINGS** Amiloride and triamterene: hyperkalemia (K > 5.5 mEq/L) – more likely in patients with diabetes, renal impairment, or elderly patients **CONTRAINDICATIONS** Do not use if hyperkalemia, severe renal impairment, Addison's disease (spironolactone) or taking strong CYP3A4 inhibitors (eplerenone)
Triamterene (*Dyrenium*) **+ HCTZ (*Dyazide*, Maxzide,*** Maxzide-25)*	100-300 mg daily in 1-2 divided doses + HCTZ: 37.5 mg/25 mg daily or BID + HCTZ: 75 mg/50 mg daily	**SIDE EFFECTS** Hyperkalemia, ↑ SCr, dizziness, hyperchloremic metabolic acidosis (rare) Spironolactone: gynecomastia, breast tenderness, impotence, irregular menses, amenorrhea Eplerenone: ↑ TGs
Amiloride	5-20 mg daily	**MONITORING** BP, K, renal function, fluid status, s/sx of HF
Eplerenone (*Inspra*)	50 mg daily or BID	**NOTES** *CaroSpir* suspension (also approved for use in heart failure and edema due to cirrhosis) is not therapeutically equivalent to *Aldactone* and dosing recommendations differ; doses > 100 mg can cause unexpectedly high concentrations; use a different formulation in this case

Brand discontinued but name still used in practice

Potassium-Sparing Diuretic Drug Interactions

- Potassium-sparing diuretics ↑ the risk of hyperkalemia. Additive potassium accumulation can occur when these medications are used with other potassium-sparing drugs (see Drug Interactions chapter).

- Diuretics can ↓ lithium renal clearance and ↑ the risk of lithium toxicity.

- Eplerenone is a major substrate of CYP3A4; do not use with strong CYP3A4 inhibitors (e.g., ketoconazole, itraconazole, clarithromycin, ritonavir).

BETA-BLOCKERS

Beta-blockers mostly end in "-olol." They are no longer recommended first-line for treating hypertension unless the patient has a comorbid condition for which beta-blockers are indicated (e.g., post-MI, stable ischemic heart disease, heart failure). Selection of a specific beta-blocker will depend on the condition being treated. For example, bisoprolol, carvedilol or metoprolol succinate should be used if treating chronic heart failure.

Beta-blockers decrease BP by competitively blocking beta-1 and/or beta-2 adrenergic receptors, resulting in decreases in HR and myocardial contractility. Carvedilol and labetalol are beta-blockers with alpha-1 blocking properties. Alpha-1 blockers decrease peripheral vasoconstriction, lowering BP. Beta-blockers with intrinsic sympathomimetic activity (ISA) (acebutolol, penbutolol and pindolol) partially stimulate beta receptors while blocking the effects of catecholamines (e.g., norepinephrine). They do not decrease HR to the same degree as beta-blockers without ISA and are not recommended in post-MI patients. If a beta-blocker is needed in a patient with bronchospastic disease (e.g., asthma, COPD), a beta-1 selective agent is preferred.

DRUG	DOSING	SAFETY/SIDE EFFECTS/MONITORING
Beta-1 Selective Blockers		
Atenolol *(Tenormin)*	25-100 mg daily	**BOXED WARNINGS** Do not discontinue abruptly (particularly in patients with CAD/IHD); gradually taper dose over 1-2 weeks to avoid acute tachycardia, hypertension, and/or ischemia **CONTRAINDICATIONS** Severe bradycardia; 2nd or 3rd degree AV block or sick sinus syndrome (unless a permanent pacemaker is in place); overt cardiac failure or cardiogenic shock
Esmolol *(Brevibloc)* Injection	0.5-1 mg/kg IV bolus followed by 50-150 mcg/kg/min via continuous IV infusion, titrate as needed to a maximum of 300 mcg/kg/min	Esmolol: pulmonary hypertension; use of IV non-DHP CCBs **WARNINGS** Use caution in patients with diabetes: can worsen hyperglycemia or hypoglycemia and mask hypoglycemic symptoms (see Diabetes chapter)
Metoprolol tartrate *(Lopressor)* Tablet, injection **Metoprolol succinate extended release *(Toprol XL, Kapspargo Sprinkle)*** Tablet, capsule sprinkle	IR: 100-450 mg daily in 2-3 divided doses XL: 25-100 mg daily; max dose is 400 mg daily	Use caution with bronchospastic diseases (e.g., asthma, COPD), beta-1 selective preferred Use caution with Raynaud's/other peripheral vascular diseases, pheochromocytoma and heart failure (slow dose titration required if used in these conditions) Can mask signs of hyperthyroidism (e.g., tachycardia), can worsen CNS depression **SIDE EFFECTS** Bradycardia, fatigue, hypotension, dizziness, depression, impotence (less than thiazides), cold extremities (can exacerbate Raynaud's)
Acebutolol	200-800 mg daily in 1-2 divided doses	**MONITORING** HR (↓ dose if HR < 55 BPM), BP **NOTES** Oral drugs: titrate doses every 1-2 weeks (as tolerated), take without regard to meals (except *Lopressor* and *Toprol XL* should be taken with or immediately following food)
Betaxolol *Betoptic S* – ophthalmic solution	5-20 mg daily	Metoprolol tartrate IV is not equivalent to PO (IV:PO ratio is 1:2.5) When switching from metoprolol tartrate to metoprolol succinate, the same total daily dose of metoprolol should be used
Bisoprolol	2.5-20 mg daily	*Kapspargo Sprinkle* should be swallowed whole; for patients with difficulty swallowing, the capsule can be opened and the contents sprinkled on 1 teaspoonful of soft food (e.g., applesauce, yogurt or pudding) – the mixture must be swallowed within 60 mins *Toprol XL* can be split in half For beta-1 selective drugs, remember: "AMEBBA" – Atenolol, Metoprolol, Esmolol, Bisoprolol, Betaxolol, Acebutolol
Beta-1 Selective Blocker with Nitric Oxide-Dependent Vasodilation		
Nebivolol *(Bystolic)*	5-40 mg daily CrCl < 30 mL/min or moderate liver impairment, start at 2.5 mg daily	Same as above plus: **CONTRAINDICATIONS** Severe liver impairment (Child-Pugh > class B) **SIDE EFFECTS** Fatigue, nausea, ↑ TGs, ↓ HDL **NOTES** Nitric oxide causes peripheral vasodilation

CARDIOVASCULAR CONDITIONS

DRUG	DOSING	SAFETY/SIDE EFFECTS/MONITORING
Beta-1 and Beta-2 Blockers (Non-Selective)		
Propranolol (Inderal LA, Inderal XL, InnoPran XL, Hemangeol) Tablet, ER capsule, oral solution, injection	IR: 80-160 mg BID, max dose is 640 mg daily LA: 80-160 mg daily, same max dose as IR XL: 80 mg daily; max dose is 120 mg daily	Same as for beta-1 selective blockers plus: **NOTES** Propranolol has high lipid solubility (lipophilic) and crosses the blood-brain barrier; it is associated with more CNS side effects, but this makes it useful for other conditions (e.g., migraine prophylaxis, essential tremor) Non-selective beta-blockers are used in portal hypertension (see Hepatitis & Liver Disease chapter)
Nadolol (Corgard)	40-320 mg daily	
Pindolol	5-30 mg BID	
Timolol Timoptic – ophthalmic solution	10-30 mg BID	
Non-Selective Beta-Blocker and Alpha-1 Blockers		
Carvedilol (Coreg, Coreg CR) Tablet, ER capsule	IR: 6.25-25 mg BID CR: 20-80 mg daily	Same as for beta-1 selective and non-selective blockers plus: **CONTRAINDICATIONS** Severe hepatic impairment **WARNINGS** Intraoperative floppy iris syndrome has occurred in cataract surgery patients who were on or were previously treated with an alpha-1 blocker **SIDE EFFECTS** Edema, weight gain **NOTES** Take all forms of carvedilol with food to ↓ the rate of absorption and the risk of orthostatic hypotension Carvedilol CR has less bioavailability than carvedilol IR; dosing conversions are not 1:1 (e.g., Coreg 3.125 mg BID = Coreg CR 10 mg daily)
Labetalol Tablet, injection	PO: 100-1,200 mg BID	Same as above for carvedilol plus: **SIDE EFFECTS** Dizziness, fatigue, nausea **NOTES** Drug of choice in pregnancy Injection is commonly used in the hospital setting and can be administered by repeated IV push or slow continuous infusion

Beta-Blocker Drug Interactions

- Beta-blockers can enhance the hypoglycemic effects of insulin and sulfonylureas and mask some of the symptoms of hypoglycemia (e.g., shakiness, palpitations, anxiety); symptoms of sweating and hunger are not masked. Beta-blockers can ↓ insulin secretion, causing hyperglycemia. Monitor blood glucose in diabetes.

- Use caution when administering other drugs that ↓ HR, including diltiazem, verapamil, digoxin, clonidine, amiodarone and dexmedetomidine (Precedex).

- Carvedilol, propranolol and metoprolol are major substrates of CYP2D6, and nebivolol is a minor substrate of CYP2D6. Monitor for drug interactions.

- Carvedilol and propranolol are inhibitors of P-gp and can increase the serum concentration of P-gp substrates (e.g., cyclosporine, dabigatran, digoxin, ranolazine).

CENTRALLY-ACTING ALPHA-2 ADRENERGIC AGONISTS

These drugs decrease BP by stimulating alpha-2 adrenergic receptors in the brain and reducing sympathetic outflow of norepinephrine, which decreases SVR and HR. Clonidine is commonly used for resistant hypertension and in patients who can not swallow (e.g., due to dysphagia, dementia) since it is available as a patch formulation. Since the patch is changed weekly, it can help with adherence.

DRUG	DOSING	SAFETY/SIDE EFFECTS/MONITORING
Clonidine (Catapres*, Catapres-TTS patch, *Duraclon* inj) **Kapvay** – for ADHD Tablet, patch, injection	0.1-0.2 mg PO BID, max dose is 2.4 mg daily **Weekly patch** *Catapres-TTS-1* = 0.1 mg/24 hr *Catapres-TTS-2* = 0.2 mg/24 hr *Catapres-TTS-3* = 0.3 mg/24 hr	**CONTRAINDICATIONS** Methyldopa: concurrent use with MAO inhibitors and active liver disease **WARNINGS** Do not discontinue abruptly (can cause rebound hypertension, sweating, anxiety, tremors); must taper gradually over 2-4 days Methyldopa: risk for hemolytic anemia (detected by a positive Coombs test), hepatic necrosis **SIDE EFFECTS** Dry mouth, somnolence, fatigue, dizziness, constipation, ↓ HR, hypotension, impotence, headache, depression, behavioral changes (irritability, confusion, anxiety, nightmares) Clonidine patch: skin rash, pruritus, erythema
Guanfacine IR (*Tenex**) **Guanfacine ER (Intuniv)** – for ADHD	1-2 mg QHS	Methyldopa: hypersensitivity reactions [e.g., drug-induced lupus erythematosus (DILE)], edema or weight gain (control with diuretics), ↑ prolactin levels **MONITORING** BP, HR, mental status
Methyldopa Tablet, injection	250 mg BID-TID; max dose is 3 grams daily	**NOTES** Clonidine patch: apply weekly to a clean, dry and hairless area of skin on the upper outer arm or upper chest; remove before MRI; can apply the adhesive cover over the patch if it loosens Methyldopa is a preferred drug in pregnancy

Brand discontinued but name still used in practice.

DIRECT VASODILATORS

These drugs cause direct vasodilation of arterioles, with little effect on veins. The result is a decrease in SVR and a reduction in BP.

DRUG	DOSING	SAFETY/SIDE EFFECTS/MONITORING
Hydralazine Tablet, injection	PO: 10-50 mg QID, max dose is 300 mg daily IM, IV: 10-20 mg Q4-6H PRN	**CONTRAINDICATIONS** Mitral valvular rheumatic heart disease, CAD **WARNINGS** Drug-induced lupus erythematosus (DILE – dose and duration related), peripheral neuritis, blood dyscrasias, hypotension **SIDE EFFECTS** Peripheral edema/headache/flushing/palpitations/reflex tachycardia, nausea/vomiting **MONITORING** HR, BP, ANA titer
Minoxidil *Men's Rogaine, Women's Rogaine* – OTC topical for hair growth	5-40 mg daily in 1-2 divided doses, max dose is 100 mg daily	**BOXED WARNING** Potent antihypertensive – can cause pericardial effusion and angina exacerbations; administer with a beta-blocker and loop diuretic **CONTRAINDICATION** Pheochromocytoma **SIDE EFFECTS** Fluid retention, tachycardia, hair growth

ALPHA-BLOCKERS

Alpha-blockers (e.g., doxazosin, prazosin, terazosin) bind to alpha-1 adrenergic receptors, which results in peripheral vasodilation of arterioles and veins. They are not recommended for hypertension but may be used in men who have hypertension and benign prostatic hyperplasia (see Benign Prostatic Hyperplasia chapter).

HYPERTENSIVE CRISES: URGENCIES AND EMERGENCIES

A hypertensive crisis is defined as a rapidly accelerating BP (generally ≥ 180/120 mmHg). The two types of crises are:

- Hypertensive emergency: patient has acute target organ damage that may be life-threatening (e.g., encephalopathy, stroke, acute kidney injury, acute coronary syndrome, aortic dissection, acute pulmonary edema).
  - ❏ Treat with IV medications (see Key Drugs Guy).
  - ❏ Decrease BP by no more than 25% (within the first hour), then if stable, decrease to ~160/100 mmHg in the next 2 – 6 hours.
- Hypertensive urgency: no evidence of acute target organ damage.
  - ❏ Treat with any oral medication that has a short onset of action (e.g., 15 – 30 minutes).
  - ❏ Decrease BP gradually over 24 – 48 hours.

KEY IV HYPERTENSION MEDICATIONS	
Chlorothiazide	Metoprolol tartrate
Clevidipine	Nicardipine
Diltiazem	Nitroglycerin*
Enalaprilat	Nitroprusside*
Esmolol	Propranolol
Hydralazine	Verapamil
Labetalol	

Vasodilators (discussed in the Acute & Critical Care Medicine chapter)

KEY COUNSELING POINTS

See the Drug Formulations and Patient Counseling chapter for counseling language/layman's terminology.

ALL HYPERTENSION PRODUCTS

- Can cause orthostasis.
- Check your blood pressure regularly.
- Take this medication as directed, even if you feel well.
  - ❏ Lowering blood pressure helps ↓ risk of complications such as heart disease, kidney disease and stroke.

Thiazide-Type Diuretics

- Take this medication early in the day (no later than 4 PM) to avoid getting up at night to go to the bathroom.
- Can cause:
  - ❏ Hyperglycemia.
  - ❏ Photosensitivity.
  - ❏ Sexual dysfunction.

Calcium Channel Blockers

- Can cause:
  - ❏ Peripheral edema.
  - ❏ Gingival hyperplasia.
- Take *Adalat CC* on an empty stomach.
- Ghost tablet in stool (*Adalat CC* and *Procardia XL*).

ACE Inhibitors, ARBs and Aliskiren

- Avoid in pregnancy (teratogenic).
- Allergy/anaphylaxis (angioedema).
- ACE inhibitors: dry, hacking cough.

Beta-Blockers

- Do not abruptly discontinue without consulting your healthcare provider.
- This medication can mask symptoms of low blood sugar. If you have diabetes, check blood sugar if you notice symptoms of sweating or hunger.
- Can cause sexual dysfunction.
- Take *Coreg/Coreg CR* with food.
- Take *Lopressor/Toprol XL* with or immediately after meals.

Clonidine

- Do not abruptly discontinue without consulting your healthcare provider.
- Patch: apply weekly to upper outer arm or chest. The white adhesive cover can be applied over the patch to keep it in place. Remove before an MRI.
- Can cause sexual dysfunction.

Select Guidelines/References

2017 ACC/AHA/AAPA/ABC/ACPM/AGS/APhA/ASH/ASPC/. NMA/PCNA guideline for the prevention, detection, evaluation, and management of high blood pressure: a report of the American College of Cardiology/American Heart Association Task Force on Clinical Pactice Guidelines. *Hypertension* 2018;71:e13-e115.

Management of Stage 1 Hypertension in Adults With a Low 10-Year Risk for Cardiovascular Disease: Filling a Guidance Gap: A Scientific Statement From the American Heart Association. *Hypertension* 2021;77(6):e58-e67.

CONTENT LEGEND

💡 = Study Tip Gal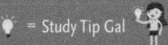

iStock.com/monkeybusinessimages

CHAPTER 29
STABLE ISCHEMIC HEART DISEASE

BACKGROUND

Angina is chest pain, pressure, tightness or discomfort, usually caused by ischemia of the heart muscle or spasm of the coronary arteries. The chest pain is described as "squeezing," "grip-like," "heavy" or "suffocating," and typically does not vary with position or respiration. Stable angina, also known as stable ischemic heart disease (SIHD), is associated with predictable chest pain, often brought on by exertion or emotional stress and relieved within minutes by rest or with nitroglycerin. Unstable angina (UA) is a type of acute coronary syndrome (ACS); this is a medical emergency where the chest pain increases (in frequency, intensity or duration) and is not relieved with nitroglycerin or rest (see Acute Coronary Syndromes chapter).

The classic anginal symptoms of SIHD may not be present in women, elderly patients or those with diabetes; this can lead to misdiagnosis (e.g., GERD) or a delay in treatment.

When chest pain is caused by vasospasm of the coronary arteries, it is called Prinzmetal's (variant or vasospastic) angina. This type of angina can occur at rest and can be caused by illicit drug use, particularly cocaine.

PATHOPHYSIOLOGY

Chest pain occurs when there is an imbalance between myocardial oxygen demand (workload) and supply (blood flow). Myocardial oxygen demand increases when the heart is working harder due to an increased heart rate, contractility or left ventricular wall tension [caused by increased preload (volume of blood returning to the heart) and/or afterload (systemic vascular resistance, or SVR)]. In SIHD, myocardial oxygen supply is often decreased due to plaque build up (atherosclerosis) within the inner walls of the coronary arteries. This is known as coronary artery disease (CAD); it causes narrowing of the arteries and reduced blood flow to the heart.

DIAGNOSIS

The risk factors for SIHD are similar to other types of heart disease, vascular disease and stroke, and include hypertension, smoking, dyslipidemia, diabetes, obesity and physical inactivity. To assess the likelihood of CAD and diagnose SIHD, a cardiac stress test is performed.

The cardiac stress test increases myocardial oxygen demand with either exercise (e.g., walking on a treadmill or pedaling a stationary exercise bicycle) or intravenous medications [adenosine, dipyridamole, dobutamine or regadenoson (Lexiscan)]. As myocardial oxygen demand increases, the patient is monitored for the development of symptoms (e.g., chest pain, dyspnea, lightheadedness), changes in heart rate and blood pressure, transient rhythm disturbances or ST segment abnormalities on an ECG.

When the diagnosis of SIHD is certain, coronary angiography can be performed to assess the extent of atherosclerosis and need for revascularization.

EVALUATION OF SIHD

History and physical

CBC, CK-MB, troponins (I or T), aPTT, PT/INR, lipid panel, glucose

ECG (at rest and during chest pain)

Cardiac stress test/stress imaging

Cardiac catheterization/angiography

NON-DRUG TREATMENT

Patients should be encouraged to follow a heart healthy diet (e.g., saturated fats < 7% and *trans* fats < 1% of total calories, adequate intake of fresh fruits and vegetables, selection of low-fat dairy products), maintain a BMI of 18.5 – 24.9 kg/m², and maintain a waist circumference < 35 inches in females and < 40 inches in males.

Patients should engage in 30 – 60 minutes of moderate-intensity aerobic activity 5 – 7 days per week, supplemented by an increase in daily lifestyle activities (e.g., walking breaks at work, gardening). Medically supervised programs, such as cardiac rehabilitation, are encouraged for at-risk patients.

Patients who smoke should quit, and secondhand smoke should be avoided. Alcohol intake should be limited to 1 drink/day (4 oz wine, 12 oz beer or 1 oz of spirits) for women and 1 – 2 drinks/day for men.

DRUG TREATMENT

The treatment goals for SIHD are to improve function (by eliminating chest pain), prevent future cardiovascular events (e.g., MI, heart failure) and reduce the risk of cardiovascular death. An antiplatelet and an antianginal drug regimen are used together. Antiplatelet treatment prevents platelets from sticking together and forming a clot that can block an artery and reduce blood flow to the heart. Aspirin is the recommended antiplatelet; clopidogrel (*Plavix*) is used when there is an allergy or other contraindication to aspirin.

The combination of aspirin and clopidogrel is only beneficial in SIHD when there is a history of stent placement or recent CABG (see Dual Antiplatelet Therapy section on next page). Low-dose rivaroxaban (*Xarelto*) in combination with aspirin is FDA-approved to reduce the risk of cardiovascular events in patients with CAD or peripheral artery disease (PAD).

Antianginal treatment decreases myocardial oxygen demand or increases myocardial oxygen supply (see Antianginal Treatment table). Beta-blockers are first line; calcium channel blockers (CCBs), both dihydropyridine (DHP) and non-dihydropyridine (non-DHP), or long-acting nitrates should be used when beta-blockers are contraindicated or when additional symptomatic relief is needed. Ranolazine can be used as a substitute for, or in addition to, beta-blockers. Short-acting nitroglycerin, as a sublingual (SL) tablet, powder or translingual (TL) spray, is recommended for immediate relief of angina in all patients.

SIHD is one of the atherosclerotic cardiovascular diseases (ASCVD). Patients should be treated with a high-intensity statin (see Dyslipidemia chapter). Hypertension, heart failure and diabetes should be aggressively managed with guideline-recommended treatments, including the use of an ACE inhibitor or ARB to manage hypertension in patients with CAD and diabetes. An annual influenza vaccine is recommended; pneumococcal vaccines should be administered per ACIP recommendations for patients with heart disease (see Immunizations chapter).

TREATMENT APPROACH FOR STABLE ISCHEMIC HEART DISEASE

A – Antiplatelet and antianginal drugs

B – Blood pressure and beta-blockers

C – Cholesterol (statins) and cigarettes (cessation)

D – Diet and diabetes

E – Exercise and education

ANTIPLATELET DRUGS

Aspirin irreversibly inhibits cyclooxygenase-1 and 2 (COX-1 and COX-2) enzymes, which results in decreased prostaglandin (PG) and thromboxane A2 (TXA2) production; TXA2 is a potent vasoconstrictor and inducer of platelet aggregation. Clopidogrel is a prodrug that irreversibly inhibits P2Y12 ADP-mediated platelet activation and aggregation. Refer to the Acute Coronary Syndromes chapter for an image depicting antiplatelet drug mechanisms of action.

DRUG	DOSING	SAFETY/SIDE EFFECTS/MONITORING
Aspirin (Bayer, Bufferin, Ecotrin, Ascriptin, Durlaza, Vazalore, others) + omeprazole (Yosprala) OTC: tablet, chewable tablet, enteric-coated tablet, liquid-filled capsule, suppository Rx: ER capsule (Durlaza), delayed-release tablet (Yosprala) See Pain chapter for more information on aspirin products	75-162 mg daily 70-100 mg daily when used in combination with rivaroxaban 2.5 mg BID (see Notes)	**CONTRAINDICATIONS** NSAID or salicylate allergy; children and teenagers with viral infection due to the risk of Reye's syndrome (symptoms include somnolence, N/V, confusion); rhinitis, nasal polyps or asthma (due to the risk of urticaria, angioedema or bronchospasm) **WARNINGS** Bleeding [including GI bleed/ulceration, ↑ risk with heavy alcohol use or when used with other drugs that have bleeding risk (e.g., NSAIDs, anticoagulants, other antiplatelets)], tinnitus (salicylate overdose) **SIDE EFFECTS** Dyspepsia, heartburn, bleeding, nausea **MONITORING** Symptoms of bleeding, bruising **NOTES** Used indefinitely in SIHD (unless contraindicated); ↓ incidence of MI, CV events and death Used with low-dose rivaroxaban to reduce the risk of major cardiovascular events (e.g., MI, stroke) Non-enteric coated, chewable aspirin is preferred in ACS; if only enteric-coated (EC) aspirin is available, it should be chewed (325 mg) Durlaza and Yosprala should not be used when rapid onset is needed (e.g., ACS, pre-PCI) To ↓ nausea, use EC or buffered product or take with food PPIs may be used to protect the gut with chronic aspirin use (e.g., Yosprala is indicated for those at risk of developing aspirin-associated gastric ulcers); consider the risks from chronic PPI use (↓ bone density, ↑ infection risk)
Clopidogrel (Plavix) Tablet Indicated for ACS (in combination with aspirin), or in patients with recent MI, stroke or PAD	75 mg daily	**BOXED WARNING** Clopidogrel is a prodrug. Effectiveness depends on the conversion to an active metabolite, mainly by CYP450 2C19. Poor metabolizers of CYP2C19 exhibit higher cardiovascular events than patients with normal CYP2C19 function. Tests to check CYP2C19 genotype can be used as an aid in determining a therapeutic strategy. Consider alternative treatments in patients identified as CYP2C19 poor metabolizers. See the Pharmacogenomics chapter. **CONTRAINDICATIONS** Active serious bleeding (e.g., GI bleed, intracranial hemorrhage) **WARNINGS** Bleeding risk (stop 5 days prior to elective surgery), do not use with omeprazole or esomeprazole (see Drug Interactions section), premature discontinuation (↑ risk of thrombosis), thrombotic thrombocytopenic purpura (TTP) **SIDE EFFECTS** Generally well tolerated, unless bleeding occurs **MONITORING** Symptoms of bleeding, Hgb/Hct as necessary **NOTES** Used in SIHD when there is a contraindication to aspirin; can be used in combination with aspirin (see Dual Antiplatelet Therapy section)

Dual Antiplatelet Therapy

SIHD is usually treated with a single antiplatelet drug (aspirin or clopidogrel). Dual antiplatelet therapy (DAPT) with aspirin and clopidogrel is reserved for those who have had placement of a bare metal stent (DAPT for at least one month), a drug-eluting stent (DAPT for at least six months) or post-CABG (DAPT for 12 months). Aspirin is dosed at 81 mg daily in DAPT regimens and is continued indefinitely at 75 – 162 mg daily after the course of DAPT is complete. Refer to the Acute Coronary Syndromes chapter for a discussion of DAPT in ACS.

Antiplatelet Drug Interactions

- Most drug interactions are due to <u>additive effects</u> when used with other drugs that can ↑ <u>bleeding risk</u> (e.g., <u>anticoagulants</u>, <u>NSAIDs, SSRIs, SNRIs, some dietary supplements</u>). See the Drug Interactions chapter.

- Aspirin: use caution in combination with other ototoxic drugs (see the Drug Interactions chapter).

- Clopidogrel: <u>avoid</u> in combination with the <u>CYP2C19 inhibitors omeprazole and esomeprazole</u> (other PPIs interact less) and use caution with other CYP2C19 inhibitors.

ANTIANGINAL TREATMENT

DRUG	MECHANISM OF CLINICAL BENEFIT	CLINICAL NOTES
Beta-Blockers 1st line in SIHD See the Hypertension chapter for a complete review of beta-blockers	Reduce myocardial oxygen demand: ↓ HR, ↓ contractility and ↓ left ventricular wall tension	Start low, go slow; <u>titrate to resting HR of 55-60 BPM</u>; avoid abrupt withdrawal Beta-blockers without ISA are preferred (e.g., metoprolol, carvedilol); can be used as monotherapy or in combination with DHP CCBs, long-acting nitrates and/or ranolazine Provide mortality reduction and symptom improvement More effective than nitrates and CCBs for silent ischemia; <u>avoid in Prinzmetal's angina</u>
Calcium Channel Blockers <u>Preferred for Prinzmetal's (variant) angina</u> See the Hypertension chapter for a complete review of calcium channel blockers	Reduce myocardial oxygen demand: <u>non-DHPs</u> ↓ HR and contractility; <u>DHPs</u> ↓ SVR (afterload) Increase myocardial oxygen supply: all CCBs ↑ blood flow through coronary arteries	Generally used when beta-blockers are contraindicated or as an add-on to beta-blockers if symptoms persist Slow-release or long-acting DHPs and non-DHPs are effective; <u>avoid</u> short-acting DHPs (e.g., <u>nifedipine IR</u>) <u>DHPs</u> are <u>preferred</u> when CCBs are used <u>in combination with beta-blockers</u> (due to the risk of excessive bradycardia when non-DHPs are used with beta-blockers)
Nitrates	Reduce myocardial oxygen demand: ↓ preload (free radical nitric oxide produces <u>vasodilation of veins more than arteries</u>) Increases myocardial oxygen supply: ↑ blood flow through collateral (non-atherosclerotic) arteries	**SL tablets, SL powder or TL spray** Recommended for <u>all patients</u> for <u>fast relief</u> of angina **Long-acting nitrates** <u>Long-acting nitrates</u> are used when <u>beta-blockers</u> are <u>contraindicated</u> or as <u>add-on</u> therapy if symptoms persist; a nitrate-free interval is required to prevent tolerance (see Nitroglycerin Formulations table on next page)
Ranolazine (*Ranexa*)	Selectively inhibits the late phase Na current and ↓ intracellular Ca; can decrease myocardial oxygen demand by decreasing ventricular tension and oxygen consumption	**CONTRAINDICATIONS** Liver cirrhosis, do not use with <u>strong CYP3A4 inhibitors or inducers</u> **WARNINGS** Can cause <u>QT prolongation</u> Acute renal failure observed when CrCl < 30 mL/min **SIDE EFFECTS** Dizziness, headache, constipation, nausea **MONITORING** ECG, K, renal function **NOTES** <u>Not for acute treatment of chest pain</u> Can use in place of beta-blockers or as add-on treatment <u>Has little to no clinical effects on HR or BP</u>

Nitroglycerin Formulations Used in SIHD

FORMULATIONS*	SAFETY/SIDE EFFECTS/MONITORING
Short-Acting Nitrates	**CONTRAINDICATIONS** Hypersensitivity to organic nitrates, do not use with PDE-5 inhibitors or riociguat (see Nitrate Drug Interactions)
Nitroglycerin SL tablet *(Nitrostat)* 0.3 mg, 0.4 mg, 0.6 mg	Short-acting nitrates: ↑ intracranial pressure, severe anemia, circulatory failure and shock (SL powder only)
Nitroglycerin TL spray *(NitroMist, Nitrolingual)* 0.4 mg/spray	**WARNINGS** Hypotension, headache, tachyphylaxis (↓ effectiveness/tolerance with long-acting products), can aggravate angina caused by hypertrophic cardiomyopathy
Nitroglycerin SL powder *(GoNitro)* 0.4 mg/packet	**SIDE EFFECTS** Headache, flushing, syncope, dizziness **MONITORING** BP, HR, chest pain
Long-Acting Nitrates	**NOTES** **Short-acting nitrates** Used PRN for immediate relief of chest pain
Nitroglycerin ointment 2% *(Nitro-Bid)*	Store nitroglycerin SL tablets in the original amber glass bottle and keep tightly capped after each use (to maintain potency) Nitrate tolerance does not develop with SL/TL products
Nitroglycerin transdermal patch *(Nitro-Dur)* 0.1, 0.2, 0.3, 0.4, 0.6, 0.8 mg/hr	**Long-acting nitrates** Require a 10-12 hour nitrate-free interval to ↓ tolerance (longer for some products) ■ Patch: wear on for 12-14 hours, off for 10-12 hours; rotate sites; dispose of safely, away from children and pets
Nitroglycerin ER capsule *(Nitro-Time)* 2.5 mg, 6 mg, 9 mg	■ Ointment: dosed BID, 6 hours apart with a 10-12 hour nitrate-free interval
Isosorbide mononitrate IR/ER tablet IR: 10 mg, 20 mg ER: 30 mg, 60 mg, 120 mg	■ Isosorbide mononitrate: IR dosed BID, 7 hours apart (e.g., 8 AM and 3 PM); ER dosed once daily in the AM ■ Isosorbide dinitrate: IR dosed BID (same as above) or TID, take at 8 AM, 12 PM and 4 PM for a 14-hour nitrate-free interval (or similar)
Isosorbide dinitrate IR *(Isordil Titradose)* IR: 5 mg, 10 mg, 20 mg, 30 mg, 40 mg	Isosorbide dinitrate in combination with hydralazine is the preferred combination for HFrEF

IV nitroglycerin is discussed in the Acute & Critical Care Medicine chapter.

Nitrate Drug Interactions

- Do not use long-acting nitrates in combination with PDE-5 inhibitors and riociguat; use caution with other antihypertensive medications and alcohol, as these combinations can cause a significant decrease in BP.

  ❑ Short-acting nitrates should not be used if a PDE-5 inhibitor was taken recently (avanafil in the past 12 hours, sildenafil or vardenafil in the past 24 hours or tadalafil in the past 48 hours). Occasionally, and with careful monitoring, nitrates can be used for an emergency (e.g., acute MI) in a patient who has recently taken a PDE-5 inhibitor.

Ranolazine Drug Interactions

- Ranolazine is a major substrate of CYP3A4 and a minor substrate of CYP2D6 and P-gp. It is a weak inhibitor of CYP3A4, 2D6 and P-gp. Do not use with strong CYP3A4 inhibitors or inducers. Limit the dose to 500 mg BID if taking moderate CYP3A4 inhibitors (e.g., diltiazem, verapamil). Limit simvastatin to 20 mg/day if used together.

KEY COUNSELING POINTS

See the Drug Formulations and Patient Counseling chapter for counseling language/layman's terminology.

ASPIRIN

- Can cause:
  - ❏ Bleeding/bruising.
  - ❏ Dyspepsia.
  - ❏ Allergy.
  - ❏ Tinnitus or loss of hearing with overdose.

CLOPIDOGREL

- Can cause:
  - ❏ Bleeding/bruising.
  - ❏ Thrombotic thrombocytopenic purpura (TTP).

ALL NITROGLYCERIN PRODUCTS

- Can cause:
  - ❏ Orthostasis.
  - ❏ Flushing and headache. Often a sign the medication is working. Usually goes away with time.
- Nitrate-free interval required with long-acting products.
- Drug interactions with phosphodiesterase-5 inhibitors.

SHORT-ACTING NITRATES

- Take one dose at first sign of chest pain.
- Call 911 immediately if chest pain persists after the first dose. Continue to take two additional doses at five minute intervals while waiting for the ambulance to arrive. Do not take more than three doses within 15 minutes.

Nitroglycerin SL Tablets

- Place the tablet under the tongue or between the inside of the cheek and the gums/teeth, and let it dissolve. Do not chew, crush or swallow.
- Slight burning or tingling sensation is not a sign of how well the medication is working.
- Keep tightly capped in the original amber glass bottle and store at room temperature. Shake out one tablet only; do not let the other tablets get wet.

Nitroglycerin TL Spray

- Prime before first use and if not used within six weeks.
- Do not shake. Press the button firmly to release the spray onto or under the tongue. Close your mouth after the spray. Do not inhale the spray, and try not to swallow too quickly afterward. Do not spit or rinse the mouth for 5 – 10 minutes after the dose.

NITROGLYCERIN PATCH

- The chest is the preferred application site, though any area can be selected except the extremities below the knees or elbows.

NITROGLYCERIN OINTMENT

- Measure the dose of ointment with the dose-measuring applicator provided (see image below). Place the applicator on a flat surface, squeeze the ointment onto the applicator and place the applicator (ointment side down) on the chest or other desired area of the skin.
- Spread the ointment, using the dose-measuring applicator, lightly onto the skin. Do not rub into the skin. Tape the applicator into place.
- Can stain clothing. Cover the applicator completely.

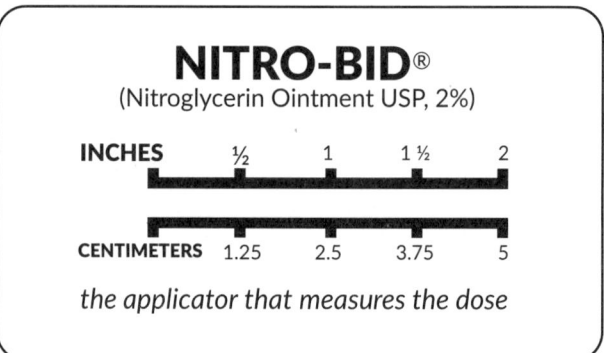

NITRO-BID®
(Nitroglycerin Ointment USP, 2%)

| INCHES | ½ | 1 | 1 ½ | 2 |

| CENTIMETERS | 1.25 | 2.5 | 3.75 | 5 |

the applicator that measures the dose

Select Guidelines/References

2014 ACC/AHA/AATS/PCNA/SCAI/STS focused update of the guideline for the diagnosis and management of patients with stable ischemic heart disease. *Circulation.* 2014;130:1749-1767.

2012 ACCF/AHA/ACP/AATS/PCNA/SCAI/STS guideline for the diagnosis and management of patients with stable ischemic heart disease. *Circulation.* 2012;126(25):e354-e471.

CHAPTER CONTENT

CONTENT LEGEND

💡 = Study Tip Gal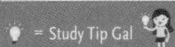

Ⓒ visona29/Shutterstock.com

CHAPTER 30

ACUTE CORONARY SYNDROMES

BACKGROUND

An acute coronary syndrome (ACS) results from plaque buildup (atherosclerosis) in the coronary arteries. The plaques are made up of fatty deposits that cause the arteries to narrow, making blood flow more difficult. The plaque can rupture, leading to clot (thrombus) formation and sudden, reduced blood flow (ischemia) to the heart. This causes an imbalance between myocardial oxygen supply and demand, resulting in symptoms (see the section below) and/or cardiac muscle cell death (myocardial necrosis). Various risk factors can lead to the plaque buildup, many of which are modifiable (see the box below).

RISK FACTORS	
Age: men > 45 years, women > 55 years (or early hysterectomy)	Known coronary artery disease
	Dyslipidemia
Family history: first-degree relative with a coronary event before 55 years (men) or 65 years (women)	Diabetes
	Chronic stable angina
Smoking	Lack of exercise
Hypertension	Excessive alcohol

SIGNS AND SYMPTOMS

The classic symptoms of an ACS include chest pain (often described as discomfort, pressure or squeezing) lasting ≥ 10 minutes, severe dyspnea, diaphoresis, syncope/presyncope and/or palpitations. The pain can radiate to the arms, back, neck, jaw or epigastric region. Females, the elderly and patients with diabetes are less likely to experience the classic symptoms. Symptoms can occur at rest, or may be precipitated by minimal exertion, exercise, cold weather, extreme emotions, stress or sexual intercourse. ACS is a medical emergency. Patients with a prescription for sublingual nitroglycerin (NTG) should use one dose every five minutes for up to three doses to relieve chest pain. If chest pain is not improved or is worse five minutes after the first dose, they should call 911 immediately.

DIAGNOSIS

ACS encompasses non-ST segment elevation acute coronary syndromes (NSTE-ACS) and ST-segment elevation myocardial infarction (STEMI). NSTE-ACS describes both unstable angina (UA) and non-ST segment elevation myocardial infarction (NSTEMI), which are indistinguishable upon presentation. The types of ACS are differentiated based on ECG findings, the detection of cardiac enzymes and the extent of blockage in the affected artery (see the Study Tip Gal below).

A 12-lead ECG should be performed and evaluated within ten minutes at the site of first medical contact (which could be in an ambulance). Patients with an acute MI (STEMI or NSTEMI) should be urgently transported to a hospital with percutaneous coronary intervention (PCI) capability, if possible.

The measurement of biochemical markers (cardiac enzymes), released into the bloodstream when myocardial cells die, helps establish the diagnosis. Cardiac troponins I and T (TnI and TnT) are the most sensitive and specific biomarkers for ACS. Levels should be obtained at presentation and 3 – 6 hours after symptom onset in all patients with ACS symptoms. Creatine kinase myocardial isoenzyme (CK-MB) and myoglobin are less sensitive markers but may still be monitored in clinical practice.

COMPARING UA, NSTEMI AND STEMI

	UA	NSTEMI	STEMI
Symptoms	Chest pain (described in text)		
Cardiac Enzymes	Negative	Positive	Positive
ECG Changes	None or transient ischemic changes*		ST segment elevation**
Blockage	Partial blockage		Complete blockage

*ST segment depression or prominent T-wave inversion
**Meeting defined criteria in ≥ 2 contiguous leads (e.g., leads looking at the same area of the heart)

TREATMENT

Treatment is aimed at providing immediate relief of ischemia and preventing MI expansion and death.

PCI OR MEDICAL MANAGEMENT

PCI is a coronary revascularization procedure that involves inflating a small balloon inside a coronary artery to widen it and improve blood flow. Usually, a stent (metal mesh) is placed to keep the artery open.

- NSTE-ACS can be treated with medications alone (medical management) or with PCI (an early invasive strategy).

- A STEMI requires that the blocked arteries be opened as quickly as possible with PCI or fibrinolysis.

  - PCI is preferred if it can be performed within 90 minutes (optimal door-to-balloon time) or within 120 minutes of first medical contact (which could be in an ambulance).

  - If PCI is not possible within 120 minutes of first medical contact, fibrinolytic therapy is recommended and should be given within 30 minutes of hospital arrival (door-to-needle time).

DRUG TREATMENT

A combination of antianginal, antiplatelet and anticoagulant medications are used in addition to PCI or fibrinolytics (see the Study Tip Gal below and the summary table on the following page). These work by different mechanisms:

- Antianginals: decrease myocardial oxygen demand or increase supply (blood flow) to relieve ischemia.

- Antiplatelets: inhibit platelet aggregation to prevent clot formation/growth.

- Anticoagulants: inhibit clotting factors to prevent clot formation/growth.

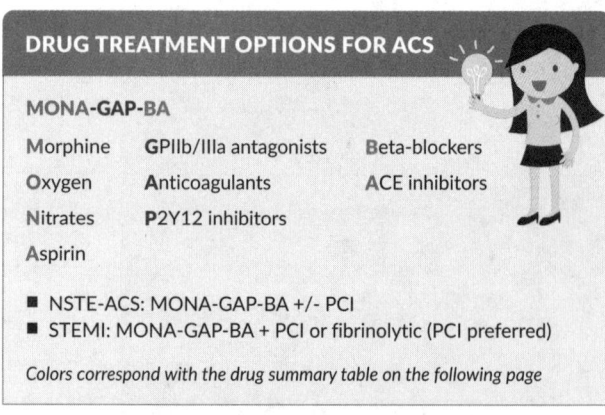

DRUG TREATMENT OPTIONS FOR ACS

MONA-GAP-BA

Morphine	GPIIb/IIIa antagonists	Beta-blockers
Oxygen	Anticoagulants	ACE inhibitors
Nitrates	P2Y12 inhibitors	
Aspirin		

- NSTE-ACS: MONA-GAP-BA +/- PCI
- STEMI: MONA-GAP-BA + PCI or fibrinolytic (PCI preferred)

Colors correspond with the drug summary table on the following page

DRUGS FOR ACS (MONA-GAP-BA)

DRUG	CLINICAL BENEFIT	CLINICAL COMMENTS
Give these immediately (as needed)		
Morphine sulfate	Provides pain relief and helps anxiety	Not for routine use (has been shown to diminish antiplatelet effects); reserve for patients with unacceptable chest discomfort despite other treatments. Dose: 2-5 mg IV repeated at 5- to 30-minute intervals PRN. Monitor for hypotension, bradycardia, N/V, sedation and respiratory depression. See the Pain chapter for additional information.
Oxygen		Administer to patients with arterial oxygen saturation < 90% (SaO2 < 90%) or those with respiratory distress.
Nitrates	Antianginal: dilate coronary arteries and improve collateral blood flow; ↓ preload and afterload (modestly); reduces chest pain	Sublingual NTG (0.4 mg every 5 minutes x 3 doses) if not already administered and the patient has persistent chest pain, hypertension or heart failure. IV NTG can be considered if symptoms persist. Do not use IV NTG if SBP < 90 mmHg, HR < 50 BPM or the patient is experiencing a right ventricular infarction. PDE-5 inhibitors are contraindicated with NTG. See the Stable Ischemic Heart Disease and Sexual Dysfunction chapters for additional details.
Aspirin	See the Antiplatelet Drugs section and image on the following page	Non-enteric-coated, chewable aspirin (162-325 mg) should be given to all patients immediately if no contraindications are present (do not use extended-release aspirin products). A maintenance dose of aspirin 81-162 mg daily should be continued indefinitely. If intolerant to aspirin, clopidogrel or ticagrelor (discussed later in this chapter) may be used.
Give these next [choice of drug/s relates to plan (PCI vs. CABG vs. medical management)]		
GPIIb/IIIa receptor antagonists	See the Antiplatelet Drugs section and image on the following page	Drugs include abciximab, eptifibatide and tirofiban.
Anticoagulants	Inhibit clotting factors and can reduce infarct size	Drugs include LMWHs (e.g., enoxaparin, dalteparin), UFH and bivalirudin (preferred for STEMI). See the Anticoagulation chapter.
P2Y12 Inhibitors	See the Antiplatelet Drugs section and image on the following page	Drugs include clopidogrel, prasugrel and ticagrelor.
Give within 24 hours (as needed); Continue as an outpatient		
Beta-Blockers	Antianginal: ↓ BP, HR and contractility; ↓ ischemia, reinfarction and arrhythmias; prevent cardiac remodeling; ↑ long-term survival	An oral, low dose beta-blocker (beta-1 selective blocker without intrinsic sympathomimetic activity preferred) should be started within the first 24 hours unless contraindicated (e.g., decompensated heart failure, cardiogenic shock, HR < 45 bpm). If the patient has concomitant HFrEF that is stable, choose bisoprolol, metoprolol succinate or carvedilol (see the Chronic Heart Failure chapter). An IV beta-blocker or an oral long-acting nondihydropyridine calcium channel blocker (verapamil or diltiazem) are alternative options used in some situations.
ACE Inhibitors	Inhibit angiotensin-converting enzyme (ACE) and block the production of angiotensin II; prevent cardiac remodeling; ↓ preload and afterload	An oral ACE inhibitor should be started within the first 24 hours and continued indefinitely in all patients with left ventricular ejection fraction (LVEF) < 40%), hypertension, diabetes or stable CKD, unless contraindicated (use an ARB if the patient is ACE inhibitor intolerant). Use of an ACE inhibitor in other patients may be reasonable. Do not use an IV ACE inhibitor within the first 24 hours due to the risk of hypotension. See the Hypertension chapter.

Medications to Avoid in the Acute Setting

- NSAIDs (except aspirin), whether nonselective or COX-2-selective, should not be administered during hospitalization due to ↑ risk of mortality, reinfarction, hypertension, cardiac rupture, renal insufficiency and heart failure.

- Immediate-release nifedipine should not be used due to ↑ risk of mortality.

ANTIPLATELET DRUGS

The antiplatelet drugs used in ACS <u>inhibit platelet aggregation</u> and clot formation by different mechanisms (see the platelet image to the right):

- Aspirin: <u>irreversibly inhibits COX-1</u> and <u>COX-2</u>, which <u>decreases</u> the production of <u>thromboxane A2 (TXA2)</u> (an inducer of platelet aggregation).

- P2Y12 inhibitors: <u>bind</u> to the platelet <u>adenosine diphosphate (ADP) P2Y12 receptor</u>, preventing ADP-mediated activation of the GPIIb/IIIa receptor complex.

- GPIIb/IIIa receptor antagonists: <u>block</u> the <u>platelet glycoprotein IIb/IIIa receptor</u>, which is the binding site for fibrinogen, von Willebrand factor and other ligands

- Protease-activated receptor-1 antagonist: <u>binds</u> to the <u>PAR-1</u> receptor, preventing thrombin- and thrombin receptor agonist peptide-induced platelet aggregation.

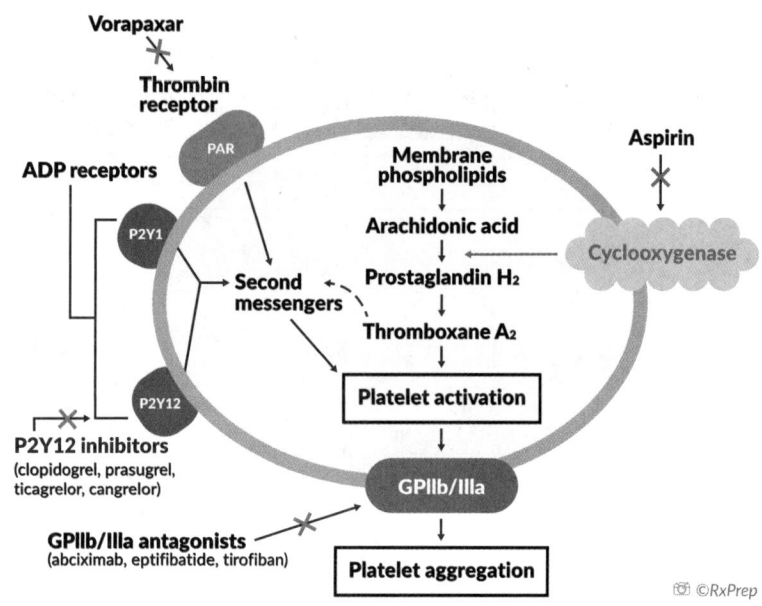

P2Y12 Inhibitors

<u>Clopidogrel and prasugrel</u> are structurally similar and are classified as <u>thienopyridines</u>. They are <u>prodrugs</u> that <u>irreversibly bind</u> to the <u>P2Y12 receptor</u>. Ticagrelor is not a prodrug and has reversible binding to the receptor. P2Y12 inhibitors are commonly <u>used with aspirin</u> after an ACS, which is called <u>dual antiplatelet therapy (DAPT)</u>. A higher one-time <u>loading dose</u> is required for P2Y12 inhibitors, either prior to PCI or at the time of diagnosis if PCI is not being performed, followed by a <u>maintenance dose</u>.

DRUG	DOSING	SAFETY/SIDE EFFECTS/MONITORING
Clopidogrel (Plavix) Tablet Indicated for ACS or as secondary prevention in patients with a history of MI, stroke or PAD	LD: 300-600 mg PO (600 mg for PCI) MD: <u>75 mg PO daily</u> If age > 75 years and fibrinolytic therapy administered for STEMI, omit the loading dose and start 75 mg daily	**BOXED WARNINGS** Clopidogrel is a <u>prodrug</u>. Effectiveness depends on the <u>conversion</u> to an <u>active metabolite</u>, mainly by <u>CYP450 2C19</u>. Poor metabolizers of CYP2C19 exhibit higher cardiovascular events than patients with normal CYP2C19 function. <u>Tests to check CYP2C19 genotype</u> can be used as an aid in determining a therapeutic strategy. Consider alternative treatments in patients identified as CYP2C19 poor metabolizers. See the Pharmacogenomics chapter. **CONTRAINDICATIONS** Active <u>serious bleeding</u> (e.g., GI bleed, intracranial hemorrhage) **WARNINGS** <u>Bleeding risk (stop 5 days prior to elective surgery)</u>, do not use with <u>omeprazole or esomeprazole</u> (see P2Y12 Drug Interactions on the following page), premature discontinuation (↑ risk of thrombosis), thrombotic thrombocytopenic purpura (<u>TTP</u>) **SIDE EFFECTS** Generally well tolerated, unless <u>bleeding</u> occurs

CARDIOVASCULAR CONDITIONS

DRUG	DOSING	SAFETY/SIDE EFFECTS/MONITORING
Prasugrel (*Effient*) Tablet Indicated for ACS managed with PCI	LD: 60 mg PO (no later than 1 hour after PCI) MD: 10 mg PO daily with ASA (5 mg daily if patient weighs < 60 kg) Once PCI is planned, give the dose promptly and no later than 1 hour after the PCI Protect from moisture; dispense in the original container	**BOXED WARNINGS** Significant, sometimes fatal, bleeding Not recommended in patients ≥ 75 years due to high bleeding risk, unless patient is considered high risk (DM or prior MI) Do not initiate if CABG likely, stop at least 7 days prior to elective surgery **CONTRAINDICATIONS** Active serious bleeding, history of TIA or stroke **WARNINGS** Bleeding risk, premature discontinuation (↑ risk of thrombosis), thrombotic thrombocytopenic purpura (TTP) **SIDE EFFECTS** Generally well-tolerated, unless bleeding occurs (higher risk than clopidogrel)
Ticagrelor (*Brilinta*) Tablet Indicated for ACS	LD: 180 mg MD: 90 mg PO BID for 1 year, then 60 mg BID Tablets can be crushed and mixed with water (to be swallowed or given via an NG tube)	**BOXED WARNINGS** Significant, sometimes fatal, bleeding After the initial dose of 162-325 mg, do not exceed a maintenance dose of aspirin 100 mg daily because higher daily doses reduce the effectiveness of ticagrelor Avoid use when CABG likely, stop 5 days before any surgery **CONTRAINDICATIONS** Active serious bleeding, history of intracranial hemorrhage **WARNINGS** Bleeding risk, severe hepatic impairment, bradyarrhythmias, premature discontinuation (↑ risk of thrombosis), thrombotic thrombocytopenic purpura (TTP) **SIDE EFFECTS** Bleeding, dyspnea (> 10%), ↑ SCr, ↑ uric acid
Cangrelor (*Kengreal*) Injection Indicated as an adjunct to PCI in patients who are P2Y12 inhibitor naïve and are not receiving a GPIIb/IIIa inhibitor	30 mcg/kg IV bolus prior to PCI, then 4 mcg/kg/min IV infusion for 2 hours or for the duration of the procedure (whichever is longer)	**CONTRAINDICATIONS** Significant active bleeding **SIDE EFFECTS** Bleeding **NOTES** Effects are gone 1 hour after drug discontinuation Transition to one of the oral P2Y12 inhibitors after PCI

LD = loading dose, MD = maintenance dose

P2Y12 Inhibitor Drug Interactions

- All P2Y12 inhibitors: most drug interactions are due to additive effects when used with other drugs that ↑ bleeding risk. If an ACS patient experiences bleeding while on a P2Y12 inhibitor, it should be managed without discontinuing the P2Y12 inhibitor, if possible. Stopping the P2Y12 inhibitor (particularly within the first few months after ACS) ↑ the risk of subsequent cardiovascular events.

    - NSAIDs, warfarin, SSRIs and SNRIs increase bleeding risk. See the Drug Interactions chapter.

- Clopidogrel: avoid in combination with the CYP2C19 inhibitors esomeprazole and omeprazole due to the risk of a decreased antiplatelet effect. Use caution with other CYP2C19 inhibitors.

- Ticagrelor is a major CYP3A4 substrate; avoid use with strong CYP3A4 inhibitors or inducers. See the Drug Interactions chapter for more information. Avoid simvastatin and lovastatin doses greater than 40 mg/day.

- Monitor digoxin levels with initiation of or any change in ticagrelor dose.

- Clopidogrel increases the effects of repaglinide, which can cause hypoglycemia. Avoid using this combination.

Glycoprotein IIb/IIIa Receptor Antagonists

Eptifibatide and tirofiban have reversible blockade of the GPIIb/IIIa receptor. They are an option for medical management of ACS or patients receiving a PCI ± stent. Abciximab has irreversible blockade of the receptor and is only indicated for PCI ± stent. If used in PCI, the GPIIb/IIIa receptor antagonist is given with heparin.

DRUG	DOSING	SAFETY/SIDE EFFECTS/MONITORING
Abciximab (ReoPro)* Injection	LD: 0.25 mg/kg IV bolus MD: 0.125 mcg/kg/min (max 10 mcg/min) IV infusion for 12 hrs (PCI, STEMI with PCI) or 18-24 hrs (NSTE-ACS unresponsive to conventional medical therapy, when PCI planned within 24 hrs) Not recommended for medical management (NSTE-ACS without PCI)	**CONTRAINDICATIONS** Thrombocytopenia (platelets < 100,000 cells/mm³) History of bleeding diathesis (i.e., a bleeding predisposition) Active internal bleeding Severe uncontrolled HTN Recent major surgery or trauma (within the past 4 weeks for tirofiban and past 6 weeks for abciximab/eptifibatide) History of stroke within 2 years (abciximab); history of stroke within 30 days or any history of hemorrhagic stroke (eptifibatide)
Eptifibatide (Integrilin**) Injection	LD: 180 mcg/kg IV bolus (max 22.6 mg), repeat bolus in 10 min if undergoing PCI MD: 2 mcg/kg/min (max 15 mg/hr) IV infusion started after the first bolus; continue for 18-24 hrs after PCI or for 12-72 hrs if PCI was not performed CrCl < 50 mL/min: same LD, reduce MD to 1 mcg/kg/min (max 7.5 mg/hr)	**For abciximab** Recent (within 6 weeks) clinically significant GI or GU bleeding ↑ prothrombin time Hypersensitivity to murine proteins Intracranial neoplasm, arteriovenous malformation or aneurysm **For eptifibatide** Dependency on renal dialysis
Tirofiban (Aggrastat) Injection	LD: 25 mcg/kg IV bolus over 5 min or less MD: 0.15 mcg/kg/min IV infusion for up to 18 hrs CrCl ≤ 60 mL/min: same LD, reduce MD to 0.075 mcg/kg/min	**SIDE EFFECTS** Bleeding, thrombocytopenia (especially abciximab) **MONITORING** Hgb, Hct, platelets, s/sx of bleeding, renal function **NOTES** Do not shake vials Must filter abciximab Platelet function returns in ~24-48 hours after stopping abciximab and ~4-8 hours after stopping eptifibatide/tirofiban

*Currently unavailable in the U.S.
**Brand discontinued but name still used in practice.
LD = loading dose, MD = maintenance dose

Protease-Activated Receptor-1 Antagonist

Vorapaxar is indicated in patients with a history of MI or peripheral arterial disease (PAD) to reduce thrombotic cardiovascular events (e.g., CV death, MI, stroke, urgent coronary revascularization). This drug was used in addition to aspirin and/or clopidogrel in clinical trials. It has not yet been incorporated into clinical guidelines.

DRUG	DOSING	SAFETY/SIDE EFFECTS/MONITORING
Vorapaxar (Zontivity) Tablet	2.08 mg (one tablet) PO daily	**BOXED WARNING** Bleeding risk (including ICH and fatal bleeding); do not use in patients with history of stroke, TIA, ICH or active serious bleeding **WARNING** Do not use in severe liver impairment **SIDE EFFECTS** Bleeding, anemia

Vorapaxar Drug Interactions

Vorapaxar is a substrate of CYP3A4 and an inhibitor of P-gp. Avoid use with strong CYP3A4 inhibitors or inducers.

FIBRINOLYTICS

These medications cause fibrinolysis (clot breakdown) by binding to fibrin and converting plasminogen to plasmin. Fibrinolytics are used only for STEMI. Once a STEMI is confirmed on a 12-lead ECG, timing is critical to open the blocked artery or arteries as quickly as possible with either PCI or fibrinolytic therapy (see PCI or Medical Management earlier in the chapter). When fibrinolytic therapy is used, it should be given within 30 minutes of hospital arrival (door-to-needle time); survival is better improved fibrinolytics are given promptly. In the absence of contraindications, and when PCI is not available, fibrinolytic therapy is reasonable in STEMI patients who are still symptomatic within 12 – 24 hours of symptom onset.

DRUG	DOSING	SAFETY/SIDE EFFECTS/MONITORING
Alteplase (Activase) Recombinant tissue plasminogen activator (tPA, rtPA)* **Cathflo Activase** (single-use 2 mg vial) used to restore function of potentially clotted central lines and devices	Accelerated Infusion > 67 kg: 100 mg IV over 1.5 hrs, given as a 15 mg bolus, 50 mg over 30 min, then 35 mg over 1 hr ≤ 67 kg: 15 mg bolus, 0.75 mg/kg (max 50 mg) over 30 min, then 0.5 mg/kg (max 35 mg) over 1 hr (max 100 mg total)	**CONTRAINDICATIONS** Active internal bleeding or bleeding diathesis History of recent stroke Any prior intracranial hemorrhage (ICH) Recent intracranial or intraspinal surgery or trauma (in the last 2-3 months) Intracranial neoplasm, arteriovenous malformation or aneurysm Severe uncontrolled hypertension (unresponsive to emergency therapy)
Tenecteplase (TNKase)	Single IV bolus dose: < 60 kg: 30 mg 60-69 kg: 35 mg 70-79 kg: 40 mg 80-89 kg: 45 mg ≥ 90 kg: 50 mg	**SIDE EFFECTS** Bleeding (including ICH) **MONITORING** Hgb, Hct, s/sx of bleeding
Reteplase (Retavase)	2 dose regimen: 10 units IV, followed by 10 units IV given 30 minutes later	**NOTES** Alteplase contraindications and dosing differ when used for ischemic stroke (refer to the Stroke chapter)

*The abbreviation "tPA" is prone to errors; though it is used commonly, it is not recommended by ISMP

SECONDARY PREVENTION AFTER ACS

ACS is one of the conditions included in the definition of atherosclerotic cardiovascular disease (ASCVD), discussed in the Dyslipidemia chapter. Taking the right medications after an ACS can reduce the risk of complications (e.g., heart failure) or future events. Many of the recommended medications will be taken indefinitely (see the Study Tip Gal below).

DRUGS FOR SECONDARY PREVENTION AFTER ACS

Aspirin
- Indefinitely (81 mg per day), unless contraindicated

P2Y12 Inhibitor
- Medical therapy patients: ticagrelor or clopidogrel* with aspirin 81 mg for at least 12 months
- PCI-treated patients (including any type of stent): clopidogrel, prasugrel or ticagrelor with aspirin 81 mg for at least 12 months
  - Continuation of DAPT beyond 12 months may be considered in patients who are tolerating DAPT and are not at high risk of bleeding following coronary stent placement

Nitroglycerin
- Indefinitely (SL tablets or spray PRN)

Beta-Blocker
- 3 years; continue indefinitely in patients with heart failure or if needed for management of hypertension

ACE Inhibitor
- Indefinitely in patients with EF < 40%, hypertension, CKD or diabetes; consider for all MI patients with no contraindications

Aldosterone Antagonist (see Chronic Heart Failure chapter)
- Indefinitely in patients with EF ≤ 40% and symptomatic heart failure or diabetes receiving target doses of an ACE inhibitor and beta-blocker
- Contraindications: significant renal impairment (SCr > 2.5 mg/dL in men, SCr > 2 mg/dL in women) or hyperkalemia (K > 5 mEq/L)

Statin (see Dyslipidemia chapter)
- Indefinitely; high-intensity statin for most patients
- Patients ≥ 75 years of age: consider moderate- or high-intensity statin

In a patient with a STEMI that received fibrinolytics, clopidogrel is the guideline-recommended P2Y12

OTHER CONSIDERATIONS

- Pain relief: patients with chronic musculoskeletal pain should use acetaminophen, nonacetylated salicylates, tramadol or small doses of narcotics before considering the use of NSAIDs. If these options are insufficient, it is reasonable to use nonselective NSAIDs such as naproxen (lowest CV risk). COX-2 selective NSAIDs have high CV risk and should be avoided.

- ACS + atrial fibrillation (AF): dual or triple antithrombotic therapy can be used in patients who require anticoagulation for AF and have had a PCI with a stent. If using triple therapy, use it for the shortest time possible. Clopidogrel is the preferred P2Y12 inhibitor for triple therapy and a transition to dual therapy (anticoagulant + P2Y12 inhibitor) can be considered after 4 – 6 weeks. Proton pump inhibitors should be prescribed in any patient with a history of GI bleeding while taking triple antithrombotic therapy.

- Lifestyle counseling should include smoking cessation, managing chronic conditions (such as hypertension and diabetes), avoiding excessive alcohol intake, encouraging physical exercise and a healthy diet.

KEY COUNSELING POINTS

Refer to the Stable Ischemic Heart Disease chapter for patient counseling on aspirin, nitrates and clopidogrel.

Select Guidelines/References

2017 ESC Guidelines for the Management of Acute Myocardial Infarction in Patients Presenting with ST-Segment Elevation. https://academic.oup.com/eurheartj/article/39/2/119/4095042 (accessed 2022 Jan 24).

2016 ACC/AHA Guideline Focused Update on Duration of Dual Antiplatelet Therapy in Patients With Coronary Artery Disease. http://www.onlinejacc.org/content/68/10/1082 (accessed 2022 Jan 24).

2014 AHA/ACC Guideline for the Management of Patients with Non-ST-Elevation Acute Coronary Syndromes. http://www.onlinejacc.org/content/64/24/e139 (accessed 2022 Jan 24).

2013 ACCF/AHA Guideline for Management of ST-Elevation Myocardial Infarction. http://www.onlinejacc.org/content/61/4/e78 (accessed 2022 Jan 24).

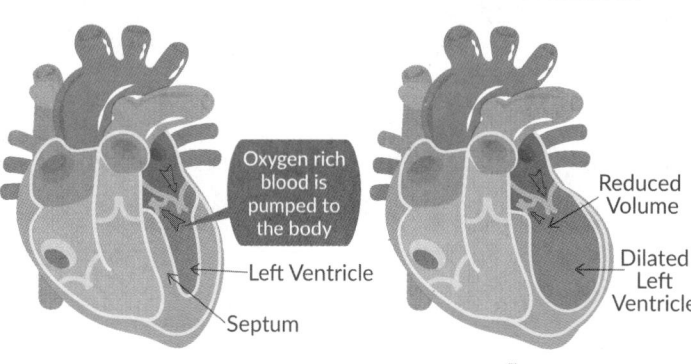

NORMAL HEART

HEART FAILURE

Oxygen rich blood is pumped to the body

Left Ventricle

Septum

Reduced Volume

Dilated Left Ventricle

CHAPTER 31
CHRONIC HEART FAILURE

BACKGROUND

Heart failure (HF) is a common condition in the U.S., especially in older adults. It is the primary diagnosis in over 1 million hospitalizations each year. Heart "failure" occurs when the heart is not able to supply sufficient oxygen-rich blood to the body, because of impaired ability of the ventricle to either fill or eject blood. HF is commonly classified as either ischemic (due to decreased blood supply, such as from an MI) or non-ischemic, such as from long-standing uncontrolled hypertension. Less common causes include valvular disease, excessive alcohol intake, illicit drug use, congenital heart defects, viral infections, diabetes and cardiotoxic drugs/chest radiation. In the U.S., most cases are due to damage from an MI or from long-standing hypertension.

DIAGNOSIS

Symptoms of HF are usually related to fluid overload, which commonly presents as shortness of breath (SOB) and edema (see Study Tip Gal on next page). Symptoms can occur due to problems with systolic (contraction) or diastolic (relaxation) functions of the heart. Patients can experience periods of stability and exacerbation (increased symptoms). Exacerbations frequently result in hospitalization and negatively impact quality of life.

An ultrasound of the heart (echocardiography or echo) is performed when HF is suspected. It provides an estimate of left ventricular ejection fraction (LVEF). LVEF is a measurement of how much blood is pumped out of the left ventricle (the main pumping chamber of the heart) with each contraction. The term LVEF is used interchangeably with ejection fraction (EF). An EF < 40% indicates systolic dysfunction, or heart failure with reduced ejection fraction (HFrEF). This type of heart failure is the focus of this chapter, since it is most widely studied and has well-defined treatment guidelines. Other types of HF are described in the Ejection Fraction table on the next page.

CHAPTER CONTENT

Background 463
Diagnosis 463
    Ejection Fraction 464
    Classification Systems 464
    Signs and Symptoms of Systolic Heart Failure 464
Pathophysiology 465
    Terminology 465
    Compensatory Mechanisms 465
Lifestyle Management 465
Drugs that Cause or Worsen Heart Failure 465
    Select Drugs that Cause or Worsen Heart Failure 465
Drug Treatment 466
    Treatment of Chronic Systolic Heart Failure 466
    Angiotensin Receptor and Neprilysin Inhibitor 467
    ACE Inhibitors and Angiotensin Receptor Blockers 467
    Beta-Blockers 469
    Loop Diuretics 470
    Aldosterone Receptor Antagonists 471
    Sodium-Glucose Cotransporter 2 Inhibitors 471
    Hydralazine/Nitrates 472
    Ivabradine 473
    Digoxin 473
    Vericiguat 474
    Potassium Oral Supplementation 475
       Potassium Chloride: A Hard Pill to Swallow 475
    Chronic Heart Failure Management/Action Plan 476
Heart Failure Exacerbations and Quality Improvement 477
Key Counseling Points 477

CONTENT LEGEND

   = Study Tip Gal   = Key Drug Guy

EJECTION FRACTION

EF	TERM	PRIMARY PROBLEM
55-70%	Normal	Normal
≥ 50%	Heart Failure with Preserved EF (HFpEF) Diastolic Dysfunction	Impaired ventricular relaxation and filling during diastole
41-49%	Heart Failure with Mildly Reduced EF (HFmrEF)	Likely mixed systolic and diastolic dysfunction
≤ 40%	Heart Failure with Reduced EF (HFrEF) Systolic Dysfunction	Impaired ability to eject blood during systole
≤ 40% at baseline, then a ≥ 10% increase and second EF > 40%	Heart Failure with Improved EF (HFimpEF)	EF improved with treatment; classified separately because treatments for HFrEF should be continued, despite higher EF

CLASSIFICATION SYSTEMS

Two classification systems are recommended for HFrEF. The American College of Cardiology and the American Heart Association (ACC/AHA), with updates from a universal consensus statement, recommend categorizing patients by HF stage (see table below). The staging system is used to guide treatment in order to slow progression of structural heart disease (LVH, low EF, valvular disease, previous MI) in asymptomatic patients (stages A and B) or in symptomatic patients (stages C and D). "Biomarkers" in the definitions refer to BNP and NT-proBNP (discussed later). HF can also be classified by the level of limitation in physical functioning using the New York Heart Association (NYHA) classification system. Many drugs were studied based on the NYHA functional classification of patients, so this remains extremely relevant to drug therapy decisions.

ACC/AHA STAGING SYSTEM		NYHA FUNCTIONAL CLASS	
A	At risk for development of HF, but without symptoms of HF and without structural heart disease or elevated biomarkers. Examples: patients with HTN, ASCVD or DM.	No corresponding category	
B	Pre-HF; structural heart disease, abnormal cardiac function or elevated biomarkers, but without signs or symptoms of HF. Examples: patients with LVH, low EF, valvular disease.	I	No limitations of physical activity. Ordinary physical activity does not cause symptoms of HF (e.g., fatigue, palpitations, dyspnea).
Clinical Diagnosis of HF			
C	Structural and/or functional cardiac abnormality with prior or current symptoms of HF. Example: a patient with known structural heart disease (e.g., LVH) plus SOB, fatigue and reduced exercise tolerance.	I	No limitations of physical activity. Ordinary physical activity does not cause symptoms of HF.
		II	Slight limitation of physical activity. Comfortable at rest, but ordinary physical activity (e.g., walking up stairs) results in symptoms of HF.
		III	Marked limitation of physical activity. Comfortable at rest but minimal exertion (e.g., bathing, dressing) causes symptoms of HF.
D	Advanced HF with severe symptoms, symptoms at rest or recurrent hospitalizations despite maximal treatment (refractory HF requiring specialized interventions).	IV	Unable to carry on any physical activity without symptoms of HF, or symptoms of HF at rest (e.g., SOB while sitting in a chair).

SIGNS AND SYMPTOMS OF SYSTOLIC HEART FAILURE

Labs/Biomarkers
↑ BNP (B-type natriuretic peptide): normal is < 100 pg/mL
↑ NT-proBNP (N-terminal pro B-type natriuretic peptide): normal is < 300 pg/mL
BNP and proBNP are used to distinguish between cardiac and non-cardiac causes of dyspnea

Left-Sided Signs and Symptoms
Orthopnea: SOB when lying flat
Paroxysmal nocturnal dyspnea (PND): nocturnal cough and SOB
Bibasilar rales: crackling lung sounds heard on lung exam
S3 gallop: abnormal heart sound
Hypoperfusion (renal impairment, cool extremities)

General Signs and Symptoms
Dyspnea (SOB at rest or upon exertion)
Cough
Fatigue, weakness
Reduced exercise capacity

Right-Sided Signs and Symptoms
Peripheral edema
Ascites: abdominal fluid accumulation
Jugular venous distention (JVD): neck vein distention
Hepatojugular reflux (HJR): neck vein distention from pressure placed on the abdomen
Hepatomegaly: enlarged liver due to fluid congestion

PATHOPHYSIOLOGY

TERMINOLOGY

Cardiac output (CO) is the volume of blood that is pumped by the heart in one minute. CO is determined by heart rate (HR) and stroke volume (SV), or the volume of blood ejected from the left ventricle during one complete heartbeat (cardiac cycle). SV depends on preload, afterload and contractility. The cardiac index (CI) relates the CO to the size of the patient, using the body surface area (BSA).

CO = HR x SV	CI = CO / BSA

COMPENSATORY MECHANISMS

HFrEF is a low cardiac output state. The body compensates by activating neurohormonal pathways to increase blood volume or the force or speed of contractions. This can temporarily increase CO, but chronically leads to myocyte damage and cardiac remodeling. This causes changes in the size, composition and shape of the heart (e.g., hypertrophy, dilatation).

The main pathways that are activated in HF are the renin-angiotensin-aldosterone system (RAAS), the sympathetic nervous system (SNS) and vasopressin (see diagram in Drug Treatment section). The neurohormones that normally balance these systems (e.g., natriuretic peptides) become insufficient.

RAAS and Vasopressin Activation

- Renin converts angiotensinogen to angiotensin I.
- Angiotensin I is converted to angiotensin II (Ang II) by angiotensin-converting enzyme (ACE).
- Ang II causes vasoconstriction and stimulates release of aldosterone from the adrenal gland and vasopressin from the pituitary gland.
- Aldosterone causes sodium and water retention and increases potassium excretion.
- Vasopressin causes vasoconstriction and water retention.

SNS Activation

- Norepinephrine (NE) and epinephrine (EPI) release cause an increase in HR, contractility (positive inotropy) and vasoconstriction.

LIFESTYLE MANAGEMENT

Patients with HF should be instructed to:

- Monitor and document body weight daily, in the morning after voiding and before eating.
- Notify the provider if weight ↑ by 2 – 4 pounds in one day or 3 – 5 pounds in one week, or if symptoms worsen (e.g., SOB

with activity, or others listed in the Study Tip Gal on the previous page). A HF action plan should be provided and explained to the patient (see example at end of chapter).

- Restrict sodium intake to ≤ 1,500 mg/day in stage A and B HF (maintain some sodium restriction in other patients).
- Restrict fluid (1.5 – 2 L/day) in stage D HF.
- Stop smoking. Limit alcohol intake. Do not use illicit drugs.
- Obtain recommended vaccines: influenza (annually) and pneumococcal vaccines per ACIP guidelines (see Immunizations chapter).
- Reduce weight to BMI < 30 kg/m² to decrease the heart's workload and preserve function.
- Exercise (or perform regular physical activity, if able).

Natural Products

- Omega-3 fatty acid (fish oil) supplementation is reasonable to ↓ mortality and cardiovascular hospitalizations.
- Hawthorn and coenzyme Q10 may improve HF symptoms.
- Avoid the use of products containing ephedra (ma huang) or ephedrine.

DRUGS THAT CAUSE OR WORSEN HEART FAILURE

Most drugs that cause or worsen HF cause fluid retention/edema, increase blood pressure or have negative inotropic effects (see Key Drugs Guy below).

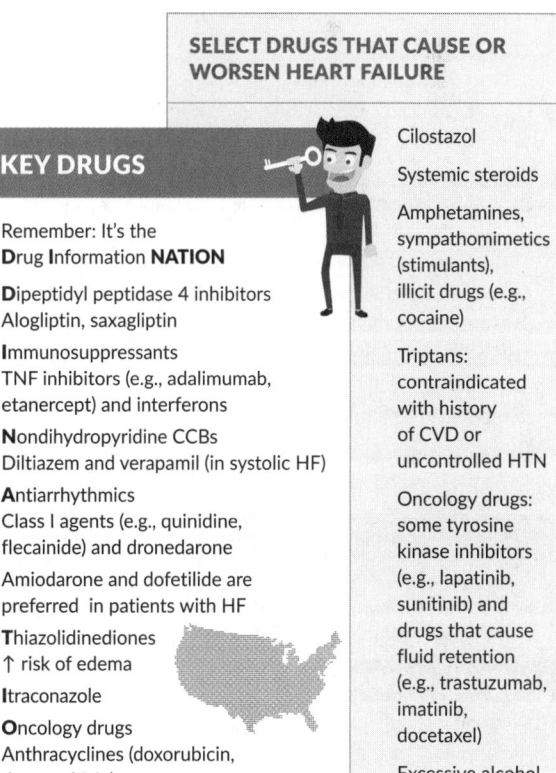

SELECT DRUGS THAT CAUSE OR WORSEN HEART FAILURE

KEY DRUGS

Remember: It's the **D**rug Information **NATION**

Dipeptidyl peptidase 4 inhibitors
Alogliptin, saxagliptin

Immunosuppressants
TNF inhibitors (e.g., adalimumab, etanercept) and interferons

Nondihydropyridine CCBs
Diltiazem and verapamil (in systolic HF)

Antiarrhythmics
Class I agents (e.g., quinidine, flecainide) and dronedarone
Amiodarone and dofetilide are preferred in patients with HF

Thiazolidinediones
↑ risk of edema

Itraconazole

Oncology drugs
Anthracyclines (doxorubicin, daunorubicin)

NSAIDs
All (including celecoxib)

Cilostazol

Systemic steroids

Amphetamines, sympathomimetics (stimulants), illicit drugs (e.g., cocaine)

Triptans: contraindicated with history of CVD or uncontrolled HTN

Oncology drugs: some tyrosine kinase inhibitors (e.g., lapatinib, sunitinib) and drugs that cause fluid retention (e.g., trastuzumab, imatinib, docetaxel)

Excessive alcohol

DRUG TREATMENT

HF is treated with a combination of an angiotensin receptor and neprilysin inhibitor (ARNI) [or an ACE inhibitor or angiotensin receptor blocker (ARB)] plus a beta-blocker (BB) and a loop diuretic (for example: *Entresto* + carvedilol + furosemide). An aldosterone receptor antagonist (ARA) is usually added next, followed by a sodium-glucose cotransporter 2 (SGLT2) inhibitor. The following diagram reviews the pathophysiology, and current treatment recommendations are summarized in the <u>Study Tip Gal</u> that follows.

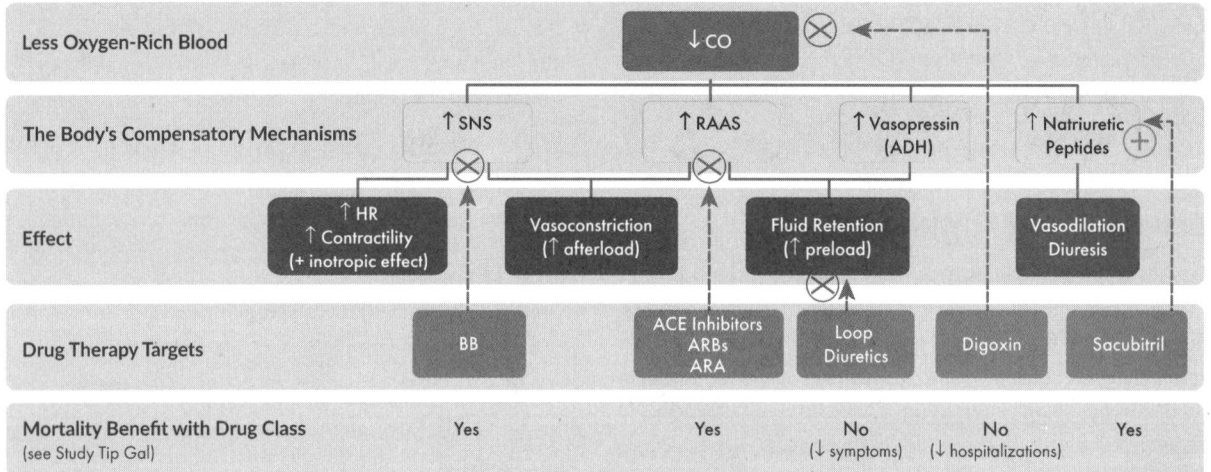

©RxPrep

TREATMENT OF CHRONIC SYSTOLIC HEART FAILURE

Initial medications, recommended for all patients without contraindications

- **Angiotensin receptor and neprilysin inhibitor (ARNI), ACE inhibitors or ARBs**
  - ❏ ↓ mortality in HFrEF
  - ❏ ARNI is preferred over an ACE inhibitor/ARB to further reduce morbidity and mortality
- **Beta-blockers (BB)**
  - ❏ Provide benefit in controlling heart rate and reducing arrhythmia risk; ↓ mortality in HFrEF
- **Loop diuretics**
  - ❏ Reduce blood volume, which ↓ edema and congestion; most HF patients need a loop diuretic for symptom relief

Secondary medications, add on in select patients

- **Aldosterone receptor antagonists (ARAs)**
  - ❏ ↓ morbidity and mortality in NYHA Class II-IV
  - ❏ Provide added diuresis; improve symptoms and EF
  - ❏ Must meet eGFR, SCr and potassium criteria for use
- **Sodium-glucose cotransporter 2 (SGLT2) inhibitors**
  - ❏ Initially approved for type 2 diabetes; select agents found to ↓ morbidity and mortality in NYHA Class II-IV HFrEF with or without diabetes
  - ❏ Must meet eGFR criteria for use
- **Hydralazine and nitrates (*BiDil*)**
  - ❏ ↓ morbidity and mortality in black patients with NYHA Class III-IV, when added to an ACE inhibitor/ARB and BB, or in other patients who cannot tolerate an ACE inhibitor or ARB
  - ❏ Recommended in persistently symptomatic black patients with NYHA Class III-IV, despite treatment with ARNI, BB, ARA, SGLT2 inhibitor
- **Ivabradine (*Corlanor*)**
  - ❏ ↓ risk of hospitalization in patients with stable NYHA Class II-III HF in normal sinus rhythm with a resting heart rate ≥ 70 BPM on maximally tolerated dose of BB

Additional medications

- **Digoxin**
  - ❏ Provides a small increase in cardiac output, improves symptoms and decreases cardiac hospitalizations (does not decrease mortality)
- **Vericiguat, a soluble guanylate cyclase (sGC) stimulator**
  - ❏ ↓ risk of hospitalization and CV death after HF hospitalization or need for IV diuretics; not yet included in treatment guidelines

ANGIOTENSIN RECEPTOR AND NEPRILYSIN INHIBITOR

Entresto is a combination of a neprilysin inhibitor (sacubitril) and an ARB (valsartan). Neprilysin is the enzyme responsible for degradation of several beneficial vasodilatory peptides, including natriuretic peptides, adrenomedullin, substance P and bradykinin. These peptides counteract the effects of RAAS activation and cause vasodilation and diuresis. An ARNI is indicated in NYHA Class II – IV patients to reduce HF hospitalizations and cardiovascular death. It is a preferred first-line treatment in all patients with HFrEF, and would be used in place of an ACE inhibitor or other ARB (*Entresto* should not be used in combination with an ACE inhibitor/ARB). Of note, *Entresto* is FDA-approved for the treatment of chronic heart failure without a specific ejection fraction cutoff indicated (e.g., approved for use in patients with an EF ≤ 40% or > 40%).

DRUG	DOSING	SAFETY/SIDE EFFECTS/MONITORING
Sacubitril/Valsartan (Entresto) Tablet	Start: 50-100 mg BID Target dose: 200 mg BID eGFR < 30 mL/min/1.73m^2: 50 mg BID The dose is the sum of the two components: 50 mg = 24/26 mg sacubitril/valsartan 100 mg = 49/51 mg sacubitril/valsartan 200 mg = 97/103 mg sacubitril/valsartan	**BOXED WARNING** Can cause injury and death to the developing fetus when used in the 2nd and 3rd trimesters; discontinue as soon as pregnancy is detected **CONTRAINDICATIONS** Do not use with or within 36 hours of ACE inhibitors Do not use with history of angioedema Do not use with aliskiren in diabetes **WARNINGS** Angioedema, hyperkalemia, hypotension, renal impairment, bilateral renal artery stenosis (avoid use) **SIDE EFFECTS** Generally well-tolerated, can cause cough, hyperkalemia, ↑ SCr, hypotension/dizziness [↑ risk if volume-depleted (e.g., with concurrent diuretic)], headache **MONITORING** BP, K, renal function, s/sx of HF and angioedema **NOTES** Do not use with an ACE inhibitor or an ARB No washout period required when switching from an ARB; take the first dose of sacubitril/valsartan when the next ARB dose was due

ACE INHIBITORS AND ANGIOTENSIN RECEPTOR BLOCKERS

ACE inhibitors block the conversion of angiotensin I to Ang II, resulting in ↓ vasoconstriction and ↓ aldosterone secretion (refer to the Hypertension chapter). They block the degradation of bradykinin, which may contribute to the vasodilatory effects and the side effects of cough and angioedema. ARBs block Ang II from binding to the angiotensin II type-1 (AT1) receptor. These drugs ↓ RAAS activation, resulting in ↓ preload and afterload. They ↓ cardiac remodeling, improve left ventricular function and ↓ morbidity and mortality. The clinical benefits are a class effect. An ARNI or ACE inhibitor or ARB is recommended for all HF patients (NYHA Class I – IV) regardless of symptoms. Other important points include:

- Clinical trials established target doses of ACE inhibitors and ARBs that improve symptoms and increase survival. The goal is to titrate to the target dose, as tolerated, not to a target BP.

- Combining an ACE inhibitor or ARB with an ARA has added survival benefits. Triple combination of an ACE inhibitor + ARB + ARA is not recommended due to a higher risk of hyperkalemia and renal insufficiency.

- Angioedema occurs more frequently with ACE inhibitors (than with ARBs) and in black patients. For testing purposes, do not use an ACE inhibitor or ARB in patients with a history of angioedema from use of any of these medications.

CARDIOVASCULAR CONDITIONS

DRUG	DOSING	SAFETY/SIDE EFFECTS/MONITORING
ACE Inhibitors – only those mentioned in the guidelines (see complete list in Hypertension chapter)		
Captopril (*Capoten*)	Start 6.25 mg TID, 1 hr before meals Target dose: 50 mg TID	**BOXED WARNING** Can cause injury and death to the developing fetus when used in the 2nd and 3rd trimesters; discontinue as soon as pregnancy is detected
Enalapril (*Vasotec*, *Epaned* oral solution)	Start 2.5 mg PO BID Target dose: 10-20 mg PO BID	**CONTRAINDICATIONS** Do not use with history of angioedema Do not use within 36 hours of sacubitril/valsartan (*Entresto*)
Fosinopril	Start 5-10 mg daily Target dose: 40 mg daily	Do not use with aliskiren in diabetes
Lisinopril (*Prinivil, Zestril*, *Qbrelis* oral solution)	Start 2.5-5 mg daily Target dose: 20-40 mg daily	**WARNINGS** Angioedema, hyperkalemia, hypotension, renal impairment, bilateral renal artery stenosis (avoid use)
Perindopril	Start 2 mg daily Target dose: 8-16 mg daily	**SIDE EFFECTS** Generally well-tolerated, can cause cough, hyperkalemia, ↑ SCr, hypotension/
Quinapril (*Accupril*)	Start 5 mg BID Target dose: 20 mg BID	dizziness [↑ risk if volume-depleted (e.g., with concurrent diuretic)], headache
Ramipril (*Altace*)	Start 1.25-2.5 mg daily Target dose: 10 mg daily	**MONITORING** BP, K, renal function, s/sx of HF and angioedema
Trandolapril	Start 1 mg daily Target dose: 4 mg daily	
ARBs – only those mentioned in the guidelines (see complete list in Hypertension chapter)		
Candesartan (*Atacand*)	Start 4-8 mg daily Target dose: 32 mg daily	Same as ACE inhibitors except: Less cough
Losartan (*Cozaar*)	Start 25-50 mg daily Target dose: 50-150 mg daily	Less angioedema
Valsartan (*Diovan*)	Start 40 mg BID Target dose: 160 mg BID	No washout period required with sacubitril/valsartan (*Entresto*)

ARNI, ACE Inhibitor and ARB Drug Interactions

- Risk of hyperkalemia; use caution with other drugs that ↑ potassium (e.g., potassium-sparing diuretics). Avoid salt substitutes that contain potassium.

- Do not use more than one RAAS inhibitor together (e.g, ACE inhibitor ± ARB/ARNI ± aliskiren) or the triple combination of ACE inhibitor + ARB/ARNI + ARA due to ↑ risk of renal impairment, hypotension and hyperkalemia.

- Use caution with other drugs that ↓ blood pressure.

- Use with NSAIDs can worsen renal function (especially if elderly, volume depleted or compromised renal function).

- Can ↓ lithium renal clearance and ↑ risk of lithium toxicity.

BETA-BLOCKERS

Beta-adrenergic receptor antagonists (beta-blockers) antagonize the effects of catecholamines (especially NE) at the beta-1, beta-2 and/or alpha-1 adrenergic receptors. They ↓ vasoconstriction, improve cardiac function and ↓ morbidity and mortality. They are recommended for all HF patients. Unlike ACE inhibitors (or ARBs), the clinical benefits of beta-blockers are not considered a class effect. Only bisoprolol, carvedilol (IR and ER) and metoprolol succinate (ER) are recommended in the guidelines. The target doses demonstrated a survival benefit in clinical trials. Do not use beta-blockers with intrinsic sympathomimetic activity (ISA). Only discontinue beta-blockers during acute decompensated HF if hypotension or hypoperfusion is present.

DRUG	DOSING	SAFETY/SIDE EFFECTS/MONITORING
Beta-1 Selective Beta-Blockers		
Metoprolol succinate extended release (*Toprol XL, Kapspargo Sprinkle*) Metoprolol tartrate (*Lopressor*) is not recommended	Start 12.5-25 mg daily Target dose: 200 mg daily Titrate every 2 weeks as tolerated	**BOXED WARNING** Do not discontinue abruptly (particularly in patients with CHD/IHD); gradually taper over 1-2 weeks to avoid acute tachycardia, HTN and/or ischemia **CONTRAINDICATIONS** Severe bradycardia; 2nd or 3rd degree AV block or sick sinus syndrome (unless a permanent pacemaker is in place); overt cardiac failure or cardiogenic shock **WARNINGS** Caution in diabetes; can worsen hyperglycemia or hypoglycemia and mask hypoglycemic symptoms (see Diabetes chapter) Use caution with bronchospastic diseases (e.g., asthma, COPD)
Bisoprolol	Start 1.25 mg daily Target dose: 10 mg daily Titrate every 2 weeks as tolerated	Use caution with Raynaud's/other peripheral vascular diseases and pheochromocytoma Can mask signs of hyperthyroidism (e.g., tachycardia), can worsen CNS depression **SIDE EFFECTS** Bradycardia, fatigue, hypotension, dizziness, depression, impotence, cold extremities (can exacerbate Raynaud's) **MONITORING** HR (↓ dose if HR < 55 BPM), BP, s/sx of HF **NOTES** Metoprolol IV is not equivalent to PO (IV:PO ratio 1:2.5) *Toprol XL*: can be cut in half; take with or immediately after meals *Kapspargo Sprinkle*: swallow whole; if needed, the capsule can be opened and the contents sprinkled on a teaspoonful of soft food (e.g., applesauce, yogurt or pudding)
Non-Selective Beta-Blocker and Alpha-1 Blocker		
Carvedilol (*Coreg, Coreg CR*)	**Immediate release** Start 3.125 mg BID Target dose: ≤ 85 kg: 25 mg BID > 85 kg: 50 mg BID **Controlled release** Start 10 mg daily Target dose: 80 mg daily Titrate every 2 weeks as tolerated	Same as above **CONTRAINDICATION** Severe hepatic impairment **WARNING** Intraoperative floppy iris syndrome has occurred in cataract surgery patients who were on or were previously treated with an alpha-1 blocker **SIDE EFFECTS** Edema, weight gain **NOTES** Take with food (all forms) to ↓ the rate of absorption and the risk of orthostatic hypotension Carvedilol CR has less bioavailability than carvedilol IR; dose conversions are not 1:1 (e.g., *Coreg* 3.125 mg BID = *Coreg CR* 10 mg daily)

Beta-Blocker Drug Interactions

- Can enhance the hypoglycemic effects of insulin and sulfonylureas and can mask some symptoms of hypoglycemia (e.g., shakiness, palpitations, anxiety).

- Use caution with other drugs that ↓ HR (e.g., digoxin, verapamil, diltiazem).

- Carvedilol and metoprolol are CYP450 2D6 substrates; monitor with CYP2D6 inhibitors or inducers.

- Carvedilol inhibits P-gp and can ↑ concentrations of P-gp substrates (e.g., digoxin, cyclosporine, dabigatran, ranolazine).

LOOP DIURETICS

Loop diuretics block sodium and chloride reabsorption in the thick ascending limb of the loop of Henle. They ↑ excretion of sodium, potassium, chloride, magnesium, calcium and water. The ↓ in fluid volume makes it easier for the heart to pump, reduces congestive symptoms (↓ preload) and restores euvolemia ("dry" weight). They do not improve survival, but are often required for symptom control. The lowest effective dose should be used to prevent over-diuresis, which can cause hypotension or renal impairment. If response to loop diuretics is poor, adding a thiazide-type diuretic, such as metolazone, can be useful.

DRUG	DOSING	SAFETY/SIDE EFFECTS/MONITORING
Furosemide *(Lasix)* Tablet, injection	Oral: 20-40 mg daily or BID Max 600 mg/day	**BOXED WARNING** Can cause profound diuresis resulting in fluid and electrolyte depletion **CONTRAINDICATIONS** Anuria **WARNINGS**
Bumetanide *(Bumex)* Tablet, injection	Oral: 0.5-1 mg daily or BID Max 10 mg/day	Sulfa allergy (not likely to cross-react – see cautionary statement in Drug Allergies & Adverse Drug Reactions chapter); warning does not apply to ethacrynic acid **SIDE EFFECTS** ↓ electrolytes: K, Mg, Na, Cl, Ca (different than thiazides which ↑ Ca) ↑ electrolytes/labs: HCO3 (metabolic alkalosis), UA, BG, TGs, total cholesterol
Torsemide Tablet	Oral: 10-20 mg daily Max 200 mg/day	Ototoxicity including hearing loss, tinnitus and vertigo (more with ethacrynic acid or rapid IV administration of any loop diuretic) Orthostatic hypotension, photosensitivity, myalgias **MONITORING** Renal function, fluid status (input/output, weight), BP, electrolytes, audiology testing (with high doses or rapid IV administration), s/sx of HF
Ethacrynic Acid *(Edecrin)* Tablet, injection	Oral: 50-200 mg daily or divided Max 400 mg/day	**NOTES** Take early in the day to avoid nocturia Furosemide injection: store at room temperature (refrigeration causes crystals to form, which may dissolve upon warming); solution must be clear, do not use if yellow in color Bumetanide and furosemide injections are light-sensitive (store in amber bottles); IV admixtures do not require light protection **Dose Conversions** Oral equivalent dosing: furosemide 40 mg = torsemide 20 mg = bumetanide 1 mg = ethacrynic acid 50 mg Furosemide IV:PO ratio 1:2 (furosemide 20 mg IV = furosemide 40 mg PO) Bumetanide and ethacrynic acid IV:PO ratio 1:1

Loop Diuretic Drug Interactions

- Avoid NSAIDs; the ↑ sodium and water retention can ↓ the effect of loop diuretics and cause renal impairment.

- Use caution with other drugs that ↓ blood pressure.

- Watch for additive diuresis and electrolyte abnormalities when used in combination with thiazide-type diuretics.

- Additive risk for ototoxicity when used with other ototoxic drugs (see the Drug Interactions chapter), especially in patients with impaired renal function.

- Diuretics can ↓ lithium renal clearance and ↑ risk of lithium toxicity.

CASE SCENARIO

A patient is being treated with furosemide 40 mg IV BID for an acute HF exacerbation. She is now ready for discharge and the team wants to send her home on bumetanide. What would be an equivalent oral dose of bumetanide?

First, determine the equivalent furosemide oral dose for the current total daily dose of IV furosemide.

$$\frac{80 \text{ mg IV}}{X \text{ mg PO}} = \frac{1 \text{ mg IV}}{2 \text{ mg PO}}$$

X = 160 mg PO furosemide

Then, determine the equivalent oral dose of bumetanide.

$$\frac{160 \text{ mg PO furosemide}}{X \text{ mg PO bumetanide}} = \frac{40 \text{ mg PO furosemide}}{1 \text{ mg PO bumetanide}}$$

X = 4 mg PO bumetanide

ALDOSTERONE RECEPTOR ANTAGONISTS

Aldosterone receptor antagonists (ARAs) compete with aldosterone at receptor sites in the distal convoluted tubule and collecting ducts of the nephron. Spironolactone is non-selective; it also blocks androgen and exhibits endocrine side effects. Eplerenone is selective and does not exhibit endocrine side effects. ARAs ↓ sodium and water retention, cardiac remodeling (especially myocardial fibrosis) and the risk of sudden cardiac death. ARAs ↓ morbidity and mortality and should be added to ARNI (or ACE inhibitors or ARBs) and beta-blockers in patients with NYHA Class II – IV HF.

DRUG	DOSING	SAFETY/SIDE EFFECTS/MONITORING
Spironolactone (**Aldactone**, *CaroSpir*) Tablet, oral suspension	Start 12.5-25 mg daily Target dose: 25 mg daily or BID *CaroSpir*: start 20 mg (4 mL) daily for eGFR > 50 mL/min/1.73m²	**CONTRAINDICATIONS** Do not use if hyperkalemia, severe renal impairment, Addison's disease (spironolactone) or taking strong CYP3A4 inhibitors (eplerenone) **WARNINGS** Do not initiate for HF if K > 5 mEq/L (> 5.5 mEq/L for eplerenone), CrCl (eGFR) ≤ 30 or SCr > 2.0 mg/dL (females) or SCr > 2.5 mg/dL (males) **SIDE EFFECTS** Hyperkalemia, ↑ SCr, dizziness, hyperchloremic metabolic acidosis (rare) Spironolactone: gynecomastia, breast tenderness, impotence, irregular menses, amenorrhea
Eplerenone (*Inspra*) Tablet	Start 25 mg daily Target dose: 50 mg daily Titrate if K remains < 5 mEq/L	Eplerenone: ↑ TGs **MONITORING** BP, K, renal function, fluid status, s/sx of HF **NOTES** *CaroSpir* suspension is not therapeutically equivalent to the tablets; *CaroSpir* doses > 100 mg can cause higher than expected concentrations; only use tablets when doses > 100 mg are needed

ARA Drug Interactions

- Risk of hyperkalemia; use caution with other drugs that ↑ potassium.
- Do not use triple combination of ACE inhibitor + ARB/ARNI + ARA due to a higher risk of hyperkalemia and renal insufficiency.
- Use caution with other drugs that ↓ blood pressure.
- Can ↓ lithium renal clearance and ↑ the risk of lithium toxicity.
- Eplerenone is a major substrate of CYP3A4. Do not use with strong CYP3A4 inhibitors (e.g., ketoconazole, itraconazole, clarithromycin, ritonavir).

SODIUM-GLUCOSE COTRANSPORTER 2 INHIBITORS

Sodium-glucose cotransporter 2 (SGLT2) inhibitors, which were originally approved for type 2 diabetes (see Diabetes chapter), have now shown benefit in treating HFrEF. They work by reducing glucose reabsorption in the proximal renal tubules. Though their mechanism in HF is not well defined, the benefits likely relate to reduced sodium reabsorption, diuresis and a decrease in preload and/or afterload. Select SGLT2 inhibitors are FDA-approved for patients with HFrEF without diabetes after demonstrating a decrease in mortality and hospitalizations in this population. SGLT2 inhibitors are recommended as add-on therapy to an ARNI (or ACE inhibitor or ARB), BB and ARA.

DRUG	DOSING	SAFETY/SIDE EFFECTS/MONITORING
Dapagliflozin (**Farxiga**)	10 mg daily in the morning eGFR < 25 mL/min/1.73m²: initiation not recommended	Refer to the Diabetes chapter
Empagliflozin (**Jardiance**)	10 mg daily in the morning eGFR < 30 mL/min/1.73m²: insufficient data for a recommendation	

HYDRALAZINE/NITRATES

Hydralazine is a direct arterial vasodilator which ↓ afterload. Nitrates ↑ the availability of nitric oxide, causing venous vasodilation and ↓ preload. The combination improves survival in HF (but to a lesser degree than ACE inhibitors) and can be used as an alternative in patients who cannot tolerate ACE inhibitors or ARBs due to poor renal function, angioedema or hyperkalemia. The combination product BiDil is indicated in self-identified black patients with NYHA Class III or IV who are symptomatic despite optimal treatment with ARNI (or ACE inhibitors or ARBs), beta-blockers, ARAs and SGLT2 inhibitors. There is no role for monotherapy with either hydralazine or oral nitrates in the treatment of HF.

DRUG	DOSING	SAFETY/SIDE EFFECTS/MONITORING
Hydralazine/Isosorbide Dinitrate (BiDil) Tablet	Start 20/37.5 mg TID (1 tab TID) Target dose: 40/75 mg TID (2 tabs TID)	See individual components below **NOTES** No nitrate tolerance
Hydralazine Tablet, injection	Start 25-50 mg TID-QID Target dose: 300 mg/day in divided doses	**CONTRAINDICATION** Mitral valve rheumatic heart disease, CAD **WARNING** Drug-induced lupus erythematosus (DILE – dose and duration related), peripheral neuritis, blood dyscrasias, hypotension **SIDE EFFECTS** Peripheral edema/headache/flushing/palpitations/reflex tachycardia, nausea/vomiting **MONITORING** HR, BP, s/sx of HF, ANA titer
Isosorbide dinitrate IR/ER (Dilatrate SR, Isordil Titradose) Preferred formulation for systolic HF Isosorbide mononitrate (Imdur*) not listed in HF guidelines	Dinitrate: Start 20-30 mg TID-QID Target dose: 120 mg daily in divided doses	**CONTRAINDICATIONS** Do not use with PDE-5 Inhibitors or riociguat **SIDE EFFECTS** Hypotension, headache, dizziness, lightheadedness, flushing, tachyphylaxis (need 10-12 hour nitrate-free interval), syncope **MONITORING** HR, BP, s/sx of HF **NOTES** Refer to Stable Ischemic Heart Disease and Acute & Critical Care Medicine chapters for further discussion of nitrates for other indications

Brand discontinued but name still used in practice.

BiDil Drug Interactions

- Do not use with PDE-5 inhibitors (e.g., avanafil, sildenafil, tadalafil, vardenafil) or riociguat. The combination can cause severe hypotension. Refer to the Sexual Dysfunction chapter for further discussion.

IVABRADINE

Ivabradine belongs to a class of drugs known as hyperpolarization-activated cyclic nucleotide-gated channel blockers. It disrupts the "funny" current (I_f) in the sinoatrial (SA) node, resulting in ↓ rate of firing and ultimately ↓ HR. Ivabradine reduces the risk of hospitalizations for worsening HF, but does not affect mortality. It is recommended as adjunct treatment in symptomatic (NYHA Class II – III) stable chronic HF (EF ≤ 35%). Patients must already be on mortality-reducing medications, including target or maximally-tolerated doses of beta-blockers (or contraindication to use), and be in sinus rhythm with a resting HR ≥ 70 BPM.

DRUG	DOSING	SAFETY/SIDE EFFECTS/MONITORING
Ivabradine *(Corlanor)*	Starting dose: 5 mg PO twice daily; after two weeks, adjust dose based on heart rate Maintenance dose: 2.5-7.5 mg PO twice daily Target: resting HR between 50-60 BPM	**CONTRAINDICATIONS** ADHF; sick sinus syndrome, SA block or 3rd degree AV block (unless a permanent pacemaker is in place); clinically significant hypotension or bradycardia; HR maintained exclusively by a pacemaker; severe hepatic impairment; use with strong CYP3A4 inhibitors **WARNINGS** Can cause bradycardia which can ↑ risk of QT prolongation and ventricular arrhythmias; not recommended in 2nd degree AV block ↑ risk of atrial fibrillation Fetal toxicity (females should use effective contraception) **SIDE EFFECTS** Bradycardia, hypertension, atrial fibrillation, luminous phenomena (phosphenes - seeing flashes of light) **MONITORING** HR, ECG, BP

Ivabradine Drug Interactions

- Do not use with moderate or strong CYP3A4 inhibitors or strong CYP3A4 inducers.
- Use caution with other drugs that ↓ HR (e.g., digoxin, beta-blockers, clonidine, non-DHP CCBs, amiodarone and dexmedetomidine).

DIGOXIN

Digoxin inhibits the Na-K-ATPase pump, causing a positive inotropic effect (↑ CO), and exerts a parasympathetic effect, which causes negative chronotropy (↓ HR). It does not improve survival, but can reduce HF related hospitalizations. It can be added to mortality-reducing drugs (e.g., ARNI, beta-blocker) to improve symptoms, exercise tolerance and quality of life. It is usually added for atrial fibrillation (AF) in those with HFrEF and low blood pressure. The starting dose is based on renal function, body size, age and gender (lower dose if renal insufficiency, smaller, older or female). The dose is adjusted to maintain a serum concentration < 1 ng/mL in HF. Since hypokalemia and hypomagnesemia ↑ the risk for digoxin toxicity, maintain potassium between 4 – 5 mEq/L and magnesium > 2 mEq/L.

DRUG	DOSING	SAFETY/SIDE EFFECTS/MONITORING
Digoxin (*Digitek, Digox, Lanoxin*) Tablet, solution, injection	Typical dose: 0.125-0.25 mg PO daily Loading dose not used in HF CrCl < 50 mL/min: ↓ dose or frequency; hold in acute renal failure ↓ dose by 20-25% when switching from PO to IV **Therapeutic range (HF)** 0.5-0.9 ng/mL (higher range used for atrial fibrillation)	**CONTRAINDICATIONS** Ventricular fibrillation **WARNINGS** $2^{nd}/3^{rd}$ degree heart block without a pacemaker, Wolff-Parkinson-White syndrome with AF, vesicant (avoid extravasation) **SIDE EFFECTS** Dizziness, mental disturbances, headache, N/V, diarrhea **MONITORING** Electrolytes, renal function, HR, ECG, BP, and digoxin level (draw 12-24 hrs after dose) **TOXICITY** Initial s/sx: N/V, loss of appetite and bradycardia Severe s/sx: blurred/double vision, greenish-yellow halos around lights or objects, altered color perception, abdominal pain, confusion, delirium, arrhythmias **NOTES** Antidote: *DigiFab*

Digoxin Drug Interactions

- Use caution with other drugs that ↓ HR (e.g., beta-blockers, clonidine, non-DHP CCBs, amiodarone, clonidine and dexmedetomidine).

- Hypokalemia, hypomagnesemia and hypercalcemia ↑ risk of digoxin toxicity.

- Hypothyroidism can ↑ digoxin levels.

- Digoxin is a substrate of P-gp and CYP3A4 (minor). P-gp inhibitors will increase digoxin levels.

  - ❑ Use caution with amiodarone, dronedarone, quinidine, verapamil, erythromycin, clarithromycin, itraconazole, cyclosporine, propafenone and others.

  - ❑ Reduce digoxin dose by 50% when starting amiodarone or dronedarone.

VERICIGUAT

Vericiguat is a soluble guanylate cyclase stimulator, which increases cyclic GMP and leads to smooth muscle relaxation and vasodilation. It is FDA-approved to reduce the risk of cardiovascular death and HF hospitalizations following a hospitalization for HF or need for IV diuretics in patients with chronic symptomatic heart failure (EF < 45%). Vericiguat can be used as add-on therapy for HF, although it is not yet included in HF guidelines.

DRUG	DOSING	SAFETY/SIDE EFFECTS/MONITORING
Vericiguat (*Verquvo*)	Initial: 2.5 mg PO daily with food; after two weeks, titrate dose as tolerated Target dose: 10 mg once daily with food	**BOXED WARNING** Do not use if pregnant. Contraception required during use and for one month after stopping treatment. **CONTRAINDICATIONS** Do not use with riociguat (another soluble guanylate cyclase stimulator) **SIDE EFFECTS** Hypotension, anemia, dyspepsia

Vericiguat Drug Interactions

- Do not use with other soluble guanylate cyclase stimulators (e.g., riociguat).

- Vericiguat may enhance the hypotensive effects of phosphodiesterase 5 (PDE-5) inhibitors; this combination should be avoided.

- Patients taking long-acting nitrates (e.g., isosorbide mononitrate, isosorbide dinitrate) were excluded from studies because of the potential for increased hypotension.

POTASSIUM ORAL SUPPLEMENTATION

Fluctuations in potassium levels are common in HF due to the use of drugs that decrease (loop diuretics) or increase (RAAS inhibitors, ARAs) potassium levels. Maintenance of normal potassium levels (3.5 – 5 mEq/L) is essential to reduce the already elevated arrhythmia risk. This can sometimes be achieved by consuming potassium-rich foods (e.g., bananas, potatoes, orange juice, beans, dark leafy greens, apricots, peaches, avocados, tomatoes). When dietary sources alone cannot maintain normal levels, oral potassium supplements can be used.

There are different potassium formulations (tablets, capsules and liquids) and salt forms (acetate, bicarbonate, citrate, chloride, gluconate and phosphate) available. Potassium chloride (KCl) is used most commonly, but some of the tablets and capsules are large and difficult to swallow (see Study Tip Gal below).

Frequency of monitoring serum potassium depends on renal function, medication regimen and clinical status. It should be checked with changes in renal function and after any change in diuretic, ACE inhibitor, ARB or ARA dose. Magnesium deficiency can aggravate hypokalemia. Magnesium should be checked and corrected (as needed) prior to correcting the potassium level.

DRUG	DOSING	SAFETY/SIDE EFFECTS/MONITORING
Potassium chloride Extended-release capsules: ***Klor-Con Sprinkle, Micro-K*** Extended-release tablets: ***K-Tab, Klor-Con 10,*** ***Klor-Con M10/M15/M20*** Oral packet: ***Klor-Con*** Oral solution: 10% (20 mEq/15 mL), 20% (40 mEq/15 mL) Injection	**Prevention of hypokalemia:** 20-40 mEq/day in 1-2 divided doses **Treatment of mild hypokalemia:** 40-100 mEq/day in 2-5 divided doses; adjust dose according to laboratory values No more than 20-25 mEq should be given as a single dose to avoid GI discomfort	**CONTRAINDICATIONS** Severe renal impairment, hyperkalemia Solid oral formulations: do not use in patients with delayed or obstructed passage through the GI tract **WARNINGS** Use caution in mild-moderate renal impairment, with disorders that alter K (untreated Addison's disease, heat cramps, severe tissue trauma/burns) and with medications that ↑ K **SIDE EFFECTS** Abdominal pain/cramping, diarrhea, nausea, flatulence, hyperkalemia **MONITORING** K, Mg, Cl, pH, urine output **NOTES** Take with meals and a full glass of water to minimize the risk of GI irritation Injection: concentrated electrolyte, high-alert medication (see Acute & Critical Care Medicine chapter for safety and key information)

POTASSIUM CHLORIDE: A HARD PILL TO SWALLOW

Extended-release capsules
- *Micro-K, Klor-Con Sprinkle:* capsule contents can be sprinkled on a small amount of applesauce or pudding

Extended-release tablets
- *K-Tab, Klor-Con:* swallow whole; do not chew, crush, cut or suck on the tablet
- *Klor-Con M:* if difficult to swallow whole, it can be cut in half or dissolved in water (stir for 2 minutes and drink immediately); do not chew, crush, or suck on the tablet

Oral packet
- Dissolve contents in water and drink immediately

Oral solution
- KCl 10% = 20 mEq/15 mL (see Case Scenario)
- Mix each 15 mL with 6 oz of water

CASE SCENARIO
A 76-year-old woman, taking furosemide for HF, recently started *Klor-Con* 20 mEq TID. She has difficulty swallowing the large tablets and would like to switch to something that is easier to take. How many milliliters of KCl 10% oral solution would provide the same amount of daily potassium that she is receiving from *Klor-Con*?

First, determine the total daily dose of potassium chloride from *Klor-Con*.

20 mEq x 3 doses/day = 60 mEq/day

Then, using the dose conversion for KCl 10% oral solution, calculate how many milliliters will provide the same total daily dose.

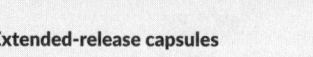
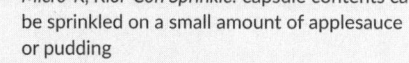

$$\frac{60\ mEq}{X\ mL} = \frac{20\ mEq}{15\ mL}$$

X = 45 mL of KCl 10% oral solution

See the Calculations II: Compounding chapter for additional examples

CHRONIC HEART FAILURE MANAGEMENT/ACTION PLAN

1. GREEN MEANS GO. FOLLOW MEDICATION, WEIGHT AND DIET ADVICE.

2. YELLOW MEANS CAUTION. YOU MAY NEED TO CHANGE YOUR MEDICATIONS.

3. RED MEANS DANGER. GET HELP FROM A DOCTOR TODAY. CALL 911.

1. GREEN – GO

- No shortness of breath
- Usual amount of swelling in legs
- No weight gain
- No chest pain
- No change in usual activity

Bring all your medications to every appointment

Weigh yourself every day

Eat a low salt diet

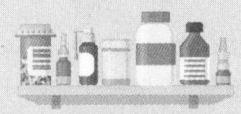

Take all your medications

Go to your doctor appointments

2. YELLOW – CAUTION

Weight gain of:
- 2-4 pounds in 1 day
- 3-5 pounds in a week

Increased swelling or coughing

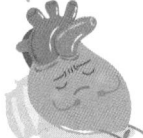

Increased number of pillows to sleep

Shortness of breath with activity

You may need to change your medications (e.g., double the dose of your loop diuretic)

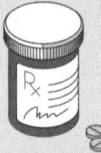

Call your doctor for instructions

3. RED – DANGER

Weight gain of more than 5 pounds in 1 week

Waking at night due to shortness of breath

Dizziness or falling

Shortness of breath at rest, chest tightness or wheezing

Call your doctor <u>today</u> to report symptoms and request an appointment

<u>Call 911 if having severe chest pain</u>

Adapted from ©www.ccwjc.com

©RxPrep

HEART FAILURE EXACERBATIONS AND QUALITY IMPROVEMENT

HF is the most common condition causing hospitalization in patients greater than 65 years old. HF admissions are caused by either new-onset HF (known as acute HF) or worsening HF (known as acute decompensated HF, or ADHF). ADHF presents with either worsening congestion and/or hypoperfusion. Treatment consists of IV loop diuretics, vasodilators and/or inotropes, which are discussed in the Acute & Critical Care Medicine chapter. Many HF hospitalizations are due to nonadherence with medications and/or lifestyle recommendations.

Avoidable HF admissions are a major cause of increased healthcare costs. Pharmacists are actively involved in quality improvement initiatives directed at decreasing hospital readmissions, such as medication optimization (ensuring the right medications are being used and harmful medications are not being used) and medication adherence strategies. Up to 25% of HF patients do not fill one or more discharge medications, and ~34% stop taking one or more medications within a month of discharge. Lifestyle adherence is essential (discussed at the beginning of the chapter), including healthy eating and sodium restriction. Patients need to know what steps to take if symptoms worsen. The steps are outlined in the sample HF action plan on the previous page.

KEY COUNSELING POINTS

See the Drug Formulations and Patient Counseling chapter for counseling language/layman's terminology.

ALL PATIENTS WITH HEART FAILURE

- Monitor and record body weight daily, in the morning after using the restroom and before eating.
- Limit salt intake. Choose foods with "no sodium added" or "low sodium." Avoid foods high in sodium, such as:
  - Prepared sauces and condiments (e.g., soy sauce, BBQ sauce, Worcestershire sauce, salsa)
  - Canned vegetables and soups
  - Frozen meals
  - Deli meat (e.g., sandwich meat, bacon, ham, hot dogs, sausage, salami)
  - Pickles, olives, cheese, nuts, chips
- Do not use NSAIDs (e.g., ibuprofen), they can worsen sodium and water retention and reduce the effectiveness of HF medications.

ARNI, ACE INHIBITORS AND ARBS

- Avoid in pregnancy (teratogenic).
- Can cause allergy/anaphylaxis.
- ACE inhibitors: tell your healthcare provider if you develop a dry, hacking cough.

BETA-BLOCKERS

- Do not suddenly stop taking this medication without consulting your healthcare provider.
- This medication can mask symptoms of low blood sugar. If you have diabetes, check your blood sugar if you notice symptoms of sweating or hunger.
- Can cause sexual dysfunction.
- Take *Coreg/Coreg CR* with food.

- Take *Toprol XL* with or immediately after meals.
- The *Coreg CR* capsule can be opened and the contents sprinkled on a small amount applesauce.
- The *Kapspargo Sprinkle* capsule can be opened and the contents sprinkled on a teaspoonful of applesauce, yogurt or pudding.

LOOP DIURETICS

- Take this medication early in the day (no later than 4 PM) to avoid getting up at night to use the bathroom.
- Can cause orthostasis.

DIGOXIN

- Digoxin levels and kidney function will be monitored regularly.
- Avoid dehydration; an overdose can occur more easily if you are dehydrated.
- Symptoms of overdose include nausea, vomiting, decreased appetite, vision changes (e.g., blurred or yellow/green vision), confusion and delirium.
- Many drug interactions.

Select Guidelines/References

2021 Update to the 2017 ACC Expert Consensus Decision Pathway for Optimization of Heart Failure Treatment: Answers to 10 Pivotal Issues About Heart Failure with Reduced Ejection Fraction. *J Am Coll Cardiol.* 2021;77(6):772-810.

2016 ACC/AHA/HFSA Focused Update on New Pharmacological Therapy for Heart Failure: An Update of the 2013 ACCF/AHA Guideline for the Management of Heart Failure. http://www.onlinejacc.org/content/68/13/1476 (accessed 2022 Jan 25).

2021 Universal Definition and Classification of Heart Failure Consensus Statement. https://www.onlinejcf.com/article/S1071-9164(21)00050-6/fulltext (accessed 2022 Jan 25).

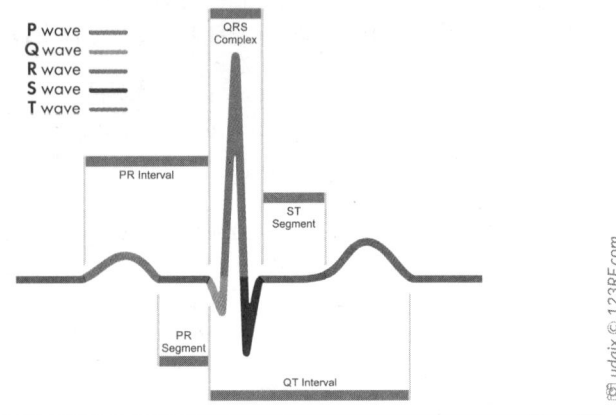

ECG SHOWING NORMAL SINUS RHYTHM

P wave
Q wave
R wave
S wave
T wave

QRS Complex

PR Interval

ST Segment

PR Segment

QT Interval

udaix © 123RF.com

CHAPTER 32

ARRHYTHMIAS

BACKGROUND

The term conduction means to transmit electrical charges (or heat) through a substance. The cardiac conduction system is the electrical signaling system that causes the atria and ventricles to contract, which pushes the blood forward. Blood flows in one direction in the body, through the heart chambers (from the atria to the ventricles), then to the lungs (to pick up oxygen) or to the body (to provide oxygen and nutrients). The "lub-dub" sounds heard through auscultation (listening to the heart with a stethoscope) are made by the closing of heart valves that occur in sequence with each heartbeat.

The first heart sound (S1) signals the beginning of ventricular systole (systole means to contract), and the second heart sound (S2) signals the end of ventricular systole. Sounds other than S1 and S2 are abnormal (e.g., S3, a murmur which is common in heart failure). Murmurs are caused by turbulent blood flow or regurgitation (i.e., blood flowing in the wrong direction).

A normal heartbeat has a relatively steady rate and a regular, coordinated rhythm. An arrhythmia is an abnormal heart rhythm, which can cause the heart to beat too slow (bradycardia) or too fast (tachycardia). Any change from the normal sequence of electrical impulses can cause an arrhythmia. When the electrical impulses are too fast, too slow, or erratic, the heart cannot pump blood efficiently, and symptoms can develop.

SYMPTOMS AND DIAGNOSIS

Some arrhythmias are silent (asymptomatic) and might only be detected during a medical exam. With other arrhythmias, patients can feel that the heart is beating very fast, "fluttering" in their chest or "skipping a beat." Symptoms can include dizziness, shortness of breath, fatigue, lightheadedness and chest pain. In severe cases, arrhythmias can lead to syncope (loss of consciousness due to decreased cardiac output), heart failure or death.

CONTENT LEGEND

= Study Tip Gal   = Key Drug Guy

An electrocardiogram (ECG) is used to diagnose arrhythmias. An ECG machine records the electrical activity of the heart using electrodes placed on the skin. An ECG recorded in a medical office will pick up an arrhythmia only if it is present while the ECG is being conducted.

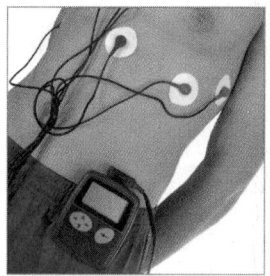

papa1266 © 123RF.com

A Holter monitor (see image to the left) is an ambulatory ECG device that records the electrical activity of the heart for 24 – 48 hours. It is used to detect arrhythmias that are intermittent [i.e., the heart goes in and out of normal sinus rhythm (NSR)]. Other monitoring devices are available, such as select smart watches and the *Zio* patch heart monitor. *Zio* is a wireless adhesive patch placed directly on the chest and worn for up to 14 days.

NORMAL SINUS RHYTHM

NSR originates (begins) in the sinoatrial (SA, or sinus) node. The SA node is the heart's natural pacemaker; this is where the electrical signal for a heartbeat begins, and the frequency of the signals determines the pace, or heart rate. A normal heart rate is 60 to 100 BPM.

A normal rhythm has the characteristic appearance shown on the ECG printout below, with a distinct pattern for each heartbeat that represents the various waves (e.g., P and T waves) and segments (e.g., the QRS complex). See the image at the beginning of the chapter.

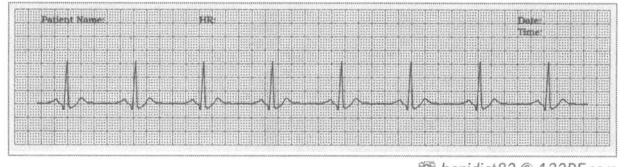

benidict83 © 123RF.com

THE CARDIAC CONDUCTION PATHWAY

The cardiac conduction pathway consists of a group of specialized cardiac cells (myocytes) that send electrical impulses (signals) to the heart muscle, causing it to contract. The main components include the SA node, AV node, bundle of His, bundle branches and Purkinje fibers. The conduction pathway can be traced by following the numbers in the next image.

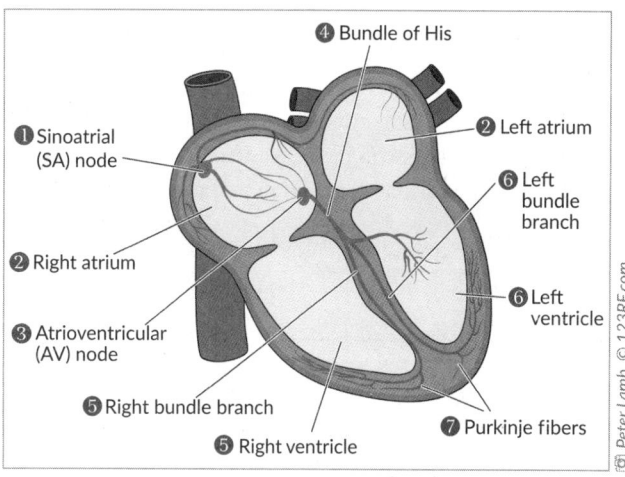

© Peter Lamb © 123RF.com

1. The electrical impulse begins in the SA node, which is a cluster of cells located at the junction of the superior vena cava and the right atrium.

2. The impulse then travels from the SA node to the right and left atria, which causes the atria to contract.

3. When the signal reaches the atrioventricular (AV) node, electrical conduction slows down.

4. The impulse continues through the bundle of His and into the ventricles.

5. The bundle of His divides into the right bundle branch for the right ventricle, and

6. The left bundle branch for the left ventricle.

7. The signal continues to spread through the ventricles via the Purkinje fibers, which causes the ventricles to contract.

Any disruption in the normal sequence of impulse conduction can result in an arrhythmia (see Study Tip Gal below).

THE HEART'S NATURAL PACEMAKER AND ARRHYTHMIAS

The rate and rhythm of the heartbeat are set by the rapidly firing cells in the sinoatrial (SA, or sinus) node. The SA node is called the heart's natural pacemaker.

An arrhythmia is caused by a disruption somewhere in the conduction (electrical signaling) system:

- The SA node can be firing at an abnormal rate or rhythm.

- Scar tissue from a prior heart attack can block and divert signal transmission.

- Another part of the heart may be acting as the pacemaker.

ELECTRICAL SIGNALING: THE CARDIAC ACTION POTENTIAL

The cardiac action potential refers to the movement of ions through channels in the myocytes that cause the electrical impulses in the cardiac conduction pathway. In essence, the action potentials provide the electricity needed to power the heart. The SA (pacemaker) cells have automaticity, which means that, unlike other myocytes, the pacemaker cells initiate their own action potential (the cells spontaneously depolarize and do not require external stimulation). The action potential of a ventricular myocyte is triggered when a threshold voltage is reached. This occurs in 5 phases (see image below labeled with Phases 0, 1, 2, 3 and 4).

- Phase 0: a heartbeat is initiated when rapid ventricular depolarization occurs in response to an influx of Na; this causes ventricular contraction (represented by the QRS complex on the ECG).

- Phase 1: early rapid repolarization (Na channels close).

- Phase 2: a plateau in response to an influx of Ca and efflux of K.

- Phase 3: rapid ventricular repolarization occurs in response to an efflux of K; this causes ventricular relaxation (represented by the T wave on the ECG).

- Phase 4: resting membrane potential is established; atrial depolarization occurs (represented by the P wave on the ECG).

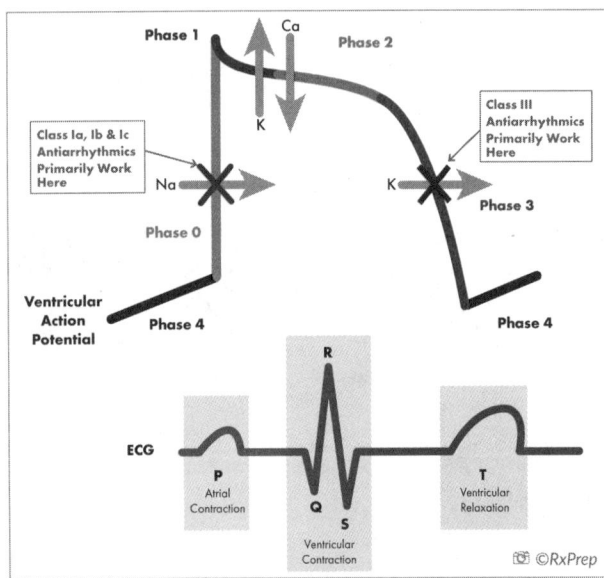

Depolarization/repolarization of cardiac cells must be properly sequenced and coordinated to produce the net ECG effects shown.

ARRHYTHMIAS

Abnormalities of the heart or its conduction system can alter the cardiac action potential and lead to arrhythmias. The most common cause of arrhythmias is myocardial ischemia or infarction. Other conditions resulting in damage to cardiac tissue can cause arrhythmias, including heart valve disorders, hypertension and heart failure.

Non-cardiac conditions that can trigger or predispose a patient to an arrhythmia include electrolyte imbalances (especially potassium, magnesium, sodium and calcium), elevated sympathetic states (e.g., hyperthyroidism, infection) and drugs (including illicit drugs, antiarrhythmics and drugs that prolong the QT interval).

Arrhythmias are generally classified into two broad categories based on their point of origin: supraventricular (originating above the AV node) and ventricular (originating below the AV node). Arrhythmias originating in or just below the atrioventricular node are called junctional rhythms, which are less common.

SUPRAVENTRICULAR ARRHYTHMIAS

These include sinus tachycardia, atrial fibrillation, atrial flutter, atrial tachycardia and supraventricular re-entrant tachycardias (formerly known as paroxysmal supraventricular tachycardias or PSVTs). Many patients have ongoing supraventricular arrhythmias (especially atrial fibrillation) without realizing it.

Atrial fibrillation (AF) is the most common type of arrhythmia. It occurs when multiple waves of electrical impulses in the atria result in an irregular (and usually rapid) ventricular response. The rapid ventricular rate can decrease cardiac output (because the ventricles do not have time to fill), which can lead to hypotension and worsen underlying ischemia and heart failure.

In addition, due to the disorganized depolarization of the atria, they cannot adequately contract. Blood becomes stagnant in the atria, which increases the risk of clot formation. A clot can embolize (break off and travel) to an artery in the brain, which can block blood flow and cause a stroke. To reduce clotting risk, patients with AF may require anticoagulation (see the Anticoagulation chapter).

Atrial flutter is more organized and regular than AF. It occurs most often in patients with underlying heart disease or COPD, and it can progress to AF.

VENTRICULAR ARRHYTHMIAS

Common ventricular arrhythmias include premature ventricular contractions (PVCs), ventricular tachycardia and ventricular fibrillation. PVCs are relatively common and occur in people both with and without heart disease. They are referred to as a skipped heartbeat. PVCs are generated from within the ventricular tissue. In some people, it can be related to stress or too much caffeine, nicotine or exercise.

A series of PVCs in a row, resulting in a heart rate of greater than 100 BPM, is known as ventricular tachycardia (VT). VT is further classified based on the presence or absence of a detectable peripheral pulse. VT with a pulse is treated with antiarrhythmics, whereas pulseless VT is a medical emergency, and advanced cardiac life support (ACLS) should be initiated. Untreated VT can degenerate into ventricular fibrillation (completely disorganized electrical activation of the ventricles), which is also a medical emergency.

QT PROLONGATION & TORSADE DE POINTES

The QT interval is measured from the beginning of the QRS complex to the end of the T wave on an ECG. It reflects ventricular depolarization and repolarization and varies with heart rate (the QT interval is longer when the heart rate is slower). A QT interval can be used if the heart rate is ≤ 60 BPM; when the heart rate is > 60 BPM, a QT interval corrected for heart rate (QTc) is used. A QTc interval is considered prolonged when it is > 440 milliseconds (msec), but is more worrisome when markedly prolonged (> 500 msec).

Prolongation of the QT interval is a risk factor for Torsade de Pointes (TdP), a particularly lethal ventricular tachyarrhythmia that can cause sudden cardiac death.

QT Prolongation Risk Factors

See the Key Drugs Guy for drugs that can prolong the QT interval. The risk of drug-induced QT prolongation increases with:

- Higher doses (risk is concentration-dependent).
- Multiple QT-prolonging drugs taken at the same time (additive effects).
- Reduced drug clearance due to renal disease, liver disease, or drug interactions (e.g., enzyme inhibitors).
- Electrolyte abnormalities, including low potassium (hypokalemia), magnesium (hypomagnesemia) and calcium (hypocalcemia).
- Other cardiac conditions; cardiac damage is a risk for arrhythmias, including TdP.
- Female gender.

QT Risk Requires Assessment

In addition to recognizing the drugs that prolong the QT interval, assessing patient risk for TdP will be required. For example, if low-dose amitriptyline is being used for neuropathic pain, the dose is not particularly risky; but if the same patient is admitted to the hospital with hypokalemia and started on fluconazole and ondansetron, the level of concern would be heightened.

SELECT DRUGS THAT CAN INCREASE OR PROLONG THE QT INTERVAL

Antiarrhythmics
Class Ia, Ic and III

Anti-infectives
Antimalarials (e.g., hydroxychloroquine)
Azole antifungals (all except isavuconazonium)
Macrolides
Quinolones
Lefamulin

Antidepressants
SSRIs (highest risk with citalopram and escitalopram)
Tricyclic antidepressants
Mirtazapine, trazodone, venlafaxine

Antiemetics
5-HT3 receptor antagonists
Droperidol, metoclopramide, promethazine

Antipsychotics
First generation (e.g., haloperidol, chlorpromazine, thioridazine)
Second generation (highest risk with ziprasidone)

Oncology medications
Androgen deprivation therapy (e.g., leuprolide)
Tyrosine kinase inhibitors (e.g., nilotinib)
Oxaliplatin

Other
Cilostazol, donepezil, fingolimod, hydroxyzine, loperamide, methadone, ranolazine, solifenacin, tacrolimus

ANTIARRHYTHMIC DRUGS

Antiarrhythmic drugs work by affecting the electrical currents in the cells of the heart. By blocking the movement of ions in different phases of the cardiac action potential (discussed previously), select drugs can reduce conduction velocity and/or automaticity, or prolong the refractory period, which can slow or terminate the abnormal electrical activity causing the arrhythmia. However, antiarrhythmic drugs are not without risk and can occasionally worsen the existing arrhythmia or cause other arrhythmias.

CARDIOVASCULAR CONDITIONS

Ventricular arrhythmias are managed in a hospital or emergent setting. Supraventricular arrhythmias (e.g., AF) are managed in both inpatient and outpatient settings, making it a commonly encountered condition by pharmacists.

Prior to starting any drug for a non-life-threatening arrhythmia, electrolytes and a toxicology screen should be checked to identify reversible causes.

VAUGHAN WILLIAMS CLASSIFICATION

The Vaughan Williams classification system is most commonly used for antiarrhythmic drugs; it splits the drugs into categories based on their dominant electrophysiological effect (see the Study Tip Gal to the right). It has the virtue of simplicity, though many drugs overlap into more than one category.

CLASSIFYING DRUGS WITH VAUGHAN WILLIAMS

CLASS I
Ia: **D**isopyramide, **Q**uinidine, **P**rocainamide
Ib: **L**idocaine, **M**exiletine
Ic: **F**lecainide, **P**ropafenone

CLASS II
Beta-blockers

CLASS III
Dronedarone, **D**ofetilide, **S**otalol, **I**butilide, **A**miodarone

CLASS IV
Verapamil, **D**iltiazem

Remember:
Double **Q**uarter **P**ounder, **L**ettuce, **M**ayo, **F**ries **P**lease!
Because **D**ieting **D**uring **S**tress **I**s **A**lways **V**ery **D**ifficult

ANTIARRHYTHMIC DRUGS: MECHANISMS OF ACTION

CLASS	MECHANISM	CONSEQUENCE
Class I	Na-channel blockers	Reduces the speed of ion conduction through sodium channels.
		Proarrhythmic (higher risk of arrhythmia) and negative inotropic potential, which ↓ the force of ventricular contraction. Use caution in patients with underlying cardiac disease.
Class II	Beta-blockers	Blocks the sympathetic activity that can trigger an arrhythmia; indirectly blocks calcium channels, which ↓ ion conduction speed. Used primarily to slow ventricular rate in AF.
Class III	K-channel blockers	Amiodarone and dronedarone block K channels (primarily), Ca channels, Na channels, and alpha- and beta-adrenergic receptors.
		Amiodarone is useful for different types of arrhythmias, including AF.
		Amiodarone and dofetilide are preferentially used for AF in patients with HF.
		Sotalol blocks K channels and is a beta-blocker.
Class IV	Ca-channel blockers, non-dihydropyridine (non-DHP)	Used primarily to slow ventricular rate in AF. Negative inotropic effect (↓ contraction force), which can cause cardiac decompensation; do not use verapamil or diltiazem in patients with heart failure and reduced ejection fraction (HFrEF).
Digoxin	Na-K-ATPase blocker	Suppresses AV node conduction (↓ heart rate) by enhancing vagal tone and ↑ force of contraction (positive inotrope).
Adenosine	Activates adenosine receptors to ↓ AV node conduction	Used for paroxysmal supraventricular tachyarrhythmias (PSVTs).

TREATMENT STRATEGIES FOR ATRIAL FIBRILLATION

There are a few different types of AF (see table below). Guideline-recommended treatment for most types of AF involves using one of two main strategies: rate control and rhythm control (see the Study Tip Gal on the following page).

TYPE OF AF	DEFINITION
Paroxysmal	AF that terminates spontaneously or with intervention within 7 days of onset; episodes may recur with variable frequency
Persistent	Continuous AF that is sustained > 7 days
Long-standing persistent	Continuous AF that is sustained > 12 months
Permanent	Term used when a joint decision has been made by the clinician and patient to cease further attempts to restore and/or maintain NSR; this is a treatment choice rather than a characteristic of the arrhythmia itself
Valvular	AF with moderate to severe mitral stenosis or with a mechanical heart valve; long-term anticoagulation with warfarin is indicated
Non-valvular	AF without moderate to severe mitral stenosis or a mechanical heart valve

Rate Control

The goal resting HR is < 80 BPM in patients with symptomatic AF; however, a more lenient goal of ≤ 110 BPM may be reasonable in patients who are asymptomatic and have preserved left ventricular function.

Beta-blockers (preferred) or non-DHP calcium channel blockers (CCBs) are recommended for controlling ventricular rate in patients with AF. Of note, patients with heart failure with reduced ejection fraction (HFrEF) should not receive a non-DHP CCB. Digoxin is not first-line for ventricular rate control, but can be added for refractory patients or used in those who cannot tolerate beta-blockers or non-DHP CCBs.

Rhythm Control

Rhythm control consists of methods for conversion to NSR and maintenance of NSR. Conversion to NSR is most effective with direct current (electrical) cardioversion, a medical procedure that delivers a high-energy shock through the chest wall. The shock breaks the incorrect cycle, stops the arrhythmia and allows the sinus node to begin firing again with a NSR (see image below).

Medications that can be used for pharmacologic cardioversion include amiodarone (oral and IV), dofetilide, flecainide, ibutilide and propafenone.

Cardioversion has a high risk of thromboembolism. If the patient is not already using therapeutic anticoagulation, it should be started at least three weeks before cardioversion and continued for at least four weeks after successful cardioversion to NSR. If using warfarin, the goal INR should be 2 – 3.

AF: RATE VS. RHYTHM CONTROL & STROKE PROPHYLAXIS

Rate Control
- Patient remains in AF and takes medications to control the ventricular rate (HR).
  - Beta-blockers or non-DHP CCBs are used (and sometimes digoxin).

Rhythm Control
- The goal is to restore and maintain NSR.
  - Class Ia, Ic or III antiarrhythmic drugs or electrical cardioversion.
- If AF is permanent, avoid a rhythm-control strategy with antiarrhythmic drugs (risk outweighs the benefit).

Stroke Prophylaxis
- Clots can form when a patient is in AF, which can embolize (causing a stroke) when the patient returns to NSR.
- For many patients, it is safer to remain in AF with rate control than to try to restore NSR. A rate control strategy may require anticoagulation for stroke prevention, depending on the CHA₂DS₂-VASc score (see the Anticoagulation chapter).
  - NOACs (e.g., apixaban, rivaroxaban) are preferred over warfarin for stroke prevention in non-valvular AF.
  - Warfarin is indicated for stroke prevention in patients with AF and a mechanical heart valve.
- When a rhythm control strategy is chosen, restoration and maintenance of NSR are not guaranteed. The decision for long-term anticoagulation will depend on the patient's clot risk.

For maintenance of NSR, recommended options include dofetilide, dronedarone, flecainide, propafenone or sotalol. Due to toxicities, amiodarone is recommended only when other drugs have failed or are contraindicated (e.g., amiodarone is used in heart failure). Despite this, amiodarone is the top-selling antiarrhythmic in the U.S.

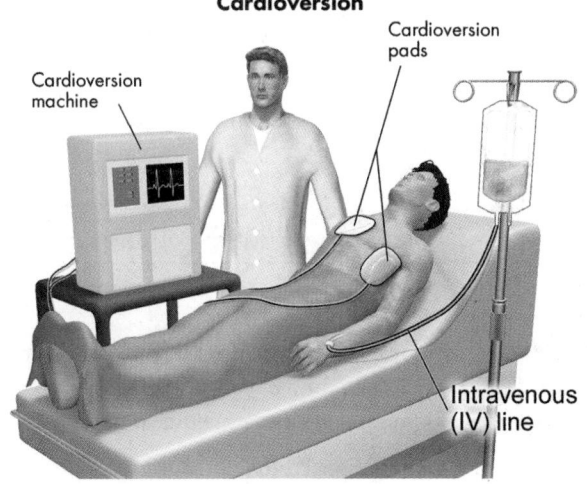

Cardioversion

© Blausen.com staff (2014)

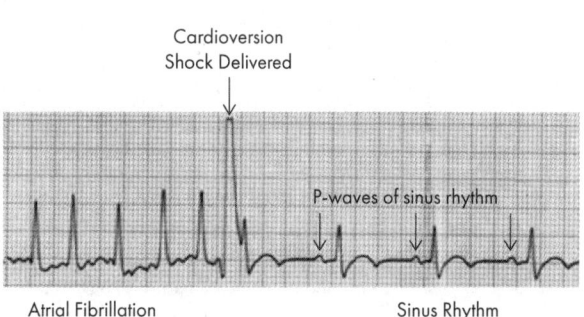

COMMON ANTIARRHYTHMICS

Drugs commonly used in the treatment of arrhythmias include amiodarone (Class III), non-DHP CCBs (diltiazem and verapamil, Class IV), beta-blockers (Class II) and digoxin. Beta-blockers are reviewed in the Hypertension and Chronic Heart Failure chapters. The other antiarrhythmics are used less commonly, but many have toxicities that require careful attention [e.g., cinchonism (another name for quinine or quinidine toxicity), DILE with procainamide]; see the Other Antiarrhythmics section.

Amiodarone

DRUG	DOSING	SAFETY/SIDE EFFECTS/MONITORING
Amiodarone (*Nexterone, Pacerone*) Tablet, injection	Pulseless VT/VF: 300 mg IV push x 1, may repeat 150 mg x 1 if needed VT with pulse: 150 mg IV bolus, then 1 mg/min x 6 hours, then 0.5 mg/min x 18 hours or longer Secondary prevention of ventricular arrhythmias: 800-1,600 mg/day x 1-3 weeks, then 600-800 mg/day x 4 weeks, then 400 mg/day AF/atrial flutter – cardioversion (off-label): 600-800 mg/day PO until a 10 gram loading dose is reached, then 200 mg daily AF/atrial flutter – maintenance of NSR (off-label): 400-600 mg/day for 2-4 weeks, then 100-200 mg daily t½ = 40-60 days Takes at least 1 week, up to 5 months, for peak response	**BOXED WARNINGS** Pulmonary toxicity: check baseline chest X-ray, PFTs Hepatotoxicity: check baseline LFTs For life-threatening arrhythmias only; proarrhythmic, must be hospitalized for IV loading dose **CONTRAINDICATIONS** Iodine hypersensitivity, severe sinus-node dysfunction causing marked ↓ HR, 2nd/3rd-degree heart block (unless using artificial pacemaker), bradycardia causing syncope, cardiogenic shock **WARNINGS** Hyper- and hypothyroidism (hypo is more common) – amiodarone partially inhibits peripheral conversion of T4 to T3, optic neuropathy (visual impairment), photosensitivity (slate-blue skin discoloration), neurotoxicity (peripheral neuropathy), severe skin reactions (SJS/TEN) Correct hypokalemia, hypomagnesemia, hypocalcemia prior to use **SIDE EFFECTS** Hypotension, bradycardia, corneal microdeposits, photosensitivity (sun protection required), dizziness, tremor/ataxia, malaise/fatigue, nausea, drug-induced lupus erythematosus (DILE) **MONITORING** ECG, BP, HR, electrolytes LFTs every 6 months, thyroid function (TSH and free T4) every 3-6 months, chest X-ray at least annually, regular eye exams **NOTES** Infusions > 2 hours require a non-PVC container (e.g., polyolefin or glass); PVC tubing is okay Premixed IV bags: longer stability, non-PVC, available in common concentrations (e.g., *Nexterone* comes in non-PVC, non-DEHP GALAXY plastic container) Antiarrhythmic drug of choice in heart failure Decrease infusion rate or discontinue as needed for hypotension or bradycardia Oral/IV can provide rate control (due to beta-blocking properties) when other measures are unsuccessful or contraindicated. IV: use 0.22 micron filter; central line preferable Incompatible with heparin (flush line with saline); many Y-site, additive incompatibilities Amiodarone (chemical structure) contains iodine Teratogenic, excreted in breast milk: avoid in pregnancy/breastfeeding when possible

Amiodarone Drug Interactions

- Amiodarone can increase the level of many other drugs; it is an inhibitor of CYP450 2C9 (moderate), 2D6 (moderate), 3A4 (weak) and P-gp.
- Amiodarone is often given with drugs that it interacts with (common cardiovascular drug interactions are reviewed in the Drug Interactions chapter). When starting amiodarone:
  - ↓ digoxin by 50%, ↓ warfarin by 30 – 50% and do not exceed 20 mg/day of simvastatin or 40 mg/day of lovastatin (consider use of alternative statin).

- Additive effects can occur when used with other drugs that decrease HR, including non-DHP CCB, digoxin, beta-blockers, clonidine and dexmedetomidine (*Precedex*).
- Sofosbuvir can enhance the bradycardic effect of amiodarone; do not use together.

Non-DHP Calcium Channel Blockers

DRUG	DOSING	SAFETY/SIDE EFFECTS/MONITORING
Diltiazem (Cardizem, Tiazac, Cardizem CD, Cardizem LA, Cartia XT, others) Tablet, capsule, injection	120-360 mg PO daily	**CONTRAINDICATIONS** HFrEF, severe hypotension (SBP < 90 mmHg), 2nd/3rd-degree heart block/sick sinus syndrome (unless the patient has a pacemaker), cardiogenic shock, Wolff-Parkinson-White syndrome with AF **WARNINGS** Hypotension, heart failure (may worsen symptoms), 1st-degree AV block with sinus bradycardia, ↑ LFTs **SIDE EFFECTS**
Verapamil (Calan SR, Verelan, Verelan PM) Tablet, capsule, injection	180-480 mg PO daily	Edema, arrhythmias, constipation (more with verapamil), gingival hyperplasia, HA, dizziness **MONITORING** ECG, BP, HR, electrolytes, LFTs **NOTES** Only non-DHP CCBs are used as antiarrhythmics

Verapamil and Diltiazem Drug Interactions

- Additive effects can occur when used with other drugs that decrease HR, including amiodarone, digoxin, beta-blockers, clonidine and dexmedetomidine (Precedex).
- Non-DHP CCBs are CYP3A4 substrates. Use strong CYP3A4 inducers/inhibitors with caution, and in some cases, avoid. Check for drug interactions when starting, and do not take with grapefruit.
- Diltiazem and verapamil are substrates of P-gp and inhibitors of CYP3A4. They can increase the concentration of many other drugs. Patients who take statins should use lower doses of simvastatin or lovastatin (see the Dyslipidemia chapter) or use a statin that is not metabolized by CYP3A4 (e.g., pitavastatin, pravastatin, rosuvastatin).

Digoxin

DRUG	DOSING	SAFETY/SIDE EFFECTS/MONITORING
Digoxin (Digitek, Digox, Lanoxin) Tablet, solution, injection Tablet strengths: 0.0625, 0.125, 0.1875, 0.25 mg	Typical dose: 0.125-0.25 mg PO daily Loading dose [called total digitalizing dose (TDD)]: 8-12 mcg/kg IBW Give ½ of the TDD as the initial dose, followed by ¼ of the TDD in 2 subsequent doses at 4-8 hour intervals (alternatively, give 0.25 mg IV and repeat dosing to a max of 1.5 mg over 24 hours) Therapeutic range = 0.8-2 ng/mL for AF (lower range for HF) CrCl < 50 mL/min: ↓ dose or ↓ frequency; hold in acute renal failure ↓ dose by 20-25% when converting from oral to IV	**CONTRAINDICATIONS** Ventricular fibrillation **WARNINGS** 2nd/3rd-degree heart block without a pacemaker, Wolff-Parkinson-White syndrome with AF, vesicant (avoid extravasation) **SIDE EFFECTS** Dizziness, mental disturbances, N/V/D **MONITORING** ECG, HR, BP, electrolytes, renal function and digoxin level (drawn 12-24 hrs after dose) **Toxicity** Initial s/sx of toxicity: N/V, loss of appetite and bradycardia Severe s/sx of toxicity: blurred/double vision, greenish-yellow halos around lights or objects, altered color perception, abdominal pain, confusion, delirium, prolonged PR interval, arrhythmias **NOTES** Not usually given alone for rate control (used in combination with a beta-blocker or non-DHP CCB) Antidote: DigiFab Hypokalemia, hypomagnesemia and hypercalcemia ↑ the risk of digoxin toxicity Hypothyroidism can ↑ digoxin levels

Digoxin Drug Interactions

- Digoxin is a substrate of P-gp. Levels ↑ with inhibitors, including amiodarone, dronedarone, diltiazem, verapamil, clarithromycin, itraconazole and many other drugs. With amiodarone or dronedarone, ↓ digoxin dose by 50%.
- Additive effects can occur when used with other drugs that decrease HR, including amiodarone, non-DHP CCB, beta-blockers, clonidine and dexmedetomidine (Precedex).

OTHER ANTIARRHYTHMICS

DRUG	DOSING	SAFETY/SIDE EFFECTS/MONITORING
Class Ia Drugs Block sodium channels		
Disopyramide *(Norpace, Norpace CR)* Capsule	400-600 mg/day Take on an empty stomach	**BOXED WARNING** Reserve use for patients with life-threatening ventricular arrhythmias **CONTRAINDICATIONS** 2nd/3rd-degree heart block (unless patient has a functional artificial pacemaker), cardiogenic shock, congenital QT syndrome, sick sinus syndrome **WARNINGS** Proarrhythmic, hypotension, HF, BPH/urinary retention/narrow-angle glaucoma, myasthenia gravis (due to anticholinergic effects) **SIDE EFFECTS** Anticholinergic effects (e.g., dry mouth, constipation, urinary retention), hypotension
Quinidine Tablet	IR: 400 mg PO Q6H ER: 300-648 mg PO Q8-12H Take with food or milk to ↓ GI upset Different salt forms are not interchangeable (267 mg of gluconate = 200 mg of sulfate form)	**BOXED WARNING** May ↑ mortality in treatment of AF or atrial flutter; control AV conduction before initiating **CONTRAINDICATIONS** Concurrent use of quinolones that prolong the QT interval or ritonavir; 2nd/3rd-degree heart block or idioventricular conduction delays (unless patient has a functional artificial pacemaker), thrombocytopenia, thrombotic thrombocytopenic purpura (TTP), myasthenia gravis **WARNINGS** Proarrhythmic, hepatotoxicity, hemolysis risk (avoid in G6PD deficiency), can cause positive Coombs test **SIDE EFFECTS** Drug-induced lupus erythematosus (DILE), diarrhea (35%), stomach cramping (22%), rash, lightheadedness Cinchonism (e.g., quinidine overdose): symptoms include tinnitus, hearing loss, blurred vision, headache, delirium) **NOTES** Avoid changes in Na intake; ↓ Na intake can ↑ quinidine levels Alkaline foods/alkaline urine ↑ quinidine levels and can lead to toxicity
Procainamide Injection Drug of choice for Wolff-Parkinson-White syndrome	Active metabolite, N-acetyl procainamide (NAPA), is renally cleared; ↓ dose when CrCl < 50 mL/min **Therapeutic levels:** Procainamide: 4-10 mcg/mL NAPA: 15-25 mcg/mL Combined: 10-30 mcg/mL Draw level 6-12 hrs after IV infusion has started	**BOXED WARNINGS** Potentially fatal blood dyscrasias (e.g., agranulocytosis); monitor patient closely in the first 3 months and periodically thereafter Long-term use leads to positive antinuclear antibody (ANA) in 50% of patients, which can result in drug-induced lupus erythematosus (DILE) in 20-30% of patients Reserve use for patients with life-threatening ventricular arrhythmias **CONTRAINDICATIONS** Heart block, systemic lupus erythematosus, TdP **WARNINGS** Proarrhythmic **SIDE EFFECTS** Hypotension, rash **NOTES** Metabolism of procainamide to NAPA occurs by acetylation: slow acetylators are at risk for drug accumulation and toxicity; fast acetylators can have subtherapeutic drug concentrations and reduced efficacy

Class Ib Drugs
Block sodium channels; useful for ventricular arrhythmias only (no efficacy in AF)

Lidocaine *(Xylocaine)* Injection Used for refractory VT/cardiac arrest	Bolus dosing: 1-1.5 mg/kg x 1, then 0.5-0.75 mg/kg every 5-10 minutes (max total dose 3 mg/kg) Continuous infusion: 1-4 mg/minute	**BOXED WARNINGS** Mexiletine: reserve use for patients with life-threatening ventricular arrhythmias, abnormal liver function seen in patients with CHF or ischemia **CONTRAINDICATIONS** 2nd/3rd-degree heart block (unless patient has a functional artificial pacemaker) Lidocaine: Wolff-Parkinson-White syndrome, Adam-Stokes syndrome, allergy to corn or corn-related products or amide-type anesthetics Mexiletine: cardiogenic shock
Mexiletine Capsule	200 mg PO Q8H; max 1.2 grams/day Take with food	**WARNINGS** Caution in the elderly, hepatic impairment and HF Mexiletine: blood dyscrasias, severe skin reactions (DRESS) **NOTES** Lidocaine is primarily used topically or locally for numbing; see the Acute & Critical Care Medicine and Pain chapters

Class Ic Drugs
Block sodium channels

Flecainide Tablet	50-100 mg PO Q12H; max 400 mg/day Store in tight, light-resistant container	**BOXED WARNINGS** When treating atrial flutter, 1:1 atrioventricular conduction may occur; pre-emptive negative chronotropic therapy (e.g., digoxin, beta-blockers) can ↓ the risk Proarrhythmic effects, especially in AF (do not use in chronic AF) Reserve use for patients with life-threatening ventricular arrhythmias **CONTRAINDICATIONS** 2nd/3rd-degree heart block (unless patient has a functional artificial pacemaker), cardiogenic shock, structural heart disease (e.g., heart failure, myocardial infarction), concurrent use of ritonavir **WARNINGS** Avoid use in severe hepatic impairment **SIDE EFFECTS** Dizziness, visual disturbances, dyspnea
Propafenone *(Rythmol SR)* IR tablet, ER capsule	Dose varies based on indication	**BOXED WARNINGS** Reserve use for patients with life-threatening ventricular arrhythmias **CONTRAINDICATIONS** Sinoatrial and atrioventricular disorders (unless patient has a functional artificial pacemaker), sinus bradycardia, cardiogenic shock, hypotension, structural heart disease (e.g., heart failure, myocardial infarction), bronchospastic disorders **WARNINGS** Proarrhythmic **SIDE EFFECTS** Taste disturbance (metallic), dizziness, visual disturbances, N/V **NOTES** Propafenone has significant beta-blocking effects, negative inotropic and proarrhythmic properties (contraindicated in HF)

Class III Drugs
Primarily block potassium channels; see the Common Antiarrhythmics section for amiodarone

Dronedarone (*Multaq*) Tablet	400 mg PO Q12H Take with meals Prior to initiation, class I or III antiarrhythmics or strong CYP3A4 inhibitors must be stopped	**BOXED WARNINGS** Increased risk of death, stroke and HF in patients with decompensated HF (NYHA Class IV, or any NYHA class with a recent hospitalization due to HF) or permanent AF **CONTRAINDICATIONS** Concurrent use of strong CYP3A4 inhibitors and QT-prolonging drugs, pregnancy, 2nd/3rd-degree heart block (unless patient has a functional artificial pacemaker), symptomatic HF, HR < 50 BPM, QTc ≥ 500 msec, PR interval > 280 msec, lung or liver toxicity from previous amiodarone use, hepatic impairment, nursing mothers **WARNINGS** Hepatic failure (especially in the first 6 months), pulmonary disease (including pulmonary fibrosis and pneumonitis), marked ↑ SCr, prerenal azotemia and ARF (usually in the setting of heart failure or hypovolemia), ↓ Mg and ↓ K with administration of K-depleting diuretics **SIDE EFFECTS** QT prolongation, ↑ SCr, diarrhea, bradycardia, asthenia **NOTES** Unlike amiodarone, dronedarone does not contain iodine and has little effect on thyroid function Dronedarone is a moderate inhibitor of CYP2D6, 3A4 and P-gp and a major substrate of CYP3A4; avoid use with strong inhibitors and inducers of CYP3A4 and with drugs that prolong the QT interval; ↓ digoxin dose by 50% and use lower doses of statins metabolized by CYP3A4, or use alternate statin; monitor INR if on warfarin
Sotalol (*Betapace AF, Betapace, Sotylize, Sorine*) Tablet, solution, injection Non-selective beta-blocker (in addition to blocking K channels)	CrCl < 60 mL/min: ↓ frequency CrCl < 40 mL/min: varies by formulation	**BOXED WARNINGS** Initiation (or reinitiation) and dosage increases should be done in a hospital with continuous ECG monitoring and experienced staff Adjust dosing interval based on CrCl to ↓ risk of proarrhythmia; QT prolongation is directly related to sotalol concentration **CONTRAINDICATIONS** 2nd/3rd-degree heart block (unless patient has a functional artificial pacemaker), congenital or acquired long QT syndrome, sinus bradycardia, uncontrolled HF, cardiogenic shock, asthma For *Betapace AF, Sotylize*, sotalol injection: QTc > 450 msec, bronchospastic conditions, CrCl < 40 mL/min, K < 4 mEq/L, sick sinus syndrome **SIDE EFFECTS** Bradycardia, palpitations, chest pain, dizziness, fatigue, dyspnea, N/V, TdP, HF, bronchoconstriction **NOTES** *Betapace* should not be substituted with *Betapace AF* since *Betapace AF* is distributed with educational information specifically for patients with AF/atrial flutter
Ibutilide (*Corvert*) Injection Indicated only for pharmacologic conversion to NSR	1 mg over 10 minutes (0.01 mg/kg < if 60 kg)	**BOXED WARNING** Proarrhythmic; confirm that benefits of maintaining NSR outweigh the risks **SIDE EFFECTS** Ventricular tachycardias (e.g., TdP), hypotension, QT prolongation **NOTES** Correct hypokalemia and hypomagnesemia prior to use and throughout treatment
Dofetilide (*Tikosyn*) Capsule	CrCl < 60 mL/min: ↓ dose CrCl < 20 mL/min: contraindicated	**BOXED WARNING** Must be initiated (or reinitiated) in a setting with continuous ECG monitoring, experienced staff and ability to assess CrCl for a minimum of 3 days; proarrhythmic (QT prolongation) **CONTRAINDICATIONS** Prolonged QTc > 440 msec at baseline; do not use with cimetidine, dolutegravir, hydrochlorothiazide, itraconazole, ketoconazole, megestrol, prochlorperazine, trimethoprim, verapamil (these drugs can inhibit renal tubular secretion of dofetilide) **SIDE EFFECTS** Ventricular tachycardias (e.g., TdP), ↑ QT interval **NOTES** Antiarrhythmic drug of choice in heart failure

Adenosine
Not Included in Vaughan Williams classification system

Adenosine (*Adenocard*) Injection	6 mg IV push (may increase to 12 mg if not responding) $t_{½}$: less than 10 sec Used in paroxysmal supraventricular tachycardia (PSVTs); do not use for ventricular tachycardia or for converting AF/atrial flutter	**CONTRAINDICATIONS** 2nd/3rd-degree heart block, sick sinus syndrome or symptomatic bradycardia (except in patients with a functional pacemaker), bronchospastic lung disease **SIDE EFFECTS** Transient new arrhythmia, facial flushing, chest pain/pressure, GI distress, transient ↓ in blood pressure, dyspnea

KEY COUNSELING POINTS

See the Drug Formulations and Patient Counseling chapter for counseling language/layman's terminology. See the Drug Interactions section for each class.

Amiodarone
- Can cause:
  - Lung damage.
  - Liver damage.
  - Eye damage (nerve damage and corneal deposits).
  - Hypothyroidism or hyperthyroidism.
  - Photosensitivity.
  - Skin discoloration to a blue-gray color. Not a harmful effect; usually goes away months after the medication is stopped.
- Avoid grapefruit.
- Many drug interactions (enzyme inhibitor).

Digoxin
- Early symptoms of overdose include loss of appetite and nausea. If this occurs, check heart rate. If bradycardic, a digoxin level should be checked.
- Symptoms of severe overdose include vision changes (e.g., blurred or yellow/green vision), confusion, hallucinations and feeling like you might pass out.
- Avoid dehydration; an overdose can occur more easily if you are dehydrated.
- Many drug interactions.

Select Guidelines/References

2019 AHA/ACC/HRS Focused Update of the 2014 AHA/ACC/HRS Guideline for the Management of Patients With Atrial Fibrillation. *J Am Coll Cardiol*. 2019; doi.org/10.1016/j.jacc.2019.01.011.

2014 AHA/ACC/HRS Guideline for the Management of Patients With Atrial Fibrillation: A Report of the American College of Cardiology/American Heart Association Task Force on Practice Guidelines and the Heart Rhythm Society. *J Am Coll Cardiol*. 2014; 64(21):2246-80.

CONTENT LEGEND

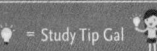
☀ = Study Tip Gal

Hemorrhagic Stroke

Hemorrhagic/blood leaks
into brain tissue

Ischemic Stroke

Clot stops blood supply
to an area of the brain

📷 *iimages © 123RF.com*

CHAPTER 33

STROKE

BACKGROUND

A stroke, or cerebrovascular accident (CVA), occurs when blood flow to an area of the brain is interrupted. There are a few different types of stroke. Acute ischemic stroke can be caused by a thrombus that forms during a cerebral atherosclerotic infarction (similar to a myocardial infarction but in the brain). This is sometimes referred to as a non-cardioembolic stroke to indicate the origin of disease as being in the brain, not the heart.

A cardioembolic stroke is an ischemic stroke that occurs when an embolus (i.e., a clot) forms in the heart and travels to the brain. A common cause of cardioembolic stroke is atrial fibrillation (see the Arrhythmias and Anticoagulation chapters). Intracerebral hemorrhage (ICH), subarachnoid hemorrhage (SAH) and subdural hematoma are all hemorrhagic strokes (bleeding in the brain due to a ruptured blood vessel).

Approximately 88% of all strokes are ischemic, and 12% are hemorrhagic. When a stroke occurs, ischemia kills brain cells in the immediate area of injury. When brain cells die, they release chemicals that set off a chain reaction. Cells in the larger, surrounding area of ischemic brain tissue (i.e., penumbra) can die, and the functions controlled by that area can be lost or impaired.

There are numerous risk factors for stroke, many of which are modifiable (see box below). Some people recover completely from less serious strokes [e.g., transient ischemic attacks, or TIAs (see Study Tip Gal on next page)], while others face chronic disability or loss of life.

RISK FACTORS FOR STROKE	
Hypertension – most important	Diabetes
Atrial fibrillation	Prior stroke or TIA
Sex (females > males)	Physical inactivity
Ethnicity (highest risk in African Americans)	Smoking
	Dyslipidemia
Age ≥ 55 years	Patent foramen ovale (PFO)
Atherosclerosis	Sickle cell disease

TIA VERSUS STROKE

Transient ischemic attack (TIA), sometimes called a "mini-stroke," is caused by a temporary clot, or block of blood flow, in the brain

Symptoms of a TIA are the same as a stroke, but disappear on their own within minutes to a few hours; there is no permanent damage

Seek immediate medical attention; TIAs are often a warning for a future full stroke

PRESENTATION AND DIAGNOSIS

The evaluation of a stroke patient must be done quickly. Early recognition of signs and symptoms by the patient or bystander is the first link in the stroke chain of survival. The American Stroke Association (ASA) and the American Heart Association (AHA) have public education campaigns to increase early recognition (see the Study Tip Gal below). Promptly calling 9-1-1 and activating the emergency medical system is essential, as brain tissue is rapidly lost as the stroke progresses (commonly stated as "time is brain").

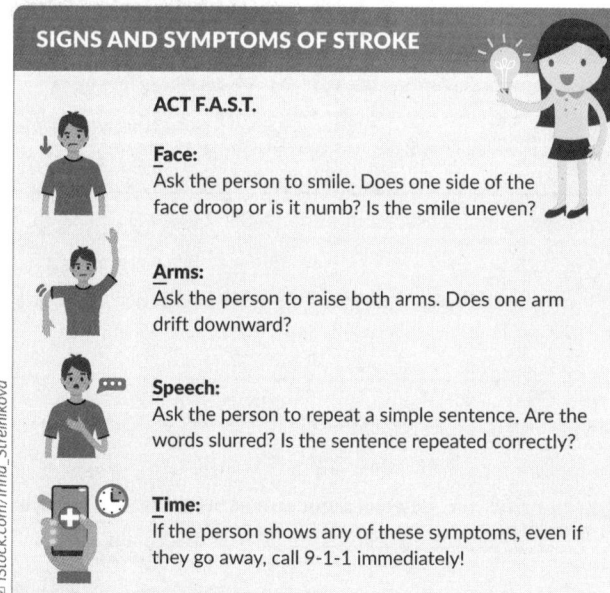

SIGNS AND SYMPTOMS OF STROKE

ACT F.A.S.T.

Face:
Ask the person to smile. Does one side of the face droop or is it numb? Is the smile uneven?

Arms:
Ask the person to raise both arms. Does one arm drift downward?

Speech:
Ask the person to repeat a simple sentence. Are the words slurred? Is the sentence repeated correctly?

Time:
If the person shows any of these symptoms, even if they go away, call 9-1-1 immediately!

iStock.com/Irina_Strelnikova

Once in the care of healthcare professionals, clinical assessment (e.g., history, physical exam, laboratory tests) and neurological assessment, using stroke scales such as the National Institutes of Health Stroke Scale (NIHSS), help determine the severity of the stroke and guide treatment.

Quickly identify whether the stroke is ischemic or hemorrhagic. It is critical to support cardiac and respiratory care. Drugs used to treat ischemic stroke can increase the risk of bleeding and can be harmful, or even fatal, in hemorrhagic stroke cases. Brain imaging using computed tomography (CT) is ideally performed within 20 minutes of arrival to the emergency department. Less commonly, magnetic resonance imaging (MRI) is performed.

ISCHEMIC STROKE: ACUTE MANAGEMENT

The immediate goal of treatment is to restore blood flow to the ischemic area of the brain to obtain complete neurological recovery. Intracranial pressure (ICP), cerebral perfusion pressure (CPP) and blood pressure (BP) should be monitored and controlled. Restoring blood flow may require mechanical removal of a clot (e.g., with stent retrievers), or the clot can be dissolved with intravenous fibrinolytic therapy if the patient arrives at the hospital in a timely manner after symptom onset.

ALTEPLASE

Alteplase is recombinant tissue plasminogen activator (tPA or rtPA). It binds to fibrin in a thrombus (clot) and converts plasminogen to plasmin, resulting in fibrinolysis. Alteplase is the only fibrinolytic drug FDA-approved to treat acute ischemic stroke. Tenecteplase, another fibrinolytic, is occasionally used off-label to treat ischemic strokes. Patients are candidates for alteplase if there is no bleeding seen on brain imaging, there are no contraindications to use (see the Study Tip Gal below and the Drug Table on the next page) and the following criteria for timing are met:

- It can be administered within 3 hours of symptom onset (FDA-approved timeline).

- It can be administered within 4.5 hours of symptom onset in select patients (guideline recommendation; not FDA-approved).

- It can be administered within 60 minutes of hospital arrival (door-to-needle time).

BP should be ≤ 185/110 mmHg before initiating alteplase; if the only contraindication to treatment is a BP > 185/110 mmHg, BP should be safely lowered so alteplase can be administered. Keep BP < 180/105 mmHg for at least the first 24 hours after treatment.

BLEEDING RISKS WITH ALTEPLASE

Alteplase breaks up existing clots → breaking up a clot increases the risk of bleeding

Before treatment, check that the patient isn't already at high bleeding risk. Conditions and drugs that increase the bleeding risk are contraindications to administering alteplase. They fit into these categories:

- Active bleed (e.g., internal bleed, ICH)

- Conditions or labs that increase bleeding risk (e.g., severe hypertension, INR > 1.7)

- Drug interactions with bleeding risk (e.g., anticoagulant use)

DRUG	DOSING	SAFETY/SIDE EFFECTS/MONITORING
Alteplase (*Activase*) Injection **Cathflo Activase** (single-use 2 mg vial) used to restore function of potentially clotted central lines and devices	0.9 mg/kg (maximum dose 90 mg); give 10% of the dose as a bolus over 1 minute then infuse the remainder over 60 minutes Must <u>rule out</u> an <u>intracranial hemorrhage before use</u>	**CONTRAINDICATIONS** <u>Active internal bleeding</u> or bleeding diathesis (predisposition) <u>History of recent stroke</u> (within the past 3 months) <u>Severe uncontrolled hypertension (BP > 185/110 mmHg)</u> Any prior intracranial hemorrhage (ICH) Other conditions that increase bleeding risk: recent intracranial or intraspinal surgery, trauma (within the past 3 months), intracranial neoplasm, arteriovenous malformation or aneurysm Labs that increase bleeding risk: <u>INR > 1.7</u>, aPTT > 40 seconds, platelet count < 100,000/mm³ Treatment dose of <u>LMWH</u> (within the previous 24 hours), use of a <u>direct thrombin inhibitor or direct factor Xa inhibitor</u> (within the previous 48 hours) Blood glucose < 50 mg/dL **SIDE EFFECTS** <u>Major bleeding</u> (e.g., ICH) **MONITORING** Hgb, Hct, s/sx of bleeding <u>Neurological assessments and BP</u> Head CT 24 hrs after treatment, before starting anticoagulants or antiplatelet drugs **NOTES** <u>Contraindications</u> and <u>dosing differ</u> when used for <u>ACS</u> (refer to the Acute Coronary Syndromes chapter) and pulmonary embolism, due to a higher risk of hemorrhagic conversion (i.e., brain bleed) in stroke If severe headache, acute hypertension, nausea, vomiting or worsening neurological function occurs, discontinue the infusion and obtain an emergent head CT The abbreviation "tPa" is prone to errors; not recommended by ISMP, but used commonly

Contraindications are summarized from the package labeling and the AHA/ASA guidelines.

Alteplase Drug Interactions

- There is a risk for <u>additive effects</u> when used in combination with other drugs that can ↑ <u>bleeding risk</u>. See the Drug Interactions chapter for further discussion.

OTHER TREATMENTS

Aspirin

<u>Aspirin 162 – 325 mg</u> PO within <u>24 – 48 hours after stroke onset</u> is recommended to prevent early recurrent stroke. Aspirin should not be given within 24 hours of fibrinolytic therapy.

Hypertension Management

Antihypertensives (e.g., IV labetalol, nicardipine or clevidipine) should be used to lower BP to <u>≤ 185/110 mmHg</u> prior to giving alteplase and maintain BP < 180/105 mmHg for at least 24 hours after the infusion. Patients who do not receive alteplase may not require treatment unless BP is severely elevated (≥ 220/120 mmHg). If treated, a 15% reduction in BP during the first 24 hours after stroke onset is considered safe. Once neurologically stable, oral antihypertensive medications may be restarted in patients with preexisting hypertension (or newly diagnosed hypertension). See the Secondary Prevention section for further discussion.

Hyperglycemia Management

Maintain blood glucose levels in the range of 140 – 180 mg/dL and closely monitor to prevent hypoglycemia.

Deep Vein Thrombosis (DVT) Prevention

DVT prophylaxis with intermittent pneumatic compression (IPC) devices is recommended. IPC devices are cuffs placed over the legs that fill with air to squeeze the legs periodically to increase blood flow. If subcutaneous anticoagulants (unfractionated heparin or LMWH) are used, they should not be started within 24 hours of receiving alteplase.

ISCHEMIC STROKE: SECONDARY PREVENTION

The recommendations below reflect secondary prevention measures after the first occurrence of stroke or TIA. Many of the same recommendations also apply to primary prevention of stroke.

TREATMENT OF MODIFIABLE RISK FACTORS

- Hypertension – blood pressure lowering treatment is often initiated after the first several days following a stroke. Thiazide diuretics, ACE inhibitors and ARBs have the best evidence for stroke risk reduction. A goal BP < 130/80 mmHg is recommended for most patients (see the Hypertension chapter). Lifestyle modifications are an important part of hypertension management (see below).

- Dyslipidemia – treat with a high-intensity statin, with atorvastatin 80 mg/day being preferred (see the Dyslipidemia chapter). In patients at higher risk, consider adding ezetimibe or a PCSK9 inhibitor to achieve an LDL < 70 mg/dL.

- Diabetes – patients with no established history should be screened for diabetes in the post-stroke period; an A1C is the preferred test. Treat diabetes according to the most recent ADA guidelines (see the Diabetes chapter).

- Atrial fibrillation – cardioembolic stroke due to atrial fibrillation requires anticoagulation to prevent future strokes (see the Anticoagulation chapter).

- Lifestyle modifications – patients should be screened for obesity and counseled on lifestyle modifications for hypertension and cardiovascular risk reduction (e.g., smoking cessation, diet, exercise, weight loss).

  - Nutrition – sodium restriction to < 2.4 grams/day, or < 1.5 grams/day for greater blood pressure reduction and a Mediterranean-type diet (emphasizing vegetables, fruits, whole grains, fish, poultry, legumes, nuts and olive oil) is recommended.

  - Physical activity – if capable, patients should engage in moderate-intensity exercise (at least 10 minutes four days per week) and avoid long periods of sitting.

  - Weight reduction – maintain a BMI 18.5 – 24.9 kg/m² and a waist circumference < 35 inches for women and < 40 inches for men.

  - Alcohol intake – limit to ≤ 2 drinks/day for males and ≤ 1 drink/day for females.

ANTIPLATELET TREATMENT

For patients with non-cardioembolic ischemic stroke or TIA, an antiplatelet, rather than oral anticoagulation, is recommended to reduce the risk of recurrent stroke, MI or death. Aspirin, aspirin/extended-release dipyridamole or clopidogrel is recommended within 24 – 48 hours after onset. Prasugrel is contraindicated in anyone with a history of TIA or stroke due to an increased risk of intracranial bleed. Other antiplatelets (e.g., ticlopidine) are not preferred due to the availability of safer options.

The combination of clopidogrel and low-dose aspirin can be initiated within 24 hours of a minor ischemic stroke and continued for 21 – 90 days, followed by antiplatelet monotherapy. This combination should not be used long-term for secondary prevention of stroke or TIA as it increases the risk of hemorrhage. This is different than the recommendations for dual antiplatelet therapy in heart disease (see the Stable Ischemic Heart Disease and Acute Coronary Syndromes chapters). Ticagrelor with aspirin can also be considered to reduce the risk of recurrent stroke following a minor to moderate stroke (i.e., NIH stroke scale score ≤ 5 or high-risk TIA); this combination should not be continued beyond 30 days.

There is no added benefit to increasing the aspirin dose in patients already taking aspirin who have an ischemic stroke or TIA. Alternative antiplatelets are often considered, though no single drug or combination has been adequately studied in patients who have had an event while receiving aspirin.

Antiplatelet Drugs

Aspirin irreversibly inhibits cyclooxygenase-1 and 2 (COX-1 and 2) enzymes, resulting in decreased prostaglandin (PG) and thromboxane A2 (TXA2) production. TXA2 is a potent vasoconstrictor and inducer of platelet aggregation. Aspirin has antiplatelet, antipyretic, analgesic and anti-inflammatory properties. Aspirin plus extended-release dipyridamole is another treatment option. Dipyridamole inhibits the uptake of adenosine into platelets and increases cAMP levels, which inhibits platelet aggregation. Clopidogrel is a prodrug that irreversibly inhibits P2Y12 ADP-mediated platelet activation and aggregation. Ticagrelor reversibly inhibits P2Y12 platelet activation and aggregation.

CARDIOVASCULAR CONDITIONS

DRUG	DOSING	SAFETY/SIDE EFFECTS/MONITORING
Aspirin (Bayer, Bufferin, Ecotrin, *Ascriptin, Durlaza*, **others)** + omeprazole *(Yosprala)* OTC: tablet, chewable tablet, enteric coated tablet, suppository Rx: ER capsule *(Durlaza)*, delayed-release tablet *(Yosprala)* See Pain chapter for more information on aspirin products	50-325 mg daily *Yosprala*: 81 mg/ 40 mg or 325 mg/ 40 mg daily Do not crush enteric-coated, delayed-release or ER products	**CONTRAINDICATIONS** NSAID or salicylate allergy; children and teenagers with viral infection due to risk of Reye's syndrome (symptoms include somnolence, N/V, confusion); rhinitis, nasal polyps or asthma (due to risk of urticaria, angioedema or bronchospasm) **WARNINGS** Bleeding [including GI bleed/ulceration, ↑ risk with heavy alcohol use or other drugs with bleeding risk (e.g., NSAIDs, anticoagulants, other antiplatelets)], tinnitus (salicylate overdose) **SIDE EFFECTS** Dyspepsia, heartburn, bleeding, nausea **MONITORING** Symptoms of bleeding, bruising **NOTES** To ↓ nausea, use EC or buffered product or take with food PPIs may be used to protect the gut with chronic NSAID use; consider the risks from chronic PPI use (↓ bone density, ↑ infection risk) *Yosprala* is indicated for those at risk of developing aspirin-associated gastric ulcers
Extended-release dipyridamole/aspirin (Aggrenox) Capsule	200 mg/25 mg BID If intolerable headache: 200 mg/ 25 mg QHS (+ low-dose aspirin daily in the morning), then resume BID dosing within 1 week	As above for aspirin component plus: **WARNINGS** Hypotension and chest pain (in patients with coronary artery disease) can occur due to the vasodilatory effects of dipyridamole **SIDE EFFECTS** Headache **NOTES** Not interchangeable with the individual components of aspirin and dipyridamole Amount of aspirin provided is not adequate for prevention of cardiac events (e.g., MI)
Clopidogrel (Plavix) Tablet Indicated for ACS, recent MI, stroke and PAD	75 mg daily	**BOXED WARNINGS** Clopidogrel is a prodrug. Effectiveness depends on the conversion to an active metabolite, mainly by CYP450 2C19. Poor metabolizers of CYP2C19 exhibit higher cardiovascular events than patients with normal CYP2C19 function. Tests to check CYP2C19 genotype can be used as an aid in determining a therapeutic strategy. Consider alternative treatments in patients identified as CYP2C19 poor metabolizers. See the Pharmacogenomics chapter. **CONTRAINDICATIONS** Active serious bleeding (e.g., GI bleed, intracranial hemorrhage) **WARNINGS** Bleeding risk: stop 5 days prior to elective surgery, do not use with omeprazole or esomeprazole (see the Drug Interactions section), premature discontinuation (↑ risk of thrombosis), thrombotic thrombocytopenic purpura (TTP) **SIDE EFFECTS** Generally well tolerated, unless bleeding occurs **MONITORING** Symptoms of bleeding, Hgb/Hct as necessary **NOTES** Drug of choice in stroke/TIA if a contraindication or allergy to aspirin; do not use in combination with aspirin long-term for stroke prevention

Antiplatelet Drug Interactions

- Most drug interactions are due to additive effects with other drugs that can ↑ bleeding risk (e.g., anticoagulants, NSAIDs, SSRIs, SNRIs, some herbals). See the Drug Interactions chapter.
- Clopidogrel: avoid in combination with omeprazole and esomeprazole (other PPIs interact less) and use caution with other CYP2C19 inhibitors.

HEMORRHAGIC STROKE

Hemorrhagic strokes result in a significant amount of morbidity and mortality. Treatment is largely supportive and includes airway management, establishing hemostasis, prevention or management of seizures, assessment for dysphagia, DVT prophylaxis and control of blood pressure and blood glucose. Hospitalized patients with hemorrhagic stroke should use IPC devices on the legs to prevent DVT. Anticoagulants should not be used while a patient is bleeding.

INTRACEREBRAL HEMORRHAGE (ICH)

There is a high risk for rapid neurological deterioration in the early hours of an ICH due to ongoing bleeding and enlargement of the brain hematoma. Patients with a severe coagulation factor deficiency or severe thrombocytopenia should receive appropriate factor replacement therapy or platelet infusions. In patients with ICH who are anticoagulated, reversal of the anticoagulant effects should be considered (see the Anticoagulation chapter for information on reversal drugs). If there is clinical evidence of seizures, they should be treated, but prophylactic anticonvulsant medication should not be used.

Increased intracranial pressure (ICP) is the primary complication in ICH. Measures should be taken to lower the ICP, including elevating the head of the bed by 30 degrees and using mannitol or hypertonic saline.

Mannitol

Mannitol produces an osmotic diuresis by increasing the osmotic pressure of the glomerular filtrate in the kidneys. This inhibits tubular reabsorption of water and electrolytes and increases urinary output. Mannitol reduces ICP by withdrawing water from the brain parenchyma and excreting it in the urine.

DRUG	DOSING	SAFETY/SIDE EFFECTS/MONITORING
Mannitol (Osmitrol, Resectisol) Injection	5%, 10%, 15%, 20%, 25% Mannitol 20%: 0.25-1 g/kg/dose IV Q6-8H PRN	**CONTRAINDICATIONS** Severe renal disease (anuria), severe hypovolemia, pulmonary edema or congestion, active intracranial bleed (except during craniotomy) **WARNINGS** CNS toxicity (can accumulate in the brain, causing rebound increases in ICP, if used for long periods of time as a continuous infusion; intermittent boluses preferred), extravasation (vesicant), nephrotoxicity, fluid and electrolyte imbalances (e.g., dehydration, hyperosmolar-induced hyperkalemia, acidosis, ↑ osmolar gap) **SIDE EFFECTS** Dehydration, headache, lethargy, ↑ or ↓ BP **MONITORING** Renal function, daily fluid intake and output, serum electrolytes, serum and urine osmolality, ICP, CPP **NOTES** Maintain serum osmolality < 300-320 mOsm/kg Inspect for crystals before administering; if crystals are present, warm the solution to redissolve Use a filter for administration

ACUTE SUBARACHNOID HEMORRHAGE (SAH)

SAH is bleeding in the space between the brain and the surrounding membrane (subarachnoid space). SAH usually results from a cerebral aneurysm rupture, and individuals frequently experience a severe headache, often described as the worst headache they have ever experienced. Surgical clipping or endovascular coiling to completely remove the aneurysm is performed when feasible to prevent rebleeding. Cerebral artery vasospasm can occur 3 - 21 days after the bleed, causing delayed cerebral ischemia. Oral nimodipine is used to prevent vasospasm. The use of prophylactic anticonvulsants may be considered in the immediate post-hemorrhagic period to prevent seizures. The routine use of long-term anticonvulsants is not recommended but may be considered for patients with known risk factors for delayed seizure disorder (e.g., prior seizure, intracerebral hematoma).

Nimodipine

Nimodipine is a <u>dihydropyridine calcium channel blocker</u> that is more selective for <u>cerebral arteries</u> due to increased <u>lipophilicity</u>. It is only indicated for SAH and is not used as an antihypertensive treatment.

DRUG	DOSING	SAFETY/SIDE EFFECTS/MONITORING
Nimodipine (Nymalize) Capsule, oral solution	60 mg PO Q4H for 21 days Start within 96 hours of SAH onset Swallow capsules whole; administer on an empty stomach, at least 1 hour before or 2 hours after meals Cirrhosis: 30 mg PO Q4H for 21 days (closely monitor)	**BOXED WARNINGS** <u>Do not administer</u> nimodipine <u>IV</u> or by other parenteral routes; <u>death and serious life-threatening adverse events</u> have occurred (including cardiac arrest, cardiovascular collapse, hypotension and bradycardia) when the <u>contents of nimodipine capsules</u> have been inadvertently <u>injected parenterally</u> (see Notes) **CONTRAINDICATIONS** ↑ risk of significant hypotension when used in combination with strong inhibitors of CYP3A4 (see the Drug Interactions section) **SIDE EFFECTS** <u>Hypotension</u> **MONITORING** CPP, ICP, BP, HR, neurological checks **NOTES** <u>If capsules cannot be swallowed</u>, contents may be <u>withdrawn with a parenteral syringe</u>, then <u>transferred to an oral syringe</u> that cannot accept a needle and that can only administer medication orally or via nasogastric tube; <u>label oral syringes "For Oral Use Only" or "Not for IV Use"</u>; the medication should be drawn up in the pharmacy to reduce medication errors

Nimodipine Drug Interactions

- Nimodipine is a major substrate of CYP3A4; strong CYP3A4 inhibitors (e.g., clarithromycin, protease inhibitors, azole antifungals) are contraindicated. Avoid grapefruit juice. Strong CYP3A4 inducers (e.g., rifampin, carbamazepine, phenytoin, St. John's wort) can decrease the levels of nimodipine and should be avoided.

KEY COUNSELING POINTS

Refer to the Stable Ischemic Heart Disease chapter for patient counseling on aspirin and clopidogrel.

Select Guidelines/References

Guidelines for the early management of patients with acute ischemic stroke: 2019 update to the 2018 guidelines for the early management of acute ischemic stroke: A guideline for healthcare professionals from the American Heart Association/American Stroke Association. *Stroke.* 2019;50:e344-e418.

2018 Guidelines for the early management of patients with acute ischemic stroke. AHA/ASA. *Stroke.* 2018;49:e46-e99.

Guidelines for the prevention of stroke in patients with stroke and transient ischemic attack. AHA/ASA. *Stroke.* 2021;52(7):e364-e467.

Guidelines for the management of spontaneous intracerebral hemorrhage. AHA/ASA. *Stroke.* 2015;41:2108-2129.

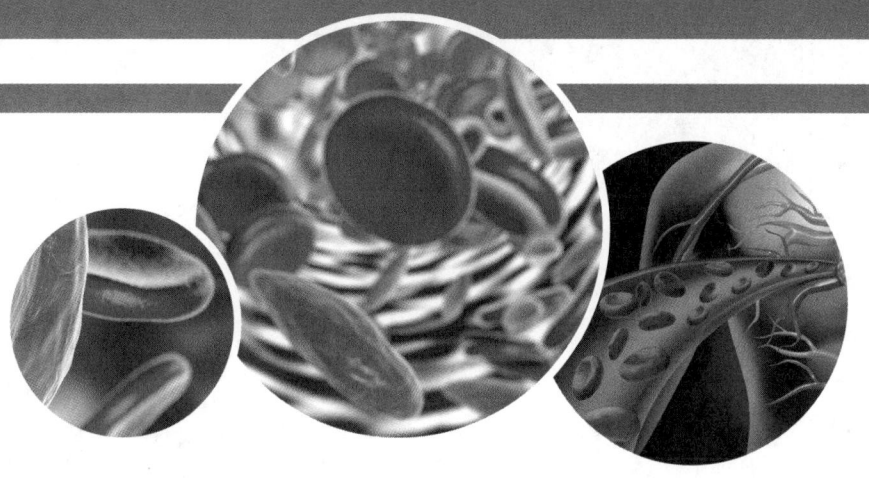

ANTICOAGULATION & BLOOD DISORDERS

CONTENTS

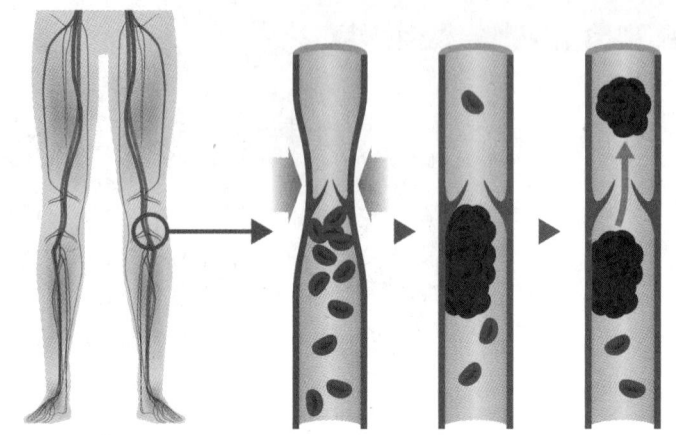

CONTENT LEGEND

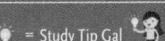 = Study Tip Gal

CHAPTER 34
ANTICOAGULATION

BACKGROUND

Anticoagulants are used to prevent blood clots from forming and to keep existing clots from becoming larger. They do not break down clots (like fibrinolytics). Anticoagulants are used in the prevention and treatment of venous thromboembolism (VTE), which refers to deep vein thrombosis (DVT) and/or pulmonary embolism (PE). Anticoagulants are also used in the immediate treatment of acute coronary syndromes (ACS) and prevention of cardioembolic stroke (see Study Tip Gal below). The most common side effect of anticoagulants is bleeding, which can be fatal. Anticoagulants are high-alert medications for this reason.

CLOT FORMATION

Coagulation is the process by which blood clots form. A number of factors can lead to activation of the coagulation process, such as blood vessel injury, blood stasis (stopping or slowing of blood flow) and pro-thrombotic conditions. Coagulation involves activation of platelets and the clotting cascade.

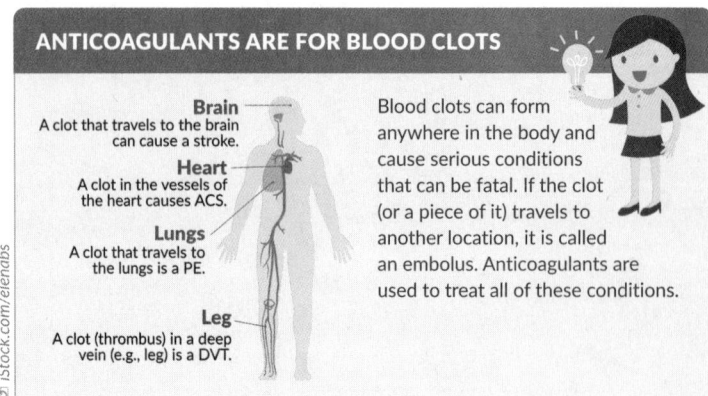

ANTICOAGULANTS ARE FOR BLOOD CLOTS

Brain A clot that travels to the brain can cause a stroke.
Heart A clot in the vessels of the heart causes ACS.
Lungs A clot that travels to the lungs is a PE.
Leg A clot (thrombus) in a deep vein (e.g., leg) is a DVT.

Blood clots can form anywhere in the body and cause serious conditions that can be fatal. If the clot (or a piece of it) travels to another location, it is called an embolus. Anticoagulants are used to treat all of these conditions.

COAGULATION CASCADE

The coagulation cascade is a process that occurs through activation of a series of clotting factors, which are proteins made (primarily) by the liver.

All of the clotting factors have an <u>inactive and an active</u> form; the "a" next to a factor means "active/activated" (e.g., factor X is inactive and factor Xa is active). Once activated, a clotting factor will activate the next clotting factor in the sequence until <u>fibrin</u> is formed. The coagulation cascade has two pathways that lead to fibrin formation: the contact activation pathway (or the intrinsic pathway) and the tissue factor pathway (or the extrinsic pathway). Anticoagulants inhibit the coagulation cascade and prevent (or stop further) clot formation (See <u>Study Tip Gal</u> below).

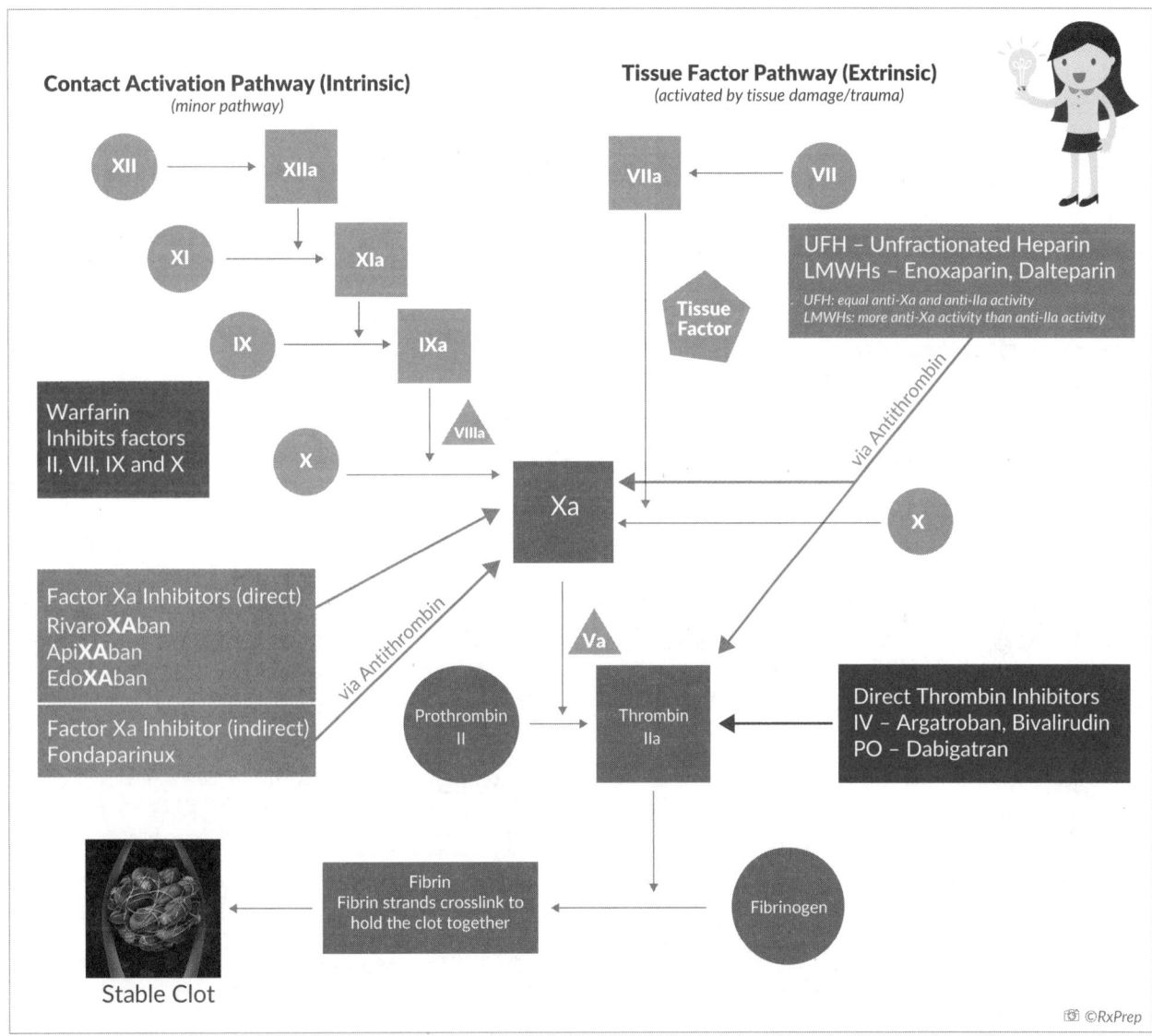

DRUG TREATMENT

Anticoagulants work by various mechanisms and different routes of administration to prevent and treat a variety of conditions. An overview of these clinical conditions is included at the end of the chapter.

Parenteral anticoagulants are used for ACS treatment and prevention/treatment of VTE. Oral anticoagulants are used mainly for VTE (treatment and prevention) and stroke prevention in patients with atrial fibrillation (AF). They include warfarin (a vitamin K antagonist), factor Xa inhibitors and thrombin inhibitors. The oral factor Xa inhibitors and thrombin inhibitors are further classified as direct-acting oral anticoagulants (DOACs). For most conditions, DOACs are preferred over warfarin (see Study Tip Gal on right).

> **DOACs VERSUS WARFARIN**
>
> DOACs have less drug-drug interactions, less or comparable bleeding and a shorter duration of action compared to warfarin
>
> DOAC dosing is based on the indication and kidney/liver function – there is no need to adjust the dose based on the INR (as with warfarin)
>
> DOACs are preferred for stroke prevention in AF
>
> - BUT – if there is moderate-to-severe mitral stenosis or a mechanical heart valve, use warfarin
>
> Use DOACs for VTE treatment
>
> - BUT – if the patient has antiphospholipid syndrome, use warfarin

Several organizations publish anticoagulation guidelines, including American College of Chest Physicians (CHEST) and the American College of Cardiology/American Heart Association (ACC/AHA).

VITAMIN K ANTAGONISM

Warfarin is a vitamin K antagonist. Vitamin K is required for the carboxylation (activation) of clotting factors II, VII, IX and X. Without adequate vitamin K, the liver produces the clotting factors, but they have reduced coagulant activity. Warfarin has a narrow therapeutic range and requires careful monitoring of the international normalized ratio (INR), which is affected by many drugs and changes in dietary vitamin K.

FACTOR Xa INHIBITION

Antithrombin (AT) is one of the body's natural anticoagulants; it inactivates thrombin (factor IIa) and other proteases (like factor Xa) involved in blood clotting. Unfractionated heparin (UFH), low molecular weight heparins (LMWHs) and fondaparinux work by binding to AT and causing a conformational change which increases AT activity 1,000-fold. LMWHs inhibit factor Xa more specifically than unfractionated heparin. Fondaparinux (Arixtra) binds to AT, resulting in selective inhibition of factor Xa.

Apixaban (Eliquis), edoxaban (Savaysa) and rivaroxaban (Xarelto) work by inhibiting factor Xa directly. These oral medications are taken once or twice daily and require no laboratory monitoring for efficacy.

THROMBIN INHIBITION

UFH and LMWH indirectly inhibit thrombin and factor Xa through AT binding. Direct thrombin inhibitors (DTIs) block thrombin directly, decreasing the amount of fibrin available for clot formation. The intravenous DTIs (e.g., argatroban) are important clinically since they do not cross-react with heparin-induced thrombocytopenia (HIT) antibodies. Dabigatran (Pradaxa) is an oral DTI.

KEY POINTS

When studying the Anticoagulation, Acute Coronary Syndromes, Stable Ischemic Heart Disease and Stroke chapters, it can be difficult to determine when a fibrinolytic, antiplatelet or anticoagulant would be appropriate.

- Oral anticoagulants are used mainly in AF (for stroke prevention) and for DVT/PE (treatment and prevention). Oral medications like *Xarelto* or *Eliquis* are not indicated for the acute management of an ACS when platelet aggregation is the main target of drug therapy.

- Fibrinolytics break down existing clots but are associated with a very high risk of bleeding. They are used to immediately treat an acute ischemic stroke or STEMI when the patient could die without rapid restoration of blood flow.

- Antiplatelet drugs (e.g., aspirin, clopidogrel, ticagrelor) are used mainly for coronary artery disease (including ACS) and to prevent recurrent ischemic stroke/TIA. Dual antiplatelet therapy (DAPT) refers to using both aspirin and a P2Y12 inhibitor (e.g., clopidogrel) together, which is very common in patients who have had an ACS. Antiplatelet drugs are not sufficient for treating DVT/PE.

HIGH-ALERT MEDICATIONS

All anticoagulants can cause significant bleeding and are classified as "high-alert" medications by the Institute for Safe Medication Practices (ISMP). Bleeding events with anticoagulants put patients at increased risk for death. The Joint Commission's National Patient Safety Goals require policies and protocols to properly initiate and manage anticoagulant therapy. Patients receiving anticoagulants should receive individualized care through a defined process that includes standardized ordering, dispensing, administration, monitoring and patient/caregiver education (for treatment doses). Refer to the Medication Safety & Quality Improvement chapter for additional information. When pharmacists are involved in managing anticoagulants, patient care and outcomes are improved and costs are decreased.

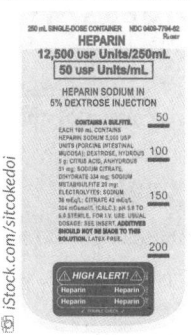

The common types of visible bleeding and select causes are reviewed in the Study Tip Gal below. In some cases, bleeding will not be visible, but can be identified from symptoms and/or labs. An acute drop in hemoglobin (e.g., ≥ 2 g/dL) could signify that bleeding is occurring (visible or not). Internal bleeding could be from anywhere, such as a retroperitoneal (behind the peritoneal space) bleed or a dissection (a tear within the wall of a blood vessel, such as an aortic dissection).

BLEEDING TYPES AND CAUSES*

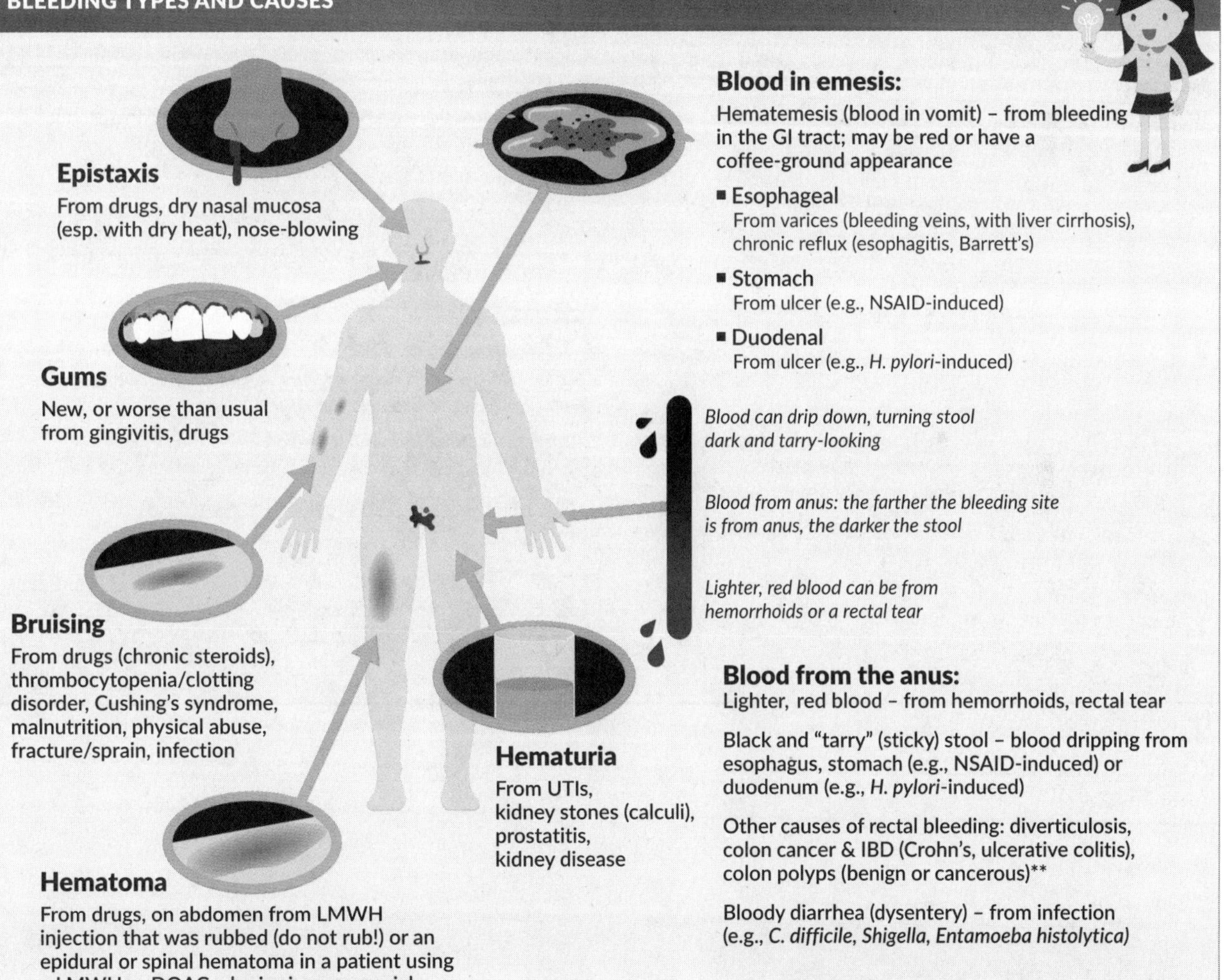

Epistaxis
From drugs, dry nasal mucosa (esp. with dry heat), nose-blowing

Gums
New, or worse than usual from gingivitis, drugs

Bruising
From drugs (chronic steroids), thrombocytopenia/clotting disorder, Cushing's syndrome, malnutrition, physical abuse, fracture/sprain, infection

Hematoma
From drugs, on abdomen from LMWH injection that was rubbed (do not rub!) or an epidural or spinal hematoma in a patient using a LMWH or DOAC who is given neuraxial anesthesia or a spinal puncture

Hematuria
From UTIs, kidney stones (calculi), prostatitis, kidney disease

Blood in emesis:
Hematemesis (blood in vomit) – from bleeding in the GI tract; may be red or have a coffee-ground appearance

- **Esophageal**
  From varices (bleeding veins, with liver cirrhosis), chronic reflux (esophagitis, Barrett's)
- **Stomach**
  From ulcer (e.g., NSAID-induced)
- **Duodenal**
  From ulcer (e.g., *H. pylori*-induced)

Blood can drip down, turning stool dark and tarry-looking

Blood from anus: the farther the bleeding site is from anus, the darker the stool

Lighter, red blood can be from hemorrhoids or a rectal tear

Blood from the anus:
Lighter, red blood – from hemorrhoids, rectal tear

Black and "tarry" (sticky) stool – blood dripping from esophagus, stomach (e.g., NSAID-induced) or duodenum (e.g., *H. pylori*-induced)

Other causes of rectal bleeding: diverticulosis, colon cancer & IBD (Crohn's, ulcerative colitis), colon polyps (benign or cancerous)**

Bloody diarrhea (dysentery) – from infection (e.g., *C. difficile, Shigella, Entamoeba histolytica*)

*Drugs that cause bleeding include anticoagulants, antiplatelets and NSAIDs. Natural products (e.g., ginkgo), SSRIs and SNRIs increase bleeding risk.
**Rectal bleeding from polyps can be occult [i.e., not visible, requires tests (e.g., FOBT) to identify]

UNFRACTIONATED HEPARIN

UFH binds to antithrombin (AT), which then inactivates thrombin (factor IIa) and factor Xa (as well as factors IXa, XIa, XIIa and plasmin) and prevents the conversion of fibrinogen to fibrin.

DRUG	DOSING	SAFETY/SIDE EFFECTS/MONITORING
Unfractionated Heparin Injection **Anticoagulation Treatment/ Prophylaxis** Treatment infusion: 25,000 units in 250 mL (concentration: 100 units/mL) in D5W, ½ NS or NS Many strengths and volumes (ranging 1 unit/mL to 20,000 units/mL), including total units of 5,000, 10,000, 12,500, 20,000, 25,000 & others **Line Flush** 10 units/mL, 100 units/mL syringes (in 1, 2, 2.5, 3, 5, 10, 30 mL), others	**Prophylaxis of VTE** 5,000 units SC Q8-12H **Treatment of VTE** 80 units/kg IV bolus; 18 units/kg/hr infusion If outpatient, 333 units/kg x 1 dose SC; 250 units/kg SC Q12H **Treatment of ACS/STEMI** 60 units/kg IV bolus; infuse 12 units/kg/hr Use total body weight for dosing Onset: IV: immediate SC: 20-30 min t½ = 1.5 hrs	**CONTRAINDICATIONS** Uncontrolled active bleed (intracranial hemorrhage), severe thrombocytopenia, history of HIT, hypersensitivity to pork products Some products contain benzyl alcohol as a preservative (do not use in neonates, infants, pregnancy and breastfeeding) **WARNING** Fatal medication errors: verify the correct concentration is chosen **SIDE EFFECTS** Bleeding (e.g., epistaxis, bruising, gingival, GI), thrombocytopenia, HIT, hyperkalemia and osteoporosis (with long-term use), alopecia **MONITORING** aPTT or anti-Xa level – check 6 hours after initiation and every 6 hrs until therapeutic, then every 24 hrs and with every dosage change aPTT therapeutic range is 1.5-2.5 x control, anti-Xa therapeutic range typically 0.3-0.7 units/mL aPTT and anti-Xa monitoring are not required for SC (prophylactic) dosing Platelets, Hgb, Hct at baseline and daily (↓ in platelets > 50% from baseline suggests possible HIT) **NOTES** Antidote: protamine (see Antidotes and Reversal section) Unpredictable anticoagulant response (has variable and extensive binding to plasma proteins and cells) Continuous IV infusions are common for treating VTE and ACS because heparin has a rapid onset and short half-life HIT antibodies have cross-sensitivity with LMWHs Do not give IM due to hematoma risk Heparin lock-flushes (*HepFlush*) are only used to keep IV lines open. Fatal errors, especially in neonates, occurred when the incorrect heparin strength (higher concentration) was chosen. Heparin injection 10,000 units/mL and flushes 10 or 100 units/mL look and sound alike.

LOW MOLECULAR WEIGHT HEPARINS

LMWHs bind to AT, which inactivates factor Xa and factor IIa. The anti-factor Xa activity is much greater than the anti-factor IIa activity.

DRUG	DOSING	SAFETY/SIDE EFFECTS/MONITORING
Enoxaparin *(Lovenox)* Multidose vial (300 mg/3 mL) and prefilled syringes: 30 mg/0.3 mL 40 mg/0.4 mL 60 mg/0.6 mL 80 mg/0.8 mL 100 mg/mL 120 mg/0.8 mL 150 mg/mL 1 mg = 100 units anti-Xa activity	**Prophylaxis of VTE** 30 mg SC Q12H or 40 mg SC daily CrCl < 30 mL/min: 30 mg SC daily **Treatment of VTE and UA/NSTEMI** 1 mg/kg SC Q12H or 1.5 mg/kg SC daily (only for inpatient VTE treatment) CrCl < 30 mL/min: 1 mg/kg SC daily Use total body weight for dosing **Treatment of STEMI in patients < 75 years of age** 30 mg IV bolus plus a 1 mg/kg SC dose followed by 1 mg/kg SC Q12H (max 100 mg for the first two SC doses only) CrCl < 30 mL/min: 30 mg IV bolus plus a 1 mg/kg SC dose, followed by 1 mg/kg SC daily **Treatment of STEMI in patients ≥ 75 years of age** 0.75 mg/kg SC Q12H (no bolus - max 5 mg for the first two SC doses only) CrCl < 30 mL/min: 1 mg/kg SC daily (no bolus)	**BOXED WARNINGS** Patients receiving neuraxial anesthesia (epidural, spinal) or undergoing spinal puncture are at risk of hematomas and subsequent paralysis **CONTRAINDICATIONS** History of HIT, active major bleed, hypersensitivity to pork **SIDE EFFECTS** Bleeding, anemia, injection site reactions (e.g., pain, bruising, hematomas), ↓ platelets (thrombocytopenia, including HIT) **MONITORING** Platelets, Hgb, Hct, SCr More predictable anticoagulant response than UFH; does not require anti-Xa level monitoring in most cases Anti-Xa level monitoring is recommended in pregnancy Monitoring may be done in obesity, low body weight, pediatrics, elderly or renal insufficiency aPTT is not used Obtain peak anti-Xa levels 4 hours post SC dose **NOTES** Antidote: protamine (see Antidotes and Reversal section) Do not expel air bubble from syringe prior to injection (can cause loss of drug) Do not administer IM Store at room temperature Patients managed with percutaneous coronary intervention (PCI): if the last SC enoxaparin dose was given 8-12 hours before balloon inflation, give 0.3 mg/kg IV bolus
Dalteparin *(Fragmin)*	**Prophylaxis of VTE** 2,500-5,000 units SC daily **Treatment of UA/NSTEMI** 120 units/kg (max 10,000 units) SC Q12H	

UFH/LMWH Drug Interactions

- Most drug interactions are due to additive effects with other drugs that can ↑ bleeding risk (other anticoagulants, antiplatelet drugs, some herbal supplements, NSAIDs, SSRIs, SNRIs, fibrinolytics). See the Drug Interactions chapter.

HEPARIN-INDUCED THROMBOCYTOPENIA OVERVIEW

Heparin-induced thrombocytopenia (HIT) is an immune-mediated IgG drug reaction that has a high risk of venous and arterial thrombosis. The immune system forms antibodies against heparin bound to platelet factor 4 (PF4), the antibodies then join with heparin and PF4 to create a complex, and this complex binds to the Fc receptors on platelets. This causes platelet activation and a release of pro-coagulant microparticles.

HIT is a prothrombotic state and, if left untreated, can cause many complications, including heparin-induced thrombocytopenia and thrombosis (HITT). HITT leads to amputations, post-thrombotic syndrome and/or death. The estimated incidence of HIT is ~3% of patients exposed to heparin for more than four days. It is lower with a shorter duration of treatment. The typical onset of HIT occurs 5 – 14 days after the start of heparin or within hours if a patient has been exposed to heparin within the past three months. A diagnosis is made by a compatible clinical picture, an unexplained drop in platelet count (defined as > 50% drop from baseline) and laboratory confirmation of antibodies (heparin-PF4 ELISA test and confirmatory serotonin release assay) or platelet activation by heparin. Thrombocytopenia is the most common sign of HIT. A thrombosis can come before thrombocytopenia in up to 25% of patients with HIT.

MANAGEMENT OF HIT COMPLICATED BY THROMBOSIS (HITT)

- If HIT is suspected or confirmed, stop all forms of heparin and LMWH, including heparin flushes and heparin-coated catheters. If the patient is on warfarin and diagnosed with HIT, the warfarin should be discontinued and vitamin K should be administered. Although the patient is at a high risk of thrombosis, warfarin use with a low platelet count has a high correlation with warfarin-induced limb gangrene and necrosis.

- For the immediate treatment of HIT, rapid-acting non-heparin anticoagulants (e.g., argatroban) are to be used.

- Do not start warfarin therapy until the platelets have recovered to $\geq$ 150,000/mm³. Warfarin should be initiated at lower doses (5 mg maximum). Overlap warfarin with a non-heparin anticoagulant for a minimum of five days and until the INR is within target range for 24 hours. Argatroban can increase the INR; the value must be interpreted cautiously.

- If urgent cardiac surgery or PCI is required, bivalirudin is the preferred anticoagulant.

FACTOR Xa INHIBITORS

Apixaban (Eliquis), edoxaban (Savaysa) and rivaroxaban (Xarelto) are direct factor Xa inhibitors that are available orally. Fondaparinux (Arixtra) is an injectable synthetic pentasaccharide that selectively inhibits factor Xa via antithrombin (AT), making it an indirect inhibitor of factor Xa. Fondaparinux is used off-label for HIT.

DRUG	DOSING	SAFETY/SIDE EFFECTS/ MONITORING
Oral Direct Factor Xa Inhibitors		
Apixaban (Eliquis) Tablet *Eliquis DVT/PE Starter Pack:* 30-day blister pack (for ease of prescribing for DVT/PE treatment) Missed Dose: Take immediately on the same day, then twice daily administration should be resumed; the dose should not be doubled to make up for a missed dose	**Nonvalvular AF (stroke prophylaxis)** <u>5 mg PO BID</u> Unless patient has at least <u>2 of the following</u>: age ≥ 80 years, body weight ≤ 60 kg, or SCr ≥ 1.5 mg/dL, then <u>give 2.5 mg BID</u> **Treatment of DVT/PE** <u>Initial: 10 mg PO BID x 7 days, then 5 mg PO BID</u> Extended phase: 2.5 mg PO BID after at least 3 months of initial treatment dosing **Prophylaxis for DVT (after knee/hip replacement)** 2.5 mg PO BID (for 12 days after knee or 35 days after hip replacement surgery); give first dose 12-24 hours after surgery	**BOXED WARNINGS** All: patients receiving <u>neuraxial anesthesia (epidural, spinal)</u> or undergoing spinal puncture are at <u>risk of hematomas and subsequent paralysis</u> Premature discontinuation ↑ risk of thrombotic events Edoxaban only: reduced efficacy in nonvalvular AF patients with <u>CrCl > 95 mL/min</u>; do not use **CONTRAINDICATIONS** Active pathological bleeding
Rivaroxaban (Xarelto) Tablet *Xarelto Starter Pack:* 30-day blister pack containing 15 mg and 20 mg tablets (for ease of prescribing for DVT/PE treatment) Missed Dose: Administer the dose as soon as possible on the same day as follows: If taking 15 mg twice daily: take immediately to ensure intake of 30 mg/day (in this particular instance, <u>two 15 mg tablets may be taken at once</u>); then resume regular schedule on the following day <u>If taking 10, 15 or 20 mg once daily</u>: take immediately on the same day; otherwise skip	<u>Doses ≥ 15 mg</u> must be taken <u>with food</u>; 10 mg dose can be taken without regard to meals **Nonvalvular AF (stroke prophylaxis)** CrCl > 50 mL/min: 20 mg PO daily <u>with evening meal</u> CrCl 15-50 mL/min: 15 mg PO daily <u>with evening meal</u> CrCl < 15 mL/min: avoid use **Treatment of DVT/PE** <u>Initial: 15 mg PO BID x 21 days, then 20 mg PO daily with food</u> Extended phase: 10 mg PO daily after at least 3 months of initial treatment dosing <u>CrCl < 30 mL/min: avoid use</u> **Prophylaxis for DVT (after knee/hip replacement) and VTE (in acutely ill medical patients)** 10 mg PO daily for: 31 to 39 days (acutely ill medical patients) 35 days (hip replacement) 12 days (knee replacement) Give first dose 6-10 hours after knee/hip replacement surgery CrCl < 30 mL/min: avoid use **Reduction in the Risk of Major CVD Events in CAD/PAD** 2.5 mg PO BID in combination with low-dose aspirin CrCl < 15 mL/min: avoid use	**WARNINGS** <u>Not recommended with prosthetic heart valves or antiphospholipid syndrome</u>, avoid in patients with moderate to severe hepatic impairment **SIDE EFFECTS** Generally well-tolerated, unless <u>bleeding</u> occurs Edoxaban: rash, ↑ LFTs **MONITORING** Hgb, Hct, SCr, LFTs; <u>no monitoring of efficacy required</u> **NOTES** <u>Antidote for apixaban</u> and <u>rivaroxaban:</u> <u>andexanet alfa (Andexxa)</u> All: can be crushed and put on applesauce or suspended in water to administer by NG tube Apixaban only: can be crushed and mixed in water, D5W or apple juice Betrixaban is no longer available in the U.S. **Elective Surgery** Discontinue 24 hours prior to elective surgery (rivaroxaban, edoxaban) Discontinue 48 hours prior to elective surgery with moderate-high bleeding risk or 24 hours prior with a low bleeding risk (apixaban)
Edoxaban (Savaysa) Tablet Missed Dose: Take immediately on the same day; the dose should not be doubled to make up for a missed dose	**Nonvalvular AF (stroke prophylaxis)** <u>CrCl > 95 mL/min: do not use</u> CrCl 51-95 mL/min: 60 mg daily CrCl 15-50 mL/min: 30 mg daily CrCl < 15 mL/min: not recommended **Treatment of DVT/PE** 60 mg daily, <u>start after 5-10 days of parenteral anticoagulation</u> CrCl 15-50 mL/min, body weight ≤ 60 kg or on certain P-gp inhibitors: 30 mg daily CrCl < 15 mL/min: not recommended	

ANTICOAGULATION & BLOOD DISORDERS

DRUG	DOSING	SAFETY/SIDE EFFECTS/MONITORING
Injectable Indirect Factor Xa Inhibitor (SC)		
Fondaparinux (*Arixtra*) Prefilled syringes: 2.5 mg/0.5 mL 5 mg/0.4 mL 7.5 mg/0.6 mL 10 mg/0.8 mL Store at room temperature	**Prophylaxis of VTE** ≥ 50 kg: 2.5 mg SC daily < 50 kg: contraindicated **Treatment of VTE** < 50 kg: 5 mg SC daily 50-100 kg: 7.5 mg SC daily > 100 kg: 10 mg SC daily **Both Indications** CrCl 30-50 mL/min: use caution CrCl < 30 mL/min: contraindicated	**BOXED WARNINGS** Patients receiving neuraxial anesthesia (epidural, spinal) or undergoing spinal puncture are at risk of hematomas and subsequent paralysis **CONTRAINDICATIONS** Severe renal impairment (CrCl < 30 mL/min), active major bleed, bacterial endocarditis, thrombocytopenia with positive test for anti-platelet antibodies in presence of fondaparinux **SIDE EFFECTS** Bleeding (e.g., epistaxis, bruising, gingival, GI), anemia, local injection site reactions (rash, pruritus, bruising), thrombocytopenia, hypokalemia, hypotension **MONITORING** Anti-Xa levels (3 hrs post-dose), platelets, Hgb, Hct, SCr **NOTES** Do not expel air bubble from syringe prior to injection No antidote Do not administer IM

Factor Xa Inhibitor Drug Interactions

- Avoid using with other anticoagulants (unless benefit outweighs risk). Monitor for additive effects with other drugs that can ↑ bleeding risk (antiplatelet drugs, some herbals, NSAIDs, SSRIs, SNRIs, fibrinolytics). See the Drug Interactions chapter.

- Apixaban is a substrate of CYP450 3A4 (major) and P-gp. Avoid use with strong dual inducers of CYP3A4 and P-gp (e.g., carbamazepine, phenytoin, rifampin, St. John's wort). For patients receiving doses > 2.5 mg BID, the dose of apixaban should be decreased by 50% when coadministered with drugs that are strong dual inhibitors of CYP3A4 and P-gp (e.g., clarithromycin, itraconazole, ketoconazole, ritonavir). For patients taking 2.5 mg BID, avoid these strong dual inhibitors.

- Rivaroxaban is a substrate of CYP3A4 (major) and P-gp. Avoid use with drugs that are combined P-gp and strong CYP3A4 inducers (e.g., carbamazepine, phenytoin, rifampin, St. John's wort) or combined P-gp and strong CYP3A4 inhibitors (e.g., ketoconazole, itraconazole, lopinavir/ritonavir, ritonavir, conivaptan). The benefit must outweigh the potential risks in these situations: CrCl 15 – 80 mL/min who are receiving combined P-gp and moderate CYP3A4 inhibitors (e.g., diltiazem, verapamil, dronedarone, erythromycin).

- Edoxaban is a substrate of P-gp; avoid use with rifampin. When treating DVT/PE, reduce dose to 30 mg daily with verapamil, macrolides (azithromycin, clarithromycin, erythromycin) and oral itraconazole or ketoconazole.

- Cobicistat (*Tybost*), *Stribild* and *Genvoya* (each containing cobicistat) can increase exposure to the factor Xa inhibitors. Rivaroxaban should not be used with any of these medications. Recommendations are product-specific for the other anticoagulants.

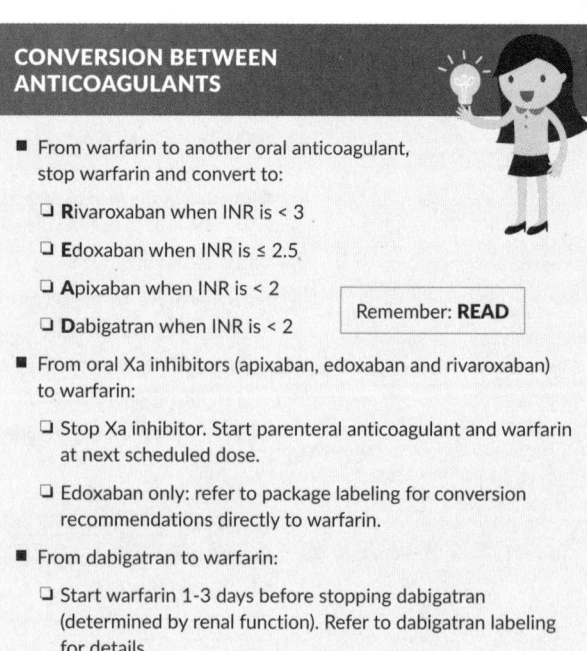

CONVERSION BETWEEN ANTICOAGULANTS

- From warfarin to another oral anticoagulant, stop warfarin and convert to:
  - ❏ **R**ivaroxaban when INR is < 3
  - ❏ **E**doxaban when INR is ≤ 2.5
  - ❏ **A**pixaban when INR is < 2
  - ❏ **D**abigatran when INR is < 2

  Remember: **READ**

- From oral Xa inhibitors (apixaban, edoxaban and rivaroxaban) to warfarin:
  - ❏ Stop Xa inhibitor. Start parenteral anticoagulant and warfarin at next scheduled dose.
  - ❏ Edoxaban only: refer to package labeling for conversion recommendations directly to warfarin.

- From dabigatran to warfarin:
  - ❏ Start warfarin 1-3 days before stopping dabigatran (determined by renal function). Refer to dabigatran labeling for details.

DIRECT THROMBIN INHIBITORS

These agents directly inhibit thrombin (factor IIa); they bind to the active thrombin site of free and clot-associated thrombin.

DRUG	DOSING	SAFETY/SIDE EFFECTS/MONITORING
Oral Direct Thrombin Inhibitor		
Dabigatran (Pradaxa) Capsule **Missed Dose:** Take immediately unless it is within 6 hours of next scheduled dose; the dose should not be doubled to make up for a missed dose	**Nonvalvular AF (stroke prophylaxis)** 150 mg BID CrCl 15-30 mL/min: 75 mg BID CrCl < 15 mL/min: avoid use **Treatment of DVT/PE and Reduction in the Risk of Recurrence of DVT and PE** 150 mg BID, start after 5-10 days of parenteral anticoagulation CrCl ≤ 30 mL/min: avoid use **Prophylaxis of DVT/PE Following Hip Replacement Surgery** 110 mg on day 1, then 220 mg daily CrCl ≤ 30 mL/min: avoid use	**BOXED WARNINGS** Patients receiving neuraxial anesthesia (epidural, spinal) or undergoing spinal puncture are at risk of hematomas and subsequent paralysis Premature discontinuation ↑ risk of thrombotic events **CONTRAINDICATIONS** Active pathological bleeding, treatment of patients with mechanical prosthetic heart valves **WARNINGS** Not recommended for antiphospholipid syndrome **SIDE EFFECTS** Dyspepsia, gastritis-like symptoms, bleeding (including more GI bleeding) **MONITORING** Hgb, Hct, SCr; no monitoring of efficacy required **NOTES** Antidote: idarucizumab (Praxbind) Protect from moisture; dispense in original container and discard 4 months after opening Blister packs are good until the date on the pack Swallow capsules whole (do not break, chew, crush or open); do not administer by NG tube Can ↑ aPTT, PT/INR Discontinue if undergoing invasive surgery (1-2 days before if CrCl ≥ 50 mL/min, 3-5 days before if CrCl < 50 mL/min)
Injectable Direct Thrombin Inhibitors (IV)		
Argatroban Injection Indicated for HIT and in patients undergoing PCI who are at risk for HIT **Bivalirudin (Angiomax)** Injection Indicated for patients with ACS undergoing PCI, including those with HIT	**HIT** Argatroban: start at 2 mcg/kg/min, then titrate to target aPTT Max: 10 mcg/kg/min **PCI** IV bolus followed by an infusion; all are weight-based Used in patients at risk for HIT Argatroban: ↓ dose in hepatic impairment Bivalirudin: ↓ dose when CrCl < 30 mL/min	**CONTRAINDICATIONS** Active major bleeding **SIDE EFFECTS** Bleeding (mild to severe), anemia **MONITORING** aPTT and/or activated clotting time, platelets, Hgb, Hct, renal function **NOTES** Safe with active HIT or history of HIT; no cross-reaction with HIT antibodies No antidote Argatroban can ↑ INR; if starting on warfarin concurrently, dose cautiously and do not use a loading dose of warfarin

Dabigatran Drug Interactions

- Avoid using with other anticoagulants (unless benefit outweighs risk). Monitor for additive effects with other drugs that can ↑ bleeding risk (antiplatelet drugs, some herbals, NSAIDs, SSRIs, SNRIs, fibrinolytics).

- Dabigatran is a substrate of P-gp; avoid use with rifampin.

- Nonvalvular AF: if CrCl 30 – 50 mL/min and patient is taking P-gp inhibitors (dronedarone or systemic ketoconazole), reduce dose to 75 mg BID. In severe renal impairment (CrCl 15 – 30 mL/min), avoid use with any P-gp inhibitors.

- Other indications: avoid use with P-gp inhibitors in patients with CrCl < 50 mL/min.

- Cobicistat (Tybost) and cobicistat-containing Stribild and Genvoya can increase exposure to dabigatran. Recommendations depend on renal function and indication for dabigatran.

ANTICOAGULATION & BLOOD DISORDERS

WARFARIN

Warfarin competitively inhibits the C1 subunit of the multi-unit vitamin K epoxide reductase (VKORC1) enzyme complex. This reduces the regeneration of vitamin K epoxide and causes depletion of active clotting factors II, VII, IX and X and proteins C and S.

DRUG	DOSING	SAFETY/SIDE EFFECTS/MONITORING
Warfarin (Coumadin,* **Jantoven)** Tablet Missed Dose: Take immediately on the same day; do not double the dose the next day to make up for a missed dose	Healthy outpatients: ≤ 10 mg daily for first 2 days, then adjust dose per INR Lower doses (≤ 5 mg) for elderly, malnourished, taking drugs which can ↑ warfarin levels, liver disease, heart failure, or have a high risk of bleeding Take at the same time each day Highly protein bound (99%) See Study Tip Gal on the next page for tablet colors	**BOXED WARNINGS** Major or fatal bleeding **CONTRAINDICATIONS** Pregnancy (except with mechanical heart valves at high risk for thromboembolism), hemorrhagic tendencies, blood dyscrasias, uncontrolled hypertension, noncompliance, recent or potential surgery of the eye or CNS, major regional lumbar block anesthesia or traumatic surgery resulting in large open surfaces, pericarditis or pericardial effusion, bacterial endocarditis, preeclampsia/eclampsia, possible miscarriage **WARNINGS** Tissue necrosis/gangrene, HIT (contraindicated as monotherapy in the initial treatment of active HIT), systemic atheroemboli and cholesterol microemboli, presence of CYP2C9*2 or *3 alleles and/or polymorphism of VKORC1 gene may increase bleeding risk (routine genetic testing is not currently recommended; see Pharmacogenomics chapter) **SIDE EFFECTS** Bleeding/bruising (mild to severe), skin necrosis, purple toe syndrome **MONITORING** Goal INR 2-3 (target 2.5): most indications (VTE, AF, bioprosthetic mitral valve, mechanical aortic valve, antiphospholipid syndrome) Goal INR 2.5-3.5 (target 3): high-risk indications such as a mechanical mitral valve or 2 mechanical heart valves Begin INR monitoring after the initial 2 or 3 doses, or if on a chronic, stable dose of warfarin, monitor every 4-12 weeks Hct, Hgb, signs of bleeding **NOTES** Antidote: vitamin K (see Antidotes and Reversal section for details) Dental cleanings and single tooth extraction do not generally require a change in warfarin dosing, if INR is in therapeutic range

*Brand discontinued but name still used in practice.

WARFARIN DRUG INTERACTIONS

Warfarin is a racemic mixture of two active enantiomers (R-warfarin and S-warfarin). Both enantiomers undergo CYP-mediated metabolism by several CYP enzymes. S-warfarin is primarily metabolized via CYP2C9, while R-warfarin is primarily metabolized via CYP3A4. S-warfarin is 3 – 5 times more potent than R-warfarin in producing an anticoagulant response. This is why drugs that interact via CYP2C9 have a greater impact on the anticoagulant effect of warfarin.

Pharmacokinetic Interactions

- Warfarin is a substrate of CYP2C9 (major), 1A2 (minor), 2C19 (minor) and 3A4 (minor), and an inhibitor of CYP2C9 (weak) and 2C19 (weak). See Drug Interactions chapter.

- CYP2C9 inducers can ↓ INR; includes aprepitant, bosentan, carbamazepine, phenobarbital, phenytoin, primidone, rifampin (large ↓ in INR), licorice and St. John's wort.

- CYP2C9 inhibitors can ↑ INR; includes amiodarone, azole antifungals (e.g., fluconazole, ketoconazole, voriconazole), capecitabine, cimetidine, fluvastatin, fluvoxamine, metronidazole, tamoxifen, tigecycline, TMP/SMX and zafirlukast.

  - When starting amiodarone, ↓ the dose of warfarin by 30 – 50%.

  - Avoid use with tamoxifen.

- Other antibiotics: penicillins, including amoxicillin, some cephalosporins, quinolones and tetracyclines can ↑ the anticoagulant effect of warfarin – monitor INR.

- Check for CYP1A2, 2C19 and 3A4 interactions; these occur, but usually have less of an effect on INR.

Pharmacodynamic Drug Interactions

- The most common pharmacodynamic interactions are with NSAIDs, antiplatelet agents, other anticoagulants, SSRIs and SNRIs. These interactions ↑ bleeding risk, but the INR may not be increased.
- Drugs that ↑ clotting risk (e.g., estrogen and SERMs) should be discontinued if possible.

Dietary Supplements/Food Interactions

- Monitor the INR closely if patients are taking natural products with warfarin, but understand that some natural products contain plant salicylates (e.g., willow bark) which increase the risk of bleeding without increasing the INR.
  - ❑ ↑ bleeding risk with warfarin: "the 5 G's" (garlic, ginger, ginkgo, ginseng, glucosamine), bromelain, dong quai, vitamin E, evening primrose oil, high doses of fish oils, goldenseal, grapefruit, policosanol, willow bark and wintergreen oil.
  - ❑ ↓ effectiveness of warfarin: alfalfa, green tea, coenzyme Q10 and St. John's wort. American ginseng may decrease the effects of warfarin, but there is evidence that both American and Panax ginseng inhibit platelet aggregation (listed above), which potentially has the opposite effect.
- Any additions of vitamin K will ↓ the INR. Check any nutritional products (including enteral nutrition) for vitamin K content. Stay consistent with the amount of vitamin K in the diet (see Foods High in Vitamin K box). Tube feeds should be held one hour before and after warfarin.

WARFARIN TABLET COLORS

Pink (1 mg)	**P**each (5 mg)
Lavender (2 mg)	**T**eal (6 mg)
Green (2.5 mg)	**Y**ellow (7.5 mg)
Brown/Tan (3 mg)	**W**hite (10 mg)
Blue (4 mg)	

Remember:

Please **L**et **G**reg **B**rown **B**ring **P**eaches **T**o **Y**our **W**edding

FOODS HIGH IN VITAMIN K

Spinach	Kale
Broccoli	Mustard greens
Brussel sprouts	Swiss chard
Cabbage	Collard greens
Beef liver	Parsley

Others: canola oil, cauliflower, chickpeas, cole slaw, coriander, endive, lettuce (red leaf or butterhead), soybean oil, some teas

WARFARIN USE – KEY POINTS

- In healthy outpatients, the suggested initial starting dose of warfarin is ≤ 10 mg daily for the first two days, then adjust per INR values.
- In patients with acute DVT/PE, start warfarin on the same day as the parenteral anticoagulant (e.g., enoxaparin or UFH) and continue both anticoagulants for a minimum of 5 days and until the INR is ≥ 2 for at least 24 hours. Both criteria must be met.
- Routine pharmacogenomic testing is not recommended.
- Routine use of vitamin K supplementation is not recommended in patients taking warfarin.
- For patients with stable therapeutic INRs presenting with a single subtherapeutic (low) INR value, routinely bridging with UFH or LMWH is not recommended.
- For patients with previously stable therapeutic INRs who present with a single out-of-range INR of ≤ 0.5 below or above the therapeutic range, continue current dose and obtain another INR within 1 – 2 weeks.
- For patients with consistently stable INRs on warfarin therapy, INR testing can be done up to every 12 weeks rather than every 4 weeks.
- Warfarin is highly protein bound. Caution is advised with other highly protein bound drugs that may displace warfarin such as phenytoin, valproic acid and others.

ANTIDOTES FOR REVERSAL

Bleeding is the major adverse effect of anticoagulants. Bleeding can be serious and fatal. Anticoagulation needs to be reversed if a patient experiences life-threatening bleeding or requires surgery.

Protamine combines with strongly acidic heparin to form a stable salt complex, neutralizing the anticoagulant activity of UFH and LMWH. Other drug-specific antidotes include: phytonadione (vitamin K), *Praxbind* and *Andexxa*. *Kcentra* is indicated for the urgent reversal of warfarin. Prothrombin complex concentrates (PCCs) are sometimes used (off-label) for reversal of factor Xa inhibitors. If PCCs are used in this manner, monitoring clotting tests (PT, PTT, INR, anti-Xa) to assess reversal is not useful and is not recommended.

ANTIDOTE	DOSING	SAFETY/SIDE EFFECTS/MONITORING
For UFH/LMWH reversal		
Protamine sulfate Injection 10 mg/mL (5 mL, 25 mL)	**For IV UFH Reversal** 1 mg protamine will reverse ~100 units of heparin Since UFH has a very short half-life, reverse the amount of heparin given in the last 2-2.5 hours; max dose: 50 mg **For LMWH Reversal** Enoxaparin given within the last 8 hours: 1 mg protamine per 1 mg of enoxaparin (can neutralize ~60% of the anti-Xa activity of LMWH) Enoxaparin given > 8 hours ago: 0.5 mg protamine per 1 mg of enoxaparin Dalteparin: 1 mg protamine for each 100 anti-Xa units of dalteparin	**BOXED WARNINGS** Hypersensitivity: hypotension, cardiovascular collapse, non-cardiogenic pulmonary edema, pulmonary vasoconstriction **SIDE EFFECTS** Hypotension, bradycardia, flushing, anaphylaxis **MONITORING** aPTT, anti-Xa levels, cardiac monitoring (ECG, BP, HR) **NOTES** Rapid IV infusion causes hypotension Administer slow IV push (50 mg over 10 minutes) Inject without further dilution over 1-3 minutes
For dabigatran reversal		
Idarucizumab (Praxbind) Injection 2.5 g/50 mL single-use vial	5 grams IV (given as 2 separate 2.5 gram doses no more than 15 minutes apart)	**WARNINGS** Thromboembolic risk, risk of serious adverse reactions due to sorbitol excipient **SIDE EFFECTS** Headache, ↓ K, delirium, constipation, fever **NOTES** Do not confuse with Idarubicin
For reversal of the Factor Xa inhibitors apixaban and rivaroxaban		
Andexanet alfa (Andexxa) Injection	Bolus, followed by infusion Dosing is specific to the Xa inhibitor, the dose and when the last Xa inhibitor dose was taken	**BOXED WARNINGS** Thromboembolic risks, ischemic events, cardiac arrest, sudden death **SIDE EFFECTS** Injection site reaction, DVT, ischemic stroke, UTI, pneumonia **NOTES** Not indicated for reversal of factor Xa inhibitors other than apixaban and rivaroxaban

ANTIDOTE	DOSING	SAFETY/SIDE EFFECTS/MONITORING
For warfarin reversal		
Vitamin K or phytonadione (Mephyton) 5 mg tablets 1 mg/0.5 mL, 10 mg/mL injection	1-10 mg PO/IV If given IV, infuse slowly; rate of infusion should not exceed 1 mg/min To ↓ risk of anaphylaxis, dilute dose in a minimum of 50 mL of compatible solution and administer using an infusion pump over at least 20 minutes	**BOXED WARNINGS** Severe reactions resembling hypersensitivity reactions (e.g., anaphylaxis) have occurred rarely during or immediately after IV administration (even with proper dilution and rate of administration); some patients had no previous exposure to phytonadione **SIDE EFFECTS** Anaphylaxis, flushing, rash, dizziness **NOTES** Requires light protection during administration SC route not recommended due to variable absorption; IM route not recommended due to risk of hematoma Orlistat and mineral oil ↓ absorption of oral vitamin K See specific dosing recommendations in Warfarin Reversal section
Four Factor Prothrombin Complex Concentrate (Human) (Kcentra) Injection Factors II, VII, IX, X, Protein C, Protein S	IV dose is based on units of Factor IX per kg of body weight and patient's INR Do not repeat dose	**BOXED WARNINGS** Arterial and venous thromboembolic complications have been reported **CONTRAINDICATIONS** Disseminated intravascular coagulation (DIC) and known HIT (contains heparin) **WARNINGS** Made from human blood and may carry risk of transmitting infectious agents **SIDE EFFECTS** Headache, N/V/D, arthralgia, hypotension, ↓ K, thrombotic events **NOTES** Administer with vitamin K Do not let drug back-up into line; will clot Refrigerate; allow to reach room temp prior to administration Each vial can have a different potency of multiple coagulation factors; actual potency is stated on the vial
Three Factor Prothrombin Complex Concentrate (Human) (Profilnine) Off-label	Weight-based dosing; give IV slowly Given with fresh frozen plasma (FFP) or factor VIIa	**WARNINGS** Contains factors II, IX and X but low or nontherapeutic levels of factor VII and should not be confused with Kcentra, which contains therapeutic levels of factor VII Made from human blood and may carry risk of transmitting infectious agents (e.g., viruses) **SIDE EFFECTS** Chills, fever, flushing, nausea, headache, risk of thrombosis **NOTES** Slow infusion and give antihistamine to minimize side effects Administer with vitamin K
Factor VIIa Recombinant (NovoSeven RT) Off-label	10-20 mcg/kg IV bolus over 5 minutes	**BOXED WARNINGS** Serious thrombotic events are associated with the use of factor VIIa

WARFARIN REVERSAL

Variable INRs are common in clinical practice. Elevated INRs are concerning due to an increased risk of bleeding. Vitamin K is used to reverse warfarin (to ↓ the INR more quickly); it can be used by itself or with other medications for life-threatening bleeding. Bleeding (regardless of the INR) will warrant more serious intervention.

Oral formulations of vitamin K (generally at doses of 2.5 – 5 mg) are preferred for reversal in patients without significant or major bleeding. Vitamin K given subcutaneously (SC) has a slow onset and a variable response; avoid SC injections. Avoid the intramuscular (IM) route due to the risk of hematoma formation. Intravenous vitamin K should be used only when the patient is experiencing serious bleeding. IV injection is reported to cause anaphylaxis in 3 out of 100,000 patients, so infuse slowly.

Use of Vitamin K for Overanticoagulation

SYMPTOMS/INR VALUE	WHAT TO DO
INR above therapeutic range but < 4.5 without bleeding	Reduce or skip warfarin dose. Monitor INR. Resume warfarin when INR therapeutic. Dose reduction may not be needed if only slightly above therapeutic range.
Supratherapeutic INR of 4.5-10 without bleeding	Routine use of vitamin K is not recommended if no evidence of bleeding. Hold 1-2 doses of warfarin. Monitor INR. Resume warfarin at lower dose when INR therapeutic. Vitamin K can be used if urgent surgery needed (≤ 5 mg, with additional 1-2 mg in 24 hours if needed) or bleeding risk is high (1-2.5 mg).
INR > 10 without bleeding	Hold warfarin. Give oral vitamin K 2.5-5 mg even if not bleeding. Monitor INR. Resume warfarin at a lower dose when INR is therapeutic.
Major bleeding	Hold warfarin. Give vitamin K 5-10 mg by slow IV injection and four-factor prothrombin complex concentrate (PCC). PCC suggested over fresh frozen plasma (FFP) due to risks of allergic reactions, infection transmission, longer preparation time, slower onset and higher volume.

PERIOPERATIVE MANAGEMENT OF PATIENTS ON WARFARIN

- Stop warfarin therapy approximately five days before major surgery. In patients with a mechanical heart valve, AF or VTE at high risk for thromboembolism, bridging therapy with LMWH or UFH is recommended (bridging means stopping the warfarin and using anticoagulant doses of the LMWH or UFH for a short period to prevent clotting). Discontinue therapeutic-dose SC LMWH 24 hours before surgery (stop the UFH IV therapy 4 – 6 hours before surgery). Patients at low risk for thromboembolism do not require bridging; stop the warfarin and restart after surgery when hemostasis is achieved.
- If INR is still elevated 1 – 2 days before surgery, give low-dose vitamin K (1 – 2 mg).
- If reversal of warfarin is needed in a patient requiring an urgent surgical procedure, give low-dose (2.5 – 5 mg) IV or oral vitamin K.
- Resume warfarin therapy 12 – 24 hours after the surgery, when there is adequate hemostasis.

VENOUS THROMBOEMBOLISM (VTE)

DIAGNOSIS

Symptoms of a DVT include pain in the affected limb and unilateral lower extremity swelling. DVTs can be diagnosed with an ultrasound (or MRI or venography, in some cases). A D-dimer (a lab test) can aid in the diagnosis. If a PE is suspected, it is diagnosed with a pulmonary CT angiogram.

VTE PROPHYLAXIS

Risk factors for the development of VTE are shown below. Various guidelines provide specific recommendations for the prevention of VTE depending on the patient's level of risk. UFH, LMWHs, fondaparinux, rivaroxaban, apixaban and dabigatran are all approved for VTE prophylaxis (refer to the recommended doses in the drug tables). If patients have a contraindication to anticoagulants (such as an active bleed) or have a high risk for bleeding, they will need non-drug alternatives to prevent VTE. These options include intermittent pneumatic compression (IPC) devices or graduated compression stockings.

RISK FACTORS FOR THE DEVELOPMENT OF VENOUS THROMBOEMBOLISM

Modifiable:	Non-modifiable:
Acute medical illness	Increasing age
Immobility	Cancer or chemotherapy
Medications (SERMs, drugs containing estrogen, erythropoiesis-stimulating agents)	Previous VTE
Obesity (BMI ≥ 30 kg/m²)	Inherited or acquired thrombophilia (e.g., antithrombin deficiency, factor V Leiden, antiphospholipid syndrome, protein C or S deficiency)
Pregnancy and postpartum period	Central venous catheterization
Recent surgery or major trauma	Certain disease states (e.g., heart failure, nephrotic syndrome, respiratory failure)
	Venous compression (tumor, hematoma, arterial abnormality)

For <u>long-distance travelers</u> at risk for VTE (previous VTE, recent surgery or trauma, active malignancy, pregnancy, estrogen use, advanced age, limited mobility, severe obesity or known thrombophilic disorder), the following recommendations will ↓ VTE risk: <u>frequent ambulation, calf muscle exercises,</u> sitting in an aisle seat and <u>using graduated compression stockings</u> with 15 – 30 mmHg of pressure at the ankle during travel. Aspirin or anticoagulants should <u>not</u> be used.

VTE TREATMENT

Any VTE that is caused by surgery or a reversible risk factor should be <u>treated for three months</u>. If the VTE is unprovoked (unknown cause), extending therapy longer than three months is recommended, as long as the patient's bleeding risk is low-to-moderate. If the risk of bleeding is high, limit the treatment to three months. If a patient has two unprovoked VTE episodes, long-term treatment can be considered. <u>Estrogen-containing medications</u> and <u>selective estrogen receptor modulators</u> (SERMs) are <u>contraindicated</u> in patients with <u>history of, or current, VTE and should be discontinued</u>.

- For patients <u>without cancer, dabigatran and the oral factor Xa inhibitors</u> (rivaroxaban, apixaban and edoxaban) <u>are preferred over warfarin for the first three months</u> of treatment for a DVT in the leg or a PE.

- For patients <u>with cancer, the oral factor Xa inhibitors are preferred over other oral anticoagulants and LMWH</u>.

- In patients with an unprovoked DVT or PE who are stopping anticoagulation, aspirin is recommended to prevent recurrence (if there are no contraindications).

ATRIAL FIBRILLATION/FLUTTER

Patients with atrial fibrillation (AF) or atrial flutter can form clots in the heart. Clots that are ejected from the heart can travel to the brain and cause a stroke (cardioembolic stroke) or transient ischemic attack (TIA). Stroke prevention is an important goal in patients with AF/atrial flutter (see Arrhythmias chapter).

AF and atrial flutter are common in patients with heart valve problems. Some of these patients require valve replacement surgery. This involves replacing the damaged valve with a mechanical (prosthetic) or animal (sometimes called a bioprosthetic) valve. Patients with <u>mechanical heart valves</u> have the <u>highest risk for clotting/strokes</u> and are treated with <u>warfarin only</u>. <u>Factor Xa inhibitors</u> and <u>DTIs</u> are <u>not approved</u> for this population.

ANTICOAGULATION FOR PATIENTS WITH AF WHO WILL UNDERGO CARDIOVERSION

- AF > 48 hours or unknown duration: anticoagulation (if warfarin, target INR 2–3) for at least <u>3 weeks prior to and 4 weeks after cardioversion</u> (regardless of method – electrical or pharmacologic) when normal sinus rhythm is restored.

- AF ≤ 48 hours duration undergoing elective cardioversion: start full therapeutic anticoagulation at presentation, perform cardioversion, and <u>continue full anticoagulation for at least 4 weeks</u> while patient is in normal sinus rhythm.

- For patients staying in AF, chronic anticoagulation therapy may be needed for stroke prevention. Treatment depends on the number of risk factors present. See text.

The majority of patients with AF/atrial flutter do not have heart valve involvement (called <u>nonvalvular</u> AF), but they still require evaluation of their stroke risk. The <u>CHA$_2$DS$_2$-VASc scoring system</u> is used to <u>estimate the risk of stroke in AF/atrial flutter</u> and guide therapy (see next page). In previous guidelines the simpler CHADS$_2$ scoring system was used but this did not take into account additional factors such as vascular disease, age and sex.

The HAS-BLED scoring system is used to assess bleeding risk for patients being anticoagulated for stroke prevention with AF. The decision to anticoagulate is individualized based on the risk of stroke (CHA$_2$DS$_2$-VASc) when compared to the risk of bleeding (HAS-BLED).

CHA$_2$DS$_2$-VASc Scoring System

Count the number of risk factors the patient has, then select the recommended therapy. The higher the score, the greater the stroke risk and the more intensive the anticoagulant recommendations.

CHA$_2$DS$_2$-VASc SCORING SYSTEM
Add up the total number of risk factors for a given patient.
C – CHF..1
H – HTN..1
A – Age ≥ 75 Years...2
D – Diabetes...1
S$_2$ – Prior Stroke/TIA 2
V – Vascular Disease ....1 (prior MI, PAD, aortic plaque)
A – Age 65-74 Years..1
S – Sex Category, Female..................................1

CHA$_2$DS$_2$-VASC SCORE	RISK OF STROKE	RECOMMENDED THERAPY
0 (males) 1 (females)	Low	No anticoagulation recommended.
≥ 1 (males) ≥ 2 (females)	Moderate	Oral anticoagulation may be considered.
≥ 2 (males) ≥ 3 (females)	High	Oral anticoagulation is recommended. Non-vitamin K oral anticoagulant (DOAC*) is recommended over warfarin.

*DOAC: apixaban, rivaroxaban, edoxaban, dabigatran

HAS-BLED Scoring System

Count the number of risk factors the patient has. The higher the score, the greater the risk of bleeding.

HAS-BLED SCORING SYSTEM
Add up the total number of risk factors for a given patient.
H – HTN (SBP > 160 mmHg).............................1
A – Abnormal Liver or Kidney Function.............1-2
S – Prior Stroke..1
B – Bleeding Tendency or Predisposition.........1
L – Labile INR (if on warfarin)..........................1
E – Elderly (age > 65 years).............................1
D – Drugs (aspirin or NSAIDs), excess alcohol use..1-2

ANTICOAGULATION IN PREGNANCY

For prevention and treatment of VTE in pregnant women, LMWH is preferred over UFH. Pneumatic compression devices can be used alone or with LMWH in select patients. Since warfarin is teratogenic, women who require chronic warfarin therapy for mechanical heart valves or inherited thrombophilias are generally converted to LMWH during pregnancy. They may be switched back to warfarin after the 13th week of pregnancy (i.e., after the first trimester), then back to LMWH close to delivery. When LMWH is used in pregnancy, anti-Xa levels are recommended to monitor therapy. The oral factor Xa inhibitors and direct thrombin inhibitors have not been adequately studied in pregnancy and are not recommended.

KEY COUNSELING POINTS

See the Drug Formulations and Patient Counseling chapter for counseling language/layman's terminology.

FOR ALL ANTICOAGULANTS

- Can cause serious and life-threatening bleeding/bruising.

- Tell physicians and dentists that you are using this medication before any surgery is performed.

- Call your healthcare provider right away if you fall or injure yourself, especially if you hit your head.

- Avoid alcohol.

- Many drug interactions.

- Missed dose: take as soon as possible on the same day. Do not take a double dose the next day to make up for a missed dose.

Dabigatran

- Take with a full glass of water; swallow capsules whole.

- Can cause dyspepsia.

- Only open one bottle of dabigatran at a time. After opening a bottle of dabigatran, use within four months.

- Keep dabigatran in the original bottle or blister package. Do not put dabigatran in pill boxes or pill organizers.

- Missed dose: if your next dose is less than six hours away, skip the missed dose.

Rivaroxaban

- Atrial fibrillation: take once daily with the evening meal.

- Blood clots in the veins of your legs or in the lungs: take once or twice daily as prescribed with food at the same time each day.

- Missed dose: if taken twice daily, can take two doses at the same time to make up for the missed dose.

Enoxaparin

- Subcutaneous injection; choose an area on the <u>right or left side of your abdomen, at least two inches from the belly button</u> (see image). Wash your hands and clean the site.

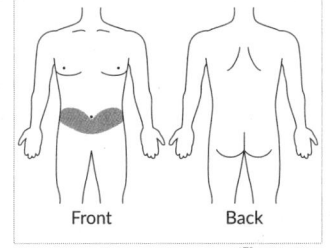

Front   Back

©RxPrep

- Remove the needle cap by pulling it straight off the syringe. Do not twist the cap off as this can bend the needle.

- <u>Do not expel the air bubble in the syringe prior to injection unless your healthcare provider has advised you to do so.</u>

- Hold the syringe like a pencil. Pinch an inch of skin to make a fold. Insert the full length of the needle straight down at a 90-degree angle into the fold of the skin.

- Press the plunger with your thumb until the syringe is empty.

- Pull the needle straight out at the same angle that it was inserted, and release the skin fold.

- Point the needle down and away from yourself and others, and push down on the plunger to activate the safety shield.

- <u>Do not rub the site of injection</u> as this can lead to bruising. Place the used syringe in the sharps collector.

Warfarin

- Take at the same time every day.

- Ask your pharmacist if your tablet looks different.

- Can rarely cause:
  - Purple toe syndrome (painful toes and purple discoloration).
  - Death of skin tissue (with pain).

- Frequent blood monitoring required (INR).

- Consistent intake of vitamin K required (mainly found in green, leafy vegetables).

Select Guidelines/References

Antithrombotic Therapy for VTE Disease: Second Update of the CHEST Guideline and Expert Panel Report. CHEST 2021;160(6):2247-2259.

Antithrombotic Therapy for VTE Disease: CHEST Guideline Expert Panel Report. CHEST 2016;149(2):315-352.

Antithrombotic Therapy for Atrial Fibrillation: CHEST Guideline Expert Panel Report. CHEST 2018;154(2):1121-1201.

CONTENT LEGEND

  💡 = Study Tip Gal   🔑 = Key Drug Guy

Normal Amount of Red Blood Cells   Anemic Amount of Red Blood Cells

— Red Blood Cell
— Platelet
— White Blood Cell

© Balint Roxana © 123RF.com

CHAPTER 35
ANEMIA

BACKGROUND

Anemia is the most common blood disorder worldwide and it affects approximately 3.5 million Americans. Anemia is a decrease in hemoglobin (Hgb) and hematocrit (Hct) concentrations below the normal range for age and gender. Hgb is an iron-rich protein found in red blood cells (RBCs); its main purpose is to carry oxygen from the lungs to the tissues. RBCs are formed in the bone marrow, where they take up Hgb and iron before being released into the circulation as immature RBCs, known as reticulocytes. After 1 – 2 days, the reticulocytes mature into erythrocytes, which have a lifespan of about 120 days. Erythrocytes are removed from circulation by macrophages, mainly in the spleen.

Anemia can occur due to impaired RBC production, increased RBC destruction (hemolysis) or blood loss. A decrease in Hgb or RBC volume results in decreased oxygen carrying capacity of the blood. Diagnosis of the underlying cause is essential. Anemia can result from nutritional deficiencies (e.g., iron, folate, vitamin B12) or it can occur as a complication of another medical disorder, such as chronic kidney disease (CKD) or a malignancy.

SYMPTOMS OF ANEMIA

Most patients with mild or early stage anemia are asymptomatic. If anemia becomes severe and/or prolonged, the lack of oxygen in the blood can lead to classic symptoms of fatigue, weakness, shortness of breath, exercise intolerance, headache, dizziness, anorexia and/or pallor. If sudden blood loss occurs, the patient can experience acute symptoms, such as chest pain, fainting, palpitations and tachycardia. Glossitis (an inflamed, sore tongue), koilonychias (thin, concave, spoon-shaped nails) or pica (craving and eating non-foods such as chalk or clay) can develop with iron deficiency anemia. Patients with vitamin B12 (cobalamin) deficiency can present with neurologic symptoms, including peripheral neuropathies, visual disturbances and/or psychiatric symptoms.

A decreased oxygen supply can cause ischemic damage to many organs. In chronic anemia, the heart tries to compensate for low oxygen levels by pumping faster (tachycardia). This can increase the mass of the ventricular wall (hypertrophy) and lead to heart failure.

TYPES OF ANEMIA

The type and cause of anemia cannot be determined based on signs and symptoms alone. The mean corpuscular volume (MCV), which reflects the size or average volume of RBCs, can help determine the type of anemia and the possible underlying cause. A low MCV means that RBCs are smaller than normal (microcytic) and a high MCV means that RBCs are larger than normal (macrocytic). These findings correlate with different causes of anemia. Certain genetic conditions can cause anemia due to dysfunctional RBCs (see the Sickle Cell Disease chapter).

Identifying the Cause of Anemia

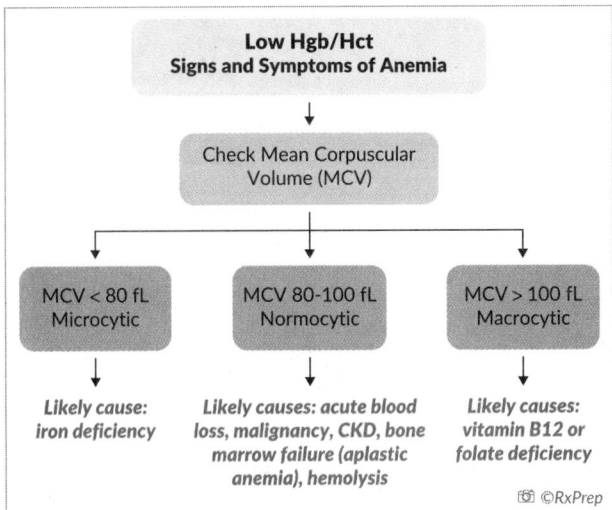

Laboratory tests are used to determine the type and cause of anemia.

- Iron studies further evaluate microcytic anemia; they include serum iron (bound to transferrin), serum ferritin (iron stores), transferrin saturation (amount of transferrin binding sites occupied by iron) and total iron binding capacity (amount of transferrin binding sites available to bind iron or unbound sites).

- Vitamin B12 and folate levels further evaluate macrocytic anemia. Vitamin B12 is required for enzyme reactions involving methylmalonic acid and homocysteine, making these tests potentially useful in confirming a diagnosis.

- A reticulocyte count measures production of RBCs. The reticulocyte count is low in untreated anemia due to iron, folate or B12 deficiency and with bone marrow suppression. The reticulocyte count is high in acute blood loss or hemolysis.

COMMON LABORATORY TESTS IN ANEMIA*

Relevant CBC Components
Hemoglobin (Hgb)

Hematocrit (Hct)

Red Blood Cell (RBC) Count

Reticulocyte Count

RBC Indices
Mean Corpuscular Volume (MCV)

Mean Corpuscular Hemoglobin (MCH)

Mean Corpuscular Hemoglobin Concentration (MCHC)

Red Blood Cell Distribution Width (RDW)

Iron Studies
Serum Iron

Serum Ferritin

Total Iron Binding Capacity (TIBC)

Transferrin Saturation (TSAT)

Additional Tests
Serum Folate

Serum Vitamin B12

Methylmalonic Acid

Homocysteine

Refer to the Lab Values & Drug Monitoring chapter for normal laboratory ranges in adults.

IRON DEFICIENCY ANEMIA

Iron deficiency is the most common nutritional deficiency in the United States. Common causes are shown in the box below. Dietary iron is available in two forms: heme iron (found in meat and seafood) and non-heme iron (found in nuts, beans, vegetables and fortified grains, such as cereals). Heme iron is more readily absorbed than non-heme iron, which is affected by gastric pH and other foods being consumed. Meat, seafood, poultry and ascorbic acid increase the absorption of non-heme iron, while foods that contain phytate and polyphenols (e.g., grains, beans, cereals and legumes) can decrease non-heme iron absorption. This is particularly important for patients who follow a vegetarian diet, since they are more likely to consume foods with a less absorbable form of iron along with foods that decrease the absorption of iron. Vegetarians may require iron supplementation, even if dietary intake of iron seems adequate.

CAUSES OF IRON DEFICIENCY

Inadequate Dietary Intake
- Iron-poor diets (e.g., vegetarian, vegan), malnutrition, disease-related (e.g., dementia, psychosis)

Blood Loss
- Acute (e.g., GI hemorrhage), chronic (e.g., heavy menses, blood donations, peptic ulcer disease, inflammatory bowel disease) or drug-induced (e.g., NSAIDs, steroids, antiplatelets, anticoagulants)

Decreased Iron Absorption
- High gastric pH (e.g., PPIs), GI diseases (e.g., celiac disease, inflammatory bowel disease, gastrectomy, gastric bypass)

Increased Iron Requirements
- Pregnancy, lactation, infants*, rapid growth (e.g., adolescence)

See the Dietary Supplements, Natural & Complimentary Medicine chapter for infant iron requirements.

Preventative measures can be used for some of the at-risk patient populations. For example, women who use hormonal contraception may experience less bleeding during menstrual periods and their risk of developing iron deficiency may be lower. The CDC recommends low-dose iron supplementation (30 mg/day) for all pregnant women, beginning at the first prenatal visit; this is usually provided in the prenatal vitamin. Larger doses of iron are required if iron deficiency anemia (IDA) is diagnosed in pregnancy.

DIAGNOSIS AND TREATMENT OF IRON DEFICIENCY ANEMIA

The Study Tip Gal below summarizes the laboratory findings that are consistent with a diagnosis of IDA as well as important treatment information.

ASSESSING AND TREATING IRON DEFICIENCY ANEMIA

LABORATORY FINDINGS
- ↓ Hgb, MCV < 80 fL, ↓ RBC production (low reticulocyte count)
- ↓ serum iron, ferritin and TSAT
- ↑ TIBC

TREATMENT: ORAL IRON THERAPY
- Recommended dose: 100-200 mg elemental iron per day*
- Take iron on an empty stomach**
- Avoid H2RAs and PPIs; separate from antacids
- Sustained-release or enteric-coated formulations cause less GI irritation but are not recommended due to poor absorption

GOALS
- ↑ in serum Hgb by 1 g/dL every 2-3 weeks; continue treatment for 3-6 months after anemia has resolved until iron stores return to normal

% ELEMENTAL IRON IN ORAL PRODUCTS

Ferrous gluconate	12%
Ferrous sulfate	20%
Ferrous sulfate, dried	30%
Ferrous fumarate	33%
Carbonyl iron, polysaccharide iron complex, ferric maltol	100%

*One oral formulation is not better than another if dosed appropriately based on elemental iron needs.
**1 hr before or 2 hrs after meals; can be taken with food if GI upset occurs.

Oral Iron

Most IDA is adequately treated with oral iron supplements. Parenteral iron is primarily used in dialysis. Many iron products contain "fe," "fer" or "ferr" in the drug name.

DRUG	DOSING	SAFETY/SIDE EFFECTS/MONITORING
Ferrous sulfate (FeroSul, Fer-In-Sol, many OTC multivitamins with iron) Tablet, elixir, oral solution, syrup	325 mg (65 mg elemental iron) PO daily to TID Most commonly prescribed and the least expensive	**BOXED WARNING** Accidental overdose of iron-containing products is a leading cause of fatal poisoning in children under 6; keep iron out of the reach of children; in the case of an accidental overdose, go to the emergency department or call a poison control center immediately (even if asymptomatic)
Ferrous sulfate, dried (Slow Fe, Slow Iron) ER tablet	160 mg (50 mg elemental iron) PO daily to TID	**CONTRAINDICATIONS** Hemochromatosis, hemolytic anemia, hemosiderosis
Ferrous fumarate (Ferretts, Ferrimin 150, Hemocyte)	324 mg (106 mg elemental iron) PO daily to TID	**SIDE EFFECTS** Constipation (dose-related), dark and tarry stools, nausea, stomach upset
Ferrous gluconate (Ferate)	324 mg (38 mg elemental iron) PO daily to TID	**MONITORING** Hgb, iron studies, RBC indices, reticulocyte count
Carbonyl iron (FerraPlus 90, Ferralet 90, Iron Chews)	90 mg (90 mg elemental iron) PO daily or as directed	**NOTES** A stool softener such as docusate is often recommended to prevent iron-induced constipation
Polysaccharide iron complex (Ferrex 150, others) Capsules, liquid	150 mg (150 mg elemental iron) PO daily	The antidote for iron overdose is deferoxamine (Desferal)
Ferric maltol (Accrufer)	30 mg (30 mg elemental iron) PO BID	

Oral Iron Drug Interactions

- Antacids, H2RAs and PPIs ↓ iron absorption by ↑ gastric pH. Patients should take iron 2 hours before or 4 hours after taking antacids. H2RAs and PPIs raise gastric pH for up to 24 hours; separating the administration of these agents from iron supplements does not improve absorption.

- Iron is a polyvalent cation that can ↓ the absorption of other drugs by binding with them in the GI tract to form nonabsorbable complexes. Separate administration of iron supplements from the following agents (consult prescribing information for exact details):

  ❑ Quinolone and tetracycline antibiotics (less of a concern with doxycycline and minocycline): take iron two hours before or 4 – 8 hours after these agents.

  ❑ Bisphosphonates: take iron 60 minutes after oral ibandronate or 30 minutes after alendronate/risedronate.

  ❑ Cefdinir, dolutegravir, levothyroxine, levodopa and methyldopa: separate from iron by 2 – 4 hours.

- Vitamin C ↑ the absorption of iron (by providing an acidic environment). Giving iron with ascorbic acid (vitamin C 200 mg) may enhance the absorption to a minimal extent.

Intravenous (Parenteral) Iron

Parenteral iron increases Hgb faster than oral iron and reduces gastrointestinal issues seen with oral administration. The total dose needed to replenish iron stores (e.g., 1,000 mg) can be provided in a single infusion, if desired. Due to the risk of more severe adverse reactions, as well as the cost of therapy, IV iron administration is typically restricted to the following patients:

- CKD on hemodialysis (most common use of IV iron).

- CKD receiving erythropoiesis-stimulating agents (ESAs).

- Unable to tolerate oral iron or failure of oral therapy (e.g., IBD, celiac disease, certain gastric bypass procedures, achlorhydria and bacterial overgrowth syndromes such as *H. pylori*).

- Losing iron too fast for oral replacement.

- As an alternative when blood transfusions are not accepted by the patient (e.g., for religious reasons).

DRUG	SAFETY/SIDE EFFECTS/MONITORING
Iron sucrose (Venofer)	**BOXED WARNING (IRON DEXTRAN AND FERUMOXYTOL)** Serious and sometimes fatal anaphylactic reactions have occurred with the use of iron dextran or ferumoxytol; all patients receiving iron dextran should be given a test dose prior to the first full therapeutic dose; fatal reactions have occurred even in patients who tolerated the test dose; a history of drug allergy or multiple drug allergies may ↑ this risk
Ferumoxytol (Feraheme)	
Iron dextran complex (INFeD)	**SIDE EFFECTS** Muscle aches, flushing, hypotension, hypertension, tachycardia, chest pain and peripheral edema
Sodium ferric gluconate (Ferrlecit)	All parenteral iron products carry a risk for hypersensitivity reactions (including anaphylaxis)
Ferric carboxymaltose (Injectafer)	**MONITORING** Hgb, iron studies, reticulocyte count, vital signs, signs and symptoms of anaphylaxis
Ferric derisomaltose (Monoferric)	**NOTES** Give by slow IV injection or infusion to ↓ the risk of hypotension All agents are stable in NS; *Feraheme* is stable in NS or D5W
Ferric pyrophosphate citrate (Triferic)	*Triferic* is only indicated for iron replacement in patients with hemodialysis-dependent CKD; it should be added to the bicarbonate concentrate of the hemodialysate for patients receiving hemodialysis

MACROCYTIC ANEMIA

Macrocytic anemia is caused by vitamin B12 or folate deficiency, or both. Pernicious anemia, the most common cause of vitamin B12 deficiency, occurs due to a lack of intrinsic factor (IF). IF is required for adequate vitamin B12 absorption in the small intestine; without IF, vitamin B12 deficiency will occur. If pernicious anemia is suspected, patients can be diagnosed with a positive test for autoantibodies to IF. Testing for autoantibodies has replaced the Schilling test, which was previously used to diagnose pernicious anemia. Of note, this type of anemia requires lifelong parenteral vitamin B12 replacement.

Other causes of macrocytic anemia include alcoholism, poor nutrition, gastrointestinal disorders (e.g., Crohn's disease, celiac disease) and pregnancy. The long-term use (≥ 2 years) of metformin, H2RAs or PPIs can decrease the absorption of vitamin B12. Vitamin B12 deficiency can result in serious neurologic dysfunction, including cognitive impairment and peripheral neuropathies. If vitamin B12 deficiency goes undiagnosed for more than three months, neurologic symptoms can become irreversible. Folic acid deficiency does not result in neurologic symptoms; it causes ulcerations of the tongue and oral mucosa and changes to skin, hair and fingernail pigmentation.

DIAGNOSIS OF MACROCYTIC ANEMIA

In addition to low Hgb and high MCV, reticulocyte counts and serum levels of vitamin B12 and/or folate will be low. Since vitamin B12 is required for enzyme reactions involving methylmalonic acid and homocysteine, they accumulate when vitamin B12 is deficient. Homocysteine levels can also be elevated in folate deficiency.

TREATMENT OF MACROCYTIC ANEMIA

The initial treatment of vitamin B12 deficiency typically involves vitamin B12 injections, to bypass absorption barriers, followed by oral supplements, if appropriate. Vitamin B12 injections are recommended first-line for anyone with a severe deficiency or neurological symptoms.

Vitamin B12 and Folic Acid Products

DRUG	DOSING	SAFETY/SIDE EFFECTS/MONITORING
Cyanocobalamin, vitamin B12 (*B-12 Compliance, Nascobal, Physicians EZ Use B-12*, oral generics) Injection, lozenge, tablets (including ER and SL forms), SL liquid, nasal solution	IM or deep SC: 100-1,000 mcg daily/weekly/monthly (varies depending on severity of deficiency) Oral/sublingual: 1,000-2,000 mcg daily *Nascobal*: 500 mcg in one nostril once weekly	**CONTRAINDICATIONS** Allergy to cobalt or vitamin B12 (an intradermal test dose is recommended for any patient suspected of vitamin B12 sensitivity prior to intranasal or injectable administration) **WARNINGS** Parenteral products may contain aluminum (which can accumulate and cause CNS and bone toxicity if renal function is impaired) or benzyl alcohol (which can cause fatal toxicity and "gasping syndrome" in neonates) **SIDE EFFECTS** Pain with injection Rash, polycythemia vera, pulmonary edema (all rare) **MONITORING** Hgb, Hct, vitamin B12, reticulocyte count
Folic acid, folate, vitamin B9 (*FA-8*) Tablet, capsule, injection	0.4-1 mg daily	**WARNINGS** As above for cyanocobalamin **SIDE EFFECTS** Bronchospasm, flushing, rash, pruritus, malaise (all rare) **MONITORING** Hgb, Hct, folate, reticulocyte count

Vitamin B12 and Folic Acid Drug Interactions

- Chloramphenicol can ↓ the efficacy of vitamin B12. Colchicine can ↓ the absorption of vitamin B12.

- The efficacy of raltitrexed (a chemotherapeutic agent) can be ↓ by folic acid; avoid combination.

- Folic acid can ↓ the serum concentration of fosphenytoin, phenytoin, primidone and phenobarbital.

- Green tea and sulfasalazine may ↓ the serum concentration of folic acid.

NORMOCYTIC ANEMIA

ANEMIA OF CHRONIC KIDNEY DISEASE

Erythropoietin (EPO) is a hormone produced by the kidneys that stimulates the bone marrow to produce RBCs. A deficiency of EPO causes anemia of chronic kidney disease (CKD). Iron therapy and erythropoiesis-stimulating agents (ESAs) are the treatments for anemia of CKD.

IV iron is first-line for hemodialysis (HD) patients. Non-HD CKD patients with anemia can be treated with oral iron supplements. The KDIGO (Kidney Disease Improving Global Outcomes) guidelines recommend iron therapy in both non-HD and HD patients if TSAT is ≤ 30% and ferritin levels are ≤ 500 ng/mL. The KDOQI (Kidney Disease Outcomes Quality Initiative) guidelines recommend iron therapy if TSAT is ≤ 20% (non-HD and HD patients) and ferritin levels are ≤ 100 ng/mL in non-HD patients and ≤ 200 ng/mL in HD patients. These criteria are important when using ESAs. ESAs help maintain Hgb levels and reduce the need for blood transfusions, but they are ineffective if iron stores are low.

Erythropoiesis-Stimulating Agents (ESAs)

DRUG	DOSING	SAFETY/SIDE EFFECTS/MONITORING
Epoetin alfa **(Epogen, Procrit,** *Retacrit*-biosimilar) IV, SC Single dose and multidose vials	**Chronic Kidney Disease** 50-100 units/kg IV or SC 3x/week Initiate when Hgb < 10 g/dL ↓ or interrupt dose when Hgb approaches or exceeds 11 g/dL (CKD on HD), or > 10 g/dL (CKD not on HD) **Cancer (taking chemotherapy)** 150 units/kg SC 3x/week or 40,000 units SC weekly Initiate when Hgb < 10 g/dL and when at least 2 additional months of chemotherapy are planned **All Indications:** Titrate dose up or down based on Hgb levels; do not ↑ the dose more frequently than once every 4 weeks	**BOXED WARNINGS** ↑ risk of death, MI, stroke, VTE, thrombosis of vascular access Use the lowest effective dose to reduce the need for blood transfusions Chronic Kidney Disease: ↑ risk of death, serious cardiovascular events and stroke when Hgb level > 11 g/dL Cancer: shortened overall survival and/or ↑ risk of tumor progression or recurrence in clinical studies of patients with some cancers. Not indicated when the anticipated outcome is cure; discontinue when chemotherapy completed Perisurgery (epoetin alfa): DVT prophylaxis is recommended due to ↑ risk of DVT **CONTRAINDICATIONS** Uncontrolled hypertension, pure red cell aplasia (PRCA) that begins after treatment Epoetin alfa: multidose vials contain benzyl alcohol (contraindicated in neonates, infants, pregnancy and lactation) **WARNINGS** Hypertension, seizures, serious allergic reactions, serious skin reactions (SJS/TEN) Epoetin alfa: contains albumin from human blood (remote risk for transmission of viral diseases)
Darbepoetin **(Aranesp)** IV, SC Single dose vial Single dose prefilled syringe (needle included)	**Chronic Kidney Disease** HD: 0.45 mcg/kg IV or SC weekly or 0.75 mcg/kg IV or SC every 2 weeks Non-HD: 0.45 mcg/kg IV or SC every 4 weeks **Cancer (taking chemotherapy)** 2.25 mcg/kg SC weekly or 500 mcg SC every 3 weeks **All Indications:** Initiation and titration criteria are the same as for epoetin alfa	**SIDE EFFECTS** Arthralgia/bone pain, fever, headache, pruritus/rash, N/V, cough, dyspnea, edema, injection site pain, dizziness **MONITORING** Hgb, Hct, TSAT, serum ferritin, BP **NOTES** IV route is recommended for patients on hemodialysis Store in the refrigerator; protect from light; discard multidose vials 21 days after initial entry Do not shake The darbepoetin t½ is 3-fold longer than epoetin alfa (it can be given weekly)

APLASTIC ANEMIA

Aplastic anemia (AA) occurs when the bone marrow fails to make enough RBCs, WBCs and platelets. It can be caused by drugs, infectious diseases, hereditary conditions or autoimmune disorders. Patients with AA are at risk for life-threatening infections or bleeding. Treatment can include immunosuppressants, blood transfusions or a stem cell transplant. Eltrombopag *(Promacta)*, a thrombopoietin nonpeptide agonist, increases platelet counts and is approved for the treatment of severe aplastic anemia in patients who are unresponsive to immunosuppressive therapy.

HEMOLYTIC ANEMIA

Hemolytic anemia develops when RBCs are destroyed and removed from the bloodstream before their normal lifespan of 120 days. This type of anemia can be acquired (e.g., drug-induced or associated with an immune disorder) or inherited (e.g., sickle cell disease, G6PD deficiency). There is more than one mechanism of drug-induced hemolytic anemia, but most often the medication binds to the RBC surface and triggers the development of antibodies that attack the RBC. The direct Coombs test is used to detect antibodies that are stuck to the surface of RBCs. See the Key Drugs Guy for medications that can cause hemolytic anemia.

Glucose-6-phosphate dehydrogenase (G6PD) deficiency is an X-linked inherited disorder that most commonly affects persons of African, Asian, Mediterranean or Middle Eastern descent. The G6PD enzyme protects RBCs from harmful substances (e.g., reactive oxygen species). Without sufficient levels of G6PD, RBCs hemolyze (break apart) 24 – 72 hours after exposure to oxidative stress. Infections, certain foods (e.g., fava beans), severe stress and certain drugs can increase the risk of hemolysis in a patient with G6PD deficiency. Most individuals do not need treatment but should be instructed to avoid certain high-risk medications (see Key Drugs Guy), foods or other known triggers. Not all medications that can cause drug-induced hemolysis are prohibited in patients with G6PD deficiency. If a high-risk drug is used, monitor closely and discontinue immediately if hemolysis develops.

SELECT DRUGS THAT CAN CAUSE HEMOLYTIC ANEMIA

Cephalosporins	Pegloticase*
Dapsone*	Penicillins
Isoniazid	Primaquine*
Levodopa	Quinidine
Methyldopa	Quinine
Methylene blue*	Rasburicase*
Nitrofurantoin*	Rifampin
	Sulfonamides*

*Avoid in G6PD deficiency

KEY COUNSELING POINTS

See the Drug Formulations and Patient Counseling chapter for counseling language/layman's terminology.

Oral Iron

- Take on an empty stomach. If stomach upset occurs, it can be taken with food, but avoid cereals, tea, coffee, eggs, milk and high-fiber products, as these decrease iron absorption.
- Drug interactions due to:
  - ❑ Binding.
  - ❑ High gastric pH.
- Can cause:
  - ❑ Dark stools, which is expected.
  - ❑ Constipation.

ESAs

- Can cause:
  - ❑ Blood clots.
  - ❑ Hypertension.
- Do not shake the vial or syringe; this will ruin the medication and it will not work.
- ESA injection sites:

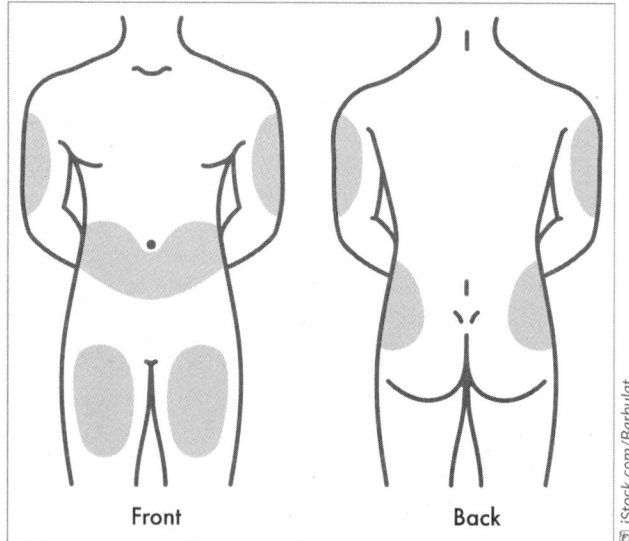

Front   Back

© iStock.com/Barbulat

Select Guidelines/References

Short MW, Domaglaski JE. Iron deficiency anemia: evaluation and management. *Am Fam Physician*. 2013:87:98-104.

Kidney Disease: Improving Global Outcomes (KDIGO) Anemia Work Group. KDIGO Clinical Practice Guideline for Anemia in Chronic Kidney Disease. Kidney Int Suppl. 2012;2:279-335.

Normal red blood cell (RBC)

Normal red blood cell section

Normal hemoglobin

RBCs flow freely within blood vessel

Abnormal sickle red blood cell section

Sticky sickle cells

Sickle cells blocking blood flow

Abnormal hemoglobin form strands that cause sickle shape

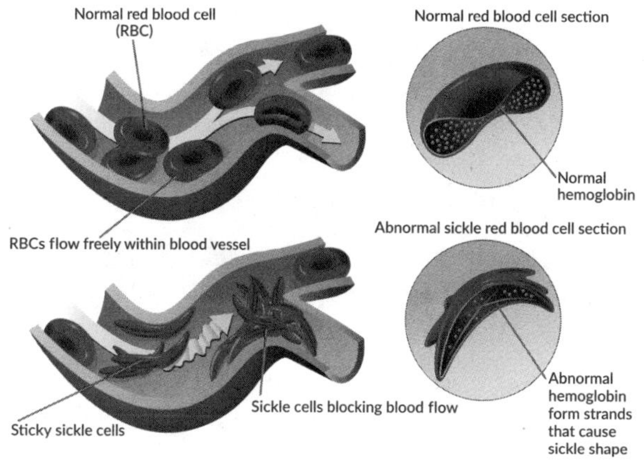

© Roberto Biasini © 123RF.com

CHAPTER 36
SICKLE CELL DISEASE

BACKGROUND

Red blood cells (RBCs) contain adult hemoglobin (HgbA) and are shaped like a donut (without the hole). They have the flexibility to move through large and small blood vessels to deliver oxygen to the tissues. RBCs have a lifespan of 90 – 120 days.

Sickle cell disease (SCD) is a group of inherited RBC disorders that most commonly affects the African American population. It results from a genetic mutation in the genes that encode hemoglobin (see the Pharmacogenomics chapter for a discussion on genetic inheritance). Patients with homozygous inheritance of the sickle cell gene (i.e., they have two copies of the mutated gene) have RBCs that contain abnormal hemoglobin, called hemoglobin S (i.e., HgbS or sickle hemoglobin). This causes RBCs to be rigid with a concave "sickle" shape. Sickled RBCs burst (hemolyze) after 10 – 20 days, which causes anemia and fatigue.

The irregularly shaped RBCs are unable to transport oxygen effectively, and they stick together, blocking smaller blood vessels (vascular occlusion) and causing a wide array of complications. Symptoms of SCD develop approximately 2 – 3 months after birth. This is because a fetus and young infants have RBCs with fetal hemoglobin (HgbF), which blocks the sickling of RBCs. A hemoglobin electrophoresis test or high-performance liquid chromatography (HPLC) can be used to measure the amount of each Hgb (A, F and S) in the blood.

ACUTE AND CHRONIC COMPLICATIONS

Vascular occlusion prevents oxygen from reaching the tissues, causing them to become ischemic. This can lead to different types of sickle cell crises (see the box on the following page), the most common of which is vaso-occlusive crisis (VOC), or acute pain crisis. VOC most commonly occurs in the lower back, legs, hips, abdomen and chest, and can last for days or weeks. If the pain is in the chest and there is evidence of a pulmonary infection, it is called acute chest syndrome. Acute chest

CONTENT LEGEND

= Key Drug Guy

syndrome is life-threatening and is the leading cause of death in SCD. Due to the risk of acute stroke, females with SCD should not use estrogen; progestin-only contraceptives, levonorgestrel intrauterine devices (IUDs) and barrier methods are preferred for contraception.

The most common chronic complications of SCD are chronic pain, avascular necrosis (bone death), pulmonary hypertension and renal impairment.

SICKLE CELL DISEASE COMPLICATIONS

Acute	Chronic
Acute chest syndrome	Avascular necrosis (bone death)
Anemia	Leg ulcers
Cholecystitis (gallbladder infection)	Gallstones
	Pain
Infection	Pregnancy complications (including fetal death)
Multiorgan failure (kidneys, liver, lung)	
	Pulmonary hypertension
Priapism (painful and prolonged erection)	Renal impairment
	Retinopathy
Spleen sequestration	Recurrent priapism
Stroke	
Vaso-occlusive crisis (acute pain crisis)	

INFECTION RISK

A healthy spleen has several physiologic roles, including the removal of old or damaged RBCs. It aids in immune function, making and storing white blood cells and clearing some types of bacterial pathogens from the body, particularly the encapsulated organisms *Streptococcus pneumoniae*, *Haemophilus influenzae* and *Neisseria meningitidis*. In SCD, the spleen becomes fibrotic and shrinks in size due to repetitive sickling and infarctions. This causes functional asplenia (decreased or absent spleen function), typically within the first year of life. Patients with functional asplenia are at an increased risk for serious infections; they require immunizations and prophylactic antibiotics and should seek medical attention for a temperature > 101.3°F.

NON-DRUG TREATMENT

Blood transfusions protect against many of the life-threatening complications of SCD by providing RBCs with HgbA. Stroke, acute chest syndrome and severe anemia are acute complications that warrant treatment with blood transfusions. When administering chronic (monthly) blood transfusions, the goal Hgb level should be no higher than 10 g/dL post-infusion. One of the risks of blood transfusions is iron overload, which can lead to hemosiderosis (excess iron that impairs organ function). Chelation therapy to remove excess iron is discussed later in the chapter.

The only cure for SCD is bone marrow transplantation. Due to the high risks involved with such invasive treatment, as well as the substantial cost, it is not a widely used approach. Children are more likely to tolerate bone marrow transplantation than adults, who have accumulated organ damage.

DRUG TREATMENT

The major drug classes used in SCD are immunizations and antibiotics to reduce infection risk, analgesics to control pain, and chelation therapy to manage iron overload from blood transfusions.

Hydroxyurea is the primary disease-modifying therapy for SCD. Other treatments include L-glutamine, voxelotor and crizanlizumab.

IMMUNIZATIONS AND ANTIBIOTICS

Infections are a major cause of death, especially in children < 5 years of age. Sepsis and meningitis, due to *S. pneumoniae*, *H. influenzae*, *N. meningitidis* and *Salmonella* spp., can occur. The risk of infections caused by atypical organisms (*Chlamydophila* and *Mycoplasma pneumoniae*) is increased. Vaccinations are essential to prevent infection (see the Key Drugs Guy).

Prophylactic penicillin, given orally, reduces the risk of death from invasive pneumococcal infections in young children. Infants who screen positive for SCD at birth should be initiated on twice daily penicillin and treated until age five years. If a patient undergoes surgical removal of the spleen, or if invasive pneumococcal infection develops despite penicillin prophylaxis, it should be continued indefinitely.

KEY VACCINES IN SICKLE CELL DISEASE

Routine Childhood Series

- *Haemophilus influenzae* type B (Hib)
- Pneumococcal conjugate (PCV13, *Prevnar 13*)

Additional Vaccines For Functional Asplenia

- Meningococcal conjugate series plus routine boosters
- Meningococcal serogroup B (*Bexsero, Trumenba*)*
- Pneumococcal vaccines - give one of the following regimens**:
  - ❑ PCV20 (*Prevnar 20*) x 1, or
  - ❑ PCV15 (*Vaxneuvance*) x 1 followed by PPSV23 (*Pneumovax 23*) ≥ 8 weeks later

*At age ≥ 10 years
**At age ≥ 19 years

ANALGESICS

Mild to moderate pain can often be managed at home with rest, fluids, application of warm compresses to affected areas and the use of NSAIDs or acetaminophen. For severe pain and VOC, management must be guided by the patient's self-reported pain severity. Outpatient analgesic use should be reviewed and a treatment plan initiated within 30 minutes of triage. Patients with severe pain and VOC will require IV administration of opioids or patient-controlled analgesia (PCA). Refer to the Pain chapter for a detailed discussion of analgesics.

HYDROXYUREA

Hydroxyurea is a disease-modifying drug that stimulates production of HgbF. Long-term use of hydroxyurea reduces the frequency of acute pain crises, episodes of acute chest syndrome and the need for blood transfusions. It is indicated for adults with ≥ 3 moderate-to-severe pain crises in one year, patients with severe or recurrent acute chest syndrome, chronic symptomatic anemia or disability. Use should be considered in all children > 9 months of age regardless of disease severity.

DRUG	DOSE	SAFETY/SIDE EFFECTS/MONITORING
Hydroxyurea (Droxia, Hydrea, Siklos) Capsule, tablet	Start: Droxia: 15 mg/kg/day as a single dose Siklos: 20 mg/kg/day as a single dose ↑ by 5 mg/kg/day every 8-12 weeks to a goal absolute neutrophil count (ANC) of 2,000-4,000/mm³ Max: 35 mg/kg/day Use IBW or TBW, whichever is less, when calculating daily dose Round doses up to the nearest capsule size CrCl < 60 mL/min: adjustment required	**BOXED WARNINGS** Myelosuppression (↓ WBCs and platelets), malignancy (leukemia, skin cancer) **WARNINGS** Fetal toxicity, avoid live vaccinations, skin ulcers, macrocytosis, pulmonary toxicity Increased risk of pancreatitis, hepatotoxicity and peripheral neuropathy when used with antiretroviral drugs **SIDE EFFECTS** ↑ LFTs, uric acid, BUN and SCr; mouth ulcers, N/V/D, alopecia, hyperpigmentation or atrophy of skin and nails, low sperm counts (males) **MONITORING** CBC with differential every 2-4 weeks during treatment initiation and titration, then every 2-3 months once a stable dose is achieved; if toxicity occurs (ANC < 2,000/mm³, platelets < 80,000/mm³), hold hydroxyurea until the bone marrow recovers, then restart at a dose 5 mg/kg/day lower HgbF, uric acid, renal function, LFTs, baseline pregnancy test **NOTES** Contraception required during treatment and after discontinuation (6 months for females, 12 months for males) Hazardous drug – wear gloves when dispensing and wash hands before and after contact (see the Compounding chapters) Folic acid supplementation is recommended to prevent macrocytosis Clinical response can take 3-6 months

Hydroxyurea Drug Interactions

- There is a higher risk for potentially fatal pancreatitis, hepatotoxicity, hepatic failure and severe peripheral neuropathy when used in combination with antiretrovirals (especially didanosine and stavudine).

- Do not use hydroxyurea with pimecrolimus, tacrolimus (topical) and other drugs that cause myelosuppression (e.g., clozapine, deferiprone, leflunomide, natalizumab, tofacitinib).

ANTICOAGULATION & BLOOD DISORDERS

L-GLUTAMINE

L-glutamine oral powder (*Endari*) is FDA-approved for adults and children age ≥ 5 years with SCD. L-glutamine is an amino acid shown to reduce acute complications of SCD (e.g., number of pain crises requiring parenteral analgesics, number and duration of hospitalizations and occurrence of acute chest syndrome). The mechanism of action is not fully known, but it is thought to decrease oxidative stress, which can damage sickled RBCs.

DRUG	DOSE	SAFETY/SIDE EFFECTS/MONITORING
L-glutamine (*Endari*) Oral powder (5 grams per package)	TBW < 30 kg: 5 grams twice daily	**SIDE EFFECTS** Constipation, flatulence, nausea, headache, pain (abdominal, extremities, back, chest), cough
	TBW 30-65 kg: 10 grams twice daily	**NOTES** Mix each dose in 8 oz. of a cold or room temperature beverage (e.g., water, milk or apple juice),
	TBW > 65 kg: 15 grams twice daily	or 4-6 oz. of food (e.g., applesauce or yogurt); medication does not have to be completely dissolved prior to administration

VOXELOTOR

Voxelotor (*Oxbryta*) is the first FDA-approved drug that works by inhibiting hemoglobin S (HgbS) polymerization, which is the cause of SCD. It is approved for patients age ≥ 4 years with SCD and can be given with or without hydroxyurea.

DRUG	DOSE	SAFETY/SIDE EFFECTS/MONITORING
Voxelotor (*Oxbryta*) Tablet	1.5 grams once daily ↓ dose if taking with strong CYP450 3A4 inhibitors, ↑ if taking CYP3A4 inducers	**WARNINGS** Hypersensitivity reactions, lab test interference with measurement of Hgb subtypes (A, F, S) by HPLC **SIDE EFFECTS** Headache, fatigue, abdominal pain, diarrhea, nausea **NOTES** Swallow tablets whole – do not crush, chew or cut tablet

CRIZANLIZUMAB

Crizanlizumab is a monoclonal antibody that is FDA-approved to reduce the frequency of VOC in SCD. It works by binding to and inhibiting P-selectin, which is involved in adhesion of sickled erythrocytes to vessels (causing vaso-occlusion).

DRUG	DOSE	SAFETY/SIDE EFFECTS/MONITORING
Crizanlizumab (*Adakveo*) Injection	5 mg/kg IV every 2 weeks x 2 doses, then 5 mg/kg every 4 weeks	**WARNINGS** Infusion-related reactions **SIDE EFFECTS** Nausea, arthralgias, fever

IRON CHELATION TREATMENT

Chronic blood transfusions cause iron overload, which damages the liver, heart and other organs. Chelation therapy is used to remove excess iron stores from the body. Historically, deferoxamine (the antidote for iron toxicity) was used, but it has significant toxicities, is not available in oral formulation and requires slow, prolonged infusions over 8 – 12 hours when administered by IV or SC routes. Oral chelating drugs, such as deferasirox (*Exjade, Jadenu*) and deferiprone (*Ferriprox*), are now more commonly used. Due to the side effect profile of both drugs, treatment is typically prescribed, dispensed and monitored by specialty clinics and pharmacies.

KEY COUNSELING POINTS

See the Drug Formulations and Patient Counseling chapter for counseling language/layman's terminology.

HYDROXYUREA

- Anyone handling the capsules (patient or caregiver) should wear disposable gloves to reduce the risk of exposure. Wash hands before and after handling. The capsules should not be opened.

- Can cause infections.

- Avoid in pregnancy (teratogenic). Effective contraception required for sexually active men and women of reproductive potential, both during and after treatment.

- Live vaccines must be avoided. Check with your physician before getting any vaccines.

Select Guidelines/References

National Heart, Lung, and Blood Institute. Evidence-based management of sickle cell disease. Expert panel report, 2014. https://www.nhlbi.nih.gov/sites/default/files/media/docs/sickle-cell-disease-report%20020816_0.pdf (accessed 2022 Feb 4).

EYES, EARS, NOSE
& SKIN CONDITIONS

CONTENTS

CONTENT LEGEND

☀ = Study Tip Gal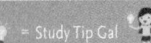

iStock.com/Photodjo

CHAPTER 37

ALLERGIC RHINITIS, COUGH & COLD

ALLERGIC RHINITIS

BACKGROUND

Allergic rhinitis, commonly called hay fever or simply "allergies," causes cold-like symptoms [congestion, rhinorrhea (runny nose), sneezing, sinus pressure and itchy eyes]. Colds are caused by a virus; allergic rhinitis is caused by exposure to an allergen (e.g., pollen, dust, pet dander). Refer to the figure below that distinguishes between colds and allergic rhinitis. Allergic rhinitis can be easily spotted when a person has a few quick sneezes in succession (due to an exposure to an allergen) with watery, itchy red eyes and an itchy nose and throat.

Allergic rhinitis symptoms can be intermittent (e.g., exposure to animal dander when visiting a friend's home) or chronic (e.g., symptoms that last for months whenever the pollen count is elevated).

Allergic rhinitis can cause discomfort, missed days at school and work and lost productivity. Untreated symptoms can lead to chronic sinusitis, otitis media (in children) and asthma exacerbations.

Many patients with asthma have allergic rhinitis; both are inflammatory reactions to some type of trigger.

COLDS VS. ALLERGIES
The symptoms of the common cold and allergies are very similar, which can make it difficult to tell the difference between the two.

COLD		ALLERGY
Sneezing		Sneezing
Runny nose		Runny nose
Thick, dark mucus		Thin, clear mucus
Sore throat		Wheezing
Body aches		Red, watery eyes
Symptoms take about three days to appear and usually last for about a week		Symptoms can last for days or months after contact with allergens

iStock.com/AnnaViolet

NON-DRUG TREATMENT

<u>Avoiding exposure to known or suspected allergens</u>, if possible, will reduce symptoms (e.g., it might be possible to avoid triggers from dust mites, but it may not be possible to avoid chronic exposure to air pollution). An <u>IgE-mediated skin prick test</u> (see picture) or blood test can determine patient-specific allergens.

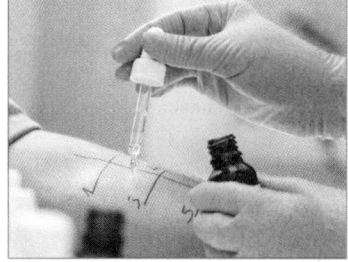
iStock.com/AlexRaths

<u>Common allergens</u> include:

- <u>Pollens</u> from trees, grasses and weeds
- <u>Molds</u>, both indoor and outdoor
- <u>Dust mites</u> that live in bedding, carpeting and other items that hold moisture
- <u>Animal dander</u> from furred animals such as cats, dogs, horses and rabbits

Ventilation systems with high-efficiency particulate air (HEPA) filters reduce some allergens (pollen, mold), but these systems can be expensive and are not effective for everyone.

<u>Vacuuming</u> carpets, drapes and upholstery with a HEPA vacuum cleaner often (at least weekly) reduces allergens. Dust mites can be reduced by <u>removing carpets</u> and <u>upholstered furniture, encasing pillows, mattresses</u> and box springs in allergen-impermeable covers and washing bedding and soft toys in <u>hot water</u> weekly.

When air pollutants are triggers, outdoor activities may need to be limited when air is unhealthy. The <u>air quality index (AQI)</u> rates the local air as good to hazardous. The AQI is useful for other conditions in which the air quality can affect breathing, including asthma, other types of lung disease and heart disease.

<u>Pollen counts</u> can be monitored when pollen is a trigger. When the pollen count is high, it is best to have patients stay indoors, with the windows closed and with the air conditioner on.

Nasal Irrigation and Wetting Agents

<u>Nasal irrigations</u> and <u>wetting agents</u> provide symptom relief by reducing nasal stuffiness, runny nose and sneezing. Nasal gels with petrolatum (*Allergen Block*) can be applied around the nostrils to physically block pollens and allergens from entering the nose. These products are considered <u>safe</u> for most populations, including <u>children</u> and <u>pregnant</u> women.

Wetting agents are commercially available (e.g., *Ocean*, *Little Remedies*, *Simply Saline*) and contain saline, propylene or polyethylene glycol, which provide moisture and reduce irritation to the nasal passages. Nasal irrigation (e.g., *NeilMed Sinus Rinse*) uses an <u>isotonic</u> (0.9%) or <u>hypertonic</u> (2 – 3.5%) saline solution, made with salt and water, to rinse out allergens and mucus, improve ciliary function and reduce swelling. Premixed saline packets are commercially available or a salt solution can be prepared at home. A homemade or store-bought saline mixture must be combined with <u>distilled, sterile or previously boiled</u> and cooled water. <u>Tap water</u> (known as drinking, or potable, water) should not be used; it contains organisms that are safe to ingest orally (killed by stomach acid) but can cause <u>infections</u> when used for nasal irrigation.

iStock.com/rob_lan

Nasal irrigations can be administered using a syringe or <u>neti pot</u>. A neti pot is a popular product that looks like a small genie lamp or a teapot (see above). The prepared saline solution is placed in the neti pot, then <u>poured</u> into <u>one nostril</u> and <u>drained out</u> of the <u>other nostril</u> while breathing through the mouth. The most common side effects are mild nasal stinging or burning which are increased at higher concentrations of saline. After each use, the neti pot should be rinsed out with distilled, sterile or previously boiled water and allowed to air dry. Pots should never be shared with others.

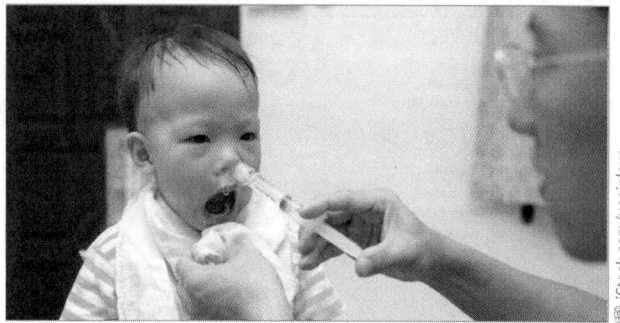
iStock.com/yaoinlove

EYES, EARS, NOSE & SKIN CONDITIONS

DRUG TREATMENT

Selecting appropriate medication treatment depends on the severity of illness and symptoms. Intranasal steroids are first line for chronic, moderate-to-severe symptoms. Milder, intermittent symptoms can be treated with oral antihistamines. Decongestants can be used if congestion is present. Antihistamines and decongestants are available in both oral and nasal formulations. Ophthalmic medications for red, itchy eyes (e.g., allergic conjunctivitis) can be found in the Common Conditions of the Eyes & Ears chapter.

Eric Glenn/Shutterstock.com

Intranasal Steroids

Intranasal steroids work by decreasing inflammation. They are considered first-line treatment for moderate-severe symptoms. They are especially effective in reducing the nasal symptoms of allergic rhinitis (e.g., sneezing, itching, rhinorrhea, congestion). Several intranasal steroids come OTC for use in adults and pediatric patients. Note that the same steroids used to treat allergic rhinitis and asthma have different brand names and delivery systems. For example, fluticasone for allergic rhinitis comes in a nasal inhaler as *Flonase* ("-nase" for nasal), and for asthma it comes in an oral inhaler as *Flovent*.

DRUG	DOSING	SAFETY/SIDE EFFECTS/MONITORING
Budesonide (Rhinocort Allergy) OTC	Adult: 1 spray per nostril daily (max 4 sprays per nostril daily) Age ≥ 6 yrs: 1 spray per nostril daily (max 2 sprays per nostril daily)	**WARNINGS** Avoid use if recent nasal septal ulcers, nasal surgery, or recent nasal trauma due to delayed wound healing High doses for prolonged periods can cause: adrenal suppression, ↓ growth velocity (pediatrics) and immunosuppression Use caution in patients with cataracts and/or glaucoma; ↑ intraocular pressure (IOP), open-angle glaucoma and cataracts have occurred with prolonged use
Fluticasone (Flonase Allergy Relief, Flonase Sensimist, Children's Flonase, Xhance) Rx and OTC + azelastine (Dymista)	Adult and children ≥ 12 yrs: 1-2 sprays per nostril daily Age 2-11 yrs: 1 spray per nostril daily	**SIDE EFFECTS** Epistaxis (nose bleeds), headache, dry nose, unpleasant taste, localized infection
Triamcinolone (Nasacort Allergy 24HR, Nasacort Allergy 24HR Children, Nasal Allergy 24HR) OTC	Adult and children age ≥ 6 yrs: 1-2 sprays per nostril daily Age 2-5 yrs: 1 spray per nostril daily	**MONITORING** Growth (pediatrics), vision changes, eye exams in long-term use, signs/symptoms of oral thrush and/or adrenal suppression
Beclomethasone (Beconase AQ, Qnasl, Qnasl Children's)	Adult: 1-2 sprays per nostril BID (Beconase AQ); 2 sprays per nostril daily (Qnasl)	If using regularly for several months, recommend periodic nasal exams to evaluate for nasal septal perforation or ulcers
Ciclesonide (Omnaris, Zetonna)	Adult: 2 sprays per nostril daily (Omnaris); 1 spray per nostril daily (Zetonna)	**NOTES** Can take up to one week to get full relief Budesonide and beclomethasone are the preferred nasal steroids in pregnancy
Flunisolide	Adult: 2 sprays per nostril BID or TID	Shake bottle well before each use Discard device after total number of labeled doses, even if the bottle does not feel completely empty
Mometasone (Nasonex) Nasal implant: Sinuva + olopatadine (Ryaltris)	Adult: 2 sprays per nostril daily	

532

Antihistamines

Oral antihistamines are commonly used for <u>mild-moderate disease</u>. They are effective in reducing symptoms of itching, sneezing, rhinorrhea and other types of immediate hypersensitivity reactions, but have <u>little effect on nasal congestion</u>. Antihistamines work by blocking histamine at the <u>histamine-1 (H1) receptor site</u>. <u>First-generation</u> antihistamines, including hydroxyzine and meclizine, cause <u>more sedation</u> than second-generation antihistamines. The <u>second-generation</u> agents are generally <u>preferred</u> since they cause less sedation and cognitive impairment. Promethazine is a first-generation antihistamine that can be seen in cough and cold combination products (see later in chapter). Antihistamines can help if symptoms of allergic conjunctivitis (e.g., itchy, red eyes) are present (see the Common Conditions of the Eyes & Ears chapter for more information).

DIPHENHYDRAMINE IN PHARMACY; IT'S EVERYWHERE

Diphenhydramine is a first-generation antihistamine, but it is used for many indications, such as:

- Treatment of acute allergic reactions (+/- epinephrine, depending on severity)
- Prevention of allergic reactions (included in most premedication regimens for high-risk drugs)
- Allergic rhinitis
- Cough (has antitussive properties)
- Sleep (sedating)
- Dystonic reactions (anticholinergic properties)
- Motion sickness

Because of its wide range of effects, it can worsen some disease states (e.g., BPH, constipation, dementia, glaucoma)

Keith Homan/Shutterstock.com

DRUG	DOSING	SAFETY/SIDE EFFECTS/MONITORING
Select First-Generation Oral Antihistamines		
Diphenhydramine (Benadryl, many others) Capsule, tablet, chewable, elixir, strip, syrup, injection, cream, gel, solution, spray Rx and OTC	Adult: 25 mg PO Q4-6H or 50 mg PO Q6-8H (max 300 mg/day) Age 6-11 yrs: 12.5-25 mg PO Q4-6H (max 150 mg/day) Age < 6 yrs: do not use OTC unless directed by a healthcare provider	**CONTRAINDICATIONS** Neonates or premature infants, breastfeeding **WARNINGS** Avoid in the elderly (due to strong anticholinergic effects; Beers criteria) and in children < 2 years Can cause CNS depression/sedation
Chlorpheniramine (Aller-Chlor, Chlor-Trimeton,* others) Tablet, syrup OTC	IR (adult): 4 mg PO Q4-6H (max 24 mg/day) ER (adult): 12 mg PO Q12H (max 24 mg/day)	Use with caution in patients with cardiovascular disease, prostate enlargement, glaucoma, asthma, pyloroduodenal obstruction and thyroid disease Do not use with MAO inhibitors (especially clemastine or carbinoxamine)
Doxylamine Unisom SleepTabs - for sleep Tablet OTC	Adult: 12.5-25 mg PO Q4-6H (max 75 mg/day)	Age restrictions vary for OTC use, check the product labeling (e.g., do not use diphenhydramine in children < 6 years or doxylamine in children < 12 years) **SIDE EFFECTS** Somnolence, cognitive impairment, strong anticholinergic effects (dry mouth, blurred vision, urinary retention, constipation) and seizures/arrhythmias at higher doses
Clemastine (Dayhist Allergy 12 HR Relief) Tablet, syrup OTC	Adult: 1.34-2.68 mg PO Q8-12H (max 8.04 mg/day)	**NOTES** First-generation antihistamines should not be taken by lactating women; second-generation agents preferred Should be discontinued ≥ 72 hours prior to allergy skin testing
Carbinoxamine (Karbinal ER, RyVent) Tablet, liquid	IR (adult): 4-8 mg PO Q6-8H ER (adult): 6-16 mg PO Q12H	Can cause photosensitivity; use sunscreens and wear protective clothing while taking FDA issued a Safety Alert regarding reports of abuse/misuse of diphenhydramine by teenagers leading to serious heart problems, seizures, coma or death

Brand discontinued but name still used in practice.

DRUG	DOSING	SAFETY/SIDE EFFECTS/MONITORING
Second-Generation Oral Antihistamines		
Cetirizine (Zyrtec, Zyrtec Allergy Childrens, *All Day Allergy*, others**)** Capsule, tablet, solution, syrup, chewable, ODT, injection OTC and Rx **+ pseudoephedrine (Zyrtec-D)** OTC	Adult and children ≥ 6 yrs: 5-10 mg PO daily (max 5 mg daily in elderly) Age 2-5 yrs: 2.5-5 mg PO daily	**CONTRAINDICATIONS** Levocetirizine: end-stage renal disease (CrCl < 10 mL/min), hemodialysis, infants and children 6 months to 11 years of age with renal impairment **WARNINGS** Can cause CNS depression/sedation, especially when used with other sedating drugs Use with caution in the elderly and in renal or hepatic impairment **SIDE EFFECTS** Somnolence can still be seen (more with cetirizine and levocetirizine), headache **NOTES** Fexofenadine: take with water (not fruit juice due to ↓ absorption); avoid administration with aluminum or magnesium-containing products Should be discontinued ≥ 72 hours prior to allergy skin testing If using in pregnancy, loratadine and cetirizine are preferred Cetirizine and levocetirizine have a fast onset and may work best for some patients More sedating: cetirizine and levocetirizine Less sedating: fexofenadine and loratadine Some formulations of fexofenadine, loratadine and desloratadine contain phenylalanine (avoid with PKU)
Levocetirizine (Xyzal Allergy 24HR, Xyzal Allergy 24HR Childrens) Tablet, solution OTC	Adult and children ≥ 12 yrs: 5 mg PO QHS Age 6-11 yrs: 2.5 mg PO QHS Age 6 mos-5 yrs: 1.25 mg PO QHS	
Fexofenadine (Allegra Allergy, Allegra Allergy Childrens) Tablet, suspension, ODT OTC **+ pseudoephedrine (Allegra-D)** OTC	Adult and children ≥ 12 yrs: 60 mg PO BID or 180 mg PO daily Age 2-11 yrs: 30 mg PO BID	
Loratadine (Claritin, Claritin Childrens, *Alavert***)** Tablet, capsule, chewable, solution, syrup, ODT OTC **+ pseudoephedrine (Claritin-D)** OTC	Adult and children ≥ 6 yrs: 10 mg PO daily or 5 mg PO BID (*RediTabs*) Age 2-5 yrs: 5 mg PO daily	
Desloratadine (*Clarinex*) Tablet, ODT + pseudoephedrine (*Clarinex-D 12 Hour*)	Adult: 5 mg PO daily	
Intranasal Antihistamines		
Azelastine (*Astelin, Astepro, Astepro Allergy*) OTC and Rx + fluticasone (*Dymista*)	Adult: 1-2 sprays per nostril BID	**SIDE EFFECTS** Bitter taste, headache, somnolence, nasal irritation, epistaxis, sinus pain **NOTES** Helps with nasal congestion; can be combined with an intranasal steroid (increases cost and risk for side effects)
Olopatadine (*Patanase*)	Adult: 2 sprays per nostril BID	

Decongestants

Decongestants are <u>alpha-adrenergic agonists</u> (sympathomimetics). They cause <u>vasoconstriction</u>, which decreases sinus vessel engorgement and mucosal edema and makes them effective at reducing sinus and nasal congestion. If a product contains a <u>D after the name</u> (such as *Mucinex D*), it usually <u>contains</u> a decongestant such as <u>phenylephrine or pseudoephedrine</u> (see <u>Study Tip Gal</u> on combination products later in chapter). <u>Phenylephrine</u> has <u>poor</u> oral absorption. It comes as a <u>nasal spray</u>, but lasts for a <u>shorter time</u> and causes more side effects than the popular <u>oxymetazoline spray</u>. <u>Pseudoephedrine</u> is an <u>effective systemic decongestant</u>; pseudoephedrine is a <u>precursor</u> to <u>methamphetamine</u>, and has restricted distribution (see box to the right).

COMBAT METHAMPHETAMINE EPIDEMIC ACT 2005

To combat the methamphetamine epidemic, there are restricted sales of <u>non-prescription</u> products containing <u>pseudoephedrine, phenylpropanolamine</u> and <u>ephedrine</u>, since these can all be <u>converted</u> easily to <u>methamphetamine</u>.

Products must be kept <u>behind the counter</u> or in a locked cabinet, usually located in the pharmacy.

A logbook of any sale more than a single-dose package (maximum of 60 mg) is kept. For any sale above this amount, the customer must show a government-issued photo ID (e.g., driver's license, ID card or US passport).

Customers record their name, date and time of sale and signature in the logbook. Staff must verify that the name matches the photo ID, the date and time are correct, record the customer address (can be done by swiping the driver's license electronically) and what the person received as well as the quantity purchased.

Under federal law <u>the maximum amount allowed for purchase is 3.6 grams per day, and 9 grams in a 30-day period</u>.

Logbook must be kept secured for a minimum of 2 years and be readily available upon request by board inspectors or law enforcement. It cannot be shared with the public.

Many states have their own restrictions in addition to the federal restrictions, such as age restrictions, prescription required or stricter quantity limits.

DRUG	DOSING	SAFETY/SIDE EFFECTS/MONITORING
Systemic (Oral)		
Phenylephrine (**Sudafed PE,** others) Tablet, liquid, solution OTC Injection: used as a vasopressor (see Acute & Critical Care Medicine chapter)	Adult: 10 mg PO Q4H PRN (max 60 mg/day) Age 6-11 yrs: 5 mg PO Q4H PRN (max 30 mg/day) Age 4-5 yrs: 2.5 mg PO Q4H PRN (max 15 mg/day)	**CONTRAINDICATIONS** Do not use within 14 days of MAO inhibitors **WARNINGS** Avoid in children < 2 years (FDA), < 4 years (package labeling) Use with <u>caution</u> in patients with <u>CV disease</u> and uncontrolled hypertension (can ↑ BP), hyperthyroidism (can worsen), diabetes (can ↑ BG), bowel obstruction, glaucoma (can ↑ IOP), <u>BPH</u> (can cause <u>urinary retention</u>), renal impairment, seizure disorder, the elderly
Pseudoephedrine (**Sudafed, Nexafed, Zephrex-D,** others) Tablet, liquid, syrup Rx and <u>non-prescription behind the counter</u> (see box above)	Adult: 60 mg PO Q4-6H PRN, or 120 mg ER PO Q12H, or 240 mg ER PO daily (max 240 mg/day) Age 6-11 yrs: 30 mg PO Q4-6H PRN (max 120 mg/day) Age 4-5 yrs: 15 mg PO Q4-6H PRN (max 60 mg/day)	**SIDE EFFECTS** Cardiovascular stimulation (<u>tachycardia, palpitations, ↑ BP</u>), CNS stimulation (anxiety, tremors, <u>insomnia</u>, nervousness, restlessness, fear, hallucinations), ↓ appetite, dizziness, headache **NOTES** Phenylephrine has low bioavailability (≤ 38%); pseudoephedrine is more effective Onset of 15-60 minutes
Topicals (Intranasal)		
Oxymetazoline 0.05% (**Afrin,** Vicks Sinex 12 Hour, Zicam Extreme Congestion Relief) OTC	Adult and Children ≥ 6 yrs: 2-3 sprays per nostril Q12H PRN	**CONTRAINDICATIONS** Oxymetazoline: do not use for more than 3 days **WARNINGS** Do not use with MAO inhibitors Use with caution in patients with CV disease and uncontrolled hypertension, thyroid disease, diabetes and <u>BPH</u>
Phenylephrine 0.25%, 0.5%, 1% (Little Noses Decongestant Drops, Neo-Synephrine, others) OTC	Adult: 2-3 sprays of 0.25% to 1% per nostril Q4H PRN	**SIDE EFFECTS** <u>Rhinitis medicamentosa</u> (rebound congestion if used <u>longer than 3 days</u>), nasal stinging, burning and dryness (vehicle-related), sneezing, trauma from the tip of the device **NOTES** Fast onset (5-10 minutes)

Additional Allergy Medications

Intranasal Cromolyn

Intranasal cromolyn (NasalCrom) is an OTC mast cell stabilizer used for treatment and prophylaxis of allergic rhinitis. It must be started at the onset of allergy season and used regularly (not PRN) to be effective. Symptoms will start to improve in 3 – 7 days, but maximal effect can take ≥ 2 – 4 weeks of continued use. Intranasal cromolyn is not as effective as other agents but it is safe to use in children ≥ 2 years old and in pregnancy.

Oral Leukotriene Receptor Antagonist

Montelukast (Singulair) is the only leukotriene modifying agent indicated for the treatment of both allergic rhinitis and asthma. It is commonly used in children. The FDA issued a boxed warning for montelukast, resulting from the risk of serious neuropsychiatric side effects. For allergic rhinitis, montelukast should be reserved for those who are unable to be treated effectively with other medications. See the Asthma chapter for more information.

Intranasal Ipratropium

This drug is effective for decreasing rhinorrhea by causing nasal dryness (it is not effective for other nasal symptoms).

Immunotherapy

Immunotherapy is a preventative treatment for allergies, either through subcutaneous (SC) injections or sublingual (SL) treatments. They work by slowly increasing exposure to the allergen, making the immune system less sensitive to the substance. Long-term immunotherapy can improve the underlying allergic disease and relieve symptoms even after stopping treatment. It is recommended to treat for a minimum of three years.

SC allergy shots are the traditional method of treatment, which must be given in a medical office. An alternative option is SL treatment. The four FDA-approved SL treatments for allergic rhinitis are tailored to specific allergens. The first dose must be given in a medical office where the patient can be monitored for at least 30 minutes afterward for signs of an allergic reaction (boxed warning). If tolerated, subsequent doses can be taken at home. The patient should have an epinephrine auto-injector while on SL immunotherapy.

- *Oralair* contains five different grass pollen extracts.
- *Grastek* contains Timothy grass pollen extract.
- *Ragwitek* contains ragweed pollen extract.
- *Odactra* contains house dust mite allergen extract.

COUGH AND COLD

BACKGROUND

The common cold, a viral infection of the upper respiratory tract, is caused by over 200 viruses, including rhinoviruses and coronaviruses. It is transmitted by mucus secretions (via patient's hands) or by the air (from coughing or sneezing). Coughing or sneezing into the elbow or into a tissue is preferable over coughing into a hand, which can then touch surfaces and spread illness. Transmission is best prevented by frequent hand washing with soap or soap substitutes (e.g., hand sanitizer). Refer to the Medication Safety & Quality Improvement chapter for correct hand washing technique, and to the Infectious Diseases II chapter for a table of common upper and lower respiratory infections. Colds are usually self-limiting, but are a leading cause of absenteeism in work and school due to bothersome symptoms.

DRUG TREATMENT

Treatment of cough and cold is based on the presenting symptoms; each patient will present differently and require different treatment. The goal of treatment is to reduce duration and frequency of symptoms to allow the patient to feel better and return to normal activities.

Natural Products Used for Colds

Zinc, in various formulations including lozenges, is used for cold prevention and treatment. Zinc lozenges or syrup might decrease cold duration if used correctly and at first signs of symptoms (taken every two hours while awake, starting 24 – 48 hours of symptom onset). For this purpose zinc supplements are rated as "possibly effective" by the *Natural Medicines Database*. Zinc lozenges can cause mouth irritation, a metallic taste and nausea. They should not be used for more than five to seven days, as long-term use can cause copper deficiency. Zinc nasal formulations were removed from the market due to causing loss of smell.

Vitamin C (ascorbic acid) supplements are commonly used, but they have little to no efficacy for cold prevention. Some data has shown a decrease in the duration of the cold by 1 – 1.5 days at doses of 1 – 3 grams/day. There might also be a dose-dependent response; doses of at least 2 grams/day appear to work better than 1 gram/day. Vitamin C is rated as "possibly effective" for cold treatment by the *Natural Medicines Database*. High doses of vitamin C (4 g/day or greater) can cause diarrhea and possibly kidney stones. Echinacea is rated as "possibly effective" for cold treatment.

With any of these products, it is important to use the correct dose from a reputable manufacturer. *Airborne* and *Emergen-C, Immune+* are popular products that contain a variety of ingredients, including vitamin C, vitamin E, zinc and echinacea.

Expectorants

Cough associated with colds is usually nonproductive (i.e., a dry cough). If productive cough is present, expectorants can be used to thin mucus and move secretions up and out of the respiratory tract.

DRUG	DOSING	SAFETY/SIDE EFFECTS/MONITORING
Guaifenesin *(Mucinex, Robitussin Mucus + Chest Congestion, Robafen)* Tablet, liquid, syrup, packet + dextromethorphan *(Robafen DM, Robitussin DM)* OTC	Adult: 200-400 mg PO Q4H PRN, or 600-1,200 mg ER PO Q12H (max 2.4 g/day) Age 6-11 yrs: 1,200 mg/day (max) Age 4-5 yrs: 600 mg/day (max)	**SIDE EFFECTS** Nausea (dose-related), vomiting, dizziness, headache, rash, diarrhea, stomach pain **NOTES** OTC: do not use ER tablets in children < 12 years of age Some formulations contain phenylalanine (avoid with PKU)

Cough Suppressants

Cough suppressants are used for dry, nonproductive cough or to suppress productive cough at night to allow for restful sleep. Dextromethorphan and opioids, such as codeine and hydrocodone, have a high affinity for several regions of the brain, including the medullary cough center, suppressing the cough reflex. Benzonatate suppresses cough by a topical anesthetic action on the respiratory stretch receptors.

Opioids and dextromethorphan have abuse potential (see the Pain chapter for opioid boxed warnings). Dextromethorphan acts as a serotonin reuptake inhibitor. At usual antitussive doses, it does not have addictive properties, but at high doses it acts as an NMDA-receptor blocker leading to euphoria and hallucinations similar to PCP, termed "robo-tripping." Due to its abuse potential, many states ban the sale of dextromethorphan to minors < 18 years of age. Codeine products containing one or more non-codeine active ingredient (e.g., guaifenesin) and no more than 200 mg of codeine/100 mL are scheduled as C-V drugs. Codeine is abused, particularly in combination with promethazine, known by the street names "purple drank" and "lean."

DRUG	DOSING	SAFETY/SIDE EFFECTS/MONITORING
Dextromethorphan *(Delsym, Robafen Cough, Robitussin Cough)* Capsule, liquid, lozenge, suspension, strips OTC + guaifenesin *(Robafen DM, Robitussin DM)* OTC	Adult: 10-20 mg PO Q4H PRN, or 30 mg PO Q6-8H PRN, or 60 mg ER PO Q12H PRN (max 120 mg/day) Age 6-12 yrs: max 60 mg/day Age 4-6 yrs: max 30 mg/day	**CONTRAINDICATIONS** Do not use within 14 days of an MAO inhibitor **WARNINGS** Serotonin syndrome (if co-administered with other serotonergic drugs), use with caution in patients who are CYP450 2D6 poor metabolizers or with CYP2D6 inhibitors, debilitated (e.g., sedated, confined to a supine position) **SIDE EFFECTS** N/V, drowsiness, CNS depression (especially when used with other sedating drugs) **NOTES** If the product name has DM at the end, such as *Robitussin DM*, it contains dextromethorphan OTC: do not use in children < 4 years
Codeine C-II (single entity used for pain) C-V (combination products used for cough and cold: see table on following page)	Adult: 7.5-120 mg PO as single dose or divided doses	**BOXED WARNING** Respiratory depression and death have occurred in children who received codeine following tonsillectomy and/or adenoidectomy and had evidence of being ultra-rapid metabolizers of codeine due to a CYP450 2D6 polymorphism; deaths have also occurred in nursing infants after being exposed to high concentrations of morphine from mothers who were ultra-rapid metabolizers **CONTRAINDICATIONS** Do not use in children < 12 years of age (any indication) or in children < 18 years of age after tonsillectomy and/or adenoidectomy **NOTES** The FDA recommends to avoid codeine-containing cough and cold products for patients < 18 years of age (see the Pain and Pediatric Conditions chapters)
Benzonatate *(Tessalon Perles)*	Adult: 100-200 mg PO TID PRN (max 600 mg/day)	**WARNINGS** Do not use in children < 10 years of age; accidental ingestion and fatal overdose has been reported **SIDE EFFECTS** Somnolence, confusion, hallucinations
Diphenhydramine *(Benadryl)* Rx and OTC	Adult: 25 mg PO Q4H PRN (max 150 mg/day)	See First-Generation Oral Antihistamines table

Decongestants

Systemic and nasal decongestants, discussed previously, are used to relieve congestion and rhinorrhea.

Analgesics/Antipyretics

Analgesics and antipyretics such as acetaminophen and ibuprofen are used to relieve sore throat, body malaise and fever. They are often added to combination products for cough/cold. Use caution <u>not</u> to <u>exceed the maximum</u> daily dosing for acetaminophen or ibuprofen if multiple medications are being used. See the Pain chapter for more information.

Select Cough and Cold Combination Products

See the <u>Study Tip Gal</u> below for methods to help recognize the ingredients in combination products.

DRUG	ADULT DOSING
Dextromethorphan/promethazine	15 mg/6.25 mg per 5 mL; 5 mL PO Q4-6H PRN (max 30 mL/day)
Brompheniramine/pseudoephedrine/dextromethorphan **(Bromfed DM)** Rx and OTC	2 mg/30 mg/10 mg per 5 mL; 10 mL PO Q4H PRN (max 60 mL/day)
Promethazine/codeine <u>C-V</u>	6.25 mg/10 mg per 5 mL; 5 mL PO Q4-6H PRN (max 30 mL/day)
Promethazine/phenylephrine/codeine (Promethazine VC/Codeine) <u>C-V</u>	6.25 mg/5 mg/10 mg per 5 mL; 5 mL PO Q4-6H PRN (max 30 mL/day)
Guaifenesin/codeine (G Tussin AC, Virtussin A/C) <u>C-V</u>	100 mg/10 mg per 5 mL; 10 mL PO Q4H PRN (max 60 mL/day)
Guaifenesin/codeine/pseudoephedrine (Coditussin DAC, Virtussin DAC) <u>C-V</u>	100 mg/10 mg/30 mg per 5 mL; 10 mL PO Q4H PRN (max 40 mL/day)
Chlorpheniramine/hydrocodone **(TussiCaps, Tussionex*)** <u>C-II</u>	Capsule: 8 mg/10 mg per capsule; 1 capsule PO Q12H PRN (max 2 caps/day) Suspension: 8 mg/10 mg ER per 5 mL; 5 mL PO Q12H PRN (max 10 mL/day)
Chlorpheniramine/codeine (Tuzistra XR) <u>C-III</u>	4 mg/20 mg ER per 5 mL; 10 mL PO Q12H PRN (max 20 mL/day)

*Brand discontinued but name still used in practice.

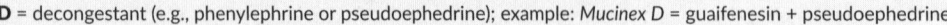

COUGH AND COLD COMBINATION PRODUCTS: WHAT'S IN A NAME?

The name of a combination cough/cold product can tell you what it contains. This is based on either the symptom it treats or the abbreviation included in the name (e.g., *Robitussin Cough + Chest Congestion DM* contains dextromethorphan, a cough suppressant identified with the abbreviation DM and guaifenesin, an expectorant for chest congestion). Some commonly used abbreviations are:

D = decongestant (e.g., phenylephrine or pseudoephedrine); example: *Mucinex D* = guaifenesin + pseudoephedrine

PE = **p**henyl**e**phrine; example: *Sudafed PE* = phenylephrine

DM = **d**extro**m**ethorphan; example: *Robafen DM* = guaifenesin + dextromethorphan

AC = contains codeine; example: *G Tussin AC* = guaifenesin + codeine

Guaifenesin is a mucolytic (thins out mucus); example: *Mucinex*

Analgesic in combination cough and cold products is usually acetaminophen

Antihistamines (e.g., diphenhydramine, chlorpheniramine, brompheniramine) are common and cause sedation; the night-time products, and some anytime products, contain an antihistamine

Cough and Cold Products in Children

If a young child has a cold, it is safe and useful to recommend proper hydration, nasal bulbs for gentle suctioning, saline drops/sprays (*Ocean* and generics) and vaporizers/humidifiers. Ibuprofen and acetaminophen can be used, if needed, for fever or pain (see the Pain and Pediatric Conditions chapters for more information).

PEDIATRIC COUGH AND COLD TREATMENT – CAUTION NEEDED

CHILDREN < 18 YEARS
- Avoid codeine and hydrocodone-containing cough and cold products (FDA)

CHILDREN < 4 YEARS
- Avoid OTC cough and cold products (package labeling)

CHILDREN < 2 YEARS
- Avoid OTC cough and cold products (FDA)
- Avoid promethazine (FDA)
- Avoid topical menthol and camphor (package labeling)

Cough and cold products generally do not offer much symptom relief to young children, while having potentially serious side effects. Many of the products contain multiple ingredients, which increases the risk of accidental overdose if combined with other medications. Symptoms due to cough and cold are self-limiting and drug treatment is often not necessary. The FDA does not recommend OTC drug treatment for cough and cold symptoms in children ≤ 2 years old, but most manufacturers include product labeling to avoid in children ≤ 4 years old. Some combination products have additional labeling restrictions for use only in children ≥ 6 years of age.

Do not use promethazine in any form in children < 2 years old because of the risk of fatal respiratory depression. Due to the risk of adverse events (e.g., slowed breathing, overdose, misuse), the FDA recommends against using prescription cough and cold products containing codeine or hydrocodone in patients ≤ 18 years old. Manufacturers have not yet included this contraindication in prescription labeling. When used to treat pain, codeine and hydrocodone do not have the same restrictions (see the Pain and Pediatric Conditions chapters for more complete information).

Topical products containing menthol (e.g., *Vicks VapoRub*) can be applied to the chest and neck (never directly to the nose) to help open the airways and suppress cough. Such products should not be used in children < 2 years of age, as menthol can cause cardiac and CNS toxicity if ingested. Camphor is generally considered safe but lacks sufficient data. *Vick's BabyRub* contains petrolatum, eucalyptus oil, lavender oil, rosemary oil and aloe extract and is considered relatively safe, but lacks sufficient efficacy data.

KEY COUNSELING POINTS

See the Drug Formulations and Patient Counseling chapter for nasal spray administration instructions.

ANTIHISTAMINES

- Some formulations contain phenylalanine. Do not use if you have phenylketonuria (PKU).

Select Guidelines/References

Seidman MD, Gurgel RK, Lin SY et al. Clinical Practice Guideline: Allergic Rhinitis. *Otolaryngology-Head and Neck Surgery.* 2015;152(IS):S1-S43.

Krinsky DL, Berardi RR, Ferreri SP, eds. Handbook of Nonprescription Drugs. 19th ed. Washington DC: APhA; 2015:189-230.

CONTENT LEGEND

  = Study Tip Gal   = Key Drug Guy

GLAUCOMA

damage to
optic nerve

abnormal
pressure
inside eye

iStock.com/TefiM

CHAPTER 38

COMMON CONDITIONS
OF THE EYES & EARS

BACKGROUND

Many eye and ear conditions can be treated with topical medications that are applied directly to the eye or ear. By applying the medication directly to the specific location, instead of systemically, adverse effects are minimized.

The various formulations of topical eye and ear medications are shown in the box below. The eyes are more sensitive than the ears. Eye drops can be used in the ear, but never use ear drops in the eyes. The ear drops may not have an appropriate pH, may not be isotonic and may not be sterile. Correct administration technique is key for each medication to work.

EYE & EAR PRESCRIPTION INTERPRETATION

ABBREV.	MEANING	CAUTION
AD AS AU	Right Ear Left Ear Each Ear	These abbreviations can be mistaken (interchanged) for each other and can mean other things; know how to interpret them, but it is safer to write them out (e.g., use right eye instead of OD)
OD OS OU	Right Eye Left Eye Each Eye	

Memory tip: A is from the Latin for ear (auris), O is for eye (oculus), D is for right (dextra) and S is for left (sinistra)

iStock.com/Sudowoodo

EYE AND EAR FORMULATIONS

- Solutions: 1 drop = 0.05 mL.
- Suspensions: shake well.
- Ointments: apply to the conjunctival sac or over lid margins (for blepharitis). Ointments can make vision blurry. Do not use with contact lenses.
- Gels: with cap on, invert and shake once to get the medication into the tip before instilling into the eye.

GLAUCOMA

Glaucoma is a disease of the eye that results in <u>damage to the optic nerve</u> and <u>loss of the visual field</u> (i.e., the vision straight ahead and the peripheral vision, measured by the <u>visual field test</u>). In most cases, the intraocular pressure (<u>IOP) is above the normal range</u> of 12 – 22 mmHg. IOP can be increased from genetics, age and medications (see <u>Key Drugs Guy</u>). The goal of treatment is to <u>reduce IOP</u>.

There are two main forms of glaucoma. <u>Open-angle glaucoma</u> is the most common type. It often presents without symptoms and is treated with eye drops or surgery. Angle-closure, or <u>closed-angle glaucoma</u>, is a sharp, <u>sudden increase in IOP</u> due to a <u>blockage</u>. This type of glaucoma usually presents with eye pain, headaches and decreased vision and is a <u>medical emergency</u> that is treated <u>surgically</u>.

DRUGS THAT CAN INCREASE IOP

Anticholinergics (e.g., antihistamines, oxybutynin, tolterodine, benztropine, scopolamine, trihexyphenidyl, tricyclic antidepressants)

Decongestants (e.g., pseudoephedrine)

Chronic steroids, especially eye drops such as prednisolone (*Pred Forte*)

Topiramate (*Topamax*)

DRUG TREATMENT

Glaucoma treatments decrease IOP by targeting the <u>aqueous humor (fluid in the eye)</u> in two main ways (see <u>Study Tip Gal</u>). <u>Prostaglandin (PG) analogs</u> are used commonly as initial treatment. PG analogs are the <u>most effective</u> drugs at decreasing IOP (~30%); they are safe and are used <u>once daily</u>. Ophthalmic <u>beta-blockers</u> (e.g., timolol), another common class of drugs, decrease IOP by ~22%. A beta-blocker is <u>preferable</u> if the pressure is high in <u>one eye only</u> because the darkening of the iris and eyelash thickening seen with PG analogs is not desirable in only one eye (see drug table below). If monotherapy does not sufficiently decrease IOP, consider switching to a different medication or using combination therapy.

GLAUCOMA TREATMENT GOAL: DECREASE IOP

Strategies:

■ Reduce aqueous humor production (make less fluid)
- ❏ Beta-blockers, like timolol
- ❏ Carbonic anhydrase inhibitors, like dorzolamide

■ Increase aqueous humor outflow (move fluid out)
- ❏ Prostaglandin analogs, like latanoprost

■ Or, do both: often achieved with add-on treatment
- ❏ Alpha-2 agonists, like brimonidine

Adequate treatment requires good eye drop technique and a high level of adherence. The correct way to administer eye drops is described in the Drug Formulations and Patient Counseling chapter. Because glaucoma often presents with no symptoms, adherence can be a major issue. Counseling on proper administration technique and the importance of adherence is critical.

DRUG	DOSING	SIDE EFFECTS/CLINICAL CONCERNS
Prostaglandin Analogs: increase aqueous humor outflow		
Bimatoprost (*Lumigan*) **Latanoprost (*Xalatan, Xelpros*)** + netarsudil (*Rocklatan*) **Travoprost (*Travatan Z*)** Latanoprostene bunod (*Vyzulta*) Tafluprost (*Zioptan*) **Bimatoprost (*Latisse*)** is indicated for eyelash hypotrichosis (inadequate growth of eyelashes) to ↑ <u>eyelash growth</u>; do <u>not</u> use with <u>prostaglandin analogs</u> indicated for <u>glaucoma</u>	1 drop QHS Do not exceed once daily dosing; can decrease efficacy Select products contain the preservative benzalkonium chloride (BAK); remove contact lenses before use	**WARNINGS** Ocular effects: <u>darkening of the iris</u>, eyelid skin and <u>eyelashes</u>; eyelash <u>length and number can increase</u>; contamination of multiple-dose ophthalmic solutions can cause bacterial keratitis **SIDE EFFECTS** <u>Blurred vision, stinging, increased pigmentation</u> of the <u>iris/eyelashes</u>, eyelash <u>growth</u>/thickening, foreign body sensation **NOTES** *Travatan Z* and *Xelpros* do not contain BAK (a different preservative is used); can be used in patients with a past reaction to BAK or dry eye *Zioptan* comes as 10 single-use, preservative-free containers in a foil pouch; discard each container after use Latanoprost, latanoprostene bunod and tafluprost should be stored in the <u>refrigerator before opening</u>; once opened, store at room temperature Naming tip: –<u>prost</u> = <u>prost</u>aglandin analog

DRUG	DOSING	SIDE EFFECTS/CLINICAL CONCERNS
Beta-Blockers: reduce aqueous humor production		
Timolol 0.25% and 0.5% (Timoptic, Timoptic-XE, Istalol, Timolol GFS, Betimol, Timoptic Ocudose) **+ dorzolamide (Cosopt, Cosopt PF)** + brimonidine (Combigan) Betaxolol (Betoptic S) Carteolol Levobunolol (Betagan)	Timolol: 1 drop daily or BID Timoptic-XE, Timolol GFS (gels): daily Gels: shake once before use; wait 10 minutes after administering other eye drops before inserting gel Select products contain the preservative BAK; remove contact lenses before use	**CONTRAINDICATIONS** Sinus bradycardia; heart block > 1st degree (except in patients with a pacemaker); cardiogenic shock; uncompensated cardiac failure; bronchospastic disease **SIDE EFFECTS** Burning, stinging, bradycardia/fatigue, bronchospasm with non-selective agents, itching of the eyes or eyelids, changes in vision, increased light sensitivity **NOTES** All are non-selective beta-blockers except betaxolol; betaxolol is less likely to cause pulmonary adverse effects in patients with chronic lung disease (e.g., asthma/COPD) Cosopt PF (the PF stands for "preservative-free") is packaged in single-use containers Some products contain sulfites, which can cause allergic reactions
Cholinergics (Miotics): increase aqueous humor outflow		
Carbachol (Miostat)	1-2 drops up to TID	**SIDE EFFECTS** Poor vision at night (due to pupil constriction), corneal clouding, burning (transient), hypotension, bronchospasm, abdominal cramps/GI distress
Pilocarpine (Isopto Carpine)	Solution: 1-2 drops up to 4 times per day Select products contain the preservative BAK; remove contact lenses before use	**NOTES** Use with caution in patients with a history of retinal detachment or corneal abrasion
Carbonic Anhydrase Inhibitors: reduce aqueous humor production		
Dorzolamide (Trusopt) **+ timolol (Cosopt, Cosopt PF)** Brinzolamide (Azopt) + brimonidine (Simbrinza) Acetazolamide – oral, injection Methazolamide – oral	Trusopt: 1 drop TID Cosopt: 1 drop BID Azopt: 1 drop TID Acetazolamide 250 mg PO 1-4 times per day, or 500 mg ER PO BID Select ophthalmic products contain the preservative BAK; remove contact lenses before use	**WARNINGS** Sulfonamide allergy: caution due to the risk of systemic exposure and cross reactivity (especially with oral formulations) **SIDE EFFECTS** Eye drops: burning, blurred vision, blepharitis, dry eye Oral (acetazolamide): CNS effects (ataxia, confusion), photosensitivity/skin rash (including risk of SJS and TEN), anorexia, nausea, risk of hematological toxicities **NOTES** Acetazolamide is used infrequently for glaucoma; it is used for the prevention and treatment of acute mountain (altitude) sickness Naming Tip: –zolamide = caution with sulfonamide allergy
Adrenergic Alpha-2 Agonists: increase aqueous humor outflow, reduce aqueous humor production		
Brimonidine (Alphagan P) + timolol (Combigan) + brinzolamide (Simbrinza) Apraclonidine (Iopidine) Brimonidine (Lumify) (OTC) is indicated for ocular redness	Alphagan P and Iopidine are dosed TID Select products contain the preservative BAK; remove contact lenses before use	**WARNINGS** CNS depression: caution with heavy machinery, driving **SIDE EFFECTS** Sedation, dry mouth, dry nose
Rho Kinase Inhibitors: increase aqueous humor outflow		
Netarsudil (Rhopressa) + latanoprost (Rocklatan)	1 drop daily in the evening Contains the preservative BAK; remove contact lenses before use	**SIDE EFFECTS** Burning/eye pain, corneal disease, conjunctival hemorrhage and conjunctival hyperemia (excess blood vessels) **NOTES** Store in the refrigerator before opening; once opened, store at room temperature for ≤ 6 weeks

CONJUNCTIVITIS

Conjunctivitis, also known as "pink eye," occurs in one or both eyes. Symptoms include swelling, itching, burning and redness of the conjunctiva, the protective membrane that lines the eyelids and covers the white part of the eye (the sclera). Conjunctivitis can be due to a virus, bacteria, an allergen or some type of ocular irritant, such as a chemical or contact lenses. In most cases, conjunctivitis causes only mild discomfort, does not harm vision and will clear without medical treatment. In some cases, treatment is required.

Viral and bacterial conjunctivitis occur mostly in young children and are highly contagious. Infected children should stay at home and only return to school once treatment begins, unless there are systemic symptoms. To prevent the spread of the infection, any patient with viral or bacterial conjunctivitis should be instructed to:

- Avoid touching their eyes
- Use proper hand hygiene and wash their hands thoroughly and frequently
- Change towels and washcloths daily, and do not share towels with others
- Discard eye cosmetics, particularly mascara

Chemical conjunctivitis has no specific drug treatment and is not described in the following table. The irritant should be flushed out of the eyes with saline, and inflammation can be reduced with an NSAID or a steroid eye drop. If contact lenses caused the irritation, they should not be used until the condition clears. It might be helpful to change the type of contact lenses or the brand of disinfectant solution. If the condition is severe, such as a burn, or the chemical is dangerous or unknown, refer for emergency care.

TREATMENT OF CONJUNCTIVITIS BY TYPE

Conjunctivitis is usually viral and self-limiting. With bacterial or allergic conjunctivitis, treatments are helpful. Antibiotics are only indicated for bacterial conjunctivitis. If antibiotics are used, the full treatment course should be completed. These treatments can be combined with symptomatic treatment (see Symptom-Based Ophthalmic Treatments on the following page).

TYPE	CAUSES	TREATMENT
Viral	Adenovirus (most common), other viruses Most infections are mild, but some can be severe (e.g., caused by zoster virus or HIV)	No topical treatment for common viral conjunctivitis; the infection runs its course over several days to three weeks
Bacterial	*Staphylococcus aureus, Streptococcus pneumoniae, Haemophilus influenzae, Moraxella catarrhalis* More severe cases caused by *Neisseria gonorrhoeae* or *Chlamydia*, which requires systemic treatment	Select topical antibiotic eye drops or ointments: **Moxifloxacin (*Vigamox*, *Moxeza*)** **Neomycin/Polymyxin B/Dexamethasone (*Maxitrol*)** **Ofloxacin (*Ocuflox*)** **Trimethoprim/Polymyxin B (*Polytrim*)** Azithromycin (*AzaSite*) – store in the refrigerator, stable for 14 days at room temperature Besifloxacin (*Besivance*) Ciprofloxacin (*Ciloxan*) Erythromycin Gentamicin (*Gentak*) Neomycin/Bacitracin/Polymyxin B (*Neo-Polycin*) Tobramycin (*Tobrex*) Tobramycin/Dexamethasone (*TobraDex*, *TobraDex ST*) Sulfacetamide (*Bleph-10*)
Allergic	Common allergens include pollen, dust mites, animal dander, molds **USAGE NOTES:** Prednisolone/steroid eye drops are often used acutely for a severe reaction, but not long term due to risk of ↑ IOP Ophthalmic decongestants can be used to decrease redness caused by allergic conjunctivitis (see Symptom-Based Ophthalmic Treatments on the next page)	**MAST CELL STABILIZERS** Cromolyn Lodoxamide (*Alomide*) Nedocromil (*Alocril*) **ANTIHISTAMINES** **Azelastine** **Olopatadine (*Pataday*)** (OTC) Cetirizine (*Zerviate*) Epinastine (*Elestat*) **ANTIHISTAMINE/MAST CELL STABILIZER** **Ketotifen (*Alaway*, *Zaditor*)** (OTC) Alcaftadine (*Lastacaft*)

BLEPHARITIS

Blepharitis (eyelid inflammation) most commonly involves the eyelid margins (where the eyelashes come out of the skin). In many patients, the condition is chronic and difficult to treat, and in others, it is an acute, short-term condition. The primary symptoms are inflamed, irritated and itchy eyelids. The preferred treatment includes application of a warm compress over the eye for a few minutes to loosen the crusty deposits, then use of a warm, moist washcloth (water plus a few drops of baby shampoo) to wipe away the debris. In some cases, antibiotic ointments, steroid eye drops and/or artificial tears are helpful.

OTHER OCULAR CONDITIONS

SYMPTOM-BASED OPHTHALMIC TREATMENTS

Symptoms can accompany the diseases previously discussed (e.g., conjunctivitis) or they can occur independently. Common ophthalmic symptoms include inflammation, dry eye and eye redness. Inflammation can be reduced with a cold compress and either an NSAID eye drop (if mild) or a steroid eye drop (if severe). Artificial tears can help with a "gritty" feeling and alleviate dryness. Chronic dry eye requires more aggressive treatment. Instruct patients to return for follow-up if they do not recover within a few days.

WHY DO MOST EYE DROPS BURN?

Most bottles of eye drops contain multiple doses. Since the drops are being put into the eyes, the bottle must remain free from contamination. A preservative is often added to prevent the growth of microorganisms. The most common preservative used in eye drops is benzalkonium chloride (BAK).

- Preservatives are toxic to bacteria and are irritating to the sensitive tissues in the eyes, which leads to burning/stinging after administration.
  - ❏ Some drugs found in eye drops can also cause irritation.
- Contact lenses trap the drug and preservatives against the surface of the eye, making irritation worse.
  - ❏ Lenses should be removed before using eye drops and wait 15 minutes after administration before reinserting.
  - ❏ This is especially important with drops containing BAK as these can damage the eyes when used with contacts.
- Some eye drops have preservative-free formulations for those unable to tolerate the side effects.
  - ❏ Example: *Cosopt PF* (the PF stands for preservative-free).

See the Drug Formulations and Patient Counseling chapter for eye drop administration instructions.

SYMPTOM	EXAMPLES OF TREATMENT	USAGE NOTES
Inflammation	**STEROIDS** **Prednisolone (*Pred Forte, Pred Mild,* Omnipred*)** Dexamethasone (*Maxidex, Ozurdex*) Fluorometholone (*Flarex, FML Forte, FML Liquifilm* suspension, ointment) Loteprednol (*Alrex, Lotemax* suspension, ointment, gel) **NSAIDS** **Ketorolac (*Acular,* Acular LS, Acuvail)** Nepafenac (*Ilevro, Nevanac*) Bromfenac Diclofenac Flurbiprofen	Steroid eye drops should be used short-term due to risk of ↑ IOP
Dryness	***Refresh*** (OTC) ***Systane*** (OTC) *Liquifilm Tears* (OTC) Others	Often referred to as Artificial Tears Contain common lubricants – mineral oil, glycerin, propylene glycol, dextran, hypromellose Administered multiple times daily, as needed
Chronic Dry Eye Disease	**Cyclosporine Emulsion Eye Drops (*Restasis*)** Lifitegrast (*Xiidra*) Loteprednol (*Eysuvis*) Varenicline nasal spray (*Tyrvaya*)	*Restasis* is indicated for keratoconjunctivitis sicca (severe, chronic dry eye syndrome)
Redness	**Naphazoline (*Clear Eyes Redness Relief*) (OTC)** **Naphazoline/Pheniramine (*Naphcon A, Visine A*) (OTC)** **Tetrahydrozoline (*Visine*) (OTC)** Brimonidine (*Lumify*) (OTC)	Can be used to treat allergic conjunctivitis

Brand discontinued but name still used in practice.

MEDICATION INDUCED OPHTHALMIC ISSUES

Medications can cause ocular adverse effects. Most disappear once the drug is discontinued (such as blurry vision from an anticholinergic). In other cases, the damage can be permanent (such as vision loss with a PDE-5 inhibitor). Patients must be instructed to report visual changes immediately; in most cases, the damage is reversible if the medication is stopped quickly. See the Key Drugs Guy below for specific medications and their effects.

COMMON DRUGS KNOWN TO CAUSE VISION CHANGES OR DAMAGE

Retinal changes/retinopathy
Chloroquine

Hydroxychloroquine

Optic neuropathy
Amiodarone (plus corneal deposits)

Ethambutol

Linezolid

Intraoperative floppy iris syndrome (IFIS); causes difficulty in cataract surgery
Alpha-blockers (e.g., tamsulosin)

Color discrimination
Digoxin (with toxicity) – yellow/green vision

PDE-5 inhibitors (e.g., sildenafil) – greenish tinge around objects

Voriconazole – color vision changes

Vision loss/abnormal vision
Digoxin (with toxicity) – blurriness, halos

PDE-5 inhibitors – vision loss (one or both eyes; can be permanent)

Isotretinoin – ↓ night vision (can be permanent), dryness, irritation

Topiramate – visual field defects

Vigabatrin – permanent vision loss (high risk)

Voriconazole – abnormal vision, photophobia

COMMON EAR CONDITIONS

Common conditions treated in the ear include pain, such as from an outer ear infection (otitis externa) and ear wax (cerumen) impaction. Tinnitus (ringing, roaring or buzzing sounds) is caused by drug toxicity (e.g., salicylates), noise exposure, or it can be idiopathic. There is no effective drug treatment for tinnitus.

OTITIS EXTERNA

Ear drops with antibiotics can be used for outer ear infections. Pain can be treated with systemic analgesics (e.g., ibuprofen, acetaminophen). During treatment, patients should stay out of the water, avoid flying due to the pressure changes and avoid the use of headphones and earplugs. A few common antibiotic products include:

- Ciprofloxacin and dexamethasone (Ciprodex)
- Ciprofloxacin and hydrocortisone (Cipro HC)
- Neomycin, colistin, hydrocortisone and thonzonium (Cortisportin-TC)

EAR WAX (CERUMEN) BLOCKAGE

Ear blockage occurs when wax (cerumen) accumulates in the ear or becomes too hard to wash away naturally. For patients with symptoms (e.g., earache, hearing loss), it is removed in a medical office (manually or with irrigation) or with the use of cerumenolytics in a medical office or at home. Cerumenolytics soften ear wax, allowing it to be cleared from the ear more easily. Examples include water, saline solution, mineral oil, hydrogen peroxide and carbamide peroxide (Debrox). Use should be limited to 3 – 5 days, with follow-up after this time (see the Drug Formulations and Patient Counseling chapter for administration instructions).

KEY COUNSELING POINTS

See the Drug Formulations and Patient Counseling chapter for counseling language/layman's terminology and eye drop and ear drop administration instructions.

ALL EYE DROPS

- Can cause stinging/burning (except for preservative-free).
- Wait five minutes in between two drops of the same medication.
- Wait 5 – 10 minutes in between drops of two different medications.
- Apply gels last. Wait 10 minutes after the last eye drop before use.
- Remove contact lenses prior to using eye drops. Wait 15 minutes to reinsert.

Prostaglandin Analogs

- Darkening of the iris and an increase in eyelash growth can occur.
- Do not use with bimatoprost (Latisse). Latisse can reduce the effectiveness of other prostaglandins.

Select Guidelines/References

American Academy of Ophthalmology Glaucoma Committee. Preferred Practice Pattern Guidelines. Primary Open-Angle Glaucoma 2020. https://www.aao.org/preferred-practice-pattern/primary-open-angle-glaucoma-ppp (accessed 2022 Feb 7).

CHAPTER CONTENT

CONTENT LEGEND

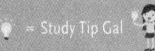 = Study Tip Gal    = Required Formula

THE STRUCTURE OF THE SKIN

sterger hair
corneal layer
root hair
sebaceous gland
sweat gland
nerve ending
granular layer
basal layer
surface vascular plexus
Epidermis
hair bulb
hair papilla
Dermis
hair muscle
nerve fiber
deep vascular plexus
subcutaneous fat
Hypodermis

© Yelena Bushtarenko © 123RF.com

CHAPTER 39

COMMON SKIN CONDITIONS

BACKGROUND

Patients in the community setting often ask pharmacists for recommendations for a variety of skin conditions. A pharmacist should be able to identify certain skin conditions, such as a blemish that could be skin cancer (see the Oncology I chapter) or the discoloration of skin and secretions caused by certain medications (see Study Tip Gal below). *The Handbook of Nonprescription Drugs* has pictures of common conditions, and many more are available at www.dermnet.com. If recommending OTC treatment, the patient should be counseled to seek further help if the condition does not improve or worsens.

NATURAL PRODUCTS

Aloe is a natural product produced from the aloe vera plant that is used for many skin conditions, including sunburn and psoriasis. It has little proven efficacy, but if used as a gel or lotion, it may provide a soothing effect. Tea tree oil is used for a variety of skin conditions, such as acne. It may be helpful for onychomycosis symptoms (depending on the dose and application schedule) but will not eradicate the infection in most patients. Lysine, taken as a tablet, capsule or applied topically, is used for cold sore (herpes simplex labialis) prevention and treatment. Biotin is a vitamin used for hair loss and brittle nails. Topical vitamin D is used in skin conditions, such as diaper rash and psoriasis.

DRUGS THAT CAN DISCOLOR SKIN AND SECRETIONS

BROWN
Entacapone
Levodopa
Methyldopa

BROWN/BLACK/GREEN
Iron (black stool)
Methocarbamol

BROWN/YELLOW
Nitrofurantoin
Metronidazole
Tinidazole
Riboflavin (B2)

PURPLE/ORANGE/RED
Chlorzoxazone

ORANGE/YELLOW
Sulfasalazine

YELLOW-GREEN
Propofol
Flutamide

RED-ORANGE
Phenazopyridine
Rifampin
Rifapentine

RED
Anthracyclines
Deferasirox (urine)

BLUE
Methylene blue
Mitoxantrone

BLUE-GRAY
Amiodarone
Chloroquine

ACNE

Most people, from infants to adults, develop acne at some point. It primarily develops in adolescents during puberty. Androgens (male sex hormones) are the primary determinant of acne, along with the presence of the bacteria, *Cutibacterium acnes* (formerly known as *Propionibacterium acnes*), and fatty acids (sebum) present in oil (sebaceous) glands. Acne mainly appears on the face, chest, shoulders and back. Diets with a high glycemic index or dairy can worsen acne.

Acne lesions are classified as whiteheads (closed comedones), blackheads (open comedones), papules, pustules and nodules (sometimes called "cysts"). Treatment is determined by severity: mild (few, occasional pimples), moderate (inflammatory papules) or severe (nodules). Acne is treated with these primary groups of medications: OTC benzoyl peroxide and salicylic acid, retinoids, topical or systemic (oral) antibiotics and systemic isotretinoin (see Study Tip Gal on the following page).

- Benzoyl peroxide (BPO) is an effective OTC medication and is recommended for most patients with acne. It is also available by prescription, including in combinations with hydrocortisone, the retinoid adapalene or with the antibiotics erythromycin or clindamycin.

- Salicylic acid is available OTC and is supplied in several different formulations, including washes, "medicated pads" and lotions.

- Retinoids, primarily topical tretinoin and derivatives, are the usual prescription drug of choice and are also used to reduce wrinkles. Retinoids are vitamin A derivatives that primarily work by reducing adherence of the keratinocytes (outer skin cells) in the oil gland.

  - Retinoids are teratogenic. They must be avoided in pregnancy or breastfeeding (see Drug Use in Pregnancy and Lactation chapter).

  - They are well-tolerated when used topically, with mild skin irritation (redness, drying) and photosensitivity possible. Retinoids should be applied daily at night with the correct (pea-sized) amount. This can be decreased to every other night if irritation occurs. A moisturizer, followed by sunscreen, should be used each morning.

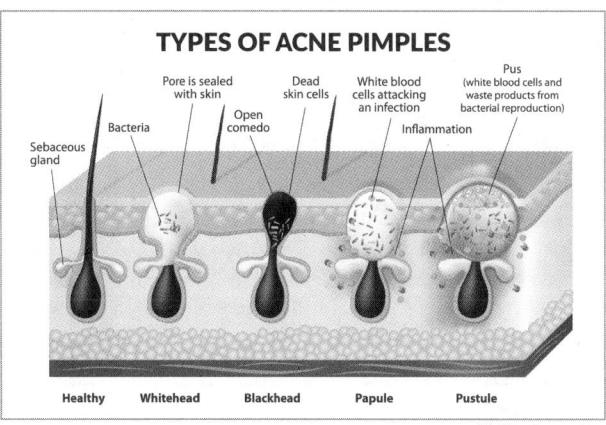

TYPES OF ACNE PIMPLES

Sebaceous gland | Bacteria | Pore is sealed with skin | Open comedo | Dead skin cells | White blood cells attacking an infection | Inflammation | Pus (white blood cells and waste products from bacterial reproduction)

Healthy | Whitehead | Blackhead | Papule | Pustule

iStock.com/ttsz

- Retinoids take 4 – 12 weeks to work, and acne can worsen initially. Minocycline can be used with topical retinoids to help reduce worsening. Tazarotene often works better than tretinoin; it is used for difficult cases.

- The oral retinoid isotretinoin has many safety considerations. Isotretinoin is FDA-approved for severe, recalcitrant nodular acne only, though it is also used off-label for moderate, treatment-resistant acne. Cholesterol and pregnancy tests are required, among other monitoring.

- Some women find benefit with oral contraceptive pills, especially if the acne occurs around the menstrual cycle or if irregular menses or symptoms of androgenic excess are present.

- Spironolactone is an aldosterone receptor antagonist with antiandrogen effects. It is not FDA-approved for acne, but is recommended as a useful treatment for some females.

- Azelaic acid (*Azelex, Finacea*) is a topical dicarboxylic acid cream or gel available OTC and prescription for acne and rosacea.

- Clascoterone (*Winlevi*) is a topical androgen receptor inhibitor. It can be used as an alternative for the treatment of mild acne in patients age 12 and older.

ACNE TREATMENT SUMMARY

ACNE TREATMENT IS DETERMINED BY ACNE SEVERITY AND SUCCESS OF PAST TREATMENTS.

	MILD	MODERATE	SEVERE
FIRST-LINE TREATMENT	Topicals: BPO and/or retinoid	Topicals: combination* or PO antibiotic + BPO + topical retinoid (+/− topical antibiotic)	Topicals: combination* + PO antibiotic or PO isotretinoin
ALTERNATIVE TREATMENT	Add topical retinoid or BPO, switch to another retinoid, topical dapsone or clascoterone	Other combination*, switch PO antibiotic, add combined OCP or spironolactone (females) or PO isotretinoin	Switch PO antibiotic, add combined OCP or spironolactone (females) or PO isotretinoin (if not previously tried)

Topical combination therapy includes the following combinations: BPO + topical antibiotic, BPO + retinoid or BPO + retinoid + topical antibiotic.

DRUGS	NOTES	SAFETY/COUNSELING
Topical Retinoids		
Tretinoin (Atralin, Renova, Retin-A, Retin-A Micro, Altreno, Avita, Refissa) Rx: cream, gel, lotion Clindamycin/tretinoin gel (Veltin, Ziana) **Adapalene (Differin)** OTC: gel (Differin gel 0.1%) Rx: adapalene/BPO gel (Epiduo, Epiduo Forte) Tazarotene Rx: cream (Tazorac), foam (Fabior), gel (Tazorac), lotion (Arazlo) Halobetasol/tazarotene lotion (Duobrii) Trifarotene Rx: cream (Aklief)	Topical retinoids should be avoided in pregnancy Retin-A Micro (microsphere gel) and Avita (polymerized cream or gel): slower release, less skin irritation Tazarotene: contraindicated in pregnancy, lotion (Arazlo) is approved in individuals aged 9 years and older Altreno: 0.05% lotion form of tretinoin, less irritating Fabior: stronger, more irritating	Limit sun exposure. Apply daily, usually at bedtime, about 20 minutes after washing face. If irritation occurs, use lower strength or decrease frequency to every other night. May need to reduce contact initially (wash off if skin is irritated). A pea-sized amount is sufficient (for facial application); it should be smoothed over the entire surface of the face, not just on acne. Avoid salicylic acid scrubs or astringents; will worsen irritation. Wash only with mild soap twice daily. Takes 4-12 weeks to see response; may worsen acne initially.
Other Topical Acne Products		
Benzoyl peroxide (BPO) OTC: many products including Benzac, Clearasil, PanOxyl Rx: BPO/hydrocortisone (Vanoxide-HC)	Start with 2.5-5% BPO, generally adequate and less irritating than the higher strengths	Can bleach clothing and hair. Limit sun exposure.
TOPICAL ANTIBIOTICS AND COMBINATIONS (All available as Rx only) Erythromycin/BPO (Benzamycin) Clindamycin/BPO (BenzaClin, Acanya, Neuac, Onexton) Minocycline foam (Amzeeq) **OTHERS** OTC: **Salicylic acid** (Clearasil, and others) OTC: **Azelaic acid** lower strengths (Paula's Choice, The Ordinary, and others) Rx: **Azelaic acid** cream, gel, lotion (Azelex 15%, Finacea 20%) Rx: Dapsone gel (Aczone) Rx: Clascoterone cream (Winlevi)	Benzamycin and BenzaClin: Add indicated amount of purified water to the vial (70% ethyl alcohol for Benzamycin) and immediately shake to completely dissolve medication (use additional purified water to bring level up to the mark if needed) Add the solution in the vial to the gel; stir until homogenous (1 to 1.5 minutes) Place a 3-month expiration date on the label following mixing Benzamycin is kept refrigerated BenzaClin is kept at room temp Winlevi: Keep refrigerated before dispensing; store at room temperature after dispensing	Clindamycin topicals: Clean face, shake (if lotion), apply a thin layer once or twice daily. Avoid contact with eyes; if contact, rinse with cold water. Takes 2-6 weeks for effect and up to 12 weeks for full benefit. Minocycline topical: See oral antibiotics section (next page) Dapsone gel: Avoid in G6PD deficiency. Clascoterone: HPA axis suppression may occur during or after treatment; more likely with use over a large surface area, prolonged use, and use with occlusive dressings. Apply a thin layer twice daily after washing and drying the skin.

EYES, EARS, NOSE & SKIN CONDITIONS

DRUGS	NOTES	SAFETY/COUNSELING
Oral Retinoids		
Isotretinoin (Absorica, Amnesteem, Claravis, Myorisan, Zenatane) Rx: capsules 0.5-1 mg/kg/day, divided BID with food for 15-20 weeks.	Only FDA-approved for severe, refractory nodular acne. Patients who can get pregnant must sign patient information/informed consent form about birth defects if the fetus is exposed to isotretinoin. Must have had 2 negative pregnancy tests prior to starting treatment. Do not get pregnant for 1 month before, while taking the drug, or for 1 month after the drug is stopped. Do not breastfeed or donate blood until at least 1 month has passed after the drug is stopped. Do not use with vitamin A supplements, tetracyclines, steroids, progestin-only contraceptives or St. John's wort. Must swallow capsule whole, or puncture and sprinkle on applesauce or ice cream – this may irritate the esophagus.	**BOXED WARNING** Birth defects have been documented; must not be used by patients who are pregnant or may become pregnant. Can only be dispensed by a pharmacy registered and activated with the pregnancy REMS (iPLEDGE) program. 1-month Rx at a time, fill within 7 days with yellow sticker attached. **WARNINGS** Dry skin, chapped lips, dry eyes/eye irritation (may cause difficulty wearing contact lenses), ↓ night vision (may be permanent), arthralgias, skeletal hyperostosis (calcification of ligaments that attach to the spine), osteoporosis, psychiatric issues (depression, psychosis, risk of suicide), ↑ cholesterol (TG) and BG. **Counseling:** pregnancy testing must be repeated on a monthly basis. 2 forms of birth control are required (cannot use a progestin-only pill). Carry bottled water, eye drops and lip balm.
Oral Antibiotics Used for Acne		
Minocycline (Minocin, Solodyn, CoreMino, Minolira, Ximino) Rx: capsule, tablet IR formulations: 50-100 mg PO BID; may be used by patients ≥ 8 years XR formulations: 1 mg/kg PO daily; only approved for use in patients ≥ 12 years Sarecycline (Seysara) Rx: tablet	Doxycycline and minocycline are more effective than tetracycline in eradicating C. acnes. Sulfamethoxazole/trimethoprim is also used. Erythromycin is used less commonly due to resistance. Sarecycline is a tetracycline derivative for non-nodular moderate to severe acne.	Can cause photosensitivity, rash in susceptible patients, dizziness, diarrhea, somnolence. Like other tetracyclines, can cause fetal harm if administered during pregnancy. May cause permanent discoloration in teeth if used when teeth are forming (up to 8 years of age).

COLD SORES

- Cold sores (herpes simplex labialis) are common and highly contagious. Infection is usually due to herpes simplex virus type 1 (HSV-1) but can be caused by HSV-2 when due to oral/genital sex. The virus spreads mostly with active lesions; kissing and sharing drinks can transmit the infection.

- Sore eruption is preceded by prodromal symptoms (e.g., tingling, itching, soreness). In most patients, the sore appears in the same location repeatedly. The most common site is the junction between the upper and lower lip. Triggers that instigate sore outbreaks include fatigue, stress, stress to the skin (e.g., sun exposure, acid peels) and dental work.

- The prodromal period is the optimal time to start treatment (topical or oral) to reduce blister duration. If recurrences are frequent (> 4 times/year), chronic suppression, taken daily, can be used. OTC and prescription topicals shorten the duration by up to one day; oral (systemic) antivirals shorten the duration by up to two days.

- The natural product lysine is used commonly for cold sore prevention and treatment.

DRUGS	NOTES	SAFETY/COUNSELING
OTC **Docosanol (Abreva)** **Rx** **Acyclovir topical cream/ointment (Zovirax)** Acyclovir buccal tablets (Sitavig) Penciclovir topical cream (Denavir)	Oral antivirals are more effective (see Infectious Diseases III chapter). 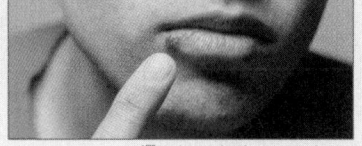 Ⓒ Lolostock/Shutterstock.com	Abreva cream: apply 5x daily at first sign of outbreak, continue until healed. Zovirax cream: apply 5x daily for 4 days (can be used on genital sores). Sitavig tablet: apply one 50 mg tablet as a single dose to the upper gum region. Denavir cream: apply every 2 hours during waking hours for 4 days.

DANDRUFF

- Dandruff occurs when the scalp is itchy and/or scaling with white oily flakes (dead skin) in the hair and on the shoulders, back or clothing.

- Dandruff can be due to either eczema or fungal (yeast) overgrowth, and is worsened by hormones, the weather or shampoo. Seborrheic dermatitis is a common form of eczema that causes flaking, itchy skin on the face, back, chest or head. If it is on the scalp, it is commonly referred to as dandruff. Patients are not likely to know the cause of dandruff.

- A store-brand, inexpensive dandruff shampoo can be tried first, and if this is ineffective, the ketoconazole antifungal shampoo can be used.

DRUGS	NOTES	SAFETY/COUNSELING
OTC **Ketoconazole 1% shampoo (Nizoral A-D), selenium sulfide (Selsun, Dandrex), pyrithione zinc (Head & Shoulders), coal tar shampoos (T/Gel),** *Suave* or store brands "dandruff" shampoos **Rx** **Ketoconazole 2% shampoo (Nizoral)** Ketoconazole topical comes in many formulations for dandruff or seborrheic dermatitis (see notes above): cream, foam, gel & shampoo	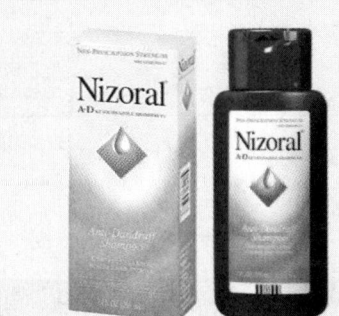	Rub shampoo in well, leave in for 5 minutes, then rinse out. Shampoo daily. If the shampoo stops working, switch products. **Nizoral A-D** Apply twice weekly, for up to 8 weeks. Do not use if open sores on scalp. Can cause skin irritation.

ALOPECIA (HAIR LOSS)

As people age, hair tends to gradually thin. Other causes of hair loss include hormonal factors, medical conditions and medications.

- The most common cause of hair loss is hereditary male-pattern baldness, and less commonly, female-pattern baldness.

- Hormonal changes in women that can result in hair loss are usually associated with pregnancy, childbirth or menopause.

- Medical conditions that cause hair loss include hypothyroidism, alopecia areata (an autoimmune condition), scalp infections and some other conditions, including lupus.

- Drugs that can contribute to alopecia include various chemotherapeutics (primarily because hair cells are rapidly dividing and are affected by the treatment) and infrequently with the following: valproate, spironolactone, heparin, warfarin, clomiphene, hydroxychloroquine, interferons, lithium, some types of oral contraceptives, levonorgestrel and procainamide.

- Zinc and vitamin D deficiency can contribute to hair loss.

- Medications work modestly for hair loss; many people will seek surgical intervention.

DRUGS	NOTES	SAFETY/COUNSELING
Finasteride (Propecia) Rx: tablet 1 mg daily; can take ≥ 3 months to begin to see effect **Finasteride (Proscar)** is a 5-alpha reductase type 2 inhibitor approved for BPH	Must be used indefinitely or condition reappears Do not dispense to patients taking finasteride (Proscar) for BPH	**CONTRAINDICATION** Pregnancy **WARNING** Hazardous drug for females of childbearing potential, can harm a male fetus **SIDE EFFECTS** Lower dose than *Proscar*; lower risk of sexual side effects; see the Benign Prostatic Hyperplasia (BPH) chapter for further details

DRUGS	NOTES	SAFETY/COUNSELING
Minoxidil topical (_Rogaine,_ others) OTC: 5% foam, 2% and 5% solution Minoxidil tablets (Rx) <u>indicated for hypertension</u> (very rarely used)	5% strength is more effective but causes more facial hair growth Must be used indefinitely or condition reappears	Flammable; do not use near a heat source Can be used by males or females
Bimatoprost (_Latisse_) Rx: solution <u>For thinning eyelashes (hypotrichosis)</u> 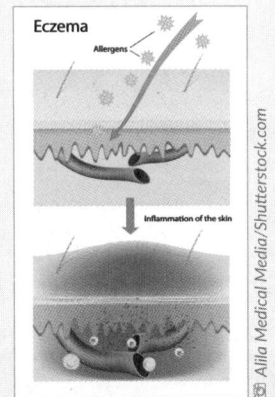	<u>Do not use with prostaglandin analogs</u> used for <u>glaucoma (IOP may increase)</u>	May cause itchy eyes and/or eye redness. Eyelid skin darkening may occur, may be reversible. Hair growth may occur in other skin areas that the solution frequently touches. <u>Apply nightly</u>, with applicator brush, to the <u>skin at the base</u> of the <u>upper eyelashes</u> only (do not apply to the lower lid). Blot any excess. Repeat on other eye. Dispose of applicator after one use. If stopped, lashes will return to their previous appearance.

ECZEMA (ATOPIC DERMATITIS)

Eczema is a general term for many types of skin inflammation, and is used interchangeably with the term atopic dermatitis.

- Eczema is most common in young children and infants, but can occur at any age.

- Eczema presents as <u>skin rashes</u> which become <u>crusty</u> and <u>scaly</u>; blisters can develop. The <u>rash is itchy, red, dry</u> and sore.

- Common sites affected include the elbows, behind the knees/ears, face (often the cheeks), buttocks, hands and feet.

- Patients should avoid triggers such as environmental irritants, allergens (soaps, perfumes), pollution, stress or weather changes.

- <u>Hydration is essential</u> to reduce disease severity. Use <u>moisturizers</u>. Maintain adequate humidity in the home.

- Treatment can include <u>topical steroids (occasional oral courses</u>, if needed), <u>antihistamines</u> (for itching) or immunosuppressant <u>calcineurin inhibitors (if topical steroids</u> with hydration <u>are not adequate</u>).

- In severe, refractory cases, oral immunosuppressants (cyclosporine, methotrexate) or monoclonal antibody drugs can be used. Dupilumab (_Dupixent_) is approved for moderate to severe eczema and is administered by subcutaneous injection every other week; other systemic immunosuppressants (used off-label) are discussed in the Systemic Steroids & Autoimmune Conditions chapter.

DRUGS	NOTES	SAFETY/COUNSELING
OTC Moisturizers with petrolatum, lanolin (_Aquaphor, Eucerin, Keri_ or store brands) **Rx** Treat first with topical steroids (see Inflammation and Rash and Potencies of Topical Steroids sections in this chapter). Only use the drugs below if steroids failed: **Topical Calcineurin Inhibitors** Tacrolimus (_Protopic_) – ointment Pimecrolimus (_Elidel_) – cream **Topical Phosphodiesterase-4 Inhibitor** Crisaborole (_Eucrisa_) – 2% ointment **Monoclonal Antibody (IL-4 antagonist)** Dupilumab (_Dupixent_) – injection **Janus Kinase Inhibitors** Ruxolitinib (_Opzelura_) – cream Upadacitinib (_Rinvoq_) – oral tablet	Eczema Allergens Inflammation of the skin © Alila Medical Media/Shutterstock.com	**All topical products:** <u>Wash hands after application</u> Apply a thin layer only to the affected skin twice a day Use the smallest amount needed to control symptoms **Topical calcineurin inhibitors:** <u>Do not use in children < 2 years of age; associated with lymphoma and skin cancer; use only as second-line drugs</u> for short-term, intermittent treatment Avoid exposure to natural or artificial sunlight Side effects can include headache, skin burning, itching, cough and flu-like symptoms **Dupilumab:** Avoid use of live vaccines Injection site reactions are the most common side effect **Janus kinase inhibitors:** Boxed warnings include serious infections (e.g., herpes zoster) and higher rates of malignancy, thrombosis, major cardiovascular events and mortality

HYPERHIDROSIS

Hyperhidrosis is excessive sweating. Diagnosis is based on physical exam and thorough medical history. Treatment depends on where the excessive sweating on the body is noticed (e.g., underarms, hands, feet).

DRUGS	NOTES	SAFETY/COUNSELING
OTC Antiperspirants (*Secret Clinical Strength, Certain Dri* and others) **Rx** Glycopyrronium topical (*Qbrexza*)	*Qbrexza* is a topical anticholinergic.	Do not use *Qbrexza* in medical conditions that can be exacerbated by anticholinergics (e.g., glaucoma, ulcerative colitis, myasthenia gravis). *Qbrexza*: wipe dry skin in the underarm area with a single-use, premoistened cloth. Wash hands with soap and water afterward.

FUNGAL INFECTIONS: SKIN

Tinea pedis, cruris, corporis and topical Candida infections are covered here. For vaginal infections, onychomycosis and diaper rash, see separate sections in this chapter.

ATHLETE'S FOOT (*TINEA PEDIS*)

- A fungal infection of the foot caused by various fungi (commonly *trichophyton rubrum*).

- Symptoms include feet itching, peeling, redness, mild burning and sometimes sores. This is a common infection, particularly among those using public pools, showers and locker rooms.

- Diagnosis is usually by symptoms, but if unclear (psoriasis and other conditions can cause itchy skin), the skin can be scraped off and viewed under a microscope.

- Treated topically with antifungals, except in severe cases.

JOCK ITCH (*TINEA CRURIS*)

- Affects the genitals, inner thighs and buttocks.

- The rash is red, itchy and can be ring-shaped.

- Jock itch is not very contagious, but can be spread person-to-person with close contact.

- Keep the skin dry (use a clean towel after showering) and treat with a topical antifungal. Creams work best.

- Change underwear at least daily.

RINGWORM (*TINEA CORPORIS*)

- Not a worm, but a fungal skin infection.

- Ringworm can appear anywhere on the body and typically looks like circular, red, flat sores (one or more, may overlap), usually with dry, scaly skin. Occasionally the ring-like presentation is not present – just itchy red skin. The outer part of the sore can be raised while the skin in the middle appears normal.

- Can spread person-to-person or by contact with infected animals.

- Most cases are treated topically.

- *Tinea capitis* is "ringworm" on the scalp. This affects primarily young children, mostly in crowded, lower-income situations and requires systemic therapy, with the same drugs used for onychomycosis.

CUTANEOUS (SKIN) *CANDIDA* INFECTIONS

- Topical *Candida* infections cause red, itchy rashes, most commonly in the groin, armpits or anywhere the skin folds.

- More likely in obese persons because they will have more skin with folds; the infection can be in unusual places, such as under the breasts, if the skin is moist. Diabetes is another risk factor.

- Occasionally, fungal infections appear in the corner of nails (on the skin, not in the nail bed). If this is a suspected bacterial infection, OTC antibiotic topicals or mupirocin can be used.

- *Candida* can cause diaper rash in infants (discussed under Diaper Rash section).

FUNGAL TREATMENTS FOR THE SKIN

DRUGS	NOTES	SAFETY/COUNSELING
OTC **Terbinafine (Lamisil AT)** Cream, gel, spray **Butenafine (Lotrimin Ultra)** Cream **Clotrimazole (Lotrimin AF,** Pro-Ex Antifungal, Shopko Athletes Foot**)** Cream **Miconazole (Lotrimin AF,** Cruex, Desenex Jock Itch Powder, spray Miconazole/petrolatum (Baza) – for moisture barrier, used in geriatrics **Tolnaftate (Tinactin)** Cream, powder, spray **Undecylenic acid** (Toelieva, others) **Rx** **Betamethasone/Clotrimazole (Lotrisone):** used for tinea with inflammation/itching Cream, lotion **Ketoconazole** (Extina) Cream, foam Luliconazole (Luzu) 1% cream	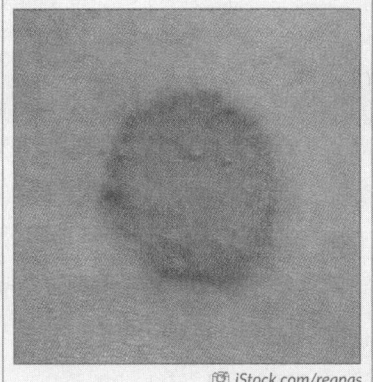 ⓘ iStock.com/reanas *Tinea corporis* (ringworm) – the name "ringworm" is a misnomer; this is a fungal infection. The rings can be single or overlap. Topical antifungals come in creams, ointments, gels and solutions.	If infection is on the foot, do not walk barefoot (to avoid spreading it); wear sandals in public showers (to avoid catching it). Apply medicine 1-2 inches beyond the rash. Use for at least 2-4 weeks, even if it appears healed. Reduce moisture to the infected area. Creams work best and are used in most cases. Solutions can be easier to apply in hairy areas. Powders do not work well for treatment but may be used for prevention, such as in shoes after a gym workout; use cotton socks. Note the same name in OTC products (Lotrimin AF) can refer to different active ingredients; be careful with recommendations to avoid mix-ups.

FUNGAL INFECTIONS: TOENAIL & FINGERNAIL

- Onychomycosis, a fungal infection of the nail, often caused by *tinea unguium,* can cause pain, discomfort and disfigurement and lead to physical limitations (e.g., difficulty standing, walking).

- Topical drugs are limited to mild cases and patients who cannot tolerate systemic therapies, in combination with systemic treatment or as prophylaxis. They are not potent enough to cure most infections.

- Itraconazole and terbinafine are approved for this use and most commonly used; fluconazole and posaconazole are used off-label. Griseofulvin is rarely used.

- It takes a long time for the nail bed to look better – sometimes up to a year in toenails. Toenails take longer to treat than fingernails and are more commonly infected.

- Pulse therapy (intermittent) can be used to reduce costs and possibly toxicity, but may not be as effective.

- A 20% potassium hydroxide (KOH) smear is essential for diagnosis as other conditions can produce a similar presentation.

DRUGS	NOTES	SAFETY/COUNSELING
Rx **Terbinafine** (*Lamisil**) – oral (topical is **Lamisil AT**; used for fungal skin infections) 250 mg PO daily for 6 weeks (fingernail) or 12 weeks (toenail) Itraconazole (*Sporanox*) – oral 200 mg PO daily x 12 weeks or "pulse-dosing" (fingernails only): 200 mg BID x 1 week, 3 weeks off then repeat 1-week course Ciclopirox (*Loprox*) – topical, used QHS Tavaborole (*Kerydin*) – topical oxaborole antifungal Efinaconazole (*Jublia*) – topical azole antifungal	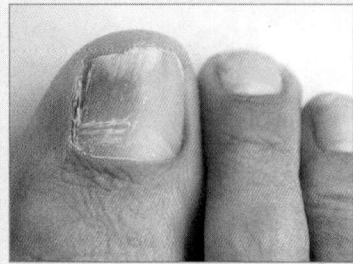 📷 *iStock.com/Manuel-F-O* Ciclopirox (*Loprox*) – used in combination with orals; poor efficacy when used alone Tavaborole (*Kerydin*) – applied topically x 48 weeks Efinaconazole (*Jublia*) – applied topically x 48 weeks	Systemic drugs used for nail fungal infections are hepatotoxic (monitor LFTs), QT-prolonging (avoid in QT risk) and CYP450 3A4 substrates and inhibitors (see Infectious Diseases III chapter for systemic azoles). Nausea and diarrhea are common. Itraconazole (*Sporanox*): boxed warning to <u>avoid use in heart failure</u>. Requires gastric acid for absorption; cannot use with strong acid-suppressing drugs. Terbinafine (*Lamisil*) – oral: primarily headache, rash, nausea, risk of <u>hepatotoxicity</u>. Recurrence is common. Practice proper foot care and keep the nails dry. Keep blood glucose controlled. Do not smoke.

Brand name discontinued but still used in practice.

FUNGAL INFECTIONS: VAGINAL

Vaginal fungal infections are common. Approximately 75% of women will have at least one episode, and half of these women will have recurrence. In a small percentage of women, infections occur chronically. Fungal vaginal infections are uncommon before a female begins menstruating. Hormones impact the pH of the vagina, making menstruating women more susceptible. Infections occur most commonly during the week before menstruation, making treatment decisions around the menses important. Women can begin treatment during menses or wait until the bleeding stops. Tampons should not be used when medication is applied.

- Vaginal fungal infections are more common during pregnancy. Pregnant patients should consult their physician. Longer (7 – 10 day) treatment is required.

- Symptoms are primarily itching with possible soreness and pain (burning) during urination or sex. Some women have a cottage-cheese like discharge (white, thick, clumpy).

- Diagnosis can be confirmed with a vaginal culture to check for fungal growth, while a pH test can be used to help rule out other conditions. A <u>pH > 4.5 is consistent with bacterial vaginosis or trichomoniasis infection</u>.

  - ❏ <u>OTC test kits</u> are available to <u>test vaginal pH</u>.

- Testing is not necessary if the woman has been seen by a physician for the initial infection and is able to recognize the symptoms. Self-treatment with OTC products is appropriate.

- If there are more than four infections in a year, or if symptoms recur within two months, refer to the physician to rule out an underlying condition that could be causative (e.g., diabetes, HIV, receiving steroids or other immune-suppressing drugs, pregnancy or irritation from repeated douching or use of lubricants).

- Women taking high-dose estrogen, hormone replacement therapy or antibiotics are at elevated risk. Antibiotic use can kill the normal flora and lead to fungal overgrowth.

- <u>Lactobacillus or yogurt with active cultures</u> is thought to <u>reduce infection occurrence</u>; however, this is rated as "possibly ineffective" by the *Natural Medicines Database*.

- If self-treating, counsel that condoms and diaphragms do not provide adequate pregnancy protection; the oil in OTC antifungals weakens the latex.

- To avoid future infections, keep the vaginal area clean, wipe from front to back after using the restroom, use cotton underwear, avoid tight-fitting clothing (including panty hose), change pads/tampons often, change out of wet swimsuits or clothing quickly and recommend against use of vaginal douches, sprays and deodorant tampons (these can alter the vaginal pH and contribute to infection).

DRUGS	NOTES	SAFETY/COUNSELING
Mild-moderate, infrequent infection: <u>1, 3 or 7 day treatment with vaginal cream, ointment or vaginal suppository/tab</u> **OTC, topical** **Clotrimazole** (*Gyne-Lotrimin**, others) **Miconazole (*Monistat 3*, others)** **Rx, topical** **Butoconazole (*Gynazole-1*, others)** Terconazole (*Terazol 7**, others) **Rx, oral** **Fluconazole (*Diflucan*) <u>150 mg PO x 1</u>** Ibrexafungerp (*Brexafemme*) 300 mg PO BID x 1 day <u>Complicated infections, pregnancy: 7–10 days treatment, or refer to healthcare provider</u>	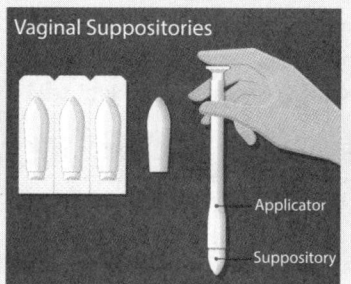 **Vaginal Suppositories** Applicator Suppository *rumruay/stock.adobe.com* Always counsel on ways to avoid future infections (see previous text) A male sexual partner can be tested if female partner's infections are recurrent (not common)	**Counseling for OTC antifungals:** Prior to using the product, wash the external genital area with mild soap and water, and pat dry with a towel. Insert applicator, suppository or vaginal tab at night before bed. Lying down immediately after insertion helps retain the medicine inside the vagina; a protective pad can be used. The creams and suppositories are oil-based medications that can weaken latex condoms and diaphragms; avoid sexual intercourse. If you get your menstrual cycle during treatment, you may continue the treatment. Do not use tampons during treatment. Complete entire course of treatment. Medical care is warranted if symptoms persist/return within 2 months after using an OTC product, or if > 4/year.

*Brand name discontinued but still used in practice.

DIAPER RASH

Diaper rash is very common in babies. The skin is sensitive, and when exposed to urine, stools and friction from a diaper moving back and forth, a rash appears. Once the skin is damaged, it is susceptible to bacteria and yeast overgrowth.

Prevention

- Change diapers often; do not cover diapers with plastic.
- Wipe well with unscented wipes or plain water.
- Leave the diaper off, when possible, to let the skin air-dry.
- Use a skin protectant:
  - ❑ Petrolatum ointment (*A & D Ointment*, store brands) is a good preventative ointment containing vitamins A & D.
  - ❑ Petrolatum with <u>zinc oxide (a desiccant</u>, used to dry out the skin) may be preferable for babies prone to rash.

Treatment

- Clotrimazole, miconazole, <u>nystatin</u>: for stubborn rashes, if <u>yeast</u> is thought to be involved.
- Hydrocortisone 0.5 – 1% cream can be applied twice a day, but not for more than several days at a time. Hydrocortisone can be used in combination with topical antifungals.

DRUGS	SAFETY/COUNSELING
OTC **Petrolatum/zinc oxide (*Desitin*, Boudreaux's Butt Paste, Triple Paste)** Petrolatum (*A&D Ointment*, others) **Rx** Miconazole/zinc oxide/petrolatum (*Vusion*)	Infants should be referred to the physician (especially if under 6 months); refer older babies if condition appears serious or worsens. Diaper rashes can have more than one contributing organism. Topical antibiotics can be needed if bacterial involvement is suspected. Topical antifungals can be needed if fungal involvement is suspected. Low-potency topical steroids may be used short-term.

HEMORRHOIDS

Hemorrhoids are swollen blood vessels in the lower rectum. They are often the result of constipation and straining to have a bowel movement. Rectal tissue is sensitive with a rich blood vessel supply making it susceptible to engorgement. Common symptoms are pruritus, burning and rectal bleeding. The blood is usually bright red.

- If dietary fiber intake is not optimal, increasing fiber intake can help reduce straining. Products such as psyllium will mix with the stool to make it easier to push out. A stool softener (such as docusate) will reduce straining.

- Phenylephrine (Preparation H, others) is a vasoconstrictor that shrinks the hemorrhoid and reduces burning and itching.

- Hydrocortisone (Anusol-HC, Preparation H, others) comes in anal suppositories and various topicals, including creams and wipes. These reduce itching and inflammation.

- Witch hazel (Tucks Medicated Cooling Pads) is a mild astringent that can relieve mild itching.

- Barriers (skin protectants) to reduce irritation from stool/urine are helpful in some cases (petrolatum, others – see Diaper Rash section).

- There are many combination products. Some contain mineral oil (skin protectant), zinc oxide (desiccant) or pramoxine (anesthetic).

DRUGS	NOTES	SAFETY/COUNSELING
OTC **Phenylephrine topical** (**Preparation H**, Anusol*, others)	Recommend suppositories for internal hemorrhoids and topical creams/ointments/wipes for external symptoms.	Clean the skin first with mild soap and warm water. Gently pat dry. Apply ointment externally up to 5 times daily. For suppository: hold wrapped suppository container with rounded end up, separate the foil tabs and slowly peel apart, remove from the wrapper, insert into the rectum up to 4 times daily, especially at night and after bowel movements.

Brand name discontinued but still used in practice.

PINWORM (VERMICULARIS)

Pinworm infection most commonly occurs in children and presents as anal itching. Anthelmintics (i.e., drugs used to kill parasitic worms), such as mebendazole, pyrantel pamoate and albendazole, are active against Enterobius vermicularis. The "tape" test is used to identify eggs: stick a piece of tape around the anus in the morning prior to voiding/defecating. The tape is removed and brought to a healthcare provider, who examines it under a microscope to look for eggs. It can take up to three morning tape tests to identify the eggs. Pinworms are often resistant to treatment; reinfection is common. Wash hands frequently and treat the entire household.

DRUGS	NOTES	SAFETY/COUNSELING
OTC **Pyrantel pamoate** (Reese's Pinworm Medicine, Pamix*, Pin-X*) Suspension **Rx** (systemic worm infections, many types) Albendazole (Albenza) Mebendazole (Emverm)		Pyrantel causes headaches and dizziness. It is given as a single dose and repeated in 2 weeks to eliminate reinfection. Mebendazole and albendazole cause headache, nausea and are hepatotoxic. Treatments for systemic worm infections are toxic. In some cases, such as treating CNS infections, steroids and AEDs will be given with the anthelmintic. When treating systemic infections, albendazole must be taken with a high-fat meal (to increase absorption).

Brand name discontinued but still used in practice.

LICE AND SCABIES

Scabies (mites) and lice are spread mainly through close body contact and treated with some of the same medications. For example, permethrin can be used to treat either of these conditions, though the concentrations and formulations are different. *Elimite* is a 5% permethrin cream used to treat scabies, while *Nix* is a 1% lotion (available OTC) used to treat lice. *Nix* can also be purchased in shampoo and spray formulations. Topical ivermectin (*Sklice*) is approved to treat head lice and is now available without a prescription. Oral ivermectin (*Stromectol*) can be used in patients who weigh at least 15 kg, though use is off-label for both conditions, and it can be difficult to tolerate. Possible adverse effects of oral ivermectin include lymph node enlargement, arthralgias, skin tenderness, pruritus and fever.

- Lice, *Pediculus humanus capitis*, occurs most commonly in elementary school-age children.

- Topical OTC drugs are generally first-line, such as pyrethrins and permethrin, though the efficacy of pyrethrins has decreased due to resistance. Avoid these products with a chrysanthemum or ragweed allergy.

- Malathion lotion 0.5% (*Ovide*) is an organophosphate only for use on persons 6 years of age and older. Can irritate the skin and is flammable; do not smoke or use electrical heat sources, including hair dryers, curlers, curling irons or flat irons near hair that is saturated with malathion.

- Benzyl alcohol 5% lotion kills live lice but not nits. Can irritate the skin and eyes; avoid eye contact.

- Lindane shampoo 1% (previously branded as *Kwell*) is no longer recommended due to neurotoxicity and is reserved for refractory cases. Lindane is never used in pregnancy, on irritated skin, in infants, children or the elderly.

- If the same medication has been used several times, it may not be working.

- Repeating the procedure and removing the nits from hair, bedding and elsewhere is essential:

  ❑ Wash clothes and bedding in hot water, followed by a hot dryer.

  ❑ If something cannot be washed, seal it in an air-proof bag for two weeks or dry clean. Vacuum the carpet well. Soak combs and brushes in hot water for 10 minutes. Make sure to check other family members in the household.

  ❑ Do not use conditioner (including combination shampoo + conditioner) before using lice medicine. Do not re-wash the hair for 1 – 2 days after treatment.

  ❑ Most products must be left on the hair for 10 minutes before rinsing to be effective; malathion should be left on for 8 – 12 hours.

  ❑ After treatment, use a nit comb to remove nits and lice every 2 – 3 days. Continue to check for 2 – 3 weeks to be sure all lice and nits are gone.

  ❑ Re-treatment is needed for most products (exceptions: *Sklice, Xeglyze*) on days 7 – 10 (they vary; check the product) to kill any surviving hatched lice before they produce new eggs.

DRUGS	NOTES	SAFETY/COUNSELING
LICE **OTC** **Permethrin (*Nix*),** ages 2 + months **Pyrethrin/Piperonyl butoxide (*RID*,** *LiceMD*), ages 2 + years Ivermectin *lotion (Sklice)*, ages 6 + months Rx Spinosad (*Natroba*), ages 6 + months Malathion (*Ovide*), ages 6 + years Benzyl alcohol lotion (*Ulesfia**), ages 6 + months Abametapir lotion (*Xeglyze*), ages 6 + months **SCABIES** **Rx** Permethrin cream (*Elimite*) Ivermectin oral (*Stromectol*)	 📷 iStock.com/wildpixel	DOC for lice: OTC topical treatment such as permethrin or pyrethrin/piperonyl butoxide. Repeat treatment on day 9. Malathion: flammable, do not use near heat source or open flame. Spinosad: works well, expensive. In addition to OTC treatment, remove the live lice and nits by inspecting the hair in 1-inch segments and using a lice comb. Nits are "cemented" to the hair shaft and do not fall off after treatment. Many OTC products require removal of live lice and nits for maximum efficacy. Nit removal requires multiple efforts, which should be continued for at least 2 weeks after treatment. See above.

Brand name discontinued but still used in practice.

MINOR WOUNDS

The basic types of minor wounds are cuts, abrasions, bites and burns. Some can be effectively treated with simple first aid and others, depending on the severity, may need more medical attention than first aid can provide. Puncture wounds should be referred to a medical provider. Make sure tetanus vaccine is current (booster every 10 years, after series has been completed). If the wound is dirty, a repeat tetanus vaccine may be required if it is > 5 years since vaccination. If wounds lead you to suspect abuse, contact authorities.

Some chronic wounds (e.g., pressure ulcers) require management by wound care providers. Debridement of chronic wounds is often needed to remove the dead, devitalized or contaminated tissue that prevents healing. There are several methods of debridement, but the most common method is enzymatic debridement, which is done with the application of collagenase ointment (Santyl). Other debridement methods, including surgical debridement, are considered for more complicated wounds.

CUTS, LACERATIONS AND ABRASIONS

- Lacerations are defined as irregular wounds with ragged edges, with the potential for deeper skin damage and bruising under the skin.

- A cut is different than a laceration because the edges will be more uniform or regular.

- After cleaning, if the bleeding does not stop, or it extends far below the surface layers of the skin, seek medical attention because it may require stitching to get the wound to close. If not, regular bandaging should close the wound over time.

- Antibiotic ointment can be applied prior to bandaging.

- Tissue adhesives (Band-Aid Liquid Bandage, Nexcare Skin Crack Care, others) create a polymer layer, which binds to the skin, keeping the wound clean and keeping moisture out. Some contain topical analgesics.

- *Wound Seal* is a topical powder that can be used over a bleeding wound to quickly form a scab and reduce the risk of infection.

- Abrasions are minor injuries to the top layer of skin and are primarily treated with simple first aid.

- Abrasions such as a skinned knee should be cleaned thoroughly; apply antibiotic ointment and bandage if desired.

BITES

- Bites (except minor insect bites) should never be treated with only first aid because of the high risk of infection, especially with animal or human bites.

- Certain spider bites in the U.S. can be deadly, such as the brown recluse, black widow and hobo spiders. See the Toxicology & Antidotes chapter.

- Spiders tend to stay hidden and are not aggressive; bites can usually be avoided by inspecting and shaking out clothing or equipment prior to use and wearing protective clothing. If bitten, stay calm, identify the type of spider if possible, wash with soap and cold water, apply a cold compress with ice, elevate the extremity and get emergency medical care.

- Minor, harmless insect bites can be treated with a topical steroid or oral antihistamine (such as diphenhydramine) to reduce itching.

BURNS

- Burns are characterized as <u>first degree</u> (red/painful, minor swelling), <u>second degree</u> (thicker, very painful, produce blisters) or <u>third degree</u> (damage to all layers of skin, appears white or charred).

- Burns from chemical exposure or in immunosuppressed patients should be referred for emergency medical care.

- If the burn is first or second degree, OTC treatment is acceptable if the area is less than two inches in diameter and not located on the face, over a major joint or on the feet or genitals. In diabetes, a burn on a foot, even mild, could lead to an amputation. Vigilance is required.

- Minor burns should be treated first by running the burn under cool water or soaking in cool water for 5 – 20 minutes.

- Do not apply ice as it can further damage injured skin. Bandages should be applied if the skin is broken, or if blisters pop.

- Burned skin itches as it heals; the fingernails of children may need to be cut short and filed, or covered. The skin that has been burned will be more sensitive to the sun for up to a year.

- <u>Ointments (80% oil/20% water, such as *Aquaphor*)</u> should be <u>used for skin protection</u> over a <u>minor burn</u> to <u>hold in moisture and reduce scarring risk</u>.

- <u>Silver sulfadiazine (*Silvadene; SSD*)</u> can be used topically to <u>reduce infection risk</u> and <u>promote healing</u>. If the skin is broken, systemic toxicity could occur. Do not use with sulfa allergy or G6PD deficiency (due to hemolysis risk).

DRUGS	NOTES	SAFETY/COUNSELING
OTC **Polymyxin/bacitracin/neomycin,** triple antibiotic ointment **(Neosporin Original,** store brands) For neomycin allergy, use *Polysporin* (bacitracin and polymyxin) or bacitracin alone; either is sufficient **Rx** **Mupirocin (Bactroban*)** is an <u>antibiotic</u> cream or ointment; <u>very good staph and strep coverage</u>, including MRSA **Bacitracin/neomycin/polymyxin B/ hydrocortisone (Cortisporin** ointment) is a popular Rx topical used for superficial skin infections Collagenase *(Santyl)* – topical debriding drug for chronic wounds	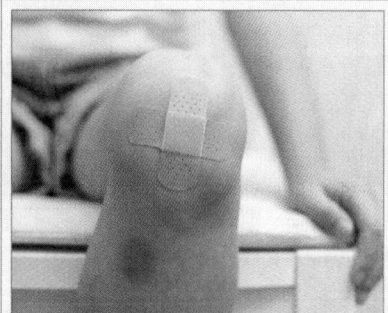 📷 *iStock.com/DmitriMaruta* If the wound is not in an area that will get dirty or be rubbed by clothing, it does not need to be covered. Leaving a wound uncovered helps it stay dry and heal.	**Application of topical antibiotics** Clean the affected area and apply a small amount of medication (an amount equal to the surface area of the tip of a finger) to the affected area 1 to 3 times daily. If the area can get dirty (such as a hand) or be irritated by clothing, cover with an adhesive strip (e.g., *Band-Aid)* or with sterile gauze and adhesive tape +/– antibiotic ointment. Change dressing/s daily. Burns require a moist (but not wet) environment for healing. Apply either an ointment or a bandage designed for burns.

Brand name discontinued but still used in practice.

POISON IVY, OAK AND SUMAC

- <u>Poison ivy, oak or sumac poisoning</u> is an <u>allergic reaction</u> that results from <u>touching the sap</u> of these plants, which <u>contain the toxin urushiol</u>.

- See the image below for the appearance of each of the leaves. Poison oak and ivy are known for leaves in clusters of three.

- The sap may be on the plant, in the ashes of burned plants, on an animal or on other objects that came in contact with the plant (e.g., clothing, garden tools and sports equipment).

- Small amounts of urushiol can remain under a person's fingernails for days unless removed with good cleaning.

DRUGS	NOTES	SAFETY/COUNSELING
OTC Aluminum acetate solution *(Boro-Packs, Domeboro Soothing Soak)* Colloidal oatmeal *(Aveeno)* Calamine lotion/pramoxine (anesthetic): *(Caladryl, IvaRest)* *Zanfel* works by binding urushiol (this is the toxin) – low evidence for efficacy	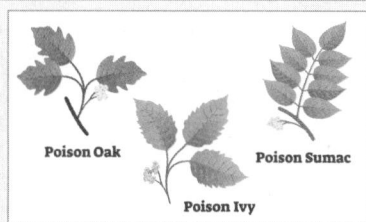 *"Leaves of three, let it be."*	Aluminum acetate is an <u>astringent</u> (drying agent). Wash the urushiol off with soap and water carefully, including under fingernails and on clothing. <u>Topical or oral steroids will help (oral needed in severe rash)</u>. Cold compresses can help.

📷 *VectorMine/stock.adobe.com*

INFLAMMATION AND RASH

- The primary treatment for skin irritation is topical steroids. Two strengths of hydrocortisone (HC) are available OTC, 0.5% and 1%; all other topical steroids are prescription only.

- The steroid vehicle influences the strength of the medication. Usual potency, from highest to lowest: ointment > creams > lotions > solutions > gels > sprays.

- Thin skin on the face, eyelids and genitals is highly susceptible to topical steroid side effects; low potency steroids should be used on these areas and skin folds (armpits, groin, under the breasts) where the absorption is higher.

- Local (skin) steroid side effects, if used long-term, include skin thinning, pigment changes (lighter or darker), telangiectasia (i.e., spider veins or small blood vessels visible through the skin), rosacea, perioral dermatitis and acne, increased risk of skin infections, delayed wound healing, irritation/burning/peeling and possibly contact dermatitis.

- For urticaria (hives), second-generation antihistamines (e.g., cetirizine) are preferred over first-generation antihistamines (e.g., diphenhydramine) due to better tolerability. Higher doses are used. The "non-sedating" antihistamines can still cause sedation at higher doses. First-generation antihistamines can be given at bedtime. See the Allergic Rhinitis, Cough & Cold chapter.

- Histamine-2 receptor antagonists (e.g., famotidine) are helpful in some patients with urticaria/hives. Hydroxyzine is often prescribed (see table).

DRUGS	NOTES	SAFETY/COUNSELING
OTC Lowest potency: **Hydrocortisone** 0.5% (infants) and 1% for mild conditions, thin skin (groin area, elderly) and for children HC 1% lotion (*Aquanil HC*) **Rx** Higher potency: see chart on the next page Apply the high-potency Rx steroids once daily Apply OTC/lower potency steroids 1-2x daily. It is common to see a higher potency product, followed by a lower potency product, to treat acute inflammation.	Common topical steroids, ranked by potency, are included in the table on the following page. Use ointments for thick or dry skin. Ointments have low water content (reduced absorption) and form a skin barrier. See the Compounding II chapter. Use lotions, gels and foams for hairy skin. No evidence for use of topical diphenhydramine, can use systemic but caution due to side effects. Skin should be lubricated (hydrated) with moisturizers for most conditions. The steroid vehicle can lubricate. Camphor, menthol, local anesthetics (often in combo creams with HC) can help relieve itching. Severe rash will likely require oral steroids for 1-2 weeks.	 The "fingertip" unit is used to estimate amount: from the fingertip to the 1st joint provides enough medication to cover one adult hand (about ½ g). Encourage patient not to use more than directed as overuse has risks (see above). Do not apply for longer than 2 weeks.
Hydroxyzine (*Vistaril*)	Used for general urticaria (hives) with severe itching. Dose is 25 mg PO TID-QID.	Anticholinergic side effects, primarily sedation and dry mouth.

POTENCIES OF TOPICAL STEROIDS

Very High Potency
Clobetasol propionate 0.05% Lotion/Shampoo/Spray (Clobex), Cream/ Ointment (Temovate), Foam (Olux), Gel
Fluocinonide 0.1% Cream (Vanos)
Betamethasone dipropionate 0.05% Ointment (Diprolene), Gel/Lotion
Halobetasol propionate 0.05% Lotion (Ultravate), Cream/Ointment
Diflorasone diacetate 0.05% Ointment

High Potency
Betamethasone dipropionate 0.05% Cream (Diprolene AF)
Fluocinonide 0.05% Ointment (Lidex*)
Mometasone furoate 0.1% Ointment (Elocon*)
Desoximetasone 0.05% Gel (Topicort), 0.25% Cream (Topicort)
Diflorasone diacetate 0.05% Cream (Psorcon*)
Halcinonide 0.1% Cream (Halog)

High-Medium Potency
Fluocinonide 0.05% Cream (Lidex-E*)
Betamethasone valerate 0.12% Foam (Luxiq)
Desoximetasone 0.05% Cream (Topicort)
Fluticasone propionate 0.005% Ointment

Medium Potency
Mometasone furoate 0.1% Cream (Elocon*)
Triamcinolone acetonide 0.1% Cream (Triderm), 0.147 mg/g Spray (Kenalog)
Fluocinolone acetonide 0.025% Cream/Ointment (Synalar)
Flurandrenolide 0.05% Ointment (Cordran)

Lower Potency
Desonide 0.05% Lotion (DesOwen)
Fluocinolone acetonide 0.01% Shampoo (Capex), 0.025% Cream (Synalar), 0.01% Cream
Flurandrenolide 0.05% Cream, Lotion/Tape (Cordran)
Fluticasone propionate 0.05% Cream/Lotion (Cutivate)
Hydrocortisone butyrate 0.1% Cream/Lotion/Ointment/Solution (Locoid)
Hydrocortisone probutate 0.1% Cream (Pandel)
Prednicarbate 0.1% Cream (Dermatop*)

Mild Potency
Alclometasone dipropionate 0.05% Cream/Ointment (Aclovate*)
Desonide 0.05% Gel (Desonate), Cream (Tridesilon), Foam (Verdeso)
Fluocinolone acetonide 0.01% Oil (Derma-Smoothe/FS), Solution (Synalar), Cream

Lowest Potency
Hydrocortisone Cream: 0.5%, **1% (Cortaid*, Cortisone*, Cortizone-10),** 2.5% (MiCort-HC); Lotion: 1%/2%; Ointment: 0.5%/1%/2.5%

Brand discontinued but still used in practice.

SUNSCREENS AND SUN PROTECTION

- Applying sunscreen is important due to the risk of sun damage and skin cancer. Keep in mind that sunscreen blocks vitamin D production in the skin, and many Americans are vitamin D deficient.

- It is advisable to stay out of the sun when it is strongest (between 10AM - 4PM). The damaging ultraviolet (UV) rays penetrate clouds; this applies to overcast days as well. Another way to avoid the sun is to wear protective clothing.

- Where skin is exposed, sunscreen can be applied that provides both UVA (A for aging - causes damage below the skin surface) and UVB (B for burning) protection. Both UVA and UVB contribute to skin cancer. A "broad-spectrum" sunscreen should be chosen that protects against both UVA and UVB.

- SPF stands for sun protection factor, which is a measure of how well the sunscreen deflects UVB rays.

- Some dermatologists and the American Academy of Pediatrics (AAP) recommend a minimum SPF 15 and others like the American Academy of Dermatology (AAD) recommend a minimum SPF 30. The key is to apply liberally and at least every two hours and reapply after swimming or sweating. The AAP recommends keeping babies less than 6 months old out of the sun.

TIME TO BURN (TTB)

TTB (with sunscreen in min) = SPF X TTB (without sunscreen)

- How SPF works: if someone would normally burn in 10 minutes, an SPF of 5 would extend the time they would burn to 50 minutes (5 x 10 = 50). Regardless of the SPF and calculated TTB, sunscreens do not last more than a couple of hours and need to be reapplied frequently.

- Sunscreen labeling is no longer permitted to use "waterproof" or "sweatproof" since they all wash off, at least partially, in the water. A sunscreen can claim to be "water-resistant," but only for 40 - 80 minutes. Always reapply after swimming or sweating.

- The AAD recommends chemical sunscreens with any of the following ingredients: oxybenzone, avobenzone, octisalate, octocrylene, homosalate or octinoxate.

  - Oxybenzone can be irritating to the skin (uncommon).

- Physical sunscreens may be used as an alternative to chemical sunscreens. Zinc oxide and titanium dioxide are recommended by the AAD.

- Products claiming to be oral sunscreens are not effective substitutes for topical sunscreen and should not be recommended.

Select Guidelines/References

Zaenglein AL, Pathy AL, Schlosser BJ, et al. Guidelines of care for the management of acne vulgaris. *J Am Acad Derm* 2016; 74:945-973.

Sidbury R, Davis DM, Cohen DE, et al. Guidelines of care for the managemet of atopic dermatitis, section 3: management and treatment with phototherapy and systemic agents. *J Am Acad Derm* 2014; 71:327-349.

Devore CD and Schutze GE. Head lice. *Pediatrics* 2015; 135: e1355-e1365.

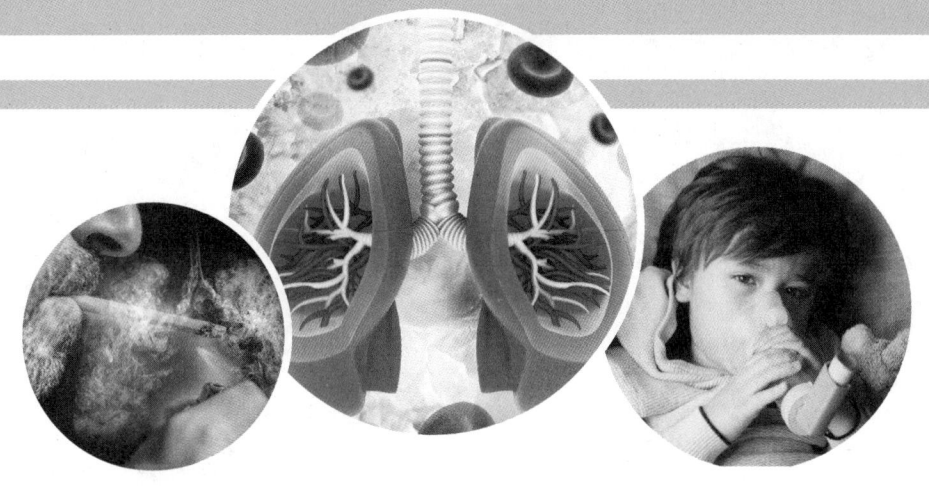

PULMONARY CONDITIONS & TOBACCO CESSATION

CONTENTS

CHAPTER CONTENT

WORLD HEALTH ORGANIZATION (WHO) CLINICAL CLASSIFICATION OF PULMONARY HYPERTENSION

Group 1: pulmonary arterial hypertension (PAH) – includes idiopathic, heritable, drug- and toxin-induced, disease-associated (e.g., connective tissue diseases, HIV infection, portal hypertension) and persistent pulmonary hypertension of a newborn

Group 2: pulmonary hypertension due to left heart disease

Group 3: pulmonary hypertension due to lung diseases and/or hypoxia

Group 4: chronic thromboembolic pulmonary hypertension (CTEPH)

Group 5: pulmonary hypertension with unclear or multifactorial mechanisms

CONTENT LEGEND

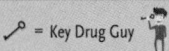 = Key Drug Guy

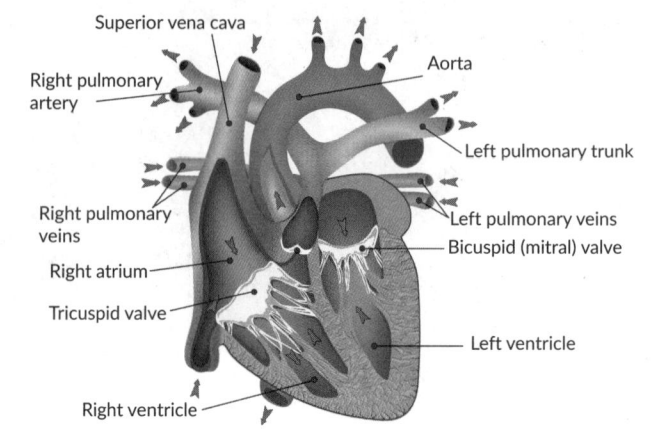

Superior vena cava
Right pulmonary artery
Aorta
Left pulmonary trunk
Right pulmonary veins
Left pulmonary veins
Bicuspid (mitral) valve
Right atrium
Tricuspid valve
Left ventricle
Right ventricle

© iStock.com/ElenBushe

CHAPTER 40

PULMONARY ARTERIAL HYPERTENSION

BACKGROUND

Pulmonary hypertension (PH) is characterized by continuous high blood pressure in the pulmonary arteries. A normal pulmonary artery pressure (PAP) ranges from 8 – 20 mmHg when resting. PH is defined as a mean PAP (mPAP) ≥ 25 mmHg in the setting of normal fluid status. Other hemodynamic parameters are affected as well.

CLASSIFICATION

PH may occur secondary to various disease states. The World Health Organization (WHO) classifies PH into five groups (see the box to the left). The primary focus of this chapter is Group 1, pulmonary arterial hypertension (PAH). When there is no identifiable cause, it is called primary, or idiopathic, PAH. Secondary causes include genetic inheritance, connective tissue diseases, advanced liver disease and HIV. Less commonly, medications can be the causative factor (see the Key Drugs Guy on the following page).

Treatment of PH groups 2 – 5 is aimed at the underlying causes. Group 2 is pulmonary venous hypertension, which arises from left-sided heart disease (e.g., left ventricular systolic or diastolic dysfunction, valvular disease, congenital heart disease). Group 3 is PH due to hypoxia or chronic lung diseases, such as COPD, pulmonary fibrosis or emphysema. Group 4 is chronic thromboembolic PH (CTEPH), which occurs in a minority of pulmonary embolism (PE) survivors. Warfarin, with an INR goal of 2 – 3, is recommended for CTEPH. Group 5 is PH caused by conditions that do not fit in the above categories (e.g., sarcoidosis).

SELECT DRUGS THAT CAN CAUSE PAH

KEY DRUGS

Cocaine

SSRI use during pregnancy
↑ risk of persistent
pulmonary hypertension
of a newborn (PPHN)

Weight-loss drugs (diethylpropion,
phendimetrazine, phentermine)

Methamphetamines/Amphetamines

Others:

Dasatinib
(Sprycel)

Diazoxide
(Proglycem)

Fenfluramine
(Fintepla)

PATHOPHYSIOLOGY

PAH stems from an imbalance in vasoconstrictor and vasodilator substances. Vasoconstrictor substances [e.g., endothelin-1 and thromboxane A2 (TXA2)] are increased, and vasodilating substances (e.g., prostacyclins) are decreased. Vasoconstriction results in reduced blood flow and high pressure within the pulmonary vasculature. In addition, there is an imbalance between cell proliferation and apoptosis (cell death) in the walls of the pulmonary arteries. The increasing amount of pulmonary artery smooth muscle cells causes pulmonary artery walls to thicken and form scar tissue (vasoproliferation). As the walls thicken and scar, the arteries become increasingly narrower. These changes make it difficult for the right ventricle to pump blood through the pulmonary arteries and into the lungs due to the increased pressure. As a result of working harder, the right ventricle becomes enlarged, and right heart failure develops. Heart failure is the most common cause of death in people who have PAH.

Symptoms of PAH include fatigue, dyspnea, chest pain, syncope, edema, tachycardia and/or Raynaud's phenomenon. In Raynaud's, reduced blood supply causes discoloration and coldness in the fingers, toes and occasionally other areas. The WHO also has a functional classification system for PAH, similar to the NYHA classification used in heart failure.

There is no cure for PAH, but in the last decade, knowledge of the disease has increased significantly and many more treatment options have become available. Without treatment, life expectancy is three years. In some cases, a lung or heart-lung transplant may be an option for younger patients.

NON-DRUG TREATMENT

Patients with PAH should follow a sodium-restricted diet of ≤ 2.4 grams/day to help manage volume status, especially if they have right ventricular failure. Medications like NSAIDs, which increase sodium and water retention, should be avoided. Routine immunizations against influenza and pneumococcal pneumonia are advised. Exposure to high altitudes may contribute to hypoxic pulmonary vasoconstriction and may not be tolerated. Oxygen is used when needed to maintain oxygen saturation above 90%.

DRUG TREATMENT

A right heart catheterization is performed to confirm the diagnosis of PAH. During the right heart catheterization, short-acting vasodilators (e.g., inhaled nitric oxide, IV epoprostenol or IV adenosine) are administered for vasoreactivity testing. The response to acute vasoreactivity testing determines which vasodilator medications should be used (see the PAH Treatment Algorithm on the next page). If the mPAP falls by at least 10 mmHg to an absolute value less than 40 mmHg, the patient is considered a responder and should be initially treated with an oral calcium channel blocker (CCB). Approximately 10% of patients are candidates for CCB therapy, though only half of these will have a sustained response. The CCBs used most frequently are long-acting nifedipine, diltiazem and amlodipine. The use of verapamil is not recommended due to its more pronounced negative inotropic effects relative to diltiazem.

Non-responders to vasoreactivity testing and positive responders who fail CCB therapy need to be treated with more potent vasodilating drugs. These include prostacyclin analogues and receptor agonists, endothelin receptor antagonists (ERAs), phosphodiesterase-5 (PDE-5) inhibitors and/or a soluble guanylate cyclase (sGC) stimulator. In most cases, drug therapy will reduce symptoms and improve exercise tolerance. Parenteral prostacyclin analogues, specifically IV epoprostenol, have been shown to decrease mortality. Some patients will require combination therapy.

Supportive therapies for PAH are similar to those used in systolic heart failure. They include loop diuretics (for volume overload) and digoxin (to improve cardiac output or control heart rate in atrial fibrillation). Biochemical changes (↑ TXA2, ↓ prostacyclin), along with other altered pathways, lead to a pro-thrombotic state and increased risk of blood clots. If warfarin is used for PAH, it should be titrated to an INR goal of 1.5 – 2.5. The lower than usual INR goal is based on observational evidence and expert opinion. Referral to a PAH specialty center is important to assess the feasibility of transplantation.

PAH TREATMENT ALGORITHM

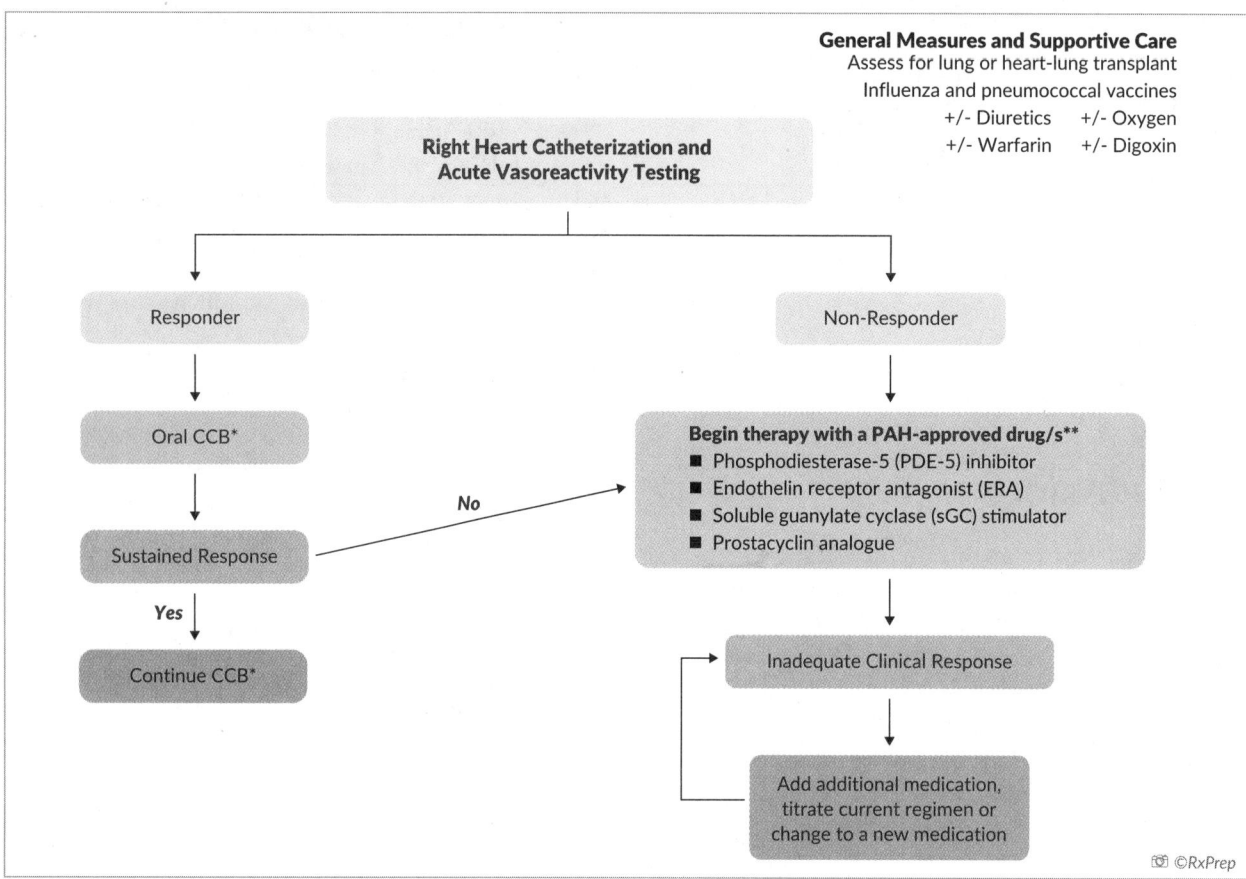

*Usually amlodipine, long-acting nifedipine or diltiazem.

**When selecting medication/s, consider disease severity and patient-specific factors (e.g., drug interactions, compliance, suitability for home IV therapy). For World Health Organization Functional Classification (WHO-FC) Class IV (i.e., unable to be physically active and with signs of right heart failure, which may be present at rest), first-line treatment is an IV prostacyclin analogue.*

CASE SCENARIO

AM is a 42-year-old female (weight 85 kg) in the ICU with pulmonary arterial hypertension. At home she mixes 9.5 mL of 1 mg/mL treprostinil (*Remodulin*) with 40.5 mL of sterile water. She sets her pump to 0.06 mL/hr.

■ **What is her dose in ng/kg/min? Round to the nearest tenth.**

Step 1: determine how many milligrams of treprostinil (*Remodulin*) are mixed with sterile water.

$$9.5 \text{ mL} \quad \times \quad \frac{1 \text{ mg}}{\text{mL}} \quad = \quad 9.5 \text{ mg}$$

Step 2: calculate the concentration by dividing the milligrams of treprostinil (*Remodulin*) by the total volume (drug plus diluent).

$$\frac{9.5 \text{ mg}}{(40.5 \text{ mL} + 9.5 \text{ mL})} = 0.19 \text{ mg/mL}$$

Step 3: calculate the dose in ng/kg/min using dimensional analysis.

$$\left[\frac{0.06 \text{ ml}}{\text{hr}} \times \frac{1 \text{ hr}}{60 \text{ min}} \times \frac{0.19 \text{ mg}}{\text{mL}} \times \frac{1,000,000 \text{ ng}}{1 \text{ mg}} \right] \bigg/ 85 \text{ kg} = 2.2 \text{ ng/kg/min}$$

■ **The pharmacy has treprostinil (*Remodulin*) 2.5 mg/mL in stock. How many milliliters of the pharmacy stock supply should be used to prepare the same treprostinil (*Remodulin*) concentration AM uses at home?**

$$9.5 \text{ mg} \quad \times \quad \frac{\text{mL}}{2.5 \text{ mg}} \quad = \quad 3.8 \text{ mL treprostinil (Remodulin)}$$

PROSTACYCLIN ANALOGUES (OR PROSTANOIDS) AND RECEPTOR AGONISTS

Prostacyclin synthase is reduced in PAH, causing decreased production of prostacyclin I2 (a vasodilator with anti-proliferative effects) in pulmonary artery smooth muscle cells. Prostacyclin analogues (prostanoids) are potent vasodilators (of both pulmonary and systemic vascular beds) and inhibitors of platelet aggregation. The prostacyclin receptor agonist selexipag *(Uptravi)* is structurally different but works similarly. Epoprostenol and treprostinil can be administered by continuous IV infusion at home using an ambulatory infusion pump.

DRUG	DOSING	SAFETY/SIDE EFFECTS/MONITORING
Epoprostenol *(Flolan, Veletri)* AKA prostacyclin Continuous IV infusion via central venous catheter	Start at 2 ng/kg/min and ↑ by 1-2 ng/kg/min in 15 minute intervals based on clinical response; usual dose is 25-40 ng/kg/min (can be higher)	**CONTRAINDICATIONS** Epoprostenol: heart failure with ↓ left ventricular ejection fraction Treprostinil (oral): severe hepatic impairment (Child-Pugh Class C) **WARNINGS** Vasodilation reactions (hypotension, flushing, headache, dizziness) Rebound PH (with interruption or large decrease in dose), which can be fatal Increased risk of bleeding Chronic IV infusions: sepsis and bloodstream infections Treprostinil *(Orenitram)*: oral tablet shell does not dissolve (ghost tablet) and can lodge in a diverticulum.
Treprostinil *Remodulin:* continuous SC or IV (central venous catheter) infusion *Tyvaso:* inhalation *Orenitram:* oral, ER tablet	*Remodulin:* start at 1.25 ng/kg/min and ↑ at weekly intervals, up to 40 ng/kg/min (and possibly more) *Tyvaso:* start with 18 mcg (3 inhalations) 4 times/day and ↑ every 1-2 weeks to target of 54 mcg (9 inhalations) 4 times/day; doses should be taken Q4H during waking hours *Orenitram:* start at 0.25 mg BID or 0.125 mg TID, ↑ every 3-4 days up to the maximum tolerated dose; take with food	**SIDE EFFECTS** Hypotension, flushing, jaw pain, headache, dizziness, N/V/D, edema, musculoskeletal pain (e.g., myalgias), tachycardia, flu-like syndrome, anxiety, tremor, thrombocytopenia IV/SC infusions: infusion-site pain, especially with SC *Remodulin* (~85%) Treprostinil (inhaled) and iloprost: cough and mouth/throat irritation **NOTES** Parenteral agents *(Flolan, Veletri, Remodulin)* are very potent vasodilators; avoid interruptions and sudden, large dose reductions
Iloprost *(Ventavis)* Inhalation	2.5-5 mcg/inhalation given 6-9 times/day, no more than once every 2 hours	Due to short half-lives of epoprostenol (~6 minutes) and parenteral treprostinil (~4 hours), it is essential to have immediate access to a backup pump, infusion sets and medication Epoprostenol: must protect from light before reconstitution and during infusion
Selexipag *(Uptravi)* Tablet	Start with 200 mcg BID and ↑ at weekly intervals to maximum dose of 1600 mcg BID	Reconstituted solutions of *Flolan* require use of ice packs for stability; *Veletri* and *Remodulin* are thermostable (no need for ice packs) To ↓ infections, instruct patients on how to care for infusion sites and use sterile technique when preparing the drug for parenteral use

Prostacyclin Analogue and Receptor Agonist Drug Interactions

- The effects of antihypertensive, antiplatelet and anticoagulant agents can be increased.

- Treprostinil levels are increased by CYP450 2C8 inhibitors (e.g., gemfibrozil) and decreased by CYP2C8 inducers (e.g., rifampin). Strong CYP2C8 inhibitors should be avoided with selexipag.

ENDOTHELIN RECEPTOR ANTAGONISTS

Endothelin is a vasoconstrictor with cellular proliferative effects. ERAs block endothelin receptors on pulmonary artery smooth muscle cells.

DRUG	DOSING	SAFETY/SIDE EFFECTS/MONITORING
Bosentan (*Tracleer*) Tablet	< 40 kg: 62.5 mg BID ≥ 40 kg: 62.5 mg BID (for 4 weeks), then 125 mg BID	**BOXED WARNINGS** Teratogenic (women of childbearing potential must have a negative pregnancy test prior to initiation of therapy and monthly thereafter) Bosentan: hepatotoxicity (↑ ALT/AST and liver failure) Available only through individual REMS programs (Bosentan REMS Program, Ambrisentan REMS Program and *Opsumit* REMS Program); prescribers, pharmacies and patients must enroll (only female patients required to be enrolled in the Ambrisentan and *Opsumit* REMS programs)
Ambrisentan (*Letairis*) Tablet	5 mg daily, may ↑ to 10 mg daily after 4 weeks if tolerated	**CONTRAINDICATIONS** Pregnancy Bosentan: use with cyclosporine or glyburide Ambrisentan: idiopathic pulmonary fibrosis **WARNINGS** Hepatotoxicity, ↓ Hgb/Hct, fluid retention (e.g., pulmonary edema, peripheral edema), decreased sperm counts Bosentan: hypersensitivity reactions (e.g., rash, angioedema, anaphylaxis, DRESS)
Macitentan (*Opsumit*) Tablet	10 mg daily	**SIDE EFFECTS** Headache, upper respiratory tract infections (e.g., nasal congestion, cough, bronchitis), flushing, hypotension **MONITORING** LFTs, bilirubin, Hgb/Hct, pregnancy tests **NOTES** Bosentan approved for children 3 and older

Endothelin Receptor Antagonist Drug Interactions

- Bosentan is a substrate and inducer of CYP3A4 and 2C9; monitor for drug interactions. Levels of bosentan can increase with CYP2C9 (e.g., amiodarone, fluconazole) and CYP3A4 (e.g., ritonavir) inhibitors. Concurrent use of cyclosporine or glyburide is contraindicated. Bosentan can decrease the effectiveness of hormonal contraceptives (at least one barrier method of contraception, if not two, is recommended).

- Ambrisentan is a substrate of CYP3A4 (major), CYP2C19 (minor) and P-gp. Cyclosporine can increase the serum concentration of ambrisentan; limit the dose of ambrisentan to 5 mg daily when given with cyclosporine.

- Macitentan is a substrate of CYP3A4 (major) and CYP2C19 (minor). Strong CYP3A4 inhibitors and inducers should be avoided with macitentan.

PHOSPHODIESTERASE-5 INHIBITORS

PDE-5 is responsible for the degradation of cyclic guanosine monophosphate (cGMP). Increased cGMP concentrations lead to pulmonary vasculature relaxation and vasodilation.

DRUG	DOSING	SAFETY/SIDE EFFECTS/MONITORING
Sildenafil (Revatio) Tablet, oral suspension, injection **Viagra** – erectile dysfunction	IV: 2.5-10 mg TID Oral: 5-20 mg TID, taken 4-6 hours apart	**CONTRAINDICATIONS** Use with nitrates or riociguat *Revatio*: avoid taking with protease inhibitors (e.g., atazanavir, ritonavir, others) **WARNINGS** Hearing loss (with or without tinnitus and dizziness), vision loss [rare but may be due to nonarteritic anterior ischemic optic neuropathy (NAION)], hypotension, priapism (seek emergency medical care if erection lasts > 4 hours), pulmonary edema
Tadalafil (Adcirca, Alyq) Tablet **Cialis** – erectile dysfunction, BPH	40 mg daily 20 mg daily if mild-mod renal or hepatic impairment CrCl < 30 mL/min: avoid use Severe hepatic impairment: avoid use	*Revatio*: not recommended for pediatric use due to increased mortality **SIDE EFFECTS** Headache, epistaxis, flushing, dyspepsia, extremity or back pain, N/D

PDE-5 Inhibitor Drug Interactions

- Do not give with other PDE-5 inhibitors used for erectile dysfunction.

- Do not use with nitrate medications (see Stable Ischemic Heart Disease chapter) or the sGC stimulator riociguat as the potential for excessively low blood pressure is increased. Taking nitrates is an absolute contraindication to the use of PDE-5 inhibitors; this includes illicit drugs such as amyl nitrate and butyl nitrate ("poppers").

- Use caution with alpha-blocker therapy (or other antihypertensives) as PDE-5 inhibitors can increase the risk of hypotension. When tadalafil is used for PAH, alpha 1-blockers are not recommended for the treatment of BPH. Alcohol can enhance hypotension with PDE-5 inhibitors.

- PDE-5 inhibitors are major substrates of CYP3A4; avoid use of strong CYP3A4 inhibitors and inducers.

SOLUBLE GUANYLATE CYCLASE STIMULATOR

Soluble guanylate cyclase (sGC) is a receptor for endogenous nitric oxide. Riociguat (Adempas) sensitizes sGC to endogenous nitric oxide and directly stimulates the receptor at a different binding site. This increases cGMP, leading to relaxation and antiproliferative effects in the pulmonary artery smooth muscle cells. Riociguat is approved for use in both PAH and CTEPH.

DRUG	DOSING	SAFETY/SIDE EFFECTS/MONITORING
Riociguat (Adempas) Tablet	Start with 0.5-1 mg TID, increasing by 0.5 mg TID every 2 weeks if SBP > 95 mmHg; max dose is 2.5 mg TID	**BOXED WARNINGS** Teratogenic (women of childbearing potential must have a negative pregnancy test prior to initiation of therapy and monthly thereafter) Available only through the *Adempas* REMS Program; prescribers, pharmacies and female patients must enroll **CONTRAINDICATIONS** Pregnancy, use of PDE-5 inhibitors or nitrates **WARNINGS** Hypotension, bleeding, pulmonary edema **SIDE EFFECTS** Headache, dyspepsia, dizziness, N/V/D

Riociguat Drug Interactions

- Do not use with nitrate medications (any formulation – see Stable Ischemic Heart Disease chapter) or PDE-5 inhibitors as the potential for excessively low blood pressure is increased. Specifically, riociguat should not be administered within 24 hours of sildenafil, or within 24 hours before or 48 hours after tadalafil.

- Smoking increases riociguat clearance; the dose may need to be decreased with smoking cessation.

- Separate from antacids by > 1 hour.

- Riociguat is a major substrate of CYP3A4, 2C8 and P-gp; monitor for drug interactions and dose adjustments.

PULMONARY FIBROSIS

Pulmonary fibrosis (PF) is scarred and damaged lung tissue. The common presentation is exertional dyspnea with a nonproductive cough. As the condition worsens, breathing becomes more labored. There are various of causes of PF, including toxin exposure (e.g., asbestos, silica), medical conditions, and drugs (see Key Drugs Guy), among others. Often the contributing factor is not identified, and the PF is called idiopathic pulmonary fibrosis (IPF).

If the condition is drug-induced, the offending drug should be discontinued. Aside from treatment with chronic oxygen supplementation, two drugs are now available for IPF. Both pirfenidone (*Esbriet*) and nintedanib (*Ofev*) slow the rate of decline in lung function. In addition to these two drugs, several of the drugs approved for PAH (particularly sildenafil) may be used off-label for IPF. The prognosis of IPF is poor; five-year survival is approximately 20 – 30% once diagnosed.

SELECT DRUGS THAT CAN CAUSE PULMONARY FIBROSIS

KEY DRUGS

Amiodarone/dronedarone

Bleomycin

Busulfan

Carmustine

Lomustine

Others:

Nitrofurantoin

Sulfasalazine

Select Guidelines/References

Therapy for pulmonary arterial hypertension in adults. *Chest*. 2019;155:565-586.

2015 ESC/ERS guidelines for the diagnosis and treatment of pulmonary hypertension. *Eur Heart J*. 2016;37:67-119.

CONTENT LEGEND

💡 = Study Tip Gal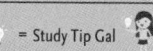

HEALTHY LUNGS
Relaxed smooth muscles
Normal airway

ASTHMA
Tightened smooth muscles
Inflammation — Mucus
Narrowed airway

© iStock.com/ttsz

CHAPTER 41

ASTHMA

BACKGROUND

Asthma is a disease that affects the airways (bronchi) of the lungs. It is a common chronic disease among children. Asthma is characterized by chronic airway inflammation and bronchoconstriction (narrowed airways). The inflammation and bronchoconstriction cause airflow obstruction, which results in expiratory airflow limitation (difficulty with exhalation). This results in recurrent episodes of wheezing, breathlessness, chest tightness and coughing, which are the classic symptoms of asthma. The symptoms can vary over time and in intensity, often occurring more frequently at night or on awakening. They can also be triggered by various factors (see Environmental Triggers and Comorbid Conditions on the following page).

The inflammation and bronchoconstriction in asthma are reversible with medication (and sometimes spontaneously). Patients with asthma can live successful and active lives if they adhere to treatment and follow an asthma action plan. The most common complication is exacerbations, which can range from mild to severe, and in some cases, can be fatal. There is no cure for asthma, but it can be controlled.

DIAGNOSIS AND ASSESSMENT

There are many types of asthma. When classic symptoms are present, a detailed history and physical examination can help define the type, along with triggers, environmental factors and comorbid conditions that can contribute to disease severity (see the table on the following page). Most types of asthma result from the activation of inflammatory mediators (e.g., histamine, leukotrienes, cytokines) and an increase in inflammatory cells (e.g., mast cells, eosinophils) that contribute to the disease process. Some patients have a genetic predisposition for severe allergic asthma, which is mediated by immunoglobulin E (IgE), or severe eosinophilic asthma. Both can require specialized treatments in addition to the use of routine inhaled medications.

An asthma diagnosis is confirmed with spirometry and pulmonary function tests (see the Study Tip Gal on the following page). These should be measured at baseline and after use of a short-acting bronchodilator (e.g., albuterol) to test for reversibility (i.e., if the FEV1 increases by more than 12% with the use of the bronchodilator). Spirometry is performed in a medical facility (not at home).

SPIROMETRY: TESTS LUNG FUNCTION (HOW WELL THE LUNGS WORK)

FEV1
How much air can be forcefully exhaled in one second.

FVC
After taking a deep breath, the maximum volume of air that is exhaled (how much air is exhaled).

FEV1/FVC
The percentage of total air capacity ("vital capacity") that can be forcefully exhaled in one second (the speed of the exhale).

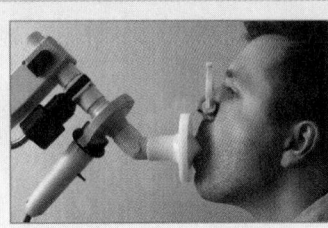

iStock.com/Koldunova_Anna

Other tests that may be involved in diagnosing asthma include fractional exhaled nitric oxide (FeNO) and the <u>peak expiratory flow rate (PEFR)</u>. FeNO measures nitric oxide in exhaled breath and can indicate the level of airway inflammation. It can be used as an additional test to diagnose asthma or for ongoing monitoring in difficult cases (it should not be used independently).

<u>PEFR</u> is measured using a <u>peak flow meter</u>. This is typically used for monitoring control as part of the asthma action plan, but it can be used at initial diagnosis to test for variability in expiratory airflow limitation. PEFR and peak flow meters are described in more detail later in the chapter.

ENVIRONMENTAL TRIGGERS AND COMORBID CONDITIONS

The triggers that cause an asthma attack vary; some people will have bronchoconstriction from a pet, and others will not. Patients need to learn their personal triggers and avoid them when possible. If the trigger cannot be avoided, acute treatment may be needed. Some of the most <u>common triggers</u> are listed below. Coughing and laughter are other triggers that are often underappreciated. Common comorbid conditions that can trigger an attack are also listed.

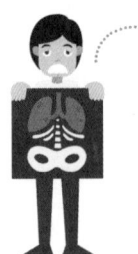

TRIGGERS

GENETICS POLLUTION CIGARETTES COLD AIR/ CHANGES IN WEATHER PETS DUST, POLLEN & COCKROACHES PERFUME & COSMETICS DRUGS Aspirin, NSAIDs, non-selective beta-blockers

COMORBID CONDITIONS

Infections (Colds and Viruses), Allergic Rhinitis, GERD, Obesity, Obstructive Sleep Apnea, Anxiety, Stress and Depression

©RxPrep

jehsomwang © 123RF.com

TREATMENT PRINCIPLES

Long-term asthma management should focus on reducing impairment (e.g., symptoms, frequency of rescue inhaler use, limitations to normal activity) and risks (exacerbations, hospitalizations and medication adverse events). Initiating, monitoring and adjusting treatment follows a step-wise and continuous process.

There are two major guidelines used for treating asthma: the <u>Global Initiative for Asthma (GINA)</u> and the NHLBI's Expert Panel Report (EPR). The GINA guidelines are considered the gold standard, as they are published annually; they are "global" guidelines, so are not specific to the United States. The treatment recommendations in this chapter follow the GINA guidelines.

CLASSIFYING ASTHMA SEVERITY

The classification of asthma severity guides the intensity (or step) of <u>initial treatment</u> and is primarily based on the frequency of daytime symptoms and nighttime awakenings. The table below describes the clinical assessment for each step. The Asthma Treatment Algorithm discussed later in the chapter provides the corresponding treatment.

Components of Severity	Classification of Asthma Severity			
	Step 1	Step 2	Step 3	Step 4 and 5
Daytime symptoms	< 2x/month	≥ 2x/month but ≤ 4-5 days/week	Most days	Daily
Nighttime awakenings	None	None	≥ 1x/week	≥ 1x/week

GENERAL TREATMENT APPROACH

- Select treatment according to the initial assessment of asthma severity (see the table on the previous page and the Asthma Treatment Algorithm later in the chapter).

- Follow up in 2 – 6 weeks. At each visit:

  ❏ Assess adherence to medications.

  ❏ Perform medication counseling (confirm appropriate inhaler technique and understanding of maintenance versus rescue treatment). See the detailed instructions on technique, priming and cleaning of select inhalers at the end of the chapter.

  ❏ Assess control of risk factors, triggers and comorbid conditions.

  ❏ Review the asthma action plan (see example later in the chapter).

  ❏ Address patient concerns.

  ❏ Assess asthma control/severity and step up, maintain or step down treatment (see next section). Do not step up therapy until the items above have been addressed; there might be other factors contributing to poor asthma control (e.g., incorrect inhaler technique or lack of adherence) and increasing doses of medications and/or adding other drugs can increase side effects without providing additional benefit.

- Follow up visits can decrease to 1 – 6 months once control is gained, and to every three months if a step down in treatment is planned.

CONTROLLING RISK FACTORS

Patients with asthma should avoid exposure to tobacco smoke and those who smoke should quit, or be strongly encouraged to quit at each healthcare visit. Physical activity should not be avoided, even in those with exercise-induced bronchospasm.

iStock.com/jehsomwang

Triggers should be identified and avoided, if possible. Some triggers should not be avoided (e.g., laughter) and others are difficult to avoid (e.g., stress, infections). Comorbid conditions should be treated to improve asthma control.

An annual influenza vaccine is recommended in all patients ≥ 6 months of age, including those with asthma. Refer to the Immunizations chapter for details on the criteria for pneumococcal vaccination in patients with asthma.

Any patient with persistent asthma and a clear connection between symptoms and exposure to an allergen should have skin or in vitro testing performed to assess sensitivity. Treatment with subcutaneous allergen immunotherapy should be used, if indicated, based on the test results.

ASSESSING ASTHMA CONTROL

Asthma control should be assessed at each visit to decide if adjustments in treatment are needed. The assessment is based on yes/no answers to the following four questions:

- Daytime asthma symptoms > twice/week?

- Any nighttime awakenings due to asthma?

- Short-acting beta-2 agonist (SABA) reliever treatment used > twice/week? (Note: only for patients using SABA therapy.)

- Is activity limited due to asthma?

Asthma control is desribed as:

- Well-controlled: if no questions are answered "yes."

- Partly controlled: if 1 – 2 questions are answered "yes."

- Uncontrolled: if 3 – 4 questions are answered "yes."

DRUG TREATMENT

Asthma drugs come in <u>oral, inhaled and injectable</u> formulations. <u>Inhaled forms</u> deliver drugs directly into the <u>lungs</u>, have <u>reduced toxicity</u> and are the <u>preferred</u> delivery vehicle. Drugs used to treat asthma long-term are classified as relievers (rescue inhalers) or controllers (maintenance drugs). The table below describes the different classes of asthma medications and the primary role or place in treatment for each.

<u>Relievers, or rescue inhalers, rapidly open airways</u> within minutes of inhalation to treat <u>acute symptoms</u> (i.e., they make breathing easier). If an <u>inhaled corticosteroid (ICS) + formoterol</u> combination inhaler is used as the reliever, asthma control is assessed based on the frequency of <u>symptoms</u> (e.g., <u>> 2 days per week</u>). If a SABA is used as the reliever, the frequency of <u>SABA</u> use (e.g., <u>> 2 days per week</u>) can be incorporated into the assessment of asthma control (see previous page). In addition to treating acute asthma symptoms, relievers can be used preventively for <u>exercise-induced bronchospasm</u> (EIB).

<u>Controllers, or maintenance inhalers</u>, are taken on a <u>daily basis</u> to <u>reduce inflammation</u> and maintain asthma control. <u>ICS</u> are the <u>mainstay of treatment</u>. Doses are categorized as low, medium or high and can be escalated (by increasing the number of inhalations per dose or increasing to a higher strength inhaler), if indicated, based on asthma severity.

ASTHMA MEDICATION CLASS	NOTES
Relievers (Rescue Drugs)	
Low-dose <u>ICS + formoterol</u> (combination inhaler)	Used intermittently (<u>as needed</u>) for acute asthma <u>symptoms</u>
	Formoterol is a long-acting beta-2 agonist (LABA) with fast onset; this combination <u>reduces</u> the risk of <u>exacerbations</u> compared to a SABA alone
	Max total daily dose of formoterol is 72 mcg, including the total combined formoterol dose when ICS-formoterol is used as both a controller (maintenance drug) and reliever (see the Asthma Treatment Algorithm)
Inhaled <u>short-acting beta-2 agonist (SABA)</u>	Used intermittently (<u>as needed</u>) for acute asthma <u>symptoms</u> (an alternative to the preferred therapy of ICS-formoterol)
	Quickly <u>reverses bronchoconstriction</u>
Systemic steroids	Injections: used during exacerbations
	Oral: used during <u>exacerbations</u> or for <u>severe asthma</u> that is difficult to control with other drug combinations
	Use should be limited as much as possible due to the risk of adverse effects (see the Systemic Steroids & Autoimmune Conditions chapter)
Inhaled epinephrine	Available OTC; can be used intermittently for acute treatment of mild asthma only
	Not included in asthma guidelines
Inhaled short-acting muscarinic antagonists (SAMAs); also called inhaled anticholinergics	Can be used in combination with a SABA during exacerbations
Controllers (Maintenance Drugs)	
Inhaled corticosteroids (ICS)	<u>First-line for all patients</u> with persistent asthma; the most effective anti-inflammatory drugs
Inhaled long-acting beta-2 agonists (LABAs)	Used <u>in combination with ICS</u> (should <u>never</u> be used <u>alone</u> due to increased risk of serious adverse outcomes)
	<u>Preferred add-on</u> agents to ICS
Oral leukotriene receptor antagonists (<u>LTRAs</u>)	Alternative option to LABA in combination with ICS; can also be added to ICS/LABA treatment
	Most commonly used in <u>children</u>
Theophylline (oral or IV)	Least desirable option for add-on treatment due to significant adverse effects, drug interactions and the need to <u>monitor serum drug concentrations</u>
Inhaled long-acting muscarinic antagonists (LAMAs); also called inhaled anticholinergics	Can be used as add-on treatment in patients with a history of exacerbations despite ICS/LABA treatment
Injectable <u>monoclonal antibodies</u> (SC or IV)	Add-on treatment in persistent severe asthma of a specific type:
	<u>Omalizumab</u>: for <u>severe allergic asthma</u>
	Mepolizumab, reslizumab, benralizumab and dupilumab: for severe eosinophilic asthma

ASTHMA TREATMENT ALGORITHM

The <u>algorithm</u> below shows the recommended treatment of asthma at each step of therapy per the GINA guidelines, with as-needed rescue inhalers shown in blue (left side) and maintenance inhalers show in green (right side). The <u>preferred regimens</u> are those that <u>use low-dose ICS-formoterol rescue therapy</u>. For steps 3 and higher, ICS-formoterol is used for rescue therapy if the same combination is also used for maintenance therapy; this is called maintenance and reliever therapy (MART). If a different LABA is used for maintenance, then a SABA is used as the reliever.

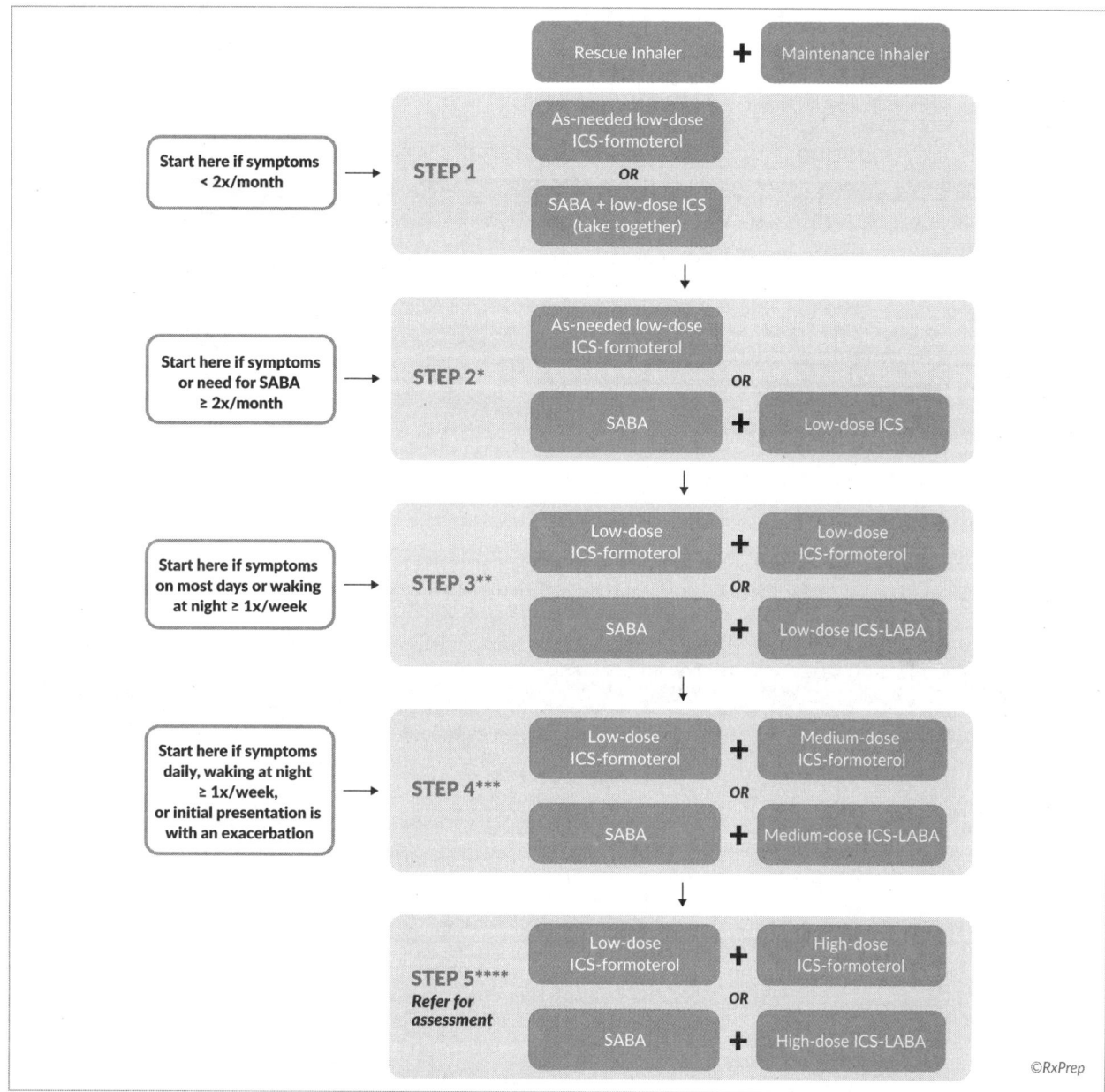

Step 2 alternative treatment: LTRA, or low-dose ICS taken whenever SABA is taken.
**Step 3 alternative treatment: low-dose ICS + LTRA or medium-dose ICS.*
***Step 4 alternative treatment: high-dose ICS, add on tiotropium or LTRA.*
****Step 5: consider adding tiotropium, oral steroid, omalizumab for patients with severe allergic asthma or mepolizumab, reslizumab, benralizumab or dupilumab for patients with severe eosinophilic asthma.*

Assess Asthma Control at Each Follow-Up Visit

Well-controlled: maintain current step (if controlled for at least 3 months, may step down treatment)

Partly controlled: step up 1 step

Uncontrolled: step up 1–2 steps (consider a short course of oral steroid)

BETA-2 AGONISTS

These medications bind to beta-2 receptors, causing relaxation of bronchial smooth muscle, which leads to bronchodilation. SABAs are used as needed (rescue therapy) for acute asthma symptoms. Traditionally, they were used as monotherapy in Step 1 of the treatment algorithm, but due to an increased risk of exacerbations, they are no longer recommended this way. SABAs should only be used with an ICS (either taken as needed, at the same time as the SABA, or daily). They can also be used for other reversible airway diseases, such as colds, allergies and bronchitis.

LABAs are used as part of rescue therapy (e.g., ICS + formoterol) or as maintenance therapy beginning in Step 3 of treatment. LABAs should be used only in combination with an ICS. If not already part of the treatment regimen, a LABA should be added to medium-dose ICS before increasing to high-dose ICS, as this leads to more rapid improvement in symptoms and lung function, and a reduction in exacerbations.

DRUG	DOSING	SAFETY/SIDE EFFECTS/MONITORING
Short-Acting Beta-2 Agonists (SABAs)		
Albuterol (ProAir HFA, ProAir RespiClick, Proventil HFA, Ventolin HFA, ProAir Digihaler) 90 mcg/inh, 0.5% and 0.083% nebulizer solution, oral syrup	MDI/DPI: 1-2 inhalations Q4-6H PRN Nebulizer: 1.25-5 mg Q4-8H PRN PO forms are available but not recommended	**WARNINGS** Caution in CVD, glaucoma, hyperthyroidism, seizures, diabetes **SIDE EFFECTS** Nervousness, tremor, tachycardia, palpitations, cough, hyperglycemia, ↓ K **MONITORING** Number of days of SABA use, symptom frequency, peak flow, pulmonary function tests, BP, HR, blood glucose, K
Levalbuterol (Xopenex, Xopenex Concentrate, Xopenex HFA) 45 mcg/inh, nebulizer solution	MDI: 1-2 inhalations Q4-6H PRN Nebulizer: 0.63-1.25 mg Q6-8H PRN (max = 1.25 mg three times daily)	**NOTES** MDIs (HFA products): shake well before use Levalbuterol contains the R-isomer of albuterol
Epinephrine (Asthmanefrin Refill) OTC	Should not be used since it is non-selective	Epinephrine inhaler: FDA-approved for mild symptoms in intermittent asthma only Most albuterol inhalers contain 200 inhalations/canister; the exception is Ventolin HFA, which is available as 200 inhalations/canister and 60 inhalations/canister EIB: use 2 inhalations 5 minutes prior to exercise
Long-Acting Beta-2 Agonists (LABAs)		
Salmeterol (Serevent Diskus) 50 mcg/inh	DPI: 1 inhalation BID	Side effects and monitoring are the same as SABAs plus: **BOXED WARNINGS** ↑ risk of asthma-related deaths; should only be used in asthma patients who are currently receiving but are not adequately controlled on an inhaled corticosteroid ↑ risk of asthma-related hospitalizations in pediatric and adolescent patients **NOTES** Maintenance inhaler only; not for acute bronchospasm

INHALED CORTICOSTEROIDS

<u>Corticosteroids inhibit the inflammatory response</u>. They block the late-phase reaction to allergens, reduce airway hyper-responsiveness and are potent and effective anti-inflammatory medications. ICSs reduce symptoms, increase lung function, improve quality of life and reduce the risk of exacerbations. They are used <u>as needed</u> in <u>combination</u> with <u>formoterol</u> or a <u>SABA</u> for acute symptoms (<u>rescue treatment</u>), and as <u>monotherapy or combination therapy</u> (<u>with a LABA</u>) to control symptoms (<u>maintenance treatment</u>).

DRUG	DOSING	SAFETY/SIDE EFFECTS/MONITORING
Beclomethasone (QVAR RediHaler) 40, 80 mcg/inh	MDI: 1-4 inhalations BID	**CONTRAINDICATIONS** Primary treatment of status asthmaticus or acute episodes of asthma
Budesonide		**WARNINGS** High doses for prolonged periods of time can cause adrenal suppression, ↑ risk of fractures, growth retardation (in children) and immunosuppression
Pulmicort Flexhaler: 90, 180 mcg/inh	DPI: 1-4 inhalations BID	
Pulmicort Respules: nebulizer suspension	Nebulizer: 0.25-0.5 mg daily or BID in children age 1-8 years	
+ formoterol (Symbicort)		**SIDE EFFECTS** Dysphonia (difficulty speaking), oral candidiasis (thrush), cough, headache, hoarseness, URTIs, hyperglycemia
Fluticasone		
Flovent HFA: 44, 110, 220 mcg/inh	MDI: 2 inhalations BID	**MONITORING** Use of SABA/rescue inhaler, symptom frequency, peak flow; growth (children/adolescents), s/sx adrenal insufficiency; s/sx of thrush; bone mineral density
Flovent Diskus: 50, 100, 250 mcg/inh	DPI: 1-2 inhalations BID	
Arnuity Ellipta: 100, 200 mcg/inh	DPI: 1-2 inhalations daily	
ArmonAir Digihaler: 55, 113, 232 mcg/inh	DPI: 1 inhalation BID	**NOTES** <u>Rinse mouth with water and spit out</u> after each use to <u>prevent thrush</u>; can use a <u>spacer device</u> with an MDI to decrease risk
+ salmeterol (Advair Diskus, Advair HFA, AirDuo RespiClick, AirDuo Digihaler, Wixela Inhub)		<u>Alvesco</u>: MDI that does <u>not need to be shaken</u> before use
+ vilanterol (Breo Ellipta)		Budesonide: only ICS available as a <u>nebulized solution</u>; used commonly in young children
Mometasone		<u>Pulmicort Respules: only use</u> with a <u>jet nebulizer</u> connected to an air compressor; do not use an ultrasonic nebulizer
Asmanex HFA: 100, 200 mcg/inh	MDI: 1-2 inhalations BID	
Asmanex: 110, 220 mcg/inh	DPI: 1-2 inhalations daily	<u>QVAR RediHaler</u>: breath-activated aerosol with characteristics of a DPI and MDI; <u>do not shake</u> or use with a spacer; does not need priming or activation
+ formoterol (Dulera)		ArmonAir and AirDuo Digihalers: contain a built-in electronic module that detects, records and stores data (detects when the inhaler is used and measures inspiratory flow)
Ciclesonide (Alvesco): 80, 160 mcg/inh	MDI: 1-2 inhalations BID	

Categorization of Inhaled Corticosteroid Daily Doses

DRUG	LOW DAILY DOSE	MEDIUM DAILY DOSE	HIGH DAILY DOSE
Beclomethasone MDI 40 or 80 mcg/inh	100-200 mcg	> 200-400 mcg	> 400 mcg
Budesonide DPI 90 or 180 mcg/inh	200-400 mcg	> 400-800 mcg	> 800 mcg
Ciclesonide MDI 80, 160 mcg/inh	80-160 mcg	> 160-320 mcg	> 320 mcg
Fluticasone MDI: 44, 110 or 220 mcg/inh	100-250 mcg	> 250-500 mcg	> 500 mcg
DPI: 50, 100 or 250 mcg/inh	100-250 mcg	> 250-500 mcg	> 500 mcg
Mometasone MDI: 100 or 200 mcg/inh	200-400 mcg	200-400 mcg	> 400 mcg
DPI: 110 or 220 mcg/inh	110-220 mcg	> 220-440 mcg	> 440 mcg

CONTROLLER (MAINTENANCE) INHALERS

There are many inhaled products available to treat respiratory conditions. This can create confusion in terms of proper use for specific disease states. The table below categorizes the different classes of controller medications for asthma and chronic obstructive pulmonary disease (COPD). ICS and ICS/LABA combinations are preferred for asthma, whereas LABA, LAMA or LAMA/LABA combinations are preferred for COPD. Some ICS/LABA combinations are approved for COPD and can be used in select patients (see the COPD chapter for treatment recommendations).

Combination inhalers increase adherence to treatment which improves disease control. Combination ICS/LABA products are considered safer for asthma, as they reduce the risk of using a LABA alone. Because of this, combination ICS/LABA inhalers do not have the boxed warning for asthma-related deaths that single-entity LABAs have. Note that this table does not include short-acting (rescue) medications.

DRUG CLASS	ASTHMA	COPD
ICS	**Beclomethasone (QVAR RediHaler)** **Budesonide (Pulmicort Flexhaler)** **Fluticasone (Flovent HFA, Flovent Diskus, Arnuity Ellipta, ArmonAir Digihaler)** Ciclesonide (Alvesco) Mometasone (Asmanex HFA, Asmanex)	No single ICS product is FDA-approved for COPD
LABA	**Salmeterol (Serevent Diskus)**	**Salmeterol (Serevent Diskus)** Formoterol (Perforomist – nebulizer) Arformoterol (Brovana – nebulizer) Olodaterol (Striverdi Respimat)
LAMA	**Tiotropium (Spiriva Respimat** only)	**Tiotropium (Spiriva HandiHaler, Spiriva Respimat)** Aclidinium (Tudorza Pressair) Glycopyrrolate (Lonhala Magnair – nebulizer) Revefenacin (Yupelri – nebulizer) Umeclidinium (Incruse Ellipta)
ICS/LABA	**Budesonide/formoterol (Symbicort)** **Fluticasone/salmeterol (Advair Diskus, Advair HFA,** AirDuo RespiClick, AirDuo Digihaler, Wixela Inhub**)** **Mometasone/formoterol (Dulera)** **Fluticasone/vilanterol (Breo Ellipta)**	**Budesonide/formoterol (Symbicort)** **Fluticasone/salmeterol (Advair Diskus,** Wixela Inhub**)** **Fluticasone/vilanterol (Breo Ellipta)**
LAMA/LABA	No combination LAMA/LABA products are FDA-approved for asthma	Aclidinium/formoterol (Duaklir Pressair) Glycopyrrolate/formoterol (Bevespi Aerosphere) Tiotropium/olodaterol (Stiolto Respimat) Umeclidinium/vilanterol (Anoro Ellipta)
LAMA/LABA/ICS	Umeclidinium/vilanterol/fluticasone (Trelegy Ellipta)	Umeclidinium/vilanterol/fluticasone (Trelegy Ellipta) Glycopyrrolate/formoterol/budesonide (Breztri Aerosphere)

RECOGNIZING AND UNDERSTANDING INHALED DELIVERY DEVICES

Inhaled devices come as metered-dose inhalers (MDIs) or dry powder inhalers (DPIs), including breath-actuated DPIs. Recognizing the type of inhaler is important as it impacts the technique the patient needs to use and how they should be educated (see the Patient Self-Management and Education section later in the chapter).

KEY DIFFERENCES BETWEEN MDIs AND DPIs

FEATURES	MDIs	DPIs
Brand name identifiers	*HFA, Respimat* or no suffix (e.g., *Alvesco*)	*Diskus, Ellipta, Pressair, HandiHaler, RespiClick, Flexhaler*
Dose delivery	Aerosolized liquid	Fine powder
Propellant	Some use a propellant (HFA)	No propellant
Administration	Slow, deep inhalation while pressing the canister (hand-breath coordination)	Quick, forceful inhalation (breath activated dose delivery; no need to press anything)
Spacer	Can be used Helpful in patients incapable of hand-breath coordination and decreases risk of thrush (with ICS)	Cannot be used
Shaking prior to use	Required for all products except: *QVAR RediHaler, Alvesco* and *Respimat* products	Do not shake
Priming	Before first use and if not used for a certain period of time (see the Key Counseling Points section later in the chapter)	Not needed except for *Flexhaler* (prior to first use)

Note: QVAR RediHaler is a breath-activated aerosol, which has characteristics of both a DPI and MDI (see the ICS table).

LEUKOTRIENE MODIFYING AGENTS

Leukotrienes are mediators of airway inflammation. Leukotriene receptor antagonists (LTRAs) reduce airway edema, constriction and inflammation. Montelukast inhibits leukotriene D4 (LTD4), while zafirlukast inhibits both LTD4 and LTE4. Zileuton, a 5-lipoxygenase inhibitor, inhibits leukotriene formation.

DRUG	DOSING	SAFETY/SIDE EFFECTS/MONITORING
Montelukast *(Singulair)* Tablet, chewable tablet, packet Also approved for allergic rhinitis and exercise-induced bronchoconstriction	10 mg daily in the evening Age 6-14 years: 5 mg daily in the evening Age 1-5 years: 4 mg daily in the evening EIB: 5 mg (6-14 years) or 10 mg (≥ 15 years) 2 hours before exercise	**BOXED WARNINGS** Montelukast: neuropsychiatric events (e.g., serious behavior and mood-related changes, including suicidal thoughts or actions) **CONTRAINDICATIONS** Zafirlukast and zileuton: hepatic impairment **WARNINGS** Neuropsychiatric events; monitor for signs of aggressive behavior, hostility, agitation, hallucinations, depression, suicidal thinking Systemic eosinophilia, sometimes presenting with features of vasculitis consistent with Churg-Strauss syndrome (rare)
Zafirlukast *(Accolate)* Tablet	20 mg BID Age 5-11 years: 10 mg BID Take 1 hour before or 2 hours after meals (empty stomach)	**SIDE EFFECTS** Headache, dizziness, abdominal pain, ↑ LFTs, URTIs **MONITORING** LFTs (zafirlukast and zileuton), mood or behavior changes (montelukast)
Zileuton *(Zyflo)* Tablet, ER tablet	*Zyflo:* 600 mg QID ER tablet: 1,200 mg BID within 1 hour after morning and evening meals Age < 12 years: not recommended	**NOTES** Montelukast granules: can be administered directly in the mouth, dissolved in a small amount (5 mL) of breast milk or formula or mixed with a spoonful of applesauce, carrots, rice or ice cream (do not mix with anything else); use within 15 minutes of opening the packet Zafirlukast: protect from moisture and light; dispense in original container

Leukotriene Modifying Agents Drug Interactions

- Montelukast is a minor substrate of CYP450 3A4 and 2C8/9 and a weak inhibitor of CYP2C8/9.

  - Gemfibrozil can ↑ levels of montelukast; lumacaftor can ↓ levels of montelukast.

- Zafirlukast is a major substrate of CYP2C9. It inhibits CYP2C9 (moderate) and CYP2C8 (weak).

- Zafirlukast can ↑ levels of theophylline and CYP2C9 substrates (e.g., warfarin).

  - Erythromycin and theophylline ↓ zafirlukast levels.

- Zileuton is a minor substrate of CYP1A2, 2C9 and 3A4, and a weak inhibitor of CYP1A2. It can ↑ levels of theophylline, propranolol and warfarin.

THEOPHYLLINE

Theophylline blocks phosphodiesterase, causing an increase in cyclic adenosine monophosphate (cAMP) and release of epinephrine from adrenal medulla cells. This results in bronchodilation, but it also causes diuresis, CNS and cardiac stimulation and gastric acid secretion. Use of theophylline is limited by ↓ effectiveness, drug interactions and adverse effects.

DRUG	DOSING	SAFETY/SIDE EFFECTS/MONITORING
Theophylline *(Elixophyllin, Theo-24)* ER capsule, ER tablet, elixir, oral solution, injection Active metabolites are caffeine and 3-methylxanthine	Oral loading dose: 5 mg/kg IBW (or TBW if < IBW) Oral maintenance dose: 300-600 mg daily **Therapeutic range** 5-15 mcg/mL Measure peak level at steady state, after 3 days of oral dosing	**WARNINGS** Can exacerbate cardiovascular arrhythmias, peptic ulcer disease and seizure disorders **SIDE EFFECTS** Nausea, vomiting, headache, insomnia, ↑ HR, tremor, nervousness Toxicity: persistent vomiting, arrhythmias, seizures **MONITORING** Theophylline levels, HR, CNS effects (insomnia, irritability), use of rescue inhaler **NOTES** Aminophylline contains 2:1 theophylline and ethylenediamine To convert aminophylline to theophylline, multiply by 0.8*; to convert theophylline to aminophylline, divide by 0.8 *Remember: ATM (Aminophylline → Theophylline Multiply)

Theophylline Interactions

Theophylline has saturable kinetics (first-order kinetics, followed by zero-order kinetics). In the higher end of the therapeutic range, small dose increases can result in large increases in theophylline concentrations (see the Pharmacokinetics chapter).

- Theophylline is a substrate of CYP1A2 (major), 3A4 and 2E1 (minor).

- CYP1A2 inhibitors that ↑ theophylline levels: cimetidine, ciprofloxacin, fluvoxamine, propranolol and zileuton.

- CYP3A4 inhibitors that ↑ theophylline levels: clarithromycin and erythromycin.

- Other drugs that ↑ theophylline levels: zafirlukast, alcohol, allopurinol, disulfiram, estrogen-containing oral contraceptives, methotrexate, pentoxifylline, propafenone and verapamil.

- Drugs that ↓ theophylline levels: carbamazepine, fosphenytoin, phenobarbital, phenytoin, primidone, rifampin, ritonavir, levothyroxine, St. John's wort and tobacco/marijuana smoking.

- Theophylline can ↓ lithium (via ↑ renal excretion) and zafirlukast.

- Conditions/foods that ↑ theophylline levels (due to ↓ theophylline clearance): CHF, cirrhosis or liver disease, acute pulmonary edema, cor pulmonale, fever, hypothyroidism, shock and high carb/low protein diet.

- Conditions/foods that can ↓ theophylline levels (due to ↑ theophylline clearance): low carb/high-protein diet, daily consumption of charbroiled beef, cystic fibrosis and hyperthyroidism.

ANTICHOLINERGICS

Anticholinergics inhibit muscarinic cholinergic receptors and reduce the intrinsic vagal tone of the airway, leading to bronchodilation. Short-acting anticholinergics (e.g., ipratropium) are sometimes used in combination with SABAs in hospitalized patients experiencing an acute exacerbation. A long-acting anticholinergic, tiotropium (*Spiriva Respimat*), is FDA-approved for asthma in patients ≥ 6 years of age with a history of exacerbations despite ICS/LABA therapy. Refer to the COPD chapter for more information on anticholinergics.

OMALIZUMAB *(XOLAIR)*

Omalizumab is a monoclonal antibody that inhibits IgE binding to the IgE receptor on mast cells and basophils. It is indicated for moderate-severe persistent, allergic asthma in patients ≥ 6 years of age who have a positive skin test to a perennial aeroallergen and inadequate symptom control on Step 5 treatment.

DRUG	DOSING	SAFETY/SIDE EFFECTS/MONITORING
Omalizumab *(Xolair)*	Administer SC every 2 or 4 weeks Dose and frequency based on pretreatment IgE serum levels and body weight Initiate in a healthcare setting under medical supervision (≥ 3 doses) Criteria for self-administration: no anaphylaxis after ≥ 3 doses, can recognize and manage anaphylaxis, uses proper injection technique Doses > 150 mg should be divided over more than one injection site	**BOXED WARNING** Anaphylaxis has occurred as early as after the first dose and has occurred beyond 1 year after beginning treatment; closely observe patients after administration and be prepared to manage anaphylaxis that can be life-threatening **WARNINGS** ↑ risk of serious cardiovascular and cerebrovascular adverse events; malignancies have been observed in clinical studies (rare) **SIDE EFFECTS** Injection site reactions, headache, dizziness, fatigue, arthralgias, pain **MONITORING** Baseline IgE, FEV1, peak flow, s/sx of anaphylaxis and infection

INTERLEUKIN RECEPTOR ANTAGONISTS

Interleukin is a cytokine responsible for the growth, differentiation, recruitment, activation and survival of eosinophils (a cell type associated with inflammation and the cause of some types of asthma). Monoclonal antibodies can be used to inhibit interleukin from binding to receptors. Mepolizumab, reslizumab and benralizumab are IL-5 receptor antagonists. Dupilumab is an IL-4 and IL-3 receptor antagonist. All are indicated for the management of severe asthma with an eosinophilic phenotype. When used, they should be added to maintenance inhaler treatment.

- Mepolizumab *(Nucala):* for patients ≥ 6 years; it is given SC once every four weeks. It can be administered at home by the patient or caregiver. Side effects are minor.

- Reslizumab *(Cinqair):* for adults only; it is given IV once every four weeks. It has a boxed warning for anaphylaxis. After administration, patients should be observed by a healthcare professional who is able to manage anaphylaxis.

- Benralizumab *(Fasenra, Fasenra Pen):* for patients ≥ 12 years; it is given SC once every four weeks for three doses, then every eight weeks. The *Fasenra Pen* can be administered at home by the patient or caregiver. Side effects are minor.

- Dupilumab *(Dupixent):* for patients ≥ 12 years of age; it is given SC every other week.

OTHER MONOCLONAL ANTIBODIES

Tezepelumab *(Tezspire)* is indicated for patients ≥ 12 years; it is given SC every 4 weeks. Its novel mechanism, blocking human thymic stromal lymphopoietin, reduces multiple biomarkers of inflammation. Its role in severe asthma has not yet been incorporated into treatment guidelines.

SPECIAL SITUATIONS

EXERCISE-INDUCED BRONCHOSPASM: *PREVENT IT*

A SABA or low-dose ICS plus formoterol, taken 5 – 15 minutes before exercise, is preferred to prevent most EIB. The effects of the SABA will last 2 – 3 hours, while the duration of the ICS plus formoterol can last up to 12 hours. Salmeterol (a LABA) can be used as an alternative to a SABA if a longer duration of symptom control is needed; it should be taken 30 minutes before exercise. If the patient is using a LABA for asthma maintenance, they should not use additional doses for EIB. LABAs should never be used alone for persistent asthma.

Montelukast can be taken two hours prior to exercise and lasts up to 24 hours. It is effective in only 50% of patients. Patients taking montelukast for asthma, or any other indication, should not take an additional dose to prevent EIB.

EIB is often a marker of inadequate asthma control. It might be necessary to start or increase a controller medication (e.g., an ICS) to control the EIB.

PREGNANCY: *KEEP CONTROL*

Asthma control can worsen during pregnancy. To ensure oxygen supply to the fetus, it is safer to treat asthma with medications than to have poorly controlled asthma. Down-titration of medications is not recommended, and exacerbations should be treated aggressively. An ICS should be continued during pregnancy and is still the preferred controller (either as needed or daily).

CASE SCENARIO

SG is a 35-year-old female with asthma. She brings a prescription for *Advair Diskus* to the pharmacy and requests a refill on her *ProAir RespiClick*. You review her medication refill history and see that she filled prescriptions for *Pulmicort Flexhaler* 3 weeks ago and *ProAir RespiClick* approximately 2 months ago.

SG tells you that she is stopping her *Pulmicort Flexhaler* and starting the *Advair Diskus* instead. She says she uses her *ProAir RespiClick* about 3 times a day, on at least 3 days of the week. She feels like she cannot have as active of a social life as she would like due to asthma attacks.

How would you assess SG's asthma control?

SG is not well controlled, as she uses her SABA inhaler *(ProAir RespiClick)* more than 2 days a week and has limitations to normal activity.

Is the change in treatment appropriate?

A step up in treatment is needed. The change from an ICS to an ICS/LABA combination product is appropriate.

What counseling points about her treatment are important for SG?

- Follow the specific instructions for inhaler technique.
- Use *Advair Diskus* twice daily to help control asthma symptoms. It is not a rescue medication.
- Rinse the mouth and spit after each dose of *Advair Diskus* to prevent thrush (an infection in the mouth).
- Use *ProAir RespiClick* as needed for shortness of breath. Using it more than twice weekly means asthma is not well controlled. If *ProAir RespiClick* is used too often, it can cause palpitations, nervousness or tremor.
- Monitor the counter on the *ProAir RespiClick* to make sure it does not run out before the next refill.
- Avoid triggers known to make asthma worse.

PATIENT SELF-MANAGEMENT AND EDUCATION

INHALERS

Most patients (up to 80%) cannot use their inhaler correctly, which results in little or no medication reaching the lungs. This contributes to poor symptom control and increased exacerbations. Patient counseling and assessing inhaler technique is essential. Up to 50% of adults and children do not take their controller medications as prescribed. Many times, this is unintentional and due to a lack of education, cost or forgetfulness. Assessing adherence is important when evaluating asthma control.

Patients should be aware of how to monitor the doses remaining in an inhaler. Some inhalers have an internal dose counter. Most controller inhalers are designed to last one month when the patient is adherent to therapy. SABA rescue inhalers can last a varying amount of time depending on use, but for a patient with good asthma control, an albuterol inhaler should last about 12 months (or 3 – 4 months for the smaller *Ventolin HFA* inhaler with 60 inhalations/canister). It is useful for patients to know when the inhaler should run out. Refer to the table below for examples of the number of days that commonly used inhalers will last.

DRUG	INHALATIONS	EXAMPLE DOSAGE	SUPPLY
Maintenance Inhalers			
Advair Diskus	60	1 inhalation BID	30 days (60/2 inhalations daily)
QVAR Redil Ialer	120	1-2 inhalations BID	30 days (120/4 inhalations daily)
Asmanex	60	2 inhalations daily	30 days (60/2 inhalations daily)
SABA Rescue Inhalers			
Albuterol MDI	200	2 inhalations per dose, used twice weekly (4 inhalations/week)	50 weeks (200/4 inhalations weekly)
Ventolin HFA	60		15 weeks (60/4 inhalations weekly)

Timing and Order of Use

If prescribed > 1 inhalation of medication at a time, the patient should wait 60 seconds between each one. If using more than one inhaler, the sequence of inhalers is important. Bronchodilators (beta-2 agonists and anticholinergics) work faster than ICS. Using bronchodilators first will open the airways quickly, allowing the ICS to travel deeper into the lungs.

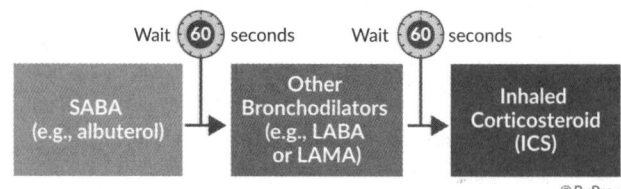

NEBULIZERS

A nebulizer is a device that turns liquid medication into a fine mist. The fine mist can be inhaled through a face mask or mouthpiece into the lungs. Nebulizers use natural breathing, making medication delivery easy for infants, children and the elderly. There are three types of nebulizers: jet, ultrasound and mesh. Check the medication information to see which nebulizer device is recommended.

Albuterol comes as a nebulizer solution in both unit dose packaging and a 20 mL vial. The two common concentrations are 0.083% solution, containing 2.5 mg/3 mL, and 0.5% solution, containing 2.5 mg/0.5 mL. The 0.083% solution is a ready-to-use preparation that can be placed directly into the nebulizer; no dilution is required. The 0.5% concentrated solution must be diluted with 2.5 mL of normal saline prior to use.

SPACERS

Spacer is a generic term for different types of open tubes that are placed between the mouthpiece of an MDI and the mouth of the patient to help with medication delivery. Spacers are used for children and anyone with dexterity issues (i.e., difficulty pressing down and breathing in at the same time with an MDI). Spacers reduce the risk of thrush (see the Study Tip Gal). They should never be used with a DPI. Clean spacers at least once a week (in warm, soapy water).

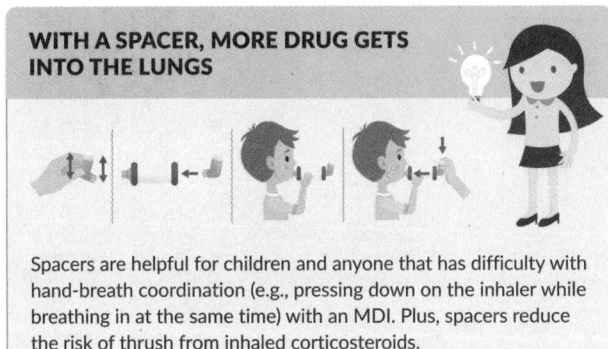

WITH A SPACER, MORE DRUG GETS INTO THE LUNGS

Spacers are helpful for children and anyone that has difficulty with hand-breath coordination (e.g., pressing down on the inhaler while breathing in at the same time) with an MDI. Plus, spacers reduce the risk of thrush from inhaled corticosteroids.

Common spacers: *AeroChamber, OptiHaler, OptiChamber*

PEAK FLOW METERS

Peak flow meters are handheld devices that measure the peak expiratory flow rate (PEFR). The PEFR is the maximum flow rate from a forceful exhalation, starting from fully inflated lungs. The patient's best PEFR is called their personal best (PB), which can be measured by spirometry. The measurement takes into account the patient's height, gender and age because the PEFR depends on the muscular strength of the patient. Patients can measure their PB themselves by taking peak flow readings twice a day (morning and evening) for 2 – 3 weeks when asthma is in good control. The highest reading that occurs most frequently is the PB.

Peak flow meters are beneficial in patients with frequent asthma exacerbations, persistent asthma (Step 3 – 5), poor perception of airflow obstruction and unexplained response to environmental factors. When used correctly, peak flow meters can identify exacerbations early (even before the patient is symptomatic), allowing treatment to begin sooner.

An asthma action plan is developed by the healthcare provider so the patient knows how to manage symptoms at home and avoid hospitalizations due to an exacerbation. The action plan uses the patient's PB and outlines "zones" of control (based on the percentage of their PB). Each "zone" is then given a specific action to follow (see the example on the next page).

Peak Flow Meter Technique

- Use the peak flow meter every morning upon awakening and before the use of any asthma medications. Proper technique and best effort are essential. Less than the best effort can lead to taking unnecessary medication.

- Move the indicator to the bottom of the numbered scale. Stand up straight. Exhale comfortably.

- Inhale as deeply as possible. Place lips firmly around the mouthpiece, creating a tight seal.

- Blow out as hard and as fast as possible. Write down the PEFR.

- Repeat steps two more times, with enough rest in between. Record the highest value.

- Compare the peak flow value to your personal asthma action plan and follow the steps as instructed.

Peak Flow Meter Care

- Always use the same brand of peak flow meter.

- Clean at least once a week using warm water and mild soap; if you have an infection, clean the meter more frequently. Rinse gently; do not use brushes to clean the inside of the peak flow meter. Do not place peak flow meters in boiling water. Allow the meter to air dry before using again.

ZONES OF AN ASTHMA ACTION PLAN

Green zone (> 80 – 100% of personal best)
- Indicates "all clear" – good control
- Patients are instructed to follow routine maintenance plan

Yellow zone (50 – 80% of personal best)
- Indicates "caution" – worsening lung function
- Patient-specific intervention required (action plan) – usually an increase in rescue inhaler use and the addition or increase of other medications

Red zone (< 50% of personal best)
- Indicates "medical alert" – seek medical attention
- Action plan includes using a rescue inhaler, possibly steroids or going to the emergency department

SAMPLE ASTHMA ACTION PLAN (ADULT)

Asthma Action Plan

For: _____ Doctor: _____ Date: _____

Doctor's Phone Number _____ Hospital/Emergency Department Phone Number _____

GREEN ZONE

Doing Well

- No cough, wheeze, chest tightness, or shortness of breath during the day or night
- Can do usual activities

And, if a peak flow meter is used,

Peak flow: more than _____
(80 percent or more of my best peak flow)

My best peak flow is: _____

Take these long-term control medicines each day (include an anti-inflammatory).

Medicine	How much to take	When to take it
_____	_____	_____
_____	_____	_____
_____	_____	_____
_____	_____	_____

Before exercise	☐ _____	☐ 2 or ☐ 4 puffs _____	5 minutes before exercise

YELLOW ZONE

Asthma is Getting Worse

- Cough, wheeze, chest tightness, or shortness of breath, or
- Waking at night due to asthma, or
- Can do some, but not all, usual activities

-Or-

Peak flow: _____ to _____
(50 to 79 percent of my best peak flow)

First Add: quick-relief medicine—and keep taking your GREEN ZONE medicine.

_____ (rescue inhaler) ☐ 2 or ☐ 4 puffs, every 20 minutes for up to 1 hour
☐ Nebulizer, once

Second If your symptoms (and peak flow, if used) return to GREEN ZONE after 1 hour of above treatment:
☐ Continue monitoring to be sure you stay in the green zone.

-Or- _____

If your symptoms (and peak flow, if used) do not return to GREEN ZONE after 1 hour of above treatment:

☐ Take: _____ (rescue inhaler) ☐ 2 or ☐ 4 puffs or ☐ Nebulizer

☐ Add: _____ (oral steroid) mg per day For _____ (3–10) days

☐ Call the doctor ☐ before/ ☐ within _____ hours after taking the oral steroid.

RED ZONE

Medical Alert!

- Very short of breath, or
- Quick-relief medicines have not helped, or
- Cannot do usual activities, or
- Symptoms are same or get worse after 24 hours in Yellow Zone

-Or-

Peak flow: less than _____
(50 percent of my best peak flow)

Take this medicine:

☐ _____ (rescue inhaler) ☐ 4 or ☐ 6 puffs or ☐ Nebulizer

☐ _____ (oral steroid) mg

Then call your doctor NOW. Go to the hospital or call an ambulance if:
- You are still in the red zone after 15 minutes AND
- You have not reached your doctor.

DANGER SIGNS
- **Trouble walking and talking due to shortness of breath**
- **Lips or fingernails are blue**

- **Take ☐ 4 or ☐ 6 puffs of your quick-relief medicine AND**
- **Go to the hospital or call for an ambulance _____ NOW!** (phone)

See the reverse side for things you can do to avoid your asthma triggers.

Adapted from ©**www.nhlbi.nih.gov**

CASE SCENARIO

ES is a 29-year-old male with asthma. He comes into the pharmacy asking for help interpreting his peak flow readings. He states that he feels fine, but is worried that his peak flow readings are declining. ES is able to demonstrate appropriate use of the peak flow meter, and reports that he has been checking at the appropriate time (first thing in the morning, before medications and taking the best of three readings). His personal best (PB) is 480 mL, and his readings from the last few days are as follows:

> Monday: 400 mL (83% PB)
> Tuesday: 388 mL (81% PB)
> Wednesday: 420 mL (88% PB)

What zone is ES in?

ES is in the green zone. All readings fall within 80–100% of his personal best.

What steps should ES take today?

ES should be advised to follow the instructions in his specific asthma action plan. Make sure this is filled out to include his medications (rescue and maintenance) and personal range of each zone:

- Green Zone (> 80%) = > 384 mL
- Yellow Zone (50–80%) = 240 mL–384 mL
- Red Zone (< 50%) = < 240 mL

Since he feels well and his peak flow readings are in the green zone, he should continue his maintenance medications. His action plan might include using a rescue inhaler prior to exercise. For anyone with asthma, it is important to avoid triggers and monitor for symptoms, regardless of peak flow readings.

KEY COUNSELING POINTS

SELECT METERED-DOSE INHALERS

Albuterol *(Ventolin HFA, ProAir HFA)*, budesonide/formoterol *(Symbicort)*, fluticasone *(Flovent HFA)*, mometasone/formoterol *(Dulera)*, others

STEP 1	STEP 2	STEP 3

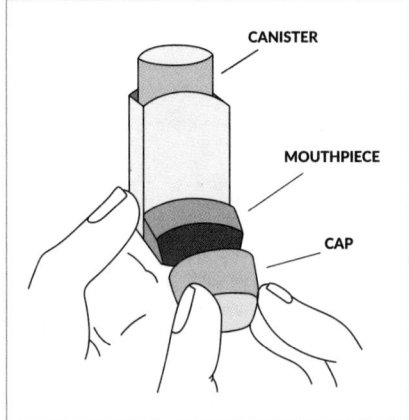 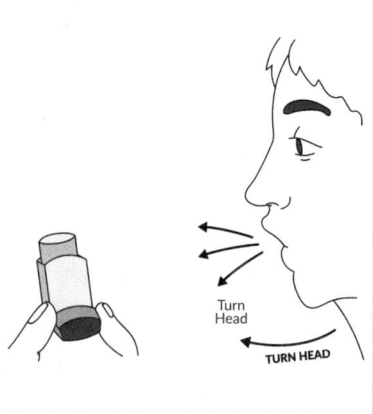 

©RxPrep

Make sure the canister is fully inserted into the actuator (if it comes separately). Always use the actuator that came with the canister. Shake the inhaler well for 5 seconds immediately before each spray (except for *QVAR RediHaler* or *Alvesco*, which do not need to be shaken). Remove cap from the mouthpiece and check mouthpiece for foreign objects prior to use.	Breathe out fully through your mouth, expelling as much air from your lungs as possible. Holding the inhaler upright (as shown in the picture), place the mouthpiece into your mouth and close your lips around it.	While breathing in slowly and deeply through your mouth, press the top of the canister all the way down with your index finger. Right after the spray comes out, take your finger off the canister. After you have inhaled all the way, take the inhaler out of your mouth and close your mouth. Hold your breath as long as possible, up to 10 seconds, then breathe normally. If another inhalation is needed, wait 1 minute and repeat Steps 1-3. Place cap back on the mouthpiece after use.

TO PRIME	**TO CLEAN**
Ventolin HFA, ProAir HFA Spray 4 times (3 for *ProAir*) away from the face, shaking between sprays. Prime again if > 14 days from last use or if you drop it.	***Ventolin HFA, ProAir HFA*** To prevent medication buildup and blockage, remove the metal canister (do not let this get wet) and rinse the mouthpiece only under warm running water for 30 seconds, then turn upside down and rinse under warm water for another 30 seconds. Shake to remove excess water and let air dry. Clean at least weekly.
Flovent HFA, Dulera Spray 4 times away from the face, shaking between sprays. Prime again with just 1 spray if > 7 days from last use (> 5 days for *Dulera*).	***Flovent HFA*** Use a clean cotton swab dampened with water to clean the small circular opening where the medication sprays out. Gently twist the swab in a circular motion to remove any medication buildup. Do not take the canister out of the plastic actuator. Wipe the inside of the mouthpiece with a damp tissue. Let air dry overnight.
Symbicort Spray 2 times away from the face, shaking between sprays. Prime again if > 7 days from last use.	***Symbicort, Dulera*** Wipe the inside and outside of the mouthpiece opening with a clean, dry cloth. Do not put into water.

SELECT DRY POWDER INHALERS

Fluticasone/salmeterol (*Advair Diskus*)

STEP 1	STEP 2	STEP 3	STEP 4	STEP 5
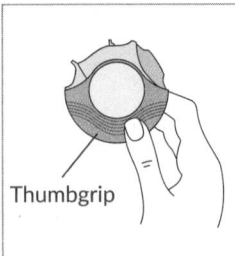	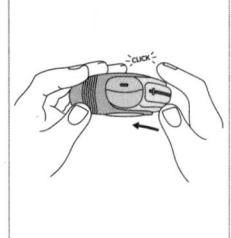	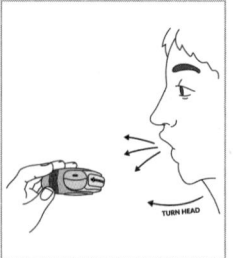	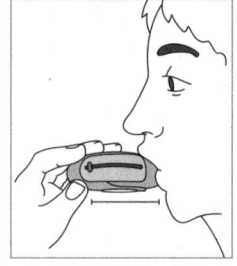	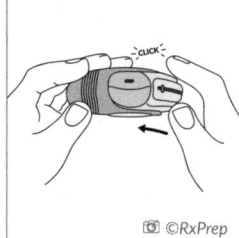
Hold the *Diskus* in your left hand and put the thumb of your right hand in the thumb grip. Push the thumb grip away from you as far as it will go until the mouthpiece appears and the *Diskus* snaps into position.	Hold the *Diskus* in a level, flat position with the mouthpiece towards you. Slide the lever away from the mouthpiece until it clicks.	Before using, breathe out fully while holding the *Diskus* <u>away from your mouth</u>. Do not tilt the *Diskus*.	Put the mouthpiece to your lips. Breathe in <u>quickly</u> and <u>deeply</u> through the inhaler. <u>Do not breathe in through your nose</u>. Remove the *Diskus* from your mouth and hold your breath as long as possible, up to 10 seconds. Then, breathe out slowly.	Close the *Diskus* by putting your thumb in the thumb grip and sliding it as far back towards you as it will go, until the *Diskus* clicks shut. <u>Rinse your mouth with water and spit out</u> the water to prevent thrush. Do not swallow the water.

TO CLEAN
Do not wash the *Diskus*. Store in a dry place.

Budesonide (*Pulmicort Flexhaler*)

STEP 1	STEP 2	STEP 3
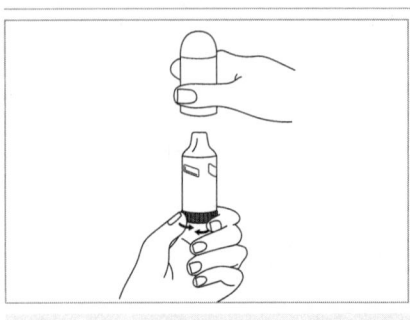	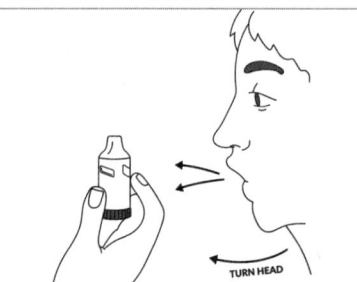	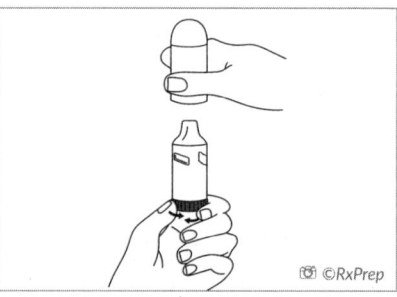
Twist off the white cover. Holding the middle of the inhaler with one hand, twist the brown base fully in one direction as far as it will go with the other hand. Twist it fully back again in the other direction as far as it will go. You will hear a "click" during one of the twisting movements. The dose is now loaded. Do not shake the inhaler after it is loaded (note: only one dose is loaded at a time, no matter how often you twist the brown base, but the dose counter will continue to advance).	Turn your head away from the inhaler and breathe out fully.	Place the mouthpiece in your mouth and close your lips around the mouthpiece. Breathe in <u>deeply</u> and <u>forcefully</u> through the inhaler. Remove the inhaler from your mouth and breathe out. Replace the white cover on the inhaler and twist shut. <u>Rinse your mouth with water and spit out the water</u> to prevent thrush.

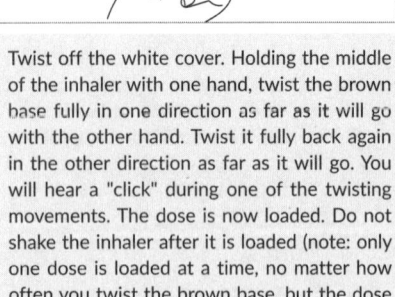

TO PRIME
Twist off the white cover. Holding the inhaler upright, twist the brown base fully in one direction as far as it will go and then fully back. You will hear a click during one of the twisting motions. Repeat twisting motion again (back and forth). The inhaler is now primed and ready to load your first dose. This inhaler does not need to be primed again (even after long periods of no use).

TO CLEAN
Wipe the mouthpiece with a dry tissue weekly. Do not use water or immerse it in water.

Albuterol *(ProAir RespiClick)*, fluticasone/salmeterol *(AirDuo RespiClick)*

STEP 1	STEP 2	STEP 3
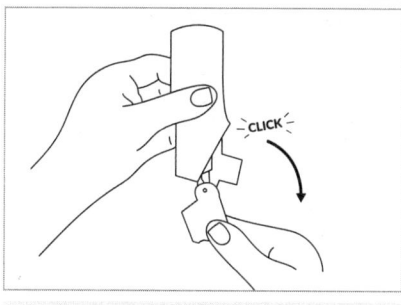	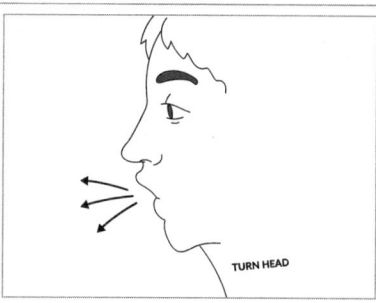	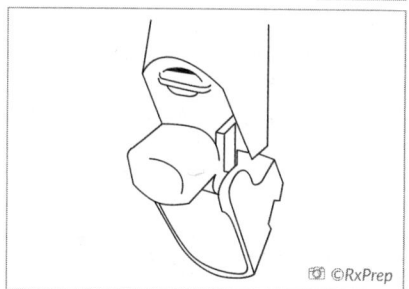
Make sure the cap is closed before each dose. Hold the inhaler upright as you open the cap fully. Open the cap all the way back until you hear a "click." Your inhaler is now ready to use. Do not open the cap unless you are taking a dose. Note: opening and closing the cap without inhaling a dose will waste medication and can damage your inhaler.	Breathe out through your mouth and push as much air from your lungs as you can. Turn your head away from the inhaler so you do not breathe into the mouthpiece.	Put the mouthpiece in your mouth and close your lips around it. Breathe in deeply through your mouth, until your lungs feel completely full of air. Do not let your lips or fingers block the vent above the mouthpiece. Hold your breath for as long as possible, up to 10 seconds. Remove the inhaler from your mouth. Check the dose counter on the back of the inhaler to make sure you received the dose. Close the cap over the mouthpiece after each use of the inhaler. Make sure the cap closes firmly into place. For *AirDuo RespiClick*: rinse your mouth with water and spit out the water to prevent thrush. Do not swallow the water.

TO PRIME
None needed.

TO CLEAN
Keep your inhaler dry and clean at all times. Do not wash or put any part of your inhaler in water. If the mouthpiece needs cleaning, gently wipe it with a dry cloth or tissue after using.

ALL PATIENTS WITH ASTHMA

See the Drug Formulations and Patient Counseling chapter for language/layman's terminology.

- Always have your rescue inhaler with you for asthma attacks.
- If asthma symptoms get worse, or if you increase the use of your rescue inhaler for asthma attacks, contact your healthcare provider right away.

MONTELUKAST *(SINGULAIR)*

- Take in the evening.
- Can cause suicidal ideation, behavior and mood changes.
- Do not use more than one dose within 24 hours. If using daily for another indication, do not take another dose to prevent exercise-induced asthma.
- Oral granules:
  - Administer within 15 minutes of opening the packet.
  - Can be mixed with a teaspoonful of baby formula, breast milk, applesauce, mashed carrots, rice or ice cream or given directly in the mouth.

BUDESONIDE *(PULMICORT RESPULES)*

- Store upright, protected from light, at room temperature.
- Ampules should be used within two weeks of opening the aluminum package.
- Gently swirl the ampule in a circular motion before use.
- Rinse mouth with water and spit it out after each dose. If a face mask was used, wash face after each treatment.

Select Guidelines/References

Global Initiative for Asthma (GINA). Global Strategy for Asthma Management and Prevention, 2021. http://www.ginasthma.org (accessed 2022 Feb 7).

National Heart, Lung and Blood Institute. Expert Panel Report 3: Guidelines for the Diagnosis and Management of Asthma. August 2007.

National Heart, Lung and Blood Institute. 2020 Focused Updates to the Asthma Management Guidelines: A Report from the National Asthma Education and Prefention Program Coordinating Committee Expert Panel Working Group. December 2020.

CHAPTER CONTENT

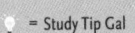

Chronic Bronchitis

Healthy — Inflammation & excess mucus

Emphysema

Healthy — Alveolar membranes break down

jehsomwang © 123RF.com

CHAPTER 42

CHRONIC OBSTRUCTIVE PULMONARY DISEASE

BACKGROUND

Chronic obstructive pulmonary disease (COPD) is a respiratory disease that causes obstructed airflow from the lungs. It is one of the leading causes of death worldwide. Symptoms include chronic and progressive dyspnea (shortness of breath), chronic cough, sputum production and wheezing.

COPD is most commonly caused by tobacco smoke, but can be caused by other air pollutants (e.g., noxious particles, smoke from fires, cigars, pipes and marijuana). Long-term exposure to these gases or particles causes chronic inflammation in the lungs, eventually resulting in emphysema and/or bronchitis. Emphysema is the destruction of the small passages in the lungs, called alveoli. Bronchitis is inflammation and narrowing of the bronchial tubes; it results in mucus production and a chronic cough.

Individuals with alpha-1 antitrypsin (AAT) deficiency are at a higher risk of developing COPD because AAT helps to protect the lungs from damage caused by inflammation.

DIAGNOSIS

COPD should be suspected in any patient with symptoms (described above) and a history of exposure to risk factors (e.g., tobacco smoke). Other common reasons for shortness of breath and cough should be ruled out, such as asthma, chronic heart failure and other pulmonary conditions (e.g., tuberculosis). Asthma is the most difficult to differentiate from COPD (see Study Tip Gal on the following page).

The limitation of airflow in asthma is reversible with medication. In COPD, the limitation of airflow is not fully reversible and progresses over time, leading to a gradual loss of lung function.

CONTENT LEGEND

= Study Tip Gal

Spirometry is required to assess lung function and make a diagnosis of COPD. It is an objective measurement of airflow limitation and the most reproducible test available. Spirometry measures the total amount of air a person can breathe out (forced vital capacity, or FVC) and the amount of air exhaled in one second (forced expiratory volume, or FEV1). A post-bronchodilator FEV1/FVC < 0.70 confirms a diagnosis of COPD.

KEY DIFFERENCES OF COPD VS. ASTHMA

FEATURE	COPD	ASTHMA
Age of onset	Usually > 40 years	Usually < 40 years
Smoking history	Usually > 10 years	Uncommon
Sputum production	Common	Infrequent
Allergies	Uncommon	Common
Symptoms	Persistent	Intermittent and variable
Disease process	Progressive, worsens over time	Stable, does not worsen over time
Exacerbations	A common complication	A common complication
First-line treatment	Bronchodilators	Inhaled corticosteroids

COPD ASSESSMENT

COPD assessment includes the following four components:

- Degree of airflow limitation (disease severity)
- Symptoms
- Risk of exacerbations
- Presence of comorbidities

DEGREE OF AIRFLOW LIMITATION

The post-bronchodilator FEV1 is assessed using spirometry and helps determine disease severity. The GOLD guidelines use a grading system of 1 – 4 to classify patients based on spirometry results. The grade assignment is used to assess prognosis and disease progression.

Severity of Post-Bronchodilator Airflow Limitation

GRADE	SEVERITY	AIRFLOW LIMITATION
In patients with FEV1/FVC < 0.70		
GOLD 1	Mild	FEV1 ≥ 80% predicted
GOLD 2	Moderate	50% ≤ FEV1 < 80% predicted
GOLD 3	Severe	30% ≤ FEV1 < 50% predicted
GOLD 4	Very Severe	FEV1 < 30% predicted

SYMPTOMS

The classic symptoms of chronic cough, sputum production and dyspnea can appear years before airflow limitation is recognized. For this reason, scoring systems are used for symptom assessment, and are integral to selecting drug treatment. The two most commonly used scoring systems are the:

- Modified British Medical Research Council (mMRC) dyspnea scale – available at: https://www.verywell.com/guidelines-for-the-mmrc-dyspnea-scale-914740

- COPD Assessment Test (CAT) – available at: https://www.catestonline.org/patient-site-test-page-english.html

The mMRC dyspnea scale assesses breathlessness. Scores range from 0 (only breathless with strenuous exercise) to 4 (too breathless to leave the house or breathless with normal daily activities, such as dressing and undressing). The CAT is a comprehensive assessment of symptoms (e.g., cough, mucus production, chest tightness, energy level, breathlessness, sleep patterns, limitations to normal activity), with possible scores ranging from 0 – 40; higher scores indicate worse symptoms.

The application of these two scoring systems is shown in the Combined Assessment of COPD chart and the case scenarios that follow.

RISK OF EXACERBATIONS

A COPD exacerbation is an acute worsening of respiratory symptoms beyond normal day-to-day variation. If a patient has two or more exacerbations per year, they are considered to be frequent exacerbators. The risk of exacerbations increases as airflow limitation worsens. Hospitalization for an exacerbation is associated with an increased risk of death. Taking measures to prevent and quickly treat exacerbations is an important component in the management of COPD.

COMORBIDITIES

Comorbid conditions, such as cardiovascular diseases, osteoporosis, diabetes, depression, anxiety, skeletal muscle dysfunction, respiratory infections and lung cancer should be monitored and treated appropriately. Poor control of comorbid conditions can independently influence mortality and hospitalizations.

COMBINED ASSESSMENT OF COPD

The combined assessment of COPD has been simplified to focus on symptom assessment and risk of exacerbations as the critical components that drive treatment. At each follow-up visit, symptoms should be assessed using the mMRC or CAT, and history of exacerbations in the past year should be documented. The patient is then assigned to a group (ABCD), which determines the initial treatment warranted (see Initial Pharmacologic Therapy).

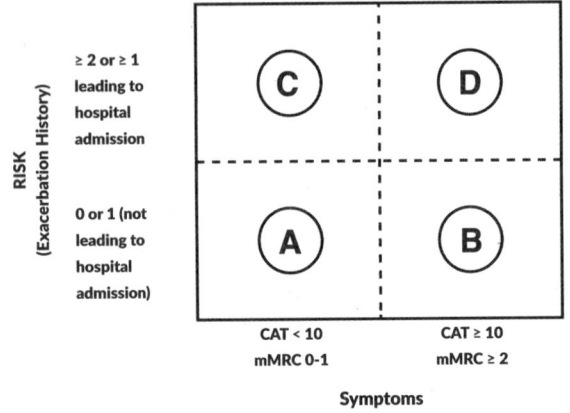

NON-DRUG TREATMENT

Smoking cessation is the only management strategy proven to slow the progression of COPD. Healthcare providers should encourage all tobacco users to quit using proven strategies (see Tobacco Cessation chapter). Vaccinations reduce the risk of hospitalizations due to serious respiratory illness and the risk of death. Patients with COPD should receive an annual influenza vaccine, pneumococcal vaccinations and Tdap per ACIP recommendations (see Immunizations chapter).

To improve outcomes, it is essential to routinely assess inhaler technique (see detailed instructions on inhaler use, priming and cleaning at the end of the chapter) and adherence. Pulmonary rehabilitation programs help improve quality of life and symptoms. Long-term oxygen treatment has been shown to increase survival in patients with severe resting hypoxemia (PaO2 < 55 mmHg or SaO2 < 88%).

DRUG TREATMENT

The medications used in COPD do not modify the long-term decline in lung function or reduce mortality. They decrease symptoms and/or prevent complications, such as exacerbations and hospitalizations. Each treatment regimen should be patient-specific, based on CAT and/or mMRC score and risk of exacerbations (see the ABCD assessment tool and treatment recommendations in the table to the right).

Bronchodilators are the first-line treatment for all patients. A short-acting beta-2 agonist (SABA) and/or short-acting muscarinic antagonist (SAMA) can be used as needed. If regular use is required, long-acting beta-2 agonists (LABAs) and/or long-acting muscarinic antagonists (LAMAs) are preferred. Combination treatment is often required; in this case, use of two bronchodilators (e.g., LABA plus LAMA) is generally preferred.

An inhaled corticosteroid (ICS) is only recommended in select patients with a history of exacerbations and high eosinophil counts (a marker of inflammation). ICS products are discussed in the Asthma chapter. Adding an ICS has been shown to improve symptoms, lung function, quality of life and exacerbation frequency, though there is a risk of pneumonia. The combination of ICS/LAMA/LABA has mortality benefit compared to LABA/LAMA in patients with symptomatic COPD and a history of exacerbations. Other, less commonly used treatments include the phosphodiesterase-4 (PDE-4) inhibitor (roflumilast) and azithromycin, which are used in only the most severe cases. Theophylline is not recommended unless long-acting bronchodilators are unavailable or unaffordable. Similarly, long-term monotherapy with oral steroids is not recommended.

INITIAL PHARMACOLOGIC THERAPY

The ABCD assessment determines the patient's group and initial treatment.

PATIENT GROUP	RECOMMENDED TREATMENT
A	A bronchodilator: SABA* PRN, SAMA* PRN, LABA or LAMA
B	LAMA or LABA
C	LAMA**
D	LAMA or LAMA + LABA (if highly symptomatic) or LABA + ICS (if eosinophils ≥ 300 cells/μL)

*Combination treatment with SABA/SAMA improves FEV1 and symptoms compared to monotherapy with either agent.

**LAMAs are preferred over LABAs in group C as they have been shown to have a greater impact on exacerbation rates.

ESCALATION OF TREATMENT

An assessment of inhaler use, non-pharmacologic approaches, symptoms and exacerbations is repeated at each follow-up visit. If there was an appropriate response to treatment, no medication changes are necessary. If the response was not appropriate, treatment should be escalated based on the primary concern (dyspnea or exacerbations).

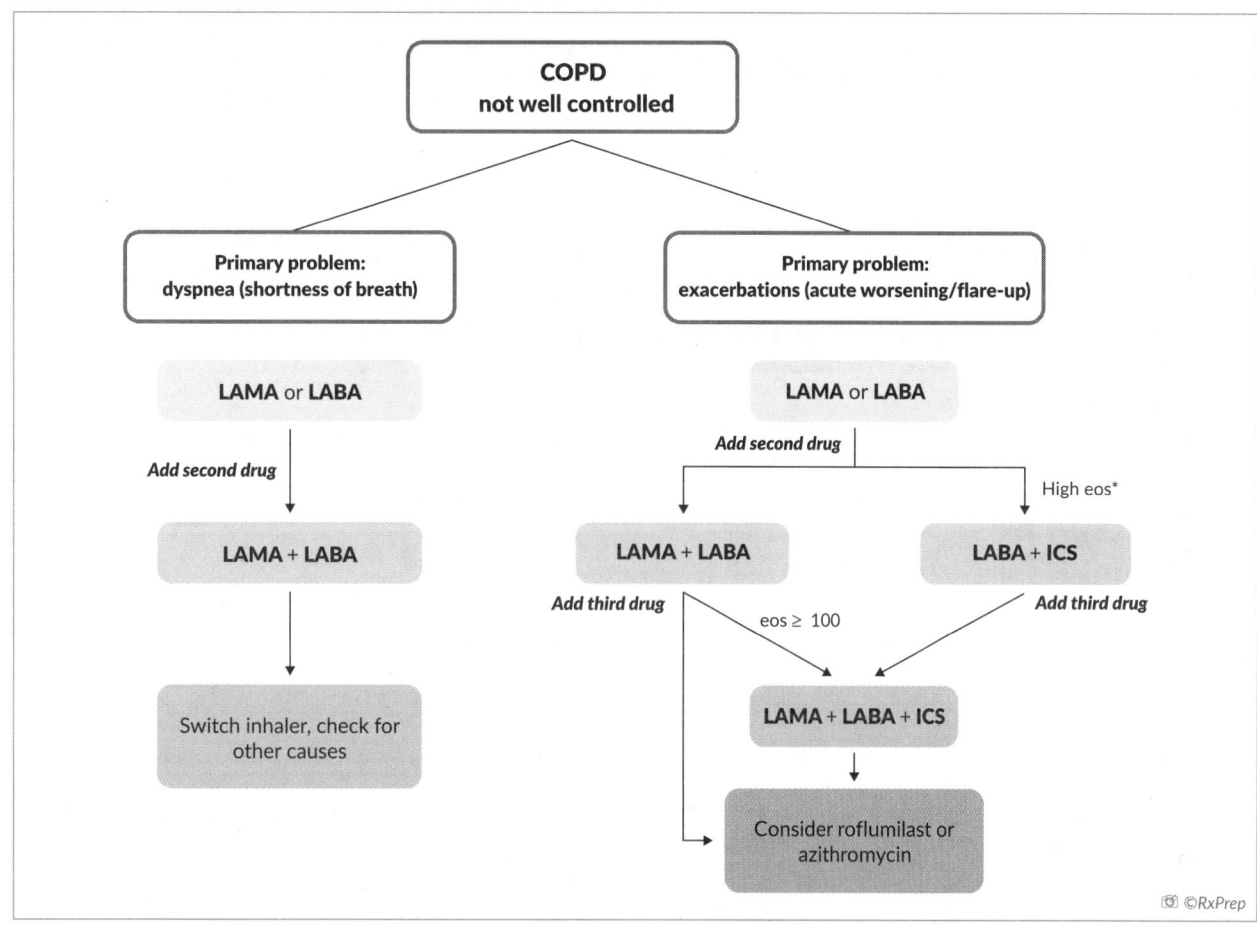

Eos = blood eosinophils (cells/ µL)
*eos ≥ 300, or eos ≥ 100 with ≥ 2 moderate exacerbations/1 hospitalization

COPD EXACERBATIONS

COPD exacerbations can be caused by respiratory tract infections (viral or bacterial) or other factors, such as increased air pollution. They are typically treated with a SABA, with or without a SAMA, plus an injectable or oral systemic steroid. If there is increased sputum purulence, sputum volume or dyspnea, or if mechanical ventilation is required, antibiotics should be used (see the Infectious Diseases II chapter).

INHALER PRODUCTS

There are two categories of inhalers: metered-dose inhalers (MDIs) and dry powder inhalers (DPIs). The difference between these two types is reviewed in the Asthma chapter. Poor adherence and incorrect use of inhalers are common concerns in the management of COPD and can lead to decreased quality of life, worsened health outcomes and increased frequency of exacerbations and hospitalizations. To improve adherence, many inhaled medications are available in combination products. Consult the Asthma chapter for a list of maintenance inhalers that are indicated in asthma vs. COPD. A comprehensive review of appropriate technique is shown for select inhalers at the end of this chapter and the Asthma chapter.

MUSCARINIC ANTAGONISTS/ANTICHOLINERGICS

Muscarinic antagonists (also called anticholinergics) cause <u>bronchodilation</u> by blocking the constricting action of acetylcholine at M3 muscarinic receptors in bronchial smooth muscle. Medications in this class are generally well tolerated.

DRUG	DOSING	SAFETY/SIDE EFFECTS/MONITORING
Short-acting muscarinic antagonist (SAMA)		**WARNINGS** Use with caution in patients with narrow-angle glaucoma, myasthenia gravis, urinary retention, benign prostatic hyperplasia and bladder neck obstruction
Ipratropium bromide *(Atrovent HFA)* 17 mcg/inh	<u>MDI: 2 inhalations QID</u>	
Nebulizer solution 0.02%	Nebulizer: 0.5 mg TID-QID	**SIDE EFFECTS** <u>Dry mouth</u>, upper respiratory tract infections (nasopharyngitis, sinusitis), cough, bitter taste
+ albuterol *(Combivent Respimat)* 20 mcg ipratropium + 100 mcg albuterol/inh	<u>MDI: 1 inhalation QID</u>	**MONITORING** S/sx at each visit, <u>smoking status</u>, <u>COPD questionnaires, annual spirometry</u>
Nebulizer solution 0.5 mg ipratropium + 2.5 mg albuterol per 3 mL	Nebulizer: 3 mL QID	
Long-acting muscarinic antagonists (LAMAs)		**NOTES** Avoid spraying in the eyes
Tiotropium		*HandiHaler* devices are <u>DPIs</u> that come with a <u>capsule</u> that is placed into the device; <u>do not swallow the capsules</u> by mouth
Spiriva HandiHaler 18 mcg capsule	<u>DPI: 1 capsule via *HandiHaler* device daily</u> (requires 2 puffs)	
Spiriva Respimat 2.5 mcg/inh	<u>MDI: 2 inhalations daily</u>	*Pressair* devices are <u>DPIs</u> that have an indicator window that turns from <u>green to red</u> if the dose was inhaled properly
+ olodaterol *(Stiolto Respimat)*		
Aclidinium *(Tudorza Pressair)* 400 mcg/inh	<u>DPI: 1 inhalation BID</u>	
+ formoterol *(Duaklir Pressair)*		
Glycopyrrolate *(Lonhala Magnair)* 25 mcg/inh nebulizer solution	Nebulizer: 25 mcg BID	
+ formoterol *(Bevespi Aerosphere)*	MDI: 2 inhalations BID	
+ formoterol/budesonide *(Breztri Aerosphere)*		
Revefenacin *(Yupelri)* 175 mcg/inh nebulizer solution	Nebulizer: 175 mcg (1 unit-dose vial) daily	
Umeclidinium *(Incruse Ellipta)* 62.5 mcg/inh	<u>DPI: 1 inhalation daily</u>	
+ vilanterol *(Anoro Ellipta)*		
+ vilanterol/fluticasone *(Trelegy Ellipta)*		

BETA-2 AGONISTS

These bind to beta-2 receptors in the lung, causing <u>relaxation of bronchial smooth muscle and bronchodilation</u>. LABAs can be used as <u>monotherapy only for COPD</u> due to the serious risks associated with use in asthma (see Boxed Warning). SABAs, which are frequently used for other reversible airway diseases, are discussed in more detail in the Asthma chapter.

DRUG	DOSING	SAFETY/SIDE EFFECTS/MONITORING
Long-acting beta-2 agonists (LABAs)		**BOXED WARNINGS** LABAs increase the risk of asthma-related deaths when used alone; they should only be used in asthma patients who are currently taking an inhaled corticosteroid but are not adequately controlled
Salmeterol (Serevent Diskus) 50 mcg/inh **+ fluticasone (Advair Diskus,** Wixela Inhub**)**	<u>DPI</u>: 1 inhalation BID	
Formoterol (Perforomist) 20 mcg/2 mL nebulizer solution **+ budesonide (Symbicort)** + aclidinium (Duaklir Pressair) + glycopyrrolate (Bevespi Aerosphere) + glycopyrrolate/budesonide (Breztri Aerosphere)	Nebulizer: 20 mcg BID <u>MDI</u>: 2 inhalations BID DPI: 1 inhalation BID	**CONTRAINDICATIONS** Status asthmaticus, acute episodes of asthma or COPD, monotherapy in the treatment of asthma **SIDE EFFECTS** <u>Nervousness, tremor, tachycardia, palpitations, hyperglycemia, ↓ K, cough</u>
Arformoterol (Brovana) 15 mcg/2 mL nebulizer solution	Nebulizer: 15 mcg BID	**MONITORING** S/sx at each visit, <u>smoking status, COPD questionnaires, annual spirometry</u>
Olodaterol (Striverdi Respimat) 2.5 mcg/inh + tiotropium (Stiolto Respimat)	<u>MDI</u>: 2 inhalations daily	**NOTES** <u>Arformoterol</u> contains the <u>R-isomer of formoterol</u>
Vilanterol (only in combination products) 25 mcg/inh **+ fluticasone (Breo Ellipta)** + umeclidinium (Anoro Ellipta) + umeclidinium/fluticasone (Trelegy Ellipta)	DPI: 1 inhalation daily	<u>ICS-containing products: rinse mouth with water and spit</u> to <u>prevent oral candidiasis</u> (thrush)

PHOSPHODIESTERASE-4 INHIBITOR

<u>Roflumilast</u> is a <u>PDE-4 inhibitor</u> that ↑ cAMP levels, leading to a <u>reduction in lung inflammation</u>. This medication should always be used in combination with at least one long-acting bronchodilator; its use is reserved for patients with very severe COPD, chronic bronchitis and a history of exacerbations.

DRUG	DOSING	SAFETY/SIDE EFFECTS/MONITORING
Roflumilast (Daliresp) Tablet	Start 250 mcg PO daily for 4 weeks (to improve tolerability), then 500 mcg PO daily	**CONTRAINDICATIONS** <u>Moderate to severe liver impairment</u> **WARNINGS** Psychiatric events (depression, mood changes) including suicidality **SIDE EFFECTS** <u>Diarrhea, weight loss</u>, nausea, ↓ appetite, insomnia, HA **MONITORING** S/sx at each visit, LFTs, smoking status, COPD questionnaires, annual spirometry

Roflumilast Drug Interactions

Roflumilast is a substrate of CYP450 3A4 and 1A2. Use with strong enzyme inducers (e.g., carbamazepine, phenobarbital, phenytoin, rifampin) is not recommended. Use with CYP3A4 inhibitors or dual CYP3A4 and CYP1A2 inhibitors (e.g., erythromycin, ketoconazole, fluvoxamine, cimetidine) will ↑ roflumilast levels.

KEY COUNSELING POINTS

SELECT METERED-DOSE INHALERS

Ipratropium bromide (Atrovent HFA)

STEP 1	STEP 2	STEP 3
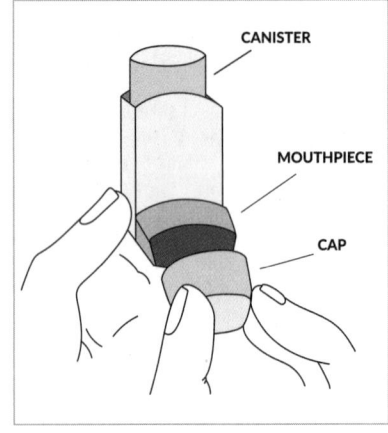	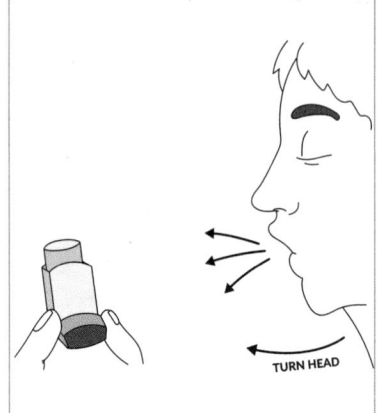	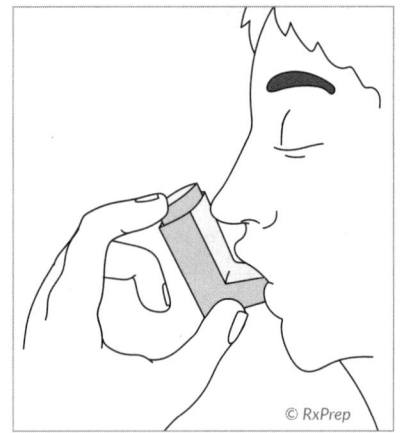
Make sure the canister is fully inserted into the actuator (if it comes separately). The *Atrovent HFA* plastic actuator should only be used with the *Atrovent HFA* canister. Remove the protective dust cap from the mouthpiece and check mouthpiece for foreign objects prior to use. You do not have to shake *Atrovent HFA* before using it.	Breathe out fully through your mouth. Holding the inhaler upright (as shown in the picture), place the mouthpiece into your mouth and close your lips around it. Keep your eyes closed so that no medication will be sprayed into your eyes.	While breathing in slowly and deeply through your mouth, press the top of the canister all the way down with your index finger. Hold your breath as long as possible, up to 10 seconds, then breathe normally. If another inhalation is needed, wait at least 15 seconds and repeat Steps 1-3. Place cap back on the mouthpiece after use.

TO PRIME

Spray 2 times away from the face. Prime again if > 3 days from last use.

TO CLEAN

To prevent medication buildup and blockage, remove the metal canister (do not let this get wet) and rinse the mouthpiece only under warm running water for 30 seconds. Shake to remove excess water and let air dry. Clean at least weekly.

Respimat products:

- **Albuterol/Ipratropium (*Combivent Respimat*)**

- **Olodaterol (*Striverdi Respimat*)**

- **Olodaterol/Tiotropium (*Stiolto Respimat*)**

- **Tiotropium (*Spiriva Respimat*)**

STEP 1	STEP 2	STEP 3
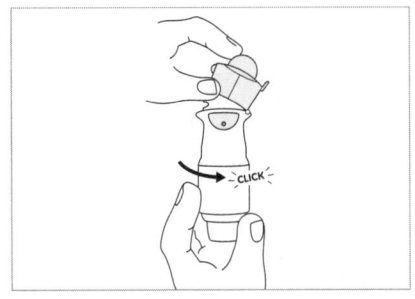	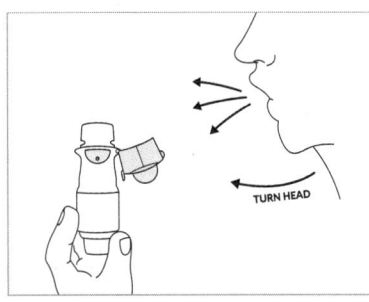	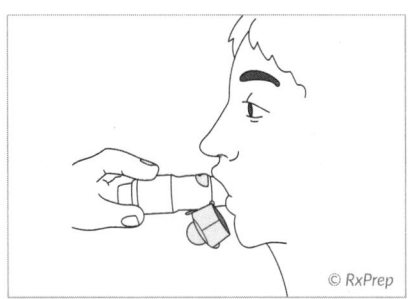
Hold the inhaler upright with the cap closed. Turn the clear base in the direction of the arrows on the label until it clicks (half a turn).	Open the cap until it snaps fully open. Turn head away from the inhaler and breathe out slowly and fully.	Close lips around the end of the mouthpiece without covering the air vents. While taking a slow, deep breath through your mouth, press the dose release button and continue to breathe in slowly. Hold your breath as long as possible, up to 10 seconds. Close the cap when finished.

To simplify these steps for patient counseling, think: *TOP*

T	**O**	**P**
TURN	**OPEN**	**PRESS**
the clear base	the cap and close your lips around the mouthpiece	the dose-release button and inhale

TO ASSEMBLE DEVICE FOR FIRST USE	TO PRIME	TO CLEAN
With the cap closed, press the safety catch while pulling off the clear base. Do not touch the piercing element located inside the bottom of the clear base. Write the discard by date on the inhaler's label (which is 3 months from the date the cartridge is inserted). Push the narrow end of the cartridge into the inhaler and push down firmly until it clicks into place. Put the clear base back into place until it clicks. Do not remove the clear base or the cartridge once assembled.	Hold the inhaler upright with the cap closed. Turn the clear base in the direction of the arrows on the label until it clicks (half a turn). Flip the cap until it snaps fully open. Point the inhaler toward the ground away from your face. Press the dose release button. Close cap. Repeat these steps over again until a spray is visible. Once the spray is visible, repeat the steps 3 more times to make sure the inhaler is prepared for use. If inhaler is not used for > 3 days, release 1 spray toward the ground to prepare the inhaler. If inhaler has not been used for > 21 days, follow priming instructions above for initial use.	Clean the mouthpiece, including the metal part inside the mouthpiece, with a damp cloth or tissue weekly.

SELECT DRY POWDER INHALERS

Tiotropium (Spiriva HandiHaler)

STEP 1	STEP 2	STEP 3	STEP 4	STEP 5
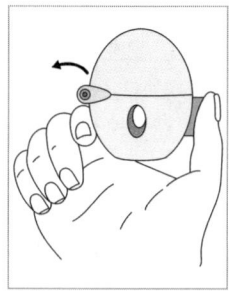	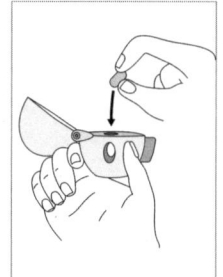	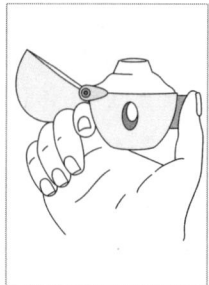	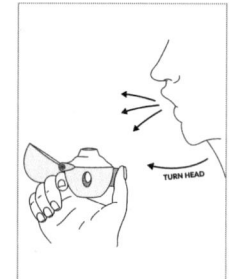	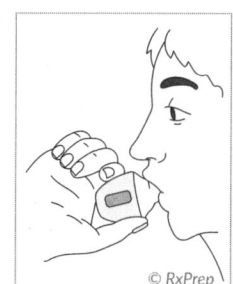
Open the HandiHaler device by pressing on the green button and lifting the cap upwards. Open the mouthpiece by pulling the mouthpiece ridge up and away from the base so the center chamber is showing.	Remove the Spiriva capsule from the blister pack and insert it into the chamber. Close the mouthpiece firmly against the gray base until you hear a click.	Press the green piercing button once until it is flat (flush) against the base, then release. Do not shake the device.	Turn head away from the inhaler and breathe out fully.	Raise the HandiHaler to your mouth in a horizontal position and close your lips around the mouthpiece. Breathe in deeply and fully. You should hear or feel the Spiriva capsule vibrate (rattle). Remove inhaler from your mouth and hold your breath for a few seconds. Breathe normally. To get the full dose, you must inhale twice from each capsule. Repeat the last two steps, breathing out fully again and breathing in deeply and fully through the inhaler. Tip out the used capsule into a trash can after 2 inhalations. Do not touch the capsule. Close the lid of the device.

© RxPrep

TO CLEAN

Clean inhaler as needed. Rinse inhaler with warm water, pressing the green button a few times so the chamber and piercing needle are under the running water. Make sure any powder build-up is removed. Let air dry. It takes 24 hours to air dry the HandiHaler device after it is cleaned.

Aclidinium *(Tudorza Pressair)*

STEP 1	STEP 2	STEP 3	STEP 4
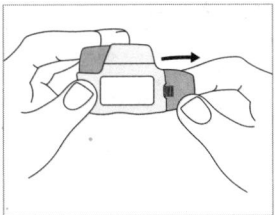	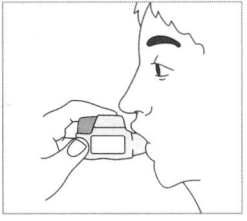	(illustration)	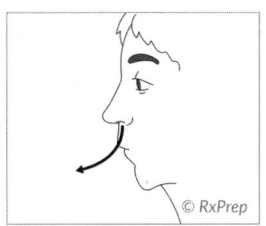
Remove the protective cap by lightly squeezing the arrows marked on each side of the cap and pulling outwards. Check the mouthpiece for foreign objects.	Hold the inhaler with the mouthpiece facing you and the green button straight above. Before putting into your mouth, press the green button all the way down and release. Check the control window; the dose is ready for inhalation if it changed from red to green. Breathe out completely, away from the inhaler.	Put your lips tightly around the mouthpiece. Breathe in quickly and deeply through your mouth. Breathe in until you hear a "click" sound and keep breathing in to get the full dose. Do not hold down the green button while breathing in.	Remove the inhaler from your mouth and hold your breath for as long as comfortable. Then breathe out slowly through your nose. Place the protective cap on the inhaler. Check that the control window has turned to red which indicates the full dose has been inhaled correctly.

TO CLEAN

Routine cleaning is not required. If needed, wipe the outside of the mouthpiece with a dry tissue or paper towel.

Ellipta products:

- **Fluticasone *(Arnuity Ellipta)***
- **Fluticasone/Vilanterol *(Breo Ellipta)***
- **Umeclidinium *(Incruse Ellipta)***
- **Umeclidinium/Vilanterol *(Anoro Ellipta)***
- **Umeclidinium/Vilanterol/Fluticasone *(Trelegy Ellipta)***

STEP 1	STEP 2	STEP 3
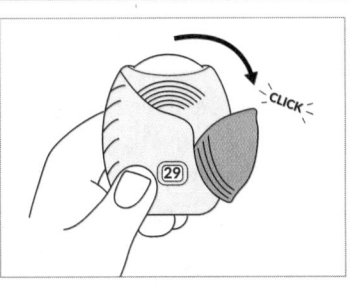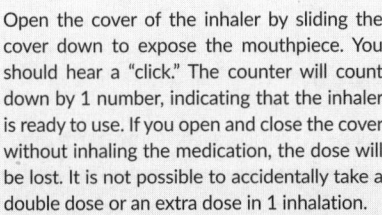	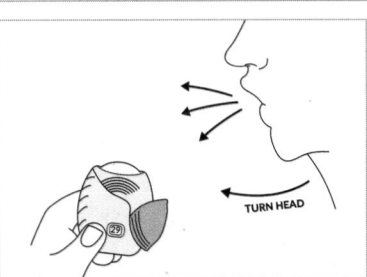	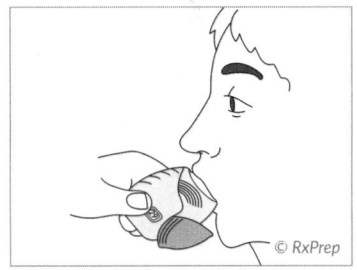
Open the cover of the inhaler by sliding the cover down to expose the mouthpiece. You should hear a "click." The counter will count down by 1 number, indicating that the inhaler is ready to use. If you open and close the cover without inhaling the medication, the dose will be lost. It is not possible to accidentally take a double dose or an extra dose in 1 inhalation.	While holding the inhaler away from your mouth, breathe out fully. Do not breathe out into the mouthpiece.	Put the mouthpiece between your lips and close your lips firmly around it. Take one long, steady, deep breath in through your mouth. Do not block the air vent with your fingers. Remove inhaler from mouth and hold your breath for 3-4 seconds or as long as comfortable. Breathe out slowly and gently. Close the inhaler. For ICS products: rinse your mouth with water and spit out the water to prevent thrush.

TO CLEAN

Routine cleaning is not required. If needed, you can clean the mouthpiece using a dry tissue before you close the cover.

Select Guidelines/References

Global Strategy for the Diagnosis, Management and Prevention of COPD, 2022 Report. Global Initiative for Chronic Obstructive Lung Disease (GOLD). http://www.goldcopd.org (accessed 2022 Feb 2).

THE "5 A'S" MODEL FOR TREATING TOBACCO USE AND DEPENDENCE

Ask about tobacco use
Identify and document tobacco use status for every patient at every visit.

Advise to quit
In a clear, strong and personalized manner, urge every tobacco user to quit.

Assess willingness to make a quit attempt
Is the tobacco user willing to make a quit attempt at this time (e.g., in the next month)?

Assist in quit attempt
For the patient willing to make a quit attempt, offer medication (if appropriate) and provide, or refer for, behavioral counseling.

For patients unwilling to quit at this time, provide motivational interventions designed to encourage a future quit attempt.

For the recent quitter, or any patient with remaining challenges, provide relapse prevention.

Arrange follow up
For the patient willing to make a quit attempt, arrange for follow up visits within the first week after the quit date.

For patients unwilling to make a quit attempt at this time, address tobacco dependence and willingness to quit at the next clinic visit.

CONTENT LEGEND

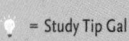 = Study Tip Gal   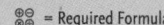 = Required Formula

iStock.com/vchal

CHAPTER 43
TOBACCO CESSATION

BACKGROUND

Smoking is the leading cause of preventable death in the U.S. and a known risk factor for heart disease, stroke, pregnancy complications, COPD, multiple cancers and many other diseases. In some cases, disease risk (e.g., lung cancer) is related to an individual's pack-year smoking history, which can be calculated using the formula below (e.g., a patient who has smoked 2 packs of cigarettes per day for 10 years has a 20 pack-year smoking history).

Pack-year smoking history	=	cigarette packs / day x number of years smoked

Tobacco dependence is a chronic disease that often requires repeated interventions and multiple attempts to quit. Effective treatments exist that can significantly increase the rates of long-term abstinence. It is essential for healthcare providers to ask patients about tobacco use, document the response and provide treatment (see the "5 A's" Model). A national network of tobacco quitlines is available by telephone for patients at 1-800-QUIT-NOW (1-800-784-8669).

TREATMENT PRINCIPLES

Counseling is an important component of tobacco cessation treatment, and two methods that are especially effective are behavioral counseling (e.g., problem-solving skills training) and social support. There is a strong correlation between counseling intensity (length and number of counseling sessions) and quitting success.

Medications should be encouraged for all patients attempting to quit, except when medically contraindicated. Medications reduce withdrawal symptoms, including anxiety, irritability, depression, insomnia, poor concentration, restlessness, increased appetite and an urge to smoke (cravings). The combination of counseling and medication is more effective than using either one alone.

There are several effective, first-line options:

- Five nicotine replacement therapies (NRTs): patch, gum, lozenge, inhaler or nasal spray.

- Two non-nicotine drugs: bupropion and varenicline.

Combining two drugs, such as using a long-acting nicotine patch with a short-acting NRT product (e.g., gum, lozenge, inhaler or spray) or a nicotine patch with bupropion sustained-release (SR), is effective and can be used first-line.

ELECTRONIC CIGARETTES

The risks and benefits of electronic nicotine delivery systems (e.g., electronic cigarettes or e-cigarettes) continue to be investigated. The nicotine content varies between products, and there is a risk for nicotine addiction. Carcinogens and other damaging chemicals can be present in the e-cigarette vapors. There is a strong link, for example, between vitamin E acetate exposure and the outbreaks of e-cigarette, or vaping, product-use associated lung injury (EVALI).

Due to health concerns, e-cigarettes are not recommended for smoking cessation. The FDA recommends the use of smoking cessation medications to help quit the use of tobacco products.

EXCEPTIONS TO DRUG TREATMENT

Treatment guidelines recommend behavioral counseling over drugs for several patient populations: pregnant women, adolescents, smokeless tobacco users (e.g., chewing tobacco) and "light" smokers (e.g., < 10 cigarettes a day).

SMOKING AND DRUG INTERACTIONS

The non-nicotine chemicals in tobacco smoke induce CYP450 enzymes, primarily CYP450 1A2. Smokers who quit no longer have CYP1A2 induction and, as a result, can experience side effects from supratherapeutic levels of caffeine, theophylline, fluvoxamine, olanzapine, clozapine and the R-isomer (less potent isomer) of warfarin. Smoking increases the risk of bleeding with warfarin and clopidogrel.

Women ≥ 35 years of age who smoke should not take estrogen-containing oral contraceptives due to an increased risk of cardiovascular events.

VACCINATIONS IN SMOKERS

Smokers age 19 – 64 years should receive a pneumococcal vaccine and an annual influenza vaccine. Additional immunizations depend on age or other risk factors (see the Immunizations chapter).

DRUG TREATMENT

NICOTINE REPLACEMENT THERAPY (NRT)

DRUG	DOSING	SAFETY/SIDE EFFECTS/MONITORING
Nicotine patch (**NicoDerm CQ**, others) OTC	Initial dose is based on the number of cigarettes smoked per day See Study Tip Gal on the following page	**WARNINGS** Avoid in immediate post-MI period, life-threatening arrhythmias, severe or worsening angina and pregnancy* Inhaler/nasal spray: avoid in asthma, COPD and other chronic respiratory diseases
Nicotine gum (**Nicorette**, others) OTC	Initial dose is based on the timing of the first cigarette smoked upon waking	**SIDE EFFECTS** Insomnia, headache, dizziness, nervousness, dyspepsia Patch: vivid dreams, skin irritation
Nicotine lozenge (**Nicorette Mini**, others) OTC	See Study Tip Gal on the following page	Inhaler: mouth and throat irritation, cough, rhinitis Nasal spray: nasal irritation, watery eyes, sneezing, transient changes in taste and smell
Nicotine inhaler (*Nicotrol*) Rx	6-16 cartridges daily for up to 12 wks, then taper frequency of use over 6-12 wks Use up to 6 months	**NOTES** The FDA prohibits sale of nicotine products to individuals < 18 years of age; identification required to purchase Combination therapy with the patch and short-acting NRT (e.g., gum or lozenge) to reduce cravings is most effective
Nicotine nasal spray (*Nicotrol NS*) Rx	1 dose = 1 spray in each nostril; use 1-2 doses per hour, ↑ PRN for symptom relief Min: 8 doses/day Max: 5 doses/hr or 40 doses/day Use up to 3 months	Patch: highest adherence rate; remove before an MRI Gum and lozenge (sugar free): 4 mg strength can reduce or delay weight gain; acidic beverages/foods ↓ buccal absorption, do not eat/drink 15 minutes before or during use Inhaler: mimics the hand to mouth smoking action, providing a coping mechanism Nasal spray: fastest delivery and is useful for rapid relief of withdrawal symptoms; has the highest risk of dependence

*Package labeling warns of NRT use in these situations, but in practice, the decision is based on comparing the risks of smoking to the potential risks of NRT.

NICOTINE PATCH, GUM AND LOZENGE DOSING

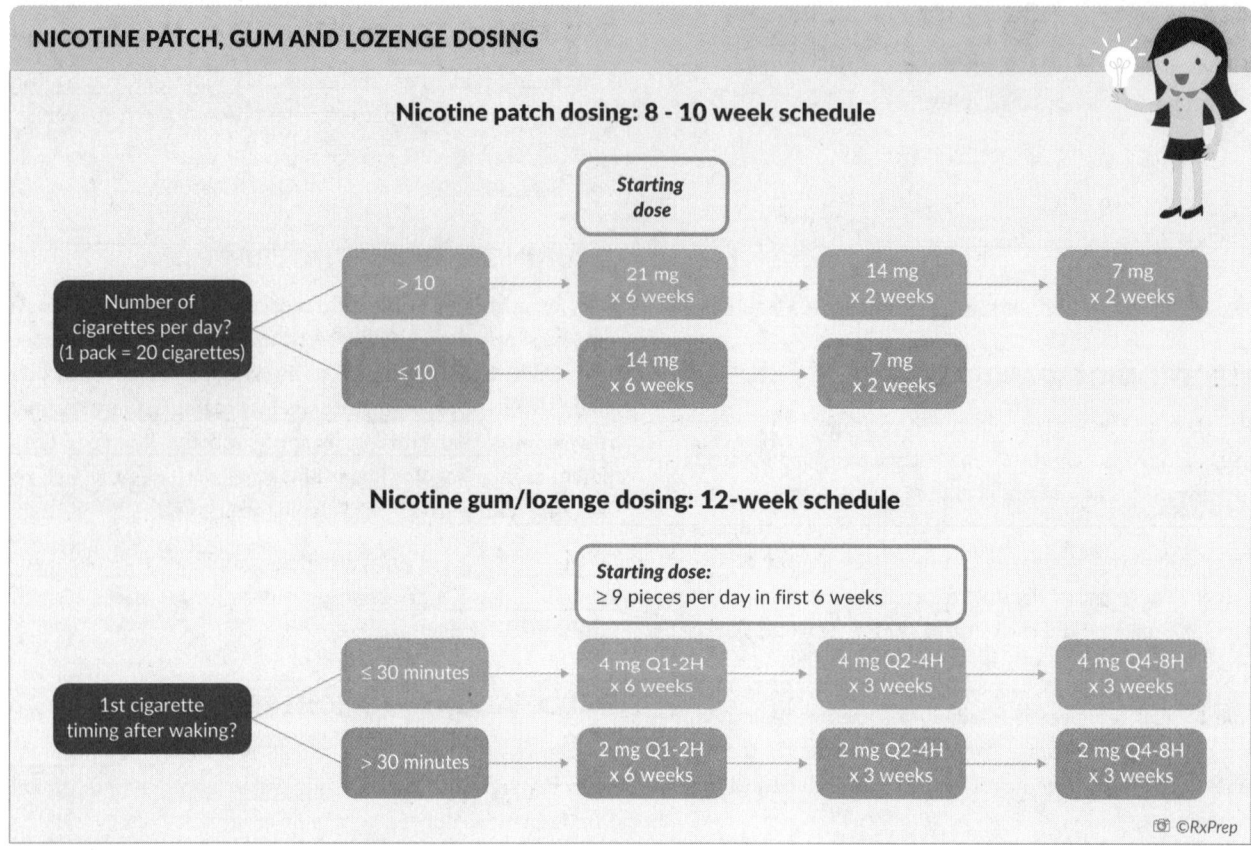

Nicotine patch dosing: 8 - 10 week schedule

Starting dose

Number of cigarettes per day? (1 pack = 20 cigarettes)

> 10 → 21 mg x 6 weeks → 14 mg x 2 weeks → 7 mg x 2 weeks

≤ 10 → 14 mg x 6 weeks → 7 mg x 2 weeks

Nicotine gum/lozenge dosing: 12-week schedule

Starting dose: ≥ 9 pieces per day in first 6 weeks

1st cigarette timing after waking?

≤ 30 minutes → 4 mg Q1-2H x 6 weeks → 4 mg Q2-4H x 3 weeks → 4 mg Q4-8H x 3 weeks

> 30 minutes → 2 mg Q1-2H x 6 weeks → 2 mg Q2-4H x 3 weeks → 2 mg Q4-8H x 3 weeks

©RxPrep

BUPROPION AND VARENICLINE

Bupropion blocks neuronal reuptake of dopamine and/or norepinephrine, resulting in reduced cravings and other withdrawal symptoms. Varenicline is a partial neuronal alpha-4 beta-2 nicotinic receptor agonist. It causes low-level stimulation of the receptor while blocking the ability of nicotine to bind. This relieves symptoms of nicotine withdrawal and inhibits the surges of dopamine responsible for the reinforcement and reward associated with smoking. Since both drugs work by reducing cravings, they are started before the quit date. These drugs do not need to be tapered when they are discontinued.

DRUG	DOSING	SAFETY/SIDE EFFECTS/MONITORING
Bupropion SR (Zyban*) Tablet For depression: **Wellbutrin SR,** **Wellbutrin XL,** *Aplenzin, Forfivo XL,* bupropion IR For seasonal affective disorder (SAD): **Wellbutrin XL,** *Aplenzin*	Start at least 1 week before quit date SR: 150 mg QAM for 3 days, then 150 mg BID Max dose: 300 mg/day Use up to 6 months	**BOXED WARNING** Increased risk of suicidal thinking and behavior in children, adolescents and young adults taking antidepressants **CONTRAINDICATIONS** Seizure disorder; history of anorexia/bulimia; concurrent use with MAO inhibitors, linezolid or IV methylene blue; abrupt discontinuation of ethanol or sedatives **WARNINGS** Serious neuropsychiatric events (e.g., mood changes, hallucinations, paranoia, aggression, anxiety), activation of mania/hypomania, hypertension, angle-closure glaucoma, rash (including SJS) **SIDE EFFECTS** Dry mouth, insomnia, tremors, weight loss, agitation, anxiety, tachycardia, headache, sweating, nausea/vomiting, constipation **NOTES** Do not use with other forms of bupropion (see Depression chapter for more information) Delays weight gain To ↓ insomnia, take the 1st dose upon waking up and the 2nd dose 8 hours after the 1st dose If no significant progress by week 7, consider discontinuation

DRUG	DOSING	SAFETY/SIDE EFFECTS/MONITORING
Varenicline (Chantix) Tablet *Chantix Starting Month Pak:* contains 0.5 mg tablets (11) and 1 mg tablets (42) *Chantix Continuing Month Pak:* contains 1 mg tablets *Tyrvaya* - nasal spray for dry eyes	<u>Start 1 week before quit date</u> Days 1-3: 0.5 mg daily Days 4-7: 0.5 mg BID Day 8 (quit date) and beyond: 1 mg BID CrCl < 30 mL/min: 0.5 mg daily titrated to max 0.5 mg BID Use for 12 weeks; can use another 12 weeks to maintain success	**WARNINGS** <u>Serious neuropsychiatric events</u> (e.g., agitation, depression, suicidal thoughts/behaviors), <u>seizures</u>, ↑ effects of alcohol, somnambulism (sleepwalking), accidental injury (e.g., traffic accidents), CVD risk, hypersensitivity reactions (e.g., angioedema, SJS) **SIDE EFFECTS** <u>Nausea</u> (~30%, dose-dependent), <u>insomnia, abnormal dreams, headache</u>, constipation, flatulence, vomiting **NOTES** To ↓ nausea, <u>take after eating with a full glass of water</u>; can reduce dose if needed To ↓ insomnia, take 2nd dose earlier than bedtime If unable to quit abruptly on day 8, decrease smoking by 50% in the first 4 weeks, an additional 50% in weeks 5-8, with complete cessation by week 12 Efficacy has not been demonstrated in those ≤ 16 years old (not recommended)

Brand discontinued but name still used in practice.

TREATMENT CONSIDERATIONS FOR TOBACCO CESSATION

- All smokers should be offered medications unless it is contraindicated, they are pregnant or they are an adolescent.
- The combination of the nicotine patch + gum, lozenge or bupropion is more effective than the patch alone.

WEIGHT GAIN	DEPRESSION	DENTURES	ASTHMA/COPD	SKIN CONDITION	SEIZURES
Use	**Use**	**Avoid**	**Avoid**	**Avoid**	**Avoid**
Gum, lozenge and bupropion SR (all delay weight gain)	Bupropion SR	Gum	Inhaler or spray	Patch	Bupropion, varenicline

---

KEY COUNSELING POINTS

See the Drug Formulations and Patient Counseling Chapter for counseling language/layman's terminology.

NICOTINE PATCH

NICOTINE PATCH ADMINISTRATION

- At the start of each day, remove a new patch from the pouch; save the pouch to throw away used patches.
- Remove the backing and apply the sticky side of the patch to a clean, dry and relatively hairless area of the skin; press the patch firmly onto the skin for ~10 seconds.
- Wear for 24 hours (especially if cravings begin when you wake up). If vivid dreams or trouble sleeping occur, remove the patch prior to bedtime (after about 16 hours) and apply a new one in the morning.
- Discard the patch by folding the sticky ends together, place it back in the pouch and put it in a trash can with a lid to keep away from children and pets.
- Wash your hands after applying (and removing) the patch.
- Rotate the application site; do not apply to the same site for at least one week. Skin reactions can occur but generally go away in a few days.
- Never cut the patch or wear more than one patch at a time.

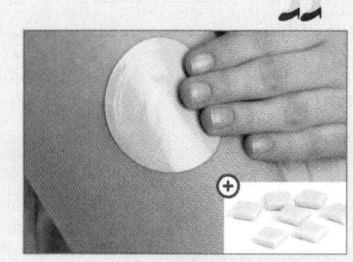

Use gum or lozenges to help with cravings while using the patch

NICOTINE GUM

HOW TO CHEW NICOTINE GUM
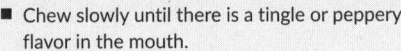

- Chew slowly until there is a tingle or peppery flavor in the mouth.
- Park it between the cheek and gum.
- When the tingle or flavor goes away, begin chewing slowly again until it returns, then park the gum again.
- Repeat until most of the flavor or tingle is gone (~30 minutes).
- Do not eat or drink 15 minutes before or during chewing.

NICOTINE LOZENGE

- Do not eat or drink for 15 minutes before or during use.
- Do not chew or swallow. Allow it to dissolve slowly. Move the lozenge from one side of the mouth to the other until it has completely dissolved (~20 – 30 minutes).
- May cause a warm or tingling sensation.
- Do not use more than one lozenge at a time or continuously use one lozenge after another.

NICOTINE INHALER

- Inhale deeply into the back of the throat or puff in short breaths.
- Each cartridge provides about 20 minutes of active puffing and is only good for one day after opening.
- Clean the mouthpiece with soap and water regularly.
- Keep at room temperature; cold temperatures reduce the amount of nicotine inhaled.

NICOTINE NASAL SPRAY

- Tilt head back slightly and spray once in each nostril while breathing through the mouth. Do not sniff, swallow or inhale through the nose.
- Can cause sneezing, coughing, watery eyes, runny nose and a hot peppery feeling in the back of the throat.

BUPROPION

- MedGuide required.
- Start taking one week before desired quit date.
- Can cause:
  - ❏ Suicidal ideation.
  - ❏ Insomnia (avoid near bedtime).
- Do not use if you have a seizure disorder, anorexia or bulimia.

VARENICLINE

- MedGuide required.
- Start taking one week before desired quit date.
- Can cause:
  - ❏ Suicidal ideation.
  - ❏ Insomnia.
  - ❏ Nausea.
- Can increase the effects of alcohol. Reduce the amount of alcohol consumed.

Select Guidelines/References

Barua RS, Rigotti NA, et al. 2018 ACC Expert Consensus Decision Pathway on Tobacco Cessation Treatment. *J Am Coll of Cardiol.* 2018;72:3332-65.

Treating Tobacco Use and Dependence: 2008 Update. Content last reviewed February 2020. Agency for Healthcare Research and Quality, Rockville, MD. http://www.ahrq.gov/prevention/guidelines/tobacco/index.html (accessed 2022 Jan 13).

ENDOCRINE CONDITIONS

CONTENTS

CONTENT LEGEND

  = Study Tip Gal   = Key Drug Guy   = Required Formula

CHAPTER 44
DIABETES

BACKGROUND

Diabetes is a common condition in the United States, affecting > 30 million Americans (just over 1 in 10). The central problem in all types of diabetes is that blood glucose (BG) remains high (hyperglycemia) due to decreased insulin secretion from the pancreas, decreased insulin sensitivity (i.e., how responsive cells are to insulin) or both. Chronic hyperglycemia can lead to damage throughout the body, including organ and nerve damage.

Patients with diabetes have abnormalities in how insulin is produced and used in the body. Insulin is a hormone produced by beta-cells (also called islet cells) in the pancreas. It is responsible for moving glucose out of the blood and into body cells to be used as energy. The glucose is either moved to muscle cells (primarily) for immediate use or stored for later use by liver cells (as glycogen, the quick glucose reserve) or adipose (fat) cells.

Insulin is counter-balanced by glucagon; they have opposite effects, as shown in the diagram below. Glucagon is produced by alpha-cells in the pancreas and works when BG is low. Glucagon pulls glucose back into the circulation by releasing glucose from glycogen. If glycogen is depleted, glucagon will signal fat cells to make ketones as an alternative energy source.

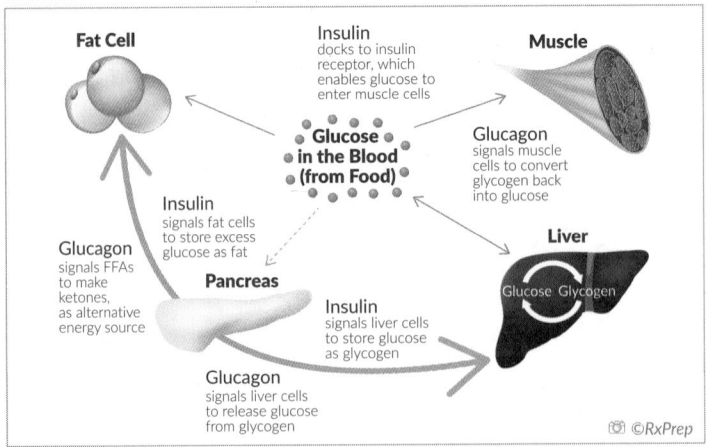

iStock.com/ttsz

TYPES OF DIABETES

TYPE 1 DIABETES

Type 1 diabetes (T1D) accounts for ~5% of all cases. It is caused by an autoimmune destruction of beta-cells in the pancreas. Once the beta-cells are destroyed, insulin cannot be produced. Without insulin, glucose cannot enter muscle cells. The body goes into starvation mode and starts to metabolize fat into ketones to use as an alternative energy source. Ketones are acidic. Very high ketone levels can cause diabetic ketoacidosis (DKA), which is a medical emergency (discussed later in this chapter).

Most T1D is diagnosed in children, but it can develop at any age. Family history is the biggest risk factor. In some patients, it is difficult to distinguish between type 1 and type 2 diabetes, especially early in the disease. The C-peptide test is used to determine if the patient is still producing insulin. C-peptide is released by the pancreas only when insulin is released. T1D is diagnosed when there is a very low or absent (undetectable) C-peptide level.

Patients with T1D must be treated with insulin and should be screened for other autoimmune disorders (e.g., thyroid disorders, celiac disease).

TYPE 2 DIABETES

Type 2 diabetes (T2D) accounts for ~95% of all cases and is due to both insulin resistance (decreased insulin sensitivity) and insulin deficiency. The pancreatic beta-cells produce less insulin over time as they become damaged. Hyperglycemia develops gradually, which is why the onset of T2D often goes unnoticed. T2D is strongly associated with obesity, physical inactivity, family history and the presence of other comorbid conditions (see Risk Factors section). T2D is usually diagnosed in older patients and can be managed with lifestyle modifications alone (in a small number of patients) or in combination with oral and/or injectable medications.

PREDIABETES

Prediabetes means there is an increased risk of developing diabetes. In prediabetes the BG is higher than normal, but not high enough for a diabetes diagnosis. Following dietary and exercise recommendations reduces the risk of progression from prediabetes to diabetes.

Metformin can be used to help improve BG levels, especially in patients with a BMI ≥ 35 kg/m², age < 60 years and women with a history of gestational diabetes mellitus (GDM). Annual monitoring for development of diabetes and treatment of modifiable cardiovascular disease (CVD) risk factors are recommended.

DIABETES IN PREGNANCY

There are two types of diabetes in pregnancy:

- Diabetes that was present prior to becoming pregnant, or
- Diabetes that developed during pregnancy (GDM)

In both types, the BG goals during pregnancy are more stringent than the non-pregnant population with diabetes (see Study Tip Gal titled Glycemic Targets in Diabetes). Babies born to mothers with hyperglycemia during pregnancy are larger than normal (macrosomia) and are at high risk for developing obesity and diabetes later in life. Women with GDM are at a higher risk of developing T2D later in life.

Most pregnant women are tested for GDM at 24 – 28 weeks gestation using the oral glucose tolerance test (OGTT) (see Diagnosis section). Hyperglycemia, if present, should be treated first with lifestyle modifications (diet and exercise). If medication is needed, insulin is preferred. Metformin and glyburide are sometimes used.

SCREENING & DIAGNOSIS

RISK FACTORS

The presence of multiple risk factors increases the likelihood of prediabetes and T2D. Major risk factors include:

- Physical inactivity
- Overweight (BMI ≥ 25 kg/m² or ≥ 23 in Asian-Americans)
- High-risk race or ethnicity: African-American, Asian-American, Latino/Hispanic-American, Native American or Pacific Islander
- History of gestational diabetes
- A1C ≥ 5.7%
- First-degree relative with diabetes (sibling or parent)
- HDL < 35 mg/dL or TG > 250 mg/dL
- Hypertension (≥ 140/90 mmHg or taking BP medication)
- CVD history or smoking history
- Conditions that cause insulin resistance (e.g., acanthosis nigricans, polycystic ovary syndrome)

SYMPTOMS

The classic symptoms of hyperglycemia include:

- Polyuria (excessive urination)
- Polyphagia (excessive hunger or increased appetite)
- Polydipsia (excessive thirst)

Other symptoms include fatigue, blurry vision, erectile dysfunction and vaginal fungal infections.

In T1D, DKA is commonly the initial presentation due to the total deficiency in insulin.

SCREENING

Risk for diabetes increases with age. Everyone, even those with no other risk factors, should be tested beginning at 35 years old.

All asymptomatic children, adolescents and adults who are overweight (BMI ≥ 25 or ≥ 23 in Asian-Americans) with at least one other risk factor (e.g., physical inactivity) should be tested. If the result is normal, repeat testing every 3 years.

DIAGNOSIS

There are three types of tests used to identify if prediabetes or diabetes is present:

1. Hemoglobin A1C (or simply A1C) indicates the average BG over approximately the past 3 months.

2. Fasting plasma glucose (FPG) gives the BG at that moment, and is taken after fasting for ≥ 8 hours.

3. The OGTT determines how well glucose is tolerated by measuring the BG level 2 hours after drinking a liquid that is high in sugar (glucose).

No single test is preferred. The criteria for diagnosing diabetes are shown in the Study Tip Gal below. A positive test should be confirmed with a second abnormal test result from either the same sample or a new sample, unless there is a clear clinical diagnosis (e.g., classic symptoms of hyperglycemia plus a random BG ≥ 200 mg/dL).

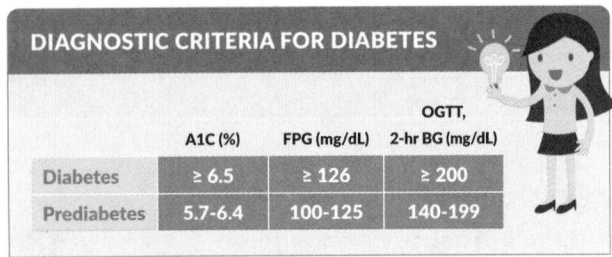

DIAGNOSTIC CRITERIA FOR DIABETES

	A1C (%)	FPG (mg/dL)	OGTT, 2-hr BG (mg/dL)
Diabetes	≥ 6.5	≥ 126	≥ 200
Prediabetes	5.7-6.4	100-125	140-199

TREATMENT GOALS

The treatment goals for A1C, preprandial glucose (before meals) and postprandial glucose (PPG, which is BG measured after eating) are shown in the Study Tip Gal below.

GLYCEMIC TARGETS IN DIABETES

	A1C (%)	Preprandial (mg/dL)	1-hr PPG (mg/dL)	2-hr PPG (mg/dL)
Not Pregnant	< 7*	80-130		< 180
Pregnant		≤ 95	≤ 140	≤ 120

*An A1C goal of < 6.5% may be acceptable if it can be reached without significant hypoglycemia. A less-stringent goal of < 8% may be appropriate (e.g., if patient has severe hypoglycemia, or a limited life-expectancy).

Typically, the A1C is measured with a blood sample sent to a lab. Point-of-care A1C test kits provide immediate results and can be used to assess blood glucose control but are not recommended for diagnosis. Patients can measure their own BG using a glucose meter or with a continuous glucose monitoring (CGM) device (discussed later).

Testing Frequency

Glycemic control (A1C or another test) should be measured:

- Quarterly (every 3 months) if not yet at goal

- Biannually (every 6 months, or twice per year) if at goal

Interpreting the A1C with the eAG

It can be difficult to understand how an A1C value correlates with BG values measured on a glucose meter. The estimated average glucose (eAG) is an interpretation of the A1C value that makes it appear similar to a glucose meter value.

- An A1C of 6% is equivalent to an eAG of 126 mg/dL. Each additional 1% increases the eAG by ~28 mg/dL.

Example: an A1C of 7% is 126 + 28 ≅ 154 eAG.

LIFESTYLE MODIFICATIONS

Lifestyle modifications, used alone or in combination with medications, are an essential component of all diabetes care plans. The modifications and goals listed below help lower BG, blood pressure and cholesterol.

Weight Loss

- Goal waist circumference is < 35 inches for females and < 40 inches for males.

- Overweight or obese patients should be encouraged to lose > 5% of their body weight. Medications and/or surgery may be needed to achieve this (see Weight Loss chapter).

Individualized Medical Nutrition Therapy

- Consume natural forms of carbohydrates and sugars (i.e., from vegetables, fruits, whole grains, legumes, dairy).

- Avoid alcohol or drink in moderation.

- Patients with T1D should use carbohydrate-counting, where the prandial (mealtime) insulin dose is adjusted to the carbohydrate intake. A carbohydrate serving is measured as 15 grams, which is approximately one small piece of fruit, 1 slice of bread or ⅓ cup of cooked rice/pasta.

Physical Activity

- Perform at least 150 minutes of moderate-intensity aerobic activity per week spread over at least 3 days.

- Reduce sedentary (long hours of sitting) habits by standing every 30 minutes, at a minimum.

Smoking Cessation

- Encourage all patients who smoke to quit (see Tobacco Cessation chapter).

COMPREHENSIVE CARE

In addition to glycemic control, treatment is aimed at preventing the long-term complications of diabetes. Left untreated, diabetes damages nearly all parts of the body. Complications are categorized as microvascular (small vessel) or macrovascular (large vessel), as shown in the Study Tip Gal to the right.

Diabetes is the top cause of lower-extremity amputations, kidney failure and blindness. The primary cause of death is cardiovascular disease, which occurs at a 2 – 4 times higher incidence than in the general population.

The American Diabetes Association (ADA) provides recommendations for monitoring, preventing and treating complications of uncontrolled diabetes (see diagram below).

DIABETES COMPLICATIONS

Microvascular Disease
Retinopathy

Diabetic kidney disease (i.e., nephropathy)

Peripheral neuropathy (i.e., loss of sensation, often in the feet), ↑ risk of foot infections and amputations

Autonomic neuropathy (gastroparesis, loss of bladder control, erectile dysfunction)

Macrovascular Disease*
Coronary artery disease (CAD), including MI

Cerebrovascular disease, including stroke (CVA)

Peripheral artery disease (PAD)

*Macrovascular disease is the same as atherosclerotic cardiovascular disease (ASCVD)

Antiplatelet Therapy (Aspirin)

- Aspirin 75-162 mg/day (usually given as 81 mg/day) is recommended for ASCVD secondary prevention (e.g., post-MI).
  - If allergy: use clopidogrel 75 mg/day.
- Not recommended for primary prevention (in most); the risk of bleeding is about equal to the benefit. Can consider if high risk.
- CAD/PAD: aspirin + low-dose rivaroxaban can be added.
- Used in pregnancy to ↓ risk of preeclampsia.

Diabetic Retinopathy

- T2D: eye exam with dilation at diagnosis.
  - If retinopathy, repeat annually. If not, repeat every 1-2 yrs.

Vaccinations

Required, in addition to all childhood vaccines:
- Hepatitis B virus (HBV) series.
- Influenza, annually.
- Pneumococcal vaccines per ACIP guidelines (see Immunizations chapter).

Neuropathy

- Annually: a 10-g monofilament test and 1 other test (e.g., pinprick, temperature, vibration) to assess sensation (feeling).
- Comprehensive foot exam at least annually. If high-risk, refer to podiatrist.

Treatment options: pregabalin, duloxetine or gabapentin.

Foot Care Counseling

- Every day: wash, dry and examine feet. Moisturize the top and bottom of feet, but not between the toes.
- Each office visit: take off shoes to have feet checked.
- Annual foot exam by a podiatrist (for most).
- Trim toenails with nail file; do not leave sharp edges from the clipper.
- Wear socks and shoes. Elevate feet when sitting.

Cholesterol Control

Statin Treatment
- High-intensity statin (atorvastatin 40-80 mg or rosuvastatin 20-40 mg daily) for:
  - Diabetes + ASCVD
  - Age 50-75 years with multiple ASCVD risk factors
- Moderate-intensity statin for:
  - Diabetes + age 40-75 years (no ASCVD)
  - Diabetes + age < 40 years + ASCVD risk factors

Add-On Treatment (to Maximally Tolerated Statin)
- Ezetimibe if ASCVD 10-yr risk > 20%.
- Icosapent ethyl (Vascepa) if LDL is controlled but TGs are 135–499 mg/dL.

Monitoring: lipid panel annually and 4-12 weeks after starting a statin or increasing the dose.

Diabetic Kidney Disease

- Monitor urine albumin and eGFR annually if normal kidney function; twice yearly if reduced kidney function (eGFR 30-60 mL/min/1.73 m² or urine albumin ≥ 300).

Treatment
- Albuminuria*: ACE inhibitor or ARB.
- eGFR ≥ 25 mL/min/1.73 m² and urine albumin ≥ 300: SGLT2 inhibitor.**

*Albuminuria is either a urine albumin ≥ 30 mg/24 hours or a urine albumin-to-creatinine ratio (UACR) ≥ 30 mg/g
**Finerenone is recommended for those unable to use SGLT2 inhibitor

Blood Pressure Control

BP Goal
- < 130/80 mmHg (esp. if ASCVD or 10-year risk ≥ 15%).
- < 140/90 mmHg acceptable if ASCVD risk < 15%.

Treatment
- No albuminuria: thiazide, DHP CCB, ACE inhibitor or ARB.
- Albuminuria: ACE inhibitor or ARB.
- CAD: ACE inhibitor or ARB.

NATURAL PRODUCTS

Natural products are commonly used for T2D, with low or minimal efficacy. Products used to decrease BG include cassia cinnamon, alpha lipoic acid, chromium, magnesium and Panax/American ginseng. Most patients will still require the use of prescription drugs.

TREATMENT FOR TYPE 2 DIABETES

The goals of treatment are to maintain BG levels in the target range (while avoiding hypoglycemia) and to reduce long-term complications of hyperglycemia. The ADA guidelines provide recommendations for initial treatment and add-on therapy (see Study Tip Gal below). Initial treatment depends on comorbidities and patient-specific factors, but metformin is generally the first-line treatment along with lifestyle modifications. It is used indefinitely unless contraindications are present or it is not tolerated. Another drug, from a different class, is recommended in the following instances:

- Start a GLP-1 agonist or SGLT2 inhibitor with proven benefit at baseline regardless of A1C (with or without metformin) if the patient has ASCVD, heart failure or chronic kidney disease.

- Start two drugs at baseline if the A1C is 8.5 – 10% (metformin + non-insulin drug).

- Insulin can be used initially if hyperglycemia is severe (A1C > 10% or BG ≥ 300 mg/dL); see Insulin section.

- Add medications if the A1C remains above goal and continue until A1C goal is met. In this case, treatment is driven by patient-specific factors (e.g., cost, risk of hypoglycemia and weight). If injectable medications are needed for A1C lowering, GLP-1 agonists are preferred to insulin.

TREATMENT ALGORITHM

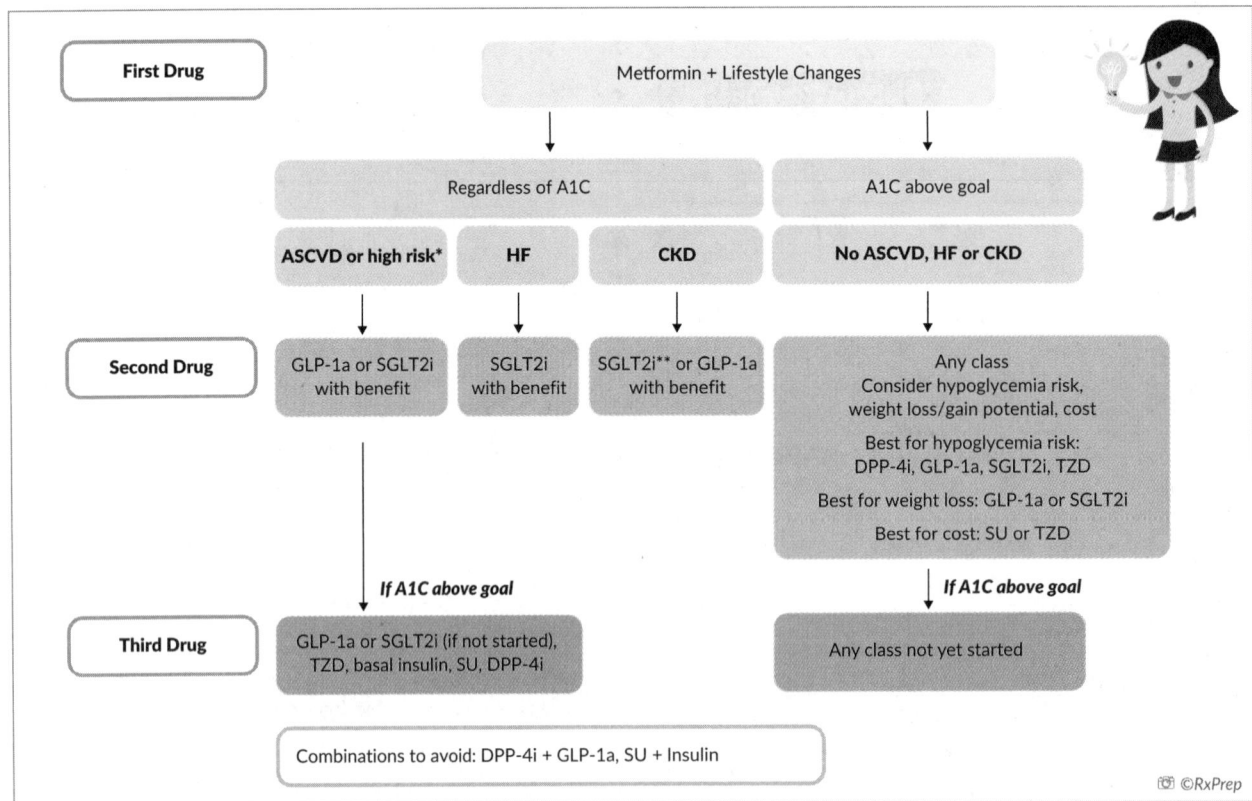

ASCVD = atherosclerotic cardiovascular disease, HF = heart failure, CKD = chronic kidney disease, GLP-1a = glucagon-like peptide 1 receptor agonist, SGLT2i = sodium-glucose cotransporter 2 inhibitor, TZD = thiazolidinedione, SU = sulfonylurea, DPP-4i = dipeptidyl peptidase 4 inhibitor

*High risk: age ≥ 55 with coronary, carotid or lower extremity artery stenosis > 50%, or LVH
**SGLT2i preferred for albuminuria

NON-INSULIN MEDICATIONS FOR TYPE 2 DIABETES

BIGUANIDE

Metformin primarily works by ↓ hepatic glucose production, ↑ insulin sensitivity and ↓ intestinal absorption of glucose. Metformin is usually the first-line treatment for T2D and can be used in prediabetes. Use of metformin is dependent on eGFR.

DRUG	DOSING	SAFETY/SIDE EFFECTS/MONITORING
Metformin *(Glucophage, Glucophage XR, Fortamet, Glumetza, Riomet)* IR: 500, 850, 1,000 mg ER: 500, 750, 1,000 mg *Riomet* liquid: 500 mg/5 mL	IR: 500 mg daily or BID ER: 500-1,000 mg daily (usually with dinner) Titrate weekly, usual maintenance dose: 1,000 mg BID Max dose: 2,000-2,550 mg/day (varies by product) Give with a meal to ↓ GI upset	**BOXED WARNING** Lactic acidosis – risk ↑ with renal impairment, radiological studies with contrast, excessive alcohol or certain drugs (see Drug Interactions) **CONTRAINDICATIONS** eGFR < 30, acute or chronic metabolic acidosis (includes DKA) **WARNINGS** Not recommended to start if eGFR 30-45; reassess if already taking and eGFR falls < 45 Vitamin B12 deficiency **SIDE EFFECTS** GI effects: diarrhea, nausea, flatulence, cramping; usually transient (resolve over time) **NOTES** ↓ A1C 1-2%, weight neutral, no hypoglycemia ER: swallow whole; can leave a ghost tablet (empty shell) in the stool Dose titration recommended to reduce GI effects; glucose-lowering effect may not be seen with initial doses

eGFR units: mL/min/1.73 m²

Metformin Drug Interactions

- Intra-arterial iodinated contrast media (used for imaging studies) can ↑ the risk of lactic acidosis. Discontinue metformin before the imaging procedure. Metformin can be restarted 48 hours after the procedure if eGFR is stable.

- Alcohol can ↑ the risk for lactic acidosis; excessive intake, acute or chronic, should be avoided.

- The combination of metformin and topiramate can ↑ the risk of metabolic acidosis.

SODIUM-GLUCOSE COTRANSPORTER 2 INHIBITORS

The sodium-glucose cotransporter 2 (SGLT2) protein, expressed in the proximal renal tubules, is responsible for the reabsorption of filtered glucose. By inhibiting SGLT2, these drugs reduce reabsorption of glucose and ↑ urinary glucose excretion, which ↓ BG concentrations. SGLT2 inhibitors are dosed based on eGFR. SGLT2 inhibitor names end in "-gliflozin."

DRUG	DOSING	SAFETY/SIDE EFFECTS/MONITORING
Canagliflozin *(Invokana)*	100 mg daily prior to the first meal of the day; can ↑ to 300 mg daily eGFR 30-59: max dose 100 mg/day eGFR < 30: not recommended, unless albuminuria > 300 mg/day	**CONTRAINDICATIONS** Dialysis **WARNINGS** Ketoacidosis (can occur with BG < 250 mg/dL, D/C prior to surgery due to risk) Genital mycotic infections, urosepsis, pyelonephritis, necrotizing fasciitis (perineum) Hypotension, AKI and renal impairment (due to intravascular volume depletion)
Dapagliflozin *(Farxiga)*	5 mg daily in the morning; can ↑ to 10 mg daily eGFR 25-45: not recommended for glycemic control eGFR < 25: initiation is not recommended	Canagliflozin: ↑ risk of leg and foot amputations, higher risk with history of amputation, PAD, peripheral neuropathy and/or diabetic foot ulcers; hyperkalemia risk when used with other drugs that increase potassium; risk of fractures
Empagliflozin *(Jardiance)*	10 mg daily in the morning; can ↑ to 25 mg daily eGFR < 30: not recommended for glycemic control	**SIDE EFFECTS** Weight loss, ↑ urination, ↑ thirst, hypoglycemia, ↑ Mg/PO4 **NOTES** ↓ A1C 0.7-1%, low hypoglycemia risk (unless used with insulin)
Ertugliflozin *(Steglatro)*	5 mg daily in the morning; can ↑ to 15 mg daily eGFR < 45: not recommended	SGLT2 inhibitors have shown reductions in HF, CKD progression and ASCVD; select drugs are now approved for HF and CKD in patients without diabetes. See Renal Disease and Chronic Heart Failure chapters. Dosing depends on indication

eGFR units: mL/min/1.73 m²

SGLT2 Inhibitor Drug Interactions

- ↑ risk of intravascular volume depletion (causing hypotension and acute kidney injury) if used in combination with diuretics, RAAS inhibitors or NSAIDs.

- Uridine diphosphate glucuronosyltransferase (UGT) inducers (e.g., rifampin, phenytoin, phenobarbital) can ↓ levels of canagliflozin; consider using 300 mg dose if used in combination and eGFR ≥ 60 mL/min/1.73 m².

GLUCAGON-LIKE PEPTIDE 1 AGONISTS

Glucagon-like peptide 1 (GLP-1) agonists are analogs of the incretin hormone GLP-1, which ↑ glucose-dependent insulin secretion, ↓ glucagon secretion, slows gastric emptying, improves satiety and can result in weight loss. They are all subcutaneous injections available in either single-dose or multidose pens, except semaglutide also comes as an oral tablet. Some are available in combination with long-acting insulin. GLP-1 agonist names end in "-tide."

DRUG	DOSING	SAFETY/SIDE EFFECTS/MONITORING
Liraglutide (*Victoza*) **Saxenda** – for weight loss	0.6 mg SC daily x 1 week, then ↑ to 1.2 mg SC daily; can ↑ to 1.8 mg SC daily	**BOXED WARNING** All (except *Byetta* and *Adlyxin*): risk of thyroid C-cell carcinomas; do not use if personal or family history of medullary thyroid carcinoma (MTC) or with Multiple Endocrine Neoplasia syndrome type 2 (MEN 2)
Dulaglutide (*Trulicity*)	0.75 mg SC once weekly; can ↑ to 1.5 mg SC once weekly	**WARNINGS** Pancreatitis (can be fatal, risk factors: gallstones, alcoholism or ↑ TGs)
Exenatide (*Byetta*)	5 mcg SC BID for 1 month; can ↑ to 10 mcg SC BID CrCl < 30: not recommended	Not recommended in patients with severe GI disease, including gastroparesis *Bydureon*: serious injection-site reactions (e.g., abscess, cellulitis, necrosis) with or without SC nodules
Exenatide ER (*Bydureon*, *Bydureon BCise*)	2 mg SC once weekly eGFR < 45: not recommended	*Ozempic*: ↑ complications with diabetic retinopathy **SIDE EFFECTS** Weight loss, nausea (reduced with dose titration), vomiting, diarrhea, hypoglycemia, injection site reactions
Lixisenatide (*Adlyxin*)	10 mcg SC daily x 14 days, then ↑ to 20 mcg SC daily eGFR < 15: not recommended	**NOTES** ↓ A1C 0.5-1.5%; ↓ postprandial BG, low hypoglycemia risk Do not use with DPP-4 inhibitors (overlapping mechanism)
Semaglutide (*Ozempic* – SC, *Rybelsus* – oral) **Wegovy** – for weight loss	SC: 0.25 mg SC once weekly x 4 weeks, then ↑ to 0.5 mg SC weekly; can ↑ to 1 mg SC weekly PO: 3 mg PO daily x 30 days, then ↑ to 7 mg daily; can ↑ to 14 mg	Liraglutide, dulaglutide and SC semaglutide have demonstrated ASCVD benefit *Byetta* and *Adlyxin*: give dose within 60 minutes of meals; others anytime Pen needles are not provided with *Byetta*, *Victoza*, or *Adlyxin*; provided with all others (which are the weekly injections) Dose titration recommended to reduce nausea; glucose-lowering effect may not be seen with initial doses

eGFR units: mL/min/1.73 m², CrCl units: mL/min

GLP-1 Agonist Drug Interactions

- These drugs slow gastric emptying and can reduce the absorption of orally administered drugs. Use caution with narrow therapeutic index drugs or drugs that require threshold concentrations for efficacy (e.g., antibiotics, oral contraceptives). Take oral contraceptives at least one hour before exenatide or *Adlyxin* and at least 11 hours after *Adlyxin*.

- Can ↑ the INR in patients on warfarin, monitor INR.

GLP-1 Agonist Injection Counseling

Injection technique is similar to insulin administration (see Insulin Injection Counseling later in the chapter).

- Injectable GLP-1 agonists are administered subcutaneously in the abdomen (alternatively in the back of the upper arms, outer thighs or upper buttocks).

- Attach a new pen needle for each injection (if not already attached). Follow the manufacturer's instructions for priming the pen (e.g., once for each new pen).

- After cleaning the hands and injection site, pinch a portion of the injection area and insert the pen needle at 90 degrees.

- Press the injection button and count 5 – 10 seconds before removing the needle.

- Rotate injection sites with each injection.

- Properly dispose of needles in a sharps disposal container. Do not store pens with a needle attached to reduce the risk of contamination or drug leakage.

INSULIN SECRETAGOGUES

Sulfonylureas (SUs) and meglitinides are known as insulin secretagogues; they work by stimulating insulin secretion from the pancreatic beta-cells to decrease postprandial BG. Meglitinides have a faster onset (15 – 60 minutes) and a shorter duration of action compared to the SUs. Older, first generation SUs (chlorpropamide, tolazamide and tolbutamide) should not be used as they can cause prolonged hypoglycemia. Meglitinide names end in "-glinide" and sulfonylurea names start with "G" and end in "-ide."

Sulfonylureas

DRUG	DOSING	SAFETY/SIDE EFFECTS/MONITORING
Glipizide **(Glucotrol, Glucotrol XL,** *Glipizide XL)*	IR: 5 mg daily, titrate to a max dose of 40 mg/day Doses > 15 mg should be divided BID XL: 5 mg daily, titrate to a max dose of 20 mg/day	**CONTRAINDICATIONS** Sulfa allergy (not likely to cross-react, see Drug Allergies & Adverse Drug Reactions chapter) **WARNINGS** Hypoglycemia **SIDE EFFECTS** Weight gain, nausea
Glimepiride **(Amaryl)**	1-2 mg daily, titrate to a max dose of 8 mg/day	**NOTES** ↓ A1C 1-2%; ↓ efficacy after long-term use (as pancreatic beta-cell function declines)
Glyburide **Micronized glyburide** **(Glynase)**	Glyburide: 2.5-5 mg daily, titrate to a max dose of 20 mg/day *Glynase:* 1.5-3 mg daily, titrate to a max dose of 12 mg/day	Glipizide IR: take 30 minutes before a meal; all other products are taken with breakfast or the first meal of the day; may need to hold doses if NPO *Glucotrol XL* is an OROS formulation and can leave a ghost tablet (empty shell) in the stool Glimepiride, glyburide not preferred in elderly (on the Beers criteria) due to hypoglycemia risk Patients with G6PD deficiency can be at increased risk of hemolytic anemia with sulfonylureas

Meglitinides

DRUG	DOSING	SAFETY/SIDE EFFECTS/MONITORING
Repaglinide	0.5-2 mg TID AC Max dose: 16 mg daily Take 15-30 minutes before meals	**CONTRAINDICATIONS** Type 1 diabetes, DKA **WARNINGS** Hypoglycemia, caution with severe liver/renal impairment
Nateglinide *(Starlix)*	60-120 mg TID AC Take 1-30 minutes before meals	**SIDE EFFECTS** Weight gain, headache, upper respiratory tract infections (URTIs) **NOTES** ↓ A1C 0.5-1.5%

Sulfonylurea and Meglitinide Drug Interactions

- Insulin in combination with either SUs or meglitinides ↑ risk of hypoglycemia and should be avoided. Use caution with other drugs that can decrease BG (see Hypoglycemia section).

- SUs are CYP2C9 substrates; use caution with 2C9 inducers or inhibitors.

- Gemfibrozil and clopidogrel can ↑ repaglinide, leading to ↓ BG. Repaglinide is contraindicated with gemfibrozil.

- Alcohol can ↑ the risk for delayed hypoglycemia when taking insulin or insulin secretagogues.

DIPEPTIDYL PEPTIDASE 4 INHIBITORS

Dipeptidyl peptidase 4 (DPP-4) inhibitors prevent the enzyme DPP-4 from breaking down incretin hormones, glucagon-like peptide 1 (GLP-1) and glucose-dependent insulinotropic polypeptide (GIP). These hormones help to regulate BG levels by ↑ insulin release from the pancreatic beta-cells and ↓ glucagon secretion (which ↓ hepatic glucose production) from pancreatic alpha-cells. These drugs enhance the effects of the body's own incretins. DPP-4 inhibitor names end in "-gliptin."

DRUG	DOSING	SAFETY/SIDE EFFECTS/MONITORING
Sitagliptin (*Januvia*)	100 mg daily eGFR 30-45: 50 mg daily eGFR < 30: 25 mg daily	**WARNINGS** Pancreatitis, severe arthralgia (joint pain), acute renal failure, hypersensitivity reactions, bullous pemphigoid (blisters/erosions requiring hospitalization)
Linagliptin (*Tradjenta*)	5 mg daily No renal dose adjustments	Risk of heart failure seen with saxagliptin and alogliptin, but warning added for class Alogliptin: hepatotoxicity
Saxagliptin (*Onglyza*)	2.5-5 mg daily eGFR < 45: 2.5 mg daily	**SIDE EFFECTS** Generally well tolerated, can cause nasopharyngitis, URTIs, UTIs, peripheral edema, rash
Alogliptin (*Nesina*)	25 mg daily CrCl 30-59: 12.5 mg daily CrCl < 30: 6.25 mg daily	**NOTES** ↓ A1C 0.5-0.8%, weight neutral, low hypoglycemia risk Do not use with GLP-1 agonists (overlapping mechanism)

CrCl units: mL/min, eGFR units: mL/min/1.73 m²

DPP-4 Inhibitor Drug Interactions

- Saxagliptin is a major substrate of CYP450 3A4 and P-gp. Limit the dose to 2.5 mg with strong CYP3A4 inhibitors, including protease inhibitors (e.g., atazanavir, ritonavir), clarithromycin, itraconazole, ketoconazole.

- Linagliptin is a major substrate of CYP3A4 and P-gp. Linagliptin levels are ↓ by strong CYP3A4 inducers (e.g., carbamazepine, phenytoin, rifampin, St. John's wort).

THIAZOLIDINEDIONES

Thiazolidinediones (TZDs) are peroxisome proliferator-activated receptor gamma (PPARγ) agonists that ↑ peripheral insulin sensitivity (↑ uptake and utilization of glucose by the peripheral tissues, also known as insulin sensitizers). Names of TZDs end in "-glitazone."

DRUG	DOSING	SAFETY/SIDE EFFECTS/MONITORING
Pioglitazone (*Actos*)	Initial: 15-30 mg daily Max dose: 45 mg daily	**BOXED WARNINGS** Can cause or exacerbate heart failure, do not use with NYHA Class III/IV heart failure Rosiglitazone: increased risk of MI **WARNINGS** Edema (including macular edema), risk of fractures, hepatic failure Can stimulate ovulation, which can lead to unintended pregnancy; may need contraception
Rosiglitazone (*Avandia*)	4-8 mg daily Max dose: 8 mg daily	Pioglitazone: ↑ risk of bladder cancer; do not use in patients with a history of bladder cancer **SIDE EFFECTS** Peripheral edema, weight gain, URTIs, myalgia Rosiglitazone: ↑ LDL, HDL and total cholesterol **NOTES** ↓ A1C 0.5-1.4%, low risk of hypoglycemia Pioglitazone has beneficial effects (e.g., reduces inflammation) in nonalcoholic steatohepatitis (NASH)

Thiazolidinedione Drug Interactions

- TZDs are major substrates of CYP2C8; use caution with CYP2C8 inducers (e.g., rifampin) or inhibitors (e.g., gemfibrozil).

OTHER MEDICATIONS

The following classes of drugs can be used in specific situations, but given their modest efficacy, side effects and/or frequency of administration, they are not used routinely for the treatment of T2D.

DRUG CLASS	COMMENTS
Alpha-Glucosidase Inhibitors Acarbose (Precose) Miglitol (Glyset)	MOA: inhibit the metabolism of intestinal sucrose, which delays glucose absorption. Do not cause hypoglycemia alone, but if hypoglycemia occurs due to another drug, it cannot be treated with sucrose (present in fruit juices, table sugar or candy); glucose tablets or gel need to be purchased to treat hypoglycemia. Each dose should be taken with the first bite of each meal. GI side effects are common (flatulence, diarrhea, abdominal pain).
Bile Acid Binding Resins Colesevelam (Welchol)	Also indicated for Dyslipidemia (see Dyslipidemia chapter). Constipation is the most common side effect. Can bind and decrease absorption of other drugs and fat-soluble vitamins (A, D, E, K).
Dopamine Agonist Bromocriptine (Cycloset)	Contraindicated in patients with syncopal migraines (can cause hypotension and orthostasis) and those who are breastfeeding (inhibits lactation). Should not be used with metoclopramide or other dopamine agonists.
Amylin Analog Pramlintide (Symlin) SC injection	MOA: helps control postprandial glucose by slowing gastric emptying, which suppresses glucagon secretion following a meal and ↑ satiety. Can be used in type 1 or type 2 diabetes, administered SC prior to each major meal. Skip dose if skipping meal. Contraindicated in gastroparesis. Significant hypoglycemia risk; must reduce mealtime insulin dose by 50% when starting. Side effects include nausea, vomiting, anorexia and weight loss.

COMBINATIONS

METFORMIN + SU
Metformin/glipizide
Metformin/glyburide

METFORMIN + TZD
Metformin/pioglitazone (Actoplus Met)

METFORMIN + DPP-4 INHIBITOR
Metformin/alogliptin (Kazano)
Metformin/linagliptin (Jentadueto, Jentadueto XR)
Metformin/sitagliptin (Janumet, Janumet XR)
Metformin/saxagliptin (Kombiglyze XR)

METFORMIN + SGLT2 INHIBITOR
Metformin/canagliflozin (Invokamet, Invokamet XR)
Metformin/dapagliflozin (Xigduo XR)
Metformin/empagliflozin (Synjardy, Synjardy XR)
Metformin/ertugliflozin (Segluromet)

METFORMIN + SGLT2 INHIBITOR + DPP-4 INHIBITOR
Metformin/dapagliflozin/ saxagliptin (Qternmet XR)
Metformin/empagliflozin/linagliptin (Trijardy XR)

METFORMIN + MEGLITINIDE
Metformin/repaglinide (PrandiMet)

SULFONYLUREA + TZD
Glimepiride/pioglitazone (Duetact)

DPP-4 INHIBITOR + TZD
Alogliptin/pioglitazone (Oseni)

DPP-4 INHIBITOR + SGLT2 INHIBITOR
Linagliptin/empagliflozin (Glyxambi)
Saxagliptin/dapagliflozin (Qtern)
Sitagliptin/ertugliflozin (Steglujan)

GLP-1 AGONIST + LONG-ACTING INSULIN
Liraglutide/insulin degludec (Xultophy)
Lixisenatide/insulin glargine (Soliqua)

Does not include premixed insulins - see Insulin section

INSULIN

In an individual without diabetes, the pancreas controls the release of insulin in the body. It provides a consistent level (or basal amount) of insulin at all times, then releases more insulin when the BG is elevated postprandially (after meals). In a patient with diabetes, insulin can be administered to mimic the normal physiologic process. Insulin cannot be given orally; it is given as a subcutaneous injection (most common), intravenously (less often, usually for acutely high BG) or inhaled (uncommon).

Insulin is a high-alert medication, which means it has a high risk of causing patient harm and requires extra care during handling and administration. Insulin is high-alert primarily due to human errors, such as misreading measurements, using the wrong insulin type, strength, dose or frequency and skipping meals.

INSULIN PROPERTIES AND TYPES

The graph below shows the onset, peak and duration of action of the common insulin types, which must be understood in order to design an insulin regimen and to make adjustments when the BG trends too high or too low. The table that follows describes how the different types of insulins are used and their major safety issues. Basal and rapid-acting insulins are called insulin analogs; when basal insulin is used with mealtime rapid-acting insulin, the profile is analogous (similar) to the natural pattern of insulin secretion from the pancreas.

Basal Insulin

- Basal insulin includes glargine (red line), detemir (blue line) and ultra-long acting degludec (pink line). These insulins are "peakless" with an onset of 3 – 4 hours and duration ≥ 24 hours. They mainly impact fasting glucose.

Intermediate-Acting Insulin

- Insulin NPH (yellow line) is intermediate-acting but it can be used as a basal insulin. NPH has an onset of 1 – 2 hours, and it peaks at 4 – 12 hours, which can cause hypoglycemia. BG control is further complicated by the variable, unpredictable duration of action (14 – 24 hours).

- The P in NPH is for protamine, which helps to delay absorption/extend the duration of effect. Protamine also comes in lispro-protamine and aspart-protamine, which have the same onset, peak and duration as NPH. These come in premixed solutions only and are combined with standard rapid-acting insulin (aspart and lispro).

Rapid-Acting and Short-Acting Insulin

- Rapid-acting insulin (purple line) includes aspart, lispro and glulisine. These provide a bolus dose, similar to the pancreas releasing a burst of insulin in response to food. They have a fast onset (~15 min), peak in 1 – 2 hours and a duration of 3 – 5 hours (gone by the next meal).

- Regular insulin U-100 (green line) is considered a short-acting insulin; it can be given as a bolus at mealtimes like rapid-acting insulin, but has a slower onset and lasts longer than needed for a meal. Regular insulin has an onset of 30 minutes, peaks at ~2 hours and lasts 6 – 10 hours.

Other Insulins (Not Included in Graph)

- Regular U-500 is a very concentrated insulin. The onset is the same as regular insulin U-100, but the duration is closer to NPH; it can last up to 24 hours. It is often dosed twice daily or TID, before meals.

- Inhaled insulin is not used commonly. It is a mealtime insulin with fast absorption through the lungs.

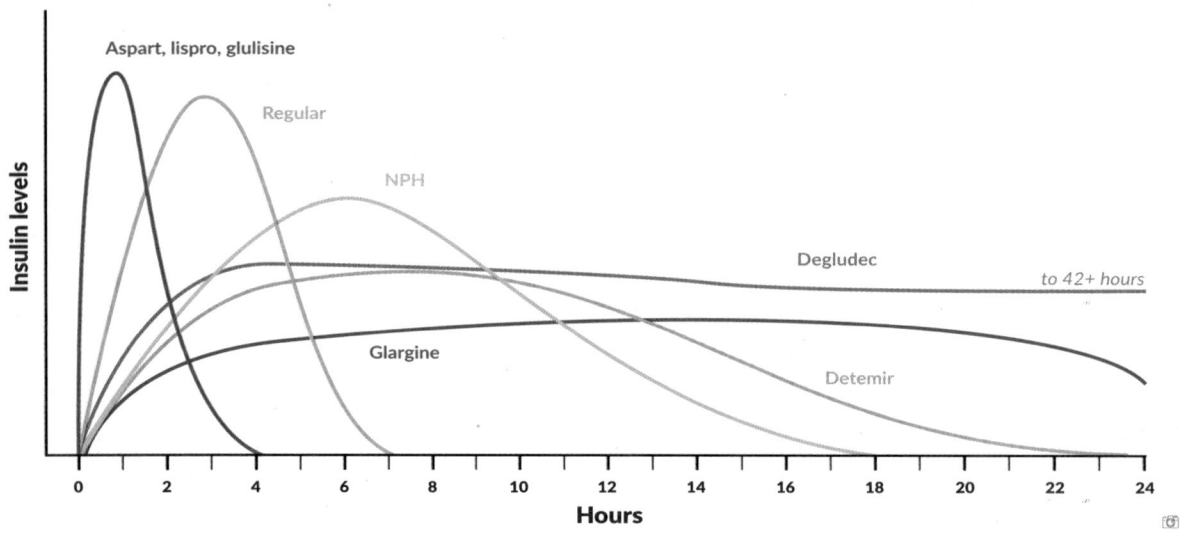

©RxPrep

INSULIN SAFETY ISSUES AND NOTES; APPLIES TO ALL INJECTABLE INSULIN, EXCEPT WHERE NOTED

CONTRAINDICATIONS
- Do not administer during episodes of hypoglycemia.

WARNINGS
- Hypoglycemia, hypokalemia (insulin facilitates K+ entry into cells, and is used to treat hyperkalemia).

SIDE EFFECTS
- Weight gain: insulin causes excess glucose to move into adipose cells, and increases body fat, lean mass and appetite stimulation.

- Lipoatrophy: loss of SC fat at the injection site (which disfigures skin) and lipohypertrophy: accumulation of fat lumps under injection site. Avoid both by rotating injection sites and using analog insulins (lower risk than with older insulins).

STORAGE AND ADMINISTRATION NOTES
- Most vials are 10 mL and most pens are 3 mL. Insulin concentrations are 100 units/mL, unless noted otherwise (discussed later in the chapter).

- Do not shake; turn suspensions (NPH, protamine mixes) up and down slowly or roll between hands. Do not freeze or expose to extreme heat.

- Unopened insulin vials and pens are stored in the refrigerator. Open vials and pens can be kept at room temperature (see Room Temperature Stability of Insulin chart later in the chapter). It is more painful/uncomfortable to inject cold insulin.

- Pen devices should never be shared (even if the needle is changed) due to the risk for transmission of blood-borne pathogens.

- Any percentage mixture of NPH and regular (or rapid-acting) insulins can be made by mixing the two insulins in the same syringe; regular insulin (or rapid-acting) is clear and is drawn up (into the syringe) first, before the NPH, which is cloudy.

Rapid-Acting (Bolus) Insulin	

Aspart (Novolog, Fiasp)
Lispro (Humalog, Admelog, Lyumjev)
Lispro U-200 (Humalog U-200)
Insulin glulisine (Apidra)
 	
Clear and colorless
 	
Apidra SoloStar pens contain glulisine
Humalog KwikPens contain lispro
Novolog FlexPens contain aspart
	■ Inject SC 5-15 minutes before meals to have insulin available when glucose from the meal is absorbed.
	  ❑ Lispro can also be administered right after eating.
	  ❑ Fiasp and *Lyumjev* can be injected with the first bite or within 20 minutes of starting a meal.
	■ Used as prandial insulin (to prevent high BG from a meal) and for correction doses when BG is high (often by sliding scale).
	■ Preferred insulin type for insulin pumps (discussed later in the chapter).
	■ Aspart and lispro insulins come in premixed insulins with intermediate-acting protamine insulin.
	■ Co-formulations with faster absorption: *Fiasp* is formulated with niacinamide (vitamin B3) and *Lyumjev* is formulated with treprostinil and citrate.

Inhaled insulin (Afrezza)	■ Contraindicated in any lung disease, including asthma and COPD; do not use *Afrezza* in smokers. ■ Can cause acute bronchospasm, cough and throat pain. ■ Requires lung monitoring with pulmonary function tests (FEV1). Replace inhaler every 15 days.

Short-Acting (Bolus) Insulin	
Regular (Humulin R, Novolin R) Clear and colorless Rx and OTC *Myxredlin* is a ready-to-use (RTU) regular insulin IV solution (100 mL bag)	■ Inject SC 30 minutes before meals to have insulin available when the glucose from the next meal is absorbed. ■ Used as prandial insulin and for correction doses when BG is high (often by sliding scale). ■ Regular insulin is preferred for IV infusions, including in parenteral nutrition; it is less expensive than other insulins and when administered as a continuous IV infusion, the onset is immediate. IV regular insulin should be prepared in a non-PVC container. ■ Often given with NPH twice daily, 30 min before breakfast and dinner. Lunch is covered by the NPH, and possibly some residual regular insulin. This regimen requires just 2 injections per day (since the insulins can be mixed).
Concentrated Regular U-500 (*Humulin R U-500*)	■ Five times as concentrated as regular insulin; many safety risks. Recommended only when patients require > 200 units of insulin per day. ■ The prescribed dose of *Humulin R U-500* should always be expressed in units of insulin. ■ All patients using the U-500 insulin vial must be prescribed U-500 insulin syringes to avoid dosing errors; see the Syringes and Needles section for details. ■ Do not mix with any other insulin; only administer as SC injection (not IV, IM or in an insulin pump).

ENDOCRINE CONDITIONS

Intermediate-Acting (Basal) Insulin	
NPH (Humulin N, Novolin N) Cloudy Rx and OTC	▪ Given as a basal insulin, typically dosed <u>twice daily</u> as an add-on to oral drugs. Can be a less expensive alternative, but has more <u>hypoglycemia</u>. ▪ If nocturnal hypoglycemia occurs with NPH dosed once daily QHS, the dose can be split (e.g., 2/3 QAM, 1/3 QHS).
Long-Acting (Basal) Insulin	
Insulin detemir (Levemir) **Insulin glargine (Lantus, Toujeo, Basaglar, Rezvoglar, Semglee)** Clear and colorless	▪ Usually injected <u>once daily</u>; detemir may need to be given twice daily. ▪ Caution required: *Lantus* is <u>100 units/mL</u> and *Toujeo* is a <u>concentrated</u> insulin glargine with <u>300 units/mL</u> (an option when > 20 units/day of insulin glargine is needed). ▪ *Toujeo* has max effect by the 5th day; the coverage may not be adequate initially. ▪ *Lantus* and *Toujeo* [and the rapid-acting insulins *Admelog* (lispro) and *Apidra* (glulisine)] are made by the same manufacturer and all of them use the same *SoloStar* pen. ▪ <u>Do not mix</u> with any other insulins. ▪ *Semglee* is FDA-approved as an interchangeable biosimilar to glargine. Pending state law restrictions, it can be substituted without a separate prescription or provider intervention. *Rezvoglar* is a biosimilar to glargine; a separate prescription is needed.
Ultra-Long-Acting (Basal) Insulin	
Insulin degludec (Tresiba)	▪ Insulin degludec comes in a vial and the *Tresiba FlexTouch* pen. The vial has 100 units/mL. *Tresiba FlexTouch* pens come in 100 units/mL <u>and</u> 200 units/mL. ▪ *Tresiba* can be useful when insulin detemir or glargine causes nocturnal hypoglycemia.
Premixed Insulin	
70/30 MIXES **70% NPH/30% regular (Humulin 70/30, Novolin 70/30)** 70% aspart protamine/30% aspart (Novolog Mix 70/30) Rx and OTC **75/25 MIX** 75% lispro protamine/25% lispro (Humalog Mix 75/25) **50/50 MIX** 50% lispro protamine/50% lispro (Humalog Mix 50/50)	▪ Given BID (before breakfast and dinner), or sometimes TID (with rapid-acting insulin). ❑ If the mixture contains <u>rapid-acting</u> insulin: inject <u>15 minutes</u> before a meal. ❑ If the mixture contains <u>regular</u> insulin: inject <u>30 minutes</u> before a meal. ▪ In premixed insulins, the percentage of NPH or protamine insulin is listed <u>first</u> and the percentage of short-acting or rapid-acting insulin is listed <u>second</u> (e.g., *Humulin 70/30* contains 70% NPH and 30% regular). ▪ NPH or protamine (which are both cloudy) make the mixes cloudy. **CASE SCENARIO** A 35-year-old female injects *Humulin 70/30* 60 units before breakfast and 20 units before dinner. **What is her TDD of regular insulin?** *Humulin 70/30* is 70% NPH and 30% regular. The regular dose in the morning is 60 units x 0.3 = 18 units. The regular dose in the evening is 20 units x 0.3 = 6 units. The TDD of regular insulin is 24 units.

DRUG INTERACTIONS

▪ <u>Avoid</u> the combination of insulin with <u>sulfonylureas or meglitinides</u> (monitor closely if used together). May need to ↓ insulin dose when used with drugs that can cause hypoglycemia, including SGLT2 inhibitors, GLP-1 agonists, TZDs and DPP-4 inhibitors.

▪ Rosiglitazone: ↑ <u>risk of heart failure</u> when taken with insulin; do not use together.

▪ Pramlintide: <u>must reduce mealtime insulin by 50%</u> when <u>starting</u> pramlintide to avoid <u>severe hypoglycemia</u>.

▪ May need to ↓ insulin dose when used with direct acting antivirals (DAAs) for hepatitis C treatment due to risk of hypoglycemia.

INSULIN AVAILABLE OTC

<u>Regular, NPH and premixed 70% NPH/30% Regular insulins</u> can be sold <u>OTC</u> or can be dispensed with a prescription for insurance coverage. All basal and rapid-acting insulins are available by prescription only.

INSULIN DOSING AND CALCULATIONS

STARTING INSULIN IN TYPE 2 DIABETES

If an injectable medication is needed to reduce the A1C in T2D, a GLP-1 receptor agonist is preferred and should be considered first. If the patient is already on a GLP-1 agonist (or a GLP-1 agonist is not appropriate), insulin should be started. An exception is when using insulin initially to treat very high BG at diagnosis (A1C > 10% or BG ≥ 300 mg/dL) or if symptoms of catabolism are present (e.g., DKA). If insulin is required, combination with a GLP-1 agonist is recommended for greater efficacy. Starting insulin in T2D should follow a step-wise approach (see image below).

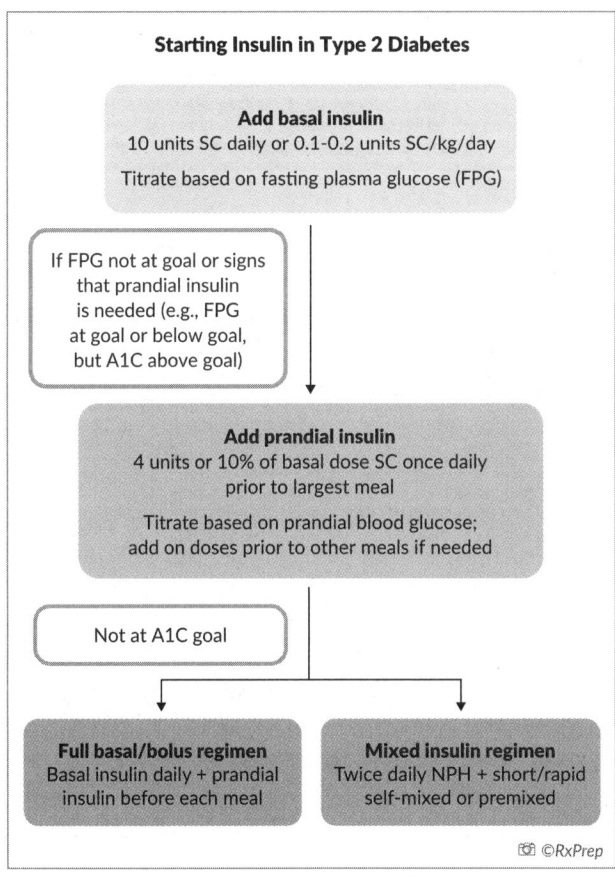

STARTING INSULIN IN TYPE 1 DIABETES

All people with T1D require insulin. Most are treated with an insulin pump or multiple daily injections of insulin designed to mimic the normal pattern of insulin secretion. Rapid-acting injectable insulins and long-acting basal insulins are preferred (over short- and intermediate-acting insulins), because they have less hypoglycemia risk and better mimic the physiologic pattern of insulin made by the body.

CASE SCENARIO

Start a basal-bolus regimen with *Lantus* and *Humalog* in a patient with type 1 diabetes that weighs 84 kg.

1. Calculate the TDD:
   0.5 units/kg/day x 84 kg = 42 units
2. Split the dose in half for basal and rapid-acting insulin:
   21 units Lantus and 21 units Humalog
3. Split rapid-acting insulin into 3 even doses:
   7 units Humalog TID AC

Answer: 21 units *Lantus* daily and 7 units *Humalog* TID AC

Starting a Regimen with NPH and Regular Insulin

NPH and regular insulin regimens are not preferred; neither insulin has a profile that can mimic the natural insulin release from the pancreas as well as basal and rapid-acting insulin combinations. However, the lower cost and ability to use less injections (since these insulins can be mixed) make this type of regimen more feasible for some.

The starting TDD of insulin is the same as with basal-bolus regimens, but ⅔ of the TDD is given as NPH and ⅓ is given as regular insulin.

TREATMENT WITH AN INSULIN PUMP

Pumps can provide excellent BG control and require less daily insulin injections. Users must be motivated, willing to test their BG frequently and be able to understand the pump's operation. Prior experience with multiple daily injections is a requirement for switching to a pump.

Pumps hold insulin in a reservoir (see image on the next page). The insulin runs out of the pump through tubing to a small infusion set placed on the skin, usually on the abdomen, through a small cannula (needle) that inserts under the skin. The cannula tip rests in subcutaneous fatty tissue, where the insulin is released. The insulin reservoir, tubing and infusion set need to be replaced regularly.

ENDOCRINE CONDITIONS

Insulin pumps deliver rapid-acting insulin (preferred) by two complementary methods, continuous and bolus dosing.

1. Continuous doses: small amounts of insulin are released every few minutes to provide a basal insulin level.

2. Bolus doses: pumps can be programmed to release a number of insulin units to match the carbohydrates in a meal. The bolus dose is calculated by the patient's insulin to carbohydrate ratio (ICR), see Mealtime Insulin Dosing Options section. The bolus dose is adjusted based on the current BG level (e.g., if low, use less insulin).

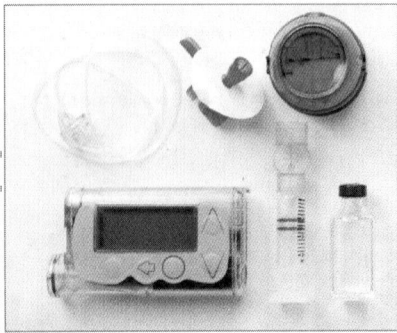

© iStock.com/Click_and_Photo

The insulin is held in a reservoir that is inserted into the pump.
The tubing connects the pump to the infusion set, which has a cannula that inserts under the skin.

ADJUSTING INSULIN BASED ON BLOOD GLUCOSE TRENDS

BG readings from a meter can be written on a paper log or downloaded from a meter's memory (see later section on Blood Glucose Monitoring). Changes to an insulin dose are not based on single measurements; there needs to be a trend showing that the BG runs too high or too low. BG is ideally checked before breakfast (FPG), lunch and dinner and at bedtime. A high or low BG reading is reflective of the insulin dose prior to that reading; look backwards to see which insulin/s are active and could be contributing to the trend.

Adjusting Basal Insulin

Fasting BG highs or lows, and/or similar trends that last most of the day (except with BG spikes after eating), typically indicate that the basal insulin dose needs to be changed.

- Low BG trend: ↓ the basal or NPH insulin dose.
- High BG trend: ↑ the basal or NPH insulin dose.

Adjusting Mealtime Insulin

If the postprandial BG is high or low following the same meal on most days, the regular or rapid-acting insulin dose taken prior to that meal should be increased for high BG, or decreased for low BG.

If the preprandial BG is high or low before the same meal (e.g., lunch) on most days, the regular or rapid-acting insulin dose taken before the previous meal (e.g., breakfast) should be increased for high BG, or decreased for low BG.

CASE SCENARIO

RC, a 47-year-old male with type 2 diabetes, takes *Toujeo* 18 units SC QHS and *Novolog* 5 units SC TID AC. He presents with two days of BG readings, taken before meals and at bedtime.

	BREAKFAST	LUNCH	DINNER	BED
Day 1 (mg/dL)	105	118	200	126
Day 2 (mg/dL)	97	115	197	122

What adjustment should be made to RC's insulin regimen?
The *Novolog* dose taken prior to lunch should be increased.

Explanation: the goal range for preprandial blood glucose is 80-130 mg/dL. The readings are all within the normal range except for the readings before dinner. The high readings before dinner indicate that RC is not taking enough insulin before lunch. The lunchtime dose should be increased.

Fasting BG is most affected by the basal insulin. If the pre-breakfast readings were high, the *Toujeo* dose should be increased.

If the readings at dinner were taken postprandially (instead of preprandially), the *Novolog* dose before dinner should be increased.

MEALTIME INSULIN DOSING OPTIONS

Option 1: Use the Same Insulin Dose Every Time

The mealtime (rapid-acting or regular) insulin can be set at the same dose everyday for a meal (e.g., 20 units of insulin lispro before dinner).

- This assumes that about the same grams of carbohydrates are eaten at dinner every day.
- This method results in high or low BG when the carbohydrate intake is higher or lower, respectively.

Option 2: Calculate an Insulin Dose at Each Meal

When different amounts of carbohydrates are eaten at each meal (which is common), a simple calculation can provide the right amount of rapid-acting or regular insulin needed.

- The bolus dose is calculated with the insulin-to-carbohydrate ratio (ICR).
- The ICR indicates the grams of carbohydrates covered by 1 unit of insulin.
- There are two variations of the ICR formula, depending on the type of insulin being used. Regular insulin uses the Rule of 450, and rapid-acting insulin uses the Rule of 500. The TDD of insulin used in the formula should account for both long-acting and short- or rapid-acting insulins included in the regimen.

ICR: Rule of 450 *for REGULAR*

$$\frac{450}{\text{total daily dose of insulin (TDD)}} = \text{grams of carbohydrates covered by 1 unit of regular insulin}$$

ICR: Rule of 500 *for RAPID-ACTING*

$$\frac{500}{\text{total daily dose of insulin (TDD)}} = \text{grams of carbohydrate covered by 1 unit of rapid-acting insulin}$$

CASE SCENARIO

ST is a 70 kg female with T1D who uses an insulin lispro pump. The continuous (basal) dose delivered by the pump in a 24 hour period is 26 units insulin lispro. The average daily amount of insulin lispro administered as bolus doses with meals is 24 units.

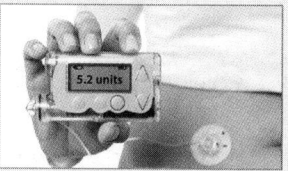

Click and Photo/Shutterstock.com

Calculate the ICR.

ST uses rapid-acting insulin. Use the Rule of 500.

$$\frac{500}{\text{total daily dose of insulin (TDD)}} = \text{grams of carbohydrate covered by 1 unit of rapid-acting insulin}$$

$$\frac{500}{50 \text{ units}} = 10$$

She has an ICR of 1:10, which means 1 unit of rapid-acting insulin covers 10 grams of carbohydrates.

ST will eat a hamburger (24 g carbohydrate) and fries (28 g carbohydrate) for lunch. She adds up the total carbohydrates and divides by 10 to calculate the bolus dose:

$$\frac{24 \text{ g (bun)} + 28 \text{ g (fries)}}{10 \text{ (her ICR)}} = 5.2 \text{ units}$$

ST enters 5.2 units on the pump. If she was using a syringe or pen to inject, she would round to the nearest whole number.

CORRECTION DOSES FOR ELEVATED BLOOD GLUCOSE

BG that is higher than the targeted range can be corrected with a bolus called a correction dose.

1. The first step is to calculate the correction factor, which indicates how much the BG will be lowered (in mg/dL) by 1 unit of insulin.

   ❑ To calculate the correction factor, use the 1,500 Rule for regular insulin and the 1,800 Rule for rapid-acting insulin. The TDD of insulin used in the formula should account for both long-acting and short- or rapid-acting insulins included in the regimen.

Calculate the Correction Factor

Correction Factor – 1,500 Rule *for REGULAR*

$$\frac{1,500}{\text{total daily dose of insulin (TDD)}} = \text{correction factor for 1 unit of regular insulin}$$

Correction Factor – 1,800 Rule *for RAPID-ACTING*

$$\frac{1,800}{\text{total daily dose of insulin (TDD)}} = \text{correction factor for 1 unit of rapid-acting insulin}$$

2. Next, calculate the correction dose, which is the total units of insulin needed to return the BG to the target range. The formula for the correction dose is the same for both regular and rapid-acting insulin.

Calculate the Correction Dose *BOTH TYPES*

$$\frac{(\text{blood glucose now}) - (\text{target blood glucose})}{\text{correction factor}} = \text{correction dose}$$

CASE SCENARIO

JJ is a 35-year-old male with T2D, currently treated with *Lantus* 50 units SC QHS and *Novolog* 15 units SC TID AC.

1. What is JJ's correction factor?

Since *Novolog* is a rapid-acting insulin, use the Rule of 1,800 to calculate JJ's correction factor.

$$\frac{1,800}{\text{total daily dose of insulin (TDD)}} = \text{correction factor for 1 unit of rapid-acting insulin}$$

50 units Lantus + 45 units Novolog = 95 units ← TDD

$$\frac{1,800}{95 \text{ units}} = 18.947 = 19 \leftarrow \text{Round to the nearest whole \#}$$

He has a correction factor of 19, which means 1 unit of rapid-acting insulin will lower the BG by 19 mg/dL.

2. JJ has a target premeal BG of 120 mg/dL. He checks his BG before dinner and it is 200 mg/dL. What dose of *Novolog* should JJ administer before dinner?

Determine the correction dose using the formula

$$\frac{(\text{blood glucose now}) - (\text{target blood glucose})}{\text{correction factor}} = \text{correction dose}$$

$$\frac{200 \text{ mg/dL} - 120 \text{ mg/dL}}{19} = 4 \text{ units}$$

Add the correction dose to the number of units he usually administers before meals to get the dose he needs before dinner: 4 units + 15 units = 19 units *Novolog*

INSULIN CONVERSIONS

Most insulin conversions are 1:1 (the same dose is used), but the regimen might need to be split up differently. The exceptions involve converting twice daily NPH and different forms of glargine; see the Study Tip Gal on the next page.

CONVERTING BETWEEN INSULINS

Most insulin conversions are 1:1
- The dose of the new insulin is usually the same as the old insulin*

Exception #1
NPH dosed BID → insulin glargine (e.g., *Lantus, Toujeo*) dosed daily

- Use 80% of the NPH dose

  Example: NPH 30 units AC breakfast and 20 units AC dinner = 50 units NPH daily

  50 x 0.8 = 40 units insulin glargine once daily

Exception #2
Toujeo → insulin glargine (e.g., *Lantus, Basaglar*) or insulin detemir (*Levemir*)

- Use 80% of the *Toujeo* dose

The dose of the new insulin might need to be adjusted when the BG is not controlled (e.g., using a higher dose for hyperglycemia).

INSULIN ADMINISTRATION

INSULIN STRENGTHS AND CONTAINERS

Most insulin products contain 100 units/mL of insulin. Some insulins have > 100 units/mL; these are concentrated insulins (see below). Insulin is available in:

- Vials (usually 10 mL), ready to be drawn up with an insulin syringe. *Humulin R U-500* comes in a 20 mL vial.

- Pens, ready to inject once a needle is attached. Pens are dialed to the number of units needed. All pens contain 3 mL of insulin, except *Toujeo*, which is available in two sizes: 1.5 mL and 3 mL.

All insulin pens are multi-dose; needles must be dispensed with all insulin pens. Some pens are disposable, and others have replaceable cartridges.

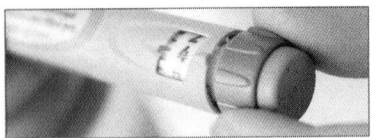

Insulin pens are easy to use; simply dial the units to inject.

Orawan Pattarawimonchai/Shutterstock.com

Example of providing a 20-unit dose of *Lantus* 100 units/mL with a pen or with a vial and syringe:

- The *Lantus Solostar* pen would be dialed to 20 units, which would provide 0.2 mL.

- The *Lantus* 10 mL vial provides the same dose by drawing up 0.2 mL with a U-100 syringe.

Concentrated Insulin

Injecting high doses of U-100 insulin requires a volume that can feel uncomfortable and, with very high doses (> 100 units), can require more than one syringe. Concentrated insulin is useful to reduce the volume of the injection, but can

be fatal when used incorrectly. Fortunately, most concentrated insulin comes in pens, which are simply dialed to the correct dose. The concentrated insulin that comes in both a pen and a vial is regular insulin U-500, which has higher risk.

INSULIN THAT COMES CONCENTRATED

Rapid-Acting Insulin
Humalog KwikPen, Lyumjev KwikPen (lispro): 200 units/mL

Regular-Acting Insulin
Humulin R U-500 KwikPen and vial: 500 units/mL

Long-Acting Insulin
Tresiba FlexTouch pen (degludec): 200 units/mL
Toujeo SoloStar, Toujeo Max SoloStar pens (glargine): 300 units/mL

Example of providing an 80-unit dose with *Tresiba FlexTouch* U-100 and U-200:

Pens of either strength would be dialed to 80 units. The difference is the volume of the injection.

- An 80-unit dose with U-100 is 0.8 mL.

- An 80-unit dose with U-200 is 0.4 mL (half the volume).

Very Concentrated Regular U-500

Humulin R U-500 is five times as concentrated as U-100 insulin. It is useful for patients taking > 200 units/day, but has a high risk for dosing errors.

Methods to avoid dosing errors with U-500 insulin:

- The prescribed dose of *Humulin R U-500* should always be expressed in units of insulin. Only dispense with U-500 syringes (see Selecting an Insulin Syringe section).

- *Humulin R U-500 KwikPen* provides up to 300 units with one injection and has a lower risk of dosing errors.

DISPENSING INSULIN

Dispensing insulin in an outpatient pharmacy requires a calculation of the days' supply and rounding up to the nearest vial/pen size.

For example, if a patient is taking 35 units of *Lantus* daily, how many *Lantus SoloStar* pens would be dispensed to provide a 30-day supply?

Step 1: calculate the total number of units needed.
35 units/day x 30 days = 1,050 units of insulin needed

Step 2: calculate the number of units per insulin pen, based on the concentration of insulin.
Lantus 100 units/mL x 3 mL per pen = 300 units per pen

Step 3: calculate the number of pens to be dispensed. Remember, pens cannot be broken, so round up.
1,050 units needed x (1 pen / 300 units) = 3.5 pens

Answer: 4 pens must be dispensed to provide enough insulin

Remember, insulin pens require priming with 2 units prior to each dose. Some pharmacists account for this in their calculation of days' supply, but it is not a standard practice to do so.

INSULIN STABILITY

<u>Unused</u> insulin vials, pens and cartridges are <u>stored in the refrigerator</u>. The expiration date of refrigerated insulin is the <u>manufacturer's expiration date</u> on the <u>label</u>. Once the insulin is in use it can be kept at <u>room temperature</u>, but the expiration date no longer applies. The insulin must be <u>used within a specific number of days</u> based on the type of insulin (see <u>Study Tip Gal</u> below). This is an important counseling point for patients.

Notice in the table that <u>most</u> insulin is stable at room temperature for <u>28 days</u> including <u>all rapid-acting insulin</u>. The insulins with shorter stability are typically pens.

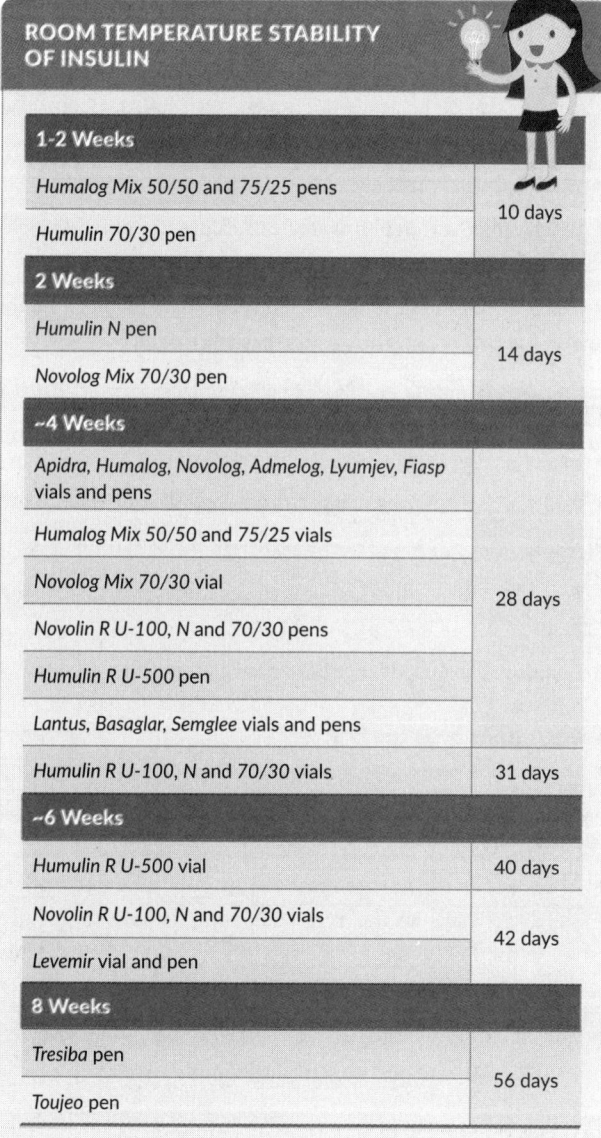

ROOM TEMPERATURE STABILITY OF INSULIN	
1-2 Weeks	
Humalog Mix 50/50 and 75/25 pens	10 days
Humulin 70/30 pen	
2 Weeks	
Humulin N pen	14 days
Novolog Mix 70/30 pen	
~4 Weeks	
Apidra, Humalog, Novolog, Admelog, Lyumjev, Fiasp vials and pens	28 days
Humalog Mix 50/50 and 75/25 vials	
Novolog Mix 70/30 vial	
Novolin R U-100, N and 70/30 pens	
Humulin R U-500 pen	
Lantus, Basaglar, Semglee vials and pens	
Humulin R U-100, N and 70/30 vials	31 days
~6 Weeks	
Humulin R U-500 vial	40 days
Novolin R U-100, N and 70/30 vials	42 days
Levemir vial and pen	
8 Weeks	
Tresiba pen	56 days
Toujeo pen	

SYRINGES AND NEEDLES

Selecting an Insulin Syringe

Use the smallest syringe that will hold the units of insulin. It is easier to read the unit markings on smaller syringes, which makes them more accurate.

- <u>0.3 mL</u> syringe for <u>up to 30 units</u>
- <u>0.5 mL</u> syringe for <u>30 – 50 units</u>
- <u>1 mL</u> syringe for <u>51 – 100 units</u>

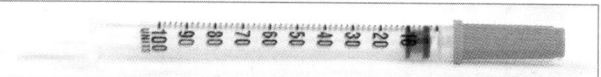

A 1 mL U-100 insulin syringe holds up to 100 units. Use smaller syringes to inject up to 50 units. khuntapol/Shutterstock.com

<u>Humulin R U-500 insulin vials</u> can <u>only</u> be dispensed with <u>U-500 syringes</u>. The U-500 vials have a dark <u>green</u> cap and the U-500 syringes (Rx only) have dark <u>green</u> needle covers. In contrast, <u>U-100 syringes</u> have <u>orange</u> caps. A U-500 syringe holds up to 250 units; a U-100 1 mL syringe holds up to 100 units.

Selecting an Insulin Pen Needle

Needles are chosen by the length and the <u>gauge</u> (thickness). The <u>higher</u> the <u>gauge</u>, the <u>thinner</u> the <u>needle</u> [e.g., 28G (thickest) – 32G (thinnest)]. The 32G cannula is thinnest and has a width of ~2 human hairs. <u>Shorter</u> needles and <u>higher-gauge</u> needles cause <u>less pain</u>.

- The shortest needles are <u>4 mm</u> and <u>5 mm</u> in length and are preferred for most pens. They <u>do not</u> require the <u>skin to be pinched</u> during administration and are good for thinner patients and children.

- 8 mm needles are long enough for <u>most</u> patients; <u>pinch up</u> the skin before injecting.

- 12.7 mm (1/2 inch) needles may be needed for obese patients; <u>pinch up</u> the skin before injecting.

Common brands for needles and syringes include *BD*, *Comfort EZ* and *Easy Touch*. Needles require a prescription in some states.

INSULIN INJECTION COUNSELING

1. Get supplies. Wash hands.

2. Check insulin for discoloration and particles. Discard if present.

3. If insulin contains NPH or protamine, it is a suspension and needs to be resuspended (do not shake):

   - Vials: roll the bottle gently between the hands.

   - Pens: <u>invert</u> (turn up/down) 4 – 5 times.

4. Clean injection site (area of the skin). If using a vial, wipe the top (after removing the plastic cover) with an alcohol swab.

5. Pens:

   ❏ Use a new needle for each injection. Prior to each injection, prime the needle by turning the knob to 2 units (can vary based on the insulin), face the needle away from you and press the injection button.

   ❏ Turn the dosing knob to the correct number of units, then inject (see number 7, below).

6. Vials:

   ❏ Use a new syringe for each injection; syringes come with a needle already attached. Inject an equal volume of air into the vial before withdrawing the insulin. Limit bubbles in the syringe.

   ❏ If mixing NPH and regular or rapid-acting insulin in the same syringe, the clear insulin (regular or rapid-acting) should be drawn into the syringe before the cloudy (NPH) insulin. Tip: inject air into the cloudy insulin first, then inject air into the clear insulin before withdrawing it out.

7. Insulin is best absorbed in the abdomen (preferred). Alternative sites for injection: posterior upper arm, superior buttocks and lateral thigh area (shaded areas of image).

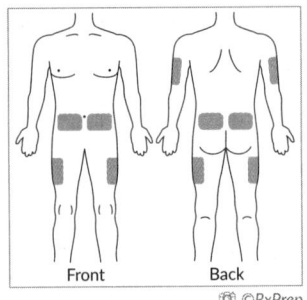

Front   Back

📷 ©RxPrep

8. With needles > 5 mm, gently pinch a 2-inch portion of skin between your thumb and first finger first (typically not required with shorter needles).

9. Insert the needle all the way in. Pens are injected straight down (at a 90-degree angle). Syringes are injected at 90 degrees for most or 45 degrees if the patient is thin.

10. Press the injection button (pen) or plunger (syringe) all the way down to inject the insulin. Count 5 – 10 seconds before removing the needle.

11. Rotate injection sites around the abdomen regularly to prevent skin damage.

12. Properly dispose of needles or entire syringes (see below). Do not store pens with needle attached.

DEVICE DISPOSAL

Used needles, syringes, single-dose pens (with needles attached) and lancets should be placed in a sharps disposal container and taken to a disposal site. Locations are provided by the local public health agency. Alternatively, a heavy plastic milk bottle (not glass) or metal coffee can works well.

BLOOD GLUCOSE MONITORING

Blood glucose monitoring (BGM), sometimes referred to as self monitoring BG (SMBG), refers to patients tracking their BG using a glucose meter or a continuous glucose monitor (CGM). CGMs are taped to the skin and have a probe that passes through the skin and into the fatty tissue. The probe provides measurements of the glucose level in the interstitial fluid between the cells.

PREPARING TO USE A GLUCOSE METER

- If the meter requires calibration, recalibrate each time a new canister of test strips is opened, if the meter was left in extreme cold or heat, if it was dropped or if the BG value does not match what the patient is feeling.

- Keep the test strips in the original container, with the cap closed. Light and air damage test strips. Check the expiration date; expired test strips can give false results.

- Wash hands vigorously, using warm water.

- Dry hands thoroughly; water can dilute the blood sample and give a false result.

- Allow arm to hang down for 30 seconds so blood can pool into the fingertips. Do not squeeze the finger.

TESTING WITH A GLUCOSE METER

- Insert test strip into meter.

- Prick side of fingertip (side is less painful) with a lancet.

- Apply a drop of blood to the test strip.

- Record the result in a logbook, or the meter might store the results.

- Dispose of the used lancet in a sharps container.

Alternative Site Testing

- Some meters are approved to test blood from both the fingertip and alternative sites (forearm, palm or thigh), which can hurt less than the side of a fingertip.

- Alternative testing sites are useful only when the BG is steady. The BG level can be ~20 minutes old. Do not use when the BG is changing quickly (e.g., after eating, after exercise and when hypoglycemia is suspected).

- The lancing device might need to have a special cap screwed onto the tip to use on an alternative site.

HYPOGLYCEMIA

Hypoglycemia is defined as a BG < 70 mg/dL. Low BG can have severe consequences, including falls, motor vehicle accidents and death. Each episode contributes to irreversible cognitive impairment. More stringent A1C goals can be overly aggressive in some cases and cause hypoglycemia (e.g., an A1C goal of < 6.5% for an elderly patient with recurrent hypoglycemia would be too aggressive).

HYPOGLYCEMIA SYMPTOMS

Symptoms include dizziness, anxiety/irritability, shakiness, headache, diaphoresis (sweating), hunger, confusion, nausea, ataxia, tremors, palpitations/tachycardia and blurred vision.

Severe hypoglycemia can cause seizures, coma and death. All episodes of hypoglycemia are dangerous and should be reported to the prescriber. Monitoring with a CGM can help by displaying the BG every few minutes and sounding an alert when the BG level falls too low.

HYPOGLYCEMIA TREATMENT

Treatment if Conscious and Able to Swallow

Pure glucose, in tablets or gel, is preferred, but any form of carbohydrate that contains glucose will work (see image). Added fat (e.g., a chocolate candy bar) is not recommended; it slows absorption and prolongs the hypoglycemia. To treat, follow the "rule of 15":

1. Take 15 – 20 grams of glucose or simple carbohydrates.

2. Recheck BG after 15 minutes.

3. If hypoglycemia continues, repeat steps 1 & 2.

4. Once BG is normal, eat a small meal or snack.

Treatment if Unconscious

When oral treatment is not possible, treat with dextrose (if there is IV access) or with glucagon. Caregivers of someone at high risk for hypoglycemia should know how to use a glucagon 1 mg SC injection (GlucaGen, Gvoke), dasiglucagon injection (Zegalogue) or glucagon nasal spray (Baqsimi). If using glucagon, place the patient in a lateral recumbent position (on side) to protect the airway and prevent choking when consciousness returns.

DRUG-INDUCED HIGH OR LOW BLOOD GLUCOSE

DRUGS THAT CAUSE HYPOGLYCEMIA

- Insulin is the primary cause of drug-induced hypoglycemia.
- Sulfonylureas and meglitinides ("insulin secretagogues"), and pramlintide are high-risk.
  - Glyburide, glimepiride and first-generation sulfonylureas (e.g., chlorpropamide) are not recommended in the elderly due to this risk.
- GLP-1 agonists, DPP-4 inhibitors, SGLT2 inhibitors and TZDs have a low risk for hypoglycemia when used alone. When used in combination with insulin or a sulfonylurea, the risk is higher, and the insulin or sulfonylurea dose may need to be lowered.

Raise Blood Sugar with 15 Grams of Simple Carbs

4 oz. (1/2 cup) of Juice

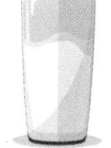

8 oz. (1 cup) Milk

4 oz. Regular Soda (not diet)

1 Tablespoon Sugar, Honey or Corn Syrup

3-4 Glucose Tablets or 1 Serving Glucose Gel (follow package instructions)

©RxPrep
iStock.com/Taisiia Iaremchuk, pioner2_001, AnnaSqBerg, Vasilyevalara, blueringmedia

- Alcohol, especially if taken on an empty stomach, can cause hypoglycemia when used with insulin or sulfonylureas.
- Caution: beta-blockers, especially if non-selective, can cause hypoglycemia and mask adrenergic symptoms of hypoglycemia (e.g., shakiness, palpitations, anxiety). Sweating and hunger are not masked. Counsel to recognize symptoms and test BG if unsure.

DRUGS THAT CAUSE HYPERGLYCEMIA

It is preferable, but not always possible, to avoid drugs that increase BG (see Key Drugs Guy). If not avoidable (e.g., using tacrolimus post-transplant), the increase in BG will need to be managed.

DRUGS THAT AFFECT BLOOD GLUCOSE

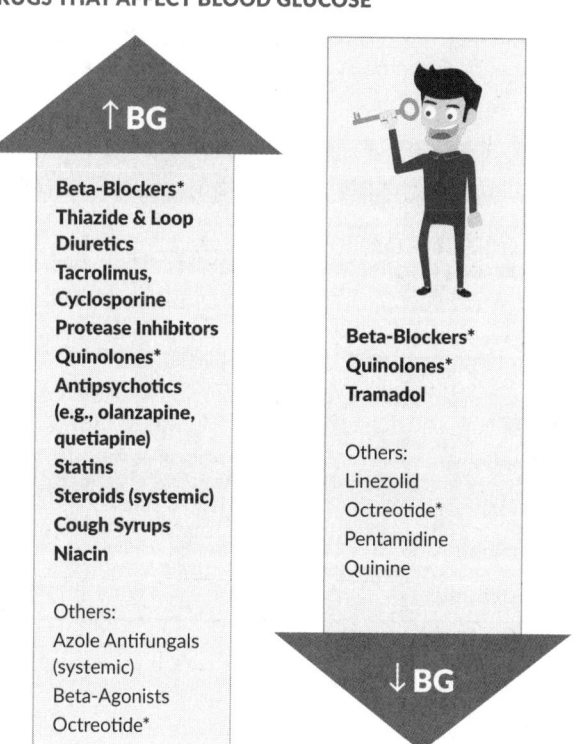

↑ BG

Beta-Blockers*
Thiazide & Loop Diuretics
Tacrolimus, Cyclosporine
Protease Inhibitors
Quinolones*
Antipsychotics (e.g., olanzapine, quetiapine)
Statins
Steroids (systemic)
Cough Syrups
Niacin

Others:
Azole Antifungals (systemic)
Beta-Agonists
Octreotide*

Beta-Blockers*
Quinolones*
Tramadol

Others:
Linezolid
Octreotide*
Pentamidine
Quinine

↓ BG

*Can cause hypo or hyperglycemia

ENDOCRINE CONDITIONS

INPATIENT GLUCOSE CONTROL

The target BG range for most non-critical and critical care patients in the hospital is between 140 – 180 mg/dL. More stringent goals might be appropriate for select patients. Treatment should be proactive and attempt to maintain BG in this range, rather than treating BG when it is high.

The use of sliding scale insulin (SSI) alone to control BG in the hospital setting is strongly discouraged. This method of administering insulin in response to elevated BG levels is reactionary (treats BG after it becomes elevated, rather than preventing elevated BG) and leads to poor outcomes. In addition, most sliding scales used are not patient-specific. See the Sliding Scale Example below.

- Insulin is used for most hospitalized patients; the regimen depends primarily on oral intake.

- If oral intake is adequate, a regimen with basal, bolus (prandial) and correction doses (usually added to the mealtime bolus dose) is preferred.

- A basal and correction dose strategy is recommended if the patient is not eating well (poor intake).

- Correction dose insulin is given when BG is already high. Like sliding scale insulin, the insulin dose given will correlate with the BG, on a scale. The difference is that the correction dose scale is designed for a specific patient. It is based on the patient's insulin sensitivity factor (same as the correction factor), which indicates how much the BG will drop with each unit of insulin.

Sliding scales, like the one below, and correction dose insulin use rapid-acting or regular insulin. Rapid-acting insulin will lower the BG quicker, and is preferable.

SLIDING SCALE EXAMPLE	
BLOOD GLUCOSE READING (MG/DL)	**INSTRUCTION**
< 60	Hold insulin; contact MD
150-200	Give 2 units of insulin
201-250	Give 4 units of insulin
251-300	Give 6 units of insulin
301-350	Give 8 units of insulin
351-400	Give 10 units of insulin
401-450	Call MD

HYPERGLYCEMIC CRISES

DIABETIC KETOACIDOSIS

Diabetic ketoacidosis (DKA) is a life-threatening crisis with high BG, ketoacidosis and ketonuria (i.e., ketones in the urine). DKA is most common in T1D, but can occur in T2D. DKA is commonly the initial presentation in T1D or caused by insulin non-adherence (e.g., a mechanical pump failure) or subtherapeutic insulin dosing (e.g., increased insulin requirements due to a stressor, like an infection).

In DKA, ketones are present because triglycerides and amino acids are used for energy, which produces free fatty acids (FFAs) and glucagon converts the FFAs into ketones. Insulin normally prevents this conversion, but in DKA, insulin is absent or severely lacking. DKA can be recognized by:

- BG > 250 mg/dL

- Ketones (urine and serum, can be recognized as "fruity" breath), abdominal pain, nausea and vomiting, dehydration

- Anion gap acidosis (arterial pH < 7.35, anion gap > 12)

HYPEROSMOLAR HYPERGLYCEMIC STATE

Hyperosmolar hyperglycemic state (HHS) has a higher mortality rate than DKA, but is less common. HHS is most common in T2D. The primary cause is illness (e.g., infection, stroke) that leads to less fluid intake. This, along with fluid shifts and osmotic diuresis, leads to severe dehydration with altered consciousness. Ketones are not present because in T2D the patient still makes insulin. HHS is recognized by:

- Confusion, delirium

- BG > 600 mg/dL, with high serum osmolality > 320 mOsm/L

- Extreme dehydration

- pH > 7.3, bicarbonate > 15 mEq/L

DKA AND HHS TREATMENT
The primary treatment is aggressive fluids (first) and insulin to treat the hyperglycemia
FLUIDS first for all patients Start with NS When blood glucose reaches 200 mg/dL, change to D5W½NS
REGULAR insulin infusion (regular is preferable in IV solutions) 1) 0.1 units/kg bolus, then 0.1 units/kg/hr continuous infusion OR 2) 0.14 units/kg/hr continuous infusion
PREVENT hypokalemia Insulin shifts K+ into the cells; the K+ will fall Monitor K+ and keep serum level between 4-5 mEq/L
TREAT acidosis if pH < 6.9; acidosis may be corrected by fluids Give sodium bicarbonate if needed

SELECTING DRUG TREATMENT

The Study Tip Gal below summarizes some of the key safety issues seen with medications for diabetes, and the following Case Scenario highlights how these safety issues could appear in exam questions. More examples can be found in the QBank.

SUMMARY OF DRUG SAFETY ISSUES

IF PRESENT	AVOID
Cancer	GLP-1 agonists (thyroid, including medullary thyroid carcinoma)
Gastroparesis, GI disorders	GLP-1 agonists, pramlintide
Genital infection/UTI	SGLT2 inhibitors
Heart failure	TZDs, alogliptin, saxagliptin
Hypoglycemia	Insulin, sulfonylureas, meglitinides and pramlintide
Hypotension/dehydration	SGLT2 inhibitors
Hypokalemia	Insulin
Ketoacidosis	SGLT2 inhibitors (can occur when BG < 250 mg/dL); ↑ risk with acute illness, dehydration, renal impairment. Discontinue SGLT2 inhibitors prior to surgery to reduce risk.
Lactic acidosis	Metformin; ↑ risk with renal impairment, alcoholism, hypoxia
Osteopenia/osteoporosis	Canagliflozin (↓ BMD, fractures), TZDs (fractures)
Pancreatitis	DPP-4 inhibitors, GLP-1 agonists
Peripheral neuropathy, PAD, foot ulcers	Canagliflozin
Sulfa allergy, severe	Consider avoiding sulfonylureas, or use cautiously
Renal insufficiency (eGFR or CrCl < 30)	Metformin, SGLT2 inhibitors, exenatide, glyburide; may need to start insulin at a lower dose
Weight gain/obesity	Sulfonylureas, meglitinides, TZDs, insulin

CASE SCENARIO

CS is a 56-year-old female with hypertension, diabetes and a past MI. At her last clinic visit 3 months ago, her A1C was 8.6% despite treatment with metformin ER 2,000 mg PO daily and *Januvia* 100 mg PO daily. At that time, *Invokana* 100 mg PO daily was added to her regimen. CS also takes aspirin, rosuvastatin, lisinopril, *Coreg CR* and hydrochlorothiazide for her hypertension and ASCVD.

At the current visit, CS complains of dry mouth, weakness, dizziness and lightheadedness. On a couple of occasions she has nearly fainted. These symptoms began approximately 2 months ago.

What do CS's symptoms likely describe?
CS has symptoms of dehydration and hypotension.

Which medications could be associated with these symptoms?
The addition of *Invokana* (canagliflozin) to her medication regimen put CS at risk for these adverse effects. *Invokana* decreases blood glucose by excreting it in the urine; water is also excreted with glucose. The use of diuretics and antihypertensive medications could be contributing to the problem due to additive effects.

What laboratory abnormalities could occur with this combination of medications?
CS is at risk for acute kidney injury. Evaluate for elevated BUN, SCr and assess the eGFR. Check an anion gap and ketones; if they are elevated, this is a sign of ketoacidosis, which can occur with *Invokana*.

If asked to select an alternative diabetes medication, what should be selected?
There are a number of treatment options for diabetes management. CS's history of ASCVD will dictate the next treatment option. An SGLT2 inhibitor was appropriate, but due to side effects, she should be switched to a GLP-1 agonist with benefit (e.g., dulaglutide, liraglutide or SC semaglutide).

KEY COUNSELING POINTS

See the Drug Formulations and Patient Counseling chapter for counseling language/layman's terminology.

Metformin

- Can cause:
  - ❏ Lactic acidosis.
  - ❏ Diarrhea, nausea; usually goes away. Taking with food and using long-acting metformin will help.
- With long-term metformin, take a vitamin B12 supplement.
- Long-acting formulations of metformin can leave a ghost tablet in the stool.

SGLT2 Inhibitors

- Can cause:
  - ❏ Hypotension.
  - ❏ Ketoacidosis. Stop prior to surgery to reduce risk.
  - ❏ Severe UTIs and genital fungal infections.
  - ❏ Canagliflozin: amputation risk (avoid if foot problems, neuropathy), fractures.

GLP-1 Receptor Agonists

- Subcutaneous injection (except *Rybelsus*). Rotate injections sites. See GLP-1 Agonist Injection Counseling section for details.
- *Byetta, Adlyxin:* give within 60 minutes of meals; others can be taken anytime.
- *Trulicity, Bydureon, Bydureon BCise, Ozempic:* inject once a week. The needles are inside the box.
- *Byetta, Victoza, Adlyxin:* needles need to be purchased.
- If injection has been in the refrigerator, leave at room temperature 15 minutes before using.
- *Bydureon BCise:* shake the injection well to mix the medication. Look in the window to check for drug particles; if present, shake again.
- Can cause:
  - ❏ Nausea, diarrhea, decrease in appetite, weight loss.
  - ❏ Pancreatitis and gallbladder disease.
  - ❏ Kidney damage, especially from dehydration due to severe vomiting or diarrhea.
  - ❏ *Bydureon:* injection-site reactions (abscesses, nodules).
  - ❏ *Ozempic:* diabetic retinopathy.

Thiazolidinediones

- Can cause:
  - ❏ Heart failure (cause or worsen).
  - ❏ Weight gain.
  - ❏ Bone fractures.

DPP-4 Inhibitors

- Can cause:
  - ❏ Pancreatitis.
  - ❏ Renal impairment.
  - ❏ Severe arthralgia.
  - ❏ Saxagliptin and alogliptin: heart failure.

Sulfonylureas/Meglitinides

- Take sulfonylureas with breakfast, except glipizide IR: take 30 minutes before breakfast.
- Take meglitinides 15 – 30 minutes before meals. Do not take if skipping the meal.
- Can cause:
  - ❏ Hypoglycemia.
  - ❏ Weight gain.

Insulins

- Subcutaneous injection (except *Afrezza*). Rotate injections sites. See Insulin Injection Counseling section for details.
- Can cause:
  - ❏ Hypoglycemia.
  - ❏ Hypokalemia.
  - ❏ Weight gain.
- Store unopened insulin pens/vials in the refrigerator. Once opened, store at room temperature and discard after the designated number of days (for that type of insulin).

Pramlintide

- When starting, reduce dose of mealtime insulin by 50%. Inject before meals. Do not mix with insulin.

Alpha Glucosidase Inhibitors

- Can cause flatulence and diarrhea.
- Do not cause hypoglycemia. If you get hypoglycemia (from another medication), treat with glucose tablets or gel.

Select Guidelines/References

American Diabetes Association (ADA). Standards of Medical Care in Diabetes. *Diabetes Care.* 2022;45 (suppl 1):S1-S264.

AACE Consensus Statement on the Comprehensive Type 2 Diabetes Management Algorithm - Executive Summary. *Endocr Pract.* 2020 Jan;26(1):107-139.

CHAPTER CONTENT

CONTENT LEGEND

= Study Tip Gal   = Key Drug Guy

Thyroid Gland (front view)

Larynx

Thyroid Gland

Right Lobe

Left Lobe

Isthmus

Trachea

Parathyroid Glands

Back View

iStock.com/VectorMine

CHAPTER 45

THYROID DISORDERS

BACKGROUND

The thyroid gland is located in the neck, below the Adam's apple and in front of the trachea (windpipe). The gland is shaped like a butterfly, with two symmetrical lobes. The lobes sit on each side of the trachea, connected by a stretch of tissue called the isthmus. The thyroid gland produces thyroid hormones, which regulate metabolism, including the chemical processes needed to maintain life: cardiac and nervous system functions, body temperature, muscle strength, skin dryness, menstrual cycles, weight and cholesterol levels. Hyperthyroidism (overactive thyroid) and hypothyroidism (underactive thyroid) are the most common thyroid disorders.

PATHOPHYSIOLOGY

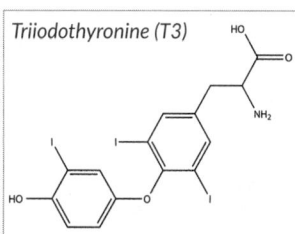

Triiodothyronine (T3)

iStock.com/chromatos

The two thyroid hormones produced by the thyroid gland are triiodothyronine, known as T3, and thyroxine, known as T4. The thyroid gland is the only organ that can absorb iodine, which is required for the production of both hormones (see T3 structure). T3 is primarily formed from the breakdown of T4. A small percentage (< 20%) is produced by the thyroid gland directly. T3 is more potent than T4 but has a shorter half-life.

Thyroid hormone production is regulated by thyroid-stimulating hormone (TSH), also referred to as thyrotropin. TSH is secreted by the pituitary gland, which is located in the brain and regulates growth and development.

ENDOCRINE CONDITIONS

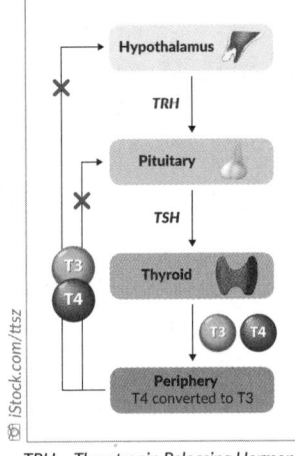

iStock.com/ttsz

TRH = Thyrotropin Releasing Hormone
TSH = Thyroid-Stimulating Hormone

Negative Feedback Loop

Feedback loops are used to regulate the production of hormones secreted by the pituitary and thyroid glands, including T3 and T4. When the level of circulating (free) T4 increases, it inhibits the secretion of TSH. Less TSH will lead to a decrease in T4 production.

T3 and T4 are transported in the blood and are largely bound to proteins. Free T4 (FT4) is the unbound, active form that is monitored in patients with thyroid disorders.

SELECT DRUGS AND CONDITIONS THAT CAN CAUSE HYPOTHYROIDISM

KEY DRUGS

Remember: **I TALC**

Interferons*

Tyrosine kinase inhibitors (e.g., sunitinib)

Amiodarone*

Lithium

Carbamazepine

Conditions:
Hashimoto's Disease

Others:
Oxcarbazepine
Eslicarbazepine
Phenytoin

Conditions:
Iodine deficiency
Pituitary failure
Surgical removal of thyroid gland
Congenital hypothyroidism
Thyroid gland ablation with radioactive iodine
External irradiation

*Can also cause hyperthyroidism (see Hyperthyroidism section)

HYPOTHYROIDISM

Hypothyroidism is a deficiency in T4, and consequently, an elevation in TSH. Hypothyroidism occurs more commonly in females (~80% of cases) and with increased age. When T4 decreases, the body slows down and the classic symptoms of low metabolism (e.g., fatigue and weight gain) appear. Hypothyroidism can cause depression, infertility, cardiovascular disease and other symptoms related to slow metabolism (see Study Tip Gal below).

The most common cause of hypothyroidism is Hashimoto's disease, an autoimmune condition in which a patient's own antibodies attack the thyroid gland. Drugs and conditions can cause hypothyroidism (see Key Drugs Guy).

Myxedema coma is an uncommon but potentially fatal complication of hypothyroidism that can occur when hypothyroidism is left untreated for a long time, or when hypothyroidism decompensates. It is a life-threatening emergency characterized by poor circulation, hypothermia and hypometabolism. The initial treatment for myxedema coma is IV levothyroxine.

S/SX OF HYPOTHYROIDISM

Cold intolerance/sensitivity	Myalgias
Dry skin	Weakness
Fatigue	Depression
Muscle cramps	Bradycardia
Voice changes	Coarse hair or loss of hair
Constipation	Menorrhagia (heavier than normal menstrual periods)
Weight gain	Memory and mental impairment
Goiter (possible; can be due to low iodine intake)	

DIAGNOSIS

A diagnosis of hypothyroidism is made using two laboratory test results:

- Low free T4: normal range 0.9 – 2.3 ng/dL
- High TSH: normal range 0.3 – 3 mIU/L

Screening should be considered in patients > 60 years old.

MONITORING

Thyroid function tests include TSH, FT4 and total T3. TSH is the primary test to monitor thyroid function in those receiving thyroid hormone replacement with drug treatment (occasionally FT4 is ordered with TSH). The TSH level and symptoms should be monitored every 4 – 6 weeks until levels are normal, then 4 – 6 months later, then yearly. It is important to monitor thyroid function as the patient ages because a reduction in thyroid hormone replacement dose can be required. Too high of a thyroid hormone replacement dose in elderly patients can cause atrial fibrillation and fractures. Serum FT4 is monitored in addition to TSH in central hypothyroidism (rare), which is a defect in pituitary production of TSH. FT4 is also monitored when treating hypothyroidism in pregnancy.

DRUG TREATMENT

The goals of treatment are to resolve symptoms, achieve euthyroid state (i.e., normal levels of thyroid hormones) and avoid over-treatment; excessive doses of thyroid hormone will cause hyperthyroidism. Patients should be counseled on symptoms of both hypo- and hyperthyroidism. Levothyroxine (T4) is the drug of choice for hypothyroidism. A consistent preparation (i.e., the same formulation and manufacturer) is preferred to minimize variability from refill to refill. Some patients state they feel better using other thyroid hormone formulations, including liothyronine (T3, such as *Cytomel*) or desiccated thyroid (T3 and T4, such as *Armour Thyroid*), although these are generally not recommended. Desiccated thyroid is called "natural thyroid" and is dosed in grains. It is not recommended because it can contain variable amounts of T3 and T4.

Levothyroxine has many drug interactions and unique administration recommendations due to binding; see the table below and the Drug Interactions section for details.

Iodine supplementation with kelp or other iodine-containing functional foods is not required in the U.S. because most table salt has iodine added (iodized salt). This has eliminated almost all U.S. cases of iodine deficiency goiter. Individuals who are restricting salt intake can consume foods high in iodine (e.g., dairy, seafood, meat, some breads) and can take a multivitamin containing iodine.

Hypothyroidism Treatment

DRUG	DOSING	SAFETY/SIDE EFFECTS/MONITORING
Levothyroxine (T4) **(Synthroid, Levoxyl, Unithroid,** *Euthyrox, Tirosint, Tirosint-SOL)* Capsule, tablet, injection, oral solution Drug of choice Check the therapeutic equivalence of a generic to a brand in the *Orange Book*. Not all generic levothyroxine formulations are A-rated to various brands.	Full replacement dose = 1.6 mcg/kg/day (IBW) Start with full replacement dose in otherwise healthy, young (< 50 years of age) patients with markedly ↑ TSH Start with partial replacement dose in milder hypothyroidism and those with comorbidities If known CAD, start with 12.5-25 mcg daily Elderly patients often need 20-25% less per kg; may require < 1 mcg/kg/day	**BOXED WARNING** Ineffective and potentially toxic when used for obesity or weight reduction, especially in euthyroid patients; high doses can cause serious, life-threatening toxic effects, particularly when used with some anorectic drugs (e.g., sympathomimetic amines) **CONTRAINDICATIONS** Uncorrected adrenal insufficiency **WARNINGS** ↓ dose in cardiovascular disease (chronic hypothyroidism predisposes to coronary artery disease), ↓ bone mineral density which can lead to osteoporosis
Thyroid, Desiccated USP (T3 and T4) (Armour Thyroid, *Nature-Throid, NP Thyroid, Westhroid, WP Thyroid)* Tablet	Start 15-30 mg daily (15 mg in cardiac disease); titrate in 15 mg increments Usual dose is 60-120 mg daily	**SIDE EFFECTS** Hyperthyroid symptoms can occur when the dose is too high: ↑ HR, palpitations, sweating, weight loss, arrhythmias, irritability **MONITORING** TSH levels and clinical symptoms every 4-6 weeks until levels are normal, then 4-6 months later, then yearly; serum FT4 in select patients **NOTES** Highly protein bound (> 99%)
Liothyronine (T3) **(Cytomel,** *Triostat)* Tablet, injection	Start 25 mcg daily; titrate in 12.5-25 mcg increments Usual dose is 25-75 mcg daily	Dose reduction may be necessary as the patient ages **Levothyroxine PO** Should be taken with water at the same time each day for consistent absorption, at least 60 minutes before breakfast or at bedtime (at least three hours after the last meal) Levothyroxine tablet colors are standard; they do not change between manufacturers (see Study Tip Gal on tablet colors) **Levothyroxine IV** IV to PO ratio is 0.75:1; use immediately upon reconstitution
Liotrix (T3 and T4 in 1:4 ratio) *(Thyrolar)* Tablet	Start 25 mcg levothyroxine/6.25 mcg liothyronine daily Usual dose is 50-100 mcg levothyroxine/ 12.5-25 mcg liothyronine	**Levothyroxine oral solution** Can be given undiluted or diluted (in water only); store in original container **Thyroid, Desiccated USP** Natural porcine-derived thyroid that contains both T3 and T4; less predictable potency and stability **Liothyronine** Shorter half-life causes fluctuations in T3 levels

ENDOCRINE CONDITIONS

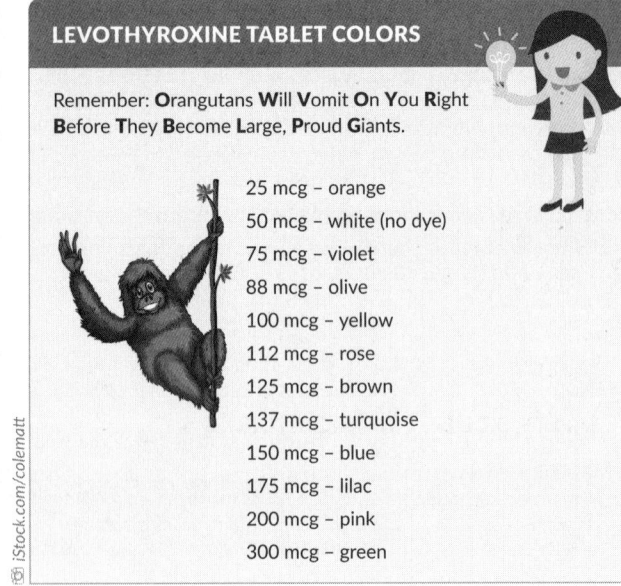

LEVOTHYROXINE TABLET COLORS

Remember: **O**rangutans **Wi**ll **V**omit **O**n **Y**ou **R**ight **B**efore **T**hey **B**ecome **L**arge, **P**roud **G**iants.

25 mcg – orange
50 mcg – white (no dye)
75 mcg – violet
88 mcg – olive
100 mcg – yellow
112 mcg – rose
125 mcg – brown
137 mcg – turquoise
150 mcg – blue
175 mcg – lilac
200 mcg – pink
300 mcg – green

© iStock.com/colematt

DRUG INTERACTIONS

Drugs that ↓ the effect of thyroid replacement hormone treatment:

- Drugs that ↓ levothyroxine absorption:
  - Antacids and polyvalent cations containing iron, calcium, aluminum or magnesium, multivitamins (containing ADEK, folate, iron), cholestyramine, orlistat *(Xenical, Alli)*, sevelamer and sucralfate: separate doses by four hours from thyroid replacement therapy.
  - Sodium polystyrene sulfonate and patiromer *(Veltassa)*: separate doses by three hours from thyroid replacement therapy.
  - Lanthanum: separate doses by two hours from thyroid replacement therapy.
- Estrogen, SSRIs and hepatic inducers ↓ thyroid hormone levels.
- Beta-blockers, amiodarone, propylthiouracil (PTU) and systemic steroids can ↓ the effectiveness of levothyroxine by ↓ the conversion of T4 to T3.
- Thyroid hormone is highly protein bound (> 99%). Drugs can cause protein-binding site displacement (e.g., phenytoin).

Thyroid hormone replacement treatment can change the concentration or effect of these drugs:

- ↑ effect of warfarin (e.g., ↑ PT/INR)
- ↓ levels of theophylline

KEY COUNSELING POINTS

See the Drug Formulations and Patient Counseling chapter for counseling language/layman's terminology.

LEVOTHYROXINE

- Drug interactions due to binding.
- Take this medication with water, 60 minutes before breakfast or at bedtime (at least three hours after your last meal). Take this medication every day, even if you feel well.
- If you get a prescription refill and your new pills look different, speak to the pharmacist.
- Tell your prescriber if you become pregnant; it is likely that your dose will need to be increased during pregnancy or if you plan to breastfeed.
- Requires blood work on a regular basis (at least annually).

HYPERTHYROIDISM

Hyperthyroidism (overactive thyroid or thyrotoxicosis) occurs when there is over-production of thyroid hormones. FT4 is high, TSH is low, and symptoms are nearly opposite of those seen in hypothyroidism. Hyperthyroidism can significantly accelerate metabolism, causing weight loss, agitation, heat intolerance and other symptoms (see Study Tip Gal below).

Left untreated, hyperthyroidism can cause tachycardia, arrhythmias, heart failure and osteoporosis.

S/SX OF HYPERTHYROIDISM

Heat intolerance or increased sweating	Insomnia
Weight loss	Tremor
Agitation, nervousness, irritability, anxiety	Thinning hair
Palpitations and tachycardia	Goiter (possible)
Fatigue and muscle weakness	Exophthalmos (protrusion of the eyeballs), diplopia
Frequent bowel movements or diarrhea	Light or absent menstrual periods

Causes

The most common cause of hyperthyroidism is <u>Graves' disease</u>, which most commonly occurs in females aged 30 – 50 years. Graves' disease is an <u>autoimmune</u> disorder (like Hashimoto's), but instead of destroying the thyroid gland, the <u>antibodies stimulate the thyroid</u> to produce too much T4. Less common causes include thyroid nodules and thyroiditis (inflammation of the thyroid). <u>Drug-induced causes</u> of <u>hyperthyroidism</u> include <u>iodine, amiodarone and interferons</u>. Excess iodine increases the synthesis and release of thyroid hormone. Iodine-induced hyperthyroidism can be due to excess iodine in the diet or <u>exposure to radiographic contrast media</u>. Excessive doses of thyroid hormone can cause hyperthyroidism.

DRUG TREATMENT

Treatment involves antithyroid <u>medications</u>, destroying part of the gland via <u>radioactive iodine</u> (RAI-131) or <u>surgery</u>. RAI-131 has historically been considered the preferred treatment in Graves' disease, but all three treatment options are effective and relatively safe. With any option, the patient can be treated with <u>beta-blockers</u> first for <u>symptom control</u> (to reduce <u>palpitations, tremors and tachycardia</u>). Propylthiouracil (PTU) or methimazole can be used as a temporary measure until surgery is complete. It takes <u>1 – 3 months of treatment</u> with antithyroid medications at <u>high doses</u> to <u>control symptoms</u>. Once symptoms are controlled, <u>the dose</u> should be <u>reduced</u> to <u>prevent hypothyroidism</u> from occurring.

Hyperthyroidism Treatment

DRUG	DOSING	SAFETY/SIDE EFFECTS/MONITORING
Thionamides – <u>inhibit synthesis of thyroid</u> hormones by blocking the oxidation of iodine in the thyroid gland; PTU also inhibits **peripheral conversion** of T4 to T3		
Propylthiouracil (PTU) Tablet	50-150 mg Q8H initially until euthyroid (higher doses for more severe hyperthyroidism), followed by dose reduction	**BOXED WARNINGS (PTU)** <u>Severe liver injury and acute liver failure</u> <u>Pregnancy: PTU preferred in 1st trimester</u> (due to increased risk of fetal abnormalities from methimazole) **WARNINGS** <u>Hepatotoxicity</u>, bone marrow suppression (rare, includes <u>agranulocytosis</u>), drug-induced lupus erythematosus (<u>DILE</u>), vasculitis **SIDE EFFECTS** <u>GI upset</u>, headache, rash (exfoliative dermatitis, pruritus), fever, constipation, loss of taste/taste perversion, lymphadenopathy, bleeding
Methimazole *(Tapazole)* Tablet	Mild hyperthyroidism: 5 mg Q8H initially until euthyroid (↑ doses for more severe hyperthyroidism), then 5-15 mg daily	**MONITORING** FT4 and T3 every 4-6 weeks until euthyroid, TSH, CBC, LFTs and PT Patient must monitor for liver toxicity (abdominal pain, yellow skin/eyes, dark urine, nausea, weakness) and infection (high fever or severe sore throat) **NOTES** Take with food to reduce GI upset <u>Methimazole</u> is the <u>drug of choice</u> (due to a lower risk of liver damage) except in certain situations, noted below <u>PTU</u> is preferred in <u>thyroid storm</u> and if methimazole is not tolerated Pregnancy: PTU is preferred in the <u>1st trimester</u> (see Boxed Warning); <u>methimazole</u> can be used in the <u>2nd and 3rd trimesters</u> (to ↓ the risk of liver toxicity from PTU)

ENDOCRINE CONDITIONS

DRUG	DOSING	SAFETY/SIDE EFFECTS/MONITORING
Iodides – temporarily inhibit secretion of thyroid hormones; T4 and T3 levels will be reduced for several weeks but effect will not be maintained		
Potassium iodide and iodine solution (*Lugol's Solution*) Oral solution	Preparation for thyroidectomy: 5-7 drops Q8H for 10 days prior to surgery (off-label)	**CONTRAINDICATIONS** Hypersensitivity to iodide or iodine, dermatitis herpetiformis, hypocomplementemic vasculitis, nodular thyroid condition with heart disease **SIDE EFFECTS** Rash, metallic taste, sore throat/gums, GI upset, urticaria, hypo/hyperthyroidism with prolonged use
Saturated solution of potassium iodide (*SSKI, ThyroSafe*) Oral solution	Preparation for thyroidectomy: 1-2 drops Q8H for 10 days prior to surgery (off-label)	**MONITORING** Thyroid function tests, s/sx of hyperthyroidism **NOTES** Dilute in a glassful of water, juice, or milk; take with food or milk to ↓ GI upset *SSKI* is also used as an expectorant

POTASSIUM IODIDE USE AFTER EXPOSURE TO RADIATION

Potassium iodide (KI) blocks the accumulation of radioactive iodine in the thyroid gland, thus preventing thyroid cancer. Potassium iodide should be taken as soon as possible after radiation exposure on the advice of public health or emergency management personnel only. The correct dose must be used; higher doses do not offer greater protection. Refer to the CDC website for age-specific dosing based on the duration of radiation exposure (https://emergency.cdc.gov/radiation/ki.asp). Iodized salt and foods do not contain enough iodine to block radioactive iodine and are not recommended.

THYROID STORM

Thyroid storm is a life-threatening medical emergency characterized by decompensated hyperthyroidism that can be precipitated by infection, trauma, surgery, radioactive iodine treatment or non-adherence to antithyroid medication. It is important to recognize symptoms so that treatment can be implemented promptly (see Study Tip Gal).

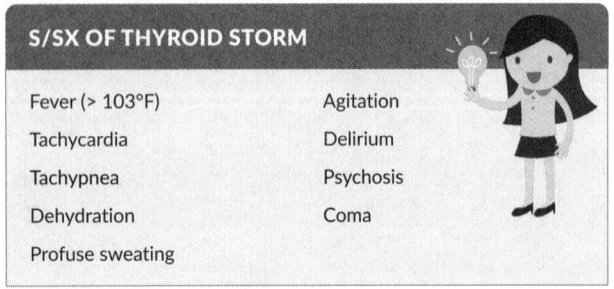

S/SX OF THYROID STORM	
Fever (> 103°F)	Agitation
Tachycardia	Delirium
Tachypnea	Psychosis
Dehydration	Coma
Profuse sweating	

DRUG TREATMENT

- Antithyroid drug therapy (PTU is preferred; 500 – 1,000 mg loading dose, then 250 mg PO Q4H)

  PLUS

- Inorganic iodide therapy such as *SSKI* 5 drops (in water or juice) PO Q6H or *Lugol's Solution* 4 – 8 drops PO Q6 – 8H

  PLUS

- Beta-blocker (e.g., propranolol 40 – 80 mg PO Q6H)

  PLUS

- Systemic steroid (e.g., dexamethasone 2 – 4 mg PO Q6H)

  PLUS

- Aggressive cooling with acetaminophen and cooling blankets and other supportive treatments (e.g., antiarrhythmics, insulin, fluids, electrolytes)

The antithyroid drug should be given ≥ 1 hour before iodide to block synthesis of thyroid hormone. PTU tablets can be crushed and administered through an NG tube if needed.

THYROID DISEASE AND PREGNANCY

PREGNANCY AND HYPOTHYROIDISM

Untreated maternal hypothyroidism has been associated with loss of pregnancy, low birth weight, premature birth and lower IQ in children. Levothyroxine is safe in pregnancy and is the recommended treatment. Pregnant women treated with thyroid hormone replacement will require a 30 – 50% increase in the dose throughout the course of their pregnancy and for several months after giving birth. Aggressive control of hypothyroidism in pregnancy is recommended. Treatment should ideally be started prior to the pregnancy.

PREGNANCY AND HYPERTHYROIDISM

Poor control of hyperthyroidism in pregnancy is associated with pregnancy loss, prematurity and low birth weight, like hypothyroidism, as well as thyroid storm, maternal hypertension and congestive heart failure. There can be lasting effects in the baby, including seizure disorders and neurobehavioral disorders. Pregnancy should be postponed until a stable euthyroid state is reached. If a woman with hyperthyroidism becomes pregnant, she should be evaluated to see if treatment can be stopped (mild disease). If treatment is needed, it should be with antithyroid drugs based on the trimester. For the first trimester, PTU should be used (due to fetal toxicity with methimazole). After that, the decision is individualized, as both PTU and methimazole carry potential risks. Historically, the patient would be switched to methimazole for the remainder of the pregnancy.

Select Guidelines/References

2016 American Thyroid Association Guidelines for Diagnosis and Management of Hyperthyroidism and Other Causes of Thyrotoxicosis. *Thyroid.* 2016;26(10):1343-1422.

Guidelines for the Treatment of Hypothyroidism: Prepared by the American Thyroid Association Task Force on Thyroid Hormone Replacement. *Thyroid.* 2014;24(12):1670-1751.

2017 Guidelines of the American Thyroid Association for the Diagnosis and Management of Thyroid Disease During Pregnancy and the Postpartum. *Thyroid.* 2017;27(3):315-389.

CONTENT LEGEND

 = Study Tip Gal    = Key Drug Guy

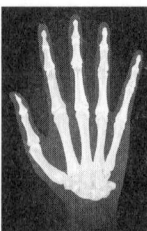
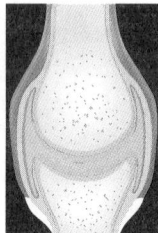
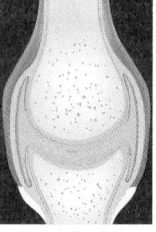
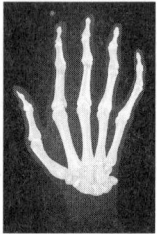
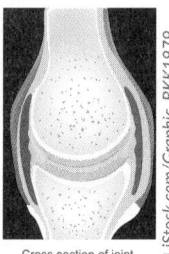

Hand normal joint   Cross section of joint   Hand with Rheumatoid arthritis   Cross section of joint with Rheumatoid arthritis

iStock.com/Graphic_BKK1979

CHAPTER 46

SYSTEMIC STEROIDS & AUTOIMMUNE CONDITIONS

SYSTEMIC STEROIDS

There are several drug classes that can be used to treat inflammation, including drugs that target the chemical pathway of inflammation (e.g., various biologics), cancer drugs that have strong anti-inflammatory properties, steroids and NSAIDs. Steroids and NSAIDs are used commonly; of these two classes, steroids are stronger anti-inflammatory drugs. Both have serious adverse effects, but chronic use of NSAIDs is considered to be safer than long-term use of steroids. See the Pain chapter for a review of NSAIDs.

Steroids are used for a variety of conditions, including inflammatory conditions (e.g., rheumatoid arthritis, psoriasis, acute asthma exacerbation), immune suppression post-transplant and adrenal insufficiency [to replace endogenous (naturally produced in the body) steroids that the adrenal gland is not producing in adequate amounts]. The two primary endogenous steroids that can require replacement are:

- Cortisol: replaced by giving any of the steroids.

- Aldosterone: replaced by giving fludrocortisone.

Fludrocortisone mimics aldosterone. It has mineralocorticoid activity, which is used to maintain a balance of water and electrolytes. This helps to keep blood pressure stable. Fludrocortisone is FDA-approved for Addison's disease but is also used off-label for orthostatic hypotension. Other commonly used steroids (e.g., prednisone, hydrocortisone) have more glucocorticoid activity, which has more anti-inflammatory effects. The rest of this section discusses only the commonly used glucocorticoids, which will be referred to simply as steroids. Systemic steroids can cause the adrenal gland to stop producing cortisol due to feedback inhibition. This is called suppression of the hypothalamic-pituitary-adrenal (HPA) axis (see diagram on the following page). When long-term steroids are discontinued, they need to be tapered off to give the adrenal gland time to resume cortisol production.

CUSHING'S SYNDROME

Cushing's syndrome can develop when the adrenal gland produces too much cortisol, or if exogenous (i.e., taken, as a drug) steroids are taken in doses higher than the normal amount of endogenous cortisol. See the diagram below for the adverse effects of long-term steroids and Cushing's syndrome.

Addison's disease can be thought of as the opposite of Cushing's. In Addison's disease, the adrenal gland is not making enough cortisol. If exogenous steroids are stopped suddenly, it can cause an "Addisonian Crisis." Hallmarks of an Addisonian Crisis are volume depletion and hypotension, which can be fatal.

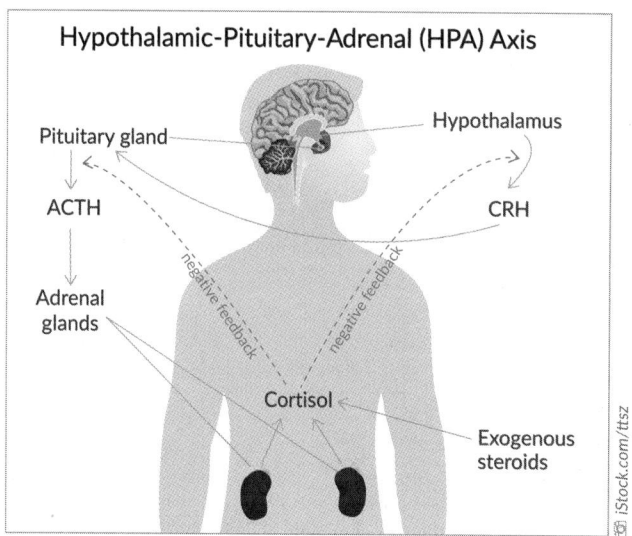

Hypothalamic-Pituitary-Adrenal (HPA) Axis

CRH = Corticotropin Releasing Hormone;
ACTH = Adrenocorticotropic Hormone, also called corticotropin

iStock.com/ttsz

Long-Term Effects of Steroids (e.g., Cushing's Syndrome)

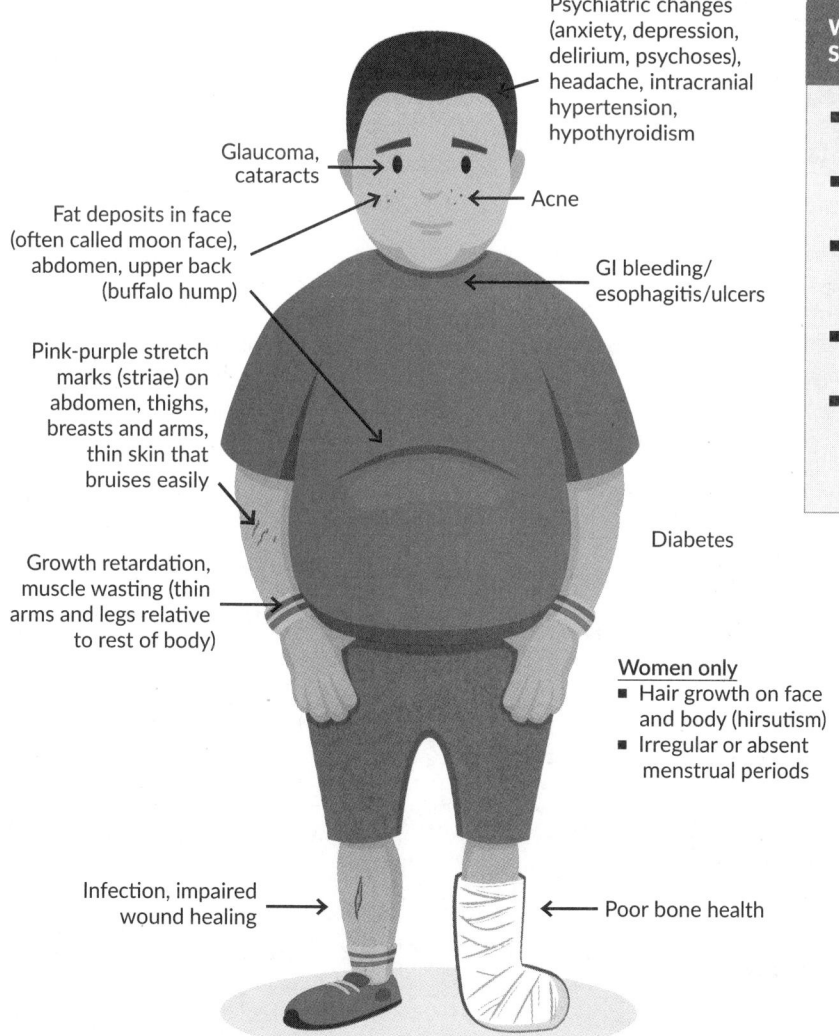

Psychiatric changes (anxiety, depression, delirium, psychoses), headache, intracranial hypertension, hypothyroidism

Glaucoma, cataracts

Fat deposits in face (often called moon face), abdomen, upper back (buffalo hump)

Acne

GI bleeding/ esophagitis/ulcers

Pink-purple stretch marks (striae) on abdomen, thighs, breasts and arms, thin skin that bruises easily

Growth retardation, muscle wasting (thin arms and legs relative to rest of body)

Diabetes

Women only
- Hair growth on face and body (hirsutism)
- Irregular or absent menstrual periods

Infection, impaired wound healing

Poor bone health

iStock.com/ttsz

WAYS TO REDUCE SYSTEMIC STEROID RISKS

- Use alternate day dosing (skip every other day); this decreases Cushing-like side effects.

- For joint inflammation, inject into the joint so the drug stays local.

- For a condition in the gut, use a steroid with low systemic absorption, such as budesonide (Entocort EC).

- For treatment of asthma, use inhaled steroids that mostly stay in the lungs.

- For conditions that require long-term steroids (e.g., transplant, a severe autoimmune condition), use the lowest possible dose for the shortest possible time.

SYSTEMIC STEROIDS (PO, IV) DOSE EQUIVALENCE

Cortisone	25 mg	Short-acting
Hydrocortisone	20 mg	
Prednisone	5 mg	Intermediate-acting
Prednisolone	5 mg	
Methylprednisolone	4 mg	
Triamcinolone	4 mg	
Dexamethasone	0.75 mg	Long-acting & highest potency
Betamethasone	0.6 mg	

STEROIDS: LEAST POTENT TO MOST POTENT

Remember: **C**ute **H**ot **P**harmacists and **P**hysicians **M**arry **T**ogether & **D**eliver **B**abies

© iStock.com/aleksey-martynyuk

CASE SCENARIO

AS is a 30-year-old female who presented to the hospital with an acute flare of her Crohn's disease. She was started on *Solu-Medrol* 40 mg IV BID. The medical team is now ready to transition her to oral prednisone at an equivalent dose. Assuming the IV:PO ratio of *Solu-Medrol* is 1:1, what is the equivalent daily dose?

$$\frac{\text{Methylprednisolone 4 mg}}{\text{Prednisone 5 mg}} = \frac{\text{Methylprednisolone 80 mg}}{\text{Prednisone X mg}}$$

X = 100 mg Prednisone

GLUCOCORTICOIDS (SYSTEMIC STEROIDS)

DRUG	DOSING	SAFETY/SIDE EFFECTS/MONITORING
Dexamethasone (***DexPak 6, 10 or 13 day, Decadron**, Dexamethasone Intensol, DoubleDex*, others)	Dosing varies by condition Many formulations: liquids, ODT (children), injections [fast-acting, long-acting (for joints usually)], tablets, others If once daily, take between 7-8 AM to mimic the natural diurnal cortisol release Take oral doses <u>with food</u> to decrease GI upset	**CONTRAINDICATIONS** Live vaccines, serious systemic infections **WARNINGS** <u>Adrenal suppression</u> – HPA axis suppression may lead to adrenal crisis and death; if taking longer than 14 days, <u>must taper slowly</u> Immunosuppression, psychiatric disturbances, Kaposi sarcoma, can worsen other conditions (use with caution in heart failure, diabetes, hypertension, osteoporosis)
Hydrocortisone (***Solu-Cortef**, Cortef*)		
Methylprednisolone (***Medrol, Solu-Medrol**, Depo-Medrol*, others)		**SIDE EFFECTS** **Short-term side effects (used < 1 month)** ↑ <u>appetite/weight gain, emotional instability</u> (euphoria, mood swings, irritability), <u>insomnia</u>, ↑ intraocular pressure, fluid retention, indigestion, bitter taste, ↑ in blood pressure and blood glucose with higher doses
Prednisone (***Deltasone**, Prednisone Intensol, Rayos*)		**Long-term side effects** See previous Long-Term Effects of Steroids figure
Prednisolone (***Millipred, Orapred ODT***)		**MONITORING** BP, weight, appetite, mood, growth (children/adolescents), bone mineral density, blood glucose, electrolytes, infection, IOP if > 6 weeks
Triamcinolone (***Kenalog**, Pro-C-Dure 5, Pro-C-Dure 6*, others)		**NOTES** <u>Cortisone</u> is a <u>prodrug of cortisol</u>
Betamethasone (*Celestone Soluspan, ReadySharp Betamethasone*)		<u>Prednisone</u> is a <u>prodrug of prednisolone</u> <u>Methylprednisolone</u> is available in a therapy pack (commonly called a "Medrol Dose Pack," see <u>Study Tip Gal</u> on next page) and as an <u>injection</u>
Cortisone		Prednisolone is used commonly in children (many formulations)

Topical steroids are discussed in the Common Skin Conditions chapter.

IMMUNOSUPPRESSION FROM STEROIDS

A patient is immunosuppressed when using ≥ 2 mg/kg/day or ≥ 20 mg/day of prednisone or prednisone equivalent (see potency table) for > 2 weeks.

Immunosuppressed patients cannot receive live vaccines and have a high risk of infection.

Due to HPA axis suppression, the steroid will need to be tapered slowly to allow the adrenal gland to resume normal cortisol production; otherwise, the patient is at risk for Addisonian Crisis.

There are many ways to taper steroids; a common method is to reduce the dose by ~10-20% every few days. Tapers can last 7-14 days (or longer or shorter), depending on the condition being treated.

TREATING ACUTE INFLAMMATION WITH STEROIDS

Give a high dose initially (to quickly reduce inflammation), then taper the dose down to treat the remaining inflammation while preventing a rebound attack.

The *Medrol* **therapy pack*** provides a tapering system that is convenient for the patient. The pack includes 21 x 4 mg tablets used in a tapered dose schedule over 6 days:

Day 1: 2 tablets before breakfast, 1 tablet after lunch, 1 tablet after dinner, 2 tablets at bedtime

Day 2: 1 tablet before breakfast, 1 tablet after lunch, 1 tablet after dinner, 2 tablets at bedtime

Day 3: 1 tablet before breakfast, 1 tablet after lunch, 1 tablet after dinner, 1 tablet at bedtime

Day 4: 1 tablet before breakfast, 1 tablet after lunch, 1 tablet at bedtime

Day 5: 1 tablet before breakfast, 1 tablet at bedtime

Day 6: 1 tablet before breakfast

*Will not be appropriate for all patients (e.g., may need a longer taper or a higher starting dose)

AUTOIMMUNE CONDITIONS

Autoimmune diseases are conditions that occur when the body's immune system attacks and destroys healthy body tissue. The immune system is a complex organization of cells and antibodies designed to "seek and destroy" invaders of the body, particularly infections. Symptoms vary based on the type of autoimmune disease and the location of the immune response. Common symptoms of most autoimmune diseases include fatigue, weakness and pain. Nonspecific laboratory blood tests that can be useful in detecting inflammation include erythrocyte sedimentation rate (ESR), C-reactive protein (CRP), rheumatoid factor (RF) and anti-nuclear antibody (ANA).

Rheumatoid arthritis (RA), systemic lupus erythematosus (SLE), multiple sclerosis (MS), celiac disease, Sjögren's syndrome, Raynaud's, myasthenia gravis and psoriasis are discussed in this chapter. Other autoimmune diseases covered elsewhere in the book include type 1 diabetes (see the Diabetes chapter) and Hashimoto's thyroiditis and Graves disease (see the Thyroid Disorders chapter).

TREATMENT

Treatment of autoimmune diseases typically involves drugs that suppress the immune system (e.g., steroids, disease-modifying antirheumatic drugs), which decrease the immune response (see Study Tip Gal for steroid immunosuppression overview). The use of strong immunosuppressants can increase the risk of certain conditions including:

- Re-activation of tuberculosis and hepatitis B and C (if present): testing (and treatment, if needed) must be done prior to the start of immunosuppressive drugs.

- Viruses: if the virus can be prevented by a live vaccine, the vaccine must be given prior to the start of immunosuppressive treatment.

- Lymphomas and certain skin cancers: these cancer types are normally suppressed by a competent immune system.

- Infections of various types (e.g., bacterial, fungal): this requires monitoring of symptoms (by the patient), complete blood counts (CBC), and may require infection control measures.

RHEUMATOID ARTHRITIS

Rheumatoid arthritis (RA) is a chronic, progressive autoimmune disorder that primarily affects joints. Other organs in the body, including the kidneys, eyes, heart and lungs can be affected. Like many of the autoimmune conditions discussed in this chapter, the disease course is highly variable and some patients have much more aggressive disease than others.

CLINICAL PRESENTATION

RA typically results in warm, tender, swollen and painful joints. Articular (i.e., joint) pain usually presents in the smaller joints of the fingers, wrist, ankles and feet first. Bilateral, symmetrical disease is consistent with an RA diagnosis, in contrast to osteoarthritis (OA), which presents unilaterally (on one side of the body, such as the right hand).

The classic symptoms of RA are shown in the box to the right. RA is a systemic disease and has systemic symptoms, such as fever, weakness and loss of appetite. Stiffness and pain are worse after rest, which is why "morning stiffness" is a common complaint. In contrast, OA does not cause prolonged stiffness. Diagnosis will depend on a combination of signs, symptoms, lab tests and x-rays.

When a patient presents with joint pain and swelling, it can be challenging to identify the type of arthritis that is causing the symptoms. Joint erosion and rheumatoid nodules can be absent if RA is caught early. Anti-citrullinated peptide antibody (ACPA) and rheumatoid factor (RF) are useful laboratory tests in diagnosing RA. RF has lower specificity for RA and can be positive due to another autoimmune disorder (see the Biostatistics chapter).

NON-DRUG TREATMENT

Non-drug treatments include rest, physical therapy, occupational therapy, exercise, diet and weight control and surgical intervention (e.g., a joint replacement).

DRUG TREATMENT

RA is classified as low, moderate or high disease activity. Patients with symptomatic RA should be started on a disease-modifying antirheumatic drug (DMARD), regardless of the severity of disease. DMARDs work via various mechanisms to slow the disease process and help prevent further joint damage. The treatment goal is remission of the disease (or low disease activity). Methotrexate (MTX) is the preferred initial therapy for most patients. For patients with moderate or high disease activity despite MTX (with or without a systemic steroid), a combination of DMARDs or a tumor necrosis

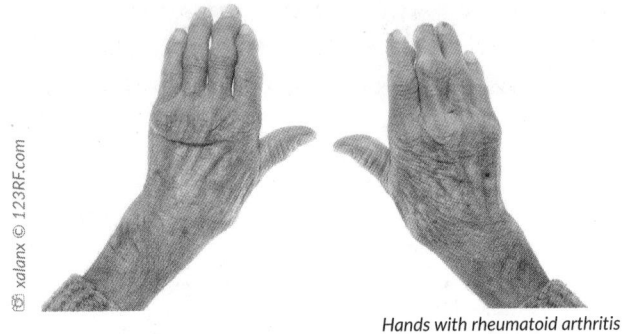

Hands with rheumatoid arthritis

ARTICULAR SYMPTOMS OF RA

Joint swelling	Weakness
Pain	Difficult to move
Stiffness	Edema
Bone deformity	Redness

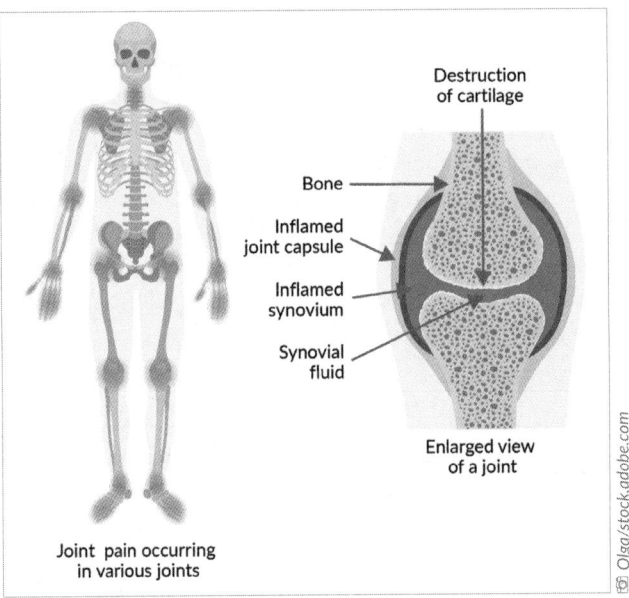

Joint pain occurring in various joints

factor (TNF) inhibitor biologic or a non-TNF biologic, with or without MTX, is recommended. Never use two biologic DMARDs in combination due to the risk of serious (fatal) infections.

Low-dose steroids (defined as ≤ 10 mg/day of prednisone or equivalent) can be added in patients with moderate or high disease activity when starting a DMARD (as a "bridging" option to provide relief while waiting for the DMARD to take effect) and in patients with DMARD failure. Steroids are commonly used in RA flares and should be used at the lowest dose and for the shortest duration possible. Compared to steroids, NSAIDs are a weaker, less toxic option for bridging. For the anti-inflammatory effect, high doses are required. NSAID toxicity (e.g., GI bleeds, CVD risk) must be considered.

Traditional (Non-Biologic) Disease-Modifying Antirheumatic Drugs (DMARDs)

DRUG	DOSING	SAFETY/SIDE EFFECTS/MONITORING
Methotrexate **(Trexall,** Otrexup, Rasuvo, Xatmep) _Trexall_ is an oral tablet _Otrexup_ and _Rasuvo_ are single-dose (needle included) SC auto-injectors _Xatmep_ is an oral solution for use in pediatric patients Injection (IV/IT) – for oncology use Irreversibly binds and inhibits dihydrofolate reductase, inhibiting folate, thymidylate synthetase and purine; has immune modulator and anti-inflammatory activity	7.5-20 mg once weekly (PO, SC, IM) Low weekly doses are used for RA; to avoid error, it is safest to take as a single dose (rather than divided oral dosages of 2.5 mg Q12H x 3 doses per week – see below) Never dose daily for RA; numerous incidences of adverse events (e.g., mouth sores, intestinal bleeding, liver damage) have occurred due to patients taking daily	**BOXED WARNINGS** Hepatotoxicity, myelosuppression, mucositis/stomatitis, pregnancy (teratogenic), acute renal failure, pneumonitis, GI toxicity, dermatologic reactions, malignant lymphomas, potentially fatal opportunistic infections; renal and lung toxicity are more likely when using higher oncology doses **CONTRAINDICATION** Pregnancy, breastfeeding, alcoholism, chronic liver disease, blood dyscrasias, immunodeficiency syndrome **SIDE EFFECTS** Vary by route and dosage N/V/D, ↑ LFTs, stomatitis, alopecia, photosensitivity, arthralgia, myalgia **MONITORING** CBC, LFTs (at baseline, every 2-4 weeks for first 3 months or following dose increases, every 8-12 weeks for 3-6 months, then less frequently), chest X-ray, hepatitis B and C serologies (if at high risk), SCr, PFTs (if lung-related symptoms), TB test **NOTES** Folate can be given to ↓ hematological, GI and hepatic side effects; give 5 mg PO weekly on the day following MTX administration (some take 1 mg daily on non-MTX days) _Xatmep_ requires no preparation; eliminates the need for needles, crushing or splitting tablets, or compounding tablets into a liquid formulation
Hydroxychloroquine **(Plaquenil)** Tablet +/- MTX Immune modulator	400-600 mg/day initially, then 200-400 mg/day for maintenance dose Take with food or milk	**WARNINGS** Irreversible retinopathy, myopathy and neuropathy, cardiomyopathy and QT prolongation, hypoglycemia, psychiatric events (including suicidal behaviors) **SIDE EFFECTS** N/V/D, abdominal pain, rash, pruritus, headache, vision changes (dose-related), pigmentation changes of the skin and hair (rare), bone marrow suppression (anemia, leukopenia, thrombocytopenia) and hemolysis in patients with G6PD deficiency, hepatotoxicity **MONITORING** CBC, LFTs and ECG at baseline and periodically; eye exam and muscle strength at baseline and every 3 months during prolonged therapy **NOTES** Lower risk of liver toxicity than MTX, can use as an alternative when there is a concern for liver disease Monotherapy: if low disease activity and symptoms < 24 months If inadequate or no response after 6 months, consider alternative
Sulfasalazine (_Azulfidine, Azulfidine EN-tabs_) Tablet +/- MTX Immune modulator	500-1,000 mg/day initially, then 1,000 mg BID (max is 3 grams/day) Take with food and 8 oz. of water to prevent crystalluria	**CONTRAINDICATION** Patients with a sulfa or salicylate allergy, GI or GU obstruction, porphyria **WARNINGS** Blood dyscrasias, severe skin reactions (SJS/TEN), hepatic failure and pulmonary fibrosis; use caution in patients with G6PD deficiency **SIDE EFFECTS** Headache, rash, anorexia, dyspepsia, N/V/D, oligospermia (reversible), folate deficiency, arthralgia, crystalluria **MONITORING** CBC and LFTs (baseline, then every other week for first 3 months, then monthly for 3 months, then once every 3 months), renal function **NOTES** Can cause yellow-orange coloration of skin/urine Impairs folate absorption, can give 1 mg/day folate supplement

ENDOCRINE CONDITIONS

DRUG	DOSING	SAFETY/SIDE EFFECTS/MONITORING
Leflunomide (*Arava*) Tablet +/- MTX Inhibits pyrimidine synthesis resulting in anti-proliferative and anti-inflammatory effects Prodrug of teriflunomide	100 mg PO x 3 days, then 20 mg PO daily (can use 10 mg PO daily if unable to tolerate 20 mg) May omit loading dose if at higher risk of liver toxicity or myelosuppression	**BOXED WARNINGS** Do not use in pregnancy (teratogenic); must test for and rule out pregnancy prior to starting therapy Hepatotoxicity: avoid in pre-existing liver disease or ALT > 2x upper limit of normal (ULN) **CONTRAINDICATION** Pregnancy, severe hepatic impairment, current teriflunomide therapy **WARNINGS** Severe infections, serious skin reactions (SJS/TEN), peripheral neuropathy, interstitial lung disease, hypertension Upon discontinuation of treatment, use accelerated drug elimination procedure (see Notes) to reduce levels of active metabolite, teriflunomide **SIDE EFFECTS** ↑ LFTs, nausea, diarrhea, respiratory infections, rash, headache **MONITORING** LFTs and CBC at baseline and monthly for first 6 months, BP at baseline and regularly, screen for TB and pregnancy prior to starting therapy **NOTES** Accelerated drug elimination options: 1. Cholestyramine 8 grams PO TID x 11 days (use 4 g if 8 g dose not tolerated) 2. Activated charcoal suspension 50 grams PO Q12H x 11 days Must have negative pregnancy test prior and use 2 forms of birth control during treatment; if pregnancy is desired, must wait 2 years after discontinuation or use accelerated drug elimination procedure

Janus Kinase Inhibitors: inhibits janus kinase (JAK) enzymes, which stimulate immune cell function

DRUG	DOSING	SAFETY/SIDE EFFECTS/MONITORING
Tofacitinib (*Xeljanz, Xeljanz XR*) Tablet +/- non-biologic DMARDs (MTX)	5 mg PO BID XR: 11 mg PO daily Dose adjustments with moderate-strong CYP 450 3A4 inducers and hepatic or renal impairment Do not start if: absolute lymphocyte count < 500 cells/mm^3, Hgb < 9 g/dL, or ANC < 1,000 cells/mm$_3$	**BOXED WARNINGS** Serious infections including tuberculosis (TB), fungal, viral, bacterial or other opportunistic infections; screen for active and latent TB and treat before starting Malignancy: ↑ risk for lymphomas and other malignancies Thrombosis: ↑ risk of serious (sometimes fatal) blood clots, including pulmonary embolism (PE), deep vein thrombosis (DVT) and arterial thrombosis Mortality and major adverse cardiovascular events: ↑ risk in patients ≥ 50 years of age with ≥ 1 cardiovascular risk factor **WARNINGS** GI perforation, ↑ LFTs, hematologic toxicities, avoid live vaccines
Baricitinib (*Olumiant*) Tablet +/- non-biologic DMARDs (MTX)	2 mg PO daily GFR < 30 mL/min/1.73m^2: not recommended Do not start if: absolute lymphocyte count < 500 cells/mm^3, Hgb < 8 g/dL, or ANC < 1,000 cells/mm^3	**SIDE EFFECTS** Upper respiratory tract infections (URTIs), urinary tract infections (UTIs), diarrhea, HA, hypertension, ↑ lipids **MONITORING** CBC (for lymphopenia, neutropenia and anemia) and lipids at baseline, then 4-8 weeks later, then every 3 months, LFTs (at baseline and periodically thereafter), new-onset abdominal pain, signs of infection
Upadacitinib (*Rinvoq*) Tablet +/- non-biologic DMARDs (MTX)	15 mg daily Do not start if: absolute lymphocyte count < 500 cells/mm^3, Hgb < 8 g/dL, or ANC < 1,000 cells/mm^3	**NOTES** Do not use with biologic DMARDs or potent immunosuppressants Caution in patients of Asian descent (↑ frequency of side effects)

Methotrexate Drug Interactions

- Methotrexate should <u>not</u> be taken <u>with alcohol</u>; this combination ↑ the risk of liver toxicity.

- Renal elimination is ↓ by <u>aspirin/NSAIDs</u>, beta-lactams and probenecid, resulting in methotrexate toxicity; caution if using together.

- Sulfonamides and topical tacrolimus ↑ adverse effects of methotrexate. Avoid using together.

- Methotrexate can ↓ effectiveness of loop diuretics; loop diuretics can ↑ the methotrexate concentration. Use caution if using together.

- Methotrexate and cyclosporine levels will both ↑ when used together, leading to toxicity; avoid using together.

Anti-TNF Biologic DMARDs

<u>Tumor necrosis factor (TNF) alpha inhibitors</u> (also called anti-TNF biologics) are used for a variety of diseases. Dosing for RA is provided below. Recommended dosing for psoriatic arthritis, plaque psoriasis, Crohn's disease, ulcerative colitis and other indications may vary. Each drug has a <u>pregnancy registry</u> due to the unknown risks to the fetus. When the anti-TNF inhibitor is supplied as a single-dose prefilled syringe, auto-injector or vial kit for subcutaneous (SC) injection, <u>needles</u> are <u>included</u> with the device and do not require a separate purchase.

DRUG	DOSING	SAFETY/SIDE EFFECTS/MONITORING
Etanercept (Etanercept, Enbrel, *Enbrel Mini, Enbrel SureClick*) Biosimilars: *Erelzi, Eticovo* Single-dose prefilled syringe or auto-injector, multidose vial +/- MTX	50 mg <u>SC weekly</u>	**BOXED WARNINGS** <u>Serious infections</u>, some fatal, including TB, fungal, viral, bacterial or opportunistic; screen for <u>latent TB</u> (and <u>treat</u> if needed) prior to therapy Lymphomas and other <u>malignancies</u> **CONTRAINDICATIONS** Active systemic infection, doses > 5 mg/kg in moderate-severe heart failure (infliximab), sepsis (etanercept) **WARNINGS** Can cause <u>demyelinating disease</u>, <u>hepatitis B reactivation</u>, <u>heart failure, hepatotoxicity, lupus-like syndrome</u>, seizures, myelosuppression and severe infections <u>Do not use with other biologic DMARDs or live vaccines</u>
Adalimumab (Humira, *Humira Pen*) Biosimilars: *Abrilada, Amjevita, Cyltezo, Hadlima, Hulio, Hyrimoz* Single-dose prefilled syringe or pen +/- MTX	40 mg <u>SC every other week</u> (if not taking MTX, can ↑ dose to 40 mg SC weekly)	
Infliximab (Remicade) Biosimilars: *Avsola, Renflexis, Inflectra* Injection (IV) + MTX	3 mg/kg <u>IV</u> at weeks 0, 2 and 6, then every 8 weeks (can ↑ dose to 10 mg/kg or treat as often as every 4 weeks based on need, but infection risk will ↑) Requires a filter and is stable in <u>NS only</u> Infusion reactions: hypotension, fever, chills, pruritus (can premedicate with acetaminophen, antihistamine, steroids) <u>Delayed hypersensitivity reaction</u> 3-12 days after administration (fever, rash, myalgia, HA, sore throat)	**SIDE EFFECTS** Infections and injection site reactions (redness, rash, swelling, itching, or bruising), positive anti-nuclear antibodies, headache, nausea, ↑ CPK (adalimumab) **MONITORING** Prior to initiation: <u>TB test</u> and <u>treat</u> if positive <u>before starting therapy</u> (see the Infectious Disease II chapter); test for <u>HBV</u> (HBsAg and anti-HBc) Routine: <u>signs of infection</u>, CBC, LFTs, HBV, TB (annually if risk factors for TB are present), symptoms of heart failure, malignancies, vitals (during infliximab infusion)
Certolizumab pegol (Cimzia, *Cimzia Prefilled, Cimzia Starter Kit*) Single-dose prefilled syringe and vial starter kit +/- MTX	400 mg SC at weeks 0, 2 and 4, then 200 mg <u>SC every other week</u> (can consider 400 mg every 4 weeks)	**NOTES** <u>Do not shake or freeze</u>; requires <u>refrigeration</u> (biologics will denature if hot); allow to reach room temperature before injecting (15-30 minutes); etanercept and adalimumab can be stored at room temperature for a maximum of 14 days; do not refrigerate once warmed <u>MTX is used 1st line</u> and anti-TNF biologics are <u>add-on therapy</u>; however, if the initial presentation is <u>severe</u>, they can be started as <u>initial therapy</u> (with or without MTX)
Golimumab (Simponi, *Simponi Aria*) Single-dose prefilled syringe or auto-injector (SC), injection (IV) + MTX	<u>SC</u> (Simponi): 50 mg <u>monthly</u> IV (Simponi Aria): 2 mg/kg infused over 30 minutes at weeks 0 and 4, then every 8 weeks IV golimumab requires a <u>filter</u>	Antibody induction can occur and will ↓ usefulness of the drug Rotate injection sites *Cyltezo* is FDA-approved as an interchangeable biosimilar to *Humira*. It can be substituted without a separate prescription or provider intervention.

Other Biologic DMARDs (Non-TNF Inhibitors)

The following drugs are biologics that affect the immune system by mechanisms other than TNF inhibition. Safety data on the use of non-TNF biologics in pregnancy is limited. Pregnant patients exposed to these drugs are encouraged to register in a pregnancy exposure registry so that pregnancy outcomes can be monitored. When the agent is supplied as a single-dose prefilled syringe, auto-injector or vial kit for SC injection, needles are included with the device and do not require a separate purchase.

DRUG	DOSING	SAFETY/SIDE EFFECTS/MONITORING
Rituximab *(Rituxan)* Biosimilars: *Riabni, Ruxience, Truxima* Injection (IV) + MTX Depletes CD20 B cells believed to have a role in RA development and progression	1,000 mg IV on day 1 and day 15 (in combination with MTX for both doses) Can repeat treatment if needed at 16-24 weeks Premedicate with a steroid, acetaminophen and an antihistamine Start infusion at 50 mg/hr; can ↑ by 50 mg/hr every 30 minutes if no reaction (max 400 mg/hr) Gently invert the bag to mix the solution, do not shake	**BOXED WARNINGS** Serious, and fatal, infusion-related reactions (usually with the first infusion), progressive multifocal leukoencephalopathy (PML) due to JC virus infection (can be fatal), serious skin reactions (SJS/TEN) HBV reactivation, some cases resulting in fulminant hepatitis, hepatic failure and death; screen high-risk groups for HBV and HCV prior to initiating therapy; monitor patients for clinical and laboratory signs (HBsAg and anti-HBc) several months after treatment **WARNINGS** Infections; do not give with other biologic DMARDs or live vaccines **SIDE EFFECTS** In patients treated for RA: infusion-related reactions, URTIs, UTIs, N/V/D, peripheral edema, weight gain, hypertension, headache, angioedema, fever, insomnia, pain **MONITORING** ECG, vitals, infusion reactions, CBC, SCr, electrolytes, screen for HBV before treatment
Anakinra *(Kineret)* Single-dose prefilled syringe +/- MTX IL-1 receptor antagonist; IL-1 mediates immunologic reactions in RA; not recommended first-line per guidelines	100 mg SC daily (same time each day) Give only after failure of one or more DMARDs CrCl < 30 mL/min: 100 mg SC every other day	**WARNINGS** Malignancies and serious infections, discontinue if a serious infection develops, screen for TB prior to initiating therapy, do not give with other biologics or live vaccines **SIDE EFFECTS** URTIs, headache, N/D, abdominal pain, injection site reactions, antibody development, arthralgias **MONITORING** CBC, SCr, signs of infection **NOTES** Do not shake or freeze; refrigerate and protect from light
Abatacept *(Orencia, Orencia ClickJect)* Single-dose prefilled syringe or auto-injector (SC), injection (IV) +/- MTX Inhibits T-cell activation by binding to CD80 and CD86 on antigen presenting cells (blocking interaction with CD28)	IV: 500-1,000 mg (based on TBW) at 0, 2 and 4 weeks, then every 4 weeks Infuse over 30 minutes SC: 125 mg weekly SC with IV loading dose: give first IV dose as above, then 125 mg SC within 24 hours, then 125 mg SC weekly	**WARNINGS** Same warnings as above for anakinra plus: caution in patients with COPD – may worsen symptoms **SIDE EFFECTS** Headache, nausea, injection site reactions, infections, nasopharyngitis, antibody development **MONITORING** Signs of infection, hypersensitivity **NOTES** Stable in NS only Requires a filter and light protection during administration; do not shake

DRUG	DOSING	SAFETY/SIDE EFFECTS/MONITORING
Tocilizumab (*Actemra, Actemra ACTPen*) Single-dose prefilled syringe (SC), injection (IV) +/- MTX IL-6 receptor antagonist; IL-6 mediates immunologic reactions in RA	IV: 4 mg/kg every 4 weeks given over 60 minutes (can ↑ to 8 mg/kg) Max dose per infusion: 800 mg SC: If < 100 kg: 162 mg every other week (can ↑ to weekly) If ≥ 100 kg: 162 mg weekly	**BOXED WARNING** Serious infections, discontinue if a serious infection develops, screen for TB prior to initiating therapy **WARNINGS** ↑ LFTs, neutropenia and thrombocytopenia, GI perforation, can cause demyelinating diseases, hypersensitivity reactions, lipid abnormalities, do not give with other biologic DMARDs or live vaccines **SIDE EFFECTS** URTIs, headache, hypertension, injection site reactions, ↑ LDL and total cholesterol
Sarilumab (*Kevzara*) Single-dose prefilled syringe +/- MTX IL-6 receptor antagonist	200 mg SC every 2 weeks	**MONITORING** LFTs, CBC (baseline, 4-8 weeks after start of therapy, and every 3 months thereafter), lipid panel, signs of infection **NOTES** Do not use SC injection for IV infusion; SC products contain polysorbate 80 Do not start if: ALT or AST are > 1.5 times ULN, ANC < 2,000 cells/mm³, or platelets < 100,000 cell/mm³

KEY COUNSELING POINTS

See the Drug Formulations and Patient Counseling chapter for counseling language/layman's terminology.

METHOTREXATE

- Dosed once weekly for rheumatoid arthritis and psoriasis. Do not use daily or double-up on doses. Choose a day of the week to take your medication that you can remember.

- Can cause:
  - ❏ Liver damage.
  - ❏ Infection.
  - ❏ Mouth sores.
  - ❏ Stomach bleeding, when used with aspirin/NSAIDs.

- Avoid in pregnancy (teratogenic). Use an effective form of birth control, whether you are male or female.

- Avoid alcohol.

- Take folic acid to decrease side effects.

Rasuvo and *Otrexup* single-use auto-injectors:

- Administer by subcutaneous injection into the abdomen (two inches away from the navel) or upper thigh only. Do not inject in the arms or any other areas of the body.

- Pinch the skin and inject at a 90° angle. Press firmly until you hear a click. Hold three seconds for *Otrexup* and five seconds for *Rasuvo*.

ADALIMUMAB, ETANERCEPT AND GOLIMUMAB

- Administer by subcutaneous injection as prescribed (once weekly for etanercept, every 1 – 2 weeks for adalimumab, monthly for golimumab).

- Can cause:
  - ❏ Injection site reactions.
  - ❏ Infection.
  - ❏ Liver damage.
  - ❏ Heart failure.

- Store the medication (single-dose syringes or multidose vials) in the refrigerator with protection from light and sources of heat. Etanercept and adalimumab can be stored at room temperature for a maximum of 14 days. Allow the medication to warm to room temperature before injecting.

- For adalimumab (*Humira*): inject SC into the abdomen or thigh.

- For etanercept (*Enbrel*) syringe or auto-injector: inject SC into the abdomen, thigh or upper arm.

- For golimumab (*Simponi*): inject SC into the abdomen, thigh or upper arm.

SYSTEMIC LUPUS ERYTHEMATOSUS

BACKGROUND

Systemic lupus erythematosus (SLE) is an autoimmune disease commonly referred to as lupus. SLE primarily affects young women, with a female-to-male ratio of 10:1. The disease predominantly occurs in people age 15 – 45 years, and it is more common in women of African-American and Asian descent. Patients experience flare-ups of varying degrees, as well as periods of disease remission. Factors such as sunlight, certain drugs and viral infections are known to trigger SLE, but the underlying cause is not fully understood. As the disease progresses, it can affect almost every organ system, with the heart, lungs, kidneys and brain being most affected. Drug-induced lupus erythematosus (DILE) can have similar clinical and laboratory features as SLE, but usually resolves within weeks after drug discontinuation. A few common DILE drugs are listed in the Key Drugs Guy below.

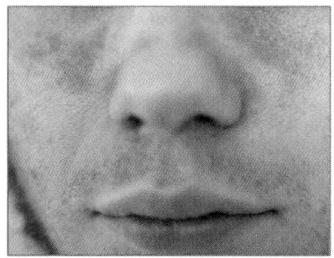
velimir/stock.adobe.com

CLINICAL PRESENTATION

The most common symptoms include fatigue, depression, anorexia, weight loss, muscle pain, discoid rash, malar rash (butterfly rash), photosensitivity and joint pain and stiffness (e.g., arthritis). Over half of the people with SLE develop a characteristic red, flat, facial rash over the bridge of their nose and cheeks. It is frequently referred to as the SLE "butterfly rash" because of its shape. Usually, the rash is not painful or itchy. The facial rash, along with inflammation in other organs, can be precipitated or worsened by exposure to sunlight.

Arthritis and cutaneous manifestations are most common, but renal, hematologic and neurologic manifestations contribute largely to morbidity and mortality. Lupus nephritis (kidney disease) develops in over 50% of patients with SLE. Common laboratory findings may include positive antinuclear antibodies (ANA – with titers ≥ 1:160), positive anti-single stranded DNA (anti-ssDNA), positive anti-double stranded DNA (anti-dsDNA), positive anti-Sm, positive antiphospholipid antibodies, low complement (C3, C4, CH50) and elevated acute phase reactants (such as ESR, CRP).

SELECT DRUGS THAT CAN CAUSE DRUG-INDUCED LUPUS ERYTHEMATOSUS (DILE)

Methimazole	Anti-TNF agents
Propylthiouracil	Terbinafine
Methyldopa	Isoniazid
Minocycline	Quinidine
Procainamide	Remember: **M**y **P**retty **M**alar
Hydralazine (alone, and in *BiDil*)	**M**arking **P**robably **H**as **A** **T**ransient **Q**uality

NON-DRUG TREATMENT

Non-drug treatment consists of rest and proper exercise to manage the fatigue. Smoking cessation is encouraged since tobacco smoke can be a trigger for disease flares. Photosensitivity is common with the condition and is also a risk with some treatments; sunscreens and sun protection/avoidance are required.

DRUG TREATMENT

Treatment approaches emphasize using a combination of drugs to minimize chronic exposure to steroids. Patients with mild disease may do well on an NSAID (dosed at anti-inflammatory doses to decrease swelling and pain), but use caution since the doses are high and these patients are more sensitive to the GI and renal side effects. Use with a proton pump inhibitor is generally recommended to reduce GI risk.

Many patients with SLE will require one or more immunosuppressants or cytotoxic agents to control the disease. Hydroxychloroquine, cyclophosphamide, azathioprine, mycophenolate mofetil and cyclosporine are all options for chronic therapy. In some cases, it may take up to six months to see maximal benefit from treatment. Except for hydroxychloroquine, these drugs do not have an FDA indication for SLE and are discussed in detail in other chapters (see the Transplant, Oncology II and Inflammatory Bowel Disease chapters). Anifrolumab (*Saphnelo*) is a recent FDA-approved treatment for lupus that works by inhibiting type 1 interferons. Belimumab is approved for the treatment of lupus and lupus nephritis and voclosporin, a drug related to cyclosporine, is approved only for the treatment of lupus nephritis.

DRUG	DOSING	SAFETY/SIDE EFFECTS/MONITORING
IgG1-lambda monoclonal antibody: prevents the survival of B lymphocytes by blocking the binding of soluble human B lymphocyte stimulator protein (BLyS) to receptors on B lymphocytes; this reduces the activity of B-cell mediated immunity and the autoimmune response		
Belimumab *(Benlysta)* Single-dose prefilled syringe or auto-injector (SC), injection (IV)	IV: 10 mg/kg every 2 weeks x 3 doses, then every 4 weeks thereafter; infuse over 1 hour Consider giving pre-medication for infusion reactions and hypersensitivity reactions SC: 200 mg once weekly	**WARNINGS** Serious (sometimes fatal) infections, PML, acute hypersensitivity reactions, malignancy, psychiatric events, do not give with other biologic DMARDs or live vaccines **SIDE EFFECTS** Nausea, diarrhea, fever, depression (including suicidal ideation), insomnia **NOTES** Crosses the placenta - caution with use in pregnancy African-American patients may have a lower response rate; use with caution
Calcineurin inhibitor: suppresses immune system by inhibiting T-lymphocyte activation		
Voclosporin *(Lupkynis)* Capsule	23.7 mg BID in combination with steroids and mycophenolate	**BOXED WARNINGS** Serious (sometimes fatal) infections; malignancies **WARNINGS** Nephrotoxicity, neurotoxicity, hypertension, hyperkalemia, QT prolongation, red cell aplasia, do not give with live vaccines **SIDE EFFECTS** Hypertension, diarrhea, headache, anemia, cough, UTI, abdominal pain, dyspepsia, fatigue, renal impairment **NOTES** Avoid use in pregnancy; breastfeeding is not recommended by the manufacturer

MULTIPLE SCLEROSIS

BACKGROUND

Multiple sclerosis (MS) is a chronic, progressive autoimmune disease in which the patient's immune system attacks the myelin sheath, the fatty substance that surrounds and insulates nerve fibers of the brain and spinal cord axons. As demyelination progresses, symptoms worsen because the nerves can no longer properly conduct electrical impulses. Similar to other autoimmune conditions, most patients experience periods of disease activity followed by intervals of remission.

CLINICAL PRESENTATION

The presentation of MS is highly variable, with some patients having a much more aggressive course while others have occasional discrete attacks. Early symptoms include fatigue, weakness, tingling, numbness and blurred vision. As the condition worsens, a variety of physical and psychological issues can make life very challenging, including deterioration of cognitive function, muscle spasms, pain, incontinence, depression, heat sensitivity, sexual dysfunction, difficulty walking with gait instability and visual disturbances.

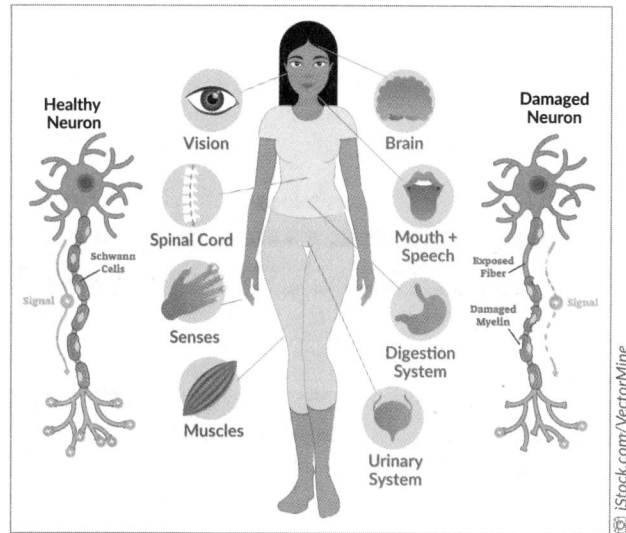

iStock.com/VectorMine

ENDOCRINE CONDITIONS

If left untreated, about 30% of patients will develop significant physical disability. Up to 10% of patients have a milder phenotype in which no significant physical disability develops, although these patients may develop mild cognitive dysfunction. Male patients can have a more progressive form of the disease and generally have the worst prognosis. Symptoms are characterized as:

- Primary: muscle weakness

- Secondary: result from primary symptoms, such as incontinence due to muscle impairment

- Tertiary: involve psychological and social concerns, such as depression

MS occurs in both men and women, but as with other autoimmune conditions, it is more common in women (ratio 2:1). The typical onset is between 20 – 40 years of age. Various tests are performed to make a diagnosis, including magnetic resonance imaging (MRI), spinal fluid analysis and evoked potentials (tests that measure electrical conduction of the brain). A primary goal of therapy is prevention of disease progression; what is lost in neuronal function cannot be regained. The agents that can modify disease progression are costly, ranging from approximately $65,000 – $80,000/year.

TREATMENT

Treating MS requires a holistic approach. Promoting functional rehabilitation and emotional health are important for all stages of MS. Programs exist to support cognitive and vocational rehabilitation. Physical and occupational therapy programs are available for motor functions, speech and swallowing. Medications are used to modify disease, treat relapses and manage symptoms.

Steroids are used to treat relapses. Usually, 3 – 7 days of IV methylprednisolone is given, with or without an oral steroid

taper afterwards. Occasionally, corticotropin (HP Acthar), also called ACTH (see HPA axis diagram earlier in the chapter), is administered SQ or IM for 2 – 3 weeks. The use of corticotropin is limited by its high cost.

Disease-Modifying Therapies

Disease-modifying therapies are used to reduce the frequency and severity of relapses. There are many drugs used for the treatment of MS (see the Drug Tables below). The selection of a drug is based on patient factors (e.g., type of MS, insurance, PMH), the route of administration, efficacy and adverse effects.

Interferon beta formulations (Betaseron, Avonex, Rebif, Extavia, Plegridy) and glatiramer acetate (Copaxone, Glatopa) are parenteral drugs that have been the mainstay of treatment for patients with relapsing forms of MS. Pegylated interferon beta (Plegridy) allows for more convenient SC dosing every 14 days. For SC injections, the site of administration should be rotated to prevent lipoatrophy and rare necrosis. When the medication is supplied as a single-dose prefilled syringe, auto-injector or vial kit for SC injection, needles are included with the device and do not require a separate purchase.

A few injectable drugs are supplied as a powder that requires reconstitution, and some of these contain albumin. Some patients will not wish to use, or cannot use, albumin-containing products.

Fingolimod (Gilenya) and teriflunomide (Aubagio) were the first oral disease-modifying agents approved for MS. More have since been approved. Other options include certain monoclonal antibodies and chemotherapy drugs. Mitoxantrone is a chemotherapeutic agent approved for MS; a review of mitoxantrone can be found in the Oncology II chapter. Monoclonal antibodies and chemotherapy drugs are considered second- or third-line options for most MS patients due to the risk of significant toxicities.

DRUG	DOSING	SAFETY/SIDE EFFECTS/MONITORING
Glatiramer acetate: an immune modulator thought to induce and activate T-lymphocyte suppressor cells in relapsing forms of MS (exact mechanism is not well defined)		
Glatiramer acetate **(Copaxone**, Glatopa) Prefilled syringes 20 and 40 mg/mL concentrations are not interchangeable	20 mg SC daily or 40 mg SC 3 times per week (at least 48 hours apart) If increasing dose to 40 mg, start 48 hrs after the 20 mg dose	**WARNINGS** Chest pain, immediate post-injection reaction, lipoatrophy **SIDE EFFECTS** Injection site reactions (inflammation, erythema, pain, pruritus, residual mass), flushing, diaphoresis, dyspnea, infection, pain, weakness, anxiety, rash, nausea, nasopharyngitis, vasodilation, antibody development **NOTES** Preferred agent if treatment is necessary during pregnancy Check solution for discoloration and discard if present Can be kept at room temperature for up to one month, or in the refrigerator (preferred); if cold, let it stand at room temperature for 20 minutes prior to injecting

DRUG	DOSING	SAFETY/SIDE EFFECTS/MONITORING
Interferon beta products: alter the expression and response to surface antigens, enhancing immune cell function (exact mechanism in MS is not well defined)		
Interferon beta-1a (*Avonex, Avonex Pen, Rebif, Rebif Rebidose*) Powder (for reconstitution), prefilled syringe and pen	*Avonex:* 30 mcg <u>IM weekly</u> *Rebif:* 22 mcg or 44 mcg <u>SC three times per week</u> (at least 48 hours apart)	**WARNINGS** <u>Psychiatric disorders</u> (depression/suicide), <u>injection site necrosis</u>, myelosuppression, ↑ LFTs, thyroid dysfunction (hyper and hypo-), infections, anaphylaxis, worsening cardiovascular disease, seizure risk **SIDE EFFECTS** <u>Flu-like symptoms</u> following administration (lasting minutes to hours); ↓ with continued treatment – can use acetaminophen or NSAIDs prior to injection or start with lower doses and titrate weekly to target dose
Interferon beta-1b (*Betaseron, Extavia*) Powder (for reconstitution), and auto-injector	SC: 0.25 mg <u>every other day</u> (use within 3 hrs of reconstitution)	Visual disturbances, fatigue, depression, pain, urinary tract infections, HA **MONITORING** LFTs, CBC (at 1, 3 and 6 months, then periodically); thyroid function every 6 months (in patients with thyroid dysfunction or as clinical necessary)
Peginterferon beta-1a (*Plegridy, Plegridy Starter Pack*) Prefilled syringe and pen	SC: 63 mcg on day 1, 94 mcg on day 15, then 125 mcg <u>every 14 days</u> starting on day 29	**NOTES** Refrigerate all except *Betaseron* and *Extavia* (which can be stored at room temperature). If refrigerated, let stand at <u>room temperature</u> prior to injection. <u>Do not expel</u> the small <u>air bubble</u> in prefilled syringes <u>due to loss of dose</u> Do not shake *Avonex, Betaseron* or *Extavia* Some formulations contain <u>albumin</u> which can increase the risk of Creutzfeldt-Jakob disease transmission (rare); avoid in albumin-sensitive patients

DRUG	SAFETY/SIDE EFFECTS/MONITORING
Pyrimidine synthesis inhibitor: anti-inflammatory; may reduce the number of activated lymphocytes in the CNS	
Teriflunomide (*Aubagio*) Tablet Active metabolite of leflunomide	Severe hepatotoxicity and teratogenicity – <u>contraindicated in pregnancy</u> and with severe hepatic impairment Can use accelerated elimination to remove drug - see leflunomide
Sphingosine 1-phosphate receptor modulators: block lymphocytes from exiting lymph nodes, reducing lymphocytes in the periphery; may limit lymphocyte migration into the CNS (exact mechanism in MS is not well defined)	
Fingolimod (*Gilenya*) Capsule	**CONTRAINDICATIONS** Some arrhythmias, or any of the following in the past 6 months: MI, unstable angina, stroke/TIA or some HF (decompensation requiring hospitalization, or Class III/IV) Ozanimod: severe untreated sleep apnea, concomitant <u>use of an MAO inhibitor</u>
Ozanimod (*Zeposia*) Capsule	Siponimod: <u>CYP2C9*3/*3 genotype</u> (testing required before use) **WARNINGS** Can cause bradycardia or other bradyarrhythmias – use caution with other drugs that <u>slow HR</u>; patients starting
Ponesimod (*Ponvory*) Tablet	fingolimod must be <u>monitored for at least 6 hours</u> after the first dose (<u>ECG</u> required at baseline and at end of initial observation period or if treatment course is interrupted) Other significant adverse effects: malignancies, ↑ risk of infection (monitor <u>CBC</u>), macular edema (monitor with <u>eye exams</u>), hepatotoxicity (monitor <u>LFTs</u>), ↑ BP, ↓ pulmonary function, fetal risk (women of childbearing potential should use effective contraception during and for a period time after stopping therapy)
Siponimod (*Mayzent*) Tablet	**NOTES** MS can become much <u>worse</u> when treatment is stopped
Nuclear factor (erythroid-derived 2)-like 2 (Nrf2) activators: anti-inflammatory and cytoprotective (exact mechanism in MS is not well defined)	
Dimethyl fumarate (*Tecfidera*) Capsule	Hepatotoxicity (monitor LFTs), neutropenia (reversible, but monitor CBC), PML Can cause flushing (prevent with aspirin 30 minutes prior to dose and administer with food) <u>Do not crush, chew or sprinkle capsule contents on food</u>
Diroximel fumarate (*Vumerity*) Capsule	Diroximel fumarate and dimethyl fumarate have the same active metabolite

ENDOCRINE CONDITIONS

DRUG	SAFETY/SIDE EFFECTS/MONITORING
Potassium channel blocker: may increase nerve signal conduction; indicated to improve walking	
Dalfampridine (*Ampyra*) Tablet	Contraindicated in patients with a history of seizures Takes up to 6 weeks to show efficacy; most patients do not respond
Monoclonal antibodies	
Natalizumab (*Tysabri*) Injection (IV) Monoclonal antibody that binds to the alpha-4 subunit of integrins expressed on the surface of leukocytes	See Inflammatory Bowel Disease chapter **BOXED WARNINGS** Progressive multifocal leukoencephalopathy (PML); only available through the REMS TOUCH Prescribing Program
Ofatumumab (*Kesimpta*) Injection (SC) *Arzerra* – for CLL Injection (IV) Anti-CD20 monoclonal antibody	**CONTRAINDICATIONS** Active hepatitis B infection **WARNINGS** ↑ risk of serious and potentially fatal infections, including PML
Recombinant humanized monoclonal antibodies	
Alemtuzumab (*Lemtrada*) *Campath* – for CLL Injection (IV) CD52-directed cytolytic monoclonal antibody	**BOXED WARNINGS** Alemtuzumab: REMS program required; serious, sometimes fatal, autoimmune conditions and infusion reactions, malignancies, stroke, **CONTRAINDICATIONS** Alemtuzumab: HIV (causes prolonged ↓ in CD4 count) Ocrelizumab: active hepatitis B infection
Ocrelizumab (*Ocrevus*) Injection (IV) Anti-CD20 monoclonal antibody	**NOTES** Indicated when there is an inadequate response to ≥ 2 MS drugs Complete all vaccinations 6 weeks before treatment Premedicate with a steroid, an antihistamine and/or acetaminophen (varies by drug) Ocrelizumab requires a 0.22-micron in-line filter, has similar safety issues as other drugs that target CD20 (e.g., rituximab)
Oral anti-neoplastic	
Cladribine (*Mavenclad*) Tablet	Boxed warning for malignancies, teratogenicity Contraindicated in patients with current malignancy, HIV or active chronic infections Contraception must be used for males and females of reproductive potential during treatment and for 6 months after the last dose

Drugs Used for Symptom Control

Patients with MS may need a variety of medications for symptom control. The individual drugs used can be found in different chapters in this book. Drugs commonly used for symptom control in MS include anticholinergics for incontinence, laxatives for constipation (or loperamide if diarrhea), skeletal muscle relaxants for muscle spasms/ spasticity, or analgesics for muscle spasms and pain. For localized pain and spasms, botulinum toxin (*Botox*) injections can provide relief for up to three months. Propranolol can help with tremor. For depression, many antidepressants can be used. An SNRI may be chosen to help with neuropathic pain. Fatigue is often treated with modafinil or stimulants used for ADHD, such as methylphenidate. Meclizine and scopolamine are used for dizziness and vertigo. Acetylcholinesterase inhibitors, including donepezil, are used to help cognitive function. Erectile dysfunction can be treated with phosphodiesterase-5 inhibitors.

Notice that <u>drugs used for symptom control can worsen other symptoms</u>. For example, anticholinergics can worsen cognitive function (not all of them do; it is patient-specific). Drugs for vertigo and propranolol can worsen cognitive function. Propranolol has added concerns for worsening depression and causing problems with sexual performance. The SSRI and SNRI antidepressants can worsen sexual dysfunction. Opioids, if used for pain, will worsen constipation, can decrease cognition and have dependence concerns. Managing the various medications used for MS requires competent pharmacists.

KEY COUNSELING POINTS

See the Drug Formulations and Patient Counseling chapter for counseling language/layman's terminology.

GLATIRAMER ACETATE

- Subcutaneous injection.

- Available in two different doses; depending on your dose, inject daily or three times a week at least 48 hours apart. Administer consistently on the same three days each week (e.g., a M, W, F schedule).

- Can cause:

  - Injection site reactions.

  - Chest pain.

  - Shortness of breath and flushing.

- Store in the refrigerator before use. The syringes can be kept at room temperature for up to one month. Allow to warm to room temperature before injecting.

INTERFERON BETA PRODUCTS

- Injected subcutaneously except for *Avonex* (IM).

- Can cause:

  - Injection site reactions.

  - Flu-like symptoms (e.g., fever, chills, myalgias); can use acetaminophen or OTC NSAIDs for prevention prior to injecting.

  - New or worsening depression.

- *Betaseron* and *Extavia* may be stored at room temperature

  - All other interferons should be stored in the refrigerator prior to use. Allow drug to reach room temperature before injecting.

RAYNAUD'S PHENOMENON

Raynaud's is a common condition that is triggered by exposure to <u>cold and/or stress</u>, leading to <u>vasospasm</u> in the extremities (most commonly in the <u>fingers and/or toes</u>). The vasospasm causes the skin to turn <u>white</u> and then <u>blue</u>, which is followed by painful swelling when the affected areas warm and can result in amputation in severe cases. Laboratory findings that can signify other autoimmune conditions are generally absent.

Prevention and treatment involve <u>vasodilation</u> to improve blood flow to the affected areas. The <u>calcium channel blocker</u> (CCB) <u>nifedipine</u> is commonly used for prevention but other CCBs can be used. Additional drugs used for vasodilation include iloprost, topical nitroglycerin and the phosphodiesterase-5 inhibitors. See <u>Study Tip Gal</u>.

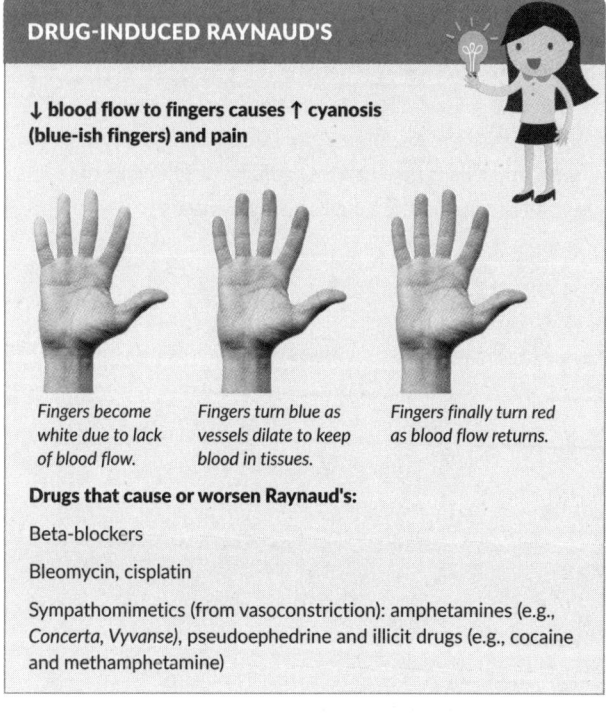

DRUG-INDUCED RAYNAUD'S

↓ **blood flow to fingers causes ↑ cyanosis (blue-ish fingers) and pain**

Fingers become white due to lack of blood flow.

Fingers turn blue as vessels dilate to keep blood in tissues.

Fingers finally turn red as blood flow returns.

Drugs that cause or worsen Raynaud's:

Beta-blockers

Bleomycin, cisplatin

Sympathomimetics (from vasoconstriction): amphetamines (e.g., *Concerta, Vyvanse*), pseudoephedrine and illicit drugs (e.g., cocaine and methamphetamine)

CELIAC DISEASE

BACKGROUND

Celiac disease (celiac sprue) is an immune response to eating gluten, a protein found in wheat, barley and rye. The primary and most effective treatment is to avoid gluten entirely. Gluten is present in many foods, food additives and many drug excipients. Pharmacists can assist patients in avoiding gluten-containing drugs completely, as even a small exposure will trigger a reaction. The FDA permits food products to be labeled "gluten-free" only if the food contains less gluten than 20 parts per million.

Gluten protein

© iStock.com/ttsz

CLINICAL PRESENTATION

The common symptoms of celiac disease are diarrhea, abdominal pain, bloating and weight loss. Constipation (rather than diarrhea) can be present and is more common in children. In celiac disease, antibodies attack and damage the lining of the small intestine, which can lead to vitamin and nutritional deficiencies as a result of decreased absorption. Other complications include small bowel ulcers, amenorrhea and infertility, as well as an increased risk of cancer (primarily lymphomas). Ninety-five percent of cases will respond well to dietary changes, although avoiding gluten entirely is not a simple task.

Dermatitis herpetiformis is an extremely itchy, blistery skin rash with chronic eruptions that occurs in 20 – 25% of patients with celiac disease, more often in males. The rash can be present with or without overt intestinal symptoms and is often mistaken for eczema or psoriasis, which leads to a delay in diagnosis and treatment.

TREATMENT

The FDA has strict regulations regarding the active ingredients in drug formulations, but there is little oversight for the excipients, making the identification of gluten difficult. The active drug is gluten-free, but the excipients may contain gluten. It is not safe to assume that generic formulations will have the same excipients as the brand, and there is no legal requirement to match the excipients.

Package inserts might contain information on the excipient components. Look for the keyword "starch," which will be either corn, potato, tapioca or wheat. If the package insert lists "starch" alone, the manufacturer must be consulted to determine if the starch is wheat. The manufacturer might report that they do not use gluten in the manufacturing process, but they cannot state whether the excipients purchased from outside vendors are gluten-free. The risk of cross-contamination is low but not absent, and this information should be provided to the patient. It is ultimately up to the patient, hopefully in consult with the prescriber, whether to take the drug or not.

MYASTHENIA GRAVIS

BACKGROUND

Myasthenia gravis is an autoimmune disease that attacks the connections between nerves and muscles, resulting in weakness in skeletal muscles (e.g., muscles that control the eyes, face, neck and limbs). In most cases, the immune system targets the acetylcholine (ACh) receptor. Symptoms often include changes to the eyes/vision [e.g., double vision (diplopia), drooping eyelid (ptosis)], problems with chewing/swallowing and weakness in the neck and jaw. This condition affects women more than men, and average onset is age 28.

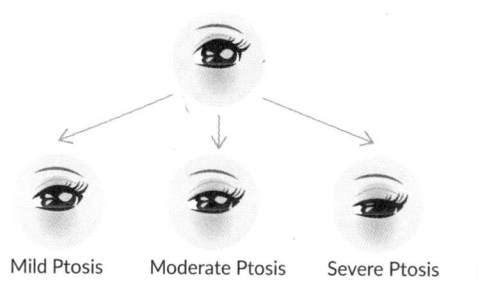

Mild Ptosis   Moderate Ptosis   Severe Ptosis

DRUGS THAT CAN WORSEN MYASTHENIA GRAVIS

Many drugs can worsen or unmask myasthenia gravis. This includes:

- Antibiotics: aminoglycosides and quinolones

- Magnesium salts

- Select antiarrhythmics

- Beta-blockers and calcium channel blockers

- Select antipsychotics

- Muscle relaxants

- Local anesthetics

These drugs should be avoided in patients with the disease, or used cautiously if the benefit outweighs the risk.

TREATMENT

Cholinesterase inhibitors are the mainstay of treatment in myasthenia gravis, specifically pyridostigmine (Mestinon). Cholinesterase inhibitors increase ACh levels and help reduce muscle weakness. Most people also require immunosuppressant medications for sufficient symptom control (e.g., steroids, azathioprine). Some severe cases require treatment with plasmapheresis or intravenous immunoglobulin (IVIG), or even thymectomy (removal of the thymus gland). Efgartigimod alfa (Vyvgart) is a recent FDA-approved treatment for myasthenia gravis in adults who are antiacetylcholine receptor antibody positive.

DRUG	DOSING	SAFETY/SIDE EFFECTS/MONITORING
Cholinesterase inhibitors: block the breakdown of acetylcholine by acetylcholinesterase, which improves neuromuscular transmission and increases muscle strength		
Pyridostigmine (Mestinon) Tablet IV and IM forms used for myasthenia gravis crisis, nerve gas exposure and reversal of nondepolarizing muscle relaxants	60-1,500 mg/day (usually 600 mg/day) divided into 5-6 doses	**CONTRAINDICATIONS** Mechanical intestinal or urinary obstruction **WARNINGS** Cholinergic effects: symptoms of excess ACh can occur (e.g., salivation, lacrimation, excessive urination, diarrhea); refer to the Basic Science Concepts chapter CVD, glaucoma, bronchospastic respiratory disease (e.g., COPD or asthma)

ENDOCRINE CONDITIONS

iStock.com/Lin Shao-hua

SJÖGREN'S SYNDROME

Sjögren's syndrome is an autoimmune disease most often characterized by severe <u>dry eyes</u> and <u>dry mouth</u>. Many other symptoms can be associated with Sjögren's, including thyroiditis, Raynaud's phenomenon, neuropathy and lymphadenopathy. Sjögren's syndrome can be primary or <u>secondary</u> (e.g., associated with <u>another autoimmune disease</u>, such as RA or SLE). Dry mouth and dry eyes are a source of significant morbidity for these patients and can lead to complications, such as <u>dental caries, corneal ulceration and chronic oral infections</u>. There is no known cure for Sjögren's; treatment focuses on reducing the symptoms of dry eyes and dry mouth.

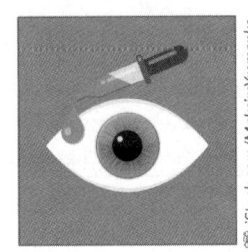

DRY EYES TREATMENT

The use of artificial teardrops is the primary treatment for xerophthalmia (i.e., dry eyes). <u>Popular OTC artificial teardrops</u> available are *Systane, Refresh, Clear Eyes* and *Liquifilm*. It may be necessary to try a couple of different OTC eye drops before finding one that provides the most comfort. If the preservative (e.g., <u>benzalkonium chloride</u>) is irritating, preservative-free artificial tear drops packaged in individual use containers are available. If the eyes dry out while sleeping, an ointment is preferable.

<u>Cyclosporine eye drops</u> *(Restasis)* can be used in patients who do not have satisfactory relief from other measures, including ductal occlusion (lacrimal duct plugs). *Restasis* provides benefit for a small percentage of users, but it is expensive. Patients should be instructed to monitor for a reduction in symptoms and a reduction in the use of OTC eye drops. Counsel patients to use *Restasis* <u>properly to avoid infection</u> and that it may take up to 3 – 6 months to notice an increase in tear production. Lifitegrast *(Xiidra)*, a first-in-class drug, is approved for the treatment of signs and symptoms of dry eye disease. Refer to the Drug Formulations and Patient Counseling chapter for detailed patient counseling information for eye drops.

Eye Drops for Dry Eyes

DRUG	DOSING	SAFETY/SIDE EFFECTS/MONITORING
Cyclosporine Emulsion *(Restasis, Cequa)* Ophthalmic	1 drop in each eye Q12H	**SIDE EFFECTS** Ocular (burning, stinging, redness, pain, blurred vision, foreign body sensation, discharge, itching eye)
		NOTES Prior to use, invert the vial several times to make the emulsion uniform
Lifitegrast *(Xiidra)* Ophthalmic	1 drop in each eye Q12H	**SIDE EFFECTS** Unusual taste, eye irritation, discomfort, blurred vision
		NOTES Store in the original foil pouch to protect from light

DRY MOUTH TREATMENT

Non-drug treatment for xerostomia (i.e., dry mouth) includes salivary stimulation, using <u>sugar-free chewing gum</u> (with <u>xylitol</u>) or <u>lozenges</u>, and daily <u>rinses with antimicrobial mouthwash</u>. Salivary substitutes are available in lozenges, rinses, sprays and swabs *(Aquoral, Mouth Kote, Biotene Oral Balance)*. These contain carboxymethylcellulose or glycerin. If OTC treatments do not provide sufficient relief, prescription oral <u>muscarinic agonists</u>, such as <u>pilocarpine</u> *(Salagen)* or <u>cevimeline</u> *(Evoxac)*, can be used. These drugs are <u>contraindicated</u> in patients with uncontrolled asthma and narrow-angle glaucoma, due to cholinergic properties and associated side effects.

PSORIASIS

BACKGROUND

Psoriasis is a chronic, autoimmune disease that appears on the skin. There are several types of psoriasis. The most common is plaque psoriasis, which appears as raised, red patches covered with a silvery-white buildup of dead skin cells, on any part of the body. Treatments can be divided into three main types: light therapy, topical and systemic medications. Most psoriasis is treated with topical medication and UV light therapy. Soaking can also help loosen and remove the plaques.

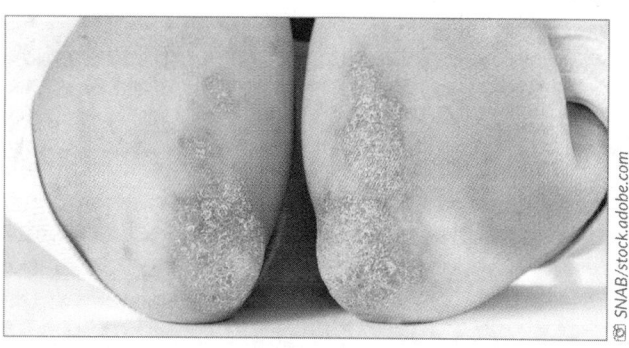

© SNAB/stock.adobe.com

NON-DRUG TREATMENT

Ultraviolet (UV) light exposure causes activated T-cells in the skin to die. This slows skin turnover and decreases scaling and inflammation. Brief, daily exposures to small amounts of sunlight can improve psoriasis, but intense sun exposure can worsen symptoms and cause skin damage. UVB phototherapy, in controlled doses from an artificial source, can improve mild to moderate psoriasis symptoms. Other non-drug treatments include photochemotherapy (ultraviolet A light with psoralen, a light sensitizer) and laser light therapy.

DRUG TREATMENT

There are many topical options for treating psoriasis, including steroids, a vitamin D analog (calcipotriene), anthralin, retinoids (some of the same drugs used for acne), salicylic acid (primarily in medicated shampoo), coal tar and moisturizers. Calcipotriene, tazarotene and salicylic acid are used in combination with topical steroids. If these fail, topical calcineurin inhibitors (Protopic, Elidel) can be tried; these are the preferred agents when applying to the face. Treatment for more severe symptoms can require immunosuppressants, including methotrexate, cyclosporine, hydroxyurea or immunomodulators (e.g., etanercept, infliximab, adalimumab or certolizumab). Newer systemic drugs approved for plaque psoriasis include Otezla and monoclonal antibodies that have interleukin receptor antagonist actions.

Topical Psoriasis Treatment

DRUG/DRUG CLASS	COMMENTS
Steroids	Use high-potency steroids only short-term due to risk of side effects
	Can be used as monotherapy or with other therapies
	See Common Skin Conditions chapter
Tazarotene (Tazorac) – a topical retinoid + halobetasol (Duobrii)	See Common Skin Conditions chapter
Coal Tar products (many, including DHS Tar, Ionil-T, Psoriasin, Pentrax Gold) + salicylic acid (Tarsum) OTC Also used for dandruff and dermatitis	Coal tar products are messy, time-consuming and can stain clothing and bedding, but some patients get relief at a reasonable cost
	There are many topical formulations available (cream, foam, emulsion, ointment, oil, shampoo), bath products (e.g., bar soap)
	Do not use salicylic acid products with other salicylates as systemic absorption can occur
	Can cause skin irritation and photosensitivity
Anthralin (Dritho-Crème HP, Zithranol)	Keratolytic containing salicylic acid with irritant potential, ↑ contact time as tolerated up to 30 min
Calcipotriene (Calcitrene, Dovonex, Sorilux) Cream, foam, ointment, solution + betamethasone (Taclonex ointment, Taclonex scalp suspension, Enstilar foam)	Vitamin D analog – contraindicated and should be avoided in hypercalcemia or vitamin D toxicity
	If using a suspension, shake well
	Do not apply to face, axillae or groin

Systemic Psoriasis Treatment

DRUG/DRUG CLASS	COMMENTS
Retinoid	
Acitretin *(Soriatane)* Tablet	Boxed warning for hepatotoxicity and pregnancy (female must sign informed consent before dispensing) Used only in severe cases when patient is unresponsive to other therapies due to numerous contraindications and side effects
Phosphodiesterase-4 inhibitor	
Apremilast *(Otezla)* Tablet	Warnings: weight loss, depression and suicidal ideation Most common side effects are diarrhea, N/V, headache
Interleukin Receptor Antagonists: monoclonal antibodies that bind to and interfere with proinflammatory cytokines	
Brodalumab *(Siliq)* Guselkumab *(Tremfya)* Ixekizumab *(Taltz)* Risankizumab *(Skyrizi)* Secukinumab *(Cosentyx)* Tildrakizumab *(Ilumya)* Ustekinumab *(Stelara)* All available in single-dose prefilled syringes, auto-injectors or vials for subcutaneous injection	Like other monoclonal antibodies, these can cause serious infections (including active TB); screen for latent TB (and treat if needed) before starting, avoid live vaccines, may exacerbate Crohn's disease, latex hypersensitivity Other common side effects include diarrhea and URTIs Brodalumab: boxed warning for suicidal ideation and behavior; REMS program required

Select Guidelines/References

2021 American College of Rheumatology Guideline for the Treatment of Rheumatoid Arthritis.
https://www.rheumatology.org/Practice-Quality/Clinical-Support/Clinical-Practice-Guidelines/Rheumatoid-Arthritis (accessed 2022 Feb 4).

American College of Rheumatology Guidelines for Screening, Treatment and Management of Lupus Nephritis.
https://www.rheumatology.org/Practice-Quality/Clinical-Support/Clinical-Practice-Guidelines/Lupus-Nephritis (accessed 2022 Feb 4).

American Academy of Dermatology. Psoriasis Clinical Guidelines. Section 1-6.
https://www.aad.org/practicecenter/quality/clinical-guidelines/psoriasis (accessed 2022 Feb 4).

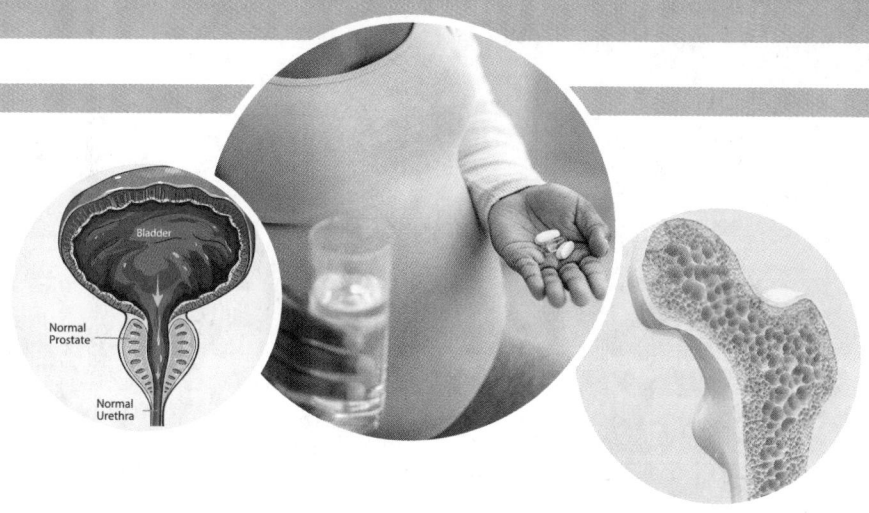

MALE & FEMALE HEALTH

CONTENTS

CONTENT LEGEND

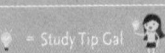 = Study Tip Gal

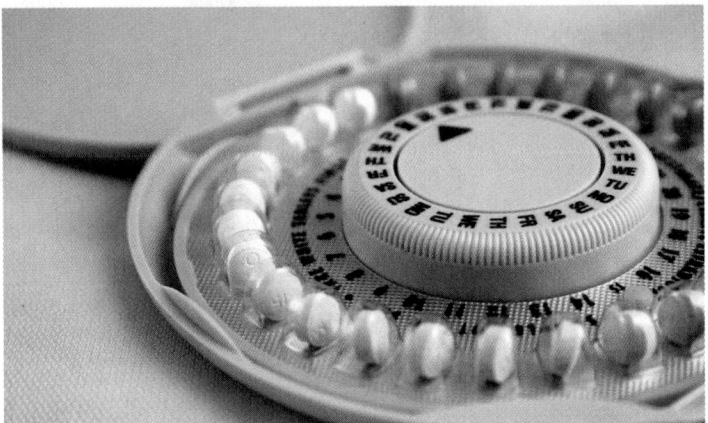

CHAPTER 47
CONTRACEPTION & INFERTILITY

BACKGROUND

According to the CDC, 65% of women between the ages of 15 and 49 currently use contraception.

Contraception is available in many different forms, including OTC and prescription options. Proper use is essential to prevent unintended pregnancy. With so many forms of contraception available, patient-specific factors should drive decisions on which product to use. Pharmacists are in a unique position to increase the appropriate use of contraceptive methods, access to contraception and prevention of unintended pregnancies.

On the other hand, many people struggle with becoming pregnant. Infertility treatments can be invasive and expensive. Pharmacists (usually in specialty settings) play an essential role in gaining access to and assisting with the appropriate use of infertility treatments.

MENSTRUAL CYCLE PHASES

A normal menstrual cycle ranges from 23 – 35 days (average 28 days). The start of bleeding (menses) indicates that the next cycle has begun and is counted as day 1 of the cycle; the remnants of the previous cycle (the thick, bloody endometrial lining) are sloughing off. Menstruation typically lasts a few days. Changes in hormone levels cause the events that characterize the different phases of the menstrual cycle (see next page). Menses occurs during the follicular phase, when the estrogen and progesterone levels start off low.

PHASES OF THE MENSTRUAL CYCLE

Follicular	Each follicle in an ovary contains an oocyte (immature egg). Follicle stimulating hormone (FSH) spurs follicle development and causes estrogen to surge. Estrogen peaks by the end of the phase.* The surge in estrogen causes luteinizing hormone (LH) and FSH to increase.
Ovulatory	The LH surge triggers ovulation 24-36 hours later. Ovulation is the release of the egg (ova) from the ovary.**
Luteal	The start of ovulation begins the luteal (last) phase, which lasts ~14 days. Progesterone is dominant in this phase.

*Estrogen and progesterone cause the endometrium (the lining of the uterus) to thicken to prepare for an embryo, and progesterone causes the cervical mucus to thicken and body temperature to increase. When estrogen and/or progesterone are low during the cycle, blood can drip off the lining, causing spotting (which can require an increase in estrogen or progesterone in birth control pills).

**Luteinizing hormone causes corpus luteum development in the ovary. LH and FSH work together in the ovulatory phase to trigger ovulation.

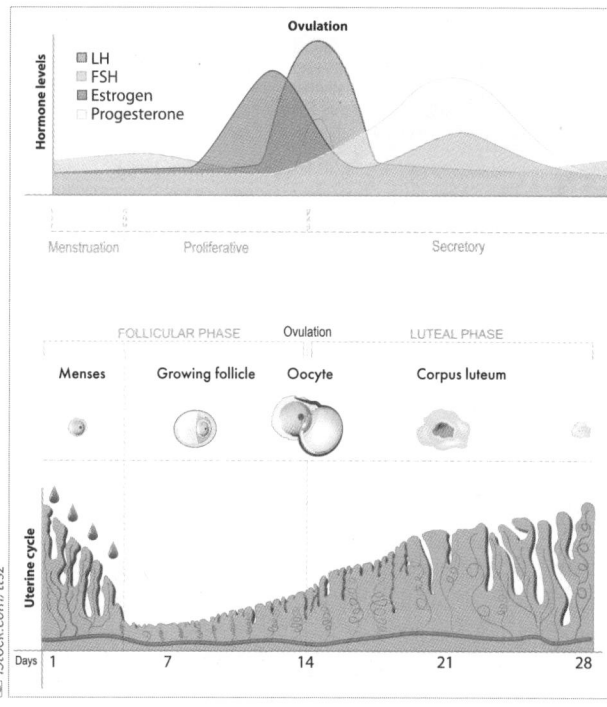

FERTILITY AWARENESS

The mid-cycle luteinizing hormone (LH) surge results in release of the oocyte (egg) from the ovary into the fallopian tube. The oocyte lives for 24 hours once released, and sperm can survive for ~3 days. Ovulation kits predict the best time for intercourse based on ovulation in order to try to conceive (get pregnant). Some kits test for LH in the urine and are positive if LH is present. A person wishing to conceive should have intercourse when the LH surge is detected, and for the following 2 days (based on sperm survival of ~3 days).

Alternative methods to test for ovulation include monitoring body temperature and cervical mucus (discussed on the next page).

PREGNANCY

Human chorionic gonadotropin (hCG) is released when a fertilized egg attaches to the lining of the uterus (called implantation). Detecting hCG in the urine or blood indicates pregnancy. A home urine test can detect pregnancy sooner if the woman tests the first urine in the morning, when the hCG level is highest.

PRECONCEPTION HEALTH

Preconception health focuses on steps to take to protect the health of a baby in the future. Any woman planning to conceive (and all women of childbearing age) should:

- Increase their folic acid (folate, vitamin B9) consumption from a combination of dietary supplements and fortified foods (e.g., dried beans, leafy green vegetables, oranges). Folate deficiency can cause birth defects of the brain and spinal cord (neural tube defects). Adults are recommended to take 400 mcg of dietary folate equivalents (DFE) per day, and this folate requirement increases during pregnancy to 600 mcg DFE/day).

- Stop smoking, using illicit drugs and drinking excessive amounts of alcohol.

- Keep vaccinations current. Attempt to avoid illnesses that will adversely affect the baby (e.g., toxoplasmosis).

- Avoid toxic chemicals, including drugs on the Hazardous Drugs List developed by NIOSH; see the Compounding chapters.

The general health of the male partner is important.

CONTRACEPTION

Contraception can be used until ready to conceive. A prompt return to fertility occurs when most contraceptives are discontinued. The only reversible contraceptive method that has a delay in return to fertility is the medroxyprogesterone injection.

Contraceptive preferences vary markedly with age. For women in their teens and 20s, the pill is the leading method. More women 35 years and older rely on sterilization, which is often performed immediately postpartum (following a birth). Male contraception options are limited. Presently, male condoms and vasectomy are the only options.

MALE & FEMALE HEALTH

EFFECTIVENESS OF CONTRACEPTIVE METHODS

The figure below provides a comparison of the efficacy of contraceptive methods that are available as OTC or prescription products. Contraceptive methods, except for condoms, do not provide protection from sexually transmitted diseases (STDs). Condoms provide protection from some infections – female internal condoms provide more protection than male external condoms.

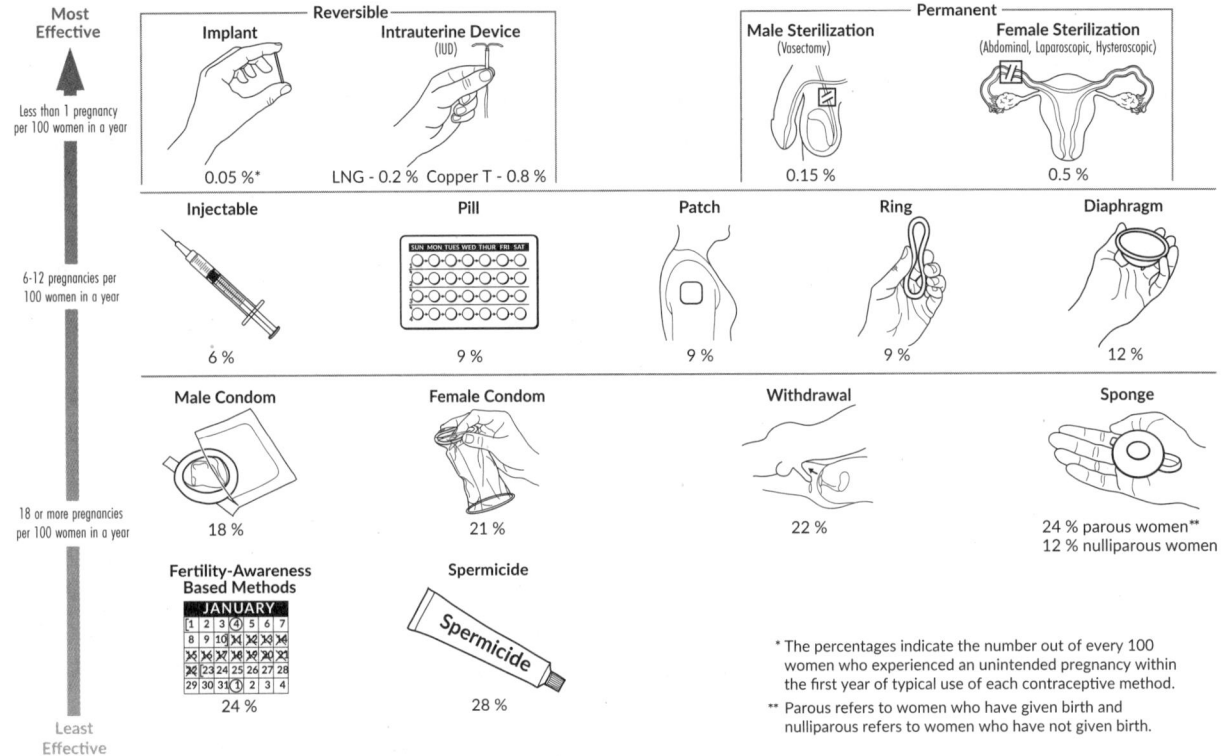

© https://www.cdc.gov/reproductivehealth/unintendedpregnancy/pdf/Contraceptive_methods_508.pdf

NON-PHARMACOLOGIC AND OTC CONTRACEPTIVE METHODS

Abstinence is the only 100% effective way to prevent pregnancy and STDs. Other non-pharmacologic methods of contraception include temperature and cervical mucus tracking and the use of barrier methods. Spermicide can be used alone or with other barrier methods as another OTC option for contraception.

The temperature needs to be taken first thing each morning, prior to any other activity. A small (~1° increase) can be missed; temperature methods work best when done in conjunction with tracking changes in the cervical mucus (i.e., vaginal discharge), which has slight changes in color, texture and volume during ovulation.

TEMPERATURE AND CERVICAL MUCUS METHODS

Keeping track of body temperature and cervical mucus are used primarily to avoid pregnancy by abstaining from intercourse on days when a woman is fertile. Tracking basal body temperature is used to predict ovulation. The typical temperature prior to ovulation is 96 – 98°F. The temperature increases to 97 – 99°F during ovulation. The changes are recorded on a calendar and used to predict ovulation (i.e., fertility) in the following months. There is an FDA-approved app, *Natural Cycles*, which can aid in tracking and predicting ovulation.

BARRIER METHODS

Barrier methods of contraception include condoms, diaphragms, caps and shields. They are non-pharmacologic options that form a physical barrier preventing passage of sperm to the oocyte.

Diaphragms, Caps and Shields

These options are soft latex or silicone barriers that cover the cervix and prevent sperm passage. They can be used with or without spermicide. The *Caya* diaphragm is a single size and does not require fitting (some diaphragms do require a prescription for fitting).

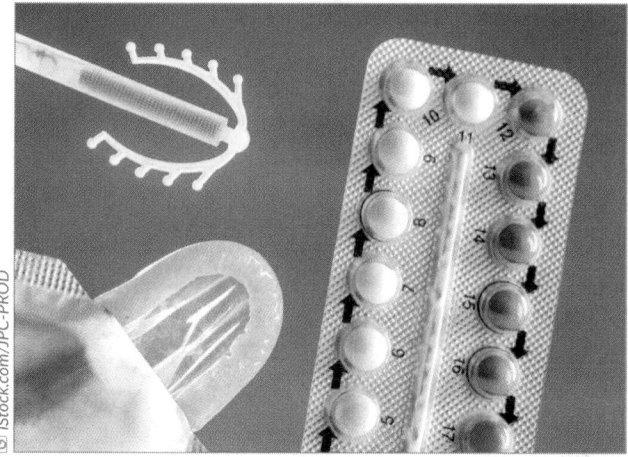

iStock.com/JPC-PROD

Condoms

Male condoms are a thin latex or plastic sheath worn on the penis. Female condoms are inserted into the vagina. Both are OTC. Condoms help protect against many STDs (only if latex or synthetic condoms, not "natural" sheepskin).

- Use with nonoxynol-9 spermicide can cause irritation and increase risk of STD/HIV transmission.

- Lubricant makes condoms less likely to break by reducing dry friction. Never recommend oil-based lubricant for use with a latex or non-latex synthetic condom; only recommend water or silicone-based lubricants. These products are discussed in the Osteoporosis, Menopause and Testosterone Use chapter.

OTHER CONTRACEPTIVE METHODS

Other OTC contraceptive methods include foams, film, creams, suppositories, sponges and jellies. These contain the spermicide nonoxynol-9. Do not use spermicide with anal sex. It is irritating and can increase the risk of STDs. The sponge is a round piece of white, plastic foam that is inserted prior to intercourse and continuously releases spermicide. It is removed and discarded after use.

A prescription-only option is *Phexxi*, a vaginal gel that maintains an acidic pH (range 3.5-4.5), which is inhospitable to sperm and reduces their mobility. It should not be used with vaginal rings or in those with a history of recurrent UTIs or urinary tract abnormalities.

HORMONAL CONTRACEPTIVES

Hormonal contraceptives work by inhibiting the production of FSH and LH, which prevents ovulation. They alter cervical mucus, which inhibits the sperm from penetrating the egg. If implantation of the fertilized egg in the uterus has already taken place, none of these methods are effective, and the pregnancy will proceed normally.

Available treatments include progestin-only options (pill, injectable, implant and IUD) or estrogen/progestin combinations (pill, patch and vaginal ring). The estrogen/progestin combination pills are called combination oral contraceptives (COCs). Non-oral contraceptives that contain both estrogen and progestin are referred to as combined hormonal contraceptives (CHC). The patch and the ring have unique considerations (such as instructions for use) but contain hormones similar to pill formulations. Contraindications are the same for the COCs and the patch or vaginal ring.

Hormonal contraceptives provide health benefits, including a decrease in menstrual pain, menstrual irregularity, endometriosis, acne, ectopic pregnancy, noncancerous breast cysts/lumps and risk of endometrial and ovarian cancer.

The FDA requires that the Patient Package Insert (PPI) be dispensed with oral contraceptives – it will be in the product packaging. The PPI has important safety information, instructions on proper use and what to do if pills are missed.

ESTROGEN AND PROGESTIN COMBINATION ORAL CONTRACEPTIVES

Most COCs contain the estrogen ethinyl estradiol (EE) and a progestin [e.g., norethindrone, levonorgestrel (LNG), drospirenone]. There are different formulations of COCs.

- Monophasic COCs have the same dose of estrogen and progestin throughout the pill pack.

- Biphasic, triphasic and quadriphasic pill packs mimic the estrogen and progesterone levels during a menstrual cycle. The type of formulation (e.g., triphasic) refers to the number of times the amounts of the hormones change (e.g., three times). The name of the pill can reflect the type (e.g., *Tri-Sprintec* is triphasic, with three different hormone "cycles").

Drospirenone is a unique progestin that is used in some COCs to reduce adverse effects commonly seen with oral contraceptives. It is a mild potassium-sparing diuretic which decreases bloating, PMS symptoms and weight gain; drospirenone-containing products are also associated with less acne, as they have anti-androgenic activity. Other progestins with low androgenic activity include norgestimate, desogestrel and dienogest.

Treatment of Other Indications

COCs are used for other indications besides pregnancy prevention, including dysmenorrhea (menstrual cramps), premenstrual syndrome (PMS), acne (in females), anemia, (by reducing blood loss), peri-menopausal symptoms (hot flashes, night sweats) and menstrual-associated migraine prophylaxis. The use of COCs to regulate menses is first-line treatment for polycystic ovary syndrome (PCOS), a common condition (~5 – 10% of women), where infrequent, irregular or prolonged menstrual periods are common. Some women with PCOS will have hirsutism, acne, excessive weight and insulin resistance, and most women experience fatigue.

COCs are used as first-line treatment for endometriosis (10 – 20% of women) in which endometrial tissue grows outside of the uterus. COCs reduce the symptoms of dysmenorrhea and heavy bleeding. Elagolix (Orilissa) is FDA-approved for moderate to severe pain associated with endometriosis.

The COC Natazia and the levonorgestrel-releasing IUD Mirena are indicated for heavy menstrual bleeding (menorrhagia). Oriahnn, which contains estradiol, norethindrone and elagolix, is indicated for heavy menstrual bleeding associated with uterine fibroids, but is not a contraceptive (not intended to prevent pregnancy). Lysteda, an oral formulation of tranexamic acid (antifibrinolytic), is a nonhormonal treatment for menorrhagia.

PROGESTIN-ONLY PILLS

Progestin-only pills (POPs, mini-pills) contain no estrogen and have 28-days of active pills in each pack. POPs prevent pregnancy by suppressing ovulation, thickening the cervical mucus to inhibit sperm penetration and thinning the endometrium. POPs are primarily used in women who are lactating (breastfeeding), because estrogen decreases milk production. POPs can be useful for women with a contraindication or intolerance to estrogen and can be started soon after delivery (3 – 6 weeks postpartum). It is not safe to use estrogen this soon after delivery because of an increased risk of thrombosis. POPs require good adherence; the pill must be taken within three hours of the scheduled time. POPs are sometimes used for migraine prophylaxis, and are safe in women who have migraines with aura; estrogen cannot be used with this type of migraine due to the risk of stroke.

NON-ORAL HORMONAL CONTRACEPTIVES

Contraceptive Patch

The patch has the same side effects, contraindications and drug interactions as COCs, but the patch causes a higher systemic estrogen exposure. It should not be used in anyone with clotting risk factors. The patch is less effective in women > 198 pounds (Xulane) or BMI > 30 kg/m² (Twirla). Do not use the patch in women > 35 years old who smoke.

Vaginal Contraceptive Rings

The vaginal rings have the same side effects, contraindications and drug interactions as oral contraceptives. These are small, flexible rings that are inserted into the vagina once a month. The exact position of the ring in the vagina does not matter.

Injectable Contraception

The injection (Depo-Provera, Depo-subQ Provera 104) is depot medroxyprogesterone acetate (DMPA), a progestin. It suppresses ovulation, thickens cervical mucus and causes thinning of the endometrium. DMPA is given by IM (150 mg) or SC (104 mg) injection every 3 months.

Intrauterine Devices (IUDs)

IUDs are long-acting, reversible forms of contraception. Some IUDs contain hormones to enhance their effects. IUDs are discussed in more detail later in the chapter, in the Long-Acting Reversible Contraceptives section.

CONTRACEPTION AND MENSTRUAL PERIODS

Most COC formulations involve 28 days (4 weeks) of pills, with 21 – 24 pills containing active hormone and the remaining pills containing no hormone (many use placebo pills, some contain iron or folate). During week 4 (the inactive pills), bleeding (menses) occurs for 3 – 7 days. Fewer inactive pills results in a shorter hormone-free interval and shorter bleeding time. Women who take COCs often have lighter bleeding because the endometrium remains relatively thin. For the contraceptive patch or vaginal ring, bleeding occurs during the patch-free or ring-free interval (week 4). About half of medroxyprogesterone acetate users will be amenorrheic (no menses) after 1 year of use.

Extended-cycle COCs involve 84 days of active hormonal pills followed by 7 days of inactive or very low-dose estrogen pills. With this schedule, bleeding occurs every 3 months rather than every month. By taking continuous contraception, it is possible to suppress menses altogether. This involves taking hormonal pills only (no placebo pills). Amethyst is approved for this; other COCs and CHCs are used in this way, though it is off-label. With continuous use, it can be difficult to tell if a woman becomes pregnant. Spotting (breakthrough bleeding) occurs commonly with continuous contraception, which can lead to discontinuation. It is important to counsel patients that this typically resolves after 3 – 6 months. There are benefits to continuous use, such as less anemia and menstrual migraines.

SELECT CONTRACEPTIVE TYPES

This is not a comprehensive list. For exam purposes, consider patient-specific factors that help in selecting a medication and understand the counseling points that are unique to each formulation.

PRODUCT TYPE	DESCRIPTION
General tips for contraceptive names: ■ "Lo" indicates ≤ 35 mcg of estrogen; less estrogen causes less estrogenic side effects. Ex: *Loestrin* ■ "Fe" indicates an iron supplement is included. Ex: *Loestrin Fe* ■ "24" indicates a shorter placebo time: 24 active + 4 placebo = 28 day cycle. Ex: *Minastrin 24 Fe*	
Pills	
Monophasic Formulations	Provides the same dose of progestin and estrogen throughout the active pill days. Example: *Junel 1/20* contains 1 mg norethindrone and 20 mcg EE
Junel Fe 1/20, Microgestin Fe 1/20, Sprintec 28, Loestrin 1/20, Yasmin 28, *Apri, Aviane, Cryselle-28, Levora, Nortrel 1/35, Ocella, Portia-28, Zovia 1/35E*	21/7 pill pack contains 21 active hormonal pills, 7 inactive pills
Loestrin 24 Fe, Yaz, *Beyaz, Minastrin 24 Fe, Nikki*	24/4 pill pack contains 24 active hormonal pills, 4 inactive pills
Lo Loestrin Fe	24/2/2 pill pack contains 24 active combined hormonal pills, 2 pills of just EE, and 2 inactive pills (with iron); very low dose estrogen used (EE 10 mcg)
Biphasic, Triphasic Formulations	"Phasic" in the name refers to the hormone dose being delivered in phases. The beginning of the name indicates the number of phases throughout the cycle (e.g., biphasic has two phases)
Ortho Tri-Cyclen Lo*, **Tri-Sprintec**, *Nortrel 7/7/7, Trivora, Velivet*	3 different weeks (7/7/7) or "tri" indicates a triphasic formulation
Quadriphasic Formulations *Natazia*	Hormone doses change over 26 days (four phases of estradiol valerate and progestin dienogest) followed by 2 placebo pills to mimic menstrual cycle and minimize menstrual bleeding
Extended Cycle Formulations	Period occurs every 3 months
Jolessa	84 days of EE + LNG followed by 7 days of placebo
Seasonique, *Camrese, Camrese Lo, Amethia*	84 days of EE + LNG followed by 7 days of low dose EE
Continuous Formulations	No inactive pills (taken continuously); no period occurs
Amethyst	28 days of EE + LNG with no placebo pills
Drospirenone Containing Formulations	Mild potassium-sparing diuretic to reduce bloating and other effects
Yasmin 28, Yaz, *Loryna, Ocella, Zarah, Nextstellis, Nikki, Safyral, Syeda, Beyaz* (Safyral & Beyaz contain folate)	Contraindicated in renal or liver disease Monitor potassium, kidney function during use
Patches	
Transdermal patch **Xulane**, *Twirla*	Higher AUC than pills Weeks 1-3: apply once weekly; week 4: off
Rings	
Vaginal ring **NuvaRing**, *EluRyng, Annovera*	Lower AUC than pills Insert monthly: in x 3 weeks; remove x 1 week *Annovera*: reusable vaginal ring; wash and store when it is removed, then reinsert; used for 1 year
Progestin-Only Pills (Mini-Pill/POP)	
Errin, Camila, Nora-BE, *Incassia*	*Errin, Camila, Nora-BE* contain a fixed dose of norethindrone; take active tablet daily (no placebo days); "Nor" in the name indicates it contains norethindrone
Slynd	*Slynd* is drospirenone-only
Injection	
Depo-Provera	Contains depot medroxyprogesterone (DMPA); injected every 3 months (150 mg IM or 104 mg SC) "Pro" in the name indicates it contains a progestin

* Brand discontinued but name still used in practice

ADVERSE EFFECTS OF HORMONAL CONTRACEPTIVES

Estrogen

Side effects of estrogen can include:

- Nausea

- Breast tenderness/fullness, bloating, weight gain and increased blood pressure (which can all be partially due to fluid retention)

- Melasma (dark skin patches, most often on the face)

Reducing the estrogen dose reduces the side effects, but a dose that is too low will cause breakthrough bleeding (spotting), especially during the early to mid-part of the cycle.

Serious adverse effects are rare, but can include thrombosis, including heart attack, stroke and DVT/PE (see Study Tip Gal). The risk for clots increases as the woman ages, if she smokes, if she has diabetes or hypertension, if she requires prolonged bed rest and if she is overweight. The higher the estrogen dose or exposure (e.g., with Xulane transdermal patch), the higher the clotting risk. When evaluating risks from use of the pill, also consider risks with an unintended pregnancy. The risk of blood clots during pregnancy and postpartum is higher than the clotting risk with any birth control pill formulation.

SEVERE & RARE ADVERSE EFFECTS OF ESTROGEN

The dose of estrogen in birth control pills used to be much higher – with a higher risk of clotting. Current formulations have lower estrogen doses and lower risk of clotting. To be safe, patients should be able to recognize symptoms of a DVT, PE and less common clots.

Remember: **ACHES**

Abdominal (stomach) pain that is severe
- ❏ Can indicate a ruptured liver tumor or cyst, mesenteric or pelvic vein thrombosis, or the pain could be due to liver or gallbladder problems or an ectopic pregnancy.

Chest pain
- ❏ Sharp, crushing, or heavy pain can indicate a heart attack. Shortness of breath can indicate a PE (a blood clot in the lungs).

Headaches
- ❏ Sudden and severe with vomiting or weakness/numbness on one side of the body can indicate a stroke.

Eye problems
- ❏ Blurry vision, flashing lights or partial/complete vision loss can indicate a blood clot in the eye.

Swelling or sudden leg pain
- ❏ Can indicate a DVT (a blood clot in the leg).

Progestin

Progestin can cause breast tenderness, headache, fatigue and depression.

Drospirenone has a slightly higher risk of clotting, and should not be used in women with clotting risk. It can also result in increased potassium; do not use with kidney, liver or adrenal gland disease as these can increase potassium. On a patient case, review the potassium level. It should be in the normal range (3.5 – 5 mEq/L).

The injectable depot medroxyprogesterone acetate can cause a loss in bone mineral density. This can be especially important for teens and young women who are still accumulating bone mass. Minimally, women should be taking adequate calcium and vitamin D (see recommendations in the Osteoporosis, Menopause & Testosterone Use chapter).

Breakthrough Bleeding

Breakthrough bleeding (i.e., spotting) usually resolves within 2 – 3 months. Continuous contraception has more breakthrough bleeding, especially during the first few months.

Always check adherence; spotting can be due to a fast drop in estrogen from missing a pill.

If spotting persists:

- And currently taking < 30 mcg estrogen daily: increase estrogen dose.

- And currently taking ≥ 30 mcg estrogen daily: try a different progestin.

RISKS OF HORMONAL CONTRACEPTIVES

BOXED WARNINGS
All estrogen-containing products (pills, ring, patch)
- Do not use in women > 35 years old who smoke due to risk of serious cardiovascular events

Estrogen + progestin transdermal patch
- Increased risk of venous thromboembolism (DVT/PE) compared to COCs

Depo-Provera
- Loss of bone mineral density with long-term use

DO NOT USE ESTROGEN WITH THESE CONDITIONS
History of DVT/PE, stroke, CAD, thrombosis of heart valves or acquired hypercoagulopathies

History of breast, ovarian, or liver cancer; liver disease; uncontrolled hypertension (e.g., > 160/100 mmHg); severe headaches or migraines with aura (especially if > 35 years of age); diabetes with vascular disease; unexplained uterine bleeding; others (vary by formulation)

CONSIDERATIONS FOR DRUG SELECTION

TYPE OF PATIENT	PRODUCT SELECTION CONSIDERATIONS
Acne or hirsutism	Use COC with a progestin that has lower androgenic activity [e.g., norgestimate (Sprintec 28)] or no androgenic activity [e.g., drospirenone (Yaz, Yasmin)].
Breastfeeding	Choose POPs or nonhormonal method. See Postpartum below.
Estrogen contraindication (including clotting risk)	Choose POPs or nonhormonal method.
Migraine	If with aura, choose POPs or nonhormonal method; do not use estrogen. If no aura, choose any method.
Fluid retention/bloating	Choose a product containing drospirenone.
Heavy menstrual bleeding (menorrhagia)	The COC Natazia and the levonorgestrel-releasing IUD Mirena are indicated for this condition. COCs with only 4 placebo pills (rather than 7) or continuous/extended regimens will minimize bleeding time.
Hypertension	If BP is uncontrolled, some estrogen formulations are contraindicated. Choose POPs or nonhormonal method.
Mood changes or disorder	Use monophasic COC – extended cycle or continuous with drospirenone is preferred.
Nausea	Take at night, with food; consider decreasing estrogen dose or switching to POP, vaginal ring or nonhormonal method (ideally after a 3 month trial).
Overweight	Choose any method. Counsel patient about the possibility of reduced effectiveness with the contraceptive patch. Do not use DMPA if trying to avoid further weight gain.
Postpartum	Do not use CHCs for 3 weeks, or for 6 weeks if patient has additional risk factors for VTE. Can use POPs or nonhormonal method during this time.
Premenstrual dysphoric disorder	Choose Yaz or antidepressant; see Depression chapter.
Spotting/"breakthrough bleeding"	Common when initiating extended cycles or continuous regimens; usually resolves within 3-6 months. When starting conventional formulations, wait 3 cycles before switching. If early or mid-cycle spotting occurs, the estrogen dose may need to be increased. If later in the cycle, the progestin dose may need to be increased.
Wishes to avoid monthly cycle/menses	Use extended (91-day) or continuous formulations. Alternative: monophasic 28-day formulation and skip placebo pills.

DRUG INTERACTIONS WITH HORMONAL CONTRACEPTIVES

Some forms of contraception can have decreased efficacy when used with other drugs; this can require use of a back-up contraception method such as condoms/spermicide. If the interaction is long-term in nature, consider an IUD or the birth control injection. The birth control injection has lower drug interaction risk as it bypasses first-pass metabolism and achieves higher serum concentrations. With all new drugs being dispensed to contraception users, the package insert should be checked for interactions that could decrease the contraceptive efficacy. If in doubt, it is safest to use back-up.

Drug Interactions that Decrease Hormonal Contraception Efficacy

- Some antibiotics (e.g., rifampin, rifabutin and rifapentine; these are all strong inducers).
  - With rifampin, the induction can be prolonged; a back-up contraception method is needed for 6 weeks after rifampin has been discontinued.
- Anticonvulsants (carbamazepine, oxcarbazepine, phenytoin, primidone, topiramate, lamotrigine, barbiturates and perampanel).
- St. John's wort.
- Smoking tobacco.
- Ritonavir-boosted protease inhibitors (PIs), bosentan (Tracleer), mycophenolate (CellCept, Myfortic).
- Colesevelam: separate by at least 4 hours.
- Byetta: take contraceptive at least one hour prior to injection.

Risks with Hepatitis C Treatment

- Mavyret and Viekira Pak cannot be used with any formulation containing ethinyl estradiol due to the risk of liver toxicity.
- With all new hepatitis C drugs being dispensed to a patient using contraception, the package insert should be checked to avoid missing an interaction that could cause toxicity.

Drospirenone Drug Interactions

- Risk of increased potassium; caution must be used with potassium-sparing drugs, including aldosterone antagonists, potassium supplements, salt substitutes (KCl), ACE inhibitors, angiotensin receptor blockers, heparin, canagliflozin and calcineurin inhibitors (see hyperkalemia discussion in Renal Disease chapter).

MALE & FEMALE HEALTH

STARTING BIRTH CONTROL PILLS

Combination Oral Contraception

In general, it takes seven days of hormonal pills to achieve contraceptive efficacy.

- Start today (also called "quick start"). Best practice recommendation. Maximizes time protected from unintended pregnancy. This method requires back-up (nonhormonal) contraception for seven days.

- Sunday start. Starts the Sunday after onset of menstruation. This is commonly used if the patient prefers that menstruation occur during the week and is complete before the following weekend. It can lead to missed doses if the patient inadvertently runs out of refills over the weekend. This method requires back-up (nonhormonal) contraception for seven days.

COCs can also be started on the first day of menses. If started within five days after the start of the period, no back-up method of birth control is needed; protection is immediate. If not within five days, use back-up for seven days.

Progestin-Only Pills

- Start at any time. Use another method of birth control for the first 48 hours of progestin-pill use – protection begins after two days. All come in 28-day packs and all pills are active.

LATE OR MISSED PILLS – INSTRUCTIONS FOR TYPICAL FORMULATIONS

Missed pills are a common cause of contraceptive failure, particularly if the hormone-free interval is extended. These are the standard instructions from the CDC; when answering questions in practice, check the package insert for the individual product. For the exam, you should know the general approach to missed doses:

- Start as soon as remembered.

- If more than one COC pill is missed, back-up contraception is required.

- If missed pills/days are in the third week of the cycle, omit the hormone-free week and start the next package of pills right away without skipping any days; back-up contraception should be used for seven days.

Missed Doses for Standard Cycle (28 days)

		WEEK 1	WEEK 2	WEEK 3	WEEK 4
COCs	**1 late or missed pill** (< 48 hours since last dose)	Take missed pill as soon as possible and take next dose on schedule (even if that makes 2 pills in 1 day).			
		Back-up contraception required? No			
		EC*: Not usually needed. Consider if missed doses earlier in the same cycle or in week 3 of the previous cycle.			
	2 missed pills (≥ 48 hours since last dose)	Take the most recent missed pill as soon as possible (discard any other missed pills). Take next dose on schedule (even if that makes 2 pills in 1 day).			
				Omit hormone-free week: start next pack of pills right after finishing current pack.**	
		Back-up contraception required? Yes, x 7 days			
		EC*: Consider if unprotected sex in last 5 days.	EC*: Can be considered.		
POPs	**If > 3 hours past scheduled time**	Take pill as soon as possible and take next dose on schedule.			
		Back-up contraception required? Yes, x 48 hours			
		EC*: Consider if unprotected sex in last 5 days.			

*EC = emergency contraception
**If unable to start a new pack right away, use back-up contraception until 7 days of the new pack have been taken

MALE & FEMALE HEALTH

LONG-ACTING REVERSIBLE CONTRACEPTIVES

These devices are generally not dispensed from community pharmacies. They must be placed and removed by trained healthcare professionals. They are the most effective forms of reversible contraception, and are as effective as sterilization.

- Intrauterine devices (*Mirena, Skyla, Kyleena, Liletta*) are hormonal IUDs that contain the progestin levonorgestrel. These cause lighter menstrual bleeding and minor or no cramping. *Mirena* is FDA-approved for heavy menstrual bleeding. After insertion, the IUD is left in place for several years before it is replaced; the specific timing is product-dependent (e.g., *Mirena* – 7 years, *Liletta* – 6 years, *Kyleena* – 5 years, *Skyla* – 3 years). About 20% of women using *Mirena* will become amenorrheic.

- The copper-T IUD (*Paragard*) can be used for emergency contraception (EC) and/or regular birth control. It can be used for up to 10 years, but causes heavier menstrual bleeding and cramping. Some women prefer this nonhormonal method.

- The implant (*Nexplanon*) is a plastic rod placed subdermally in the arm. It releases the progestin etonogestrel for three years.

CASE SCENARIO

KL is a 37-year-old female (G2 P2)* with antiphospholipid syndrome, diagnosed 2 years ago after a second DVT. She takes aspirin daily. Her last pregnancy was difficult. She requests contraception that is highly effective.

KL is 5 feet, 4 inches; 145 pounds; BP 111/77 mmHg

- Assess her medical history:
  - ❏ Estrogen is contraindicated with antiphospholipid syndrome or any clotting condition. She cannot use COCs, a vaginal ring or transdermal patch.
  - ❏ She could use POPs (the mini-pill), but the risk of unplanned pregnancy is high with missed or even late pills.
  - ❏ Another hormonal option is the *Depo-Provera* injection. Her bone health should be considered prior to use.
  - ❏ IUD placement or sterilization may be acceptable to KL.

*G2 P2 is an abbreviation for gravida and para. She has been pregnant twice and has had 2 deliveries after 24 weeks gestation.

EMERGENCY CONTRACEPTION (EC)

EMERGENCY CONTRACEPTIVE	EFFECTIVENESS	TIMING	CONSIDERATIONS
Copper IUD (*Paragard*)	Most effective (99.9%)	Within 5 days	Must be placed in the uterus by a doctor or nurse Lasts for up to 10 years
Ulipristal (*Ella*)	More effective than *Plan B* Less effective if > 195 pounds or BMI > 30 kg/m² (consider IUD)	ASAP, within 5 days	Prescription required Must be taken after every episode of unprotected sex
Levonorgestrel (*Plan B One-Step* or a generic)	Less effective if > 165 pounds or BMI > 25 kg/m² (consider *Ella* or IUD)	ASAP, within 3 days	Available OTC Must be taken after every episode of unprotected sex

Emergency contraception (EC) is a form of contraception that prevents pregnancy after unprotected intercourse. The copper IUD (*Paragard*) is the most effective form of EC if inserted within five days. There are two oral EC (also known as the "morning after pill") options, levonorgestrel (*Plan B One-Step*) and ulipristal acetate (*Ella*). Ulipristal acetate is best used within five days; levonorgestrel is best used within three days (guidelines recommend within five days), with effectiveness diminishing over time. The sooner EC is used, the higher the efficacy. The use of higher doses of combination oral contraceptives is no longer a common practice as it is less effective than these options, leads to more nausea/vomiting and has more contraindications.

EC can be an important resource after unprotected sex, such as from missed pills, a condom breaking, a diaphragm or cap moving out of place during intercourse or if a female has been sexually assaulted. If sexual assault has occurred, empiric STD treatment (chlamydia, gonorrhea, trichomoniasis), HIV post-exposure prophylaxis, HBV and HPV vaccines may be required. Pharmacists should have referrals for other providers available to provide to patients.

EC after sex might be used as a regular method of birth control. This can be done with occasional (not regular) sexual activity if the effectiveness of the method is acceptable (as well as the potential increased cost).

LEVONORGESTREL

Plan B One-Step and generics are packaged as one 1.5 mg tab of levonorgestrel. This EC formulation reduces the risk of pregnancy by up to 89% if started within 72 hours (3 days) after unprotected intercourse. The sooner it is taken, the higher the efficacy.

Plan B One-Step and generics (*Take Action, Aftera, My Way, React*) are available OTC with no age or other restrictions. These products can be sold in stores without a pharmacy. Per the FDA, these should be placed in the OTC aisles with the other family-planning products, such as condoms and spermicides. The generics cost $35 – $45, about $10 less than the brand *Plan B One-Step*. There is no reason to use a prescription with the formulations available OTC, except to use insurance coverage.

If the EC is purchased OTC, there is no requirement for purchasers to sign a registry. They can purchase multiple doses and the American College of Obstetrics and Gynecologists (ACOG) recommends an additional dose for future use, if needed, since EC is more effective the sooner it is used.

- Mechanism of action: primarily works by preventing or delaying ovulation and thickens cervical mucus.

- Preferred regimen is 1.5 mg as a single dose (*Plan B One-Step*).

- This type of EC can be used for up to five days (the sooner, the better) after unprotected intercourse. The package indicates to use within three days, but is used up to five days off-label according to evidence-based guidelines.

- The primary side effect is nausea, which occurs in 23% of women, and 6% have vomiting. If the woman is easily nauseated, an OTC antiemetic (one hour prior to use, and caution if driving due to sedation) should be recommended to avoid losing the dose. If a patient vomits within two hours of taking the medication, she should consider repeating the dose.

ULIPRISTAL ACETATE *(ELLA)*

Some patients may not wish to use ulipristal because it is a chemical cousin to mifepristone (*Mifeprex*), also known as the "abortion pill" or RU-486. They are not the same drug and are used differently. The mifepristone product available in the U.S. is used primarily for pregnancy terminations and other non-contraceptive uses. Ulipristal has a lower potency and is used to delay ovulation. It may also prevent implantation in the uterus and this is controversial for some patients.

- Given as a single 30 mg dose. Requires a prescription.

- Indicated for up to five days after unprotected intercourse. More effective than levonorgestrel if 72 – 120 hours since unprotected intercourse or if the woman is overweight.

- Primary side effects are headache, nausea and abdominal pain. Some women have changes in their menstrual cycle, but all should get their period within a week. Can only use once per cycle. Use a barrier method of contraception the rest of the cycle as ovulation may occur later than normal.

KEY COUNSELING POINTS

See the Drug Formulations and Patient Counseling chapter for counseling language/layman's terminology.

OTC CONTRACEPTIVE METHODS

Diaphragm

- Wash hands thoroughly. Place one tablespoon of spermicide in the diaphragm and disperse inside and around the rim.

- Pinch the ends of the cup and insert the pinched end into the vagina.

- Leave in for six hours after intercourse. Diaphragms should not be in place greater than 24 hours.

- Reapply spermicide if intercourse is repeated or diaphragm is in place for more than two hours before sex, by inserting jelly with applicator.

- Wash with mild soap and warm water after removal, air dry.

- Can be used for up to two years.

Foams, Creams, Suppositories and Jellies

- Place deep into the vagina right before intercourse where they melt (except for foam, which bubbles).

Sponge

- Place deep into the vagina right before intercourse.

- Leave in place for at least six hours after intercourse, but it can be used for up to 24 hours. Remove and discard after use.

COMBINATION ORAL CONTRACEPTIVES

- Can increase risk of blood clots.

- Can cause nausea, weight gain and breast tenderness. Side effects often improve after three months of use. Taking the pill with food or at night helps to reduce nausea.

- Take the pill at the same time each day; pick a time of day that you will remember.

- Many drug interactions.

Drospirenone Formulations
- Can increase potassium.

NON-ORAL FORMULATIONS

Contraceptive Patch
- Apply to clean, dry skin of <u>buttocks, stomach, upper arm or upper torso</u> once a week for 21 out of 28 days. Do not apply to breasts.

- Start on either <u>day 1</u> (no back-up needed) or <u>Sunday</u> (back-up seven days if not day 1).

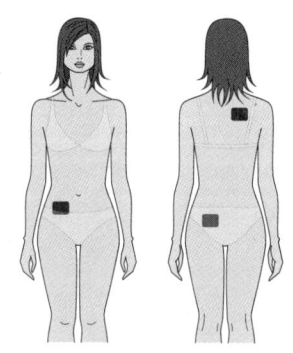

Xulane, Twirla (back, abdomen, arm or buttock)
📷 *pushinka © 123RF.com*

- If the patch becomes loose or falls off for > 24 hours during the three weeks of use, or if > 7 days have passed during the fourth week where no patch is required, there is a risk of pregnancy. A back-up method should be used for one week after starting a new patch.

NuvaRing Vaginal Contraceptive Ring
- The ring is inserted into the vagina once a month. It is <u>kept in</u> place for <u>three weeks</u> and taken <u>out for one week</u> before replacement with a new ring. The ring is effective for up to four weeks and, though not FDA-approved, can be kept in place to prevent a period. If the ring is <u>kept in</u> place for <u>> 4 weeks</u>: confirm no pregnancy, then insert a new ring and use <u>back-up contraception</u> until the new ring has been in place for seven continuous days.

- The exact position of the ring in the vagina does not matter.

- Starting therapy and no hormonal contraceptive use in preceding cycle: <u>insert</u> the ring the <u>first day</u> of menstrual bleeding. If inserted on days 2 – 5 of cycle, <u>back-up contraception</u> should be used for the first <u>seven days</u> in the first cycle.

- If the ring is expelled or removed:
  - ❑ Weeks 1 and 2: if ring is out > 3 hours, rinse with cool to lukewarm water and reinsert. Use back-up contraception for seven days while the ring is in place, consider EC if intercourse within last five days.
  - ❑ Week 3: discard and insert a new ring. Use back-up contraception for seven days while the ring is in place.

- Store for up to four months at room temperature (refrigerate prior to dispensing).

Injectable Contraception (Medroxyprogesterone)
- Can decrease bone density. Take the recommended daily intake of calcium and vitamin D.

- You might experience a change in your normal menstrual cycle.

EMERGENCY CONTRACEPTION

- Can cause nausea/vomiting. OTC antiemetics can help. If you vomit after taking the dose, contact your healthcare provider (may need to take another dose).

- If you do not get your period in three weeks (or it is more than a week late), a pregnancy test should be taken. Severe abdominal pain or irregular bleeding requires immediate medical attention.

- Visit your healthcare provider for a regular birth control method and information about preventing sexually transmitted infections. If you may have contracted an infection, you should get care right away.

- You may wish to get a <u>package of EC for future use</u>, if needed.

- Regular hormonal contraceptives (OCs, shot, ring, patch) should be started on the same or the following day as taking the EC.

- You should only use one type of oral EC pill. Do not use two different types together.

MALE & FEMALE HEALTH

INFERTILITY

Infertility is defined as not being able to get pregnant (conceive) after <u>one year</u> or longer of unprotected sex. Infertility can be due to either the male or female. This section covers drugs used in females.

The treatment choice for females depends on the cause of the infertility (e.g., absent ovulation). <u>Clomiphene</u>, a <u>selective estrogen receptor modulator</u> (SERM), and letrozole, an aromatase inhibitor, are oral tablets used to induce ovulation. Drugs that are SERMs act as estrogen <u>agonists</u> in some tissues and estrogen <u>antagonists</u> in other tissues. Clomiphene, like estrogen, causes LH and FSH to surge, which triggers ovulation. The surge in LH commonly causes <u>hot flashes</u>. SERMs, including clomiphene, have <u>clotting risks</u>. Letrozole impacts ovulation primarily through estrogen negative feedback (estrogen production is suppressed resulting in an initial FSH surge that leads to follicle development and ovulation).

<u>Gonadotropins</u> trigger ovulation by acting similar to the endogenous (naturally produced) gonadotropins <u>FSH</u> or <u>LH</u>. Gonadotropins are used after a poor response to clomiphene, or to spur egg release for procedures such as intrauterine insemination and *in vitro* fertilization.

Alternatively, human chorionic gonadotropin (hCG) or gonadotropin releasing hormone agonists (GnRHA), such as leuprolide (*Lupron*), can be used to trigger ovulation. The hCG hormone is important in pregnancy <u>and</u> in ovulation, where it binds to the LH receptor with a similar effect. Leuprolide and other GnRHAs are more commonly used to decrease hormone levels in breast or prostate cancer treatment.

Fertility medications, including <u>gonadotropins</u> and <u>clomiphene</u>, can cause multiple eggs to be released, which causes a <u>risk</u> of <u>multiple births</u> (see <u>Study Tip Gal</u>). Gonadotropins, similar to the majority of drugs that are hormones, cannot be taken orally. They are administered by <u>SC</u> or <u>IM injection</u>. This is one of the rare times a patient (or their partner) could be injecting IM, which is more painful than SC administration.

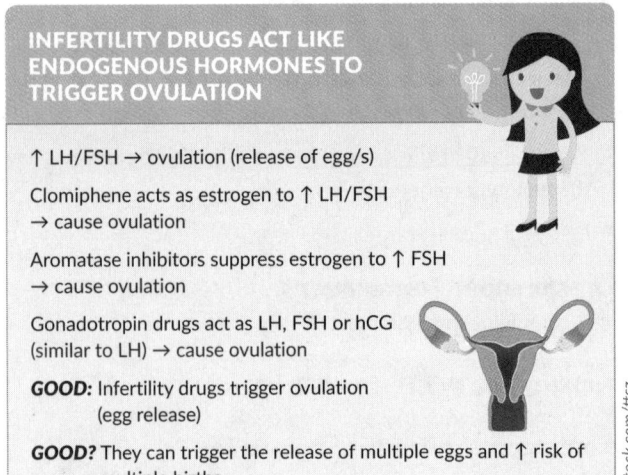

INFERTILITY DRUGS ACT LIKE ENDOGENOUS HORMONES TO TRIGGER OVULATION

↑ LH/FSH → ovulation (release of egg/s)

Clomiphene acts as estrogen to ↑ LH/FSH → cause ovulation

Aromatase inhibitors suppress estrogen to ↑ FSH → cause ovulation

Gonadotropin drugs act as LH, FSH or hCG (similar to LH) → cause ovulation

GOOD: Infertility drugs trigger ovulation (egg release)

GOOD? They can trigger the release of multiple eggs and ↑ risk of multiple births

iStock.com/ttsz

GONADOTROPIN DRUG NAMES

<u>Generic</u> names include chorionic gonadotropin-recombinant, follicle stimulating hormone-recombinant, human chorionic gonadotropin-recombinant and menotropin, which contains LH and FSH extracted from the urine of menopausal females.

<u>Brand</u> names can include parts of the words <u>repro</u>duce, men(strual), <u>follicle</u>, <u>gonadotropin</u>, <u>preg</u>nancy and <u>ovary</u>, including *Menopur, Follistim AQ, Gonal-f, Pregnyl, Novarel* and *Ovidrel*.

Select Guidelines/References

US Selected Practice Recommendations (US SPR) for Contraceptive Use, 2016 https://www.cdc.gov/reproductivehealth/contraception/mmwr/spr/combined.html (accessed 2022 Feb 8).

CONTENT LEGEND

🔑 = Key Drug Guy

© iStock.com/microgen

CHAPTER 48

DRUG USE IN PREGNANCY & LACTATION

PREGNANCY

BACKGROUND

Pregnancy typically lasts 37 – 40 weeks and is divided into three trimesters. A positive human chorionic gonadotropin (hCG+) lab result confirms pregnancy. The first trimester (0 – 12 weeks) is when most organ development occurs, making the embryo most susceptible to birth defects caused by teratogens during this time (though they can occur later). For a drug to be teratogenic, the drug has to cross the placenta into the fetal circulation. Teratogenic drugs should be discontinued prior to pregnancy, if possible.

Pharmacokinetic changes during pregnancy can require dose and regimen changes. For example, in women being treated for hypothyroidism, an increased dose of levothyroxine will be required in order to keep thyroid hormones within normal ranges. The American College of Obstetricians and Gynecologists (ACOG) is an organization that publishes guidelines for safe and effective drug use in conditions impacting women, including pregnancy.

A patient's obstetric history can be described using gravida and para. Gravida (G) is the number of times the person has been pregnant. Para (P) is the number of times a patient has given birth. For example, a patient that is gravida 2, para 1 (or G2, P1 for short), has been pregnant twice and given birth once.

LIFESTYLE MANAGEMENT

Lifestyle modifications should always be considered first when treating pregnant patients. This includes encouragement to stop using recreational drugs, alcohol and tobacco, each of which is teratogenic. Behavioral intervention is a safe and sometimes effective strategy for prenatal smoking cessation. See the Tobacco Cessation chapter for more information.

Vitamin and Mineral Supplementation

Folate deficiency causes birth defects of the brain and spinal cord (neural tube defects). Folate (folic acid, vitamin B9) is found in many healthy foods, including fortified flour and cereals, dried beans, green leafy vegetables and orange juice.

Adults should consume 400 mcg of dietary folate equivalents (DFE) per day. During pregnancy, folate requirements increase to 600 mcg DFE/day. Females of childbearing potential should increase their folic acid consumption from a combination of dietary supplements, fortified foods and their regular diet.

The baby's skeleton requires adequate calcium and vitamin D. If deficient in calcium, the mother's bone health will be sacrificed to provide for the baby. Pregnant women from 19 – 50 years old require 1,000 mg/day of calcium and 15 mcg/day (600 IU/day) of vitamin D.

Prenatal vitamins are available by prescription and OTC. Most contain 800 – 1,000 mcg DFE, 10 mcg (400 IU) vitamin D and ~200 mg calcium, though composition varies. Calcium is bulky and the prenatal vitamin would be too large if it contained more calcium. If the woman's dietary intake is insufficient, a separate calcium and vitamin D supplement may be needed.

CHANGES TO FDA PREGNANCY CATEGORIES

The old pregnancy categories were viewed as confusing and overly simplistic. Categories were difficult to interpret, leading physicians to unintentionally apply the provided information incorrectly. The updated labeling is intended to provide patients and clinicians with more detailed benefit/risk data on prescription drugs in order to make informed decisions. See the new pregnancy package insert requirements in the table to the right.

The deadline for the transition to the new pregnancy and lactation labeling format was June 2020. The package labeling for most drugs has been updated, but some drugs may still retain the old categories. Drugs approved before 2001 are exempt from adopting the new labeling requirements but are required to remove the old categories. The manufacturers of these older drugs are not required to replace the old categories with new information.

Despite the updated labeling, prescribers will likely continue to use the traditional terminology in practice. For this reason, it is important to remain familiar with the traditional categories. Drugs with known risk from the old categories should be considered to have the same risk unless known otherwise. If a drug was Pregnancy Category X, it is contraindicated in pregnancy, which means it cannot be used in pregnancy for any reason.

Previous Pregnancy Categories & Interpretation

A	Controlled studies in animals & women show no risk in the first trimester. Risk of fetal harm is remote.
B	Animal studies have not demonstrated a fetal risk, but no well-controlled studies are available in pregnant women.
C	Animal studies have shown harm to the fetus, but there are no well-controlled studies in pregnant women. Use only if potential benefit outweighs the risk.
D	Positive evidence of risk to the human fetus is available, but the benefits may outweigh the risk with life-threatening or serious diseases.
X	Studies in animals or humans show fetal abnormalities. The risks involved clearly outweigh potential benefits; use in pregnancy is contraindicated.

Updated Pregnancy Sections in Package Inserts

8.1 Pregnancy	A pregnancy risk summary is required for all medications that includes the risk of adverse developmental outcomes based on human and animal data and the drug's pharmacology. Includes any dose adjustments, maternal/fetal adverse reactions and disease risks. Includes pregnancy exposure registry information. Pregnant women should be encouraged to participate in registries, which exist for select disease states and drugs. The registries collect health information from women who take prescription drugs and vaccines when pregnant and breastfeeding. Information is also collected on the newborn baby.
8.2 Lactation	Includes whether the drug/metabolites are present in human milk, the effects on the breastfed infant, and the effects on milk production. If applicable, ways to minimize exposure and monitor for adverse reactions are included.
8.3 Females & Males of Reproductive Potential	Includes any effects on fertility and requirements for pregnancy testing and contraception.

DRUG TREATMENT

If possible, use lifestyle measures to treat medical conditions in pregnant women. When this is impossible or ineffective, choose drugs carefully.

There are two immunizations that are routinely recommended for pregnant patients. The inactivated influenza vaccine (not live) is recommended during any trimester at the beginning of flu season. A single dose of Tdap should be administered during each pregnancy. All live vaccines are contraindicated in pregnant patients. See the Immunizations chapter for more information on vaccination in pregnancy.

Common Teratogens

Teratogenic drugs should be discontinued prior to pregnancy, if possible, but about half of pregnancies are not planned. Once pregnancy is confirmed, medical providers should switch patients from teratogenic drugs to safer options.

In the RxPrep course book, medications with boxed warnings and contraindications associated with teratogenicity are noted in the drug tables. The medications in the Key Drugs Guy to the right are a summary and should be known for the exam. Many of the medications included are commonly used drugs with teratogenic risk. Others are well-documented teratogens, and use in a pregnant patient is rarely, if ever, appropriate. Some drugs with significant teratogenic risk have REMS requirements due to potential harm to the fetus (see the Drug Allergies & Adverse Drug Reactions chapter). Watch for these important teratogens when evaluating medication profiles on the exam.

Teratogens are hazardous drugs according to the National Institute for Occupational Safety and Health (NIOSH), and require special handling to avoid risk to healthcare workers; see the Compounding chapters.

Use of some medications in pregnant patients is debatable, and many medications have limited data regarding safety in pregnancy. With any medication, the drug's potential harm must be weighed against the risk of the condition not being adequately treated. For example, the use of lamotrigine in pregnancy carries a risk of congenital malformations, but seizures cause damage to both the mother and child. In some cases, a switch to a safer drug is possible, while in other situations the risk of switching is high. A pregnant woman may need to remain on lamotrigine if she has a history of poor seizure control before being placed on the drug.

Always check reputable, up-to-date resources when prescribing/dispensing to pregnant women. *Briggs' Drugs in Pregnancy and Lactation* and other resources are reviewed in the Drug References chapter.

KEY DRUGS

TERATOGENS: DANGER IN PREGNANCY

Acne
Isotretinoin, topical retinoids

Antibiotics*
Quinolones, tetracyclines

Anticoagulants
Warfarin; see discussion of anticoagulation in pregnancy in this chapter

Dyslipidemia, Heart Failure and Hypertension
Statins, RAAS inhibitors (ACE inhibitors, ARBs, aliskiren, sacubitril/valsartan)

Hormones
Most, including estradiol, progesterone (including megestrol), raloxifene, *Duavee*, testosterone, contraceptives

Migraine
Dihydroergotamine, ergotamine

Other important teratogens

Hydroxyurea	Ribavirin
Lithium	Thalidomide
Methotrexate	Topiramate
Misoprostol	Weight loss drugs
NSAIDs	
Paroxetine	Valproic Acid/Divalproex

Others:
Amiodarone
Aminoglycosides
Dronedarone
Atenolol
Benzodiazepines
Carbamazepine
Dutasteride
Finasteride
Fluconazole
Voriconazole
ERAs (e.g., bosentan)
Griseofulvin
Leflunomide
Lenalidomide
Lomitapide
Methimazole
Propylthiouracil
Radioactive iodine
Phenobarbital
Phenytoin

See Infectious Diseases I chapter for information on metronidazole, nitrofurantoin, sulfamethoxazole/trimethoprim and telavancin.

Preeclampsia

Preeclampsia is a complication of pregnancy that presents with elevated blood pressure and evidence of organ damage, most often to the kidneys or liver. It usually presents after the first trimester of pregnancy and can occur in women with previously normal blood pressure. If not treated, preeclampsia can progress to eclampsia, which can lead to seizures and death. The only cure for preeclampsia is delivery of the baby.

To prevent preeclampsia, ACOG and American Diabetes Association (ADA) guidelines recommend adding daily low-dose aspirin at the end of the first trimester for pregnant women at risk for preeclampsia (e.g., type 1 or 2 diabetes, renal disease, history of preeclampsia, chronic hypertension). See the Hypertension chapter for more information.

MALE & FEMALE HEALTH

Select Conditions and Preferred Management During Pregnancy

CONDITION	PREFERRED MANAGEMENT	NOTES
Morning Sickness, Nausea, Vomiting	Lifestyle first: eat smaller, more frequent meals, drink plenty of water, avoid spicy or odorous foods, take more frequent naps, and reduce stress, including working long hours. If lifestyle measures fail, ACOG recommends pyridoxine (vitamin B6) +/- doxylamine first line. Rx: doxylamine/pyridoxine (Bonjesta, Diclegis).	Ginger is rated "possibly effective" for treating morning sickness. Hyperemesis gravidarum is severe N/V, causing weight loss, dehydration and electrolyte imbalance. It will be treated under the care of an obstetrician and may require hospitalization.
GERD/Heartburn	Lifestyle first: eat smaller, more frequent meals, avoid foods that worsen GERD. If symptoms occur while sleeping, recommend elevating the head of the bed and not eating 3 hours prior to sleep. If lifestyle measures fail, recommend antacids. Calcium antacids, such as calcium carbonate (Tums), are a good choice since calcium intake is often deficient.	If heartburn symptoms are not relieved by Tums, H2 receptor antagonists or PPIs can be considered for add-on therapy.
Flatulence	Simethicone (Gas-X, Mylicon).	
Constipation	Lifestyle first: ↑ fluid intake, ↑ dietary fiber intake and ↑ physical activity. If lifestyle measures fail, fiber (psyllium, calcium polycarbophil, methylcellulose), with adequate amounts of fluids, is preferred. Docusate and polyethylene glycol are used to prevent and treat constipation.	Constipation is such a prevalent issue in pregnancy that many prenatal vitamins contain docusate.
Cough, Cold, Allergies	First line: cromolyn. Second line: first-generation antihistamines. Chlorpheniramine (drug of choice) and diphenhydramine are commonly used. The non-sedating second-generation agents loratadine and cetirizine are often recommended by obstetricians during the second and third trimesters. If nasal steroids are needed for chronic allergy symptoms, all intranasal steroids are considered to be safe. Budesonide (Rhinocort Allergy) and beclomethasone (Beconase AQ) are preferred.	Oral decongestants should not be recommended during the first trimester. The cough-suppressant dextromethorphan and the mucolytic guaifenesin have limited safety data in pregnancy/lactation, but are sometimes used. Avoid liquid formulations that contain alcohol.
Pain	Non-drug options such as hot/cold packs, light massage or physical therapy can help limit or avoid the use of analgesics. ACOG recommends acetaminophen first-line for mild pain during pregnancy because it has a better safety profile than NSAIDs and opioids. A proposed link between acetaminophen use during pregnancy and ADHD/autism was investigated by the FDA, but insufficient evidence was found. Surveillance is ongoing.	Avoid NSAIDs, including aspirin (except for low-dose aspirin for preeclampsia prevention), especially at 20 weeks gestation or later. During pregnancy, NSAID use can cause premature closure of the fetal ductus arteriosus and kidney problems in the fetus (leading to low amniotic fluid). Opioid metabolism can affect safety risk (see the Drug Interactions and Pain chapters).
Asthma	Maintenance therapy: budesonide is preferred but all inhaled corticosteroids are considered safe for use in pregnancy. Rescue therapy (short-acting beta agonist): inhaled albuterol.	Budesonide is also the preferred steroid for infants; the Respules are used in a nebulizer.
Iron Deficiency Anemia	Supplemental iron, prenatal vitamins with iron.	Iron worsens constipation.
Hypertension*	Labetalol, methyldopa, nifedipine.	ACE inhibitors, ARBs, aliskiren and Entresto are contraindicated in pregnancy. Low-dose aspirin is recommended for preeclampsia prevention in high-risk groups.
Diabetes*	Insulin is preferred if not controlled with lifestyle. Metformin and glyburide are commonly used.	Low-dose aspirin is recommended for preeclampsia prevention in both type 1 and 2 diabetes. If diabetes develops during pregnancy it is called gestational diabetes.

CONDITION	PREFERRED MANAGEMENT	NOTES
Infection*	Generally considered safe to use: penicillins (including amoxicillin and ampicillin), cephalosporins, erythromycin and azithromycin. **VAGINAL FUNGAL INFECTIONS** Topical antifungals (creams, suppositories) x 7 days. **URINARY TRACT INFECTIONS** Cephalexin 500 mg PO Q6H x 7 days. Ampicillin 500 mg PO Q6H x 7 days. Nitrofurantoin and SMX/TMP should be considered last line during the 1st trimester, and should not be used in the last 2 weeks of pregnancy. Must treat bacteriuria, even if asymptomatic with negative urinalysis. Untreated bacteriuria can lead to premature birth, pyelonephritis and neonatal meningitis. **TOXOPLASMOSIS** Many people are infected with toxoplasmosis, and are asymptomatic. If a woman contracts toxoplasmosis during pregnancy, it can cause miscarriage, stillbirth or damage to the baby's brain and eyes. Women can be tested prior to pregnancy with an IgG test. If unsure of the status, it is best to avoid dirty food and water (uncommon in the U.S.), unpasteurized dairy products and cat feces (including contact with cat litter boxes), which can contain the parasite.	Do not use: quinolones (due to cartilage damage) and tetracyclines (due to teeth discoloration). **VAGINAL FUNGAL INFECTIONS** Avoid fluconazole. **URINARY TRACT INFECTION** SMX/TMP has mixed data for use in pregnancy; per ACOG, use in pregnancy (if necessary) may be acceptable. See the Infectious Diseases II chapter for STI/STD management in pregnancy.
Conditions requiring anticoagulation	**VENOUS THROMBOEMBOLISM (VTE)** Treatment: low molecular weight heparin (LMWH) is preferred over unfractionated heparin (UFH). Prophylaxis: pneumatic compression devices ± LMWH (preferred over UFH). **MECHANICAL VALVE** Women who require chronic warfarin therapy for mechanical heart valves or inherited thrombophilias are generally converted to LMWH during pregnancy. They may be switched back to warfarin after the 13th week of pregnancy, then back to LMWH close to delivery.	The risk of developing a VTE is increased during pregnancy and for the first six weeks postpartum. Warfarin is teratogenic. The oral factor Xa inhibitors and direct thrombin inhibitors have not been adequately studied in pregnancy and are not recommended. Monitor peak anti-Xa levels, drawn 4 hours post-dose (LMWH), or aPTT (heparin).
Hypothyroidism	Levothyroxine (will require a 30-50% dose increase during pregnancy).	Hypothyroidism must be treated during pregnancy; if left untreated, severe consequences could include miscarriage or stillbirth, preeclampsia, low birth weight, cognitive impairment and growth retardation.
Hyperthyroidism	Mild cases will not require treatment. Preferable to normalize the mother's thyroid function prior to pregnancy. Contraception should be used until the condition is controlled. If drugs are necessary (i.e., Graves' disease): propylthiouracil (PTU) is preferred if trying to conceive or in the 1st trimester. After that, the decision is individualized, as both PTU and methimazole carry potential fetal risks. Historically, the patient would be switched to methimazole for the remainder of the pregnancy.	Both PTU and methimazole have a high risk for liver damage, readily cross the placenta and can cause congenital defects. Uncontrolled maternal hyperthyroidism can cause premature delivery and low birth weight. Radioactive iodine is teratogenic and not used in pregnancy.

*Managing hypertension, diabetes, HIV and certain infections during pregnancy are discussed in detail in the respective chapters.

MALE & FEMALE HEALTH

LACTATION

The American Academy of Pediatrics (AAP) recommends that babies be exclusively breastfed for the first six months of life, as long as it is mutually desired by the mother and baby and if safety risks are not present. Babies receiving breast milk partially or exclusively should receive 10 mcg (400 IU) of vitamin D daily until they are consuming at least one liter of vitamin D-fortified formula/day. Human milk contains very little iron (unlike formula), so breastfed babies require 1 mg/kg daily of iron during months 4 – 6. Most newborns have adequate iron stores in the body for at least the first 4 months of life. Iron supplementation is needed after 4 months of age until the infant can obtain adequate iron from eating iron-rich solid foods, which usually occurs at 6 months old. See the Dietary Supplements, Natural & Complementary Medicine chapter for more information. Mothers who are breastfeeding should increase their diet by 450 – 500 kcal/day and continue prenatal vitamins and omega-3 supplements.

Excretion into breast milk is higher with drugs that are non-ionized, have a small molecular weight, a low volume of distribution and high lipid solubility. The majority of medications have low excretion into breast milk, and can be taken safely while breastfeeding. Additionally, breastfeeding can continue when the mother has a cold, influenza and with the majority of other infections. *LactMed* (http://toxnet.nlm.nih.gov) or *Briggs' Drugs in Pregnancy and Lactation* can be used to check for drug safety during breastfeeding. Refer to the Drug References chapter for more information.

TREATING PAIN

Postpartum pain can often be adequately treated with acetaminophen or ibuprofen, which are safe to use while breastfeeding. Codeine and tramadol should not be used by breastfeeding mothers due to risk of excessive sleepiness, breathing difficulty and/or death in the infant. Breastfed infants have died, especially in mothers taking codeine who were CYP450 2D6 ultra-rapid metabolizers. Because of the importance, this is discussed further in the Drug Interactions, Pharmacogenomics and Pain chapters. Even small doses of opioids taken by the mother can cause serious side effects for the infant.

KNOWN OR SUSPECTED HIV

Breastfeeding is not recommended for women with documented HIV infection in the United States, including those women receiving antiretroviral therapy. Any woman with suspected HIV infection, should stop breastfeeding until HIV is ruled out with proper testing.

SPECIFIC MEDICATIONS

Drugs that should be avoided completely during lactation include chemotherapy, illicit drugs and radioactive compounds used for treatment and diagnostic studies (e.g., iodine).

Some medications should be avoided during lactation, if possible. Use of these drugs while breastfeeding is not without significant risk and a decision must be made based on a discussion between patient and provider. In some cases, patients may be able to pump and dispose of the breastmilk when drug concentrations are at the highest. Examples of these medications include amphetamines, amiodarone, ergotamines, lithium, metronidazole, phenobarbital and statins. Most often, safer alternatives are available.

For all drugs taken during lactation, the infant should be monitored for adverse effects caused by maternal medication use.

Select Guidelines/References

American College of Obstetricians and Gynecologists (ACOG) Practice Guidelines, available at www.acog.org (accessed 2022 Feb 9).

CDC Recommendations for STI/STD, available at www.cdc.gov (accessed 2022 Feb 9).

CONTENT LEGEND

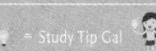 ❀ = Study Tip Gal

NORMAL BONE

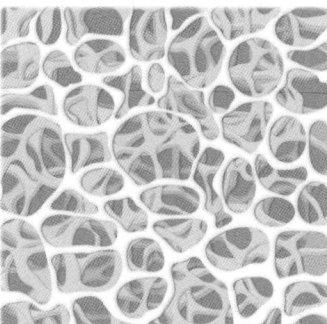

OSTEOPOROSIS

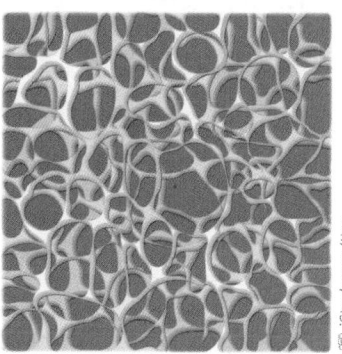

© iStock.com/ttsz

CHAPTER 49

OSTEOPOROSIS, MENOPAUSE & TESTOSTERONE USE

OSTEOPOROSIS

BACKGROUND

Osteoporosis ("porous bones") is a condition that causes bones to become weak and fragile. It is estimated that more than one-quarter of all adults in the U.S., and over half of those > 50 years of age, have osteoporosis, low bone density or low bone mass. Osteoporosis can occur in both men and women of all races. It is most common in postmenopausal females. About one in two women and one in five men will have an osteoporosis-related fracture during their lifetime. Falls are the most common cause of fractures, but with extremely porous bones, they can be caused by coughing or rolling over in bed.

The most common locations for fractures are the vertebrae (spine), proximal femur (hip) and distal forearm (wrist). Vertebral fractures can occur without a fall and can initially be painless (the only clue may be a gradual loss of height). Hip fractures are the most devastating type of fractures, with higher costs, disability and mortality than all other fractures combined. Hip fractures are more common after the age of 75 years. Wrist fractures, and other types of fractures, appear in younger people and serve as an early indicator of poor bone health.

RISK FACTORS

Osteoporosis can occur as a result of normal age-related bone loss. Bone accumulates until approximately age 30. After that, men lose bone at a rate of 0.2 – 0.5% per year, and women lose bone at a similar rate, except in the 10 years after menopause when bone loss is accelerated (1 – 5% per year). Patient-specific characteristics that can contribute to osteoporosis risk include lifestyle habits, diseases and medications (see the Study Tip Gal on the following page).

SELECT FACTORS AND CONDITIONS WITH OSTEOPOROSIS RISK

Patient Characteristics
Advanced age
Ethnicity (Caucasian and Asian are at ↑ risk)
Family history
Sex (females > males)
Low body weight

Medical Diseases/Conditions
Diabetes
Eating disorders (e.g., anorexia nervosa)
Gastrointestinal diseases (e.g., IBD, celiac disease, gastric bypass, malabsorption syndromes)
Hyperthyroidism
Hypogonadism in men
Menopause
Rheumatoid arthritis, autoimmune diseases
Others (e.g., epilepsy, HIV/AIDS, Parkinson disease)

Lifestyle Factors
Smoking
Excessive alcohol intake (≥ 3 drinks per day)
Low calcium intake
Low vitamin D intake
Physical inactivity

Medications
Anticonvulsants (e.g., carbamazepine, phenytoin, phenobarbital)
Aromatase inhibitors
Depo-medroxyprogesterone
GnRH (gonadotropin-releasing hormone) agonists
Lithium
PPIs (↑ gastric pH decreases Ca absorption)
Steroids* (≥ 5 mg daily of prednisone or prednisone equivalent for ≥ 3 months)
Thyroid hormones (in excess)
Others (e.g., loop diuretics, SSRIs, TZDs)

Long-term use of steroids is the major drug-contributing factor to poor bone health.

DIAGNOSIS

Bone Mineral Density

Bone is not "dead tissue"; it is living and undergoes constant remodeling. Osteoblasts are the cells involved in bone formation. Osteoclasts are the cells involved in bone resorption; they break down tissue in the bone. Bone health is evaluated by measuring bone mineral density (BMD). The gold standard to measure BMD and diagnose osteoporosis is a dual-energy X-ray absorptiometry (DEXA or DXA) scan. This measures BMD of the spine and hip and calculates a T-score or a Z-score. See the Study Tip Gal for interpreting T-scores for the diagnosis of osteoporosis and osteopenia.

All women ≥ 65 years and men ≥ 70 years should have BMD measured. BMD can be checked earlier if there is a history of a fragility fracture (e.g., a fall from standing height or lower that results in a fracture) after age 50, risk for disease or drug-induced bone loss, a parental history of hip fracture or other clinical risk factors (e.g., smoking, alcoholism, low body weight).

If a DXA scan is unavailable, an ultrasound may be performed. Ultrasounds are less expensive, portable and do not emit radiation, but they are less than optimal. Ultrasound readings provide bone density in one location, such as the heel. If low, the patient should be encouraged to get a DXA scan. Since vertebral fractures are so common in older adults and usually lack symptoms, vertebral imaging may be performed if height loss is observed or if BMD testing indicates osteopenia.

Fracture Risk Assessment Tool (FRAX)

The FRAX tool is a computer-based algorithm developed by the World Health Organization (WHO) that estimates the

DIAGNOSIS OF OSTEOPOROSIS

WHAT IS A T-SCORE?
It compares the patient's measured BMD to the average peak BMD of a healthy, young, white adult of the same sex.*

A DEXA (or DXA) measures BMD so a T-score can be determined.

T-scores are negative: a score at or above -1 correlates with stronger (denser) bones, which are less likely to fracture.**

WHO SHOULD HAVE BMD MEASURED?
Women ≥ 65 years and men ≥ 70 years.

Younger patients at high risk for fracture (see text).

INTERPRETING T-SCORE RESULTS
Normal: ≥ -1

Osteopenia (low bone mass): -1 to -2.4

Osteoporosis: ≤ -2.5

A Z-score is calculated the same way, but compares the patient's measured BMD to the mean BMD of an age, sex and ethnicity-matched population.
**Scores less than -1 reflect the standard deviation from the comparator group (e.g., a T-score of < -2.5 means the patient's BMD is at least 2.5 standard deviations below the average BMD for healthy, young, white adults).*

risk of osteoporotic fracture in the next 10 years (available at www.nof.org or www.shef.ac.uk/FRAX). It has been well-validated, and the U.S. tool has adapted versions available for White, Black, Asian and Hispanic women. Clinical risk factors included in the tool are age, sex, weight, height, previous fracture, parental hip fracture, femoral neck BMD, smoking status, steroid use, alcohol intake, disorders strongly associated with osteoporosis (e.g., type 1 diabetes, chronic liver disease, premature menopause) and diagnosis of rheumatoid arthritis. The tool is intended for postmenopausal women and men > 50 years of age.

PREVENTION

Fall Prevention Measures

If the bone density is low, care must be taken to avoid falls. Factors that put a patient at increased fall risk include a history of recent falls, medications that cause sedation or orthostasis (e.g., antihypertensives, sedatives, hypnotics, narcotic analgesics, psychotropics), neurologic disorders, conditions causing physical instability or poor coordination (e.g., Parkinson disease, dementia, prior stroke, peripheral neuropathy), impaired vision or hearing, poor health/frailty and urinary or fecal urgency. A home safety assessment should ensure that lighting is appropriate, floors are safe (throw rugs/clutter/cords have been removed), storage is at reasonable heights, bathrooms have safety bars and non-skid floors, handrails are present on all stairs and the stairs are well-lit with non-skid treads or carpet.

Preventing falls requires measures to improve muscle strength, balance and vision. Adequate corrective lenses, safe shoes and appropriate clothing (that will not cause falls) are required. If a disability is present, canes or walkers should be strongly recommended.

Lifestyle Measures

Patients with low bone density should perform regular weight-bearing exercise (e.g., walking, jogging, Tai-Chi) and muscle-strengthening exercise (e.g., weight training, yoga). They should be encouraged to stop smoking and avoid secondhand smoke, reduce alcohol intake and adopt fall prevention strategies, as described above.

Calcium and Vitamin D Intake

Adequate calcium intake is required throughout life. It is critically important in children (who can build bone stores), in pregnancy (when the fetus can deplete the mother's stores) and during the years around menopause when bone loss is rapid. Dietary intake of calcium is preferred, with supplements used if needed. Intake in excess of the recommended allowances may contribute to kidney stones, cardiovascular disease and stroke, though the evidence remains controversial.

Vitamin D is required for calcium absorption, and low levels contribute to various health conditions, including autoimmune conditions and cancer. Vitamin D deficiency in children causes rickets, and in adults, it causes osteomalacia (softening of the bones). The National Osteoporosis Foundation (NOF) recommends 20 – 25 mcg [800 – 1,000 international units (IU)] of vitamin D daily for adults age ≥ 50 years. Other organizations recommend 15 mcg (600 IU) daily for people ≥ 71 years. Many endocrinologists suggest a higher intake of 25 – 50 mcg (800 – 2,000 IU) daily. The

Institute of Medicine considers a safe upper limit to be 100 mcg (4,000 IU) daily for adolescents and adults. Higher doses are needed if a vitamin D deficiency is present (see the Study Tip Gal below).

Calcium and Vitamin D Supplementation

Calcium obtained through the diet is generally not enough; most women need an additional 600 – 900 mg daily (2 to 3 servings of dairy products) to reach recommended levels.

Calcium absorption is saturable; doses above 500 – 600 mg of elemental calcium should be divided. Calcium products are available in many forms (e.g., capsules, tablets, chewables, liquids, granules/powder). There is no known benefit of using more expensive formulations.

- Calcium carbonate has more elemental calcium per unit compared to calcium citrate, but requires an acidic environment for absorption

- Calcium citrate has better absorption with an increased gastric pH (e.g., elderly patients, use of PPIs)

Vitamin D deficiency can be treated with high doses of vitamin D2 (ergocalciferol) or vitamin D3 (cholecalciferol) for 8 to 12 weeks, followed by maintenance therapy. Maintenance therapy is 25 – 50 mcg (1,000 – 2,000 IU) daily, or dosed to maintain target levels. See the Renal Disease chapter for information on vitamin D analogs (e.g., calcitriol).

Sunlight is another source of vitamin D3 but is not ideal due to the risk of skin cancer. Dietary intake and supplements are the preferred sources of vitamin D.

CALCIUM AND VITAMIN D

CALCIUM
- Recommended daily intake for most adults is 1,000-1,200 mg elemental calcium
  - Do not exceed 500-600 mg of elemental calcium per dose
- Calcium carbonate (e.g., *Tums*, *Oscal*)
  - 40% elemental calcium
  - Absorption: acid-dependent
  - Must take with meals
- Calcium citrate (e.g., *Citracal*)
  - 21% elemental calcium
  - Absorption: not acid-dependent
  - Can take with or without food

VITAMIN D
- Required for calcium absorption
- Deficiency: serum vitamin D [25(OH)D] < 30 ng/mL
- Treat deficiency with cholecalciferol (vitamin D3) or ergocalciferol (vitamin D2), 125-175 mcg (5,000-7,000 IU) daily or 1,250 mcg (50,000 IU) weekly

Avoid low bone density later in life by building strong bones in children

MALE & FEMALE HEALTH

DRUG	DOSING	SAFETY/SIDE EFFECTS/MONITORING
Calcium Supplements		
Calcium Carbonate (*Os-Cal, Tums*, *Caltrate*, *Maalox*, *Oysco*, others) 40% elemental calcium	500 mg PO TID with meals (can vary with formulation used) Total daily dose of elemental calcium should be < 2,000 mg (diet and supplements)	**SIDE EFFECTS** Constipation, hypercalcemia, nausea **MONITORING** Ca, PO4, PTH **NOTES** Hypercalcemia is especially problematic with concomitant use of vitamin D (due to increased calcium absorption)
Calcium Citrate (*Calcitrate, Citracal*, others) 21% elemental calcium	1 g calcium carbonate = 400 mg elemental calcium 1 g calcium citrate = 210 mg elemental calcium	Calcium carbonate: take with food; do not use with PPIs Calcium citrate: take with or without food

DRUG TREATMENT

There are a number of FDA-approved options for the treatment and prevention of osteoporosis. Medications approved for prevention include bisphosphonates (except IV ibandronate) and the estrogen-based therapies, raloxifene and *Duavee*. Bisphosphonates, denosumab, parathyroid hormone analogs (e.g., teriparatide, abaloparatide) and calcitonin are indicated for treatment. These medications have primarily been studied in postmenopausal women with osteoporosis, and there is limited data in men or in those with glucocorticoid-induced osteoporosis. Regardless of drug selection, treatment must include adequate calcium and vitamin D intake, with levels evaluated before initiating therapy. See the Study Tip Gal below for important facts about each drug/drug class.

Criteria for Initiating Treatment

Osteoporosis	■ T-score ≤ -2.5 in the spine, femoral neck, total hip or 1/3 radius, OR ■ Presence of a fragility fracture, regardless of BMD
Osteopenia, if high risk	■ Low bone density (T-score between -1 and -2.5) AND ■ FRAX score indicates a 10-year probability of a major osteoporosis-related fracture ≥ 20% or a 10-year hip fracture probability ≥ 3%

DRUG SUMMARY FOR OSTEOPOROSIS TREATMENT AND PREVENTION

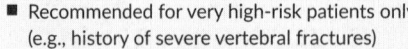

BISPHOSPHONATES
■ First-line for treatment or prevention in most patients
■ PO administration: must stay upright for 30 minutes (60 minutes for ibandronate) and drink 6-8 oz of plain water
■ Side effects: esophagitis, hypocalcemia, GI effects
■ Rare (but serious) side effects:
 ❑ Atypical femur fractures
 ❑ Osteonecrosis of the jaw (ONJ): jaw bone becomes exposed and cannot heal due to decreased blood supply
■ Formulations:
 ❑ PO: given weekly/monthly
 ❑ IV: given quarterly/yearly (if GI side effects or adherence issues with PO formulation)
■ Treatment duration: 3-5 years in patients with a low risk of fracture (due to the risk of femur fractures and ONJ)

DENOSUMAB (*PROLIA*)
■ Alternative to bisphosphonates
■ SC administration every 6 months
■ Side effect: hypocalcemia

TERIPARATIDE (*FORTEO*), ABALOPARATIDE (*TYMLOS*)
■ Recommended for very high-risk patients only (e.g., history of severe vertebral fractures)
■ SC administration daily
■ Side effect: hypercalcemia

RALOXIFENE (*EVISTA*), BAZEDOXIFENE/ESTROGENS (*DUAVEE*)
■ Alternative to bisphosphonates if high risk of vertebral fractures
■ Increased risk for VTE and stroke
■ Raloxifene can be used if low VTE risk or high breast cancer risk
 ❑ Side effect: vasomotor symptoms
■ Bazedoxifene/estrogens can be used in women with an intact uterus for prevention of osteoporosis
 ❑ Also used as treatment for vasomotor symptoms
 ❑ Side effect: increased risk of breast cancer

LAST LINE OR NOT RECOMMENDED
■ Estrogen (with or without progestin) for prevention only in postmenopausal women with vasomotor symptoms; use lowest possible dose for shortest duration of time
■ Calcitonin for treatment only if other options are not suitable (less effective and has a risk of cancer with long-term use)

Bisphosphonates

Bisphosphonates increase bone density by <u>inhibiting osteoclast activity and bone resorption</u>. They reduce vertebral and hip fracture risk (<u>except ibandronate</u>, which only reduces vertebral fractures). Bisphosphonates are <u>first-line</u> for most patients for the <u>prevention or treatment</u> of osteoporosis. A drug holiday (i.e., time off of the drug) should be considered for low-risk patients after <u>3 – 5 years</u> of treatment. Bisphosphonates are also used to treat Paget's disease, glucocorticoid-induced osteoporosis (in patients taking ≥ 7.5 mg daily of prednisone or prednisone equivalent) and hypercalcemia of malignancy.

DRUG	DOSING	SAFETY/SIDE EFFECTS/MONITORING
Oral Bisphosphonates		
Alendronate (Fosamax, *Binosto*) Tablet, oral solution, effervescent tablet (*Binosto*) + cholecalciferol (*Fosamax Plus D*) Tablet	**Prevention (postmenopausal females)** 5 mg PO daily or 35 mg PO weekly **Treatment (males and postmenopausal females)** 10 mg PO <u>daily</u> or 70 mg PO <u>weekly</u> *Fosamax Plus D:* 70 mg/2,800 IU or 70 mg/5,600 IU PO weekly **Glucocorticoid-Induced Osteoporosis** 5 mg PO daily Postmenopausal women not on estrogen: 10 mg PO daily	**CONTRAINDICATIONS** <u>Hypocalcemia; inability to stand or sit upright for at least 30 minutes</u> (60 minutes for *Boniva*); abnormalities of the esophagus (e.g., stricture, achalasia); high risk of aspiration (effervescent tablet or oral solution) **WARNINGS** <u>ONJ:</u> ↑ risk with invasive dental procedures, poor dental hygiene, cancer diagnosis, use with chemotherapy or corticosteroids and duration of exposure Atypical <u>femur fractures</u>; bone, joint or muscle pain (may be severe) Esophagitis, esophageal ulcers, erosions, stricture or perforation (rare): <u>follow administration instructions</u> (see Key Counseling Points section) <u>Hypocalcemia</u> must be corrected prior to use <u>Renal impairment:</u> do not use if CrCl < 35 mL/min (alendronate) or CrCl < 30 mL/min (ibandronate, risedronate)
Risedronate (*Actonel, Atelvia*) Tablet, delayed-release tablet (*Atelvia*)	**Prevention and Treatment (postmenopausal females)** 5 mg PO <u>daily</u>, 35 mg PO <u>weekly</u>, or 150 mg PO <u>monthly</u> **Treatment (males)** 35 mg PO weekly **Glucocorticoid-Induced Osteoporosis** 5 mg PO daily	**SIDE EFFECTS** Dyspepsia, dysphagia, heartburn, N/V, hypocalcemia, hypophosphatemia (mild, transient), abdominal pain, musculoskeletal pain Risedronate: headache, hypertension, skin rash, UTI, infection **NOTES** Check calcium and vitamin D levels prior to initiating treatment Due to the risk of jaw decay/necrosis, <u>dental work</u> should be completed <u>prior to starting treatment</u> Use caution with aspirin or NSAIDs (can worsen GI irritation) <u>Separate from calcium, antacids, iron and magnesium by at least 2 hours</u>
Ibandronate (*Boniva*) Tablet	**Prevention and Treatment (postmenopausal females)** PO: 150 mg <u>monthly</u> (on the same date every month)	Separate at least 30 minutes from food and beverages (except water) *Atelvia* (delayed-release): requires an <u>acidic gut</u> for absorption; <u>do not use with H2RAs and PPIs</u>
Injectable Bisphosphonates		
Ibandronate (*Boniva*) Injection	**Treatment (postmenopausal females)** 3 mg IV <u>every 3 months</u> Administer over 15-30 seconds	**CONTRAINDICATIONS** Hypocalcemia Zoledronic acid: CrCl < 35 mL/minute or evidence of acute renal impairment
Zoledronic Acid (Reclast) *Zometa** – for hypercalcemia of malignancy	**Prevention (postmenopausal females)** 5 mg IV every 2 years **Treatment (males and postmenopausal females)** 5 mg IV <u>once yearly</u> **Glucocorticoid-Induced Osteoporosis** 5 mg IV once yearly Administer over ≥ 15 minutes	**WARNINGS** Same as oral bisphosphonates (except no GI problems) plus: <u>Renal impairment:</u> monitor SCr before each dose; use caution if dehydrated and with comorbid conditions or medications that can cause renal impairment Ibandronate: do not use if CrCl < 30 mL/min Zoledronic acid: use caution in aspirin-sensitive asthma (risk of bronchoconstriction), avoid in pregnancy (teratogenic) **SIDE EFFECTS** Same as oral bisphosphonates (except no esophageal problems) plus: Acute-phase reaction (flu-like symptoms: fever, achiness, runny nose, headache) Zoledronic acid: edema, hypotension, fatigue, dehydration, ↓ PO4, K and Mg **NOTES** <u>Preferred if esophagitis is present</u> (due to <u>risk for esophageal cancer</u>)

Brand discontinued but name still used in practice.

MALE & FEMALE HEALTH

Estrogen Agonist/Antagonist-Containing Products

Raloxifene is an estrogen agonist/antagonist [a selective estrogen receptor modulator (SERM)] that ↓ bone resorption. Conjugated estrogens/bazedoxifene (*Duavee*) is an equine (horse) estrogen/SERM combination indicated for osteoporosis prevention in postmenopausal women with a uterus.

DRUG	DOSING	SAFETY/SIDE EFFECTS/MONITORING
Raloxifene (*Evista*) Tablet	**Prevention and Treatment (postmenopausal females)** 60 mg PO daily	**BOXED WARNINGS** ↑ risk of VTE (DVT/PE); ↑ risk of death due to stroke in women with CHD or at risk for coronary events **CONTRAINDICATIONS** History of or current VTE, pregnancy **SIDE EFFECTS** Hot flashes, peripheral edema, arthralgia, leg cramps/muscle spasms, flu symptoms, infection **NOTES** Separate raloxifene and levothyroxine by several hours Discontinue 72 hours prior to and during prolonged immobilization
Conjugated Estrogens/ Bazedoxifene (*Duavee*)	**Prevention (postmenopausal females with a uterus)** 1 tablet (0.45/20 mg) PO daily Other indications: treatment of moderate-severe vasomotor symptoms associated with menopause (same dose)	**BOXED WARNINGS** Endometrial cancer (due to unopposed estrogen); ↑ risk of DVT and stroke in postmenopausal women 50-79 years of age (do not use to prevent CVD); dementia (women ≥ 65 years); use lowest effective dose for shortest duration possible **CONTRAINDICATIONS** Breast cancer (any history); pregnancy; undiagnosed uterine bleeding; history of or active VTE, MI or stroke; protein C, S or antithrombin deficiency; hepatic impairment **WARNINGS** ↑ risk of breast cancer (due to unopposed estrogen) and ovarian cancer; ↑ risk of retinal vascular thrombosis; lipid effects (↑ HDL, ↑ TG, ↓ LDL) **SIDE EFFECTS** Nausea, diarrhea, dyspepsia, abdominal pain, muscle spasms **NOTES** Not recommended for women > 75 years of age Use estrogen-containing products for the shortest duration possible

Calcitonin

Calcitonin inhibits bone resorption by osteoclasts. It is less effective than other agents for the treatment of osteoporosis and, with long-term use, the risk of cancer is increased. It is rarely used for this indication.

DRUG	DOSING	SAFETY/SIDE EFFECTS/MONITORING
Calcitonin (*Miacalcin*) Nasal spray, injection	**Treatment (females > 5 years postmenopause)** Nasal spray: 1 spray (200 units) in one nostril daily (alternate nostril daily) SC or IM: 100 units daily	**WARNINGS** Hypocalcemia (associated with tetany and seizures); ↑ risk of malignancy with long-term use; hypersensitivity reactions to salmon-derived products (e.g., bronchospasm, anaphylaxis, swelling of the tongue or throat); antibody formation Nasal spray: can cause nasal ulceration, epistaxis and rhinitis; nasal exams are recommended **SIDE EFFECTS** Back pain, myalgia, nausea, dizziness Injection: flushing, injection site reactions **NOTES** Keep the injection and unopened nasal spray bottles refrigerated Can be used in the management of hypercalcemia of malignancy (see the Oncology I chapter)

Parathyroid Hormone 1-34

Teriparatide and abaloparatide are analogs of human parathyroid hormone, which stimulates osteoblast activity and increases bone formation. They are used to treat osteoporosis when there is a very high risk of fracture (e.g., previous history of vertebral fracture). Due to safety issues, the cumulative lifetime treatment duration is restricted to two years or less.

DRUG	DOSING	SAFETY/SIDE EFFECTS/MONITORING
Teriparatide (Forteo) Injection (prefilled multi-dose pen; needles not included)	**Treatment (males and postmenopausal females)** 20 mcg SC daily **Glucocorticoid-Induced Osteoporosis** 20 mcg SC daily	**WARNINGS** Osteosarcoma (bone cancer): risk dependent on dose and duration of use, do not use in bone malignancy or metabolic bone diseases Hypercalcemia; orthostatic hypotension; use caution with urolithiasis (urinary stones) **SIDE EFFECTS** Arthralgias, leg cramps, nausea, orthostasis/dizziness Tymlos: ↑ uric acid, antibody development, erythema at injection site (58%)
Abaloparatide (Tymlos) Injection (prefilled multi-dose pen; needles not included)	**Treatment (postmenopausal females)** 80 mcg SC daily	**NOTES** Keep refrigerated Forteo: protect from light

Receptor Activator of Nuclear Factor kappa-B Ligand (RANKL) Inhibitor

Denosumab is a monoclonal antibody that binds to RANKL and blocks its interaction with RANK (a receptor on osteoclasts) to prevent osteoclast formation; this leads to ↓ bone resorption and ↑ bone mass. It is used for the treatment of osteoporosis when there is a high risk of fracture.

DRUG	DOSING	SAFETY/SIDE EFFECTS/MONITORING
Denosumab (Prolia) Injection **Xgeva** – hypercalcemia of malignancy, bone cell tumor, prevention of bone metastasis Other indications: treatment of bone loss in men on androgen deprivation therapy for prostate cancer and women on aromatase inhibitor therapy for breast cancer	**Treatment (males and postmenopausal females)** 60 mg SC every 6 months Must be administered by a healthcare professional	**CONTRAINDICATIONS** Hypocalcemia (correct prior to using); pregnancy **WARNINGS** ONJ: ↑ risk with invasive dental procedures, poor dental hygiene, cancer diagnosis, use of chemotherapy or corticosteroids and duration of exposure Atypical femur fractures; bone, joint or muscle pain (may be severe) Hypocalcemia: use caution in predisposed patients (e.g., hypoparathyroidism, thyroid surgery, malabsorption syndromes, CrCl < 30 mL/min) Infections (e.g., skin, abdomen, urinary tract); dermatologic reactions (e.g., dermatitis, eczema, rash) **SIDE EFFECTS** Hypertension, fatigue, edema, dyspnea, headache, N/V/D, ↓ PO4 **NOTES** If discontinued, bone loss can be rapid; consider alternative agents to maintain BMD

Romosozumab

Romosozumab is indicated for postmenopausal females with a history of an osteoporotic fracture or multiple risk factors. It is recommended as an alternative to other treatments. It inhibits sclerostin, a protein that blocks bone formation. Treatment duration is limited to 12 months due to a decrease in efficacy.

DRUG	DOSING	SAFETY/SIDE EFFECTS/MONITORING
Romosozumab (Evenity) Injection	**Treatment** 210 mg SC (administered in two separate injections) once a month Duration of therapy is limited to 12 months	**BOXED WARNINGS** Increased risk of MI, stroke and cardiovascular death **CONTRAINDICATIONS** Hypocalcemia **SIDE EFFECTS** Arthralgia, headache, injection site reactions **NOTES** Keep refrigerated; let sit at room temperature for 30 min before administration

MALE & FEMALE HEALTH

OSTEOPOROSIS KEY COUNSELING POINTS

See the Drug Formulations and Patient Counseling chapter for counseling language/layman's terminology.

All Osteoporosis Medications

- Must supplement with calcium and vitamin D.
  - ❏ Do not take calcium carbonate with proton pump inhibitors (acidic gut is needed for absorption).
  - ❏ Switch to calcium citrate if use of a proton pump inhibitor is required.

Bisphosphonates

- Oral formulations (except *Atelvia*): take in the morning with 6 – 8 oz of plain water at least 30 minutes before first food. Take *Atelvia* with ≥ 4 oz of water immediately after breakfast.
  - ❏ Must stay sitting or standing upright for at least 30 minutes after taking (at least 60 minutes with *Boniva*) and until after first food of the day.
  - ❏ Separate from calcium, iron, magnesium, antacids and multivitamin supplements.
- *Dissolve Binosto* in 4 oz of plain water (room temperature). Wait five minutes to dissolve, then stir for 10 seconds.
- Do not take *Atelvia* with acid-suppressing medications.
- Can cause dyspepsia.
- Missed dose:
  - ❏ Daily dosing: skip missed dose; take next dose at regularly scheduled time.
  - ❏ Weekly dosing: take missed dose the next morning; do not take two doses on the same day.
  - ❏ Monthly dosing: take missed dose the morning after you remember, unless it is less than one week from the next dose, then skip it; do not take two doses in the same week.

Raloxifene

- Can cause blood clots.
- Discontinue at least 72 hours prior to and during prolonged immobilization (e.g., surgery requiring bed rest).

Teriparatide and Abaloparatide

- Can cause:
  - ❏ Dizziness.
  - ❏ Orthostasis.

Calcitonin Nasal Spray

- Refrigerate unused bottles.
- Allow bottle to reach room temperature prior to use, then store at room temperature. Discard after 30 doses.
- Prime the pump before first use by pressing the two white side arms toward the bottle, releasing at least five sprays, until a full spray is produced.
- Alternate nostrils each day.

MENOPAUSE

BACKGROUND

Menopause is reached when the last menstrual period was over 12 months ago. Menopause usually occurs between the ages of 40 – 58 years (average age is 52 years). A decrease in estrogen and progesterone causes an increase in follicle stimulating hormone (FSH), resulting in vasomotor symptoms. Many women experience these symptoms during the menopause transition period (perimenopause) as estrogen production by the ovaries declines. These are often described as hot flashes (transient episodes of flushing and a sensation of heat in the upper body and face, sometimes followed by chills) and night sweats (hot flashes that occur during sleep). Sleep can be disturbed, and mood changes may be present. Due to a decline in estrogen in the vaginal mucosa, vaginal dryness, burning and painful intercourse can occur (called the genitourinary syndrome of menopause).

Some women remain largely asymptomatic during menopause, while others suffer from severe symptoms that significantly impact quality of life. Vasomotor symptoms can last up to seven years. Women who have both ovaries removed, or receive chemotherapy or radiation for cancer, will experience induced menopause. The symptoms are similar but often more acute initially due to a sudden rather than a gradual decline in estrogen.

ESTROGEN-PROGESTIN PRODUCTS

The most effective treatment for vasomotor symptoms is systemic hormone therapy with estrogen. Estrogen causes a decrease in luteinizing hormone (LH) and more stable temperature control. It improves bone density as well, but has a number of safety issues to consider before initiating. The North American Menopause Society (NAMS) and the American Association of Clinical Endocrinologists (AACE) provide criteria for the use of estrogen to control vasomotor symptoms. See the Study Tip Gal below for the appropriate use and health risks associated with hormone therapy.

Formulation Considerations

Transdermal, local (topical) and low-dose oral estrogen products are associated with a lower risk of venous thromboembolism (VTE) and stroke than standard doses of oral estrogen. Estrogen is generally well tolerated but can cause nausea, dizziness, headaches, mood changes, vaginal bleeding, bloating and breast tenderness/fullness. Topical formulations (e.g., patch, gel, emulsion) bypass first-pass metabolism and lower doses can be used. They may decrease systemic exposure, resulting in fewer side effects.

Local estrogen products are preferred for patients who have vaginal symptoms only (vaginal dryness and/or painful intercourse). Any of the vaginal products in this chapter (creams, tablets, rings) or OTC lubricants can be helpful. Common OTC lubricants and moisturizers include *Replens* and *Luvena*. *Astroglide* is a lubricant marketed specifically for dyspareunia (painful intercourse). Oil-based lubricants should not be used with condoms as they can cause the condom to tear. *Astroglide* or silicone-based lubricants are safe to recommend with condoms.

HORMONE THERAPY: HEALTH RISKS AND APPROPRIATE USE

Estrogen
- Most effective treatment for vasomotor symptoms.
- Women with a uterus: use in combination with a form of progesterone (e.g., a progestin). Unopposed estrogen increases the risk of endometrial cancer.
- Associated with significant safety risks (see the drug table on the following page), including boxed warnings for VTE, stroke, dementia and breast cancer (bigger concern in the elderly).

Progestin
- Progestins (e.g., norethindrone, levonorgestrel, drospirenone) can be given as part of a combination pill (with estrogen) or as a separate tablet, most commonly medroxyprogesterone (MPA).
- Can cause mood disturbances, which may be intolerable; if taken intermittently (e.g., for two weeks per month as with *Premphase*), spotting can occur.
- Micronized progestins (e.g., *Prometrium*) are considered to be safer than synthetic progestins (e.g., medroxyprogesterone).

CRITERIA FOR USE OF HORMONE THERAPY
- Healthy, symptomatic women who are within 10 years of menopause, ≤ 60 years of age and have no contraindications to use.
- Extending treatment beyond age 60 years may be acceptable (e.g., patient has osteoporosis) if the lowest possible dose is used and the woman is advised of the safety risks.
- Consider quality-of-life priorities and personal risk factors (e.g., age, time since menopause, risk of blood clots, heart disease, stroke and breast cancer) before use. Patients with risk factors should use non-hormonal treatments (e.g., SSRIs, SNRIs, gabapentin or pregabalin).

Common Hormone Therapy Products

Estradiol-containing products and conjugated estrogens are used primarily for vasomotor symptoms, vaginal atrophy and osteoporosis prevention. Oral contraceptives, used for contraception, contain ethinyl estradiol (discussed in the Contraception & Infertility chapter).

COMPONENTS	FORMULATION	SAFETY/SIDE EFFECTS/MONITORING
Local Hormone Therapies		
17-Beta-Estradiol	Vaginal cream (*Estrace*) Vaginal ring (*Estring*) Vaginal tablet (*Vagifem*) Vaginal insert (*Imvexxy*)	**NOTES** Topical (vaginal) hormone products may have lower systemic absorption, but some may still occur; the safety issues below should be considered
Conjugated Equine Estrogens	Vaginal cream (*Premarin*): 0.625 mg/gram	
Systemic Hormone Therapies		
Estradiol	Topical gel (*Elestrin*) Transdermal patch (*Alora, Climara, Vivelle-Dot, Menostar, Minivelle*) Vaginal ring (*Femring*)	**BOXED WARNINGS** Endometrial cancer (if estrogen used without progestin in women with a uterus); dementia (women ≥ 65 years); ↑ risk of VTE and stroke in postmenopausal women 50-79 years of age (do not use to prevent CVD); breast cancer; use lowest effective dose for shortest duration possible
17-Beta-Estradiol	Oral tablet, micronized (*Estrace*) Topical gel (*Divigel, Estrogel*) Topical spray (*Evamist*)	*Evamist*: secondary exposure can cause breast budding and breast masses in prepubertal females, and gynecomastia and breast masses in prepubertal males; keep children away from spray/application site
Estradiol and Levonorgestrel	Transdermal patch (*ClimaraPro*) "Pro" indicates it contains a progestin	**CONTRAINDICATIONS** Estrogen-containing products: breast cancer (any history); undiagnosed uterine bleeding; active VTE, arterial thromboembolic disease, or known protein C, S or antithrombin deficiency; hepatic impairment; pregnancy
Estradiol and Norethindrone	Transdermal patch (*CombiPatch*) Oral tablet (*Activella, Amabelz*)	**WARNINGS** ↑ risk of breast cancer (from use of estrogen alone) and ovarian cancer; ↑ risk of retinal vascular thrombosis; lipid effects (↑ HDL, ↑ TG, ↓ LDL)
Estradiol and Norgestimate	Oral tablet (*Prefest*): cyclic treatment – estradiol x 3 days, estradiol + norgestimate x 3 days, then repeat	**SIDE EFFECTS** Edema, hypertension, headache, weight gain, depression, nausea, abdominal pain
Estradiol and Drospirenone	Oral tablet (*Angeliq*)	Patch: redness/irritation of the skin
Conjugated Equine Estrogens	Oral tablet (*Premarin*): 0.3, 0.45, 0.625, 0.9, 1.25 mg Injection (*Premarin*)	Remove transdermal patches prior to an MRI
Conjugated Equine Estrogens and Medroxyprogesterone (MPA)	Oral tablet (*Prempro*): 0.3/1.5, 0.45/1.5, 0.625/2.5, 0.625/5 mg Oral tablet (*Premphase*): phasic dosing – 0.625 mg on days 1-14, then 0.625/5 mg on days 15-28	*CombiPatch*: store in the refrigerator prior to dispensing; once dispensed, it can be kept at room temperature for up to 6 months *Vivelle-Dot, Alora,* and *Minivelle* patches are applied twice weekly; *Climara* and *Menostar* patches are once weekly
Medroxyprogesterone *Depo-Provera* – SC or IM for contraception	Oral tablets (*Provera*): 2.5, 5, 10 mg	Gels and *Evamist* spray are flammable
Micronized progesterone	Oral tablet (*Prometrium*)	Micronized progestin (in combination with estrogen) may have a lower risk of breast cancer and cardiovascular events than synthetic progestin, medroxyprogesterone (in combination with estrogen)
Conjugated Estrogens/ Bazedoxifene	Oral tablet (*Duavee*)	

"Bioidentical" Nomenclature

Some females prefer to use bioidentical hormones to treat symptoms, including commercially available products approved by the FDA or compounded preparations. *Bijuva* is an oral capsule and the first FDA-approved bioidentical estradiol and progesterone combination for the treatment of moderate-severe hot flashes. The term "bioidentical" has different meanings; some use it to refer to hormones that have an identical structure to those found in the female body, while others use it to refer to plant-derived hormones that are compounded.

Some people believe that bioidentical hormone therapy is safer, but there are no well-designed studies to confirm risk or benefit, and the FDA does not regulate compounded preparations. Compounded products allow for patient-specific formulations when needs are not met by the FDA-approved commercially available products. The AACE does not recommend bioidentical hormones to treat menopausal symptoms.

ESTROGEN-PROGESTIN KEY COUNSELING POINTS

See the Drug Formulations and Patient Counseling chapter for counseling/layman's terminology.

- Topical gels: apply once daily; wash hands after applying.
  - Apply *Divigel* to the upper thigh (alternate legs daily).
  - Apply *Elestrin* to the upper arm and shoulder.
  - Apply *Estrogel* to the entire arm from wrist to shoulder.
- *Evamist* spray: spray on the inside of the forearm (between elbow and wrist) every morning.
- Patch: apply to the lower abdomen, below the waistline.

OTHER PRODUCTS FOR MENOPAUSE

Natural Products

Natural products used for vasomotor symptoms include black cohosh, evening primrose oil, red clover, soy, flaxseed, dong quai, St. John's wort and chasteberry. The mild "plant estrogens" found in soy and red clover are called phytoestrogens; phyto means plant. These natural products may help with mild symptoms but do not usually provide the same benefit seen with estrogens.

SSRIs and Other Drugs

Paroxetine *(Brisdelle)* is a non-hormonal treatment for moderate-severe vasomotor symptoms associated with menopause. The dose of paroxetine used is lower than the recommended dose for depression. *Brisdelle* should not be used with tamoxifen or warfarin. Paroxetine is a CYP450 2D6 inhibitor, and it will block the effectiveness of tamoxifen (a prodrug). SSRIs can increase the risk of bleeding in patients using warfarin. SNRIs (e.g., venlafaxine, desvenlafaxine), clonidine, gabapentin and pregabalin have shown effectiveness for treating vasomotor symptoms related to menopause, but they are not FDA-approved for this indication.

Ospemifene

Ospemifene *(Osphena)* is an oral estrogen agonist/antagonist indicated for dyspareunia (painful intercourse) and moderate-severe vaginal dryness, which are symptoms of vulvar and vaginal atrophy due to menopause. It has risks associated with use and is not indicated for mild symptoms (topical vaginal products are safer for this purpose). Ospemifene should be used short-term for moderate-severe symptoms. *Intrarosa* (prasterone), a vaginally inserted steroid, is another treatment for moderate-severe dyspareunia.

SSRIs and Ospemifene

DRUG	DOSING	SAFETY/SIDE EFFECTS/MONITORING
Paroxetine *(Brisdelle)* Capsule **Paxil**, Paxil CR, Pexeva – for depression, panic disorder	7.5 mg PO QHS	**BOXED WARNING** Suicide risk (same as with other SSRIs – see the Depression chapter) **CONTRAINDICATIONS/WARNINGS** Same as with other SSRIs (see the Depression chapter) **SIDE EFFECTS** Same sexual side effects as other SSRIs (see the Depression chapter); *Brisdelle* trials showed > 10% incidence of sedation, insomnia, restlessness, tremor, dizziness/weakness, nausea, dry mouth, constipation, diaphoresis **NOTES** Lag time to effect (~4 weeks) Do not use with warfarin (↑ bleeding risk) or tamoxifen (↓ tamoxifen efficacy)
Ospemifene *(Osphena)* Tablet	60 mg PO daily Take with food	**BOXED WARNINGS/CONTRAINDICATIONS** Same as for other estrogen-containing products (see the Common Hormone Therapy Products table on the previous page) **WARNING** Should not be used in women with severe hepatic impairment **SIDE EFFECTS** Hot flashes, vaginal discharge, hyperhidrosis, muscle spasms

HYPOGONADISM IN MALES

Hypogonadism in older males can be due to a normal age-related decline in testosterone, or it can be secondary to a medical condition, surgical procedure or medications that lower testosterone. Medications that can lower testosterone include opioids (especially methadone when used for opioid dependence), chemotherapy drugs used for prostate cancer (see the Oncology II chapter), cimetidine and spironolactone.

TESTOSTERONE USE

In recent years, the increased use of testosterone is largely due to older males requesting treatment for "Low T" symptoms to increase sexual interest (libido), sexual performance, muscle mass, bone density, energy, memory and concentration. The use of testosterone replacement for conditions other than the accepted medical uses is controversial, and a clear benefit of improved sexual function has not been established. The FDA has released a warning about the cardiovascular risks associated with testosterone use, and they recommend treatment only in men with low testosterone levels caused by certain medical conditions and confirmed by laboratory tests.

There have been reports of increased clotting risk in men using testosterone therapy. Most men who experienced clotting may have had a higher risk at baseline, and the link to testosterone use is unclear. Testosterone increases hematocrit, which can cause polycythemia and an increase in clotting risk.

Testosterone can cause noncancerous prostate growth and use is restricted in men with severe BPH. If dispensing a 5-alpha-reductase inhibitor for BPH (e.g., finasteride) that blocks the conversion of testosterone to an active form, it would not make sense to dispense another drug that provides testosterone directly. Common side effects of testosterone include increased male pattern baldness, acne and gynecomastia.

Testosterone and anabolic androgenic steroids (AAS) carry a warning for abuse potential and risk of serious adverse events. When used at higher than prescribed doses, serious adverse outcomes can occur, including myocardial infarction, heart failure, stroke, depression, hostility, aggression, liver toxicity and male infertility. Individuals abusing high doses of testosterone can have withdrawal symptoms, such as depression, fatigue, irritability, loss of appetite, decreased libido and insomnia.

Testosterone Formulations

Testosterone comes in many formulations, including parenteral (IM or SC) injections, topical gels and solutions, buccal tablets and transdermal patches. The injections are painful, and patients may report feeling symptomatic when it is getting close to the time for the next dose. The injections can increase hematocrit more than topical formulations. *Testopel* is a small SC pellet that is implanted under the skin. Testosterone undecanoate (*Jatenzo*) is an oral formulation FDA-approved for hypogonadism due to medical conditions, not age-related.

The gel formulations (*AndroGel* and other topical gels) are popular and relatively well tolerated. *AndroGel* is applied to the upper body. Men who use the gel need to let it dry prior to dressing and be careful not to let others touch the application area, as this increases the risk of drug transfer. If the drug transfers to a female or male child, it can cause "early virilization," and depending on the dose received, the child could have enlarged genital organs, aggressive behavior and premature pubic hair growth. The risk of early virilization is a boxed warning and requires counseling (see the Testosterone Key Counseling Points section). There are new topical formulations that reduce accidental exposure risk (e.g., *Fortesta* and *Natesto*).

Testosterone Products: C-III

TESTOSTERONE	DOSING/COUNSELING	SAFETY/SIDE EFFECTS/MONITORING
Topical Gels and Solutions		**BOXED WARNINGS**
Testosterone gel [AndroGel (1%, 1.62%), **AndroGel Pump** (1.62%)]	*AndroGel* 1%: apply daily to upper arms, shoulders and/or abdomen 1.62%: apply to upper arms or shoulders (not the abdomen)	Topical gel/solution: <u>secondary exposure</u> to testosterone <u>in children</u> can result in virilization; children should avoid contact with any unwashed or unclothed application sites in men using topical testosterone *Jatenzo* and SC testosterone ethanate: can increase blood pressure which increases the risk of major adverse cardiovascular events
Testosterone gel 1% (*Vogelxo, Vogelxo Pump*)	Apply to upper arms and shoulders daily	*Aveed:* pulmonary oil microembolism reactions (cough, dyspnea, throat tightening, anaphylaxis) can be life-threatening; observe in a healthcare setting for 30 minutes after each injection
Testosterone gel 1% (*Testim*)	Apply to arms and shoulders daily	**CONTRAINDICATIONS** Breast cancer, prostate cancer, pregnancy, breastfeeding
Testosterone gel 2% (*Fortesta*)	Apply to front and inner thighs daily	*Aveed:* allergy to castor oil or benzyl benzoate
Testosterone solution	Apply to armpits daily	*Depo-Testosterone:* serious cardiac, hepatic or renal disease
Testosterone nasal gel (*Natesto*)	1 spray per nostril TID	**WARNINGS** ↑ risk of breast cancer, prostate cancer, cardiovascular events, VTE, dyslipidemia, gynecomastia, polycythemia, priapism; use caution in hepatic impairment; may worsen BPH (↑ PSA)
Alternative Formulations		
Injections:		**SIDE EFFECTS** ↑ appetite, acne, edema, hepatotoxicity, reduced sperm count, ↑ SCr, sensitive nipples, sleep apnea
Testosterone cypionate (*Depo-Testosterone*)	IM every 4 weeks (2 doses), then every 10 weeks	*Androderm:* <u>skin irritation</u>
Testosterone undecanoate (*Aveed*)	IM every 2-4 weeks	*Natesto:* <u>nasal irritation</u>
Testosterone enanthate	IM every 2-4 weeks	Injections: pain at the site of injection
Testosterone enanthate (*Xyosted*)	SC auto-injector every week	**MONITORING** Testosterone levels, PSA, liver function, cholesterol, hematocrit (some products)
Transdermal patch (*Androderm*)	2 mg, 4 mg Apply to back, abdomen, thighs or upper arms <u>each night</u>	**NOTES** Gels: apply at the <u>same time each morning</u>; flammable until dry
Implantable pellets (*Testopel*)	SC every 3-6 months	*Androderm:* do not use two 2 mg patches for a 4 mg dose; after removal, OTC <u>hydrocortisone</u> can be used to treat any irritation; <u>remove the patch before an MRI</u>
Testosterone ointment/cream (*First-Testosterone*)	Apply as directed	*Xyosted* contains sesame oil
Testosterone undecanoate oral capsule (*Jatenzo*)	158-396 mg PO BID	

MALE & FEMALE HEALTH

MALE & FEMALE HEALTH

TESTOSTERONE KEY COUNSELING POINTS

See the Drug Formulations and Patient Counseling chapter for counseling/layman's terminology.

- Topical gels/solutions: do not let others come in contact with the application site (can cause secondary exposure, leading to adverse effects). Keep application site covered by clothing.

- For maximal absorption, wait at least 2 - 6 hours after applying gels/solutions before showering or swimming.

- Gels are flammable while wet; do not smoke or go near an open flame until dry.

- Apply deodorant prior to applying solutions to the underarms.

- *AndroGel Pump:* before first use, prime the device by pushing the pump down three times. Do not apply the gel released during priming.

- *Androderm:* do not apply patch to the same site for at least seven days. Remove patch before an MRI.

- *Natesto:* prime the pump ten times, then insert the actuator into the nostril, depress slowly until the pump stops, remove from the nose while wiping the tip to transfer gel to the lateral side of the nostril, then press on the nose and lightly massage. Do not blow your nose or sniff for one hour after administration.

Select Guidelines/References

American Association of Clinical Endocrinologists/American College of Endocrinology Clinical Practice Guidelines for the Diagnosis and Treatment of Postmenopausal Osteoporosis. *Endocrine Practice.* 2020;26(1).

Management of Osteoporosis in Postmenopausal Women: the 2021 Position Statement of the North American Menopause Society. *Menopause.* 2021;28(9):973-997.

American Association of Clinical Endocrinologist and American College of Endocrinology Clinical Position Statement on Menopause-2017 Update. *Endocr Pract.* 2017;23(No. 7).

Testosterone Therapy in Men With Hypogonadism: An Endocrine Soceity Clinical Practice Guideline. *J Clin Endocrinolo Metab.* 2018;103:1715-1744.

CHAPTER CONTENT

ileezhun © 123RF.com

CHAPTER 50
SEXUAL DYSFUNCTION

BACKGROUND

This chapter focuses on erectile dysfunction in males and hypoactive sexual desire disorder in females. Erectile dysfunction (impotence) refers to difficulty getting or sustaining an erection that is firm enough for sex. This is a common type of sexual dysfunction in males and can generally be treated with phosphodiesterase-5 inhibitors (PDE-5 inhibitors). Males can experience other types of sexual dysfunction, including problems with ejaculation and low libido, which is sometimes due to low testosterone levels. Testosterone treatment is discussed in the Osteoporosis, Menopause & Testosterone Use chapter.

In women, sexual dysfunction can be due to either an inability to reach orgasm (anorgasmia), painful intercourse or hypoactive (i.e., lower than normal) sexual desire disorder (HSDD). Flibanserin (*Addyi*) and bremelanotide (*Vyleesi*) are FDA-approved to treat HSDD for premenopausal women only.

In both males and females, sexual dysfunction can be due to the use of an SSRI or SNRI, or less commonly, another antidepressant. An alternate antidepressant can be tried that does not cause sexual side effects, such as bupropion.

ERECTILE DYSFUNCTION

The most common cause of erectile dysfunction (ED) is reduced blood flow to the penis. This can be common in patients with cardiovascular diseases, such as hypertension and atherosclerosis, and conditions that cause neuropathy, such as diabetes. Since the arteries supplying blood to the penis are smaller than those supplying blood to the heart, they can become restricted sooner than the larger vessels. ED can be considered an early warning indicator of cardiovascular disease, and

CONTENT LEGEND

 = Study Tip Gal    = Key Drug Guy

males with ED who have cardiovascular disease risk factors should be referred for cardiac evaluation. Psychological issues (including <u>depression</u> and <u>stress</u>) and neurological illness (<u>spinal cord injury, stroke</u>) can be contributory. Medications used for other conditions, including <u>blood pressure lowering drugs</u> used in cardiovascular diseases, can contribute to erectile dysfunction (see <u>Key Drugs Guy</u>).

DRUGS THAT CAN CAUSE ERECTILE/SEXUAL DYSFUNCTION

KEY DRUGS

Alcohol

Antidepressants
Especially SSRIs and SNRIs (including ↓ libido)

Antihypertensives
Beta-blockers, clonidine, thiazides

Antipsychotics
First-generation (e.g., chlorpromazine)

Prolactin-raising second-generation (e.g., risperidone, paliperidone)

BPH medications
Finasteride, dutasteride, and silodosin (mostly retrograde ejaculation)

Others

Anticancer drugs: Leuprolide, flutamide

Anticholinergics

Atomoxetine

Digoxin

H2RAs: Cimetidine, ranitidine

Nicotine

Opioids (chronic use, especially methadone)

NON-DRUG TREATMENT

Lifestyle changes, including weight loss, quitting tobacco and reducing alcohol intake, can improve ED. Underlying diseases that can contribute to the condition should be properly managed, and any offending agents should be discontinued, if possible. Non-drug options that are beneficial in some males are vacuum erection devices, penile implants and surgery.

NATURAL PRODUCTS

Natural products used to treat ED include <u>yohimbe</u>, <u>L-arginine and panax ginseng</u>. *The Natural Medicines Database* rates L-arginine (taken in high doses) and panax ginseng as "possibly effective" for this purpose. L-arginine can cause dizziness, headaches and flushing. The same side effects are caused by PDE-5 inhibitors, and the additive effects should be avoided. Yohimbe is rated as "insufficient evidence to date." Yohimbe causes gastrointestinal side effects, anxiety and more severe health concerns, including tachycardia and arrhythmias. Ginseng can increase the risk of <u>bleeding</u>.

There are many products marketed to "treat" ED. It is important to recognize that the majority of these products contain a false list of ingredients, have not been tested and are not regulated by the FDA.

DRUG TREATMENT

<u>PDE-5 inhibitors (sildenafil, vardenafil, tadalafil and avanafil)</u> are <u>first-line</u> for the treatment of ED. These are often started at a low dose, then <u>titrated</u> as tolerated and to desired effect. Treatment success is defined by the patient and partner. Treatment failure could be due to a number of factors, such as lack of sexual stimulation, <u>timing of the dose</u> and eating a large meal with the dose. Efficacy appears to be similar among the most common PDE-5 inhibitors (sildenafil, vardenafil and tadalafil), but patients could consider switching between drugs if they do not achieve desired effect. See the PDE-5 Inhibitor table on the next page for details.

If a patient cannot tolerate or has a contraindication to PDE-5 inhibitors, alprostadil can be used instead. Alprostadil is either injected into the penis or inserted into the penis with a urethral suppository. This treatment is invasive, painful and short-acting.

Two of the PDE-5 inhibitors used for ED are indicated for other conditions. <u>Tadalafil *(Cialis)* is used for benign prostatic hyperplasia (BPH)</u> at a dose of 5 mg daily, which could <u>treat</u> concurrent <u>ED</u>. Sildenafil *(Revatio)* and tadalafil *(Adcirca, Alyq)* are indicated for <u>pulmonary arterial hypertension</u> (PAH). Patients should not be using two PDE-5 inhibitors concurrently due to the risk of additive side effects.

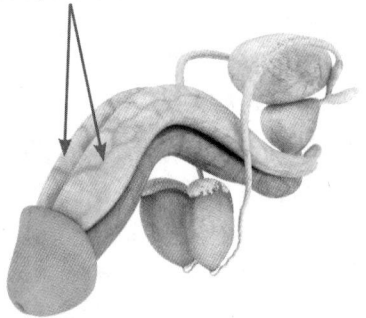

The corpora cavernosa (plural) are the two spongy tubular vessels that run down the length of the penis. When the vessels are filled with blood, the penis is hard and erect.

Nitric oxide (NO) → guanylate cyclase → ↑ cGMP → relaxes the smooth muscle in the arteries → blood flows into the vessels → erection.

Phosphodiesterase type 5 (PDE-5) degrades cGMP.

Phosphodiesterase Type 5 (PDE-5) Inhibitors

Following sexual stimulation, there is a local release of nitric oxide, which increases cGMP and causes smooth muscle relaxation. This permits blood to flow in, resulting in an erection (see figure on previous page). PDE-5 inhibitors block PDE-5 from degrading cGMP. PDE-5 inhibitors do not increase libido (sexual interest), which must be present for the drugs to work.

DRUG	DOSING	SAFETY/SIDE EFFECTS/MONITORING
Sildenafil (*Viagra*) *Revatio* – PAH	On-demand dosing: 25-100 mg daily PRN Start at 50 mg, take ~1 hr before sexual activity Start at 25 mg in select conditions (see Study Tip Gal)	**CONTRAINDICATIONS** Do not use with nitrates or riociguat (a guanylate cyclase stimulator). **WARNINGS** Impaired color discrimination (dose-related) – patients with retinitis pigmentosa may have higher risk. Hearing loss, with or without tinnitus/dizziness. Vision loss – rare, but can be due to nonarteritic anterior ischemic optic neuropathy (NAION). Risk factors: low cup-to-disc ratio, CAD and other vascular conditions, age > 50 yrs, Caucasian ethnicity. Avoid with retinal disorders.
Vardenafil (*Levitra, Staxyn*)	On-demand dosing: 5-20 mg daily PRN Start at 10 mg, take ~1 hr before sexual activity Start with a lower dose of *Levitra* in select conditions (see Study Tip Gal) *Staxyn* is an ODT and only available as 10 mg (max dose)	Hypotension, due to vasodilation. Higher risk with fluid depletion, resting BP < 90/50 mmHg or autonomic dysfunction. Priapism, seek emergency medical care if erection lasts > 4 hrs. CVD, caution with low or very high BP or recent cardiac events. If chest pain occurs, seek immediate medical help.
Tadalafil (*Cialis*) ***Cialis*** – also used for BPH ***Adcirca***, *Alyq* – PAH Lasts the longest – known as the "weekend pill"	Daily dosing: 2.5-5 mg daily Start at 2.5 mg; do not use daily dosing with severe renal or liver impairment On-demand dosing: 5-20 mg daily PRN Start at 10 mg, at least 30 min before sexual activity Start at 5 mg in select conditions (see Study Tip Gal) CrCl 30-50 mL/min: 5 mg PRN CrCl < 30 mL/min: 5 mg PRN Q72H	**SIDE EFFECTS** Headache, flushing, dizziness, dyspepsia, blurred vision, difficulty with color discrimination, increased sensitivity to light, epistaxis, diarrhea, myalgia, muscle/back pain (mostly with tadalafil). **NOTES** Take with or without food. Sildenafil and vardenafil can have decreased efficacy if taken with a high-fat or large meal (common cause of treatment failure per guidelines).
Avanafil (*Stendra*)	On-demand dosing: 50-200 mg daily PRN Start at 100 mg, take 15-30 min before sexual activity Start at 50 mg in select conditions (see Study Tip Gal)	For ED, no more than one dose per day is recommended. *Stendra* can be taken closest to sexual activity.

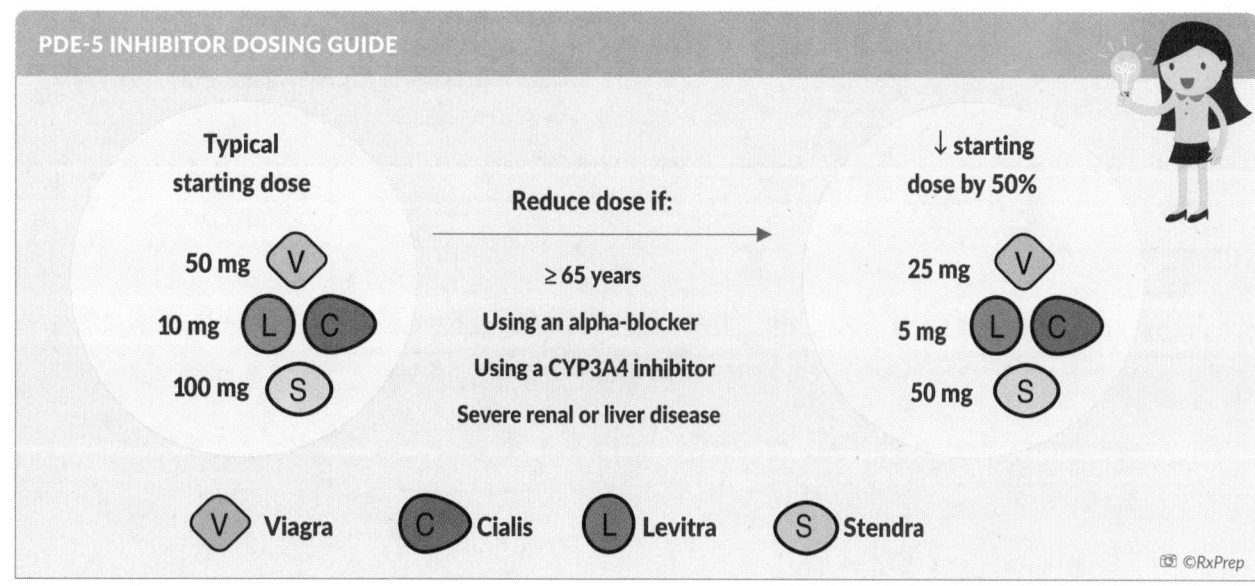

PDE-5 INHIBITOR DOSING GUIDE

Typical starting dose
- 50 mg V
- 10 mg L C
- 100 mg S

Reduce dose if:
- ≥ 65 years
- Using an alpha-blocker
- Using a CYP3A4 inhibitor
- Severe renal or liver disease

↓ starting dose by 50%
- 25 mg V
- 5 mg L C
- 50 mg S

V Viagra   C Cialis   L Levitra   S Stendra

©RxPrep

PDE-5 Inhibitor Drug Interactions

- It is an <u>absolute contraindication</u> to use <u>nitrates</u> or riociguat with PDE-5 inhibitors. These combinations can cause <u>severe hypotension</u>. This includes any prescription nitrates (e.g., *Nitrostat*, *Nitrolingual Pumpspray,* and *BiDil*) or illicit alkyl nitrates ("poppers" such as amyl nitrate and butyl nitrate).

  - ❏ Avoid long-acting nitrates completely. If a patient with ED has taken a PDE-5 inhibitor and develops angina, short-acting nitroglycerin should not be used until after 12 hours for avanafil, after 24 hours for sildenafil or vardenafil, and after 48 hours for tadalafil. Occasionally, if needed, nitrates are used in an acute emergency with careful monitoring.

  - ❏ Riociguat should not be administered within 24 hours of sildenafil, or within 24 hours before or 48 hours after tadalafil.

- Use caution with other agents that cause hypotension, including <u>alpha-blockers</u> and <u>antihypertensive drugs</u>.

  - ❏ PDE-5 inhibitors can enhance the hypotensive effects of alpha-1 blockers. The patient should be <u>stable on the alpha-1 blocker</u> (without excessive dizziness/hypotension) <u>before</u> starting the <u>PDE-5 inhibitor</u>. If *Cialis* is being used to treat BPH, do not use alpha-1 blockers concurrently.

  - ❏ Alcohol can enhance hypotension with PDE-5 inhibitors.

- Moderate and strong CYP450 <u>3A4 inhibitors</u> (e.g., grapefruit juice, protease inhibitors, azole antifungals) increase the drug levels of PDE-5 inhibitors; <u>lower starting doses</u> and/or extended dosing intervals are required. Strong CYP3A4 <u>inducers decrease drug levels; monitor effectiveness</u>.

Alprostadil (Prostaglandin E1)

Alprostadil is <u>prostaglandin E1</u>, a <u>vasodilator</u> that allows blood to flow into the cavernosal arteries, which then enlarges the penis. It is either <u>injected into the penis, or a pellet is inserted</u> through the urethra. This treatment is invasive, painful and does not last as long as the PDE-5 inhibitors. Alprostadil is used in some men who cannot tolerate or have contraindications to PDE-5 inhibitors.

DRUG	DOSING	SAFETY/SIDE EFFECTS/MONITORING
Alprostadil (*Caverject, Caverject Impulse, Edex*) Intracavernous injection Reconstitute prior to use	Inject 1.25-2.5 mcg into the base of the penis; titrate until desired response is achieved Appropriate dose should cause erection 5-10 min after injection; lasts ~1 hr Max 1x/day, 3x/week	**CONTRAINDICATIONS** Conditions that predispose the patient to priapism (e.g., sickle cell anemia, multiple myeloma, leukemia) Intracavernous injection: anatomical deformation or fibrotic conditions of the penis, penile implants Urethral pellets: urethral stricture, balanitis, severe hypospadias and curvature, urethritis, venous thrombosis
Alprostadil (*Muse*) Urethral pellets	Insert 125-250 mcg pellet into urethra Urinate before administration Max 2x/day <u>Refrigerate</u>	**SIDE EFFECTS** <u>Penile pain, priapism</u>, headache, dizziness Intracavernous injection: hematoma, bruising at injection site Urethral pellets: urethral burning or bleeding

HYPOACTIVE SEXUAL DESIRE DISORDER

Hypoactive sexual desire disorder (HSDD) is characterized by a low sexual desire that causes marked distress or interpersonal difficulty. The low sexual desire is not due to a health condition or drug.

DRUG TREATMENT

Flibanserin exhibits agonist activity at 5-HT1A and antagonist activity at 5-HT2A receptors. Bremelanotide is a nonselective melanocortin receptor agonist. The exact mechanism of how either of these medications treat HSDD is unknown. They are both indicated for use in premenopausal females only.

DRUG	DOSING	SAFETY/SIDE EFFECTS/MONITORING
Flibanserin (Addyi)	100 mg QHS Discontinue if no benefit after 8 weeks	**BOXED WARNINGS** Contraindicated: with alcohol due to an ↑ risk of severe hypotension and syncope (REMS program required); in combination with moderate or strong CYP3A4 inhibitors; in patients with hepatic impairment **WARNINGS** Hypotension, syncope, CNS depression **SIDE EFFECTS** Dizziness, somnolence, nausea, fatigue, insomnia, dry mouth **NOTES** Avoid in pregnancy or if breastfeeding
Bremelanotide (Vyleesi) Injection	1.75 mg SC PRN, injected ≥ 45 minutes before sexual activity Maximum dose: 1.75 mg/ 24 hours; no more than 8 doses per month Discontinue if no benefit after 8 weeks	**CONTRAINDICATIONS** Do not use with uncontrolled hypertension or known cardiovascular disease **WARNINGS** ↑ BP and ↓ HR after each dose, skin hyperpigmentation, nausea, delayed gastric emptying **NOTES** Avoid in pregnancy; effective contraception should be used

Flibanserin Drug Interactions

- Use with CNS depressants will ↑ the risk of hypotension and syncope.
- Flibanserin is a major substrate of CYP3A4 and inhibits P-gp. Concurrent moderate-strong CYP3A4 inhibitors are contraindicated.

KEY COUNSELING POINTS

See the Drug Formulations and Patient Counseling chapter for counseling language/layman's terminology.

ALL PDE-5 INHIBITORS

- Take approximately 15 minutes (avanafil), 30 minutes (tadalafil, when taken as needed) or 1 hour (sildenafil and vardenafil) before sexual activity.
- Sexual activity can put an extra strain on your heart. Stop sexual activity and get medical help right away if you have chest pain, dizziness or nausea during sexual activity.
- Can cause:
  - Priapism.
  - Orthostasis and decreased blood pressure. Do not take with nitrates; they worsen this effect.
  - Dizziness, headache, flushing and indigestion.
  - Ringing in the ears (tinnitus) or loss of hearing in one or both ears.
  - Vision changes, including blurry vision and changes to the look of colors (blue color tinge). Sudden vision loss in one or both eyes is a rare but serious side effect. Get medical help right away if this occurs.

Tadalafil (Cialis)

- Can cause muscle or back pain. This usually occurs 12 to 24 hours after taking, and can last up to two days.

Select Guidelines/References

Erectile Dysfunction: AUA Guideline (2018). http://www. auanet.org/guidelines/male-sexual-dysfunction-erectile-dysfunction-(2018) (accessed 2022 Feb 8).

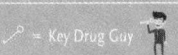

Normal Prostate

Prostate Hypertrophy

Bladder

Bladder

Urine

Normal Prostate

Enlarged Prostate

Normal Urethra

Compressed Urethra

© Hakan çorbaci © 123RF.com

CHAPTER 51

BENIGN PROSTATIC HYPERPLASIA (BPH)

BACKGROUND

The prostate is a walnut-sized gland that surrounds the male urethra at the base of the bladder. As part of the male reproductive system, the main function of the prostate is to secrete fluid that becomes part of the seminal fluid carrying sperm.

The prostate is dependent on androgens (mainly testosterone) for development, maintenance of size and function. Testosterone is metabolized to dihydrotestosterone (DHT) by 5 alpha-reductase. DHT is responsible for normal and hyperplastic growth (increase in the number of cells). Benign prostatic hyperplasia (BPH) results from overgrowth of the stromal and epithelial cells of the prostate gland.

The layer of tissue surrounding the enlarged prostate stops it from expanding, causing the gland to press against or pinch the urethra. This contributes to lower urinary tract symptoms (LUTS) via direct bladder outlet obstruction and increased smooth muscle tone and resistance. The bladder wall becomes thicker and irritated. It begins to contract even when it contains small amounts of urine, causing frequent urination. Eventually, the bladder weakens and loses the ability to empty itself.

Prostate gland enlargement does not typically cause problems until after 65 years of age. Diagnosis requires assessment of the medical history (surgeries, trauma and medications, including herbal and OTC

DRUGS THAT CAN WORSEN BPH

Centrally-acting anticholinergics (e.g., benztropine)

Drugs with anticholinergic effects:
Antihistamines (e.g., diphenhydramine)
Decongestants (e.g., pseudoephedrine)
Phenothiazines (e.g., prochlorperazine)
TCAs (e.g., amitriptyline)

Caffeine

Diuretics

SNRIs

Testosterone products

drugs) and a physical exam. The physical exam should include a digital rectal exam (DRE) to determine the size of the prostate and identify any lumps or nodules. A urinalysis and serum prostate-specific antigen (PSA) are used to rule out conditions other than BPH. PSA, a protein produced by prostate cells, is frequently increased in prostate cancer. It can increase when the prostate becomes larger due to BPH, though BPH is a benign (non-cancerous) condition and does not increase prostate cancer risk.

SYMPTOMS AND COMPLICATIONS

The signs and symptoms of BPH are mainly LUTS, which include:

- Hesitancy, intermittent urine flow, straining or a weak stream of urine.
- Urinary urgency and leaking or dribbling.
- Urinary frequency, especially nocturia (urination at night).
- Incomplete emptying of the bladder (bladder feels full).
- Bladder outlet obstruction.

Symptoms can significantly impact quality of life. BPH rarely causes more severe symptoms, but if the blockage is severe, the urine could back up into the kidneys and result in acute renal failure. Urinary tract infections can also be present but are uncommon. Symptoms can be similar to prostate cancer, so all patients should be referred to a physician for an appropriate evaluation prior to starting treatment.

TREATMENT PRINCIPLES

The severity of reported BPH symptoms guides selection of treatment. Questionnaires, such as the American Urological Association Symptom Score (AUASS) or the International Prostate Symptom Score (I-PSS), are used to quantify symptoms. The scoring systems rate how bothersome the symptoms are, with higher scores indicating more severe symptoms. Treatment options can include watchful waiting, pharmacologic therapy or surgical intervention. Mild disease is generally treated with watchful waiting and yearly reassessments. Moderate/severe disease is generally treated with medications or a minimally invasive procedure or surgery, such as transurethral resection of the prostate (TURP).

NATURAL PRODUCTS

The American Urological Association (AUA) guidelines do not recommend natural products for the treatment of BPH symptoms, though various natural products have been investigated. Saw palmetto has been used for BPH, but it is unlikely to be effective based on contradictory and inconsistent data. Pygeum, pumpkin seed (beta-sitosterol)

and rye pollen are other natural products that have shown some improvement in BPH symptoms. Lycopene is used for prostate cancer prevention, but there is no good evidence for use in BPH. Pharmacists should not recommend natural products until the patient has seen a healthcare provider, as prostate cancer symptoms present similarly to BPH.

DRUG TREATMENT

Medications include alpha-blockers (selective and non-selective), used alone or in combination with a 5 alpha-reductase inhibitor. The 5 alpha-reductase inhibitors work by decreasing prostate size, but they have a delayed onset. They should not be used in men who have bladder outlet obstruction symptoms without prostate enlargement. Alpha-blockers work quickly, but do not shrink the prostate. The two classes are often used together to get the benefits of each.

Peripherally-acting anticholinergic drugs (e.g., tolterodine) or beta-3 receptor agonist (e.g., mirabegron) in combination with alpha-blockers are sometimes a reasonable option for men without an elevated post void residual (PVR) urine and when LUTS are predominately irritative. If anticholinergics are used, the PVR should be < 250 – 300 mL. These medications are used for overactive bladder and discussed in the Urinary Incontinence chapter.

Another treatment option is the phosphodiesterase-5 (PDE-5) inhibitor tadalafil, with or without finasteride. This can be used in men with BPH alone, and can be an attractive option for men with both BPH and erectile dysfunction (ED).

ALPHA-BLOCKERS

Alpha-1 blockers are first-line treatment for moderate-to-severe symptoms. They inhibit alpha-1 adrenergic receptors, causing relaxation of smooth muscle in the prostate and bladder neck. This reduces bladder outlet obstruction and improves urinary flow. There are three types of alpha-1 receptors. Alpha-1A receptors are primarily found in the prostate. Alpha-1B and alpha-1D receptors are dominant in the heart and arteries. The non-selective alpha-1 blockers (terazosin, doxazosin) have more side effects (e.g., orthostasis, dizziness, headache) than the selective alpha-1A blockers (tamsulosin, alfuzosin, silodosin).

Intraoperative Floppy Iris Syndrome

Alpha-blockers relax the smooth muscle of the prostate and bladder neck. The same receptors are present on the iris dilator muscle in the eye. Patients using alpha-blockers are at risk of developing intraoperative floppy iris syndrome (IFIS) during cataract surgery. With alpha-1 blockade, the iris becomes floppy, has a risk of prolapse and the pupils do not dilate well, complicating the procedure. If cataract surgery is planned, alpha-blocker treatment should be delayed until the surgery has been completed.

MALE & FEMALE HEALTH

DRUG	DOSING	SAFETY/SIDE EFFECTS/MONITORING
Non-Selective Alpha-1 Blockers		**CONTRAINDICATIONS** Concurrent use of silodosin or alfuzosin with strong CYP3A4 inhibitors; hepatic impairment (Child-Pugh class C for silodosin, class B/C for alfuzosin); severe renal impairment (silodosin)
Doxazosin *(Cardura, Cardura XL)*	IR: start 1 mg at bedtime; titrate slowly up to 4-8 mg at bedtime XL: start 4 mg daily with breakfast; max 8 mg daily	**WARNINGS** Orthostatic hypotension/syncope, typically with the first dose, if therapy is interrupted for several days, if the dosage is increased too rapidly, or if another antihypertensive drug or PDE-5 inhibitor is started Intraoperative floppy iris syndrome (IFIS) can occur in cataract surgery if currently on or previously treated with an alpha-1 blocker
Terazosin	Start 1 mg at bedtime; titrate slowly to a max of 20 mg at bedtime (10 mg generally effective)	Priapism, seek medical attention if an erection lasts > 4 hours Angina, discontinue if symptoms of angina begin or worsen **SIDE EFFECTS** Dizziness, fatigue, headache, abnormal ejaculation (especially with tamsulosin and silodosin), fluid retention, rhinitis (tamsulosin)
Selective Alpha-1A Blockers		**MONITORING** BP, PSA, urinary symptoms
Tamsulosin *(Flomax)* + dutasteride *(Jalyn)*	0.4 mg daily, 30 min after the same meal each day; max 0.8 mg daily	**NOTES** The non-selective drugs are often given at bedtime to help minimize the initial "first-dose" effect of orthostasis/dizziness. This requires careful counseling, as nocturia is common, and getting up at night to use the bathroom can be dangerous if dizziness and orthostasis occur. Alpha-blockers work right away, but 4-6 weeks may be required to assess whether beneficial effects have been achieved; they do not shrink the prostate and do not change PSA levels.
Alfuzosin *(Uroxatral)*	10 mg daily, immediately after the same meal each day CrCl < 30 mL/min: use with caution	*Cardura XL* is an OROS formulation (see Drug Formulations and Patient Counseling chapter) and can leave a ghost tablet (empty shell) in the stool. Silodosin can cause retrograde ejaculation in ~30% of patients. It is reversible upon drug discontinuation.
Silodosin *(Rapaflo)*	8 mg daily with a meal CrCl 30-50 mL/min: 4 mg daily CrCl < 30 mL/min: do not use	Do not use alfuzosin if at risk for QT prolongation. Alpha-blockers can be used for bladder outlet obstruction in women (off-label).

Alpha-Blocker Drug Interactions

- Use caution when co-administered with PDE-5 inhibitors used for erectile dysfunction (sildenafil, tadalafil, vardenafil, avanafil) due to additive hypotensive effects. See the Sexual Dysfunction chapter. If tadalafil *(Cialis)* is being used to treat BPH, do not use in combination with alpha-1 blockers.

- Use caution with other drugs that lower BP.

- Tamsulosin, alfuzosin and silodosin are major CYP450 3A4 substrates; do not use with strong CYP3A4 inhibitors.

- Silodosin cannot be used with strong P-gp inhibitors, such as cyclosporine.

- Alfuzosin can cause QT prolongation; do not use with other QT-prolonging drugs. Use with caution in patients with cardiovascular disease.

5 ALPHA-REDUCTASE INHIBITORS

These medications inhibit the <u>5 alpha-reductase enzyme</u>, which <u>blocks</u> the conversion of <u>testosterone to dihydrotestosterone</u> (<u>DHT</u>). Finasteride is selective for the 5 alpha-reductase type II enzyme (the more prevalent type within the prostate), while dutasteride inhibits both type I and type II. This class of medications is indicated for the treatment of symptomatic BPH in men <u>with an enlarged prostate</u>. They are used in combination with alpha-blockers to <u>improve symptoms, decrease the risk</u> of acute <u>urinary retention</u> and <u>decrease</u> the need for <u>surgery</u> (e.g., TURP, prostatectomy).

DRUG	DOSING	SAFETY/SIDE EFFECTS/MONITORING
Finasteride (*Proscar*) ***Propecia*** – for alopecia (hair loss) at lower doses (1 mg daily) + tadalafil (*Entadfi*)	5 mg daily	**CONTRAINDICATIONS** <u>Women of child-bearing potential, pregnancy</u>, children **WARNINGS** May ↑ risk of high-grade prostate cancer **SIDE EFFECTS** <u>Impotence, ↓ libido, ejaculation disturbances, breast enlargement and tenderness</u>, rash; sexual SEs ↓ with time and return to baseline at one year of use in some men
Dutasteride (*Avodart*) + tamsulosin (*Jalyn*)	0.5 mg daily Take *Jalyn* 30 min after the same meal each day	**MONITORING** PSA, urinary symptoms **NOTES** <u>Pregnant women should not take or handle these medications</u> as they can be absorbed through the skin and can be detrimental to the fetus. They are on the NIOSH list of hazardous drugs. Delayed onset, <u>treatment for 6 months</u> (or longer) may be required for <u>maximal efficacy</u>. 5 alpha-reductase inhibitors <u>shrink the prostate</u> and <u>↓ PSA levels</u>. Swallow dutasteride whole. Do not chew or open as contents can cause oropharyngeal irritation.

5 Alpha-Reductase Inhibitor Drug Interactions

- Finasteride and dutasteride are minor CYP3A4 substrates; strong CYP3A4 inhibitors can ↑ levels.
- Do not use *Proscar* if using *Propecia* for hair loss.

MALE & FEMALE HEALTH

PHOSPHODIESTERASE-5 INHIBITORS

The mechanism of action of PDE-5 inhibitors in treating BPH symptoms is not well known. They likely decrease smooth muscle and endothelial cell proliferation, decrease nerve activity, increase smooth muscle relaxation and tissue perfusion of the prostate and bladder. Tadalafil is the only PDE-5 inhibitor that is FDA-approved for the treatment of BPH with or without erectile dysfunction. It has been studied alone and in combination with finasteride. Due to the risks for hypotension, tadalafil should not be used in combination with an alpha-blocker for the treatment of BPH.

DRUG	DOSING	SAFETY/SIDE EFFECTS/MONITORING
Tadalafil (Cialis) Cialis – also for ED **Adcirca,** Alyq – for pulmonary arterial hypertension (PAH) + finasteride (Entadfi)	5 mg daily, at the same time each day CrCl 30-50 mL/min: 2.5 mg initially, max of 5 mg daily CrCl < 30 mL/min: do not use Use 2.5 mg if taking a strong CYP3A4 inhibitor	**CONTRAINDICATIONS** Do not use with nitrates or riociguat (a guanylate cyclase stimulator) **WARNINGS** Impaired color discrimination (dose-related), higher risk with retinitis pigmentosa Hearing loss, with or without tinnitus/dizziness Vision loss, rare, can be due to nonarteritic anterior ischemic optic neuropathy (NAION); risk factors: low cup-to-disc ratio, CAD, vascular conditions, age > 50 yrs, Caucasian ethnicity; avoid with retinal disorders Hypotension, due to vasodilation; higher risk with resting BP < 90/50 mmHg, fluid depletion or autonomic dysfunction CVD, caution with low or very high BP or recent CV events; seek immediate medical help for chest pain Priapism, seek emergency medical care if an erection lasts > 4 hrs **SIDE EFFECTS** Headache, flushing, dizziness, dyspepsia, muscle/back pain, myalgia, blurred vision, increased sensitivity to light, epistaxis, diarrhea **MONITORING** BP, PSA, urinary symptoms

- For drug interactions and key counseling points for tadalafil, see the Sexual Dysfunction chapter.

KEY COUNSELING POINTS

See the Drug Formulations and Patient Counseling chapter for counseling language/layman's terminology.

ALPHA-BLOCKERS

- Can cause orthostasis.
- Tell your healthcare provider about the use of this medication if having cataract surgery.

Doxazosin and Terazosin (Non-Selective)

- Take at bedtime.
- Ghost tablet in stool (Cardura XL).

Silodosin

- Can cause sexual dysfunction (retrograde ejaculation).

5 ALPHA-REDUCTASE INHIBITORS

- Can cause sexual dysfunction (decreased libido, ejaculation disturbances and erectile dysfunction).
- Avoid in pregnancy (teratogenic). Women who are or may become pregnant should not handle the tablets.

Select Guidelines/References

AUA Management of Lower Urinary Tract Symptoms Attributed to Benign Prostatic Hyperplasia. Published 2021; http://www.auanet.org/guidelines/benign-prostatic-hyperplasia-(bph)-guideline (accessed 2022 Feb 8).

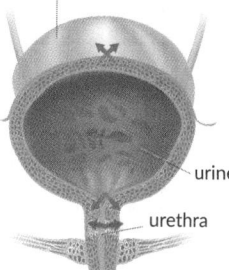 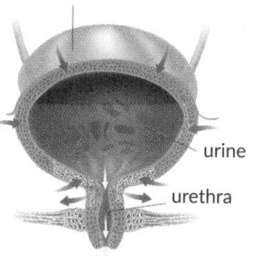

Normal Bladder detrusor muscle contracting when bladder is full — urine, urethra

Overactive Bladder detrusor muscle contracting before bladder is full — urine, urethra

iStock.com/Graphic_BKK1979

CHAPTER 52
URINARY INCONTINENCE

BACKGROUND

Urinary incontinence is a common and debilitating urinary disorder that affects many people. It is not a normal sign of aging. Overactive bladder (OAB) is a syndrome of bothersome urinary symptoms, including:

- Urinary urgency: a sudden feeling of needing to urinate. This is the primary symptom of OAB; it can occur with or without incontinence and is usually accompanied by urinary frequency and nocturia.

- Urinary frequency: voiding ≥ 8 times during waking hours.

- Nocturia: ≥ 2 awakenings in the night to urinate.

- Urinary incontinence: involuntary leakage of urine (see table for different forms).

About 1/3 of patients with OAB have incontinent episodes (OAB wet) and the other 2/3 of patients do not (OAB dry). Urge incontinence is a form of OAB wet that can be treated with the medications discussed in this chapter.

FORMS OF URINARY INCONTINENCE

Urge	A sudden and unstoppable urge to urinate. Associated with neuropathy and often present in those with diabetes, strokes, dementia, Parkinson disease or multiple sclerosis (although people without comorbidities can be affected).
Stress	Urine leaks out during any form of exertion (e.g., exercise, coughing, sneezing, laughing) as a result of pressure on the bladder.
Mixed	Combination of urge and stress incontinence.
Functional	There is no abnormality in the bladder, but the patient may be cognitively, socially or physically impaired thus hindering access to a toilet (e.g., patients in wheelchairs).
Overflow	Leakage that occurs when the quantity of urine stored in the bladder exceeds its capacity. Often occurs without the urge to urinate (BPH is the most common cause).

Many comorbidities exist in patients with OAB, including falls and fractures, skin breakdown and skin infections, UTIs, depression and sexual dysfunction. Due to the embarrassment of the condition, there are many social implications of OAB, including low self-esteem, lack of sexual intimacy, social and physical isolation, sleep disturbances, limits on travel and dependence on caregivers. These can lead to a reduced quality of life. Many patients become dehydrated because they limit fluid intake. The cost of pads and adult diapers can cause a financial burden.

PATHOPHYSIOLOGY AND ETIOLOGY

The bladder is commonly referred to as a "balloon" with an outer muscular layer known as the detrusor muscle. The detrusor muscle and the bladder outlet functions are neurologically coordinated to store and expel urine. The detrusor muscle is innervated mainly by the parasympathetic nervous system (acetylcholine acting on muscarinic receptors), while the bladder neck is innervated by the sympathetic nervous system. The internal sphincter is innervated by the sympathetic nervous system and the external sphincter is innervated by the somatic nervous system. Both voluntary and involuntary contractions of the detrusor muscle are mediated by acetylcholine activation of muscarinic receptors.

In OAB, there is inappropriate stimulation of the muscarinic receptors on the detrusor muscle causing involuntary contractions and the feeling of urinary urgency. This is a contraction of the bladder even when it is not full. Of the five known muscarinic receptor subtypes, the human bladder is comprised of M2 and M3 receptors in a 3:1 ratio. The M3 receptor is responsible for both emptying contractions as well as involuntary bladder contractions. Anticholinergic drugs inhibit the effects of acetylcholine on the M2 and M3 receptors. Similar to anticholinergics, the other drug used for OAB, mirabegron, causes relaxation of the detrusor muscle (prevents contraction) but it does so by acting as a beta-3 receptor agonist.

RISK FACTORS FOR OVERACTIVE BLADDER

Age > 40 years	Drugs that increase incontinence (e.g., alcohol, cholinesterase inhibitors, diuretics, sedatives)
Diabetes	
Prior vaginal delivery	
Obesity	Restricted mobility
Neurologic conditions (e.g., Parkinson disease, stroke, dementia)	Hysterectomy
	Pelvic injury

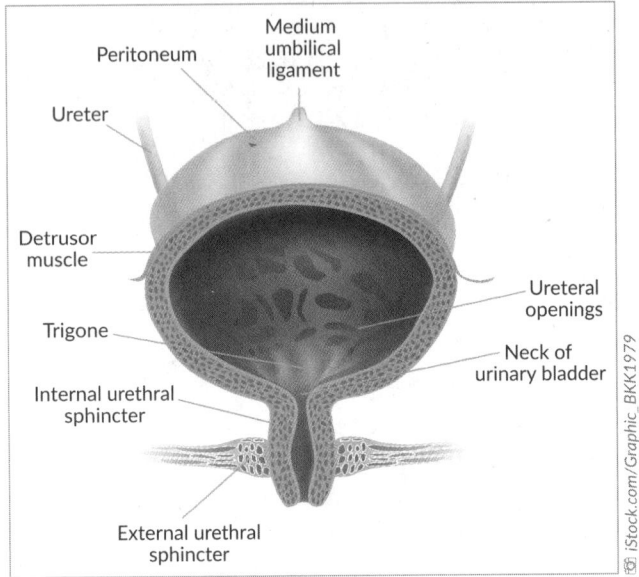

© iStock.com/Graphic_BKK1979

NON-DRUG TREATMENT

Behavioral therapies are considered first-line to improve OAB symptoms. These include bladder training, delayed or scheduled voiding, pelvic floor muscle exercises (Kegel exercises), urge control techniques (distraction, self-assertions), fluid management, dietary changes (avoiding bladder irritants, such as caffeine), weight loss and other lifestyle measures (e.g., stopping medications that can worsen OAB; or with diuretics, changing the time of administration to avoid nocturia).

Behavioral therapies can be combined with other treatment modalities, such as medications. Surgical intervention should be reserved for the rare non-neurogenic patient who has failed all other therapeutic options and whose symptoms are intolerable.

Proper technique of Kegel exercises is key. Instruct the patient to imagine that they are trying to stop urination midstream. Squeeze the muscles they would use. If they sense a "pulling" feeling, those are the correct muscles for pelvic exercise. Pull in the pelvic muscles and hold for a count of three, then relax for a count of three. Patients should work up to three sets of ten exercises per day to reduce wetting episodes.

DRUG TREATMENT

A step-wise approach is recommended that begins conservatively with behavioral therapy (see previous section). Treatment depends on the degree of severity felt by the patient; with severe symptoms, treatment can begin at a higher level (see algorithm). Drugs are added to the behavioral recommendations (e.g., Kegel exercises, bladder training, weight loss), when needed.

URGE INCONTINENCE/MIXED INCONTINENCE

Mixed incontinence has an urge incontinence component and is treated in a similar manner. First-line drugs include anticholinergics (e.g., oxybutynin) or a beta-3 receptor agonist (e.g., mirabegron). OnabotulinumtoxinA (*Botox*) has higher efficacy but is not first-line due to cost and the route of administration through the urethra and into the detrusor muscle. Nerve stimulation or surgical intervention is used last.

Women with postmenopausal symptoms of vulvar and vaginal atrophy can use vaginal estrogen in a cream or a ring, which may provide modest relief of symptoms. Estrogen is not FDA-approved for this purpose. See the Osteoporosis, Menopause & Testosterone Use chapter.

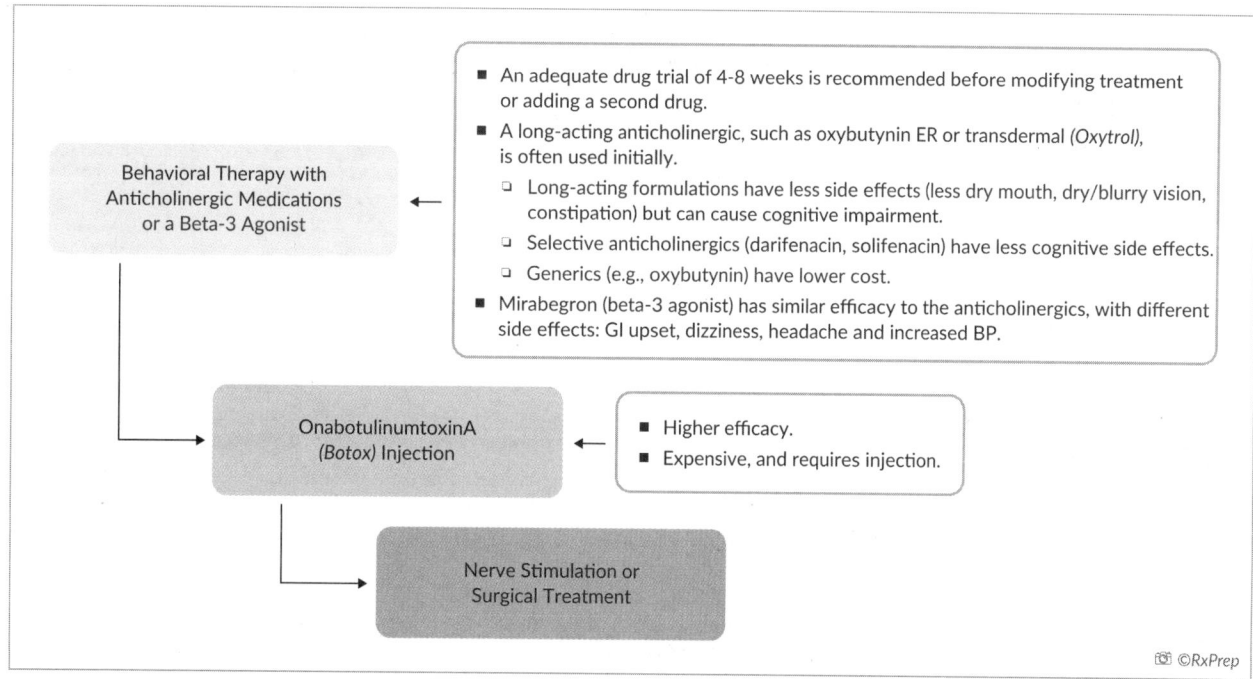

- An adequate drug trial of 4-8 weeks is recommended before modifying treatment or adding a second drug.
- A long-acting anticholinergic, such as oxybutynin ER or transdermal *(Oxytrol)*, is often used initially.
  - Long-acting formulations have less side effects (less dry mouth, dry/blurry vision, constipation) but can cause cognitive impairment.
  - Selective anticholinergics (darifenacin, solifenacin) have less cognitive side effects.
  - Generics (e.g., oxybutynin) have lower cost.
- Mirabegron (beta-3 agonist) has similar efficacy to the anticholinergics, with different side effects: GI upset, dizziness, headache and increased BP.

Behavioral Therapy with Anticholinergic Medications or a Beta-3 Agonist

OnabotulinumtoxinA *(Botox)* Injection
- Higher efficacy.
- Expensive, and requires injection.

Nerve Stimulation or Surgical Treatment

©RxPrep

STRESS INCONTINENCE

The medications used for stress incontinence are not FDA-approved for this use and have minimal efficacy, but there is a lack of more effective options. Pseudoephedrine, an agonist of norepinephrine (NE) and epinephrine (Epi), causes adrenaline-type effects, including tachycardia, palpitations, nervousness/anxiety, headache and insomnia. Duloxetine is commonly chosen when it is possible to treat two conditions with one drug (e.g., incontinence/depression), though it has little efficacy for incontinence (see the Depression chapter).

MALE & FEMALE HEALTH

ANTICHOLINERGIC DRUGS

Anticholinergic drugs, also called <u>antimuscarinic drugs</u>, competitively bind to muscarinic receptors and <u>block acetylcholine</u> from binding. This limits contractions of the detrusor muscle. <u>Extended-release formulations are preferred</u> over immediate-release formulations due to a <u>lower risk of dry mouth</u>. Drugs that are more <u>selective</u> for the <u>M3</u> receptor (solifenacin, darifenacin and fesoterodine) have <u>fewer CNS side effects</u> than the older, non-selective drugs, such as oxybutynin. The <u>Beers Criteria</u> recommend <u>avoiding anticholinergics</u> in patients aged <u>65 years and older</u>, due to a risk of <u>delirium and cognitive impairment</u>.

DRUG	DOSING	SAFETY/SIDE EFFECTS/MONITORING
Oxybutynin IR	5 mg PO BID-QID	**CONTRAINDICATIONS** Uncontrolled <u>narrow angle glaucoma</u>, urinary retention, gastric retention, decreased gastric motility *Oxytrol for Women* OTC: pain or burning when urinating, blood in urine, unexplained lower back or side pain, cloudy or foul-smelling urine, male sex, age < 18 years, urinary or gastric retention, glaucoma, accidental urine loss only due to coughing, sneezing or laughing **WARNINGS** <u>Agitation, confusion, drowsiness, dizziness, blurred vision</u>, hallucinations, and/or headache, which may impair physical or mental abilities; use <u>caution</u> if performing <u>tasks which require mental alertness</u> (e.g., operating machinery, driving) Angioedema of the face, lips, tongue and/or larynx **SIDE EFFECTS** <u>Dizziness and drowsiness</u> (greatest with <u>oxybutynin</u> and less with the newer, selective drugs), <u>xerostomia</u> (dry mouth), <u>constipation</u>, dry eyes/blurred vision, urinary retention, application site reactions (with topical gel and patch) **NOTES** ↓ dose in renal impairment (CrCl < 30 mL/min) with fesoterodine, solifenacin, tolterodine, and trospium (do not use trospium XR) *Ditropan XL* is an <u>OROS formulation</u> (see the Drug Formulations and Patient Counseling chapter) and can leave a <u>ghost shell</u> (empty shell) in the stool Oxybutynin <u>patch</u> and <u>gel</u> cause <u>less dry mouth</u> and constipation than oral forms *Oxytrol* patch should be placed on dry, intact skin on the abdomen, hips or buttocks; avoid reapplication to the same site within 7 days; available <u>OTC</u> for women ≥ 18 years Package labeling is not clear if metals may be present in *Oxytrol* patch (Rx and OTC); consider removing before MRI *Gelnique* should be applied to dry, intact skin on the abdomen, thighs or upper arms/shoulders; rotate application sites (do not use same site on consecutive days)
Oxybutynin ER (*Ditropan XL*)	5-30 mg PO daily	
Oxybutynin patch (*Oxytrol* – Rx, *Oxytrol for Women* – OTC)	Apply one patch (3.9 mg/day) <u>twice weekly</u> (every 3-4 days; OTC patch is changed every 4 days)	
Oxybutynin 10% topical gel (*Gelnique, Gelnique Pump*)	Apply contents of 1 sachet (or 1 pump) daily	
Tolterodine (*Detrol*)	1-2 mg PO BID	
Tolterodine ER (*Detrol LA*)	2-4 mg PO daily	
Trospium IR	20 mg PO BID	
Trospium XR	60 mg PO daily	
	Take on an <u>empty stomach</u>	
Solifenacin (*Vesicare*)	5-10 mg PO daily	
Darifenacin (*Enablex*)	7.5-15 mg PO daily	
Fesoterodine (*Toviaz*)	4-8 mg PO daily	

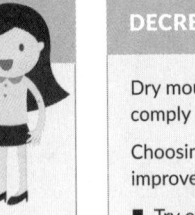

ANTICHOLINERGIC SIDE EFFECTS

Peripheral:
- Dry mouth
- Dry eyes/blurred vision
- Urinary retention
- Constipation
- Tachycardia

Central:
- Sedation
- Dizziness
- Cognitive impairment

Anticholinergic Drug Interactions

- Additive effects can be seen when used with other medications that have anticholinergic side effects.

- The lowest dose of tolterodine, solifenacin, darifenacin and fesoterodine should be used if the patient is taking strong CYP450 3A4 inhibitors.

- Acetylcholinesterase inhibitors used for dementia (e.g., donepezil) increase acetylcholine in the CNS. Although OAB drugs primarily stay in the periphery (outside the

DECREASING RISK OF DRY MOUTH

Dry mouth is a major reason that patients fail to comply with anticholinergic treatment.

Choosing a treatment that minimizes dry mouth can improve adherence.

- Try extended-release formulations (lower risk than IR formulations).

- Try oxybutynin gel or patch (lower risk than oral formulations).

- Mirabegron has a lower incidence of dry mouth and can be helpful in patients who cannot tolerate anticholinergics.

- Try non-drug options to help with symptoms: avoid mouthwashes with alcohol, use ice chips, water, sugar-free candy or gum.

CNS), some patients can experience CNS side effects (e.g., memory impairment). While this is not a drug interaction, use of anticholinergic drugs can worsen dementia symptoms. The risk versus benefit must be considered.

BETA-3 AGONISTS

Beta-3 agonists <u>relax the detrusor muscle</u> and increase bladder capacity by <u>activating beta-3 receptors</u>. Mirabegron and Vibegron have similar efficacy to anticholinergic drugs but cause <u>less dry mouth</u>. They can be used in combination with anticholinergic drugs or as monotherapy.

DRUG	DOSING	SAFETY/SIDE EFFECTS/MONITORING
Mirabegron (*Myrbetriq*)	25-50 mg PO daily CrCl 15-29 mL/min: 25 mg daily CrCl < 15 mL/min: not recommended	**WARNINGS** <u>Urinary retention</u> in patients with BPH and when used with anticholinergic drugs; ↑ BP Mirabegron: angioedema of the face, lips, tongue and/or larynx **SIDE EFFECTS** Nasopharyngitis, headache, constipation, diarrhea, dizziness
Vibegron (*Gemtesa*)	75 mg PO daily	Mirabegron: UTI **MONITORING** Urinary symptoms Mirabegron: BP **NOTES** Efficacy seen within 8 weeks

Beta-3 Agonist Drug Interactions

- Mirabegron is a moderate CYP2D6 inhibitor. Use caution in combination with narrow therapeutic drugs metabolized by CYP2D6. Levels of metoprolol are increased when co-administered with mirabegron. Levels of tamoxifen are decreased when co-administered with mirabegron. Use caution in combination with digoxin (use lowest digoxin dose and monitor levels).

ONABOTULINUMTOXINA (*BOTOX*)

Botox is a <u>third-line treatment</u> for patients who are <u>refractory</u> to first- and second-line treatment options. It affects the detrusor activity by inhibiting the release of acetylcholine.

DRUG	DOSING	SAFETY/SIDE EFFECTS/MONITORING
OnabotulinumtoxinA (*Botox*)	100 units total dose, administered as 0.5 mL (5 units) injections, across 20 sites (given intradetrusor) – repeat no sooner than 12 weeks from previous administration In adults treated with *Botox* for more than one indication, do not exceed a total dose of 360 units in a 3-month interval	**BOXED WARNING** All botulinum toxin products may spread from the area of injection to produce symptoms consistent with botulinum toxin effects; swallowing and breathing difficulties can be life-threatening **CONTRAINDICATIONS** Infection at the targeted injection site, urinary tract infection, urinary retention **SIDE EFFECTS** Urinary tract infection, urinary retention, dysuria **MONITORING** Post void residual volume, symptoms of OAB **NOTES** Potency units of *Botox* are not interchangeable with other preparations of botulinum toxin products Prophylactic antimicrobial therapy (excluding aminoglycosides) should be administered 1-3 days prior to, on the day of, and for 1-3 days following *Botox* administration

Botox Drug Interactions

- Aminoglycosides and drugs affecting neuromuscular transmission can increase the side effects of *Botox*.

NOCTURIA TREATMENT

The only medication FDA-approved for the treatment of nocturia in adults is <u>desmopressin</u>, an <u>antidiuretic hormone</u> analog that temporarily <u>decreases urine production</u>. It is administered before bed to prevent patients from having to urinate during the night.

DRUG	DOSING	SAFETY/SIDE EFFECTS/MONITORING
Desmopressin tablet (DDAVP)	0.2-0.6 mg at bedtime	**BOXED WARNING** Severe, life-threatening <u>hyponatremia</u> can develop **CONTRAINDICATIONS** Patients with increased risk of severe hyponatremia (e.g., excessive fluid intake, illnesses or drugs that can cause fluid or electrolyte imbalances, including chronic kidney disease, SIADH, loop diuretics, systemic or inhaled glucocorticoids) and patients with increased risk of <u>fluid retention</u> (e.g., uncontrolled hypertension, heart failure) **WARNINGS** Do not use with nasal conditions (nasal spray) **SIDE EFFECTS** Hyponatremia, headache, hypertension, xerostomia (Nocdurna) **MONITORING** <u>Serum Na</u> (baseline, 1 week and 1 month)
SL tablet (Nocdurna)	Females: 27.7 mcg 1 hour before bedtime Males: 55.3 mcg 1 hour before bedtime	
Nasal spray (DDAVP, DDAVP Rhinal Tube, Stimate)		
Injection (DDAVP)		
Diabetes insipidus – DDAVP Rhinal Tube, DDAVP tablet, nasal spray, injection		
Hemophilia A – DDAVP injection, Stimate		
von Willebrand's disease – DDAVP injection, Stimate		

KEY COUNSELING POINTS

See the Drug Formulations and Patient Counseling chapter for counseling language/layman's terminology.

ANTICHOLINERGICS

- Can cause:
    - Dry mouth.
    - Constipation.
    - Dizziness.
- Avoid mouthwashes with alcohol, and use ice chips, sugar-free candy or gum to help with dry mouth symptoms.

Oxybutynin XL (Ditropan XL)
- Ghost tablet in stool.

Oxytrol Patch

- Open one pouch and apply one patch to clean, dry, intact skin on the abdomen, hips or buttocks. Avoid applying the patch on your waistline, since tight clothing can rub the patch off.
- Apply a new patch twice weekly. Select a new site for each new patch (avoid reapplication to the same site within seven days).

DESMOPRESSIN

- Can cause low sodium.

Select Guidelines/References

AUA/SUFU Guideline: Diagnosis and Treatment of Overactive Bladder (Non-Neurogenic) In Adults. https://www.auanet.org/guidelines/overactive-bladder-(oab)-guideline (accessed 2022 Feb 12).

SPECIAL POPULATIONS

CONTENTS

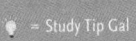

© iStock.com/shironosov

CONTENT LEGEND

 ☀ = Study Tip Gal   ⚏ = Required Formula

CHAPTER 53

ACUTE & CRITICAL CARE MEDICINE

BACKGROUND

When a patient is sick enough to require an advanced level of care, they are assessed for risk and admitted to either the hospital general medical unit (acute care) or the critical care/intensive care unit (ICU). If their illness has a high probability of imminent or life-threatening deterioration, treatment in the ICU is needed. The goal of critical care treatment is stabilization. If the illness is not as life-threatening, treatment in a general medical (acute care) unit is acceptable. The goal of acute care treatment is to diagnose and treat the illness, and return the patient to their normal state of health.

Common conditions and associated medications used in hospitalized general medical and critically ill patients are addressed in this chapter.

FLUIDS

CRYSTALLOIDS VS COLLOIDS

Intravenous (IV) fluids, used to replace fluid losses and treat various conditions, are categorized as crystalloids or colloids. Crystalloids contain various concentrations of sodium and/or dextrose that pass freely between semipermeable membranes. Most of the administered volume does not remain in the intravascular space (inside the blood vessels), but moves into the extravascular or interstitial space. Crystalloids are less costly and generally have fewer adverse reactions than colloids. Balanced solutions (e.g., Lactated Ringer's) may be preferred in certain disease states, such as sepsis, since the chloride load from a sodium chloride solution can be high enough to contribute to cellular injury, including renal damage.

Colloids are large molecules (typically protein or starch) dispersed in a solution; they primarily remain in the intravascular space and ↑ oncotic pressure. Colloids provide greater intravascular volume expansion than equal volumes of crystalloids, but are more expensive and have not shown a clear clinical benefit over crystalloids.

Many different crystalloid and colloid products are available, including combination formulations (e.g., D5NS). Dextrose-containing products contain "free water" and are used when water is needed intracellularly. Lactated Ringer's and normal saline are the most common fluids used for volume resuscitation in shock states (see the Types of Shock section). Albumin is the most commonly used colloid and is particularly useful when there is significant edema (e.g., cirrhosis); albumin should not be used for nutritional supplementation when serum albumin is low. Hydroxyethyl starch should only be used if other treatments are unavailable due to its boxed warning for mortality, renal injury and coagulopathy (bleeding).

CLASS	COMMON FLUIDS
Crystalloids	5% Dextrose (D5W)*
	0.9% NaCl (normal saline, NS)*
	Lactated Ringer's (LR) – contains NaCl, KCl, CaCl$_2$, Na-lactate (lactate is converted to bicarbonate)
	Multiple electrolyte injection (*Plasma-Lyte A,* others)
Colloids	Albumin 5%, 25% (*Albutein, AlbuRx,* others)
	Dextran
	Hydroxyethyl starch (*Hespan, Hextend*)

There are various crystalloid concentrations and combinations including: D50, D5NS, D5½NS, ½NS

ELECTROLYTE DISORDERS

Electrolyte abnormalities are common in hospitalized general medical and critically ill patients, though they can also occur in nonhospitalized patients. There are many causes (see specific electrolyte sections that follow). Electrolyte abnormalities can lead to severe complications (e.g., seizures, cardiac arrhythmias, coma, death). Electrolyte replacement protocols, used to correct deficiencies, should be followed to avoid toxicity. Electrolytes and their reference ranges are discussed in the Lab Values & Drug Monitoring chapter.

SODIUM

Hyponatremia

Hyponatremia (Na < 135 mEq/L) is usually not symptomatic until the sodium is ≤ 120 mEq/L, unless the serum level falls rapidly (e.g., acute hyponatremia). Symptoms most often result from cerebral edema, and an increased intracranial pressure, and can range from mild-moderate (e.g., headache, confusion, lethargy, gait disturbances) to severe (e.g., seizures, coma, respiratory arrest).

Hyponatremia is classified according to serum osmolality and volume status:

- Hypotonic hypervolemic hyponatremia is caused by fluid overload (e.g., cirrhosis, heart failure, renal failure). Diuresis with fluid restriction is the preferred treatment.

- Hypotonic isovolemic (euvolemic) hyponatremia can be caused by the syndrome of inappropriate antidiuretic hormone (SIADH). Treatment includes diuresis, restricting fluids and stopping drugs that can induce SIADH. Demeclocycline can be used off-label for SIADH.

- Hypotonic hypovolemic hyponatremia can be caused by diuretics, salt-wasting syndromes, adrenal insufficiency, blood loss or vomiting/diarrhea. The treatment is to correct any underlying causes and stop intake of hypotonic solutions; patients with acute hyponatremia, severe symptoms and/or Na < 120 mEq/L are candidates for hypertonic (3%) sodium chloride IV (see correction goals and risks below).

Hyponatremia should not be corrected too quickly (a typical goal is 4 – 8 mEq/L/24 hours). Correcting sodium more rapidly than 12 mEq/L/24 hours can cause osmotic demyelination syndrome (ODS) or central pontine myelinolysis, which can cause paralysis, seizures and death. Administration of desmopressin reduces water diuresis and can help avoid overcorrection.

The arginine vasopressin (AVP) receptor antagonists (conivaptan and tolvaptan) may be used to treat SIADH and hypervolemic hyponatremia. They increase excretion of free water while maintaining sodium. The role of these drugs is still being determined, as they are more expensive than 3% saline and use beyond 30 days with the oral product, tolvaptan (*Samsca*), is not recommended.

Arginine Vasopressin Receptor Antagonists

DRUG	DOSE	SAFETY/SIDE EFFECTS/MONITORING
Conivaptan *(Vaprisol)* Injection Dual AVP antagonist [vasopressin 1A (V1A) and vasopressin 2 (V2)]	LD: 20 mg IV over 30 minutes MD: 20 mg continuous IV infusion over 24 hours; can ↑ to 40 mg IV daily if Na does not ↑ at desired rate; do not use > 4 days CrCl < 30 mL/min: avoid ↓ dose in moderate and severe hepatic impairment	**CONTRAINDICATIONS** Hypovolemic hyponatremia, concurrent use with strong CYP450 3A4 inhibitors, anuria **WARNING** Overly rapid correction of hyponatremia (> 12 mEq/L/24 hours) is associated with ODS (life-threatening) **SIDE EFFECTS** Orthostatic hypotension, fever, hypokalemia, infusion site reactions (> 60%) **MONITORING** Rate of Na increase, BP, volume status, urine output
Tolvaptan *(Samsca)* Tablet Selective AVP antagonist [vasopressin 2 (V2) only]	15 mg PO daily; max 60 mg PO daily; limited to ≤ 30 days due to hepatotoxicity CrCl < 10 mL/min: avoid Avoid fluid restriction in the first 24 hours of therapy	**BOXED WARNINGS** Should be initiated and re-initiated in a hospital with close monitoring of serum Na Overly rapid correction of hyponatremia (> 12 mEq/L/24 hours) is associated with ODS (life-threatening); consider slower correction with severe malnutrition, alcoholism or advanced liver disease **CONTRAINDICATIONS** Patients who are unable to sense or respond appropriately to thirst, urgent need to raise Na, hypovolemic hyponatremia, use with strong CYP3A4 inhibitors, anuria **WARNINGS** Hepatotoxicity (avoid use > 30 days and in liver disease/cirrhosis) **SIDE EFFECTS** Thirst, nausea, dry mouth, polyuria, weakness, hyperglycemia, hypernatremia **MONITORING** Rate of Na increase, BP, volume status, urine output, signs of drug-induced hepatotoxicity

LD = loading dose, MD = maintenance dose

Hypernatremia

Hypernatremia (Na > 145 mEq/L) is associated with a water deficit and hypertonicity.

- Hypovolemic hypernatremia is caused by dehydration, vomiting or diarrhea and is treated with fluids.

- Hypervolemic hypernatremia is caused by intake of hypertonic fluids and is treated with diuresis.

- Isovolemic (euvolemic) hypernatremia is frequently caused by diabetes insipidus (DI), which can ↓ antidiuretic hormone (ADH). It is treated with desmopressin.

POTASSIUM

Hyperkalemia is often due to chronic kidney disease, discussed in the Renal Disease chapter. This section discusses hypokalemia.

Hypokalemia, or potassium (K) < 3.5 mEq/L, is a common occurrence in hospitalized patients. In general, a drop of 1 mEq/L in serum K below 3.5 mEq/L represents a total body deficit of 100 - 400 mEq. Management includes treating the underlying cause [e.g., metabolic alkalosis, overdiuresis, medications (such as amphotericin, insulin)] and administering oral or IV potassium. The oral route is preferred for potassium replacement when feasible. Oral potassium salt formulations are reviewed in the Chronic Heart Failure chapter. Some hospitals use potassium sliding scales that allow a healthcare provider (usually a nurse) to administer a certain dose of potassium based on the serum potassium level in patients with normal kidney function (see example protocol below).

EXAMPLE POTASSIUM REPLACEMENT PROTOCOL

Step 1: check phosphate level. If > 2.5 mg/dL, proceed to step 2. If ≤ 2.5 mg/dL, use separate potassium phosphate replacement protocol.

Step 2: provide replacement doses as follows.

SERUM POTASSIUM (MEQ/L)	INSTRUCTION
< 2.6	100 mEq KCl IV; contact MD
2.6-2.9	80 mEq KCl IV; contact MD
3.0-3.2	60 mEq KCl PO/IV
3.3-3.5	40 mEq KCl PO/IV

Step 3: order follow-up labs. For K < 3.2 mEq/L, recheck immediately and with AM labs. For K ≥ 3.2 mEq/L, recheck with AM labs only.

Potassium chloride premixed IV solutions are generally used for IV replacement. Safe recommendations for administration of IV potassium through a peripheral line include a maximum infusion rate ≤ 10 mEq/hr and a maximum concentration of 10 mEq/100 mL. More rapid infusions and higher concentrations may be warranted in severe or symptomatic hypokalemia; these require a central line and cardiac monitoring. IV potassium can be fatal if administered undiluted or via IV push. When hypokalemia is resistant to treatment, serum magnesium should be checked. Magnesium is necessary for potassium uptake; hypomagnesemia can worsen and/or prevent correction of hypokalemia. Magnesium should be replaced first when both hypokalemia and hypomagnesemia are present.

MAGNESIUM

Hypomagnesemia, or magnesium (Mg) < 1.3 mEq/L, is more common than hypermagnesemia, which is most often due to renal insufficiency. Common causes of hypomagnesemia include chronic alcohol use, diuretics, vomiting and diarrhea. When serum Mg is ≤ 1 mEq/L with life-threatening symptoms (e.g., seizures, arrhythmias), IV magnesium sulfate replacement is recommended. When serum Mg is < 1 mEq/L without life-threatening symptoms, therapy can be administered IV or IM. When serum Mg is > 1 mEq/L and < 1.5 mEq/L, magnesium is replaced orally, most commonly with magnesium oxide. Magnesium replacement regimens should continue for 5 days to fully replace body stores.

PHOSPHORUS

Hyperphosphatemia is often due to chronic kidney disease, and is discussed in the Renal Disease chapter. This section discusses hypophosphatemia.

Hypophosphatemia is considered severe and is usually symptomatic when serum phosphate (PO4) is < 1 mg/dL. Symptoms can include muscle weakness and respiratory failure. Hypophosphatemia can be caused by phosphate-binding drugs (e.g., calcium salts, sevelamer), chronic alcohol intake and hyperparathyroidism. When serum PO4 is ≤ 1 mg/dL, IV phosphorus is used for replacement. Many regimens can be used, but 0.08 - 0.16 mmol/kg in 500 mL of NS or D5W over 6 hours is common. Patients must be carefully monitored and additional doses may be necessary. Patients with hypophosphatemia often have hypokalemia and hypomagnesemia that will require correction. Less severe hypophosphatemia can be treated orally and full replacement often takes one week or longer.

OTHER DRUG TREATMENTS IN HOSPITALIZED PATIENTS

VTE PROPHYLAXIS

People in the hospital often have limited mobility and other risk factors for developing a venous thromboembolism (VTE). For this reason, the need for VTE prophylaxis should be evaluated in all inpatients. Refer to the Anticoagulation chapter for a discussion on VTE prophylaxis treatment.

INTRAVENOUS IMMUNOGLOBULIN

Intravenous immune globulin (IVIG or IGIV) contains pooled immunoglobulin (IgG) that is administered intravenously. The IgG is extracted from the plasma of a thousand or more blood donors (this is the FDA's minimum; typically the IVIG is derived from between 3,000 – 10,000 donors). IVIG is given as plasma protein replacement therapy for immune-deficient patients who have decreased or abolished antibody production capabilities. Initially, IVIG was used only for immunodeficiency conditions. Currently, IVIG has several FDA-approved indications and is used for a variety of off-label indications (e.g., multiple sclerosis, myasthenia gravis, Guillain-Barré syndrome) with varying results. IVIG treatment can impair the response to vaccination (refer to the Immunizations chapter for a discussion on the timing of vaccinations and antibody-containing products).

DRUG	DOSING	SAFETY/SIDE EFFECTS/MONITORING
Intravenous immunoglobulin (*Gammagard, Gamunex-C, Octagam, Privigen,* others)	Indication and product specific IBW or AdjBW is usually used to calculate the dose Use a slower infusion rate in renal and CV disease patients Do not freeze, shake or heat	**BOXED WARNINGS** Acute renal dysfunction can occur (rare) and has been associated with fatalities; it usually occurs within 7 days (more likely with products stabilized with sucrose); use caution in the elderly, those with renal disease, diabetes, volume depletion, sepsis, paraproteinemia or taking nephrotoxic medications Thrombosis can occur even without risk factors; for patients at risk, administer the minimum dose **CONTRAINDICATIONS** IgA deficiency (use the product with the lowest amount of IgA) **WARNINGS** Use with caution in CV disease (use isotonic products and a lower infusion rate) **SIDE EFFECTS** Headache, nausea, diarrhea, injection site reaction, infusion reaction (facial flushing, chest tightness, fever, chills, hypotension – slow/stop infusion), renal failure or blood dyscrasias (both rare) **MONITORING** Renal function, urine output, volume status, Hgb **NOTES** Patients should be asked about past IVIG infusions, including product used and any reactions that occurred; a slower titration and premedication may be needed Lot numbers of administered IVIG products must be tracked (it is a blood product)

CRITICAL CARE

For life-threatening injuries or illnesses that require specialized care, treatment is often initiated pre-hospital or in an emergency department and continued in the ICU. Large hospitals have specialized ICUs for different types of care (e.g., medical, surgical, cardiovascular, trauma, pediatric, neonatal). Many medications in the ICU are administered IV with an infusion pump, which bypasses gut/absorption issues and allows for a rapid onset of effect, easy titration and continuous administration. Often, a central line is used; this is especially important with vesicants and IV solutions that can contribute to phlebitis.

The ICU mortality rate in the U.S. is ~15%. The Acute Physiologic Assessment and Chronic Health Evaluation II (APACHE II) is a scoring tool used to determine prognosis and estimate ICU mortality risk. With adequate care, most patients will recover and return home. Conditions that commonly require ICU care are addressed in the rest of this chapter.

ICU MEDICATIONS THAT TARGET THE SYMPATHETIC NERVOUS SYSTEM

VASOPRESSORS

Most vasopressors work by stimulating alpha receptors; this causes peripheral vasoconstriction (think "pressing down on the vasculature") and increases systemic vascular resistance (SVR), which increases blood pressure (BP). Vasopressors that stimulate beta receptors can increase heart rate (HR) and cardiac output (CO). Phenylephrine is a pure alpha-agonist that increases SVR without increasing HR. Epinephrine and norepinephrine are mixed alpha- and beta-agonists, causing both an increase in SVR as well as an increase in CO and HR. Dopamine is a natural precursor of norepinephrine and has dose-dependent receptor effects. Vasopressin and angiotensin II both increase SVR by unique mechanisms. Vasopressin acts directly on vasopressin receptors. Angiotensin II *(Giapreza)* raises blood pressure by vasoconstriction and aldosterone release, which results in sodium and water retention. Angiotensin II, a natural hormone produced in the renin-angiotensin-aldosterone system, is discussed in detail in the Hypertension chapter. A review of the nervous system and receptor pharmacology can be found in the Basic Science Concepts chapter.

DOPAMINE DOSING

Dopamine stimulates different receptors depending on the dose.

- Low (renal) dose: 1-4 mcg/kg/min
  - ❑ Dopamine-1 agonist
- Medium dose: 5-10 mcg/kg/min
  - ❑ Beta-1 agonist
- High dose: 10-20 mcg/kg/min
  - ❑ Alpha-1 agonist

DRUG	MOA	SAFETY/SIDE EFFECTS/MONITORING
Dopamine	Dose-dependent, see Study Tip Gal	**BOXED WARNING** Dopamine and norepinephrine have a boxed warning regarding extravasation; all vasopressors are vesicants when administered IV; treat extravasation with phentolamine **WARNINGS** Use extreme caution in patients taking an MAO inhibitor; prolonged hypertension may result (dopamine, epinephrine and norepinephrine)
Epinephrine *(Adrenalin)* **EpiPen**, others – for anaphylaxis	Alpha-1, beta-1, beta-2 agonist	**SIDE EFFECTS** Arrhythmias, tachycardia (especially dopamine, epinephrine), necrosis (gangrene), bradycardia (phenylephrine), hyperglycemia (epinephrine), tachyphylaxis, peripheral and gut ischemia
Norepinephrine *(Levophed)*	Alpha-1 agonist activity is > beta-1 agonist activity	**MONITORING** Continuous BP monitoring (with continuous infusions), HR, mean arterial pressure (MAP), ECG, urine output, infusion site for extravasation
Phenylephrine	Alpha-1 agonist	**NOTES** Solutions should not be used if they are discolored or contain a precipitate All vasopressors are Y-site compatible with each other (except angiotensin II) Some institutions use non-weight-based infusions (mcg/min) instead of weight-based infusions (mcg/kg/min)
Vasopressin *(Vasostrict)* Known as arginine vasopressin (AVP) and antidiuretic hormone (ADH)	Vasopressin receptor agonist Vasoconstrictor, no inotropic or chronotropic effects	All vasopressors should be administered via central IV line There is no clear evidence that low dose dopamine (renal dosing) provides benefit Epinephrine used for IV push is 0.1 mg/mL (1:10,000 ratio strength); epinephrine used for IM injection or compounding IV products is 1 mg/mL (1:1,000 ratio strength); ratio strength has been removed from labeling per the FDA

Extravasation

Many drugs used in the ICU, including vasopressors, are vesicants that cause severe tissue damage/necrosis with extravasation (leakage of drug from the blood vessel into the surrounding tissue). This is a medical emergency. To reduce the risk, every attempt should be made to infuse vasopressors through a central line. Vasopressor extravasation should be treated with phentolamine, an alpha-1 blocker that antagonizes the effects of the vasopressor. If extravasation occurs with norepinephrine, epinephrine or phenylephrine, stop the infusion but do not disconnect the needle/cannula and do not flush the line; instead, gently aspirate (remove) the drug. Nitroglycerin ointment is sometimes used topically as an alternative if phentolamine is unavailable.

VASODILATORS

Vasodilators administered by continuous IV infusion include nitroglycerin (NTG) and nitroprusside. Frequent or continuous BP monitoring is required when using IV vasodilators, and doses must be decreased if there is hypotension or worsening renal function. NTG is often used when there is active myocardial ischemia or uncontrolled hypertension, but effectiveness may be limited to 24 – 48 hours due to tachyphylaxis (tolerance).

Nitroprusside is a mixed (equal) arterial and venous vasodilator at all doses. It has a greater effect on BP than NTG. It should not be used in active myocardial ischemia because it can cause blood to be diverted away from the diseased coronary arteries ("coronary steal"). The metabolism of nitroprusside results in thiocyanate and cyanide formation, which can cause toxicity in patients with renal or hepatic insufficiency, respectively. Hydroxocobalamin can be administered to reduce the risk of thiocyanate toxicity or to treat cyanide toxicity. Sodium thiosulfate + sodium nitrite (Nithiodote) is used for cyanide toxicity (see the Toxicology & Antidotes chapter).

DRUG	MOA	SAFETY/SIDE EFFECTS/MONITORING
Nitroglycerin See the Stable Ischemic Heart Disease chapter for other formulations	Low doses: venous vasodilator High doses: arterial vasodilator	**CONTRAINDICATIONS** SBP < 90 mmHg, use with PDE-5 inhibitors or riociguat **WARNINGS** Severe hypotension and ↑ intracranial pressure (ICP) **SIDE EFFECTS** Headache, tachycardia, tachyphylaxis (within 24-48 hours of continuous administration), lightheadedness **MONITORING** BP, HR **NOTES** Requires a non-PVC container (e.g., glass, polyolefin); use administration sets (tubing) intended for NTG
Nitroprusside **(Nipride)**	Mixed (equal) arterial and venous vasodilator	**BOXED WARNINGS** Metabolism produces cyanide (use the lowest dose for the shortest duration necessary), excessive hypotension (continuous BP monitoring required), not for direct injection (must be further diluted; D5W preferred) **WARNINGS** ↑ ICP **SIDE EFFECTS** Headache, tachycardia, thiocyanate/cyanide toxicity (risk ↑ in renal and hepatic impairment) **MONITORING** BP (continuous), HR, renal/hepatic function, urine output, s/sx of thiocyanate/cyanide toxicity, acid-base status, venous oxygen concentration **NOTES** Requires light protection during administration; use only clear solutions, a blue color indicates degradation to cyanide – do not use

INOTROPES

Intravenous inotropes <u>increase the contractility</u> of the heart. <u>Dobutamine</u> is a <u>beta-1 agonist</u> that increases HR and the force of myocardial contraction, which increases CO. It has weak beta-2 (vasodilation) and alpha-1 agonist activity. <u>Milrinone</u> is a selective <u>phosphodiesterase-3 inhibitor</u> in cardiac and vascular tissue. It produces inotropic effects with <u>significant vasodilation</u>. Dobutamine and milrinone should only be used when BP is adequate because they produce vasodilation.

DRUG	MOA	SAFETY/SIDE EFFECTS/MONITORING
Dobutamine	<u>Beta-1 agonist</u> with some beta-2 and alpha-1 agonism	**SIDE EFFECTS** Dobutamine: hyper/hypotension, ventricular arrhythmias, tachycardia, angina Milrinone: ventricular arrhythmias, hypotension **MONITORING** Continuous BP and ECG monitoring, HR, central venous pressure (CVP), MAP, urine output, LFTs and renal function (with milrinone)
Milrinone	<u>Phosphodiesterase-3 (PDE-3) inhibitor</u>	**NOTES** Milrinone: dose must be reduced for renal impairment Dobutamine may turn <u>slightly pink due to oxidation</u>, but potency is not lost Dobutamine and milrinone are often referred to as "inodilators" Risk of hypotension; use for inotropic effect only after adequate perfusion is achieved

TYPES OF SHOCK

Shock is a medical emergency common in ICU patients. It is characterized by <u>hypoperfusion</u>, usually in the setting of <u>hypotension</u>, defined as SBP < 90 mmHg or MAP < 70 mmHg. There are four main types of shock:

- Hypovolemic (e.g., hemorrhagic)
- Distributive (e.g., septic, anaphylactic)
- Cardiogenic (e.g., post-myocardial infarction)
- Obstructive (e.g., massive pulmonary embolism)

The diagnosis of shock is based on hemodynamic parameters, and more than one type of shock can occur at the same time. Drugs used for shock may also be used for advanced cardiac life support (ACLS)/cardiac arrest, hypotension during surgery/anesthesia, acute decompensated heart failure (ADHF) and other critical conditions.

HYPOVOLEMIC SHOCK

To treat hypovolemic shock, restore intravascular volume, and improve oxygen-carrying capacity. <u>Fluid resuscitation</u> with <u>crystalloids</u> is generally recommended <u>first-line</u> for <u>hypovolemic shock</u> that is <u>not caused by hemorrhage</u>. Blood products (e.g., packed red blood cells, fresh frozen plasma) should be administered in hypovolemic shock with intravascular depletion due to bleeding. If the patient does not respond to the initial crystalloid or blood product therapy ("fluid challenge"), then vasopressors may be indicated. <u>Vasopressors</u> will not be effective unless the <u>intravascular volume</u> is <u>adequate</u>.

DISTRIBUTIVE SHOCK

Distributive shock is characterized by low SVR, and initially high CO followed by low or normal CO. <u>Septic</u>, anaphylactic and neurogenic shock are examples of distributive shock.

Sepsis and Septic Shock

<u>Sepsis</u> is defined as <u>life-threatening organ dysfunction</u> caused by a <u>dysregulated host response to infection</u> (see the <u>Study Tip Gal</u> on the next page for common causes of ICU infections). Several screening tools, each using some different combination of criteria (e.g., tachypnea, tachycardia, hypotension, fever, decreased mental status), are available to evaluate for sepsis and infection-induced organ dysfunction. Tools such as the National Early Warning Score (NEWS) and systemic inflammatory response syndrome (SIRS) criteria are recommended over the quick Sequential Organ Failure Assessment (qSOFA).

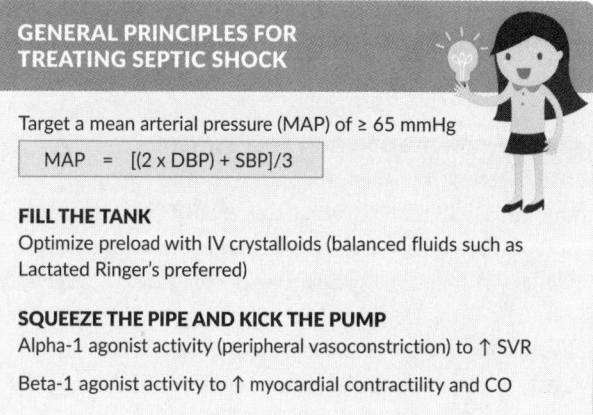

GENERAL PRINCIPLES FOR TREATING SEPTIC SHOCK

Target a mean arterial pressure (MAP) of ≥ 65 mmHg

$$MAP = [(2 \times DBP) + SBP]/3$$

FILL THE TANK
Optimize preload with IV crystalloids (balanced fluids such as Lactated Ringer's preferred)

SQUEEZE THE PIPE AND KICK THE PUMP
Alpha-1 agonist activity (peripheral vasoconstriction) to ↑ SVR

Beta-1 agonist activity to ↑ myocardial contractility and CO

TWO COMMON CAUSES OF ICU INFECTIONS

Mechanical ventilation: pushes air into the lungs for patients who cannot breathe on their own.

Mechanical ventilators are called respirators. Air flows into the trachea through an endotracheal tube (ET tube) placed through the mouth or nose. This is called intubation. "Weaning" refers to the process of getting the patient off the ventilator when they are ready to breathe on their own again.

↑ *time on ventilator* = ↑ *risk of infection, including lung infections*

Pseudomonas (and a few other organisms) thrive in the moist air in the ventilator.

Indwelling urinary catheter.

Intubated patients have an indwelling catheter that is inserted into the bladder to drain urine.

Foley catheters are the most common type.

↑ *time with foley catheter* = ↑ *risk of bladder infection*

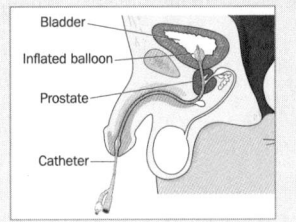

Bladder
Inflated balloon
Prostate
Catheter

© Blamb/Shutterstock.com

Septic shock is sepsis in the presence of persistent hypotension, requiring a vasopressor to maintain MAP ≥ 65 mmHg, and a serum lactate level ≥ 2 mEq/L despite adequate fluid resuscitation.

The Surviving Sepsis Campaign is an initiative that prompts the use of selected evidence-based interventions (called "bundles") to reduce mortality from sepsis and septic shock. These bundles include early administration of broad-spectrum antibiotics and fluid resuscitation with IV crystalloids. When combined with additional measures, this is associated with lower overall mortality. If adequate perfusion cannot be maintained with IV crystalloids, vasopressors are used. Norepinephrine is considered the vasopressor of choice in septic shock. Vasopressin is commonly used in addition to norepinephrine.

ACUTE DECOMPENSATED HEART FAILURE AND CARDIOGENIC SHOCK

Patients with heart failure may experience episodes of worsening symptoms, such as sudden weight gain, an inability to lie flat without becoming short of breath, decreasing functionality (e.g., unable to perform their daily routine), increasing shortness of breath and fatigue. This is called acute decompensated heart failure (ADHF); when hypotension and hypoperfusion are also present, it is called cardiogenic shock.

Clinical Presentation and Assessment

ADHF is caused by worsening HF, a cardiac event (e.g., MI, arrhythmia, valvular disease, uncontrolled hypertension) or a non-cardiac cause (e.g., non-adherence with medications or dietary restrictions, worsening renal function, infection, illicit drug use). Negative inotropes (e.g., non-DHP CCBs), drugs that cause fluid retention (e.g., NSAIDs) and cardiotoxic drugs can worsen cardiac function and cause/exacerbate HF.

ADHF presents with volume overload, hypoperfusion or both. Some patients require invasive monitoring with a catheter

that is guided through the right side of the heart into the pulmonary artery, called a Swan-Ganz or pulmonary artery catheter. The catheter provides hemodynamic measurements of congestion (pulmonary capillary wedge pressure, or PCWP), hypoperfusion (cardiac output) and other measurements (e.g., SVR, CVP) useful for guiding treatment. Treatment of ADHF generally consists of diuretics, inotropes and vasodilators, used in various combinations depending on the patient's symptoms (see the Study Tip Gal below). Beta-blockers should only be stopped in an ADHF episode if hypotension or hypoperfusion is present.

Treating Volume Overload

ADHF most commonly presents with volume overload. Volume overload is treated with diuretics and possibly IV vasodilators. Loop diuretics are initially given IV since volume overload also affects the vessels of the gut and can decrease their oral absorption. If diuretic resistance develops, the dose can be increased or a thiazide-type diuretic (e.g., metolazone, chlorothiazide) can be added to the loop diuretic.

TREATING ADHF

Patients with edema (pulmonary or lower extremity), jugular venous distention (JVD) and/or ascites are **VOLUME OVERLOADED**; treatment options include:

- Loop diuretics

- Vasodilators can be added (NTG, nitroprusside)

Patients with ↓ renal function, altered mental status and/or cool extremities have **HYPOPERFUSION***; treatment options include:

- Inotropes (dobutamine, milrinone)

- If the patient becomes hypotensive, consider adding a vasopressor (dopamine, norepinephrine, phenylephrine)

Some patients experience both **VOLUME OVERLOAD** and **HYPOPERFUSION**; treatment options include:

- A combination of agents above

*Avoid vasodilators; these can ↓ BP and worsen hypoperfusion

Treating Hypoperfusion

The most common cause of cardiogenic shock (or ADHF with hypoperfusion) is an MI, with resulting failure of the left ventricle. Cardiogenic shock requires treatment with vasopressors and/or inotropes. The vasodilatory and inotropic properties of dobutamine and milrinone make them uniquely suited to treat ADHF in patients with adequate BP and symptoms of both congestion and hypoperfusion. If BP is inadequate, inotropes will often be used in combination with vasopressors. Inotropes are associated with worse heart failure outcomes and should be stopped as soon as the patient is stabilized.

OTHER COMMON ICU CONDITIONS

PAIN

IV opioids (e.g., morphine, hydromorphone, fentanyl) are first-line for analgesia (to reduce pain) in the ICU, but the principles of pain management are the same for everyone (see the Pain chapter for a full discussion of opioids). The pharmacokinetic properties of the drug and the renal/hepatic function of the patient will dictate the choice of agent because all IV opioids exhibit similar analgesic efficacy when dosed correctly. Adjuvants (e.g., acetaminophen, NSAIDs) may be appropriate depending on the type of pain. An assessment of pain (with a validated pain scale) should be performed at least every 2 – 4 hours in the ICU, and all ICU patients should be evaluated for pain at rest. Analgesia-based sedation or "analgosedation" is a sedation strategy that uses analgesia first to relieve pain and discomfort, which are the primary causes of agitation. Compared to benzodiazepines, analgosedation is associated with less time on the ventilator and shorter ICU length of stay (LOS).

AGITATION

Sedation is necessary for some ICU patients to maintain synchronized breathing with the ventilator (prevent "bucking" the ventilator) and to limit suffering in the harsh ICU environment. Agitation is managed with benzodiazepines (lorazepam, midazolam) and/or non-benzodiazepine hypnotics (propofol, dexmedetomidine). Non-benzodiazepines (propofol and dexmedetomidine) are preferred for sedation and are associated with improved ICU outcomes, shorter mechanical ventilation duration and decreased LOS. Dexmedetomidine (Precedex) is the only sedative approved for use in intubated and non-intubated patients. Benzodiazepines have an important role in sedation in the presence of seizures or alcohol/benzodiazepine withdrawal. Benzodiazepines are discussed in the Anxiety chapter.

Sedatives are used with validated sedation scales that allow for titration to light or deep sedation. Light sedation (unless contraindicated) is preferred. Some commonly used sedation scales are the Richmond Agitation Sedation Scale (RASS – see table below), the Ramsay Agitation Scale (RAS) and the Riker Sedation-Agitation Scale (SAS). In some situations, the Glasgow Coma Scale is used to determine the level of consciousness (often after traumatic brain injury). Patients should be monitored every 2 – 3 hours while receiving sedation to make sure they are receiving the least amount of drug to keep them calm and pain-free. Daily interruptions ("sedation vacations") of continuous infusions of sedative drugs are used to assess the readiness to wean off/stop the sedative as soon as possible.

DELIRIUM

Delirium assessment is required, as it affects up to 80% of ventilated ICU patients and is associated with increased mortality and LOS. Early mobilization and control of the patient's environment (light, noise, stimuli) are recommended to decrease delirium incidence, but no medications are recommended for prevention. Providing sedation with non-benzodiazepines may reduce the incidence of delirium and/or shorten the duration in patients who already have it. There is little evidence to support the use of haloperidol for treatment of ICU delirium, although this is common in practice. Atypical antipsychotics, primarily quetiapine, which is mildly sedating and has little risk for movement disorders, can be useful (see the Schizophrenia/Psychosis chapter).

RICHMOND AGITATION AND SEDATION SCALE (RASS)

SCORE	TERM	DESCRIPTION
+4	Combative	Overtly combative, violent, immediate danger to staff
+3	Very agitated	Pulls or removes tube(s) or catheter(s); aggressive
+2	Agitated	Frequent, non-purposeful movement, fights ventilator
+1	Restless	Anxious, but movements not aggressive or vigorous
0	Alert and calm	
-1	Drowsy	Not fully alert, but has sustained awakening (eye opening/eye contact) to voice (≥ 10 seconds)
-2	Light sedation	Briefly awakens with eye contact to voice (< 10 seconds)
-3	Moderate sedation	Movement or eye opening to voice (but no eye contact)
-4	Deep sedation	No response to voice, but movement or eye opening to physical stimulation
-5	Unarousable	No response to voice or physical stimulation

DRUG	SAFETY/SIDE EFFECTS/MONITORING
Pain/Analgesia	
Fentanyl (Sublimaze) **Hydromorphone (Dilaudid)** **Morphine (Duramorph, Infumorph)** Remifentanil (Ultiva) Oliceridine (Olinvyk)	See the Pain chapter for additional information In critical care patients, monitor BP, HR, respiration, pain and sedation Fentanyl: less hypotension (no histamine release) than morphine; 100x more potent than morphine; rapid onset and short duration of action (half-life increases with duration of infusion); can accumulate in hepatic impairment; CYP3A4 substrate and potential for numerous drug interactions Hydromorphone: very potent, dose carefully
Agitation/Sedation	
Dexmedetomidine (Precedex) Alpha-2 adrenergic agonist	**WARNINGS** Use with caution in patients with hepatic impairment, diabetes, heart block, bradycardia, severe ventricular dysfunction, hypovolemia or chronic hypertension **SIDE EFFECTS** Hypo/hypertension, bradycardia, dry mouth, nausea, constipation **MONITORING** BP, HR, sedation scale **NOTES** Does not require refrigeration Duration of infusion should not exceed 24 hours per FDA labeling Used for sedation in intubated and non-intubated patients; patients are arousable and alert when stimulated (less respiratory depression than other sedatives)
Propofol (Diprivan) Short-acting general anesthetic	**CONTRAINDICATIONS** Hypersensitivity to egg, egg product, soy or soy product **SIDE EFFECTS** Hypotension, apnea, hypertriglyceridemia, green urine/hair/nail beds, propofol-related infusion syndrome (PRIS – rare, but can be fatal), myoclonus, pancreatitis, pain on injection (particularly peripheral vein), QT prolongation **MONITORING** BP, HR, RR, sedation scale, triglycerides (if administered longer than 2 days), signs and symptoms of pancreatitis **NOTES** Shake well before use; do not use if there is separation of phases in the emulsion Use strict aseptic technique due to potential for bacterial growth; discard vial and tubing within 12 hours of use If transferred to a syringe prior to administration, must discard syringe within 6 hours Do not use a filter < 5 microns for administration Does not require refrigeration Oil-in-water emulsion (opaque, white solution); provides 1.1 kcal/mL
Lorazepam (Ativan, Lorazepam Intensol) Benzodiazepine	**NOTES** Injection is formulated in propylene glycol; total daily dose as low as 1 mg/kg/day can cause propylene glycol toxicity (acute renal failure and metabolic acidosis) In critical care patients, monitor BP, HR, RR, sedation scale, s/sx of propylene glycol toxicity (BUN, SCr, lactate, anion gap) if receiving continuous infusion; limit use for delirium See the Anxiety chapter for additional information

DRUG	SAFETY/SIDE EFFECTS/MONITORING
Midazolam (Versed*, Nayzilam) Benzodiazepine Used specifically in acute care settings	**BOXED WARNINGS** Respiratory depression, respiratory arrest, apnea; start at lower end of dosing range in debilitated patients and geriatric population; do not administer by rapid IV injection in neonates **CONTRAINDICATIONS** Intrathecal or epidural administration (benzyl alcohol in formulation), acute narrow-angle glaucoma, do not use with potent CYP3A4 inhibitors **SIDE EFFECTS** Hypotension **MONITORING** BP, HR, RR, sedation scale **NOTES** Shorter acting than lorazepam if patient has normal organ function (no hepatic or renal impairment or HF) Can accumulate in obese patients (highly lipophilic) and renal impairment (active metabolite) – caution with continuous infusion
Etomidate (Amidate) Nonbarbiturate hypnotic Ultra short-acting; used as an induction agent for intubation	**WARNING** Inhibits 11-B-hydroxylase which can lead to ↓ cortisol production for up to 24 hours **MONITORING** S/sx of adrenal insufficiency (hypotension, hyperkalemia), respiratory status, BP, HR, infusion site, sedation scale
Ketamine (Ketalar) NMDA receptor antagonist Used as an induction agent for intubation; used off-label for continuous sedation, pain and other indications	**WARNINGS** Emergence reactions (vivid dreams, hallucinations, delirium), cerebrospinal fluid (CSF) pressure elevation, respiratory depression/apnea, dependence/tolerance **MONITORING** BP, HR, respiratory status, emergence reactions, sedation scale **NOTES** Pretreatment with benzodiazepine can ↓ incidence of emergence reactions (see warnings) by 50%
Delirium	
Haloperidol (Haldol*)	See the Schizophrenia/Psychosis chapter Commonly used, but not recommended for treatment of delirium in current guidelines
Quetiapine (Seroquel)	See the Schizophrenia/Psychosis chapter May decrease duration of delirium

*Brand discontinued but name still used in practice.

STRESS ULCERS

In patients with critical illness, blood flow is diverted to the body's major organs and there is reduced blood flow to the gut. This results in a breakdown of gastric mucosal defense mechanisms, including prostaglandin synthesis, bicarbonate production and cell turnover, which can lead to stress ulcers.

Histamine-2 receptor antagonists (H2RAs) and proton pump inhibitors (PPIs) are recommended to prevent stress-related mucosal damage in patients with risk factors (see box).

RISK FACTORS FOR THE DEVELOPMENT OF STRESS ULCERS	
Mechanical ventilation > 48H	Major burns
Coagulopathy	Acute renal failure
Sepsis	High dose systemic steroids
Traumatic brain injury	

H2RAs can cause thrombocytopenia and mental status changes in the elderly or those with renal impairment. Tachyphylaxis has also been reported. PPIs are associated with an increased risk of GI infections (C. difficile), fractures and nosocomial pneumonia. These drugs are discussed further in the Gastroesophageal Reflux Disease & Peptic Ulcer Disease chapter.

ADDITIONAL DRUGS USED IN THE ICU AND OPERATING ROOM

ANESTHETICS

Anesthetics are used for a variety of effects, including to numb an area (local anesthesia), block pain (regional anesthesia) or cause a reversible loss of consciousness and sleepiness during surgery (general anesthesia). Anesthetics can be given via several routes of administration: topical, inhaled, intravenous, epidural or spinal.

Increasingly, anesthetics are being used with opioids to reduce the opioid requirement for pain control. They work by decreasing the neuronal permeability to sodium ions, which blocks the initiation and conduction of nerve impulses. Most patients receiving anesthetics must have vital signs (especially respiration) continuously monitored. The main

COMMONLY USED ANESTHETICS
LOCAL
■ Lidocaine *(Xylocaine)*, benzocaine, liposomal bupivacaine *(Exparel)*
INHALED
■ Desflurane *(Suprane)*, sevoflurane *(Ultane)*, isoflurane *(Forane)*, nitrous oxide
INJECTABLE
■ Bupivacaine *(Marcaine, Sensorcaine)*, lidocaine *(Xylocaine)*, ropivacaine *(Naropin)*

side effects of anesthetics include hypotension, bradycardia, nausea, vomiting and a mild drop in body temperature that can cause shivering. Overdose can cause respiratory depression. Allergic reactions are possible, and though rare, inhaled anesthetics can cause malignant hyperthermia.

It is important to verify use of the correct anesthetic product, concentration and route of administration. Bupivacaine, commonly used in epidurals, can be fatal if administered intravenously. Lidocaine should not be given by dual routes of administration (e.g., IV and topical). Lidocaine/epinephrine combination products are used for some local procedures that require an anesthetic, such as inserting an IV line. The epinephrine is added for vasoconstriction, which keeps the lidocaine localized to the area where the numbing is needed. Deaths have occurred due to mix-ups with epinephrine products and lidocaine/epinephrine products.

NEUROMUSCULAR BLOCKING AGENTS

Patients can require the use of a neuromuscular blocking agent (NMBA) in surgery conducted under general anesthesia, to facilitate mechanical ventilation, to treat muscle spasms (tetany) or to prevent shivering when undergoing therapeutic hypothermia after cardiac arrest. The use of NMBAs is typically recommended when other methods have proven ineffective; they are not routinely used in all critically ill patients. NMBAs cause paralysis of the skeletal muscle, including those used for respiration (e.g., the diaphragm), and patients must be mechanically ventilated. Since they have no effect on pain or sedation, patients should receive adequate sedation and analgesia prior to starting an NMBA. NMBAs are considered high-risk medications by ISMP; all agents should be labeled with a colored auxiliary label stating "WARNING, PARALYZING AGENT" and care should be taken to separate NMBAs from other solutions to avoid confusion and inadvertent administration to a patient for whom it was not intended.

There are two types of NMBAs: depolarizing and non-depolarizing. Succinylcholine is the only available depolarizing agent; resembling ACh, succinylcholine binds to and activates the ACh receptors and desensitizes them. It is typically reserved for intubation and is not used for continuous neuromuscular blockade. Succinylcholine has been associated with causing malignant hyperthermia (particularly when used with inhaled anesthetics).

The non-depolarizing NMBAs work by binding to the ACh receptor, blocking the actions of endogenous ACh. Patients receiving NMBAs are unable to breathe, move, blink or cough. Special care must be taken to protect the skin, lubricate the eyes and suction the airway frequently to clear secretions while NMBAs are being used. Glycopyrrolate is an anticholinergic drug that can be used to reduce secretions. Numerous medications can enhance the neuromuscular blocking activity of the NMBAs, leading to toxicity (e.g., aminoglycosides, calcium channel blockers, polymyxins, cyclosporine, inhaled anesthetics, lithium, quinidine, vancomycin). Monitoring for the appropriate depth of paralysis is recommended (see the Toxicology & Antidotes chapter for NMBA antidotes).

DRUG	SAFETY/SIDE EFFECTS/MONITORING
Depolarizing NMBA	
Succinylcholine (*Quelicin Anectine*)	Short-acting, fast onset (30-60 seconds)
Non-Depolarizing NMBAs	
For all non-depolarizing NMBAs	**SIDE EFFECTS** Flushing, bradycardia, hypotension, tachyphylaxis, acute quadriplegic myopathy syndrome with long-term use **MONITORING** Peripheral nerve stimulator to assess depth of paralysis during continuous infusions [also called train-of-four (TOF)], vital signs (BP, HR, RR)
Atracurium	Short t½; intermediate-acting; metabolized by Hofmann elimination (independent of renal and hepatic function)
Cisatracurium (*Nimbex*)	Short t½; intermediate-acting; metabolized by Hofmann elimination (independent of renal and hepatic function)
Pancuronium	Long-acting; can accumulate in renal or hepatic dysfunction; ↑ HR
Rocuronium	Intermediate-acting
Vecuronium	Intermediate-acting; can accumulate in renal or hepatic dysfunction

HEMOSTATIC AGENTS

The term hemostasis means causing bleeding to stop. Hemostatic methods include simple manual pressure with one finger, electrical tissue cauterization, or the systemic administration of blood products (transfusions) or hemostatic agents. The systemic hemostatic drugs work by inhibiting fibrinolysis or enhancing coagulation. Several factor products are available to treat hemorrhage in patients with hemophilia or rare factor deficiencies (*FEIBA, Coagadex, Adynovate*). Some hemostatic drugs (e.g., *Praxbind, Andexxa*) have been approved as reversal agents for specific anticoagulants (see the Anticoagulation chapter).

There are many topical hemostatic agents, most of which are used surgically. These include thrombin in bandages, liquids and sprays, fibrin sealants, acrylates and a few others (names often include "throm": *Recothrom, Thrombin-JMI*). A few topical hemostatics are OTC.

DRUG	SAFETY/SIDE EFFECTS/MONITORING
Aminocaproic acid (*Amicar*) Tablet, solution, injection	**CONTRAINDICATIONS** Disseminated intravascular coagulation (without heparin); active intravascular clotting process **SIDE EFFECTS** Injection-site reactions, thrombosis **NOTES** FDA-approved for excessive bleeding associated with cardiac surgery, liver cirrhosis and urinary fibrinolysis. Do not use in patients with active clots, and do not give with factor IX complex concentrates due to ↑ risk for thrombosis.
Tranexamic acid (***Cyklokapron***, injection) (***Lysteda***, tablet)	**CONTRAINDICATIONS** IV: acquired defective color vision, active intravascular clotting, subarachnoid hemorrhage Oral: previous or current thromboembolic disease, current use of combination hormonal contraception **SIDE EFFECTS** Injection: vascular occlusion, thrombosis Oral: retinal clotting **NOTES** *Lysteda* (oral) is approved for heavy menstrual bleeding (menorrhagia). The injection is approved for bleeding with hemophilia and is often used off-label to control surgical bleeding and trauma-associated hemorrhage.
Recombinant Factor VIIa (*NovoSeven RT*) Injection	**BOXED WARNING** Risk of thrombotic events, particularly when used off-label **NOTES** FDA-approved for hemophilia and factor VII deficiency; has been used successfully off-label for patients with hemorrhage from trauma and warfarin-related bleeding events.

Select Guidelines/References

Singer M, Deutschman CS, Seymour CW, et al. The Third International Consensus Definitions for Sepsis and Septic Shock (Sepsis-3). *JAMA*. 2016;315(8):801-10.

Evans LE, Rhodes A, Alhazzani W, et al. Surviving Sepsis Campaign: International Guidelines for Management of Severe Sepsis and Septic Shock: 2021. *Crit Care Med*. 2021;49(11):e1063-e1143.

Devlin J, Skrobik, Y, Gelinas C et al. Clinical Practice Guidelines for the Prevention and Management of Pain, Agitation/Sedation, Delirium, Immobility, and Sleep Disruption in Adult Patients in the ICU. Crit Care Med. 2018;46(9):1532-48.

PEDIATRIC TOPIC	CHAPTER
Vaccines	Immunizations
Infections (including acute otitis media)	Infectious Diseases
Cough and cold	Allergic Rhinitis, Cough & Cold
Pediculosis (lice) and diaper rash	Common Skin Conditions
Asthma	Asthma
Diabetes	Diabetes
Seizures	Seizures/Epilepsy
Iron and vitamin D recommendations	Dietary Supplements, Natural & Complementary Medicine

CONTENT LEGEND

 = Study Tip Gal

© iStock.com/blueringmedia

CHAPTER 54
PEDIATRIC CONDITIONS

BACKGROUND

Pediatric patients have unique and important differences in drug dosing and metabolism due to physiologic differences that change as they mature. See the table below for age classifications.

AGE CLASSIFICATIONS

Neonate	0 – 28 days
Infant	1 month – 12 months
Toddler	1 – 2 years
Child	2 – 12 years
Adolescent	13 – 18 years

Infants can become seriously ill very quickly. Children must be referred to urgent care in certain situations (see box below). Rectal temperature cut-offs are used because conversion between the various measuring methods (e.g., oral, axillary, ear, forehead) is not standardized.

Several conditions common in younger patients are covered in this chapter. Additional pediatric topics are covered elsewhere in this course book (see table to the left).

WHEN TO SEEK URGENT CARE FOR A CHILD

- Age < 3 months with a temperature of 100.4°F/38°C (rectal)
- Age 3 – 6 months with a temperature of 101°F/38.3°C (rectal)
- Age > 6 months with a temperature of 103°F/ 39.4°C (rectal)
- Any cough/cold that worsens or does not improve in several days
- Unusual, severe or persistent pain that does not go away after several hours
- Blood in the urine or stool
- Inability to sleep or drink
- Rash that looks severe or any rash with fever
- Abrasions/cuts that are dirty or deep (requiring sutures)
- Limping or unable to move an extremity
- Seizure

SAFE MEDICATION ADMINISTRATION

Household spoons should not be used for measuring medication. All liquid medications should be dispensed with an oral dosing syringe or dosing cup (oral syringes preferred; can decrease measuring errors). The parent or caregiver should be able to read the markings on the device when it contains medication. Instruct the caregiver on how to draw up the correct dose. When dispensing liquid medications that carry high risk, follow safe practice recommendations:

- Stock only one strength if a dangerous drug comes in a variety of strengths. Place the container in a high-risk bin with instructions attached to the container.

- The dose should be written in terms of total mg and in mg/kg per dose.

- The pharmacist should check that the dose is appropriate for the child's weight. Ask the caregiver for the child's weight if it is not available.

- The container label should include the dose (mg) and the volume (mL). Dispense with a measuring device.

With some high-risk drugs, it is preferable to administer at a medical facility, where help is available if needed.

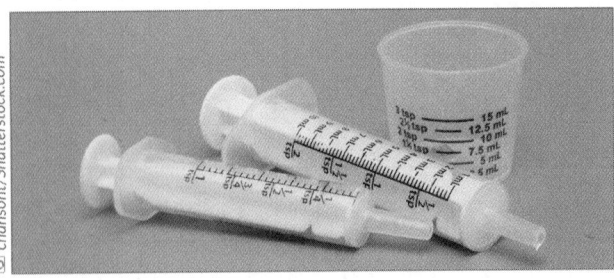

© chansont/Shutterstock.com

NEWBORN BABY HEALTH

APGAR SCORING

A newborn's general condition is assessed with an Apgar score, which is taken at one minute and again at five minutes after birth. The Apgar score measures performance in five categories: heart rate, respiratory effort, color, muscle tone and reflex irritability (the baby's response to stimulation). Each category is rated from 0 (worst score) to 2 (best score). The values are added together for a maximum score of 10. A healthy infant will initially score between 7 – 10. An infant with a lower score requires more medical care.

SCREENING AND MEDICATIONS

Shortly after birth, newborns are screened for congenital illnesses, such as phenylketonuria and cystic fibrosis. Standard medications given at birth include: intramuscular vitamin K to prevent bleeding, ophthalmic erythromycin to prevent conjunctivitis and the first dose of the hepatitis B

vaccine. Other treatments may be given for certain patient conditions (e.g., analgesia if being circumcised, light therapy for jaundice).

PRE-TERM BABY CONDITIONS

Low Apgar scores in pre-term infants are usually due to immature lung and heart development. Support for inadequate respiration can include oxygen delivered with a face mask, continuous positive airway pressure (CPAP) or full ventilator support with endotracheal (mechanical) intubation. Patients on ventilators require sedatives and analgesics; see the Acute & Critical Care Medicine chapter.

Cardiovascular conditions that are common in pre-term infants include hypotension, patent ductus arteriosus (PDA) and persistent pulmonary hypertension of the newborn (PPHN).

Hypotension is treated primarily with IV fluids. Hypotension due to intraventricular hemorrhage (IVH) (i.e., blood from a cranial hemorrhage seeping into the ventricles of the brain) may require a blood transfusion. IVH is more common in premature neonates.

PATENT DUCTUS ARTERIOSUS

The ductus arteriosus is a normal opening between the aorta and pulmonary artery in an unborn fetus. After delivery, the ductus arteriosus should close naturally. If this does not occur, it remains open (patent). This is referred to as a PDA and requires medical attention with surgery or drugs. NSAIDs (such as IV indomethacin or ibuprofen) can help the PDA to close by blocking the prostaglandins that keep the PDA open. NSAIDs must be administered within 14 days of birth to be effective. NSAIDs should not be used in the third trimester of pregnancy because they can cause the PDA to close prematurely.

PERSISTENT PULMONARY HYPERTENSION OF THE NEWBORN

When an infant is born, blood vessels in the lungs normally relax, which allows blood flow into the lungs. When this process fails, it can lead to PPHN. In addition to supportive care, inhaled nitric oxide (NO) to dilate the pulmonary arterioles is the standard treatment. Some drugs used to treat pulmonary arterial hypertension (PAH) can be used for PPHN, including prostacyclin analogues and PDE-5 inhibitors (see the Pulmonary Arterial Hypertension chapter). PPHN may be linked to in utero SSRI exposure.

Pre-term infants have lungs that have not yet fully developed, which increases the risk for pulmonary conditions, including respiratory distress syndrome (RDS) and respiratory syncytial virus (RSV).

RESPIRATORY DISTRESS SYNDROME

Respiratory Distress Syndrome (RDS) is caused by a deficiency of surfactant production in lungs that are not fully developed. Fetuses begin to produce surfactant around week 24, and by week 35, are producing an adequate amount. Inadequate surfactant in pre-term infants causes the alveoli to collapse, which causes RDS, followed by respiratory failure and death. Most babies born < 35 weeks gestation will receive surfactant immediately after birth or within the first few days of life. Surfactant products can be recognized by either "surf" or "actant" in the name, such as poractant alfa (Curosurf) and calfactant (Infasurf).

OVER-THE-COUNTER PRODUCTS FOR CHILDREN < 12 MONTHS OLD

If a condition does not require urgent care, there are several over-the-counter (OTC) products that are deemed generally safe for use in infants. See the box on the first page for when to refer a pediatric patient for urgent care.

MILD PAIN AND FEVER

Aspirin and salicylate-containing products (e.g., bismuth subsalicylate) have been associated with Reye's syndrome when used in children recovering from viral infections (especially influenza and chickenpox). Do not recommend aspirin or salicylates for patients < 16 years old, as it may not be apparent that they are recovering from a viral illness.

Acetaminophen infant drops and children's suspension are the same concentration to help reduce dosing errors. Acetaminophen is the most common cause of liver failure when used in doses above the safe amount. Accidental overdose can be due to the inadvertent use of multiple combination products containing acetaminophen. Caregivers should be counseled about this danger and the various names in which acetaminophen is packaged. Avoid ibuprofen in infants age < 6 months for pain/fever due to the risk of nephrotoxicity. To prevent dosing errors, pharmacists and caregivers should be aware that ibuprofen products are supplied in different dosage strengths for infants and children.

In children 6 months of age or older, acetaminophen or ibuprofen are appropriate for treating pain and fever. Some physicians may recommend that these are given together in alternating doses (e.g., acetaminophen given first, then ibuprofen given three hours later; each drug is dosed every six hours). Ibuprofen has a longer duration of action and may provide benefit if given before sleep.

With either acetaminophen or ibuprofen infant drops, the medicine can be placed into the child's mouth. It is acceptable to mix with a small amount of formula, but if the child does not drink the entire dose, it will be difficult to know how much of the dose was taken.

INTESTINAL GAS

Intestinal gas is a common condition with infants and causes distress post-feedings. Simethicone drops can offer mild, if any, benefit. The drug is not absorbed and is safe to use. As the child's digestive tract grows, the crying and fussiness will resolve. Caregivers can be comforted that symptoms will generally dissipate when the child is around 6 – 8 months old.

NASAL CONGESTION

Nasal congestion is very common in babies and is generally not serious. Children < 2 years old breathe mostly through their nose; they have not yet learned to breathe through their mouths. Smoke, including that from e-cigarettes, causes irritation; do not permit anyone to smoke near children. A cool-mist humidifier near the bedside can reduce congestion, especially in the winter when the home is heated. To relieve congestion, a caregiver can sit with the child in the bathroom while a hot shower creates steam in the room. Avoid hot water or steam getting near the child's skin, as burns could result. Gentle suction with saline drops or spray to loosen the mucus can provide relief.

The FDA does not recommend OTC cough and cold medications in children ≤ 2 years old, but most manufacturers include product labeling to avoid in children under age 4. Some combination products have additional labeling restrictions for use only in children ≥ 6 years old.

CONSTIPATION

Oral polyethylene glycol 3350 (MiraLax) is recommended for the treatment of intermittent constipation at a dose of 0.2 – 0.8 g/kg/day. Prunes or pears, as the fruit or juice, can be helpful. OTC pediatric-size glycerin suppositories are commonly used for quick relief of constipation in an uncomfortable baby, although the FDA-approved indication is for children age 2 years and older. Any child with ongoing constipation issues should be seen by a pediatrician.

DIARRHEA

Dehydration can occur as a result of significant diarrhea and can be dangerous in infants. Fluid and electrolytes should be replaced with oral rehydration solutions, such as Pedialyte and Enfamil Enfalyte, which are available over-the-counter. Antidiarrheal medications, such as bismuth subsalicylate, should not be used due to the risk of Reye's syndrome. Loperamide is not recommended for over-the-counter use in children under the age of 6 years.

SPECIAL POPULATIONS

Select OTC Products for Infants

DRUG	DOSING	SAFETY/SIDE EFFECTS/MONITORING	
Fever			
Acetaminophen (*Children's Tylenol, PediaCare Infants' Fever Reducer/Pain Reliever*, others)	<u>10-15 mg/kg/dose every 4-6 hours</u> (max 75 mg/kg/day) All acetaminophen oral liquid formulations (infants and children) are the same concentration: <u>160 mg/5 mL</u>	For simplicity, age and weight-based dosing for infants is on the side of the dropper container Caution for incorrect dosing or overdose from use of multiple products	
Ibuprofen (*Infants' Advil Drops, Motrin Infant Drops, Advil* or *Motrin* children's suspension, others)	<u>5-10 mg/kg/dose every 6-8 hours</u> (max 40 mg/kg/day) Infant drops: 50 mg/1.25 mL Children's suspension: 100 mg/5 mL	Indicated for infants ≥ 6 months old Caution for nausea	
Intestinal gas			
Simethicone (*Mylicon Infants' Gas Relief Drops, Gas Relief Infant*)	20 mg, 1-4 times/day PRN	Administer after meals and at bedtime for mild gas pains Shake drops before using; can mix with water, formula or other liquids	
Nasal dryness/congestion			
Intranasal saline solution (*Little Remedies Saline Nasal Drops, Ocean for Kids*)	2-6 drops per nostril PRN	See the Allergic Rhinitis, Cough & Cold chapter; saline can be used with a suction bulb	
Constipation			
Polyethylene glycol (*MiraLax*)	Age ≥ 6 months starting dose: 0.4 gram/kg Dose range: 0.2-0.8 gram/kg/day (max 17 grams) Dissolve in 4-8 oz water or other fluid A capful (filled to the indicated line) contains ~17 grams	Instruct caregivers to discuss with the pediatrician if using more than occasionally	
Glycerin suppositories (*Pedia-Lax*)	1 pediatric suppository per dose Insert high into the rectum; retain for ~15 minutes	Instruct caregivers to discuss with the pediatrician if using more than occasionally	

CASE SCENARIO

The father of LC, a 9-month-old female patient, presents to a community pharmacy stating that she has a rectal temperature of 102°F. The father asks for a treatment recommendation for LC. He states that the child weighs 18.5 lbs.

Can this patient be treated OTC?

Yes, LC can be treated OTC based on her age (9 months) and temperature (below 103°F). No alarm symptoms are noted (e.g., if the case mentions that the patient has a rash with the fever or has not been able to sleep or drink).

What medication/s and dose/s would be appropriate?

Acetaminophen or ibuprofen (based on her age and no past medical history). Both can safely be given, and can be used together (in alternating doses).

To find the dose, first calculate LC's weight in kg: 18.5 lbs / 2.2 = 8.409 kg

Next, calculate LC's dose range for each medication:

Acetaminophen: 10-15 mg/kg/dose every 4-6 hours	Ibuprofen: 5-10 mg/kg/dose every 6-8 hours
LC's dose: 84.09-126.14 mg every 4-6 hours	LC's dose: 42.05-84.09 mg every 6-8 hours

How should the father be instructed to give these medications?

Determine a dose within the range that can easily be given based on the products available:

Acetaminophen: 160 mg/5 mL	Ibuprofen Infants Drops: 50 mg/1.25mL
LC's dose: 96 mg (3 mL) every 4-6 hours	LC's dose: 80 mg (2 mL) every 6-8 hours

The father can alternate between the two medications, keeping at least 3 hours between any doses and at least 6 hours between doses of the same medication. Ibuprofen can be given before bed to help with sleep (lasts longer).

COMMON CONDITIONS IN YOUNG CHILDREN

BACTERIAL MENINGITIS

This topic is included in the Infectious Diseases II chapter, but is emphasized here because of the unique aspects of neonatal meningitis. If untreated, the fatality rate is close to 100%, and the treatment recommendations are different than in other age groups because the common pathogens differ. The classic signs of meningitis are uncommon in neonates (age 0 – 28 days). Bulging fontanelles (swelling between the bones of the skull) and nuchal rigidity (inability to bend the neck) will be present in < 25% of cases; otherwise, the symptoms are non-specific. A definitive diagnosis in a suspected case can be made with a lumbar puncture.

The likely pathogens causing bacterial meningitis in a neonate differ from other age groups due to the vertical transmission of organisms from the mother to the baby in the birth canal. The predominant pathogens are Group B *Streptococcus* (GBS), *Escherichia coli*, *Listeria* and *Klebsiella*. Empiric treatment in neonates consists of ampicillin plus either cefotaxime or gentamicin.

Ceftriaxone, which is used in adults, is generally avoided in neonates. Ceftriaxone displaces bilirubin from albumin, which can cause bilirubin-induced brain damage (kernicterus). Ceftriaxone and calcium-containing solutions can precipitate, causing an embolus and death. Concurrent use in neonates is contraindicated. See the Infectious Diseases II chapter for more information on empiric treatment of bacterial meningitis.

AGE	COMMON BACTERIAL PATHOGENS	EMPIRIC TREATMENT
< 1 month	*Streptococcus agalactiae* (Group B strep), *Escherichia coli*, *Listeria monocytogenes*, *Klebsiella*	Ampicillin + cefotaxime or Ampicillin + aminoglycoside (gentamicin)
1 – 23 months	*Streptococcus pneumoniae*, *Neisseria meningitidis*, *S. agalactiae*, *Haemophilus influenzae*, *E. coli*	Vancomycin + 3rd generation cephalosporin (ceftriaxone or cefotaxime)
2+ years	*N. meningitidis*, *S. pneumoniae*	Vancomycin + 3rd generation cephalosporin (ceftriaxone or cefotaxime)

RESPIRATORY SYNCYTIAL VIRUS (RSV)

Respiratory Syncytial Virus (RSV) infection occurs commonly and nearly all children have been infected by the age of two years. In older, healthy children, the symptoms mimic the common cold, but in premature babies and neonates, RSV can be deadly. Good hand hygiene can reduce the spread of RSV.

RSV is a common cause of bronchiolitis (swelling and mucus build up in the bronchioles). Symptoms include low-grade fever, cough, dyspnea and cyanosis (bluish skin due to lack of oxygen). Similar to other viral infections, the treatment is primarily supportive (supplemental oxygen, IV fluids, suction of secretions). In patients with severe lower respiratory tract RSV infections with an underlying compromising condition (prematurity, cardiopulmonary disease or immunosuppression), treatment with inhaled ribavirin (*Virazole*) can be considered. This drug should not be used for routine cases.

RSV Prophylaxis

No vaccine is available for RSV and no lasting immunity develops after infection. Palivizumab (*Synagis*) is a humanized monoclonal antibody indicated for the prevention of serious lower respiratory tract disease caused by RSV in children at high risk of the disease.

Palivizumab is used for premature infants and children < 24 months with select medical conditions that affect respiration (see the box below). RSV prophylaxis is recommended by the American Academy of Pediatrics (AAP) during RSV season (late fall, winter, early spring).

Palivizumab is dosed monthly at 15 mg/kg per dose by intramuscular (IM) injection. In neonates and infants, the IM injection site is the anterolateral thigh muscle. The deltoid can be used in children once the muscle mass is adequate, which usually does not occur until at least 3 years of age. Infants should not receive more than five monthly doses during the RSV season. If the baby becomes infected with RSV, no further doses of palivizumab should be given.

WHO SHOULD RECEIVE PALIVIZUMAB (SYNAGIS)?

In the first year of life:

- Premature infants born at < 29 weeks gestation
- Premature infants born < 32 weeks gestation with chronic lung disease (CLD) who are < 12 months of age
- Infants < 12 months of age with certain heart conditions

CROUP

Croup, or laryngotracheobronchitis, is usually due to a <u>viral</u> infection which causes <u>inflammation</u> of the <u>upper airway</u>, larynx, trachea and bronchi. Bacterial infections are less common and are often associated with severe symptoms. The inflammation results in the hallmark signs of <u>inspiratory stridor (high pitched breathing sound), barking cough and hoarseness</u>. Croup is most common in children <u>< 6 years old</u> and is often worse at night. The illness is classified and treated by the severity of the symptoms.

Non-Drug Treatment

In mild cases, a child can present with only a croupy cough, which can be managed at home and should resolve within a few days. Cool mist or steam and adequate hydration may help alleviate symptoms, although evidence of benefit is lacking.

Drug Treatment for Mild, Moderate or Severe Illness

<u>Systemic steroids</u> (usually <u>dexamethasone</u> 0.6 mg/kg) are a mainstay of croup treatment for mild, moderate and severe cases. In a typical croup case presenting to an acute care setting with moderate to severe symptoms, a patient having difficulty breathing will be given a systemic steroid and then <u>nebulized racemic epinephrine</u>, if needed. Nebulized racemic epinephrine is a 1:1 mixture of dextro (D) and levo (L) isomers (<u>the L-isomer is the active component</u>). If racemic epinephrine is not available, L-epinephrine is used; this is half of the drug (one of the isomers) and the dose is half of the racemic formulation.

Epinephrine is an <u>adrenergic agonist</u> that relaxes the bronchial smooth muscle and causes <u>bronchodilation</u>. When administered using a nebulizer, the onset of action is fast but the duration of action is short; it lasts up to about 2 hours. A child receiving epinephrine should be monitored for up to four hours for recurrence of symptoms. The child should not be discharged until breathing is easy with no stridor at rest and after receiving steroids to reduce the inflammation.

Some severe symptoms (e.g., stridor at rest, respiratory distress, severe retractions, mental status changes) can require respiratory support such as intubation. Antibiotics are used only if a bacterial infection is present.

Systemic Steroids and Nebulized Epinephrine

DRUG	DOSING	SAFETY/SIDE EFFECTS/MONITORING
Dexamethasone Oral solution, injection (other forms not used in infants)	0.6 mg/kg PO/IM/IV x 1; max 16 mg/dose	See the Asthma chapter for steroid safety issues; this refers to acute use only
Nebulized: Racemic epinephrine 2.25% solution or L-epinephrine 1 mg/mL solution (10 mg racemic epinephrine = 5 mg L-epinephrine)	Racemic epinephrine dose: 0.05-0.1 mL/kg (max 0.5 mL) diluted in 2 mL NS, can repeat Q20 min PRN L-epinephrine dose: 0.5 mL/kg of 1 mg/mL solution (max dose: 5 mL) diluted in NS, can repeat Q20 min PRN	**WARNINGS** Caution with cardiovascular disease, cerebrovascular disease, thyroid disease, diabetes (can ↑ blood glucose) **SIDE EFFECTS** ↑ BP, ↑ HR, anxiety, arrhythmia **NOTES** Monitor for recurrent bronchospasm

NOCTURNAL ENURESIS

Nocturnal enuresis, or bed-wetting, is a normal part of a child's development and is not generally treated before age 5 years. Boys (more often than girls) can be developing nighttime bladder control until 7 years of age.

Non-Drug Treatment

Behavioral approaches are used first. Practices that can be effective include positive reinforcement, establishing a normal daytime voiding pattern and a normal bowel pattern, and establishing a normal hydration pattern. Fluid intake should be limited prior to bedtime. Bladder training exercises (such as attempting to hold the urine during the day for a set time period) are not recommended. Embarrassment should be minimized. Behavioral approaches are effective in many children and should be tried for up to three months. If behavioral methods do not result in dryness, either alarm therapy or alarm therapy with drug treatment (desmopressin) can be tried. There are numerous alarms available that attach to the underwear or pajamas and sound an alarm when wet. The child may sleep through the alarm, but generally stops voiding. When the alarm sounds a caregiver should wake the child and escort him or her to the bathroom.

Alarm therapy can be useful and should be considered for a minimum of three consecutive months. If unsuccessful initially, alarm therapy might work when the child is older and more motivated. Alarm therapy is effective in about two out of three children initially; many will relapse and require the intervention repeated.

Drug Treatment

Desmopressin (oral tablet) is the only preferred medication for enuresis. Desmopressin is a synthetic analog of antidiuretic hormone (ADH); simulating ADH will ↓ nocturnal urine production. Desmopressin can be used in combination with alarm therapy.

DRUG	DOSING	SAFETY/SIDE EFFECTS/MONITORING
Desmopressin (*DDAVP*) Tablets used for enuresis Tablets, nasal spray or injection used for diabetes insipidus and hemophilia A (to control bleeding)	Start 0.2 mg PO QHS, can titrate to 0.6 mg max	**BOXED WARNINGS** Severe, life-threatening hyponatremia can develop **CONTRAINDICATIONS** Hyponatremia, history of hyponatremia CrCl < 50 mL/min **WARNINGS** Hyponatremia, water intoxication **SIDE EFFECTS** Headache, fatigue, possible ↓ Na due to water retention **NOTES** Limit fluid intake starting 1 hour before dose and until the next morning

SPECIAL POPULATIONS

DRUGS NOT GENERALLY RECOMMENDED IN PEDIATRICS

- Codeine is metabolized to morphine by the CYP2D6 enzyme; certain children over-express this enzyme and consequently, produce a higher than expected amount of morphine. This can result in respiratory depression and a possible lethal overdose. Codeine use is contraindicated in all patients age < 12 years and in those < 18 years after tonsillectomy/adenoidectomy. In January 2018, the FDA changed the labeling for all prescription cough and cold medications that contain codeine or hydrocodone; they are no longer indicated in patients < 18 years old.

- Promethazine is contraindicated in children < 2 years of age due to the potential for severe and potentially fatal respiratory depression.

- Quinolones are not recommended in pediatric patients due to the possibility of adverse effects on cartilage, bone and muscle. In special cases, such as anthrax treatment, they are used on a case-by-case basis.

- Tetracyclines are not recommended in children < 8 years of age because they stain teeth and deposit into mineralizing (i.e., growing) bone and cartilage, which weakens it. One notable exception is in tick-borne Rickettsial diseases (Rocky Mountain spotted fever, ehrlichiosis and anaplasmosis). Doxycycline is the most effective treatment, and is recommended in pediatric patients, as the risk of severe illness or death outweighs the risk of tooth discoloration. See the Infectious Diseases II chapter.

- Topical teething products containing benzocaine increase the risk of methemoglobinemia. The FDA now recommends against their use in children < 2 years of age.

- At the wrong dose, many OTC products are not safe in young children.

AVOID IN PEDIATRICS

Contraindicated
- Codeine in age < 12 years
- Tramadol in age < 12 years
- Promethazine in age < 2 years
- Ceftriaxone in neonates (1-28 days)

Not generally recommended
- Aspirin in children and teenagers
- Quinolones
- Tetracyclines in age < 8 years
- OTC teething medications containing benzocaine in age < 2 years
- OTC cough and cold preparations in age < 2 years (per FDA)

PRIMARY TOXICITIES FROM ACCIDENTAL OVERDOSE IN CHILDREN

Iron and acetaminophen are two common culprits of accidental overdose in children. Toddlers put anything in their mouths, especially if it looks like it could be candy. One tablet of several drug classes, including sulfonylureas, can be fatal to an infant. It is important to counsel older patients about the safe storage of medications to prevent accidental overdoses. If the child has ingested anything that could be toxic (even if the ingestion is suspected only) the poison control center should be contacted immediately for advice. Review the Toxicology & Antidotes chapter for further information on pediatric poisoning.

VACCINE-PREVENTABLE CHILDHOOD DISEASES

Vaccine-preventable diseases occur more commonly than in previous years due to lower immunization rates in some areas. Vaccine information is found in the Immunizations chapter. The symptoms of the more common vaccine-preventable diseases are important for a pharmacist to recognize if it presents in a child. Each of the conditions below can lead to severe, permanent damage. Although chickenpox (an acute illness) generally dissipates without long-term consequences, any person who has had chickenpox is at risk for developing shingles later in life. This is a painful condition that results from reactivation of the virus in some nerves. It occurs most commonly in patients > 50 years of age and can lead to postherpetic neuralgia and chronic pain. For additional information, see the Infectious Diseases III chapter.

VACCINE-PREVENTABLE CHILDHOOD DISEASES

ILLNESS	CLASSIC SYMPTOMS	NOTES
Measles	Koplik spots are small white spots on the inside of the cheeks (inside the mouth) that appear 2-5 days prior to the rash seen below © phichet chaiyabin/Shutterstock.com	Koplik spots in mouth, maculopapular rash, fever, malaise, cough, rhinitis, conjunctivitis. Transmission is airborne and measles are highly contagious. If not immune, 90% of people who are in contact with an infected person will also become infected. Prevention: MMR vaccine
Mumps	Swollen and tender salivary glands under the ears (parotitis) © airdone/Shutterstock.com	Swollen salivary glands, fever, headache, myalgia, fatigue, loss of appetite; up to 50% of patients have mild or no symptoms. Prevention: MMR vaccine
Rubella	A fine, pink rash that begins on the face and quickly spreads to the rest of the body © Akkalak Aiempradit/Shutterstock.com	Fever, rash, swollen glands, cold-like symptoms, aching joints; up to 50% of patients have mild or no symptoms. Can cause birth defects if contracted by a pregnant woman. Prevention: MMR vaccine

ILLNESS	CLASSIC SYMPTOMS	NOTES
Polio	Child with poliomyelitis _© podsy/Shutterstock.com_	Fever, sore throat, fatigue, nausea, headache, abdominal pain; the majority have no symptoms and never know they were infected – others get severe nerve damage (paralytic polio) and later in life, post-polio syndrome, which causes progressive weakness and cognitive issues. Prevention: IPV vaccine
Pertussis (Whooping cough)	"Whoop" sounding cough	Sudden cough outbursts, fever, rhinitis, bluish skin (cyanosis), vomiting, fatigue. Can cause respiratory failure and death, especially in infants. Prevention: DTaP vaccine
Rotavirus	Diarrhea, fever, vomiting	Severe, watery diarrhea that can lead to dehydration and death. Children are most likely to get rotavirus in the winter and spring (December through June). Prevention: RV vaccine
Chickenpox (Varicella)	Chickenpox rash (spots) _© John-Kelly/Shutterstock.com_	Itchy rash, fever, malaise. The rash appears as crops of sores (head, then trunk, then arms & legs), that turn into blisters, burst, then form crusts. Long-term implications include shingles (herpes zoster) with risk of ophthalmic involvement and postherpetic neuralgia (severe pain after the infection). Prevention: varicella vaccine

Select Guidelines/References

Smith DK, McDermott AJ, Sullivan JF. Croup: diagnosis and management. *Am Fam Physician*. 2018; 97:575-1073.

Vande Walle J, Rittig S, Tekgul S, et al. Enuresis: practical guidelines for primary care. *Br J Gen Pract*. 2017; 67(660):328-329.

Tabbers MM, DiLorenzo C. et al. Evaluation and treatment of functional constipation in infants and children. *JPGN*. 2014; 58:258–274.

CONTENT LEGEND

= Study Tip Gal

© iStock.com/nata_zhekova

CHAPTER 55

CYSTIC FIBROSIS

BACKGROUND

Cystic fibrosis (CF) is an incurable, hereditary disease caused by a mutation in the gene for the protein cystic fibrosis transmembrane conductance regulator (CFTR). The mutation causes abnormal transport of chloride, bicarbonate and sodium ions across the epithelium, leading to thick, viscous secretions. The thick mucus affects the lungs, pancreas, liver and intestines, which causes difficulty breathing, lung infections and digestive complications. The name cystic fibrosis refers to the characteristic scarring (fibrosis) and cyst formation that occurs within the pancreas. The average life expectancy of a person with CF is 35 – 40 years with more than 75% of patients being diagnosed by 2 years of age. The disease is progressive, with some eventually qualifying for lung transplantation.

DIAGNOSIS

Newborn screening is performed in the U.S. in the first 2 – 3 days after a baby is born and includes testing for CF and other conditions. If the initial screening identifies a risk of CF, then a sweat chloride test (or "sweat test") is performed to confirm the diagnosis. The sweat test measures the amount of salt (chloride) in the sweat, which is high in patients with CF.

SIGNS AND SYMPTOMS

The classic symptoms of CF are salty tasting skin, poor growth and poor weight gain (despite adequate food intake), thick and sticky mucus production, frequent lung infections, coughing and shortness of breath. Patients experience obstruction of pancreatic ducts causing steatorrhea (fatty stools) and poor absorption of nutrients, including fat-soluble vitamins. Clubbing of the fingers may be present. Malnutrition and a failure to thrive can result if CF is not treated.

DRUG TREATMENT

The primary goals of therapy include preventing/treating lung infections, maintaining adequate nutrition and optimizing quality of life. Most patients will receive airway clearance therapies (see drug table on the next page), inhaled antibiotics targeting *Pseudomonas aeruginosa* and pancreatic enzyme replacement. Targeted CFTR modulators reduce the frequency of exacerbations and may be appropriate for some patients. Early diagnosis and a comprehensive treatment plan can improve survival and quality of life. Specialty clinics for CF can be found in many communities.

LUNG COMPLICATIONS

Multiple medications are used to help manage the thick mucus and reduce the risk of lung infections. Administering the inhaled medications in the correct order is critical to maximize absorption and effect. Airway clearance therapies (e.g., bronchodilators, hypertonic saline and dornase alfa) are given before inhaled antibiotics (see Study Tip Gal to the right).

Inhaled therapies are the foundation of treatment in CF. The drug is delivered directly to the lungs, resulting in minimal systemic absorption (reducing the risk of toxicity). Although inhaled medications are an effective form of drug delivery, the average patient with CF receives up to 10 doses of inhaled medications daily, which can take 2 – 3 hours to administer. This requires lifestyle modification since dosing must be scheduled around work, school and other activities.

INFECTIONS

Intermittent Infection

Impaired mucus clearance causes bacterial colonization and lung infections. The most common organisms seen early in the disease are *Staphylococcus aureus* and *Haemophilus influenzae*, followed by *Pseudomonas aeruginosa* in adolescents and adults. Acute pulmonary exacerbations are characterized by an increase in cough, sputum production with a change in sputum color (greenish), shortness of breath and a rapid decline in FEV1. Treatment often includes an extended course of antibiotics (2 – 4 weeks) and modalities to increase airway clearance.

For infections caused by *Pseudomonas aeruginosa*, two IV drugs are recommended to provide potential synergy and prevent resistance. These include aminoglycosides, beta-lactams, quinolones and others that cover *Pseudomonas aeruginosa*. See the Infectious Diseases I chapter for a complete discussion of treatment options for *Pseudomonas aeruginosa*. Doses tend to be larger than normal to address altered pharmacokinetics in patients with CF, to obtain therapeutic drug concentrations in lung tissue, and to overcome reduced susceptibility of the bacteria chronically colonizing the airways.

INHALED MEDICATIONS FOR CF

ORDER	INTERVENTION	PURPOSE
1st	Inhaled bronchodilators (e.g., albuterol)	Opens the airways
2nd	Hypertonic saline (e.g., *HyperSal*)	Mobilizes mucus to improve airway clearance
3rd	Dornase alfa (*Pulmozyme*)	Decreases viscosity of (thins) mucus to promote airway clearance
4th	Chest physiotherapy	Mobilizes mucus to improve airway clearance
5th	Inhaled antibiotics	Controls airway infection

Most patients will require oral medications (e.g., pancreatic enzyme products, azithromycin). These can be given at any time.

Chronic Infection

Lung infections occur intermittently at first, but eventually become chronic. Chronic lung infections with *Pseudomonas aeruginosa* are associated with a more rapid decline in pulmonary function. Inhaled antibiotics are recommended for patients with chronic *Pseudomonas aeruginosa* lung infections to reduce the bacterial burden. Treatment is cycled with 28 days on therapy, followed by 28 days off. This is associated with an improvement in lung function and a reduction in the frequency of acute pulmonary exacerbations. The frequency of exacerbations is strongly associated with lung function decline and shortened survival in CF. If a patient is using a bronchodilator and/or mucolytic, these should be given prior to the antibiotic inhalation (see Study Tip Gal above).

Inhaled antibiotics should be taken as prescribed in order to reduce the risk of developing antibiotic resistance. Inhaled aztreonam (*Cayston*), an antibiotic used for chronic suppression (see drug table on the next page), is dosed TID and should be scheduled as close to every 8 hours as possible. This dosing provides optimal bacterial killing around the clock, while minimizing the time when the antibiotic concentration is low (which can worsen resistance). Dosing every 8 hours requires waking up in the middle of the night, so it is usually more convenient to give doses during waking hours (e.g., before school, after school and before bed). The doses must be at least 4 hours apart to provide adequate drug concentrations throughout the day. Similarly, inhaled tobramycin (*TOBI, TOBI Podhaler*) is dosed every 12 hours and should be scheduled as close to every 12 hours as possible with at least 8 hours in between doses.

A six month trial of oral azithromycin can be considered for patients with chronic infection who are worsening on conventional treatment. Azithromycin has no direct bactericidal activity against *Pseudomonas*, but disrupts biofilm formation by the bacteria which can improve lung function and decrease exacerbations.

Treatment for Lung Complications and Infections

DRUG	DOSING	SAFETY/SIDE EFFECTS/MONITORING
Airway Clearance Therapies, Inhaled		
Bronchodilator (e.g., albuterol)	2-4 times daily	See Asthma chapter
Hypertonic saline *(HyperSal, PulmoSal)* 4 mL unit-dose vial	4 mL via nebulizer 2-4 times daily	Hypertonic saline is supplied as small ready-to-use vials that are <u>delivered via a nebulizer</u> *PulmoSal* is buffered to match physiologic pH of the airway surface Hypertonic saline is a high-alert drug, especially with IV administration
Dornase alfa (Pulmozyme) 2.5 mg single-use ampule	2.5 mg daily with recommended nebulizer and compressor system	Works by degrading extracellular DNA in the lungs to <u>decrease viscosity of mucus</u> (i.e., thin the mucus) **CONTRAINDICATIONS** Hypersensitivity to Chinese Hamster Ovary (CHO) products **SIDE EFFECTS** Chest pain, fever, rash, rhinitis, laryngitis, voice alteration, throat irritation **NOTES** <u>Store ampules in the refrigerator</u> (do not expose to room temperature ≥ 24 hours) <u>Protect from light</u> <u>Do not mix with any other drug in the nebulizer</u>
Antibiotics, Inhaled – via <u>inhalation</u> to target *Pseudomonas aeruginosa* colonization to ↓ infections/hospitalization		
Tobramycin (*TOBI, TOBI Podhaler*, Bethkis, Kitabis Pak) Solution for inhalation: *TOBI, Kitabis:* 300 mg/ 5 mL single-use ampule *Bethkis:* 300 mg/4 mL single-use ampule <u>Capsule for inhalation:</u> *TOBI Podhaler:* 28 mg capsules in blister card	Age ≥ 6 years: **Solution for inhalation** *TOBI, Bethkis, Kitabis Pak:* 300 mg via nebulizer Q12H **Capsule for inhalation** *TOBI Podhaler:* 112 mg (4 x 28 mg caps) via inhalation Q12H	**SIDE EFFECTS** <u>Ototoxicity, tinnitus, voice alteration, mouth and throat pain,</u> dizziness, bronchospasm **NOTES** Give for <u>28 days, followed by 28 days off</u> cycle Dosed every 12 hours, but must be at least <u>6 hours apart</u> *TOBI, Bethkis, Kitabis:* <u>refrigeration recommended</u> (can be kept at <u>room temperature up to 28 days</u>); store in foil pouch to protect from light; <u>do not mix with any other drug in the nebulizer</u> *TOBI:* use with *PARI LC Plus* nebulizer and *DeVilbiss Pulmo-Aide* air compressor *Bethkis:* use with *PARI LC Plus* nebulizer and *PARI Vios* air compressor *TOBI Podhaler:* store capsules at <u>room temperature</u> in a dry place; <u>use with *Podhaler*</u> (device dispensed with the capsules); <u>do not swallow</u> capsules
Aztreonam *(Cayston)* Solution for inhalation **Azactam** (IV) – for acute infection	Age ≥ 7 years: 75 mg via nebulizer TID	**SIDE EFFECTS** <u>Allergic reactions (may be severe), bronchospasm, fever, wheezing, cough, chest discomfort</u> **NOTES** Give for <u>28 days, followed by 28 days off</u> cycle Dosed every 8 hours, but must be at least <u>4 hours apart</u> <u>Refrigeration recommended</u> (can be kept at <u>room temperature</u> up to <u>28 days</u>) <u>Do not mix with any other drug in the nebulizer</u> Use with *Altera* nebulizer system Protect from light
Antibiotic, <u>Oral</u> – to ↓ inflammation and ↓ exacerbations		
Azithromycin (Zithromax) Off-label	Age ≥ 6 years: < 40 kg: 250 mg 3 times/week ≥ 40 kg: 500 mg 3 times/week	**SIDE EFFECTS** In CF: tinnitus, nausea, risk of QT prolongation **NOTES** Do not use as monotherapy in individuals with nontuberculous mycobacteria lung infections

WHAT'S IN A NAME?

Enzymes are proteins that break bonds and speed up chemical reactions (in addition to other functions). You can spot an enzyme because the generic name usually ends in "-ase."

Lungs: Dor__nase__ alfa / *Pulmo__zyme__* indicates that it is an en__zyme__

■ Breaks DNA strands into smaller pieces, thinning the mucus to make it easier to cough up

GI Tract: Pancreli__pase__

■ Pancreli__pase__ contains the enzymes li__pase__, prote__ase__ and amyl__ase__ that are needed to break down fats, proteins and starches

　❏ *Zenpep* identifies that it is a pancreatic enzyme product (PEP)

　❏ *Creon* comes from the generic name pan__crelipase__

　❏ *Vio__kace__* indicates that it is an enzyme by the suffix (slightly different spelling)

PANCREATIC ENZYME PRODUCTS

The thick mucus in CF obstructs pancreatic enzyme flow, resulting in a lack of these enzymes reaching the gastrointestinal tract and subsequent malabsorption. Frequent, greasy, oily, foul-smelling stools are manifestations of pancreatic insufficiency. Most patients with CF need to supplement their diet with pancreatic enzyme products (PEPs) to help break down fat, starches and protein. This is called pancreatic enzyme replacement therapy (PERT).

Pancrelipase is a natural product harvested from porcine pancreatic glands which contains a combination of lipase, amylase and protease. PEPs are formulated to dissolve in the more basic pH of the duodenum. The dose is individualized for each patient and is based on the lipase component. Once PEP therapy is started, the dose is adjusted every 3 – 4 days until stools are normalized.

DRUG	DOSING	SAFETY/SIDE EFFECTS/MONITORING
Pancrelipase (Creon, Viokace, Zenpep, Lip-Prot-Amyl, Pancreaze, Pertzye)	**Initial** Age < 1 year: varies by product Age 1-3 years: lipase 1,000 units/kg/meal Age ≥ 4 years: lipase 500 units/kg/meal **Max (all ages)** Lipase ≤ 2,500 units/kg/meal or ≤ 10,000 units/kg/day; doses > 6,000 units/kg/meal are associated with colonic stricture	**WARNINGS** Fibrosing colonopathy advancing to colonic strictures (rare: higher risk with doses > 10,000 lipase units/kg/day), mucosal irritation, hyperuricemia **SIDE EFFECTS** Abdominal pain, flatulence, nausea, HA, neck pain **MONITORING** Abdominal symptoms, nutritional intake, weight, height (children), stool, fecal fat **NOTES** See Study Tip Gal below

COMMON ISSUES WITH PANCREATIC ENZYME PRODUCTS

Pancreatic enzyme replacement helps patients with CF digest food, maintain weight and improve nutrient absorption.

■ PEP formulations are not interchangeable. Commonly used products are *Creon*, *Viokace* and *Zenpep*.

■ *Viokace* is the only PEP that is a tablet. It is non-enteric coated and must be given with a PPI.

■ All other PEPs are capsules.

　❏ Do not crush or chew the contents of the capsules.

　❏ Delayed-release capsules with enteric-coated microspheres or microtablets may be opened and sprinkled on soft, acidic foods (pH ≤ 4.5) like applesauce. Avoid foods with high pH such as dairy.

　❏ Do not retain the capsule contents in the mouth. Swallow immediately and follow with water to avoid mucosal irritation and stomatitis.

■ Take PEPs before or with all meals and snacks. High-fat meals may require higher doses.

　❏ Use 50% of the mealtime dose with snacks.

■ Protect from moisture; dispense in original container (exceptions: *Zenpep* and some *Creon* strengths). Do not refrigerate.

CYSTIC FIBROSIS TRANSMEMBRANE CONDUCTANCE REGULATOR (CFTR) MODULATORS

Ivacaftor works by increasing the time the CFTR channels remain open, which enhances chloride transport activity. Lumacaftor, tezacaftor and elexacaftor help correct the CFTR folding defect, which increases the amount of CFTR delivered to the cell surface. Because each drug is approved for very specific mutations, genotype testing must be performed prior to initiation.

The most common mutation in the CFTR gene is a homozygous F508del mutation (two copies of the same allele). Combination products (*Orkambi, Symdeko* and *Trikafta*) are approved for the most common CF mutation.

DRUG	APPROVED MUTATION	SAFETY/NOTES
Ivacaftor (*Kalydeco*) Tablet, oral granules	Not approved for use in the homozygous F508del mutation; approved for use in other responsive mutations	**WARNINGS** ↑ LFTs, cataracts in children **NOTES** Take with high-fat containing food Approved ages for use: ■ *Kalydeco*: ≥ 4 months of age ■ *Orkambi*: ≥ 2 years of age ■ *Symdeko, Trikafta*: ≥ 6 years of age
Lumacaftor/ivacaftor (*Orkambi*) Tablet, oral granules	Approved for use in the homozygous F508del mutation and additional responsive mutations	
Tezacaftor/ivacaftor (*Symdeko*) Co-packaged tablets		
Elexacaftor/tezacaftor/ivacaftor (*Trikafta*) Co-packaged tablets		

CFTR Modulator Drug Interactions

■ Ivacaftor is a substrate of CYP450 3A4 (major) and should be avoided with strong CYP3A4 inducers. Dosage adjustments may be required when CFTR modulators are used with CYP3A4 inhibitors.

OTHER CONCERNS

CF is usually diagnosed in very young children. Appropriate measures to address the patient's growth, nutrition, bone health and other CF complications are critical.

■ A high-fat and calorically dense diet is recommended to help with nutrition, normal weight and growth, increased energy needs and to prolong survival.

■ Vitamin supplements are required, especially the fat-soluble vitamins A, D, E and K for normal cellular function. Calcium and vitamin D intake/absorption should be monitored to maximize bone health.

■ Many patients with CF will eventually require insulin for treatment of CF-related diabetes mellitus.

■ If the patient maintains good health, the chances of qualifying for a transplant are improved.

KEY COUNSELING POINTS

See the Drug Formulations and Patient Counseling chapter for counseling language/layman's terminology.

TOBI Podhaler

■ Do not swallow capsules.

■ Use only the provided *Podhaler* device.

■ Take doses as close to 12 hours but no less than six hours apart.

Pancreatic Enzyme Products

■ Take at the beginning of a meal or snack. Take half of the meal-time dose with snacks.

■ Swallow whole.

■ Contents can be sprinkled on a spoonful of soft food (e.g., applesauce, pureed bananas or pears). Use right away.

■ Do not mix with dairy products.

■ Drink plenty of non-caffeinated liquids every day.

Select Guidelines/References

ECFS Best Practice Guidelines: The 2018 Revision. *J Cyst Fibros* 2018;17:153-78.

Cystic Fibrosis Foundation: Clinical Care Guidelines. https://www.cff.org/Care/Clinical-Care-Guidelines/ (accessed 2022 Feb 14).

CHAPTER CONTENT

AVOIDING AN "ABO MISMATCH" OR INCOMPATIBILITY REACTION

Type O blood = "universal donor"
Type O blood does not cause an immune response when received by people with type A, B or AB blood. It can given to patients of any blood type.

People with type O blood will react against type A, B or AB blood. People with type O can only receive type O.

Type AB blood = "universal receiver"
People with type AB blood can safely receive type A, B, AB or O blood.

People with type A blood will react against type B or AB blood.

People with type B blood will react against type A or AB blood.

CONTENT LEGEND

 = Study Tip Gal

© iStock.com/kgtoh

CHAPTER 56

TRANSPLANT

BACKGROUND

Transplantation is one of the most challenging and complex areas of modern medicine. The main goal of transplantation is to prolong patient and graft (i.e., the transplanted organ or tissue) survival. United Network for Organ Sharing (UNOS) is the organization responsible for organ allocation in the U.S. Organs that have been successfully transplanted include the kidney, liver, pancreas, heart and lungs, with kidney and liver transplants being most common. Bone marrow transplantation has been used successfully for certain hematological and immunodeficiency conditions.

PREVENTION OF GRAFT REJECTION

An allograft is the transplant of an organ or tissue from one individual to another of the same species with a different genotype. This can also be called an allogenic transplant. A transplanted organ from a genetically identical donor (such as an identical twin) is called an isograft. An autograft (also called autologous transplant) is a transplant in the same patient, from one site to another (e.g., autologous stem cell transplant or skin grafting).

Rejection occurs when the body has an immune response to the allograft. This response may lead to transplant failure, the need for organ failure support (e.g., dialysis) or removal of the transplanted organ.

Prior to any transplant, tissue typing or crossmatching is performed to assess donor-recipient compatibility for human leukocyte antigen (HLA) and ABO blood group. A mismatch in either instance would lead to a fast, acute rejection (see box on the left). A Panel Reactive Antibody (PRA) test can be used to gauge the degree to which the recipient is "sensitized" to foreign (or "non-self") proteins. A high PRA score correlates with the likelihood of graft rejection and could necessitate a desensitization protocol before the transplant.

Immunosuppressants are given just prior to transplant (induction immunosuppression), chronically after transplant (maintenance immunosuppression) and in the event of acute rejection. These medications prevent or stop the patient's own immune system from attacking the new organ.

INDUCTION IMMUNOSUPPRESSION

Induction immunosuppression is given immediately before or at the time of transplant to prevent acute rejection during the early post-transplant period. It consists of a short course of effective intravenous (IV) medication, either a polyclonal or monoclonal antibody (these end in "-mab"), most often combined with high-dose IV steroids. In some cases, high-dose IV steroids may be given alone.

A commonly used induction drug is basiliximab, an interleukin-2 (IL-2) receptor antagonist. The IL-2 receptor is expressed on activated T-lymphocytes and is a critical pathway for activating T-lymphocytes to attack and reject the organ. Basiliximab does not deplete immature T-lymphocytes and therefore cannot be used to treat rejection (only for prevention). Because the protein is humanized, infusion-related reactions are unlikely, and pre-medication is not necessary.

As an alternative to basiliximab, patients at higher risk of rejection can receive a lymphocyte-depleting medication, antithymocyte globulin. These drugs are made by injecting human T-lymphocytes into animals, allowing the animals to make antibodies against the T-lymphocytes, and then administering the animal's purified antibodies back to the human transplant recipients. Because they deplete both mature and immature T-lymphocytes, they can be used for both induction and treatment of rejection. Alemtuzumab, a monoclonal antibody usually used for leukemia and multiple sclerosis, can also be used off-label for induction. Induction immunosuppression may not be required if the transplant is from an identical twin.

DRUG	SAFETY/SIDE EFFECTS/MONITORING
Antithymocyte globulins – Bind to antigens on T-lymphocytes and interfere with their function.	
Antithymocyte Globulin (**Atgam** – Equine) (**Thymoglobulin** – Rabbit) Injection Dosing: normal equine doses are approximately 10-fold greater than the rabbit product (5-15 mg/kg/day vs. 1-1.5 mg/kg/day IV, respectively)	**BOXED WARNINGS** Administer under the supervision of a physician experienced in immunosuppressive therapy. Adequate laboratory and supportive medical resources must be readily available (e.g., epinephrine). Anaphylaxis can occur; intradermal skin testing recommended prior to the 1st dose of *Atgam*. **SIDE EFFECTS** Infusion-related reactions/cytokine release syndrome (fever, chills, pruritus, rash, ↓ BP; particularly common with the first dose), infections, leukopenia, thrombocytopenia, chest pain, ↑ BP, edema. **MONITORING** Lymphocyte profile (T-cell count), CBC with differential, vital signs during administration. **NOTES** Premedicate (diphenhydramine, acetaminophen and steroids) to lessen infusion-related reactions. Epinephrine and resuscitative equipment should be nearby. Administer over at least 4 hours (6 hours for the first dose of *Thymoglobulin*) to minimize infusion reactions. Infuse with an in-line filter.
Interleukin-2 (IL-2) receptor antagonist – Chimeric (murine/human) monoclonal antibody that inhibits the IL-2 receptor on the surface of activated T-lymphocytes.	
Basiliximab (*Simulect*) Injection Dosing: 20 mg IV on the day of transplant (day 0) then repeat dose on post-operative day 4	**BOXED WARNINGS** Use only by physicians experienced in immunosuppressive therapy. **SIDE EFFECTS** ↑ BP, fever, stomach upset/nausea/vomiting/cramping, peripheral edema, dyspnea, upper respiratory irritation/infection, tremor, painful urination. **MONITORING** Signs and symptoms of hypersensitivity and infection.

MAINTENANCE IMMUNOSUPPRESSION

Maintenance immunosuppression is generally provided by the combination of:

- A calcineurin inhibitor (CNI) such as cyclosporine or tacrolimus. Tacrolimus is the first-line CNI.
  - Belatacept may be used as an alternative to a CNI.
- An antiproliferative agent such as mycophenolate or azathioprine. Mycophenolate is first line in most protocols.
  - Mammalian target of rapamycin (mTOR) inhibitors (everolimus and sirolimus) may be used as an alternative.
- With or without steroids (typically prednisone). If the patient is low immunological risk, the steroids can be discontinued; otherwise, the long-term adverse effects need to be considered.

Suppressing the immune system via multiple mechanisms with different drug classes is designed to both lower toxicity risk of the individual immunosuppressants and reduce the risk of graft rejection. Doses and goal blood levels of maintenance immunosuppression vary depending on the type of transplant, drug interactions, time from transplant, risk for rejection and specific transplant center protocols. The following drug tables contain some dosing and blood level information, but remember that this varies in practice.

DRUG	DOSING	SAFETY/SIDE EFFECTS/MONITORING
Systemic steroids – Naturally occurring hormones that prevent or suppress inflammatory and cytokine gene expression.		
Prednisone, others	2.5-20 mg PO daily, or on alternate days	**SHORT-TERM SIDE EFFECTS** Fluid retention, stomach upset, emotional instability (euphoria, mood swings, irritability), insomnia, ↑ appetite, weight gain, acute rise in blood glucose and blood pressure with high doses. **LONG-TERM SIDE EFFECTS** Adrenal suppression/Cushing's syndrome, impaired wound healing, ↑ BP, diabetes, acne, osteoporosis, impaired growth in children. See Systemic Steroids & Autoimmune Conditions chapter for further information on chronic steroid use.
Antiproliferative agents – Inhibit T- and B-lymphocyte proliferation by altering purine nucleotide synthesis.		
Mycophenolate Mofetil (CellCept) Tablet, Capsule, Suspension, Injection **Mycophenolic Acid (Myfortic)** Delayed-Release Tablet	1-1.5 g PO/IV BID (CellCept) or 360-720 mg PO BID (Myfortic)	**BOXED WARNINGS** ↑ risk of infection, lymphoma and skin malignancies; ↑ risk of congenital malformations and spontaneous abortions when used during pregnancy; should only be prescribed by healthcare providers experienced in immunosuppressive therapy. **SIDE EFFECTS** Diarrhea, GI upset, vomiting, leukopenia, ↑ or ↓ BP, edema, tachycardia, pain, ↑ BG, hypo/hyperkalemia, hypomagnesemia, hypocalcemia, hypercholesterolemia, tremor, acne, infections. **MONITORING** CBC, intolerable diarrhea, renal function, LFTs, signs of infection. **NOTES** REMS drug. CellCept and Myfortic are not interchangeable due to differences in absorption (CellCept 500 mg ≅ to Myfortic 360 mg). Myfortic is enteric coated to decrease diarrhea (1% absolute difference with CellCept vs. Myfortic). Tablets must be protected from light; dispense in a light-resistant container, such as the manufacturer's original container. CellCept IV is stable in D5W only. Do not use IV if allergy to polysorbate 80. Begin infusion within 4 hours of reconstitution. Decreases efficacy of oral contraceptives.

DRUG	DOSING	SAFETY/SIDE EFFECTS/MONITORING
Azathioprine *(Azasan, Imuran)* Tablet, Injection	1-3 mg/kg PO daily, for maintenance CrCl < 50 mL/min: adjustment required	**BOXED WARNINGS** ↑ risk of malignancy (e.g., lymphomas); hematologic toxicities (leukopenia, thrombocytopenia) and mutagenic potential. **WARNINGS** Patients with genetic deficiency of thiopurine methyltransferase (TPMT) are at ↑ risk for myelosuppression and may require lower dose; GI (severe N/V/D), hematologic (leukopenia, thrombocytopenia, anemia) and hepatotoxicity. **SIDE EFFECTS** GI upset (N/V), rash, ↑ LFTs, myelosuppression. **MONITORING** LFTs, CBC, renal function.

Calcineurin inhibitors – Suppress cellular immunity by inhibiting T-lymphocyte activation.

Tacrolimus *(Prograf)* Capsule, Granules for Oral Solution, Injection Extended-Release Capsule – *Astagraf XL* Extended-Release Tablet – *Envarsus XR* *Protopic* – topical for eczema	Initial: 0.1-0.2 mg/kg/day PO (depending on transplant type) For *Prograf*, give in 2 divided doses, every 12 hours For *Astagraf XL* and *Envarsus XR*, give as a single dose, every 24 hours PO IR doses are 3-4 times that of IV; start oral dosing 8-12 hours after last IV dose	**BOXED WARNINGS** ↑ susceptibility to infection; possible development of lymphoma; administer under the supervision of a physician experienced in organ transplantation in a facility appropriate for monitoring and managing therapy. Extended-release tacrolimus (*Astagraf XL*) associated with ↑ mortality in female liver transplant recipients. **SIDE EFFECTS** ↑ BP, nephrotoxicity, ↑ BG, neurotoxicity (tremor, headache, dizziness, paresthesia), hypo/hyperkalemia, hypomagnesemia, hypo/hyperphosphatemia, hyperlipidemia, QT prolongation, alopecia, edema, chest pain, insomnia, generalized pain, rash/pruritus, diarrhea, abdominal pain, nausea, dyspepsia, anorexia, constipation, urinary tract infection, anemia, leukopenia, leukocytosis, thrombocytopenia, elevated liver enzymes, arthralgia. **MONITORING** Specific trough level goal (usually within the range of 3-15 ng/mL) varies based on the type of transplant, time since transplant, concomitant immunosuppression and history of rejection. Serum electrolytes (K, Phos and Mg), renal function, LFTs, BP, blood glucose, lipid profile. **NOTES** Do not interchange XL to immediate-release (IR). IV is administered as a continuous infusion; must use non-PVC bag and tubing. Numerous drug interactions: this is a CYP450 3A4 and P-gp substrate; avoid alcohol. *Prograf*: take consistently with or without food; food decreases absorption, higher fat food decreases absorption the most. *Astagraf XL*: take every morning on an empty stomach (1 hour before or 2 hours after a meal). *Envarsus XR*: take once daily on an empty stomach, preferably in the morning.

DRUG	DOSING	SAFETY/SIDE EFFECTS/MONITORING
Cyclosporine (modified: **Gengraf, Neoral;** non-modified: **Sandimmune**) Capsule, Oral Solution, Injection **Restasis** drops for dry eyes	Cyclosporine (modified): initial dosing of ~8 ± 4 mg/kg/day, divided BID and then individualized to achieve target trough level Cyclosporine (non-modified): 3-10 mg/kg/day, divided BID, for maintenance, individualized to achieve target trough level IV cyclosporine (Sandimmune) dose is ⅓ of the PO dose Goal trough 100-400 ng/mL (nephrotoxicity can occur at any level)	**BOXED WARNINGS** Nephrotoxicity; ↑ risk of lymphoma and other malignancies, including skin cancer; ↑ risk of infection; can cause ↑ BP; only experienced providers should prescribe cyclosporine, cyclosporine (modified – Gengraf/Neoral) has 20-50% greater bioavailability compared to cyclosporine (non-modified – Sandimmune) and cannot be used interchangeably. **SIDE EFFECTS** ↑ BP, nephropathy, hyperkalemia, hypomagnesemia, hirsutism, gingival hyperplasia, edema, ↑ BG, neurotoxicity (tremor, headache, paresthesia), abdominal discomfort/nausea/diarrhea, ↑ triglycerides, viral infections, QT prolongation. **MONITORING** Trough levels, serum electrolytes (K and Mg), renal function, LFTs, BP, blood glucose, lipid profile. **NOTES** Numerous drug interactions: CYP3A4 inhibitor, and a CYP3A4 and P-gp substrate. Do not administer oral liquid from a plastic or styrofoam cup. Use the syringe provided and do not rinse before or after use. IV: non-PVC sets should be used to minimize leaching of DEHP.

Mammalian target of rapamycin (mTOR) kinase inhibitors – Inhibit T-lymphocyte activation/proliferation; may be synergistic with CNIs.

Everolimus (Zortress) Tablet Afinitor and Afinitor Disperz for treatment of breast, pancreatic, neuroendocrine and renal cancers; tuberous sclerosis complex associated cancers and partial seizures	Initial: 0.75-1 mg PO BID; adjust maintenance dose if needed to reach serum trough of 3-8 ng/mL	**BOXED WARNINGS** Only experienced prescribers should prescribe everolimus, ↑ risk of infection and cancers; when used with cyclosporine, reduced doses are recommended; ↑ risk of renal and hepatic artery thrombosis can result in graft loss; not recommended in heart transplant. **WARNINGS** Hyperlipidemia/hypertriglyceridemia, angioedema, impaired wound healing, fluid accumulation, pneumonitis (discontinue drug if this develops), proteinuria, anemia, lymphocytopenia, thrombocytopenia, new-onset diabetes, male infertility. **SIDE EFFECTS** Peripheral edema, ↑ BP, constipation, N/V/D, headache, ↑ BG, fatigue, fever, rash/pruritus, xeroderma, acne, onychoclasis (nail disease), abdominal discomfort, stomatitis, dysgeusia, weight loss, dry mouth, risk of renal and hepatic artery thrombosis (do not use within 30 days of transplant). **MONITORING** Trough levels, renal function, LFTs, lipids, blood glucose, BP, CBC, signs of infection. **NOTES.** Numerous drug interactions: CYP3A4 and P-gp substrate. Must be protected from light and moisture.
Sirolimus (Rapamune) Tablet, Oral Solution	Usually 1-5 mg/day Serum trough concentrations are determined 3-4 days after loading doses and 7-14 days after dosage adjustments; approximate range 4-12 ng/mL, level dependent on concurrent drug use, including potent inhibitors or inducers of CYP3A4 or P-gp	**BOXED WARNINGS** ↑ risk of infection; ↑ risk of lymphoma; only experienced prescribers should prescribe sirolimus; not recommended for use in liver or lung transplantation. **WARNINGS** Impaired wound healing, angioedema, fluid accumulation, decline in renal function, hyperlipidemia, latent viral infections, ↑ risk of hemolytic uremic syndrome when used with a CNI. **SIDE EFFECTS** Irreversible pneumonitis/bronchitis/cough (discontinue therapy if this develops), ↑ BG, peripheral edema, ↑ BP, headache, pain, insomnia, acne, constipation, abdominal pain, diarrhea, nausea, anemia, thrombocytopenia, arthralgia. **MONITORING** Trough levels, renal function, LFTs, lipids, blood glucose, BP, CBC, signs of infection. **NOTES** Tablets and oral solution are not bioequivalent. Numerous drug interactions: CYP3A4 and P-gp substrate.

DRUG	DOSING	SAFETY/SIDE EFFECTS/MONITORING

Belatacept – Inhibits T-lymphocyte activation and production of inflammatory mediators by binding to CD80 and CD86 on antigen presenting cells, blocking costimulation with CD28 on T-lymphocytes.

Belatacept *(Nulojix)*

Injection

Initial: 10 mg/kg on days 1, 5 and then at the end of weeks 2, 4, 8, and 12 after transplantation

Maintenance: 5 mg/kg at the end of week 16 after transplantation and then monthly thereafter

Dose using TBW and round dose to the nearest 12.5 mg

BOXED WARNINGS

↑ risk of post-transplant lymphoproliferative disorder (PTLD) with the highest risk in recipients without immunity to Epstein-Barr Virus (EBV); use in EBV seropositive patients only.

↑ risk of infection and malignancies; avoid use in liver transplant patients due to risk of graft loss and death; administer under the supervision of a prescriber experienced in immunosuppressive therapy.

WARNINGS

↑ risk of opportunistic infections, sepsis and/or fatal infections, ↑ risk of tuberculosis (TB); test for latent TB prior to initiation and treat latent TB prior to use.

SIDE EFFECTS

Headache, anemia, leukopenia, constipation, diarrhea, nausea, peripheral edema, ↑ or ↓ BP, cough, photosensitivity, insomnia, urinary tract infection, pyrexia, ↑ or ↓ K, hypophosphatemia.

MONITORING

Neurological, cognitive or behavioral signs/symptoms [consider progressive multifocal leukoencephalopathy (PML), PTLD or CNS infection]; signs/symptoms of infection, TB screening prior to initiation, EBV seropositive verification prior to initiation.

NOTES

Use silicone-free disposable syringe (comes with drug).

TRANSPLANT DRUGS: WHAT'S USED, WHEN

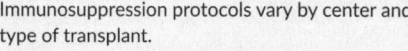

Immunosuppression protocols vary by center and type of transplant.

Induction Immunosuppressants
- Basiliximab, an interleukin-2 (IL-2) receptor antagonist
- Antithymocyte globulin in patients at higher risk of rejection
- High-dose IV steroids

Maintenance Immunosuppressants
- The calcineurin inhibitors (CNIs) [tacrolimus (primarily) or cyclosporine]
  - Belatacept as an alternative to a CNI
- Adjuvant medications given with a CNI (to achieve adequate immunosuppression while decreasing the dose and toxicity of the individual agents)
  - Antiproliferative agents (mycophenolate or azathioprine)
  - mTOR inhibitors (everolimus or sirolimus)
- Steroids at lower or tapering doses

DRUG INTERACTIONS

- Cyclosporine inhibits CYP3A4. Both cyclosporine and tacrolimus are CYP3A4 and P-glycoprotein (P-gp) substrates. Inducers of either enzyme (e.g., carbamazepine, nafcillin, rifampin) decrease the CNI concentration, and inhibitors (e.g., azole antifungals, diltiazem, erythromycin) increase the CNI concentration. Both interact with the majority of drugs.

- Cyclosporine can ↓ mycophenolate and ↑ sirolimus, everolimus and some statins (which transplant patients are usually taking).

- Tacrolimus absorption is decreased by food.

- Azathioprine is metabolized by xanthine oxidase. Avoid using azathioprine with xanthine oxidase inhibitors (allopurinol or febuxostat). Febuxostat is contraindicated. If allopurinol is used, reduce the azathioprine dose by 75%.

- Use of azathioprine with other drugs that can cause myelosuppression should be done cautiously.

- Mycophenolate can ↓ levels of hormonal contraception; mycophenolate can be ↓ by antacids and multivitamins, cyclosporine, metronidazole, PPIs, quinolones, sevelamer, bile acid resins and rifampin and derivatives. Monitor for additive myelosuppression when using mycophenolate with other marrow suppressing drugs.

- Avoid grapefruit juice and St. John's wort with either CNI.

- Caution with additive drugs that are nephrotoxic with tacrolimus and cyclosporine.

- Caution with additive drugs that raise blood glucose with tacrolimus, steroids, cyclosporine and the mTOR inhibitors (everolimus/sirolimus).

- Caution with additive drugs that worsen lipids with the mTOR inhibitors, steroids and cyclosporine.

- Caution with additive drugs that raise blood pressure with steroids, cyclosporine and tacrolimus.

ORGAN TRANSPLANT COMPLICATIONS

MONITORING BY PATIENT & HEALTH CARE TEAM

In addition to symptoms of drug toxicity, patients need to monitor for symptoms of organ rejection.

> **Monitoring Questions**
> Is it a symptom of drug **toxicity**?
> Is it a symptom of **organ rejection**?
> Is it a symptom of an **infection**?

Common symptoms of acute rejection include flu-like symptoms, such as chills, body aches, nausea, cough, shortness of breath and organ-specific symptoms that depend on the transplant type.

Examples include:

- Heart failure symptoms or a new arrhythmia could be due to heart transplant rejection.

- A decrease in urine output, fluid retention, blood pressure elevation or graft tenderness could be due to kidney transplant rejection.

Immunosuppressive medications require careful monitoring (including drug trough levels for some) to minimize toxicities and the incidence of rejection. Trough levels should be drawn 30 minutes before a scheduled dose.

Keep in mind which maintenance immunosuppressants have the highest incidence of certain adverse effects:

- Nephrotoxicity (tacrolimus and cyclosporine)

- Worsening or new-onset diabetes (tacrolimus, steroids and cyclosporine)

- Worsening lipid parameters (mTOR inhibitors, steroids and cyclosporine)

- Hypertension (steroids, cyclosporine and tacrolimus)

All transplant recipients must self-monitor for symptoms of infection:

- Fever of 100.4°F (38°C) or higher (lower if elderly), chills

- Cough, more sputum or change in color of sputum, sore throat

- Pain with passing urine, ear or sinus pain

- Mouth sores or a wound that does not heal

BOXED WARNINGS FOR TRANSPLANT DRUGS: THERE'S A LOT OF OVERLAP

Infection Risk
Transplant drugs suppress the immune system to prevent it from attacking the transplanted organ. The flip side is that the immune system is suppressed, and this increases the risk of different types of infections.

Sometimes, infection prophylaxis is needed, which can include the same drugs used for opportunistic infection in HIV when the CD4+ count is low.

Cancer Risk
A healthy immune system suppresses some types of cancers, including lymphomas, melanoma and non-melanoma skin cancers. Kaposi's sarcoma is another type of cancer that occurs with a severely depressed immune system but is mostly seen in HIV.

"Only Experienced Prescribers..."
Transplant drugs require experienced physicians. This is especially important when the drugs are started. The transplant team includes several types of highly skilled practitioners, including pharmacists who have specialized in managing transplant drugs.

ACUTE REJECTION

Acute rejection of the transplanted organ arises from either T-cell (cellular) or B-cell (humoral or antibody) mediated mechanisms. Both types can occur simultaneously (mixed rejection). Distinguishing the type of rejection via biopsy is essential to determine treatment.

An initial approach to treating acute cellular rejection (ACR) is the administration of high-dose steroids and increased levels of maintenance immunosuppression. For steroid-resistant or more aggressive ACR, antithymocyte globulin is administered. Another option for steroid-resistant ACR is off-label use of alemtuzumab.

Antibody-mediated rejection (AMR), sometimes referred to as humoral rejection, is more challenging to treat as the antibodies against the graft must be removed and then suppressed from recurring. This is accomplished with plasmapheresis and administration of intravenous immunoglobulin (IVIG) and steroids, followed by a dose of rituximab (see the Acute & Critical Care Medicine chapter for more information on IVIG). Rituximab, a monoclonal antibody against the CD20 antigen on B-cells, will prevent further antibody development. See the Systemic Steroids & Autoimmune Conditions and Oncology II chapters.

REDUCING INFECTION RISK

The use of strong immunosuppressants has made solid organ transplant widely available and successful but correlates with infection risk. The majority of infections are opportunistic, and these are a major cause of death in transplant recipients. Opportunistic infections caused by organisms that are ubiquitous (everywhere) in the environment rarely cause disease in the immunocompetent host (persons with a functional immune system). See the Infectious Diseases IV chapter.

Infection prophylaxis is essential. Infection control must include reducing risk from transmission, such as proper hand-washing techniques (see the Medication Safety & Quality Improvement chapter), air filtration systems, keeping the mouth clean and keeping away from dusty, crowded areas and sick people.

Prophylactic drug use is often needed. The drugs used for opportunistic infection prophylaxis are often the same as those used for treatment, but treatment usually requires larger doses, IV administration and a combination of drugs. Vaccine-preventable illness is an important consideration pre-transplant since live vaccines cannot be given post-transplant (see Study Tip Gal below).

CANCER

Cancer risk is higher in transplant recipients compared to the general population. The cancer risk is similar to that seen with the use of immunosuppressant medications used for autoimmune conditions.

Some cancer types are viral-mediated and related to immunosuppression, which causes increased cancer incidence. For example, the Epstein-Barr virus infects most people without serious consequences. In transplant recipients, there is a marked increase in the risk of malignancies associated with the infection.

Age-appropriate cancer screening is performed as part of the transplant candidate work-up. Screening for common cancers is routine, along with lifestyle measures known to reduce risk. Skin cancer is common following a transplant. Sunscreen must be used routinely, along with sun avoidance or sun protection with clothing. The skin should be assessed professionally at least annually.

CARDIOVASCULAR DISEASE

Many of the medications used to prevent transplant rejection can cause metabolic syndrome. These patients are among the highest risk for cardiovascular disease (CVD), so blood pressure, blood glucose, cholesterol and weight must be tightly controlled. Specific goals based on transplant protocols are managed by specialists, including pharmacists, who have received transplant medicine training. Blood glucose is managed according to the ADA guidelines and cholesterol to the ACC/AHA guidelines. Weight is measured at each visit, and weight loss programs are used as-needed. Refer to the individual chapters for treatment of these conditions, but keep in mind that drug interactions and adverse effects may limit the use of standard first-line therapies in some transplant patients.

VACCINE-PREVENTABLE ILLNESS IN TRANSPLANT RECIPIENTS

Required vaccines are given pre-transplant if not up-to-date (see the Immunizations chapter for additional information).

Inactivated vaccines can be given 3-6 months post-transplant (once the immune system recovers from the induction immunosuppression), except for the influenza vaccine, which can be administered 1 month post-transplant.

Live vaccines cannot be given post-transplant.

Important vaccines for transplant recipients:
- Influenza (inactivated, not live) annually
- Pneumococcal vaccine in adults ≥ 19 years. Give one of the following:
  - PCV20 (*Prevnar 20*) x 1 or
  - PCV15 (*Vaxneuvance*) x 1 followed by PPSV23 (*Pneumovax 23*) x 1 ≥ 8 weeks later.

- Varicella vaccine
  - High risk for serious varicella infections, with a very high risk of disseminated disease if infection occurs.
  - Vaccinate pre-transplant.
  - Vaccinate close contacts. Although there is a small risk that transmission could occur (from the vaccine recipient to the transplant recipient), ACIP states that the benefits outweigh the risk of transmission.
  - If a vaccinated household contact develops a rash they are considered contagious, and must avoid contact with the transplant recipient and contact their physician.
  - If the transplant patient develops a rash, they need to be seen right away.

KEY COUNSELING POINTS

See the Drug Formulations and Patient Counseling chapter for counseling language/layman's terminology.

See the Drug Interactions section.

ALL IMMUNOSUPPRESSANTS

- Take the medication <u>exactly as prescribed</u> by your healthcare provider, at the same time every day. <u>Stay consistent on how you take your medication.</u>
- If getting a blood test to measure the drug level, take your medication after you have your blood drawn (not before). It is important to measure the <u>lowest (trough) level</u> of drug in your blood (30 minutes before a scheduled dose).
- Can increase risk of:
  - ❑ Infection.
  - ❑ Cancer, particularly lymphoma and skin cancer.
- Many drug interactions (including natural products and OTC medications).
- Live vaccines must be avoided. Check with your transplant physician before getting any vaccines.

Mycophenolate

- Mycophenolic acid (*Myfortic*) and mycophenolate mofetil (*CellCept*) are not interchangeable. Do not switch between products unless directed by your prescriber.
- Can cause diarrhea.
- Avoid in pregnancy (teratogenic). Birth control pills do not work as well with this drug.
- Drug interactions due to binding. Avoid taking antacids and vitamins at the same time.

Tacrolimus

- Take <u>every 12 hours or once daily in the morning for XL or XR formulations.</u>
- Taking on an <u>empty stomach</u> is best for absorption. However it is taken, consistency is important (with food or without food).
- Can cause:
  - ❑ Nephrotoxicity.
  - ❑ Increased blood pressure.
  - ❑ Hyperglycemia.
  - ❑ QT prolongation.
  - ❑ Alopecia.
- Avoid grapefruit.

Cyclosporine

- Do not administer oral liquid from a plastic or styrofoam cup. Use the measuring device provided and do not rinse it before or after the dose. Use only recommended liquids for dilution (i.e., orange juice).
- Different brands deliver different amounts of medication; do not switch brands of cyclosporine unless directed by your prescriber.
- Can cause:
  - ❑ Nephrotoxicity.
  - ❑ Increased blood pressure.
  - ❑ Hyperglycemia.
  - ❑ Gingival hyperplasia.
  - ❑ Hirsutism.
- Avoid grapefruit.

Select Guidelines/References

Kidney Disease: Improving Global Outcomes (KDIGO) Transplant Work Group. KDIGO Clinical Practice Guideline for the Care of Kidney Transplant Recipients. *Am J Transplant*. 2009; 9 (Suppl 3):S1-155.

Lucey MR, Terrault N, Ojo L et al. Long-Term Management of the Successful Adult Liver Transplant: 2012 Practice Guideline by AASLD and the American Society of Transplantation. https://www.aasld.org/sites/default/files/2019-06/2013PracticeGuidelineLongTermManagmentofSuccessfulLT.pdf (accessed 2022 Feb 28).

Costanzo MR, Dipchand A, Starling R et al. The International Society of Heart and Lung Transplantation Guidelines for the Care of Heart Transplant Recipients. *J Heart Lung Transplant*. 2010; 29:914-56.

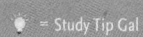 = Study Tip Gal   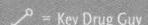 = Key Drug Guy

© iStock.com/shironosov

CHAPTER 57

WEIGHT LOSS

BACKGROUND

The conditions of overweight and obesity are national health threats and a major public health challenge. Data from the CDC estimates that ~74% of U.S. adults and ~40% of children and adolescents are overweight (BMI 25 – 29.9 kg/m^2) or obese (BMI ≥ 30 kg/m^2). A person who is overweight is at a higher risk for coronary heart disease, hypertension, stroke, type 2 diabetes, certain types of cancer and premature death. In addition to the health risks, being overweight can reduce quality of life and cause social stigmatization and discrimination.

Weight loss must involve an "energy deficit." Calories must be decreased and/or energy expenditure increased to force the body to use fat as an energy source. If someone is hungry, it is difficult not to eat. Many weight loss drugs work by increasing satiety (feeling full) or decreasing appetite.

MEDICAL CONDITIONS, DRUGS AND WEIGHT

Prior to starting a weight loss treatment plan, other causes of weight gain should be evaluated and managed, as appropriate. Select drugs and medical conditions can cause weight gain (see Key Drugs Guy on top of the following page). Weight will increase when a medication known to cause weight loss is discontinued, when a medication that causes weight gain is started or if a condition with weight gain is left untreated. Weight will decrease when a condition known to cause weight gain is treated.

When treating other medical conditions in patients who are overweight or obese, medications that cause weight gain should be avoided (if able) and preference should be given to medications that can cause weight loss (see Key Drugs Guy on the bottom of the following page).

SELECT DRUGS/CONDITIONS THAT CAN CAUSE WEIGHT GAIN

KEY DRUGS

Antipsychotics
(e.g., clozapine, olanzapine, risperidone, quetiapine)

Diabetes drugs (insulin, meglitinides, sulfonylureas, thiazolidinediones)

Divalproex/valproic acid

Gabapentin, pregabalin

Lithium

Mirtazapine

Steroids

TCAs (e.g., amitriptyline, nortriptyline)

Conditions:
Hypothyroidism

Others:

Beta-blockers

Dronabinol

Hormones (e.g., estrogen, megestrol)

MAO inhibitors

SSRIs (paroxetine, others may be weight neutral)

Vasodilators (e.g., minoxidil)

TREATMENT PRINCIPLES

The American Association of Clinical Endocrinologists/American College of Endocrinology (AACE/ACE) obesity guidelines recommend various eating plans that are either reduced-calorie (daily deficit ~500 – 750 kcal) or individualized, based on personal and cultural preferences. These include Mediterranean, DASH, low-carbohydrate, low-fat, volumetric, high protein and vegetarian diets. Select patients may be candidates for very low-calorie diets.

Physical activity should increase to ≥ 150 minutes per week, performed on three to five separate days. This should include resistance exercises two or three times weekly. Behavioral interventions should be used to assist patients, depending on factors that are hindering successful weight loss. These can include self-monitoring (of food intake, exercise, weight), goal setting, stress reduction, stimulus control, use of social support structures and/or guidance by trained educators.

Weight loss medications should only be added when lifestyle measures alone have failed to achieve adequate weight loss, maintain weight loss or prevent continued weight gain. In patients with weight-related complications (e.g., diabetes, dyslipidemia, hypertension, sleep apnea), weight loss medications may be started at the same time as lifestyle measures. As weight decreases, these conditions can improve. Treatment may need to be reevaluated and possibly decreased to prevent adverse effects (e.g., hypoglycemia, hypotension).

DRUG TREATMENT

OTC SUPPLEMENTS

OTC weight loss supplements commonly contain stimulants, such as bitter orange (see the Dietary Supplements, Natural & Complementary Medicine chapter) and/or excessive amounts of caffeine, which can be packaged under different names (e.g., yerba mate, guarana and concentrated green tea powder). OTC supplements are generally ineffective and are not recommended, as they can be harmful, especially in patients with cardiovascular disease.

PRESCRIPTION WEIGHT LOSS MEDICATIONS

Prescription drugs are not appropriate for patients with small amounts of weight to lose. They are indicated with a BMI ≥ 30 kg/m², or a BMI ≥ 27 kg/m² with at least one weight-related condition, such as dyslipidemia, hypertension or diabetes. Weight loss medications are only used in addition to a dietary plan and increased physical activity. Selection of a medication is based on the patient's comorbid conditions. Treatments can worsen other conditions and must be avoided in certain populations (see Study Tip Gal on the following page).

Older stimulant drugs (e.g., phentermine, diethylpropion) are only used short-term to "jump-start" a diet. The newer drugs Qsymia, Contrave, Saxenda, Wegovy and the orlistat formulations can be continued long-term for weight maintenance. Weight loss drugs should be discontinued if they do not produce at least a 5% weight loss at 12 weeks.

SELECT DRUGS/CONDITIONS THAT CAN CAUSE WEIGHT LOSS

KEY DRUGS

ADHD drugs
(e.g., amphetamine, methylphenidate)

Bupropion

GLP-1 agonists
(e.g., exenatide, liraglutide)

Pramlintide

Roflumilast

SGLT2 inhibitors (e.g., canagliflozin, empagliflozin)

Topiramate

Conditions:
Hyperthyroidism
Celiac disease
Inflammatory bowel disease

Others:
Acetylcholinesterase inhibitors
(e.g., donepezil, rivastigmine, galantamine)

Antiepileptic drugs
(zonisamide, ethosuximide)

Interferons

Thyroid drugs (e.g., levothyroxine)

Conditions:
Cystic fibrosis
GERD or peptic ulcer disease
Lupus
Tuberculosis (active disease)

PRESCRIPTION WEIGHT LOSS DRUGS: AVOID OR USE CAUTION

PREGNANCY	HYPERTENSION	DEPRESSION	SEIZURES	TAKING OPIOIDS
Avoid all weight loss drugs	**Avoid** *Contrave* – contraindicated with uncontrolled BP (contains bupropion) **Caution** *Qsymia* – monitor HR (contains phentermine)	**Caution in young adults and adolescents** *Contrave* – suicide risk (contains bupropion)	**Avoid** *Contrave* – lowers seizure threshold (contains bupropion) **Caution** *Qsymia* – must taper off slowly if used (contains topiramate)	**Avoid** *Contrave* – blocks opioid receptors (contains naltrexone)

WEIGHT LOSS DRUGS

DRUG	DOSING	SAFETY/SIDE EFFECTS/MONITORING
Phentermine: sympathomimetic (stimulant); release of norepinephrine stimulates the satiety center which ↓ appetite **Topiramate: ↑ satiety and ↓ appetite, possibly by ↑ GABA, blocking glutamate receptors and/or inhibition of carbonic anhydrase**		
Phentermine/Topiramate ER *(Qsymia)* C-IV REMS drug due to teratogenic risk; pregnancy test needed before treatment and monthly thereafter; use effective contraception during treatment	Start: 3.75 mg/23 mg PO QAM x 14 days; titrate up based on weight loss Max dose: 15 mg/92 mg PO QAM CrCl < 50 mL/min: max dose is 7.5 mg/46 mg/day	**CONTRAINDICATIONS** Pregnancy, glaucoma, hyperthyroidism, MAO inhibitor use within past 14 days **SIDE EFFECTS** Tachycardia, CNS effects [e.g., insomnia (take in the morning to ↓ risk), depression, anxiety, suicidal thoughts, headache, paresthesias], vision problems, constipation, dry mouth, ↓ HCO3, upper respiratory tract infection, ↑ SCr **NOTES** Taper off due to seizure risk
Naltrexone: ↓ food cravings Bupropion: ↓ appetite		
Naltrexone/Bupropion *(Contrave)*	ER tablet: 8 mg/90 mg Week 1: 1 tab PO QAM Week 2: 1 tab PO QAM, 1 tab PO QPM Week 3: 2 tabs PO QAM, 1 tab PO QPM Week 4+: 2 tabs PO QAM, 2 tabs PO QPM Do not cut, chew or crush; swallow whole Fatty food increases drug levels; do not take with high-fat meal	**BOXED WARNING** Not approved for treatment of major depressive disorder (MDD) or psychiatric disorders; antidepressants (bupropion) can increase the risk of suicidal thinking and behavior in children, adolescents and young adults; not approved for use in pediatric patients **CONTRAINDICATIONS** Pregnancy, chronic opioid use or acute opiate withdrawal, uncontrolled hypertension, seizure disorder, use of other bupropion-containing products, bulimia/anorexia, abrupt discontinuation of alcohol, benzodiazepines, barbiturates, antiepileptic drugs, use of MAO inhibitors within 14 days **WARNINGS** Use caution with psychiatric disorders, discontinue with s/sx of hepatotoxicity, can ↑ HR and BP, glaucoma **SIDE EFFECTS** N/V, constipation, headache, dizziness, dry mouth, insomnia, ↑ SCr **NOTES** Naltrexone blocks opioids and buprenorphine, which blocks analgesia and can induce withdrawal; discontinue opioids or buprenorphine 7-14 days prior to use of *Contrave*

SPECIAL POPULATIONS

DRUG	DOSING	SAFETY/SIDE EFFECTS/MONITORING
Glucagon-Like Peptide 1 (GLP-1) Agonists: ↑ satiety		
Liraglutide (Saxenda) Injection **Victoza** – for diabetes Approved for use in children age ≥ 12 years with weight > 60 kg and BMI corresponding to ≥ 30 kg/m² for adults	Start: 0.6 mg SC daily x 1 week, titrate up by 0.6 mg SC daily at weekly intervals Target dose: 3 mg SC daily	**BOXED WARNING** Risk of thyroid C-cell carcinomas – seen in animal studies; risk to humans unknown **CONTRAINDICATIONS** Personal or family history of medullary thyroid carcinoma (MTC) or patients with Multiple Endocrine Neoplasia syndrome type 2 (MEN 2) *Saxenda*: pregnancy **WARNINGS** Pancreatitis, hypoglycemia, acute gallbladder disease, gastroparesis (slows gastric emptying)
Semaglutide (*Wegovy*) Injection *Ozempic* – for diabetes	Start: 0.25 mg SC weekly x 4 weeks, titrate up every 4 weeks Target dose: 2.4 mg SC weekly	**SIDE EFFECTS** Nausea (primary side effect), vomiting, diarrhea, constipation, injection site reactions **NOTES** May need to ↓ insulin or sulfonylurea/meglitinide doses to ↓ risk of hypoglycemia (see the Diabetes chapter)
Lipase inhibitor: ↓ absorption of dietary fats by ~30%		
Orlistat Rx – **Xenical** OTC – **Alli**	*Xenical:* 120 mg PO w/ each meal containing fat; take with meal or up to 1 hr after eating Indicated in ages > 12 years *Alli:* 60 mg PO w/each meal containing fat Must be used with a low-fat diet plan	**CONTRAINDICATIONS** Pregnancy, chronic malabsorption syndrome, cholestasis **WARNINGS** Liver damage (rare), cholelithiasis, ↑ urinary oxalate/kidney stones, hypoglycemia (in patients with diabetes) **SIDE EFFECTS** GI (flatus with discharge, fatty stool, fecal urgency) **NOTES** Take multivitamin with A, D, E, K and beta carotene at bedtime or separated by ≥ 2 hours; do not use with cyclosporine or separate by ≥ 3 hours; separate levothyroxine by ≥ 4 hours Must stick to dietary plan for both weight improvement and to help lessen GI side effects (max 30% of kcals from fat)
Appetite suppressants: sympathomimetics (stimulants), release of norepinephrine stimulates the satiety center which ↓ appetite		
Phentermine (Adipex-P, *Lomaira)* C-IV	15-37.5 mg PO daily, before or after breakfast, or in divided doses	**CONTRAINDICATIONS** Cardiovascular disease (e.g., uncontrolled hypertension, arrhythmias, heart failure, CAD), hyperthyroidism, glaucoma, pregnancy, breast feeding, history of drug abuse, MAO inhibitors within the past 14 days
Diethylpropion C-IV	IR: 25 mg PO TID, 1 hour before meals and mid-evening SR: 75 mg PO once at mid-morning	**SIDE EFFECTS** Tachycardia, agitation, ↑ BP, insomnia, dizziness, tremor, psychosis **MONITORING** HR, BP
Phendimetrazine C-III	IR: 35 mg PO BID-TID, 1 hr before meals ER: 105 mg PO daily, 30-60 minutes before the morning meal	**NOTES** Used short-term, up to 12 weeks, to "jump-start" a diet Stimulants taken later in the day can cause insomnia Potential for misuse/dependence
Benzphetamine C-III	25-50 mg PO daily to TID; avoid late afternoon administration	

BARIATRIC SURGERY

Guidelines recommend weight loss or bariatric surgery for adults when <u>BMI ≥ 40 kg/m²</u> or when <u>BMI ≥ 35 kg/m² with an obesity-related condition</u>. Traditional bariatric surgery restricts food intake, which leads to weight loss. Patients must commit to a lifetime of healthy eating and regular exercise to sustain the weight loss. Some common issues associated with bariatric surgery are described below.

COMMON NUTRIENT DEFICIENCIES

- Calcium is mostly absorbed in the duodenum, which may be bypassed. <u>Calcium citrate</u> supplementation is <u>preferred</u> as it has <u>non-acid-dependent absorption</u>.

- Anemia can result from <u>vitamin B12</u> and <u>iron deficiency</u>; both may require supplementation.

- <u>Iron</u> and <u>calcium</u> supplements should be taken <u>two hours prior or four hours after</u> antacids.

- Patients may require life-long supplementation of the <u>fat-soluble vitamins A, D, E and K</u> due to fat malabsorption.

MEDICATION CONCERNS

- Medications may require dose reduction and may need to be <u>crushed</u> and <u>put in liquid</u> or used in <u>transdermal form</u> for up to <u>two months post-surgery</u>. Pharmacists need to assess which drugs can be safely crushed and provide alternatives to drugs that cannot be crushed (i.e., extended-release formulations).

- Rapid weight loss can cause gallstones. <u>Ursodiol</u> (*Actigall, Urso 250, Urso Forte*) dissolves gallstones and may be needed, unless the gallbladder has been removed.

KEY COUNSELING POINTS

See the Drug Formulations and Patient Counseling chapter for counseling language/layman's terminology.

ALL WEIGHT LOSS MEDICATIONS

- Weight loss can improve diabetes and hypertension. Monitor these conditions closely; dose reductions may be needed for medications.

Phentermine/Topiramate (*Qsymia*)

- Take this medication in the morning. Avoid taking this medication in the evening, to prevent insomnia.

- Phentermine can cause increased heart rate.

Naltrexone/Bupropion (*Contrave*)

- Do not take with opioids or with a history of seizures.

- Can cause increased blood pressure.

GLP-1 Agonists

- Subcutaneous injection.

- Can cause:
  - Hypoglycemia.
  - Pancreatitis.
  - Nausea.

- Do not take with other GLP-1 agonists (used for diabetes).

Orlistat (*Xenical* and *Alli*)

- Take one capsule at each main meal, or up to one hour after a meal that contains fat.

- You should be eating a healthy diet that is low in fat in order to reduce GI side effects.

- Can cause stomach issues (e.g., fatty/oily stool, oily spotting, intestinal gas with discharge, need to have a bowel movement right away, increased number of bowel movements or poor bowel control).

Appetite Suppressants

- Can cause:
  - Increased blood pressure.
  - Increased heart rate.

Select Guidelines/References

US DHHS/ODPHP's 2020 – 2025 Dietary Guidelines for Americans, 8th Ed. Available at https://health.gov/our-work/food-nutrition (accessed 2022 Feb 15).

AACE/ACE Comprehensive clinical practice guidelines for medical care of patients with obesity. *Endoc Pract*. 2016; 22(3):1-203.

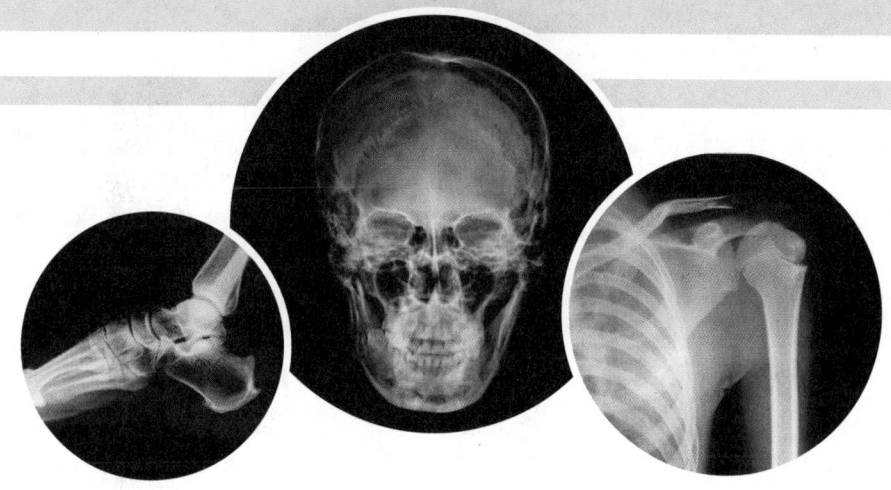

PAIN/RELATED CONDITIONS

CONTENTS

CHAPTER CONTENT

CONTENT LEGEND

 = Study Tip Gal

---

iStock.com/yaom

CHAPTER 58

PAIN

BACKGROUND

Pain can be defined as the physical suffering caused by an illness or injury. Pain can lead to a significant decrease in quality of life and ability to carry out daily tasks. In 2019, the Centers for Disease Control estimated that 20.4% of adults had chronic pain.

PATHOPHYSIOLOGY

Pain is classified into two main categories (nociceptive pain and pathophysiologic pain) based on the underlying cause of the pain. Nociceptive pain occurs when sensory nerves (nociceptors) identify tissue damage. Injured tissue releases substances [e.g., prostaglandins (PGs), substance P, histamine] which stimulate the nociceptors to send impulses to the brain that result in feeling pain. Nociceptive pain results from injury to internal organs (visceral pain) or from an injury to the skin, muscles, bones, joints or ligaments (somatic pain, which is commonly referred to as musculoskeletal pain).

Pathophysiologic pain is different from nociceptive pain as it does not result from tissue injury or damage but from damage or malfunction of the nervous system. This is commonly referred to as neuropathic pain. Various pain syndromes are considered pathophysiologic pain, such as fibromyalgia, diabetic neuropathy, chronic headaches, drug-induced toxicities (e.g., vinca alkaloids) and others.

ACUTE AND CHRONIC PAIN

The difference between acute and chronic pain is important because it impacts treatment decisions. Acute pain begins suddenly and usually feels sharp. It is typically nociceptive in nature, such as a fracture, burn, acute illness, surgery or childbirth. The pain can last just a few moments or longer, and usually goes away when the cause of the pain has resolved. Acute pain can cause anxiety and physical symptoms, including sweating and tachycardia. If acute pain goes untreated, it has been shown to increase the risk for the development of chronic pain.

Chronic pain has been described as pain that persists beyond the normal healing time (or three months), but for some conditions, there is no acute injury. It can persist with a visible injury (such as crushed lumbar vertebrae, causing lower back pain) or when no visible injury is present, such as with osteoarthritis (OA) or diabetic neuropathy (see the Diabetes chapter). OA is a common type of chronic pain caused by a breakdown in the cartilage that pads the joint, which results in stiffness, pain and/or swelling. Chronic pain is divided into cancer pain or chronic non-cancer pain, which have separate treatment guidelines. Poorly managed chronic pain is miserable and can cause depression and physical symptoms, including muscle tension and fatigue.

TREATMENT PRINCIPLES

Pain is subjective. It is primarily measured by the patient's own description, along with observations. Patients with chronic pain should be taught to monitor and document their pain by recording the pain level, the type or quality (using words such as burning, shooting, stabbing, aching) and the time of day that the pain is better or worse. Anything that worsens or lessens the pain should be noted. This helps to evaluate pain control and give guidance on pain medication changes.

Pain scales are useful to assess pain severity. Pain is commonly rated using a numeric scale (0 = no pain, 10 = worst pain) or with the visual analog scale (see figure below). The Joint Commission (TJC) standards require that pain be assessed and managed while patients are hospitalized. Hospitals must inquire about, assess, treat and re-assess pain in a timely manner using non-pharmacologic and/or pharmacologic treatments.

0 Pain Free	1 Very Mild	2 Discomforting	3 Tolerable	4 Distressing	5 Very Distressing	6 Intense	7 Very Intense	8 Utterly Horrible	9 Excruciating Unbearable	10 Unimaginable Unspeakable

© Vectoral/Shutterstock.com

SELECTING AN ANALGESIC REGIMEN

Choosing the correct analgesic regimen is important. Pain can be treated using a stepwise approach, where the choice of drug depends on the patient's self-reported pain severity. Generally, non-opioid analgesics [e.g., acetaminophen, non-steroidal anti-inflammatory drugs (NSAIDs)] are recommended for many types of acute and chronic pain. When initially using any class of analgesic (including opioids), start low and stop at the lowest dose that adequately reduces the pain. Using medicines with multiple mechanisms of action (multimodal pain control) often produces improved pain control via additive or synergistic effects. Non-opioid analgesics are most commonly used for mild pain but can be added to an opioid-based regimen to reduce the total opioid dose required and provide better pain relief. Opioids are, in general, strong analgesics, most appropriate for moderate to severe pain. Adjuvants [e.g., antidepressants, antiepileptic drugs (AEDs), muscle relaxants] should be considered for all severities of pain.

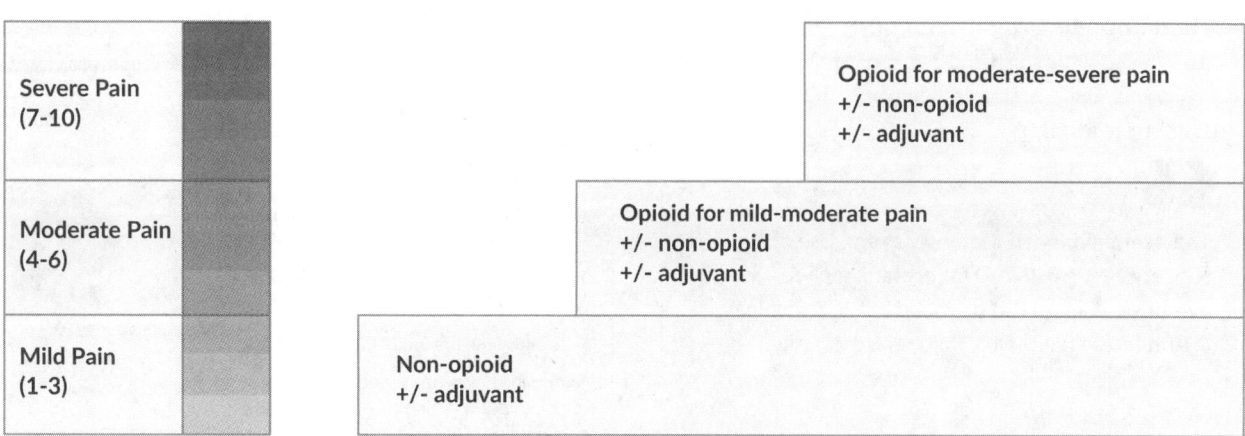

Severe Pain (7-10)

Moderate Pain (4-6)

Mild Pain (1-3)

Opioid for moderate-severe pain
+/- non-opioid
+/- adjuvant

Opioid for mild-moderate pain
+/- non-opioid
+/- adjuvant

Non-opioid
+/- adjuvant

PAIN/RELATED CONDITIONS

NON-OPIOID ANALGESICS

ACETAMINOPHEN

Acetaminophen <u>reduces pain</u> and <u>fever</u> (is an <u>antipyretic</u>) but does <u>not</u> provide an <u>anti-inflammatory</u> effect. The mechanism of action is not well defined but is thought to involve <u>inhibition of PG synthesis</u> in the central nervous system (CNS), resulting in reduced pain impulse generation.

DRUG	DOSING	SAFETY/SIDE EFFECTS/MONITORING
Acetaminophen *(Tylenol, FeverAll, Ofirmev,* most "Non-Aspirin" pain relievers) Tablet/caplet, chewable tablet, ODT, suspension, suppository, injection **FeverAll:** rectal suppository **Ofirmev:** injection Rx and OTC **+ hydrocodone** *(Lorcet,* Lortab,* Norco, Vicodin,* Verdrocet, Xodol)* **+ oxycodone** *(Endocet,* Percocet, Primlev)* **+ codeine** *(Tylenol #2,* 3, 4)* + tramadol *(Ultracet)* **+ caffeine** *(Excedrin Tension Headache)* **+ aspirin/caffeine** *(Excedrin Extra Strength, Excedrin Migraine, Goody's Powder)* **+ caffeine/pyrilamine** *(Midol Complete)* + butalbital/caffeine *(Fioricet)* +/– codeine + diphenhydramine *(Tylenol PM Extra Strength)* + ibuprofen *(Advil Dual Action)* And in multiple cough & cold products and OTC combinations	**Adults** Maximum < 4,000 mg/day from all sources Maximum of 325 mg per prescription dosing unit in combo products, per the FDA Dosing ranges and maximum doses depend on the formulation 325 mg: max 2 tabs Q4H/10 tabs per 24 hr (3,250 mg) 500 mg: max 2 tabs Q6H/6 tabs per 24 hr (3,000 mg) 650 mg ER: max 2 tabs Q8H/6 tabs per 24 hr (3,900 mg) Rectal suppository 650 mg: max 1 PR Q4H/6 per 24 hr (3,900 mg) IV max: 650 mg Q4H or 1,000 mg Q6H/4-6 injections per 24 hr (4,000 mg) **Pediatrics (< 12 yrs)** <u>10-15 mg/kg Q4-6H</u> Max: 5 doses/day OTC: use weight and age based dosing table on label Infant and children's suspension; use dosing syringe or dosing cup: <u>160 mg/5 mL</u>	**BOXED WARNINGS** Severe <u>hepatotoxicity</u> (can require liver transplant or result in death); associated with doses <u>> 4 grams/day</u> or use of <u>multiple acetaminophen-containing products</u>, risk of 10-fold dosing errors with injection **WARNINGS** Severe skin reactions including SJS, TEN (rare) Renal impairment: use cautiously **SIDE EFFECTS** Generally well-tolerated with oral administration **NOTES** <u>Avoid</u> the "APAP" abbreviation **Injection** Concentration is 10 mg/mL (in 100 mL vials); use caution with dosing Prescribe in mg, not mL All IV acetaminophen doses should be prepared in the pharmacy

*Brand name discontinued but still used in practice.

Acetaminophen Drug Interactions

- Can be used with warfarin, but if used chronically (doses > 2 grams/day), acetaminophen can increase the INR. Monitor accordingly.

- Avoid or limit alcohol use due to the risk of hepatotoxicity.

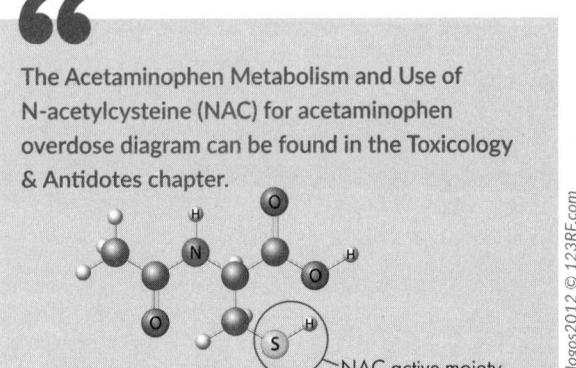

> The Acetaminophen Metabolism and Use of N-acetylcysteine (NAC) for acetaminophen overdose diagram can be found in the Toxicology & Antidotes chapter.

NAC active moiety

© logos2012 © 123RF.com

ACETAMINOPHEN OVERDOSE

The antidote for acetaminophen overdosage is N-acetylcysteine (NAC, *Acetadote*).

- Glutathione precursor (↑ glutathione).

- Administered intravenously or orally (using the solution for inhalation or injectable formulation).

The Rumack-Matthew nomogram uses the serum acetaminophen level and the time since ingestion to determine whether hepatotoxicity is likely (and the need for NAC).

NON-STEROIDAL ANTI-INFLAMMATORY DRUGS

NSAIDs include the traditional non-selective agents (e.g., ibuprofen and aspirin) and the selective cyclooxygenase (COX) 2 inhibitors. The COX-1 and 2 enzymes catalyze the conversion of arachidonic acid to PGs and thromboxane A2 (TxA2). All NSAIDs decrease the formation of PGs, which results in decreased inflammation, alleviation of pain and reduced fever. Non-selective NSAIDs block the synthesis of both COX enzymes. COX-2 selective NSAIDs block the synthesis of COX-2 only, which decreases GI risk because COX-1 protects the gastric mucosa. Blocking COX-1 decreases the formation of TxA2, which is required for both platelet activation and aggregation. Aspirin is an irreversible COX-1 and 2 inhibitor and is an effective antiplatelet agent that provides cardiovascular (CV) benefit, often referred to as cardioprotection.

Non-Aspirin Boxed Warnings

All prescription non-aspirin NSAIDs require a MedGuide due to the risks listed below. These warnings are not repeated in the drug tables.

- **GI Risk**: NSAIDs can increase the risk of serious GI adverse events, including bleeding and ulceration. Patients who are elderly, have a history of GI bleed or are taking systemic steroids, SSRIs or SNRIs are at the greatest risk. Aspirin and OTC NSAIDs do not carry a boxed warning but still have this risk.

- **CV Risk**: NSAIDs can increase the risk of MI and stroke. Avoid use in patients with CV disease or risk factors. This warning includes all OTC non-selective NSAIDs except aspirin.

- **Coronary Artery Bypass Graft (CABG) Surgery**: NSAID use is contraindicated after CABG surgery. Antiplatelet therapy (commonly aspirin) is recommended after CABG surgery.

Side Effects of All NSAIDs

- Can decrease renal clearance by reducing blood flow to the glomerulus; additional nephrotoxic agents or dehydration increases the risk. All NSAIDs should be used cautiously (or avoided) in renal failure.

- Can increase blood pressure. Use cautiously in patients with controlled hypertension, and avoid in patients with uncontrolled hypertension.

- Can cause premature closure of the ductus arteriosus, which can lead to heart failure in the baby. Do not use NSAIDs in the third trimester of pregnancy (≥ 30 weeks). See the Study Tip Gal below.

- NSAIDs can cause rare, but serious, renal impairment if used around 20 weeks gestation or later in pregnancy.

- NSAIDs can cause nausea. Salicylates cause worse nausea compared to other NSAIDs. Nausea can be minimized by taking with food, switching to an enteric-coated or buffered product or changing to a different NSAID.

- Can cause photosensitivity. Avoid the sun during mid-day hours, use sun-protective clothing and broad-spectrum sunscreen with an SPF of at least 30.

NSAIDS AND THE DUCTUS ARTERIOSUS

Before birth, the ductus arteriosus (DA) connects the pulmonary artery to the aorta, allowing oxygenated blood to flow to the baby, bypassing the immature lungs.

Do not use NSAIDs in the third trimester of pregnancy. NSAIDs can prematurely close the DA.

After birth, the DA should close on its own. In some cases, it remains patent (open) and NSAIDs can be used to help it close.

IV NSAIDs (indomethacin, ibuprofen) can be used within 14 days after birth to close a patent ductus arteriosus (PDA).

Non-Aspirin NSAIDs

DRUG	DOSING	SAFETY/SIDE EFFECTS/MONITORING
COX-1 and COX-2 Non-selective NSAIDs: all agents have GI risk, CV risk and risk in post-operative CABG setting		
Ibuprofen (Advil, Caldolor, Motrin IB, NeoProfen) Tablet, capsule, chewable tablet, suspension, injection Rx and OTC	**Adults** OTC: 200-400 mg Q4-6H Max: 1.2 grams/day Rx: 400-800 mg Q6-8H Max: 3.2 grams/day **Pediatrics** 5-10 mg/kg/dose Q6-8H (as an antipyretic) Max: 40 mg/kg/day	**SIDE EFFECTS** All NSAIDs: dyspepsia, abdominal pain, nausea (see above text) **NOTES** NeoProfen injection is indicated for closure of PDA in premature infants OTC: limit self-treatment to < 10 days Severe skin reactions, including SJS/TEN
Indomethacin (Indocin, Tivorbex) Capsule, oral suspension, suppository, injection	IR: 25-50 mg BID-TID CR: 75 mg daily-BID Tivorbex: 20 mg TID or 40 mg BID-TID	**NOTES** High risk for CNS side effects (avoid in psych conditions) The IR formulation is an older NSAID approved for gout Tivorbex is micronized for faster dissolution IV injection is indicated for closure of PDA in premature infants

DRUG	DOSING	SAFETY/SIDE EFFECTS/MONITORING
Naproxen (Aleve, Naprelan, Naprosyn) Tablet, capsule, suspension Rx and OTC + sumatriptan (Treximet) + esomeprazole **(Vimovo)** And in OTC combos with diphenhydramine and pseudoephedrine	OTC (pain, fever): 200 mg Q8-12H (1st dose can take 2 tabs) Max: 3 tabs in 24 hours (600 mg) Rx (inflammation, mild-mod pain): 500 mg Q12H (or 250 mg Q6-8H) Max: 1,000 mg/day (1,250 mg day 1)	**NOTES** Prescribers and patients sometimes prefer naproxen since it can be <u>dosed BID</u> Naproxen base 200 mg = Naproxen Na 220 mg PPI in Vimovo is used to protect the GI tract
Ketorolac (Toradol,* Acular, Sprix) Tablet, injection, nasal spray, ophthalmic Acular: ophthalmic Sprix: nasal spray	Oral: 10-20 mg x 1, then 10 mg Q4-6H PRN (max: 40 mg/day) IV (≥ 50 kg): 30 mg x 1 or 30 mg Q6H (↓ dose if ≥ 65 yrs) IM (≥ 50 kg): 60 mg x 1 or 30 mg Q6H (↓ dose if ≥ 65 yrs) Nasal spray: < 65 yrs and ≥ 50 kg: 1 spray in <u>each</u> nostril Q6-8H ≥ 65 yrs or < 50 kg: 1 spray in <u>one</u> nostril Q6-8H	**BOXED WARNINGS** Oral ketorolac: for short-term moderate to severe acute pain only as continuation of IV or IM ketorolac (<u>max combined duration</u> IV/IM and PO/nasal is <u>5 days</u> in adults); not for intrathecal or epidural use; avoid in patients with advanced renal disease or at risk for renal impairment due to volume depletion; hypersensitivity reactions to ketorolac or other NSAIDs; avoid use in labor and delivery and use with aspirin or NSAIDs; dose adjustments needed in ≥ 65 yrs or < 50 kg **WARNINGS** ↑ bleeding, <u>acute renal failure, liver failure</u> and anaphylactic shock **SIDE EFFECTS** Headache, injection site pain (often given IM) **NOTES** Usually used after surgery, never before <u>Nasal</u> spray: <u>prime</u> five times <u>before use.</u> No additional priming is needed if additional doses are used. Discard 24 hours after opening.
Piroxicam (Feldene)	10-20 mg daily	**NOTES** High risk for GI toxicity and severe skin reactions, including SJS/TEN Used when other NSAIDs have failed; may need protective agent for the gut (PPI, misoprostol)
Sulindac	150-200 mg BID	**NOTES** Sometimes used with reduced renal function, and in patients on lithium who require an NSAID

Other less commonly used NSAIDs include: meclofenamate, mefenamic acid (Ponstel), ketoprofen, fenoprofen (Nalfon), flurbiprofen, oxaprozin (Daypro – caution similar to piroxicam – higher risk of side effects)

Increased COX-2 Selectivity: lower risk for GI complications (but still present), ↑ risk MI/stroke (avoid with CV risk, avoid ↑ doses and longer duration in patients at risk for CV disease), <u>same risk for renal complications</u>

DRUG	DOSING	SAFETY/SIDE EFFECTS/MONITORING
Celecoxib (Celebrex) Capsule + amlodipine (Consensi) + tramadol (Seglentis)	OA: 100 mg BID or 200 mg daily RA: 100-200 mg BID Indications: OA, RA, juvenile RA, acute pain, primary dysmenorrhea, ankylosing spondylitis Consensi: OA pain and HTN Seglentis: acute pain	**CONTRAINDICATIONS** <u>Sulfonamide allergy</u> **NOTES** <u>Highest COX-2 selectivity</u> Avoid in pregnancy; risk greatest at ≥ 30 weeks gestation Severe skin reactions, including SJS/TEN
Diclofenac (Voltaren, Cambia, Flector, Pennsaid, Xrylix, Zipsor, Zorvolex) Tablet, capsule, cream, packet, gel (OTC), kit, patch, topical solution, injection **Voltaren** (OTC): gel Rx and OTC + misoprostol (Arthrotec)	Oral tablets: 50-75 mg BID-TID Voltaren gel: 2-4 g to affected joint four times per day (<u>total body max 32 grams/day</u>) Flector: 1 patch (180 mg) to most painful area BID Cambia: 1 packet (50 mg) mixed in water for acute migraine Zipsor: 25 mg four times per day Zorvolex: 18 mg or 35 mg TID	**BOXED WARNINGS** Arthrotec: <u>avoid in females of childbearing potential</u> unless the female is capable of complying with effective contraceptive measures **SIDE EFFECTS** Topical: occasional application site reactions (rash/pruritus) **NOTES** Has some COX-2 selectivity Oral diclofenac formulations are not bioequivalent, even if same mg strength <u>Misoprostol</u> is used to replace the gut-protective prostaglandins to ↓ GI risk; can ↑ uterine contractions (which can terminate pregnancy) and causes cramping and diarrhea Remove Flector patch before an MRI

*Brand name discontinued but still used in practice.

DRUG	DOSING	SAFETY/SIDE EFFECTS/MONITORING
Meloxicam *(Mobic, Vivlodex)* Tablet, capsule, ODT, oral suspension	7.5-15 mg once daily Capsule: 5-10 mg once daily	**NOTES** These agents have <u>some COX-2 selectivity</u> Capsules and ODT are not interchangeable with other meloxicam formulations
Etodolac Tablet, capsule, ER tablet	300-500 mg Q6-8H	
Nabumetone Tablet	1,000-2,000 mg daily (can be divided BID)	

Salicylate NSAIDs

DRUG	DOSING	SAFETY/SIDE EFFECTS/MONITORING
Aspirin/Acetylsalicylic Acid *(Ascriptin, **Bufferin**, **Ecotrin**, Durlaza, Vazalore)* Tablet, caplet, chewable tablet, liquid-filled capsule, suppository ***Ascriptin, Bufferin, Ecotrin***: EC/buffered *Durlaza* (Rx): ER capsule Rx and OTC **+ acetaminophen/caffeine *(Excedrin, Excedrin Migraine*,** *Goody's Powder)* + antacid *(Alka-Seltzer)* + caffeine *(BC Powder)* + calcium *(Bayer Women's Low Dose)* + dipyridamole *(Aggrenox)* for stroke + omeprazole *(Yosprala)* And in multiple other OTC combinations	Cardioprotection dosing: <u>81-162 mg once daily</u> *Durlaza*: 162.5 mg once daily Analgesic dosing: 325-650 mg Q4-6H *Goody's Powder*: 520 mg per packet BC: 845-1000 mg per packet	**WARNINGS** Avoid with NSAID hypersensitivity (past reaction with trouble breathing), nasal polyps, asthma <u>Avoid aspirin in children</u> and <u>teenagers</u> with any <u>viral infection</u> due to potential risk of <u>Reye's syndrome</u> (symptoms include somnolence, N/V, lethargy, confusion); other NSAIDs can be used in pediatrics Severe skin rash (rare) including SJS/TEN GI ulceration and bleeding can occur Avoid in the third trimester of pregnancy due to fetal harm **SIDE EFFECTS** <u>Dyspepsia, heartburn, bleeding</u>, nausea **NOTES** To ↓ nausea, use EC or buffered product or take with food <u>PPIs may be used to protect the gut</u> with chronic NSAID use; <u>consider the risks from chronic PPI use</u> (↓ bone density, ↑ infection risk) Do not use *Durlaza* or *Yosprala* when immediate effect is needed (e.g., myocardial infarction) Salicylate <u>overdose</u> can cause <u>tinnitus</u> <u>Methyl salicylate</u> is a popular OTC topical found in *BenGay*, *IcyHot*, *Thera-Gesic*, *Salonpas*; see Topical Adjuvants Aspirin has risk of gastritis/ulceration; the benefit of chronic (daily) use must outweigh the risk of GI bleeding
NON-ACETYLATED SALICYLATES		
Salsalate	Up to 3 grams/day, divided BID-TID	
Magnesium Salicylate *(Doan's Extra Strength)*	580 mg ES tab: 2 tablets Q6H Max: 8 tablets/day	
Choline Magnesium Trisalicylate	1 gram BID-TID or 3 grams QHS	
Diflunisal	500 mg BID-TID Max 1.5 grams daily	
Salicylate salts	No longer commonly used	

NSAID Drug Interactions

- Additive bleeding risk with other agents that can ↑ bleeding risk, such as steroids. See the Drug Interactions chapter.

- Caution using aspirin with other ototoxic agents (e.g., aminoglycosides, IV loop diuretics).

- Multiple NSAIDs should not be used together, except the addition of low dose aspirin for cardioprotection when indicated. If using <u>aspirin</u> for cardioprotection <u>and ibuprofen</u> for pain, take <u>aspirin one hour before</u> or <u>eight hours after</u> ibuprofen.

- <u>NSAIDs</u> can ↑ the levels of <u>lithium</u> and methotrexate.

OPIOID ANALGESICS

Opioid drugs interact in a variety of ways with the three primary types of opioid receptors: μ (mu), κ (kappa) and δ (delta). Opioids are mu receptor agonists in the CNS, which primarily produce pain relief, but also cause euphoria and respiratory depression. These agents are primarily used to treat moderate to severe acute pain and chronic pain.

SAFETY CONCERNS

A risk evaluation and mitigation strategy (REMS) exists for all opioid medications. Primary components of the REMS include prescriber education and counseling requirements. Opioid medications have several boxed warnings (see Study Tip Gal to the right); these are not repeated in the drug tables that follow. Periodically, patients should be assessed and educated on opioid safety.

Elderly, debilitated, cachectic patients and patients with chronic pulmonary disease (conditions associated with hypoxia) or head injury/increased intracranial pressure should be monitored closely. All are at increased risk of respiratory depression. In addition, opioids have a risk of hypotension.

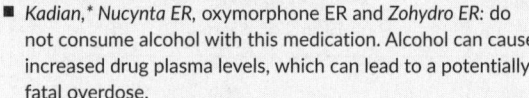

OPIOID BOXED WARNINGS

- Addiction, abuse and misuse can lead to overdose and death.
- Respiratory depression, which can be fatal.
- Use of any opioid with benzodiazepines or other CNS depressants, including alcohol, can increase the risk of death.
- *Kadian,** Nucynta ER*, oxymorphone ER and *Zohydro ER*: do not consume alcohol with this medication. Alcohol can cause increased drug plasma levels, which can lead to a potentially fatal overdose.
- Accidental ingestion/exposure of even one dose in children can be fatal. Never give this medication to anyone else (includes patches).
- Crushing, dissolving or chewing of the long-acting products can cause the delivery of a potentially fatal dose.
- Life-threatening neonatal opioid withdrawal with prolonged use during pregnancy.

Brand name discontinued but still used in practice.

TERMINOLOGY

TERM	DEFINITION
Physiological Adaptation (Physical Dependence)	Almost all patients using chronic opioids, including abusers, become physiologically adapted to the opioid, and experience physical withdrawal symptoms when the opioid is stopped or a dose is late or missed. The symptoms include anxiety, tachycardia, shakiness and shortness of breath. The withdrawal causes much suffering. Physiological adaptation is not addiction.
Addiction	A strong desire or compulsion to take the drug despite harm. Involves drug-seeking behavior, including exaggerating the pain or physical problems, getting prescriptions from multiple prescribers and/or prescription forgery.
Pseudo-Addiction	On occasion, a patient is seen at the pharmacy who appears anxious and states they ran out of medication or are afraid of running out too early. The person seems similar to an addict but is actually a legitimate pain patient with poorly controlled pain. The remedy is adequate analgesics, such as extended-release (ER) opioids, for pain control.
Tolerance	A higher opioid dose is needed to produce the same level of analgesia that a lower dose previously provided. Tolerance develops over time with chronic opioid use. It is important to distinguish whether the higher pain severity is due to a condition (e.g., cancer that has spread), or a decrease in the drug's effectiveness due to tolerance, or both. If tolerance develops, it can be preferable to switch to another opioid rather than increase the dose.
Opioid Hyperalgesia	Present when the opioid dose is increased to treat the pain, but the pain becomes worse rather than better. This occurs occasionally. If suspected, a different class of analgesic or a switch to another opioid should be tried.
Break-Through Pain [(BTP), end of dose pain]	Sharp spikes of severe pain that occur despite the use of an ER opioid. Must be treated with a fast-acting pain agent, such as an injection, transmucosal immediate-release fentanyl (TIRF) drugs (for cancer BTP only) or immediate-release (IR) opioids (less expensive, but not preferable). When multiple doses are required for BTP, a higher baseline dose can be required, or possibly a switch to a different opioid. Baseline opioids are dispensed with a BTP medication until the dose of the scheduled opioid is adequate.
Opioid-Induced Respiratory Depression (OIRD)	The usual cause of fatality in opioid overdose. Hospitalized patients receiving IV opioids must be carefully monitored for sedation and oxygen saturation.
Centrally-Acting Opioid Antagonists	There are two drugs in this group; both block opioids from binding to the mu receptor. Naloxone is used to reverse respiratory depression. Naltrexone is most commonly used in combination with an opioid to block the use of other opioids that may be taken (inappropriately) at the same time.

COMMON OPIOIDS

DRUG	DOSING	SAFETY/SIDE EFFECTS/MONITORING
ALL OPIOIDS		
C-II (except where noted otherwise)		
Constipation, nausea/vomiting (especially with acute, high-dose use), somnolence, dizziness/lightheadedness and risk of respiratory depression (see Study Tip Gal on previous page). Pruritus is common, especially in opioid-naïve patients; diphenhydramine can be used (especially with morphine) to reduce rash and itching.		
Codeine C-II: codeine tablet C-III: tablet/capsule combination products **+ acetaminophen (Tylenol #2,* 3,* 4*)** C-V: oral solution combination products (e.g., cough syrups) Select combo products: + chlorpheniramine/ pseudoephedrine + promethazine + promethazine/ phenylephrine *(Promethazine VC/ Codeine)*	15-60 mg Q4H PRN *Tylenol #3:* codeine 30 mg + acetaminophen 300 mg *Tylenol #4:* codeine 60 mg + acetaminophen 300 mg Q4-6H PRN, range 15-120 mg codeine	**BOXED WARNINGS** Respiratory depression and death have occurred in children following tonsillectomy and/or adenoidectomy found to have evidence of being ultra-rapid metabolizers of codeine due to a CYP450 2D6 polymorphism; deaths have also occurred in nursing infants after being exposed to high concentrations of morphine because the mothers were ultra-rapid metabolizers; use with CYP3A4 inducers/inhibitors or CYP2D6 inhibitors should be carefully considered due to variable effects; refer to the acetaminophen drug table for boxed warning **CONTRAINDICATIONS** Do not use in children < 12 years (any indication) and < 18 years following tonsillectomy/ adenoidectomy surgery; FDA recommends to avoid codeine-containing cough and cold products for children < 18 years of age **WARNINGS** Adolescents between 12-18 years who are obese or have sleep apnea or severe lung disease are at ↑ risk of breathing problems **SIDE EFFECTS** Codeine has a high degree of GI side effects including constipation **NOTES** Codeine-containing cough and cold preparations are no longer indicated in patients < 18 years of age – do not use Codeine, a prodrug, is metabolized to morphine via CYP2D6 (See Drug Interactions chapter)
Fentanyl (Duragesic, Sublimaze, others) Injection, patch *Actiq:* oral transmucosal lozenge on a stick ("lollipop") *Lazanda:* nasal spray *Fentora:* buccal tabs *Subsys:* spray, SL	Patch: apply 1 patch Q72H (can be Q48H) Available in 12 (delivers 12.5 mcg/ hr), 25, 50, 75, and 100 mcg/hr patch strengths Lozenge: always start with 200 mcg, can titrate to 4 BTP episodes/day. Only for cancer BTP.	**BOXED WARNINGS** Potential for medication errors when converting between dosage forms, use with strong or moderate CYP3A4 inhibitors can result in ↑ effects and potentially fatal respiratory depression, avoid exposing transdermal fentanyl to external heat **SIDE EFFECTS** Hyperhidrosis (excessive sweating), dry mouth, asthenia, loss of appetite, application site redness/erythema (patch) **NOTES** Outpatient use of fentanyl is for chronic pain management only Fentanyl is not used in opioid-naïve patients; a patient who has been using equivalent to morphine 60 mg/day or more for at least 7 days can be converted to a fentanyl patch *Actiq:* cut off stick and flush unused/unneeded doses Short t½ when given IV (boluses given Q1-2H); continuous infusion or PCA are most common Similar drugs (IV only) include alfentanil (*Alfenta*), remifentanil (*Ultiva*), sufentanil (*Dsuvia*) REMS program for transmucosal immediate-release fentanyl requires documentation of patient's opioid tolerance with each prescription **Fentanyl Patch** Analgesic effect can be seen 8-16 hrs after application; discontinue all around-the-clock opioid drugs when the patch is applied Apply to hairless skin (cut hair short if necessary) Do not apply > 1 patch each time Can be covered only with the permitted adhesive film dressings *Bioclusive* or *Tegaderm* Do not cover with a heating pad or any other bandage Some patches need to be removed before MRI (specific to each formulation and manufacturer); check the individual manufacturer package insert Dispose of patch in toilet Keep away from children and pets

DRUG	DOSING	SAFETY/SIDE EFFECTS/MONITORING
Hydrocodone IR (combination products only)	2.5-10 mg Q4-6H PRN	**BOXED WARNINGS** Refer to the acetaminophen drug table for boxed warning, initiation of CYP3A4 inhibitors (or stopping CYP3A4 inducers) can cause fatal overdose **WARNINGS** Acetaminophen and opioids: respiratory and/or CNS depression, constipation, hypotension, skin reactions (rare), caution in liver disease (avoid or limit alcohol intake) and in CYP2D6 poor metabolizers **SIDE EFFECTS** Pruritus, dry mouth **NOTES** Hydrocodone containing cough and cold preparations are no longer indicated in patients < 18 years of age – do not use
+ acetaminophen (***Lorcet,*** **Lortab,*** **Norco, Vicodin,*** *Verdrocet, Xodol*)	2.5, 5, 7.5, 10 mg hydrocodone + 325 mg acetaminophen	
Select combo products:	Usual starting dose: 5/325 mg Q6H	
+ chlorpheniramine (*TussiCaps*)		
+ chlorpheniramine/ pseudoephedrine		
+ homatropine (*Hycodan*)		
+ ibuprofen		
Hydrocodone ER (*Zohydro ER, Hysingla ER*) *Zohydro ER*: capsule *Hysingla ER*: tablet	Capsule: start at 10 mg Q12H (opioid-naïve), range 10-50 mg Tablet: start at 20 mg Q24H (opioid-naïve), range 20-120 mg	**BOXED WARNINGS** Initiation of CYP3A4 inhibitors (or stopping CYP3A4 inducers) can cause fatal overdose **NOTES** Substrate of CYP3A4 (major) and CYP2D6 (minor) Preferably avoid use if breastfeeding Abuse-deterrent formulations *Hysingla ER*: QT prolongation has occurred at doses > 160 mg/day
Hydromorphone (*Dilaudid*) Tablet, injection, solution, suppository	Initial (opioid-naïve) Oral: 2-4 mg Q4-6H PRN IV: 0.2-1 mg Q2-3H PRN	**BOXED WARNINGS** Risk of medication error with high potency (HP) injection (use in opioid-tolerant patients only) **SIDE EFFECTS** Pruritus, dry mouth, hyperhidrosis **NOTES** Potent: start low, convert carefully; high risk for overdose Commonly used in PCAs and epidurals HP injection (10 mg/mL) is a higher potency injection than *Dilaudid* (1 mg/mL) ER tablet: abuse-deterrent formulation (crush and extraction resistant) contraindicated in opioid-naïve patients Two-week washout required between hydromorphone and MAO inhibitors
Methadone (***Dolophine,*** *Methadose, Methadone Intensol*) Tablet, soluble tablet, solution, oral concentrate *Methadose* 40 mg soluble tablet; for detox and maintenance treatment in opioid addicted patients only	Initial: 2.5-10 mg Q8-12H	**BOXED WARNINGS** Life-threatening QT prolongation and serious arrhythmias (e.g., Torsades de Pointes) have occurred during treatment (most involve large, multiple daily doses), should be prescribed by professionals who know requirements for safe use, initiation of CYP450 inhibitors (or stopping inducers) can cause fatal overdose **WARNINGS** Combination with other serotonergic drugs or MAO inhibitors can ↑ the risk of serotonin syndrome, methadone also blocks reuptake of norepinephrine **SIDE EFFECTS** Hyperhidrosis **NOTES** Due to variable half-life, methadone is hard to dose safely Can ↓ testosterone and contribute to sexual dysfunction Methadone is a major CYP3A4 substrate; avoid use with inhibitors or lower methadone dose

Brand name discontinued but still used in practice.

DRUG	DOSING	SAFETY/SIDE EFFECTS/MONITORING
Meperidine (Demerol) Tablet, solution, injection	Oral/IM/SC: 50-150 mg Q3-4H PRN	**WARNINGS** Renal impairment/elderly at risk for CNS toxicity, avoid with or within 2 weeks of MAO inhibitor **SIDE EFFECTS** Hyperhidrosis **NOTES** No longer recommended as an analgesic (especially in elderly and renally impaired); avoid for chronic pain and even short-term in elderly If cannot avoid use for acute pain, use short-term or single use (e.g., sutures in ER) Used off-label for post-operative rigors (shivering) Short duration of action (pain controlled for max 3 hrs) Normeperidine (metabolite) is renally cleared and can accumulate and cause CNS toxicity, including seizures In combination with other drugs, it is serotonergic and can ↑ risk of serotonin syndrome
Morphine ER: **MS Contin, Kadian,*** *Roxanol** Injection: **Duramorph, Infumorph** Tablet (IR/ER), ER capsule, injection, solution, suppository	IR (including solution): 10-30 mg Q4H PRN ER: 15, 30, 60, 100, 200 mg Q8-12H *Kadian* can be given daily or BID IV (opioid-naïve): 2.5-5 mg Q3-4H PRN	**BOXED WARNINGS** Medication errors with oral solution (note strength), appropriate staff and equipment needed for intrathecal/epidural administration **SIDE EFFECTS** Pruritus, dry mouth, hyperhidrosis **NOTES** Do not use MSO4 or MS abbreviations for morphine or magnesium Do not crush or chew any ER products; *Kadian** can be opened and sprinkled on applesauce or soft food If renally impaired, start at a lower dose, or avoid morphine, due to accumulation of parent drug and/or active metabolite Diphenhydramine or similar can be given to block histamine-induced pruritus
Oliceridine (Olinvyk) Solution	IV: 1.5 mg bolus, 0.75 mg can be given 1 hour after bolus Max: 27 mg/day (3 mg/dose)	**WARNINGS** QT prolongation with daily doses > 27 mg **SIDE EFFECTS** Pruritus, hyperhidrosis
Oxycodone IR: **Roxicodone,** *Oxaydo* CR: **OxyContin** ER: *Xtampza ER* Tablet (IR/ER), capsule (IR/ER), solution **+ acetaminophen (Endocet,* Percocet)**	IR: 5-20 mg Q4-6H CR: 10-80 mg Q12H (60, 80 mg only for opioid-tolerant patients)	**BOXED WARNINGS** Initiation of CYP3A4 inhibitors (or stopping CYP3A4 inducers) can cause fatal overdose, caution with oxycodone oral solution and oral concentrate (confusion between mg and mL and different concentrations) **SIDE EFFECTS** Pruritus, dry mouth, hyperhidrosis **NOTES** Abuse-deterrent formulations: *Oxaydo, OxyContin* and *Xtampza ER* *Xtampza ER* capsules can be opened and contents administered with soft food or through a gastric tube Avoid high fat meals with higher doses (except re-formulated *OxyContin*) If renally impaired, start at a lower dose, or avoid oxycodone, due to accumulation of parent drug and/or active metabolite
Oxymorphone (Opana*) Tablet (IR/ER), injection	IR (opioid-naïve): 5-10 mg Q4-6H PRN	**NOTES** Do not use with moderate-to-severe liver impairment Use low doses in elderly, renal or mild liver impairment; there will be higher drug concentrations in these patients Take on empty stomach

Brand name discontinued but still used in practice.

PAIN/RELATED CONDITIONS

Opioid Drug Interactions

- Caution with other CNS depressants: additive somnolence, dizziness, confusion, increased risk of respiratory depression. These include alcohol, hypnotics, benzodiazepines and muscle relaxants. Avoid alcohol with all opioids, especially ER formulations.

- Increased risk of hypoxemia with underlying respiratory disease (e.g., COPD) and sleep apnea.

- Methadone: caution with agents that worsen cardiac function or increase arrhythmia risk. Caution with other serotonergic agents. Caution with agents that worsen renal function, elderly patients and those with seizure history.

- Hydrocodone, fentanyl, methadone and oxycodone are CYP3A4 substrates. Avoid use with CYP3A4 inhibitors. Analgesic effect is decreased with CYP3A4 inducers.

DOSING CONVERSIONS

The correct dose is the lowest dose that provides effective pain relief. If the medicine is effective, but runs out too fast, do not increase the dose. This can cause respiratory depression. Rather, give the same dose more frequently. If the medication is not effective, consider increasing the dose. It is appropriate to consider switching to a different agent if:

- The dose has been increased or the interval shortened and the pain relief is not adequate

- The side effects are intolerable (patients react differently to different opioids)

- The drug is unaffordable or not included on formulary

- Changing formulations from IV to PO

For opioid conversions (not methadone) you can use ratio conversion (see table below). When converting one opioid to another, round down (do not round up) and use breakthrough doses. A patient may respond better to one agent than another (likely due to less tolerance) and rounding the dose down will reduce the risk of overdose.

DRUG	IV/IM (MG)	ORAL (MG)
Morphine	10	30
Hydromorphone	1.5	7.5
Oxycodone	–	20
Hydrocodone	–	30
Codeine	130	200
Fentanyl	0.1	–
Meperidine	75	300
Oxymorphone	1	10

Steps to Convert

- Calculate total 24-hour dose of the current drug.

- Use ratio-conversion to calculate the dose of the new drug. (Refer to the Calculations I chapter for a review).

- Calculate the 24-hour dose of the new drug and reduce the dose at least 25% for cross-tolerance (if the exam does not specify to reduce, calculate the equivalent dose and do not reduce).

- Divide for new drug's appropriate interval and dose.

- Always have medication available for BTP while making changes. Guideline recommendation for BTP dosing ranges from 5 – 17% (typically 10 – 15%) of the total daily baseline opioid dose.

Example of Opioid Conversion

A hospice patient has been receiving 12 mg/day of IV hydromorphone. The pharmacist will convert the hydromorphone to morphine ER to be given Q12H. The hospice policy for opioid conversion is to reduce the new dose by 50%, and to use 5 – 17% of the total daily dose for BTP.

The conversion factors (the left side of the ratio-conversion below) are taken from the table on this same page. The right side of the ratio-conversion has the patient's current total daily hydromorphone IV dose in the denominator, and the total daily dose of morphine in the numerator:

$$\frac{30 \text{ mg oral morphine}}{1.5 \text{ mg IV hydromorphone}} = \frac{X \text{ mg oral morphine}}{12 \text{ mg IV hydromorphone}} \qquad X = 240 \text{ mg of oral morphine}$$

Reduce by 50%, as instructed in the problem:

50% of 240 mg = 120 mg, the correct dose of morphine ER would be 60 mg BID

Whenever possible, use an IR version of the long-acting opioid for BTP. Any drug that requires oral absorption will take time for the onset of action. For cancer pain (in which case the BTP is likely to be quite severe), a sublingual form of fentanyl may be preferred due to the faster onset. BTP medication is typically administered Q1 – 2H as needed. For the elderly, ~5% of the total daily baseline opioid dose is administered Q4H as needed.

- Using the BTP range provided by the hospice policy in the example, a dose of 15 mg IR morphine Q1 – 2H as needed for BTP could be used with morphine ER 60 mg BID.

Combination agents, such as hydrocodone/acetaminophen, can be used for BTP. Monitor the total acetaminophen intake (given alone or in combination). In an inpatient setting, injections can be given. Injections have a faster onset and can be preferred for severe BTP. However, if the patient does not have an existing IV line, the injection itself will cause discomfort.

Exception: Fentanyl Patches

Converting to a fentanyl patch is most commonly done using a dosing table provided in the package insert (see table and example). If converting to fentanyl using the previous chart, remember that you are finding the total daily dose in mg, and will then need to convert it to mcg (multiply by 1,000) and then divide by 24 to get the patch dose; the fentanyl patch is dosed in mcg per hour (no oral dose conversion is listed on the conversion chart because fentanyl is not absorbed orally). Some clinicians use this estimation: morphine 60 mg total daily dose = 25 mcg/hr fentanyl patch. These methods can provide different answers. For the exam, follow the specific instructions given when converting to or from fentanyl patches.

Example of Conversion to Fentanyl Patch using a Conversion Table

MJ is a 52-year-old male patient who has been using *OxyContin* 40 mg BID and *Endocet* 5-325 mg as needed for BTP. He uses the BTP medication 2 – 3 times weekly. Using the *OxyContin* dose only, select the fentanyl patch strength that should be chosen for this patient, using the following table:

Fentanyl Conversion Table

Table 1: DOSE CONVERSION TO DURAGESIC

Current Analgesic	Daily Dosage (mg/day)			
Oral morphine	60–134	135–224	225–314	315–404
Intramuscular or Intravenous morphine	10–22	23–37	38–52	53–67
Oral oxycodone	30–67	67.5–112	112.5–157	157.5–202
Oral codeine	150–447			
Oral hydromorphone	8–17	17.1–28	28.1–39	39.1–51
Intravenous hydromorphone	1.5–3.4	3.5–5.6	5.7–7.9	8–10
Intramuscular meperidine	75-165	166-278	279-390	391-503
Oral methadone	20–44	45–74	75–104	105–134
	↓	↓	↓	↓
Recommended DURAGESIC Dose	25 mcg/hour	50 mcg/hour	75 mcg/hour	100 mcg/hour

Table 1 should not be used to convert from DURAGESIC to other therapies because this conversion to DURAGESIC is conservative. Use of Table 1 for conversion to other analgesic therapies can overestimate the dose of the new agent. Overdosage of the new analgesic agent is possible.

Answer: Oxycodone 80 mg daily is in the range of 67.5 – 112 mg daily which correlates to the 50 mcg/hr patch.

Methadone Conversion: Not Straight-Forward; Should Be Done By Pain Specialists

Morphine to methadone conversion ranges from 3:1 – 20:1; this is highly variable due to patient tolerance and duration of therapy. The half-life of methadone varies widely. There are separate conversion charts for pain specialists to estimate methadone dosing. This should be done only by specialists with experience in using methadone.

Methadone is used both for the treatment of opioid addiction and for chronic pain. When used for chronic pain syndromes, it is administered 2 – 3 times per day after the proper dose is determined by titration. It should be started at very low doses of no more than 2.5 mg PO BID or TID, and escalated slowly.

OPIOIDS & CHRONIC NON-CANCER PAIN

Opioids are not first-line for chronic pain treatment and should not be used routinely. In some cases, they have benefit. When used, follow safe use recommendations:

- Establish and measure goals for pain and function. Reaching low pain rather than no pain may be reasonable.
- If using opioids, start with immediate release. *Start low and go slow.*
- Evaluate risk factors for opioid-related harm routinely.
- Pharmacists should check their state's Prescription Drug Monitoring Program (PDMP) database. *Look for high dosages and multiple prescribers.*
- Use urine drug testing, and watch for false positives and negatives.
- Use adjunctive medications to enable a lower opioid dose.
- Avoid benzodiazepines and opioids given together, except in rare cases. *This quadruples the risk of overdose death.*
- Follow-up, taper the dose, consider discontinuation.

ALLERGY

True opioid allergies are rare. Most complaints of itching or rash are not a true allergic reaction. Symptoms of an opioid allergy (rare but dangerous if present) include difficulty breathing, severe drop in blood pressure, serious rash, swelling of face, lips, tongue and larynx. In a true opioid allergy, use an agent in a different chemical class (see Study Tip Gal below).

Tramadol package labeling warns of increased risk of reactions to tramadol in those with previous anaphylactic reactions to opioids. Tapentadol does not have this warning in the U.S., though tramadol and tapentadol are structurally similar. If allergic to tramadol, an allergy to tapentadol is likely, and vice versa.

OPIOID ALLERGY

The common drugs in the same chemical class that cross-react with each other have **cod** or **morph** in the name. Buprenorphine has **norph** instead of **morph**.

Codeine   **Morph**ine

Hydro**cod**one   Hydro**morph**one   Bupre**norph**ine

Oxy**cod**one   Oxy**morph**one   Heroin (diacetyl-morphine)

What to do if a morphine-type allergy is reported? In practice, make sure it is an actual allergy, and not nausea or itching. If it seems to be accurate, choose a drug in a different chemical class, such as methadone or fentanyl. Meperidine is also in a different class, but is no longer recommended as an analgesic.

SIDE EFFECTS AND MANAGEMENT

Opioid side effects usually lessen over time, except for constipation (see Study Tip Gal below). If a patient has a problem that persists or is bothersome, such as pruritus, switching to another opioid is reasonable. Hydroxyzine and diphenhydramine can be used for pruritus. Postoperative nausea and vomiting (PONV) occurs in surgical patients due primarily to the use of anesthesia and opioids. PONV is treated in the hospital with a 5HT3-receptor antagonist, such as ondansetron, or a phenothiazine, such as prochlorperazine. All oral opioids (except oxymorphone) should be taken with food to lessen nausea.

Sedation and cognitive effects occur when the opioid is started, or the dose is increased, and generally lessen over time. Pharmacists should advise patients not to drive or do anything potentially hazardous until they are accustomed to the medication. The use of other CNS depressants should be minimized. Alcohol should not be used with opioids.

OPIOID-INDUCED CONSTIPATION

All opioids cause constipation, referred to as opioid-induced constipation (OIC).

Opioids reduce GI tract peristalsis, making it difficult to pass a bowel movement.

Unlike CNS depression, OIC does not improve over time without treatment; it **must be anticipated and treated**.

When opioids are dosed around-the-clock, such as with an ER opioid, prophylaxis for constipation is required.

Stimulant laxatives, including senna, are the typical first-line laxative, with or without a stool softener. The stimulant laxative bisacodyl comes as a tablet (for prophylaxis) or suppository (for treatment).

If laxatives are not sufficient, specific medications for OIC that counteract the effects of the opioid receptor in the gut (PAMORAs) can be used.

Lubiprostone, which is used for different types of constipation, could be considered following trial of laxatives or PAMORAs.

TREATMENT OF OPIOID-INDUCED CONSTIPATION

DRUG	DOSING	SAFETY/SIDE EFFECTS/MONITORING
Peripherally-acting mu-opioid receptor antagonists (PAMORAs) - block opioid receptors in the gut to <u>reduce constipation</u> without affecting analgesia. PAMORAs are indicated for OIC and are only effective when constipation is secondary to use of an opioid.		
Methylnaltrexone (Relistor) Injection, tablet	OIC with chronic non-cancer pain: 12 mg SC daily or 450 mg PO once daily OIC with advanced illness: weight-based dose SC every other day CrCl < 30 mL/min: ↓ dose	**CONTRAINDICATIONS** GI obstruction **WARNINGS** Risk of <u>GI perforation</u> (rare reports; monitor for severe abdominal symptoms), risk of opioid withdrawal (evaluate risk vs benefit and monitor), use > 4 months has not been studied, discontinue if opioid is discontinued or if severe/persistent diarrhea **SIDE EFFECTS** <u>Abdominal pain, flatulence</u>, diarrhea, nausea, dizziness **NOTES** Stay close to toilet after injecting Discontinue all laxatives prior to use Only for patients on opioids who have <u>failed OTC laxatives</u> Do not use routinely; can often increase laxative to obtain effect
Naloxegol (Movantik) Tablet	OIC with chronic non-cancer pain: 25 mg once daily in the morning on empty stomach CrCl < 60 mL/min: 12.5 mg once daily	**CONTRAINDICATIONS** GI obstruction, use with strong CYP3A4 inhibitors **WARNINGS** Risk of <u>GI perforation</u> (rare reports; monitor for severe abdominal symptoms), risk of opioid withdrawal (evaluate risk vs benefit and monitor) **SIDE EFFECTS** <u>Abdominal pain, flatulence</u>, diarrhea, nausea **NOTES** Discontinue all laxatives prior to use; can reintroduce laxatives if suboptimal response after 3 days Do not use with strong CYP3A4 inhibitors (e.g., grapefruit juice); avoid use or reduce dose to 12.5 mg daily with moderate CYP3A4 inhibitors
Naldemedine (Symproic) Tablet	OIC with chronic non-cancer pain: 0.2 mg daily	**CONTRAINDICATION** GI obstruction **WARNINGS** Risk of <u>GI perforation</u> (rare reports; monitor for severe abdominal symptoms), risk of opioid withdrawal (evaluate risk vs benefit and monitor) **SIDE EFFECTS** <u>Abdominal pain</u>, diarrhea, nausea
Chloride channel activator - approved for other indications in addition to OIC		
Lubiprostone (Amitiza) Capsule	OIC: 24 mcg BID	See the Constipation & Diarrhea chapter

CENTRALLY ACTING ANALGESICS

Both tramadol and tapentadol are <u>mu-opioid receptor agonists</u> and <u>inhibitors of norepinephrine reuptake</u>. <u>Tramadol</u> also inhibits reuptake of <u>serotonin</u>. Both tapentadol and tramadol have the <u>same boxed warnings as opioids</u> (see Opioid Analgesics, Safety Concerns).

DRUG	DOSING	SAFETY/SIDE EFFECTS/MONITORING
Tramadol (Ultram, ConZip) <u>C-IV</u> Tablet (IR/ER), ER capsule, solution + acetaminophen (Ultracet) + celecoxib (Seglentis)	IR: 50-100 mg Q4-6H, max 400 mg/day ER: 100 mg once daily, max 300 mg/day CrCl < 30 mL/min: IR: increase dosing interval to Q12H ER: do not use	**BOXED WARNINGS** <u>Respiratory depression</u> and <u>death</u> have occurred in <u>children</u> following <u>tonsillectomy and/or adenoidectomy</u> found to have evidence of being <u>ultra-rapid metabolizers</u> of tramadol due to a <u>CYP450 2D6 polymorphism</u>; use with CYP3A4 inducers/inhibitors or CYP2D6 inhibitors should be carefully considered due to variable effects; refer to the acetaminophen drug table for boxed warning **WARNINGS** <u>Seizure risk</u> (avoid in patients with seizure history, head trauma), risk of <u>serotonin syndrome</u> when used alone or with other serotonergic drugs or <u>inhibitors of CYP2D6 or 3A4</u>, CNS depression, <u>hypoglycemia</u>, respiratory depression (rare), avoid in patients who are suicidal, risk of serious breathing problems in adolescents age 12-18 years with obesity, sleep apnea or lung disease, breastfeeding mothers should avoid due to ↑ risk of serious breathing problems in breastfed infants **CONTRAINDICATIONS** Do not use in <u>children < 12 years</u> of age; or in <u>children < 18 years</u> of age following tonsillectomy/adenoidectomy surgery Do not use with concurrent <u>MAO inhibitors</u> or within 14 days **SIDE EFFECTS** <u>Dizziness, constipation, nausea, somnolence</u> or insomnia, dry mouth, pruritus, flushing, headache, asthenia Lower severity of GI side effects versus strong opioids On the Beers list: postmarketing reports of hyponatremia and SIADH **NOTES** Tramadol <u>requires conversion</u> to active metabolite <u>by CYP2D6</u>; use with <u>CYP2D6 inhibitors has variable effects</u> due to mixed mechanism of action of tramadol
Tapentadol (Nucynta, Nucynta ER) <u>C-II</u> Tablet (IR/ER)	IR: 50-100 mg Q4-6H ER: 50-250 mg BID CrCl < 30 mL/min: Use not recommended (not studied)	**CONTRAINDICATIONS** Do not use with concurrent MAO inhibitors or within 14 days **WARNINGS** Can increase <u>seizure risk</u> (avoid in patients with seizure history or seizure risk), risk of <u>serotonin syndrome</u> when used with other serotonergic drugs **SIDE EFFECTS** <u>Dizziness, constipation, nausea, somnolence</u> or insomnia, dry mouth, pruritus Lower severity of GI side effects versus strong opioids **NOTES** Tapentadol is a stronger analgesic than tramadol

Centrally Acting Analgesic Drug Interactions

- Caution with other agents that <u>lower seizure</u> threshold.

- Caution with other <u>serotonergic drugs</u>.

- <u>Avoid</u> tramadol with <u>CYP2D6 inhibitors</u>.

- Possibility of increased INR with warfarin; monitor.

- Tapentadol can enhance the adverse/toxic effect of MAO inhibitors; avoid use with MAO inhibitors.

OPIOID ABUSE

Opioid overdose-related deaths have more than quadrupled since 1999. Opioid abuse is now an epidemic in the U.S. This addiction referred to as opioid use disorder (OUD) can be lethal. The U.S. government has created five strategies to prevent overdose death:

- Educate providers and general public about how to prevent and manage opioid overdose.

- Ensure access to treatment for patients addicted to opioids.

- Ensure ready access to naloxone (see Study Tip Gal below). Encourage providers to discuss the availability of naloxone with all patients prescribed opioids or medications to treat OUD.

- Encourage the public to call 911.

- Encourage prescribers to use state Prescription Drug Monitoring Programs (PDMPs).

Additionally, there have been a number of FDA-approved opioids designed to help mitigate drug abuse and misuse. It is important to note that these formulations do not eliminate the ability to abuse or misuse opioids. Some opioid combination products such as *Suboxone* and *Bunavail* are formulated with the abuse-deterrent medication naloxone, while others such as *OxyContin* and *Hysingla ER* are manufactured using specific technology designed to deter crushing, dissolving or other modifications.

OPIOID ABUSE AGENTS

Buprenorphine is a partial mu-opioid agonist. It is an agonist at low doses and an antagonist at higher doses. It is used in lower doses to treat pain and higher doses to treat addiction. Naloxone is an opioid antagonist; it replaces the opioid on the mu receptor. Given by itself, naloxone (injection or nasal spray) is used for opioid overdose. Buprenorphine/naloxone combination products are used as alternatives to methadone for opioid dependence (buprenorphine suppresses withdrawal symptoms and naloxone helps prevent misuse).

Naltrexone is an opioid antagonist normally used to help treat alcohol and opioid dependence. It is available as a daily oral formulation and a monthly IM injection *(Vivitrol)*. Lofexidine *(Lucemyra)*, a non-opioid, alpha-2 adrenergic agonist was approved to treat withdrawal symptoms in patients who wish to abruptly stop use of opioids altogether. While not a treatment for OUD, it is used as part of a long-term treatment plan. The non-pharmacologic treatment *reSET-O* is a digital technology FDA-cleared for OUD treatment.

Naloxone can be given if opioid overdose is suspected due to respiratory symptoms and/or symptoms of CNS depression (see Study Tip Gal below). All approved naloxone formulations can be administered for prevention of opioid overdose death. Many states have made naloxone readily available by allowing first responders and laymen to obtain naloxone in case they see someone overdosing.

OPIOID-INDUCED RESPIRATORY DEPRESSION (OIRD) RISKS

An opioid prescription requires a risk/benefit assessment, and monitoring.

A prescription for naloxone should be offered to patients with elevated risk factors for OIRD.

Risk factors include:

- History of previous overdose
- Substance abuse
- Using large doses (≥ 50 morphine milligram equivalent dose)
- Using with benzodiazepines, gabapentin or pregabalin
- Comorbid illness such as respiratory and psychiatric disease

---

OPIOID OVERDOSE MANAGEMENT

S/Sx of overdose: extreme sleepiness, slow or shallow breathing, fingernails or lips turning blue or purple, extremely small "pinpoint" pupils, slow heartbeat and/or blood pressure.

If overdose is suspected, give naloxone and call 911.

If an individual is not breathing or struggling to breathe, life support measures should be performed.

If there is a question about whether to give naloxone, give it, because fatality could result from not giving it.

Opioids last longer than naloxone, so monitor closely for respiratory depression and provide repeat doses, as needed.

Naloxone is available in two options:

- *Narcan* (nasal spray): onset of action is slower than injection, a single-use nasal spray is 4 mg administered in 1 nostril, repeat doses in alternating nostrils may be needed

- Naloxone (injection): generic formulation provided in multiple size vials, separate syringe will be needed, may need to repeat doses every 2-3 minutes until emergency medical assistance arrives

---

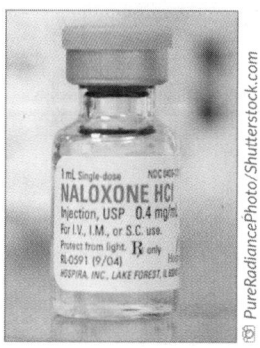

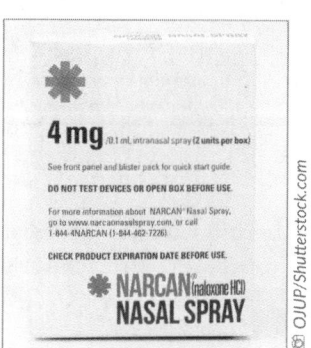

TREATMENT OF OPIOID ABUSE

DRUG	DOSING	SAFETY/SIDE EFFECTS/MONITORING
Naloxone (Narcan) Injection, nasal spray *Narcan:* nasal spray	IV/IM/SC: 0.4-2 mg Q2-3 min or IV infusion at 0.4 mg/hr IM: Give in thigh through clothing, hold for 5 seconds, then call 911 Nasal spray: 1 spray (4 mg), can repeat Repeat dosing can be required (opioid can last longer than blocking agent)	**SIDE EFFECTS** Opioid-dependent: acute withdrawal symptoms (pain, anxiety, tachypnea) Injection: site reactions (erythema/irritation) Nasal: nasal dryness/congestion/swelling
Buprenorphine C-III Injection, patch, buccal film, sublingual tablet **Belbuca:** buccal film **Butrans:** patch (only for mod-severe pain in patients who need ATC opioid) *Buprenex:* injection *Probuphine* implant kit *Sublocade:* once-monthly injection **+ naloxone (Suboxone:** sublingual film, **Zubsolv:** sublingual tablets, *Bunavail:* buccal film)	*Butrans* (opioid-naïve): 5 mcg/hr patch once weekly *Belbuca* (opioid-naïve): 75 mcg daily or Q12H *Bunavail, Suboxone, Zubsolv:* used daily for addiction and used off-label for pain **Patch Application** Apply to upper outer arm, upper chest, side of chest, upper back. Change weekly. Do not use same site for at least 3 weeks. Disposal: fold sticky sides together, flush or put in disposal unit that comes with drug **Film Application** *Belbuca* is a small film that has one white side and one yellow side. The white side should be placed on fingertip, and the film is inserted between gum and cheek on the cheek. The cheek must be wet from saliva or water, and patient should be instructed not to eat or drink for 30 minutes after placement of film.	**BOXED WARNINGS** Refer to the opioid boxed warnings Serious harm (e.g., thromboembolic events, tissue damage) or death when extended-release injection administered intravenously **WARNINGS** CNS depression, QT prolongation (do not exceed one 20 mcg/hr patch), severe dental adverse events with buccal or sublingual formulations **SIDE EFFECTS** Sedation, dizziness, headache, confusion, mental and physical impairment, diaphoresis, QT prolongation, respiratory depression (dose-dependent) Patch: dizziness, headache, application site reactions (pruritus/erythema/rash), nausea/vomiting, constipation, somnolence, dry mouth *Suboxone* SL film: headache, constipation, abdominal pain, nausea, hyperhidrosis **NOTES** Do not expose patch to heat To prescribe for opioid dependence: prescribers need a Drug Addiction Treatment Act (DATA 2000) waiver; if they have it, the DEA will issue a unique identification number to the prescriber, which will start with X *Sublocade:* patients must have been taking a stable dose of transmucosal buprenorphine for 7 days prior to initiation *Butrans* can be covered only with the permitted adhesive film dressings *Bioclusive* or *Tegaderm*
Lofexidine (*Lucemyra*) Tablet	Initial: 0.54 mg four times daily in 5 to 6 hour intervals. Maximum duration of treatment 14 days	**WARNINGS** Risk of hypotension, bradycardia and syncope, QT prolongation, ↑ CNS depression, ↑ risk of opioid overdose after discontinuation, risk of discontinuation symptoms; must taper when discontinuing over 2 to 4 days **SIDE EFFECTS** Orthostatic hypotension, dizziness and dry mouth **NOTES** Can reduce efficacy of oral naltrexone Paroxetine and other CYP2D6 inhibitors can ↑ risk of orthostatic hypotension and bradycardia, monitor closely

Buprenorphine Drug Interactions

- Use caution with CNS depressants: additive sedation (somnolence), dizziness and confusion. These include alcohol, hypnotics, benzodiazepines and skeletal muscle relaxants.
- Use cautiously in patients taking other QT-prolonging drugs or with arrhythmia risk.

COMMON ADJUVANTS FOR PAIN MANAGEMENT

Adjuvants [e.g., muscle relaxants, antiepileptic drugs (AEDs), antidepressants, topical anesthetics] are useful in pain management though they are not classified as analgesics. They can be added to opioid or non-opioid analgesics (multimodal treatment).

Adjuvants are commonly used in pain associated with neuropathy (from diabetes or spinal cord injury), postherpetic neuralgia (PHN), fibromyalgia, osteoarthritis (OA) and others. AEDs (e.g., pregabalin, gabapentin), tricyclic antidepressants (TCAs) and SNRIs are useful for neuropathic pain (note: TCAs and SNRIs block norepinephrine uptake, which has shown to be beneficial in neuropathic pain; SSRIs do not have this effect). Some adjuvants are being developed and labeled for specific indications. For example, a lidocaine 1.8% patch formulation, *ZTlido*, was developed and approved for PHN. In severe cases, other classes of agents, including opioids, can provide benefit.

Muscle relaxants have various, poorly understood mechanisms of action. Some work predominantly by CNS depression leading to relaxation of skeletal muscles (e.g., carisoprodol, chlorzoxazone, metaxalone, methocarbamol), while others work by decreasing transmission of reflexes at the spinal level.

Injectable adjuvants can be used in specific cases by pain specialists. For example, clonidine injection can be added to opioids in intrathecal (epidural) pain infusion pumps for patients with cancer pain when other agents are insufficient. Only analgesics approved by the FDA for intrathecal administration should be used. Some other common injectable adjuvants include anesthetics like lidocaine injected locally to a small area for pain, for example, before a dental procedure or before placing stitches (see a list of these agents in the Acute & Critical Care Medicine chapter) or steroid injections for temporary relief in some conditions. Triamcinolone acetonide extended-release (*Zilretta*) was approved for OA knee pain and is administered by injection into the knee joint (intra-articular) to provide 12 weeks of pain relief without opioids.

ORAL ADJUVANTS FOR NEUROPATHIC PAIN

DRUG	DOSING	SAFETY/SIDE EFFECTS/MONITORING
Antiepileptic drugs (AEDs)		
Gabapentin (*Neurontin,* *Fanatrex* compounding kit) Capsule, tablet, solution, suspension *Gralise*: tablet – for PHN Gabapentin enacarbil (*Horizant*): ER tablet – for PHN and restless legs syndrome	Initial: 300 mg TID Max 3,600 mg/day CrCl < 60 mL/min: ↓ dose and/or extend interval	**WARNINGS** Angioedema/anaphylaxis, multiorgan hypersensitivity (DRESS) reactions, suicidal thoughts or behavior (all AEDs), ↑ seizure frequency if rapidly discontinued in those with seizures, CNS depression (if possible, avoid other CNS depressants; if prescribed with an opioid, use the lowest possible dose) **SIDE EFFECTS** Dizziness, somnolence, peripheral edema/weight gain, ocular effects (diplopia, blurred vision), ataxia, nystagmus, tremor, dry mouth, mild anxiolytic (scheduled in some states) **NOTES** Used most commonly off-label for fibromyalgia, pain (neuropathic), headache, drug abuse, alcohol withdrawal Take ER formulation with food IR, ER and gabapentin enacarbil are not interchangeable
Pregabalin (*Lyrica*) C-V Capsule, solution, ER tablet	Initial: 75 mg BID or 50 mg TID Max 450 mg/day CrCl < 60 mL/min: ↓ dose and/or extend interval	**WARNINGS** Angioedema, hypersensitivity reactions, risks of suicidal thoughts or behavior (all AEDs), ↑ seizure frequency if rapidly discontinued in those with seizures; can cause peripheral edema, CNS depression such as dizziness and somnolence (if possible, avoid other CNS depressants; if prescribed with an opioid, use the lowest possible dose) **SIDE EFFECTS** Dizziness, somnolence, peripheral edema/weight gain, mild anxiolytic, diplopia, ataxia **NOTES** Approved for use in fibromyalgia, PHN and neuropathic pain associated with diabetes and spinal cord injury

PAIN/RELATED CONDITIONS

DRUG	DOSING	SAFETY/SIDE EFFECTS/MONITORING
Carbamazepine (Tegretol, Tegretol XR, Carbatrol, Epitol) Tablet (IR/ER), ER capsule, chewable tablet, suspension, injection	Initial: 100 mg BID Max 1,200 mg/day	**NOTES** Only FDA-approved medication for the treatment of trigeminal neuralgia See the Seizures/Epilepsy chapter

SNRIs and TCAs

DRUG	DOSING	SAFETY/SIDE EFFECTS/MONITORING
Milnacipran (Savella, Savella Titration Pack) Tablet	Day 1: 12.5 mg daily Days 2-3: 12.5 mg BID Days 4-7: 25 mg BID Then 50 mg BID CrCl < 30 mL/min: max dose is 25 mg BID	**BOXED WARNINGS** Milnacipran is an SNRI. Antidepressants ↑ the risk of suicidal thoughts and behavior in children, adolescents and young adults with depression and other psychiatric disorders (do not use in pediatric patients) **CONTRAINDICATIONS** Use with or within 2 weeks of MAO inhibitors, avoid with linezolid or IV methylene blue **SIDE EFFECTS** Nausea, headache, constipation, dizziness, insomnia, hot flashes **NOTES** Indicated for fibromyalgia only (not approved for depression) Do not use IV digoxin with milnacipran; milnacipran can ↑ the toxic effect of digoxin including postural hypotension and tachycardia (particularly IV digoxin) Increased bleeding risk with anticoagulants or antiplatelets
Amitriptyline (Elavil*) Tablet Desipramine (Norpramin) Tablet **Duloxetine (Cymbalta,** Drizalma Sprinkle) Capsule	10-50 mg QHS, sometimes higher Initial: 25 mg daily Max 150 mg/day 30-60 mg/day	**NOTES** See the Depression chapter Desipramine: titrate every 3-7 days Duloxetine approved for the treatment of neuropathic and musculoskeletal pain

ORAL ADJUVANTS FOR MUSCULOSKELETAL PAIN/SPASMS

DRUG	DOSING	SAFETY/SIDE EFFECTS/MONITORING
Antispasmodics (muscle relaxants) with analgesic effects. Use caution with other CNS depressants (e.g., alcohol, benzodiazepines and opioids) due to the additive risk of CNS depression		
Baclofen (Lioresal) Tablet, solution, injection, oral suspension, granules	5-20 mg TID-QID PRN Injection given via intrathecal pump for severe spasticity	**BOXED WARNINGS** Abrupt withdrawal of intrathecal baclofen has resulted in severe effects (high fever, lethargy, rebound/↑ spasticity, muscle rigidity and rhabdomyolysis), leading to organ failure and death **SIDE EFFECTS** All muscle relaxants: excessive sedation, dizziness, confusion, asthenia (muscle weakness) Baclofen: nausea, headache, constipation, hypotension **NOTES** Do not overdose in elderly (e.g., start low, titrate carefully), watch for additive side effects
Cyclobenzaprine (Amrix, Fexmid, Flexeril*) Tablet, capsule	IR: 5-10 mg TID PRN ER: 15-30 mg once daily	**SIDE EFFECTS** Dry mouth **NOTES** Can have efficacy with fibromyalgia Serotonergic: do not combine with other serotonergic agents Can precipitate or exacerbate cardiac arrhythmias; caution in elderly or those with heart disease (similar to TCAs chemically a tricyclic almost identical to amitriptyline)

*Brand name discontinued but still used in practice.

PAIN/RELATED CONDITIONS

DRUG	DOSING	SAFETY/SIDE EFFECTS/MONITORING
Tizanidine *(Zanaflex)* Tablet, capsule	2-4 mg Q6-8H PRN (max 36 mg/day)	**CONTRAINDICATIONS** Use with strong CYP1A2 inhibitors (e.g., fluvoxamine, ciprofloxacin) **SIDE EFFECTS** Hypotension, dry mouth, ↑ LFTs **NOTES** Centrally acting alpha-2 agonist

Antispasmodics (muscle relaxants) that exert their effects by sedation

Carisoprodol *(Soma)* C-IV	250-350 mg QID PRN	**NOTES** Poor CYP2C19 metabolizers will have ↑ carisoprodol concentrations (up to 4-fold) Rapid CYP2C19 metabolizers will convert to the active metabolite meprobamate (↑ toxicity/sedation)
Metaxalone *(Skelaxin)*	800 mg TID-QID PRN	**SIDE EFFECTS** Hepatotoxicity
Methocarbamol *(Robaxin, Robaxin-750)*	1,500-2,000 mg QID PRN	**SIDE EFFECTS** Sedation

Rarely used muscle relaxants include dantrolene *(Dantrium* used for malignant hyperthermia*)*, chlorzoxazone *(Lorzone)* and orphenadrine *(Norflex)*.

TOPICAL ADJUVANTS

DRUG	DOSING/NOTES	SAFETY/SIDE EFFECTS/MONITORING
Lidocaine topical Cream, gel, patch Rx and OTC **Lidocaine 5%** *[Lidoderm* (Rx)]: **patch** **Lidocaine viscous** (Rx): **gel** Lidocaine 1.8% *[ZTlido* (Rx)]: patch for PHN Lidocaine 4% and lower strengths *[LidoPatch, Lidocare,* others (OTC)]: patch	*Lidoderm:* Apply to painful area 1-3 patches/day and worn for up to 12 hrs/day Approved for PHN (shingles) pain	**SIDE EFFECTS** Patch: minor application site reactions (slight burning/pruritus/rash) **NOTES** Can cut into smaller pieces (before removing backing) *Lidoderm:* do not apply more than 3 patches at one time Caution with used patches; can harm children and pets; fold patch in half and discard safely Do not cover with heating pads/electric blankets Do not use on broken, abraded, severely burned or skin with open lesions (can significantly increase amount absorbed)
Capsaicin topical Cream, gel, patch, stick, lotion Rx and OTC **Capsaicin 0.025% and 0.075%** *[Zostrix, Zostrix HP* (OTC)]: cream Capsaicin 8% *[Qutenza* (Rx)]: patch	Apply to affected area TID-QID	**SIDE EFFECTS** Topical burning, which dissipates with continued use **NOTES** ↓ TRPV1-expressing nociceptive nerve endings (↓ substance P) Onset of pain relief takes 2-4 weeks of continuous application for OTC products and 1 week for *Qutenza* Do not touch genitals, nasal area, mouth or eyes after application; wash hands after application *Qutenza* is applied in the healthcare provider's office for PHN pain. It works in ~40% of patients to reduce pain. Causes topical burning and requires pre-treatment with lidocaine. Applied for 1 hour and effect lasts for months.
Methyl salicylate topical Patch, cream, stick OTC *BenGay, IcyHot, Salonpas, Thera-Gesic,* store brands Methyl salicylate plus other ingredients **Trolamine** *(Aspercreme)*	Apply to affected area TID-QID	**NOTES** Occasionally, topicals have caused first to third-degree burns, mostly in patients with neuropathic damage: discontinue use and seek medical attention if signs of skin injury (pain, swelling, or blistering) occur following application

KEY COUNSELING POINTS

See the Drug Formulations and Patient Counseling chapter for counseling language/layman's terminology.

ACETAMINOPHEN

- The <u>total daily dose</u> of all products containing acetaminophen should <u>not exceed 4,000 mg</u>.
- Can cause hepatotoxicity.

NSAIDS

- Requires a MedGuide.
- Can cause:
  - ❏ Stomach bleeding.
  - ❏ Increased blood pressure.
  - ❏ Edema.
  - ❏ Photosensitivity.
- Do not use this medicine if you have experienced breathing problems or allergic-type reactions after taking aspirin or other NSAIDs.
- Avoid in pregnancy (teratogenic).

Diclofenac Gel

- Use the reusable dosing card inside the package to correctly measure each dose. Apply diclofenac gel onto the dosing card evenly to cover the dosing area up to the correct dosing line.
  - ❏ The dose for hands, wrists or elbows is 2 grams applied four times daily. Do not exceed 8 grams each day to these areas.

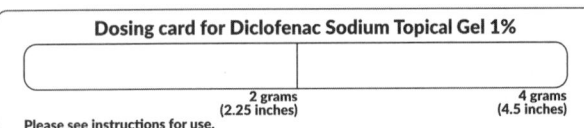

Dosing card for Diclofenac Sodium Topical Gel 1%

2 grams (2.25 inches)   4 grams (4.5 inches)

Please see instructions for use.

  - ❏ The dose for feet, ankles or knees is 4 grams applied four times daily. Do not exceed more than 16 grams each day to these areas.
- Do not shower, bathe or wash your treated hands for at least one hour after application.

OPIOIDS

- Can cause:
  - ❏ Drowsiness.
  - ❏ Constipation.
- Take with food or milk if stomach upset occurs. Exception: oxymorphone should be taken on an empty stomach.
- Do not consume alcohol with *Kadian*, *Nucynta ER*, oxymorphone ER or *Zohydro ER*.
- *Kadian* can be opened and the contents sprinkled on applesauce immediately before ingestion.

MUSCLE RELAXANTS

- Can cause drowsiness.

CAPSAICIN TOPICAL

- Unless treating hand pain, wash hands thoroughly with soap and water immediately after use.
- If treating hands, leave on for 30 minutes, then wash hands as above.
- Do not touch genitals, nasal area, mouth or eyes with the medicine; it will burn the sensitive skin.
- The burning pain should dissipate with continual use; starting at the lower strength will help.
- Do not cover with heating pads/electric blankets or bandages; serious burning can occur.

Select Guidelines/References

CDC Guideline for Prescribing Opioids for Chronic Pain. https://www.cdc.gov/mmwr/volumes/65/rr/rr6501e1.htm (accessed 2022 Feb 17).

SAMHSA Opioid Overdose Prevention Toolkit. https://store.samhsa.gov/system/files/sma18-4742.pdf (accessed 2022 Feb 17).

Use of Opioids for the Treatment of Chronic Pain: a Statement from the American Academy of Pain Medicine. http://www.painmed.org/files/use-of-opioids-for-the-treatment-of-chronic-pain.pdf (accessed 2022 Feb 17).

American Academy of Neurology. Oral and Topical Treatment of Painful Diabetic Polyneuropathy Practice Guideline Update. https://www.aan.com/Guidelines/home/GuidelineDetail/1037 (accessed 2022 Feb 17).

CONTENT LEGEND

 = Study Tip Gal

© iStock.com/Siphotography

CHAPTER 59
MIGRAINE

BACKGROUND

Headache treatment is a common concern in the community pharmacy. It is one of the most frequent complaints in neurologists' offices and the most common pain complaint seen in family practice. Most headaches are migraine and tension-type headaches.

Migraines are chronic headaches that cause significant pain for hours or days. Most migraines cause nausea, vomiting and sensitivity to light and sound. Some migraines are preceded or accompanied by sensory warning symptoms or signs (auras), such as flashes of light, blind spots or tingling in the arms or legs. Most migraines do not have an aura.

A headache accompanied by fever, stiff neck, rash, confusion, seizures, double vision, weakness, numbness, chest pain, shortness of breath or aphasia (trouble speaking) could indicate a serious cardiovascular, cerebrovascular or infectious event. Patients with these symptoms should seek immediate medical attention.

CAUSES

The cause of migraines is not well understood. They may be caused by changes in the trigeminal nerve or imbalances in neurotransmitters, including serotonin. A decrease in neurotransmitters causes a release of neuropeptides that trigger vasodilation in cranial blood vessels.

Patients should identify and avoid "triggers" to reduce migraine incidence (see Study Tip Gal on the following page). A common type of migraine is menstrual-associated migraine (MAM) in women. These can be treated with oral contraceptives, the estradiol patch or creams to decrease their frequency. Women who have migraine with aura are at higher risk for stroke and should not use estrogen-containing contraceptives.

COMMON MIGRAINE TRIGGERS

Hormonal Changes in Women
Fluctuations in estrogen can trigger headaches. Monophasic oral contraceptives can keep estrogen levels more constant and help reduce MAM.

Progestin-only pills are recommended for migraine with aura due to stroke risk with estrogen-containing contraceptives.

Foods
Common offending agents include alcohol, especially beer and red wine, aged cheeses, chocolate, aspartame, overuse of caffeine, monosodium glutamate (MSG), salty foods and processed foods.

Stress
Stress is a major cause of migraines.

Sensory Stimuli
Bright lights, sun glare, loud sounds and certain scents (which may be pleasant or unpleasant odors).

Changes in Wake-Sleep Pattern
Either missing sleep or getting too much sleep (including jet lag).

Changes in the Environment
A change of weather or barometric pressure.

DIAGNOSIS

Migraines can be diagnosed when an adult has at least five attacks (not attributed to another disorder) fulfilling the following criteria:

1. Headaches last 4 – 72 hours and recur sporadically.

2. Headaches have ≥ 2 of the following characteristics: unilateral location, pulsating, moderate-severe pain and aggravated by (or causing avoidance of) routine physical activity.

3. One of the following occurs during the headache: nausea and/or vomiting, photophobia (sensitivity to light) and phonophobia (sensitivity to sound).

NON-DRUG TREATMENT

A headache diary can assist patients in identifying triggers. Non-pharmacologic interventions involve avoiding triggers, stress management, massage, spinal manipulation or applying cold compresses/ice to the head. Acupuncture can be helpful for reducing migraines in some patients.

There are several transcutaneous electrical nerve stimulation (TENS) units approved for the prevention and/or treatment of migraines. These devices, such as Cephaly and Relivion, are worn by the patient and provide small electrical pulses that ultimately block pain signals. The gammaCore Sapphire device is approved for both migraines and cluster headaches.

NATURAL PRODUCTS

Caffeine is effective in combination with acetaminophen or aspirin to treat migraine headaches; several combination products are available for this purpose. Butterbur, feverfew, magnesium, riboflavin, peppermint (applied topically) and coenzyme Q10 (each alone or in combination) have been used for prevention of migraines.

ACUTE DRUG TREATMENT

Acute (abortive) treatment is used for a headache that is already present. OTC options include: acetaminophen, *Advil Migraine* (which contains only ibuprofen), *Excedrin Migraine* (aspirin, acetaminophen and caffeine), *Aleve* (naproxen) or other drugs, including store brands of these options. OTC drugs can be tried for migraines that are mild to moderate. Refer to the Pain chapter for a more detailed discussion of these medications.

Prescription options for acute treatment include: serotonin receptor agonists (triptans), ergotamine- and butalbital-containing medications, opioids, opioid-combination products and diclofenac (*Cambia*), a packet formulation that is specifically indicated for migraine treatment. Lasmiditan (*Reyvow*) is a serotonin receptor agonist specific for the 5-HT1F receptor. Lasmiditan and two oral calcitonin gene-related peptide (CGRP) receptor antagonists, ubrogepant (*Ubrelvy*) and rimegepant (*Nurtec ODT*) are FDA-approved for acute treatment of migraines. The CGRP receptor antagonists used for migraine prevention are discussed later in this chapter.

Opioids, butalbital-containing products, tramadol and tapentadol are not recommended due to abuse/dependence issues. If other drugs have failed, these are used in select cases.

Some patients get more relief from OTC products, some from triptans and others need to use combinations of both. Always ask the patient what they have tried in the past, and if it was useful. Patients with nausea/vomiting may benefit from combined treatment with an antiemetic.

TRIPTANS

<u>Triptans</u> are selective <u>agonists for the 5-HT1 receptor</u> (1B/1D subtypes) and cause <u>vasoconstriction of cranial blood vessels</u>, inhibit neuropeptide release and decrease pain transmission. They are <u>first-line</u> for <u>acute treatment</u>. Triptans should be taken at the <u>first sign of a migraine</u> for best efficacy. The safety of treating more than 3 – 5 headaches per month (product-specific) has not been established.

DRUG	DOSING	SAFETY/SIDE EFFECTS/MONITORING
Almotriptan Tablet	Initial: 6.25-12.5 mg, can repeat x 1 after 2 hrs (max 25 mg/day)	**CONTRAINDICATIONS** <u>Cerebrovascular disease</u> (stroke/TIA), <u>uncontrolled hypertension</u>, <u>ischemic heart disease</u>, peripheral vascular disease, history of hemiplegic or basilar migraine, use <u>within 24 hrs</u> of another triptan or ergotamine-type medication. See Drug Interactions for products contraindicated with MAO inhibitors and CYP450 3A4 inhibitors.
Eletriptan *(Relpax)* Tablet	Initial: 20-40 mg, can repeat x 1 after 2 hrs (max 80 mg/day)	
Frovatriptan *(Frova)* Tablet	Initial: 2.5 mg, can repeat x 1 after 2 hrs (max 7.5 mg/day)	**WARNINGS** Risk of ↑ blood pressure, serotonin syndrome, cardiac and cerebrovascular events, arrhythmias, medication overuse headache (MOH), seizures (sumatriptan only); caution in hepatic or renal impairment (product specific).
Naratriptan *(Amerge)* Tablet	Initial: 1-2.5 mg, can repeat x 1 after 4 hrs (max 5 mg/day)	
Rizatriptan *(Maxalt-MLT,* Maxalt) Tablet, <u>ODT</u>	Initial: 5-10 mg, can repeat x 1 after 2 hrs (max 30 mg/day)	**SIDE EFFECTS** Paresthesia (tingling/numbness), dizziness, hot/cold sensations, chest pain/tightness, dry mouth, somnolence, nausea.
Sumatriptan Tablet, <u>SC</u> (autoinjector, prefilled syringe and solution), nasal spray ***Imitrex*** Tablet, nasal spray, SC injection ***Imitrex STATdose System, Zembrace SymTouch*** SC autoinjector ***Onzetra Xsail*** <u>Nasal powder</u> *Tosymra* Nasal spray	PO: 25, 50 or 100 mg, can <u>repeat x 1 after 2 hrs</u> (max 200 mg/day) **Subcutaneous:** *Imitrex, Imitrex STATdose System:* 4 or 6 mg, can <u>repeat x 1 after 1 hr</u> (max 12 mg/day) *Zembrace SymTouch:* 3 mg, can repeat up to <u>4 times per day</u> [wait a minimum of 1 hr between doses or 1 hr following use of another sumatriptan product (max 12 mg/day)] **Intranasal:** Spray *(Imitrex):* 5, 10, or 20 mg in <u>one nostril</u> can <u>repeat x 1 after 2 hrs</u> (max 40 mg/day) Spray *(Tosymra):* 10 mg in one nostril can repeat x 1 after 1 hr (max 30 mg/day) <u>Powder *(Onzetra Xsail):*</u> 11 mg in <u>each nostril</u> using nosepiece, can repeat x 1 after 2 hrs (max 44 mg/day)	Triptan sensations (pressure or heaviness in the chest or pressure in the neck region) usually dissipate after administration. **NOTES** <u>ODTs, nasal sprays and injections</u> are useful <u>if nausea</u> is <u>present</u>. No water is required for ODTs. Nasal sprays and injections <u>work faster</u>. <u>Nasal sprays</u> contain only <u>1 dose</u> (<u>do not prime</u>). *Treximet:* protect from moisture; <u>dispense in original container</u>. *Treximet* carries all warnings associated with naproxen (see Pain chapter). *Maxalt-MLT, Zomig* ZMT ODTs contain phenylalanine and should <u>not be used</u> in patients with <u>phenylketonuria</u>. **Children and Adolescents** <u>Almotriptan tablets, zolmitriptan nasal spray</u> and *Treximet* are approved for children and adolescents ≥ 12 years of age; <u>rizatriptan</u> is approved for children and adolescents 6-17 years of age.
+ naproxen *(Treximet)* Tablet Adult: 85/500 mg Pediatric: 10/60 mg	***Treximet*** Adults: 1 tab, can repeat x 1 after 2 hrs (max 2 tabs/24 hrs) Pediatric (12-17 yrs): 1 tab x 1 dose	**Duration of Action** <u>Frovatriptan</u> has the <u>longest half-life</u> (26 hrs). Both frovatriptan and naratriptan are considered <u>long-acting</u>, but <u>onset is slower</u>. These can be chosen if headache recurs after dosing, lasts a long time or can be anticipated (e.g., MAM). Triptans with a <u>shorter half-life have a faster onset</u>: almotriptan, eletriptan, rizatriptan, sumatriptan and zolmitriptan.
Zolmitriptan *(Zomig ZMT,* Zomig) Tablet, <u>ODT, nasal spray</u>	PO: 1.25-5 mg, can repeat x 1 after 2 hrs Intranasal: 2.5-5 mg in <u>one nostril</u>, can repeat x 1 after 2 hrs [max 10 mg/day (all formulations)]	**Sumatriptan Injections** All are injected <u>SC</u>. Preferred site is <u>lateral thigh or upper arm</u>. Protect from light. Available as: prefilled syringe and single-dose vial (sumatriptan) and prefilled autoinjector *(Zembrace).* Needle shield of the prefilled syringe contains a latex derivative. This has the potential to cause allergic reactions in latex-sensitive individuals.

TRIPTAN FORMULATIONS

TABLET	ODT	NASAL SPRAY/ POWDER	SC INJECTION
All triptans	Rizatriptan (*Maxalt-MLT*) Zolmitriptan (*Zomig ZMT*)	**SPRAY** Sumatriptan (*Imitrex*) Zolmitriptan (*Zomig*) **POWDER** Sumatriptan (*Onzetra Xsail*)	**PREFILLED SYRINGE** Sumatriptan **AUTOINJECTOR** Sumatriptan (*Imitrex STATdose System, Zembrace SymTouch*)

Triptan Drug Interactions

- The risk of serotonin syndrome may be increased when combining a triptan with other serotonergic drugs, such as SSRIs or SNRIs. Many patients take both safely since triptans are only used as needed, but there is an FDA warning regarding this combination.

- Sumatriptan, rizatriptan and zolmitriptan are contraindicated with MAO inhibitors (or within two weeks of stopping), the other triptans are not.

- Use with strong CYP3A4 inhibitors: eletriptan is contraindicated; reduce the dose of almotriptan.

ERGOTAMINE DRUGS

Ergotamine is a nonselective agonist of serotonin receptors, which causes cerebral vasoconstriction. In patients who do not find benefit with a triptan, ergotamine is generally used next.

DRUG	DOSING	SAFETY/SIDE EFFECTS/MONITORING
Dihydroergotamine (*D.H.E. 45, Migranal*, *Trudhesa*) Injection (IM/SC/IV), nasal spray	IM/SC/IV (*D.H.E. 45*): 1 mg at first sign of headache, repeat hourly to a max dose of 2 mg/day (IV) or 3 mg/day (IM/SC) Weekly max: 6 mg Intranasal (*Migranal*): 1 spray (0.5 mg) into each nostril, can repeat after 15 minutes, up to a total of 4 sprays (2 mg/day)	**BOXED WARNING** Contraindicated with potent CYP3A4 inhibitors due to serious and life-threatening peripheral ischemia. **CONTRAINDICATIONS** Uncontrolled hypertension, pregnancy, ischemic heart disease, angina, MI, peripheral vascular disease, hemiplegic or basilar migraine, renal/hepatic impairment, sepsis, use with pressors/vasoconstrictive drugs, use within 24 hours of serotonin agonists (triptans) or other ergotamine-type drugs. Dihydroergotamine: avoid use during or within 2 weeks of discontinuing MAO inhibitors.
Ergotamine + caffeine (*Cafergot, Migergot*) Tablet, suppository	*Cafergot* (1 mg ergotamine + 100 mg caffeine): take 2 tablets at onset of migraine, then 1 tablet every 30 min PRN to a max of 6 tablets per attack *Migergot*: 1 suppository at first sign of migraine, may repeat x 1 after 1 hr to a max of 2 suppositories per attack	**WARNINGS** Cardiovascular effects (avoid in any patient with baseline risk), cerebrovascular events, ergotism (intense vasoconstriction resulting in peripheral vascular ischemia and possible gangrene), cardiac valvular fibrosis, potentially serious drug interactions. **SIDE EFFECTS** Nasal spray: rhinitis, dysgeusia, nausea, dizziness. **NOTES** Nasal spray: prime by pumping 4 times. Do not inhale deeply (to let drug absorb into skin in nose). Recommended to use at first sign of attack, but can be used at any time during migraine.

OTHER ABORTIVE AGENTS

Rimegepant (*Nurtec ODT*) and ubrogepant (*Ubrelvy*) are oral CGRP receptor antagonists. Ubrogepant is approved to treat acute migraine attacks, and rimegepant is approved to both prevent and treat acute migraine attacks. CGRP is thought to play a role in migraine by transmitting pain signals from the trigeminal nerve. Blocking the CGRP receptor blocks these signals, reducing or eliminating migraine pain.

Lasmiditan (*Reyvow*) is a first-in-class serotonin agonist that is selective for the 5-HT1F receptor subtype. Unlike the triptans and ergotamine drugs, lasmiditan does not cause vasoconstriction. It is not contraindicated in patients with CVD, though it has not been studied in this population.

DRUG	DOSING	SAFETY/SIDE EFFECTS/MONITORING
Rimegepant (*Nurtec ODT*) ODT	75 mg PO once Max dose 75 mg/24 hours	**CONTRAINDICATIONS** Do not use with strong CYP3A4 inhibitors. Do not use rimegepant with strong P-gp inhibitors. **WARNINGS** Rimegepant: hypersensitivity reactions, including delayed serious reactions.
Ubrogepant (*Ubrelvy*)	50-100 mg PO, can repeat x 1 after 2 hrs Max dose 200 mg/24 hours Severe hepatic impairment (Child-Pugh Class C): 50 mg (can repeat x 1) CrCl 15-29 mL/min: 50 mg (can repeat x 1) CrCl < 15 mL/min: do not use	**SIDE EFFECTS** Nausea, somnolence. **NOTES** The starting dose of ubrogepant is based on the patient's other medications; see Drug Interactions, below. The safety of treating > 8 migraines/month (ubrogepant) or using > 18 doses/month (rimegepant) has not been established.
Lasmiditan (*Reyvow*) C-V	50-200 mg PO as a single dose Max 1 dose/24 hours	**CONTRAINDICATIONS** None. **WARNINGS** CNS depression, including significant driving impairment; use caution if patient is taking other CNS depressants. May cause serotonin syndrome with or without other serotonergic drugs. **SIDE EFFECTS** Dizziness, fatigue, paresthesia. **NOTES** Strong inhibitor of P-gp; do not use with P-gp substrates. May ↓ HR; use with caution if using other drugs that ↓ HR. Lasmiditan should not be used if the patient cannot wait at least 8 hrs between dosing and driving or operating heavy machinery. The safety of treating > 4 migraines/month has not been established.

CGRP Receptor Antagonist Drug Interactions

- Rimegepant and ubrogepant are substrates of CYP3A4 and P-gp. Both are contraindicated in patients taking strong 3A4 inhibitors, and neither is recommended in patients taking strong 3A4 inducers (possible lack of efficacy of CGRP receptor antagonist).

  ❏ The starting dose of ubrogepant is 50 mg in patients taking a moderate or weak 3A4 inhibitor or a P-gp inhibitor.

  ❏ Start at 100 mg of ubrogepant if the patient is taking a moderate or weak 3A4 inducer.

  ❏ Avoid using a second dose of rimegepant within 48 hours if the patient is taking a moderate 3A4 inhibitor.

BUTALBITAL-CONTAINING PRODUCTS

Butalbital is a barbiturate. Acetaminophen/butalbital/caffeine (*Fioricet*) and aspirin/butalbital/caffeine (*Fiorinal*) are both available in combinations with codeine: *Fioricet with Codeine* and *Fiorinal with Codeine*. All of these products are federally classified as schedule III, except *Fioricet* (which is exempt). *Fioricet* remains a popular drug, but butalbital-containing products are not recommended for treating acute migraines due to abuse/dependence issues and lower efficacy. If used regularly and long-term, they must be tapered off or the patient will get worsening of headache, tremors and be at risk for delirium and seizures. Pharmacists should make sure patients do not exceed safe doses of acetaminophen and counsel on the potential for nausea and constipation with the codeine-containing formulations and additive sedation with alcohol.

PROPHYLACTIC DRUG TREATMENT

Some patients require a prophylactic (preventative) medication to decrease the frequency of migraines. These medications are taken when the patient feels well and are not effective for the treatment of acute migraine. Consider a prophylactic medication if the patient requests it, if they use acute treatments ≥ 2 days/week or ≥ 3 times per month, if the migraines decrease their quality of life or if acute treatments are ineffective or contraindicated.

Choose a prophylactic drug based on patient characteristics and the medication's side effect profile; efficacy data is similar for all (~50% reduction in headache days). A full trial, at a reasonable dose, should be 2 – 6 months. Many patients try more than one drug before finding one that works well for them. Oral prophylactic therapies include:

- Antihypertensives: most experience is with beta-blockers (best evidence with propranolol, timolol and metoprolol, though others have been used). Lisinopril and verapamil are alternatives.

- Antiepileptic drugs: topiramate *(Topamax* and other brands) and valproic acid. Topiramate causes weight loss in many patients, making it a popular choice for migraine prophylaxis.

- Antidepressants: tricyclic antidepressants (most evidence with amitriptyline) are effective. TCAs are used at lower doses for migraine prophylaxis. Venlafaxine can also be effective.

- MAM: monophasic and extended-cycle oral contraceptives can be used (if no aura). NSAIDs or a triptan (specifically those with a longer half-life: frovatriptan or naratriptan) can be started prior to menses and continued for 5 - 7 days.

- Natural products (discussed at the beginning of the chapter).

ORAL PROPHYLACTIC DRUGS

DRUG	TYPICAL DOSING	COMMENTS/SIDE EFFECTS
Beta-Blockers (see Hypertension chapter for complete discussion)		
Propranolol *(Inderal, Inderal LA)*	IR: 80-240 mg, divided Q6-8H LA: 80 -240 mg once daily	**WARNINGS** Use caution with bronchospastic diseases (e.g., asthma, COPD), especially with non-selective propranolol and timolol
Metoprolol tartrate *(Lopressor)* **Metoprolol succinate extended release *(Toprol XL,* Kapspargo Sprinkle)**	100-200 mg, divided BID	**SIDE EFFECTS** Bradycardia, fatigue, hypotension, dizziness, depression (more so with propranolol, the most lipophilic), impotence, cold extremities (can exacerbate Raynaud's)
Timolol	10 mg twice daily	**NOTES** Propranolol XL formulations *(Inderal XL, InnoPran XL)* are not FDA-approved for migraine prophylaxis Metoprolol is beta-1 selective

DRUG	TYPICAL DOSING	COMMENTS/SIDE EFFECTS
Antiepileptic Drugs (see Seizures/Epilepsy chapter for complete discussion)		
Divalproex (Depakote, Depakote ER, Depakote Sprinkle) **Valproic acid** (Depakene*)	*Depakote:* 250-500 mg twice daily *Depakote ER:* 500-1,000 mg once daily	**BOXED WARNINGS** Fetal harm, hepatic failure, pancreatitis **WARNINGS AND SIDE EFFECTS** Weight gain, thrombocytopenia, ↑ ammonia, alopecia, N/V, somnolence, tremor, polycystic ovarian syndrome
Topiramate (Topamax, Topamax Sprinkle) Topiramate extended release (Qudexy XR, Trokendi XR)	*Topamax:* start 25 mg QHS, titrate to 50 mg BID	**WARNINGS** Fetal harm, metabolic acidosis, nephrolithiasis, ↑ ammonia, open angle glaucoma and visual field defects, oligohidrosis **SIDE EFFECTS** Weight loss (6-13%), somnolence, cognitive impairment, paresthesia, reduced efficacy of oral contraceptives

Brand discontinued but name still used in practice.

OTHER PROPHYLACTIC DRUGS

CGRP Receptor Antagonists

Rimegepant *(Nurtec ODT)* is approved for the treatment and prevention of migraines. Atogepant *(Qulipta)* is a recently FDA-approved oral tablet for migraine prevention. The injectable CGRP antagonists listed below are monoclonal antibodies that are approved for migraine prophylaxis. These drugs target high levels of CGRP in patients with migraine headaches.

DRUG	TYPICAL DOSING RANGE	COMMENTS/SIDE EFFECTS
Atogepant *(Qulipta)* Tablet	10, 30 or 60 mg PO daily	**WARNINGS** *Aimovig:* latex allergy Rimegepant: hypersensitivity reactions, including delayed serious reactions
Eptinezumab-jjmr *(Vyepti)* IV injection	100 mg IV once every 3 months; some patients benefit from 300 mg	**SIDE EFFECTS** Injection site reaction, antibody development, constipation Atogepant, rimegepant: nausea, somnolence
Erenumab-aooe *(Aimovig)* SC autoinjector	70 mg SC once monthly; some patients benefit from two 70 mg injections (140 mg)	**NOTES** Approved for prevention of migraine headache in adults
Fremanezumab-vfrm *(Ajovy)* Prefilled syringe	225 mg SC once monthly or 675 mg SC every 3 months	SC injection: self-administer in the abdomen, thigh or upper arm; store refrigerated in the original carton prior to use; allow to sit at room temperature for at least 30 min before injecting
Galcanezumab-gnlm *(Emgality)* SC autoinjector, prefilled syringe	240 mg SC as loading dose, then 120 mg SC once monthly	Atogepant: dose adjustments depend on concurrent use with strong CYP3A4 inhibitors or inducers or OATP inhibitors
Rimegepant *(Nurtec ODT)* ODT	75 mg PO every other day	Rimegepant: do not use with strong CYP3A4 inhibitors or P-gp inhibitors Galcanezumab: approved for cluster headache prevention

Botulinum Toxin

Botulinum toxin type A *(Botox)* injections are used for prophylaxis. *Botox* is for chronic migraines only (≥ 15 headache days per month).

MEDICATION-OVERUSE ("REBOUND") HEADACHES

Medication overuse headaches (MOH) result from overuse of most headache medications (e.g., NSAIDs, opioids, the butalbital-containing drugs, analgesic combination products, triptans and ergotamines, except DHE) and are characterized by headaches that occur more than 10 – 15 days per month. Pharmacists are in a position to see many patients who chronically use headache medications and have daily headaches. It may be best to consult with another healthcare provider if the patient seems at risk or is unlikely to successfully reduce analgesic use independently. To prevent MOH, educate patients to limit acute treatment medications to 2 – 3 times per week, at most. The most important thing is to stop the "over-used" medication. If the drug is an opioid or contains butalbital *(Fioricet, Fiorinal)*, a slow taper is needed.

KEY COUNSELING POINTS

See the Drug Formulations and Patient Counseling chapter for counseling language/layman's terminology and for instructions on self-administered injections, nasal sprays/powder and ODTs.

ALL TRIPTANS

- Can cause serotonin syndrome if taken with other medications that can increase serotonin.
- If your symptoms are only partly relieved, or if your headache comes back, you may take a second dose in the time period explained to you by the pharmacist.
- If you use migraine treatments more than twice a week or if your migraines are severe, you should be using a daily medication for prevention. Discuss this with your healthcare provider.

Imitrex STATdose System

- Includes a carrying case, a *STATdose* pen and two syringe cartridges.

Maxalt-MLT, Zomig ZMT ODT

- Contains phenylalanine. Do not use if you have phenylketonuria (PKU).

Onzetra Xsail Nasal Powder

- Open the pouch and remove the first nosepiece. Insert the nosepiece into the device until you hear it click.
- Press and release the white button to pierce the medication capsule.
- Insert the nosepiece deeply into the nose (first nostril). Rotate the device to place the mouthpiece into your mouth.
- Blow into the device with your mouth for 2 – 3 seconds to deliver medication into your nose.
- Press the clear tab to remove the first nosepiece. Check the capsule to be sure the medication is gone. Discard the first nosepiece.
- Insert the second nosepiece into the device and repeat the steps above using the second nostril.

Select Guidelines/References

Evidence-Based Guideline Update: Pharmacologic Treatment for Episodic Migraine Prevention in Adults. http://www.neurology.org/content/78/17/1337.full.pdf+html (accessed 2022 January 5).

CHAPTER CONTENT

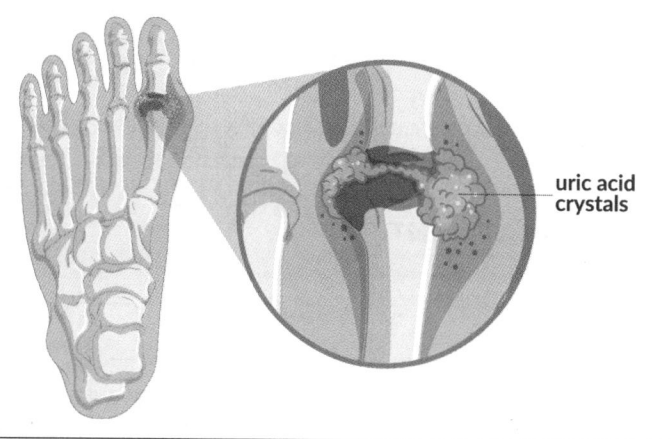

uric acid crystals

📷 iStock.com/colematt

CHAPTER 60

GOUT

BACKGROUND

Gout is a type of arthritis caused by a buildup of uric acid (UA) crystals, primarily in the joints. UA is produced as an end-product of purine metabolism (see adenosine metabolism later in the chapter). Purines are present in many foods, and they make up one of the base pairs of DNA. Under normal conditions, UA is excreted renally (mainly) and via the GI tract.

A normal serum UA level is 2 – 6.5 mg/dL in females and 3.5 – 7.2 mg/dL in males. When UA builds up in the blood, the patient can remain asymptomatic (many people with high UA, or hyperuricemia, never get gout), or the UA can crystallize in the joints (called tophi), resulting in a severe, painful gout attack with burning and swelling of the affected joint. Gout attacks have a sudden onset. Gout typically occurs in one joint, most often the metatarsophalangeal joint (MTP, the big toe). If left untreated, the attacks can occur repeatedly and damage the joints, tendons and other tissues.

In addition to a UA level, a sample of synovial (joint) fluid can be evaluated to identify if UA crystals are present. Various imaging studies (X-ray, US, MRI, CT) can provide an image of the affected joint.

RISK FACTORS

Risk factors for gout include male sex, obesity, excessive alcohol consumption (particularly beer), hypertension, chronic kidney disease (CKD), lead intoxication, advanced age and using medications that increase UA (see Key Drugs Guy below).

DRUGS THAT INCREASE URIC ACID

Aspirin, lower doses
Calcineurin inhibitors (tacrolimus and cyclosporine)
Diuretics (loops and thiazides)
Niacin
Pyrazinamide
Select chemotherapy (with tumor lysis syndrome; see end of chapter)
Select pancreatic enzyme products

CONTENT LEGEND

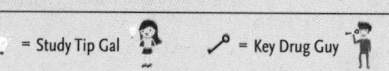

💡 = Study Tip Gal   🔑 = Key Drug Guy

Changing the diet can lower the risk of gout. Foods to <u>avoid</u> include <u>organ meats, high-fructose corn syrup and alcohol</u>. Foods that should be limited include fruit juices, table sugar, sweetened drinks, desserts, salt, beef, lamb, pork and seafood with high purine content (sardines, shellfish). A healthy diet, including low-fat dairy products and vegetables, reduces gout risk. Weight control, smoking cessation, exercise and hydration are other ways to reduce risk.

DRUG TREATMENT

<u>Asymptomatic hyperuricemia</u> is <u>not</u> treated with <u>drugs</u>. Once a gout attack occurs, anti-inflammatory drugs are used to treat the acute attack. If certain criteria are met, drugs may be started to prevent future attacks. Preventative medications are considered after multiple/frequent gout attacks have occurred, if there is radiographic evidence of advanced disease or if there are tophi present. See <u>Study Tip Gal</u> for an overview of treatments.

The drugs used for <u>acute attacks</u> target <u>pain and inflammation</u> (e.g., colchicine, NSAIDs and steroids). The <u>prophylactic drugs</u> are used to <u>lower UA levels</u>, with a goal UA level of <u>< 6 mg/dL</u>.

GOUT TREATMENT BASICS

Treat acute pain with anti-inflammatory drugs:

- Colchicine

- Steroids (including intra-articular injections)

- NSAIDs (often with a high starting dose)

Treat chronically to prevent future attacks:

- Xanthine oxidase inhibitor (XOI): allopurinol (preferred) or febuxostat

  An acute gout flare can occur when an XOI is started, so give initially with colchicine or an NSAID

If XOI didn't work well enough and UA remains > 6 mg/dL:

- Add on probenecid or lesinurad to daily XOI

- Replace the XOI with IV pegloticase (*Krystexxa*)

ACUTE GOUT ATTACK TREATMENT

Gout attacks are extremely painful; acute treatment should begin as soon as possible. A single drug is recommended, which is either an <u>NSAID</u>, a systemic <u>steroid</u> or <u>colchicine</u>. In more severe disease, combination treatment usually includes colchicine with either an NSAID or an oral steroid. If the gout attack is localized to one or two joints, an <u>intra-articular steroid</u> injection (injected into the joint/s) can be helpful. If an acute attack occurs in a patient using chronic urate-lowering therapy (ULT), such as allopurinol or febuxostat, they should <u>continue the ULT</u> during the acute attack. Topical ice applied to the affected joints reduces pain and inflammation.

Acute Gout Attack Therapy

DRUG	DOSING	SAFETY/SIDE EFFECTS/MONITORING
Colchicine		
Colchicine (*Colcrys*, *Gloperba, Mitigare*) Tablet, liquid, capsule + probenecid	**Treatment** 1.2 mg PO (this is <u>two 0.6 mg tablets</u>) followed by <u>0.6 mg in 1 hr</u> (do not exceed a total of <u>1.8 mg in 1 hr</u> or 2.4 mg/day) CrCl < 30 mL/min: the treatment dose is the same, but do not give again for 2 weeks **Prophylaxis** 0.6 mg once or twice daily CrCl < 30 mL/min: ↓ to 0.3 mg/day	**CONTRAINDICATIONS** Do not use in combination with a <u>P-gp</u> or <u>strong CYP3A4 inhibitor</u> with renal and/or hepatic impairment **WARNINGS** <u>Myelosuppression</u>, neuromuscular toxicity (including rhabdomyolysis), if possible, do not use with cyclosporine, diltiazem, verapamil, gemfibrozil or statins as these drugs ↑ <u>myopathy risk</u> **SIDE EFFECTS** <u>Diarrhea, nausea, myopathy, neuropathy</u> (dose-dependent), ↓ vitamin B12 **NOTES** Start <u>within 36 hours</u> of symptom onset (for treatment) Wait <u>12 hours</u> after a treatment dose before resuming prophylaxis dosing ↑ risk of myelosuppression, GI and neuromuscular adverse effects in elderly with CrCl < 30 mL/min; ↓ dose and monitor, or use steroid as an alternative Maintain adequate fluid intake

DRUG	DOSING	SAFETY/SIDE EFFECTS/MONITORING
NSAIDs		
Indomethacin (*Indocin*)	50 mg PO TID until attack resolved	See Pain chapter for more information
Naproxen (*Aleve*, *Naprosyn*, others)	500 mg PO BID until attack resolved	**NOTES** Avoid use in severe renal disease (UA is renally cleared and patients with gout often have renal insufficiency) and CVD risk, bleeding (risk is lower with short duration of use)
Sulindac	200 mg PO BID until attack resolved	
Celecoxib (*Celebrex*)	200 mg PO BID, discontinue 2-3 days after attack resolved	Indomethacin, naproxen and sulindac are approved for gout; other NSAIDs can be used
Steroids: given PO, IM, IV, intra-articular or as ACTH (adrenocorticotropic hormone), which triggers endogenous glucocorticoid secretion		
Prednisone/ Prednisolone	30-40 mg/day given daily or BID until attack resolved, then taper (reduce dose by 5 mg each day) over 7-10 days	See Systemic Steroids & Autoimmune Disease chapter for more information **NOTES** Acute side effects of steroids, including ↑ BG, ↑ BP, insomnia, ↑ appetite
Methylprednisolone (*Medrol, Solu-Medrol*)	Intra-articular: if 1-2 large joints involved Oral: methylprednisolone dose pack	Intra-articular steroid injections stay localized and do not cause systemic side effects; repeat injections can cause joint damage
Triamcinolone	If 1-2 joints: intra-articular 10-40 mg If polyarticular, IM 60 mg, may repeat once or twice Q48H	

Colchicine Drug Interactions

- Colchicine is a major substrate of CYP450 3A4 and P-gp. Fatal toxicity can occur if colchicine is combined with strong CYP3A4 inhibitors, such as clarithromycin, or a strong inhibitor of P-gp, such as cyclosporine. Check for inhibitors prior to dispensing. If colchicine is used with a strong CYP3A4 inhibitor, the dose is reduced and repeated no earlier than three days. If using a moderate CYP3A4 inhibitor, the maximum dose for acute treatment is 1.2 mg (2 tablets).

PROPHYLACTIC TREATMENT

Chronic ULT should be started in all patients with gout who have experienced multiple or frequent gout attacks, have evidence of joint damage or have tophi (UA crystals that form under the skin in long-term gout). When starting chronic ULT, colchicine, steroids or NSAIDs should be used as prophylaxis to reduce the risk of attacks, which can occur when UA is lowered rapidly (possibly due to mobilization of the urate crystals).

The first-line ULT is allopurinol, a xanthine oxidase inhibitor (XOI). Blocking the xanthine oxidase enzyme stops the production of UA and produces a non-toxic end product. Patients at high risk of a severe allopurinol hypersensitivity reaction (including certain Asian groups) should be screened for the HLA-B*5801 allele prior to use. Another XOI, febuxostat, is available as an alternative treatment option. XOIs are titrated up slowly to lower the UA to a target level of < 6 mg/dL. Allopurinol is started at a lower dose with moderate or severe CKD.

Probenecid is a uricosuric and a second-line treatment that can be used if XOIs are contraindicated or not tolerated, or can be added when the UA level is not at goal despite maximal doses of XOIs. Probenecid inhibits reabsorption of UA in the proximal tubule of the nephron, which increases UA excretion. It requires adequate renal function to be effective, which many patients with gout do not have. Another option when the XOI treatment is inadequate (UA remains above 6 mg/dL) is lesinurad, a uricosuric that is taken with the XOI. Pegloticase is a recombinant uricase enzyme, which converts UA to an inactive metabolite that can be easily excreted. Pegloticase is reserved for severe, refractory disease.

PAIN/RELATED CONDITIONS

Uric Acid Production and Drug Treatment

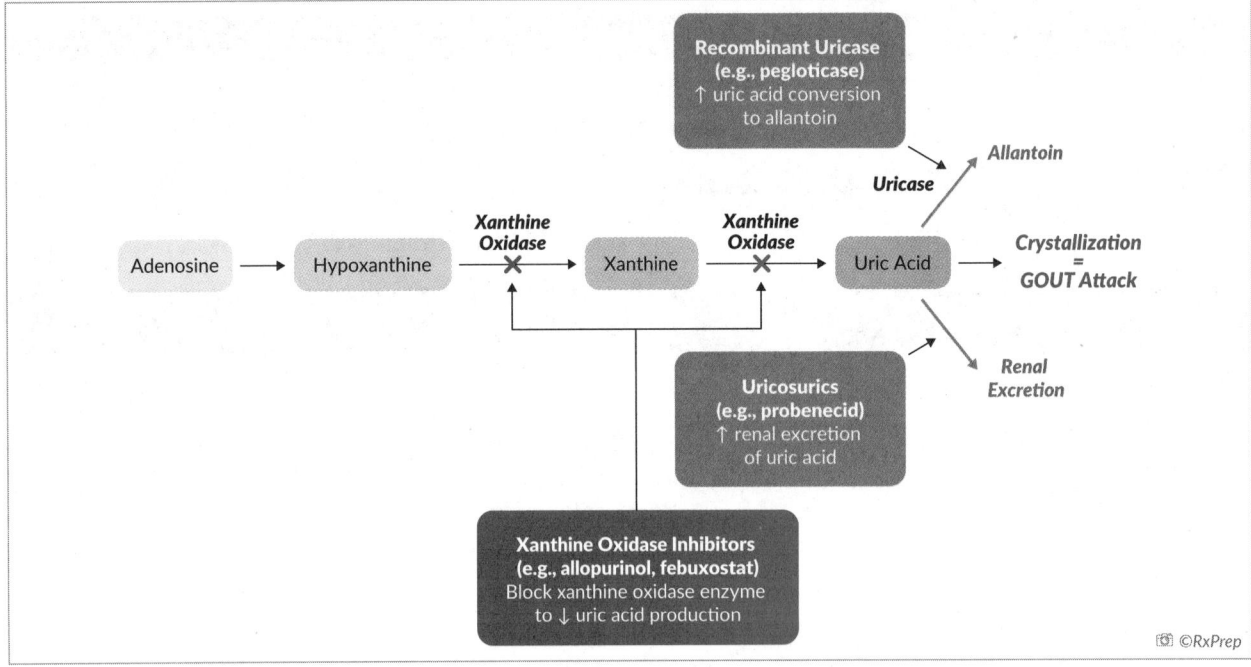

Chronic Urate Lowering Therapy

DRUG	DOSING	SAFETY/SIDE EFFECTS/MONITORING
Xanthine Oxidase Inhibitors: decrease uric acid production		
Allopurinol **(Zyloprim, Aloprim)** Tablet, injection	Start at 100 mg daily, then slowly titrate up until UA is < 6 mg/dL (doses > 300 mg can be necessary and should be divided BID) CrCl ≤ 30 mL/min: Start at 50 mg daily, increase gradually up 300 mg/day Take after a meal (with food in stomach) to ↓ nausea	**WARNINGS** Hypersensitivity reactions, including severe rash (SJS/TEN, DRESS); HLA-B*5801 testing prior to use if high risk (especially for patients of Asian descent) and do not use drug if positive, hepatotoxicity, bone marrow suppression **SIDE EFFECTS** Rash, acute gout attacks, nausea, diarrhea, ↑ LFTs **MONITORING** CBC, LFTs, renal function **NOTES** Higher doses used for tumor lysis syndrome (see Oncology I chapter) Due to the high rate of gout attacks when beginning ULT, use with colchicine (0.6 mg once or twice daily) or an NSAID for the first 3-6 months
Febuxostat (Uloric) Tablet	Start at 40 mg daily, ↑ to 80 mg if UA not < 6 mg/dL at 2 weeks; can increase to 120 mg/day if needed CrCl < 30 mL/min: max dose 40 mg daily	**BOXED WARNING** Increased risk of cardiovascular (CV) death compared to allopurinol in patients with established CV disease; use should be limited to those who cannot tolerate allopurinol (e.g., hypersensitivity) or if allopurinol is not effective **CONTRAINDICATIONS** Do not use with mercaptopurine or azathioprine **WARNINGS** Hepatotoxicity, possible MI or stroke, gout attack, hypersensitivity and serious skin reactions including SJS/TEN, DRESS **SIDE EFFECTS** Rash, nausea, ↑ LFTs, arthralgia **MONITORING** LFTs **NOTES** Due to the high rate of gout attacks when beginning ULT, use with colchicine (0.6 mg once or twice daily) or an NSAID for the first 3-6 months

DRUG	DOSING	SAFETY/SIDE EFFECTS/MONITORING
Uricosurics: inhibit reabsorption of uric acid in the kidneys, which ↑ uric acid excretion		
Lesinurad (*Zurampic*)* Tablet	200 mg daily, in the morning, with allopurinol or febuxostat; if XOI stopped, stop lesinurad Only initiate if CrCl ≥ 45 mL/min CrCl < 30 mL/min: contraindicated	**BOXED WARNINGS** Acute renal failure, more common if used alone; only use with XOI **NOTES** Use only with XOI if UA goals not reached with XOI alone; keep hydrated
Probenecid Tablet + colchicine	Start 250 mg BID, can increase to 2 g/day CrCl < 30 mL/min: avoid	**CONTRAINDICATIONS** Do not use with aspirin therapy, blood dyscrasias, UA kidney stones (nephrolithiasis), children < 2 years, initiation in acute gout attack **WARNINGS** ↓ effectiveness with CrCl < 30 mL/min (ACR guidelines: do not use if CrCl < 50 mL/min), do not use with G6PD deficiency **SIDE EFFECTS** Hypersensitivity reactions, hemolytic anemia **NOTES** Probenecid can be used to ↑ beta-lactam levels by ↓ beta-lactam renal excretion
Recombinant Uricase: converts uric acid to allantoin, which is excreted		
Pegloticase (*Krystexxa*) Injection	8 mg IV every 2 weeks	**BOXED WARNINGS** Anaphylactic reactions – monitor and premedicate with antihistamines and steroids, risk is highest if UA is > 6 mg/dL; life-threatening hemolytic reactions and methemoglobinemia may occur with G6PD deficiency **CONTRAINDICATIONS** G6PD deficiency **WARNINGS** Acute gout flares can occur upon initiation; an NSAID or colchicine should be given 1 week prior to infusion and continued for at least 6 months **SIDE EFFECTS** Antibody formation, gout flare, infusion reactions, nausea, bruising, urticaria, erythema, pruritus **NOTES** Do not use in combination with allopurinol, febuxostat or probenecid (↑ risk of anaphylaxis)

*Currently unavailable in the U.S.

Xanthine Oxidase Inhibitor Drug Interactions

- Allopurinol and febuxostat ↑ the concentration of mercaptopurine, the active metabolite of azathioprine. Do not use either drug with allopurinol or febuxostat, or ↓ dose and monitor for toxicity.

- Avoid use with didanosine; allopurinol and febuxostat can ↑ didanosine levels.

- Antacids ↓ allopurinol absorption.

Probenecid Drug Interactions

- Probenecid decreases the renal clearance of other medications when taken together, including aspirin (do not use salicylates concurrently), methotrexate, penicillins, cephalosporins and carbapenems.

- Probenecid is sometimes used with beta-lactams to ↑ the concentration of the antibiotic; this will ↑ the risk of adverse reactions. This is occasionally done with penicillin when treating neurosyphilis or other penicillin-treated infections.

- Probenecid decreases the efficacy of loop diuretics, but increases the risk of loop diuretic toxicity.

TUMOR LYSIS SYNDROME

Tumor lysis syndrome (TLS) is an acute, potentially life-threatening complication of some types of chemotherapy. When cells are "lysed" open, purines are released into the blood and quickly converted to UA. This can cause acute gout and significant electrolyte abnormalities, which can lead to renal failure, cardiac arrhythmias, seizures and potential death. See the Oncology I chapter for more on TLS.

Rasburicase (Elitek) is a urate-oxidase enzyme used in the treatment of TLS. It is contraindicated with G6PD deficiency. Discontinue immediately and permanently in any patient developing hemolysis.

KEY COUNSELING POINTS

See the Drug Formulations and Patient Counseling chapter for counseling language/layman's terminology.

COLCHICINE

- At the first sign of an attack, take two tablets. Take one more tablet in one hour.
    - Do not use more than three tablets in an hour, and do not use more than four tablets in 24 hours.
    - Do not take the second dose if you have upset stomach, nausea or diarrhea.
- Can cause:
    - Nausea and diarrhea.
    - Muscle damage.

ALLOPURINOL

- Can cause:
    - Mild or severe rash.
    - Liver damage.
    - Nausea.
- Take after a meal to reduce stomach upset (higher doses can be divided). Drink plenty of fluids.

Select Guidelines/References

Fitzgerald JD, Dalbeth N, Mikuls T, et al. 2020 American College of Rheumatology Guideline for the Management of Gout. *Arthritis Care & Research.* 2020;0:1-17.

Richette P, Doherty M, Pascual E, et al. 2016 updated EULAR evidence-based recommendations for the management of gout. *Ann Rheum Dis.* 2017;76:29-42.

ONCOLOGY

CONTENTS

CHAPTER CONTENT

CONTENT LEGEND

💡 = Study Tip Gal 🧑

© Sebastian Kaulitzki © 123RF.com

CHAPTER 61

ONCOLOGY I: OVERVIEW & SIDE EFFECT MANAGEMENT

BACKGROUND

Cancer is uncontrolled cell growth. A tumor (mass of cells) can be malignant (cancerous) or benign (non-cancerous, relatively harmless). Cells that continue to grow will infiltrate normal body tissue, causing organ dysfunction, pain and death.

Cancer is caused by both external factors (e.g., chemicals, radiation, bacteria, viruses) and internal factors [genetic disorders (e.g., BRCA genes, reviewed in Oncology II), hormones (e.g., estrogen, required for most breast tumors to grow) and immune disorders]. Sunlight exposure, tobacco use, excessive alcohol intake, obesity, older age, poor diet and low physical activity increase the risk for certain cancers.

Approximately one-third of cancer cases result in fatality, though the death rate has declined due to better screening, tobacco cessation efforts and improved treatments.

CANCER TYPES AND TERMS

There are hundreds of cancer types. Cancers are often named for the organs or tissues where the cancer forms; cancers based on the tissue type are classified as epithelial (e.g., squamous cell), connective (e.g., sarcoma), lymphoid or nerve. Diagnosis and classification are based on a sample of tissue that is excised in a biopsy. The assessment of the cancer will be aided by some type of imaging, including an X-ray, CT scan, PET scan or MRI. Blood work can identify cancers in the circulatory system (e.g., leukemia), the presence of tumor markers (i.e., chemicals produced by the tumor) and other markers (e.g., altered immunoglobulins can indicate a possibility of multiple myeloma).

SELECT CANCER TYPES

NAME	CHARACTERISTICS
Carcinoma	Cancer that starts in skin or in the tissues that line or cover internal organs.
Leukemia	Cancer of the leukocytes (WBCs); leukemia is referred to as blood cancer.
Lymphoma	Cancer of the lymphatic system.
Multiple myeloma	A type of bone marrow cancer.
Sarcoma	Cancer in connective tissue (tissue that connects, supports, binds or separates other tissues), including fat, muscle, blood vessels and bone. Osteosarcoma is a type of bone cancer.
Skin cancers: Basal cell & squamous cell carcinomas and melanoma	Basal cell and squamous cell carcinoma: common, unlikely to metastasize, simple to remove surgically or with topical treatment. Melanoma: skin cancer that forms in the melanocytes [the skin cells that produce the pigment (melanin) that colors skin]. The least prevalent type of skin cancer (2%), but the most deadly.

CANCER TERMS

TERM	DEFINITION
Adjuvant	Treatment given after the primary therapy (usually surgery) or concurrent with other therapy (usually radiation) to eradicate residual disease and ↓ recurrence.
Benign	A tumor that is not cancerous.
Biopsy	The excision (removal, by cutting out) of a slice of tissue for microscopic examination to see if it is cancerous. A pathologist identifies if any abnormal cancer cells are present. The biopsy results are used to make a definitive diagnosis.
Curative	Treatment given with the intention of curing the cancer.
Hormone (endocrine) therapy	Treatment that removes, blocks or provides hormones that slow down or kill cancer cells.
Imaging tests	Used to make images (pictures) of internal body parts, tissues or organs (e.g., X-rays, MRIs, PET scans, CT scans).
Immunotherapy	Cancer treatment designed to boost the body's natural defenses to fight cancer, including monoclonal antibodies (drugs that end in "mab") and interferons.
Metastatic	The term for cancer that has spread to a different part of the body from the primary (starting) location.
Neoadjuvant	Treatment given before the primary therapy (which is usually surgery) to shrink the size of the tumor and make surgery more effective.
Palliative	Treatment given with the intention of reducing symptoms and/or slowing the growth of the cancer (rather than curing it).
Polyp	A growth of normal tissue that sticks out from the lining of an organ, such as the colon. Polyps in the colon can become cancerous.
Radiation therapy	The use of high-energy X-rays or other particles to destroy cancer cells.
Recurrence	Cancer that has returned after a period during which it could not be detected.
Remission	The disappearance of the signs and symptoms of cancer, but not necessarily the presence of the disease (cancer could be undetectable but still present).
Staging	A ranking system used to describe a cancer, such as how large the tumor is (the size), and if it has metastasized. The ranking can be simple, such as 0-4, or the common TNM staging where T refers to the tumor size and extent, N is the spread of cancer to lymph nodes and M refers to whether the cancer has metastasized. The letters have numbers after them that provide more details.
Terminal	Cancer that cannot be cured and leads to death. Can be referred to as end-stage cancer.
Tumor markers	Substances at higher than normal levels in the blood, urine or body tissue that identify cancer. For example, the carcinoembryonic antigen (CEA) test is one type of tumor marker common in colon cancer.

ONCOLOGY

METASTATIC CANCER HAS THE HIGHEST FATALITY

Metastases form when malignant cells from the primary cancer (the original site of the cancer) travel through the lymph or blood to form new tumors in other parts of the body (see figure). A metastasis (secondary malignancy) will be the same cancer type as the primary tumor. Metastatic cancer is often not curable and may be treated palliatively (see the Cancer Terms table on the previous page) to reduce symptoms and control further growth. If aggressively treated, an otherwise healthy patient will need to tolerate significant toxicities.

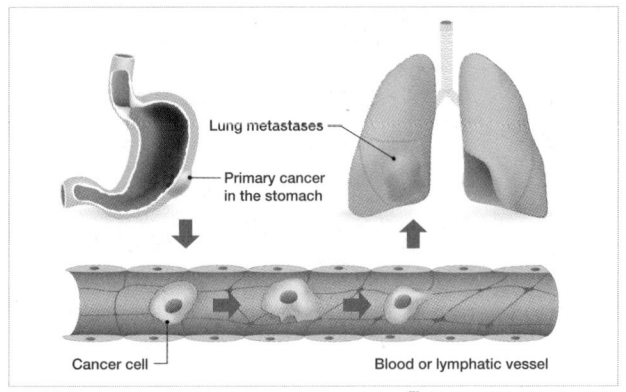

© Designua/Shutterstock.com

WARNING SIGNS OF CANCER

The American Cancer Society (ACS) lists seven warning signs of cancer in an adult. Any of the CAUTION warning signs warrant referral to a physician.

Change in bowel or bladder habits

A sore that does not heal

Unusual bleeding or discharge

Thickening or lump in breast or elsewhere

Indigestion or difficulty swallowing

Obvious change in wart or mole

Nagging cough or hoarseness

© nicoelnino © 123RF.com

HEALTHY LIFESTYLES LOWER CANCER RISK

Cancer can appear for no apparent reason, such as cancer in a child with no known heredity or other risk factors. Other cancers have risk that increases with some type of exposure, such as lung cancer from smoking or skin cancer from sun exposure. A healthy lifestyle lowers the risk of different types of cancer.

- Avoid tobacco (enroll in a tobacco cessation program if needed).
- Maintain a healthy weight.
- Exercise regularly.
- Eat healthy (e.g., plenty of fruits and vegetables).
- Avoid alcohol intake.
- Protect skin from harmful UV rays.
- Assess cancer risk, family history and individual history.

- Have regular check-ups and cancer screening tests.
- Low-dose aspirin is recommended for prevention of colorectal cancer.

SKIN PROTECTION LOWERS SKIN CANCER RISK

Recommendations for reducing the risk of developing skin cancer include:

- Seek shade, especially between 10 AM and 4 PM.
- Wear a shirt, tightly woven fabrics are best.
- Use a broad-spectrum sunscreen, at least SPF 15 – 30, and reapply every 2 hours.
- Wear a hat with at least a 2 – 3" brim.
- Wear sunglasses to protect the skin around the eyes and help prevent cataracts.

CANCER SCREENING GUIDELINES FOR AVERAGE RISK PATIENTS

CANCER	SEX	AGE	SCREENING
Breast	F	40-44 years	Annual mammograms are optional
		45-54 years	Begin yearly mammograms
		≥ 55 years	Mammograms every 2 years or continue yearly
Cervical	F	21-29 years	Pap smear every 3 years
		30-65 years	Pap smear + HPV (Human papillomavirus) DNA test every 5 years
Colon	M/F	≥ 45 years	Stool-based tests (if positive, follow-up with a colonoscopy) ■ Highly sensitive fecal immunochemical test (FIT) yearly ■ Highly sensitive guaiac-based fecal occult blood test (gFOBT) yearly ■ Multi-targeted stool DNA test (MT-sDNA) every 3 years Visual exams of the colon and rectum: ■ Colonoscopy every 10 years ■ CT colonography (virtual colonoscopy) every 5 years ■ Flexible sigmoidoscopy (FSIG) every 5 years
Lung	M/F	55-74 years	Annual CT scan of chest if all of the following: ■ In good health ■ Have at least a 30 pack-year smoking history ■ Still smoking or quit smoking within the past 15 years
Prostate	M	≥ 50 years	If a patient chooses to be tested: ■ Prostate specific antigen (PSA) blood test ■ +/– digital rectal exam (DRE)

PREGNANCY & BREASTFEEDING

Chemotherapy can be highly teratogenic. All patients, regardless of gender, must avoid conceiving during treatment. Contraception should include barrier methods to prevent a partner from having contact with body fluids.

Pregnant patients should not handle chemotherapy drugs. All patients should be informed when a medication can cause long-term sterility.

CHEMOTHERAPY DRUG TOXICITY

Treatment regimens are designed to be toxic to the cancer cells, but they can also be highly toxic to the patient and require careful management. For select drugs (see the Study Tip Gal below), limiting lifetime, per cycle or single doses can aid in reducing toxicity.

DOSING CONSIDERATIONS FOR SELECT HIGHLY TOXIC DRUGS

DRUG	MAXIMUM DOSES	REASON
Bleomycin	Lifetime cumulative dose: 400 units	Pulmonary toxicity
Doxorubicin	Lifetime cumulative dose: 450-550 mg/m²	Cardiotoxicity
Cisplatin	Dose per cycle not to exceed 100 mg/m²	Nephrotoxicity
Vincristine	Single dose "capped" at 2 mg	Neuropathy

ONCOLOGY

SUMMARY OF TOXICITIES

All pharmacists should know the major toxicities of common chemotherapeutics, and the drugs most commonly associated with a specific toxicity. An IV room pharmacist might dispense a drug that requires a chemoprotectant (i.e., an antidote to reverse a toxic effect, such as dexrazoxane to prevent cardiac damage from doxorubicin) and will need to know when the chemoprotectant should be dispensed with the toxic drug. The maximum lifetime dose that can be given for select drugs is important to check before dispensing (see the Study Tip Gal on the previous page). The common toxicities are discussed here, and the drugs are discussed in more detail in the Oncology II chapter.

Doxorubicin has a range of maximum doses to limit cardiac toxicity. Radiation given to the sternal (i.e., chest) region will damage the heart, which lies under the sternum. In a patient who received sternal radiation, it is safer to use the lower end of the dose range.

Mark_Kostich/Shutterstock.com

Common Toxicities of Select Chemotherapeutic Agents

TOXICITY	COMMON DRUGS	MONITORING	MANAGEMENT
Myelosuppression	Almost all chemotherapy drugs, except: Asparaginase, bleomycin, vincristine, most monoclonal antibodies (MAbs), many tyrosine kinase inhibitors (TKIs)	Complete blood count (CBC) with differential, temperature, bleeding, fatigue, shortness of breath	Neutropenia: colony-stimulating factors (CSFs) Anemia: RBC transfusions, and (in palliation only) erythropoiesis-stimulating agents (ESAs) Thrombocytopenia: platelet transfusions (when very low, especially if bleeding)
Nausea and vomiting	Cisplatin, cyclophosphamide, ifosfamide, doxorubicin, epirubicin	Patient symptoms of nausea, vomiting and dehydration	Neurokinin-1 receptor antagonist (NK1-RA), Serotonin-3 receptor antagonist (5HT3-RA), dexamethasone, olanzapine, metoclopramide, prochlorperazine IV/PO fluid hydration
Mucositis	Fluorouracil, methotrexate, capecitabine, irinotecan, many TKIs	S/sx of an oral ulcer superinfection from herpes simplex virus or thrush (*Candida* species)	Symptomatic treatment [e.g., mucosal coating agents, topical local anesthetics (such as lidocaine viscous)], antifungals, antivirals
Diarrhea	Irinotecan, capecitabine, fluorouracil, methotrexate, many TKIs	Frequency of bowel movements, hydration status, potassium and other electrolytes	IV/PO fluid hydration, antimotility medications (e.g., loperamide) Irinotecan: atropine for early-onset diarrhea
Constipation	Vincristine, pomalidomide, thalidomide	Frequency of bowel movements	Stimulant laxatives, polyethylene glycol (PEG 3350, *Miralax*)
Xerostomia	Caused by radiation therapy to the head or neck regions	Dry mouth	Artificial saliva substitutes, pilocarpine, amifostine
Cardiotoxicity	**Cardiomyopathy** Anthracyclines, HER2 inhibitors (ado-trastuzumab, trastuzumab, pertuzumab, lapatinib), fluorouracil **QT prolongation** Arsenic trioxide, many TKIs, leuprolide	**Cardiomyopathy** Left ventricular ejection fraction (LVEF), lifetime cumulative dose of anthracycline **QT prolongation** ECG, K, Mg, Ca	**Cardiomyopathy** Do not exceed recommended lifetime cumulative dose of 450-550 mg/m² for doxorubicin; give dexrazoxane prophylactically in select patients receiving doxorubicin **QT prolongation** Keep K, Mg, Ca within normal limits, consider holding therapy if QTc > 500 msec
Pulmonary toxicity (pulmonary fibrosis or pneumonitis)	**Pulmonary fibrosis** Bleomycin, busulfan, carmustine, lomustine **Pneumonitis** Methotrexate (with chronic use) and MAbs targeting CTLA-4 or PD-1	Oxygen saturation, ABGs, symptoms (shortness of breath, dyspnea on exertion)	Symptomatic management Stop therapy Steroids (if an autoimmune mechanism is suspected) for immunotherapy agents Do not exceed recommended lifetime cumulative dose of 400 units for bleomycin

ONCOLOGY

TOXICITY	COMMON DRUGS	MONITORING	MANAGEMENT
Hepatotoxicity	Antiandrogens (bicalutamide, flutamide, nilutamide), folate antimetabolites (e.g., methotrexate), pyrimidine analog antimetabolites (e.g., cytarabine), many TKIs, some MAbs	LFTs, jaundice, ascites	Symptomatic management Consider stopping therapy Steroids, if an autoimmune mechanism is suspected as with CTLA-4 or PD-1 immune therapy MAbs – atezolizumab, durvalumab, ipilimumab, nivolumab and pembrolizumab
Nephrotoxicity	Cisplatin Methotrexate (high doses), pemetrexed, pralatrexate, some MAbs	BUN, SCr, urinalysis, urine output, creatinine clearance	Amifostine (Ethyol) can be given prophylactically with cisplatin to reduce the risk of nephrotoxicity Ensure adequate hydration Do not exceed maximum dose of 100 mg/m²/cycle for cisplatin
Hemorrhagic Cystitis	Ifosfamide (all doses), cyclophosphamide (higher doses > 1 gram/m²)	Urinalysis for blood, symptoms of dysuria	Mesna (Mesnex) is always given prophylactically with ifosfamide (and sometimes with cyclophosphamide) to reduce the risk of hemorrhagic cystitis Ensure adequate hydration
Neuropathy	**Peripheral Neuropathy** Vinca alkaloids (vincristine, vinblastine, vinorelbine) Platinums (cisplatin, oxaliplatin) Taxanes (paclitaxel, docetaxel, cabazitaxel) Proteasome inhibitors (bortezomib, carfilzomib), thalidomide, ado-trastuzumab, cytarabine (high doses), brentuximab **Autonomic Neuropathy** Vinca alkaloids	S/sx of paresthesias (pain, tingling, numbness) Constipation	Symptomatic treatment with drugs for neuropathic pain **Vincristine** Limit dose of vincristine to 2 mg per dose (regardless of BSA calculated dose) **Oxaliplatin** Causes an acute cold-mediated sensory neuropathy; instruct patients to avoid cold temperatures and avoid drinking cold beverages **Bortezomib** SC administration is associated with less peripheral neuropathy than IV administration
Thromboembolic risk (clotting)	Aromatase inhibitors (e.g., anastrozole, letrozole), SERMs (e.g., tamoxifen, raloxifene), immunomodulators (thalidomide, lenalidomide, pomalidomide)	S/sx of DVT/PE, stroke, MI	Consider thromboprophylaxis based on the patient's risk factors

CHEMOMAN AND MAJOR TOXICITIES OF COMMON CHEMOTHERAPY DRUGS

Chemoman helps with learning the major toxicities of some of the common chemotherapy drugs. Use the blank version on the next page to practice by filling in the body parts with the drugs and associated toxicities.

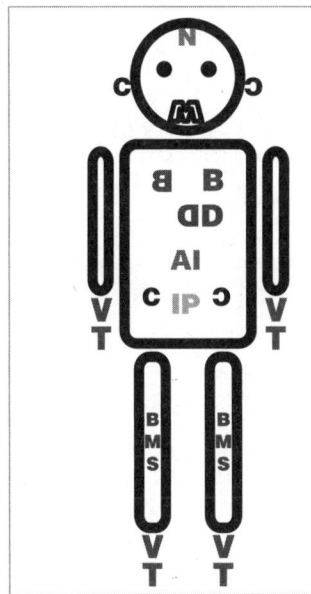

N **Nitrosoureas** (Lomustine, Carmustine) Neurotoxicity

C **Platinum-Based (Cisplatin, Carboplatin)** Nephrotoxic/Ototoxic

Ⓜ **Methotrexate** Mucositis

B **Bleomycin, Busulfan, Carmustine, Lomustine** Pulmonary Fibrosis

D **Doxorubicin & other Anthracyclines** Cardiotoxic

AI **Immunotherapy** targeting CTLA-4 or PDL-1: ipilimumab, atezolizumab, durvalumab, nivolumab, pembrolizumab Autoimmune Syndromes (widespread effects)

IP **Ifosfamide & Cyclophosphamide** Hemorrhagic Cystitis

VT **Vinca Alkaloids** (Vincristine, Vinblastine & Vinorelbine) and **Taxanes** (Paclitaxel, Docetaxel) Peripheral Neuropathy

BMS **Bone marrow suppression** is a common toxicity of many chemotherapy agents including: alkylators, anthracyclines, platinum based compounds (cisplatin), taxanes, topoisomerase I and II inhibitors, antimetabolites and vinca alkaloids (vinblastine and vinorelbine)

ONCOLOGY

TEST YOURSELF!

LABEL (on Chemoman)	DRUGS	TOXICITY
AI		
B		
BMS		
C		
D		
IP		
M		
N		
V T		

©RxPrep

CHEMOTHERAPY ADJUNCTIVE TREATMENT

CHEMOTHERAPEUTIC DRUG	ADJUNCTIVE TREATMENT	INDICATION FOR ADJUNCTIVE TREATMENT
Cisplatin	Amifostine (Ethyol) and hydration	Prophylaxis to prevent nephrotoxicity
Doxorubicin	Dexrazoxane (Totect)	Prophylaxis to prevent cardiomyopathy
Fluorouracil	Leucovorin or levoleucovorin	Given with fluorouracil to enhance efficacy (as a cofactor)
Fluorouracil or capecitabine	Uridine triacetate	Antidote: use within 96 hours for an overdose or to treat severe, life-threatening or early-onset toxicity
Ifosfamide	Mesna (Mesnex) and hydration	Prophylaxis to prevent hemorrhagic cystitis
Irinotecan	Atropine	Prevent or treat acute diarrhea
	Loperamide	Treat delayed diarrhea
Methotrexate	Leucovorin or levoleucovorin	Given prophylactically after high-dose methotrexate to ↓ myelosuppression and mucositis
	Glucarpidase	An antidote to ↓ excessive methotrexate levels due to acute renal failure

MANAGEMENT OF SIDE EFFECTS

MYELOSUPPRESSION OVERVIEW

Myelosuppression (↓ in bone marrow activity, resulting in fewer RBCs, WBCs and platelets) is a complication of most chemotherapy regimens (see figure below).

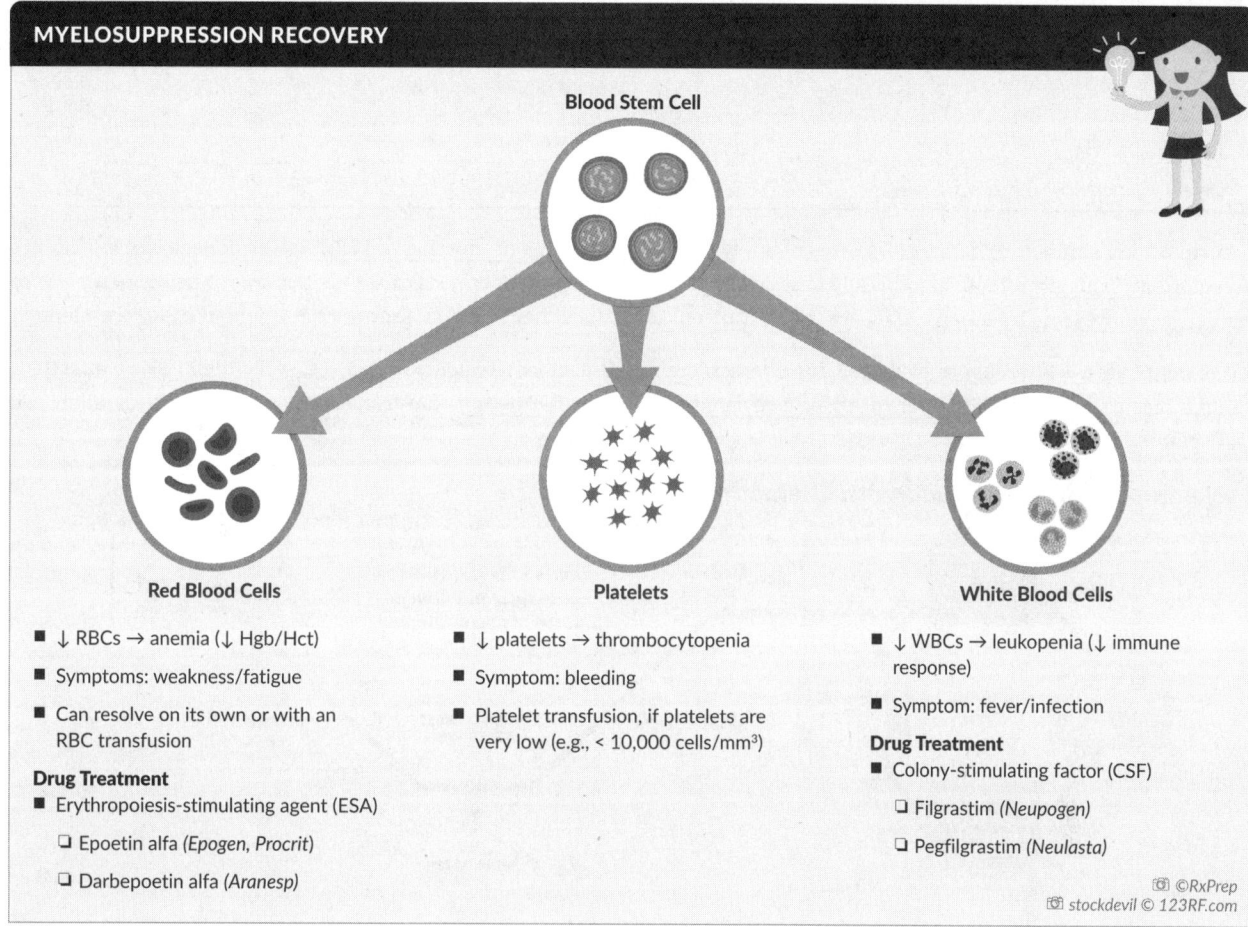

MYELOSUPPRESSION RECOVERY

Blood Stem Cell

Red Blood Cells

- ↓ RBCs → anemia (↓ Hgb/Hct)
- Symptoms: weakness/fatigue
- Can resolve on its own or with an RBC transfusion

Drug Treatment
- Erythropoiesis-stimulating agent (ESA)
  - ❑ Epoetin alfa *(Epogen, Procrit)*
  - ❑ Darbepoetin alfa *(Aranesp)*

Platelets

- ↓ platelets → thrombocytopenia
- Symptom: bleeding
- Platelet transfusion, if platelets are very low (e.g., < 10,000 cells/mm³)

White Blood Cells

- ↓ WBCs → leukopenia (↓ immune response)
- Symptom: fever/infection

Drug Treatment
- Colony-stimulating factor (CSF)
  - ❑ Filgrastim *(Neupogen)*
  - ❑ Pegfilgrastim *(Neulasta)*

©RxPrep
stockdevil © 123RF.com

Myelosuppression Recovery

The lowest point that WBCs and platelets reach is called the nadir, which occurs (with most drugs) about 7 – 14 days after chemotherapy. The RBC nadir is much later, generally after several months of treatment, due to the long life span of RBCs (~120 days).

- WBCs and platelets generally recover 3 – 4 weeks post treatment. The next dose of chemotherapy is given after the WBCs and platelets have returned to a safe level.

- The next cycle of chemotherapy may need to be delayed to give more time for recovery.

- Drugs that hasten recovery can be needed. Severe cases can require a transfusion (e.g., giving packed RBCs for severe anemia).

In early 2021, the kinase-inhibitor trilaciclib *(Cosela)* was approved to decrease myelosuppression from extensive-stage small cell lung cancer treatment. It is given as an IV infusion within four hours prior to the start of platinum/etoposide or topotecan-containing chemotherapy regimens.

NEUTROPENIA

Neutropenia, a type of leukopenia, is a low neutrophil count that is assessed by calculating an absolute neutrophil count (ANC). The more significant the neutropenia (i.e., the lower the ANC), the higher the risk of infection. The ANC calculation can be found in the Calculations IV chapter.

Neutropenia Definitions (American Society of Clinical Oncology)

CATEGORY	ABSOLUTE NEUTROPHIL COUNT (ANC)
Neutropenia	< 1,000 cells/mm^3
Severe Neutropenia	< 500 cells/mm^3
Profound Neutropenia	< 100 cells/mm^3

Growth colony stimulating factors (G-CSFs, or simply CSFs) stimulate the production of WBCs in the bone marrow. They are given prophylactically after chemotherapy to shorten the time that a patient is at risk for infection due to neutropenia and to reduce mortality from infections. They are used to prevent (or reduce) neutropenia; they are not used for acute treatment.

All patients with > 20% chance of developing chemotherapy-induced febrile neutropenia (i.e., very high risk of infection) should receive either G-CSF (filgrastim) or pegylated G-CSF (pegfilgrastim). Sargramostim is used only for stem cell transplants.

Development of Neutropenia with Chemotherapy

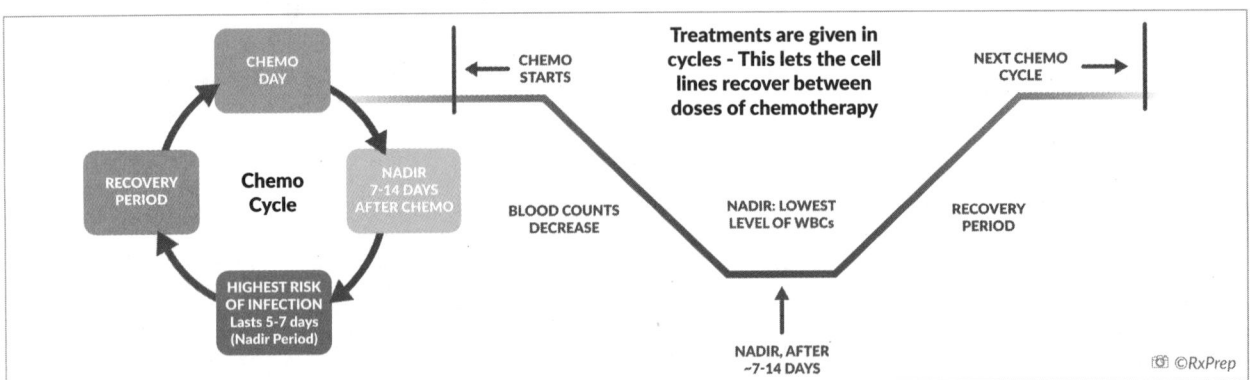

Colony Stimulating Factors

DRUG	DOSING	SAFETY/SIDE EFFECTS/MONITORING
G-CSF **Filgrastim (Neupogen,** *Nivestym, Zarxio)* Biosimilar: tbo-filgrastim *(Granix)*	5 mcg/kg/day given IV/SC daily (round to the nearest 300 mcg or 480 mcg vial size); treat through post-nadir recovery (until ANC > 2,000-3,000 cells/mm^3) 10 mcg/kg/day used for bone marrow transplant	**SIDE EFFECTS** Filgrastim/pegfilgrastim/tbo-filgrastim: bone pain, fever, glomerulonephritis, generalized rash, injection site reaction Sargramostim: fever, bone pain, arthralgias, myalgias, rash, dyspnea, peripheral edema, pericardial effusion, hypertension, chest pain **MONITORING** CBC with differential, pulmonary function, weight, vital signs
Pegylated G-CSF **Pegfilgrastim (Neulasta)** Biosimilars: pegfilgrastim -apgf *(Nyvepria)* -bmez *(Ziextenzo)* -cbqv *(Udenyca)* -jmdb *(Fulphila)*	1 prefilled syringe (6 mg) SC once per chemo cycle (pegfilgrastim is pegylated, extending the half-life)	**NOTES** Store in refrigerator; protect vials from light Administer first dose no sooner than 24 hours after chemotherapy; can be up to 96 hours after Patients should report any signs of enlarged spleen (pain in left upper abdomen or respiratory distress syndrome)
GM-CSF Sargramostim *(Leukine)* Limited to use in stem cell transplantation	250 mcg/m^2/day given IV/SC; treat through post-nadir recovery	Pegfilgrastim: must document when given; should have at least 12 days before the next chemotherapy cycle

Febrile Neutropenia

Patients receiving cytotoxic chemotherapy are at risk for infections from their own normal flora, including enteric bacteria and fungi, due to alterations in the GI mucosa. Infections can also occur due to the use of a central venous access device (i.e., a central line), whereby organisms on the skin are introduced into a sterile space (e.g., the blood).

If neutropenia occurs, the ability to fight infections is low, and the risk of death from sepsis increases. Infection can be difficult to diagnose; fever may be the only sign of infection in a neutropenic patient (i.e., the increase in WBC count will not be present). Empiric antibiotics are started immediately if a fever occurs.

Neutropenia Diagnosis Requirements

FEVER	NEUTROPENIA
Oral temperature > 38.3° C (101° F) x 1 reading, or	Absolute neutrophil count (ANC) < 500 cells/mm³, or
Oral temperature > 38.0° C (100.4° F) sustained for > 1 hour	ANC that is expected to ↓ to < 500 cells/mm³ during the next 48 hours

Gram-positive and Gram-negative bacteria cause infections in febrile neutropenia, but Gram-negative bacteria have the highest risk for causing sepsis. The initial empiric antibiotics must provide adequate activity against Gram-negative bacteria, including _Pseudomonas aeruginosa_. Modification of the initial empiric antibiotic regimen can be required, based on the culture results or if the clinical situation does not improve (e.g., persistent fever).

PATIENT RISK	RISK DEFINITION	INITIAL EMPIRIC ANTIBIOTICS
Low-risk	Expected ANC < 500 cells/mm³ for ≤ 7 days No comorbidities	**Oral anti-pseudomonal antibiotics** Ciprofloxacin or levofloxacin, PLUS Amoxicillin/clavulanate (for adequate gram-positive coverage) or clindamycin (if allergic to penicillin)
High-risk	Expected ANC ≤ 100 cells/mm³ for > 7 days Presence of comorbidities Evidence of renal or hepatic impairment (CrCl < 30 mL/min or LFTs > 5x ULN)	**Intravenous anti-pseudomonal beta-lactams** Cefepime or Ceftazidime or Meropenem or Imipenem/cilastatin or Piperacillin/tazobactam

ANEMIA

Hemoglobin (Hgb) levels are used to assess anemia. Normal Hgb levels are 12 – 16 g/dL for females and 13.5 – 18 g/dL for males. Anemia can resolve without treatment or can be treated with an RBC transfusion. Rarely, an erythropoiesis-stimulating agent is used. ESAs include epoetin alfa _(Epogen, Procrit)_, epoetin alfa-epbx _(Retacrit)_ and the longer-acting darbepoetin alfa _(Aranesp)_. ESAs can shorten survival and ↑ tumor progression (i.e., they can contribute to cancer growth). Therefore, they are for palliation only and are not recommended in patients receiving chemotherapy with curative intent.

To minimize the risks of ESAs, a MedGuide must be dispensed at the start of treatment and the following requirements must be met:

- Use is only for patients with non-myeloid malignancies where anemia is due to the effect of the chemotherapy.
- Upon initiation, there must be a minimum of two additional months of planned chemotherapy.
- Initiate only when the Hgb is < 10 g/dL.
- Use the lowest dose needed to avoid RBC transfusions.

Serum ferritin, transferrin saturation (TSAT) and total iron-binding capacity (TIBC) must be assessed since ESAs will not work well to correct the anemia if iron levels are inadequate. Levels of folate and vitamin B12 may need to be evaluated, especially if there is a poor response to the ESA. For further information regarding ESAs, see the Anemia chapter.

THROMBOCYTOPENIA

Low platelets (thrombocytes) can result in spontaneous, uncontrolled bleeding. The normal range for platelets is 150,000 – 450,000/mm³. The risk for spontaneous bleeding is increased when the platelet count is < 10,000 cells/mm³, which is the threshold at which a platelet transfusion is indicated (or < 30,000 cells/mm³ if active bleeding is present). Chemotherapy doses may be reduced or placed on hold until the platelet count recovers. Intramuscular injections and medications that affect platelet functioning, such as NSAIDs, should be avoided in patients who are thrombocytopenic.

CHEMOTHERAPY-INDUCED NAUSEA AND VOMITING (CINV)

Nausea and vomiting are common with chemotherapy. Patient factors that increase the risk of nausea and vomiting include female gender, age < 50 years, anxiety, depression, dehydration, history of motion sickness and history of nausea and vomiting with prior regimens. For chemotherapy-induced nausea and vomiting (CINV), administer antiemetics at least 30 minutes prior to chemotherapy and provide take-home antiemetic medication (e.g., ondansetron, prochlorperazine or metoclopramide) for breakthrough nausea and vomiting. There are 3 subtypes of CINV: acute, delayed and anticipatory.

SUBTYPE	ONSET	RISK FACTORS	MAJOR NEURO-TRANSMITTERS	DRUG THERAPY*
Acute	Within 24 hours after chemotherapy	See text above for patient risk factors	Serotonin and substance P	5HT-3 receptor antagonists (5HT3-RAs), NK1 receptor antagonists (NK1-RAs), dexamethasone, olanzapine
Delayed	> 24 hours after chemotherapy	Anthracyclines, platinum analogs, cyclophosphamide, ifosfamide, any regimens with a high risk for causing acute CINV	Substance P and dopamine	NK1-RA, corticosteroids, palonosetron, granisetron ER SC, olanzapine
Anticipatory	Before chemotherapy	History of CINV with previous regimen	Gamma aminobutyric acid (GABA)	Benzodiazepines; start the evening prior to chemotherapy to alleviate anxiety and N/V

*Most antiemetics are started at least 30 minutes prior to the chemotherapy regimen.

Nausea/Vomiting (Emesis) Treatment

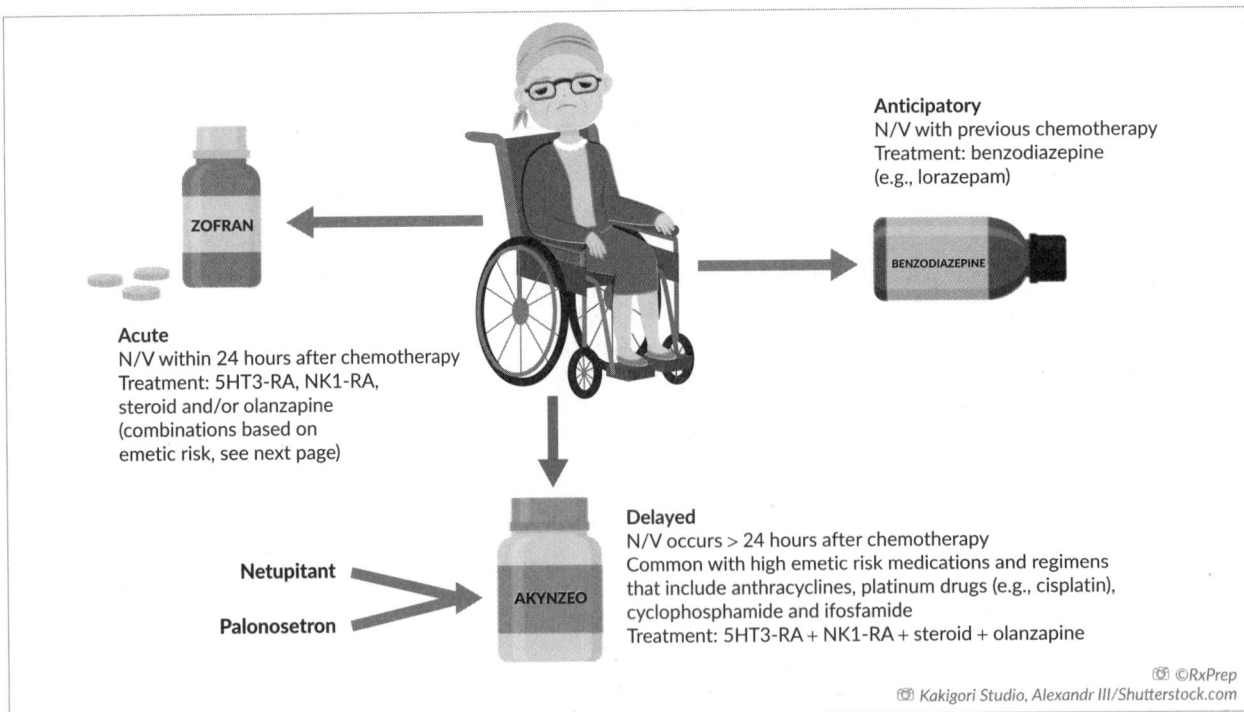

Anticipatory
N/V with previous chemotherapy
Treatment: benzodiazepine
(e.g., lorazepam)

Acute
N/V within 24 hours after chemotherapy
Treatment: 5HT3-RA, NK1-RA, steroid and/or olanzapine
(combinations based on emetic risk, see next page)

Delayed
N/V occurs > 24 hours after chemotherapy
Common with high emetic risk medications and regimens that include anthracyclines, platinum drugs (e.g., cisplatin), cyclophosphamide and ifosfamide
Treatment: 5HT3-RA + NK1-RA + steroid + olanzapine

Netupitant

Palonosetron

©RxPrep
Kakigori Studio, Alexandr III/Shutterstock.com

Emetic Risk Potential

Chemotherapy regimens are divided into risk groups for emetogenicity. Regimens with high emetic risk cause emesis at a frequency > 90%. Cisplatin is a high emetic risk drug; see the Common Toxicities of Select Chemotherapeutic Agents table earlier in the chapter for additional medications. Other categories include moderate (30 – 90%), low (10 – 30%) and minimal (< 10%) emetic risk. The majority of the MAbs and TKIs have minimal emetic risk.

Antiemetic Regimens for Acute/Delayed Nausea & Vomiting

Since the goal is to <u>prevent</u> nausea and vomiting, antiemetic regimens are started <u>before chemotherapy</u>. The risk of nausea and vomiting persists for three days after receiving the last dose of a high emetic risk chemotherapy drug and for at least two days following the last dose of a moderate emetic risk drug.

5HT3-RA	NK1-RA	COMBINATION	OTHER	STEROID
Ondansetron	Aprepitant PO	Netupitant/palonosetron PO *(Akynzeo)*	Olanzapine	Dexamethasone
Granisetron	Fosaprepitant IV			
Palonosetron	Rolapitant	Fosnetupitant/palonosetron IV *(Akynzeo)*		

CHEMOTHERAPY REGIMEN	ANTIEMETIC REGIMEN

<u>High emetic risk*</u>	**3 or 4 drugs**
	■ <u>NK1-RA + 5HT3-RA + olanzapine + dexamethasone</u> (preferred)
	  ❑ Olanzapine + netupitant or fosnetupitant/palonosetron *(Akynzeo)* + dexamethasone
	■ <u>Palonosetron + olanzapine + dexamethasone</u>
	■ <u>NK1-RA + 5HT3-RA + dexamethasone</u>
	  ❑ Netupitant or fosnetupitant/palonosetron *(Akynzeo)* + dexamethasone

Moderate emetic risk*	**2 or 3 drugs** ■ NK1-RA + 5HT3-RA + dexamethasone ❑ Netupitant or fosnetupitant/palonosetron *(Akynzeo)* + dexamethasone ■ 5HT3-RA + dexamethasone ■ Palonosetron + olanzapine + dexamethasone
Low emetic risk	**1 drug (any except NK1-RA)** ■ 5HT3-RA** ■ Dexamethasone ■ Prochlorperazine ■ Metoclopramide

Can add lorazepam PRN, H2RA or PPI
**Granisetron or ondansetron*

Antiemetics for Breakthrough CINV

Despite receiving antiemetic prophylaxis for acute and/or delayed CINV, some patients may experience breakthrough nausea and vomiting. <u>Various medications</u> may be beneficial, including <u>5HT3-RAs, dopamine receptor antagonists, cannabinoids, olanzapine</u>, lorazepam, dexamethasone or scopolamine.

Medications for CINV

<u>5HT3-RAs</u> are usually well-tolerated by most patients, with <u>migraine-like headaches and constipation</u> being common side effects. They also cause <u>minimal sedation</u> compared to dopamine receptor antagonists and cannabinoids. <u>Dopamine receptor antagonists</u> such as <u>prochlorperazine, promethazine and metoclopramide</u> commonly cause <u>sedation</u> and some anticholinergic side effects. <u>Extrapyramidal symptoms</u> (EPS) such as acute dystonic reactions can also occur, especially in younger patients. <u>Acute dystonic reactions</u> should be <u>treated with anticholinergics (benztropine, diphenhydramine)</u>.

<u>Droperidol</u> is an antiemetic in the same class as haloperidol (i.e., butyrophenones). Droperidol has restricted use (or has been removed entirely) in most hospitals due to <u>QT-prolongation</u> and the risk of Torsades de Pointes. Droperidol used to be commonly used for postoperative nausea and vomiting (not for CINV).

<u>Cannabinoids, such as dronabinol</u> and <u>nabilone</u>, can be used as <u>second-line agents</u>. These are <u>synthetic</u> analogs of <u>delta-9-tetrahydrocannabinol</u>, a naturally occurring component of *Cannabis sativa* <u>(marijuana)</u>. Although these agents may be legally prescribed, they may cause side effects similar to *Cannabis*, such as <u>increased appetite, sedation, dysphoria or euphoria</u>. The DEA classifies *Cannabis* (marijuana, used in the plant form) as a schedule I drug, however it can be purchased for medical and nonmedical use in some states, and for medical use only in other jurisdictions.

Antiemetics

DRUG	DOSING	SAFETY/SIDE EFFECTS/MONITORING
Substance P/Neurokinin-1 Receptor Antagonists: inhibit the substance P/neurokinin 1 receptor, therefore augmenting the antiemetic activity of 5HT-3 receptor antagonists and corticosteroids to inhibit acute and delayed phases of chemotherapy-induced emesis.		
Aprepitant (Emend, Emend Tri-Pack, Cinvanti) Capsule, injection (Cinvanti), oral suspension	PO: 125 mg 1 hour before chemotherapy on day 1, then 80 mg daily x 2 days	**CONTRAINDICATIONS** Aprepitant/fosaprepitant: do not use with pimozide or cisapride (CYP3A4 substrates) Rolapitant: do not use with thioridazine or pimozide (CYP2D6 substrates)
Fosaprepitant (Emend) Injection	IV: 150 mg 30 minutes before chemotherapy	**SIDE EFFECTS** Dizziness, fatigue, constipation, weakness, hiccups
Netupitant + palonosetron (Akynzeo) Capsule	PO: 300/0.5 mg 1 hour before chemotherapy	Fosaprepitant: infusion site reactions **NOTES** Aprepitant/fosaprepitant/netupitant are CYP3A4 inhibitors;
Fosnetupitant + palonosetron (Akynzeo) Injection	IV: 235/0.25 mg 1 hour before chemotherapy	a decreased dexamethasone dose (CYP3A4 substrate) may be needed when used concurrently as an antiemetic
Rolapitant (Varubi) Tablet, injection	PO: 180 mg 1-2 hours before chemotherapy	Rolapitant is a CYP2D6 inhibitor; the dose of dexamethasone should not be decreased when used concurrently as an antiemetic
5HT-3 Receptor Antagonists: work by blocking serotonin, both peripherally on vagal nerve terminals and centrally in the chemoreceptor trigger zone. All may be given once prior to chemotherapy on day 1, with the exception of the granisetron transdermal patch which is started prior to day 1 of chemotherapy.		
Ondansetron (Zofran, Zuplenz film) Tablet, ODT, oral solution, oral film, injection	PO: 8-24 mg IV: 8-16 mg	**CONTRAINDICATIONS** Do not use with apomorphine (Apokyn) due to severe hypotension and loss of consciousness
Granisetron (Sancuso, Sustol) Tablet, injection, transdermal patch	PO: 1-2 mg IV: 10 mcg/kg or 1 mg SC (Sustol): 10 mg over 20-30 seconds Patch (Sancuso): 3.1 mg/24 hour, apply 24-48 hours before chemotherapy; may leave in place up to 7 days	**WARNINGS** Dose-dependent ↑ in QT interval (Torsades de Pointes) - more common with IV Serotonin syndrome when used in combination with other serotonergic agents Constipation, progressive ileus and gastric distension (Sustol)
Palonosetron (Aloxi) Injection + netupitant (Akynzeo) + fosnetupitant (Akynzeo)	IV (Aloxi): 0.25 mg PO (Akynzeo): 0.5/300 mg 1 hour before chemotherapy IV (Akynzeo): 0.25/235 mg 1 hour before chemotherapy	**SIDE EFFECTS** Headache, constipation, fatigue, dizziness, injection site reactions (Sustol) **NOTES** Palonosetron PO only available in combination with netupitant (Akynzeo). Of the 5HT3-RAs, only palonosetron and Sustol have FDA-approval for delayed CINV
Corticosteroids		
Dexamethasone (Decadron) Tablet, oral solution, injection	All off-label dosing High risk: 12 mg PO/IV on day 1 of chemotherapy, then 8 mg PO daily days 2-4 Moderate risk: 12 mg PO/IV on day 1 of chemotherapy, then 8 mg PO/IV days 2-3 Low risk: 8-12 mg PO/IV on chemotherapy days	**CONTRAINDICATIONS** Systemic fungal infections, cerebral malaria **SIDE EFFECTS** Short-term side effects include ↑ appetite/weight gain, fluid retention, emotional instability (euphoria, mood swings, irritability, acute psychosis), insomnia, GI upset Higher doses ↑ BP and blood glucose (especially in patients with diabetes)

DRUG	DOSING	SAFETY/SIDE EFFECTS/MONITORING
Dopamine Receptor Antagonists: work by <u>blocking dopamine receptors</u> in the CNS, including the <u>chemoreceptor trigger zone</u>.		
Prochlorperazine (_Compazine*_, _Compro_) Tablet, suppository, injection	10 mg IV/PO Q6H PRN May give 25 mg suppository PR Q12H PRN	**BOXED WARNINGS** Prochlorperazine: ↑ mortality in elderly patients with dementia-related psychosis. Promethazine: <u>do not use in children < 2 years</u> of age (risk of respiratory depression). <u>Do not give via intra-arterial or SC</u> administration. IV route can cause <u>serious tissue injury if extravasation</u> occurs. Deep IM injection is preferred.
Promethazine (_Phenergan_, _Promethegan_) Tablet, oral solution, suppository, injection	12.5-25 mg PO/IM/IV/PR Q4-6H PRN	Metoclopramide: <u>tardive dyskinesia (TD) that can be irreversible</u>. Discontinue metoclopramide if signs or symptoms of TD occur. Risk is ↑ with ↑ duration of treatment and total cumulative dose. Avoid treatment with metoclopramide for > 12 weeks. <u>↓ dose with renal impairment</u>.
Metoclopramide (_Reglan_) Tablet, ODT, injection _Gimoti_ nasal spray – diabetic gastroparesis	10-20 mg PO/IV Q4-6H PRN For highly emetic regimens: 0.5-2 mg/kg/dose PO/IV Q6H PRN CrCl < 40 mL/min: give 50% of the dose	Droperidol: <u>QT prolongation and serious arrhythmias</u>. All patients should have a 12-lead ECG prior to receiving droperidol and continue for 2-3 hours after completing treatment. Contraindicated if baseline QT interval is prolonged.
Olanzapine (_Zyprexa_) Tablet, ODT, injection Works through several mechanisms (e.g., dopamine, 5HT, histamine)	10 mg PO on the day of chemotherapy, and on days 2-4 5 mg PO Q4H PRN, max of 20 mg/day	**WARNINGS** Symptoms of <u>Parkinson disease</u> may be <u>exacerbated</u>. Avoid use in patients with Parkinson disease. **SIDE EFFECTS** <u>Sedation, lethargy, acute EPS</u> (common in children; antidote is diphenhydramine or benztropine), can ↓ <u>seizure</u> threshold, hypotension, neuroleptic malignant syndrome (NMS), QT prolongation.
Droperidol Injection	Indicated only for post-operative N/V, not for CINV	Strong anticholinergic side effects (e.g., constipation) except with metoclopramide (diarrhea). **Olanzapine Side Effects** Mild (sedation, orthostasis, others) when used for CINV; see Schizophrenia chapter for details. **NOTES** Droperidol is not used for CINV. It is included here due to <u>high QT risk</u>, and for completeness of the antiemetic discussion.
Cannabinoids: may work by activating cannabinoid receptors within the central nervous system and/or by inhibiting the vomiting control mechanism in the medulla oblongata.		
Dronabinol (_Marinol_, _Syndros_) Capsules: C-III Solution: C-II <u>Refrigerate</u>	Labeled dosing: 5 mg/m² PO prior to chemotherapy and Q2-4H after chemotherapy for up to 6 doses/day. Most patients respond to 5 mg 3-4 times/day.	**SIDE EFFECTS** <u>Somnolence, euphoria, ↑ appetite</u>, orthostatic hypotension, dysphoria, lowering of the seizure threshold, use with caution in patients with histories of substance abuse or psychiatric disorders. **NOTES** Solution contains 50% alcohol.
Nabilone (_Cesamet*_) C-II No refrigeration needed	1-2 mg PO BID, continue for up to 48 hours after the last chemotherapy dose	
Benzodiazepines: <u>enhance GABA</u> (an inhibitory neurotransmitter) to decrease neuronal excitability, which results in alleviation of anxiety and suppression of anticipatory nausea and vomiting.		
Lorazepam (_Ativan_) C-IV	0.5-2 mg PO or IV Q6H PRN Start the <u>evening prior</u> to chemotherapy	See the Anxiety Disorders chapter for details.

*Brand discontinued but name still used in practice.

ONCOLOGY

OTHER GASTROINTESTINAL COMPLICATIONS

Cells of the GI tract are rapidly dividing and are therefore susceptible to being killed by chemotherapy agents that interfere with DNA replication or cell division. Damage to the epithelium of the GI tract results in diarrhea. Damage to oral mucosal epithelial cells leads to painful oral ulcerations, also called oral mucositis. Damage to the salivary glands usually caused by radiation therapy to the head or neck regions may cause dry mouth, also called xerostomia.

Chemotherapy-Induced Diarrhea

Chemotherapy-induced diarrhea can lead to life-threatening dehydration and electrolyte imbalances. Antimotility agents, such as loperamide and diphenoxylate/atropine, may be prescribed to treat chemotherapy-induced diarrhea. The usual maximum dose of loperamide is 16 mg/day when treating diarrhea under medical supervision. Fluorouracil, capecitabine and irinotecan commonly cause diarrhea that occurs several days after chemotherapy. The risk of diarrhea is increased when fluorouracil (or the prodrug capecitabine) is used in combination with leucovorin, or when used in patients with dihydropyrimidine dehydrogenase (DPD) deficiencies (not common). Irinotecan also causes early-onset diarrhea that occurs during the infusion of the drug and is often accompanied by symptoms of cholinergic excess such as abdominal cramping, rhinitis, lacrimation and salivation. Treatment for cholinergic excess is the anticholinergic drug atropine. Many TKIs, especially those targeting VEGF or EGF, such as sorafenib and sunitinib, commonly cause diarrhea.

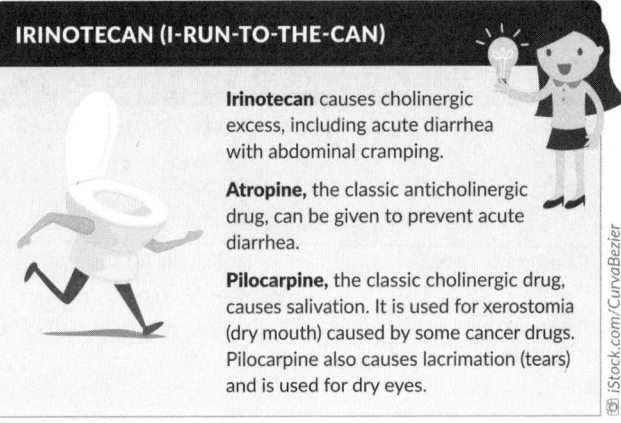

IRINOTECAN (I-RUN-TO-THE-CAN)

Irinotecan causes cholinergic excess, including acute diarrhea with abdominal cramping.

Atropine, the classic anticholinergic drug, can be given to prevent acute diarrhea.

Pilocarpine, the classic cholinergic drug, causes salivation. It is used for xerostomia (dry mouth) caused by some cancer drugs. Pilocarpine also causes lacrimation (tears) and is used for dry eyes.

© iStock.com/CurvaBezier

Oral Mucositis

Chemotherapy-induced oral mucositis causes painful ulcers to form in the mouth. Symptoms begin about a week after chemotherapy (e.g., 5-FU, methotrexate). Oral mucositis symptoms can be severe (e.g., difficulty eating, drinking, talking and cleaning the teeth) and require treatment. Good oral hygiene, brushing with a very soft toothbrush, is important.

Viscous lidocaine 2%, magic mouthwash (i.e., various compounded preparations) and systemic analgesics will lessen pain and make it possible to talk, eat and drink, thought parenteral nutrition or IV fluids may be needed in some cases. Frequent rinsing with NaCl solution (i.e., salt water) helps retain moisture. Oral mucositis increases the risk of oral *Candida* infection (thrush). Nystatin oral suspension or clotrimazole troches are used for treatment.

MEDICATIONS FOR ORAL COMPLICATIONS OF CHEMOTHERAPY

DRUG	DOSING	SAFETY/SIDE EFFECTS/MONITORING
Oral Mucositis		
Mucosal Barrier Agents (*Episil, Gelclair, Mucotrol, MuGard, Orafate, ProThelial*) Gel, spray, solution, wafer	Varies depending on product. Most are applied to the oral mucosa several times per day.	**SIDE EFFECTS** Burning, stinging sensation in the mouth
Lidocaine, Viscous 2% topical solution for mouth/throat	15 mL swish and spit/swallow Q3H PRN	**BOXED WARNING** Avoid use in patients < 3 years of age due to reports of seizures, cardiopulmonary arrest and death **WARNINGS** Exceeding the recommended dose can result in high plasma levels and serious adverse effects (seizures, cardiopulmonary arrest), methemoglobinemia **SIDE EFFECTS** Dizziness, drowsiness, confusion, hypotension **NOTES** Avoid ingestion of food for 60 minutes following dose due to risk of impaired swallowing and aspiration

DRUG	DOSING	SAFETY/SIDE EFFECTS/MONITORING
Xerostomia		
Artificial Saliva Substitutes (*Aquoral, Biotene, Mouth Kote, NeutraSal, SalivaSure*, others) Spray, solution, lozenge	Varies depending on product. Most can be applied to oral mucosa PRN.	
Pilocarpine (*Salagen*)	5-10 mg PO TID Hepatic impairment: Moderate: 5 mg BID Severe: avoid use	**WARNINGS** Use with caution in patients with cholelithiasis, nephrolithiasis, cardiovascular disease, asthma, bronchitis, COPD **SIDE EFFECTS** Cholinergic side effects: flushing, sweating, nausea, urinary frequency **NOTES** Avoid administering with a high-fat meal

HAND-FOOT SYNDROME

Hand-foot syndrome (also known as palmar-plantar erythrodysesthesia, or PPE) frequently occurs following treatment with capecitabine, fluorouracil, cytarabine, liposomal doxorubicin and the tyrosine kinase inhibitors (TKIs) sorafenib and sunitinib.

PPE occurs when small amounts of the chemotherapy drug leak out of capillaries and into the palms of the hands and soles of the feet. Heat and friction on the palms and soles increases the amount of drug in the capillaries and the amount of drug leakage. This causes tenderness, pain, inflammation and possibly peeling of the palms and soles. See the Hand-Foot Syndrome Management box for methods to manage PPE. Dose reductions or treatment delays may be needed if symptoms do not adequately improve.

Cooling hands/feet with cold compresses provides temporary relief of pain and tenderness.

Emollients (*Aquaphor, Udder Cream, Bag Balm*) are used to retain moisture in the hands and feet. Steroids and pain medications can be helpful to lessen inflammation and pain.

HAND-FOOT SYNDROME MANAGEMENT

- Limit daily activities to reduce friction and heat exposure to hands and feet.
- Avoid prolonged exposure to hot water (washing dishes, showers). Take shorter showers in lukewarm water.
- Avoid use of dishwashing gloves as the rubber will hold in heat.
- Avoid increased pressure on the soles of the feet (no jogging, aerobics, power walking or jumping).
- Avoid increased pressure on the palms of the hands (no use of garden tools, screwdrivers, knives for chopping or performing other tasks that require squeezing hands on a hard surface).

ONCOLOGY

TUMOR LYSIS SYNDROME

Chemotherapy that causes tumor cell death can cause the cell wall and/or membrane to disintegrate (lyse), which releases the intracellular contents into the bloodstream (see image). Tumor lysis syndrome (TLS) has occurred with most cancer types, but most commonly occurs with leukemia and non-Hodgkins lymphoma.

When the cell is lysed, the intracellular components that enter the bloodstream include potassium, phosphate, purines and pyrimidines (the base pairs that compose DNA). The phosphate that is released into the bloodstream will bind to calcium, which can cause hypocalcemia. Calcium and phosphate can also precipitate in soft tissues. TLS causes acute <u>hyperkalemia</u> (which can cause <u>arrhythmias</u>), hyperphosphatemia, <u>hypocalcemia</u> (which can cause anorexia, nausea and <u>seizures</u>) and hyperuricemia.

The xanthine oxidase enzyme is present in the blood and can readily convert large amounts of purines into uric acid, causing acute <u>hyperuricemia</u>, which <u>crystallizes</u>, as with gout. The uric acid crystals <u>damage the kidneys</u>, which can progress to acute renal failure.

<u>Allopurinol</u> is a <u>xanthine oxidase inhibitor</u> that blocks the conversion of purines into uric acid. The usual initial dose of allopurinol for gout is ~100 mg daily. For tumor lysis syndrome, higher doses (400 – 800 mg/day) are used and continued for 10 – 14 days after chemotherapy. Allopurinol is reviewed in detail in the Gout chapter.

<u>Rasburicase</u> is an expensive medication that is added to allopurinol when allopurinol and hydration fail to control the uric acid level or is not a reasonable option (e.g., with risk of <u>allopurinol</u>-induced <u>rash/severe skin</u> reactions). It converts uric acid to a more water-soluble metabolite (allantoin), which is easily excreted. Rasburicase is contraindicated in G6PD deficiency. Discontinue immediately and permanently in any patient who develops hemolysis.

Both allopurinol and rasburicase are initially given with IV normal saline, which increases urine output and speeds up excretion of some of the excess intracellular components.

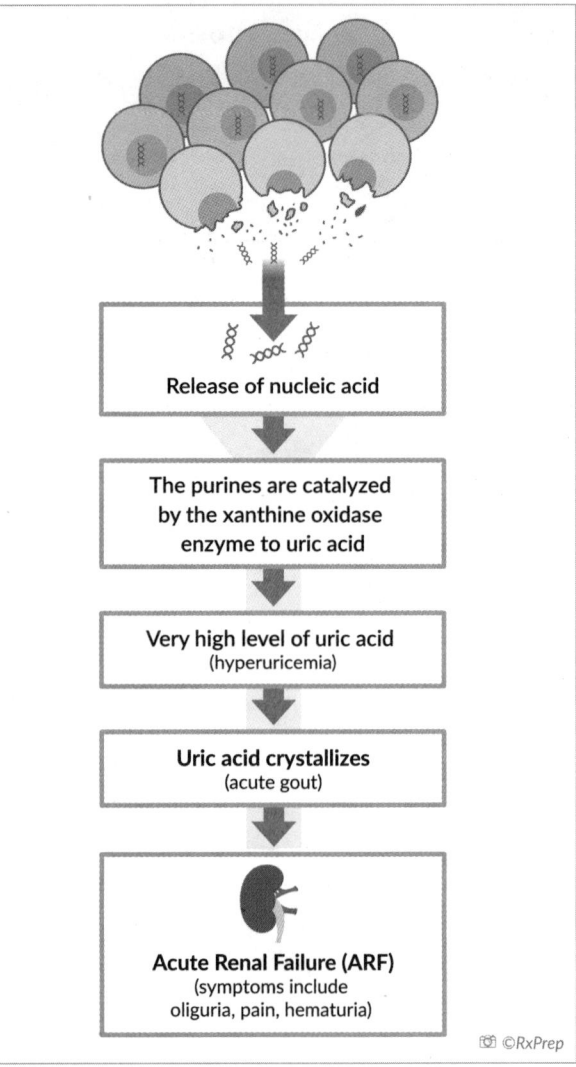

Release of nucleic acid

The purines are catalyzed by the xanthine oxidase enzyme to uric acid

Very high level of uric acid (hyperuricemia)

Uric acid crystallizes (acute gout)

Acute Renal Failure (ARF) (symptoms include oliguria, pain, hematuria)

©RxPrep

HYPERCALCEMIA OF MALIGNANCY

Certain cancers cause calcium to leach from bone, causing hypercalcemia and bones that are weak and prone to fracture. Mild hypercalcemia is typically asymptomatic and can be treated with hydration and loop diuretics.

Moderate to severe hypercalcemia (calcium > 12 mg/dL) can be symptomatic, with nausea, vomiting, fatigue, dehydration and confusion. Treatment includes IV hydration with normal saline and medication to lower calcium levels. Calcitonin is sometimes used initially for up to 48 hours; the treatment duration is short because tachyphylaxis (tolerance) develops quickly.

An IV bisphosphonate (e.g., pamidronate, zoledronic acid) is generally considered first-line, and may be given with calcitonin in severe cases. An alternative to IV bisphosphonates is denosumab. IV bisphosphonates and denosumab are common treatment options for osteoporosis (at different doses). They have the added benefit of building bone density and reducing fractures.

Hypercalcemia of Malignancy Treatment

TREATMENT	MOA	ONSET	DEGREE OF HYPERCALCEMIA*
Hydration with normal saline and loop diuretics	↑ renal calcium excretion	Minutes to hours	Mild (oral or IV hydration) Moderate Severe
Calcitonin (Miacalcin) 4-8 units/kg IM/SC Q12H	Inhibits bone resorption, ↑ renal calcium excretion	2-6 hours	Moderate Severe
IV Bisphosphonates **Zoledronic acid (Zometa)** 4 mg IV once, may repeat in 7 days if needed; do not infuse over < 15 minutes due to increased risk of renal toxicity; dose does not need to be adjusted for mild-moderate renal insufficiency when used for hypercalcemia. Do not confuse with Reclast, which is dosed at 5 mg IV yearly for osteoporosis - see Osteoporosis chapter. Pamidronate 60-90 mg IV over 2-24 hrs once, may repeat in 7 days if needed	Inhibits bone resorption by stopping osteoclast function	24-72 hours	Mild Moderate Severe
Denosumab (Xgeva) 120 mg SC on days 1, 8 and 15 of the first month, then monthly. Do not confuse with Prolia, which is dosed at 60 mg SC every 6 months for osteoporosis - see Osteoporosis chapter	Monoclonal antibody that blocks the interaction between RANKL and RANK (a receptor on osteoclasts), preventing osteoclast formation	24-72 hours	Moderate Severe

*Degree of hypercalcemia – mild: corrected calcium < 12 mg/dL, moderate: corrected calcium 12-14 mg/dL, severe: corrected calcium > 14 mg/dL, or presence of symptoms. Corrected calcium (mg/dL) = calcium (reported) + [(4 – albumin) x 0.8]

ONCOLOGY

IMMUNOLOGIC REACTIONS TO MONOCLONAL ANTIBODIES

Immunologic reactions commonly occur with virtually every monoclonal antibody (MAb). This is due to two main reasons:

- MAbs are proteins and can be recognized by the human immune system as a foreign substance. This risk is higher if there is a murine (i.e., mouse) component.

- Cytokine release syndrome (CRS) frequently occurs with the initial few doses of a MAb. CRS is related to cytokine release (e.g., TNF-alpha, IL-2, IL-6, interferon-gamma) that peaks about 1 – 4 hours after administration of the MAb. MAbs that target B- or T- lymphocytes and leukocytes are likely to cause CRS. Risk factors for CRS include a high WBC tumor burden, pre-existing cardiac or pulmonary conditions and prior infusion reactions.

Treatment of Immunologic Reactions

To prevent immunologic reactions, most MAbs require the following premedications:

- Acetaminophen (usually 650 mg PO)

- Diphenhydramine (IV or PO) or another antihistamine

Additional medications can be needed based on severity of the reaction or treatment guidelines. This can include H2 blockers, steroids and/or meperidine (for rigors).

CHEMOTHERAPY HANDLING, ADMINISTRATION AND EXTRAVASATION

IV ADMINISTRATION AND EXTRAVASATION

All chemotherapy drugs are hazardous, which means they are carcinogenic, mutagenic or teratogenic and can harm healthcare staff if they are exposed to the drug. Pharmacists, technicians, nurses and other healthcare personnel must use protective measures to limit exposure. The Compounding chapters provide detailed information on USP 800 requirements for the compounding environment and necessary equipment.

Many chemotherapy agents are vesicants, which means they may cause tissue necrosis if the IV drug accidentally leaks from the vein into the surrounding tissue (also called extravasation). Major vesicants include anthracyclines and vinca alkaloids. Care should be taken to avoid extravasation by administering these drugs through central venous catheters or freshly started peripheral IV lines with confirmed patency. If extravasation occurs, apply cold compresses (except with the vinca alkaloids and etoposide, use warm compresses) and the antidotes below depending on the drug extravasated:

- Anthracyclines: dexrazoxane (*Totect*) or dimethyl sulfoxide

- Vinca alkaloids and etoposide: hyaluronidase

Based on clinical experience, a limited number of chemotherapy agents can be given intrathecally (administered into the cerebrospinal fluid), including cytarabine, methotrexate, hydrocortisone and thiotepa. They must be preservative-free. Unfortunately, accidental intrathecal administration of vincristine has been reported, which is fatal.

TIMING OF VACCINATIONS

Vaccination during chemotherapy should be avoided because the antibody response is suboptimal. When chemotherapy is being planned, vaccination should precede chemotherapy by ≥ 2 weeks. Patients on chemotherapy may receive the inactivated seasonal influenza vaccine in between cycles of chemotherapy. The administration of live vaccines to immunocompromised patients must be avoided. Live vaccines can generally be administered at least three months after discontinuation of chemotherapy.

Select Guidelines/References

- American Cancer Society. Cancer Screening Guidelines http://www.cancer.org/healthy/findcancerearly/cancerscreeningguidelines/american-cancer-society-guidelines-for-the-early-detection-of-cancer (accessed 2022 Feb 13)

- National Comprehensive Cancer Network (NCCN). www.nccn.org (accessed 2022 Feb 13)

- American Society of Clinical Oncology (ASCO). www.asco.org (accessed 2022 Feb 13)

CONTENT LEGEND

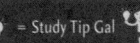 = Study Tip Gal   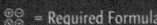 = Required Formula

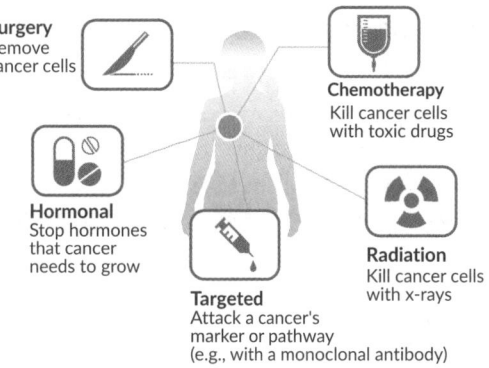

Cancer Treatments

Surgery
Remove cancer cells

Chemotherapy
Kill cancer cells with toxic drugs

Hormonal
Stop hormones that cancer needs to grow

Targeted
Attack a cancer's marker or pathway
(e.g., with a monoclonal antibody)

Radiation
Kill cancer cells with x-rays

©RxPrep

📷 iStock.com/ArnaPhoto, newannyart; 📷 kanate/stock.adobe.com

CHAPTER 62

ONCOLOGY II: COMMON CANCER TYPES & TREATMENT

BACKGROUND

The five most common types of cancer are basal and squamous cell skin cancer (i.e., non-melanoma), breast, lung, prostate and colorectal cancer.

The majority of this chapter reviews the use of chemotherapeutic drugs that either kill tumor cells directly (e.g., cytotoxic drugs) or prevent cell division and growth (e.g., hormone-blocking drugs).

TREATMENT OVERVIEW

Cancer can be treated with surgery, radiation, chemotherapy, hormone (endocrine) therapy, biological therapy, targeted therapy and/or immunotherapy. Complementary therapy (e.g., acupuncture, medical marijuana) is commonly used among cancer patients to manage treatment side effects.

Cancer treatment decisions should involve the patient, their family and the healthcare team, and are based on:

- The cancer type and characteristics (e.g., a breast tumor that is estrogen-receptor positive will receive different treatment than a breast tumor that is estrogen-receptor negative).

- The stage of cancer (i.e., the size and how far it has metastasized, or spread).

- Patient characteristics, such as acceptable tolerability to chemotherapy.

The adverse effects of chemotherapy range from relatively mild to severe (e.g., the drug is highly toxic); a cancer patient should have greater benefit than harm from a selected regimen.

ONCOLOGY

TREATMENT GOALS

The patient's physical functioning is assessed with rating systems, such as the Karnofsky or Eastern Cooperative Oncology Group (ECOG), and reported as performance status. Performance status can help determine the treatment goal. The treatment goal could be to achieve remission (with curative intent) or be palliative, where cure is not the focus of care and the primary intent is to provide comfort, support and control of symptoms, such as pain.

The response to treatment can be complete or partial:

- A complete response, or complete remission, means that the treatment has destroyed all known tumors.

- A partial response, or partial remission, means that at least 30% of the tumor was eliminated.

Some types of cancer have a higher rate of recurrence than others. If a patient remains cancer-free for five years, it is unlikely that the cancer will recur.

TREATMENT TYPES

Patient factors including age, comorbidities and past treatments are considered when selecting a regimen. A patient's quality of life may lead the clinician and family to choose palliative measures over a more aggressive treatment plan that could have intolerable side effects.

If the cancer is resectable, the primary treatment is often surgery to remove the bulk of the tumor. Surgery and radiation target cancer that is confined locally. Other treatments can target both localized cancer and cancer cells that have spread.

Neoadjuvant therapy (e.g., radiation or chemotherapy) can be used before surgery to shrink the tumor in order to make complete resection more likely.

Adjuvant therapy (e.g., radiation and/or chemotherapy) is given after surgery in an attempt to eradicate residual disease and decrease recurrence.

LUNG CANCER

Lung cancer is the most common type of cancer worldwide. In the United States, there are ~235,000 new cases of lung cancer annually. The three main types are non-small cell (~85%), small cell (~10 – 15%) and carcinoid (< 5%). Non-small cell and small cell are distinguished by the cell size; as the name implies, small cell lung cancer has smaller cells.

Smoking causes ~80% of lung cancers. The other 20% are attributed to exposure to radon, asbestos fibers and various other types of chemicals and pollution. A chronic cough with dyspnea can indicate lung cancer and necessitates a visit to a healthcare provider.

Typical treatment includes surgery, followed by radiation and/or chemotherapy to destroy the remaining cancer cells. The chemotherapy drugs described in this chapter are used in various combination regimens.

The survival odds substantially increase when smoking is discontinued, yet 10% of cancer patients continue to smoke.

STAGES OF LUNG CANCER

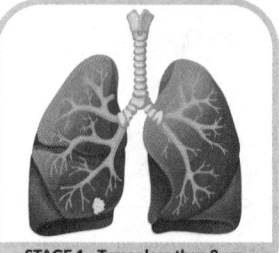

STAGE 1 - Tumor less than 3 cm. There is no metastasis.

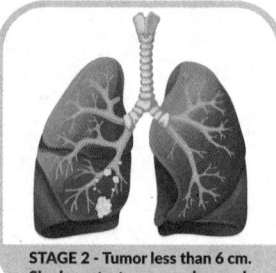

STAGE 2 - Tumor less than 6 cm. Single metastases are observed.

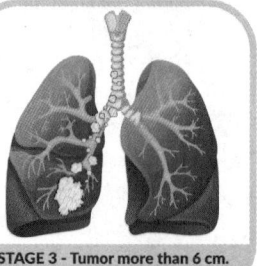

STAGE 3 - Tumor more than 6 cm. Metastases in the lymph nodes.

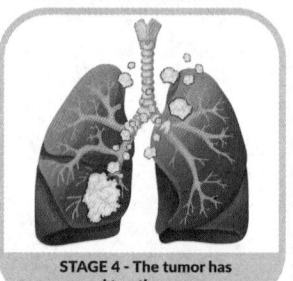

STAGE 4 - The tumor has spread to other organs.

© Valadzionak Volha/Shutterstock.com

SKIN CANCER

Skin cancer is the most common cancer in the United States. Risk factors include a history of UV light exposure (sun or tanning beds), light skin that burns easily, light hair color, immunosuppressant drugs or diseases, and a past history of skin cancer. The immune system can eliminate some early cancers. Suppressing the immune system, such as with immunosuppressants post-transplant, can increase the risk of skin cancer.

The three types of skin cancer are basal cell, squamous cell and melanoma. Basal cell and squamous cell are common and survivable if treated early. Melanoma is less common but often invasive, and accounts for ~7,000 skin cancer-related deaths each year.

Recommendations for reducing the risk of skin cancer:

- Seek shade, especially between 10 AM and 4 PM.
- Wear a shirt, tightly woven fabrics are best.
- Use a broad-spectrum sunscreen, at least SPF 15 – 30, and reapply every 2 hours.
- Wear a hat with at least a 2 – 3" brim.
- Wear sunglasses to protect the skin around the eyes and help prevent cataracts.

The "ABCDE" mnemonic below is used to educate patients about suspicious skin spots. A spot that is changing over time or looks different from other spots should be examined.

ABCDE – WARNING SIGNS OF MELANOMA SKIN CANCER

A	B	C	D	E
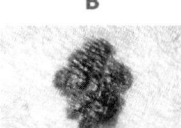	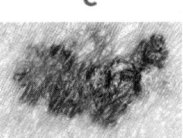	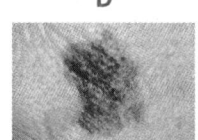	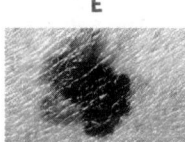	
ASYMMETRY One half of the mole does not match the other.	**BORDER** Edges are irregular, notched.	**COLOR** Color is not the same all over.	**DIAMETER** Larger than 6 mm, or the size of the tip of a pencil eraser.	**EVOLVING** Mole is changing in size, color, shape or symptoms (itching, bleeding, tenderness).

Skin Cancer Foundation, National Cancer Institute

BREAST CANCER

After skin cancer, breast cancer is the most common cancer diagnosed in the United States. The biggest risk factor for developing breast cancer is female gender. Females produce more estrogen than males, and many breast cancer tumors have estrogen receptors that require estrogen to grow. Female breast cells are more likely to mutate because they are more active than male breast cells (largely inactive). Risk factors can also be present at the cellular level, with genetic mutations that alter protein expression and cellular replication. Modifiable risk factors include being overweight (in postmenopausal females), low physical activity, poor nutrition and tobacco use.

Males have a higher risk of breast cancer when they have a condition that increases estrogen production, including Klinefelter syndrome, described later in this section.

IDENTIFYING BREAST CANCER

Breast Self-Exams

Breast self-exams are not used for screening, but can help identify a change in the look or feel of the breast or nipple, or nipple discharge, which would warrant follow-up screening.

Breast Imaging Studies

The recommended imaging schedule varies by organization but is typically annually or every other year beginning at age 40 or 45. Mammograms use low-dose x-rays to identify abnormal breast tissue. A few images are taken in a screening mammogram, and if they look suspicious, a diagnostic mammogram is performed. An ultrasound is useful to differentiate between a benign fluid-filled cyst and a cancerous tumor; it can also be used to guide the needle during a biopsy. High-risk females can receive an MRI, in addition to an annual mammogram.

Following an abnormal test (e.g., mammogram, MRI), a biopsy is performed. A small sample of tissue is excised (removed) with a biopsy needle and sent to pathology to identify if cancer cells are present.

Weight and Breast Cancer Risk

Overweight postmenopausal females have a higher breast cancer risk than lean females. Fat cells contain androgens (i.e., male sex hormones), which are converted to estrogens by the aromatase enzyme. The decline in estrogen after menopause causes abdominal cells to store more fat. Most females gain 5 – 10 pounds in the first ten years after menopause.

ONCOLOGY

BRCA1 and BRCA2 Gene Mutations

The BRCA1 and BRCA2 genes normally suppress tumor growth. The genes contain instructions for the production of proteins that repair damaged DNA. Inherited mutations in either gene prevents cell repair and causes a dramatic increase in breast cancer incidence. BRCA mutations were first linked to breast cancer (BR for breast, CA for cancer) but are now also linked with an increased risk for ovarian and prostate cancer.

In a female without either mutation, the lifetime risk of developing breast cancer is ~12%; with either BRCA mutation, the risk can increase up to ~70%. Fortunately, the risk of either mutation is low in the general population. Ethnic groups at high risk for mutations include Ashkenazi Jewish (8 – 10%), non-Ashkenazi Jewish (2 – 3%) and Hispanic (4%) populations. African-American and Asian-American females have a lower risk (< 1%).

MEN AND BREAST CANCER RISK

Less than 1% of breast cancer occurs in males. The risk increases in men with a BRCA mutation, and with the presence of any condition that increases estrogen production (e.g., Klinefelter syndrome). Similar to postmenopausal females, males who are overweight have increased estrogen production, which increases risk.

Klinefelter Syndrome and Male Breast Cancer Risk

Normally, males have one X and one Y chromosome. Klinefelter syndrome is a congenital condition in which males have one Y chromosome and two or more X chromosomes.

Males with Klinefelter syndrome produce more estrogen than is typical; they have small testicles, develop gynecomastia and are usually infertile. Males with Klinefelter syndrome have a higher breast cancer risk.

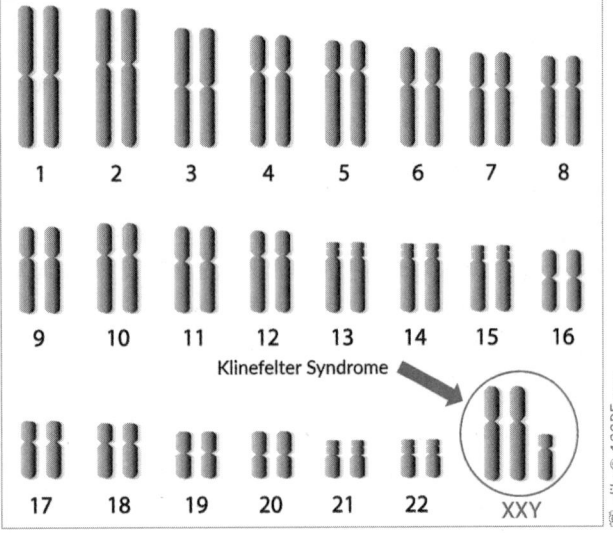

BREAST CANCER TREATMENT

Breast cancer treatment includes some combination of surgery, chemotherapy and/or radiation. Cancers that express markers on the cell surface that contribute to tumor growth will receive therapy that targets the markers.

Hormone-Sensitive Cancer Treatment

All breast tumors express some estrogen and progesterone receptors. If a tumor expresses a high percentage of either receptor type, the tumor is referred to as hormone-sensitive, and classified as estrogen receptor positive (ER+), progesterone receptor positive (PR+) or both (ER+/PR+).

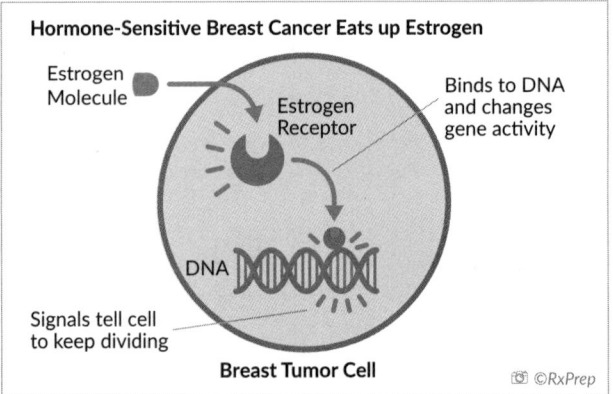

Hormone-sensitive cancers will be treated with adjuvant hormone (endocrine) therapy for 5 – 10 years to suppress cancer recurrence. The choice of treatment depends on the menopausal status of the patient.

Selective Estrogen Receptor Modulators and Aromatase Inhibitors

The first-line treatment for premenopausal females with hormone-sensitive cancer is tamoxifen, a selective estrogen receptor modulator (SERM) and antagonist in breast cells.

Premenopausal females produce estradiol, the most potent estrogen, in the ovaries. Postmenopausal females produce very little estradiol and instead get most of their estrogen from the peripheral conversion of androgens. Aromatase inhibitors (AIs) reduce estrogen production by blocking the aromatase enzyme that catalyzes this conversion. AIs do not block ovarian estradiol production, which is why they are not useful in premenopausal females (see diagram on the following page).

Raloxifene is a SERM used for breast cancer prophylaxis, not treatment. Raloxifene increases bone density and is indicated for osteoporosis prevention and treatment; most commonly, it is used in postmenopausal females who also wish to prevent breast cancer. Raloxifene is not first-line for osteoporosis because it causes hot flashes and has a risk of blood clots. The other SERMS, fulvestrant and toremifene, are used when tamoxifen is not a reasonable option.

In some circumstances, a premenopausal female will have menopause induced by taking a gonadotropin-releasing hormone (GnRH) agonist (goserelin or leuprolide). GnRH agonist treatment decreases LH and FSH, which suppresses ovarian estradiol production. This then makes AI treatment a reasonable option.

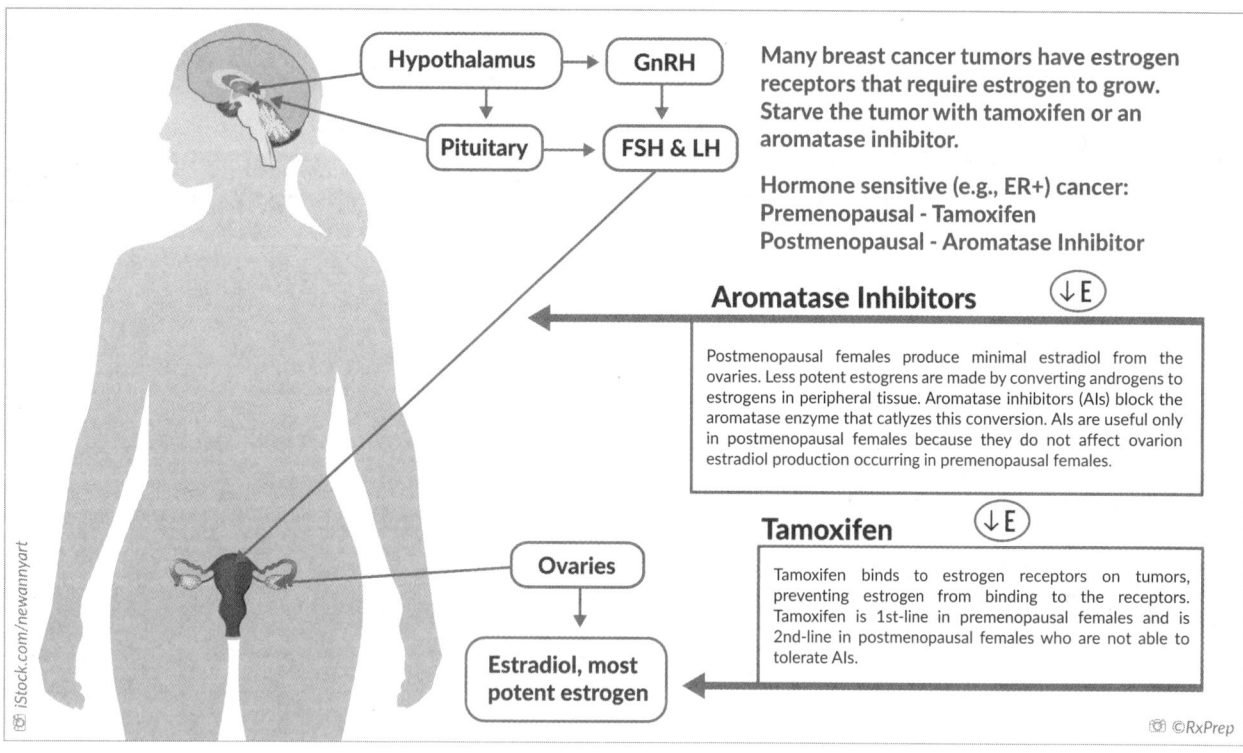

HER2 Overexpression

An oncogene is a protein that can turn a normal cell into a cancer cell; the HER2/NEU (typically referred to as HER2) oncogene promotes breast tumor growth. Approximately 20% of breast tumors overexpress HER2 on the cell surface, which makes the tumor grow quickly (i.e., it is an aggressive malignancy). Fortunately, there are drugs that are very effective in treating tumors that over-express HER2. The HER2 proteins on the cell surface must be coupled (dimerized) to send signals that accelerate cell division and tumor growth. Trastuzumab (Herceptin), and other monoclonal antibodies in its class, bind to the HER2 receptor, preventing dimerization. The HER2 inhibitors are used for multiple cancers that over-express HER2, and are described later in this chapter.

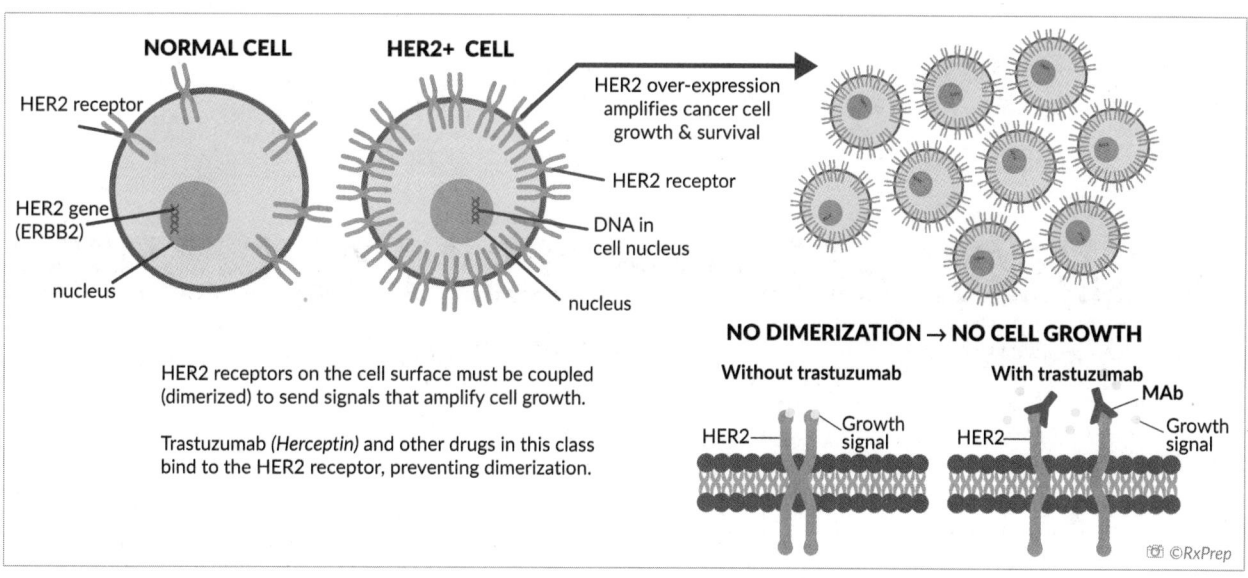

ONCOLOGY

CDK4/6 Inhibitors and Other Targeted Therapy for Breast Cancer

The CDK4/6 inhibitors in the following table are preferred, in combination with hormone (endocrine) therapy, for metastatic breast cancer. Abemaciclib is also approved for early-stage hormone-sensitive, HER2-negative breast cancer. Another targeted treatment used in hormone-sensitive breast cancer is the mTOR inhibitor everolimus, described later in this chapter.

Breast Cancer Hormonal (Endocrine) Treatment and CDK4/6 Inhibitors

DRUG	UNIQUE CONCERNS	SAFETY/SIDE EFFECTS/MONITORING
Selective Estrogen Receptor Modulators (SERMs) Estrogen antagonist in breast tissue.		
Tamoxifen (*Soltamox*) Oral Raloxifene (*Evista*) Oral Toremifene (*Fareston*) Oral	Tamoxifen: a prodrug converted via CYP2D6 to the potent metabolite endoxifen; slow CYP2D6 metabolizers or those taking CYP2D6 inhibitors have decreased efficacy Causes hot flashes/night sweats; estrogen (the usual treatment) and fluoxetine and paroxetine (CYP2D6 inhibitors) cannot be used to treat these symptoms; venlafaxine is preferred Toremifene: an alternative option in a person with slow CYP2D6 metabolism or if a drug interaction is present Raloxifene: for breast cancer prophylaxis (not treatment); it increases bone density, and is indicated for osteoporosis prevention and treatment in select postmenopausal females who need breast cancer prophylaxis	**BOXED WARNINGS** ↑ risk of uterine or endometrial cancer (tamoxifen), ↑ risk of thromboembolic events (tamoxifen, raloxifene), QT prolongation (toremifene) **CONTRAINDICATIONS** Do not use with warfarin (tamoxifen), history of DVT/PE (tamoxifen, raloxifene), pregnancy or breastfeeding (raloxifene), QT prolongation, hypokalemia, hypomagnesemia (toremifene) **SIDE EFFECTS** Hot flashes/night sweats, vaginal bleeding/spotting, vaginal discharge/dryness/pruritus, ↓ libido, edema, weight gain, hypertension, mood changes, amenorrhea, arthralgia/myalgia, cataracts (tamoxifen) Tamoxifen: ↓ bone density (premenopausal females); supplement with calcium/vitamin D Tamoxifen is teratogenic; contraception should be used in premenopausal females; raloxifene is also unsafe in pregnancy, but is only used in postmenopausal females
Selective Estrogen Receptor Degrader (SERD) Estrogen receptor antagonist that causes receptor degradation and downregulation.		
Fulvestrant (*Faslodex*) IM injection		**SIDE EFFECTS** ↑ LFTs, injection site pain, hot flashes, arthralgia/myalgia, nausea, headache, cough, dyspnea
Aromatase Inhibitors Block conversion of androgens to estrogens.		
Anastrozole (*Arimidex*) **Oral** Letrozole (*Femara*) Oral Exemestane (*Aromasin*) Oral	Higher risk of osteoporosis due to decreased bone mineral density; consider Ca and vitamin D supplementation, weight-bearing exercise, DEXA screening Higher risk of CVD compared to SERMs	**CONTRAINDICATIONS** Pregnancy **SIDE EFFECTS** Hot flashes/night sweats, arthralgia/myalgia, lethargy/fatigue, N/V, rash, hepatotoxicity, hypertension, dyslipidemia
Cyclin-Dependent Kinase (CDK4/6) Inhibitors Inhibit downstream signaling and tumor growth.		
Palbociclib (*Ibrance*) Oral Abemaciclib (*Verzenio*) Oral Ribociclib (*Kisqali*) Oral	Avoid or reduce dose with CYP3A4 inhibitors or inducers	**WARNINGS** Interstitial lung disease **SIDE EFFECTS** Neutropenia, anemia, nausea, diarrhea, fatigue, alopecia, blurred vision Risk of thromboembolic events

METASTATIC BREAST CANCER

Breast cancer metastases are often located in the bone, lungs, liver and brain. Hormone (endocrine) treatment or a HER2 inhibitor will still be used, if the cancer is ER+/PR+ or HER2 positive, respectively. Chemotherapy is given to shrink tumors and reduce further growth. Radiation is useful only for local palliation. Both chemotherapy and radiation have considerable side effects, which must be managed to reduce the impact on the patient's quality of life. Primary chemotherapy drugs used for breast cancer include capecitabine, carboplatin, cyclophosphamide, docetaxel, paclitaxel, doxorubicin and methotrexate. These are many of the potent chemotherapy drugs that are described in this chapter.

KEY COUNSELING POINTS

See the Drug Formulations and Patient Counseling chapter for counseling language/layman's terminology.

ALL PATIENTS WITH BREAST CANCER

- Do not take any estrogen-containing medications. Estrogen is <u>contraindicated</u> with any history of breast cancer.
- Take adequate calcium and vitamin D (unless calcium level is high from metastases).

TAMOXIFEN

- Avoid in pregnancy (teratogenic).
- Can cause:
  - ❑ Blood clots.
  - ❑ Endometrial cancer.
  - ❑ Hot flashes and night sweats, vaginal bleeding and discharge, and a lower sex drive.
  - ❑ Eye damage (cataracts).

RALOXIFENE

- Can cause blood clots.

AROMATASE INHIBITORS

- Can cause:
  - ❑ Hot flashes and night sweats.
  - ❑ Muscle damage.

PROSTATE CANCER

Prostate cancer is the most common cancer in males in the U.S. (lung cancer is the most common in the world). Fortunately, most prostate cancers are identified before the cancer has metastasized.

Early, non-metastatic prostate cancer can be treated with surgery, radiation, hormonal treatment or watchful waiting. Unlike breast cancer, in which treatment is almost always used, prostate cancer might not be treated, especially in an elderly male with a slow-growing tumor. In such a case, the male might die of an alternate condition before the prostate cancer causes considerable harm.

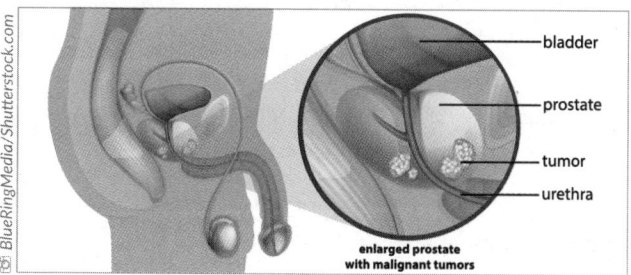

enlarged prostate
with malignant tumors

IDENTIFYING PROSTATE CANCER

Digital Rectal Exam

Most prostate cancers develop near the side of the prostate and can be felt with a <u>digital rectal exam (DRE)</u>, whereby a healthcare provider inserts a gloved, lubricated finger into the rectum to palpate the prostate. If abnormal lumps or masses are felt, tissue from the prostate will be excised and sent to pathology to assess if cancerous cells are present.

Prostate-Specific Antigen

<u>Prostate-specific antigen (PSA)</u>, produced in the prostate gland by normal and cancerous cells, <u>increases</u> with most prostate cancers. PSA is measured with a blood test. A level above 4 ng/mL can indicate prostate cancer. PSA is also increased in BPH; a PSA level of 4 – 10 ng/mL overlaps for the two diseases. A PSA > 10 ng/mL likely indicates prostate cancer.

HORMONAL THERAPIES FOR PROSTATE CANCER

Similar to blocking estrogen for breast cancer, the primary hormones which are blocked when treating prostate cancer are testosterone and the active metabolite dihydrotestosterone (DHT), otherwise known as androgens or male sex hormones. The hormonal treatment is called androgen deprivation therapy (ADT), or sometimes chemical castration.

ADT has considerable adverse effects, including impotence, weakness, hot flashes and loss of bone density. ADT is achieved with either a gonadotropin-releasing hormone (GnRH) antagonist (alone) or a GnRH agonist (initially taken with an antiandrogen). Metastatic prostate cancer that has failed to respond to ADT is called "castration-resistant" and may be treated with chemotherapy.

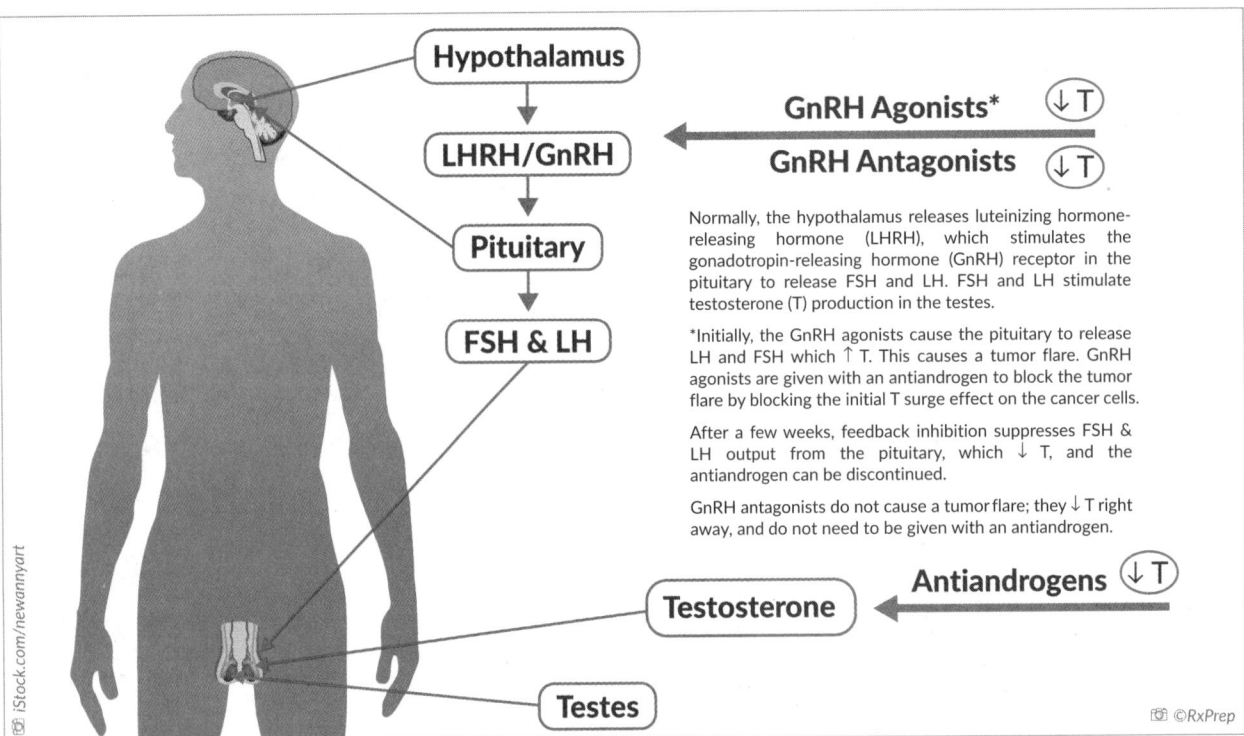

Hormonal Therapies for Prostate Cancer

DRUG	UNIQUE CONCERNS	SAFETY/SIDE EFFECTS/MONITORING
Gonadotropin-Releasing Hormone (GnRH) Agonists Also referred to as luteinizing hormone-releasing hormone (LHRH) agonists, they reduce testosterone through a negative feedback mechanism, causing an initial surge in testosterone, followed by a gradual reduction.		
Leuprolide (Lupron Depot, *Eligard, Fensolvi)* IM injection	↓ bone density; supplement with calcium/vitamin D, perform weight-bearing exercise, DEXA screening can identify if treatment (e.g., with a bisphosphonate) would be useful Leuprolide and goserelin can be used to treat breast cancer in females (by ovarian ablation) Tumor flare: prevent with concurrent use of an antiandrogen (e.g., bicalutamide) for several weeks	**CONTRAINDICATIONS** Pregnancy, breastfeeding **SIDE EFFECTS** Hot flashes, impotence, gynecomastia, bone pain, injection site pain, osteoporosis, shrunken testicles, anxiety, peripheral edema First few weeks of treatment: bone pain, difficulty urinating QT prolongation, dyslipidemia, hyperglycemia Loss of muscle mass
Goserelin (Zoladex) SC injection Histrelin *(Supprelin LA)* SC injection Triptorelin *(Trelstar)* IM injection		

DRUG	UNIQUE CONCERNS	SAFETY/SIDE EFFECTS/MONITORING
Gonadotropin-Releasing Hormone (GnRH) Antagonists Block GnRH receptors directly causing a rapid decrease in testosterone production.		
Degarelix (*Firmagon*) SC injection	<u>Osteoporosis risk</u>: consider calcium/ vitamin D supplementation, weight-bearing exercise, DEXA screening	**CONTRAINDICATIONS** Pregnancy (degarelix) **SIDE EFFECTS** Similar to GnRH agonists
Relugolix (*Orgovyx*) Oral	<u>No tumor flare</u>; antiandrogen not needed	Hypersensitivity reactions (degarelix)
Antiandrogens, First-Generation Competitively inhibit testosterone from binding to prostate cancer cells. They are only used in <u>combination</u> with a <u>GnRH agonist</u>.		
Bicalutamide (*Casodex*) Oral		**BOXED WARNINGS** Hepatotoxicity (flutamide), interstitial pneumonitis (nilutamide)
Flutamide Oral	Causes more diarrhea than others in class	**CONTRAINDICATIONS** Do not use in females, especially in pregnancy (bicalutamide); severe hepatic impairment (flutamide, nilutamide)
Nilutamide (*Nilandron*) Oral	Can cause night blindness Disulfiram reactions (avoid alcohol)	**SIDE EFFECTS** <u>Hot flashes, gynecomastia</u>, edema, asthenia, hepatotoxicity, ↑ risk of CVD, N/V/D
Antiandrogen, Second-Generation Unlike first-generation antiandrogens, they do not cause upregulation of androgen receptors, and can be used as a single treatment.		
Apalutamide (*Erleada*) Oral		**WARNINGS** Seizures (apalutamide, enzalutamide), myocardial ischemia, <u>QT prolongation</u> (apalutamide), neutropenia (darolutamide)
Darolutamide (*Nubeqa*) Oral		Can cause fetal harm; patients with partners who may become pregnant should use effective contraception
Enzalutamide (*Xtandi*) Oral		**SIDE EFFECTS** Hypertension, peripheral edema, hot flashes, fatigue
Androgen Biosynthesis Inhibitor Interferes with a specific CYP-17 enzyme involved in the synthesis of steroid hormones in the testes and adrenal glands to decrease testosterone production. Must be taken with prednisone to cause negative feedback on the production of aldosterone and prevent symptoms of hyperaldosteronism (hypertension, fluid retention, hypokalemia).		
Abiraterone (*Zytiga*) Oral	Avoid concurrent use with strong CYP3A4 inducers; if used with a strong CYP3A4 inducer, dose adjustment required	**WARNINGS** Can cause fetal harm; patients with partners who may become pregnant should use effective contraception **SIDE EFFECTS** Mineralocorticoid excess: fluid retention, ↑ BP, hypokalemia (reduce excess with concurrent prednisone) Hepatotoxicity, hyperglycemia, ↑ TGs, hypophosphatemia, hot flashes

KEY COUNSELING POINTS

See the Drug Formulations and Patient Counseling chapter for counseling language/layman's terminology.

LEUPROLIDE FOR PROSTATE CANCER

- Can cause:
  - Hot flashes, weakness and impotence.
  - Bone pain and difficulty urinating.

- This medication is taken initially with another drug called an antiandrogen.

CHEMOTHERAPY

Chemotherapy regimens for all types of cancer are usually given in combinations to take advantage of synergistic relationships, by targeting cells with different resistance mechanisms and at different stages of replication. This can also increase efficacy and decrease toxicity.

REGIMENS ARE GIVEN IN CYCLES

Chemotherapy regimens are usually administered in 2 – 6 week cycles, followed by days or weeks without treatment. The break in treatment allows the patient time to recover from the adverse effects, including myelosuppression (decreased platelets, white blood cells and red blood cells).

Example Breast Cancer Regimen

AC is a combination of two drugs:

- Doxorubicin (*Adriamycin,* an anthracycline with multiple mechanisms, cell-cycle independent)

- Cyclophosphamide (an alkylating agent, cell-cycle independent)

AC is given on day one of a 2 or 3-week treatment cycle. The cycle is repeated 4 times every 2 – 3 weeks for ~3 months. This regimen is highly emetogenic, requiring an aggressive antiemetic regimen, and filgrastim is needed to prevent myelosuppression.

CANCER TREATMENTS

Traditional Chemotherapy

Traditional cancer drugs kill cancer cells (i.e., they are cytotoxic) by interfering with cell division (replication). Cell-cycle specific agents kill cancer cells during a specific phase of the cell cycle. Cell-cycle independent agents kill cancer cells in any phase of the cell cycle (see the figure below).

Regardless of cell cycle specificity, traditional cytotoxic cancer drugs are more effective at killing cells undergoing cell division. Cancers that are characterized by more rapid cell growth, such as acute leukemias, are very susceptible to the cytotoxic effects of traditional cytotoxic drugs.

Cells in the body that are also rapidly dividing, including cells in the gastrointestinal tract, hair follicles and bone marrow, are susceptible to the damaging effects of cytotoxic drugs. This is why many cytotoxic drugs cause diarrhea, mucositis, nausea, alopecia and myelosuppression. The Oncology I chapter reviews side effect management.

Targeted Treatment

Targeted treatment, such as the monoclonal antibodies (MAbs) and tyrosine kinase inhibitors (TKIs) discussed later in the chapter, recognize biomarkers present on cancer cells or on other cells that are essential for tumor growth.

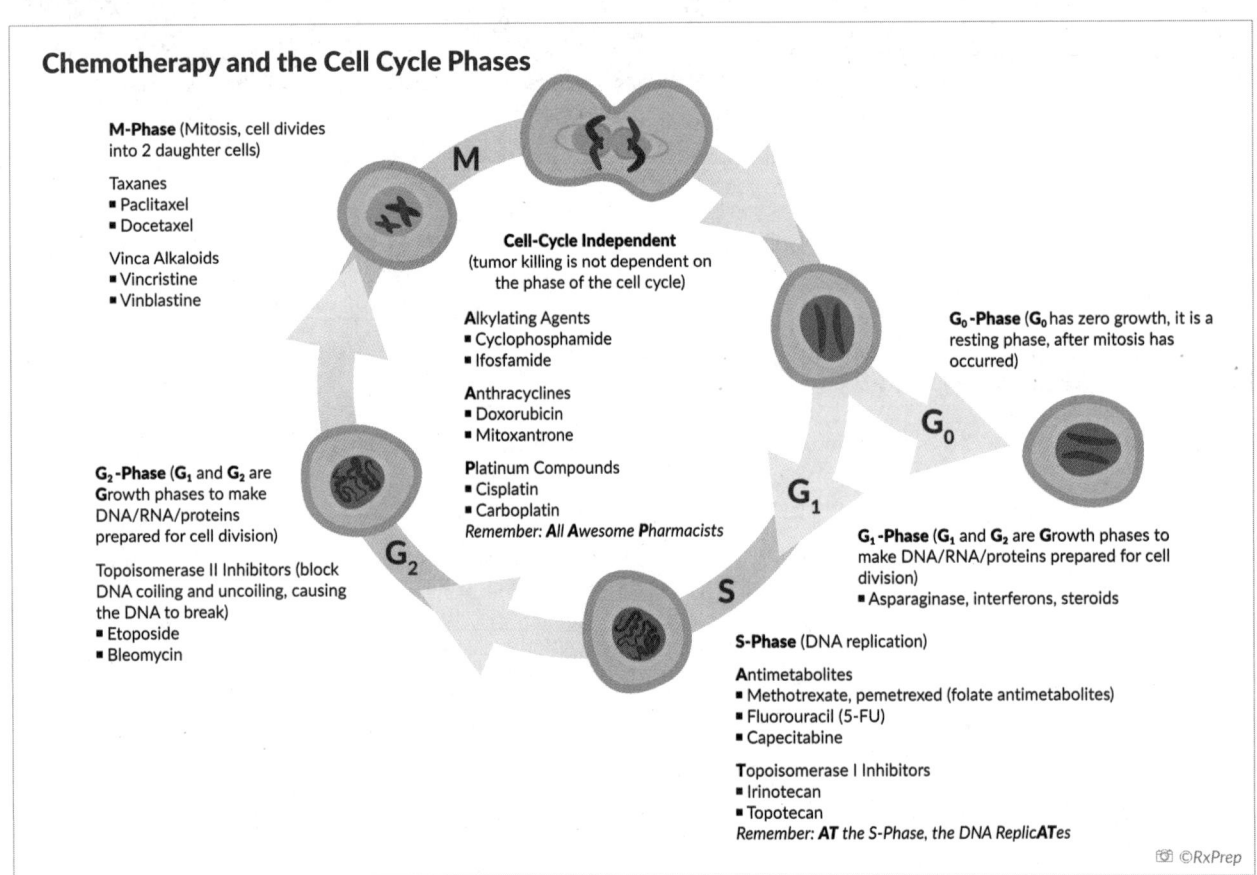

Chemotherapy and the Cell Cycle Phases

M-Phase (Mitosis, cell divides into 2 daughter cells)

Taxanes
- Paclitaxel
- Docetaxel

Vinca Alkaloids
- Vincristine
- Vinblastine

Cell-Cycle Independent
(tumor killing is not dependent on the phase of the cell cycle)

Alkylating Agents
- Cyclophosphamide
- Ifosfamide

Anthracyclines
- Doxorubicin
- Mitoxantrone

Platinum Compounds
- Cisplatin
- Carboplatin
Remember: **All Awesome Pharmacists**

G₀-Phase (G₀ has zero growth, it is a resting phase, after mitosis has occurred)

G₂-Phase (G₁ and G₂ are **G**rowth phases to make DNA/RNA/proteins prepared for cell division)

Topoisomerase II Inhibitors (block DNA coiling and uncoiling, causing the DNA to break)
- Etoposide
- Bleomycin

G₁-Phase (G₁ and G₂ are **G**rowth phases to make DNA/RNA/proteins prepared for cell division)
- Asparaginase, interferons, steroids

S-Phase (DNA replication)

Antimetabolites
- Methotrexate, pemetrexed (folate antimetabolites)
- Fluorouracil (5-FU)
- Capecitabine

Topoisomerase I Inhibitors
- Irinotecan
- Topotecan
Remember: **AT** *the S-Phase, the DNA ReplicATes*

©RxPrep

BODY SURFACE AREA (BSA) CALCULATIONS

Chemotherapy can be dosed using flat or fixed dosing, weight-based dosing (mg/kg) or dosing based on body surface area (BSA). There are several BSA formulas. The ones most commonly used are <u>Mosteller</u> and DuBois and DuBois. Actual (or total) body weight is commonly used for calculating the dose in oncology. Use the patient's <u>actual body weight for BSA</u>, unless instructed otherwise.

Mosteller Equation

$$BSA\ (m^2) = \sqrt{\frac{Ht\ (cm) \times Wt\ (kg)}{3,600}}$$

Examples

A patient has a weight of 175 pounds and height of 6'1". Calculate the patient's BSA using the Mosteller formula. Round to the nearest hundredth.

Convert weight in pounds to kilograms by dividing by 2.2: 175 lbs/2.2 = 79.5 kg

Convert height in inches to centimeters by multiplying by 2.54: 73 inches x 2.54 = 185.4 cm

$$BSA\ (m^2) = \sqrt{\frac{185.4\ cm \times 79.5\ kg}{3,600}} = 2.02\ m^2$$

A patient with a BSA of 2.02 m² is going to receive paclitaxel at a dose of 175 mg/m². Calculate the dose of paclitaxel that this patient will receive. Round to the nearest whole number.

$$175\ mg/m^2 \times 2.02\ m^2 = 354\ mg$$

A patient with a BSA of 2.02 m² is going to receive paclitaxel at a dose of 175 mg/m². Paclitaxel is available as a 6 mg/mL solution. If the patient's dose is 354 mg, how many milliliters will be needed for the dose?

$$354\ mg \times \frac{1\ mL}{6\ mg} = 59\ mL$$

AVERAGE BODY SURFACE AREA (BSA) FOR MEN AND WOMEN

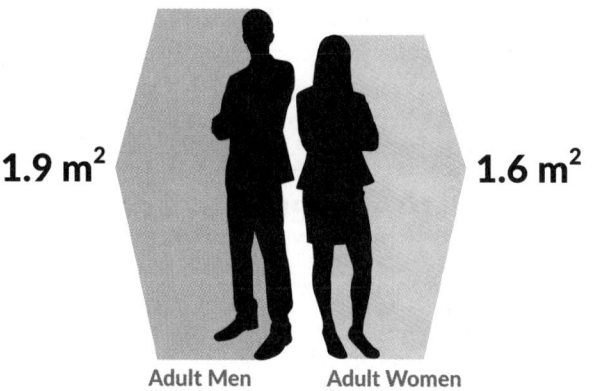

1.9 m² 1.6 m²

Adult Men Adult Women

©RxPrep
Bokica/stock.adobe.com

Dubois and Dubois Equation

$$BSA\ (m^2) = 0.007184 \times [Height\ (cm)]^{0.725} \times [Weight\ (kg)]^{0.425}$$

Example

A patient has a weight of 175 pounds and height of 6'1". Calculate the patient's BSA using the DuBois and DuBois formula. Round to the nearest hundredth.

Convert weight in pounds to kilograms by dividing by 2.2: 175 lbs/2.2 = 79.5 kg

Convert height in inches to centimeters by multiplying by 2.54: 73 inches x 2.54 = 185.4 cm

$$BSA\ (m^2) = 0.007184 \times (185.4)^{0.725} \times (79.5)^{0.425}$$

$$BSA\ (m^2) = 2.03\ m^2$$

ONCOLOGY

TRADITIONAL CYTOTOXIC CHEMOTHERAPY DRUGS

Included below are the commonly encountered "prototype drugs" in each class, with safety and administration information. The drugs are divided into cell-cycle independent (i.e., the cell cycle does not affect the drug's killing) and cell-cycle specific (i.e., the drugs work in a specific phase or phases of the cell cycle).

Most drugs are more effective at killing rapidly dividing cancer cells since they work by interfering with DNA replication.

CELL-CYCLE INDEPENDENT AGENTS

ALKYLATING AGENTS

Alkylating agents work by cross-linking DNA strands and inhibiting protein synthesis and DNA synthesis.

- Can cause DNA mutations that lead to "secondary malignancies" (e.g., leukemias and lymphomas).

- Cyclophosphamide and ifosfamide produce a metabolite, acrolein, that concentrates in the bladder and can cause hemorrhagic cystitis. The chemoprotectant mesna inactivates this toxic metabolite in the bladder without interfering with the cytotoxic efficacy. Ifosfamide is always dispensed with mesna. High doses of cyclophosphamide may require mesna.

DRUG	UNIQUE CONCERNS	SAFETY/SIDE EFFECTS/MONITORING
Cyclophosphamide **Ifosfamide** (*Ifex*)	Hemorrhagic cystitis: ensure adequate hydration and give mesna Mesna (*Mesnex*) is a chemoprotectant that must be given prophylactically with ifosfamide and with high doses of cyclophosphamide	**BOXED WARNINGS** Myelosuppression Hemorrhagic cystitis (ifosfamide, cyclophosphamide) Pulmonary toxicity (carmustine) Neurotoxicity (ifosfamide) Hepatic necrosis (dacarbazine) **WARNINGS** Severe skin reactions, including SJS/TEN Reactivation of infections, including HBV, CMV, TB, HSV Hepatotoxicity (bendamustine)
Carmustine (*BiCNU, Gliadel Wafer*) Lomustine (*Gleostine*)	Carmustine: use non-PVC bag and tubing Lomustine: fatal toxicity occurs with overdosage; do not dispense more than one dose at a time; both the prescriber and pharmacist should emphasize to the patient that only one dose of lomustine is taken every 6 weeks	
Dacarbazine Temozolomide (*Temodar*)	Dacarbazine: protect from light to avoid drug degradation	
Altretamine Bendamustine (*Belrapzo, Bendeka, Treanda*) **Busulfan** (*Myleran*) Mechlorethamine (*Valchlor* topical gel) Melphalan (*Evomela*) Procarbazine (*Matulane*)	Procarbazine: MAO inhibitor, avoid interacting drugs/foods	**SIDE EFFECTS** Pulmonary toxicity (busulfan, carmustine, lomustine) SIADH (cyclophosphamide) Mucositis, alopecia, secondary malignancies, neurotoxicity Moderate-high emetic potential Hypertensive crisis, serotonin syndrome with food/drug interactions (procarbazine)
Mitomycin Free radical formation and alkylator	Vesicant, do not extravasate; antidote is dimethyl sulfoxide (DMSO) and cool compresses Mitomycin IV solutions are a hazy blue in color and can make the urine blue-green	**BOXED WARNINGS** Bone marrow suppression, hemolytic uremic syndrome **CONTRAINDICATIONS** Thrombocytopenia, coagulopathy, bleeding **SIDE EFFECTS** Leukopenia, thrombocytopenia, N/V, fatigue, alopecia, mucous membrane toxicity, cystitis or dysuria (from intravesical administration into the bladder)

PLATINUM-BASED COMPOUNDS

Similar to alkylating agents in that they cross-link DNA and interfere with DNA synthesis and cell replication.

- Due to the platinum content, they can cause a few toxicities with symptoms that are similar to heavy metal poisoning, such as peripheral sensory neuropathy, ototoxicity and nephrotoxicity.

- Cisplatin is associated with the highest incidence of nephrotoxicity and chemotherapy-induced nausea and vomiting (CINV).

- All platinum-based compounds are renally eliminated and require dose adjustments for renal impairment.

DRUG	UNIQUE CONCERNS	SAFETY/SIDE EFFECTS/MONITORING
Cisplatin	Nephrotoxicity, ototoxicity (both cumulative) Nephrotoxicity: monitor renal function, intake/output, Mg and K (levels may decrease) and ensure adequate IV hydration (1-2 L) before each dose Amifostine *(Ethyol)* is a chemoprotectant that can be given prophylactically to prevent nephrotoxicity Ototoxicity: perform audiograms at baseline and before each dose Highly emetogenic: see Oncology I chapter for emesis prevention	**BOXED WARNINGS** Anaphylactic-like reactions – risk increases with repeated exposure; caution when > 6 cycles of carboplatin are used Cisplatin: due to the risk for renal toxicity and ototoxicity, doses > 100 mg/m²/cycle must be confirmed with the prescriber Myelosuppression (carboplatin and cisplatin) **CONTRAINDICATIONS** Pre-existing renal impairment, hearing impairment (cisplatin) Myelosuppression (cisplatin and carboplatin)
Carboplatin	Myelosuppression is dose-related Doses for adults are commonly calculated by target AUC using the Calvert Formula: Total carboplatin dose (mg) = (Target AUC) x (GFR + 25) where: - AUC can range from 2-8 mg/mL x min - GFR is commonly "capped" at 125 mL/min/1.73 m²	**SIDE EFFECTS** Peripheral neuropathy (cumulative, dose-related) ↑ LFTs N/V (cisplatin, carboplatin) QT prolongation (oxaliplatin)
Oxaliplatin	Acute sensory neuropathy: occurs 1-7 days after administration and can be exacerbated by exposure to cold, including drinking cold beverages	

ONCOLOGY

ANTHRACYCLINES

These work by several mechanisms, including intercalation into DNA, inhibition of topoisomerase II and creation of oxygen-free radicals that damage cells.

- All anthracyclines are associated with cardiotoxicity, which manifests as cardiomyopathy and heart failure. The risk for cardiotoxicity is related to the total lifetime cumulative dose the patient receives (see the recommended dose for doxorubicin in the Study Tip Gal). Dexrazoxane (Totect) is a chemoprotectant indicated for prevention of doxorubicin-induced cardiotoxicity.

- Anthracyclines are strong vesicants, except for the liposomal formulations. Dexrazoxane (Totect) is also used as an antidote for accidental doxorubicin extravasation.

- Protect from light during administration.

REDUCE DOXORUBICIN CARDIOTOXICITY

1. Keep track of the lifetime cumulative doxorubicin dose for each patient

   [Doxorubicin dose in mg/m²/cycle] x [total number of cycles received] = cumulative doxorubicin dose in mg/m²

   Example: (Doxorubicin 50 mg/m²/cycle) x (6 cycles) = 300 mg/m²

2. Lifetime maximum cumulative doxorubicin dose = 450-550 mg/m²

3. Monitor left ventricular ejection fraction (LVEF) before and after treatment (using echocardiogram or MUGA scan)

4. Dexrazoxane (Totect) may be considered when the doxorubicin cumulative dose > 300 mg/m²

DRUG	UNIQUE CONCERNS	SAFETY/SIDE EFFECTS/MONITORING
Doxorubicin (*Adriamycin*) Daunorubicin Epirubicin (*Ellence*) Idarubicin (*Idamycin PFS*) Valrubicin (*Valstar*) – only used as a bladder instillation, but can have systemic toxicity	Potent vesicants (tissue necrosis if extravasated) Drug is red, and causes red discoloration of urine, tears, sweat and saliva Doxorubicin: do not exceed 450-550 mg/m² (total lifetime cumulative dose) Dexrazoxane (*Totect*) for extravasation and cardioprotection (at higher doses)	**BOXED WARNINGS** Myocardial (cardiovascular) toxicity, vesicant, myelosuppression, secondary malignancy Hepatotoxicity (daunorubicin), reduce dose if impairment (except valrubicin) Renal impairment (daunorubicin, idarubicin) **CONTRAINDICATIONS** Pre-existing myocardial insufficiency, severe hepatic impairment **SIDE EFFECTS** N/V – give antiemetics
Daunorubicin and cytarabine liposomal (*Vyxeos*) Doxorubicin liposomal (*Doxil*)	Liposomal formulations are not interchangeable with non-liposomal formulations	**BOXED WARNINGS** Myocardial (cardiovascular) toxicity, infusion-related reactions, myelosuppression **SIDE EFFECTS** Hand-foot syndrome
Mitoxantrone An anthracenedione, related to the anthracyclines	Irritant with vesicant-like properties Drug is blue, and causes blue discoloration of urine, sclera and other body fluids	**BOXED WARNINGS** Myocardial (cardiovascular) toxicity, myelosuppression, secondary malignancy

CELL-CYCLE SPECIFIC AGENTS

TOPOISOMERASE I INHIBITORS

Topoisomerase I inhibitors block the coiling and uncoiling of the double-stranded DNA helix during the S phase of the cell cycle. This causes single and double-strand breaks in the DNA and prevents religation (sealing the DNA strands back together again) of single-strand breaks.

DRUG	UNIQUE CONCERNS	SAFETY/SIDE EFFECTS/MONITORING
Irinotecan (*Camptosar*) *"I run to the can" (acute diarrhea)*	Acute cholinergic symptoms: flushing, sweating, abdominal cramps, diarrhea (treat with atropine) Delayed diarrhea: treat with loperamide (up to 24 mg/day) Pharmacogenomics: patients homozygous for the UGT1A1*2B allele are at ↑ risk for neutropenia and delayed diarrhea	**BOXED WARNINGS** Myelosuppression Use only when ANC > 1,500 cells/mm³ and platelets > 100,000 cells/mm³ (topotecan) Diarrhea (early and late) (irinotecan) **SIDE EFFECTS** N/V/D, alopecia, diarrhea, abdominal pain
Topotecan (*Hycamtin*)		

TOPOISOMERASE II INHIBITORS

Topoisomerase II inhibitors work in the same way as topoisomerase I inhibitors, but at a different phase of the cell cycle. They block the coiling and uncoiling of double-stranded DNA during the G2 phase; this causes single and double-strand breaks in the DNA and prevents religation (sealing the DNA strands back together again) of single-strand breaks.

DRUG	UNIQUE CONCERNS	SAFETY/SIDE EFFECTS/MONITORING
Etoposide intravenous	Infusion rate-related hypotension: infuse over at least 30-60 minutes IV preparation: prepare solution to a concentration ≤ 0.4 mg/mL to avoid precipitation (due to poor water solubility) Use non-PVC IV bag and tubing due to leaching of DEHP	**BOXED WARNING** Myelosuppression **SIDE EFFECTS** Hypersensitivity reactions, anaphylaxis, secondary malignancies
Etoposide phosphate (*Etopophos*)	Does not have solution concentration limits like etoposide (primarily used if the concentration needs to be ≥ 0.4 mg/mL) Helpful in patients with fluid restriction	
Etoposide capsules	Refrigerate capsules Etoposide IV:PO ratio is 1:2 (50% bioavailability) Doses > 200 mg need to be divided due to reduced bioavailability	
Bleomycin Also an intercalating agent	Due to risk of anaphylactoid reactions, a test dose should be given May premedicate with acetaminophen to ↓ incidence of fever or chills ↑ risk of pulmonary fibrosis when given with G-CSF (filgrastim) Not myelosuppressive Maximum lifetime dose of 400 units due to pulmonary toxicity risk	**BOXED WARNINGS** Pulmonary fibrosis, anaphylaxis **SIDE EFFECTS** Hypersensitivity reaction, pulmonary reactions (including pneumonitis, which may progress to pulmonary fibrosis), mucositis, hyperpigmentation, fever, chills, N/V (mild)

VINCA ALKALOIDS

Vinca alkaloids inhibit the function of microtubules during the M phase of the cell cycle.

- Peripheral sensory and autonomic neuropathies (constipation) are common because microtubules play an important role in axonal transport in neurons.

   - VinCristine is associated with more CNS toxicity (neuropathy) than the other vinca alkaloids.

- VinBlastine and vinorelBine are associated with more Bone marrow suppression (myelosuppression) than vincristine.

- Vinca alkaloids are potent vesicants. Use warm compresses and hyaluronidase if extravasation occurs.

- Accidental intrathecal administration will cause progressive paralysis and death. Label products to prevent accidental intrathecal administration (see the Intravenous Medication Principles chapter).

> FOR INTRAVENOUS USE ONLY.
> FATAL IF GIVEN BY OTHERS ROUTES.

- Vincristine is a major substrate of CYP3A4; when given with azole antifungals there is a high risk of severe toxicities (e.g., peripheral neuropathy, seizures, paralytic ileus).

DRUG	UNIQUE CONCERNS	SAFETY/SIDE EFFECTS/MONITORING
Vincristine Vincristine liposomal (*Marqibo*)	Not myelosuppressive Often "capped" at 2 mg/dose, regardless of the calculated mg/m² dose; higher doses may be associated with ↑ risk of neuropathy Lipsomal and non-liposomal forms are not interchangeable	**BOXED WARNINGS** Vesicants For IV administration only (intrathecal administration is fatal) **SIDE EFFECTS** Peripheral sensory neuropathy (paresthesias), autonomic neuropathy (gastroparesis, constipation), SIADH
Vinblastine Vinorelbine	Myelosuppressive	**NOTES** To prevent inadvertent intrathecal administration, prepare vincristine in a small IV bag (a piggyback) rather than in a syringe

TAXANES

Taxanes inhibit the function of microtubules during the M phase of the cell cycle.

- Peripheral sensory neuropathies are common side effects since the microtubules play an important role in axonal transport in neurons.

- Severe infusion-related hypersensitivity reactions (HSR) and fatal anaphylaxis can occur with all taxanes. Premedication regimens vary depending on the specific taxane.

- All taxanes are metabolized by the liver and require adjustment for hepatic impairment.

- Drug interaction: elimination of taxanes is reduced when given after cisplatin/carboplatin. Give taxanes before platinum-based compounds.

DRUG	UNIQUE CONCERNS	SAFETY/SIDE EFFECTS/MONITORING
Paclitaxel Paclitaxel albumin-bound (*Abraxane*)	HSR: premedicate with diphenhydramine, steroid, H2RA	**BOXED WARNINGS** Severe hypersensitivity reactions (except *Abraxane*), myelosuppression Fluid retention (docetaxel)
Docetaxel	HSR: premedicate with steroids for 3 days, starting 1 day prior to docetaxel Causes severe fluid retention (e.g., pleural effusion, cardiac tamponade, edema) Some formulations contain alcohol and may cause symptoms of alcohol intoxication	**SIDE EFFECTS** Peripheral sensory neuropathy, myalgias, arthralgias, hepatotoxicity, alopecia (less with cabazitaxel) **NOTES** Hypersensitivity reactions are due to the solvent systems, not the taxane
Cabazitaxel (*Jevtana*)	HSR: premedicate with diphenhydramine, steroid, H2RA	*Abraxane*, paclitaxel bound to albumin without a solvent system, has only isolated case reports of allergic reactions; no need to premedicate Use non-PVC bag and tubing (except *Abraxane*) Paclitaxel and cabazitaxel: use 0.22-micron filter

PYRIMIDINE ANALOG ANTIMETABOLITES

These agents inhibit pyrimidine synthesis during the S phase of the cell cycle; an active metabolite (F-UMP) is incorporated into RNA to replace uracil and inhibits cell growth, while another active metabolite (5-dUMP) inhibits thymidylate synthetase.

DRUG	UNIQUE CONCERNS	SAFETY/SIDE EFFECTS/MONITORING
Fluorouracil, "5-FU" *Efudex, Carac, Tolak* and *Fluoroplex* are topical formulations used for actinic keratosis *Efudex* is also used for basal cell carcinoma	Leucovorin is given with fluorouracil to ↑ the efficacy; it helps fluorouracil bind more tightly to its target enzyme, thymidylate synthetase Pharmacogenomics: dihydropyrimidine dehydrogenase (DPD) deficiency ↑ risk of severe toxicity	**BOXED WARNINGS** Significant ↑ in INR during and up to 1 month after treatment, monitor INR frequently (capecitabine) **CONTRAINDICATIONS** Severe renal impairment (CrCl < 30 mL/min) (capecitabine) **SIDE EFFECTS** Hand-foot syndrome, diarrhea, mucositis, cardiotoxicity, photosensitivity, dermatitis **NOTES** Uridine triacetate *(Vistogard)* can be given as an antidote for overdose or toxicity due to DPD deficiency
Capecitabine *(Xeloda)* 2 divided doses 12 hrs apart, given with water within 30 min after a meal	Oral prodrug of fluorouracil Pharmacogenomics: dihydropyrimidine dehydrogenase (DPD) deficiency ↑ risk of severe toxicity	
Cytarabine conventional (also called "ara-C")	Cytarabine syndrome: fever, flu-like symptoms, myalgia, bone pain, rash; responds to steroids Given via intrathecal (IT) administration for CNS leukemias/lymphomas	**BOXED WARNINGS** Myelosuppression, hepatotoxicity and GI toxicities **SIDE EFFECTS** Pulmonary toxicity, encephalopathy, hand-foot syndrome, neuropathy, conjunctivitis (higher doses require use of steroid eye drops) IT administration can cause nausea, vomiting, fever and headache
Gemcitabine	Infusion rate affects efficacy and toxicity; infuse per institutional protocol	**SIDE EFFECTS** Myelosuppression, flu-like symptoms, hepatotoxicity, pulmonary toxicity

---

CASE SCENARIO

LK is a 34-year-old male with testicular cancer, hypertension and chronic back pain. His current medications include: hydrochlorothiazide 25 mg PO daily, naproxen 500 mg PO BID, hydrocodone/acetaminophen 5/325 mg PO Q4H PRN pain. He received his 4th cycle of chemotherapy with:

> Paclitaxel 250 mg/m^2 IV on day 1
> Ifosfamide 1,000 mg/m^2 IV on days 2-5 (along with mesna)
> Cisplatin 25 mg/m^2 IV on days 2-5

He returns to the clinic to receive his 5th cycle of chemotherapy and complains of numbness and tingling pain in his fingertips. His laboratory values are within normal limits with the exception of: BUN = 22 mg/dL, SCr = 2.4 mg/dL. His vital signs are within normal limits and stable.

■ **How would you characterize the type of pain LK describes?** It is consistent with sensory peripheral neuropathy.

■ **What could be causing his new pain symptoms?** Paclitaxel (a taxane) is associated with sensory peripheral neuropathy, as is cisplatin (although at a lower incidence).

■ **The team rules out dehydration based on the BUN/SCr ratio and normal vital signs. What is the likely cause of his elevated SCr?**
Cisplatin-induced nephrotoxicity should be suspected. No further cisplatin should be given at this time. Naproxen and hydrochlorothiazide should be held, as NSAIDs can decrease renal blood flow and diuretics could cause dehydration and potentiate further kidney damage. An alternative medication can be chosen for BP control.

FOLATE ANTIMETABOLITES

Interfere with the enzymes involved in the folic acid cycle, blocking purine and pyrimidine biosynthesis during the S phase of the cell cycle.

- Folic acid or folic acid analogs +/- vitamin B12 may be required to reduce toxicity caused by interference with the folic acid cycle (myelosuppression, mucositis, diarrhea). With high doses of methotrexate, leucovorin (or levoleucovorin) "rescue" must be given. Leucovorin is the active form of folic acid that is able to bypass the blocked dihydrofolate reductase enzyme caused by methotrexate. Note that folic acid is ineffective for high-dose methotrexate "rescue."

- All of the folate antimetabolites are associated with nephrotoxicity, but high-dose methotrexate (≥ 1 gram/m^2) is the most frequent cause.

DRUG	UNIQUE CONCERNS	SAFETY/SIDE EFFECTS/MONITORING
Methotrexate (Trexall, Otrexup, Rasuvo, RediTrex Xatmep) Cancer doses are much higher than doses used for rheumatoid arthritis (RA) or psoriasis RA/psoriasis doses are given weekly, not daily If given intrathecally, use only the preservative-free formulation of methotrexate Avoid use of "MTX" – this is an error prone abbreviation	"High-dose" methotrexate (≥ 500 mg/m^2) requires leucovorin (folinic acid) "rescue" "Moderate-dose" methotrexate (100-499 mg/m^2) may require leucovorin rescue Levoleucovorin is the levo (L) isomer (the active biological moiety) of leucovorin and is dosed at 1/2 the dose of leucovorin; monitor methotrexate level and renal function daily and continue leucovorin until level is ≤ 0.05-0.1 micromolar Hydration and IV sodium bicarbonate must be given to alkalinize the urine and ↓ risk of nephrotoxicity caused by high doses; ensure patient does not have 3rd spacing prior to drug administration (e.g., ascites, pleural effusions, severe edema) because this will delay drug clearance Glucarpidase (Voraxaze) is an antidote that will rapidly lower methotrexate levels that remain high despite adequate hydration and urinary alkalinization (with bicarbonate) Drug interactions: NSAIDs, salicylates, beta-lactams, proton pump inhibitors, sulfonamide antibiotics, probenecid – all ↓ clearance of methotrexate IV drug solution is orangish-yellow	**BOXED WARNINGS** Myelosuppression and aplastic anemia, renal damage, hepatotoxicity (fibrosis and cirrhosis with long-term use), interstitial pneumonitis, dermatologic reactions (SJS/TEN), GI toxicity [nausea, diarrhea, oral stomatitis (with mucositis)], immunosuppression, tumor lysis syndrome, teratogenicity/fetal death Renal impairment or ascites/pleural effusions: requires dose adjustments or discontinuation **SIDE EFFECTS** Nephrotoxicity (dose related), hepatotoxicity (more common with chronic use for autoimmune disease), nausea, diarrhea, stomatitis, mucositis, dizziness, sedation, hand-foot syndrome
Pemetrexed (Alimta)	To ↓ risk of side effects, give folic acid, vitamin B12 and dexamethasone	**SIDE EFFECTS** Nephrotoxicity, hepatotoxicity, dermatologic toxicity (premedicate with dexamethasone)
Pralatrexate (Folotyn)	To ↓ risk of side effects, give folic acid and vitamin B12	**SIDE EFFECTS** Nephrotoxicity, hepatotoxicity

WHICH FOLATE ANALOG, AND WHEN?

Folic acid antagonists are used in oncology and rheumatologic diseases to alter autoimmune processes.

IN AUTOIMMUNE DISEASES:
- The dose of methotrexate is much lower (5-25 mg WEEKLY).
- Folic acid (folate) 1-5 mg daily is recommended prophylactically to reduce methotrexate side effects (GI, hematologic, hepatic).
- Leucovorin is NOT used unless the patient does not respond to the folic acid.

IN ONCOLOGIC DISEASES:
- The dose of methotrexate is much higher (40-12,000 mg/m^2) and may be given with other chemotherapy every 2-3 weeks, allowing the patient to recover between doses.
- To rescue the patient from high-dose methotrexate toxicity, a reduced form of folate must be started after the methotrexate has a chance to kill the cancer cells. Leucovorin or levoleucovorin is given (levoleucovorin is the L-isomer of leucovorin, so lower doses are used).
- Regular folate (folic acid) is NOT effective in the rescue of high-dose methotrexate.
- Folic acid is used with pemetrexed and pralatrexate to reduce side effects.

MISCELLANEOUS AGENTS

DRUG	UNIQUE CONCERNS	SAFETY/SIDE EFFECTS/MONITORING
Tretinoin, also know as All-trans Retinoic Acid (ATRA) ↓ proliferation and ↑ differentiation of acute promyelocytic leukemia (APL) cells First-line therapy for APL	Retinoids are vitamin A analogs Retinoic acid-acute promyelocytic leukemia (RA-APL) differentiation syndrome: fever, dyspnea, weight gain, edema, pulmonary infiltrates, pericardial or pleural effusions – treat with dexamethasone	**BOXED WARNINGS** RA-APL differentiation syndrome, leukocytosis, pregnancy **SIDE EFFECTS** QT prolongation, N/V/D, skin/mucous membrane dryness, hyperlipidemia, GI bleeding
Arsenic trioxide *(Trisenox)* ↑ apoptosis of APL cells and damages fusion protein PML-RAR alpha Second-line therapy for APL	QT prolongation: monitor ECG, avoid concurrent QT prolonging agents, keep Mg, Ca and K within normal range If acute vasomotor reactions (lightheadedness, dizziness, or hypotension) occur, prolong infusion	**BOXED WARNINGS** Differentiation syndrome, ECG abnormalities (AV block, QT prolongation) **SIDE EFFECTS** Leukocytosis, N/V/D, GI bleeding, stomatitis, electrolyte imbalance, acute vasomotor reactions (lightheadedness, dizziness, or hypotension), fatigue, edema, HA, insomnia, anxiety, infection
Asparaginase Pegaspargase *(Oncaspar)* – modified form of L-asparaginase (derived from *E. coli*) conjugated with polyethylene glycol	Deprives leukemia cells of asparagine, which is an essential amino acid in leukemia The pegylated form (pegaspargase) allows for less frequent dosing (every 2 weeks) and less allergic reactions	**CONTRAINDICATIONS** Bleeding, thrombosis or pancreatitis with prior asparaginase treatment **SIDE EFFECTS** Hypersensitivity reactions, pancreatitis, hyperglycemia, hepatotoxicity, CNS toxicity (lethargy, somnolence), encephalopathy, N/V, prolonged prothrombin time (PT/INR)
Mammalian Target of Rapamycin (mTOR) Inhibitors		
Inhibit downstream regulation of vascular endothelial growth factor (VEGF) reducing cell growth, metabolism, proliferation and angiogenesis.		
Everolimus *(Afinitor)* Tablet *Zortress* – for transplant	CYP3A4 major substrate	**BOXED WARNINGS** See Transplant chapter for *Zortress* **CONTRAINDICATIONS** Hypersensitivity to rapamycin derivatives **SIDE EFFECTS** Mouth ulcers/stomatitis, rash, interstitial lung disease, peripheral edema, dyslipidemia, ↑ BP, hyperglycemia, myelosuppression, rash, pruritus, hand-foot syndrome, stomatitis, fatigue, N/V/D, interstitial lung disease, renal impairment, ↑ LFTs
Temsirolimus *(Torisel)* Injection	CYP3A4 major substrate Premedicate with diphenhydramine Use non-PVC bag and tubing due to leaching of DEHP	**CONTRAINDICATIONS** Moderate to severe hepatic impairment **SIDE EFFECTS** Dyslipidemia, hyperglycemia, myelosuppression, interstitial lung disease, acute hypersensitivity reactions (polysorbate 80 solvent system), N/V/D, peripheral edema, renal impairment

ONCOLOGY

DRUG	UNIQUE CONCERNS	SAFETY/SIDE EFFECTS/MONITORING
CAR T-Cell Gene Therapy The first gene therapy approved for cancer (large B-cell lymphoma). Anti-CD19 CAR T-cell therapy involves collecting a patient's T-cells from their blood and genetically engineering them to express a specific receptor against the CD19 protein present on the lymphoma cells. These cells are then re-infused back into the patient to find and attack the lymphoma cells.		
Axicabtagene ciloleucel (*Yescarta*)	Restricted via a REMS program to patients who have not responded to or who have relapsed after at least two other treatments.	**BOXED WARNINGS** Cytokine release syndrome Neurological toxicities
Immunomodulators Oral agents that block angiogenesis and kill abnormal cells in the bone marrow while stimulating the bone marrow to produce normal healthy cells. Usually indicated for multiple myeloma.		
Lenalidomide (*Revlimid*) Pomalidomide (*Pomalyst*) Thalidomide (*Thalomid*)	Severe birth defects – only available under a restricted distribution program: patient, prescriber and pharmacist must be registered with *Revlimid*, *Pomalyst* or *Thalomid* REMS program Consider prophylactic anticoagulation due to ↑ VTE risk	**BOXED WARNINGS** Fetal risk/pregnancy, thrombosis (DVT/PE), hematologic toxicity (lenalidomide) **CONTRAINDICATIONS** Pregnancy **SIDE EFFECTS** Neutropenia, thrombocytopenia, constipation, N/V/D, fatigue, fever, cough, pruritus, rash, arthralgias, back pain, peripheral edema, DVT/PE Neuropathy, confusion, somnolence (thalidomide) Hypercalcemia (pomalidomide)
Proteasome Inhibitors Inhibit proteasomes, which help to regulate intracellular protein homeostasis by inhibiting cell cycle progression and inducing apoptosis.		
Bortezomib (*Velcade*) SC administration has less neuropathy than IV administration	An antiviral (acyclovir, valacyclovir) can be used to prevent herpes reactivation (zoster and simplex)	**CONTRAINDICATIONS** Hypersensitivity to boron or mannitol, intrathecal administration (fatal) **SIDE EFFECTS** Peripheral neuropathy, psychiatric disturbances, insomnia, weakness, paresthesias, arthralgia/myalgia, cardiotoxicity, pulmonary toxicity, hypotension, thrombocytopenia, neutropenia, N/V/D, tumor lysis syndrome
Carfilzomib (*Kyprolis*)	Premedicate with dexamethasone and fluids ↑ alkaline phosphatase correlates with ↑ efficacy	**SIDE EFFECTS** Peripheral neuropathy (less than bortezomib), fatigue, pulmonary toxicity, acute renal failure, tumor lysis syndrome, hepatotoxicity, anemia, thrombocytopenia, N/V/D, pyrexia, cardiotoxicity

TARGETED THERAPIES

MONOCLONAL ANTIBODIES

Monoclonal antibodies (MAbs) are used in oncology and many other conditions. MAbs work in various ways to inhibit cancer cell growth. Some bind to specific antigens or receptors on the surface of cancer cells and cause cell death. Other agents are conjugated to cytotoxic drugs or radioactive compounds. Some help to activate the immune system so that it recognizes and destroys tumor cells. Representative monoclonal antibody targets and associated drugs are included in the following tables (not a complete list). Some common characteristics of MAbs include:

- All are given as intravenous infusions.

- Most are associated with infusion-related reactions, including hypersensitivity reactions, anaphylaxis, hypotension and bronchospasm. Some infusion-related reactions may be fatal. Premedication is usually required.

- Agents that are conjugated to cytotoxic drugs are associated with additional side effects due to the cytotoxic conjugate.

- Agents that activate the immune system can be associated with potentially life-threatening autoimmune-mediated side effects.

Hints for Understanding Monoclonal Antibodies Used in Oncology

SUBSTEM	EXAMPLES	TARGET	MECHANISM OF ACTION	COMMON TOXICITIES
"ci" Circulatory System	Bevacizumab Ramucirumab	Vascular endothelial growth factor (VEGF) or VEGF receptor	Inhibits growth of blood vessels. Used to treat certain solid tumors, such as colon cancer and non-small cell lung cancer (NSCLC).	■ Inhibition of blood vessel growth → HTN → proteinuria ■ Hemorrhage or thrombosis may occur ■ Impaired wound healing (due to decreased blood flow)
"tu" Tumor	Cetuximab Panitumumab	Epidermal growth factor receptor (EGFR)	Inhibits growth factor from binding to surface of tumor cell and promoting cell growth. Used to treat certain solid tumors, such as colon cancer.	■ EGFR → epidermis → skin toxicity (acneiform rash) ■ Development of rash is correlated with response to therapy
"tu" Tumor	Trastuzumab Pertuzumab	Human epidermal growth factor receptor 2 (HER2)	Inhibits growth factor from binding to surface of tumor cell and promoting cell growth. Used to treat certain solid tumors, such as breast cancer.	■ Cardiotoxicity ■ Teratogenic
"tu" Tumor	Rituximab Brentuximab	Cluster of differentiation (e.g., CD20, CD22, CD30, CD38) antigens expressed on cell surface of hematopoietic cells	Binds to antigens expressed on specific hematopoietic cells and causes cell death. Used to treat certain hematologic malignancies, such as non-Hodgkin's lymphoma, Hodgkin's lymphoma, multiple myeloma.	■ CD antigens are expressed on normal, as well as malignant, hematopoietic cells → suppression of specific hematopoietic cells → bone marrow suppression, increased risk for reactivation of viral infections ■ Brentuximab vedotin is an antibody-drug conjugate (ADC); the antibody binds to the cell, which enables the cytotoxic drug to enter
"li" Immune System	Ipilimumab Pembrolizumab	Immune system (PD-1, PDL-1, CTLA-4)	Interferes with the body's ability to "down-regulate" the immune system. Results in increased immune recognition of tumor antigens. Used to treat certain solid tumors, such as NSCLC and melanoma.	■ Patient's immune system becomes overactive → potentially life-threatening immune-mediated reactions, such as colitis, hepatic toxicity, thyroid dysfunction and myocarditis can occur; requires steroid treatment

ONCOLOGY

DRUG EXAMPLES	UNIQUE CONCERNS	SAFETY/SIDE EFFECTS/MONITORING
Vascular Endothelial Growth Factor (VEGF) Inhibitors		
Bevacizumab (Avastin) Biosimilars: bevacizumab -awwb (Mvasi) -bvzr (Zirabev)	Impairs wound healing: do not administer for 28 days before or after surgery Monitor blood pressure and proteinuria prior to each dose	**BOXED WARNINGS** Severe/fatal bleeding, GI perforation, surgical wound dehiscence (splitting open) **SIDE EFFECTS** Hypertension, proteinuria, nephrotic syndrome, heart failure, thrombosis
Human Epidermal Growth Factor Receptor 2 (HER2) Inhibitors		
Trastuzumab (Herceptin) Biosimilars: trastuzumab -anns (Kanjinti) -dkst (Ogivri) -dttb (Ontruzant) -pkrb (Herzuma) -qyyp (Trazimera) Ado-Trastuzumab Emtansine (Kadcyla) Trastuzumab conjugated to a microtubule inhibitor	Pharmacogenomics: test for HER2 gene expression; must have HER2 overexpression to use Monitor LVEF (using echocardiogram or MUGA scan) at baseline and during treatment Use 0.22-micron filter for ado-trastuzumab emtansine	**BOXED WARNINGS** Heart failure, embryo-fetal death and birth defects (avoid pregnancy for 7 months after treatment) Severe infusion-related reactions and pulmonary toxicity (trastuzumab) Hepatotoxicity (ado-trastuzumab emtansine) Ado-trastuzumab emtansine and conventional trastuzumab are not interchangeable **SIDE EFFECTS** Infusion-related reactions, N/V/D, alopecia Ado-trastuzumab emtansine: myelosuppression, hepatotoxicity, neuropathy, pulmonary toxicity
Epidermal Growth Factor Receptor (EGFR) Inhibitors		
Cetuximab (Erbitux)	Premedicate 1st dose with diphenhydramine Use 0.22-micron filter Pharmacogenomics: test for EGFR gene expression and KRAS mutation; EGFR positive expression correlates with better response rates in NSCLC; must be KRAS wild type to use; KRAS mutation predicts poor response to treatment in colorectal cancer	**BOXED WARNINGS** Severe/fatal infusion-related reactions, cardiac arrest (cetuximab) **SIDE EFFECTS** Acneiform rash, serious skin toxicities (SJS/TEN), ocular toxicities, infusion-related reactions, N/V/D, Mg and Ca wasting **NOTES** Rash usually occurs within the 1st two weeks of treatment and indicates that a patient is expected to have a better response to the drug; advise patients to avoid sunlight and use sunscreen; topical emollients, including topical steroids and antibiotics, can be given prophylactically to reduce skin damage (and avoid the need for a dose reduction)
Leukocyte Cluster of Differentiation (CD) Antigens (e.g., CD20) Inhibitors		
Rituximab (Rituxan) Biosimilars: rituximab -abbs (Truxima) -arrx (Riabni) -rvvr (Ruxience)	Premedicate with diphenhydramine, acetaminophen and a steroid; slowly titrate the infusion rate to lower the risk of infusion reactions Pharmacogenomics: test for B-cell antigen CD20; must be CD20 positive to use	**BOXED WARNINGS** Hepatitis B reactivation, progressive multifocal leukoencephalopathy (PML) Serious skin reactions (SJS/TEN), severe/fatal infusion-related reactions **SIDE EFFECTS** Rash, peripheral edema, hypertension, renal impairment, tumor lysis syndrome **NOTES** Check hepatitis B panel prior to administration Can cause severe infusion-related reactions (urticaria, hypotension, angioedema, bronchospasm, hypoxia, anaphylaxis)
Others: Brentuximab Vedotin (Adcetris) Blinatumomab (Blincyto) Daratumumab (Darzalex)	Pharmacogenomics: Must be CD30 antigen positive to use Must be CD19 and CD3 antigen positive to use Must be CD38 antigen positive to use	**SIDE EFFECTS** Varies by product: myelosuppression, neuropathy, pulmonary toxicity, hepatotoxicity, infusion-related reactions, SJS/TEN

DRUG EXAMPLES	UNIQUE CONCERNS	SAFETY/SIDE EFFECTS/MONITORING
Programmed Death Receptor-1 (PD-1) Inhibitors When the programmed cell death (PD-1) receptor binds the PD-L1 ligand, the end result is decreased T-cell activation. PD-1 inhibitors are monoclonal antibodies that selectively inhibit PD-1 activity, increasing T-cell activation. Activated T-cells are capable (to some extent) of recognizing cancer cells as "non-self" or foreign, and activating the immune system against them (antitumor responses).		
Pembrolizumab (Keytruda)	Immune-mediated toxicities may require interruption or permanent discontinuation of treatment and treatment with steroids	**SIDE EFFECTS** Immune-mediated toxicities including: colitis, hepatotoxicity, pulmonary toxicity, nephrotoxicity (pembrolizumab), thyroid disorders, myocarditis, encephalitis, endocrinopathies, rash, weakness
Cytotoxic T-Lymphocyte Antigen-4 (CTLA-4) Inhibitor Monoclonal antibody that binds to the cytotoxic T-lymphocyte associated antigen 4 (CTLA-4) receptor, which effectively removes the "brake" from T-cell activation. Induces antitumor responses through increased T-cell recognition of cancer cells.		
Ipilimumab (Yervoy)	REMS program	**BOXED WARNINGS** Fatal immune-mediated reactions (enterocolitis, hepatitis, dermatitis, endocrinopathy, neuropathy) **SIDE EFFECTS** Pneumonitis, nephrotoxicity, ocular toxicity, rash **NOTES** Immune-mediated toxicities may require interruption or permanent discontinuation of treatment and administration of steroids

TYROSINE KINASE INHIBITORS

A large number of tyrosine kinase proteins play a role in the intracellular signaling pathways that control the growth and differentiation of cells. Tyrosine kinase inhibitors (TKIs) are orally administered small molecules that are often "targeted" to inhibit specific abnormal tyrosine kinases associated with certain types of cancers. Pharmacogenomic testing must be performed to identify patients likely to respond to these targeted TKIs. Other TKIs are considered to be "multi-targeted." They inhibit multiple different tyrosine kinases involved in the cell signaling pathway and/or cell growth. Many TKIs have limited distribution through specialty pharmacies. The table below is not a complete list of TKIs, but contains representative TKI targets and associated drugs. For many of the TKIs, oral bioavailability may be altered if taken with food. It is very important for patients to follow the dosing instructions with regards to taking the specific TKI with or without food (see the Administration of Oral Agents table at the end of the chapter).

DRUG EXAMPLES	MECHANISM/GENETICS	SAFETY/SIDE EFFECTS/MONITORING
Used in chronic myelogenous leukemia (CML) **BCR-ABL Inhibitors**		
Imatinib (Gleevec) Dasatinib (Sprycel) Nilotinib (Tasigna)	BCR-ABL gene translocation (Philadelphia chromosome) → abnormal tyrosine kinase (occurs in ~95% of CML patients) Pharmacogenomics: must be Philadelphia chromosome (BCR-ABL) positive to use	**BOXED WARNINGS** QT prolongation (nilotinib) Vascular occlusions (strokes, MIs), heart failure) **SIDE EFFECTS** Myelosuppression, N/V/D, fluid retention, edema, skin rash, ↑ LFTs, HF, QT prolongation; HBV reactivation
Used in melanoma **BRAF Inhibitors**		
Vemurafenib (Zelboraf) Dabrafenib (Tafinlar)	BRAF mutation → abnormal tyrosine kinase that is always "on" → melanoma (occurs in ~50% of melanoma patients) Pharmacogenomics: must be BRAF V600E or V600K mutation positive to use	**WARNINGS** New malignancies, such as squamous cell carcinoma and basal cell carcinoma, QT prolongation, serious skin reactions, hepatotoxicity **SIDE EFFECTS** Skin rash, photosensitivity, N/V/D, peripheral edema, fatigue, arthralgia

ONCOLOGY

DRUG EXAMPLES	MECHANISM/GENETICS	SAFETY/SIDE EFFECTS/MONITORING
Mitogen-Activated Extracellular Kinase (MEK) 1 and 2 Inhibitors		
Cobimetinib (Cotellic)	Inhibits MEK, a cell signaling protein downstream from RAF Used in combination with BRAF inhibitors in patients with BRAF V600E or V600K mutations	**SIDE EFFECTS** Hypertension, HF, hepatotoxicity, skin rash, N/V/D, myelosuppression Hand-foot syndrome Visual impairment
Used in non-small cell lung cancer (NSCLC)		
Epidermal Growth Factor Receptor (EGFR) Inhibitors		
Afatinib (Gilotrif) Erlotinib (Tarceva)	EGFR mutation → abnormal tyrosine kinase that is always "on" → NSCLC (occurs in ~15% of NSCLC patients) Pharmacogenomics: must be EGFR mutation positive (exon 19 or 21) to use	**WARNINGS** Interstitial lung disease, hepatotoxicity, GI perforation, skin reactions (SJS/TEN), ocular toxicity (keratitis), teratogenic, diarrhea **SIDE EFFECTS** Acneiform rash, dry skin, pruritus, N/V/D, mucositis, stomatitis **NOTES** Acneiform rash from an EGFR inhibitor indicates that a patient is expected to have a better response to the drug; advise patients to avoid sunlight and use sunscreenl; topical emollients, including topical steroids and antibiotics, can be given prophylactically to reduce skin damage (and avoid the need for a dose reduction)
Anaplastic Lymphoma Kinase (ALK) Inhibitors		
Alectinib (Alecensa) Brigatinib (Alunbrig)	ALK gene translocation → abnormal tyrosine kinase that is always "on" → NSCLC (occurs in ~5% of NSCLC patients) Pharmacogenomics: must be ALK mutation positive to use	**WARNINGS** Hepatotoxicity, bradycardia, interstitial lung disease, QT prolongation, myalgia and photosensitivity (alectinib) **SIDE EFFECTS** Skin rash, N/V/D, edema
OTHER TKIs (not a complete list)		
Lapatinib (Tykerb) Neratinib (Nerlynx)	Human epidermal growth factor receptor 2 (HER2) inhibitors (also inhibit EGFR) Pharmacogenomics: must have HER2 overexpression to use in breast cancer	**WARNINGS** Hepatotoxicity (lapatinib, neratinib), cardiotoxicity (lapatinib), GI toxicity due to severe diarrhea (neratinib requires antidiarrheal prophylaxis with loperamide) **SIDE EFFECTS** Diarrhea, N/V, skin rash, hand-foot syndrome
Sorafenib (Nexavar) Sunitinib (Sutent)	Multiple targets Useful in cancers where traditional therapy has little benefit, such as hepatocellular, renal and thyroid cancers	**BOXED WARNINGS** Hepatotoxicity (sunitinib) **WARNINGS** Hepatotoxicity, cardiac toxicity, hypertension, proteinuria, hemorrhagic events, SJS/TEN, impaired wound healing **SIDE EFFECTS** Skin changes, hand-foot syndrome, N/V/D, QT prolongation, thyroid dysfunction, mucositis

COMMON TOXICITIES OF TYROSINE KINASE INHIBITORS

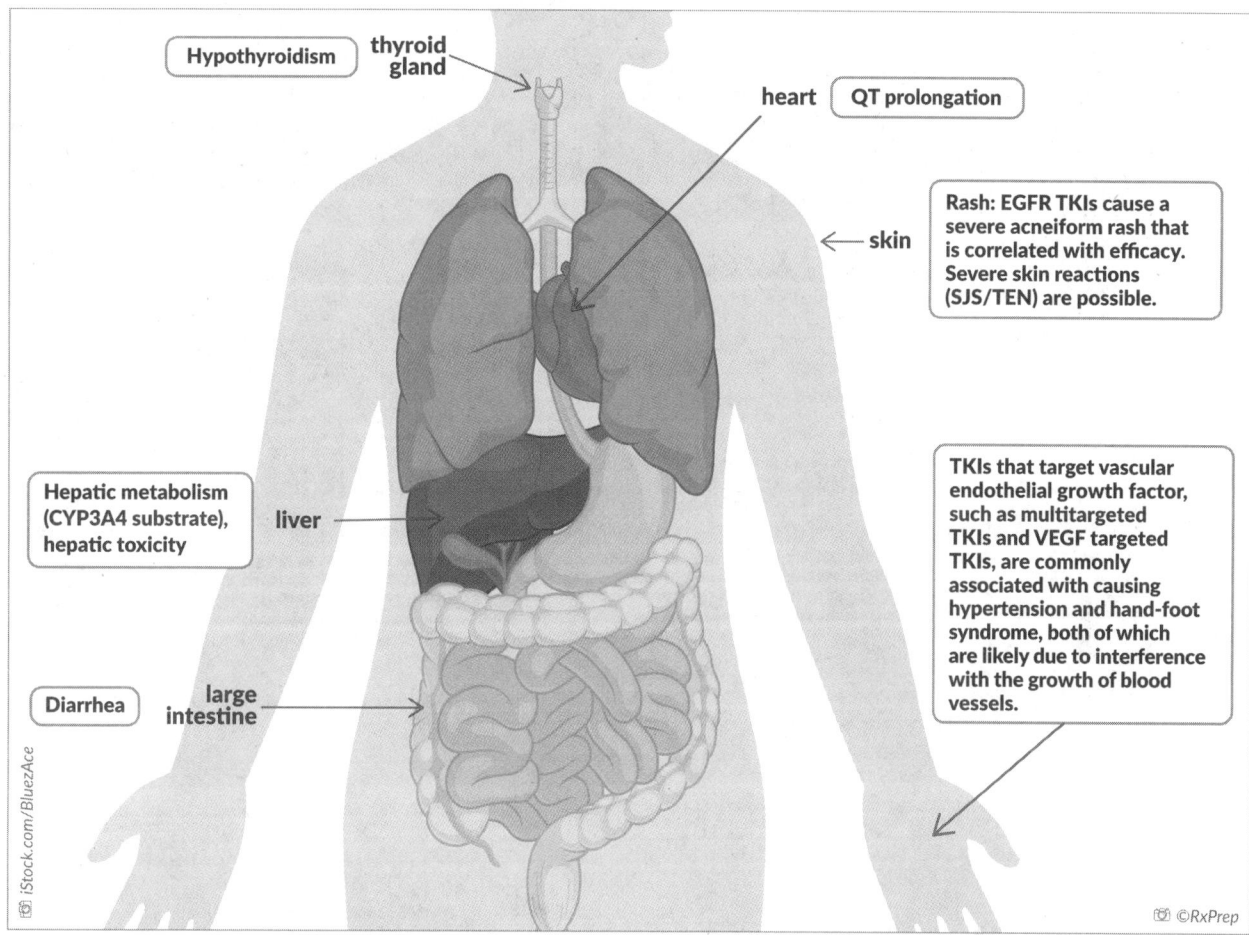

Hypothyroidism — thyroid gland

heart — QT prolongation

skin

Rash: EGFR TKIs cause a severe acneiform rash that is correlated with efficacy. Severe skin reactions (SJS/TEN) are possible.

Hepatic metabolism (CYP3A4 substrate), hepatic toxicity — liver

TKIs that target vascular endothelial growth factor, such as multitargeted TKIs and VEGF targeted TKIs, are commonly associated with causing hypertension and hand-foot syndrome, both of which are likely due to interference with the growth of blood vessels.

Diarrhea — large intestine

iStock.com/BluezAce

©RxPrep

ADMINISTRATION OF ORAL AGENTS

GENERIC (BRAND)	ADMINISTRATION	SPECIAL INSTRUCTIONS
Imatinib (Gleevec) **Capecitabine (Xeloda)** Thalidomide (Thalomid) Exemestane (Aromasin)	Take with food or within 1 hour after a meal	Thalidomide, pomalidomide and lenalidomide are teratogenic: female patients of reproductive potential must have 2 negative pregnancy tests prior to starting treatment and use 2 forms of birth control
Nilotinib (Tasigna) Erlotinib (Tarceva) Sorafenib (Nexavar) Temozolomide (Temodar) Abiraterone (Zytiga) Pomalidomide (Pomalyst)	Take on an empty stomach (1 hour before or 2 hours after food, except pomalidomide is taken 2 hours before or 2 hours after food)	REMS drugs are only available through a specialty pharmacy
Anastrozole (Arimidex) **Tamoxifen (Soltamox)** Dasatinib (Sprycel) Sunitinib (Sutent) Bicalutamide (Casodex) Lenalidomide (Revlimid) Letrozole (Femara)	Take without regard to food	

Select Guidelines/References

National Comprehensive Cancer Network (NCCN). www.nccn.org (accessed 2022 Feb 17)
American Society of Clinical Oncology (ASCO). www.asco.org (accessed 2022 Feb 17)

PSYCHIATRIC CONDITIONS

CONTENTS

CHAPTER CONTENT

CONTENT LEGEND

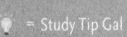 = Study Tip Gal   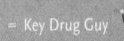 = Key Drug Guy

---

© iStock.com/kitzcorner

CHAPTER 63

DEPRESSION

BACKGROUND

Major Depressive Disorder (MDD, referred to here as "depression") is one of the most common health conditions in the world. People with depression suffer greatly with persistent feelings of hopelessness, dejection, constant worry, poor concentration, a lack of energy, an inability to sleep and, sometimes, suicidal tendencies. The statistics are sobering. In 2020, approximately 20 million adults in the United States experienced a major depressive episode (about 8.4% of the population). About 66% of the adults with a major depressive episode received treatment.

About half of those with a first depression episode recover and experience no further episodes. The remaining patients will experience persistent or recurrent depression and the risk of recurrence increases with each episode. After three episodes, recurrence risk is nearly 100% without ongoing treatment.

Treatment problems that arise include discontinuation of medication without medical advice, or continuation of medication despite an inadequate response.

CAUSES

The causes of depression are poorly understood, but involve some combination of genetic, biologic and environmental factors. Neurotransmitters believed to be involved in depression include serotonin (5-HT), norepinephrine (NE), epinephrine (Epi), dopamine (DA), glutamate and acetylcholine (ACh). 5-HT may be the most important neurotransmitter (NT) involved with feelings of well-being. Certain drugs can cause or worsen depression (see Key Drugs Guy on the following page).

DIAGNOSIS

Diagnosis and treatment of depression is difficult since it is not possible to measure brain chemical imbalances. Diagnosis relies on symptom assessment according to the Diagnostic and Statistical Manual of Mental Disorders, 5th Edition (DSM-5) (see Study Tip Gal). The Hamilton Depression Rating Scale (HDRS, also known as the Ham-D) is the most widely used depression assessment scale. It is designed to be used in a medical office. The patient rates their symptoms of depression on a numerical scale, and the total score indicates whether or not depression is present.

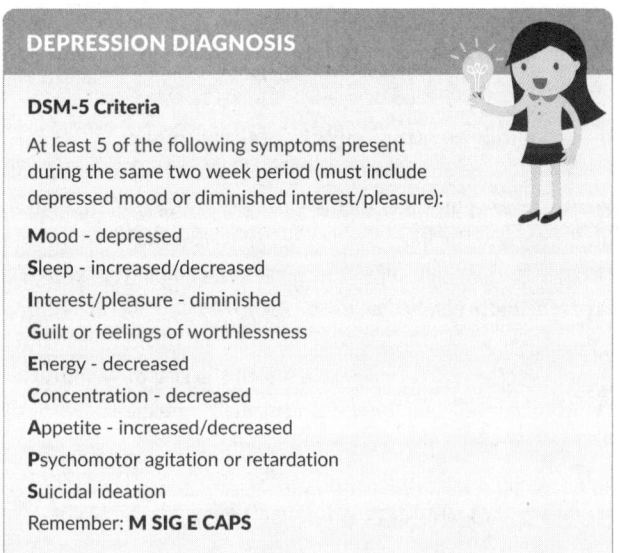

DEPRESSION DIAGNOSIS

DSM-5 Criteria

At least 5 of the following symptoms present during the same two week period (must include depressed mood or diminished interest/pleasure):

Mood - depressed
Sleep - increased/decreased
Interest/pleasure - diminished
Guilt or feelings of worthlessness
Energy - decreased
Concentration - decreased
Appetite - increased/decreased
Psychomotor agitation or retardation
Suicidal ideation
Remember: **M SIG E CAPS**

CONCURRENT BIPOLAR OR ANXIETY DISORDERS

It is necessary to rule out bipolar disorder prior to initiating antidepressant therapy to avoid inducing mania or causing rapid-cycling (cycling rapidly between bipolar depression and mania). Screening forms to assess mood and identify mania symptoms include questions such as "I get into moods where I feel very 'speeded-up' or irritable."

Benzodiazepines (BZDs) are often used to treat anxiety, though they are not first-line. When depression and anxiety occur together, BZDs should not be used alone; they can worsen and/or mask depression and can be problematic in patients with concurrent substance abuse disorders (called Dual Diagnosis). The risk for physiological dependence, withdrawal symptoms (e.g., tachycardia, anxiety) and respiratory depression and death (especially when given with opioids or other CNS depressants) is further discussed in the Anxiety Disorders chapter.

SELECT DRUGS THAT CAUSE OR WORSEN DEPRESSION

KEY DRUGS

ADHD medications
Atomoxetine (Strattera)

Analgesics
Indomethacin

Antiretrovirals (NNRTIs)
Efavirenz (in Atripla)
Rilpivirine (in Complera, Odefsey)

Cardiovascular medications
Beta-blockers (especially propranolol)

Hormones
Hormonal contraceptives
Anabolic steroids

Other
Antidepressants: see Boxed Warnings & MedGuides Section
Benzodiazepines
Systemic steroids
Interferons
Varenicline
Ethanol

Others:
Methylphenidate and other stimulants
Methadone, and possibly other chronic opioid use that can lower testosterone or estrogen levels
Clonidine
Methyldopa
Procainamide
Cyclosporine
Isotretinoin

Medical conditions such as stroke, Parkinson disease, dementia, multiple sclerosis, hypothyroidism, low vitamin D levels, metabolic conditions (e.g., hypercalcemia), malignancy, overactive bladder and infectious diseases can contribute to depression.

NATURAL PRODUCTS

St. John's wort, SAMe (S-adenosyl-L-methionine), valerian or 5-HTP (5-hydroxytryptophan) may be helpful for treating depression, but there is less evidence of efficacy than with standard treatments. St. John's wort carries a weak recommendation for use in patients who are not pregnant or breastfeeding and prefer herbal treatment. St. John's wort, SAMe and 5-HTP can increase the risk of serotonin syndrome and should not be used with other serotonergic agents. St. John's wort is a broad-spectrum CYP450 enzyme inducer with many significant drug interactions, and it can cause phototoxicity. Valerian can cause sedation.

DRUG TREATMENT

Treatment of depression can require one or more trials of medication/s. If a drug does not work after a suitable trial of at least 4 – 8 weeks, treatment should be reassessed (see Treatment-Resistant Depression). A thorough patient history is critical; what worked in the past, or did not work, should help guide therapy.

Mild depression should be treated with psychotherapy [e.g., cognitive behavioral therapy (CBT)] or medication. Moderate to severe depression should be treated with medication in addition to the option of psychotherapy. The effectiveness of the different antidepressant classes is generally comparable. The initial choice of medication should be based on the side effect profile, safety concerns and patient-specific symptoms. For most patients an SSRI or SNRI is preferred, or (with specific concurrent conditions) mirtazapine or bupropion.

DEPRESSION IN PREGNANCY AND POSTPARTUM DEPRESSION

If a woman is on antidepressants and wishes to become pregnant, it may be possible to taper the drug if the depression is mild and she has been symptom-free for the previous six months. In more severe cases, medications may need to be continued.

Depression in pregnant women often goes unrecognized and untreated. Untreated depression, especially in the late second or early third trimesters, is associated with increased rates of adverse outcomes (e.g., premature birth, low birth weight, postnatal complications). The American College of Obstetricians and Gynecologists (ACOG) guidelines for mild depression in pregnancy recommend psychotherapy first, followed by drug treatment if needed.

The initiation of drug treatment is concerning because of the risks of adverse outcomes for both the mother and the unborn baby. All drugs carry risk; the risk versus benefit must be considered individually. SSRIs are often used initially, with the exception of paroxetine, due to potential cardiac effects. Although preferred, there is a warning regarding SSRI use during pregnancy and the potential risk of persistent pulmonary hypertension of the newborn (PPHN).

Postpartum depression is often unrecognized or under-treated, and can have adverse outcomes for the mother, baby and family. Breastfeeding helps for physical and emotional symptoms, and is considered beneficial for the baby. Drug safety when breastfeeding is essential. SSRIs or tricyclics are generally preferred (with the exception of doxepin, per ACOG recommendations). Brexanolone (Zulresso), a C-IV drug, is FDA-approved for postpartum depression. It is given as a continuous IV infusion over 60 hours and can cause excessive sedation.

SAFETY ISSUES WITH ANTIDEPRESSANTS

Due to safety concerns (drug-drug and drug-food interactions) the use of oral nonselective monoamine oxidase inhibitors (MAO inhibitors) such as phenelzine, tranylcypromine and isocarboxazid is restricted to patients unresponsive to other treatments. Since many antidepressants increase serotonin levels, serotonin syndrome can occur with the administration of one or more serotonergic medications (e.g., SSRIs/SNRIs, mirtazapine, trazodone, opioids, tramadol, lithium, buspirone, triptans, dextromethorphan and St. John's wort). The risk is most severe when an MAO inhibitor is administered with another serotonergic medication. Higher doses increase the risk.

Symptoms of serotonin syndrome include severe nausea, dizziness, headache, diarrhea, agitation, tachycardia, hallucinations or muscle rigidity. Further discussion of MAO inhibitor drug interactions and serotonin syndrome can be found in the Basic Science Concepts and Drug Interactions chapters.

If an antidepressant is being discontinued, it should generally be tapered over several weeks to avoid withdrawal. Withdrawal symptoms include anxiety, agitation, insomnia, dizziness and flu-like symptoms. Paroxetine and venlafaxine carry a higher risk of withdrawal symptoms and must be tapered upon discontinuation. An exception to this rule is fluoxetine, which self-tapers because of its long half-life. Pharmacists must counsel patients on the risk of withdrawal symptoms and to not discontinue treatment without discussing with their healthcare provider.

BOXED WARNINGS & MEDGUIDES

All antidepressants carry a boxed warning of a possible increase in suicidal thoughts or actions in some children, teenagers or young adults within the first few months of treatment or when the dose is changed. MedGuides are required for all antidepressants. Patients and caregivers must be advised that mood may worsen and that they should contact a healthcare provider if changes in mood, behavior, thoughts or feelings are observed. This information is not included in the drug tables that follow.

LAG EFFECT AND SUICIDE PREVENTION

Antidepressant medication must be used daily, and will take time to work. Physical symptoms such as low energy improve within 1 – 2 weeks but psychological symptoms, such as low mood, may take a month or longer. Physicians and pharmacists must educate patients, family and caregivers about the risk of suicidality and screen for suicide risk. If a patient reports suicidal ideation, refer the patient to the emergency department, the suicide hotline or elsewhere for help. If someone has a plan to attempt suicide, it is more likely that the threat is immediate.

SELECTIVE SEROTONIN REUPTAKE INHIBITORS

Selective serotonin reuptake inhibitors (SSRIs) increase 5-HT by inhibiting its reuptake in the neuronal synapse. They weakly affect NE and DA.

DRUG	DOSING	SAFETY/SIDE EFFECTS/MONITORING
Citalopram (Celexa)	20-40 mg/day Max dose: 40 mg/day Max dose in elderly (> 60 years): 20 mg/day	**CONTRAINDICATIONS** Do not use with MAO inhibitors, linezolid, IV methylene blue or pimozide Fluoxetine, paroxetine: do not use with thioridazine Fluvoxamine: do not use with alosetron, thioridazine or tizanidine Sertraline solution: do not use with disulfiram *Brisdelle*: pregnancy
Escitalopram (Lexapro) – S-enantiomer of citalopram	10 mg/day Max dose: 20 mg/day Max dose in elderly: 10 mg/day	**WARNINGS** QT prolongation: do not exceed citalopram 20 mg/day in elderly (> 60 years), liver disease, with CYP2C19 poor metabolizers or on 2C19 inhibitors; do not exceed escitalopram 10 mg/day in elderly
Fluoxetine (Prozac) *Sarafem** – for premenstrual dysphoric disorder (PMDD) only + olanzapine (Symbyax) – for treatment-resistant depression	10-60 mg/day Max dose: 80 mg/day; 90 mg/week (delayed release) *Sarafem*: 20 mg daily or 20 mg daily starting 14 days prior to menstruation through 1st full day of bleeding *Symbyax*: initial 6 mg/25 mg QHS	SIADH/hyponatremia, fall risk (Beers criteria: use caution in elderly, avoid if history of falls/fractures or use of CNS depressants) Bleeding (additive risk; see SSRI Drug Interactions) **SIDE EFFECTS** Sexual side effects: ↓ libido, ejaculation difficulties, anorgasmia, erectile dysfunction Somnolence, insomnia, nausea, dry mouth, diaphoresis (dose-related), weakness, tremor, dizziness, headache
Paroxetine (Paxil, Paxil CR, Pexeva) *Brisdelle* – for moderate-severe vasomotor symptoms associated with menopause	IR: 10-60 mg/day CR: 12.5-62.5 mg/day 10 mg IR = 12.5 mg CR *Brisdelle*: 7.5 mg QHS	Most activating: fluoxetine; take dose in AM Most sedating: paroxetine, fluvoxamine; take dose in the PM Others: take dose in the AM; if causing sedation, take in the PM Osteopenia/osteoporosis, restless leg syndrome (assess whether the onset coincided with initiation of treatment)
Sertraline (Zoloft)	50-200 mg/day Premenstrual dysphoric disorder (PMDD): 50-150 mg daily or 50-150 mg daily starting 14 days prior to menstruation through 1st full day of bleeding	**NOTES** All approved for depression and a variety of anxiety disorders, except fluvoxamine (only approved for OCD) All available in solution except fluvoxamine
Fluvoxamine IR/ER	50-300 mg/day (daily doses > 100 mg/day should be divided BID)	Sertraline is preferred in patients with cardiac risk To switch to fluoxetine delayed release 90 mg/weekly from fluoxetine 20 mg daily, start 7 days after last daily dose

*Brand discontinued but name still used in practice

SSRI Drug Interactions

- MAO inhibitors and serotonin syndrome or hypertensive crisis:

  - Allow a two-week washout between MAO inhibitors and SSRIs. Fluoxetine is the exception; due to its long half life (4 – 6 days), a five-week washout period is required if switching from fluoxetine.

  - Do not initiate in patients receiving linezolid or IV methylene blue due to risk of serotonin syndrome.

- QT prolongation most consistently noted with citalopram and escitalopram (see max dose recommendations). Additive QT prolongation risk with SSRIs and other QT-prolonging drugs (see Arrhythmias chapter).

- ↑ bleeding risk when used with anticoagulants, antiplatelets, NSAIDs, select natural products (e.g., ginkgo, garlic, ginger, ginseng, glucosamine, fish oils), thrombolytics.

- Fluoxetine, paroxetine and fluvoxamine are CYP2D6 inhibitors.

  - Tamoxifen requires conversion to its active form by CYP2D6. Decreased tamoxifen effectiveness occurs with fluoxetine and paroxetine. Venlafaxine (an SNRI) is preferred in combination with tamoxifen.

  - Some antipsychotic drugs (e.g., aripiprazole, olanzapine) are CYP2D6 substrates and may need a lower dose when given in combination with fluoxetine and paroxetine.

- Do not use with thioridazine, pimozide or cimetidine.

- Caution with drugs that cause orthostasis or CNS depression due to risk of falls.

SSRI COMBINED MECHANISM

DRUG	DOSING	SAFETY/SIDE EFFECTS/MONITORING
SSRI and 5-HT1A Partial Agonist		**CONTRAINDICATIONS** Do not use within 14 days of MAO inhibitors; do not use with linezolid or IV methylene blue
Vilazodone *(Viibryd, Viibryd Starter Pack)*	Start at 10 mg daily x 7 days, then 20 mg daily (dosing in patient starter kit); max 40 mg/day Take with food	**WARNINGS** Seizures; avoid in patients with seizure history
SSRI, 5-HT3 Receptor Antagonist and 5-HT1A Agonist		**SIDE EFFECTS** N/V/D, insomnia, ↓ libido (less sexual SEs compared to SSRIs and SNRIs) Vortioxetine: constipation
Vortioxetine *(Trintellix)*	5-20 mg/day, with or without food	**NOTES** Vortioxetine: decrease dose by 50% when used with strong CYP2D6 inhibitors (e.g., bupropion, fluoxetine, paroxetine or quinidine)

SEROTONIN AND NOREPINEPHRINE REUPTAKE INHIBITORS

Serotonin and norepinephrine reuptake inhibitors (SNRIs) have a similar mechanism as SSRIs, in that they increase 5-HT by inhibiting its reuptake in the neuronal synapse. SNRIs also inhibit reuptake of norepinephrine (NE). This explains the differences in indications and side effect profiles compared to SSRIs.

DRUG	DOSING	SAFETY/SIDE EFFECTS/MONITORING
Venlafaxine *(Effexor XR)* Depression, generalized anxiety disorder (GAD), panic disorder, social anxiety disorder	37.5-375 mg/day Max dose: 375 mg/day (IR), 225 mg/day (ER) Different generics; check *Orange Book*	**CONTRAINDICATIONS** SNRIs and MAO inhibitors can potentially cause a lethal drug interaction: hypertensive crisis (see SNRI Drug Interactions section) Do not initiate in a patient receiving linezolid or IV methylene blue
Duloxetine *(Cymbalta, Drizalma Sprinkle)* Depression, peripheral neuropathy (pain), fibromyalgia, GAD, chronic musculoskeletal pain	40-60 mg/day (or 20-30 BID) Max dose: 120 mg/day; doses > 60 mg/day not more effective	**WARNINGS** SIADH/hyponatremia, fall risk (Beers criteria: use caution in elderly, avoid if history of falls/fractures or use of CNS depressants) Bleeding (additive risk; see SNRI Drug Interactions) **SIDE EFFECTS** Similar to SSRIs (due to ↓ 5-HT reuptake)
Desvenlafaxine *(Pristiq)* Depression	50 mg/day (can ↑ to 400 mg/day, but no benefit > 50 mg)	Side effects due to ↑ NE: ↑ HR, dilated pupils (can lead to an episode of narrow angle glaucoma), dry mouth, excessive sweating and constipation Can affect urethral resistance; caution when using SNRIs in patients prone to obstructive urinary disorders
Levomilnacipran *(Fetzima)* Depression	Start 20 mg/day x 2 days then increase to 40 mg/day; can titrate by 40 mg/day no sooner than every 2 days Max dose: 120 mg/day Do not open, chew or crush capsules; do not take with alcohol	↑ BP: risk is greatest with venlafaxine when dosed > 150 mg/day (all have risk, especially at higher doses); can ↓ dose, use antihypertensive/s or change therapy Osteopenia/osteoporosis, restless leg syndrome (assess whether the onset coincided with initiation of treatment) **NOTES** Do not use levomilnacipran with CrCl < 15 mL/min or duloxetine with CrCl < 30 mL/min *Pristiq* can leave a ghost tablet (empty shell) in the stool

SNRI Drug Interactions

- SNRIs and MAO inhibitors can cause hypertensive crisis or serotonin syndrome if used together.

  ❏ A washout period is needed if changing between SNRIs and MAO inhibitors; 14 days are recommended.

  ❏ Do not initiate in patients receiving linezolid or IV methylene blue due to risk of serotonin syndrome.

- Additive QT prolongation risk with venlafaxine.

- SNRIs can increase BP. Use caution, especially at higher doses, and monitor if on antihypertensive medications.

- Duloxetine is a moderate CYP2D6 inhibitor. Tamoxifen requires conversion to its active metabolite by CYP2D6. Decreased tamoxifen effectiveness occurs with duloxetine.

- ↑ bleeding risk with concurrent use of anticoagulants, antiplatelets, NSAIDs, select natural products (e.g., ginkgo, garlic, ginger, ginseng, glucosamine, fish oils), thrombolytics.

TRICYCLICS

Tricyclic antidepressants (TCAs) primarily inhibit NE and 5-HT reuptake. They also block ACh and histamine receptors, which contributes to the side effect profile. There are two main categories of TCAs: secondary amines and tertiary amines. Secondary amines are relatively selective for NE. Tertiary amines can be slightly more effective, but have a worse side effect profile.

DRUG	DOSING	SAFETY/SIDE EFFECTS/MONITORING
TERTIARY AMINES **Amitriptyline** (*Elavil**) **Doxepin** – for depression, all are generic; *Silenor* is for insomnia; *Zonalon* is a cream for pruritus Clomipramine (*Anafranil*) Imipramine (*Tofranil*) Trimipramine	**Amitriptyline** Depression: 100-300 mg/day QHS or in divided doses Neuropathic pain/migraine prophylaxis: 10-150 mg QHS **Doxepin** Depression: 100-300 mg/day	**CONTRAINDICATIONS** Do not use with MAO inhibitors, linezolid, IV methylene blue; myocardial infarction; glaucoma and urinary retention (doxepin) **SIDE EFFECTS** **Cardiotoxicity** QT prolongation with overdose (monitor for suicidal ideation, as overdose can quickly cause fatal arrhythmias); obtain baseline ECG if cardiac risk factors or age > 50 years old Orthostasis, tachycardia
SECONDARY AMINES **Nortriptyline (*Pamelor*)** Amoxapine Desipramine (*Norpramin*) Maprotiline Protriptyline	**Nortriptyline** Depression: 25 mg TID-QID	**Anticholinergic** Dry mouth, blurred vision, urinary retention, constipation (taper off to avoid cholinergic rebound) Vivid dreams, weight gain (varies by agent and patient), sedation, sweating, myoclonus (muscle twitching – a symptom of drug toxicity) Beers criteria (use caution in elderly): risk of falls (avoid if history of falls/fractures or use of CNS depressants) **NOTES** Low dose amitriptyline is commonly used and generally well tolerated Tertiary amines have increased anticholinergic properties, and are more likely to cause sedation and weight gain

*Brand discontinued but name still used in practice

Tricyclic Drug Interactions

- MAO inhibitors and hypertensive crisis: two-week washout if going to or from an MAO inhibitor.

- Additive QT prolongation risk with TCAs and other QT-prolonging drugs (see Arrhythmias chapter).

- Metabolized by CYP2D6; check for drug interactions.

DOPAMINE AND NOREPINEPHRINE REUPTAKE INHIBITOR

DRUG	DOSING	SAFETY/SIDE EFFECTS/MONITORING
Bupropion (*Wellbutrin SR, Wellbutrin XL*, *Aplenzin, Forfivo XL*) **Zyban*** – for <u>smoking cessation</u> **Wellbutrin XL** and *Aplenzin* are approved for seasonal affective disorder (SAD) + naltrexone (*Contrave*) – for <u>weight management</u>	150-450 mg daily Bupropion IR is TID *Wellbutrin SR* is BID (Max: 200 mg/dose) *Wellbutrin XL* is daily <u>Do not exceed 450 mg/ day</u> (up to 522 mg/day with *Aplenzin*) due to <u>seizure risk</u>	**CONTRAINDICATIONS** <u>Seizure disorder; history of anorexia/bulimia</u>, abrupt discontinuation of ethanol or sedatives; <u>do not use</u> with <u>MAO inhibitors, linezolid, IV methylene blue</u> or <u>other forms of bupropion</u> **WARNINGS** Neuropsychiatric adverse events possible when used for smoking cessation (can include mood changes, hallucinations, paranoia, aggression, anxiety) **SIDE EFFECTS** <u>Dry mouth</u>, CNS stimulation (<u>insomnia, restlessness</u>), tremors/seizures (dose-related), <u>weight loss</u>, headache/migraine, nausea/vomiting, constipation and possible blood pressure changes (more hypertension than hypotension) <u>Sexual dysfunction is rare</u> (no effect on 5-HT); can use if issues with other antidepressants

*Brand discontinued but name still used in practice

Bupropion Drug Interactions

- <u>Do not use multiple formulations of bupropion.</u>

- Increased risk of <u>hypertensive crisis</u> with <u>MAO inhibitors</u>. Allow 14-day washout when converting to an MAO inhibitor.

MONOAMINE OXIDASE INHIBITORS

Monoamine oxidase (MAO) inhibitors inhibit the enzyme <u>monoamine oxidase</u>, which breaks down catecholamines, including 5-HT, NE, Epi and DA. If these NTs ↑ dramatically, <u>hypertensive crisis</u> and death can result.

DRUG	DOSING	SAFETY/SIDE EFFECTS/MONITORING
Isocarboxazid (*Marplan*)	20 mg/day in divided doses Max dose: 60 mg/day	**CONTRAINDICATIONS** History of cardiovascular disease, cerebrovascular defect, headache, hepatic disease, pheochromocytoma Do not use with other sympathomimetics and related compounds (risk of hypertensive crisis – see Warnings and Drug Interactions below) Severe renal disease (isocarboxazid, phenelzine)
Phenelzine (*Nardil*)	15 mg TID Max dose: 60-90 mg/day	**WARNINGS** Not commonly used, but watch for <u>drug-drug and drug-food interactions – if missed could be fatal</u> <u>Hypertensive crisis or serotonin syndrome</u> can occur when taken with <u>TCAs, SSRIs, SNRIs, many other drugs and tyramine-rich foods</u> (see MAO Inhibitor Drug Interactions)
Tranylcypromine (*Parnate*)	30 mg/day in divided doses Max dose: 60 mg/day	**SIDE EFFECTS** Anticholinergic effects (taper upon discontinuation to avoid cholinergic rebound) Orthostasis Sedation (except tranylcypromine causes stimulation) Sexual dysfunction, weight gain, headache, insomnia
Selegiline <u>transdermal patch</u> (*Emsam*) <u>MAO-B selective inhibitor</u> *Zelapar* (ODT) is for Parkinson disease	Start at 6 mg patch/day, can ↑ by increments of 3 mg to 12 mg/day	**CONTRAINDICATIONS** Use with serotonergic drugs (see MAO Inhibitor Drug Interactions), pheochromocytoma **SIDE EFFECTS** Constipation, gas, dry mouth, loss of appetite, sexual dysfunction

MAO Inhibitor Drug Interactions

- To avoid <u>hypertensive crisis, serotonin syndrome</u> or psychosis, MAO inhibitors <u>cannot be used</u> with drugs or food that increase concentrations of <u>epinephrine, norepinephrine, serotonin or dopamine</u>.

  - ❏ Contraindicated drugs that increase serotonin: <u>linezolid, lithium, tramadol, opioids, St. John's wort</u>, SSRIs, SNRIs, mirtazapine, trazodone, triptans, buspirone and dextromethorphan.

  - ❏ Contraindicated drugs that increase epinephrine: bupropion, SNRIs, levodopa, linezolid, methylene blue, stimulants used for ADHD and OTC diet pills/herbal weight loss products.

  - ❏ Contraindicated to consume <u>tyramine-rich foods</u> that increase norepinephrine: <u>aged cheese, pickled herring, yeast extract, air-dried meats, sauerkraut, soy sauce</u>, fava beans and some red wines and beers (tap beer and any beer that has not been pasteurized - canned and bottled beers contain little or no tyramine). Foods can become high in tyramine when they have been <u>aged, fermented, pickled or smoked</u>.

MAO INHIBITORS – KEEP THEM SEPARATED

To avoid serotonin syndrome and hypertensive crisis*

- 2-week washout is required between MAO inhibitors and:

  - ❏ SSRIs (see fluoxetine, below)
  - ❏ SNRIs
  - ❏ TCAs
  - ❏ Bupropion

- 5-week washout is required when changing from:

  - ❏ Fluoxetine → MAO inhibitor (due to fluoxetine's long half-life)

*See Drug Interactions chapter for more information on serotonin syndrome and hypertensive crisis with MAO inhibitors

---

MISCELLANEOUS ANTIDEPRESSANTS

DRUG	DOSING	SAFETY/SIDE EFFECTS/MONITORING
Tetracyclic antidepressant: has central presynaptic alpha-2 adrenergic antagonist effects, which results in ↑ release of NE and 5-HT		
Mirtazapine (Remeron, Remeron SolTab) Used commonly in oncology and skilled nursing facilities to help with <u>sleep</u> (dosed QHS) & to ↑ <u>appetite</u> (can ↑ weight gain in frail elderly)	15-45 mg QHS	**CONTRAINDICATIONS** Do not use with <u>MAO inhibitors, linezolid or IV methylene blue</u> **WARNINGS** Anticholinergic effects, QT prolongation, blood dyscrasias, CNS depression **SIDE EFFECTS** <u>Sedation, ↑ appetite, weight gain</u>, dry mouth, dizziness, agranulocytosis (rare)
Inhibits 5-HT reuptake, blocks H1 and alpha-1 adrenergic receptors		
Trazodone Rarely used as an antidepressant due to sedation; used primarily off-label for <u>sleep</u>	IR: 150-400 mg/day in divided doses ER: 150-375 mg QHS Sleep: dosed 50-100 mg QHS	**CONTRAINDICATIONS** Do not use with <u>MAO inhibitors, linezolid or IV methylene blue</u> **SIDE EFFECTS** <u>Sedation</u> (trazodone ER may be less sedating), orthostasis (risk in elderly for falls) Sexual dysfunction and risk of <u>priapism</u> (painful erection longer than 4 hours, medical emergency)
Inhibits 5-HT and NE reuptake, blocks 5-HT2 and alpha-1 adrenergic receptors		
Nefazodone Rarely used due to <u>hepatotoxicity</u>	200-600 mg/day divided BID	**BOXED WARNING** <u>Hepatotoxicity</u> **CONTRAINDICATIONS** Hepatic disease, concurrent use with MAO inhibitors, carbamazepine, cisapride, pimozide or triazolam **SIDE EFFECTS** Similar to trazodone, but less sedating

Drug Interactions

- Additive sedation; avoid use of any other sedating medications along with mirtazapine and trazodone.

- Mirtazapine, trazodone: additive QT prolongation risk. Use caution with other medications known to prolong the QT interval (see the Arrhythmias chapter).

- Avoid use with other serotonergic drugs, due to increased risk of serotonin syndrome.

- Avoid use with MAO inhibitors due to increased risk of hypertensive crisis.

SELECTING THE BEST ANTIDEPRESSANT

General Principles
The antidepressant selected should incorporate patient-specific information and history.

Did it work? If an antidepressant was taken at a reasonable dose for 4-8 weeks and did not work well, do not use it again.

Was it well-tolerated? Do not choose a treatment that was poorly tolerated in the past.

Does the patient have co-morbid conditions that make a drug a good or a poor choice?

- Cardiac/QT risk
  - Sertraline preferred
  - Do not choose a QT-prolonging drug/dose (e.g., high doses of citalopram or escitalopram)
  - Watch for additive QT effects when SSRIs, SNRIs, TCAs, mirtazapine or trazodone are used with other QT-prolonging drugs (see Arrhythmias chapter)
- Smoker
  - Bupropion SR is FDA-approved for smoking cessation
- Peripheral neuropathy or pain
  - Consider duloxetine
- Taking serotonergic antidepressants
  - Avoid multiple serotonergic medications due to risk of serotonin syndrome (See MAO Inhibitors section and Drug Interactions chapter)
  - ↑ bleeding risk with anticoagulants, antiplatelets, NSAIDs and some natural products (e.g., ginkgo, garlic, ginger, ginseng, glucosamine, fish oils)
- Seizure disorder or at risk for seizures (bulimia/anorexia, recent alcohol or sedative withdrawal)
  - Do not use bupropion

- Pregnant
  - Do not use paroxetine
  - Mild-to-moderate depression: psychotherapy is first-line
  - Severe depression: certain SSRIs are first-line (e.g., citalopram, escitalopram, fluoxetine, sertraline)
- Daytime sedation
  - Do not take a sedating drug early in the day (e.g., paroxetine, mirtazapine, trazodone)
  - Activating medications taken in the morning are preferred (e.g., fluoxetine, bupropion)
- Insomnia
  - Do not take an activating drug later in the day (e.g., bupropion, fluoxetine)
  - Sedating medications taken at night are preferred (e.g., paroxetine, mirtazapine, trazodone)
- Sexual dysfunction
  - High risk with SSRIs and SNRIs
  - Lower risk with bupropion and mirtazapine

TREATMENT-RESISTANT DEPRESSION

Depression that does not fully respond to two full treatment trials is considered treatment-resistant. The American Psychiatric Association (APA) guidelines state that patients should receive a 4 – 8 week trial of medication at a therapeutic dose before concluding that a drug is not working. If the patient is not improving (making progress toward the treatment goal of remission) or has an incomplete response, the following should be considered:

- Change to a new antidepressant.
- Increase the antidepressant dose.
- Use a combination of antidepressants with different mechanisms of action.

- Augment with buspirone or a low dose of an atypical antipsychotic. Agents approved as augmentation therapy with antidepressants are aripiprazole (Abilify), olanzapine + fluoxetine (Symbyax), quetiapine extended release (Seroquel XR) and brexpiprazole (Rexulti). Esketamine (Spravato) is an another option.
- Augmentation with lithium, thyroid hormone (i.e., T3), or in some cases, electroconvulsive therapy (ECT).

SELECT ADJUNCTIVE THERAPY IN TREATMENT-RESISTANT DEPRESSION

DRUG	DOSING	SAFETY/SIDE EFFECTS/MONITORING
Antipsychotics		
Aripiprazole (Abilify, Abilify Maintena, Abilify MyCite) Tablet, ODT, solution, injection Only oral formulations are indicated for treatment-resistant depression	Start 2-5 mg/day (QAM), can ↑ to 15 mg/day	**BOXED WARNING** Elderly patients with dementia-related psychosis treated with antipsychotic drugs are at ↑ risk of death Antidepressants increase the risk of suicidal thinking and behavior in children, adolescents, and young adults; see Boxed Warnings and MedGuides discussion **CONTRAINDICATIONS** Olanzapine/fluoxetine (Symbyax): do not use with MAO inhibitors, linezolid, IV methylene blue, pimozide, thioridazine and caution with other drugs/conditions that cause QT prolongation
Olanzapine/fluoxetine (Symbyax)	Usually started at 6 mg/25 mg QHS (fluoxetine is activating, but olanzapine is more sedating), can ↑ cautiously	**WARNINGS** Neuroleptic malignant syndrome, tardive dyskinesia (TD), falls, leukopenia, neutropenia Multiorgan hypersensitivity (drug reaction with eosinophilia and systemic symptoms, or DRESS) reactions with olanzapine (Symbyax)
Quetiapine (Seroquel, Seroquel XR)	Start 50 mg QHS, ↑ to 150-300 mg QHS	Pathological gambling and other compulsive behaviors (aripiprazole) **SIDE EFFECTS** Each of these drugs can cause metabolic issues, including dyslipidemia, weight gain, diabetes (less with aripiprazole) All can cause orthostasis/dizziness (can lead to falls)
Brexpiprazole (Rexulti)	Start 0.5-1 mg/day, can ↑ to 3 mg/day (titrate weekly)	**Aripiprazole:** anxiety, insomnia, akathisia, constipation, agitation **Olanzapine:** sedation, weight gain, ↑ lipids, ↑ glucose, EPS, QT prolongation (lower risk) **Quetiapine:** sedation, orthostasis, weight gain, ↑ lipids, ↑ glucose, EPS (lower risk) **Brexpiprazole:** weight gain, dyspepsia, diarrhea, agitation
NMDA Receptor Antagonist		
Esketamine (Spravato) C-III Nasal spray Treatment-resistant depression and depression with suicidality	Start 56 mg intranasally twice weekly, can ↑ to 84 mg twice weekly if tolerated Must be administered under the supervision of a health care provider; monitor for adverse effects for at least 2 hours following administration	**BOXED WARNING** Sedation and dissociative or perceptual changes, potential for abuse and misuse Antidepressants increase the risk of suicidal thinking and behavior in children, adolescents, and young adults; see Boxed Warnings and MedGuides discussion **NOTES** Due to risks, only available through a restricted distribution system under the Spravato REMS program

KEY COUNSELING POINTS

See the Drug Formulations & Patient Counseling chapter for counseling language/layman's terminology.

All Antidepressants

- Can cause suicidal ideation.
- MedGuide required.
- Can take 1 – 2 weeks to feel a benefit from this drug and 6 – 8 weeks to feel the full effect on mood.

SSRIs

- Can cause:
  - ❑ Sexual dysfunction.
  - ❑ Serotonin syndrome.
- Fluoxetine: take in the morning.

SNRIs

- Can cause:
  - ❑ Increased blood pressure.
  - ❑ Increased sweating.
  - ❑ Sexual dysfunction.
  - ❑ Serotonin syndrome.
- Ghost tablet in stool *(Pristiq)*.

Tricyclics

- Can cause:
  - ❑ Anticholinergic effects.
  - ❑ Orthostasis.

Bupropion

- Can cause insomnia.

MAO Inhibitors

- Can cause serotonin syndrome.
- Many drug interactions.

Other Antidepressants

- Trazodone: take at bedtime.
  - ❑ Can cause priapism.
- Mirtazapine: take at bedtime.

Select Guidelines/References

Practice Guideline for the Treatment of Patients with Major Depressive Disorder, 2010. https://psychiatryonline.org/pb/assets/raw/sitewide/practice_guidelines/guidelines/mdd.pdf (accessed 2022 Feb 14)

VA/DoD Clinical Practice Guideline for the Management of Major Depressive Disorder, 2016. https://www.healthquality.va.gov/guidelines/MH/mdd/MDDCPGClinicianSummaryFINAL1.pdf (accessed 2022 Feb 14)

Diagnostic and Statistical Manual of Mental Disorders (DSM-5).

DEFINITIONS: EXTRAPYRAMIDAL SIDE EFFECTS (EPS)

Extrapyramidal side effects (EPS) are a group of side effects related to irregular movements.

Dystonias: prolonged contraction of muscles during drug initiation, including painful muscle spasms; life-threatening if airway is compromised. Higher risk with younger males. Centrally-acting anticholinergics (diphenhydramine, benztropine) can be used for prophylaxis or treatment.

Akathisia: restlessness with anxiety and an inability to remain still; treated with benzodiazepines or propranolol.

Parkinsonism: looks similar to Parkinson disease, with tremors, abnormal gait and bradykinesia; treat with anticholinergics or propranolol if tremor is the main symptom.

Tardive dyskinesias (TD): abnormal facial movements, primarily in the tongue or mouth; higher risk with elderly females. TD can be irreversible. Must stop the drug and replace with an SGA with low EPS risk (e.g., quetiapine, clozapine).

Dyskinesias: abnormal movements; more common with dopamine replacement for Parkinson disease.

CONTENT LEGEND

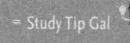 = Study Tip Gal 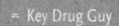 = Key Drug Guy

---

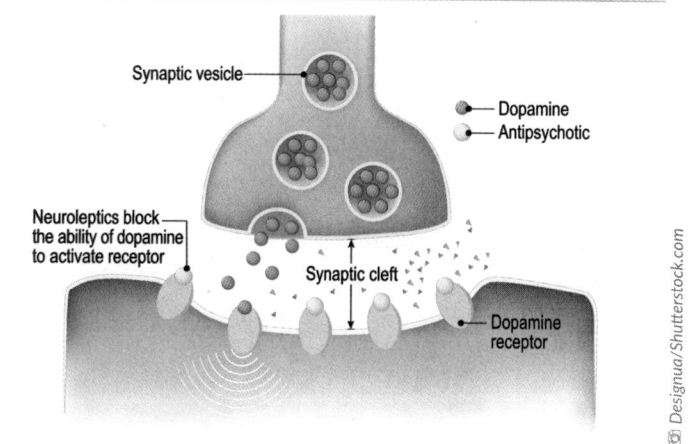

Synaptic vesicle

Dopamine
Antipsychotic

Neuroleptics block the ability of dopamine to activate receptor

Synaptic cleft

Dopamine receptor

© Designua/Shutterstock.com

CHAPTER 64
SCHIZOPHRENIA/PSYCHOSIS

BACKGROUND

Schizophrenia is a chronic, severe and disabling thought disorder that occurs in ~1% of all societies regardless of class, color, religion or culture.

Common symptoms of schizophrenia include:

- Hallucinations: sensing something that is not present, such as imaginary voices.

- Delusions: a belief about something real that is not true, such as imagining that your family (which is real) wishes to hurt you (delusion).

- Disorganized thinking/behavior: inability to focus attention and communicate organized thoughts.

Schizophrenia ranges from relatively mild to severe. Some people can function adequately in daily life, while others need specialized, intensive care. Treatment adherence is important and often difficult to obtain, primarily due to a lack of insight (i.e., inability of the patient to recognize the illness). Schizophrenia can cause a life of torment and is associated with a high suicide rate.

The onset of symptoms usually begins in young adulthood. A diagnosis is not based on lab tests, but on behavior, which includes both negative and positive signs and symptoms (described on the following page). The Diagnostic and Statistical Manual of Mental Disorders, 5th Edition (DSM-5) sets the diagnostic criteria for psychiatric conditions.

PATHOPHYSIOLOGY

Schizophrenia's pathophysiology is multifactorial and includes altered brain structure and chemistry, primarily involving dopamine, serotonin and glutamine. Genetics (inherited susceptibility) and environmental factors (e.g., stress) contribute to disease risk. In addition to neurotransmitter imbalances and stressors, psychosis can be caused or exacerbated by drug use, including both recreational drugs and prescription drugs (see Key Drugs Guy).

Medical conditions besides schizophrenia can cause psychosis. Dopamine is critical to many central nervous system functions, including movement. Parkinson medications increase dopamine in the brain, which relieves the motor symptoms. Increased dopamine can trigger hallucinations or delusions. Up to 50% of patients with Parkinson disease will experience hallucinations or delusions.

MEDICATIONS/RECREATIONAL DRUGS THAT CAN CAUSE PSYCHOTIC SYMPTOMS

Anticholinergics (centrally-acting, high doses)

Dextromethorphan

Dopamine or dopamine agonists (e.g., *Requip, Mirapex, Sinemet*)

Interferons

Stimulants, especially if already at risk (includes amphetamines)

Systemic steroids (typically with lack of sleep – ICU psychosis)

Illicit/recreational substances
Bath salts (synthetic cathinones, MDPV)

Cannabis

Cocaine, especially "crack" cocaine

Lysergic acid diethylamide (LSD, hallucinogenics)

Methamphetamine, ice, crystal

Phencyclidine (PCP)

DSM-5 DIAGNOSTIC CRITERIA FOR SCHIZOPHRENIA

Note: delusions, hallucinations or disorganized speech must be present

Negative signs and symptoms	Positive signs and symptoms
Loss of interest in everyday activities	Hallucinations: can be auditory (hearing voices), visual or somatic
Lack of emotion (apathy)	Delusions: beliefs held by the patient that are without a basis in reality
Inability to plan or carry out activities	Disorganized thinking/behavior, incoherent speech, often on unrelated topics, purposeless behavior, or difficulty speaking and organizing thoughts, such as stopping in mid-sentence or jumbling together meaningless words
Poor hygiene	
Social withdrawal	
Loss of motivation (avolition)	
Lack of speech (alogia)	Difficulty paying attention

NATURAL PRODUCTS

Fish oils are used for psychosis and other psychiatric disorders (e.g., ADHD, depression). Considering the debilitating nature of schizophrenia, prescription medications are usually required.

DRUG TREATMENT

Antipsychotics primarily block dopamine receptors. Newer antipsychotics also block serotonin and other receptors. Decreasing dopamine activity helps control psychosis, but negatively affects dopamine pathways involved in focus, attention and movement.

- Drugs can effectively treat positive symptoms (e.g., hallucinations, delusions).

- The negative symptoms (e.g., lack of motivation, cognitive and functional impairment) are more difficult to treat.

- Currently, second-generation antipsychotics (SGAs) are used first-line due to a lower incidence of extrapyramidal symptoms (EPS), yet there are many patients who are stabilized on first-generation antipsychotics (FGAs) and in some initial cases, they may be preferable.

- FGAs have a high incidence of EPS (see expanded EPS definitions on the previous page), including painful

dystonias (muscle contractions), dyskinesias (abnormal movements), tardive dyskinesias (repetitive, involuntary movements, such as grimacing and eye blinking) and akathisia (restlessness, inability to remain still).

- Tardive dyskinesia (TD) can be irreversible; the drug causing the TD should be discontinued.

FORMULATIONS

Adherence to antipsychotics is poor, primarily due to lack of insight (i.e., inability of the patient to recognize the illness). Formulations are used to increase adherence and help when dysphagia (i.e., difficulty swallowing) is present.

- Long-acting injections eliminate the need for daily oral tablets or capsules. They are given intramuscularly (IM).

- Orally Disintegrating Tablets (ODTs) are useful with dysphagia (difficulty swallowing) and prevents cheeking (when tablets are hidden inside the cheek and spit out later). ODTs dissolve quickly in the mouth.

- Oral solutions/suspensions are useful for children and people with a feeding tube (e.g., PEG tube).

- Acute IM Injections provide "stat" relief to calm down an agitated, psychotic patient for their own safety and the safety of others.

  - IM antipsychotics are often mixed with other drugs (in "cocktails"), such as benzodiazepines for anxiolytic/sedative effects, and anticholinergics to reduce dystonias (e.g., the "Haldol cocktail" contains haloperidol, lorazepam and diphenhydramine).

  - Olanzapine and benzodiazepines should not be given together (i.e., in an injection) due to risk of excessive sedation and breathing difficulty.

BOXED WARNINGS/OTHER WARNINGS

Antipsychotics are <u>not</u> indicated for <u>agitation</u> control in <u>elderly</u> patients with <u>dementia-related psychosis</u>. There is an <u>increased</u> risk of <u>mortality</u> when used for this purpose, mostly due to cardiovascular conditions (e.g., heart failure, sudden death) and infection. Several antipsychotics also carry a warning for an increased risk of <u>stroke</u> in patients with dementia. All antipsychotics carry a warning for falls.

FIRST-GENERATION ANTIPSYCHOTICS

First-generation antipsychotics (FGAs) work mainly by <u>blocking dopamine-2</u> (D2) receptors, with minimal serotonin (5-HT2A) receptor blockade. Many of the FGAs are in the <u>phenothiazine</u> class; they can be easily recognized because their names end in "-azine" (e.g., thioridazine, fluphenazine).

First-Generation Antipsychotics (FGAs)

DRUG	DOSING	SAFETY/SIDE EFFECTS/MONITORING
Low Potency		**BOXED WARNINGS** <u>Elderly</u> patients with <u>dementia-related psychosis</u>: ↑ risk <u>death</u> from antipsychotics
Chlorpromazine	300-1,000 mg/day, divided	Thioridazine: QT prolongation
Thioridazine	300-800 mg/day, divided	*Adasuve*: bronchospasm (REMS program)
Mid potency		**WARNINGS** Cardiovascular effects: <u>QT prolongation</u> (especially with <u>thioridazine, haloperidol, chlorpromazine</u>), orthostasis/falls, tachycardia
Loxapine (*Adasuve*-inhalation powder for acute agitation)	30-100 mg/day, divided	Anticholinergic effects: constipation, xerostomia, blurred vision, urinary retention
Perphenazine	8-64 mg/day, divided	<u>CNS depression</u>
High Potency		<u>Extrapyramidal</u> symptoms (EPS): including Parkinsonism, dystonic reactions, akathisia, tardive dyskinesia (↑ EPS with injections)
Haloperidol (*Haldol*, *Haldol Decanoate*) Oral, injection Class: <u>butyrophenone</u> Also used for Tourette syndrome (for tics and vocal outbursts)	Oral (tablet, solution): start 0.5-2 mg BID-TID, up to 30 mg/day IV: usually 5-10 mg Decanoate (<u>monthly</u>): <u>IM</u> only; for conversion from PO, use 10-20x the PO dose	Hyperprolactinemia: infertility, oligomenorrhea/amenorrhea (less or no menstrual periods), galactorrhea (abnormal breast discharge), erectile dysfunction/↓ libido Neuroleptic malignant syndrome (NMS): use may be associated with NMS; monitor for mental status changes, fever, muscle rigidity, autonomic instability Blood dyscrasias (leukopenia, neutropenia and agranulocytosis), ocular effects
Fluphenazine Tablet, elixir, injection	6-12 mg/day, divided Decanoate (<u>every 2 weeks</u>): <u>IM</u> only	**SIDE EFFECTS** <u>Sedation, dizziness, anticholinergic effects</u> (see Warnings), ↑ prolactin (see Warnings) EPS (see Warnings): can give <u>anticholinergic</u> (e.g., benztropine, diphenhydramine) to <u>limit/avoid</u> painful <u>dystonic</u> reactions
Thiothixene	15-60 mg/day, divided	*Adasuve*: dysgeusia (bad, bitter, or metallic taste in mouth) Injections (haloperidol, fluphenazine): injection site pain/redness
Trifluoperazine	15-50 mg/day, divided	**NOTES** Sedation and EPS: <u>lower potency</u> drugs have ↑ sedation and ↓ EPS, and <u>higher potency</u> drugs have ↓ sedation and ↑ EPS (all cause sedation and EPS)

SECOND-GENERATION ANTIPSYCHOTICS

Second-generation antipsychotics (SGAs) block dopamine (D2) and serotonin (5-HT2A) receptors. Aripiprazole, brexpiprazole and cariprazine are unique: they are D2 and 5-HT1A partial agonists, and brexpiprazole is also a 5-HT2A antagonist.

Second-Generation Antipsychotics (SGAs)

DRUG	DOSING	SAFETY/SIDE EFFECTS/MONITORING
Aripiprazole (Abilify, *Abilify Maintena, Aristada* injection) Tablet, ODT, IM suspension Also approved for irritability with autism and Tourette disorder	10-30 mg PO QAM *Abilify Maintena*-IM suspension, give monthly *Aristada*-IM suspension, give every 4-8 weeks	**SIDE EFFECTS** Akathisia, activating or sedating, headache, anxiety, constipation Lower risk of weight gain, some QT prolongation, EPS (in children) **NOTES** *Aristada* frequency dependent on dose
Clozapine (Clozaril, *Versacloz* suspension) Only if failed to respond to treatment with 2 standard AP treatments, or had significant ADRs	300-900 mg/day, divided (start at 12.5 mg and titrate; titrate off since abrupt discontinuation can cause seizures) Clozapine is very effective and has ↓ risk of EPS/TD, but used no sooner than 3rd-line due to severe side effect potential (metabolic effects, neutropenia)	**BOXED WARNINGS** Significant risk of potentially life-threatening neutropenia/agranulocytosis (REMS program) Bradycardia, orthostatic hypotension, syncope and cardiac arrest; risk is highest during the initial titration period, especially with rapid dose increases; titrate slowly Myocarditis and cardiomyopathy; discontinue if suspected Seizures, dose related; start at no higher than 12.5 mg once or twice daily, titrate slowly, using divided doses; use with caution in patients at seizure risk (e.g., seizure history, head trauma, alcoholism or taking medications which lower seizure threshold) **SIDE EFFECTS** Agranulocytosis, seizures, constipation, somnolence, metabolic syndrome (↑ weight, ↑ BG, ↑ lipids), sialorrhea (hypersalivation), hypotension **MONITORING** REMS: prescribers and pharmacies must be certified and patients must be enrolled with the Clozapine REMS To start treatment, baseline ANC must be ≥ 1,500/mm³ Check ANC weekly x 6 months, then every 2 weeks x 6 months, then monthly; stop therapy if ANC < 1,000/mm³ **NOTES** Smoking reduces drug levels
Lurasidone (Latuda)	40-160 mg/day, divided Take with food ≥ 350 kcal	**CONTRAINDICATIONS** Use with strong CYP450 3A4 inducers and inhibitors **SIDE EFFECTS** Somnolence, EPS (dystonias), nausea Risk of metabolic syndrome, but lower risk than other SGAs – minimal effect on weight, lipid and blood glucose
Olanzapine (Zyprexa, *Zyprexa Zydis* ODT, *Zyprexa Relprevv* injection) + fluoxetine (*Symbyax*) for treatment-resistant depression + samidorphan (*Lybalvi*) for treatment of schizophrenia and bipolar disorder	10-20 mg QHS IM Injection (acute agitation) *Relprevv* inj suspension lasts 2-4 weeks; restricted use	**BOXED WARNING** *Zyprexa Relprevv*: sedation (including coma) and delirium (including agitation, anxiety, confusion, disorientation) have been observed following injection; must be administered in a registered healthcare facility and patients are monitored for 3 hours post-injection (*Zyprexa Relprevv* REMS program requirements). **SIDE EFFECTS** Somnolence, metabolic syndrome (↑ weight, ↑ blood glucose, ↑ lipids), orthostasis **NOTES** Smoking reduces drug levels *Lybalvi*: samidorphan is an opioid receptor antagonist that may help mitigate weight gain from olanzapine; use is contraindicated in anyone taking opioids or undergoing acute opioid withdrawal

DRUG	DOSING	SAFETY/SIDE EFFECTS/MONITORING
Paliperidone (Invega, *Invega Sustenna, Invega Trinza, Invega Hafyera)* Active metabolite of risperidone; SEs similar	PO: 3-12 mg daily CrCl < 50 mL/min: 3 mg daily CrCl < 10 mL/min: Not recommended OROS delivery enables once daily dosing-do not break or crush *Invega Sustenna*, IM injection, give <u>monthly</u> *Invega Trinza*, IM injection, give <u>every 3 months</u> (start only after receiving *Invega Sustenna* x 4 months) *Invega Hafyera*, IM injection, give <u>every 6 months</u> (start only after receiving *Invega Sustenna* x 4 months or *Invega Trinza* x 1 dose)	**SIDE EFFECTS** ↑ prolactin – sexual dysfunction, galactorrhea, irregular/missed periods <u>EPS, especially at higher doses</u> Tachycardia, QT prolongation <u>Metabolic syndrome (↑ weight, ↑ blood glucose, ↑ lipids)</u> Somnolence **NOTES** *Invega* can leave a ghost tablet (empty shell) in the stool
Quetiapine (Seroquel, *Seroquel XR)*	400-800 mg/day, divided BID or XR QHS	**SIDE EFFECTS** <u>Somnolence, metabolic syndrome (↑ weight, ↑ blood glucose, ↑ lipids), orthostasis, possible ocular effects (cataracts)</u> <u>Low EPS</u> risk – often used for <u>psychosis in Parkinson disease</u> **NOTES** Take XR at night, <u>without food</u> or with a <u>light meal</u> (≤ 300 kcal)
Risperidone (Risperdal, *Risperdal Consta, Perseris)* Also approved for irritability associated with autism	2-16 mg/day, divided *Risperdal Consta*: IM injection, give <u>every 2 weeks</u>, 25-50 mg *Perseris*: SC injection, give monthly	**SIDE EFFECTS** ↑ prolactin – sexual dysfunction, galactorrhea, irregular/missed periods <u>EPS, especially at higher doses</u> Tachycardia, QT prolongation <u>Metabolic syndrome (↑ weight, ↑ blood glucose, ↑ lipids)</u> Somnolence
Ziprasidone (Geodon)	40-160 mg/day, divided BID <u>Take with food</u> Acute injection: *Geodon* IM 10 mg Q2H or 20 mg Q4H Max: 40 mg/day IM	**CONTRAINDICATIONS** QT prolongation; do <u>not use</u> with <u>QT risk</u> **SIDE EFFECTS** Somnolence, EPS, dizziness, nausea
Asenapine *(Saphris, Secuado)* *Saphris:* <u>sublingual tablet</u> *Secuado:* patch	10-20 mg/day, divided BID <u>No food/drink</u> for <u>10 min</u> after dose *Secuado:* 3.8-7.6 mg applied daily	**CONTRAINDICATIONS** Severe hepatic impairment **SIDE EFFECTS** Somnolence, <u>tongue numbness</u> (sublingual tablet), EPS (5% more than placebo), QT prolongation
Brexpiprazole *(Rexulti)*	2-4 mg daily	**SIDE EFFECTS** Weight gain, dyspepsia, diarrhea, akathisia
Cariprazine *(Vraylar)*	1.5-6 mg daily	**SIDE EFFECTS** EPS, dystonias, headache, insomnia
Iloperidone *(Fanapt)*	12-24 mg/day, divided Titrate slowly due to orthostasis/dizziness	**SIDE EFFECTS** Dizziness, somnolence, orthostasis, tachycardia QT prolongation
Lumateperone *(Caplyta)*	42 mg daily	**SIDE EFFECTS** Somnolence, EPS

PSYCHIATRIC CONDITIONS

SELECTING AN ANTIPSYCHOTIC

Antipsychotics are chosen based on several considerations, including past medication history and side effects. SGAs have variable degrees of metabolic side effects, including weight gain, increased cholesterol, increased triglycerides (TGs) and increased blood glucose (BG). Drugs with higher metabolic risk should be monitored during treatment and avoided if diabetes or cardiovascular disease is present. Although at a lower incidence than FGAs, some of the SGAs can cause dose-related EPS. Prolactin levels can increase, causing gynecomastia (painful, swollen breast tissue), galactorrhea, sexual dysfunction and oligomenorrhea/amenorrhea. Clozapine has the highest efficacy, but has multiple boxed warnings (e.g., agranulocytosis, seizures, myocarditis). Clozapine can be tried after failure with at least two other antipsychotics (at least one SGA). The Study Tip Gal lists the drugs most likely to cause major adverse effects; avoid using them in an at-risk patient.

TREATMENT CONSIDERATIONS

When assessing treatment resistance or evaluating the best option for a partial response, it is important to evaluate whether the patient has had an adequate trial (at least 6 weeks) of an antipsychotic, including whether the dose is adequate and whether the patient has been taking the medication as prescribed.

Did it work (e.g., quieted the voices down) and was it well-tolerated
If the drug was being taken (at a reasonable dose and for a long-enough trial period) and did not work well, do not use it again.

Do not choose a treatment that was poorly tolerated in the past (e.g., painful dystonia or tardive dyskinesia with haloperidol, painful gynecomastia with paliperidone/risperidone).

Cardiac risk/QT risk
Do not choose a QT-prolonging drug like ziprasidone, haloperidol, thioridazine or chlorpromazine.

History of movement disorder (e.g., Parkinson disease)
Do not choose a drug with high risk of EPS [e.g., FGAs, risperidone, paliperidone (at higher doses)]. Quetiapine is preferred.

Overweight/metabolic risk (e.g., ↑ TG)
Do not choose a drug that worsens metabolic issues like olanzapine or quetiapine. There is a lower metabolic risk with aripiprazole, ziprasidone, lurasidone and asenapine.

Nonadherence or experiencing homelessness
Choose a long-acting injection (see algorithm below).

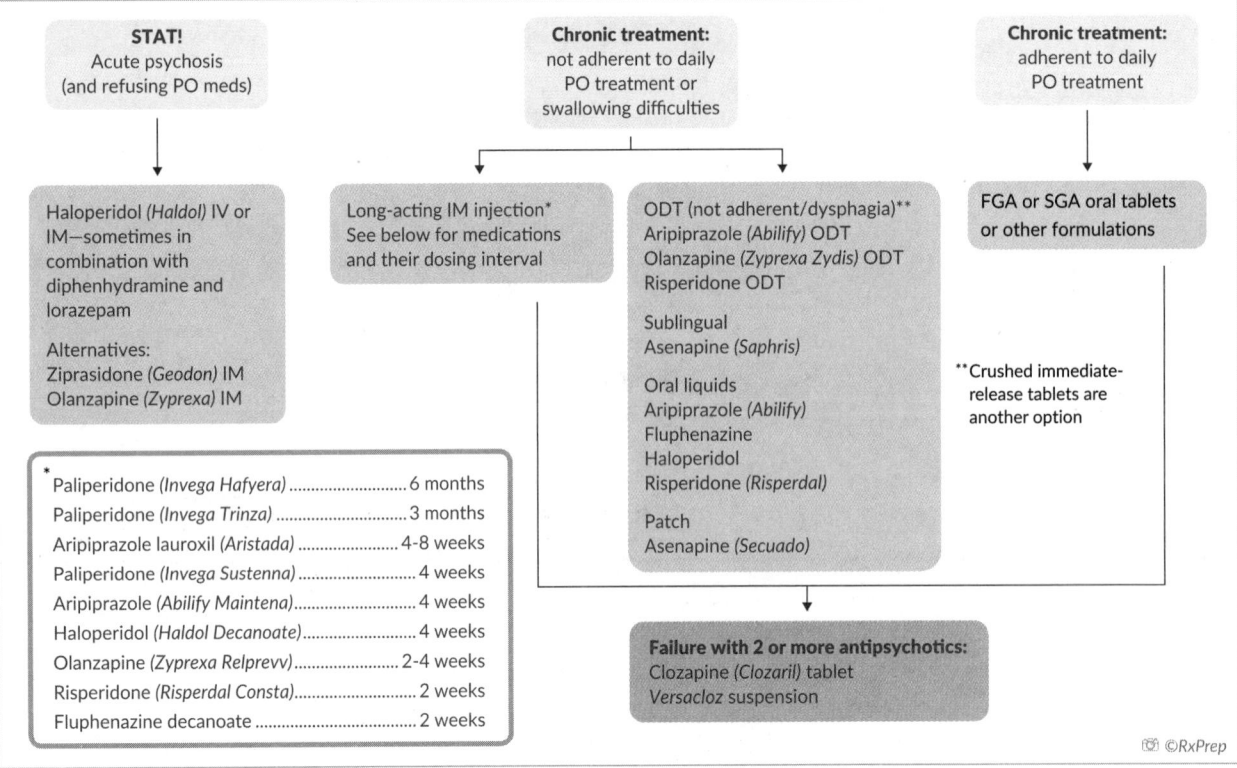

PSYCHOSIS IN PARKINSON DISEASE

Commonly, quetiapine is used to treat psychosis in Parkinson disease because it has a low risk of causing extrapyramidal effects. Pimavanserin *(Nuplazid)* is approved for psychosis with Parkinson disease. It is an inverse agonist and antagonist at serotonin 5-HT2A receptors and a lesser extent at serotonin 5-HT2C receptors. It does not affect dopamine receptors and does not worsen motor symptoms of Parkinson disease.

DRUG	DOSING	SAFETY/SIDE EFFECTS/MONITORING
Pimavanserin *(Nuplazid)*	34 mg PO daily (two 17 mg tablets)	**WARNINGS** Not approved for dementia-related psychosis. See Boxed Warnings discussion. QT prolongation; avoid use with drugs that also increase the QT interval and in patients with risk factors for prolonged QT interval. **SIDE EFFECTS** Peripheral edema, confusion.

ANTIPSYCHOTIC DRUG INTERACTIONS

- All antipsychotics can prolong the QT interval. Some are considered higher risk than others. The higher risk QT-prolonging SGAs are noted previously. Thioridazine, a FGA, is high-risk for QT prolongation (boxed warning). Use caution with other medications that increase risk.

- Smoking can reduce plasma levels of olanzapine and clozapine; patients who smoke can require higher doses.

- High plasma levels of risperidone and paliperidone can increase prolactin and cause EPS. Caution when using risperidone with CYP2D6 inhibitors, including paroxetine and fluoxetine.

- Avoid concurrent drugs that lower the seizure threshold with clozapine.

- Monitor for respiratory depression and hypotension when antipsychotics are given with benzodiazepines.

- Caution with other dopamine blocking agents (e.g., metoclopramide), as EPS and TD risk may be increased.

KEY COUNSELING POINTS

See the Drug Formulations and Patient Counseling chapter for counseling language/layman's terminology.

ALL ANTIPSYCHOTICS

- MedGuide required.
- Can cause:
  - Drowsiness.
  - Orthostasis.
  - Unusual body movements. Symptoms include shakiness, stiffness, or uncontrollable movements of the mouth, tongue, cheeks, jaw, arms or legs. Contact your healthcare provider immediately.
  - Fever, sweating, severe muscle stiffness (rigidity) and confusion. Contact your healthcare provider immediately.

Olanzapine, Risperidone, Paliperidone and Quetiapine

- Can cause hyperglycemia and weight gain.

Clozapine

- Can cause low white blood cell count; requires monitoring via REMS program.

Risperidone

- *Risperdal* oral solution: administered directly from the calibrated pipette, or mixed with water, coffee, orange juice or low-fat milk; it cannot be mixed with cola or tea.

Asenapine Sublingual

- Can cause tongue numbness.

TARDIVE DYSKINESIA

Tardive dyskinesia (TD) is a complication that can occur with dopamine receptor blockade, as with antipsychotics. TD can cause irreversible symptoms that include uncontrollable movements in the tongue, face, trunk and extremities and can interfere with walking, talking and breathing. Valbenazine was the first medication approved for the treatment of TD. It reversibly inhibits vesicular monoamine transporter 2 (VMAT2), a transporter that regulates monoamine uptake from the cytoplasm to the synaptic vesicle for storage and release. Deutetrabenazine is another VMAT2 inhibitor that is approved for TD.

DRUG	DOSING	SAFETY/SIDE EFFECTS/MONITORING
Valbenazine (*Ingrezza*)	Start 40 mg PO daily, increase in 1 week to 80 mg PO daily; maintenance dose of 60-80 mg daily Moderate-severe hepatic impairment: adjustment required CYP2D6 poor metabolizer: consider dose reduction	**WARNINGS** Somnolence, QT prolongation (avoid in long QT syndrome)
Deutetrabenazine (*Austedo*) Also approved for chorea associated with Huntington's disease	Start 6 mg PO BID, increase weekly based on response (max 48 mg/day) Concurrent strong CYP2D6 inhibitors or CYP2D6 poor metabolizer: max dose 36 mg/day	**CONTRAINDICATIONS** Hepatic impairment, administration with tetrabenazine or valbenazine, administration with an MAO inhibitor (within 14 days) **WARNINGS** Somnolence, QT prolongation (avoid in long QT syndrome)

Drug Interactions

■ Avoid use with MAO inhibitors.

■ Valbenazine and deutetrabenazine are substrates of CYP3A4 and 2D6. Dose reduction is required when given with strong inhibitors of CYP3A4 (e.g., itraconazole, clarithromycin) or 2D6 (e.g., paroxetine, fluoxetine).

■ Valbenazine is a P-gp inhibitor and can increase digoxin concentrations. Dosage adjustment of digoxin may be required.

NEUROLEPTIC MALIGNANT SYNDROME

Antipsychotics used to be called neuroleptics. Neuroleptic malignant syndrome (NMS) is rare but is highly lethal. It occurs most commonly with the FGAs and is due to D2 blockade. NMS is less common with SGAs and with other dopamine blocking agents, including metoclopramide (*Reglan*). The majority of cases occur within two weeks of starting treatment or immediately following high doses of injectables given alongside multiple oral doses. Occasionally, patients develop NMS after years of antipsychotic use. NMS is a medical emergency. Intense muscle contractions can lead to acute renal injury (due to rhabdomyolysis from the destruction of muscle tissue), suffocation and death.

Signs

■ Hyperthermia (high fever, with profuse sweating)

■ Extreme muscle rigidity (called "lead pipe" rigidity), which can lead to respiratory failure

■ Mental status changes

■ Tachycardia, tachypnea and blood pressure changes

Laboratory Results

■ ↑ creatine phosphokinase and ↑ white blood cells

Treatment

■ Stop the antipsychotic and provide supportive care: cardiorespiratory and hemodynamic support and manage electrolytes

■ Control the patient's temperature: cooling bed, antipyretics, cooled IV fluids

■ Relax the muscles: benzodiazepines, dantrolene (*Ryanodex, Dantrium, Revonto*) or some cases may require a dopamine agonist (e.g., bromocriptine)

■ After resolution of the symptoms, consider a different antipsychotic (e.g., quetiapine or clozapine)

Select Guidelines/References

American Psychiatric Association. (2013). Diagnostic and Statistical Manual of Mental Disorders: DSM-5. Washington, D.C: American Psychiatric Association

The American Psychiatric Association Practice Guideline for the Treatment of Patients with Schizophrenia. Third Ed. American Psychiatric Association; 2021. https://doi.org/10.1176/appi. books.9780890424841 (accessed 2022 Feb 17).

BIPOLAR CLASSIFICATIONS AND DEFINITIONS

BIPOLAR I

At least one episode of mania, and usually, bouts of intense depression (a depressive episode is not required for diagnosis).

Mania is associated with at least one of the following: significant impairment in social/work functioning, psychosis/delusions or requires hospitalization.

BIPOLAR II

At least one episode of hypomania (lasting ≥ 4 consecutive days) and at least one depressive episode (lasting ≥ 2 weeks).

Hypomania does not affect social/work functioning, does not cause psychosis nor require hospitalization.

BIPOLAR DEPRESSION

Predominant symptoms of a depressive episode include feelings of sadness or depressed mood and/or loss of interest in previously enjoyed activities (see Depression chapter).

PSYCHOSIS

Severe mental condition where there is a loss of contact with reality, involves abnormal thinking and perception (e.g., hallucinations and delusions).

CONTENT LEGEND

☀ = Study Tip Gal

© iStock.com/Siphotography

CHAPTER 65

BIPOLAR DISORDER

BACKGROUND

Bipolar disorder occurs in ~2.6% of adults. It is characterized by fluctuations in mood from an extremely sad or hopeless state to an abnormally elevated, overexcited or irritable mood called mania or hypomania (a milder form of mania). Each mood episode represents a drastic change from an individual's usual mood and behavior. Some episodes include symptoms of both mania and depression, which is called a mixed state. Individuals may seek help during a depressive episode, which can lead to a misdiagnosis of depression only.

Bipolar disorder is classified as bipolar I or bipolar II, which differ primarily by the severity of mania experienced (see Bipolar Classifications and Definitions to the left). Cyclothymia is a related disorder consisting of periods of hypomanic and depressive symptoms without meeting criteria for a major depressive, manic or hypomanic episode. Bipolar disorder can reduce quality of life or cause problems with relationships and employment. It can also lead to drug abuse, anxiety disorders and suicide.

DIAGNOSTIC CRITERIA

Diagnostic and Statistical Manual of Mental Disorders, Fifth Edition (DSM-5) criteria are used to diagnose bipolar disorders. A toxicology screen should be done prior to starting treatment to rule out drug-induced mania.

WHAT IS MANIA?

Symptoms
- Inflated self-esteem
- Needs less sleep
- More talkative than normal
- Jumping from topic to topic
- Easily distracted
- Increase in goal-directed activity
- High-risk, pleasurable activities (e.g., buying sprees, sexual indiscretions, gambling)

Definition
Abnormally elevated or irritable mood for at least a week (or any duration if hospitalization is needed)

Diagnosis
Exhibits ≥ 3 symptoms (if mood is only irritable, exhibits ≥ 4 symptoms)

DRUG TREATMENT

Patients with bipolar disorder usually cycle between mania and depression. The goal of treatment is to stabilize the mood without inducing a depressive or manic state. The traditional mood stabilizers, such as lithium and antiepileptic drugs (valproate, lamotrigine and carbamazepine), treat both mania and depression without inducing either state. Antipsychotics, while not traditional mood stabilizers, can help stabilize the mood when mania occurs with psychosis. Antidepressants can induce or exacerbate a manic episode when used as monotherapy, so they should only be used in combination with a mood stabilizer.

To select treatment, consider the following:

- The side effect profile of the drug.
- The patient's medication history and first-degree relatives' medication history; if the patient or a family member responded well to a drug, the same drug might be a reasonable option.
- The drug formulations available and cost.

ACUTE TREATMENT

Acute treatment will depend on the type of episode (mania vs. depression).

- Manic episode: first-line treatment is valproate, lithium or an antipsychotic. A combination of an antipsychotic + lithium or valproate is preferred for severe episodes.
- Depressive episode: first-line treatment is an antipsychotic (e.g., quetiapine, lurasidone). Lithium, valproate or lamotrigine can be added or used as alternatives.

MAINTENANCE

Medications that were effective for acute episodes should be continued as maintenance treatment to prevent relapse. These include lithium, antiepileptic drugs and second-generation antipsychotics (SGAs). Combination treatment might be more effective than monotherapy at preventing relapse.

MedGuides are required with all antidepressants (primarily due to suicide risk) and antipsychotics (due to increased risk of death in elderly patients with dementia-related psychosis).

PREGNANCY

Treating bipolar disease in pregnancy is complex since the common mood stabilizers have known teratogenic effects.

- Valproate exposure in pregnancy can increase the risk of fetal anomalies, including neural tube defects, fetal valproate syndrome and long-term adverse cognitive effects. Avoid in pregnancy, if possible, especially during the first trimester.

- Carbamazepine exposure in pregnancy can cause fetal carbamazepine syndrome, which can result in facial abnormalities and other significant issues. Avoid in pregnancy, if possible, especially during the first trimester.
- Lithium exposure in pregnancy can cause an increase in congenital cardiac malformations and other abnormalities.

During pregnancy, lamotrigine is a safer option relative to the other mood stabilizers mentioned in this section. SGAs are safer choices than valproate, carbamazepine or lithium. Lurasidone has the most favorable safety profile in pregnancy, but its use is limited since it is only approved for bipolar depression.

ANTIEPILEPTIC DRUGS

Several anticonvulsants are used for the treatment of bipolar disorder. See the Seizures/Epilepsy chapter for a detailed review of these medications:

- **Lamotrigine (Lamictal, Lamictal ODT, Lamictal XR, Lamictal Starter Kit):** requires a slow titration due to the risk of a severe rash. Do not use for acute mania.
- **Valproate/Valproic Acid Derivatives (Depakote, Depacon*, Depakene*)**
- **Carbamazepine (Equetro)**

Brand discontinued but name still used in practice.

SECOND-GENERATION ANTIPSYCHOTICS

Antipsychotics can be used alone or in combination with one of the traditional mood stabilizers. A major concern with antipsychotics is the risk of extrapyramidal symptoms (EPS). The first-generation antipsychotics (e.g., haloperidol) have a higher incidence of EPS than SGAs, so SGAs are preferred. The following are the more common SGAs that can be used alone or in combination with mood stabilizers for acute mania and/or maintenance treatment:

- **Aripiprazole (Abilify, Abilify Maintena)**
- **Olanzapine (Zyprexa, Zyprexa Relprevv, Zyprexa Zydis)**
- **Quetiapine (Seroquel, Seroquel XR)**
- **Risperidone (Risperdal, Risperdal Consta, Perseris)**
- **Ziprasidone (Geodon)**

Other common SGAs used for bipolar disorders include:

- **Lurasidone (Latuda):** can use alone or in combination with mood stabilizers for bipolar depressive episodes.
- Olanzapine/Fluoxetine (Symbyax): can use alone for acute depressive episodes.

See the Schizophrenia/Psychosis chapter for a detailed review of the SGAs.

LITHIUM

Lithium is proposed to work by influencing the reuptake of serotonin and/or norepinephrine or by moderating glutamate levels in the brain. Glutamate is the primary excitatory neurotransmitter, so high levels could cause mania.

DRUG	DOSING	SAFETY/SIDE EFFECTS/MONITORING
Lithium (Lithobid) Tablet, capsule, syrup	Start: 300-900 mg/day, divided BID-TID Usual range: 900-1,800 mg/day, divided BID-TID Extended-release: take BID Titrate slowly, as tolerated Take with or after meals to reduce nausea **Therapeutic Range** 0.6-1.2 mEq/L (trough level) Acute mania may require up to 1.5 mEq/L initially	**BOXED WARNING** Serum lithium levels should be monitored to avoid toxicity **WARNINGS** Renal impairment, hyponatremia and dehydration (↑ lithium toxicity) Serotonin syndrome (see Drug Interactions) **SIDE EFFECTS** **Within therapeutic range:** GI upset (nausea/diarrhea), cognitive effects, cogwheel rigidity, fine hand tremor, thirst, polyuria/polydipsia, weight gain, hypothyroidism, hypercalcemia, cardiac abnormalities, edema, anorexia, worsening psoriasis, blue-gray skin pigmentation, impotence **Toxicity:** > 1.5 mEq/L: ataxia, coarse hand tremor, vomiting, persistent diarrhea, confusion, sedation > 2.5 mEq/L: CNS depression, arrhythmia, seizure, coma **MONITORING** Serum lithium levels, renal function, thyroid function (TSH, FT4), electrolytes (calcium, potassium, sodium) **NOTES** Renally cleared; no CYP450 interactions Avoid in pregnancy; associated with cardiac malformations in first trimester; avoid in breastfeeding

Lithium Drug Interactions

- Lithium levels ↑ with:

    - ↓ salt intake, sodium loss (e.g., with ACE inhibitors, ARBs, thiazide diuretics)

    - NSAIDs: aspirin and sulindac are safer options

- Lithium levels ↓ with:

    - ↑ salt intake, caffeine and theophylline

- ↑ risk of serotonin syndrome if lithium is taken with:

    - SSRIs, SNRIs, triptans, linezolid and other serotonergic drugs (see Drug Interactions chapter)

- ↑ risk of neurotoxicity (e.g., ataxia, tremors, nausea) if lithium is taken with:

    - Verapamil, diltiazem, phenytoin and carbamazepine

CONVERTING BETWEEN LITHIUM FORMULATIONS

5 mL lithium citrate syrup = 8 mEq of lithium ion

8 mEq of lithium ion = 300 mg lithium carbonate tabs/caps

CASE SCENARIO

A patient is taking 450 mg lithium carbonate BID, but reports difficulty swallowing the capsules. How many milliliters of lithium citrate syrup should be given for each dose? (Round to the nearest TENTH.)

Determine how many milliequivalents of lithium are required for each dose.

$$\frac{300 \text{ mg lithium carbonate}}{8 \text{ mEq lithium ion}} = \frac{450 \text{ mg lithium carbonate}}{X \text{ mEq lithium ion}}$$

$$X = 12 \text{ mEq lithium ion}$$

Next determine how many milliliters of lithium citrate syrup are required.

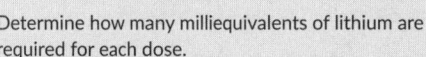

$$\frac{12 \text{ mEq}}{X \text{ mL}} = \frac{8 \text{ mEq}}{5 \text{ mL}}$$

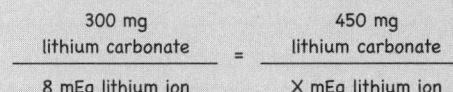

7.5 mL of lithium citrate syrup per dose

This problem can also be solved using the milliequivalent formula. Refer to the Calculations II chapter for additional examples.

KEY COUNSELING POINTS

See the Drug Formulations and Patient Counseling chapter for counseling language/layman's terminology.

LITHIUM

- Take with food or at end of meal to reduce nausea.

- Maintain consistent salt intake. Changes in salt intake can alter lithium levels in the body.

- Maintain adequate hydration with non-caffeinated fluids.

- Avoid dehydration (e.g., excessive sweating, diarrhea, vomiting and prolonged heat/sun exposure). Can increase lithium levels and side effects.

- Avoid in pregnancy/breastfeeding.

- Notify healthcare provider immediately for worsening nausea or diarrhea, slurred speech or confusion.

- Can impair alertness, use caution while driving or during other tasks requiring you to be alert.

Select Guidelines/References

Diagnostic and Statistical Manual of Mental Disorders, Fifth Edition (DSM-5). Arlington VA, American Psychiatric Association, 2013.

Bobo WV. The Diagnosis and Management of Bipolar I and II Disorders: Clinical Practice Update. Mayo Clin Proc. 2017;92(10):1532-1551.

WFSBP: Update 2012 on the long-term treatment of bipolar disorder. The World Journal of Biological Psychiatry. 2013;14:154–219.

APA, Treatment of Patients with Bipolar Disorder. http://psychiatryonline.org/pb/assets/raw/sitewide/practice_guidelines/guidelines/bipolar.pdf (accessed 2022 Feb 17).

© iStock.com/Slphotography

CHAPTER 66

ATTENTION DEFICIT HYPERACTIVITY DISORDER (ADHD)

BACKGROUND

ADHD is the most common neurodevelopmental disorder in children, occurring almost twice as often in boys compared to girls. This is a chronic illness that frequently continues to cause symptoms throughout adolescence and adulthood.

ADHD is characterized by symptoms of inattention, hyperactivity and impulsivity. Patients often have difficulty focusing, are easily distracted, have trouble staying still and are frequently unable to control impulsive behavior. The primary presenting symptoms can vary; some individuals are more inattentive, and others are more impulsive. With increasing age, inattention and impulsivity can remain, and hyperactivity can decrease.

Defects in the dopamine pathways that regulate reward anticipation and emotional self-regulation can play a role in ADHD. This is why the primary focus of ADHD research is on the catecholamine system (dopamine is metabolized to epinephrine and norepinephrine). The primary treatment for ADHD is stimulant medications (e.g., methylphenidate, amphetamine) because they raise dopamine and norepinephrine levels.

Treatment of ADHD includes a combination of medication and behavioral therapy. The decision to medicate should be weighed against the risks, especially in young children. A child with untreated ADHD can have impaired academic standing, poor social skills and risky behavior. Medications are beneficial, but they have side effects. For this reason, first-line treatment for preschool aged children (age 4 – 5 years) is parent training in behavior management and/or behavioral classroom intervention. Methylphenidate can be considered if moderate-severe symptoms persist despite behavioral interventions.

ADHD medications are considered first line in patients ≥ 6 years old and should be used with behavioral interventions when available.

DIAGNOSTIC CRITERIA

The Diagnostic and Statistical Manual of Mental Disorders (DSM-5) provides definitions and diagnostic criteria for various mental disorders. The DSM-5 diagnostic criteria for ADHD are based on an assessment of the primary symptoms, inattention and/or hyperactivity and impulsivity, as described below.

INATTENTION

≥ 6 symptoms of inattention for children up to age 16 (≥ 5 symptoms for ages 17 and older); symptoms must have been present for at least 6 months and are inappropriate for the developmental level.

Symptoms:
Fails to pay attention, has trouble holding attention, does not pay attention when someone is talking, does not follow through on instructions, fails to finish schoolwork, has difficulty organizing tasks, avoids or dislikes tasks which require mental effort, loses things, is easily distracted, is forgetful.

HYPERACTIVITY & IMPULSIVITY

≥ 6 symptoms of hyperactivity-impulsivity for children up to age 16 (≥ 5 symptoms for ages 17 and older); symptoms must have been present for at least 6 months and are inappropriate for the developmental level.

Symptoms:
Often fidgets or squirms, leaves seat unexpectedly, runs about when not appropriate, unable to play quietly, is "on the go" as if "driven by a motor," talks excessively, blurts out answers, has trouble waiting his/her turn, interrupts or intrudes on others.

THE FOLLOWING CONDITIONS MUST BE MET:

■ Several inattentive or hyperactive-impulsive symptoms were present before age 12.

■ Symptoms must have been present in 2 or more settings (e.g., at home, school, work, with friends, relatives or babysitters).

■ Symptoms interfere with functioning and are not caused by another disorder.

NATURAL PRODUCTS

Fish oils are increasingly used for various psychiatric conditions and have been shown to modestly improve cognitive function and behavior in children with ADHD. Melatonin is used to help with sleep onset in individuals taking stimulants.

DRUG TREATMENT

Stimulants are the first-line medications for ADHD. Some stimulant medications come in formulations that are easier for children to swallow (see Study Tip Gal to the right) or more difficult to abuse. Long-acting formulations are preferred for children, to help maintain more steady symptom control and avoid the need for a dose during the day at school.

Atomoxetine (*Strattera*), a non-stimulant medication, can be tried when stimulants do not work well enough (after trials of 2 – 3 medications). *Strattera* can be used first line when prescribers are concerned about the possibility of abuse by the patient or family.

Guanfacine ER (*Intuniv*) and clonidine ER (*Kapvay*) are non-stimulant medications that can be used alone or in combination with stimulants.

Almost all ADHD medications are approved for use in adults and children ≥ 6 years of age, with a few exceptions, as noted in the drug tables in this chapter.

PATIENT-FRIENDLY FORMULATIONS FOR STIMULANTS

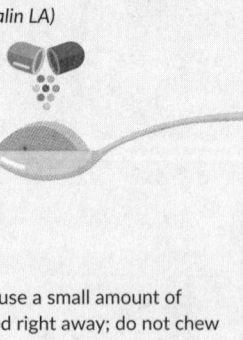

Young children (and others) who cannot swallow capsules or tablets can use these long-acting formulations:

■ Capsule

❑ Some capsule contents can be sprinkled on a small amount of applesauce (e.g., *Adderall XR, Ritalin LA*)

❑ *Vyvanse* capsule contents can be mixed in water, orange juice or yogurt

■ Chewable tablet

■ Orally-disintegrating tablet

■ Patch

■ Suspension

When putting capsule contents in food, use a small amount of food (do not warm the food). Eat the food right away; do not chew the beads.

PSYCHIATRIC CONDITIONS

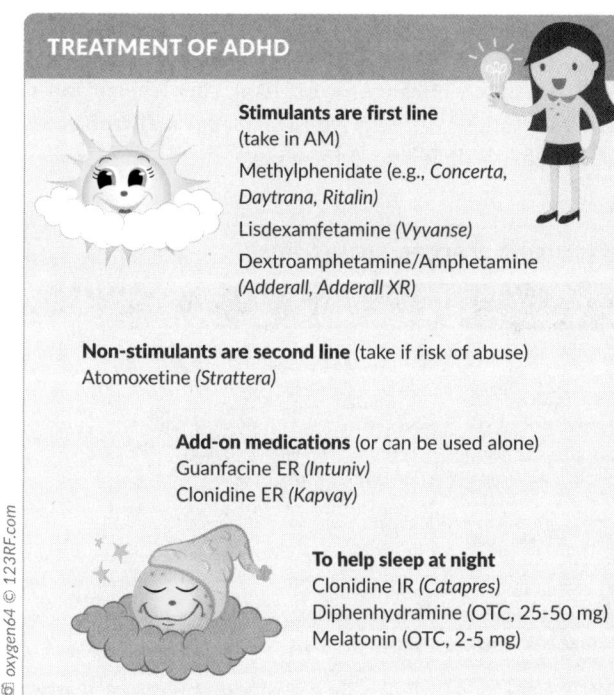

TREATMENT OF ADHD

Stimulants are first line (take in AM)
Methylphenidate (e.g., *Concerta, Daytrana, Ritalin*)
Lisdexamfetamine (*Vyvanse*)
Dextroamphetamine/Amphetamine (*Adderall, Adderall XR*)

Non-stimulants are second line (take if risk of abuse)
Atomoxetine (*Strattera*)

Add-on medications (or can be used alone)
Guanfacine ER (*Intuniv*)
Clonidine ER (*Kapvay*)

To help sleep at night
Clonidine IR (*Catapres*)
Diphenhydramine (OTC, 25-50 mg)
Melatonin (OTC, 2-5 mg)

© oxygen64 © 123RF.com

STIMULANT SAFETY CONCERNS

All stimulants are C-II medications and must be dispensed with a MedGuide. The Boxed Warnings, Contraindications and Warnings discussed on this page are common to most stimulant drugs and will not be repeated in the stimulant drug tables that follow. Additional safety issues unique to specific products are noted in the drug tables.

Boxed Warnings

Stimulant medications have a high potential for abuse and dependence. Risk for abuse (e.g., history of alcohol or drug abuse) should be assessed prior to dispensing. Symptoms of abuse (e.g., dilated pupils, increased heart rate and blood pressure, sweating, tremor, anxiety) should be monitored during treatment. When abused long-term, tolerance and psychological dependence can occur, with varying degrees of abnormal behavior (including psychotic episodes when injected). When withdrawing treatment from someone abusing a stimulant, severe depression can occur.

Contraindications

- Do not use within 14 days of an MAO inhibitor due to the risk of hypertensive crisis when used together.
- Due to the risk of cardiovascular events, some stimulants are contraindicated with comorbid heart failure, recent myocardial infarction, arrhythmias or moderate-severe hypertension.
- Most stimulants are contraindicated in patients with marked anxiety, tension, agitation, glaucoma, hyperthyroidism, or a history of Tourette's syndrome or other tic disorders.

Warnings

- Increased levels of dopamine and norepinephrine can increase heart rate and blood pressure. This can cause serious cardiovascular events in children and adults with or without preexisting cardiac disease. Assess for cardiac disease at baseline and avoid stimulants when cardiac abnormalities are present, due to an increased risk of sudden death.
- Other vascular problems (e.g., priapism, Raynaud's disease) can occur and may require a dose reduction or discontinuation.
- New-onset psychosis or mania, or an exacerbation of preexisting psychosis (e.g., a mixed/manic episode in bipolar disorder) can occur. Caution should be used when prescribing stimulants in patients with a preexisting psychiatric condition.
- Some stimulants can lower the seizure threshold, which increases the risk for seizures.
- A loss of appetite is common. This is especially concerning in children, as it can contribute to a decrease in the child's growth trajectory.
- The risk of serotonin syndrome is increased when stimulants are used in combination with other serotonergic drugs (e.g., SSRIs, SNRIs, TCAs, buspirone). Refer to the Drug Interactions chapter.
- Visual disturbances (e.g., difficulty with accommodation and blurry vision) can occur.

STIMULANTS

Stimulants <u>block</u> the <u>reuptake</u> of <u>norepinephrine</u> and <u>dopamine</u>; they are highly effective for ADHD and are recommended <u>first line</u>. Most stimulants are dosed every morning (IR products and some others can be given in divided doses) with doses <u>titrated up every seven days</u>, as needed, to reduce adverse effects. Stimulants <u>do not need to be tapered off</u> when used as directed (i.e., not abused).

DRUG	DOSING	SAFETY/SIDE EFFECTS/MONITORING
Methylphenidate		
IR tablet: *Ritalin* IR oral solution: *Methylin* IR chewable tablet	<u>Start 5 mg BID</u>, 30 min before breakfast and lunch Max: 60 mg/day	See Stimulant Safety Concerns **WARNINGS** *Daytrana*: loss of skin pigmentation at application site and areas distant from the application site (can resemble vitiligo); allergic contact dermatitis with local reactions (e.g., edema, papules) *Concerta*: do not use with GI narrowing conditions (e.g., motility issues, small bowel disease)
ER tablet: *Concerta* (<u>OROS delivery</u>)	*Concerta*: <u>start 18-36 mg QAM</u> Max: 72 mg/day	
ER capsule: *Ritalin LA, Adhansia XR, Aptensio XR, Jornay PM*	*Ritalin LA*: start 10-20 mg QAM *Aptensio XR*: start 10 mg QAM Max: 60 mg/day *Adhansia XR*: start 25 mg QAM *Jornay PM*: start 20 mg <u>QPM</u> Max: 100 mg/day	**SIDE EFFECTS** <u>Insomnia, ↓ appetite/weight loss, headache, irritability</u>, nausea/vomiting, blurry vision, dry mouth **MONITORING** Consider <u>ECG prior</u> to treatment; <u>monitor BP and HR</u>, cardiac symptoms, CNS effects, abuse potential and <u>height and weight</u> (children)
ER oral suspension: *Quillivant XR* ER chewable tablet: *QuilliChew ER*	Start 20 mg QAM Start 20 mg QAM Max: 60 mg/day	**NOTES** *Concerta* <u>OROS delivery</u>: the <u>outer coat dissolves fast</u> to provide immediate action, and the <u>rest is released slowly</u>; can see a <u>ghost tablet</u> in stool; harder to crush, which <u>decreases abuse potential</u> *Jornay <u>PM</u>*: outer coating delays initial drug release 10 hours to allow for <u>evening dosing</u>; inner coating controls the slow release of the drug during the day
ER orally-disintegrating tablet: *Cotempla XR-ODT*	Start 17.3 mg QAM for ages 6-17 years Max: 51.8 mg/day	*Daytrana*: apply <u>2 hrs before desired effect</u> (or as soon as the child awakens so it starts to deliver prior to school); <u>remove after 9 hrs</u>; <u>alternate hips daily</u>
Transdermal patch: *Daytrana*	Start 10 mg/9 hr patch <u>QAM</u> Max: 30 mg/9 hr	Chewable tablets: contain phenylalanine (avoid with PKU)
Dexmethylphenidate		
Dexmethylphenidate (*Focalin, Focalin XR*) IR tablet, ER capsule	IR: start 2.5 mg BID, given at least 4 hrs apart Max: 20 mg/day ER: start 5 mg (children) or 10 mg (adults) QAM Max: 30 mg/day (children) or 40 mg/day (adults)	See Stimulant Safety Concerns **NOTES** <u>Active isomer of methylphenidate</u>; to convert from methylphenidate to dexmethylphenidate use one-half of the total daily dose of methylphenidate Serdexmethylphenidate: prodrug to dexmethylphenidate, provides extended duration of action following faster-acting dexmethylphenidate
Serdexmethylphenidate/Dexmethylphenidate (*Azstarys*) Capsule	Start 39.2 mg/7.8 mg QAM Max: 52.3 mg/10.4 mg daily	

PSYCHIATRIC CONDITIONS

DRUG	DOSING	SAFETY/SIDE EFFECTS/MONITORING
Amphetamine, Dextroamphetamine and Combinations		
Dextroamphetamine/Amphetamine		See Stimulant Safety Concerns
IR tablet: **Adderall**	Start 5 mg QAM or BID, with 2nd dose 4-6 hrs after 1st dose	**BOXED WARNINGS** Misuse can cause sudden death and serious CV events
	Max: 40 mg/day	**NOTES** IR products approved for children ≥ 3 years of age (except *Evekeo ODT*)
ER capsules: **Adderall XR,** *Mydayis*	Start 5-10 mg (6-12 yrs), 10 mg (13-17 yrs) or 10-20 mg (adults) QAM	AAP guidelines do not recommend dextroamphetamine in children ≤ 5 years of age
	Max: 30 mg/day (children) or 60 mg/day (adults)	ER formulations cannot be substituted for other amphetamine products on a mg-per-mg basis; follow dosing schedule provided by manufacturer
Amphetamine ER orally-disintegrating tablet: *Adzenys XR-ODT*	*Adzenys XR-ODT:* start 6.3 mg (children) or 12.5 mg (adults) QAM	Conversion from *Adderall XR* to *Adzenys XR-ODT:* use 3.1 mg for each 5 mg dose of *Adderall XR*
	Max: varies based on age	*Dyanavel XR:* shake suspension prior to use
ER oral suspension: *Dyanavel XR*	*Dyanavel XR:* start 2.5-5 mg QAM	Do not take with acidic foods such as juice or vitamin C (↓ absorption)
	Max: 20 mg/day	
IR tablet: *Evekeo* IR orally-disintegrating tablet: *Evekeo ODT*	*Evekeo* and *Evekeo ODT:* start 5 mg QAM or BID, with 2nd dose 4-6 hrs after 1st dose (6-17 yrs)	
	Max: 40 mg/day	
Dextroamphetamine ER capsule: *Dexedrine* IR oral solution: *ProCentra* IR tablet: *Zenzedi*	All formulations: start 5 mg QAM or BID, with 2nd dose 4-6 hrs after 1st dose Max: 40 mg/day	
Lisdexamfetamine (prodrug of dextroamphetamine)		
Lisdexamfetamine (Vyvanse) Capsule, chewable tablet	Start 20-30 mg (children) or 30 mg (adults) QAM Max: 70 mg/day	See Stimulant Safety Concerns **NOTES** Low abuse potential; prodrug composed of l-lysine (amino acid) bonded to dextroamphetamine; it is hydrolyzed in the blood to active dextroamphetamine; if injected or snorted, the fast effect (rush) is muted
Methamphetamine		
Methamphetamine *(Desoxyn)* Tablet	Start 5 mg QAM or BID Max: 20-25 mg daily	See Stimulant Safety Concerns

NON-STIMULANTS

These medications are used <u>second line</u> after trials of <u>stimulant medications</u> have <u>failed</u>. They can be used first line if the prescriber is concerned about <u>abuse potential</u>. Non-stimulant medications for ADHD are not controlled and therefore do not have the same potential for abuse and dependence as stimulants. Clonidine and guanfacine are antihypertensive drugs and are marketed in longer-acting formulations for ADHD (clonidine IR can still be used to help with sleep). Viloxazine *(Qelbree)* is a new selective norepinephrine reuptake inhibitor FDA-approved for ADHD treatment in pediatric patients 6 – 17 years of age.

DRUG	DOSING	SAFETY/SIDE EFFECTS/MONITORING
Selective Norepinephrine Reuptake Inhibitor		
Atomoxetine *(Strattera)* Capsule	> 70 kg: start 40 mg daily ≤ 70 kg: start 0.5 mg/kg/day Max: 100 mg/day Can take in divided doses if needed (morning and late afternoon/early evening) Strong CYP450 2D6 inhibitors (e.g., paroxetine): max dose is 80 mg daily	**BOXED WARNINGS** Risk of <u>suicidal ideation</u>; monitor for suicidal thinking or behavior, worsening mood, or unusual behavior **CONTRAINDICATIONS** <u>MAO inhibitor use within the past 14 days</u>, glaucoma, pheochromocytoma, severe cardiovascular disorders **WARNINGS** Aggressive behavior, treatment-emergent psychotic or manic symptoms, orthostasis and syncope, allergic reactions, priapism, urinary hesitancy and retention Rare but severe hepatotoxicity (most often within 120 days of starting treatment) Serious cardiovascular events; assess at baseline and as needed during treatment and avoid use if known cardiac disease Projected height and weight can be reduced in children **SIDE EFFECTS** ↓ appetite, insomnia, somnolence, dry mouth, hypertension, tachycardia, headache, nausea, abdominal pain, erectile dysfunction, ↓ libido **MONITORING** BP, HR, ECG, mood, height and weight (children) **NOTES** Do not open the capsule – ocular irritant
Central Alpha-2A Adrenergic Receptor Agonists		
Clonidine ER *(Kapvay)* Tablet **Clonidine IR** *(Catapres*)* – for hypertension	Start 0.1 mg <u>QHS</u>, increase by 0.1 mg weekly Max: 0.4 mg/day Take BID; if uneven dosing take the higher dose QHS	**WARNINGS** <u>Dose-dependent cardiovascular effects</u> (bradycardia, hypotension, orthostasis, syncope), <u>sedation and drowsiness</u> <u>Do not discontinue abruptly</u> (can cause <u>rebound hypertension</u>) Guanfacine: skin rash (rare, discontinue if occurs); dose adjustments required with CYP3A4 inducers and inhibitors (see Drug Interactions section) **SIDE EFFECTS** Dry mouth, somnolence, fatigue, dizziness, constipation, ↓ HR, hypotension, headache, nausea, abdominal pain
Guanfacine ER *(Intuniv)* Tablet IR tablet – for hypertension	Start 1 mg <u>daily</u> and increase by ≤ 1 mg weekly Max: varies based on age Do not take with high-fat meal (↑ absorption)	**MONITORING** BP, HR **NOTES** <u>Must be tapered</u> off to decrease the risk of rebound hypertension: decrease dose (≤ 0.1 mg/day for clonidine and ≤ 1 mg/day for guanfacine) every 3-7 days Do not substitute IR clonidine or guanfacine for ER formulations

*Brand discontinued but name still used in practice.

Atomoxetine Drug Interactions

- Atomoxetine is a CYP2D6 substrate; CYP2D6 inducers or inhibitors can necessitate a change in atomoxetine dose.

Clonidine and Guanfacine Drug Interactions

- Watch for additive sedation when used in combination with other CNS depressants.

- Use caution with other drugs that decrease blood pressure and heart rate (e.g., beta-blockers, non-DHP CCBs).

- Guanfacine:

  - Double the dose if used with strong CYP3A4 inducers.

  - Decrease the dose by 50% if used with strong CYP3A4 inhibitors.

KEY COUNSELING POINTS

See the Drug Formulations and Patient Counseling chapter for counseling language/layman's terminology and formulation-specific administration instructions.

STIMULANTS

- MedGuide required.
- Can cause:
  - Increased heart rate and blood pressure
  - Serious cardiovascular events
  - Insomnia
  - Psychosis
  - Priapism
- Decreased appetite: eat a larger breakfast to prevent weight loss; check height and weight regularly in children.
- Ghost tablet in stool *(Concerta)*.
- Some formulations contain phenylalanine. Do not use if you have phenylketonuria (PKU).

ATOMOXETINE

- MedGuide required.
- Can cause:
  - Liver damage
  - Suicidal ideation
  - Somnolence

Select Guidelines/References

Diagnostic and Statistical Manual of Mental Disorders, Fifth Edition. Arlington, VA, American Psychiatric Association, 2013.

Clinical Practice Guideline for the Diagnosis, Evaluation, and Treatment of Attention-Deficit/Hyperactivity Disorder in Children and Adolescents. Pediatrics 2019;144 (4):1-19.

SELECT DRUGS THAT CAUSE ANXIETY

Albuterol (if used too frequently or incorrectly)

Antipsychotics (e.g., aripiprazole, haloperidol)

Bupropion

Caffeine, in high doses

Decongestants (e.g., pseudoephedrine)

Illicit drugs (e.g., cocaine, LSD, methamphetamine)

Levothyroxine (if therapeutic overdose occurs)

Steroids

Stimulants (e.g., amphetamine, methylphenidate)

Theophylline

CONTENT LEGEND

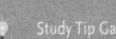 Study Tip Gal    Key Drug Guy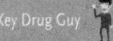

iStock.com/Malombra76

CHAPTER 67
ANXIETY DISORDERS

BACKGROUND

The general population can experience occasional anxiety when faced with challenging issues at work, home or school. The symptoms of occasional anxiety (fear, worry) and any physical symptoms (tachycardia, palpitations, shortness of breath, stomach upset, chest pain or other pain, insomnia or fatigue) resolve once the issue is gone.

With an anxiety disorder, the symptoms are chronic, severe and cause great distress. The disorder can interfere with the ability to do well at school or work and can harm relationships. The major types of anxiety disorders are generalized anxiety disorder (GAD), panic disorder (PD) and social anxiety disorder (SAD). Other disorders that have symptoms of anxiety include obsessive compulsive disorder (OCD) and posttraumatic stress disorder (PTSD). These are classified differently by the Diagnostic and Statistical Manual of Mental Disorders, Fifth Edition (DSM-5). OCD is categorized as "obsessive-compulsive and related disorders," and PTSD is categorized under "trauma and stressor-related disorders."

NON-DRUG TREATMENT

Patients with an anxiety disorder should be assessed for comorbid conditions (e.g., hyperthyroidism) or medications that could be contributing to the problem (see Key Drugs Guy). Comorbid conditions should be treated and medications that worsen anxiety should be discontinued if possible.

Lifestyle changes can improve symptoms. Increasing physical activity, helping others, community involvement, yoga and meditation are some of the methods that can reduce stress. Cognitive Behavioral Therapy (CBT) is a type of mental health treatment in which a trained clinician helps the patient explore patterns of thinking that lead to problem-solving, relaxation techniques, worry exposure and more. In some cases, CBT provides adequate relief without the need for chronic medications.

NATURAL PRODUCTS

Some natural products may provide benefit when treating anxiety, but their use is generally limited by safety issues. St. John's wort, used for depression and anxiety, is a strong CYP3A4 inducer and can decrease the concentration of other medications. St. John's wort also causes photosensitivity and is serotonergic, which increases the risk of serotonin syndrome when used in combination with other serotonergic medications. Valerian is used for anxiety and sleep, but some products may be contaminated with liver toxins; if used, liver function should be monitored. Passionflower appears to be safe and is rated as "possibly effective" by the *Natural Medicines Database*. Kava is a relaxant, but it can cause severe liver damage and is not recommended.

DRUG TREATMENT

A number of medications can be used long-term to manage anxiety. Some antidepressants are FDA-approved for anxiety and other drugs are used off-label. The selection of a drug is based on both the efficacy and the risk of adverse effects. The table below summarizes the first and second-line options to consider. Benzodiazepines (BZDs) should only be used short-term and are discussed in-depth later in the chapter.

Drugs Used for Anxiety

DRUG/DRUG CLASS	COMMENTS
First-Line: selective serotonin reuptake inhibitors (SSRIs) and serotonin and norepinephrine reuptake inhibitors (SNRIs)	
Escitalopram (*Lexapro*) **Fluoxetine (*Prozac*)** **Paroxetine (*Paxil*, Paxil CR, Pexeva)** **Sertraline (*Zoloft*)** **Duloxetine (*Cymbalta*, Drizalma Sprinkle)** **Venlafaxine XR (*Effexor XR*)**	Start at half the initial dose used for depression and slowly titrate to minimize anxiousness and jitteriness (common during the first couple of weeks) Will not provide immediate relief; takes at least four weeks at higher doses for a noticeable effect Other SSRIs and SNRIs may be used off-label for anxiety disorder Refer to the Depression chapter for more information on antidepressants
Second-Line	
Buspirone	Can use in combination with antidepressants (e.g., when there is a poor response) Considered a more favorable add-on medication than benzodiazepines in elderly patients (less sedating) or if there is a risk for benzodiazepine abuse Does not provide immediate relief; takes 2-4 weeks for effect
Tricyclic Antidepressants **Amitriptyline** **Nortriptyline (*Pamelor*)** Imipramine	Not FDA-approved for anxiety Risk of adverse effects (e.g., anticholinergic side effects) limit use (see the Depression chapter)
Hydroxyzine (Vistaril)	Sedating antihistamine with anticholinergic activity FDA-approved for anxiety but does not treat the underlying condition Should not be used long-term; use only short-term, as needed, as an alternative to benzodiazepines See the Common Skin Conditions chapter for more information
Pregabalin (*Lyrica*, Lyrica CR) C-V **Gabapentin (*Neurontin*, Gralise)**	Not FDA-approved for anxiety but has shown benefit in patients with anxiety and neuropathic pain Has immediate anxiolytic effects similar to benzodiazepines
Special Situations	
Propranolol (*Inderal LA, Inderal XL*, others)	Not FDA-approved for anxiety but can reduce symptoms of stage fright or performance anxiety (e.g., tremor, tachycardia) Dose: 10-40 mg one hour prior to an event (such as a public speech) Can cause CNS side effects (e.g., dizziness, confusion) See Hypertension chapter for more information

BUSPIRONE

The mechanism of action of buspirone is unknown, but its effects may be due to its affinity for <u>5-HT1A and 5-HT2 receptors</u>.

DRUG	DOSING	SAFETY/SIDE EFFECTS/MONITORING
Buspirone Tablet	Start 7.5 mg PO BID Can increase by 5 mg/day every 2-3 days, to a max dose of 30 mg PO BID Take with or without food, but must be consistent	**CONTRAINDICATIONS** <u>Do not use with MAO inhibitors</u> (or within 14 days of discontinuation), linezolid or IV methylene blue **WARNINGS** Risk of <u>serotonin syndrome</u> alone or in combination with other serotonergic drugs **SIDE EFFECTS** Dizziness, drowsiness, headache, lightheadedness, nausea, excitement **NOTES** <u>No potential for abuse, tolerance or physiological dependence</u> When switching from a benzodiazepine to buspirone, the benzodiazepine must be tapered off slowly Avoid use in severe kidney or liver impairment

Buspirone Drug Interactions

- Risk of <u>serotonin syndrome</u> is ↑ when used in combination with other serotonergic drugs. See the Drug Interactions chapter.

- Avoid grapefruit and grapefruit juice as they may ↑ buspirone levels.

- Buspirone is a major substrate of CYP3A4.

  ❏ Decrease the dose if used in combination with moderate and strong CYP3A4 inhibitors (e.g., erythromycin, diltiazem, verapamil, itraconazole).

  ❏ An increase in the buspirone dose may be required with CYP3A4 inducers (e.g., rifampin).

BENZODIAZEPINES

- BZDs <u>enhance</u> gamma aminobutyric acid (<u>GABA</u>), an <u>inhibitory neurotransmitter</u>. This causes CNS depression, resulting in anxiolytic, anticonvulsant, sedative and/or muscle relaxant properties.

- They provide <u>fast relief</u> of symptoms (antidepressants have a longer onset of action), but they do not treat the underlying causes of anxiety.

- BZDs can be useful for <u>short-term</u> treatment of <u>acute anxiety</u> that is preventing restful sleep and disrupting life. This can be due to the recent death of a loved one, a natural disaster or another stressful situation.

- If taken long-term, patients can become addicted to BZDs and develop tolerance. Due to the risk of <u>dependence</u>, they should only be used for <u>1 – 2 weeks</u> and then <u>discontinued</u>. If used for longer periods of time, they must be <u>tapered off slowly</u> to <u>prevent withdrawal</u> symptoms.

- <u>Beers Criteria</u>: BZDs are <u>potentially inappropriate</u> in patients ≥ 65 years old. BZDs have a high risk of <u>confusion</u>, <u>dizziness and falls</u> in the <u>elderly</u>, which is <u>increased</u> if used with other <u>CNS depressants</u>. The elderly also have a higher risk of having a "paradoxical" reaction (hyperactivity, aggression, agitation). If a BZD is used in an elderly patient, the <u>L-O-T drugs</u> (see <u>Study Tip Gal</u>) are preferred due to the lower risk of adverse reactions.

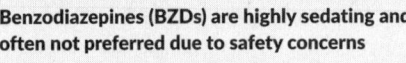

SAFE USE OF BENZODIAZEPINES

Benzodiazepines (BZDs) are highly sedating and often not preferred due to safety concerns

Anxiety
- Most anxiety is due to depression; SSRIs and SNRIs are preferred
- If used, consider a BZD with a longer half-life and less risk of abuse (e.g., clonazepam, lorazepam, diazepam)

Sleep
- First-line: non-pharmacologic treatment
- Second-line: non-BZD hypnotics, like zolpidem (fewer safety issues than BZDs)
- If used, consider temazepam

Elderly or Patients with Liver Impairment
- If used, consider BZDs that undergo glucuronidation; **L-O-T** drugs (**L**orazepam, **O**xazepam, **T**emazepam)

Seizures
- Injectable BZDs or diazepam rectal gel (*Diastat AcuDial*); diazepam rectal gel can be administered by a caregiver at home

DRUG	DOSING	SAFETY/SIDE EFFECTS/MONITORING
Alprazolam (Xanax, Xanax XR, Alprazolam Intensol) Tablet, ODT, oral solution	0.25-0.5 mg PO TID	**BOXED WARNING** Use with opioids can result in sedation, respiratory depression, coma and death Risk for abuse, misuse and addiction, which can lead to overdose or death Continued use can lead to physical dependence; abrupt discontinuation can cause withdrawal symptoms (taper off slowly)
Clonazepam (Klonopin) Tablet, ODT	0.25-0.5 mg PO BID	**CONTRAINDICATIONS** Acute narrow-angle glaucoma, sleep apnea, severe respiratory insufficiency, severe liver disease (clonazepam and diazepam), myasthenia gravis (diazepam), not for use in infants < 6 months of age (diazepam oral), premature infants (lorazepam parenteral products)
Diazepam (Valium, Diastat AcuDial, Diazepam Intensol) Tablet, injection, oral solution, rectal gel, intranasal	2-10 mg PO BID-QID	**WARNINGS** CNS depression, anterograde amnesia, potential for abuse, safety risks in patients age 65 years and older (impaired cognition, delirium, falls/fractures), extravasation with IV use, paradoxical reactions, severe renal or hepatic impairment Pregnancy: crosses placenta; can cause birth defects and neonatal withdrawal syndrome
Lorazepam (Ativan, Lorazepam Intensol, Loreev XR) Tablet, injection, oral solution	2-3 mg PO daily in divided doses	
Chlordiazepoxide Capsule	5-25 mg TID-QID	**SIDE EFFECTS** Somnolence, dizziness, ataxia, weakness, lightheadedness **NOTES** C-IV
Clorazepate (Tranxene-T) Tablet	30 mg PO daily in divided doses	Diazepam: lipophilic, fast onset, long half-life, high abuse potential Alprazolam: fast onset, often abused due to its quick action Commonly used for alcohol withdrawal syndrome: lorazepam, diazepam, chlordiazepoxide
Oxazepam Capsule	10-30 mg PO TID-QID	Midazolam (Versed) used in acute care (see the Acute & Critical Care Medicine chapter) Antidote: flumazenil (refer to the Toxicology & Antidotes chapter)

Benzodiazepine Drug Interactions

- Additive effects with CNS depressants (e.g., alcohol, anticonvulsants, antihistamines, antipsychotics, opioids, mirtazapine, skeletal muscle relaxants, trazodone).

- Diazepam, clonazepam, chlordiazepoxide and clorazepate: use cautiously with CYP3A4 inhibitors.

- Alprazolam is contraindicated with strong CYP3A4 inhibitors (e.g., ketoconazole, itraconazole). Use caution with moderate CYP3A4 inhibitors.

- Valproate increases the serum concentration of lorazepam.

KEY COUNSELING POINTS

See the Drug Formulations and Patient Counseling chapter for counseling language/layman's terminology.

BUSPIRONE

- The tablets are scored to easily break in half or into thirds.
- Can cause:
  - Dizziness.
  - Drowsiness.
  - Nausea.

BENZODIAZEPINES

- If used regularly for > 10 days, do not stop suddenly. Taper off slowly to avoid withdrawal symptoms (e.g., anxiety, shakiness, fast heart rate, difficulty sleeping, muscle pain).
- To reduce the risk of addiction, do not take doses more frequently or for a longer period than prescribed.
- Can cause drowsiness.

- Do not use with opioid medications (can cause profound sedation, respiratory depression, coma and death).
- Do not use with alcohol (can increase risk of CNS depression).

Select Guidelines/References

American Psychiatric Association: Diagnostic and Statistical Manual of Mental Disorders, Fifth Edition. Arlington VA, American Psychiatric Association, 2013.

Locke AB, Kirst N, Shultz CG. Diagnosis and management of generalized anxiety disorder and panic disorder in adults. Am Fam Physician 2015;91:617-624.

Anxiety and Depression Association of America. Clinical practice review for GAD. Revised 2015. https://adaa.org/resources-professionals/practice-guidelines-gad (accessed 2022 Feb 15).

CONTENT LEGEND

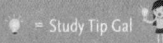 = Study Tip Gal   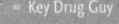 = Key Drug Guy

© iStock.com/OcusFocus

CHAPTER 68

SLEEP DISORDERS

BACKGROUND

There are several types of sleep disorders. This chapter discusses the primary types managed with medications: chronic insomnia, restless legs syndrome (RLS) and narcolepsy. Another common sleep disorder is obstructive sleep apnea, which is primarily treated with non-drug measures, including continuous positive airway pressure (CPAP). A lack of restful sleep contributes to poor health and is linked to the development of a number of chronic conditions, including cardiovascular disease, mood disorders, alcoholism and depression. Patients who chronically use OTC medications for sleep should be referred to a healthcare provider.

INSOMNIA

Insomnia is the most common sleep condition and is characterized by difficulty falling asleep (sleep initiation or sleep latency), reduced sleep duration and/or poor sleep quality (e.g., awakenings after sleep onset). A diagnosis of chronic insomnia occurs when the patient has symptoms at least three times per week for at least three months, despite adequate opportunity to sleep. This often causes daytime impairment, such as being absent from work or experiencing accidents due to fatigue, somnolence, poor memory and decreased concentration.

NON-DRUG TREATMENT

Cognitive behavioral therapy for insomnia (CBT-I) is preferred and includes changes to sleep hygiene that can reduce the need for drugs (see the flow diagram on the following page).

It is important to treat any underlying medical conditions that may be contributing (e.g., pain, shortness of breath due to heart failure, anxiety, bipolar disorder, depression, alcoholism) and discontinue medications that can worsen insomnia (see Key Drugs Guy on next page), if possible.

NATURAL PRODUCTS

Melatonin (3 – 5 mg in the evening) or valerian are used by some patients. Melatonin is also used for jet lag and can cause additive adverse effects (e.g., drowsiness, daytime somnolence) if used with other CNS depressants. It is a substrate of CYP450 1A2, and prolonged effects may be observed with CYP1A2 inhibitors (e.g., ciprofloxacin, fluvoxamine). Valerian is considered to have few adverse risks, but there have been isolated reports of liver toxicity. Kava is another supplement used by patients, but is not recommended due to risk of hepatotoxicity. Drinking chamomile tea in the evening to feel calmer can help some patients with insomnia.

DRUG TREATMENT

Sedative-hypnotics are the mainstay of insomnia treatment, but they are over-prescribed, and there is a concern for adverse effects associated with even occasional use. It is preferable to reserve use for when non-drug treatments have failed, and to select drugs with the best evidence for sleep onset and/or sleep maintenance depending on the problem identified (see diagram below).

SELECT DRUGS THAT CAN WORSEN INSOMNIA

Acetylcholinesterase inhibitors (e.g., donepezil)

Alcohol

Antiretrovirals (e.g., emtricitabine, INSTIs)

Aripiprazole

Atomoxetine

Bupropion

Caffeine

Decongestants (e.g., pseudoephedrine)

Diuretics (due to nocturia)

Fluoxetine, if taken late in the day

Steroids

Stimulants (e.g., methylphenidate, phentermine)

Varenicline

Insomnia Guideline Recommendations

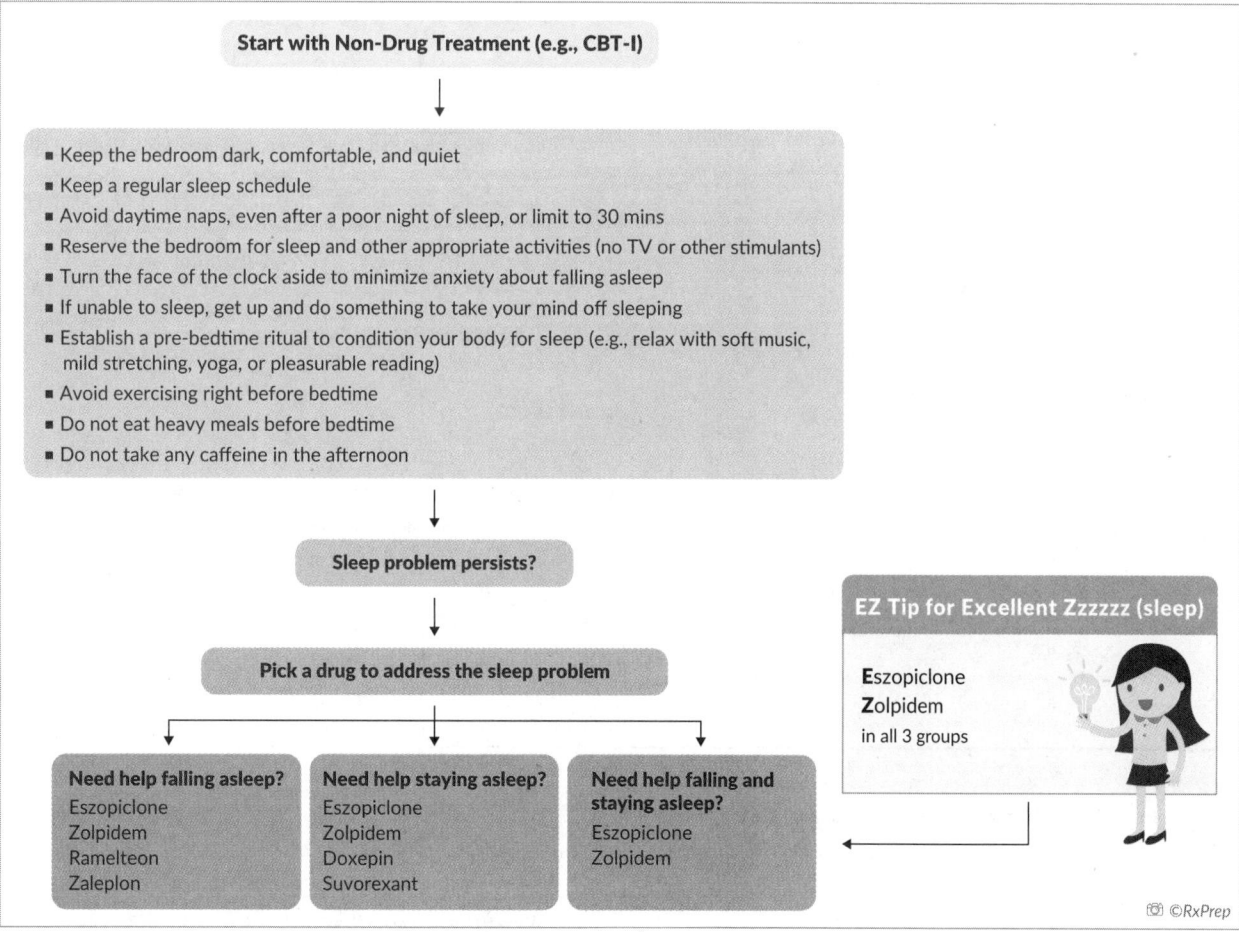

CASE SCENARIO

A retired elderly male presents to his healthcare provider complaining of trouble sleeping. He has a daily routine that includes watching television and napping for much of the day.

Patient Solution: eliminate or reduce napping during the day and try taking a brisk walk earlier in the day, before starting a medication.

In patients using prescription drugs long-term, non-benzodiazepines are preferred over benzodiazepines due to a decreased risk of physical dependence and fewer daytime cognitive effects. The lowest effective dose should be used for all medications to minimize adverse effects, and treatment should be limited to the shortest duration possible.

Patients may self-treat insomnia with OTC first-generation antihistamines, such as diphenhydramine or doxylamine. While these can help short-term, they should not be used long-term for the treatment of insomnia. The American Academy of Sleep Medicine (AASM) guidelines state that the following treatments are not recommended for chronic use: diphenhydramine, melatonin, tiagabine, trazodone and valerian.

Benzodiazepines (e.g., temazepam) can be tried for short-term treatment (such as from acute trauma) if there is no substance abuse history or current use of opioids. According to Beers Criteria, benzodiazepines, non-benzodiazepine hypnotics (e.g., zolpidem) and first-generation antihistamines are considered potentially inappropriate in patients aged 65 years and older. If benzodiazepines are used, lorazepam, oxazepam and temazepam (L-O-T) are preferred in the elderly due to the lower risk of adverse reactions; see the Anxiety Disorders chapter for more details.

Hypnotics

The non-benzodiazepines act selectively at benzodiazepine receptors to increase GABA, an inhibitory neurotransmitter. This causes CNS depression.

DRUG	DOSING	SAFETY/SIDE EFFECTS/MONITORING
Eszopiclone *(Lunesta)* C-IV	1-3 mg PO QHS Start with 1 mg immediately before bed and increase to 2 mg or 3 mg if necessary	**BOXED WARNINGS** Complex sleep behavior (e.g., sleep-walking, sleep-driving and engaging in other activities while not fully awake) can lead to serious injury or death **WARNINGS** ↑ risk of CNS depression and next-day impairment with < 7-8 hours of sleep (especially with higher doses or coadministration of CNS depressants or alcohol), abnormal thinking and behavioral changes (can worsen depression), respiratory depression, increased risk for hazardous sleep-related activities (e.g., sleep-driving)
Zolpidem **Ambien, Ambien CR** IR and ER tablets *Zolpimist* Oral spray (5 mg/spray) **Edluar**, *Intermezzo** SL tablets C-IV	*Ambien, Edluar, Zolpimist* Female/Elderly: 5 mg PO/SL/spray QHS Male: 5-10 mg PO/SL/spray QHS *Ambien CR:* Female/Elderly: 6.25 mg PO QHS Male: 6.25-12.5 mg PO QHS *Intermezzo:* Female/Elderly: 1.75 mg SL QHS Male: 1.75-3.5 mg SL QHS	Potential for abuse and dependence (can cause withdrawal symptoms if used longer than 2 weeks) **CONTRAINDICATIONS** History of complex sleep behavior **SIDE EFFECTS** Somnolence, dizziness, ataxia, headache, can cause parasomnias (unusual actions while sleeping, which the patient may be unaware of), lightheadedness, "pins and needles" feeling on the skin Eszopiclone: dysgeusia (altered sense of taste)
Zaleplon *(Sonata)* C-IV	5-20 mg PO QHS	**NOTES** These are C-IV drugs; there is a risk of physical (physiological) dependence, abuse (addiction) and tolerance Preferred over benzodiazepines for first-line treatment due to ↓ abuse, dependence and tolerance Do not take with fatty food, a heavy meal or alcohol

*Brand discontinued but name still used in practice.

Eszopiclone, Zaleplon and Zolpidem Drug Interactions

- Use caution in combination with potent CYP3A4 inhibitors (e.g., protease inhibitors, ketoconazole, itraconazole, erythromycin and clarithromycin).

- Can cause additive effects when used with other sedating drugs, including most pain medications, muscle relaxants, antihistamines, mirtazapine *(Remeron)*, trazodone and alcohol.

Orexin Receptor Antagonists

The orexin neuropeptide signaling system promotes wakefulness. Orexin receptor antagonists block the orexin neuropeptide signaling system, resulting in drowsiness.

DRUG	DOSING	SAFETY/SIDE EFFECTS/MONITORING
Lemborexant (*DayVigo*) C-IV	5-10 mg PO QHS if at least 7 hours of sleep remaining Use 5 mg with weak CYP3A4 inhibitors Avoid use with strong or moderate CYP3A4 inhibitors	**CONTRAINDICATIONS** Narcolepsy **WARNINGS** Worsening depression/suicidal ideation, sleep paralysis, hallucinations, cataplexy-like symptoms (sudden loss of muscle tone), increased risk for complex sleep behavior, daytime impairment (risk ↑ with other CNS depressants)
Suvorexant (*Belsomra*) C-IV	10-20 mg PO QHS if at least 7 hours of sleep remaining Use 5 mg with moderate CYP3A4 inhibitors and do not exceed 10 mg daily Avoid use with strong CYP3A4 inhibitors	**SIDE EFFECTS** Somnolence, headache, dizziness, abnormal dreams **NOTES** Should be taken on an empty stomach (food delays absorption) Not recommended in patients with severe hepatic impairment

Melatonin Receptor Agonists

These drugs are agonists at the melatonin receptors, MT1 and MT2. This promotes sleepiness and regulates the circadian rhythm to coordinate the sleep-wake cycle.

DRUG	DOSING	SAFETY/SIDE EFFECTS/MONITORING
Ramelteon (*Rozerem*)	8 mg PO QHS	**SIDE EFFECTS** Somnolence, dizziness **NOTES** Not a controlled substance
Tasimelteon (*Hetlioz, Hetlioz LQ*)	20 mg PO QHS	Do not take with fatty food Contraindicated with fluvoxamine (increases serum concentration of ramelteon) Tasimelteon (*Hetlioz*) is indicated for non-24 hour sleep-wake disorder; *Hetlioz LQ* is an oral suspension that may be used in children as young as 3 years of age

Tricyclic Antidepressant

Tricyclic antidepressants inhibit norepinephrine and 5-HT reuptake. They also block acetylcholine and histamine receptors which contribute to side effects (e.g., somnolence). *Silenor* is the branded formulation of doxepin that is FDA-approved for insomnia.

DRUG	DOSING	SAFETY/SIDE EFFECTS/MONITORING
Doxepin (*Silenor*)	3-6 mg PO QHS 3 mg if ≥ 65 years	**BOXED WARNINGS** Increase in suicidal thoughts or actions in some children, teenagers or young adults within the first few months of treatment or when the dose is changed (see Depression chapter) **CONTRAINDICATIONS** Requires a 2-week washout for MAO inhibitors **SIDE EFFECTS** Somnolence, possibility of anticholinergic side effects **NOTES** Generic doxepin, trazodone and mirtazapine may be used off-label for sleep (not recommended by guidelines)

Benzodiazepines

These drugs enhance GABA, an inhibitory neurotransmitter, causing CNS depression. A brief summary of the drugs that are FDA-indicated for insomnia is provided below; consult the Anxiety Disorders chapter for a full discussion.

DRUG	DOSING	SAFETY/SIDE EFFECTS/MONITORING
Temazepam (*Restoril*)	7.5-30 mg PO QHS	**ALL** C-IV drugs; there is a risk of physical (physiological) dependence, abuse (addiction) and tolerance
Estazolam	1-2 mg PO QHS	Increased risk of falls, use with caution in those at high risk Cross the placenta; contraindicated in pregnancy due to observed teratogenicity
Quazepam (*Doral*)	7.5-15 mg PO QHS	Lorazepam, oxazepam and temazepam (L-O-T) are preferred for elderly patients; temazepam can be used for sleep; lorazepam and oxazepam are indicated for anxiety **WARNINGS** Complex sleep behaviors (e.g., sleep-driving) have been noted
Flurazepam	15-30 mg PO QHS	**SIDE EFFECTS** Drowsiness, dizziness/↑ fall risk, cognitive impairment
Triazolam (*Halcion*)	0.125-0.5 mg PO QHS	**NOTES** Estazolam: do not use with potent CYP3A4 inhibitors (e.g., ketoconazole, itraconazole) Triazolam: associated with higher rebound insomnia and daytime anxiety; contraindicated with azole antifungals, protease inhibitors and other CYP3A4 Inhibitors

Antihistamines

These drugs compete with (i.e., block) histamine H1 receptors.

DRUG	DOSING	SAFETY/SIDE EFFECTS/MONITORING
Diphenhydramine (*Benadryl*, store brands) Rx and OTC	50 mg PO QHS	**SIDE EFFECTS** Sedation (tolerance to sedative effects can develop after 10 days of use), confusion (can exacerbate memory/cognition difficulty) Antihistamines may cause paradoxical excitation in young children; do not use doxylamine in children < 12 years
Doxylamine (*Unisom SleepTabs*, *Sleep Aid*, store brands) OTC	25 mg PO QHS	Peripheral anticholinergic side effects: dry mouth, urinary retention (makes it very difficult for males with BPH to urinate), dry/blurry vision, constipation Best to avoid use in BPH (can worsen symptoms) and glaucoma (can elevate IOP) **NOTES** Risk of mix-up; some OTC *Unisom* branded-products are diphenhydramine

RESTLESS LEGS SYNDROME

Restless legs syndrome (RLS) is an urge to move the lower legs, which is sometimes described as a "creeping" sensation. It is worse at night and is relieved with movement. RLS is thought to be due to a dysfunction of dopamine in the brain's basal ganglia circuits.

DRUG TREATMENT

The primary treatment of RLS includes dopamine agonists and the anticonvulsant gabapentin. Pramipexole (*Mirapex*) and ropinirole (*Requip*) are dopamine agonists primarily used in longer-acting formulations for Parkinson disease (PD). For RLS, the immediate-release (IR) formulation is taken 1 – 3 hours before bedtime. Rotigotine (*Neupro*) is a dopamine agonist that comes in a patch formulation (used for both PD and RLS). The patch is applied once daily, and patients must be counseled on appropriate use (e.g., do not apply a heat source over the patch, remove the patch before an MRI procedure, rotate sites to avoid skin irritation).

Dopamine agonists cause <u>orthostasis, somnolence</u> and nausea that is dose-related. Even when used for RLS, the dose should be titrated up slowly. Patients should be monitored for psychiatric side effects (e.g., hallucinations, abnormal dreams) and movement disorders.

<u>Gabapentin</u> enacarbil *(Horizant)* is an extended-release form of gabapentin approved for <u>postherpetic neuralgia (PHN) and RLS</u>. The tablet is taken with food and must be swallowed whole (it cannot be crushed or chewed). For RLS, it is taken at ~5:00 PM daily. The IR formulation of gabapentin is used off-label as a less expensive alternative. Refer to the Parkinson Disease chapter for additional information on the dopamine agonists and the Seizures/Epilepsy chapter for additional information on gabapentin.

NARCOLEPSY

Narcolepsy is <u>excessive daytime sleepiness with cataplexy</u> (sudden loss of muscle tone) and sleep paralysis. Narcolepsy causes sudden daytime "sleep attacks" due to poor control of normal sleep-wake cycles. The sleep attacks last a few seconds to several minutes. Patients have difficulty managing daily activities with narcolepsy; they can fall asleep while at work, school or in the middle of a conversation. Sleep quality at night is poor.

DRUG TREATMENT

Narcolepsy is treated with <u>stimulants</u>, such as <u>modafinil</u> or armodafinil, or with <u>sodium oxybate *(Xyrem)*</u> or <u>calcium, magnesium, potassium and sodium oxybate *(Xywav)*</u>, both of which are derived from the inhibitory neurotransmitter GABA. Several of the stimulants used for ADHD have an indication for narcolepsy, including <u>dextroamphetamine</u> *(Dexedrine, ProCentra and Zenzedi)*, <u>dextroamphetamine/amphetamine</u> *(Adderall)* and various <u>methylphenidate</u> formulations (e.g., *Methylin* and *Ritalin)*.

Stimulants for Wakefulness

DRUG	DOSING	SAFETY/SIDE EFFECTS/MONITORING
Modafinil *(Provigil)* C-IV	200 mg PO QAM	**WARNINGS** Avoid with pre-existing cardiac conditions, caution with hepatic or renal dysfunction, psychiatric disorders and Tourette's syndrome **SIDE EFFECTS** Severe <u>rash, can be life-threatening</u> (e.g., Stevens-Johnson syndrome), headache, insomnia, anxiety, nausea
Armodafinil *(Nuvigil)* R-isomer of modafinil C-IV	150-250 mg PO QAM	**NOTES** Other indications include obstructive sleep apnea (to help with excessive daytime sleepiness) and shift work disorder

Sodium Oxybates

These drugs are <u>derived from GABA</u> and are indicated for <u>narcolepsy with cataplexy</u>. They help with sleep at night and are generally used with daytime stimulants.

DRUG	DOSING	SAFETY/SIDE EFFECTS/MONITORING
Sodium oxybate *(Xyrem)* Calcium, magnesium, potassium and sodium oxybates *(Xywav)* Oral solution C-III (narcolepsy) C-I (illicit use) These are "<u>date rape</u>" <u>drugs</u> (the sedative GHB); a REMS program is required to ensure use only by patients with narcolepsy with cataplexy	Start 2.25 grams PO QHS and take again 2.5-4 hours later Titrate to effect; dosing range ~6-9 grams/night Take in ¼ cup water at least 2 hours after eating; lie down immediately after taking and stay in bed; sleep onset typically occurs within 5-15 minutes after taking the first dose	**BOXED WARNINGS** Strong CNS depressant; respiratory depression, coma and death can result; risk is increased when taken with other CNS depressants <u>Restricted access through the *Xywav* and *Xyrem* REMS Program</u> **CONTRAINDICATIONS** Use with sedative-hypnotics or alcohol **WARNINGS** Depression, suicide, psychosis, anxiety, sleepwalking **SIDE EFFECTS** Dizziness, confusion, nausea **NOTES** High sodium content; limiting dietary sodium intake may be required

Other Oral Medications for Narcolepsy

Other available treatments shown in the table below are approved by FDA to improve wakefulness in narcolepsy.

DRUG CLASS	SAFETY/SIDE EFFECTS/MONITORING
Histamine-3 (H3) Receptor Antagonist/Inverse Agonist Pitolisant *(Wakix)* Approved for adult patients with excessive daytime sleepiness associated with narcolepsy	**CONTRAINDICATIONS** Severe hepatic impairment **WARNINGS** QT prolongation **SIDE EFFECTS** Insomnia, nausea, anxiety, headache
Dopamine and Norepinephrine Reuptake Inhibitor (DNRI) Solriamfetol *(Sunosi)* Approved for adult patients with excessive daytime sleepiness associated with narcolepsy or obstructive sleep apnea	**CONTRAINDICATIONS** Concomitant MAO inhibitors or within 14 days of discontinuation **WARNINGS** Increase in blood pressure and heart rate, psychiatric symptoms (e.g., anxiety, irritability) **SIDE EFFECTS** Headache, nausea, decreased appetite, insomnia, anxiety

KEY COUNSELING POINTS

See the Drug Formulations and Patient Counseling chapter for counseling language/layman's terminology.

Eszopiclone, Zaleplon, Zolpidem and Suvorexant

- Can cause:
  - Drowsiness, lightheadedness, dizziness and headache. You may still feel drowsy the day after taking this medication. Use caution when driving a car or operating dangerous machinery.
  - Paresthesia.
  - Abnormal thoughts and behavior (e.g., more outgoing or aggressive behavior than usual, confusion, agitation, hallucinations, worsening depression and suicidal thoughts or actions).
  - Withdrawal symptoms (e.g., cramps, nausea, sweating and shakiness) if abruptly stopped.
- This medication is a federally controlled substance (C-IV) because it can be abused or lead to dependence. Keep the bottle in a safe place to prevent misuse and abuse.

Antihistamines

- Can cause anticholinergic effects.

Stimulants for Wakefulness

- Take in the morning to avoid difficulty falling asleep at night.

Select Guidelines/References

Clinical practice guideline for the pharmacologic treatment of chronic insomnia in adults: an American Academy of Sleep Medicine clinical practice guideline. *J Clin Sleep Med.* 2017;13(2):307-349.

Practice guideline summary: Treatment of restless legs syndrome in adults: Report of the American Academy of Neurology. *Neurology.* 2016;87:2585-2593.

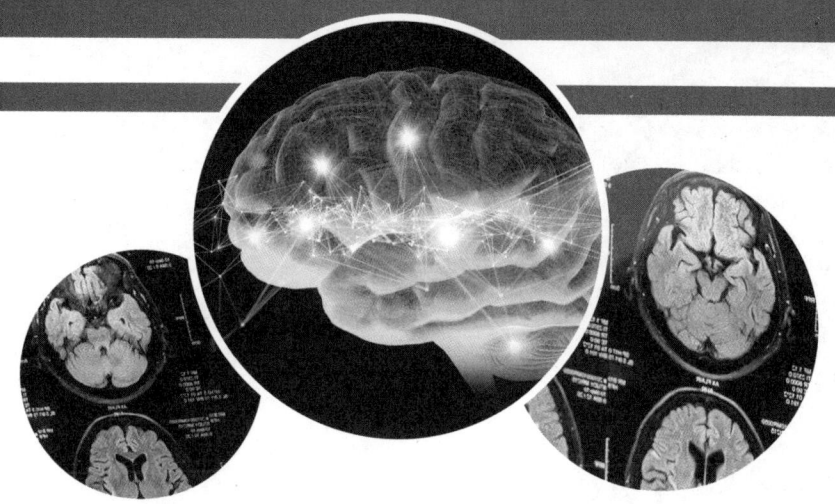

NEUROLOGIC CONDITIONS

CONTENTS

Stooped posture

Masked Face

Back rigidity

Forward tilt of trunk

Flexed elbows and wrists

Reduced arm swing

Hand tremor

Tremors in the legs

Slightly flexed hip and knees

Shuffling, short stepped gait

iStock.com/ttsz

CHAPTER 69

PARKINSON DISEASE

BACKGROUND

Parkinson disease (PD) is a <u>neurological disorder</u>. It usually develops after age 65, though 15% of cases are diagnosed under age 50. PD occurs when <u>neurons</u> in the <u>substantia nigra</u> (a part of the brain) <u>die</u> or become impaired. The cause of neuronal death is not well understood, but is multi-factorial. These cells <u>produce</u> the neurotransmitter <u>dopamine</u> (DA), which allows smooth, <u>coordinated function</u> and <u>movement</u> of body muscles. When ~80% of the dopamine-producing cells are damaged, the motor symptoms of the disease appear (see <u>Study Tip Gal</u> below).

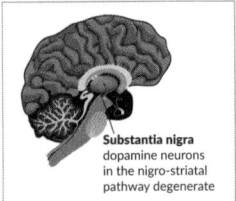

Substantia nigra
dopamine neurons in the nigro-striatal pathway degenerate

iStock.com/CurvaBezier

PARKINSON DISEASE SYMPTOMS

Pathophysiology:
Less dopamine → less instructions to the brain → movement problems (called the **TRAP** major symptoms)

TRAP Major Symptoms:

Tremor: when resting

Rigidity: in legs, arms, trunk and face (mask-like face)

Akinesia/bradykinesia: lack of/ slow start in movement

Postural instability: imbalance, falls

Additional Symptoms:

Small, cramped handwriting (micrographia)

Shuffling walk, stooped posture

Muffled speech, drooling, dysphagia

Depression, anxiety (psychosis in advanced disease)

Constipation, incontinence

Tremor is often the first noticeable symptom, and usually starts in one hand or foot (on just one side, unilateral) and eventually spreads to both sides (bilateral). *Resting* tremor means it appears when the hand is not moving, such as when a person's hand is resting in their lap.

Medications can cause similar symptoms, and can mimic PD or make PD worse (see <u>Key Drugs Guy</u> on the following page). The <u>Abnormal Involuntary Movement Scale (AIMS)</u> can be used to measure involuntary movements (e.g., tardive dyskinesias) from medications.

CHAPTER CONTENT

CONTENT LEGEND

🔆 = Study Tip Gal   🔑 = Key Drug Guy

DOPAMINE BLOCKING DRUGS THAT CAN WORSEN PD

- Phenothiazines (e.g., prochlorperazine) used for psychosis, nausea, agitation
- Butyrophenones (e.g., haloperidol, droperidol) used for psychosis and behavior disorders or nausea
- First and second-generation antipsychotics (e.g., risperidone at higher doses, paliperidone); lowest risk with quetiapine
- Metoclopramide, a renally-cleared drug that can accumulate in elderly patients

Non-motor symptoms can precede motor symptoms and may appear much earlier in the disease process. These include a loss of smell (anosmia), constipation, sleep difficulties, low mood/depression and orthostasis. Biomarkers that can identify early disease prior to visible symptoms are a focus of research.

Even with high doses of PD drugs and various combinations, the disease will progress, including extended periods of "off time." This is when symptoms of the disease worsen before the next dose of medication is due. An "off" episode, with muscle stiffness, slow movements and difficulty starting movement, is one of the most frustrating aspects of living with the disease. Symptoms can progress to severe disability, and patients can lose the ability to walk, feed themselves and swallow food.

RELATED PSYCHIATRIC CONDITIONS

Patients with PD have a high incidence of depression. SSRIs or SNRIs are commonly used for treatment. There is some concern that they may contribute to tremor or an increased risk of serotonin syndrome in patients who are taking other serotonergic drugs. Tricyclic antidepressants, preferably the secondary amines (such as desipramine and nortriptyline), and the dopamine agonist pramipexole (reported to provide antidepressant effects), are other options.

Psychosis can occur with advanced disease or can be due to side effects of drug treatment. Quetiapine is the preferred antipsychotic due to a low risk of movement disorders, but it can cause metabolic complications, including increased cholesterol and blood glucose. Clozapine has a low risk of worsening movement disorders but has a high risk of seizures, agranulocytosis (requires frequent monitoring and reporting of white blood cells) and other serious complications. Pimavanserin (Nuplazid), a 5HT2A/2C receptor inverse agonist, is FDA-approved to treat hallucinations and delusions in PD. Refer to the Schizophrenia/Psychosis chapter for a discussion of antipsychotic drugs.

Rapid withdrawal of levodopa or dopamine agonists can lead to a condition similar to neuroleptic malignant syndrome (NMS), which is a life-threatening condition sometimes seen with antipsychotics. These medications must be tapered off slowly when discontinued to prevent this condition.

DRUG TREATMENT

Medications are used to improve movement, which also helps related issues, such as psychosis and constipation. Levodopa, a prodrug of dopamine, is the most effective agent. Carbidopa is given with levodopa (in the combination product Sinemet) to prevent the peripheral (i.e., outside of the CNS) metabolism of levodopa, which would destroy most of the drug before it crosses the blood-brain barrier. It is important to provide the right amount of carbidopa without causing excess side effects (see the drug table on the following page). Initial treatment with carbidopa/levodopa is sometimes better tolerated in the elderly than the dopamine agonists.

Dopamine agonists are eventually used in most patients. As the disease progresses, treatment will be directed at both reducing "off" periods and limiting dyskinesias (abnormal movement). This will require multiple therapies, such as catechol-o-methyltransferase (COMT) inhibitors and MAO-B inhibitors.

Tremor-predominant disease in younger patients can be treated with a centrally-acting anticholinergic (e.g., benztropine). The considerable side effects of these drugs make them difficult to use in elderly patients (the Beers criteria for potentially inappropriate medication use in older adults recommends to "avoid" use). Amantadine, or a selective monoamine oxidase (MAO) inhibitor, are other options for initial treatment of tremor. Note that for PD, selective MAO inhibitors are used; the non-selective inhibitors that are used for depression are contraindicated with dopaminergic drugs because they would block drug metabolism.

Amantadine can be useful to help with dyskinesias, in addition to tremor. Apomorphine treats severe "freezing" episodes that usually occur in more advanced disease, but it requires subcutaneous (SC) administration, has worrisome side effects and provides increased movement for just about an hour. Droxidopa (Northera) is a newer drug indicated for orthostatic hypotension, which can affect PD patients.

PARKINSON DISEASE TREATMENT PRINCIPLES

Primary treatment: replace dopamine
✓ Give a precursor to dopamine that becomes dopamine in the brain (that's levodopa, in Sinemet).
✓ Give a dopamine agonist that acts like dopamine.
✓ Give other drugs for specific symptoms (e.g., benztropine for resting tremor).

DOPAMINE REPLACEMENT DRUGS & AGONISTS

DRUG	DOSING	SAFETY/SIDE EFFECTS/MONITORING
Carbidopa/levodopa: levodopa is a <u>precursor</u> of <u>dopamine</u>. Carbidopa <u>inhibits dopa decarboxylase enzyme</u>, preventing peripheral <u>metabolism</u> of levodopa.		
Carbidopa/Levodopa IR tablet, ER tablet, ODT **Sinemet** Tablet *Dhivy* Scored IR tablet to facilitate titration *Rytary* ER capsule *Duopa* Enteral suspension given via J-tube *Inbrija* Levodopa capsule for oral inhaler, used as needed for symptoms during off periods	<u>Titrate cautiously</u> IR (starting dose): <u>25/100 mg PO TID</u> ER (starting dose): 50/200 mg PO BID <u>ER tab can be cut in half</u> – do not crush or chew Rytary: start at 23.75/95 mg PO TID if levodopa-naive; <u>take whole or sprinkle</u> on a small amount of applesauce Inbrija: 84 mg (2 capsules) inhaled up to 5 times daily as needed, max dose: 420 mg/day	**CONTRAINDICATIONS** <u>Non-selective MAO inhibitors</u> within 14 days, narrow angle glaucoma **SIDE EFFECTS** Nausea, dizziness, orthostasis, dyskinesias, hallucinations, psychosis, xerostomia (dry mouth), dystonias (occasional, painful), confusion Can cause brown, <u>black</u> or dark discoloring of <u>urine</u>, saliva or sweat and can discolor clothing; positive <u>Coombs test: discontinue drug (hemolysis risk)</u>; unusual sexual urges, priapism; ↑ uric acid *Rytary:* suicidal ideation and attempts *Duopa:* GI complications **NOTES** <u>70-100 mg/day of carbidopa required</u> to inhibit dopa decarboxylase <u>Long-term</u> use can lead to <u>fluctuations</u> in response and <u>dyskinesias</u> Separate from oral iron and high protein foods <u>Do not discontinue abruptly</u>; must be tapered *Duopa* cassettes: store in freezer, thaw in refrigerator prior to dispensing (good for 12 weeks upon refrigeration)
COMT inhibitors: <u>increase the duration of action of levodopa</u>; <u>inhibit</u> the enzyme <u>catechol-O-methyltransferase</u> (COMT) to prevent peripheral conversion of levodopa. COMT inhibitors should <u>only</u> be used <u>with levodopa</u>.		
Entacapone (*Comtan*) + carbidopa/levodopa (*Stalevo*)	<u>200 mg PO with each dose</u> of carbidopa/levodopa (max = 1,600 mg/day) *Stalevo:* carbidopa/levodopa in a ratio of 1:4 with 200 mg of entacapone in each tablet (example: 12.5/50/200 mg)	**SIDE EFFECTS** Similar to levodopa, due to extending its duration **NOTES** ↓ in levodopa dose of 10-30% is usually necessary when adding on a COMT inhibitor Dyskinesias can occur earlier with COMT inhibitors Tolcapone: rarely used due to hepatotoxicity risk
Opicapone (*Ongentys*)	50 mg PO QHS Dose ↓ needed in liver disease	
Tolcapone (*Tasmar*)		
Dopamine agonists: act <u>similar to dopamine</u> at the <u>dopamine receptor</u>.		
Pramipexole (*Mirapex, Mirapex ER*) IR formulation also approved for restless legs syndrome (RLS)	IR: start with 0.125 mg PO TID, titrate weekly to max of 1.5 mg TID ER: start with 0.375 mg PO daily, titrate weekly to max of 4.5 mg daily ↓ dose if CrCl < 50 mL/min (90% renally excreted)	**WARNINGS** <u>Somnolence</u> (including <u>sudden daytime sleep attacks</u>), orthostasis, hallucinations, <u>dyskinesias</u>, impulse control disorders Rotigotine patch: <u>application site (skin) reactions</u> Pramipexole: postural deformity (e.g., bent spine, dropped head), rhabdomyolysis **SIDE EFFECTS** Dizziness, nausea, vomiting, dry mouth, peripheral edema, constipation Rotigotine: hyperhidrosis
Ropinirole (*Requip XL**) IR formulation also approved for RLS	IR: start with 0.25 mg PO TID, titrate weekly to max of 8 mg TID XL: start with 2 mg PO daily, titrate weekly to max of 24 mg daily	**NOTES** A slow titration (no more than weekly) is required due to orthostasis, dizziness, sleepiness; <u>do not discontinue abruptly</u> Ropinirole: CYP450 1A2 substrate; caution with CYP1A2 inhibitors Bromocriptine is another drug in the class that is no longer recommended
Rotigotine (*Neupro*) Patch Also approved for RLS	Patch: start with 2 mg/24 hrs (early PD) Max dose: 8 mg/24 hours	**Patch** Apply <u>once daily</u> at the same time each day to the stomach, thigh, hip, side of the body, shoulder or upper arm; do <u>not</u> use the <u>same site</u> for at least <u>14 days</u> Remove the patch before an MRI; do not apply a heat source over the patch; avoid if sensitivity/allergy to <u>sulfites</u>

Brand discontinued but name still used in practice.

DRUG	DOSING	SAFETY/SIDE EFFECTS/MONITORING
Dopamine agonist use as a "rescue" movement drug for "off" periods.		
Apomorphine *Apokyn* Injection *Kynmobi* Sublingual film Taken in addition to other PD medications	**Injection:** Start with 0.2 mL (2 mg) SC PRN (up to 5x/day); titrate by 1 mg every few days Max single dose: 0.6 mL (6 mg) Lasts 45-90 minutes Must be started with a test dose in a medical office **Sublingual film:** 10-30 mg PRN; max of 5 doses/day	**CONTRAINDICATION** Do not use with 5HT-3 antagonists (e.g., ondansetron) due to severe hypotension and loss of consciousness **SIDE EFFECTS** Severe nausea/vomiting, hypotension, yawning, dyskinesias, somnolence, dizziness, QT prolongation Sublingual film: dry mouth, tongue pain **NOTES** Monitor supine and standing blood pressure For emesis prevention: give trimethobenzamide *(Tigan)* 300 mg PO TID, or a similar antiemetic, started 3 days prior to the initial dose

Carbidopa/Levodopa *(Sinemet)* Drug Interactions

- Contraindicated with non-selective MAO inhibitors (a two-week separation is required).

- Iron and protein-rich foods can ↓ absorption.

- Do not use with dopamine blockers, which will worsen Parkinson symptoms (e.g., phenothiazines, metoclopramide).

OTHER DRUGS FOR PARKINSON DISEASE

DRUG	DOSING	SAFETY/SIDE EFFECTS/MONITORING
Amantadine: blocks dopamine reuptake into presynaptic neurons and increases dopamine release from presynaptic fibers. Primarily used to treat dyskinesias associated with peak-dose of carbidopa/levodopa.		
Amantadine IR: tablet, capsule, syrup Amantadine extended-release *(Gocovri, Osmolex ER)*	IR: 100 mg PO BID *Osmolex ER:* 137 mg PO daily, increase after 1 week to 274 mg daily *Gocovri:* 129 mg daily, increase weekly to max dose of 322 mg daily ↓ dose in renal impairment eGFR < 15 mL/min/1.73 m²: ER products contraindicated	**WARNINGS** Somnolence (including falling asleep without warning during activities of daily living), compulsive behaviors, psychosis (hallucinations, delusions, paranoia) **SIDE EFFECTS** Dizziness, orthostatic hypotension, syncope, insomnia, abnormal dreams, dry mouth, constipation Cutaneous reaction called livedo reticularis (reddish skin mottling – can require drug discontinuation) **NOTES** *Gocovri* is indicated for the treatment of dyskinesia in patients receiving levodopa-based therapy
Selective MAO-B inhibitors: block the breakdown of dopamine which increases dopaminergic activity. Primarily used as adjunctive treatment to carbidopa/levodopa; rasagiline has an indication for monotherapy.		
Selegiline Capsule, tablet (generics) *Zelapar* – ODT *Emsam* – patch; only indicated for depression	Capsule, tablet: 5 mg PO BID, with breakfast and lunch ODT: 1.25-2.5 mg daily (not recommended if CrCl < 30 mL/min) Selegiline can be activating; do not take dose at bedtime; if dosed twice daily, take the 2nd dose at midday	**CONTRAINDICATIONS** Use in combination with other MAO inhibitors (including linezolid), opioids, SNRIs, TCAs, others (see Drug Interactions) *Xadago:* severe hepatic impairment **WARNINGS** Serotonin syndrome, hypertension, nausea, CNS depression, dyskinesias, impulse control disorders, caution in patients with psychotic disorders (may exacerbate) or ophthalmic disorders *(Xadago)* Rasagiline (monotherapy): headache, joint pain, indigestion
Rasagiline *(Azilect)*	0.5-1 mg PO daily	
Safinamide *(Xadago)* Adjunctive treatment to carbidopa/levodopa in patients experiencing "off" episodes	Start with 50 mg once daily; after 2 weeks may increase to 100 mg once daily When stopping treatment: decrease the dose to 50 mg for one week before discontinuing	**MONITORING** BP, signs of serotonin syndrome, visual changes *(Xadago)* **NOTES** May need to reduce levodopa dose when beginning treatment with a selective MAO-B inhibitor

DRUG	DOSING	SAFETY/SIDE EFFECTS/MONITORING
Centrally-acting anticholinergics: have <u>anticholinergic</u> and antihistamine effects. Primarily used for tremor.		
Benztropine *(Cogentin)*	0.5-2 mg TID (start QHS)	**SIDE EFFECTS** High incidence of peripheral and central anticholinergic effects: <u>dry mouth</u>, <u>constipation, urinary retention, blurred vision, mydriasis, somnolence, confusion</u>, tachycardia
Trihexyphenidyl	1-5 mg TID (start 1 mg QHS)	**NOTES** Avoid use in elderly patients
Adenosine receptor antagonist: used in combination with carbidopa/levodopa to reduce "off" episodes.		
Istradefylline *(Nourianz)*	20 mg PO daily, can titrate to a max of 40 mg daily Dose must be adjusted if used with CYP3A4 inhibitors or tobacco smoking	**WARNINGS** Hallucinations, dyskinesias, impulse control disorders **SIDE EFFECTS** Nausea, constipation
Alpha/beta agonist: used for neurogenic orthostatic hypotension.		
Droxidopa *(Northera)*	Start at 100 mg PO TID, can titrate every 24-48 hour to a max of 1800 mg/day Take the last dose at least 3 hours prior to bedtime (to avoid supine hypertension during sleep)	**BOXED WARNING** Supine hypertension: monitor supine BP prior to and during treatment; elevate the head of the bed and measure BP in this position; if supine hypertension cannot be managed by elevation of the head of the bed, reduce dose or discontinue **SIDE EFFECTS** <u>Syncope, falls, headache</u>

MAO-B Inhibitor Drug Interactions

- While taking, do not eat <u>foods high in tyramine</u>, including <u>aged or matured cheese, air-dried or cured meats</u> (e.g., sausages, salamis), <u>sauerkraut</u>, fava or broad bean pods, tap/draft beers, Marmite concentrate, soy sauce or other soybean condiments. Avoid these foods during and for two weeks after discontinuation of the medication.

- Do not use with products containing dopamine, tyrosine, phenylalanine, tryptophan or caffeine.

- Do not use with other drugs that increase the risk of <u>serotonin syndrome</u>. See the Drug Interactions chapter.

- Rasagiline is a CYP1A2 substrate; limit dose to 0.5 mg daily with ciprofloxacin or other CYP1A2 inhibitors.

KEY COUNSELING POINTS

See the Drug Formulations and Patient Counseling chapter for counseling language/layman's terminology.

ALL PARKINSON DISEASE PATIENTS

- Increased risk of:
  - ❑ Irregular movements, psychosis, suicidal ideation or depression.
- Treatments have many drug interactions.
- Avoid alcohol.

CARBIDOPA/LEVODOPA

- Can cause:
  - ❑ Nausea, dizziness, orthostasis or psychosis.
  - ❑ Body fluid discoloration (e.g., dark brown urine, saliva or sweat).
  - ❑ Priapism.
- Drug interactions due to binding; specifically with iron and high-protein foods.

DOPAMINE AGONISTS

- Can cause orthostasis, drowsiness or psychosis.

Rotigotine *(Neupro)* Patch

- Can cause skin irritation.
- Patch application:
  - ❑ Wear for 24 hours. Rotate where you place the patch. Wait at least 14 days before applying in the same location. Remove patch before an MRI.

Select Guidelines/References

International Parkinson and Movement Disorder Society Evidence-Based Review: Update on Treatments for the Motor Symptoms of Parkinson's Disease. *Movement Disorders.* 2018 Feb;00:1-19.

Update on Treatments for Nonmotor Symptoms of Parkinson's Disease-An Evidence-Based Medicine Review. *Movement Disorders.* 2019 Feb;34(2):180-198.

CONTENT LEGEND

= Key Drug Guy

iStock.com/KatarzynaBialasiewicz

CHAPTER 70

ALZHEIMER'S DISEASE

BACKGROUND

Mild age-associated cognitive decline is normal and can cause bothersome symptoms, such as losing the car keys more often. Mild cognitive impairment (MCI) is a condition of measurable decreases in memory and mental function, but it is not severe enough to significantly interfere with daily functioning.

With dementia, the decline is more severe. Intellectual and social abilities progressively worsen, and functioning becomes impaired. The most noticeable symptom initially is <u>memory loss</u>. As dementia worsens, problems develop with judgment, attention, planning and personal grooming. Agitation, aggression and depression can be present and are difficult challenges for patients and caregivers.

ALZHEIMER'S DISEASE SYMPTOMS
Memory loss, getting lost
Difficulty communicating, repeating words and information
Inability to learn or remember new information
Difficulty with planning and organizing
Poor coordination and motor function
Personality changes
Inappropriate behavior
Paranoia, agitation, hallucinations

DEMENTIA TYPES

There are different types of dementia, including Alzheimer's disease, vascular dementia and Lewy body dementia. The clinical findings in a patient can help the clinician characterize the dementia type. Alzheimer's is the most common type of dementia and has well-defined treatment, though the benefits are modest. The pathophysiology of Alzheimer's dementia involves neuritic plaques (clusters of beta-amyloid protein) and tangles (accumulation of tau protein) in brain tissue, which interrupt neuron signaling, and/or alteration of neurotransmitters (e.g., decreased acetylcholine).

SCREENING AND DIAGNOSIS

A definitive diagnosis of the cause and type of dementia cannot be made unless an autopsy is conducted post-mortem (after death). Researchers are developing markers and tests that can identify dementia at an early stage. The FDA approved flortaucipir F18 *(Tauvid)* as a radioactive imaging drug to estimate the tau protein tangles in adult patients being evaluated for Alzheimer's disease. With dementia that worsens over time, such as Alzheimer's disease, an early diagnosis provides a person time to plan for the future while he or she can still participate in decision making.

Initial screening should attempt to rule out causes of memory impairment that could be reversible, such as vitamin B12 deficiency, depression and infection. In some patients, the use of analgesics, benzodiazepines or other centrally-acting medications can cause or exacerbate memory loss (see Key Drugs Guy to the right). Anticholinergics are particularly concerning and are discussed below.

SCREENING TOOLS

Assessments used to identify or screen for dementia include the Folstein Mini-Mental State Exam (MMSE, max score is 30, score < 24 indicates a memory disorder), the Montreal Cognitive Assessment (MoCA) and DSM-5 criteria. Functional abilities can be assessed using the Alzheimer's Disease Cooperative Study – Activities of Daily Living (ADCS-ADL) tool. These screening tools ask the patient a series of questions to evaluate cognitive impairment (e.g., to spell a word backwards or count backwards from 100 by sevens) and/or assess functional abilities with activities of daily living (e.g., bathing, dressing, using a telephone, housekeeping).

ANTICHOLINERGICS & MEMORY IMPAIRMENT

Anticholinergics are used to treat incontinence (e.g., oxybutynin), allergies or insomnia (e.g., diphenhydramine), dystonic reactions (e.g., benztropine, diphenhydramine) and other conditions. A drug with strong centrally-acting anticholinergic effects can cause acute cognitive impairment and, occasionally, psychosis and hallucinations. The effect depends on the patient's baseline cognitive function, sensitivity to the drug, drug clearance, the number of drugs with additive effects and the dosing schedule. Centrally-acting anticholinergics should be avoided in the elderly due to these risks. This is a key point of the Beers Criteria (the guidance on potentially inappropriate medications in the elderly, published by the American Geriatrics Society).

KEY DRUGS THAT CAN WORSEN DEMENTIA

Antiemetics (e.g., promethazine)
Antihistamines (e.g., diphenhydramine, doxylamine)
Antipsychotics (e.g., chlorpromazine, aripiprazole)
Barbiturates (e.g., phenobarbital, butalbital)
Benzodiazepines (e.g., alprazolam, clonazepam)
Central anticholinergics (e.g., benztropine)
Peripheral anticholinergics (including incontinence and IBS drugs)
Skeletal muscle relaxants (e.g., baclofen)
Other CNS depressants (e.g., opioids, sedative hypnotics)

While anticholinergics can affect cognition, they are sometimes needed to treat urinary incontinence. If a drug is used to treat incontinence, the reduction in symptoms should be evaluated at six weeks. If there is a lack of improvement, the drug should be discontinued.

NATURAL PRODUCTS

Supplements with possible benefit for Alzheimer's dementia include Vitamin E (2,000 IU daily) and ginkgo. Both of these can increase bleeding risk; ginkgo especially should be discontinued in patients at high risk (e.g., taking warfarin or aspirin) and prior to elective surgical procedures. Other natural products that may be helpful include acetyl-L-carnitine, which acts as an acetylcholine precursor, and vinpocetine. Older adults with low vitamin D levels may have an increased risk of cognitive decline, including memory loss. If vitamin D levels are low, supplementation should be provided.

NON-DRUG TREATMENT

The vascular health of the blood vessels in the brain is vital for cognitive function. To promote vascular health:

- Keep blood glucose, blood pressure and cholesterol well-controlled.

- Engage in "thinking" activities and regular physical activity (in all age groups, physical activity enhances the growth and survival of brain cells).

- Eat a healthy diet, with fruits, vegetables, nuts, fish and with a low intake of red meat and alcohol.

DRUG TREATMENT

Acetylcholinesterase inhibitors (e.g., donepezil) are the mainstay of treatment. They are used alone or with memantine in more advanced stages of the disease. Clinical improvement with these medications is usually modest, but at a minimum, the patient can have a slower clinical progression than with no treatment. For family members and caregivers, this may mean that the patient can feed themselves for a little while longer or use the bathroom independently for several more months. Some patients will not have noticeable improvement and can experience side effects (nausea, diarrhea, dizziness).

Patients receiving acetylcholinesterase inhibitors should be monitored for both improvement and side effects; if there is no improvement, or if side effects are intolerable, the drug can be discontinued. Discontinuation is advisable if the dementia has advanced to the point where the drug lacks clinical benefit, though this may not be acceptable to the family and in some patients, there will be a noticeable deterioration when the medication is stopped.

The timing of medication administration can help reduce adverse effects. If nausea is present, administration in the evening can help. Donepezil is taken at bedtime for this reason. If insomnia is a concern, the patient can take the dose in the morning.

Memantine (Namenda) is approved for use alone or with donepezil for moderate-to-severe disease. Namzaric is a combination of donepezil and memantine. Patients stabilized on donepezil 10 mg can be switched to Namzaric.

Aducanumab (Aduhelm) is a novel monoclonal antibody approved for treating mild Alzheimer's disease. It has been shown to reduce amyloid plaques, which is likely to predict clinical benefit (though this has not been proven yet). Aducanumab is given as an intravenous infusion every four weeks (after an initial titration).

Antidepressants (e.g., sertraline, citalopram, escitalopram) can be used to treat related depression and anxiety. Antipsychotics are used off-label for delusions and agitation, but there is an increased risk of death in elderly patients (see Boxed Warning in the Schizophrenia/Psychosis chapter).

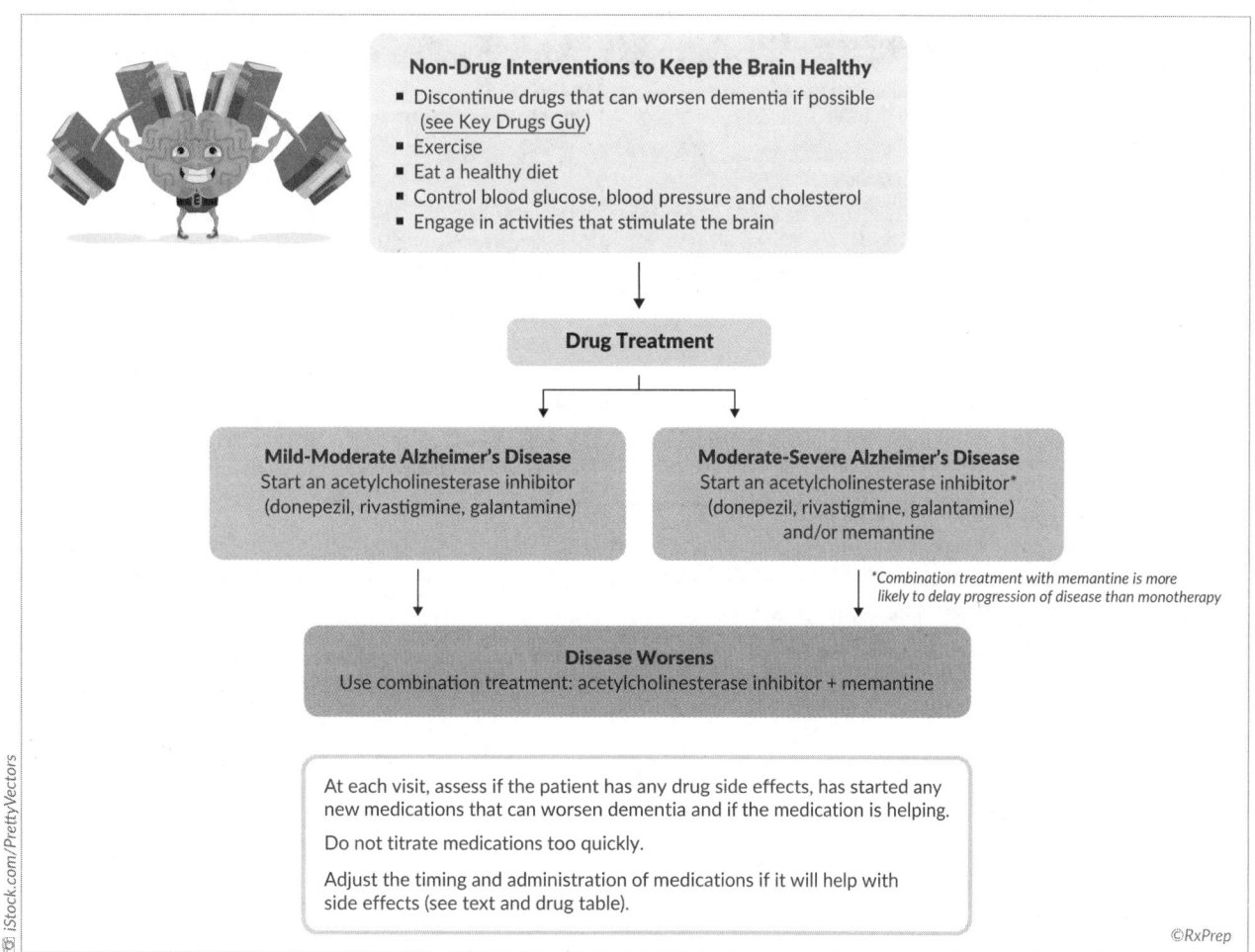

Non-Drug Interventions to Keep the Brain Healthy
- Discontinue drugs that can worsen dementia if possible (see Key Drugs Guy)
- Exercise
- Eat a healthy diet
- Control blood glucose, blood pressure and cholesterol
- Engage in activities that stimulate the brain

Drug Treatment

Mild-Moderate Alzheimer's Disease
Start an acetylcholinesterase inhibitor (donepezil, rivastigmine, galantamine)

Moderate-Severe Alzheimer's Disease
Start an acetylcholinesterase inhibitor* (donepezil, rivastigmine, galantamine) and/or memantine

*Combination treatment with memantine is more likely to delay progression of disease than monotherapy

Disease Worsens
Use combination treatment: acetylcholinesterase inhibitor + memantine

At each visit, assess if the patient has any drug side effects, has started any new medications that can worsen dementia and if the medication is helping.

Do not titrate medications too quickly.

Adjust the timing and administration of medications if it will help with side effects (see text and drug table).

©RxPrep

ALZHEIMER'S DISEASE DRUGS

DRUG	DOSING	SAFETY/SIDE EFFECTS/MONITORING
Acetylcholinesterase inhibitors: <u>inhibit</u> centrally-active <u>acetylcholinesterase</u>, the enzyme responsible for hydrolysis (breakdown) of acetylcholine; this causes an ↑ in acetylcholine		
Donepezil (*Aricept*) ODT, tablet + memantine (*Namzaric*)	Start: 5 mg <u>QHS</u>, can increase to 10 mg QHS after 4-6 weeks Moderate-to-severe disease: can increase to 23 mg QHS after ≥ 3 months of 10 mg QHS	**WARNINGS** <u>Cardiac</u> effects, including <u>bradycardia</u>, syncope, QT prolongation Anorexia/weight loss Patients < 55 kg can have more nausea and weight loss Neuroleptic malignant syndrome and rhabdomyolysis (both rare)
Rivastigmine (*Exelon*) Capsule, <u>patch</u>	Capsule: start 1.5 mg BID, can increase every 2 weeks to 6 mg BID Patch: start with 4.6 mg/24 hrs, can increase every 4 weeks to 13.3 mg/24 hrs (<u>patch</u> is changed <u>daily</u>) Hepatic impairment: max patch dose is 4.6 mg/24 hrs	**SIDE EFFECTS** <u>Nausea, diarrhea</u> (both dose-related, transient), insomnia, ↓ appetite/weight loss **NOTES** <u>Donepezil</u> is dosed QHS to help ↓ nausea <u>*Exelon* patch and donepezil ODT have less GI side effects</u>
Galantamine (*Razadyne, Razadyne ER*) Tablet, capsule, solution	IR tablet or solution: start 4 mg BID, can increase every 4 weeks to 12 mg BID ER capsule: start 8 mg daily, can increase every 4 weeks to 24 mg daily Severe hepatic/renal impairment: do not use	*Exelon* patch: apply first patch the day after last oral dose; <u>rotate</u> sites – do not use same site for 14 days. Does not contain metal (i.e., will not burn skin in MRI) *Exelon* capsules and galantamine IR should be taken with breakfast and dinner; galantamine ER should be taken with breakfast Galantamine solution can be mixed with liquid; drink immediately If <u>stable on donepezil 10 mg, can switch to *Namzaric*</u> (memantine 7 mg/donepezil 10 mg QHS) and titrate weekly (minimally)
Memantine: <u>blocks NMDA</u> (N-methyl-D-aspartate) receptors, which inhibits glutamate (an excitatory neurotransmitter) from binding and ↓ abnormal neuron activation		
Memantine (*Namenda*, *Namenda XR, Namenda Titration Pack*) Tablet, capsule, oral solution + donepezil (*Namzaric*)	IR: start with 5 mg PO daily, titrate weekly to 10 mg PO BID ER: start with 7 mg PO daily, titrate weekly to 28 mg PO daily Can switch IR 10 mg BID to ER 28 mg daily; begin ER the day after the last IR dose CrCl < 30 mL/min: max dose 5 mg PO BID (IR) or 14 mg PO daily (ER)	**WARNINGS** Caution with drugs/conditions that ↑ urine pH, which ↓ clearance of memantine (e.g., Na bicarbonate, acetazolamide, renal tubular acidosis) **SIDE EFFECTS** Generally well-tolerated, can cause <u>dizziness, confusion, headache,</u> constipation, syncope **NOTES** ER capsule and *Namzaric*: <u>do not crush or chew</u>; capsules can be opened and <u>sprinkled on applesauce</u> (swallow immediately) Oral solution: use provided dosing device and squirt into mouth The brand name NaMenDA has NMDA embedded in the name

Acetylcholinesterase Inhibitor Drug Interactions

- Use <u>caution</u> with <u>other drugs</u> that can <u>lower heart rate</u> (e.g., beta-blockers, diltiazem, verapamil, digoxin) and with drugs that cause dizziness (e.g., antipsychotics, alpha-blockers, skeletal muscle relaxants, hypnotics, opioids).

- Drugs that have <u>anticholinergic</u> effects can <u>reduce</u> the <u>efficacy</u> of acetylcholinesterase inhibitors. Discontinue incontinence drugs if there is no benefit.

- These drugs can increase gastric acid secretion; use cautiously with NSAIDs due to the risk of GI bleeding.

KEY COUNSELING POINTS

See the Drug Formulations and Patient Counseling chapter for counseling language/layman's terminology.

ALL ALZHEIMER'S DISEASE MEDICATIONS

- Tell your healthcare provider which prescription and over-the-counter medications you are taking; other drugs can worsen memory problems.

ACETYLCHOLINESTERASE INHIBITORS

- Can cause:
  - Nausea. Taking donepezil at bedtime can help.
  - Diarrhea.
  - Decreased heart rate.

Exelon Patch

- Apply a new patch at the same time each day to the upper or lower back (preferred sites if patient might remove patch), or on the upper arm or chest.
- Rotate application sites. Do not use the same site within 14 days.
- After 24 hours, remove the used patch. Do not touch the sticky side. Fold the patch in half with the sticky sides together and dispose of it safely.

Select Guidelines/References

Rabins PV, Rovner BW, Rummans T, et al. APA Guideline Watch (October 2014): Practice Guideline for the Treatment of Patients with Alzheimer's Disease and Other Dementias. https://psychiatryonline.org/pb/assets/raw/sitewide/practice_guidelines/guidelines/alzheimerwatch.pdf (accessed 2022 Feb 21).

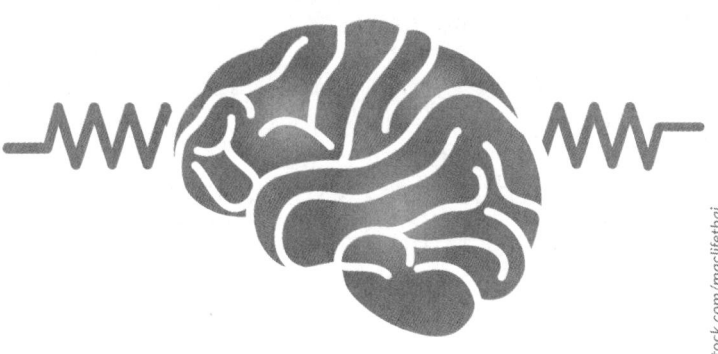

© iStock.com/maclifethai

CHAPTER 71
SEIZURES/EPILEPSY

BACKGROUND

A seizure occurs when excitatory neurons produce a sudden surge of electrical activity in the brain. Seizures can be caused by temporary conditions such as fever (common in children), infection, alcohol withdrawal, hypoglycemia or electrolyte abnormalities; in these cases, treating the underlying cause stops the seizure. Some drugs can lower the threshold for seizures and this makes a person more susceptible to a seizure. These drugs should be avoided in a person with a history of seizures. See the <u>Key Drug Guy</u> on the next page.

<u>Epilepsy</u> is a <u>chronic</u> seizure <u>disorder</u>. This is a broad-spectrum condition; there are different types of seizures, and different types of medications are used to treat them. Seizure medications are called antiepileptic drugs (AEDs). <u>Seizure types vary</u> from <u>uncontrolled jerking movements (tonic-clonic seizures)</u> to a subtle <u>momentary loss of awareness (absence seizures)</u>. Seizures can damage and destroy neurons, which causes brain damage and can be life-threatening.

The incidence of epilepsy is highest in the young and the elderly. One-third of new cases in the U.S. each year (50,000 of 150,000) are in children and adolescents. Seizures caused by a high fever in infants and young children do not usually lead to epilepsy. The elderly are at risk for seizures due to conditions that are more prevalent in the elderly, including dementia, brain tumors and, most commonly, damage from a stroke.

Motor vehicle accidents, gunshot wounds and other causes of severe head trauma damage the brain and can trigger seizures; emergency room treatment for severe head injuries often includes seizure prophylaxis or treatment. There is no identifiable cause or event that leads to seizures in half of all cases; these are attributable to some combination of genes and environment. About 500 genes have been linked to specific seizure types.

Individuals with epilepsy are evaluated for age of onset, seizure type, seizure frequency, description of witnessed seizure, identifiable causes or triggers and a thorough neurologic (brain and brain function)

FIRST AID FOR SEIZURES

First aid for seizures involves responding in ways that can keep the person safe until the seizure stops by itself:

■ Prevent injury by clearing the area around the person of anything hard or sharp.

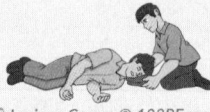
© Luciano Cosmo © 123RF.com

■ Ease the person to the floor and put something soft and flat, like a folded jacket, under the head. Turn the person gently onto one side. This will help keep the airway clear.

■ Remove eyeglasses and loosen ties or anything around the neck that may make breathing difficult.

■ Time the seizure. If the seizure continues for longer than five minutes without signs of slowing down, or if the person has trouble breathing, appears to be injured, in pain or has an unusual recovery, call 911.

■ Do not hold people down or try to stop their movements.

■ Contrary to popular belief, it is not true that people having a seizure can swallow their tongue. Do not put anything in the person's mouth.

■ Do not attempt artificial respiration except in the unlikely event that a person does not start breathing after the seizure has stopped.

CONTENT LEGEND

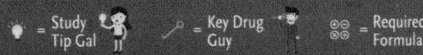

= Study Tip Gal   = Key Drug Guy   = Required Formula

exam. An electroencephalogram (EEG), the most common test used to diagnose epilepsy, records electrical activity in the brain. An EEG can show abnormal patterns even when the patient is not having a seizure. Brain imaging with a CT or MRI can identify some conditions that can provoke seizures, including brain tumors or damage from a stroke.

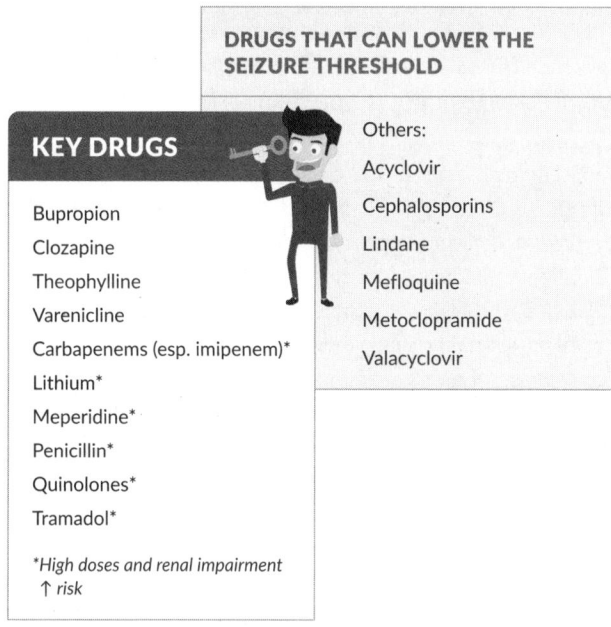

DRUGS THAT CAN LOWER THE SEIZURE THRESHOLD

KEY DRUGS

Bupropion
Clozapine
Theophylline
Varenicline
Carbapenems (esp. imipenem)*
Lithium*
Meperidine*
Penicillin*
Quinolones*
Tramadol*

High doses and renal impairment ↑ risk

Others:
Acyclovir
Cephalosporins
Lindane
Mefloquine
Metoclopramide
Valacyclovir

CLASSIFICATION OF SEIZURE TYPES

Seizures are classified into three main types based on where the seizure starts in the brain: focal seizures, generalized seizures and unknown onset seizures.

Focal seizures start on one side of the brain but can spread to the other side. Generalized seizures start on both sides of the brain. Seizures are classified as unknown onset if the location of the beginning of the seizure is not known (e.g., the seizures are unwitnessed or occur during the night).

Focal seizures are further classified based on the patient's awareness during the seizure. If a focal seizure results in no loss of consciousness, it is called a focal aware seizure, previously known as a simple partial seizure. If the patient experiences loss of consciousness, it is called a focal seizure with impaired awareness, previously known as a complex partial seizure. Patients with generalized seizures experience loss of consciousness or are unaware during the seizure event.

All seizure types can be described based on the patient's symptoms. Motor symptoms include sustained rhythmical jerking movements (clonic), limp or weak muscles (atonic), muscle twitching (myoclonus) and rigid or tense muscles (tonic). Non-motor symptoms include changes in sensation, emotions, thinking or cognition. Generalized seizures with non-motor symptoms are called absence seizures, which typically present as staring spells.

ACUTE SEIZURE MANAGEMENT

Most seizures last less than two minutes and do not require medical intervention. Seizures that continue longer cause more brain damage and can be fatal. Status epilepticus (SE) is a seizure that lasts five minutes or more because the normal mechanisms that terminate seizures are not working. At 30 minutes, long-term damage can occur. This is a medical emergency, and emergency treatment should begin with any seizure that lasts longer than five minutes.

SE management is divided into phases (see figure below). Initial treatment is a benzodiazepine injection. Intravenous (IV) access can be difficult during a seizure; if it is not possible to connect an IV line, midazolam can be given intramuscularly (IM).

If the patient is not receiving urgent medical care (i.e., not in a medical facility), diazepam rectal gel (Diastat AcuDial), or intranasal or buccal midazolam are non-injectable options. The Diastat AcuDial is given to patients (or caregivers, such as parents) who are at risk of long-lasting seizures; dispensing and counseling requirements are essential (see Study Tip Gal on the following page).

Status Epilepticus Treatment

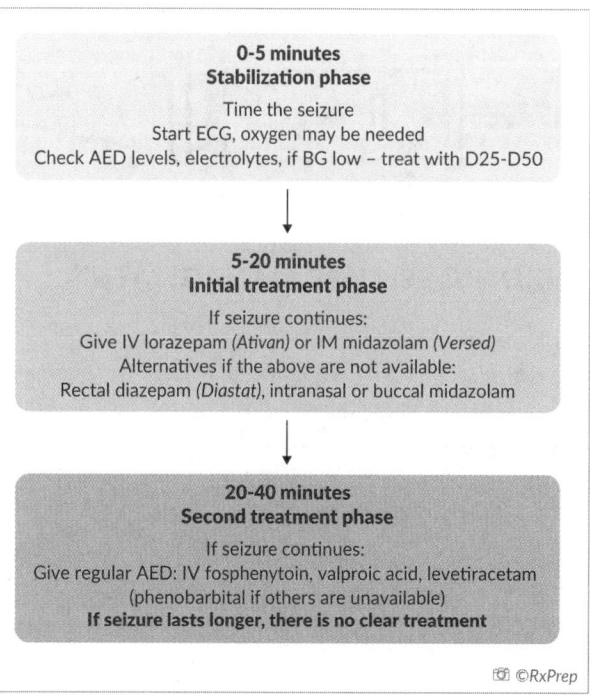

0-5 minutes
Stabilization phase

Time the seizure
Start ECG, oxygen may be needed
Check AED levels, electrolytes, if BG low – treat with D25-D50

5-20 minutes
Initial treatment phase

If seizure continues:
Give IV lorazepam (Ativan) or IM midazolam (Versed)
Alternatives if the above are not available:
Rectal diazepam (Diastat), intranasal or buccal midazolam

20-40 minutes
Second treatment phase

If seizure continues:
Give regular AED: IV fosphenytoin, valproic acid, levetiracetam
(phenobarbital if others are unavailable)
If seizure lasts longer, there is no clear treatment

©RxPrep

DIASTAT ACUDIAL DISPENSING

Each package contains two rectal syringes prefilled with diazepam rectal gel.

Syringes MUST be dialed to the right dose and locked BEFORE DISPENSING. Syringes come in 2.5, 10 and 20 mg.

Pharmacist instructions for locking in the dose are included on a card in the package:

STOP
PHARMACIST MUST
DIAL AND LOCK
CORRECT PRESCRIBED DOSE

1. Hold the barrel of the syringe in one hand with the cap facing down and the dose window visible. Do not remove the cap.

2. Use the other hand to grab the cap firmly and turn to adjust the dose.

3. Confirm the correct dose shows in the window. Hold the locking ring at the bottom of the syringe barrel and push upward to lock both sides of the ring.

4. Repeat these steps with the second syringe in the case.

Once locked, the green band should say "READY," and the syringe cannot be unlocked (see image below).

When counseling, check both syringes with the patient before they leave the pharmacy to ensure they are dialed and locked. See the Key Counseling Points section for administration instructions.

Confirm the dose and green band are visible

Dose Display Window   Green "READY" Band

Rvector/Shutterstock.com

CHRONIC SEIZURE MANAGEMENT

AEDs are first-line treatment for epilepsy. The initial one or two drugs will provide adequate control in approximately 70% of cases. Seizures that are resistant to AEDs need to be addressed another way; uncontrolled seizures cause brain damage and can be fatal. AEDs should not be stopped abruptly as this can lead to seizures.

NON-DRUG AND ALTERNATIVE TREATMENTS

Non-drug and alternative options for chronic seizure treatment include medical marijuana (cannabis), a ketogenic diet, vagal nerve stimulation or surgical intervention. The *Embrace2* smartwatch is an FDA-cleared medical device that monitors seizures in adults and children 6 years of age and older.

Medical Marijuana (Cannabis)

There are patients with resistant seizures who have received some degree of seizure control with medical cannabis. Cannabidiol, or CBD *(Epidiolex)*, was the first cannabis-derived medication approved by the FDA to treat rare forms of epilepsy. *Epidiolex* does not contain tetrahydrocannabinol (THC), but there are other CBD and medical marijuana products available that contain varying amounts of THC. Pharmacists should consider the impact of additive CNS side effects, particularly with THC-containing products (e.g., somnolence, euphoria, possible anxiety and paranoia), and the potential for drug interactions from the THC and CBD components.

Ketogenic Diet

A ketogenic diet can be used in patients with refractory seizures (not responding to medications). The diet contains high fats, normal protein and low carbohydrates (usually a 4:1 ratio of fats to combined protein and carbohydrates). This forces the body to break down fatty acids into ketone bodies as an energy source. Ketone bodies pass into the brain and replace glucose. This elevated ketone state is called ketosis, and can lead to a reduction in seizure frequency.

ANTIEPILEPTIC DRUGS

A few AEDs are used for isolated conditions, such as ethosuximide for absence seizures. Broad-spectrum AEDs treat different seizure types. Lamotrigine, levetiracetam, topiramate and valproic acid treat focal and generalized seizures. Several narrow-spectrum AEDs are used commonly, including carbamazepine, lacosamide, oxcarbazepine, phenobarbital, phenytoin and fosphenytoin. Pregabalin and gabapentin are not listed with common AEDs. Pregabalin and gabapentin are used commonly, but not for epilepsy; they are used to treat neuropathic pain. The other AEDs are used less commonly, but there are some important issues, such as vision loss with vigabatrin.

AED MECHANISMS OF ACTION

Benzodiazepines	↑ GABA
Valproic acid	↑ GABA
Phenobarbital	Enhance/potentiate GABA effect
Levetiracetam	Ca channel blocker and ↑ GABA
Ethosuximide	T-type Ca channel blocker
Pregabalin/ Gabapentin	Ca channel blocker
Oxcarbazepine	Na and Ca channel blocker
Carbamazepine	Na channel blocker
Lamotrigine	Na channel blocker
Phenytoin/ Fosphenytoin	Na channel blocker
Topiramate	Na channel blocker

A seizure occurs when excitatory (activating) neurons produce a sudden surge of electrical activity in the brain. The sudden electrical surge is caused by a receptor malfunction or an imbalance of neurotransmitters (NTs).

A deficiency of the inhibitory NT, gamma-aminobutyric acid (GABA), or an excess of the excitatory NT, glutamate, can result in a seizure, as shown here:

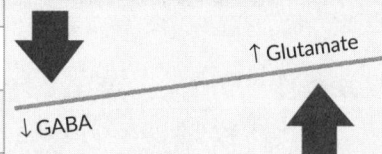

↑ Glutamate

↓ GABA

AEDs ↓ abnormal electrical activity by either:

- ↑ GABA
- ↓ Glutamate
- Blocking (or altering) Ca channels, which slows down or stops transmission of the electrical signal
- Blocking Na channels, which decreases the neurons firing rate

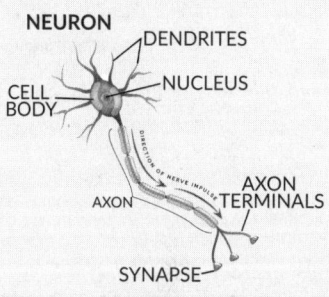

NEURON
DENDRITES
NUCLEUS
CELL BODY
AXON
AXON TERMINALS
SYNAPSE

iStock.com/TefiM

AED COUSINS

Some AEDs have "family members" with similar side effects and safety considerations.

- Carbamazepine, Oxcarbazepine and Eslicarbazepine
  - ❑ Hyponatremia, rash, enzyme induction
- Gabapentin and Pregabalin
  - ❑ Weight gain, peripheral edema, mild euphoria
  - ❑ Used primarily for neuropathic pain

- Phenobarbital and Primidone (prodrug of phenobarbital)
  - ❑ Sedation, dependence/tolerance/overdose risk, enzyme induction
- Topiramate and Zonisamide
  - ❑ Weight loss, metabolic acidosis
  - ❑ Nephrolithiasis and oligohidrosis/hyperthermia (in children)

TAKE YOUR VITAMINS ON AEDs!

Supplement with:

- ALL AEDs: calcium and vitamin D
- Women of childbearing age: folate
- Valproic acid: possibly carnitine (see drug table)
- Lamotrigine and valproic acid: if alopecia develops, supplement with selenium and zinc

COMMON BROAD-SPECTRUM ANTIEPILEPTIC DRUGS

Lamotrigine

DRUG	DOSING	SAFETY/SIDE EFFECTS/MONITORING
Lamotrigine (Lamictal, Lamictal ODT, Lamictal Starter Kit, Lamictal XR, *Subvenite, Subvenite Starter Kit-Blue, Green, Orange)* Tablet, chewable, ODT	**Initial:** Weeks 1 and 2: 25 mg daily Weeks 3 and 4: 50 mg daily Week 5 and on: can ↑ by 50 mg daily every 1-2 weeks **Maintenance Dose:** 300-400 mg daily, divide BID, unless using XR (daily)	**BOXED WARNING** Serious skin reactions, including SJS/TEN (rate of rash is greater in pediatrics than adults); ↑ risk with higher than recommended starting doses, dose escalation or when used with valproic acid **WARNINGS** Risk of aseptic meningitis, blood dyscrasias, cardiac rhythm abnormalities, multiorgan hypersensitivity (DRESS) reactions, serious rare immune system reaction [hemophagocytic lymphohistiocytosis (HLH)] that can be fatal **SIDE EFFECTS** Alopecia (supplement selenium and zinc), N/V, somnolence, rash, tremor, ataxia, impaired coordination, dizziness, diplopia, blurred vision **MONITORING** Rash **NOTES** Discontinue if there is any sign of hypersensitivity reaction or unspecified rash Use starter kit packaging when starting to ensure correct dosing (see Study Tip Gal below)

Lamotrigine Drug Interactions

- Valproic acid ↑ lamotrigine concentrations more than two-fold. Use lower dose starter kit (blue box).

- Oral estrogen-containing contraceptives ↓ lamotrigine; higher maintenance doses of lamotrigine may be needed.

- Carbamazepine, phenytoin, phenobarbital, primidone, lopinavir/ritonavir, atazanavir/ritonavir and rifampin ↓ lamotrigine levels by 40%. Use the higher dose starter kit (green box).

LAMICTAL STARTER KITS BY COLOR

Lamotrigine doses need to be just right.

- Too much leads to a higher risk of severe rash.
- Too little leads to seizures.

The colored starter kits are helpful to make sure the right dose is selected.

ORANGE	BLUE	GREEN
■ Standard starting dose ■ Use if no interacting medications	■ Lower starting dose ■ Use if taking valproic acid (enzyme inhibitor)	■ Higher starting dose ■ Use if taking an enzyme inducer (e.g., carbamazepine, phenytoin, phenobarbital, primidone), and not taking valproic acid

Levetiracetam

DRUG	DOSING	SAFETY/SIDE EFFECTS/MONITORING
Levetiracetam (*Keppra*, *Keppra XR*, *Roweepra, Spritam)* Tablet, ODT, oral solution, injection	**Initial:** 500 mg BID or 1,000 mg daily (XR) **Maximum:** 3,000 mg/day **CrCl ≤ 80 mL/min:** ↓ dose IV:PO ratio 1:1	**WARNINGS** Psychiatric reactions, including psychotic symptoms, somnolence, fatigue, suicidal behavior, anaphylaxis, angioedema, coordination difficulties, severe skin reactions (SJS/TEN), hematologic abnormalities (mainly anemias), ↑ BP, loss of seizure control during pregnancy **SIDE EFFECTS** Irritability, dizziness, weakness, asthenia, vomiting (children and adolescents) **NOTES** No significant drug interactions

Topiramate

DRUG	DOSING	SAFETY/SIDE EFFECTS/MONITORING
Topiramate (*Topamax*, *Topamax Sprinkle)* Topiramate extended-release (*Qudexy XR, Trokendi XR)* Capsule, extended-release capsule, tablet Also used for migraine prophylaxis	**Initial:** Week 1: 25 mg BID (IR) or 50 mg daily (XR) Weeks 2-4: ↑ by 25 mg BID (IR) or 50 mg daily (XR) each week Week 5 and on: ↑ by 100 mg weekly until max dose or therapeutic effect **Maximum:** 400 mg/day **CrCl < 70 mL/min:** ↓ dose by 50%	**CONTRAINDICATIONS** *Trokendi XR* only: alcohol use 6 hours before or after dose, *Qudexy XR* only: patients with metabolic acidosis who are taking metformin **WARNINGS** Hyperchloremic nonanion gap metabolic acidosis, oligohidrosis (reduced perspiration)/hyperthermia (mostly in children), nephrolithiasis (kidney stones), acute myopia and secondary angle-closure glaucoma, hyperammonemia (alone and with valproic acid), visual problems (reversible), fetal harm **SIDE EFFECTS** Somnolence, dizziness, psychomotor slowing, difficulty with memory/concentration/attention, weight loss, anorexia, paresthesia **MONITORING** Electrolytes (especially bicarbonate), renal function, hydration status, eye exam (intraocular pressure) **NOTES** *Topamax Sprinkle*: swallow whole or open and sprinkle on a small amount of soft food (do not chew; swallow immediately)

Topiramate Drug Interactions

- Topiramate is a weak inhibitor of CYP2C19 and inducer of CYP3A4.

- Phenytoin, carbamazepine, valproic acid and lamotrigine can ↓ topiramate levels.

- Topiramate can ↓ oral contraceptive effectiveness, (especially doses ≥ 200 mg/day). Non-hormonal contraception is recommended.

- Topiramate can ↓ the INR in patients on warfarin; monitor closely.

Valproic Acid

DRUG	DOSING	SAFETY/SIDE EFFECTS/MONITORING
Valproic acid (*Depakene**) Capsule, syrup **Valproate sodium** (*Depacon**) IV **Divalproex (Depakote, Depakote ER, Depakote Sprinkle)** *Depakote* – delayed-release (DR) tablet *Depakote ER* – extended-release (ER) tablet *Depakote Sprinkle* – capsules can be opened and sprinkled on food Also used for bipolar disorder and migraine prophylaxis	**Initial:** 10-15 mg/kg/day **Maximum:** 60 mg/kg/day **Therapeutic Range:** 50-100 mcg/mL (total level) If the albumin is low (< 3.5 g/dL), the true valproic acid level will be higher than it appears – adjust with the same formula used for phenytoin. DR and ER formulations are not bioequivalent, ↑ total daily dose 8-20% when converting from DR to ER tablets	**BOXED WARNINGS** Hepatic failure: usually during first 6 months of therapy, children < 2 years old and patients with mitochondrial disorders [mutations in mitochondrial DNA polymerase gamma gene (POLG)] are at ↑ risk; fetal harm (neural tube defects and ↓ IQ scores); pancreatitis **CONTRAINDICATIONS** Hepatic disease, urea cycle disorders, prophylaxis of migraine in pregnancy, known POLG-related disorder or suspected if < 2 years of age **WARNINGS** Hyperammonemia (treat with carnitine in symptomatic adults only), hypothermia, dose-related thrombocytopenia (↑ bleeding risk), multiorgan hypersensitivity (DRESS) reactions **SIDE EFFECTS** Alopecia (supplement selenium and zinc), weight gain, N/V, headache, anorexia, abdominal pain, dizziness, somnolence, tremor, edema, polycystic ovary syndrome, diplopia, blurred vision **MONITORING** LFTs (baseline and frequently in the first 6 months), CBC with differential, platelets **NOTES** Divalproex is a valproic acid derivative with the same side effect profile and CYP enzyme/protein binding interactions as the valproic acid formulations

* Brand discontinued but name still used in practice.

Valproic Acid Drug Interactions

- Valproic acid is an inhibitor of CYP2C9 (weak) and a substrate of CYP2C19 and 2E1 (minor).

- Valproic acid can ↑ levels of lamotrigine, phenobarbital, phenytoin, warfarin and zidovudine.

- Salicylates displace valproic acid from albumin (↑ levels).

- Carbapenem antibiotics can ↓ the levels of valproic acid.

- Estrogen-containing hormonal contraceptives can ↓ valproic acid levels.

- Use caution with valproic acid and lamotrigine due to risk of serious rash; use lower starting dose of lamotrigine and titrate slowly.

- Use with topiramate can lead to hyperammonemia with or without encephalopathy.

COMMON NARROW-SPECTRUM ANTIEPILEPTIC DRUGS

Carbamazepine

DRUG	DOSING	SAFETY/SIDE EFFECTS/MONITORING
Carbamazepine (Tegretol, Tegretol XR, Carbatrol, Epitol) Capsule, tablet, chewable, oral suspension Equetro – for bipolar disorder Also used for trigeminal neuralgia	**Initial:** 200 mg BID (or divided QID for suspension) **Maximum:** 1,600 mg/day (some patients can require more) **Therapeutic Range:** 4-12 mcg/mL	**BOXED WARNINGS** Serious skin reactions, including SJS/TEN: patients of Asian descent should be tested for HLA-B*1502 allele prior to initiation; if positive for this allele, carbamazepine cannot be used (unless benefit clearly outweighs risk); aplastic anemia and agranulocytosis; discontinue if significant myelosuppression occurs **CONTRAINDICATIONS** Myelosuppression, hypersensitivity to TCAs, use of MAO inhibitors within past 14 days, use with nefazodone or non-nucleoside reverse transcriptase inhibitors (NNRTIs) that are substrates of CYP3A4 **WARNINGS** Risk of developing a hypersensitivity reaction can be ↑ in patients with the variant HLA-A*3101 allele, multiorgan hypersensitivity (DRESS) reactions, hyponatremia (SIADH), hypothyroidism, mild anticholinergic effects, cardiac conduction abnormalities, liver damage, fetal harm **SIDE EFFECTS** Dizziness, drowsiness, ataxia, N/V, pruritus, photosensitivity, blurred vision, rash, ↑ LFTs, alopecia **MONITORING** CBC with differential and platelets prior to and during therapy, LFTs, rash, eye exam, thyroid function tests, electrolytes (especially Na), renal function Monitor levels within 3-5 days of initiation and after 4 weeks due to autoinduction **NOTES** Enzyme inducer, autoinducer – ↓ level of other drugs and itself

Carbamazepine Drug Interactions

- Carbamazepine is an autoinducer and will ↓ its own levels.

- Carbamazepine is a strong inducer of many enzymes (CYP1A2, 2C19, 2C8/9, 3A4) and P-glycoprotein (P-gp). It will ↓ the levels of many drugs, including other seizure medications, aripiprazole, levothyroxine, warfarin and hormonal contraceptives. Use of an alternative, non-hormonal contraceptive is recommended.

- Carbamazepine is a major CYP3A4 substrate; inhibitors will ↑ carbamazepine levels and inducers will ↓ carbamazepine levels. Do not use with nefazodone or NNRTIs.

- Carbamazepine suspension should not be taken with other liquid medications (especially chlorpromazine) or diluents, as precipitates can form.

Lacosamide

DRUG	DOSING	SAFETY/SIDE EFFECTS/MONITORING
Lacosamide (Vimpat) C-V Tablet, oral solution, injection	**Initial:** 50-100 mg BID **Maximum:** 400 mg/day **CrCl < 30 mL/min:** maximum dose is 300 mg/day IV:PO ratio 1:1	**WARNINGS** Prolongs PR interval and ↑ risk of arrhythmias; obtain an ECG prior to use and after titrated to steady state in patients with or at risk of cardiac conduction problems; multiorgan hypersensitivity (DRESS) reactions, syncope, dizziness, ataxia **SIDE EFFECTS** Dizziness, headache, diplopia, blurred vision, ataxia, tremor, euphoria **MONITORING** ECG (baseline and at steady state) in at-risk patients

Lacosamide Drug Interactions

- Lacosamide is a substrate of CYP2C19 (minor), 2C9 (minor), 3A4 (minor) and an inhibitor of CYP2C19 (weak). Caution with inhibitors of CYP2C19, 2C9 and 3A4 as they can ↑ lacosamide levels.

- Use caution with medications that prolong the PR interval (e.g., beta-blockers, calcium channel blockers, digoxin) due to the risk of AV block and bradycardia.

Oxcarbazepine

DRUG	DOSING	SAFETY/SIDE EFFECTS/MONITORING
Oxcarbazepine (*Trileptal, Oxtellar XR*) Tablet, oral suspension (*Trileptal*) Extended-release tablet (*Oxtellar XR*)	**Initial:** 300 mg BID (*Trileptal*); 600 mg daily (*Oxtellar XR*) **Maximum:** 2,400 mg/day **CrCl < 30 mL/min:** start 300 mg daily Carbamazepine to oxcarbazepine dose conversion: 1.2-1.5x carbamazepine dose	**CONTRAINDICATIONS** Hypersensitivity to eslicarbazepine **WARNINGS** ↑ risk for serious skin reactions (SJS/TEN), consider screening patients of Asian descent for HLA-B*1502 prior to initiating therapy, multiorgan hypersensitivity (DRESS) reactions, hypersensitivity reactions to carbamazepine have 25-30% cross-sensitivity to oxcarbazepine Hyponatremia, hypothyroidism, potential worsening of seizures **SIDE EFFECTS** Somnolence, dizziness, N/V, abdominal pain, diplopia, visual disturbances, ataxia, tremor **MONITORING** Serum Na levels, especially during first 3 months of therapy, thyroid function, CBC **NOTES** *Trileptal* oral suspension: must be used within 7 weeks once original container is opened XR tablet: take on empty stomach 1 hour before or 2 hours after a meal

Oxcarbazepine Drug Interactions

- Oxcarbazepine is a weak CYP3A4 inducer and CYP2C19 inhibitor, but is <u>not an autoinducer</u>. Strong CYP3A4 inducers can ↓ oxcarbazepine levels. Oxcarbazepine and its active metabolite, MHD, can ↑ levels of fosphenytoin, phenytoin and phenobarbital.

- Oxcarbazepine doses ≥ 1200 mg/day can significantly ↑ phenytoin levels. Phenytoin levels should be monitored carefully as dose reductions may be needed.

- Oxcarbazepine can ↓ hormonal contraceptive levels significantly. Use of a <u>non-hormonal contraceptive</u> is recommended.

Phenobarbital

DRUG	DOSING	SAFETY/SIDE EFFECTS/MONITORING
Phenobarbital C-IV Tablet, oral solution, elixir, injection	**Initial:** 50-100 mg BID or TID **Therapeutic Range:** <u>20-40 mcg/mL</u> <u>(adults)</u> 15-40 mcg/mL (children)	**CONTRAINDICATIONS** Severe hepatic impairment, dyspnea or airway obstruction, previous addiction to sedative-hypnotics, intraarterial administration **WARNINGS** <u>Habit-forming, respiratory depression, fetal harm</u>, paradoxical reactions including hyperactive or aggressive behavior (in acute pain and pediatric patients), hypotension when given IV, serious skin reactions (SJS/TEN) **SIDE EFFECTS** <u>Physiological dependence, tolerance, hangover effect</u>, somnolence, cognitive impairment, dizziness, ataxia, depression, folate deficiency **MONITORING** LFTs, CBC with differential **NOTES** Primidone is a prodrug of phenobarbital

Phenobarbital Drug Interactions

- Phenobarbital (and primidone, which is the prodrug) is a <u>strong inducer</u> of most enzymes, including CYP1A2, 2C8/9, 3A4 and P-gp. These two drugs can ↓ the levels of many drugs metabolized by these enzymes.

- Phenobarbital and primidone can ↓ hormonal contraceptive levels significantly. Use of an alternative, <u>non-hormonal contraceptive</u> is recommended.

Phenytoin/Fosphenytoin

DRUG	DOSING	SAFETY/SIDE EFFECTS/MONITORING
Phenytoin **(Dilantin, Dilantin Infatabs,** *Phenytek)* Capsule, chewable, oral suspension, injection (IV only)	**Loading dose:** 15-20 mg/kg **Maintenance dose:** up to 300-600 mg/day Fosphenytoin is dosed in phenytoin equivalents (PE): 1 mg PE = 1 mg phenytoin (fosphenytoin 1.5 mg = 1 mg PE) IV:PO ratio 1:1	**BOXED WARNINGS** Phenytoin IV administration rate should not exceed 50 mg/minute and fosphenytoin IV should not exceed 150 mg PE/minute or 2 mg PE/kg/min (use the slower rate); if given faster, hypotension and cardiac arrhythmias can occur **CONTRAINDICATIONS** Previous hepatotoxicity due to phenytoin **WARNINGS** Extravasation (leading to purple glove syndrome, characterized by edema, pain and bluish discoloration of the skin, which can sometimes lead to tissue necrosis), avoid phenytoin in patients with a positive HLA-B*1502 and in patients who have had a severe rash with carbamazepine, multiorgan hypersensitivity (DRESS) reactions, fetal harm, bradycardia, ↑ risk of serious skin reactions (SJS/TEN), fraction of unbound (free) drug is higher with renal or hepatic failure or ↓ albumin, blood dyscrasias, caution in cardiac disease, hepatic and renal impairment, hypothyroidism
Fosphenytoin *(Cerebyx,* *Sesquient)* Injection (IV/IM) Prodrug of phenytoin	**Therapeutic Range:** 10-20 mcg/mL (total level) 1-2.5 mcg/mL (free level)	**SIDE EFFECTS** **Dose-related (toxicity):** Nystagmus, ataxia, diplopia/blurred vision, slurred speech, dizziness, somnolence, lethargy, confusion **Chronic:** Gingival hyperplasia, hair growth, hepatoxicity, skin thickening (children), morbilliform rash (measles-like), rash, peripheral neuropathy,↑ BG, metallic taste, connective tissue changes, enlargement of facial features (lips) **MONITORING** Serum phenytoin concentration, LFTs, CBC with differential IV: continuous cardiac (ECG, BP, HR) and respiratory monitoring **NOTES** See adjusting phenytoin doses for low albumin later in the chapter

Phenytoin/Fosphenytoin Drug Interactions

- Phenytoin and fosphenytoin are strong inducers of several enzymes, including CYP2B6, 2C19, 2C8/9, 3A4, P-gp and UGT1A1; they are substrates of CYP2C19 (major), 2C9 (major) and 3A4 (minor). Phenytoin and fosphenytoin can ↓ the concentration of many drugs including other AEDs, contraceptives and warfarin.

- Use of an alternative, non-hormonal contraceptive is recommended with chronic phenytoin.

- Both have high protein binding and can displace other highly protein-bound drugs or be displaced by other highly protein-bound drugs, causing an ↑ in levels that can lead to toxicity.

PHENYTOIN/FOSPHENYTOIN ADMINISTRATION

IV Phenytoin
- Do not exceed 50 mg/minute (slow infusion)
- Monitor BP, respiratory function and ECG
- Requires a filter
- Dilute in NS, stable for 4 hours, do not refrigerate

NG-tube Phenytoin
- Enteral feedings (e.g., tube feeds) ↓ phenytoin absorption
- Hold feedings 1-2 hours before and after administration

IV Fosphenytoin
- Do not exceed 150 mg PE/minute
- Monitoring same as above
- Lower risk of purple glove syndrome than phenytoin

NEUROLOGIC CONDITIONS

OTHER ANTIEPILEPTIC DRUGS

DRUG	SAFETY/SIDE EFFECTS/MONITORING
Benzodiazepines, including: Clobazam (Onfi, Sympazan) Tablet, oral suspension, oral film Diazepam (Valtoco) Midazolam (Nayzilam) Nasal spray C-IV	**BOXED WARNINGS** Use with <u>opioids</u> can result in profound sedation, <u>respiratory depression and death</u> **WARNINGS** Serious skin reactions (SJS/TEN), paradoxical reactions including hyperactive or aggressive behavior, anterograde amnesia **NOTES** Causes physiological dependence, tolerance, drooling, pyrexia, nasal/throat irritation (nasal formulations)
Brivaracetam (Briviact) Tablet, oral solution, injection C-V	**WARNINGS** Behavioral reactions including psychotic symptoms, irritability, depression, aggressive behavior and anxiety; bronchospasm and angioedema **MONITORING** Somnolence and fatigue, caution driving or operating machinery **NOTES** No added therapeutic benefit when used in combination with levetiracetam
Cannabidiol (Epidiolex) Oral solution	**WARNINGS** Somnolence and sedation; hepatotoxicity (monitor LFTs), risk is ↑ when used with valproic acid **NOTES** For treatment of seizures associated with Lennox-Gastaut syndrome, Dravet syndrome or tuberous sclerosis complex Can cause ↓ appetite
Cenobamate (Xcopri) Tablet C-V	**WARNINGS** Multiorgan hypersensitivity (DRESS) reactions, shortening of the QT interval, somnolence, gait disturbance, visual changes (diplopia, blurred vision) **MONITORING** Eye exam, serum K (can become elevated)
Eslicarbazepine (Aptiom) Tablet <u>Oxcarbazepine – active metabolite</u>	**NOTES** Same warnings/side effects as oxcarbazepine including ↓ Na (monitor) plus a warning for drug-induced liver injury, (monitor LFTs) Inducer of CYP3A4 (moderate)
Ethosuximide (Zarontin) Capsule, oral solution Used for <u>absence</u> seizures	**WARNINGS** Serious skin rash (<u>SJS/TEN</u>), <u>blood dyscrasias</u>, multiorgan hypersensitivity (DRESS) reactions **SIDE EFFECTS** N/V, abdominal pain, weight loss, hiccups, dizziness, somnolence **MONITORING** LFTs, CBC with differential, urinalysis, platelets, signs of rash, trough serum concentration
Felbamate (Felbatol) Tablet, oral suspension	**BOXED WARNINGS** <u>Hepatic failure, aplastic anemia</u> **MONITORING** LFTs, CBC, serum levels of other AEDs **NOTES** Informed consent needs to be signed by patient and prescriber prior to dispensing
Fenfluramine (Fintepla) Oral solution C-IV	**BOXED WARNING** <u>Valvular heart disease, pulmonary hypertension</u> (available only through a restricted distribution program/REMS) **WARNINGS** <u>↓ appetite/weight loss</u>, serotonin syndrome (contraindicated with MAO inhibitors), ↑ BP, angle-closure glaucoma **MONITORING** Echocardiogram required before, during and after treatment, weight, BP

DRUG	SAFETY/SIDE EFFECTS/MONITORING
Gabapentin *(Neurontin)* Capsule, tablet, oral solution, oral suspension *(Fanatrex* compounding kit) *Gralise* – postherpetic neuralgia (PHN) *Horizant* (gabapentin enacarbil) – PHN and restless legs syndrome	**WARNINGS** Angioedema **SIDE EFFECTS** Dizziness, somnolence, peripheral edema, weight gain, ataxia, diplopia, blurred vision, dry mouth, mild euphoria **MONITORING** Edema/weight gain **NOTES** Often used for neuropathic pain treatment See the Pain chapter for more details
Perampanel *(Fycompa)* Tablet, oral suspension C-III	**BOXED WARNING** Neuropsychiatric events (dose-related) including irritability, aggression, anger and paranoia, mostly in the first 6 weeks **NOTES** Substrate of CYP3A4 (major)
Pregabalin *(Lyrica)* C-V	**NOTES** Warnings, side effects and monitoring are the same as gabapentin Also used for diabetic or spinal cord injury neuropathic pain, PHN, fibromyalgia See the Pain chapter for more details
Primidone *(Mysoline)*	**NOTES** Prodrug of phenobarbital and phenylethylmalonamide (PEMA) – both are active metabolites See phenobarbital drug table for more details
Rufinamide *(Banzel)* Tablet, oral suspension	**CONTRAINDICATIONS** Patients with familial short QT syndrome due to QT shortening (dose-related) **NOTES** Take with food
Stiripentol *(Diacomit)* Capsule, oral suspension	**WARNINGS** Loss of appetite/weight loss, delirium/hallucinations (rare) **MONITORING** CBC and hepatic function, weight, mood **NOTES** To be taken with clobazam
Tiagabine *(Gabitril)* Tablet	**WARNINGS** Worsening of seizures/new-onset seizures when used off-label for other indications, serious skin reactions (SJS/TEN) **NOTES** Take with food
Vigabatrin *(Sabril, Vigadrone)* Tablet, packet for solution	**BOXED WARNING** Causes permanent vision loss (≥ 30% of patients) **MONITORING** Eye exam at baseline, every 3 months during therapy and 3-6 months after discontinuation **NOTES** Only available through a restricted program called the Vigabatrin REMS Program
Zonisamide *(Zonegran)* Capsule	**CONTRAINDICATIONS** Hypersensitivity to sulfonamides **WARNINGS** Same as topiramate except no hyperammonemia warning and there is a risk of serious skin reactions (SJS/TEN); multiorgan hypersensitivity (DRESS) reactions **SIDE EFFECTS** Side effects similar to topiramate, including oligohidrosis/hyperthermia (mostly in children) and risk of nephrolithiasis

NEUROLOGIC CONDITIONS

CONCERNS WITH AEDs

AEDs should be selected based on individual patient factors, including seizure type, age, childbearing potential and school and career requirements. The right AED for one patient may not be appropriate for another patient with the same seizure type. Below are factors to consider when selecting an AED for a particular patient.

Monitoring

All AEDs require monitoring of seizure frequency (to ensure efficacy) and mental status (to minimize adverse effects). Some AEDs (e.g., phenytoin, valproic acid, carbamazepine and phenobarbital) have therapeutic drug level ranges that are monitored to control seizures and keep the toxic effects to a minimum. Drug levels are commonly obtained when treatment is started, with dose adjustments, with suspected toxicity and to check adherence. The metabolism of phenytoin can become saturated; when there are no enzymes left to metabolize the drug, a small increase in the dose can lead to a large increase in the drug concentration. See the Study Tip Gal below on Adjusting Phenytoin Doses. It is important to monitor levels and make dose changes carefully.

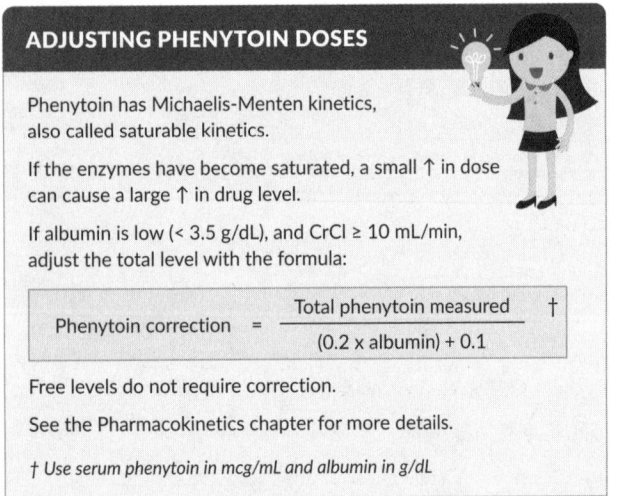

ADJUSTING PHENYTOIN DOSES

Phenytoin has Michaelis-Menten kinetics, also called saturable kinetics.

If the enzymes have become saturated, a small ↑ in dose can cause a large ↑ in drug level.

If albumin is low (< 3.5 g/dL), and CrCl ≥ 10 mL/min, adjust the total level with the formula:

$$\text{Phenytoin correction} = \frac{\text{Total phenytoin measured}}{(0.2 \times \text{albumin}) + 0.1} \quad \dagger$$

Free levels do not require correction.

See the Pharmacokinetics chapter for more details.

† Use serum phenytoin in mcg/mL and albumin in g/dL

CASE SCENARIO

A patient has a total phenytoin level of 13 mcg/mL and recent labs as follows: SCr 1.1 mg/dL, albumin 3.1 g/dL. What is the corrected phenytoin level (round to the nearest TENTH)?

Phenytoin correction = 13 / (0.2 x 3.1) + 0.1

Phenytoin correction = 18.1 mcg/mL

Drug Interactions

Many AEDs are enzyme inducers and lower the concentration of other medications, including other AEDs (see Study Tip Gal below). Valproic acid is an enzyme inhibitor, which is usually not a big issue, except with lamotrigine. The two are often used together. Higher lamotrigine levels increase the risk of severe rash.

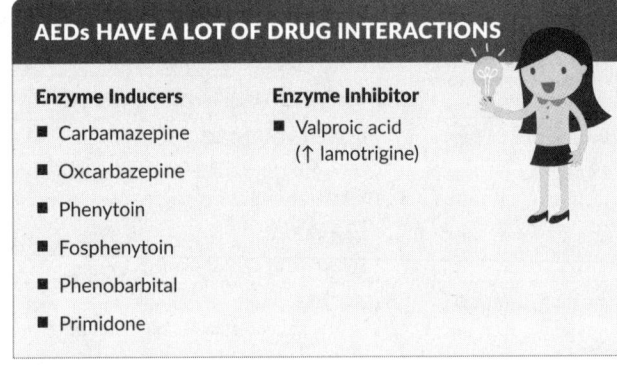

AEDs HAVE A LOT OF DRUG INTERACTIONS

Enzyme Inducers
- Carbamazepine
- Oxcarbazepine
- Phenytoin
- Fosphenytoin
- Phenobarbital
- Primidone

Enzyme Inhibitor
- Valproic acid
  (↑ lamotrigine)

CNS Depression

All AEDs have to cross the blood-brain barrier to prevent seizures. Regardless of the specific mechanism of action, all AEDs depress electrical activity in the brain. All AEDs cause CNS depression (e.g., dizziness, confusion, sedation and ataxia/coordination difficulties) and increase risk for impairment, falls and injuries. The degree of CNS depression is an important consideration when selecting treatment for adults, who need to perform well at work, and for children, who need to perform well in school.

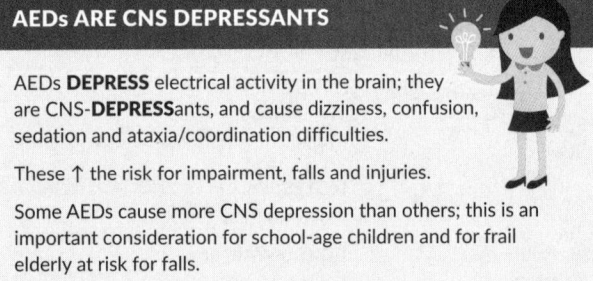

AEDs ARE CNS DEPRESSANTS

AEDs **DEPRESS** electrical activity in the brain; they are CNS-**DEPRESS**ants, and cause dizziness, confusion, sedation and ataxia/coordination difficulties.

These ↑ the risk for impairment, falls and injuries.

Some AEDs cause more CNS depression than others; this is an important consideration for school-age children and for frail elderly at risk for falls.

Bone Loss

AEDs can cause bone loss and increase fracture risk. All patients on AEDs should be supplemented with calcium and vitamin D. Bone loss can occur as soon as two years after the start of an AED. Modifiable factors that affect bone density should be addressed (see the Osteoporosis, Menopause & Testosterone Use chapter).

Suicide Risk and Rash

All AEDs have a warning for suicide risk and require monitoring of mood by the patient and caregivers. Many AEDs can cause serious skin rash, including risk for Stevens-Johnson syndrome (SJS) and toxic epidermal necrolysis (TEN). Higher blood levels increase the risk.

Use in Pregnancy

Several of the older AEDs (e.g., clonazepam, phenobarbital, primidone, phenytoin, fosphenytoin, carbamazepine and valproic acid) have known teratogenic risk. Valproic acid has the highest risk, including neural tube defects and impaired cognitive function in the child (decreased IQ). The risk profiles of newer AEDs are not well defined, and most have some degree of risk.

Congenital malformations occur more commonly in children exposed to AEDs *in utero*. Most are minor, but some are not, including cardiac defects (e.g., atrial septal defect, Tetralogy of Fallot, patent ductus arteriosus and pulmonary stenosis), urogenital defects and neural tube defects. Neural tube defects occur most commonly in children born to mothers taking carbamazepine or valproic acid. Women of childbearing age on AEDs should receive daily folate supplementation.

Women of childbearing age on AEDs should avoid unplanned pregnancy. Pre-pregnancy counseling should be done to ensure that a plan is in place to maintain good seizure control. Many AEDs reduce efficacy of oral contraceptives (see the Contraception & Infertility chapter).

AEDs contribute to bone loss, as discussed previously. In pregnancy, the mother provides calcium for the baby to grow bone. This leads to an additive need for extra calcium. The mother must receive adequate supplementation of calcium and vitamin D while pregnant and taking an AED.

Blood levels of AEDs can change throughout pregnancy and postpartum. Monitoring drug levels throughout this time frame is very important. The levels of all AEDs decline during pregnancy, with some being more affected than others. Low AED levels can lead to seizures, which can be harmful to the baby. Dose increases can be needed. In the postpartum period, AED levels increase, and decreased doses are commonly needed. Monitoring levels in the postpartum period is necessary to minimize side effects.

Use in Children

In addition to cognitive impairment and coordination difficulty, there are drug-specific risks in children taking AEDs. Topiramate and zonisamide can cause reduced or lack of sweating (i.e., hypohidrosis) in young children. This means that exposure to the sun should be limited, which affects playtime and sports. Lamotrigine-induced rash, with risk of fatality, occurs more commonly in children.

Administering medications to children can be difficult as many are unable to swallow tablets and capsules. AEDs that are often used in children come in formulations that are easy to swallow, including lamotrigine (ODT, chewable tablets) and levetiracetam (ODT, oral solution).

Half of the children with epilepsy outgrow the condition. A child who remains seizure-free for one to two years can often be tapered off AEDs safely without repercussions.

KEY COUNSELING POINTS

See the Drug Formulations and Patient Counseling Chapter for counseling language/layman's terminology.

ALL ANTIEPILEPTIC DRUGS

- Can cause:
    - Suicidal ideation.
    - Drowsiness.
- Seizures can become worse when the drug is suddenly stopped. The dose must be gradually decreased.
- Many drug interactions, including drugs that worsen drowsiness (e.g., benzodiazepines and opioids) and drugs that lower the seizure threshold.
- Supplement with calcium and vitamin D while taking this medication.

Carbamazepine

- Can cause:
    - Severe rash.
    - Rare but serious blood problems. You will need to have your blood checked while on this medication.
- Avoid in pregnancy (teratogenic).

NEUROLOGIC CONDITIONS

Diazepam Rectal Gel

- The green "READY" band should be visible before leaving the pharmacy.
- Administration instructions (detailed administration instructions can be found at https://diastat.com/):
  - ❑ Put the person on their side in a safe location (where they can't fall).
  - ❑ Get medication syringe and lubricating jelly.
  - ❑ Remove syringe cap (and seal pin) by pushing up with thumb.
  - ❑ Apply lubricating jelly to syringe tip.
  - ❑ Turn the person on their side facing you and bend upper leg forward to expose the rectum.
  - ❑ Separate buttocks and gently insert syringe tip into the rectum. The syringe rim should be snug against the rectal opening.
  - ❑ Slowly count to 3 while gently pushing the plunger until it stops.
  - ❑ Count to 3 before removing syringe from rectum.
  - ❑ Count to 3 again while holding buttocks together to prevent leakage.
  - ❑ Make note of the time given and observe.
- Call 911 if the seizure continues 15 minutes after giving the medication.
- Dispose of any remaining medication in the sink or toilet.

Lamotrigine

- Can cause:
  - ❑ Severe rash (most likely in the first 2 to 8 weeks of treatment).
- Chewable tablets can be swallowed whole, chewed or mixed in water or diluted fruit juice. If mixed, take the whole amount right away.

Oxcarbazepine

- Can cause:
  - ❑ Low sodium concentrations in the blood. Contact your healthcare provider if you experience fatigue, headache, nausea or confusion.
  - ❑ Severe rash.
- Take extended-release (*Oxtellar XR*) on an empty stomach at least one hour before or two hours after food.
- Oral suspension must be shaken for 10 seconds before using and can be mixed in a small glass of water. Discard any unused portion after seven weeks.

Phenobarbital

- Abuse and dependence can occur.
- Avoid in pregnancy (teratogenic).

Phenytoin

- Can cause:
  - ❑ Severe rash.
  - ❑ Gingival hyperplasia.
  - ❑ Hair growth.
- Avoid in pregnancy (teratogenic).

Topiramate

- Can cause:
  - ❑ Problems with concentration, attention, memory or speech.
  - ❑ Eye damage.
  - ❑ Decreased sweating and increased body temperature (especially in children).
  - ❑ Weight loss.
- Sprinkle capsules can be swallowed whole or opened and sprinkled on a teaspoon of soft food. Swallow whole, do not chew. Follow with a glass of water.
- Drink plenty of fluids to prevent kidney stones.
- Avoid in pregnancy (teratogenic).

Valproic Acid

- Can cause:
  - ❑ Liver damage.
  - ❑ Weight gain.
- Avoid in pregnancy (teratogenic).
- Take with food to help avoid stomach upset.

Select Guidelines/References

Evidence-Based Guideline: Treatment of Convulsive Status Epilepticus in Children and Adults: Report of the Guideline Committee of the American Epilepsy Society. *Epilepsy Curr*. 2016;16(1):48-61.

Operational Classification of Seizure Types by the International League Against Epilepsy. 2017 Update. https://www.ilae.org/files/dmfile/Operational-Classification--Fisher_et_al-2017-Epilepsia.pdf (accessed 2022 Feb 22).

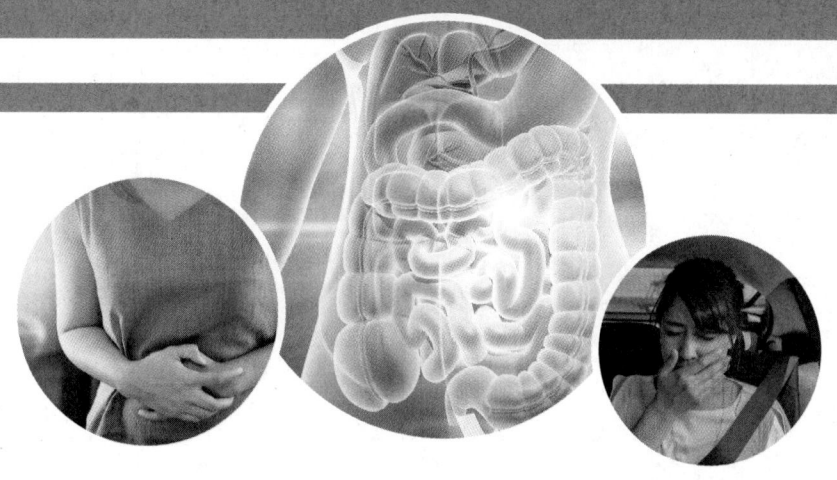

GASTROINTESTINAL CONDITIONS

CONTENTS

CONTENT LEGEND

  = Study Tip Gal   = Key Drug Guy

© iStock.com/Tharakorn

CHAPTER 72

GASTROESOPHAGEAL REFLUX DISEASE & PEPTIC ULCER DISEASE

GASTROESOPHAGEAL REFLUX DISEASE

BACKGROUND

Parietal cells in the epithelial lining of the stomach secrete hydrochloric acid (HCl) through the H^+/K^+-adenosine triphosphatase (ATPase) pump, known as the proton pump. The pump, and secretion of HCl, is stimulated by histamine, acetylcholine and the hormone gastrin, which has the added role of stimulating stomach muscle contractions to aid in digestion. Acidic gastric contents are normally prevented from backflow into the esophagus by a protective ring of muscle fibers called the lower esophageal sphincter (LES). Patients with gastroesophageal reflux disease (GERD) have reduced LES pressure (muscle tone), and gastric contents can backflow into the esophagus.

SCREENING AND DIAGNOSIS

Typical GERD symptoms include heartburn (daytime or nocturnal), hypersalivation and regurgitation of acidic contents into the mouth or throat. Less common symptoms include epigastric pain, nausea, cough, sore throat, hoarseness or chest pain, which can be difficult to distinguish from cardiac pain.

Diagnosis is based on patient-reported symptoms (duration, daytime and/or nocturnal occurrence), frequency ($\geq$ 2 times per week) and risk factors (e.g., family history, diet and eating habits, sleep position); invasive testing is not required when typical symptoms are present.

GERD can decrease quality of life and lead to esophageal erosion, strictures, bleeding and Barrett's esophagus (abnormal cell growth in the esophageal lining which can lead to esophageal cancer). If a patient has alarm symptoms (see next page) or there is concern for a more serious condition, endoscopy can be performed to further investigate the problem. Patients who are refractory to GERD treatment may benefit from 24-hour esophageal pH monitoring.

KEY DRUGS THAT CAN WORSEN GERD SYMPTOMS

Aspirin/NSAIDs	Iron supplements
Bisphosphonates	Nicotine replacement therapy
Dabigatran	Steroids
Estrogen products	Tetracyclines
Fish oil products	

GERD Treatment Algorithm

Lifestyle Modifications

- <u>Weight loss</u> (if overweight or recently gained weight)*
- Elevate the head of the bed with foam wedges or blocks
- Avoid eating high fat meals within 2-3 hours of bedtime
- Avoid foods/beverages that trigger reflux (patient-specific): caffeine, chocolate, acidic/spicy foods, carbonated beverages

Initial Drug Treatment

PPI once daily for 8 weeks

- Can increase to twice daily if partial response or if nocturnal symptoms are present

Stop treatment at 8 weeks; if symptoms return, start maintenance therapy

Maintenance Treatment

- 1st line: <u>PPI at the lowest effective dose</u>**
- Alternative: H2RA, if there is no erosive esophagitis and it relieves symptoms
- Not recommended: metoclopramide or sucralfate

*Weight loss has the best evidence for improvement of symptoms
**Can include intermittent or on-demand dosing (see PPI section of text)

TREATMENT PRINCIPLES

The vast majority of patients self-treat GERD symptoms with OTC products and do not seek medical attention unless this fails. It is common for a pharmacist to be the first healthcare encounter for a patient with GERD symptoms. Patients should be <u>referred for further evaluation</u> if they do not respond to lifestyle modifications and/or <u>two weeks</u> of self-treatment with <u>OTC products</u>, or if <u>alarm symptoms</u> are present [odynophagia (painful swallowing), dysphagia, frequent nausea and vomiting, hematemesis, black bloody stools, unintentional weight loss].

Treatment should include lifestyle modifications and drugs. <u>Infrequent heartburn</u> (< 2 times per week) can be treated with as needed (<u>PRN</u>) OTC <u>antacids</u> or <u>histamine-2 receptor antagonists (H2RAs)</u>. An <u>eight-week</u> course of a <u>proton pump inhibitor</u> (PPI) is the <u>initial drug</u> treatment of choice for <u>GERD</u> and is used to heal any erosive esophagitis. There are no major differences in efficacy between the available PPIs. After eight weeks, treatment should be interrupted; if symptoms return, maintenance therapy is needed.

DRUG TREATMENT

Antacids

<u>Antacids work by neutralizing gastric acid</u> (producing salt and water), which <u>increases gastric pH</u>. Since antacids do not require systemic absorption, they provide <u>relief within minutes</u>, but the <u>duration</u> of relief is <u>short (30 – 60 minutes)</u>. Antacids can be purchased <u>OTC</u> and are suitable for mild, infrequent symptoms. Patients using <u>antacids containing aspirin</u> (e.g., *Alka-Seltzer*) should be made aware of the serious <u>bleeding</u> risk if used too frequently.

DRUG	DOSING	SAFETY/SIDE EFFECTS/MONITORING
Calcium carbonate (*Tums*, others) **+ magnesium (*Mylanta Supreme*,** others) **+ simethicone (anti-gas) (*Maalox Advanced Maximum Strength*,** others) **Magnesium hydroxide (*Milk of Magnesia*,** others) + aluminum (*Gaviscon, Mag-Al*, others) **+ aluminum + simethicone (*Mylanta Classic*,** others) **Sodium bicarbonate/aspirin/ citric acid (*Alka-Seltzer*,** others)	Many formulations including suspensions, chewable tablets, capsules Dosing varies by product; many require administration 4-6 times per day	**WARNINGS** <u>Aluminum and magnesium</u>: can <u>accumulate</u> with severe <u>renal dysfunction</u> (not recommended if CrCl < 30 mL/min); risk of bleeding with aspirin-containing products **SIDE EFFECTS** Unpleasant taste <u>Calcium: constipation</u>, bloating, belching <u>Aluminum: constipation</u>, hypophosphatemia <u>Magnesium: loose stools</u> (use with aluminum may counter-balance) **NOTES** <u>Calcium</u>-containing antacids may be <u>preferred in pregnancy</u> (see Drug Use in Pregnancy and Lactation chapter) *Alka-Seltzer* contains > 500 mg Na per tablet which can worsen edema in patients with heart failure or cirrhosis

Histamine-2 Receptor Antagonists

H2RAs reversibly inhibit H2 receptors on gastric parietal cells, which decreases gastric acid secretion. They are used PRN for infrequent or mild heartburn but have a slower onset than antacids. H2RAs can be used as maintenance treatment for GERD, after the initial eight weeks of PPI therapy, if there are no esophageal erosions and the patient can remain symptom-free. Use of an H2RA for maintenance treatment could decrease side effects associated with long-term use of PPIs (see Risks Associated with PPI section). If H2RAs are used for ulcer healing or hypersecretory conditions (e.g., Zollinger-Ellison syndrome), higher doses are needed.

DRUG	DOSING	SAFETY/SIDE EFFECTS/MONITORING
Famotidine (**Pepcid AC, Zantac 360,** others) Rx and OTC: tablet, chewable tablet, suspension Rx: injection + calcium carbonate and magnesium hydroxide (*Pepcid Complete*) OTC: chewable tablet + ibuprofen (*Duexis*) Rx: tablet	**OTC** 10-20 mg 1-2 times daily PRN **Rx** 20 mg BID CrCl < 60 mL/min: decrease dose	**WARNINGS** Confusion, usually reversible [risk factors: elderly, severely ill, renal impairment (see Notes)]; vitamin B12 deficiency with prolonged use (≥ 2 years) Famotidine: ECG changes (QT prolongation) with renal dysfunction Ranitidine: ↑ ALT **SIDE EFFECTS** Headache, agitation/vomiting in children < 1 year Cimetidine (high doses): gynecomastia, impotence
Ranitidine* (**Zantac, Ranitidine Acid Reducer,** others) Rx and OTC: tablet, capsule, syrup Rx: injection	**OTC** 75-150 mg 1-2 times daily PRN **Rx** 150 mg BID	**NOTES** Onset of relief: within 60 minutes Duration: 4-10 hours May be used in pregnancy when clinically indicated Decrease dose when CrCl < 50 mL/min (ranitidine, nizatidine) or CrCl < 30 mL/min (cimetidine)
Nizatidine Rx: capsule, oral solution	**Rx** 150 mg BID	Cimetidine can ↑ SCr, without causing renal impairment Avoid cimetidine due to drug interactions and side effects
Cimetidine (*Tagamet HB*) Rx and OTC: tablet, oral solution	**OTC** 200 mg 1-2 times daily PRN **Rx** 400 mg Q6H	To relieve symptoms, take PRN; to prevent symptoms, take PRN 30-60 minutes before food or beverages that cause heartburn Tachyphylaxis (tolerance to effects) can occur if used on a scheduled basis

*All ranitidine products were removed from the market in April 2020

Proton Pump Inhibitors

PPIs irreversibly bind to the gastric H⁺/K⁺-ATPase pump (the proton pump) in parietal cells. This shuts down the pump and blocks gastric acid secretion. PPIs are the most effective medications for GERD, and an eight-week course of treatment is recommended for relief of symptoms and to heal erosions that may be present. All PPIs have similar efficacy, though an individual patient may respond better to one drug over another. If used long-term as maintenance treatment, the lowest effective dose should be used and the need for treatment should be assessed regularly. Intermittent use (PPI taken for a short time after relapse of GERD symptoms) and on-demand use (PPI taken only when symptoms occur) are additional options.

Recommended Administration of Oral PPIs

DRUG	MEAL	TIMING
Esomeprazole (*Nexium*)	Before breakfast	At least 60 minutes before
Lansoprazole (*Prevacid, Prevacid SoluTab*)		Time not specified
Omeprazole (*Prilosec*)		Time not specified
Omeprazole + sodium bicarbonate (*Zegerid*)		60 minutes before (can control nocturnal symptoms if given at bedtime)
Dexlansoprazole (*Dexilant*)	Formulation-specific	Without regard to meals
Pantoprazole (*Protonix*)		Tablet: without regard to meals Oral suspension: 30 minutes before a meal
Rabeprazole (*Aciphex, AcipHex Sprinkle*)		Tablet: without regard to meals Capsule sprinkles: 30 minutes before meal

Proton Pump Inhibitor Products

DRUG	DOSING	SAFETY/SIDE EFFECTS/MONITORING
Dexlansoprazole (Dexilant) Rx: capsule	**Rx** 30-60 mg daily	**WARNINGS** _C. difficile_-associated diarrhea (CDAD), hypomagnesemia, vitamin B12 deficiency with prolonged use (≥ 2 years), osteoporosis-related bone fractures with high doses or long-term (≥ 1 year) use, acute interstitial nephritis (hypersensitivity reaction), cutaneous and systemic lupus erythematosus
Esomeprazole (Nexium, Nexium 24HR, Nexium I.V., _Esomep-EZS_, others) Rx and OTC: capsule, tablet Rx: injection, packet for oral suspension **+ naproxen (Vimovo)** Rx: tablet	**OTC** 20 mg daily **Rx** 20-40 mg daily	PPIs may diminish the therapeutic effect of clopidogrel, do not use omeprazole and esomeprazole while taking clopidogrel; rabeprazole or pantoprazole have less risk IV _Protonix_: thrombophlebitis, severe skin reactions (SJS/TEN)
Lansoprazole (Prevacid, Prevacid SoluTab, Prevacid 24HR, _First-Lansoprazole_, others) Rx and OTC: capsule, ODT Rx: suspension	**OTC** 15 mg daily **Rx** 15-30 mg daily	**SIDE EFFECTS** Generally well-tolerated, can cause headache, abdominal pain, nausea, diarrhea **NOTES** Onset: 1-3 hours; duration > 24 hrs for most PPIs
Omeprazole (Prilosec, Prilosec OTC, _First-Omeprazole, Omeprazole+Syrspend SF Alka_) Rx and OTC: capsule, tablet Rx: packet for oral suspension OTC: ODT + sodium bicarbonate (Zegerid, Zegerid OTC) Rx and OTC: capsule, packet for oral suspension + aspirin (Yosprala) Rx: tablet	**OTC** 20 mg daily **Rx** 20-40 mg daily	May be used in pregnancy when clinically indicated Pantoprazole and esomeprazole are the only PPIs available IV Do not crush, cut, or chew tablets or capsules Dexlansoprazole, esomeprazole, lansoprazole, omeprazole and rabeprazole capsules can be opened (not crushed), mixed in applesauce and swallowed immediately (without chewing) _Zegerid_ 20 mg and 40 mg have the same Na bicarbonate content (1,100 mg); do not substitute two 20 mg capsules/packets for one 40 mg capsule/packet because the patient will receive twice the amount of Na; caution in patients on Na-restricted diet (e.g., heart failure, cirrhosis)
Pantoprazole (Protonix) Rx: tablet, injection, packet for oral suspension	**Rx** 40 mg daily	_First-Omeprazole, Omeprazole+Syrspend SF Alka_ and _First-Lansoprazole_ are suspension compounding kits that contain pre-measured powdered drug, suspension liquid (with flavoring) and mixing tools
Rabeprazole (Aciphex, AcipHex Sprinkle) Rx: tablet, capsule sprinkle	**Rx** 20 mg daily	_Esomep-ESZ_ is a kit that contains capsules with Pill Swallowing Spray

---

H2RA AND PPI FORMULATIONS TO KNOW

- H2RAs and PPIs are very common medications. Sometimes suspensions, solutions or ODT formulations are needed (e.g., infants, children, adults unable to swallow tablets/capsules). Non-oral formulations are used when patients are NPO.

	OTC	ODT	ORAL SOLUTION/SUSPENSION	INJECTION
H2RA	Cimetidine Famotidine Ranitidine*		Cimetidine Famotidine Nizatidine Ranitidine*	Famotidine Ranitidine*
PPI	Esomeprazole Lansoprazole Omeprazole	Lansoprazole Omeprazole	Lansoprazole **Packets for suspension:** Esomeprazole Omeprazole Pantoprazole	Esomeprazole Pantoprazole

*All ranitidine products were removed from the market in April 2020

Risks Associated with PPI Therapy

Long-term use of PPIs causes chronic changes in gastric pH. This can promote growth of microorganisms and increase the risk of GI infections, including _C. difficile_ and possibly pneumonia (due to reflux of gastric contents beyond the oral cavity). PPIs also increase the risk of osteoporosis and fractures. The Beers Criteria recommend that PPIs not be used beyond eight weeks in elderly patients unless there is a clear indication (e.g., high risk for GI bleed due to chronic NSAID use, demonstrated need for maintenance treatment).

Metoclopramide and Other Medications

Other medications historically used for GERD treatment include the cytoprotective drugs, misoprostol and sucralfate, and the prokinetic drug, metoclopramide. There is currently no role for these medications in the management of GERD and they are not recommended by guidelines. Misoprostol and sucralfate can be used for peptic ulcer disease, which is discussed later in the chapter. Metoclopramide and erythromycin are most commonly used when patients have coexisting gastroparesis.

Metoclopramide is a dopamine antagonist. At higher doses, it blocks serotonin receptors in the chemoreceptor zone of the CNS which helps nausea and vomiting (see the Oncology I chapter). Metoclopramide enhances the response to acetylcholine in the upper GI tract, causing increased motility, accelerated gastric emptying (peristaltic speed) and ↑ LES tone.

DRUG	DOSING	SAFETY/SIDE EFFECTS/MONITORING
Metoclopramide **(Reglan)** Tablet, ODT, oral solution, injection, nasal solution	10-15 mg QID 30 min before meals and at bedtime Has a short duration of action (food must be present in the gut) Not recommended for use > 12 weeks CrCl < 60 mL/min: decrease dose 50% (to avoid side effects, including CNS/EPS side effects)	**BOXED WARNING** Can cause tardive dyskinesia (a serious movement disorder, often irreversible); there is increased risk with high doses, long-term treatment (> 12 weeks) and in elderly patients **CONTRAINDICATIONS** GI obstruction, perforation or hemorrhage, history of seizures, pheochromocytoma, use in combination with other drugs likely to increase extrapyramidal symptoms (EPS) **WARNINGS** EPS (including acute dystonia), parkinsonian-like symptoms, rare neuroleptic malignant syndrome (NMS), depression, suicidal ideation Avoid use in patients with Parkinson disease **SIDE EFFECTS** Drowsiness, restlessness, fatigue, hypertension, pro-arrhythmic, diarrhea

DRUG INTERACTIONS

There are many types of interactions between acid-suppressing drugs and other medications. This section highlights the most important interactions for antacids, H2RAs and PPIs, but it is not all-inclusive. As appropriate, refer to other chapters (e.g., HIV, Hepatitis & Liver Disease, Infectious Diseases).

Antacids, H2RAs and PPIs

- Some drugs require an acidic gut for absorption, including enteric-coated or delayed-release products that can dissolve and release drug prematurely if the gastric pH is increased. The Key Drugs Guy to the right shows some important drugs that can have decreased absorption when given concurrently with antacids, H2RAs and PPIs.

  - ❑ Due to the short duration of action of antacids, this type of interaction can often be alleviated by separating administration of the interacting drugs (see Antacids section on next page).

  - ❑ The following should be avoided completely when taking H2RAs or PPIs: dasatinib, pazopanib and the delayed-release formulation of risedronate (Atelvia). Erlotinib, rilpivirine and velpatasvir/sofosbuvir (Epclusa) are additional medications that should be avoided in combination with PPIs.

KEY DRUGS WITH DECREASED ABSORPTION

Drugs that require an acidic gut (absorption ↓ by antacids, H2RAs and PPIs)
- Antiretrovirals: rilpivirine (NNRTI*), atazanavir (PI*)
- Antivirals: ledipasvir, velpatasvir/sofosbuvir
- Azole antifungals: *Sporanox* (itraconazole capsules), ketoconazole, posaconazole oral suspension**
- Cephalosporins (oral): cefpodoxime, cefuroxime
- Iron products
- Mesalamine
- Risedronate delayed-release
- Tyrosine kinase inhibitors: dasatinib, erlotinib, pazopanib

Oral drugs/drug classes that antacids bind
- Antiretrovirals (INSTIs*): bictegravir, dolutegravir, elvitegravir, raltegravir
- Bisphosphonates
- Isoniazid
- Levothyroxine
- Mycophenolate
- Quinolones
- Sotalol
- Steroids (especially budesonide)
- Tetracyclines

*NNRTI = non-nucleoside reversetranscriptase inhibitor, PI = protease inhibitor, INSTI = integrase strand transfer inhibitor
**Absorption decreased by H2RAs and PPIs only

Antacids

- Antacids can decrease the absorption of some drugs by binding or adsorbing to them. It is necessary to separate administration of antacids from select drugs (see Key Drugs Guy on previous page). The timing of separation varies; for most products, avoiding antacids 2 – 4 hours before or 2 – 6 hours after is recommended.

H2RAs

- Use caution with CNS depressants (especially in the elderly) due to the risk of additive delirium, dementia and cognitive impairment. Use lower doses in patients with renal impairment.

- Do not use famotidine with highest risk QT-prolonging drugs (see the Arrhythmias chapter).

- Cimetidine is an inhibitor of CYP450 enzymes (e.g., CYP2C19, CYP3A4 and CYP1A2). Avoid use with dofetilide and use caution with other drugs, including amiodarone, calcium channel blockers, clopidogrel, phenytoin, SSRIs, theophylline and warfarin.

PPIs

- All PPIs inhibit CYP2C19; most are weak inhibitors but omeprazole and esomeprazole are moderate inhibitors. PPIs can ↑ the levels of citalopram, phenytoin, tacrolimus, voriconazole and warfarin. Do not use PPIs with nelfinavir.

- Omeprazole and esomeprazole can ↓ the effectiveness of clopidogrel (a prodrug) through CYP2C19 inhibition. Do not use these drugs together.

- PPIs can inhibit renal elimination of methotrexate, leading to ↑ serum levels and risk of methotrexate toxicities.

Metoclopramide

- Do not use in patients receiving medications for Parkinson disease (antagonistic effect). Do not use in combination with antipsychotic drugs, droperidol and promethazine due to an increased risk of adverse effects. When used in combination with SSRIs, SNRIs or TCAs, monitor for possible EPS, NMS and serotonin syndrome.

PEPTIC ULCER DISEASE

BACKGROUND

Peptic ulcer disease (PUD) occurs when there is mucosal erosion within the gastrointestinal tract. Unlike gastritis, the ulcers in PUD extend deeper into the mucosa. Most ulcers occur in the duodenum, but a small percentage occur in the stomach. Ulcers can be observed with an upper gastrointestinal endoscopy. The three most common causes of PUD are *Helicobacter pylori (H. pylori)*-positive ulcers, non-steroidal anti-inflammatory drug (NSAID)-induced ulcers and stress ulcers, which occur in critically ill and mechanically-ventilated patients (see the Acute & Critical Care Medicine chapter). *H. pylori*, a spiral-shaped, pH-sensitive, gram-negative bacterium that lives in the acidic environment of the stomach, is responsible for the majority of peptic ulcers (70 – 95%). Less common causes of PUD are hypersecretory states (e.g., increased gastric acid in Zollinger-Ellison syndrome), viral infections (e.g., cytomegalovirus), radiation therapy and infiltrative diseases (e.g., Crohn's Disease).

Under normal conditions, a physiologic balance exists between gastric acid secretion and the gut's mucosal defense and repair mechanisms, which include mucus and bicarbonate secretion, mucosal blood flow, prostaglandin synthesis, cellular regeneration and epithelial cell renewal. These mechanisms protect the GI mucosa from damage caused by NSAIDs (including aspirin), *H. pylori*, acid, pepsin and other GI irritants.

Symptoms

The primary symptom of PUD is dyspepsia, a gastric pain that can feel like a gnawing or burning sensation in the middle or upper stomach. If the ulcer is duodenal (usually caused by *H. pylori*), pain is typically worse 2 – 3 hours after eating (when the stomach is empty); eating food or taking antacids lessens the pain. With gastric ulcers (primarily from NSAIDs), eating generally worsens the pain. Other symptoms include heartburn, belching, bloating, cramping, nausea and anorexia.

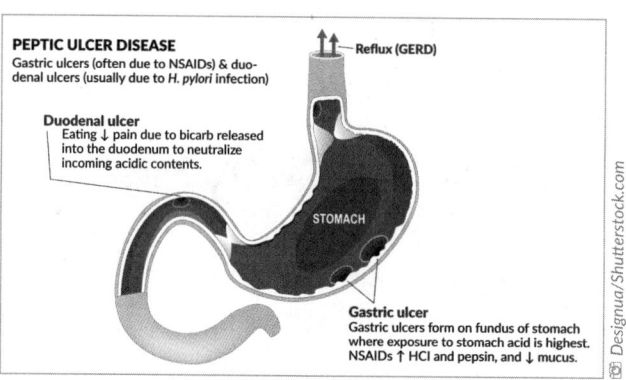

PEPTIC ULCER DISEASE
Gastric ulcers (often due to NSAIDs) & duodenal ulcers (usually due to *H. pylori* infection)

Reflux (GERD)

Duodenal ulcer
Eating ↓ pain due to bicarb released into the duodenum to neutralize incoming acidic contents.

STOMACH

Gastric ulcer
Gastric ulcers form on fundus of stomach where exposure to stomach acid is highest. NSAIDs ↑ HCl and pepsin, and ↓ mucus.

© Designua/Shutterstock.com

H. PYLORI DETECTION AND MANAGEMENT

Diagnostic Tests

Common, non-invasive, diagnostic tests for *H. pylori* include the urea breath test (UBT), which detects gas (CO_2) produced by the bacteria, and the fecal antigen test, which detects *H. pylori* in the stool. PPIs, bismuth and antibiotics should be discontinued two weeks prior to these tests to avoid false negative results. The infection should be treated if testing is positive.

Drug Treatment

H. pylori infection, if left untreated, can lead to gastric cancer. There are several combination regimens available to treat *H. pylori* (see the table below). Due to failure rates with triple therapy (often caused by clarithromycin resistance), the American College of Gastroenterology (ACG) guidelines recommend quadruple therapy first-line. The use of triple therapy first-line is only recommended if clarithromycin resistance rates are low (< 15%) and the patient has no previous history of taking a macrolide antibiotic (for any reason).

Do not make drug substitutions in *H. pylori* eradication regimens. H2RAs should not be substituted for a PPI, unless the patient cannot tolerate a PPI. Other antibiotics within a class should not be substituted (for example, do not use ampicillin instead of amoxicillin). If the PPI is continued beyond 14 days, this is to help ulcer healing; it should not be continued indefinitely.

First-Line *H. pylori* Treatment Regimens

DRUG REGIMEN	NOTES
Bismuth Quadruple Therapy: Take for 10-14 Days Use first-line, especially if local resistance rates to clarithromycin are high (≥ 15%), the patient has had a previous macrolide exposure or a penicillin allergy, or triple therapy failed (if used first)	
Bismuth subsalicylate 300 mg QID + **Metronidazole 250-500 mg QID +** **Tetracycline 500 mg QID +** **PPI BID** Or use a (3-in-1) combination product + PPI: ***Pylera* (bismuth subcitrate potassium 420 mg + metronidazole 375 mg + tetracycline 375 mg) QID + PPI BID**	Tinidazole may be substituted for metronidazole If the patient cannot tolerate a PPI, substitute an H2RA (e.g., famotidine 40 mg daily, nizatidine 150 mg BID) Swallow all capsules in the *Pylera* regimen (3 capsules per dose) **Alcohol Use** Do not use metronidazole **Pregnancy/Children** Do not use tetracycline during pregnancy or in children < 8 years of age **Salicylate Allergy** Do not use bismuth subsalicylate
Concomitant Therapy: Take for 10-14 Days Use only if local resistance rates to clarithromycin are low (< 15%) and the patient has had no previous exposure to a macrolide; preferred over clarithromycin triple therapy if previous macrolide exposure	
Amoxicillin 1,000 mg BID + **Clarithromycin 500 mg BID +** **Metronidazole 250-500 mg QID +** **PPI BID**	Tinidazole may be substituted for metronidazole
Clarithromycin Triple Therapy: Take for 14 Days Use only if local resistance rates to clarithromycin are low (< 15%) and the patient has had no previous exposure to a macrolide	
Amoxicillin 1,000 mg BID + **Clarithromycin 500 mg BID +** **PPI BID (or esomeprazole 40 mg daily)** Or use a (3-in-1) combination product with PPI: ***Prevpac* (amoxicillin + clarithromycin + lansoprazole)** *Omeclamox-Pak* (amoxicillin + clarithromycin + omeprazole)	Penicillin allergy: replace amoxicillin with metronidazole 500 mg TID or use quadruple therapy (see above) *Prevpac* contains all medications on one blister card; take the entire contents of one card (divided BID) every day for 14 days *Omeclamox-Pak* is a combination package, swallow capsules and tablets whole

Other *H. pylori* Treatments

Sequential therapy (PPI plus amoxicillin for 5 – 7 days, followed by a PPI, clarithromycin and metronidazole for the remaining 5 – 7 days), hybrid therapy (PPI plus amoxicillin for seven days, followed by a PPI, amoxicillin, clarithromycin and metronidazole for seven days) and quinolone-based regimens are other options presented in the guidelines, though the level of evidence for these treatment recommendations is weaker.

Talicia is the first FDA-approved rifabutin-based treatment for *H. pylori*. It is a combination capsule that contains rifabutin, amoxicillin and omeprazole.

NON-STEROIDAL ANTI-INFLAMMATORY DRUG-INDUCED ULCERS

Background

NSAIDs, including aspirin, can cause gastric mucosal damage by two mechanisms: direct irritation of the gastric epithelium and systemic inhibition of prostaglandin synthesis (by inhibiting COX-1). The chronic use of NSAIDs increases the risk for gastric (GI) ulcers. Patients are at high risk if they have any of the risk factors shown in the box to the right.

RISK FACTORS FOR NSAID-INDUCED ULCERS
Age > 60 years
History of PUD (including *H. pylori*-induced)
High-dose NSAIDs
Using > 1 NSAID (e.g., ibuprofen plus aspirin)
Concomitant use of anticoagulants, steroids, SSRIs or SNRIs

Prevention and Treatment

All NSAIDs elevate blood pressure and decrease renal blood flow; they should be used with caution in any person with cardiovascular or renal disease. When selecting an NSAID, it is important to weigh these risks with the risks for GI ulcers and bleeding. NSAIDs with selective inhibition of COX-2 (e.g., celecoxib) have decreased GI risk but increased cardiovascular (CV) risk compared to non-selective NSAIDs. NSAIDs that approach the selectivity of celecoxib are meloxicam, nabumetone, diclofenac and etodolac.

Patients with high GI risk (or a history of ulcers) who take non-selective NSAIDs can use PPI to prevent or decrease the risk of ulcers and bleeding, but the long-term risks need to be considered (see Risks of PPI Therapy section). The cytoprotective drug, misoprostol, is an alternative option to a PPI, but diarrhea, cramping and its four times per day dosing contribute to poor patient compliance. Combination products specifically marketed to reduce the risk of NSAID-induced ulcers include naproxen/esomeprazole (*Vimovo*), ibuprofen/famotidine (*Duexis*) and diclofenac/misoprostol (*Arthrotec*); these are indicated to relieve symptoms of osteoarthritis and rheumatoid arthritis in patients at risk of GI ulcers. *Yosprala*, a combination of aspirin and omeprazole, is approved for secondary prevention of cardiovascular and cerebrovascular events in patients at risk for aspirin-associated ulcers.

If possible, both non-selective NSAIDs and COX-2 selective drugs should be avoided in patients with both high GI and high CV risk. Naproxen may be the preferred NSAID in patients with low-moderate GI risk and high CV risk. A COX-2 selective drug, with or without a PPI, can be used in patients who do not have CV risk factors.

If an ulcer develops, it should be treated with a PPI for eight weeks, and NSAIDs should be discontinued. If PPIs cannot be used, high-dose H2RAs or sucralfate are other options.

Cytoprotective Drugs

Misoprostol is a prostaglandin E1 analog that replaces the gastro-protective prostaglandins removed by NSAIDs. Sucralfate is a sucrose-sulfate-aluminum complex and can interact with albumin and fibrinogen to form a physical barrier over an open ulcer. This protects the ulcer from further insult by HCl acid, pepsin and bile, and allows it to heal.

DRUG	DOSING	SAFETY/SIDE EFFECTS/MONITORING
Misoprostol (*Cytotec*) + diclofenac 50 mg (*Arthrotec*)	200 mcg PO QID with food; if not tolerated, may ↓ to 100 mcg QID; take with meals and at bedtime	**BOXED WARNING** Misoprostol: an abortifacient, do not use to ↓ NSAID-induced ulcers in females of childbearing potential unless capable of complying with effective contraceptive measures; warn patients not to give this drug to others *Arthrotec*: NSAIDs ↑ risk of serious GI events (e.g., bleeding and ulceration) and CV disease (e.g., MI and stroke) **SIDE EFFECTS** Diarrhea, abdominal pain **NOTES** Use of psyllium (*Metamucil*) can help decrease diarrhea
Sucralfate (*Carafate*) Tablet, suspension	1 gram PO QID before meals (empty stomach) and at bedtime	**WARNING** Caution in renal impairment; sucralfate is in an aluminum complex and can accumulate **SIDE EFFECTS** Constipation **NOTES** Drink adequate fluids and use laxatives PRN for constipation Difficult to use due to binding interactions (separate antacids by 30 minutes and take other drugs 2 hrs before or 4 hrs after)

KEY COUNSELING POINTS

See the Drug Formulations and Patient Counseling chapter for counseling language/layman's terminology.

ANTACIDS, H2RAs AND PPIs

- Seek urgent or emergency care if you have trouble or pain when swallowing, bloody stools or vomit with blood or material that looks like coffee grounds.
- Drug interactions due to binding and high gastric pH.

Antacids

- Can cause bleeding [antacids with aspirin (e.g., *Alka Seltzer)*].

H2RAs

- These medications can cause confusion, dizziness or memory loss in the elderly, especially with kidney disease.

PPIs

- Can cause diarrhea.
- Can increase the risk of bone fractures, especially if taking longer than a year. Supplemental calcium and vitamin D may be needed. Calcium citrate is the preferred calcium supplement.

Prevacid SoluTab

- Contains phenylalanine. Do not use if you have phenylketonuria (PKU).

METOCLOPRAMIDE

- Can cause drowsiness.
- Can cause unusual body movements. Contact your healthcare provider immediately if you have symptoms that include shakiness, stiffness or uncontrollable movements of the mouth, tongue, cheeks, jaw, arms or legs.

H. PYLORI TREATMENTS

- Some components can cause:
  - Allergy/anaphylaxis (antibiotics).
  - Bleeding/bruising (bismuth subsalicylate).
  - Diarrhea (antibiotics, PPIs).
  - Headache (PPIs).
  - Bad taste in the mouth (metronidazole).
  - Dark tongue and stool (bismuth subsalicylate).
- If treatment includes metronidazole, avoid alcohol during treatment and for at least three days after stopping, as you may have headaches, flushing, cramps and an upset stomach.

Prevpac

- Each card has your dose (four pills) for the morning and the evening. Take your dose before breakfast and before dinner.

Pylera

- Use *Pylera* with a separate acid-reducing medication.
- Take *Pylera* (three capsules) four times each day with a full glass of water (after breakfast, lunch, dinner and at bedtime). Swallow the capsules whole.

Select Guidelines/References

Katz PO, Dunbar KB, Schnoll-Sussman FH, et al. American Colleg of Gastroenterology (ACG) clinical guideline for the diagnosis and management of gastroesophageal reflux disease. *Am J Gastroenterol.* 2022;177:27-56.

Chey, WD, Leontiadis, G, Howden, CW. American College of Gastroenterology (ACG) clinical guideline: treatment of *Helicobacter pylori* infection. *Am J Gastroenterol.* 2017;112:212-238.

CONTENT LEGEND

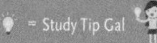 = Study Tip Gal    = Key Drug Guy

© iStock.com/Tharakorn

CHAPTER 73
CONSTIPATION & DIARRHEA

CONSTIPATION

BACKGROUND

Constipation is defined as infrequent bowel movements (less than three per week) or difficulty in passing stools (e.g., straining, lumpy/hard stools, pushing for more than 10 minutes, stool requiring digital evacuation or the sensation of incomplete evacuation). Constipation can be caused by diet, lifestyle, drugs (see Key Drugs Guy on the next page), pregnancy, GI disorders and other medical conditions (see box below). When constipation persists for several weeks or longer, and the cause is unknown, it is termed chronic idiopathic constipation (CIC). Idiopathic constipation associated with chronic or recurrent abdominal discomfort that is relieved by defecation is termed irritable bowel syndrome with constipation (IBS-C).

MEDICAL CONDITIONS THAT CAN CAUSE CONSTIPATION	
Irritable bowel syndrome (constipation-predominant)	Cerebrovascular events
	Parkinson disease
Anal disorders (fissures, fistulae, rectal prolapse)	Spinal cord tumors
	Diabetes
Multiple sclerosis	Hypothyroidism

NON-DRUG TREATMENT

Non-drug treatments are preferred for constipation. These include increasing fluid intake (64 oz daily recommended), limiting caffeine and alcohol intake (to avoid dehydration) and increasing physical activity. Replacing refined foods with whole grain products, bran, fruits, vegetables, beans and other foods high in fiber is useful. It is important to avoid delays in going to the bathroom when the urge to defecate is present (young children may need a scheduled time to use the bathroom). If possible, drugs that are constipating should be discontinued.

GASTROINTESTINAL CONDITIONS

DRUG TREATMENT

If constipation does not improve with lifestyle measures, or if a constipating drug cannot be stopped, one or more drug treatments can be used. Most medications are available OTC and can be tried for the initial treatment of IBS-C, CIC or opioid-induced constipation (OIC). If constipation is not improved after seven days of OTC treatment, a healthcare provider should be consulted for further evaluation and, if appropriate, prescription medication can be considered (see the Other Drugs Used for Constipation section).

Most drug treatments act to stimulate the muscles of the digestive tract or soften the stool, often speeding up the time for bowel movements; thus, the most common side effects are diarrhea and abdominal cramping.

- Bulk-forming drugs (e.g., soluble fiber such as psyllium) and dietary fiber are the first-line treatments in most cases and the treatment of choice in pregnancy. They absorb water in the intestine, soaking up fluid and adding bulk to the stool. This increases peristalsis and decreases stool transit time.

- Osmotics [e.g., polyethylene glycol (PEG)] contain large ions or molecules that are poorly absorbed. They draw fluid into the bowel lumen through osmosis, which distends the colon and increases peristalsis.

- Stimulants (e.g., senna, bisacodyl) directly stimulate neurons in the colon, causing peristaltic activity. Patients using chronic opioids, all of which are constipating, often require a stimulant laxative, because opioids reduce peristalsis and prolong stool transit time. The stool softener docusate can be given with the stimulant laxative if the stool is hard. If the stool is not hard, but the patient cannot push it out ("mush with no push"), a stimulant alone is the usual treatment.

- Stool softeners (e.g., docusate) are emollients that reduce the surface tension of the stool oil-water interface, allowing more water and fat to mix with the stool. This softens the fecal mass making defecation easier. These can be used by patients using iron supplements, which make the stool hard and compact.

- Lubricants (e.g., mineral oil) coat the bowel and stool with a waterproof film. This keeps moisture in the stool and makes defecation easier.

DRUGS THAT ARE CONSTIPATING

KEY DRUGS

Antacids (aluminum- and calcium-containing)

Antidiarrheals

Clonidine

Colesevelam

Drugs with anticholinergic effects:
Antihistamines (e.g., diphenhydramine)
Antispasmodics (e.g., baclofen)
Phenothiazines (e.g., prochlorperazine)
TCAs (e.g., amitriptyline)
Urge incontinence drugs (e.g., oxybutynin)

Iron

Non-DHP calcium channel blockers (especially verapamil)

Opioids

Sucralfate (contains an aluminum complex)

Others:
5HT-3 receptor antagonists (e.g., ondansetron)

Aripiprazole

Clozapine

Milnacipran

Phentermine/topiramate

Ranolazine

Tramadol, tapentadol

Varenicline

WHICH OTC TO RECOMMEND FOR CONSTIPATION

Most adults
Fiber

Iron-induced or hard stool
Docusate (stool softener)

Opioid-induced
Senna or bisacodyl (stimulants)

Pregnancy
Fiber

Fast relief needed
Adults: bisacodyl or glycerin (more gentle) suppository
Children: glycerin suppository

If no improvement in 7 days, refer patient to a healthcare provider.

COMMON DRUGS USED FOR CONSTIPATION

DRUG	DOSING	SAFETY/SIDE EFFECTS/MONITORING
Bulk-Forming Drugs		
Psyllium (*Metamucil,* others) Capsule, powder OTC	2.5-30 g/day in divided doses	**CONTRAINDICATIONS** Fecal impaction and GI obstruction (psyllium) **SIDE EFFECTS** Flatulence, abdominal cramping, bloating, bowel obstruction (if strictures present), choking (if powder forms are not taken with enough liquid) **NOTES** Onset of action 12-72 hrs
Calcium polycarbophil (*FiberCon,* others) Caplet, chewable tablet OTC	1,250 mg 1-4 times/day	
Methylcellulose (*Citrucel,* others) Caplet, powder OTC	1-6 g/day	Adequate fluids are required; use caution if fluid restricted (e.g., heart failure), if difficulty swallowing (e.g., Parkinson disease) or if at risk for fecal impaction (e.g., intestinal ulcerations, stenosis)
Wheat dextrin (*Benefiber*) Tablet, chewable tablet, powder OTC	4 g (2 teaspoons) in 4-8 oz of liquid or soft food TID	Calcium is a polyvalent cation; separate calcium polycarbophil from select drugs due to a binding interaction Sugar-free options available Psyllium modestly improves cholesterol and blood glucose levels
Osmotics		
Magnesium hydroxide (*Milk of Magnesia,* others), magnesium citrate, magnesium sulfate Chewable tablet, suspension OTC	Magnesium hydroxide: 2.4-4.8 g QHS or in divided doses	**CONTRAINDICATIONS** Anuria (sorbitol), low galactose diet (lactulose), GI obstruction (*MiraLax,* lactitol), galactosemia (lactitol) **SIDE EFFECTS** Electrolyte imbalance, abdominal cramping, abdominal distention, flatulence, dehydration, rectal irritation (suppository) Lactitol: upper respiratory tract infections, increased blood pressure, increased blood creatinine phosphokinase
Polyethylene glycol 3350 (*MiraLax, GaviLax, GlycoLax,* others) Powder OTC	17 g in 4-8 oz of water daily	
Glycerin (*Fleet Liquid Glycerin Supp, Pedia-Lax,* others) Suppository: adult & pediatric sizes OTC	PR: insert 1 daily	**NOTES** Onset of action 30 mins to 96 hrs (oral), 5-30 mins (rectal) Magnesium-containing products: caution with renal impairment and do not use if severe renal impairment
Lactulose (*Constulose, Enulose, Generlac, Kristalose*) Crystal packet, solution Rx	PO: 10-20 g daily Oral solution can be diluted and administered rectally	Lactulose: used commonly for hepatic encephalopathy Glycerin suppository used commonly in children who need to defecate quickly
Sodium phosphates (*Fleet Enema,* others) Enema OTC	PR: insert contents of one 4.5 oz enema as a single dose	
Lactitol (*Pizensy*) Powder Rx	20 g in 4-8 oz of water, juice or other beverage (e.g., coffee, tea, soda) daily, preferably taken with a meal	
Sorbitol Enema, oral solution OTC	PO: 30-150 mL (70% solution) as a single dose PR (enema): 120 mL (25-30% solution)	

GASTROINTESTINAL CONDITIONS

DRUG	DOSING	SAFETY/SIDE EFFECTS/MONITORING
Stimulants		
Senna (*Ex-Lax, Senokot*, others) Tablet, chewable tablet, liquid, syrup OTC **+ docusate (*Senna S, Senokot S, Senna Plus*, others)** Capsule, tablet OTC	17.2-50 mg daily-BID	**WARNINGS** Avoid use with stomach pain, N/V or a sudden change in bowel movements that lasts > 2 weeks **SIDE EFFECTS** Abdominal cramping, electrolyte imbalance, rectal irritation (suppository) **NOTES** Onset of action 6-12 hrs (oral), 15-60 mins (rectal) Take oral products at bedtime to induce a bowel movement the following morning; can give 30 mins after a meal to enhance peristalsis Chronic opioid use often requires a stimulant laxative
Bisacodyl Enteric-coated tablet, suppository (*Dulcolax*, others) Enema (*Fleet Bisacodyl*, others) OTC	PO: 5-15 mg daily, do not take within 1 hr of dairy products or antacids PR (enema, suppository): 10 mg daily, cool suppository in the fridge or cold water first if too soft to insert	
Emollients (Stool Softeners)		
Docusate sodium (*Colace*, others), docusate calcium, docusate potassium Capsule, tablet, enema, liquid, syrup OTC **+ senna (*Senna S, Senokot S, Senna Plus*, others)** Capsule, tablet OTC	Docusate sodium: PO: 50-360 mg daily or in divided doses PR (enema): 283 g/5 mL daily-TID	**CONTRAINDICATIONS** Abdominal pain, N/V, use with mineral oil, OTC use > 1 week **SIDE EFFECTS** Abdominal cramping, throat irritation (liquid) **NOTES** Onset of action 12-72 hrs (oral), 2-15 mins (rectal) Preferred when straining should be avoided (e.g., postpartum, post-MI, anal fissures, hemorrhoids) Use when stool is hard or dry Do not take docusate and mineral oil together (it increases the absorption of mineral oil)
Lubricants		
Mineral oil Oral liquid, enema OTC	PO: 15-45 mL daily or in divided doses PR (enema): 118 mL as a single dose	**CONTRAINDICATIONS** Age < 6 years, pregnancy, bedridden patients, elderly, use > 1 week, difficulty swallowing **SIDE EFFECTS** Abdominal cramping, nausea, incontinence, rectal discharge **NOTES** Onset of action 6-8 hrs (oral), 2-15 mins (rectal) Oral formulation generally not recommended due to safety concerns (e.g., risk of aspiration and lipid pneumonitis) Take a multivitamin at a different time due to malabsorption of fat-soluble vitamins Do not take docusate and mineral oil together (it increases the absorption of mineral oil)

OTHER DRUGS USED FOR CONSTIPATION

Prescription medications can be used if constipation is not relieved with OTC drugs or lifestyle modifications.

- The chloride channel activator <u>lubiprostone</u> acts on chloride channels in the gut, leading to increased fluid and peristalsis.

- Guanylate cyclase C agonists (e.g., <u>linaclotide</u>) increase chloride and bicarbonate secretion into the lumen of the intestines, increasing the speed of GI transit and reducing abdominal pain.

- <u>Peripherally-acting mu-opioid receptor antagonists (PAMORAs)</u> (e.g., <u>alvimopan</u>) act on mu-opioid receptors in the <u>GI tract</u>, decreasing constipation.

- Serotonin 5HT-4 receptor agonists (e.g., prucalopride) release acetylcholine which causes muscle contractions and increases gastrointestinal motility.

PRESCRIPTION DRUGS BY INDICATION

	CIC	IBS-C	OIC	Surgery
Lubiprostone	X	X*	X	
Linaclotide, Plecanatide	X	X		
Alvimopan				X
Methylnaltrexone, Naloxegol, Naldemedine			X	
Prucalopride	X			
Tegaserod		X**		

*IBS-C in adult women
**IBS-C in adult women < 65 years

DRUG	DOSING	SAFETY/SIDE EFFECTS/MONITORING
Chloride Channel Activator		
Lubiprostone (*Amitiza*) Capsule CIC, OIC, IBS-C in adult women	CIC & OIC: 24 mcg BID IBS-C: 8 mcg BID ↓ dose with moderate-severe liver impairment	**CONTRAINDICATIONS** Mechanical bowel obstruction **SIDE EFFECTS** Nausea, diarrhea, abdominal pain, abdominal distension, headache **NOTES** Take with food and water to decrease nausea Consider alternative treatment with methadone (↓ lubiprostone effects)
Guanylate Cyclase C Agonists		
Linaclotide (*Linzess*) Capsule CIC, IBS-C	CIC: 145 mcg daily IBS-C: 290 mcg daily Take at least 30 mins before breakfast on an empty stomach	**BOXED WARNING** Do not use in pediatric patients; high risk of dehydration that can cause death **CONTRAINDICATIONS** Age < 6 years, mechanical GI obstruction **SIDE EFFECTS** Diarrhea, abdominal pain, flatulence
Plecanatide (*Trulance*) Tablet CIC, IBS-C	3 mg daily	**NOTES** Swallow *Linzess* capsules whole; if needed, the capsule can be opened and the contents mixed with 1 teaspoonful of applesauce or 30 mL of room temperature water; the mixture must be swallowed immediately *Trulance* tablets can be crushed *Linzess*: protect from moisture; original container has a desiccant

GASTROINTESTINAL CONDITIONS

Peripherally-Acting Mu-Opioid Receptor Antagonists (PAMORAs)		
Alvimopan (Entereg) Capsule For hospitalized surgery patients to decrease risk of post-operative ileus	12 mg, 30 min-5 hrs prior to surgery, then 12 mg BID for up to 7 days total (maximum 15 doses)	**BOXED WARNING** Potential risk of MI with long-term use Available only for short-term inpatient use through a REMS program **CONTRAINDICATIONS** Therapeutic doses of opioids for > 7 consecutive days immediately prior to use **SIDE EFFECTS** Dyspepsia
Methylnaltrexone (Relistor) **Naloxegol (Movantik)** Naldemedine (Symproic)		**NOTES** Only used in patients taking opioids who have OIC (see Pain chapter)

Serotonin 5HT-4 Receptor Agonists		
Prucalopride (Motegrity) Tablet CIC, used off-label for OIC	CIC: 2 mg daily CrCl < 30 mL/min: 1 mg daily Avoid use in ESRD with HD	**CONTRAINDICATIONS** Gastrointestinal obstruction Prucalopride: bowel perforation, ileus, severe inflammatory conditions of the GI tract (Crohn's disease, ulcerative colitis, toxic megacolon) Tegaserod: intestinal ischemia (e.g., ischemic colitis), history of cardiovascular events (e.g., myocardial infarction, stroke or TIA, angina), severe renal impairment or ESRD, hepatic impairment (Child-Pugh class B or C), gallbladder disease, sphincter of Oddi dysfunction, abdominal adhesions
Tegaserod (Zelnorm) Tablet IBS-C in adult women < 65 years	6 mg BID eGFR < 15 mL/min/1.73 m²: avoid Take 30 mins before meals Discontinue if no improvement after 4-6 weeks	**WARNINGS** Suicidal ideation **SIDE EFFECTS** Diarrhea, headache, nausea, abdominal pain **MONITORING** Worsening of depression or emergence of suicidal thoughts; rectal bleeding, blood in stool, severe abdominal pain

LAXATIVES USED FOR WHOLE BOWEL IRRIGATION

Several laxatives are specifically designed to prep the bowel before a colonoscopy. Some of these drugs contain the same active ingredients as those used for constipation (e.g., PEG has the brand name *MiraLax* to treat constipation, but formulations such as *GoLytely* are used for bowel prep before a colonoscopy). Although usually safe and well-tolerated, laxatives for whole bowel irrigation can cause fluid and electrolyte losses. These can be critical in some patients and with select products (e.g., oral sodium phosphates such as *OsmoPrep*). Use extra caution in patients with cardiovascular disease, renal insufficiency or if taking loop diuretics (due to additional fluid loss) or NSAIDs.

DRUG	DOSING	SAFETY/SIDE EFFECTS/MONITORING
Polyethylene glycol-electrolyte solution (*Colyte, GoLytely, NuLytely,* *GaviLyte-C, GaviLyte-G, GaviLyte-N, MoviPrep, Plenvu, TriLyte*)	Drink 240 mL every 10 mins until 4 liters are consumed *MoviPrep:* the evening before, drink 240 mL every 15 mins until 1 liter is consumed, then drink 480 mL clear liquid; repeat in the morning *Plenvu:* the evening before, drink 480 mL over 30 mins, then drink 480 mL clear liquid over 30 mins; repeat in the morning	**BOXED WARNING** *OsmoPrep:* nephropathy **CONTRAINDICATIONS** Ileus, gastrointestinal obstruction, gastric retention, bowel perforation, toxic colitis, toxic megacolon *OsmoPrep:* acute phosphate nephropathy, gastric bypass or stapling surgery *Prepopik, Clenpiq:* severe renal impairment **WARNINGS** Arrhythmias, electrolyte abnormalities, seizures **SIDE EFFECTS** Abdominal discomfort, bloating, N/V **NOTES** Onset of action 1-6 hrs
Sodium phosphates (*OsmoPrep*)	Take 4 tablets (with 8 oz of clear liquid) every 15 mins (5 doses the evening before and 3 doses 3-5 hrs before the procedure)	
Sodium sulfate, potassium sulfate and magnesium sulfate (*Suprep Bowel Prep Kit*)	Evening before: drink 480 mL followed by 960 mL clear liquid over 1 hr; repeat in the morning	Bowel prep regimens typically require doses the evening before colonoscopy and the morning of colonoscopy to completely evacuate the bowel A clear liquid diet is required the day prior to colonoscopy and can include: water, clear broth (beef or chicken), juices without pulp (apple, white cranberry, white grape, lemonade), soda, coffee or tea (without milk or cream), clear gelatin (without fruit pieces), popsicles (without fruit pieces or cream)
Sodium picosulfate, magnesium oxide, and citric acid (*Prepopik, Clenpiq*)	*Prepopik:* the evening before, drink 150 mL; repeat 5 hrs before the procedure	
Combination of a stimulant and osmotic laxative (enables lower fluid intake)	*Clenpiq:* the evening before, drink 160 mL; repeat 5 hrs before the procedure	Do not consume the following: solid or semi-solid foods, anything with red or blue/purple food coloring (including gelatin and popsicles), milk, cream, tomato, orange or grapefruit juice, alcoholic beverages, cream soups

DIARRHEA

BACKGROUND

Diarrhea is an increase in the number of bowel movements or stools that are more watery and loose than normal. When the intestines push stools through the bowel before the water in the stool can be reabsorbed, diarrhea occurs. Abdominal cramps, nausea, vomiting or fever can be present.

Diarrhea can be idiopathic, caused by diseases, drugs (see Key Drugs Guy on following page) or by consuming contaminated food/water. *E. coli* is the most common bacterial cause. Most cases of diarrhea are viral, have a quick onset and resolve within a few days without treatment. Infectious diarrhea is discussed in the Travelers and Infectious Diseases II chapters.

Recurrent idiopathic diarrhea associated with chronic or reoccurring abdominal discomfort that is relieved by defecation is termed irritable bowel syndrome with diarrhea (IBS-D).

Diarrhea that occurs after consuming milk or milk products could be due to lactose intolerance. Lactose intolerance can be confirmed through testing or eliminating dairy intake to see if diarrhea resolves.

NON-DRUG TREATMENT

Management of diarrhea includes fluid and electrolyte replacement, especially in moderate-severe cases and in the elderly, children or adults with chronic medical conditions. Dehydration from diarrhea in infants is dangerous; care should be overseen by a healthcare provider (see Pediatrics chapter for more information). Replace fluid and electrolytes with oral rehydration solutions (ORS), such as *Pedialyte* or *Enfamil Enfalyte*, which are available over the counter. *Gatorade* or similar products can be used as alternatives.

DRUG TREATMENT FOR DIARRHEA

Most patients with non-infectious diarrhea who require symptomatic relief can use short-term bismuth subsalicylate (*Pepto-Bismol*) or loperamide as needed. Bismuth subsalicylate has both antisecretory and antimicrobial effects when used as an antidiarrheal. Loperamide and diphenoxylate are antimotility drugs that slow intestinal motility, prolonging the time for water absorption. Pain and abdominal discomfort associated with IBS-D can be managed with antispasmodics (e.g., dicyclomine) and antidepressants in select cases.

Eluxadoline *(Viberzi)* is a mixed mu-opioid receptor agonist (in contrast to the PAMORAs, which are mu-receptor antagonists). While the PAMORAs compete and displace the binding of opioids to receptors in the periphery to reduce constipation, eluxadoline binds to the opioid receptors as an agonist to treat diarrhea. It is indicated for IBS-D when diarrhea is difficult to treat with usual measures.

SELECT DRUGS THAT CAN CAUSE DIARRHEA

Acetylcholinesterase inhibitors (e.g., donepezil)

Antacids containing magnesium

Antibiotics (especially broad-spectrum drugs), diarrhea may be infectious (e.g., *C. difficile*)

Antidiabetics (e.g., metformin, GLP-1 agonists)

Antineoplastics (e.g., irinotecan, capecitabine, fluorouracil, methotrexate, TKIs)

Colchicine

Drugs used for constipation (e.g., laxatives)

Misoprostol

Mycophenolate

Prokinetic drugs (e.g., metoclopramide, cisapride)

Protease inhibitors (especially nelfinavir)

Quinidine

Roflumilast

DRUG	DOSING	SAFETY/SIDE EFFECTS/MONITORING
Antidiarrheals		
Bismuth subsalicylate (*Pepto-Bismol*, others) Suspension (262 mg/15 mL) Chewable tablet (262 mg) OTC	524 mg (30 mL or 2 tablets) every 30-60 mins PRN or 1,050 mg (60 mL or 4 tablets) every 60 mins PRN Max: 4,200 mg/day for up to 2 days	**CONTRAINDICATIONS** Salicylate allergy, taking other salicylates (e.g., aspirin), GI ulcer, bleeding problems, black/bloody stool **WARNINGS** Children and teenagers who are recovering from the flu, chickenpox or other viral infections should not use this drug due to the risk of Reye's syndrome **SIDE EFFECTS** Black tongue/stool (temporary and harmless), salicylate toxicity if used excessively (tinnitus, metabolic acidosis), nausea, abdominal pain **NOTES** Can cause an increased risk of bleeding when used with anticoagulants, antiplatelets (e.g., aspirin) or NSAIDs Use caution in those with renal insufficiency or in combination with other nephrotoxic drugs
Loperamide (*Imodium A-D*, *Anti-Diarrheal*, *Diamode*) Capsule, tablet, liquid, suspension OTC 1 tab/cap = 2 mg	4 mg PO after the first loose stool, then 2 mg after each subsequent loose stool Max: 8 mg/day (self-care) or 16 mg/day (under healthcare supervision)	**BOXED WARNING** Torsades de pointes, cardiac arrest and sudden death with doses higher than recommended; do not exceed the recommended dose Do not use in children < 2 years **CONTRAINDICATIONS** Acute dysentery (bloody diarrhea and high fever), pseudomembranous colitis (*C. difficile*), bacterial enterocolitis caused by invasive organisms (toxigenic *E. coli*, *Salmonella*, *Shigella*), abdominal pain without diarrhea, acute ulcerative colitis **SIDE EFFECTS** Constipation, abdominal cramping, nausea, QT prolongation **NOTES** Self-treatment: do not use > 48 hrs Loperamide can be abused, as it causes a mild opioid-like "high" in large quantities To encourage safe use, the FDA requires use of blister packs or other single-dose packaging for tablets and capsules, and the number of doses per package is limited to no more than 48 mg (24 tablets/capsules)

DRUG	DOSING	SAFETY/SIDE EFFECTS/MONITORING
Diphenoxylate/atropine *(Lomotil)* Liquid, tablet <u>C-V</u> Diphenoxylate inhibits excessive GI motility and propulsion; atropine is used to discourage abuse	Diphenoxylate 5 mg (2 tablets) up to 4 times daily Max: 20 mg/day Improvement is usually seen within 48 hrs; if not seen within 10 days, discontinue	**CONTRAINDICATIONS** Risk of respiratory and CNS depression in children [do not use if <u>< 2 years</u> of age (or <u>< 6 years of age for tablets</u>)], diarrhea caused by enterotoxin-producing bacteria or pseudomembranous colitis *(C. difficile)*, obstructive jaundice **SIDE EFFECTS** Mild euphoria due to diphenoxylate, possible anticholinergic effects (see Notes) **NOTES** <u>Liquid</u> formulation is recommended in children <u>< 13 years</u> <u>Anticholinergic</u> effects due to <u>atropine</u> (e.g., constipation, dry mouth, sedation, tachycardia, flushing, urinary retention, blurred vision); these are mild at recommended doses
Antispasmodic		
Dicyclomine *(Bentyl)* Capsule, injection, solution, tablet	20 mg QID Max: 80 mg/day for < 2 weeks (can increase to 40 mg QID after 1 week, if symptoms respond)	**CONTRAINDICATIONS** Gastrointestinal obstruction, severe ulcerative colitis, reflux esophagitis, acute hemorrhage with cardiovascular instability, obstructive uropathy, narrow-angle glaucoma, myasthenia gravis, breastfeeding women, infants < 6 months of age **WARNINGS** <u>Anticholinergic</u> (caution in <u>patients ≥ 65 years</u>, per Beer's Criteria), caution in mild-moderate ulcerative colitis (can cause <u>toxic megacolon or paralytic ileus</u>) **SIDE EFFECTS** <u>Dizziness, dry mouth, nausea, blurred vision</u>, somnolence, weakness, nervousness
Peripherally-Acting Mixed Mu-Opioid Receptor Agonist		
Eluxadoline *(Viberzi)* Tablet <u>C-IV</u> IBS-D	100 mg PO BID Decrease to 75 mg BID if unable to tolerate 100 mg dose Take with food	**CONTRAINDICATIONS** <u>Patients without a gallbladder</u>, biliary duct obstruction, sphincter of Oddi dysfunction/disease, pancreatic disease (including history of pancreatitis), alcoholism or > 3 alcoholic drinks/day, severe hepatic impairment (Child-Pugh class C), history of severe constipation, gastrointestinal obstruction **WARNINGS** CNS depression **SIDE EFFECTS** Constipation, nausea, abdominal pain **MONITORING** S/sx of pancreatitis or sphincter of Oddi spasm (e.g., abdominal pain that radiates to the back or shoulder, nausea and vomiting), LFTs

OTHER ORAL MEDICATIONS FOR DIARRHEA

Other available treatments shown in the table below have advantages and disadvantages and are used less commonly.

DRUG CLASS	COMMENTS
Antibiotic Rifaximin *(Xifaxan)* IBS without constipation	Costly, and relapse often occurs within several months of treatment.
Serotonin 5HT-3 Receptor Antagonist Alosetron *(Lotronex)* IBS-D	Approved for women only, but has restricted use due to the risk of ischemic colitis.

KEY COUNSELING POINTS

See the Drug Formulations and Patient Counseling chapter for counseling language/layman's terminology.

ALL CONSTIPATION PRODUCTS

- Can cause diarrhea and/or abdominal cramping.
- If no improvement after one week of OTC treatment, contact a healthcare provider.

Bulk-Forming Drugs

- Drug interactions due to binding.

ALL DIARRHEA PRODUCTS

- Contact a healthcare provider for any of the following: age < 6 months, pregnant, high fever (> 101°F), severe abdominal pain or blood in the stool.
- Can cause constipation.

Bismuth Subsalicylate

- Do not take for longer than two days without the approval of your healthcare provider.
- Can cause:
  - ❏ Bleeding/bruising.
  - ❏ Dark tongue and stool; this is normal.

Loperamide

- Do not take for longer than two days without the approval of your healthcare provider.

Diphenoxylate/Atropine

- Can cause anticholinergic effects.

Dicyclomine

- Can cause anticholinergic effects.

Select Guidelines/References

American Gastroenterological Association (AGA) Medical Position Statement on Constipation. *Gastroenterology.* 2013;144:211–217.

American College of Gastroenterology (ACG) Clinical Guideline: Management of Irritable Bowel Syndrome. *Gastroenterology.* 2021;116:17-44.

CHAPTER CONTENT

CONTENT LEGEND

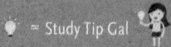 ☀ ≈ Study Tip Gal

Small intestine

Colon

Large intestine

Sigmoid colon

Cecum

Rectum

Appendix

Anus

📷 iStock.com/BluezAce

CHAPTER 74

INFLAMMATORY BOWEL DISEASE

BACKGROUND

Inflammatory bowel disease (IBD) is a group of inflammatory conditions of the colon and small intestine. The major types of IBD are ulcerative colitis and Crohn's disease. The classic symptom is bloody diarrhea. Other symptoms include rectal urgency, tenesmus (a feeling of having to pass stools, even if the colon is empty), abdominal pain, fatigue and, in some cases, weight loss, night sweats, nausea, vomiting and constipation. IBD is a chronic, intermittent disease; symptoms can be mild to severe during flares (or exacerbations) and minimal or absent during periods of remission. Flares can occur at any time and can be triggered by infections, use of NSAIDs or certain foods. Food triggers are patient-specific but can include fatty foods and gas-producing foods (e.g., lentils, beans, legumes, cabbage, broccoli, onions). Food triggers can be avoided or food can be prepared in a way that improves tolerability.

IBD can be mistaken for irritable bowel syndrome (IBS), as they have similar symptoms (e.g., abdominal pain, bloating, gas, and either constipation or diarrhea). Unlike IBD, IBS does not cause inflammation and is not as serious of a condition. Drugs used to treat IBS primarily treat constipation or diarrhea; refer to the Constipation & Diarrhea chapter for drug specifics.

ULCERATIVE COLITIS

Ulcerative colitis (UC) is characterized by mucosal inflammation confined to the rectum and colon with superficial ulcerations. When UC is limited to the descending colon and rectum, it is called distal disease and can be treated with topical (rectal) treatment. Inflammation limited to the rectum is called proctitis. The larger the affected area (e.g., extensive UC), the worse the symptoms. When the disease flares, patients can have numerous stools per day, often with pain, which can significantly decrease quality of life. UC is classified as mild, moderate, severe or fulminant. Moderate disease is characterized by > 4 stools per day with minimal signs of toxicity, and patients with severe disease have ≥ 6 bloody stools per day with evidence of toxicity [fever, tachycardia, anemia, or an elevated erythrocyte sedimentation rate (ESR)]. Fulminant disease refers to patients with > 10 stools per day and severe symptoms (e.g., continuous bleeding, abdominal pain, distension and acute, severe toxic symptoms including fever and anorexia). These patients are at risk of progressing to toxic megacolon and bowel perforation.

CROHN'S DISEASE

Crohn's disease (CD) is characterized by deep, transmural (through the bowel wall) inflammation that can affect any part of the GI tract. The ileum and colon are most commonly affected. Damage to the bowel wall can cause strictures (narrowing of the bowel) and fistulas (abnormal connections or openings in the bowel). Symptoms of CD include chronic diarrhea (often nocturnal), abdominal pain and weight loss. Perianal symptoms [e.g., bleeding, fissures (tears)] can be present before bowel symptoms.

CD AND UC COMPARISON

CLINICAL FEATURES	CD	UC
Diarrhea	Bloody or non-bloody	Bloody
Fistulas/ Strictures	Common	Uncommon
Location	Entire GI tract (especially the ileum & colon)	Colon (especially the rectum)
Depth	Transmural	Superficial
Pattern	Non-continuous, "cobblestone" appearance	Continuous
Smoking	Risk factor	Protective

DIAGNOSIS

IBD can be difficult to diagnose because the symptoms mimic other common conditions (e.g., constipation, diarrhea, infections, anorexia/bulimia and peptic ulcer disease). These conditions must be ruled out before a diagnosis is made. Laboratory blood tests (for inflammatory markers, such as CRP) and stool testing (e.g., fecal calprotectin test) can be helpful, but usually a colonoscopy with tissue biopsy is needed to make the diagnosis. A colonoscopy allows the healthcare provider to visualize the entire colon. A sigmoidoscopy might be used for UC, which is similar to a colonoscopy but only evaluates the end part of the intestine, closest to the rectum. Endoscopy (scope through the mouth) might be used if upper GI symptoms are present. Imaging tests (e.g., CT, MRI) can be helpful for diagnosis as well.

LIFESTYLE MEASURES, SUPPORTIVE CARE AND NATURAL PRODUCTS

As previously mentioned, patients with IBD should adapt their diet to avoid foods that are more likely to trigger flares. In general, eating smaller, more frequent meals that are low in fat and dairy products can be helpful. Fiber should be added to the diet, as tolerated. It is usually best to drink plenty of water. Alcohol and caffeinated beverages that can stimulate the GI tract should be avoided, as well as carbonated beverages that can be gas-producing. The patient should watch for avoidable problems; both sorbitol and lactose are classified as excipients (or binders) and are present in various medications to help hold tablets together. Sorbitol is also used as a sweetener in some diet foods; it has laxative properties and can cause considerable GI distress in some patients. Lactose will worsen GI symptoms if the patient is lactose-intolerant.

Some patients may use antidiarrheals or antispasmodic drugs [e.g., dicyclomine (Bentyl)] to help manage symptoms of diarrhea; these should be used cautiously, and under the supervision of a healthcare provider, as they need to be avoided in select patients with IBD (e.g., severe disease, acute exacerbations, post-bowel resection). See the Constipation & Diarrhea chapter for more information on these products. Vitamin supplements (e.g., B12, folate, vitamin D, calcium, iron, zinc) can help prevent deficiencies related to malabsorption. Nicotine has been shown to worsen CD but can be protective in UC. Nicotine patches have been used as an adjunct therapy for UC, but adverse effects (e.g., nausea, dizziness) limit the benefits.

The probiotics Lactobacillus or Bifidobacterium infantis can reduce abdominal pain, bloating, urgency, constipation or diarrhea in some patients. Fish oils with EPA and DHA (omega-3 fatty acids) can help fight inflammation, although the evidence for benefit is minimal. Some natural products that might be useful include peppermint (in oils or teas), chamomile, horehound and wheatgrass.

DRUG TREATMENT

Treatments for IBD are used for induction of remission (they treat exacerbations or active disease) and/or maintenance of remission. Short courses of oral or IV steroids are commonly used to treat acute exacerbations in both UC and CD. Systemic steroids are not recommended for maintenance of remission and will usually be tapered over 8 – 12 weeks once remission is achieved.

In UC, aminosalicylates (active component is 5-aminosalicylic acid, or 5-ASA) are used for maintenance therapy in most patients with distal UC or mild extensive disease. For patients with moderate-severe UC that extends beyond the colon and rectum, other immunosuppressive medications [e.g., thiopurines, anti-tumor necrosis factor (TNF) drugs, tofacitinib and cyclosporine] can be used (see Study Tip Gal below).

For mild CD that is limited to the ileum and proximal colon, oral budesonide can be used to induce remission, then tapered to discontinue. In moderate-severe cases, immunosuppressive medications [e.g., thiopurines, anti-TNF agents, methotrexate, interleukin (IL) receptor antagonists] can be used. Steroids might be needed for severe cases of CD. Integrin receptor antagonists (e.g., vedolizumab) are used in patients with IBD that is refractory to other therapies, or that is steroid-dependent.

Some of the more common drugs used to treat UC and CD are shown in the tables below. Additional medications [e.g., IV steroids, anti-TNF agents (infliximab, adalimumab, certolizumab), methotrexate, interleukin receptor antagonists (ustekinumab)] are discussed fully in the Systemic Steroids & Autoimmune Conditions chapter.

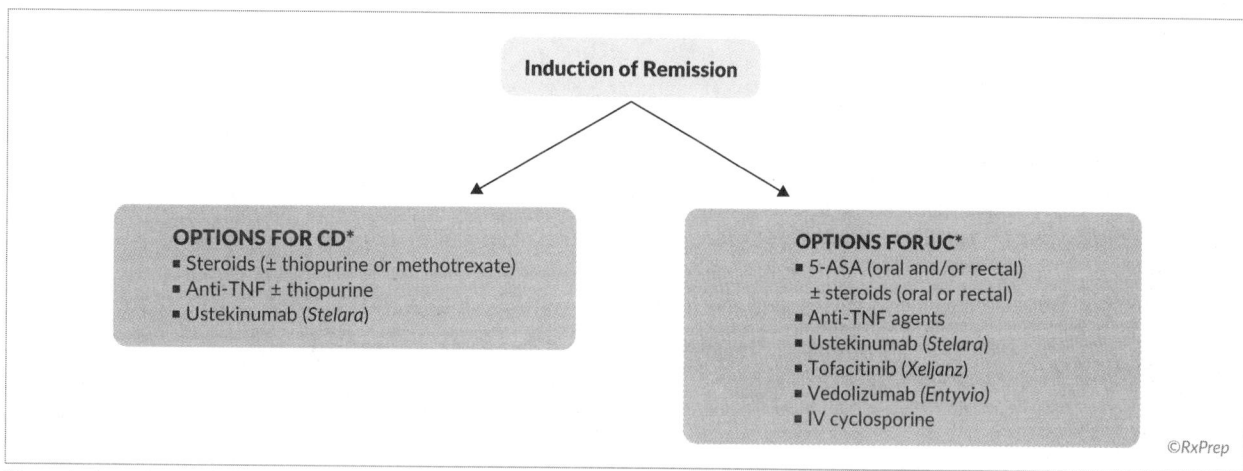

Induction of Remission

OPTIONS FOR CD*
- Steroids (± thiopurine or methotrexate)
- Anti-TNF ± thiopurine
- Ustekinumab (*Stelara*)

OPTIONS FOR UC*
- 5-ASA (oral and/or rectal) ± steroids (oral or rectal)
- Anti-TNF agents
- Ustekinumab (*Stelara*)
- Tofacitinib (*Xeljanz*)
- Vedolizumab (*Entyvio*)
- IV cyclosporine

©RxPrep

Drug selection and route of administration are based on the clinical status of the patient (e.g., severity of illness, location of disease), past treatments (successful and failed therapies), inpatient versus outpatient status and more.

MAINTENANCE OF REMISSION: COMPARISON OF COMMON CD AND UC TREATMENTS

CROHN'S DISEASE
Mild disease of the ileum and/or right colon
- Oral budesonide for ≤ 3 months; after this course, discontinue treatment or change to thiopurine or methotrexate

Moderate-severe disease*
- Anti-TNF agents**
    - Adalimumab (*Humira*)
    - Infliximab (*Remicade*)
    - Certolizumab (*Cimzia*)
- Thiopurine (azathioprine, mercaptopurine)
- Methotrexate
- IL receptor antagonist
    - Ustekinumab (*Stelara*)

Refractory to above treatments and/or steroid dependent
- Integrin receptor antagonists
    - Vedolizumab (*Entyvio*)
    - Natalizumab (*Tysabri*)

ULCERATIVE COLITIS
Mild disease
- Mesalamine (5-ASA) rectal and/or oral preferred

Moderate-severe disease*
- Anti-TNF agents**
    - Adalimumab (*Humira*)
    - Infliximab (*Remicade*)
    - Golimumab (*Simponi*)
- Thiopurine (azathioprine, mercaptopurine)
- Cyclosporine
- IL receptor antagonist
    - Ustekinumab (*Stelara*)
- Janus kinase inhibitor
    - Tofacitinib (*Xeljanz*) – not first-line

Refractory to above treatments and/or steroid dependent
- Integrin receptor antagonists
    - Vedolizumab (*Entyvio*)

Agents can be used as monotherapy or in combination.
**Select anti-TNF biosimilars are also FDA-approved for IBD.*

STEROIDS

DRUG	DOSING	SAFETY/SIDE EFFECTS/MONITORING
Oral Steroids		
Prednisone Tablet *(Deltasone*)* Oral solution *(Prednisone Intensol)* Delayed-release tablet *(Rayos)*	5-60 mg PO daily	**CONTRAINDICATIONS** Systemic fungal infections, live vaccines **SIDE EFFECTS** Short-term: ↑ appetite/weight gain, emotional instability (euphoria, mood swings, irritability), insomnia, fluid retention, indigestion, higher doses can cause an ↑ in BP and blood glucose Long-term: adrenal suppression/Cushing's syndrome, impaired wound healing, ↑ BP, ↑ blood glucose, cataracts, osteoporosis, others; refer to the Systemic Steroids & Autoimmune Conditions chapter **NOTES** **All Steroids** For management of acute flares; avoid long-term use if possible
Budesonide **(Entocort EC, Uceris)** *Entocort EC:* 3 mg extended release capsule (for CD only) *Uceris:* 9 mg extended release tablet (for UC only)	**Induction (CD and UC):** 9 mg PO once daily in the morning for up to 8 weeks **Maintenance (CD only):** 6 mg PO once daily for 3 months, then taper	Can use alternate day therapy (ADT) to ↓ adrenal suppression and other adverse effects If used longer than 2 weeks, must taper to avoid withdrawal symptoms If long-term use is required, assess bone density (optimize calcium and vitamin D intake and consider bisphosphonates if needed) **Budesonide** Undergoes extensive first-pass metabolism; ↓ systemic exposure than other oral steroids Swallow whole – do not crush or chew; can open *Entocort EC* capsules and sprinkle on applesauce
Rectal Steroids		
Hydrocortisone *(Cortenema, Cortifoam)* Enema, rectal foam	**Induction and/or Maintenance** *Cortenema:* 1 enema (100 mg) QHS for 21 days or until remission, then taper *Cortifoam:* 1 applicatorful (90 mg) 1-2 times daily for 2-3 weeks, then every other day thereafter; taper after long-term therapy	**CONTRAINDICATIONS** *Cortifoam:* obstruction, abscess, perforation, peritonitis, fresh intestinal anastomoses, extensive fistulas and sinus tracts *Cortenema:* ileocolostomy in immediate/early post-op period **NOTES** Rectal steroids are indicated for UC only Not proven effective for maintenance of remission; maintenance use is limited to mild-moderate distal UC as an alternative to rectal and/or oral aminosalicylates
Budesonide rectal foam *(Uceris)*	**Induction** 1 metered dose PR BID x 2 weeks, then 1 metered dose daily x 4 weeks (1 metered dose = 2 mg budesonide)	Budesonide rectal foam: propellant is flammable; avoid fire and smoking during and after use

*Brand discontinued but name still used in practice.

Budesonide Drug Interactions

- Budesonide is a major substrate of CYP450 3A4. Avoid strong and moderate inhibitors of CYP3A4, including grapefruit juice and grapefruit products.

- Use of steroids with other immunosuppressants can increase the risk of serious adverse events.

- Antacids can cause enteric coated oral budesonide to dissolve prematurely due to ↑ gastric pH. Separate administration of antacids by two hours.

AMINOSALICYLATES

Aminosalicylates are indicated for treatment of UC; the mechanism of action is unknown, but they appear to have a topical anti-inflammatory effect in the gastrointestinal tract. Mesalamine (5-ASA) is the primary aminosalicylate used in the U.S.; it is well tolerated and available in both oral and rectal formulations. The other aminosalicylates (sulfasalazine, balsalazide, olsalazine) are available in oral form only and must be converted to mesalamine to have an effect. Sulfasalazine is used less commonly due to the many side effects associated with the sulfapyridine component.

DRUG	DOSING	SAFETY/SIDE EFFECTS/MONITORING
Mesalamine ER ER capsules **(Pentasa,** Apriso, Delzicol) ER tablets **(Asacol HD,** Lialda) Enema **(Rowasa)** Suppository **(Canasa)**	**Induction** (oral therapy for 6-8 weeks and/or rectal therapy for 3-6 weeks) Asacol HD: 1.6 g PO TID Delzicol: 800 mg PO TID Lialda: 2.4-4.8 g PO daily Pentasa: 1 g PO QID Suppository: 1 g rectally QHS, retain for at least 1-3 hours Enema: 4 g rectally QHS, retain in the rectum overnight for approximately 8 hours **Maintenance** Apriso: 1.5 g PO daily Delzicol: 1.6 g PO in 2-4 divided doses Lialda: 2.4 g PO daily Pentasa: 1 g PO QID Enema: 2 g rectally QHS, or 4 g QHS every 2-3 days	**CONTRAINDICATIONS** Hypersensitivity to salicylates or aminosalicylates **WARNINGS** Acute intolerance syndrome (cramping, acute abdominal pain, bloody diarrhea); caution in patients with renal or hepatic impairment; delayed gastric retention (e.g., due to pyloric stenosis) can delay release of oral products in the colon; hypersensitivity reactions (including myocarditis, pericarditis, nephritis, hematologic abnormalities and other internal organ damage) – more likely with sulfasalazine than mesalamine; ↑ risk of blood dyscrasias in patients > 65 years of age, photosensitivity Apriso contains phenylalanine; do not use in patients with phenylketonuria (PKU) Rowasa enema contains potassium metabisulfite, may cause an allergic-type reaction **SIDE EFFECTS** Abdominal pain, nausea, headache, flatulence, eructation (belching), nasopharyngitis **MONITORING** Renal function, CBC, hepatic function, s/sx of IBD **NOTES** Mesalamine is better tolerated than other aminosalicylates Rectal mesalamine is more effective than oral mesalamine and rectal steroids for distal disease/proctitis in UC; can use oral and topical formulations together Asacol and Delzicol: can leave a ghost tablet in the stool Swallow capsules/tablets whole; do not crush, chew or break due to delayed-release coating Apriso: do not use with antacids (dissolution is pH-dependent)
Sulfasalazine Tablets (Azulfidine) ER tablets (Azulfidine EN-tabs)	**Induction** 3-4 g PO divided TID or QID, titrate to 4-6 g PO daily divided QID **Maintenance** 2 g PO daily divided TID or QID	Refer to the Systemic Steroids & Autoimmune Conditions chapter **CONTRAINDICATIONS** Salicylate allergy, sulfa allergy, intestinal or urinary obstruction, porphyria **NOTES** Doses should be taken at ≤ 8 hour intervals Can reduce dose if GI intolerance occurs
Balsalazide (Colazal) Capsule	**Induction** Colazal: 2.25 g (three 750 mg capsules) PO TID for 8-12 weeks	**CONTRAINDICATION** Salicylate allergy **WARNINGS** Gastric retention (e.g., due to pyloric stenosis) can delay release of drug in the colon; acute intolerance syndrome; caution in patients with renal or hepatic impairment, photosensitivity **SIDE EFFECTS** Headache, abdominal pain, N/V/D **MONITORING** Renal function, LFTs, s/sx of IBD **NOTES** Colazal capsule can be opened and sprinkled on applesauce; beads are not coated, so mixture can be chewed if needed; when used this way, it can cause staining of the teeth/tongue
Olsalazine (Dipentum) Capsule	**Maintenance** 500 mg PO BID Take with food	**CONTRAINDICATION** Salicylate allergy **SIDE EFFECTS** Diarrhea, abdominal pain **MONITORING** CBC, LFTs, renal function, symptoms of IBD

THIOPURINES

The thiopurines, azathioprine and mercaptopurine, are immunosuppressive drugs, sometimes referred to as "immunomodulators." They do not have an FDA indication for IBD but are recommended as an option in guidelines for induction and maintenance of remission, often in combination with other drugs.

DRUG	DOSING	SAFETY/SIDE EFFECTS/MONITORING
Azathioprine (Azasan, Imuran) Tablet, injection	1.5-2.5 mg/kg/day IV or PO CrCl < 50 mL/min: adjustment required PO: taking after meals or in divided doses may ↓ GI side effects	**BOXED WARNINGS** Chronic immunosuppression ↑ risk of malignancy in patients with IBD (especially lymphomas); mutagenic potential; risk for hematologic toxicities **WARNINGS** Hematologic toxicities (e.g., leukopenia, thrombocytopenia, anemia); patients with a genetic deficiency of thiopurine methyltransferase (TPMT) are at ↑ risk for myelosuppression GI hypersensitivity reactions (severe N/V/D, rash, fever, ↑ LFTs), serious infections, hepatotoxicity **SIDE EFFECTS** N/V/D, rash, ↑ LFTs **MONITORING** LFTs, CBC (weekly for 1st month), renal function, s/sx of malignancy **NOTES** Consider TPMT genetic testing before starting (see Pharmacogenomics chapter) Azathioprine is metabolized to mercaptopurine; do not use the thiopurines in combination Aminosalicylates inhibit TPMT; caution with use in combination Allopurinol inhibits a pathway for inactivation of azathioprine; azathioprine dose reduction required if used in combination
Mercaptopurine (Purixan) Tablet, oral suspension	1-1.5 mg/kg/day CrCl ≤ 50 mL/min: adjustment required	Same as azathioprine above (except no boxed warning) plus: **NOTES** Take on an empty stomach Avoid old terms "6-mercaptopurine" and "6-MP"; they ↑ the risk of overdose due to administration of doses 6-fold higher than normal

METHOTREXATE AND CYCLOSPORINE

Methotrexate is an immunosuppressive drug with anti-inflammatory properties. It does not have an FDA indication for IBD, but it is recommended by the guidelines for induction and maintenance of remission in moderate-severe CD in patients who cannot tolerate azathioprine. It is dosed once weekly by IM or SC injection. See the Systemic Steroids & Autoimmune Conditions chapter for information on methotrexate.

Cyclosporine is an immunosuppressive drug recommended for severe UC. It can be given orally or via IV continuous infusion. See the Transplant chapter for more information on cyclosporine.

ANTI-TNF AGENTS, INTERLEUKIN RECEPTOR ANTAGONISTS AND JANUS KINASE INHIBITORS

The anti-TNF agents (e.g., infliximab) are monoclonal antibodies that bind to human TNF-alpha, preventing induction of proinflammatory cytokines (e.g., interleukins). They are used in patients with moderate-severe UC or CD, often in combination with a thiopurine. See the Study Tip Gal earlier in the chapter for information on which specific anti-TNF agents are FDA-approved for UC and CD.

Ustekinumab (Stelara) is an interleukin receptor antagonist that binds to and interferes with IL-12 and IL-23. It is FDA-approved for moderate-severe UC or CD and can be used in patients who have not yet failed or are intolerant to anti-TNF treatment. Tofacitinib (Xeljanz) is an oral tablet that inhibits janus kinase (JAK) enzymes, which are involved in stimulating immune cell function. It is FDA-approved to treat moderate-severe UC, but is not considered first-line due to risks. These medications are discussed further in the Systemic Steroids & Autoimmune Conditions chapter.

GASTROINTESTINAL CONDITIONS

INTEGRIN RECEPTOR ANTAGONISTS

Natalizumab and vedolizumab are <u>monoclonal antibodies</u> that bind to subunits of integrin molecules, blocking the ability of integrin to interact with adhesion molecules and preventing inflammatory cells from migrating into gastrointestinal tissue. They are indicated for <u>induction</u> and <u>maintenance of remission</u> in patients with IBD who have <u>responded inadequately</u> or cannot tolerate conventional therapies, or in patients who are <u>steroid-dependent</u>.

DRUG	DOSING	SAFETY/SIDE EFFECTS/MONITORING
Natalizumab (Tysabri) <u>Injection</u> Approved for <u>Crohn's disease</u> and multiple sclerosis	300 mg IV over 1 hour <u>every 4 weeks</u> <u>Discontinue if no response by 12 weeks</u>	**BOXED WARNING** <u>Progressive multifocal leukoencephalopathy [(PML), an opportunistic viral infection of the brain that leads to death or severe disability]; monitor for mental status changes;</u> risk factors include: anti-JCV antibodies, ↑ treatment duration and prior immunosuppressant use <u>Only available through the REMS TOUCH Prescribing Program</u> **WARNINGS** Herpes encephalitis and meningitis, hepatotoxicity, hypersensitivity (antibody formation), immunosuppression/infections **SIDE EFFECTS** Infusion reactions, headache, fatigue, arthralgia, nausea, rash, depression, gastroenteritis, abdominal/back pain **NOTES** Cannot be used with other immunosuppressants Stable in NS only; do not shake If taking steroids when initiating *Tysabri*, begin tapering when the onset of benefit is observed; stop *Tysabri* if patient cannot taper steroids within 6 months of initiation
Vedolizumab (Entyvio) <u>Injection</u> Approved for <u>Crohn's disease and ulcerative colitis</u>	300 mg IV over 30 min at 0, 2, and 6 weeks, then every 8 weeks <u>Discontinue if no benefit by week 14</u>	**WARNINGS** Infusion reactions, hypersensitivity reactions, infections, liver injury, PML All immunizations must be up to date before starting; should not receive live vaccines during treatment unless benefit outweighs risk **SIDE EFFECTS** Headache, nasopharyngitis, arthralgia, antibody development **MONITORING** LFTs, s/sx of infection, hypersensitivity, neurological symptoms (to monitor for PML), routine TB screening **NOTES** Refrigerate and store in original packaging to protect from light Swirl during reconstitution, do not shake; after reconstitution, use immediately or refrigerate up to 4 hours (do not freeze) Cannot be used with other immunosuppressants

KEY COUNSELING POINTS

See the Drug Formulations and Patient Counseling chapter for counseling language/layman's terminology and instructions for suppository and enema administration.

MESALAMINE

- Select ER products can cause a ghost tablet.

Mesalamine Enemas and Suppositories

- Administer in the evening, just before bedtime. Try not to have a bowel movement until morning.

- Can cause staining of surfaces, including clothing and other fabrics.

Select Guidelines/References

Bowel Disease. Updated 2015. http://www.worldgastroenterology.org/guidelines/global-guidelines/inflammatory-bowel-disease-ibd (accessed 2022 Feb 24).

American College of Gastroenterology (ACG) Clinical Guideline: Management of Crohn's Disease in Adults. Am J Gastroenterol 2018;113:481–517.

American Gastroenterological Association (AGA) Clinical Practice Guidelines on the Management of Mild-to-Moderate Ulcerative Colitis. Gastroenterology 2019;156:748-764.

American Gastroenterological Association (AGA) Clinical Practice Guidelines on the Management of Moderate-to-Severe Ulcerative Colitis. Gastroenterology 2020;158:1450-1461.

CHAPTER CONTENT

DEFINITIONS

Nausea

The uncomfortable, queasy feeling that one may vomit.

Treatment

The chemoreceptor trigger zone (CTZ) in the CNS contains receptors for dopamine (DA), serotonin (5HT) and acetylcholine (Ach). Each receptor can set off a chemical pathway leading to nausea and vomiting. Blocking the receptors reduces nausea, such as:

- Blocking 5HT with 5HT-3 receptor antagonists (e.g., ondansetron)

- Blocking DA with phenothiazines (e.g., prochlorperazine)

- Blocking 5HT and DA with metoclopramide (a prokinetic that moves food through the gut)

Nausea due to chemotherapy is treated with 5HT-3 receptor antagonists and various other medications; see Oncology I chapter.

Vertigo

Dizziness, with the sensation that the environment is moving or spinning. Vertigo is typically due to an inner-ear condition that affects balance.

Treatment
- Vestibular (inner-ear) suppressants, including antihistamines (e.g., meclizine, dimenhydrinate) and benzodiazepines

5HT-3 receptor antagonists are not useful for vertigo because they do not affect the inner ear.

Motion Sickness

Dizziness, with a sensation of being off-balance and woozy due to repetitive motions, such as a boat moving over waves or an airplane flying in turbulent weather.

Treatment
- Anticholinergics (e.g., scopolamine) and antihistamines (e.g., meclizine)

🖾 iStock.com/NiwatSingsamarn

CONTENT LEGEND

 ♀ = Study Tip Gal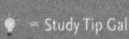

🖾 iStock.com/djedzura

CHAPTER 75
MOTION SICKNESS

BACKGROUND

Motion sickness (kinetosis) is a common condition that is also called travel/car sickness, seasickness or airsickness. Symptoms include nausea, dizziness and fatigue. People can get motion sickness on a moving boat, airplane, car or amusement park ride. Symptoms can be triggered in some patients by movies or video games.

NON-DRUG TREATMENT

Some patients find benefit with a wrist band that presses on an acupuncture point located on the inside of the wrist, about the length of 2 fingernails up the arm from the center of the wrist crease. One popular brand is *Sea-Band*.

Ginger, in teas or supplements, is used commonly for nausea. Some people also find it helpful for motion sickness. Peppermint may also be helpful. The best way to stop motion sickness, if possible, is to stop the motion.

DRUG TREATMENT

Antihistamines and anticholinergics are recommended for motion sickness. Scopolamine *(Transderm Scop)*, an anticholinergic, is most commonly prescribed. It is not more effective than generically-available OTC drugs, but is applied topically (behind the ear) and is taken less frequently (lasts three days).

Antihistamines used for motion sickness include diphenhydramine (Benadryl), dimenhydrinate (Dramamine) and meclizine (Dramamine All Day Less Drowsy, Bonine). Oral medications must be taken 30 - 60 minutes prior to the needed effect.. Dimenhydrinate and meclizine are long-acting piperazine antihistamines and are a little less sedating than other antihistamines. All of the antihistamines have anticholinergic effects similar to scopolamine.

Medications for motion sickness cause drowsiness and impair judgment. Pilots, ship crew members, or anyone operating heavy equipment or driving a car should not take them. Sometimes combinations of products (such as scopolamine to reduce nausea, taken with a stimulant, such as dextroamphetamine, to counteract the drowsiness from the scopolamine) are used, but these combinations have significant risk and should not be routinely recommended.

Traditional antiemetics are discussed in the Oncology I chapter. Promethazine is prescription only and should not be used in children due to the risk of respiratory depression. All promethazine products carry a boxed warning to avoid use in children less than 2 years old and strongly caution against use in children age 2 and older (see Pediatric Conditions and Allergic Rhinitis, Cough & Cold chapters). Metoclopramide and the 5HT-3 receptor antagonists (e.g., ondansetron) are generally not effective for motion sickness.

MOTION SICKNESS DRUGS

DRUG	DOSING	SAFETY/SIDE EFFECTS/MONITORING
Scopolamine (Transderm Scop)	**Motion Sickness** Apply 1 patch behind the ear at least 4 hrs before the effect is needed. May use a new patch every 3 days PRN. **Preoperative (e.g., cesarean section)** Apply 1 patch the night before surgery or 1 hr prior to surgery. Remove patch 24 hrs after surgery.	**CONTRAINDICATIONS** Hypersensitivity to belladonna alkaloids, closed-angle glaucoma **SIDE EFFECTS** Dry mouth, CNS effects [drowsiness, dizziness, confusion (can be significant in elderly, frail), hallucinations (rare)], stinging of the eyes and pupil dilation (if eyes are touched after handling), risk of ↑ IOP, tachycardia (rare) **NOTES** Refer to counseling section (on the following page) Remove the patch before an MRI (contains metal) Avoid alcohol while wearing the patch Primarily for motion sickness, occasionally used inpatient Do not use in children
Dimenhydrinate (Dramamine) Tablet, injection	**Motion Sickness** Oral: 50-100 mg Q4-6 hrs **Nausea and Vomiting** IM, IV: 50-100 mg Q4 hrs	**WARNINGS** CNS depression (may impair physical or mental abilities, caution in elderly), worsening of BPH symptoms, ↑ IOP (glaucoma) **SIDE EFFECTS** Dizziness, drowsiness, dry mouth, blurry vision, tachycardia **NOTES** There are various OTC formulations of Dramamine with different ingredients. Dramamine Original Formula contains only dimenhydrinate. Dramamine All Day Less Drowsy contains only meclizine.
Meclizine (Dramamine All Day Less Drowsy, Bonine, Motion-Time, Travel Sickness)	25-50 mg PO 1 hour before travel, can repeat Q24 hrs PRN	**WARNINGS** CNS depression (may impair physical or mental abilities, caution in elderly), worsening of BPH symptoms, ↑ IOP (glaucoma) **SIDE EFFECTS** Sedation, dry mouth, dry/blurry vision, tachycardia **NOTES** Meclizine is commonly used for vertigo; it was previously branded as Antivert

KEY COUNSELING POINTS

See the Drug Formulations and Patient Counseling chapter for counseling language/layman's terminology.

SCOPOLAMINE PATCH *(TRANSDERM SCOP)*

- See <u>Study Tip Gal</u> to the right for application instructions.
- Can cause:
    - ❏ Drowsiness.
    - ❏ Dry mouth.
    - ❏ Vision changes, such as blurry vision and widening of the pupils.
- Remove patch before an MRI.

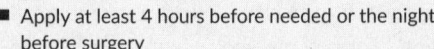

SCOPOLAMINE *(TRANSDERM SCOP)* PATCH

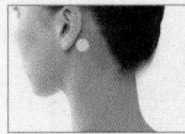

For N/V due to motion sickness or anesthesia/ surgery

- Apply at least 4 hours before needed or the night before surgery
- Press firmly to skin behind ear for 30 seconds
- Try to avoid placing the patch over hair, or when the patch is removed, the hair may be removed, too
- Lasts 3 days; if continued treatment needed, remove the first patch and place a new patch behind the other ear
- Wash hands after applying

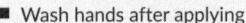

Do not drive: high level of sedation, dizziness, confusion - these anticholinergic side effects are worse, and not well-tolerated, in elderly patients (avoid use when possible)

PHARMACY FOUNDATIONS
PART 2

CONTENTS

CONTENT LEGEND

✿ = Study Tip Gal

© iStock.com/peshkov

CHAPTER 76
MEDICATION SAFETY & QUALITY IMPROVEMENT

BACKGROUND

A report published by the Institute of Medicine (IOM), *To Err is Human* (1999), increased awareness of the prevalence of medical errors. The study found that up to 98,000 Americans die each year in U.S. hospitals due to preventable medical errors, with 7,000 from medication errors alone. These numbers understated the problem because they did not include preventable deaths due to medical treatments outside of hospitals. Since the release of the IOM study, there has been a greater focus on the quality of healthcare provided in the U.S. The Joint Commission (TJC) and the Institute for Safe Medication Practices (ISMP) are two organizations actively involved in improving medication safety.

HOW TO APPROACH MEDICATION SAFETY

The term "medication safety" is defined as freedom from preventable harm due to medication use. It is an essential component of all areas of pharmacy practice and is therefore encompassed throughout most chapters in this course book (see examples in the table below). This chapter is intended to set the foundation and discuss some of the core elements of medication safety.

TOPIC*	CHAPTER
Collaborative practice	Immunizations
	Anticoagulation
	Contraception & Infertility
Transitions of care and continuity of care	Answering Case-Based Exam Questions
	Drug Formulations & Patient Counseling
Disease prevention and stewardship	Infectious Diseases I-IV
	Human Immunodeficiency Virus
	Hypertension
Vulnerable populations	Drug Use in Pregnancy & Lactation
	Pediatrics
	Oncology I and II
Pharmacy informatics	Drug References
	Lab Values & Drug Monitoring

*Adapted from Area 6 of the NAPLEX Competency Statements

MEDICATION ERRORS

The formal <u>definition</u> of a medication error developed by the National Coordinating Council for Medication Error Reporting and Prevention (NCC MERP) is "any <u>preventable event</u> that may cause or lead to <u>inappropriate medication use</u> or <u>patient harm</u> while the medication is in the control of the healthcare professional, patient, or consumer." This can include errors made in prescribing, order communication, product labeling and packaging, compounding, dispensing, administration, education or monitoring.

<u>Do not confuse</u> medication errors with <u>adverse drug reactions</u> (<u>ADRs</u>). ADRs are usually <u>not avoidable</u>, although they may be <u>more likely</u> to occur if the drug is given to a <u>patient at high risk</u> for certain complications. Refer to the Drug Allergies & Adverse Drug Reactions chapter for a discussion of ADRs.

EXAMPLE OF AN ADR (NOT A MEDICATION ERROR)

A 55-year-old female has a history of herpes zoster. She reports considerable "shingles pain" and received a prescription for pregabalin. She returned to the clinic with complaints of ankle swelling, which required drug discontinuation.

This is not a medication error made by the prescriber of pregabalin or by the pharmacist who dispensed it. Rather, this is a side effect that can occur with the use of this drug.

A <u>sentinel event</u> is an unexpected occurrence involving <u>death</u> or <u>serious</u> physical or psychological <u>injury</u> of a patient. When a sentinel event occurs, it is important to find out what went wrong and implement measures to prevent it from happening again.

SYSTEM-BASED CAUSES

Experts in medication safety agree that the most common cause of medication errors is a <u>problem</u> with the <u>design</u> of the <u>medical system itself</u>, not usually the healthcare worker making an error. Instead of placing blame on individuals, healthcare professionals should find ways to improve the system (referred to as a "just culture"). This creates an environment where individual workers feel more comfortable disclosing errors. Errors will always occur, but the goal is to design systems to prevent medication errors from reaching the patient. Some "at-risk" behaviors that can compromise patient safety are included in the box that follows.

AT-RISK BEHAVIORS THAT CAN COMPROMISE PATIENT SAFETY

Drug and Patient-Related
- Failure to check/reconcile home medications and doses
- Dispensing medications without complete drug knowledge
- Not questioning unusual doses
- Not checking/verifying allergies

Communication
- Not addressing questions/concerns
- Rushed communication

Technology
- Overriding computer alerts without proper consideration
- Not using available technology

Work Environment
- Trying to do multiple things vs. focusing on a single complex task
- Inadequate supervision and orientation/training

RESPONSE

Institutions should have a plan in place for responding to medication errors. The plan should address the following:

- Internal notification: who should be notified within the institution and within what time frame?
- External reporting: who should be notified outside of the institution?
- Disclosure: what information should be shared with the patient/family? Who will be present when this occurs?
- Investigation: what is the process for immediate and long-term internal investigation of an error?
- Improvement: what process will ensure that immediate and long-term preventative actions are taken?

ERRORS OF OMISSION AND COMMISSION

Error of Omission
Something was <u>left out</u> that is needed for safety

Example: failing to use a pharmacist double-check system for chemotherapy orders

Error of Commission
Something was done <u>incorrectly</u>

Example: prescribing bupropion to a patient with a history of seizures

REPORTING

Medication errors, preventable adverse drug reactions, hazardous conditions and "close calls" or "near misses" should be reported. Medication errors are reported so that changes can be made to the system to prevent similar errors in the future. Without reporting, these events may go unrecognized and will likely happen again because others will not learn from the incident.

In a pharmacy, the staff member who discovers the error should immediately report it to the appropriate authority (e.g., corporate office, the owner of an independent pharmacy, designated hospital office) using the established reporting structure. Many state boards of pharmacy require quality assurance programs to promote pharmacy processes that prevent medication errors. Error investigations need to take place quickly (within 48 hours of the incident) so that the sequence of events remains clear to those involved. Many states mandate the ethical requirement that errors be reported to the patient and the prescriber as soon as possible.

Most medication error reporting systems within hospitals are electronic. The hospital's Pharmacy and Therapeutics (P&T) committee and Medication Safety Committee (or similar entity) should be informed of the error.

ORGANIZATIONS THAT SPECIALIZE IN ERROR PREVENTION

Organizations that specialize in error prevention can analyze the system-based causes of errors and make recommendations. The ISMP National Medication Errors Reporting Program (MERP) is a confidential, voluntary reporting program. It provides expert analysis of the system causes of medication errors and provides recommendations for prevention.

Medication errors and close calls can be reported on the ISMP website (www.ismp.org). Professionals and consumers should be encouraged to report medication errors using this site even if the error was reported internally. When there are

many reports of a particular error, the manufacturer may be required to take measures to increase drug safety (e.g., REMS program, name change, packaging change).

Every pharmacist should make it a practice to read medication error reports, such as the ISMP Medication Safety Alert newsletters, and use the information to improve their own practice setting.

EVALUATION AND QUALITY IMPROVEMENT

Evaluation and quality improvement can be performed prospectively, retrospectively or continuously.

- Prospective
  - Failure mode and effects analysis (FMEA) is a proactive method used to reduce the frequency and consequences of errors. FMEA is used to analyze the design of the system in order to evaluate the potential for failures and to determine what potential effects could occur when the medication delivery system changes in any substantial way or if a potentially dangerous new drug will be added to the formulary.
- Retrospective
  - A root cause analysis (RCA) is a retrospective investigation of an event that has already occurred, which includes reviewing the sequence of events that led to the error. The information obtained in the analysis is used to design changes that will hopefully prevent future errors.
- Continuous
  - Continuous quality improvement (CQI) is the goal for most healthcare settings. CQI programs improve efficiency, quality and patient satisfaction while reducing costs. Examples include Lean and Six Sigma, which are often used together. Lean focuses on minimizing waste, while Six Sigma focuses on reducing defects. Six Sigma uses the DMAIC (define, measure, analyze, improve, control) process.

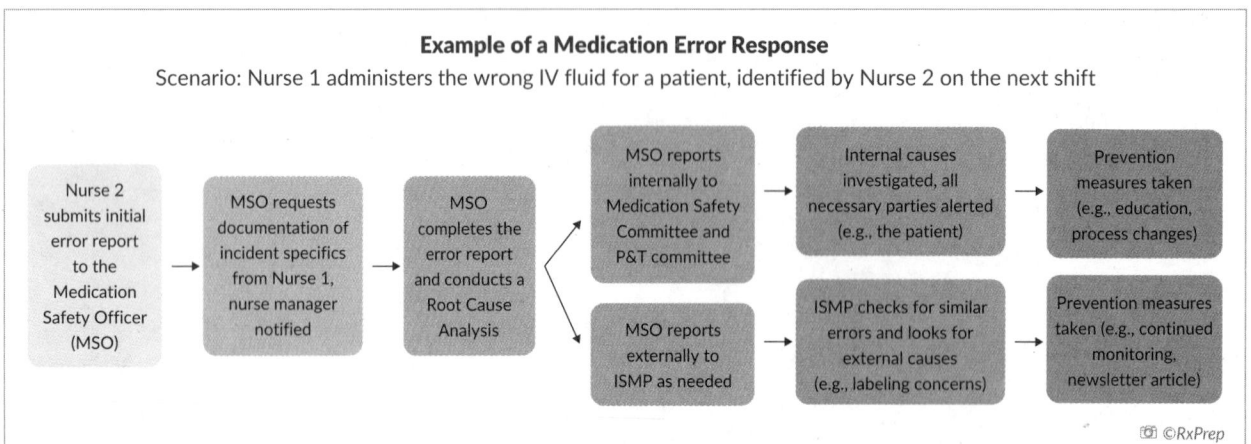

Example of a Medication Error Response
Scenario: Nurse 1 administers the wrong IV fluid for a patient, identified by Nurse 2 on the next shift

Nurse 2 submits initial error report to the Medication Safety Officer (MSO) → MSO requests documentation of incident specifics from Nurse 1, nurse manager notified → MSO completes the error report and conducts a Root Cause Analysis → MSO reports internally to Medication Safety Committee and P&T committee → Internal causes investigated, all necessary parties alerted (e.g., the patient) → Prevention measures taken (e.g., education, process changes)

MSO reports externally to ISMP as needed → ISMP checks for similar errors and looks for external causes (e.g., labeling concerns) → Prevention measures taken (e.g., continued monitoring, newsletter article)

©RxPrep

PHARMACY FOUNDATIONS PART 2

THE JOINT COMMISSION (TJC)

The Joint Commission on Accreditation of Healthcare Organizations (TJC) is an independent, not-for-profit organization that accredits and certifies more than 20,000 healthcare organizations and programs in the U.S., including hospitals, healthcare networks, long-term care facilities, home care organizations, office-based surgery centers and independent laboratories. TJC focuses on the highest quality and safety of care and sets standards that institutions must meet to be accredited. An accredited organization must undergo an on-site survey at least every three years, and surveys can be unannounced.

NATIONAL PATIENT SAFETY GOALS

National Patient Safety Goals (NPSGs) are set annually by TJC for different types of healthcare settings (e.g., ambulatory care, behavioral health, hospital). Each goal includes defined measures called "Elements of Performance" that must be met. These will be included in institutional protocols. Important NPSGs for pharmacists are described below.

- Use at least two patient identifiers when providing care, treatment and services.
  - Appropriate patient identifiers include name, medical record number and date of birth.
  - Inappropriate patient identifiers include zip code, room number and physician name.
- Reduce the likelihood of patient harm associated with the use of anticoagulant therapy.
  - There are many important elements to this goal, including the requirements to use approved dosing protocols and programmable pumps (e.g., for heparin) and to provide education to patients and families. Protocols should include starting dose ranges, alternate dosing strategies to address drug-drug interactions, communication with the dietary department to address drug-food interactions, general monitoring requirements and monitoring for bleeding and heparin-induced thrombocytopenia (HIT).

- Maintain and communicate accurate patient medication information.
  - This includes medication reconciliation, providing written information to the patient and conducting discharge counseling. The medication name, dose, frequency, route and indication (at a minimum) should be confirmed. Refer to the section on Medication Reconciliation later in this chapter.

SELECT NATIONAL PATIENT SAFETY GOALS

NPSG 01.01.01: Use at least two patient identifiers when providing care, treatment and services (see text).

NPSG 02.03.01: Report critical results of tests and diagnostic procedures on a timely basis.

NPSG 03.04.01: Label all medications, medication containers (e.g., syringes) and other solutions on and off the sterile field in perioperative and other procedural settings.

NPSG 03.05.01: Reduce the likelihood of patient harm associated with the use of anticoagulant therapy (see text).

NPSG 03.06.01: Maintain and communicate accurate patient medication information (see text).

NPSG 06.01.01: Improve the safety of clinical alarm systems.

NPSG 07.01.01: Comply with either the Centers for Disease Control (CDC) or World Health Organization (WHO) hand hygiene guidelines.

OTHER ACCREDITING ORGANIZATIONS

While TJC is the most recognized accreditation body, three other organizations accredit and certify healthcare programs. These organizations include DNV GL Healthcare, Healthcare Facilities Accreditation Program-Accreditation Association for Hospitals/Health Systems (HFAP/AAHHS) and the Center for Improvement in Healthcare Quality (CIHQ). Similar to TJC, each organization has specific standards that must be met to obtain accreditation. The approaches to accreditation are different, and institutions can select the accrediting organization that best matches their population and needs.

COMMON METHODS TO REDUCE MEDICATION ERRORS

AVOID "DO NOT USE" ABBREVIATIONS

Abbreviations are unsafe and contribute to many medical errors. The minimum list of "Do Not Use" abbreviations per TJC is shown in the table below. ISMP also publishes a list of error-prone abbreviations, symbols and dosage designations which includes those on TJC's list and many others. All institutions accredited by TJC are required to have a list of abbreviations that should not be used in the facility. This list must include all of the abbreviations from the TJC "Do Not Use" list and any additional abbreviations selected by the institution (e.g., those that have resulted in significant errors in the past). The unapproved abbreviation list should be readily accessible in the institution (e.g., wall charts, pocket cards). It is best to try to avoid abbreviations entirely. Electronic prescribing can virtually eliminate errors associated with poor handwriting. See the Study Tip Gal at the bottom of the page.

DO NOT USE	POTENTIAL PROBLEM	USE INSTEAD
U, u (unit)	Mistaken for "O" (zero), the number "4" (four) or "cc"	Write "unit"
IU (international unit)	Mistaken for IV (intravenous) or the number 10 (ten)	Write "international unit"
Q.D., QD, q.d., qd (daily)	Mistaken for each other	Write "daily"
Q.O.D., QOD, q.o.d., qod (every other day)	Period after the Q mistaken for "I" and the "O" mistaken for "I"	Write "every other day"
Trailing zero (X.0 mg)	Decimal point is missed resulting in a 10-fold dosing error	Write X mg
Lack of leading zero (.X mg)		Write 0.X mg
MS	Can mean morphine sulfate or magnesium sulfate	Write "morphine sulfate"
MSO$_4$ and MgSO$_4$	Confused with one another	Write "magnesium sulfate"

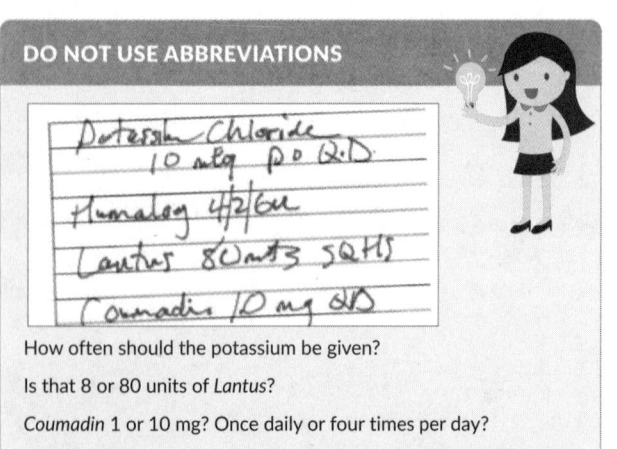

DO NOT USE ABBREVIATIONS

How often should the potassium be given?

Is that 8 or 80 units of *Lantus*?

Coumadin 1 or 10 mg? Once daily or four times per day?

TALL MAN LETTERING

Look-alike, sound-alike medications are a common cause of medication errors. Poor handwriting and similar product labeling aggravate the problem. Drugs that are easily mixed up should be labeled with tall man letters. Here are two examples:

- *CeleXA, CeleBREX*
- predniSONE, prednisoLONE

Using tall man letters, which mix upper and lower case letters, draws attention to the dissimilarities in the drug names. The letters that are upper cases are the ones that are different between the two look-alike, sound-alike drugs. Safety-conscious organizations (e.g., ISMP, FDA, TJC) have promoted the use of tall man letters as one means of reducing confusion between similar drug names. The FDA's and ISMP's approved tall man lettering information is available at: http://www.ismp.org/tools/tallmanletters.pdf.

Drug dictionaries within computer systems and automated dispensing cabinets (ADC) often have alerts that prompt the provider to confirm that the correct medication is being ordered or withdrawn. For example, a warning may appear on the screen of the ADC that will state: "This is *DILAUDID*. Did you want HYDROmorphone?" to avoid confusion with morphine.

HIGH-ALERT MEDICATIONS

Drugs with a heightened risk of causing significant patient harm if used in error should be designated as high-alert (see Study Tip Gal on the next page). The ISMP "high-alert" list for acute care settings is available online. ISMP's list represents the most common agents that are high risk, but an institution's list may include additional drugs based on experience in that setting.

High-alert medications can be used safely by developing protocols or order sets for use, using premixed products whenever possible, limiting concentrations available in the institution and stocking high-alert products only in the pharmacy. See examples of safe use precautions for insulin and potassium chloride below. Protocols for high-alert drugs increase appropriate prescribing and reduce the chance of errors from inappropriate prescribing.

SELECT HIGH-ALERT MEDICATIONS

- Anesthetics, inhaled or IV (e.g., propofol)
- Antiarrhythmics, IV (e.g., amiodarone)
- Anticoagulants/antithrombotics (e.g., heparin, warfarin)
- Chemotherapeutics (e.g., methotrexate)
- Epidural/intrathecal drugs
- Hypertonic saline (greater than 0.9% NaCl)
- Immunosuppressants (e.g., cyclosporine)
- Inotropics (e.g., digoxin)
- Insulins (e.g., insulin aspart, insulin U-500)
- Magnesium sulfate injection
- Neuromuscular blocking agents (e.g., vecuronium)
- Opioids
- Oral hypoglycemics (e.g., sulfonylureas)
- Parenteral nutrition
- Potassium chloride and phosphates for injection
- Sterile water for injection

Examples of Safe-Use Precautions

DRUG	PRECAUTIONS
Insulin	Do not place insulin in automated dispensing cabinets; all insulin orders should be reviewed by a pharmacist prior to dispensing
	Standardize all insulin infusions to one concentration
	Develop protocols for insulin infusions, transition from infusion to SC and sliding scale orders; use standard orders for management of hypoglycemia
	Do not use "U" for units; always label with "units" or "units = mL," but never just "mL"
	If U-500 is stocked, specify conditions under which it is to be used, which product will be stocked (vials and U-500 syringes vs. pens), and how doses will be supplied
Potassium Chloride	Remove all KCl vials from floor stock; prepare all KCl infusions in the pharmacy
	Use premixed containers
	Use protocols for KCl delivery which include indications for IV administration, maximum rate of infusion, maximum allowable concentration, guidelines for when cardiac monitoring is required, a stipulation that all KCl infusions must be given via a pump, prohibition of multiple simultaneous KCl solutions (e.g., no IV KCl while KCl is being infused in another IV)
	Allow for automatic substitution of oral KCl for IV KCl, when appropriate
	Label all fluids containing potassium with a "Potassium Added" sticker

Any drug that is high-risk for significant harm if dispensed incorrectly can be placed in a medication bin that provides a visual alert to the person accessing the medication. The bin can be labeled with warnings and include materials (placed inside the bin) that should be dispensed with the drug (such as oral syringes or MedGuides).

MEDICATION THERAPY MANAGEMENT

Errors may be discovered during a medication therapy review (MTR), through the process of medication therapy management (MTM). A personal medication record (PMR) is prepared, and a medication-related action plan (MAP) is developed, preferably by a pharmacist-led team. The next steps involve interventions or referrals, documentation and plans for follow-up. Patients targeted for MTM include those with multiple chronic conditions who are taking multiple drugs and are likely to incur annual costs for covered drugs that exceed a predetermined level. Computer databases are used to identify patients with certain high-risk conditions (such as heart failure or uncontrolled diabetes) and assign a pharmacist (preferably) to review profiles for proper medication use.

The pharmacist can form a partnership with the patient and prescriber to remedy any issues or lapses. Often, these reviews identify missed therapy such as lack of an ACE inhibitor or ARB in patients with diabetes and albuminuria, missing beta-blocker therapy post-MI, or missing bisphosphonate therapy with high-dose chronic steroids. A popular MTM initiative is to improve nonadherence in patients with heart failure due to the high rate of ED visits for decompensated heart failure. MTM is also used to identify cost savings, by promoting switches to generics or more affordable brands, or by suggesting patient assistance programs or low-income subsidies for eligible members.

MEDICATION RECONCILIATION

Medication reconciliation involves comparing a patient's new medication orders to all of the medications that the patient has been taking at home (including OTC and dietary supplements). This reconciliation is done to avoid medication errors such as omissions, duplications, dosing errors or drug interactions during transitions of care.

Medication reconciliation ("med rec") is now usually performed within the electronic health record (EHR). Prescribers can view side-by-side lists of home medications and ordered medications, and address any discrepancies. This process is most effective when complete and accurate information is entered into the patient's medical record. For this reason, pharmacy departments are often actively involved in documenting home medication use and performing medication reconciliation. In many hospitals, admission orders for a patient cannot be entered into the electronic system until medication reconciliation is completed by a prescriber, pharmacist, pharmacy technician or nurse.

Medication reconciliation should be completed at every transition of care in which new medications are ordered or existing orders are rewritten. Transitions of care include changes in setting, service, practitioner or level of care. Common examples are hospital admission, transfer into or out of an ICU and hospital discharge. The medication reconciliation process comprises five steps:

- Develop a list of current medications
- Develop a list of medications to be prescribed
- Compare the medications on the two lists
- Note discrepancies and make clinical decisions based on the comparison
- Communicate the new list to appropriate caregivers and to the patient

Discharge medication reconciliation is an opportunity for the prescriber to address any of the patient's home medications that were "on hold" during the hospitalization and which medications used during the hospitalization should be continued when the patient goes home. Discrepancies are addressed, and the patient is educated. Though most often discussed in the hospital context, medication reconciliation can be equally important in ambulatory care, as many patients receive prescriptions from more than one outpatient provider and may go to several pharmacies.

EXAMPLE OF THE BENEFIT OF MEDICATION RECONCILIATION

AN is an 82-year-old female. Her only medication for the previous ten years has been atenolol 25 mg daily. She recently developed influenza, began to have trouble breathing and was taken to the hospital. It was discovered that she had pneumonia and heart failure. She was prescribed lisinopril, carvedilol and furosemide. AN was discharged to transitional care and received the new medications plus her home medication (atenolol). The consultant pharmacist conducted a medication review to reconcile the medications and, after discussion with the physician, the pharmacist wrote an order to discontinue the atenolol.

INDICATIONS AND PROPER INSTRUCTIONS ON PRESCRIPTIONS

An indication for use written on the prescription (such as lisinopril 10 mg once daily for hypertension) helps pharmacists ensure appropriate prescribing and drug selection.

Using the term "as directed" is not acceptable on prescriptions because the patient often has no idea what this means, and the pharmacist cannot verify a proper dosing regimen. Occasionally, this term is used on the bottle along with a separate dosing calendar, such as with warfarin. It would be preferable to write "use per instructions on the dosing calendar" since the patient may not understand how to take the medication and may not be aware that a separate dosing calendar exists.

USE OF THE METRIC SYSTEM

Measurements should be recorded using the metric system only. Prescribers should use metric units to express all weights and volumes. Computer systems generally have a drop-down menu for selecting the correct units (e.g., lb vs. kg) and easily converting between units. It is critical to record the correct units since many calculations (CrCl or eGFR) and dosing checks are performed automatically by the EHR system based on the height and/or weight recorded for the patient. With the increasing prevalence of obesity in the U.S., it is not uncommon to care for patients weighing 100 kg (or more), but serious errors can occur if this weight was intended to be 100 lb.

DO NOT IDENTIFY MEDICATIONS BASED ON PACKAGING ALONE

Look-alike packaging can contribute to errors. If unavoidable, separate look-alike drugs in the pharmacy and patient care units, or repackage. Never rely on the package appearance (e.g., color, design) to identify the right drug product. Pharmacies frequently have to purchase products from different manufacturers (and these may look vastly different).

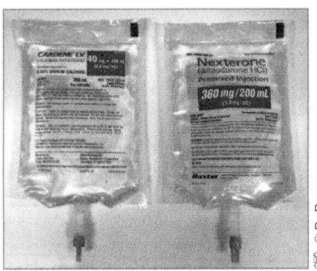

Example of Similar Drug Packaging

EXAMPLE OF AN ERROR DUE TO MISIDENTIFICATION OF A CONCENTRATION BASED ON THE PACKAGING

The intravenous catheters of three neonates in a NICU were flushed with the adult therapeutic dose of heparin (10,000 units/mL) rather than the heparin flush dose of 10 units/mL. This accident did not result in fatalities, although two of the babies required the reversal agent protamine. Three babies died from a similar incident the previous year at a different hospital. The wrong product was accidentally selected and administered because the packaging for the two concentrations looked similar and the products were stored in the same location.

Due to the high risk associated with heparin overdose, high concentration heparin vials should not be present in patient care areas. Instead, therapeutic doses should be sent by the pharmacy department.

AVOID MULTIPLE-DOSE VIALS

Multiple-dose vials pose a risk for cross-contamination (infection) and overdosing. If used, they should (ideally) be designated for a single patient and labeled appropriately. The remainder should be discarded when the medication is discontinued or the patient is discharged.

SAFE PRACTICES FOR EMERGENCY MEDICATIONS/CRASH CARTS

Staff must be properly trained to handle emergencies and use crash cart medications. The medications should be in unit-dose packaging (e.g., contains a single dose) and be age-specific, including doses for pediatric patients. A quick reference with weight-based dosing (e.g., Broselow tape) should be placed in the trays used in the pediatric units. If a unit-dose medication is not available, it is best to have prefilled syringes and premixed drips in the cart (to the extent possible) because it is easy to make a mistake under the stress of a code. The emergency medications should be stored in sealed or locked containers in a locked room and replaced as soon as possible after use (through a cart exchange so that the area is not left without required medications). Drug expiration dates should be monitored. Trained pharmacists should be present at codes when possible.

> **CODE BLUE**
>
> A code blue refers to a patient requiring emergency medical care, typically for cardiac or respiratory arrest. The overhead announcement and/or paging system will provide the patient's location. The code team (often including a pharmacist) will rush to the room and begin immediate resuscitative efforts.

DEDICATE PHARMACISTS TO HIGH-RISK AREAS

Intensive care units (ICUs), pediatric units and emergency departments are units with a high incidence of preventable medication errors. Pharmacists working in these units can assist in identifying and preventing medication errors by developing process improvements designed to reduce errors.

MONITOR FOR DRUG-FOOD INTERACTIONS

Check for drug-food interactions routinely and involve the nutrition department (also called "dietary") when the profile includes drugs with a high rate of food interactions (e.g., warfarin) or medications that interact with enteral feedings (i.e., tube feedings). For example, phenytoin administration via feeding tube requires that enteral feeding be held for 1 – 2 hours before and after the dose.

EDUCATION

Staff education programs such as "in-services" should be provided whenever new high-alert drugs are being used in the facility, to introduce new guidelines and procedural changes aimed at preventing medication errors. The information provided in these "in-services" should be unbiased and should not be provided in a skewed manner by drug company representatives. Many hospitals now limit access of pharmaceutical companies and representatives due to the inherent bias.

Patients can play a vital role in preventing medication errors when they have been encouraged to ask questions and seek satisfactory answers about their medications before drugs are dispensed at a pharmacy. If a patient questions any part of the medication dispensing process, whether it is about the drug's appearance, dose or something else, the pharmacist must be receptive and responsive (not defensive). All patient inquiries should be thoroughly investigated before the medication is dispensed. The written information about the medications should be at a reading level that is appropriate for the patient.

It may be necessary to provide pictures or other means of instruction to patients who do not speak English or are unable to read English. Attempts must be made to communicate to the patient in their language, using on-site staff or dial-in translation services.

FIVE RIGHTS OF MEDICATION ADMINISTRATION

The "five rights" are a quick double-check that should be performed by a healthcare professional every time a medication is administered (see figure below). They are an example of a best practice in medication safety that helps prevent medication errors, but must be combined with other system-based error prevention methods. Barcoding (discussed later in this chapter) is an example of a technological tool that has been implemented in medication administration to assist in ensuring the "five rights."

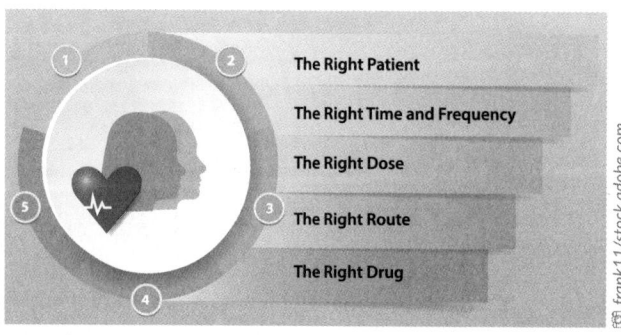

The Right Patient

The Right Time and Frequency

The Right Dose

The Right Route

The Right Drug

© frank11/stock.adobe.com

USE OF TECHNOLOGY AND AUTOMATED SYSTEMS

The integration of healthcare knowledge with technology and automation is called pharmacy informatics. Some of the more common systems integrated into the medication-use process are described in the sections below. In most institutions, pharmacists are actively involved in creating, monitoring and improving use of these tools.

COMPUTERIZED PRESCRIBER ORDER ENTRY AND CLINICAL DECISION SUPPORT

Computerized physician/provider order entry (CPOE) is a process that allows direct entry of medical orders by prescribers into the computer system. This has the benefit of reducing errors by minimizing the ambiguity resulting from handwritten orders. A much greater benefit is seen with the combination of CPOE and clinical decision support (CDS) tools. Clinical guidelines and patient labs can be built into the CPOE system, and alerts can notify a prescriber if the drug is inappropriate, or if labs indicate that the drug could be unsafe (such as a high potassium level and a new order for a potassium-sparing agent). For example, one of the ISMP's best practice recommendations is to program the computer system to automatically select a weekly frequency for oral methotrexate orders to prevent accidental selection of daily dosing.

CPOE can include standard order sets and protocols. An example of an on-screen alert from a CDS system is shown below. This alert appears when a prescriber attempts to order citalopram with a dose greater than 40 mg/day. In addition to medication orders, CPOE is used for laboratory orders and procedures. One aspect of CQI is monitoring, reporting trends and addressing alert overrides.

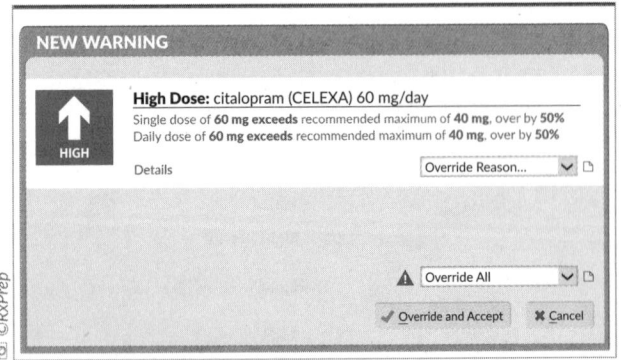

BARCODING

Barcoding may be the most important medication error reduction tool currently available. The barcode follows the drug through the medication-use process to make sure it is properly stocked (such as in the right space in the pharmacy or in the right pocket in the dispensing cabinet), through compounding (if required) and administered to the right patient. It also helps to prevent diversion of drugs that are commonly abused.

The barcode is used at the bedside to identify that the correct drug (by scanning the barcode on the drug's packaging) is going to the right patient (by scanning the barcode on the patient's wristband) and confirms that the dose is being given at the right time by matching to the order in the system. The nurse is often signed into the electronic medical record (or scans the barcode on their name tag) while barcode scanning, which records who administered the dose.

Barcodes are now on many infusion pumps and can prevent errors involving medications being given IV. This includes identifying drugs that are not meant to be administered via this route, auto-programming (which pulls infusion parameters from the electronic health record) and auto-documentation (which records dose/rate changes for confirmation).

When a medication is scanned and administered using barcode technology, the administration can automatically populate on the medication administration record (MAR), thus avoiding the time associated with manually charting medication administration.

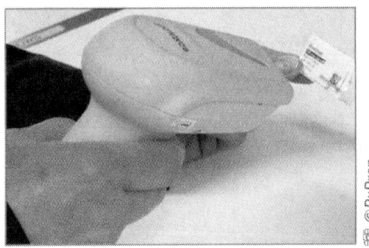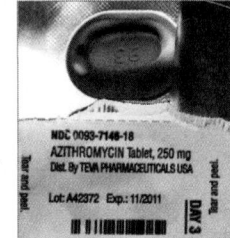

AUTOMATED DISPENSING CABINETS

Most hospitals in the U.S. now use automated dispensing cabinets (ADCs). Common names of ADCs are *Pyxis, Omnicell, ScriptPro* and *Accudose*. In many hospitals, they have replaced patient cassettes that had to be filled at least once daily and exchanged.

Practical Benefits of ADCs

Drug inventory and medication replenishment can be automated when drugs are placed into the cabinet and removed. ADCs provide enhanced security of controlled drugs by recording detailed information about transactions (e.g., who gained access to the controlled medications). The drugs are easily available at the unit and do not require individual delivery from the pharmacy. ADCs permit barcoding and provide alerts and usage reports.

Methods to Improve ADC Safety

- TJC requires that the pharmacist review the order before the medication can be removed from the ADC for a patient, except in special circumstances (an override). The override function should be limited to a select list of medications. Overrides for medications used for reversal of adverse events (e.g., naloxone, flumazenil) should be investigated.

- The most common error associated with ADC use is giving the wrong drug or dose to a patient. The patient's MAR should be accessible to practitioners while they are removing medications from the ADC. The use of barcode scanning improves ADC safety.

- Look-alike, sound-alike medications should be stored in different locations within the ADC. Using computerized alerts can help reduce error risk (e.g., require confirmation when selecting drugs with high potential for mix-up).

- Certain medications should not be put into ADCs, including insulin, warfarin and high-dose narcotics (such as hydromorphone 10 mg/mL and morphine 25 mg/mL).

- Nurses should not be permitted to put medications back into the medication compartment because they might be placed in the wrong area; it is best to have a separate drawer for all "returned" medications.

- If the machine is in a busy, noisy environment, or in one with poor lighting, errors increase.

PATIENT CONTROLLED ANALGESIA DEVICES

Opioids are effective medications for moderate to severe post-surgical pain. They may be administered with patient-controlled analgesia (PCA) devices, where the patient can self-administer doses of medication with the push of a button (see image to the right). The dose and dose limits are ordered by the physician. The PCA will not allow the patient to take more medication than ordered. PCAs allow the patient to treat pain quickly (there is no need to call the nurse and wait for the dose to arrive) and allow the administration of small doses, which helps reduce side effects (particularly over-sedation). PCA drug delivery can mimic the pain pattern more closely and provide good pain control. PCAs can be administered with anesthetics for a synergistic benefit in pain relief.

PCA Safety Considerations

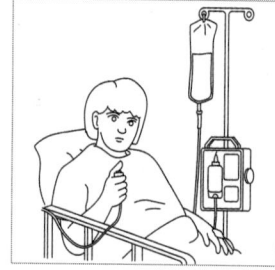

- The devices can be complex and require setup and programming. This is a significant cause of preventable medication errors. PCAs should be used only by well-coordinated healthcare teams.

- Patients may not be appropriate candidates for PCA treatment. They should be cooperative and should have a cognitive assessment prior to using the PCA to ensure that they can follow instructions.

- Friends and family members should not administer PCA doses. This is a TJC requirement.

- PCAs do not frequently cause respiratory depression, but the risk is present. Advanced age, obesity and concurrent use of CNS depressants (in addition to higher opioid doses) increase the risk.

PCA Safety Steps

- Limit the opioids available outside of ADCs. Use standard order sets (set drug dosages, especially for opioid-naïve patients) so that safe doses of drugs are selected.

- Educate staff about HYDROmorphone and morphine mix-ups.

- Implement PCA protocols that include independent double-checking of the drug, pump setting and dosage. The concentration on the MAR should match the PCA label.

- Use barcoding technology. Some infusion pumps incorporate barcoding technology. Scanning the barcode on the PCA would help ensure the correct concentration is entered during PCA programming. It will also ensure that the right patient is getting the medication.

- Assess the patient's pain, sedation and respiratory rate on a scheduled basis.

SUMMARY OF STEPS AND SAFETY CHECKS IN THE INPATIENT MEDICATION USE PROCESS

Drug ordered from supplier

- Limit available drugs to those on formulary (P&T committee)
- Limit the concentrations stocked

Drug arrives in pharmacy and is checked into inventory

- Barcode scanning ensures the correct drug was received and allows for inventory tracking

Drug added to pharmacy stock

- Separate look-alike, sound-alike drugs and use tall man lettering
- High-alert medications should be labeled

Medication order placed for patient

- CPOE and CDS decrease errors – verbal or handwritten orders can be misinterpreted
- Avoid abbreviations

Pharmacist reviews drug order

- The patient-specific dose, frequency, route and risk for drug interactions are assessed for appropriateness
- CDS provides safety double-check

RISK POINT: errors can occur if a CDS safety alert is ignored or if this step is skipped completely (e.g., nurse removes drug from an ADC without an order or before the order is reviewed)

Drug compounding (if needed)

- Use good compounding practices (see Compounding chapters)

Drug delivered to patient care unit

- Several routes for drug delivery
  - ❏ Drug prepared and labeled in pharmacy, checked by pharmacist, then delivered to the unit (pneumatic tube systems can be used for some medications)
  - ❏ Drug stocked by pharmacy in ADC on unit; nurse removes drug from ADC once the order is approved/verified
- Barcode scanning ensures correct drug/dose was selected for the correct patient

Drug administered to patient

- 5 rights checked (typically with barcode scanning): right patient (2 identifiers needed), right drug, right route, right dose, right time

ADC = automated dispensing cabinet, CDS = clinical decision support,
CPOE = computerized physician/provider order entry,
P&T = Pharmacy and Therapeutics

SUMMARY OF STEPS AND SAFETY CHECKS IN THE OUTPATIENT MEDICATION USE PROCESS

Drug ordered from supplier

Drug arrives in pharmacy and is checked into inventory
- Barcode scanning ensures the correct drug was received and allows for inventory tracking

Drug added to pharmacy stock
- Separate look-alike, sound-alike drugs and use tall man lettering
- High-alert medications should be labeled

Prescription is received
- CPOE and CDS decrease errors – verbal or handwritten orders can be misinterpreted
- Avoid abbreviations

Pharmacy staff processes order
- CDS provides safety double-check

RISK POINT: not all information available outpatient (e.g., weight, past medical history)

Drug compounding (if needed)
- Use good compounding practices (see Compounding chapters)

Prescription filled
- Barcode scanning used to make sure the correct drug was pulled from pharmacy stock
- Drugs may be stored in an ADS in the pharmacy; drug counted and vial filled using automated technology to reduce errors

Pharmacist reviews drug order
- The patient-specific dose, frequency, route and risk for drug interactions are assessed for appropriateness
- CDS and barcode scanning provide safety double-checks

Drug dispensed to patient
- Proper counseling needed to decrease error risk
- 2 identifiers needed for pick up to ensure delivery to correct recipient

RISK POINT: if counseling is skipped (or abbreviated) patient understanding decreases

ADS = automated dispensing system, CDS = clinical decision support, CPOE = computerized physician/provider order entry

INFECTION CONTROL IN HOSPITALS

More than one million infections are acquired in hospitals annually – about one infection for every thirty patients. Hospital infections cause avoidable illness and death, and add enormous financial costs. Many of these infections are preventable if proper techniques are followed. Many states now require hospitals to report infection rates, and Medicare can refuse reimbursement for hospital-acquired infections that are largely avoidable.

It is important to properly clean surfaces, including bed rails, eating trays and other room surfaces. Healthcare professionals should be careful not to be sources of infection from contaminated clothing (including white coats and ties). Organisms that spread via surface contact include VRE, *C. difficile*, noroviruses and other intestinal tract pathogens.

COMMON TYPES OF HOSPITAL-ACQUIRED (NOSOCOMIAL) INFECTIONS

- Urinary tract infections from indwelling catheters (very common); remove the catheter as soon as possible
- Bloodstream infections from IV lines (central lines have the highest risk) and catheters
- Surgical site infections (see Infectious Diseases II chapter)
- Decubitus ulcers
- Hepatitis
- *Clostridioides difficile*, other GI infections
- Pneumonia (mostly due to ventilator use)

UNIVERSAL PRECAUTIONS TO PREVENT TRANSMISSION

Universal precautions is an approach to infection control that treats human blood and bodily fluids as if they are infectious with HIV, HBV and other bloodborne pathogens. Contact with bodily fluids should be avoided by wearing gloves, performing good hand hygiene and, in select cases, the use of gowns, masks or patient isolation.

The following sections describe the three categories of transmission-based precautions defined by the CDC.

Contact Precautions

- Intended to prevent transmission of infectious agents which are spread by direct and indirect contact with the patient and the patient's environment.
- Single patient rooms are preferred. If not available, keep ≥ 3 feet spatial separation between beds to prevent inadvertent sharing of items between patients.
- Healthcare personnel caring for these patients wear a gown and gloves for all interactions that may involve contact with the patient or contaminated areas in the patient's room.
- Contact precautions are recommended for patients colonized or infected with MRSA and VRE and patients with *C. difficile* infection.

Droplet Precautions

- Intended to prevent transmission of pathogens spread through close respiratory contact with respiratory secretions.
- Single patient rooms are preferred. If not available, keeping ≥ 3 feet spatial separation and drawing a curtain between beds is especially important for diseases transmitted via droplets.
- Healthcare personnel wear a mask (a respirator is not necessary) for close contact with the patient. The mask is donned upon entry to the patient's room.
- Droplet precautions are recommended for patients with active *B. pertussis*, influenza virus, respiratory syncytial virus (RSV), adenovirus, rhinovirus, *N. meningitidis*, and group A streptococcus (for the first 24 hours of antimicrobial therapy).

Airborne Precautions

- Intended to prevent transmission of infectious agents that remain infectious over long distances when suspended in the air.
- The patient should be placed in an airborne infection isolation room (AIIR). An AIIR is a single-patient room that is equipped with special air and ventilation handling systems. The air is exhausted directly to the outside or re-circulated through HEPA filtration before being returned.
- Healthcare personnel wear a mask or respirator (N95 level or higher), depending on the disease, which is donned prior to room entry.
- Airborne precautions are recommended for patients with active pulmonary tuberculosis, measles or varicella virus (chickenpox).

CATHETER-RELATED BLOODSTREAM INFECTIONS

- The most important and cost-effective strategy to minimize catheter-related bloodstream infections (CRBSI) is use of aseptic technique during catheter insertion, including proper handwashing and utilization of standard protocols/catheter insertion checklist.

- It is also important to minimize use of intravascular catheters, if possible, through intravenous to oral route conversion protocols and setting appropriate time limits for catheter use. For example, peripheral catheters should be removed/replaced every 2 – 3 days to minimize risk for infection.

- Other strategies shown to reduce the risk of CRBSI include the use of skin antiseptics (2% chlorhexidine), antibiotic impregnated central venous catheters, and antibiotic/ethanol lock therapy, but use must be weighed against the potential risk for increased rates of resistance.

HAND HYGIENE

Numerous studies show that proper hand hygiene by those working in healthcare settings reduces the spread of nosocomial infection. Alcohol-based hand rubs (gel, rinse or foam) are considered more effective in the healthcare setting than plain soap or antimicrobial soap and water, but soap and water are preferable in some situations (see next page). Fingernails should be clipped short, and no jewelry should be worn under gloves (this can harbor bacteria and tear the gloves).

Antimicrobial hand soaps that contain chlorhexidine (Hibiclens, others) may be preferable to reduce infections in healthcare facilities. Triclosan may also be beneficial, but this compound gets into the water supply and has environmental concerns.

When to Perform Hand Hygiene

- Before entering and after leaving patient rooms and between patient contacts if there is more than one patient per room.

- Before donning and after removing gloves (use new gloves with each patient).

- Before handling invasive devices, including injections.

- After coughing or sneezing.

- Before handling food and oral medications.

📷 ©RxPrep

Use Soap and Water (not Alcohol-Based Rubs) in These Situations

- Before eating.

- After using the restroom.

- Anytime there is visible soil (anything noticeable on the hands).

- After caring for a patient with diarrhea or known *C. difficile* or spore-forming organisms; alcohol-based hand rubs have poor activity against spores. Handwashing physically removes spores.

- Before caring for patients with food allergies.

Soap and Water Technique

- Wet both sides of hands, apply soap, rub together for at least 15 seconds.

- Rinse thoroughly.

- Dry with paper towel and use the towel to turn off the water.

Alcohol-Based Hand Rubs Technique

- Use enough gel (2 – 5 mL or about the size of a quarter).

- Rub hands together until the gel dries (15 – 25 seconds).

- Hands should be completely dry before putting on gloves.

Hand-Hygiene for Sterile Compounding

- Refer to the Compounding chapters.

SAFE INJECTION PRACTICES

Outbreaks involving the transmission of bloodborne pathogens (e.g., HIV, hepatitis B or C) or other microbial pathogens to patients (and occasionally to healthcare workers) continue to occur due to unsafe injection techniques. The majority of safety breaches involve the reuse of syringes in multiple patients, contamination of IV bags with used syringes, failure to follow basic injection safety when administering IV medications and inappropriate care or maintenance of glucometer equipment that is used on multiple patients. See the Study Tip Gal below for safe injection practices.

If a needle-stick (percutaneous exposure) occurs with a used needle, contact the proper department at a healthcare facility immediately. If post-exposure prophylaxis (PEP) is required (for HIV and/or hepatitis), acting quickly is important. PEP regimens are more likely to be effective the sooner they are started. In the outpatient setting, instruct the patient to wash the area right away with soap and water and contact their healthcare provider. See the Human Immunodeficiency Virus chapter for details on PEP medication regimens.

SAFE INJECTION PRACTICES FOR HEALTHCARE FACILITIES

- Never administer an oral solution/suspension intravenously; fatal errors have occurred. Use oral syringes (which are difficult or impossible to attach to a needle for IV injection) and label oral syringes "for oral use only."

- Never reinsert used needles into a multiple-dose vial or solution container. Single-dose vials are preferred over multiple-dose vials, especially when medications will be administered to multiple patients.

- Needles used for withdrawing blood or any other bodily fluid, or used for administering medications or other fluids should preferably have "engineered sharps protection," which reduces the risk of an exposure incident by a mechanism such as drawing the needle into the syringe barrel after use.

- Never touch the tip or plunger of a syringe.

- Disposable needles that are contaminated (e.g., with drugs, chemicals or blood products) should never be removed from their original syringes, unless no other option is available. Throw the entire needle/syringe assembly (needle attached to the syringe) into the red plastic sharps container.

- Immediately discard used disposable needles or sharps into a sharps container without recapping.

- Sharps containers should be easily accessible and not allowed to overfill; they should be routinely replaced.

SHARPS DISPOSAL

Patients who use injectable medications should have a disposal container and be instructed to put needles and other sharps in the container immediately after use (see Study Tip Gal). Sharps should be disposed of in an FDA-cleared sharps container, which is puncture resistant, labeled or color-coded appropriately, closeable and leak-proof. They come marked with a line that indicates when the container should be considered full (about ¾ full). Never compress or "push down" on the contents of any sharps container.

If an FDA-cleared container is not available, some community guidelines recommend using a heavy-duty plastic household container as an alternative (e.g., a plastic laundry detergent container). The container must be leak and puncture-resistant with a tight-fitting lid.

The entire needle/syringe assembly is discarded. The only time that recapping a needle is permitted is when the sharps container is not immediately available; in that case, use the one-hand method to recap until the sharps container can be reached: (1) Place the cap on a table or counter next to something firm to push the cap against; (2) Hold the syringe with the needle attached and slip the needle into the cap without using the other hand. Push the capped needle on the firm surface to "seat" the cap onto the needle using only the one hand. Sharps disposal guidelines and programs vary. The local trash removal services or health department should have the available service/s, and the pharmacy can provide this information to patients. Services include drop boxes or supervised collection sites (such as in a hospital, pharmacy, police or fire station), household hazardous waste collection sites, mail-back programs and residential special waste services pick-up.

Select Guidelines/References

Institute for Safe Medication Practices. www.ismp.org (accessed 2022 Feb 23).

The Joint Commission. www.jointcommission.org (accessed 2022 Feb 23).

MMWR Guideline for Hand Hygiene in Health-Care Settings October 25, 2002, 51(RR16);1-44.

CHAPTER CONTENT

DEFINITIONS

Mild or Severe Reactions to Histamine Release

Urticaria (hives)
A rash with red/pinkish raised patches. The patches have varied shapes and sizes.

Pruritus (itching)
Any rash or reaction that causes itching can be referred to as pruritus.

Erythema
Redness on the skin from superficial (near the surface) capillaries, often due to inflammation with pruritus. When pressed down, the red skin will blanch (whiten) temporarily because the blood flow is blocked. Erythematous refers to an area on the skin, such as a patch, with erythema.

Angioedema
Swelling caused by edema in the deeper dermal, cutaneous and submucosal tissue.

Morbilliform
Macular or maculopapular rash (or both), with 1-10 mm lesions and healthy skin between the lesions.

CONTENT LEGEND

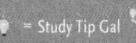 = Study Tip Gal  = Key Drug Guy

---

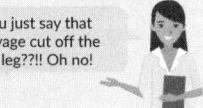

designua © 123RF.com

CHAPTER 77

DRUG ALLERGIES & ADVERSE DRUG REACTIONS

BACKGROUND

Adverse drug reaction (ADR) is a term that encompasses all unintended pharmacologic effects of a drug when it is administered correctly and used at recommended doses. ADRs should not be confused with medication errors, which can include overdose and administration mistakes, and are discussed in the Medication Safety & Quality Improvement chapter. ADRs result in substantial morbidity and mortality, and ADR reports are increasing; over one million reports with serious outcomes were logged with the FDA in 2021 (including over 180,000 deaths).

Although side effects or adverse effects can occur in anyone, some patients are more susceptible than others. For example, some degree of renal damage can occur with use of an aminoglycoside for longer than seven days. However, in patients with underlying renal impairment, nephrotoxicity is more likely to occur and may happen after a shorter duration of treatment.

ADVERSE DRUG REACTIONS VS. ERRORS

Adverse Drug Reaction (ADR)
Effects from a drug when it is administered correctly. ADRs are typically dose-related; the ADR severity increases with higher doses/reduced clearance.

The new drug you are taking causes "urinary retention" which means it can take longer to pee when you use the restroom.

Medication Error
Something wrong occurred, such as giving a medication dose to the wrong person.

Did you just say that Dr. Savage cut off the wrong leg??!! Oh no!

Hi Mrs. Apple Cake! Dr. Savage sent over a prescription for you for *Celebrex* for joint pain. Weren't you hospitalized recently for a stroke?

iStock.com/Irina_Strelnikova

ADVERSE DRUG REACTIONS

ADRs are categorized into two types: predictable (Type A) and unpredictable (Type B) reactions.

TYPE A REACTIONS

Type A reactions are dose-dependent, related to the known pharmacologic actions of the drug, can occur in any patient and can range from mild to severe. Type A reactions are most common and account for an estimated 80% of ADRs. An example of a Type A reaction is orthostatic hypotension with doxazosin. If a patient starts doxazosin at 1 mg QHS, they will have much less orthostatic hypotension and dizziness than if the medication is started at a 4 mg dose. Because of this risk, the dose should be slowly titrated upward.

TYPE B REACTIONS

Type B reactions are generally not dose-dependent, are unrelated to the pharmacologic actions of the drug and can be influenced by patient-specific factors. Type B reactions include:

- Drug allergies [immune-mediated responses to a medication or excipient (inactive ingredient)]. The four types are described in the box below.
- Pseudoallergic reactions (e.g., itching after administration of an opioid, vancomycin infusion reaction)
- Drug intolerances (e.g., nausea with codeine)
- Idiosyncratic reactions (e.g., Stevens-Johnson syndrome)

TYPES OF DRUG ALLERGIES

Type I Reactions
- IgE-mediated and immediate (within 60 minutes of drug exposure), ranging from minor local reactions to severe systemic reactions
  - Examples: urticuria, bronchospasm, angioedema, anaphylaxis

Type II Reactions
- Antibody-mediated, occurring several days (usually 5-8 days) after drug exposure
  - Examples: hemolytic anemia, thrombocytopenia

Type III Reactions
- Immune-complex reactions, occurring ≥ 1 week after drug exposure
  - Example: drug-induced lupus erythematosus

Type IV Reactions
- Cell-mediated or delayed hypersensitivity reactions, occurring anytime from 48 hours to several weeks after drug exposure
  - Example: Stevens-Johnson syndrome

FDA TOOLS TO REDUCE ADVERSE DRUG REACTIONS

BOXED WARNINGS

A boxed warning indicates a risk of death or permanent disability from a drug (e.g., increased risk of venous thromboembolism and death from stroke with raloxifene).

The risk of fatality can be due to prescribing or dispensing errors. For example, conventional amphotericin B deoxycholate has a boxed warning not to exceed 1.5 mg/kg. Fatalities have been caused by using the lipid amphotericin dosing (typically 3 – 6 mg/kg) for conventional amphotericin.

CONTRAINDICATIONS, WARNINGS AND PRECAUTIONS

Contraindications indicate that the drug cannot be used in that patient. The risk will outweigh any possible benefit (e.g., a history of venous thromboembolism is a contraindication to the use of raloxifene). If there are no known contraindications for a drug, the section of the package insert will state "None."

> Mrs. Jones, you cannot get *Evista* because you had a DVT in the past.

Warnings and precautions include serious reactions that can result in death, hospitalization, medical intervention, disability or teratogenicity (e.g., raloxifene has a warning for venous thromboembolism). Warnings and precautions may or may not change a prescribing decision.

> Mrs. Smith, you could get a DVT from *Evista* if you are immobile most of the day.

ADVERSE REACTIONS

Adverse reactions refer to undesirable, uncomfortable or dangerous effects from a drug (e.g., arthralgia from raloxifene). The risk-benefit assessment is patient-specific (e.g., arthralgia from raloxifene will be more of a concern in a patient with chronically sore joints versus a patient with no sore joints).

> Mrs. Ngo, you are starting *Evista*. You might get hot flashes and achy joints.

RISK EVALUATION AND MITIGATION STRATEGIES

Risk Evaluation and Mitigation Strategies (REMS) are required by the FDA for some drugs. They are developed by the manufacturer and approved by the FDA to ensure the benefits of a drug outweigh the risks. REMS programs can include a medication guide or patient package insert, communication plan, elements to assure safe use (ETASU) or an implementation system.

For example, the REMS for a drug could require prescribers or pharmacies to have a special certification to prescribe or dispense the drug, enroll patients in a registry so that ADRs can be tracked, or evaluate lab tests before dispensing. Examples include the clozapine REMS, the isotretinoin iPLEDGE program and the REMS to reduce misuse of long-acting opioids.

MEDICATION GUIDES

Medication Guides (or MedGuides) are FDA-approved patient handouts that detail a drug's important adverse events in non-technical language; they are considered part of the drug's labeling. If a medication has a MedGuide, it should be dispensed with the original prescription and with each refill. It is not necessary to dispense a drug's MedGuide for hospitalized patients because the patient is being monitored, though the MedGuide should be available to the patient or family upon request.

There are required MedGuides for many individual drugs and, in some cases, entire classes of medications (e.g., anticonvulsants, antidepressants, long-acting opioids, NSAIDs, ADHD stimulants).

ASSESSING CAUSALITY OF AN ADVERSE DRUG REACTION

When an ADR occurs, the Naranjo Scale (a validated causality assessment scale) can help determine the likelihood that a drug caused the adverse reaction. Based on the questionnaire, a probability score is calculated. A score ≥ 9 = definite ADR; 5 – 8 = probable ADR; 1 – 4 = possible ADR; 0 = doubtful ADR.

QUESTION	YES	NO	DO NOT KNOW
Are there previous conclusive reports on this reaction?	+1	0	0
Did the adverse event appear after the suspected drug was given?	+2	–1	0
Did the adverse reaction improve when the drug was discontinued or a specific antagonist was given?	+1	0	0
Did the adverse reaction appear when the drug was readministered?	+2	–1	0
Are there alternative causes that could (on their own) have caused the reaction?	–1	+2	0
Did the reaction reappear when a placebo was given?	–1	+1	0
Was the drug detected in any body fluid in toxic concentrations?	+1	0	0
Was the reaction more severe when the dose was increased or less severe when the dose was decreased?	+1	0	0
Did the patient have a similar reaction to the same or similar drugs in any previous exposure?	+1	0	0
Was the adverse event confirmed by any objective evidence?	+1	0	0

CHARACTERIZING AN ADVERSE DRUG REACTION

When patients report an adverse drug reaction, pharmacists must ask the right questions in order to determine whether an adverse reaction is an intolerance or drug allergy:

- What reaction occurred (e.g., mild rash, severe rash with blisters, trouble breathing)?
- When did it occur? About how old were you?

- Can you use similar drugs in the class? For example, for a penicillin allergy, ask if cephalexin has ever been used.
- Do you have any food allergies or a latex allergy?

Some food allergies (e.g., soy, peanut) have implications for certain drugs or formulations. Latex allergies should be documented because some drugs require tubing, have latex vial stoppers or require gloves for administration. All allergies should be noted in the patient medical record.

ADR REPORTING

Side effects, adverse events and allergies should be reported to the FDA's MedWatch program, which is called the FDA Adverse Event Reporting System (FAERS) and provides a central collection point for problems caused by drugs, biologics, medical devices, some dietary supplements and cosmetics. Vaccines are an exception and are reported under a different program called VAERS (see the Immunizations chapter for more information).

When drugs are studied in clinical trials, high-risk patients are typically excluded, though in a real-life setting, high-risk patients may receive the medication. The FDA can require Phase IV trials (post-marketing safety surveillance programs) for approved drugs and biologics, to collect and analyze ADR reports and better understand a drug's safety profile in a real-world setting. Post-marketing reports also help identify side effects that occur less frequently. If a drug causes a reaction in 1 out of every 3,000 people, the problem may not be apparent in a smaller clinical trial. For this reason, community-based ADR reporting is critical.

EXAMPLE: ADR INCIDENCE IN REAL LIFE VS. A CLINICAL TRIAL

When spironolactone was studied in heart failure patients during the RALES trial, patients with renal insufficiency or elevated potassium levels were excluded due to the known risk of additional hyperkalemia from the use of spironolactone. The drug was found to have benefit in advanced heart failure patients and doctors in the community began to use it in their heart failure patients. In this real-life setting, patients with renal insufficiency or elevated potassium were occasionally prescribed spironolactone, and arrhythmias and sudden death due to hyperkalemia were reported.

Reporting is voluntary but has important implications for safe medication use. Healthcare professionals and patients can report adverse events to the drug manufacturer, who is required by law to send the report to the FDA. The MedWatch form used for reporting can be found online. Reports can also be made by calling the FDA directly.

If the FDA receives enough reports that a drug is linked to a particular problem, the manufacturer can be required to update the labeling (e.g., package insert). In especially risky cases, a drug safety alert is issued to prescribers, usually before the labeling is changed.

EXAMPLE: ADR REPORTS LEAD TO FDA REQUIREMENT FOR SAFETY LABELING CHANGES

Oseltamivir (Tamiflu) was initially marketed without any warning of unusual behavior in children. The FDA received enough reports that they issued a warning to prescribers in 2006. In 2008, after many more reports, the FDA required the manufacturer to update the prescribing information to include a precaution about hallucinations, confusion and other strange behavior in children.

Example of a Posting on the FDA Website of Phase IV Monitoring

DRUG	USAGE	ADVERSE EVENT REPORTS	NOTES
Dulaglutide (Trulicity)	Diabetes mellitus, type 2	Serious hypersensitivity reactions	FDA is evaluating the need for regulatory action

INTOLERANCES, SENSITIVITIES AND IDIOSYNCRATIC REACTIONS

STOMACH UPSET/NAUSEA

Stomach upset or nausea is often incorrectly reported as an allergy. It should be listed on the patient profile because the drug bothered the patient and, if possible, should be avoided in the future, but this is not an allergy and should not prevent drugs in the same class from being used. This is more accurately categorized as an intolerance. Electronic medical records allow for documentation of intolerances separate from allergies. An example of an intolerance is the patient who has stomach upset with codeine (but not hydrocodone or other drugs in the morphine class) or erythromycin (but not azithromycin or other macrolides).

EXAMPLE: INTOLERANCE REPORTED INCORRECTLY AS A DRUG ALLERGY

CG received acetaminophen 300 mg/codeine 30 mg for pain relief after a dental extraction. She got very nauseated from the medication. When she was admitted to the hospital several years later for a left hip replacement, she reported that she was "allergic" to codeine. The reaction was not clarified. The hospital's pain management protocol used hydromorphone in a patient-controlled analgesia device for postoperative pain control. The prescriber used a less desirable option for pain control due to the reported allergy.

INTOLERANCE OR ALLERGY?

Gather enough information to determine the type of reaction.

Example:
A patient reports getting a stomach ache from Chantix.

Scenarios:
I did not eat anything until dinner because Chantix made me nauseous. (Intolerance)

I got nauseous, felt dizzy and had trouble breathing. (Allergy)

Intolerances are less serious complaints, such as nausea or constipation. Since the drug bothers the patient, it should be avoided, if possible.

Allergies are an immune system response and range from mild (e.g., pruritus) to severe (e.g., anaphylaxis). Allergies can present in different ways, for example:

- Facial swelling, bronchoconstriction and a severe drop in BP
- Weakness, fever and severe rash

MILD RASH

Opioids cause a <u>non-allergic release of histamine</u> from mast cells in the skin, causing <u>itching and hives</u> in some patients. This is particularly problematic in the inpatient setting after surgery, when opioid-naïve patients receive the medication or when non-naïve patients receive higher than normal doses. This type of reaction, if not severe, can be reduced or avoided if the patient is premedicated with an antihistamine, such as diphenhydramine.

PHOTOSENSITIVITY

Photosensitivity can occur when sunlight reacts with a drug in the skin and causes tissue damage that looks like a severe sunburn on sun-exposed areas; this occurs within hours of sun exposure. A type IV (delayed hypersensitivity) reaction can also occur with sun exposure and some medications. It appears as a red, itchy rash that can spread to areas that were not exposed to sun and occurs within days of sun exposure.

When dispensing medications that can cause photosensitivity (see <u>Key Drugs Guy</u> below), it is important to advise the patient and/or their caregivers to limit sun exposure and to <u>use broad-spectrum sunscreen that blocks both UVA and UVB</u> radiation.

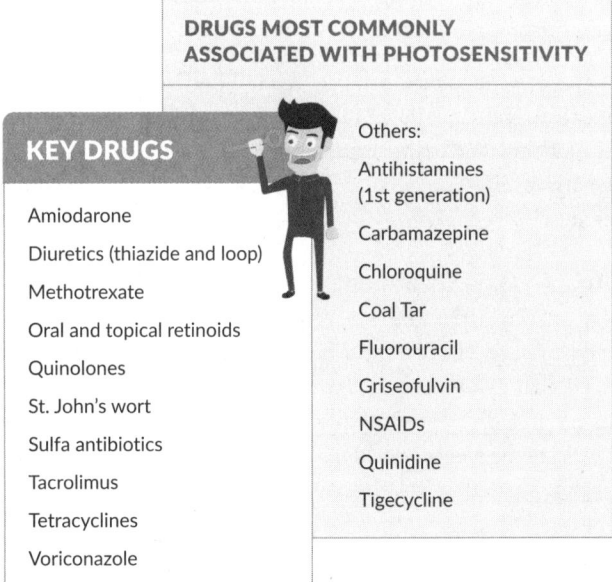

DRUGS MOST COMMONLY ASSOCIATED WITH PHOTOSENSITIVITY

KEY DRUGS

Amiodarone
Diuretics (thiazide and loop)
Methotrexate
Oral and topical retinoids
Quinolones
St. John's wort
Sulfa antibiotics
Tacrolimus
Tetracyclines
Voriconazole

Others:
Antihistamines (1st generation)
Carbamazepine
Chloroquine
Coal Tar
Fluorouracil
Griseofulvin
NSAIDs
Quinidine
Tigecycline

THROMBOTIC THROMBOCYTOPENIC PURPURA

Thrombotic thrombocytopenic purpura (<u>TTP</u>) is a blood disorder in which clots form throughout the body. The clotting process consumes platelets and leads to bleeding under the skin and the formation of purpura (bruises) and petechiae (dots) on the skin. TTP can be fatal and should be treated immediately with plasma exchange. See the <u>Key Drugs Guy</u> for common drugs that can cause TTP.

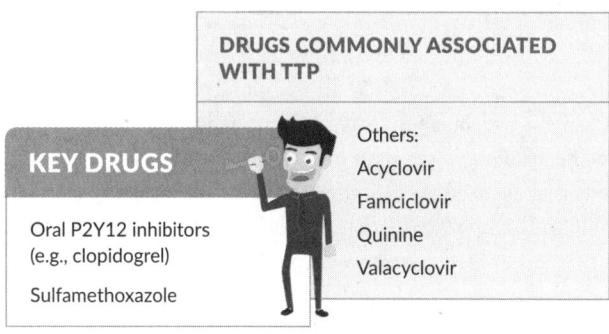

DRUGS COMMONLY ASSOCIATED WITH TTP

KEY DRUGS

Oral P2Y12 inhibitors (e.g., clopidogrel)
Sulfamethoxazole

Others:
Acyclovir
Famciclovir
Quinine
Valacyclovir

SPOTS AND RASHES

Papules Raised spots **Macules** Flat spots

Purpura
Red/purple skin spots (lesions) due to bleeding underneath the skin. Purpura includes small and large spots:

Petechiae Smaller lesions < 3 mm
Ecchymoses Larger lesions > 5 mm

Hematoma
A collection of blood under the skin due to trauma (injury) to a blood vessel, resulting in blood leaking into the surrounding tissue. Drugs that can cause a hematoma include heparin, low molecular weight heparin (LMWH), other anticoagulants and phytonadione (vitamin K) if given mistakenly as an IM injection.

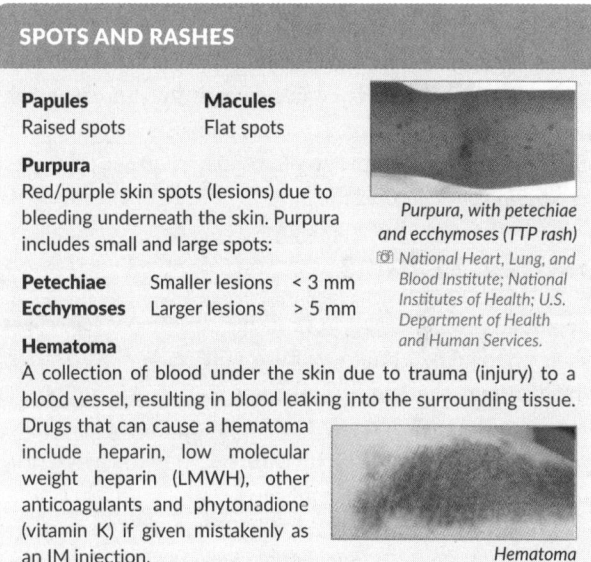

Purpura, with petechiae and ecchymoses (TTP rash)
National Heart, Lung, and Blood Institute; National Institutes of Health; U.S. Department of Health and Human Services.

Hematoma
SneSivan/Shutterstock.com

SEVERE SKIN REACTIONS

There are several severe skin reactions that can be caused by drugs, including <u>Stevens-Johnson syndrome (SJS)</u>, <u>toxic epidermal necrolysis (TEN)</u> and <u>drug reaction with eosinophilia and systemic symptoms (DRESS)</u>. All of these can be <u>life-threatening and require prompt treatment</u>. Although the OTC analgesics acetaminophen and ibuprofen are generally considered safe, cases of severe reactions have been reported, which highlights the unpredictable nature of these reactions. Drugs most commonly associated with severe skin reactions are listed in the <u>Key Drugs Guy</u> on the following page.

Stevens-Johnson Syndrome and Toxic Epidermal Necrolysis

SJS and TEN involve epidermal detachment and skin loss that is equivalent to third-degree burns. They generally occur 1 – 3 weeks after drug administration and can result in severe mucosal erosions, a high body temperature, major fluid loss and organ damage (eyes, liver, kidney, lungs).

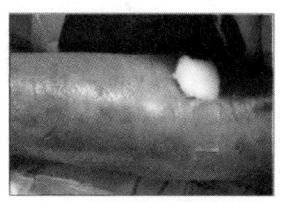

Patient with Stevens-Johnson syndrome
Pawarit Khunkrai/Shutterstock.com

SJS and TEN are commonly classified by the percent of skin detachment. The key to treating both is to stop the offending agent as soon as possible. In addition, patients will receive fluid and electrolyte replacement, wound care and pain medications. Systemic steroids are contraindicated with TEN, but may be used for SJS, though the benefit is controversial. Due to the severity of the mucosal involvement, antibiotics are often necessary to prevent or treat an infection.

Drug Reaction with Eosinophilia and Systemic Symptoms

DRESS can include a variety of skin eruptions accompanied by systemic symptoms such as fever, hepatic dysfunction, renal dysfunction and lymphadenopathy, but it rarely involves mucosal surfaces. Treatment consists of stopping the offending drug, although symptoms may continue to worsen for a period of time after the drug has been discontinued.

DRUG ALLERGIES

For a true drug allergy to occur, the drug must have been taken previously. Initial exposure will cause sensitization, which primes the body to release excessive histamine the next time the individual is exposed to the drug, causing a type I hypersensitivity reaction. This section describes drug allergy reactions and treatment, but keep in mind that similar treatment can be used for non-drug allergies. A pharmacist who is dispensing an epinephrine auto-injector for other types of allergies will provide the same instructions.

Some medications (e.g., phytonadione, contrast media) are associated with a pseudoallergic reaction, sometimes called an anaphylactoid reaction. It is not IgE-mediated, but the clinical appearance and treatment are similar to anaphylaxis.

A reaction without breathing difficulty can sometimes be treated by stopping the offending drug. Antihistamines can be used to counteract the histamine release that causes itching, swelling and rash. Systemic steroids, and sometimes NSAIDs, can be used to decrease swelling. Severe swelling may necessitate a steroid injection. Epinephrine is used to reverse bronchoconstriction if the patient is wheezing or has other signs of trouble breathing.

ANAPHYLAXIS

Anaphylaxis is a severe, life-threatening allergic reaction that usually happens within 1 hour of drug exposure, but may occur much more rapidly (e.g., within seconds). Anaphylaxis typically occurs after an initial exposure and subsequent immune response, but some drugs can cause anaphylaxis with the first exposure. A patient experiencing anaphylaxis may have generalized urticaria (hives), swelling of the mouth and throat, difficulty breathing or wheezing sounds, abdominal cramping or hypotension (which can

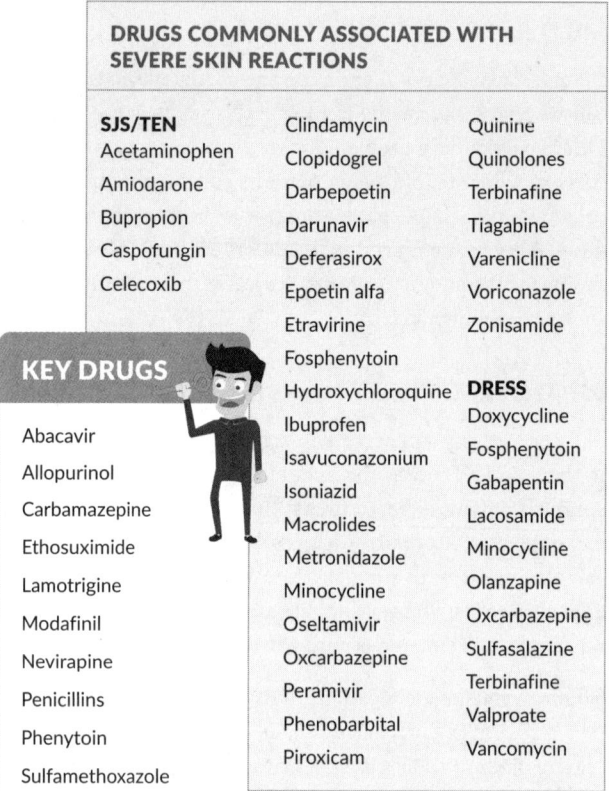

DRUGS COMMONLY ASSOCIATED WITH SEVERE SKIN REACTIONS

SJS/TEN		
Acetaminophen	Clindamycin	Quinine
Amiodarone	Clopidogrel	Quinolones
Bupropion	Darbepoetin	Terbinafine
Caspofungin	Darunavir	Tiagabine
Celecoxib	Deferasirox	Varenicline
	Epoetin alfa	Voriconazole
	Etravirine	Zonisamide
	Fosphenytoin	
	Hydroxychloroquine	**DRESS**
	Ibuprofen	Doxycycline
	Isavuconazonium	Fosphenytoin
	Isoniazid	Gabapentin
	Macrolides	Lacosamide
	Metronidazole	Minocycline
	Minocycline	Olanzapine
	Oseltamivir	Oxcarbazepine
	Oxcarbazepine	Sulfasalazine
	Peramivir	Terbinafine
	Phenobarbital	Valproate
	Piroxicam	Vancomycin

KEY DRUGS

Abacavir
Allopurinol
Carbamazepine
Ethosuximide
Lamotrigine
Modafinil
Nevirapine
Penicillins
Phenytoin
Sulfamethoxazole

cause dizziness, lightheadedness or loss of consciousness). Because symptoms can develop quickly, treatment must be administered immediately.

Anyone with severe drug or food allergies should wear a medical identification bracelet. This will alert emergency responders, and many bracelets can be linked to the patient's health profile accessible through a 24-hour information center.

Anaphylaxis Treatment

An anaphylactic reaction requires immediate emergency medical care. The patient or family should be instructed to call 911 if anaphylaxis occurs. Treatment includes an epinephrine injection ± diphenhydramine ± steroids ± IV fluids. To avoid blocking the airway, nothing should be placed under the head or in the mouth. Swollen airways can be quickly fatal.

Patients who have had such a reaction should carry a single-use epinephrine auto-injector (EpiPen, EpiPen Jr, Auvi-Q, Symjepi or a generic equivalent) as they may be at future risk. These are generally available as epinephrine 1 mg/mL (previously labeled as 1:1000) in doses of 0.3 mg (adult dose) or 0.15 mg (pediatric dose). The 0.15 mg dose is for patients 15 – 30 kg (EpiPen Jr). Auvi-Q is also available in 0.1 mg (for patients weighing 7.5 – 14 kg). The patient's emergency kit should also include emergency contact information and diphenhydramine tablets (25 mg x 2), which should be taken only if there is no tongue/lip swelling.

KEY COUNSELING POINTS FOR EPINEPHRINE AUTO-INJECTORS

EPINEPHRINE AUTO-INJECTOR ADMINISTRATION

EpiPen:
- Remove from the carrying case and pull off the blue safety release.
- Keep thumb, fingers and hand away from the orange (needle) end of the device.
- Inject into the middle of the outer thigh at a 90 degree angle.
- Hold the needle firmly in place while counting to 3.
- Remove the needle and massage the area for 10 seconds.
- After the injection, the orange tip will extend to cover the needle. If the needle is visible, it should not be reused.

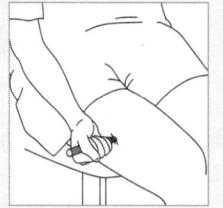

All epinephrine auto-injectors:
- It is normal to see liquid remaining in the device after injecting.
- Call for emergency help, because additional care may be needed.
- A second dose (in the opposite leg) may be given, if needed, prior to the arrival of medical help.
- Refrigeration is not required.
- All products can be injected through clothing.
- Check the device periodically to make sure the medication is clear and not expired.

- Tell family, caregivers and others where the epinephrine auto-injector is kept and how to use it, as you may not be able to speak in an emergency.
- It is important to keep the thumb, fingers and hand away from the needle end of the device, as accidental injection can cause vasoconstriction and necrosis.
- When injecting an uncooperative child, hold the leg firmly to avoid bending or breaking the needle.
- Skin infections can occur. Report any prolonged redness, swelling, warmth or tenderness at the injection site.

For *Symjepi:*
- Pull off the cap, holding the syringe with the fingers (avoiding the needle).
- Inject in the middle of the outer thigh, hold needle firmly in place for two seconds, then massage area for 10 seconds.
- After injection, slide the safety guard out over the needle.

For *Auvi-Q:*
- Pull off the outer case, then follow the voice instructions to administer. Hold the needle firmly in place on the thigh for five seconds.

DRUGS COMMONLY ASSOCIATED WITH ALLERGIC REACTIONS

While any drug can lead to an allergic reaction, some are known to do so more than others. Penicillins and sulfonamides cause the most drug allergies. These and other drugs that commonly cause allergies are discussed below. Often the drug that caused a reaction can be replaced with another drug. Patch testing by an allergist is the most reliable way to determine if a person is truly allergic to a drug, but it does not provide any information regarding the type of reaction that would occur.

BETA-LACTAMS

Penicillins are beta-lactam antibiotics with many related compounds within the class (e.g., nafcillin, ampicillin, piperacillin). Anyone who is allergic to one of the penicillins is typically presumed to be allergic to all penicillins and should avoid the entire group, unless they have been specifically evaluated by a healthcare provider.

Cephalosporins and carbapenems are structurally related to penicillin. People with a penicillin allergy history have a risk of also having an allergic reaction to a cephalosporin or carbapenem. The risk of cross-reactivity is low, but it is prudent on the NAPLEX to avoid any beta-lactam with a stated allergy to another, unless there is no acceptable alternative. A notable exception is in acute otitis media (AOM); the American Academy of Pediatrics recommends a 2nd- or 3rd-generation cephalosporin in patients with a non-severe penicillin allergy, due to the toxicities and decreased efficacy of alternative AOM therapies in children. Aztreonam (a monobactam) is considered safe in patients with a penicillin allergy.

A PENICILLIN ALLERGY, OR NOT?

Although 10% of people report a penicillin "allergy," the CDC reports the true incidence of IgE-mediated (type I hypersensitivity) reactions to penicillin as < 1%. When a "penicillin allergy" is reported, other broad-spectrum antibiotics are often used, which increases resistance, cost and possible side effects.

A skin test can assess risk:

- Patients with a negative result should be given an oral drug "challenge" dose before the full treatment dose.
- Patients with a positive test or a past severe skin reaction (e.g., SJS/TEN) should avoid use of the drug.
  - ❑ Remember: penicillin is the only acceptable treatment in pregnant or non-adherent patients with syphilis. If a skin test is positive, temporarily desensitize and administer penicillin.

Many cephalosporins can be safely tolerated in patients with a mild penicillin allergy. In acute otitis media patients with an allergy to penicillin/amoxicillin, give cefdinir, cefpodoxime, ceftriaxone or cefuroxime.

SULFA DRUGS

Sulfa reactions are most commonly reported with sulfamethoxazole (in *Bactrim*). Other drugs that should be avoided in patients with a sulfa allergy include sulfasalazine, sulfadiazine and sulfisoxazole. The package labeling for "non-arylamine" sulfonamides [thiazide diuretics, loop diuretics (except ethacrynic acid), sulfonylureas, acetazolamide, zonisamide and celecoxib], as well as cidofovir, darunavir (*Prezista*), fosamprenavir and tipranavir contain warnings or contraindications for use in patients with a sulfa allergy, although they usually do not cross-react with a sulfamethoxazole allergy.

The risk of cross-reactivity with sulfamethoxazole, thiazides and loop diuretics is very low, and in clinical practice the reaction is usually not considered significant. Even so, the patient should be aware to watch for a possible reaction and on the NAPLEX, you should recognize the possible interaction. Sulfite or sulfate allergies do not cross react with sulfonamides.

OPIOIDS

Opioid intolerance due to histamine release is common; however, a true opioid allergy is uncommon. See the Pain chapter for information on treatment options in patients with opioid allergies.

HEPARIN

See the Anticoagulation chapter for information on heparin-induced thrombocytopenia (HIT).

BIOLOGICS

Biologics (e.g., rituximab) can cause hypersensitivity reactions and other ADRs. Desensitization to some agents is possible in patients who need a biologic but have had a prior reaction. See the following page for more information regarding desensitization processes.

NSAIDs

Reactions to NSAIDs, including aspirin, can either be a drug sensitivity or a true allergic reaction. A drug sensitivity can cause rhinitis, mild asthmatic-type reactions or skin reactions. If a true allergy is present, the patient will experience urticaria, angioedema and occasionally anaphylaxis.

CONTRAST MEDIA

Contrast media (used in some imaging studies) can cause anaphylactoid reactions and delayed skin reactions. Systemic steroids and antihistamines can be used to prevent reactions if contrast media is needed in a patient who has had a prior reaction.

PEANUTS AND SOY

It is important for pharmacists to be aware if a patient has a peanut allergy. Parents of children with peanut allergies should be CPR-trained and have ready access to an epinephrine auto-injector. An oral immunotherapy [peanut allergen powder (*Palforzia*)] is indicated to mitigate allergic reactions to peanuts, including anaphylaxis. Soy is used in some medications; peanuts and soy are in the same family and can have cross-reactivity. Drugs that are contraindicated with a soy allergy include clevidipine (*Cleviprex*) and propofol (*Diprivan*).

EGGS

If a patient has a true allergy to eggs, they cannot use clevidipine (*Cleviprex*), propofol (*Diprivan*) or the yellow fever vaccine (chicken eggs are used in vaccine production). For influenza vaccines, ACIP states that even patients who have had more severe symptoms when consuming eggs can receive any indicated inactivated vaccine. *Flublok* and *Flucelvax Quadrivalent* contain no egg protein and are options in patients with a severe egg allergy. If a severe reaction to an influenza vaccine occurs, regardless of which ingredient is suspected, that patient should not receive further doses of any influenza vaccine formulation. For further discussion, refer to the Immunizations chapter.

SKIN TESTING AND DESENSITIZATION

PENICILLIN SKIN TESTING

Some patients report a penicillin "allergy" when their reaction was more properly categorized as an intolerance (e.g., nausea, diarrhea). In other cases, patients may have had a true allergic reaction to penicillin in the past, but over time, the antibodies can wane and the patient may be able to safely receive penicillins. Due to concerns of cross-reactivity with cephalosporins and carbapenems, a penicillin allergy can severely limit the selection of antibiotics available to treat infectious diseases, leading to use of broad-spectrum antibiotics that have an increased risk for *C. difficile* (e.g., quinolones) or other toxicities (e.g., vancomycin). The goal of penicillin skin testing is to identify patients who are at the greatest risk of a type I hypersensitivity reaction if exposed to a systemic penicillin.

The penicillin skin test uses the components of penicillin that most often cause an immune (allergic) response, such as the diagnostic agent *Pre-Pen* (benzylpenicilloyl polylysine injection), with very dilute solutions of penicillin G. A step-wise skin test is performed, beginning with a skin prick test followed by intradermal testing. A localized reaction around the *Pre-Pen* or penicillin G test site indicates a high risk of a reaction to systemic penicillin and the patient should not receive it. A patient with a negative skin test (no reaction to the test solutions) can be considered to be at the same risk as a patient in the general population who does not report a penicillin allergy. Skin testing only predicts an IgE-mediated reaction. Regardless of skin test results, a patient should never be re-challenged with an agent that caused SJS or TEN.

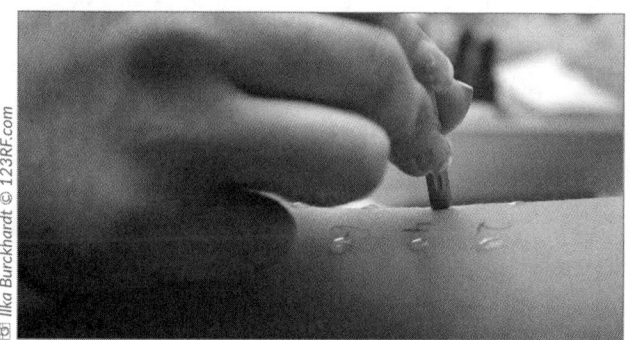

© Ilka Burckhardt © 123RF.com

INDUCTION OF DRUG TOLERANCE (DESENSITIZATION)

In many cases when a drug allergy is present, an alternative medication can be chosen. When no acceptable alternative is available, induction of drug tolerance (often referred to as desensitization) may be recommended. For example, if a pregnant patient has syphilis and a penicillin allergy, the CDC recommends desensitization and penicillin treatment (see Infectious Diseases II chapter).

Desensitization is a step-wise process that begins by administering a very small dose of the medication and then incrementally increasing the dose at regular time intervals up to a target dose. This modifies the patient's response to the medication and temporarily allows safe treatment. The desensitization procedure must take place in a medical setting where emergency care can be provided if a serious reaction occurs. Treatment with the drug must start immediately following desensitization and must not be interrupted. If doses are missed, the drug-free period allows the immune system to re-sensitize to the drug and serious hypersensitivity reactions (including anaphylaxis) could occur with subsequent doses.

Desensitization does not "cure" the patient of an allergy, and the reaction should not be removed from the patient's medical record. If the drug is required on a separate occasion, the desensitization process must be repeated. Desensitization protocols exist for a number of antimicrobial agents, some biologics and a few other medications (e.g., aspirin). Desensitization should never be attempted if a drug has previously caused SJS or TEN.

Select Guidelines/References

Food and Drug Administration MedWatch program http://www.fda.gov/Safety/MedWatch/ (accessed 2022 Feb 23)

Drug Allergy: An Updated Practice Parameter. *Ann Allergy Asthma Immunol.* 2010 Oct;105:259-273.

CHAPTER CONTENT

CONTENT LEGEND

 = Study Tip Gal   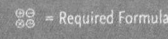 = Required Formula

---

The figure at the top of the right column shows a concentration versus time curve with two lines labeled "With Loading Dose," "No Loading Dose (Maintenance Dose Only)," and a bracket marking "Steady State." The x-axis is labeled "Time" and the y-axis is labeled "Concentration."

CHAPTER 78

PHARMACOKINETICS

BACKGROUND

Pharmacokinetics is what the human body does to a drug during the processes of drug absorption, distribution, metabolism and excretion (often abbreviated ADME). Mathematical relationships are used to describe these processes, which clinicians use to assess drug levels and optimize drug therapy. Pharmacodynamics, what the drug does to the human body, refers to the relationship between the drug concentration at the site of action, and both therapeutic and adverse effects.

ABSORPTION

When a drug is given intravascularly (e.g., intravenously or intra-arterially), absorption is not required because the drug enters directly into the bloodstream (systemic circulation). If a drug is administered extravascularly, drug absorption occurs as the drug moves from the site of administration to the bloodstream (see the Study Tip Gal on the next page). Some examples of drug formulations with extravascular administration include oral, sublingual, buccal, intramuscular, subcutaneous, transdermal, inhaled, topical, ocular, intraocular, intrathecal and rectal products.

When a drug is given orally, it passes from the stomach to the intestine. Most oral drug absorption occurs in the small intestine because of the large surface area and permeable membrane. After gut absorption, the drug enters the portal vein and travels to the liver. Some drugs are extensively metabolized in the liver before reaching the systemic circulation; this is called first-pass metabolism (discussed later). Some drugs are transported through the bile back to the gut where they can be reabsorbed. This is called enterohepatic recycling (see the Drug Interactions chapter).

Absorption of oral drugs occurs via two primary processes: passive diffusion across the gut wall or active transport. Passive diffusion is movement of drugs from an area of high concentration (e.g., the gut lumen) to an area of lower concentration (e.g., the blood). Energy is not required for passive diffusion. Active transport occurs when drugs are moved across the gut wall via transporter proteins that are normally used to absorb nutrients from food.

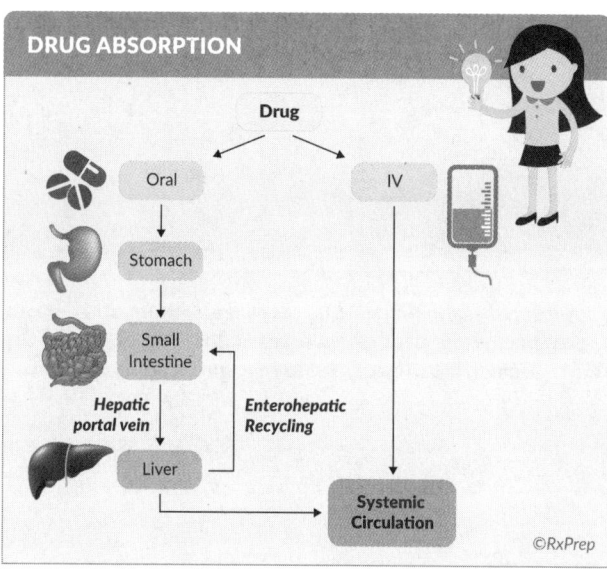

DRUG ABSORPTION

LOCAL VS. SYSTEMIC EFFECTS

Drugs administered extravascularly can be divided into two categories: drugs intended for local effects and drugs intended for systemic effects. Drugs intended for local effects are often applied topically where the drug effect is needed. Examples of this include eye drops for glaucoma (e.g., latanoprost), dermal preparations for psoriasis (e.g., coal tar preparations) and nasal sprays for allergies (e.g., fluticasone nasal spray). Topical administration of a drug can produce therapeutic effects while minimizing systemic toxicity due to lower systemic exposure.

Drugs intended for systemic effects are formulated to facilitate some percentage of drug absorption from the site of administration into the circulatory system. Examples include oral tablets for seasonal allergies (e.g., loratadine), suppositories for fever (e.g., acetaminophen), sublingual tablets for angina (e.g., nitroglycerin SL) and transdermal patches for pain (e.g., fentanyl patch).

DISINTEGRATION, DISSOLUTION AND DRUG SOLUBILITY

When a solid oral dosage form is ingested, it breaks into smaller pieces in the gastrointestinal (GI) tract, which is called disintegration. The smaller pieces then dissolve, and the active ingredient is released from the dosage form (typically a compressed tablet or a capsule). This is called dissolution. The rate of dissolution is described by the Noyes-Whitney equation. The rate of disintegration and dissolution depend on the inactive ingredients used to make the dosage form. Some drugs are made using polymers that help slow down the release of the drug in a controlled way. This can provide less variability in drug concentrations and reduce the dosing frequency.

Sublingual (SL) and orally-disintegrating tablet (ODT) formulations generally have fast absorption. In general, the rate of absorption by dosage form will follow this order (fastest to slowest): IV, SL, ODT, immediate-release tablet, extended-release tablet.

Most immediate-release formulations dissolve and get absorbed rapidly, but some can be destroyed in the gut (primarily by hydrolysis, or lysis with water) making them less available for absorption. Drug formulations have been developed with protective coatings to limit drug degradation in the stomach (acidic) and permit dissolution in the intestine (basic). Drugs with this type of enteric-coated formulation include *Dulcolax* and budesonide.

If a drug has poor absorption, one of the methods used to increase the dissolution rate is to reduce particle diameter, which increases surface area. Drugs with very small particle diameters are referred to as micronized, which usually means the diameter was measured in micrometers but sometimes refers to even smaller particle sizes measured in nanometers. Progesterone and fenofibrate are examples of drugs with poor oral absorption that have been developed in micronized formulations.

Following disintegration, the released drug can dissolve in GI fluids. The rate and extent to which the drug dissolves depends on the drug's solubility. Poorly soluble drugs are generally lipophilic, or lipid-loving. Freely soluble drugs are generally hydrophilic, or water-loving. As a drug moves through the GI tract, only dissolved drug is absorbed into the bloodstream. Poorly soluble drugs generally have poor systemic absorption, and highly soluble drugs often have good systemic absorption.

BIOAVAILABILITY

The extent of drug absorption into the systemic circulation is called bioavailability. Bioavailability is reported as a percentage (from 0 to 100%) and reflects the percentage of drug absorbed from extravascular (e.g., oral) compared to intravascular administration (e.g., IV). Bioavailability is affected by solubility, dissolution, route of administration and other factors.

A drug with good absorption has high bioavailability (> 70%), while a drug with poor absorption has low bioavailability (≤ 10%). For example, levofloxacin and linezolid have high bioavailability; nearly 100% of the oral dose is absorbed, and the oral and IV doses are the same. In many hospitals, these drugs are automatically converted from IV to the same oral dose using a therapeutic interchange or IV to PO protocol. Bisphosphonates, like ibandronate, have low oral bioavailability, so the oral dose (150 mg PO monthly) is much higher than the IV dose (3 mg IV every 3 months) to produce a similar therapeutic effect.

Bioavailability can be calculated using the area under the plasma concentration time curve, or AUC. The AUC represents the total systemic exposure to the drug following administration.

Absolute bioavailability, represented by F, is calculated using the following equation:

$$F\,(\%) \;=\; 100 \;\times\; \frac{AUC_{extravascular}}{AUC_{intravenous}} \;\times\; \frac{Dose_{intravenous}}{Dose_{extravascular}}$$

1. **A pharmacokinetic study of an investigational drug was conducted in healthy volunteers. Following an IV bolus dose of 15 mg, the AUC was determined to be 4.2 mg x hr/L. Subjects were later given an oral dose of 50 mg and the AUC was determined to be 8 mg x hr/L. Calculate the absolute bioavailability of the investigational drug. Round to the nearest whole number.**

$$F\,(\%) \;=\; 100 \;\times\; \frac{\dfrac{8 \text{ mg} \times \text{hr}}{L}}{\dfrac{4.2 \text{ mg} \times \text{hr}}{L}} \;\times\; \frac{15 \text{ mg}}{50 \text{ mg}} \;=\; 57\%$$

Different dosage forms of the same drug (e.g., tablet vs. solution) may have different bioavailabilities. The formula below can be used to calculate an equivalent dose of a drug when the dosage form is changed:

$$\frac{\text{Dose of New}}{\text{Dosage Form}} \;=\; \frac{\text{Amount Absorbed from Current Dosage Form}}{\text{F of New Dosage Form}}$$

DISTRIBUTION

Distribution is the process by which drug molecules move from the systemic circulation to various tissues and organs. Distribution can occur with intravascular and extravascular routes of administration and depends on the physical and chemical properties of the drug molecule and interactions with membranes and tissues throughout the body. Factors that impact distribution include drug lipophilicity, molecular weight, solubility, ionization status and the extent of protein binding. Factors that favor passage across membranes and greater drug distribution to the tissues include high lipophilicity, low molecular weight, unionized status and low protein binding.

Human plasma contains many proteins, and albumin is the primary protein responsible for drug binding. Only the unbound (free) form of a drug can interact with receptors, exert therapeutic or toxic effects and be cleared from the body. If a drug is highly protein-bound (> 90%) and serum albumin is low (< 3.5 g/dL), then a higher percentage of the drug will be in the unbound form and the patient may experience therapeutic or even adverse effects at what appears to be a normal or subtherapeutic level.

Many drug assays cannot differentiate between bound and unbound (active) drug. When assessing levels of highly protein bound compounds (e.g., phenytoin, calcium) in a patient with low serum albumin, an adjustment (correction) of the total level is required. The correction formulas allow us to determine what the concentration would be if albumin was normal. With hypoalbuminemia, the corrected level of a highly protein bound drug will be higher than the total level reported by the lab. This is discussed further in the Calculations III and Seizures/Epilepsy chapters.

The issue described above can be overcome by obtaining a "free" phenytoin level or ionized calcium level. Free phenytoin and ionized calcium only measure the unbound portion, so no adjustment is required for hypoalbuminemia.

CALCIUM AND PHENYTOIN CORRECTION FORMULAS

$$Ca_{corrected} \ (mg/dL) = calcium_{reported \ (serum)} + [(4.0 - albumin) \times (0.8)] \ \dagger$$

$$Phenytoin \ corrected \ (mcg/mL) \ = \frac{Total \ phenytoin \ measured}{(0.2 \times albumin) + 0.1} \ \ddagger$$

† Use serum calcium in mg/dL and albumin in g/dL (standard units in the U.S.) in the corrected calcium formula.
‡ Use serum phenytoin in mcg/mL and albumin in g/dL (standard units in the U.S.) in the corrected phenytoin formula.

2. **A pharmacist receives a call from a provider asking for assistance with two patients in the clinic. Both patients have a seizure disorder and are taking phenytoin. Patient A is seizure free, but is experiencing symptoms of toxicity. Patient B has a higher phenytoin level and is doing fine. Both patients have normal renal function. Which of the following statements is/are true of this scenario? (Select ALL that apply.)**

LAB	REFERENCE RANGE	PATIENT A	PATIENT B
Phenytoin level (total)	10-20 mcg/mL	14.3	17.8
Albumin	3.5-5 g/dL	2.1	4.2

A. Patient B's corrected phenytoin level will be lower than the total level reported.
B. Patient A's corrected phenytoin level will be lower than the total level reported.
C. Patient A's corrected phenytoin level will be higher than the total level reported.
D. Patient A has a greater percentage of bound phenytoin.
E. Patient A has a greater percentage of unbound phenytoin.

The correct answers are (C) and (E). The corrected phenytoin level for Patient A (using the formula provided) is 27.5 mcg/mL. Increased unbound phenytoin is contributing to the patient's side effects.

VOLUME OF DISTRIBUTION

The volume of distribution (V or Vd) reflects how large of an area in the patient's body the drug has distributed into and is based on the properties of the drug (discussed previously). The volume of distribution relates the amount of drug in the body to the concentration of the drug measured in plasma (or serum). The equation for volume of distribution is:

SUBSCRIPTS IN FORMULAS

Vd can be written as V_d and ke can be written as k_e. Subscripts are not used in this chapter for simplicity.

$$Vd = \frac{Amount \ of \ drug \ in \ body}{Concentration \ of \ drug \ in \ plasma}$$

The Vd is determined from the amount of drug in the body immediately after an IV dose is given.

3. **A 500 mg dose of gentamicin is administered to a patient, and a blood sample is drawn. The concentration of gentamicin is measured as 25 mcg/mL (which is the same as 25 mg/L). What is the volume of distribution of gentamicin in this patient?**

$$Vd = \frac{500 \ mg}{25 \ mg/L} = 20 \ L$$

Vd is a theoretical value, which is why it is sometimes called the "apparent" volume of distribution. Vd is not an exact physical volume that is measured, but is a helpful parameter used to make inferences regarding how widely a drug distributes throughout the body.

METABOLISM

Metabolism is the process by which a drug is converted from its original chemical structure into other forms to facilitate elimination from the body. The original chemical form is called the parent drug and the additional forms are called metabolites. Metabolism can occur throughout the body. The gut and liver are primary sites for drug metabolism due to high levels of metabolic enzymes in these tissues.

Blood from the gut travels to the liver before it reaches the rest of the body. First-pass metabolism is the metabolism of a drug before it reaches the systemic circulation, which can dramatically reduce the bioavailability of an oral formulation. First-pass metabolism of lidocaine is so extensive that the drug cannot be given orally – it must be given IV. Some drugs with extensive first-pass metabolism can be given orally, but in much higher doses than IV doses (e.g., propranolol). Many non-oral, extravascular methods of administration (e.g., transdermal, buccal, sublingual) bypass first-pass metabolism entirely. Rectal administration partially avoids first-pass metabolism.

Drug metabolism involves Phase I reactions (oxidation, reduction and hydrolysis), followed by Phase II reactions (e.g., conjugation). Phase I reactions provide a reactive functional group on the compound that permits the drug to be attacked by Phase II enzymes. For example, breaking carbon bonds or adding a hydroxyl group to a drug makes the drug more hydrophilic – this means more of the drug stays in the blood; the blood then passes through the kidneys, and the drug is renally excreted. Glucuronidation and other Phase II reactions create compounds that are more readily excreted in the urine and bile. Cytochrome P450 (CYP450) enzymes, located mainly in the liver and intestines, metabolize the majority of drugs. Refer to the Compounding II chapter for further discussion of hydrolysis and oxidation as they relate to drug degradation.

EXCRETION

Excretion is the process of irreversible removal of drugs from the body. Excretion can occur through the kidneys (urine), liver (bile), gut (feces), lungs (exhaled air) and skin (sweat). The primary route of excretion for most drugs is the kidneys (renal excretion). Renal excretion can be increased by adjusting the acidity of the urine. For a weak base, increase excretion by acidifying the urine. For a weak acid, increase excretion by alkalinizing the urine.

P-glycoprotein (P-gp) efflux pumps in the gut play a role in the absorption and excretion of many drugs (see the Drug Interactions chapter). Renal excretion is discussed in the Renal Disease and Calculations IV chapters.

CLEARANCE AND AREA UNDER THE CURVE

Clearance (Cl) describes the rate of drug removal in a certain volume of plasma over a certain amount of time. Since the liver and kidneys clear most of the drug (and these organs do not usually speed up or slow down), most drug elimination occurs at a steady rate (called the rate of elimination). This is true of drugs that follow first-order kinetics (discussed later in the chapter). Clearance is the efficiency of drug removal from the body and is described by the following equation:

$$Cl = \frac{\text{Rate of Elimination (Re)}}{\text{Drug Concentration}}$$

4. **A dose of gentamicin is given to a patient, and urine is collected from the patient for 4 hours after drug administration. It is determined that 300 mg of gentamicin was eliminated during that time period, and the measured plasma concentration at the midpoint of the collection was 12.5 mg/L. Calculate the patient's gentamicin clearance.**

$$Cl = \frac{300 \text{ mg of gentamicin} / 4 \text{ hours}}{12.5 \text{ mg/L}} = 6 \text{ L/hr}$$

or

$$Cl = \frac{300 \text{ mg of gentamicin}}{4 \text{ hours}} \times \frac{L}{12.5 \text{ mg}} = 6 \text{ L/hr}$$

The rate of elimination (Re) has units of mass per time (e.g., mg/hr), and drug concentration has units of amount per volume (e.g., mg/L); units of mass (mg) cancel out and clearance has units of volume per time (e.g., L/hr). Because the rate of elimination is difficult to assess clinically, another method is used to calculate the clearance of a drug from the body:

$$F \times Dose = Cl \times AUC$$

The AUC is the most reliable measurement of a drug's bioavailability because it directly represents the amount of the drug that has reached the systemic circulation. The clearance for extravascular administration is calculated with this formula:

$$Cl = \frac{F \times Dose}{AUC}$$

Following IV administration, bioavailability (F) = 1, which can be inserted into the previous equation to determine clearance for a drug given intravenously:

$$Cl = \frac{Dose}{AUC}$$

5. **A patient is currently receiving 400 mg of gentamicin IV once daily and, based on measured serum concentrations, the AUC is determined to be 80 mg x hr/L. Calculate the patient's gentamicin clearance.**

$$Cl = \frac{400 \text{ mg}}{80 \frac{\text{mg x hr}}{L}} = 5 \text{ L/hr}$$

ZERO VS. FIRST-ORDER PHARMACOKINETICS

Most drugs follow first-order elimination or "first-order kinetics," where a constant percentage of drug is removed per unit of time. For example, a 325 mg dose of acetaminophen is eliminated at the same rate as a 650 mg dose. With zero-order elimination, a constant amount of drug (mg) is removed per unit of time, no matter how much drug is in the body. The following table provides an example of zero-order and first-order elimination of a 2 gram dose of a drug.

	ZERO-ORDER			FIRST-ORDER		
Hour	Amount of Drug (mg)	Percent Removed in Previous Hour	Amount (mg) Removed in Previous Hour	Amount of Drug (mg)	Percent Removed in Previous Hour	Amount (mg) Removed in Previous Hour
0	2,000			2,000		
1	1,700	15	300	1,600	20	400
2	1,400	17.65	300	1,280	20	320
3	1,100	21.43	300	1,024	20	256

MICHAELIS-MENTEN KINETICS

Phenytoin, theophylline and voriconazole exhibit Michaelis-Menten kinetics (also called saturable, mixed order or non-linear kinetics). The maximum rate of metabolism is defined as the Vmax (see figure on the right). The concentration at which the rate of metabolism is half maximal is defined as the Michaelis-Menten constant (Km). At very low concentrations (much less than the Km), the rate of metabolism mimics a first-order process.

At most concentrations approaching and exceeding the Km, the rate of metabolism becomes mixed. At even higher concentrations relative to the Km, the rate of metabolism approaches zero-order (e.g., Vmax). Throughout this process, an increase in dose leads to a disproportionate increase in drug concentration at steady state. The rate of phenytoin metabolism approaches the maximum at accepted therapeutic concentrations. Because of this, phenytoin dose adjustments should be made in small increments (30 – 50 mg) when the serum concentration is > 7 mcg/mL. See the Study Tip Gal.

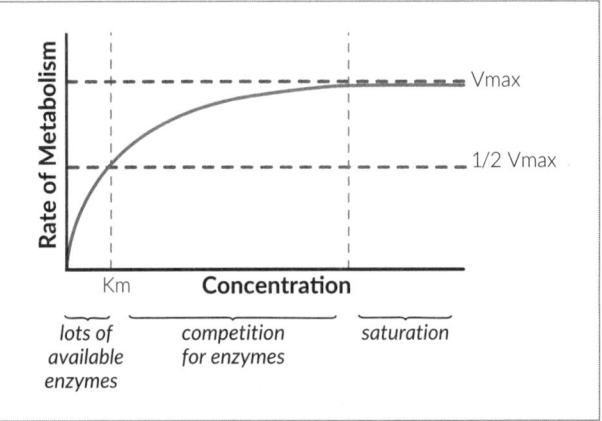

DOSE ADJUSTMENTS FOR MICHAELIS-MENTEN KINETICS

Most drugs follow first-order (linear) kinetics.

- At steady state, doubling the dose approximately doubles the serum concentration.

Some drugs (phenytoin, theophylline and voriconazole) follow Michaelis-Menten (also called non-linear, saturable or mixed-order) kinetics.

- Doubling the dose of these drugs can more than double the serum concentration.
  - Using a proportion to calculate a new dose is not appropriate.
  - Dosing adjustments must be made cautiously to avoid toxicity.

6. **A patient has been using phenytoin 100 mg three times daily. A phenytoin level was drawn and found to be 8.8 mcg/mL (reference range 10 – 20 mcg/mL). The dose was doubled to 200 mg three times daily. The patient started to slur her words, felt fatigued and returned to the clinic. The level was repeated and found to be 23.7 mcg/mL. Which of the following statements is accurate regarding the most likely reason for the change in phenytoin level?**

 A. Phenytoin half-life is reduced at higher doses.
 B. Phenytoin volume of distribution increases at higher doses.
 C. The patient's serum albumin level likely increased.
 D. Phenytoin bioavailability can decrease at higher doses.
 E. Phenytoin metabolism can become saturated at higher doses.

The correct answer is (E). The most likely explanation for the increase in phenytoin level is that when the dose was doubled, the metabolism became partially or completely saturated, and the steady-state level increased dramatically.

ELIMINATION RATE CONSTANT

The <u>elimination rate constant (ke)</u> is the fraction of the drug that is eliminated (cleared) per unit of time. It is calculated from the Vd and the clearance:

$$ke = \frac{Cl}{Vd}$$

7. **A drug has the following pharmacokinetic parameters: Vd = 50 liters and Cl = 5,000 mL/hour. Calculate the elimination rate constant of the drug.**

$$ke = \frac{5\ L/hr}{50\ L} = 0.1\ hr^{-1}$$

Be certain that the values are converted to units that properly cancel out in the equation. The ke is 0.1 hr^{-1} (meaning that <u>10% of the drug remaining is cleared per hour</u>).

Predicting Drug Concentrations

The ke can be used to predict the concentration of a drug at any time (t) after the dose using the calculations below. The second formula is derived from the first.

$$C_2 = C_1 \times e^{-kt}$$

$$ke = \frac{\ln(C_1/C_2)}{t}$$

Where C1 = the first or higher drug concentration (sometimes the peak concentration), C2 = the second (or lower) drug concentration (at time = t) and e = the base of the natural log.

8. **A patient received a dose of gentamicin. A short time after the end of the infusion, it is known that the drug level was 10 mg/L, and the patient's ke = 0.22 hr^{-1}. Calculate the predicted concentration after 8 hours.**

$$C_2 = 10\ mg/L \times e^{-0.22 \times 8}$$

$$C_2 = 10\ mg/L \times 0.172 = 1.72\ mg/L$$

9. A patient being treated with vancomycin had a supratherapeutic trough level of 28 mcg/mL. If ke = 0.15 hr^{-1}, predict how long it will take for the trough to decrease to the goal therapeutic trough (15 mcg/mL). Round to the nearest hour.

$$0.15 \text{ hr}^{-1} = \frac{\ln(28/15)}{t} = 4.16 \text{ hr, or 4 hours}$$

HALF-LIFE (T½) AND STEADY STATE

The time required for a drug concentration (and drug amount) to <u>decrease by 50%</u> is called the elimination <u>half-life</u> ($t_{1/2}$). For example, it takes 5 hours for theophylline concentrations to fall from 16 to 8 mg/L. The half-life of theophylline is 5 hours. It takes 5 more hours for the drug concentration to fall from 8 mg/L to 4 mg/L. Half-life is independent of the drug concentration for drugs exhibiting first-order kinetics.

Half-life is more clinically meaningful than ke. The half-life of a drug can be calculated from the ke:

$$t_{1/2} = \frac{0.693}{ke}$$

The half-life of a drug can be used to calculate the time required for drug washout (complete elimination) or the time required to achieve steady-state (refer to the table below). When a fixed dose is administered at regular intervals, the drug accumulates until it reaches steady state where the rate of <u>drug intake equals</u> the rate of <u>drug elimination</u>. The time required to reach steady state depends on the elimination half-life of the drug. It takes <u>~5 half-lives to reach steady state</u>, assuming the drug follows first-order kinetics (described previously) in a one-compartment distribution model (the drug is rapidly and evenly distributed throughout the body) and no loading dose has been given. Similarly, <u>5 half-lives are required to eliminate more than 95% of the drug</u> if no additional doses are given. The most clinically useful information is obtained from drug levels collected at <u>steady state</u>.

# OF HALF-LIVES	ELIMINATION (NO ADDITIONAL DOSES GIVEN) % OF DRUG REMAINING IN THE BODY	ACCUMULATION (MULTIPLE DOSES GIVEN) % OF STEADY-STATE ACHIEVED
1	50	50
2	25	75
3	12.5	87.5
4	6.25	93.8
5	3.13	96.9

10. Tetracycline has a clearance of 7.014 L/hr and a Vd of 105 L. Calculate the half-life of tetracycline (round to the nearest tenth) and the time required for elimination of greater than 95% of the drug from the body.

$$ke = \frac{Cl}{Vd} = \frac{7.014 \text{ L/hr}}{105 \text{ L}} = 0.0668 \text{ hr}^{-1}$$

$$t_{1/2} = \frac{0.693}{ke} = \frac{0.693}{0.0668 \text{ hr}^{-1}} = 10.4 \text{ hours}$$

The time required is 10.4 hours × 5 half-lives = 52 hours

11. **The serum concentration of Drug A over time is plotted in the figure below. What is the half-life of Drug A?**

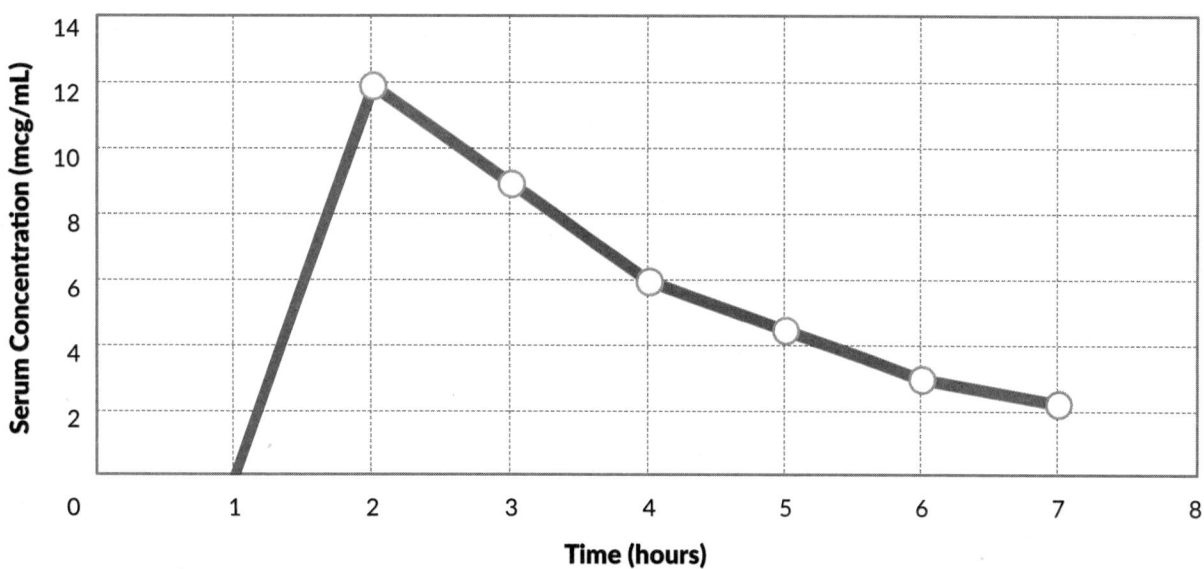

The drug concentrations can be presented in a figure (as shown) or in a list. <u>Identify two times</u> (in hours) where the <u>drug concentration has decreased by half</u> to find the half-life:

- At 2 hours the concentration is 12 mcg/mL and at 4 hours the concentration is 6 mcg/mL.

- It takes 2 hours for the concentration to decrease by 50%, so the half-life is 2 hours.

The equations under "Predicting Drug Concentrations" can also be used to calculate half-life and drug levels on a concentration curve like this. Plotting out the levels and time can be useful for solving many types of pharmacokinetic problems.

---

12. **A patient was receiving Drug B for 1 week. The drug was held on June 1st due to an elevated serum concentration. Based on the serum concentrations obtained after the drug was held (shown below), what is the half-life of Drug B?**

TIME	CONCENTRATION OF DRUG B
1400	12 mcg/mL
1500	8.5 mcg/mL
1600	6 mcg/mL
1700	4.3 mcg/mL
1900	2.1 mcg/mL

The drug concentration fell by 50% (from 12 mcg/mL to 6 mcg/mL) in 2 hours, so the half-life of Drug B is 2 hours. This is a different way of presenting the same information from the previous problem.

---

13. **A patient receives 200 mg of a drug with a half-life of 5 hours. How much of the drug remains after 10 hours?**

- 10 hours = 2 half-lives

- 50 mg of the drug remains after 10 hours

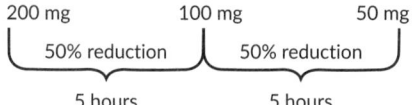

LOADING DOSE

Administration of a loading dose can be necessary to rapidly achieve therapeutic concentrations of a drug. When the half-life of a drug is long relative to the frequency of administration, several doses must be administered before steady state is achieved.

14. **A patient will be started on daily oral digoxin for management of atrial fibrillation. The following pharmacokinetic parameters for oral digoxin are known: F = 0.6, Vd = 500 L and Cl = 120 L/day. When would steady state be reached? Round to the nearest day.**

$$ke = \frac{Cl}{Vd} = \frac{120\ L/day}{500\ L} = 0.24\ days^{-1} \qquad t_{1/2} = \frac{0.693}{ke} = \frac{0.693}{0.24\ days^{-1}} = {\sim}2.89\ days$$

$$Steady\ State = 5\ half\text{-}lives \times 2.89\ days = {\sim}14\ days$$

It is beneficial to administer a loading dose to achieve the targeted levels more quickly in this case. The loading dose can be determined with the following equation:

$$Loading\ Dose = \frac{Desired\ Concentration \times Vd}{F}$$

15. **Using the pharmacokinetic parameters provided in the previous question, what oral loading dose of digoxin is appropriate to rapidly achieve a peak concentration of 1.5 mcg/L?**

$$Loading\ Dose = \frac{Desired\ Concentration \times Vd}{F} = \frac{1.5\ mcg/L \times 500\ L}{0.6} = 1,250\ mcg\ or\ 1.25\ mg$$

THERAPEUTIC DRUG MONITORING

Some medications are monitored with drug levels to reach dosing goals and avoid toxicity (see the Lab Values & Drug Monitoring chapter). If drug levels are too high, toxicity can occur. If drug levels are too low, the patient's condition might not be treated adequately. To prevent either toxicity or inadequate treatment, an adjustment of the dosing regimen is needed.

The peak level is the highest concentration in the blood the drug will reach. With intravenous drugs, peaks are typically drawn 30 minutes after the end of the infusion to allow for drug distribution to occur (e.g., aminoglycosides). The trough level is the lowest concentration reached by the drug before the next dose is given; it is drawn immediately before (or within 30 minutes before) the dose is due. When adjusting a dosing regimen, changing the dose generally affects the peak, and changing the interval/frequency generally affects the trough.

Therapeutic drug monitoring optimizes drug therapy by enhancing efficacy (e.g., overcoming resistance) and reducing toxicity associated with overdosing or drug accumulation. Antibiotic dosing strategies are dictated by certain pharmacodynamic parameters [e.g., peak to minimum inhibitory concentration (MIC) ratio, AUC to MIC ratio or time above the MIC]. This is discussed in the Infectious Diseases I chapter.

16. A patient is receiving tobramycin 120 mg IV every 8 hours at 0600, 1400 and 2200. The drug is being infused over 30 minutes. A tobramycin level drawn at 1500 was 9.8 mcg/mL. A trough level scheduled for 2200 was inadvertently drawn at 1830 and was 5.6 mcg/mL. What would the expected level (extrapolated trough) be at 2200? Round to the nearest tenth.

$$ke = \frac{\ln(9.8 / 5.6)}{3.5} = 0.1599 \text{ hr}^{-1}$$

$$C_2 = 5.6 \text{ mcg/mL} \times e^{-0.1599 \times 3.5}$$

$$C_2 = 5.6 \text{ mcg/mL} \times 0.5714 = 3.2 \text{ mcg/mL}$$

CALCULATING TIME (t)

Determining the correct value to use for time (t) can be challenging. Try creating your own concentration-time curve and plotting the values you are given.

Either measured level (9.8 mcg/mL or 5.6 mcg/mL) can be used in the second step of the problem. If 9.8 mcg/mL was used, time (t) would be 7 hours. In this case, the regimen should be adjusted due to an elevated trough (goal < 2 mcg/mL) by increasing the dosing interval.

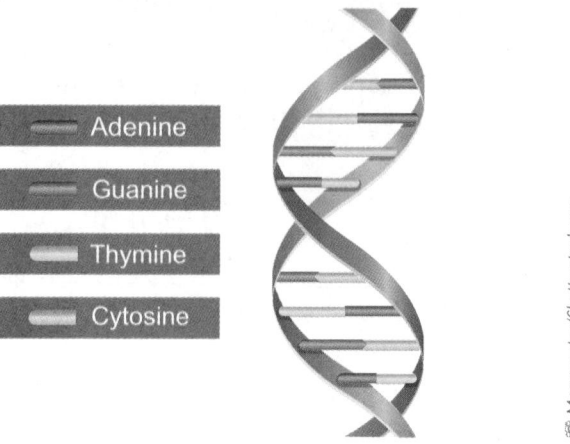

CHAPTER 79

PHARMACOGENOMICS

BACKGROUND

Pharmacogenomics is the science of examining inherited variations in genes that determine a patient's response to a drug. It is estimated that genetic factors are responsible for 20 – 40% of the differences in drug metabolism and response between patients. The goal of pharmacogenomics is to identify these factors and design treatments with improved efficacy and reduced adverse reactions.

Pharmacogenomics is called "personalized medicine" because drugs can be avoided entirely or used preferentially, based on a person's genotype. The genotype is an individual's unique genetic instructions (the coding in the DNA), which determines response and tolerability of drugs.

Pharmacogenomics is Becoming Mainstream

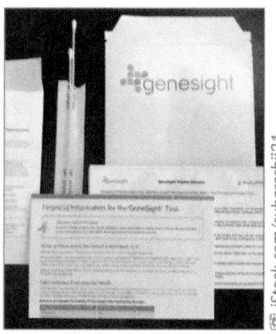

Medication prescribing has historically been hit-or-miss (e.g., it has not always been possible to predict a patient's response to or tolerability of medications). Today, pharmacogenomic testing is more accessible, and assessing the presence or lack of genes that influence efficacy (response) and the likelihood of adverse events can guide prescribing.

Many tests are conducted on DNA extracted from a sample of saliva. Health insurance plans cover the cost of some pharmacogenetic tests if prescribed by a healthcare provider.

CONTENT LEGEND

= Study Tip Gal   = Key Drug Guy

DOMINANT AND RECESSIVE TRAITS

Dominant and recessive genotypes describe the inheritance patterns of certain traits. They can be used to determine how likely it is for a certain phenotype (an observable trait) to pass from parent to offspring.

Each parent contributes one copy (an allele) of each gene to the offspring. The differences in each allele cause variations in protein production (expression), which determines the phenotype (e.g., brown or blonde hair). The phenotype will also be influenced by the offspring's environment.

A <u>dominant</u> allele produces a dominant phenotype in individuals who have <u>one copy</u> of the allele from one parent. For a <u>recessive</u> allele to produce a recessive phenotype, the individual must have <u>two copies</u>, one from each parent (see figure).

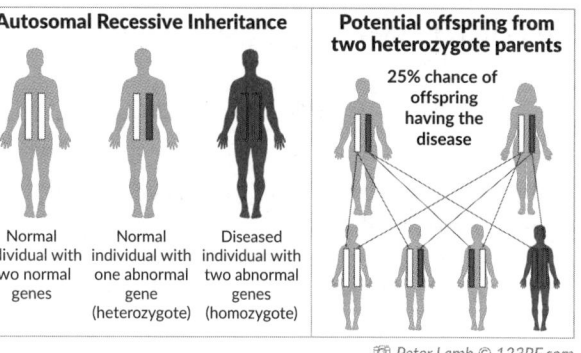

Peter Lamb © 123RF.com

DEFINITIONS

TERM	DEFINITION
Deoxyribonucleic acid (DNA)	The genetic information inherited from both parents that is present in <u>two long chains of nucleotides</u>, joined together by hydrogen bonds and twisted into a <u>double helix</u>. DNA is the main component of chromosomes.
Nucleotide	A subunit of the nucleic acids DNA and RNA (ribonucleic acid). Each nucleotide contains a nitrogen base, a five-carbon sugar (deoxyribose in DNA, and ribose in RNA) and a phosphate group. In DNA, the <u>bases</u> consist of two purines (<u>adenine and guanine</u>) and two pyrimidines (<u>thymine and cytosine</u>). In RNA, uracil is present instead of thymine.
Chromosome	A tightly packed structure within the cell nucleus, consisting of DNA and proteins. Chromosomes contain genes. Human cells contain <u>23 pairs</u> of chromosomes.
Gene	A specific <u>sequence of nucleotides that code</u> (i.e., provide instructions) for a <u>single protein</u>. A gene is similar to a recipe, or a set of instructions, on how to make a protein. Since proteins make up the entire life form, genes are referred to as the "blueprint" of life.
Allele	The specific form of a gene. Alleles are either wild-type or variants. <u>Wild-type</u> is usually the <u>most commonly occurring</u> allele. <u>Two identical alleles</u> make up a <u>homozygous</u> genotype (e.g., CYP450 2C19 *1/*1) and <u>two different alleles</u> make up a <u>heterozygous</u> genotype (e.g., CYP2C19 *1/*3).
Genotype	The set of <u>unique genes</u> that determine a <u>specific trait</u> in an individual.
Phenotype	An <u>observable trait</u> (outward expression) <u>of the genotype</u>, such as hair color, or an inherited trait that is not outwardly visible, such as sickle cell disease.
Haplotype	A group of genes or DNA variations inherited from a single parent that exist on the same chromosome and are likely to be inherited together.
Single nucleotide polymorphism (SNP)	A <u>change</u> in a <u>single nucleotide</u> in a genetic sequence (e.g., C replaced by G). SNPs are the <u>most common</u> genetic alteration in DNA. A SNP can be harmless, or it can result in a disease. SNPs are responsible for the <u>majority</u> of <u>individual variability in response to a drug</u>. Example: in cystic fibrosis, a SNP results in defective coding for a protein involved in sweat and mucus production.
Structural variation (SV)	SVs are polymorphisms, like SNPs, except that they are longer. They involve a large portion of DNA. SVs, like SNPs, can be harmless or associated with a certain risk or disease.
Polymorphism	An <u>inherited variation</u> in the DNA sequence (such as a SNP or SV).
Poor metabolizer	A person with significantly reduced or <u>no enzyme activity</u>. This would lead to reduced or no metabolism (breakdown) of a drug through a particular enzyme. This might mean a patient should avoid drugs metabolized by that enzyme or use a modified dose to prevent adverse effects.
Ultra-rapid metabolizer	A person with <u>high enzyme activity</u>. This leads to fast metabolism of a drug through that particular enzyme. This means a patient would quickly metabolize a prodrug to its active form and/or eliminate an active drug faster than expected.

CYTOCHROME P450 ENZYMES

CYP ENZYMES ARE POLYMORPHIC

The CYP450 enzymes are polymorphic, which means there are different forms of the same enzyme (due to a SNP in the DNA that codes for the enzyme). A SNP can cause the enzyme production in an individual to increase or decrease, which will increase or decrease the rate of drug metabolism and, consequently, the serum level of the substrate drug. The major types of CYP enzyme variations are classified into 4 groups, based on the effect on the rate of metabolism: ultra-rapid metabolizer (UM), extensive metabolizer (EM), intermediate metabolizer (IM) and poor metabolizer (PM).

EMs have normal enzyme activity, which typically results in an expected drug response. PMs have fewer functional enzymes to metabolize a drug substrate. This can cause drug levels to increase (or in the case of a prodrug, less will be metabolized to the active form). This is similar to the effects seen with drug enzyme inhibitors. UMs have more enzymes to metabolize a substrate drug. This causes drug levels to decrease (or in the case of a prodrug, more rapid metabolism to the active form). This is similar to the effects seen with drug enzyme inducers. Enzyme inhibitors and inducers are discussed in more detail in the Drug Interactions chapter.

CYP Enzymes Vary by Ethnicity and Among Individuals

Gene variants are most often inherited, and the variant enzyme expression can be measured among ethnic groups. Using CYP2D6 as an example, 6 – 10% of Caucasians are PMs and produce little or no CYP2D6, while 30% of Ethiopians are UMs and produce about double the usual amount (see table below).

GENETIC TYPE	CYP2D6 ACTIVITY	ETHNIC DIFFERENCES (APPROX.)
Poor metabolizers	Very low or none	Caucasians 6-10% Mexican Americans 3-6% African Americans 2-5% Asians ~1%
Intermediate metabolizers	Low	Not established
Extensive metabolizers	Normal	Includes most people
Ultra-rapid metabolizers	High	Finns and Danes 1% North Americans (white) 4% Greeks 10% Portuguese 10% Saudis 20% Ethiopians 30%

Reprinted with Permission from Dr. John Horn

PHARMACOGENOMIC TESTING AND PHARMACIST ACTION

DRUG	TEST	SIGNIFICANCE/POPULATION	RESULT/ACTION
Human leukocyte antigen (HLA) testing: the major histocompatibility complex, class I, B (HLA-B) is an important gene in the immune system.			
Abacavir *(Ziagen)* and abacavir-containing combination drugs (e.g., **Triumeq, Epzicom**)	HLA-B*5701	Patients who are HLA-B*5701 positive are at ↑ risk for a hypersensitivity reaction. Test all patients prior to starting. Serious and fatal hypersensitivity reactions have occurred.	If positive, do not use.
Allopurinol *(Zyloprim, Aloprim)*	HLA-B*5801	Patients testing positive for HLA-B*5801 have an increased risk of Stevens-Johnson syndrome (SJS). Discontinue at the first sign of an allergic reaction, including skin rash. Consider testing high-risk individuals (Korean patients with renal impairment or those with Han Chinese or Thai ancestry).	If positive, do not use.
Carbamazepine (Tegretol, others) **Oxcarbazepine (Trileptal) Phenytoin (Dilantin,** others) **Fosphenytoin (Cerebyx)**	HLA-B*1502	The HLA-B*1502 allele (more common in Asian populations) ↑ the risk of serious skin reactions including SJS and toxic epidermal necrolysis (TEN). Test all Asian patients before starting carbamazepine; testing is suggested for oxcarbazepine and is optional for phenytoin and fosphenytoin.	If positive, do not use (unless benefit clearly outweighs risk).
Select drugs with CYP450 polymorphisms: polymorphisms of various CYP450 enzymes may be responsible for much of the variability in medication response. These polymorphisms could affect any population, but are not yet routinely tested.			
Clopidogrel *(Plavix)*	CYP2C19	Clopidogrel is a prodrug. It must be converted to an active metabolite by CYP2C19. The CYP2C19*1 allele is fully functional, whereas the *2 and *3 alleles indicate reduced metabolism (less active metabolite formed). Patients with CYP2C19*2 or *3 alleles are poor metabolizers and have ↑ cardiovascular events.	If the patient is known to have the CYP2C19*2 or *3 alleles, consider alternative treatment.
Codeine	CYP2D6	Codeine (a prodrug) is metabolized to morphine via CYP2D6. Ultra-rapid metabolizers are at ↑ risk of opioid overdose due to extensive conversion to morphine. Over-production of morphine can cause ↑ CNS effects, including respiratory depression. Infant deaths have occurred when nursing mothers who were ultra-rapid metabolizers took codeine for pain. Excessive morphine was passed to the infant through breast milk.	If a known CYP2D6 ultra-rapid metabolizer, do not use (toxicity risk). If a known CYP2D6 poor metabolizer, do not use (lack of efficacy).
Warfarin *(Coumadin*, Jantoven)*	CYP2C9*2 and *3, VKORC1	Increased bleeding risk due to reduced function of alleles and haplotypes (CYP2C9*2 and *3) and VKORC1 G > A variant.	If these allele variations are known to be present, start with a lower dose.

Brand discontinued but name still used in practice.

DRUG	TEST	SIGNIFICANCE/POPULATION	RESULT/ACTION
Other Pharmacogenomic Tests			
Trastuzumab *(Herceptin)* and other HER2 inhibitors (see Oncology II chapter)	HER2 gene expression	These drugs require overexpression of HER2 for efficacy. HER2 negative status and those with weakly positive (1+) tumors do not respond well to treatment.	If tumor is HER2 negative, drugs are not effective.
Cetuximab *(Erbitux)* and other EGFR inhibitors (see Oncology II chapter)	KRAS mutation	Only patients who are KRAS mutation-negative (i.e., are wild-type) should receive these medications. They are not effective in patients with colorectal cancer who are positive for the KRAS mutation (~40% of patients).	If positive for a KRAS mutation, do not use.
Azathioprine *(Azasan, Imuran)*	Thiopurine methyltransferase (TPMT)	Low/absent TPMT activity ↑ the risk of severe, life threatening myelosuppression (↓ WBCs, ↓ RBCs, ↓ platelets); patients with intermediate TPMT activity are also at ↑ risk for myelosuppression, but with lower severity.	If TPMT activity is low/absent, start at a very low dose or use an alternative treatment.
Capecitabine *(Xeloda)* **Fluorouracil**	DPD deficiency	Dihydropyrimidine dehydrogenase (DPD) deficiency ↑ risk of severe toxicity (diarrhea, neutropenia, neurotoxicity).	If DPD deficient, do not use.

Refer to the Key Drugs Guy below for drugs with required or strongly recommended pharmacogenomic testing per the package labeling.

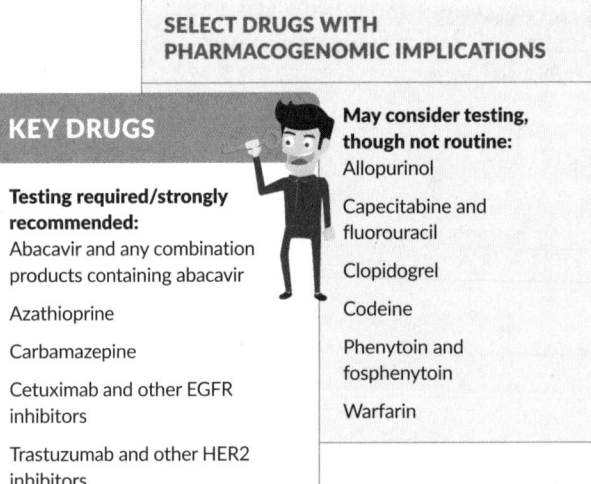

DOES A POSITIVE OR NEGATIVE TEST REQUIRE ACTION?

Avoid the drug when these pharmacogenomic tests are POSITIVE

- HLA-B: a positive test indicates ↑ risk of hypersensitivity
- KRAS mutation: a positive test (often called "KRAS mutant") predicts a poor response

Avoid the drug when this pharmacogenomic test is NEGATIVE

- HER2 expression: a negative result indicates a poor response

SELECT DRUGS WITH PHARMACOGENOMIC IMPLICATIONS

KEY DRUGS

Testing required/strongly recommended:
Abacavir and any combination products containing abacavir

Azathioprine

Carbamazepine

Cetuximab and other EGFR inhibitors

Trastuzumab and other HER2 inhibitors

May consider testing, though not routine:
Allopurinol

Capecitabine and fluorouracil

Clopidogrel

Codeine

Phenytoin and fosphenytoin

Warfarin

Select Guidelines/References

Clinical Pharmacogenetics Implementation Consortium (CPIC) Guidelines. https://cpicpgx.org/guidelines (accessed 2022 Feb 23).

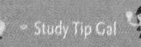
= Study Tip Gal

© iStock.com/ChamilleWhite

CHAPTER 80

DIETARY SUPPLEMENTS, NATURAL & COMPLEMENTARY MEDICINE

BACKGROUND

Complementary medicine refers to health practices (e.g., dietary supplements and acupuncture) that are used with conventional medicine (e.g., healthcare provider visits and prescription medications). In the last decade, yoga and meditation had the largest increases in use. Complementary medicine is used commonly in the United States.

The term alternative medicine is used when conventional medicine is not used.

NATURAL MEDICINE

'Natural medicine' is a general umbrella term that includes herbals (plant products), vitamins, minerals and many substances that are not plant-derived but exist in nature, such as glucosamine from shellfish. The FDA uses the term "dietary supplements," which will be used here.

Dietary supplements are regulated by the Dietary Supplement Health and Education Act (DSHEA) of 1994. DSHEA requires the manufacturer to ensure that their products are safe before they are marketed. In contrast, drugs must be proven safe and effective before they can be sold. Once the supplement is marketed, the FDA must show it is "unsafe" before it can restrict use or remove it from the marketplace. The company selling or distributing the supplement must forward adverse event reports to the FDA. Adverse events from supplements can be reported to the FDA's Safety Reporting Portal, which sorts safety issues to the correct FDA site. FDAble is a searchable database of adverse events caused by dietary supplements, medications, devices and tobacco products. Information on natural medicines can be found in general drug references and the *Natural Medicines Database*.

DIFFERENCES BETWEEN DIETARY SUPPLEMENTS AND DRUGS

Supplement safety is the manufacturer's responsibility, which should be proven prior to release. After release, the FDA can remove a supplement if it is found to be unsafe.

- In contrast, drugs must be proven safe and effective to the FDA prior to release.

Supplements cannot claim to treat, cure or mitigate (lessen) a condition (e.g., "melatonin treats insomnia" is not appropriate).

- In contrast, drug claims are based on FDA approval (e.g., "zolpidem treats insomnia" is appropriate).

SUPPLEMENTS
- The Supplement Facts label is similar to the label required on food products. It includes the ingredients, quantities, serving size, servings/container, calories, calories from fat, total fat and saturated fat, cholesterol, sodium, carbohydrate, dietary fiber, sugars, protein, vitamin A, vitamin C, calcium and iron, when present in measurable amounts.

OTC DRUGS
- The OTC Drug Facts label includes ingredients, purpose, uses, warnings, instructions, excipients and how to avoid an allergic reaction. OTC drugs can include a package insert similar to prescription drugs; this depends on the product's approval process.

PRESCRIPTION DRUGS
- Much more detailed information, which is in the package insert; see the Drug References chapter.

Manufacturers cannot make claims that the product treats or cures a condition. Health claims are limited to the nutrient content, the relationship to health and the impact on normal body structure or function, such as "calcium builds strong bones," and "fiber maintains bowel regularity." Products that make claims on the structure or function of the body (e.g., antioxidants maintain cell integrity) must state in a "disclaimer" that the FDA has not evaluated the claim. The United States Pharmacopeia (USP) establishes standards for dietary supplements. Pharmacists can help consumers choose a reputable product with the USP Verified Mark on the product label.

Risks with natural products are usually dose-dependent; higher doses have a higher risk. Supplements can pose safety risks in certain patients. Four areas of particular concern are supplements that interact with prescription drugs, increase bleeding risk or cause hepatotoxicity or cardiotoxicity.

DIETARY SUPPLEMENT LABELING

The claims on supplement labels are limited (see Study Tip Gal above) because the supplements have not had rigorous trials to determine safety and efficacy. The Supplement Facts label includes the recommended daily intake (RDI) and the amount of each ingredient in the product.

Label Updates

The RDIs have been changed for some common vitamins and minerals. Additionally, some of the products will have new measurement units. The labeling is not yet required, but some labeling has been updated already.

- One that will cause confusion is folic acid, which will have units listed on labels in DFE instead of in micrograms.
  - Folic acid 600 mcg DFE ≅ 360 mcg of folic acid daily, the RDA for women in child-bearing years.

INTERACTIONS WITH PRESCRIPTION DRUGS

St. John's Wort

St. John's wort (SJW) has several important drug interactions to be aware of.

- SJW induces the CYP450 3A4, 2C19, 2C9 and 1A2 enzymes and p-glycoprotein (P-gp), which lowers levels of other drugs (with possible treatment failures).
  - Do not use with many drugs, including oral contraceptives, transplant drugs and warfarin.
- SJW is serotonergic and is often implicated in serotonin syndrome.
  - Do not use with MAO inhibitors, including linezolid.
  - Concurrent use with other serotonergic drugs can be dangerous, especially at higher doses, including SSRIs and SNRIs.
- SJW causes photosensitivity and requires counseling on sun protection and avoidance.
  - Photosensitivity risk increases when taken with other photosensitizing drugs, including diuretics, retinoids, quinolones, sulfamethoxazole, tetracyclines and transplant drugs (e.g., tacrolimus); see Drug Allergies & Adverse Drug Reactions chapter.
- SJW may lower the seizure threshold. Caution is required when taking drugs that lower the seizure threshold (e.g., bupropion, quinolones, tramadol, penicillin and carbapenems) or in anyone with a history of seizures; see Seizures/Epilepsy chapter.

SUPPLEMENTS THAT INCREASE BLEEDING RISK

Several natural medicines have the potential to increase bleeding risk.

- The "5 Gs": garlic, ginger, ginkgo, ginseng and glucosamine
- Fish oils (at higher doses)
- Vitamin E
- Dong quai
- Willow bark (a salicylate); do not use with anticoagulants. Other supplements should not be given concurrently with warfarin; see Anticoagulation chapter

SUPPLEMENTS WITH RISK OF LIVER TOXICITY

Natural products can be hepatotoxic.

- Black cohosh (used for menopausal symptoms)
- Kava (used for stress/anxiety)
- Chaparral, comfrey
- Green tea "extracts" may be a health concern; see below

SUPPLEMENTS WITH RISK OF CARDIAC TOXICITY

Cardiotoxic supplements will have a higher risk in patients with cardiac conditions, but can cause toxicity in anyone.

- Ephedra was removed from the market due to reports of cardiac toxicity. Bitter orange (Citrus aurantium or synephrine) replaced ephedra in many products.
  - ❏ Ephedra and bitter orange/synephrine are stimulants with dose-dependent cardiac toxicity. They increase blood pressure and heart rate. There are reports of myocardial infarction, stroke and arrhythmias.
- DMAA (dimethylamylamine) is an amphetamine derivative used in body-building or performance-enhancement products, including powdered supplement mixtures.
  - ❏ DMAA has cardiac toxicity, including increasing blood pressure and heart rate.
- Licorice contains glycyrrhizin; artificially flavored licorice products do not contain this compound.
  - ❏ Glycyrrhizin, taken in excess, can lower potassium and increase blood pressure.
- Yohimbe is used to increase libido and for erectile dysfunction.
  - ❏ Yohimbe raises blood pressure, increases heart rate and has a risk of seizures.

Caffeine and Health Risks

Caffeine taken in usual doses is not harmful; in excessive doses, caffeine can raise blood pressure and increase heart rate.

- Caffeine is present in supplements for weight loss, energy and body-building. Many have high caffeine content.
- Caffeine is present in black tea, green tea, cocoa (including chocolate), yerba mate, guarana and kombucha (fermented tea).
- Green tea "extract" (with various unknown contents) has been linked to liver damage in body-building products.

Caffeine and Health Benefits

Caffeine is not all bad; it is the most popular drug in the world, with several benefits.

- Caffeine increases alertness, helps with weight management and can be useful in treating headaches.
- Green tea, in reasonable amounts, helps lower LDL and triglycerides. The table on the following page includes other supplements with beneficial cardiovascular effects.

MEDICAL FOODS

Medical foods are not medications, nor are they supplements. They are compounds used to meet a nutritional need, which should be used under medical supervision, yet not all require a prescription. Medical foods are not covered by most insurance plans.

FDA Requirements for Medical Foods

The FDA requires medical foods to be:

- Taken enterally (i.e., by mouth or with an enteral feeding tube).
- Taken under the supervision of a healthcare professional.
- Intended to treat a condition with a known nutritional requirement.

Medical Food Use is Increasing

Commonly used medical foods include L-methylfolate, an active form of folate (Deplin) used for depression, L-methylfolate, B6 and B12 (Metanx) used for neuropathic pain and phosphatidylserine conjugated to different forms of enriched omega-3 fatty acids used for mild cognitive impairment and ADHD, respectively.

Generally Recognized As Safe

Some of the supplements in the following table (e.g., chamomile, cinnamon, synephrine) are used in food products. The FDA labels food additives as Generally Recognized As Safe (GRAS) when the additive is considered safe when used as intended. When used in doses that are higher than the intended dose, the safety profile will change and could include toxicity. All ingredients in a medical food must be GRAS.

PHARMACY FOUNDATIONS PART 2

COMMONLY USED SUPPLEMENTS

CONDITION	TREATMENT
Anxiety	Valerian
	Passionflower
	Kava
	St. John's wort
	Chamomile
	5-Hydroxytryptophan (5-HTP)
ADHD	Omega-3 fatty acids, "fish oils," polyunsaturated fatty acids (PUFAs), contains docosahexaenoic acid (DHA) and eicosapentaenoic acid (EPA)
Cold Sores (Aphthous Ulcers/Canker Sores)	L-lysine
Colds and Flu	Echinacea
	Zinc
	Vitamin C (ascorbic acid)
	Eucalyptus oil, used for nasal congestion, allergies
	Probiotics (e.g., *Bifidobacterium animalis*, *Lactobacillus acidophilus*)
Dementia/ Memory	Ginkgo
	Vitamin E (alpha-tocopherol)
	Vitamin D
	Acetyl-L-carnitine
	Vinpocetine, used for memory, neuroprotection, weight loss
Depression	St. John's wort
	SAMe (S-adenosyl-L-methionine), used for depression, osteoarthritis
	Valerian
	5-HTP
Diabetes	Alpha lipoic acid, used for diabetic neuropathy, memory, neuroprotection
	Chromium
	Cassia cinnamon
	Magnesium
	American ginseng
	Panax ginseng

CONDITION	TREATMENT
Dyslipidemia	Red yeast rice (contains a natural form of lovastatin)
	Omega-3 fatty acids, "fish oils"
	Garlic (controversial benefit; small ↓ TC and LDL)
	Plant sterol (beta-sitosterol)
	Fibers (barley, psyllium and oat bran)
	Artichoke extract
Dyspepsia	Calcium
	Magnesium
	Peppermint
	Chamomile
Energy/Weight Loss	Bitter orange (synephrine component)
	Caffeine
	Guarana, green tea powder (contain caffeine)
Erectile Dysfunction	Ginseng
	L-arginine
	Yohimbe
Heart Failure, Heart Health (general)	Coenzyme Q10 (ubiquinone), used as adjunctive treatment with HF medications
	Hawthorn
	Omega-3 fatty acids, "fish oils"
Hypertension	Omega-3 fatty acids, "fish oils"
	L-arginine
	Coenzyme Q10
	Garlic (controversial benefit; small ↓ in systolic BP)
	Fiber (psyllium, oats and wheat bran)
	Potassium
Gastrointestinal Health	Fibers [for diarrhea, constipation; examples: psyllium (in *Metamucil*, barley and oat bran)]
	Chamomile
	Probiotics (*Lactobacillus, Saccharomyces boulardii, Bifidobacterium infantis* strains)
	Peppermint
	Horehound (GI health, constipation)
	Wheatgrass (GI health, detoxification)
Inflammation	Omega-3 fatty acids, "fish oils"
	Flax seeds/oil, converted to DHA and EPA
	Turmeric

CONDITION	TREATMENT
Insomnia/Sleep	Melatonin used for sleep (taken QHS) and to help prevent/treat jetlag (0.5 to 2 mg taken pre-flight and higher doses, such as 5 mg, post-flight)
	Valerian
	Chamomile
	Lemon balm
	Passionflower
	Coenzyme Q10 (if due to heart failure)
	5-HTP and L-tryptophan
Liver Disease	Milk thistle
Menopause	Black cohosh
	Dong quai
	Evening primrose oil; provides essential fatty acids (gamma-lineloic acid, or GLA)
	Soy, red clover, Panax ginseng contain mild phyto-(plant) estrogens
Migraine, Prophylaxis	Feverfew
	Butterbur
	Magnesium
	Riboflavin (vitamin B2)
	Coenzyme Q10
	Guarana (for caffeine) or other caffeine sources
Motion Sickness	Ginger
	Peppermint

CONDITION	TREATMENT
Osteoarthritis	Glucosamine (best evidence with sulfate salts)
	Chondroitin
	SAMe (S-adenosyl-L-methionine), used for depression, osteoarthritis
	Turmeric (↓ inflammation/pain)
Osteoporosis	Calcium
	Vitamin D
	Soy
	Ipriflavone
Prostate Health	Saw palmetto (used often, may be ineffective)
	Lycopene
	Pygeum
	Pumpkin seed (contains beta-sitosterol)
Skin Conditions	Tea tree oil (for acne, dandruff, fungal infections)
	Aloe vera (for lichen planus, psoriasis, HSV, burns)
	Topical vitamin D (for psoriasis, seborrheic keratosis, diaper rash-vitamin A & D ointment)
	Biotin (hair loss, ↑ nail and hair thickness)
UTI	Cranberry
	Yogurt
	Probiotics (*Bifidobacteria, Lactobacillus* strains)
Weight Loss	Garcinia cambogia

SAFETY ISSUES WITH COMMON SUPPLEMENTS

TREATMENT	NOTES, SAFETY ISSUES
5-HTP	Serotonergic, ↑ risk with other serotonergic drugs
Artichoke extract	Allergic reactions (uncommon), cross-sensitivity with other members of Asteraceae family (e.g., asters, chamomile, chrysanthemum, echinacea, ragweed)
Bitter melon	↓ blood glucose (BG); caution with hypoglycemic drugs
Bitter orange (synephrine component)	Stimulant; dose-related ↑ BP, ↑ HR, arrhythmia risk
Black cohosh	May be hepatotoxic Do not use with medications for heart failure: ACE inhibitors, ARBs, beta-blockers, amiodarone
Caffeine	Dose-related (with high doses) dizziness, agitation, irritability, ↑ BP, ↑ HR
Chamomile	Allergic reactions (uncommon), cross-sensitivity with other members of Asteraceae family (e.g., ragweed, asters, chrysanthemums, artichoke)
Chondroitin	Bleeding risk at higher doses, ↑ INR with warfarin
Dong quai	Increased bleeding risk (e.g., with concurrent use of anticoagulants, antiplatelets, salicylates)

TREATMENT	NOTES, SAFETY ISSUES
Echinacea	Controversial safety with autoimmune disorders; use cautiously with other members of Asteraceae family (e.g. ragweed, asters, chamomile, chrysanthemums, artichoke)
Feverfew	Mouth ulceration (inflammation of the oral cavity/tongue), increased bleeding risk (e.g., with concurrent use of anticoagulants, antiplatelets, salicylates)
Fibers (barley, psyllium, oat bran)	GI effects, if not used to fiber intake
Garcinia cambogia	May be serotonergic
Garlic	↑ bleeding risk
Ginger	↑ bleeding risk
Ginkgo	↑ bleeding risk; discontinue in advance of surgery
Ginseng	↑ bleeding risk
Glucosamine	↑ bleeding risk
Guarana, green tea powder (contains caffeine)	See caffeine
Hawthorn	Positive inotrope; avoid concurrent use with digoxin (additive effect), ↓ BP; caution for additive effect with BP-lowering drugs
Kava	Avoid due to hepatotoxicity
L-arginine	L-arginine converts into nitric oxide, ↓ BP and ↑ dizziness, caution for additive effect with BP-lowering drugs; avoid concurrent use with nitrates
Melatonin	When used chronically for sleep, endogenous melatonin can be decreased, resulting in dependency for sleep
Omega-3 fatty acids, "fish oils"	↑ bleeding risk with high doses, can ↑ LDL
Passionflower	QT prolongation; avoid with QT risk/other QT-prolonging drugs
Potassium	Potassium levels should be measured in a lab, and dosed accordingly (not with OTC supplements)
Probiotics	Separate use from oral antibiotics, safety concern with use of live bacteria in immunocompromised states
Red yeast rice (contains a natural form of lovastatin)	CYP450 inhibitors (e.g., amiodarone) will ↑ red yeast rice level; red yeast rice ↓ coenzyme Q10, which may ↑ myopathy risk; do not use with statins
SAMe (S-adenosylmethionine), used for depression, osteoarthritis	Serotonergic, ↑ risk with other serotonergic drugs ↑ bleeding risk, do not use in bipolar disorder due to ↑ risk manic behavior
Soy, red clover, Panax ginseng mild phyto-(plant) estrogens	Soy might increase breast cancer risk in postmenopausal women who are not producing estradiol
St. John's wort	Many drug interactions, mainly due to enzyme induction (results in ↓ levels of other drugs, except ↑ levels of prodrugs); serotonergic, photosensitivity
Valerian	Sedation, CNS depressant; risk with concurrent CNS depressants
Vinpocetine	Vinpocetine is semi-synthetic and derived from a plant product; FDA issued a warning for fetal harm
Vitamin C (ascorbic acid)	Nephrolithiasis with high doses, false-negative stool occult blood 48 to 72 hours after ascorbic acid ingestion
Vitamin E (alpha-tocopherol)	Do not exceed 400 IU daily; bleeding risk, CVD risk
Yohimbe	↑ BP, ↑ HR, seizure risk
Zinc	Nasal products can cause loss of smell

VITAMIN SUPPLEMENTATION

People who consume a balanced diet typically do not require supplementation with vitamins. Many people have poor diets that are low in nutritional value and may require a vitamin supplement to prevent nutrient deficiencies. Calcium and vitamin D intake remains insufficient for the majority of adults and children. Folate intake among women of childbearing age can be

VITAMINS	NAMES
Vitamin A	Retinol
Vitamin B1	Thiamine
Vitamin B2	Riboflavin
Vitamin B3	Niacin
Vitamin B6	Pyridoxine
Vitamin B9	Folic Acid
Vitamin B12	Cobalamin
Vitamin C	Ascorbic Acid
Vitamin D2	Ergocalciferol
Vitamin D3	Cholecalciferol
Vitamin E	Alpha-tocopherol

insufficient. Thiamine (vitamin B1) deficiency is common in alcoholism and malabsorptive states, such as Crohn's disease, following bariatric surgery, advanced HIV and several other conditions. Thiamine deficiency can cause Wernicke's encephalopathy. Symptoms of Wernicke's include mental confusion, ataxia, tremor and vision changes. As the symptoms of Wernicke's fade, Korsakoff syndrome tends to develop (also called Korsakoff psychosis), which is permanent neurologic (mental) damage. Pharmacists are part of the solution to problems associated with vitamin deficiencies. Anticonvulsants can contribute to calcium deficiency; supplementation with calcium and vitamin D is required for most patients. Some drugs may deplete nutrients, require a supplement to work properly or require a supplement to reduce toxicity (see table on the following page).

CALCIUM & VITAMIN D

For all prescription medications for low bone density (osteopenia or osteoporosis), adequate calcium and vitamin D supplementation should be recommended if dietary intake is inadequate. Low levels of vitamin D impairs calcium absorption. Patients who do not receive enough vitamin D from the sun or diet can benefit from supplementation with both calcium and vitamin D. Calcium and vitamin D supplementation is an essential topic for pharmacists since they often recommend OTC products. Product type and selection are discussed in the Osteoporosis, Menopause & Testosterone Use chapter.

The American Academy of Pediatrics (AAP) makes the following recommendations for infants and children:

- Exclusively breastfed infants or babies drinking less than 1 liter of baby formula need 400 IU of vitamin D daily. *Poly-Vi-Sol* products (discussed later) or generics are acceptable.

- Older children who do not drink at least 4 cups of vitamin D fortified milk also need vitamin D supplementation.

FOLIC ACID (FOLATE)

Folate deficiency causes birth defects of the brain and spinal cord (neural tube defects). All women of childbearing age should obtain 400 mcg/day of folic acid. During pregnancy, folate requirements increase to 600 mcg/day. Folate should be taken at least one month before pregnancy and continued for the first 2 – 3 months of pregnancy. Once pregnant, the woman will likely take a prescription prenatal vitamin which is continued throughout the pregnancy since it also contains calcium (not enough, about 200 mg) and some iron. Folate is in many healthy foods, including fortified cereals (some of which are not healthy), dried beans, leafy green vegetables and orange juice. Multivitamins usually contain an amount in the recommended range. Prescription prenatal vitamins usually contain 1,000 mcg, or 1 mg, of folate. The newer birth control pills *Beyaz* and *Safyral* contain folate, however, it is less expensive to use a different birth control pill with a supplement. *Beyaz* and *Safyral* contain the potassium-sparing progestin drospirenone, with ethinyl estradiol and levomefolate.

VITAMIN E

It is unusual to have a vitamin E deficiency since it is present in many foods. Vitamin E in foods is considered healthy, but excess intake of supplements is considered a health risk (particularly CVD risk); patients should not exceed 400 IU daily.

IRON

AAP Iron Recommendations

AGE	TREATMENT
0 – 4 months	Supplemental iron is not required.
4 – 6 months	Formulas contain adequate iron; supplementation is not required. Breastfed babies need 1 mg/kg/day from 4-6 months old and until consuming iron-rich foods. At about 6 months, most breastfed babies get about half their calories from other foods, which may be adequate.
6 – 12 months	Need 11 mg/day of iron. Food sources are preferred; supplement as-needed.
1 – 3 years	Need 7 mg/day of iron. Food sources are preferred; supplement as-needed.

Pre-Term Infants

- Preterm (< 37 weeks) breastfed infants should receive 2 mg/kg/day of elemental iron supplementation from age 1 – 12 months. Most preterm formula-fed infants receive enough iron from formula, but some still require supplementation.

Adolescent Girls

■ Adolescent girls are at risk of anemia once menstruation begins. During this time, females should consume a diet high in iron-rich foods such as beans, eggs, fortified cereals and meats. Some will need an oral iron supplement.

Iron-Only Supplements (generics available)

Check the label on iron drops because the amount of iron provided by the dropper ranges from 10 – 15 mg.

■ *Fer-In-Sol* Iron Supplement Drops

■ *Feosol* tablets and caplets

Vitamin Supplements with Iron

■ *Poly-Vi-Sol* Vitamin Drops with Iron: use if both vitamin D and iron are needed

■ Others: *Flintstones* Children's Chewable Multivitamin plus Iron, *Pokemon* Children's Multiple Vitamin with Iron, store brands

DRUGS THAT CAUSE NUTRIENT DEPLETION

DRUG	DEPLETED NUTRIENT	CHAPTER
Acetazolamide	Calcium, potassium	Travelers, Common Conditions of the Eyes & Ears
Antiepileptics (including carbamazepine, lamotrigine, oxcarbazepine, phenobarbital/primidone, phenytoin, topiramate, valproic acid/divalproex, zonisamide)	Calcium*	Seizures/Epilepsy, Bipolar Disorder, others
Amphotericin B	Magnesium, potassium	Infectious Diseases III
Isoniazid	Vitamin B6	Infectious Diseases II (for neuropathy prevention)
Loop Diuretics	Potassium	Hypertension, Chronic Heart Failure
Metformin	Vitamin B12	Diabetes
Methotrexate	Folate	Systemic Steroids & Autoimmune Conditions, Oncology II
Orlistat	Beta-carotene, fat-soluble vitamins	Weight Loss
Proton Pump Inhibitors	Magnesium, vitamin B12 (> 2 years of treatment)	GERD
Sulfamethoxazole	Folate	Infectious Diseases I

*A supplement is needed for most patients using these drugs. Calcium should be given with vitamin D, if needed.

CONDITIONS WITH RECOMMENDED SUPPLEMENTS

CONDITION	RECOMMENDED SUPPLEMENT	CHAPTER
Alcoholism	Vitamin B1, folate	Hepatitis & Liver Disease
Goiter	Iodine (iodized salt)	Thyroid Disorders
Microcytic Anemia	Ferrous sulfate	Anemia
Macrocytic Anemia	Vitamin B12 and/or folate	Anemia
Pregnancy	Folate, calcium, vitamin D, pyridoxine (for nausea)	Pregnancy
Osteopenia/Osteoporosis	Calcium, vitamin D	Osteoporosis, Pregnancy
Osteomalacia (Rickets)	Calcium, vitamin D	
Chronic Kidney Disease	Vitamin D	Renal Disease, Bipolar Disorder (for lithium side effect)
Scurvy	Vitamin C	
Crohn's Disease (possibly ulcerative colitis)	Patient-specific, depends on levels; can require iron, zinc, folate, calcium, vitamin D, B vitamins	Inflammatory Bowel Disease
Bariatric Surgery	Various; patient-specific	Weight Loss

CANNABIDIOL (CBD)

Cannabidiol (CBD) is one cannabinoid found in the cannabis plant (marijuana is a type of cannabis plant). CBD does not cause the "high" that can come from marijuana use, and it does not appear to cause physical or psychological dependence. Tetrahydrocannabinol (THC) is generally extracted from marijuana; ingestion of THC may result in a "high." CBD is used in a variety of health issues (some with proof of efficacy and some without), including childhood epilepsy (Dravet syndrome and Lennox-Gastaut syndrome), anxiety, insomnia and chronic pain. While generally well-tolerated, it can cause nausea, diarrhea, fatigue and irritability.

The legality of CBD is evolving and can be confusing. Currently, it is illegal to market CBD as a food or dietary supplement because it is available as a prescription drug (*Epidiolex* used in certain childhood seizures). This means nonprescription CBD products are not FDA-approved. CBD can be extracted from the hemp plant, and federal law removed hemp from the definition of marijuana. Hemp-derived CBD products are still considered illegal in some states, while some states have legalized marijuana (and CBD) with various restrictions.

HOMEOPATHIC PRODUCTS

Homeopathy is based on "the law of similars" or the concept that "like is cured by like." This is when very small amounts of an active substance are given to stimulate the body to react against similar symptoms produced by that same substance when given at a higher dose. For example, homeopathic medicine made from the coffee bean relieves sleeplessness with agitation and racing thoughts. There is some evidence supporting the clinical use of homeopathic medicines. More research is needed before it can be considered a conventional medicine option.

Most homeopathic medicines are made from diluted amounts of the active substance, reported in X or C dilution scales. An X represents a 1:10 dilution, and C represents a 1:100 dilution of solute:solvent. The number in front of the X or C is the number of dilutions. A low dilution (e.g., 6C) could be seen to treat more localized symptoms such as a sore throat. A high dilution (e.g., 30C) could be seen in the treatment of more systemic symptoms (e.g., fever) or psychologic or behavioral symptoms (e.g., insomnia). The more dilute a substance is, the more "potent" it is considered.

The official compendium for homeopathic medicines is the Homeopathic Pharmacopoeia of the United States (HPUS), which is recognized by the FDA and equivalent to the United States Pharmacopoeia (USP). The HPUS publishes standards for homeopathic substances, including the identity, origin and quality assurance methods. The HPUS also determines what dilution of each medicine can be sold over the counter or with a prescription.

Since homeopathic medicines do not require FDA approval, manufacturers could distribute products with false claims, poor quality, measurable concentrations of drugs, nutrients or dietary supplements. In 2010, *Hyland's Teething Tablets* were recalled due to cases of belladonna toxicity. The amount of belladonna could be measured and was unsafe.

Select Guidelines/References

National Center for Complementary and Integrative Health (NCCIH). National Health Interview Survey 2017. https://nccih.nih.gov/research/statistics/NHIS/2017 (accessed 2022 Feb 28).

Baker RD, Greer FR. Diagnosis and prevention of iron deficiency and iron-deficiency anemia in infants and young children (0-3 years of age). *Pediatrics*. 2010;126(5):1040-50.

CONTENT LEGEND

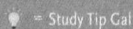 = Study Tip Gal

Lost_in_the_Midwest/Shutterstock.com

CHAPTER 81
TOXICOLOGY & ANTIDOTES

EMERGENCY PREPAREDNESS

Pharmacy staff can be involved in the response to a disaster (e.g., natural disasters, industrial accidents, biological and chemical threats). Pharmacists are primarily involved in the planning and execution of drug distribution and medication management during a disaster. Legal issues regarding dispensing a drug during an emergency are discussed in RxPrep's MPJE and CPJE Courses.

Pharmacy staff involved in emergency preparation should be well-informed about likely threats in their locality. They coordinate the drug components, such as appropriate drug stockpiling, included in the emergency response plans with the federal, regional/state and local agencies responsible for the plan development and maintenance. Pharmacists should be familiar with emergency protocols for their institution or workplace, including those for evacuation, disaster preparedness, mass dispensing (if required) and poisoning emergencies.

Communication concerning emergency planning and response requires an electronic network that includes the hospital pharmacy department directors and local pharmacies that can serve the needs of the community. Pharmacists involved from a hospital setting should be familiar with the recommendations of the American Society of Health-System Pharmacists (ASHP). The CDC pages on Emergency Preparedness and Response include recommendations for exposure to biological agents, information on current disease outbreaks and treatment for chemical and radiation exposure. One of the antidotes for exposure to radioactive iodine (KI, potassium iodide) is reviewed in the Thyroid Disorders chapter.

TOXICOLOGY

Toxicology is the study of poisonous chemicals, including drugs at unsafe doses. Children are the most common victims of accidental poisoning in the U.S. The top categories of exposures in children are to cosmetics/personal care products, analgesics and cleaning substances. Accidental poisoning is common among the elderly, primarily due to mental or physical impairment, the use of multiple drugs and reduced elimination of the drug from the body. Poisoning can be due to illicit (i.e., illegal) drug use, or the use of FDA-approved drugs (e.g., opioids) taken alone or in combination with other drugs, including fixed-dose combinations (e.g., hydrocodone and acetaminophen). Poisoning can be intentional, such as with attempted suicide, an act of revenge or in situations such as drug-facilitated sexual assault. General drug information resources often contain information on toxicology (e.g., Micromedex contains POISONDEX and Lexi-Comp contains Lexi-Tox).

PREVENTION OF ACCIDENTAL OVERDOSE

To reduce accidental poisoning in children, child-resistant (C-R) containers are helpful, but are not foolproof. These are required for most prescription drugs unless waived by the patient or the provider (for a single exception). Some drugs are excluded from this requirement, such as nitroglycerin sublingual tablets. Non-prescription (OTC) drugs that require C-R containers include iron, acetaminophen, salicylates, NSAIDs, diphenhydramine and drugs that have been switched from Rx to OTC status. Non-drug compounds that are dangerous if swallowed require C-R packaging, such as turpentine. A list of drugs that must have C-R packaging is provided in the RxPrep MPJE Course, since this is a federal legal requirement. Common C-R packaging includes:

- Screw caps that require more than a simple turn to open (such as pressing down with the palm when turning to open)

📷 Jorge Salcedo/Shutterstock.com

- Unit-dose packaging

- Card adherence (e.g., multiple medication blister packs)

- Safety packaging (*Optilock*) requires the user to press on one side while pulling the medication card out of the other side. *Optilock* packaging can also help with adherence; each dose is labeled with the day it should be taken.

INITIAL OVERDOSE MANAGEMENT

If poisoning is suspected, anyone can contact Poison Control by phone (1-800-222-1222) to receive guidance and recommendations. Basic first aid for poisonings should be initiated immediately after the exposure.

- For topical exposure, remove contaminated clothing and wash skin with soap and water for 10 minutes to remove the poison from the skin.

- For ocular exposure, remove contact lenses and rinse eye/s with a gentle stream of water for at least 15 minutes.

- For oral ingestion, remove any remaining substance/s from the mouth. If there are symptoms of burning or irritation, drink a small amount of water or milk immediately.

- For inhaled exposure, move to fresh air immediately. Stay away from toxic fumes and/or gases.

- For ingestion of button batteries (commonly found in electronics), give two teaspoons of honey every 10 minutes while seeking immediate medical care. Ingestion can be fatal within hours, and honey or sucralfate can slow damage to the esophagus and airway.

Ipecac syrup, used previously to induce emesis for certain exposures, is no longer recommended or commercially available but remains in many home medicine cabinets. Instruct others not to give ipecac syrup or use any other mechanism to induce vomiting.

If the patient is unconscious, having difficulty breathing, appears agitated or is having a seizure, call 911. Patients must be transported to the nearest hospital to receive specialized care for the overdose. While waiting for emergency help to arrive, initiate basic life support (BLS). The first step to the "CABs" (circulation, airway, breathing), previously called the ABCs, is to evaluate if the patient has a pulse. If pulseless, immediately start cardiopulmonary resuscitation (CPR) with chest compressions. During BLS, give two breaths for every 30 chest compressions. At a minimum, bystander hands-only CPR is encouraged. In transit to the hospital and at the hospital, supportive care (e.g., blood pressure support, airway management) will be initiated.

HOSPITAL OVERDOSE MANAGEMENT

Correct identification of the ingested substance/s is helpful to correctly treat and support the patient. Pharmacists can assist in identifying ingested substances by interviewing family members or calling the patient's pharmacy. For some substances, specific antidotes or dialysis may be used. Antidotes for common overdoses are discussed later in the chapter. In many cases of overdose, more than one drug is involved and more than one antidote may be required.

If the specific cause of the overdose remains unknown, patients are treated with supportive care and symptomatic treatment to minimize symptoms of the overdose. Some overdoses have specific symptoms that can help healthcare providers identify the exposure or ingestion (see Additional Antidotes table).

Several of the most dangerous compounds do not cause immediate symptoms when toxic. The clinician should consider the formulation, quantity and timing of ingestion of these substances. For example, in an acetaminophen overdose the patient can remain asymptomatic or have non-specific symptoms (such as nausea, abdominal pain, fatigue) until end organ toxicity (liver failure) becomes apparent.

DECONTAMINATION WITH ACTIVATED CHARCOAL

Activated charcoal is used in the emergency treatment of certain orally ingested drugs and is an early step in some overdose protocols. Activated charcoal is most effective when used within one hour of ingestion to stop or decrease the absorption of as much of the drug as possible while it is still in the gut. The charcoal adsorbs the drug, which prevents GI absorption and systemic toxicity. The dose of activated charcoal is 1 g/kg. Typically, only one dose of activated charcoal is administered. Multiple doses should only be considered if a patient has ingested a life-threatening amount of carbamazepine, dapsone, phenobarbital, quinine or theophylline.

Prior to using activated charcoal, the airway should be protected (with intubation, if needed) to prevent aspiration. Aspiration is the inhalation of foreign material, usually vomit, and can cause lung irritation leading to respiratory failure or respiratory infections. Some ingested compounds, such as hydrocarbons (petroleum products including gasoline and paint thinner) can increase the risk of aspiration. Care must be taken to protect the airway from these ingestions.

Activated charcoal is contraindicated in these situations:

- When the airway is unprotected, including when the patient:
    - ❑ Is unconscious
    - ❑ Cannot clear their throat
    - ❑ Cannot hold their head upright
- With intestinal obstruction
- When the gastrointestinal tract is not intact or when there is decreased peristalsis

Potential complications include transient constipation, bowel obstruction and regurgitation. If administered via an incorrectly placed nasogastric tube, there is an increased risk of aspiration, with consequent pulmonary complications (including death).

ANTIDOTES FOR COMMON POISONINGS

Antidotes are substances that stop the harmful effects of the poison or overdosed drug. Many are used off-label in the management of poisonings. According to 2020 American Association of Poison Control Centers (AAPCC) data, the most commonly ingested substances by adults are analgesics, sedative hypnotics, antipsychotics and antidepressants. Analgesics include both prescription (e.g., opioids) and non-prescription (e.g., acetaminophen) pain medications. The most commonly ingested substances by children are cosmetic products, cleaning substances, analgesics and dietary/herbal supplements. The antidotes for acetaminophen and opioid overdoses are reviewed individually since these are frequent overdoses.

ACETAMINOPHEN

Acetaminophen is the most common cause of drug-induced liver injury (DILI); excessive ingestion can lead to hepatotoxicity. Limiting acetaminophen from all sources to < 4,000 mg per day can reduce the risk of hepatotoxicity. Hepatotoxicity is a dose-dependent adverse effect caused by the increased metabolism of acetaminophen by CYP450 2E1 to N-acetyl-p-benzoquinone imine (NAPQI). NAPQI can covalently bind to liver cell proteins and cause liver injury, and ultimately, liver failure (see figure below). Acetaminophen overdose presents in four phases:

- Phase 1 (1 – 24 hours): commonly asymptomatic or non-specific symptoms, such as nausea and vomiting.

- Phase 2 (24 – 48 hours): hepatotoxicity evident on labs (e.g., elevated INR, AST/ALT); any symptoms from phase 1 usually subside.

- Phase 3 (48 – 96 hours): fulminant hepatic failure (e.g., jaundice, coagulopathy, renal failure and/or death).

- Phase 4 (> 96 hours): the patient recovers or receives a liver transplant.

In order to prevent hepatotoxicity, acetaminophen overdose must be identified early and the antidote, N-acetylcysteine (NAC), given quickly. See the Study Tip Gal and image below for NAC's mechanism of action.

The acetaminophen level (drawn 4 – 24 hours after ingestion) is used as the basis for treatment. The levels are plotted on the Rumack–Matthew nomogram to determine the risk of

N-ACETYLCYSTEINE (NAC) TREATMENT

- N-acetylcysteine (*Acetadote*) mechanism: free radical scavenger and precursor to glutathione (GSH), ultimately increasing GSH. GSH converts NAPQI to mercapturic acid, which can safely be excreted.

- Treatment: use the Rumack-Matthew nomogram to determine the need for NAC (IV or oral).

   ❏ Oral NAC (using injectable or inhalation solution): high dose given once, then lower dose for 17 doses. Repeat the dose if emesis occurs within 1 hour of administration.

   ❏ IV NAC: three infusions over a total of 21 hours.

hepatotoxicity. If there is possible or probable hepatotoxicity, NAC should be started (see Study Tip Gal). NAC is available in both oral and IV formulations.

OPIOIDS

Opioid abuse, overdose and related deaths have become an epidemic in the U.S. Acute opioid overdose can lead to life-threatening respiratory depression and sedation. The depressant effects of opioids can easily be reversed if the appropriate antidote, naloxone, is administered quickly. There are minimal to no adverse effects associated with giving naloxone to a patient who did not ingest any opioids. In many states, pharmacists can dispense naloxone without a prescription to patients at risk for opioid-induced respiratory depression. Various naloxone products are currently available and are covered in the Pain chapter.

Acetaminophen Metabolism and Use of N-acetylcysteine (NAC)

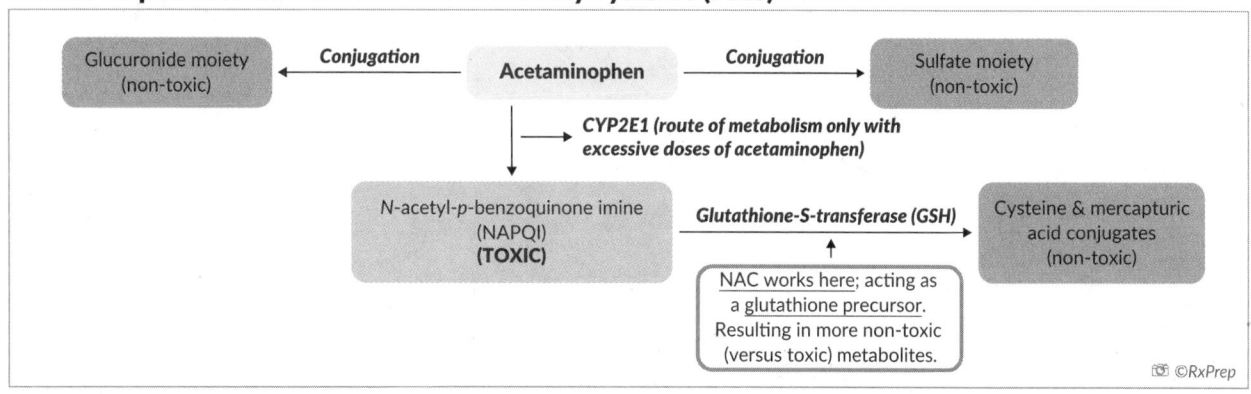

ADDITIONAL ANTIDOTES

DRUG OVERDOSE/POISON	SYMPTOMS/TREATMENT
Anticholinergics: atropine, diphenhydramine, dimenhydrinate, scopolamine, *Atropa belladonna* (deadly nightshade), jimson weed	Symptoms: "red as a beet": flushing, "dry as bone": dry skin and mucous membranes, "blind as a bat": mydriasis with double or blurry vision, "mad as a hatter": altered mental status, "hot as a hare": fever Primarily supportive care, rarely physostigmine is given; physostigmine inhibits the enzyme that breaks down acetylcholine (ACh), acetylcholinesterase, which ↑ ACh and ↓ anticholinergic toxicity
Anticoagulants: warfarin, direct thrombin inhibitors, factor Xa inhibitors, heparin, low molecular weight heparins	Symptoms: bleeding Agent specific: see Anticoagulation chapter for more details Andexanet alfa *(Andexxa)*: apixaban, rivaroxaban Idarucizumab *(Praxbind)*: dabigatran Phytonadione (vitamin K): warfarin Protamine: heparin, low molecular weight heparin Prothrombin complex concentrate *(Kcentra)*: warfarin, factor Xa inhibitors
Antipsychotics	Primarily supportive care, benztropine can be given for dystonias and bicarbonate can be given if there is QRS-interval widening
Benzodiazepines	Flumazenil: can cause seizures when used in patients on benzodiazepines chronically; sometimes used off-label for non-benzodiazepine hypnotic overdose (e.g., zolpidem), but not routinely recommended
Beta-blockers	Glucagon (if unresponsive to symptomatic treatment) High-dose insulin with glucose may be used in patients refractory to glucagon Lipid emulsion to enhance elimination of some lipophilic drugs
Calcium channel blockers	Same as beta-blockers plus: Calcium (chloride or gluconate): administer calcium IV only, avoid fast infusion, monitor ECG, do not infuse calcium in same line as phosphate-containing solutions
Cyanide: smoke inhalation, nitroprusside in high doses/long durations/renal impairment	Hydroxocobalamin *(Cyanokit)* Sodium thiosulfate + sodium nitrite *(Nithiodote)*
Digoxin, oleander, foxglove	Digoxin Immune Fab *(DigiFab)* Each *DigiFab* 40 mg vial binds ~0.5 mg digoxin; when the amount ingested or digoxin level is unknown, the max adult dose is 20 vials Interferes with digoxin levels drawn after it has been given
Ethanol (alcoholic drinks)	If suspected to be a chronic alcohol user, administer thiamine (vitamin B1) to prevent Wernicke's encephalopathy (neurological damage) Can cause an ↑ anion gap
5-fluorouracil (5-FU), capecitabine	Uridine triacetate *(Vistogard, Xuriden)*
Heavy metals: arsenic, copper, gold, lead, mercury, thallium	Dimercaprol: arsenic, gold, mercury Dimercaprol + calcium disodium edetate (CaNa2 EDTA) or succimer *(Chemet)* + dimercaptosuccinic acid *(DMSA)*: lead Ferric hexacyanoferrate, ["Prussian blue" *(Radiogardase)*]: thallium Penicillamine: copper
Hydrocarbons: petroleum products, gasoline, kerosene, mineral oil, paint thinners	Do not induce vomiting; keep patient NPO due to aspiration risk
Insulin or other hypoglycemics	Dextrose injection or infusion (drip), oral glucose (do not administer if the patient is unconscious) Glucagon (when IV or oral dextrose cannot be administered) Sulfonylurea-induced hypoglycemia: octreotide *(Sandostatin)*
Isoniazid	Pyridoxine (vitamin B6), benzodiazepines and/or barbiturates For acute neurotoxicity (seizure, coma), administer IV pyridoxine Oral pyridoxine 10–50 mg is used daily with isoniazid to prevent neuropathies
Iron and aluminum	Deferoxamine *(Desferal)*: iron and aluminum Deferiprone *(Ferriprox)* or deferasirox *(Exjade, Jadenu)*: iron overload from blood transfusions
Local anesthetics (bupivacaine, mepivacaine, ropivacaine) and other lipophilic drugs	IV lipid emulsion 20% Symptomatic treatment for seizures (benzodiazepines)

DRUG OVERDOSE/POISON	SYMPTOMS/TREATMENT
Organophosphates (OPs), including industrial insecticides (malathion, others) and nerve (warfare) gases (sarin, others)	OPs block acetylcholinesterase, which ↑ ACh levels and causes cholinergic "SLUDD" symptoms: salivation, lacrimation, urination, diarrhea/defecation Atropine: anticholinergic which blocks the effects of ACh to reduce the cholinergic SLUDD symptoms. Pralidoxime (Protopam): treats muscle weakness and relieves paralysis of respiratory muscles by reactivating cholinesterase that was inactivated by exposure to the OPs Atropine and pralidoxime may be used combination (DuoDote)
Methotrexate	Leucovorin (folinic acid), levoleucovorin (Fusilev), glucarpidase (Voraxaze): for rescue after high dose in cancer treatment, after an accidental overdose, or to ↓ toxicity and counteract the effects of impaired elimination
Methemoglobinemia from topical benzocaine (in OraGel or teething products), dapsone, nitrates or sulfonamides	Methylene blue (ProvayBlue) Methylene blue is contraindicated in patients with G6PD deficiency; avoid administration with SSRIs and SNRIs
Mushrooms (amatoxin-containing)	Treat severe muscarinic symptoms (bradycardia) with atropine
Naphthalene, from mothballs	Methylene blue (ProvayBlue)
Neostigmine, pyridostigmine	Pralidoxime (Protopam): counteracts the muscle weakness and/or respiratory depression secondary to overdose of acetylcholinesterase medications used to treat myasthenia gravis Atropine or glycopyrrolate can be given to prevent bradycardia from neostigmine
Nicotine, including e-cigarettes	Early symptoms: abdominal pain, nausea, diaphoresis, tachycardia, tremors Later symptoms: bradycardia, dyspnea, lethargy, coma, seizures Supportive care (e.g., atropine for symptomatic bradycardia, benzodiazepines for seizures)
Paralytics (e.g., rocuronium bromide, vecuronium bromide, pancuronium bromide)	For reversal of the effects of neuromuscular blockade in adults undergoing surgery: Neostigmine methylsulfate (Bloxiverz): rocuronium, vecuronium and pancuronium Sugammadex (Bridion): rocuronium and vecuronium
Salicylates	General concept: for a weak base, ↑ excretion by acidifying the urine, and for a weak acid, ↑ excretion by alkalinizing the urine Salicylates are acidic. Sodium bicarbonate is an alkalinizing agent and is given to alkalinize the urine; this will ↓ drug reabsorption and ↑ the excretion of the salicylates and other weak acids
Stimulant overdose: amphetamines, including ADHD and weight loss drugs, cocaine, ephedrine, caffeine, theophylline, MDMA (ecstasy)	Supportive care for agitation or seizures (benzodiazepines)
Toxic alcohols: ethylene glycol (antifreeze), diethylene glycol, methanol	Can cause an ↑ anion gap Fomepizole is preferred; ethanol (2nd line)
Tricyclic antidepressants (TCAs)	Overdose can quickly cause fatal arrhythmias Sodium bicarbonate: to ↓ a widened QRS complex Supportive care for agitation or seizures (benzodiazepines), if present Vasopressors may be needed for hypotension
Valproic acid or topiramate-induced hyperammonemia	Levocarnitine (Carnitor)

ORGANOPHOSPHATE OVERDOSE

SLUDD SYMPTOMS	TREATMENT	CAUSES
Salivation **L**acrimation **U**rination **D**iarrhea **D**efecation	Atropine: blocks the effects of acetylcholine Pralidoxime (Protopam): reactivates cholinesterase Atropine and pralidoxime may be used in combination (DuoDote)	Organophosphates include pesticides. People working on farms are at risk.

OVERDOSE? MIXED OVERDOSE? MATCHING THE SYMPTOMS TO THE ANTIDOTE

In overdose situations, it is not always known what substance was taken or if it was more than one substance. Symptoms and labs (sometimes referred to as toxidromes) guide the treatment until more information is known.

Possible Actions

- Always treat the most life-threatening overdose first (the substance causing impaired circulation, airway, or breathing).

  ❑ Somnolence, shallow labored breathing or pinpoint pupils could be an opioid overdose. Naloxone should be administered.

  ❑ If opioids and acetaminophen were both ingested, naloxone is given first.

- Check an acetaminophen level and use the Rumack-Matthew nomogram to determine if NAC should be given.

- Check glucose level and if hypoglycemic, give dextrose injection or (if a family member is providing) can inject glucagon. Oral carbohydrates can be given if alert and conscious.

- Tachycardia, seizures or severe agitation can be from multiple causes. Give benzodiazepines.

- QT prolongation can be caused by TCAs. Check ECG and give sodium bicarbonate if QRS is widened.

ANTIDOTES FOR COMMON BITES AND STINGS

TOXIN	ANTIDOTE	COMMENTS
Animal bites	Rabies vaccine (RabAvert, Imovax Rabies) + Human rabies immune globulin (HyperRAB S/D, Imogam Rabies HT)	High-risk animal bites or exposure (no previous rabies vaccination): give vaccine and human rabies immune globulin (HRIG). Vaccine given 1 mL IM in the deltoid (adults) or thigh (children, infants) on days 0, 3, 7, 14 and immune globulin is given 20 units/kg on day 0, infiltrated around wound site and a location separate from vaccine site. HRIG is not useful after day 7 of vaccine or in previously immunized individuals. Clean wound with soap and water. Tetanus shot is required if it has been at least 10 years since the last booster shot. See the Immunizations chapter for more details.
Black Widow spider bites	Antivenin for Latrodectus mactans	Predominantly found in southern and western states. Children and frail elderly are at highest risk for severe injury. The primary treatment is supportive care (opioids for pain management and benzodiazepines for muscle spasms). Antivenin is made by injecting a small amount of venom into an animal, then collecting and purifying the antibodies the animal produces.
Scorpion stings	Antivenin immune FAB Centruroides (Anascorp)	Scorpions with venom potent enough to cause clinically severe symptoms are found mainly in the southwest.
Snake bites: eastern coral snake, Texas coral snake, copperhead snake, rattlesnake	Crotalidae polyvalent immune FAB (CroFab) for copperhead and rattlesnake bites. Crotalidae Immune F(ab')$_2$ (Anavip) for rattlesnake bites	Do not use ice; do not cut/suck out venom; transport patient to healthcare facility.

Select Guidelines/References

American Heart Association. Update for cardiopulmonary resuscitation and emergency cardiovascular care. Circulation. 2020;142:S337-S357.
Lexi-Comp Toxicology Online. http://online.lexi.com/lco/action/home/tox (accessed 2022 Feb 24).
CDC, Emergency Preparedness. http://emergency.cdc.gov (accessed 2022 Feb 24).

PATIENT CASES

CONTENTS

iStock.com/SbytovaMN

CHAPTER 82
CASES, EXAM-STYLE PRACTICE

CASE #1

History of Present Illness: DD is a 67-year-old white male who works as a manager in a shipping and receiving department. He presents for follow-up of fatigue, right and left-sided finger stiffness/soreness, and right-sided hip stiffness/pain. He recently had a rheumatoid factor level ordered that was reported as 86 IU/mL. Other complaints include decreased sexual desire, productive cough, dyspnea on exertion and poor sleep quality.

Past Medical History: hypertension, depression, anxiety, COPD

Family History: father deceased (stroke), mother still living with dementia

Social History: drinks alcohol socially on weekends, former smoker (quit approximately 4 years ago)

Allergies: *Vasotec* (cough)

Vitals: height 5' 11", weight 168 lbs, BP 148/88 mmHg, HR 88 BPM, RR 18 BPM

Physical Exam: rhonchi bilaterally, some SOB. Pain as described in the history of present illness. Active bowel sounds, last bowel movement earlier today. Some lower extremity edema.

MEDICATIONS:	NEW PRESCRIPTIONS:
Amlodipine 10 mg PO daily	Methotrexate 7.5 mg PO weekly
Atenolol 25 mg PO daily	Topical Pain Gel (Compound)
Celexa 40 mg PO daily	Ketamine HCl ....20 g
Zolpidem 10 mg PO QHS	Lidocaine HCl .... 8 g
Spiriva Respimat 2 inhalations daily	Ketoprofen...20 g
Welchol 3.75 grams PO daily	Polyethylene glycol ....15 g
Omeprazole 20 mg PO daily	*Span 80* ....7.5 g
	Sorbic acid...400 mg
	Poloxamer 30% gel........................qs ad 175 g

Assessment and Plan: rheumatoid arthritis. See medication orders above. Follow up in 6 – 8 weeks for clinical assessment and laboratory monitoring. Add a long-acting beta-2 agonist for COPD.

Labs (6 weeks later):

Na (135-146 mEq/L)	133	WBC (4-11 x 10³ cells/mm³)	3.1
K (3.5-5.3 mEq/L)	4.3	Hgb (13-17 g/dL)	11.8
Cl (98-110 mEq/L)	102	Hct (38-50%)	35
HCO3 (24-30 mEq/L)	26	Platelets (150-450 x 10³ cells/mm³)	198
BUN (7-25 mg/dL)	14	PMNs (45-73%)	21
Creatinine (0.6-1.2 mg/dL)	0.9	Bands (3-5%)	25
Glucose (65-99 mg/dL)	122	Lymphocytes (20-40%)	40
Ca (8.5-10.5 mg/dL)	8.8	Monocytes (2-8%)	10
A1C (%)	6.2	Eosinophils (0-5%)	3
AST (10-40 units/L)	23	Basophils (0-1%)	1
ALT (10-40 units/L)	34	Total cholesterol (< 200 mg/dL)	168
BNP (< 100 pg/mL)	92	HDL (> 50 mg/dL)	38
Albumin (3.5-5 g/dL)	3.6	LDL (< 100 mg/dL)	120
RF (< 60 IU/mL)	44	TG (< 150 mg/dL)	188
CCP Ab Ig (< 20 units)	43	10-year ASCVD risk (%)	22

Test your knowledge on this case with the questions on the following page.

CASE #1 QUESTIONS

1. Which of DD's medications can decrease A1C?

    A. Amlodipine

    B. *Celexa*

    C. Methotrexate

    D. *Spiriva Respimat*

    E. *Welchol*

2. Which medication is indicated for DD?

    A. Calcium carbonate

    B. Glipizide

    C. Iron dextran

    D. Lisinopril

    E. Rosuvastatin

3. Place the instructions for use of DD's current COPD maintenance inhaler in the correct order.

    A. Breathe out fully away from the inhaler

    B. Hold your breath as long as possible

    C. Open the cap

    D. Press the dose release button and breathe in slowly

    E. Turn the clear base until it clicks

4. What change in COPD treatment is most appropriate for the pharmacist to recommend for DD?

    A. Add *Combivent Respimat*

    B. Add *Flovent HFA*

    C. Add *Serevent Diskus*

    D. Switch to *Breo Ellipta*

    E. Switch to *Proventil HFA*

5. What is the percentage strength (w/w) of lidocaine in the compounded topical pain gel? (Round to the nearest TENTH.)

6. What is the purpose of *Span 80* in the compounded topical pain gel?

    A. Acidifier

    B. Emollient

    C. Preservative

    D. Surfactant

    E. Sweetener

7. What is the most likely role of sorbic acid in the compounded topical pain gel?

    A. Diluent

    B. Levigating agent

    C. Lubricant

    D. Preservative

    E. Thickening agent

8. What would be an appropriate beyond use date for the compounded topical pain gel?

    A. 7 days

    B. 14 days

    C. 30 days

    D. 3 months

    E. 6 months

9. Which medication is most likely causing DD's complaint of decreased sexual desire?

    A. Amlodipine

    B. *Celexa*

    C. Methotrexate

    D. *Welchol*

    E. Zolpidem

10. Calculate DD's absolute neutrophil count. (Round to the nearest WHOLE number.)

CASE #2

History of Present Illness: HG is a 69-year-old female who was admitted to the hospital on January 5th with fever, chills, shortness of breath and right lower extremity swelling. Her initial work up revealed the following:

EF: 25%; CXR: bilateral fluid overload but no consolidations or infiltrates; Lower Extremity Ultrasound: positive right popliteal DVT; Urine Culture: > 100,000 CFUs/mL gram negative rods

Past Medical History: hypertension, dyslipidemia, type 2 diabetes, heart failure, peripheral neuropathy

Allergies: *Bactrim* (hives)

Home Medications: metformin 1,000 mg PO BID, *Altace* 5 mg PO BID, furosemide 20 mg PO daily, *Coreg* 6.25 mg PO BID, *Cymbalta* 30 mg PO daily, St. John's wort, cassia cinnamon 3 grams PO daily

ADMISSION ORDERS AND NOTES (JANUARY 5TH)

Continue all home medications except metformin and furosemide	*Lasix* 40 mg IV Q12H
Lantus 20 units SC daily	Enoxaparin – pharmacy to dose per protocol
Humalog 6 units SC TID-AC	Warfarin – pharmacy to dose per protocol
Humalog SC PRN per correction dose protocol	*Unasyn* 1.5 g IV Q6H
(Blood glucose goal = 140 mg/dL)	Nitroglycerin 100 mg/250 mL x 12 hours, titrate per protocol

Vitals (January 7th): height 5' 1", weight 126 lbs, BP 144/92 mmHg, HR 87 BPM, RR 18 BPM, T 98.7°F

Labs (January 7th):

Glu (65-99 mg/dL)	154	WBC (4-11 x 10³ cells/mm³)	8.2
A1C (%)	7.5	RBC (3.8-5.1 x 10⁶ cells/mcL)	4.6
Na (135-146 mEq/L)	133	Hgb (12-16 g/dL)	12.1
K (3.5-5.3 mEq/L)	3.1	Hct (36-46%)	38
Cl (98-110 mEq/L)	102	Plt (150-450 x 10³ cells/mm³)	150
HCO3 (24-30 mEq/L)	24	Anti-Xa (units/mL)	Pending
BUN (7-25 mg/dL)	12	Total cholesterol (< 200 mg/dL)	166
Creatinine (0.6-1.2 mg/dL)	1.4	HDL (> 50 mg/dL)	38
INR	1.8	TG (< 150 mg/dL)	188

Urine Culture: *Klebsiella pneumoniae*

ANTIBIOTIC	MIC DILUTION	MIC INTERPRETATION
Amoxicillin/Clavulanate	< 8/4	S
Cefazolin	< 2	S
Ciprofloxacin	< 1	S
Gentamicin	< 2	S
Nitrofurantoin	< 32	S
Piperacillin/Tazobactam	< 16	S
Trimethoprim/Sulfamethoxazole	< 2/38	S

INR Report

DATE	INR
January 5	1.2
January 6	1.6
January 7	1.8
January 8	2.1

Test your knowledge on this case with the questions on the following page.

CASE #2 QUESTIONS

1. Which medication has the same mechanism of action as the beta-blocker HG takes at home?

    A.   Atenolol

    B.   Esmolol

    C.   Labetalol

    D.   Nadolol

    E.   Nebivolol

2. The medical team wants to switch HG's IV *Lasix* to an equivalent oral dose. What dose should be recommended?

    A.   20 mg twice daily

    B.   40 mg once daily

    C.   40 mg twice daily

    D.   80 mg once daily

    E.   80 mg twice daily

3. Once stable, which intervention should be made to HG's home medication list?

    A.   Add *Entresto*

    B.   Add lisinopril

    C.   Add *Norvasc*

    D.   Change furosemide to chlorthalidone

    E.   Increase the dose of *Coreg*

4. If the enoxaparin doses are administered at 0600 and 1800, what time should the anti-Xa level have been drawn?

    A.   0530

    B.   0630

    C.   1000

    D.   1400

    E.   1800

5. How many milliliters of *Lantus* will be administered with each dose? (Round to the nearest TENTH.)

6. Which of the following statements is true regarding *Lantus*?

    A.   It can be given at bedtime

    B.   It can be mixed with regular insulin

    C.   It is available as 500 units/mL

    D.   It is stable at room temperature for 42 days

    E.   It peaks at approximately 18 hours

7. The hospital uses *Lantus* vials and *Humalog KwikPen* 200 units/mL. How many milliliters are contained in each *Humalog KwikPen* device?

    A.   0.03 mL

    B.   0.09 mL

    C.   1.5 mL

    D.   3 mL

    E.   10 mL

8. Based on HG's current insulin regimen, what is her correction factor? (Round to the nearest WHOLE number.)

9. Which of HG's medications can increase the risk of bleeding when used with warfarin?

    A.   *Altace*

    B.   *Coreg*

    C.   *Cymbalta*

    D.   Metformin

    E.   St. John's wort

10. HG is most likely using cinnamon to treat:

    A.   Anxiety

    B.   Depression

    C.   Diabetes

    D.   Dyslipidemia

    E.   Heart failure

CASE #3

PATIENT PROFILE

Patient Name:	EG						
Address:	1365 Stephens Avenue						
Age:	48	**Sex:**	M	**Race:** African American	**Height:** 5'10"	**Weight:**	143 pounds
Allergies:	Morphine – itching, Sulfa – rash						

DIAGNOSES	HOME MEDICATIONS
Epilepsy	Phenytoin 300 mg PO nightly
Barrett's esophagus	

MEDICATIONS

Date	Prescriber	Drug/Strength/Sig
10/9	Marks	Phenytoin 100 mg IV Q8 hours
10/9	Smith	D5NS IV infusion at 50 mL/hour
10/9	Smith	Propofol IV infusion, starting at 5 mcg/kg/min. Titrate by 5 mcg/kg/min every 10 minutes to achieve a RASS of -2. Max dose 40 mcg/kg/min.
10/9	Smith	Morphine 2.5 mg IV Q3 hours PRN severe pain
10/15	Smith	NS bolus 1,000 mL IV x 1
10/15	Smith	Meropenem 1 gram IV Q8 hours
10/15	Smith	Tobramycin IV per pharmacy protocol (Hartford Nomogram)
10/15	Smith	Dexmedetomidine IV infusion, starting at 0.2 mcg/kg/hour. Titrate by 0.1 mcg/kg/hour every 30 minutes to achieve a RASS of -1. Max dose 0.7 mcg/kg/hour.
10/15	Taylor	Parenteral nutrition IV per pharmacy protocol
10/25	Doner	Enteral nutrition (Jevity 1.5) at 10 mL/hour
10/25	Doner	Phenytoin 100 mg via PEG tube Q8 hours

LAB/DIAGNOSTIC TESTS

Test	Normal Value	Results Date: 10/9	Date: 10/15	Date: 10/19	Date: 10/25
Glu	65-99 mg/dL	102	118	101	110
Na	135-146 mEq/L	137	140	143	138
K	3.5-5.3 mEq/L	4.4	4.6	6.1	4.2
Cl	98-110 mEq/L	106	107	108	102
CO2	24-30 mEq/L	26	26	24	24
BUN	7-25 mg/dL	14	17	45	15
Creatinine	0.6-1.2 mg/dL	1.2	1.3	3.1	1.1
Albumin	3.5-5 g/dL	2.9		3.2	
TG	< 150 mg/dL		507		
AST	10-40 units/L	23	40		
ALT	10-40 units/L	27	52		
WBC	4-11 x 10^3 cells/mm^3	6.2	14.6	8.9	
PLT	150-450 x 10^3 cells/mm^3	250	267	258	
Hgb	13-17 g/dL	11.3	10.8	10.6	
Hct	40-52%	43	37	38	
MCV	80-100 fL	65			
MRSA nasal swab		Positive			
Pheytoin, total (mcg/mL)				9	

PROGRESS NOTES

10/9 at 1700	Vitals: BP 144/88 mmHg, HR 86 BPM, T 37°C; patient admitted to the ICU s/p esophageal surgery. Plan: patient will remain intubated, sedated and NPO x 14 days. Will convert home medications to IV and start IV fluids.
10/15 at 1300	Vitals: BP 90/46 mmHg, HR 92 BPM, T 39°C; patient remains intubated and sedated on propofol. Patient noted to have increased sputum production with increased purulence and increasing oxygen requirements. Plan: obtain chest X-ray, send blood and sputum cultures to evaluate for infection and start broad-spectrum antibiotics. DC propofol and start dexmedetomidine. DC IV fluids and start parenteral nutrition.
10/19 at 1100	Vitals: BP 130/76 mmHg, HR 56 BPM, T 36.5°C; patient is less responsive and noted to have some seizure like activity. Urine output has decreased overnight. Peaked T-waves are noted on EKG. Plan: obtain EEG, BMP and phenytoin level.
10/25 at 1400	Vitals: BP 131/72 mmHg, HR 80 BPM, T 37°C; patient remains stable; percutaneous G-tube (PEG) placed; extubated. Plan: DC parenteral nutrition and start enteral nutrition. DC IV phenytoin and administer medications via PEG.

Test your knowledge on this case with the questions on the following page.

CASE #3 QUESTIONS

1. Based on his admission labs on 10/9, EG likely has a diagnosis of:

    A. Diabetes

    B. Dyslipidemia

    C. Gout

    D. Iron deficiency anemia

    E. Osteoporosis

2. The hospital stocks 500 mg/50 mL bottles of propofol. At what rate (mL/hour) should the nurse start the infusion on 10/9? (Round to the nearest HUNDREDTH.)

3. The medical team asks about a recommendation for VTE prophylaxis. Which of the following would be appropriate for EG? (Select **ALL** that apply.)

    A. Enoxaparin 40 mg subcutaneously daily

    B. Heparin 5,000 units subcutaneously Q8 hours

    C. *Lovenox* 1 mg/kg subcutaneously Q12 hours

    D. Rivaroxaban 15 mg PO BID

    E. Unfractionated heparin 80 units/kg IV once, followed by an infusion starting at 18 units/kg/hr

4. By 10/15, EG's propofol has been titrated up to 40 mcg/kg/min to achieve adequate sedation. Propofol is changed to dexmedetomidine. What adverse effect of propofol is the team concerned about?

    A. Anemia

    B. Emergence reaction

    C. Hyponatremia

    D. Pancreatitis

    E. Propylene glycol toxicity

5. On 10/15, EG's chest X-ray shows a focal opacity in the right upper lobe. The gram stain of the respiratory culture shows numerous white blood cells with many gram-positive cocci in clusters. Meropenem and tobramycin are ordered. What additional antibiotic should be recommended?

    A. Ciprofloxacin

    B. Daptomycin

    C. Linezolid

    D. Nafcillin

    E. *Unasyn*

Questions 6-7 relate to the Hartford nomogram for tobramycin dosing discussed in the Infectious Diseases I chapter.

6. The hospital uses a policy of rounding tobramycin doses to the nearest 20 mg. What dose of tobramycin should EG receive based on the order from 10/15?

7. A tobramycin level was drawn 9 hours after the start of the infusion and the result was 4.8 mcg/mL. Based on the Hartford nomogram, what dosing interval should be ordered for EG?

    A. Q12H

    B. Q24H

    C. Q36H

    D. Q48H

    E. Q72H

8. Based on the parenteral nutrition order on 10/15, the pharmacist calculates EG's protein requirement to be 80 grams daily. Using a 15% amino acid solution, how many milliliters will be required to provide the daily protein requirement? (Round to the nearest WHOLE number.)

9. On 10/19, EG experiences seizure-like activity. Which of his medications can lower the seizure threshold?

    A. *Dilantin*

    B. *Diprivan*

    C. Meropenem

    D. Morphine

    E. Tobramycin

10. What is EG's corrected phenytoin level on 10/19? (Round to the nearest TENTH.)

11. Which of the following can be used for the electrolyte abnormality on 10/19? (Select **ALL** that apply.)

    A. IV albumin

    B. IV calcium gluconate

    C. IV conivaptan

    D. IV insulin

    E. IV pamidronate

ANSWERS TO CASE QUESTIONS

CASE #1 ANSWERS

1-**E**, refer to the Diabetes chapter

2-**E**, refer to the Dyslipidemia chapter

3-**E,C,A,D,B**, refer to the Chronic Obstructive Pulmonary Disease chapter

4-**C**, refer to the Chronic Obstructive Pulmonary Disease and Asthma chapters

5-**4.6%**, refer to the Calculations II chapter

6-**D**, refer to the Compounding chapters

7-**D**, refer to the Compounding chapters

8-**C**, refer to the Compounding chapters

9-**B**, refer to the Depression and Sexual Dysfunction chapters

10-**1426**, refer to the Calculations IV chapter

CASE #2 ANSWERS

1-**C**, refer to the Hypertension chapter

2-**E**, refer to the Chronic Heart Failure chapter

3-**E**, refer to the Chronic Heart Failure chapter

4-**C**, refer to the Anticoagulation chapter

5-**0.2 mL**, refer to the Diabetes chapter

6-**A**, refer to the Diabetes chapter

7-**D**, refer to the Diabetes chapter

8-**47**, refer to the Diabetes chapter

9-**C**, refer to the Drug Interactions and Anticoagulation chapters

10-**C**, refer to the Dietary Supplements, Natural & Complementary Medicine chapter

CASE #3 ANSWERS

1-**D**, refer to the Anemia chapter

2-**1.95 mL/hour**, refer to the Calculations IV chapter

3-**A,B**, refer to the Anticoagulation chapter

4-**D**, refer to the Acute & Critical Care Medicine chapter

5-**C**, refer to the Infectious Diseases II chapter

6-**460 mg**, refer to the Infectious Diseases I chapter

7-**B**, refer to the Infectious Diseases I chapter

8-**533 mL**, refer to the Calculations III chapter

9-**C**, refer to the Seizures/Epilepsy chapter

10-**12.2 mcg/mL**, refer to the Seizures/Epilepsy chapter

11-**B,D**, refer to the Renal Disease chapter

© Lisa-S/Shutterstock.com

INDEX

INDEX

INDEX

INDEX

Image Credits

Some images have been modified from their original state. All images are being used for illustrative purposes only. Any person depicted in the content is a model.

Front cover:

iStock.com/da-vooda

Kdonmuang/Shutterstock.com

bukhta79/stock.adobe.com

Mangostar/stock.adobe.com

StratfordProductions/stock.adobe.com

For images used in the design of the book:

iStock.com/Ae11615

iStock.com/Chaliya

iStock.com/bearsky23

iStock.com/blueringmedia

iStock.com/Christoph Burgstedt

iStock.com/Dr_Microbe

iStock.com/francescoch

iStock.com/_human

iStock.com/image_jungle

iStock.com/ipopba

iStock.com/jacklooser

iStock.com/Kateryna Kon

iStock.com/metamorworks

iStock.com/Mohammed Haneefa Nizamudeen

iStock.com/Olivier Le Moal

iStock.com/scyther5

iStock.com/stockdevil

iStock.com/Sudowoodo

iStock.com/SbytovaMN

iStock.com/t:yodiyim

iStock.com/Tharakorn

iStock.com/VolodymyrV

Sebastian Kaulitzki © 123FR.com

Ann in the uk/Shutterstock.com

Buravleva stock/Shutterstock.com

Crevis/Shutterstock.com

David Fossler/Shutterstock.com

Explode/Shutterstock.com

hernan ceballos/Shutterstock.com

Mark Mondaini/Shutterstock.com

metamorworks/Shutterstock.com

Motortion Films/Shutterstock.com

PopTika/Shutterstock.com

Prostock-studio/Shutterstock.com

Roman Zaiets/Shutterstock.com

sciencepics/Shutterstock.com

thodonal88/Shutterstock.com

Tyler Olson/Shutterstock.com

7activestudio/stock.adobe.com

Chinnapong/stock.adobe.com

freshidea/stock.adobe.com

lufeethebear/stock.adobe.com

MarekPhotoDesign.com/stock.adobe.com

pathdoc/stock.adobe.com

peterschreiber.media/stock.adobe.com

SciePro/stock.adobe.com

Sondem/stock.adobe.com

sudok1/stock.adobe.com

topvectors/stock.adobe.com